Hoover's MasterList of U.S. Companies

2016

MERGENT
BUSINESS PRESS

Hoover's MasterList of U.S. Companies is intended to provide readers with accurate and authoritative information about the enterprises covered in it. The information contained herein is as accurate as we could reasonably make it. In many cases we have relied on third-party material that we believe to be trustworthy but were unable to independently verify. We do not warrant that the book is absolutely accurate or without error. Readers should not rely on any information contained herein in instances where such reliance might cause financial loss.

The publisher, the editors, and their data suppliers specifically disclaim all warranties, including the implied warranties of merchantability and fitness for a specific purpose. This book is sold with the understanding that neither the publisher, the editors, nor any content contributors are engaged in providing investment, financial, accounting, legal, or other professional advice.

Mergent Inc., provided financial data for most public companies in this book. For private companies and historical information on public companies prior to their becoming public, we obtained information directly from the companies or from third-party material that we believe to be trustworthy. Hoover's, Inc., is solely responsible for the presentation of all data.

Many of the names of products and services mentioned in this book are the trademarks or service marks of the companies manufacturing or selling them and are subject to protection under U.S. law. Space has not permitted us to indicate which names are subject to such protection, and readers are advised to consult with the owners of such marks regarding their use. Hoover's is a trademark of Hoover's, Inc.

Copyright © 2016 by Hoover's, Inc. All rights reserved. No part of this book may be reproduced or transmitted in any form or by any means, electronic or mechanical, including by photocopying, facsimile transmission, recording, rekeying, or using any information storage and retrieval system, without permission in writing from Hoover's, except that brief passages may be quoted by a reviewer in a magazine, in a newspaper, online, or in a broadcast review.

10 9 8 7 6 5 4 3 2 1

Publishers Cataloging-in-Publication Data

Hoover's MasterList of U.S. Companies 2016, Vol. 2

    Includes indexes.

    ISBN: 978-1-63053-826-2

    ISSN 1549-6457

    1. Business enterprises — Directories. 2. Corporations — Directories.

HF3010 338.7

U.S. AND WORLD BOOK SALES

Mergent Inc.
444 Madison Ave
New York, NY 10022
Phone: 800-342-5647

e-mail: orders@mergent.com
Web: www.mergentbusinesspress.com

Mergent Inc.

CEO: Jonathan Worrall

Executive Managing Director: John Pedernales

Executive Vice President of Sales: Fred Jenkins

Managing Director of Relationship Management: Chris Henry

Managing Director of Print Products: Thomas Wecera

Senior Product Manager: Neel Gandhi

Director of Print Products: Charlot Volny

Director of Data: Mohamed Hanif

Quality Assurance Editor: Wayne Arnold

Production Research Assistant: Wayne Arnold

MERGENT CUSTOMER SERVICE

Support and Fulfillment Manager: Melanie Horvat

ABOUT MERGENT, INC.

Mergent, Inc. is a leading provider of business and financial data on global publicly listed companies. Based in the U.S, the company maintains a strong global presence, with offices in New York, Charlotte, San Diego, London, Tokyo and Melbourne.

Founded in 1900, Mergent operates one of the longest continuously collected databases of: descriptive and fundamental information on domestic and international companies; pricing and terms and conditions data on fixed income and equity securities; and corporate action data.

In addition, Mergent's Indxis subsidiary develops and licenses equity and fixed income investment products based on its proprietary investment methodologies. Our licensed products have over $9 billion in assets under management and are offered by major investment management firms. The Indxis calculation platform is the chosen technology for some of the world's largest index companies. Its index calculation and pricing distribution protocols are used to administer index rules and distribute real-time pricing data.

Abbreviations

AFL-CIO – American Federation of Labor and Congress of Industrial Organizations
AMA – American Medical Association
AMEX – American Stock Exchange
ARM – adjustable-rate mortgage
ASP – application services provider
ATM – asynchronous transfer mode
ATM – automated teller machine
CAD/CAM – computer-aided design/computer-aided manufacturing
CD-ROM – compact disc – read-only memory
CD-R – CD-recordable
CEO – chief executive officer
CFO – chief financial officer
CMOS – complementary metal oxide silicon
COO – chief operating officer
DAT – digital audiotape
DOD – Department of Defense
DOE – Department of Energy
DOS – disk operating system
DOT – Department of Transportation
DRAM – dynamic random-access memory
DSL – digital subscriber line
DVD – digital versatile disc/digital video disc
DVD-R – DVD-recordable
EPA – Environmental Protection Agency
EPROM – erasable programmable read-only memory
EPS – earnings per share
ESOP – employee stock ownership plan
EU – European Union
EVP – executive vice president
FCC – Federal Communications Commission
FDA – Food and Drug Administration
FDIC – Federal Deposit Insurance Corporation
FTC – Federal Trade Commission
FTP – file transfer protocol
GATT – General Agreement on Tariffs and Trade
GDP – gross domestic product
HMO – health maintenance organization
HR – human resources
HTML – hypertext markup language
ICC – Interstate Commerce Commission
IPO – initial public offering
IRS – Internal Revenue Service
ISP – Internet service provider
kWh – kilowatt-hour
LAN – local-area network
LBO – leveraged buyout
LCD – liquid crystal display

LNG – liquefied natural gas
LP – limited partnership
Ltd. – limited
mips – millions of instructions per second
MW – megawatt
NAFTA – North American Free Trade Agreement
NASA – National Aeronautics and Space Administration
NASDAQ – National Association of Securities Dealers Automated Quotations
NATO – North Atlantic Treaty Organization
NYSE – New York Stock Exchange
OCR – optical character recognition
OECD – Organization for Economic Cooperation and Development
OEM – original equipment manufacturer
OPEC – Organization of Petroleum Exporting Countries
OS – operating system
OSHA – Occupational Safety and Health Administration
OTC – over-the-counter
PBX – private branch exchange
PCMCIA – Personal Computer Memory Card International Association
P/E – price to earnings ratio
RAID – redundant array of independent disks
RAM – random-access memory
R&D – research and development
RBOC – regional Bell operating company
RISC – reduced instruction set computer
REIT – real estate investment trust
ROA – return on assets
ROE – return on equity
ROI – return on investment
ROM – read-only memory
S&L – savings and loan
SCSI – Small Computer System Interface
SEC – Securities and Exchange Commission
SEVP – senior executive vice president
SIC – Standard Industrial Classification
SOC – system on a chip
SVP – senior vice president
USB – universal serial bus
VAR – value-added reseller
VAT – value-added tax
VC – venture capitalist
VP – vice president
VoIP – Voice over Internet Protocol
WAN – wide-area network
WWW – World Wide Web

CONTENTS

Volume 1

About Hoover's MasterList of
U.S. Companies 2016 .... **vii**

Company Lists **2a-21a**
    Top 500 Companies By Sales **2a**
    Top 500 Companies By Employer **7a**
    Top 500 Companies by Net Profit **12a**
    Mergent Top 500 Public Companies 17a

Company Listings A – L **2**

Volume 2

Company Listings M – Z **944**

Indexes **1745**
    By Industry **1747**
    By Headquarters Location **1791**

About Hoover's MasterList of U.S. Companies 2016

This edition of *Hoover's MasterList of U.S. Companies* is packed with information, and we believe, represents a true value for the information seeker. We have worked hard to ensure that this edition of the *MasterList* retains its position as one of the most comprehensive, but still affordable, sources for information on the vast array of enterprises that power the U.S. economy.

In this two-volume set, we feature our capsule summaries for each company. Additionally, we have included lists of the Top 500 companies in this book, organized by sales, employees, five-year annualized sales growth, and market value.

Hoover's MasterList of U.S. Companies 2016 contains essential information on about 10,000 companies taken from our internal database. We supplemented and expanded that database by obtaining sales information on most public companies from Morningstar, Inc.

In our selection process, we have endeavored to cover all US companies traded on the major stock exchanges and the largest and most important private enterprises in the US, as well as many other organizations that contribute to our economy, including government-owned enterprises (the United States Postal Service), foundations (the Bill & Melinda Gates Foundation), and major subsidiaries of US and non-US corporations.

We selected companies using the following criteria:

Public Companies (4,719)

We've included all US companies that trade on the New York Stock Exchange (NYSE), the NYSE Alternext, and the NASDAQ Global (NASDAQ GM) and Global Select Markets (NASDAQ GS), as well as many of the companies in Hoover's database that trade on the NASDAQ Capital Market (NASDAQ CM), OTC, or Pink Sheets.

Private and Other Enterprises (5,640)

Our coverage of privately held businesses and other non-public entities includes:

- the largest privately held companies in the US;
- hundreds of the largest mutual insurance companies, agricultural co-ops, foundations, sports teams and leagues, universities, and not-for-profits;
- major subsidiaries of US and non-US corporations that have strong identities independent of the parent organizations;
- major government-owned enterprises.

INFORMATION PROVIDED ABOUT THE COMPANIES

Each entry contains a description of the company's products and operations, ownership, and market position if available, as well as the basic information that most people need to locate, communicate with, and evaluate a company. We have included each company's legal name at the top of the entry (or in the text if it is too long), and if available:

- The street address, phone number, fax number, and Web site address;
- The names of the chief executive officer (CEO), chief financial officer (CFO), and human resources (HR) contact;
- The company's status (privately held, public, subsidiary, etc.).

Headquarters for companies that are incorporated in Bermuda, but whose operational headquarters are in the US, are listed under their US address. The same applies for companies with joint US and non-US headquarters (such as KPMG International).

For public companies, we have provided trading symbols and exchanges. Sales numbers are provided for all companies, if available, with generally two major exceptions: Corporate parents do not break out sales for many subsidiaries or business segments, and venture capital firms and investment bankers do not provide revenue numbers. Sales for private companies are the most recent available; some are estimated or approximate, as the companies would not divulge exact figures. (Estimated sales numbers are identified as such.)

Some companies have joint CEOs or even no one with the title CEO, although there is someone who functions as the chief executive. In these cases, we have listed after the CEO heading the name of the person who appears first in the company's materials. In smaller companies, sometimes no one individual has the official title of CFO. In those cases, we have listed after the CFO heading the name of the principal financial officer (i.e., the officer who signs off on the company's financial statements).

INDEXES

To help readers easily locate information, we have included three indexes: companies by headquarters location, by industry, and by stock exchange symbol. The indexes for the two volumes are combined and are located at the end of each volume.

Hoover's MasterList of U.S. Companies

Company Rankings

Top 500 Companies by Sales in Hoover's MasterList of U.S. Companies 2016

Rank	Company	Headquarters	Sales ($ bil)
1	Wal-Mart Stores, Inc.	AR	$485,651
2	Exxon Mobil Corp.	TX	$411,939
3	Apple Inc	CA	$233,715
4	Chevron Corporation	CA	$211,970
5	Berkshire Hathaway Inc.	NE	$194,673
6	McKesson Corp.	CA	$179,045
7	Phillips 66	TX	$164,093
8	UnitedHealth Group Inc	MN	$157,107
9	CVS Health Corp	RI	$153,290
10	General Motors Co.	MI	$152,356
11	Ford Motor Co. (DE)	MI	$149,558
12	General Electric Co	CT	$148,589
13	AmerisourceBergen Corp.	PA	$135,962
14	AT&T Inc	TX	$132,447
15	Valero Energy Corp.	TX	$130,844
16	Verizon Communications Inc	NY	$127,079
17	Fannie Mae	DC	$116,461
18	Costco Wholesale Corp	WA	$116,199
19	Federal Reserve System	DC	$114,299
20	Kroger Co (The)	OH	$108,465
21	Amazon.com Inc.	WA	$107,006
22	Walgreens Boots Alliance Inc	IL	$103,444
23	HP Inc	CA	$103,355
24	Cardinal Health, Inc.	OH	$102,531
25	JPMorgan Chase & Co	NY	$102,102
26	Express Scripts Holding Co	MO	$101,752
27	Marathon Petroleum Corp.	OH	$98,102
28	Boeing Co.	IL	$96,114
29	Bank of America Corp.	NC	$95,181
30	Microsoft Corporation	WA	$93,580
31	International Business Machi	NY	$92,793
32	Citigroup Inc	NY	$90,572
33	Wells Fargo & Co.	CA	$88,372
34	Home Depot Inc	GA	$83,176
35	Archer Daniels Midland Co.	IL	$81,201
36	Philip Morris International	NY	$80,106
37	Procter & Gamble Co	OH	$76,279
38	Alphabet Inc	CA	$74,989
39	Comcast Corp	PA	$74,510
40	Johnson & Johnson	NJ	$74,331
41	Anthem Inc	IN	$73,874
42	MetLife Inc	NY	$73,316
43	Target Corp	MN	$72,618
44	Freddie Mac	VA	$69,367
45	Federal Reserve Bank Of New Y	NY	$68,824
46	American International Group	NY	$64,406
47	Pepsico Inc.	NY	$63,056
48	United Parcel Service Inc	GA	$58,232
49	Aetna Inc.	CT	$58,003
50	Lowe's Companies Inc	NC	$56,223
51	United Technologies Corp	CT	$56,098
52	Energy Transfer Equity L P	TX	$55,691
53	ConocoPhillips	TX	$55,517
54	Intel Corp	CA	$55,355
55	Prudential Financial, Inc.	NJ	$54,105
56	Disney (Walt) Co. (The)	CA	$52,465
57	Hewlett Packard Enterprise C	CA	$52,107
58	Energy Transfer Partners LP	TX	$51,158
59	Pfizer Inc	NY	$49,605
60	Cisco Systems, Inc.	CA	$49,161
61	Dow Chemical Co.	MI	$48,778
62	Sysco Corp.	TX	$48,681
63	Humana, Inc.	KY	$48,500
64	Enterprise Products Partners	TX	$47,951
65	FedEx Corp	TN	$47,453
66	Caterpillar Inc.	IL	$47,011
67	Ingram Micro Inc.	CA	$46,487
68	Coca-Cola Co (The)	GA	$45,998
69	Lockheed Martin Corp.	MD	$45,600
70	Plains GP Holdings, L.P	TX	$43,464
71	Plains All American Pipeline	TX	$43,464
72	World Fuel Services Corp.	FL	$43,386
73	American Airlines Group Inc	TX	$42,650
74	Merck & Co., Inc	NJ	$42,237
75	Tyson Foods, Inc.	AR	$41,373
76	Delta Air Lines, Inc. (DE)	GA	$40,704
77	Tesoro Corporation	TX	$40,633
78	Best Buy Inc	MN	$40,339
79	Goldman Sachs Group, Inc.	NY	$40,085
80	United Continental Holdings	IL	$38,901
81	Honeywell International Inc	NJ	$38,581
82	Oracle Corp.	CA	$38,226
83	Morgan Stanley	NY	$37,953
84	Johnson Controls Inc	WI	$37,179
85	HCA Holdings Inc	TN	$36,918
86	American Express Co.	NY	$35,999
87	Allstate Corp.	IL	$35,239
88	UNITED NETWORK FOR ORGAN SHA	VA	$35,112
89	Cigna Corp	CT	$34,914
90	INTL FCStone Inc.	NY	$34,676
91	CHS Inc	MN	$34,582
92	Sprint Corp (New)	KS	$34,532
93	Mondelez International Inc	IL	$34,244
94	General Dynamics Corp.	VA	$31,469
95	Sears Holdings Corp	IL	$31,198
96	Publix Super Markets, Inc.	FL	$30,802
97	NIKE Inc	OR	$30,601
98	3M Co	MN	$30,274
99	T-Mobile US Inc	WA	$29,564
100	Exelon Corp.	IL	$29,447
101	TJX Companies, Inc.	MA	$29,078
102	Twenty-First Century Fox Inc	NY	$28,987
103	Deere & Co.	IL	$28,863
104	Macy's Inc	NY	$28,105
105	Avnet Inc	AZ	$27,925
106	Tech Data Corp.	FL	$27,671
107	McDonald's Corp	IL	$27,441
108	Time Warner Inc	NY	$27,359
109	Travelers Companies Inc (The	NY	$26,800
110	Rite Aid Corp.	PA	$26,528
111	Teachers Insurance & Annuity	NY	$26,197
112	Qualcomm, Inc.	CA	$25,281
113	Du Pont (E.I.) de Nemours &	DE	$25,130
114	Gilead Sciences, Inc.	CA	$24,890
115	Baker Hughes Inc.	TX	$24,551
116	Altria Group Inc	VA	$24,522
117	EMC Corp. (MA)	MA	$24,440
118	Duke Energy Corp	NC	$23,925
119	Alcoa, Inc.	NY	$23,906
120	Capital One Financial Corp	VA	$23,869

Top 500 Companies by Sales in Hoover's MasterList of U.S. Companies 2016 (continued)

Rank	Company	Headquarters	Sales ($ bil)
121	Time Warner Cable Inc	NY	$23,697
122	Halliburton Company	TX	$23,633
123	International Paper Co	TN	$23,617
124	Northrop Grumman Corp	VA	$23,526
125	Arrow Electronics, Inc.	CO	$23,282
126	Raytheon Co.	MA	$23,247
127	AFLAC Inc.	GA	$22,728
128	MAKE CORPORATION	IL	$22,725
129	Burlington Northern & Santa F	TX	$22,714
130	Staples Inc	MA	$22,492
131	Emerson Electric Co.	MO	$22,304
132	Occidental Petroleum Corp	TX	$21,947
133	Union Pacific Corp	NE	$21,813
134	CANDID COLOR SYSTEMS INC.	OK	$21,742
135	Amgen Inc	CA	$21,662
136	Fluor Corp.	TX	$21,532
137	National Oilwell Varco Inc	TX	$21,440
138	Freeport-McMoRan Inc	AZ	$21,438
139	U.S. Bancorp (DE)	MN	$21,392
140	Nucor Corp.	NC	$21,105
141	Chesapeake Energy Corp.	OK	$20,951
142	Whirlpool Corp	MI	$20,891
143	AutoNation, Inc.	FL	$20,862
144	ManpowerGroup	WI	$20,763
145	Abbott Laboratories	IL	$20,247
146	AbbVie Inc.	IL	$19,960
147	Danaher Corp.	DC	$19,914
148	PBF Energy Inc	NJ	$19,828
149	Southwest Airlines Co	TX	$19,820
150	HollyFrontier Corp.	TX	$19,764
151	Lilly (Eli) & Co.	IN	$19,616
152	Devon Energy Corp.	OK	$19,566
153	Xerox Corp	CT	$19,540
154	Progressive Corp. (OH)	OH	$19,391
155	Starbucks Corp.	WA	$19,163
156	Icahn Enterprises LP	NY	$19,157
157	Paccar Inc.	WA	$19,115
158	Cummins, Inc.	IN	$19,110
159	Kohl's Corp.	WI	$19,023
160	Dollar General Corp	TN	$18,910
161	Community Health Systems, In	TN	$18,639
162	Hartford Financial Services	CT	$18,614
163	Kimberly-Clark Corp.	TX	$18,591
164	Southern Co.	GA	$18,467
165	Lear Corp.	MI	$18,211
166	Sunoco Logistics Partners L.	PA	$18,088
167	EOG Resources, Inc.	TX	$18,035
168	CenturyLink, Inc.	LA	$18,031
169	AECOM	CA	$17,990
170	Facebook, Inc.	CA	$17,928
171	Jabil Circuit, Inc.	FL	$17,899
172	Supervalu Inc.	MN	$17,820
173	General Mills, Inc.	MN	$17,630
174	United States Steel Corp.	PA	$17,507
175	Exelon Generation Co LLC	PA	$17,393
176	Colgate-Palmolive Co.	NY	$17,277
177	Global Partners LP	MA	$17,270
178	Murphy USA Inc	AR	$17,210
179	Penske Automotive Group Inc	MI	$17,177
180	AES Corp.	VA	$17,146
181	PG&E Corp. (Holding Co.)	CA	$17,090
182	NextEra Energy Inc	FL	$17,021
183	American Electric Power Co.,	OH	$17,020
184	Thermo Fisher Scientific Inc	MA	$16,890
185	VENTURE ELECTRICAL CONTRACTO	WI	$16,837
186	NGL Energy Partners LP	OK	$16,802
187	Baxter International Inc.	IL	$16,671
188	Tenet Healthcare Corp.	TX	$16,615
189	Centene Corp	MO	$16,560
190	Bristol-Myers Squibb Co.	NY	$16,560
191	Goodyear Tire & Rubber Co.	OH	$16,443
192	The Gap, Inc.	CA	$16,435
193	PNC Financial Services Group	PA	$16,281
194	Micron Technology Inc.	ID	$16,192
195	Office Depot, Inc.	FL	$16,096
196	Bank of New York Mellon Corp	NY	$16,046
197	NRG Energy Inc	NJ	$15,868
198	ConAgra Foods, Inc.	NE	$15,832
199	Whole Foods Market, Inc.	TX	$15,389
200	PPG Industries, Inc.	PA	$15,360
201	Genuine Parts Co.	GA	$15,342
202	Performance Food Group Co	VA	$15,270
203	Western Refining Inc	TX	$15,154
204	Omnicom Group, Inc.	NY	$15,134
205	FirstEnergy Corp.	OH	$15,026
206	Monsanto Co.	MO	$15,001
207	Land O' Lakes Inc	MN	$14,966
208	KAISER FOUNDATION HOSPITALS	CA	$14,795
209	Dish Network Corp	CO	$14,643
210	Las Vegas Sands Corp	NV	$14,584
211	Kellogg Co	MI	$14,580
212	Western Digital Corp.	CA	$14,572
213	Kinder Morgan Inc.	TX	$14,403
214	Aramark	PA	$14,329
215	Loews Corp.	NY	$14,325
216	Ecolab, Inc.	MN	$14,281
217	Carmax Inc.	VA	$14,269
218	Health Net, Inc.	CA	$14,009
219	Waste Management, Inc. (DE)	TX	$13,996
220	WellCare Health Plans Inc	FL	$13,890
221	CBS Corp	NY	$13,886
222	Visa Inc	CA	$13,880
223	Textron Inc.	RI	$13,878
224	Apache Corp.	TX	$13,851
225	Marriott International, Inc.	MD	$13,796
226	Lincoln National Corp.	PA	$13,554
227	Nordstrom, Inc.	WA	$13,506
228	Robinson (C.H.) Worldwide, I	MN	$13,470
229	Edison International	CA	$13,413
230	Illinois Tool Works, Inc.	IL	$13,405
231	Southern California Edison C	CA	$13,380
232	Synnex Corp	CA	$13,338
233	Viacom Inc	NY	$13,268
234	Yum! Brands, Inc.	KY	$13,105
235	Texas Instruments, Inc.	TX	$13,045
236	Marsh & McLennan Companies I	NY	$12,951
237	Consolidated Edison, Inc.	NY	$12,919
238	DaVita HealthCare Partners I	CO	$12,795
239	CST Brands Inc	TX	$12,758
240	Synchrony Financial	CT	$12,727

Top 500 Companies by Sales in
Hoover's MasterList of U.S. Companies 2016 (continued)

Rank	Company	Headquarters	Sales ($ bil)	Rank	Company	Headquarters	Sales ($ bil)
241	Parker Hannifin Corp.	OH	$12,712	301	Becton, Dickinson & Co.	NJ	$10,282
242	Entergy Corp. (New)	LA	$12,495	302	Core Mark Holding Co Inc	CA	$10,280
243	Dominion Resources Inc	VA	$12,436	303	Cognizant Technology Solutio	NJ	$10,263
244	VF Corp.	NC	$12,282	304	AutoZone, Inc.	TN	$10,187
245	Praxair, Inc.	CT	$12,273	305	Navistar International Corp.	IL	$10,140
246	Ameriprise Financial Inc	MN	$12,268	306	MGM Resorts International	NV	$10,082
247	Penney (J.C.) Co.,Inc. (Hold	TX	$12,257	307	HOVENSA LLC	VI	$10,048
248	Oneok Inc.	OK	$12,195	308	Grainger (W.W.), Inc.	IL	$9,965
249	ONEOK Partners LP	OK	$12,192	309	Stryker Corp.	MI	$9,946
250	Computer Sciences Corp.	VA	$12,173	310	Group 1 Automotive, Inc.	TX	$9,938
251	L-3 Communications Holdings,	NY	$12,124	311	BB&T Corp.	NC	$9,926
252	Jacobs Engineering Group, In	CA	$12,115	312	Air Products & Chemicals, In	PA	$9,895
253	CDW Corp	IL	$12,075	313	Advance Auto Parts Inc	VA	$9,844
254	Principal Financial Group, I	IA	$11,964	314	Charter Communications Inc	CT	$9,754
255	Santander Holdings USA Inc.	MA	$11,919	315	AGCO Corp.	GA	$9,724
256	Bed, Bath & Beyond, Inc.	NJ	$11,881	316	CNA Financial Corp.	IL	$9,692
257	CSX Corp	FL	$11,811	317	MasterCard Inc	NY	$9,667
258	Federal Reserve Bank of San F	CA	$11,704	318	Ally Financial Inc	MI	$9,667
259	Xcel Energy, Inc.	MN	$11,686	319	Molina Healthcare Inc	CA	$9,667
260	Donnelley (R. R.) & Sons Co.	IL	$11,603	320	Applied Materials, Inc.	CA	$9,659
261	PPL Corp	PA	$11,499	321	Discover Financial Services	IL	$9,611
262	Leucadia National Corp.	NY	$11,486	322	Genworth Financial, Inc. (Ho	VA	$9,565
263	WAKEFERN FOOD CORP.	NJ	$11,456	323	Eastman Chemical Co.	TN	$9,527
264	L Brands, Inc	OH	$11,454	324	Dean Foods Co.	TX	$9,503
265	Hess Corp	NY	$11,439	325	Lennar Corp.	FL	$9,474
266	Florida Power & Light Co.	FL	$11,421	326	Owens & Minor, Inc. (New)	VA	$9,440
267	WestRock Co	VA	$11,381	327	GameStop Corp	TX	$9,296
268	Stanley Black & Decker Inc	CT	$11,339	328	Hormel Foods Corp.	MN	$9,264
269	TRAMMO INC.	NY	$11,315	329	Celgene Corp.	NJ	$9,256
270	Marathon Oil Corp.	TX	$11,258	330	PayPal Holdings Inc	CA	$9,248
271	First Data Corp (New)	NY	$11,152	331	Autoliv Inc.		$9,241
272	Sherwin-Williams Co.	OH	$11,130	332	CenterPoint Energy, Inc	TX	$9,226
273	BlackRock, Inc.	NY	$11,081	333	Priceline Group Inc. (The)	CT	$9,224
274	Voya Financial Inc	NY	$11,071	334	Sonic Automotive, Inc.	NC	$9,197
275	Hertz Global Holdings Inc	FL	$11,046	335	Toyota Motor Credit Corp.	CA	$9,142
276	Ross Stores, Inc.	CA	$11,042	336	Republic Services, Inc.	AZ	$9,115
277	Sempra Energy	CA	$11,035	337	Corning, Inc.	NY	$9,111
278	Tennessee Valley Authority	TN	$11,003	338	CVR Energy Inc	TX	$9,110
279	Automatic Data Processing In	NJ	$10,939	339	Crown Holdings Inc	PA	$9,097
280	Reinsurance Group of America	MO	$10,904	340	U.S. VENTURE INC.	WI	$9,089
281	Public Service Enterprise Gr	NJ	$10,886	341	Mosaic Co. (The)	MN	$9,056
282	Horton (D.R.) Inc.	TX	$10,824	342	CBRE Group Inc	CA	$9,050
283	Consolidated Edison Co. of N	NY	$10,786	343	Georgia Power Co.	GA	$8,988
284	Lauder (Estee) Cos., Inc. (T	NY	$10,780	344	HD Supply Holdings Inc	GA	$8,882
285	Biogen Inc	MA	$10,764	345	Avon Products, Inc.	NY	$8,851
286	State Street Corp.	MA	$10,687	346	Qwest Corp	LA	$8,838
287	Reynolds American Inc	NC	$10,675	347	CVR Refining, LP	TX	$8,830
288	Schein (Henry), Inc.	NY	$10,630	348	THE PRIDDY FOUNDATION	TX	$8,792
289	Norfolk Southern Corp.	VA	$10,511	349	Cameron International Corp	TX	$8,782
290	Unum Group	TN	$10,510	350	Steel Dynamics Inc.	IN	$8,756
291	Hilton Worldwide Holdings In	VA	$10,502	351	Suntrust Banks, Inc.	GA	$8,707
292	Liberty Interactive Corp	CO	$10,499	352	Anadarko Petroleum Corp	TX	$8,698
293	Reliance Steel & Aluminum Co	CA	$10,452	353	News Corp (New)	NY	$8,633
294	ALLEGIS GROUP INC.	MD	$10,440	354	Targa Resources Corp	TX	$8,617
295	Univar Inc	IL	$10,374	355	Dollar Tree, Inc.	VA	$8,602
296	GROWMARK INC.	IL	$10,372	356	eBay Inc.	CA	$8,592
297	DTE Energy Co.	MI	$10,337	357	Pilgrims Pride Corp.	CO	$8,583
298	Assurant Inc	NY	$10,325	358	Caesars Entertainment Corp	NV	$8,516
299	TENASKA MARKETING VENTURES	NE	$10,310	359	Avis Budget Group Inc	NJ	$8,485
300	Huntsman Corp	UT	$10,299	360	Tenneco Inc	IL	$8,420

Top 500 Companies by Sales in
Hoover's MasterList of U.S. Companies 2016 (continued)

Rank	Company	Headquarters	Sales ($ bil)	Rank	Company	Headquarters	Sales ($ bil)
361	ASSOCIATED WHOLESALE GROCERS	KS	$8,380	421	LKQ Corp	IL	$6,740
362	Delek US Holdings Inc	TN	$8,324	422	UGI Corp.	PA	$6,691
363	Jarden Corp	FL	$8,287	423	Expedia Inc	WA	$6,672
364	PVH Corp	NY	$8,241	424	Spirit AeroSystems Holdings	KS	$6,644
365	United Natural Foods Inc.	RI	$8,185	425	Buckeye Partners, L.P.	TX	$6,620
366	Campbell Soup Co.	NJ	$8,082	426	Dana Holding Corp	OH	$6,617
367	Universal Health Services, I	PA	$8,065	427	NCR Corp.	GA	$6,591
368	Fidelity National Financial	FL	$8,024	428	Ryder System, Inc.	FL	$6,572
369	BorgWarner Inc	MI	$8,023	429	Expeditors International of	WA	$6,565
370	HY-VEE INC.	IA	$8,014	430	Symantec Corp.	CA	$6,508
371	Ball Corp	CO	$7,997	431	AK Steel Holding Corp.	OH	$6,506
372	Enbridge Energy Partners, L.	TX	$7,965	432	Fifth Third Bancorp (Cincinn	OH	$6,504
373	Franklin Resources, Inc.	CA	$7,949	433	Seaboard Corp.	KS	$6,473
374	FMC Technologies, Inc.	TX	$7,943	434	Calpine Corp	TX	$6,472
375	SpartanNash Co.	MI	$7,916	435	NiSource Inc. (Holding Co.)	IN	$6,471
376	Wesco International, Inc.	PA	$7,890	436	Cablevision Systems Corp.	NY	$6,461
377	Quanta Services, Inc.	TX	$7,851	437	CMS Energy Corp	MI	$6,456
378	Mohawk Industries, Inc.	GA	$7,803	438	Anixter International Inc	IL	$6,446
379	TravelCenters of America LLC	OH	$7,779	439	Chemours Co (The)	DE	$6,432
380	Casey's General Stores, Inc.	IA	$7,767	440	EMCOR Group, Inc.	CT	$6,425
381	Sealed Air Corp.	NC	$7,751	441	Fidelity National Informatio	FL	$6,414
382	Eversource Energy	MA	$7,742	442	Sanmina Corp	CA	$6,375
383	CFJ PROPERTIES LLC	TN	$7,672	443	CenterPoint Energy Resources	TX	$6,367
384	Williams Cos Inc (The)	OK	$7,637	444	KBR Inc	TX	$6,366
385	Ralph Lauren Corp	NY	$7,620	445	Avery Dennison Corp.	CA	$6,330
386	Virginia Electric & Power Co	VA	$7,579	446	iHeartMedia Inc	TX	$6,319
387	ZEN-NOH GRAIN CORPORATION	LA	$7,550	447	Rockwell Automation, Inc.	WI	$6,308
388	Interpublic Group of Compani	NY	$7,537	448	Discovery Communications, In	MD	$6,265
389	Visteon Corp.	MI	$7,509	449	Harley-Davidson Inc	WI	$6,229
390	Blackstone Group LP	NY	$7,485	450	Trinity Industries, Inc.	TX	$6,170
391	Quest Diagnostics, Inc.	NJ	$7,435	451	Hunt (J.B.) Transport Servic	AR	$6,165
392	Hershey Company (The)	PA	$7,422	452	Consumers Energy Co.	MI	$6,165
393	Veritiv Corp	GA	$7,407	453	Owens-Illinois, Inc.	OH	$6,156
394	Weyerhaeuser Co	WA	$7,403	454	Harman International Industr	CT	$6,155
395	Boston Scientific Corp.	MA	$7,380	455	Federal Reserve Bank of Richm	VA	$6,148
396	Duke Energy Carolinas LLC	NC	$7,351	456	Santander Consumer USA Holdi	TX	$6,127
397	Federal-Mogul Holdings Corp	MI	$7,317	457	Erie Indemnity Co.	PA	$6,124
398	Terex Corp. (New)	CT	$7,309	458	Netapp Inc	CA	$6,123
399	Newmont Mining Corp. (Holdin	CO	$7,292	459	Dr Pepper Snapple Group Inc	TX	$6,121
400	CGB ENTERPRISES INC.	LA	$7,228	460	Oshkosh Corp (New)	WI	$6,098
401	O'Reilly Automotive, Inc.	MO	$7,216	461	A-Mark Precious Metals, Inc	CA	$6,070
402	Foot Locker, Inc.	NY	$7,151	462	Barnes & Noble Inc	NY	$6,069
403	Masco Corp.	MI	$7,142	463	Schwab (Charles) Corp.	CA	$6,058
404	Berkley (W. R.) Corp.	CT	$7,129	464	Ameren Corp.	MO	$6,053
405	CONSOLIDATED GRAIN & BARGE	IL	$7,093	465	VMware Inc	CA	$6,035
406	Pacific Mutual Holding Compa	CA	$7,073	466	Constellation Brands Inc	NY	$6,028
407	Coca-Cola Enterprises Inc	GA	$7,011	467	Mattel Inc	CA	$6,024
408	Huntington Ingalls Industrie	VA	$6,957	468	Laboratory Corporation of Am	NC	$6,012
409	Dover Corp	IL	$6,956	469	Tegna Inc	VA	$6,008
410	MetLife Insurance Company of	NC	$6,903	470	Commercial Metals Co.	TX	$5,989
411	Live Nation Entertainment, I	CA	$6,867	471	Starwood Hotels & Resorts Wo	CT	$5,983
412	Federal Reserve Bank Of Atlan	GA	$6,861	472	PulteGroup, Inc.	GA	$5,982
413	Dick's Sporting Goods, Inc	PA	$6,814	473	General Cable Corp. (DE)	KY	$5,980
414	Peabody Energy Corp	MO	$6,792	474	Graybar Electric Co., Inc.	MO	$5,979
415	Dillard's Inc.	AR	$6,780	475	Energy Future Holdings Corp	TX	$5,978
416	Netflix Inc.	CA	$6,780	476	Baxalta Inc	IL	$5,952
417	Alon USA Energy Inc	TX	$6,779	477	Alabama Power Co.	AL	$5,942
418	Level 3 Communications, Inc.	CO	$6,777	478	MRC Global Inc	TX	$5,933
419	Darden Restaurants, Inc. (Un	FL	$6,764	479	Spectra Energy Corp	TX	$5,903
420	MORTGAGE INVESTORS CORPORAT	FL	$6,746	480	Midcoast Energy Partners LP	TX	$5,894

Top 500 Companies by Sales in Hoover's MasterList of U.S. Companies 2016 (continued)

Rank	Company	Headquarters	Sales ($ bil)
481	Motorola Solutions Inc.	IL	$5,881
482	Asbury Automotive Group, Inc	GA	$5,868
483	Packaging Corp of America	IL	$5,853
484	Windstream Holdings Inc	AR	$5,830
485	United Rentals, Inc.	CT	$5,817
486	JetBlue Airways Corp	NY	$5,817
487	HRG Group Inc	NY	$5,816
488	Calumet Specialty Product Pa	IN	$5,791
489	Southern Copper Corp	AZ	$5,788
490	Quintiles Transnational Hold	NC	$5,738
491	HanesBrands Inc	NC	$5,732
492	Newell Rubbermaid, Inc.	GA	$5,727
493	American Financial Group Inc	OH	$5,713
494	Tractor Supply Co.	TN	$5,712
495	Smucker (J.M.) Co.	OH	$5,693
496	Celanese Corp (DE)	TX	$5,674
497	Regions Financial Corp	AL	$5,674
498	HILL/AHERN FIRE PROTECTION LLC	IL	$5,669
499	Ingredion Inc	IL	$5,668
500	Clorox Co (The)	CA	$5,655

Top 500 Companies by Employees in Hoover's MasterList of U.S. Companies 2016

Rank	Company	Headquarters	Employees
1	Wal-Mart Stores, Inc.	AR	2,200,000
2	Kelly Services, Inc.	MI	563,300
3	Yum! Brands, Inc.	KY	505,000
4	United Parcel Service Inc	GA	435,000
5	McDonald's Corp	IL	420,000
6	Kroger Co (The)	OH	400,000
7	International Business Machi	NY	379,592
8	Home Depot Inc	GA	371,000
9	Walgreens Boots Alliance Inc	IL	360,000
10	Target Corp	MN	347,000
11	Berkshire Hathaway Inc.	NE	316,000
12	General Electric Co	CT	305,000
13	HP Inc	CA	287,000
14	Lowe's Companies Inc	NC	266,000
15	Aramark	PA	265,500
16	Wells Fargo & Co.	CA	264,500
17	Pepsico Inc.	NY	263,000
18	AT&T Inc	TX	253,000
19	CVS Health Corp	RI	243,000
20	JPMorgan Chase & Co	NY	241,359
21	Citigroup Inc	NY	241,000
22	Hewlett Packard Enterprise C	CA	240,000
23	Starbucks Corp.	WA	238,000
24	Amazon.com Inc.	WA	230,800
25	HCA Holdings Inc	TN	225,000
26	Robert Half International In	CA	225,000
27	Bank of America Corp.	NC	224,000
28	General Motors Co.	MI	215,000
29	Cognizant Technology Solutio	NJ	211,500
30	Costco Wholesale Corp	WA	205,000
31	UnitedHealth Group Inc	MN	200,000
32	Ford Motor Co. (DE)	MI	199,000
33	TJX Companies, Inc.	MA	198,000
34	United Technologies Corp	CT	197,200
35	Sears Holdings Corp	IL	196,000
36	Disney (Walt) Co. (The)	CA	185,000
37	Starwood Hotels & Resorts Wo	CT	180,400
38	Verizon Communications Inc	NY	177,300
39	KAISER FOUNDATION HOSPITALS	CA	175,668
40	Publix Super Markets, Inc.	FL	175,000
41	Community Health Systems, In	TN	167,000
42	Macy's Inc	NY	166,900
43	FedEx Corp	TN	166,000
44	Boeing Co.	IL	161,400
45	Jabil Circuit, Inc.	FL	161,000
46	Hilton Worldwide Holdings In	VA	157,000
47	Corporate Resource Services	NY	150,800
48	Darden Restaurants, Inc. (Un	FL	150,000
49	Xerox Corp	CT	147,500
50	Comcast Corp	PA	141,000
51	The Gap, Inc.	CA	141,000
52	Johnson Controls Inc	WI	139,000
53	Kohl's Corp.	WI	137,000
54	Lear Corp.	MI	136,200
55	Oracle Corp.	CA	132,000
56	Coca-Cola Co (The)	GA	129,200
57	Honeywell International Inc	NJ	129,000
58	Johnson & Johnson	NJ	126,500
59	Best Buy Inc	MN	125,000
60	Convergys Corp.	OH	125,000
61	Marriott International, Inc.	MD	123,500
62	ABM Industries, Inc.	NY	120,000
63	Microsoft Corporation	WA	118,000
64	Penney (J.C.) Co.,Inc. (Hold	TX	114,000
65	American Airlines Group Inc	TX	113,300
66	Tyson Foods, Inc.	AR	113,000
67	Lockheed Martin Corp.	MD	112,000
68	Emerson Electric Co.	MO	110,800
69	Apple Inc	CA	110,000
70	Procter & Gamble Co	OH	110,000
71	Tenet Healthcare Corp.	TX	108,989
72	Intel Corp	CA	107,300
73	Caterpillar Inc.	IL	105,700
74	Dollar General Corp	TN	105,500
75	Mondelez International Inc	IL	104,000
76	Bloomin' Brands Inc.	FL	100,000
77	DAKOTA ELECTRIC ASSOCIATION	MN	100,000
78	General Dynamics Corp.	VA	99,900
79	Whirlpool Corp	MI	97,000
80	Barrett Business Services, I	WA	93,040
81	AECOM	CA	92,000
82	Whole Foods Market, Inc.	TX	90,900
83	Dollar Tree, Inc.	VA	90,000
84	3M Co	MN	89,446
85	Rite Aid Corp.	PA	89,000
86	ALLEGIS GROUP INC.	MD	85,000
87	United Continental Holdings	IL	84,000
88	Delta Air Lines, Inc. (DE)	GA	83,000
89	Philip Morris International	NY	82,500
90	Brookdale Senior Living Inc	TN	81,300
91	AutoZone, Inc.	TN	81,000
92	L Brands, Inc	OH	80,100
93	Staples Inc	MA	79,075
94	Pfizer Inc	NY	78,300
95	Abbott Laboratories	IL	77,000
96	Western Digital Corp.	CA	76,449
97	Exxon Mobil Corp.	TX	75,300
98	Omnicom Group, Inc.	NY	74,900
99	Advance Auto Parts Inc	VA	73,000
100	GameStop Corp	TX	73,000
101	Synnex Corp	CA	72,500
102	Cracker Barrel Old Country S	TN	72,000
103	Cisco Systems, Inc.	CA	71,833
104	Ross Stores, Inc.	CA	71,400
105	Danaher Corp.	DC	71,000
106	McKesson Corp.	CA	70,400
107	Merck & Co., Inc	NJ	70,000
108	EMC Corp. (MA)	MA	70,000
109	Computer Sciences Corp.	VA	70,000
110	Universal Health Services, I	PA	68,700
111	MGM Resorts International	NV	68,100
112	MetLife Inc	NY	68,000
113	Donnelley (R. R.) & Sons Co.	IL	68,000
114	Caesars Entertainment Corp	NV	68,000
115	O'Reilly Automotive, Inc.	MO	67,926
116	Nordstrom, Inc.	WA	67,000
117	U.S. Bancorp (DE)	MN	66,750
118	Icahn Enterprises LP	NY	66,559
119	Baxter International Inc.	IL	66,000
120	Goodyear Tire & Rubber Co.	OH	66,000

Top 500 Companies by Employees in Hoover's MasterList of U.S. Companies 2016 (continued)

Rank	Company	Headquarters	Employees	Rank	Company	Headquarters	Employees
121	HanesBrands Inc	NC	65,300	181	Interpublic Group of Compani	NY	47,400
122	American International Group	NY	65,000	182	Regis Corp.	MN	47,000
123	Halliburton Company	TX	65,000	183	Capital One Financial Corp	VA	46,000
124	Northrop Grumman Corp	VA	65,000	184	TeleTech Holdings, Inc.	CO	46,000
125	Chevron Corporation	CA	64,700	185	Panera Bread Co.	MO	45,400
126	Brinks Co (The)	VA	64,100	186	Marathon Petroleum Corp.	OH	45,340
127	Jacobs Engineering Group, In	CA	64,000	187	T-Mobile US Inc	WA	45,000
128	National Oilwell Varco Inc	TX	63,642	188	CenturyLink, Inc.	LA	45,000
129	Abercrombie & Fitch Co.	OH	63,000	189	L-3 Communications Holdings,	NY	45,000
130	NIKE Inc	OR	62,600	190	Quest Diagnostics, Inc.	NJ	45,000
131	Baker Hughes Inc.	TX	62,000	191	Hyatt Hotels Corp	IL	45,000
132	HY-VEE INC.	IA	62,000	192	Foot Locker, Inc.	NY	44,568
133	Alphabet Inc	CA	61,814	193	PPG Industries, Inc.	PA	44,400
134	Kindred Healthcare Inc	KY	61,500	194	Cedar Fair LP	OH	44,100
135	Raytheon Co.	MA	61,000	195	Lauder (Estee) Cos., Inc. (T	NY	44,000
136	Bed, Bath & Beyond, Inc.	NJ	60,000	196	Sanmina Corp	CA	43,854
137	Autoliv Inc.		60,000	197	Texas Roadhouse Inc	KY	43,300
138	THE SALVATION ARMY NATIONAL	VA	60,000	198	Kimberly-Clark Corp.	TX	43,000
139	Chipotle Mexican Grill Inc	CO	59,330	199	General Mills, Inc.	MN	42,000
140	Alcoa, Inc.	NY	59,000	200	WestRock Co	VA	41,400
141	VF Corp.	NC	59,000	201	Barnes & Noble Inc	NY	41,000
142	Jones Lang LaSalle Inc	IL	58,100	202	Six Flags Entertainment Corp	TX	40,900
143	International Paper Co	TN	58,000	203	Allstate Corp.	IL	40,200
144	DaVita HealthCare Partners I	CO	57,900	204	Dillard's Inc.	AR	40,000
145	Deere & Co.	IL	57,200	205	Fidelity National Informatio	FL	40,000
146	Humana, Inc.	KY	57,000	206	LifePoint Health Inc	TN	40,000
147	Marsh & McLennan Companies I	NY	57,000	207	Waste Management, Inc. (DE)	TX	39,800
148	Fidelity National Financial	FL	56,883	208	Sherwin-Williams Co.	OH	39,674
149	Time Warner Cable Inc	NY	56,600	209	Lilly (Eli) & Co.	IN	39,135
150	Office Depot, Inc.	FL	56,000	210	Genuine Parts Co.	GA	39,000
151	Morgan Stanley	NY	55,802	211	Supervalu Inc.	MN	38,500
152	Cummins, Inc.	IN	55,200	212	Huntington Ingalls Industrie	VA	38,000
153	Automatic Data Processing In	NJ	55,000	213	American Eagle Outfitters, I	PA	38,000
154	Parker Hannifin Corp.	OH	54,754	214	Colgate-Palmolive Co.	NY	37,700
155	American Express Co.	NY	54,000	215	Wyndham Worldwide Corp	NJ	37,700
156	PNC Financial Services Group	PA	53,587	216	Dick's Sporting Goods, Inc	PA	37,600
157	Brinker International, Inc.	TX	53,000	217	Fluor Corp.	TX	37,508
158	Du Pont (E.I.) de Nemours &	DE	52,000	218	On Assignment, Inc.	CA	37,500
159	CBRE Group Inc	CA	52,000	219	Cigna Corp	CT	37,200
160	Sysco Corp.	TX	51,700	220	Buffalo Wild Wings Inc	MN	37,200
161	Anthem Inc	IN	51,500	221	Quintiles Transnational Hold	NC	36,100
162	Thermo Fisher Scientific Inc	MA	51,000	222	Big Lots, Inc.	OH	36,100
163	Michaels Companies Inc	TX	51,000	223	Laboratory Corporation of Am	NC	36,000
164	Amphenol Corp.	CT	50,700	224	Corning, Inc.	NY	35,700
165	Sykes Enterprises, Inc.	FL	50,450	225	Cheesecake Factory Inc. (The	CA	35,700
166	Stanley Black & Decker Inc	CT	50,400	226	Freeport-McMoRan Inc	AZ	35,000
167	RMR Group Inc (The)	MA	50,400	227	Pilgrims Pride Corp.	CO	35,000
168	Bank of New York Mellon Corp	NY	50,300	228	BANNER HEALTH	AZ	35,000
169	Southwest Airlines Co	TX	49,583	229	MAXIM HEALTHCARE SERVICES INC.	MD	35,000
170	Becton, Dickinson & Co.	NJ	49,517	230	Cardinal Health, Inc.	OH	34,500
171	Dow Chemical Co.	MI	49,500	231	PVH Corp	NY	34,100
172	Aetna Inc.	CT	48,800	232	Goldman Sachs Group, Inc.	NY	34,000
173	Federal-Mogul Holdings Corp	MI	48,600	233	Textron Inc.	RI	34,000
174	Las Vegas Sands Corp	NV	48,500	234	Burlington Stores Inc	NJ	34,000
175	Prudential Financial, Inc.	NJ	48,331	235	Apollo Education Group, Inc.	AZ	34,000
176	Burlington Northern & Santa F	TX	48,000	236	Archer Daniels Midland Co.	IL	33,900
177	Illinois Tool Works, Inc.	IL	48,000	237	Envision Healthcare Holdings	CO	33,748
178	Ascena Retail Group Inc	NJ	48,000	238	BB&T Corp.	NC	33,400
179	Union Pacific Corp	NE	47,457	239	Avon Products, Inc.	NY	33,200
180	Ecolab, Inc.	MN	47,430	240	Ryder System, Inc.	FL	33,100

Top 500 Companies by Employees in Hoover's MasterList of U.S. Companies 2016 (continued)

Rank	Company	Headquarters	Employees
241	Qualcomm, Inc.	CA	33,000
242	Hertz Global Holdings Inc	FL	33,000
243	Republic Services, Inc.	AZ	33,000
244	Jarden Corp	FL	33,000
245	YRC Worldwide Inc	KS	33,000
246	ConAgra Foods, Inc.	NE	32,900
247	Bob Evans Farms, Inc.	OH	32,341
248	Mohawk Industries, Inc.	GA	32,300
249	Command Center, Inc.	ID	32,210
250	Ruby Tuesday, Inc.	TN	32,100
251	Cintas Corp.	OH	32,000
252	HEARTLAND HEALTH	MO	32,000
253	UNIVERSITY OF WISCONSIN SYS	WI	31,992
254	Micron Technology Inc.	ID	31,800
255	Casey's General Stores, Inc.	IA	31,766
256	Select Medical Holdings Corp	PA	31,400
257	Tegna Inc	VA	31,250
258	Wendy's Co (The)	OH	31,200
259	Texas Instruments, Inc.	TX	31,003
260	Sprint Corp (New)	KS	31,000
261	Mattel Inc	CA	31,000
262	Travelers Companies Inc (The	NY	30,900
263	Norfolk Southern Corp.	VA	30,456
264	NCR Corp.	GA	30,200
265	Avis Budget Group Inc	NJ	30,000
266	BorgWarner Inc	MI	30,000
267	UNIVERSITY HOSPITALS HEALTH S	OH	30,000
268	State Street Corp.	MA	29,970
269	Kellogg Co	MI	29,790
270	Exelon Corp.	IL	29,762
271	LKQ Corp	IL	29,500
272	CSX Corp	FL	29,000
273	Tenneco Inc	IL	29,000
274	LIFE CARE CENTERS OF AMERICA IN	TN	29,000
275	Duke Energy Corp	NC	28,344
276	Sally Beauty Holdings Inc	TX	28,330
277	NYSARC INC.	NY	28,000
278	Praxair, Inc.	CT	27,780
279	Energy Transfer Equity L P	TX	27,605
280	Red Robin Gourmet Burgers In	CO	27,543
281	Volt Information Sciences, I	NY	27,400
282	Genesco Inc.	TN	27,325
283	UNIVERSITY OF WASHINGTON INC	WA	27,228
284	Civitas Solutions Inc	MA	27,100
285	Stryker Corp.	MI	27,000
286	EMCOR Group, Inc.	CT	27,000
287	Owens-Illinois, Inc.	OH	27,000
288	Cooper-Standard Holdings, In	MI	27,000
289	Universal Corp.	VA	27,000
290	PROGRESS WEST HEALTHCARE CEN	MO	27,000
291	Williams Sonoma Inc	CA	26,800
292	Progressive Corp. (OH)	OH	26,501
293	ALLINA HEALTH SYSTEM	MN	26,400
294	Southern Co.	GA	26,369
295	Tailored Brands Inc	TX	26,100
296	AutoNation, Inc.	FL	26,000
297	ManpowerGroup	WI	26,000
298	AbbVie Inc.	IL	26,000
299	Dover Corp	IL	26,000
300	CH2M HILL COMPANIES LTD.	CO	26,000
301	OREGON UNIVERSITY SYSTEM	OR	26,000
302	Express Scripts Holding Co	MO	25,900
303	Energy Transfer Partners LP	TX	25,682
304	Time Warner Inc	NY	25,600
305	Monsanto Co.	MO	25,500
306	Visteon Corp.	MI	25,500
307	AMERCO	NV	25,400
308	Bright Horizons Family Solut	MA	25,400
309	Bon-Ton Stores Inc	PA	25,200
310	Bristol-Myers Squibb Co.	NY	25,000
311	News Corp (New)	NY	25,000
312	Ralph Lauren Corp	NY	25,000
313	Masco Corp.	MI	25,000
314	KBR Inc	TX	25,000
315	Avery Dennison Corp.	CA	25,000
316	CH2M Hill Companies Ltd	CO	25,000
317	Ingles Markets, Inc.	NC	25,000
318	Five Star Quality Care Inc	MA	25,000
319	SCHOOL BOARD OF ORANGE COUN	FL	25,000
320	CHRISTUS HEALTH	TX	25,000
321	Suntrust Banks, Inc.	GA	24,638
322	Quanta Services, Inc.	TX	24,600
323	Syntel Inc.	MI	24,553
324	ON Semiconductor Corp	AZ	24,500
325	Cinemark USA, Inc.	TX	24,500
326	Cinemark Holdings Inc	TX	24,500
327	Harman International Industr	CT	24,197
328	BG Staffing Inc	TX	24,170
329	Quad/Graphics, Inc.	WI	24,100
330	Regal Beloit Corp	WI	24,100
331	HealthSouth Corp	AL	24,100
332	SP Plus Corp	IL	24,030
333	Sealed Air Corp.	NC	24,000
334	Boston Scientific Corp.	MA	24,000
335	Urban Outfitters, Inc.	PA	24,000
336	Pier 1 Imports, Inc	TX	24,000
337	Regions Financial Corp	AL	23,916
338	Biglari Holdings Inc.	TX	23,851
339	Charter Communications Inc	CT	23,800
340	Chico's FAS Inc	FL	23,800
341	Service Corp. International	TX	23,662
342	Nucor Corp.	NC	23,600
343	Grainger (W.W.), Inc.	IL	23,600
344	Unisys Corp.	PA	23,200
345	Regal Entertainment Group	TN	23,168
346	Paccar Inc.	WA	23,000
347	United States Steel Corp.	PA	23,000
348	First Data Corp (New)	NY	23,000
349	Crown Holdings Inc	PA	23,000
350	Qwest Corp	LA	23,000
351	Cameron International Corp	TX	23,000
352	INTERMOUNTAIN HEALTH CARE INC	UT	23,000
353	HENRY FORD HEALTH SYSTEM	MI	23,000
354	ExlService Holdings Inc	NY	22,800
355	Dana Holding Corp	OH	22,600
356	Vishay Intertechnology, Inc.	PA	22,600
357	PG&E Corp. (Holding Co.)	CA	22,581
358	Rockwell Automation, Inc.	WI	22,500
359	Booz Allen Hamilton Holding	VA	22,500
360	Hershey Company (The)	PA	22,450

Top 500 Companies by Employees in Hoover's MasterList of U.S. Companies 2016 (continued)

Rank	Company	Headquarters	Employees	Rank	Company	Headquarters	Employees
361	Ulta Salon Cosmetics & Fragr	IL	22,400	421	American Electric Power Co.,	OH	18,529
362	TravelCenters of America LLC	OH	22,330	422	Arrow Electronics, Inc.	CO	18,500
363	Harris Corp.	FL	22,300	423	AES Corp.	VA	18,500
364	Rent-A-Center Inc.	TX	22,200	424	SkyWest Inc.	UT	18,500
365	Penske Automotive Group Inc	MI	22,100	425	Fifth Third Bancorp (Cincin	OH	18,351
366	Carmax Inc.	VA	22,064	426	Citizens Financial Group Inc	RI	18,310
367	SENTARA HEALTHCARE	VA	22,000	427	Boyd Gaming Corp.	NV	18,290
368	Trinity Industries, Inc.	TX	21,950	428	Weis Markets, Inc.	PA	18,200
369	Amkor Technology Inc.	AZ	21,900	429	ESSENTIA HEALTH	MN	18,177
370	THE GOLUB CORPORATION	NY	21,741	430	Addus HomeCare Corp	IL	18,054
371	Ingram Micro Inc.	CA	21,700	431	Party City Holdco Inc	NY	18,027
372	Papa John's International, I	KY	21,700	432	VMware Inc	CA	18,000
373	Vail Resorts Inc.	CO	21,613	433	Flowserve Corp.	TX	18,000
374	Gallagher (Arthur J.) & Co.	IL	21,500	434	Fortune Brands Home & Securi	IL	18,000
375	ST. JOSEPH HEALTH SYSTEM	CA	21,500	435	Express, Inc.	OH	18,000
376	Swift Transportation Co	AZ	21,274	436	FAIRVIEW HEALTH SERVICES	MN	18,000
377	Tractor Supply Co.	TN	21,100	437	PRINCE GEORGE"S COUNTY PUBLIC	MD	18,000
378	Aeropostale Inc	NY	21,007	438	WHEATON FRANCISCAN SERVICES.	IL	18,000
379	Fiserv, Inc.	WI	21,000	439	OCEAN BEAUTY SEAFOODS LLC	WA	18,000
380	Weight Watchers Internationa	NY	21,000	440	Amgen Inc	CA	17,900
381	AGCO Corp.	GA	20,800	441	UNIVERSITY OF GEORGIA	GA	17,800
382	Sonoco Products Co.	SC	20,800	442	Loews Corp.	NY	17,510
383	Education Management Corp	PA	20,800	443	AmerisourceBergen Corp.	PA	17,500
384	Fastenal Co.	MN	20,746	444	Hartford Financial Services	CT	17,500
385	Hormel Foods Corp.	MN	20,700	445	Molson Coors Brewing Co.	Quebec	17,500
386	Jack in the Box, Inc.	CA	20,700	446	Geo Group Inc (The) (New)	FL	17,479
387	DST Systems Inc. (DE)	MO	20,525	447	Newell Rubbermaid, Inc.	GA	17,400
388	Twenty-First Century Fox Inc	NY	20,500	448	Frontier Communications Corp	CT	17,400
389	Terex Corp. (New)	CT	20,400	449	PPL Corp	PA	17,391
390	McGraw Hill Financial, Inc.	NY	20,400	450	Dean Foods Co.	TX	17,246
391	Carrols Restaurant Group Inc	NY	20,400	451	INDIANA UNIVERSITY HEALTH INC.	IN	17,242
392	FMC Technologies, Inc.	TX	20,300	452	Team Health Holdings Inc	TN	17,200
393	Hunt (J.B.) Transport Servic	AR	20,158	453	First American Financial Cor	CA	17,103
394	Liberty Interactive Corp	CO	20,078	454	ADT Corp	FL	17,100
395	Iron Mountain Inc (New)	MA	20,000	455	Sempra Energy	CA	17,046
396	STAFF FORCE INC.	TX	20,000	456	Airgas Inc.	PA	17,000
397	Air Products & Chemicals, In	PA	19,700	457	Bemis Co Inc	WI	17,000
398	AMC Entertainment Holdings I	KS	19,700	458	Sprouts Farmers Market Inc	AZ	17,000
399	Gannett Co Inc (New)	VA	19,600	459	MAXIMUS Inc.	VA	17,000
400	Rockwell Collins, Inc.	IA	19,500	460	WAKE COUNTY PUBLIC SCHOOL SY	NC	17,000
401	DeVry Education Group Inc	IL	19,404	461	SPECTRUM HEALTH SYSTEM	MI	16,996
402	Cabelas Inc	NE	19,300	462	ClubCorp Holdings Inc	TX	16,900
403	iHeartMedia Inc	TX	19,200	463	TTM Technologies Inc	CA	16,857
404	ConocoPhillips	TX	19,100	464	PayPal Holdings Inc	CA	16,800
405	Dish Network Corp	CO	19,000	465	Wynn Resorts Ltd	NV	16,800
406	Schein (Henry), Inc.	NY	19,000	466	Assurant Inc	NY	16,700
407	Symantec Corp.	CA	19,000	467	Penn National Gaming, Inc.	PA	16,650
408	Dr Pepper Snapple Group Inc	TX	19,000	468	CACI International Inc.	VA	16,650
409	Leidos Holdings Inc	VA	19,000	469	MEMORIAL HERMANN HEALTHCARE	TX	16,505
410	Leidos, Inc.	VA	19,000	470	GNC Holdings Inc	PA	16,500
411	Leggett & Platt, Inc.	MO	19,000	471	Ensign Group Inc	CA	16,494
412	BON SECOURS HEALTH SYSTEM INC	MD	19,000	472	Old Dominion Freight Line, I	NC	16,443
413	IOWA HEALTH SYSTEM	IA	18,923	473	CBS Corp	NY	16,260
414	Avnet Inc	AZ	18,800	474	THE SALVATION ARMY	GA	16,168
415	Expedia Inc	WA	18,730	475	UNIVERSITY OF SOUTH FLORIDA	FL	16,165
416	BJ's Restaurants Inc	CA	18,700	476	SpartanNash Co.	MI	16,100
417	Stericycle Inc.	IL	18,656	477	Baxalta Inc	IL	16,000
418	Campbell Soup Co.	NJ	18,600	478	St. Jude Medical, Inc.	MN	16,000
419	PAREXEL International Corp.	MA	18,600	479	Salesforce.Com Inc	CA	16,000
420	Ignite Restaurant Group Inc	TX	18,600	480	Berry Plastics Group Inc	IN	16,000

Top 500 Companies by Employees in Hoover's MasterList of U.S. Companies 2016 (continued)

Rank	Company	Headquarters	Employees
481	Timken Co. (The)	OH	16,000
482	Diebold, Inc.	OH	16,000
483	Children's Place, Inc. (The)	NJ	16,000
484	DEKALB COUNTY BOARD OF EDU	GA	16,000
485	HRG Group Inc	NY	15,922
486	Coach, Inc.	NY	15,800
487	Cerner Corp.	MO	15,800
488	M & T Bank Corp	NY	15,782
489	FirstEnergy Corp.	OH	15,781
490	MasTec Inc. (FL)	FL	15,550
491	Applied Materials, Inc.	CA	15,500
492	Priceline Group Inc. (The)	CT	15,500
493	Spectrum Brands Holdings Inc	WI	15,500
494	Acadia Healthcare Company In	TN	15,500
495	Northern Trust Corp.	IL	15,400
496	AMETEK, Inc.	PA	15,400
497	Hubbell Inc.	CT	15,400
498	JetBlue Airways Corp	NY	15,334
499	SolarCity Corp	CA	15,273
500	Ball Corp	CO	15,200

Top 500 Companies by Net Profit in Hoover's MasterList of U.S. Companies 2016

($Bil)

Rank	Company	Headquarters	Net Income	Rank	Company	Headquarters	Net Income
1	Apple Inc	CA	$53,394	60	Burlington Northern & Santa F	TX	$4,397
2	Exxon Mobil Corp.	TX	$32,520	61	Federal Reserve System	DC	$4,363
3	Wells Fargo & Co.	CA	$23,057	62	Walgreens Boots Alliance Inc	IL	$4,220
4	JPMorgan Chase & Co	NY	$21,762	63	PNC Financial Services Group	PA	$4,207
5	Berkshire Hathaway Inc.	NE	$19,872	64	Time Warner Inc	NY	$3,827
6	Chevron Corporation	CA	$19,241	65	MasterCard Inc	NY	$3,808
7	Wal-Mart Stores, Inc.	AR	$16,363	66	Facebook, Inc.	CA	$3,688
8	Alphabet Inc	CA	$16,348	67	Valero Energy Corp.	TX	$3,630
9	Johnson & Johnson	NJ	$16,323	68	Lockheed Martin Corp.	MD	$3,614
10	General Electric Co	CT	$15,233	69	Biogen Inc	MA	$3,547
11	Fannie Mae	DC	$14,208	70	Morgan Stanley	NY	$3,467
12	Microsoft Corporation	WA	$12,193	71	Travelers Companies Inc (The	NY	$3,439
13	Gilead Sciences, Inc.	CA	$12,101	72	BlackRock, Inc.	NY	$3,294
14	International Business Machi	NY	$12,022	73	NIKE Inc	OR	$3,273
15	Merck & Co., Inc	NJ	$11,920	74	Reynolds American Inc	NC	$3,253
16	Intel Corp	CA	$11,420	75	Marathon Oil Corp.	TX	$3,046
17	Oracle Corp.	CA	$9,938	76	United Parcel Service Inc	GA	$3,032
18	General Motors Co.	MI	$9,687	77	General Dynamics Corp.	VA	$2,965
19	Verizon Communications Inc	NY	$9,625	78	AFLAC Inc.	GA	$2,951
20	Pfizer Inc	NY	$9,135	79	EOG Resources, Inc.	TX	$2,915
21	Cisco Systems, Inc.	CA	$8,981	80	Micron Technology Inc.	ID	$2,899
22	Goldman Sachs Group, Inc.	NY	$8,477	81	American Airlines Group Inc	TX	$2,882
23	Disney (Walt) Co. (The)	CA	$8,382	82	Allstate Corp.	IL	$2,850
24	Twenty-First Century Fox Inc	NY	$8,306	83	Las Vegas Sands Corp	NV	$2,841
25	Comcast Corp	PA	$8,163	84	Enterprise Products Partners	TX	$2,834
26	Freddie Mac	VA	$7,690	85	Texas Instruments, Inc.	TX	$2,821
27	Dow Chemical Co.	MI	$7,685	86	Starbucks Corp.	WA	$2,757
28	United Technologies Corp	CT	$7,608	87	EMC Corp. (MA)	MA	$2,714
29	American International Group	NY	$7,529	88	Emerson Electric Co.	MO	$2,710
30	Yahoo! Inc.	CA	$7,522	89	Lowe's Companies Inc	NC	$2,698
31	Philip Morris International	NY	$7,493	90	Danaher Corp.	DC	$2,598
32	Ford Motor Co. (DE)	MI	$7,373	91	Anthem Inc	IN	$2,570
33	Citigroup Inc	NY	$7,313	92	Bank of New York Mellon Corp	NY	$2,567
34	Coca-Cola Co (The)	GA	$7,098	93	Priceline Group Inc. (The)	CT	$2,551
35	Procter & Gamble Co	OH	$7,036	94	CANDID COLOR SYSTEMS INC.	OK	$2,535
36	Amgen Inc	CA	$6,939	95	Marathon Petroleum Corp.	OH	$2,524
37	ConocoPhillips	TX	$6,869	96	National Oilwell Varco Inc	TX	$2,502
38	Home Depot Inc	GA	$6,345	97	Baxter International Inc.	IL	$2,497
39	Visa Inc	CA	$6,328	98	Express Scripts Holding Co	MO	$2,476
40	MetLife Inc	NY	$6,309	99	NextEra Energy Inc	FL	$2,469
41	AT&T Inc	TX	$6,224	100	Hewlett Packard Enterprise C	CA	$2,461
42	American Express Co.	NY	$5,885	101	Federal Reserve Bank Of New Y	NY	$2,398
43	U.S. Bancorp (DE)	MN	$5,851	102	Lilly (Eli) & Co.	IN	$2,391
44	UnitedHealth Group Inc	MN	$5,813	103	Costco Wholesale Corp	WA	$2,377
45	Pepsico Inc.	NY	$5,452	104	Santander Holdings USA Inc.	MA	$2,335
46	Qualcomm, Inc.	CA	$5,271	105	Discover Financial Services	IL	$2,323
47	CVS Health Corp	RI	$5,237	106	Hess Corp	NY	$2,317
48	Boeing Co.	IL	$5,176	107	Monsanto Co.	MO	$2,314
49	Altria Group Inc	VA	$5,070	108	Voya Financial Inc	NY	$2,300
50	Bank of America Corp.	NC	$4,833	109	Abbott Laboratories	IL	$2,284
51	3M Co	MN	$4,833	110	Exelon Corp.	IL	$2,250
52	Union Pacific Corp	NE	$4,772	111	Archer Daniels Midland Co.	IL	$2,248
53	Honeywell International Inc	NJ	$4,768	112	BB&T Corp.	NC	$2,226
54	Phillips 66	TX	$4,762	113	TJX Companies, Inc.	MA	$2,215
55	McDonald's Corp	IL	$4,758	114	Mondelez International Inc	IL	$2,184
56	HP Inc	CA	$4,554	115	Southwest Airlines Co	TX	$2,181
57	Delta Air Lines, Inc. (DE)	GA	$4,526	116	Colgate-Palmolive Co.	NY	$2,180
58	ALASKA PERMANENT FUND CORP	AK	$4,520	117	Williams Cos Inc (The)	OK	$2,114
59	Capital One Financial Corp	VA	$4,428	118	Rite Aid Corp.	PA	$2,109

Top 500 Companies by Net Profit in Hoover's MasterList of U.S. Companies 2016 (continued)

Rank	Company	Headquarters	Net Income ($Bil)	Rank	Company	Headquarters	Net Income ($Bil)
119	Synchrony Financial	CT	$2,109	178	Cummins, Inc.	IN	$1,399
120	Caterpillar Inc.	IL	$2,102	179	CF Industries Holdings Inc	IL	$1,390
121	Cigna Corp	CT	$2,102	180	Plains All American Pipeline	TX	$1,384
122	PPG Industries, Inc.	PA	$2,102	181	Prudential Financial, Inc.	NJ	$1,381
123	Raytheon Co.	MA	$2,074	182	Applied Materials, Inc.	CA	$1,377
124	Aetna Inc.	CT	$2,041	183	Ford Motor Credit Company LL	MI	$1,363
125	State Street Corp.	MA	$2,037	184	THE SALVATION ARMY NATIONAL	VA	$1,350
126	Franklin Resources, Inc.	CA	$2,035	185	Corning, Inc.	NY	$1,339
127	Southern Co.	GA	$2,031	186	Energy Transfer Partners LP	TX	$1,336
128	Northrop Grumman Corp	VA	$1,990	187	Southern Copper Corp	AZ	$1,333
129	CSX Corp	FL	$1,968	188	Schwab (Charles) Corp.	CA	$1,321
130	Du Pont (E.I.) de Nemours &	DE	$1,953	189	Dominion Resources Inc	VA	$1,310
131	Deere & Co.	IL	$1,940	190	Motorola Solutions Inc.	IL	$1,299
132	Viacom Inc	NY	$1,922	191	Waste Management, Inc. (DE)	TX	$1,298
133	Chesapeake Energy Corp.	OK	$1,917	192	Graham Holdings Co.	VA	$1,294
134	Illinois Tool Works, Inc.	IL	$1,899	193	Yum! Brands, Inc.	KY	$1,293
135	Thermo Fisher Scientific Inc	MA	$1,894	194	Progressive Corp. (OH)	OH	$1,281
136	Duke Energy Corp	NC	$1,883	195	Air Products & Chemicals, In	PA	$1,278
137	HCA Holdings Inc	TN	$1,875	196	Intercontinental Exchange In	GA	$1,274
138	Time Warner Cable Inc	NY	$1,844	197	The Gap, Inc.	CA	$1,262
139	Weyerhaeuser Co	WA	$1,826	198	Sempra Energy	CA	$1,262
140	AbbVie Inc.	IL	$1,774	199	Georgia Power Co.	GA	$1,242
141	Suntrust Banks, Inc.	GA	$1,774	200	Principal Financial Group, I	IA	$1,234
142	PPL Corp	PA	$1,737	201	Best Buy Inc	MN	$1,233
143	Baxalta Inc	IL	$1,737	202	PayPal Holdings Inc	CA	$1,228
144	Publix Super Markets, Inc.	FL	$1,735	203	T Rowe Price Group, Inc.	MD	$1,223
145	Kroger Co (The)	OH	$1,728	204	General Mills, Inc.	MN	$1,221
146	eBay Inc.	CA	$1,725	205	Tyson Foods, Inc.	AR	$1,220
147	Baker Hughes Inc.	TX	$1,719	206	Cardinal Health, Inc.	OH	$1,215
148	Praxair, Inc.	CT	$1,694	207	Noble Energy, Inc.	TX	$1,214
149	Simon Property Group, Inc.	IN	$1,652	208	Ecolab, Inc.	MN	$1,203
150	American Electric Power Co.,	OH	$1,634	209	Federal Reserve Bank of Richm	VA	$1,202
151	Ameriprise Financial Inc	MN	$1,619	210	Toyota Motor Credit Corp.	CA	$1,197
152	Edison International	CA	$1,612	211	AutoZone, Inc.	TN	$1,160
153	Devon Energy Corp.	OK	$1,607	212	McGraw Hill Financial, Inc.	NY	$1,156
154	Paccar Inc	WA	$1,604	213	ST. LUKE"S HEALTH SYSTEM	TX	$1,156
155	Celgene Corp.	NJ	$1,602	214	Ally Financial Inc	MI	$1,150
156	Blackstone Group LP	NY	$1,585	215	Navient Corp	DE	$1,149
157	Bristol-Myers Squibb Co.	NY	$1,565	216	Humana, Inc.	KY	$1,147
158	Southern California Edison C	CA	$1,565	217	Public Storage	CA	$1,144
159	Johnson Controls Inc	WI	$1,563	218	Discovery Communications, In	MD	$1,139
160	Norfolk Southern Corp.	VA	$1,556	219	United Continental Holdings	IL	$1,132
161	INTERMOUNTAIN HEALTH CARE INC	UT	$1,546	220	CIT Group, Inc.	NY	$1,130
162	Macy's Inc	NY	$1,526	221	CME Group Inc	IL	$1,127
163	Public Service Enterprise Gr	NJ	$1,518	222	Tennessee Valley Authority	TN	$1,111
164	Florida Power & Light Co.	FL	$1,517	223	Omnicom Group, Inc.	NY	$1,094
165	Lincoln National Corp.	PA	$1,515	224	Consolidated Edison, Inc.	NY	$1,092
166	Macerich Co. (The)	CA	$1,499	225	Lauder (Estee) Cos., Inc. (T	NY	$1,089
167	International Finance Corp.	DC	$1,483	226	Spectra Energy Corp	TX	$1,082
168	Fifth Third Bancorp (Cincinn	OH	$1,481	227	Duke Energy Carolinas LLC	NC	$1,072
169	McKesson Corp.	CA	$1,476	228	M & T Bank Corp	NY	$1,066
170	Western Digital Corp.	CA	$1,465	229	Dollar General Corp	TN	$1,065
171	Marsh & McLennan Companies I	NY	$1,465	230	Tegna Inc	VA	$1,062
172	Automatic Data Processing In	NJ	$1,453	231	Regions Financial Corp	AL	$1,062
173	PG&E Corp. (Holding Co.)	CA	$1,450	232	Consolidated Edison Co. of N	NY	$1,058
174	Cognizant Technology Solutio	NJ	$1,439	233	FedEx Corp	TN	$1,050
175	Stryker Corp.	MI	$1,439	234	VF Corp.	NC	$1,048
176	CBS Corp	NY	$1,413	235	Macquarie Infrastructure Cor	NY	$1,042
177	MAKE CORPORATION	IL	$1,400	236	L Brands, Inc	OH	$1,042

Top 500 Companies by Net Profit in Hoover's MasterList of U.S. Companies 2016 (continued)

Rank	Company	Headquarters	Net Income ($Bil)
237	Mosaic Co. (The)	MN	$1,029
238	Xcel Energy, Inc.	MN	$1,021
239	Kimberly-Clark Corp.	TX	$1,013
240	Parker Hannifin Corp.	OH	$1,013
241	Spectra Energy Partners LP	TX	$1,004
242	St. Jude Medical, Inc.	MN	$1,002
243	USG Corp	IL	$991
244	Moody's Corp.	NY	$989
245	Teachers Insurance & Annuity	NY	$984
246	Continental Resources Inc.	OK	$977
247	Qwest Corp	LA	$970
248	Xerox Corp	CT	$969
249	RiverSource Life Insurance C	MN	$965
250	Entergy Corp. (New)	LA	$960
251	Radian Group, Inc.	PA	$960
252	Bed, Bath & Beyond, Inc.	NJ	$957
253	Dish Network Corp	CO	$945
254	Pioneer Natural Resources Co	TX	$930
255	Ross Stores, Inc.	CA	$925
256	Southwestern Energy Company	TX	$924
257	THE WASHINGTON UNIVERSITY	MO	$918
258	Vornado Realty L.P.	NY	$912
259	ONEOK Partners LP	OK	$910
260	Murphy Oil Corp	AR	$906
261	KeyCorp	OH	$900
262	Newfield Exploration Co.	TX	$900
263	Taubman Centers, Inc.	MI	$893
264	VMware Inc	CA	$886
265	Symantec Corp.	CA	$878
266	Electronic Arts	CA	$875
267	Dover Corp	IL	$870
268	Kohl's Corp.	WI	$867
269	Sherwin-Williams Co.	OH	$866
270	Citizens Financial Group Inc	RI	$865
271	SENTARA HEALTHCARE	VA	$862
272	Virginia Electric & Power Co	VA	$858
273	BANNER HEALTH	AZ	$855
274	Western Union Co.	CO	$852
275	Alaska Air Group, Inc.	WA	$848
276	Hershey Company (The)	PA	$847
277	CA Inc	NY	$846
278	Harley-Davidson Inc	WI	$845
279	Tesoro Corporation	TX	$843
280	Magellan Midstream Partners	OK	$840
281	Constellation Brands Inc	NY	$839
282	Exelon Generation Co LLC	PA	$835
283	Activision Blizzard, Inc.	CA	$835
284	Rockwell Automation, Inc.	WI	$828
285	American Tower Corp (New)	MA	$825
286	Eversource Energy	MA	$820
287	TD Ameritrade Holding Corp	NE	$813
288	Northern Trust Corp.	IL	$812
289	Edwards Lifesciences Corp	CA	$811
290	STAPLE COTTON CO-OPERATIVE AS	MS	$807
291	Lennar Corp.	FL	$803
292	Grainger (W.W.), Inc.	IL	$802
293	Alabama Power Co.	AL	$800
294	Skyworks Solutions, Inc.	MA	$798
295	Hartford Financial Services	CT	$798
296	Spirit AeroSystems Holdings	KS	$789
297	QEP Resources Inc	CO	$784
298	Whirlpool Corp	MI	$783
299	CHS Inc	MN	$781
300	O'Reilly Automotive, Inc.	MO	$778
301	CenturyLink, Inc.	LA	$772
302	AES Corp.	VA	$769
303	Santander Consumer USA Holdi	TX	$766
304	Expedia Inc	WA	$764
305	Chemtura Corp	PA	$763
306	LUDWIG INSTITUTE FOR CANCER	NY	$761
307	Stanley Black & Decker Inc	CT	$761
308	Vornado Realty Trust	NY	$760
309	PSEG Power LLC	NJ	$760
310	Fiserv, Inc.	WI	$754
311	Marriott International, Inc.	MD	$753
312	Eastman Chemical Co.	TN	$751
313	Horton (D.R.) Inc.	TX	$751
314	Republic Services, Inc.	AZ	$750
315	Lear Corp.	MI	$746
316	Enbridge Energy Partners, L.	TX	$740
317	Host Hotels & Resorts Inc	MD	$732
318	Wynn Resorts Ltd	NV	$732
319	EP Energy Corp.	TX	$731
320	DTE Energy Co.	MI	$727
321	DaVita HealthCare Partners I	CO	$723
322	Zimmer Biomet Holdings Inc	IN	$720
323	Nordstrom, Inc.	WA	$720
324	Mead Johnson Nutrition Co	IL	$720
325	Nucor Corp.	NC	$714
326	Pilgrims Pride Corp.	CO	$712
327	Genuine Parts Co.	GA	$711
328	Darden Restaurants, Inc. (Un	FL	$710
329	Amphenol Corp.	CT	$709
330	Dr Pepper Snapple Group Inc	TX	$703
331	Ralph Lauren Corp	NY	$702
332	FMC Technologies, Inc.	TX	$700
333	Pacificorp	OR	$698
334	Analog Devices, Inc.	MA	$697
335	Becton, Dickinson & Co.	NJ	$695
336	CNA Financial Corp.	IL	$691
337	Campbell Soup Co.	NJ	$691
338	Sysco Corp.	TX	$687
339	Hormel Foods Corp.	MN	$686
340	Rockwell Collins, Inc.	IA	$686
341	Reinsurance Group of America	MO	$684
342	Brown-Forman Corp.	KY	$684
343	AvalonBay Communities, Inc.	VA	$684
344	THE METHODIST HOSPITAL	TX	$684
345	Alleghany Corp. (New)	NY	$679
346	Fidelity National Informatio	FL	$679
347	Westlake Chemical Corp	TX	$679
348	Trinity Industries, Inc.	TX	$678
349	Hartford Life Insurance Co	CT	$676
350	Paychex Inc	NY	$675
351	Antero Resources Corp	CO	$674
352	Hilton Worldwide Holdings In	VA	$673
353	SM Energy Co.	CO	$666
354	General Growth Properties In	IL	$666

Top 500 Companies by Net Profit in Hoover's MasterList of U.S. Companies 2016 (continued)

Rank	Company	Headquarters	Net Income ($Bil)	Rank	Company	Headquarters	Net Income ($Bil)
355	L-3 Communications Holdings,	NY	$664	414	Torchmark Corp.	TX	$543
356	Equity Residential	IL	$659	415	Boston Properties L.P.	MA	$541
357	ERP OPERATING LIMITED PARTNER	IL	$659	416	Pacific Mutual Holding Compa	CA	$540
358	WILLIAM MARSH RICE UNIVERSITY	TX	$658	417	Concho Resources Inc	TX	$538
359	ERP Operating L.P.	IL	$656	418	SCANA Corp	SC	$538
360	Lam Research Corp	CA	$656	419	Liberty Interactive Corp	CO	$537
361	Berkley (W. R.) Corp.	CT	$650	420	Whole Foods Market, Inc.	TX	$536
362	Xilinx, Inc.	CA	$648	421	Caterpillar Financial Servic	TN	$535
363	Roper Technologies Inc	FL	$646	422	DTE Electric Company	MI	$532
364	Prologis LP	CA	$638	423	Mohawk Industries, Inc.	GA	$532
365	Wells Fargo Real Estate Inve	MN	$638	424	NiSource Inc. (Holding Co.)	IN	$530
366	Prologis Inc	CA	$636	425	Cerner Corp.	MO	$525
367	Regeneron Pharmaceuticals, I	NY	$636	426	CMS Energy Corp	MI	$525
368	Denbury Resources, Inc. (DE)	TX	$635	427	Cincinnati Financial Corp.	OH	$525
369	Range Resources Corp	TX	$634	428	HSBC Finance Corp	IL	$523
370	Energy Transfer Equity L P	TX	$633	429	Linear Technology Corp.	CA	$521
371	Starwood Hotels & Resorts Wo	CT	$633	430	Foot Locker, Inc.	NY	$520
372	Huntington Bancshares, Inc	OH	$632	431	Flowserve Corp.	TX	$519
373	Kellogg Co	MI	$632	432	SL Green Realty Corp.	NY	$518
374	NVIDIA Corp	CA	$631	433	Fastenal Co.	MN	$516
375	Adobe Systems, Inc.	CA	$630	434	Keysight Technologies Inc	CA	$513
376	Occidental Petroleum Corp	TX	$616	435	Welltower Inc	OH	$512
377	Wyndham Worldwide Corp	NJ	$612	436	SECURITIES INVESTOR PROTECTION	DC	$512
378	LITTLE COMPANY OF MARY HOSPIT	IL	$612	437	Laboratory Corporation of Am	NC	$511
379	CenterPoint Energy, Inc	TX	$611	438	Fluor Corp.	TX	$511
380	BorgWarner Inc	MI	$610	439	Sirius XM Holdings Inc	NY	$510
381	VANGUARD CHARITABLE ENDOW	PA	$608	440	Newmont Mining Corp. (Holdin	CO	$508
382	LLOG EXPLORATION COMPANY L.L.C.	LA	$601	441	Cimarex Energy Co	CO	$507
383	Textron Inc.	RI	$600	442	WestRock Co	VA	$507
384	Dollar Tree, Inc.	VA	$599	443	Oasis Petroleum Inc.	TX	$507
385	Carmax Inc.	VA	$597	444	Alliance Data Systems Corp.	TX	$506
386	Amazon.com Inc.	WA	$596	445	OneMain Holdings Inc	IN	$505
387	Coca-Cola Enterprises Inc	GA	$596	446	UNIVERSITY OF WISCONSIN SYS	WI	$503
388	THE NEW YORK AND PRESBYTERIAN	NY	$595	447	Raymond James Financial, Inc	FL	$502
389	Consumers Energy Co.	MI	$594	448	Cameron International Corp	TX	$501
390	DST Systems Inc. (DE)	MO	$593	449	Mattel Inc	CA	$499
391	Comerica, Inc.	TX	$593	450	Keurig Green Mountain Inc	VT	$498
392	Loews Corp.	NY	$591	451	John Deere Capital Corp.	NV	$498
393	Chimera Investment Corp	NY	$589	452	Arrow Electronics, Inc.	CO	$498
394	Intuitive Surgical Inc	CA	$589	453	Alliance Resource Partners L	OK	$497
395	WEC Energy Group Inc	WI	$588	454	Starwood Property Trust Inc.	CT	$495
396	Ameren Corp.	MO	$586	455	PulteGroup, Inc.	GA	$494
397	THE PEW CHARITABLE TRUSTS	PA	$585	456	Advance Auto Parts Inc	VA	$494
398	United Rentals, Inc.	CT	$585	457	Protective Life Insurance Co	AL	$492
399	AMETEK, Inc.	PA	$584	458	TIAA REAL ESTATE ACCOUNT	NY	$490
400	Fidelity National Financial	FL	$583	459	First Republic Bank (San Fra	CA	$487
401	Zoetis Inc	NJ	$583	460	TUDOR INVESTMENT CORPORATION	CT	$486
402	Clorox Co (The)	CA	$580	461	New York Community Bancorp I	NY	$485
403	FirstEnergy Corp.	OH	$578	462	CBRE Group Inc	CA	$485
404	Avnet Inc	AZ	$572	463	Tiffany & Co.	NY	$484
405	UNIVERSITY OF PITTSBURGH	PA	$570	464	Ambac Financial Group, Inc.	NY	$484
406	MBIA, Inc.	NY	$569	465	Kansas City Southern	MO	$484
407	Western Refining Inc	TX	$560	466	Monster Beverage Corp (New)	CA	$483
408	Netapp Inc	CA	$560	467	Schein (Henry), Inc.	NY	$479
409	Quest Diagnostics, Inc.	NJ	$556	468	SVB Financial Group	CA	$479
410	International Paper Co	TN	$555	469	Snap-On, Inc.	WI	$479
411	Florida Power Corp.	FL	$548	470	KKR & Co LP (DE)	NY	$478
412	Universal Health Services, I	PA	$545	471	Interpublic Group of Compani	NY	$477
413	Scripps Networks Interactive	TN	$545	472	Tribune Media Co.	IL	$477

Top 500 Companies by Net Income in Hoover's MasterList of U.S. Companies 2016 (continued)

Rank	Company	Headquarters	Net Income ($Bil)	Rank	Company	Headquarters	Net Income ($Bil)
473	Chipotle Mexican Grill Inc	CO	$476	487	AutoNation, Inc.	FL	$443
474	Block (H. & R.), Inc.	MO	$474	488	New Residential Investment C	NY	$442
475	Federal Reserve Bank of San F	CA	$470	489	PVH Corp	NY	$439
476	Autoliv Inc.	MN	$468	490	Atwood Oceanics, Inc.	TX	$433
477	Polaris Industries Inc.	MN	$454	491	Waters Corp.	MA	$432
478	Affiliated Managers Group In	FL	$452	492	Domtar Corp	SC	$431
479	American Financial Group Inc	OH	$452	493	Cintas Corp.	OH	$431
480	Oncor Electric Delivery Co	TX	$450	494	KAISER FOUNDATION HOSPITALS	CA	$429
481	Robinson (C.H.) Worldwide, I	MN	$450	495	HanesBrands Inc	NC	$429
482	Springleaf Finance Corp	IN	$448	496	Oceaneering International, I	TX	$428
483	TransDigm Group Inc	OH	$447	497	ManpowerGroup	WI	$428
484	AmTrust Financial Services I	NY	$447	498	CYS Investments	MA	$426
485	KBS Real Estate Investment T	CA	$446	499	UNIVERSITY OF WASHINGTON INC	WA	$425
486	Boston Properties, Inc.	MA	$444	500	Kimco Realty Corp.	NY	$424

The Mergent 500 Largest US Public Corporations

Rank	Company	Sales ($ bil.)
1	Wal-Mart Stores, Inc.	$485,651
2	Exxon Mobil Corp.	$411,939
3	Apple Inc	$233,715
4	Chevron Corporation	$211,970
5	Berkshire Hathaway Inc.	$194,673
6	McKesson Corp.	$179,045
7	Phillips 66	$164,093
8	UnitedHealth Group Inc	$157,107
9	CVS Health Corp	$153,290
10	General Motors Co.	$152,356
11	Ford Motor Co. (DE)	$149,558
12	General Electric Co	$148,589
13	AmerisourceBergen Corp.	$135,962
14	AT&T Inc	$132,447
15	Valero Energy Corp.	$130,844
16	Verizon Communications Inc	$127,079
17	Fannie Mae	$116,461
18	Costco Wholesale Corp	$116,199
19	Federal Reserve System	$114,299
20	Kroger Co (The)	$108,465
21	Amazon.com Inc.	$107,006
22	Walgreens Boots Alliance Inc	$103,444
23	HP Inc	$103,355
24	Cardinal Health, Inc.	$102,531
25	JPMorgan Chase & Co	$102,102
26	Express Scripts Holding Co	$101,752
27	Marathon Petroleum Corp.	$98,102
28	Boeing Co.	$96,114
29	Bank of America Corp.	$95,181
30	Microsoft Corporation	$93,580
31	International Business Machi	$92,793
32	Citigroup Inc	$90,572
33	Wells Fargo & Co.	$88,372
34	Home Depot Inc	$83,176
35	Archer Daniels Midland Co.	$81,201
36	Philip Morris International	$80,106
37	Procter & Gamble Co	$76,279
38	Alphabet Inc	$74,989
39	Comcast Corp	$74,510
40	Johnson & Johnson	$74,331
41	Anthem Inc	$73,874
42	MetLife Inc	$73,316
43	Target Corp	$72,618
44	Freddie Mac	$69,367
45	Federal Reserve Bank Of New Y	$68,824
46	American International Group	$64,406
47	Pepsico Inc.	$63,056
48	United Parcel Service Inc	$58,232
49	Aetna Inc.	$58,003
50	Lowe's Companies Inc	$56,223
51	United Technologies Corp	$56,098
52	Energy Transfer Equity L P	$55,691
53	ConocoPhillips	$55,517
54	Intel Corp	$55,355
55	Prudential Financial, Inc.	$54,105
56	Disney (Walt) Co. (The)	$52,465
57	Hewlett Packard Enterprise C	$52,107
58	Energy Transfer Partners LP	$51,158
59	Pfizer Inc	$49,605
60	Cisco Systems, Inc.	$49,161
61	Dow Chemical Co.	$48,778
62	Sysco Corp.	$48,681
63	Humana, Inc.	$48,500
64	Enterprise Products Partners	$47,951
65	FedEx Corp	$47,453
66	Caterpillar Inc.	$47,011
67	Ingram Micro Inc.	$46,487
68	Coca-Cola Co (The)	$45,998
69	Lockheed Martin Corp.	$45,600
70	Plains GP Holdings, L.P	$43,464
71	Plains All American Pipeline	$43,464
72	World Fuel Services Corp.	$43,386
73	American Airlines Group Inc	$42,650
74	Merck & Co., Inc	$42,237
75	Tyson Foods, Inc.	$41,373
76	Delta Air Lines, Inc. (DE)	$40,704
77	Tesoro Corporation	$40,633
78	Best Buy Inc	$40,339
79	Goldman Sachs Group, Inc.	$40,085
80	United Continental Holdings	$38,901
81	Honeywell International Inc	$38,581
82	Oracle Corp.	$38,226
83	Morgan Stanley	$37,953
84	Johnson Controls Inc	$37,179
85	HCA Holdings Inc	$36,918
86	American Express Co.	$35,999
87	Allstate Corp.	$35,239
88	Cigna Corp	$34,914
89	INTL FCStone Inc.	$34,676
90	CHS Inc	$34,582
91	Sprint Corp (New)	$34,532
92	Mondelez International Inc	$34,244
93	General Dynamics Corp.	$31,469
94	Sears Holdings Corp	$31,198
95	Publix Super Markets, Inc.	$30,802
96	NIKE Inc	$30,601
97	3M Co	$30,274
98	T-Mobile US Inc	$29,564
99	Exelon Corp.	$29,447
100	TJX Companies, Inc.	$29,078
101	Twenty-First Century Fox Inc	$28,987
102	Deere & Co.	$28,863
103	Macy's Inc	$28,105
104	Avnet Inc	$27,925
105	Tech Data Corp.	$27,671
106	McDonald's Corp	$27,441
107	Time Warner Inc	$27,359
108	Travelers Companies Inc (The	$26,800
109	Rite Aid Corp.	$26,528
110	Teachers Insurance & Annuity	$26,197
111	Qualcomm, Inc.	$25,281
112	Du Pont (E.I.) de Nemours &	$25,130
113	Gilead Sciences, Inc.	$24,890
114	Baker Hughes Inc.	$24,551
115	Altria Group Inc	$24,522
116	EMC Corp. (MA)	$24,440
117	Chesapeake Energy Corp.	$20,951
118	Whirlpool Corp	$20,891
119	AutoNation, Inc.	$20,862
120	ManpowerGroup	$20,763
121	Duke Energy Corp	$23,925
122	Alcoa, Inc.	$23,906
123	Capital One Financial Corp	$23,869
124	Time Warner Cable Inc	$23,697
125	Halliburton Company	$23,633
126	International Paper Co	$23,617
127	Northrop Grumman Corp	$23,526
128	Arrow Electronics, Inc.	$23,282
129	Raytheon Co.	$23,247
130	AFLAC Inc.	$22,728
131	Burlington Northern & Santa F	$22,714
132	Staples Inc	$22,492
133	Emerson Electric Co.	$22,304
134	Occidental Petroleum Corp	$21,947
135	Union Pacific Corp	$21,813
136	Amgen Inc	$21,662
137	Fluor Corp.	$21,532
138	National Oilwell Varco Inc	$21,440
139	Freeport-McMoRan Inc	$21,438
140	U.S. Bancorp (DE)	$21,392
141	Nucor Corp.	$21,105
142	Abbott Laboratories	$20,247
143	AbbVie Inc.	$19,960
144	Danaher Corp.	$19,914
145	PBF Energy Inc	$19,828
146	Southwest Airlines Co	$19,820
147	HollyFrontier Corp.	$19,764
148	Lilly (Eli) & Co.	$19,616
149	Devon Energy Corp.	$19,566
150	Xerox Corp	$19,540
151	Progressive Corp. (OH)	$19,391
152	Starbucks Corp.	$19,163
153	Icahn Enterprises LP	$19,157
154	Paccar Inc.	$19,115
155	Cummins, Inc.	$19,110
156	Kohl's Corp.	$19,023
157	Dollar General Corp	$18,910
158	Community Health Systems, In	$18,639
159	Hartford Financial Services	$18,614
160	Kimberly-Clark Corp.	$18,591
161	Southern Co.	$18,467
162	Lear Corp.	$18,211
163	Sunoco Logistics Partners L.	$18,088
164	EOG Resources, Inc.	$18,035
165	CenturyLink, Inc.	$18,031
166	AECOM	$17,990
167	Facebook, Inc.	$17,928
168	Jabil Circuit, Inc.	$17,899
169	Supervalu Inc.	$17,820
170	General Mills, Inc.	$17,630
171	United States Steel Corp.	$17,507
172	Exelon Generation Co LLC	$17,393
173	Colgate-Palmolive Co.	$17,277
174	Global Partners LP	$17,270
175	Murphy USA Inc	$17,210
176	Penske Automotive Group Inc	$17,177
177	AES Corp.	$17,146
178	PG&E Corp. (Holding Co.)	$17,090
179	NextEra Energy Inc	$17,021
180	American Electric Power Co.,	$17,020
181	Thermo Fisher Scientific Inc	$16,890
182	NGL Energy Partners LP	$16,802
183	Baxter International Inc.	$16,671
184	Tenet Healthcare Corp.	$16,615
185	Centene Corp	$16,560
186	Bristol-Myers Squibb Co.	$16,560
187	Goodyear Tire & Rubber Co.	$16,443
188	The Gap, Inc.	$16,435
189	PNC Financial Services Group	$16,281
190	Micron Technology Inc.	$16,192
191	Office Depot, Inc.	$16,096
192	Bank of New York Mellon Corp	$16,046
193	NRG Energy Inc	$15,868
194	ConAgra Foods, Inc.	$15,832
195	Whole Foods Market, Inc.	$15,389
196	PPG Industries, Inc.	$15,360
197	Genuine Parts Co.	$15,342
198	Performance Food Group Co	$15,270
199	Western Refining Inc	$15,154
200	Omnicom Group, Inc.	$15,134
201	FirstEnergy Corp.	$15,026

17a

The Mergent 500 Largest US Public Corporations

Rank	Company	Sales ($ bil.)
202	Monsanto Co.	$15,001
203	Land O' Lakes Inc	$14,966
204	Dish Network Corp	$14,643
205	Las Vegas Sands Corp	$14,584
206	Kellogg Co	$14,580
207	Western Digital Corp.	$14,572
208	Kinder Morgan Inc.	$14,403
209	Aramark	$14,329
210	Loews Corp.	$14,325
211	Ecolab, Inc.	$14,281
212	Carmax Inc.	$14,269
213	Health Net, Inc.	$14,009
214	Waste Management, Inc. (DE)	$13,996
215	WellCare Health Plans Inc	$13,890
216	CBS Corp	$13,886
217	Visa Inc	$13,880
218	Textron Inc.	$13,878
219	Apache Corp.	$13,851
220	Marriott International, Inc.	$13,796
221	Lincoln National Corp.	$13,554
222	Nordstrom, Inc.	$13,506
223	Robinson (C.H.) Worldwide, I	$13,470
224	Edison International	$13,413
225	Illinois Tool Works, Inc.	$13,405
226	Southern California Edison C	$13,380
227	Synnex Corp	$13,338
228	Viacom Inc	$13,268
229	Yum! Brands, Inc.	$13,105
230	Texas Instruments, Inc.	$13,045
231	Marsh & McLennan Companies I $12,951	
232	Consolidated Edison, Inc.	$12,919
233	DaVita HealthCare Partners I	$12,795
234	CST Brands Inc	$12,758
235	Synchrony Financial	$12,727
236	Parker Hannifin Corp.	$12,712
237	Entergy Corp. (New)	$12,495
238	Dominion Resources Inc	$12,436
239	VF Corp.	$12,282
240	Praxair, Inc.	$12,273
241	Ameriprise Financial Inc	$12,268
242	Penney (J.C.) Co.,Inc. (Hold	$12,257
243	Oneok Inc.	$12,195
244	ONEOK Partners LP	$12,192
245	Computer Sciences Corp.	$12,173
246	L-3 Communications Holdings, $12,124	
247	Jacobs Engineering Group, In	$12,115
248	CDW Corp	$12,075
249	Principal Financial Group, I	$11,964
250	Santander Holdings USA Inc.	$11,919
251	Bed, Bath & Beyond, Inc.	$11,881
252	CSX Corp	$11,811
253	Federal Reserve Bank of San F	$11,704
254	Xcel Energy, Inc.	$11,686
255	Donnelley (R. R.) & Sons Co.	$11,603
256	PPL Corp	$11,499
257	Leucadia National Corp.	$11,486
258	L Brands, Inc	$11,454
259	Hess Corp	$11,439
260	Florida Power & Light Co.	$11,421
261	WestRock Co	$11,381
262	Stanley Black & Decker Inc	$11,339
263	Marathon Oil Corp.	$11,258
264	First Data Corp (New)	$11,152
265	Sherwin-Williams Co.	$11,130
266	BlackRock, Inc.	$11,081
267	Voya Financial Inc	$11,071
268	Hertz Global Holdings Inc	$11,046
269	Ross Stores, Inc.	$11,042
270	Sempra Energy	$11,035
271	Tennessee Valley Authority	$11,003
272	Automatic Data Processing In	$10,939
273	Reinsurance Group of America	$10,904
274	Public Service Enterprise Gr	$10,886
275	Horton (D.R.) Inc.	$10,824
276	Consolidated Edison Co. of N	$10,786
277	Lauder (Estee) Cos., Inc. (T	$10,780
278	Biogen Inc	$10,764
279	State Street Corp.	$10,687
280	Reynolds American Inc	$10,675
281	Schein (Henry), Inc.	$10,630
282	Norfolk Southern Corp.	$10,511
283	Unum Group	$10,510
284	Hilton Worldwide Holdings In	$10,502
285	Liberty Interactive Corp	$10,499
286	Reliance Steel & Aluminum Co	$10,452
287	Univar Inc	$10,374
288	DTE Energy Co.	$10,337
289	Assurant Inc	$10,325
290	Huntsman Corp	$10,299
291	Becton, Dickinson & Co.	$10,282
292	Core Mark Holding Co Inc	$10,280
293	Cognizant Technology Solutio	$10,263
294	AutoZone, Inc.	$10,187
295	Navistar International Corp.	$10,140
296	MGM Resorts International	$10,082
297	Grainger (W.W.), Inc.	$9,965
298	Stryker Corp.	$9,946
299	Group 1 Automotive, Inc.	$9,938
300	BB&T Corp.	$9,926
301	Air Products & Chemicals, In	$9,895
302	Advance Auto Parts Inc	$9,844
303	Charter Communications Inc	$9,754
304	AGCO Corp.	$9,724
305	CNA Financial Corp.	$9,692
306	MasterCard Inc	$9,667
307	Ally Financial Inc	$9,667
308	Molina Healthcare Inc	$9,667
309	Applied Materials, Inc.	$9,659
310	Discover Financial Services	$9,611
311	Genworth Financial, Inc. (Ho	$9,565
312	Eastman Chemical Co.	$9,527
313	Dean Foods Co.	$9,503
314	Lennar Corp.	$9,474
315	Owens & Minor, Inc. (New)	$9,440
316	GameStop Corp	$9,296
317	Hormel Foods Corp.	$9,264
318	Celgene Corp.	$9,256
319	PayPal Holdings Inc	$9,248
320	Autoliv Inc.	$9,241
321	CenterPoint Energy, Inc	$9,226
322	Priceline Group Inc. (The)	$9,224
323	Sonic Automotive, Inc.	$9,197
324	Toyota Motor Credit Corp.	$9,142
325	Republic Services, Inc.	$9,115
326	Corning, Inc.	$9,111
327	CVR Energy Inc	$9,110
328	Crown Holdings Inc	$9,097
329	Mosaic Co. (The)	$9,056
330	CBRE Group Inc	$9,050
331	Georgia Power Co.	$8,988
332	HD Supply Holdings Inc	$8,882
333	Avon Products, Inc.	$8,851
334	Qwest Corp	$8,838
335	CVR Refining, LP	$8,830
336	Cameron International Corp	$8,782
337	Steel Dynamics Inc.	$8,756
338	Suntrust Banks, Inc.	$8,707
339	Anadarko Petroleum Corp	$8,698
340	News Corp (New)	$8,633
341	Targa Resources Corp	$8,617
342	Dollar Tree, Inc.	$8,602
343	eBay Inc.	$8,592
344	Pilgrims Pride Corp.	$8,583
345	Caesars Entertainment Corp	$8,516
346	Avis Budget Group Inc	$8,485
347	Tenneco Inc	$8,420
348	Delek US Holdings Inc	$8,324
349	Jarden Corp	$8,287
350	PVH Corp	$8,241
351	United Natural Foods Inc.	$8,185
352	Campbell Soup Co.	$8,082
353	Universal Health Services, I	$8,065
354	Fidelity National Financial	$8,024
355	BorgWarner Inc	$8,023
356	Ball Corp	$7,997
357	Enbridge Energy Partners, L.	$7,965
358	Franklin Resources, Inc.	$7,949
359	FMC Technologies, Inc.	$7,943
360	SpartanNash Co.	$7,916
361	Wesco International, Inc.	$7,890
362	Quanta Services, Inc.	$7,851
363	Mohawk Industries, Inc.	$7,803
364	TravelCenters of America LLC	$7,779
365	Casey's General Stores, Inc.	$7,767
366	Sealed Air Corp.	$7,751
367	Eversource Energy	$7,742
368	Williams Cos Inc (The)	$7,637
369	Ralph Lauren Corp	$7,620
370	Virginia Electric & Power Co	$7,579
371	Interpublic Group of Compani	$7,537
372	Visteon Corp.	$7,509
373	Blackstone Group LP	$7,485
374	Quest Diagnostics, Inc.	$7,435
375	Hershey Company (The)	$7,422
376	Veritiv Corp	$7,407
377	Weyerhaeuser Co	$7,403
378	Boston Scientific Corp.	$7,380
379	Duke Energy Carolinas LLC	$7,351
380	Federal-Mogul Holdings Corp	$7,317
381	Terex Corp. (New)	$7,309
382	Newmont Mining Corp. (Holdin	$7,292
383	O'Reilly Automotive, Inc.	$7,216
384	Foot Locker, Inc.	$7,151
385	Masco Corp.	$7,142
386	Berkley (W. R.) Corp.	$7,129
387	Pacific Mutual Holding Compa	$7,073
388	Coca-Cola Enterprises Inc	$7,011
389	Huntington Ingalls Industrie	$6,957
390	Dover Corp	$6,956
391	MetLife Insurance Company of	$6,903
392	Live Nation Entertainment, I	$6,867
393	Federal Reserve Bank Of Atlan	$6,861
394	Dick's Sporting Goods, Inc	$6,814
395	Peabody Energy Corp	$6,792
396	Dillard's Inc.	$6,780
397	Netflix Inc	$6,780
398	Alon USA Energy Inc	$6,779
399	Level 3 Communications, Inc.	$6,777
400	Darden Restaurants, Inc. (Un	$6,764

The Mergent 500 Largest US Public Corporations

Rank	Company	Sales ($ bil.)
403	Expedia Inc	$6,672
404	Spirit AeroSystems Holdings	$6,644
405	Buckeye Partners, L.P.	$6,620
406	Dana Holding Corp	$6,617
407	NCR Corp.	$6,591
408	Ryder System, Inc.	$6,572
409	Expeditors International of	$6,565
410	Symantec Corp.	$6,508
411	AK Steel Holding Corp.	$6,506
412	Fifth Third Bancorp (Cincinn	$6,504
413	Seaboard Corp.	$6,473
414	Calpine Corp	$6,472
415	NiSource Inc. (Holding Co.)	$6,471
416	Cablevision Systems Corp.	$6,461
417	CMS Energy Corp	$6,456
418	Anixter International Inc	$6,446
419	Chemours Co (The)	$6,432
420	EMCOR Group, Inc.	$6,425
421	Fidelity National Informatio	$6,414
422	Sanmina Corp	$6,375
423	CenterPoint Energy Resources	$6,367
424	KBR Inc	$6,366
425	Avery Dennison Corp.	$6,330
426	iHeartMedia Inc	$6,319
427	Rockwell Automation, Inc.	$6,308
428	Discovery Communications, In	$6,265
429	Harley-Davidson Inc	$6,229
430	Trinity Industries, Inc.	$6,170
431	Hunt (J.B.) Transport Servic	$6,165
432	Consumers Energy Co.	$6,165
433	Owens-Illinois, Inc.	$6,156
434	Harman International Industr	$6,155
435	Federal Reserve Bank of Richm	$6,148
436	Santander Consumer USA Holdi	$6,127
437	Erie Indemnity Co.	$6,124
438	Netapp Inc	$6,123
439	Dr Pepper Snapple Group Inc	$6,121
440	Oshkosh Corp (New)	$6,098
441	A-Mark Precious Metals, Inc	$6,070
442	Barnes & Noble Inc	$6,069
443	Schwab (Charles) Corp.	$6,058
444	Ameren Corp.	$6,053
445	VMware Inc	$6,035
446	Constellation Brands Inc	$6,028
447	Mattel Inc	$6,024
448	Laboratory Corporation of Am	$6,012
449	Tegna Inc	$6,008
450	Commercial Metals Co.	$5,989
451	Starwood Hotels & Resorts Wo	$5,983
452	PulteGroup, Inc.	$5,982
453	General Cable Corp. (DE)	$5,980
454	Graybar Electric Co., Inc.	$5,979
455	Energy Future Holdings Corp	$5,978
456	Baxalta Inc	$5,952
457	Alabama Power Co.	$5,942
458	MRC Global Inc	$5,933
459	Spectra Energy Corp	$5,903
460	Midcoast Energy Partners LP	$5,894
461	Motorola Solutions Inc.	$5,881
462	Asbury Automotive Group, Inc	$5,868
463	Packaging Corp of America	$5,853
464	Windstream Holdings Inc	$5,830
465	United Rentals, Inc.	$5,817
466	JetBlue Airways Corp	$5,817
467	HRG Group Inc	$5,816
468	Calumet Specialty Product Pa	$5,791
469	Southern Copper Corp	$5,788
470	Quintiles Transnational Hold	$5,738
471	HanesBrands Inc	$5,732
472	Newell Rubbermaid, Inc.	$5,727
473	American Financial Group Inc	$5,713
474	Tractor Supply Co.	$5,712
475	Smucker (J.M.) Co.	$5,693
476	Celanese Corp (DE)	$5,674
477	Regions Financial Corp	$5,674
478	Ingredion Inc	$5,668
479	Clorox Co (The)	$5,655
480	Navient Corp	$5,637
481	St. Jude Medical, Inc.	$5,622
482	Western Union Co.	$5,607
483	Alaska Air Group, Inc.	$5,598
484	SanDisk Corp.	$5,565
485	Domtar Corp	$5,563
486	Kelly Services, Inc.	$5,563
487	Northern Tier Energy LP	$5,556
488	Wyndham Worldwide Corp	$5,536
489	Old Republic International C	$5,531
490	Advanced Micro Devices, Inc.	$5,506
491	Murphy Oil Corp	$5,476
492	CH2M Hill Companies Ltd	$5,468
493	PSEG Power LLC	$5,434
494	Wynn Resorts Ltd	$5,434
495	Jones Lang LaSalle Inc	$5,430
496	Gallagher (Arthur J.) & Co.	$5,392
497	Lithia Motors, Inc.	$5,390
498	Ashland Inc	$5,387
499	Salesforce.Com Inc	$5,374
500	Host Hotels & Resorts Inc	$5,354

Hoover's MasterList of U.S. Companies

Company Listings

1 SOURCE CONSULTING INC.

1250 H St. NW Ste. 575
Washington DC 20005
Phone: 202-624-0800
Fax: 202-624-0810
Web: www.1-sc.com

CEO: William Teel Jr
CFO: Warren Goldman
HR: Scott Rutherford
FYE: December 31
Type: Private

1 Source Consulting isn't the only company to provide information technology and strategic consulting services to the US government but it would like to be at the top of the list. The company offers IT systems design development and integration services as well as security management program management infrastructure and operations consulting and systems development. 1 Source has served federal agencies such as the departments of Homeland Security Energy Transportation as well as the ATF and SEC. The company operates from offices in Germantown Maryland and Washington D.C. 1 Source was founded in 1999 by CEO William R. Teel Jr.

1-800 CONTACTS INC.

66 E. Wadsworth Park Dr. 3rd Fl.
Draper UT 84020
Phone: 801-924-9800
Fax: 801-924-9905
Web: www.1800contacts.com

CEO: –
CFO: Robert G Hunter
HR: Max Neves
FYE: December 31
Type: Private

Lose a contact? If you can still find your telephone or computer you can get replacement lenses from 1-800 CONTACTS. Through its website and over the phone the company offers contact lenses from major manufacturers and distributors. Its most popular brands include Acuvue Air Optix Biomedics Focus FreshLook and Proclear. To ensure order accuracy 1-800 CONTACTS verifies prescription information with eye doctors. The company was founded in 1995 by entrepreneurs Jonathan Coon and John Nichols. It was bought by WellPoint for an undisclosed amount in mid-2012 as the health insurance giant looks to grow its direct-to-consumer operations.

1-800 FLOWERS.COM, INC.

One Old Country Road
Carle Place, NY 11514
Phone: 516 237-6000
Fax: –
Web: www.1800flowers.com

NMS: FLWS
CEO: James F. (Jim) McCann
CFO: William E. Shea
HR: –
FYE: June 28
Type: Public

Some say it's all in the name but 1-800-FLOWERS.COM does more than deliver the daisies. The company sells fresh-cut flowers floral arrangements and plants through its toll-free number and websites; it also markets gifts for every occasion via catalog TV and radio ads and third-party online affiliates. Through subsidiaries 1-800-FLOWERS.COM offers gift baskets gourmet foods chocolates and candies cookies and popcorn. Its BloomNet service provides products and services to florists too. Inspired by the emergence of toll-free calling founder and CEO James McCann launched the flower business in 1976 and over time established a national brand that was further fueled by the evolution of the Internet.

	Annual Growth	07/11	07/12*	06/13	06/14	06/15
Sales ($ mil.)	12.9%	689.8	716.3	735.5	756.3	1,121.5
Net income ($ mil.)	37.2%	5.7	17.6	12.3	15.4	20.3
Market value ($ mil.)	34.8%	204.2	227.0	402.5	373.3	675.0
Employees	18.4%	2,300	2,200	2,150	2,034	4,524

*Fiscal year change

1105 MEDIA INC.

9121 Oakdale Ave. Ste. 101
Chatsworth CA 91311
Phone: 818-734-1520
Fax: 818-734-1522
Web: www.101com.com

CEO: –
CFO: Richard Vitale
HR: –
FYE: December 31
Type: Private

1105 Media has a myriad of ways to distribute business-to-business information. The company covers markets such as IT and computing office technology home medical equipment and the public sector. Its products and operations include publications (Redmond Magazine for the Microsoft IT community) e-newsletters (Federal Employees News Digest) websites (CampusTechnology.com) and conferences and events (The Defense Systems Conference). Its 1105 Government Information Group subsidiary covers the government information technology market. 1105 Media was founded in 2006 by Nautic Partners Alta Communications and publishing and marketing executive Neal Vitale.

1MAGE SOFTWARE INC.

384 Inverness Pkwy. Ste. 206
Englewood CO 80112
Phone: 800-844-1468
Fax: 303-796-0587
Web: www.1mage.com

CEO: David R Deyoung
CFO: –
HR: –
FYE: December 31
Type: Private

For 1mage Software images are everything. 1mage helps organizations manage their paper and electronic files by providing software that captures stores and displays documents as electronic images. The company's software handles a wide range of documents including e-mails scanned forms memos letters spreadsheets databases multimedia documents faxes and maps. Add-on modules include tools for faxing printing workflow searching reporting and remote access. 1mage licenses its software to a wide range of clients including energy manufacturing transportation and real estate firms as well as government agencies and organizations.

1ST CENTURY BANCSHARES, INC.

1875 Century Park East, Suite 1400
Los Angeles, CA 90067
Phone: 310 270-9500
Fax: –
Web: www.1cbank.com

NAS: FCTY
CEO: Alan I Rothenberg
CFO: Bradley S Satenberg
HR: –
FYE: December 31
Type: Public

Where would Jesus bank? Probably at 1st Century Bank the operating subsidiary of 1st Century Bancshares. Not to be confused with First Century Bank of West Virginia 1st Century Bank is a one-branch commercial bank located in western Los Angeles near Beverly Hills. It caters to small businesses entrepreneurs and high-net-worth professionals. 1st Century Bank offers checking money market accounts CDs trusts debit and credit cards and online banking to more than 2300 account holders. Commercial loans make up about half of its loan portfolio with real estate loans accounting for most of the rest. 1st Century Bancshares was founded in 2004 not the 1st century.

	Annual Growth	12/10	12/11	12/12	12/13	12/14
Assets ($ mil.)	17.4%	308.4	405.3	499.2	538.1	585.2
Net income ($ mil.)	–	(2.0)	1.0	2.9	6.9	2.4
Market value ($ mil.)	11.5%	41.6	35.9	46.8	72.5	64.4
Employees	14.7%	41	49	56	63	71

1ST COLONIAL BANCORP INC   NBB: FCOB

210 Lake Drive East, Suite 300
Cherry Hill, NJ 08002
Phone: 856 858-2042
Fax: 856 321-8272
Web: www.1stcolonial.com/

CEO: Gerald M Banmiller
CFO: Robert Faix
HR: –
FYE: December 31
Type: Public

1st Colonial Bancorp is the holding company for 1st Colonial National Bank. Founded in 2000 the bank serves Camden County in southern New Jersey through branches in the communities of Cinnaminson Collingswood and Westville. With an emphasis on personalized service it caters to small and midsized businesses professional practices and local government entities as well as consumers. The bank provides traditional deposit products such as checking savings and money market accounts and certificates of deposit. Additional services include check cards online banking and safe deposit boxes.

	Annual Growth	12/10	12/11	12/12	12/13	12/14
Assets ($ mil.)	10.7%	272.6	290.8	304.2	336.2	409.0
Net income ($ mil.)	53.3%	0.2	0.7	1.1	0.9	1.3
Market value ($ mil.)	10.2%	17.1	15.3	18.3	24.6	25.2
Employees	–	–	–	–	–	–

1ST CONSTITUTION BANCORP   NMS: FCCY

2650 Route 130, P.O. Box 634
Cranbury, NJ 08512
Phone: 609 655-4500
Fax: –
Web: www.1stconstitution.com

CEO: Robert F Mangano
CFO: Stephen J Gilhooly
HR: –
FYE: December 31
Type: Public

In order to "secure the blessings of liberty" the founding fathers established the US Constitution. As for promoting the general welfare some banks share the same dedication to "We the people." 1st Constitution Bancorp is the parent of 1st Constitution Bank which serves consumers small businesses and not-for-profits through more than a dozen branches in Middlesex Mercer and Somerset counties in New Jersey. Services and products include demand savings and time deposits as well as loans and mortgages. Commercial mortgages business loans and construction loans make up more half of the bank's lending portfolio.

	Annual Growth	12/10	12/11	12/12	12/13	12/14
Assets ($ mil.)	10.4%	644.4	791.7	841.0	742.3	956.8
Net income ($ mil.)	7.1%	3.3	3.9	5.1	5.8	4.4
Market value ($ mil.)	6.2%	64.1	52.3	65.6	82.4	81.6
Employees	8.1%	137	150	152	173	187

1ST FRANKLIN FINANCIAL CORP.

P.O. Box 880, 135 East Tugalo Street
Toccoa, GA 30577
Phone: 706 886-7571
Fax: –
Web: www.1ffc.com

CEO: Virginia C Herring
CFO: A Roger Guimond
HR: –
FYE: December 31
Type: Public

Benjamin Franklin was known for doling out sage financial advice to "common folk." Today 1st Franklin Financial is known for doling out direct cash loans and first and second home mortgages to a similar demographic. Secured direct cash loans make up the lion's share of the company's lending activity; finance charges on loans account for the majority of its revenues. 1st Franklin also offers credit insurance to borrowers and supplements its business by purchasing and servicing sales finance contracts from retailers. The firm operates through about 250 branch offices in the Southeast. Chairman and CEO Ben Cheek III and his family own 1st Franklin which was founded by his father in 1941.

	Annual Growth	12/10	12/11	12/12	12/13	12/14
Assets ($ mil.)	9.4%	422.1	464.9	518.3	561.8	605.6
Net income ($ mil.)	12.7%	20.7	29.1	32.7	34.4	33.3
Market value ($ mil.)	–	–	–	–	–	–
Employees	4.0%	1,042	1,074	1,092	1,146	1,217

1ST SOURCE CORP.   NMS: SRCE

100 North Michigan Street
South Bend, IN 46601
Phone: 574 235-2000
Fax: –
Web: www.1stsource.com

CEO: Christopher J. (Chris) Murphy
CFO: Andrea G. Short
HR: Abigail Zaher
FYE: December 31
Type: Public

Need a bank? Don't give it a 2nd thought. Contact 1st Source Corporation parent of 1st Source Bank which provides commercial and consumer banking services through nearly 80 branches in northern Indiana and southwestern Michigan. The bank offers deposit accounts; business agricultural and consumer loans; residential and commercial mortgages; credit cards; and trust services. Its specialty finance group provides financing for aircraft automobile fleets trucks and construction and environmental equipment through about two-dozen offices nationwide; such loans account for nearly half of 1st Source's portfolio.

	Annual Growth	12/10	12/11	12/12	12/13	12/14
Assets ($ mil.)	2.1%	4,445.3	4,374.1	4,550.7	4,722.8	4,830.0
Net income ($ mil.)	8.9%	41.2	48.2	49.6	55.0	58.1
Market value ($ mil.)	14.1%	531.3	664.9	579.8	838.4	900.6
Employees	(1.3%)	1,160	1,160	1,180	1,100	1,100

1ST UNITED BANCORP, INC.   NMS: FUBC

One North Federal Highway
Boca Raton, FL 33432
Phone: 561 362-3400
Fax: 561 362-3439
Web: www.1stunitedbankfl.com

CEO: –
CFO: –
HR: –
FYE: December 31
Type: Public

1st United Bancorp is the holding company for 1st United Bank a community-based retail bank with 15 branches in the greater Miami area of Broward Brevard Indian River Miami-Dade and Palm Beach counties plus another handful of branches in Central Florida. 1st United Bank offers checking savings money market and NOW accounts as well as debit and credit cards. It caters mostly to professionals entrepreneurs and high-net-worth individuals. 1st United Bancorp has a mortgage-heavy loan portfolio; some 75% consists of commercial and residential real estate loans. 1st United Bancorp was founded in 2000 as Advantage Bancorp the holding company for Advantage Bank.

	Annual Growth	12/08	12/09	12/10	12/11	12/12
Assets ($ mil.)	26.2%	617.8	1,015.6	1,267.8	1,421.2	1,566.8
Net income ($ mil.)	–	–	(1.4)	4.7	2.2	3.7	4.7
Market value ($ mil.)	1.0%	204.4	243.3	235.4	189.1	212.9
Employees	18.1%	153	229	301	291	298

1SYNC INC.

Princeton Pike Corporate Center 1009 Lenox Dr. Ste. 115
Lawrenceville NJ 08648
Phone: 312-463-4000
Fax: 609-620-4601
Web: www.1sync.org

CEO: Nihat Arkan
CFO: Gary Lo
HR: –
FYE: December 31
Type: Subsidiary

1SYNC hopes to help you synchronize all sorts of trading relationships and product information. The company provides collaborative software used to synchronize data in multiple locations formats and languages. 1SYNC's products are used for functions such as supply chain management business intelligence collaborating with trading partners and managing catalog and pricing information. The company also offers services such as consulting implementation maintenance support and training. Its customers include manufacturers membership organizations and retailers. The company was formed in 2005 when the operations of Transora and UCCnet were combined. 1SYNC is a not-for-profit subsidiary of GS1 US.

21ST CENTURY NORTH AMERICA INSURANCE COMPANY

3 Beaver Valley
Wilmington DE 19803
Phone: 800-443-3100
Fax: 330-668-7204
Web: www.aschulman.com

CEO: Bruce W Marlow
CFO: –
HR: –
FYE: December 31
Type: Subsidiary

Cutting out the middleman — that's how 21st Century Insurance grew in the 20th century. The company's primary subsidiaries provide inexpensive auto and personal umbrella insurance for customers by selling directly rather than through brokers which eliminates the cost of agents and commissions. 21st Century Insurance limits sales of its auto policies to preferred-risk applicants (good drivers). The company has historically been most active in California but has been actively expanding into other states including Texas. 21st Century Insurance is part of the Farmers Group of Zurich Financial Services.

24/7 REAL MEDIA INC.

132 W. 31st St.
New York NY 10001
Phone: 212-231-7100
Fax: 212-760-1774
Web: www.247realmedia.com

CEO: Brian Lesser
CFO: Christina Van Tassell
HR: –
FYE: December 31
Type: Subsidiary

Keeping it real — 24/7. 24/7 Real Media provides key elements in the rapidly changing Internet advertising arena: search marketing services software to host and manage digital ads (including mobile Web ads) and a network of websites that run the ads. The company's Advertiser Solutions segment provides advertisers access to its network of websites and permission-based e-mail marketing database. 24/7 also offers search engine optimization services. Technology offerings revolve around its ad delivery and management software which allows advertisers to plan manage and measure their online campaigns. Operating through 18 offices across 12 countries 24/7 is a subsidiary of communications conglomerate WPP.

30DC INC

NBB: TDCH

80 Broad Street, 5th Floor
New York, NY 10004
Phone: 212 962-4400
Fax: –
Web: www.30dcinc.com

CEO: Henry Pinskier
CFO: Theodore A Greenberg
HR: –
FYE: June 30
Type: Public

30DC offers digital marketing platforms tools services and training through four business units. Its original product was a free 30 day challenge (30DC) training program for Internet marketers. The company also offers digital publishing and marketing tools with MagCast a platform that enables online content to be published and delivered via Apple's Newstand application and Market ProMax a comprehensive online marketing platform that aids in the creation of digital products and e-commerce sites. Formerly a business development company named Infinity Capital Group the company completed a reverse merger with 30DC in 2010 and adopted its name business and management team.

	Annual Growth	06/11	06/12	06/13	06/14	06/15
Sales ($ mil.)	(21.0%)	1.9	2.9	2.0	2.8	0.7
Net income ($ mil.)	–	(1.4)	0.0	(0.4)	0.1	(1.6)
Market value ($ mil.)	(50.3%)	13.1	7.7	4.6	10.0	0.8
Employees	2.4%	10	10	14	11	11

360I LLC

1 Peachtree Pointe 1545 Peachtree St. Ste. 450
Atlanta GA 30309
Phone: 404-876-6007
Fax: 404-876-9097
Web: www.360i.com

CEO: William Margiloff
CFO: –
HR: –
FYE: March 31
Type: Subsidiary

If you are ready for a revolution in your online marketing campaign keep this company on your short list. 360i provides search engine optimization paid placement management and performance analytics services for US and international clients including H&R Block NBCUniversal and Office Depot. In addition to turning Web searches into marketing opportunities (through optimization and paid placement) the company provides development and management services for targeted marketing campaigns using banner ads e-mails and websites. A subsidiary of Innovation Interactive 360i got off the ground in 1998. In 2010 Innovation Interactive was acquired by Japanese advertising conglomerate Dentsu.

3D SYSTEMS CORP. (DE)

NYS: DDD

333 Three D Systems Circle
Rock Hill, SC 29730
Phone: 803 326-3900
Fax: –
Web: www.3dsystems.com

CEO: Andrew M. Johnson
CFO: David R. Styka
HR: Amy Decker
FYE: December 31
Type: Public

3D Systems helps product designers and engineers bring their concepts to life. The company's stereolithography apparatuses (SLAs) and other machines create 3-D prototypes of everything from toys to airplane parts. Its SLAs rapidly produce 3-D objects designed in CAD/CAM software in a process called solid imaging which uses a laser to sculpt plastic resin materials into physical models. Its ThermoJet solid object printer also fabricates plastic models using a modified ink jet printing system. Additionally 3D Systems sells the raw plastic and metal consumable material used in its machinery. Customers have included General Electric Hasbro and Texas Instruments.

	Annual Growth	12/10	12/11	12/12	12/13	12/14
Sales ($ mil.)	42.2%	159.9	230.4	353.6	513.4	653.7
Net income ($ mil.)	(12.2%)	19.6	35.4	38.9	44.1	11.6
Market value ($ mil.)	1.1%	3,511.9	1,605.9	5,949.8	10,363.9	3,665.8
Employees	44.9%	484	714	1,010	1,388	2,136

3M CO

NYS: MMM

3M Center
St. Paul, MN 55144
Phone: 651 733-1110
Fax: 651 733-9973
Web: www.3m.com

CEO: Inge G. Thulin
CFO: Nicholas C. Gangestad
HR: Philip Hanson
FYE: December 31
Type: Public

Loath to be stuck on one thing 3M makes everything from tape to high-tech security gear. The diversified company makes products through five operating segments: Industrial; Safety and Graphics; Electronics and Energy; Health Care; and Consumer. Well-known brands include Post-it notes Scotch tapes Scotchgard fabric protectors Scotch-Brite scouring pads and Filtrete home air filters. 3M sells products directly to users and through numerous wholesalers retailers distributors and dealers worldwide. Industrial its largest segment accounted for about 34% of 3M's total revenues in 2014.

	Annual Growth	12/11	12/12	12/13	12/14	12/15
Sales ($ mil.)	0.6%	29,611.0	29,904.0	30,871.0	31,821.0	30,274.0
Net income ($ mil.)	3.1%	4,283.0	4,444.0	4,659.0	4,956.0	4,833.0
Market value ($ mil.)	16.5%	49,800.6	56,576.3	85,458.5	100,125.1	91,789.5
Employees	1.5%	84,198	87,677	88,667	89,800	89,446

3M COGENT INC.

639 N. Rosemead Blvd.
Pasadena CA 91107
Phone: 626-325-9600
Fax: 626-325-9700
Web: www.cogentsystems.com

CEO: Ming Hsieh
CFO: Paul Kim
HR: –
FYE: December 31
Type: Subsidiary

3M Cogent knows security. The company provides Automated Fingerprint Identification Systems (AFIS) that governments law enforcement agencies and companies use to capture analyze and compare fingerprints. 3M Cogent's offerings include proprietary biometrics access control software hardware (including mobile systems) system maintenance and services that include consulting implementation and systems integration. It also enjoys an alliance with Northrop Grumman for design development and sale of biometric ID systems. 3M Cogent operates in Austria Canada China Taiwan the UK and the US where the Department of Homeland Security is a core customer. In 2010 3M purchased the company for $943 million.

3M PURIFICATION INC.

400 Research Pkwy.
Meriden CT 06450
Phone: 203-237-5541
Fax: 203-238-8977
Web: www.3mpurification.com

CEO: Inge Thulin
CFO: Frederick C Flynn Jr
HR: –
FYE: October 31
Type: Subsidiary

3M Purification looks at liquids and gases through rose-colored filters. The company a unit of 3M's Industrial and Transportation segment makes a full line of filtration products for the health care fluid-processing and potable-water markets. Its filters remove contaminants as small as molecules and particles as large as sand from liquids and gases. They are used to purify drugs paints and resins oil and gas and home drinking water. 3M Purification assigns its own scientists to work with customers when creating new products. The company which was known as CUNO until 2009 operates sales offices worldwide and eight manufacturing plants in Australia Europe Japan South America and the US.

454 LIFE SCIENCES

20 Commercial St.
Branford CT 06405
Phone: 203-871-2300
Fax: 203-481-2075
Web: www.454.com

CEO: Christopher K Mc Leod
CFO: –
HR: –
FYE: December 31
Type: Subsidiary

454 Life Sciences wants to give drug developers and other gene researchers the 411 on entire genomes. The company has developed computer-controlled instruments and related software that enable scientists to analyze whole genomes in one fell swoop rather than a few hundred genes at a time. Parent company Roche Diagnostics distributes 454 Life Sciences' Genome Sequencing systems (GS Junior and GS FLX) to clinical laboratories medical research institutes drugmakers and other scientific customers worldwide. Research fields include cancer infectious disease drug discovery agriculture and paleontology.

4LICENSING CORP

NBB: FOUR

5 Penn Plaza
New York, NY 10001
Phone: 646 931-1022
Fax: –
Web: www.4kidsentertainment.com

CEO: Bruce R Foster
CFO: Bruce R Foster
HR: –
FYE: December 31
Type: Public

If your kids are into Yu-Gi-Oh! thank (or blame) 4Kids Entertainment. The company licenses the rights to third-party entertainment properties for use in cartoons games toys and apparel. It also uses those properties to produce TV shows videos films music and websites for kids. Its youth-oriented portfolio includes Chaotic Yu-Gi-Oh! Cabbage Patch Kids Dinosaur King and Viva Piñata. 4Kids also handles licensing for the American Kennel Club the Cat Fanciers' Association and the UK's Royal Air Force. It has a five-year partnership with The CW Network (ending in 2013) to program its Saturday morning The CW4Kids lineup. In 2011 4Kids voluntarily filed for Chapter 11 bankruptcy protection.

	Annual Growth	12/10	12/11	12/12	12/13	12/14
Sales ($ mil.)	(46.7%)	14.5	12.3	3.3	1.2	1.2
Net income ($ mil.)	–	(27.2)	(15.2)	9.5	(3.2)	(0.9)
Market value ($ mil.)	4.2%	–	–	–	9.5	9.9
Employees	(49.0%)	89	71	16	10	6

5LINX ENTERPRISES INC.

275 KENNETH DR STE 100
ROCHESTER, NY 146234277
Phone: 585-359-2922
Fax: –
Web: www.5linx.com

CEO: Craig Jerabeck
CFO: –
HR: –
FYE: December 31
Type: Private

You won't see 5LINX stores popping up anytime soon but the telecommunications company is still a fast growing enterprise. Relying on a network of independent marketing representatives to sell its products (similar to the model employed by Mary Kay) 5LINX provides an array of telecommunications products and services. Among these are cellular phones and plans from major US carriers; satellite TV service from DISH Network and DIRECTV; and broadband Internet and home security services. Representatives also sell GLOBALINX VoIP services for residential and business customers; a subsidiary of 5LINX GLOBALINX products include Wi-Fi phones and digital phone services.

	Annual Growth	12/09	12/10	12/11	12/12	12/13
Sales ($ mil.)	30.8%	–	50.0	81.4	103.6	112.1
Net income ($ mil.)	(10.4%)	–	–	1.5	3.8	1.2
Market value ($ mil.)	–	–	–	–	–	–
Employees	–	–	–	–	–	275

7-ELEVEN INC.

1722 Routh St. Ste. 1000 1 Arts Plz
Dallas TX 75201
Phone: 972-828-7011
Fax: 972-828-7848
Web: www.7-eleven.com

CEO: Joseph M Depinto
CFO: Stanley Reynolds
HR: –
FYE: December 31
Type: Subsidiary

"If convenience stores are open 24 hours why the locks on their doors?" If anyone knows it's 7-Eleven. The North American subsidiary of Seven-Eleven Japan 7-Eleven operates more than 7200 company-owned or franchised stores in the US and Canada under the 7-Eleven name. Globally 7-Eleven licenses more than 24000 stores in about a dozen countries mostly in the Asia Pacific and Nordic regions. Its stores range from 2400 to 3000 sq. ft. and sell about 2500 items. The world's leading convenience store company is owned by the Japanese retail conglomerate Seven & i Holdings which is the holding company for Seven-Eleven Japan Ito-Yokado Denny's restaurants and other businesses.

800-JR CIGAR INC.

301 Rte. 10 East
Whippany NJ 07981
Phone: 973-884-9555
Fax: 973-884-9556
Web: www.jrcigars.com

CEO: Lew Rothman
CFO: Michael E Colleton
HR: Karen Dallesondro
FYE: December 31
Type: Subsidiary

800-JR Cigar would like to give that man (or woman) a cigar. Doing business as JR Cigars the company that began as a small Manhattan cigar shop is now a leading distributor and retailer of premium cigars. It also sells pipe tobacco lighters humidors and other smoking accessories as well as coffee. JR Cigars' retail operations include three discount outlet stores in North Carolina a catalog and an e-commerce site. The company's website also features regular auctions and a section called JR Cigar University where tobacco aficionados can read up on all things stogie related. 800-JR Cigar is a subsidiary of Altadis itself owned by Imperial Tobacco Group.

84 LUMBER COMPANY

1019 Rte. 519
Eighty Four PA 15330-2813
Phone: 724-228-8820
Fax: 310-319-0310
Web: www.amark.com

CEO: Joe Hardy
CFO: Paul Lentz
HR: –
FYE: December 31
Type: Private

With its utilitarian stores (most don't have heat or A/C) 84 Lumber has built itself up to be a leading low-cost provider of lumber building materials and related services. Through about 250 stores in 30 states the company (which is the nation's largest privately held building materials retailer) sells lumber siding drywall windows and other supplies as well as plans to construct decks garages and houses. Its 84 Components subsidiary operates plants that make floor and roof trusses and wall panels. In addition 84 Lumber provides insurance travel and professional installation services. CEO Joseph Hardy Sr. founded 84 Lumber in 1956.

8X8 INC.
NMS: EGHT

2125 O'Nel Drive
San Jose, CA 95131
Phone: 408 727-1885
Fax: 408 980-0432
Web: www.8x8.com

CEO: Vikram (Vik) Verma
CFO: Mary Ellen P. Genovese
HR: –
FYE: March 31
Type: Public

8x8 is counting on Internet telephony usage to multiply. The company provides services powered by its software that enable voice and video communication over Internet Protocol (IP) networks. Its services are used primarily by business subscribers in the US to make phone calls over broadband connections and access other functions including voice mail caller ID call waiting call forwarding and conferencing. 8x8 sells directly and through resellers and retailers to businesses government agencies and educational institutions as well as a dwindling number of residential subscribers. 8x8's MobileTalk service targets mobile phone users who want to lower their rates by making international calls over the Web.

	Annual Growth	03/11	03/12	03/13	03/14	03/15
Sales ($ mil.)	23.3%	70.2	85.8	107.6	128.6	162.4
Net income ($ mil.)	(26.2%)	6.5	69.2	13.9	2.5	1.9
Market value ($ mil.)	31.5%	247.5	369.9	603.2	952.0	739.8
Employees	22.1%	254	301	357	484	565

99 CENTS ONLY STORES
NYSE: NDN

4000 Union Pacific Ave.
Los Angeles CA 90023
Phone: 323-980-8145
Fax: 323-980-8160
Web: www.99only.com

CEO: Geoffrey Covert
CFO: Christopher A Laurence
HR: –
FYE: March 31
Type: Private

Pass the buck get a penny back. 99 Cents Only Stores sells closeout and regular general merchandise for 99 cents or less. With about 300 stores the company sells name-brand and private-label food and beverages (more than 50% os sales) health and beauty aids household and seasonal goods hardware toys and more. Nearly three-quarters of its stores are in California; other stores are located in Arizona Nevada and Texas. The company's Bargain Wholesale unit distributes discounted merchandise to retailers distributors and exporters. Founded in 1982 99 Cents Only Stores was taken private by Ares Management Canada Pension Plan Investment and the Gold/Schiffer family in 2012.

A & H SPORTSWEAR CO. INC.

500 William St.
Pen Argyl PA 18072
Phone: 610-863-4176
Fax: 630-467-3010
Web: www.necdisplay.com

CEO: Mark Waldman
CFO: Mark Greenberg
HR: –
FYE: October 31
Type: Private

When swimsuit season rolls around Houdini has nothing on A & H Sportswear. The company's Miraclesuit makes 10 pounds disappear! The Miraclesuit bathing suits suck in that tummy using three times as much Lycra as most other swimwear. The firm also makes shapewear jeans and other casual apparel using its patented Miratex fabric. A & H Sportswear's clothing and swimsuits are sold in the US through finer retailers (such as Bloomingdale's Nordstrom Saks Fifth Avenue) catalogs (Eddie Bauer Norm Thompson and Spiegel) and online. A & H Sportswear's offerings are also marketed internationally through independent dealers.

A&E TELEVISION NETWORKS LLC

235 E. 45th St.
New York NY 10017
Phone: 212-210-1400
Fax: 212-210-1308
Web: www.aetn.com

CEO: –
CFO: Gerard Gruosso
HR: –
FYE: December 31
Type: Joint Venture

You might say this company gives viewers a lifetime dose of television. A&E Television Networks (AETN) owns and operates a portfolio of ten cable TV channels including Lifetime Television the flagship network of AETN subsidiary Lifetime Entertainment that targets women with a variety of lifestyle and entertainment content. Its A&E network offers a mix of reality-based programming and documentaries while its HISTORY channel airs original programs on historical topics. The company also operates sister networks such as Crime & Investigation Network and The Biography Channel. AETN is a joint venture between Hearst Walt Disney and NBCUniversal (NBCU).

A&R LOGISTICS INC.

8440 S. Tabler Rd.
Morris IL 60450
Phone: 815-941-5200
Fax: 800-406-5703
Web: www.artransport.com

CEO: Mark R Holden
CFO: Anthony W Lenhart
HR: –
FYE: December 31
Type: Private

Through its subsidiaries A&R Logistics offers a diverse menu of transportation and logistics services. A&R Transport is a bulk plastic and dry flowable transportation provider with about 25 terminals and 10 warehouses throughout the US; its fleet includes 770 tractors and about 1100 trailers. A&R Global Logistics arranges freight transportation (mostly bulk shipments of dry plastic pallets in hopper trucks for chemical companies) through a network of independent carriers and A&R Packaging & Distribution operates warehouses and provides packaging services. UTC Overseas provides freight-forwarding and door-to-door services in Europe.

A&W RESTAURANTS INC.

1648 McGrathiana Pkwy.
Lexington KY 40511
Phone: 859-219-0019
Fax: 770-448-7726
Web: www.presidio.com/presidio_tech_cap

CEO: Kevin Bazner
CFO: –
HR: –
FYE: December 31
Type: Private

The old-fashioned root beer stand lives on thanks to this business. A&W Restaurants franchises more than 1200 quick-service restaurants in the US and unaffiliated restaurants in about 15 other countries. The eateries many of which still offer drive-up service in addition to dine-in seating offer a menu featuring hamburgers hot dogs onion rings and fries along with its signature root beer. A&W traces its roots back to a California root beer stand business started by Roy Allen in 1919. It belonged to YUM! Brands the world's largest fast-food franchisor until late 2011 when a group of franchisees purchased it.

A. B. BOYD COMPANY

600 S. McClure Rd.
Modesto CA 95357
Phone: 209-236-1111
Fax: 209-236-0154
Web: www.boydcorp.com

CEO: –
CFO: Kurt Wetzel
HR: –
FYE: December 31
Type: Private

A. B. Boyd Company puts a little zip in rubber manufacturing. Initially a zipper distributor the company has evolved to operate as Boyd Corporation and manufacture rubber plastic and fiber products that offer environmental sealing and energy-efficient solutions. The custom-designed and manufactured products meet requirements for acoustic thermal shock and shielding systems among others. Boyd uses a range of specialized materials from silicone to Mylar polypropylene copper and aluminum foils and coated fabrics to deliver a low-cost engineered lineup. It caters to OEMs in aerospace electronics medical equipment telecommunications and transportation. Boyd is held by Stonebridge Partners Management.

A. DUIE PYLE INC.

650 Westtown Rd.
West Chester PA 19381-0564
Phone: 610-696-5800
Fax: 610-696-3768
Web: www.aduiepyle.com

CEO: Peter Latta
CFO: –
HR: –
FYE: December 31
Type: Private

A. Duie Pyle has piled up a collection of transportation-related businesses. The company's services include less-than-truckload (LTL) and truckload freight hauling warehousing third-party logistics and equipment leasing. (LTL carriers consolidate freight from multiple shippers into a single trailer.) A. Duie Pyle's LTL business operates primarily in the Northeast US and in Canada from a network of more than 15 service depots. The LTL unit maintains a fleet of about 790 tractors and 1800 trailers; another 325 tractors for heated truckload hauling. The company offers service outside its core region through alliances with other carriers. A. Duie Pyle maintains about 2 million sq. ft. of warehouse space.

A. EICOFF & COMPANY

401 N. Michigan Ave.
Chicago IL 60611
Phone: 312-527-7100
Fax: 312-527-7192
Web: www.eicoff.com

CEO: Bill McCabe
CFO: Pat Sacony
HR: –
FYE: December 31
Type: Subsidiary

This firm's business is getting couch potatoes to take action. A. Eicoff & Company is a leading advertising agency specializing in direct response television marketing. It helps create TV spots and campaigns that not only highlight a product or brand but also urge consumers to call write or log onto the Internet for more information. In addition to creative work A. Eicoff provides monitoring and measuring services to track the effectiveness of its campaigns and it offers planning services to help its clients target specific consumer groups. The company was founded in 1965 by Alvin Eicoff and now operates as part of OgilvyOne the marketing services arm of global advertising agency network Ogilvy & Mather.

A. FINKL & SONS COMPANY

2011 N. Southport Ave.
Chicago IL 60614
Phone: 773-975-2510
Fax: 773-348-5347
Web: www.finkl.com

CEO: –
CFO: Joseph E Curci
HR: –
FYE: January 31
Type: Private

Thanks to Mrs. O'Leary's cow A. Finkl & Sons has chiseled a niche for itself in the steel industry. The company was founded in 1879 when Anton Finkl developed a chisel to clean bricks rescued from buildings destroyed in the Great Chicago Fire. Since then Finkl has forged ahead to become a leading global supplier of forging die steels. (A forging die is a steel block used in a hammer or press for shaping metal.) The firm also produces plastic mold steels die casting tool steels and custom open-die forging. German steel company SCHMOLZ+BICKENBACH owns Finkl.

A. P. HUBBARD WHOLESALE LUMBER CORPORATION

1027 ARNOLD ST
GREENSBORO, NC 274057101
Phone: 336-275-1343
Fax: –
Web: www.hubbardlumber.com

CEO: –
CFO: –
HR: –
FYE: March 31
Type: Private

A.P. Hubbard Lumber manufactures lumber and lumber products for the construction industry. Its offerings include air- and kiln-dried lumber made from cypress hardwoods softwoods and eastern white pine as well as engineered wood products such as glue-laminated timber rim board wood deckinh sheathing and framing lumber. The company distributes its products in the Carolinas Virginia and Maryland. A.P. Hubbard Lumber was founded in Greensboro North Carolina in 1952.

	Annual Growth	03/08	03/09	03/10	03/11	03/12
Sales ($ mil.)	20.2%	–	8.8	8.8	11.7	15.3
Net income ($ mil.)	96.7%	–	–	0.0	0.0	0.1
Market value ($ mil.)	–	–	–	–	–	–
Employees	–	–	–	–	–	5

A.C. MOORE ARTS & CRAFTS INC.

NASDAQ: ACMR

130 A.C. Moore Dr.
Berlin NJ 08009
Phone: 856-768-4930
Fax: 856-753-4723
Web: www.acmoore.com

CEO: Joseph A Jeffries
CFO: David Stern
HR: –
FYE: December 31
Type: Private

Some are content to collect and dust their tchotchkes but others are compelled to make them. A.C. Moore Arts & Crafts is eager to serve them all (focusing on women 35 and older). The chain's 130-plus superstores (up from 17 in 1997) sell crafts and art and scrapbooking supplies which account for about 60% of sales as well as yarn seasonal items fashion crafts home decor and picture frames and everything else needed to glue paint or arrange. A.C. Moore also offers in-store arts-and-crafts classes. Its stores are located in more than a dozen states along the East Coast. Founded in 1985 A.C. Moore was acquired in late 2011 by affiliates of arts and crafts distributor Sbar's Inc. for about $41 million.

A.P. PHARMA INC.

NASDAQ: APPA

123 Saginaw Dr.
Redwood City CA 94063
Phone: 650-366-2626
Fax: 650-365-6490
Web: www.appharma.com

CEO: Barry D Quart
CFO: Brian G Drazba
HR: –
FYE: December 31
Type: Public

A.P. Pharma wants to hit you where it hurts. The firm develops bioerodible polymers for injectable and implantable drug delivery. Its Biochronomer technology delivers medication directly to the site where the drug is needed. A.P. Pharma's leading drug candidate APF530 could ease chemotherapy-induced nausea and vomiting. A second candidate in clinical trials is a post-surgical pain management product that delivers pain relief right to the surgical site. A.P. Pharma is also developing therapies for inflammation and chronic pain using its Biochronomer technology. Its drug candidates combine approved therapeutics with its bioerodible polymers.

A.V. THOMAS PRODUCE INC.

3900 SULTANA AVE
ATWATER, CA 953019605
Phone: 209-394-7514
Fax: –
Web: www.avthomasproduce.com

CEO: –
CFO: Dana Miller
HR: –
FYE: December 31
Type: Private

A.V. Thomas Produce knows a sweet potato is not just a yam by another name. The California grower produces packages and sells several varieties of yams and the yam's sweeter cousin the sweet potato. (Though the names are used interchangeably in this country most US-grown "yams" are actually sweet potatoes.) With 1700 acres in production its brands include Best West Court House Nature's Pride Oriental Beauty Royal Flush Sweetie Pie Thomas and Winner; it is also a major US producer of organic sweet potatoes which it sells under the Natural Beauty label. Founded in 1960 by Antonio Vieira Tomas an immigrant from the Azores Islands A.V. Thomas is owned and run by Tomas's nephew CEO Manuel Vieira.

	Annual Growth	12/09	12/10	12/11	12/12	12/13
Sales ($ mil.)	12.8%	–	48.5	60.8	65.5	69.7
Net income ($ mil.)	16.6%	–	–	10.6	9.0	14.5
Market value ($ mil.)	–	–	–	–	–	–
Employees	–	–	–	–	–	8

A2D TECHNOLOGIES

2345 Atascocita Rd.
Humble TX 77396
Phone: 281-319-4944
Fax: 281-319-4945
Web: www.tgsnopec.com

CEO: –
CFO: –
HR: –
FYE: December 31
Type: Subsidiary

Less talkative than Star Wars' R2-D2 A2D Technologies nevertheless communicates well by providing digital well log data interpretive software and data management services. A2D's LOG-LINE system allows geoscientists to access and download well log data from their workstations. Customers use its well log data to calibrate seismic data to known geologic conditions in well bores. A2D Technologies has data coverage worldwide including the US Canada the Gulf of Mexico offshore Northwest Europe Russia West Africa and Madagascar. Parent TGS-NOPEC Geophysical is one of the largest owners of digital well log data in North America.

AAA COOPER TRANSPORTATION

1751 KINSEY RD
DOTHAN, AL 363035877
Phone: 334-793-2284
Fax: –
Web: www.aaacooper.com

CEO: –
CFO: Steve Roy
HR: Preston Warren
FYE: December 29
Type: Private

They might not give you a map like that other AAA but AAA Cooper Transportation can freight your cargo from point A to point B. A non-union regional less-than-truckload (LTL) freight hauler AAA Cooper (ACT) operates in a dozen southeastern US states as well as Puerto Rico; it also maintains facilities in Chicago and a few other industrial crossroads. (LTL carriers combine freight from multiple shippers into a single truckload.) ACT operates a fleet of approximately 2400 tractors and 6000 trailers. ACT also offers freight brokerage services and dedicated contract carriage.

	Annual Growth	01/10	01/11	01/12*	12/12	12/13
Sales ($ mil.)	10.7%	–	468.9	520.9	553.4	575.0
Net income ($ mil.)	170.0%	–	–	7.6	20.8	20.4
Market value ($ mil.)	–	–	–	–	–	–
Employees	–	–	–	–	–	4,193

*Fiscal year change

AAC GROUP HOLDING CORP.

7211 Circle S Rd.
Austin TX 78745
Phone: 512-444-0571
Fax: 512-443-5213
Web: www.cbi-rings.com

CEO: –
CFO: Kris G Radhakrishnan
HR: –
FYE: August 31
Type: Subsidiary

School spirit tops the shopping list of customers of AAC Group. Doing business as American Achievement the company manufactures and supplies class rings yearbooks and letter athletic jackets as well as graduation items such as caps and gowns diplomas and announcements for the US elementary through high school and college markets. Its ring and accessory brands include Art-Carved Balfour and Keepsake. Although scholastic products account for most of its sales AAC Group also makes commemorative jewelry for families bridal jewelry personalized rings for the military bowling tournaments and pro sports such as World Series Super Bowl and Stanley Cup. The memorabilia maker is owned by Fenway Partners.

AAMCO TRANSMISSIONS INC.

201 Gibraltar Rd.
Horsham PA 19044
Phone: 215-643-5885
Fax: 215-956-0340
Web: www.aamco.com

CEO: Keith A Morgan
CFO: Jim Gregory
HR: –
FYE: December 31
Type: Private

AAMCO Transmissions is geared for transmission repair. The company is a leading franchiser of transmission fix-it facilities with about 900 independently owned and operated shops throughout the US Canada and Puerto Rico. In addition to transmission work AAMCO locations provide automotive cooling and electrical system repairs as well as other general maintenance services. The company was established in 1963 by Robert Morgan and MAACO founder Anthony Martino. Today it operates alongside sister franchiser Cottman Transmission under holding company American Driveline Systems itself a subsidiary of investment firm American Capital.

AAON, INC.

2425 South Yukon
Tulsa, OK 74107
Phone: 918 583-2266
Fax: 918 583-6094
Web: www.aaon.com

NMS: AAON
CEO: Norman H. (Norm) Asbjornson
CFO: Scott M. Asbjornson
HR: Martha Lenard
FYE: December 31
Type: Public

Some like it hot some like it cold; AAON keeps it just right. Operating through its subsidiaries the company makes and markets air conditioning and heating equipment for commercial and industrial buildings primarily in the US and some provinces in Canada. AAON's products include rooftop units air-handling and make-up air units chillers and heat recovery units condensing as well as commercial self-contained units and coils. Units range in size from one ton to 230 tons. (Most commercial buildings require one ton of cool air for every 300 to 400 sq. ft.) AAON sells to property owners and contractors in the new construction and replacement market via a network of OEM representatives and its own sales force.

	Annual Growth	12/10	12/11	12/12	12/13	12/14
Sales ($ mil.)	9.9%	244.6	266.2	303.1	321.1	356.3
Net income ($ mil.)	19.2%	21.9	14.0	27.4	37.5	44.2
Market value ($ mil.)	(5.6%)	1,524.5	1,107.3	1,127.9	1,726.6	1,210.0
Employees	3.1%	1,420	1,506	1,396	1,167	1,604

AAR CORP

One AAR Place, 1100 N. Wood Dale Road
Wood Dale, IL 60191
Phone: 630 227-2000
Fax: 630 227-2019
Web: www.aarcorp.com

NYS: AIR
CEO: David P. Storch
CFO: Michael J. Sharp
HR: Maryanne Cipperly
FYE: May 31
Type: Public

On much more than a wing and a prayer AAR provides a wide variety of aviation services and technology products primarily for the aerospace and defense industries. The company supplies commercial customers and the US government and its contractors with aircraft components such as transportation pallets containers shelters mobility systems and control systems used in support of the deployment of military and humanitarian activities. AAR also provides inventory management and parts distribution; aircraft maintenance repair and overhaul; and expeditionary airlift services. The company traces its historical roots to 1955 when it was founded as Allen Aircraft Radio.

	Annual Growth	05/11	05/12	05/13	05/14	05/15
Sales ($ mil.)	(2.7%)	1,775.8	2,065.0	2,137.3	2,035.0	1,594.3
Net income ($ mil.)	(38.2%)	69.8	67.7	55.0	72.9	10.2
Market value ($ mil.)	2.9%	934.8	426.8	710.6	860.8	1,046.4
Employees	(4.4%)	6,870	7,600	7,200	6,400	5,750

AARON AND COMPANY INC.

30 TURNER PL
PISCATAWAY, NJ 088543839
Phone: 732-752-8200
Fax: –
Web: www.aaronco.com

CEO: –
CFO: Victor De Rosa
HR: –
FYE: December 31
Type: Private

Aaron & Company knows a thing or two about staying cool. Catering primarily to contractors in New Jersey and eastern Pennsylvania the wholesaler offers plumbing and HVAC supplies through more than five locations in the Garden State. Three of these outlets house Aaron Kitchen & Bath Design Galleries which feature complete kitchen and bathroom set-ups to help customers with building and remodeling plans. Aaron & Company is served by a single 120000-sq.-ft. distribution center that is stocked with more than 15000 items.

	Annual Growth	12/08	12/09	12/11	12/12	12/13
Sales ($ mil.)	9.9%	–	54.6	68.4	68.4	79.6
Net income ($ mil.)	9.2%	–	–	0.8	0.8	1.0
Market value ($ mil.)	–	–	–	–	–	–
Employees	–	–	–	–	–	188

AARON'S, INC.

309 E. Paces Ferry Road, N.E.
Atlanta, GA 30305-2377
Phone: 404 231-0011
Fax: –
Web: www.aarons.com

NYS: AAN
CEO: John W. Robinson
CFO: Steven A. (Steve) Michaels
HR: –
FYE: December 31
Type: Public

For customers who desire a desk seek a sofa or lust for an LCD TV Aaron's rents — and sells — all of these and more. One of the nation's top furniture rental and rent-to-own companies (behind industry leader Rent-A-Center) Aaron's purveys home furnishings electronics computers and appliances through more than 2100 Aaron's stores and more than 80 HomeSmart locations in the US and Canada. Its Woodhaven Furniture Industries unIt makes most of the firm's furniture and bedding at more than a dozen plants in the US. Founded in 1955 Aaron's has exited the office furniture rental business to focus on household goods.

	Annual Growth	12/10	12/11	12/12	12/13	12/14
Sales ($ mil.)	9.8%	1,876.8	2,024.0	2,222.6	2,234.6	2,725.2
Net income ($ mil.)	(9.8%)	118.4	113.8	173.0	120.7	78.2
Market value ($ mil.)	10.7%	1,478.0	1,934.0	2,050.0	2,131.2	2,216.0
Employees	4.5%	10,400	11,200	11,900	12,600	12,400

AARP INC.

601 E St. NW
Washington DC 20049
Phone: 202-434-2277
Fax: 202-434-7710
Web: www.aarp.org

CEO: Jo Ann Jenkins
CFO: Robert R Hagans
HR: –
FYE: December 31
Type: Private - Not-for-Pr

Turn 50 and the doors of the AARP will open for you as they have for 37 million current members. On behalf of its members the not-for-profit AARP acts as an advocate on public policy issues such as health care and financial security publishes information (the monthly "AARP Bulletin" and the bimonthly "AARP The Magazine" and through Spanish language media) promotes community service and works with business partners to offer products and services (including discounts on insurance and travel). The group is organized into some 2400 local chapters throughout the US. Royalties from businesses eager to reach AARP members account for about half of the group's revenue.

AASTRA INTECOM INC.

2811 Internet Blvd.
Frisco TX 75034
Phone: 469-365-3237
Fax: 469-365-3533
Web: www.aastraintecom.com

CEO: –
CFO: –
HR: –
FYE: December 31
Type: Subsidiary

Aastra Intecom also known as Aastra USA is the US division of Canada's Aastra Technologies. The company provides IP telephony systems and contact center services to enterprise and government customers. Its products include the Clearspan line of IP communications equipment as well as its Centergy virtual contact center for managing agents across multiple sites. The company also offers professional services such as project management system installation and technical support. It targets such industry sectors as education government health care and insurance. Aastra USA represents less than 15% of its parent's overall sales.

ABATIX CORP.

PINK SHEETS: ABIX

2400 Skyline Dr. Ste. 400
Mesquite TX 75149
Phone: 214-381-0222
Fax: 214-388-0443
Web: www.abatix.com

CEO: Terry W Shaver
CFO: Frank J Cinatl IV
HR: –
FYE: December 31
Type: Private

Following a huff and a puff Abatix cleans up. The company distributes more than 30000 personal protection and safety equipment products to environmental contractors as well as construction and industrial safety companies. Abatix's lineup is used by workers involved in cleanup projects such as asbestos and lead abatement and natural disasters. Products include sheeting and bags dehumidifiers air scrubbers and filters and germicidals. Subsidiary International Enviroguard Systems imports fire retardant and disposable protective clothing. Abatix serves some 6000 customers located throughout the US. It operates sales and distribution centers in Texas Arizona Nevada California Washington and Florida.

ABAXIS, INC.

NMS: ABAX

3240 Whipple Road
Union City, CA 94587
Phone: 510 675-6500
Fax: –
Web: www.abaxis.com

CEO: Clinton H. (Clint) Severson
CFO: Ross Taylor
HR: –
FYE: March 31
Type: Public

Abaxis makes a praxis of analyzing blood. Its two types of point-of-care blood analyzers (one for animals and one for humans) can each perform more than a dozen tests on their respective veterinary and human health patients. The analyzers are portable require little training provide on-the-spot results and offer built-in quality control and calibration. Abaxis also sells compatible chemical reagent supplies. In the veterinary market its systems bear the VetScan name; in the human medical market Piccolo Xpress. Abaxis sells to veterinarians hospitals managed care organizations and the military.

	Annual Growth	03/11	03/12	03/13	03/14	03/15
Sales ($ mil.)	9.0%	143.7	156.6	186.0	171.9	202.6
Net income ($ mil.)	17.1%	14.5	13.1	27.5	14.2	27.3
Market value ($ mil.)	22.1%	650.0	656.6	1,066.5	876.3	1,445.0
Employees	10.7%	388	491	535	520	582

ABBOTT LABORATORIES

NYS: ABT

100 Abbott Park Road
Abbott Park, IL 60064-6400
Phone: 224 667-6100
Fax: –
Web: www.abbott.com

CEO: Miles D. White
CFO: Thomas C. (Tom) Freyman
HR: Stephen R. (Steve) Fussell
FYE: December 31
Type: Public

Filling baby bottles and treating disease... these are the habits of Abbott. Abbott Laboratories is a top health care products manufacturer. Its nutritional products division makes such well-known brands as Similac infant formula and the Ensure line of nutrition supplements while its drug division sells branded generic medicines (such as antibiotics and gastroenterology medicines) in international markets. The company also makes diagnostic instruments (including tests and assays) vascular medical devices such as its Xience drug-eluting stents and the FreeStyle diabetes care line as well as eye care products. Abbott spun off its non-generic pharmaceutical operations into AbbVie in 2013.

	Annual Growth	12/10	12/11	12/12	12/13	12/14
Sales ($ mil.)	(12.9%)	35,166.7	38,851.3	39,873.9	21,848.0	20,247.0
Net income ($ mil.)	(16.2%)	4,626.2	4,728.4	5,962.9	2,576.0	2,284.0
Market value ($ mil.)	(1.5%)	72,250.0	84,796.8	98,776.3	57,803.0	67,891.8
Employees	(3.8%)	90,000	91,000	91,000	69,000	77,000

ABBVIE INC.

NYS: ABBV

1 North Waukegan Road
North Chicago, IL 60064-6400
Phone: 847 932-7900
Fax: –
Web: www.abbvie.com

CEO: Richard A. (Rick) Gonzalez
CFO: William J. Chase
HR: Leanna Walther
FYE: December 31
Type: Public

AbbVie came from Abbott but is making a life of its own. The biopharmaceutical research company was spun off from its former parent health care products maker Abbott Labs in 2013. AbbVie has seven facilities making products that are available in more than 170 countries. Its key drugs include arthritis and Crohn's disease treatment Humira; TriCor Trilipix Simcor and Niaspan for high cholesterol; HIV drugs Kaletra and Norvir; and low testosterone treatment AndroGel among others. Humira which is best known as a rheumatoid arthritis drug accounts for more than 60% of AbbVie's sales. With its main product's patent protection expiring in 2016 the R&D firm is looking for the next big thing.

	Annual Growth	12/10	12/11	12/12	12/13	12/14
Sales ($ mil.)	6.3%	15,637.7	17,444.0	18,380.0	18,790.0	19,960.0
Net income ($ mil.)	(19.3%)	4,177.9	3,433.1	5,275.0	4,128.0	1,774.0
Market value ($ mil.)	23.9%	–	–	–	84,041.3	104,140.5
Employees	(4.7%)	–	30,000	21,500	25,000	26,000

ABC APPLIANCE INC.

1 Silverdome Industrial Park
Pontiac MI 48343-6001
Phone: 248-335-4222
Fax: 248-335-2568
Web: www.abcwarehouse.com

CEO: –
CFO: Paul Black
HR: Sarah Burger
FYE: October 31
Type: Private

When customers have to buy retail they turn to ABC Appliance for "the closest thing to wholesale." The company sells audio equipment electronics computers home appliances and other products at more than 60 stores in Michigan Ohio and Indiana as well as online. ABC Appliance's inventory includes products from manufacturers such as LG General Electric Sony and Whirlpool. The company's retail stores operate under the ABC Warehouse Mickey Shorr (mobile electronics) and Hawthorne Appliance banners. US-Appliance.com is the firm's online-only consumer electronics and appliance sales business. CEO Gordy Hartunian founded ABC Appliance in 1964 and the chain remains owned by his family.

ABC CABLE NETWORKS GROUP

3800 W. Alameda Ave.
Burbank CA 91505
Phone: 818-569-7500
Fax: +972-9-956-1610
Web: www.onsettechnology.com

CEO: –
CFO: –
HR: –
FYE: September 30
Type: Subsidiary

ABC Cable Networks Group wants to work a little magic on the television dial. The unit of Disney/ABC Television Group owns and operates a portfolio of cable television networks including entertainment channels ABC Family. It also owns Disney Channels Worldwide which operates kids' networks the Disney Channel and Disney XD; other kids' programming is distributed under Disney Junior (launched in 2012) and Jetix. (Through ABC Family ABC Cable Networks owns animation distributor Jetix Europe.) In addition ABC Cable Networks holds a 42% stake in A&E Television. Disney/ABC Television Group oversees the television broadcasting production and distribution operations of media giant Walt Disney.

ABC INC.

77 W. 66th St.
New York NY 10023-6298
Phone: 212-456-7777
Fax: 212-456-1424
Web: abc.go.com

CEO: Robert A Iger
CFO: –
HR: –
FYE: September 30
Type: Subsidiary

Some Desperate Housewives a Modern Family and a group of doctors schooled in Grey's Anatomy call this network home. ABC operates the #3 television network in the US (behind CBS and FOX) with more than 230 affiliates (including 10 corporate-owned stations). ABC also owns an 80% stake in ESPN a leader in cable sports broadcasting with a stable of channels including ESPN2 ESPN Classic and ESPN News as well as its flagship channel. (Publisher Hearst owns the remaining 20% of ESPN.) In addition the company operates mass-market publisher Hyperion. ABC is the cornerstone of Disney-ABC Television Group the TV division of parent Walt Disney.

ABDON CALLAIS OFFSHORE LLC

1300 N ALEX PLISANCE BLVD
GOLDEN MEADOW, LA 703572612
Phone: 985-475-7111
Fax: –
Web: www.acoboats.com

CEO: –
CFO: Lionel Largared
HR: –
FYE: December 31
Type: Private

Abdon Callais Offshore provides freight and passenger transportation services to the offshore oil and gas industry. The company operates its fleet of about 75 supply vessels utility vessels and crew boats in the Gulf of Mexico serving coastal shelf and deepwater projects. It counts both production companies and service companies among its customers. The company was founded in 1945 by Abdon Callais grandfather of president and CEO Peter Callais. The Callais family controls the company; other backers have included private equity firm Stonehenge Capital.

	Annual Growth	12/07	12/08	12/09	12/10	12/12
Sales ($ mil.)	15.8%	–	–	–	75.5	101.2
Net income ($ mil.)	65.1%	–	–	–	14.4	39.3
Market value ($ mil.)	–	–	–	–	–	–
Employees	–	–	–	–	–	430

ABEONA THERAPEUTICS INC

3333 Lee Parkway, Suite 600
Dallas, TX 75219
Phone: 214 665-9495
Fax: –
Web: www.abeonatherapeutics.com

NAS: ABEO
CEO: Tim Miller
CFO: Harrison Wehner
HR: –
FYE: December 31
Type: Public

Abeona Therapeutics (formerly PlasmaTech Pharmaceuticals) is developing treatments to tap into the cancer therapy market. The company makes pharmaceutical products based on nanopolymer chemistry and other drug delivery technologies. Its FDA-approved MuGard is a prescription oral rinse for the treatment of mucositis or mouth ulceration a common side effect of chemotherapy or radiation. MuGard has marketing approval in the US and it is available in Europe through partner SpePharm. MuGard is also awaiting regulatory approvals for certain markets in Asia. Other Abeona products including ovarian cancer candidate ProLindac and treatments and drug delivery technologies for solid tumors and diabetes are in clinical and preclinical development.

	Annual Growth	12/10	12/11	12/12	12/13	12/14
Sales ($ mil.)	17.8%	0.5	1.8	4.4	2.0	0.9
Net income ($ mil.)	–	(7.5)	(2.5)	(10.5)	4.4	(26.8)
Market value ($ mil.)	8.6%	49.5	28.7	4.8	5.0	68.9
Employees	(14.3%)	13	14	8	6	7

ABERCROMBIE & FITCH CO.

6301 Fitch Path
New Albany, OH 43054
Phone: 614 283-6500
Fax: –
Web: www.abercrombie.com

NYS: ANF
CEO: Arthur C. Martinez
CFO: Joanne C. Crevoiserat
HR: John (Jack) Gabrielli
FYE: January 31
Type: Public

Trading on its century-old name Abercrombie & Fitch (A&F) sells upscale men's women's and kids' casual clothes and accessories — quite a change from when the company outfitted Ernest Hemingway and Teddy Roosevelt for safari. A&F operates about 950 stores in Asia Europe and North America and also sells via catalog and online. Its carefully selected college-age sales staff and All-American models imbue its stores with an upscale fraternity-house feel. In addition to its namesake stores A&F runs a chain of teen stores called Hollister and a chain targeted at boys and girls ages 7 to 14 called abercrombie kids; locations of the Aussie-inspired just-for-girls brand Gilly Hicks have been closed.

	Annual Growth	01/11	01/12*	02/13	02/14*	01/15
Sales ($ mil.)	1.9%	3,468.8	4,158.1	4,510.8	4,116.9	3,744.0
Net income ($ mil.)	(23.4%)	150.3	127.7	237.0	54.6	51.8
Market value ($ mil.)	(14.8%)	3,353.9	3,275.5	3,541.8	2,453.7	1,769.9
Employees	(7.2%)	85,000	90,000	98,000	75,000	63,000

*Fiscal year change

ABF FREIGHT SYSTEM INC.

3801 Old Greenwood Rd.
Fort Smith AR 72903
Phone: 479-785-6000
Fax: 800-599-2810
Web: www.abfs.com

CEO: –
CFO: –
HR: –
FYE: December 31
Type: Subsidiary

ABF Freight System knows the ABCs of freight transportation. The largest subsidiary of Arkansas Best ABF Freight System offers national and regional less-than-truckload (LTL) transportation of general commodities such as apparel appliances chemicals food furniture metal plastics and textiles. LTL carriers generally combine freight from multiple shippers into a single truckload. The company operates a fleet of more than 17000 trailers and about 1600 tractors from a network of some 275 terminals. It ships throughout the US and to Canada Mexico Guam and Puerto Rico. Beyond its core LTL business ABF is expanding with end-to-end supply chain management services.

ABILENE CHRISTIAN UNIVERSITY INC

1600 CAMPUS CT
ABILENE, TX 796013761
Phone: 325-674-2000
Fax: –
Web: www.acu.edu

CEO: –
CFO: –
HR: –
FYE: May 31
Type: Private

Abilene was once the home where the buffalo roamed but now it's where the Abilene Christian University Wildcats play. The private Church of Christ-affiliated university which requires Bible study courses and daily chapel attendance has an enrollment of about 4600 students. By 2020 the school intends to be the world's premier Christ-centered university. It offers some 70 baccalaureate majors that include more than 125 areas of study in addition to about 25 graduate academic programs one doctoral program and study abroad programs in Oxford England; Montevideo Uruguay; and Leipzig Germany. The student-teacher ratio is 15:1. Abilene Christian was founded in 1906.

	Annual Growth	05/10	05/11	05/12	05/13	05/14
Sales ($ mil.)	(6.8%)	–	144.9	112.0	111.8	117.1
Net income ($ mil.)	436.0%	–	–	2.7	34.8	77.4
Market value ($ mil.)	–	–	–	–	–	–
Employees	–	–	–	–	–	675

ABINGTON MEMORIAL HOSPITAL INC

1200 OLD YORK RD
ABINGTON, PA 190013788
Phone: 215-481-2000
Fax: –

CEO: –
CFO: –
HR: Hans Kim
FYE: June 30
Type: Private

Abington Memorial Hospital brings health care to residents of southeastern Pennsylvania. The not-for-profit community hospital has some 670 beds. In addition to general medical and surgical care the hospital offers specialized care centers for cancer and cardiovascular conditions operates high-tech orthopedic and neurological surgery units and serves as a regional trauma care facility. It also runs an inpatient pediatric unit in affiliation with The Children's Hospital of Philadelphia. Abington Memorial also known as Abington Health operates the neighboring 125-bed Lansdale Hospital and several area outpatient facilities.

	Annual Growth	06/07	06/08	06/09	06/10	06/13
Sales ($ mil.)	0.1%	–	–	704.7	783.1	708.5
Net income ($ mil.)	–	–	–	(36.8)	16.3	20.9
Market value ($ mil.)	–	–	–	–	–	–
Employees	–	–	–	–	–	4,018

ABIOMED, INC.   NMS: ABMD

22 Cherry Hill Drive
Danvers, MA 01923
Phone: 978 646-1400
Fax: 978 777-8411
Web: www.abiomed.com

CEO: Michael R. Minogue
CFO: Michael Tomsicek
HR: Franky Leblanc
FYE: March 31
Type: Public

ABIOMED gives weary hearts a rest. The medical device maker has developed a range of cardiac assist devices and is developing a self-contained artificial heart. Its Impella micro heart pumps can temporarily take over blood circulation during surgery or catheterization. Its AB5000 ventricular assist device temporarily takes over the heart's pumping function and improves circulatory flow in patients with acute heart failure thus allowing their hearts to rest and recover. ABIOMED markets its products through both a direct sales force and distributors.

	Annual Growth	03/11	03/12	03/13	03/14	03/15
Sales ($ mil.)	22.8%	101.2	126.4	158.1	183.6	230.3
Net income ($ mil.)	–	(11.8)	1.5	15.0	7.4	113.7
Market value ($ mil.)	49.0%	600.6	917.2	771.7	1,076.4	2,958.8
Employees	12.0%	374	397	467	511	589

ABM INDUSTRIES, INC.   NYS: ABM

551 Fifth Avenue, Suite 300
New York, NY 10176
Phone: 212 297-0200
Fax: –
Web: www.abm.com

CEO: Scott Salmirs
CFO: D. Anthony Scaglione
HR: Angelique Carbo
FYE: October 31
Type: Public

Many businesses hope to clean up but diversified facilities services contractor ABM counts on it. The company primarily offers janitorial services to owners and operators of office buildings hospitals manufacturing plants schools shopping centers and transportation facilities throughout the US and in Canada and Puerto Rico. Through other units ABM provides security services and maintains mechanical electrical and plumbing systems. Its Ampco System Parking operates more than 1800 parking lots and garages mainly at airports across 35 states while ABM Security Services provides security officers and security systems monitoring services.

	Annual Growth	10/11	10/12	10/13	10/14	10/15
Sales ($ mil.)	3.6%	4,246.8	4,300.3	4,809.3	5,032.8	4,897.8
Net income ($ mil.)	2.7%	68.5	62.6	72.9	75.6	76.3
Market value ($ mil.)	8.9%	1,134.5	1,066.0	1,543.5	1,550.8	1,593.4
Employees	5.7%	96,000	95,000	110,000	118,000	120,000

ABM SECURITY SERVICES

7324 Southwest Fwy. Ste. 1400
Houston TX 77074
Phone: 713-926-4453
Fax: 713-926-2435
Web: www.abm.com/services/security/pages/commercial

CEO: –
CFO: –
HR: Janice Smith
FYE: October 31
Type: Subsidiary

ABM Security Services keeps its eagle eyes on guard. The company provides uniformed security officers security systems monitoring and consulting services through a variety of subsidiaries and brand names such as Security Services of America (SSA) Silverhawk Security and Elite Protection. All told the company maintains about 70 branch offices in more than 30 states. Its guards protect high-rise buildings high-tech computer facilities financial institutions data centers and other commercial and industrial locations. ABM Security is a subsidiary of ABM Industries. The parent company also provides parking janitorial and engineering services.

ABP CORPORATION

1 Au Bon Pain Way
Boston MA 02210
Phone: 617-423-2100
Fax: 617-423-7879
Web: www.aubonpain.com

CEO: Susan Morelli
CFO: –
HR: –
FYE: September 30
Type: Private

To make dough in the bistro business it helps to start with good bread. ABP Corporation operates the Au Bon Pain bakery cafe chain with more than 250 company-owned and franchised locations in the US Kuwait Japan Thailand South Korea and Taiwan. The bistros offer a wide range of sandwiches soups salads and baked goods as well as coffee and other cafe beverages. Most of the restaurants are located in urban areas but ABP also has on-site locations in airports shopping malls and on university campuses. The company also does catering and sells gift baskets. The Au Bon Pain chain was started in 1978 by Louis Kane. ABP is controlled by LNK Partners a Boston-based private equity firm.

ABS CAPITAL PARTNERS L.P.

400 E. Pratt St. Ste. 910
Baltimore MD 21202-3116
Phone: 410-246-5600
Fax: 410-246-5606
Web: www.abscapital.com

CEO: –
CFO: –
HR: –
FYE: December 31
Type: Private

ABS Capital Partners seeks out companies that have learned their business ABCs. The firm typically invests $10 million to $30 million per transaction in late-stage (but growing) US companies in the business services health care media and communications and technology sectors. It provides capital for expansions acquisitions management buyouts and recapitalizations. In addition to taking a seat on the boards of its portfolio companies the firm also provides strategic and financial advice to them but usually does not get involved with their day-to-day operations. ABS Capital Partners has interests in more than two dozen companies including Liquidity Services Rosetta Stone and Vibrant Media.

ABRA INC.

6601 Shingle Creek Pkwy. Ste. 200
Brooklyn Center MN 55430
Phone: 763-561-7220
Fax: 763-561-7433
Web: www.abraauto.com

CEO: Duane Rouse
CFO: Brent A Moen
HR: –
FYE: December 31
Type: Private

ABRA Auto Body & Glass offers more than just an incantation to get your wrecked car back on the road. Through more than 105 company-owned and franchised shops in a dozen states the company provides collision repair services as well as paintless dent removal and glass repair. The majority of ABRA's stores are in Colorado Georgia and Minnesota. Almost all of the company's services are paid for by insurance companies. Insurance agents can earn continuing education credits for ABRA's classes on issues relating to car repair. Founded in 1984 ABRA Auto Body & Glass is owned by investors and employees.

ABT ASSOCIATES INC.

55 Wheeler St.
Cambridge MA 02138-1168
Phone: 617-492-7100
Fax: 617-492-5219
Web: www.abtassociates.com

CEO: Kathleen L Flanagan
CFO: Richard Small
HR: –
FYE: March 31
Type: Private

Abt Associates offers a wide array of research-based consulting services to government agencies businesses and other organizations worldwide. The firm specializes in issues related to social economic and health policy; clinical research; and international development. Its services include consulting implementation and technical assistance; research and evaluation; survey data collection management and analysis (through Abt SRBI); and strategy planning and policy. Abt Associates has served the US Departments of Agriculture Education and Defense and does business from four US offices and from 40 project sites around the globe. Employees own the company which was founded in 1965 by Clark Abt.

ABRAXAS PETROLEUM CORP.   NAS: AXAS

18803 Meisner Drive
San Antonio, TX 78258
Phone: 210 490-4788
Fax: –
Web: www.abraxaspetroleum.com

CEO: Robert L. G. (Bob) Watson
CFO: Geoffrey R. King
HR: –
FYE: December 31
Type: Public

Abraxas is a mythical Gnostic symbol that represents the number 365 in Greek and Abraxas Petroleum is working hard as a 365-days-a-year oil and gas company. The independent energy company is engaged in natural gas and crude oil exploration development and production. It operates primarily in Texas (in the South along the Gulf Coast and in the Permian Basin) the Rocky Mountains and the Mid-Continent and in 2013 the company reported estimated proved reserves of 31 million barrels of oil equivalent. That year Abraxas Petroleum also owned interests in more than 132880 net acres (primarily in mature fields) and in 1059 gross producing wells.

	Annual Growth	12/10	12/11	12/12	12/13	12/14
Sales ($ mil.)	22.7%	59.0	64.6	68.6	94.3	133.8
Net income ($ mil.)	144.7%	1.8	13.7	(18.8)	38.6	63.3
Market value ($ mil.)	(10.4%)	485.3	350.4	232.5	346.3	312.2
Employees	14.8%	74	104	101	112	–

ACACIA RESEARCH CORP   NMS: ACTG

520 Newport Center Drive
Newport Beach, CA 92660
Phone: 949 480-8300
Fax: 949 480-8301
Web: www.acaciaresearch.com

CEO: Marvin E. Key
CFO: Clayton J. Haynes
HR: –
FYE: December 31
Type: Public

Acacia Research provides protection under its canopy for intellectual property. The company acquires develops licenses and protects patented technologies for individual inventors and small companies that have limited resources to protect against infringement. The company owns or controls the rights to more than 180 patent portfolios in the US and abroad. It typically buys portfolios and pays its clients an upfront fee or becomes the exclusive licensing agent and doles out royalties. It has out-licensed to such companies as 3M Dell IBM Texas Instruments and Walt Disney Company. Acacia Research primarily operates through its Acacia Research Group (formerly Acacia Technologies) and Acacia Global Acquisition subsidiaries.

	Annual Growth	12/10	12/11	12/12	12/13	12/14
Sales ($ mil.)	(0.2%)	131.8	172.3	250.7	130.6	130.9
Net income ($ mil.)	–	34.1	21.1	59.5	(56.4)	(66.0)
Market value ($ mil.)	(10.1%)	1,298.7	1,827.9	1,284.6	728.0	848.1
Employees	4.4%	48	55	55	68	57

ACACIA TECHNOLOGIES LLC

500 Newport Center Dr. 7th Fl.
Newport Beach CA 92660
Phone: 949-480-8300
Fax: 949-480-8301
Web: www.acaciatechnologies.com

CEO: Paul R Ryan
CFO: Clayton J Haynes
HR: –
FYE: December 31
Type: Subsidiary

Acacia Technologies offers shade to more than 150 patent portfolios. The company (which is the primary subsidiary of Acacia Research) acquires and licenses patent rights to various technologies related to digital audio-on-demand and video-on-demand transmission. It markets many of these patents under the DMT brand to makers of electronics gear who incorporate the technologies into applications for cable satellite and Internet distribution of digital content. Acacia Technologies has reached licensing agreements with Fujitsu Pioneer Sony and Union Pacific among other companies.

ACADEMY LTD.

1800 N. Mason Rd.
Katy TX 77449
Phone: 281-646-5200
Fax: 281-646-5000
Web: www.academy.com

CEO: David E Gochman
CFO: –
HR: –
FYE: January 31
Type: Private

Academy is near the head of the class among sporting goods retailers. It's one of the leading full-line sporting goods chains in the US with more than 150 Academy Sports + Outdoors stores in Texas and about a dozen other southeastern states. Academy's low-frills stores carry clothing shoes and equipment for almost any sport and outdoor activity including camping golf hunting fishing and boating. The company which also operates a catalog and e-commerce site dates back to a San Antonio tire shop opened by Max Gochman in 1938. The business moved into military surplus items and during the 1980s began focusing on sports and outdoor goods. Academy was acquired by the investment firm KKR in 2011.

ACADEMY OF MOTION PICTURE ARTS & SCIENCES

8949 WILSHIRE BLVD
BEVERLY HILLS, CA 902111907
Phone: 310-247-3000
Fax: –
Web: www.oscars.org

CEO: –
CFO: Andy Horn
HR: Kim Congdon
FYE: June 30
Type: Private

And the Oscar goes to ... the Academy of Motion Picture Arts and Sciences (AMPAS). The not-for-profit organization promotes the movie industry by recognizing excellence fostering cultural progress providing a forum for various crafts and cooperating in technical research. It is best known for the annual Academy Awards in which a Britannia metal trophy (known as the Oscar) is awarded for outstanding achievement in the motion picture industry. The more than 6000 AMPAS members (who pick the Oscar winners) represent 15 branches of the industry including actors directors producers and executives. The organization was founded in 1927 and is governed by seven officers and a board of governors.

	Annual Growth	06/06	06/07	06/08	06/09	06/10
Sales ($ mil.)	–	–	–	0.0	80.5	97.7
Net income ($ mil.)	4167.4%	–	–	0.0	(6.5)	29.8
Market value ($ mil.)	–	–	–	–	–	–
Employees	–	–	–	–	–	174

ACADEMY OF TELEVISION ARTS & SCIENCES INC.

5220 Lankershim Blvd.
North Hollywood CA 91601-3109
Phone: 818-754-2800
Fax: 818-761-2827
Web: www.emmys.org

CEO: Dick Askin
CFO: –
HR: –
FYE: December 31
Type: Private - Not-for-Pr

And the award for best organization that honors the television industry goes to: the Academy of Television Arts & Sciences (ATAS). ATAS which has more than 13000 members presents the annual Emmy Awards and sponsors various television-related conferences and activities. The organization also oversees the Daytime and L.A. Area Emmy Awards publishes "emmy" magazine manages archival and educational programs through its ATAS Foundation and operates Web sites such as emmys.tv and emmys.com. The Emmy statuette features a winged woman holding an atom aloft to symbolize the melding of art and science. The award's name is a deviation of "Immy" an early television camera. ATAS was founded in 1946.

ACADIA HEALTHCARE COMPANY INC. — NMS: ACHC

6100 Tower Circle, Suite 1000
Franklin, TN 37067
Phone: 615 861-6000
Fax: –
Web: www.acadiahealthcare.com

CEO: Joey A. Jacobs
CFO: David Duckworth
HR: –
FYE: December 31
Type: Public

Acadia Healthcare help people to be mentally healthy. Acadia operates more than 200 behavioral health facilities with 8600 licensed beds in 21 US states the UK and Puerto Rico. Its mental health and addiction treatment services include adult geriatric and adolescent inpatient residential and partial hospitalization programs. The company also offers treatment options for children with autism eating disorders fetal alcohol syndrome substance abuse and traumatic brain injury as well as for sexually abused children. Acadia offers services nationwide.

	Annual Growth	12/10	12/11	12/12	12/13	12/14
Sales ($ mil.)	98.8%	64.3	221.4	407.5	713.4	1,004.6
Net income ($ mil.)	91.2%	6.2	(34.9)	20.4	42.6	83.0
Market value ($ mil.)	83.1%	–	590.3	1,382.6	2,802.5	3,624.4
Employees	33.7%	4,857	5,820	7,200	11,000	15,500

ACADIA PHARMACEUTICALS INC — NMS: ACAD

3611 Valley Centre Drive, Suite 300
San Diego, CA 92130
Phone: 858 558-2871
Fax: –
Web: www.acadia-pharm.com

CEO: Stephen R. (Steve) Davis
CFO: Stephen R Davis
HR: –
FYE: December 31
Type: Public

ACADIA Pharmaceuticals develops small molecule drugs for the treatment of central nervous system disorders. The biopharmaceutical company's most advanced compound pimavanserin is in clinical trials as a treatment for Parkinson's disease psychosis a common development with the disease. Two other clinical-stage candidates are being developed in collaboration with Allergan to treat patients with chronic pain and glaucoma. The company's pipeline also includes preclinical candidates in development for chronic pain and Parkinson's disease. All candidates are birthed from ACADIA's own R-SAT drug discovery platform.

	Annual Growth	12/10	12/11	12/12	12/13	12/14
Sales ($ mil.)	(76.9%)	42.1	2.1	4.9	1.1	0.1
Net income ($ mil.)	–	15.1	(22.8)	(20.8)	(37.9)	(92.5)
Market value ($ mil.)	126.8%	120.1	108.1	465.2	2,500.2	3,176.5
Employees	37.7%	27	24	26	48	97

ACADIA REALTY TRUST
NYS: AKR

411 Theodore Fremd Avenue, Suite 300
Rye, NY 10580
Phone: 914 288-8100
Fax: –
Web: www.acadiarealty.com

CEO: Kenneth F. Bernstein
CFO: Jonathan (Jon) Grisham
HR: –
FYE: December 31
Type: Public

A self-managed real estate investment trust (REIT) Acadia Realty acquires redevelops and manages retail properties in the Northeast Mid-Atlantic and Midwest. The REIT specializes in community shopping centers and mixed-use properties in urban areas. Acadia owns or has interests in more than 80 properties — mostly shopping centers anchored by a grocery store drug store or big box store — that contain more than 8 million sq. ft. of leasable space. It also has investments in self-storage properties mortgage loans and other real estate interests. The company's largest tenants include SUPERVALU Stop & Shop A&P and Walgreen.

	Annual Growth	12/10	12/11	12/12	12/13	12/14
Sales ($ mil.)	6.4%	152.0	150.2	134.4	168.3	195.0
Net income ($ mil.)	24.0%	30.1	51.6	39.7	40.1	71.1
Market value ($ mil.)	15.1%	1,242.3	1,371.7	1,708.2	1,691.2	2,181.5
Employees	(0.4%)	116	114	126	120	114

ACADIAN AMBULANCE SERVICE INC.

130 E KALISTE SALOOM RD
LAFAYETTE, LA 705088308
Phone: 337-291-3333
Fax: –
Web: www.acadian.com

CEO: Richard E Zuschlag
CFO: David L Kelly
HR: –
FYE: December 31
Type: Private

From ground to air and back again Acadian Ambulance Service is all about getting Southerners to the hospital safe and sound. The company provides ground and air medical transportation service to millions of residents in Louisiana Mississippi and Texas. Along with its ground ambulances the company operates a handful of helicopter ambulances through affiliate Metro Aviation. Its many subsidiaries provide a broad array of additional services including telemedicine (remote patient monitoring) paramedic training services chartered transportation and emergency medical services to offshore oil projects. Established in 1971 Acadian Ambulance Service is owned by its employees through a private stock option plan.

	Annual Growth	12/07	12/08	12/09	12/10	12/11
Sales ($ mil.)	(45.1%)	–	–	1,264.3	358.3	380.6
Net income ($ mil.)	21794.4%	–	–	0.0	7.2	9.3
Market value ($ mil.)	–	–	–	–	–	–
Employees	–	–	–	–	–	2,385

ACCEL PARTNERS

428 University Ave.
Palo Alto CA 94301
Phone: 650-614-4800
Fax: 650-614-4880
Web: www.accel.com

CEO: –
CFO: –
HR: –
FYE: December 31
Type: Private

How fast can you make money? Venture capital and growth equity investment firm Accel Partners hopes to accelerate that. Founded in 1983 the firm which has more than $6 billion under management makes early-stage investments mostly in software and networking companies. Accel also targets more established companies in IT internet digital media mobile networking software and services. After making an investment Accel typically provides its companies with strategic financing recruiting and business development among other services. Its strategy has helped grow some of the most powerful and influential tech companies in the world including Macromedia Riverbed Groupon and Facebook.

ACCELERATE DIAGNOSTICS INC
NAS: AXDX

3950 South Country Club, Suite 470
Tucson, AZ 85714
Phone: 520 365-3100
Fax: –
Web: www.accelr8.com

CEO: Lawrence (Larry) Mehren
CFO: Steve Reichling
HR: –
FYE: December 31
Type: Public

Accelerate Diagnostics (formerly Accelr8 Technology) wants to speed up your lab results. Using its ID/AST system the company is working on quicker methods for identifying bacterial infections. The system is being designed for use in clinical settings to provide bacterial identification within two hours. If successful it will be an improvement over existing methods that depend upon identifying bacteria in a culture grown over two to five days from a patient sample. Instead ID/AST will look directly at the sample itself sort through the tens of thousands of bacterial cells to identify any pathogenic bacteria and determine if any are resistant to antibiotics. Investment group Crabtree Partners owns a controlling stake in the firm.

	Annual Growth	07/11	07/12*	12/12	12/13	12/14
Sales ($ mil.)	(52.3%)	1.1	0.2	0.0	0.0	0.1
Net income ($ mil.)	–	(0.4)	(5.3)	(3.4)	(15.3)	(30.9)
Market value ($ mil.)	70.2%	173.6	146.0	179.9	544.6	856.6
Employees	109.0%	8	6	15	47	73

*Fiscal year change

ACCELERON PHARMA, INC.
NMS: XLRN

128 Sidney Street
Cambridge, MA 02139
Phone: 617 649-9200
Fax: –
Web: www.acceleronpharma.com

CEO: John L. Knopf
CFO: Kevin F. McLaughlin
HR: –
FYE: December 31
Type: Public

Acceleron Pharma is ready to accelerate the treatment of cancer. The biopharmaceutical company is developing protein therapies to treat certain types of cancer and rare diseases such as the blood diseases beta-thalassemia and myelodysplastic syndromes (MDS). It has collaboration agreements with pharmaceutical giants Alkermes Celgene and Shire but its work with Celgene shows the most promise. The two companies are developing sotatercept and ACE-536 to treat anemia and associated complications in patients with other blood diseases. Acceleron Pharma raised $83 million in its 2013 IPO which it will use to fund clinical trials for its drug candidates.

	Annual Growth	12/10	12/11	12/12	12/13	12/14
Sales ($ mil.)	–	0.0	80.9	15.3	57.2	14.6
Net income ($ mil.)	–	0.0	36.3	(32.6)	(21.9)	(51.3)
Market value ($ mil.)	–	0.0	–	–	1,284.3	1,263.6
Employees	2.5%	–	–	79	80	83

ACCELPATH INC
NBB: ACLP

137 National Plaza, Suite 300
National Harbor, MD 20745
Phone: 240 273-3295
Fax: –

CEO: Janon Costley
CFO: –
HR: –
FYE: June 30
Type: Public

Technest Holdings can help you get a better picture of your security efforts or better diagnose your patients. The company makes 3-D modeling and imaging software and equipment primarily for the security and health care industries. Technest's products include intelligent surveillance 3-D facial recognition and 3-D imaging devices and systems. The company's customers have included the Department of Defense and the National Institute of Health.

	Annual Growth	06/10	06/11	06/12	06/13	06/14
Sales ($ mil.)	(21.7%)	–	0.4	0.6	0.3	0.2
Net income ($ mil.)	–	(0.3)	(2.9)	(2.1)	(2.0)	(2.5)
Market value ($ mil.)	–	0.8	1.3	0.2	0.0	0.0
Employees	(55.0%)	–	11	5	1	1

ACCELRYS INC   NMS: ACCL

5005 Wateridge Vista Drive   CEO: Max Carnecchia
San Diego, CA 92121   CFO: Michael Piraino
Phone: 858 799-5000   HR: –
Fax: –   FYE: December 31
Web: www.accelrys.com   Type: Public

Accelrys feels strongly that nothing speeds up research like good software. The company develops business intelligence applications used in the development of new drugs and medical technologies. Its software is designed to enable and automate the collection aggregation and analysis of scientific data and include tools for reporting documentation modeling database access and collaboration. Accelrys also offers consulting software integration contract research and training services. While its customers come primarily from the pharmaceutical life sciences and biotech industries Accelrys also serves clients in industries with significant R&D efforts such as aerospace consumer packaged goods and energy.

	Annual Growth	03/09	03/10*	12/10	12/11	12/12
Sales ($ mil.)	26.1%	81.0	83.0	80.2	144.3	162.5
Net income ($ mil.)	–	0.1	1.2	(20.6)	1.8	(10.4)
Market value ($ mil.)	31.5%	222.4	344.2	463.8	375.5	505.7
Employees	21.1%	364	362	580	601	647

*Fiscal year change

ACCENTIA BIOPHARMACEUTICALS INC   NBB: ABPI

324 South Hyde Park Avenue, Suite 350   CEO: –
Tampa, FL 33606   CFO: Garrison J Hasara
Phone: 813 864-2554   HR: –
Fax: –   FYE: September 30
Web: www.accentia.net   Type: Public

Accentia Biopharmaceuticals is accentuating its positives and eliminating its negatives. The drug development company is focused on two development-stage drugs multiple sclerosis drug Revimmune and BiovaxID a possible vaccine for non-Hodgkin's lymphoma being developed by majority-owned subsidiary BioVest International. BioVest also sells cell growth instruments and offers contract manufacturing of cell cultures. The company and its subsidiaries (including BioVest) filed for Chapter 11 bankruptcy protection in late 2008 and emerged in late 2010.

	Annual Growth	09/08	09/09	09/10	09/11	09/12
Sales ($ mil.)	(29.0%)	15.9	10.6	10.5	4.0	4.1
Net income ($ mil.)	–	(60.8)	(5.3)	(47.8)	(11.6)	(9.2)
Market value ($ mil.)	(26.6%)	47.9	18.6	89.5	40.7	13.9
Employees	(16.3%)	110	80	67	68	54

ACCESS NATIONAL CORP   NMS: ANCX

1800 Robert Fulton Drive, Suite 300   CEO: Michael W. Clarke
Reston, VA 20191   CFO: Margaret M. Taylor
Phone: 703 871-2100   HR: Doris Hambright
Fax: –   FYE: December 31
                                                  Type: Public

Enabling easy access to your money is Access National's aim. The holding company owns Access National Bank a thrift founded in 1999 that serves the suburbs of Washington DC in Northern Virginia through about five branches. The bank offers credit deposit mortgage services and wealth management services to middle market commercial businesses and associated professionals primarily in the greater Washington D.C. Metropolitan Area. Commercial Real Estate Loans-Owner Occupied and Commercial Real Estate Loans-Owner Occupied make up some 40% of the company's portfolio; residential real estate another 25%; and Commercial Loans 26.5%.

	Annual Growth	12/10	12/11	12/12	12/13	12/14
Assets ($ mil.)	6.1%	831.8	809.8	863.9	847.2	1,052.9
Net income ($ mil.)	16.4%	7.6	11.4	17.7	13.2	13.9
Market value ($ mil.)	27.2%	67.6	92.1	136.1	156.5	177.1
Employees	(5.6%)	277	286	305	215	220

ACCESS SYSTEMS AMERICAS INC.

1188 E. Arques Ave.   CEO: Kiyo Oishi
Sunnyvale CA 94085-4602   CFO: Jeanne Seeley
Phone: 408-400-3000   HR: –
Fax: 408-400-1500   FYE: May 31
Web: www.access-company.com   Type: Private

ACCESS Systems Americas wants to help you step away from your desk. The company develops software for mobile products and the networking infrastructure needed to support them. Its software makes it possible for netbook computers laptops and notebooks and smartphones to access the Internet through wireless communications systems. Along with its IP Infusion subsidiary ACCESS also develops software to run the networks and servers in the wireless infrastructure. The company provides the Garnet operating system the successor to the OS that powered the Palm Pilot PDA and a commercial-grade platform based on the open-source Linux OS for mobile phones. ACCESS Systems Americas is a subsidiary of Japan's ACCESS Co. Ltd.

ACCIDENT FUND HOLDINGS INC.

200 N. Grand Ave.   CEO: –
Lansing MI 48901   CFO: –
Phone: 517-342-4200   HR: –
Fax: 480-609-6520   FYE: December 31
Web: www.peterpiperpizza.com   Type: Subsidiary

Accident Fund Holdings wants to keep your workplace safe. Founded in 1912 the company is the largest non-governmental specialty writer of workers' compensation insurance in the US; it serves more than 50000 businesses nationwide. Its main subsidiary Accident Fund Insurance Company of America does business with small and midsized companies but also provides third-party administration (TPA) and loss prevention services. Three other subsidiaries — CompWest Third Coast Underwriters and United Heartland provide regional coverage. Accident Fund sells its products through a network of independent agents. Formerly state-owned Accident Fund operates as a for-profit subsidiary of Blue Cross Blue Shield of Michigan.

ACCO BRANDS CORP   NYS: ACCO

Four Corporate Drive   CEO: Boris Elisman
Lake Zurich, IL 60047   CFO: Neal V. Fenwick
Phone: 847 541-9500   HR: –
Fax: –   FYE: December 31
Web: www.accobrands.com   Type: Public

ACCO Brands solves one of the more common workplace indignities: taking a co-worker's stapler. The company makes and markets a slew of traditional brand name office and computer-related products including Swingline staplers Kensington keyboards Wilson Jones binders and ledger paper and Day-Timer personal organizers and more. It also offers private-label supplies. ACCO sells mostly to businesses through retail superstores mass merchandisers commercial stationers wholesalers mail order and internet catalogs and club stores and dealers. In 2012 ACCO merged with the Consumer & Office Products business spun off by MeadWestvaco.

	Annual Growth	12/10	12/11	12/12	12/13	12/14
Sales ($ mil.)	6.1%	1,330.5	1,318.4	1,758.5	1,765.1	1,689.2
Net income ($ mil.)	64.9%	12.4	56.7	115.4	77.1	91.6
Market value ($ mil.)	1.4%	953.5	1,079.9	821.4	752.0	1,008.3
Employees	5.7%	4,200	3,800	5,850	5,470	5,240

ACCOR NORTH AMERICA

4001 International Pkwy.
Carrollton TX 75007
Phone: 972-360-9000
Fax: 703-834-3593
Web: www.airbusnorthamerica.com

CEO: Olivier Poirot
CFO: Didier Bosc
HR: –
FYE: December 31
Type: Business Segment

This company is keeping the light on for North American travelers. A division of global hotel giant Accor Accor North America operates a total of 17 upscale Sofitel and midscale Novotel hotels in the US and Canada. In order to reduce its debt and fund international expansion parent Accor sold Accor North America's economy division which included 1100 US and Canadian hotels under the Motel 6 and Studio 6 brands to private equity giant Blackstone Group for $1.9 billion in October 2012. Accor North America has operational and development teams in Dallas and New York.

ACCREDO HEALTH INCORPORATED

1640 Century Center Pkwy.
Memphis TN 38134
Phone: 901-385-3688
Fax: 901-385-3689
Web: www.accredo.com

CEO: David D Stevens
CFO: Joel Kimbrough
HR: –
FYE: December 30
Type: Subsidiary

Accredo Health doesn't stock aspirin in its medicine cabinet. As part of the specialty pharmacy segment of pharmacy benefits manager Express Scripts Accredo dispenses high-tech injectable and infusion drugs for chronic and serious illnesses such as cancer multiple sclerosis hemophilia pulmonary arterial hypertension (PAH) and certain autoimmune disorders. Under contracts with managed care organizations and drugmakers it delivers drugs and related supplies in temperature-controlled packaging to patient homes or clinics. It also provides consulting and monitoring services to make sure patients are complying with their drug regimens and it files claims on behalf of patients and doctors.

ACCRETIVE HEALTH, INC.   NBB: ACHI

401 North Michigan Avenue Suite 2700
Chicago, IL 60611
Phone: 312 324-7820
Fax: –
Web: www.accretivehealth.com

CEO: Emad Rizk
CFO: Peter Csap
HR: –
FYE: December 31
Type: Public

You could say Accretive Health makes sure hospitals don't leave money on the operations table. The company provides its own employees and management systems to improve back-office operations for health care providers and specializes in maximizing profits while reducing costs. Services include benefit coordination coding billing and collection management. Typical customers are not-for-profit and for-profit hospital systems as well as independent medical centers such as Ascension Health; it also serves physician groups and home health agencies. Accretive was founded in 2003 and went public in 2010.

	Annual Growth	12/10	12/11	12/12	12/13	12/14
Sales ($ mil.)	(23.3%)	606.3	826.3	72.3	504.8	210.1
Net income ($ mil.)	–	12.6	29.2	(119.7)	130.1	(79.6)
Market value ($ mil.)	(19.4%)	1,594.3	2,254.6	1,136.1	898.7	673.0
Employees	8.1%	2,222	3,063	–	2,900	3,030

ACCUCODE INC.

6886 S. Yosemite St. Ste. 100
Centennial CO 80112
Phone: 303-639-6111
Fax: 303-639-6178
Web: www.accucode.com

CEO: Kevin Price
CFO: –
HR: Casey Roberts
FYE: December 31
Type: Private

AccuCode designs and installs customized asset-tracking systems that combine mobile computing with automated data collection tools such as bar codes and radio-frequency identification (RFID). The company's offerings include hardware from manufacturers such as Datalogic Scanning Intermec Motorola Solutions and Psion Teklogix as well as proprietary software. Its customers — which include airlines delivery service providers retail stores manufacturers and health care providers — use AccuCode's systems to track warehouse inventory and corporate assets monitor patients and manage assembly-line efficiency. The company counts British Airways Corporate Express DHL and Kroger among its clients.

ACCURAY INC (CA)   NMS: ARAY

1310 Chesapeake Terrace
Sunnyvale, CA 94089
Phone: 408 716-4600
Fax: –
Web: www.accuray.com

CEO: Joshua H. Levine
CFO: Kevin Waters
HR: Theresa Dadone
FYE: June 30
Type: Public

Accuray gets an A not a C for accuracy. Its radiosurgery CyberKnife system uses precisely aimed high-dose radiation and improves upon older radio-surgery systems that have limited mobility and are mostly used to treat brain tumors. Doctors can use CyberKnife to treat tumors anywhere in the body; the system tracks and adjusts for movement in real time allowing for patient and tumor movement. Accuray also offers the TomoTherapy systems which allow doctors to change the intensity of the radiation beam to adapt to the shape location and size of a tumor. Together the two products have an installed base of more than 700 units in about 40 countries.

	Annual Growth	06/11	06/12	06/13	06/14	06/15
Sales ($ mil.)	14.3%	222.3	409.2	316.0	369.4	379.8
Net income ($ mil.)	–	(26.7)	(72.0)	(103.2)	(35.4)	(40.2)
Market value ($ mil.)	(4.2%)	636.6	541.6	456.2	699.4	535.7
Employees	(2.1%)	1,100	1,100	989	1,026	1,010

ACCURIDE CORP   NYS: ACW

7140 Office Circle
Evansville, IN 47715
Phone: 812 962-5000
Fax: –
Web: www.accuridecorp.com

CEO: Richard F. (Rick) Dauch
CFO: Michael A. (Mike) Hajost
HR: –
FYE: December 31
Type: Public

If you're driving a big rig Accuride offers the goods to keep you rolling — or to stop you in your tracks. The company is a leading manufacturer of steel and forged aluminum wheels for commercial trucks and trailers pickups and military vehicles. It also makes truck body and chassis parts brake systems seating assemblies aftermarket components and non-powered farm equipment. Customers include commercial vehicle OEM Navistar trailer manufacturers (Great Dane and Wabash National) and automaker General Motors. Accuride's brands include Accuride AOT Brillion Gunite and Accuride Wheel end Solutions.

	Annual Growth	12/10	12/11	12/12	12/13	12/14
Sales ($ mil.)	1.7%	659.9	936.1	929.8	642.9	705.2
Net income ($ mil.)	–	(126.5)	(17.0)	(178.0)	(38.3)	(2.3)
Market value ($ mil.)	(27.7%)	757.8	339.8	153.2	178.0	207.1
Employees	(6.4%)	2,927	3,280	2,752	2,056	2,247

ACCURIDE INTERNATIONAL INC.

12311 Shoemaker Ave.
Santa Fe Springs CA 90670
Phone: 562-903-0200
Fax: 562-903-0208
Web: www.accuride.com

CEO: Scott E Jordan
CFO: –
HR: –
FYE: December 31
Type: Private

Business at Accuride International is on a finely crafted roll. The company is the world's largest manufacturer of ball bearing slides. Its lineup makes it easy every time to open and close drawers in residential and office furniture or the doors of appliances and electronic enclosures or rack mounts. The company's slides are also made for automotive accessories including storage units and arm rests and industrial equipment such as cash registers and assembly lines. Accuride International builds and maintains its own tools and machinery for manufacturing its products. Its operations dot China Germany Japan Mexico the UK and the US. Founded in 1962 by Fred Jordan the company remains family owned.

ACCUVANT INC.

1125 17th St. Ste. 1700
Denver CO 80202
Phone: 303-298-0600
Fax: 303-298-0868
Web: www.accuvant.com

CEO: –
CFO: –
HR: –
FYE: December 31
Type: Private

Data security consultant Accuvant likes to get it right for its customers. The company helps businesses assess risk improve regulatory compliance and protect data and network infrastructure through needs assessment systems design and compliance management. Accuvant identifies vulnerabilities in enterprise applications and tests network security after which it procures and implements the necessary technology to protect digital assets. The company also provides managed security services training and consulting. Accuvant operates nationwide from more than 30 offices. Customers have included Piper Jaffray BSML and Union Bank. The company was founded in 2002 by CEO Dan Burns COO Scott Walker and SVP Dan Wilson.

ACE HARDWARE CORPORATION

2200 Kensington Ct.
Oak Brook IL 60523-2100
Phone: 630-990-6600
Fax: 630-990-6838
Web: www.acehardware.com

CEO: John Venhuizen
CFO: Bill Guzik
HR: –
FYE: December 31
Type: Private - Cooperativ

In an age of big-box home improvement centers (Home Depot Lowes) Ace makes the case for the local hardware store. By sales it is the #1 hardware cooperative in the US ahead of Do It Best. Ace dealer-owners operate more than 4000 Ace Hardware stores home centers and lumber and building materials locations in all 50 US states and about 60 other countries. Stores range in size from small urban shops to large rural locations. From about 15 warehouses Ace distributes such products as electrical and plumbing supplies garden equipment hand tools housewares and power tools. Its paint division is also a major paint manufacturer in the US. Ace was founded in 1924 by a group of Chicago hardware store owners.

ACE PARKING MANAGEMENT INC.

645 Ash St.
San Diego CA 92101
Phone: 619-233-6624
Fax: 619-233-0741
Web: www.aceparking.com

CEO: John Baumgardner
CFO: Charles Blottin
HR: –
FYE: December 31
Type: Private

When you're betting on finding a convenient parking spot in the western US your chances of drawing an Ace are pretty good. Controlling about 70% of the San Diego parking market Ace Parking Management oversees more than 450 parking locations in eight states including Arizona California Oregon Texas and Washington. The company manages facilities at locations such as airports hospitals hotels medical centers office and retail buildings and stadiums. It serves almost 200000 customers per day including Bank of America and the San Diego Padres baseball team. Chairman Scott Jones owns Ace Parking which was founded in San Diego by his father in 1950.

ACE RELOCATION SYSTEMS INC.

5608 EASTGATE DR
SAN DIEGO, CA 921212816
Phone: 858-677-5500
Fax: –
Web: www.acerelocation.com

CEO: Lawrence R Lammers
CFO: Paul Sanford
HR: –
FYE: December 31
Type: Private

Hoping to trump the kings and queens of the moving industry Ace Relocation Systems provides corporate and household relocation services. The family owned company operates from more than half a dozen offices spread throughout the US. Ace Relocation Systems is an agent of Atlas Van Lines; as an agent Ace Relocation Systems operates within its assigned geographic territories and cooperates with other Atlas agents on interstate moves. In addition the company can arrange international moves and provide transportation of items such as trade show exhibits through the Atlas network. Ace Relocation Systems was founded in 1968.

	Annual Growth	12/09	12/10	12/11	12/12	12/13
Sales ($ mil.)	9.6%	–	40.8	46.3	50.2	53.8
Net income ($ mil.)	(7.7%)	–	–	2.5	1.8	2.2
Market value ($ mil.)	–	–	–	–	–	–
Employees	–	–	–	–	–	255

ACE USA

436 Walnut St.
Philadelphia PA 19106-3703
Phone: 215-640-1000
Fax: 215-640-2489
Web: www.aceusa.com

CEO: –
CFO: Joe Cavolo
HR: –
FYE: December 31
Type: Subsidiary

ACE USA's deck is stacked with insurance cards. The company is the US retail operating division of Swiss insurance firm ACE Limited. ACE USA provides a comprehensive range of property/casualty risk management accident disaster professional lines workers' compensation and health insurance products to individuals and businesses throughout the US. It sells these through licensed insurance brokers. ACE USA has dedicated efforts to tailor its services to four specialized industries: construction health care energy and public entities. It also has an arm dedicated to merger and acquisition underwriting practices.

ACELRX PHARMACEUTICALS INC
NMS: ACRX

351 Galveston Drive
Redwood City, CA 94063
Phone: 650 216-3500
Fax: –
Web: www.acelrx.com

CEO: Howard B Rosen
CFO: Timothy E Morris
HR: –
FYE: December 31
Type: Public

For patients with acute pain a slip of the tongue could be a useful thing. AcelRx is developing the Sufentanil NanoTab PCA System which administers pain medication sublingually or under the tongue. Designed for patients with post-operative pain the system administers measured doses of the opioid sufentanil in the form of tiny tablets which quickly dissolve and are absorbed into the body through the lining under the tongue. Currently in late-stage of development its NanoTab system is also being developed to treat cancer-related pain or provide sedation and pain relief to patients having procedures at doctors' offices. Founded in 2005 AcelRx went public in 2011 through a $40 million IPO.

	Annual Growth	12/10	12/11	12/12	12/13	12/14
Sales ($ mil.)	69.5%	–	1.1	2.4	29.5	5.2
Net income ($ mil.)	–	(14.3)	(20.1)	(33.4)	(23.4)	(33.4)
Market value ($ mil.)	51.9%	–	83.9	186.2	494.4	294.2
Employees	27.4%	19	21	25	27	50

ACENTO ADVERTISING INCORPORATED

2254 S. Sepulveda Blvd.
Los Angeles CA 90064
Phone: 310-943-8300
Fax: 310-943-8330
Web: www.acento.com

CEO: Roberto Orci
CFO: –
HR: –
FYE: December 31
Type: Private

Founded in 1983 Acento Advertising offers advertising and marketing services geared toward the Hispanic market. Acento provides such services as creative development in broadcast print and interactive media as well as TV production facilities in the US and Latin America. The agency also offers expertise in market research public relations and direct marketing. The company's clients have included Alaska Airlines Wells Fargo and Staples.

ACER AMERICA CORPORATION

333 W. San Carlos St. Ste. 1500
San Jose CA 95110
Phone: 408-533-7700
Fax: 408-533-4555
Web: www.acer.us

CEO: Emmanuel Fromont
CFO: Ming Wang
HR: –
FYE: December 31
Type: Subsidiary

Whether it's laptops in Los Angeles or servers in Saskatchewan Acer America has North America covered. The company a subsidiary of Taiwanese computer giant Acer sells to businesses government agencies schools and consumers. Its core products are desktop and portable PCs with consumer models sold under the Aspire brand and professional models marketed under the Veriton banner. Acer America also supports the eMachines Gateway and Packard Bell PC brands. Other Acer products include smartphones network servers LCD monitors data storage systems and video projectors. Acer's sales in North America account for less than one quarter of its total revenue. Acer America was established in 1976.

ACETO CORP
NMS: ACET

4 Tri Harbor Court
Port Washington, NY 11050
Phone: 516 627-6000
Fax: –
Web: www.aceto.com

CEO: Salvatore J. Guccione
CFO: Douglas Roth
HR: –
FYE: June 30
Type: Public

Distributor Aceto (pronounced "a-seat-o") is getting bigger through chemicals — primarily specialty chemicals and pharmaceuticals. It sources and distributes more than 1100 chemical products through three segments. Its largest segment is Performance Chemicals which sources and distributes specialty chemicals and agricultural protection products. Aceto's other business segments include Pharmaceutical Ingredients (active pharmaceutical ingredients or APIs and pharmaceutical intermediates) and Human Health (generic drugs and nutraceutical products). Aceto sources about two-thirds of its products from Asia mostly China and India and turns around to sell more than half of them in the US.

	Annual Growth	06/11	06/12	06/13	06/14	06/15
Sales ($ mil.)	7.3%	412.4	444.4	499.7	510.2	547.0
Net income ($ mil.)	39.0%	9.0	17.0	22.3	29.0	33.5
Market value ($ mil.)	38.4%	195.6	263.2	406.0	528.7	717.9
Employees	3.2%	238	233	234	270	270

ACF INDUSTRIES LLC

101 Clark St.
St. Charles MO 63301
Phone: 636-949-2399
Fax: 636-949-2825
Web: www.acfindustries.com

CEO: James E Bowles
CFO: –
HR: –
FYE: December 31
Type: Private

After more than a century ACF Industries is still on track making railcars and railcar components. ACF (originally The American Car and Foundry Co.) manufactures and fabricates an array of transportation equipment for the new railcar and repair railcar markets as well as custom steel parts for non-rail customers. Operations include facilities in Pennsylvania and West Virginia which churn out related products such as weld sub-assemblies pressure vessels and wheel and axle machining and mounting. ACF is owned by financier Carl Icahn who serves as chairman. Icahn is a major stockholder and chairman of American Railcar Industries and American Railcar Leasing trade affiliates of ACF railcar components.

ACH FOOD COMPANIES INC.

7171 Goodlett Farms Pkwy.
Memphis TN 38016
Phone: 901-381-3000
Fax: 901-381-2968
Web: www.achfood.com

CEO: Richard Rankin
CFO: Stephen Zaruba
HR: –
FYE: September 30
Type: Subsidiary

ACH Food Companies is ACH-ing to help the cook. The company markets sells and produces a variety of cooking oils and other food ingredients such as cornstarch syrup spices and sauces. Its lineup is led by well-known brands including Mazola (the #1 corn oil brand in North America) Argo corn starch Fleischmann's yeast Karo corn syrup and Spice Islands seasonings. The company also offers private-label and custom manufacture services. Operating through two divisions consumer products and commercial products it caters to the retail and industrial food and foodservice industries in the US Canada and Mexico. ACH is a subsidiary of UK food giant Associated British Foods which purchased ACH in 1995.

ACHILLION PHARMACEUTICALS INC.

NMS: ACHN

300 George Street
New Haven, CT 06511
Phone: 203 624-7000
Fax: –
Web: www.achillion.com

CEO: Milind S Deshpande
CFO: Mary Kay Fenton
HR: –
FYE: December 31
Type: Public

Achillion Pharmaceuticals is looking for the Achilles heel of infectious disease. The firm is developing treatments for infectious diseases including antiviral treatments for HIV infection and hepatitis C as well as antibacterials for fighting drug-resistant hospital-based infections. Achillion is focused on the development of three hepatitis C treatments. It has out-licensed elvucitabine a late-stage treatment of HIV and hepatitis B to GCA Therapeutics and sent its eye and skin infection treatment to Ora Inc. Achillion has other candidates aimed at combating drug-resistant staph. The company was formed in 1998 and went public in 2006.

	Annual Growth	12/08	12/09	12/10	12/11	12/12
Sales ($ mil.)	–	(0.2)	(0.3)	2.4	0.2	2.6
Net income ($ mil.)	–	(28.2)	(25.9)	(25.5)	(44.2)	(47.1)
Market value ($ mil.)	85.3%	54.1	247.6	330.4	606.8	637.8
Employees	1.4%	54	43	42	50	57

ACI WORLDWIDE INC

NMS: ACIW

3520 Kraft Rd, Suite 300
Naples, FL 34105
Phone: 239 403-4600
Fax: –
Web: www.aciworldwide.com

CEO: Philip G. (Phil) Heasley
CFO: Scott W. Behrens
HR: Shirley Guidroz
FYE: December 31
Type: Public

ACI Worldwide helps money go mobile. The company develops e-payment and electronic funds transfer (EFT) software for companies around the world. Customers use its software to process transactions involving ATMs credit and debit cards online banking and payment processing point-of-sale terminals smart cards and wire transfers. ACI also makes network integration software and it offers services such as design implementation and facilities management. The company serves the financial services and retail industries with more than 750 customers in some 80 countries. ACI agreed to sell its community bank-oriented community financial services business to Fiserv for $200 million in early 2016.

	Annual Growth	12/10	12/11	12/12	12/13	12/14
Sales ($ mil.)	24.8%	418.4	465.1	666.6	864.9	1,016.1
Net income ($ mil.)	25.5%	27.2	45.9	48.8	63.9	67.6
Market value ($ mil.)	(6.9%)	3,107.2	3,311.9	5,052.2	7,516.5	2,332.4
Employees	20.3%	2,134	2,131	3,530	4,329	4,472

ACMAT CORP.

NBB: ACMT A

30 South Road
Farmington, CT 06032
Phone: 860 946-4800
Fax: –
Web: www.acmatcorp.com

CEO: Henry W Nozko Jr
CFO: –
HR: –
FYE: December 31
Type: Public

ACMAT does its part to wipe out asbestos. Originally a contracting firm focused on asbestos abatement the company moved into the insurance industry when it was dropped by its own insurer. Through its ACSTAR Insurance subsidiary the company handles liability insurance and supply bonds to customers such as general specialty trade environmental and asbestos and lead abatement contractors. ACMAT's insurance products are sold nationwide. AMCAT still provides design and construction contracting services for commercial and government customers through its ACMAT Contracting division.

	Annual Growth	12/07	12/10	12/11	12/12	12/13
Sales ($ mil.)	(20.5%)	22.0	8.1	6.4	6.0	5.5
Net income ($ mil.)	(21.0%)	4.1	0.9	1.2	1.2	1.0
Market value ($ mil.)	0.7%	24.7	27.9	26.8	23.6	25.7
Employees	–	–	–	–	–	–

ACME COMMUNICATIONS INC

NBB: ACME

2101 E. Fourth Street, Suite 202
Santa Ana, CA 92705
Phone: 714 245-9499
Fax: 714 245-9494
Web: www.acmecommunications.com

CEO: Jamie Kellner
CFO: Thomas Allen
HR: –
FYE: December 31
Type: Public

ACME Communications' relationship with Warner Bros. has nothing to do with a wily coyote rockets or any other explosives. The company owns and operates three television stations in midsized markets (KWBQ and KASY in Albuquerque/Santa Fe New Mexico and WBUW in Madison Wisconsin) most of which are affiliated with The CW Network a joint venture between Time Warner's Warner Bros. Entertainment and CBS Corporation. In addition to its stations ACME Communications produces a syndicated morning program called The Daily Buzz that airs on about 150 TV stations throughout the country.

	Annual Growth	12/09	12/10	12/11	12/12	12/13
Sales ($ mil.)	(61.0%)	26.8	14.6	12.9	14.7	0.6
Net income ($ mil.)	–	(8.7)	(8.5)	12.4	4.9	0.3
Market value ($ mil.)	(50.0%)	8.0	18.0	10.8	2.2	0.5
Employees	–	–	–	–	–	–

ACME MARKETS INC.

75 Valley Stream Pkwy.
Malvern PA 19355
Phone: 610-889-4000
Fax: 610-889-3039
Web: www.acmemarkets.com

CEO: –
CFO: –
HR: –
FYE: February 28
Type: Subsidiary

Wile E. Coyote has nothing to fear from this Acme company. Regional grocery chain Acme Markets operates about 115 supermarkets under the Acme and Acme Sav-on banners in Delaware Maryland New Jersey and Pennsylvania. It's the #2 food and drug retailer (behind Wakefern Food-owned ShopRite) in the competitive Philadelphia market where it competes with local chains including A&P-owned Pathmark and Giant. In addition to its bricks-and-mortar operations Acme offers online grocery ordering for its customers in and around Philadelphia. Founded in 1891 Acme Markets is a division of grocery-retailer-and-wholesaler SUPERVALU.

ACME UNITED CORP.

ASE: ACU

55 Walls Drive
Fairfield, CT 06824
Phone: 203 254-6060
Fax: –
Web: www.acmeunited.com

CEO: Walter C Johnsen
CFO: Paul G. Driscoll
HR: –
FYE: December 31
Type: Public

Acme United has the goods for measuring twice and cutting once ... even if you cut yourself in the process. The company supplies measuring instruments (including rulers protractors tape measures) cutting devices (scissors paper trimmers) and safety items (first-aid kits personal protection products) under the Westcott Camillus Clauss PhysiciansCare and Pac-Kit brands as well as under private labels. Acme's products are sold to stationery and industrial supply distributors office supply stores drugstores hardware chains mass merchants and florists. Its operations span Canada Germany Hong Kong China and the US (its biggest market). Chairman and CEO Walter Johnsen owns about 15% of the company.

	Annual Growth	12/10	12/11	12/12	12/13	12/14
Sales ($ mil.)	14.2%	63.1	73.3	84.4	89.6	107.2
Net income ($ mil.)	16.8%	2.6	2.8	3.5	4.0	4.8
Market value ($ mil.)	20.4%	31.3	31.3	36.3	49.0	65.8
Employees	23.1%	132	157	171	180	303

ACNB CORP.

NAS: ACNB

16 Lincoln Square
Gettysburg, PA 17325
Phone: 717 334-3161
Fax: –
Web: www.acnb.com

CEO: Thomas A Ritter
CFO: David W Cathell
HR: –
FYE: December 31
Type: Public

Seven score and a few years ago ACNB Corporation's fathers brought forth a small-town bank. Now ACNB is dedicated to the proposition of being the holding company for Adams County National Bank operating more than 20 branches in the Gettysburg and Newville areas of Pennsylvania. It is altogether fitting and proper that the bank offers traditional retail banking services. The world may long note and remember that the bank also provides residential mortgage (about 60% of the portfolio) commercial real estate consumer and business loans. In addition ACNB gives a full measure of devotion to insurance products; provides trust services; and hopes that community banking shall not perish from the earth.

	Annual Growth	12/10	12/11	12/12	12/13	12/14
Assets ($ mil.)	3.0%	968.7	1,004.8	1,050.0	1,046.0	1,089.8
Net income ($ mil.)	5.1%	8.4	8.5	8.9	9.3	10.3
Market value ($ mil.)	8.5%	94.4	83.2	97.3	108.6	130.8
Employees	1.4%	281	291	283	290	297

ACO HARDWARE INC.

23333 Commerce Dr.
Farmington Hills MI 48335
Phone: 248-471-0100
Fax: 248-615-2696
Web: www.acohardware.com

CEO: –
CFO: –
HR: Jayne Polisano
FYE: February 28
Type: Private

ACO Hardware can provide both the food and the supplies if you want to get your floor clean enough to eat off. Michigan's largest independent hardware chain sells automotive supplies electrical goods food and beverages hardware housewares paint lawn and garden necessities apparel furniture and tools. It also sharpens knives refills propane tanks and rents equipment for carpet cleaning plumbing and home maintenance. ACO Hardware operates about 70 stores in southeastern Michigan primarily in the Detroit area. Customers can view weekly specials and find hardware tips on the company's Web site. Founded in 1946 by Ted Traskos and his four brothers ACO Hardware is still owned by the Traskos family.

ACORDA THERAPEUTICS INC

NMS: ACOR

420 Saw Mill River Road
Ardsley, NY 10502
Phone: 914 347-4300
Fax: 914 347-4560
Web: www.acorda.com

CEO: Ron Cohen
CFO: Michael W. Rogers
HR: Denise Duca
FYE: December 31
Type: Public

Acorda Therapeutics hopes its products really get on your nerves. The company is developing prescription drugs that aim to restore neurological function for patients with central nervous system disorders. The company's marketed drugs include Ampyra which enhances conduction in nerves damaged from multiple sclerosis (MS) and Zanaflex a muscle spasm controller. Acorda is working with Biogen Idec to market Ampyra outside the US. Acorda's other drug candidates include potential new therapies for MS and other central nervous system disorders as well as cardiac conditions.

	Annual Growth	12/10	12/11	12/12	12/13	12/14
Sales ($ mil.)	20.4%	191.0	292.2	305.8	336.4	401.5
Net income ($ mil.)	–	(11.8)	30.6	155.0	16.4	17.7
Market value ($ mil.)	10.7%	1,141.4	998.2	1,040.9	1,222.6	1,711.3
Employees	12.5%	305	328	378	421	489

ACORN ENERGY INC

NBB: ACFN

3844 Kennett Pike
Wilmington, DE 19807
Phone: 302 656-1707
Fax: –
Web: www.acornenergy.com

CEO: Jan H. Loeb
CFO: Michael Barth
HR: –
FYE: December 31
Type: Public

Acorn Energy is hopeful that its seedling energy technology companies might one day grow into big trees. The company has controlling or equity positions in four energy infrastructure firms — Energy & Security Sonar Solutions GridSense Systems OmniMetrix US Sensor Systems (USSI). Its largest company Israel-based Energy & Security Sonar Solutions offers underwater acoustic and sonar security systems for the military and offshore oil rigs through 84%-owned DSIT Solutions. GridSense makes electronic monitoring systems for utility companies and USSI designs fiber optic sensing systems for energy companies. OmniMetrix is engaged in remote monitoring of emergency back-up power generation systems.

	Annual Growth	12/10	12/11	12/12	12/13	12/14
Sales ($ mil.)	(14.0%)	35.7	18.9	19.4	21.8	19.6
Net income ($ mil.)	–	(25.1)	35.4	(16.7)	(29.7)	(27.1)
Market value ($ mil.)	(33.2%)	102.7	159.9	206.8	107.8	20.4
Employees	(8.0%)	228	159	218	205	163

ACOSTA INC.

6600 Corporate Center Pkwy.
Jacksonville FL 32216
Phone: 904-281-9800
Fax: 904-281-9966
Web: www.acosta.com

CEO: Robert Hill
CFO: Gregory Delaney
HR: –
FYE: October 31
Type: Private

Acosta spends a lot of time thinking about which products are top-shelf. The company (which does business as Acosta Sales and Marketing Company) offers sales and marketing services that reach consumers from the shelves of North American retail food service and grocery businesses. Major consumer products manufacturers call on Acosta to help them position their products in grocery and convenience stores drug stores and mass merchandisers. The company which operates through 75 locations in the US and Canada specializes in inventory and merchandising services and business consulting for promotions marketing campaigns and sales. Established in 1927 Acosta is owned by Thomas H. Lee Partners.

ACQUITY GROUP L.L.C.

NYSE: AQ

500 W. Madison St. Ste. 2200
Chicago IL 60661
Phone: 312-427-2470
Fax: 403-266-6259
Web: www.crewenergy.com

CEO: Chris Dalton
CFO: –
HR: Kimberly Magner
FYE: December 31
Type: Public

Acquity Group thinks the digital sphere is the best place to get a brand name out into the world. A marketing and e-commerce company Acquity offers digital marketing services primarily to multinational companies operating in the US and Asia. It provides digital marketing analysis and strategy as well as marketing services targeted to Internet mobile devices and social media channels. In addition Acquity designs and implements e-commerce websites such as online stores and other points of sale for its clients. Its core clients have included Adobe Systems Inc. Allstate American Express GM and HTC. Acquity Group went public in 2012.

ACRE REALTY INVESTORS INC
ASE: AIII

c/o Avenue Capital Group, 399 Park Avenue, 6th Floor
New York, NY 10022
Phone: 212-878-3504
Fax: –

CEO: Edward Gellert
CFO: Mark E Chertok
HR: –
FYE: December 31
Type: Public

Roberts Realty Investors really wants to get it REIT. A self-administered real estate investment trust (REIT) Roberts Realty owns and operates commercial real estate and land primarily in metropolitan Atlanta. The company sold a 400-unit apartment community in 2008; it followed that sale with a handful of other property divestitures. The REIT now owns about five retail and office assets and approximately 150 acres of land which it plans to develop into residential and mixed-use properties. Roberts Realty Investors operates through its majority-owned Roberts Properties Residential partnership.

	Annual Growth	12/10	12/11	12/12	12/13	12/14
Sales ($ mil.)	(75.7%)	1.8	1.3	1.4	0.0	0.0
Net income ($ mil.)	–	(9.4)	(9.1)	(6.9)	(0.5)	(2.4)
Market value ($ mil.)	(7.8%)	13.7	12.0	11.0	8.4	9.9
Employees	(15.9%)	2	1	1	1	1

ACSIS INC.

9 E. Stow Rd.
Marlton NJ 08053
Phone: 856-673-3000
Fax: 856-810-3597
Web: www.acsisinc.com

CEO: Jeremy Coote
CFO: Stephanie Seibel
HR: –
FYE: December 31
Type: Private

Acsis connects the shop floor with the top floor by helping customers keep track of their products. The company provides supply chain software and services to help large manufacturers make the most of their SAP-based supply chain systems. Its products and services improve data collection and help users integrate supply chain and enterprise resource planning (ERP) systems. Acsis's ProducTrak software makes supply chain data accessible throughout an organization; its online TrakExchange service lets customers share information with trading partners. Clients have included BASF Coca Cola and Wyeth. The company has partnered with Cisco Systems (hardware) Accenture (systems integration) and WaveLink (software).

ACT INC.

500 ACT Dr.
Iowa City IA 52245
Phone: 319-337-1000
Fax: 319-339-3021
Web: www.act.org

CEO: Jon Whitmore
CFO: Thomas J Goedken
HR: –
FYE: August 31
Type: Private - Not-for-Pr

A C and T... three little letters that can strike fear in the hearts of high school students across the US. ACT most notably develops and administers the ACT national college admission exam with more than 1.6 million high school seniors taking the test each year but it also designs other educational assessment tests and programs as well as career planning and workforce development programs for people of all ages around the world. Its Workforce Solutions provides assessment training and consulting to employers. The not-for-profit organization was founded in 1959 by E. F. Lindquist and Ted McCarrel who sought to create an exam to measure potential college students' capacity for critical thinking.

ACTAVIS U.S.

60 Columbia Rd. Bldg. B
Morristown NJ 07960
Phone: 973-993-4500
Fax: 973-993-4303
Web: www.actavis.us

CEO: Paul M Bisaro
CFO: R Todd Joyce
HR: –
FYE: December 31
Type: Subsidiary

As its name implies the Actavis U.S. is the US manufacturing and marketing unit of global generics firm Actavis. The company makes some 150 generic equivalents of both prescription and OTC drugs in a number of forms including liquids tablets creams and suppositories. Actavis U.S. has manufacturing and distribution facilities in Florida Maryland New Jersey and North Carolina. The group also provides contract manufacturing services to third parties. Actavis U.S. accounts for a quarter of its parents revenues. The parent has agreed to be acquired by US rival Watson Pharmaceuticals. Following the acquisition Watson will likely integrate Actavis U.S.' products and pipeline into its existing operations.

ACTELIS NETWORKS INC.

6150 Stevenson Blvd.
Fremont CA 94538
Phone: 510-545-1045
Fax: 510-545-1075
Web: www.actelis.com

CEO: Tuvia Barlev
CFO: Stephen Cordial
HR: Carmel Lewis
FYE: December 31
Type: Private

Actelis Networks prefers copper over glass. The company's transmission equipment enables carriers and telecommunications providers to deliver Ethernet services over copper wires. Its products are intended to increase the data-carrying capacity of the copper lines and eliminate the need for installing fiber optics in the "last mile" between service providers' networks and their subscribers. Actelis targets regional Bell telephone companies independent and competitive local exchange carriers and alternative carriers worldwide. The company has received financial backing from investors including The Carlyle Group Innovacom Venture Capital and New Enterprise Associates.

ACTION FOR BOSTON COMMUNITY DEVELOPMENT REAL ESTATE CORP.

178 TREMONT ST
BOSTON, MA 021111006
Phone: 617-357-6000
Fax: –
Web: www.bostonabcd.org

CEO: –
CFO: Marjorie Lombard
HR: –
FYE: August 31
Type: Private

Action For Boston Community Development (ABCD) strives to make helping others as easy as 1-2-3. The not-for-profit serves more than 100000 low-income people in New England in areas such as advocacy child care consumer services education health and housing. The group operates through a decentralized model that utilizes a citywide network of Area Planning Action Councils Neighborhood Service Centers and Family Service Centers. It partners with more than a dozen programs like SUMMERWORKS (work experience for low-income teens) Foster Grandparents Urban College of Boston and another 10 or so government agencies. ABCD was established in 1962 as one of several national programs to combat poverty.

	Annual Growth	08/06	08/07	08/08	08/09	08/10
Sales ($ mil.)	5.6%	–	–	–	143.5	151.5
Net income ($ mil.)	–	–	–	–	0.3	(0.0)
Market value ($ mil.)	–	–	–	–	–	–
Employees	–	–	–	–	–	1,000

ACTIONET INC.

2600 PARK TWR DR STE 1000
VIENNA, VA 22180
Phone: 703-204-0090
Fax: -
Web: www.actionet.com

CEO: Ashley W Chen
CFO: Kendra Leser
HR: -
FYE: December 31
Type: Private

ActioNet provides information technology services such as custom software development computer security assessment network design consulting project management systems integration and design and training. Customers come from industries such as manufacturing retail transportation telecommunications financial services and the public sector. ActioNet was founded in 1998 by president and CEO Ashley Chen. Key customers have included Qwest the Department of Energy and the Department of Labor.

	Annual Growth	12/05	12/06	12/07	12/08	12/13
Sales ($ mil.)	(19.7%)	-	1,392.4	15.6	23.4	298.5
Net income ($ mil.)	53.0%	-	-	1.9	3.1	23.8
Market value ($ mil.)	-	-	-	-	-	-
Employees	-	-	-	-	-	1,352

ACTIONTEC ELECTRONICS INC.

760 N MARY AVE
SUNNYVALE, CA 940852908
Phone: 408-752-7700
Fax: -
Web: www.actiontec.com

CEO: Dean Chang
CFO: Brian Paul
HR: -
FYE: December 31
Type: Private

Actiontec Electronics aims to broaden your approach to networking. The company makes gateways routers modems and other broadband connection equipment used to create wireless home networks. Its fiber optic routers allow broadband television and other content to be distributed to multiple devices throughout the home over coaxial cables. Actiontec sells its equipment through partnerships with broadband service providers and equipment makers such as Qwest Verizon Cisco and Entropic. It also sells directly through retailers including Amazon.com Best Buy and Wal-Mart.

	Annual Growth	12/04	12/05	12/06	12/07	12/10
Sales ($ mil.)	-	-	-	(1,449.1)	183.1	162.3
Net income ($ mil.)	225.5%	-	-	0.0	0.0	1.8
Market value ($ mil.)	-	-	-	-	-	-
Employees	-	-	-	-	-	350

ACTIVE DAY INC.

400 Redland Ct. Ste. 114
Owings Mills MD 21117
Phone: 443-548-2200
Fax: 443-548-2280
Web: www.activeday.com

CEO: Jim Donnelly
CFO: Craig O Mehnert
HR: -
FYE: December 31
Type: Private

From dawn to dusk and back again Active Day sees no rest until it has cared for the needs of its elderly and disabled clients. The company operates about 50 adult day care centers in more than half a dozen states. Visitors to its centers participate in social gatherings crafts exercise and other activities. The centers also provide medical care (such as physical therapy and nursing care) and assistance with personal care including feeding and bathing. Active Day offers its patients transportation to and from home as well. It also provides therapeutic services to independent clients and operates home health agencies. Active Day is a subsidiary of Senior Care Centers of America.

ACTIVE MEDIA SERVICES INC.

1 Blue Hill Plaza
Pearl River NY 10965
Phone: 845-735-1700
Fax: 845-735-0717
Web: www.activeinternational.com

CEO: Alan Elkin
CFO: -
HR: -
FYE: June 30
Type: Private

Take a pawn shop cross it with a factoring service and you have Active Media Services. Doing business as Active International the corporate trading firm acquires underperforming assets including surplus inventory capital equipment real estate and receivables. It exchanges these for cash and/or trade credit which is used to offset expenses or purchase such services as advertising freight printing shipping event planning and travel. Clients may barter future manufacturing capacity for services including advertising across all mediums. Active International also provides traditional marketing services. Alan Elkin and Art Wagner founded the employee-owned company in 1984.

ACTIVE POWER INC

NAS: ACPW

2128 W. Braker Lane, BK 12
Austin, TX 78758
Phone: 512 836-6464
Fax: -
Web: www.activepower.com

CEO: Mark A Ascolese
CFO: Jay Powers
HR: -
FYE: December 31
Type: Public

Active Power keeps the juices flowing. The company's UPS (uninterruptible power system) products use a flywheel that stores kinetic energy by spinning converting the kinetic energy into electricity when power quality problems are detected. It was developed in partnership with heavy equipment maker Caterpillar which markets the product with its generator sets. Active Power also makes PowerHouse a continuous power system that combines the company's flywheel UPS products with switchgear and a generator which is sold primarily for military utility and data center applications. Customers in North America account for about 64% of sales.

	Annual Growth	12/10	12/11	12/12	12/13	12/14
Sales ($ mil.)	(6.7%)	65.0	75.5	76.3	61.7	49.1
Net income ($ mil.)	-	(3.9)	(7.1)	(1.9)	(8.4)	(12.8)
Market value ($ mil.)	(7.0%)	56.8	15.2	77.4	77.8	42.5
Employees	3.0%	181	226	216	234	204

ACTIVECARE, INC.

NBB: ACAR

1365 West Business Park Drive
Orem, UT 84058
Phone: 877 219-6050
Fax: 855 864-2511
Web: www.activecare.com

CEO: Michael Z Jones
CFO: Marc C Bratsman
HR: -
FYE: September 30
Type: Public

ActiveCare (formerly known as Volu-Sol Reagents) deals in two very different areas of the health care industry. The company manufactures diagnostic products for use by clinical laboratories; it also provides personal emergency response products and services for consumers. The company's diagnostic business develops and manufactures chemical reagents stains and related equipment used by hematology and microbiology laboratories to detect certain properties in biological samples. The company's ActiveOne services employ biosensors cell phone and GPS technology to remotely monitor a client's vital signs and provide assistance.

	Annual Growth	09/11	09/12	09/13	09/14	09/15
Sales ($ mil.)	71.0%	0.8	1.5	11.4	6.1	6.6
Net income ($ mil.)	-	(7.9)	(12.4)	(25.6)	(13.5)	(11.5)
Market value ($ mil.)	(29.2%)	37.5	5.5	113.3	18.7	9.4
Employees	7.2%	28	148	65	49	37

ACTIVEVIDEO NETWORKS INC.

333 W. San Carlos St. Ste. 400
San Jose CA 95110
Phone: 408-931-9200
Fax: 408-931-9100
Web: www.avnetworks.com

CEO: Jeff Miller
CFO: John Taft
HR: –
FYE: December 31
Type: Private

ActiveVideo Networks bridges the gap between the TV and the Internet. The company creates software that allows cable system operators to offer advanced interactive services to their subscribers. Its technology delivers new applications to digital set-top boxes eliminating the need for costly equipment upgrades. ActiveVideo Networks also provides a variety of professional services such as consulting planning deployment implementation maintenance support and training. Customers include Cablevision Systems and Time Warner Cable. The company's majority investor is Lauder Partners an investment fund managed by the Estee Lauder family.

ACTIVIDENTITY CORPORATION

6623 Dumbarton Cir.
Fremont CA 94555
Phone: 510-574-0100
Fax: 510-574-0101
Web: www.actividentity.com

CEO: Grant Evans
CFO: Jacques Kerrest
HR: –
FYE: September 30
Type: Subsidiary

ActivIdentity isn't passive about data security. The company provides a variety of authentication and user management products including smart cards biometric readers tokens and USB keys. Its products are used to control and monitor access to intranets extranets and the Internet enabling businesses to digitally authenticate and manage the identities of employees customers and trading partners. The company's commercial customers have included Citibank Novell and Oracle; the US Department of Defense is also a client. About half of ActivIdentity's business is done outside of North America. It also offers services such as consulting support and training. The company is a subsidiary of ASSA ABLOY.

ACTIVISION BLIZZARD, INC.   NMS: ATVI

3100 Ocean Park Boulevard
Santa Monica, CA 90405
Phone: 310 255-2000
Fax: –
Web: www.activisionblizzard.com

CEO: Robert A. (Bobby) Kotick
CFO: Dennis Durkin
HR: –
FYE: December 31
Type: Public

When it comes to making cool video games Activision Blizzard aims to be subzero. The leading global video game publisher is best known for industry-dominating franchises such as World of Warcraft from Blizzard Entertainment and Call of Duty through Activision. The latter division also makes games based on licensed properties from Marvel (Spider-Man and X-Men) DreamWorks Animation (Shrek) MGM and the UK's EON Productions (James Bond) Hasbro (Transformers). Other popular franchises include Diablo III and the children's hit Skylanders. The company boosted its mobile gaming presence with a $5.9 billion bid to buy King Digital Entertainment maker of Candy Crush and other mobile games.

	Annual Growth	12/10	12/11	12/12	12/13	12/14
Sales ($ mil.)	(0.2%)	4,447.0	4,755.0	4,856.0	4,583.0	4,408.0
Net income ($ mil.)	18.9%	418.0	1,085.0	1,149.0	1,010.0	835.0
Market value ($ mil.)	12.8%	8,980.8	8,894.2	7,666.9	12,872.0	14,546.9
Employees	(2.7%)	7,600	7,300	6,700	6,900	6,800

ACTUA CORP   NMS: ACTA

555 East Lancaster Ave., Suite 640
Radnor, PA 19087
Phone: 610 727-6900
Fax: –
Web: www.actua.com

CEO: Walter W. Buckley
CFO: R Kirk Morgan
HR: –
FYE: December 31
Type: Public

Actua Corporation (formerly ICG Group) actually invests in companies in the business-to-business (B2B) market working with its holdings to develop strategy. It owns stakes in roughly a handful of cloud-based companies involved in technology-enabled business process outsourcing cloud-based software and software as a service (SaaS) including government-focused communications provider GovDelivery wealth management platform FolioDynamix EHS compliance software provider MSDSonline and property & casualty insurance distribution platform Bolt Solutions. Actua works closely with its companies often helping in day-to-day management.

	Annual Growth	12/10	12/11	12/12	12/13	12/14
Sales ($ mil.)	(7.5%)	115.7	140.5	166.6	59.2	84.8
Net income ($ mil.)	–	46.6	27.6	23.0	209.1	(23.6)
Market value ($ mil.)	6.7%	493.4	267.3	395.7	645.0	639.5
Employees	0.5%	747	829	1,125	551	761

ACTUANT CORP.   NYS: ATU

N86 W12500 Westbrook Crossing
Menomonee Falls, WI 53051
Phone: 262 293-1500
Fax: –
Web: www.actuant.com

CEO: Mark E. Goldstein
CFO: Andrew G. (Andy) Lampereur
HR: Sheri Grissom
FYE: August 31
Type: Public

A diversified industrial company Actuant makes electrical and industrial devices such as wire connectors switches transformers and tools (for wholesale and retail distribution) under such brand names as Acme Electric Gardner Bender Hydratight and Kopp. Actuant's engineered solutions product line includes Power-Packer brand drive technology used in the hydraulic cab-tilt systems of heavy-duty trucks and automotive convertible tops. The company also offers cable synthetic rope pipeline connectors and rental equipment for the energy industry. Customers have included such heavy hitters as Caterpillar BorgWarner BP Petrofac and West Marine.

	Annual Growth	08/11	08/12	08/13	08/14	08/15
Sales ($ mil.)	(3.6%)	1,445.3	1,605.3	1,279.7	1,399.9	1,249.3
Net income ($ mil.)	(35.0%)	111.6	87.3	30.0	163.6	19.9
Market value ($ mil.)	1.7%	1,188.9	1,664.9	2,114.8	1,997.0	1,269.4
Employees	(2.5%)	6,200	6,700	6,700	5,800	5,600

ACTUATE CORP.   NMS: BIRT

951 Mariners Island Boulevard
San Mateo, CA 94404
Phone: 650 645-3000
Fax: –
Web: www.actuate.com

CEO: Mark J Barrenechea
CFO: John Doolittle
HR: Sokha Khun
FYE: December 31
Type: Public

Actuate accentuates reporting. The company provides enterprise reporting and analytics software that corporations use to analyze business data and design publish and distribute content over company networks and the Internet. Actuate's customers which include HSBC Johnson Controls State Street Bank and PNC Bank use the company's software to publish financial statements performance metrics manufacturing and distribution reports and customer account information; that information is pulled from databases and displayed in easily digestible interactive Web pages Excel spreadsheets and other formats. Founded in 1993 Actuate operates in North America Europe and the Asia Pacific region.

	Annual Growth	12/08	12/09	12/10	12/11	12/12
Sales ($ mil.)	1.5%	131.0	119.3	131.5	134.9	138.8
Net income ($ mil.)	(6.7%)	13.6	12.2	10.6	12.0	10.3
Market value ($ mil.)	17.3%	142.7	206.4	274.9	282.6	270.0
Employees	3.9%	533	497	569	553	622

ACUATIVE CORPORATION

30 TWO BRIDGES RD STE 240
FAIRFIELD, NJ 070041550
Phone: 973-227-8040
Fax: –
Web: www.acuative.com

CEO: Vincent Sciarra
CFO: Patrick Danna
HR: –
FYE: December 31
Type: Private

This company helps businesses stay in touch. Acuative builds and manages voice and data networks for business clients. It provides network integration and field engineering services utilizing equipment from third-party vendors such as Aruba Networks Cisco Systems and HP. The company also offers managed services including network administration performance monitoring and security. Its areas of focus include data security unified communications and infrastructure. Acuative serves customers in the financial services insurance retail and manufacturing sectors among others.

	Annual Growth	12/09	12/10	12/11	12/12	12/13
Sales ($ mil.)	4.5%	–	75.2	75.2	61.3	85.9
Net income ($ mil.)	80.2%	–	–	0.5	0.3	1.5
Market value ($ mil.)	–	–	–	–	–	–
Employees	–	–	–	–	–	325

ACUITY A MUTUAL INSURANCE COMPANY

2800 S. Taylor Dr.
Sheboygan WI 53082
Phone: 920-458-9131
Fax: 920-458-1618
Web: https://www.acuity.com

CEO: –
CFO: –
HR: –
FYE: December 31
Type: Private - Mutual Com

For Acuity A Mutual Insurance Company keeping its eye on the prize means meeting its customers' insurance needs. The company writes a variety of personal and commercial property/casualty insurance plans for policyholders in 20 states primarily in the Midwest. Its products include automobile homeowners liability marine umbrella and workers' compensation coverage. Acuity provides policies for such businesses as construction contractors manufacturers trucking and small service businesses. Some 1000 independent agencies sell the company's policies. Acuity was founded in 1925 as Mutual Auto Insurance Company of the Town of Herman. As a mutual insurance firm the company is owned by its policyholders.

ACUITY BRANDS INC (HOLDING COMPANY)   NYS: AYI

1170 Peachtree Street, N.E., Suite 2300
Atlanta, GA 30309-7676
Phone: 404 853-1400
Fax: 404 853-1300
Web: www.acuitybrands.com

CEO: Vernon J. (Vern) Nagel
CFO: Richard K. (Ricky) Reece
HR: –
FYE: August 31
Type: Public

And a booming voice cried out "Let there be light" and Acuity Brands replied "Okay sure." Acuity Brands through its subsidiaries manufactures and distributes a range of indoor/outdoor lighting fixtures and control systems. Applications include residential as well as commercial and institutional buildings industrial facilities and infrastructure projects (highways airports and tunnels). Its services provide wireless and network control-based lighting energy audits and turn-key labor renovation. The company's 13 plants in the US and Mexico one in Canada and two in Europe turn out offerings under such brands as Holophane Gotham Lithonia ROAM Sensor Switch and Tersen.

	Annual Growth	08/11	08/12	08/13	08/14	08/15
Sales ($ mil.)	10.8%	1,795.7	1,933.7	2,089.1	2,393.5	2,706.7
Net income ($ mil.)	20.5%	105.5	116.3	127.4	175.8	222.1
Market value ($ mil.)	43.4%	1,993.8	2,778.5	3,702.6	5,364.6	8,438.9
Employees	6.8%	6,000	6,000	6,500	7,000	7,800

ACUMEN SOLUTIONS INC.

1660 International Dr. Ste. 500
McLean VA 22102
Phone: 703-600-4000
Fax: 703-600-4001
Web: www.acumensolutions.com

CEO: David Joubran
CFO: Erfan Kabir
HR: –
FYE: December 31
Type: Private

Acumen Solutions has keen insight into IT services. The company offers such services as enterprise architecture systems integration program management data warehousing and application development. Acumen also offers services focused on customer relationship management including salesforce.com optimization and customer analytics. Its clients include companies in the communications media consumer products and financial services industries as well as schools and government agencies. Customers have included American Express Comcast Sprint Nextel and the SEC. Acumen was founded by David Joubran and Stacy Reed in 1999.

ACURA PHARMACEUTICALS, INC.   NAS: ACUR

616 N. North Court, Suite 120
Palatine, IL 60067
Phone: 847 705-7709
Fax: –
Web: www.acurapharm.com

CEO: Robert B. (Bob) Jones
CFO: Peter A. Clemens
HR: –
FYE: December 31
Type: Public

Acura Pharmaceuticals is working to provide accurate dosages of powerful drugs while preventing drug abuse. The company has developed a technology to add abuse-deterring agents to commonly abused pharmaceuticals. If a drug with these agents (what Acura calls Aversion Technology) is crushed and inhaled certain ingredients will cause nasal irritation and if an abuser attempts to dissolve the powder it will form a non-injectable gel. Its Impede Technology works with pseudoephedrine to disrupt the process used to turn the decongestant into meth. Acura's approved products include prescription Aversion oxycodone and over-the-counter Nexafed (pseudoephedrine with Impede ingredients).

	Annual Growth	12/10	12/11	12/12	12/13	12/14
Sales ($ mil.)	(31.0%)	3.3	20.5	–	0.1	0.8
Net income ($ mil.)	–	(12.7)	10.4	(9.7)	(13.9)	(13.2)
Market value ($ mil.)	(39.2%)	32.3	34.1	21.7	16.3	4.4
Employees	0.0%	–	15	15	15	15

ACUSHNET COMPANY

333 Bridge St.
Fairhaven MA 02719-0965
Phone: 508-979-2000
Fax: 508-979-3927
Web: www.acushnet.com

CEO: Walter R Uihlein
CFO: –
HR: –
FYE: December 31
Type: Subsidiary

Acushnet stays teed off all the time. The company is a top maker of golf balls clubs shoes gloves and other golfing equipment and accessories. Its Titleist golf balls and FootJoy golf shoes and gloves are #1 sellers in the US. Acushnet also makes value-priced Pinnacle golf balls Titleist golf clubs Scotty Cameron putters and Vokey Design wedges as well as golf bags and outerwear. Products are sold worldwide through golf pro shops specialty sporting goods stores and mass merchants. PGA players who have used Acushnet's equipment include Adam Scott Davis Love III Geoff Ogilvy and Mark O'Meara. Global Fila brand owner Fila Korea bought Acushnet from spirits maker Beam Inc. (formerly Fortune Brands) for $1.2 billion in mid-2011.

ACXIOM CORP.

NMS: ACXM

P.O. Box 8190, 601 E. Third Street
Little Rock, AR 72203-8190
Phone: 501-342-1000
Fax: –
Web: www.acxiom.com

CEO: Scott E. Howe
CFO: Warren C. Jenson
HR: Jennifer (Jen) Compton
FYE: March 31
Type: Public

Acxiom will help you make sense of customer information. The provider of data and software used for direct marketing and customer relationship management (CRM) collects and maintains a storehouse of consumer information covering nearly every household in the US. It has real estate records on millions of properties that it offers to clients needing contact and demographics for direct mail and telemarketing. Acxiom helps companies manage customer data and integrate that information into marketing systems. It draws clients from various sectors including financial services packaged goods automotive health care and telecommunications. Acxiom has operations in Australia Canada China Europe and the US.

	Annual Growth	03/11	03/12	03/13	03/14	03/15
Sales ($ mil.)	(3.2%)	1,160.0	1,130.6	1,099.4	1,097.5	1,020.1
Net income ($ mil.)	–	(23.1)	77.3	57.6	8.9	(11.0)
Market value ($ mil.)	6.5%	1,116.9	1,142.6	1,587.9	2,677.2	1,439.2
Employees	(10.1%)	6,600	6,175	6,300	5,555	4,320

ADA-ES INC.

NASDAQ: ADES

8100 SouthPark Way Unit B
Littleton CO 80120-4527
Phone: 303-734-1727
Fax: 303-734-0330
Web: www.adaes.com

CEO: Michael D Durham
CFO: Mark H McKinnies
HR: –
FYE: December 31
Type: Public

ADA-ES wants to make "clean coal" more than just a marketing term. The company makes environmental technology systems and specialty chemicals to reduce emissions at coal-burning power plants. It offers integrated mercury control systems as well as flue gas conditioning and combustion aid chemicals. ADA-ES provides consulting and testing services and mercury measurement equipment. It also has a joint venture with NexGen Refined Coal to market technology that reduces emissions of nitrogen oxides and mercury from some treated coals. The company has withdrawn plans to reorganize its operations under the name Advanced Emissions Solutions in 2012. ADA-ES was created after being spun off from Earth Sciences in 2003.

ADAC PLASTICS INC.

5920 TAHOE DR SE
GRAND RAPIDS, MI 495467123
Phone: 616-957-0311
Fax: –
Web: www.adacplastics.com

CEO: Jim Teets
CFO: Jeff Dolbee
HR: –
FYE: December 31
Type: Private

ADAC Plastics which does business as ADAC Automotive has a handle on what automakers need. The company (privately owned by the Teets and Hungerford families) supplies automakers and tier 1 suppliers worldwide with door handles and components exterior trim and marker lighting. Other products include cowl vent grilles and fuel filler doors. Services provided by ADAC Automotive include design molding painting and assembly. Its ADAC Technologies subsidiary is a leading supplier of plastic moldings subassemblies and decorative finishes. It is part of the VAST (Vehicle Access Systems Technology) Alliance along with fellow automotive suppliers STRATTEC SECURITY and WITTE Automotive of Velbert Germany.

	Annual Growth	12/04	12/05	12/06	12/07	12/12
Sales ($ mil.)	–	–	(1,820.3)	177.2	177.2	226.9
Net income ($ mil.)	11.1%	–	–	3.8	25.8	7.2
Market value ($ mil.)	–	–	–	–	–	–
Employees	–	–	–	–	–	800

ADAMIS PHARMACEUTICALS CORPORATION

OTC: ADMP

2658 Del Mar Heights Rd. No. 555
Del Mar CA 92014
Phone: 858-401-3984
Fax: +852-2810-6963
Web: www.chnr.net

CEO: Dennis J Carlo
CFO: Robert O Hopkins
HR: –
FYE: March 31
Type: Public

Adamis Pharmaceuticals adamantly develops and markets specialty prescription drugs for respiratory ailments allergies viral infections and other medical conditions. Subsidiary Adamis Labs develops and markets allergy respiratory and pediatric prescription medicines to physicians in the US. Its products include a pre-filled epinephrine syringe for severe allergic reactions dubbed Epi PFS. Adamis Viral Therapies is developing vaccine technologies for ailments such as influenza and hepatitis. The company is also developing Savvy a contraceptive gel and other candidates to potentially treat prostate cancer.

ADAMS FAIRACRE FARMS INC.

765 DUTCHESS TPKE
POUGHKEEPSIE, NY 126032000
Phone: 845-454-4330
Fax: –
Web: www.adamsfarms.com

CEO: –
CFO: –
HR: –
FYE: January 31
Type: Private

From seeds to seafood and fertilizer to fencing Adams Fairacre Farms has a few things covered. The company's four locations in New York's Hudson River Valley offer groceries including fresh produce power equipment (John Deere tractors and mowers chippers chain saws) fencing supplies landscaping materials and gifts and gardening supplies (plants seeds soil pest control). Adams Fairacre Farms was founded in 1919 by Ralph Adams Sr. as a roadside produce stand where the Adams family sold the excess from its 50-acre farm. The company added other items as customers requested them. Descendants of Adams including some third-generation members own and run the family business.

	Annual Growth	01/07	01/08	01/09	01/11	01/12
Sales ($ mil.)	–	–	–	(1,039.1)	115.6	122.1
Net income ($ mil.)	1968.7%	–	–	0.0	1.6	0.8
Market value ($ mil.)	–	–	–	–	–	–
Employees	–	–	–	–	–	550

ADAMS GOLF INC.

NASDAQ: ADGF

2801 E. Plano Pkwy.
Plano TX 75074
Phone: 972-673-9000
Fax: 972-398-8818
Web: www.adamsgolf.com

CEO: –
CFO: –
HR: –
FYE: December 31
Type: Public

Like any golfer Adams Golf says the problem isn't in the swing it's in the clubs. The company's Speedline fairway woods are designed to lift a golf ball from any lie — even bunkers rough or divots — and send it farther. Adams Golf also develops drivers wedges irons putters and accessories (golf bags and hats). A Women's Golf Unlimited subsidiary caters to women golfers with irons in various colors clubs balls and other gear. Specialty retailers mass merchants pro shops and sporting goods stores account for about 80% of Adams' sales. In addition to endorsing Adams Golf's products pro golfer Tom Watson assists in design and testing. The company was founded by chairman Barney Adams in 1987.

ADAMS MEDIA

57 Littlefield St.
Avon MA 02322
Phone: 508-427-7100
Fax: 508-427-6790
Web: www.adamsmedia.com

CEO: –
CFO: –
HR: –
FYE: December 31
Type: Business Segment

Adams Media publishes everything. The company publishes trade paperback books including titles in its Everything series (Everything Parenting Everything Pets Everything Health). Adams Media primarily covers non-fiction topics such as cooking pets health careers parenting and travel. Other imprints include Platinum Press (business) Polka Dot Press (for women) and Provenance Press (new age). The company publishes some 140 new titles per year with a total catalog of about 700 titles. Other series include "Streetwise Cup of Comfort Small Miracles" and Knock 'Em Dead. Adams Media is a unit of niche magazine publisher F+W Media.

ADB AIRFIELD SOLUTIONS LLC

977 Gahanna Pkwy.
Columbus OH 43230
Phone: 614-861-1304
Fax: 614-864-2069
Web: www.adb-airfield.com

CEO: Joe Pokoj
CFO: Michael Morrow
HR: Rita Maruscak
FYE: September 30
Type: Business Segment

ADB Airfield Solutions (formerly Siemens Airfield Solutions) can shed some light on landings takeoffs and other aircraft endeavors. The company makes products that illuminate approach zones aprons main runways and taxiways. From the largest freight hub in the world to small regional airports ADB's products can be found in virtually any airport. Other products include externally lighted wind cones guidance and control monitoring systems and cables and connectors. ADB also acts as a turnkey contractor for a variety of airport projects. Montagu Private Equity acquired ADB in November 2009 for E45 million ($60 million) from German giant Siemens AG which had owned the airfield lighting business since 1987.

ADAMS RESOURCES & ENERGY, INC.   ASE: AE

17 South Briar Hollow Lane, Suite 100
Houston, TX 77027
Phone: 713 881-3600
Fax: –
Web: www.adamsresources.com

CEO: Thomas S. (Tommy) Smith
CFO: Richard B. (Rick) Abshire
HR: Lisa Carrizales
FYE: December 31
Type: Public

The late Bud Adams may have moved his NFL team to Tennessee years ago but the company he founded (Adams Resources & Energy) remains a Houston oiler with interests in oil and gas exploration transportation and marketing. Its primary operations are all within a 1000-mile radius of Houston. Subsidiary Gulfmark Energy buys crude oil at the wellhead for transport to refiners and other customers via trucks and barges and the company's Ada Resources subsidiary markets refined petroleum products such as gasoline and diesel fuel. With exploration and production mainly in Texas and Louisiana in 2014 Adams Resources had proved reserves of 5.6 billion cu. ft. of natural gas and 318000 barrels of oil.

	Annual Growth	12/10	12/11	12/12	12/13	12/14
Sales ($ mil.)	16.9%	2,212.0	3,214.4	3,381.0	3,946.0	4,132.8
Net income ($ mil.)	(6.8%)	8.6	22.9	27.8	21.6	6.5
Market value ($ mil.)	19.7%	102.6	122.8	147.9	288.9	210.7
Employees	4.1%	740	780	925	821	870

ADCARE HEALTH SYSTEMS, INC.   ASE: ADK

1145 Hembree Road
Roswell, GA 30076
Phone: 678 869-5116
Fax: –
Web: www.adcarehealth.com

CEO: William McBride III
CFO: Allan J Rimland
HR: –
FYE: December 31
Type: Public

Retirement keeps AdCare Health Systems working. The company buys leases and manages some 50 nursing homes assisted-living facilities and independent retirement communities in Alabama Arkansas Georgia Missouri North Carolina Ohio and Oklahoma with a total of more than 4800 beds in service. It owns all or part of about half of its facilities including the Hearth & Home assisted living facilities. Services include Alzheimer's and subacute care. AdCare also operates a home health care business Assured Health Care which offers nursing therapy and living assistance services as well as administrative services for insurance coordination and caregiver hiring.

	Annual Growth	12/10	12/11	12/12	12/13	12/14
Sales ($ mil.)	38.0%	53.2	151.4	201.7	222.8	193.3
Net income ($ mil.)	–	(2.7)	(6.2)	(6.9)	(12.6)	(13.6)
Market value ($ mil.)	0.7%	74.7	76.2	91.0	82.3	76.8
Employees	11.5%	2,210	3,800	4,400	3,368	3,414

ADAMS-COLUMBIA ELECTRIC COOPERATIVE

401 E LAKE ST
FRIENDSHIP, WI 539348050
Phone: 800-831-8629
Fax: –
Web: www.acecwi.com

CEO: Martin Hillard Jr
CFO: John West
HR: –
FYE: December 31
Type: Private

With a name that harkens back to Christopher Columbus and the Founding Fathers Adams-Columbia Electric Cooperative provides power to more than 36000 member-owners in 12 counties in central Wisconsin. The rural distribution cooperative operates nearly 5300 miles of transmission and distribution lines. Adams-Columbia Electric was formed through the merger of Adams-Marquette Electric Cooperative and Columbus Rural Electric Cooperative in 1987. The utility expanded further through its 1992 acquisition of Waushara Electric Cooperative. The cooperative covers a 2500 sq. mi. geographic service area.

	Annual Growth	12/98	12/99	12/01	12/08	12/13
Sales ($ mil.)	(20.7%)	–	1,620.1	29.0	56.3	63.4
Net income ($ mil.)	(7.0%)	–	–	1.9	0.0	0.8
Market value ($ mil.)	–	–	–	–	–	–
Employees	–	–	–	–	–	115

ADDUS HOMECARE CORP   NMS: ADUS

2300 Warrenville Rd.
Downers Grove, IL 60515
Phone: 630 296-3400
Fax: –
Web: www.addus.com

CEO: Mark S. Heaney
CFO: Dennis B. Meulemans
HR: Jessica Vandyke
FYE: December 31
Type: Public

Addus HomeCare is there for those who need in-home personal and medical care services. Doing business through subsidiary Addus HealthCare it serves the elderly and disabled. Its home and community unit provides long-term non-medical social services such as bathing grooming housekeeping meal preparation and transportation. State and county government payors generate most of its revenues. Addus divested its home health division which provided skilled nursing and rehabilitative therapies typically on a short-term recovery basis in 2013.

	Annual Growth	12/10	12/11	12/12	12/13	12/14
Sales ($ mil.)	3.6%	271.7	273.1	244.3	265.9	312.9
Net income ($ mil.)	19.4%	6.0	(2.0)	7.6	19.1	12.2
Market value ($ mil.)	56.0%	45.1	39.3	78.7	247.2	267.2
Employees	8.0%	13,284	13,602	14,528	16,585	18,054

ADDVANTAGE TECHNOLOGIES GROUP, INC.   NMS: AEY

1221 E. Houston
Broken Arrow, OK 74012
Phone: 918 251-9121
Fax: –
Web: www.addvantagetechnologies.com

CEO: David L Humphrey
CFO: Scott A Francis
HR: –
FYE: September 30
Type: Public

ADDvantage Technologies uses change to its advantage. The company took its present form in 1999 when it bought Oklahoma-based cable TV parts and services provider TULSAT in a deal that gave TULSAT's owners control over the company. ADDvantage sells new and remanufactured cable TV equipment and provides repair services to cable operators. Its products include headend equipment (satellite receivers amplifiers and antennas) fiber products (couplers optical transmitters) and distribution gear (directional taps line extenders). ADDvantage gets most of its sales in the US with a small portion in Central America and South America. Its biggest supplier is Cisco Systems.

	Annual Growth	09/11	09/12	09/13	09/14	09/15
Sales ($ mil.)	3.5%	38.1	35.2	33.4	35.9	43.7
Net income ($ mil.)	(12.3%)	2.5	1.3	1.7	(0.0)	1.5
Market value ($ mil.)	(0.2%)	22.7	22.1	24.7	23.4	22.5
Employees	5.5%	126	123	122	159	156

ADELPHI UNIVERSITY

1 S AVE LVH 310 310 LVH
GARDEN CITY, NY 11530
Phone: 516-877-3000
Fax: –
Web: www.libraries.adelphi.edu

CEO: –
CFO: –
HR: –
FYE: August 31
Type: Private

It may not house an oracle but Adelphi University hopes to provide answers to students' questions about their future. Founded in 1896 the university has about 7700 students enrolled at its four campuses located in New York (Garden City Hauppage Manhattan and the Hudson Valley). Adelphi University a private institution offers graduate undergraduate and continuing education programs in areas including business management education nursing and social work. Its Swirbul Library contains about 600000 books and documents and 33000 audiovisual materials. The school counts Nextel co-founder Brian McAuley US Chamber of Commerce CEO Thomas Donahue and author Alice Hoffman among its alumni.

	Annual Growth	08/08	08/09	08/10	08/13	08/14
Sales ($ mil.)	6.0%	–	157.5	175.9	195.4	210.7
Net income ($ mil.)	15.7%	–	–	13.1	13.7	23.4
Market value ($ mil.)	–	–	–	–	–	–
Employees	–	–	–	–	–	1,400

ADENA HEALTH SYSTEM

272 HOSPITAL RD
CHILLICOTHE, OH 456019031
Phone: 740-779-7360
Fax: –
Web: www.adena.org

CEO: Mark H. Shuter
CFO: Dawn Bennett Johnson
HR: –
FYE: December 31
Type: Private

Adena Health System hopes to be an Eden for those seeking health care. The system serves the residents of some 10 counties in southern and central Ohio centered on the city of Chillicothe. Its main facility is the 261-bed Adena Regional Medical Center which provides general medical and surgical care as well as specialty care in a number of areas including cardiology women's health oncology and rehabilitation. The health system also features two smaller hospitals outpatient clinics surgery centers and a counseling center among other facilities. The history of the Adena Health System goes back to 1895 when a group of local women established an emergency hospital in the wake of a fatal train wreck.

	Annual Growth	12/04	12/05	12/06	12/07	12/09
Sales ($ mil.)	11.1%	–	207.2	231.4	252.1	315.4
Net income ($ mil.)	(1.5%)	–	–	16.6	9.7	15.8
Market value ($ mil.)	–	–	–	–	–	–
Employees	–	–	–	–	–	2,700

ADEONA PHARMACEUTICALS INC.   NYSE AMEX: AEN

3930 Varsity Dr.
Ann Arbor MI 48108
Phone: 734-332-7800
Fax: 775-358-4458
Web: www.alliednevada.com

CEO: Jeff Riley
CFO: Steven A Shallcross
HR: –
FYE: December 31
Type: Public

Adeona Pharmaceuticals is developing drugs for the treatment of serious central nervous system disorders. In its pipeline are a prescription medical food — specifically an oral tablet of zinc and an amino acid called cysteine — for Alzheimer's disease and drugs for age-related macular degeneration (loss of vision) fibromyalgia (arthritis-related muscle pain) multiple sclerosis and rheumatoid arthritis. The company generally prefers to in-license product candidates that have already shown certain clinical efficacy and then either develop them to commercialization or attract development partners such as it did with Meda which holds rights to complete development of Adeona's fibromyalgia drug Effirma.

ADEPT TECHNOLOGY INC.   NAS: ADEP

5960 Inglewood Drive
Pleasanton, CA 94588
Phone: 925 245-3400
Fax: 925 960-0590
Web: www.adept.com

CEO: Rob Cain
CFO: Seth Halio
HR: Kent Yeun
FYE: June 30
Type: Public

Within 25-plus years Adept Technology has evolved from making industrial robots to a lineup of intelligent automation products. Its robots are designed to handle assemble test inspect and package goods in the electronics food processing automotive component packaging and pharmaceutical industries. Adept Technology's robots can replicate the movements of human shoulders elbows and wrists. The company also makes vision guidance and inspection systems as well as software that allows operators to control robots from a PC. Adept Technology targets a diverse group of Global 1000 companies including Procter & Gamble Johnson & Johnson Seagate Boeing and General Motors.

	Annual Growth	06/10	06/11	06/12	06/13	06/14
Sales ($ mil.)	2.7%	51.6	57.5	66.2	46.8	57.5
Net income ($ mil.)	–	(1.4)	(6.8)	(3.7)	(10.0)	(0.3)
Market value ($ mil.)	20.1%	65.8	52.9	56.8	50.8	136.9
Employees	(1.7%)	163	183	183	139	152

ADEXA INC.

5933 W. Century Blvd. 12th Fl.
Los Angeles CA 90045
Phone: 310-642-2100
Fax: 310-338-9878
Web: www.adexa.com

CEO: Khosrow Cyrus Hadavi
CFO: –
HR: –
FYE: January 31
Type: Private

Adexa gives businesses a bit more digital dexterity. The company's Enterprise Global Planning System (eGPS) software includes components designed to help manufacturers manage a wide range of operations including costs factory scheduling sales inventory and materials management and supply chain planning. The application suite also includes tools for managing product information and collaborating with suppliers distributors and customers. Adexa targets clients in the semiconductor aerospace soft goods industrial automotive electronics chemicals and consumer packaged goods industries; its customers have included Advanced Micro Devices Boeing General Motors and Samsung.

ADHEREX TECHNOLOGIES INC.

PINK SHEETS: ADHXF

501 Eastowne Dr. Ste. 140
Chapel Hill NC 27514
Phone: 919-636-4530
Fax: 604-689-9022
Web: www.pacificgeoinfo.com

CEO: Rostislav Raykov
CFO: Krysia Lynes
HR: –
FYE: December 31
Type: Public

Working nimbly with a very sticky subject Adherex Technologies researches and develops cancer treatments. One of its lead drug candidates targets a tumor's blood supply and makes those blood vessels weak and leaky by disrupting a key protein. Other potential therapies could make cancer cells more vulnerable to anti-cancer drugs or help prevent hearing loss in children undergoing certain types of chemotherapy. Adherex Technologies' pipeline is strongly based on compounds that disrupt cadherins proteins that adhere similar molecules together in cell adhesion. Southpoint Capital Advisors owns a controlling stake in the company.

ADIRONDACK PARK AGENCY

PO Box 99 1133 NYS Rte. 86
Ray Brook NY 12977
Phone: 518-891-4050
Fax: 518-891-3938
Web: www.apa.state.ny.us

CEO: –
CFO: –
HR: –
FYE: December 31
Type: Government Agency

In the Northeastern corner of New York state campers hikers and nature lovers of all sorts flock to Adirondack Park. The park is the largest publicly protected area in the lower 48 bigger than Yellowstone Glacier Everglades and Grand Canyon National Parks combined. New York's Adirondack Park Agency (APA) oversees the 2.6 million acres that belong to the state; the total acreage is 6 million acres and includes more than 3000 lakes and 30000 miles of rivers and streams. The agency develops long-range plans for use of the entire area protects the public land and manages the development of private lands within the park. The New York State Legislature created the APA in 1971.

ADM INVESTOR SERVICES INC.

141 W. Jackson Blvd. Suite 1600A
Chicago IL 60604
Phone: 312-242-7000
Fax: 312-242-7045
Web: www.admis.com

CEO: –
CFO: –
HR: –
FYE: June 30
Type: Subsidiary

ADM Investor Services is a sprout off of agribusiness giant Archer Daniels Midland. The commodities brokerage offers market research and trade clearing and execution services to retail commercial and institutional customers for trading conducted on all major commodities exchanges. It also performs business consulting marketing and investment analysis. The company's ADM Derivatives division provides foreign exchange services via an electronic trading platform. ADM Investor Services serves international markets through affiliates in Hong Kong London and Taiwan. Through a joint venture the company also operates in Mumbai India.

ADM TRONICS UNLIMITED, INC.

NBB: ADMT

224-S Pegasus Ave.
Northvale, NJ 07647
Phone: 201 767-6040
Fax: 201 784-0620
Web: www.admtronics.com

CEO: Andre' Dimino
CFO: Andre' Dimino
HR: –
FYE: March 31
Type: Public

ADM Tronics has had its own Industrial Revolution. While the company previously focused on the making of medical devices ADM has shifted its main focus to water-based chemical products for industrial use. These products include coatings resins primers and additives primarily for the printing and packaging industries. The firm licenses many of its medical products which include the Sonotron line of devices (used to treat osteoarthritis and inflammatory joint ailments with radio waves). Its Pros-Aide unit makes adhesives used in professional makeup products. ADM spun off Ivivi Technologies in 2006 but still owns about a third of the company. The founding DiMino family owns nearly half of ADM Tronics.

	Annual Growth	03/11	03/12	03/13	03/14	03/15
Sales ($ mil.)	24.2%	1.2	2.3	1.6	1.8	2.9
Net income ($ mil.)	–	(0.6)	(0.0)	(0.5)	(0.2)	0.4
Market value ($ mil.)	68.8%	1.6	1.4	1.3	1.6	13.0
Employees	7.5%	15	18	13	16	20

ADOBE SYSTEMS, INC.

NMS: ADBE

345 Park Avenue
San Jose, CA 95110-2704
Phone: 408 536-6000
Fax: –
Web: www.adobe.com

CEO: Shantanu Narayen
CFO: Mark S. Garrett
HR: –
FYE: November 27
Type: Public

Adobe Systems is the house that desktop publishing software built and now it helps customers create distribute and manage digital content in a variety of ways. Among the company's marquee brands are Acrobat Photoshop Flash and Dreamweaver. Adobe serves customers such as content creators and Web application developers with its digital media products and marketers advertisers publishers and others with its digital marketing business. It not only offers products in traditional software packages but some such as its Creative Suite (which combines many of its digital media products) are available as cloud-based versions. Adobe operates worldwide but the US accounts for nearly half of sales.

	Annual Growth	12/11*	11/12	11/13	11/14	11/15
Sales ($ mil.)	3.3%	4,216.3	4,403.7	4,055.2	4,147.1	4,795.5
Net income ($ mil.)	(6.8%)	832.8	832.8	290.0	268.4	629.6
Market value ($ mil.)	35.8%	13,495.6	17,229.2	28,265.6	36,678.6	45,883.1
Employees	8.8%	9,925	11,144	11,847	12,499	13,893

*Fiscal year change

ADT CORP

NYS: ADT

1501 Yamato Road
Boca Raton, FL 33431
Phone: 561 988-3600
Fax: –
Web: www.adt.com

CEO: Naren K. Gursahaney
CFO: Michael S. Geltzeiler
HR: Elizabeth Marston
FYE: September 25
Type: Public

Burglar at your window? ADT wants you to be armed and calm with its alarms. The company provides products and services used for fire protection access control alarm monitoring medical alert system monitoring video surveillance and intrusion detection. It divides its security operations across four disciplines: Residential Security (provides burglar fire carbon dioxide alarms) Small Business (intruder detection and cameras) ADT Pulse (allows users to access and control security systems remotely) and Home Health (emergency response in the case of medical emergencies).

	Annual Growth	09/11	09/12	09/13	09/14	09/15
Sales ($ mil.)	3.5%	3,110.0	3,228.0	3,309.0	3,408.0	3,574.0
Net income ($ mil.)	(5.8%)	376.0	394.0	421.0	304.0	296.0
Market value ($ mil.)	(13.7%)	–	–	6,843.0	5,905.9	5,091.6
Employees	2.2%	–	16,000	17,000	17,500	17,100

ADTRAN, INC.

NMS: ADTN

901 Explorer Boulevard
Huntsville, AL 35806-2807
Phone: 256 963-8000
Fax: –
Web: www.adtran.com

CEO: Thomas R Stanton
CFO: Roger D. Shannon
HR: –
FYE: December 31
Type: Public

ADTRAN turns copper into gold. The company offers more than 1700 network access products and systems used to enable Internet access telephony data transport and video over voice and data networks from traditional copper wire to optical. ADTRAN sells its switches routers multiplexing systems and other carrier-grade equipment to wireline and wireless service providers such as AT&T and CenturyLink. Its enterprise networking equipment ranges from modems to larger integrated access devices for multiple users access routers multiplexers firewalls and radio equipment. ADTRAN sells directly and through a network of distributors to a mostly US-based clientele.

	Annual Growth	12/10	12/11	12/12	12/13	12/14
Sales ($ mil.)	1.0%	605.7	717.2	620.6	641.7	630.0
Net income ($ mil.)	(20.9%)	114.0	138.6	47.3	45.8	44.6
Market value ($ mil.)	(11.9%)	1,934.7	1,611.5	1,044.0	1,443.2	1,164.8
Employees	5.8%	1,663	1,737	2,045	2,010	2,080

ADVANCE AMERICA CASH ADVANCE CENTERS INC.

NYSE: AEA

135 N. Church St.
Spartanburg SC 29306
Phone: 864-342-5600
Fax: 864-342-5612
Web: www.advanceamerica.net

CEO: Patrick O'Shaughnessy
CFO: James A Ovenden
HR: Charlotte Bergman
FYE: December 31
Type: Subsidiary

Advance America Cash Advance Centers is one of the largest payday advance firms in the US. Active in nearly 30 states it operates more than 2100 locations under the Advance America brand and more than 400 more under the National Cash Advance Check Advance First American Cash Advance First American Cash Loans Purpose Financial and Purpose Money banners; California Florida and Texas are its largest markets. At its branches or online customers provide proof of identification source of income bank account and references and Advance America loans them from $50 to $1000 (plus fees and interest) to cover unexpected expenses. Grupo Elektra acquired Advance America in 2012 for some $780 million.

ADVANCE AUTO PARTS INC

NYS: AAP

5008 Airport Road
Roanoke, VA 24012
Phone: 540 362-4911
Fax: –
Web: www.advanceautoparts.com

CEO: Darren R. Jackson
CFO: Michael A. (Mike) Norona
HR: Chip Grubb
FYE: January 03
Type: Public

Advance Auto Parts (AAP) has taken the lead in the race to become the #1 provider of automotive aftermarket parts in North America. Serving both the do-it-yourself (DIY) and professional installer markets AAP operates nearly 5300 stores under the Advance Auto Parts Autopart International (AI) Carquest and Worldpac banners in the US and Canada. Its stores carry brand-name replacement parts batteries maintenance items and automotive chemicals for individual car owners. AAP's Carquest AI and Worldpac stores cater to commercial customers including garages service stations and auto dealers. AAP acquired General Parts International in 2014.

	Annual Growth	01/11*	12/11	12/12	12/13	01/15
Sales ($ mil.)	13.5%	5,925.2	6,170.5	6,205.0	6,493.8	9,843.9
Net income ($ mil.)	9.3%	346.1	394.7	387.7	391.8	493.8
Market value ($ mil.)	24.4%	4,833.8	5,088.1	5,225.5	8,032.3	11,586.6
Employees	9.4%	51,000	53,000	55,000	71,867	73,000

*Fiscal year change

ADVANCE DISPLAY TECHNOLOGIES INC.

7334 S. Alton Way Ste. F
Centennial CO 80112-2320
Phone: 303-267-0111
Fax: 303-267-0330

CEO: Matthew W Shankle
CFO: –
HR: –
FYE: June 30
Type: Private

Advance Display Technologies (ADTI) develops large-screen fiber-optic video displays. The company plans to license or sell its intellectual property assets. After a brief foray into theater operations ADTI is looking to raise capital and restructure its debt in order to continue development of its displays. It acquired the rights to light-emitting diode (LED) display technologies that are patented as SkyNet. Affiliate ADTI Media agreed to pay ADTI a 20% royalty on revenues from the patents after ADTI's lender foreclosed on its assets. In 2010 a group of stockholders including majority owner Lawrence DeGeorge formed GLSD Holdings and acquired the company in a going private transaction.

ADVANCE MAGAZINE PUBLISHERS INC.

4 Times Square
New York NY 10036
Phone: 212-286-2860
Fax: 952-944-7869
Web: www.datalink.com

CEO: Charles Townsend
CFO: David Geithner
HR: –
FYE: December 31
Type: Subsidiary

While being Wired may hold a certain Allure traditional publishing will always be in Vogue at Advance Magazine Publishers doing business as Conde Nast. Owned by newspaper publisher Advance Publications Conde Nast publishes one of the most recognizable magazine portfolios in the industry including fashion bible Vogue and cybermag Wired as well as stalwarts GQ The New Yorker and Vanity Fair and newer shopping title "Lucky". Conde Nast Digital runs websites such as Epicurious (food) and Concierge (travel) while Conde Nast International produces foreign versions of its titles for readers across the globe. In addition Conde Nast oversees fashion and trade magazine unit Fairchild Fashion Group.

ADVANCE PUBLICATIONS INC.

950 Fingerboard Rd.
Staten Island NY 10305
Phone: 718-981-1234
Fax: 718-981-1456
Web: www.advance.net

CEO: –
CFO: Tom Summer
HR: –
FYE: December 31
Type: Private

The drumbeat urging this company forward is the drone of printing presses. Advance Publications is a leading newspaper and magazine publisher with several dozen titles. Its portfolio of about 25 newspapers includes The Star-Ledger (New Jersey) The Cleveland Plain Dealer and namesake Staten Island Advance as well as more than 40 weekly titles published by American City Business Journals. Through Advance Magazine Publishers (DBA Conde Nast) the company owns magazines including The New Yorker Vanity Fair and Wired. Other operations and interests include online content and cable television. Patriarch Sam Newhouse started the family-owned business with the purchase of the Staten Island Advance in 1922.

ADVANCED ANALOGIC TECHNOLOGIES INCORPORATED — NASDAQ: AATI

3230 Scott Blvd.
Santa Clara CA 95054
Phone: 408-330-1400
Fax: 408-737-4611
Web: www.analogictech.com

CEO: David J Aldrich
CFO: Ashok Chandran
HR: –
FYE: December 31
Type: Subsidiary

Advanced Analogic Technologies tries to take an advanced approach to its chip technology. The company known as AnalogicTech provides specialized power management semiconductors for use in a variety of computing communications and consumer electronics applications. AnalogicTech's chips go into portable media players digital cameras netbook and notebook computers smartphones and wireless handsets. The company's customers include Samsung Electronics and LG Electronics. AnalogicTech gets most of its revenues from the Asia/Pacific region; South Korea makes up about two-thirds of sales. In 2012 the company was acquired by Skyworks Solutions in a deal valued at about $260 million in cash.

ADVANCED HEALTH MEDIA LLC

300 Somerset Corporate Blvd.
Bridgewater NJ 08807
Phone: 908-393-8700
Fax: 908-393-8701
Web: www.ahmdirect.com

CEO: Nigel J Whitehead
CFO: Christine Croft
HR: Renee Defranco
FYE: December 31
Type: Private

Advanced Health Media (AHM) keeps biotech and pharma companies' operations from going astray. The company provides hosted sales force logistics and compliance management tools that clients use to manage their interactions with healthcare professionals. Its offerings are focused on logistics (venue management travel meeting coordination) finances (budgeting travel reimbursement reporting) and compliance (attendee tracking healthcare provider eligibility). It also serves venues through its VenueVantage program. Chairman Kevin McMurtry and founding partner Joseph Luzi formed the company in 1999.

ADVANCED ENERGY INDUSTRIES INC. — NMS: AEIS

1625 Sharp Point Drive
Fort Collins, CO 80525
Phone: 970 221-4670
Fax: –
Web: www.advancedenergy.com

CEO: Yuval Wasserman
CFO: Thomas (Tom) Liguori
HR: Randall S. Hester
FYE: December 31
Type: Public

Advanced Energy Industries advances ordinary electrical power to the head of the high-tech class. The company's power conversion products transform raw electricity making it uniform enough to ensure consistent production in high-precision manufacturing. Semiconductor and solar manufacturing equipment maker Applied Materials (14% of sales) is its top customer. Advanced Energy's gear also is used in the production of solar panels and other thin-film products such as cell phones computers cars and glass panels for windows and electronic devices. The company gets around 70% of sales from the US.

	Annual Growth	12/10	12/11	12/12	12/13	12/14
Sales ($ mil.)	6.1%	459.4	516.8	451.9	547.0	583.1
Net income ($ mil.)	(9.9%)	71.2	36.3	20.6	32.1	47.0
Market value ($ mil.)	14.8%	554.0	435.8	560.8	928.4	962.5
Employees	(1.9%)	1,788	1,471	1,354	1,504	1,656

ADVANCED LIGHTING TECHNOLOGIES INC.

32000 Aurora Rd.
Solon OH 44139
Phone: 440-519-0500
Fax: 440-519-0501
Web: www.adlt.com

CEO: Wayne R Hellman
CFO: Wayne J Vespoli
HR: –
FYE: June 30
Type: Private

And then there was light the metal halide kind. Made by Advanced Lighting Technologies (ADLT) metal halide simulates sunlight more closely and efficiently than other technologies. ADLT subsidiary Venture Lighting produces metal halide lamps and ballast systems. Its lineup includes lamp components power supplies and lamp-making equipment for commercial and industrial markets. ADLT's APL Engineered Materials business makes the metal halide salts used in its products as well as sells the salts to other manufacturers. Via Deposition Sciences ADLT also produces durable thin-film optical coatings for industrial medical and biological sciences instrumentation. ADLT is owned by private equity Saratoga Partners.

ADVANCED ENVIRONMENTAL RECYCLING TECHNOLOGIES INC — NBB: AERT

914 N. Jefferson Street
Springdale, AR 72764
Phone: 479 756-7400
Fax: –
Web: www.aert.com

CEO: Timothy D Morrison
CFO: J R Brian Hanna
HR: –
FYE: December 31
Type: Public

It may not turn straw into gold but Advanced Environmental Recycling Technologies (AERT) does turn recycled waste into building materials. The company specializes in processing and converting scrap plastic and wood fiber waste into outdoor decking and fencing systems and window and door components. Its products are mainly used in residential renovation and remodeling by homeowners homebuilders and contractors as a greener alternative to traditional wood and plastic products. AERT markets its products under such names as ChoiceDek and MoistureShield; ChoiceDek is sold to home improvement retailers such as Lowe's through an agreement with distributor BlueLinx. H.I.G. Capital acquired 80% of AERT in 2011.

	Annual Growth	12/10	12/11	12/12	12/13	12/14
Sales ($ mil.)	2.1%	69.8	59.3	74.6	68.8	76.0
Net income ($ mil.)	–	(5.1)	(6.9)	(0.7)	(0.1)	0.4
Market value ($ mil.)	(19.7%)	16.1	6.3	8.3	9.9	6.7
Employees	(0.4%)	403	427	371	415	397

ADVANCED MICRO DEVICES, INC. — NAS: AMD

One AMD Place
Sunnyvale, CA 94088
Phone: 408 749-4000
Fax: –
Web: www.amd.com

CEO: Lisa Su
CFO: Devinder Kumar
HR: Robert (Bob) Gama
FYE: December 27
Type: Public

Advanced Micro Devices (AMD) makes well-regarded processors for customers such as Hewlett-Packard Sony and Dell but it remains a distant #2 in PC and server microprocessors behind Intel. AMD in the past has at times eroded Intel's market share thanks to the popularity of its PC-powering Athlon and Opteron processor families as well as its newer A-series of processors that combine computing and graphics on a chip. In addition to its computing solutions the company generates more than 40% of sales from embedded processors and other chips for enterprise and semi-customized design. Most of AMD's sales are from international customers with China as its single biggest market.

	Annual Growth	12/10	12/11	12/12	12/13	12/14
Sales ($ mil.)	(4.0%)	6,494.0	6,568.0	5,422.0	5,299.0	5,506.0
Net income ($ mil.)	–	471.0	491.0	(1,183.0)	(83.0)	(403.0)
Market value ($ mil.)	(24.2%)	6,239.0	4,190.4	1,769.3	2,933.3	2,056.4
Employees	(3.3%)	11,100	11,100	10,340	10,671	9,700

ADVANCED MP TECHNOLOGY INC.

1010 CALLE SOMBRA
SAN CLEMENTE, CA 92673-6227
Phone: 949-492-3113
Fax: –
Web: www.advancedmp.com

CEO: Jafar Yassai
CFO: Mehdi Taghiei PHD
HR: H Tom
FYE: December 31
Type: Private

Advanced MP Technology advances the cause of global electronic components distribution services for high-tech manufacturers. The company distributes linear and digital integrated circuits such as logic devices; DRAMs static random-access memories (SRAMs) and flash memories; and microprocessors. It also distributes passive components such as capacitors. The company which was founded by CEO Jeff Yassai in 1978 offers inventory management services including inventory reduction programs designed to keep customers from getting stuck with excess inventory during industry downturns. Yassai owns half of the company while president Homey Shorooghi owns the other half.

	Annual Growth	12/98	12/99	12/00	12/01	12/11
Sales ($ mil.)	(3.0%)	–	167.0	455.0	227.0	115.7
Net income ($ mil.)	(15.6%)	–	21.7	147.0	31.0	2.8
Market value ($ mil.)	–	–	–	–	–	–
Employees	–	–	–	–	–	274

ADVANCED PHOTONIX, INC. ASE: API

2925 Boardwalk Drive
Ann Arbor, MI 48104
Phone: 734 864-5600
Fax: –
Web: www.advancedphotonix.com

CEO: Richard D Kurtz
CFO: Jeff Anderson
HR: Charu Gulati
FYE: March 31
Type: Public

Advanced Photonix Inc. (API) senses more with light. The company makes devices that detect light and radiation including photodiodes photo detectors and optoelectronic assemblies which are used by manufacturers in analysis and imaging equipment for applications ranging from missile guidance and satellite positioning to baggage scanning and blood analysis. API's large-area avalanche photodiodes (LAAPDs) are used to sense low levels of light and radiation. Its FILTRODE technology applies optical coatings to photodiode chips to filter out bright background light. About 25% of its sales are to federal government contractors.

	Annual Growth	03/10	03/11	03/12	03/13	03/14
Sales ($ mil.)	8.3%	21.1	28.8	29.5	23.6	29.0
Net income ($ mil.)	–	(3.7)	(1.9)	(2.1)	(4.4)	(4.3)
Market value ($ mil.)	2.7%	17.5	62.7	20.8	14.7	19.5
Employees	(5.5%)	153	185	157	134	122

ADVANCED PROTEOME THERAPEUTICS INC. TSX VENTURE: APC

650 Albany St. Ste. 113
Boston MA 02118
Phone: 617-638-0340
Fax: 617-638-0341
Web: www.advancedproteome.com

CEO: –
CFO: –
HR: –
FYE: July 31
Type: Public

Advanced Proteome Therapeutics (APT) has the technology to help biopharmaceutical developers place their therapeutic proteins in exactly the right spot. However it's taking a while to find those developers and those right spots. One of its applications will enhance the usefulness of existing polyethylene glycol-based drug delivery technology. The company is housed with other research firms on the campus of Boston University but is technically a Canadian company. APT's technology is based upon the work of its founder and CEO Dr. Allen Krantz.

ADVANCED TECHNOLOGIES GROUP LTD. OTC: AVGG

331 Newman Springs Rd. Bldg. 1 Ste. 143
Red Bank NJ 07701
Phone: 732-784-2801
Fax: 732-784-2850
Web: www.atgworld.com

CEO: Alex J Stelmak
CFO: Alex J Stelmak
HR: –
FYE: January 31
Type: Public

Advanced Technologies Group (ATG) is a holding company that owns Internet and software assets. Its MoveIdiot.com subsidiary offers a free Web-based service that enables users to track expenses shipments tasks and lists of goods during the process of moving from one location to the next. ATG also owns software assets designed to monitor Internet traffic for marketing purposes (PromotionStat) and for digital threat detection (Cyber-Fence) but the company said in 2010 that it could not afford to develop those products to bring them to market. ATG was compelled to pay about $19 million to settle a civil action brought against it by the SEC in 2010 regarding securities violations that allegedly took place between 1997 and 2006.

ADVANCEPIERRE FOODS INC.

9990 Princeton Rd.
Cincinnati OH 45246
Phone: 513-874-8741
Fax: 513-874-8395
Web: www.pierrefoods.com

CEO: John N Simons
CFO: Michael B Sims
HR: –
FYE: February 28
Type: Private

AdvancePierre Foods takes the prep out of preparing a meal. The company is a top US supplier of packaged sandwiches fully-cooked chicken and beef items veggie patties breaded meats and bakery products. It caters to several sectors such as schools vending wholesale clubs and grocery and convenience stores. As part of its business it operates meat processing plants sandwich assembly facilities and bakeries across five mostly Midwestern states. AdvancePierre Foods was formed by the 2010 merger of Pierre Foods Advance Food Company and Advance Brands. The company is owned by Oaktree Capital Management along with shareholders and managers of its predecessor companies.

ADVANSOURCE BIOMATERIALS CORP NBB: ASNB

229 Andover Street
Wilmington, MA 01887
Phone: 978 657-0075
Fax: 978 657-0074

CEO: Michael F Adams
CFO: –
HR: –
FYE: March 31
Type: Public

If artificial blood becomes a reality the manufacturers can hook up with AdvanSource Biomaterials maker of synthetic blood vessels. The company's products replace or bypass damaged and diseased arteries and provide access for dialysis needles in kidney disease patients undergoing hemodialysis. These man-made blood vessels also called vascular grafts are made of ChronoFlex the company's polyurethane-based biomaterial. Its CardioPass product candidate is a synthetic coronary artery bypass graft. AdvanSource's HydroThane polymer-based biomaterial mimics living tissue and is marketed for use by other medical device makers.

	Annual Growth	03/11	03/12	03/13	03/14	03/15
Sales ($ mil.)	11.5%	1.7	1.9	2.2	2.6	2.6
Net income ($ mil.)	–	(3.2)	(1.8)	(1.0)	(0.5)	(0.3)
Market value ($ mil.)	(11.4%)	1.3	0.7	1.1	1.0	0.8
Employees	(7.5%)	15	15	13	12	11

ADVANT-E CORPORATION

NBB: ADVC

2434 Esquire Dr.
Beavercreek, OH 45431
Phone: 937 429-4288
Fax: –
Web: www.advant-e.com

CEO: Jason K Wadzinski
CFO: James E Lesch
HR: –
FYE: December 31
Type: Public

Advant-e makes B2B e-commerce EZ. Through subsidiaries Edict Systems and Merkur Group the holding company offers Electronic Data Interchange (EDI) and electronic document management software for small and midsized businesses. More than half of Advant-e's sales come from Edict Systems' GroceryEC.com which helps suppliers such as Associated Grocers do business with retailers by automating invoices and purchase orders. Merkur Group which accounts for less than 20% of sales sells document management software that works within a company's Oracle SAP or Microsoft application. President and CEO Jason Wadzinski who founded Edict System when he was 25 controls more than 54% of Advant-e's stock.

	Annual Growth	12/08	12/09	12/10	12/11	12/12
Sales ($ mil.)	3.3%	8.9	8.6	9.3	9.6	10.1
Net income ($ mil.)	17.1%	1.1	1.2	1.6	1.7	2.0
Market value ($ mil.)	(34.4%)	81.1	16.2	13.2	13.3	15.0
Employees	4.4%	59	66	65	68	70

ADVANTAGE SALES AND MARKETING LLC

18100 Von Karman Ave. Ste. 900
Irvine CA 92612
Phone: 949-797-2900
Fax: 949-797-9112
Web: www.asmnet.com

CEO: Tanya Domier
CFO: Brian Stevens
HR: –
FYE: December 31
Type: Private

Making consumer products is one thing but selling them is another and that's where Advantage Sales & Marketing (ASM) comes in. The company provides outsourced sales merchandising and marketing services to consumer goods and food product manufacturers and suppliers. It works to win optimal placement of clients' products at retail locations throughout the US and Canada and it offers a variety of promotional programs aimed at boosting sales. Owning more than 65 offices in the US and Canada ASM does merchandising for 1200 clients — including Johnson & Johnson Mars Unilever Energizer. Investment group Apax Partners owns a controlling stake in the company which was established in 1987.

ADVENT INTERNATIONAL CORPORATION

75 State St.
Boston MA 02109
Phone: 617-951-9400
Fax: 617-951-0566
Web: www.adventinternational.com

CEO: –
CFO: –
HR: –
FYE: December 31
Type: Private

Buyout firm Advent International invests in mid-market companies in the Americas Europe and Japan. The active investor focuses on business and financial services health care industrial consumer and technology and media. Advent provides its portfolio companies with capital infusions (up to $1.25 billion) for international expansion restructuring or to fuel growth. In developing markets in Central Europe and Latin America Advent finances companies with up to $200 million per transaction. Founded in 1984 Advent has backed more 500 companies and has raised some $26 billion in capital. Investors include pension funds funds of funds financial institutions university endowments and foundations.

ADVENT SOFTWARE, INC.

NMS: ADVS

600 Townsend Street
San Francisco, CA 94103
Phone: 415 543-7696
Fax: –
Web: www.advent.com

CEO: David Peter Hess Jr
CFO: James Cox
HR: –
FYE: December 31
Type: Public

Advent Software manages investments from beginning to end. A provider of investment management software for advisers brokers funds and other financial firms Advent offers applications for managing everything from client relationships to trade order executions. The company's products (marketed under the APX Geneva Black Diamond and Tamale brands among others) are used to manage portfolio accounting trading and order execution hedge and venture fund allocation reconciliation and other functions. Advent also offers services such as consulting hosting support and maintenance. More than 80% of sales come from customers in the US including TIAA CREF Merrill Lynch and Wells Capital Management.

	Annual Growth	12/09	12/10	12/11	12/12	12/13
Sales ($ mil.)	10.2%	259.5	283.5	326.2	358.8	383.0
Net income ($ mil.)	(6.0%)	36.9	24.2	30.2	30.4	28.8
Market value ($ mil.)	(3.8%)	2,087.7	2,968.9	1,248.6	1,095.9	1,791.6
Employees	3.6%	998	1,051	1,201	1,222	1,151

ADVENTIST HEALTH SYSTEM SUNBELT HEALTHCARE CORPORATION

900 Hope Way
Altamonte Springs FL 32714
Phone: 407-357-1000
Fax: 248-594-3190
Web: www.us.belfor.com

CEO: –
CFO: Terry D Shaw
HR: –
FYE: December 31
Type: Private - Not-for-Pr

Adventist Health System Sunbelt Healthcare's mission is to serve the community and boy does it! One of the country's largest faith-based hospital systems not-for-profit Adventist Health runs about 45 hospitals 20 nursing homes and 25 home health care agencies. Its acute care hospitals have some 7600 beds combined; its long-term care facilities offer 1900 beds. It operates in about a dozen states mostly in the Southeast. The organization's Florida Hospital division includes about two dozen hospitals as well as home health agencies and nursing homes. Adventist Health is sponsored by the Seventh-Day Adventist Church as part of that denomination's legacy of providing health care.

ADVENTIST HEALTH SYSTEM/WEST

2100 Douglas Blvd.
Roseville CA 95661-9002
Phone: 916-781-2000
Fax: 916-783-9909
Web: www.adventisthealth.org

CEO: –
CFO: –
HR: –
FYE: December 31
Type: Private - Not-for-Pr

Not content to wait around for the advent of good health Adventist Health System/West operates 18 hospital systems (with about 2800 beds) in the western US. Its health care facilities sprinkled throughout California Hawaii Oregon and Washington also include 100 physicians' clinics and outpatient centers. The not-for-profit organization also runs more than a dozen home health care agencies and has established a handful of joint-venture nursing homes in California Oregon and Washington. Adventist Health maintains strong ties to the Seventh-Day Adventist Church but is independently owned. A sister organization Adventist Health System operates in the central and southern parts of the country.

ADVENTIST HEALTHCARE INC.

1801 RES BLVD STE 400
ROCKVILLE, MD 20850
Phone: 301-315-3030
Fax: –
Web: www.adventisthealthcare.com

CEO: –
CFO: James Lee
HR: –
FYE: December 31
Type: Private

From the newest newborn to the most senior senior Adventist HealthCare takes care of residents living throughout Maryland the metropolitan Washington DC-area and northwestern New Jersey. The not-for-profit network with its more than 2000 physicians is home to three acute care hospitals two specialty care hospitals that offer inpatient and outpatient behavioral health care and more than a dozen home health and rehabilitation operations. Its acute care hospitals include Hackettstown Regional Medical Center Shady Grove Adventist Hospital and Washington Adventist Hospital which combined have 1045 beds. Founded in 1907 Adventist HealthCare is affiliated with the Seventh-Day Adventist Church.

	Annual Growth	12/01	12/02	12/09	12/10	12/11
Sales ($ mil.)	4.3%	–	521.7	852.1	785.3	760.7
Net income ($ mil.)	–	–	0.0	35.3	62.5	15.8
Market value ($ mil.)	–	–	–	–	–	–
Employees	–	–	–	–	–	5,236

ADVENTRX PHARMACEUTICALS INC.   NYSE AMEX: ANX

6725 Mesa Ridge Rd. Ste. 100
San Diego CA 92121
Phone: 858-552-0866
Fax: 858-552-0876
Web: www.adventrx.com

CEO: Brian M Culley
CFO: Brandi L Roberts
HR: –
FYE: December 31
Type: Public

Mast Therapeutics (formerly ADVENTRX Pharmaceuticals) steers its R&D ship towards investigational drug treatments for genetic disease and cancer. The company is focused on developing a late-stage treatment for sickle-cell disease patients. The drug aims to reduce tissue and organ damage by repairing microvascular function and is being explored as a treatment for other inflammatory and circulatory disorders. The company also has some candidates in development to treat cancer. To reflect its focus on its MAST (molecular adhesion and sealant technology) platform the company changed its name to Mast Therapeutics in 2013.

ADVENTURELAND PARK

305 34th NW
Altoona IA 50009
Phone: 515-266-2121
Fax: 515-266-9831
Web: www.adventureland-usa.com

CEO: –
CFO: –
HR: –
FYE: December 31
Type: Private

Adventureland is indeed a land within itself. The 180-acre family resort boasts an amusement park with more than 100 attractions (Adventureland Park) an inn (Adventureland Inn) and a full-service campground (Adventureland Campground). Rides range from roller coasters to kiddie-sized fun and shows include live music magic and musicals. The Adventureland Inn features a tropical themed pool and free shuttle service to and from the amusement park. Adventureland Campground offers its own pool along with RV and tent camping spots. The company opened a new water area Adventure Island in 2008. Former CEO John Krantz founded Adventureland in 1974. Krantz died in 2006.

ADVISORY BOARD COMPANY (THE)   NMS: ABCO

2445 M Street N.W.
Washington, DC 20037
Phone: 202 266-5600
Fax: –
Web: www.advisory.com

CEO: Robert W. Musslewhite
CFO: Michael T. Kirshbaum
HR: –
FYE: December 31
Type: Public

Here's where a hospital might go for a second opinion. The Advisory Board Company specializes in providing best practices consulting to member-clients in the health care and education industries. Members include some 4500 hospitals pharmaceutical and insurance companies universities and related organizations. The Advisory Board offers more than 60 programs across three key areas: best practices research software tools and management and advisory services. Members buy subscriptions to its programs and participate in research efforts. Programs typically include research studies seminars customized reports and decision-support tools. The firm was founded in 1979 as the Research Council of Washington.

	Annual Growth	03/11	03/12	03/13	03/14*	12/14
Sales ($ mil.)	14.5%	290.2	370.3	450.8	520.6	436.2
Net income ($ mil.)	(37.4%)	18.5	25.3	22.1	24.6	4.6
Market value ($ mil.)	(1.7%)	1,858.5	3,198.1	1,895.3	2,318.6	1,767.6
Employees	24.7%	1,600	1,850	2,400	2,800	3,100

*Fiscal year change

ADVIZEX TECHNOLOGIES LLC

6480 Rockside Woods Blvd. South Ste. 190
Independence OH 44131
Phone: 216-901-1818
Fax: 216-901-1447
Web: www.advizex.com

CEO: Fred Traversi
CFO: Mark Woelke
HR: –
FYE: December 31
Type: Private

AdvizeX Technologies marks the spot where hardware meets IT. The value-added reseller provides information technology (IT) products including servers enterprise storage systems workstations and database applications. It works with such vendors as EMC Hewlett-Packard Cisco Systems Microsoft Oracle and VMware. The company's services range from implementation and support to business process consulting and performance management. AdvizeX serves clients in banking and financial services education government health care manufacturing and retail sectors. Its offices are located primarily in the Midwest and East Coast regions of the US.

ADVOCATE HEALTH AND HOSPITALS CORPORATION

1775 DEMPSTER ST
PARK RIDGE, IL 600681143
Phone: 847-723-6105
Fax: –
Web: www.advocatehealth.com

CEO: –
CFO: –
HR: –
FYE: December 31
Type: Private

Advocate Lutheran General Hospital also known simply as Lutheran General provides acute and long-term medical and surgical care to the residents of Park Ridge Illinois and the surrounding northern suburban Chicago area. As one of the largest hospitals in the region Lutheran General boasts nearly 640 beds and a Level I trauma center. Its operations also include a complete children's hospital and pediatric critical care center. Lutheran General serves as a teaching hospital and its specialized programs include oncology cardiology women's health emergency medicine and hospice care. Lutheran General is part of the Advocate Health Care network.

	Annual Growth	12/0-1	12/00	12/01	12/02	12/12
Sales ($ mil.)	(12.4%)	–	–	–	2,603.6	692.0
Net income ($ mil.)	–	–	–	–	(6.8)	102.1
Market value ($ mil.)	–	–	–	–	–	–
Employees	–	–	–	–	–	4,818

ADVOCATE HEALTH CARE NETWORK

2025 Windsor Dr.
Oak Brook IL 60523-1586
Phone: 630-572-9393
Fax: 630-990-4752
Web: www.advocatehealth.com

CEO: James H Skogsbergh
CFO: Dominic J Nakis
HR: –
FYE: December 31
Type: Private - Not-for-Pr

Advocating wellness in Chicagoland from Palos Heights to Palatine Advocate Health Care is a not-for-profit integrated health care network with more than 250 care sites serving the Chicago and surrounding areas. Advocate's operations include about a dozen acute and specialty care hospitals (including Christ Medical Center Hope Children's Hospital Advocate BroMenn Medical Center and Lutheran General Hospital) with more than 3400 beds as well as community health clinics and home health care and hospice services. The health system includes the largest physician network of primary care physicians specialists and sub-specialists in the state.

AEA INVESTORS LP

65 E. 55th St.
New York NY 10022
Phone: 212-644-5900
Fax: 212-888-1459
Web: www.aeainvestors.com

CEO: John Garcia
CFO: –
HR: Sandra L Petruzzelli
FYE: December 31
Type: Private

AEA Investors is in business to make its group of rich investors even richer by buying midsized companies improving their operations and eventually selling them at a profit if all goes to plan. With an exclusive club-like reputation the company has interests in some two dozen firms in the consumer products specialty chemicals and industrial sectors in the US Asia and Europe. It seeks out established enterprises with strong management and competitive position. Holdings include roofing products manufacturer Henry Company and industrial insulation maker Unifrax.

AEARO TECHNOLOGIES LLC

5457 W. 79th St.
Indianapolis IN 46268
Phone: 317-692-6666
Fax: 317-692-6772
Web: www.aearo.com

CEO: –
CFO: –
HR: –
FYE: December 31
Type: Subsidiary

When the sparks fly it helps to be under the aegis of Aearo Technologies. The company manufactures and sells a slew of personal protection and energy-absorbing equipment to the do-it-yourself retail market in more than 70 countries. Sold under brand names such as AOSafety E-A-R Peltor and Safe-Waze its products include earplugs goggles face shields respirators hard hats safety clothing first-aid kits and communication headsets. Aearo also supplies safety prescription eyewear and makes energy-absorbing foams that control noise vibration and shock. The company operates as part of 3M Company's Safety Security and Protection Services business segment.

AECOM

1999 Avenue of the Stars, Suite 2600
Los Angeles, CA 90067
Phone: 213 593-8000
Fax: –
Web: www.aecom.com

NYS: ACM
CEO: Christopher O. (Chris) Ward
CFO: W. Troy Rudd
HR: Rick Heinick
FYE: September 30
Type: Public

AECOM means never having to say Architecture Engineering Consulting Operations and Maintenance. One of the world's top engineering and design groups AECOM (formerly AECOM Technology) provides planning consulting and construction management services for civil and infrastructure construction to government and private clients in 150 countries. The company also provides facilities management and maintenance logistics IT services and systems integration services. AECOM projects have included project management for the Saadiyat Island Cultural District in Abu Dhabi and master planning for the 2012 London Olympics. AECOM acquired competitor URS Corp and homebuilder Hunt Construction Group in late 2014.

	Annual Growth	09/11	09/12	09/13	09/14	09/15
Sales ($ mil.)	22.3%	8,037.4	8,218.2	8,153.5	8,356.8	17,989.9
Net income ($ mil.)	–	275.8	(58.6)	239.2	229.9	(154.8)
Market value ($ mil.)	11.7%	2,672.8	3,200.7	4,730.0	5,105.1	4,161.3
Employees	19.6%	45,000	46,800	45,500	43,300	92,000

AEGERION PHARMACEUTICALS INC

One Main Street, Suite 800
Cambridge, MA 02142
Phone: 617 500-7867
Fax: –
Web: www.aegerion.com

NMS: AEGR
CEO: Mary T. Szela
CFO: Gregory D. (Greg) Perry
HR: Mary Weger
FYE: December 31
Type: Public

Bad cholesterol beware! Aegerion Pharmaceuticals is hot on your trail. The biopharmaceutical company develops cholesterol-lowering drugs for the treatment of cardiovascular and metabolic disease specifically targeting elevated LDL (low-density lipoprotein also known as "bad" cholesterol) levels. Aegerion's first approved drug is Juxtapid (lomitapide branded Lojuxta in Europe) a protein inhibitor that blocks cholesterol production in the liver and intestine. The company is working on getting Juxtapid an oral once-daily medication approved in Japan and for children and teens. Aegerion also markets Myalept a treatment for leptin deficiency.

	Annual Growth	12/10	12/11	12/12	12/13	12/14
Sales ($ mil.)	226.2%	–	–	–	48.5	158.4
Net income ($ mil.)	–	(14.3)	(39.5)	(62.3)	(63.4)	(39.4)
Market value ($ mil.)	10.3%	403.3	476.5	722.4	2,019.9	596.1
Employees	107.2%	16	33	98	217	295

AEGION CORP

17988 Edison Avenue
Chesterfield, MO 63005-1195
Phone: 636 530-8000
Fax: –
Web: www.insituform.com

NMS: AEGN
CEO: Charles R. (Chuck) Gordon
CFO: David A. Martin
HR: –
FYE: December 31
Type: Public

Aegion owns a legion of companies that aim to prop up aging highways bridges and pipes. Its energy- and mining-focused companies —Bayou Corrpro CCSI CRTS and United Pipeline — rehab pipelines and provide corrosion protection for pipes storage tanks and water treatment facilities. Insituform the water and wastewater unit refurbishes water distribution stormwater and wastewater pipes in situ that is without digging them up. Its commercial and structural reinforcement firm Fyfe makes the Tyfo and Fibrwrap brands of support and strengthening systems for masonry steel concrete and wooden structures. Aegion which has more than 20 global offices was formed in 2011 as a holding company.

	Annual Growth	12/10	12/11	12/12	12/13	12/14
Sales ($ mil.)	9.8%	915.0	938.6	1,028.0	1,091.4	1,331.4
Net income ($ mil.)	–	61.9	27.7	56.8	45.5	(35.4)
Market value ($ mil.)	(8.5%)	990.4	573.1	829.0	817.8	695.3
Employees	18.0%	3,200	3,000	3,400	5,400	6,200

AEGIS COMMUNICATIONS GROUP INC.

8201 Ridgepoint Dr.
Irving TX 75063
Phone: 972-830-1800
Fax: 972-868-0220
Web: www.aegiscomgroup.com

CEO: -
CFO: -
HR: -
FYE: December 31
Type: Subsidiary

This is not a pre-recorded message. Aegis Communications Group (which does business as Aegis BPO) provides outsourced telemarketing and customer care services through about 50 facilities in Africa the Asia/Pacific Costa Rica India and the US. Through its operations (which includes Aegis PeopleSupport) it handles both inbound and outbound calling services order provisioning and multilingual communications programs. Besides teleservices Aegis offers online customer services such as e-mail responses real-time chat and data collection. Major clients have included AT&T Qwest Communications and Western Union. India-based conglomerate Essar Group owns Aegis which was established in 1985.

AEGON USA LLC

4333 Edgewood Rd. NE
Cedar Rapids IA 52499
Phone: 319-398-8511
Fax: 319-369-2209
Web: www.aegonins.com

CEO: Donald J Shepard
CFO: -
HR: -
FYE: December 31
Type: Subsidiary

If AEGON USA were an Argonaut its quest would be to conquer the US insurance market. The company a subsidiary of Dutch insurance giant AEGON that operates under the AEGON Americas moniker provides life insurance and accident and health insurance (such as cancer and long-term care policies) to some 30 million customers throughout the US. Its products include traditional whole life universal life variable universal life and term life insurance for individuals and groups. AEGON USA also offers annuity and investment products such as mutual funds as well as asset management services. Subsidiaries include Monumental Life Transamerica Life and Western Reserve Life.

AEHR TEST SYSTEMS

NAS: AEHR

400 Kato Terrace
Fremont, CA 94539
Phone: 510 623-9400
Fax: 510 623-9450
Web: www.aehr.com

CEO: Gayn Erickson
CFO: Kenneth B Spink
HR: -
FYE: May 31
Type: Public

Aehr Test Systems' products don't test air but rather silicon. Aehr (pronounced "air") makes gear that tests logic and memory semiconductors to weed out defective devices. Its burn-in systems test chips' reliability under stress by exposing them to high temperatures and voltages. Aehr also makes massively parallel test systems for handling thousands of chips simultaneously die carriers for testing unpackaged chips custom-designed fixtures for test equipment and other memory test products. Top customers include Spansion (about 80% of sales) and Texas Instruments. Aehr gets more than one-third of its business outside the US.

	Annual Growth	05/11	05/12	05/13	05/14	05/15
Sales ($ mil.)	(7.6%)	13.7	15.5	16.5	19.7	10.0
Net income ($ mil.)	–	(3.4)	(3.4)	(3.4)	0.4	(6.6)
Market value ($ mil.)	12.9%	19.0	16.3	18.5	29.1	30.9
Employees	(1.9%)	82	84	72	76	76

AEOLUS PHARMACEUTICALS INC

NBB: AOLS

26361 Crown Valley Parkway, Suite 150
Mission Viejo, CA 92691
Phone: 949 481-9825
Fax: -
Web: www.aolsrx.com

CEO: John L McManus
CFO: David Cavalier
HR: -
FYE: September 30
Type: Public

Aeolus Pharmaceuticals wants to put an end to free radicals' free-wheeling cell-damaging fun. The development-stage company is focusing its attention on developing catalytic antioxidant drugs which can neutralize free radicals. Aeolus' drug candidates could battle amyotrophic lateral sclerosis (ALS better known as Lou Gehrig's disease) stroke Parkinson's disease and other neurodegenerative conditions. The company is also developing antioxidant drugs to treat respiratory conditions and protect healthy tissue from cancer-fighting radiation. Chairman David Cavalier controls about half of the company through investment company XMark Asset Management.

	Annual Growth	09/11	09/12	09/13	09/14	09/15
Sales ($ mil.)	(10.4%)	4.8	7.3	3.9	9.6	3.1
Net income ($ mil.)	–	0.3	1.7	(3.2)	(0.1)	(2.6)
Market value ($ mil.)	(13.0%)	57.1	50.3	38.1	34.0	32.7
Employees	(9.6%)	6	5	4	4	4

AEP INDUSTRIES INC.

NMS: AEPI

95 Chestnut Ridge Road
Montvale, NJ 07645
Phone: 201 641-6600
Fax: -
Web: www.aepinc.com

CEO: J. Brendan Barba
CFO: Paul M. Feeney
HR: -
FYE: October 31
Type: Public

Making plastic cling is this company's thing! AEP Industries manufactures plastic packaging films — more than 15000 types — including stretch wrap for industrial pallets packaging for foods and beverages and films for agricultural uses such as wrap for hay bales. AEP also makes dispenser-boxed plastic wraps which are sold to consumers as well as institutions ranging from schools to hospitals. Other industries courted by AEP are packaging transportation food autos chemicals textiles and electronics. The company operates in the US and in Canada.

	Annual Growth	10/11	10/12	10/13	10/14	10/15
Sales ($ mil.)	4.0%	974.8	1,152.5	1,143.9	1,193.0	1,141.4
Net income ($ mil.)	23.5%	12.4	23.2	10.7	(5.5)	28.8
Market value ($ mil.)	31.2%	137.9	326.2	303.2	234.7	408.2
Employees	0.0%	2,600	2,600	2,600	2,500	2,600

AERO SYSTEMS ENGINEERING INC.

358 E. Fillmore Ave.
St. Paul MN 55107-1289
Phone: 651-227-7515
Fax: 651-227-0519
Web: www.aerosysengr.com

CEO: Thomas G Moll
CFO: Steven R Hedberg
HR: -
FYE: December 31
Type: Private

But will it fly? Aero Systems Engineering (AeroSystems) answers that question by designing and building engine and aerodynamic testing components and facilities. Besides its turbine and wind-tunnel facilities AeroSystems makes test equipment for turbine engines and aircraft control and instrumentation systems. Customers can buy the equipment or test at the company's Minnesota lab. AeroSystems also offers design installation and engineering support as well as acoustic measurement processes to measure noise levels; it serves OEMs MROs (maintenance repair and overhaul) the military and researchers. Investment firms Tonka Bay Equity Partners and Centerfield Capital Partners own AeroSystems.

AEROCENTURY CORP.
ASE: ACY

1440 Chapin Avenue, Suite 310
Burlingame, CA 94010
Phone: 650 340-1888
Fax: -
Web: www.aerocentury.com

CEO: -
CFO: Toni M Perazzo
HR: -
FYE: December 31
Type: Public

With a high-flyin' inventory AeroCentury leases used turboprop aircraft and engines to domestic and foreign regional airlines and other commercial customers. The company buys equipment from an airline and then either leases it back to the seller buys assets already under lease and assumes the obligations of the seller or makes a purchase and then immediately enters into a new lease with a third-party lessee (when it has a customer committed to a lease). Typically lessees are responsible for any maintenance costs. AeroCentury owns over 40 aircraft mainly deHavilland and Fokker models. Almost 90% of the company's lease revenues come from airlines headquartered outside the US.

	Annual Growth	12/10	12/11	12/12	12/13	12/14
Sales ($ mil.)	(1.7%)	30.7	24.6	29.4	32.2	28.7
Net income ($ mil.)	-	1.6	(1.5)	5.2	3.2	(11.3)
Market value ($ mil.)	(16.8%)	27.9	9.5	21.7	26.5	13.4
Employees	-	-	-	-	-	-

AEROFLEX HOLDING CORP.
NYS: ARX

35 South Service Road, P.O. Box 6022
Plainview, NY 11803-0622
Phone: 516 694-6700
Fax: -
Web: www.aeroflex.com

CEO: Leonard Borow
CFO: John Adamovich Jr
HR: -
FYE: June 30
Type: Public

Aeroflex flexes its high-tech muscle with aerospace and communications components. Its Aeroflex Microelectronic Solutions (AMS) division offers integrated circuits radio-frequency (RF) components and microwave assemblies for use in military aircraft satellites and wireless communications networks. The company also provides test and measurement equipment used in avionics military and mobile radio applications through its Aeroflex Test Solutions (ATS) unit. Customers include the US government and such blue-chip clients as Boeing Cisco Alcatel Lucent and Lockheed Martin. It generates most of its sales in the US.

	Annual Growth	06/09	06/10	06/11	06/12	06/13
Sales ($ mil.)	1.9%	599.3	655.0	729.4	673.0	647.1
Net income ($ mil.)	-	(76.7)	(12.3)	(34.7)	(53.6)	(104.2)
Market value ($ mil.)	(34.1%)	-	-	1,541.6	513.9	670.1
Employees	(2.9%)	-	2,950	2,900	2,800	2,700

AEROGROUP INTERNATIONAL LLC

201 Meadow Rd.
Edison NJ 08817
Phone: 732-985-6900
Fax: 732-985-3697
Web: www.aerosoles.com

CEO: R Shawn Neville
CFO: -
HR: -
FYE: June 30
Type: Private

Aerogroup International wants ladies to feel like they're walking on air or at least feel like buying a pair of its Aerosoles. The company designs and peddles women's footwear sold under the Aerosoles What's What A2 Aerology Sole A and Flexation brands. Aerogroup's shoes are sold in more than 100 Aerosoles stores in the US located mostly in New York and California and abroad. The shoe maker also sells shoes by catalog website and through thousands of department and specialty stores (such as Kohl's Macy's and Boscov's). Originally a division of Kenneth Cole CEO Jules Schneider got together a group of investors and took the business private in 1987.

AEROGROW INTERNATIONAL, INC.
NBB: AERO

6075 Longbow Drive, Suite 200
Boulder, CO 80301
Phone: 303 444-7755
Fax: 303 444-0406
Web: www.aerogrow.com

CEO: -
CFO: H. MacGregor (Greg) Clarke
HR: Mercedes Chansisourath
FYE: March 31
Type: Public

No time or space for a garden? AeroGrow may be able to cultivate your inner indoor gardener self. The company develops and manufactures a line of indoor gardening products and seed kits for both amateur and experienced gardeners. Using a self-contained light source and hydroponics technologies (water in place of soil) AeroGrow's products are capable of growing a variety of vegetables herbs and flowers. It offers more than 15 garden models and 50 seed kits which are sold in the US through retailers such as Target Kohl's and Bed Bath & Beyond as well as through its own website. Aerogrow was founded in 2002 by former CEO and chairman Michael Bissonnette.

	Annual Growth	03/11	03/12	03/13	03/14	03/15
Sales ($ mil.)	12.2%	11.3	8.2	7.3	9.4	17.9
Net income ($ mil.)	-	(7.9)	(3.6)	(8.3)	(2.4)	(0.2)
Market value ($ mil.)	184.7%	0.3	0.1	7.2	48.0	19.7
Employees	(5.6%)	34	21	22	23	27

AEROJET ROCKETDYNE HOLDINGS INC
NYS: AJRD

2001 Aerojet Road
Rancho Cordova, CA 95742
Phone: 916 355-4000
Fax: -
Web: www.gencorp.com

CEO: Scott J. Seymour
CFO: Kathleen E. (Kathy) Redd
HR: Bryan Ramsey
FYE: November 30
Type: Public

Aerojet Rocketdyne (formerly GenCorp) wants to take you higher — if you're a rocket that is. The company is one of the largest manufacturers and suppliers of propulsion systems for defense and space applications in the US. These systems are used in missiles maneuvering systems launch vehicles spacecraft and satellites. Virtually all its revenue comes from aerospace and defense. Principal customers include the US Department of Defense NASA and Lockheed Martin. In 2015 the company changed its name to Aerojet Rocketdyne Holdings. Aerojet refers to a longtime part of the company and Rocketdyne to a significant acquisition. The company also has a much smaller business segment that deals in real estate.

	Annual Growth	11/10	11/11	11/12	11/13	11/14
Sales ($ mil.)	16.8%	857.9	918.1	994.9	1,383.1	1,597.4
Net income ($ mil.)	-	6.8	2.9	(2.6)	167.9	(53.0)
Market value ($ mil.)	35.8%	288.7	319.9	541.0	1,078.4	982.0
Employees	12.8%	3,135	3,268	3,391	5,386	5,071

AEROJET-GENERAL CORPORATION

2001 Aerojet Rd.
Rancho Cordova CA 95742-6418
Phone: 916-355-4000
Fax: 916-351-8667
Web: www.aerojet.com

CEO: Warren M Boley Jr
CFO: Kathleen E Redd
HR: -
FYE: November 30
Type: Subsidiary

They say it doesn't take a rocket scientist to figure this out. But in the case of Aerojet-General it actually did. Founded by a professor and his colleagues at Caltech the company today develops and manufactures propulsion systems for defense and space applications including tactical missiles and space launch vehicles. It is the largest provider of propulsion systems in the US serving the likes of the US Army the Missile Defense Agency (MDA) and NASA. Aerojet in fact is the only domestic supplier of all four propulsion types: solid liquid air-breathing and electric. The company is the primary operating subsidiary of GenCorp.

AEROKOOL AVIATION CORPORATION

1495 SE 10TH AVE
HIALEAH, FL 330105916
Phone: 305-887-6912
Fax: –
Web: www.aerokool.com

CEO: John N Bambacus
CFO: Steven Favazza
HR: –
FYE: December 31
Type: Private

Aero Kool makes sure aircraft pilots are not left out in the cold□. The aircraft maintenance company which has its own engineering and manufacturing departments□, provides airframe and engine accessory repair and overhaul services. Aero Kool works on a wide range of equipment including air cycle machines air starters fuel heaters heat exchangers oil tanks and coolers refrigeration packs valves (both electro mechanical and electro pneumatic) and water separators. The company also sells airframe and engine accessories and designs and manufactures replacement parts. Aero Kool□, was founded in 1959.

	Annual Growth	12/04	12/05	12/06	12/08	12/09
Sales ($ mil.)	(75.7%)	–	–	642.6	9.5	9.2
Net income ($ mil.)	1335.8%	–	–	0.0	0.4	0.3
Market value ($ mil.)	–	–	–	–	–	–
Employees	–	–	–	–	–	50

AERONET INC.

42 CORP PARK STE 100
IRVINE, CA 92606
Phone: 949-474-3000
Fax: –
Web: www.aeronet.com

CEO: Anthony N. Pereira
CFO: –
HR: –
FYE: April 30
Type: Private

Aeronet is casting a wide net for its logistics business. The company provides a full range of logistics services both in the US and overseas. Offerings include time-guaranteed domestic freight delivery (ranging from same-day to five-day) air and ocean freight forwarding customs brokerage shipment tracking supply chain management and warehousing and distribution. As a freight forwarder the company purchases transportation capacity from carriers and resells it to customers. Aeronet maintains 10 offices near major trade gateways throughout the US and operates through agents in other regions.

	Annual Growth	04/06	04/07	04/08	04/09	04/14
Sales ($ mil.)	0.6%	–	64.1	70.5	70.1	66.6
Net income ($ mil.)	(10.9%)	–	–	0.8	0.1	0.4
Market value ($ mil.)	–	–	–	–	–	–
Employees	–	–	–	–	–	140

AEROPOSTALE INC

NYS: ARO

112 W. 34th Street
New York, NY 10120
Phone: 646 485-5410
Fax: –
Web: www.aeropostale.com; www.ps4u.com

CEO: Julian R. Geiger
CFO: David J. Dick
HR: –
FYE: January 31
Type: Public

Aéropostale operates more than 850 mostly mall-based stores under the Aéropostale and P.S. from Aéropostale (for kids) banners in 50 US states Puerto Rico and Canada. It stocks the usual teen outerwear (jeans T-shirts accessories) mostly under the Aéropostale and Aéro names. The retailer designs and sources its own merchandise so that it can quickly respond to trends but has been struggling in a competitive environment in the aftermath of the US recession. The Aéropostale name originated from a 1920s airmail firm Compagnie Generale Aéropostale. The brand was created by R.H. Macy & Co. as a private label in the 1980s and later became a specialty store concept.

	Annual Growth	01/11	01/12*	02/13	02/14*	01/15
Sales ($ mil.)	(6.4%)	2,400.4	2,342.3	2,386.2	2,090.9	1,838.7
Net income ($ mil.)	–	231.3	69.5	34.9	(141.8)	(206.5)
Market value ($ mil.)	(43.7%)	1,926.3	1,304.3	1,068.4	558.0	193.1
Employees	4.2%	17,828	25,766	26,279	29,337	21,007

*Fiscal year change

AEROTEK INC.

7301 PARKWAY DR
HANOVER, MD 210761159
Phone: 410-694-5100
Fax: –
Web: www.aerotek.com

CEO: –
CFO: Thomas B. (Tom) Kelly
HR: Tanya Axenson
FYE: December 31
Type: Private

Aerotek a unit of staffing powerhouse Allegis Group offers commercial and technical staffing services throughout North America. Through several divisions Aerotek staffs workers such as engineers mechanics scientists and technical professionals as well as administrative staff members general laborers and tradespeople. The company also provides training and support services. Along with aerospace auto and engineering companies Aerotek's clients include companies from the construction energy manufacturing health care and finance industries.

	Annual Growth	12/09	12/10	12/11	12/12	12/13
Sales ($ mil.)	15.2%	–	3,446.5	4,481.3	5,119.0	5,268.7
Net income ($ mil.)	–	–	–	226.2	307.3	0.0
Market value ($ mil.)	–	–	–	–	–	–
Employees	–	–	–	–	–	4,200

AEROVIRONMENT, INC.

NMS: AVAV

900 Innovators Way
Simi Valley, CA 93065
Phone: 626 357-9983
Fax: –
Web: www.avinc.com

CEO: Timothy E. (Tim) Conver
CFO: Raymond D. Cook
HR: –
FYE: April 30
Type: Public

AeroVironment (AV) gives soldiers a birds-eye view of their mission. The company designs and manufactures a line of small unmanned aircraft systems (UAS) for the Department of Defense (DoD). Small enough for one-man transport and launch and operable through a hand-held control AV's UAS provide intelligence surveillance and reconnaissance for small tactical units. Through its Efficient Energy Systems (EES) unit AV produces PosiCharge fast-charge systems for industrial equipment batteries and electric vehicles (EV) as well as EV testing systems used by auto defense and utility markets.

	Annual Growth	04/11	04/12	04/13	04/14	04/15
Sales ($ mil.)	(3.0%)	292.5	325.0	240.2	251.7	259.4
Net income ($ mil.)	(42.2%)	25.9	30.5	10.4	13.7	2.9
Market value ($ mil.)	(2.8%)	668.0	567.0	451.4	787.3	596.9
Employees	(3.6%)	768	817	768	625	663

AERUS LLC

5956 Sherry Ln.
Dallas TX 75225
Phone: 214-378-4000
Fax: 214-378-4053
Web: www.aerusonline.com

CEO: Joseph P Urso
CFO: Brett Holland
HR: Rene Bartcher
FYE: December 31
Type: Private

A pioneer in the vacuum business Aerus has been dirt's worst enemy since 1924. The company manufactures and sells vacuums air and water purification systems cleansers and allergy-control products. Its brands include Guardian Lux and Epic. Aerus' products are marketed through in-home demonstrations more than 500 Aerus sales centers in the US and Canada and online. The company formerly named Electrolux sold the brand's North American rights to AB Electrolux in 2000. Aerus is a subsidiary of Aerus Holdings. It is owned by investment firm Engles Urso Follmer Capital.

AES CORP.
NYS: AES

4300 Wilson Boulevard
Arlington, VA 22203
Phone: 703 522-1315
Fax: 703 528-4510
Web: www.aes.com

CEO: Andrés R. Gluski
CFO: Thomas M. (Tom) O'Flynn
HR: Paritosh Mishra
FYE: December 31
Type: Public

AES is out to please power customers around the world. A leading independent power producer the company has interests in 137 generation facilities in 18 countries throughout the Americas Asia Africa Europe and the Middle East that gave it a net generating capacity of 35000 MW in 2014. (It also has one coal-fired project under development with a total capacity of 1320 MW). AES sells electricity to utilities and other energy marketers through wholesale contracts or on the spot market. AES also sells power directly to customers worldwide through stakes in distribution utilities mainly in Latin America and the US.

	Annual Growth	12/10	12/11	12/12	12/13	12/14
Sales ($ mil.)	0.7%	16,647.0	17,274.0	18,141.0	15,891.0	17,146.0
Net income ($ mil.)	204.0%	9.0	58.0	(912.0)	114.0	769.0
Market value ($ mil.)	3.1%	8,572.9	8,333.6	7,531.2	10,212.9	9,692.0
Employees	(10.6%)	29,000	27,000	25,000	22,000	18,500

AETEA INFORMATION TECHNOLOGY INC.

1445 RES BLVD STE 300
ROCKVILLE, MD 20850
Phone: 301-721-4200
Fax: -
Web: www.aetea.com

CEO: -
CFO: Charles V Brown III
HR: -
FYE: December 31
Type: Private

AETEA knows information technology backward and forward. The company provides systems integration enterprise resource management software consulting and other IT services. It also offers IT staffing services to a variety of customers ranging from large global enterprises to small and midsized companies. Industries served include financial services pharmaceuticals and health care. AETEA also has a unit devoted to public sector clients which targets the US Department of Defense as well as civilian agencies. Clients have included ADP BNP Paribas and Bristol-Myers Squibb. The company operates from offices in Maryland New Jersey New York Pennsylvania and Washington. AETEA was established in 1979.

	Annual Growth	12/02	12/03	12/04	12/06	12/07
Sales ($ mil.)	(2.6%)	-	-	74.2	73.8	68.5
Net income ($ mil.)	(20.2%)	-	-	7.7	0.6	3.9
Market value ($ mil.)	-	-	-	-	-	-
Employees	-	-	-	-	-	350

AETNA INC.
NYS: AET

151 Farmington Avenue
Hartford, CT 06156
Phone: 860 273-0123
Fax: -
Web: www.aetna.com

CEO: Nancy J. Ham
CFO: Shawn M. Guertin
HR: Anna Gill
FYE: December 31
Type: Public

Life death health or injury — Aetna's got an insurance policy to cover it. The company one of the largest health insurers in the US also offers life and disability insurance as well as retirement savings products. Its health care division offers HMO PPO point of service (POS) health savings account (HSA) and traditional indemnity coverage along with dental vision behavioral health and Medicare and Medicaid plans to groups and individuals. The health care segment covers some 24 million medical members. Aetna's group insurance segment sells life and disability insurance nationwide and its large case pensions segment offers pensions annuities and other retirement savings products.

	Annual Growth	12/10	12/11	12/12	12/13	12/14
Assets ($ mil.)	9.1%	37,739.4	38,593.1	41,494.5	49,871.8	53,402.1
Net income ($ mil.)	3.7%	1,766.8	1,985.7	1,657.9	1,913.6	2,040.8
Market value ($ mil.)	30.6%	10,672.4	14,758.1	16,199.2	23,992.8	31,072.7
Employees	9.5%	34,000	33,300	35,000	48,600	48,800

AFFILIATED COMPUTER SERVICES INC.

2828 N. Haskell Ave.
Dallas TX 75204
Phone: 214-841-6111
Fax: 732-205-8237
Web: www.mack-cali.com

CEO: Lynn R Blodgett
CFO: Kevin Kyser
HR: -
FYE: December 31
Type: Subsidiary

Affiliated Computer Services (ACS) handles jobs its clients would rather hand off. The company provides business process outsourcing (BPO) services for commercial enterprises and government agencies focusing on markets such as communications health care and transportation. As an outsourcer ACS handles functions such as administration including health care claims processing; finance and accounting; human resources; payment processing; sales marketing and customer care call centers; and supply chain management. BPO services account for most of the company's sales. ACS also offers information technology and systems integration services. In early 2010 ACS was acquired by printing equipment giant Xerox.

AFFILIATED FOODS MIDWEST COOPERATIVE INC.

1301 W OMAHA AVE
NORFOLK, NE 687015872
Phone: 402-371-0555
Fax: -
Web: www.afmidwest.com

CEO: -
CFO: Duane Severson
HR: -
FYE: June 28
Type: Private

Affiliated Foods Midwest Cooperative is a wholesale food distribution cooperative that supplies more than 800 independent grocers in some 15 states in the Midwest. From its handful of distribution centers in Kansas Nebraska and Wisconsin the co-op distributes fresh produce meats deli items baked goods dairy products and frozen foods as well as general merchandise and equipment. It distributes goods under the Shurfine brand (from Topco Associates) and IGA labels. Additionally Affiliated Foods Midwest provides marketing merchandising and warehousing support services for its members. The cooperative was formed in 1931 to make wholesale purchases for a group of retailers in Nebraska.

	Annual Growth	06/10	06/11	06/12	06/13	06/14
Sales ($ mil.)	2.9%	-	1,356.2	1,486.3	1,391.7	1,477.5
Net income ($ mil.)	0.7%	-	-	2.8	2.7	2.8
Market value ($ mil.)	-	-	-	-	-	-
Employees	-	-	-	-	-	850

AFFILIATED MANAGERS GROUP INC.
NYS: AMG

777 South Flagler Drive
West Palm Beach, FL 33401
Phone: 800 345-1100
Fax: -
Web: www.amg.com

CEO: Sean M. Healey
CFO: Jay C. Horgen
HR: -
FYE: December 31
Type: Public

AMG knows a good asset when it sees one. Affiliated Managers Group (AMG) is an asset management company that owns interests in more than 30 boutique investment management firms in the North America Europe and Asia. Together the company's affiliates manage approximately $625 billion in assets and offer more than 400 investment products including more than 200 mutual funds. AMG typically acquires majority stakes in its affiliates which cater to institutional investors and wealthy individuals. The structure allows affiliates to retain partial ownership of their firms and operate with relative autonomy. AMG usually allocates a percentage of revenues to affiliates for operating expenses such as compensation.

	Annual Growth	12/10	12/11	12/12	12/13	12/14
Sales ($ mil.)	16.6%	1,358.2	1,704.8	1,805.5	2,188.8	2,510.9
Net income ($ mil.)	34.4%	138.6	164.9	174.0	360.5	452.1
Market value ($ mil.)	20.9%	5,417.4	5,238.9	7,106.2	11,841.6	11,588.3
Employees	11.0%	1,910	2,020	2,230	2,500	2,900

AFFINIA GROUP HOLDINGS INC.

1101 Technology Dr.
Ann Arbor MI 48108
Phone: 734-827-5400
Fax: 814-278-7286
Web: www.rexenergy.com

CEO: Terry R McCormack
CFO: Thomas H Madden
HR: –
FYE: December 31
Type: Private

Affinia Group caters to car drivers with a natural affinity for parts. The company is a leading designer manufacturer and distributor of aftermarket vehicular components. The aftermarket comprises a global network of suppliers that sell automotive goods intended to replace a manufacturer's stock parts. Affinia's slew of products — primarily brake filtration and chassis parts — are made for passenger cars; SUVs; light medium and heavy trucks; and off-highway vehicles. Its well-known brand names including AIMCO McQuay-Norris Nakata Raybestos and WIX are sold in 70-plus countries. The Cypress Group and OMERS Administration are Affinia's largest stakeholders. In mid-2010 Affinia filed to go public.

AFFINION GROUP HOLDINGS INC   NL:

6 High Ridge Park
Stamford, CT 06905
Phone: 203 956-1000
Fax: –

CEO: Todd H Siegel
CFO: Gregory S Miller
HR: –
FYE: December 31
Type: Public

Through its partners and affiliations Affinion Group aims to make fans of its customers' customers. The company operates membership and loyalty programs on behalf of corporate clients seeking to strengthen their ties to consumers. It specializes in launching a variety of media services — through direct mail and the Internet — and packaging these benefits to its clients' customers. Programs overseen include AutoVantage Buyers Advantage and Travelers Advantage. Overall the group offers its programs to some 65 million members worldwide through more than 5700 partners.

	Annual Growth	12/10	12/11	12/12	12/13	12/14
Sales ($ mil.)	(2.5%)	1,376.3	1,535.2	1,494.6	1,334.7	1,242.8
Net income ($ mil.)	–	(191.1)	(156.9)	(139.6)	(135.5)	(428.7)
Market value ($ mil.)	–	–	–	–	–	–
Employees	(6.3%)	–	4,500	4,300	3,925	3,700

AFFIRMATIVE INSURANCE HOLDINGS INC   NBB: AFFM Q

4450 Sojourn Drive, Suite 500
Addison, TX 75001
Phone: 972 728-6300
Fax: –

CEO: –
CFO: Earl R Fonville
HR: Jacqueline Debowski
FYE: December 31
Type: Public

If you've got an iffy driving record or let your insurance lapse can you still get auto coverage? This company answers in the Affirmative. Affirmative Insurance Holdings through its subsidiaries writes nonstandard auto insurance policies — that is coverage for drivers in high-risk categories due to their age driving records and other factors. It sells its policies through about 5300 independent agents in seven southern and mid-western states. Affirmative sold its nearly 200 company-owned retail locations (including A-Affordable Driver's Choice InsureOne and USAgencies stores) in late 2013. Investment firm J.C. Flowers controls more than half of the company.

	Annual Growth	12/10	12/11	12/12	12/13	12/14
Assets ($ mil.)	(18.0%)	745.7	444.8	338.4	386.8	337.7
Net income ($ mil.)	–	(88.9)	(164.2)	(51.9)	30.7	(32.2)
Market value ($ mil.)	(17.5%)	43.1	8.6	2.3	41.2	20.0
Employees	(21.2%)	1,268	1,078	949	522	489

AFFYMAX INC   NBB: AFFY

19200 Stevens Creek Blvd. Suite 240
Cupertino, CA 95014
Phone: 650 812-8700
Fax: –
Web: www.affymax.com

CEO: Jonathan M Couchman
CFO: Mark G Thompson
HR: –
FYE: December 31
Type: Public

Affymax is training peptides to give red blood cells a pep talk. The biotechnology firm is researching and developing drugs based upon peptides which can help regulate biological processes. Its leading drug candidate Omontys (peginesatide) was approved by the FDA in 2012 as a treatment for anemia due to chronic kidney disease. Affymax believes Omontys which was developed and commercialized through a partnership with Japan's Takeda Pharmaceutical will prove to be cheaper and longer lasting than the EPO stimulants currently used on dialysis patients. However the product was recalled in 2013 due to adverse reactions to the drug.

	Annual Growth	12/09	12/10	12/11	12/12	12/13
Sales ($ mil.)	(67.0%)	114.9	112.5	47.7	94.4	1.4
Net income ($ mil.)	–	(76.5)	(14.1)	(61.4)	(93.4)	(14.4)
Market value ($ mil.)	(57.9%)	927.5	249.3	247.8	711.9	29.2
Employees	(59.1%)	143	140	130	304	4

AFFYMETRIX, INC.   NMS: AFFX

3420 Central Expressway
Santa Clara, CA 95051
Phone: 408 731-5000
Fax: –
Web: www.affymetrix.com

CEO: Frank R. Witney
CFO: Gavin Wood
HR: Tracy Ting
FYE: December 31
Type: Public

Affymetrix detects the secrets of human genetics. Its GeneChip system and other products are used to identify analyze and manage genetic data and disease characteristics in the development of new treatments for infectious diseases cancer and other ailments. Affymetrix sells its products directly to drugmakers academic research labs and government agencies primarily in North American and European markets. It also provides outsourced genotyping research services and it has partnerships and licensing agreements with such pharmaceutical companies as BGI and Roche to develop new disease diagnostics and instrumentation systems.

	Annual Growth	12/10	12/11	12/12	12/13	12/14
Sales ($ mil.)	2.9%	310.7	267.5	295.6	330.4	349.0
Net income ($ mil.)	–	(10.2)	(28.2)	(10.7)	(16.3)	(3.8)
Market value ($ mil.)	18.4%	373.7	303.8	235.5	636.6	733.2
Employees	4.6%	918	875	1,100	1,100	1,100

AFLAC INC.   NYS: AFL

1932 Wynnton Road
Columbus, GA 31999
Phone: 706 323-3431
Fax: 706 596-3488
Web: www.aflac.com

CEO: Daniel P. (Dan) Amos
CFO: Frederick J. (Fred) Crawford
HR: Chad Melvin
FYE: December 31
Type: Public

Would you buy insurance from a duck? Aflac counts on it! To soften the financial stresses during periods of disability or illness Aflac sells supplemental health and life insurance policies including coverage for accidents intensive care dental vision and disability as well as for specific conditions (primarily cancer) and general life policies. It is a leading supplier of supplemental insurance in the US and is an industry leader in Japan's life and cancer insurance markets. Aflac which is marketed through — and is an acronym for — American Family Life Assurance Company sells policies that pay cash benefits for hospital confinement emergency treatment and medical appliances.

	Annual Growth	12/10	12/11	12/12	12/13	12/14
Assets ($ mil.)	4.3%	101,039.0	117,102.0	131,094.0	121,307.0	119,767.0
Net income ($ mil.)	5.9%	2,344.0	1,964.0	2,866.0	3,158.0	2,951.0
Market value ($ mil.)	2.0%	24,967.2	19,140.2	23,502.7	29,555.3	27,029.0
Employees	3.8%	8,211	8,562	8,965	9,141	9,525

AFRICARE

440 R ST NW
WASHINGTON, DC 200011961
Phone: 202-328-5320
Fax: –
Web: www.africare.org

CEO: –
CFO: –
HR: –
FYE: June 30
Type: Private

Africare helps Africans help themselves. The not-for-profit organization provides support to communities in Africa in areas such as health care and HIV/AIDS prevention food security agriculture education environmental management and water resource development. It also works to help people create small businesses such as growing sunflowers and pressing the seeds into cooking oil and to provide emergency humanitarian aid when needed. Africare has given more than $800 million in aid to some 35 countries in Africa funding more than 2500 projects. William and Barbara Kirker founded the organization in 1970.

	Annual Growth	06/06	06/07	06/08	06/10	06/11
Sales ($ mil.)	–	–	–	(40.8)	54.8	76.9
Net income ($ mil.)	5821.0%	–	–	0.0	(1.1)	0.8
Market value ($ mil.)	–	–	–	–	–	–
Employees	–	–	–	–	–	1,000

AG INTERACTIVE INC.

1 American Rd.
Cleveland OH 44144
Phone: 216-889-5000
Fax: 216-889-5371
Web: www.aginteractive.com

CEO: –
CFO: Michael Waxman-Lenz
HR: –
FYE: February 28
Type: Subsidiary

This company has just the thing for those special occasions when an e-mail just won't do. AG Interactive represents the electronic greetings and other digital content of its parent company American Greetings. The subsidiary offers e-cards to nearly 4 million subscribers through a variety of electronic channels including websites Internet portals instant messaging services and mobile devices. AG Interactive's portfolio of e-card websites includes AmericanGreetings.com BlueMountain.com Egreetings.com. In addition the company operates Kiwee.com (graphics animations emoticons text generators) Cardstore.com (custom physical greeting cards) and Webshots.com (photo sharing).

AG MORTGAGE INVESTMENT TRUST INC

245 Park Avenue, 26th Floor
New York, NY 10167
Phone: 212 692-2000
Fax: –

NYS: MITT

CEO: David N. Roberts
CFO: Brian C. Sigman
HR: –
FYE: December 31
Type: Public

AG Mortgage Investment Trust invests in acquires and manages a diverse portfolio of residential mortgage assets as well as other real estate-related securities and financial assets. Residential mortgage-backed securities backed by US government agencies including Fannie Mae Freddie Mac and Ginnie Mae known as "Agency RMBS" make up about 70% of the mortgage real estate investment trust's (REIT) portfolio. Credit assets including RMBS not issued or backed by the government account for most of the rest. Formed in 2011 by executives of investment adviser Angelo Gorden looking to profit from a recovery in the US mortgage bond market the mortgage REIT is managed by a subsidiary of Angelo Gordon.

	Annual Growth	04/11*	12/11	12/12	12/13	12/14
Sales ($ mil.)	96.2%	–	18.7	96.4	151.0	141.6
Net income ($ mil.)	79.3%	–	19.0	134.9	(31.6)	109.4
Market value ($ mil.)	(2.7%)	–	571.4	666.5	444.0	527.1
Employees	–	–	–	–	–	–

*Fiscal year change

AG PROCESSING INC. A COOPERATIVE

12700 W. Dodge Rd.
Omaha NE 68154
Phone: 402-496-7809
Fax: 402-498-2215
Web: www.agp.com

CEO: Martin P Reagan
CFO: J Keith Spackler
HR: –
FYE: August 31
Type: Private - Cooperativ

Soy far soy good for Ag Processing (AGP) the largest farmer-owned soybean processor in the world and roughly the fourth-largest soybean processor in the US based on capacity. It purchases and processes more than 5.5 million acres of members' soybeans per year. The farmer-owned cooperative is also a leading supplier of refined vegetable oil in the US. It procures processes markets and transports grains and grain products ranging from human food ingredients to livestock feed to renewable fuels. AGP is owned by about 180 local and regional cooperatives and represents more than 250000 farmers in 15 states throughout the US.

AG&E HOLDINGS INC

9500 West 55th Street, Suite A
McCook, IL 60525-3605
Phone: 708 290-2100
Fax: –
Web: www.agegaming.com

ASE: WGA

CEO: Anthony Spier
CFO: James F. (Jim) Brace
HR: –
FYE: December 31
Type: Public

Wells-Gardner Electronics puts on quite a display in the world of games. The company's video products and accessories include LCD-based displays and monitors. In addition to its standard products Wells-Gardner customizes displays and optically bonds touchscreen sensors to the face of monitors. The company also provides refurbished gaming machines parts and related installation services to more than 700 casinos in North America. Most manufacturing of its products is contracted to factories in China. Aristocrat Leisure accounts for 35% of sales. Customers located in the US provide around three-quarters of sales.

	Annual Growth	12/10	12/11	12/12	12/13	12/14
Sales ($ mil.)	(16.8%)	45.7	42.9	51.1	57.9	21.9
Net income ($ mil.)	–	0.2	0.0	0.2	0.7	(5.5)
Market value ($ mil.)	(24.8%)	25.9	23.6	20.8	20.8	8.3
Employees	(20.2%)	69	64	75	69	28

AGAR SUPPLY CO. INC.

Myles Standish Industrial Park 225 John Hancock Rd.
Taunton MA 02780-7318
Phone: 508-821-2060
Fax: 617-880-5113
Web: www.agarsupply.com

CEO: –
CFO: –
HR: –
FYE: September 30
Type: Private

Agar Supply is a leading independent wholesale foodservice supplier serving restaurants and other hospitality operators in New England. Recognized for its assortment of meats poultry and seafood the company also distributes a variety of produce dairy items and herbs as well as non-food products (such as kitchenware and cleaning supplies). In addition Agar Supply provides retailers with grocery goods. Karl Bressler founded the family-owned business in 1940.

AGC AMERICA INC.

11175 Cicero Dr. Ste. 400
Alpharetta GA 30022
Phone: 404-446-4200
Fax: 404-446-4295
Web: us.agc.com

CEO: William Dankmyer
CFO: Toshihiko Uchida
HR: –
FYE: December 31
Type: Subsidiary

AGC America is a wholly owned subsidiary of Asahi Glass the world's #1 maker of flat glass. AGC America is the holding company for more than 10 of Asahi's major subsidiaries in North America that manufacture products for the automotive chemicals glass and electronics industries. It makes architectural automotive flat float figured solar and other processed glass. AGC Chemicals Americas manufactures and markets fluorochemicals caustic soda specialty chemicals and soda ash for glass production. AGC Electronics America makes high-purity silicon carbide and synthetic quartz glass for semiconductors and glass substrates for LCDs.

AGC FLAT GLASS NORTH AMERICA INC.

11175 Cicero Dr. Ste. 400
Alpharetta GA 30022
Phone: 404-446-4200
Fax: 404-446-4221
Web: www.na.agc-flatglass.com

CEO: D Roger Kennedy
CFO: Doris Ladd
HR: –
FYE: December 31
Type: Subsidiary

In this company's line of work if the boss catches you staring out the window you can say that you're doing research. AGC Flat Glass North America (formerly AFG Industries) is one of North America's largest manufacturers of construction/specialty glass and the continent's second-largest maker of flat glass. AGC North America offers its coated insulated solar laminated store-front and fire-rated glass products to customers in the residential/commercial building products specialty solar and automotive glass markets. AFG Industries was formed via the 1978 merger of Fourco Glass and ASG. AGC North America is a subsidiary of AGC America which is a subsidiary of Japan's glass-making giant Asahi Glass.

AGCO CORP.

NYS: AGCO

4205 River Green Parkway
Duluth, GA 30096
Phone: 770 813-9200
Fax: –
Web: www.agcocorp.com

CEO: Martin H. Richenhagen
CFO: Andrew H. (Andy) Beck
HR: Lucinda Smith
FYE: December 31
Type: Public

AGCO's annual harvests may be smaller than those of major rivals John Deere and CNH but it reaps some healthy profits. AGCO makes tractors combines hay and forage tools sprayers grain storage and protein production systems seeding and tillage implements and replacement parts for agricultural end uses. It sells through a global network of some 3100 dealers and distributors spanning 140 countries. It also builds diesel engines gears and generators through its AGCO Sisu Power unit. Core brands include Massey Ferguson GSI Challenger Valtra (Finland-based) and Fendt (Germany). The company offers financing services to retail customers and dealers via a venture with Dutch company Rabobank.

	Annual Growth	12/10	12/11	12/12	12/13	12/14
Sales ($ mil.)	9.0%	6,896.6	8,773.2	9,962.2	10,786.9	9,723.7
Net income ($ mil.)	16.4%	220.2	585.3	516.4	592.3	404.2
Market value ($ mil.)	(2.8%)	4,516.1	3,830.6	4,378.9	5,276.6	4,029.4
Employees	9.8%	14,300	17,400	20,300	22,100	20,800

AGE GROUP LTD.

180 MADISON AVE STE 401
NEW YORK, NY 100165267
Phone: 212-213-9500
Fax: –
Web: www.agegroup.com

CEO: –
CFO: –
HR: –
FYE: December 31
Type: Private

People like to be comfy under there no matter what their age group. Age Group makes and markets sleepwear lingerie and underwear under the brand name Of the Moment as well as apparel and accessories under licensed names including Hello Kitty Disney Roca Wear and American Tourister and others. A leading wholesaler Age Group also manufactures and designs pet accessories including an exclusive line of pet apparel bedding and grooming supplies under the Martha Stewart brand for sale in PetSmart stores. The company's products are distributed through large-scale department stores nationwide. Age Group's age? The company has been in the design and manufacturing business for more than 25 years.

	Annual Growth	12/01	12/02	12/04	12/09	12/13
Sales ($ mil.)	–	–	(83.3)	60.0	69.8	84.3
Net income ($ mil.)	(1.5%)	–	–	5.8	5.1	5.0
Market value ($ mil.)	–	–	–	–	–	–
Employees	–	–	–	–	–	65

AGENT INFORMATION SOFTWARE INC

NBB: AIFS

430 N Vineyard Ave. Ste. 100
Ontario, CA 91764
Phone: 909 595-7004
Fax: 909 595-3506
Web: www.auto-graphics.com

CEO: –
CFO: –
HR: –
FYE: December 31
Type: Public

Agent Information Software (AIS) seeks to organize information on your behalf. A holding company AIS owns two niche information management software subsidiaries: Auto-Graphics and AgentLegal. Auto-Graphics which primarily serves public libraries offers hosted software used to manage share (e.g. interlibrary loans) and search library resources. On the other hand AgentLegal's software caters to law firm professionals including firm CFOs looking to manage the cost of search resources; law librarians and IT departments who manage and protect information; and researchers who gather information. AIS was formed in 2009 to take over Auto-Graphics' stock.

	Annual Growth	12/07	12/11	12/12	12/13	12/14
Sales ($ mil.)	(3.1%)	5.6	4.8	5.0	4.7	4.5
Net income ($ mil.)	(9.9%)	0.2	0.1	(0.4)	0.0	0.1
Market value ($ mil.)	(19.9%)	3.3	0.9	0.4	0.7	0.7
Employees	–	–	–	–	–	–

AGENUS INC

NAS: AGEN

3 Forbes Road
Lexington, MA 02421
Phone: 781 674-4400
Fax: –
Web: www.agenusbio.com

CEO: Garo H Armen
CFO: Shalini Sharp
HR: –
FYE: December 31
Type: Public

Cancer and other diseases had better beware — Agenus (formerly Antigenics) is packing heat. The firm develops heat shock proteins which are related to the immune system's response to disease. Its patient-specific vaccines work on the theory that each person's cancer has a unique signature that can be derived from the tumor after it has been removed. The company refers to these vaccines as its Prophage Series the lead drug candidate in the series Oncophage is the first personalized cancer vaccine to receive FDA fast track status and is being developed to treat kidney and skin cancers. Agenus is also developing viral vaccines and QS-21 Stimulon an improved vaccine adjuvant to make vaccines more effective.

	Annual Growth	12/10	12/11	12/12	12/13	12/14
Sales ($ mil.)	20.0%	3.4	2.8	16.0	3.0	7.0
Net income ($ mil.)	–	(21.9)	(23.3)	(11.3)	(30.1)	(42.5)
Market value ($ mil.)	40.8%	63.3	125.4	257.2	165.6	249.0
Employees	23.7%	56	54	53	114	131

AGFIRST FARM CREDIT BANK

1401 Hampton St.
Columbia SC 29201
Phone: 803-799-5000
Fax: 803-254-1776
Web: www.agfirst.com

CEO: Tim Amerson
CFO: Charl Butler
HR: –
FYE: December 31
Type: Private - Cooperativ

The expenses involved in equipping and operating a farm add up quickly which is where AgFirst Farm Credit Bank comes in. AgFirst is one of a half-dozen members of the Farm Credit System a federally chartered network of agricultural and rural lending cooperatives. It provides financing to 20 farmer-owned agricultural credit associations which in turn offer mortgages and loans to some 80000 farmers agribusinesses and rural homowners in 15 eastern states and Puerto Rico. They also offer crop insurance credit-related life insurance and financial planning services. AgFirst does not accept deposits; it raises money by selling bonds and notes on the capital markets.

AGILENT TECHNOLOGIES, INC.   NYS: A

5301 Stevens Creek Blvd.
Santa Clara, CA 95051
Phone: 408 345-8886
Fax: –
Web: www.investor.agilent.com

CEO: Michael R. (Mike) McMullen
CFO: Didier Hirsch
HR: –
FYE: October 31
Type: Public

Products from Agilent Technologies have a measurable effect on the scientific world. A leading maker of scientific testing equipment Agilent supplies a slew of analytical and measurement instruments including oscilloscopes gas and liquid chromatographs mass spectrometers vacuum pumps anatomic pathology workflows and nuclear magnetic resonance imaging systems. Its operations include products used in electronic test and measurement life sciences chemical analysis and diagnostics and genomics. Agilent's customers include such global giants as Cisco Dow Chemical Merck and Samsung. The company which gets most of sales outside the US spun off its electronic measurement business in late 2014.

	Annual Growth	10/11	10/12	10/13	10/14	10/15
Sales ($ mil.)	(11.6%)	6,615.0	6,858.0	6,782.0	6,981.0	4,038.0
Net income ($ mil.)	(20.7%)	1,012.0	1,153.0	724.0	504.0	401.0
Market value ($ mil.)	0.5%	12,287.2	11,929.2	16,824.9	18,323.1	12,515.9
Employees	(10.9%)	18,700	20,500	20,600	21,400	11,800

AGILYSYS INC   NMS: AGYS

425 Walnut Street, Suite 1800
Cincinnati, OH 45202
Phone: 770 810-7800
Fax: –
Web: www.agilysys.com

CEO: James H. Dennedy
CFO: Janine Seebeck
HR: Richard A Sayers
FYE: March 31
Type: Public

Agilysys serves as an agile ally for systems procurement. The company provides IT services to enterprise and government customers in North America implementing hardware and software from primary partners Hewlett-Packard IBM and Oracle. Services range from disaster planning to document and storage management. Agilysys also provides industry-specific software tools such as property management applications. Specializing in the retail and hospitality sectors Agilysys also markets to the education financial services government health care manufacturing and transportation industries. Verizon Communications is the company's top customer representing 23% of overall sales and 32% of technology segment sales.

	Annual Growth	03/11	03/12	03/13	03/14	03/15
Sales ($ mil.)	(37.4%)	675.5	208.9	236.1	101.3	103.5
Net income ($ mil.)	–	(55.5)	(22.8)	(1.3)	17.1	(11.5)
Market value ($ mil.)	14.4%	130.8	204.9	226.5	305.4	224.2
Employees	(19.1%)	1,179	751	765	474	504

AGIOS PHARMACEUTICALS INC   NMS: AGIO

88 Sidney Street
Cambridge, MA 02139
Phone: 617 649-8600
Fax: –
Web: www.agios.com

CEO: David P Schenkein
CFO: –
HR: –
FYE: December 31
Type: Public

Agios Pharmaceuticals wants to say "adios" to cancer. The biopharmaceutical company is developing metabolic treatments for certain types of cancer and rare genetic diseases. Its lead drug candidates AG-221 and AG-120 are oral tablets that apply cellular metabolism to treat patients with cancers that harbor certain mutations. Agios has a development collaboration agreement with Celgene for its cancer metabolism program. Another drug candidate AG-348 would treat a form of hemolytic anemia known as pyruvate kinase deficiency or PK deficiency. Agios went public in 2013 raising about $106 million in its IPO which it plans to use to further fund clinical development for its drug candidates.

	Annual Growth	12/10	12/11	12/12	12/13	12/14
Sales ($ mil.)	–	0.0	21.8	25.1	25.5	65.4
Net income ($ mil.)	–	0.0	(23.7)	(20.1)	(39.4)	(53.5)
Market value ($ mil.)	–	0.0	–	–	888.6	4,156.7
Employees	22.7%	–	–	85	96	128

AGL RESOURCES INC.   NYS: GAS

Ten Peachtree Place N.E.
Atlanta, GA 30309
Phone: 404 584-4000
Fax: –
Web: www.aglresources.com

CEO: Andrew W. (Drew) Evans
CFO: Elizabeth W. (Beth) Reese
HR: Dave Smith
FYE: December 31
Type: Public

AGL Resources brings its resources to customers in seven states through its fleet of utilities. Its Nicor Gas unit has 2.2 million customers in Illinois; Atlanta Gas Light 1.5 million natural gas customers in Georgia. AGL also distributes natural gas to 4.5 million customers in half a dozen states. Through its nonregulated subsidiaries AGL markets natural gas to retail and wholesale customers stores and transports gas and offers asset and risk management services. The company serves 628000 energy customers and 1.2 million service contracts across through its SouthStar unit. In 2015 the company agreed to be bought by Southern Company for $8 billion.

	Annual Growth	12/11	12/12	12/13	12/14	12/15
Sales ($ mil.)	13.9%	2,338.0	3,922.0	4,617.0	5,385.0	3,941.0
Net income ($ mil.)	19.7%	172.0	271.0	313.0	482.0	353.0
Market value ($ mil.)	10.9%	5,087.1	4,811.5	5,685.4	6,561.7	7,681.2
Employees	(5.0%)	6,400	6,121	6,094	5,165	5,203

AGNES SCOTT COLLEGE INC.

141 E COLLEGE AVE
DECATUR, GA 300303797
Phone: 404-471-6000
Fax: –
Web: www.asccomnet.agnesscott.edu

CEO: Elizabeth Kiss
CFO: John Hegman
HR: William Gailey
FYE: June 30
Type: Private

Great Scott Agnes it's a liberal arts college for women! Agnes Scott College (ASC) offers bachelor of arts degrees in 33 majors and 27 minors with pre-law and pre-medicine programs and dual degree programs in architecture engineering and nursing as well as post-baccalaureate programs. The school also grants master of arts in teaching degrees in English biology chemistry physics and mathematics. Enrollment in 2008 was about 850 students. Founded in 1889 ASC is affiliated with the Presbyterian Church and has an endowment of about $300 million. Tuition fees room and board cost $39000 per year. The 100-acre campus rated one of the most beautiful in the country is in Decatur Georgia.

	Annual Growth	06/07	06/08	06/09	06/10	06/11
Sales ($ mil.)	–	–	–	0.0	51.9	62.2
Net income ($ mil.)	–	–	–	0.0	5.1	(3.6)
Market value ($ mil.)	–	–	–	–	–	–
Employees	–	–	–	–	–	350

AGREE REALTY CORP.

NYS: ADC

70 E. Long Lake Road
Bloomfield Hills, MI 48304
Phone: 248 737-4190
Fax: 248 737-9110
Web: www.agreerealty.com

CEO: Joey Agree
CFO: Matthew M. Partridge
HR: –
FYE: December 31
Type: Public

Shopping sprees really agree with Agree Realty. The self-managed real estate investment trust (REIT) owns develops and manages retail real estate primarily freestanding big-box properties. It owns approximately 100 retail properties in mostly Midwestern states. A dozen of the REIT's properties are anchored strip malls. Altogether Agree Realty owns a total of more than 3 million sq. ft. of leasable space. Its largest tenants include Borders Kmart and Walgreen. National tenants make up 90% of Agree's revenues. Agree considers acquisitions to diversify its portfolio and grow its stable of long-term tenants. The REIT was founded in 1971 by CEO Richard Agree.

	Annual Growth	12/10	12/11	12/12	12/13	12/14
Sales ($ mil.)	10.4%	36.1	36.3	35.8	43.5	53.6
Net income ($ mil.)	5.2%	15.1	9.6	18.0	19.7	18.5
Market value ($ mil.)	4.4%	459.4	427.6	469.9	509.0	545.3
Employees	6.2%	11	13	14	14	14

AGRI-MARK INC.

100 Milk St.
Methuen MA 01844-4665
Phone: 978-689-4442
Fax: 978-794-8304
Web: www.agrimark.net

CEO: –
CFO: –
HR: –
FYE: November 30
Type: Private - Cooperativ

Cheese lovers who make a habit of Cabot ought to know about Agri-Mark. The northeastern US dairy cooperative makes Cabot-brand Vermont cheddar cheese butter and cultured dairy products as well as McCadam-branded and European cheeses. The co-op boasts more than 1200 member-owners who operate farms throughout New England and New York producing 300 million gallons of milk a year. Agri-Mark also sells milk to bottlers and manufacturers in the eastern US and dairy ingredients to foodservice and industrial clients. It owns processing plants in Vermont Massachusetts and New York. The co-op was formed in 1916 as the New England Milk Producers Association and became Agri-Mark in 1980.

AGRIBANK FCB

30 E. 7th St. Ste. 1600
St. Paul MN 55101
Phone: 651-282-8800
Fax: 651-282-8666
Web: www.agribank.com

CEO: –
CFO: –
HR: –
FYE: December 31
Type: Private - Cooperativ

AgriBank puts the "green" in green acres. The borrower-owned bank provides wholesale lending and business services to Farm Credit System (FCS) associations in America's heartland. Established by Congress in 1916 the FCS is a nationwide network of cooperatives that provide loans and financial services for farmers ranchers agribusiness timber producers and rural homeowners. The co-ops write loans for homes land equipment and other farm operating costs. AgriBank also provides credit to rural electric water and telephone systems. The largest bank in the FCS its footprint includes more than half of the cropland in the US covering 15 states from Ohio to Wyoming and Minnesota to Arkansas.

AGY HOLDING CORP.

2556 Wagener Rd.
Aiken SC 29801
Phone: 803-648-8351
Fax: 803-643-1180
Web: www.agy.com

CEO: Patrick J Burns
CFO: Jay W Ferguson
HR: –
FYE: December 31
Type: Private

Glass and yarns usually go together in a pub frequented by sailors but AGY Holding Corp. (formerly Advanced Glassfiber Yarns and its subsidiaries) brings them together in a business. The company produces glass yarns (thin filaments of glass twisted together to form advanced yarn or fiber) which are used in myriad aerospace automotive construction defense electronics industrial and recreational applications. The US military for example reinforces Humvees and other armored vehicles with AGY's proprietary glass fiber. AGY products are differentiated by glass chemistry coating technology and form; brands include L Glass S-2 Glass and S-1 HM Glass. Private equity Kohlberg & Co. owns AGY Holding.

AH BELO CORP

NYS: AHC

P.O. Box 224866
Dallas, TX 75222-4866
Phone: 214 977-8200
Fax: –
Web: www.ahbelo.com

CEO: James M. (Jim) Moroney
CFO: Mary Kathryn Murray
HR: –
FYE: December 31
Type: Public

This company gives the Big D a helping of news with breakfast. A. H. Belo is a leading newspaper publisher with a portfolio of three daily newspapers anchored by The Dallas Morning News one of the country's top papers with a circulation of about 260000. It also owns The Press-Enterprise (Riverside California). In addition to its flagship papers A. H. Belo publishes the Denton Record-Chronicle (Texas) and several niche papers such as the Spanish-language paper Al Dia (Dallas) along with websites serving most of its publications. The company was spun off from TV station operator Belo Corp. in 2008.

	Annual Growth	12/10	12/11	12/12	12/13	12/14
Sales ($ mil.)	(13.5%)	487.3	461.5	440.0	366.3	272.8
Net income ($ mil.)	–	(124.2)	(10.9)	0.5	16.1	92.9
Market value ($ mil.)	4.5%	189.5	103.5	101.3	162.7	226.1
Employees	(16.8%)	2,480	2,160	2,050	1,560	1,190

AHOLD U.S.A. INC.

1149 Harrisburg Pike
Carlisle PA 17013
Phone: 717-249-4000
Fax: 801-569-6045
Web: www.kennecott.com

CEO: Dick Boer
CFO: Bob Fishbune
HR: –
FYE: December 31
Type: Subsidiary

Ahold USA is the American arm of Netherlands-based Royal Ahold — one of the world's leading grocery retailers. The subsidiary oversees some 750 supermarkets in about 10 states — from Massachusetts to Virginia. Ahold USA's four divisions include: Stop & Shop New England Stop & Shop Metro New York Giant-Landover and Giant-Carlisle each with its own support business. Its online grocery ordering and delivery service Peapod serves Giant Food and Stop & Shop customers in select markets. Ahold USA accounts for about 60% of its Dutch parent's group sales. After nearly a decade of retrenchment Royal Ahold is growing again on both sides of the Atlantic.

AHS HILLCREST MEDICAL CENTER LLC

1120 S. Utica Ave.
Tulsa OK 74104
Phone: 918-579-1000
Fax: 918-579-1024
Web: www.hillcrest.com

CEO: Kevin Gross
CFO: Donald Baker
HR: Carrie Brannon
FYE: December 31
Type: Subsidiary

Hillcrest Medical Center as part of the Hillcrest HealthCare System provides a helping hand to health care patients in northeastern Oklahoma. The medical center operates health care facilities in Tulsa and surrounding areas. The main hospital facility has about 690 beds and offers emergency cancer cardiology neurology rehabilitation and other acute and specialty care services. Hillcrest Medical Center also operates outpatient and extended care facilities including general health and specialty clinics and provides home health foster care and hospice services. The health care organization is part of Ardent Health Services.

AHS MEDICAL HOLDINGS LLC

1 Burton Hills Blvd. Ste. 250
Nashville TN 37215
Phone: 615-296-3000
Fax: 615-296-6351
Web: www.ardenthealth.com

CEO: -
CFO: -
HR: -
FYE: December 31
Type: Private

AHS Medical Holdings (doing business as Ardent Health Services) is passionate about healing the body. The company operates about 10 acute care hospitals a rehab hospital a heart hospital and a number of specialty care facilities through health systems in the southern US. Its facilities are primarily located in New Mexico where it operates as the Lovelace Health System and in Oklahoma where it operates as Hillcrest HealthCare System. Ardent Health Services' operations also include physician practices about a dozen pharmacies and the Lovelace Health Plan which serves some 240000 members in New Mexico. Welsh Carson Anderson & Stowe owns a controlling stake in Ardent Health Services.

AIMCO PROPERTIES L.P.

4582 S. Ulster Street Pkwy. Ste. 1100
Denver CO 80237
Phone: 303-757-8101
Fax: 502-347-6001
Web: www.northamericanstainless.com

CEO: Terry Considine
CFO: Ernest M Freedman
HR: -
FYE: December 31
Type: Subsidiary

AIMCO Properties' aim is true. The company is the operating arm of multi-family real estate giant Apartment Investment and Management Company (AIMCO) which owns and/or manages some 500 apartment properties (with nearly 94000 individual units) throughout the US. AIMCO Properties holds most of AIMCO's assets and manages its day-to-day operations including property management and asset management. Its portfolio includes suburban apartment communities urban high-rise properties and government-subsidized affordable housing properties. Investment management operations include management of its own portfolio as well as services for affiliated partnerships. AIMCO controls more than 90% of AIMCO Properties.

AIR LEASE CORP

NYS: AL

2000 Avenue of the Stars, Suite 1000N
Los Angeles, CA 90067
Phone: 310 553-0555
Fax: -
Web: www.airleasecorp.com

CEO: Steven F. Udvar-Házy
CFO: Gregory B. Willis
HR: -
FYE: December 31
Type: Public

Air Lease doesn't really lease air unless of course you include the air inside the cabins of its fleet of airplanes. An aircraft leasing company Air Lease buys new and used commercial aircraft from manufacturers and airlines and then leases to airline carriers in Europe the Asia-Pacific region and the Americas. Its fleet is primarily made up of about 45 narrowbody and widebody Boeing and Airbus passenger airplanes that it leases to Air China (15% of revenues) Air Italy (11%) Air France (10%) and other major carriers. In addition to leasing Air Lease also offers fleet management services such as lease management and sales.

	Annual Growth	12/10	12/11	12/12	12/13	12/14
Sales ($ mil.)	106.0%	58.4	336.7	655.7	858.7	1,050.5
Net income ($ mil.)	-	(52.0)	53.2	131.9	190.4	256.0
Market value ($ mil.)	13.1%	-	2,427.7	2,201.4	3,182.3	3,513.1
Employees	17.6%	34	47	52	63	65

AIR METHODS CORP.

NMS: AIRM

7301 South Peoria
Englewood, CO 80112
Phone: 303 792-7400
Fax: -
Web: www.airmethods.com

CEO: Aaron D. Todd
CFO: Trent J. Carman
HR: Allison Farish
FYE: December 31
Type: Public

It's a bird it's a plane ... it's an ambulance! With a fleet of more than 400 medically equipped aircraft mainly helicopters Air Methods is the largest provider of emergency medical air-transportation services in the US. The company operates through three divisions. A community-based operating segment which represents roughly 85% of revenues offers transportation and in-flight medical care from hubs in some two dozen states. It also provides tourism operations around the Grand Canyon and Hawaiian Islands. The smallest division United Rotorcraft designs manufactures and installs aircraft medical-transport products.

	Annual Growth	12/10	12/11	12/12	12/13	12/14
Sales ($ mil.)	15.6%	562.0	660.5	850.8	881.6	1,004.8
Net income ($ mil.)	21.1%	44.1	46.6	93.2	62.3	94.9
Market value ($ mil.)	(5.9%)	2,207.4	3,312.9	1,447.9	2,285.5	1,727.3
Employees	11.4%	2,960	3,935	3,961	4,227	4,556

AIR PRODUCTS & CHEMICALS, INC.

NYS: APD

7201 Hamilton Boulevard
Allentown, PA 18195-1501
Phone: 610 481-4911
Fax: 610 481-5900
Web: www.airproducts.com

CEO: Seifi Ghasemi
CFO: M. Scott Crocco
HR: Jennifer (Jen) Woo
FYE: September 30
Type: Public

Air Products and Chemicals looks for its profits to expand like the gases it sells. The company provides gases such as argon hydrogen nitrogen and oxygen to manufacturers health care facilities and energy markets. Air Products' largest segment (through fiscal 2014) was Merchant Gases which manufactures atmospheric process and specialty gases delivered from tanker truck trailer or on-site. The company's Tonnage Gases segment serves the global refining and chemical industries while its Electronics and Performance Materials unit serves electronics and other manufacturing companies. Air Products also makes gas containers and equipment that separates air purifies hydrogen and liquefies gas.

	Annual Growth	09/11	09/12	09/13	09/14	09/15
Sales ($ mil.)	(0.5%)	10,082.0	9,611.7	10,180.4	10,439.0	9,894.9
Net income ($ mil.)	1.1%	1,224.2	1,167.3	994.2	991.7	1,277.9
Market value ($ mil.)	13.7%	16,447.0	17,810.2	22,950.8	28,035.4	27,475.5
Employees	1.0%	18,900	21,300	21,600	21,200	19,700

AIR T INC
NAS: AIRT

3524 Airport Road
Maiden, NC 28650
Phone: 828 464-8741
Fax: –
Web: www.airt.net

CEO: –
CFO: Candice L Otey
HR: –
FYE: March 31
Type: Public

Air T helps FedEx deliver the goods. The company owns two overnight air cargo subsidiaries — Mountain Air Cargo (MAC) and CSA Air — which operate under contracts with FedEx. MAC and CSA Air fly mainly in the Eastern and Midwest regions of the US as well as the Caribbean and South America. Its combined fleet consists of about 80 turboprop Cessna aircraft most of which are leased from FedEx. Air Cargo Services accounts for about half of its sales. Air T's Aircraft Ground Service Equipment and Service business comprises Global Ground Support (GGS; de-icing and scissor-lift equipment used at airports) and Global Aviation Services (GAS; provides related maintenance services).

	Annual Growth	03/11	03/12	03/13	03/14	03/15
Sales ($ mil.)	7.7%	83.4	89.4	103.1	100.8	112.2
Net income ($ mil.)	3.8%	2.1	1.4	1.7	1.5	2.5
Market value ($ mil.)	27.2%	22.3	22.7	22.5	28.7	58.4
Employees	8.5%	433	508	519	576	600

AIR TRANSPORT SERVICES GROUP, INC.
NMS: ATSG

145 Hunter Drive
Wilmington, OH 45177
Phone: 937 382-5591
Fax: –
Web: www.atsginc.com

CEO: Joseph C. (Joe) Hete
CFO: Quint O. Turner
HR: John (Jack) Starkovich
FYE: December 31
Type: Public

Air Transport Services Group (ATSG) has a lease on (aircraft) life. Through its subsidiaries the company provides aircraft leases maintenance operations and other support services to the cargo transportation and package delivery industries. The company's largest segment ACMI Services provides aircraft crew maintenance and insurance operations to the company's largest customers DHL and the US military through airline subsidiaries Ohio-based ABX Air Inc. and Arkansas-based ATI. ATSG's Cargo Aircraft Management (CAM) subsidiary leases converted cargo Boeing 767 and 757 aircraft internally to ATSG airlines and to external customers through multiyear agreements.

	Annual Growth	12/10	12/11	12/12	12/13	12/14
Sales ($ mil.)	(3.1%)	667.4	730.1	607.4	580.0	589.6
Net income ($ mil.)	(7.0%)	39.8	23.2	40.9	(19.6)	29.9
Market value ($ mil.)	2.0%	512.4	306.1	260.1	524.7	555.2
Employees	(3.2%)	2,065	2,010	1,900	1,800	1,810

AIR2WEB INC.

3424 Peachtree Rd. NE Ste. 400
Atlanta GA 30326
Phone: 404-942-5300
Fax: 202-692-2901
Web: www.peacecorps.gov

CEO: Jim Continenza
CFO: –
HR: –
FYE: December 31
Type: Private

Air2Web believes that marketers should take a flying leap. The company provides mobile markeing software and related managed services under the Air-CARE banner which are used by customers to wirelessly reach potential clients on the go. Other products include customer service-oriented messaging applications (DirectTEXT) and mobile and Web accessible customer data access tools (Enterprise Agent). Air2Web targets industries such as insurance financial services food and retail. Customers include enterprises phone companies marketing agences and content providers such as Office Depot Dominos and Axciom. Mobile marketing and advertising technology firm Velti acquired Air2Web for $19 million in 2011.

AIRBAND COMMUNICATIONS HOLDINGS INC.

14800 Landmark Pkwy. Ste. 500
Dallas TX 75254
Phone: 469-791-0000
Fax: 469-374-0741
Web: www.airband.com

CEO: Michael Ruley
CFO: Timothy Kinnear
HR: –
FYE: December 31
Type: Private

There are no air guitarists in this band. Wireless communications provider airBand Communications offers broadband Internet and data services as well as computer telephony connections to businesses in about 14 US cities. The company's fixed-wireless services include data colocation Internet access virtual private networks wireless private lines and Web hosting. airBand operates networks in select cities in Arizona California Georgia Maryland North Carolina Pennsylvania and Texas. The company serves clients in such industries as financial services and health care; customers have included CoStar Group Medifast and WakeMed.

AIRCASTLE LIMITED
NYSE: AYR

300 First Stamford Pl. 5th Fl.
Stamford CT 06902
Phone: 203-504-1020
Fax: 203-504-1021
Web: www.aircastle.com

CEO: Ron Wainshal
CFO: Michael J. Inglese
HR: Jill Saverine
FYE: December 31
Type: Public

Not to be confused with the inflatable palaces that parents rent for kids' birthday parties Aircastle Limited is an aircraft leasing concern. The company owns a lineup of utility jet aircraft that it adds to leases and sells to passenger and cargo markets. Aircastle touts a portfolio of 130-plus aircraft which are leased to about 60 different businesses. Lessees of Aircastle's aircraft maintain the planes as well as pay operating and insurance expenses. The company's leases are managed from offices in Ireland Singapore and the US. Aircastle also invests in industry-related assets such as financing vehicles secured by commercial aircraft. Its three largest customers are US Airways Martinair and Emirates.

AIRCRAFT SERVICE INTERNATIONAL INC.

201 S. Orange Ave. Ste. 1100-A
Orlando FL 32801
Phone: 407-648-7373
Fax: 407-206-5391
Web: www.asig.com

CEO: Keith P Ryan
CFO: Sami Teittinen
HR: –
FYE: December 31
Type: Subsidiary

Rather than soaring through the skies the company (dba Aircraft Service International Group or "ASIG") offers flight support services to commercial planes on the ground. It provides refueling as well as ground handling services including baggage and cargo handling and transfer cabin and lounge cleaning and other related services. Technical services include de-icing and jetway maintenance. ASIG operates at about 70 airports worldwide primarily in the US and the UK but also in Europe Central America and Asia/Pacific. Sister company Signature Flight Support serves the general aviation community as a leading fixed-base operator (FBO). ASIG was founded in 1947 and acquired by UK-based BBA Aviation in 2001.

AIRGAS INC.

NYS: ARG

259 North Radnor-Chester Road, Suite 100
Radnor, PA 19087-5283
Phone: 610 687-5253
Fax: 610 687-1052
Web: www.airgas.com

CEO: Michael L. (Mike) Molinini
CFO: Robert M. (Bob) McLaughlin
HR: –
FYE: March 31
Type: Public

Airgas has floated to the top of the industrial gas distribution industry. Its North American network of more than 1100 locations includes retail stores gas fill plants specialty gas labs production facilities (16 air separation plants) and distribution centers. Airgas distributes argon carbon dioxide hydrogen nitrogen oxygen and a variety of medical and specialty gases as well as dry ice and protective equipment (hard hats goggles). Its gases production unit operates air-separation plants that produce oxygen nitrogen and argon. The company also sells welding machines. In 2015 France's Air Liquide SA agreed to buy Airgas for $13.4 billion.

	Annual Growth	03/11	03/12	03/13	03/14	03/15
Sales ($ mil.)	5.7%	4,251.5	4,746.3	4,957.5	5,072.5	5,304.9
Net income ($ mil.)	10.2%	249.8	313.4	340.9	350.8	368.1
Market value ($ mil.)	12.4%	5,005.2	6,704.5	7,472.4	8,026.3	7,996.1
Employees	5.0%	14,000	15,000	15,000	16,000	17,000

AIRTRAN AIRWAYS INC.

9955 AirTran Blvd.
Orlando FL 32827
Phone: 407-318-5600
Fax: 407-318-5900
Web: www.airtran.com

CEO: –
CFO: –
HR: –
FYE: December 31
Type: Subsidiary

Need to be transported by air with a low fare? AirTran Airways offers low-cost passenger transportation to almost 70 cities mainly in the eastern US but also in Aruba the Bahamas Jamaica Mexico and Puerto Rico. The airline operates from a primary hub in Atlanta and secondary hubs in Baltimore; Milwaukee; and Orlando Florida. AirTran maintains a fleet of about 140 Boeing aircraft (717s and 737s). It is a leading carrier in the Atlanta market behind Delta which handles the largest share of the traffic at Hartsfield-Jackson Atlanta International Airport. AirTran Airways was acquired by Southwest Airlines in 2011.

AIRVANA INC.

19 Alpha Rd.
Chelmsford MA 01824
Phone: 978-250-3100
Fax: 978-250-3910
Web: www.airvana.com

CEO: –
CFO: David Gamache
HR: –
FYE: December 31
Type: Private

Airvana makes a technology called femtocells which are basically 3G network cell phone transmitters that improve weak signal reception indoors. Airvana's femtocell products sold under the HubBub brand bring better voice service and speed up data downloads and uploads for 3G network users in homes and small offices. The company has partnered with several telecommunications and IT manufacturers to integrate femtocell technology with their equipment. These companies include Alcatel-Lucent Ericsson Freescale Semiconductor and Hitachi. Sprint Nextel and KDDI provide service powered by Airvana femtocells.

AK STEEL HOLDING CORP.

NYS: AKS

9227 Centre Pointe Drive
West Chester, OH 45069
Phone: 513 425-5000
Fax: 513 425-5220
Web: www.aksteel.com

CEO: Roger K. Newport
CFO: Jaime Vasquez
HR: Larry Zizzo
FYE: December 31
Type: Public

Automobile sales help AK Steel's business keep rolling though it also has operations in the infrastructure and manufacturing industries. The company manufactures carbon stainless and electrical steel. It sells hot- and cold-rolled carbon steel to construction companies steel distributors and service centers and automotive and industrial machinery producers. AK Steel also sells cold-rolled and aluminum-coated stainless steel to automakers. The company produces electrical steels (iron-silicon alloys with unique magnetic properties) for makers of power transmission and distribution equipment.

	Annual Growth	12/10	12/11	12/12	12/13	12/14
Sales ($ mil.)	2.2%	5,968.3	6,468.0	5,933.7	5,570.4	6,505.7
Net income ($ mil.)	–	(128.9)	(155.6)	(1,027.3)	(46.8)	(96.9)
Market value ($ mil.)	(22.4%)	2,901.0	1,463.8	815.2	1,453.2	1,052.7
Employees	4.9%	6,600	6,600	6,400	6,400	8,000

AKAL SECURITY INC.

7 INFINITY LOOP
ESPANOLA, NM 875326737
Phone: 505-753-7832
Fax: –
Web: www.akalsecurity.com

CEO: Matthew Branigan
CFO: Dave Garlock
HR: –
FYE: December 31
Type: Private

Unarmed? Akal Security provides contract security guard services for customers in the US and abroad. Akal's Judicial Security division specializes in security services for protecting federal courthouses in 40 states. It also transports prisoners and illegal aliens for homeland security efforts. In addition Akal supplies security officers for detention facilities and military installations and offers electronic security surveillance and access control system design installation and integration. The company serves federal agencies as well as commercial clients and state and local government facilities. Clients have included the US Army the Department of Homeland Security the US Marshals Service and NASA.

	Annual Growth	12/07	12/08	12/09	12/10	12/11
Sales ($ mil.)	(18.7%)	–	–	698.9	466.2	461.5
Net income ($ mil.)	29351.6%	–	–	0.0	2.5	3.6
Market value ($ mil.)	–	–	–	–	–	–
Employees	–	–	–	–	–	15,000

AKAMAI TECHNOLOGIES INC

NMS: AKAM

150 Broadway
Cambridge, MA 02142
Phone: 617 444-3000
Fax: 617 444-3001
Web: www.akamai.com

CEO: Tom (Tom) Leighton
CFO: Jim Benson
HR: Susan (Sue) LaPointe
FYE: December 31
Type: Public

For companies who provide and use cloud computing Akamai moves the data back and forth. The company's hardware software and algorithms enables corporations and government agencies to deliver digital content and applications such as ads business transaction tools streaming video and websites over the Internet. It also offers applications that supply network data feeds and website analytics to customers. With a network of more than 107000 servers in 102 countries around the world Akamai analyzes and manages Web traffic transmitting content from servers that are geographically closest to end users. In addition to its 11 US offices the company has more than 25 international locations. Customers include Apple Hitachi and SAP.

	Annual Growth	12/10	12/11	12/12	12/13	12/14
Sales ($ mil.)	17.7%	1,023.6	1,158.5	1,373.9	1,577.9	1,963.9
Net income ($ mil.)	18.2%	171.2	200.9	204.0	293.5	333.9
Market value ($ mil.)	7.6%	8,389.0	5,755.5	7,294.3	8,412.2	11,225.8
Employees	23.4%	2,200	2,380	3,074	3,908	5,105

AKELA PHARMA INC.

TORONTO: AKL

11501 Domain Dr. Ste. 130
Austin TX 78758
Phone: 512-834-0449
Fax: 512-834-2105
Web: akelapharma.com

CEO: Rudy Emmelot
CFO: –
HR: –
FYE: December 31
Type: Private

Drug developer Akela Pharma is hoping to be there before the last dose of pain meds wears off and the next dose kicks in. The company's lead product candidate is Fentanyl Taifun an inhaled formulation of cancer pain fighter fentanyl to be used in conjunction with other drugs to manage severe pain. Akela Pharma is also working on research in areas not related to pain relief; it is developing a growth hormone stimulator to help treat frailty and malnutrition in patients with kidney failure. Akela Pharma's subsidiary PharmaForm provides contract drug development services and specializes in controlled-release drug delivery technology.

AKERS BIOSCIENCES INC.

LONDON: AKR

201 Grove Rd.
Thorofare NJ 08086
Phone: 856-848-8698
Fax: 856-848-0269
Web: www.akersbiosciences.com

CEO: John J Gormally
CFO: –
HR: –
FYE: December 31
Type: Public

When there's no time to send a sample off to the lab Akers Biosciences (ABI) steps up. The company manufactures a variety of point-of-care rapid diagnostic tests. In addition to tests for such diseases as malaria it has produced screening tools to detect drug and enzyme levels in blood. ABI has also developed sniffing devices to detect breath alcohol as well as diseases such as lung disease and diabetes through breath analysis. Another product whiffs for biological warfare agents in the air. Its Tri-Cholesterol product is a home-use test kit. ABI customers include healthcare facilities (hospitals physicians' offices) as well as the US military and aid organizations.

AKIBIA INC.

4 Technology Dr.
Westborough MA 01581
Phone: 508-621-5100
Fax: 508-621-5205
Web: www.akibia.com

CEO: Thomas Tucker
CFO: Thomas Tucker
HR: –
FYE: March 31
Type: Private

Akibia provides information technology (IT) consulting systems integration and technical support services for a variety of computing environments. Its areas of specialty include data security data storage and infrastructure design and maintenance. The company also offers consulting related to customer relationship management (CRM) software installation and customization as well as network planning and support. Akibia's outsourced services include technical support and training for corporate call centers. It serves such industries as financial services consumer electronics and retail. Clients have included Bose Atmel and Egenera. Founded in 1988 Akibia is a subsidiary of India-based Zensar Technologies.

AKORN INC

NMS: AKRX

1925 W. Field Court, Suite 300
Lake Forest, IL 60045
Phone: 847 279-6100
Fax: –
Web: www.akorn.com

CEO: Raj Rai
CFO: Duane A. Portwood
HR: –
FYE: December 31
Type: Public

Akorn has its roots firmly planted in the pharmaceutical industry. The firm makes and sells branded and generic drugs in therapeutic and diagnostic categories including ophthalmology injectables and specialty therapeutics. Akorn's ophthalmic segment includes antibiotics steroids glaucoma treatments and diagnostic stains and dyes as well as prescription and OTC eye care products. The firm's injectable and hospital-administered therapeutics segment includes anti-infectives antidotes anesthesia agents pain management drugs and other specialty substances. Akorn also provides contract drug manufacturing services. Chairman John Kapoor is the company's largest shareholder owning a one-third stake in Akorn.

	Annual Growth	12/10	12/11	12/12	12/13	12/14
Sales ($ mil.)	61.9%	86.4	136.9	256.2	317.7	593.1
Net income ($ mil.)	12.8%	21.8	43.0	35.4	52.4	35.3
Market value ($ mil.)	56.3%	678.2	1,242.5	1,492.8	2,750.9	4,044.8
Employees	46.4%	410	564	767	1,462	1,881

AKRON GENERAL MEDICAL CENTER

400 Wabash Ave.
Akron OH 44307
Phone: 330-344-6000
Fax: 330-344-2300
Web: www.agmc.org

CEO: –
CFO: –
HR: –
FYE: December 31
Type: Subsidiary

Akron General Medical Center the flagship hospital of Akron General Health System is a not-for-profit teaching hospital that boasts more than 500 acute care beds. The hospital serves the residents of Northeast Ohio as a regional referral center in a number of medical specialties including cardiovascular disease heart surgery cancer care orthopedics sports medicine and trauma care. Akron General Medical also operates Edwin Shaw Rehab the area's only hospital specializing in rehabilitation. Edwin Shaw with 35 beds treats patients who have experienced stroke head trauma and other critical injuries. Akron General Medical was founded in 1914 as Peoples Hospital.

ALABAMA FARMERS COOPERATIVE INC.

121 SOMERVILLE RD NE
DECATUR, AL 356012659
Phone: 256-353-6843
Fax: –
Web: www.alafarm.com

CEO: Tommy Paulk
CFO: W Dan Groscost
HR: –
FYE: July 31
Type: Private

Alabama Farmers Cooperative (AFC) provides farmers in the Yellowhammer state with a range of agricultural supplies and services. The co-op offers animal feed crop fertilizer and home-gardening items such as seed and hand tools as well as grain storage and hardware. AFC comprises 37 member associations including about 90 retail locations. Expanding through joint ventures it boasts one of the largest farmer-owned agriculture businesses in the southeastern US. Its Bonnie Plants is one of the biggest suppliers of vegetable and herb plants for home gardeners. BioLogic makes forage products for wild game. AFC supplies the foodservice industry with fresh fish through its SouthFresh Farms catfish farm.

	Annual Growth	07/08	07/09	07/10	07/11	07/13
Sales ($ mil.)	10.8%	–	393.6	401.0	450.8	592.6
Net income ($ mil.)	28.6%	–	–	8.1	9.2	17.3
Market value ($ mil.)	–	–	–	–	–	–
Employees	–	–	–	–	–	3,000

ALABAMA GAS CORPORATION

605 Richard Arrington Jr. Blvd. North
Birmingham AL 35203-2707
Phone: 205-326-2700
Fax: 205-326-2590
Web: www.alagasco.com

CEO: Steven L Lindsey
CFO: Steven P Rasche
HR: –
FYE: December 31
Type: Subsidiary

With all the gas a customer could possibly need Alagasco is THE gas co. in Alabama. A unit of Birmingham Alabama-based oil and gas company Energen utility Alabama Gas Corporation (Alagasco) distributes natural gas to about 395770 residential and 31840 commercial and industrial customers in about half of the counties in the state. The utility also provides gas transportation services to large end users who purchase wholesale gas from suppliers. Alagasco has seven operating districts: Anniston Birmingham Gadsden Montgomery Opelika Selma and Tuscaloosa. The Alagasco distribution system includes 11225 miles of mains and more than 11980 miles of service lines.

ALABAMA POWER CO.
NYS: ALP PRO

600 North 18th Street
Birmingham, AL 35203
Phone: 205 257-1000
Fax: –
Web: www.alapower.com

CEO: Mark A Crosswhite
CFO: Philip C Raymond
HR: –
FYE: December 31
Type: Public

Alabama Power powers up Southern Rockers and many others in the heart of Dixie. The Southern Company subsidiary provides electricity to 1.4 million residential and business customers in a 44500 sq. mi. service area in Alabama. The utility operates more than 83000 miles of power lines and it has nuclear hydroelectric and fossil-fueled power plant interests that give it a generating capacity of more than 12000 MW. Alabama Power sells wholesale power to more than 15 municipal and rural distribution utilities; it also provides steam transmission (used for heating and cooling buildings) in downtown Birmingham Alabama and sells electric appliances (such as thermostats ovens and washing machines).

	Annual Growth	12/10	12/11	12/12	12/13	12/14
Sales ($ mil.)	(0.1%)	5,976.0	5,702.0	5,520.0	5,618.0	5,942.0
Net income ($ mil.)	1.8%	746.0	747.0	743.0	751.0	800.0
Market value ($ mil.)	1.9%	765.1	805.6	857.8	776.9	823.6
Employees	1.4%	6,552	6,632	6,778	6,896	6,935

ALACRA INC.

100 Broadway Ste. 1101
New York NY 10005
Phone: 212-363-9620
Fax: 212-363-9630
Web: www.alacra.com

CEO: Steve Goldstein
CFO: Craig Kissel
HR: –
FYE: December 31
Type: Private

Those who lack business knowledge may want to consult Alacra. The company gathers business and financial information from about 200 sources (such as Thomson Reuters Dow Jones and LexisNexis) and feeds it to some 400 knowledge-hungry clients including investment and commercial banks management consulting firms law firms and other corporations. The company's Alacra Book searches for and collects company and industry information relevant to the customer's query and publishes it for the customer as a single PDF or Word file. The firm was founded in 1996 by former Knight-Ridder execs Steven Goldstein (chairman and CEO) and Michael Angle (president and COO).

ALAMO GROUP, INC.
NYS: ALG

1627 East Walnut
Seguin, TX 78155
Phone: 830 379-1480
Fax: 830 372-9683
Web: www.alamo-group.com

CEO: Ronald A. (Ron) Robinson
CFO: Dan E. Malone
HR: Janet Pollock
FYE: December 31
Type: Public

Remember the Alamo Group for tractor-mounted mowing equipment — rotary flail and sickle-bar! The company designs manufactures and distributes a slew of right-of-way maintenance and agricultural equipment. Its branded lines Alamo Industrial and Tiger hydraulically powered tractor-mounted mowers serve US government agencies. Rhino Products and M&W Gear subsidiaries sell rotary cutters and other equipment to farmers for pasture upkeep. UK McConnel and Bomford and France's S.M.A. subsidiaries market vegetation maintenance equipment such as hydraulic boom-mounted hedge and grass mowers.

	Annual Growth	12/10	12/11	12/12	12/13	12/14
Sales ($ mil.)	12.5%	524.5	603.6	628.4	676.8	839.1
Net income ($ mil.)	18.2%	21.1	32.1	28.9	36.1	41.2
Market value ($ mil.)	14.9%	313.4	303.3	367.7	683.6	545.6
Employees	7.5%	2,300	2,500	2,470	2,550	3,070

ALANCO TECHNOLOGIES INC
NBB: ALAN

7950 E. Acoma Drive, Suite 111
Scottsdale, AZ 85260
Phone: 480 607-1010
Fax: –
Web: www.alanco.com

CEO: John A Carlson
CFO: Danielle L Haney
HR: Stacey Maroney
FYE: June 30
Type: Public

Having failed to strike gold and feeling lost Alanco Technologies is looking for a new business venture. The company once made pollution control systems owned gold mines and made unsuccessful forays into both the data storage and restaurant fryer businesses. It also made radio-frequency ID (RFID) tracking devices for correctional facilities through its TSI PRISM subsidiary until that line of business was sold in 2010 to Alabama-based Black Creek Integrated Systems for about $2 million in cash. Alanco then offered subscription-based GPS tracking data services for the refrigerated transport industry through StarTrak Systems (acquired for $15 million in 2006) but sold that business to ORBCOMM in 2011.

	Annual Growth	06/11	06/12	06/13	06/14	06/15
Sales ($ mil.)	41.8%	–	–	0.4	0.6	0.8
Net income ($ mil.)	–	(0.1)	(0.6)	(0.7)	(0.1)	(0.9)
Market value ($ mil.)	(38.4%)	9.7	7.4	2.2	2.4	1.4
Employees	25.7%	2	–	2	1	5

ALASKA AIR GROUP, INC.
NYS: ALK

19300 International Boulevard
Seattle, WA 98188
Phone: 206 392-5040
Fax: –
Web: www.alaskaair.com

CEO: Bradley D. (Brad) Tilden
CFO: Lorraine Hurt
HR: Tammy Young
FYE: December 31
Type: Public

Whether you want to capture a "Kodiak" moment or down a daiquiri by the Sea of Cortez an Alaska Air Group airplane can fly you there. Operating through primary subsidiary Alaska Airlines and regional carrier Horizon Air the group flies more than 29 million passengers to more than 100 destinations in the US (mainly western states including Alaska and Hawaii) Canada and Mexico. The group's primary hub is Seattle (accounting for almost two-thirds of passengers) but it also flies out of key markets such as Portland Oregon; Los Angeles; and Anchorage Alaska. Alaska Airlines has a fleet of about 140 Boeing 737 jets. Horizon Air operates more than 50 Bombardier Q400 turboprops.

	Annual Growth	12/11	12/12	12/13	12/14	12/15
Sales ($ mil.)	6.7%	4,317.8	4,657.0	5,156.0	5,368.0	5,598.0
Net income ($ mil.)	36.5%	244.5	316.0	508.0	605.0	848.0
Market value ($ mil.)	1.8%	9,399.4	5,393.8	9,184.1	7,480.5	10,077.9
Employees	4.3%	12,806	12,932	13,177	13,952	15,143

ALASKA COMMUNICATIONS SYSTEMS GROUP INC   NMS: ALSK

600 Telephone Avenue
Anchorage, AK 99503-6091
Phone: 907 297-3000
Fax: –
Web: www.alsk.com

CEO: Anand Vadapalli
CFO: Wayne P Graham
HR: Debra English
FYE: December 31
Type: Public

Alaska Communications Systems Group keeps customers in the largest US state connected. Through subsidiaries the telecom carrier operates the leading local-exchange network in the state providing wired local and long-distance voice and data services mostly to enterprise customers. It also offers wireless phone service through a joint venture with GCI that offers mobile devices from Apple HTC and Samsung. The company has about 130000 wired phone lines in service about 110000 wireless subscribers and about 55000 Internet customers. Alaska Communications sells to consumers in part through its network of retail stores.

	Annual Growth	12/10	12/11	12/12	12/13	12/14
Sales ($ mil.)	(2.0%)	341.5	349.3	367.8	348.9	314.9
Net income ($ mil.)	–	(30.7)	0.5	17.4	156.4	(2.8)
Market value ($ mil.)	(36.6%)	551.2	149.5	96.3	105.3	88.9
Employees	(0.2%)	855	855	830	826	848

ALASKA CONSERVATION FOUNDATION

441 W. 5th Ave. Ste. 402
Anchorage AK 99501-2340
Phone: 907-276-1917
Fax: 907-274-4145
Web: www.akcf.org

CEO: –
CFO: –
HR: –
FYE: June 30
Type: Private - Not-for-Pr

Whales and otters and bears oh my! The Alaska Conservation Foundation strives to protect the environment (and all its inhabitants) in Alaska as well as help the state's native people retain their cultural connections to the land. The foundation has awarded more than $22 million in grants to about 200 organizations. Its projects include the Alaska Coalition (national parks wildlife refuges and other federal lands) Alaska Oceans Program (conservation and sustainable fishing) Alaska Conservation for the Majority (finding common ground between conservationists and state residents) and Climate Change Program (minimizing individual impact). The Alaska Conservation Foundation was formed in 1980.

ALASKA NATIVE TRIBAL HEALTH CONSORTIUM

4000 AMBASSADOR DR
ANCHORAGE, AK 995085909
Phone: 907-729-1900
Fax: –

CEO: –
CFO: Garvin Federenko
HR: –
FYE: September 30
Type: Private

The Alaska Native Tribal Health Consortium (ANTHC) brings good health to Alaska Natives. The company is a not-for-profit statewide health care organization managed by regional tribal governments and their respective regional health organizations. The organization connects disparate medical providers by providing a range of health programs and services including community health care public health advocacy and education initiatives health research (including water and sanitation) and medical supply distribution. The 150-bed Alaska Native Medical Center (ANMC) a native-owned hospital is jointly managed by ANTHC and Southcentral Foundation a regional health corporation based in the Cook Inlet region.

	Annual Growth	09/09	09/10	09/11	09/12	09/13
Sales ($ mil.)	3.5%	–	414.9	427.8	447.1	459.8
Net income ($ mil.)	(6.8%)	–	–	24.6	21.7	21.4
Market value ($ mil.)	–	–	–	–	–	–
Employees	–	–	–	–	–	1,850

ALASKA PACIFIC BANCSHARES INC.   OTC: AKPB

2094 Jordan Ave.
Juneau AK 99801
Phone: 907-789-4844
Fax: 907-790-5110
Web: www.alaskapacificbank.com

CEO: –
CFO: –
HR: –
FYE: December 31
Type: Public

If you hail from Alaska Juneau about Alaska Pacific Bancshares. It is the holding company for Alaska Pacific Bank which serves the communities of Juneau Ketchikan and Sitka through about a half-dozen branches. The bank offers deposit products including checking and savings accounts CDs IRAs and check cards. Single- to four-family residential mortgages and commercial real estate loans each account for about a quarter of the company's loan portfolio. The bank also originates construction business and consumer loans. Alaska Pacific Bank was founded in 1935.

ALASKA USA FEDERAL CREDIT UNION

4000 Credit Union Dr.
Anchorage AK 99503
Phone: 907-563-4567
Fax: +44-1962-867-037
Web: www.basepoint.co.uk

CEO: William B Eckhardt
CFO: Norman P West
HR: –
FYE: December 31
Type: Private - Not-for-Pr

Alaska USA is no half-baked financial institution. The member-owned credit union provides financial services to more than 435000 members from about 65 branch locations in Alaska Washington and California. Serving consumers and small businesses Alaska USA offers deposit accounts loans credit cards insurance and trust and investment management services. Loans for automobiles and RVs account for nearly two-thirds of the credit union's lending portfolio; it also originates real estate consumer and commercial loans. Alaska USA was founded in 1948 as the Alaskan Air Depot Federal Credit Union.

ALBANY COLLEGE OF PHARMACY AND HEALTH SCIENCES

106 NEW SCOTLAND AVE
ALBANY, NY 12208-3425
Phone: 518-694-7200
Fax: –
Web: www.acphs.edu

CEO: –
CFO: –
HR: –
FYE: June 30
Type: Private

Rather than touting their love for the Big Apple students at this school "heart" medicine. Located in New York's capital city Albany College of Pharmacy offers a half dozen degree programs with an emphasis in health care including pharmacy pre-med and biomedical technology. The school also provides a home for the Pharmaceutical Research Institute a not-for-profit drug discovery and development facility. Albany College of Pharmacy has an enrollment of more than 1200 students and was founded in 1881.

	Annual Growth	06/08	06/09	06/09	06/11	06/12
Sales ($ mil.)	8.7%	–	43.9	50.9	53.0	56.4
Net income ($ mil.)	–	–	0.0	9.6	6.0	6.2
Market value ($ mil.)	–	–	–	–	–	–
Employees	–	–	–	–	–	110

ALBANY INTERNATIONAL CORP
NYS: AIN

216 Airport Drive
Rochester, NH 03867
Phone: 518 445-2200
Fax: 603 994-3835
Web: www.albint.com

CEO: Joseph G. Morone
CFO: John B. Cozzolino
HR: –
FYE: December 31
Type: Public

Albany International's products look good on paper and on papermaking machines. The company makes paper machine clothing (PMC custom-made fabrics and belts that move paper stock through each phase of production). It markets these products to paper mills worldwide through a direct sales staff and also provides woven/non-woven fabrics for paper/tannery/textile industries and building products. Its other business segment Engineered Composites (AEC) makes engineered composite parts for the aerospace industry and high-tech applications. Over the years the company has been selling off former units and operations to focus on its PMC and AEC segments.

	Annual Growth	12/10	12/11	12/12	12/13	12/14
Sales ($ mil.)	(5.0%)	914.4	814.7	760.9	757.4	745.3
Net income ($ mil.)	2.5%	37.6	34.9	31.0	17.5	41.6
Market value ($ mil.)	12.5%	754.8	736.6	722.6	1,144.8	1,210.4
Employees	(5.4%)	5,000	4,300	4,000	4,100	4,000

ALBANY MEDICAL CENTER

43 NEW SCOTLAND AVE
ALBANY, NY 122083478
Phone: 518-262-3125
Fax: –
Web: www.amc.edu

CEO: James J. Barba
CFO: William C. Hasselbarth
HR: Thomas (Thom) Murphy
FYE: December 31
Type: Private

Albany Medical Center (AMC) provides upscale medical care in upstate New York. Serving residents of northeastern New York and western New England the health system has at its heart the 730-bed Albany Medical Center Hospital. The general medical-surgical facility also provides specialty care in such areas as oncology rehabilitation and organ transplantation. AMC also features a children's hospital an outpatient surgery center and a group medical practice. It employs some 400 full-time physicians. Its Albany Medical College is one of the nation's first private medical schools. It offers undergraduate and graduate medical degrees and residency programs as well as fellowships and continuing medical education.

	Annual Growth	12/04	12/05	12/11	12/12	12/13
Sales ($ mil.)	9.3%	–	480.7	–	935.2	980.6
Net income ($ mil.)	51.1%	–	–	–	76.2	115.1
Market value ($ mil.)	–	–	–	–	–	–
Employees	–	–	–	–	–	7,000

ALBANY MOLECULAR RESEARCH, INC.
NMS: AMRI

26 Corporate Circle
Albany, NY 12212
Phone: 518 512-2000
Fax: –
Web: www.amriglobal.com

CEO: William S. Marth
CFO: Felicia Ladin
HR: –
FYE: December 31
Type: Public

Albany Molecular Research dba AMRI pushes drug development efforts along from start to finish. The company provides contract research and manufacturing services to pharmaceutical and biotechnology firms. The company's services run the gamut — from compound screening and other drug discovery services to the contract manufacturing of existing and experimental drugs and drug ingredients for clinical trials and commercial sale. The company has R&D locations and manufacturing plants in the US Europe and Asia. Historically AMRI has leveraged its drug-discovery expertise to conduct some of its own research with the goal of licensing its compounds to other firms for further development.

	Annual Growth	12/10	12/11	12/12	12/13	12/14
Sales ($ mil.)	8.7%	198.1	207.6	226.7	246.6	276.6
Net income ($ mil.)	–	(62.9)	(32.3)	(3.8)	12.7	(3.3)
Market value ($ mil.)	30.5%	183.4	95.6	172.3	328.9	531.3
Employees	4.1%	1,421	1,389	1,329	1,282	1,668

ALBEMARLE CORP.
NYS: ALB

451 Florida Street
Baton Rouge, LA 70801
Phone: 225 388-8011
Fax: –
Web: www.albemarle.com

CEO: Luther C. (Luke) Kissam
CFO: Scott A. Tozier
HR: Linda Lopez
FYE: December 31
Type: Public

When it comes to chemistry Albemarle does it all. The company develops makes and sells specialty chemicals for a range of markets including automotive construction consumer electronics crop protection food safety lubricants pharmaceuticals plastics and refining. Its products include polymer additives (flame retardant chemicals antioxidants to extend fuel storage life and curatives that improve reaction time in coatings adhesives and elastomers) as well as catalysts surface treatment products and fine chemicals. Albemarle also offers fine chemistry services which include custom manufacturing R&D and scale-up for companies that are developing new products like drugs or agrichemicals.

	Annual Growth	12/10	12/11	12/12	12/13	12/14
Sales ($ mil.)	0.9%	2,362.8	2,869.0	2,745.4	2,616.4	2,445.5
Net income ($ mil.)	(19.9%)	323.7	436.3	311.5	413.2	133.3
Market value ($ mil.)	1.9%	4,352.5	4,019.4	4,847.3	4,946.4	4,692.0
Employees	(2.6%)	4,020	4,260	4,304	4,231	3,625

ALBERICI CORPORATION

8800 PAGE AVE
SAINT LOUIS, MO 631146106
Phone: 314-733-2000
Fax: –
Web: www.alberici.com

CEO: –
CFO: –
HR: –
FYE: December 31
Type: Private

Alberici helped shape the St. Louis skyline; it now sets its sights — or its construction sites — across North America. As the parent company of Alberici Constructors the company encompasses a group of enterprises with a presence in North America Central America South America and Europe. Operations include construction services building materials and steel fabrication and erection units. Alberici offers general contracting design/build construction management demolition and specialty contracting services while also offering facilities management. Founded in 1918 the Alberici family still holds the largest share of the employee-owned firm.

	Annual Growth	12/09	12/10	12/11	12/12	12/13
Sales ($ mil.)	56.0%	–	–	713.9	772.2	1,736.5
Net income ($ mil.)	–	–	–	0.0	0.0	0.0
Market value ($ mil.)	–	–	–	–	–	–
Employees	–	–	–	–	–	2,080

ALBERTSON'S LLC

250 Parkcenter Blvd.
Boise ID 83706
Phone: 208-395-6200
Fax: 208-395-6349
Web: albertsonsmarket.com

CEO: Robert Miller
CFO: Rick Navarro
HR: –
FYE: February 28
Type: Private

Call it the incredible shrinking grocery chain. Albertson's LLC runs about 190 Albertsons supermarkets in Arizona Arkansas Colorado Florida Louisiana New Mexico and Texas. That's all that remains of what was once the nation's #2 supermarket operator with about 2500 stores. Stung by competition the firm sold itself to a consortium that included rival grocer SUPERVALU drugstore chain CVS investment firm Cerberus Capital Management and Kimco Realty for about $9.7 billion in 2006. SUPERVALU and CVS cherry-picked the company's best supermarket and drugstore assets. Subsequent closings and divestments including 132 stores in Northern California and most of its Florida locations further shrunk the firm.

ALBION COLLEGE

611 E PORTER ST
ALBION, MI 492241887
Phone: 517-629-1000
Fax: –
Web: www.albion.edu

CEO: –
CFO: Marilyn Wieschowski
HR: –
FYE: June 30
Type: Private

Albion College is a private co-educational liberal arts college in Michigan associated with the Methodist church. The college offers Bachelor of Arts in about 30 subjects and Bachelor of Fine Arts degrees in art and art history. It employs some 130 full-time faculty members and has an enrollment of almost 2000. Albion can trace its roots to 1835 when early Methodist settlers of the Michigan Territory worked to get the college a charter from the Michigan Territorial Legislature. Notable alumni include chairman and editor-in-chief of Newsweek magazine Richard Smith and Broadway producer Michael David founder of Dodger Theatricals.

	Annual Growth	06/09	06/10	06/11	06/12	06/13
Sales ($ mil.)	4.0%	–	45.7	50.5	49.9	51.4
Net income ($ mil.)	(40.3%)	–	–	32.0	(15.0)	11.4
Market value ($ mil.)	–	–	–	–	–	–
Employees	–	–	–	–	–	600

ALBRIGHT COLLEGE

1621 N 13TH ST
READING, PA 196041708
Phone: 610-921-7520
Fax: –
Web: www.albright.edu

CEO: –
CFO: –
HR: Katherine Shilenok-Wright
FYE: May 31
Type: Private

Students' futures are bright at Albright College. The school is a private liberal arts university that offers bachelor's of arts and science degrees as well as masters in education degrees. More than 1600 students study at Albright College which offers programs in areas such as art biology English psychology mathematics and communications. The college employs about 110 faculty members. Affiliated with the United Methodist Church Albright College was established in 1856 and sits upon 118 acres in Reading Pennsylvania. The College is named for Jacob Albright a German evangelical preacher.

	Annual Growth	05/09	05/10	05/11	05/12	05/13
Sales ($ mil.)	(2.9%)	–	59.0	61.1	59.3	54.0
Net income ($ mil.)	(31.7%)	–	–	18.4	0.3	8.6
Market value ($ mil.)	–	–	–	–	–	–
Employees	–	–	–	–	–	394

ALCATEL-LUCENT USA INC.

600 Mountain Ave.
Murray Hill NJ 07974
Phone: 908-582-6173
Fax: 908-508-2576
Web: www.usa.alcatel.com

CEO: Michel Combes
CFO: –
HR: Jodie Toolen
FYE: December 31
Type: Subsidiary

Alcatel-Lucent USA may be headquartered in New Jersey but that doesn't mean it's not as technologically sophisticated as its Parisian parent. The US subsidiary of France-based Alcatel-Lucent designs develops and builds wireline wireless and converged communications networks. It supplies equipment software applications and related services to telecom carriers and network service providers such as 360networks AT&T and Verizon as well as enterprise customers. Government customers are served through DC-based subsidiary LGS Innovations which works with federal agencies including the US Army and major contractors such as Raytheon. Alcatel-Lucent USA accounts for almost 30% of its parent's overall revenues.

ALCO STORES INC

751 Freeport Parkway
Coppell, TX 75019
Phone: 469 322-2900
Fax: –
Web: www.alcostores.com

NBB: ALCS Q
CEO: Stanley B Latacha
CFO: –
HR: –
FYE: February 02
Type: Public

Some retailers prize locations where they can battle competitors toe-to-toe; ALCO Stores (formerly Duckwall-ALCO) covets locations big national discounters such as Wal-Mart and Target won't even consider. The retailer runs some 200 ALCO and ALCO Market Place discount stores in small towns in some two dozen states primarily in the central US. Situated in towns with populations of 5000 or fewer ALCO stores offer a broad line of merchandise that includes automotive apparel consumables crafts electronics fabrics furniture hardware health and beauty aids toys and more. The company closed all of its smaller Duckwall stores to focus on growing its larger and more profitable ALCO chain.

	Annual Growth	01/10	01/11	01/12*	02/13	02/14
Sales ($ mil.)	(0.8%)	488.7	465.2	482.8	492.6	474.1
Net income ($ mil.)	–	3.0	(4.6)	1.7	1.3	(26.4)
Market value ($ mil.)	(7.1%)	39.7	44.2	28.3	27.6	29.6
Employees	(5.6%)	4,150	3,460	3,700	3,400	3,300

*Fiscal year change

ALCOA, INC.

390 Park Avenue
New York, NY 10022-4608
Phone: 212 836-2732
Fax: –
Web: www.alcoa.com

NYS: AA
CEO: Klaus Kleinfeld
CFO: William F. (Bill) Oplinger
HR: Vas Nair
FYE: December 31
Type: Public

While many of its aluminum products may be lightweight Alcoa is anything but. It is one of the world's top producers of alumina (aluminum's principal ingredient from bauxite) and aluminum. Operations include bauxite mining alumina refining and aluminum smelting; products include alumina and alumina-based chemicals automotive components and sheet aluminum for beverage cans. Markets include the aerospace automotive and construction industries. Non-aluminum products include precision castings and aerospace and industrial fasteners. In 2015 the company announced plans to separate into two public companies — an upstream company (aluminum production) and a value-add company (aluminum products) — by mid-2016.

	Annual Growth	12/10	12/11	12/12	12/13	12/14
Sales ($ mil.)	3.3%	21,013.0	24,951.0	23,700.0	23,032.0	23,906.0
Net income ($ mil.)	1.4%	254.0	611.0	191.0	(2,285.0)	268.0
Market value ($ mil.)	0.6%	18,724.5	10,524.1	10,560.6	12,933.1	19,211.1
Employees	0.0%	59,000	61,000	61,000	60,000	59,000

ALDA OFFICE PROPERTIES INC.

315 S. Beverly Dr. Ste. 211
Los Angeles CA 90212
Phone: 310-734-2300
Fax: 925-474-2599
Web: www.coolsculpting.com

CEO: Richard S Ackerman
CFO: –
HR: –
FYE: December 31
Type: Private

California just may be the land of opportunity for ALDA Office Properties. The real estate company is focused on acquiring owning and operating office properties primarily in Northern and Southern California. Having formed as a new business in 2011 it filed to go public that same year with the intent of acquiring office properties that are 300000 sq. ft. or smaller in such markets as Los Angeles Orange County and San Francisco. Upon completion of its $18 million IPO ALDA Office Properties' initial portfolio will consist of a leasehold interest in a property in Beverly Hills California totaling 68000 sq. ft. The company intends to eventually qualify as an office real estate investment trust (REIT).

ALDAGEN INC.

2810 Meridian Pkwy. Ste. 148
Durham NC 27713
Phone: 919-484-2571
Fax: 919-484-8792
Web: www.aldagen.com

CEO: –
CFO: –
HR: –
FYE: December 31
Type: Subsidiary

Aldagen's work stems from the need for tissue repair. The biopharmaceutical company develops cell regeneration therapies using adult stem cells. It uses a proprietary technology that isolates an enzyme known as aldehyde dehydrogenase or ALDH which it believes can target a number of diseases. Aldagen hopes its products will be used to treat ailments such as cardiovascular conditions hereditary metabolic diseases in children and leukemia; all its drugs are in the development stage. The company does its own manufacturing and plans to do its own marketing. The company was acquired by Cytomedix in 2012.

ALDRIDGE ELECTRIC INC.

844 E ROCKLAND RD
LIBERTYVILLE, IL 600483358
Phone: 847-680-5200
Fax: –
Web: www.aldridge-electric.com

CEO: Steven Rivi
CFO: –
HR: –
FYE: March 31
Type: Private

Aldridge Electric powers up the Windy City and other parts of the Midwest. The electrical contractor divides its business into six main areas: airport industrial power drilling highway and transit. It works on projects ranging from Chicago's subway system to its airport runways. Additional activities include services for street lighting traffic signals high-voltage cabling and splicing and foundation drilling. Aldridge Electric has worked for clients such as Commonwealth Edison Company and Exelon Corporation. It sister companies in the family-owned AldridgeGroup include Aldridge Construction GFS Construction and Woodward Brothering.

	Annual Growth	03/07	03/08	03/09	03/10	03/11
Sales ($ mil.)	(23.2%)	–	–	–	272.2	208.9
Net income ($ mil.)	(79.8%)	–	–	–	10.5	2.1
Market value ($ mil.)	–	–	–	–	–	–
Employees	–	–	–	–	–	500

ALERE INC.

51 Sawyer Road, Suite 200
Waltham, MA 02453
Phone: 781 647-3900
Fax: 781 647-3939
Web: www.alere.com

NYS: ALR
CEO: Namal Nawana
CFO: James F. (Jim) Hinrichs
HR: –
FYE: December 31
Type: Public

When you really need an answer — fast — toss out the crystal ball and bring in Alere. The company offers both professional and consumer diagnostic tests. Its professional diagnostic products include tests for cancers cardiovascular disease drugs of abuse infectious diseases and women's health including pregnancy tests and fertility monitors. Alere also makes consumer diagnostics including First Check drug tests through a venture with Procter & Gamble. Branded products include Actim (early pregnancy detection) Cholestech (lipid and cholesterol testing) and Determine (HIV tuberculosis hepatitis B and syphilis detection). Abbott Laboratories is buying Alere for $5.8 billion.

	Annual Growth	12/10	12/11	12/12	12/13	12/14
Sales ($ mil.)	4.7%	2,155.3	2,386.5	2,818.8	3,029.4	2,586.7
Net income ($ mil.)	–	(1,017.3)	(133.5)	(78.2)	(71.3)	9.9
Market value ($ mil.)	0.9%	3,069.0	1,936.2	1,551.3	3,035.5	3,186.4
Employees	(4.7%)	11,900	14,500	17,400	17,600	9,800

ALERIS CORP

25825 Science Park Drive, Suite 400
Cleveland, OH 44122-7392
Phone: 216 910-3400
Fax: –
Web: www.aleris.com

NL:
CEO: Sean M. Stack
CFO: Eric M. Rychel
HR: Thomas W. Weidenkopf
FYE: December 31
Type: Public

Aleris (which conducts its business through Aleris International) wants you to use your blue recycling bin so that it can turn your world (and its world) green. The company's rolled and extruded products unit makes aluminum products for manufacturers operating in most major industries (including aerospace automotive building and construction distribution molding and tooling and transportation). Aleris operates some 39 production facilities across North America Europe and China. To raise cash in 2015 the company sold its North American and European Recycling and Specification Alloys businesses to an affiliate of Signature Group Holdings for $525 million.

	Annual Growth	12/10	12/11	12/12	12/13	12/14
Sales ($ mil.)	3.9%	2,474.1	4,826.4	4,412.4	4,332.5	2,882.4
Net income ($ mil.)	5.1%	71.4	161.6	107.5	(37.1)	87.1
Market value ($ mil.)	–	–	–	–	–	–
Employees	(15.8%)	–	–	7,200	7,200	5,100

ALERIS CORPORATION

25825 Science Park Dr. Ste. 400
Beachwood OH 44122-7392
Phone: 216-910-3400
Fax: 216-910-3650
Web: www.aleris.com

CEO: –
CFO: –
HR: –
FYE: December 31
Type: Private

Aleris Corporation (formerly Aleris International) wants you to use your blue recycling bin so that it can turn your world (and its world) green. The company's rolled and extruded products unit makes aluminum products for manufacturers operating in most major industries (including aerospace automotive building and construction distribution molding and tooling and transportation) while its recycling unit processes recycled aluminum alloys and other scrap metals. Aleris operates more than 40 production facilities across North America Europe and China.

ALEX LEE INC.

120 4th St. SW
Hickory NC 28602
Phone: 828-725-4424
Fax: 828-725-4435
Web: www.alexlee.com

CEO: Boyd L George
CFO: Ronald W Knedlik
HR: –
FYE: September 30
Type: Private

The business of wholesaling groceries is only part of the bigger picture for Alex Lee. The company is a leading distributor of food and other products to retailers and foodservice operators. Its primary Merchants Distributors Inc. (MDI) subsidiary supplies food and general merchandise to more than 600 retailers in nearly a dozen mostly southeastern states. MDI's own Consolidation Services business provides warehousing and logistics services. As part of its business Alex Lee also operates Lowe's Food Stores a chain of more than 100 grocery stores located in the Carolinas and Virginia. Alex and Lee George started the company in 1931. The George family continues to control Alex Lee.

ALEXANDER & BALDWIN INC.

NYS: ALEX

822 Bishop Street
Honolulu, HI 96813
Phone: 808 525-6611
Fax: -
Web: www.alexanderbaldwin.com

CEO: Stanley M. Kuriyama
CFO: Paul K. Ito
HR: Son-Jai Paik
FYE: December 31
Type: Public

Alexander & Baldwin (A&B) is all about its real estate and agribusiness operations in The Aloha State. Its A&B Properties subsidiary engages in real estate development and property management for commercial properties both in Hawaii and eight states on the US mainland. It owns 87000 acres of land in Hawaii primarily on the islands of Maui and Kauai. In addition the company produces sugarcane molasses and sugar products (under the Maui Brand) through its Hawaiian Commercial & Sugar Company. In mid-2012 A&B separated from its former ocean transportation subsidiary Matson which carries freight mainly between ports in Hawaii Guam China Alaska and Puerto Rico and the continental US.

	Annual Growth	12/10	12/11	12/12	12/13	12/14
Sales ($ mil.)	20.8%	263.0	268.7	296.7	365.2	560.0
Net income ($ mil.)	16.7%	33.1	23.5	20.5	36.9	61.4
Market value ($ mil.)	15.6%	-	-	1,433.3	2,036.4	1,915.9
Employees	16.1%	-	961	946	1,446	1,502

ALEXANDER AND HORNUNG INC.

20643 STEPHENS ST
SAINT CLAIR SHORES, MI 480801047
Phone: 586-771-9880
Fax: -
Web: www.alexanderhornung.com

CEO: -
CFO: -
HR: -
FYE: December 31
Type: Private

You might say this company is trying to be the best of the wurst. Alexander & Hornung is a popular sausage maker that has been serving the Detroit area since 1945. The company makes a variety of bratwursts knockwursts and hot dogs as well as Polish sausages bologna and salami. It also offers bacon ham and deli meats. In addition it owns Brookside Foods (deli meats) Bosell Foods (deli salads) and Gateway Specialty Foods (meat brokerage). Alexander & Hornung distributes its food products to retail grocers and deli stores throughout the US; it also operates a retail meat store in Detroit. The family-owned business was started by butchers Erich and Willie Alexander and sausage maker Otto Hornung.

	Annual Growth	12/09	12/10	12/11	12/12	12/13
Sales ($ mil.)	11.3%	-	-	-	26.4	29.3
Net income ($ mil.)	(40.5%)	-	-	-	0.6	0.4
Market value ($ mil.)	-	-	-	-	-	-
Employees	-	-	-	-	-	100

ALEXANDER'S, INC.

NYS: ALX

210 Route 4 East
Paramus, NJ 07652
Phone: 201 587-8541
Fax: 201 708-6214
Web: www.alx-inc.com

CEO: Steven Roth
CFO: Joseph Macnow
HR: -
FYE: December 31
Type: Public

Alexander's knows what's great about real estate. The real estate investment trust (REIT) owns manages and leases about a half-dozen properties totaling about 2.2 million sq. ft. of leasable space in metropolitan New York City. Once a department store chain Alexander's held on to its property interests including the site of its erstwhile flagship store — an entire block on Manhattan's Lexington Avenue. The REIT leases space at the mixed-use site to tenants such as Bloomberg The Home Depot The Container Store and Hennes & Mauritz. The Lexington site is also home to about 105 condominiums. Bloomberg accounts for about a third of the REIT's revenues. Vornado Realty Trust owns 32% of the company.

	Annual Growth	12/11	12/12	12/13	12/14	12/15
Sales ($ mil.)	(4.9%)	254.3	191.3	196.5	200.8	207.9
Net income ($ mil.)	(0.8%)	79.4	674.4	56.9	67.9	76.9
Market value ($ mil.)	0.9%	1,889.4	1,689.1	1,685.0	2,232.3	1,961.3
Employees	(8.7%)	105	72	72	68	73

ALEXANDRIA EXTRUSION COMPANY

401 COUNTY ROAD 22 NW
ALEXANDRIA, MN 563084974
Phone: 320-762-7657
Fax: -
Web: www.alexandriaindustries.com

CEO: Tom Schabel
CFO: Marc Illies
HR: Deb Moorman
FYE: December 31
Type: Private

Alexandria Extrusion Company (doing business as Alexandria Industries) makes precision aluminum extruded products such as custom front panels and heat sinks. The company's services include assembly CNC (computerized numerical control) machining finishing stretch forming and welding. Alexandria Industries markets its products to companies in a variety of industries such as electronics medical equipment power tools telecommunications and transportation. The company has expanded its offerings through acquisitions including those of aluminum specialty extruder M&M Metals and precision component maker Doege Precision Machining both in 2008. CEO Tom Schabel owns the company which was founded in 1966.

	Annual Growth	12/09	12/10	12/11	12/12	12/13
Sales ($ mil.)	18.5%	-	62.5	72.2	85.3	104.0
Net income ($ mil.)	-	-	-	0.0	0.0	0.0
Market value ($ mil.)	-	-	-	-	-	-
Employees	-	-	-	-	-	350

ALEXANDRIA INOVA HOSPITAL

4320 SEMINARY RD
ALEXANDRIA, VA 223041535
Phone: 703-504-3000
Fax: -
Web: www.inova.org

CEO: -
CFO: Thomas Knight
HR: Bernardine Dunn
FYE: December 31
Type: Private

Inova Alexandria Hospital provides medical surgical and therapeutic services in northeastern Virginia. The hospital was founded in 1872 and became part of the not-for-profit Inova Health System in 1997. Inova Alexandria Hospital has about 320 beds. The hospital offers specialty services such as heart and cancer treatment women's and children's health care emergency medicine vascular procedures interventional radiology and sleep disorder and heartburn treatment services. The Inova Health System provides health care services in northern Virginia through a network of hospitals clinics assisted living centers and other provider facilities.

	Annual Growth	12/00	12/01	12/05	12/06	12/08
Sales ($ mil.)	6.2%	-	180.9	233.8	247.1	276.2
Net income ($ mil.)	2.8%	-	-	22.9	22.7	24.9
Market value ($ mil.)	-	-	-	-	-	-
Employees	-	-	-	-	-	1,750

ALEXANDRIA REAL ESTATE EQUITIES, INC.

NYS: ARE

385 East Colorado Boulevard, Suite 299
Pasadena, CA 91101
Phone: 626 578-0777
Fax: -
Web: www.are.com

CEO: Joel S. Marcus
CFO: Dean A. Shigenaga
HR: -
FYE: December 31
Type: Public

The pearl of the Mediterranean might be found in Egypt but the pearls of science are typically found in the lab. Alexandria Real Estate Equities owns develops and operates offices and labs to life science tenants including biotech and pharmaceutical companies universities research institutions medical office developers and government agencies. A real estate investment trust (REIT) Alexandria owns approximately 170 specialized properties with more than 15 million sq. ft. of rentable space in the US and Canada. Its portfolio is largely located in high-tech hotbeds such as Boston greater New York City the San Francisco Bay area San Diego Seattle and suburban Washington DC.

	Annual Growth	12/11	12/12	12/13	12/14	12/15
Sales ($ mil.)	10.1%	573.4	586.1	631.2	726.9	843.5
Net income ($ mil.)	1.6%	135.4	105.5	140.2	106.8	144.2
Market value ($ mil.)	7.0%	5,003.7	5,029.1	4,615.5	6,438.0	6,555.5
Employees	7.0%	212	217	215	243	278

ALEXION PHARMACEUTICALS INC.

NMS: ALXN

100 College Street
New Haven, CT 06510
Phone: 203 272-2596
Fax: –
Web: www.alxn.com

CEO: David L. Hallal
CFO: Vikas Sinha
HR: Clare M. Carmichael
FYE: December 31
Type: Public

Alexion Pharmaceuticals can't suppress its enthusiasm for treating immune functions gone awry. The firm develops drugs that inhibit certain immune system functions that cause rare hematology nephrology oncology neurology inflammatory and metabolic disorders. The company's first marketed antibody product Soliris has won approval in the US Canada and some European and Asian countries for the treatment of two rare genetic blood disorders known as paroxysmal nocturnal hemoglobinuria (PNH) and atypical hemolytic uremic syndrome (aHUS). Alexion is also developing Soliris as a potential treatment for other kidney and neurology conditions and it has development programs for other disease-fighting antibodies.

	Annual Growth	12/11	12/12	12/13	12/14	12/15
Sales ($ mil.)	35.0%	783.4	1,134.1	1,551.3	2,233.7	2,604.0
Net income ($ mil.)	(4.7%)	175.3	254.8	252.9	656.9	144.4
Market value ($ mil.)	27.8%	16,133.8	21,152.1	29,984.9	41,751.5	43,042.2
Employees	30.5%	1,008	1,373	1,774	2,273	2,924

ALEXZA PHARMACEUTICALS INC

NAS: ALXA

2091 Stierlin Court
Mountain View, CA 94043
Phone: 650 944-7000
Fax: –
Web: www.alexza.com

CEO: Thomas B King
CFO: Mark K Oki
HR: –
FYE: December 31
Type: Public

Alexza Pharmaceuticals has found that its inhalation technologies can lead to swifter drug absorption. That is the basis for the company's primary product Staccato inhalers which it is developing to treat central nervous system (CNS) disorders. The inhalers contain a heating element coated with a thin layer of medicine. Before use the patient triggers the heating element which vaporizes the medicine allowing the patient to inhale it. The medicine is then rapidly absorbed through the lungs at a rate typically faster than oral and intravenous applications. Alexza Pharmaceuticals targets neurological disorders including addiction and anxiety.

	Annual Growth	12/10	12/11	12/12	12/13	12/14
Sales ($ mil.)	(40.0%)	42.9	5.7	4.1	47.8	5.6
Net income ($ mil.)	–	(1.5)	(40.5)	(28.0)	(39.6)	(36.7)
Market value ($ mil.)	4.4%	24.3	16.1	96.1	91.8	28.9
Employees	(4.4%)	97	44	63	90	81

ALFA CORPORATION

2108 E. South Blvd.
Montgomery AL 36116
Phone: 334-288-3900
Fax: 334-613-4709
Web: www.alfains.com

CEO: Jerry A Newby
CFO: Stephen G Grutledge
HR: –
FYE: December 31
Type: Private

Alfa Corporation wants to be top dog in Alabama's insurance pack. As part of the Alfa Mutual group of companies (Alfa Mutual Insurance Alfa Mutual Fire Insurance and Alfa Mutual General Insurance) Alfa Corporation primarily provides auto homeowners and other personal property/casualty insurance in about a dozen central and southeastern states. It also offers life insurance policies in its core markets of Alabama Georgia and Mississippi. The company which has nearly 400 office locations enjoys a pooling arrangement between all of the Alfa companies.

ALFRED UNIVERSITY

1 SAXON DR
ALFRED, NY 148021232
Phone: 607-871-2963
Fax: –
Web: www.alfred.edu

CEO: –
CFO: –
HR: –
FYE: June 30
Type: Private

Alfred University was a progressive bastion of learning from the start. A private university in Western New York the small non-sectarian school serves about 2400 students. Its academic programs range from the liberal arts and sciences to engineering business and art and design with degrees from a bachelor's to a Ph.D. The school also houses the New York State College of Ceramics. The student-faculty ratio is 12-to-1. The university was founded as the Select School in 1836 providing a coeducational environment from the school's beginnings. Alfred University (and the village it's in) is named for Alfred the Great ninth-century ruler of southern England. Its mascot is of course the Saxons.

	Annual Growth	06/10	06/11	06/12	06/13	06/14
Sales ($ mil.)	(2.5%)	–	68.6	64.7	64.2	63.5
Net income ($ mil.)	103.1%	–	–	2.7	12.5	11.1
Market value ($ mil.)	–	–	–	–	–	–
Employees	–	–	–	–	–	530

ALICO, INC.

NMS: ALCO

10070 Daniels Interstate Court, Suite 100
Fort Myers, FL 33913
Phone: 239 226-2000
Fax: –
Web: www.alicoinc.com

CEO: Clayton G. (Clay) Wilson
CFO: W. Mark Humphrey
HR: –
FYE: September 30
Type: Public

Alico is bullish on cattle but citrus generates more revenue. The agribusiness company which owns more than 130000 acres of farm land in Florida dabbles in sugarcane citrus and sod and native plant production as well as land leasing and conservation. Alico's citrus is packed or processed with fruit from other growers through produce marketer Ben Hill Griffin. It has a breeding herd of approximately 8700 cows and bulls and it sells stock primarily to meat packing and processing plants. Alico's sugarcane is sold through a pooling agreement with a nearby sugar mill; sod is marketed through a US wholesaler. Alico is majority owned by the New York investment firm 734 Agriculture LLC and the Arlon Group.

	Annual Growth	09/11	09/12	09/13	09/14	09/15
Sales ($ mil.)	11.6%	98.6	127.2	101.7	88.7	153.1
Net income ($ mil.)	22.0%	7.1	18.5	19.6	8.1	15.7
Market value ($ mil.)	19.9%	163.5	260.0	342.8	317.2	337.9
Employees	26.8%	134	157	154	128	346

ALIENWARE CORPORATION

14591 SW 120th St.
Miami FL 33186-8638
Phone: 305-251-9797
Fax: 305-259-9874
Web: www.alienware.com

CEO: Arthur R Lewis Jr
CFO: –
HR: –
FYE: December 31
Type: Subsidiary

Aliens have landed in Florida and they're spreading! Relax they come in peace. Based in Miami Alienware caters to consumer video game enthusiasts in the market for high-performance gaming PCs with striking case designs. Sporting names like Area-51 and Aurora the company's colorfully appointed systems utilize processors video cards and storage components optimized for gaming applications. Its PC's are further differentiated by customized cases upgraded power supplies and multiple cooling fans. The company has branch facilities in Australia Costa Rica and Ireland. Alienware is a subsidiary of Dell.

ALIGN AEROSPACE LLC

21123 Nordhoff St.
Chatsworth CA 91311
Phone: 818-727-7800
Fax: 818-773-5493
Web: www.alignaero.com

CEO: -
CFO: -
HR: -
FYE: December 31
Type: Private

Align Aerospace (formerly Anixter Aerospace Hardware) isn't deploying any troops just scads of aircraft fasteners. The company distributes threaded fasteners for Airbus Boeing and military planes and related components such as bolts nuts screws and studs. In addition to distribution services the company also offers testing supply chain management inventory management kitting assembly and related services. Its customers are primarily aerospace and military manufacturers. The company has distribution hubs in Canada France and the US and a sales office in the UK. Former parent Anixter International sold the company to investment firm Greenbriar Equity Group in 2011.

ALIGN TECHNOLOGY INC

NMS: ALGN

2560 Orchard Parkway
San Jose, CA 95131
Phone: 408 470-1000
Fax: -
Web: www.aligntech.com

CEO: Joseph M. (Joe) Hogan
CFO: David L. White
HR: -
FYE: December 31
Type: Public

Brace-face begone! Align Technology produces and sells the Invisalign system which corrects malocclusion or crooked teeth. Instead of using metal or ceramic mounts that are cemented on the teeth and connected by wires (traditional braces) the system involves using an array of clear and removable dental Aligners to move a patient's teeth into a desired alignment. The company markets its products to orthodontists and dentists worldwide. Align also provides training for practitioners to model treatment schemes using its online ClinCheck application which simulates tooth movement and suggests the appropriate Aligner. It also makes and sells orthodontic scanning and CAD (computer-assisted design) devices.

	Annual Growth	12/10	12/11	12/12	12/13	12/14
Sales ($ mil.)	18.4%	387.1	479.7	560.0	660.2	761.7
Net income ($ mil.)	18.4%	74.3	66.7	58.7	64.3	145.8
Market value ($ mil.)	30.1%	1,567.2	1,902.9	2,225.7	4,582.9	4,484.3
Employees	14.3%	2,097	2,593	3,176	3,420	3,580

ALIMERA SCIENCES, INC.

NMS: ALIM

6120 Windward Parkway, Suite 290
Alpharetta, GA 30005
Phone: 678 990-5740
Fax: -
Web: www.alimerasciences.com

CEO: C. Daniel (Dan) Myers
CFO: Richard S. (Rick) Eiswirth
HR: -
FYE: December 31
Type: Public

Alimera Sciences wants to see clear into the future. The biopharmaceutical company is developing prescription ophthalmic pharmaceuticals particularly those aimed at treating ocular diseases affecting the retina. Alimera's most advanced product candidate Iluvien is an insert smaller than a grain of rice that slowly releases a corticosteroid to the back of the eye to treat diabetic macular edema (DME). DME a retinal disease affecting diabetics can lead to severe vision loss and blindness. The company had hoped to gain FDA approval for the drug in 2011; however a major setback occurred late that year when federal regulators chose to delay approval and request more expensive clinical trials.

	Annual Growth	12/10	12/11	12/12	12/13	12/14
Sales ($ mil.)	349.9%	-	-	-	1.9	8.4
Net income ($ mil.)	-	(13.9)	(22.5)	(19.7)	(46.2)	(35.9)
Market value ($ mil.)	(14.5%)	460.0	55.4	69.6	208.3	245.5
Employees	40.4%	27	21	25	31	105

ALINABAL HOLDINGS CORPORATION

28 WOODMONT RD
MILFORD, CT 064602872
Phone: 203-877-3241
Fax: -
Web: www.alinabal.com

CEO: -
CFO: Kevin M Conlisk
HR: Steve Bennett
FYE: December 28
Type: Private

Alinabal Holdings operates through its individual business units that serve the automotive aerospace and printing industries. Alinabal Motion Transfer Devices manufactures spherical bearings stamped molded bearing and linkage assemblies and standard/custom rod ends. Alinabal Engineered Products produces complex mechanical assemblies and precision stampings. Its Alinabal Practical Automation unit provides printers (for use in ticket kiosks and ATMs) and the company also makes aircraft instrumentation (desiccators and dehumidifiers) and optical shutters (aka "beam blockers") through its DACO Instrument subsidiary. Alinabal was founded in 1913.

	Annual Growth	01/10	01/11*	12/11	12/12	12/13
Sales ($ mil.)	7.7%	-	47.7	52.8	58.4	55.4
Net income ($ mil.)	(54.7%)	-	-	1.4	0.8	0.3
Market value ($ mil.)	-	-	-	-	-	-
Employees	-	-	-	-	-	340

*Fiscal year change

ALION SCIENCE AND TECHNOLOGY CORPORATION

1750 Tysons Blvd. Ste. 1300
McLean VA 22102
Phone: 703-918-4480
Fax: 703-714-6508
Web: www.alionscience.com

CEO: Bahman Atefi
CFO: Barry Broadus
HR: -
FYE: September 30
Type: Private

Alion creates alliances between science and big government. Alion Science and Technology is an employee-owned development and research company that provides scientific engineering and information technology research and consulting services primarily to federal agencies. More than 90% of its revenue comes from contracts with the US Department of Defense (DOD) especially the Navy. Focusing on national defense homeland security energy and the environment Alion specializes in naval architecture and marine engineering defense operations modeling and simulations technology integration and wireless communications.

ALIXPARTNERS LLP

2000 Town Center Ste. 2400
Southfield MI 48075
Phone: 248-358-4420
Fax: 248-358-1969
Web: www.alixpartners.com

CEO: Fred Crawford
CFO: Doug Barnett
HR: -
FYE: October 1/
Type: Private

Company headed in the wrong direction? AlixPartners would like to try to help you turn things around. The consulting firm provides operational and financial advisory services to underperforming companies worldwide. Specialties include assistance with bankruptcy reorganizations and litigation. AlixPartners also offers performance improvement and strategic consulting services for healthy companies. The firm operates from more than a dozen offices not only in the US but also in Europe and the Asia/Pacific region. Private equity firm Hellman & Friedman together with AlixPartners employees owns a controlling stake in the turnaround firm.

ALJ REGIONAL HOLDINGS INC
NBB: ALJJ

244 Madison Avenue, PMB #358
New York, NY 10016
Phone: 212 883-0083
Fax: 606 929-1261

CEO: John Scheel
CFO: T Robert Christ
HR: –
FYE: September 30
Type: Public

ALJ Regional Holdings owns a steel mini-mill in Kentucky which it acquired in 2005. The mill is operated by Kentucky Electric Steel which produces bar flat products that it sells to service centers as well as makers of truck trailers steel springs and cold drawn bars. Kentucky Electric Steel produces steel in both Merchant Bar Quality and Special Bar Quality. The company also recycles steel from scrap to produce steel. Kentucky Electric Steel operates mainly in the US Canada and Mexico.

	Annual Growth	09/05	09/06	09/10	09/11	09/12
Sales ($ mil.)	12.6%	69.2	139.8	112.8	162.0	158.8
Net income ($ mil.)	–	(3.4)	2.4	5.7	11.4	13.3
Market value ($ mil.)	22.2%	5.7	9.7	14.8	25.2	23.2
Employees	0.9%	143	146	–	–	152

ALL AMERICAN CONTAINERS INC.

9330 NW 110TH AVE
MEDLEY, FL 331782519
Phone: 305-913-0620
Fax: –
Web: www.allamericancontainers.com

CEO: Fausto Diaz-Oliver
CFO: Amparo Alvarez
HR: –
FYE: December 31
Type: Private

It has become an All American pastime to put liquid consumer products (everything from beer to honey to cleaning products) in safe sturdy and attractive containers. All American Containers supports this tradition by making containers for the beverage chemical cosmetic food liquor perfume and pharmaceutical industries. The manufacturer's range of products includes glass plastic and metal tubes and dispensers and plastic and metal closures. The company exports its products to more than 50 countries around the world. Major customers include Coca-Cola McCormick PepsiCo and Seven-Up. All American Containers was founded by female Floridian and CEO Remedios Diaz-Oliver in 1991.

	Annual Growth	12/01	12/02	12/03	12/06	12/07
Sales ($ mil.)	2.7%	–	96.0	104.0	102.1	109.7
Net income ($ mil.)	14.5%	–	–	2.3	5.9	4.0
Market value ($ mil.)	–	–	–	–	–	–
Employees	–	–	–	–	–	202

ALL AMERICAN GROUP INC.

2831 Dexter Dr.
Elkhart IN 46514
Phone: 574-266-2500
Fax: 574-266-2559
Web: www.allamericangroupinc.com

CEO: –
CFO: –
HR: –
FYE: December 31
Type: Private

All American Group makes modular housing and other structures. The company's residential housing segment includes the All American Homes and Mod-U-Kraf Homes subsidiaries which build one-story ranch homes and two-story colonials. Its Ameri-Log Homes brand makes log homes and a line of energy-efficient houses are sold under the Solar Village banner. Subsidiary Innovative Design and Building Serives specializes in larger-scale housing projects such as apartments hotels and military and student housing. All American Group also sells a line of wheelchair-accessible buses through a joint venture with ARBOC Mobility. H.I.G. Capital acquired All American Group in 2011.

ALL AMERICAN SEMICONDUCTOR LLC

16115 NW 52nd Ave.
Miami FL 33014-9317
Phone: 305-621-8282
Fax: 305-620-7831
Web: www.allamerican.com

CEO: –
CFO: –
HR: Jeff Siegelman
FYE: December 31
Type: Private

They couldn't be more patriotic at All American Semiconductor. They take pride in distributing electronic components from more than 55 suppliers. The company primarily sells active semiconductor components such as transistors diodes integrated circuits microprocessors and memory products; it also offers passive components including capacitors resistors and switches. After filing for Chapter 11 protection from creditors All American sold substantially all of its assets to Rock River Capital for about $15 million. In 2008 Rock River Capital brought in new management to run the company.

ALL POINTS COOPERATIVE

120 8TH ST
GOTHENBURG, NE 691381006
Phone: 308-537-7141
Fax: –
Web: www.allpoints.coop

CEO: Ed E Foster
CFO: Michael Schroeder
HR: –
FYE: September 30
Type: Private

All Points Cooperative provides agricultural support services to farmers and ranchers in central Nebraska. The cooperative offers seed energy fuel agronomy storage and purchasing services along with financial credit marketing and purchasing assistance for its member/farmers. Its agronomy services include fertilizer application soil sampling and crop planning and management. Its energy division offers bulk fuel bulk oil heating oil and propane delivery. It also operates retail outlets including two Ampride Convenience Stores and the Trustworthy Feed and Hardware Store. In addition to its headquarters in Gothenburg Nebraska All Points has cooperative operations in 12 other communities.

	Annual Growth	09/04	09/05	09/06	09/08	09/12
Sales ($ mil.)	–	–	0.0	91.7	192.9	236.1
Net income ($ mil.)	–	–	–	0.0	10.8	7.6
Market value ($ mil.)	–	–	–	–	–	–
Employees	–	–	–	–	–	150

ALL-AMERICAN SPORTPARK INC.
NBB: AASP

6730 South Las Vegas Boulevard
Las Vegas, NV 89119
Phone: 702 798-7777
Fax: 702 896-9754

CEO: –
CFO: –
HR: –
FYE: December 31
Type: Public

If golf is your sport then this company has a park for you. All-American Sport-Park operates Callaway Golf Center (CGC) a 42-acre golf practice facility located at the end of the famous Las Vegas Strip. Amenities include 110 driving stations in two tiers and a lighted nine-hole par-three golf course called the Divine Nine. The center also features a restaurant and St. Andrews Golf Shop where customers can buy golf equipment and related merchandise. The founding Boreta family owns more than 20% of the company. Tennis pro Andre Agassi and partner Perry Rogers together also own almost 20% of All-American SportPark.

	Annual Growth	12/10	12/11	12/12	12/13	12/14
Sales ($ mil.)	2.1%	2.0	2.1	2.1	2.1	2.1
Net income ($ mil.)	–	(0.9)	(0.7)	(0.9)	(0.9)	(0.7)
Market value ($ mil.)	38.7%	1.0	0.7	0.5	4.7	3.7
Employees	57.8%	5	35	30	30	31

ALLEGHANY CORP.

7 Times Square Tower, 17th Floor
New York, NY 10036
Phone: 212 752-1356
Fax: 212 759-8149
Web: www.alleghany.com

CEO: Stephen J. Sills
CFO: John L. (Jack) Sennott
HR: –
FYE: December 31
Type: Public

NYS: Y

After a spell as a conglomerate with interests ranging from minerals to steel fasteners Alleghany found that it really prefers property/casualty insurance with a smattering of good old real estate. Alleghany's subsidiaries include Transatlantic Holdings (TransRe) which offers property/casualty reinsurance (risk coverage for insurers) globally through Transatlantic Reinsurance Fair American and Trans Re Zurich. The company also issues specialty property/casualty insurance policies through RSUI Group and Capitol Transamerica (CATA). Alleghany's offerings are marketed in the US and abroad.

	Annual Growth	12/10	12/11	12/12	12/13	12/14
Assets ($ mil.)	38.2%	6,431.7	6,478.1	22,808.0	23,361.1	23,489.4
Net income ($ mil.)	36.0%	198.5	143.3	702.2	628.4	679.2
Market value ($ mil.)	10.9%	4,918.6	4,580.1	5,384.9	6,421.1	7,441.2
Employees	29.1%	745	763	1,506	1,985	2,067

ALLEGHENY COLLEGE

520 N MAIN ST
MEADVILLE, PA 163353902
Phone: 814-332-3100
Fax: –
Web: www.allegheny.edu

CEO: –
CFO: David McInally
HR: –
FYE: June 30
Type: Private

Allegheny College ranks among the oldest colleges and universities in the US. The private co-educational liberal arts school was founded in 1815 with a class of just four students. Today approximately 2100 enrolled students can pursue Bachelor of Arts and Bachelor of Science degrees in more than 50 academic programs including art biology communications computer science English history math music philosophy psychology and religious studies. It also offers accelerated master's and doctorate programs in partnership with other universities. Though the college is non-sectarian it maintains a historic affiliation with the United Methodist Church.

	Annual Growth	06/09	06/10	06/11	06/12	06/13
Sales ($ mil.)	(9.4%)	–	111.9	130.6	78.8	83.3
Net income ($ mil.)	(9.0%)	–	–	23.4	(9.8)	19.4
Market value ($ mil.)	–	–	–	–	–	–
Employees	–	–	–	–	–	479

ALLEGHENY TECHNOLOGIES, INC

1000 Six PPG Place
Pittsburgh, PA 15222-5479
Phone: 412 394-2800
Fax: –
Web: www.atimetals.com

CEO: Richard J. (Rich) Harshman
CFO: Patrick J. DeCourcy
HR: –
FYE: December 31
Type: Public

NYS: ATI

Allegheny Technologies Inc. (ATI) is on a roll when it comes to producing metals. The company manufactures stainless and specialty steels nickel- and cobalt-based alloys and superalloys titanium and titanium alloys tungsten materials and such exotic alloys as niobium and zirconium. The company's flat-rolled products (sheet strip and plate) accounted for 52% of its sales in 2014. Its high-performance metals unit produces metal bar coil foil ingot plate rod and wire. ATI's largest markets include the aerospace chemical process and oil and gas industries.

	Annual Growth	12/10	12/11	12/12	12/13	12/14
Sales ($ mil.)	1.1%	4,047.8	5,183.0	5,031.5	4,043.5	4,223.4
Net income ($ mil.)	–	70.7	214.3	158.4	154.0	(2.6)
Market value ($ mil.)	(10.9%)	5,998.7	5,196.4	3,300.5	3,873.4	3,779.9
Employees	1.3%	9,200	11,400	11,200	9,500	9,700

ALLEGIANT TRAVEL COMPANY

1201 North Town Center Drive
Las Vegas, NV 89144
Phone: 702 851-7300
Fax: –
Web: www.allegiant.com

CEO: Maurice J. (Maury) Gallagher
CFO: D. Scott Sheldon
HR: –
FYE: December 31
Type: Public

NMS: ALGT

Allegiant Travel pledges to serve the vacation needs of residents of more than 60 small US cities in 35 states. Through Allegiant Air the company provides nonstop service to tourist destinations such as Las Vegas Los Angeles and Orlando Florida from places such as Cedar Rapids Iowa; Fargo North Dakota; and Toledo Ohio. It maintains a fleet of about 50 MD-80 series aircraft. Besides scheduled service Allegiant Air offers charter flights for casino operators Caesars Entertainment (formerly Harrah's Entertainment) and MGM MIRAGE in addition to other customers. Sister company Allegiant Vacations works with partners to allow customers to book hotel rooms and rental cars along with their airline tickets.

	Annual Growth	12/10	12/11	12/12	12/13	12/14
Sales ($ mil.)	14.4%	663.6	779.1	908.7	996.2	1,137.0
Net income ($ mil.)	7.2%	65.7	49.4	78.6	92.3	86.7
Market value ($ mil.)	32.2%	857.4	928.8	1,278.3	1,836.1	2,617.7
Employees	8.9%	1,826	1,719	1,938	2,235	2,564

ALLEGIS GROUP INC.

7301 PARKWAY DR
HANOVER, MD 210761159
Phone: 410-579-3000
Fax: –
Web: www.allegisgroup.com

CEO: Michael (Mike) Salandra
CFO: Paul J. Bowie
HR: Connie Lee
FYE: December 31
Type: Private

Clients in need of highly skilled technical and other personnel might want to take the pledge of Allegis. The group is one of the world's largest staffing and recruitment firms. Among its companies are Aerotek (engineering automotive and scientific professionals) Stephen James Associates (recruitment for accounting financial and cash management positions) and TEKsystems (information technology staffing and consulting). Other Allegis units include sales support outsourcer MarketSource. Chairman Jim Davis helped found the company (originally known as Aerotek) in 1983 to provide contract engineering personnel to two clients in the aerospace industry.

	Annual Growth	12/09	12/10	12/11	12/12	12/13
Sales ($ mil.)	17.7%	–	6,406.0	8,275.5	9,544.3	10,440.0
Net income ($ mil.)	–	–	–	438.0	0.0	0.0
Market value ($ mil.)	–	–	–	–	–	–
Employees	–	–	–	–	–	85,000

ALLEN & COMPANY LLC

711 5th Ave. 9th Fl.
New York NY 10022
Phone: 212-832-8000
Fax: 212-832-8023

CEO: –
CFO: –
HR: –
FYE: November 30
Type: Private

For Allen & Company there's no business like financing show business. The investment bank serves variously as investor underwriter and broker to some of the biggest names in entertainment technology and information. Viewed as something of a secret society the firm has had a quiet hand in such hookups as Seagram (now part of Vivendi) and Universal Studios Hasbro and Galoob Toys and Disney and Capital Cities/ABC. The notoriously secretive firm's famous annual retreat in Sun Valley Idaho attracts more moguls than a double-black ski run (Warren Buffett Bill Gates Rupert Murdoch and Oprah Winfrey have attended). Brothers Herbert and Charles Allen founded the company in 1922.

ALLEN COMMUNICATION LEARNING SERVICES INC.

55 W 900 S
SALT LAKE CITY, UT 841012931
Phone: 801-537-7800
Fax: -
Web: www.allencomm.com

CEO: Ron Zamir
CFO: Paul Zackrison
HR: -
FYE: December 31
Type: Private

Allen Communication Learning Services helps improve organizations' performance and productivity by developing customized training offerings. Founded in 1981 the employee-owned company provides systems like e-learning courseware and multimedia instruction (i.e. combining electronic courseware with Web meetings podcasts and e-mail) as well as related consulting presentation preparation and technical support services. The company's training courses address issues such as compliance ethics safety and management effectiveness. Catering to a variety of industries Allen has served clients such as Deutsche Bank Avon American Express Rockwell Collins Northrop Grumman and Pfizer.

	Annual Growth	12/08	12/09	12/10	12/12	12/13
Sales ($ mil.)	11.7%	-	6.4	7.5	9.9	10.0
Net income ($ mil.)	(16.3%)	-	-	1.0	0.9	0.6
Market value ($ mil.)	-	-	-	-	-	-
Employees	-	-	-	-	-	53

ALLEN HARIM FOODS LLC

126 N. Shipley St.
Seaford DE 19973
Phone: 302-629-9163
Fax: 541-608-4519
Web: www.asante.org

CEO: Gary Gladys
CFO: Brian G Hildreth
HR: -
FYE: March 31
Type: Private

The Allen family counts its chickens before and after they hatch. Allen Harim Foods (formerly Allen Family Foods) is a vertically-integrated poultry operation that includes breeding hatching feed milling and processing of its chickens. It operates nearly 30 of its own "growout" farms and contracts with about 270 independent farms to raise the rest of its chickens. Allen Harim offers whole frying roasting and rotisserie chickens chicken parts and tray packs. It sells 600 million pounds of chicken a year to food retailers in the US and throughout the rest of the world. Founded in 1919 Allen Family Foods filed for Chapter 11 bankruptcy protection in 2011 and sold its assets to Korea's Harim Group.

ALLEN LUND COMPANY LLC

4529 ANGELES CREST HWY # 300
LA CANADA FLINTRIDGE, CA 910113247
Phone: 818-790-1110
Fax: -

CEO: -
CFO: Steve Doerfler
HR: -
FYE: December 31
Type: Private

The Allen Lund Company (ALC) knows loads; it matches shippers' loads with a network of truckload and less-than-truckload (LTL) carriers. (LTL carriers collect consolidate and haul freight from multiple shippers.) The brokerage firm arranges the transport of dry refrigerated (predominantly produce) and flatbed cargo. It operates from 30 offices throughout more than 20 US states. ALC Logistics ALC Perishable Logistics and ALC International (an international division) assist shippers in managing transportation costs tracking and tracing shipments managing appointments and executing freight forward management services overseas. The company was founded in 1976 by Allen Lund and his wife Kathie Lund.

	Annual Growth	10/10	10/11	10/12*	12/12	12/13
Sales ($ mil.)	15.9%	-	313.7	313.7	355.3	421.5
Net income ($ mil.)	(58.1%)	-	-	3.1	3.1	1.3
Market value ($ mil.)	-	-	-	-	-	-
Employees	-	-	-	-	-	310

*Fiscal year change

ALLEN ORGAN COMPANY

150 Locust St.
Macungie PA 18062-0036
Phone: 610-966-2202
Fax: 610-965-3098
Web: www.allenorgan.com

CEO: Steven Markowitz
CFO: -
HR: Walt Sloyer
FYE: December 31
Type: Private

Allen Organ's musical instruments may inspire hymns of praise but the company has faith in technology too. The company which introduced the world's first commercially available electronic organ in 1939 makes electronic keyboards including digital organs and accessories for use in churches theaters and other venues. Subsidiary Allen Integrated Assemblies performs contract manufacturing of electronic assemblies while Allen Audio makes PA systems for churches or social halls. Allen Organ sold its Eastern Research subsidiary to Sycamore Networks a provider of optical switching products in 2006. Allen Organ was founded by the late Jerome Markowitz (father of president Steven) in 1937.

ALLEN SYSTEMS GROUP INC.

1333 3rd Ave. South
Naples FL 34102
Phone: 239-435-2200
Fax: 239-263-3692
Web: www.asg.com

CEO: -
CFO: Ernest J Scheidemann
HR: -
FYE: December 31
Type: Private

When it comes to enterprise computing Allen Systems Group (ASG) strives to make all systems go. The company provides a wide range of business automation software to clients worldwide. Its products are used for functions such as legacy data migration business performance management and business applications development and content management. ASG also offers business information portals and applications for identity and user access management in addition to consulting implementation and training services. The company serves such industries as transportation manufacturing financial services and retail. Customers have included Coca-Cola General Electric Societe Generale and Procter & Gamble.

ALLEN-EDMONDS SHOE CORPORATION

201 E. Seven Hills Rd.
Port Washington WI 53074-0998
Phone: 262-235-6000
Fax: 262-268-7427
Web: www.allenedmonds.com

CEO: Paul D Grangaard
CFO: Jay Schauer
HR: Elizabeth Gregoire
FYE: December 31
Type: Private

Allen-Edmonds' shoes stand their ground in the US. Maker of high-end men's dress and casual shoes boots belts leather care goods and hosiery Allen-Edmonds makes most of its shoes in Maine and Wisconsin resisting the trend of moving production abroad. Its shoes are handmade by skilled craftsmen and Allen-Edmonds is known for its full range of shoe sizes for men. Its footwear is sold in more than 25 company-owned stores in the US Belgium and Italy as well as in department stores (Nordstrom) and specialty shops in more than 20 countries in Europe and Latin America and online and by catalog. Founded by Elbert Allen in 1922 the iconic American shoemaker is owned by Goldner Hawn Johnson & Morrison.

ALLERGAN, INC   NYS: AGN

2525 Dupont Drive
Irvine, CA 92612
Phone: 714 246-4500
Fax: –
Web: www.allergan.com
CEO: –
CFO: –
HR: Shauna Crossan
FYE: December 31
Type: Public

Vanity thy true name be Profits — at least for Allergan. The company is a leading maker of eye care skin care and aesthetic products including best-selling pharmaceutical Botox. Originally used to treat muscle spasms (as well as eye spasms and misalignment) Botox found another more popular application in diminishing facial wrinkles. Allergan's eye care products include medications for glaucoma allergic conjunctivitis and chronic dry eye. Skin care products include treatments for acne wrinkles and psoriasis. Allergan also sells breast augmentation implants and other surgical devices. Its products are sold in more than 100 countries. Pharmaceutical giant Actavis is buying Allergan in a $66 billion deal.

	Annual Growth	12/09	12/10	12/11	12/12	12/13
Sales ($ mil.)	8.8%	4,503.6	4,919.4	5,419.1	5,806.1	6,300.4
Net income ($ mil.)	12.2%	621.3	0.6	934.5	1,098.8	985.1
Market value ($ mil.)	15.2%	18,752.2	20,436.7	26,112.0	27,299.5	33,058.2
Employees	8.3%	8,300	9,200	10,000	10,800	11,400

ALLETE INC.   NYS: ALE

30 West Superior Street
Duluth, MN 55802-2093
Phone: 218 279-5000
Fax: –
Web: www.allete.com
CEO: Alan R. Hodnik
CFO: Steven Q. (Steve) DeVinck
HR: Brenda Flayton
FYE: December 31
Type: Public

ALLETE provides light to the northern climes. Most of its business is classified within its regulated operations which include electric gas and water utilities located in northeastern Minnesota and northwestern Wisconsin. Those operations are conducted through subsidiaries Minnesota Power (about 144000 customers) and Superior Water Light and Power (37000 electric gas and water customers). ALLETE's other segment includes coal mining operations emerging technologies related to electric utilities and a real estate business (large land tracts in Florida). Subsidiary BNI Coal operates a mine in North Dakota that supplies primarily two generating co-ops Minnkota Power and Square Butte.

	Annual Growth	12/10	12/11	12/12	12/13	12/14
Sales ($ mil.)	5.8%	907.0	928.2	961.2	1,018.4	1,136.8
Net income ($ mil.)	13.5%	75.3	93.8	97.1	104.7	124.8
Market value ($ mil.)	10.3%	1,710.2	1,926.9	1,881.0	2,289.5	2,530.9
Employees	2.6%	1,465	1,371	1,361	1,560	1,625

ALLEY-CASSETTY COMPANIES INC.

2 OLDHAM ST
NASHVILLE, TN 372131107
Phone: 615-244-7077
Fax: –
Web: www.alley-cassetty.com
CEO: Fred Cassetty
CFO: –
HR: Teresa Roberts
FYE: April 30
Type: Private

Some build with blood sweat and tears; Alley-Cassetty Companies do it with trucks bricks and coal. The company's trucking division specializes in hauling liquid- and dry-bulk cargo including hazardous materials while the Alley-Cassetty Truck Center sells and services commercial trucks. The building supply division which operates in Georgia Kentucky and Tennessee produces and distributes bricks and other masonry products. Alley-Cassetty also provides coal to commercial and industrial users arranging its transportation via barge train and truck. Originally a coal company Alley-Cassetty was formed in 1964 through the merger of two Nashville residential coal delivery companies dating to the 1880s.

	Annual Growth	03/06	03/07	03/08	03/09*	04/10
Sales ($ mil.)	(28.5%)	–	–	–	114.0	81.5
Net income ($ mil.)		–	–	–	1.0	(0.3)
Market value ($ mil.)		–	–	–	–	–
Employees		–	–	–	–	180

*Fiscal year change

ALLIANCE BANCORP INC. OF PENNSYLVANIA   NASDAQ: ALLB

541 Lawrence Rd.
Broomall PA 19008
Phone: 610-353-2900
Fax: 610-359-6908
Web: www.allianceanytime.com
CEO: –
CFO: –
HR: –
FYE: December 31
Type: Public

Alliance Bancorp Inc. of Pennsylvania is the holding company for Alliance Bank (formerly Greater Delaware Valley Savings Bank). The bank has about 10 branch offices that serve individuals and local businesses in suburban Philadelphia's Delaware and Chester counties. It offers standard deposit products such as checking and savings accounts money market accounts CDs and IRAs. Commercial real estate loans (more than 45% of the company's loan portfolio) and residential mortgages (more than 40%) comprise most of the bank's lending activities. Alliance Bancorp was formed in 2007 when the bank converted from mutual ownership to a mid-tier stock holding company structure.

ALLIANCE DATA SYSTEMS CORP.   NYS: ADS

7500 Dallas Parkway, Suite 700
Plano, TX 75024
Phone: 214 494-3000
Fax: –
Web: www.alliancedata.com
CEO: Edward J. (Ed) Heffernan
CFO: Charles L. Horn
HR: –
FYE: December 31
Type: Public

Hoping to forge an alliance between consumers and retailers Alliance Data Systems provides private-label credit card financing and processing and database and direct marketing services to more than 1500 companies. Its client base includes retailers like ANN J. Crew Pottery Barn and Victoria's Secret as well as banks (Bank of America) grocery and drugstore chains gas stations and hospitality media and pharmaceutical companies. Alliance Data's Epsilon unit develops customer loyalty programs and performs database marketing and strategic consulting services while LoyaltyOne operates the AIR MILES rewards and data-driven marketer BrandLoyalty. About 90% of Alliance Data's business is in North America.

	Annual Growth	12/10	12/11	12/12	12/13	12/14
Sales ($ mil.)	17.4%	2,791.4	3,173.3	3,641.4	4,319.1	5,302.9
Net income ($ mil.)	27.1%	193.7	315.3	422.3	496.2	506.3
Market value ($ mil.)	41.7%	4,532.6	6,626.2	9,237.4	16,778.1	18,253.4
Employees	18.5%	7,600	8,600	10,700	12,000	15,000

ALLIANCE ENTERTAINMENT LLC

4250 Coral Ridge Dr.
Coral Springs FL 33065
Phone: 954-255-4000
Fax: 954-255-4078
Web: www.aent.com
CEO: Jeff Walker
CFO: George Campagna
HR: –
FYE: January 31
Type: Private

Alliance Entertainment rolls out the rock 'n' roll to retailers colleges and public libraries. The company is a distributor of some 400000 CDs DVDs videogames and related products to some 3000 merchants including Target Best Buy Barnes and Noble and Borders Group as well as Internet retailers such as Amazon.com. Alliance also provides fulfillment e-commerce and related support services through its AEC Direct division. Its NCircle Entertainment unit licenses and distributes family entertainment titles based on such characters as Super Mario Bros. and My Little Pony. Alliance Entertainment founded in 1990 is owned by investment firms Platinum Equity and The Gores Group.

ALLIANCE FIBER OPTIC PRODUCTS INC.

NMS: AFOP

275 Gibraltar Drive
Sunnyvale, CA 94089
Phone: 408 736-6900
Fax: 408 736-4882
Web: www.afop.com

CEO: Peter C Chang
CFO: Anita K Ho
HR: –
FYE: December 31
Type: Public

Alliance Fiber Optic Products (AFOP) is no light weight in light waves. Communications equipment designers and manufacturers plug AFOP's fiber-optic components into products used to build networks that connect cities regions within cities and telecommunications service providers with their individual customers. Its optical path integration and optical fiber amplifier components which include attenuators couplers depolarizers multiplexers and splitters account for most of sales. The company sells directly to telecom equipment makers primarily in North America where it gets about half of sales. AFOP has more than 200 customers.

	Annual Growth	12/10	12/11	12/12	12/13	12/14
Sales ($ mil.)	17.3%	45.4	42.0	46.6	76.1	86.0
Net income ($ mil.)	24.6%	6.0	4.4	9.6	18.8	14.5
Market value ($ mil.)	(1.9%)	281.3	137.4	215.7	270.0	260.3
Employees	5.3%	1,137	1,037	1,063	1,514	1,397

ALLIANCE HEALTHCARE SERVICES, INC.

NMS: AIQ

100 Bayview Circle, Suite 400
Newport Beach, CA 92660
Phone: 949 242-5300
Fax: –
Web: www.alliancehealthcareservices-us.com

CEO: Tom C. (Tom) Tomlinson
CFO: Howard K. Aihara
HR: Alex Hurtado
FYE: December 31
Type: Public

Alliance HealthCare Services has a lead apron ready for you. Through its Alliance Imaging division the company operates some 500 diagnostic imaging systems for more than 1000 hospitals and other health care providers throughout the US. For most customers the company provides imaging systems and the staff to run and maintain them as well as marketing and billing support. In addition to MRI equipment and services (its largest revenue source) Alliance offers positron emission tomography (PET) computed tomography (CT) combination scanning X-rays and ultrasound among other imaging services. The company's Alliance Oncology unit runs about 30 cancer centers that provide radiation therapy.

	Annual Growth	12/10	12/11	12/12	12/13	12/14
Sales ($ mil.)	(2.3%)	478.9	493.7	472.3	448.8	436.4
Net income ($ mil.)	–	(32.7)	(160.1)	(11.9)	(21.5)	10.6
Market value ($ mil.)	49.1%	44.8	13.3	67.3	261.1	221.6
Employees	(5.1%)	1,952	1,909	1,720	1,504	1,582

ALLIANCE HOLDINGS GROUP LP

NMS: AHGP

1717 South Boulder Avenue, Suite 400
Tulsa, OK 74119
Phone: 918 295-1415
Fax: –
Web: www.ahgp.com

CEO: Joseph W. Craft
CFO: Brian L. Cantrell
HR: –
FYE: December 31
Type: Public

When it comes to coal mining it takes more than one company to make this Alliance work. Alliance Holdings GP owns Alliance Resource Management GP which is the managing general partner of major coal mining company Alliance Resource Partners L.P. That operational company company has seven coal mining complexes in Illinois Indiana Kentucky and Maryland plus other coal interests in West Virginia. Alliance Holdings GP generates all of its revenues from its general partnership interest and its ownership stake in Alliance Resource Partners L.P.

	Annual Growth	12/10	12/11	12/12	12/13	12/14
Sales ($ mil.)	9.3%	1,609.7	1,843.2	2,033.9	2,205.2	2,300.3
Net income ($ mil.)	13.0%	174.3	214.1	196.1	233.9	284.4
Market value ($ mil.)	6.1%	2,881.4	3,111.7	2,848.3	3,509.8	3,651.0
Employees	5.7%	3,558	3,832	4,345	4,313	4,439

ALLIANCE LAUNDRY HOLDINGS LLC

119 Shepard St.
Ripon WI 54971
Phone: 920-748-3121
Fax: 202-962-4601
Web: www.icmarc.org

CEO: –
CFO: –
HR: –
FYE: December 31
Type: Private

Laundry day can't come often enough for Alliance Laundry Holdings (ALH). Through its wholly owned subsidiary Alliance Laundry Systems the company makes commercial laundry equipment used in Laundromats multi-housing laundry facilities (such as apartments dormitories and military bases) and on-premise laundries (hotels hospitals and prisons). Its washers and dryers are made under the brands Speed Queen UniMac Huebsch IPSO and Cissell. They're sold primarily in the US and Canada but also internationally. Investment firm Teachers' Private Capital (private equity arm of Ontario Teachers' Pension Plan) acquired more than 91% of ALH for about $450 million in 2005. The company was founded in 1908.

ALLIANCE OF PROFESSIONALS & CONSULTANTS INC.

8200 BROWNLEIGH DR
RALEIGH, NC 276177411
Phone: 919-510-9696
Fax: –
Web: www.apc-services.com

CEO: –
CFO: –
HR: Karin Pillow
FYE: December 31
Type: Private

Alliance of Professionals & Consultants (APC) provides information technology and other technical staffing services for clients in the telecommunications financial manufacturing e-commerce pharmaceutical and health care industries. The company offers temp-to-hire and permanent placement — as well as total outsourcing arrangements — in such areas as application development quality assurance and testing network engineering and security and project management. It also operates staffing and consulting practices in engineering and business services. APC which was founded in 1993 uses subcontractors to supply its clients with personnel for some projects.

	Annual Growth	12/09	12/10	12/11	12/12	12/13
Sales ($ mil.)	19.1%	–	40.7	60.4	60.1	68.8
Net income ($ mil.)	(19.8%)	–	–	1.9	1.5	1.2
Market value ($ mil.)	–	–	–	–	–	–
Employees	–	–	–	–	–	735

ALLIANCE ONE INTERNATIONAL INC

NYS: AOI

8001 Aerial Center Parkway
Morrisville, NC 27560-8417
Phone: 919 379-4300
Fax: –
Web: www.aointl.com

CEO: J. Pieter Sikkel
CFO: Joel L. Thomas
HR: –
FYE: March 31
Type: Public

Alliance One International keeps one eye on the world's tobacco farmers and the other eye on the cigarette makers. The company is a leading global leaf-tobacco merchant behind its slightly larger rival Universal Corporation. Alliance One purchases leaf tobacco directly from more than 35 countries buying more than 20% of its tobacco from South American farmers alone. It also processes flue-cured burley and oriental tobaccos and sells them to large multinational cigarette and cigar manufacturers including Philip Morris International (PMI) and Japan Tobacco in some 90 countries. Alliance One was formed by the merger of tobacco processor DIMON and Standard Commercial.

	Annual Growth	03/11	03/12	03/13	03/14	03/15
Sales ($ mil.)	(0.3%)	2,094.1	2,150.8	2,243.8	2,355.0	2,065.9
Net income ($ mil.)	–	(71.6)	29.5	24.0	(86.7)	(15.4)
Market value ($ mil.)	(27.7%)	38.8	36.4	37.5	28.2	10.6
Employees	(0.1%)	3,300	3,255	3,330	3,574	3,281

ALLIANCE RESOURCE PARTNERS LP

NMS: ARLP

1717 South Boulder Avenue, Suite 400
Tulsa, OK 74119
Phone: 918 295-7600
Fax: –
Web: www.arlp.com

CEO: Joseph W Craft III
CFO: Brian L Cantrell
HR: –
FYE: December 31
Type: Public

Coal is the main resource of Alliance Resource Partners which operates in the Illinois Basin Central Appalachia and Northern Appalachia. The company has 11 underground coal mining complexes in Illinois Indiana Kentucky Maryland Pennsylvania and West Virginia. Alliance controls about 650 million tons of reserves. Approximately 205 million tons of these reserves located in Hamilton County Illinois are leased to independent coal company White Oak Resources. Alliance produces about 32 million tons of coal annually nearly all of which is sold to electric utilities.

	Annual Growth	12/10	12/11	12/12	12/13	12/14
Sales ($ mil.)	9.3%	1,610.1	1,843.6	2,034.3	2,205.6	2,300.7
Net income ($ mil.)	11.6%	321.0	389.4	335.6	393.5	497.2
Market value ($ mil.)	(10.0%)	4,870.2	5,597.5	4,299.8	5,702.7	3,188.3
Employees	(2.8%)	3,558	3,832	4,345	4,313	3,177

ALLIANCEBERNSTEIN HOLDING L P

NYS: AB

1345 Avenue of the Americas
New York, NY 10105
Phone: 212 969-1000
Fax: –
Web: www.alliancebernstein.com

CEO: –
CFO: –
HR: –
FYE: December 31
Type: Public

The raison d'etre of AllianceBernstein Holding is its more than 35% stake in investment manager AllianceBernstein. (French insurer AXA through its AXA Financial unit owns a majority of the subsidiary.) AllianceBernstein which has more than $420 million of client assets under management administers about 200 mutual funds invested in growth and value equities fixed-income securities and index and blended strategies. The subsidiary also offer separately managed accounts closed-end funds structured financial products and alternative investments such as hedge funds. It mainly serves institutional clients such as pension funds corporations and not-for-profits in addition to retail investors.

	Annual Growth	12/11	12/12	12/13	12/14	12/15
Sales ($ mil.)	–	(65.6)	70.8	185.9	203.3	212.5
Net income ($ mil.)	–	(93.3)	51.1	165.5	180.8	188.2
Market value ($ mil.)	16.2%	1,308.6	1,743.8	2,134.9	2,584.1	2,386.1
Employees	(1.1%)	3,764	3,318	3,295	3,487	3,600

ALLIANT CREDIT UNION

11545 W. Touhy Ave.
Chicago IL 60666
Phone: 773-462-2000
Fax: 773-462-2095
Web: www.alliantcreditunion.org

CEO: –
CFO: Mona Leung
HR: –
FYE: December 31
Type: Private - Not-for-Pr

Members fly high with Alliant Credit Union. Though its branch total may be small — about 15 locations in or near major US airports — Alliant is one of the largest credit unions in the country with some $8 billion in assets and more than 275000 members. Its financial products and services include checking and savings accounts credit cards investments and insurance. Alliant also offers mortgages as well as home equity auto and student loans. Membership is open to all residents of the Chicago area as well as current and retired employees (and their family members) of firms such as United Airlines Google Kaiser Permanente and more than a hundred other qualifying companies and organizations.

ALLIANT ENERGY CORP.

NYS: LNT

4902 N. Biltmore Lane
Madison, WI 53718
Phone: 608 458-3311
Fax: 608 458-4824
Web: www.alliantenergy.com

CEO: Patricia L. (Pat) Kampling
CFO: Thomas L. (Tom) Hanson
HR: Wayne Reschke
FYE: December 31
Type: Public

Alliant Energy is reliant on its business model of delivering regulated and non regulated electric and natural gas services to homes businesses and industries across the Midwest at the lowest costs it can support. The company's operating utilities Interstate Power and Light (IP&L) and Wisconsin Power and Light (WPL) provide electricity to about 1 million customers and natural gas to 420000 customers in four states; the utility's generation division produces electricity at more than 34 power plants with a total generating capacity of more than 6290 MW. Non-regulated operations include rail and marine transportation services and independent power production (including wind farms).

	Annual Growth	12/10	12/11	12/12	12/13	12/14
Sales ($ mil.)	(0.5%)	3,416.1	3,665.3	3,094.5	3,276.8	3,350.3
Net income ($ mil.)	6.4%	306.3	321.9	335.7	376.2	393.3
Market value ($ mil.)	15.9%	4,079.1	4,893.4	4,871.2	5,724.3	7,368.3
Employees	(2.7%)	4,704	4,262	4,055	3,945	4,212

ALLIANT INTERNATIONAL UNIVERSITY

1 BEACH ST STE 100
SAN FRANCISCO, CA 941331221
Phone: 415-955-2000
Fax: –
Web: www.catalog.alliant.edu

CEO: –
CFO: Tarun Bhatia
HR: –
FYE: June 30
Type: Private

Alliant International University churns out mental health professionals lawyers teachers businessmen and forensic specialists. The university prepares students (graduates and undergraduates who've completed at least two years of college) for careers in psychology and applied social sciences. Alliant International University consists of five graduate schools specializing in psychology business management forensics law and education. It also operates two undergraduate educational centers and has an affiliation with the Presidio Graduate School which focuses on sustainable management. It serves more than 4000 students from its seven campus locations in California as well as three satellite locations overseas.

	Annual Growth	06/06	06/07	06/08	06/09	06/10
Sales ($ mil.)	–	–	–	0.0	78.3	76.3
Net income ($ mil.)	10937.9%	–	–	0.0	8.5	1.9
Market value ($ mil.)	–	–	–	–	–	–
Employees	–	–	–	–	–	471

ALLIANZ LIFE INSURANCE COMPANY OF NORTH AMERICA

5701 Golden Hills Dr.
Minneapolis MN 55416
Phone: 763-765-6500
Fax: 212-771-9884
Web: www.cit.com/products-and-services/corporate-fi

CEO: Walter White
CFO: Giulio Terzariol
HR: –
FYE: December 31
Type: Subsidiary

There's more to Allianz Life than life. The subsidiaries and affiliates of Allianz Life Insurance Company of North America (Allianz Life) offer a range of insurance investment and savings products to individuals throughout the US. Allianz Life boasts a network of more than 100000 independent agents and financial planners selling such products as life insurance variable and fixed life annuity products and long-term care insurance. It offers mutual funds and other broker-dealer services through its Questar Capital affiliate. Allianz Life operates in New York through its Allianz Life Insurance Company of New York unit. Allianz Life became a subsidiary of Allianz SE in 1979.

ALLIED BUILDING PRODUCTS CORP.

15 E. Union Ave.
East Rutherford NJ 07073
Phone: 201-507-8400
Fax: 201-507-3842
Web: www.alliedbuilding.net

CEO: Bob Feury Jr
CFO: –
HR: –
FYE: December 31
Type: Subsidiary

Allied Building Products counts home builders and contractors as part of its circle of friends. Serving the commercial and residential construction markets the company distributes exterior and interior building materials including roofing siding drywall and acoustical tile from major manufacturers. Allied also markets products under its own Cutting Edge and Tri-Bilt brands. The firm operates about 180 branches in 30 states and it maintains a fleet of more than 2700 vehicles including cranes and delivery trucks. Allied is a subsidiary of Oldcastle (itself a subsidiary of CRH). The company was founded in 1950 as a family-operated roofing and custom sheet metal fabrication business.

ALLIED ELECTRONICS INC.

7151 Jack Newell Blvd. S.
Fort Worth TX 76118
Phone: 817-595-3500
Fax: 817-595-6444
Web: www.alliedelec.com

CEO: –
CFO: Gavin Robinson
HR: –
FYE: March 31
Type: Subsidiary

Allied Electronics is an engineer's ally. The company distributes electronic and electromechanical products including test and measurement equipment (analyzers meters and oscilloscopes) cables power supplies interconnects active and passive components tools and racks and cabinets. Its products come from more than 300 suppliers including the likes of Agilent Honeywell Dialight Cornell Dubilier National Semiconductor and Panduit. Allied Electronics also offers services such as assembly labeling packaging and inventory management. Founded in 1928 as Allied Radio (the radio parts distribution arm of Columbia Radio) Allied Electronics is a subsidiary of UK-based Electrocomponents.

ALLIED HEALTHCARE INTERNATIONAL INC.

245 Park Ave.
New York NY 10167
Phone: 212-750-0064
Fax: 212-750-7221
Web: www.alliedhealthcare.com

CEO: Alexander Young
CFO: Paul Weston
HR: Louise Cherry
FYE: September 30
Type: Subsidiary

Allied Healthcare International offers temporary staffing services to the UK health care industry. The company operates through a network of about 110 branches across the UK. Allied Healthcare places its staff which includes more than 10000 nurses nurses aides and home health aides in hospitals nursing homes care homes and private homes. Customers affiliated with the British government such as the UK National Health Service and local social service departments account for a sizeable portion of the company's sales each year. Allied Healthcare International was established in 1981. In late 2011 it was acquired by Saga Group Limited.

ALLIED HEALTHCARE PRODUCT, INC.   NMS: AHPI

1720 Sublette Avenue
St. Louis, MO 63110
Phone: 314 771-2400
Fax: –
Web: www.alliedhpi.com

CEO: Earl R Refsland
CFO: Daniel C Dunn
HR: –
FYE: June 30
Type: Public

Allied Healthcare Products helps medical workers get oxygen flowing. The medical equipment maker produces respiratory equipment used in hospitals surgery centers ambulances and other medical facilities as well as in patient homes. Its products include anesthesia equipment oxygen cylinders and nebulizers used in home respiratory therapy as well as emergency resuscitation products. It also makes medical gas system components installed in hospital walls during construction as well as spine immobilization backboards and other items used in trauma situations. Allied Healthcare sells directly to hospitals and through equipment dealers in the US and abroad.

	Annual Growth	06/11	06/12	06/13	06/14	06/15
Sales ($ mil.)	(6.7%)	46.8	43.4	38.6	36.4	35.5
Net income ($ mil.)	–	0.2	(0.4)	(1.3)	(2.8)	(1.8)
Market value ($ mil.)	(21.0%)	32.4	25.0	22.1	19.4	12.6
Employees	(7.2%)	313	289	276	243	232

ALLIED INTERNATIONAL CORPORATION OF VIRGINIA

101 DOVER RD NE STE 2
GLEN BURNIE, MD 210606561
Phone: 410-424-4003
Fax: –
Web: www.alliedint.com

CEO: –
CFO: –
HR: –
FYE: December 31
Type: Private

Allied International imports packed food products from more than 35 countries for distribution to grocery retailers throughout the US. Its product portfolio includes breakfast cereals candy condiments cookies and crackers as well as pasta products oils and salad dressings. It distributes such brands as Forrelli Smith & Johnson and Sunrise Valley. In addition Allied International imports and distributes kosher products and general merchandise including cleaning products and personal care items. The family-owned company was formed in 1980.

	Annual Growth	12/05	12/06	12/07	12/08	12/09
Sales ($ mil.)	(99.2%)	–	–	302,448.6	17.4	17.5
Net income ($ mil.)	(83.5%)	–	–	16.4	0.4	0.4
Market value ($ mil.)	–	–	–	–	–	–
Employees		–	–	–	–	19

ALLIED MOTION TECHNOLOGIES INC   NMS: AMOT

495 Commerce Drive, Suite 3
Amherst, NY 14228
Phone: 716 242-8634
Fax: –
Web: www.alliedmotion.com

CEO: Richard S. (Dick) Warzala
CFO: Michael R. (Mike) Leach
HR: –
FYE: December 31
Type: Public

Allied Motion Technologies has the motor to control your drive. The company makes specialized motors optical encoders and brushless drives used in mechanical motion control applications. Its products are incorporated into a number of end products including high-definition printers barcode scanners surgical tools robotic systems wheelchairs and satellite tracking systems. Allied Motion targets applications in the alternative energy automotive aerospace and defense industrial automation medical printing and imaging and semiconductor equipment markets.

	Annual Growth	12/10	12/11	12/12	12/13	12/14
Sales ($ mil.)	32.7%	80.6	110.9	102.0	125.5	249.7
Net income ($ mil.)	40.2%	3.6	7.0	5.4	4.0	13.9
Market value ($ mil.)	36.2%	63.4	52.0	60.8	114.7	218.3
Employees	21.0%	456	476	418	942	977

ALLIED RESOURCES INC
NBB: ALOD

1403 East 900 South
Salt Lake City, UT 84105
Phone: 801-582-9609
Fax: –
Web: www.allied-resources-inc.com

CEO: Ruairidh Campbell
CFO: Ruairidh Campbell
HR: –
FYE: December 31
Type: Public

Allied Resources has allied with Allstate Energy to get the most out of its Appalachian energy resources. The company is an oil and natural gas exploration and production enterprise with primary operations in West Virginia (in Calhoun and Ritchie counties). Allied Resources produces oil and natural gas from 145 wells which are maintained and operated by Allstate Energy. The depth at which the wells produce ranges from 1730 feet to more than 5470 feet. The company also owns 13 gross wells in Goliad Edwards and Jackson counties Texas. In 2008 Allied Resources reported proved reserves of 18950 barrels of oil and 1.4 billion cu. ft. of natural gas. CEO Ruairidh Campbell owns 27% of the company

	Annual Growth	12/10	12/11	12/12	12/13	12/14
Sales ($ mil.)	(3.3%)	0.7	0.6	0.5	0.6	0.6
Net income ($ mil.)	–	(0.1)	(1.0)	(0.1)	(0.0)	(0.0)
Market value ($ mil.)	(26.6%)	3.1	2.3	2.5	2.1	0.9
Employees	0.0%	2	2	2	2	2

ALLIED SYSTEMS HOLDINGS INC.

2302 Parklake Dr. Bldg. 15 Ste. 600
Atlanta GA 30345
Phone: 404-373-4285
Fax: 404-370-4206
Web: www.alliedholdings.com

CEO: Mark J Gendregske
CFO: Thomas H King
HR: Paul Books
FYE: December 31
Type: Private

Allied Systems Holdings is busting to "get a move on." Carrying millions of cars trucks and SUVs every year Allied Systems Holdings leads the North American vehicle-hauling market. Through subsidiary Allied Automotive Group Allied Systems moves approximately 9 million vehicles annually with a fleet of about 4000 tractor-trailer rigs which it operates from about 90 terminals in the US and Canada. Assembled vehicles are transported from manufacturing plants railway distribution points ports and auctions to auto dealers and car rental companies. Customers have included major auto OEMs Chrysler Ford General Motors Honda and Toyota. In mid-2012 Allied Systems filed for Chapter 11 bankruptcy protection.

ALLINA HEALTH SYSTEM

2925 CHICAGO AVE
MINNEAPOLIS, MN 554071321
Phone: 612-262-5000
Fax: –
Web: www.allinahealth.org

CEO: Penny Ann Wheeler
CFO: Duncan P. Gallagher
HR: Margaret Butler
FYE: December 31
Type: Private

Allina Health System (aka Allina Hospitals and Clinics) is a not-for-profit health care system that goes all in to protect people's #1 asset — their good health. The health system owns and operates more than a dozen hospitals a network of nearly one hundred clinics and specialty centers and a whole bunch of pharmacies. Its vast system of provider locations serve residents throughout Minnesota and western Wisconsin providing disease prevention programs along with specialized inpatient and outpatient services. Allina's Aspen Medical Group division also operates a range of outpatient clinics providing primary and specialty care.

	Annual Growth	12/08	12/09	12/11	12/12	12/13
Sales ($ mil.)	3.5%	–	2,978.9	2,743.2	3,246.4	3,420.6
Net income ($ mil.)	28.7%	–	–	226.0	154.3	374.2
Market value ($ mil.)	–	–	–	–	–	–
Employees	–	–	–	–	–	26,400

ALLIS-CHALMERS ENERGY INC.

11125 Equity Dr. Ste. 200
Houston TX 77041
Phone: 713-856-4222
Fax: 713-856-4246
Web: www.alchenergy.com/profiles/investor/fullpage.

CEO: Munawar H Hidayatallah
CFO: Victor M Perez
HR: –
FYE: December 31
Type: Subsidiary

This company knows the drill. Allis-Chalmers Energy provides drilling and oil field services to oil and gas exploration companies operating primarily Argentina and in the western and southern US. It operates in three segments: Drilling and Completion; Oilfield Services (underbalanced drilling directional drilling tubular services and production services); and Rental Services. Its Strata Directional Technology subsidiary offers directional drilling services to clients in conventional and unconventional hydrocarbon plays. In 2011 Archer Limited (formerly Seawell) acquired debt-laden Allis-Chalmers for some $890 million including assumed debt.

ALLISON TRANSMISSION HOLDINGS INC
NYS: ALSN

One Allison Way
Indianapolis, IN 46222
Phone: 317-242-5000
Fax: –
Web: www.allisontransmission.com

CEO: Lawrence E. (Larry) Dewey
CFO: David S. Graziosi
HR: –
FYE: December 31
Type: Public

In the world of automatics Allison Transmission has pull. The company builds automatic transmissions for medium- and heavy-duty commercial vehicles and hybrid-propulsion systems for city buses. Allison's customers include OEMs of garbage trucks and city transit buses military transports and dump trucks. The company also makes electric drives for buses and shuttles (it is the world's #1 heavy-duty hybrid producer) and remanufactures transmissions for aftermarket customers. The US accounts for nearly 75% of its total revenues. Allison serves customers in Europe Asia South America and Africa in more than 80 countries.

	Annual Growth	12/10	12/11	12/12	12/13	12/14
Sales ($ mil.)	2.5%	1,926.3	2,162.8	2,141.8	1,926.8	2,127.4
Net income ($ mil.)	66.7%	29.6	103.0	514.2	165.4	228.6
Market value ($ mil.)	28.8%	–	–	3,665.2	4,955.7	6,084.7
Employees	(1.2%)	–	2,800	2,800	2,700	2,700

ALLOS THERAPEUTICS INC.
NASDAQ: ALTH

11080 CirclePoint Rd. Ste. 200
Westminster CO 80020
Phone: 303-426-6262
Fax: 303-426-4731
Web: www.allos.com

CEO: Abraham N Oler
CFO: –
HR: –
FYE: December 31
Type: Public

Drug developer Allos Therapeutics has worked to make a big breakthrough in the fight against cancer. The company's first FDA-approved drug Folotyn (pralatrexate) was launched commercially in the US in 2010 to treat a relatively rare blood cancer called peripheral T-cell lymphoma (PTCL). Allos Therapeutics is also investigating the compound as a potential treatment in other oncology applications including additional forms of lymphoma. Spectrum Pharmaceuticals acquired Allos Therapeutics in 2012.

ALLOY INC.

151 W. 26th St. 11th Fl.
New York NY 10001
Phone: 212-244-4307
Fax: 212-244-4311
Web: www.alloy.com

CEO: Matthew C Diamond
CFO: –
HR: William Cunningham
FYE: January 31
Type: Subsidiary

Alloy has its eye on the next generation. Through its Alloy Media + Marketing division the company provides advertising and marketing services for online and print media designed to help customers reach the attractive yet elusive youth market of people between the ages of 10 and 24. Its Alloy Entertainment develops TV shows (Gossip Girl) while its Alloy Digital broadcasts content online including original sponsored Web series (Private). In addition the company's Channel One TV network broadcasts daily newscasts and educational videos at junior and senior high schools across the country. Investment firm ZelnickMedia Corporation owns Alloy. Warner Bros. Television Group is buying Alloy Entertainment.

ALLSCRIPTS HEALTHCARE SOLUTIONS, INC.   NMS: MDRX

222 Merchandise Mart, Suite 2024
Chicago, IL 60654
Phone: 312 506-1200
Fax: –
Web: www.allscripts.com

CEO: Paul Black
CFO: Richard J. (Rick) Poulton
HR: –
FYE: December 31
Type: Public

Jokes about doctors' handwriting may go the way of house calls thanks to Allscripts Healthcare Solutions. The company provides software as either onsite or hosted options and services that automate common healthcare data flow tasks such as entering prescription information managing orders for lab tests and other medical workflows and records. Allscripts software includes tools that give doctors access (via desktop or wireless handheld devices) to patient drug history drug interactions and generic alternatives. Its products also help hospitals and healthcare organizations manage financial and operational functions. Physician practices make up nearly half of Allscripts' business.

	Annual Growth	12/10	12/11	12/12	12/13	12/14
Sales ($ mil.)	22.4%	613.3	1,444.1	1,446.3	1,373.1	1,377.9
Net income ($ mil.)	–	(5.6)	73.6	(1.2)	(104.0)	(66.5)
Market value ($ mil.)	(9.8%)	3,477.6	3,418.0	1,700.0	2,790.0	2,304.6
Employees	6.6%	5,580	6,300	7,100	7,200	7,200

ALLSTATE CORP.   NYS: ALL

2775 Sanders Road
Northbrook, IL 60062
Phone: 847 402-5000
Fax: –
Web: www.allstate.com

CEO: Thomas J. Wilson
CFO: Steven E. (Steve) Shebik
HR: Harriet Harty
FYE: December 31
Type: Public

Ya gotta hand it to Allstate. The "good hands" company has managed to work its way towards the top of the property/casualty insurance pile. The company is the second-largest personal lines insurer in the US just behind rival State Farm. Its Allstate Protection segment sells auto homeowners and other property/casualty insurance products in Canada and the US. Allstate Financial provides life insurance through subsidiaries including Allstate Life and American Heritage Life. It also provides investment products targeting affluent and middle-income consumers. Allstate Motor Club provides emergency road service.

	Annual Growth	12/10	12/11	12/12	12/13	12/14
Assets ($ mil.)	(4.6%)	130,874.0	125,563.0	126,947.0	123,520.0	108,533.0
Net income ($ mil.)	32.4%	928.0	788.0	2,306.0	2,280.0	2,850.0
Market value ($ mil.)	21.8%	13,325.8	11,457.4	16,791.1	22,797.7	29,364.5
Employees	3.0%	35,700	37,600	38,600	39,400	40,200

ALLSTEEL INC.

2210 2nd Ave.
Muscatine IA 52761
Phone: 563-262-4800
Fax: 563-272-7812
Web: www.allsteeloffice.com

CEO: –
CFO: –
HR: –
FYE: December 31
Type: Subsidiary

Allsteel believes that the best offices are filled with Energy. The company makes office systems desks seating storage products tables and accessories under names such as Energy Stride Align Concensys Scout and Terrace. Allsteel sells its products through dealers and its own sales force. Its customers originate in the corporate government and educational markets. The company operates about 10 showrooms in the US and Canada. Founded in 1912 as All-Steel-Equip Allsteel invented the lateral file in 1967. The company is a subsidiary of HNI.

ALLY COMMERCIAL FINANCE LLC

3000 Town Center Ste. 280
Southfield MI 48075
Phone: 248-356-4622
Fax: 248-350-2733
Web: www.allycf.com

CEO: –
CFO: –
HR: –
FYE: December 31
Type: Subsidiary

In the market for some cash for your business? Ally Commercial Finance provides funding to large and middle-market businesses in a variety of industries. The company's product menu includes term loans letters of credit working capital asset-based lending equipment finance and leasing import/export financing equity co-investments and recapitalizations. Target industries include automotive business services consumer goods health care manufacturing and retail. Ally Commercial typically lends from $5 million to $250 million per transaction. Its portfolio entails approximately $4 billion in financing to some 125 corporate clients. A subsidiary of auto lender Ally Financial the firm has five US offices.

ALLY FINANCIAL INC   NYS: ALLY

200 Renaissance Center, P.O. Box 200
Detroit, MI 48265-2000
Phone: 866 710-4623
Fax: –
Web: www.ally.com

CEO: Jeffrey J. (JB) Brown
CFO: Christopher A. Halmy
HR: –
FYE: December 31
Type: Public

Ally Financial wants to be your friend in the financing business. In addition to owning the branchless Ally Bank the company provides auto financing for almost 17000 auto dealerships (mostly GM and Chrysler) and their customers. Ally Financial also provides financing services for large- and mid-market companies through Ally Corporate Finance (formerly GMAC Commercial Finance). It exited the mortgage business in 2013 when Residential Capital (ResCap) went bankrupt. Formerly known as GMAC and once majority-owned by US taxpayers following a federal bailout in 2008 Ally Financial went public in 2014.

	Annual Growth	12/10	12/11	12/12	12/13	12/14
Assets ($ mil.)	(3.1%)	172,008.0	184,059.0	182,347.0	151,167.0	151,828.0
Net income ($ mil.)	1.7%	1,075.0	(157.0)	1,196.0	361.0	1,150.0
Market value ($ mil.)	–	–	–	–	–	11,339.8
Employees	(16.8%)	14,400	14,800	10,600	7,100	6,900

ALMA COLLEGE

614 W SUPERIOR ST
ALMA, MI 488011599
Phone: 989-463-7111
Fax: –
Web: www.events.alma.edu

CEO: –
CFO: –
HR: –
FYE: June 30
Type: Private

Alma College is glad to show off its Gaelic garb. The school is a undergraduate liberal arts college situated on 100 acres in central Michigan and has an enrollment of about 1400 students. Founded in 1886 by Presbyterians the college has several Scottish traditions including a marching band clad in Kilts a Scottish dance troupe and its own official registered tartan. Each year Alma College hosts the Alma Highland Festival and Games which feature traditional Scottish games and revelry.

	Annual Growth	06/10	06/11	06/12	06/13	06/14
Sales ($ mil.)	9.5%	–	38.7	43.2	44.0	50.8
Net income ($ mil.)	–	–	–	(5.9)	5.7	14.9
Market value ($ mil.)	–	–	–	–	–	–
Employees	–	–	–	–	–	300

ALMOST FAMILY INC

NMS: AFAM

9510 Ormsby Station Road, Suite 300
Louisville, KY 40223
Phone: 502 891-1000
Fax: –
Web: www.almostfamily.com

CEO: William B. Yarmuth
CFO: –
HR: Mark Sutton
FYE: December 31
Type: Public

Almost Family steps in when you're more than an arm's reach from family members with health needs. With its home health nursing services Almost Family offers senior citizens in 15 states (including Florida) an alternative to institutional care. Its Visiting Nurse unit provides skilled nursing care and therapy services at home under a variety of names including Apex Caretenders Community Home Health and Mederi-Caretenders. Its Personal Care Services segment operating under the Almost Family banner offers custodial care such as housekeeping meal preparation and medication management. Almost Family operates 175 Visiting Nurse agencies and about 65 Personal Care Services locations.

	Annual Growth	12/10	12/11	12/12	12/13	12/14
Sales ($ mil.)	10.1%	336.9	339.9	348.5	357.8	495.8
Net income ($ mil.)	(18.2%)	30.7	20.8	17.3	8.2	13.8
Market value ($ mil.)	(6.8%)	364.2	157.2	192.1	306.5	274.4
Employees	14.2%	6,400	9,000	8,000	11,500	10,900

ALNYLAM PHARMACEUTICALS INC

NMS: ALNY

300 Third Street
Cambridge, MA 02142
Phone: 617 551-8200
Fax: 617 551-8101
Web: www.alnylam.com

CEO: –
CFO: –
HR: Karen Anderson
FYE: December 31
Type: Public

Like a genetic linebacker Alnylam Pharmaceuticals runs interference with RNA to prevent the forward progress of disease. RNA interference (RNAi) technology developed by the biotech firm can selectively shut off harmful genes. The company is developing a pipeline of candidates both individually and through collaborations with other drugmakers. Its disease targets include neurological ailments hypercholesterolemia and hemophilia. Alnylam has additional partner-based programs in clinical or development stages including candidates targeting respiratory syncytial virus (RSV) infection and liver cancers.

	Annual Growth	12/10	12/11	12/12	12/13	12/14
Sales ($ mil.)	(15.7%)	100.0	82.8	66.7	47.2	50.6
Net income ($ mil.)	–	(43.5)	(57.6)	(106.0)	(89.2)	(360.4)
Market value ($ mil.)	77.1%	761.2	629.2	1,409.0	4,964.1	7,488.7
Employees	10.5%	172	116	129	165	256

ALOHA PETROLEUM LTD.

1132 Bishop St. Suite 1700
Honolulu HI 96813-2820
Phone: 808-522-9700
Fax: 808-522-9707
Web: www.alohagas.com

CEO: Richard Parry
CFO: –
HR: –
FYE: December 31
Type: Private

Aloha Petroleum has focused on fueling its convenience store business through its longtime island heritage. The company provides fuel to its customers through 30-plus company-operated convenience store and gasoline facilities that operate under the Aloha Petroleum and Island Mini-Mart banners. Overall Aloha Petroleum counts about 50 retail fuel locations among its retail portfolio on the Big Island and on Oahu. As part of its business the retail and gas company also provides fuel storage and transportation services between its locations. Aloha Petroleum was established in the early 1900s as Associated Oil a division of Tidewater Oil which was then owned by J. Paul Getty.

ALON USA ENERGY INC

NYS: ALJ

12700 Park Central Dr., Suite 1600
Dallas, TX 75251
Phone: 972 367-3600
Fax: –
Web: www.alonusa.com

CEO: W. Paul Eisman
CFO: Shai Even
HR: –
FYE: December 31
Type: Public

Could anything be finer than FINA? Perhaps Alon is. Alon USA Energy is the driving force behind Alon (formerly FINA)-branded marketing and refining operations throughout the US Southwest. The Delek US Holdings unit provides fuel to 640 Alon-branded retail sites. It owns or operates about 300 convenience stores under the 7-Eleven and Alon brands. It also sub-licenses the Alon brand to distributors supplying 115 additional locations. Alon USA Energy's refineries in California (two) Louisiana (one) and Oregon (one) have a combined throughput capacity of 144000 barrels per day. It also indirectly owns a 70000 barrels-per-day refinery in Texas. The company is also a top asphalt producer.

	Annual Growth	12/10	12/11	12/12	12/13	12/14
Sales ($ mil.)	13.9%	4,030.7	7,186.3	8,017.7	7,046.4	6,779.5
Net income ($ mil.)	–	(132.6)	43.7	90.6	48.1	38.5
Market value ($ mil.)	20.7%	416.2	606.3	1,259.2	1,151.3	881.9
Employees	(0.7%)	2,821	2,824	2,824	2,740	2,745

ALON USA PARTNERS LP

NYS: ALDW

12700 Park Central Dr., Suite 1600
Dallas, TX 75251
Phone: 972 367-3600
Fax: –
Web: www.alonpartners.com

CEO: Paul Eisman
CFO: –
HR: –
FYE: December 31
Type: Public

The crude oil refinery of Alon USA Partners doesn't exactly stand alone seeing as how it's situated right in the middle of the West Texas oil patch. Located in Big Spring with a capacity of 70000 barrels per day it powers the company's petroleum products refining and marketing business. The refinery mainly produces gasoline and diesel and jet fuel along with asphalt and petrochemicals and the company markets them in Arizona New Mexico Oklahoma and Texas. In 2012 Alon USA Partners was spun off by Alon USA Energy which in turn is majority-owned by Alon Israel Oil. The same year the company went public through an IPO that raised $184 million.

	Annual Growth	12/10	12/11	12/12	12/13	12/14
Sales ($ mil.)	18.4%	1,639.9	3,208.0	3,476.8	3,430.3	3,221.4
Net income ($ mil.)	–	(38.5)	294.4	37.1	136.2	169.1
Market value ($ mil.)	(26.8%)	–	–	1,504.5	1,041.4	807.0
Employees	–	–	–	–	–	–

ALORICA INC.

5 Park Plaza Ste. 1100
Irvine CA 92614
Phone: 949-527-4600
Fax: 301-874-5685
Web: www.canam-steeljoists.ws

CEO: Andy Lee
CFO: James Molloy
HR: –
FYE: December 31
Type: Private

Alorica is here to remedy your front- and back-office ailments. The company provides outsourced customer service operations through about 40 call centers located in the US India and the Philippines. Its contact center services include technical support customer service help desk billing and sales (inbound and outbound). The company also offers fulfillment and service logistics including returns management warranty support management and field service dispatch. Alorica caters to customers in the automotive consumer products energy and utilities financial services health care media and entertainment retail technology telecommunications and travel sectors. It was founded in 1999 by Andy Lee.

ALPHA ASSOCIATES INC.

2 Amboy Ave.
Woodbridge NJ 07095
Phone: 732-634-5700
Fax: 732-634-1430
Web: www.alphainc.com

CEO: A Louis Avallone
CFO: –
HR: –
FYE: December 31
Type: Private

Alpha Associates would like to be seen as the alpha and omega of high-performance industrial fabrics composites and elastomers. The company makes and markets coated fabrics and laminates for a myriad of products from marine insulation welding fabrics outdoor jacketing to acoustical baffles. Alpha Associates also develops and manufactures specialty materials for high temperature insulation. Within its high performance elastomer (HPE) line goods include flexible expansion joints for flue gas ducting industrial belting and gasket sheeting. Alpha Associates' plants are setup in South Carolina Nevada and New Jersey. The family-owned company is led by its co-founder chairman and CEO A. Louis Avallone.

ALPHA NATURAL RESOURCES INC

NBB: ANRZ Q

One Alpha Place, P.O. Box 16429
Bristol, VA 24209
Phone: 276 619-4410
Fax: –
Web: www.alphanr.com

CEO: Kevin S. Crutchfield
CFO: Philip J. Cavatoni
HR: –
FYE: December 31
Type: Public

The alpha and omega of Alpha Natural Resources is coal mining. One of the top coal producers in the US the company produces steam and metallurgical coal at 60 active mines and 22 coal preparation plants primarily in central and northern Appalachia and the Powder River Basin in Wyoming. Alpha's sales are split between low-sulfur steam coal used mainly for electricity generation and metallurgical coal used primarily for steelmaking. The company produces about 84 million tons of coal per year. Alpha controls about 4 billion tons of proved and probable coal reserves. Faced with increasing debt and tightening federal regulations the company entered into Chapter 11 bankruptcy protection in August 2015.

	Annual Growth	12/10	12/11	12/12	12/13	12/14
Sales ($ mil.)	2.3%	3,917.2	7,109.2	6,974.9	4,953.5	4,287.1
Net income ($ mil.)	–	95.6	(677.4)	(2,437.1)	(1,113.5)	(875.0)
Market value ($ mil.)	(59.2%)	13,302.6	4,527.3	2,158.4	1,582.2	370.1
Employees	8.2%	6,500	14,500	12,400	10,500	8,900

ALPHA PRO TECH LTD.

ASE: APT

60 Centurian Drive, Suite 112
Markham, Ontario L3R 9R2
Phone: 905 479-0654
Fax: –
Web: www.alphaprotech.com

CEO: –
CFO: –
HR: –
FYE: December 31
Type: Public

Don't look for Alpha Pro Tech's gowns on the Paris runway; this designer stresses function over fashion. The firm makes and sells protective apparel and related products used in the cleanrooms of drugmakers lab researchers and semiconductor makers as well as in hospitals nursing homes and dentists' offices. Its disposable products include coveralls gowns lab coats and shoe covers. Its infection control products include face masks eye shields and medical bed pads. Its Alpha Pro Tech Engineered Products subsidiary manufactures building supply products used to weatherize houses. The firm sells its products primarily in the US under the Alpha Pro Tech and ChemTech brands and private labels.

	Annual Growth	12/10	12/11	12/12	12/13	12/14
Sales ($ mil.)	3.3%	41.9	38.5	41.1	43.8	47.6
Net income ($ mil.)	20.5%	1.3	0.9	1.0	2.1	2.7
Market value ($ mil.)	9.6%	32.7	22.0	26.2	39.4	47.2
Employees	(0.6%)	128	110	111	121	125

ALPHA-EN CORPORATION

OTC: ALPE

120 White Plains Rd.
Tarrytown NY 10591
Phone: 914-631-5265
Fax: +41-58-158-88-89
Web: www.jetaviation.com

CEO: Jerry I Feldman
CFO: Jerry I Feldman
HR: –
FYE: December 31
Type: Public

alpha-En Corporation (formerly Avenue Entertainment) once brought entertainment to the street where you live. The company produced films such as Closer and The Merchant of Venice and made-for-TV and cable movies including Angels in America and Path To Paradise: The Untold Story of the World Trade Center Bombing both for HBO. Its Wombat Productions created one-hour profiles of Hollywood celebrities shown on networks such as PBS A&E and Bravo. The company halted production activities and sold its assets in 2007. It is seeking another business to acquire.

ALPHABET INC

NMS: GOOG

1600 Amphitheatre Parkway
Mountain View, CA 94043
Phone: 650 253-0000
Fax: –
Web: www.abc.xyz

CEO: Sundar Pichai
CFO: Ruth M Porat
HR: Amy Buchen
FYE: December 31
Type: Public

If you don't know what the term Google means there's a leading Internet search engine you can use to find out. Taking its name from "googol" — the mathematical term for the value represented by a one followed by 100 zeros — Google offers targeted search results from billions of Web pages. Results are based on a proprietary algorithm; its technology for ranking Web pages is called PageRank. The firm generates revenue through ad sales. Advertisers deliver relevant ads targeted to search queries or Web content. The Google Network is a network of third-party customers that use Google's ad programs to deliver relevant ads to their own sites. In October 2015 Google formally became part — and by far the biggest part — of the Alphabet Inc. holding company.

	Annual Growth	12/11	12/12	12/13	12/14	12/15
Sales ($ mil.)	18.6%	37,905.0	50,175.0	59,825.0	66,001.0	74,989.0
Net income ($ mil.)	13.8%	9,737.0	10,737.0	12,920.0	14,444.0	16,348.0
Market value ($ mil.)	4.8%	443,958.1	486,216.2	770,317.8	364,748.1	534,763.6
Employees	17.5%	32,467	53,861	47,756	53,600	61,814

ALPHATEC HOLDINGS INC　　　　　　　　　　　　NMS: ATEC

5818 El Camino Real　　　　　　　　　　　　CEO: James M Corbett
Carlsbad, CA 92008　　　　　　　　　　　　CFO: Michael O'Neill
Phone: 760 431-9286　　　　　　　　　　　　HR: –
Fax: –　　　　　　　　　　　　FYE: December 31
Web: www.alphatecspine.com　　　　　　　　　　　　Type: Public

Alphatec Holdings aims to help people stand up straight and keep moving. The company develops and manufactures products used to treat spinal disorders including stenosis compression fractures and degenerating discs. Through its Alphatec Spine subsidiary the company makes a variety of FDA-approved products for the spinal fusion market in the US as well as overseas. Its spinal implant products include screws plates fixation systems grafting materials and surgical instruments. Alphatec markets its products to surgeons through a network of independent but exclusive distributors as well as a direct sales force. The company develops its products through its manufacturing facilities in California and France.

	Annual Growth	12/10	12/11	12/12	12/13	12/14
Sales ($ mil.)	4.8%	171.6	197.7	196.3	204.7	207.0
Net income ($ mil.)	–	(14.4)	(22.2)	(15.5)	(82.2)	(12.9)
Market value ($ mil.)	(15.0%)	269.6	171.8	164.8	200.7	140.8
Employees	(0.5%)	460	470	490	500	450

ALPINE AIR EXPRESS INC.　　　　　　　　　　　　OTC: APNX

1177 Alpine Air Way　　　　　　　　　　　　CEO: Kenneth E Brailsford
Provo UT 84601　　　　　　　　　　　　CFO: Rick C Wood
Phone: 801-373-1508　　　　　　　　　　　　HR: –
Fax: 801-377-3781　　　　　　　　　　　　FYE: October 31
Web: www.alpine-air.com　　　　　　　　　　　　Type: Public

Alpine Air Express flies the western skies to cart cargo for its customers. The air cargo company provides scheduled transportation of mail packages and other time-sensitive freight to more than 25 cities in the western half of the US mainland and in Hawaii. Its primary customers the United States Postal Service and United Parcel Service together account for more than 85% of sales. Alpine Air operates a fleet of about 25 Beechcraft turboprop planes from bases in Hawaii Montana and Utah. Along with its cargo operations the company provides pilot training and aircraft maintenance services. CEO Eugene Mallette owns a controlling stake in Alpine Air.

ALPS HOLDINGS INC.

1290 Broadway Ste. 1100　　　　　　　　　　　　CEO: –
Denver CO 80203　　　　　　　　　　　　CFO: –
Phone: 303-623-2577　　　　　　　　　　　　HR: –
Fax: 303-623-7850　　　　　　　　　　　　FYE: December 30
Web: www.alpsinc.com　　　　　　　　　　　　Type: Subsidiary

ALPS Holdings wants to make sure fund managers can attain peak performance by keeping their focus on their investments and letting ALPS handle the rest. Through various subsidiaries the company performs a range of back-office functions for mutual funds closed-end funds hedge funds and exchange-traded funds (ETFs). Its offerings encompass fund administration and accounting shareholder servicing and legal marketing tax distribution and transfer agency services. Clients include Cohen & Steers Macquarie Group and exchange-traded Standard & Poor's Depositary Receipts (SPDR) sector funds. DST Systems acquired ALPS from Lovell Minnick Partners in 2011.

ALRO STEEL CORPORATION

3100 E HIGH ST　　　　　　　　　　　　CEO: Alvin Glick
JACKSON, MI 492036413　　　　　　　　　　　　CFO: Steve Laten
Phone: 517-787-5500　　　　　　　　　　　　HR: –
Fax: –　　　　　　　　　　　　FYE: May 31
Web: www.alro.com　　　　　　　　　　　　Type: Private

Alro Steel runs its service centers like a grocery store for metals keeping what customers need in easy reach. The service center operator which has a dozen facilities in the US Northeast Midwest and Southeast provides processing services such as aluminum circle cutting CNC flame cutting forming and machining. The company carries an extensive inventory of steel products along with industrial tools and supplies. It also offers plastic sheet rod tube and film through its Alro Plastics division and distributes industrial tools and materials through subsidiary Alro Industrial Supplies.

	Annual Growth	05/10	05/11	05/12	05/13	05/14
Sales ($ mil.)	6.2%	–	1,348.8	1,605.3	1,553.6	1,613.7
Net income ($ mil.)	–	–	–	0.0	0.0	0.0
Market value ($ mil.)	–	–	–	–	–	–
Employees	–	–	–	–	–	2,000

ALSCO INC.

505 E SOUTH TEMPLE　　　　　　　　　　　　CEO: Robert C Steiner
SALT LAKE CITY, UT 841021004　　　　　　　　　　　　CFO: James D Kearns
Phone: 801-328-8831　　　　　　　　　　　　HR: –
Fax: –　　　　　　　　　　　　FYE: December 31
Web: www.alsco.com　　　　　　　　　　　　Type: Private

Alsco has built a big business outfitting its customers in uniforms linens and related products. Operating from some 150 branches in about 10 countries worldwide the company (whose name stands for American linen supply company) rents and sells uniforms linens towels and clean room garments to more than 140000 customers in North America. It also manages janitorial services provides washroom supplies and launders and sterilizes garments. Alsco serves the automotive food processing restaurant medical and IT industries as well as the federal government. Founded in 1889 by George Steiner the company is owned and operated by the Steiner family.

	Annual Growth	12/09	12/10	12/11	12/12	12/13
Sales ($ mil.)	5.1%	–	544.9	556.2	614.3	633.1
Net income ($ mil.)	(12.7%)	–	–	43.4	35.4	33.1
Market value ($ mil.)	–	–	–	–	–	–
Employees	–	–	–	–	–	13,585

ALSERES PHARMACEUTICALS INC　　　　　　　　　　　　NBB: ALSE

275 Grove Street Suite 2-400　　　　　　　　　　　　CEO: Peter G Savas
Auburndale, MA 02466　　　　　　　　　　　　CFO: Kenneth L Rice Jr
Phone: 508 497-2360　　　　　　　　　　　　HR: –
Fax: –　　　　　　　　　　　　FYE: December 31
　　　　　　　　　　　　Type: Public

Unlike most people the folks at Alseres Pharmaceuticals (formerly Boston Life Sciences) want to get on your nerves. The biotechnology company is developing therapies and diagnostics related to nervous system conditions such as spinal cord injury Parkinson's disease and attention deficit hyperactivity disorder (ADHD). Its lead candidate is Altropane a molecular imaging agent for diagnosing Parkinson's disease and ADHD. Another candidate Cethrin aims to repair nerve damage caused by spinal cord injury; Alseres licensed Cethrin from Canadian firm BioAxone Therapeutic in 2006.

	Annual Growth	12/09	12/10	12/11	12/12	12/13
Sales ($ mil.)	(10.7%)	–	–	–	0.5	0.5
Net income ($ mil.)	–	(10.8)	0.5	(2.9)	(1.6)	(0.9)
Market value ($ mil.)	–	0.0	0.0	0.0	0.0	0.0
Employees	(12.0%)	5	4	3	3	3

ALSTON & BIRD LLP

1 Atlantic Center 1201 W. Peachtree St.
Atlanta GA 30309-3424
Phone: 404-881-7000
Fax: 404-881-7777
Web: www.alston.com

CEO: –
CFO: Richard Levinson
HR: Shana Beldick
FYE: December 31
Type: Private - Partnershi

One of the South's leading law firms Alston & Bird groups its 80-plus practices into four main areas: corporate and finance intellectual property litigation and tax. The firm's intellectual property practice group is one of the nation's largest. Overall Alston & Bird has more than 800 attorneys policy advisers and patent agents. The firm serves a wide range of domestic and international clients which have included Bank of America Duke University General Electric Mohawk Industries New Frontier Media PSS World Medical Qualstar Corporation and UPS. Alston & Bird traces its roots to a law practice founded in 1893.

ALTA BATES SUMMIT MEDICAL CENTER

2450 Ashby Ave.
Berkeley CA 94705
Phone: 510-204-4444
Fax: 510-869-8980
Web: www.altabates.com

CEO: –
CFO: Robert Petrina
HR: –
FYE: December 31
Type: Subsidiary

Alta Bates Summit Medical Center operates a private non-profit hospital system spanning three campuses in Berkeley and Oakland California. Specializing in clinical and community outreach Alta Bates offers advanced medical care services through 30 different programs located in the East Bay including behavioral health oncology orthopedics rehabilitation cardiovascular diabetes neuroscience and women's services. Its facilities have a combined capacity of more than 1000 beds and are staffed with more than 1100 physicians. The company is a Sutter Health affiliate and was formed in 1999 through the merging of Alta Bates Herrick Merritt Peralta and Providence hospitals.

ALTA MESA HOLDINGS LP

15415 Katy Fwy. Ste. 800
Houston TX 77094-1813
Phone: 281-530-0991
Fax: +44-0161-455-4079
Web: www.odeonanducicinemasgroup.com

CEO: Hal Chappelle
CFO: Michael McCabe
HR: –
FYE: December 31
Type: Private

If Alta Mesa Holdings were your dinner companion it'd ask "Are you going to finish that?" The company goes over established oil and natural gas fields looking for what's left behind. It exploits mature fields originally developed by the big boys — Shell Chevron and Exxon — using enhanced oil recovery techniques that boost the amount of extractable oil and gas. Its properties are located in South Louisiana Oklahoma the Deep Bossier resource play of East Texas Eagle Ford Shale play and Indian Point field in South Texas the Blackjack Creek field in Florida and the Marcellus Shale in West Virginia. The company reports proved reserves of 325 billion cu. ft. of natural gas and about 250 producing wells.

ALTADIS U.S.A. INC.

5900 N. Andrews Ave. Ste. 1100
Fort Lauderdale FL 33309-2369
Phone: 954-772-9000
Fax: 954-267-1198
Web: www.altadisusa.com

CEO: Gary R Ellis
CFO: –
HR: Jost L Relea
FYE: December 31
Type: Subsidiary

When the smoke clears connoisseur puffers may find themselves holding a cigar crafted by Altadis USA. Created in 2000 from the consolidation of HavaTampa Inc. and Consolidated Cigar Holdings Altadis USA has grown to rival the world's largest cigar makers and generate a considerable share of parent Altadis S.A.'s global cigar sales. Altadis USA manufactures markets and sells both premium and mass-market cigars under such well-known brand names as Montecristo Romeo y Julieta H. Upmann and Trinidad. It also sells little cigars under the Dutch Treats and Supre Sweets brands as well as humidors and cigar cases. Altadis USA's Spanish parent company was acquired by Britain's Imperial Tobacco Group in 2008.

ALTAIR NANOTECHNOLOGIES INC

NAS: ALTI

204 Edison Way
Reno, NV 89502-2306
Phone: 775 856-2500
Fax: –
Web: www.altairnano.com

CEO: Guohua Sun
CFO: Karen Werner
HR: –
FYE: December 31
Type: Public

When Altair Nanotechnologies paints the town its pigment of choice is titanium dioxide (TiO2). The company produces titanium dioxide particles used in paints coatings and sensors. Altair intends to create new applications and products with its nanocrystalline technology. Its major development thus far has been its nano lithium-titanate battery materials which offer superior performance the company says to other rechargeable batteries. In 2011 Canon Investment Holdings through a subsidiary purchased a 49% share in Altair for $57.5 million. The deal includes the transfer of Altair's lithium-titanate manufacturing process for producing battery cells to Canon's Energy Storage Technology (China) Group.

	Annual Growth	12/08	12/09	12/10	12/11	12/12
Sales ($ mil.)	(27.9%)	5.7	4.4	7.8	5.2	1.5
Net income ($ mil.)	–	(29.1)	(21.9)	(22.3)	(19.9)	(18.0)
Market value ($ mil.)	15.3%	14.1	10.2	32.0	7.6	24.9
Employees	(2.1%)	98	99	99	77	90

ALTARUM INSTITUTE

3520 GREEN CT STE 300
ANN ARBOR, MI 481051566
Phone: 734-302-4600
Fax: –
Web: www.altarum.org

CEO: Linc Smith
CFO: Mark Kielb
HR: –
FYE: December 31
Type: Private

The Altarum Institute is a not-for-profit organization that provides health care research and consulting services primarily to government agencies. Altarum's services include policy analysis program development and management business operations planning and finance clinical research support strategic communications and event design and management. Key customers include the US Department of Health and Human Services the US Department of Defense Military Health System and the US Department of Veterans Affairs. Altarum operates in California Georgia Maine Michigan Texas and the Washington DC area.

	Annual Growth	12/09	12/10	12/11	12/12	12/13
Sales ($ mil.)	2.6%	–	73.2	84.7	87.1	79.0
Net income ($ mil.)	–	–	–	(4.6)	0.1	(1.8)
Market value ($ mil.)	–	–	–	–	–	–
Employees	–	–	–	–	–	455

ALTEC LANSING LLC

535 Rte. 6 and 209
Milford PA 18337-0277
Phone: 570-296-4434
Fax: 570-296-6887
Web: www.altectlansing.com

CEO: Ross Gatlin
CFO: Richard P Horner
HR: –
FYE: March 31
Type: Private

Altec Lansing (formerly Altec Lansing Technologies) is in the business of selling sound. The company is a leading manufacturer and marketer of speaker systems for consumer PCs as well as sound accessories such as headsets headphones and docking stations for personal digital media. It also makes home entertainment systems and scales its units to accommodate large venues. Altec Lansing traces its name back to audio pioneer James B. Lansing who founded a company devoted to theater sound systems in the 1920s. Headset specialist Plantronics which acquired Altec in 2005 to strengthen its position in the PC speaker market sold the company in December 2009 to a private equity firm.

ALTERNET SYSTEMS INC.   OTC: ALYI

1 Glen Royal Pkwy. Ste. 401
Miami FL 33125
Phone: 786-265-1840
Fax: 786-513-2887
Web: www.alternetsystems.com/

CEO: Fabio Alvino
CFO: Michael Viadero
HR: –
FYE: December 31
Type: Public

Alternet Systems turns your mobile phone into a virtual wallet. The company provides mobile payment services to consumers as well as banks and financial processing institutions merchants and retailers public transportation and utilities providers telecommunications operators and government customers throughout North America Latin America and the Caribbean. Its mobile commerce and e-ticketing products and services allow for cashless transactions such as transferring and withdrawing funds receiving overseas payments and making point-of-sale purchases. Alternet Systems restructured its operations in 2008 after acquiring VoIP telecom company TekVoice Communications.

ALTEGRITY INC.

7799 Leesburg Pike Ste. 1100 North
Falls Church VA 22043-2413
Phone: 703-448-0178
Fax: 703-448-1422
Web: www.altegrity.com

CEO: David R Fontaine
CFO: Jeffrey S Campbell
HR: –
FYE: September 30
Type: Private

It doesn't take a great detective to determine that Altegrity is a leader in security services. The holding company owns Kroll Kroll Ontrack HireRight and USIS. Kroll is a risk management company offers a range of security and technology services. Kroll Ontrack provides legal technologies data recovery and information management services while HireRight specializes in employment background and drug testing services for the private sector. USIS (formerly US Investigations Services) is the largest provider of background investigations and employment screening to the federal government. Altegrity and its subsidiaries have operations in 30 countries. The company is controlled by Providence Equity Partners.

ALTEVA   ASE: ALTV

401 Market Street, 1st Floor
Philadelphia, PA 19106
Phone: 877 258-3722
Fax: –
Web: www.alteva.com

CEO: Brian J Kelley
CFO: Brian H Callahan
HR: –
FYE: December 31
Type: Public

Alteva (formerly Warwick Valley Telephone) provides communications services from its quiet niche. The independent facilities-based telecom company was established in 1902 and has about 20000 access lines in operation. It provides local and long-distance services to consumers and businesses in a mostly rural area in southeastern New York (Warwick Wallkill and Goshen) and northwestern New Jersey (Vernon and West Milford). The company's Warwick Online unit offers dial-up and DSL Internet access digital video and a VoIP computer telephony service that is sold under the VoiceNet brand. Alteva's services for business customers include hosted conferencing and wholesale voice access.

	Annual Growth	12/09	12/10	12/11	12/12	12/13
Sales ($ mil.)	5.9%	23.9	24.4	25.9	27.9	30.1
Net income ($ mil.)	–	6.8	2.9	(2.9)	(9.5)	(0.6)
Market value ($ mil.)	(11.1%)	80.4	85.7	80.4	64.1	50.2
Employees	2.3%	113	112	143	155	124

ALTERA CORP.   NMS: ALTR

101 Innovation Drive
San Jose, CA 95134
Phone: 408 544-7000
Fax: –
Web: www.altera.com

CEO: John P Daane
CFO: Ronald J Pasek
HR: –
FYE: December 31
Type: Public

Altera is a fabless semiconductor company that specializes in high-density programmable logic devices (PLDs) — integrated circuits (ICs) that OEMs can program to perform logic functions in electronic systems. PLDs are an alternative to custom-designed ICs and offer a quick reduced-cost chip. The company's products are used by its more than 13000 customers worldwide in communications network gear consumer electronics medical systems and industrial equipment. Altera outsources fabrication of the devices to top silicon foundry Taiwan Semiconductor Manufacturing Company. Customers outside the US represent most of the company's sales.

	Annual Growth	12/10	12/11	12/12	12/13	12/14
Sales ($ mil.)	(0.3%)	1,954.4	2,064.5	1,783.0	1,732.6	1,932.1
Net income ($ mil.)	(11.9%)	782.9	770.7	556.8	440.1	472.7
Market value ($ mil.)	0.9%	10,760.5	11,220.2	10,400.6	9,832.3	11,171.8
Employees	3.8%	2,666	2,884	3,129	3,094	3,091

ALTEX INDUSTRIES, INC.   NBB: ALTX

P.O. Box 1057
Breckenridge, CO 80424-1057
Phone: 303 265-9312
Fax: –

CEO: –
CFO: –
HR: –
FYE: September 30
Type: Public

More OilRockies than AllTex(as) Altex Industries buys and sells oil and gas properties participates in drilling exploratory wells and sells oil and gas production to refineries pipeline operators and processing plants. The oil and gas exploration and production independent owns interests in two gross productive oil wells and 200 gross developed acres in Utah and Wyoming. Over the last few years Altex Industries has been forced to sell most of its oil and gas assets in order to pay down debt. CEO Steven Cardin holds a majority stake in the company.

	Annual Growth	09/11	09/12	09/13	09/14	09/15
Sales ($ mil.)	(26.1%)	0.2	0.1	0.1	0.1	0.0
Net income ($ mil.)	–	(0.3)	(0.3)	(0.3)	(0.3)	(0.3)
Market value ($ mil.)	(12.4%)	1.7	1.2	1.4	1.4	1.0
Employees	0.0%	1	1	1	1	1

ALTICOR INC.

7575 Fulton St. East
Ada MI 49355-0001
Phone: 616-787-1000
Fax: 616-682-4000
Web: www.alticor.com

CEO: –
CFO: Michael Cazer
HR: –
FYE: December 31
Type: Private

At the core of Alticor there is Amway. Holding company Alticor operates direct-selling giant Amway International and North American Web sales affiliate Amway Corp. which does business as Amway Global. Its Access Business Group offers manufacturing and distribution services primarily catering to the Amway units but also to contract clients. Outside the direct-sales realm Alticor Corporate Enterprises operates resort management firm Amway Hotel upscale cosmetics maker Gurwitch Products (known for its Laura Mercier and ReVive brands) and health diagnostics developer Interleukin Genetics. Formed in 2000 Alticor is owned by Amway's founders the DeVos and Van Andel families.

ALTIGEN COMMUNICATIONS INC   NBB: ATGN

679 River Oaks Parkway
San Jose, CA 95134
Phone: 408 597-9000
Fax: 408 597-2020
Web: www.altigen.com

CEO: Jeremiah J Fleming
CFO: Philip M. (Phil) McDermott
HR: –
FYE: September 30
Type: Public

AltiGen Communications helps businesses find their calling on the Internet. The company provides Microsoft brand voice-over-IP (VoIP) telephone systems and administration software to small and midsized businesses and call centers. Its phone systems utilize both the Internet and public telephone networks to transmit voice signals. Its MaxCommunications Server (MaxCS) systems include voicemail auto attendant menus and other features of traditional business PBX systems; its AltiContact Manager product adds advanced call center functionality. AltiGen deals primarily through resellers and distributors counts more than 10000 customers worldwide and generates the majority of its revenues in the US.

	Annual Growth	09/10	09/11	09/12	09/13	09/14
Sales ($ mil.)	(12.9%)	16.6	17.7	16.9	13.1	9.6
Net income ($ mil.)	–	(1.7)	(2.7)	(1.8)	(1.3)	(0.9)
Market value ($ mil.)	(30.0%)	17.1	15.5	5.4	3.6	4.1
Employees	(22.7%)	112	115	103	93	40

ALTRA INDUSTRIAL MOTION CORP   NMS: AIMC

300 Granite Street, Suite 201
Braintree, MA 02184
Phone: 781 917-0600
Fax: –
Web: www.altramotion.com

CEO: Carl R. Christenson
CFO: Christian Storch
HR: Amy Popoff
FYE: December 31
Type: Public

Altra Industrial Motion likes to bring things to a stop. The company manufactures mechanical power transmission and motion control products. Altra specializes in industrial clutches and brakes gear drives couplings and bearings used in such diverse assemblies as elevator braking systems and wheelchairs. Its lineup is marketed under multiple brands including TB Wood's and Warner Electric both directly and through distributors to OEMs in material handling mining and transportation industries. The company also caters to customers engaged in energy food processing medical and turf and garden markets. North America accounts for more than 60% of sales.

	Annual Growth	12/10	12/11	12/12	12/13	12/14
Sales ($ mil.)	12.0%	520.2	674.8	732.0	722.2	819.8
Net income ($ mil.)	13.1%	24.5	37.7	24.3	40.3	40.2
Market value ($ mil.)	9.3%	523.4	496.2	581.1	901.8	748.2
Employees	9.2%	2,787	3,466	3,617	3,810	3,957

ALTRIA GROUP INC   NYS: MO

6601 West Broad Street
Richmond, VA 23230
Phone: 804 274-2200
Fax: –
Web: www.altria.com

CEO: Martin J. (Marty) Barrington
CFO: William F. (Billy) Gifford
HR: –
FYE: December 31
Type: Public

The house the Marlboro Man built Altria Group owns the largest cigarette company in the US. Altria operates through subsidiary Philip Morris USA which sells Marlboro — the world's #1-selling cigarette brand. Controlling about half of the US tobacco market Altria manufactures cigarettes under the Parliament Virginia Slims and Basic brands among many. Altria however has diversified from solely a cigarette maker to a purveyor of cigars and pipe tobacco through John Middleton Co. smokeless tobacco products through UST and wine through Ste. Michelle Wine Estates. Another subsidiary Philip Morris Capital Corp. holds a group of finance leases. Altria also owns a 27% stake in SABMiller.

	Annual Growth	12/10	12/11	12/12	12/13	12/14
Sales ($ mil.)	0.2%	24,363.0	23,800.0	24,618.0	24,466.0	24,522.0
Net income ($ mil.)	6.7%	3,905.0	3,390.0	4,180.0	4,535.0	5,070.0
Market value ($ mil.)	18.9%	48,537.7	58,454.2	61,983.2	75,684.9	97,134.5
Employees	(2.6%)	10,000	9,900	9,100	9,000	9,000

ALTRU HEALTH SYSTEM

1200 S. Columbia Rd.
Grand Forks ND 58206
Phone: 701-780-5000
Fax: 701-780-1093
Web: www.altru.org

CEO: David Molmen
CFO: Dwight Thompson
HR: –
FYE: December 31
Type: Private - Not-for-Pr

This much is all true: Altru Health System provides medical care throughout northeastern North Dakota and northwestern Minnesota. The integrated health care network administers everything from primary care to inpatient medical and surgical care through its Altru Hospital (with roughly 260 beds) and about a dozen primary care clinics. It also operates a cancer center a rehabilitation center dialysis facilities and home health providers. For area seniors Altru Health operates Parkwood Place a senior living facility that provides several levels of care to residents depending on need. Altru Health was formed in 1997 by the integration of Grand Forks Clinic and United Health Services.

ALTUM INCORPORATED

12100 SUNSET HILLS RD # 101
RESTON, VA 201903233
Phone: 703-657-8299
Fax: –
Web: www.altum.com

CEO: Steve Pinchotti
CFO: Wendy Fyock
HR: –
FYE: December 31
Type: Private

Altum hopes to provide alternatives to old fashioned data management solutions such as filing cabinets paper and pen. The company provides software and services that clients use to access analyze and manage enterprise data. Altum's software products include applications for data collection collaboration reporting and text searches as well as tools that enable grant-making organizations to analyze and manage their grant programs. The company also offers services such as consulting training support and maintenance. Altum was founded in 1997.

	Annual Growth	03/05	03/06	03/07	03/08*	12/12
Sales ($ mil.)	38.4%	–	–	–	2.3	8.4
Net income ($ mil.)	(47.3%)	–	–	–	2.1	0.2
Market value ($ mil.)	–	–	–	–	–	–
Employees	–	–	–	–	–	39

*Fiscal year change

ALVAREZ & MARSAL HOLDINGS LLC

600 Lexington Ave. 6th Fl.
New York NY 10022
Phone: 212-759-4433
Fax: 212-759-5532
Web: www.alvarezandmarsal.com

CEO: –
CFO: –
HR: –
FYE: December 31
Type: Private

A&M specializes in M&A along with restructuring right-sizing and other corporate turnaround processes. Alvarez & Marsal provides advisory and consulting services related to mergers and acquisitions (M&A) restructuring turnaround situations crisis and interim management divestitures performance improvement dispute resolution and strategic planning. The firm is becoming increasingly involved in private equity investing. It possesses expertise in the financial services healthcare real estate retail and public sectors. Alvarez & Marsal has some 40 offices around the world. Co-CEOs Bryan Marsal and Tony Alvarez II started the firm in 1983.

ALVERNIA UNIVERSITY

400 SAINT BERNARDINE ST
READING, PA 196071737
Phone: 610-796-8200
Fax: –
Web: www.de.alvernia.edu

CEO: –
CFO: –
HR: –
FYE: June 30
Type: Private

Alvernia University (formerly Alvernia College) is a private Catholic Franciscan liberal arts college. It offers about 40 undergraduate majors and about 20 undergraduate minors as well as associate of science degrees in business and computer information systems six master's degrees programs and a doctor of philosophy program. Its main campus is located in Reading Pennsylvania with additional courses taught in Pottsville and Philadelphia. The university has a total enrollment of some 3000 students. Alvernia was founded in 1958 by the Bernardine Franciscan Sisters. The institution gained university status in 2008.

	Annual Growth	06/08	06/09	06/10	06/11	06/13
Sales ($ mil.)	–	–	–	0.0	56.0	63.3	69.1
Net income ($ mil.)	(1.3%)	–	–	–	4.2	5.6	4.0
Market value ($ mil.)	–	–	–	–	–	–	–
Employees	–	–	–	–	–	–	293

ALVERNO COLLEGE

3400 S 43RD ST
MILWAUKEE, WI 532194844
Phone: 414-382-6000
Fax: –
Web: www.alverno.edu

CEO: –
CFO: –
HR: –
FYE: June 30
Type: Private

Alverno College is an independent liberal arts institution with an enrollment of more than 2100 undergraduates and about 500 graduate students. It confers associate's bachelor's and master's degrees in more than 60 areas of study at four schools: Arts and Sciences Business Education and Nursing. Matriculating only women in its undergraduate programs Alverno accepts men as graduate students. Alverno takes its name from a mountain in Italy (La Verna) that was given to St. Francis as a gift and used by his followers as a place of reflection. The school was founded by the School Sisters of St. Francis in 1887.

	Annual Growth	06/09	06/10	06/11	06/12	06/13
Sales ($ mil.)	4.6%	–	53.8	45.2	60.6	61.6
Net income ($ mil.)	32.9%	–	–	4.4	6.1	7.7
Market value ($ mil.)	–	–	–	–	–	–
Employees	–	–	–	–	–	1,000

ALY ENERGY SERVICES INC (DE)

NBB: ALYE

3 Riverway, Suite 920
Houston, TX 77056
Phone: 713 333-4000
Fax: –
Web: www.alyenergy.com

CEO: Munawar H Hidayatallah
CFO: Alya Hidayatallah
HR: –
FYE: December 31
Type: Public

A Preferred Voice may be one that makes life easier. Preferred Voice answers that call with a host of integrated voice-driven products and services. The company's Global Application Platform (GAP) lets telecommunications providers offer enhanced services such as ringtones and games reminders voice-activated dialing and conferencing. The company's My Phone Services Suite features a network-based address book with offerings such as its flagship Rockin' Ringback and Emma the virtual receptionist. Preferred Voice offers its services through half-a-dozen carriers but wireless service provider MetroPCS Communications is its biggest customer accounting for 52% of sales.

	Annual Growth	12/11*	03/12*	12/12	12/13	12/14
Sales ($ mil.)	130.8%	–	–	–	18.4	42.5
Net income ($ mil.)	–	(0.1)	(0.1)	(0.1)	0.7	2.6
Market value ($ mil.)	122.4%	0.3	0.3	0.2	1.3	3.3
Employees	1349.1%	–	1	1	99	210

*Fiscal year change

ALYESKA PIPELINE SERVICE COMPANY

900 E. Benson St.
Anchorage AK 99519
Phone: 907-787-8700
Fax: 907-787-8240
Web: www.alyeska-pipe.com

CEO: –
CFO: –
HR: Bryan Brown
FYE: December 31
Type: Private - Consortium

Named after the Aleut word for mainland The Alyeska Pipeline Service Company operates the 800-mile-long 48-inch-diameter pipeline that transports crude oil and natural gas liquids from Alaska's North Slope to the marine oil terminal of Valdez in Prince William Sound. Founded in 1970 to make the newly discovered finds in Prudhoe Bay commercially accessible the company was assigned the task of designing building operating and maintaining the Trans-Alaska Pipeline System (TAPS). TAPS is owned by a consortium of oil and gas firms including BP (47%) ConocoPhillips (28%) Exxon Mobil (20%) Koch (3%) and Chevron (Unocal Pipeline 1%).

ALZHEIMER''S DISEASE AND RELATED DISORDERS ASSOCIATION INC.

225 N MICHIGAN AVE FL 17
CHICAGO, IL 606017652
Phone: 312-335-8700
Fax: –
Web: www.alz.org

CEO: Harry Johns
CFO: –
HR: –
FYE: June 30
Type: Private

Alzheimer's Association wants you to "maintain your brain". The charitable organization is working to prevent treat and ultimately cure Alzheimer's a progressive brain disorder that destroys memory and the ability to learn reason and do other daily activities. The group has more than 80 local chapters throughout the US and numerous service programs including a 24-hour helpline support groups information libraries public advocacy an online community and a registration program so wandering Alzheimer patients can be returned home safely. Alzheimer's Association also funds research and hosts national and international conferences for scientists and caregivers. Its annual fund raiser is the Walk to End Alzheimer's.

	Annual Growth	06/09	06/10	06/11	06/12	06/13
Sales ($ mil.)	10.6%	–	87.9	98.7	110.1	119.0
Net income ($ mil.)	(7.1%)	–	–	10.9	2.7	9.4
Market value ($ mil.)	–	–	–	–	–	–
Employees	–	–	–	–	–	200

AM-MEX PRODUCTS INC.

3801 W. Military Hwy.
McAllen TX 78503-8810
Phone: 956-631-7916
Fax: 956-631-7999
Web: www.ammexproducts.com

CEO: –
CFO: –
HR: –
FYE: December 31
Type: Private

Am-Mex Products helps companies set up maquiladora operations in the McAllen Texas and Reynosa Mexico border region. The maquiladora program allows US firms and other foreign companies to import raw materials into Mexico duty-free for assembly there by lower-wage Mexican workers. The program also offers faster startup lower shipping costs and central distribution. Its services include contract manufacturing engineering factory management warehousing and distribution cross-border trucking training and other services required for international trade. Am-Mex has been in business since 1990 and has around 1 million sq. ft. of manufacturing and warehouse space in Mexico in addition to its US operation.

AMAG PHARMACEUTICALS, INC.

NMS: AMAG

1100 Winter Street
Waltham, MA 02451
Phone: 617 498-3300
Fax: –
Web: www.amagpharma.com

CEO: William K. Heiden
CFO: Scott A Holmes
HR: Elizabeth (Beth) Bolgiano
FYE: December 31
Type: Public

It's rare when the illness and cure are one in the same; but in AMAG Pharmaceuticals' case iron is the problem and the solution. The biopharmaceutical company is focused on the development and commercialization of an iron compound to treat iron deficiency anemia (IDA). Its primary money maker is its ferumoxytol Feraheme Injection to treat IDA in patients with chronic kidney disease (CKD). AMAG sells Feraheme in the US through its own sales force; in Europe (Switzerland) some Asian countries Canada India and Turkey through an exclusive licensing agreement with Takeda. AMAG's other product MuGard Mucoadhesive Oral Wound Rinse is marketed in the US and is used in the management of oral mucositis.

	Annual Growth	12/10	12/11	12/12	12/13	12/14
Sales ($ mil.)	17.1%	66.2	61.2	85.4	80.9	124.4
Net income ($ mil.)	–	(81.2)	(77.1)	(16.8)	(9.6)	135.8
Market value ($ mil.)	23.9%	463.4	484.1	376.6	621.6	1,091.1
Employees	3.3%	226	174	129	148	257

AMALGAMATED LIFE INSURANCE COMPANY

333 Westchester Ave.
White Plains NY 10604-2910
Phone: 914-367-5000
Fax: 404-872-0457
Web: www.arthritis.org

CEO: David J Walsh
CFO: Vinecsa Castro
HR: Clementina Todorova
FYE: December 31
Type: Private

Amalgamated Life Insurance has combined a variety of life insurance products and services to aid the working man and woman. The company provides life insurance retirement plans voluntary benefits and other products to members of some 30 different labor unions and other moderate income individuals. In addition to its group and individual products (life accident and disability) Amalgamated Life Insurance and its affiliates offer third party administration (TPA) and medical cost management to self-insured groups. The company is licensed in over 40 states and has offices nationwide. It provides coverage to some 800000 customers.

AMARILLO BIOSCIENCES INC.

NBB: AMAR Q

4134 Business Park Drive
Amarillo, TX 79110
Phone: 806 376-1741
Fax: –
Web: www.amarbio.com

CEO: Stephen Chen
CFO: Bernard Cohen
HR: –
FYE: December 31
Type: Public

Amarillo — home to cattlemen prairies and...interferon? Amarillo Biosciences hopes its low-dose interferon alpha (IFNa) which modulates the immune system will help those suffering from a range of maladies including viral and autoimmune diseases. The company's interferon technology which uses a low-dose dissolving tablet potentially offers effective treatment with fewer side effects than injectable forms of the drug. Amarillo Biosciences is developing its interferon technology as a treatment for flu oral warts in HIV patients and chronic cough. Through research partners it is also investigating the drug in relation to Behcet's disease (a severe inflammatory disorder) and hepatitis C.

	Annual Growth	12/08	12/09	12/10	12/11	12/12
Sales ($ mil.)	(73.6%)	0.1	0.1	0.0	0.1	0.0
Net income ($ mil.)	–	(1.9)	(3.0)	0.5	(1.3)	(0.7)
Market value ($ mil.)	(27.6%)	4.0	12.5	5.9	2.6	1.1
Employees	(9.6%)	6	5	4	4	4

AMAZON.COM INC.

NMS: AMZN

410 Terry Avenue North
Seattle, WA 98109-5210
Phone: 206 266-1000
Fax: 206 266-1821
Web: www.amazon.com

CEO: Jeffrey P. (Jeff) Bezos
CFO: Brian T. Olsavsky
HR: John (Jack) Olsen
FYE: December 31
Type: Public

What began as Earth's biggest bookstore has become Earth's biggest everything store. Expansion has propelled Amazon.com in innumerable directions. While the website still offers millions of books movies games and music selling other items — such as electronics apparel and accessories auto parts home furnishings health and beauty aids toys and groceries — contributes some two-thirds of sales. Shoppers can also download e-books games MP3s and films to their computers or handheld devices including Amazon's own portable e-reader the Kindle. Amazon also offers products and services such as self-publishing online advertising e-commerce platform hosting and a co-branded credit card.

	Annual Growth	12/11	12/12	12/13	12/14	12/15
Sales ($ mil.)	22.1%	48,077.0	61,093.0	74,452.0	88,988.0	107,006.0
Net income ($ mil.)	(1.4%)	631.0	(39.0)	274.0	(241.0)	596.0
Market value ($ mil.)	40.6%	81,530.1	118,159.8	187,830.1	146,174.9	318,344.2
Employees	42.4%	56,200	88,400	117,300	154,100	230,800

AMB FINANCIAL CORP

OTC: AMFC

8230 Hohman Avenue
Munster, IN 46321
Phone: 219 836-5870
Fax: 219 836-5883
Web: www..acbanker.com

CEO: Michael Mellon
CFO: Steven A Bohn
HR: –
FYE: December 31
Type: Public

AMB Financial is the holding company for American Savings a thrift serving Lake County Indiana near the southern tip of Lake Michigan. It operates four offices in Dyer Hammond Munster and Schererville. Catering to local families and businesses the bank offers checking and savings accounts money market accounts certificates of deposit and IRAs. It mainly uses these deposit funds to originate real estate construction consumer commercial land and other loans. One- to four-family residential mortgages account for approximately three-quarters of its loan portfolio. American Savings offers financial planning services through its American Financial Services division.

	Annual Growth	12/06	12/07	12/12	12/13	12/14
Assets ($ mil.)	0.2%	182.3	174.8	–	174.5	185.0
Net income ($ mil.)	6.1%	0.6	0.0	0.8	0.8	1.0
Market value ($ mil.)	(6.1%)	15.4	13.1	5.9	7.2	9.3
Employees	(5.1%)	39	37	–	–	–

AMBAC FINANCIAL GROUP, INC.   NMS: AMBC

One State Street Plaza
New York, NY 10004
Phone: 212 658-7470
Fax: –

CEO: Nader Tavakoli
CFO: David Trick
HR: –
FYE: December 31
Type: Public

Ambac Financial Group used to give an A+ to school bonds until its own ratings fell to C's. Ambac Assurance the holding company's primary subsidiary sold financial guarantee insurance and other credit enhancement products for municipal bonds in the US market. However the company has halted all new business and has placed its remaining business in "run-off" — meaning it is only taking in premium payments and paying out claims as it is able. Already operating under "rehabilitation" by Wisconsin regulators Ambac Financial filed for Chapter 11 bankruptcy in 2010.

	Annual Growth	12/11	12/12*	04/13*	12/13	12/14
Assets ($ mil.)	(2.5%)	27,113.7	27,007.2	–	27,106.9	25,159.9
Net income ($ mil.)	–	(1,960.4)	(256.7)	3,349.0	505.2	483.7
Market value ($ mil.)	(0.2%)	–	–	–	1,105.3	1,102.6
Employees	(6.1%)	227	226	–	212	188

*Fiscal year change

AMBASSADORS GROUP INC   NMS: EPAX

Dwight D. Eisenhower Building, 2001 South Flint Road
Spokane, WA 99224
Phone: 509 568-7800
Fax: –
Web: www.ambassadorsgroup.com

CEO: Philip B Livingston
CFO: –
HR: –
FYE: December 31
Type: Public

Ambassadors Group provides students and professionals with opportunities to meet their counterparts overseas. It organizes trips under contracts with the People to People organization which was founded by President Eisenhower to promote world peace. Ambassadors Group markets trips using the People to People name and makes travel arrangements for participants which include student athletes and leaders as well as professionals. It also offers international adventure travel services to students through its World Adventures Unlimited subsidiary. Outside the travel industry the firm operates BookRags.com a research website with more than 8 million pages of educational content for students and teachers.

	Annual Growth	12/09	12/10	12/11	12/12	12/13
Sales ($ mil.)	(15.1%)	98.6	76.1	66.4	58.1	51.2
Net income ($ mil.)	–	20.3	8.1	3.0	1.7	(7.1)
Market value ($ mil.)	(23.1%)	226.0	196.0	76.9	72.6	79.2
Employees	(3.5%)	251	221	240	238	218

AMBIENT CORP.   NBB: AMBT Q

7 Wells Avenue
Newton, MA 02459
Phone: 617 332-0004
Fax: –
Web: www.ambientcorp.com

CEO: –
CFO: –
HR: –
FYE: December 31
Type: Public

Ambient hopes its smart grid technology will stand out not blend in. The company develops technology that allows power lines to serve as high-speed data communications networks. Ambient's products — including nodes couplers and network management software — utilize Broadband over Power Line (BPL) and other technologies to create advanced power grids (also known as smart grids) with two-way communication capabilities. Its systems are designed to be used by utility companies for such applications as demand management direct load control meter reading and real-time pricing. Ambient has landed deals with Con Ed and Duke Energy to develop and deploy its technology.

	Annual Growth	12/09	12/10	12/11	12/12	12/13
Sales ($ mil.)	50.8%	2.2	20.4	62.3	42.8	11.4
Net income ($ mil.)	–	(14.2)	(3.2)	4.8	(5.4)	(17.7)
Market value ($ mil.)	105.9%	2.5	1.7	78.1	50.8	44.9
Employees	(1.7%)	44	59	88	105	41

AMC ENTERTAINMENT INC.

920 Main St.
Kansas City MO 64105-1977
Phone: 816-221-4000
Fax: 816-480-4617
Web: www.amcentertainment.com

CEO: Gerardo I Lopez
CFO: Craig R Ramsey
HR: –
FYE: March 31
Type: Private

AMC Entertainment shines when the lights go down. The company whose initials once stood for American Multi-Cinema is the #2 movie theater chain in the US (behind Regal Entertainment). It owns partially owns or operates about 350 theaters with 5000 screens most of which are in megaplexes (units with more than 14 screens and stadium seating). Nearly all of its theaters are in the US though it does have a few in Europe. AMC also owns about 25% of MovieTickets.com. The company is itself owned by a group that includes investment firms Apollo Management LP The Carlyle Group Bain Capital JPMorgan and Spectrum Equity Investors. Chinese investment firm Wanda Group announced plans to acquire AMC in 2012.

AMC ENTERTAINMENT HOLDINGS INC.   NYS: AMC

One AMC Way, 11500 Ash Street
Leawood, KS 66211
Phone: 913 213-2000
Fax: –
Web: www.amctheatres.com

CEO: Gerardo I. (Gerry) Lopez
CFO: Craig R. Ramsey
HR: –
FYE: December 31
Type: Public

AMC Entertainment shines when the lights go down. The company whose initials once stood for American Multi-Cinema is the #2 movie theater chain in the US (behind Regal Entertainment). It owns partially owns or operates about 350 theaters with 5000 screens most of which are in megaplexes (units with more than 12 screens and stadium seating). Nearly all of its theaters are in the US though it does have a few in Europe. AMC also owns about 25% of MovieTickets.com. Chinese investment firm Wanda Group bought AMC in 2012 and took the company public again in 2013.

	Annual Growth	03/12*	08/12*	12/12	12/13	12/14
Sales ($ mil.)	3.4%	2,522.0	1,206.1	811.5	2,749.4	2,695.4
Net income ($ mil.)	–	(94.1)	90.2	(42.7)	364.4	64.1
Market value ($ mil.)	27.4%	–	–	–	2,001.3	2,549.6
Employees	1.8%	–	–	19,000	20,600	19,700

*Fiscal year change

AMC NETWORKS INC   NMS: AMCX

11 Penn Plaza
New York, NY 10001
Phone: 212 324-8500
Fax: –
Web: www.amcnetworks.com

CEO: Joshua W. Sapan
CFO: Sean S. Sullivan
HR: Rob Doodian
FYE: December 31
Type: Public

AMC Networks is now somewhere over the rainbow. Formerly Rainbow Media Holdings the company is a leading cable television broadcaster with a portfolio of popular TV networks anchored by American Movie Classics (AMC) the cable network airing such critical hits as Mad Men and Breaking Bad that reaches more than 95 million households. It also owns The Independent Film Channel (IFC) the Sundance Channel and WE: Women's Entertainment (WE tv) one of the top networks aimed at women viewers. The company was a former subsidiary of Cablevision Systems until mid-2011 when Cablevision spun off Rainbow Media Holdings into a publicly traded company and changed its name to AMC Networks.

	Annual Growth	12/10	12/11	12/12	12/13	12/14
Sales ($ mil.)	19.2%	1,078.3	1,187.7	1,352.6	1,591.9	2,175.6
Net income ($ mil.)	34.3%	80.1	126.5	136.5	290.7	260.8
Market value ($ mil.)	19.3%	–	2,707.2	3,565.8	4,906.4	4,593.8
Employees	21.9%	876	956	1,010	2,197	1,933

AMCOL INTERNATIONAL CORP.　　　　　　　　　　NYS: ACO

2870 Forbs Avenue　　　　　　　　　　CEO: Ryan F McKendrick
Hoffman Estates, IL 60192　　　　　　　　　CFO: Donald W Pearson
Phone: 847 851-1500　　　　　　　　　　　　　　　　　　HR: –
Fax: 847 851-1699　　　　　　　　　　　　　FYE: December 31
Web: www.amcol.com　　　　　　　　　　　　　　　Type: Public

AMCOL International is nothing if not diverse with operations in minerals environmental services oilfield services and transportation. Its performance materials segment is a global supplier of bentonite products used in cat litter laundry detergent metal casting paper manufacturing and as a plastic additive. Its construction services segment provides building materials and construction services to concrete waterproofing drilling flood control and site remediation projects. AMCOL's energy services unit offers water treatment and well testing to the oil and gas industry. The company's transportation business provides long-haul trucking and freight brokerage services to AMCOL units and third parties in the US and Canada.

	Annual Growth	12/08	12/09	12/10	12/11	12/12
Sales ($ mil.)	2.8%	883.6	703.2	852.5	942.4	985.6
Net income ($ mil.)	26.6%	25.3	34.8	30.3	59.1	65.1
Market value ($ mil.)	10.0%	674.3	914.7	997.7	864.1	987.4
Employees	4.3%	2,388	2,211	2,383	2,563	2,824

AMCON DISTRIBUTING COMPANY　　　　　　　ASE: DIT

7405 Irvington Road　　　　　　　　　　CEO: Christopher H Atayan
Omaha, NE 68122　　　　　　　　　　　　CFO: Andrew C Plummer
Phone: 402 331-3727　　　　　　　　　　　　　　　　　　HR: –
Fax: 402 331-4834　　　　　　　　　　　　FYE: September 30
Web: www.amcon.com　　　　　　　　　　　　　　Type: Public

AMCON Distributing enjoys a healthy meal but the company is not without its vices. A leading consumer products wholesaler AMCON distributes more than 16000 different consumer products including cigarettes and other tobacco products as well as candy beverages groceries paper products and health and beauty aids. AMCON serves about 4500 convenience stores supermarkets drugstores tobacco shops and institutional customers in the Great Plains and Rocky Mountain regions. Throughout the Midwest and Florida the company also operates a growing chain of health food stores under the Chamberlin's Natural Foods and Akin's Natural Foods Market banners.

	Annual Growth	09/11	09/12	09/13	09/14	09/15
Sales ($ mil.)	5.3%	1,041.6	1,174.2	1,211.1	1,236.8	1,281.9
Net income ($ mil.)	(5.8%)	8.1	7.4	5.9	5.0	6.4
Market value ($ mil.)	8.9%	35.4	40.4	50.9	52.6	49.7
Employees	(2.5%)	895	875	874	840	808

AMEDICA CORP　　　　　　　　　　　　　　　　NAS: AMDA

1885 West 2100 South　　　　　　　　　　　　　CEO: B. Sonny Bal
Salt Lake City, UT 84119　　　　　　　　　　　　　CFO: Ty Lombardi
Phone: 801 839-3500　　　　　　　　　　　　　　　　　　HR: –
Fax: –　　　　　　　　　　　　　　　　　　　　FYE: December 31
Web: www.amedicacorp.com　　　　　　　　　　　　Type: Public

You can spin a disc or burn a disc but when you blow a disc (in your back) the fun stops and Amedica steps in. It develops manufactures and commercializes joint and spine implants made of silicon nitride ceramic a more durable resistant and patient-compatible alternative to traditional implant materials. Amedica's lead product candidates are its Valeo spinal implants which are intended to restore and maintain vertebrae alignment in the neck and lower back. Valeo spinal spacer implants have received FDA and EU approval for use as vertebra replacements. Amedica's other candidates include ceramic hip and knee implants with material that mimic the porous structure of natural bone. It went public in 2014.

	Annual Growth	12/10	12/11	12/12	12/13	12/14
Sales ($ mil.)	–	–	0.0	20.3	23.1	22.8
Net income ($ mil.)	–	–	0.0	(23.8)	(35.0)	(8.3)	(32.6)
Market value ($ mil.)	–	–	0.0	–	–	1.4
Employees	(8.6%)	–	–	–	79	79	66

AMEDISYS, INC.　　　　　　　　　　　　　　　NMS: AMED

5959 S. Sherwood Forest Blvd.　　　　　　　CEO: Paul B. Kusserow
Baton Rouge, LA 70816　　　　　　　　　　CFO: Ronald A. LaBorde
Phone: 225 292-2031　　　　　　　　　　HR: Martha S Williams
Fax: –　　　　　　　　　　　　　　　　　FYE: December 31
Web: www.amedisys.com　　　　　　　　　　　　Type: Public

Because the last thing you want to do when you're ailing is drive to a doctor's office Amedisys brings health care home. Through more than 300 home health care agencies located throughout the US the company provides skilled nursing and home health services primarily to geriatric patients covered by Medicare. Its range of services includes disease-specific programs that help patients recovering from stroke as well as assistance for those coping with emphysema or diabetes. In addition to home health services Amedisys owns or manages about 100 hospice agencies that offer palliative care to terminally ill patients.

	Annual Growth	12/10	12/11	12/12	12/13	12/14
Sales ($ mil.)	(7.3%)	1,634.3	1,470.4	1,487.9	1,249.3	1,204.6
Net income ($ mil.)	(42.0%)	112.6	(382.5)	(83.6)	(96.2)	12.8
Market value ($ mil.)	(3.3%)	1,125.4	366.5	379.8	491.5	986.0
Employees	(5.1%)	16,300	16,500	15,200	14,300	13,200

AMEN PROPERTIES INC　　　　　　　　　　　NBB: AMEN

303 W. Wall Street, Suite 2300　　　　　　　　　CEO: Jon M Morgan
Midland, TX 79701　　　　　　　　　　　　　　CFO: Kris Oliver
Phone: 432 684-3821　　　　　　　　　　　　　　　　　　HR: –
Fax: –　　　　　　　　　　　　　　　　　　　FYE: December 31
Web: www.amenproperties.com　　　　　　　　　Type: Public

AMEN Properties is hoping that the answer to its prayers are power and energy and a little property thrown in for good measure. The company's Priority Power subsidiary provides energy management and consulting services. This unit has current or previous business activities in Texas and 21 other states and serves more than 1200 clients (including a large number of oil and gas companies.) These activities include electricity load aggregation natural gas and electricity procurement energy risk management and energy consulting. AMEN Properties also invests in commercial real estate in secondary markets and in oil and gas royalties.

	Annual Growth	12/07	12/11	12/12	12/13	12/14
Sales ($ mil.)	(20.4%)	14.3	3.6	2.6	3.0	2.9
Net income ($ mil.)	28.7%	1.3	1.0	1.3	2.5	7.6
Market value ($ mil.)	86.0%	0.4	37.2	31.9	31.1	30.8
Employees	–	–	27	–	–	–

AMERALIA INC.　　　　　　　　　　　　　PINK SHEETS: AALA

9233 Park Meadows Dr. Ste. 431　　　　　　　　　　　　CEO: –
Lone Tree CO 80124　　　　　　　　　　　　　CFO: Bill H Gunn
Phone: 720-876-2373　　　　　　　　　　　　　　　　　　HR: –
Fax: 970-878-5866　　　　　　　　　　　　　　　FYE: June 30
Web: www.naturalsoda.com　　　　　　　　　　　Type: Public

AmerAlia is sold on soda. Through subsidiary Natural Soda Inc. AmerAlia owns sodium bicarbonate leases in the region of Colorado's Piceance Creek Basin. AmerAlia can produce about 110000 tons of various grades of sodium bicarbonate per year. Sodium bicarbonate (baking soda) is used in animal feed food and pharmaceuticals. Byproducts such as soda ash and caustic soda are used to make glass detergents and chemicals. Investment group Sentient USA Resources Fund owns about three-quarters of AmerAlia. The company's operations are handled through 18%-owned subsidiary Natural Soda Holdings which itself owns Natural Soda Inc. outright.

AMERAMEX INTERNATIONAL INC.

PINK SHEETS: AMMX

3930 Esplanade
Chico CA 95973
Phone: 530-895-8955
Fax: 530-895-8959
Web: www.ammx.net/index.htm

CEO: Lee R Hamre
CFO: Tracie Hannick
HR: –
FYE: December 31
Type: Public

Let AmeraMex take care of the heavy stuff. The company sells leases services and maintains heavy equipment to businesses such as heavy construction surface mining infrastructure logging shipping and transportation. AmeraMex has four business units: Hamre Equipment Hamre Heavy Haul Industry Hamre Parts and Service and John's Radiator. Its inventory includes front-end loaders excavators container handlers and trucks and trailers; manufacturers represented include Taylor Machine Works Terex Heavy Equipment and Barko Hydraulics. The firm is active in the Americas Europe the Middle East and Asia. AmeraMex also provides heavy hauling services throughout the US.

AMERCO

NMS: UHAL

5555 Kietzke Lane, Ste. 100
Reno, NV 89511
Phone: 775 688-6300
Fax: 775 688-6338
Web: www.amerco.com

CEO: Edward J. (Joe) Shoen
CFO: Jason A Berg
HR: –
FYE: March 31
Type: Public

U-Haul wants to know if you are sure you want to spend the extra money for a moving company? If not there's AMERCO whose principal subsidiary U-Haul International serves do-it-yourselfers with orange-and-white trucks trailers and towing devices. Founded in 1945 the company also sells packing supplies through about 18200 independent dealers and 1600 company-owned centers across the US and Canada. U-Haul's websites offer equipment reservations and moving information. AMERCO owns U-Haul-managed self-storage facilities and provides property and casualty insurance to U-Haul customers through Repwest. Its Oxford Life unit provides annuities Medicare supplement and life insurance coverage.

	Annual Growth	03/11	03/12	03/13	03/14	03/15
Sales ($ mil.)	8.2%	2,241.3	2,502.7	2,558.6	2,835.3	3,074.5
Net income ($ mil.)	18.1%	183.6	205.4	264.7	342.4	356.7
Market value ($ mil.)	35.9%	1,902.0	2,068.8	3,402.7	4,551.4	6,478.4
Employees	11.2%	16,600	17,700	21,600	24,300	25,400

AMEREN CORP.

NYS: AEE

1901 Chouteau Avenue
St. Louis, MO 63103
Phone: 314 621-3222
Fax: –
Web: www.ameren.com

CEO: Warner L. Baxter
CFO: Martin J. Lyons
HR: John (Jack) Fey
FYE: December 31
Type: Public

Ameren provides the power that makes much of the American Midwest run. The holding company distributes electricity to 2.8 million customers and natural gas to 940000 customers in Missouri and Illinois through regulated utility subsidiaries Union Electric (which does business as Ameren Missouri) and Ameren Ilinois. Ameren has a generating capacity of about 10272 MW (primarily coal-fired) most of which is controlled by Ameren Missouri). Ameren operates a nuclear power facility two hydroelectric plants and several coal-fired plants and natural gas-fired facilities. It also purchases green power including wind power and solar.

	Annual Growth	12/10	12/11	12/12	12/13	12/14
Sales ($ mil.)	(5.6%)	7,638.0	7,531.0	6,828.0	5,838.0	6,053.0
Net income ($ mil.)	43.3%	139.0	519.0	(974.0)	289.0	586.0
Market value ($ mil.)	13.1%	6,838.9	8,037.3	7,452.7	8,772.4	11,191.1
Employees	(2.6%)	9,474	9,323	9,097	8,527	8,527

AMEREN ILLINOIS CO

NBB: AILL P

6 Executive Drive
Collinsville, IL 62234
Phone: 618 343-8150
Fax: –

CEO: Richard J Mark
CFO: Martin J Lyons Jr
HR: –
FYE: December 31
Type: Public

Ameren Illinois brings gas and electric services to customers across the Land of Lincoln. The Ameren subsidiary operates a rate-regulated electric and natural gas transmission and distribution business in Illinois serving more than 1.2 million electricity and 806000 natural gas customers in 85 of Illinois' 102 counties. The multi-utility has a service area of 43700 square miles. Ameren Illinois operates 4500 miles of transmission lines 45400 miles of power distribution lines and 18000 miles of gas transmission and distribution mains. It also has 12 underground natural gas storage fields.

	Annual Growth	12/10	12/11	12/12	12/13	12/14
Sales ($ mil.)	(4.6%)	3,014.0	2,787.0	2,525.0	2,311.0	2,498.0
Net income ($ mil.)	(5.1%)	252.0	196.0	144.0	163.0	204.0
Market value ($ mil.)	2.5%	2,218.5	2,530.9	2,588.3	2,451.8	2,453.4
Employees	3.9%	2,752	2,793	2,994	3,133	3,208

AMERESCO INC.

NYS: AMRC

111 Speen Street, Suite 410
Framingham, MA 01701
Phone: 508 661-2200
Fax: –
Web: www.ameresco.com

CEO: George P. Sakellaris
CFO: John R. Granara
HR: –
FYE: December 31
Type: Public

Ameresco gives its customers alternative ways to cut their energy bills. Primarily serving commercial and industrial customers along with municipal and federal government agencies Ameresco provides development engineering and installation services to clients seeking to upgrade and improve the efficiency of their heating and air conditioning ventilation lighting and other building systems. Other services include developing and constructing small-scale onsite (or near-site) renewable energy plants for customers as well as installing solar panels wind turbines and other alternative energy sources. Founded in 2000 by CEO George Sakellaris Ameresco operates through 65 locations in the US Canada and Europe.

	Annual Growth	12/10	12/11	12/12	12/13	12/14
Sales ($ mil.)	(1.0%)	618.2	728.2	631.2	574.2	593.2
Net income ($ mil.)	(22.5%)	28.7	34.7	18.4	2.4	10.4
Market value ($ mil.)	(16.4%)	665.6	635.9	454.7	447.8	324.5
Employees	8.7%	735	947	922	976	1,026

AMERIANA BANCORP

NAS: ASBI

2118 Bundy Avenue
New Castle, IN 47362-1048
Phone: 765 529-2230
Fax: 765 529-2232
Web: www.ameriana.com

CEO: –
CFO: –
HR: –
FYE: December 31
Type: Public

Ameriana Bancorp may sound merry but it takes business seriously. It's the parent of Ameriana Bank which has about a dozen offices in central Indiana. The bank offers standard deposit products including checking savings and money market accounts; CDs; and IRAs. It focuses on real estate lending: Residential mortgages account for about half of its loan portfolio and commercial real estate loans represent about 30%. The company sells auto home life health and business coverage through its Ameriana Insurance Agency subsidiary. Another unit Ameriana Investment Management provides brokerage and investment services through an agreement with LPL Financial.

	Annual Growth	12/09	12/10	12/11	12/12	12/13
Assets ($ mil.)	1.0%	441.6	429.7	429.8	445.8	458.6
Net income ($ mil.)	–	(0.3)	0.6	1.1	1.8	2.2
Market value ($ mil.)	49.2%	8.0	12.1	11.8	24.6	39.6
Employees	–	–	–	–	–	–

AMERICA CHUNG NAM (GROUP) HOLDINGS LLC

1163 FAIRWAY DR
CITY OF INDUSTRY, CA 917892846
Phone: 909-839-8383
Fax: –
Web: www.acni.net

CEO: Teresa Cheung
CFO: Kevin Zhao
HR: –
FYE: December 31
Type: Private

Ever wondered where all that paper and plastic to be recycled goes? If this company is any indication a lot of it — some 10 million tons — goes to China. The company sells recovered fiber sources to Chinese paper mills where they can be converted into fiberboard cardboard and packaging. It also collects and exports a number of grades of post-consumer plastics. The company sources its materials through exclusive relationships with recycling facilities waste management companies and distribution centers. Founder Yan Cheung owns the company.

	Annual Growth	12/05	12/06	12/07	12/08	12/09
Sales ($ mil.)	(17.5%)	–	–	–	1,363.3	1,125.2
Net income ($ mil.)	112.4%	–	–	–	7.9	16.9
Market value ($ mil.)	–	–	–	–	–	–
Employees	–	–	–	–	–	250

AMERICA FIRST CREDIT UNION

1344 W. 4675 South
Riverdale UT 84405
Phone: 801-627-0900
Fax: 801-778-8079
Web: www.americafirst.com

CEO: –
CFO: Rex Rollo
HR: –
FYE: December 31
Type: Private - Not-for-Pr

If saving your money makes you feel like doing a little flag-waving could there be a more appropriate place for it than America First Credit Union? The institution offers deposits loans credit cards investments and other financial services to both business and consumer customers through more than 100 branches in Utah and Nevada. With more than 597000 members America First ranks among the nation's top 10 credit unions by membership and is one of the 15 largest by assets. Membership is open to residents of certain counties in Utah and Nevada food service workers in Utah employees of selected companies and family members of America First members.

AMERICA'S BODY COMPANY INC.

939 E. Starr Ave.
Columbus OH 43201
Phone: 614-299-1136
Fax: 614-299-2314
Web: www.abctruck.com

CEO: –
CFO: –
HR: –
FYE: December 31
Type: Private

America's Body Company (ABC) is one business that really wants you to get carried away with its product. Operating through some seven facilities in Florida Kentucky Ohio Oregon Maryland and Texas ABC customizes trucks with equipment and accessories for several industries including landscaping contracting distribution and manufacturing. The company also customizes trucks for special needs. ABC sells to vehicle dealers fleet operators and end users. Its products include aerial lift devices dump bodies for pickup trucks liftgates and water tanks. ABC was founded in 1976 as Great Lakes Truck Equipment. It was owned by Leggett & Platt until September 2008 when The Reading Group acquired the company.

AMERICA'S CAR-MART INC

NMS: CRMT

802 Southeast Plaza Avenue, Suite 200
Bentonville, AR 72712
Phone: 479 464-9944
Fax: –
Web: www.car-mart.com

CEO: William H. (Hank) Henderson
CFO: Jeffrey A. Williams
HR: Karen Duffy
FYE: April 30
Type: Public

No €redit? Bad Credit? No problem. America's Car-Mart targets car buyers with poor or limited credit histories. The company's subsidiaries operate more than 140 used car dealerships in 10 states primarily in smaller urban and rural markets throughout the US South Central region. Dealerships focus on selling basic and affordable transportation with an average selling price of about $9680 in 2015. It has been expanding primarily in Alabama Tennessee and Mississippi. While the company's business plan has focused on cities with up to 50000 in population (73% of sales) it sees better collection results among the smaller communities it serves. America's Car-Mart was founded in 1981 as the Crown Group.

	Annual Growth	04/11	04/12	04/13	04/14	04/15
Sales ($ mil.)	8.7%	379.3	430.2	464.7	489.2	530.3
Net income ($ mil.)	1.1%	28.2	33.0	32.2	21.1	29.5
Market value ($ mil.)	20.3%	208.8	391.8	394.6	308.2	437.9
Employees	7.3%	1,025	1,100	1,200	1,360	1,360

AMERICAN ACADEMY OF PEDIATRICS

141 NORTHWEST POINT BLVD
ELK GROVE VILLAGE, IL 600071019
Phone: 847-228-5005
Fax: –
Web: www.aap.org

CEO: –
CFO: John Miller
HR: –
FYE: June 30
Type: Private

The American Academy of Pediatrics (AAP) is a membership group of some 64000 pediatricians pediatric specialists and pediatric surgeons dedicated to improving the health and well-being of infants children teenagers and young adults. The not-for-profit organization executes research on a number of topics including school health common childhood illnesses and immunizations and acts as an advocate on behalf of children's health needs. It also provides continuing education for its members through courses scientific meetings and publications such as Pediatrics and Pediatrics in Review. The organization is funded by membership dues grants gifts and its own activities. AAP was founded in 1930.

	Annual Growth	06/09	06/10	06/11	06/12	06/13
Sales ($ mil.)	6.7%	–	87.2	93.5	104.1	105.8
Net income ($ mil.)	(20.5%)	–	–	7.3	1.9	4.6
Market value ($ mil.)	–	–	–	–	–	–
Employees	–	–	–	–	–	400

AMERICAN AGIP COMPANY INC.

485 Madison Ave.
New York NY 10022
Phone: 646-264-2100
Fax: 646-264-2222
Web: www.americanagip.com

CEO: Gian Franco Mosconi
CFO: –
HR: –
FYE: December 31
Type: Subsidiary

You might say that American Agip is as slick as a whistle. Formed in 1987 the subsidiary of Italian energy heavyweight Eni operates three major petrochemical businesses: the manufacturing and marketing of lubricants; the marketing and trading of MTBE and methanol; and the trading of refined petroleum products. American Agip supplies bulk and package customers throughout the eastern US and across Canada. It has a manufacturing center in Cabot Pennsylvania (where it has more than 1 million gallons of lubricant storage) and distribution centers located in New Jersey New York Ohio Pennsylvania and West Virginia as well as in Quebec Canada.

AMERICAN AIR LIQUIDE INC.

2700 Post Oak Blvd. Ste. 1800
Houston TX 77056
Phone: 713-624-8000
Fax: 713-624-8085
Web: www.us.airliquide.com

CEO: Pierre Dufour
CFO: Scott Krapf
HR: –
FYE: December 31
Type: Subsidiary

American Air Liquide builds up its liquid assets through the supply of gas in the US. The company supplies industrial gases (oxygen nitrogen CO2 argon etc.) to companies in the automotive chemicals food and beverage and health care industries. The US distribution arm of industrial gas provider Air Liquide the company can depending on its customers' needs it can manufacture onsite ship its product in cylinders or through more than 2000 miles of pipeline. It operates 200 locations throughout the US including 140 industrial gas plants. American Air Liquide also fulfills semiconductor companies' gas and liquid chemical requirements from its own fabrication plants.

AMERICAN AIRLINES FEDERAL CREDIT UNION

4151 Amon Carter Blvd.
Fort Worth TX 76155
Phone: 817-963-6000
Fax: 817-963-6108
Web: https://www.aacreditunion.org

CEO: Angie Owens
CFO: –
HR: –
FYE: December 31
Type: Private - Not-for-Pr

American Airlines Federal Credit Union won't hassle you about the position of your seatback or tray table. The member-owned institution (aka AA Credit Union) operates more than 40 branches in or near airports in about 20 cities in the US and Puerto Rico. It provides standard retail financial services such as checking and savings accounts loans credit cards and investments to some 237000 members who also have access to more than 6600 shared locations and 30000 ATMs. Its lending program consists of home mortgages and vehicle education and other personal loans as well as real estate equipment and vehicle loans and lines of credit for small businesses.

AMERICAN AIRLINES GROUP INC   NMS: AAL

4333 Amon Carter Blvd.
Fort Worth, TX 76155
Phone: 817 963-1234
Fax: 817 967-9641
Web: www.aa.com

CEO: W. Douglas (Doug) Parker
CFO: Derek J. Kerr
HR: –
FYE: December 31
Type: Public

American Airlines Group (AAG) knows America's spacious skies — and lots of others. After merging with US Airways in late 2013 AAG is one of the largest airlines in the world. The combined airline together with its third-party regional carriers including Air Wisconsin Chautauqua ExpressJet Mesa Republic and SkyWest operate nearly 6700 daily flights to roughly 340 destinations in more than 50 countries. American and US Airways operate 980 mainline jets and regional subsidiaries and third-party regional carriers operate nearly 565 regional jets. AAG extends its geographic reach through code-sharing arrangements and is part of the oneworld Alliance.

	Annual Growth	12/10	12/11	12/12	12/13	12/14
Sales ($ mil.)	17.8%	22,170.0	23,979.0	24,855.0	26,743.0	42,650.0
Net income ($ mil.)	–	(471.0)	(1,979.0)	(1,876.0)	(1,834.0)	2,882.0
Market value ($ mil.)	62.0%	5,433.3	244.1	554.5	17,611.2	37,405.6
Employees	9.7%	78,250	80,100	77,750	110,400	113,300

AMERICAN APPAREL, INC.   ASE: APP

747 Warehouse Street
Los Angeles, CA 90021
Phone: 213 488-0226
Fax: –
Web: www.americanapparel.com

CEO: Paula Schneider
CFO: Hassan N Natha
HR: –
FYE: December 31
Type: Public

American Apparel wants you to be hip and comfortable inside and out. It designs and makes logo-free T-shirts tanks yoga pants and more for men women and children — and does it all from its California factory rather than exporting labor overseas. Brands include Classic Girl Standard American Classic Baby and Sustainable Edition among others. American Apparel runs 250-plus retail stores in 20 countries. Known for its no-sweat factory and for paying up to $19-an-hour for manufacturers American Apparel was teetering on the brink of insolvency until it received strategically timed funding. In mid-2014 the board replaced controversial CEO Dov Charney who founded American Apparel in 1998.

	Annual Growth	12/09	12/10	12/11	12/12	12/13
Sales ($ mil.)	3.2%	558.8	533.0	547.3	617.3	633.9
Net income ($ mil.)	–	1.1	(86.3)	(39.3)	(37.3)	(106.3)
Market value ($ mil.)	(20.6%)	345.1	184.8	80.2	112.4	136.9
Employees	0.0%	10,000	11,300	10,000	10,000	10,000

AMERICAN ARBITRATION ASSOCIATION INC

120 BROADWAY FL 21
NEW YORK, NY 102710016
Phone: 212-716-5800
Fax: –
Web: www.adr.org

CEO: India Johnson
CFO: Francesco Rossi
HR: –
FYE: December 31
Type: Private

The American Arbitration Association (AAA) wants to keep things civil. The organization provides arbitration mediation and other forms of alternative dispute resolution services — alternatives that is to going to court. It maintains a panel of more than 7000 arbitrators and mediators who can be engaged to hear cases and supports their work. Every year more than 185000 cases are filed with AAA in a full range of matters including commercial construction labor employment insurance international and claims program disputes. The association's services include development of alternative dispute resolution (ADR) systems for corporations unions government agencies law firms and the courts.

	Annual Growth	12/05	12/06	12/08	12/09	12/13
Sales ($ mil.)	(36.9%)	–	1,929.9	70.7	67.9	77.2
Net income ($ mil.)	–	–	–	(23.0)	8.9	8.5
Market value ($ mil.)	–	–	–	–	–	–
Employees	–	–	–	–	–	750

AMERICAN ASSOCIATION FOR THE ADVANCEMENT OF SCIENCE

1200 NEW YORK AVE NW
WASHINGTON, DC 200053928
Phone: 202-898-0873
Fax: –
Web: www.aaas.org

CEO: Rush D. Holt
CFO: Phillip Blair
HR: –
FYE: December 31
Type: Private

The American Association for the Advancement of Science (AAAS) likes to think of itself as the voice of science. Founded in 1848 AAAS is a nonprofit that promotes scientific research and technology through educational and international programs policy support and the publication of books newsletters and weekly magazine Science (available to AAAS members and institutional subscribers). It also runs science news website EurekAlert! The association includes about 260 affiliated societies and academies of science reaching some 10 million individuals. AAAS has advised policymakers on such topics as global climate change and stem cell research and has rallied for more US research and development funding.

	Annual Growth	12/05	12/06	12/07	12/08	12/09
Sales ($ mil.)	–	–	–	(1,060.6)	89.7	87.8
Net income ($ mil.)	12856.9%	–	–	0.0	(14.4)	3.6
Market value ($ mil.)	–	–	–	–	–	–
Employees	–	–	–	–	–	360

AMERICAN AXLE & MANUFACTURING HOLDINGS INC — NYS: AXL

One Dauch Drive
Detroit, MI 48211-1198
Phone: 313 758-2000
Fax: –
Web: www.aam.com

CEO: David C. Dauch
CFO: Christopher J May
HR: –
FYE: December 31
Type: Public

American Axle & Manufacturing (AAM) is GM's right-hand man for driveline systems and forged products. AAM manufactures axles driveshafts and chassis components mainly for light trucks and SUVs but also for cars and crossover vehicles. Axles and driveshafts account for more than 80% of AAM's sales; chassis components forged products and other components make up the rest. The Tier 1 supplier gets nearly three-quarters of its business from GM; other customers include PACCAR Chrysler Harley-Davidson VW and Ford. AAM operates more than 35 manufacturing facilities around the world and earns 56% of its revenue from sales in North America.

	Annual Growth	12/11	12/12	12/13	12/14	12/15
Sales ($ mil.)	10.9%	2,585.0	2,930.9	3,207.3	3,696.0	3,903.1
Net income ($ mil.)	13.3%	142.8	367.7	94.5	143.0	235.6
Market value ($ mil.)	17.6%	752.6	852.3	1,556.2	1,719.1	1,441.3
Employees	9.1%	9,200	11,300	12,650	12,820	13,050

AMERICAN BANKERS ASSOCIATION INC

1120 CONNECTICUT AVE NW # 600
WASHINGTON, DC 200363959
Phone: 202-663-5000
Fax: –
Web: www.aba.com

CEO: Rob Nichols
CFO: Robert G Eady
HR: –
FYE: August 31
Type: Private

The American Bankers Association (ABA) brings together banks of various types and sizes. Its members include bank holding companies savings associations savings banks trust companies and community regional and money center banks. The ABA serves as an advocate for its members in legislative and regulatory arenas. It also engages in consumer education research and training efforts. The ABA's BankPac the banking industry's largest political action committee provides financial support to candidates for the US Senate and House of Representatives. The ABA was founded in 1875 and claims to represent more than 95% of banking assets. The group merged with the America's Community Bankers association in 2007.

	Annual Growth	08/06	08/07	08/08	08/09	08/10
Sales ($ mil.)	(42.0%)	–	–	239.7	64.0	80.7
Net income ($ mil.)	612.2%	–	–	0.0	(22.3)	0.8
Market value ($ mil.)	–	–	–	–	–	–
Employees	–	–	–	–	–	354

AMERICAN BAPTIST HOMES OF THE WEST

6120 STONERIDGE MALL RD # 300
PLEASANTON, CA 945883296
Phone: 925-924-7100
Fax: –
Web: www.abhow.com

CEO: David B Ferguson
CFO: –
HR: –
FYE: September 30
Type: Private

American Baptist Homes of the West (ABHOW) preaches the gospel of the active senior lifestyle operating more than 40 senior living facilities in four western states. Nearly three-fourths of ABHOW's communities are government-subsidized apartments for low-income seniors. About a dozen of its residences however are continuing care retirement communities which offer a continuum of care — residential living assisted living or skilled nursing — depending on residents' needs. The communities also schedule social activities and offer wellness programs and transportation services. Parent company Cornerstone Affiliates acquires and develops communities with ABHOW.

	Annual Growth	09/07	09/08	09/09	09/10	09/13
Sales ($ mil.)	(17.0%)	–	306.2	145.3	149.5	120.3
Net income ($ mil.)	30.2%	–	–	0.8	12.2	2.2
Market value ($ mil.)	–	–	–	–	–	–
Employees	–	–	–	–	–	2,500

AMERICAN BAR ASSOCIATION

321 N CLARK ST FL 14
CHICAGO, IL 606547598
Phone: 312-988-5000
Fax: –
Web: www.americanbar.org

CEO: –
CFO: –
HR: –
FYE: August 31
Type: Private

The world's largest voluntary professional organization American Bar Association (ABA) promotes improvements in the American justice system and develops guidelines for the advancement of the legal profession and education. The association provides law school accreditation continuing education legal information and other services to assist legal professionals. The ABA's roster of about 400000 members includes lawyers judges court administrators law librarians and law school professors and students. The organization cannot discipline lawyers nor enforce its rules; it can only develop guidelines. The ABA was founded in 1878.

	Annual Growth	08/09	08/10	08/11	08/12	08/13
Sales ($ mil.)	13.5%	–	140.8	140.7	146.3	206.0
Net income ($ mil.)	90.2%	–	–	10.9	9.1	39.4
Market value ($ mil.)	–	–	–	–	–	–
Employees	–	–	–	–	–	900

AMERICAN BILTRITE INC. — NBB: ABLT

57 River Street
Wellesley Hills, MA 02481-2097
Phone: 781 237-6655
Fax: –
Web: www.ambilt.com

CEO: –
CFO: Howard N Feist III
HR: Pauline Nadeau
FYE: December 31
Type: Public

American Biltrite (ABI) which makes and distributes commercial flooring and industrial rubber has its hand in several different pots some of which are sticky. Its Tape division makes adhesive-coated pressure-sensitive tapes and films used to protect materials during handling and storage as well as for applications in the heating ventilation and air conditioning automotive and electrical industries. ABI also designs and distributes wholesale jewelry and accessories to stores through its K&M subsidiary while its AB Canada subsidiary makes floor tile and rubber products. The founding Marcus family controls ABI.

	Annual Growth	12/10	12/11	12/12	12/13	12/14
Sales ($ mil.)	0.5%	201.6	208.7	213.7	209.3	205.6
Net income ($ mil.)	(52.2%)	57.2	(1.7)	(0.3)	3.4	3.0
Market value ($ mil.)	188.2%	0.2	0.2	14.6	13.4	13.8
Employees	(4.0%)	625	600	–	–	–

AMERICAN BIO MEDICA CORP. — NBB: ABMC

122 Smith Road
Kinderhook, NY 12106
Phone: 518 758-8158
Fax: –
Web: www.abmc.com

CEO: Melissa A Waterhouse
CFO: Melissa A Waterhouse
HR: –
FYE: December 31
Type: Public

There's a thin line between employment and unemployment and that line might just be on one of American Bio Medica's drug-testing kits. The company's Rapid Drug Screen products indicate within minutes the presence in a urine sample of such illegal substances as marijuana cocaine amphetamines and opiates. Used by employers law enforcement agencies hospitals schools and other institutions the tests offer up to 10-panel options (each panel tests for different substances). The company's Rapid One is a line of single-drug specific tests; its Rapid Tec and Rapid TOX products detect multiple drug classes on one panel. American Bio Medica also offers saliva-based tests for law enforcement customers.

	Annual Growth	12/10	12/11	12/12	12/13	12/14
Sales ($ mil.)	(8.6%)	10.4	9.3	9.3	8.9	7.3
Net income ($ mil.)	–	(0.8)	(0.3)	(1.1)	(0.8)	(0.5)
Market value ($ mil.)	10.2%	2.1	4.0	3.1	3.1	3.1
Employees	(6.2%)	88	80	88	75	68

AMERICAN BUILDINGS COMPANY

1150 State Docks Rd.
Eufaula AL 36027
Phone: 334-687-2032
Fax: 334-688-2185
Web: www.americanbuildings.com

CEO: –
CFO: –
HR: –
FYE: December 31
Type: Subsidiary

American Buildings Company can put a roof over your head quite literally. It manufactures metal buildings and roofing products for industrial institutional and commercial construction applications. From multi-story buildings to customized self-storage units to metal roof and wall panels the company's buildings and components are marketed through a network of more than 1000 authorized builders and dealers in the US and Canada. Its heavy fabrication capabilities include building custom-engineered steel mills sports stadiums and large aircraft maintenance hangars. American Buildings Company and its former parent MAGNATRAX were acquired by steelmaker Nucor Corporation in 2007.

AMERICAN BUREAU OF SHIPPING INC

16855 NORTHCHASE DR
HOUSTON, TX 770606010
Phone: 281-877-5800
Fax: –
Web: www.eagle.org

CEO: Christopher J. (Chris) Wiernicki
CFO: –
HR: –
FYE: December 31
Type: Private

One of the world's largest ship classification societies American Bureau of Shipping (ABS) offers inspection and analysis services to verify that vessels are mechanically and structurally fit. The not-for-profit company's surveyors examine ships in major ports throughout the world assessing whether the vessels comply with ABS rules for design construction and maintenance. Additionally its engineers consult with shipbuilders on proposed designs and repairs. The not-for-profit company operates from more than 150 offices in about 70 countries. For-profit subsidiaries ABS Group offers risk management consulting services while ABS Nautical Systems provides fleet management software. ABS was founded in 1862.

	Annual Growth	12/02	12/03	12/09	12/11	12/12
Sales ($ mil.)	24.4%	–	159.2	648.8	726.7	1,134.3
Net income ($ mil.)	(4.9%)	–	–	180.8	143.6	155.3
Market value ($ mil.)	–	–	–	–	–	–
Employees	–	–	–	–	–	3,000

AMERICAN CAMPUS COMMUNITIES INC

NYS: ACC

12700 Hill Country Blvd., Suite T-200
Austin, TX 78738
Phone: 512 732-1000
Fax: –
Web: www.americancampus.com

CEO: William C. Bayless
CFO: Jonathan A. Graf
HR: Brian Vogel
FYE: December 31
Type: Public

American Campus Communities (ACC) actually does most of its business off campus. The self-managed real estate investment trust (REIT) owns and operates student housing properties located at or near colleges and universities in more than 25 states. The company leases the ground for on-campus properties from the schools which in turn receive half of the net cash flow from these properties. ACC also works with schools to develop new properties and renovate existing housing and provides third-party leasing and management services for other student housing owners. In all the REIT manages about 201 properties (with some 128700 beds) at more than 85 schools in the US and Canada.

	Annual Growth	12/10	12/11	12/12	12/13	12/14
Sales ($ mil.)	20.8%	345.0	390.3	491.3	657.5	733.9
Net income ($ mil.)	40.3%	16.2	56.6	56.6	104.6	62.8
Market value ($ mil.)	6.8%	3,403.9	4,497.1	4,944.0	3,452.1	4,432.8
Employees	8.4%	2,334	2,387	2,913	3,059	3,227

AMERICAN CANNABIS CO INC

NBB: AMMJ

5690 Logan Street #A
Denver, CO 80216
Phone: 720 466-3789
Fax: –

CEO: Corey Hollister
CFO: Jesus Quintero
HR: –
FYE: December 31
Type: Public

NatureWell hopes to offer relief out of the mist to migraine sufferers in a fog. The company has developed its MICROMIST technology to deliver homeopathic and natural remedies under the tongue. Currently the company's only product is over-the-counter migraine treatment MigraSpray which can be used both as a preventative measure and to relieve the acute pain of migraines. It is only available through healthcare professionals and by mail order. NatureWell outsources manufacturing distribution and customer service functions. It is exploring new product offerings for arthritis and general pain including Arthrispray PMS Spray and Allerspray.

	Annual Growth	06/11	06/12*	12/12	12/13	12/14
Sales ($ mil.)	(83.8%)	–	–	–	7.8	1.3
Net income ($ mil.)	–	(0.2)	(0.2)	0.0	(4.5)	(3.6)
Market value ($ mil.)	–	0.0	0.0	0.0	4.7	26.3
Employees	71.0%	2	2	36	36	10

*Fiscal year change

AMERICAN CAPITAL AGENCY CORP

NMS: AGNC

2 Bethesda Metro Center, 14th Floor
Bethesda, MD 20814
Phone: 301 968-9300
Fax: 301 968-9301
Web: www.agnc.com

CEO: Malon Wilkus
CFO: John R Erickson
HR: –
FYE: December 31
Type: Public

American Capital Agency is taking on the rocky real estate market. The real estate investment trust (REIT) was created in 2008 to invest in securities backed by single-family residential mortgages and collateralized mortgage obligations guaranteed by government agencies Fannie Mae Freddie Mac and Ginnie Mae. The Maryland-based REIT is externally managed and advised by American Capital AGNC Management a subsidiary of US publicly traded alternative asset manager American Capital which spun off American Capital Agency in 2008 but retained about a 33% stake in the REIT.

	Annual Growth	12/10	12/11	12/12	12/13	12/14
Sales ($ mil.)	–	307.4	850.6	1,440.0	1,440.0	(92.0)
Net income ($ mil.)	–	288.1	770.5	1,277.0	1,259.0	(233.0)
Market value ($ mil.)	(6.6%)	10,139.5	9,906.6	10,195.9	6,805.5	7,701.6
Employees	–	–	–	–	–	–

AMERICAN CAPITAL LTD.

NASDAQ: ACAS

2 Bethesda Metro Center 14th Fl.
Bethesda MD 20814
Phone: 301-951-6122
Fax: 301-654-6714
Web: www.americancapital.com

CEO: Malon Wilkus
CFO: John R Erickson
HR: –
FYE: December 31
Type: Public

Whether you make musical instruments or mints salon appliances or safes this company has a strategy for you. Founded in 1986 American Capital invests in a diverse selection of middle-market companies both directly and through its global asset management business. It typically provides up to $300 million per transaction to companies for management and employee buyouts and private equity buyouts. The firm also directly provides capital to companies. Other investments include financial products such as commercial mortgage-backed securities and collateralized loan obligations. American Capital's portfolio consists of stakes in more than 150 companies and has a focus on manufacturing services and distribution.

AMERICAN CAPITAL MORTGAGE INVESTMENT CORP.   NMS: MTGE

2 Bethesda Metro Center, 14th Floor
Bethesda, MD 20814
Phone: 301 968-9220
Fax: –
Web: www.mtge.com

CEO: Malon Wilkus
CFO: John R Erickson
HR: –
FYE: December 31
Type: Public

When reading its name it's not difficult to figure out what American Capital Mortgage Investment does. The newly-formed real estate investment trust (REIT) invests in and manages a portfolio of residential mortgage-backed securities mostly fixed-rate pass-through certificates guaranteed by Fannie Mae Freddie Mac or Ginnie Mae. The company which is externally-managed by American Capital MTGE Management also plans to invest in adjustable-rate mortgages (ARMs) and collateralized mortgage obligations (CMOs). American Capital Mortgage was formed and went public in 2011.

	Annual Growth	12/10	12/11	12/12	12/13	12/14
Sales ($ mil.)	–	0.0	16.4	145.4	255.7	168.1
Net income ($ mil.)	–	0.0	19.7	250.2	(84.5)	159.2
Market value ($ mil.)	–	0.0	962.9	1,206.0	893.3	963.9
Employees	–	–	–	–	250	270

AMERICAN CARESOURCE HOLDINGS INC   NAS: GNOW

1170 Peachtree Street, Suite 2350
Atlanta, GA 30309
Phone: 404 465-1000
Fax: –
Web: www.anci-care.com

CEO: John Pappajohn
CFO: Adam S Winger
HR: –
FYE: December 31
Type: Public

American CareSource mends the connection between medical plan sponsors and specialty health care providers. Operating through its Ancillary Care Services subsidiary the company negotiates contracts with more than 4000 providers of supplemental health care (i.e. outpatient surgery rehabilitation hospice laboratory and other services); in turn the company offers insurance companies and other health benefit administrators access to a vast network of reduced-cost ancillary care services. American CareSource's clients include preferred provider organizations (PPOs) health maintenance organizations (HMOs) third-party administrators and self-insured employers. The company's roots go back to the mid-1990s.

	Annual Growth	12/10	12/11	12/12	12/13	12/14
Sales ($ mil.)	(18.5%)	61.2	48.9	34.9	26.8	27.1
Net income ($ mil.)	–	0.5	(7.2)	(3.1)	(3.8)	(6.8)
Market value ($ mil.)	20.0%	9.4	2.9	9.6	11.0	19.5
Employees	21.8%	64	56	56	52	141

AMERICAN CHARTERED BANCORP INC.

1199 E. Higgins Rd.
Schaumburg IL 60173
Phone: 847-517-5400
Fax: 415-675-6701
Web: www.wideorbit.com

CEO: –
CFO: –
HR: –
FYE: December 31
Type: Private

American Chartered Bancorp helps customers stay the course in the oft-choppy waters of money management. The holding company owns American Chartered Bank a commercial and retail bank that primarily serves small to midsized businesses and individuals in the Chicago area. Through about 15 branches it offers standard deposit products such as checking and savings accounts and credit cards as well as loans and leases treasury management and merchant services. American Chartered Bancorp was founded in 1987 and is locally owned and operated.

AMERICAN CHEMICAL SOCIETY

1155 16TH ST NW
WASHINGTON, DC 200364892
Phone: 202-872-4600
Fax: –
Web: www.portal.acs.org

CEO: Thomas M. (Tom) Connelly
CFO: Brian Bernstein
HR: –
FYE: December 31
Type: Private

This group has a lot of chemistry. With more than 163000 members the American Chemical Society (ACS) is the world's largest scientific society. It provides information career development and educational resources to member chemists chemical engineers and technicians. ACS also publishes dozens of magazines journals and books and its Chemical Abstracts Service provides access to an online database o more than 70 million literature and research summaries from around the world. ACS also serves as an advocate for its members on public policy issues. The ACS Member Insurance Program provides insurance plans to members. The not-for-profit organization was founded in 1876 and chartered by Congress in 1937.

	Annual Growth	12/02	12/03	12/04	12/05	12/08
Sales ($ mil.)	1.4%	–	421.4	408.5	411.7	451.5
Net income ($ mil.)	–	–	–	57.0	26.4	(38.4)
Market value ($ mil.)	–	–	–	–	–	–
Employees	–	–	–	–	–	2,000

AMERICAN CITY BUSINESS JOURNALS INC.

120 W. Morehead St. Ste. 400
Charlotte NC 28202
Phone: 704-973-1000
Fax: 704-973-1001
Web: www.acbj.com

CEO: Whitney R Shaw
CFO: George B Guthinger
HR: –
FYE: December 31
Type: Subsidiary

Cities big and small can turn to this company for coverage of US metropolitan business news. American City Business Journals (ACBJ) is a leading newspaper publisher that serves more than 500000 subscribers with local business news through more than 40 publications. Its bizjournals subsidiary also publishes news and information online for about 4 million registered users. In addition ACBJ owns The Sporting News one of the top sports magazines in the US and Hemmings Motor News a publisher of collectible-car books and magazines. Its Street & Smith's Sports Group publishes several sports publications including SportsBusiness Journal. ACBJ is a unit of newspaper and magazine publisher Advance Publications.

AMERICAN CIVIL LIBERTIES UNION FOUNDATION INC.

125 BROAD ST FL 18
NEW YORK, NY 100042454
Phone: 212-549-2500
Fax: –
Web: www.aclu.org

CEO: –
CFO: Caroline Greene
HR: –
FYE: March 31
Type: Private

The philosopher Socrates once said "I am that gadfly which God has given the state." While the American Civil Liberties Union (ACLU) might have a quarrel with the "God" part the group has at times proved a stinging critic in its efforts to defend individual rights. It acts as a legal and legislative advocate in matters related to civil liberties and the Bill of Rights. The ACLU has participated in such cases as the 1925 Scopes trial (challenged a ban on teaching evolution) Brown v. Board of Education (school desegregation) Roe v. Wade (abortion rights) and Romer v. Evans (gay and lesbian rights). The group which has more than 500000 members has offices throughout the US. It was founded in 1920.

	Annual Growth	03/05	03/06	03/07	03/13	03/14
Sales ($ mil.)	4.9%	–	48.0	67.6	69.9	70.3
Net income ($ mil.)	–	–	–	34.3	(5.7)	(19.1)
Market value ($ mil.)	–	–	–	–	–	–
Employees	–	–	–	–	–	350

AMERICAN COMMERCE SOLUTIONS INC

NBB: AACS

1400 Chamber Drive
Bartow, FL 33830
Phone: 863 533-0326
Fax: –
Web: www.aacssymbol.com

CEO: Daniel L Hefner
CFO: Frank D Puissegur
HR: –
FYE: February 28
Type: Public

Holding company American Commerce Solutions (ACS) through its International Machine and Welding subsidiary provides specialized machining and repair services for heavy equipment used in the agricultural construction forestry mining and scrap industries. Its Chariot Manufacturing Company subsidiary (which includes Chariot Trailers) manufactures open and enclosed trailers to carry motorcycles. ACS also sells aftermarket repair parts. The company also has a strategic relationship with American Fiber Green Products. The Mosaic Company generates about 36% of sales.

	Annual Growth	02/11	02/12	02/13	02/14	02/15
Sales ($ mil.)	(0.5%)	2.3	2.4	2.4	2.7	2.2
Net income ($ mil.)	–	(0.4)	0.0	(0.0)	(0.2)	(0.1)
Market value ($ mil.)	6.0%	1.9	1.2	2.9	3.9	2.4
Employees	1.3%	19	18	19	21	20

AMERICAN COMMERCIAL LINES INC.

1701 E. Market St.
Jeffersonville IN 47130
Phone: 812-288-0100
Fax: 812-288-1766
Web: www.aclines.com

CEO: Mark K Knoy
CFO: Thomas R Pilholski
HR: –
FYE: December 31
Type: Private

One of the mightiest on the mighty Mississippi barge operator American Commercial Lines (ACL) navigates the inland waterways of the US. ACL moves dry bulk commodities including grain cement fertilizer salt coal steel and pig iron. It also transports bulk liquid cargo such as chemicals ethanol and petroleum products. ACL's fleet comprises more than 2000 dry cargo barges and some 330 tank barges powered by 125 towboats. In addition to transportation its Jeffboat subsidiary designs and manufactures inland and ocean service vessels for ACL and other customers and its Elliott Bay Design Group (EBDG) provides marine engineering. ACL was acquired by an affiliate of Platinum Equity in late 2010.

AMERICAN COMMUNITY MUTUAL INSURANCE COMPANY

39201 Seven Mile Rd.
Livonia MI 48152-1094
Phone: 734-591-9000
Fax: 734-591-4628
Web: www.american-community.com

CEO: Michel Tobin
CFO: David Skup
HR: Dorothy Petro
FYE: December 31
Type: Private - Mutual Com

American Community Mutual Insurance worked to maintain the health and well-being of America's communities but failed to keep itself robust. American Community provided group and individual health care plans and life insurance plans in over a dozen states throughout the Midwest and Southwest. The company's offerings included PPO short-term health dental vision and prescription plans. Focusing largely on the small to midsized employer group market the company insured more than 165000 individuals. The company distributes its products through a force of 14000 independent agents. American Community was founded in 1938. Due to financial troubles the company entered into rehabilitation in 2010.

AMERICAN CRYSTAL SUGAR COMPANY

101 N. 3rd St.
Moorhead MN 56560
Phone: 218-236-4400
Fax: 218-236-4422
Web: www.crystalsugar.com

CEO: David A Berg
CFO: Thomas S Astrup
HR: –
FYE: August 31
Type: Private - Cooperativ

Call it saccharine but for American Crystal Sugar business is all about sharing. This sugar-beet cooperative is owned by some 2800 growers in the Red River Valley of North Dakota and Minnesota who farm more than one-half million owned and contracted acres of cropland. American Crystal formed in 1899 and converted into a co-op in 1973 divides the 35-mile-wide valley into five districts each served by a processing plant. The plants produce sugar molasses and beet pulp. American Crystal's products are sold internationally to industrial users and to retail and wholesale customers under the Crystal name as well as under private labels through marketing co-ops United Sugars and Midwest Agri-Commodities.

AMERICAN DEFENSE SYSTEMS INC.

NYSE AMEX: EAG

420 McKinney Pkwy.
Lillington NC 27546
Phone: 910-514-9701
Fax: 910-514-9702
Web: www.adsi-armor.com

CEO: Dale Scales
CFO: Gary Sidorsky
HR: –
FYE: December 31
Type: Public

American Defense Systems Inc. (ASDI) does a bang-up job of supporting our troops. The company makes custom bulletproof steel plates and glass panes that provide protection to US military vehicles in combat. It also manufactures bullet- and blast-resistant transparent armor walls and doors to protect buildings as well as barriers steel gates and bollards to keep vehicles from crashing into them. ASDI earns all of its revenues from the Departments of Defense and Homeland Security and branches of the US military. In addition the company runs the American Institute for Defense and Tactical Studies which offers tactical training courses. CEO Tony Piscitelli owns almost three-quarters of the company's stock.

AMERICAN DENTAL ASSOCIATION

211 E CHICAGO AVE
CHICAGO, IL 606112637
Phone: 312-440-2653
Fax: –
Web: www.ada.org

CEO: –
CFO: Paul Sholty
HR: –
FYE: December 31
Type: Private

Four out of five dentists recommend the ADA to their peers who join organizations. The American Dental Association is the world's oldest and largest dental association representing some 158000 dentists. The ADA provides information on oral health promotes dental science and conducts research development and testing on dental products and materials. If products are up to the organization's standards they are allowed to carry the ADA Seal of Acceptance. The group's Professional Product Review (PPR) evaluates and reports on products used by dental professionals. The ADA was founded in 1859 by 26 representatives from dental societies around the country.

	Annual Growth	12/04	12/05	12/06*	08/08*	12/08
Sales ($ mil.)	(1.2%)	–	113.9	121.6	0.5	110.0
Net income ($ mil.)	(38.5%)	–	–	10.8	0.1	4.1
Market value ($ mil.)						
Employees	–	–	–	–	–	475

*Fiscal year change

AMERICAN DENTAL PARTNERS INC.   NASDAQ: ADPI

401 Edgewater Place Ste. 430
Wakefield MA 01880
Phone: 781-224-0880
Fax: 781-224-4216
Web: www.amdpi.com

CEO: Kevin Trexler
CFO: Breht T Feigh
HR: –
FYE: December 31
Type: Private

Helping dentists focus on drilling (and not billing) is the mission of American Dental Partners. The company provides management and support services for the growing group practice segment of the dental care industry. Through long-term service agreements the company manages about 25 general and specialty dental practice groups operating some 275 dental facilities in 22 states mainly in the eastern and midwestern US. Its services include planning and budgeting facilities development and management scheduling training recruiting economic analysis financial reporting and quality assurance. American Dental Partners was acquired by private equity firm JLL Partners in 2012.

AMERICAN DG ENERGY INC   ASE: ADGE

45 First Avenue
Waltham, MA 02451
Phone: 781 522-6000
Fax: –
Web: www.americandg.com

CEO: John N Hatsopoulos
CFO: Bonnie Brown
HR: –
FYE: December 31
Type: Public

Doggone tired of high utility bills? American DG Energy wants to put an end to that. The company provides DG or distributed generation energy by installing electricity generating equipment on-site to save on energy loss during transmission. The equipment which the company owns and maintains uses clean natural gas to generate power and for heating and cooling; it captures waste heat for water chilling and heating. While the technology is in wide use by consumers of more than 10 MW of power American DG Energy targets smaller users one MW and less. The Hatsopoulos family including chairman George Hatsopoulos and CEO John Hatsopoulos control about 25% of the company.

	Annual Growth	12/10	12/11	12/12	12/13	12/14
Sales ($ mil.)	11.0%	5.6	6.0	5.6	7.5	8.6
Net income ($ mil.)	–	(1.9)	(3.8)	(6.5)	(4.9)	(5.9)
Market value ($ mil.)	(31.8%)	144.4	75.6	120.4	88.6	31.3
Employees	16.7%	14	24	27	27	26

AMERICAN EAGLE OUTFITTERS, INC.   NYS: AEO

77 Hot Metal Street
Pittsburgh, PA 15203-2329
Phone: 412 432-3300
Fax: –
Web: www.ae.com

CEO: Jay L. Schottenstein
CFO: Mary M. Boland
HR: –
FYE: January 31
Type: Public

It was once a purveyor of outdoor gear but American Eagle Outfitters now feathers its nest with jeans and polos. The mall-based retailer sells denim and other casual apparel and accessories (top categories include jeans t-shirts bras and panties) aimed at young men and women ages 15-25. The chain operates more than 1000 stores across the US Puerto Rico Canada Hong Kong China Mexico and the UK. It also has stores in 17 other countries operated under license. Direct sales come from the company's websites. Virtually all of the company's products bear its private-label brand names American Eagle Outfitters and aerie.

	Annual Growth	01/11	01/12*	02/13	02/14*	01/15
Sales ($ mil.)	2.6%	2,967.6	3,159.8	3,475.8	3,305.8	3,282.9
Net income ($ mil.)	(13.1%)	140.6	151.7	232.1	83.0	80.3
Market value ($ mil.)	(0.9%)	2,832.2	2,721.3	3,927.3	2,631.8	2,731.0
Employees	(1.2%)	39,900	39,600	44,000	40,000	38,000

*Fiscal year change

AMERICAN ELECTRIC POWER COMPANY, INC.   NYS: AEP

1 Riverside Plaza
Columbus, OH 43215-2373
Phone: 614 716-1000
Fax: 614 223-1823
Web: www.aep.com

CEO: Nicholas K. (Nick) Akins
CFO: Brian X. Tierney
HR: Dorothy Coleman
FYE: December 31
Type: Public

American Electric Power (AEP) takes its slice of the US power pie out of Middle America. The holding company is one of the largest power generators and distributors in the US. AEP owns the nation's largest electricity transmission system a network of almost 40000 miles. It also has 230000 miles of distribution lines. Its electric utilities have 5.3 million customers in 11 states and have about 32000 MW of largely coal-fired generating capacity. AEP is a top wholesale energy company; it markets electricity in the US. To raise cash in 2015 the company agreed to sell its commercial barging operations that transport liquids coal and dry bulk commodities on the Ohio Illinois and lower Mississippi Rivers.

	Annual Growth	12/10	12/11	12/12	12/13	12/14
Sales ($ mil.)	4.2%	14,427.0	15,116.0	14,945.0	15,357.0	17,020.0
Net income ($ mil.)	7.7%	1,214.0	1,946.0	1,259.0	1,480.0	1,634.0
Market value ($ mil.)	14.0%	17,608.7	20,217.2	20,887.7	22,874.7	29,716.5
Employees	(0.2%)	18,712	18,710	18,513	18,521	18,529

AMERICAN ELECTRIC TECHNOLOGIES, INC.   NAS: AETI

1250 Wood Branch Park Drive, Suite 600
Houston, TX 77079
Phone: 713 644-8182
Fax: –
Web: www.aeti.com

CEO: Charles M. Dauber
CFO: Bill Brod
HR: –
FYE: December 31
Type: Public

American Electric Technologies (AETI) tames wild and woolly wiring. Its technical products and services segment makes low- and medium-voltage switchgears for land- and offshore-based oil and gas drilling as well as refineries and municipal power companies. The electrical and instrumentation construction unit makes electric power delivery and control products and provides technical field services and electrical and instrumentation construction services. American Access Technologies makes zone-cabling cabinets for telephone lines data networking and security systems.

	Annual Growth	12/10	12/11	12/12	12/13	12/14
Sales ($ mil.)	10.1%	39.0	51.9	54.1	65.3	57.3
Net income ($ mil.)	–	(1.7)	(5.9)	2.3	4.6	(4.7)
Market value ($ mil.)	25.4%	18.3	41.6	41.3	81.7	45.3
Employees	0.0%	332	366	312	310	332

AMERICAN EQUITY INVESTMENT LIFE HOLDING CO   NYS: AEL

6000 Westown Parkway
West Des Moines, IA 50266
Phone: 515 221-0002
Fax: –
Web: www.american-equity.com

CEO: John M. Matovina
CFO: Ted M. Johnson
HR: –
FYE: December 31
Type: Public

Eagles' nests aren't particularly downy but American Equity Investment Life Holding (American Equity Life) helps middle income investors plan for a softer retirement. The company issues and administers fixed-rate and indexed annuities through subsidiaries American Equity Investment Life Insurance Eagle Life Insurance Company and American Equity Investment Life Insurance Company of New York. Licensed in 50 states and the District of Columbia the company sells its products through about 30000 independent agents and 45 national marketing associations. American Equity Life targets individuals between the ages of 45 and 75. The company also offers a variety of whole term and universal life insurance products.

	Annual Growth	12/10	12/11	12/12	12/13	12/14
Assets ($ mil.)	13.6%	26,426.8	30,874.7	35,133.5	39,621.5	43,989.7
Net income ($ mil.)	30.9%	42.9	86.2	57.8	253.3	126.0
Market value ($ mil.)	23.5%	954.6	791.0	928.7	2,006.5	2,220.3
Employees	3.8%	360	386	388	416	418

AMERICAN EUROCOPTER CORPORATION

2701 Forum Dr.
Grand Prairie TX 75052-7099
Phone: 972-641-0000
Fax: 972-641-3550
Web: www.eurocopterusa.com

CEO: Marc Paganini
CFO: Francois Bordes
HR: –
FYE: December 31
Type: Subsidiary

You've heard of An American In Paris? Well how about a Eurocopter in America? American Eurocopter is the US-based arm of European helicopter giant Eurocopter itself a subsidiary of aerospace conglomerate EADS. American Eurocopter's primary offerings include Eurocopter helicopter repair and overhaul services spares and parts support technical publications and maintenance training services. It also provides manufacturing completion and final assembly for A-Star AS350 helicopters and provides customization services for Eurocopter EC120 EC135 EC145 and EC155 helicopter models among others. American Eurocopter keeps more than 1800 helicopters flying across the US and caters to 600 customers.

AMERICAN EXPRESS CO.

200 Vesey Street
New York, NY 10285
Phone: 212 640-2000
Fax: 212 640-0404
Web: www.americanexpress.com

NYS: AXP
CEO: Kenneth I. (Ken) Chenault
CFO: Jeffrey C. (Jeff) Campbell
HR: Kent Price
FYE: December 31
Type: Public

American Express makes money even if you do leave home without it. Best known for its charge cards and revolving credit cards the company is also one of the world's largest providers of travel services. And yes the company still issues traveler's checks. Its travel agency operations have thousands of locations worldwide and its Travelers Cheque Group is the world's largest issuer of traveler's checks. Still the company's charge and credit cards are its bread and butter; American Express boasts $159 billion in assets $1 trillion in annual billed business and has more than 110 million cards in circulation in 130-plus countries worldwide.

	Annual Growth	12/10	12/11	12/12	12/13	12/14
Sales ($ mil.)	4.5%	30,242.0	32,282.0	33,808.0	34,932.0	35,999.0
Net income ($ mil.)	9.7%	4,057.0	4,935.0	4,482.0	5,359.0	5,885.0
Market value ($ mil.)	21.3%	43,907.2	48,254.9	58,802.0	92,816.8	95,179.9
Employees	(3.0%)	61,000	62,500	63,500	62,800	54,000

AMERICAN EXPRESS PUBLISHING CORPORATION

1120 Avenue of the Americas
New York NY 10036
Phone: 212-382-5600
Fax: 212-768-1568
Web: www.amexpub.com

CEO: Edward F Kelly Jr
CFO: Paul Francis
HR: –
FYE: December 31
Type: Subsidiary

American Express Publishing targets readers who enjoy the high life in their travel and culinary adventures. A division of American Express the company publishes magazines such as "Food & Wine Travel + Leisure" "Departures" Black Ink and Executive Travel. It also publishes a number of books (100 Greatest Trips) produces events (Food & Wine Classic in Aspen) and has custom publishing operations (magazines newsletters and other publications for corporate clients). American Express Publishing uses the credit card publisher's database to cull customers. The business is managed by Time Inc.; Time and American Express share its profits. American Express has been in the magazine business since 1968.

AMERICAN FAMILY MUTUAL INSURANCE COMPANY

6000 American Pkwy.
Madison WI 53783-0001
Phone: 608-249-2111
Fax: 608-243-4921
Web: www.amfam.com

CEO: David R Anderson
CFO: Jack Slazwedel
HR: –
FYE: December 31
Type: Private - Mutual Com

Even confirmed bachelors can get insured through American Family Mutual Insurance. The company and its subsidiaries specialize in personal and commercial property/casualty insurance. Its coverage products include auto homeowners farm and ranch and commercial liability. Its subsidiaries also offer life insurance and annuities and health plans. The company operates in 19 states primarily in the midwestern and western US. It is among the largest US property/casualty mutual insurance companies. Policies are underwritten by American Family Mutual and its American Standard Insurance and American Family Life Insurance Company (AFLIC) subsidiaries; together they operate as the American Family Insurance Group.

AMERICAN FEDERATION OF LABOR & CONGRESS OF INDUSTRIAL ORGANZATIO

815 16TH ST NW
WASHINGTON, DC 200064101
Phone: 202-637-5000
Fax: –
Web: www.aflcio.org

CEO: –
CFO: –
HR: –
FYE: June 30
Type: Private

Talk about spending a long time in labor: The AFL-CIO (American Federation of Labor and Congress of Industrial Organizations) has been focused on the task for more than a century. The AFL-CIO is an umbrella organization for more than 55 autonomous national and international unions. Altogether the AFL-CIO represents more than 12 million workers from actors and airline pilots to marine engineers and machinists. It fights to improve wages and working conditions. The organization charters 50-plus state federations and about 500 central labor councils. The AFL-CIO was created in 1955 by the merger of the AFL and the CIO.

	Annual Growth	06/07	06/08*	08/09*	06/11	06/13
Sales ($ mil.)	0.9%	–	150.9	0.7	168.1	158.0
Net income ($ mil.)	–	–	–	0.0	6.3	(9.4)
Market value ($ mil.)	–	–	–	–	–	–
Employees	–	–	–	–	–	380

*Fiscal year change

AMERICAN FEDERATION OF STATE COUNTY & MUNICIPAL EMPLOYEES

1625 L ST NW
WASHINGTON, DC 200365665
Phone: 202-429-1000
Fax: –

CEO: –
CFO: –
HR: –
FYE: December 31
Type: Private

American Federation of State County and Municipal Employees AFL-CIO (AFSCME) finds strength in its numbers. The 1.6 million member labor union represents public sector employees in industries such as health care education social services transportation and public works. The group advocates and seeks legislative change for issues relating to social and economic justice in the workplace. AFSCME has more than 3400 local unions in some 45 states the District of Columbia and Puerto Rico. The union is a member of The American Federation of Labor-Congress of Industrial Organizations (AFL-CIO). AFSCME began in 1932 as the Wisconsin State Administrative Clerical Fiscal and Technical Employees Association.

	Annual Growth	06/07	06/08*	12/08	12/12	12/13
Sales ($ mil.)	136.3%	–	2.5	2.3	160.2	181.9
Net income ($ mil.)	–	–	–	0.0	(15.8)	32.2
Market value ($ mil.)	–	–	–	–	–	–
Employees	–	–	–	–	–	450

*Fiscal year change

AMERICAN FIBER GREEN PRODUCTS INC   NBB: AFBG

4209 Raleigh Street
Tampa, FL 33619
Phone: 813 247-2770
Fax: -
Web: www.americanfibergreenproducts.com

CEO: Daniel L Hefner
CFO: Frank D Puissegur
HR: -
FYE: December 31
Type: Public

The recycled fiberglass molding to be made by American Fiber Green Products will come in more colors than green. American Fiber Green Products announced plans in 2008 to build the first fiberglass recycling plant in the US. Its subsidiaries including American Leisure Products and Chariot Manufacturing will incorporate the recycled resin products into their manufacturing process to build such products as picnic tables park benches trailers boats and vehicle bodies for replicas of vintage cars. American Fiber Green Products is working on other uses to circumvent fiberglass away from landfills. Company president and CEO Dan Hefner also holds those positions for American Commerce Solutions.

	Annual Growth	12/10	12/11	12/12	12/13	12/14
Sales ($ mil.)	61.9%	-	0.1	0.3	0.3	0.4
Net income ($ mil.)	-	(0.2)	(0.1)	(0.2)	(0.1)	(0.3)
Market value ($ mil.)	(29.1%)	11.1	8.8	3.5	5.3	2.8
Employees	0.0%	3	3	3	3	3

AMERICAN FIDELITY ASSURANCE COMPANY

2000 N. Classen Blvd.
Oklahoma City OK 73106-6013
Phone: 405-523-2000
Fax: 405-523-5421
Web: www.afadvantage.com

CEO: -
CFO: -
HR: Arete Muse
FYE: December 31
Type: Private

American Fidelity Assurance (AFA) puts its faith in the American people and insurance policies. It provides voluntary supplemental life and health insurance products and related services to more than 1 million customers primarily in the US and in about 23 other countries. The company's insurance plans include disability life cancer long term care and hospitalization insurance. The company also provides tax deferred annuity and flexible spending programs. It has tailored units to serve primary and secondary education employees and trade association members. Products and services are sold via worksite marketing by the company's sales force and a network of insurance brokers.

AMERICAN FINANCIAL GROUP INC   NYS: AFG

301 East Fourth Street
Cincinnati, OH 45202
Phone: 513 579-2121
Fax: -
Web: www.afginc.com

CEO: S. Craig Lindner
CFO: Joseph E. (Jeff) Consolino
HR: -
FYE: December 31
Type: Public

American Financial Group (AFG) insures American businessmen in pursuit of the great American Dream. Through the Great American Insurance Group of companies and its flagship Great American Insurance Company AFG offers commercial property/casualty insurance focused on specialties such as workers' compensation professional liability ocean and inland marine and multiperil crop insurance. The company also provides surety coverage for contractors and risk management services. For individuals and employers AFG provides a wide range of annuity policies sold through its Great American Financial Resources (GAFRI) subsidiary.

	Annual Growth	12/10	12/11	12/12	12/13	12/14
Assets ($ mil.)	10.0%	32,454.0	36,042.0	39,171.0	42,087.0	47,535.0
Net income ($ mil.)	(1.4%)	479.0	343.0	488.0	471.0	452.0
Market value ($ mil.)	17.1%	2,832.1	3,235.6	3,466.3	5,062.6	5,325.7
Employees	2.8%	6,450	6,500	6,100	6,300	7,200

AMERICAN FOODS GROUP LLC

500 So. Washington St.
Green Bay WI 54301-4219
Phone: 920-436-4229
Fax: 920-436-6466
Web: www.americanfoodsgroup.com

CEO: -
CFO: -
HR: -
FYE: December 31
Type: Subsidiary

American Foods Group is a bona fide Green Bay packer. With facilities in that Wisconsin city and cities in four other Midwestern states the company slaughters cattle to process four-plus million pounds of beef a day. Its lineup comprises an assortment of ground beef and specialty cuts such as bone-in tenderloin boneless beef roast and consumer-ready variety meats as well as specialty brands including Halal Meats and America's Heartland Organic Ground Beef. The group supplies beef to the US retail grocery and foodservice markets federal school lunch programs and American soldiers worldwide. It also exports to markets in some 38 countries. American Foods is owned by holding company Rosen's Diversified.

AMERICAN FRUIT & PRODUCE CORP.

12805 NW 42ND AVE
OPA LOCKA, FL 33054-4401
Phone: 305-681-1880
Fax: -

CEO: Hugo J Acosta
CFO: -
HR: -
FYE: December 31
Type: Private

American Fruit & Produce's (AFP) patriotic duty is to distribute fresh fruits and vegetables. The company supplies everything from apples to zucchini to US wholesale foodservice and retail customers. AFP also exports fresh fruits and vegetables from Florida ports to locations in the Americas and Europe. It is the largest US supplier of fresh produce to Caribbean countries. Hugo Acosta and his uncle Delio Medina opened their small produce outfit in Miami in 1983. The company has grown to include some 300000 sq. ft. of floor space situated on 32 acres in South Florida. American Fruit & Produce is still owned and operated by the its founders and their families.

	Annual Growth	12/06	12/07	12/08	12/09	12/11
Sales ($ mil.)	0.9%	-	-	-	83.2	84.8
Net income ($ mil.)	(9.5%)	-	-	-	1.9	1.6
Market value ($ mil.)	-	-	-	-	-	-
Employees	-	-	-	-	-	100

AMERICAN FURNITURE MANUFACTURING INC.

604 Pontotoc County Industrial Park Rd.
Ecru MS 38841
Phone: 662-489-2633
Fax: 662-488-9558
Web: americanfurn.net

CEO: Michael Thomas
CFO: -
HR: -
FYE: December 31
Type: Private

American Furniture Manufacturing (AFM) does most of its business at home. The company makes low-cost upholstered home furnishings including sofas chairs and recliners as well as accent tables. Its products are distributed to independent furniture stores in the US. AFM can ship most furniture within 48 hours and delivery is handled by its American Furniture Trucking division which maintains a fleet of trucks. The furniture maker sources wood and fabrics from the Asia/Pacific region which has also helped to keep costs down. AFM is owned by investment firm Compass Diversified Holdings.

AMERICAN FURNITURE WAREHOUSE CO INC

8820 AMERICAN WAY
ENGLEWOOD, CO 801127056
Phone: 303-799-9044
Fax: -
Web: www.afwonline.com

CEO: Jacob Jabs
CFO: -
HR: Cathy Steffes
FYE: March 31
Type: Private

Tony the Tiger hawking home furnishings might give some marketers pause but the combination seems to work for American Furniture Warehouse. American Furniture's television commercials often spotlight white-haired president and CEO Jake Jabs (who has become a well-known personality in the state as well as in the home furnishings industry) accompanied by baby exotic animals mostly tigers. The company sells furniture electronics and decor at discounted prices. It boasts about a dozen retail locations in Colorado and Arizona and sells through its website which also features bridal and gift registries. The company has built a reputation as a home-spun local furniture retailer. Jabs bought the company in 1975.

	Annual Growth	03/10	03/11	03/12	03/13	03/14
Sales ($ mil.)	10.5%	-	306.6	326.8	353.0	413.2
Net income ($ mil.)	7.1%	-	-	10.8	11.4	12.4
Market value ($ mil.)	-	-	-	-	-	-
Employees	-	-	-	-	-	1,900

AMERICAN FURUKAWA INC.

47677 Galleon Drive
Plymouth MI 48170
Phone: 734-446-2200
Fax: 734-446-2260
Web: www.americanfurukawa.com

CEO: Kazuhisa Sakata
CFO: Manuel Euyoqui
HR: -
FYE: March 31
Type: Subsidiary

American Furukawa Inc. (formerly named Furukawa Electric North America or FENA) is a subsidiary of Japan-based parent the Furukawa Electric Co. In April 2009 American Furukawa (AFI) was established to merge Furukawa Electric North America Automotive Products Division Inc. (FENA APD) and Furukawa America Inc. (FAI) to supply products for automotive electronics medical and industrial applications in North America. Products include heat sinks and thermal solutions memory disks for hard drives wire harnesses insulated wire and copper products to name a few. AFI's headquarters are now in Plymouth Michigan.

AMERICAN GENERAL LIFE INSURANCE COMPANY

2727 Allen Pkwy.
Houston TX 77019
Phone: 713-522-1111
Fax: 713-620-6653
Web: www.aigag.com

CEO: Ronald H Ridlehuber
CFO: Robert Frank Herbert Jr
HR: -
FYE: December 31
Type: Subsidiary

A-ten-schun! American General Life Insurance is still among the top brass of US life insurance and financial services firms. It anchors the domestic life insurance operations of American International Group under the AIG Life and Retirement umbrella. Serving some 13 million policyholders American General Life offers clients a variety of products to build their nest eggs including fixed and deferred annuities. Life insurance offerings include individual and group policies for families businesses and affiliation groups. Other products include accident and supplemental health insurance income protection and retirement planning programs.

AMERICAN GOLF CORPORATION

2951 28th St.
Santa Monica CA 90405
Phone: 310-664-4000
Fax: 310-664-4386
Web: www.americangolf.com

CEO: Jim Hinckley
CFO: Mike Moecker
HR: -
FYE: December 31
Type: Private

You might say this company knows to stay out of the rough. American Golf Corporation (AGC) is one of the largest golf course management firms in the world with more than 110 public private and resort properties in more than 25 states. Its portfolio of courses includes such country clubs as The Golf Club at Mansion Ridge (Monroe New York) Oakhurst Country Club (Clayton California) and Palm Valley Country Club (Palm Desert California). The company also runs the American Golf Foundation which helps promote the game through charity and education. AGC is owned by investment firms Goldman Sachs and Starwood Capital.

AMERICAN HERITAGE LIFE INSURANCE COMPANY

1776 American Heritage Life Dr.
Jacksonville FL 32224
Phone: 904-992-1776
Fax: 904-992-2658
Web: https://www.ahlcorp.com

CEO: -
CFO: -
HR: -
FYE: December 31
Type: Subsidiary

American Heritage Life Insurance Company doing business as Allstate Workplace Division offers voluntary supplemental insurance products — the ones you might pay a little extra for in addition to basic employee benefits. A wholly-owned subsidiary of Allstate American Heritage Life Insurance offers individual and group life and health insurance products including dental cancer stroke accident disability income and hospital indemnity. Its products are sold by more than 29000 exclusive and independent workplace enrollment agents to more than 20000 businesses. The company is licensed to operate in all US states as well as in Washington DC Guam Puerto Rico and the US Virgin Islands.

AMERICAN HOMEPATIENT INC.

5200 Maryland Way Ste. 400
Brentwood TN 37027-5018
Phone: 615-221-8884
Fax: 615-373-9932
Web: www.ahom.com

CEO: Mark Lamp
CFO: Stephen L Clanton
HR: Sandy Irvin
FYE: December 31
Type: Private

American HomePatient is making sure no one is home alone when it comes to health care. American HomePatient provides home health services from some 250 locations in the US. The company provides respiratory therapy and equipment including oxygen therapy sleep apnea systems and nebulizers. It also offers home infusion therapy services including feeding and intravenous drug administration. American HomePatient also rents and sells durable hospital equipment including beds and wheelchairs. Mostly it operates independently but also provides home care in a few areas through joint ventures with hospitals. Founded in 1983 American HomePatient is owned by funds of investment firm Highland Capital Management.

AMERICAN HOSPITAL ASSOCIATION

155 N WACKER DR STE 400　　　　　　　CEO: Richard J. (Rick) Pollack
CHICAGO, IL 606061719　　　　　　　　CFO: John Evans
Phone: 312-422-3000　　　　　　　　　　HR: –
Fax: –　　　　　　　　　　　　　　　　FYE: December 31
Web: www.aha.org　　　　　　　　　　　Type: Private

The American Hospital Association (AHA) represents some 5000 hospitals and other health care providers and some 43000 individuals from various health care fields. The AHA acts as an advocate in national health care policy development and provides services to its members such as helping hospitals and other health care providers form networks for patient care conducting research and development projects on the structuring and delivery of health care services and producing educational programs and publications. The AHA Resource Center maintains an extensive collection of books and documents relating to hospitals and health care. The AHA was founded in 1898.

	Annual Growth	12/07	12/08	12/10	12/11	12/13
Sales ($ mil.)	0.6%	–	120.6	107.8	113.0	124.4
Net income ($ mil.)	4.3%	–	–	6.5	7.8	7.4
Market value ($ mil.)	–	–	–	–	–	–
Employees		–	–	–	–	508

AMERICAN HOTEL REGISTER COMPANY

100 S. Milwaukee Ave.　　　　　　　　　CEO: –
Vernon Hills IL 60061-4305　　　　　　　CFO: Daniel D Potts
Phone: 847-564-4000　　　　　　　　　　HR: –
Fax: 847-743-2098　　　　　　　　　　　FYE: December 31
Web: www.americanhotel.com　　　　　　Type: Private

Delighted by the embossed soaps and sundries offered during your hotel visit? Thank American Hotel Register. The company distributes more than 50000 products in 20-plus categories including toiletries cleaning products appliances furniture carpeting drapery and linens to hotels of all sizes. It also caters to funeral homes health care facilities government offices and military institutions. American Hotel Register sells products through its 2150-page catalog and website. It operates distribution centers in the US Puerto Rico Canada and Mexico. Founded in 1865 to sell hotel guest registers the company was acquired by Thomas Leahy in the early 1900s. It is owned and operated by his descendants.

AMERICAN INDEPENDENCE CORP

485 Madison Avenue　　　　　　　　　　NAS: AMIC
New York, NY 10022　　　　　　　　　　CEO: Roy T K Thung
Phone: 212 355-4141　　　　　　　　　　CFO: Teresa A Herbert
Fax: –　　　　　　　　　　　　　　　　HR: –
Web: www.americanindependencecorp.com　FYE: December 31
　　　　　　　　　　　　　　　　　　　Type: Public

Since the name American Independence tells you nothing about the company we'll help you out. What sounds like a lone bold ideal is really a holding company which through its subsidiaries provides reinsurance and insurance coverage specializing in medical stop-loss insurance for self-insured employers. It also offers group and individual health and short-term medical insurance policies. Subsidiary Independence American is licensed to provide property/casualty insurance throughout most of the US. American Independence is majority-owned by Independence Holding which also owns Madison National Life Insurance and Standard Security Life Insurance.

	Annual Growth	12/10	12/11	12/12	12/13	12/14
Sales ($ mil.)	16.5%	89.4	88.0	101.9	153.3	164.9
Net income ($ mil.)	25.8%	2.1	2.5	9.6	3.4	5.3
Market value ($ mil.)	20.6%	39.2	31.3	40.4	97.1	82.9
Employees	38.1%	52	50	74	123	189

AMERICAN INFRASTRUCTURE INC.

1805 BERKS RD　　　　　　　　　　　　CEO: A Ross Myers
WORCESTER, PA 19490　　　　　　　　　CFO: Denis P Moore
Phone: 610-222-8800　　　　　　　　　　HR: –
Fax: –　　　　　　　　　　　　　　　　FYE: December 31
Web: www.americaninfrastructure.com　　Type: Private

American Infrastructure provides heavy civil construction services for projects in the Mid-Atlantic. Operating as Allan A. Myers in Pennsylvania and Delaware and as American Infrastructure in Maryland and Virginia the company builds and reconstructs highways water treatment plants medical facilities and shopping centers and offers site development for homebuilders. Its quarries and asphalt plants operate under the Independence Construction Materials (ICM) subsidiary which supplies aggregates asphalt and ready-mixed concrete to its construction companies. The family-run business was established in 1939 as Allan A. Myers and Son a local hauling company in the suburbs of Philadelphia.

	Annual Growth	12/08	12/09	12/10	12/10	12/11
Sales ($ mil.)	–	–	–	(1,363.0)	476.4	545.6
Net income ($ mil.)	523392.7%	–	–	0.0	20.2	1.6
Market value ($ mil.)	–	–	–	–	–	–
Employees	–	–	–	–	–	1,700

AMERICAN INSTITUTE OF ARCHITECTS INC

1735 NEW YORK AVE NW　　　　　　　　CEO: Robert Ivy Jr
WASHINGTON, DC 200065209　　　　　　CFO: Tracy Harris
Phone: 202-626-7300　　　　　　　　　　HR: –
Fax: –　　　　　　　　　　　　　　　　FYE: December 31
Web: www.aia.org　　　　　　　　　　　Type: Private

The American Institute of Architects (AIA) knows how to raise the roof. The group represents the interests of some 83000 professional architects through more than 300 chapters in every state in the US and in Asia Europe and South America. Members adhere to a code of ethics and the AIA disciplines members who break the rules with censure admonition suspension of membership or permanent termination of membership. The organization's member benefits include educational programs referrals discounted contract documents and job search assistance. It also lobbies government bodies on behalf of its members and provides media relations support.

	Annual Growth	12/05	12/06	12/07	12/08	12/10
Sales ($ mil.)	(1.1%)	–	60.1	64.9	59.5	57.3
Net income ($ mil.)	(22.6%)	–	–	5.6	2.3	2.6
Market value ($ mil.)	–	–	–	–	–	–
Employees		–	–	–	–	185

AMERICAN INSTITUTE OF CERTIFIED PUBLIC ACCOUNTANTS

220 LEIGH FARM RD　　　　　　　　　　CEO: Barry C. Melancon
DURHAM, NC 277078110　　　　　　　　CFO: Tim LaSpaluto
Phone: 919-402-0682　　　　　　　　　　HR: –
Fax: –　　　　　　　　　　　　　　　　FYE: July 31
Web: www.aicpa.org　　　　　　　　　　Type: Private

When you add it all up the American Institute of Certified Public Accountants (AICPA) makes perfect sense. One of the nation's leading nonprofit professional associations the AICPA has more than 400000 members from more than 145 countries who are involved in public accounting business education law and government. The group which generates just more than half of its revenues from membership dues promotes awareness of the accounting profession; identifies financial trends; sets certification licensing and professional standards; and provides information and advice to CPAs. The AICPA distributes its information through websites conferences and forums and publications.

	Annual Growth	07/06	07/07	07/08	07/09	07/13
Sales ($ mil.)	1.0%	–	–	209.4	199.8	219.9
Net income ($ mil.)	8.9%	–	–	9.9	(13.6)	15.2
Market value ($ mil.)	–	–	–	–	–	–
Employees		–	–	–	–	400

AMERICAN INSTITUTE OF PHYSICS INCORPORATED

1 PHYSICS ELLIPSE
COLLEGE PARK, MD 20740-3841
Phone: 301-209-3100
Fax: –
Web: www.aip.org

CEO: Dr Robert G W Brown
CFO: Catherine Swartz
HR: –
FYE: December 31
Type: Private

Who says scientists don't know how to get physical? The American Institute of Physics (AIP) publishes magazines (Physics Today) journals (Journal of Applied Physics) conference proceedings online products and other publications in the sciences of physics and astronomy. The company provides publishing services for its own publications as well as for its member societies and other publishers. Scitation AIP's online publishing platform hosts 1.6 million articles from 190 sources. AIP was founded in New York in 1931 by a group of American physical science societies. It was chartered as a membership corporation to advance and diffuse knowledge of the science of physics and its applications to human welfare.

	Annual Growth	12/08	12/09	12/10	12/11	12/12
Sales ($ mil.)	(2.3%)	–	77.4	76.0	73.1	72.3
Net income ($ mil.)	(4.5%)	–	23.0	8.6	(8.3)	20.0
Market value ($ mil.)	–	–	–	–	–	–
Employees	–	–	–	–	–	273

AMERICAN INSTITUTES FOR RESEARCH IN THE BEHAVIORAL SCIENCES

1000 THMAS JFFERSON ST NW
WASHINGTON, DC 200073835
Phone: 202-403-5000
Fax: –
Web: www.air.org

CEO: David Myers
CFO: Marijo Ahlgrimm
HR: Kiane Hutchins
FYE: December 31
Type: Private

The American Institutes for Research (AIR) lives and breathes to enhance human performance. The not-for-profit organization conducts behavioral and social science research on topics related to education and educational assessment health international development and work and training. Clients including several federal agencies use AIR's research in developing policies. As a major ongoing initiative the organization provides tools to improve education both in the US and internationally particularly in disadvantaged areas. John C. Flanagan who developed the Critical Incident Technique personnel-selection tool to identify human success indicators in the workplace founded the organization in 1946.

	Annual Growth	12/09	12/10	12/11	12/12	12/13
Sales ($ mil.)	7.7%	–	285.3	300.0	326.5	356.3
Net income ($ mil.)	36.4%	–	–	13.0	22.5	24.2
Market value ($ mil.)	–	–	–	–	–	–
Employees	–	–	–	–	–	1,589

AMERICAN INTERNATIONAL INDUSTRIES INC   NBB: AMIN

601 Cien Street, Suite 235
Kemah, TX 77565-3077
Phone: 281 334-9479
Fax: 281 334-9508
Web: www.americanii.com

CEO: Daniel Dror
CFO: Charles R Zeller
HR: –
FYE: December 31
Type: Public

Nothing says Texas like oil and real estate. American International Industries (AII) covers those bases — and more — from its home in the Houston metro area. The company typically takes a controlling interest in undervalued companies; it holds investments in oil wells real estate and various industrial manufacturers. AII owns Delta Seaboard International (formerly Hammonds Industries) which operates technical services fuel additives and water treatment systems divisions. Its Northeastern Plastics subsidiary makes automotive after-market products. International Diversified Corporation (a firm connected with the brother of chairman and CEO Daniel Dror) owns 27% of the firm.

	Annual Growth	12/10	12/11	12/12	12/13	12/14
Sales ($ mil.)	(80.8%)	24.3	21.7	8.0	7.2	0.0
Net income ($ mil.)	–	0.1	(3.3)	(2.1)	(1.8)	(2.4)
Market value ($ mil.)	6.1%	1.5	0.6	5.8	4.2	1.9
Employees	(22.9%)	51	60	18	18	18

AMERICAN ITALIAN PASTA COMPANY

4100 N. Mulberry Dr. Ste. 200
Kansas City MO 64116
Phone: 816-584-5000
Fax: 816-584-5100
Web: www.aipc.com

CEO: –
CFO: –
HR: Janet Hopkins
FYE: September 30
Type: Subsidiary

American Italian Pasta Company (AIPC) uses its noodle in many ways. The company is one of the biggest makers of dry pasta in North America by volume offering some 300 different pasta shapes and 3100 stock-keeping units or SKUs from angel hair to ziti. Its name brands such as Golden Grain Heartland and Mueller's are staples on retail shelves in the US and overseas. The company's regional private-label customers include most major US grocers and club stores. It also serves the institutional market comprising foodservice operators that supply restaurants and schools and food manufacturers that use pasta as an ingredient. AIPC is owned by private-label giant Ralcorp which acquired the company in 2010.

AMERICAN LAFRANCE LLC

1090 Newton Way
Summerville SC 29483
Phone: 843-486-7400
Fax: 843-486-7417
Web: www.americanlafrance.com

CEO: –
CFO: –
HR: –
FYE: December 31
Type: Subsidiary

The flashing lights in your rear-view mirror just might be an American LaFrance product. The company manufactures emergency vehicle equipment for fire medical and rescue services. Signals of public safety its custom and commercial red offerings include fire trucks tankers ambulances tractor drawn aerial ladders fire pumps and fire rescue boats. A former subsidiary of DaimlerChrysler's Freightliner American LaFrance has roots that date back to 1832 and has operated under the management of private equity group Patriarch Partners since 2005.

AMERICAN LAND LEASE INC.

380 Park Place Blvd. Ste. 200
Clearwater FL 33759
Phone: 727-726-8868
Fax: 727-725-4391
Web: www.americanlandlease.com

CEO: Terry Considine
CFO: Shannon E Smith
HR: –
FYE: December 31
Type: Private

American Land Lease wants to make the American Dream an American Reality especially during the golden years. The self-managed real estate investment trust (REIT) owns develops renovates and manages manufactured housing communities for active adults. It owns about 35 communities in Arizona and Florida; properties include some 9000 leased developed and undeveloped homesites and RV parks. In light of growing senior demographics American Land Lease operates its properties primarily as retirement communities. The REIT's communities often feature swimming pools golf courses and clubhouses. American Land Lease was acquired by Chicago private equity firm Green Courte Partners in 2009.

AMERICAN LEARNING CORPORATION   NASDAQ: ALRN

1 Jericho Plaza
Jericho NY 11753
Phone: 516-938-8000
Fax: 516-938-0405
Web: www.americanlearningcorporation.com

CEO: Gary Gelman
CFO: Gary J Knauer
HR: –
FYE: March 31
Type: Public

American Learning (formerly American Claims Evaluation) has undergone a transition. The company historically provided vocational rehabilitation and disability management services through its RPM Rehabilitation & Associates subsidiary; but in 2008 it sold those operations and got into the business of helping kids with developmental delays and disabilities. It acquired private New York-based Interactive Therapy Group Consultants which provides comprehensive therapy services including early intervention programs preschool programs and school staffing services to developmentally delayed and disabled children primarily in New York. Chairman president and CEO Gary Gelman owns two-thirds of the company.

AMERICAN LICORICE COMPANY

2796 NW Clearwater Dr.
Bend OR 97701
Phone: 541-617-0800
Fax: 541-617-0224
Web: www.americanlicorice.com

CEO: John R Kretchmer
CFO: –
HR: –
FYE: October 31
Type: Private

American Licorice makes candy concoctions using one of America's favorite flavorings — licorice. The company manufactures licorice twists pieces and ropes in various flavors (including original red original black strawberry and cherry). It also makes sour hard candies and drinking straws packed with sour candy. American's brand names include Red Vines Natural Vines (sweetened with brown rice syrup instead of high-fructose corn syrup) Snaps Super Ropes Sour Punch Sip-n-Chew and Extinguisher. The company's products can be purchased at retail food outlets grocery chains club dollar and drug stores and specialty venues throughout the US as well as online through its CandyCabinet.com division.

AMERICAN LEATHER

4501 Mountain Creek Pkwy.
Dallas TX 75236
Phone: 972-296-9599
Fax: 972-296-8859
Web: www.americanleather.com

CEO: Robert Duncan
CFO: –
HR: –
FYE: December 31
Type: Private

It may not be as American as apple pie but American Leather hopes to make itself into a household name. The company a manufacturer of custom-made leather and upholstered furniture offers furnishing pieces such as sofas sleepers beds recliners chairs and ottomans in more than a dozen styles (including traditional transitional and contemporary) and nearly 300 colors and textures. American Leather sells its products through independent retailers located throughout the US and has showrooms in Dallas San Francisco and High Point North Carolina. It also makes exclusive styles for Crate & Barrel Design Within Reach and Room & Board. CEO Bob Duncan has a controlling interest in the company.

AMERICAN LIFE INSURANCE COMPANY

1 ALICO Plaza 600 King St.
Wilmington DE 19899
Phone: 302-594-2000
Fax: 408-428-3732
Web: www.ss8.com

CEO: Marlene Debel
CFO: –
HR: –
FYE: December 31
Type: Subsidiary

Belying its moniker American Life Insurance Company (ALICO) provides life and health insurance only "outside" the US. (Fairness dictates noting that ALICO was named Asia Life Insurance Company for its first three decades dating from its 1921 founding in Shanghai.) The company operates in more than 50 countries worldwide; Japan is ALICO's largest single market. ALICO sells such individual and group products as life insurance and annuities accident and health coverage and pensions. The company markets its products through a network of some 40000 agents and brokers and banks. US insurance giant American International Group (AIG) sold ALICO to MetLife in 2010.

AMERICAN LIBRARY ASSOCIATION

50 E HURON ST
CHICAGO, IL 606112788
Phone: 312-944-6780
Fax: –
Web: www.americanlibrariesmagazine.org

CEO: –
CFO: –
HR: –
FYE: August 31
Type: Private

Shhhh! The American Library Association (ALA) is a not-for-profit that works to develop promote and improve library and information services. Governed by an elected council the ALA works with libraries of all types from public to academic to prison. The more than 67000-member organization consists of 11 divisions as well as affiliated organizations and chapters in all 50 states all working to advance ALA causes such as Banned Books Week an annual event promoting awareness about efforts to ban certain books from libraries. The ALA's Washington DC branch office tries to influence federal legislative policy to ensure the public's right to free access to information. The group was founded in 1876.

	Annual Growth	08/05	08/06	08/07	08/08	08/09
Sales ($ mil.)	(83.2%)	–	–	1,762.1	57.2	50.0
Net income ($ mil.)	–	–	–	0.0	3.0	(7.4)
Market value ($ mil.)	–	–	–	–	–	–
Employees	–	–	–	–	–	275

AMERICAN LOCKER GROUP, INC.   NBB: ALGI

2701 Regent Blvd., Suite 200
DFW Airport, TX 75261
Phone: 817 329-1600
Fax: –
Web: www.americanlocker.com

CEO: –
CFO: –
HR: –
FYE: December 31
Type: Public

Ever carried around one of those orange plastic-capped locker keys at the theme park? That's American Locker Group. The company sells and rents coin- key- and electronically controlled lockers used by health clubs amusement parks ski resorts bus stations and employee locker rooms. Customers include SeaWorld Vail Resorts Walt Disney World The UPS Store and the University of Colorado. Postal mailboxes such as those used by apartment complexes make up about a third of sales. Besides the US American Locker Group serves customers in Canada Chile Greece India Mexico and the UK (less than 20% of sales in 2009). The company was founded in 1958.

	Annual Growth	12/09	12/10	12/11	12/12	12/13
Sales ($ mil.)	4.0%	12.5	12.1	13.4	13.7	14.6
Net income ($ mil.)	–	(0.4)	0.1	0.0	(0.6)	(2.8)
Market value ($ mil.)	5.1%	2.7	1.9	2.5	2.9	3.3
Employees	(3.3%)	137	103	110	108	120

AMERICAN MANAGEMENT ASSOCIATION INTERNATIONAL

1601 BROADWAY FL 7
NEW YORK, NY 100197420
Phone: 212-586-8100
Fax: –
Web: www.amanet.org

CEO: Edward T. Reilly
CFO: Vivianna Guzman
HR: –
FYE: March 31
Type: Private

American Management Association (AMA) is a not-for-profit membership association that provides a variety of educational and management development services to businesses government agencies and individuals. The associations is engaged in professional development advancing the skills of individuals. AMA offers more than 140 training seminars in more than 25 subject areas of business management and workforce development. It also sponsors conferences and workshops and provides webcasts podcasts and books in such areas as communication leadership project management sales and marketing human resources and finance and accounting.

	Annual Growth	03/08	03/09	03/10	03/11	03/13
Sales ($ mil.)	–	–	(442.0)	83.9	87.9	90.8
Net income ($ mil.)	–	–	–	(2.9)	(3.7)	1.2
Market value ($ mil.)	–	–	–	–	–	–
Employees	–	–	–	–	–	500

AMERICAN MANAGEMENT SERVICES WEST LLC

Pier 70 2801 Alaskan Way Ste. 200
Seattle WA 98121
Phone: 206-215-9700
Fax: 206-215-9777
Web: www.pinnaclerealty.com

CEO: –
CFO: John Carrosino
HR: –
FYE: December 31
Type: Private

American Management Services (which operates as Pinnacle) makes sure investment properties are in top form. Pinnacle provides property management and brokerage services for real estate investors such as financial institutions foreign investors government housing agencies pension funds and private partnerships. Its portfolio of properties — worth around $20 billion — spans 250 cities across the US as well as Asia and Canada. Its assets under management include about 175000 apartment units as well as military housing and industrial retail and office space. Pinnacle also offers such services as customized financial reporting risk management recruitment and technology planning.

AMERICAN MEDIA INC.

1000 American Media Way
Boca Raton FL 33464
Phone: 561-997-7733
Fax: 800-943-3694
Web: www.akorn.com

CEO: David Pecker
CFO: –
HR: –
FYE: March 31
Type: Private

These publications cover some American obsessions: gossip and good health. American Media is the nation's top publisher of tabloid newspapers and magazines including National Enquirer and Star. It also publishes women's health magazine Shape as well as a number of other magazines including Flex Men's Fitness and Natural Health. In addition to publishing American Media offers distribution and marketing services to other publishers to get their periodicals in the racks at supermarkets throughout the US and Canada. American Media is owned by a group of investment firms including Angelo Gordon & Co. The company emerged from Chapter 11 bankruptcy in late 2010 after it was able to restructure its debt.

AMERICAN MEDICAL ALERT CORP.

NASDAQ: AMAC

3265 Lawson Blvd.
Oceanside NY 11572
Phone: 516-536-5850
Fax: 516-536-5276
Web: www.amacalert.com

CEO: Jack Rhian
CFO: Richard Rallo
HR: –
FYE: December 31
Type: Subsidiary

It's like having a guardian angel hovering above but without the wings. American Medical Alert Corp (AMAC) provides health care communication and monitoring services. The company's Health Safety and Monitoring Services (HSMS) unit markets remote patient monitoring systems including personal emergency response systems health management and medication management systems and safety monitoring systems. Its Telephony Based Communication Services (TBCS) unit provides telephone answering services and operates clinical trial recruitment call centers. In late 2011 UK health care services company Tunstall Healthcare Group acquired AMAC for an estimated $82 million.

AMERICAN MEDICAL ASSOCIATION INC

330 N WABASH AVE # 39300
CHICAGO, IL 606113586
Phone: 312-464-5000
Fax: –
Web: www.ama-assn.org

CEO: James L. Madara
CFO: Denise M. Hagerty
HR: Robert (Bob) Davis
FYE: December 31
Type: Private

The AMA knows whether there's a doctor in the house. The American Medical Association (AMA) prescribes the standards for the medical profession. The membership group's activities include advocacy for physicians promoting ethics standards in the medical community and improving health care education. Policies are set by the AMA's House of Delegates comprised of elected representatives. The AMA is also a publisher of books for physicians and provides an online physician network through a partnership with Medfusion sells medical malpractice insurance and helps doctors fight legal claims. Founded in 1847 by a physician to establish a code of medical ethics AMA has nearly 225000 members.

	Annual Growth	12/04	12/05*	06/06*	12/08	12/13
Sales ($ mil.)	–	–	0.0	1.5	3.2	258.5
Net income ($ mil.)	–	–	–	(0.2)	(0.3)	(7.0)
Market value ($ mil.)	–	–	–	–	–	–
Employees	–	–	–	–	–	1,150

*Fiscal year change

AMERICAN MEDICAL RESPONSE AMBULANCE SERVICE INC.

6200 S. Syracuse Way #200
Greenwood Village CO 80111
Phone: 303-495-1200
Fax: 303-495-1295
Web: www.amr.net

CEO: –
CFO: Randy Owen
HR: –
FYE: December 31
Type: Subsidiary

Because driving yourself to the emergency room isn't always the best plan there is American Medical Response (AMR). With thousands of vehicles in some 40 states AMR is the largest contract provider of emergency and non-emergency ambulance services in the US. Non-emergency services include transportation for medically unstable patients and such non-medical transport services as transfers to and from health care facilities. The company provides around 3 million transports annually for customers that also include hospitals and local government agencies. AMR is a subsidiary of Emergency Medical Services Corporation (EMSC).

AMERICAN MEDICAL SYSTEMS HOLDINGS INC.

10700 Bren Rd. West
Minnetonka MN 55343
Phone: 952-930-6000
Fax: 952-930-6373
Web: www.americanmedicalsystems.com

CEO: –
CFO: Mark A Heggestad
HR: –
FYE: December 31
Type: Subsidiary

Purchasing American Medical Systems' products could make a few of us blush but they are important nonetheless. AMS is a leading maker of urological devices including products to help with erectile dysfunction such as inflatable penile implants as well as urinary incontinence devices for men and women. Its other products treat such conditions as menorrhagia (excessive uterine bleeding) enlarged prostate and fecal incontinence. AMS has around 80 independent distributors in addition to a global sale and marketing force of about 500 employees. Marketing efforts target urologists gynecologists and colorectal surgeons. The company was acquired by Endo Pharmaceuticals in 2011 for $2.9 billion.

AMERICAN MIDSTREAM PARTNERS LP   NYS: AMID

1400 16th Street, Suite 310
Denver, CO 80202
Phone: 720 457-6060
Fax: –
Web: www.americanmidstream.com

CEO: Lynn L. Bourdon
CFO: Dan C. Campbell
HR: –
FYE: December 31
Type: Public

If natural gas exploration and production companies are hunters then American Midstream Partners is a gatherer. Serving oil and gas companies American Midstream gathers treats processes and transports natural gas through a network of 1400 miles of pipeline stretching across Alabama Louisiana Mississippi Tennessee and Texas. Its owned and operated assets include eight interstate or intrastate pipelines nine gathering systems and three processing facilities. The company has counted Exxon ConocoPhillips and Dow Hydrocarbons as customers. Formed in 2009 American Midstream went public in 2011 through a $73 million IPO.

	Annual Growth	12/10	12/11	12/12	12/13	12/14
Sales ($ mil.)	9.8%	211.9	244.7	210.6	292.7	308.4
Net income ($ mil.)	–	(8.6)	(11.7)	(6.5)	(34.0)	(98.0)
Market value ($ mil.)	2.8%	–	441.8	331.7	658.5	479.3
Employees	–	–	–	–	–	–

AMERICAN NATIONAL BANKSHARES, INC. (DANVILLE, VA)   NMS: AMNB

628 Main Street
Danville, VA 24541
Phone: 434 792-5111
Fax: –
Web: www.amnb.com

CEO: Jeffrey V. Haley
CFO: William W. Traynham
HR: –
FYE: December 31
Type: Public

American National Bankshares with total assets of about $1.3 billion is the holding company for American National Bank and Trust. Founded in 1909 the bank operates some 25 locations that serve southern and central Virginia and north central North Carolina. Operating through two segments — Community Banking and Trust and Investment Services — it offers checking and savings accounts CDs IRAs and insurance. Lending activities primarily consist of real estate loans: Commercial mortgages account for about one-third of its loan portfolio; residential mortgages bring in another quarter. American National Bankshares' trust and investment services division manages nearly $610 million in assets.

	Annual Growth	12/10	12/11	12/12	12/13	12/14
Assets ($ mil.)	12.7%	833.7	1,304.7	1,283.7	1,307.5	1,346.5
Net income ($ mil.)	11.4%	8.3	11.6	16.0	15.7	12.7
Market value ($ mil.)	1.3%	185.4	153.5	159.0	206.7	195.3
Employees	4.1%	242	315	307	290	284

AMERICAN NATIONAL INSURANCE CO. (GALVESTON, TX)   NMS: ANAT

One Moody Plaza
Galveston, TX 77550-7999
Phone: 409 763-4661
Fax: 409 766-6502
Web: www.anico.com

CEO: Gregory V. Ostergren
CFO: John J. Dunn
HR: Jeanette Cernosek
FYE: December 31
Type: Public

True to its name American National Insurance Company (ANICO) offers agricultural commercial and personal property/casualty insurance as well as life insurance annuities supplemental health credit and other types of insurance throughout the US Puerto Rico and other territories. It subsidiaries include Garden State Life Insurance Standard Life and Accident Insurance and Farm Family Holdings. It markets its products through independent and career agents broker-dealers employee benefit advisors financial representatives and managing general underwriters. Variable products are securities products distributed through ANICO Financial Services Inc.

	Annual Growth	12/10	12/11	12/12	12/13	12/14
Assets ($ mil.)	2.4%	21,413.0	22,524.3	23,107.1	23,324.9	23,552.0
Net income ($ mil.)	14.5%	144.0	192.2	191.0	268.4	247.2
Market value ($ mil.)	7.5%	2,300.8	1,962.5	1,835.1	3,077.9	3,070.4
Employees	(0.9%)	3,251	3,207	3,075	3,078	3,138

AMERICAN NATURAL ENERGY CORP.   TVX: ANR U

One Warren Place, 6100 South Yale, Suite2010
Tulsa, OK 74136
Phone: 918 481-1440
Fax: 918 481-1473
Web: www.annrg.com

CEO: –
CFO: Steven P Ensz
HR: –
FYE: December 31
Type: Public

American Natural Energy Corp. is not selling organic food and dietary supplements to boost metabolism it is tapping into that other American natural energy source — hydrocarbons. Doing business as ANEC the company is an oil and natural gas exploration and production company which focuses its operations on a property in St. Charles Parish Louisiana. ANEC works in tandem with partner Exxon Mobil to develop this Louisiana project. In 2007 the company sold 75% of ANEC's development rights in this project to Dune Energy.

	Annual Growth	12/09	12/10	12/11	12/12	12/13
Sales ($ mil.)	32.3%	1.1	2.6	2.0	2.1	3.3
Net income ($ mil.)	–	24.0	(2.1)	(0.9)	(3.3)	(3.1)
Market value ($ mil.)	(26.9%)	0.7	6.3	2.2	2.0	0.2
Employees	0.0%	6	7	7	7	6

AMERICAN NUTRITION INC.

2813 Wall Ave.
Odgen UT 84401
Phone: 801-394-3477
Fax: 801-394-3674
Web: www.anibrands.com

CEO: –
CFO: Raymond Bialick
HR: Patty Valentine
FYE: June 30
Type: Private

American Nutrition (ANI) is looking out for your canine and feline friends — er family members. The company makes more than 300000 tons of dry and wet food and snacks for dogs and cats annually. Its products are sold under such brand names as Atta Boy Atta Cat Basic Plus Natural Harmony and Vita Bone. ANI also produces premium biodegradable cat litter. In addition to making its own products for dogs and cats the company provides contract pet food manufacturing services. It operates production facilities in Arizona Utah and Washington. ANI was founded in 1972 by the late Jack Behnken.

AMERICAN OIL & GAS INC.

1050 17th St. Ste. 2400
Denver CO 80265
Phone: 303-991-0173
Fax: 303-595-0709
Web: www.americanoilandgasinc.com

CEO: Timothy B Goodell
CFO: –
HR: –
FYE: December 31
Type: Subsidiary

Deep in the heart of the North American continent lie untapped natural gas deposits and American Oil & Gas is searching for them. The exploration and production company is focusing its efforts on the Rocky Mountains a region with one of the largest underdeveloped natural gas fields in the US (the Bakken Shale formation). American Oil & Gas in 2009 reported that it had estimated proved reserves of about 64420 barrels of oil and 645.3 million cu. ft. of natural gas. The company is developing its position in the Bakken and Three Forks plays in the Williston Basin in North Dakota. In 2010 American Oil & Gas was acquired by Hess in a $450-million stock deal that grew Hess' Bakken holdings.

AMERICAN PACIFIC CORP.

NMS: APFC

3883 Howard Hughes Parkway, Suite 700
Las Vegas, NV 89169
Phone: 702 735-2200
Fax: –
Web: www.apfc.com

CEO: Joseph Carleone
CFO: Dana M Kelley
HR: –
FYE: September 30
Type: Public

American Pacific (AMPAC) manufactures and markets a potent mix of Specialty Chemicals and Fine Chemicals mainly for pharmaceutical uses. Its largest unit makes and supplies active pharmaceutical ingredients and advanced intermediates to the pharmaceutical industry. AMPAC's specialty chemicals also include sodium azide an airbag deployment chemical also used in pharmaceuticals; and Halotron an ozone-friendly fire suppressant. The company also makes and environmental protection products including electro-chemical equipment for the water treatment.

	Annual Growth	09/09	09/10	09/11	09/12	09/13
Sales ($ mil.)	2.2%	197.1	176.2	209.7	185.6	215.1
Net income ($ mil.)	–	(6.0)	(3.3)	(7.2)	25.3	23.2
Market value ($ mil.)	63.6%	60.8	35.1	58.3	95.0	435.3
Employees	(2.6%)	589	595	653	494	530

AMERICAN PETROLEUM INSTITUTE INC

1220 L ST NW STE 900
WASHINGTON, DC 200054070
Phone: 202-682-8000
Fax: –
Web: www.recycleoil.org

CEO: Jack N Gerard
CFO: Brenda Hargett
HR: –
FYE: December 31
Type: Private

The American Petroleum Institute (API) is a trade association for the oil and natural gas industry. The group represents more than 625 corporate members including such industry giants as BP and Exxon Mobil as well as small independent companies with offices in more than 20 state capitals and overseas. Besides serving as an advocate in legislative regulatory and media arenas the API compiles data on industry operations. The organization's members come from several segments of the petroleum industry including upstream (exploration and production) downstream (refining and marketing) pipeline operations marine transportation and oil field service. The API was founded in 1919.

	Annual Growth	12/06	12/07	12/08	12/09	12/13
Sales ($ mil.)	(27.4%)	–	1,529.2	204.2	197.4	224.4
Net income ($ mil.)	–	–	–	(10.4)	19.0	1.0
Market value ($ mil.)	–	–	–	–	–	–
Employees	–	–	–	–	–	250

AMERICAN PLASTIC TOYS INC.

799 LADD RD
WALLED LAKE, MI 483903025
Phone: 248-624-4881
Fax: –
Web: www.americanplastictoys.com

CEO: –
CFO: –
HR: –
FYE: December 31
Type: Private

If your child spends hours applying pretend makeup at her Enchanted Beauty Salon or hammering away at his Build & Play Tool Bench or digging in the sand with her Castle Pail of Toys you can thank American Plastic Toys for the much-needed break. The company manufactures plastic toys including doll accessories (strollers nurseries) children's furniture role-playing items (kitchen sets tool benches) riding toys (trikes wagons) seasonal toys (pail and shovel sets) and vehicles (dump trucks airplanes). Products are sold by such retailers as Wal-Mart Kmart and Toys "R" Us across the US as well as in Canada the Caribbean Central and South America and Mexico. The company was founded in 1962.

	Annual Growth	12/09	12/10	12/11	12/12	12/13
Sales ($ mil.)	(1.7%)	–	51.1	45.4	51.0	48.5
Net income ($ mil.)	–	–	–	(1.5)	5.2	3.0
Market value ($ mil.)	–	–	–	–	–	–
Employees	–	–	–	–	–	300

AMERICAN POP CORN COMPANY

1 Fun Place
Sioux City IA 51108
Phone: 712-239-1232
Fax: 712-239-1268
Web: www.jollytime.com

CEO: –
CFO: Connie Deharty
HR: Rosa Bailey
FYE: December 31
Type: Private

Settle down with a bowl of Jolly Time a bottle of pop and prepare yourself for a jolly popping-good time. Founded in 1914 when Cloid Smith and his son Howard set up shop in their basement the American Pop Corn Company still makes the traditional American treat in bagged unpopped kernel form for the purists among us. For those with less time than purists it makes microwave popcorn in lots of varieties and flavors. American's brands include AMERICAN'S BEST (kernals) and Jolly Time (microwave and kernals). The family-owned company is run by Carlton (chairman) and Garrett (president) Smith the great-grandsons of Cloid. Jolly Time popcorn is distributed throughout the US and overseas.

AMERICAN POWER GROUP CORP

NBB: APGI

7 Kimball Lane
Lynnfield, MA 01940
Phone: 781 224-2411
Fax: –
Web: www.americanpowergroupinc.com

CEO: Lyle Jensen
CFO: Charles E Coppa
HR: –
FYE: September 30
Type: Public

Wish your engine ran on natural gas instead of diesel? American Power Group Corporation (formerly GreenMan Technologies) makes and sells dual-fuel energy technology that allows for the easy conversion of diesel engines to liquid and compressed natural gas as well as well-head gas or biomethane. This technology is specifically designed for aftermarket vehicular and diesel engines and diesel generators. The former GreenMan Technologies changed its name to American Power Group Corporation in mid-2012 after acquiring American Power Group in mid-2009.

	Annual Growth	09/11	09/12	09/13	09/14	09/15
Sales ($ mil.)	13.7%	1.8	2.6	7.0	6.3	3.0
Net income ($ mil.)	–	(6.8)	(4.6)	(2.0)	(2.3)	0.5
Market value ($ mil.)	(22.4%)	44.2	35.4	37.6	33.2	16.0
Employees	1.4%	18	14	20	21	19

AMERICAN PSYCHOLOGICAL ASSOCIATION INC.

750 1ST ST NE STE 605
WASHINGTON, DC 200028009
Phone: 202-336-5500
Fax: –
Web: www.apa.org

CEO: Norman B Anderson
CFO: Archie L Turner
HR: –
FYE: December 31
Type: Private

The American Psychological Association (APA) works to advance mental health: yours and that of its members. The APA is the largest scientific and professional organization representing psychology in the US as well as the world's largest association of psychologists. The association seeks to advance the study and practice of psychology in the US. It is also vocal about the role of psychological services in health care reform. It offers members career resources insurance and financial and other services. The APA has more than 134000 members including researchers educators clinicians consultants and students as well some 55 professional divisions.

	Annual Growth	12/04	12/05	12/06	12/11	12/12
Sales ($ mil.)	–	–	–	0.0	5.5	130.0	118.8
Net income ($ mil.)	–	–	–	–	0.3	(7.2)	(0.8)
Market value ($ mil.)	–	–	–	–	–	–	–
Employees	–	–	–	–	–	–	550

AMERICAN PUBLIC EDUCATION INC   NMS: APEI

111 West Congress Street
Charles Town, WV 25414
Phone: 304 724-3700
Fax: –
Web: www.americanpubliceducation.com

CEO: Harry T. Wilkins
CFO: Richard W. Sunderland
HR: –
FYE: December 31
Type: Public

American Public Education (APE) promotes military intelligence. The company offers online postsecondary education to those in the military and other public servants such as police and firefighters. Its American Military University and American Public University make up the American Public University System which offers roughly 90 degree programs and 70 certificate programs in such disciplines as business administration criminal justice intelligence technology liberal arts and homeland security. Enrollment in the online university consists of more than 100000 students from all 50 states and about 100 foreign countries. More than 60% of APE's students serve in the US military on active duty.

	Annual Growth	12/10	12/11	12/12	12/13	12/14
Sales ($ mil.)	15.3%	198.2	260.4	313.5	329.5	350.0
Net income ($ mil.)	8.2%	29.9	40.8	42.3	42.0	40.9
Market value ($ mil.)	(0.2%)	638.7	742.3	619.5	745.6	632.4
Employees	23.6%	1,500	1,790	2,950	3,492	3,500

AMERICAN RAILCAR INDUSTRIES INC   NMS: ARII

100 Clark Street
St. Charles, MO 63301
Phone: 636 940-6000
Fax: –
Web: www.americanrailcar.com

CEO: Jeffrey S. Hollister
CFO: Luke M. Williams
HR: Tim Lograsso
FYE: December 31
Type: Public

American Railcar Industries (ARI) doesn't make the little engine that could but it does make the cars that the engine pulls. A North American manufacturer of railcars and railcar components the company also provides maintenance and fleet management services to freight shippers railcar leasing companies and railroads. Its two Arkansas manufacturing facilities make several types of railcars including covered hoppers for grains cement and other dry bulk and tank cars for liquid and gas commodities. The company also serves non-rail industries with industrial products such as steel and aluminum casting machining stamping welding and fabrication.

	Annual Growth	12/10	12/11	12/12	12/13	12/14
Sales ($ mil.)	27.9%	273.6	519.4	711.7	750.6	733.0
Net income ($ mil.)	–	(27.0)	4.3	63.8	86.9	99.5
Market value ($ mil.)	23.5%	472.5	511.0	677.5	976.9	1,099.6
Employees	15.7%	1,598	2,413	2,643	2,663	2,865

AMERICAN REALTY CAPITAL TRUST INC.   NASDAQ: ARCT

106 York Rd.
Jenkintown PA 19046
Phone: 215-887-2189
Fax: +66-2-661-6664
Web: www.indorama.net

CEO: William M Kahane
CFO: Brian D Jones
HR: –
FYE: December 31
Type: Public

American Realty Capital Trust (ARCT) isn't afraid to stand alone. The self-administered and self-advised real estate investment trust (REIT) owns a portfolio of more than 480 single-tenant free-standing commercial properties (as opposed to strip malls or shopping centers with multiple tenants) located in 43 states and Puerto Rico. Almost half of its properties are leased by top tenants Bridgestone CVS Dollar General FedEx PNC Bank and Walgreens. Formed by American Realty Capital in 2007 the REIT went public via an initial public offering in February 2012. Later that year Realty Income Corporation arranged to acquire ARCT for nearly $3 billion in cash stock and debt.

AMERICAN REALTY INVESTORS, INC.   NYS: ARL

1603 Lyndon B. Johnson Freeway, Suite 800
Dallas, TX 75234
Phone: 469 522-4200
Fax: 469 522-4299
Web: www.amrealtytrust.com

CEO: Daniel J Moos
CFO: Gene S Bertcher
HR: –
FYE: December 31
Type: Public

American Realty Investors (ARI) invests in develops and operates commercial properties and land in growing suburban markets. The company's portfolio includes approximately 60 apartment communities about 20 office buildings and about five each of industrial retail and hotel properties. It also owns a trade show and exhibit hall as well as undeveloped land. ARI has properties in about 20 states but most of its holdings are located in Texas. The company is part of a complex web of ownership that includes Prime Income Asset Management which manages ARI and owns about 15% of it. Through various entities Texas real estate mogul Gene Phillips and his family control around three-quarters of ARI.

	Annual Growth	12/10	12/11	12/12	12/13	12/14
Sales ($ mil.)	(15.7%)	157.0	118.4	119.5	89.6	79.4
Net income ($ mil.)	–	(94.7)	0.3	(5.6)	41.3	30.9
Market value ($ mil.)	(9.0%)	111.5	26.2	38.3	73.6	76.6
Employees	–	–	–	–	–	–

AMERICAN RESIDENTIAL SERVICES L.L.C.

965 Ridge Lake Blvd. Ste. 201
Memphis TN 38120
Phone: 901-271-9700
Fax: 703-873-2100
Web: www.lcc.com

CEO: Don Karnes
CFO: James McMahon
HR: –
FYE: December 31
Type: Private

For those whose home maintenance skills don't rival Bob Vila's there's American Residential Services (operating as ARS/Rescue Rooter). The company is an amalgamation of some 100 firms combined to create a national home improvement services company specializing in heating ventilation air-conditioning plumbing sewer and rain services and electricity as well as major home appliance installation maintenance repair and replacement. With some more than 60 locations across the US ARS/Rescue Rooter services homes as well as small commercial buildings. The company is owned by CI Capital Partners Royal Palm Capital Partners and its management.

AMERICAN RESTAURANT GROUP INC.

4410 El Camino Real Ste. 201
Los Altos CA 94022
Phone: 650-949-6400
Fax: 650-917-9207
Web: www.blackangus.com

CEO: Meredith Taylor
CFO: Rick Rokson
HR: Mike Turner
FYE: December 31
Type: Private

As far as this company is concerned Angus beef is as American as apple pie. American Restaurant Group owns and operates the Black Angus Steakhouse chain with about 45 locations in half a dozen western states. The upscale casual dinnerhouses offer a menu of Black Angus steaks and prime rib along with chicken seafood and pasta dishes. Some locations also offer happy hour specials. In addition to dine-in seating the chain provides drive-up take-out service at many of its units. Rancher and entrepreneur Stuart Anderson opened the first Black Angus restaurant in Seattle in 1964. The chain was acquired in 2009 by affiliates of private equity firm Versa Capital Management.

AMERICAN RIVER BANKSHARES   NMS: AMRB

3100 Zinfandel Drive, Suite 450
Rancho Cordova, CA 95670
Phone: 916 851-0123
Fax: –
Web: www.americanriverbank.com

CEO: David T. Taber
CFO: Mitchell A. (Mitch) Derenzo
HR: Anneliese Hein
FYE: December 31
Type: Public

American River Bankshares' family is growing. The holding company is the parent of American River Bank which has about a dozen branches in Central California. About half of the bank's offices are operating under the North Coast Bank or Bank of Amador names. The bank serves area small to midsized businesses and individuals offering traditional deposit products such as checking and savings accounts and CDs. It offers commercial and residential mortgages as well as business construction and consumer loans and lease financing for business equipment.

	Annual Growth	12/10	12/11	12/12	12/13	12/14
Assets ($ mil.)	1.6%	578.9	581.5	596.4	592.8	617.8
Net income ($ mil.)	74.0%	0.5	2.5	3.2	3.1	4.4
Market value ($ mil.)	12.0%	48.5	36.8	55.9	76.4	76.2
Employees	(1.1%)	111	110	112	101	106

AMERICAN SAVINGS BANK FSB

1001 Bishop St.
Honolulu HI 96813
Phone: 808-523-6844
Fax: 808-531-7292
Web: www.asbhawaii.com

CEO: Richard Wacker
CFO: Heather Schwarm
HR: –
FYE: December 31
Type: Subsidiary

You might say this bank is a real powerhouse — American Savings Bank is owned by Hawaiian Electric Industries which supplies power to almost all of the state's residents. Hawaii's third-largest financial institution (behind Bankoh and First Hawaiian Bank) the bank operates more than 50 branches across the state's five main islands; many of its locations have extended hours and are open on weekends. In addition to traditional products such as deposit accounts mortgages credit cards and business and consumer loans the bank also offers insurance investments and financial planning. Residential mortgages secured by Hawaiian real estate comprise the majority of its loan portfolio.

AMERICAN SCIENCE & ENGINEERING INC   NMS: ASEI

829 Middlesex Turnpike
Billerica, MA 01821
Phone: 978 262-8700
Fax: –
Web: www.as-e.com

CEO: Charles P. (Chuck) Dougherty
CFO: Diane Basile
HR: George S Peterman
FYE: March 31
Type: Public

You can't hide from American Science and Engineering (AS&E). The company makes X-ray detection systems for inspection and security at airports border stations military situations shipping ports high-security facilities and law enforcement scenarios. Using a lower radiation dose than typical systems AS&E's Z Backscatter technology detects organic materials such as illegal drugs plastic explosives and plastic weapons. AS&E also makes scanning equipment for detecting contraband on persons in aircraft vehicles and in luggage and packages. About 40% of sales are to the US government and its contractors; top customers include Al Hamra Group Sal Offshore and US Customs and Border Protection.

	Annual Growth	03/11	03/12	03/13	03/14	03/15
Sales ($ mil.)	(17.9%)	278.6	203.6	186.7	190.2	126.8
Net income ($ mil.)	(61.1%)	42.8	21.4	17.5	15.1	1.0
Market value ($ mil.)	(14.7%)	664.4	482.3	438.7	483.2	351.5
Employees	(7.2%)	420	415	347	344	311

AMERICAN SEAFOODS GROUP LLC

Marketplace Tower 2025 1st Ave. Ste. 900
Seattle WA 98121-3119
Phone: 206-374-1515
Fax: 206-374-1516
Web: www.americanseafoods.com

CEO: Bernt O Bodal
CFO: Brad Bodenman
HR: –
FYE: December 31
Type: Private

With operations in the northern Pacific (i.e. in the Bering Sea and Aleutian Islands) American Seafoods Group casts a bountiful net. The vertically integrated company offers frozen and processed fish such as Alaska pollock Pacific whiting Pacific cod sea and bay scallops haddock sole and farm-raised tilapia and catfish. It operates its own fleet of ships that process and freeze the catch while at sea as well as a fleet of transport trucks. American Seafoods' land-based operation in Massachusetts makes breaded seafood products. The company sells its fish under the American Pride brand name in North America Asia and Europe.

AMERICAN SHARED HOSPITAL SERVICES   ASE: AMS

Four Embarcadero Center, Suite 3700
San Francisco, CA 94111
Phone: 415 788-5300
Fax: –
Web: www.ashs.com

CEO: Ernest A Bates
CFO: Craig K Tagawa
HR: –
FYE: December 31
Type: Public

Business is brain surgery for American Shared Hospital Services (ASHS). The company owns 81% of GK Financing (GKF) which installs finances and services the Leksell Gamma Knife a noninvasive surgical device that uses gamma rays to destroy brain tumors without harming surrounding tissue. Sweden-based Elekta which makes the Gamma Knife owns the other 19% of GKF. GKF usually leases the Gamma Knife units on a per-use basis to major urban medical centers; it has contracts for units installed in about 20 hospitals in the US; it markets the product in the US and Brazil.

	Annual Growth	12/10	12/11	12/12	12/13	12/14
Sales ($ mil.)	(1.9%)	16.7	22.2	17.0	17.6	15.4
Net income ($ mil.)	–	0.1	0.5	0.0	(0.3)	(1.0)
Market value ($ mil.)	0.0%	15.1	14.3	14.6	14.9	15.1
Employees	(4.9%)	11	9	10	9	9

AMERICAN SNUFF COMPANY LLC

813 Ridge Lake Blvd. #100
Memphis TN 38120
Phone: 901-761-2050
Fax: 901-767-1302
Web: https://www.americansnuff.com

CEO: –
CFO: –
HR: –
FYE: January 31
Type: Subsidiary

American Snuff Company loves a bear market when it comes to moist snuff and other smokeless tobacco products. It makes the Grizzly Kodiak Hawken and Cougar brands of moist tobacco and is the second-largest manufacturer of smokeless tobacco products in the US. American Snuff also makes loose-leaf tobacco (including Morgan's Levi Garrett and Taylor's Pride brands) snuff (Garrett and Dental brands) and a variety of other smokeless tobacco (including twist moist and plug). Its Lane unit sold in 2011 made little cigars and roll-your-own tobacco. Purchased by Reynolds American for $3.5 billion in 2006 the firm generates about 8% of its parent's annual revenue and took its existing name in 2010.

AMERICAN SOCIETY FOR TESTING AND MATERIALS

100 BARR HARBOR DR
CONSHOHOCKEN, PA 194282951
Phone: 610-832-9500
Fax: –
Web: www.astm.org

CEO: –
CFO: –
HR: –
FYE: December 31
Type: Private

The American Society for Testing and Materials — which does business as ASTM International — is a not-for-profit standards organization focused on developing voluntary codes and regulations for technical materials products systems and services. Established in 1898 to set standards for railroad steel the organization also works in such areas as petroleum medical devices consumer products and environmental assessment. ASTM International publishes its technical specifications in the Annual Book of ASTM Standards a more than 70-volume set. Its income is derived from selling its publications and through annual administrative fees. The organization has more than 30000 members in over 120 countries.

	Annual Growth	12/09	12/10	12/11	12/12	12/13
Sales ($ mil.)	5.3%	–	54.0	55.2	58.9	63.1
Net income ($ mil.)	–	–	–	(9.5)	23.6	67.5
Market value ($ mil.)	–	–	–	–	–	–
Employees	–	–	–	–	–	185

AMERICAN SOCIETY FOR THE PREVENTION OF CRUELTY TO ANIMALS (INC)

424 E 92ND ST
NEW YORK, NY 101286804
Phone: 212-876-7700
Fax: –
Web: www.aspca.org

CEO: Matthew Bershadker
CFO: Julia Nelson
HR: –
FYE: December 31
Type: Private

This group watches out for Fidos Fluffies and other furry friends all across the country. The ASPCA (American Society for the Prevention of Cruelty to Animals) is a nonprofit organization dedicated to promoting the humane treatment of non-humans. The society's aim is to save the lives of homeless pets and help victims of animal cruelty. It engages in education public awareness and government advocacy efforts and supports the work of independent humane societies throughout the US. It provides medical services and animal placement from facilities in New York City. The privately-funded organization was established in 1866 by Henry Bergh.

	Annual Growth	12/03	12/04	12/05	12/08	12/13
Sales ($ mil.)	–	–	0.0	66.9	127.9	171.7
Net income ($ mil.)	–	–	–	19.7	34.2	(1.4)
Market value ($ mil.)	–	–	–	–	–	–
Employees	–	–	–	–	–	350

AMERICAN SOFTWARE INC

NMS: AMSW A

470 East Paces Ferry Road, N.E.
Atlanta, GA 30305
Phone: 404 261-4381
Fax: –
Web: www.amsoftware.com

CEO: J. Michael (Mike) Edenfield
CFO: Vincent C. (Vince) Klinges
HR: –
FYE: April 30
Type: Public

American Software sells business software from sea to shining sea. The company's cloud-based andn on-premise supply chain management and enterprise resource planning (ERP) software is used by manufacturers and distributors to manage back-office operations including global supply chain warehouse and transportation operations. Its Logility subsidiary makes collaborative applications that connect buyers with suppliers and help in planning transportation and logistics. American Software also provides IT staffing and consulting services. The company's customers come from a wide range of industries worldwide and have included The Home Depot Avery Dennison Tiffany and Ingram Micro.

	Annual Growth	04/11	04/12	04/13	04/14	04/15
Sales ($ mil.)	4.7%	85.6	102.6	100.5	100.6	102.9
Net income ($ mil.)	2.5%	7.4	11.3	10.4	10.3	8.1
Market value ($ mil.)	5.7%	222.4	236.7	237.5	275.6	277.6
Employees	7.9%	297	332	377	383	402

AMERICAN SOIL TECHNOLOGIES INC

NBB: SOYL

9018 Balboa Ave., #558
Northridge, CA 91304
Phone: 818 899-4686
Fax: –
Web: www.americansoiltech.com

CEO: Carl P Ranno
CFO: Carl P Ranno
HR: –
FYE: September 30
Type: Public

American Soil Technologies works to make sure your farmland isn't dirt poor. The company manufactures agricultural chemicals that help retain water in soil the direct benefit of which is manifold. In addition to minimizing the frequency of irrigation the chemicals also decrease the likelihood of erosion and reduce other damage. Its products are used by agricultural residential and recreational clients. Subsidiary Smart World Organics gives American Soil entrance to the organic turf and horticultural markets. Though primarily operating in the US it also distributes internationally to the Middle East North Africa and China. The family of the late chairman Louie Visco controls 30% of the company.

	Annual Growth	09/11	09/12	09/13	09/14	09/15
Sales ($ mil.)	(61.5%)	0.1	0.1	0.1	0.0	0.0
Net income ($ mil.)	–	(0.7)	(0.6)	(0.5)	0.1	(0.6)
Market value ($ mil.)	(29.3%)	1.2	0.3	1.5	0.8	0.3
Employees	0.0%	3	3	3	3	3

AMERICAN SPECTRUM REALTY, INC.

ASE: AQQ

2401 Fountain View, Suite 750
Houston, TX 77057
Phone: 713 706-6200
Fax: –
Web: www.americanspectrum.com

CEO: William J Carden
CFO: –
HR: –
FYE: December 31
Type: Public

American Spectrum Realty invests in and manages commercial real estate primarily multitenant office and industrial space. The company and its subsidiaries own manage or lease 90 properties valued at more than $1 billion. Most properties are located in Texas but it also owns assets in California and 20 other states. Since 2010 subsidiary American Spectrum Realty Management has owned the property and asset management assets of Evergreen Realty Group. The deal brought contracts for 80 properties ranging from storage units to student housing and has helped American Spectrum expand its third-party management and leasing capabilities across the US. CEO William Carden controls about 40% of the company.

	Annual Growth	12/09	12/10	12/11	12/12	12/13
Sales ($ mil.)	6.4%	33.3	55.6	69.4	55.1	42.7
Net income ($ mil.)	–	(8.3)	(8.0)	4.0	1.4	(13.8)
Market value ($ mil.)	(46.6%)	82.5	64.9	18.0	12.7	6.7
Employees	(12.6%)	283	219	183	180	165

AMERICAN STANDARD ENERGY CORP
NBB: ASEN

4800 North Scottsdale Road, Suite 1400
Scottsdale, AZ 85251
Phone: 480 371-1929
Fax: –
Web: www.asenergycorp.com

CEO: –
CFO: –
HR: –
FYE: December 31
Type: Public

Famous Uncle Al's Hot Dogs & Grille operates a chain of about 10 franchised quick-service restaurants in Arizona Connecticut Florida Nevada and Virginia that specialize in hot dogs and sausage sandwiches. The eateries also serve a variety of Italian-style sandwiches burgers and fries. CEO Paul Esposito and president Dean Valentino together control more than 30% of the company.

	Annual Growth	12/08	12/09	12/10	12/11	12/12
Sales ($ mil.)	259.6%	0.1	0.0	1.4	12.4	19.7
Net income ($ mil.)	–	(0.6)	(0.1)	(5.5)	(13.7)	(93.7)
Market value ($ mil.)	73.9%	2.6	0.3	194.0	162.9	23.8
Employees	(9.6%)	3	1	5	5	2

AMERICAN STATES WATER CO.
NYS: AWR

630 E. Foothill Blvd
San Dimas, CA 91773-1212
Phone: 909 394-3600
Fax: –
Web: www.aswater.com

CEO: Robert J. Sprowls
CFO: Eva G. Tang
HR: –
FYE: December 31
Type: Public

American States Water holds the essence of life for Californians. Its main subsidiary regulated public utility Golden State Water Company (GSWC) which was formerly known as Southern California Water Company supplies water to more than 255650 customers in 75 communities primarily in Los Angeles San Bernardino and Orange counties. GSWC's Bear Valley Electric subsidiary distributes electricity to almost 23380 Californians in the Big Bear area. American States Water operates in nonregulated water markets through American States Utility Services (ASUS) which offers billing and meter reading services and contracts to operate water and wastewater systems.

	Annual Growth	12/10	12/11	12/12	12/13	12/14
Sales ($ mil.)	3.9%	398.9	419.3	466.9	472.1	465.8
Net income ($ mil.)	16.5%	33.2	45.9	54.1	62.7	61.1
Market value ($ mil.)	2.2%	1,319.7	1,336.2	1,837.0	1,100.0	1,441.9
Employees	53.6%	127	732	728	722	707

AMERICAN SUPERCONDUCTOR CORP.
NMS: AMSC

64 Jackson Road
Devens, MA 01434
Phone: 978 842-3000
Fax: –
Web: www.amsc.com

CEO: Daniel P McGahn
CFO: David (Dave) Henry
HR: –
FYE: March 31
Type: Public

American Superconductor (AMSC) gets a charge out of carrying a heavy load. The company has two units: wind and grid. The wind segment licenses highly engineered wind turbine designs and supplies wind turbine makers with advanced power electronics and control systems. The grid segment offers grid interconnection systems for wind farms solar power plants and transmission cable systems. Austrian subsidiary AMSC Windtec designs wind turbines. Customers in the Asia/Pacific region account for about two-thirds of sales. MIT professors Gregory Yurek and John Vander Sande formed AMSC in 1987.

	Annual Growth	03/11	03/12	03/13	03/14	03/15
Sales ($ mil.)	(29.6%)	286.6	76.5	87.4	84.1	70.5
Net income ($ mil.)	–	(186.3)	(136.8)	(66.1)	(56.3)	(48.7)
Market value ($ mil.)	(28.7%)	238.5	39.5	25.6	15.4	61.8
Employees	(21.7%)	848	446	362	269	318

AMERICAN SYSTEMS CORPORATION

14151 PK MADOW DR STE 500
CHANTILLY, VA 20151
Phone: 703-968-6300
Fax: –
Web: www.americansystems.com

CEO: –
CFO: –
HR: Bob Hedgpeth
FYE: December 31
Type: Private

American Systems provides government and commercial clients with IT management and consulting services including custom engineering and application development. Its consulting division advises clients on such issues as network access and identity management data security and process optimization. The company also provides managed technical support and staffing. American Systems works with government customers to develop systems related to command and control logistics and national security functions. Its commercial-focused operations serve the energy financial services retail and telecom industries among others.

	Annual Growth	12/09	12/10	12/11	12/12	12/13
Sales ($ mil.)	5.8%	–	273.9	250.2	242.0	324.1
Net income ($ mil.)	(44.8%)	–	–	16.8	10.5	5.1
Market value ($ mil.)	–	–	–	–	–	–
Employees	–	–	–	–	–	1,480

AMERICAN TECHNICAL CERAMICS CORP.

1 Norden Ln.
Huntington Station NY 11746
Phone: 631-622-4700
Fax: 631-622-4748
Web: www.atceramics.com

CEO: John Lawing
CFO: –
HR: –
FYE: June 30
Type: Subsidiary

American Technical Ceramics (ATC) isn't into pottery. The company makes ceramic and porcelain single- and multilayer capacitors that store and discharge precise amounts of electrical current. The company's radio-frequency (RF) microwave and millimeter-wave capacitors are key components in mobile phones instruments radar and navigation systems and broadcast satellites. Its high-reliability products are used in critically sensitive military and aerospace applications. ATC also makes resistors as well as custom thin-film substrates for microwave and fiber-optic telecommunications devices. In 2007 rival AVX acquired ATC for about $231 million in cash.

AMERICAN TERRAZZO COMPANY LTD.

309 GOLD ST
GARLAND, TX 750426648
Phone: 972-272-8084
Fax: –
Web: www.americanterrazzo.com

CEO: –
CFO: –
HR: –
FYE: December 31
Type: Private

If you walk all over American Terrazzo's handiwork well that's really kind of the point. The company installs mural-like terrazzo flooring in public commercial and residential facilities. Terrazzo derived from the word for terraces in Italian is made from discarded marble remnants or cement and is used in a wide range of applications including sidewalks plazas terraces and stairways. American Terrazzo does most of its business in Texas primarily in Dallas. The company's handiwork can be found anywhere from homes schools and churches to offices airports and arenas. Mattia "Mike" Flabiano founded the family-owned firm in 1931.

	Annual Growth	12/05	12/06	12/07	12/08	12/12
Sales ($ mil.)	(46.8%)	–	666.0	9.2	8.0	15.1
Net income ($ mil.)	61.0%	–	–	0.1	0.3	1.5
Market value ($ mil.)	–	–	–	–	–	–
Employees	–	–	–	–	–	133

AMERICAN TIRE DISTRIBUTORS HOLDINGS INC.

12200 Herbert Wayne Ct. Ste. 150
Huntersville NC 28078-3145
Phone: 704-992-2000
Fax: 704-992-1384
Web: www.atd-us.com

CEO: William E Berry
CFO: Jason T Yaudes
HR: –
FYE: December 31
Type: Private

Business for American Tire Distributors Holdings starts where the rubber meets the road. The company through its American Tire Distributors (ATD) unit is one of the largest independent tire wholesalers in the US. Its offerings include flagship brands Bridgestone Continental Goodyear Pirelli and Michelin as well as budget brands and private-label tires. ATD also markets custom wheels and tire service equipment. Its roughly 100 distribution centers serve independent tire dealers retail chains and auto service centers in some 40 states. The company is owned by privated equity firm TPG Capital.

AMERICAN TOWER CORP (NEW)

116 Huntington Avenue
Boston, MA 02116
Phone: 617 375-7500
Fax: –
Web: www.americantower.com

NYS: AMT
CEO: James D. (Jim) Taiclet
CFO: Thomas A. (Tom) Bartlett
HR: –
FYE: December 31
Type: Public

Growth in wireless communications is taking American Tower to new heights. The tower management company operates more than 27700 broadcast and wireless communications towers and distributed antenna systems in the US and nearly 40000 more in emerging markets in Asia and Central and South America. It rents space on towers and rooftop antenna systems to wireless carriers and radio and TV broadcasters who use the infrastructure to enable their services. American Tower also offers some tower-related services: construction site acquisition structural analyses to determine support for additional equipment and zoning and permitting management services. Its top tenants include AT&T Sprint Nextel and Verizon.

	Annual Growth	12/10	12/11	12/12	12/13	12/14
Sales ($ mil.)	19.9%	1,985.3	2,443.5	2,876.0	3,361.4	4,100.0
Net income ($ mil.)	22.0%	372.9	396.5	637.3	551.3	824.9
Market value ($ mil.)	17.6%	20,485.5	23,805.9	30,652.9	31,664.5	39,213.7
Employees	14.5%	1,729	2,122	2,432	2,716	2,974

AMERICAN TRANSMISSION COMPANY LLC

W234N2000 RDGVIEW PKY CT
WAUKESHA, WI 53188-1022
Phone: 262-506-6700
Fax: –
Web: www.atcllc.com

CEO: John C Procario
CFO: Michael Hofbauer
HR: –
FYE: December 31
Type: Private

American Transmission Company is an entrepreneur in the US power grid business — a for-profit multi-state transmission-only utility. Connecting electricity producers to distributors American Transmission owns operates monitors and maintains 9440 miles of high-voltage electric transmission lines and 525 substations in portions of Illinois Michigan Minnesota and Wisconsin. The company a member of the Midwest Independent Transmission System Operator regional transmission organization operates the former transmission assets of some of its shareholders. About 30 utilities municipalities electric companies and cooperatives in its service area have an ownership stake in American Transmission.

	Annual Growth	12/08	12/09	12/10	12/11	12/12
Sales ($ mil.)	5.0%	–	521.5	556.7	567.2	603.3
Net income ($ mil.)	3.6%	–	213.4	219.7	223.9	237.4
Market value ($ mil.)	–	–	–	–	–	–
Employees	–	–	–	–	–	547

AMERICAN TRIM LLC

1005 W. Grand Ave.
Lima OH 45801-3429
Phone: 419-228-1145
Fax: 419-996-4850
Web: www.amtrim.com

CEO: Jeffrey A Hawk
CFO: Dana Morgan
HR: –
FYE: December 31
Type: Private

American Trim is not a new fad diet but a company that manufactures metal components for the automotive appliance and furniture industries. American Trim's automotive products include bumper beams frame members and interior and exterior trim. Other products include office furniture doors and shelves appliance handles and hinges support members and decorative metal tiles. The company also provides services such as product design tooling and process development metal forming metal finishing and assembly. The company has manufacturing facilities in Alabama Ohio and Pennsylvania as well as in Mexico. Founded in 1948 by the Hawk family American Trim is a subsidiary of Superior Metal Products.

AMERICAN TV & APPLIANCE OF MADISON INC.

2404 W. Beltline Hwy.
Madison WI 53713
Phone: 608-271-1000
Fax: 608-275-7339
Web: www.americantv.com

CEO: Douglas G Reuhl
CFO: Steve Mixtacki
HR: –
FYE: June 30
Type: Private

American TV & Appliance of Madison is happy to outfit your entire house including your upscale kitchen. The company sells appliances electronics and furniture in Illinois Iowa Michigan and Wisconsin. Its 11 plus retail outlets offer such products as recliners dining room sets mattresses car stereos CD players dishwashers refrigerators personal computers digital cameras plasma and LCD TVs and DVD players. The company also has a distribution center and a service center offering parts and repairs. American TV even makes house calls to fix large appliances regardless of where they were purchased. Ferd Mattioli founded the company in 1954.

AMERICAN UNIVERSITY

4400 MASSACHUSETTS AVE NW
WASHINGTON, DC 200168200
Phone: 202-885-1000
Fax: –
Web: www.american.edu

CEO: –
CFO: Douglas Kudravetz
HR: –
FYE: April 30
Type: Private

Fulfilling the vision of George Washington for a national university in the country's capital American University was chartered by an Act of Congress in 1893 as a private independent co-educational institution under the auspices of the United Methodist Church. Today the school offers a broad range of undergraduate and graduate degree programs to more than 12000 students from 140 countries. Its student-teacher ratio is 12:1. American University has schools devoted to arts and sciences business communications international service public affairs and law. It is one of the top producers of Peace Corps volunteers serving overseas. Nine US presidents have served on American University's Board of Trustees.

	Annual Growth	04/07	04/08	04/09	04/12	04/13
Sales ($ mil.)	5.0%	–	398.1	54.2	605.3	507.2
Net income ($ mil.)	–	–	–	(108.7)	55.1	90.5
Market value ($ mil.)	–	–	–	–	–	–
Employees	–	–	–	–	–	2,000

AMERICAN VANGUARD CORP.   NYS: AVD

4695 MacArthur Court
Newport Beach, CA 92660
Phone: 949 260-1200
Fax: –

CEO: Eric G. Wintemute
CFO: David T. Johnson
HR: –
FYE: December 31
Type: Public

American Vanguard Corporation (AMVAC) bugs bugs roots out roots weeds out weeds and helps people take care of their health and personal appearance. The company makes specialty chemicals designed to protect the health of animals crops and people. Products made by its AMVAC Chemical subsidiary include pesticides plant-growth regulators herbicides and soil fumigants. Its GemChem subsidiary distributes the company's chemicals nationally to the cosmetic nutritional and pharmaceutical industries. AMVAC also has marketing subsidiaries in the UK and Mexico.

	Annual Growth	12/10	12/11	12/12	12/13	12/14
Sales ($ mil.)	6.8%	229.6	304.4	366.2	381.0	298.6
Net income ($ mil.)	(18.5%)	11.0	22.1	36.9	34.4	4.8
Market value ($ mil.)	8.0%	248.5	388.2	904.1	706.8	338.1
Employees	2.2%	350	390	504	499	382

AMERICAN WATER WORKS CO, INC.   NYS: AWK

1025 Laurel Oak Road
Voorhees, NJ 08043
Phone: 856 346-8200
Fax: –
Web: www.amwater.com

CEO: –
CFO: Susan N. Story
HR: Lorraine Cecil
FYE: December 31
Type: Public

Water water everywhere — and American Water Works wants to own it. The company is the largest US public water utility. Its regulated utilities provide water and wastewater services in 16 states. Its market-based operations include a broad range of water and wastewater services and products including water and sewer line maintenance services for homeowners water and wastewater facility operations and granular carbon technologies for water treatment. Overall it serves 15 million people in 47 states. Regulated operations account for 88% of sales. Subsidiary American Water Works Service provides shared services and a central administration of water and wastewater systems.

	Annual Growth	12/10	12/11	12/12	12/13	12/14
Sales ($ mil.)	2.7%	2,710.7	2,666.2	2,876.9	2,901.9	3,011.3
Net income ($ mil.)	12.1%	267.8	309.6	358.1	369.3	423.1
Market value ($ mil.)	20.5%	4,538.6	5,717.7	6,663.4	7,584.1	9,565.3
Employees	(4.2%)	7,600	7,000	6,700	6,600	6,400

AMERICAN WOODMARK CORP.   NMS: AMWD

3102 Shawnee Drive
Winchester, VA 22601
Phone: 540 665-9100
Fax: –
Web: www.americanwoodmark.com

CEO: S. Cary Dunston
CFO: M. Scott Culbreth
HR: Brenda Dean
FYE: April 30
Type: Public

American Woodmark has more cabinet selections than the prime minister of Russia. A top maker of home cabinets in the US the company makes and distributes about 500 styles of low- to mid-priced kitchen cabinets and vanities. Styles vary by finish (oak cherry hickory maple as well as laminate) and door design. Brands include American Woodmark Shenandoah Cabinetry Timberlake and Waypoint. Targeting the remodeling and new home construction markets American Woodmark sells its lineup through home centers and independent dealers and distributors; it also sells directly to major builders. American Woodmark was established through a leveraged buyout of Boise Cascade's cabinet division.

	Annual Growth	04/11	04/12	04/13	04/14	04/15
Sales ($ mil.)	16.2%	452.6	515.8	630.4	726.5	825.5
Net income ($ mil.)	–	(20.0)	(20.8)	9.8	20.5	35.5
Market value ($ mil.)	25.7%	326.6	288.6	541.1	482.6	815.2
Employees	8.2%	3,693	3,791	4,537	4,916	5,070

AMERICARES FOUNDATION INC.

88 HAMILTON AVE
STAMFORD, CT 069023100
Phone: 203-658-9500
Fax: –
Web: www.americares.org

CEO: Curtis Welling
CFO: –
HR: –
FYE: June 30
Type: Private

AmeriCares Foundation provides emergency medical aid around the world. The not-for-profit charitable organization helps victims of natural disasters and supports long-term humanitarian programs by collecting medical supplies in the US and overseas and delivering them to places where they are needed. AmeriCares has provided aid in more than 90 countries worldwide. In the US the organization offers medical assistance runs a camp for kids with HIV/AIDS and conducts HomeFront a program that renovates housing for the needy in parts of Connecticut and New York. Robert C. Macauley founded AmeriCares in 1982.

	Annual Growth	06/09	06/10	06/11	06/12	06/13
Sales ($ mil.)	(7.9%)	–	795.1	671.6	526.1	621.9
Net income ($ mil.)	–	–	–	(0.7)	6.0	(38.3)
Market value ($ mil.)	–	–	–	–	–	–
Employees	–	–	–	–	–	125

AMERICA'S HOME PLACE INC.

2144 HILTON DR
GAINESVILLE, GA 305016172
Phone: 770-532-1128
Fax: –
Web: www.americashomeplace.com

CEO: Barry G Conner
CFO: –
HR: Vicki Ryan
FYE: December 31
Type: Private

America's Home Place builds custom homes on its customers' land. The company builds single-family detached houses with more than 100 custom floor plans and designs. Its two- to five-bedroom cabin chalet ranch two-story and split-level houses range in price from about $80000 to more than $300000. Sizes start at about 900 sq. ft. and go up to to 4000 sq. ft. America's Home Place operates nearly 40 home building and model centers in the southeastern US. Buyers typically already own their land from a single lot to many acres. The company also assists buyers who are not landowners in locating available property. President Barry Conner owns the company he founded in 1972.

	Annual Growth	12/05	12/06	12/07	12/11	12/12
Sales ($ mil.)	(2.9%)	–	184.8	173.4	125.6	155.3
Net income ($ mil.)	(3.3%)	–	–	8.4	4.6	7.1
Market value ($ mil.)	–	–	–	–	–	–
Employees	–	–	–	–	–	275

AMERICO LIFE INC.

300 West 11th Street
Kansas City MO 64105
Phone: 937-492-6129
Fax: 937-498-4554
Web: peoplesfederalsandl.com

CEO: –
CFO: Mark K Fallon
HR: –
FYE: December 31
Type: Private

Americo Life sells insurance to cover American lives. The holding company sells life insurance and annuities to individuals families and groups mainly through its Americo Financial Life and Annuity Insurance unit. Americo Life companies also offer insurance policies that cover funeral expenses and mortgages. Policies are distributed through 13000 independent agents nationwide to about 800000 policyholders. The firm is a wholly owned subsidiary of Financial Holding Corporation which the family of chairman Michael Merriman controls. Other Financial Holding business interests include real estate ventures in the Southeast and a 50% stake in Argus Health Systems a processor of prescription drug claims.

AMERICOLD REALTY TRUST

10 Glenlake Pkwy. South Tower Ste. 800
Atlanta GA 30328
Phone: 678-441-1400
Fax: 678-441-6824
Web: www.americold.com

CEO: Tony Schnug
CFO: Edward F Lange Jr
HR: –
FYE: December 31
Type: Subsidiary

Americold Realty Trust keeps temperatures low to make revenues grow. The company which is controlled by The Yucaipa Companies owns more than 180 temperature-controlled warehouses that are part of the supply chain serving food producers distributors and retailers who rent space to store frozen and perishable food. Distribution services are handled by subsidiary AmeriCold Logistics. A majority of Americold's warehouse facilities are located in the US with other properties in Argentina Australia Canada China and New Zealand. Its portfolio represents more than 1 billion cu. ft. of cold storage. Americold operates in three main segments: warehousing; transportation; and web-based inventory tracking services.

AMERICUS MORTGAGE CORPORATION

6110 PINEMONT DR STE 215
HOUSTON, TX 770923216
Phone: 713-684-0725
Fax: –
Web: www.alliedhomenet.com

CEO: –
CFO: James Hagen
HR: –
FYE: June 30
Type: Private

Need someone on your side while seeking a home loan? Americus Mortgage (formerly Allied Home Mortgage Capital) wants to be your ally. The company is a privately held mortgage banker and broker with offices and representatives located throughout the US and the Virgin Islands. Through its history it has brokered a variety of mortgages including conventional loans jumbo loans reverse mortgages FHA loans and VA loans. At its peak (in 2003) Americus Mortgage originated more than $15 billion in loans in a single year; however the company has had trouble in recent years following the housing crisis of 2008.

	Annual Growth	06/05	06/06	06/07	06/08	06/09
Assets ($ mil.)	0.7%	–	–	16.4	15.6	16.6
Net income ($ mil.)	–	–	–	(2.5)	0.2	0.1
Market value ($ mil.)	–	–	–	–	–	–
Employees	–	–	–	–	–	2,500

AMERIFLIGHT LLC

Burbank-Glendale-Pasadena Airport Hangar #1 4700 W. Empire Ave.
Burbank CA 91505-1098
Phone: 818-980-5005
Fax: 818-980-5105
Web: www.ameriflight.com

CEO: Brian Randow
CFO: David W Moore
HR: Jody Garrick
FYE: December 31
Type: Private

Ameriflight takes flight across the Americas delivering time-sensitive packages for banks and for other air cargo carriers. The company serves some 200 communities primarily in the western US but also elsewhere in the US and in Canada and Mexico. Managing 75000 packages a day it operates a fleet of about 170 aircraft consisting of small jets and turboprops from several manufacturers from about a dozen hubs. The company serves other air cargo carriers by meeting their larger air freighters at major airports and distributing cargo to markets not easily served by big aircraft. Ameriflight is owned by its management team.

AMERIGAS PARTNERS, L.P.

NYS: APU

460 North Gulph Road
King of Prussia, PA 19406
Phone: 610 337-7000
Fax: –
Web: www.amerigas.com

CEO: Jerry E Sheridan
CFO: Hugh J Gallagher
HR: –
FYE: September 30
Type: Public

America has a gas with AmeriGas Partners. Purveying propane has propelled the company to its position as the top US retail propane marketer (besting Ferrellgas). It serves more than 2 million residential commercial industrial agricultural motor fuel and wholesale customers from 2000 locations in 50 states. AmeriGas also sells propane-related supplies and equipment and exchanges prefilled portable tanks for empty ones. The company stores propane in Arizona California and Virginia and distributes its products through an interstate carrier structure that runs across the US and in Canada.

	Annual Growth	09/11	09/12	09/13	09/14	09/15
Sales ($ mil.)	3.3%	2,538.0	2,921.6	3,166.5	3,712.9	2,885.3
Net income ($ mil.)	11.1%	138.5	11.0	221.2	289.9	211.2
Market value ($ mil.)	(1.4%)	4,086.2	4,055.6	4,000.8	4,237.6	3,857.7
Employees	10.0%	5,800	9,200	8,500	8,400	8,500

AMERIGROUP CORPORATION

NYSE: AGP

4425 Corporation Ln.
Virginia Beach VA 23462
Phone: 757-490-6900
Fax: +33-1-49-02-27-41
Web: www.coface.com

CEO: James G Carlson
CFO: James W Truess
HR: –
FYE: December 31
Type: Public

AMERIGROUP looks after the health of America's needy. The managed health care provider targets people eligible for Medicaid the State Children's Health Insurance Program (SCHIP) FamilyCare and other government special needs plans. Its top Medicaid plans include a product for families receiving temporary assistance to needy families (TANF) benefits and one for aged blind or disabled (ABD) persons receiving supplemental income. AMERIGROUP's SCHIP programs cover uninsured kids ineligible for Medicaid. The company contracts with about 135000 primary care doctors and specialists as well as 800 hospitals to serve some 2.7 million members in more than a dozen states. The company is owned by WellPoint.

AMERIPATH INC.

7111 Fairway Dr. Ste. 400
Palm Beach Gardens FL 33418
Phone: 561-712-6200
Fax: 561-845-0129
Web: www.ameripath.com

CEO: –
CFO: –
HR: –
FYE: December 31
Type: Subsidiary

Pickled organs and preserved tissues are AmeriPath's favorite things. The firm provides anatomic pathology dermatopathology and esoteric testing services to hospitals doctors clinics and clinical laboratories in about 20 states across the US. Some 400 pathologists in AmeriPath's network diagnose conditions such as cancer and kidney disease by examining tissue samples; work is performed in more than 70 outpatient labs and in about 200 hospitals. The company's esoteric testing operations involve complex specialized clinical tests (including DNA analysis and molecular diagnostics) that doctors use to diagnose and treat disease. AmeriPath is a subsidiary of Quest Diagnostics.

AMERIPRISE FINANCIAL INC
NYS: AMP

1099 Ameriprise Financial Center
Minneapolis, MN 55474
Phone: 612 671-3131
Fax: –
Web: www.ameriprise.com

CEO: James M. (Jim) Cracchiolo
CFO: Walter S. Berman
HR: Kelli A. Hunter
FYE: December 31
Type: Public

What combines the spark of American enterprise with financial advisor services? Ameriprise Financial Inc. Ameriprise provides a variety of financial products including mutual funds savings plans personal trust services retail brokerage and insurance products through its various brands and affiliates — which include Ameriprise Financial Columbia Management RiverSource and others. Ameriprise has more than $806 billion in assets under management and distributes its products primarily through a network of 10000 financial advisors. Founded in 1894 Ameriprise Financial was spun off from American Express.

	Annual Growth	12/10	12/11	12/12	12/13	12/14
Sales ($ mil.)	5.3%	9,976.0	10,192.0	10,217.0	11,199.0	12,268.0
Net income ($ mil.)	10.2%	1,097.0	1,076.0	1,029.0	1,334.0	1,619.0
Market value ($ mil.)	23.1%	10,538.0	9,089.6	11,468.1	21,066.7	24,216.2
Employees	3.9%	10,472	11,139	12,235	12,039	12,209

AMERIQUEST TRANSPORTATION SERVICES INC.

457 Haddonfield Rd. Ste. 220
Cherry Hill NJ 08002
Phone: 856-773-0600
Fax: 856-773-0609
Web: www.ameriquestcorp.com

CEO: Douglas Clark
CFO: Mark Joyce
HR: –
FYE: December 31
Type: Private

AmeriQuest Transportation Services makes money helping its clients save on transportation costs. AmeriQuest offers fleet management services touted for cost-savings and expertise to the commercial trucking industry. Through its primary businesses of AmeriQuest Transportation Services NationaLease CURE and Corcentric it offers supply and asset management truck rental and leasing fleet maintenance materials handling purchasing programs and logistics services. It also arranges dedicated contract carriage where drivers and equipment are assigned to a customer long-term. Founded in 1996 AmeriQuest offers more than 600 facilities and 700000 vehicles in the US and Canada.

AMERIS BANCORP
NMS: ABCB

310 First Street S.E.
Moultrie, GA 31768
Phone: 229 890-1111
Fax: –
Web: www.amerisbank.com

CEO: Edwin W. (Ed) Hortman
CFO: Dennis J. Zember
HR: Cindi H. Lewis
FYE: December 31
Type: Public

Ameris Bancorp enjoys the financial climate of the Deep South. It is the holding company of Ameris Bank which holds roughly $3.6 billion in assets and serves retail and consumer customers through more than 75 full-service and mortgage branches in Alabama Georgia South Carolina and northern Florida. In addition to its standard banking products and services the bank also provides treasury services mortgage and refinancing solutions and investment services through an agreement with Raymond James Financial. Loans secured by commercial real estate accounted for approximately 45% of the company's loan portfolio while 1-4 family residential and construction & land development mortgages accounted for nearly a quarter and about 10% respectively.

	Annual Growth	12/10	12/11	12/12	12/13	12/14
Assets ($ mil.)	8.0%	2,972.2	2,994.3	3,019.1	3,667.6	4,037.1
Net income ($ mil.)	—	(4.0)	21.1	14.4	20.0	38.7
Market value ($ mil.)	24.9%	282.2	275.2	334.4	565.2	686.5
Employees	9.7%	709	746	866	984	1,027

AMERISAFE INC
NMS: AMSF

2301 Highway 190 West
DeRidder, LA 70634
Phone: 337 463-9052
Fax: –
Web: www.amerisafe.com

CEO: –
CFO: Michael F. Grasher
HR: Cynthia Harris
FYE: December 31
Type: Public

AMERISAFE has what it takes to insure roughnecks and truckers. AMERISAFE specializes in providing workers' compensation insurance for businesses in hazardous industries including agriculture manufacturing construction logging and sawmill oil and gas maritime and trucking. Through its subsidiaries American Interstate Insurance Silver Oak Casualty and American Interstate Insurance of Texas the company writes coverage for more than 7900 employers (mainly small and midsized firms). In addition AMERISAFE offers worksite safety reviews loss prevention and claims management services. AMERISAFE sells its products in more than 30 states and the District of Columbia.

	Annual Growth	12/10	12/11	12/12	12/13	12/14
Assets ($ mil.)	6.6%	1,128.1	1,148.5	1,220.9	1,329.0	1,457.2
Net income ($ mil.)	12.6%	33.4	24.1	29.4	43.6	53.7
Market value ($ mil.)	24.7%	330.7	439.4	515.0	798.2	800.5
Employees	1.2%	424	428	429	437	445

AMERISERV FINANCIAL INC.
NMS: ASRV

Main & Franklin Streets,, P.O. Box 430
Johnstown, PA 15907-0430
Phone: 814 533-5300
Fax: –
Web: www.ameriserv.com

CEO: Jeffrey A Stopko
CFO: Michael D Lynch
HR: –
FYE: December 31
Type: Public

AmeriServ Financial offers up a smorgasbord of banking services for Pennsylvanians. The company owns AmeriServ Financial Bank which primarily serves the southwestern portion of the state through some 20 branches. Targeting individuals and local businesses the bank offers standard services such as deposits credit cards and loans. Commercial mortgages account for more than half of its loan portfolio; other real estate loans including residential mortgage and construction loans make up about 30%. One of a handful of unionized banks in the US AmeriServ also manages union pension funds through its AmeriServ Trust and Financial Services subsidiary which provides trust and wealth management services as well.

	Annual Growth	12/10	12/11	12/12	12/13	12/14
Assets ($ mil.)	3.5%	949.0	979.1	1,001.0	1,056.0	1,089.3
Net income ($ mil.)	23.9%	1.3	6.5	5.0	5.2	3.0
Market value ($ mil.)	18.6%	29.7	36.7	56.6	56.9	58.8
Employees	(2.6%)	374	372	374	377	336

AMERISOURCEBERGEN CORP.
NYS: ABC

1300 Morris Drive
Chesterbrook, PA 19087-5594
Phone: 610 727-7000
Fax: 610 647-0141
Web: www.amerisourcebergen.com

CEO: Steven H. Collis
CFO: Tim G. Guttman
HR: Jay Webster
FYE: September 30
Type: Public

AmerisourceBergen is the source for many of North America's pharmacies and health care providers. The distribution company serves as a go-between for drug makers and the pharmacies doctors' offices hospitals and other health care providers that dispense drugs. Operating primarily in the US and Canada it distributes generic branded and over-the-counter pharmaceuticals as well as some medical supplies and other products using its network of more than two dozen facilities. Its specialty distribution unit focuses on sensitive and complex biopharmaceuticals. Other operations include pharmaceutical packaging. AmerisourceBergen also provides commercialization and consulting services to its customers.

	Annual Growth	09/11	09/12	09/13	09/14	09/15
Sales ($ mil.)	14.1%	80,217.6	79,489.6	87,959.2	119,569.1	135,961.8
Net income ($ mil.)	—	706.6	719.0	433.7	276.5	(134.9)
Market value ($ mil.)	26.4%	7,710.9	8,008.8	12,641.1	15,992.7	19,652.7
Employees	14.2%	10,300	14,500	13,000	14,000	17,500

AMERISURE MUTUAL INSURANCE COMPANY

26777 Halsted Rd.
Farmington Hills MI 48331-3586
Phone: 248-615-9000
Fax: 248-615-8548
Web: www.amerisure.com

CEO: Gregory J Crabb
CFO: –
HR: Carrie Henry
FYE: December 31
Type: Private - Mutual Com

This company wants to help all businesses rest Amerisured. Amerisure Mutual Insurance Company provides a range of commercial property/casualty products with a special focus on the manufacturing health care and construction contracting industries. Coverage includes general and employee benefits liability workers compensation property auto inland marine and equipment insurance. The mutual firm is licensed in all US states and operates out of about a dozen offices across the nation. It uses a network of independent agents and brokers to distribute its products. Amerisure was founded as Michigan Workmen's Compensation Mutual Insurance in 1912.

AMERITAS MUTUAL HOLDING COMPANY

5900 O St.
Lincoln NE 68510
Phone: 402-467-1122
Fax: 402-467-7335
Web: www.ameritas.com

CEO: Joann M Martin
CFO: –
HR: –
FYE: December 31
Type: Private - Mutual Com

Ameritas Mutual Holding takes the task of providing life insurance to its members seriously. The company primarily operates through Ameritas Life Insurance and Ameritas Life Insurance of New York which provide life insurance and annuity products to about 430000 policyholders nationwide. In addition to managing some $80 billion in life insurance policies in force its subsidiaries also offer such services as financial planning and workplace investing. Ameritas' investment firms boast more than $30 billion of assets under management. Other companies under its umbrella include mutual fund manager Calvert Group.

AMERITRANS CAPITAL CORPORATION

830 3rd Ave. Ste. 830
New York NY 10022
Phone: 212-355-2449
Fax: 212-759-3338
Web: www.ameritranscapital.com

NASDAQ: AMTC
CEO: –
CFO: Robert C Ammerman
HR: –
FYE: June 30
Type: Public

Ameritrans Capital Corporation has switched off the meter on its taxi cab medallion business. The company previously provided financing to taxicab drivers in Boston Chicago Miami and New York City to acquire medallions or city-granted operating licenses. Medallion loans accounted for about half of Ameritrans' lending portfolio. However in 2008 it sold its portfolio of medallion loans held by subsidiary Elk Associates Funding to Medallion Financial for $31 million. Since then Ameritrans has focused on real estate mortgages corporate loans and equity investments in real estate while Elk Associates originates small business loans.

AMERITYRE CORPORATION

1501 Industrial Road
Boulder City, NV 89005
Phone: 702 293-1930
Fax: –
Web: www.amerityre.com

NBB: AMTY
CEO: Michael F Sullivan
CFO: Lynda R Keeton-Cardno
HR: –
FYE: June 30
Type: Public

Amerityre makes polyurethane foam tires which are unable to go flat for the bicycle and lawn equipment industries. The company also offers composite tires pneumatic tires and solid tires along with tire-filling materials. Central Purchasing accounts for one-fifth of Amerityre's sales. In 2008 the company acquired the manufacturing assets of a competitor KIK Technology International and KIK went out of business.

	Annual Growth	06/11	06/12	06/13	06/14	06/15
Sales ($ mil.)	6.8%	3.7	4.4	3.6	4.3	4.8
Net income ($ mil.)	–	(0.8)	(1.2)	(1.1)	(1.3)	(0.3)
Market value ($ mil.)	(45.8%)	10.4	12.1	1.2	2.2	0.9
Employees	1.4%	18	28	21	17	19

AMERON INTERNATIONAL CORPORATION

245 S. Los Robles Ave.
Pasadena CA 91101-3638
Phone: 626-683-4000
Fax: 626-683-4060
Web: www.ameron.com

CEO: Thomas Charles Zyroll Jr
CFO: Gary Wagner
HR: –
FYE: November 30
Type: Subsidiary

Oil water and other liquids need a place to flow and that's where Ameron International comes in. The firm designs makes and markets fiberglass-composite pipes for transmitting oil chemicals corrosive liquids and other specialty materials. Ameron also makes and sells concrete and fabricated steel products used for water transmission and wind towers. Additionally its infrastructure unit supplies ready-mix concrete and aggregates box culverts and sand for construction projects in Hawaii. The firm's pole products division makes concrete and steel poles for lighting and traffic signals. Oilfield equipment maker National Oilwell Varco bought Ameron for some $777 million in 2011.

AMERY REGIONAL MEDICAL CENTER INC.

265 GRIFFIN ST E
AMERY, WI 54001-1292
Phone: 715-268-8000
Fax: –
Web: www.amerymedicalcenter.org

CEO: Michael Karuschak Jr
CFO: Scott D Edin
HR: –
FYE: April 30
Type: Private

Amery Regional Medical Center provides medical care for the residents of Wisconsin. Among its specialized services are emergency medicine obstetrics home and hospice care physical therapy surgery and pain management. The not-for-profit hospital also provides wellness classes nutritional counseling and support groups. Its affiliates include Clear Lake Clinic Regions Hospital and Luck Medical Clinic.

	Annual Growth	12/07	12/08*	04/10	04/11	04/12
Sales ($ mil.)	3.2%	–	44.8	48.1	50.8	50.9
Net income ($ mil.)	–	–	(1.3)	0.7	0.7	1.6
Market value ($ mil.)	–	–	–	–	–	–
Employees	–	–	–	–	–	480

*Fiscal year change

AMES CONSTRUCTION INC.

14420 COUNTY ROAD 5
BURNSVILLE, MN 553066997
Phone: 952-435-7106
Fax: –
Web: www.amesconstruction.com

CEO: Raymond G Ames
CFO: Michael J Kellen
HR: –
FYE: November 30
Type: Private

Ames Construction aims right for the heart of heavy construction. The company is a general contractor providing heavy civil and industrial construction services to the transportation mining and power industries mainly in the West and Midwest. The family-owned company works on highways airports bridges rail lines mining facilities power plants and other infrastructure projects. Ames also performs flood control environmental remediation reclamation and landfill work. Additionally the firm builds golf courses and undertakes commercial and residential site development projects. Ames typically partners with other companies to perform the engineering and design portion of construction jobs.

	Annual Growth	11/08	11/09	11/10*	12/12*	11/14
Sales ($ mil.)	8.6%	–	712.8	685.4	582.3	1,074.6
Net income ($ mil.)	8.4%	–	–	18.8	5.7	26.0
Market value ($ mil.)	–	–	–	–	–	–
Employees	–	–	–	–	–	2,200

*Fiscal year change

AMES NATIONAL CORP.

405 Fifth Street
Ames, IA 50010
Phone: 515 232-6251
Fax: 515 663-3033
Web: www.amesnational.com

NAS: ATLO
CEO: Thomas H Pohlman
CFO: John P. Nelson
HR: –
FYE: December 31
Type: Public

This company aims to please citizens of Ames... and central Iowa. Ames National Corporation is the multi-bank holding company for flagship subsidiary First National Bank Ames Iowa as well as Boone Bank & Trust Reliance State State Bank & Trust and United Bank & Trust. Boasting over $1 billion in assets and 15 branches the banks provide area individuals and businesses with standard services such as deposit accounts IRAs and credit and debit cards. Commercial-related loans account for about 50% of Ames' loan portfolio while agricultural loans make up another 20%. The banks also write residential construction consumer and business loans and offer trust and financial management services.

	Annual Growth	12/10	12/11	12/12	12/13	12/14
Assets ($ mil.)	7.8%	963.0	1,035.6	1,217.7	1,233.1	1,301.0
Net income ($ mil.)	4.1%	13.0	13.9	14.2	14.0	15.3
Market value ($ mil.)	4.6%	201.8	181.6	203.9	208.5	241.5
Employees	4.6%	187	193	209	210	224

AMES TRUE TEMPER INC.

465 Railroad Ave.
Camp Hill PA 17011
Phone: 717-737-1500
Fax: 717-730-2552
Web: www.ames.com

CEO: –
CFO: Marcus Hamilton
HR: Bobbi Clay
FYE: September 30
Type: Subsidiary

It could be said that Ames True Temper is at the root of all lawn and garden tool manufacturers in the US. Tracing its history to 1774 the firm was founded as a shovel maker by John Ames. Today it's one of the largest suppliers of non-powered yard equipment in North America. Its product portfolio includes long-handle tools planters pruning and striking tools wheelbarrows hoses and hose reels and snow tools. Products are marketed under the Ames True Temper Hound Dog Jackson Professional Razor-Back and Union Tools brand names. They are sold in North America Europe and Australia via mass merchandisers wholesalers and distributors. Ames True Temper is owned by plastics maker Griffon Corporation.

AMETEK, INC.

1100 Cassatt Road
Berwyn, PA 19312-1177
Phone: 610 647-2121
Fax: 610 647-0211
Web: www.ametek.com

NYS: AME
CEO: Frank S. Hermance
CFO: Robert R. Mandos
HR: Paul Melniczek
FYE: December 31
Type: Public

You might say that AMETEK is powerfully instrumental. Its Electronic Instruments Group (EIG) makes monitoring calibration and display devices for the aerospace heavy equipment and power generation markets among others. Its Electromechanical Group (EMG) makes air-moving electric motors for vacuum cleaners and other floor care equipment blowers and heat exchangers connectors for moisture-proof applications and specialty metals for the aerospace mass transit medical and office products markets. AMETEK has some 120 manufacturing facilities throughout the world; most of its sales are to international customers.

	Annual Growth	12/10	12/11	12/12	12/13	12/14
Sales ($ mil.)	13.0%	2,471.0	2,989.9	3,334.2	3,594.1	4,022.0
Net income ($ mil.)	19.8%	283.9	384.5	459.1	517.0	584.5
Market value ($ mil.)	7.6%	9,472.4	10,160.2	9,067.0	12,711.1	12,701.5
Employees	7.3%	11,600	12,200	13,700	14,500	15,400

AMEXDRUG CORP.

7251 Condor Street
Commerce, CA 90040
Phone: 323 725-3100
Fax: –
Web: www.amexdrug.com

NBB: AXRX
CEO: Jack Amin
CFO: Jack Amin
HR: –
FYE: December 31
Type: Public

Amexdrug through subsidiaries Allied Med and Dermagen is a wholesale distributor of pharmaceuticals nutritional supplements and beauty products to pharmacies and other retailers. The company allows small pharmacies to get the lower prices that large pharmaceutical chains such as Walgreen and CVS enjoy. Its customers are primarily located in California. Part of Allied Med's growth strategy includes increasing its online traffic so it is increasing its name recognition and branding efforts. Top executive Jack Amin and his wife own more than 90% of the company.

	Annual Growth	12/08	12/09	12/10	12/11	12/12
Sales ($ mil.)	12.6%	5.7	9.8	11.5	12.4	9.1
Net income ($ mil.)	60.6%	0.0	0.0	0.2	0.1	0.1
Market value ($ mil.)	(52.9%)	172.5	372.1	338.2	338.2	8.5
Employees	(3.5%)	15	14	11	9	13

AMGEN INC

One Amgen Center Drive
Thousand Oaks, CA 91320-1799
Phone: 805 447-1000
Fax: 805 447-1010
Web: www.amgen.com

NMS: AMGN
CEO: Robert (Bob) Bradway
CFO: Jennifer Swiecki
HR: Ted Bagley
FYE: December 31
Type: Public

Amgen is among the biggest of the biotech big'uns and it's determined to get even bigger. The company uses cellular biology and medicinal chemistry to target cancers kidney ailments inflammatory disorders and metabolic diseases. Its top protein-based therapeutic products include Neulasta and Neupogen (both used as anti-infectives in cancer patients) Aranesp and Epogen (used to fight anemia in chronic kidney disease and cancer patients) and Enbrel for rheumatoid arthritis. In addition Amgen has extensive drug research and development programs. Its products are marketed in 75 countries to doctors hospitals pharmacies and other health care providers.

	Annual Growth	12/11	12/12	12/13	12/14	12/15
Sales ($ mil.)	8.6%	15,582.0	17,265.0	18,676.0	20,063.0	21,662.0
Net income ($ mil.)	17.2%	3,683.0	4,345.0	5,081.0	5,158.0	6,939.0
Market value ($ mil.)	26.1%	48,414.3	64,994.8	86,016.3	120,104.7	122,396.8
Employees	0.1%	17,800	18,000	20,000	17,900	17,900

AMICUS THERAPEUTICS INC
NMS: FOLD

1 Cedar Brook Drive
Cranbury, NJ 08512
Phone: 609-662-2000
Fax: -
Web: www.amicusrx.com

CEO: John F. Crowley
CFO: William D. (Chip) Baird
HR: -
FYE: December 31
Type: Public

Amicus Therapeutics develops drugs that treat rare genetic diseases known as lysosomal storage disorders. Unlike other treatments which replace defective enzymes Amicus uses small molecule pharmacological "chaperones" which bind to a patient's own defective proteins and restore their functions a process it calls Chaperone-Advanced Replacement Therapy (CHART). Its lead drug candidate migalastat HCl is aimed at aiding patients with Fabry disease. Other candidates are in development to treat Gaucher disease and Pompe disease. The company is also researching treatments for neurodegenerative diseases including Parkinson's.

	Annual Growth	12/10	12/11	12/12	12/13	12/14
Sales ($ mil.)	7.3%	0.9	21.4	18.4	0.4	1.2
Net income ($ mil.)	-	(54.9)	(44.4)	(48.8)	(59.6)	(68.9)
Market value ($ mil.)	15.3%	449.1	328.7	256.1	224.6	795.0
Employees	(0.5%)	99	96	112	92	97

AMKOR TECHNOLOGY INC.
NMS: AMKR

2045 East Innovation Circle
Tempe, AZ 85284
Phone: 480-821-5000
Fax: -
Web: www.amkor.com

CEO: Stephen D. (Steve) Kelley
CFO: Joanne Solomon
HR: -
FYE: December 31
Type: Public

Amkor is the technology version of a finishing school for the electronic products that contain computer chips. A top contractor in chip assembly and testing services for semiconductor manufacturers it handles chips that end up in PCs handheld devices TVs gaming machines routers automobiles and in communications and industrial settings. The company's some 250 customers worldwide include big semiconductor companies and electronics makers such as Altera Broadcom IBM QUALCOMM Texas Instruments and Toshiba. Founder and chairman James Kim and his family control Amkor.

	Annual Growth	12/10	12/11	12/12	12/13	12/14
Sales ($ mil.)	1.6%	2,939.5	2,776.4	2,759.5	2,956.5	3,129.4
Net income ($ mil.)	(13.4%)	232.0	91.8	41.8	109.3	130.4
Market value ($ mil.)	(1.1%)	1,753.4	1,031.7	1,003.5	1,450.5	1,680.1
Employees	2.4%	19,900	18,300	18,900	20,900	21,900

AML COMMUNICATIONS INC.

1000 Avenida Acaso
Camarillo CA 93012
Phone: 805-388-1345
Fax: 805-484-2191
Web: www.amlj.com

CEO: Jacob Inbar
CFO: Heera Lee
HR: Martha Lozano
FYE: March 31
Type: Subsidiary

AML Communications wants to pump up the volume with its microwave amplifiers for wireless communications. The amplifiers support defense-related radar satellite and surveillance systems as well as commercial wireless applications. AML also makes higher-power microwave amplifiers for the defense market through subsidiary Microwave Power. AML's customers include defense equipment manufacturers (such as Raytheon and Boeing) systems integrators and commercial wireless operators (AT&T Mobility and Verizon Wireless). In 2011 AML was acquired by Microsemi for about $28 million in cash to complement its existing defense-related product portfolio and to expand its wireless communications business.

AMN HEALTHCARE SERVICES, INC.
NYS: AHS

12400 High Bluff Drive, Suite 100
San Diego, CA 92130
Phone: 866-871-8519
Fax: -
Web: www.amnhealthcare.com

CEO: Susan R. Salka
CFO: Brian M. Scott
HR: Julie Fletcher
FYE: December 31
Type: Public

Understaffed hospitals say "amen" for AMN Healthcare Services. Operating under such brands as American Mobile Healthcare Medical Express Nurse-Choice NursesRx Medfinders Med Travelers Staff Care and O'Grady-Peyton International the firm is one of the leading temporary health care staffing companies in the world. It places nurses technicians and therapists for 13-week stints at hospitals clinics and schools nationwide. With professionals recruited from Australia Canada South Africa the UK and the US AMN provides travel reimbursement and housing for its nurse and health care workers on assignment. The majority of temporary assignments for its clients are at acute-care hospitals in the US.

	Annual Growth	12/10	12/11	12/12	12/13	12/14
Sales ($ mil.)	10.7%	689.2	887.5	954.0	1,011.8	1,036.0
Net income ($ mil.)	-	(52.0)	(26.3)	17.1	32.9	33.2
Market value ($ mil.)	33.7%	286.4	206.6	538.7	685.6	914.1
Employees	(0.5%)	1,833	1,840	1,700	1,900	1,800

AMOS PRESS INC.

911 Vandemark Rd.
Sidney OH 45365
Phone: 937-498-2111
Fax: 937-498-0812
Web: www.amospress.com

CEO: Bruce Boyd
CFO: -
HR: -
FYE: December 31
Type: Private

Amos Press (also known as Amos Publishing) is something of a hobby horse. The company publishes more than 15 niche titles that provide news information and entertainment pieces for collectors. Initially a daily newspaper publishing company Amos expanded into the collectibles business in 1960 with its launch of Coin World a weekly national news magazine for coin collectors. It later acquired Linn's Stamp News a weekly periodical serving stamp collectors and Cars & Parts a publication designed for automotive fans with a focus on authentic collector cars. In 1984 Amos bought Scott Publishing Company another publisher of content for stamp collectors. Amos Press was founded by James Amos in 1876.

AMPACET CORPORATION

660 White Plains Rd.
Tarrytown NY 10591
Phone: 914-631-6600
Fax: 914-631-7278
Web: www.ampacet.com

CEO: -
CFO: Joel Slutsky
HR: Robert K Oaes
FYE: December 31
Type: Private

Ampacet helps manufacturers of plastic products show their true hues with custom color and additive concentrates. Using polyethylene polypropylene polyamide and polyester resins Ampacet makes compounds concentrates and masterbatches that enable those manufacturers to produce consistent colors and chemical characteristics for their extruded and molded products. Globally the company competes with firms such as BASF and Clariant in the color concentrates market. Its additives are used in food and industrial packaging pipe and conduit wire and cable and other plastic products.

AMPCO-PITTSBURGH CORP.

NYS: AP

726 Bell Avenue, Suite 301
Pittsburgh, PA 15106
Phone: 412 456-4400
Fax: 412 456-4404
Web: www.ampcopittsburgh.com

CEO: John S. Stanik
CFO: Marliss D. (Dee Ann) Johnson
HR: –
FYE: December 31
Type: Public

Steel giant Ampco-Pittsburgh keeps its worth by never losing its temper. Among the leaders in steel producers the company divides its work in two segments: The forged and cast steel roll arm comprising subsidiaries Union Electric Steel and Union Electric Steel UK makes forged hardened-steel rolling mill rolls and cast rolls for steel and aluminum manufacturers. The air and liquid processing unit has three divisions: Buffalo Pumps which makes centrifugal pumps for refrigeration marine defense and power generation industries; Aerofin highly-engineered heat-exchange coils and Buffalo Air Handling air-handling systems for defense power generation and construction customers.

	Annual Growth	12/10	12/11	12/12	12/13	12/14
Sales ($ mil.)	(4.4%)	326.9	344.8	292.9	281.1	272.9
Net income ($ mil.)	–	15.5	21.3	8.4	12.4	(1.2)
Market value ($ mil.)	(9.0%)	292.4	201.6	208.3	202.8	200.7
Employees	(3.9%)	1,264	1,240	1,178	1,109	1,076

AMPHENOL CORP.

NYS: APH

358 Hall Avenue
Wallingford, CT 06492
Phone: 203 265-8900
Fax: 203 265-8746
Web: www.amphenol.com

CEO: Richard A. (Adam) Norwitt
CFO: Craig A. Lampo
HR: Jerome Monteith
FYE: December 31
Type: Public

Amphenol knows it's all about connections. A leading manufacturer of connector and interconnect products its serves the communications industrial medical and military markets. Amphenol's interconnect products are used to conduct electrical and optical signals in computers wired and wireless communications and networking equipment medical instruments office equipment aircraft and spacecraft and energy applications. Its Times Fiber Communications subsidiary is a leading maker of coaxial cable for the cable TV industry and flat-ribbon cable for computer and telecommunications products. With customers in about 70 countries more than two thirds of its sales come from outside the US led by customers in China.

	Annual Growth	12/10	12/11	12/12	12/13	12/14
Sales ($ mil.)	10.7%	3,554.1	3,939.8	4,292.1	4,614.7	5,345.5
Net income ($ mil.)	9.3%	496.4	524.2	555.3	635.7	709.1
Market value ($ mil.)	0.5%	16,355.7	14,065.7	20,049.5	27,635.5	16,674.9
Employees	6.7%	39,100	39,100	41,600	44,500	50,700

AMPIO PHARMACEUTICALS INC

ASE: AMPE

373 Inverness Parkway, Suite 200
Englewood, CO 80112
Phone: 720 437-6500
Fax: –
Web: www.ampiopharma.com

CEO: Michael Macaluso
CFO: Gregory A Gould
HR: –
FYE: December 31
Type: Public

With hopes one day of taking in revenues somewhere between ample and copious Ampio Pharmaceuticals is a development-stage company that focuses on repositioning existing drugs for new uses. Drugs in formulation for new indications include candidates for treating eye and kidney disorders inflammatory conditions and metabolic disease. In addition the company is working on diagnostic devices for measuring levels of oxidation in the bloodstream. Ampio is conducting clinical trials for two drugs: Ampion (for osteoarthritis of the knee) and Optina (for diabetic macular edema). In late 2013 it announced plans to spin off its sexual dysfunction business (Zertane and Zertane-ED).

	Annual Growth	12/10	12/11	12/12	12/13	12/14
Sales ($ mil.)	60.0%	–	0.0	0.1	0.1	0.1
Net income ($ mil.)	–	(8.1)	(18.4)	(11.6)	(24.0)	(38.1)
Market value ($ mil.)	9.4%	124.7	221.9	186.6	370.6	178.3
Employees	20.2%	11	12	13	16	23

AMPLIPHI BIOSCIENCES CORP

ASE: APHB

800 East Leigh Street, Suite 209
Richmond, VA 23219
Phone: 804 827-2524
Fax: 206 223-0288
Web: www.campliphibio.com

CEO: M Scott Salka
CFO: Steve R. Martin
HR: –
FYE: December 31
Type: Public

AmpliPhi Biosciences (formerly called Targeted Genetics) is amping up the fight against bacterial infections. The drug developer focuses on anti-bacterial (bacteriophage) therapeutics. It was after the 2011 acquisition of Biocontrol that AmpliPhi reorganized itself; going from being focused on developing DNA-based gene therapies to encourage (or sometimes inhibit) the production of proteins associated with disease to its current focus of treatments for antibiotic-resistant bacterial infections. The field for anti-infective treatments is receiving great attention these days with the spread of antibiotic-resistant infections such as the deadly methicillin-resistant Staphylococcus aureus aka MRSA.

	Annual Growth	12/09	12/10	12/12	12/13	12/14
Sales ($ mil.)	(49.3%)	12.2	2.1	0.7	0.3	0.4
Net income ($ mil.)	23.8%	7.9	(2.6)	(1.1)	(58.4)	23.1
Market value ($ mil.)	(6.2%)	1.1	1.4	0.7	2.0	0.8
Employees	35.7%	5	–	–	12	23

AMREIT INC.

NYSE: AMRE

8 Greenway Plaza Ste. 1000
Houston TX 77046
Phone: 713-850-1400
Fax: 713-850-0498
Web: www.amreit.com

CEO: –
CFO: –
HR: –
FYE: December 31
Type: Private

AmREIT is tuned in to its own shopping network. A self-managed real estate investment trust (REIT) the company invests in develops and manages retail properties primarily lifestyle centers grocery store-anchored strip centers and single-tenant retail properties. It owns some 30 properties with more than 1 million sq. ft. of leasable space; more than half are located in Texas. The company's preferred assets are located in dense high-traffic areas in the suburbs of Houston Dallas and San Antonio. The REIT's largest tenants are Kroger H-E-B and CVS Care; together they account for about 20% of its rental revenues. After a brief stint off the public markets AmREIT went public again in 2012.

AMREP CORP.

NYS: AXR

300 Alexander Park, Suite 204
Princeton, NJ 08540
Phone: 609 716-8200
Fax: –
Web: www.amrepcorp.com

CEO: –
CFO: Peter M Pizza
HR: –
FYE: April 30
Type: Public

Mailing magazines and developing land in New Mexico keep AMREP hopping. About 80% of the company's sales come from newsstand distribution and subscription and product fulfillment services it provides through its Kable Media Services and Palm Coast Data subsidiaries. The units serve about 200 publishing clients by managing subscriptions and mailing 900-plus magazine titles. Through its AMREP Southwest subsidiary the company develops its Rio Rancho property (roughly 17300 acres) as well as certain parts of Sandoval County outside Albuquerque New Mexico. AMREP was founded in 1961. Its largest shareholder in 2010 scrapped plans to take AMREP private and merge it with another firm.

	Annual Growth	04/11	04/12	04/13	04/14	04/15
Sales ($ mil.)	(15.3%)	96.8	85.4	83.0	87.3	49.8
Net income ($ mil.)	–	(7.6)	(1.1)	(2.8)	(2.9)	11.3
Market value ($ mil.)	(15.4%)	80.6	62.6	72.5	43.8	41.2
Employees	(17.5%)	1,230	1,100	1,200	1,278	570

AMRON INTERNATIONAL INC.

1380 ASPEN WAY
VISTA, CA 920818349
Phone: 760-208-6500
Fax: –
Web: www.wk101649566.company.weiku.com

CEO: Debra L Ritchie
CFO: –
HR: –
FYE: December 31
Type: Private

Talk about being under pressure. Amron International is a manufacturer and supplier of specialized diving and hyperbaric equipment. Its underwater products include helium unscramblers oxygen treatment panels and hoods chamber conditioning systems diver communication systems and vulcanized rubber dry suits. The company also distributes tactical and outdoor gear from such brands as Patagonia Slumberjack and Suunto. Amron International is a prime vendor for the US military. Other customers include commercial business with many in the oil industry. The company has facilities in Vista California and in Virginia Beach Virginia. Amron International was founded in 1978 by Norma Ockwig.

	Annual Growth	12/04	12/05	12/06	12/07	12/08
Sales ($ mil.)	–	–	–	(1,073.2)	63.4	79.4
Net income ($ mil.)	20730.4%	–	–	0.0	3.1	4.6
Market value ($ mil.)	–	–	–	–	–	–
Employees	–	–	–	–	–	80

AMS HEALTH SCIENCES INC.

4000 N. Lindsay
Oklahoma City OK 73105
Phone: 405-842-0131
Fax: 405-843-4935
Web: www.amsonline.com

CEO: –
CFO: Randy Webb
HR: –
FYE: December 31
Type: Private

Combine green algae ionized silver shark cartilage and pomegranate juice and you might find the fountain of youth or at least the ingredients for a multi-level marketing company like AMS Health Sciences. The company's 60 products consist of dietary supplements weight management products and hair and skin care products — all of which are manufactured by third parties. A network of 7000 independent distributors sell the products in Canada and the US. Its products are sold under the Advantage AMS Prime One and ToppFast brands. The company also markets and sells promotional material to its distributors. AMS has restructured and emerged from Chapter 11 bankruptcy protection.

AMSCAN HOLDINGS INC.

80 Grasslands Rd.
Elmsford NY 10523
Phone: 914-345-2020
Fax: 541-774-7617
Web: www.lithiainvestorrelations.com

CEO: Gerald C Rittenberg
CFO: Michael A Correale
HR: Laura Bucci
FYE: December 31
Type: Private

Amscan Holdings caters to the party animal in all of us. The vertically-integrated company operates a wholesale business Amscan Inc. that manufactures and distributes party goods such as balloons invitations pi?atas favors stationery and tableware. It also sells its party supplies to its own growing chain of retail stores including nearly 500 Party City superstores as well as those operated by rival party chains discount and grocery stores dollar stores and gift shops. Amscan has production and distribution facilities in North America Europe and the Asia/Pacific region. It is a subsidiary of Party City Holdingswhich is owned by Berkshire Partners Weston Presidio and Advent International.

AMSTED INDUSTRIES INCORPORATED

2 Prudential Plaza 180 N. Stetson St. Ste. 1800
Chicago IL 60601
Phone: 312-645-1700
Fax: 312-819-8494
Web: www.amsted.com

CEO: W Robert Reum
CFO: Tomas Bergmann
HR: –
FYE: September 30
Type: Private

Wilbur and Orville Wright's first flight might never have succeeded without an assist from Amsted Industries' Diamond Chain subsidiary. A maker of bicycle and industrial roller chains Diamond produced the propeller chain for the Wright brothers' aircraft. Amsted Industries' three different segments manufacture highly engineered industrial components for locomotive and railcar makers automotive OEMs and construction and building suppliers. It is a major force in making freight car undercarriages too. Main subsidiaries include ASF-Keystone Griffin Pipe Products Griffin Wheel and Means Industries. Employee-owned Amsted Industries runs about 50 plants in 11 countries.

AMSURG CORP

1A Burton Hills Boulevard
Nashville, TN 37215
Phone: 615 665-1283
Fax: –
Web: www.amsurg.com

NMS: AMSG
CEO: Christopher A. Holden
CFO: Claire M. Gulmi
HR: –
FYE: December 31
Type: Public

It's not quite an assembly line but AmSurg aims to make outpatient surgeries more efficient cost effective and up to date. The company operates ambulatory surgery centers that specialize in a few high-volume low-risk procedures with no overnight stays. Its specialties include gastroenterology (colonoscopy and endoscopy) orthopedics (knee scopes and carpal tunnel repair) ophthalmology (cataracts and laser eye surgery) otolaryngology (earn nose and throat) and urology. It also provides multi-specialty services primarily in anesthesiology children's services radiology and emergency medicine to health care facilities. Each of its centers are affiliated with a physicians practice group.

	Annual Growth	12/10	12/11	12/12	12/13	12/14
Sales ($ mil.)	22.9%	710.4	786.9	928.5	1,079.3	1,621.9
Net income ($ mil.)	1.9%	49.8	50.0	62.6	72.7	53.7
Market value ($ mil.)	27.1%	1,008.0	1,252.9	1,443.9	2,209.3	2,633.2
Employees	35.7%	3,100	5,500	6,100	6,200	10,500

AMTEC PRECISION PRODUCTS INC.

1875 Holmes Rd.
Elgin IL 60123-1298
Phone: 847-622-2686
Fax: 847-695-8295
Web: www.amtecprecision.com

CEO: –
CFO: –
HR: –
FYE: May 31
Type: Private

Liking neither Dr. Seuss' Sam-I-am nor green eggs and ham AMTEC would like precision components here or there. Its products include precision-machined metals injection-molded plastics and mechanical electromechanical and electronic assemblies. Clients for its precision products include Bosch Caterpillar Copeland Ford and General Motors. Its clients for molded plastics include Barber Coleman Bergstrom Ecolab and Kysor Westran. The company maintains three manufacturing plants in Illinois. AMTEC Precision Products was founded in 1954. Since 2005 the company has operated as a subsidiary of India-based Ucal Fuel Systems Ltd.

AMTECH SYSTEMS, INC.   NMS: ASYS

131 South Clark Drive
Tempe, AZ 85281
Phone: 480 967-5146
Fax: –
Web: www.amtechsystems.com

CEO: Fokko Pentinga
CFO: Bradley C Anderson
HR: –
FYE: September 30
Type: Public

Amtech Systems furnishes fabs with furnaces and more. The company operates through four subsidiaries: Tempress Systems makes diffusion furnaces for semiconductor and solar cell fabrication as well as for precision thermal processing (annealing brazing silvering sealing and soldering) of electronic devices including optical components and photovoltaic (PV) solar cells. P.R. Hoffman Machine Products makes equipment used to polish items such as silicon wafers precision optics ceramic components and disk media. Bruce Technologies makes horizontal diffusion furnace systems and R2D Automation makes wafer automation and handling equipment for the solar and semiconductor sectors and is based in France.

	Annual Growth	09/11	09/12	09/13	09/14	09/15
Sales ($ mil.)	(19.3%)	246.7	81.5	34.8	56.5	104.9
Net income ($ mil.)	–	22.9	(23.0)	(20.1)	(13.0)	(7.8)
Market value ($ mil.)	(14.4%)	105.2	43.5	96.0	140.7	56.5
Employees	4.6%	420	350	267	262	503

AMTRUST FINANCIAL SERVICES INC   NMS: AFSI

59 Maiden Lane, 43rd Floor
New York, NY 10038
Phone: 212 220-7120
Fax: –
Web: www.amtrustgroup.com

CEO: Barry D. Zyskind
CFO: Ronald E. Pipoly
HR: Kevin Oxley
FYE: December 31
Type: Public

Insurance holding company AmTrust Financial Services likes a mix of businesses on its plate. Its subsidiaries offer a range of commercial property/casualty insurance products for small and midsized customers including workers' compensation products auto and general liability workplace and agricultural coverage and extended service and warranty coverage of consumer and commercial goods. It also provides a small amount of personal auto reinsurance. It operates in Bermuda Ireland the UK and the US and distributes its products through brokers agents and claims administrators. The firm's customers include restaurants retailers physicians' offices auto and electronics manufacturers and trucking operations.

	Annual Growth	12/10	12/11	12/12	12/13	12/14
Assets ($ mil.)	34.9%	4,182.5	5,682.6	7,417.2	11,257.4	13,847.4
Net income ($ mil.)	33.1%	142.5	170.4	178.0	290.9	447.0
Market value ($ mil.)	33.9%	2,720.9	3,692.6	4,460.7	5,082.6	8,745.6
Employees	38.2%	1,400	1,900	2,100	3,238	5,100

AMWAY INTERNATIONAL INC.

7575 Fulton St. East
Ada MI 49355-0001
Phone: 616-787-6000
Fax: 616-682-4000
Web: www.amway.com

CEO: –
CFO: Russ Evans
HR: –
FYE: August 31
Type: Subsidiary

Selling makeup and vitamins to friends and family is a way of life at Amway International. One of the world's largest direct-sales businesses Amway boasts more than 3 million independent consultants who sell its catalog of more than 450 personal care household nutrition and cleaning products. It also sells the products and services of other companies in 80-plus markets worldwide. Revival-like techniques are used to motivate distributors (mostly part-timers) to sell products and find new recruits to build the multi-level marketing platform. Operations outside of the US generate about 80% of sales mainly in Asia. Founder Richard DeVos and the Van Andel family own Amway and its parent company Alticor.

AMX LLC

3000 Research Dr.
Richardson TX 75082
Phone: 469-624-8000
Fax: 469-624-7153
Web: www.amxcorp.com

CEO: Rashid Skap
CFO: C Chris Apple
HR: –
FYE: December 31
Type: Subsidiary

Like a football fan on Sunday AMX really knows how to work the remote control. The company designs and sells systems that control devices such as lights audio and video equipment and security cameras from a common remote interface. Its systems are used in corporate educational entertainment industrial and government settings. AMX also offers residential systems that control security systems lighting and electronic devices. The company sells through distributors and manufacturers including Tech Data and Dell; it also has partnerships with a number of Asian vendors including Fujitsu Hitachi NEC Samsung and Sony. Founded in 1982 AMX is a subsidiary of The Duchossois Group.

AMY'S KITCHEN INC.

Corporate Circle Ste. 200
Petaluma CA 94954
Phone: 707-578-7270
Fax: 310-752-4444
Web: www.thephelpsgroup.com

CEO: Andy Berliner
CFO: Andrew Koprel
HR: –
FYE: June 30
Type: Private

Amy's Kitchen helps you stock your own with lots of vegetarian options. The company makes and markets more than 170 frozen and pre-packaged vegetarian meals and other food products using all-natural and organic ingredients. Foods from Amy's Kitchen are also a popular option for non-vegetarian health-conscious consumers. The company's products include more than 88 frozen entrees including pizzas pocket sandwiches pot pies snacks toaster pops and veggie burgers as well as canned soups beans chili jarred pasta sauces and salsa. Founded in 1987 Amy's Kitchen distributes specialty foods in North America through supermarkets natural food and grocery stores warehouse stores and college campuses.

AMYLIN PHARMACEUTICALS INC.   NASDAQ: AMLN

9360 Towne Centre Dr.
San Diego CA 92121
Phone: 858-552-2200
Fax: 858-552-2212
Web: www.amylin.com

CEO: Daniel M Bradbury
CFO: Mark G Foletta
HR: –
FYE: December 31
Type: Public

Amylin Pharmaceuticals helps diabetics gain the upper hand in their battle with the disease. The company makes and markets injectable diabetes drugs Byetta and Symlin which are approved as adjunct therapies to other diabetes treatments such as metformin and insulin. Byetta is also approved as a stand-alone diabetes therapy. Amylin gained FDA approval for Bydureon a once-weekly version of Byetta in 2012 and it is developing additional drugs for metabolic conditions. The company's US sales force markets its products to patients and physicians; development partner Eli Lilly markets Byetta internationally although Amylin and Lilly are ending their partnership. Amylin was acquired by Bristol-Myers Squibb in 2012.

AMYRIS, INC.
NMS: AMRS

5885 Hollis Street, Suite 100
Emeryville, CA 94608
Phone: 510 450-0761
Fax: –
Web: www.amyris.com

CEO: John G Melo
CFO: Raffi Asadorian
HR: –
FYE: December 31
Type: Public

Amyris Biotechnologies is engineering yeast in the hopes to rise above the world's dependence on petroleum by creating alternative fuels. The company has developed a process that uses genetically modified molecules from yeast to create biofuels and other renewable chemicals as an alternative to petroleum products. Amyris uses fermented yeast from Brazilian sugarcane to produce Biofene a chemical that can replace petroleum as the basis for such products as detergent cosmetics perfume industrial lubricants and fuel. The company has operations in the US and in Brazil through a joint venture with sugar giant Grupo S⎵⎵o Martinho.

	Annual Growth	12/10	12/11	12/12	12/13	12/14
Sales ($ mil.)	(14.3%)	80.3	147.0	73.7	41.1	43.3
Net income ($ mil.)	–	(82.8)	(178.9)	(205.1)	(235.1)	2.2
Market value ($ mil.)	(47.3%)	2,113.6	914.2	247.2	419.1	163.2
Employees	2.2%	371	489	397	392	404

ANACOR PHARMACEUTICALS INC
NMS: ANAC

1020 East Meadow Circle
Palo Alto, CA 94303-4230
Phone: 650 543-7500
Fax: –
Web: www.anacor.com

CEO: Paul L. Berns
CFO: Graeme Bell
HR: Anh Antonio
FYE: December 31
Type: Public

Anacor is hardcore about curing skin conditions. The company is developing boron-based drug compounds for use as topical treatments of bacterial fungal and inflammatory conditions. Its lead candidates aim to treat onychomycosis (a kind of toenail fungus) psoriasis and hospital-acquired bacterial infections. Anacor has focused on topical treatments for the time being because they are relatively easy to develop and market but it believes its boron chemistry can produce drugs in therapeutic fields such as viral and parasitic infections and rare infectious diseases. The company went public in 2010.

	Annual Growth	12/10	12/11	12/12	12/13	12/14
Sales ($ mil.)	(7.1%)	27.8	20.3	10.7	17.2	20.7
Net income ($ mil.)	–	(10.1)	(47.9)	(56.1)	84.8	(87.1)
Market value ($ mil.)	56.5%	232.4	268.3	225.0	726.1	1,395.6
Employees	11.4%	65	80	85	79	100

ANADARKO PETROLEUM CORP
NYS: APC

1201 Lake Robbins Drive
The Woodlands, TX 77380-1046
Phone: 832 636-1000
Fax: –
Web: www.anadarko.com

CEO: R. A. (Al) Walker
CFO: Robert G. (Bob) Gwin
HR: –
FYE: December 31
Type: Public

Anadarko Petroleum has ventured beyond its original area of operation — the Anadarko Basin — to explore for develop produce and market oil natural gas natural gas liquids and related products worldwide. In 2014 the large independent company reported proved reserves (92% of which is located in the US) of 2.9 billion barrels of oil equivalent. Additional assets include coal trona (natural soda ash) and other minerals. Anadarko operates a handful of gas-gathering systems in the Mid-Continent. Internationally the company has substantial oil and gas interests in Algeria. It also has holdings in Brazil China Indonesia Mozambique and West Africa.

	Annual Growth	12/11	12/12	12/13	12/14	12/15
Sales ($ mil.)	(11.2%)	13,967.0	13,411.0	14,581.0	18,470.0	8,698.0
Net income ($ mil.)	–	(2,649.0)	2,391.0	801.0	(1,750.0)	(6,692.0)
Market value ($ mil.)	(10.7%)	38,798.5	37,771.8	40,318.4	41,934.8	24,693.2
Employees	4.8%	4,800	5,200	5,700	6,100	5,800

ANADIGICS INC
NAS: ANAD

141 Mt. Bethel Road
Warren, NJ 07059
Phone: 908 668-5000
Fax: –
Web: www.anadigics.com

CEO: Ronald Michels
CFO: Terrence G. (Terry) Gallagher
HR: Rachel Braverman
FYE: December 31
Type: Public

ANADIGICS makes chips that cook with GaAs. The company makes gallium arsenide (GaAs) radio-frequency integrated circuits for cellular wireless WiFi and infrastructure applications. GaAs ICs may be costlier than silicon but their physical properties allow the compound materials to be used for chips that are smaller and faster or more energy-efficient than silicon chips. ANADIGICS' power amplifiers switches and other chips can be found in the cable modems set-top boxes wireless devices and other gear of companies including Samsung Huawei and ZTE. The majority of customers come from Asia. In late 2015 ANADIGICS agreed to be acquired by GaAs Labs a venture capital firm.

	Annual Growth	12/10	12/11	12/12	12/13	12/14
Sales ($ mil.)	(20.6%)	216.7	152.8	112.6	134.2	86.3
Net income ($ mil.)	–	1.3	(49.3)	(69.9)	(54.0)	(38.9)
Market value ($ mil.)	(42.6%)	601.3	190.0	218.6	159.6	65.1
Employees	(16.1%)	590	540	504	477	293

ANADYS PHARMACEUTICALS INC.
NASDAQ: ANDS

5871 Oberlin Dr. Ste. 200
San Diego CA 92121
Phone: 858-530-3600
Fax: 858-527-1540
Web: www.anadyspharma.com

CEO: –
CFO: –
HR: –
FYE: December 31
Type: Public

Anadys Pharmaceuticals has hepatitis and cancer in the crosshairs. The biotechnology company is developing new therapeutic treatments for those infected with hepatitis C (HCV) and other bacterial infections as well as for applications in oncology. Anadys is exploring compounds that either act as direct antivirals or that stimulate the body's immune system responses to fight disease. In addition Anadys Pharmaceuticals explores potential strategic alliances with other pharmaceutical firms for collaborative development or licensing arrangements. In late 2011 the company agreed to be acquired by Roche Holding in a deal worth about $230 million.

ANALOG DEVICES, INC.
NMS: ADI

One Technology Way
Norwood, MA 02062-9106
Phone: 781 329-4700
Fax: –
Web: www.analog.com

CEO: Vincent T. Roche
CFO: David A. (Dave) Zinsner
HR: –
FYE: October 31
Type: Public

Analog Devices' name tells just half its story. It's a leading maker of linear and mixed-signal analog integrated circuits (ICs) as well as digital ICs. Its line of 20000 devices includes converters amplifiers power management products and digital signal processors (DSPs). Its linear ICs translate real-world phenomena such as pressure temperature and sound into digital signals. ADI's chip designs are used in industrial process controls medical and scientific instruments communications gear computers automobiles and consumer electronics. Its chips operate in high-tech goods from more than 100000 companies. Customers outside the US account for most of the company's sales. ADI marks its 50th year in 2015.

	Annual Growth	10/11*	11/12	11/13	11/14*	10/15
Sales ($ mil.)	3.5%	2,993.3	2,701.1	2,633.7	2,864.8	3,435.1
Net income ($ mil.)	(5.3%)	867.4	651.2	673.5	629.3	696.9
Market value ($ mil.)	12.4%	11,764.7	12,426.3	15,503.2	15,484.5	18,761.1
Employees	1.3%	9,200	9,200	9,100	9,600	9,700

*Fiscal year change

ANALOGIC CORP

NMS: ALOG

8 Centennial Drive
Peabody, MA 01960
Phone: 978 326-4000
Fax: -
Web: www.analogic.com

CEO: James W. (Jim) Green
CFO: Mark T. Frost
HR: Douglas Rosenfeld
FYE: July 31
Type: Public

Analogic envisions a logical use for data — health care and airport security. The company's data acquisition conversion and signal processing gear converts analog signals such as pressure temperature and X-rays into digital computer data. Its medical image processing systems and security imaging products are used in equipment such as CT and MRI scanners and other diagnostic screeners as well as luggage inspection systems. The company also makes ultrasound systems under the brands BK Medical and Sonix for the surgery anesthesia and general imaging markets among others. Analogic has facilities in Asia Europe and North America and generates more than 60% of its sales outside the US.

	Annual Growth	07/11	07/12	07/13	07/14	07/15
Sales ($ mil.)	3.3%	473.6	516.6	550.4	517.5	540.3
Net income ($ mil.)	17.1%	17.8	43.1	31.1	34.5	33.5
Market value ($ mil.)	10.6%	668.8	796.0	887.7	894.1	1,001.6
Employees	2.9%	1,500	1,600	1,700	1,700	1,679

ANCESTRY.COM INC.

NASDAQ: ACOM

360 W. 4800 North
Provo UT 84604
Phone: 801-705-7000
Fax: 801-705-7001
Web: corporate.ancestry.com

CEO: Timothy Sullivan
CFO: Howard Hochhauser
HR: -
FYE: December 31
Type: Private

For those with the urge to unearth and discover their roots Ancestry.com helps people research and share family histories as well as create family trees. Users can search through a variety of documents photographs maps and newspapers on its website. In addition to this data Ancestry.com relies on user-generated content and social networking activities — including uploading and sharing family trees photographs and documents and written stories — to encourage collaboration among users. Ancestry.com also provides family-history desktop software Family Tree Maker and offers research services. Ancestry.com was taken private in late 2012 by Permira.

ANCHIN BLOCK & ANCHIN LLP

1375 Broadway
New York NY 10018
Phone: 212-840-3456
Fax: 212-840-7066
Web: www.anchin.com

CEO: -
CFO: -
HR: -
FYE: September 30
Type: Private - Partnershi

Einstein knew that logic will get you from A to B and Anchin Block & Anchin is no exception. The regional accounting and consulting firm concentrates on serving privately held businesses in a number of industries. It offers audits financial statements reviews and compilations tax preparation and other advisory services. Its Anchin Wealth Management unit serves wealthy clients with investment estate and other financial services while Anchin Capital Advisors specializes in mergers and acquisitions. Anchin Block & Anchin which was founded in 1923 as a three-man partnership has grown to number more than 50 partners and principals.

ANCHOR BANCORP WISCONSIN INC (DE)

NMS: ABCW

25 West Main Street
Madison, WI 53703
Phone: 608 252-8700
Fax: 608 252-8783
Web: www.anchorbank.com

CEO: Chris M. Bauer
CFO: Thomas G Dolan
HR: -
FYE: December 31
Type: Public

Anchor BanCorp Wisconsin is the holding company for AnchorBank which has more than 50 branches across the Badger State. The thrift courts individuals and local businesses offering checking and savings accounts credit cards CDs and IRAs as well as insurance and investment products. Founded in 1919 AnchorBank is predominantly a real estate lender with residential and commercial mortgages and construction and land loans accounting for the majority of its loan portfolio. Like many other banks though AnchorBank is struggling with its capital levels due to real estate-related losses. The company has sold some of its branches to raise capital.

	Annual Growth	03/11	03/12	03/13*	12/13	12/14
Assets ($ mil.)	(15.0%)	3,394.8	2,789.5	2,367.6	2,112.5	2,082.4
Net income ($ mil.)	-	(41.2)	(36.7)	(34.2)	111.6	14.6
Market value ($ mil.)	-	-	-	-	-	328.8
Employees	(7.1%)	817	738	690	693	656

*Fiscal year change

ANCHOR GLASS CONTAINER CORPORATION

401 E. Jackson St. Ste. 2800
Tampa FL 33602
Phone: 813-884-0000
Fax: 212-549-2646
Web: www.aclu.org

CEO: James J Fredlake
CFO: Wilkes G Kenneth
HR: Mark Karrenbauer
FYE: December 31
Type: Private

In a sea of options Anchor Glass Container anchors its business on manufacturing sustainable safe attractive glass packaging. One the leading glass container-makers in the US — it ranks behind Owens-Illinois and Saint-Gobain Containers Anchor Glass Container serves primarily manufacturers of beverages beer and liquor and foods and other consumer goods. It produces clear and colored-glass containers in a myriad of sizes via eight glassmaking plants and one for making moulds. For years the company's largest customer has included beer giant Anheuser-Busch. Anchor Glass Container's lineup also caters to Snapple LiDestri Foods and High Falls Brewing. The company is controlled by Wayzata Investment Partners.

ANDALAY SOLAR INC

NBB: WEST

2721 Shattuck Avenue, #305
Berkeley, CA 94705
Phone: 408 402-9400
Fax: -
Web: www.andalaysolar.com

CEO: Steven Chan
CFO: -
HR: -
FYE: December 31
Type: Public

Ask anyone at Akeena about their company's name and they'll tell you Akeena was the mistress of the Greek sun god Apollo. The company (which does business under the Westinghouse Solar name as the result of a 2010 partnership agreement) designs markets and sells solar power systems for residential and small commercial customers. Akeena was founded in 2001 and by early 2009 had installed more than 3000 solar power systems at schools wineries restaurants housing developments and other locations. However the company exited the installation business in 2009 to concentrate on manufacturing and distribution. Previously limited to six states the company now distributes in some 34 states and in Canada.

	Annual Growth	12/10	12/11	12/12	12/13	12/14
Sales ($ mil.)	(37.9%)	8.7	11.4	5.2	1.1	1.3
Net income ($ mil.)	-	(12.9)	(4.6)	(8.6)	(2.8)	(1.9)
Market value ($ mil.)	(55.9%)	131.9	89.4	12.6	6.1	5.0
Employees	(26.4%)	34	31	7	9	10

ANDERSEN CONSTRUCTION COMPANY

6712 N CUTTER CIR
PORTLAND, OR 972173933
Phone: 503-283-6712
Fax: -
Web: www.andersen-const.com

CEO: -
CFO: Bill Eckhardt
HR: -
FYE: January 31
Type: Private

Andersen Construction Company focuses on commercial and industrial construction in the Western US. The group which introduced concrete tilt-up construction to the Pacific Northwest builds everything from parking structures to medical facilities manufacturing plants and industrial complexes. It also works on institutional projects for the government and education markets. Other projects include tenant improvements seismic upgrades and remediation construction. The company provides construction management (which accounts for 80% of its work) as well as general contracting and design/build delivery. It also offers startup and commissioning services. Chairman and CEO Andy Andersen founded the company in 1950.

	Annual Growth	01/04	01/05	01/06	01/11	01/14
Sales ($ mil.)	-	-	(274.1)	198.2	279.0	329.5
Net income ($ mil.)	(8.8%)	-	-	1.0	1.0	0.5
Market value ($ mil.)	-	-	-	-	-	-
Employees	-	-	-	-	-	150

ANDERSEN CORPORATION

100 4th Ave. North
Bayport MN 55003-1096
Phone: 651-264-5150
Fax: 651-264-5107
Web: www.andersenwindows.com

CEO: Jay Lund
CFO: Philip E Donaldson
HR: -
FYE: December 31
Type: Private

Windows of opportunity abound for Andersen a maker of wood-clad windows and patio doors in North America. Andersen offers window designs from hinged bay and double-hung to skylight gliding and picture windows. Its Renewal by Andersen subsidiary provides start-to-finish window renewal services in more than 100 markets in the US. Anderson Storm Doors makes storm and screen doors. Through independent and company-owned distributorships (including its Andersen Logistics division) Andersen sells to homeowners architects builders designers and remodelers. The company which builds some 12 million doors and windows each year at more than 15 factories is owned by the Andersen family and company employees.

ANDERSON AND DUBOSE INC.

5300 TOD AVE SW
WARREN, OH 444819767
Phone: 440-248-8800
Fax: -
Web: www.anderson-dubose.com

CEO: -
CFO: -
HR: Linsey Gray
FYE: December 30
Type: Private

You might say this company keeps the Big Mac big and the Happy Meals happy. Anderson-DuBose Pittsburgh is a leading wholesale distributor that supplies food and non-food items to McDonald's and Chipotle fast-food restaurants in Ohio Pennsylvania New York and West Virginia. It serves about 500 Golden Arches locations with frozen meat and fish dairy products and paper goods and packaging as well as toys for Happy Meals. One of the largest black-owned companies in the US Anderson-DuBose was started in 1991 by Warren Anderson and Stephen DuBose who purchased control of a McDonald's distributorship from Martin-Brower. Anderson became sole owner in 1993 when he bought out his partner's stake in the business.

	Annual Growth	12/07	12/08	12/09	12/10	12/11
Sales ($ mil.)	-	-	-	(757.8)	341.7	372.9
Net income ($ mil.)	7130.5%	-	-	0.0	1.7	1.2
Market value ($ mil.)	-	-	-	-	-	-
Employees	-	-	-	-	-	100

ANDERSON KILL & OLICK P.C.

1251 Avenue of the Americas
New York NY 10020
Phone: 212-278-1000
Fax: 212-278-1733
Web: www.andersonkill.com

CEO: Robert M Horkovich
CFO: -
HR: -
FYE: December 31
Type: Private - Partnershi

Law firm Anderson Kill & Olick is well known for representing policyholders in recovery claims against insurance companies. Other practice areas include anti-counterfeiting bankruptcy business litigation financial services employment and labor law and real estate and construction. The firm represents businesses governmental entities nonprofits and personal estates. Its 100 attorneys practice from offices in Greenwich Connecticut; Newark New Jersey; New York; Philadelphia; Ventura California; and Washington DC. Anderson Kill was founded in 1969.

ANDERSON TRUCKING SERVICE INC.

725 Opportunity Dr.
St. Cloud MN 56301
Phone: 320-255-7400
Fax: 320-255-7438
Web: www.atsinc.com

CEO: Rollie Anderson
CFO: Scott Fuller
HR: Joyce Steussy
FYE: December 31
Type: Private

Anderson Trucking Service (ATS) moves cargo that ranges from cranes to chairs. The company's ATS Specialized unit transports heavy equipment and other cargo requiring flatbed trailers; an offshoot concentrates on wind energy equipment. Its ATS Van Solutions unit offers dry van truckload transportation and other operations transport new furniture for manufacturers. Overall the company's trucking units operate a fleet of some 2400 tractors and 8600 trailers. ATS also offers logistics services including international freight forwarding. Harold Anderson established the family-owned business in 1955.

ANDERSONS, INC.

480 W. Dussel Drive
Maumee, OH 43537
Phone: 419 893-5050
Fax: -
Web: www.andersonsinc.com

NMS: ANDE
CEO: Patrick E. (Pat) Bowe
CFO: John J. Granato
HR: Chuck Gallagher
FYE: December 31
Type: Public

The Andersons earns its daily bread on a mix of grains trains and corncobs. The agricultural company's main business — its Grain and Ethanol segments — consists of the buying conditioning and reselling of corn soybeans and wheat which it acquires from US grain farmers and stores. To support the operation it uses a system of elevators and terminals located in the Midwest. Its Grain and Ethanol units account for more than 75% of annual sales. The Andersons also boasts a Plant Nutrient/Turf & Specialty Group a Retail Group and a Rail Group. The agricultural firm operates in the US in 16 states as well as in Puerto Rico. The company also has rail-leasing interests in Canada and Mexico.

	Annual Growth	12/10	12/11	12/12	12/13	12/14
Sales ($ mil.)	7.5%	3,393.8	4,576.3	5,272.0	5,604.6	4,540.1
Net income ($ mil.)	14.1%	64.7	95.1	79.5	89.9	109.7
Market value ($ mil.)	10.0%	1,052.8	1,264.5	1,242.5	2,582.6	1,539.1
Employees	3.3%	2,943	2,985	3,111	3,238	3,345

ANDREA ELECTRONICS CORP.
NBB: ANDR

620 Johnson Avenue Suite 1-B
Bohemia, NY 11716
Phone: 631 719-1800
Fax: –

CEO: –
CFO: Corisa L Guiffre
HR: Vicki Tursi
FYE: December 31
Type: Public

Andrea Electronics wants to make a big noise with its Anti-Noise technology. The company's Anti-Noise products include software that increases voice clarity and reduces background noise plus headsets that enhance audio in high-noise environments. Andrea Electronics also offers voice recognition products for voice-activated computing applications such as word processing. The company designs its products for audio- and videoconferencing call centers in-vehicle communications and personal computing. Andrea Electronics sells directly and through distributors software publishers ISPs and other resellers. The company gets most of its sales in the US.

	Annual Growth	12/10	12/11	12/12	12/13	12/14
Sales ($ mil.)	(19.1%)	6.5	5.5	3.3	3.3	2.8
Net income ($ mil.)	–	(0.1)	(0.5)	(1.5)	(1.1)	(2.9)
Market value ($ mil.)	2.2%	4.5	3.8	2.0	3.5	4.9
Employees	(6.9%)	20	19	18	17	15

ANGELICA CORPORATION

1105 Lakewood Pkwy. Ste. 210
Alpharetta GA 30009
Phone: 678-823-4100
Fax: 678-823-4165
Web: www.angelica.com

CEO: David A Van Vliet
CFO: –
HR: –
FYE: January 31
Type: Private

Hospitals don't have to move heaven and earth to get clean sheets — Angelica will do it for them. The firm provides laundry services and rents linens to more than 4200 health care providers including dentists medical clinics hospitals and nursing homes. It rents and cleans scrubs bed sheets towels gowns and surgical linens. Angelica also provides mops mats sterile surgical packs and on-site linen room management. The firm operates about 30 laundry service centers across the US. Angelica traces its roots back to 1878 when it was established as a uniform manufacturer. It is owned by private equity firm Trilantic Capital Partners.

ANGELO STATE UNIVERSITY

2601 W AVENUE N
SAN ANGELO, TX 769095099
Phone: 325-942-2555
Fax: –
Web: www.angelo.edu

CEO: –
CFO: Sharon Meyer
HR: –
FYE: August 31
Type: Private

Out in the West Texas town of San Angelo (a community of 100000) more than 6000 students attend Angelo State University (ASU). The school offers approximately 45 undergraduate programs of study at its College of Liberal and Fine Arts College of Education College of Business and College of Sciences. ASU also has a School of Graduate Studies that offers nearly 30 master's degree programs. It also offers one doctorate program. With more than 330 faculty members its student-teacher ratio is 20:1. ASU is part of the Texas Tech University System.

	Annual Growth	08/10	08/11	08/12	08/13	08/14
Sales ($ mil.)	0.2%	–	60.6	64.0	64.7	60.9
Net income ($ mil.)	164.8%	–	–	0.7	12.1	5.2
Market value ($ mil.)	–	–	–	–	–	–
Employees	–	–	–	–	–	550

ANGELS BASEBALL LP

2000 Gene Autry Way
Anaheim CA 92806
Phone: 714-940-2000
Fax: 714-940-2001
Web: www.angelsbaseball.com

CEO: –
CFO: Andrew Roundtree
HR: –
FYE: December 31
Type: Private

Los Angeles' other baseball team actually resides in Anaheim California. Angels Baseball owns and operates the Los Angeles Angels of Anaheim professional baseball franchise. The team originally owned by cowboy actor Gene Autry joined Major League Baseball as an expansion franchise in 1960 and has boasted such Hall of Fame talent as Rod Carew and Nolan Ryan. However Angels fans had to wait until 2002 for the team to win its first American League pennant and World Series title. Phoenix businessman Arturo Moreno who has owned the team since 2003 was the first Hispanic to own a major sports franchise in the US.

ANGIE'S LIST INC.
NMS: ANGI

1030 E. Washington Street
Indianapolis, IN 46202
Phone: 888 888-5478
Fax: –
Web: www.angieslist.com

CEO: Scott Durschslag
CFO: Thomas R. Fox
HR: Christine Grebenc
FYE: December 31
Type: Public

Better not get on Angie's bad side — she's got a list. Angie's List provides consumer ratings on companies in the service industry. Consumers rate local providers in more than 550 business service categories including roofing plumbing home remodeling and doctors. The company has amassed a collection of some 2.2 million reviews receiving about 40000 new reviews each month from consumers in 175 markets across the US. Revenues come from ads and subscription fees. Angie's List has more than 1 million paying members who access ratings and reviews via AngiesList.com and Angie's List Magazine. The firm was founded by Angie Hicks and Bill Oesterle in 1995. It filed to go public in 2011.

	Annual Growth	12/10	12/11	12/12	12/13	12/14
Sales ($ mil.)	52.0%	59.0	90.0	155.8	245.6	315.0
Net income ($ mil.)	–	(27.2)	(49.0)	(52.9)	(33.0)	(12.1)
Market value ($ mil.)	(27.1%)	–	942.1	701.6	886.5	364.6
Employees	26.4%	726	349	1,158	1,637	1,852

ANGIODYNAMICS INC
NMS: ANGO

14 Plaza Drive
Latham, NY 12110
Phone: 518 795-1400
Fax: –
Web: www.angiodynamics.com

CEO: Joseph M. (Joe) DeVivo
CFO: Michael Trimarchi
HR: –
FYE: May 31
Type: Public

AngioDynamics makes therapeutic and diagnostic medical devices for veins that have become a pain. Doctors use its array of devices in minimally invasive procedures to treat cancer; peripheral vascular disease (PVD) in which arteries or veins in the arms legs or kidneys become blocked or restricted by plaque; and other non-coronary diseases. Products include laser systems that ablate varicose veins angiographic catheters that deliver drugs and contrast agents for imaging dialysis catheters for those with renal failure abscess drainage devices and radiofrequency ablation devices that help destroy tumors. AngioDynamics markets and sells directly in the US and through distributors and directly internationally.

	Annual Growth	05/11	05/12	05/13	05/14	05/15
Sales ($ mil.)	13.4%	215.8	221.8	342.0	354.5	357.0
Net income ($ mil.)	–	8.1	(5.1)	(0.6)	3.1	(3.3)
Market value ($ mil.)	0.5%	563.7	432.3	390.6	514.5	576.2
Employees	15.8%	722	1,400	1,330	1,300	1,300

ANGSTROM GRAPHICS INC.

2025 McKinley St.
Hollywood FL 33020
Phone: 954-920-7300
Fax: 212-613-9565
Web: www.redcats.com

CEO: Wayne R Angstrom
CFO: Rachel Malakoff
HR: —
FYE: July 31
Type: Private

Angstrom Graphics loves it when its customers get graphic. The company provides prepress printing finishing and fulfillment services for catalogs magazines and newspapers. It also prints annual reports brochures and marketing materials. Angstrom Graphics also offers graphic arts and digital photography production services including redesigns copywriting and image retouching. The firm operates facilities in Ohio and Florida. In 2009 Angstrom Graphics formerly named St Ives US Division was sold by European printing group St Ives through a management-led buyout.

ANHEUSER-BUSCH COMPANIES INC.

1 Busch Place
St. Louis MO 63118-1852
Phone: 314-577-2000
Fax: 314-577-2900
Web: www.anheuser-busch.com

CEO: Carlos Brito
CFO: W Randolph Baker
HR: —
FYE: December 31
Type: Subsidiary

Anheuser-Busch (A-B) has brewed up a billion-dollar business with its Buds. The company is best known for brewing Budweiser one of the world's largest-selling beers by volume. Other A-B labels include Bud Light Busch Michelob O'Doul's and Kirin under license. As part of its business the company also owns a 50% stake in Mexico's GRUPO MODELO maker of beers under the Corona and Negra Modelo names. Besides beer A-B produces distilled beverages energy drinks and non-alcoholic malt beverages. The company has operated as a subsidiary of Anheuser-Busch InBev (AB InBev) the world's largest beer maker since the Belgium brewer acquired A-B for $52 billion in 2008.

ANI PHARMACEUTICALS, INC.   NMS: ANIP

210 Main Street West
Baudette, MN 56623
Phone: 218 634-3500
Fax: —
Web: www.biosantepharma.com

CEO: Arthur S. Przybyl
CFO: Phillip B. Donenberg
HR: Patricia M Adams
FYE: December 31
Type: Public

ANI Pharmaceuticals (formerly BioSante) wants to stabilize hormonal ups and downs. The firm is developing topical hormone therapy gels to deliver supplemental estrogen progestogen and testosterone. Its Elestrin product is a transdermal estrogen gel used to treat menopausal symptoms while its Bio-T-Gel treats hypogonadism a form of testosterone deficiency in men that can cause impotence and bone or muscle weakness. The company's development-stage candidates include a gel to treat female sexual dysfunction (LibiGel) as well as contraceptive-compatible hormone therapies (Pill-Plus). The firm is also developing potential cancer vaccine therapies. BioSante acquired drug manufacturer ANI Pharmaceuticals in 2013 and took its name.

	Annual Growth	12/10	12/11	12/12	12/13	12/14
Sales ($ mil.)	118.1%	2.5	0.4	2.3	30.1	56.0
Net income ($ mil.)	—	(46.2)	(51.6)	(27.7)	0.3	28.7
Market value ($ mil.)	142.1%	18.7	5.7	14.0	228.9	642.8
Employees	19.6%	45	54	23	81	92

ANIKA THERAPEUTICS INC.   NMS: ANIK

32 Wiggins Avenue
Bedford, MA 01730
Phone: 781 457-9000
Fax: —
Web: www.anikatherapeutics.com

CEO: Charles H. Sherwood
CFO: Sylvia Cheung
HR: Steven Cyr
FYE: December 31
Type: Public

Anika Therapeutics uses hyaluronic acid (HA) a natural polymer extracted from rooster combs and other sources to make products that treat bone cartilage and soft tissue. Anika's Orthovisc treats osteoarthritis of the knee and other joints and is available in the US and overseas. (DePuy Mitek sells the product in the US.) The company also makes and sells products that maintain eye shape and protect tissue during eye surgery some of which are marketed by Bausch & Lomb. Other items include surgical anti-adhesive products veterinary osteoarthritis therapies and dermatology products. The US accounts for about three-fourths of sales.

	Annual Growth	12/10	12/11	12/12	12/13	12/14
Sales ($ mil.)	17.4%	55.6	64.8	71.4	75.1	105.6
Net income ($ mil.)	72.6%	4.3	8.5	11.8	20.6	38.3
Market value ($ mil.)	57.2%	99.1	145.5	147.6	566.7	605.1
Employees	(2.7%)	114	129	106	102	102

ANIXTER INTERNATIONAL INC   NYS: AXE

2301 Patriot Blvd.
Glenview, IL 60026
Phone: 224 521-8000
Fax: —
Web: www.anixter.com

CEO: Robert J. (Bob) Eck
CFO: Theodore A. (Ted) Dosch
HR: Rodney A. Smith
FYE: January 02
Type: Public

When it comes to getting wired Anixter International's got the connections. The company is a distributor of communication products used to connect voice video data and security systems. It sells 400000-plus products including electrical and electronic wire cable and security system components to some 125000 customers in a host of industries. Anixter operates primarily through special sales forces — Electric and Electronic Wire and Cable and Enterprise Cabling and Security Solutions — operating from about 250 warehouses and sales centers in 50 countries. Although Anixter gets its products from thousands of suppliers almost one-third come from just five companies.

	Annual Growth	12/10	12/11	12/12*	01/14	01/15
Sales ($ mil.)	3.3%	5,472.1	6,146.9	6,253.1	6,226.5	6,445.5
Net income ($ mil.)	12.4%	108.5	188.2	124.8	200.5	194.8
Market value ($ mil.)	8.1%	1,979.6	1,976.6	2,076.0	2,969.9	2,922.5
Employees	2.6%	7,989	8,200	8,300	8,200	9,100

*Fiscal year change

ANN & ROBERT H. LURIE CHILDREN'S HOSPITAL OF CHICAGO

225 E CHICAGO AVE
CHICAGO, IL 606112991
Phone: 312-227-4000
Fax: —
Web: www.luriechildrens.org

CEO: Patrick M Magoon
CFO: Paula Noble
HR: —
FYE: August 31
Type: Private

When it comes to caring for kids Ann & Robert H. Lurie Children's Hospital of Chicago has the Windy City covered. Founded in 1882 the not-for-profit hospital provides a full range of pediatric services with acute and specialty care. Lurie Children's provides services through its main hospital campus with about 300 beds and outpatient centers in Chicago's Lincoln Park neighborhood and through more than a dozen suburban outpatient centers and outreach partner locations in the greater Chicago area. A leader in pediatric research the hospital operates the Children's Hospital of Chicago Research Center and is the pediatric teaching facility of Northwestern University's Feinberg School of Medicine.

	Annual Growth	08/07	08/08	08/09	08/10	08/13
Sales ($ mil.)	11.1%	—	410.3	534.0	599.3	694.2
Net income ($ mil.)	—	—	—	(5.2)	53.0	28.8
Market value ($ mil.)	—	—	—	—	—	—
Employees	—	—	—	—	—	2,800

ANN INC
NYS: ANN

7 Times Square
New York, NY 10036
Phone: 212 541-3300
Fax: –
Web: www.anntaylor.com

CEO: Kay Krill
CFO: Michael J Nicholson
HR: –
FYE: February 01
Type: Public

ANN: a name favored by royalty and commoners as well as a company recognized for its aspirational luxury and feminine wear-to-work style. The national retailer specializes in women's clothing shoes and accessories designed and sold exclusively under its Ann Taylor and LOFT monikers. The Ann Taylor brand targets fashion-conscious career women through about 375 namesake stores (about 110 of which are "Factory" outlets) while the LOFT brand offers moderate-to-more priced casual apparel through some 650 stores (110 of which are outlets). ANN also moves merchandise for both brands through its fast-growing online business. ANN has favored its own name since changing from AnnTaylor Stores Corporation in 2011.

	Annual Growth	01/10	01/11	01/12*	02/13	02/14
Sales ($ mil.)	8.1%	1,828.5	1,980.2	2,212.5	2,375.5	2,493.5
Net income ($ mil.)	–	(18.2)	73.4	86.6	102.6	102.4
Market value ($ mil.)	26.7%	580.5	1,009.9	1,129.1	1,426.8	1,494.7
Employees	1.3%	18,800	19,400	19,900	19,600	19,800

*Fiscal year change

ANNALY CAPITAL MANAGEMENT INC
NYS: NLY

1211 Avenue of the Americas
New York, NY 10036
Phone: 212 696-0100
Fax: 212 696-9809
Web: www.annaly.com

CEO: Kevin G. Keyes
CFO: Glenn A. Votek
HR: –
FYE: December 31
Type: Public

Annaly cannily invests its capital. A real estate investment trust (REIT) Annaly Capital Management invests in and manages a portfolio of mortgage-backed securities including mortgage pass-through certificates collateralized mortgage obligations and agency callable debentures. Commencing operations in 1997 the firm primarily invests in high-quality securities issued or guaranteed by the likes of Freddie Mac Fannie Mae and Ginnie Mae and backed by single-family residential mortgages. More than 95% of Annaly's assets are agency mortgage-backed securities which carry an implied AAA rating. The firm is externally managed by Annaly Management Company LLC.

	Annual Growth	12/10	12/11	12/12	12/13	12/14
Assets ($ mil.)	1.6%	83,026.6	109,630.0	133,452.3	81,922.5	88,355.4
Net income ($ mil.)	–	1,267.3	344.5	1,735.9	3,729.7	(842.1)
Market value ($ mil.)	(11.9%)	16,981.8	15,124.4	13,304.9	9,448.0	10,244.0
Employees	(31.6%)	114	147	147	48	25

ANNE ARUNDEL MEDICAL CENTER INC.

2001 MEDICAL PKWY
ANNAPOLIS, MD 214013280
Phone: 443-481-1000
Fax: –
Web: www.annearundeldiagnostics.com

CEO: –
CFO: –
HR: –
FYE: June 30
Type: Private

The ill and infirm get the royal treatment at Anne Arundel Medical Center. The full-service acute-care hospital serves the residents of Anne Arundel Calvert Prince George's and Queen Anne counties in Maryland. With about 425 beds the hospital administers care for women's health oncology pediatrics (it has a level III neonatal intensive care unit) neurology orthopedics and cardiovascular care. The medical center also has weight loss sleep disorder and rehabilitation centers. Anne Arundel which opened its doors in 1902 and is part of the Anne Arundel Health System has expanded its service offerings through various affiliations with regional specialty and primary care clinics. It also has a partnership with Johns Hopkins Medicine.

	Annual Growth	06/08	06/09	06/10	06/11	06/13
Sales ($ mil.)	–	–	–	0.0	413.9	445.3	493.1
Net income ($ mil.)	(6.1%)	–	–	20.3	24.1	16.8
Market value ($ mil.)	–	–	–	–	–	–
Employees	–	–	–	–	–	1,890

ANNIE'S INC
NYS: BNNY

1610 Fifth Street
Berkeley, CA 94710
Phone: 510 558-7500
Fax: –
Web: www.annies.com

CEO: John Foraker
CFO: Kelly J Kennedy
HR: –
FYE: March 31
Type: Public

While doing what it loves Annie's also wouldn't mind taking a bite out of Kraft's business. An organic and natural food producer Annie's makes about 125 products consisting of pastas cereals dressings condiments and snacks through its Annie's Homegrown and Annie's Naturals units. Annie's Homegrown banner includes boxed organic macaroni and cheese breakfast cereals (Cinna Bunnies) fruit snacks (Bunny Fruit) organic granola bars and organic ready meals. Under the Annie's Naturals name the company offers organic and natural salad dressings condiments (marinades sauces mustard ketchup) and olive oil. Annie's which began trading in 2012 is 63%-owned by private equity firm Solera Capital.

	Annual Growth	03/09	03/10	03/11	03/12	03/13
Sales ($ mil.)	16.1%	93.6	96.0	117.6	141.3	170.0
Net income ($ mil.)	–	(1.0)	6.0	20.2	9.6	11.6
Market value ($ mil.)	9.8%	–	–	–	587.0	644.6
Employees	15.1%	–	–	86	93	114

ANOMATIC CORPORATION

1650 Tamarack Rd.
Newark OH 43055
Phone: 740-522-2203
Fax: 740-522-3339
Web: www.anomatic.com

CEO: William B Rusch
CFO: –
HR: Kristen Marinzel
FYE: December 31
Type: Private

Anomatic has made anodizing aluminum into an art form. The company anodizes stamps and packages small aluminum parts which are made into such products as cosmetics containers and packaging hand tools jewelry musical instruments and plumbing fittings. Its Anomatic anodizing process (by which an oxide coating is formed on aluminum to provide a corrosive resistant and decorative finish) was the first automated belt conveyor system built for high speed high volume anodizing of small aluminum parts. Anomatic operates eight anodizing lines which run two shifts per day and generate a monthly production of 80 million anodized components. Customers include Estee Lauder Mary Kay and Revlon.

ANR PIPELINE COMPANY

717 Texas Ave.
Houston TX 77002
Phone: 832-320-5000
Fax: 805-445-4925
Web: www.harborfreight.com

CEO: Lee Hobbs
CFO: –
HR: –
FYE: December 31
Type: Subsidiary

ANR Pipeline keeps natural gas in line a pipeline that is. The company operates one of the largest interstate natural gas pipeline systems in the US. A subsidiary of TransCanada Corp. ANR controls about 10350 miles of pipeline and delivers more than 1 trillion cu. ft. of natural gas per year. The company primarily serves customers in the Midwest but through its network is capable of connecting to all major gas basins in North America. In tandem with its ANR Storage and Blue Lake Gas Storage subsidiaries ANR Pipeline also provides natural gas storage services and has ownership interests in more than 250 billion cu. ft. of underground natural gas storage capacity.

ANSCHUTZ COMPANY

555 17th St. Ste. 2400
Denver CO 80202
Phone: 303-298-1000
Fax: 303-298-8881

CEO: Phillip Anschutz
CFO: Wayne Barnes
HR: –
FYE: December 31
Type: Private

Denver multibillionaire Philip Anschutz is a man of varied interests. His holding company includes an eclectic stable of entertainment media and sports businesses in addition to telecom and energy development. Through Anschutz Entertainment Group (AEG) Anschutz promotes concerts and other events and owns 120 sports and entertainment centers such as Staples Center and Best Buy Theater. It also owns soccer and other pro teams in the US and Europe (including the NHL's Los Angeles Kings and a stake in the Los Angeles Lakers). Other Anschutz holdings include movie chain Regal Entertainment Group the family-oriented Anschutz Film Group and the San Francisco Examiner newspaper.

ANSEN CORPORATION

100 Chimney Point Dr.
Ogdensburg NY 13669-2289
Phone: 315-393-3573
Fax: 315-393-7638
Web: www.ansencorp.com

CEO: James Kingman
CFO: –
HR: Tim Perry
FYE: March 31
Type: Private

Ansen offers electronics design and manufacturing services to makers of microelectronics systems and components. Ansen provides services such as printed circuit board surface mounting and assembly from manufacturing facilities in China Hong Kong and the US. It also offers design prototyping and engineering services as well as packaging distribution warranty and support. The company's products are used in medical instruments computers telecommunications gear and industrial controls. Ansen was taken private by management in 2003 and then combined with fellow EMS firm InnerStep in 2004. Ansen divested two US plants in 2005 in favor of expanding Chinese operations.

ANSYS INC.

2600 ANSYS Drive
Canonsburg, PA 15317
Phone: 724 746-3304
Fax: –
Web: www.ansys.com

NMS: ANSS
CEO: James E. (Jim) Cashman
CFO: Maria T. Shields
HR: –
FYE: December 31
Type: Public

It's good to look before you leap – and even before you make. That's why ANSYS helps designers and engineers see how their ideas play out even before a prototype is built by simulating designs on a computer. The company's software analyzes the models for their response to combinations of such physical variables as stress pressure impact temperature and velocity. Ranging from small consulting firms to multinational enterprises its customers come from a broad range of industries and have included Delphi Airbus Invensys and Plexus. ANSYS generates two-thirds of its revenue from outside the US with Japan and Germany among its leading international markets.

	Annual Growth	12/10	12/11	12/12	12/13	12/14
Sales ($ mil.)	12.7%	580.2	691.4	798.0	861.3	936.0
Net income ($ mil.)	13.6%	153.1	180.7	203.5	245.3	254.7
Market value ($ mil.)	12.0%	4,726.2	5,199.0	6,112.1	7,914.7	7,442.8
Employees	12.9%	1,660	2,100	2,400	2,600	2,700

ANTARES PHARMA INC.

100 Princeton South, Suite 300
Ewing, NJ 08628
Phone: 609 359-3020
Fax: –
Web: www.antarespharma.com

NAS: ATRS
CEO: Robert F. Apple
CFO: James E. (Jim) Fickenscher
HR: –
FYE: December 31
Type: Public

Antares Pharma understands antagonism towards needles. The company develops needle-free systems for administering injectable drugs. Its Medi-Jector Vision system for instance injects a thin high-pressure stream of liquid eliminating the need for a needle. The Vision system is used primarily for the delivery of insulin and of human growth hormones (hGH) and Vibex disposable pen injectors carry epinephrine and other products. The products are available in the US and overseas. In addition to its needle-free systems the company develops other drug-delivery platforms including topical gels orally administered disintegrating tablets and mini-needle injection systems.

	Annual Growth	12/10	12/11	12/12	12/13	12/14
Sales ($ mil.)	19.9%	12.8	16.5	22.6	20.6	26.5
Net income ($ mil.)	–	(6.1)	(4.4)	(11.4)	(20.5)	(35.2)
Market value ($ mil.)	10.9%	224.0	289.8	501.9	589.0	338.6
Employees	45.1%	21	29	42	60	93

ANTERO RESOURCES CORP

1615 Wynkoop Street
Denver, CO 80202
Phone: 303 357-7310
Fax: –
Web: www.anteroresources.com

NYS: AR
CEO: Paul M. Rady
CFO: Glen C. Warren
HR: –
FYE: December 31
Type: Public

While Mount Antero is located more than 14000 feet about sea level in Colorado Antero Resources is more concerned with what's beneath the earth's surface. The company explores for and produces oil natural gas and natural gas liquids (NGLs) across more than 400000 acres in the Appalachian Basin in West Virginia Ohio and Pennsylvania. It reports proved reserves of almost 5 trillion cu. ft. of natural gas. In 2013 the company produced an average of 383 million cu. ft. of natural gas per day including almost 2400 barrels per day of oil and NGLs using horizontal drilling and hydraulic fracturing techniques. Founded in 2002 Antero Resources went public in 2013 raising more than $1.5 billion in its IPO.

	Annual Growth	12/10	12/11	12/12	12/13	12/14
Sales ($ mil.)	116.0%	125.0	691.4	735.7	1,313.1	2,720.6
Net income ($ mil.)	31.0%	228.6	392.7	(285.1)	(18.9)	673.6
Market value ($ mil.)	(36.0%)	–	–	–	16,625.8	10,634.9
Employees	55.3%	–	–	184	233	444

ANTHELIO HEALTHCARE SOLUTIONS INC.

5400 LBJ Fwy. Ste. 200
Dallas TX 75240
Phone: 214-257-7000
Fax: 214-257-7042
Web: www.antheliohealth.com

CEO: Asif Ahmad
CFO: Jeff Robertson
HR: –
FYE: September 30
Type: Private

Anthelio (formerly PHNS) provides IT consulting and cloud computing services to hospitals private physicians and other health care businesses across the US. Its offerings provide assistance with admission/registration medical records management and electronic medical records implementations coding and transcription and revenue cycle management. The company also provides data center services network security protection disaster recovery and electronic data backup and recovery. Anthelio counts Symantec Healthland and Microsoft among its technology partners. Clients include Fairfield California-based NorthBay Healthcare and Plano Texas-based Legacy Hospital Partners.

ANTHEM INC NYS: ANTM

120 Monument Circle
Indianapolis, IN 46204-4903
Phone: 317 488-6000
Fax: –
Web: www.antheminc.com

CEO: Joseph R. Swedish
CFO: Wayne S. DeVeydt
HR: Jose D. Tomas
FYE: December 31
Type: Public

Health benefits provider Anthem (formerly WellPoint) is the king of the Blues. Through its subsidiaries the firm provides health coverage to nearly 40 million members. One of the largest health insurers in the US it is a Blue Cross and Blue Shield Association (BCBSA) licensee in more than a dozen states (where it operates under the Anthem Empire and BCBS monikers) and provides plans under the Unicare Amerigroup and CareMore names in other parts of the country. Plans include PPO HMO indemnity and hybrid plans offered to employers individuals and Medicare and Medicaid recipients. It also provides administrative services to self-insured groups as well as specialty insurance products. In mid-2015 Anthem agreed to acquire rival Cigna.

	Annual Growth	12/10	12/11	12/12	12/13	12/14
Sales ($ mil.)	5.9%	58,801.8	60,710.7	61,711.7	71,023.5	73,874.1
Net income ($ mil.)	(2.9%)	2,887.1	2,646.7	2,655.5	2,489.7	2,569.7
Market value ($ mil.)	21.9%	15,244.7	17,762.3	16,333.3	24,770.7	33,693.4
Employees	8.3%	37,500	37,700	43,500	48,200	51,500

ANTHERA PHARMACEUTICALS INC. NASDAQ: ANTH

25801 Industrial Blvd. Ste. B
Hayward CA 94545
Phone: 510-856-5600
Fax: 510-856-5597
Web: www.anthera.com

CEO: Paul F Truex
CFO: –
HR: –
FYE: December 31
Type: Public

Anthera Pharmaceuticals is involved in some very complicated sounding (not to mention hard to say) drug development. Its lead product varespladib methyl is in late stage clinical trials to treat acute coronary syndrome. Other candidates include A-623 to treat lupus and varespladib sodium to treat acute chest syndrome. Varespladib is designed to inhibit an enzyme called sPLA2 that is implicated in a variety of acute inflammatory conditions such as cardiovascular disease sickle cell disease and coronary artery disease. Since its founding in 2004 Anthera's operations have consisted primarily of research and development activities. The company went public in early 2010 in an IPO worth about $37 million.

ANTHONY & SYLVAN POOLS CORPORATION

Mt. Vernon Sq. 6690 Beta Dr. Ste. 300
Mayfield Village OH 44143
Phone: 440-720-3301
Fax: 440-720-3303
Web: www.anthonysylvan.com

CEO: Stuart D Neidus
CFO: Martin Iles
HR: –
FYE: December 31
Type: Private

Pooling resources is second nature to Anthony & Sylvan Pools Corporation. The company created through the 1996 union of industry leaders Anthony Pools and Sylvan Pools installs custom in-ground concrete swimming pools for private residences. The company has roots dating back to 1946 and has installed more than 360000 pools during its history. It operates a network of more than 35 company-owned locations consisting of sales and design centers pool and spa renovation centers and retail service centers that sell pool accessories such as chemicals heaters filters pumps and pool toys. The company is active in Texas Nevada and 10 East Coast states.

ANTHONY DOORS INC.

12391 Montero Ave.
Sylmar CA 91342
Phone: 818-365-9451
Fax: 818-361-9611
Web: www.anthonydoors.com

CEO: Jeffrey Clark
CFO: David Lautenschaelger
HR: –
FYE: December 31
Type: Private

Anthony Doors can shed a little light on things that are pretty cool. The company makes glass refrigerator/freezer doors display case doors shelving mounts and lighting systems and display equipment for commercial refrigeration and merchandising end-use. Anthony Doors also offers custom glass units replacement parts and installation manuals and it manufactures custom-fabricated curved/bent glass used in display cases. The company primarily caters to grocery stores convenience stores and specialty retailers. Besides the US it has offices in Canada China and Italy. Founded in 1958 as Anthony's Refrigerations Service Company the company was sold to Dover Corporation in 2012.

ANTS SOFTWARE INC. OTC: ANTS

71 Stevenson St. Ste. 400
San Francisco CA 94105
Phone: 650-931-0500
Fax: 650-931-0510
Web: www.ants.com

CEO: Rik Sanchez
CFO: Elise Vetula
HR: –
FYE: December 31
Type: Public

ANTs software hopes to help your data march about in perfect order with no locking up. The company develops and markets software used to improve the performance of database-driven enterprise applications. ANTs' technology is designed to process and manipulate data with no database locking. Its primary product is its ANTs Compatibility Server which enables customers to move software applications from one company's database product to another. ANTs markets its products to information technology departments application developers and database architects. The company also provides professional services such as consulting training support implementation and maintenance.

ANVIL INTERNATIONAL INC.

110 Corporate Dr. Ste. 10
Portsmouth NH 03802-6822
Phone: 603-422-8000
Fax: 603-422-8033
Web: www.anvilint.com

CEO: Thomas E Fish
CFO: –
HR: –
FYE: December 31
Type: Subsidiary

In the hot red glow of industrial competition Anvil International hammers out its profits by making a comprehensive range of pipe fittings pipe hangers and related products and services. Anvil International (Anvil) manufactures cast iron fittings couplings pipe fittings pipe hangers seamless pipe nipples and valves. The company also provides basic design services such as fabrication drawings to extended design services for air handling units commercial piping oilfield piping and single-line routing systems. Anvil has 11 manufacturing facilities in the US and Canada. The company is a subsidiary of Atlanta-based Mueller Water Products which was spun off by Walter Industries in 2006.

ANWORTH MORTGAGE ASSET CORP.   NYS: ANH

1299 Ocean Avenue, Second Floor
Santa Monica, CA 90401
Phone: 310 255-4493
Fax: 310 434-0070
Web: www.anworth.com

CEO: Joseph Lloyd McAdams
CFO: Charles J. Siegel
HR: –
FYE: December 31
Type: Public

What's an Anworth? Depends on the mortgage market. An externally managed real estate investment trust (REIT) Anworth Mortgage invests in mortgage-related assets primarily mortgage-backed securities (MBS) guaranteed by the US government or federally sponsored entities Fannie Mae Freddie Mac and Ginnie Mae. As a REIT the trust is exempt from paying federal income tax so long as it distributes dividends back to shareholders. Anworth Mortgage funds its investment activities mainly through short-term loans.

	Annual Growth	12/10	12/11	12/12	12/13	12/14
Assets ($ mil.)	(1.6%)	7,790.2	8,813.8	9,285.1	8,619.5	7,298.3
Net income ($ mil.)	(28.7%)	110.5	122.9	100.2	75.7	28.6
Market value ($ mil.)	(6.9%)	764.6	686.0	631.4	459.9	573.5
Employees	–		12			

ANXEBUSINESS CORP.

2000 Town Center Ste. 2050
Southfield MI 48075
Phone: 248-263-3400
Fax: 248-356-9380
Web: www.anx.com

CEO: Rich Stanbaugh
CFO: –
HR: –
FYE: January 31
Type: Private

ANXeBusiness provides secure business-to-business network management and security services to companies worldwide. The company specializes in building and maintaining virtual private networks (VPN) for customers who want to outsource their data and security management operations in order to cut costs. It also implements networking software and offers managed services related to data translation business-to-business transactions and e-commerce systems under the ANXVelocity brand. ANXeBusiness is a subsidiary of equity investor One Equity Partners.

AOL ADVERTISING INC.

1020 Hull St. Ivory Bldg.
Baltimore MD 21230
Phone: 410-244-1370
Fax: 410-244-1699
Web: advertising.aol.com

CEO: Scott Ferber
CFO: Don Neff
HR: –
FYE: December 31
Type: Subsidiary

AOL Advertising (formerly Platform-A) offers a host of digital marketing and advertising services including display video mobile contextual and search marketing. Its sponsored listing network allows advertisers to target an ad's placement whether it be by site section or page. Its flagship product ADTECH is an ad serving platform enabling users to manage campaigns across various mediums including display video and mobile. As a whole AOL Advertising reaches more than 180 million consumers and its Advertising.com network is comprised of 6000 sites. Operating as a wholly owned subsidiary of AOL the company operates from a dozen offices in the US the UK and Japan.

AOL INC.   NYS: AOL

770 Broadway
New York, NY 10003
Phone: 212 652-6400
Fax: –
Web: www.corp.aol.com

CEO: Tim M Armstrong
CFO: Karen Dykstra
HR: –
FYE: December 31
Type: Public

Though it's no longer a part of Time Warner AOL is still serving America online. The Web portal serves users with an array of content and communication tools including sites for news (TheHuffingtonPost.com) maps (MapQuest) entertainment (Moviephone) local information (Patch) and technology (Engadget and TechCrunch). AOL primarily earns revenues through display search and contextual advertising (AOL Advertising) sales. It sells ads on AOL Properties as well as its Third Party Network (third-party sites). Search is provided through a deal with Google. AOL still offers dial-up Internet access to 3.3 million subscribers in the US. Time Warner spun off AOL to shareholders at the tail end of 2009.

	Annual Growth	12/09	12/10	12/11	12/12	12/13
Sales ($ mil.)	(8.1%)	3,257.4	2,416.7	2,202.1	2,191.7	2,319.9
Net income ($ mil.)	(21.9%)	248.8	(782.5)	13.1	1,048.4	92.4
Market value ($ mil.)	19.0%	1,843.8	1,877.8	1,195.9	2,345.1	3,692.3
Employees	(6.6%)	6,700	5,860	5,660	5,600	5,100

AON BENFIELD INC.

200 E. Randolph St.
Chicago IL 60601
Phone: 312-381-5300
Fax: 312-381-0160
Web: www.aonbenfield.com

CEO: –
CFO: –
HR: –
FYE: December 31
Type: Subsidiary

Aon Benfield is ensuring that those who are insuring won't go broke. The company is one of the world's leading reinsurance brokerages. It operates in more than 50 countries placing reinsurance coverage (protection for insurance companies against excessive losses on traditional insurance policies) as well as providing investment banking risk management consulting and catastrophe information forecasting services. The company's client services unit also offers accounting market security contract writing and claims processing services. Aon Benfield is a subsidiary of top global insurance broker Aon Corporation.

AOXING PHARMACEUTICALS CO., INC.   ASE: AXN

444 Washington Blvd, Suite 3338
Jersey City, NJ 07310
Phone: 646 367-1747
Fax: –
Web: www.aoxingpharma.com

CEO: Zhenjiang Yue
CFO: James Chen
HR: –
FYE: June 30
Type: Public

Narcotics are the name of the game for Aoxing Pharmaceutical which makes Naloxone and oxycodone products. Opioids are relatively new to China and the company has one of the only government-sanctioned manufacturing facilities; it is also the largest. Like many pharma companies Aoxing operates through many joint ventures and partnerships including a JV with pharmaceutical ingredient maker Johnson Matthey Plc and strategic alliances with American Oriental Bioengineering QRxPharma and Phoenix PharmaLabs. In addition to narcotics the company offers OTC pain relievers some based on traditional Chinese medicine. Aoxing which traces its roots to 1600 became a public company in 2006 through a reverse merger.

	Annual Growth	06/11	06/12	06/13	06/14	06/15
Sales ($ mil.)	39.9%	6.7	8.1	10.8	12.7	25.5
Net income ($ mil.)	–	(4.9)	(15.8)	(16.8)	(8.2)	5.5
Market value ($ mil.)	6.1%	96.4	22.7	15.0	22.3	122.2
Employees	(4.1%)	400	375	589	481	339

APAC CUSTOMER SERVICES INC.

2201 Waukegan Rd. Ste. 300
Bannockburn IL 60015
Phone: 847-374-4980
Fax: 847-374-4989
Web: www.apaccustomerservices.com

CEO: –
CFO: Andrew B Szafran
HR: Mary Wagner
FYE: December 31
Type: Private

The telephone isn't the instrument of choice for APAC Customer Services anymore. The company provides outsourced customer-management and acquisition services using the telephone and the Internet. APAC's customer management services include customer retention help-line information direct mail response training recruitment and order entry services. Clients include companies in the communications government health care insurance retail technology utility and education sectors. Through its affiliation with sister company NCO Group the company operates through more than 100 facilities around the globe. In late 2011 APAC was acquired by investment firm One Equity Partners.

APACHE CORP.   NYS: APA

One Post Oak Central, 2000 Post Oak Boulevard, Suite 100
Houston, TX 77056-4400
Phone: 713 296-6000
Fax:
Web: www.apachecorp.com

CEO: John J. Christmann
CFO: Stephen J. Riney
HR: Margery M. (Margie) Harris
FYE: December 31
Type: Public

There's more than only a patch of oil for Apache. The oil and gas exploration and production company has onshore and offshore operations in major oil patches around the world including in North America as well as in Australia Egypt and the UK North Sea. In North America it is active in the Gulf of Mexico the Gulf Coast of Texas and Louisiana the Permian Basin in West Texas the Anadarko Basin in Oklahoma and Canada's Western Sedimentary Basin. In 2014 the company reported worldwide estimated proved reserves of 2.4 billion barrels of oil equivalent. In 2015 Anadarko Petroleum made a bid to acquire Apache which was rebuffed.

	Annual Growth	12/10	12/11	12/12	12/13	12/14
Sales ($ mil.)	3.5%	12,092.0	16,888.0	17,078.0	16,054.0	13,851.0
Net income ($ mil.)	–	3,032.0	4,584.0	2,001.0	2,288.0	(5,060.0)
Market value ($ mil.)	(14.9%)	44,890.7	34,103.8	29,555.6	32,356.8	23,595.6
Employees	2.7%	4,449	5,299	5,976	5,342	4,950

APACHE DESIGN SOLUTIONS INC.

2645 Zanker Rd.
San Jose CA 95134
Phone: 408-457-2000
Fax: 408-428-9569
Web: www.apache-da.com

CEO: Andrew T Yang
CFO: Emily Chang
HR: –
FYE: December 31
Type: Subsidiary

Apache Design Solutions makes sure new semiconductor designs have integrity — power and signal integrity that is. Its physical design and verification software packages enable engineers to design integrated circuits (ICs) that use less power ensure reliable power delivery and reduce signal interference or noise that can lead to poor performance in mobile electronics. Clients have included Intel Texas Instruments Toshiba STMicroelectronics and Samsung Electronics. The company gets more than half of its sales from customers in the US. Apache Design was acquired by rival ANSYS for $310 million in mid-2011 following an IPO filing earlier that year.

APARTMENT INVESTMENT & MANAGEMENT CO.   NYS: AIV

4582 South Ulster Street, Suite 1100
Denver, CO 80237
Phone: 303 757-8101
Fax: 303 759-3226
Web: www.aimco.com

CEO: Terry Considine
CFO: Paul L. Beldin
HR: –
FYE: December 31
Type: Public

Apartment Investment and Management Company (AIMCO) is the host with the most — apartment units that is. A self-managed real estate investment trust (REIT) AIMCO owns manages and redevelops multifamily residential properties throughout the US. It is one of the nation's largest apartment owner/managers (surpassed by Sam Zell's Equity Residential) with nearly 220 properties in about two dozen states in its portfolio. Operating arm AIMCO Properties holds and manages most of AIMCO's assets which include suburban communities high-rises and subsidized affordable housing. The REIT targets the largest multifamily markets in the US namely coastal cities Los Angeles Washington DC Philadelphia and Boston.

	Annual Growth	12/10	12/11	12/12	12/13	12/14
Sales ($ mil.)	(3.7%)	1,144.9	1,079.6	1,033.2	974.1	984.4
Net income ($ mil.)	–	(71.7)	(57.1)	132.5	207.3	309.2
Market value ($ mil.)	9.5%	3,783.1	3,354.1	3,961.7	3,793.3	5,438.9
Employees	(14.0%)	3,100	2,640	2,150	1,932	1,693

APELON INC.

100 Danbury Rd.
Ridgefield CT 06877
Phone: 203-431-2530
Fax: 203-431-2523
Web: www.apelon.com

CEO: Stephen F Coady
CFO: –
HR: –
FYE: December 31
Type: Private

If it sometimes sounds like your doctor is speaking a foreign language Apelon is trying to make sure that she's at least speaking the same language as all the other doctors. Founded in 1999 Apelon provides software and services that health care providers use to create maintain and standardize medical terminology. The company offers medical terminology databases concept-based indexing and retrieval applications vocabulary information authoring applications and tools for integrating standard vocabularies into health care software products. Apelon's technologies have been used by the American Medical Association and the College of American Pathologists to create consistent terminology.

APEX TOOL GROUP LLC

14600 York Rd. Ste. A
Sparks MD 21152
Phone: 800-688-8949
Fax: 800-234-0472
Web: www.apextoolgroup.com

CEO: Thomas Wroe Jr
CFO: –
HR: –
FYE: December 31
Type: Joint Venture

Apex Tool Group is near the top of the heap among global producers of hand power and electronic tools. Geared at industrial commercial and do-it-yourself (DIY) markets the group manufactures and markets more than 30 leading tool brands including Crescent wrenches Jobox storage boxes Lufkin measuring tools and Weller soldering equipment. Directly and through subsidiaries Apex serves a range of markets including automotive aerospace electronics energy industrial and consumer retail. Apex Tool Group was formed in 2010 as a joint venture between Danaher and Cooper Industries (now Eaton). In February 2013 Danaher and Eaton sold Apex to global private investment firm Bain Capital for about $1.6 billion.

API GROUP INC.

1100 OLD HIGHWAY 8 NW
SAINT PAUL, MN 551126447
Phone: 651-636-4320
Fax: –
Web: www.apigroupinc.com

CEO: Russell Becker
CFO: Gregory Keup
HR: –
FYE: December 31
Type: Private

Holding company APi Group has a piece of the action in two main sectors: fire protection systems and industrial and specialty construction services. APi boasts about 40 subsidiaries which operate as independent companies across the US (nearly half of them in Minnesota) the UK and Canada. Services provided by the company's construction subsidiaries include HVAC and plumbing system installation; electrical industrial and mechanical contracting; industrial insulation; and garage door installation. Safety-focused units install a host of fire sprinkler detection security and alarm systems. The family-owned company was founded in 1926 by Reuben Anderson father of chairman Lee Anderson.

	Annual Growth	12/09	12/10	12/11	12/12	12/13
Sales ($ mil.)	18.3%	–	1,238.7	1,484.9	1,731.4	2,049.1
Net income ($ mil.)	32.9%	–	–	52.9	62.3	93.5
Market value ($ mil.)	–	–	–	–	–	–
Employees	–	–	–	–	–	4,237

API TECHNOLOGIES CORP NAS: ATNY

4705 S. Apopka Vineland Rd., Suite 210
Orlando, FL 32819
Phone: 855 294-3800
Fax: –
Web: www.apitech.com

CEO: Robert E. Tavares
CFO: Eric F. Seeton
HR: Laura Reeder
FYE: November 30
Type: Public

API Technologies is good at defense. Through various operating subsidiaries the company designs and manufactures highly-engineered electronic components and robotics as well as secure communications systems for military and aerospace applications. It develops products for missile electronic warfare flight control and range finder systems as well as devices that remotely manage critical IT and communications systems. With manufacturing facilities in North America and the UK API maintains a direct sales and marketing team and primarily sells to defense prime contractors and contract manufacturers. Roughly half of its revenues are generated by US Department of Defense subcontractors.

	Annual Growth	05/11*	11/11	11/12	11/13	11/14
Sales ($ mil.)	28.0%	108.3	144.3	280.8	244.3	226.9
Net income ($ mil.)	–	(26.2)	7.9	(148.7)	(7.2)	(18.9)
Market value ($ mil.)	(32.6%)	380.6	181.7	145.7	210.5	116.6
Employees	43.5%	630	2,140	2,234	1,975	1,862

*Fiscal year change

APOGEE ENTERPRISES, INC. NMS: APOG

4400 West 78th Street - Suite 520
Minneapolis, MN 55435
Phone: 952 835-1874
Fax: –
Web: www.apog.com

CEO: Joseph F. (Joe) Puishys
CFO: James S. (Jim) Porter
HR: Audrey Hyland
FYE: February 28
Type: Public

Apogee Enterprises goes to great panes for its glass customers. Te company designs and develops value-added glass products primarily for the US market. Its architectural products and services segment fabricates and installs glass that features specialized colors or coatings and aluminum framing systems for commercial and institutional buildings. Customers include architects general contractors glazing subcontractors and building owners. Its large-scale optical (LSO) technologies segment manufactures anti-reflective UV-protected glass and acrylic under the Tru Vue brand for custom picture framing. Tru Vue products are sold through independent distributors and mass merchandisers.

	Annual Growth	02/11*	03/12	03/13	03/14*	02/15
Sales ($ mil.)	12.5%	582.8	662.5	700.2	771.4	933.9
Net income ($ mil.)	–	(10.3)	4.6	19.1	28.0	50.5
Market value ($ mil.)	34.7%	404.4	366.0	761.4	994.4	1,331.9
Employees	7.8%	3,555	3,636	3,871	4,266	4,802

*Fiscal year change

APOLLO COMMERCIAL REAL ESTATE FINANCE INC. NYS: ARI

c/o Apollo Global Management, LLC, 9 West 57th Street, 43rd Floor
New York, NY 10019
Phone: 212 515-3200
Fax: –
Web: www.apolloreit.com

CEO: Stuart A. Rothstein
CFO: Megan Gaul
HR: –
FYE: December 31
Type: Public

Apollo Commercial Real Estate Finance invests in buys and manages commercial real estate mortgage loans and other real estate-related debt investments. The company was formed in 2009 by Apollo Global Management to be a mortgage real estate investment trust (REIT). Externally managed by ACREFI Management (an indirect subsidiary of Apollo Global Management) the firm is using proceeds from its 2009 IPO to invest in performing non-distressed US commercial real estate loans; commercial mortgage-backed securities (CMBS); and other commercial real estate debt investments. Apollo Commercial Real Estate Finance expects its average investment to range between $25 million and $75 million.

	Annual Growth	12/10	12/11	12/12	12/13	12/14
Sales ($ mil.)	39.6%	32.5	52.9	57.1	77.5	123.3
Net income ($ mil.)	65.6%	11.0	25.9	40.2	52.5	82.7
Market value ($ mil.)	0.0%	766.8	615.8	761.2	762.1	767.3
Employees	–	–	–	–	–	–

APOLLO EDUCATION GROUP, INC. NMS: APOL

4025 S. Riverpoint Parkway
Phoenix, AZ 85040
Phone: 480 966-5394
Fax: 480 929-7499
Web: www.apollo.edu

CEO: Gregory W. Cappelli
CFO: Joseph L. DÂ'Amico
HR: Frederick J Newton
FYE: August 31
Type: Public

Apollo's creed could be that we all deserve the chance to advance. The for-profit Apollo Education Group provides educational programs through a number of subsidiaries including online stalwart University of Phoenix. The largest private university in the US the University of Phoenix accounts for about 85% of Apollo's sales and has an enrollment of more than 900000 students in degree programs ranging from associate's to doctoral. Other schools include Western International University (graduate and undergraduate courses) South Africa's MBA-grantor Milpark Education and UK-based BPP Holdings a provider of legal and financial professional training. Apollo is going private in a $1.1 billion transaction.

	Annual Growth	08/11	08/12	08/13	08/14	08/15
Sales ($ mil.)	(14.2%)	4,733.0	4,253.3	3,681.3	3,024.2	2,566.3
Net income ($ mil.)	(52.3%)	572.4	422.7	248.5	209.3	29.8
Market value ($ mil.)	(30.2%)	5,075.8	2,910.5	2,013.0	3,010.3	1,204.3
Employees	(12.0%)	56,743	49,992	44,000	39,000	34,000

APOLLO GLOBAL MANAGEMENT LLC NYS: APO

9 West 57th Street, 43rd Floor
New York, NY 10019
Phone: 212 515-3200
Fax: –
Web: www.apolloic.com

CEO: Leon Black
CFO: Martin Kelly
HR: –
FYE: December 31
Type: Public

In Greek and Roman mythology Apollo is the god of light medicine arts and archery but Apollo Global Management is even more diverse. The alternative asset manager invests in across a range of nine core industries including chemicals commodities consumer and retail and media on behalf of institutional and individual investors. Apollo has some $160 billion of assets under management spread among its private equity capital markets and real estate segments. It specializes in buying distressed businesses and debt and has had some of its biggest successes investing during economic downturns. The publicly-traded firm has offices in the US Europe and Asia and is run by billionaire Leon Black.

	Annual Growth	12/10	12/11	12/12	12/13	12/14
Sales ($ mil.)	(7.3%)	2,109.9	171.6	2,860.0	3,733.6	1,560.1
Net income ($ mil.)	15.5%	94.6	(468.8)	311.0	659.4	168.2
Market value ($ mil.)	23.9%	–	2,023.4	2,830.5	5,153.9	3,844.6
Employees	14.9%	485	548	634	710	845

APOLLO RESIDENTIAL MORTGAGE, INC.

c/o Apollo Global Management, LLC, 9 West 57th Street, 43rd Floor
New York, NY 10019
Phone: 212 515-3200
Fax: -
Web: www.apolloresidentialmortgage.com

NYS: AMTG
CEO: Michael A. Commaroto
CFO: Teresa D. Covello
HR: -
FYE: December 31
Type: Public

The gods at Apollo Global Management are trying their luck with the residential mortgage market. The alternative asset manager formed Apollo Residential Mortgage to invest in residential mortgage-backed securities (MBS) and collateralized mortgage obligations (CMOs) guaranteed by Fannie Mae Freddie Mac and Ginnie Mae. A real estate investment trust the company is externally managed by ARM Manager an indirect subsidiary of Apollo Global Management. Formed in March 2011 Apollo Residential Mortgage went public later that year via a $205 million initial public offering (IPO).

	Annual Growth	12/10	12/11	12/12	12/13	12/14
Sales ($ mil.)	-	0.0	10.7	94.4	154.7	154.2
Net income ($ mil.)	-	0.0	4.5	172.8	(47.2)	96.1
Market value ($ mil.)	-	0.0	489.7	647.9	474.3	506.0
Employees	-	-	-	-	2	2

APPALACHIAN POWER CO.

1 Riverside Plaza
Columbus, OH 43215-2373
Phone: 614 716-1000
Fax: -
Web: www.appalachianpower.com

CEO: Nicholas K Akins
CFO: -
HR: -
FYE: December 31
Type: Public

When they're not out enjoying the scenery Virginians and West Virginians count on Appalachian Power to keep indoor temperatures stable. A subsidiary of American Electric Power Appalachian Power serves about 960000 residential and business customers in southwestern Virginia and southern West Virginia and a small portion of northwestern Tennessee. The electric utility operates about 53300 miles of distribution and transmission lines. It operates coal-fired gas-fired and hydroelectric plants that give it about 8020 MW of capacity and it markets power to wholesale customers in the region.

	Annual Growth	12/10	12/11	12/12	12/13	12/14
Sales ($ mil.)	(1.7%)	3,275.1	3,205.2	3,276.9	3,417.4	3,053.1
Net income ($ mil.)	12.0%	136.7	162.8	257.5	193.2	215.4
Market value ($ mil.)	-	-	-	-	-	-
Employees	(3.4%)	2,186	2,176	2,128	1,967	1,902

APPALACHIAN REGIONAL HEALTHCARE INC.

2285 Executive Dr. Ste. 400
Lexington KY 40505
Phone: 859-226-2440
Fax: 309-749-2064
Web: www.uhcrivervalley.com

CEO: Jerry W Haynes
CFO: Christopher Ellington
HR: -
FYE: December 31
Type: Private - Not-for-Pr

Under-the-weather coal miners (and their daughters) can turn to Appalachian Regional Healthcare (ARH) for medical services. The not-for-profit health system serves residents of eastern Kentucky and southern West Virginia through nine hospitals with more than 1000 beds as well as dozens of clinics home health care agencies and retail pharmacies. Its largest hospital in Hazard Kentucky has 310 beds and features an inpatient psychiatric unit that serves as the state mental health facility. Several of the system's hospitals are Critical Access Hospitals a federal government designation for rural community hospitals that operate in medically underserved areas.

APPLABS INC.

3170 Fairview Park Dr.
Falls Church VA 22042
Phone: 703-876-1000
Fax: +47-24-13-47-01
Web: www.birdstep.com

CEO: -
CFO: -
HR: -
FYE: December 31
Type: Private

AppLabs made its living by getting more than a little testy when it comes to computer software. The software testing firm provided a variety of software testing third-party validation and custom application development services for customers in such industries as information technology life sciences financial services and health care. AppLabs largely US customer base has included Avis. The vast majority of its employees worked at the company's offices in India. AppLabs was acquired by Computer Sciences Corporation (CSC) in 2011 for $171 million.

APPLE AMERICAN GROUP LLC

6200 OAK TREE BLVD # 250
CLEVELAND, OH 441316933
Phone: 216-525-2775
Fax: -
Web: www.appleamerican.com

CEO: -
CFO: -
HR: Yolanda Means
FYE: December 29
Type: Private

This company must really enjoy casual dining in its neighborhood. Apple American Group is the largest franchisee of Applebee's with about 450 Applebee's Neighborhood Grill & Bar locations in about two dozen states. The #1 casual dining chain in the US Applebee's restaurants offer a full-service menu of beef chicken and seafood entrees along with a wide selection of appetizers. Apple American's restaurants are found from coast to coast with large concentrations in the Midwest (Ohio Indiana Pennsylvania) and on the West Coast (California Washington). Founded in 1998 by CEO Greg Flynn Apple American is controlled by private equity firm Weston Presidio Service.

	Annual Growth	12/06	12/07	12/08	12/09	12/13
Sales ($ mil.)	21.7%	-	339.0	431.1	479.8	1,098.8
Net income ($ mil.)	12.7%	-	-	9.9	19.3	18.0
Market value ($ mil.)	-	-	-	-	-	-
Employees	-	-	-	-	-	5,500

APPLE FINANCIAL HOLDINGS INC.

122 E. 42nd St. 9th Fl.
New York NY 10168
Phone: 212-224-6400
Fax: 212-224-6589
Web: www.theapplebank.com

CEO: -
CFO: -
HR: Susan B Goro
FYE: December 31
Type: Private

Helping customers manage their money is at the core of Apple Financial Holdings. It is the holding company of Apple Bank for Savings which serves the New York metropolitan area from about 50 branches throughout New York City Long Island and Westchester County. Catering to retail and commercial customers the bank offers savings checking amd retirement accounts certificates of deposit and credit cards. Subsidiary ABS Associates markets life insurance products and fixed annuities to bank customers. Apple Bank traces its roots back to 1863.

APPLE INC
NMS: AAPL

1 Infinite Loop
Cupertino, CA 95014
Phone: 408 996-1010
Fax: 408 974-2483
Web: www.apple.com

CEO: Timothy D. (Tim) Cook
CFO: Luca Maestri
HR: Ann Bowers
FYE: September 26
Type: Public

Apple has an "i" for revolutionary technology. Since release the company's iPhone — which accounts for the largest portion of its sales — has spurred a revolution in cell phones and mobile computing. Apple also continues to innovate its core Mac desktop and laptop computers all of which feature its OS X operating system including the iMac all-in-one desktop for the consumer and education markets the MacBook Air ultra-portable laptop and the high-end Mac Pro and MacBook Pro for consumers and professionals. The company's popular iPad tablet computer has become another game-changer in the consumer market. It generates nearly two-thirds of sales outside the US.

	Annual Growth	09/11	09/12	09/13	09/14	09/15
Sales ($ mil.)	21.2%	108,249.0	156,508.0	170,910.0	182,795.0	233,715.0
Net income ($ mil.)	19.8%	25,922.0	41,733.0	37,037.0	39,510.0	53,394.0
Market value ($ mil.)	–	0.0	0.0	0.0	0.0	0.0
Employees	14.8%	63,300	76,100	84,400	97,000	110,000

APPLETON COATED LLC

569 Carter Ct.
Kimberly WI 54136
Phone: 920-968-3999
Fax: 920-968-3950
Web: www.appletoncoated.com

CEO: Douglas Ostrberg
CFO: –
HR: Brad Reinke
FYE: December 31
Type: Subsidiary

Curious paper buyers may find that Appleton Coated has the ticket to Utopia. The company manufactures and markets coated free-sheet carbonless paper products under brands names including Altima Curious and Utopia. The company's products are used to make such goods as books magazines corporate annual reports and consumer product packaging. Its Curious products include metallic tactile and translucent sheets. Appleton Coated primarily serves printers and paper merchants and produces about 400000 tons of paper per year. The company is a subsidiary of France-based paper manufacturer ArjoWiggins which is in turn owned by Sequana Capital.

APPLETON PAPERS INC.

825 E. Wisconsin Ave.
Appleton WI 54912-0359
Phone: 920-734-9841
Fax: 972-830-2619
Web: www.tm.com

CEO: Mark R Richards
CFO: Thomas J Ferree
HR: –
FYE: December 31
Type: Private

Paper is the apple of Appleton Papers' eye. The company manufactures specialty coated paper products including carbonless and security papers and thermal papers. It is the world's #1 producer of carbonless paper. Sold under the NCR Paper brand carbonless paper is used in multi-part business forms (such as invoices). Appleton makes security papers for government documents and coated products for point-of-sale displays. Its thermal papers are used in coupons gaming and transportation tickets and medical charts. The company's Encapsys segment makes microencapsulation (the process of inserting a microscopic wall around a substance) materials.

APPLIANCE RECYCLING CENTERS OF AMERICA
NAS: ARCI

175 Jackson Avenue North Suite 102
Minneapolis, MN 55343
Phone: 952 930-9000
Fax: –

CEO: Edward R Cameron
CFO: Jeffery Ostapeic
HR: –
FYE: January 03
Type: Public

Appliance Recycling Centers of America (ARCA) retrieves recycles repairs and resells household appliances. The company's retail business operates 20 ApplianceSmart Factory Outlet stores in Minnesota Georgia Ohio and Texas that sell new reconditioned and "special-buy" appliances from manufacturers such as Electrolux GE and Whirlpool. ARCA provides recycling and replacement services for appliance makers electric utilities and energy-efficiency programs in North America. The firm also cashes in on byproducts collecting fees for appliance disposal and selling scrap metal and reclaimed chlorofluorocarbon refrigerants from processed appliances. ARCA was founded in 1976 as a used appliance retailer.

	Annual Growth	12/11	12/11	12/12	12/13*	01/15
Sales ($ mil.)	0.8%	–	126.7	114.3	129.1	130.9
Net income ($ mil.)	(35.5%)	–	4.5	(3.9)	3.3	0.8
Market value ($ mil.)	(14.6%)	28.9	28.9	7.5	16.8	15.4
Employees	(2.0%)	–	379	351	340	349

*Fiscal year change

APPLIED CARD SYSTEMS INC.

5401 BROKEN SOUND BLVD NW
BOCA RATON, FL 334873512
Phone: 561-995-8820
Fax: –
Web: www.appliedcard.com

CEO: Rocco A Abessinio
CFO: –
HR: Angela Quattrocki
FYE: December 31
Type: Private

Applied Card Systems is the servicing arm for Applied Bank a subprime consumer lender that issues secured and unsecured credit cards to customers with little or no credit history. Applied Card Systems processes payments from and provides customer service to more than 500000 holders of subprime Visa and MasterCard accounts. Applied Card Systems also services credit card accounts for third-party issuers primarily small and midsized financial institutions. Chairman Rocco Abessinio is the founder of both Applied Card Bank and Applied Card Systems which was formed in 1987. The company has offices in Florida and Pennsylvania.

	Annual Growth	12/05	12/06	12/07	12/08	12/09
Sales ($ mil.)	(67.4%)	–	–	1,520.1	251.2	162.0
Net income ($ mil.)	23844.9%	–	–	0.0	145.4	21.8
Market value ($ mil.)	–	–	–	–	–	–
Employees	–	–	–	–	–	126

APPLIED CONCEPTS INC.

2609 Technology Dr.
Plano TX 75074-7467
Phone: 972-398-3750
Fax: 972-398-3751
Web: www.stalkerradar.com

CEO: Alan Mead
CFO: –
HR: –
FYE: December 31
Type: Private

Your Speed Is: Below the posted speed limit we hope for your own safety. Applied Concepts (dba Stalker Radar) makes radar speed detectors and in-car video camera systems used largely by law enforcement agencies. The branded Stalker Radar Speed Sensor garners about 40% of the law enforcement market. The company also caters to sports and OEM testing applications making laser-based speed measuring devices and display equipment (including roadside signs that signal vehicle speed) and accessories (cables and power supplies). Stalker Radar products are marketed in the US and more than 100 countries. Co-founders CEO Alan Mead and president Stan Partee started the company in 1977; they are its majority owners.

APPLIED DISCOVERY INC.

13427 NE 16th St. Ste. 200
Bellevue WA 98005-2307
Phone: 425-467-3000
Fax: 425-467-3010
Web: www.applieddiscovery.com

CEO: –
CFO: Gregg Harmon
HR: –
FYE: December 31
Type: Subsidiary

This firm helps you find that information and apply it to the real world. Applied Discovery (aka LexisNexis Applied Discovery) provides electronic discovery services to law firms and corporate clients. A division of information provider LexisNexis the company offers document management services such as data collection legacy media restoration data processing and format conversion as well as document production and reporting. Applied Discovery has worked with such big name law firms as Akin Gump Clifford Chance and Morrison & Foerster. Its corporate clients have included 3M Honeywell and Pfizer. Founded in 1998 Applied Discovery was acquired in 2003 by LexisNexis a unit of Reed Elsevier Group.

APPLIED DNA SCIENCES INC — NAS: APDN

50 Health Sciences Drive
Stony Brook, NY 11790
Phone: 631 240-8800
Fax: –
Web: www.adnas.com

CEO: James A Hayward
CFO: Beth Jantzen
HR: –
FYE: September 30
Type: Public

Counterfeiters needn't apply here. Applied DNA Sciences makes anti-counterfeiting and product authentication solutions. Its products are encoded with botanical DNA sequences that can distinguish counterfeits from the genuine article. The DNA markers (which hold the SigNature DNA brand) can be employed in ink glue holograms microchips and paint and are then used to tag documents currency event tickets and clothing labels. The company applies its SigNature markers to art and collectibles fine wine consumer products digital recording media pharmaceuticals and homeland security products.

	Annual Growth	09/11	09/12	09/13	09/14	09/15
Sales ($ mil.)	74.6%	1.0	1.9	2.0	2.7	9.0
Net income ($ mil.)	–	(10.5)	(7.2)	(17.7)	(13.1)	(11.9)
Market value ($ mil.)	209.5%	1.2	5.5	1.9	2.0	110.1
Employees	30.0%	21	29	49	59	60

APPLIED ENERGETICS INC — NBB: AERG

2480 W. Ruthrauff Road, Suite 140 Q
Tucson, AZ 85705
Phone: 520 628-7415
Fax: –
Web: www.appliedenergetics.com

CEO: George P Farley
CFO: Thomas C Dearmin
HR: –
FYE: December 31
Type: Public

Bullets?!! We don't need no stinkin' bullets — not with the Buck Rogers technology of Applied Energetics. The company is developing Laser Guided Energy and Laser Induced Plasma Channel directed-energy weapons for sale to the US government. In plain English? Laser-guided man-made lightning! Applied Energetics is developing more compact laser sources and field testing its technology for mobile platforms such as tanks Humvees and personnel carriers. Depending on the military situation the charge can be set to stun or kill people or to disable vehicles. Applied Energetics also develops technology for neutralizing car bombs and other explosives.

	Annual Growth	12/10	12/11	12/12	12/13	12/14
Sales ($ mil.)	(78.0%)	13.1	5.1	1.3	0.0	0.0
Net income ($ mil.)	–	(2.9)	(6.4)	(3.5)	(1.4)	(0.7)
Market value ($ mil.)	(75.1%)	78.1	6.7	2.6	0.9	0.3
Employees	(51.5%)	54	27	10	4	3

APPLIED INDUSTRIAL TECHNOLOGIES, INC. — NYS: AIT

One Applied Plaza
Cleveland, OH 44115
Phone: 216 426-4000
Fax: –
Web: www.applied.com

CEO: Neil A. Schrimsher
CFO: Mark O Eisele
HR: –
FYE: June 30
Type: Public

Just imagine getting lost in this distributor's warehouse. Applied Industrial Technologies distributes 5 million industrial parts made by more than 4000 manufacturers. The short list includes bearings power transmission components hydraulic and pneumatic components industrial rubber products and linear motion components. Customers are concentrated in maintenance/repair/operations (MRO) and OEM markets. Applied also manages regional mechanical rubber and fluid power shops that offer a slate of services from engineering design to conveyor belt repair.

	Annual Growth	06/11	06/12	06/13	06/14	06/15
Sales ($ mil.)	5.6%	2,212.8	2,375.4	2,462.2	2,459.9	2,751.6
Net income ($ mil.)	4.5%	96.8	108.8	118.1	112.8	115.5
Market value ($ mil.)	2.7%	1,421.0	1,470.5	1,928.6	2,024.4	1,582.2
Employees	5.9%	4,640	4,664	5,109	5,472	5,839

APPLIED MATERIALS, INC. — NMS: AMAT

3050 Bowers Avenue, P.O. Box 58039
Santa Clara, CA 95052-8039
Phone: 408 727-5555
Fax: –
Web: www.appliedmaterials.com

CEO: Gary E. Dickerson
CFO: Robert J. (Bob) Halliday
HR: Blake Wolfe
FYE: October 25
Type: Public

Applied Materials makes the machines that make computer chips flat panel TVs and solar energy devices. The company's equipment vies for supremacy in many segments of the chip-making process including deposition (layering film on wafers) etching (removing portions of chip material to allow precise construction of circuits) and semiconductor metrology and inspection equipment. The company's plan to acquire its rival Tokyo Electron the second biggest equipment maker died in 2015 due to antitrust concern from US regulators.

	Annual Growth	10/11	10/12	10/13	10/14	10/15
Sales ($ mil.)	(2.1%)	10,517.0	8,719.0	7,509.0	9,072.0	9,659.0
Net income ($ mil.)	(8.0%)	1,926.0	109.0	256.0	1,072.0	1,377.0
Market value ($ mil.)	6.8%	14,639.2	12,354.0	20,537.8	24,348.4	19,070.4
Employees	2.8%	13,900	15,000	14,500	14,950	15,500

APPLIED MICRO CIRCUITS CORP. — NMS: AMCC

4555 Great America Parkway, 6th Floor
Santa Clara, CA 95054
Phone: 408 542-8600
Fax: 408 542-8601
Web: www.apm.com

CEO: Paramesh Gopi
CFO: Martin S. McDermut
HR: Michael (Mike) Major
FYE: March 31
Type: Public

For Applied Micro Circuits X marks the spot for its chips. The company's lines of chips bearing the "X" are aimed at data centers scientific and high-performance computing and enterprise applications. The X-Gene and X-Weave families of chips based on the ARM architecture provide computing power and high-speed connectivity for telecommunications applications while operating on a low-level of energy. The company outsources manufacturing to TSMC and UMC. Its top customers include Avnet (26% of sales) and Wintec (20%). Applied Micro gets 57% of its sales from outside the US.

	Annual Growth	03/11	03/12	03/13	03/14	03/15
Sales ($ mil.)	(9.7%)	247.7	230.9	195.6	216.2	165.0
Net income ($ mil.)	–	(1.0)	(82.7)	(134.1)	(5.7)	(52.1)
Market value ($ mil.)	(16.3%)	838.9	560.9	599.7	800.1	412.2
Employees	(6.8%)	672	728	649	591	507

APPLIED MINERALS INC NBB: AMNL

110 Greene Street a Suite 1101
New York, NY 10012
Phone: 212 226-4265
Fax: –
Web: www.appliedminerals.com

CEO: Andre M Zeitoun
CFO: Chris Carney
HR: –
FYE: December 31
Type: Public

Applied Minerals (formerly Atlas Mining) develops the Dragon mine in Utah. The 230-acre site contains a deposit of halloysite clay a substance used as an intermediate ingredient in chemicals manufacturing as well as in making bone china fine china and porcelain. The mine is believed to be the only source of halloysite clay in the Western Hemisphere suitable for large-scale commercial production. In addition to halloysite the Dragon mine contains other clays including kaolinite ilite and smectite as well as iron oxide ores such as hematite goethite and manganese. The Dragon property contains a measured resource of nearly 600000 tons of clay and more than 2 million tons of iron ore.

	Annual Growth	12/10	12/11	12/12	12/13	12/14
Sales ($ mil.)	–	0.0	0.1	0.2	0.1	0.2
Net income ($ mil.)	–	(4.8)	(7.5)	(9.7)	(13.1)	(10.3)
Market value ($ mil.)	(2.2%)	76.0	120.7	146.4	104.6	69.4
Employees	36.0%	12	17	27	27	41

APPLIED MOLECULAR EVOLUTION INC.

10300 Campus Point Dr. Ste. 200
San Diego CA 92121
Phone: 858-597-4990
Fax: 858-597-4950
Web: www.amevolution.com

CEO: –
CFO: –
HR: Sarah Novicki
FYE: December 31
Type: Subsidiary

Natural selection doesn't happen fast enough for Applied Molecular Evolution (AME). The biotech firm uses its AMEsystem technology to customize antibodies and proteins for medical uses. Employing what AME calls directed evolution the company adjusts a protein's amino acids one at a time until the protein acquires the desired therapeutic characteristics. AME's biopharmaceuticals have increased the potency of MedImmune's anti-tumor drug Vitaxin (which AME helped developed). The system has also been used to customize a protein which may ultimately help lymphoma patients who otherwise don't respond to Rituxin. The company is a subsidiary of Eli Lilly

APPLIED OPTOELECTRONICS INC NMS: AAOI

13115 Jess Pirtle Blvd.
Sugar Land, TX 77478
Phone: 281 295-1800
Fax: –
Web: www.ao-inc.com

CEO: Lin (Thompson) Chih-Hsiang
CFO: Stefan J. Murry
HR: –
FYE: December 31
Type: Public

When it comes to making lasers Applied Optoelectronics stays on the beam. The company designs and makes fiber-optic networking components that go into communications equipment used by cable-TV providers broadband network providers and Internet data centers to allow for faster network connections. Applied Optoelectronics makes laser chips components subassemblies and modules using its proprietary Molecular Beam Epitaxy (MBE) fabrication process. Customers include Arris Group Aurora Networks Cisco Systems Harmonic and Motorola. Founded in 1997 the company went public in 2013 raising $36 million in its IPO.

	Annual Growth	12/10	12/11	12/12	12/13	12/14
Sales ($ mil.)	34.0%	40.5	47.8	63.4	78.4	130.4
Net income ($ mil.)	–	(3.4)	(5.3)	(0.9)	(1.4)	4.3
Market value ($ mil.)	(25.3%)	–	–	–	222.5	166.3
Employees	24.9%	–	–	927	1,146	1,447

APPLIED RESEARCH ASSOCIATES INC.

4300 SAN MATEO BLVD NE A220
ALBUQUERQUE, NM 871101229
Phone: 505-883-3636
Fax: –
Web: www.ara.com

CEO: Robert H Sues
CFO: –
HR: –
FYE: September 30
Type: Private

Applied Research Associates (ARA) has defense down to a science. The research and engineering contractor develops tests and manages software and equipment for the aerospace and defense civil and commercial sectors. From more than 70 offices laboratories and testing and manufacturing facilities primarily in the US ARA provides expertise in system analysis blast testing environmental site characterization pavement evaluation robotic vehicles and other technologies and technical fields. The federal government including various US Department of Defense agencies is ARA's primary client. Founded in 1979 the company is owned by its employees.

	Annual Growth	09/07	09/08	09/11	09/12	09/13
Sales ($ mil.)	1.7%	–	196.4	232.1	226.8	213.7
Net income ($ mil.)	1.3%	–	–	6.0	2.8	6.1
Market value ($ mil.)	–	–	–	–	–	–
Employees	–	–	–	–	–	1,235

APPLIED SYSTEMS INC.

200 Applied Pkwy.
University Park IL 60484
Phone: 708-534-5575
Fax: 708-534-8016
Web: www.appliedsystems.com

CEO: Reid French Jr
CFO: Colleen Mikuce
HR: –
FYE: December 31
Type: Private

Applied Systems applies technology to automate the insurance industry — from lone agent to large agency. The company helps independent insurance agents become more efficient by minimizing paperwork streamlining workflows and improving access to information. Its main product The Agency Manager (TAM) system assists with client management policy pricing electronic data interchange policy and claims servicing and office administration. Its Vision system provides large carriers with automated billing policy and claims processing and reports. DORIS provides small brokers with a hosted system. Applied Systems is owned by chairman and CEO James Kellner and Bain Capital.

APPLIED VISUAL SCIENCES INC. OTC: APVS

250 Exchange Place Ste. H
Herndon VA 20170
Phone: 703-464-5495
Fax: 703-464-8530
Web: www.guardiantechintl.com

CEO: William J Donovan
CFO: Gregory E Hare
HR: –
FYE: December 31
Type: Public

Applied Visual Sciences sees a new future for itself. Formerly Guardian Technologies the company changed its name and restructured its operations in July 2010. It primarily operates through two subsidiaries: Guardian Technologies (homeland security and defense technology) and Signature Mapping Medical Sciences (health care technology). Its security and defense products include threat identification and screening software for airlines while its health care offerings include medical image processing applications.

APPRISS INC.

10401 Linn Station Rd. Ste. 200
Louisville KY 40223-3842
Phone: 502-561-8463
Fax: 502-561-1825
Web: www.appriss.com

CEO: Michael Davis
CFO: Rick Simpson
HR: –
FYE: December 31
Type: Private

Appriss aptly observes offenders. The company's flagship product Victim Information & Notification Everyday or VINE makes information about offenders' custody or court status available to victims of crime as well as the general public. It also offers automated notification services to victims of federal crimes in partnership with AT&T and the US Department of Justice. Appriss' ancillary products include JusticeXchange a tool that enables law enforcement officials to track offenders in jail and investigate crimes; MethCheck a program that helps track and report pseudoephedrine purchases; and AlertXpress which enables government agencies to deliver mass notifications to via phone fax or e-mail.

APPTIS INC.

4800 Westfields Blvd.
Chantilly VA 20151
Phone: 703-745-6016
Fax: 210-366-4722
Web: www.mysiriuszone.com

CEO: Albert Notini
CFO: Francis Meyer
HR: –
FYE: December 31
Type: Subsidiary

Apptis — 'tis an appropriate name for a company that provides many apps for its customers. The company offers a wide range of information technology services including network engineering software development and systems integration for US federal agencies and commercial clients. It also distributes and integrates equipment from such vendors as Cisco Dell and Hewlett-Packard. Apptis provides such other services as maintenance support and training. Clients have included the FAA and the Department of Defense (DOD). Apptis has several offices in its home state of Virginia and several more in five other states. The company was acquired by URS Corporation in 2011 for about $260 million.

APPROACH RESOURCES INC

NMS: AREX

One Ridgmar Centre, 6500 West Freeway, Suite 800
Fort Worth, TX 76116
Phone: 817 989-9000
Fax: –
Web: www.approachresources.com

CEO: J. Ross Craft
CFO: Sergei Krylov
HR: –
FYE: December 31
Type: Public

Approach Resources takes a different approach to natural gas and oil exploration development and production. Specializing in finding and exploiting unconventional reservoirs the company operates primarily in West Texas' Permian Basin. It also has operations in East Texas. The company's unconventional designation results from a focus on developing natural gas reserves in tight gas sands and shale areas necessitating a reliance on advanced completion fracturing and drilling techniques. In 2012 Approach Resources reported proved reserves of 95.5 million barrels of oil equivalent.

	Annual Growth	12/10	12/11	12/12	12/13	12/14
Sales ($ mil.)	45.6%	57.6	108.4	128.9	181.3	258.5
Net income ($ mil.)	65.6%	7.5	7.2	6.4	72.3	56.2
Market value ($ mil.)	(27.5%)	919.7	1,170.9	995.8	768.4	254.4
Employees	26.8%	55	81	95	135	142

APPTIX INC.

OSLO: APP

13461 Sunrise Valley Dr. Ste. 300
Herndon VA 20171
Phone: 703-890-2800
Fax: 703-890-2801
Web: www.apptix.com

CEO: David Ehrhardt
CFO: Chris Mack
HR: –
FYE: December 31
Type: Public

Apptix has an appetite for e-mail. The company provides hosted communications services including Microsoft Exchange e-mail mobile e-mail SharePoint collaboration VoIP (Voice over Internet Protocol) phone services Web conferencing website hosting online backup and other services. In addition to Microsoft the company counts Mozy Global Relay PARALLELS and Research In Motion among its technology partners. Its channel partners include Bell Canada Fujitsu IBM Global Services and SAVVIS. Once a provider of services to small businesses Apptix has added midsized and large enterprise subscribers. The company operates in the US.

APPTECH CORP

NBB: APCX

2011 Palomar Airport Road, Suite 102
Carlsbad, CA 92011
Phone: 760 707-5959
Fax: –

CEO: –
CFO: –
HR: –
FYE: December 31
Type: Public

When nutritional supplements didn't transform its fortunes AppTech decided to apply itself elsewhere. Formerly known as Natural Nutrition the company it lost its primary customer in 2009 and switched its focus to mobile device applications. AppTech plans to create an online marketplace for not just Apple apps but apps that will run on Motorola Mobility's Android the BlackBerry Palm smartphones and China Mobile's new OPhone. The company plans to act a middleman for US-based app developers and mobile users in the emerging markets of Brazil China India. The company will translate English-based apps and sell them to wireless carriers overseas.

	Annual Growth	12/07	12/11	12/12	12/13	12/14
Sales ($ mil.)	(41.8%)	9.6	0.0	0.0	0.9	0.2
Net income ($ mil.)	–	(14.7)	(0.6)	(0.2)	(0.7)	(1.8)
Market value ($ mil.)	8.6%	3.2	0.0	0.0	12.7	5.7
Employees	–	2	–	–	–	–

APRIA HEALTHCARE GROUP INC.

26220 Enterprise Ct.
Lake Forest CA 92630
Phone: 949-639-2000
Fax: 516-593-7039
Web: www.biospecifics.com

CEO: John G Figueroa
CFO: Peter A Reynolds
HR: Howard Derman
FYE: December 31
Type: Private

When an apple a day doesn't keep the illness away perhaps Apria Healthcare Group can help. With about 540 branches nationwide Apria is one of the country's largest home health firms. The company provides supplemental oxygen ventilators nebulizers and sleep monitoring equipment and medication to patients with emphysema sleep apnea and other respiratory conditions. Its infusion therapy nurses administer intravenous or injectable therapies — including pain drugs chemotherapy and parenteral nutrition — at home or in one of the company's outpatient infusion clinics. Apria also delivers home medical equipment such as walkers and hospital beds. The company is owned by the Blackstone Group.

APRICUS BIOSCIENCES INC
NAS: APRI

11975 El Camino Real, Suite 300
San Diego, CA 92130
Phone: 858 222-8041
Fax: –
Web: www.apricusbio.com

CEO: Richard W Pascoe
CFO: –
HR: –
FYE: December 31
Type: Public

Apricus Biosciences (formerly NexMed) wants you to rub it in. The drug development company uses its NexACT technology to deliver drugs through the skin; it is developing topical formulations with improved absorption rates using already-proven drug ingredients. One of the company's products is a treatment for erectile dysfunction Vitaros that is sold in select international markets. Another offering Totect works to detoxify tissue that has been accidentially exposed to chemotherapy agents. Apricus Biosciences is also working on a topical product called Femprox that treats female sexual arousal disorder as well as a topical nail fungus treatment called MycoVa.

	Annual Growth	12/10	12/11	12/12	12/13	12/14
Sales ($ mil.)	16.8%	5.0	4.1	8.4	2.5	9.3
Net income ($ mil.)	–	(29.5)	(18.1)	(31.8)	(16.9)	(21.8)
Market value ($ mil.)	(26.7%)	153.8	228.7	88.2	117.5	44.3
Employees	(10.0%)	35	25	114	21	23

APRISO CORPORATION

301 E. Ocean Blvd. Ste. 1200
Long Beach CA 90802
Phone: 562-951-8000
Fax: 562-951-9000
Web: www.apriso.com

CEO: James Henderson
CFO: Carey Tokirio
HR: –
FYE: December 31
Type: Private

Apriso helps companies size up their manufacturing activities. The company's FlexNet product which works with languages and currencies from around the world is a suite of manufacturing operations management applications. The FlexNet suite addresses plant activities such as production supply chain warehousing labor and maintenance. In more than 40 countries spread across the Americas Europe Africa and Asia Apriso's more than 200-strong client list includes British American Tobacco General Motors Lockheed Martin and Microsoft. The company was founded in 1992.

APS HEALTHCARE INC.

44 S. Broadway Ste. 1200
White Plains NY 10601
Phone: 800-305-3720
Fax: +44-2079227789
Web: www.northernandshell.com

CEO: Greg Scott
CFO: John McDonough
HR: –
FYE: December 31
Type: Private

At APS Healthcare attitude is everything. What started out as a behavioral health services provider has morphed into a full-service health management firm aiming to reduce health care costs and improve wellness through lifestyle changes. APS provides disease and care management wellness and prevention clinical quality reviews and mental health services to Medicaid agencies state and local governments health plans and employers. The company which serves some 17 million members in 25 US states plus Puerto Rico also provides employee assistance and work-life programs. APS which was previously owned by private equity firm GTCR Goldner Rauner was acquired by Medicare provider Universal American in 2012.

APTALIS PHARMA INC.

22 Inverness Center Pkwy. Ste. 310
Birmingham AL 35242
Phone: 205-991-8085
Fax: 604-688-7168
Web: www.ivanhoe-energy.com

CEO: Frank Verwiel
CFO: Steve Gannon
HR: –
FYE: September 30
Type: Private

Aptalis Pharma knows its ABCs when it comes to treating CF and GI ailments. The company formerly named Axcan Intermediate Holdings develops and sells drugs mainly to treat cystic fibrosis (CF) and gastrointestinal (GI) conditions. Its Urso line treats liver disease; Carafate and Sulcrate treat ulcers; and Canasa and Salofalk offer relief for inflammatory bowel diseases. In addition Aptalis Pharma markets Zenpep a digestive aids for patients with exocrine pancreatic insufficiency a condition associated with cystic fibrosis. The firm's products are primarily sold in North America and the European Union. Aptalis Pharma is a subsidiary of Axcan Holdings which is controlled by TPG Capital.

APTARGROUP INC.
NYS: ATR

475 West Terra Cotta Avenue, Suite E
Crystal Lake, IL 60014
Phone: 815 477-0424
Fax: 815 477-0481
Web: www.aptar.com

CEO: Stephen J. Hagge
CFO: Robert W. Kuhn
HR: Ursula Saint-leger
FYE: December 31
Type: Public

AptarGroup hopes its dispensers are well indispensable. The company's pump dispensers are used for fragrances and cosmetics food and pharmaceuticals and a myriad of other personal care items. AptarGroup also makes dispensing closures for plastic-capped squeezable containers holding toiletries and to a lesser extent food and beverage and household goods. The company offers aerosol valves in both continuous-spray and metered-dose options. Lines are sold under the AptarGroup subsidiary brands that produce them: Emsar Pfeiffer Seaquist and Valois. AptarGroup operates on five continents selling dispensers worldwide through an in-house sales network.

	Annual Growth	12/10	12/11	12/12	12/13	12/14
Sales ($ mil.)	5.8%	2,076.7	2,337.2	2,331.0	2,520.0	2,597.8
Net income ($ mil.)	2.5%	173.5	183.7	162.6	172.0	191.7
Market value ($ mil.)	8.9%	2,946.1	3,230.9	2,955.4	4,199.5	4,139.5
Employees	10.9%	8,600	10,900	12,000	12,400	13,000

APTIFY

1850 K St. NW 3rd Fl.
Washington DC 20006-1605
Phone: 202-223-2600
Fax: 202-223-8800
Web: www.aptify.com

CEO: Amith Nagarajan
CFO: Chris Frederick
HR: –
FYE: December 31
Type: Private

Aptify hopes to help the disorganized masses. The company develops data management software used by customers for the automation of a variety of back-office functions such as accounting order entry fundraising marketing membership renewal and polling and surveying. Aptify serves a range of industries including education health care and manufacturing. It also has products tailored for religious groups and other non-profit organizations. Clients have included Publishing Technology and The Catholic Health Association of the United States. The company has additional offices in California Illinois and Pennsylvania. Chairman and CEO founded Aptify in 1993.

APTIMUS INC.

199 Fremont St. Ste. 1800
San Francisco CA 94105
Phone: 415-896-2123
Fax: 415-896-2561
Web: www.aptimus.com

CEO: Joseph L D'Amico
CFO: John A Wade
HR: –
FYE: December 31
Type: Subsidiary

Aptimus thinks it's the most qualified to bring you online shopping deals. The company whose name is derived from the Latin words "aptus" (unusually qualified) and "optimus" (most beneficial) operates an ad network that showcases free trial and promotional offers from a variety of corporate clients. Serving primarily the education sector Aptimus provides banner ads hyperlinks and pop-ups across its network of sites as part of its clients' marketing campaigns and coordinates mailings using its database of e-mail addresses of people who have opted to receive promotional offers. Owning offices in Seattle and San Francisco Aptimus is a subsidiary of education services company Apollo Group.

APTINA LLC

3080 N. 1st St.
San Jose CA 95134
Phone: 408-660-2699
Fax: 408-660-2674
Web: www.aptina.com

CEO: –
CFO: –
HR: –
FYE: December 31
Type: Private

For Aptina image is everything. The company is a leader in CMOS (complementary metal-oxide-semiconductor) imaging technology. Its digital image sensor components and processors are used in standard digital still and video cameras as well as cameras built into mobile phones PCs and surveillance equipment. The company also makes sensors for medical imaging scopes (used in colonoscopies for example) and automobile cameras that enable rear view images. Aptina partners with mobile handset makers and camera component designers and distributes its products from offices in North America Europe and Asia. Memory chip maker Micron Technology formed Aptina in 2008 and spun it off in 2009.

APTIUM ONCOLOGY INC.

8201 Beverly Blvd.
Los Angeles CA 90048-4505
Phone: 323-966-3400
Fax: 323-966-3685
Web: www.aptiumoncology.com

CEO: Wesley Scruggs
CFO: –
HR: –
FYE: December 31
Type: Subsidiary

The side effects of cancer treatment can be nearly as devastating as the disease itself but Aptium Oncology offers treatment variations to make the best of a bad situation for patients. Aptium Oncology manages hospital-based outpatient and comprehensive cancer treatment centers for patients with all types of cancer. It operates a network of 24-hour cancer treatment centers in hospitals in California Florida New York and New Jersey. Aptium Oncology provides consulting management information technology and research coordination services to its clients. The company is a subsidiary of UK-based AstraZeneca a top maker of cancer drugs.

AQUA AMERICA INC

762 W. Lancaster Avenue
Bryn Mawr, PA 19010-3489
Phone: 610 527-8000
Fax: –
Web: www.aquaamerica.com

NYS: WTR
CEO: Christopher H. (Chris) Franklin
CFO: David P. Smeltzer
HR: Susan Brouard
FYE: December 31
Type: Public

Aqua America helps keep water clean and people quenched. It is a holding company for regulated utilities that provide water distribution and wastewater services to about 3 million US residents as well as commercial and industrial customers. The company now operates in 10 states. After a swap of operations with American Water Works in 2012 Aqua America's regulated utilities spread across nine states mainly along the East Coast and in the South. The company also owns a nonregulated wastewater utility in Georgia. Its operating subsidiaries manage the utilities.

	Annual Growth	12/10	12/11	12/12	12/13	12/14
Sales ($ mil.)	1.8%	726.1	712.0	757.8	768.6	779.9
Net income ($ mil.)	17.1%	124.0	143.1	196.6	221.3	233.2
Market value ($ mil.)	4.4%	3,973.4	3,897.4	4,493.1	4,169.6	4,719.3
Employees	(0.2%)	1,632	1,615	1,619	1,553	1,617

ARADIGM CORP.

3929 Point Eden Way
Hayward, CA 94545
Phone: 510 265-9000
Fax: –
Web: www.aradigm.com

NAS: ARDM
CEO: Igor Gonda
CFO: Nancy E Pecota
HR: –
FYE: December 31
Type: Public

Aradigm helps the medicine go down for people who swoon at the sight of a needle. Aradigm develops orally inhaled drug delivery systems that treat respiratory diseases. Its lead delivery technology AERx (an aerosol created from liquid drug formulations) is being adapted to deliver a variety of drugs to treat pulmonary diseases. Aradigm has focused its efforts on developing respiratory treatments for conditions such as cystic fibrosis bronchiectasis inhaled anthrax smoking cessation and asthma. Aradigm typically elects to reformulate already-approved drugs (such as antibiotic ciprofloxacin) and combine them with its inhalation delivery technologies in order to speed up the regulatory process.

	Annual Growth	12/10	12/11	12/12	12/13	12/14
Sales ($ mil.)	66.3%	4.4	0.8	1.0	9.7	33.6
Net income ($ mil.)	–	(5.4)	(9.3)	(8.2)	(21.6)	4.7
Market value ($ mil.)	70.3%	13.3	13.3	13.3	2.6	111.9
Employees	10.7%	12	11	11	12	18

ARAMARK

Aramark Tower, 1101 Market Street
Philadelphia, PA 19107
Phone: 215 238-3000
Fax: –
Web: www.aramark.com

NYS: ARMK
CEO: Eric J. Foss
CFO: Stephen P. (Steve) Bramlage
HR: Lynn B. McKee
FYE: October 02
Type: Public

Keeping employees fed and clothed is one mark of this company. ARAMARK is the world's #3 contract foodservice provider (behind Compass Group and Sodexo) and the #2 uniform supplier (behind Cintas) in the US. It offers corporate dining services and operates concessions at many sports arenas and other entertainment venues while its ARAMARK Refreshment Services unit is a leading provider of vending and beverage services. The firm also provides facilities management services. Through ARAMARK Uniform and Career Apparel the company supplies uniforms for healthcare public safety and technology workers. Founded in 1959 ARAMARK became a public company again in 2013.

	Annual Growth	09/11	09/12	09/13*	10/14	10/15
Sales ($ mil.)	2.3%	13,082.4	13,505.4	13,945.7	14,832.9	14,329.1
Net income ($ mil.)	29.5%	83.8	103.6	69.4	149.0	235.9
Market value ($ mil.)	16.6%	–	–	–	6,343.4	7,396.7
Employees	(1.2%)	–	–	272,000	269,500	265,500

*Fiscal year change

ARAMARK REFRESHMENT SERVICES LLC

ARAMARK Tower 1101 Market St.
Philadelphia PA 19107-2934
Phone: 215-238-3000
Fax: 215-238-3333
Web: www.aramarkrefreshments.com
CEO: –
CFO: –
HR: –
FYE: September 30
Type: Subsidiary

You might say this company facilitates water cooler discussions and breakroom meetings. ARAMARK Refreshment Services is a leading supplier of vending machines and office coffee and water services. The subsidiary of foodservices firm ARAMARK Corporation serves its customers through about 90 distribution facilities that cater to more than 100000 locations in North America. Its "Complete Breaktime Experience" offers an array of coffee and brewing systems along with water dispensing equipment and other supplies. In addition the firm's vending unit stocks and maintains vending machines mainly in workplaces. In 2011 it picked up Van Houtte US Coffee Service or Filterfresh from Green Mountain Coffee Roasters.

ARBELLA MUTUAL INSURANCE COMPANY

1100 Crown Colony Dr.
Quincy MA 02169
Phone: 617-328-2800
Fax: 617-328-2970
Web: www.arbella.com
CEO: –
CFO: Christopher E Hall
HR: Ellen Mann
FYE: December 31
Type: Private

The ship Arbella carried the Puritan settlers of the Massachusetts Bay Colony but Arbella Mutual Insurance would insure their worldly goods. The New England company provides consumer and personal property/casualty insurance in Massachusetts and is one of the state's top auto insurers. Operating through Arbella Mutual and Commonwealth Mutual it underwrites auto homeowners and other personal insurance products in Massachusetts. The group also provides business insurance products (auto fleet coverage and workers' compensation for instance) in its home state New Hampshire and Rhode Island. Arbella's Covenant Insurance affiliate writes personal insurance policies in Connecticut.

ARAMARK UNIFORM AND CAREER APPAREL LLC

115 N. 1st St.
Burbank CA 91502
Phone: 818-973-3700
Fax: 818-973-2848
Web: www.aramark-uniform.com
CEO: –
CFO: Bruce Hausman
HR: Patricia Cadogan
FYE: September 30
Type: Subsidiary

What do butchers chefs municipal workers nurses and supermarket clerks have in common? Their uniforms may all be provided by ARAMARK Uniform and Career Apparel. The company makes rents and sells professional uniforms and workplace apparel to businesses in 45 US states Puerto Rico and Ontario Canada. ARAMARK Uniform and Career Apparel also sells or leases workplace supplies including floor mats mops towels and dispensers. Divisions of the company include ARAMARK Uniform Services Galls and WearGuard and Crest. A subsidiary of the world's third-largest food service provider ARAMARK ARAMARK Uniform and Career Apparel is the #2 uniform rental company in the US (behind rival Cintas).

ARBINET CORPORATION

460 Herndon Parkway
Herndon VA 20170
Phone: 703-456-4100
Fax: 703-456-4123
Web: www.arbinet.com
CEO: Shawn F O'Donnell
CFO: Gary G Brandt
HR: –
FYE: December 31
Type: Subsidiary

Arbinet makes communications capacity a tradable commodity. The company operating as PTGi International Carrier Services created and operates the leading electronic marketplace for communications trading. Used by roughly 1100 members primarily communications services providers its automated platform offers anonymous buying and selling of wholesale voice and data traffic capacity. The company targets customers in the Americas Asia Europe and the Middle East. Arbinet was acquired by Primus Telecommunications (PTGi) in 2011. Primus integrated Arbinet's business brand and technology into a division called PTGi International Carrier Services (PTGi ICS).

ARATANA THERAPEUTICS, INC

1901 Olathe Boulevard
Kansas City, KS 66103
Phone: 913 353-1000
Fax: –
Web: www.aratana.com
NMS: PETX
CEO: Steven St. Peter
CFO: Craig A. Tooman
HR: –
FYE: December 31
Type: Public

If you can't teach old dogs new tricks you can at least ease their stiff joints with medications by Aratana Therapeutics. The company is developing biopharmaceuticals for dogs and cats by licensing pharmaceutical compounds already approved for human consumption and reformulating them for animal use. Aratana has three products in the works — to treat osteoarthritis pain and inflammation in dogs boost appetite in cats and dogs and alleviate post-operative pain in cats and dogs. The company expects these products to be ready for market in the US and Europe by 2016. Founded in 2010 Aratana Therapeutics went public in mid-2013 raising $57.5 million.

ARBITECH LLC

15330 BARRANCA PKWY
IRVINE, CA 926182215
Phone: 949-376-6650
Fax: –
Web: www.arbitech.com
CEO: Torin Pavia
CFO: Clarissa Zulick
HR: Bryndley Schafer
FYE: December 31
Type: Private

There's nothing arbitrary about Arbitech's business model. Arbitech sells a variety of new and used computer equipment made by such companies as Avaya Cisco Systems Hewlett-Packard IBM Microsoft Nortel and VMware. The company's wide range of products include PCs networking equipment servers storage systems components memories and software. In addition to new equipment the company deals in open-box discontinued and refurbished inventory a niche typically not served by other large distributors and resellers of computer products. Arbitech was co-founded in 2000 by CEO Torin Pavia and one of the company's partners William Poovey.

	Annual Growth	12/10	12/11	12/12	12/13	12/14
Sales ($ mil.)	–	0.0	–	–	0.1	0.8
Net income ($ mil.)	–	0.0	(3.5)	(11.6)	(4.3)	(38.8)
Market value ($ mil.)	–	–	0.0	–	652.2	608.5
Employees	52.7%	–	–	16	–	44	57

	Annual Growth	12/03	12/04	12/05	12/08	12/09
Sales ($ mil.)	5.7%	–	–	153.3	180.3	191.4
Net income ($ mil.)	–	–	–	8.4	0.0	0.0
Market value ($ mil.)	–	–	–	–	–	–
Employees	–	–	–	–	–	74

ARBOR COMMERCIAL MORTGAGE LLC

333 Earle Ovington Blvd. Ste. 900
Uniondale NY 11553
Phone: 516-832-8002
Fax: 516-832-8045
Web: www.arbor.com

CEO: Ivan Kaufman
CFO: Paul Elenio
HR: Annette Givelekian
FYE: December 31
Type: Private

Countless borrowers have sought shelter in this arbor. Arbor Commercial Mortgage originates underwrites and services real estate loans with an emphasis on multifamily housing as well as commercial health care industrial office and retail properties. It services more than 600 loans totaling about $3.5 billion for investors including Fannie Mae institutional and corporate investors and private mortgage holders. The company operates about a dozen sales and origination support offices throughout the US. CEO Ivan Kaufman founded Arbor in 1983.

ARBORGEN INC.

180 Westvaco Rd.
Summerville SC 29483
Phone: 843-851-4129
Fax: 843-832-2164
Web: www.arborgen.com

CEO: Andrew Baum
CFO: John Radak
HR: –
FYE: March 31
Type: Private

ArborGen's seedlings are a chip off the ol' bioengineering block. The company produces and markets genetically enhanced eucalyptus and pine tree seedlings designed to grow quickly and resist frigid temperatures and disease. The company which also offers conventional seedlings typically markets to customers in the US New Zealand and Australia. While sold directly to core customers like large land owners and managers its trees are ultimately used by pulp and paper products producers and companies in the biopower charcoal and biofuels industries. ArborGen operates a dozen nurseries 15 orchards three R&D facilities and several distribution centers. In mid-2011 the company shelved its plans to go public.

ARBOR NETWORKS INC.

6 Omni Way
Chelmsford MA 01824
Phone: 978-703-6600
Fax: 978-250-1905
Web: www.arbornetworks.com

CEO: Matthew Moynahan
CFO: Donald W Pratt Jr
HR: –
FYE: December 31
Type: Private

Arbor Networks provides network security software and related computing equipment intended to help businesses grow healthy secure networks. The company's Peakflow and Pravail systems are designed to recognize and respond to network threats such as denial of service attacks. Its eSeries products enable network traffic monitoring and routing among other tasks. Arbor's customers come from such industries as financial services education health care and telecommunications. Clients include Cox Communications Comerica and Tata Communcations. Arbor has international sales offices in Europe and Asia. In 2010 the company was acquired by Tektronix.

ARC DOCUMENT SOLUTIONS, INC.

NYS: ARC

1981 N. Broadway, Suite 385
Walnut Creek, CA 94596
Phone: 925 949-5100
Fax: 925 949-5101
Web: www.e-arc.com

CEO: Kumarakulasingam (Suri) Suriyakumar
CFO: Jorge Avalos
HR: –
FYE: December 31
Type: Public

This "arc" keeps builders from being flooded with too much paper. ARC Document Solutions (formerly American Reprographics Company) provides large-format document reproduction services mainly to architectural engineering and construction firms. It operates about 240 service centers under a variety of local brands and offers on-site document management services at some 5800 customer locations. In addition the company sells reprographics equipment and supplies and licenses its proprietary PlanWell offering an online document management service to independent reprographers. ARC's network of facilities extends across some 40 US states and into Canada China India and the UK.

	Annual Growth	12/10	12/11	12/12	12/13	12/14
Sales ($ mil.)	(1.0%)	441.6	422.7	406.1	407.2	423.8
Net income ($ mil.)	–	(27.5)	(133.1)	(32.0)	(15.3)	7.3
Market value ($ mil.)	7.7%	354.6	214.5	119.6	384.1	477.5
Employees	(5.1%)	3,200	2,900	2,600	2,600	2,600

ARBOR REALTY TRUST INC

NYS: ABR

333 Earle Ovington Boulevard, Suite 900
Uniondale, NY 11553
Phone: 516 506-4200
Fax: –
Web: www.arborrealtytrust.com

CEO: Ivan Kaufman
CFO: Paul Elenio
HR: –
FYE: December 31
Type: Public

Money doesn't grow on trees so Arbor Realty Trust invests in real estate-related assets. The real estate investment trust (REIT) buys structured finance assets in the commercial and multifamily real estate markets. It primarily invests in bridge loans (short-term financing) and mezzanine loans (large and usually unsecured loans) but also invests in discounted mortgage notes and other assets. The REIT targets lending and investment opportunities where borrowers seek interim financing until permanent financing is attained. Arbor Realty Trust is externally managed by financing firm Arbor Commercial Mortgage with which it also shares several key executive officers.

	Annual Growth	12/10	12/11	12/12	12/13	12/14
Sales ($ mil.)	9.2%	99.1	98.2	111.5	129.2	141.0
Net income ($ mil.)	(4.8%)	113.1	(40.1)	21.7	21.3	93.0
Market value ($ mil.)	3.2%	300.8	177.7	302.4	336.2	341.7
Employees	3.7%	32	32	30	37	37

ARC GROUP WORLDWIDE INC

NAS: ARCW

810 Flightline Blvd.
Deland, FL 32724
Phone: 303 467-5236
Fax: –
Web: www.arcgroupworldwide.com

CEO: Jason T Young
CFO: Drew M Kelley
HR: –
FYE: June 30
Type: Public

ARC Group puts a modern twist on making old-fashioned parts. The company makes industrial parts for aerospace automotive and medical uses with a 3D manufacturing process. The 3D process reduces times to prototype and make a part and helps the customer get its product to market faster. ARC offers more traditional manufacturing processes such as metal injection molding plastic injection molding and metal stamping. Those processes are ARC's biggest moneymaker accounting for more than four-fifths of revenue. The US is by far the company's biggest market. It has added to its portfolio of manufacturing processes through a series of acquisitions.

	Annual Growth	12/11*	06/12	06/13	06/14	06/15
Sales ($ mil.)	141.4%	3.3	30.4	68.5	82.9	112.5
Net income ($ mil.)	–	(0.6)	4.5	3.0	4.5	(0.2)
Market value ($ mil.)	15.0%	56.1	55.2	98.2	281.7	98.2
Employees	250.0%	4	–	450	700	600

*Fiscal year change

ARC LOGISTICS PARTNERS LP
NYS: ARCX

725 Fifth Avenue, 19th Floor
New York, NY 10022
Phone: 212-993-1290
Fax: –
Web: www.arcxlp.com

CEO: Vincent T Cubbage
CFO: Bradley K Oswald
HR: –
FYE: December 31
Type: Public

Arc Logistics Partners owns more than a dozen fuel storage terminals in 10 states that can hold almost 5 million barrels of oil ethanol and other types of petroleum products. It also owns two rail transloading facilities in Alabama that can move 23000 barrels per day and a liquefied natural gas storage facility in Mississippi. Customers include oil and gas companies refineries marketers distributors and other industrial manufacturers. Arc Logistics Partners was formed by Lightfoot Capital Partners (which is majority owned by GE). Organized as a limited partnership Arc is exempt from paying corporate income tax as long as it distributes quarterly dividends to shareholders. The partnership went public in 2013.

	Annual Growth	12/10	12/11	12/12	12/13	12/14
Sales ($ mil.)	–	0.0	21.0	22.9	47.8	54.9
Net income ($ mil.)	–	0.0	5.4	5.4	12.8	1.3
Market value ($ mil.)	–	0.0	–	–	283.6	220.9
Employees	9.0%	–	–	80	83	95

ARCA BIOPHARMA INC.
NASDAQ: ABIO

8001 Arista Place Ste. 200
Broomfield CO 80021
Phone: 720-940-2200
Fax: 720-208-9261
Web: www.arcabiopharma.com

CEO: Michael R Bristow
CFO: –
HR: –
FYE: December 31
Type: Public

ARCA biopharma is using genes to treat your heart. The biopharmaceutical company's lead candidate Gencaro is a beta-blocker being developed to treat chronic heart failure and other cardiovascular diseases. Having identified common genetic variations in the cardiac nervous system ARCA biopharma believes those variations may help predict how well patients will respond to Gencaro. Pending regulatory approval Gencaro may be marketed directly by the company or through partnerships. If approved it will be the first genetically-targeted heart failure treatment. ARCA biopharma is also collaborating with LabCorp to develop a companion genetic diagnostic test for Gencaro.

ARCBEST CORP
NMS: ARCB

3801 Old Greenwood Road
Fort Smith, AR 72903
Phone: 479-785-6000
Fax: 479-785-6004
Web: www.arkbest.com

CEO: Judy R. McReynolds
CFO: David R. Cobb
HR: Dana Deason
FYE: December 31
Type: Public

ArcBest (formerly Arkansas Best) puts its best efforts on the road to provide freight transportation services in its home state and the rest of North America. Specializing in long-haul less-than-truckload (LTL) shipments of general commodities (no hazardous waste or dangerous explosives) subsidiary ABF Freight System accounts for nearly 75% of the company's sales. (LTL carriers combine freight from multiple shippers into a single truckload.) ABF Freight System operates a fleet of about 4100 tractors and 20000 trailers from about 250 terminals in the US Canada and Puerto Rico; it offers service into Mexico via alliances. The company changed its name in 2014.

	Annual Growth	12/10	12/11	12/12	12/13	12/14
Sales ($ mil.)	12.0%	1,657.9	1,907.6	2,066.0	2,299.5	2,612.7
Net income ($ mil.)	–	(32.7)	6.2	(7.7)	15.8	46.2
Market value ($ mil.)	14.0%	714.1	501.9	248.7	877.2	1,207.7
Employees	1.7%	10,750	10,800	9,900	11,420	11,484

ARCH CHEMICALS INC.

501 Merritt 7
Norwalk CT 06856-5204
Phone: 203-229-2900
Fax: 519-888-7884
Web: www.rim.com

CEO: Richard Ridinger
CFO: –
HR: –
FYE: December 31
Type: Subsidiary

Arch Chemicals and its line of pool-cleaning products may make it safe to go back in the water but the company is after bigger (smaller) fish — dangerous microbes in the environment. Arch "The Biocides Company" makes products designed to destroy and control the growth of harmful microbes in several areas. In addition to products for the pool Arch sells chemicals for hair and skin care wood treatment preservation and protection applications for paints and building products and health and hygiene applications. The company operates two business segments: biocides products and performance products. In 2011 Swiss biopharmaceutical company Lonza Group acquired Arch in a $1.2 billion cash tender offer.

ARCH COAL, INC.
NBB: ACII Q

One CityPlace Drive, Suite 300
St. Louis, MO 63141
Phone: 314-994-2700
Fax: –
Web: www.archcoal.com

CEO: John W. Eaves
CFO: John T. Drexler
HR: –
FYE: December 31
Type: Public

What powers your power company? Perhaps Arch Coal. About half of the electricity generated in the US comes from coal and Arch Coal is one of the country's largest coal producers by volume behind industry leader Peabody Energy. Arch Coal controls a more than 5 billion ton reserve base of metallurgical and thermal coals. It sold about 130 million tons of coal in 2014 from 16 active mining complexes in every major coal supply basin in the US. It produces thermal (steam) coal used by electric utilities to produce steam in boilers and metallurgical coal used to make steel products. In 2016 the company filed for Chapter 11 bankruptcy protection in a bid to cut $4.5 billion in debt.

	Annual Growth	12/10	12/11	12/12	12/13	12/14
Sales ($ mil.)	(2.0%)	3,186.3	4,285.9	4,159.0	3,014.4	2,937.1
Net income ($ mil.)	–	158.9	141.7	(684.0)	(641.8)	(558.4)
Market value ($ mil.)	(52.5%)	744.2	308.0	155.4	94.5	37.8
Employees	1.6%	4,700	7,442	6,424	5,350	5,000

ARCH VENTURE PARTNERS

8725 W. Higgins Rd. Ste. 290
Chicago IL 60631
Phone: 773-380-6600
Fax: 773-380-6606
Web: www.archventure.com

CEO: –
CFO: Mark A Mc Donnell
HR: –
FYE: December 31
Type: Private

ARCH Venture Partners wants to catch companies on the upward curve of their development. The firm invests in startup and seed-stage companies particularly those concentrating on information technology life sciences and physical sciences. The company also specializes in the commercialization of technologies originating from academic and research institutions. ARCH launched its first fund in 1989 and now manages seven funds totaling some $1.5 billion. It has invested in more than 130 companies since its founding. Portfolio holdings include AmberWave Systems Impinj Nanosys Surface Logix and Xtera Communications.

ARCHEMIX CORP.

300 Third St.
Cambridge MA 02142
Phone: 617-621-7700
Fax: 617-621-9300
Web: www.archemix.com

CEO: Kenneth M Bate
CFO: –
HR: –
FYE: December 31
Type: Private

Monoclonal antibodies and small molecules? Feh! Archemix is focused on aptamers a type of synthetic oligonucleotide that the drug discovery company believes will trump those other cutting edge biotech tools in treating acute and chronic diseases. Aptamers bind to molecular targets much like antibodies but are more easily reproduced. It has R&D programs for potential treatments for cancers rheumatoid arthritis and multiple sclerosis. The company has partnered with larger firms including Merck Serono GlaxoSmithKline and Elan Pharmaceuticals.

ARCHER DANIELS MIDLAND CO.   NYS: ADM

77 West Wacker Drive, Suite 4600
Chicago, IL 60601
Phone: 312 634-8100
Fax: –
Web: www.adm.com

CEO: Juan R. Luciano
CFO: Ray G. Young
HR: Crocifissa Mandraccia
FYE: December 31
Type: Public

Archer-Daniels-Midland's (ADM) forges every link the food chain from field to processing to store. One of the world's largest processors of agricultural commodities the company converts corn oilseeds and wheat into products for food animal feed industrial and energy uses at some 300 processing plants worldwide. The company is also a leading manufacturer of protein meal vegetable oil corn sweeteners flour biodiesel ethanol and other value-added food and feed ingredients. ADM operates an extensive US grain elevator and global transportation network that buys stores transports and resells feed commodities for the ag processing industry connecting crops with markets on six continents.

	Annual Growth	06/11	06/12*	12/12	12/13	12/14
Sales ($ mil.)	0.2%	80,676.0	89,038.0	46,729.0	89,804.0	81,201.0
Net income ($ mil.)	3.4%	2,036.0	1,223.0	692.0	1,342.0	2,248.0
Market value ($ mil.)	19.9%	19,205.6	18,804.2	17,447.4	27,645.8	33,124.0
Employees	3.4%	30,700	30,000	30,600	31,100	33,900

*Fiscal year change

ARCHIE COMIC PUBLICATIONS INC.

325 Fayette Ave.
Mamaroneck NY 10543-2306
Phone: 914-381-5155
Fax: 914-381-2335
Web: www.archiecomics.com

CEO: –
CFO: –
HR: –
FYE: December 31
Type: Private

Throw on your letterman jacket grab Veronica and Betty (really who can choose between them?) and head to Riverdale home to Archie and friends. Archie Comic Publications (ACP) publishes the family-friendly comic book Archie in addition to titles featuring cat-suited rockers Josie and the Pussycats and Sabrina the Teenage Witch. The company's Archie Comics Entertainment division produces and distributes original projects for TV film home video music live events and the Internet and also represents ACP's licensing and merchandising. All total ACP publishes more than 10 million comics per year in a dozen languages worldwide.

ARCHIPELAGO LEARNING INC.   NASDAQ: ARCL

3232 McKinney Ave. Ste. 400
Dallas TX 75204
Phone: 800-419-3191
Fax: 877-592-1357
Web: www.archipelagolearning.com

CEO: Tim J McEwen
CFO: James Walburg
HR: –
FYE: December 31
Type: Public

Archipelago Learning is a subscription-based online education company that provides instruction assessment and productivity tools to improve student and teacher performance. Its products Study Island and EducationCity are used by more than 37000 elementary and secondary schools in the US Canada and the UK to improve student performance on standardized tests. The company's Northstar Learning products offer adult education study and exam prep services. It also distributes Reading Eggs an online reading program for younger children. Providence Equity Partners owns nearly half of the company's stock. Archipelago Learning has agreed to be acquired by PLATO Learning.

ARCHON CORPORATION   OTC: ARHN

4336 Losee Rd. Ste. 5
North Las Vegas NV 89030
Phone: 702-732-9120
Fax: 702-658-4331

CEO: Paul W Lowden
CFO: –
HR: Margaret Gabaldon
FYE: September 30
Type: Public

Archon is banking on gamblers to follow the trail of the Pioneer. Formerly Santa Fe Gaming the embattled company owns and operates one casino the Pioneer Hotel & Gambling Hall in Laughlin Nevada. The Pioneer features some 400 guest rooms and gaming operations that consist of approximately 730 slot machines six blackjack tables one craps table one roulette wheel and five other gaming tables. The hotel includes two restaurants and bars a special events area banquet rooms and a swimming pool and spa. Gaming accounts for more than half of revenues. Chairman and CEO Paul Lowden owns about 75% of the company.

ARCHON GROUP L.P.

6011 Connection Dr.
Irving TX 75039
Phone: 972-368-2200
Fax: 972-368-2290
Web: www.archongroup.com

CEO: –
CFO: –
HR: –
FYE: November 30
Type: Subsidiary

Archon Group keeps it real ... real estate that is. Archon provides portfolio management and financing services to commercial property owners and investors around the world. Its offerings include accounting legal consultation and IT services. The group also provides mortgage origination and specialty financing. Archon manages a property portfolio worth nearly $60 billion in North America Europe and Asia; property types include office buildings industrial facilities multifamily residences and retail spaces. Archon was established in 1996 by Goldman Sachs; its primary client is Whitehall Street Real Estate Funds also part of the Goldman Sachs family.

ARCHROCK INC

NYS: AROC

16666 Northchase Drive
Houston, TX 77060
Phone: 281 836-8000
Fax: –
Web: www.exterran.com

CEO: D. Bradley (Brad) Childers
CFO: Jon C. Biro
HR: Chris Michel
FYE: December 31
Type: Public

Applying pressure is Archrock's (formerly Exterran Holdings) forte — the company rents and repairs compressors and performs natural gas compression services for oil and gas companies. It's three businesses are contract operations fabrication and aftermarket services. The company serves customers in the US or customers that own compression equipment in the US. Archrock provides fabrication services and equipment for oil and natural gas processing and transportation applications. The firm's aftermarket services support the surface production and processing needs of customers. Archrock is a 31% owner of Archrock Partners which contracts compressor units in the US. In 2015 it spun off its international services and global fabrication business as Exterran Corporation.

	Annual Growth	12/10	12/11	12/12	12/13	12/14
Sales ($ mil.)	4.2%	2,461.5	2,683.5	2,803.6	3,160.4	2,899.7
Net income ($ mil.)	–	(101.8)	(340.6)	(39.5)	123.2	98.2
Market value ($ mil.)	8.0%	1,648.8	626.5	1,509.1	2,354.5	2,243.0
Employees	(0.2%)	10,100	10,400	10,000	10,000	10,000

ARCHROCK PARTNERS LP

NMS: APLP

16666 Northchase Drive
Houston, TX 77060
Phone: 281 836-8000
Fax: –
Web: www.exterran.com

CEO: D Bradley Childers
CFO: David S Miller
HR: –
FYE: December 31
Type: Public

Archrock Partners (formerly Exterran Partners) is the largest operator of contract compression equipment in the US. Its services include designing installing operating repairing and maintaining compression equipment. The company operates a fleet of more than 3950 compressor units comprising almost 1.6 million horsepower. Archrock a global leader in full-service natural gas compression equipment and services controls Archrock Partners. Archrock Partners and Archrock (formerly Exterran Holdings) manage their respective US compression fleets as one pool of compression equipment in order to more easily fulfill their respective customers' needs.

	Annual Growth	12/10	12/11	12/12	12/13	12/14
Sales ($ mil.)	25.0%	237.6	308.3	387.5	466.2	581.0
Net income ($ mil.)	–	(23.3)	6.1	10.5	64.0	61.7
Market value ($ mil.)	(5.3%)	1,525.4	1,144.4	1,151.2	1,716.8	1,227.8
Employees	–	–	–	–	–	–

ARCHWAY MARKETING SERVICES INC.

19850 S. Diamond Lake Rd.
Rogers MN 55374
Phone: 763-428-3300
Fax: 763-428-3302
Web: www.archway.com

CEO: Doug Mann
CFO: Tom Smith
HR: –
FYE: December 31
Type: Private

Archway Marketing Services provides marketing information management and customer service for clients primarily residing in the business-to-business sector. It offers such marketing services as program management for rebates sweepstakes and other promotions; fulfillment and distribution; merchandising; and customer relationship management through a dozen facilities throughout North America. It also helps clients hit by the slumping economy by providing cost-saving ideas integrating marketing programs and consolidating a number of outsourced services as they relate to marketing and merchandising. Archway traces its roots to 1952 when it began offering mailing services in Minnesota.

ARCSIGHT LLC

5 Results Way
Cupertino CA 95014
Phone: 408-864-2600
Fax: 408-342-1615
Web: www.arcsight.com

CEO: Meg Whitman
CFO: Tim Stonesifer
HR: Alan May
FYE: April 30
Type: Subsidiary

ArcSight keeps a watchful eye on business risk. The company provides security and compliance management products used to identify prioritize and respond to corporate policy violations and cyber attacks. Its business software tools and network devices handle such security functions as compliance automation event collection and management (ESM) identity monitoring (IdentityView) and log management (Logger). The company also provides consulting implementation support and training services. ArcSight markets to the aerospace and defense energy and utilities financial services food production and health care industries among others. The company is a subsidiary of Hewlett-Packard.

ARCTIC CAT INC

NMS: ACAT

505 Highway 169 North, Suite 1000
Plymouth, MN 55441
Phone: 763 354-1800
Fax: –
Web: www.arcticcat.com

CEO: Christopher T. (Chris) Metz
CFO: Christopher J. Eperjesy
HR: –
FYE: March 31
Type: Public

Prowling over hard ground or snow Arctic Cat offers drivers a purrfect ride. The company manufactures and markets about 30 types of all-terrain vehicles (ATVs) and about 60 snowmobile models. Its four-wheel recreational and utility ATVs and snowmobiles are marketed under the Arctic Cat name. Arctic Cat also supplies replacement parts and Cat-branded protective clothing and riding gear to foster its drivers' experience and loyalty. The company produces and outsources parts to other vehicle OEMs too. Products are sold through a network of independent dealers throughout North America and through representatives of dealers worldwide. The US accounts for roughly 60% of Arctic Cat's sales.

	Annual Growth	03/11	03/12	03/13	03/14	03/15
Sales ($ mil.)	10.7%	464.7	585.3	671.6	730.5	698.8
Net income ($ mil.)	(21.6%)	13.0	29.9	39.7	39.4	4.9
Market value ($ mil.)	23.6%	201.4	554.8	565.9	618.9	470.3
Employees	6.0%	1,323	1,369	1,508	1,611	1,670

ARCTIC SLOPE REGIONAL CORPORATION

3900 C ST STE 801
ANCHORAGE, AK 995035963
Phone: 907-339-6000
Fax: –
Web: www.asrc.com

CEO: Rex A. Rock
CFO: Charlie Kozak
HR: –
FYE: December 31
Type: Private

The Inupiat people have survived the rigors of the Arctic for centuries and now they're surviving in the business world. The Inupiat-owned Arctic Slope Regional Corporation (ASRC) is the largest locally owned and operated business in Alaska. It gets the bulk of its of sales from energy services (ASRC Energy Services) and petroleum refining and marketing unit (Petro Star). Other operations include construction (ASRC Construction Holding) governmental services (ASRC Federal Holding) economic development (Alaska Growth Capital BIDCO) local services (Eskimos Inc.) and tourism (Tundra Tours).

	Annual Growth	12/04	12/05	12/06	12/07	12/08
Sales ($ mil.)	13.6%	–	1,566.5	1,700.5	1,777.5	2,297.3
Net income ($ mil.)	(14.4%)	–	–	206.3	207.7	151.2
Market value ($ mil.)	–	–	–	–	–	–
Employees	–	–	–	–	–	6,000

ARDEA BIOSCIENCES INC.

NASDAQ: RDEA

4939 Directors Place
San Diego CA 92121
Phone: 858-652-6500
Fax: 858-625-0760
Web: www.ardeabiosciences.com

CEO: –
CFO: John W Beck
HR: –
FYE: December 31
Type: Public

Ardea Biosciences wants to end the ordeal painful conditions. The biotechnology company discovers and develops therapies for the treatment of ailments such as cancer gout and inflammatory diseases. The company which focuses on the development of small-molecule therapies (named as such because the molecular compounds weigh less than 1000 Daltons) has drug candidates in clinical and preclinical stages of development. The company's most advanced candidate lesinurad is in Phase III clinical development as a treatment to manage hyperuricaemia — the build up of uric acid in the bloodstream otherwise known as gout. The company was acquired by AstraZeneca for $1.26 billion in 2012.

ARES CAPITAL CORPORATION

NASDAQ: ARCC

280 Park Ave. 44th Fl.
New York NY 10167
Phone: 212-750-7300
Fax: +91-20-2747-7380
Web: www.bajajfinserv.in

CEO: R Kipp Deveer
CFO: Penni F Roll
HR: –
FYE: December 31
Type: Public

Targeting US middle-market companies Ares Capital invests in senior debt loans (secured loans that receive repayment priority over other types of debt) and mezzanine debt; it also makes equity investments. The firm which typically invests between $20 and $250 million per transaction manages a portfolio of more than 140 middle-market companies representing the health care education food service beverage financial services industries among others. Founded in 2004 Ares Capital is externally managed by Ares Capital Management a subsidiary of Ares Management LLC. Arees Capital is one of the larest development companies in the US with some $52 billion of capital under management.

ARDEN GROUP, INC.

NMS: ARDN A

2020 South Central Avenue
Compton, CA 90220
Phone: 310 638-2842
Fax: –
Web: www.ardengroupinc.com

CEO: Bernard Briskin
CFO: Laura J Neumann
HR: –
FYE: December 29
Type: Public

Glitz meets groceries at Arden Group's 18 supermarkets in Southern California (primarily in the Los Angeles area). Through its wholly-owned subsidiary Arden-Mayfair the company operates Gelson's Markets (18000 - 40000 sq. ft.) which carry traditional grocery items as well as imported foods and unusual deli selections. Most also feature coffee and gelato bars fresh pizza sushi and bakeries. While some house in-store banks and pharmacies most are too small to accommodate additional services. The company converted its last Mayfair Markets store to the Gelson's banner in 2009. Arden Group owns a shopping center in Calabasas California that houses a Gelson's supermarket.

	Annual Growth	01/09	01/10	01/11*	12/11	12/12
Sales ($ mil.)	(2.9%)	479.1	431.2	417.1	429.5	439.0
Net income ($ mil.)	(8.5%)	24.7	21.6	18.1	17.0	18.9
Market value ($ mil.)	(10.8%)	390.0	293.6	253.4	276.4	276.4
Employees	(3.0%)	2,291	2,134	2,082	2,134	2,088

*Fiscal year change

ARGAN INC

NYS: AGX

One Church Street, Suite 201
Rockville, MD 20850
Phone: 301 315-0027
Fax: –
Web: www.arganinc.com

CEO: Rainer H Bosselmann
CFO: Cynthia A Flanders
HR: –
FYE: January 31
Type: Public

Argan makes sure its customers stay all juiced up. The holding company owns subsidiaries that provide power services and products for the government telecommunications power and personal health care industries. Its main subsidiary Gemma Power Systems designs builds and maintains power plants including traditional and alternate fuel plants. The company's Southern Maryland Cable unit provides inside-premise wiring and also performs splicing and underground and aerial telecom infrastructure construction services to carriers government entities service providers and electric utilities. Argan's power industry segment accounts for more than 95% of its total revenues.

	Annual Growth	01/11	01/12	01/13	01/14	01/15
Sales ($ mil.)	20.4%	182.6	141.9	278.6	227.5	383.1
Net income ($ mil.)	40.7%	7.8	9.3	23.3	40.1	30.4
Market value ($ mil.)	34.6%	135.6	212.2	275.1	415.7	444.9
Employees	46.3%	188	239	246	359	862

ARENA PHARMACEUTICALS INC

NMS: ARNA

6154 Nancy Ridge Drive
San Diego, CA 92121
Phone: 858 453-7200
Fax: –
Web: www.arenapharm.com

CEO: Harry F. Hixson
CFO: –
HR: –
FYE: December 31
Type: Public

Arena Pharmaceuticals is working to put weight loss in the spotlight. The company is focused on developing biopharmaceutical treatments for cardiovascular central nervous system inflammatory and metabolic diseases. Its first commercial product Belviq (lorcaserin) assists in weight loss and maintenance in obese patients and patients with type 2 diabetes; the drug is marketed by Eisai in the US. In 2015 Belviq was approved for weight management in South Korea. Arena supports its operations with income from R&D partnerships and licensing agreements. From its manufacturing facility in Switzerland Arena also earns a portion of its revenues as a contract manufacturer for another pharmaceutical company.

	Annual Growth	12/10	12/11	12/12	12/13	12/14
Sales ($ mil.)	22.1%	16.6	12.7	27.6	81.4	37.0
Net income ($ mil.)	–	(124.5)	(109.2)	(85.5)	(19.4)	(60.5)
Market value ($ mil.)	19.2%	379.0	412.0	1,987.3	1,288.9	764.5
Employees	(1.9%)	351	266	293	310	325

ARGO INTERNATIONAL CORPORATION

125 CHUBB AVE FL 1
LYNDHURST, NJ 070713504
Phone: 212-431-1700
Fax: –
Web: www.argointl.com

CEO: Clyde Keaton
CFO: Wayne Ackerman
HR: –
FYE: December 31
Type: Private

Argo International is naut about Jason and the Golden Fleece but it does have a stimulating story to tell. The company distributes electrical (fuses generators motors) mechanical (cable reels pumps thrusters) and marine (controls gauges valves) equipment to industrial users in the mining oil utility marine petroleum and refining industries. Argo has more than 20 offices and warehouses throughout Asia Europe the Middle East and North and South America. The company which was established in 1952 is a subsidiary of New York-based Delcal Enterprises Inc.

	Annual Growth	12/00	12/01	12/02	12/12	12/13
Sales ($ mil.)	–	–	0.0	73.4	81.7	59.0
Net income ($ mil.)	11.6%	–	–	1.0	0.7	3.3
Market value ($ mil.)	–	–	–	–	–	–
Employees	–	–	–	–	–	150

ARGO-TECH CORPORATION

23555 Euclid Ave.
Cleveland OH 44117
Phone: 216-692-6000
Fax: 216-692-5293
Web: www.argo-tech.com

CEO: Alexander M Cutler
CFO: John S Glover
HR: —
FYE: October 31
Type: Subsidiary

Argo-Tech makes Fantasy Island's "De plane Boss de plane!" a reality; the company keeps commercial and military aircraft aloft with its high-performance fuel-flow devices. It builds main engine fuel pumps and systems airframe fuel pumps and various ground fuel distribution products. Through its Carter Ground Fueling division Argo-Tech also makes ground refueling equipment. Customers have included the US Army and Air Force; engine and airframe makers such as Airbus Boeing GE Aircraft Engines and Lockheed Martin; and aerospace distributor Upsilon International. In 2007 investment concerns Greenbriar Equity Group and Vestar Capital Partners sold AT Holdings Corp. the parent of Argo-Tech to Eaton.

ARGON ST INC.

12701 Fair Lakes Circle Ste. 800
Fairfax VA 22033
Phone: 703-322-0881
Fax: 703-322-0885
Web: www.argonst.com

CEO: —
CFO: John Holt
HR: —
FYE: September 30
Type: Subsidiary

Argon ST has the five C's of defense down: command control communications computers and combat. It also develops systems for intelligence reconnaissance and surveillance. Together these areas are known as C5ISR. Electronic systems tailored for these purposes track intercept and interpret data needed to make mission decisions on land at sea or in the air. Argon ST's portfolio includes sensors that detect hostile signals and radar; ISR force protection geo-location navigation and threat warning systems; integrated communications networks; and engineering integration and training services. The Boeing subsidiary primarily serves the US defense and homeland security markets from about a dozen US offices.

ARGOSY EDUCATION GROUP INC.

2 First National Plaza 20 S. Clark St. Fl. 3
Chicago IL 60603
Phone: 312-201-0200
Fax: 312-424-7282
Web: www.argosy.edu

CEO: —
CFO: —
HR: —
FYE: August 31
Type: Subsidiary

It's never too late for school at Argosy Education Group. Geared toward working people the for-profit school offers bachelor's master's and doctoral degrees in fields such as psychology and behavioral sciences education and human development business and information technology and the health sciences. Created with the 2001 merger of the American Schools of Professional Psychology the Medical Institute of Minnesota and the University of Sarasota the company operates nearly 20 Argosy University campuses throughout the US in more than a dozen US states. It also offers some classes on the Internet and others through intensive week-long programs.

ARI NETWORK SERVICES, INC.

NAS: ARIS

10850 West Park Place, Suite 1200
Milwaukee, WI 53224
Phone: 414 973-4300
Fax: —
Web: www.arinet.com

CEO: Roy W Olivier
CFO: William A Nurthen
HR: Angela Salsman
FYE: July 31
Type: Public

ARI Network Services helps some very manly industries attract smart shoppers. The company makes and sells software for creating electronic catalogs and e-commerce websites (together more than 80% of sales) in industries such as outdoor power equipment power sports motorcycles marine and agricultural equipment. Dealers manufacturers and distributors use its applications including its PartSmart software which allows companies to access product information for their suppliers and dealers who can use the database. In addition the company's e-commerce and communication applications process orders product registrations and warranty claims and perform search engine optimization.

	Annual Growth	07/11	07/12	07/13	07/14	07/15
Sales ($ mil.)	17.3%	21.3	22.5	30.1	33.0	40.4
Net income ($ mil.)	(18.6%)	2.4	1.1	(0.8)	(0.1)	1.1
Market value ($ mil.)	48.8%	11.1	11.1	11.1	50.8	54.4
Employees	31.4%	133	139	270	248	397

ARIAD PHARMACEUTICALS, INC.

NMS: ARIA

26 Landsdowne Street
Cambridge, MA 02139-4234
Phone: 617 494-0400
Fax: —
Web: www.ariad.com

CEO: Paris Panayiotopoulos
CFO: Edward M. (Ed) Fitzgerald
HR: —
FYE: December 31
Type: Public

ARIAD Pharmaceuticals is exploring the myriad possibilities for new cancer treatments. The firm has a handful of candidates being studied for the treatment of various types of cancer. Its drug Iclusig (ponatinib) a treatment for two rare forms of leukemia is already approved in the US and Europe though the company is seeking approvals for additional indications. ARIAD is also developing ridaforolimus with Merck for the treatment of soft tissue and bone cancers. Other drug candidates aim to treat maladies including lung cancer and lymphoma. ARIAD's drug candidates are in varying stages of preclinical research and clinical trials.

	Annual Growth	12/10	12/11	12/12	12/13	12/14
Sales ($ mil.)	(12.4%)	179.0	25.3	0.6	45.6	105.4
Net income ($ mil.)	—	85.2	(123.6)	(220.9)	(274.2)	(162.6)
Market value ($ mil.)	7.7%	955.2	2,294.4	3,592.3	1,277.3	1,286.7
Employees	32.8%	122	150	300	307	379

ARIBA INC.

NASDAQ: ARBA

910 Hermosa Ct.
Sunnyvale CA 94085
Phone: 650-390-1000
Fax: 317-392-6208
Web: www.shelbycountybank.com

CEO: Robert M Calderoni
CFO: Ahmed Rubaie
HR: —
FYE: September 30
Type: Public

Ariba helps ensure that your supplies arrive in a timely fashion. The company provides spend management software and consulting services used by manufacturers retailers and distributors to connect with suppliers and to manage procurement. Its applications automate buying help target preferred suppliers and manage enterprise sourcing. Companies use its tools to procure such services as equipment repair temporary staffing and travel. Ariba works with more than 150 million suppliers. The company gets the majority of its revenues in North America. Customers have included Bank of America Chevron FedEx Heinz and TE Connectivity. Ariba was acquired by SAP in 2012 for about $4.3 billion.

ARINC INCORPORATED

2551 Riva Rd.
Annapolis MD 21401
Phone: 410-266-4000
Fax: 410-266-2329
Web: www.arinc.com

CEO: Robert K Ortberg
CFO: Patrick E Allen
HR: –
FYE: December 31
Type: Subsidiary

ARINC is a high flyer in communications and systems integration. Commercial aviation US defense and government customers rely on its communications products IT know-how and engineering expertise to make their operations run smoothly. The company's broad range of products and services cover airport security air traffic management aircraft and satellite testing modeling and simulation network design passenger and baggage processing voice and data communications and weather reporting. ARINIC operates from more than 50 offices in the US and it does business in about 100 other countries from facilities in Europe Latin America and Asia. ARINC is owned by private investment firm The Carlyle Group.

ARISTOCRAT TECHNOLOGIES INC.

7230 Amigo St.
Las Vegas NV 89119
Phone: 702-270-1000
Fax: 702-270-1001
Web: www.aristocrat.com.au/company/about/pages/amer

CEO: Jamie Odell
CFO: Toni Korsanos
HR: –
FYE: December 31
Type: Subsidiary

Aristocrat Technologies helps casino managers tell if the house is ahead. The company is the North America Latin America and Caribbean operations of Australian gaming machine manufacturer Aristocrat Leisure. It designs manufactures and markets casino management tools and software to monitor gaming machine use and control payouts. The information systems can also monitor table games and offer additional tools for marketing and accounting. In addition the company makes a variety of gaming machines including reel slot machines video gaming systems and progressive payout machines. Aristocrat Technologies has sales and support centers in Argentina and the US (Minnesota Mississippi New Jersey and Nevada).

ARIVA DISTRIBUTION INC.

50 RiverCenter Blvd. Ste. 260
Covington KY 41011
Phone: 859-292-5000
Fax: 859-261-9777
Web: www.arivanow.com

CEO: –
CFO: –
HR: –
FYE: December 31
Type: Subsidiary

Ariva Distribution formerly known as RIS Paper doesn't mind being called a paper pusher. With approximately 20 branches dotting the US Northeast Mid-Atlantic and Midwest regions the company is a giant merchant of paper and packaging. Ariva purchases warehouses sells and distributes fine printing papers and communication products such as magnetic media copier laser and computer papers. Its lineup includes industrial and packaging products from films and tapes to corrugated strapping and packaging equipment. A branch-based sales force markets to a diverse mix of small to large commercial printers and publishing houses catalog and retail businesses and institutional and government organizations.

ARIZONA CHEMICAL HOLDINGS CORPORATION

4600 Touchton Rd. East Bldg. 100 Ste. 1500
Jacksonville FL 32246
Phone: 904-928-8700
Fax: 904-928-8779
Web: www.arizonachemical.com

CEO: –
CFO: Frederic Jung
HR: David Cowfer
FYE: December 31
Type: Private

Arizona Chemical is pining for more business. The company is among the world's largest fractionators (separators) of crude tall oil (from the Swedish talloja or pine oil). (It claims to be the world's largest producer of pine chemicals). Arizona Chemical manufactures such pine tree-based chemicals as fatty acids rosin esters and terpenes. Those chemicals are used to manufacture a wide variety of products including adhesives household cleaners hydraulic fluids inks paints personal care products and plastics. Investment firm American Securities LLC acquired a 75% stake in Arizona Chemical in 2010 though former majority owner Rhone Capital maintained a 25% stake in the company.

ARIZONA INSTRUMENT LLC

3375 N. Delaware St.
Chandler AZ 85225
Phone: 602-470-1414
Fax: 480-804-0656
Web: www.azic.com

CEO: George G Hays
CFO: –
HR: –
FYE: December 31
Type: Private

Undaunted by their amorphous character Arizona Instrument (AZI) puts the predictable in liquids and gases. The company designs manufactures and sells automated instruments for analyzing moisture content and detecting and monitoring the presence of toxic gas. The equipment is used in a range of industrial environmental and quality control applications. AZI's Jerome hand-held analyzer detects toxic substances such as mercury and hydrogen sulfide while its Computrac Vapor Pro moisture analyzer spies moisture levels key to quality control in producing cookie dough to tobacco adhesives paints and plastics. The privately held company is owned by CEO George Hays his father James Hays and Harold Schwartz.

ARIZONA PUBLIC SERVICE CO.

NL:

400 North Fifth Street, P.O. Box 53999
Phoenix, AZ 85072-3999
Phone: 602 250-1000
Fax: –
Web: www.apsc.com

CEO: Donald E. (Don) Brandt
CFO: James R. (Jim) Hatfield
HR: –
FYE: December 31
Type: Public

Arizona Public Service (APS) is a grand provider of energy in the Grand Canyon state. APS a subsidiary of Pinnacle West Capital distributes power to about 1.2 million customers in 11 of 15 Arizona counties making it the largest electric utility in the state. It operates more than 5900 miles of transmission lines and more than 28930 miles of distribution lines; it generates 6394 MW of capacity mainly from fossil-fueled and nuclear power plants. Arizona Public Service also purchases power from other suppliers to supplement its company-owned generation capacity.

	Annual Growth	12/10	12/11	12/12	12/13	12/14
Sales ($ mil.)	2.3%	3,180.8	3,237.2	3,293.5	3,451.3	3,488.9
Net income ($ mil.)	5.8%	335.7	336.2	395.5	425.0	421.2
Market value ($ mil.)	13.3%	2,953.9	3,433.5	3,633.1	3,771.3	4,868.1
Employees	(1.2%)	6,600	6,663	6,534	6,352	6,279

ARK RESTAURANTS CORP.

NMS: ARKR

85 Fifth Avenue
New York, NY 10003
Phone: 212 206-8800
Fax: 212 206-8845
Web: www.arkrestaurants.com

CEO: Michael Weinstein
CFO: Robert Stewart
HR: Jennifer Jordan
FYE: October 03
Type: Public

You might say this company floats the boat of fine dining fans. Ark Restaurants owns and manages about 20 chic eateries in New York City Las Vegas and Washington DC including the Bryant Park Grill Center Café; and V-Bar. It also operates locations under the names America and Sequoia. In addition Ark Restaurants manages food courts banquet facilities and room services at several casino resorts including the New York-New York Hotel & Casino (owned by MGM Resorts International) the Venetian Casino Resort (Las Vegas Sands) and the Foxwoods Resorts Casino (Mashantucket Pequot Tribal Nation). Founder and CEO Michael Weinstein owns about 30% of the company.

	Annual Growth	10/11*	09/12	09/13	09/14*	10/15
Sales ($ mil.)	1.1%	139.4	138.0	130.6	139.4	145.9
Net income ($ mil.)	39.7%	1.4	5.5	3.8	4.9	5.4
Market value ($ mil.)	14.8%	45.3	57.6	74.1	76.7	78.6
Employees	0.9%	1,953	1,752	1,853	1,901	2,028

*Fiscal year change

ARKANSAS CHILDREN'S HOSPITAL

1 CHILDRENS WAY
LITTLE ROCK, AR 722023500
Phone: 501-364-1100
Fax: -
Web: www.archildrens.org

CEO: Jonathan R. (Jon) Bates
CFO: Gena G. Wingfield
HR: Charlotte Johnson
FYE: June 30
Type: Private

As the only pediatric medical center in the state Arkansas Children's Hospital (ACH) serves the youngest Razorbacks from birth to age 21. The not-for-profit hospital with its 370 beds specializes in childhood cancer pediatric orthopedics and neonatology. Besides acute care services it operates more than 80 specialty clinics and outpatient centers. One of the US's largest pediatric hospitals ACH is also engaged in teaching and medical research through its affiliation with the University of Arkansas for Medical Sciences. Its Arkansas Children's Hospital Research Institute focuses on biological mechanisms underlying birth defects diabetes-related complications and childhood diseases.

	Annual Growth	06/05	06/06	06/08	06/10	06/11
Sales ($ mil.)	-	-	-	0.0	1.1	513.1	509.2
Net income ($ mil.)	-	-	-	-	(0.0)	42.9	48.6
Market value ($ mil.)	-	-	-	-	-	-	-
Employees	-	-	-	-	-	-	3,700

ARKANSAS ELECTRIC COOPERATIVE CORPORATION

1 Cooperative Way
Little Rock AR 72209
Phone: 501-570-2200
Fax: 501-570-2900
Web: www.aecc.com

CEO: Gary Voigt
CFO: -
HR: -
FYE: October 31
Type: Private - Cooperativ

Having access to power is the natural state in the Natural State thanks to Arkansas Electric Cooperative Corporation (AECC) the sole wholesale power provider for 17 Arkansas electric distribution cooperatives. The company operates power plants with about 3418 MW of generating capacity owns transmission assets and buys wholesale power to meet its members' demands. Affiliate Arkansas Electric Cooperatives Inc. (AECI) provides administrative and maintenance services to the distribution companies. The distribution utilities serve about 500000 customers in more than 60% of Arkansas. AECC and AECI along with the state's 17 electric distribution cooperatives are known as the Electric Cooperatives of Arkansas.

ARKANSAS TECH UNIVERSITY

1509 N BOULDER AVE RM 206
RUSSELLVILLE, AR 728018800
Phone: 479-968-0300
Fax: -
Web: www.atu.edu

CEO: -
CFO: -
HR: -
FYE: June 30
Type: Private

Technically Arkansas Tech University is more than a tech college. The state-supported four-year institution of higher education offers undergraduate and graduate degrees in a variety of disciplines including science business arts and humanities engineering and computer science. The school employs more than 400 faculty members and has an average enrollment of more than 11000 students. Based in Russellville Arkansas it also operates a small satellite campus in the town of Ozark. Arkansas Tech was founded in 1909 as the Second District Agricultural School. The school's purpose and name were changed in 1925 when it became Arkansas Polytechnic College; it was renamed Arkansas Tech University in 1976.

	Annual Growth	06/10	06/11	06/12	06/13	06/14
Sales ($ mil.)	6.9%	-	59.7	66.5	69.4	73.0
Net income ($ mil.)	2.1%	-	-	9.8	8.7	10.2
Market value ($ mil.)	-	-	-	-	-	-
Employees	-	-	-	-	-	1,039

ARLINGTON ASSET INVESTMENT CORP

NYS: AI

1001 Nineteenth Street North
Arlington, VA 22209
Phone: 703 373-0200
Fax: -
Web: www.arlingtonasset.com

CEO: Eric F. Billings
CFO: Richard E. (Rich) Konzmann
HR: -
FYE: December 31
Type: Public

Arlington Asset Investment invests mostly in residential mortgage-backed securities (MBS). About one-fourth of the financial firm's MBS holdings are backed by the US government through agencies such as Freddie Mac and Fannie Mae. The remainder of Arlington's MBS portfolio consists of private-label funds issued by private organizations. As part of its business Arlington also manages merchant bank holdings including interest in equity securities mezzanine debt and senior loans. Arlington Asset Investment was founded as Friedman Billings Ramsey in 1989.

	Annual Growth	12/11	12/12	12/13	12/14	12/15
Sales ($ mil.)	(49.2%)	33.4	53.4	39.3	84.9	2.2
Net income ($ mil.)	-	15.2	191.8	49.5	6.0	(69.4)
Market value ($ mil.)	(11.3%)	490.1	477.2	606.4	611.4	304.0
Employees	2.4%	10	11	11	11	11

ARLINGTON INDUSTRIES INC.

1 STAUFFER INDUSTRIAL PAR
SCRANTON, PA 185179620
Phone: 570-562-0270
Fax: -
Web: www.aifittings.com

CEO: -
CFO: -
HR: Brenda Keen
FYE: December 31
Type: Private

Thank goodness for zinc's abundance; the element has enabled Arlington Industry's dominance in manufacturing individual zinc die-cast line items. Arlington manufactures and distributes a slew of metallic and non-metallic fittings and connectors. Its lineup includes bushings cable connectors concrete pipe sleeves conduit bodies gaskets and screw couplings used in the electrical and construction markets. The company operates a sole plant in Scranton Pennsylvania. Since 2003 the privately-held manufacturing company has introduced more than 400 new products.

	Annual Growth	12/08	12/09	12/11	12/12	12/13
Sales ($ mil.)	9.0%	-	89.2	99.0	109.0	126.0
Net income ($ mil.)	-	-	-	0.0	0.0	0.0
Market value ($ mil.)	-	-	-	-	-	-
Employees	-	-	-	-	-	320

ARMANINO FOODS OF DISTINCTION, INC.   NBB: AMNF

30588 San Antonio Street
Hayward, CA 94544
Phone: 510 441-9300
Fax: -
Web: www.armaninofoods.com

CEO: Edmond J. Pera
CFO: Edgar Estonina
HR: -
FYE: December 31
Type: Public

Armanino Foods would tell us: "You're too skinny! Eat!" Armanino Foods of Distinction makes upscale frozen and refrigerated Italian-style food. Its flagship product is pesto and it makes half a dozen varieties. The company also manufactures frozen filled pastas and frozen meatballs. It counts other US food manufacturers restaurants and foodservice vendors among its customers as well as club stores and major retail food chains. Near its headquarters in Hayward California Armanino Foods operates pesto and pasta production facilities. The firm processes its meat in nearby Stockton California. It has branch offices in San Francisco Sacramento Los Angeles Las Vegas Boston and Sioux City Iowa.

	Annual Growth	12/10	12/11	12/12	12/13	12/14
Sales ($ mil.)	8.3%	22.9	24.8	28.0	28.9	31.5
Net income ($ mil.)	13.6%	2.3	2.4	2.9	3.3	3.8
Market value ($ mil.)	28.5%	24.0	25.0	29.5	62.2	65.4
Employees	1.7%	42	44	43	43	45

ARMCO METALS HOLDINGS INC   ASE: AMCO

1730 S Amphelt Blvd, #230
San Mateo, CA 94402
Phone: 650 212-7620
Fax: -
Web: www.armcometals.com

CEO: Kexuan Yao
CFO: Fengtao Wen
HR: -
FYE: December 31
Type: Public

Steel is important to China's growth and iron ore is important to steel. That's where China Armco Metals comes in. The company imports ores for sale to steel mills and other heavy industry. Its iron copper chrome and nickel ore as well as coal come from South America and Asia. Armco's largest customers include Lianyungang Jiaxin Resources Import & Export Sundial Metals and Minerals and China-Base Ningbo Foreign Trade together about two-thirds of sales. The company also imports and recycles scrap metal a cheaper replacement for iron ore in steel production. Armco was incorporated in 2001 in China as Armco & Metawise; it went public in 2008 through a reverse merger with US firm Cox Distributing.

	Annual Growth	12/10	12/11	12/12	12/13	12/14
Sales ($ mil.)	15.9%	68.8	106.2	106.6	128.7	124.2
Net income ($ mil.)	-	(2.2)	(3.3)	(2.6)	(4.1)	1.9
Market value ($ mil.)	(50.6%)	21.8	1.6	2.7	1.7	1.3
Employees	(20.2%)	131	115	98	58	53

ARMOUR RESIDENTIAL REIT INC.   NYS: ARR

3001 Ocean Drive, Suite 201
Vero Beach, FL 32963
Phone: 772 617-4340
Fax: -
Web: www.armourreit.com

CEO: Jeffrey J. Zimmer
CFO: James R. Mountain
HR: -
FYE: December 31
Type: Public

ARMOUR Residential hopes to protect its investments with the strength of the US government. A real estate investment trust or REIT ARMOUR Residential invests in single-family residential mortgage-backed securities issued or guaranteed by Fannie Mae Freddie Mac and Ginnie Mae. The company's investments include fixed-rate adjustable-rate and hybrid adjustable-rate mortgages (hybrid mortgages start off with fixed rates that may eventually increase as the loan matures). To a lesser extent the company also invests in government-issued bonds unsecured notes and other debt. Formed in 2008 ARMOUR Residential is externally managed by ARMOUR Residential Management LLC.

	Annual Growth	12/10	12/11	12/12	12/13	12/14
Sales ($ mil.)	-	8.1	0.3	247.7	(149.9)	(141.5)
Net income ($ mil.)	-	6.5	(9.4)	222.3	(187.0)	(179.0)
Market value ($ mil.)	(17.1%)	344.8	311.2	285.6	177.0	162.5
Employees	33.4%	6	8	14	19	19

ARMSTRONG ENERGY INC.

7733 Forsyth Blvd. Ste. 1625
St. Louis MO 63105
Phone: 314-721-8202
Fax: 510-632-2169
Web: www.laborbank.com

CEO: -
CFO: Jeffrey F Winnick
HR: -
FYE: December 31
Type: Private

Armstrong Energy is strong on coal. The company produces coal from Kentucky's Illinois Basin with proved and probable reserves of 319 million tons; it sells about 7 million tons of coal per year to utilities. In addition to six mines the company also owns three coal processing plants along the Green River with access to river rail and truck transportation. Armstrong Energy uses a variety of coal seams and processing techniques to deliver custom blends to its energy plant customers. The company leases the land its mine are on from its sister firm real estate management company Armstrong Resource Partners. Both are owned by investors Yorktown Partners which filed in late 2011 for both to trade publicly.

ARMSTRONG WORLD INDUSTRIES INC   NYS: AWI

2500 Columbia Avenue
Lancaster, PA 17603
Phone: 717 397-0611
Fax: -
Web: www.armstrong.com

CEO: Matthew J. (Matt) Espe
CFO: David S (Dave) Schulz
HR: -
FYE: December 31
Type: Public

Armstrong World Industries (AWI) won't mind if you walk all over it. Or to be more exact its products. AWI makes tile hardwood laminate linoleum and vinyl sheet flooring under such brands as Armstrong Bruce and Robbins. Flooring accounts for nearly half of total sales. Meanwhile AWI's building products unit produces ceilings and suspension systems. AWI operates about 35 plants in eight countries. The company announced plans to separate its flooring business from its ceilings business in 2015 via a spinoff that would result in two independent publicly-traded companies. AWI exited the cabinet making business in 2012.

	Annual Growth	12/10	12/11	12/12	12/13	12/14
Sales ($ mil.)	(2.4%)	2,766.4	2,859.5	2,618.9	2,719.9	2,515.3
Net income ($ mil.)	55.2%	11.0	112.4	131.3	94.1	63.8
Market value ($ mil.)	4.4%	2,370.4	2,418.4	2,796.5	3,175.8	2,818.0
Employees	(6.8%)	9,800	9,100	8,500	8,700	7,400

ARMY AND AIR FORCE EXCHANGE SERVICE

3911 W. Walton Walker Blvd.
Dallas TX 75236-1598
Phone: 214-312-2011
Fax: 214-312-3000
Web: www.aafes.com

CEO: Thomas Counter Shull
CFO: -
HR: -
FYE: January 31
Type: Government Agency

Be all that you can be and buy all that you can buy at the PX (Post Exchange). The Army and Air Force Exchange Service (AAFES) runs more than 3700 facilities — including PXs and BXs (Base Exchanges) — at US Army and Air Force bases in 30-plus countries (including Iraq) all 50 US states and five US territories. Its presence ranges from tents to shopping centers including 160 retail stores 2100 fast-food outlets (brands like Burger King and Taco Bell) 120 movie theaters beauty shops and gas stations. AAFES serves active-duty military personnel reservists retirees and their family members. Although it's a government agency under the DOD it receives less than 5% of its funding from the department.

ARNOLD & PORTER LLP

555 12th St. NW
Washington DC 20004-1206
Phone: 202-942-5000
Fax: 202-942-5999
Web: www.arnoldporter.com

CEO: –
CFO: –
HR: –
FYE: December 31
Type: Private - Partnershi

A tourist might go to Washington DC to see the Smithsonian's museums but an executive's agenda might include a visit to Arnold & Porter. The law firm's wide-ranging practice areas center on business transactions and public policy; its specialties include antitrust bankruptcy and corporate restructuring white collar criminal defense international trade intellectual property and litigation. The firm is also known for its strong pro bono work. Arnold & Porter has about 825 lawyers at seven offices in the US and two in Europe. The firm was established in 1946 as Arnold Fortas & Porter; Abe Fortas later a Supreme Court justice was a founding partner.

ARNOLD MACHINERY COMPANY

2955 W 2100 S
SALT LAKE CITY, UT 841191207
Phone: 801-972-4000
Fax: –
Web: www.arnoldmachinery.com

CEO: Russ Fleming
CFO: –
HR: –
FYE: September 30
Type: Private

Arnold Machinery helps keep construction on the move. Through its many divisions the company distributes construction mining industrial and material handling equipment as well as farm machinery throughout the US. Arnold Machinery also offers used equipment and provides repair and maintenance rebuild exchange and rental services. The company's divisions include General Implement Distributors Mining Equipment Construction Equipment and Material Handling. Arnold Machinery operates about 20 branch facilities covering some 15 states in the Western US.

	Annual Growth	09/09	09/10	09/11	09/12	09/13
Sales ($ mil.)	15.4%	–	191.4	235.5	307.0	294.5
Net income ($ mil.)	6.3%	–	–	11.2	13.1	12.7
Market value ($ mil.)	–	–	–	–	–	–
Employees	–	–	–	–	–	450

ARNOLD WORLDWIDE LLC

101 Huntington Ave.
Boston MA 02199
Phone: 617-587-8000
Fax: 617-587-8004
Web: www.arnoldworldwide.com

CEO: Robert Leplae
CFO: –
HR: –
FYE: December 31
Type: Business Segment

A partnership with this Arnold will get your brand promoted not terminated. Arnold Worldwide is a full-service advertising agency that offers creative ad development campaign planning and brand management services. Responsible for creating those ubiquitous "Progressive Flo" ads for Progressive Insurance its vast advertising agency network spans 15 offices in Amsterdam Canada China Italy the Czech Republic London Lisbon Spain the UK and the US. The agency's primary three East Coast offices in the US have served such brands as Titleist McDonald's Levi's and Volvo. Arnold Worldwide is a unit of Paris-based advertising conglomerate Havas.

AROTECH CORP

1229 Oak Valley Drive
Ann Arbor, MI 48108
Phone: 800 281-0356
Fax: –
Web: www.arotech.com

NMS: ARTX
CEO: Steven Esses
CFO: Thomas J Paup
HR: –
FYE: December 31
Type: Public

Arotech has broadened its horizon from making batteries and chargers in 1990 to military training simulators and aviation and vehicle armor. Subsidiary FAAC supplies simulators related software and training for the US military and various government and private industry clients. MDT Protective Industries and MDT Armor produce lightweight armor and ballistic glass for vehicles as well as aircraft armor kits under the Armour of America name. Arotech also makes lithium batteries and charging systems for military and homeland security markets via Electric Fuel Battery and Epsilor Electronic Industries. The US government (through its military branches) is Arotech's #1 customer representing about 40% of sales.

	Annual Growth	12/10	12/11	12/12	12/13	12/14
Sales ($ mil.)	8.9%	73.7	62.1	80.1	88.6	103.6
Net income ($ mil.)	–	(0.9)	(11.5)	(3.0)	2.2	3.5
Market value ($ mil.)	8.5%	41.0	29.4	25.3	85.6	56.9
Employees	6.2%	418	307	340	373	531

ARQULE INC.

One Wall Street
Burlington, MA 01803
Phone: 781 994-0300
Fax: –
Web: www.arqule.com

NMS: ARQL
CEO: Paolo Pucci
CFO: Robert J Weiskopf
HR: –
FYE: December 31
Type: Public

ArQule is pursuing drug research in the molecular biology field with a focus on cancer cell termination. The biotechnology firm works independently and with other drugmakers to discover new potential drug compounds based on its cancer-inhibiting technology platform. ArQule is developing a portfolio of oncology drugs with a handful of anti-cancer compounds undergoing clinical trials. Its lead product candidate in Phase 2 and Phase 3 clinical development together with development and commercialization partner Daiichi Sankyo is tivantinib an oral selective inhibitor of the c-MET receptor tyrosine kinase.

	Annual Growth	12/10	12/11	12/12	12/13	12/14
Sales ($ mil.)	(21.2%)	29.2	47.3	36.4	15.9	11.3
Net income ($ mil.)	–	(30.1)	(10.8)	(10.9)	(24.6)	(23.4)
Market value ($ mil.)	(32.5%)	368.8	354.3	175.3	135.1	76.6
Employees	(23.2%)	115	103	97	63	40

ARRAY BIOPHARMA INC.

3200 Walnut Street
Boulder, CO 80301
Phone: 303 381-6600
Fax: –
Web: www.arraybiopharma.com

NMS: ARRY
CEO: Ron Squarer
CFO: Patricia Hennehan
HR: –
FYE: June 30
Type: Public

Array BioPharma wants to offer sufferers of cancer inflammatory and metabolic diseases a multitude of treatment options. The development-stage biopharmaceutical company has five wholly owned programs in its development pipeline. Its seven clinical trials in progress include the wholly-owned hematology drug filanesib (ARRY-520) for multiple myeloma and two partnered cancer drugs: selumetinib (with AstraZeneca) and binimetinib or MEK162 (with Novartis). Array's agreement with Genetech includes candidates for the treatment of cancer. The company also has R&D agreements with Amgen InterMune Celgene and others. Array grants distribution rights when it partners with other companies.

	Annual Growth	06/11	06/12	06/13	06/14	06/15
Sales ($ mil.)	(7.8%)	71.9	85.1	69.6	42.1	51.9
Net income ($ mil.)	–	(56.3)	(23.6)	(61.9)	(85.3)	9.4
Market value ($ mil.)	33.9%	318.3	493.1	645.2	648.0	1,024.6
Employees	(11.9%)	259	250	265	198	156

ARRHYTHMIA RESEARCH TECHNOLOGY, INC. ASE: HRT

25 Sawyer Passway
Fitchburg, MA 01420
Phone: 978 345-5000
Fax: –
Web: www.arthrt.com

CEO: Salvatore Emma Jr
CFO: Derek T Welch
HR: –
FYE: December 31
Type: Public

It's all about heart for Arrhythmia Research Technology (ART). The company offers signal-averaging electrocardiographic (SAECG) software that collects data and analyzes electrical impulses of the heart in an effort to detect potentially lethal heart arrhythmias. The company plans to sell the products through licensing agreements with equipment makers. Until it finds a marketing partner however ART is relying on sales from its Micron Products subsidiary which makes snaps and sensors used in the manufacture and operation of disposable electrodes for electrocardiographic (ECG) equipment. Micron Products has acquired assets of several companies that enhance its metal and plastics molding capabilities.

	Annual Growth	12/10	12/11	12/12	12/13	12/14
Sales ($ mil.)	0.8%	23.4	24.3	20.6	21.3	24.1
Net income ($ mil.)	6.4%	0.5	(1.3)	(6.1)	(3.5)	0.7
Market value ($ mil.)	8.4%	15.5	9.1	6.4	8.8	21.4
Employees	0.6%	116	132	99	108	119

ARRIS GROUP INC. (NEW) NMS: ARRS

3871 Lakefield Drive
Suwanee, GA 30024
Phone: 678 473-2000
Fax: –
Web: www.arrisi.com

CEO: Robert J Stanzione
CFO: David B Potts
HR: –
FYE: December 31
Type: Public

ARRIS brings the idea of broadband home. The company makes communications equipment and components used to enable broadband voice and data transmission and to build television broadcast networks. Products include cable network headend gear Internet protocol switching systems modems and other consumer premises products. It also sells such related hardware as cable connectors and other supplies used for mounting and installation. ARRIS primarily markets to large cable-network operators. The company added cable set-top boxes digital video and Internet TV distribution systems and other products to its portfolio in 2013 with the acquisition of Motorola Mobility's Home business which more than triples its size.

	Annual Growth	12/09	12/10	12/11	12/12	12/13
Sales ($ mil.)	34.5%	1,107.8	1,087.5	1,088.7	1,353.7	3,620.9
Net income ($ mil.)	–	90.8	64.1	(17.7)	53.5	(48.8)
Market value ($ mil.)	20.8%	1,624.2	1,594.4	1,537.5	2,123.0	3,458.7
Employees	36.3%	1,884	1,942	2,211	2,175	6,500

ARROW ELECTRONICS, INC. NYS: ARW

9201 East Dry Creek Road
Centennial, CO 80112
Phone: 303 824-4000
Fax: –
Web: www.arrow.com

CEO: Michael J. (Mike) Long
CFO: Paul J. Reilly
HR: John McMahon
FYE: December 31
Type: Public

Arrow Electronics knows its target market. The company is a leading global distributor of electronic components and computer products alongside rival Avnet. It sells semiconductors passive components interconnect products and computer peripherals to more than 100000 equipment manufacturers and commercial customers. Arrow also provides value-added services such as materials planning design and engineering inventory management and contract manufacturing. It distributes products made by such manufacturers as IBM Panasonic Microsoft and Intel. The company operates from some 460 locations across the globe (serving some 56 countries); half of its sales comes from the Americas.

	Annual Growth	12/11	12/12	12/13	12/14	12/15
Sales ($ mil.)	2.1%	21,390.3	20,405.1	21,357.3	22,768.7	23,282.0
Net income ($ mil.)	(4.5%)	598.8	506.3	399.4	498.0	497.7
Market value ($ mil.)	9.7%	3,401.4	3,462.3	4,932.6	5,263.5	4,926.2
Employees	4.2%	15,700	16,500	16,500	17,000	18,500

ARROW FINANCIAL CORP. NMS: AROW

250 Glen Street
Glens Falls, NY 12801
Phone: 518 745-1000
Fax: –
Web: www.arrowfinancial.com

CEO: Thomas J. (Tom) Murphy
CFO: Terry R. Goodemote
HR: Sally Costello
FYE: December 31
Type: Public

Arrow Financial has more than one shaft in its quiver. It's the holding company for two banks: Glens Falls National Bank operates about 30 branches in five counties in eastern upstate New York while Saratoga National Bank and Trust Company has more than five locations in Saratoga County. Serving local individuals and businesses the banks offer standard deposit products like checking savings and money market accounts; CDs; and IRAs. The banks also provide retirement trust and estate planning services and employee benefit plan administration.

	Annual Growth	12/10	12/11	12/12	12/13	12/14
Assets ($ mil.)	3.8%	1,908.3	1,962.7	2,022.8	2,163.7	2,217.4
Net income ($ mil.)	1.6%	21.9	21.9	22.2	21.8	23.4
Market value ($ mil.)	(0.0%)	356.2	303.5	323.0	343.9	355.9
Employees	1.6%	481	521	518	516	513

ARROW FINANCIAL SERVICES L.L.C.

5996 W. Touhy Ave.
Niles IL 60714
Phone: 847-557-1100
Fax: 847-647-9526
Web: www.arrow-financial.com

CEO: –
CFO: –
HR: –
FYE: December 31
Type: Subsidiary

Sallie Mae giveth what Arrow Financial Services taketh back with interest. The collection services company which is majority owned by student loan provider SLM (Sallie Mae) performs contingency collection services on past-due consumer accounts. Arrow Financial works on behalf of its parent as well as credit card issuers; telecommunications providers; utility companies; and auto education and other consumer lenders. The company also purchases and services performing and nonperforming consumer debt. It has about a half-dozen call centers and other offices around the nation. Sallie Mae acquired a majority stake in Arrow Financial in 2004.

ARROW HEAD REGIONAL MEDICAL CENTER

400 N PEPPER AVE
COLTON, CA 923241801
Phone: 909-580-1000
Fax: –

CEO: –
CFO: –
HR: –
FYE: June 30
Type: Private

Find yourself dehydrated after searching the Inland Empire deserts for arrowheads? Arrowhead Regional Medical Center (ARMC) can fix you up. The San Bernardino County owned and operated hospital provides a range of health services from general medical and surgical care to emergency services rehabilitation inpatient psychiatric care pediatric and women's health services. It also serves as a Level II trauma center a regional burn center and medical training facility. ARMC with some 460 beds (370 inpatient and 90 behavioral) opened in 1999 to replace the aging San Bernardino County Hospital. The hospital also offers outpatient services on its main campus and at area clinics.

	Annual Growth	06/01	06/02	06/03	06/04	06/09
Sales ($ mil.)	(4.6%)	–	313.5	313.5	439.1	225.0
Net income ($ mil.)	–	–	–	(1.1)	3.7	25.4
Market value ($ mil.)	–	–	–	–	–	–
Employees	–	–	–	–	–	2,500

ARROWHEAD RESEARCH CORP
NMS: ARWR

225 S. Lake Avenue, Suite 1050
Pasadena, CA 91101
Phone: 626 304-3400
Fax: 626 304-3401
Web: www.arrowheadresearch.com

CEO: Christopher (Chris) Anzalone
CFO: Kenneth (Ken) Myszkowski
HR: –
FYE: September 30
Type: Public

Arrowhead Research is a development-stage holding company with several subsidiaries focused on developing and commercializing nanotechnologies. Its Agonn Systems unit is developing nanotechnology-based storage devices used for hybrid electric vehicles while Unidym focuses on the commercialization of carbon nanotube-based (sphere-like molecules that can transfer electricity heat and other forms of energy) properties. In addition Calando Pharmaceuticals develops and commercializes therapeutics. Arrowhead has also funded nanoscience research at universities (including the California Institute of Technology and Duke University) in exchange for the right to commercialize the resulting intellectual property.

	Annual Growth	09/11	09/12	09/13	09/14	09/15
Sales ($ mil.)	6.6%	0.3	0.1	0.3	0.2	0.4
Net income ($ mil.)	–	(3.1)	(21.1)	(31.1)	(58.6)	(91.9)
Market value ($ mil.)	96.1%	23.2	156.0	338.8	879.5	343.0
Employees	55.0%	18	52	54	81	104

ART CENTER COLLEGE OF DESIGN INC

1700 LIDA ST
PASADENA, CA 911031999
Phone: 626-396-2200
Fax: –
Web: www.artcenter.edu

CEO: –
CFO: Gina Luciffino
HR: Dave Di Raddo
FYE: June 30
Type: Private

Art Center College of Design (ACCD) is designing a future of creativity for its students. The college offers undergraduate and graduate degrees in such fields as advertising film fine art media graphic design illustration photography industrial design product design and transportation design. Degrees offered include 11 Bachelor of Fine Arts and Bachelor of Science programs and six Master of Fine Arts and Master of Science programs. ACCD which has an enrollment of about 1700 full-time students is ranked among top design schools in the US.

	Annual Growth	06/08	06/09	06/10	06/11	06/13
Sales ($ mil.)	52.6%	–	–	41.0	107.1	145.6
Net income ($ mil.)	420.7%	–	–	0.3	5.6	37.1
Market value ($ mil.)	–	–	–	–	–	–
Employees	–	–	–	–	–	400

ARTECH INFORMATION SYSTEMS L.L.C.

240 Cedar Knolls Rd. Ste. 100
Cedar Knolls NJ 07927
Phone: 973-998-2500
Fax: 973-998-2599
Web: www.artechinfo.com

CEO: –
CFO: –
HR: –
FYE: December 31
Type: Private

Artech Information Systems comes to the rescue for the technically unsavvy. The minority- and woman-owned company specializes in providing IT staffing and consulting project management and business process outsourcing (BPO) services. Artech Information Systems serves clients in the financial services pharmaceutical telecommunications and technology industries among others. The company which operates from more than 20 locations in China India Mexico and the US also works with federal and state government agencies. It provides its services 24 hours a day seven days a week.

ARTESIAN RESOURCES CORP.
NMS: ARTN A

664 Churchmans Road
Newark, DE 19702
Phone: 302 453-6900
Fax: 302 453-6957
Web: www.artesianresources.com

CEO: Dian C. Taylor
CFO: David B. Spacht
HR: –
FYE: December 31
Type: Public

All's well that ends in wells for Artesian Resources. Operating primarily through regulated utility Artesian Water the company provides water in parts of Delaware Maryland and Pennsylvania to a population of some 300000 (nearly 82000 metered customers). It serves residential commercial industrial municipal and utility customers; residential customers account for about 55% of the utility's water sales. Artesian pumps more than 7 billion gallons of water annually from its wells then sends it to customers through nearly 1200 miles of mains and some 5700 hydrants. The company also provides wastewater services in Delaware and Maryland.

	Annual Growth	12/10	12/11	12/12	12/13	12/14
Sales ($ mil.)	2.8%	64.9	65.1	70.6	69.1	72.5
Net income ($ mil.)	5.7%	7.6	6.7	9.8	8.3	9.5
Market value ($ mil.)	4.5%	152.3	151.3	180.3	184.5	181.6
Employees	(0.9%)	246	230	234	239	237

ARTHROCARE CORP.
NMS: ARTC

7000 W. William Cannon, Building One
Austin, TX 78735
Phone: 512 391-3900
Fax: 512 391-3901
Web: www.arthrocare.com

CEO: David Fitzgerald
CFO: Todd Newton
HR: Tiffany Raines
FYE: December 31
Type: Public

With the wave of a wand ArthroCare can make tissue disappear. The company's proprietary Coblation technology (one of several of its technologies) uses bipolar radiofrequency energy to remove and shape cartilage and tendons and other soft tissues. Its specialized wands focus the energy and minimize damage to nearby healthy tissue simultaneously sealing small bleeding vessels. First used in arthroscopic procedures to repair joints the electrosurgery system line now includes equipment used in a wide range of minimally invasive surgeries. The company also makes ligament repair spinal stabilization and wound-care products.

	Annual Growth	12/08	12/09	12/10	12/11	12/12
Sales ($ mil.)	4.1%	314.2	331.6	355.4	354.9	368.5
Net income ($ mil.)	–	(34.7)	(5.8)	37.1	(0.9)	46.4
Market value ($ mil.)	64.1%	133.5	663.1	869.0	886.3	967.7
Employees	38.4%	463	1,363	1,407	1,600	1,700

ARTISAN PARTNERS ASSET MANAGEMENT INC
NYS: APAM

875 E. Wisconsin Avenue, Suite 800
Milwaukee, WI 53202
Phone: 414 390-6100
Fax: –
Web: www.artisanpartners.com

CEO: Eric R Colson
CFO: Charles J Daley Jr
HR: –
FYE: December 31
Type: Public

These artisans are into making bread. Artisan Partners Asset Management is an institutional investment manager with $64 billion in assets under management. The firm manages a dozen funds from small- and mid-cap growth and value funds to foreign and emerging markets funds. It acts as the investment adviser to Artisan Funds mutual funds which account for about 55% of its assets under management. The remainder is made up of separate accounts for institutional investors including pension plans trusts endowments foundations not-for-profit organizations government entities and private companies. Founded in 1994 Artisan Partners Asset Management went public in 2013.

	Annual Growth	12/10	12/11	12/12	12/13	12/14
Sales ($ mil.)	–	0.0	–	–	685.8	828.7
Net income ($ mil.)	–	0.0	(0.1)	(0.0)	24.8	69.6
Market value ($ mil.)	–	0.0	–	–	4,754.1	3,685.0
Employees	12.4%	–	–	273	300	345

ARTISANAL BRANDS INC.

NBB: AHFP

483 Tenth Avenue
New York, NY 10018
Phone: 212 871-3150
Fax: –
Web: www.artisanalcheese.com

CEO: Daniel W Dowe
CFO: James Lillis
HR: –
FYE: May 31
Type: Public

American Home Food Products which does business as Artisanal Cheese aspires to be the big cheese. Formerly a building supply marketing firm the company is now active in the marketing of private-label foods. In 2007 it acquired specialty food company Artisanal Premium Cheese for about $4.5 million. At the same time the company sold its building material assets for approximately $1 million. Artisanal Cheese markets and sells specialty and handmade cheeses to upscale restaurants and retailers. In addition to wholesale and foodservice distribution the company sells products in supermarkets through catalogs and on its Web site.

	Annual Growth	05/08	05/09	05/10	05/11	05/12
Sales ($ mil.)	–	0.0	5.7	4.2	4.6	3.6
Net income ($ mil.)	–	0.0	(1.6)	(2.3)	(2.5)	(4.3)
Market value ($ mil.)	–	0.0	8.1	3.4	4.8	1.3
Employees	21.6%	–	–	23	30	34

ARTS WAY MANUFACTURING CO INC

NAS: ARTW

5556 Highway 9
Armstrong, IA 50514
Phone: 712 864-3131
Fax: 712 864-3154
Web: www.artsway-mfg.com

CEO: Carrie L Majeski
CFO: Amber J Murra
HR: –
FYE: November 30
Type: Public

Sinatra did it his way but farmers have been doing it Art's way since 1956. Art's-Way Manufacturing makes an assortment of machinery under its own label and its customers' private labels. Art's-Way equipment includes custom animal-feed processing machines high-bulk mixing wagons mowers and stalk shredders and equipment for harvesting sugar beets and potatoes. Its private-label OEM customers include CNH Global for whom Art's-Way makes and supplies hay blowers. Equipment dealers throughout the US sell Art's-Way products. Steel truck bodies are also manufactured under the Cherokee Truck Bodies name. Art's-Way owns subsidiaries Art's-Way Vessels and Art's-Way Scientific.

	Annual Growth	11/11	11/12	11/13	11/14	11/15
Sales ($ mil.)	0.3%	27.6	36.5	34.2	36.2	27.9
Net income ($ mil.)	–	1.2	2.7	1.6	0.9	(0.6)
Market value ($ mil.)	(15.8%)	24.5	22.3	25.4	21.5	12.3
Employees	1.2%	143	194	208	204	150

ARUBA NETWORKS INC

NMS: ARUN

1344 Crossman Ave.
Sunnyvale, CA 94089-1113
Phone: 408 227-4500
Fax: –
Web: www.arubanetworks.com

CEO: –
CFO: Catherine A Lesjak
HR: –
FYE: July 31
Type: Public

Aruba Networks wants to turn your business into a wireless paradise. The company offers network access equipment and software for mobile enterprise networks. Its Mobile Virtual Enterprise (MOVE) architecture unifies access between wired and wireless network infrastructures for employees both at and away from the office. Products include controllers access points and concentrators as well as operating system and management software. Aruba also provides professional and support services. It targets the corporate education and government sectors. Aruba outsources most manufacturing to partners such as Flextronics and Sercomm. The US is the company's largest market.

	Annual Growth	07/10	07/11	07/12	07/13	07/14
Sales ($ mil.)	28.6%	266.5	396.5	516.8	600.0	728.9
Net income ($ mil.)	–	(34.0)	70.7	(8.9)	(31.6)	(29.0)
Market value ($ mil.)	1.3%	1,826.3	2,468.4	1,525.2	1,912.4	1,921.0
Employees	26.7%	681	1,057	1,223	1,473	1,754

ARUP LABORATORIES INC.

500 Chipeta Way
Salt Lake City UT 84108
Phone: 801-583-2787
Fax: 800-522-2706
Web: www.aruplab.com

CEO: Edward R Ashwood
CFO: Andy Theurer
HR: –
FYE: June 30
Type: Private

The good folks at ARUP Laboratories don't grow pale at the sight of blood. The clinical reference lab performs tens of thousands of tests daily on blood body fluids and tissue for health care clients including teaching hospitals hospital groups clinics government entities and other labs across the US. Its test menu includes thousands of assays ranging from routine screenings (such as allergy and infectious diseases tests) to highly complex genetic and molecular tests. The organization also offers consulting and information services including online access to test results. ARUP Laboratories is owned by the University of Utah.

ARVEST BANK GROUP INC.

125 W. Central Ste. 218
Bentonville AR 72712
Phone: 479-750-1400
Fax: 614-716-1823
Web: www.aeptexas.com

CEO: –
CFO: –
HR: –
FYE: December 31
Type: Private

Arvest Bank Group operates more than 240 locations in Arkansas Kansas Missouri and Oklahoma. Through Arvest Bank it provides traditional services such as checking and savings accounts CDs and credit cards. The bank's lending activities mainly consist of commercial real estate loans residential mortgages and business construction and consumer loans. The group maintains a decentralized structure of about 15 individually chartered banks; local managers and directors control lending decisions and deposit rates in many communities. Descendants of Wal-Mart founder Sam Walton (including bank CEO Jim Walton a son of Sam and one of the richest men in America) control Arvest Bank Group.

ARXAN TECHNOLOGIES INC.

6903 Rockledge Dr. Ste. 910
Bethesda MD 20817
Phone: 301-968-4290
Fax: 301-968-4291
Web: www.arxan.com

CEO: Joe Sander
CFO: Michael Kelley
HR: –
FYE: December 31
Type: Private

Arxan Technologies doesn't mind being defensive when it comes to security. The company provides network security software and services for protecting computer systems from piracy and unauthorized access. Businesses in a variety of industries used its GuardIT and EnsureIT software suites to control access to their data and applications. Its TransformIT product provides cryptographic key security and BindIT application safeguards against HostID spoofing. Arxan's professional services include needs and risk assessment as well as technical consulting. The company serves clients in such industries as publishing media and telecommunications services. Arxan has satellite offices in San Francisco and London.

ASAHI/AMERICA INC.

35 Green St.
Malden MA 02148-0134
Phone: 781-321-5409
Fax: 781-321-4421
Web: www.asahi-america.com

CEO: Hidetoshi Hashimoto
CFO: Stephen Harrington
HR: –
FYE: March 31
Type: Subsidiary

Asahi/America has made it its mission in life to keep track of the ebb and flow. A subsidiary of Japan-based Asahi Organic Chemicals Industry Asahi/America makes and distributes corrosion-resistant products for fluid and gas flow such as thermoplastic valves tubing and piping systems filtration equipment flow meters and components used in mining pulp and paper chemical/petrochemical water treatment aquarium and semiconductor manufacturing applications. Asahi/America's revenues come from the distribution of valves made by its parent company pipe made by Asahi partner Austrian firm Alois-Gruber and from the sale of its own products (flow meters actuators valve controls filtration equipment).

ASARCO LLC

5285 E. Williams Cir. Ste. 2000
Tucson AZ 85711
Phone: 520-798-7500
Fax: 520-798-7780
Web: www.asarco.com

CEO: –
CFO: –
HR: –
FYE: December 31
Type: Subsidiary

Copper is king for ASARCO. A subsidiary of diversified mining firm Grupo Mexico ASARCO (American Smelting and Refining Company) operates mining and copper smelting activities primarily in the Southwestern US. Each year its mines produce from 350 million to 400 million pounds of copper as well as silver and gold as by-products of copper production. It produces copper cathode rod and cake. The company's three mines and a 720000 tons per year smelter are located in Arizona. It also operates a copper refinery with a 279.5 million pounds per year production capacity in Amarillo Texas. ASARCO was founded in 1899.

ASB FINANCIAL CORP.

NBB: ASBN

503 Chillicothe Street
Portsmouth, OH 45662
Phone: 740 354-3177
Fax: –
Web: www.bankwithasb.com

CEO: –
CFO: Michael L Gampp
HR: –
FYE: June 30
Type: Public

ASB Financial is the holding company for American Savings Bank. Operating since 1892 the bank serves Scioto and Pike counties in southern Ohio as well as communities across the Ohio River in northern Kentucky. From about five offices the thrift originates a variety of loans more than half of which are one-to four-family mortgages. Other loan products include commercial real estate construction business consumer and land loans. American Savings' deposit products include traditional checking and savings accounts NOW and money market accounts CDs IRAs and health savings accounts. The thrift also provides access to financial planning services.

	Annual Growth	06/10	06/11	06/12	06/13	06/14
Assets ($ mil.)	2.4%	229.3	229.3	238.1	260.6	252.1
Net income ($ mil.)	(8.8%)	1.9	2.0	1.7	1.6	1.3
Market value ($ mil.)	(0.5%)	25.7	23.9	23.9	26.7	25.2
Employees	–	–	–	–	–	–

ASBURY AUTOMOTIVE GROUP, INC

NYS: ABG

2905 Premiere Parkway N.W., Suite 300
Duluth, GA 30097
Phone: 770 418-8200
Fax: –
Web: www.asburyauto.com

CEO: Craig T. Monaghan
CFO: Keith R Style
HR: –
FYE: December 31
Type: Public

Asbury Automotive Group has made a living out of being large. The company oversees more than 85 dealerships which operate around 105 auto franchises in about a dozen states including the Carolinas Florida Texas and Virginia. The dealerships sell some 30 different brands of US and foreign new and used vehicles. Asbury also offer parts service and collision repair from about 30 repair centers as well as financing insurance and warranty and service contracts. The auto dealer has grown by acquiring large locally branded dealership groups as well as smaller groups and individually owned dealerships throughout the US. Customers include individual buyers and fleet operators.

	Annual Growth	12/10	12/11	12/12	12/13	12/14
Sales ($ mil.)	10.5%	3,936.0	4,276.7	4,640.3	5,334.9	5,867.7
Net income ($ mil.)	30.8%	38.1	67.9	82.2	109.1	111.6
Market value ($ mil.)	42.4%	527.1	615.0	913.6	1,532.9	2,165.5
Employees	4.0%	7,100	6,800	7,000	7,600	8,300

ASCENA RETAIL GROUP INC

NMS: ASNA

933 MacArthur Boulevard
Mahwah, NJ 07430
Phone: 551 777-6700
Fax: 845 369-8001
Web: www.ascenaretail.com

CEO: David R. Jaffe
CFO: Robb Giammatteo
HR: –
FYE: July 25
Type: Public

Ascena Retail Group (formerly Dress Barn Inc.) has left the farm for greener retail pastures. The apparel and accessories retailer operates about 5000 specialty stores throughout the US Puerto Rico and Canada. Its 900-plus dressbarn stores court women ages 35 to 55. Maurices with some 770 locations targets 17-to-34-year-old females in towns with populations between 25000 and 100000. Its largest chain Justice courts "tweens" at about 1000 stores and online. Its Charming Shoppes subsidiary operates the plus-size Lane Bryant and Catherines Plus Sizes apparel chains. Ascena Retail Group added Ann Taylor Lou & Grey and LOFT stores in 2015 with the $2 billion-plus purchase of upscale retailer ANN.

	Annual Growth	07/11	07/12	07/13	07/14	07/15
Sales ($ mil.)	13.3%	2,914.0	3,353.3	4,714.9	4,790.6	4,802.9
Net income ($ mil.)	–	170.5	162.2	151.3	133.4	(236.8)
Market value ($ mil.)	(21.0%)	5,274.6	3,086.1	3,035.5	2,630.8	2,049.8
Employees	11.6%	31,000	46,000	48,000	48,000	48,000

ASCENA RETAIL GROUP INC.

NASDAQ: ASNA

30 Dunnigan Dr.
Suffern NY 10901
Phone: 845-369-4500
Fax: 914-428-4581
Web: www.drewindustries.com

CEO: David Jaffe
CFO: Robb Giammatteo
HR: –
FYE: July 31
Type: Public

Ascena Retail Group (formerly Dress Barn Inc.) has left the farm for greener — but not leaner — retail pastures. The apparel and accessories retailer operates more than 3800 specialty stores throughout the US Puerto Rico and Canada. Its 825 Dress Barn stores cater to women ages 35 to 55. Maurices with some 830 locations targets 17-to-34-year-old females in small towns with populations between 25000 and 100000. Its Justice chain courts "tweens" at 940 stores and online. Its newly-acquired Charming Shoppes subsidiary operates the plus-size Lane Bryant and Catherines Plus Sizes apparel chains. Founded as Dress Barn in 1962 the company changed its name to Ascena Retail Group in 2011.

ASCEND HOLDINGS LLC

450 E. 1000 N.
North Salt Lake UT 84054
Phone: 801-299-6400
Fax: 801-299-6401
Web: www.ascendhr.com

CEO: –
CFO: –
HR: Josh Henderson
FYE: December 31
Type: Private

If moving up means moving human resources away then this is the company for you. Ascend HR Solutions a professional employer organization provides off-site human resources employee benefits administration and payroll services so clients can focus on their core business. The company also offers computer maintenance consulting and support services for clients of any size. The company's services include skills testing employee handbook development recruiting 401K plan administration tax filing and insurance. Ascend HR Solutions was founded in 1995.

ASCENDANT SOLUTIONS, INC.

NBB: ASDS

16250 Knoll Trail Drive, Suite 102
Dallas, TX 75248
Phone: 972 250-0945
Fax: –
Web: www.ascendantsolutions.com

CEO: –
CFO: Mark S Heill
HR: –
FYE: December 31
Type: Public

Ascendant Solutions holds stakes in companies involved in health care retailing real estate and other sectors. It seeks out opportunities among corporate divestitures distressed or bankrupt firms and entrepreneurs looking to sell their companies. Its investments include Dallas-based specialty pharmacy Dougherty's and CRESA Partners which provides tenant representation and lease management services. Ascendant Solutions also owns stakes in Ampco Safety Tools and Dallas-area mixed-use real estate development firm Frisco Square. In 2008 Ascendant Solutions sold its stake in the Medicine Man chain of pharmacies to a subsidiary of Medicine Shoppe.

	Annual Growth	12/10	12/11	12/12	12/13	12/14
Sales ($ mil.)	(0.2%)	28.7	27.6	24.7	25.2	28.5
Net income ($ mil.)	(31.4%)	2.0	(2.0)	(3.6)	1.2	0.5
Market value ($ mil.)	(1.7%)	6.2	0.9	5.5	3.9	5.8
Employees	–	–	–	–	–	–

ASCENSION HEALTH

4600 Edmundson Rd.
St. Louis MO 63134
Phone: 314-733-8000
Fax: 314-733-8013
Web: www.ascensionhealth.org

CEO: Robert J Henkel Fache
CFO: Anthony J Speranzo
HR: –
FYE: June 30
Type: Private - Not-for-Pr

Ascension Health has ascended to the pinnacle of not-for-profit health care. As the largest Catholic hospital system in the US and thus one of the top providers of charity care in the nation the organization's health care network consists of some 80 general hospitals along with a dozen long-term care acute care rehabilitation and psychiatric hospitals (combined more than 17500 beds). Ascension Health also operates nursing homes community clinics and other health care providers. Its network of medical facilities spans 20 states and the District of Columbia. Ascension Health was created in 1999 from a union of the Daughters of Charity National Health System and the Sisters of St. Joseph Health System.

ASCENT CAPITAL GROUP, INC.

NMS: ASCM A

5251 DTC Parkway, Suite 1000
Greenwood Village, CO 80111
Phone: 303 628-5600
Fax: –
Web: www.ascentcapitalgroupinc.com

CEO: William R. (Bill) Fitzgerald
CFO: Michael R. Meyers
HR: –
FYE: December 31
Type: Public

Ascent Capital Group formerly Ascent Media has a different mountain to climb. Historically the holding company operated through subsidiary Ascent Media Group (AMG) which provided an array of services for the film and TV industries in the US the UK and Singapore. However in 2010 Ascent Media switched gears and acquired security alarm monitoring company Monitronics International for about $1.2 billion. It sold AMG Creative and Media Services (primarily post-production-related businesses) in late 2010 and AMG Content Distribution-related services in 2011. Strategic alternatives are being pursued for AMG's remaining Systems Integration unit.

	Annual Growth	12/10	12/11	12/12	12/13	12/14
Sales ($ mil.)	40.2%	139.5	311.9	345.0	451.0	539.4
Net income ($ mil.)	–	(34.3)	20.6	(28.6)	(22.4)	(37.8)
Market value ($ mil.)	8.1%	525.1	687.1	839.1	1,159.0	717.0
Employees	(8.6%)	1,430	722	788	1,117	1,000

ASCENT HEALTHCARE SOLUTIONS INC.

10232 S. 51st St.
Phoenix AZ 85244
Phone: 480-763-5300
Fax: 480-763-0101
Web: ascenths.com

CEO: Brian White
CFO: Tim Einwechter
HR: –
FYE: December 31
Type: Subsidiary

Ascent Healthcare Solutions is banking on the idea that one doctor's trash could be another doctor's treasure. The company is out to help hospitals with the three "R"s — reduce reuse and recycle. Ascent focuses on reprocessing disposable medical devices for health care facilities (from small rural providers to surgery centers and group purchasing organizations). Its OR-based systems permit the collection of thousands of tons of devices marketed as "single-use" as well as a range of recyclable materials. After collecting the used devices it cleans sterilizes tests and then returns them from its centers in Florida and Arizona. The company is part of the MedSurg division of medical products maker Stryker.

ASCENT SOLAR TECHNOLOGIES INC

NAS: ASTI

12300 Grant Street
Thornton, CO 80241
Phone: 720 872-5000
Fax: –

CEO: Victor Lee
CFO: Victor Lee
HR: –
FYE: December 31
Type: Public

As long as that sun keeps ascending in the eastern skies every day there will be ventures trying to tap its enormous energy resources. Ascent Solar Technologies is a development-stage company working on photovoltaic modules for use in consumer applications as well as satellites and spacecraft. The firm aspires to make such gear smaller lighter and more flexible than existing solar cells for use in space by utilizing a thin-film absorbing layer on top of a polyimide substrate. The thin-film layer on top of the high-temperature plastic is made up of copper indium gallium and selenium which is why the technology is called CIGS. Norsk Hydro has a 39% stake in the company.

	Annual Growth	12/10	12/11	12/12	12/13	12/14
Sales ($ mil.)	21.1%	2.5	3.9	1.2	1.3	5.3
Net income ($ mil.)	–	(31.2)	(105.7)	(28.8)	(30.1)	(43.4)
Market value ($ mil.)	(24.9%)	61.2	7.1	11.3	12.8	19.5
Employees	0.4%	117	77	94	114	119

ASHFORD HOSPITALITY TRUST INC

NYS: AHT

14185 Dallas Parkway, Suite 1100
Dallas, TX 75254
Phone: 972 490-9600
Fax: 972 980-2705
Web: www.ahtreit.com

CEO: -
CFO: Deric S. Eubanks
HR: Donald (Don) Denzin
FYE: December 31
Type: Public

Ashford Hospitality is in with the inn crowd. A self-administered real estate investment trust (REIT) Ashford owns more than 85 luxury hotel properties representing 17200 rooms in states primarily on the East Coast West Coast and Texas. Most of its properties operate under the upscale and upper upscale Embassy Suites Hilton Marriott Hyatt Starwood and Intercontinental Hotels Group brands. In addition to making direct investments in hotels the REIT also originates loans secured by hotel properties. About 80% of Ashford's revenue comes from its Rooms while around 15% comes from its food and beverage services.

	Annual Growth	12/10	12/11	12/12	12/13	12/14
Sales ($ mil.)	(1.4%)	841.4	889.8	922.6	942.3	794.8
Net income ($ mil.)	-	-	(51.7)	2.1	(53.8)	(41.3)	(31.4)
Market value ($ mil.)	2.1%	863.1	715.5	940.0	740.6	937.3
Employees	8.3%	67	75	78	83	92

ASHLAND INC

NYS: ASH

50 E. RiverCenter Boulevard, P.O. Box 391
Covington, KY 41012-0391
Phone: 859 815-3333
Fax: -
Web: www.ashland.com

CEO: William A. (Bill) Wulfsohn
CFO: J. Kevin Willis
HR: Susan B Esler
FYE: September 30
Type: Public

Ashland's three business units are built on chemicals and cars. Ashland Performance Materials makes specialty resins polymers and adhesives. Specialty Ingredients makes cellulose ethers vinyl pyrrolidones and biofunctionals. It offers industry-leading products technologies and resources for solving formulation and product-performance challenges. Consumer Markets led by subsidiary Valvoline runs an oil-change chain in the US and sells Valvoline oil and Zerex antifreeze. The company's Ashland Specialty Ingredients unit produces polymers and additives for the food personal care pharmaceutical and other industries. In 2015 Ashland announced plans to spin off Valvoline.

	Annual Growth	09/11	09/12	09/13	09/14	09/15
Sales ($ mil.)	(4.6%)	6,502.0	8,206.0	7,813.0	6,121.0	5,387.0
Net income ($ mil.)	(7.1%)	414.0	26.0	683.0	233.0	309.0
Market value ($ mil.)	22.9%	2,957.4	4,797.2	6,196.2	6,974.7	6,741.5
Employees	(8.5%)	15,000	15,000	15,000	11,000	10,500

ASI COMPUTER TECHNOLOGIES INC

48289 FREMONT BLVD
FREMONT, CA 945386510
Phone: 510-353-1960
Fax: -
Web: www.asipartner.com

CEO: Christine Liang
CFO: -
HR: -
FYE: December 31
Type: Private

ASI Computer Technologies is a wholesale distributor of computer software hardware and accessories. It offers more than 15000 products including PCs modems monitors networking equipment and data storage devices. The company sells to resellers retailers systems integrators and equipment makers from offices and facilities in the US Canada and Mexico. Its vendor partners include companies the likes of AMD Intel Microsoft and Western Digital. ASI's services include custom systems integration and contract assembly. It also markets PCs and notebooks under its own brands: Pegatron IQ and Nspire. The company was established in 1987 by president and owner Cristine Liang.

	Annual Growth	12/01	12/02	12/03	12/04	12/13
Sales ($ mil.)	6.6%	-	865.6	982.5	1,057.1	1,746.9
Net income ($ mil.)	3.0%	-	-	13.1	12.2	17.6
Market value ($ mil.)	-	-	-	-	-	-
Employees	-	-	-	-	-	700

ASICS AMERICA CORPORATION

29 Parker Ste. 100
Irvine CA 92618
Phone: 949-453-8888
Fax: 949-453-0292
Web: www.asicsamerica.com

CEO: Kevin Wulff
CFO: -
HR: Delores Lay
FYE: March 31
Type: Subsidiary

With ASICS America you don't have to earn your stripes you just have to purchase them. ASICS America is the North American arm of Japanese athletic footwear apparel and accessories maker ASICS Corporation. Its shoe collection — featuring a trademarked stripe design — includes footwear for basketball racing and running track and field volleyball walking and wrestling. ASICS products which were introduced in the US in 1977 are sold at regional and national retailers throughout the country as well as through online vendors such as Zappos.com. ASICS opened its first freestanding store in the US in fall 2009.

ASK.COM

555 12th St. Ste. 500
Oakland CA 94607
Phone: 510-985-7400
Fax: 510-985-7412
Web: www.ask.com

CEO: Doug Leeds
CFO: Steven J Sordello
HR: -
FYE: December 31
Type: Subsidiary

Ask and you shall receive especially when it comes to the Internet. Ask.com (formerly Ask Jeeves) operates an online question-and-answer service. The site solicits users to ask questions as well as answer questions from other users. Results reveal answers from a variety of sources. Previously the operator of a search engine Ask.com switched gears in 2010. While it still offers search on its site it no longer compiles an index of billions of Web pages. Instead it delivers results via an agreement with search partner Google. Ask.com operates alongside websites such as CityGrid Media's Citysearch.com and Lexico Publishing Group's Dictionary.com as part of the Search holdings of IAC/InterActiveCorp (IAC).

ASPEN MARKETING SERVICES INC.

1240 North Ave.
West Chicago IL 60185
Phone: 630-293-9600
Fax: 630-293-7584
Web: www.aspenms.com

CEO: Patrick J O'Rahilly
CFO: Donald Danner
HR: -
FYE: December 31
Type: Business Segment

Need marketing services? Ask Aspen. The company provides integrated marketing services with particular expertise in serving the automotive and telecommunications industries. Aspen Marketing Services blends strategic planning public relations and brand promotion as well as event and direct marketing to provide clients in a wide range of industries unified marketing for greater results. Its digital marketing capabilities utilize Web design e-mail marketing database processing and online loyalty marketing services. Aspen was founded in 1986 and operates about 10 offices spanning North America. In mid-2011 it was acquired by Alliance Data Systems and integrated into its Epsilon Data Management unit.

ASPEN TECHNOLOGY INC
NMS: AZPN

20 Crosby Drive
Bedford, MA 01730
Phone: 781 221-6400
Fax: –
Web: www.aspentech.com

CEO: Antonio J. Pietri
CFO: Mark P. Sullivan
HR: Joana Nikka
FYE: June 30
Type: Public

Aspen Technology (AspenTech) helps its customers scale mountains of supply chain and engineering challenges. It provides supply chain manufacturing and engineering process optimization software to some 1500 companies in the energy chemical construction and pharmaceutical industries among others. The company's software — which includes supplier collaboration inventory management production planning and collaborative engineering functions — is offered under its aspenONE subscription service. AspenTech which generates most of its sales outside the US also provides related technical and professional services such as technical support training and systems implementation and integration.

	Annual Growth	06/11	06/12	06/13	06/14	06/15
Sales ($ mil.)	22.1%	198.2	243.1	311.4	391.5	440.4
Net income ($ mil.)	84.3%	10.3	(13.8)	45.3	85.8	118.4
Market value ($ mil.)	27.6%	1,451.8	1,956.3	2,432.9	3,921.0	3,849.2
Employees	2.0%	1,269	1,325	1,328	1,344	1,372

ASPIRUS INC.

333 PINE RIDGE BLVD
WAUSAU, WI 544014187
Phone: 715-298-3213
Fax: –
Web: www.aspirus.org

CEO: Matthew Heywood
CFO: Sidney Sczygelski
HR: –
FYE: June 30
Type: Private

Aspirus aspires to provide care for Midwesterners in need. The health system provides a comprehensive range of health and medical services to residents in a 14-county region of central and northern Wisconsin as well as Michigan's Upper Peninsula. Aspirus operates the Aspirus Wausau Hospital a 325-bed multi-specialty regional health center and seven smaller community hospitals. Its hospitals and network of community clinics provide specialized primary and emergency care. Aspirus also operates imaging centers hospice services home health care long-term care facilities and an outpatient dialysis center.

	Annual Growth	06/10	06/11	06/12	06/13	06/14
Sales ($ mil.)	3.8%	–	503.1	529.8	536.9	562.0
Net income ($ mil.)	72.9%	–	–	26.2	48.0	78.3
Market value ($ mil.)	–	–	–	–	–	–
Employees	–	–	–	–	–	3,900

ASPLUNDH TREE EXPERT CO.

708 Blair Mill Rd.
Willow Grove PA 19090
Phone: 215-784-4200
Fax: 215-784-4493
Web: www.asplundh.com

CEO: Christopher B Asplundh
CFO: –
HR: –
FYE: December 31
Type: Private

How much wood would a woodchuck chuck if a woodchuck could chuck wood? A lot if the woodchuck were named Asplundh. One of the world's leading tree-trimming businesses Asplundh clears tree limbs from power lines for utilities and municipalities throughout the US and in Canada Australia and New Zealand. Asplundh also offers utility-related services such as line construction meter reading and pole maintenance; in addition the company has branched out into fields such as billboard maintenance traffic signal and highway lighting construction and vegetation control for railroads and pipelines. The Asplundh family owns and manages the company which was founded in 1928.

ASRC ENERGY SERVICES

3900 C St. Ste. 701
Anchorage AK 99503
Phone: 907-339-6200
Fax: 907-339-6219
Web: www.asrcenergy.com

CEO: Jeff Kinneeveauk
CFO: Jens Beck
HR: –
FYE: December 31
Type: Subsidiary

Alaska's slippery slopes have led to financial success for ASRC Energy Services. A subsidiary of Arctic Slope Regional Corp. ASRC Energy Services provides oil and gas and other engineering services to customers operating in the North Slope region of Alaska and to other energy and communications companies around the world. The company's services include well drilling and completion well testing facilities engineering geophysical services demolition pipeline construction and maintenance module fabrication and assembly and offshore construction and maintenance.

ASSET PROTECTION & SECURITY SERVICES LP

5502 BURNHAM DR
CORPUS CHRISTI, TX 784133855
Phone: 361-906-1552
Fax: –
Web: www.asset-security-pro.com

CEO: –
CFO: –
HR: Ron Berglund
FYE: December 31
Type: Private

Asset Protection & Security Services is a leading provider of patrol and security guard services in the US. It offers both armed and unarmed guard services as well as specialized services such as executive protection movie production security and mobile command centers. In addition Asset Protection provides investigative services (computer security internal investigations loss prevention) and electronic surveillance and security as well as security consulting and training services. The company was founded in 1994 by CEO Charles Mandel.

	Annual Growth	12/03	12/04	12/05	12/06	12/07
Sales ($ mil.)	–	–	–	0.0	31.2	51.8
Net income ($ mil.)	–	–	–	0.0	3.3	10.7
Market value ($ mil.)	–	–	–	–	–	–
Employees	–	–	–	–	–	800

ASSOCIATED BANC-CORP
NYS: ASB

433 Main Street
Green Bay, WI 54301
Phone: 920 491-7500
Fax: –
Web: www.associatedbank.com

CEO: Philip B. (Phil) Flynn
CFO: Christopher J. Del Moral-Niles
HR: Judith M. Docter
FYE: December 31
Type: Public

A lot of Midwesterners are associated with Associated Banc-Corp the holding company for Associated Bank. One of the largest banks based in Wisconsin the bank operates about 200 branches in that state as well as in Illinois and Minnesota. Catering to consumers and local businesses it offers deposit accounts loans mortgage banking credit and debit cards and leasing. The bank's wealth management division offers investments trust services brokerage insurance and employee group benefits plans. Commercial loans including agricultural construction and real estate loans make up more than 60% of bank's loan portfolio. The bank also writes residential mortgages consumer loans and home equity loans.

	Annual Growth	12/11	12/12	12/13	12/14	12/15
Assets ($ mil.)	6.0%	21,924.2	23,487.7	24,226.9	26,821.8	27,715.0
Net income ($ mil.)	7.7%	139.7	179.0	188.7	190.5	188.3
Market value ($ mil.)	13.8%	1,689.3	1,984.3	2,631.6	2,817.6	2,835.7
Employees	(3.7%)	5,100	4,900	4,600	4,300	4,383

ASSOCIATED CATHOLIC CHARITIES INC.

320 CATHEDRAL ST
BALTIMORE, MD 212014421
Phone: 410-561-6363
Fax: -
Web: www.catholiccharities-md.org

CEO: -
CFO: -
HR: -
FYE: June 30
Type: Private

Catholic Charities of Baltimore (CCB) provides people in the greater Baltimore area including about a dozen Maryland counties with a wide variety of social services. The not-for-profit religious organization runs 80 programs that focus on children and families the elderly and people with developmental disabilities; offerings include adoption services child abuse prevention food immigration assistance residential facilities and services for homeless people. It serves more than 160000 people of all religions each year. Money for its operations comes mainly from government contracts and grants. In addition CCB relies on a network of about 15000 volunteers. CCB was founded in 1923.

	Annual Growth	06/04	06/05	06/06	06/08	06/09
Sales ($ mil.)	6.6%	-	92.3	108.6	115.8	119.4
Net income ($ mil.)	-	-	-	9.7	(8.0)	(11.0)
Market value ($ mil.)	-	-	-	-	-	-
Employees	-	-	-	-	-	2,000

ASSOCIATED ELECTRIC COOPERATIVE INC.

2814 S GOLDEN AVE
SPRINGFIELD, MO 658073213
Phone: 660-261-4211
Fax: -
Web: www.aeci.org

CEO: James J. Jura
CFO: David W. McNabb
HR: David P Stum
FYE: December 31
Type: Private

Associated Electric Cooperative makes the connection between power and cooperatives. The utility provides transmission and generation services to its six member/owner companies which in turn provide power supply services to 51 distribution cooperatives in three Midwest states. (The distribution cooperatives have a combined customer count of about 875000 people.) Associated Electric operates 9645 miles of power transmission lines and has about 5895 MW of generating capacity from interests in primarily coal- and gas-fired power plants and from wholesale energy transactions with other regional utilities.

	Annual Growth	12/09	12/10	12/11	12/12	12/13
Sales ($ mil.)	2.3%	-	1,055.1	1,083.7	1,081.9	1,129.8
Net income ($ mil.)	(5.6%)	-	-	46.9	50.4	41.8
Market value ($ mil.)	-	-	-	-	-	-
Employees	-	-	-	-	-	600

ASSOCIATED ENTERTAINMENT RELEASING

4401 Wilshire Blvd.
Los Angeles CA 90010
Phone: 323-556-5600
Fax: 323-556-5610
Web: www.associatedtelevision.com

CEO: -
CFO: Murray Dreschler
HR: -
FYE: December 31
Type: Private

You might say this company has a close association with the small screen. Associated Entertainment Releasing which does business as Associated Television International (ATI) produces and distributes television programming mostly for the syndication market. Its shows include American Adventurer and reality crime program Crime Strike as well as specials such as Masters of Illusion: Impossible Magic and World Magic Awards. The company also distributes a library of TV programming to the home entertainment market and it produces some radio content. ATI began producing television programming in 1967.

ASSOCIATED ESTATES REALTY CORP.   NYS: AEC

1 AEC Parkway
Richmond Hts., OH 44143-1550
Phone: 216 261-5000
Fax: 216 289-9600
Web: www.associatedestates.com

CEO: -
CFO: -
HR: -
FYE: December 31
Type: Public

The estates this corporation associates with house the multitudes. Associated Estates Realty is a self-administered real estate investment trust (REIT) that specializes in apartment communities in the Midwest Mid-Atlantic and Southeast. It invests in develops builds operates and manages multifamily real estate. More than half of the company's properties are located in Ohio and Michigan its largest markets. The REIT's portfolio includes more than 50 residential communities containing around 14000 individual units; it also owns a handful of properties under development and land. Subsidiary Merit Enterprises performs in-house general contracting and construction management services.

	Annual Growth	12/09	12/10	12/11	12/12	12/13
Sales ($ mil.)	8.6%	130.4	153.7	175.9	174.9	181.5
Net income ($ mil.)	77.2%	6.2	(8.6)	5.3	30.6	61.3
Market value ($ mil.)	9.2%	647.8	878.8	916.7	926.5	922.5
Employees	2.7%	360	390	400	410	400

ASSOCIATED FOOD STORES INC.

1850 W 2100 S
SALT LAKE CITY, UT 841191304
Phone: 801-973-4400
Fax: -
Web: www.afstores.com

CEO: Neil Berube
CFO: -
HR: -
FYE: March 31
Type: Private

This business makes sure there's plenty of grub for the Wild West. Associated Food Stores (AFS) is a leading regional cooperative wholesale distributor that supplies groceries and other products to some 500 independent supermarkets in about eight Western states. It also offers support services for its member-owners including market research real estate analysis store design technology procurement and training. In addition AFS owns a stake in Western Family Foods a grocery wholesalers' partnership that produces Western Family private-label goods. The co-op formed in 1940 also operates 40-plus corporate stores in Utah under five different banners including Fresh Market.

	Annual Growth	03/09	03/10	03/11	03/12	03/13
Sales ($ mil.)	3.1%	-	1,785.6	1,954.0	2,011.3	1,957.5
Net income ($ mil.)	-	-	-	(6.5)	5.9	2.5
Market value ($ mil.)	-	-	-	-	-	-
Employees	-	-	-	-	-	300

ASSOCIATED GROCERS OF NEW ENGLAND INC.

11 COOPERATIVE WAY
PEMBROKE, NH 032753251
Phone: 603-223-6710
Fax: -
Web: www.agne.com

CEO: Michael C Bourgione
CFO: Steven N Murphy
HR: Hope Kelly
FYE: March 30
Type: Private

AGNE gets the products you want on to grocers' shelves. Associated Grocers of New England (AGNE) is a leading wholesale grocery distributor. The retailer-owned organization supplies more than 650 independent grocers and convenience stores in six New England states and the Upstate New York and Albany area. AGNE supplies customers with baked goods fresh produce and meat as well as general grocery items and other merchandise. The grocery distributor also offers such retail support services as advertising marketing and merchandising. AGNE's retail arm operates about a half a dozen supermarkets under the Harvest Market Sully's Superette and Vista Foods banners. The cooperative was formed in 1946.

	Annual Growth	03/06	03/07	03/08	03/09	03/13
Sales ($ mil.)	-	-	(1,996.9)	315.8	340.3	480.8
Net income ($ mil.)	23.7%	-	-	0.2	0.7	0.7
Market value ($ mil.)	-	-	-	-	-	-
Employees	-	-	-	-	-	625

ASSOCIATED MATERIALS LLC

3773 State Rd.
Cuyahoga Falls OH 44223
Phone: 330-929-1811
Fax: 330-922-2354
Web: www.associatedmaterials.com

CEO: Brian C Strauss
CFO: Scott F Stephens
HR: John Fhaumesser
FYE: December 31
Type: Private

Vinyl has never gone out of style at Associated Materials (AM). The company makes and distributes vinyl aluminum and steel exterior building products as well as siding windows fencing decking and railing. Products are marketed under the brand names Alpine Alside Gentek Preservation Revere and Ultra-Guard. Its products are also sold through about 275 independent distributors in North America under brands such as Alside Revere and Gentek. The company's customer base includes contractors remodelers and architects. Private equity firm Hellman & Friedman owns a majority stake of the company.

ASSOCIATED MILK PRODUCERS INC.

315 N. Broadway
New Ulm MN 56073
Phone: 507-354-8295
Fax: 507-359-8651
Web: www.ampi.com

CEO: Paul Toft
CFO: Patricia Radloff
HR: –
FYE: December 31
Type: Private - Cooperativ

Associated Milk Producers Inc. (AMPI) might wear a cheesy grin but it churns up solid sales. The dairy cooperative transforms (a record) about 5.8 billion pounds of milk into butter cheese fluid milk and other dairy products each and every year. A regional co-op with some 2800 member/farmers in six states across the Midwest AMPI operates about a dozen manufacturing plants. In addition to its State Brand and Cass-Clay brand Associated Milk Producers also makes private-label products for food retailers fast-food restaurants (including McDonald's) and other food service operators. It also makes dairy ingredients for food manufacturers.

ASSOCIATED WHOLESALE GROCERS INC.

5000 KANSAS AVE
KANSAS CITY, KS 661061135
Phone: 913-288-1000
Fax: –
Web: www.awginc.com

CEO: –
CFO: Robert Z Walker
HR: Susan (Sue) Ott
FYE: December 28
Type: Private

Associated Wholesale Grocers (AWG) knows its customers can't live on bread and milk alone. The second-largest retailer-owned cooperative in the US (behind Wakefern Food Corporation) AWG supplies more than 2900 retail outlets in more than 30 states from nine distribution centers. In addition to its wholesale grocery operation AWG offers a variety of business services to its members including marketing and merchandising programs shelf management insurance and store design. AWG was founded by a group of independent grocers in 1924.

	Annual Growth	12/09	12/10	12/11	12/12	12/13
Sales ($ mil.)	4.9%	–	7,251.7	7,766.8	7,852.0	8,380.2
Net income ($ mil.)	6.6%	–	–	169.5	175.9	192.5
Market value ($ mil.)	–	–	–	–	–	–
Employees		–	–	–	–	5,500

ASSOCIATION OF UNIVERSITIES FOR RESEARCH IN ASTRONOMY INC.

1212 NEW YORK AVE NW # 450
WASHINGTON, DC 200053987
Phone: 202-483-2101
Fax: –
Web: www.aura-astronomy.org

CEO: –
CFO: –
HR: –
FYE: September 30
Type: Private

There is nothing quasi-scientific about this aura. The Association of Universities for Research in Astronomy (AURA) is a consortium of universities and not-for-profit organizations devoted to the study of space. The organization was founded to create astronomical observing facilities for use by qualified researchers and to serve the community by offering public outreach education and dissemination of information. AURA was founded in 1957 and operates astronomical observatories at 34 US institutions and six international affiliates including Harvard University Ohio State University and the University of Toronto.

	Annual Growth	09/07	09/08	09/09	09/10	09/13
Sales ($ mil.)	–	–	–	0.0	180.9	197.2	238.4
Net income ($ mil.)	–	–	–	(0.6)	(2.4)	2.1
Market value ($ mil.)	–	–	–	–	–	–
Employees	–	–	–	–	–	1,000

ASSURANT INC

NYS: AIZ

28 Liberty Street, 41st Floor
New York, NY 10005
Phone: 212 859-7000
Fax: –
Web: www.assurant.com

CEO: Alan B. Colberg
CFO: Christopher J. Pagano
HR: Robyn Price Stonehill
FYE: December 31
Type: Public

From credit cards to trailer parks Assurant provides a range of specialty insurance products. Through Assurant Solutions and Assurant Specialty Property the company offers such products as credit protection insurance manufactured home coverage creditor-placed homeowners insurance pre-need funeral policies and extended warranties for electronics appliances and vehicles. Individuals and small employer groups can choose from several types of health coverage offered by Assurant Health while group life dental and disability products are available through the Assurant Employee Benefits segment. Assurant's products are distributed through sales offices and independent agents across the US and abroad.

	Annual Growth	12/11	12/12	12/13	12/14	12/15
Assets ($ mil.)	2.6%	27,115.4	28,946.6	29,714.7	31,562.5	30,043.1
Net income ($ mil.)	(28.6%)	545.8	483.7	488.9	470.9	141.6
Market value ($ mil.)	18.3%	2,703.8	2,285.0	4,370.5	4,506.1	5,303.6
Employees	4.3%	14,100	14,600	16,600	17,600	16,700

ASTA FUNDING, INC.

NMS: ASFI

210 Sylvan Ave.
Englewood Cliffs, NJ 07632
Phone: 201 567-5648
Fax: –
Web: www.astafunding.com

CEO: Gary Stern
CFO: Robert J Michel
HR: –
FYE: September 30
Type: Public

Say Hasta luego to unpaid receivables. Asta Funding buys services and collects unpaid credit card debts and consumer loans. The company buys delinquent accounts at a discount directly from the credit grantors as well as indirectly through auctions brokers and other third parties. It targets credit card charge-offs from banks finance companies and other issuers of Visa MasterCard and private-label cards as well as telecom and other industry charge-offs. The company then collects on its debt balances either internally or through an outsourced agency. Asta Funding also invests in semi-performing and non-delinquent receivables. Subsidiary VATIV Recovery Solutions services bankrupt and deceased accounts.

	Annual Growth	09/11	09/12	09/13	09/14	09/15
Sales ($ mil.)	0.6%	43.2	44.5	42.4	60.1	44.2
Net income ($ mil.)	(33.8%)	10.5	10.0	2.7	5.9	2.0
Market value ($ mil.)	1.3%	104.3	120.8	114.3	105.6	109.7
Employees	14.4%	87	74	72	80	149

ASTAR USA LLC

1200 Brickell Ave. 16th Flr.
Miami FL 33131
Phone: 305-982-0500
Fax: 305-416-9564
Web: www.astaraircargo.us

CEO: John Dasburg
CFO: Stephen Dodd
HR: –
FYE: December 31
Type: Private

ASTAR USA helps DHL take on delivery giants FedEx and UPS on their own turf. Hiring the carrier's fleet of some 8 aircraft enables DHL and other customers including the US Air Force Department of Defense and the United States Postal Service to achieve overnight delivery of virtually any kind of cargo. ASTAR's service includes scheduled as well as chartered flights. In early 2009 ASTAR suffered a blow to its business when — in order to cut costs — DHL was forced to shut down its US express delivery operations. ASTAR and other carriers continue to operate DHL's international shipping services to and from the US albeit at a reduced level. An investment group led by CEO John Dasburg controls ASTAR.

ASTEA INTERNATIONAL, INC.   NBB: ATEA

240 Gibraltar Road
Horsham, PA 19044
Phone: 215 682-2500
Fax: –
Web: www.astea.com

CEO: Zack B. Bergreen
CFO: Frederic (Rick) Etskovitz
HR: –
FYE: December 31
Type: Public

Astea International keeps employees in the field connected to the home office. The company's field service management software Astea Alliance is used to automate sales and service processes manage contracts and warranties reverse logistics and distribute information to employees customers and suppliers. FieldCentrix offers mobile workforce management and its ServiceVision (launched in 2012) is cloud-based service management and mobility software suite for small to midsize businesses. Altogether it counts more than 650 customers from a range of industries. Founder and CEO Zack Bergreen owns about 45% of Astea.

	Annual Growth	12/10	12/11	12/12	12/13	12/14
Sales ($ mil.)	(0.8%)	21.4	26.6	26.4	20.3	20.7
Net income ($ mil.)	–	(1.6)	0.7	(0.2)	(3.0)	(3.4)
Market value ($ mil.)	(10.2%)	9.7	12.0	9.6	9.1	6.3
Employees	(2.9%)	179	185	182	161	159

ASTEC INDUSTRIES, INC.   NMS: ASTE

1725 Shepherd Road
Chattanooga, TN 37421
Phone: 423 899-5898
Fax: 423 899-4456
Web: www.astecindustries.com

CEO: Benjamin G. (Ben) Brock
CFO: David C. Silvious
HR: –
FYE: December 31
Type: Public

Whistle Willie Nelson's "On the Road Again" while you work at Astec Industries! The company via its dozen-plus manufacturing subsidiaries makes equipment for every phase of road building. Its lineup includes aggregate crushers pavers asphalt plants and related components. The company is comprised of three segments: road building and related equipment (Infrastructure Group); aggregate processing and mining equipment (Aggregate and Mining Group); and equipment for the extraction and production of fuels biomass production and water drilling (Energy Group). Customers are asphalt road contractors as well as utility and pipeline service providers government agencies and mine and quarry operators.

	Annual Growth	12/10	12/11	12/12	12/13	12/14
Sales ($ mil.)	6.0%	771.3	955.7	936.3	933.0	975.6
Net income ($ mil.)	1.5%	32.4	39.9	40.2	39.0	34.5
Market value ($ mil.)	4.9%	743.2	738.6	764.9	885.8	901.4
Employees	4.7%	3,284	3,885	3,860	3,708	3,952

ASTELLAS PHARMA US INC.

1 Astellas Way
Northbrook IL 60062
Phone: 847-317-8800
Fax: 248-435-1120
Web: www.axletech.com

CEO: Masao Yoshida
CFO: Shinichiro Katayanagi
HR: –
FYE: March 31
Type: Subsidiary

Astellas Pharma US pilots pharma efforts that are outta this world. The company conducts research development and marketing efforts focused on therapeutic areas including cardiology dermatology immunology infectious disease neurology oncology urology and metabolism. The company's primary products include transplant rejection therapy Prograf overactive bladder treatment Vesicare and vascular dilator Adenoscan as well as antifungals Mycamine and AmBisome and enlarged prostate treatment Flomax. Astellas Pharma US which is a subsidiary of Japan-based pharmaceutical firm Astellas Pharma uses a direct sales force to market its products to consumers and health professionals in the US market.

ASTORIA FINANCIAL CORP.   NYS: AF

One Astoria Bank Plaza
Lake Success, NY 11042-1085
Phone: 516 327-3000
Fax: 516 327-7860
Web: www.astoriabank.com

CEO: Monte N. Redman
CFO: Frank E. Fusco
HR: –
FYE: December 31
Type: Public

Astoria Financial is the holding company for Astoria Bank (formerly Astoria Federal) one of the largest thrifts in New York with deposits totaling $9.7 billion. The bank has more than 85 branches in and around New York City and on Long Island in addition to a network of third-party mortgage brokers spanning more than a dozen states and Washington DC. It offers standard deposit products such as CDs and checking savings and retirement accounts. With these funds Astoria Bank primarily writes loans and invests in mortgage-backed securities. Subsidiary AF Insurance Agency sells life and property/casualty coverage to bank customers. New York Community Bancorp agreed to acquire Astoria in late 2015.

	Annual Growth	12/10	12/11	12/12	12/13	12/14
Assets ($ mil.)	(3.6%)	18,089.3	17,022.1	16,496.6	15,793.7	15,640.0
Net income ($ mil.)	6.8%	73.7	67.2	53.1	66.6	95.9
Market value ($ mil.)	(1.0%)	1,390.2	848.5	935.4	1,382.2	1,335.2
Employees	(0.2%)	1,662	1,730	1,614	1,603	1,649

ASTORIA SOFTWARE INC.

300 Broadway St. Ste. 8
San Francisco CA 94133
Phone: 650-357-7477
Fax: 650-357-7677
Web: www.astoriasoftware.com

CEO: Michael Rosinski
CFO: –
HR: –
FYE: December 31
Type: Subsidiary

Astoria Software is a disciplinarian when it comes to content — all your documents need is a little structure. Astoria provides a content management system that enables companies to collect and manage their data and then to use that data to create and publish documents including charts images and tables. Astoria maintains partnerships with software providers including Innodata Isogen. Customers include ABB Cessna Aircraft Honeywell Lockheed Martin Nokia Texas Instruments the US Armed Forces and Xerox. In 2010 Astoria Software was acquired by TransPerfect Translations International.

ASTRAL HEALTH & BEAUTY INC.

3715 Northside Pkwy. NW Bldg. 200 Ste. 200
Atlanta GA 30327
Phone: 678-303-3088
Fax: 858-625-3010
Web: www.enterpriseinformatics.com

CEO: –
CFO: –
HR: –
FYE: December 31
Type: Private

Astral Health & Beauty believes in natural beauty. The company owns three cosmetics and skin care lines that use nature-based ingredients — Aloette CosMedix and Pur Minerals. Aloette's aloe vera-based skin care products and cosmetics are sold mainly through home parties held by Aloette's direct sales network of more than 10000 consultants in some 40 franchises across the US and Canada. CosMedix is a line of premium skin care products sold only at professional spas while Pur Minerals' mineral makeup is sold at major retailers such as Dillard's Duane Reade and Ulta. All three brands are also sold online and on television shopping channels such as QVC.

ASTRAZENECA PHARMACEUTICALS LP

1800 Concord Pike
Wilmington DE 19850-5437
Phone: 302-886-3000
Fax: 302-886-2972
Web: www.astrazeneca-us.com

CEO: Pascal Soriot
CFO: David V Elkins
HR: –
FYE: December 31
Type: Subsidiary

AstraZeneca Pharmaceuticals (which does business as AstraZeneca US) can help with a full alphabet of ailments. The company a subsidiary of global drugmaker AstraZeneca is one of the largest pharma companies in the US. Its sales represent about 5% of all the drugs sold in the US and about 40% of its parent company's revenues. AstraZeneca US' treatments focus on several therapeutic areas: cardiovascular and metabolic gastrointestinal neuroscience oncology respiratory and infection. Its best-known products include Crestor (high cholesterol) Seroquel (anti-psychotic) Nexium (acid reflux) Symbicort (asthma) and Zoladex (cancer treatment).

ASTRO-MED, INC.   NMS: ALOT

600 East Greenwich Avenue
West Warwick, RI 02893
Phone: 401 828-4000
Fax: –
Web: www.astro-medinc.com

CEO: Gregory A. Woods
CFO: Joseph P. O'Connell
HR: –
FYE: January 31
Type: Public

The sky's the limit for Astro-Med. The company makes data recorders and ruggedized printers used on commercial airplanes. Its Test & Measurement (T&M) division (30% of sales) makes products that record and monitor data for customers in the aerospace automotive metal mill power and telecommunications industries. Its QuickLabel Systems division (70% of sales) makes digital color label printers bar code printers automatic labelers and printer consumables. In 2013 Astro-Med divested its former Grass Technologies unit which made EEG equipment instruments for monitoring such conditions as epilepsy and sleep disorders and biomedical research supplies.

	Annual Growth	01/11	01/12	01/13	01/14	01/15
Sales ($ mil.)	5.6%	71.0	79.2	61.2	68.6	88.3
Net income ($ mil.)	22.6%	2.1	3.1	10.8	3.2	4.7
Market value ($ mil.)	17.5%	56.9	58.4	72.5	99.1	108.4
Employees	(5.3%)	423	372	342	304	340

ASTRONAUTICS CORPORATION OF AMERICA

4115 N TEUTONIA AVE
MILWAUKEE, WI 532096731
Phone: 414-449-4000
Fax: –
Web: www.astronautics.com

CEO: Dr Ronald E Zelazo
CFO: Steven Givant
HR: –
FYE: May 31
Type: Private

Sometimes it's hard to know which way is up but Astronautics Corporation of America gives good directions. The company makes maintains and repairs electronic components and systems that enable manned and unmanned planes ships land vehicles and spacecraft to orient themselves in time and space. Its lineup runs from integrated avionics navigation and network server systems to electronic flight bags and instruments mission and display processors and inertial navigation systems. More than 150000 aircraft rely on the hardware. Astronautics' customers include the US Departments of Defense and Homeland Security as well as NASA Boeing Lockheed Martin and Sikorsky.

	Annual Growth	05/04	05/05	05/06	05/07	05/08
Sales ($ mil.)	–	–	–	(353.4)	233.0	235.7
Net income ($ mil.)	23275.9%	–	–	0.0	20.7	19.6
Market value ($ mil.)	–	–	–	–	–	–
Employees	–	–	–	–	–	1,550

ASTRONICS CORP.   NMS: ATRO

130 Commerce Way
East Aurora, NY 14052
Phone: 716 805-1599
Fax: –
Web: www.astronics.com

CEO: Peter J Gundermann
CFO: David C. Burney
HR: –
FYE: December 31
Type: Public

In the glare of its own lights but without histrionics Astronics Corporation displays its talents daily to a specialized audience. Astronics makes external and internal lighting systems as well as power generation and distribution technology for commercial general aviation and military defense aircraft. Products include cabin emergency lighting systems (escape path markers and exit locators) cockpit lighting systems (avionics keyboards ambient light sensors annunciator panels and electronic dimmers) external lights and military test equipment. Astronics operates subsidiaries include Astronics Advanced Electronic Systems Corp. Ballard Luminescent Systems and DME Corporation.

	Annual Growth	12/10	12/11	12/12	12/13	12/14
Sales ($ mil.)	35.6%	195.8	228.2	266.4	339.9	661.0
Net income ($ mil.)	39.2%	14.9	21.6	21.9	27.3	56.2
Market value ($ mil.)	27.4%	529.6	903.1	577.0	1,286.2	1,394.9
Employees	18.6%	1,010	1,081	1,156	1,715	2,000

ASTROTECH CORP.   NAS: ASTC

401 Congress Ave. Suite 1650
Austin, TX 78701
Phone: 512 485-9530
Fax: 512 485-9531
Web: www.astrotechcorp.com

CEO: Thomas B Pickens III
CFO: Eric N Stober
HR: –
FYE: June 30
Type: Public

Astrotech is the muscle on the ground prior to satellite launch countdown. Formerly SPACEHAB the company offers services and products that aid the US government and commercial customers in preparing satellites and cargo payloads for space launch. Its Astrotech Space Operations (ASO) business unit is a contractor that provides such services as ground transportation hardware integration fueling and launch pad delivery. It also fabricates launch equipment and hardware. Astrotech's much smaller Spacetech unit is focused on using space-based technologies to develop commercial products in the chemical and biotechnology sectors. About 75% of Astrotech's revenues are made from NASA and US government contracts.

	Annual Growth	06/11	06/12	06/13	06/14	06/15
Sales ($ mil.)	(60.1%)	20.1	26.1	24.0	16.4	0.5
Net income ($ mil.)	–	(5.0)	(2.7)	(0.2)	(5.0)	10.8
Market value ($ mil.)	27.3%	21.4	22.2	14.5	66.0	56.2
Employees	(10.7%)	66	60	62	66	42

ASURE SOFTWARE INC.

NAS: ASUR

110 Wild Basin Road, Suite 100
Austin, TX 78746
Phone: 512 437-2700
Fax: –
Web: www.asuresoftware.com

CEO: Patrick Goepel
CFO: Brad Wolfe
HR: –
FYE: December 31
Type: Public

Asure Software wants to guaranty a more organized workplace. The company develops Web-based business administration software through its NetSimplicity and iEmployee divisions. NetSimplicity's offerings include Meeting Room Manager which lets users reserve meeting rooms and schedule equipment and resources. NetSimplicity also provides an asset management tool called Visual Asset Manager that tracks and manages fixed and mobile IT assets. The company's iEmployee division offers tools for managing time and attendance benefits payroll and expense information. Asure primarily sells its products directly in North America; it uses resellers for customers outside the US and for federal government sales.

	Annual Growth	12/10	12/11	12/12	12/13	12/14
Sales ($ mil.)	28.3%	10.0	10.9	20.0	25.5	27.2
Net income ($ mil.)	–	(1.1)	(0.6)	(3.0)	(1.7)	(0.3)
Market value ($ mil.)	17.8%	17.7	38.5	35.5	34.0	34.1
Employees	20.7%	56	66	120	125	119

ASURION CORPORATION

648 Grassmere Park Dr. Ste. 300
Nashville TN 37211
Phone: 615-837-3000
Fax: 615-837-3001
Web: www.asurion.com

CEO: Bret Comolli
CFO: Mark Gunning
HR: –
FYE: December 31
Type: Private

Dead battery? Would that be the battery on your car or cell phone? Either way Asurion assures that you won't be stranded. A global leader in wireless and technology insurance Asurion replaces defunct cell phones and other tech equipment but also provides specialty services such as roadside assistance to stranded motorists via their wireless phones. The firm serves about 80 million end users through partnerships with wireless carriers including Cricket T-Mobile and AT&T Mobility. In 2008 Asurion merged with extended service plan provider N.E.W. Customer Service Companies. Both companies continue to operate independently.

AT&T INC

NYS: T

208 S. Akard St.
Dallas, TX 75202
Phone: 210 821-4105
Fax: –
Web: www.att.com

CEO: F. Thaddeus Arroyo
CFO: John J. Stephens
HR: William A. (Bill) Blase
FYE: December 31
Type: Public

Through its subsidiaries affiliates and operating companies holding company AT&T is the industry-leading provider of wireline voice communications services in the US. Customers use AT&T-branded telephone Internet and VoIP services; it also sells digital TV under the U-verse brand. Key markets include California Illinois and Texas. The company's corporate government and public sector clients use its conferencing managed network and wholesale communications services. Subsidiary AT&T Mobility is the second-largest US mobile carrier by both sales and subscriptions (after Verizon Wireless). It provides mobile services to more than 126 million subscribers.

	Annual Growth	12/10	12/11	12/12	12/13	12/14
Sales ($ mil.)	1.6%	124,280.0	126,723.0	127,434.0	128,752.0	132,447.0
Net income ($ mil.)	(25.2%)	19,864.0	3,944.0	7,264.0	18,249.0	6,224.0
Market value ($ mil.)	–	0.0	0.0	0.0	0.0	0.0
Employees	(1.3%)	266,590	256,420	242,000	243,000	253,000

AT&T MOBILITY LLC

1025 Lenox Park Blvd.
Atlanta GA 30319
Phone: 866-662-4548
Fax: 914-666-2188
Web: www.curtisinst.com

CEO: Ralph De La Vega
CFO: Peter A Ritcher
HR: –
FYE: December 31
Type: Subsidiary

The second-largest wireless voice and data carrier in the US by subscribers (after Verizon) AT&T Mobility serves about 100 million mobile users over a nationwide network that spans all major metropolitan areas. The subsidiary which accounts for about half of parent AT&T's business provides a full range of wireless voice messaging and data services to consumer and enterprise customers. AT&T Mobility's services for businesses government agencies and educational institutions include e-mail wireless Internet access and private wireless networking. The company provides international network coverage for its subscribers in more than 200 countries through partnerships with other carriers.

ATALANTA CORPORATION

1 ATLANTA PLZ STE 3
ELIZABETH, NJ 072062120
Phone: 908-351-8000
Fax: –
Web: www.atalanta1.com

CEO: –
CFO: Tom Decarll
HR: –
FYE: December 31
Type: Private

Atalanta Corporation helps customers outfit any wine and cheese soirée. The company is a top specialty food importer that markets 2500 different products such as gourmet cheeses deli and canned meats and frozen seafood. Its menu of products also includes pastas rices and grains as well as coffee and a line of kosher foods. Atalanta's brands include Casa Diva Celebrity Zerto Del Destino Maria Brand Martel and Atalanta. Importing products from Europe Asia and South America Atalanta sells primarily to restaurants and other foodservice operators grocery stores and specialty food retailers. Founded in 1945 the company is controlled by the Gellert family and led by chairman George Gellert.

	Annual Growth	12/04	12/05	12/06	12/07	12/09
Sales ($ mil.)	–	–	–	0.0	348.8	384.9
Net income ($ mil.)	–	–	–	0.0	10.8	9.0
Market value ($ mil.)	–	–	–	–	–	–
Employees	–	–	–	–	–	150

ATHENAHEALTH INC

NMS: ATHN

311 Arsenal Street
Watertown, MA 02472
Phone: 617 402-1000
Fax: –
Web: www.athenahealth.com

CEO: Jonathan S. Bush
CFO: Kristi A. Matus
HR: –
FYE: December 31
Type: Public

athenahealth knows that managing physician practices can result in a splitting headache especially when patients are late paying bills or missing appointments. The company provides health care organizations with online software for cloud-based electronic health record (EHR) practice management and patient communication services. Offerings include revenue cycle management (athenaCollector) medical record automation (athenaClinicals) and patient relations and referral systems (athenaCommunicator and athenaCoordinator). Its services help health care providers streamline workflow data and billing and collection tasks. athenahealth's programs are managed through its cloud-based athenaNet network.

	Annual Growth	12/11	12/12	12/13	12/14	12/15
Sales ($ mil.)	30.0%	324.1	422.3	595.0	752.6	924.7
Net income ($ mil.)	(7.4%)	19.0	18.7	2.6	(3.1)	14.0
Market value ($ mil.)	34.5%	1,912.3	2,853.3	5,236.2	5,672.2	6,266.7
Employees	27.0%	1,795	2,339	2,966	3,676	4,668

ATHENS BANCSHARES CORP   NBB: AFCB

106 Washington Avenue
Athens, TN 37303
Phone: 423-745-1111
Fax: –
Web: www.athensfederal.com

CEO: Jeffrey L Cunningham
CFO: Michael R Hutsell
HR: Linda Morrow
FYE: December 31
Type: Public

Athens Bancshares Corporation is the holding company for Athens Federal Community Bank an eight-branch bank in Athens Tennessee. Athens is located in the southeast corner of the state halfway between Knoxville and Chattanooga. The town is home to major manufacturers such as DENSO Heil Johnson Controls and Thomas & Betts where many of the bank's customers are employed. Athens Federal offers checking and savings accounts including NOW and money market accounts as well as debit and credit cards and online banking services. Through Florida-based INVEST Financial Corporation (a subsidiary of Prudential) it offers mutual funds variable and fixed annuities and discount brokerage services.

	Annual Growth	12/10	12/11	12/12	12/13	12/14
Assets ($ mil.)	2.1%	278.0	283.7	291.6	294.8	302.4
Net income ($ mil.)	33.7%	0.8	1.9	2.6	2.3	2.7
Market value ($ mil.)	19.4%	22.5	21.6	29.7	35.7	45.8
Employees	1.5%	100	99	104	109	106

ATHEROTECH INC.

201 London Pkwy.
Birmingham AL 35211
Phone: 205-871-8344
Fax: 205-871-8392
Web: www.atherotech.com

CEO: Michael V Mullen
CFO: Charles Musial
HR: –
FYE: December 31
Type: Private

The Good the Bad and the VAP. Atherotech makes the Vertical Auto Profile (VAP) Cholesterol test a cholesterol level diagnostic that directly measures both low-density lipoprotein (LDL the "good cholesterol") and high-density lipoprotein (HDL the "bad cholesterol"). At its clinical laboratory site in Birmingham the company performs the tests on blood samples collected at doctors' offices hospitals clinics and other labs around the US. In addition to the VAP test Atherotech makes other diagnostics used to detect cardiovascular disease and is developing new tests based on its VAP technology. The company was acquired by private equity firm Behrman Capital in 2010.

ATHERSYS INC   NAS: ATHX

3201 Carnegie Avenue
Cleveland, OH 44115-2634
Phone: 216-431-9900
Fax: –
Web: www.athersys.com

CEO: Gil Van Bokkelen
CFO: –
HR: –
FYE: December 31
Type: Public

Biotechnology is all the RAGE at Athersys. The development-stage company uses its Random Activation of Gene Expression (RAGE) technology to scan the human genome identify proteins with specific biological functions and link those protein functions with gene structures (functional genomics). It is also developing therapies for oncology and vascular applications based on its MultiStem technology which uses stem cells from adult bone marrow. The firm plans to leverage its technologies by partnering with other biotechs and drugmakers but it also aims to develop its own proprietary drugs. It counts Bristol-Myers Squibb and Angiotech Pharmaceuticals among its partners.

	Annual Growth	12/10	12/11	12/12	12/13	12/14
Sales ($ mil.)	(34.7%)	8.9	10.3	8.7	2.4	1.6
Net income ($ mil.)	–	(11.4)	(13.7)	(14.7)	(30.7)	(22.1)
Market value ($ mil.)	(10.6%)	191.9	134.4	82.4	194.3	122.8
Employees	6.7%	44	48	48	56	57

ATI LADISH LLC

5481 S. Packard Ave.
Cudahy WI 53110
Phone: 414-747-2611
Fax: 414-747-2963
Web: www.ladishco.com

CEO: Gary J Vroman
CFO: –
HR: –
FYE: December 31
Type: Subsidiary

ATI Ladish started in 1905 when Herman Ladish bought a 1500-lb. steam hammer; the company's been swinging ever since. ATI Ladish (formerly Ladish Co. Inc.) designs and manufactures high-strength forged and cast metal components for aerospace and industrial markets. Complex jet engine parts missile components landing gear helicopter rotors and other aerospace products generate about 85% of company sales; general industrial components account for the remainder. Rolls-Royce (26%) United Technologies (17%) and GE (13%) collectively account for more than half of its sales. In 2011 Allegheny Technologies (ATI) acquired and renamed Ladish and joined its operations with ATI's High Performance Metals segment.

ATI TITANIUM LLC

1600 NE Old Salem Rd.
Albany OR 97321
Phone: 541-926-4211
Fax: 541-967-6994
Web: www.atimetals.com/businesses/business-units/wa

CEO: –
CFO: Dennis P Kelly
HR: –
FYE: December 31
Type: Subsidiary

ATI Titanium (doing business as ATI Wah Chang which in part means "great development") creates specialty metals and chemicals. Wah Chang principally makes zirconium mill products as well as other corrosion-resistant specialty metals such as hafnium niobium titanium and vanadium. Its products are used in industries including aerospace chemical processing energy production medical and consumer goods. It also provides laboratory services for metal testing and analysis. Its Ti Wire division makes titanium bar and wire products while business unit Midwest Laboratory performs radiological monitoring. The company now a subsidiary of Allegheny Technologies dates back to a trading company founded in 1916.

ATLANTA CLARK UNIVERSITY INC

223 JAMES P BRAWLEY DR SW
ATLANTA, GA 303144385
Phone: 404-880-8000
Fax: –
Web: www.cauaa.org

CEO: Dr Colton Brown
CFO: Lucille Mauga
HR: –
FYE: June 30
Type: Private

Clark Atlanta University (CAU) is a historically African-American liberal arts college that enrolls about 3500 students. The private school which is affiliated with the United Methodist Church offers undergraduate and graduate degrees through its four schools: Arts and Sciences Business Administration Education Social Work. It also offers professional programs and certificates. CAU is a member of the Atlanta University Center a consortium of educational institutions that includes Spelman College and Morehouse College. Clark Atlanta University was formed by the 1988 merger of two colleges founded in the 1860s — Clark College and Atlanta University.

	Annual Growth	06/07	06/08	06/09	06/10	06/13
Sales ($ mil.)	–	–	0.0	85.8	94.6	110.8
Net income ($ mil.)	–	–	–	(7.2)	5.7	3.0
Market value ($ mil.)	–	–	–	–	–	–
Employees	–	–	–	–	–	1,150

ATLANTA FALCONS FOOTBALL CLUB LLC

4400 Falcon Pkwy.
Flowery Branch GA 30542
Phone: 770-965-3115
Fax: 770-965-2766
Web: www.atlantafalcons.com

CEO: -
CFO: -
HR: -
FYE: February 28
Type: Private

These birds keep Atlanta flapping about the gridiron all year round. The Atlanta Falcons Football Club is a professional football franchise that joined the National Football League in 1966. First awarded to businessman Rankin Smith the team has made the playoffs just nine different seasons and counts only one conference championship in 1998. (Atlanta lost that year to the Denver Broncos in Super Bowl XXXIII.) The Georgia Dome has played host to Falcons games since 2002 the same year Home Depot co-founder Arthur Blank acquired the franchise from Smith's family.

ATLANTA HARDWOOD CORPORATION

5596 RIVERVIEW RD SE
MABLETON, GA 301262914
Phone: 404-792-2290
Fax: -
Web: www.hardwoodweb.com

CEO: James W Howard Jr
CFO: Paul Harris
HR: -
FYE: December 31
Type: Private

Atlanta Hardwood Corporation, carves out, its living from the trees of the Appalachian Mountains. Through its various divisions Atlanta Hardwood supplies hardwood products including lumber plywood veneer, moulding and flooring made from some, 75 varieties of wood. It, specializes in processing distributing and exporting products, made from Appalachian wood including Ash Maple Poplar and White Oak. It also imports Mahogany Teak European Beech and several other types of wood from international sources. Other offerings include custom product services that cater to architects designers and fabricators. Founded in 1952 by James Howard Sr. Atlanta Hardwood is today headed by Howard's son Jim Howard.

	Annual Growth	12/04	12/05	12/06	12/07	12/08
Sales ($ mil.)	(82.5%)	-	-	761.0	27.3	23.3
Net income ($ mil.)	-	-	-	0.0	0.6	(0.3)
Market value ($ mil.)	-	-	-	-	-	-
Employees	-	-	-	-	-	243

ATLANTA NATIONAL LEAGUE BASEBALL CLUB INC.

755 Hank Aaron Dr. SW
Atlanta GA 30315
Phone: 404-522-7630
Fax: 303-312-2116
Web: www.coloradorockies.com

CEO: -
CFO: Chip Moore
HR: -
FYE: December 31
Type: Subsidiary

America may be the land of the free but Atlanta is the home of these baseball Braves. Atlanta National League Baseball Club owns and operates the Atlanta Braves Major League Baseball franchise which boasts three World Series championships its last in 1995. A charter member of the National League the team was formed as the Boston Red Stockings in 1871 (it became the Braves in 1912) and moved to Milwaukee in the 1950s before settling in Atlanta in 1966. Under the ownership of media mogul Ted Turner the Braves won five pennants during the 1990s. The Braves play host at Turner Field. John Malone's Liberty Media has owned the team since 2007.

ATLANTIC AMERICAN CORP.

NMS: AAME

4370 Peachtree Road, N.E.
Atlanta, GA 30319
Phone: 404 266-5500
Fax: -
Web: www.atlam.com

CEO: Hilton H Howell Jr
CFO: John G Sample Jr
HR: -
FYE: December 31
Type: Public

Baseball apple pie and... insurance! Atlantic American sells a mix of property/casualty health and life insurance throughout the US. Its Bankers Fidelity Life Insurance subsidiary provides life and supplemental health insurance offerings with income primarily coming from sales of Medicare supplement policies. Its American Southern subsidiary offers commercial and personal property/casualty products including automobile insurance products targeted at large motor pools and fleets owned by local governments. The unit also offers general commercial liability coverage and surety bonds catering to niche markets such as school bus transportation and subdivision construction.

	Annual Growth	12/10	12/11	12/12	12/13	12/14
Assets ($ mil.)	3.4%	277.6	302.1	320.2	319.4	317.0
Net income ($ mil.)	15.5%	2.5	3.3	4.4	11.0	4.4
Market value ($ mil.)	18.7%	41.8	40.6	63.7	84.3	83.0
Employees	5.5%	117	121	122	133	145

ATLANTIC CITY ELECTRIC CO

500 North Wakefield Drive
Newark, DE 19702
Phone: 202 872-2000
Fax: -
Web: www.atlanticcityelectric.com

CEO: David M Velazquez
CFO: Frederick J Boyle
HR: -
FYE: December 31
Type: Public

Atlantic City Electric makes America's favorite playground shine in the nighttime. The Pepco Holdings' utility generates transmits and distributes electricity to 547000 homes and businesses in southern New Jersey. Atlantic City Electric operates more than 11000 miles of transmission and distribution lines in its 2700 sq. ml. 8-county service area. Atlantic City Electric's electricity delivery operations are regulated by the New Jersey Board of Public Utilities. In 2011 the utility distributed a total of 9683000 MWh of electricity to its customers.

	Annual Growth	12/10	12/11	12/12	12/13	12/14
Sales ($ mil.)	(4.0%)	1,430.0	1,268.0	1,198.0	1,202.0	1,213.0
Net income ($ mil.)	(4.0%)	53.0	39.0	35.0	50.0	45.0
Market value ($ mil.)	-	512.8	-	-	-	-
Employees	(0.4%)	553	558	575	544	545

ATLANTIC COAST FINANCIAL CORP

NMS: ACFC

4655 Salisbury Road, Suite 110
Jacksonville, FL 32256
Phone: 800 342-2824
Fax: -
Web: www.atlanticcoastbank.net

CEO: John K Stephens Jr
CFO: Tracy L Keegan
HR: -
FYE: December 31
Type: Public

Atlantic Coast Financial Corporation (formerly Atlantic Coast Federal Corporation) is the holding company for Atlantic Coast Bank which operates about a dozen branches in southeastern Georgia and the Jacksonville Florida area. The bank offers standard deposit lending and investment services. Residential mortgages make up around half of its loan portfolio. Atlantic Coast Bank was established in 1939 as a credit union that served Atlantic Coast Line Railroad employees. Formerly mutually owned Atlantic Coast Federal Corporation converted to a stock form of ownership in 2011 changed its name and moved its headquarters to Jacksonville where the company is focusing its growth strategy.

	Annual Growth	12/10	12/11	12/12	12/13	12/14
Assets ($ mil.)	(3.9%)	827.4	789.0	772.6	733.6	706.5
Net income ($ mil.)	-	(14.2)	(10.3)	(6.7)	(11.4)	1.3
Market value ($ mil.)	11.7%	-	44.2	31.2	67.2	61.6
Employees	(1.7%)	184	174	147	135	172

ATLANTIC DIVING SUPPLY INC.

621 LYNNHVEN PKWY STE 400
VIRGINIA BEACH, VA 23452
Phone: 757-481-7758
Fax: –
Web: www.adsinc.com

CEO: Luke M Hillier
CFO: Kiran Rai
HR: –
FYE: December 31
Type: Private

Atlantic Diving Supply (doing business as ADS Tactical) is geared toward gearing up the military. Serving agencies in the Department of Defense the company specializes in helping customers procure tactical and operational military equipment. Like a retailer it sells 160000 products manufactured by some 1500 vendors including Camelbak FLIR L-3 Communications and Oakley but its niche offering is its supply management services. These services which are tailored to military customers include kitting (packaging related products in groups) assembly training custom sourcing product research and development and quality assurance. ADS Tactical filed an IPO in early 2011 but withdrew it six months later.

	Annual Growth	12/07	12/08	12/09	12/10	12/11
Sales ($ mil.)	29.4%	–	650.8	938.9	1,327.2	1,409.9
Net income ($ mil.)	7.8%	–	40.2	54.4	77.3	50.4
Market value ($ mil.)	–	–	–	–	–	–
Employees	–	–	–	–	–	380

ATLANTIC HEALTH SYSTEM INC.

475 SOUTH ST
MORRISTOWN, NJ 079606459
Phone: 973-660-3100
Fax: –
Web: www.atlantichealth.org

CEO: –
CFO: Kevin Shanley
HR: Andrew L (Andy) Kovach
FYE: December 31
Type: Private

Got a gash or gout in the Garden State? Atlantic Health System has more than 1600 beds for you to get better in. The not-for-profit Atlantic Health System (AHS) operates five acute care hospital providing general medical and surgical services to residents of northern New Jersey. Its flagship Morristown Medical Center serves as a regional trauma center and provides specialty care in a number of areas including oncology pediatrics and cardiac care. The system's Overlook Medical Center houses the Atlantic Neuroscience Institute; home to the Comprehensive Stroke Center. Its smaller Newton Medical Center serves patients in two New Jersey counties as well as counties in Pennsylvania and New York.

	Annual Growth	12/01	12/02	12/03	12/09	12/13
Sales ($ mil.)	6.3%	–	–	883.8	0.1	1,624.9
Net income ($ mil.)	45.3%	–	–	7.0	0.0	291.9
Market value ($ mil.)	–	–	–	–	–	–
Employees	–	–	–	–	–	221

ATLANTIC METHANOL PRODUCTION COMPANY LLC

12600 NORTHBOROUGH DR # 150
HOUSTON, TX 770673200
Phone: 281-872-8324
Fax: –
Web: www.atlanticmethanol.com

CEO: –
CFO: –
HR: –
FYE: December 31
Type: Private

Atlantic Methanol Production Company (AMPCO) must have adopted "Waste not want not" as its motto. It tries not to waste the natural gas that is a by-product of its parent companies' production processes. A joint venture between Noble Energy (45% ownership) Marathon Oil (45%) and SONAGAS the National Gas Company of Equatorial Guinea (10%) the company operates one of the largest methanol plants in the world. The plant off the coast of Equatorial Guinea produces about 1 million tons of methanol annually — 2% of the global market. AMPCO also distributes using three vessels and five terminals in Europe and US where it sells most of its production.

	Annual Growth	12/05	12/06	12/07	12/08	12/10
Sales ($ mil.)	(43.4%)	–	–	1,405.6	341.1	254.2
Net income ($ mil.)	10372.8%	–	–	0.0	122.0	65.5
Market value ($ mil.)	–	–	–	–	–	–
Employees	–	–	–	–	–	342

ATLANTIC POWER CORPORATION

NYSE: AT

200 Clarendon St. 25th Fl.
Boston MA 02116
Phone: 617-977-2400
Fax: 617-977-2410
Web: www.atlanticpower.com

CEO: James J. Moore
CFO: Terrence Ronan
HR: –
FYE: December 31
Type: Public

Contrary to its name Atlantic Power works on both sides of the US. The power company has about a dozen hydro coal and natural gas power generation projects in eight states with a net generating capacity of 870 MW. Its plants are located primarily in the Northeast Southwest and Northwest. Caithness Energy Cogentrix Energy and Western Area Power Administration maintain and operate Atlantic Power's plants and its 84-mile transmission line in California. The company is also developing alternative energy including wind and biomass projects. Progress Energy Florida Tampa Electric Company and Atlantic City Electric are its leading customers. Atlantic Power was formed in 2004.

ATLANTIC PREMIUM BRANDS LTD.

1033 Skokie Blvd. Ste. 600
Northbrook IL 60062
Phone: 847-412-6200
Fax: 516-327-7461
Web: www.astoriafederal.com

CEO: Thomas M Dalton
CFO: Thomas M Dalton
HR: –
FYE: December 31
Type: Private

Atlantic Premium Brands doesn't operate along the Atlantic Ocean but it does have a boatload of premium regional meat brands. The company processes and distributes packaged value-added meats under names such as J.C. Potter Blue Ribbon Texas Traditions Richard's Cajun Foods Carlton and Cajun Favorites. It also offers its customers private-label products and services. Atlantic Premium's meats include smoked and breakfast sausages ham bacon and meat-based entrees. The Northbrook Illinois-headquartered company distributes its products to US supermarkets and discount stores.

ATLANTIC RECORDS GROUP

1290 Avenue of the Americas
New York NY 10104
Phone: 212-707-2000
Fax: 212-405-5475
Web: www.atlanticrecords.com

CEO: Ahmet M Ertegun
CFO: –
HR: –
FYE: September 30
Type: Business Segment

This record company makes sure there's music to please fans from sea to shinning sea. Atlantic Records Group is one of the top purveyors of pop music in the US promoting such artists as Southern rapper T. I. and the rock band Death Cab for Cutie. It distributes such imprints as Elektra Records as well as the venerable Atlantic Records label. Music industry mogul Ahmet Ertegun and partner Herb Abramson started Atlantic in 1947. Atlantic Records and Elektra Records merged in 2004 to form The Atlantic Records Group. Along with Warner Bros. Records today the company is one of the two flagship recorded music operations of Warner Music Group.

ATLANTIC SOUTHEAST AIRLINES INC.

A-Tech Center 990 Toffie Terrace
Atlanta GA 30354
Phone: 404-856-1000
Fax: 404-856-1203
Web: www.flyasa.com

CEO: Jerry C Atkin
CFO: Michael J Kraupp
HR: –
FYE: December 31
Type: Subsidiary

It's all about connections for Atlantic Southeast Airlines (ASA). Operating as a Delta Connection regional carrier ASA flies to smaller markets on behalf of Delta Air Lines primarily from Delta's hubs in Atlanta and Cincinnati. The carrier serves about 110 destinations mainly east of the Mississippi in the US but also in western states and in Canada Mexico and the Caribbean. ASA maintains a fleet of about 160 aircraft all of which are Canadair regional jets (CRJs) made by Bombardier. Founded in 1979 ASA is a subsidiary of SkyWest which bought the company from Delta in 2005. In late 2010 SkyWest boosted its capacity by acquiring rival ExpressJet via ASA establishing ExpressJet as a subsidiary of ASA.

ATLANTIC TELE-NETWORK, INC.   NMS: ATNI

600 Cummings Center
Beverly, MA 01915
Phone: 978 619-1300
Fax: –
Web: www.atni.com

CEO: Michael T. Prior
CFO: Justin D. Benincasa
HR: –
FYE: December 31
Type: Public

Atlantic Tele-Network (ATN) makes connections from the maple groves of Vermont to the rain forests of Guyana. In the US the company provides wholesale wireless voice and data roaming services to local and national communications carriers through subsidiary Commnet Wireless. ATN voice and broadband Internet services in New England particularly Vermont through its SoVerNet subsidiary. SoVerNet subsidiary ION offers fiber-optic transport services in New York State on a wholesale basis.

	Annual Growth	12/10	12/11	12/12	12/13	12/14
Sales ($ mil.)	(14.1%)	619.1	759.2	741.4	292.8	336.3
Net income ($ mil.)	5.8%	38.5	21.8	48.9	311.7	48.2
Market value ($ mil.)	15.2%	611.1	621.9	584.6	900.9	1,076.4
Employees	(13.2%)	1,765	1,884	1,800	1,000	1,000

ATLANTICUS HOLDINGS CORP   NMS: ATLC

Five Concourse Parkway, Suite 300
Atlanta, GA 30328
Phone: 770 828-2000
Fax: –
Web: www.atlanticus.com

CEO: David G Hanna
CFO: William R McCamey
HR: –
FYE: December 31
Type: Public

Suffering from a fiscal near-death experience? Let Atlanticus Holdings help resuscitate you. Subprime is the strategy for this company. Formerly named CompuCredit until November 2012 it traditionally issued unsecured Visa and MasterCard credit cards to customers with low credit scores and charged them more for the risk. The economic downturn compelled the firm to close most of its active credit card accounts. However Atlanticus continues to collect on portfolios of credit card receivables underlying now-closed credit card accounts. The company current portfolio offers Credit and Other Investments; and Auto Finance.

	Annual Growth	12/10	12/11	12/12	12/13	12/14
Sales ($ mil.)	(28.3%)	711.7	336.7	183.0	158.7	188.6
Net income ($ mil.)	–	(97.5)	134.0	24.5	(17.7)	7.2
Market value ($ mil.)	(23.8%)	106.9	56.6	51.3	54.3	36.1
Employees	(33.4%)	1,623	494	285	315	319

ATLANTICUS HOLDINGS CORPORATION   NASDAQ: CCRT

5 Concourse Pkwy. Ste. 400
Atlanta GA 30328
Phone: 770-828-2000
Fax: 770-870-5183
Web: atlanticusholdings.net

CEO: David G Hanna
CFO: J Paul Whitehead III
HR: –
FYE: December 31
Type: Public

Suffering from a fiscal near-death experience? Let Atlanticus Holdings resuscitate you. Subprime was the strategy for this company. Formerly named CompuCredit until November 2012 it traditionally issued unsecured Visa and MasterCard credit cards to customers with low credit scores and charged them more for the risk; however the economic downturn compelled the firm to close most of its active accounts. Subsidiary Jefferson Capital Systems collects on debt other companies have written off. Atlanticus sold its 300 US microloan retail locations — which provided payday loans under such banners as First American Cash Advance and First Southern Cash Advance — to Advance America for more than $46 million in 2011.

ATLAS AIR WORLDWIDE HOLDINGS, INC.   NMS: AAWW

2000 Westchester Avenue
Purchase, NY 10577
Phone: 914 701-8000
Fax: –
Web: www.atlasair.com

CEO: Michael T. Steen
CFO: Spencer Schwartz
HR: Adam R. Kokas
FYE: December 31
Type: Public

Atlas carried the weight of the world; Atlas Air Worldwide Holdings (AAWW) carries the freight of the world. The company leases cargo planes to customers mainly airlines under long-term ACMI (aircraft crew maintenance and insurance) contracts. The segment accounts for about 45% of AAWW's revenue. All told the company maintains a fleet of more than 35 Boeing 747 freighters. AAWW also offers dry leasing (aircraft and engines only) via its Titan division. Affiliates Atlas Air and 51% owned Polar Air Cargo provide charter services to charter brokers freight forwarders airlines and the US military (referred to as AMC) which accounts for 22% of sales.

	Annual Growth	12/10	12/11	12/12	12/13	12/14
Sales ($ mil.)	7.7%	1,337.8	1,398.2	1,646.0	1,656.9	1,799.2
Net income ($ mil.)	(6.9%)	141.8	96.1	129.9	93.8	106.8
Market value ($ mil.)	(3.1%)	1,385.0	953.4	1,099.5	1,020.8	1,223.0
Employees	3.0%	1,532	1,716	1,744	1,792	1,724

ATLAS COPCO USA HOLDINGS INC.

34 Maple Ave.
Pine Brook NJ 07058
Phone: 973-439-3400
Fax: 973-439-9455
Web: www.atlascopco.com

CEO: –
CFO: –
HR: –
FYE: May 31
Type: Subsidiary

With businesses both Swedish and American you may not think of construction and mining equipment. But you should. Atlas Copco USA Holdings operates throughout the US Canada and Mexico as an arm of Swedish manufacturing giant Atlas Copco AB. The US-based business manufactures a slew of compressors and generators construction and mining equipment and power tools. Its power tool lineup includes air assembly devices grinders drills air motors hoists and trolleys and related services. Demolition equipment rock drills blast hole drilling rigs and exploration drilling tools are part of the list of mining and construction offerings. North America generates about 18% of the parent company's total sales.

ATLAS PIPELINE PARTNERS LP — NYS: APL

Park Place Corporate Center One, 1000 Commerce Drive, 4th Floor
Pittsburgh, PA 15275-1011
Phone: 877 950-7473
Fax: –
CEO: Eugene N Dubay
CFO: Eric T Kalamaras
HR: –
FYE: December 31
Type: Public

Atlas Pipeline Partners shoulders the burden of getting natural gas from wellheads to major gas utilities such as Peoples Natural Gas National Fuel Gas and East Ohio Gas. The midstream company is engaged in the transmission gathering and processing of natural gas in the Appalachia and Mid-Continent regions. Atlas Pipeline Partners operates about 9700 miles of active intrastate gas gathering and processing pipelines in Kansas Oklahoma Tennessee and Texas. It also owns and operates five natural gas processing plants. Atlas Pipeline Partners' general partner is owned by Atlas Energy L.P (formerly Atlas Pipeline Holdings L.P.) In 2014 the company agreed to be acquired by Targa Resources Partners.

	Annual Growth	12/09	12/10	12/11	12/12	12/13
Sales ($ mil.)	23.5%	904.2	935.6	1,302.7	1,246.0	2,106.8
Net income ($ mil.)	–	62.7	280.4	295.4	68.1	(91.6)
Market value ($ mil.)	37.5%	790.5	1,988.0	2,993.7	2,544.1	2,824.5
Employees	9.8%	310	270	280	350	450

ATLAS WORLD GROUP INC.

1212 St. George Rd.
Evansville IN 47711-2364
Phone: 812-424-2222
Fax: 812-421-7125
Web: www.atlasworldgroup.com
CEO: Glen E Dunkerson
CFO: –
HR: –
FYE: December 31
Type: Private

Willing to carry the weight of a moving world Atlas World Group is the holding company for Atlas Van Lines one of the largest moving companies in the US. Atlas Van Lines transports household goods domestically and between the US and Canada; it also offers specialized transportation of items such as trade show exhibits fine art and electronics. Atlas Van Lines International provides international corporate relocation and freight forwarding services. Its Atlas Canada unit moves household goods in that country while American Red Ball International specializes in military relocations and serves van lines outside Atlas' network. Atlas World Group was formed in 1994 and is owned by its agents.

ATMEL CORP. — NMS: ATML

1600 Technology Drive
San Jose, CA 95110
Phone: 408 441-0311
Fax: –
Web: www.atmel.com
CEO: Steven A. Laub
CFO: Stephen A. (Steve) Skaggs
HR: –
FYE: December 31
Type: Public

Atmel is a leading maker of microcontrollers which are used in a wide range of products from computers and mobile devices (smartphones tablets e-readers) to automobile motor control systems television remote controls and solid-state lighting. In addition the company offers touchscreen controllers and sensors nonvolatile memory devices and radio frequency (RF) and wireless components. Its chips are used worldwide in consumer communications industrial military and networking applications. Most of Atmel's sales come from customers outside the US. In early 2016 the company agreed to be bought by Microchop a chip maker for $3.6 billion.

	Annual Growth	12/10	12/11	12/12	12/13	12/14
Sales ($ mil.)	(3.7%)	1,644.1	1,803.1	1,432.1	1,386.4	1,413.3
Net income ($ mil.)	(47.5%)	423.1	315.0	30.4	(22.1)	32.2
Market value ($ mil.)	(9.1%)	5,127.3	3,371.0	2,726.0	3,258.7	3,493.8
Employees	0.0%	5,200	5,200	5,000	5,000	5,200

ATMI, INC. — NMS: ATMI

7 Commerce Drive
Danbury, CT 06810
Phone: 203 794-1100
Fax: 203 792-8040
Web: www.atmi.com
CEO: Douglas A Neugold
CFO: Timothy C Carlson
HR: Kathleen G Mincieli
FYE: December 31
Type: Public

ATMI's original name — Advanced Technology Materials Inc. — is a pretty good summary of its business. The company provides ultrapure materials and related packaging and delivery systems used by semiconductor and flat-panel display manufacturers during copper integration deposition ion implantation photolithography and surface preparation production processes. It also offers single-use disposable storage systems mixers and bioreactors along with flexible film and cleanroom packaging to the biotechnology cell therapy laboratory and pharmaceutical industries. (This life sciences segment is being sold to Pall Corporation.) Most of its business comes from customers located in the Asia/Pacific region.

	Annual Growth	12/08	12/09	12/10	12/11	12/12
Sales ($ mil.)	4.7%	339.1	254.7	367.3	390.1	407.4
Net income ($ mil.)	6.2%	33.3	(6.7)	39.5	(20.0)	42.3
Market value ($ mil.)	7.9%	493.5	595.5	637.7	640.6	667.8
Employees	1.8%	761	693	773	814	817

ATMOS ENERGY CORP. — NYS: ATO

Three Lincoln Centre, Suite 1800, 5430 LBJ Freeway
Dallas, TX 75240
Phone: 972 934-9227
Fax: 972 855-3075
Web: www.atmosenergy.com
CEO: Kim R. Cocklin
CFO: Bret J. Eckert
HR: Kimberly Ried
FYE: September 30
Type: Public

Atmos Energy the largest gas-only utility company in the US is interested in more than atmospherics; it is focused on delivery. Through its utility units which operate under the Atmos Energy brand the holding company distributes natural gas to more than 3 million residential commercial and industrial customers in more than 1400 communities in eight Midwestern and southern states. Nonregulated subsidiary Atmos Energy Marketing sells natural gas and offers energy management services to more than 1000 utility and industrial customers in 22 states. The company also has gas transportation and storage operations.

	Annual Growth	09/11	09/12	09/13	09/14	09/15
Sales ($ mil.)	(1.2%)	4,347.6	3,438.5	3,886.3	4,940.9	4,142.1
Net income ($ mil.)	11.0%	207.6	216.7	243.2	289.8	315.1
Market value ($ mil.)	15.7%	3,293.0	3,631.9	4,322.0	4,840.5	5,904.0
Employees	(1.0%)	4,949	4,759	4,720	4,761	4,753

ATRIA SENIOR LIVING INC.

401 S. 4th St. Ste. 1900
Louisville KY 40202
Phone: 502-779-4700
Fax: 502-779-4701
Web: www.atriaseniorliving.com
CEO: John A Moore
CFO: Mark D Jesee
HR: –
FYE: December 31
Type: Private

Atria Senior Living is breathing new life as a senior living management company. It was formed in 2011 as a spinoff of Atria Senior Living Group (ASLG) formerly an owner and operator of about 120 independent and assisted living communities throughout the US. After those assets were acquired for $3.1 billion by health care real estate investment trust Ventas Atria Senior Living signed a long-term contract to manage that portfolio of communities for Ventas. Atria Senior Living also manages communities for other owners. In addition to long-term care its facilities offer temporary and short-term stay options as well as specialized assistance for residents with Alzheimer's.

ATRICURE INC

NMS: ATRC

6217 Centre Park Drive
West Chester, OH 45069
Phone: 513 755-4100
Fax: –
Web: www.atricure.com

CEO: Michael H. Carrel
CFO: M. Andrew Wade
HR: –
FYE: December 31
Type: Public

If your heart thumps to the beat of a different drummer AtriCure will help give you your rhythm back. The medical device maker markets the Synergy Ablation System used in the treatment of atrial fibrillation (AFib) a common type of heart arrhythmia. Cardiothoracic surgeons use the AtriCure Synergy Ablation System in conjunction with elective surgical ablation procedures to treat patients through minimally invasive procedures. AtriCure also sells reusable and disposable cryoablation devices (probes using extreme cold) to ablate cardiac tissue. Additionally the company offers the AtriClip Gillinov-Cosgrove Left Atrial Appendage System or AtriClip system designed to help surgeons exclude the left atrial appendage.

	Annual Growth	12/10	12/11	12/12	12/13	12/14
Sales ($ mil.)	16.2%	59.0	64.4	70.2	81.9	107.5
Net income ($ mil.)	–	(3.8)	(5.5)	(7.5)	(11.5)	(16.2)
Market value ($ mil.)	18.1%	283.2	306.1	190.3	515.2	550.5
Employees	9.8%	220	240	230	320	320

ATRION CORP.

NMS: ATRI

One Allentown Parkway
Allen, TX 75002
Phone: 972 390-9800
Fax: –

CEO: David A. Battat
CFO: Jeffery Strickland
HR: –
FYE: December 31
Type: Public

Atrion makes some nifty doo-dads for medical niches. Its products range from aortic punches used in vein graft surgeries to one-way valves used to control fluids and gasses as well as a tiny balloon catheter used to unblock tear ducts. Subsidiary Quest Medical makes intravenous and cardiovascular fluid delivery products; its MPS2 Myocardial Protection System manages fluid delivery to the heart during open-heart surgery. Its Halkey-Roberts business manufactures plastic inflation widgets used in health care equipment marine and aviation devices and other inflatable products. Subsidiary Atrion Medical Products manufactures plastic medical products and offers contract manufacturing and medical device assembly.

	Annual Growth	12/10	12/11	12/12	12/13	12/14
Sales ($ mil.)	6.7%	108.6	117.7	119.1	132.0	140.8
Net income ($ mil.)	7.3%	21.0	26.0	23.6	26.6	27.8
Market value ($ mil.)	17.3%	343.3	459.6	374.9	566.7	650.4
Employees	2.5%	437	458	459	485	483

ATRIX INTERNATIONAL INC.

1350 Larc Industrial Blvd.
Burnsville MN 55337-1412
Phone: 952-894-6154
Fax: 952-894-6256
Web: www.atrix.com

CEO: Steven Reidel
CFO: –
HR: –
FYE: June 30
Type: Private

Atrix International manufactures fine particulate vacuum cleaners and related products and accessories for use in industrial hospital office restaurant and HAZMAT applications. Atrix also makes copier control management and tracking products. Its Omega vacuum cleaner can be used to make cleanrooms for manufacturing semiconductors and other precision components even cleaner. The Omega line guards against electrostatic discharges (ESD) and is shielded against electromagnetic and radio-frequency interference. The company also offers the Windows-based ATRAX network monitoring software. Atrix was established in 1981. Steve Riedel the company's president is the majority shareholder.

ATRM HOLDINGS INC

NBB: ATRM

3050 Echo Lake Avenue, Suite 300
Mahtomedi, MN 55115
Phone: 651 704-1800
Fax: –
Web: www.aetrium.com

CEO: Daniel M Koch
CFO: Paul H Askegaard
HR: Mary Kvaal
FYE: December 31
Type: Public

Aetrium can attribute whatever success it reaps to its semiconductor testing equipment. The company makes systems used in testing integrated circuits (ICs) and other electronic components. Its main products are test handlers which work with testers to thermally condition and sort ICs. Other product lines include automated IC handling products reliability test systems and gear for adapting test handlers to different types of IC packages. Aetrium's customers include analog chip maker Maxim Integrated Products (more than half of sales). The company gets about three-quarters of its sales outside the US mostly in Asian nations.

	Annual Growth	12/10	12/11	12/12	12/13	12/14
Sales ($ mil.)	19.4%	16.3	9.0	6.2	2.7	33.1
Net income ($ mil.)	–	(1.9)	(4.7)	(6.1)	(2.9)	(8.3)
Market value ($ mil.)	5.7%	2.8	0.9	0.6	7.9	3.5
Employees	32.6%	68	59	36	19	210

ATS CORPORATION

NYSE AMEX: ATSC

7925 Jones Branch Dr.
McLean VA 22102
Phone: 571-766-2400
Fax: 571-766-2401
Web: www.atsc.com

CEO: Pamela A Little
CFO: Gerry Beard
HR: –
FYE: October 31
Type: Public

ATS Corporation knows that the key to technological success lies in the right mix of services. Doing business as ATSC the company provides a variety of IT services to the federal government and commercial organizations including consulting systems integration network design and support. ATSC which was founded in 1978 as Advanced Technology Systems went public in 2010. In April 2012 the company was bought by Salient Federal Solutions in an all-stock transaction and taken private. ATSC is now part of Salient's Civilian Mission Critical Solutions division and its System and Software Engineering Solutions division.

ATTRONICA COMPUTERS INC.

15867 GAITHER DR
GAITHERSBURG, MD 208771403
Phone: 301-417-0070
Fax: –
Web: www.attronica.com

CEO: –
CFO: –
HR: –
FYE: December 31
Type: Private

Attronica hopes to offer an alternative to chunking your old outdated computers out the window. The company provides a variety of information technology (IT) services including network and systems integration product consulting and hardware procurement to middle-market businesses in the mid-Atlantic states. Attronica also offers such services as network security support inventory management and training. The company's customers come from a wide range of industries including financial services health care manufacturing retail consumer goods and transportation. It operates from four offices in Maryland and Virginia. Attronica was co-founded by CEO Atul Tucker in 1983.

	Annual Growth	12/09	12/10	12/11	12/12	12/13
Sales ($ mil.)	3.6%	–	55.8	57.7	61.4	62.1
Net income ($ mil.)	4.3%	–	–	0.4	0.4	0.5
Market value ($ mil.)	–	–	–	–	–	–
Employees		–	–	–	–	61

ATWELL LLC

2 TOWNE SQ STE 700
SOUTHFIELD, MI 480763737
Phone: 248-447-2000
Fax: –
Web: www.atwell-group.com

CEO: Brian Wenzel
CFO: Roderick Petschauer
HR: Emilie Stawiarski
FYE: December 31
Type: Private

Atwell provides real estate and development consulting encompassing civil engineering land planning surveying and environmental services. Spanning the commercial residential corporate real estate and institutional development markets the company helps clients manage real estate development projects and navigate local regulations and planning requirements. The company's consulting services include feasibility studies and economic viability analysis. Atwell's more technical services consist of surveying civil engineering landscape architecture as well as expertise covering environmental impact water and wastewater systems and water resource management.

	Annual Growth	12/09	12/10	12/11	12/12	12/13
Sales ($ mil.)	76.5%	–	–	–	36.6	64.7
Net income ($ mil.)	(58.5%)	–	–	–	5.4	2.2
Market value ($ mil.)	–	–	–	–	–	–
Employees	–	–	–	–	–	201

ATWOOD OCEANICS, INC.   NYS: ATW

15011 Katy Freeway, Suite 800
Houston, TX 77094
Phone: 281 749-7800
Fax: 281 492-7871
Web: www.atwd.com

CEO: Robert J. (Rob) Saltiel
CFO: Mark L. Mey
HR: Luis Jimenez
FYE: September 30
Type: Public

Atwood Oceanics is at work in oceans all over the world. An offshore oil and gas drilling contractor the firm owns about a dozen drilling rigs including six semisubmersible rigs five jack-ups and one semisubmersible tender assist vessel (which places drilling equipment on permanent platforms). Its rigs operate in the Gulf of Mexico offshore Southeast Asia offshore West Africa offshore Australia and in the Mediterranean. Atwood Oceanics serves a limited number of customers at one time and generates nearly all of its sales internationally.

	Annual Growth	09/11	09/12	09/13	09/14	09/15
Sales ($ mil.)	21.3%	645.1	787.4	1,063.7	1,174.0	1,395.9
Net income ($ mil.)	12.3%	271.7	272.2	350.2	340.8	432.6
Market value ($ mil.)	(19.0%)	2,221.5	2,938.5	3,558.6	2,824.7	957.5
Employees	9.5%	1,300	1,460	1,830	1,905	1,868

ATX GROUP INC.

8550 Freeport Pkwy.
Irving TX 75063-2547
Phone: 972-753-6200
Fax: 972-753-6226
Web: www.atxg.com

CEO: –
CFO: –
HR: –
FYE: December 31
Type: Private

ATX Group takes its business in every direction. The company provides telematics services to automobile manufacturers primarily in North America including BMW Toyota Motor Sales and Rolls-Royce; in Europe it provides services for PSA Group Peugeot. Drivers of telematics-enabled vehicles can utilize ATX's collision notification emergency assistance navigation roadside diagnostics stolen vehicle tracking and traffic information services. In addition to managing a telematics service network and response centers ATX provides dealer support remote activation services and maintenance. A division of Cross Country Automotive Services the company operates from offices in Texas France and Germany.

AUBURN NATIONAL BANCORP, INC.   NMS: AUBN

100 N. Gay Street
Auburn, AL 36830
Phone: 334 821-9200
Fax: –
Web: www.auburnbank.com

CEO: Robert W. Dumas
CFO: David A. Hedges
HR: Marian Harper
FYE: December 31
Type: Public

War Eagle! Auburn National Bancorporation is the holding company for AuburnBank which operates about 10 branches and a handful of loan offices in and around its headquarters in the eastern Alabama home of Auburn University. With offices in area grocery stores and Wal-Mart locations AuburnBank offers traditional retail banking services such as checking and savings accounts and CDs. It uses funds from deposits to fund residential mortgages and other loans for individuals and businesses. Auburn Bank was founded in 1907.

	Annual Growth	12/10	12/11	12/12	12/13	12/14
Assets ($ mil.)	0.8%	763.8	776.2	759.8	751.3	789.2
Net income ($ mil.)	8.6%	5.3	5.5	6.8	7.1	7.4
Market value ($ mil.)	4.2%	73.1	67.5	76.0	91.1	86.1
Employees	0.2%	155	157	161	155	156

AUDIBLE INC.

1 Washington Park
Newark NJ 07102
Phone: 973-820-0400
Fax: 973-820-0505
Web: www.audible.com

CEO: Donald R Katz
CFO: William H Mitchell
HR: –
FYE: December 31
Type: Subsidiary

Audible has a story to tell. The subsidiary of online retail giant Amazon.com sells downloadable audio versions of books as well as radio broadcasts speeches stand-up comedy and other spoken word performances via its Audible website. Some 85000 audiobooks are available. Users can listen to programs on their computer or via wireless mobile device (iPad iPhone or Kindle to name a few) or burn to CD. Audible has distribution rights to content from some 1000 content providers including The New York Times The Wall Street Journal and Forbes. Audible also provides audiobooks for Apple's iTunes store. The company has international versions of its site for consumers in the UK France and Germany.

AUDIENCESCIENCE INC.

1110 112th Ave. NE Ste. 300
Bellevue WA 98004
Phone: 425-216-1700
Fax: 425-216-1777
Web: www.audiencescience.com

CEO: Jeff Pullen
CFO: –
HR: –
FYE: December 31
Type: Private

AudienceScience (formerly Revenue Science) has a vested interest in your behavior. The company provides behavioral targeting services that help clients determine prime audiences for specific campaigns. AudienceScience primarily serves Web publishers (such as Dow Jones FT.com and The Wall Street Journal Online) that can then offer advertisers and ad agencies with behaviorally targeted audiences. It provides search-based and rules-based targeting and segments audiences based on search terms used or other criteria such as geographic location or how often they visit a certain portion of the site. The company was established in 2000.

AUGUSTANA COLLEGE

639 38TH ST
ROCK ISLAND, IL 612012296
Phone: 309-794-3377
Fax: -
Web: www.augustanafaculty.org

CEO: -
CFO: David English
HR: -
FYE: June 30
Type: Private

Augustana College is a private liberal arts college located near the Mississippi River in northwestern Illinois. The school offers undergraduate degrees in some 50 areas of study plus pre-professional programs in fields including dentistry law medicine and veterinary medicine. It enrolls approximately 2500 students. The Swenson Center a national archive dedicated to the study of Swedish immigration to the US is housed on the Augustana campus. Augustana College is associated with the Evangelical Lutheran Church.

	Annual Growth	06/10	06/11	06/12	06/13	06/14
Sales ($ mil.)	(11.1%)	-	106.0	78.1	72.6	74.5
Net income ($ mil.)	63.0%	-	-	8.7	22.1	23.1
Market value ($ mil.)	-	-	-	-	-	-
Employees	-	-	-	-	-	650

AUGUSTANA COLLEGE ASSOCIATION

2001 S SUMMIT AVE
SIOUX FALLS, SD 571970002
Phone: 605-274-4116
Fax: -
Web: www.augie.edu

CEO: -
CFO: -
HR: Jane (Ginny) Kuper
FYE: July 31
Type: Private

Augustana College is a liberal arts college affiliated with the Evangelical Lutheran Church. It enrolls about 1800 students in more than 50 academic fields. The college focuses on its five shared core values: Christian Liberal Arts Excellence Community and Service. Augustana College was founded in 1860 in Chicago and moved to four other sites in the Midwest before settling in its current home of Sioux Falls South Dakota in 1918.

	Annual Growth	07/10	07/11	07/12	07/13	07/14
Sales ($ mil.)	3.8%	-	49.2	67.9	58.2	55.1
Net income ($ mil.)	122.7%	-	-	1.8	13.4	9.2
Market value ($ mil.)	-	-	-	-	-	-
Employees	-	-	-	-	-	400

AUNTIE ANNE'S INC.

48-50 W. Chestnut St. Ste. 200
Lancaster PA 17603
Phone: 717-435-1435
Fax: 717-435-1436
Web: www.auntieannes.com

CEO: -
CFO: -
HR: -
FYE: December 31
Type: Private

You don't have to be twisted to enjoy one of these pretzels. Auntie Anne's is a leading franchisor of snack outlets with about 1150 pretzel stores located in some 45 states and 20 other countries. The stores offer a variety of pretzel flavors including original cinnamon sugar garlic almond and sesame as well as the popular pretzel-wrapped hot dog. They are primarily found in high-traffic areas such as malls airports train stations and stadiums. Anne Beiler started the company in 1988 to help fund a faith-based family assistance foundation. Roark Capital company FOCUS Brands acquired Auntie Anne's in 2010.

AURA SYSTEMS INC

4000 Redondo Beach Ave.
Redondo Beach, CA 90278
Phone: 310 643-5300
Fax: 310 643-7457
Web: www.aurasystems.com

NBB: AUSI
CEO: Melvin Gagerman
CFO: Melvin Gagerman
HR: -
FYE: February 28
Type: Public

Aura Systems is charging ahead with its AuraGen electric generator which can produce 8500 watts of power from an idling car engine. Companies in the telecommunications utilities and oil and gas industries use the AuraGen to generate mobile power; the military version of the AuraGen is marketed as the VIPER. RV maker Country Coach announced plans in 2004 to install the AuraGen on its Prevost model. Aura Systems also is entitled to royalties from Daewoo Electronics for use of electro-optical technology found in projection TVs. The company gets about 80% of its sales in the US.

	Annual Growth	02/10	02/11	02/12	02/13	02/14
Sales ($ mil.)	(7.7%)	3.2	3.4	3.3	2.7	2.3
Net income ($ mil.)	-	(16.1)	(11.2)	(14.2)	(15.1)	(14.0)
Market value ($ mil.)	(30.0%)	66.7	51.6	56.0	44.5	16.0
Employees	(12.4%)	61	62	58	60	36

AURORA CAPITAL PARTNERS L.P.

10877 Wilshire Blvd. Ste. 2100
Los Angeles CA 90024
Phone: 310-551-0101
Fax: 310-277-5591
Web: www.auroracap.com

CEO: -
CFO: -
HR: San Diego
FYE: December 31
Type: Private

Aurora Capital Partners (or Aurora Capital Group) focuses on buyouts of mid-sized companies in the energy health care industrial services software manufacturing and transportation industries. It typically invests in companies with values between $100 million and $1 billion. Employing a buy-and-build strategy the investor works with existing management to create organic growth then adds on acquisitions to increase the value of its portfolio companies. Aurora's Resurgence Fund invests in companies that face operational or financial troubles. Holdings include Mitchell International and ADCO Global. Aurora Capital which has completed more than 100 acquisitions has some $2 billion of assets under management.

AURORA CASKET COMPANY INC.

10944 Marsh Rd.
Aurora IN 47001
Phone: 812-926-1111
Fax: 800-457-1112
Web: www.auroracasket.com

CEO: Michael Quinn
CFO: -
HR: -
FYE: December 31
Type: Private

Aurora Casket Company won't meet you at the Pearly Gates but it will get you there in style. One of the nation's largest casket and cremation urn makers it sells its products directly to licensed funeral homes via 60 US service centers. Known for its stainless-steel line Aurora Caskets makes caskets in a variety of woods and metals. Its cremation items extend beyond urns to include memorial markers tablets and plaques. It provides online advice on funeral planning and grief support and offers consulting software and website design services to funeral homes. Aurora Casket was owned and managed by the Backman and Barrott families for more than 120 years. In mid-2012 Kohlberg & Co. acquired the company.

AURORA DAIRY CORPORATION

1919 14TH ST STE 300
BOULDER, CO 803025321
Phone: 720-564-6296
Fax: -
Web: www.auroraorganic.com

CEO: Marc B Peperzak
CFO: Cammie Muller
HR: -
FYE: December 31
Type: Private

Aurora Organic Dairy suspects you've never heard of its herd. That's why the cow-to-carton company is aiming to change that situation by becoming a leader in the US organic dairy market. Aurora Organic specializes in private-label and store-brand milk and butter cream and non-fat dry milk for large grocery retailers and natural food stores. It also supplies industrial customers with bulk milk cream butter and non-fat dry milk. The company has agreements with Colorado and Texas farmers who operate 50000 acres of organic farmland and supply Aurora with organic feed and pasture for its cows. With its clean-living herds Aurora works to make organic dairy products widespread and affordable.

	Annual Growth	12/05	12/06	12/07	12/08	12/09
Sales ($ mil.)	16.2%	-	77.5	111.3	125.9	121.6
Net income ($ mil.)	-	-	-	(12.4)	(1.8)	18.1
Market value ($ mil.)	-	-	-	-	-	-
Employees	-	-	-	-	-	300

AURORA DIAGNOSTICS INC.

11025 RCA Center Dr. Ste. 300
Palm Beach Gardens FL 33410
Phone: 561-626-5512
Fax: 561-626-4530
Web: www.auroradx.com

CEO: -
CFO: -
HR: -
FYE: December 31
Type: Private

Doctors turn to Aurora Diagnostics when they need help making a diagnosis. The company performs anatomical pathology services studying organ samples and tissue biopsies to diagnose cancer and other diseases. Through a network of almost 20 labs it specializes in women's health urology gastrointestinal pathology hematopathology and dermatopathology services. The company performs more than 1.5 million tests a year and has a network of 10000 referring physicians. While the majority of its clients are clinics and doctor's offices the company does have contracts with more than 35 hospitals. Aurora Diagnostics also offers a Web-based system to report its findings. The company filed to go public in 2010.

AURORA FLIGHT SCIENCES CORP

9950 WAKEMAN DR
MANASSAS, VA 201102702
Phone: 703-369-3633
Fax: -
Web: www.aurora.aero

CEO: -
CFO: Tim Crossno
HR: -
FYE: September 30
Type: Private

Pilots? For most of its products Aurora Flight Sciences doesn't need pilots (at least not ones who sit in a cockpit of a plane). The company makes unmanned aerial vehicles (UAVs aka drones) and composite structures for aircraft with both military and scientific applications. It also provides flight operations and testing services for a variety of aircraft. Customers include major aerospace contractors such as Raytheon and US government agencies. Aurora Flight Sciences along with Georgia Institute of Technology is developing next-generation distributed controllers for turbine engines for the Air Force Research Laboratory.

	Annual Growth	09/06	09/07	09/08	09/09	09/10
Sales ($ mil.)	-	-	-	(1,111.2)	65.1	62.7
Net income ($ mil.)	1064.5%	-	-	0.0	(1.6)	0.1
Market value ($ mil.)	-	-	-	-	-	-
Employees	-	-	-	-	-	292

AURORA NETWORKS INC.

5400 Betsy Ross Dr.
Santa Clara CA 95054
Phone: 408-235-7000
Fax: 408-845-9043
Web: www.aurora.com

CEO: Guy Sucharczuk
CFO: Craig McCollam
HR: -
FYE: December 31
Type: Private

Aurora Networks wants to lighten up the atmosphere of digital broadband networks. The company manufactures optical transport systems used by cable companies to build fiber-optic networks and upgrade older hybrid fiber/coax (HFC) networks. Its products include optical nodes and headend equipment such as amplifiers transmitters receivers and switches. The company also provides engineering and field services as well as equipment repair. Aurora chief scientist Dr. Charles Barker VP Krzysztof Pradzynski and CEO Guy Sucharczuk founded the company in 1999. It counts Battery Ventures Castile Ventures Sprout Group TA Associates and Velocity Interactive Group among its backers and shareholders.

AURORA WHOLESALERS LLC

31000 AURORA RD
SOLON, OH 441392769
Phone: 440-248-5200
Fax: -
Web: www.themazelcompany.com

CEO: -
CFO: Larry Hulkama
HR: -
FYE: December 31
Type: Private

Aurora Wholesalers (dba The Mazel Company) buys a broad range of name-brand closeout consumer products from some 700 global suppliers and sells the items at below-wholesale prices. It also offers such proprietary goods as candles party goods tableware batteries and light bulbs. The company operates from offices and a warehouse distribution facility in Solon Ohio. It has buyers in Solon and in New York City and sales and marketing representation in Boston Chicago New York Philadelphia and in Solon and Columbus Ohio. CEO Reuven Dessler and EVP Jacob "Jake" Koval founded The Mazel Company as a wholesaler of closeout merchandise in 1975.

	Annual Growth	12/07	12/08	12/09	12/12	12/13
Sales ($ mil.)	(0.5%)	-	65.3	70.8	61.2	63.7
Net income ($ mil.)	(19.9%)	-	-	2.8	0.0	1.1
Market value ($ mil.)	-	-	-	-	-	-
Employees	-	-	-	-	-	100

AUSTIN INDUSTRIES INC.

3535 Travis St. Ste. 300
Dallas TX 75204-1466
Phone: 214-443-5500
Fax: 806-364-3842
Web: www.aztx.com

CEO: David B Walls
CFO: Jt Fisher
HR: -
FYE: December 31
Type: Private

Austin Industries is actually based in Dallas rather than its namesake Live Music Capital of the World. The company provides civil commercial and industrial construction services in the southern half of the US. Its oldest subsidiary Austin Bridge & Road provides road bridge and parking lot construction across Texas. (It built the longest bridge in Texas the Queen Isabella Causeway.) Subsidiary Austin Commercial builds office buildings technology sites hospitals and other commercial projects. The group's Austin Industrial arm provides construction maintenance and electrical services for the chemical refining power and manufacturing industries. The employee-owned company was founded in 1918.

AUSTIN POWDER COMPANY

25800 Science Park Dr.
Cleveland OH 44122
Phone: 216-464-2400
Fax: 216-464-4418
Web: www.austinpowder.com

CEO: David M Gleason
CFO: –
HR: –
FYE: December 31
Type: Subsidiary

Austin Powder has the original boom box. The company was founded in 1833 to manufacture black powder used to blast rocks mine coal create canals and generally move mountains. Today Austin Powder's commercial explosives are used primarily for construction mining quarrying and seismic exploration. Products include detonating cord detonator-sensitive emulsions cast boosters and high-explosive emulsions. It also makes electric and non-electric detonators. Austin International through joint ventures and partnerships provides explosives for projects outside the US mostly in other parts of the Americas.

AUSTIN RIBBON & COMPUTER SUPPLIES INC.

9211 Waterford Centre Blvd. Ste. 202
Austin TX 78758
Phone: 512-452-0651
Fax: 512-452-0691
Web: www.arc-texas.com

CEO: Laura Grant
CFO: –
HR: –
FYE: December 31
Type: Private

Nothing as archaic as ribbons and typewriters adorn the shelves at ARC (Austin Ribbon & Computer). The old-school name belies a modern firm offering IT products and services to state government education and health care customers throughout Texas. It sells more than 400 brands of computers tablets and peripherals — including Dell HP EMC Lenovo and Cisco. (The company is the largest supplier of Dell computers to Texas government.) ARC also provides IT services from single computer fixes to office-wide system design installation and maintenance. Customers have included the Texas Lottery Commission City of Dallas The University of Texas at Austin and University Health Systems San Antonio.

AUTHENTEC INC.

100 Rialto Place Ste. 100
Melbourne FL 32901
Phone: 321-308-1300
Fax: 321-308-1430
Web: www.authentec.com

NASDAQ: AUTH
CEO: Lawrence J Ciaccia
CFO: Philip L Calamia
HR: –
FYE: December 31
Type: Public

AuthenTec is good at fingering out who's using your electronic gear. The company designs biometric fingerprint sensor chips a way to digitally verify identity and to allow only authorized users to access the equipment. Electronics makers incorporate its TruePrint devices into a variety of goods such as automotive subsystems PCs and wireless devices. With most of sales made in the Asia/Pacific region the company's top three customers (Fujitsu Lenovo and Edom Technology) together account for one third of revenues. The technology was originally developed within Harris Semiconductor; AuthenTec was spun out of Harris Corporation in 1998.

AUTHENTIDATE HOLDING CORP

Connell Corporate Center, 300 Connell Drive, 5th Floor
Berkeley Heights, NJ 07922
Phone: 908 787-1700
Fax: –
Web: www.authentidate.com

NBB: ADAT
CEO: Ian C Bonnet
CFO: William A Marshall
HR: –
FYE: June 30
Type: Public

AuthentiDate Holding wants to leave its technological stamp of approval on the US health care industry. Through its subsidiaries the company provides secure workflow management software and remote patient monitoring technology to health care companies and government entities. Its hosted Inscrybe platform facilitates administrative functions like electronic signing identity management and content authentication while its ExpressMD Solutions subsidiary makes in-home patient vital signs monitoring systems. Other offerings include Inscrybe Office which extends its Web-based workflow management software to personal and business customers. Major customers include the US Department of Veterans Affairs.

	Annual Growth	06/11	06/12	06/13	06/14	06/15
Sales ($ mil.)	7.2%	2.8	3.2	4.8	5.6	3.7
Net income ($ mil.)	–	(12.6)	(8.4)	(11.3)	(7.1)	(9.7)
Market value ($ mil.)	(36.7%)	5.6	3.0	4.1	3.1	0.9
Employees	(9.3%)	37	38	37	41	25

AUTO-OWNERS INSURANCE COMPANY

6101 Anacapri Blvd.
Lansing MI 48917
Phone: 517-323-1200
Fax: 517-323-8796
Web: www.auto-owners.com

CEO: Roger L Looyenga
CFO: –
HR: –
FYE: December 31
Type: Private

There's more to Auto-Owners Insurance Group than the name implies. In addition to auto coverage the company provides a range of personal property/casualty and life insurance products to more than 3 million policyholders. Auto-Owners Insurance Group operates through subsidiaries including Auto-Owners Life Insurance Home-Owners Insurance and Property-Owners Insurance Company. Its Southern-Owners Insurance subsidiary offers property/casualty insurance in Florida. Auto-Owners Insurance also sells commercial auto liability and workers' compensation policies. Established in 1916 the company operates in 26 states nationwide and is represented by more than 6000 independent agencies.

AUTOALLIANCE INTERNATIONAL INC.

1 International Dr.
Flat Rock MI 48134-9401
Phone: 734-782-7800
Fax: 734-783-8216
Web: media.ford.com/plant_display.cfm?plant_id=62

CEO: –
CFO: –
HR: –
FYE: December 31
Type: Joint Venture

Two heads are better than one at AutoAlliance International (AAI). A 50/50 joint venture between Ford Motor and Mazda the company is a contract manufacturer of the Mazda6 and Ford Mustang. AutoAlliance's history traces back to 1984 when Mazda built a plant in Michigan to make the Mazda MX-6 and called the new company Mazda Motor Manufacturing (USA) Corporation (MMUC). In 1992 MMUC teamed up with Ford and the name of the company took its present form. In addition to its current model lineup AutoAlliance International produces the Mazda 626 and Mustang GT500. Ford and Mazda are considering (in 2011) the dissolution of AAI due to low capacity and sluggish sales.

AUTOBYTEL INC.
NAS: ABTL

18872 MacArthur Boulevard, Suite 200
Irvine, CA 92612
Phone: 949 225-4500
Fax: –
Web: www.autobytel.com

CEO: Jeffrey H Coats
CFO: Kimberly Boren
HR: –
FYE: December 31
Type: Public

Autobytel puts cars on the information superhighway. Using the company's websites a potential car buyer can research make model fuel efficiency and more then complete an online request form for the desired new or used car. The form is forwarded to local auto dealers and manufacturers who contact the shopper within 24 hours. Car buyers can also research insurance financing and other related services. Autobytel generates most of its revenue through lead referral fees it charges dealers and manufacturers (car buyers pay no fees). However the company also operates advertising-driven consumer website Car.com which offers many of the same services.

	Annual Growth	12/10	12/11	12/12	12/13	12/14
Sales ($ mil.)	19.8%	51.5	63.8	66.8	78.4	106.3
Net income ($ mil.)	–	(8.6)	0.4	1.4	38.1	3.4
Market value ($ mil.)	88.9%	7.6	6.2	35.3	134.4	96.8
Employees	5.6%	119	118	122	159	148

AUTOCAM CORPORATION

4436 Broadmoor SE
Kentwood MI 49512
Phone: 616-698-0707
Fax: 616-698-6876
Web: www.autocam.com

CEO: John C Kennedy
CFO: Warren A Veltman
HR: –
FYE: December 31
Type: Private

Members of both the UAW and the AMA are fans of Autocam. The company manufactures precision components and assemblies for the automotive as well as the medical device industries. Its automotive components are used in brake fuel and power steering systems. Customers include Bosch Hitachi and Delphi. Autocam also makes electric motors and offers machined parts for power tools. Its medical arm specializes in surgical devices implants and hand pieces which serve a range of surgical applications. Customers include Abbott Medtronic Stryker and others. Founded in 1988 the company is owned by a group of investors led by its founder and CEO John Kennedy who holds a 60% stake.

AUTODESK INC.
NMS: ADSK

111 McInnis Parkway
San Rafael, CA 94903
Phone: 415 507-5000
Fax: –
Web: www.autodesk.com

CEO: Carl Bass
CFO: R. Scott Herren
HR: Jan Becker
FYE: January 31
Type: Public

Autodesk is a pioneer in 3D design engineering and digital entertainment software. Since introducing its AutoCAD software in 1982 the company offers one of the broadest portfolios of 3D computer-aided design (CAD) software on the market. Its AutoCAD and Revit software is primarily used by architects engineers and structural designers to design draft and model buildings and other structures. Maya is a 3D animation software used in film visual effects and game development. Autodesk 360 provides cloud-based tools and services plus mobile apps for smartphones and tablets that can be used by professionals amateur designers and students. Services offered include consulting support and training.

	Annual Growth	01/11	01/12	01/13	01/14	01/15
Sales ($ mil.)	6.5%	1,951.8	2,215.6	2,312.2	2,273.9	2,512.2
Net income ($ mil.)	(21.2%)	212.0	285.3	247.4	228.8	81.8
Market value ($ mil.)	7.3%	9,234.4	8,172.0	8,825.8	11,633.8	12,259.1
Employees	6.7%	6,800	7,500	7,300	7,600	8,823

AUTOGRILL GROUP INC.

6905 Rockledge Dr.
Bethesda MD 20817
Phone: 240-694-4100
Fax: 240-694-4790
Web: www.hmshost.com

CEO: Steve Johnson
CFO: –
HR: –
FYE: December 31
Type: Subsidiary

Autogrill Group knows some travelers hunger for more than just transportation. Operating as HMSHost the company is a leading contract foodservice operator focused on the travel market. It has restaurant operations in more than 100 airports in North America Europe and parts of the Asia Pacific. Its eateries operate under such licensed brands as Burger King Chili's Too California Pizza Kitchen Quiznos and Starbucks as well as proprietary names Fresh Attractions Deli and Flatbreadz. HMSHost also has service operations at more than 80 highway rest areas and runs newsstands and other retail locations in addition to restaurants. HMSHost is a unit of Italian contract foodservices giant Autogrill.

AUTOLIV ASP INC.

3350 Airport Rd.
Ogden UT 84405
Phone: 801-625-4800
Fax: 801-625-4964
Web: www.autoliv.com

CEO: Jan Carlson
CFO: –
HR: –
FYE: December 31
Type: Subsidiary

Autoliv ASP the North American subsidiary of Sweden-based Autoliv Inc. designs and manufactures automobile safety restraint systems such as airbags and airbag inflators (the highest-cost item in making an airbag module) seatbelts night vision systems radar sensors gas generators and other airbag modules. It is credited with the invention of the side-impact airbag the Inflatable Curtain (for head protection) the Anti-Whiplash Seat and night vision systems. It also provides testing of automotive safety products for vehicle manufacturers as well as engineering design of products at its technical center and test laboratory. Autoliv ASP with 10 locations across the US was founded in 1996.

AUTOLIV INC.
NYS: ALV

Vasagatan 11, 7th Floor, SE-111 20, Box 70381
Stockholm SE-107 24
Phone: (46) 8 587 20 600
Fax: –
Web: www.autoliv.com

CEO: Jan Carlson
CFO: Mats Wallin
HR: Kim Kovac
FYE: December 31
Type: Public

Autoliv puts some drive behind the Bee Gees' jive about stayin' alive. The world's #1 manufacturer of car safety equipment aims to save lives by increasing the survivability statistics of traffic accidents. It makes components such as seat belts airbags anti-whiplash systems and safety electronics. Other products include rollover protection systems steering wheels (with airbags) night vision systems radar systems and child seats. The company caters to about every car maker in the industry and has more than 100 locations around the globe.

	Annual Growth	12/10	12/11	12/12	12/13	12/14
Sales ($ mil.)	6.5%	7,170.6	8,232.4	8,266.7	8,803.4	9,240.5
Net income ($ mil.)	(5.7%)	590.6	623.4	483.1	485.8	467.8
Market value ($ mil.)	7.7%	7,004.1	4,746.0	5,979.3	8,145.1	9,415.7
Employees	8.5%	43,300	47,900	50,900	56,500	60,000

AUTOMATIC DATA PROCESSING INC.
NMS: ADP

One ADP Boulevard
Roseland, NJ 07068
Phone: 973 974-5000
Fax: 973 974-5390
Web: www.adp.com

CEO: Carlos A. Rodriguez
CFO: Jan Siegmund
HR: Dermot J. O'Brien
FYE: June 30
Type: Public

The original outsourcer Automatic Data Processing (ADP) has still got it. ADP is one of the largest payroll and tax filing processors in the world serving about 625000 clients. Employer services (payroll processing tax and benefits administration services) account for the majority of the company's sales and its PEO (professional employer organization) services are provided through ADP TotalSource. Other offerings include accounting auto collision estimates for insurers employment background checks desktop support and business development training services. The company in 2014 spun off its former dealer services segment.

	Annual Growth	06/11	06/12	06/13	06/14	06/15
Sales ($ mil.)	2.6%	9,879.5	10,665.2	11,310.1	12,206.5	10,938.5
Net income ($ mil.)	3.7%	1,254.2	1,388.5	1,405.8	1,515.9	1,452.5
Market value ($ mil.)	11.1%	24,570.0	25,959.8	32,116.3	36,976.2	37,419.3
Employees	1.9%	51,000	57,000	60,000	61,000	55,000

AUTOMOBILE PROTECTION CORPORATION

6010 Atlantic Blvd.
Norcross GA 30071
Phone: 678-225-1000
Fax: 770-246-2468
Web: www.easycare.com

CEO: Larry I Dorfman
CFO: John Marks
HR: –
FYE: December 31
Type: Private

For those sweet cars that turn out to be sour lemons Automobile Protection Corporation (APCO) sells lemon aid. The company offers extended-care warranties (under the EasyCare brand) and service contracts for new and used vehicles including cars pickups and recreational vehicles. It has some 1.7 million active contracts which are insured by XL Capital. The warranties provide bumper-to-bumper mechanical coverage and offer rental car and towing reimbursements. The company has agreements with auto manufacturers such as Honda Jaguar Land Rover Mazda and Volvo. It sells its contracts through more than 3000 car dealers in the US and Canada.

AUTONATION, INC.
NYS: AN

200 S.W. 1st Avenue
Fort Lauderdale, FL 33301
Phone: 954 769-6000
Fax: –
Web: www.autonation.com

CEO: Michael J. (Mike) Jackson
CFO: Cheryl Miller
HR: –
FYE: December 31
Type: Public

AutoNation wants to instill patriotic fervor in the fickle car-buying public. The brainchild of entrepreneur Wayne Huizenga (Waste Management Blockbuster) AutoNation is the #1 auto dealer in the US (ahead of Penske Automotive Group and Sonic Automotive). The firm owns some 280 new-vehicle franchises (down from 300 in 2008) in 15 states and it conducts online sales through AutoNation.com and individual dealer websites. It sells 34 new brands of new vehicles. An active acquirer of local retail brands the company is in the midst of transitioning them to the AutoNation name. In addition to auto sales AutoNation provides maintenance and repair services sells auto parts and finances and insures vehicles.

	Annual Growth	12/11	12/12	12/13	12/14	12/15
Sales ($ mil.)	10.8%	13,832.3	15,668.8	17,517.6	19,108.8	20,862.0
Net income ($ mil.)	12.0%	281.4	316.4	374.9	418.7	442.6
Market value ($ mil.)	12.8%	4,085.3	4,398.9	5,505.9	6,693.7	6,610.6
Employees	7.6%	19,400	21,000	22,000	24,000	26,000

AUTOTRADER GROUP INC.

3003 Summit Blvd. Ste. 200
Atlanta GA 30319
Phone: 404-568-8000
Fax: 404-568-3060
Web: www.autotradergroup.com

CEO: Sandy Schwartz
CFO: –
HR: Portia Taylor
FYE: December 31
Type: Subsidiary

AutoTrader Group gives the Internet its very own Motor Mile. The company operates the AutoTrader.com and KBB.com websites which work to connect online buyers with those who have cars to sell. AutoTrader.com draws an average of about 29 million visitors a month who browse its extensive listings and popular features such as vehicle reviews warranty information insurance and financing. In addition to used cars and trucks the site offers listings for motorcycles and classic cars for collectors (at AutoTrader Classics) as well as some new cars. Its kbb.com website provides consumers with a ballpark car value when they set out to shop. Majority-owned by Cox Enterprises AutoTrader Group withdrew an IPO in 2013.

AUTOZONE, INC.
NYS: AZO

123 South Front Street
Memphis, TN 38103
Phone: 901 495-6500
Fax: –
Web: www.autozone.com

CEO: William C. (Bill) Rhodes
CFO: William T. (Bill) Giles
HR: Daisy L Vanderlinde
FYE: August 29
Type: Public

Imagine that you are in your garage making some weekend car repairs. The wheel cylinders are leaking ... the brake shoe adjuster nut is rusted solid ... you're about to enter ... the AutoZone. With more than 5100 stores in the US and Puerto Rico it's the nation's #1 auto parts chain. It also operates some 440 stores in Mexico and seven in Brazil. AutoZone stores sell hard parts (alternators engines batteries) maintenance items (oil antifreeze) accessories (car stereos floor mats) and non-automotive merchandise under brand names as well as under private labels. AutoZone's commercial sales program distributes parts and other products to garages dealerships and other businesses.

	Annual Growth	08/11	08/12	08/13	08/14	08/15
Sales ($ mil.)	6.0%	8,073.0	8,603.9	9,147.5	9,475.3	10,187.3
Net income ($ mil.)	8.1%	849.0	930.4	1,016.5	1,069.7	1,160.2
Market value ($ mil.)	24.6%	9,237.6	11,193.0	12,874.9	16,520.3	22,270.4
Employees	5.7%	65,000	70,000	71,000	76,000	81,000

AUVIL FRUIT COMPANY INC.

21902 STATE HIGHWAY 97
ORONDO, WA 988439759
Phone: 509-784-1033
Fax: –
Web: www.auvilfruit.com

CEO: –
CFO: –
HR: –
FYE: March 31
Type: Private

Auvil Fruit Company's products are "auvilly" tasty. The company grows apples in the US's cool misty Northwest whose climate would do Johnny Appleseed proud. Auvil markets its crops under the brand names Elite Gee Whiz and Topaz. Granny Smith Fuji Gala and Pink Lady apples are grown on one of three Auvil ranches (some 1350 acres) and sold at grocery stores throughout the US and Canada. Auvil also sells Rainier and Bing cherries. Its retail food customers include Raley's and Stop & Shop. The company was founded in 1928 by Grady Auvil who introduced the Granny Smith apple to state of Washington.

	Annual Growth	03/08	03/09	03/10	03/11	03/12
Sales ($ mil.)	16.6%	–	32.6	36.0	40.6	51.6
Net income ($ mil.)	70.7%	–	–	5.4	7.2	15.8
Market value ($ mil.)	–	–	–	–	–	–
Employees	–	–	–	–	–	575

AUXILIO INC

NBB: AUXO

26300 La Alameda, Suite 100
Mission Viejo, CA 92691
Phone: 949 614-0700
Fax: –
Web: www.auxilioinc.com

CEO: Joseph J Flynn
CFO: Paul T Anthony
HR: –
FYE: December 31
Type: Public

Hospitals count on AUXILIO to streamline their printing processes; you can print copy scan and fax that. The company is a managed print services provider meaning it does not sell printing equipment and related supplies. Rather it is vendor neutral and procures different makes and models of equipment depending on the needs of its US health care industry clients which include California Pacific Medical Center Saddleback Memorial Medical Center and St. Joseph Health System. Often working with IT departments AUXILIO's consultants assess clients' print environments and assist them with plans to minimize costs on supplies that will maximize their productivity and also reduce unnecessary paper waste.

	Annual Growth	12/10	12/11	12/12	12/13	12/14
Sales ($ mil.)	30.0%	15.4	21.8	35.6	43.0	44.0
Net income ($ mil.)	–	(1.6)	(2.6)	(2.4)	1.3	1.3
Market value ($ mil.)	2.3%	23.9	18.0	22.4	35.0	26.2
Employees	20.6%	101	112	173	196	214

AUXILIUM PHARMACEUTICALS INC

NMS: AUXL

640 Lee Road
Chesterbrook, PA 19087
Phone: 484 321-5900
Fax: –
Web: www.auxilium.com

CEO: Adrian Adams
CFO: Andrew Saik
HR: –
FYE: December 31
Type: Public

Auxilium Pharmaceuticals wants to be the wingman for patients suffering from ailments including hormonal imbalances or tissue conditions. The biopharmaceutical developer markets products that include Testim a topical testosterone gel used to treat hypogonadism (low testosterone production) and XIAFLEX an injectable enzyme approved to treat Dupuytren's contracture (a progressive disease which causes a person's fingers to permanently contract). Auxilium added several testosterone replacement and erectile dysfunction drugs through the 2013 acquisition of Actient. The company's pipeline of candidates includes potential treatments for unusual soft tissue conditions and pain.

	Annual Growth	12/08	12/09	12/10	12/11	12/12
Sales ($ mil.)	33.3%	125.4	164.0	211.4	264.3	395.3
Net income ($ mil.)	–	(46.3)	(53.5)	(51.2)	(32.9)	85.9
Market value ($ mil.)	(10.1%)	1,401.6	1,477.5	1,039.9	982.2	913.7
Employees	11.5%	340	540	565	530	526

AV HOMES INC

NMS: AVHI

8601 N. Scottsdale Rd., Suite 225
Scottsdale, AZ 85253
Phone: 480 214-7400
Fax: –
Web: www.avatarholdings.com

CEO: Roger A. Cregg
CFO: Michael S. Burnett
HR: –
FYE: December 31
Type: Public

AV Homes (formerly Avatar Holdings) aspires to be the embodiment of stylish retirement living. The company develops active adult and primary residential communities and builds homes in Florida Arizona and North Carolina. Its Joseph Carl Homes unit builds homes for people of all ages in Florida and Phoenix. AV Homes owns some 23000 acres of developed and developable land. AV Homes also operates a title insurance agency and manages the day-to-day operations of its communities' amenities. The company gets nearly 90% of its revenue from homebuilding developments while the remainder comes from land sales.

	Annual Growth	12/10	12/11	12/12	12/13	12/14
Sales ($ mil.)	48.3%	59.1	89.0	107.5	143.7	285.9
Net income ($ mil.)	–	(35.1)	(165.9)	(90.2)	(9.5)	(1.9)
Market value ($ mil.)	(7.4%)	439.7	159.3	315.4	403.1	323.2
Employees	(3.1%)	243	100	112	133	214

AVALON HOLDINGS CORP.

ASE: AWX

One American Way
Warren, OH 44484-5555
Phone: 330 856-8800
Fax: –
Web: www.avalonholdings.com

CEO: Ronald E Klingle
CFO: Bryan P Saksa
HR: –
FYE: December 31
Type: Public

The magical promise of this Avalon is waste management services and golf courses. Through its American Waste Management Services subsidiary Avalon Holdings helps customers manage and dispose of wastes. Services include hazardous and nonhazardous waste brokerage and management services and captive landfill management services — management of landfills used exclusively by their owners. The company also operates two golf courses near its headquarters. The golf operations include the management of dining and banquet facilities and a travel agency. Chairman Ronald Klingle controls a 67% voting stake in Avalon Holdings.

	Annual Growth	12/10	12/11	12/12	12/13	12/14
Sales ($ mil.)	4.3%	43.5	54.0	48.9	59.5	51.5
Net income ($ mil.)	–	(0.5)	0.8	(0.3)	0.4	(1.1)
Market value ($ mil.)	(1.0%)	10.4	11.0	14.5	19.8	10.0
Employees	13.8%	226	255	271	285	379

AVALON OIL & GAS INC

NBB: AOGN

310 Fourth Avenue South, Suite 7000
Minneapolis, MN 55415
Phone: 952 746-9652
Fax: –
Web: www.avalonoilinc.com

CEO: Kent Rodriguez
CFO: Kent Rodriguez
HR: –
FYE: March 31
Type: Public

Avalon Oil & Gas is looking for that legendary prize — making consistent profits in the oil business. The company focuses on acquiring mature oil and gas wells in Kansas Louisiana Oklahoma and Texas and in 2009 it reported proved reserves of about 45650 barrels of oil equivalent. In addition to its oil and gas assets Avalon Oil & Gas' technology segment (through majority-owned Oiltek) provides explorers with oil production enhancing technologies. To develop this segment the company has a strategic partnership with UK technology group Innovaro. In 2011 the company agreed to buy Oklahoma properties from Fossiltek. CEO Kent Rodriguez owns 46% of Avalon Oil & Gas.

	Annual Growth	03/11	03/12	03/13	03/14	03/15
Sales ($ mil.)	(12.5%)	0.2	0.3	0.2	0.2	0.1
Net income ($ mil.)	–	(1.3)	(0.7)	(0.7)	(0.8)	0.1
Market value ($ mil.)	62.7%	0.1	0.0	2.6	1.4	0.7
Employees	25.7%	2	5	5	5	5

AVALONBAY COMMUNITIES, INC.

NYS: AVB

Ballston Tower, 671 N. Glebe Road, Suite 800
Arlington, VA 22203
Phone: 703 329-6300
Fax: 703 329-9130
Web: www.avalonbay.com

CEO: Timothy J. (Tim) Naughton
CFO: Kevin P Oshea
HR: Suzanne Jakstavich
FYE: December 31
Type: Public

AvalonBay Communities has it down in the apartment department. The real estate investment trust (REIT) buys develops renovates and operates multi-family properties in the US. It specializes in upscale properties in high barrier-to-entry markets such as Boston Los Angeles New York City San Francisco Seattle and Washington DC. By providing luxury living in high-demand areas where apartment-zoned land is in low supply AvalonBay can also charge premium rent. The REIT owns about 180 apartment communities with more than 53000 units. It also has more than 30 properties under construction or redevelopment and owns rights to develop more than 30 additional ones.

	Annual Growth	12/10	12/11	12/12	12/13	12/14
Sales ($ mil.)	17.1%	895.3	968.7	1,038.7	1,462.9	1,685.1
Net income ($ mil.)	40.5%	175.3	441.6	423.9	353.1	683.6
Market value ($ mil.)	9.8%	14,862.3	17,245.8	17,904.7	15,612.3	21,575.7
Employees	10.8%	1,993	2,095	2,178	–	3,006

AVANADE INC.

818 Stewart St. Ste. 400
Seattle WA 98101
Phone: 206-239-5600
Fax: 206-239-5605
Web: www.avanade.com

CEO: Adam Warby
CFO: Ken Guthrie
HR: –
FYE: September 30
Type: Subsidiary

Avanade tries to give its customers a fresh view into their own operations. A subsidiary of Dublin-based information technology services provider Accenture the company provides IT consulting services centered mostly around Microsoft products. With offices worldwide Avanade helps large corporations with the design implementation and support of the software systems related to communications operations management resource planning and customer relationship management (CRM). A large portion of Avanade's business comes from subcontracting services provided to its parent company and minority shareholder Microsoft. The company's other clients have included European electricity company Vattenfall and EMI Music.

AVANIR PHARMACEUTICALS, INC. NMS: AVNR

20 Enterprise, Suite 200
Aliso Viejo, CA 92656
Phone: 949 389-6700
Fax: 858 453-5845
Web: www.avanir.com

CEO: Keith A Katkin
CFO: –
HR: –
FYE: September 30
Type: Public

AVANIR Pharmaceuticals doesn't have anything against tears it just wants them to be triggered by emotions instead of central nervous system disorders. Its drug NUEDEXTA has been approved as a treatment for pseudobulbar affect — the involuntary crying or laughing experienced by some people with neurological disorders such as multiple sclerosis or following brain injury or stroke. NUEDEXTA is also in late-stage trials for diabetic neuropathic pain. AVANIR had an earlier success with its development of OTC cold sore cream Abreva which GlaxoSmithKline Consumer Healthcare markets in North America. The company receives royalty revenues from GSK and other licensees around the world.

	Annual Growth	09/09	09/10	09/11	09/12	09/13
Sales ($ mil.)	106.1%	4.2	2.9	10.5	41.3	75.4
Net income ($ mil.)	–	(22.0)	(26.7)	(60.6)	(59.7)	(75.5)
Market value ($ mil.)	19.4%	316.3	485.1	434.1	486.6	643.2
Employees	91.1%	20	128	188	225	267

AVANTAIR INC NBB: AAIR

4311 General Howard Drive
Clearwater, FL 33762
Phone: 727 539-0071
Fax: –
Web: www.avantair.com

CEO: –
CFO: –
HR: –
FYE: June 30
Type: Public

Rather than fly commercial Avantair offers a little privacy. The company sells fractional ownership interests in piloted aircraft coupled with fleet maintenance. Pricier than commercial flights but cheaper than owning a jet a fractional interest allows travelers to schedule their own flights generally from smaller airports. Ownership can be purchased in increments beginning with a 1/16th share equating to 50 hours of flight time a year. Avantair also sells charter flight-cards for 15 or 25 hours and an Axis Club membership for a three-year term. Its fleet includes 55 aircraft which operate on the East and West coasts. Service extends across the US as well as Canada Mexico and the Bahamas and Caribbean.

	Annual Growth	06/08	06/09	06/10	06/11	06/12
Sales ($ mil.)	10.8%	115.6	136.8	143.0	149.0	174.0
Net income ($ mil.)	–	(18.9)	(4.5)	(4.0)	(10.8)	(6.6)
Market value ($ mil.)	(23.9%)	51.4	30.5	79.5	49.8	17.2
Employees	6.8%	403	445	450	530	525

AVAYA GOVERNMENT SOLUTIONS INC.

12730 Fair Lakes Cir.
Fairfax VA 22033
Phone: 703-653-8000
Fax: 703-653-8001
Web: www.avayagov.com

CEO: –
CFO: Mike Whyte
HR: –
FYE: December 31
Type: Subsidiary

Avaya Government Solutions is delighted when the feds come calling. The subsidiary of business communications systems maker Avaya has developed communications and networking systems for a number of government agencies including the Department of Defense the FAA and the US Treasury; other clients come from the homeland security and criminal justice sectors among others. Its services include technology consulting systems engineering and integration of older legacy systems with newer technology as well as consulting training and support. The subsidiary specializes in designing and implementing large-scale telecom systems and call centers using Avaya's extensive selection of enterprise communications products.

AVAYA INC.

211 Mt. Airy Rd.
Basking Ridge NJ 07920
Phone: 908-953-6000
Fax: 908-953-7609
Web: www.avaya.com

CEO: Kevin J Kennedy
CFO: Dave Vellequette
HR: –
FYE: September 30
Type: Subsidiary

Avaya helps to tie the corporate world together. The company's communication equipment and software integrate voice and data services for customers including large corporations government agencies and small businesses. Its office phone systems incorporate Internet protocol (IP) and Session Initiation protocol (SIP) telephony messaging Web access and interactive voice response. Avaya also offers a wide array of consulting integration and other managed IT services. The company sells directly and through distributors resellers systems integrators and telecommunications service providers; more than three-quarters of its sales are made indirectly. Parent company Avaya Holdings filed for an IPO in 2011.

AVEO PHARMACEUTICALS, INC. NMS: AVEO

One Broadway, 14th Floor
Cambridge, MA 02142
Phone: 617 588-1960
Fax: –
Web: www.aveooncology.com

CEO: Michael P Bailey
CFO: Keith S Ehrlich
HR: –
FYE: December 31
Type: Public

AVEO Pharmaceuticals' models don't pout strut or even turn heads — unless you're a cancer drug researcher. Operating as AVEO Oncology the biotech firm develops cancer models to uncover how genes mutate into tumors and how tumors progress through additional mutations. AVEO then builds genetic profiles of such tumors and applies them to antibody (protein) drug candidates in preclinical and clinical development to help predict actual human responses. In addition to its own pipeline of potential drugs AVEO has partnered with other pharmaceutical developers to apply its Human Response Platform to their drug candidates.

	Annual Growth	12/10	12/11	12/12	12/13	12/14
Sales ($ mil.)	(20.2%)	44.7	164.8	19.3	1.3	18.1
Net income ($ mil.)	–	(58.8)	30.6	(114.4)	(107.0)	(52.7)
Market value ($ mil.)	(51.0%)	764.5	899.4	420.9	95.7	43.9
Employees	(21.1%)	147	220	219	71	57

AVERA HEALTH

3900 W AVERA DR
SIOUX FALLS, SD 571085717
Phone: 605-665-8709
Fax: –
Web: www.avera.org

CEO: John T. Porter
CFO: Jim Breckenridge
HR: –
FYE: June 30
Type: Private

Avera Health provides health care services to eastern South Dakota as well as parts of Iowa Minnesota Nebraska and North Dakota. The health care system operates an extensive network of facilities including five regional hospitals and 300 other facilities including community hospitals primary care clinics nursing homes hospices urgent care clinics and home health offices. These operations are divided into five regions: Avera St. Luke's Avera Queen of Peace Avera Marshall Avera McKennan and Avera Sacred Heart. The system also operates a health care plan and a hospital purchasing organization. Avera Health is sponsored by the Benedictine Sisters and Presentation Sisters.

	Annual Growth	06/02	06/03	06/04	06/05	06/13
Sales ($ mil.)	–	–	–	0.0	5.4	9.2	125.0
Net income ($ mil.)	48.3%	–	–	1.1	4.7	37.4
Market value ($ mil.)	–	–	–	–	–	–
Employees	–	–	–	–	–	2,450

AVERITT EXPRESS INC.

1415 NEAL ST
COOKEVILLE, TN 385014328
Phone: 931-526-3306
Fax: –
Web: www.averittexpress.com

CEO: Gary D. Sasser
CFO: George Johnson
HR: –
FYE: December 31
Type: Private

Small loads add up at Averitt Express. The company provides less-than-truckload (LTL) freight transportation service. (LTL carriers combine freight from multiple shippers into a single trailer.) It operates a fleet of about 4100 tractors and 12250 trailers from a network of 80 terminals. Averitt Express directly serves the southern US and Mexico and it provides service elsewhere in North America through partnerships with other carriers such as Lakeville Motor Express and DATS. The company also offers truckload and expedited freight transportation along with logistics warehousing and international freight forwarding. Customers have included Home Depot Shoe Carnival and V.F. Corporation.

	Annual Growth	12/09	12/10	12/11	12/12	12/13
Sales ($ mil.)	6.8%	–	819.9	917.2	957.6	1,000.0
Net income ($ mil.)	14.4%	–	–	30.3	39.9	39.6
Market value ($ mil.)	–	–	–	–	–	–
Employees	–	–	–	–	–	8,208

AVERY DENNISON CORP.

NYS: AVY

207 Goode Avenue
Glendale, CA 91203
Phone: 626 304-2000
Fax: –
Web: www.averydennison.com

CEO: Dean A. Scarborough
CFO: Anne L. Bramman
HR: Anne Hill
FYE: January 03
Type: Public

Avery Dennison is easy to label: It's a global leader in the making of adhesive labels used on packaging mailers and other items. Pressure-sensitive adhesives and materials account for more than half of its sales. Its Pressure-sensitive Materials (PSM) unit is split into two other units: Label and Packaging Materials (LPM) and Graphics and Reflective Solutions (GRS). Under the Avery Dennison and Fasson brands it makes papers films and foils coated with adhesive and sold in rolls to printers. Its most widely used products are the self-adhesive stamps used by the US Postal Service. It also makes retail branding and security tags printer systems and fasteners as well as medical adhesive products.

	Annual Growth	01/11*	12/11	12/12	12/13*	01/15
Sales ($ mil.)	(0.7%)	6,512.7	6,026.3	6,035.6	6,140.0	6,330.3
Net income ($ mil.)	(5.9%)	316.9	190.1	215.4	215.8	248.9
Market value ($ mil.)	5.2%	3,830.0	2,594.4	3,111.8	4,566.4	4,684.9
Employees	(6.1%)	32,100	30,400	29,800	26,000	25,000

*Fiscal year change

AVERY WEIGH-TRONIX LLC

1000 Armstrong Dr.
Fairmont MN 56031-1439
Phone: 507-238-4461
Fax: 507-238-8258
Web: www.wtxweb.com

CEO: –
CFO: –
HR: Sarah Hughes
FYE: December 31
Type: Subsidiary

Avery Weigh-Tronix puts the whole weight of its being into its work. The company makes a full slate of industrial and retail weighing systems from bench scales to conveyor scales counting scales floor scales truck scales and weigh bars. It also produces accessories such as printers remote displays signal processors and wireless transceivers. Clients come from such sectors as transportation and logistics as well as public safety. The company operates globally through regional sales offices; much of its revenue comes from outside North America. It has about 500 locations worldwide with about half of those in the US. The company is a subsidiary of Illinois Tool Works (ITW).

AVI SYSTEMS INC.

9675 W 76TH ST STE 200
EDEN PRAIRIE, MN 553443707
Phone: 952-949-3700
Fax: –
Web: www.avisystems.com

CEO: Jeff Stoebner
CFO: Randi Borth
HR: Briana Cassidy
FYE: March 31
Type: Private

AVI Systems knows that a CEO's message is only as good as its transmission. The employee-owned company designs installs and services audiovisual systems in boardrooms classrooms hospitals hotels places of worship and sports arenas primarily in the Midwest. It specializes in broadcast and cable sales and training video production and post-production videoconferencing and rental and staging systems. AVI runs more than 15 regional offices as well as a help desk that offers remote monitoring and emergency on-site service. It also provides IT engineering support for larger-scale national or international installations. AVI was founded in 1974 by chairman and former CEO Joe Stoebner.

	Annual Growth	03/10	03/11	03/12	03/13	03/14
Sales ($ mil.)	24.4%	–	89.6	111.5	143.5	172.5
Net income ($ mil.)	25.3%	–	–	6.3	7.2	9.8
Market value ($ mil.)	–	–	–	–	–	–
Employees	–	–	–	–	–	233

AVI-SPL INC.

6301 Benjamin Rd. Ste. 101
Tampa FL 33634
Phone: 813-884-7168
Fax: 813-882-9508
Web: www.splis.com

CEO: John Zettel
CFO: Raj Dani
HR: –
FYE: December 31
Type: Private

AVI-SPL wants to win the eyes and ears of its clients. The company designs and installs videoconferencing systems and integrated multimedia audio and video systems. Customers include corporations universities and government agencies. It serves commercial clients in such industries as health care hospitality and financial services. Projects have included upgrading the audiovisual systems of the Budget Hearing Room of the US House of Representatives and the sound system at Gillette Stadium in Massachusetts. AVI-SPL also sells and rents equipment and offers event management and production through its Creative Show Services. The company has more than 30 locations across the US with an international office in Dubai.

AVIALL INC.

2750 Regent Blvd.
DFW Airport TX 75261-9048
Phone: 972-586-1000
Fax: 972-586-1361
Web: www.aviall.com

CEO: –
CFO: Colin M Cohen
HR: –
FYE: December 31
Type: Subsidiary

When it comes to aviation Aviall has all the right parts. The Boeing subsidiary is one of the top global distributors of commercial aircraft parts and aftermarket services. Through its primary operating unit Aviall Services the company markets and distributes aviation parts for 240 manufacturers and offers related aftermarket supply chain services to the aerospace and defense sectors. Its supply chain and logistics services include order processing and inventory management. Other services include repair and maintenance of components such as batteries brakes and hose assemblies. Aviall has some 40 service centers located in North America Europe the Middle East and other regions.

AVIAT NETWORKS, INC.

5200 Great America Parkway
Santa Clara, CA 95054
Phone: 408 567-7000
Fax: –
Web: www.aviatnetworks.com

NMS: AVNW

CEO: Michael A Pangia
CFO: Ralph S Marimon
HR: Cecilia Teh
FYE: July 03
Type: Public

Aviat Networks makes data fly. The company designs and manufactures wireless network transmission equipment — primarily microwave radios sold under the Eclipse and WTM 3000 brands among others — used to link and manage both fixed and wireless voice and data networks. It also provides network management and turnkey support services and sells third-party networking equipment such as antennas and routers. Aviat's customers include mobile network operators public safety agencies private network operators and utility and transportation companies in more than 140 countries; the company gets about 55% of its sales outside the US.

	Annual Growth	07/11*	06/12	06/13	06/14*	07/15
Sales ($ mil.)	(7.2%)	452.1	444.0	471.3	346.0	335.9
Net income ($ mil.)	–	(90.5)	(24.1)	(15.0)	(51.2)	(24.7)
Market value ($ mil.)	(24.1%)	247.5	175.0	163.7	78.1	82.2
Employees	(8.7%)	1,130	1,056	1,065	1,036	785

*Fiscal year change

AVID TECHNOLOGY, INC.

75 Network Drive
Burlington, MA 01803
Phone: 978 640-6789
Fax: –
Web: www.avid.com

NMS: AVID

CEO: Louis Hernandez
CFO: John Frederick
HR: –
FYE: December 31
Type: Public

Movie and music makers are keen on Avid Technology. The company provides digital media recording and editing software and hardware. Products include its Media Composer video editing systems and its ProTools professional audio recording and editing systems and are used by music and film studios post-production facilities radio broadcasters and TV stations as well as independent professionals and amateurs. Avid also makes newsroom automation systems digital storage systems and music notation and education software. With sales offices in about 20 countries about 60% of revenue comes from outside the US.

	Annual Growth	12/10	12/11	12/12	12/13	12/14
Sales ($ mil.)	(6.0%)	678.5	677.9	635.7	563.4	530.3
Net income ($ mil.)	–	(37.0)	(23.8)	92.9	21.2	14.7
Market value ($ mil.)	(5.0%)	686.1	335.2	297.8	320.2	558.4
Employees	(2.1%)	1,960	1,787	–	1,858	1,804

AVIS BUDGET GROUP INC

6 Sylvan Way
Parsippany, NJ 07054
Phone: 973 496-4700
Fax: –
Web: www.avisbudgetgroup.com

NMS: CAR

CEO: Larry De Shon
CFO: David B. Wyshner
HR: Edward P. (Ned) Linnen
FYE: December 31
Type: Public

Whether you're a business traveler on an expense account or a family on vacation counting every penny Avis Budget Group (ABG) has a car rental brand for you. The company's core brands include: Avis Rent A Car which targets corporate and leisure travelers at the high end of the market; Budget Rent A Car and Payless Car Rental both marketed to those on a budget; and Zipcar a car-sharing service. The rental car operator boasts nearly 5500 Avis and 3500 Budget branches across some 175 countries in North America Europe Australia and New Zealand and generates nearly 70% of its revenue from its on-airport locations. Avis's Budget Truck is one of the leading truck rental businesses in the US.

	Annual Growth	12/10	12/11	12/12	12/13	12/14
Sales ($ mil.)	13.1%	5,185.0	5,900.0	7,357.0	7,937.0	8,485.0
Net income ($ mil.)	45.9%	54.0	(29.0)	290.0	16.0	245.0
Market value ($ mil.)	43.7%	1,644.8	1,133.2	2,095.1	4,272.7	7,011.5
Employees	9.3%	21,000	28,000	28,000	29,000	30,000

AVIS RENT A CAR SYSTEM LLC

6 Sylvan Way
Parsippany NJ 07054
Phone: 973-496-3500
Fax: 408-990-4040
Web: www.quicklogic.com

CEO: F Robert Salerno
CFO: –
HR: –
FYE: December 31
Type: Subsidiary

A major player in the car rental industry Avis Rent A Car System maintains some 2200 locations primarily in the US and Canada but also in Australia New Zealand Latin America and the Caribbean. The company owns about 1275 of its locations; franchisees operate the rest. Together with sister company Budget Rent A Car System Avis Rent A Car System has a fleet of more than 350000 rental cars. Business travelers account for 60% of Avis' sales with leisure renters making up the rest. The company is a wholly-owned subsidiary of Avis Budget Group which is seeking to acquire UK-based Avis Europe a separately owned company with operations in Europe Africa the Middle East and parts of Asia.

AVISTA CORP.

1411 East Mission Avenue
Spokane, WA 99202-2600
Phone: 509 489-0500
Fax: 509 482-4361
Web: www.avistacorp.com

NYS: AVA

CEO: Scott L. Morris
CFO: Mark T. Thies
HR: Karen S. Feltes
FYE: December 31
Type: Public

It is no shock that Avista is a leading utility serving the northwestern US. The firm's regulated utility unit has a generation capacity of more than 1940 MW of electricity. Avista Utilities provides electric service to 700000 electric and natural gas customers. The company operates six hydroelectric projects and owns coal natural gas and wood waste plants. Avista has no natural gas reserves and purchases its supply from the wholesale market. The company also operated 79%-owned Ecova (which manages energy expenses and provides energy consulting expertise for about 700 multisite companies across the US) but sold this unit in 2014.

	Annual Growth	12/10	12/11	12/12	12/13	12/14
Sales ($ mil.)	(1.4%)	1,558.7	1,619.8	1,547.0	1,618.5	1,472.6
Net income ($ mil.)	20.1%	92.4	100.2	78.2	111.1	192.0
Market value ($ mil.)	11.9%	1,401.7	1,602.8	1,500.7	1,754.6	2,200.3
Employees	4.8%	1,554	2,809	3,179	3,310	1,874

AVISTAR COMMUNICATIONS CORPORATION — PINK SHEETS: AVSR

1875 S. Grant St. 10th Fl.
San Mateo CA 94402
Phone: 650-525-3300
Fax: 650-525-1360
Web: www.avistar.com

CEO: –
CFO: –
HR: –
FYE: December 31
Type: Public

If geography prevents you from concluding business with a firm handshake Avistar Communications is ready to furnish the next-best thing. The company provides communication software and hardware used to equip communications networks with video capabilities. Its systems enable videoconferencing content creation video broadcasting and data sharing between users over telephony networks and the Internet. Avistar markets its products primarily to corporations in the financial services industry including UBS Investment Bank Deutsche Bank and JPMorgan Chase. Chairman Gerald Burnett owns about 42% of the company.

AVIV REIT INC.

303 W. Madison St. Ste. 2400
Chicago IL 60606
Phone: 312-855-0930
Fax: 312-855-1684
Web: www.avivreit.com/

CEO: –
CFO: –
HR: –
FYE: December 31
Type: Private

Aviv REIT sees a healthy future in health care-related real estate. The self-administered real estate investment trust (REIT) invests in and owns nursing homes that provide post-acute (short-term stays) and long-term assisted living care. Its portfolio includes more than 250 properties in some 30 states. (Texas is home to about 60 facilities and California about 35.) Aviv REIT doesn't run the facilities — it leases them to more than 35 local regional and national operators including Daybreak Venture Saber Healthcare and Sun Healthcare. Aviv REIT is trying its hand at the IPO market again. It first filed an IPO back in 2008 but withdrew it a year later. The company then filed a second IPO in December 2012.

AVNET INC — NYS: AVT

2211 South 47th Street
Phoenix, AZ 85034
Phone: 480 643-2000
Fax: –
Web: www.avnet.com

CEO: Richard P. (Rick) Hamada
CFO: Kevin Moriarty
HR: MaryAnn G. Miller
FYE: June 27
Type: Public

If you need an electronic component Avnet probably has it. The company is the world's top distributor of electronic components (including connectors and semiconductors) enterprise computing and storage products and embedded subsystems ahead of Arrow Electronics and Ingram Micro. Avnet's suppliers include more than 700 component and systems makers; its largest supplier of parts for distribution is IBM. Avnet distributes these products to some 100000 manufacturers and resellers worldwide. Avnet distributes products from around 300 locations in more than 80 countries. It also offers a host of value-added design supply chain and aftermarket services.

	Annual Growth	07/11*	06/12	06/13	06/14	06/15
Sales ($ mil.)	1.3%	26,534.4	25,707.5	25,458.9	27,499.7	27,924.7
Net income ($ mil.)	(3.8%)	669.1	567.0	450.1	545.6	571.9
Market value ($ mil.)	6.6%	4,409.4	4,180.4	4,551.6	5,921.2	5,701.7
Employees	1.7%	17,600	19,100	18,500	19,000	18,800

*Fiscal year change

AVNET TECHNOLOGY SOLUTIONS

8700 S. Price Rd.
Tempe AZ 85284
Phone: 480-794-6500
Fax: 480-794-6890
Web: www.ats.avnet.com

CEO: –
CFO: –
HR: –
FYE: June 30
Type: Business Segment

Avnet Technology Solutions (ATS) distributes everything under the technology sun. A unit of electronic components and computer products distribution giant Avnet ATS sells servers networking gear data storage and software to independent software vendors equipment makers systems integrators and resellers worldwide. ATS accounts for about 40% of Avnet's revenues through two main groups. Its Enterprise Solutions unit provides resellers with computing systems and software as well as financing logistics marketing sales and technical support. Its Embedded Solutions group offers design and integration services to developers of application-specific computing systems used in medical telecom and industrial settings.

AVON PRODUCTS, INC. — NYS: AVP

777 Third Avenue
New York, NY 10017-1307
Phone: 212 282-5000
Fax: 212 282-6035
Web: www.avon.com

CEO: Sherilyn S. (Sheri) McCoy
CFO: James S. Scully
HR: –
FYE: December 31
Type: Public

Avon calling — calling for a younger crowd overseas reps and improved global operational efficiencies. Avon Products the world's top direct seller of cosmetics and beauty-related items is busy building a global brand and enticing more consumers to buy its products. Direct selling remains its modus operandi; sales also come from catalogs and a website. Its lineup includes cosmetics fragrances toiletries apparel home furnishings and more. Avon boasts more than 6 million independent representatives worldwide. With sales and distribution operations in more than 100 countries nearly 90% of sales come from outside the US. Avon is working to transform its business amid falling sales and profits.

	Annual Growth	12/10	12/11	12/12	12/13	12/14
Sales ($ mil.)	(5.0%)	10,862.8	11,291.6	10,717.1	9,955.0	8,851.4
Net income ($ mil.)	–	606.3	513.6	(42.5)	(56.4)	(388.6)
Market value ($ mil.)	(24.6%)	12,632.4	7,594.2	6,242.3	7,485.5	4,081.8
Employees	(5.7%)	42,000	40,600	39,100	36,700	33,200

AVSTAR AVIATION GROUP INC. — PINK SHEETS: AAVG

9801 Westheimer Ste. 302
Houston TX 77042
Phone: 713-706-6350
Fax: 713-706-6351
Web: avstargroup.com

CEO: Russell Ivy
CFO: Robert Wilson
HR: –
FYE: December 31
Type: Public

AvStar Aviation Group is making the switch from searching for oil and gas to investing in the aviation sector. Once known as Pangea Petroleum the company formerly specialized in oil and natural gas exploration and production in the US Gulf Coast region. In 2009 however Pangea Petroleum was acquired by AvStar Aviation Services which redirected the company's focus as a service provider to the general aviation industry. Now known as AvStar Aviation Group the company plans to acquire fixed base operations (FBOs) at airports. Its San Diego Airmotive subsidiary provides maintenance repair and overhaul services for aircraft.

AVX CORP.

NYS: AVX

1 AVX Boulevard
Fountain Inn, SC 29644
Phone: 864 967-2150
Fax: –
Web: www.avx.com

CEO: John S Gilbertson
CFO: Kurt P. Cummings
HR: –
FYE: March 31
Type: Public

AVX proves that tiny parts can add up to big business. The company's largest segment passive components makes passive electronic components for automotive braking systems copiers hearing aids locomotives and wireless phones. The KED Resale segment specializes in products made by Kyocera (which owns a controlling stake in the company) such as ceramic and tantalum capacitors that store filter and regulate electrical energy in electronic devices. The interconnect segment makes electronic connectors for automotive and medical electronics applications. Asia is its largest market.

	Annual Growth	03/11	03/12	03/13	03/14	03/15
Sales ($ mil.)	(4.9%)	1,653.2	1,545.3	1,414.4	1,442.6	1,353.2
Net income ($ mil.)	(1.9%)	244.0	152.8	(64.3)	127.0	225.9
Market value ($ mil.)	(1.1%)	2,507.7	2,230.2	2,001.5	2,216.8	2,400.1
Employees	(1.8%)	11,200	10,800	10,700	10,900	10,400

AWARE INC. (MA)

NMS: AWRE

40 Middlesex Turnpike
Bedford, MA 01730
Phone: 781 276-4000
Fax: –
Web: www.aware.com

CEO: Richard P Moberg
CFO: Richard P Moberg
HR: –
FYE: December 31
Type: Public

Aware is mindful of both the physical and intellectual aspects of its business. The company provides biometrics and imaging software to capture and verify fingerprint facial and iris images for identification purposes. The software is primarily used in law enforcement border control access control and national defense applications. Aware also offers imaging software used to process and display medical images and data. While DSL service assurance systems were once its largest product line Aware discontinued its DSL hardware business opting to focus on DSL software used by broadband service providers to manage DSL networks. The company also has a small intellectual property (IP) licensing business.

	Annual Growth	12/10	12/11	12/12	12/13	12/14
Sales ($ mil.)	0.2%	23.6	24.6	19.9	19.4	23.7
Net income ($ mil.)	124.6%	0.2	2.6	72.3	2.6	4.6
Market value ($ mil.)	12.4%	64.8	68.4	125.0	139.4	103.6
Employees	(4.2%)	83	77	73	58	70

AXA EQUITABLE LIFE INSURANCE COMPANY

1290 Avenue of the Americas
New York NY 10104
Phone: 212-554-1234
Fax: 716-823-6454
Web: www.sorrentocheese.com

CEO: Mark Pearson
CFO: Anders Malmstrom
HR: –
FYE: December 31
Type: Subsidiary

This company definitely has what it takes to be equitable. AXA Equitable Life Insurance is the US life insurance and annuities underwriting arm of its globe-spanning ultimate parent AXA. The company has some 2.3 million life insurance policies in force and is licensed throughout the US and Puerto Rico. Policies are sold through affiliates AXA Advisors (retail brokerage) and AXA Distributors (wholesale brokerage that sells to independent brokers and advisors) as well as corporate sales representatives. AXA Equitable a subsidiary of AXA Financial offers investment management services through affiliate Alliance Bernstein; together the firms have about $500 billion in assets under management.

AXA FINANCIAL INC.

1290 Avenue of the Americas
New York NY 10104
Phone: 212-554-1234
Fax: 212-314-4480
Web: www.axa-equitable.com/axa/axa-financial.html

CEO: Mark Pearson
CFO: Richard S Dziadzio
HR: –
FYE: December 31
Type: Subsidiary

A US-based subsidiary of French insurance giant AXA AXA Financial provides financial advisory and insurance services through subsidiaries such as AXA Equitable AXA Advisors and AXA Distributors. These businesses offer life insurance annuities mutual funds separate accounts and other investment products. It caters to individuals small businesses and professional organizations. AXA Financial's investment management business is anchored by majority-owned affiliate AllianceBernstein and serves institutional and retail clients including individuals with high net worth. AXA Financial and its subsidiaries have approximately $575 billion in assets under management most of it at AllianceBernstein.

AXA ROSENBERG INVESTMENT MANAGMENT LLC

4 Orinda Way Bldg. E
Orinda CA 94563
Phone: 925-254-6464
Fax: 925-253-0141
Web: www.axarosenberg.com

CEO: Jeremy Baskin
CFO: –
HR: –
FYE: December 31
Type: Subsidiary

No need for rose-colored glasses; AXA Rosenberg Group prefers a more analytical approach to equity investing. The unit of insurance giant AXA manages investment portfolios for institutional clients such as corporations pension funds endowments foundations and government entities. It also acts as a manager or subadvisor for several mutual funds with holdings in global equities; such funds are available to retail customers as well. AXA Rosenberg operates a handful of offices in financial centers around the globe and has more than $30 billion of assets under management. Established in 1985 the company became part of AXA in 1999.

AXCELIS TECHNOLOGIES INC

NMS: ACLS

108 Cherry Hill Drive
Beverly, MA 01915
Phone: 978 787-4000
Fax: 978 787-3000
Web: www.axcelis.com

CEO: Mary G. Puma
CFO: Kevin J. Brewer
HR: Lynnette C. Fallon
FYE: December 31
Type: Public

Ions are iconic at Axcelis Technologies. The company develops and makes ion implanters that semiconductor manufacturers use to insert ions into silicon wafers to change their conductive properties. Axcelis Technologies manufactures its ion implantation devices in house at its plant in Beverly Massachusetts. In addition to equipment it offers aftermarket service and support including spare parts equipment upgrades maintenance and training. While the company sells its products around the world the US accounts for about two-thirds of sales.

	Annual Growth	12/10	12/11	12/12	12/13	12/14
Sales ($ mil.)	(7.3%)	275.2	319.4	203.4	195.6	203.1
Net income ($ mil.)	–	(17.6)	5.1	(34.0)	(17.1)	(11.3)
Market value ($ mil.)	(7.3%)	390.0	149.9	155.6	275.1	288.6
Employees	(9.3%)	1,131	1,047	887	863	765

AXCESS INTERNATIONAL INC.

OTC: AXSI

16650 Westgrove Dr.
Addison TX 75001
Phone: 972-407-6080
Fax: 972-407-9085
Web: www.axcessinc.com

CEO: Allan Griebenow
CFO: Allan L Frank
HR: –
FYE: December 31
Type: Public

Axcess International can watch the door and mind the store. The company's ActiveTag radio-frequency identification (RFID) system is for tracking people vehicles inventory and equipment. Axcess International's Online Supervisor system integrates RFID data and digital video to a standard Web browser. The company has also developed a micro-wireless technology platform called Dot a small low-cost battery powered wireless computer for the automatic identification location tracking protecting and monitoring of personnel physical assets and vehicles; applications include airport school and military installations. Customers include security systems integrators and distributors in the US.

AXEL JOHNSON INC.

155 SPRING ST FL 6
NEW YORK, NY 100125254
Phone: 646-291-2445
Fax: –
Web: www.axeljohnson.com

CEO: –
CFO: Ben J Hennelly
HR: –
FYE: December 31
Type: Private

The Johnson family of Stockholm Sweden has an investment arm that stretches across the ocean. Axel Johnson owns and operates North American businesses on behalf of the Johnson dynasty. The investment firm focuses on several industries such as energy medical device manufacturing and water treatment. Its portfolio includes Sprague Energy Parkson Corp. and Kinetico Incorporated. Axel Johnson's companies boast about $4 billion in annual revenues. Axel Johnson along with Axel Johnson AB and AXFast are all affiliated with Sweden-based Axel Johnson Group but are independent. Established in 1873 the Johnson family of companies is in its fourth generation of family ownership.

	Annual Growth	12/06	12/07	12/08	12/09	12/10
Sales ($ mil.)	14.8%	–	–	–	2,598.3	2,982.1
Net income ($ mil.)	26.0%	–	–	–	11.9	15.0
Market value ($ mil.)	–	–	–	–	–	–
Employees	–	–	–	–	–	1,200

AXESSTEL INC

NBB: AXST

6815 Flanders Drive, Suite 210
San Diego, CA 92121
Phone: 858 625-2100
Fax: –

CEO: Patrick Gray
CFO: Patrick Gray
HR: –
FYE: December 31
Type: Public

Axesstel can soup up that old phone on your desk. The company designs and manufactures fixed wireless voice and broadband data systems that link stationary office phones to the communications network via cellular connections. Axesstel's products include fixed wireless telephones transmission terminals and wireless modems. The company mostly sells its products to telecommunications companies in developing countries that then resell the products to consumers. Axesstel has shifted its engineering and design operations to China in an effort to reduce operating expenses.

	Annual Growth	12/08	12/09	12/10	12/11	12/12
Sales ($ mil.)	(14.1%)	109.6	50.8	45.4	54.1	59.7
Net income ($ mil.)	32.1%	1.4	(10.1)	(6.3)	1.1	4.3
Market value ($ mil.)	50.4%	8.5	3.1	2.4	7.5	43.5
Employees	(11.8%)	71	22	34	39	43

AXIALL CORP

NYS: AXLL

1000 Abernathy Road, Suite 1200
Atlanta, GA 30328
Phone: 770 395-4500
Fax: –
Web: www.axiall.com

CEO: Timothy Mann
CFO: Gregory C. (Greg) Thompson
HR: Dean Adelman
FYE: December 31
Type: Public

Axiall's business revolves around the axis of commodity chemicals. The company makes chlorovinyls and aromatics used by the construction and housing plastics pulp and paper and pharmaceutical industries. Its primary chlorovinyl products are PVC (polyvinyl chloride) caustic soda and chlorine; this segment also makes vinyl chloride monomer (VCM) used to make PVC resins. Aromatics include phenol acetone (for makers of acrylic resins) and cumene (used to make phenol and acetone). Its building products unit makes extruded vinyl window and door profiles and moldings products. In 2016 Axiall rejected a $1.4 billion buyout from rival Westlake Chemical.

	Annual Growth	12/10	12/11	12/12	12/13	12/14
Sales ($ mil.)	12.8%	2,818.0	3,222.9	3,325.8	4,666.0	4,568.7
Net income ($ mil.)	2.1%	42.7	57.8	120.6	165.3	46.3
Market value ($ mil.)	15.3%	1,688.9	1,368.1	2,897.7	3,330.1	2,981.2
Employees	11.1%	3,932	3,744	6,000	6,000	6,000

AXION INTERNATIONAL HOLDINGS INC

NBB: AXIH Q

4005 All American Way
Zanesville, OH 43701
Phone: 740 452-2500
Fax: –
Web: www.axih.com

CEO: Claude Brown
CFO: Donald Fallon
HR: Sandra Herbold
FYE: December 31
Type: Public

Axion International Holdings surveyed the landscape and decided to shift into a new line of business. Formerly operating as Analytical Surveys the company completed a reverse merger with Axion in 2008 and adopted that company's name and line of business. Axion is a licensee of technology regarding the manufacture of plastic composites used for structural applications such as railroad crossties bridge infrastructure marine pilings. and bulk headings. While the company is initially targeting the railroad industry it has yet to generate any significant revenues.

	Annual Growth	12/10	12/11	12/12	12/13	12/14
Sales ($ mil.)	54.7%	–	3.9	5.3	6.6	14.4
Net income ($ mil.)	–	(2.3)	(8.1)	(5.4)	(24.2)	(16.3)
Market value ($ mil.)	(19.9%)	68.7	51.0	24.8	70.8	28.3
Employees	125.8%	6	12	28	120	156

AXIS CONSTRUCTION CORP.

125 LASER CT
HAUPPAUGE, NY 117883911
Phone: 631-243-5970
Fax: –
Web: www.theaxisgroup.com

CEO: –
CFO: Andrew Meyerson
HR: –
FYE: December 31
Type: Private

Axis Construction revolves around building health care facilities from operating suites and emergency rooms to outpatient treatment centers and medical imaging facilities. About 80% of the company's business comes from the health care industry but Axis also constructs commercial and retail buildings modular structures and educational and intuitional facilities. The company provides general contracting construction management design/build consulting and renovation services to clients throughout New York. Its list of clients include Brookhaven National Lab Northrop Grumman and Estée Lauder. Axis Construction was founded in 1993 by company leaders Robert Wihlborg and Roy and Ralph Lambert.

	Annual Growth	12/03	12/04	12/05	12/07	12/08
Sales ($ mil.)	13.4%	–	31.9	43.2	47.5	52.8
Net income ($ mil.)	(25.9%)	–	–	0.9	0.5	0.4
Market value ($ mil.)	–	–	–	–	–	–
Employees	–	–	–	–	–	45

AXOGEN INC

NAS: AXGN

13631 Progress Blvd., Suite 400
Alachua, FL 32615
Phone: 386 462-6800
Fax: –
Web: www.axogeninc.com

CEO: Karen Zaderej
CFO: Lee Robert Johnston Jr
HR: –
FYE: December 31
Type: Public

AxoGen formerly known as LecTec is an intellectual property licensing and holding company. It licenses topical patches that deliver over-the-counter drugs through the skin. Its patents used by pharmaceutical companies include adhesive patches wound dressings and inhalation therapies. AxoGen licenses its technology to Novartis for that company's Triaminic Vapor Patch a cough suppressant for adults and children and is pursuing additional licensing agreements with Novartis. After acquiring AxoGen Corporation in 2011 LecTec changed its name to AxoGen Inc. and became the parent of AxoGen Corporation which develops and sells peripheral nerve reconstruction and regeneration products.

	Annual Growth	12/10	12/11	12/12	12/13	12/14
Sales ($ mil.)	268.4%	0.1	4.8	7.7	10.9	16.8
Net income ($ mil.)	–	(1.3)	(9.2)	(9.4)	(14.6)	(17.7)
Market value ($ mil.)	0.7%	68.0	52.6	52.6	87.5	70.0
Employees	154.6%	2	41	57	73	84

AXSUN TECHNOLOGIES INC.

1 Fortune Dr.
Billerica MA 01821
Phone: 978-262-0049
Fax: 978-262-0035
Web: www.axsun.com

CEO: Jonathan Hartmann
CFO: Chris Baldwin
HR: –
FYE: December 31
Type: Subsidiary

AXSUN Technologies takes the ax to bulky optoelectronic subsystems. Its Axsun Packaging Platform is a suite of components and manufacturing techniques that reduce the size of photonic assemblies used in optical networking systems. The platform combines specialized lenses microelectromechanical system devices and other components into packages much smaller than the usual printed circuit boards; these units can be tailored for many combinations of active and passive optical chips. The company was founded in 1999 by optical industry veterans. In early 2009 Volcano Corp. acquired AXSUN for $21.5 million in cash.

AXT INC

NMS: AXTI

4281 Technology Drive
Fremont, CA 94538
Phone: 510 683-5900
Fax: –
Web: www.axt.com

CEO: Morris S Young
CFO: Gary L Fischer
HR: –
FYE: December 31
Type: Public

For applications in which plain silicon would get the ax AXT offers fancier fare. AXT makes semiconductor substrates from compounds such as gallium arsenide (GaAs) and indium phosphide (InP) and from single elements such as germanium. Manufacturers use AXT's substrates to make high-performance semiconductors for products — including fiber-optic devices satellite solar cells and wireless handsets — for which standard silicon microchips are not adequate. Most of its customers — and its employees — are in China. International customers include Soitec of France and IQE Group of the UK.

	Annual Growth	12/10	12/11	12/12	12/13	12/14
Sales ($ mil.)	(3.3%)	95.5	104.1	88.4	85.3	83.5
Net income ($ mil.)	–	18.7	20.3	3.1	(8.0)	(1.4)
Market value ($ mil.)	(28.0%)	342.8	136.9	92.3	85.7	91.9
Employees	(13.5%)	1,302	1,308	1,284	1,255	729

AZURE MIDSTREAM PARTNERS LP

NYS: AZUR

12377 Merit Drive, Suite 300
Dallas, TX 75251
Phone: 972 674-5200
Fax: –
Web: www.marlinmidstream.com

CEO: I J Berthelot II
CFO: Amanda Bush
HR: –
FYE: December 31
Type: Public

Marlin Midstream Partners knows how to capture and prepare the biggest of energy fish. An oil and gas company Marlin gathers transports and processes natural gas and crude oil for energy companies. It operates two natural gas facilities in East Texas with an aggregate 65 miles of natural gas pipelines a gathering capacity of 200 million cu. ft. of gas per day (MMcf/d) and a 300 MMcf/d processing capacity. It also operates crude oil transloading facilities in Wyoming and Colorado. Marlin's core customer base comprises Anadarko and Associated Energy Services. The company was formed in 2013 and went public that year using its $137.5 million in proceeds to repay debt.

	Annual Growth	12/10	12/11	12/12	12/13	12/14
Sales ($ mil.)	–	0.0	65.8	51.0	52.9	75.2
Net income ($ mil.)	–	0.0	8.5	(4.3)	1.2	22.1
Market value ($ mil.)	–	0.0	–	–	303.4	328.4
Employees	–	–	–	–	–	–

AZUSA PACIFIC UNIVERSITY

901 E ALOSTA AVE
AZUSA, CA 917022701
Phone: 626-969-3434
Fax: –
Web: www.apu.edu

CEO: –
CFO: Bob Johansen
HR: Becky Casserino
FYE: June 30
Type: Private

An evangelical Christian institution Azusa Pacific University (APU) has an enrollment of about 10300 undergraduate graduate and doctoral students. It offers approximately 70 fields of undergraduate study and about 40 graduate degree programs (including eight doctoral programs) as well as a number of certificate and credentialing programs. Undergraduate students are required to complete ministry and service credits every semester; options include participating in ministries international service experience and doing volunteer work. APU traces its roots to 1899 and the Training School for Christian Workers the West Coast's first bible college.

	Annual Growth	06/08	06/09	06/10	06/11	06/13
Sales ($ mil.)	–	–	0.0	227.4	270.1	281.7
Net income ($ mil.)	(49.6%)	–	–	8.6	26.1	1.1
Market value ($ mil.)	–	–	–	–	–	–
Employees	–	–	–	–	–	1,344

AZZ GALVANIZING SERVICES

3100 W. 7th St. Ste. 500
Fort Worth TX 76107
Phone: 817-810-0095
Fax: 817-336-5354
Web: www.azzgalvanizing.com

CEO: –
CFO: –
HR: –
FYE: December 31
Type: Subsidiary

AZZ Galvanizing Services (formerly North American Galvanizing & Coatings) is glad that rust never sleeps. Operations include hot-dip galvanizes fabricated structural iron and steel components to provide protection against corrosion. The company galvanizes its metal products by submerging them in molten zinc. Typical galvanizing customers work in the petrochemical irrigation food processing highway and transportation wastewater treatment telecommunications energy and utilities industries. It operates facilities in eight states and sells its services directly to customers primarily in the US. Texas-based galvanizer AZZ paid more than $125 million to acquire North American Galvanizing & Coatings in 2010.

AZZ INC

One Museum Place, Suite 500, 3100 West Seventh Street
Fort Worth, TX 76107
Phone: 817 810-0095
Fax: –
Web: www.azz.com

NYS: AZZ
CEO: Thomas E. (Tom) Ferguson
CFO: Paul W. Fehlman
HR: Trey Quinn
FYE: February 28
Type: Public

When companies need to power up or get "in zink" they give AZZ incorporated a buzz. The company has two business segments: galvanizing services and energy. To protect steel from environmental corrosion galvanizing services dip steel products into baths of molten zinc. The process is vital for steel fabricators who serve highway construction electrical utility transportation and water-treatment firms. Through subsidiaries AZZ makes electrical power distribution systems industrial lighting switchgear motor control centers bus duct systems and tubular goods. Industrial petrochemical and power generation and transmission companies use the company's products.

	Annual Growth	02/11	02/12	02/13	02/14	02/15
Sales ($ mil.)	21.0%	380.6	469.1	570.6	751.7	816.7
Net income ($ mil.)	16.7%	35.0	40.7	60.5	59.6	64.9
Market value ($ mil.)	1.6%	1,097.7	1,291.7	1,149.2	1,141.7	1,168.7
Employees	13.5%	1,956	2,154	2,632	2,927	3,244

B&G FOODS INC

4 Gatehall Drive
Parsippany, NJ 07054
Phone: 973 401-6500
Fax: –
Web: www.bgfoods.com

NYS: BGS
CEO: Robert C. (Bob) Cantwell
CFO: Thomas P. Crimmins
HR: Eric Hart
FYE: January 03
Type: Public

Peter Piper picks more than a peck of peppers from B&G Foods. The company makes markets and distributes jalapeños beans maple syrup fruit spreads and other shelf-stable foods and household goods. B&G's products are sold under brand names many of which are regional or national best-sellers including B&G and Trappey (beans) Ac'cent (meat flavoring) Emeril's (seasoning — under license) Ortega (Mexican condiments) Grandma's and Brer Rabbit (molasses) and Underwood (meat spread). They're sold through B&G's subsidiaries to supermarkets mass merchants warehouse clubs and drug store chains as well as institutional and food service operators in the US Canada and Puerto Rico.

	Annual Growth	01/11*	12/11	12/12	12/13*	01/15
Sales ($ mil.)	13.4%	513.3	543.9	633.8	725.0	848.0
Net income ($ mil.)	6.1%	32.4	50.2	59.3	52.3	41.0
Market value ($ mil.)	21.3%	736.8	1,291.7	1,481.1	1,820.8	1,592.7
Employees	6.3%	749	739	999	984	956

*Fiscal year change

B&R STORES INC.

4554 W. St.
Lincoln NE 68503-2831
Phone: 402-464-6297
Fax: 402-434-5733
Web: www.brstores.com

CEO: –
CFO: Kipp Utemark
HR: –
FYE: December 31
Type: Private

B&R Stores operates about 20 supermarkets in six cities across Nebraska and Iowa that operate under the Super Saver Russ's Market and ALPS (an acronym for Always Low Price Store) banners. The stores offer the usual grocery selections as well as carpet cleaner and video rentals. Other specialties include smoked meat products produced by in-store smokehouses at all Super Saver stores. The regional grocery chain was founded in 1962 by Russ Raybould (father of company president Pat Raybould) and Clayton Burnett. The Raybould family owns a majority stake in B&R Stores; employees own the rest.

B&W TECHNICAL SERVICES Y-12 LLC

Y-12 National Security Complex 301 Bear Creek Rd.
Oak Ridge TN 37830
Phone: 865-576-5454
Fax: 865-576-3806
Web: www.y12.doe.gov

CEO: –
CFO: –
HR: –
FYE: December 31
Type: Subsidiary

B&W Technical Services Y-12 (formerly BWXT Y-12) manages the Y-12 National Security Complex for the Department of Energy and the National Nuclear Security Administration (NNSA). The Y-12 National Security Complex (built as part of the Manhattan Project during WWII) makes dismantles refurbishes stores and manages nuclear weapons and weapon components; removes and secures nuclear material and equipment from foreign sources and provides fuel for research and Naval reactors; and works with the Department of Defense and Homeland Security on national security projects such as the Future Medical Shelter System and the Vulnerability Assessment Resource Center. Y-12 is a unit of Babcock & Wilcox Technical Services.

B. BRAUN MEDICAL INC.

824 12th Ave.
Bethlehem PA 18018-3524
Phone: 610-691-5400
Fax: 610-691-6249
Web: www.bbraunusa.com

CEO: Caroll H Neubauer
CFO: Bruce Heugel
HR: –
FYE: December 31
Type: Subsidiary

B. Braun Medical is the US arm of German medical supply firm B. Braun Melsungen. The company's products and services include a wide range of traditional and needleless IV systems and accessories pharmaceutical devices dialysis machines critical care products and vascular access and interventional product lines as well as continuing education and training programs. B. Braun's customers include hospitals outpatient surgery centers and home care services companies. Its network of CAPS (Central Admixture Pharmacy Services) compounding pharmacies provides IV admixtures and solutions to hospitals clinics and home care providers throughout the US.

B. L. HARBERT INTERNATIONAL L.L.C.

820 Shades Creek Pkwy. Ste. 3000
Birmingham AL 35209
Phone: 205-802-2800
Fax: 205-802-2801
Web: www.blharbert.com

CEO: Billy Harbert
CFO: R Alan Hall
HR: –
FYE: December 31
Type: Private

My way or the highway? For Harbert it's my way and the highway. B. L. Harbert International Group provides highway and heavy construction services for commercial industrial and public projects throughout the world primarily in the Southeast US. The design/build company's portfolio includes commercial and institutional buildings research facilities hotels and condominiums water and wastewater treatment plants dams and highways and pipelines. B. L. Harbert International has offices in the US and Dubai. CEO Billy Harbert Jr. leads the family-owned company which traces its roots to the 1949 founding of Harbert Construction by brothers Bill and John Harbert.

B/E AEROSPACE, INC

NMS: BEAV

1400 Corporate Center Way
Wellington, FL 33414-2105
Phone: 561 791-5000
Fax: 561 791-7900
Web: www.beaerospace.com

CEO: Werner Lieberherr
CFO: Joseph T. (Joe) Lower
HR: Jim Bennett
FYE: December 31
Type: Public

B/E Aerospace ensures that travelers truly enjoy air travel. A leading maker of cabin components for commercial business jets and military aircraft B/E's offerings include aircraft seats coffeemakers lighting refrigeration equipment galley structures and emergency oxygen systems. B/E aftermarket operations represent about 40% of its revenue. Operating through two business segments (commercial aircraft and business jet) B/E sells its products to most major airlines and aviation OEMs. The company also provides oil field equipment and services.

	Annual Growth	12/10	12/11	12/12	12/13	12/14
Sales ($ mil.)	7.0%	1,984.2	2,499.8	3,085.3	3,483.7	2,599.0
Net income ($ mil.)	(7.6%)	143.3	227.8	233.7	365.6	104.3
Market value ($ mil.)	11.9%	3,923.8	4,101.8	5,234.6	9,222.0	6,148.0
Employees	9.7%	6,650	7,700	9,500	10,825	9,617

BAB INC

NBB: BABB

500 Lake Cook Road, Suite 475
Deerfield, IL 60015
Phone: 847 948-7520
Fax: –
Web: www.babcorp.com

CEO: Michael W Evans
CFO: Geraldine Conn
HR: –
FYE: November 30
Type: Public

Bagels muffins and coffee are fueling this company. BAB operates a chain of about 110 franchised coffee and baked goods outlets under the brand names Big Apple Bagels and My Favorite Muffin. The stores offer several varieties of bagels and spreads muffins sandwiches soups salads and gourmet coffee. The company also markets a proprietary java brand Brewster's Coffee. BAB has coffee shops in more than 25 states as well as in the United Arab Emirates. An investment group controlled by CEO Michael Evans and VP Michael Murtaugh owns nearly 40% of the company.

	Annual Growth	11/10	11/11	11/12	11/13	11/14
Sales ($ mil.)	(3.4%)	2.9	3.0	2.7	2.5	2.5
Net income ($ mil.)	5.7%	0.4	0.4	0.4	0.4	0.5
Market value ($ mil.)	13.1%	3.3	4.2	4.6	6.3	5.4
Employees	(8.3%)	24	17	20	17	17

BABSON COLLEGE

231 FOREST ST
BABSON PARK, MA 02457
Phone: 781-235-1200
Fax: –
Web: www.babsonathletics.com

CEO: –
CFO: Philip Shapiro
HR: Donna Bonaparte
FYE: June 30
Type: Private

Babson students could babble on and on about business management. With an enrollment of more than 3000 students Babson College is lauded as one of the nation's leading business schools. The school's undergraduate programs combine liberal arts with business curriculum; it also grants master's degrees in business administration entrepreneurship and other fields. Babson students in their first year receive the practical experience of creating for-profit ventures. Babson's entrepreneurship program has been ranked at the top of such programs in publications including Entrepreneur and U.S. News & World Report.

	Annual Growth	06/09	06/10	06/11	06/13	06/14
Sales ($ mil.)	2.2%	–	176.4	202.8	177.6	192.4
Net income ($ mil.)	48.5%	–	–	14.5	43.3	47.4
Market value ($ mil.)	–	–	–	–	–	–
Employees	–	–	–	–	–	750

BABYCENTER L.L.C.

163 Freelon St.
San Francisco CA 94107
Phone: 415-537-0900
Fax: 415-537-0909
Web: www.babycenter.com

CEO: –
CFO: –
HR: –
FYE: December 31
Type: Subsidiary

If the parenting information you're getting from other sources is a bit too infantile turn to BabyCenter. The company operates websites for parents of infants and young children. Its BabyCenter.com Baby.com and Pregnancy.com sites contain content for parents of offspring from pre-conception through age eight. The sites also include the BabyCenter Community feature for interactive communication advice and support. BabyCenter additionally has international sites and a retail partnership with Quidsi's Diapers.com to sell clothing and baby products online. Johnson & Johnson owns BabyCenter which was founded in 1997 by Matt Glickman and Mark Selcow. The firm was acquired by Johnson & Johnson in 2001.

BACK YARD BURGERS INC.

500 Church St. Ste. 200
Nashville TN 37219
Phone: 615-620-2300
Fax: 615-620-2301
Web: www.backyardburgers.com

CEO: David McDougall
CFO: Craig Clark
HR: Charlotte Brown
FYE: December 31
Type: Private

Back Yard Burgers offers diners the chance to eat a charbroiled burger without having to slave over hot coals. The company operates and franchises about 120 quick service restaurants in Tennessee Mississippi and more than 15 other states in the Southeast and Midwest. The eateries are known for their made-to-order charbroiled hamburgers made from 100% Black Angus beef. Back Yard Burgers' menu also includes chicken sandwiches chili milkshakes salads and cobbler. The company's "Grills on the Go" team caters events by grilling food on location. The firm was ounded by Lattimore Michael in 1987. Back Yard Burgers filed for bankruptcy in 2012.

BACKUS CORPORATION

326 Washington St.
Norwich CT 06360
Phone: 860-889-8331
Fax: 860-886-1219
Web: www.backushospital.org

CEO: –
CFO: –
HR: –
FYE: September 30
Type: Private

Backus Corporation is a real part of the backbone of Norwich and its environs. Backus Corporation is the parent company of The William W. Backus Hospital which was founded in 1893 and serves eastern Connecticut. The hospital has some 210 medical surgical and critical care beds. It provides specialty services such as trauma care cancer care neurology obstetrics urology and cardiology. The Backus Corporation network also includes several community health clinics outpatient and rehabilitation centers medical labs and a hospice. The Backus Foundation is a not-for-profit affiliate that solicits and receives contributions on behalf of the hospital. Backus has agreed to join Hartford Health Care.

BACTOLAC PHARMACEUTICAL INC.

7 Oser Ave. Unit 14
Hauppauge NY 11788-3808
Phone: 631-951-4908
Fax: 631-951-4749
Web: www.bactolac.com

CEO: Pailla M Reddy
CFO: –
HR: –
FYE: September 30
Type: Private

Bactolac Pharmaceutical (formerly Advanced Nutraceuticals) makes private-label vitamins minerals herbs and other over-the-counter nutritional supplement products. The company's encapsulated and tablet-based products are available already packaged and branded or sold in bulk to customers who repackage them for private-label sale. Customers include distributors retailers and multi-level marketing companies. Its services include product formulation sample runs and product testing. Chairman and CEO Pailla Reddy holds a majority of the company.

BADGER METER, INC.

NYS: BMI

4545 W. Brown Deer Road
Milwaukee, WI 53223
Phone: 414 355-0400
Fax: –
Web: www.badgermeter.com

CEO: Richard A. Meeusen
CFO: Richard E. Johnson
HR: –
FYE: December 31
Type: Public

No Badger Meter does not measure the frequency of the appearance of a certain nocturnal carnivorous mammal. Instead it provides water utilities and industrial customers with instruments that measure and control the flow of liquids. Badger's largest segment is the manufacture of water meters and automatic meter reading (AMR) and advanced metering infrastructure (AMI) products which are mainly sold to municipalities. Its industrial business is made up of metering technologies for markets including concrete HVAC water and wastewater chemicals and food and beverage. Established in 1905 Badger also makes handheld devices that dispense and monitor oil and other fluids for the automotive market.

	Annual Growth	12/10	12/11	12/12	12/13	12/14
Sales ($ mil.)	7.2%	276.6	262.9	319.7	334.1	364.8
Net income ($ mil.)	0.9%	28.7	19.2	28.0	24.6	29.7
Market value ($ mil.)	7.6%	639.5	425.6	685.6	788.1	858.3
Employees	2.6%	1,293	1,220	1,366	1,360	1,431

BADGERLAND MEAT AND PROVISIONS LLC

1849 Wright St.
Madison WI 53704
Phone: 608-244-1934
Fax: 608-244-9162
Web: www.badgerlandmeats.com

CEO: –
CFO: –
HR: –
FYE: December 31
Type: Private

All those University of Wisconsin sports fans have a place to buy meat. Badgerland Meat and Provisions stores wholesales and distributes beef pork and poultry products in its home state as well as parts of Illinois and Michigan. It sells to grocery chains meat markets restaurants and warehouses stores. The company gets its meat from producers such as American Foods Excel Farmland Foods Gold Kist and Iowa Turkey. Badgerland also operates a case-ready business for which the company cuts packs and distributes more than 300000 pounds of pre-packaged and pre-priced pork products every week.

BAE SYSTEMS INC.

1101 Wilson Blvd. Ste. 2000
Arlington VA 22209-2444
Phone: 703-312-6100
Fax: 703-312-6111
Web: www.baesystems.com

CEO: Gerard J Demuro
CFO: –
HR: –
FYE: December 31
Type: Subsidiary

BAE Systems takes care of business in North America for UK-based parent BAE SYSTEMS plc — the largest foreign player in the US defense market. BAE Systems' military operations include the design manufacture and maintenance of armored combat vehicles weapons munitions and other defense systems. Affiliate BAE Systems also provides security information technology (IT) systems for defense commercial and law enforcement applications. It is a top supplier to the US Department of Defense (DoD) and adheres to the Pentagon's Special Security Agreement to ensure control of sensitive technology. The US division has operations in 38 states and in Germany Israel Mexico South Africa Sweden and the UK.

BAE SYSTEMS NORFOLK SHIP REPAIR INC.

750 W. Berkley Ave.
Norfolk VA 23523
Phone: 757-494-4000
Fax: 757-494-4184
Web: www.baesystems.com/productsservices/bae_eis_sh

CEO: Ian King
CFO: –
HR: –
FYE: December 31
Type: Subsidiary

A giant white whale is no match for contractor BAE Systems Norfolk Ship Repair. The company is a leading non-nuclear ship repair modernization conversion and overhaul facility which operates at one of the US Navy's principal ports at Norfolk Virginia the home of the Atlantic Fleet. Parent company UK-based BAE SYSTEMS plc a defense security and aerospace company also has ship repair operations in San Diego (home of the Pacific Fleet). BAE Systems Norfolk Ship Repair is a full-service repair facility that focuses on dry dock and ship repair for the US Navy and other defense agencies as well as commercial customers such as cruise ship owners liquefied natural gas tankers ferries and cargo ships.

BAER'S FURNITURE CO. INC.

1589 NW 12TH AVE
POMPANO BEACH, FL 330691734
Phone: 954-946-8001
Fax: –
Web: www.baers.com

CEO: Robert M Baer
CFO: –
HR: –
FYE: December 31
Type: Private

Having assembled a furniture portfolio full of big-name brands Baer's Furniture counts the likes of Lexington Home Brands and Bernhardt as family. Family-owned Baer's Furniture operates about 15 mid-priced to high-end retail furniture showrooms and two warehouses in South Florida. The company offers furnishings (living room dining room bedroom and office furniture) bedding rugs and accessories made by popular manufacturers that are designed to fit the budgets of shoppers who have a little cash tucked away. The chain was founded in 1945 by Melvin and Lucile Baer in South Bend Indiana. Their sons Robert now the company's CEO and Allan company president moved the business to Florida in 1968.

	Annual Growth	12/05	12/06	12/11	12/12	12/13
Sales ($ mil.)	–	–	0.0	138.1	143.2	160.8
Net income ($ mil.)	20.8%	–	–	7.3	9.5	10.6
Market value ($ mil.)	–	–	–	–	–	–
Employees	–	–	–	–	–	437

BAIN CAPITAL LLC

111 Huntington Ave.
Boston MA 02199
Phone: 617-516-2000
Fax: 617-516-2010
Web: www.baincapital.com

CEO: –
CFO: Jay Corrigan
HR: –
FYE: December 31
Type: Private

If you want to make a big deal out of it chances are Bain Capital will get involved. The private equity and venture capital investor acquires and owns interests in companies in the business services retail and consumer products communications health care hospitality and technology sectors. The firm has made private equity investments in more than 250 companies since its 1984 founding. Its diverse portfolio currently includes stakes in such well-known companies as American Standard Burlington Coat Factory Clear Channel Communications Dunkin' Brands SunGard Data Systems Warner Music Group The Weather Channel and HD Supply the former wholesale construction supply business of The Home Depot.

BAIRD & WARNER HOLDING COMPANY

120 S. LaSalle
Chicago IL 60603
Phone: 312-368-1855
Fax: 312-368-1490
Web: www.bairdwarner.com

CEO: Stephen W Baird
CFO: Warren Habib
HR: Audra Lapointe
FYE: December 31
Type: Private

Baird & Warner knows its Chicagoland history. It has been around to witness events from the Great Fire in 1871 to the the Cubbies' last World Series win. Illinois' largest independent real estate brokerage offers residential sales financial services and title services in the Chicago area through more than 25 branch offices and some 1600 sales agents. Its listings include foreclosed properties ultra-luxury homes and some commercial properties. The firm also maintains a directory of vetted home services providers (cleaning repair landscaping etc.) to help sellers prepare their homes for sale. Baird & Warner was founded in 1855 and has been family-owned and operated for five generations.

BAKEMARK USA LLC

7351 Crider Ave.
Pico Rivera CA 90660
Phone: 562-949-1054
Fax: 562-948-5506
Web: www.yourbakemark.com

CEO: Jim Parker
CFO: Refugio Reynoso
HR: –
FYE: December 31
Type: Subsidiary

When it comes to baking BakeMark USA has the secret ingredient. The company makes a slew of ingredients and bakery goods such as cake and cookie mixes pie and pastry fillings various flours and yeast as well as pre-baked goods and paper supplies. Its lineup is sold under brand names: Produits Marguerite (nut pastes mousses custards for French pastries); Trigal Dorado (mixes and fillings for Mexican pastries); Westco (baked good mixes and dough). Customers are mainly US retail wholesale and in-store bakeries and bakery chains. BakeMark USA and sister subsidiary BakeMark Canada are part of Dutch ingredient maker CSM's Bakery Supplies North America business which generates about half of all CSM sales.

BAKER & HOSTETLER LLP

PNC Center 1900 E. 9th St. Ste. 3200
Cleveland OH 44114-3482
Phone: 216-621-0200
Fax: 216-696-0740
Web: www.bakerlaw.com

CEO: –
CFO: Kevin L Cash
HR: –
FYE: December 31
Type: Private - Partnershi

Like Major League Baseball a longtime client law firm Baker & Hostetler has players from coast to coast. The firm's more than 800 lawyers practice from about a dozen offices in the US from New York to Los Angeles. Besides baseball and other sports and entertainment enterprises the firm's roster of clients has included leading companies in the automotive energy health care hospitality and media industries. Among Baker & Hostetler's major practice groups are teams devoted to intellectual property business employment and labor and tax and litigation.

BAKER & MCKENZIE LLP

300 E. Randolph St. Ste. 5000
Chicago IL 60601
Phone: 312-861-8000
Fax: 312-861-2899
Web: www.bakermckenzie.com

CEO: –
CFO: –
HR: –
FYE: June 30
Type: Private

Baker & McKenzie believes big is good and bigger is better. One of the world's largest law firms it has about 4000 attorneys practicing from more than 70 offices — from Bangkok to Berlin to Buenos Aires — in almost 45 countries. It offers expertise in a wide range of practice areas including antitrust intellectual property international trade mergers and acquisitions project finance and tax law. Baker & McKenzie's client list includes big companies from numerous industries including banking and finance construction and technology as well as smaller enterprises.

BAKER BOOK HOUSE COMPANY

6030 FULTON ST E
ADA, MI 493019156
Phone: 616-676-1868
Fax: –
Web: www.bakerpublishinggroup.com

CEO: Dwight Baker
CFO: –
HR: Dan Baker
FYE: April 30
Type: Private

Baker Publishing Group has a spirit in its step. The Christian publisher publishes books through seven market-focused divisions: Baker Books Baker Academic Bethany House Publishers Brazos Press Cambridge University Press Chosen Books and Revell. Its Baker Books division includes titles for pastors and church leaders featuring books on worship preaching counseling and leadership. Its Cambridge division focuses on bible publishing. Other imprints publish Christian fiction and self-help titles as well as books on subjects such as theology discipleship and Christian living. The company was founded in 1939 by Herman Baker.

	Annual Growth	04/10	04/11	04/12	04/13	04/14
Sales ($ mil.)	0.8%	–	55.1	52.2	53.2	56.4
Net income ($ mil.)	14.7%	–	–	3.6	4.0	4.7
Market value ($ mil.)	–	–	–	–	–	–
Employees	–	–	–	–	–	215

BAKER BOTTS L.L.P.

1 Shell Plaza 910 Louisiana St.
Houston TX 77002-4995
Phone: 713-229-1234
Fax: 713-229-1522
Web: www.bakerbotts.com

CEO: –
CFO: Lydia Companion
HR: –
FYE: December 31
Type: Private - Partnershi

Baker Botts is a Lone Star legal legend. The law firm's history stretches back to 1840 when founding partner Peter Gray was admitted to the bar of the Republic of Texas. The firm became Baker & Botts after Walter Browne Botts and James Addison Baker (great-grandfather of former US Secretary of State and current partner James A. Baker III) joined the partnership. The firm has some 725 lawyers in about a dozen offices worldwide. Over the years Baker Botts has represented numerous clients from the energy industry including Exxon Mobil and Halliburton. The firm practices in such areas as corporate intellectual property and tax law.

BAKER BOYER BANCORP

7 W. Main St.
Walla Walla WA 99362
Phone: 509-525-2000
Fax: 509-525-1034
Web: www.bakerboyer.com

OTC: BBBK

CEO: –
CFO: –
HR: –
FYE: December 31
Type: Public

For Baker Boyer Bancorp it "is" personal. The holding company for Baker Boyer National Bank takes pride in the personal touch it applies to its services which include standard deposit products loans financial planning and insurance services. One- to four-family residential mortgages account for the largest portion of the bank's loan portfolio. Through Baker Boyer Wealth Management Services the company offers investments private banking brokerage and trust services. Baker Boyer National Bank serves individual and business customers through about 10 branches in southern Washington and northern Oregon. Founded in 1869 the family-owned company is the oldest bank in Washington State

BAKER CAPITAL

540 Madison Ave. 29th Fl.
New York NY 10022
Phone: 212-848-2000
Fax: 212-848-0660
Web: www.bakercapital.com

CEO: –
CFO: Joseph Saviano
HR: –
FYE: December 31
Type: Private

Cream puffs and tarts need not apply at Baker Capital. This Madison Avenue private equity firm is instead looking to take controlling or significant minority stakes in mainly later-stage communication and technology companies. In addition to providing funding Baker Capital also offers post-investment consulting services in such areas as strategy executive and board recruitment and international expansion. It typically exits its investments through a sale or an IPO within five years. The firm which has approximately $1.5 billion of funds under management owns stakes in about 20 companies in the US and Europe.

BAKER COMMODITIES INC.

4020 Bandini Blvd.
Los Angeles CA 90023
Phone: 323-268-2801
Fax: 323-268-5166
Web: www.bakercommodities.com

CEO: –
CFO: –
HR: –
FYE: December 31
Type: Private

This Baker is somewhere between a butcher and a candlestick maker. Baker Commodities is a rendering company that takes unused animal byproducts from meat processing plants supermarkets restaurants and butcher shops and produces animal fats and oils poultry and bone meal and tallow. These products then can be used to make candles cosmetics paints plastics organic detergents livestock feed pet food and biodiesel. It is one of the nation's largest rendering companies with 21 plants in about a dozen US states including four in California four in New York and one in Hawaii.

BAKER DONELSON BEARMAN CALDWELL & BERKOWITZ PC

First Tennessee Bldg. Ste. 2000 165 Madison Ave.
Memphis TN 38103
Phone: 901-526-2000
Fax: 901-577-2303
Web: www.bakerdonelson.com

CEO: Ben Adams
CFO: –
HR: Kacee McCalla
FYE: January 31
Type: Private - Partnershi

Law firm Baker Donelson Bearman Caldwell & Berkowitz has grown beyond its southern roots to represent clients with stakes in national and international issues as well as local and regional matters. The firm boasts more than 630 attorneys and public policy advisers in about 15 offices which are concentrated in the southeastern US; it also operates out of Washington DC and London. Baker Donelson's practice areas focus on real estate and construction contract drafting and licensing mediation dispute resolution intellectual property financial services and tax advisory issues among others. The law firm traces its roots back to 1888 when James F. Baker established his law firm in Tennessee.

BAKER HUGHES INC.

2929 Allen Parkway, Suite 2100
Houston, TX 77019-2118
Phone: 713 439-8600
Fax: 713 439-8699
Web: www.bakerhughes.com

NYS: BHI

CEO: Martin S. Craighead
CFO: Kimberly A. Ross
HR: Murali Kuppuswamy
FYE: December 31
Type: Public

Baker Hughes cooks up dozens of products and services for the global petroleum market. Through its Drilling and Evaluation segment Baker Hughes makes products and services used to drill oil and natural gas wells. It also makes bits and drilling fluids and submersible pumps. Through its Completion and Production segment the company provides equipment and services used from the completion phase through the productive life of oil and natural gas wells. Its Industrial Service segment provides equipment and services for the refining process and pipeline industries. In 2014 the company agreed to acquired by Halliburton for about $35 billion.

	Annual Growth	12/10	12/11	12/12	12/13	12/14
Sales ($ mil.)	14.2%	14,414.0	19,831.0	21,361.0	22,364.0	24,551.0
Net income ($ mil.)	20.6%	812.0	1,739.0	1,311.0	1,096.0	1,719.0
Market value ($ mil.)	(0.5%)	24,811.8	21,109.8	17,727.9	23,982.8	24,334.4
Employees	4.0%	53,100	57,700	58,800	59,400	62,000

BAKER MICHAEL JR INC

4301 DUTCH RIDGE RD
BEAVER, PA 15009-9600
Phone: 724-495-7711
Fax: –
Web: www.mbakercorp.com

CEO: Kurt Bergman
CFO: –
HR: –
FYE: December 31
Type: Private

Michael Baker Jr. is the first-born subsidiary of engineering and construction consulting group Michael Baker. Michael Baker Jr. focuses on engineering design for civil infrastructure and transportation projects which include highways bridges airports busways corporate headquarters data centers correctional facilities and educational facilities. The unit also provides planning geotechnical and environmental services in the water/wastewater pipeline emergency and consequence management resource management and telecommunications markets. Recent projects include facilities for the US government.

	Annual Growth	12/04	12/05	12/06	12/07	12/09
Sales ($ mil.)	42.4%	–	–	144.9	351.9	418.5
Net income ($ mil.)	5327.2%	–	–	0.0	10.2	15.5
Market value ($ mil.)	–	–	–	–	–	–
Employees	–	–	–	–	–	1,798

BALCHEM CORP.
NMS: BCPC

52 Sunrise Park Road
New Hampton, NY 10958
Phone: 845 326-5600
Fax: –

CEO: Theodore L. (Ted) Harris
CFO: William A. Backus
HR: Robert (Bob) Miniger
FYE: December 31
Type: Public

Believe Balchem when they say they have it covered. The company has developed a technology that covers or encapsulates ingredients used in food and animal health products; the encapsulation improves nutritional value and shelf life and allows for controlled time release. Balchem also provides specialty gases such as ethylene oxide (used to sterilize medical instruments) propylene oxide (used to reduce bacteria in spice treating and chemical processing) and methyl chloride (a refrigerant). The company's unencapsulated feed ingredients unit (BCP Ingredients) supplies the nutrient choline chloride to poultry and swine farmers. Reashure an encapsulated choline product increases milk production in dairy cows.

	Annual Growth	12/10	12/11	12/12	12/13	12/14
Sales ($ mil.)	20.7%	255.1	291.9	310.4	337.2	541.4
Net income ($ mil.)	12.2%	33.3	38.8	40.0	44.9	52.8
Market value ($ mil.)	18.5%	1,042.9	1,250.5	1,124.3	1,810.6	2,055.5
Employees	24.6%	351	365	376	387	845

BALDOR ELECTRIC COMPANY

5711 R. S. Boreham Jr. St.
Fort Smith AR 72901
Phone: 479-646-4711
Fax: 479-648-5792
Web: www.baldor.com

CEO: Ronald E Tucker
CFO: George E Moeschner
HR: –
FYE: December 31
Type: Subsidiary

Electricity drives Baldor Electric's sales — and its products. The company manufactures industrial AC and DC electric motors controls and speed drives that power products ranging from material handling conveyors to fluid handling pumps. Other products include industrial grinders buffers polishing lathes and generators. Baldor Electric sells to OEMs primarily in the agricultural and semiconductor equipment industries and to independent distributors for resale as replacement parts. It has about two dozen plants in Canada China Mexico the UK and the US. Baldor Electric a subsidiary of ABB gets most of its sales in the US although it has customers in some 70 countries.

BALDWIN & LYONS, INC.
NMS: BWIN B

111 Congressional Boulevard
Carmel, IN 46032
Phone: 317 636-9800
Fax: –
Web: www.baldwinandlyons.com

CEO: Joseph J Devito
CFO: Patrick (Paddy) Corydon
HR: –
FYE: December 31
Type: Public

Baldwin & Lyons (B&L) insures truckers and the bad motorists who terrorize them. The company's Protective Insurance subsidiary licensed in the US and Canada writes property/casualty insurance for large to midsized trucking fleets and public transportation fleets. It also covers independent contractors in the trucking industry. B&L's Sagamore Insurance subsidiary provides insurance to high-risk private auto drivers throughout most of the US through a network of independent agents. It also markets physical-damage insurance and liability insurance for small trucking fleets and for large and midsized bus fleets. Founded in 1930 B&L also provides property/casualty reinsurance and brokerage services.

	Annual Growth	12/10	12/11	12/12	12/13	12/14
Assets ($ mil.)	8.1%	837.9	905.3	983.0	1,072.3	1,144.2
Net income ($ mil.)	4.4%	25.0	(28.2)	31.9	36.6	29.7
Market value ($ mil.)	2.3%	352.5	326.6	357.4	409.2	386.2
Employees	9.2%	299	330	360	384	425

BALDWIN FILTERS INC.

4400 E. Hwy. 30
Kearney NE 68848-6010
Phone: 308-234-1951
Fax: 800-828-4453
Web: www.baldwinfilter.com

CEO: Norman Johnson
CFO: –
HR: –
FYE: November 30
Type: Subsidiary

Baldwin Filters wants to clear the air — and the fuel and the oil and a lot more. A key subsidiary of manufacturing group CLARCOR Baldwin Filters makes thousands of different products designed for the filtration of air fuel hydraulic and transmission fluid coolant and oil for all types of off-road heavy-duty and light trucks; locomotives; industrial mining and marine equipment; heavy-duty construction and agricultural equipment; as well as for passenger cars and SUVs. Baldwin Filters sells its products through a worldwide network of distributors. Founded in 1936 the company has operations in North America and throughout the world.

BALDWIN PIANO INC.

309 Plus Park Blvd.
Nashville TN 37217
Phone: 615-871-4500
Fax: 615-889-5509
Web: www.baldwinpiano.com

CEO: Henry Juszkiewicz
CFO: –
HR: –
FYE: December 31
Type: Subsidiary

The keys to success for Baldwin alternate in color — black and white. One of the top piano manufacturers in the US Baldwin Piano is best known for making concert and upright pianos under the Baldwin Howard Hamilton Chickering and Wurlitzer names. The company also makes ConcertMaster computerized player pianos. Its custom models feature hand-painted designs including gold-leaf scrollwork and pinstripes marble finishes and exotic leopard spots and zebra stripes. Gibson Guitar which has been working to breathe new life into Baldwin bought the ailing piano maker from GE Capital in 2001. Dwight Hamilton Baldwin established the company as Baldwin Piano & Organ in 1862.

BALDWIN RICHARDSON FOODS CO.

20201 S. LaGrange Rd. Ste. 200
Frankfort IL 60423
Phone: 815-464-9994
Fax: 815-464-9995
Web: www.brfoods.com

CEO: Eric Johnson
CFO: Evelyn White
HR: –
FYE: December 31
Type: Private

Baldwin Richardson is sweet on foods. The company started out in in 1916 making dessert toppings. Today it makes many kinds of liquid products for the food industry including condiments sauces syrups and fruit fillings. Baldwin Richardson Foods sells its products such as Mrs. Richardson's toppings and Nance's condiments to retail food customers. Its consumer offerings also include Baldwin ice cream Mrs. Richardson's ice cream toppings and Nance's mustards and condiments. In addition the company has customers in the food manufacturing and foodservice sectors. Baldwin Richardson offers private-label co-packing and contract-manufacturing services.

BALDWIN TECHNOLOGY COMPANY INC.   NYSE AMEX: BLD

2 Trap Falls Rd. Ste. 402
Shelton CT 06484-0941
Phone: 203-402-1000
Fax: 203-402-5500
Web: www.baldwintech.com

CEO: Mark T Becker
CFO: Ivan R Habibe
HR: –
FYE: June 30
Type: Private

Baldwin Technology has pressing business. The company supplies an array of process automation technologies for commercial printing and newspaper publishing. It manufactures printing press equipment and control systems (such as for press cleaning ink control drying water-regulation and paper flow). Baldwin products are marketed as a premium technology via subsidiaries and distributors in about a dozen countries. Customers include printing press OEMs who bolt the products onto their own systems for sale to printers. The company also sells directly to printers wanting to upgrade their presses. Baldwin Technology was acquired by Forsyth Capital Investors in 2012.

BALKAMP INC.

2601 S. Holt Rd.
Indianapolis IN 46241
Phone: 317-244-7241
Fax: 317-381-2200
Web: www.balkamp.com

CEO: –
CFO: –
HR: –
FYE: December 31
Type: Subsidiary

A majority-owned subsidiary of Genuine Parts Balkamp distributes parts and accessories for cars trucks motorcycles and farm equipment to repair shops and retail members of the National Automotive Parts Association (NAPA). The company also provides diagnostics equipment cleaning supplies chemicals and other service-related items. Balkamp offers some 45000 items from about 600 domestic and foreign suppliers. It operates distribution centers in Indianapolis and Plainfield Indiana and West Jordan Utah. Balkamp was formed in 1936 by the NAPA board of directors. Its moniker blends the surnames of the company's first managers John Baldwin and Bob Leercamp.

BALL CORP   NYS: BLL

10 Longs Peak Drive, P.O. Box 5000
Broomfield, CO 80021-2510
Phone: 303 469-3131
Fax:
Web: www.ball.com

CEO: John A. Hayes
CFO: Scott C. Morrison
HR: Lisa A. Pauley
FYE: December 31
Type: Public

The well-rounded Ball Corporation perpetually pitches packaging to companies producing food beverage and household goods. Food and beverage packaging includes steel cans and aluminum slugs. Ball's packaging revenue derives primarily from a relatively few beverage making customers owning brands spanning Argentina Brazil China Europe and North America. Ball Aerospace & Technologies manufactures an array of aerospace systems from satellites to tactical antennas as well as providing systems engineering services. Ball Corporation operates through 90 locations around the world.

	Annual Growth	12/11	12/12	12/13	12/14	12/15
Sales ($ mil.)	(1.9%)	8,630.9	8,735.7	8,468.1	8,570.0	7,997.0
Net income ($ mil.)	(10.8%)	444.0	403.5	406.8	470.0	280.9
Market value ($ mil.)	19.5%	5,081.1	6,367.4	7,350.7	9,699.9	10,348.7
Employees	0.3%	15,000	15,000	14,600	14,500	15,200

BALL HORTICULTURAL COMPANY

622 Town Rd.
West Chicago IL 60185-2698
Phone: 630-231-3600
Fax: 630-231-3605
Web: www.ballhort.com

CEO: Anna C Ball
CFO: Todd Billings
HR: –
FYE: June 30
Type: Private

Flower power still reigns at Ball Horticultural. One of the nation's largest sellers of commercial seed for flowers and ornamental crops Ball Horticultural develops produces and distributes seeds young plants and cuttings to professional growers landscapers wholesalers and retailers. It operates in more than 20 countries through subsidiaries and joint ventures including PanAmerican Seed and Ball Seed. The firm sells through its own sales force and online. It also publishes FloraCulture International Green Profit and "GrowerTalks" magazines. Founded in 1905 by George Ball Ball Horticultural remains family owned. The Ball clan also owns W. Atlee Burpee a major seed seller to home gardeners.

BALL STATE UNIVERSITY

2000 W UNIVERSITY AVE
MUNCIE, IN 473060002
Phone: 765-289-1241
Fax:
Web: www.cms.bsu.edu

CEO: –
CFO: –
HR: –
FYE: June 30
Type: Private

Students at this university are on the ball. Ball State University (BSU) has an enrollment of about 21000 undergraduate and graduate students. It offers about 180 undergraduate majors more than 100 master's degree programs and 17 doctoral six associate and two specialist degrees in seven academic colleges. It has a Teachers College as well as colleges of applied sciences and technology; architecture and planning; business; communication information and media; fine arts; and sciences and humanities. Notable alumni include late night talk show host David Letterman and Garfield comic strip creator Jim Davis.

	Annual Growth	06/03	06/04	06/05	06/06	06/07
Sales ($ mil.)	(10.2%)	–	–	277.8	219.7	224.1
Net income ($ mil.)	53178.7%	–	–	0.0	24.5	43.4
Market value ($ mil.)	–	–	–	–	–	–
Employees	–	–	–	–	–	6,426

BALLANTYNE STRONG, INC.

ASE: BTN

13710 FNB Parkway, Suite 400
Omaha, NE 68154
Phone: 402 453-4444
Fax: –
Web: www.strong-world.com

CEO: D. Kyle Cerminara
CFO: Nathan D. (Nate) Legband
HR: –
FYE: December 31
Type: Public

Ballantyne Strong projects a lot of images. The company is an international supplier of motion picture theater equipment used by major theater chains such as AMC Entertainment and Regal Entertainment. Primary offerings include its digital projectors and accessories which it distributes through an agreement with NEC Solutions. The company also operates a cinema screen manufacturing business and offers specialty lighting equipment and services. Ballantyne Strong has international operations in Canada Hong Kong Beijing and China. The company exited the analog projector manufacturing business in early 2012.

	Annual Growth	12/10	12/11	12/12	12/13	12/14
Sales ($ mil.)	(8.6%)	136.3	184.4	169.1	103.6	95.1
Net income ($ mil.)	–	8.4	10.3	5.5	0.2	(0.0)
Market value ($ mil.)	(14.6%)	109.4	57.6	46.5	65.2	58.3
Employees	3.0%	289	236	211	298	325

BALLARD SPAHR LLP

1735 Market St. 51st Fl.
Philadelphia PA 19103-7599
Phone: 215-665-8500
Fax: 215-864-8999
Web: www.ballardspahr.com

CEO: –
CFO: –
HR: –
FYE: December 31
Type: Private - Partnershi

As a law firm Ballard Spahr employs more than 475 attorneys and operates 12 offices throughout the West and Mid-Atlantic. Ballard Spahr represents individuals and companies as well as other entitles globally in nearly 40 practice areas including construction franchise and distribution intellectual property and zoning and land use. The firm has particular expertise in climate change health care reform economic stabilization and recovery and legal guidance for distressed real estate projects. Clients have included Aetna Comcast the Philadelphia Phillies and The John Hopkins University. The firm was founded in 1886. In 2009 it shortened its name from Ballard Spahr Andrews & Ingersoll.

BALLY TECHNOLOGIES INC

NYS: BYI

6601 S. Bermuda Rd.
Las Vegas, NV 89119
Phone: 702 584-7700
Fax: 702 263-5636
Web: www.ballytech.com

CEO: –
CFO: –
HR: –
FYE: June 30
Type: Public

Bally Technologies helps keep the casinos buzzing. The firm is a leading manufacturer and supplier of casino gaming machines gaming operations and gaming information systems. Its gaming equipment segment includes both video and mechanical-reel slot machines used in gambling casinos in the US and abroad. Bally Technologies' gaming operations segment rents gaming devices and content and provides systems for linking slot machines together so players can gamble for progressively increasing jackpots. In addition the company's systems segment includes software and hardware that helps gaming operator customers with marketing player bonusing data management accounting player tracking and security services.

	Annual Growth	06/09	06/10	06/11	06/12	06/13
Sales ($ mil.)	3.1%	883.4	778.2	758.2	879.8	997.0
Net income ($ mil.)	2.9%	126.3	137.5	98.3	101.1	141.4
Market value ($ mil.)	17.2%	1,162.5	1,258.5	1,580.6	1,813.0	2,192.2
Employees	4.3%	2,907	2,620	2,827	3,146	3,443

BALTIC TRADING LIMITED

NYSE: BALT

299 Park Ave. 20th Fl.
New York NY 10171
Phone: 646-443-8550
Fax: 541-386-7316
Web: www.fullsailbrewing.com

CEO: John C Wobensmith
CFO: Apostolos D Zafolias
HR: –
FYE: December 31
Type: Public

Baltic Trading swims against the current in international shipping. While most cargo carriers look for long-term contracts to fill their holds Baltic Trading operates in the spot market immediate charters that are usually single voyages. The company was formed in 2009 by parent Genco Shipping & Trading to serve the dry bulk industry. Its initial fleet of six drybulk vessels (two Capesize and four Supramax) will have an aggregate carrying capacity of 566000 deadweight tons (DWT). Genco is providing strategic and administrative services and establishing a link to companies like Cargill COSCO and Louis Dreyfus. Baltic Trading completed an IPO in 2010 with Genco investing $75 million for majority control.

BALTIMORE ORIOLES L.P.

333 W. Camden St.
Baltimore MD 21201
Phone: 410-685-9800
Fax: 410-547-6277
Web: baltimore.orioles.mlb.com

CEO: –
CFO: –
HR: –
FYE: June 30
Type: Private

These birds are partial to Louisville timber. The Baltimore Orioles baseball team is a storied franchise of Major League Baseball boasting seven American League pennants and three World Series titles (its last in 1983). Organized as the Milwaukee Brewers in 1901 the team became the St. Louis Browns the next year and moved to Baltimore in 1954. The team's roster has boasted such Hall of Fame talent as Jim Palmer Cal Ripken Jr. and Brooks Robinson. The Orioles organization also has a controlling interest in Mid-Atlantic Sports Network a regional cable sports channel. Peter Angelos has controlled the team since 1993.

BALTIMORE RAVENS LIMITED PARTNERSHIP

1 Winning Dr.
Owings Mills MD 21117
Phone: 410-701-4000
Fax: 410-654-6239
Web: www.baltimoreravens.com

CEO: –
CFO: –
HR: –
FYE: January 31
Type: Private

Named in honor of the Edgar Allan Poe poem the Baltimore Ravens Limited Partnership owns and operates Baltimore's National Football League franchise which won its first Super Bowl following the 2000 season and its second championship after the 2012 campaign. The team was created in 1996 when former Cleveland Browns owner Art Modell relocated his franchise to Maryland. As part of the deal Modell agreed to give up all rights to the Browns' name colors and history. The team plays host at M&T Bank Stadium. Stephen Bisciotti a local businessman who founded staffing firm Allegis Group acquired control of the team from Modell in 2004.

BANANA REPUBLIC LLC

2 Folsom St.
San Francisco CA 94105
Phone: 650-952-4400
Fax: +47-24-13-47-01
Web: www.birdstep.com

CEO: Art Perck
CFO: –
HR: –
FYE: January 31
Type: Subsidiary

Banana Republic has grown from a two-store wannabe safari outfitter to an retail empire in its own right though no pith hats or fake palm trees can be seen now in its stores. Instead the well-known retailer of men's and women's mid-scale (not high-dollar but far from discount) work-to-play casual and tailored apparel has a sprawling territory some 620 stores in North American Europe and Asia and a website through which it distributes its well-put-together look. It's also expanding in Latin America and the Middle East via franchise agreements. A subsidiary of retail giant Gap Inc. since 1978 Banana Republic accounts for nearly 20% of its parent company's sales.

BANC OF AMERICA MERCHANT SERVICES LLC

1231 Durrett Ln.
Louisville KY 40213-2008
Phone: 502-315-2000
Fax: 502-315-3535
Web: corp.bankofamerica.com/public/merchant/index.j

CEO: –
CFO: David E Fountain
HR: –
FYE: December 31
Type: Joint Venture

The next time you swipe your card and it clears you might thank Banc of America Merchant Services. A 2009 joint venture between Bank of America and First Data it is one of the largest processors of electronic payments in the US. The firm handles more than 7 billion check and credit debit stored value payroll and electronic benefits transfer card transactions (worth a total of some $250 billion) annually. Its clients are small businesses and large corporations including retailers restaurants hotels supermarkets utilities gas stations convenience stores and government entities. First Data owns 51% of Banc of America Merchant Services while Bank of America owns 49%.

BANC OF CALIFORNIA INC

NYS: BANC

18500 Von Karman Ave., Suite 1100
Irvine, CA 92612
Phone: 855 361-2262
Fax: –
Web: www.bancofcal.com

CEO: Steven A. Sugarman
CFO: Ronald J. Nicolas
HR: Lisa Moss
FYE: December 31
Type: Public

Banc of California (formerly PacTrust Bank) offers deposit and loan services at 15 branches in Southern California's Los Angeles Orange County and San Diego. Customers enjoy checking savings and money market accounts as well as mobile online and card payment services telephone banking automated bill payment safe deposit boxes direct deposit and wire transfers. Customers can also access their accounts through a nationwide network of 30000 surcharge-free ATMs. In addition Banc of California operates more than 65 mortgage loan production offices in California Arizona Oregon Montana Virginia and Washington.

	Annual Growth	12/10	12/11	12/12	12/13	12/14
Assets ($ mil.)	62.3%	861.6	999.0	1,682.7	3,628.0	5,971.6
Net income ($ mil.)	81.0%	2.8	(2.7)	6.0	0.1	30.3
Market value ($ mil.)	(3.6%)	461.8	356.7	427.0	466.7	399.2
Employees	92.5%	107	147	614	1,384	1,470

BANCFIRST CORP. (OKLAHOMA CITY, OKLA)

NMS: BANF

101 North Broadway
Oklahoma City, OK 73102-8405
Phone: 405 270-1086
Fax: 405 270-1089
Web: www.bancfirst.com

CEO: David E. Rainbolt
CFO: Randy P. Foraker
HR: Mike Rogers
FYE: December 31
Type: Public

This Oklahoma bank wants to be more than OK. It wants to be super. BancFirst Corporation is the holding company for BancFirst a super-community bank that emphasizes decentralized management and centralized support. BancFirst operates about 95 locations in some 52 Oklahoma communities. It serves individuals and small to midsized businesses offering traditional deposit products such as checking and savings accounts CDs and IRAs. Commercial real estate lending (including farmland and multifamily residential loans) makes up more than a third of the bank's loan portfolio while one-to-four family residential mortgages represent about 20%. The bank also issues business construction and consumer loans.

	Annual Growth	12/10	12/11	12/12	12/13	12/14
Assets ($ mil.)	6.8%	5,060.2	5,608.8	6,022.3	6,039.0	6,575.0
Net income ($ mil.)	10.9%	42.3	45.6	51.9	54.3	63.9
Market value ($ mil.)	11.4%	638.6	582.0	656.8	869.2	982.8
Employees	2.4%	1,533	1,641	1,635	1,653	1,688

BANCINSURANCE CORPORATION

250 E. Broad St. 10th Fl.
Columbus OH 43215
Phone: 614-220-5200
Fax: 614-228-5552
Web: www.bancins.com

CEO: John S Sokol
CFO: Matthew C Nolan
HR: –
FYE: December 31
Type: Private

Insurance holding company Bancinsurance Corporation underwrites niche insurance products through its subsidiary Ohio Indemnity Company. Operating throughout the US it provides coverage to protect auto dealers banks and other lenders by insuring collateralized personal property against damage and theft. It also bonds employers that elect not to pay unemployment taxes and provides waste management coverage. Policies are sold directly to lenders through subsidiary Ultimate Services Agency; Bancinsurance also sells insurance through independent agents. CEO John Sokol (son of founder Si Sokol) and his family own a controlling stake in the firm.

BANCO POPULAR NORTH AMERICA INC.

9600 W. Bryn Mawr Ave.
Rosemont IL 60018
Phone: 847-994-5400
Fax: 847-994-6969
Web: www.bancopopular.com

CEO: –
CFO: –
HR: –
FYE: December 31
Type: Subsidiary

Banco Popular North America (BPNA) is the mainland subsidiary of Puerto Rican bank Popular. Through Popular Community Bank (formerly Banco Popular) the company provides commercial banking products and services including deposit accounts loans and mortgages and insurance and investment products from approximately 100 branches in New York California Florida Illinois and New Jersey. (It exited Texas in 2008.) Faced with losses in the global financial downturn the company sold its Popular Equipment Financing leasing portfolio and stripped down the offerings of its online unit E-LOAN in 2009.

BANCORP OF NEW JERSEY, INC.
ASE: BKJ

1365 Palisade Avenue
Fort Lee, NJ 07024
Phone: 201-944-8600
Fax: 201-944-8618
Web: www.bonj.net

CEO: Michael Lesler
CFO: Richard Capone
HR: –
FYE: December 31
Type: Public

Bancorp of New Jersey caters to individuals and small businesses on the west side of the Hudson River. It is the holding company for the Bank of New Jersey a community bank with about a half-dozen branches in Bergen County. The Bank of New Jersey offers personal and business checking and savings accounts as well as interest-bearing money market accounts CDs and IRAs. The bank's loan portfolio primarily consists of residential and commercial mortgages secured by real estate located in Bergen County. The holding company and the Bank of New Jersey were formed in 2006.

	Annual Growth	12/10	12/11	12/12	12/13	12/14
Assets ($ mil.)	19.0%	370.3	469.8	571.4	610.8	743.7
Net income ($ mil.)	15.2%	2.2	3.3	4.2	4.7	3.8
Market value ($ mil.)	0.4%	60.4	49.4	75.2	71.9	61.4
Employees	14.7%	41	51	56	66	71

BANCORPSOUTH INC.
NYS: BXS

One Mississippi Plaza, 201 South Spring Street
Tupelo, MS 38804
Phone: 662-680-2000
Fax: –
Web: www.bancorpsouth.com

CEO: James D. (Dan) Rollins
CFO: William L. (Bill) Prater
HR: –
FYE: December 31
Type: Public

Like Elvis Presley BancorpSouth has grown beyond its Tupelo roots. It's the holding company for BancorpSouth Bank which operates some 290 branches in nine southern and midwestern states. Catering to consumers and small and midszed businesses the bank offers checking and savings accounts loans credit cards and commercial banking services. BancorpSouth also sells insurance and provides brokerage investment advisory and asset management services throughout most of its market area. Real estate loans including consumer and commercial mortgages and home equity construction and agricultural loans comprise approximately three-quarters of its loan portfolio. BancorpSouth has assets of $13 billion.

	Annual Growth	12/10	12/11	12/12	12/13	12/14
Assets ($ mil.)	(0.5%)	13,615.0	12,995.9	13,397.2	13,029.7	13,326.4
Net income ($ mil.)	50.2%	22.9	37.6	84.3	94.1	116.8
Market value ($ mil.)	9.0%	1,535.3	1,060.7	1,399.5	2,446.8	2,166.7
Employees	(3.0%)	4,311	4,244	4,231	4,005	3,820

BANCTEC INC.

2701 E. Grauwyler Rd.
Irving TX 75061-3414
Phone: 972-821-4000
Fax: 972-821-4823
Web: www.banctec.com

CEO: Jim Reynolds
CFO: Jeffrey D Cushman
HR: –
FYE: December 31
Type: Private

Through its outsourced work BancTec keeps tabs on all sorts of financial transactions. The company offers electronic processing systems business process outsourcing (BPO) software hardware and services for government agencies banks utility and telecommunications companies. It serves other organizations too that do high-volume financial transactions. BancTec's systems and software capture and process checks bills and other documents. Products include digital archiving systems workflow software and scanners. Services include cost estimates and contingency planning. As part of its business BancTec operates more than 20 BPO centers globally.

BANCWEST CORPORATION

180 Montgomery St.
San Francisco CA 94104
Phone: 415-765-4800
Fax: 765-747-1473
Web: www.firstmerchants.com

CEO: J Michael Shepherd
CFO: Duke Dayal
HR: –
FYE: December 31
Type: Subsidiary

BancWest knows which direction it's heading. The subsidiary of French banking group BNP Paribas is the holding company for Bank of the West and First Hawaiian Bank. On the US mainland Bank of the West founded in 1874 has more than 700 locations in some 20 states west of the Mississippi River. Founded in 1858 First Hawaiian has about 60 branches in Hawaii Guam and Saipan. The banks' services include residential and commercial real estate lending commercial banking (with expertise in niche lending such as agricultural loans church loans and loans to RV and boat dealers) consumer finance credit cards insurance investments private banking and wealth management. BNP Paribas acquired BancWest in 2001.

BAND-IT-IDEX INC.

4799 Dahlia St.
Denver CO 80216-0307
Phone: 303-320-4555
Fax: 303-333-6549
Web: www.band-it-idex.com

CEO: –
CFO: –
HR: –
FYE: December 31
Type: Subsidiary

It's not daylight robbery but Band-It-Idex's BAND-IT brand products are a steal when it comes to holding up other equipment and components. Band-It-Idex a subsidiary of IDEX Corporation makes a wide range of stainless steel clamping bundling fastening and identification products for a variety of industrial applications. The company's fasteners include clamps buckles hose fittings and mounting hardware. It also makes related manual and power installation tools. Band-It-Idex sells its clamps and other products worldwide to the aerospace/defense agricultural automotive communications construction manufacturing mining utilities oil and gas and transportation industries among others.

BANDAI AMERICA INCORPORATED

5551 Katella Ave.
Cypress CA 90630
Phone: 714-816-9500
Fax: 714-816-6710
Web: www.bandai.com

CEO: Akihiro Sato
CFO: –
HR: –
FYE: March 31
Type: Subsidiary

Confused as to who Ben Tennyson Loula and Lion-O are? Bandai America the North American marketing arm of Japanese toy maker Namco Bandai is happy to help clear up any game character and/or action figure confusion you may have. The company's portfolio of licensed and original toy and video game brands include Ben 10 ThunderCats Dragon Ball Z Harumika Pocoyo Power Rangers Tamagotchi and Teeny Little Families. Bandai America's operations consist of toy distribution Japanese animated video distribution (through Bandai Entertainment) video game production and the development of wireless technology and content that works with existing mobile phones.

BANK LEUMI USA

579 5th Ave.
New York NY 10017
Phone: 917-542-2343
Fax: 917-542-2254
Web: www.leumiusa.com

CEO: Avner Mendelson
CFO: –
HR: –
FYE: December 31
Type: Subsidiary

Bank Leumi USA is a subsidiary of Bank Leumi le-Israel one of Israel's largest banks. It specializes in commercial and international banking services to large and midsized corporations (particularly import and export lending) as well as lending to businesses in such industries as textiles and apparel real estate diamonds technology food and entertainment. The bank which also acts as an intermediary for American firms and individuals with investments in Israel has more than a dozen offices in California Florida Illinois New York and the Cayman Islands. The bank was established in New York in 1954.

BANK MUTUAL CORP NMS: BKMU

4949 West Brown Deer Road
Milwaukee, WI 53223
Phone: 414 354-1500
Fax: –
Web: www.bankmutualcorp.com

CEO: David A. Baumgarten
CFO: Michael W. (Mike) Dosland
HR: –
FYE: December 31
Type: Public

Bank Mutual Corporation wants to be the place America's Dairyland put its moo-la. Bank Mutual Corp. is the holding company for Bank Mutual which serves consumers and businesses through about 75 branches in Wisconsin and one in Minnesota. Founded in 1892 the bank offers standard products such as checking and savings accounts CDs and credit cards. The bank mainly uses funds gathered from deposits to originate a variety of loans and to invest in mortgage-backed securities and US government securities. Bank subsidiary BancMutual Financial and Insurance Services offers mutual funds annuities insurance and brokerage and investment advisory services.

	Annual Growth	12/10	12/11	12/12	12/13	12/14
Assets ($ mil.)	(2.6%)	2,591.8	2,498.5	2,418.3	2,347.3	2,328.4
Net income ($ mil.)	–	(72.6)	(47.6)	6.8	10.8	14.7
Market value ($ mil.)	9.5%	222.6	148.1	200.2	326.4	319.5
Employees	(1.6%)	764	719	720	722	715

BANK OF AMERICA CORP. NYS: BAC

Bank of America Corporate Center, 100 N. Tryon Street
Charlotte, NC 28255
Phone: 704 386-5681
Fax: –
Web: www.bankofamerica.com

CEO: Brian T. Moynihan
CFO: Paul Donofrio
HR: Michelle (Mitch) John
FYE: December 31
Type: Public

Among the nation's largest banks by assets (alongside JPMorgan Chase and Citigroup) ubiquitous Bank of America operates one of the country's most extensive branch networks with some 4800 locations and more than 15800 ATMs. The bank's core services include consumer and small business banking corporate banking credit cards mortgage lending and asset management. Its online banking operation counts 31 million active users and 17 million-plus mobile users. Thanks largely to its acquisition of Merrill Lynch known as "The Bull" Bank of America is also one of the world's leading wealth managers — with more than $2 trillion under management — and boasts a beefed up trading and international businesses.

	Annual Growth	12/10	12/11	12/12	12/13	12/14
Assets ($ mil.)	(1.8%)	2,264,909.0	2,129,046.0	2,209,974.0	2,102,273.0	2,104,534.0
Net income ($ mil.)	–	(2,238.0)	1,446.0	4,188.0	11,431.0	4,833.0
Market value ($ mil.)	–	0.0	0.0	0.0	0.0	0.0
Employees	(6.1%)	288,000	282,000	267,000	242,000	224,000

BANK OF COMMERCE HOLDINGS (CA) NMS: BOCH

1901 Churn Creek Road
Redding, CA 96002
Phone: 530 722-3952
Fax: –
Web: www.bankofcommerceholdings.com

CEO: Randall S Eslick
CFO: James A Sundquist
HR: Donna Moore
FYE: December 31
Type: Public

Bank of Commerce Holdings provides traditional banking services through subsidiary Redding Bank of Commerce and its Roseville Bank of Commerce and Sutter Bank of Commerce divisions. It targets small to midsized businesses and medium- to high-net-worth individuals in the northern California communities of Redding Roseville and Yuba City. Through more than five branches the banks offer checking and savings accounts CDs IRAs and money market accounts. Commercial mortgages and business and industrial loans account for more than two-thirds of the company's loan portfolio.

	Annual Growth	12/10	12/11	12/12	12/13	12/14
Assets ($ mil.)	1.5%	939.1	940.7	979.4	956.3	997.2
Net income ($ mil.)	(2.0%)	6.2	7.3	7.4	7.9	5.7
Market value ($ mil.)	8.8%	56.5	44.5	61.2	75.9	79.2
Employees	(15.8%)	313	292	142	145	157

BANK OF HAWAII CORP NYS: BOH

130 Merchant Street
Honolulu, HI 96813
Phone: 888 643-3888
Fax: –
Web: www.boh.com

CEO: Peter S. Ho
CFO: Kent T. Lucien
HR: –
FYE: December 31
Type: Public

Bank of Hawaii knows there's no place like home. The firm is the holding company for Bank of Hawaii (familiarly known as Bankoh) which has about 75 branches and 460-plus ATMs in its home state plus an additional dozen in American Samoa Guam Palau and Saipan. Founded in 1897 the bank operates through four business segments: retail banking for consumers and small businesses in Hawaii; commercial banking including property/casualty insurance for middle-market and large corporations (this segment also includes the bank's activities beyond the state); investment services such as trust asset management and private banking; and treasury which performs corporate asset and liability management services.

	Annual Growth	12/10	12/11	12/12	12/13	12/14
Assets ($ mil.)	3.0%	13,126.8	13,846.4	13,728.4	14,084.3	14,787.2
Net income ($ mil.)	(3.0%)	183.9	160.0	166.1	150.5	163.0
Market value ($ mil.)	5.9%	2,064.2	1,945.3	1,926.1	2,585.8	2,593.3
Employees	(2.2%)	2,400	2,400	2,300	2,200	2,200

BANK OF KENTUCKY FINANCIAL CORP. NMS: BKYF

111 Lookout Farm Drive
Crestview Hills, KY 41017
Phone: 859 371-2340
Fax: –
Web: www.bankofky.com

CEO: –
CFO: –
HR: –
FYE: December 31
Type: Public

The Bank of Kentucky Financial Corporation is the holding company for The Bank of Kentucky which provides a variety of personal and commercial banking services from more than 30 branches in northern portions of the Bluegrass State. It attracts deposits by offering checking and savings accounts CDs and IRAs. Commercial real estate loans make up about 30% of the bank's loan portfolio while residential mortgage loans account for more than 20%. Real estate loans account for about 80% of the bank's total loan portfolio. The Bank of Kentucky also offers business and consumer loans as well as credit cards investments and trust services.

	Annual Growth	12/09	12/10	12/11	12/12	12/13
Assets ($ mil.)	4.4%	1,565.0	1,664.9	1,744.7	1,844.1	1,857.5
Net income ($ mil.)	22.6%	8.8	11.7	16.5	18.1	19.8
Market value ($ mil.)	18.4%	143.1	147.9	152.8	188.4	281.2
Employees	1.3%	352	370	387	389	371

BANK OF MARIN BANCORP

NAS: BMRC

504 Redwood Blvd., Suite 100
Novato, CA 94947
Phone: 415 763-4520
Fax: –
Web: www.bankofmarin.com

CEO: Russell A. (Russ) Colombo
CFO: Tani Girton
HR: –
FYE: December 31
Type: Public

Bank of Marin supports the wealthy enclave of Marin County north of San Francisco. The bank operates more than 20 branches in the posh California counties of Marin Sonoma and Napa as well as in San Francisco and Alameda counties. Targeting area residents and small to midsized businesses the bank offers standard retail products as checking and savings accounts CDs credit cards and loans. It also provides private banking and wealth management services to high net-worth clients. Commercial mortgages account for the largest portion of the company's loan portfolio followed by business construction and home equity loans.

	Annual Growth	12/10	12/11	12/12	12/13	12/14
Assets ($ mil.)	10.3%	1,208.2	1,393.3	1,434.7	1,805.2	1,787.1
Net income ($ mil.)	9.9%	13.6	15.6	17.8	14.3	19.8
Market value ($ mil.)	10.7%	207.9	223.3	222.5	257.7	312.4
Employees	5.7%	223	247	253	297	278

BANK OF MCKENNEY (VA)

NBB: BOMK

20718 First Street
McKenney, VA 23872
Phone: 804 478-4434
Fax: –
Web: www.bankofmckenney.com

CEO: –
CFO: James B Neville
HR: Victoria V Heller
FYE: December 31
Type: Public

This company can help you make the most of your McKenney penny or your Dinwiddie dollar. The Bank of McKenney is a community thrift serving central Virginia's Dinwiddie and Chesterfield counties the independent city of Colonial Heights and surrounding areas. The bank's six branches offer traditional deposit products including savings and checking accounts NOW accounts money markets and CDs. Commercial real estate loans make up about half of the company's lending portfolio; residential mortgages and trusts make up about 35%. Subsidiary McKenney Group provides investment services insurance products and business management services.

	Annual Growth	12/10	12/11	12/12	12/13	12/14
Assets ($ mil.)	3.0%	192.1	205.0	211.9	213.4	216.1
Net income ($ mil.)	6.5%	1.5	1.4	1.2	1.7	1.9
Market value ($ mil.)	10.1%	12.8	12.8	12.7	15.9	18.8
Employees	–	–	–	–	–	–

BANK OF NEW YORK MELLON CORP

NYS: BK

225 Liberty Street
New York, NY 10286
Phone: 212 495-1784
Fax: –
Web: www.bnymellon.com

CEO: Gerald L. Hassell
CFO: Thomas P. (Todd) Gibbons
HR: Monique R. Herena
FYE: December 31
Type: Public

Big Apple meet Iron City. The Bank of New York Mellon (BNY Mellon) is the result of the marriage of Bank of New York and Pittsburgh's Mellon Financial. BNY Mellon is one of the largest securities servicing companies in the world and a leader in asset management and corporate trust and treasury services. The firm boasts more than $28.5 trillion in assets under custody and administration and some $1.7 trillion of assets under management. BNY Mellon's state-chartered bank subsidiary Bank of New York Mellon offers asset issuer treasury broker-dealer and asset management services while BNY Mellon N.A. offers wealth management services.

	Annual Growth	12/10	12/11	12/12	12/13	12/14
Assets ($ mil.)	11.7%	247,259.0	325,266.0	358,990.0	374,310.0	385,303.0
Net income ($ mil.)	(0.1%)	2,581.0	2,569.0	2,445.0	2,111.0	2,567.0
Market value ($ mil.)	7.7%	33,770.5	22,263.9	28,738.4	39,070.9	45,366.5
Employees	1.2%	48,000	48,700	49,500	51,100	50,300

BANK OF SOUTH CAROLINA CORP.

NAS: BKSC

256 Meeting Street
Charleston, SC 29401
Phone: 843 724-1500
Fax: –
Web: www.banksc.com

CEO: Fleetwood S Hassell
CFO: Sheryl G Sharry
HR: –
FYE: December 31
Type: Public

What were you expecting something different? The Bank of South Carolina Corporation is the holding company for The Bank of South Carolina which was founded in 1987. It operates four branches in and around Charleston. Targeting individuals and small to midsized business customers the bank offers such standard retail services as checking and savings accounts credit cards and money market and NOW accounts. Real estate loans make up more than 70% of the The Bank of South Carolina's loan portfolio which also includes commercial loans (around 20%) and to a lesser extent personal loans. President and CEO Hugh Lane and his family control about 12% of the company.

	Annual Growth	12/10	12/11	12/12	12/13	12/14
Assets ($ mil.)	7.0%	280.5	334.0	325.4	340.9	367.2
Net income ($ mil.)	9.1%	3.1	3.2	3.7	4.1	4.4
Market value ($ mil.)	6.1%	57.2	50.5	52.7	78.0	72.6
Employees	1.3%	74	77	78	78	78

BANK OF THE CAROLINAS CORP

NBB: BCAR

135 Boxwood Village Drive
Mocksville, NC 27028
Phone: 336 751-5755
Fax: –
Web: www.bankofthecarolinas.com

CEO: –
CFO: –
HR: –
FYE: December 31
Type: Public

It would be more accurate to call it Bank of the North Carolina. Bank of the Carolinas Corporation was formed in 2006 to be the holding company for Bank of the Carolinas which provides traditional deposit and lending services to individuals and businesses through about 10 branches in central North Carolina. Deposit services include checking savings and money market accounts; IRAs; and CDs. Commercial real estate loans account for the largest portion of the company's loan portfolio; the bank's lending activities also include business construction and consumer loans residential mortgages and home equity lines of credit.

	Annual Growth	12/09	12/10	12/11	12/12	12/13
Assets ($ mil.)	(8.6%)	610.4	535.0	486.0	437.4	426.7
Net income ($ mil.)	–	(3.1)	(2.7)	(28.3)	(4.6)	(0.4)
Market value ($ mil.)	(36.0%)	17.3	9.7	1.1	0.8	2.9
Employees	(4.2%)	120	108	112	105	101

BANK OF THE JAMES FINANCIAL GROUP INC

NAS: BOTJ

828 Main Street
Lynchburg, VA 24504
Phone: 434 846-2000
Fax: –
Web: www.bankofthejames.com

CEO: Robert R. Chapman
CFO: J. Todd Scruggs
HR: –
FYE: December 31
Type: Public

Bank of the James Financial Group is the holding company for Bank of the James a financial institution serving central Virginia from about 10 branch locations. Catering to individuals and small businesses the bank offers standard retail products and services including checking and savings accounts CDs and IRAs. Funds from deposits are mainly used to originate residential mortgages which make up about half of the bank's loan portfolio and commercial and consumer loans. Subsidiary BOTJ Investment Group offers bank customers brokerage services annuities and related investment products through a third-party broker-dealer.

	Annual Growth	12/10	12/11	12/12	12/13	12/14
Assets ($ mil.)	2.4%	418.9	427.4	441.4	434.5	460.9
Net income ($ mil.)	17.0%	1.8	0.6	2.1	3.1	3.4
Market value ($ mil.)	12.2%	21.9	14.8	19.2	31.3	34.7
Employees	0.2%	120	120	120	120	121

BANK OF THE OZARKS, INC.
NMS: OZRK

17901 Chenal Parkway
Little Rock, AR 72223
Phone: 501 978-2265
Fax: 501 978-2224
Web: www.bankozarks.com

CEO: George Gleason
CFO: Greg McKinney
HR: –
FYE: December 31
Type: Public

Bank of the Ozarks is the holding company for the bank of the same name which has about 175 branches in Alabama Arkansas California the Carolinas Florida Georgia New York and Texas. Focusing on individuals and small to midsized businesses the $9-billion bank offers traditional deposit and loan services in addition to personal and commercial trust services retirement and financial planning and investment management. Commercial real estate and construction and land development loans make up the largest portion of Bank of the Ozarks' loan portfolio followed by residential mortgage business and agricultural loans. Bank of the Ozarks grows its loan and deposit business by acquiring smaller banks and opening branches across the US.

	Annual Growth	12/10	12/11	12/12	12/13	12/14
Assets ($ mil.)	19.9%	3,273.7	3,840.0	4,040.2	4,787.1	6,766.5
Net income ($ mil.)	16.7%	63.9	101.3	77.1	87.2	118.6
Market value ($ mil.)	(3.3%)	3,464.7	2,368.2	2,675.1	4,522.9	3,030.7
Employees	13.8%	881	1,084	1,120	1,223	1,479

BANK OF THE WEST

180 Montgomery St.
San Francisco CA 94104
Phone: 415-765-4800
Fax: 925-943-1224
Web: www.bankofthewest.com

CEO: J Michael Shepherd
CFO: Dan Beck
HR: –
FYE: December 31
Type: Subsidiary

Bank of the West can't "bear" the thought of customers banking elsewhere. The bank (which uses a bear as its logo) has more than 700 offices in some 20 states in the western and Midwestern US. Catering to consumers and small to midsized companies Bank of the West offers deposit accounts credit cards insurance investment products trust services and financial planning. It focuses its lending on residential mortgages and consumer loans which together make up about half of its loan portfolio. Parent company BancWest is owned by French bank BNP Paribas.

BANK OF VIRGINIA
NASDAQ: BOVA

11730 Hull Street Rd.
Midlothian VA 23112
Phone: 804-774-7576
Fax: 804-774-2306
Web: www.bankofva.com

CEO: Jack C Zoeller
CFO: Nancy Corsiglia
HR: –
FYE: December 31
Type: Public

Bank of Virginia helps put the Rich in Richmond. The bank serves Chesterfield and Henrico counties from a handful of branches in Richmond Chester and Midlothian. It offers standard retail and commercial deposit services such as checking and savings accounts CDs IRAs and money market accounts. Commercial mortgages account for more than half of the bank's loan portfolio which also includes business loans one-to-four-family residential mortgages and construction loans. Consumer lending accounts for less than 1% of its portfolio. Washington DC-based Cordia Bancorp bought a majority of Bank of Virginia in 2010 and plans to buy the rest.

BANKERS FINANCIAL CORPORATION

11101 Roosevelt Blvd. North
St. Petersburg FL 33716
Phone: 727-823-4000
Fax: 727-823-6518
Web: www.bankersfinancialcorp.com

CEO: Dr John A Strong
CFO: Jim D Albert
HR: –
FYE: December 31
Type: Private

Bankers Financial Corporation has more to do with extended warranties and hurricanes than it does with checking and savings accounts. The holding company operates two primary arms: Bankers Insurance Group and Bankers Business Group. The insurance group offers commercial and personal lines through a handful of property/casualty carriers an annuity company and an insurance outsourcing services provider. The business group offers a range of services from bail bonds to new-home warranties to medical plans through a handful of companies in Florida. Its diverse portfolio even includes a private hunting and sporting club in the Florida woodlands called the Gilchrist Club and a parolee monitoring company.

BANKFINANCIAL CORP
NMS: BFIN

15W060 North Frontage Road
Burr Ridge, IL 60527
Phone: 800 894-6900
Fax: –

CEO: F. Morgan Gasior
CFO: Paul A. Cloutier
HR: –
FYE: December 31
Type: Public

If you need a BankNow to handle your BankBusiness try BankFinancial. The bank serves individuals and businesses through about 20 branches in Cook DuPage Lake and Will counties in northeastern Illinois including parts of Chicago. It offers standard products such as checking and savings accounts credit cards and loans; services such as account management are available online. Investment and business loans including commercial nonresidential real estate multifamily construction and land loans account for about 80% of the company's portfolio; residential mortgages including home equity loans and lines of credit make up most of the balance.

	Annual Growth	12/10	12/11	12/12	12/13	12/14
Assets ($ mil.)	(1.1%)	1,530.7	1,563.6	1,481.2	1,453.6	1,465.4
Net income ($ mil.)	–	(4.3)	(48.7)	(27.1)	3.3	40.6
Market value ($ mil.)	5.0%	205.7	116.5	156.6	193.3	250.3
Employees	(3.7%)	337	368	356	320	290

BANKRATE INC (DE)
NYS: RATE

477 Madison Avenue, Suite 430
New York, NY 10022
Phone: 917 368-8600
Fax: –
Web: www.bankrate.com

CEO: Kenneth S. (Ken) Esterow
CFO: Steven D. Barnhart
HR: –
FYE: December 31
Type: Public

Bankrate knows there's life after budget-cutting. The firm's online network including flagship Bankrate.com provides information (including rate data and reviews) on more than 300 personal finance products including mortgages credit cards money market accounts and car and home equity loans. Bankrate culls information from about 4800 institutions covers nearly 600 local markets across the US and distributes content to about 175 media partners. Other Bankrate sites include InsureMe.com and NetQuote which sell leads to insurance agents and carriers and CreditCardGuide.com a credit card comparison website. Bankrate in 2011 filed to go public.

	Annual Growth	12/10	12/11	12/12	12/13	12/14
Sales ($ mil.)	25.4%	220.6	424.2	457.2	457.4	544.9
Net income ($ mil.)	–	(21.5)	(13.4)	29.3	(10.0)	5.2
Market value ($ mil.)	(16.7%)	–	2,181.9	1,263.5	1,820.6	1,261.5
Employees	9.9%	378	438	452	488	552

BANKUNITED INC.

14817 Oak Lane
Miami Lakes, FL 33016
Phone: 305-569-2000
Fax: –
Web: www.bankunited.com

CEO: John A Kanas
CFO: Leslie N Lunak
HR: –
FYE: December 31
Type: Public

BankUnited is uniting the north and south again. It's the bank holding company for BankUnited N.A. which provides standard banking services to individuals and businesses through about 100 branches in 15 Florida counties and six banking centers in the New York metro area (following the purchase of the New York private bank Herald National). BankUnited was formed in 2009 following the demise of the former BankUnited FSB which collapsed under the weight of bad mortgages. A team of private investors bought BankUnited from the FDIC injected $900 million in fresh capital and in 2011 took the company public via an initial public offering (IPO); it was the first IPO of a rescued bank during the economic crisis.

	Annual Growth	12/10	12/11	12/12	12/13	12/14
Assets ($ mil.)	15.3%	10,869.6	11,322.0	12,376.0	15,046.6	19,210.5
Net income ($ mil.)	2.5%	184.7	63.2	211.3	208.9	204.2
Market value ($ mil.)	9.6%	–	2,235.4	2,484.5	3,346.5	2,945.0
Employees	6.9%	1,263	1,365	1,429	1,623	1,647

BANNER CORP.

10 South First Avenue
Walla Walla, WA 99362
Phone: 509-527-3636
Fax: –
Web: www.bannerbank.com

NMS: BANR
CEO: Mark J. Grescovich
CFO: Lloyd W. Baker
HR: –
FYE: December 31
Type: Public

Flagging bank accounts? See Banner Corporation. Banner is the holding company for Banner Bank which serves the Pacific Northwest through about 100 branches and 10 loan production offices in Washington Oregon and Idaho. The company also owns Islanders Bank which operates three branches in Washington's San Juan Islands. The banks offer standard products such as deposit accounts credit cards and business and consumer loans. Commercial loans including business agriculture construction and multifamily mortgage loans account for about 90% of the company's portfolio. Bank subsidiary Community Financial writes residential mortgage and construction loans.

	Annual Growth	12/10	12/11	12/12	12/13	12/14
Assets ($ mil.)	1.8%	4,406.1	4,257.3	4,265.6	4,388.2	4,723.9
Net income ($ mil.)	–	(61.9)	5.5	64.9	46.6	54.2
Market value ($ mil.)	107.5%	45.4	335.7	601.4	877.2	842.0
Employees	2.2%	1,092	1,111	1,173	1,131	1,193

BANNER HEALTH

1441 N 12TH ST
PHOENIX, AZ 850062887
Phone: 602-747-4000
Fax: –
Web: www.bannerhealth.com

CEO: Peter S. Fine
CFO: Dennis Dahlen
HR: Diane Ekstrand
FYE: December 31
Type: Private

Hoist this Banner high! Banner Health is one of the largest secular not-for-profit health systems in the US. The organization operates 28 acute-care hospitals (with roughly 4000 beds). It also operates clinics nursing homes clinical laboratories ambulatory surgery centers home health agencies and other healthcare-related organizations including physician practices and a captive insurance company. Banner Health participates in medical research in areas such as Alzheimer's disease and spinal cord injuries through its Banner Sun Health Research division. The company which has almost 300000 members provides services in seven states in the western US; its largest concentration of facilities is in Arizona.

	Annual Growth	12/09	12/10	12/11	12/12	12/13
Sales ($ mil.)	1.5%	–	4,863.8	4,741.1	4,878.2	5,085.0
Net income ($ mil.)	12367.6%	–	–	0.1	614.8	854.9
Market value ($ mil.)	–	–	–	–	–	–
Employees	–	–	–	–	–	35,000

BANNER PHARMACAPS INC.

4100 Mendenhall Oaks Pkwy Ste 301
High Point NC 27265
Phone: 336-812-3442
Fax: 336-812-7030
Web: www.banpharm.com

CEO: –
CFO: Damien Reynolds
HR: –
FYE: December 31
Type: Subsidiary

Skip the spoonful of sugar Banner Pharmacaps uses gelatin to help the medicine go down. The company develops and makes a range of softgels for convenient oral dosage and delivery of prescription over-the-counter (OTC) and nutritional medicines and supplements. Its soft gelatin technologies are used in both branded and private-label OTC products such as pain and cold medicines. Banner also works with prescription drugmakers to enhance solubility and delivery methods for existing products as well as for compounds in clinical trial stages. It specializes in softgel technologies that control release rate and enhance performance of certain compounds. Parent company VION has agreed to sell Banner to Patheon.

BAPTIST HEALTH

9601 INTRSTATE 630 EXIT 7
LITTLE ROCK, AR 722057299
Phone: 501-202-2000
Fax: –
Web: www.baptist-health.com

CEO: –
CFO: Bob Roberts
HR: Anthony Kendall
FYE: December 31
Type: Private

For those seeking medical salvation Baptist Health may be the answer to their prayers. The organization provides health services through about 175 points of care scattered throughout in Arkansas. Its facilities include seven hospitals and a number of rehabilitation facilities family clinics and therapy and wellness centers. Arkansas Health Group a division of Baptist Health runs more than 20 physician clinics across the state. Specialized services include cardiology women's health orthopedics rehabilitation and home and hospice care. Baptist Health's Parkway Village is a 90-acre retirement community for active seniors located close to Baptist Health Medical Center - Little Rock.

	Annual Growth	12/06	12/07	12/08	12/09	12/13
Sales ($ mil.)	(0.5%)	–	–	860.2	924.0	837.0
Net income ($ mil.)	–	–	–	(204.3)	64.5	71.8
Market value ($ mil.)	–	–	–	–	–	–
Employees	–	–	–	–	–	7,000

BAPTIST HEALTH CARE

1000 W. Moreno St.
Pensacola FL 32501
Phone: 850-434-4011
Fax: 850-469-2307
Web: www.ebaptisthealthcare.org

CEO: –
CFO: Joseph Felkner
HR: –
FYE: September 30
Type: Private - Not-for-Pr

Baptist Health Care strives for coastal health excellence. The firm operates hospitals clinics and a home health agency in northern and western Florida as well as southern Alabama. Founded in 1951 the Pensacola Florida-based not-for-profit health care system operates four acute-care hospitals including the 490-bed Baptist Hospital and 65-bed Gulf Breeze Hospital. Baptist Health Care in conjunction with its affiliates provides a wide variety of services such as home health care rehabilitation services and behavioral health services. Its Baptist Manor in Pensacola provides sub-acute care and long-term care and the Andrews Institute provides sports medicine services.

BAPTIST HEALTH SOUTH FLORIDA INC.

6855 S RED RD STE 600
SOUTH MIAMI, FL 331433518
Phone: 305-596-1960
Fax: –
Web: www.baptisthealth.net

CEO: Brian E. Keeley
CFO: Ralph E. Lawson
HR: Frank Voytek
FYE: September 30
Type: Private

Baptist Health South Florida (BHSF) has a good grip on Miami's health. The faith-based not-for-profit enterprise operates seven acute-care hospitals a children's hospital and a vascular institute in the Miami area. Its flagship facility Baptist Hospital with more than 680 beds provides a comprehensive range of medical and surgical services. The system also includes South Miami Hospital with 460 beds as well as several smaller inpatient facilities in surrounding communities. In all BHSF hospitals contain about 1500 beds. In addition to inpatient services the organization provides ambulatory surgery primary and urgent care diagnostic imaging rehabilitation and home health services.

	Annual Growth	09/04	09/05	09/06*	12/08*	09/09
Sales ($ mil.)	(19.4%)	–	1,459.8	1,517.6	2.6	616.1
Net income ($ mil.)	(3.9%)	–	–	136.6	(1.0)	121.3
Market value ($ mil.)	–	–	–	–	–	–
Employees	–	–	–	–	–	9,374

*Fiscal year change

BAPTIST HEALTHCARE SYSTEM INC.

2701 EASTPOINT PKWY
LOUISVILLE, KY 402234166
Phone: 502-896-5000
Fax: –
Web: www.bhsi.com

CEO: –
CFO: –
HR: David (Dave) Rhodes
FYE: August 31
Type: Private

Baptist Healthcare System which goes by Baptist Health wants to keep all its followers healthy. The system owns eight acute-care hospitals one a long-term facility in Kentucky with a total capacity of more than 2100 beds. The not-for-profit health system's largest facility is Baptist Hospital East a 520-bed hospital in Louisville that provides a wide range of health services with special expertise in cardiology rehabilitation and women's health. In addition to its owned facilities Baptist Healthcare manages Hardin Memorial a 300-bed hospital located in Elizabethtown and Russell County Hospital with 25 beds. Founded as a single hospital in Louisville in 1924 the growing hospital system rebranded as Baptist Health in 2012.

	Annual Growth	08/08	08/09	08/10	08/11	08/12
Sales ($ mil.)	(3.8%)	–	1,448.1	1,231.4	1,317.6	1,290.4
Net income ($ mil.)	9.1%	–	–	75.8	96.8	90.2
Market value ($ mil.)	–	–	–	–	–	–
Employees	–	–	–	–	–	12,601

BAPTIST HOSPITAL OF MIAMI INC.

8900 N KENDALL DR
MIAMI, FL 331762197
Phone: 786-596-1960
Fax: –
Web: www.baptisthealth.net

CEO: Albert Boulenger
CFO: Ralph Lawson
HR: –
FYE: September 30
Type: Private

Baptist Hospital of Miami can treat many vices for Miami residents. The flagship facility of the Baptist Health South Florida health system provides residents of the city with a full range of health care services including pediatric cancer home health rehabilitation neurology and cardiovascular care. The hospital has more than 680 beds and includes the Baptist Children's Hospital which offers a pediatric emergency room and a neonatal intensive care unit. Baptist Hospital of Miami also includes the Baptist Cardiac & Vascular Institute a regional cancer program and a diabetes care center. Baptist Hospital of Miami was founded in 1960.

	Annual Growth	09/03	09/04	09/08	09/12	09/13
Sales ($ mil.)	2.5%	–	674.9	908.7	916.7	846.2
Net income ($ mil.)	4.0%	–	–	81.6	71.9	99.3
Market value ($ mil.)	–	–	–	–	–	–
Employees	–	–	–	–	–	4,200

BAPTIST MEMORIAL HEALTH CARE CORPORATION

350 N HUMPHREYS BLVD
MEMPHIS, TN 381202177
Phone: 901-227-2727
Fax: –
Web: www.baptistonline.org

CEO: Jason Little
CFO: Don Pounds
HR: Jerry Barbaree
FYE: September 30
Type: Private

Serving portions of Tennessee Mississippi and Arkansas Baptist Memorial Health Care consists of more than a dozen acute care and specialty hospitals and a network of clinic home health care and hospice operations. The health system has more than 2300 beds with more than half of which are located in the greater Memphis area. Its flagship facility is 700-bed Baptist Memorial Hospital-Memphis a tertiary care facility offering advanced care in numerous medical specialties including cardiovascular disease and pediatrics. Via an affiliation with Baptist College of Health Sciences the organization provides undergraduate education in a number of health care fields including nursing and medical radiography.

	Annual Growth	09/08	09/09	09/10	09/12	09/13
Sales ($ mil.)	97.4%	–	124.1	136.2	161.9	1,884.4
Net income ($ mil.)	–	–	–	(1.5)	1.3	28.0
Market value ($ mil.)	–	–	–	–	–	–
Employees	–	–	–	–	–	9,877

BAPTIST MEMORIAL HOSPITAL

6019 WALNUT GROVE RD
MEMPHIS, TN 381202113
Phone: 901-226-5000
Fax: –
Web: www.baptistonline.org

CEO: Jason Little
CFO: Don Pounds
HR: –
FYE: September 30
Type: Private

When most of us think of Memphis we think of Elvis Presley. When doctors think of Memphis they think of Elvis and Baptist Memorial Hospital-Memphis. As the flagship facility of Baptist Memorial Health Care the 710-bed hospital often simply called Baptist Memphis offers patients the full spectrum of health care services including cancer treatment orthopedics surgical services and neurology. The campus also features the Baptist Heart Institute for cardiovascular care and research a pediatric emergency room a skilled nursing facility and the Plaza Diagnostic Pavilion for outpatient health care. Baptist Memphis established in 1979 is one of the state's highest volume hospitals.

	Annual Growth	09/01	09/02	09/03	09/12	09/13
Sales ($ mil.)	2.7%	–	377.1	429.1	697.3	504.3
Net income ($ mil.)	(4.1%)	–	–	26.4	15.1	17.4
Market value ($ mil.)	–	–	–	–	–	–
Employees	–	–	–	–	–	6,000

BAR HARBOR BANKSHARES

ASE: BHB

P.O. Box 400, 82 Main Street
Bar Harbor, ME 04609-0400
Phone: 207 288-3314
Fax: 207 288-4560
Web: www.bhbt.com

CEO: Joseph M. Murphy
CFO: Gerald Shencavitz
HR: –
FYE: December 31
Type: Public

Bar Harbor Bankshares is a Maine-stay for communities in the Pine Tree State's Hancock Knox and Washington counties. Through more than a dozen branches subsidiary Bar Harbor Bank & Trust offers such deposit products as checking savings and money market accounts; NOW accounts; IRAs; and CDs. Real estate mortgages make up some 80% of the bank's loan portfolio which also includes consumer commercial and agricultural loans. About 10% of the bank's lending is focused on the tourist industry associated with nearby Acadia National Park. Bar Harbor Trust Services a subsidiary of the bank offers trust and estate planning services.

	Annual Growth	12/10	12/11	12/12	12/13	12/14
Assets ($ mil.)	6.9%	1,117.9	1,167.5	1,302.9	1,373.9	1,459.3
Net income ($ mil.)	8.2%	10.7	11.0	12.5	13.2	14.6
Market value ($ mil.)	2.5%	172.7	178.3	200.1	237.8	190.3
Employees	7.2%	169	168	183	185	223

BARAN TELECOM INC.

2355 Industrial Park Blvd.
Cumming GA 30041
Phone: 678-513-1501
Fax: 678-513-1501
Web: www.barantelecom.com

CEO: Eyal Cohen
CFO: Talli Shechter
HR: –
FYE: December 31
Type: Subsidiary

Baran Telecom provides network infrastructure development services to the global wireless telecommunications industry. The company specializes in the planning design deployment and maintenance of mobile phone and other wireless and broadband networks. It has undertaken projects at more than 50000 communication facilities in all states of the US and in more than 35 countries in Europe Africa and Asia. Baran Telecom primarily serves mobile phone operators and other telecom carriers tower operators and equipment vendors. Clients have included Ericsson Nokia Orange and Vodafone. It is a subsidiary of Israel's engineering construction and technology giant Baran Group.

BARCELO CRESTLINE CORPORATION

3950 University Dr. Ste. 301
Fairfax VA 22030
Phone: 571-529-6000
Fax: 571-529-6050
Web: www.barcelocrestline.com

CEO: James A Carroll
CFO: –
HR: –
FYE: December 31
Type: Subsidiary

Though some of its hotels are upscale Barcelo Crestline Corporation's clientele includes more than just the upper crust. The company primarily operates through its Crestline Hotels & Resorts hotel management subsidiary which oversees a portfolio of about 50 hotels resorts and conference centers in nearly a dozen US states and Washington DC. Properties include leading hotel brands such as Marriott Hilton and Sheraton. Barcelo Crestline also has equity interests in several upscale hotels. The company was formed in 2002 when the Spanish hotel operator Barcelo Group acquired the American hotel operator Crestline Capital the parent company of Crestline Hotels & Resorts to set up an American branch.

BARCLAYS BANK DELAWARE

125 South West St.
Wilmington DE 19801
Phone: 302-255-8000
Fax: +33-1-4070-5017
Web: www.eulergroup.com

CEO: –
CFO: Jerry Pavelich
HR: –
FYE: December 31
Type: Subsidiary

Spending money is a rewarding experience for holders of Barclays Bank Delaware cards. With co-branded credit cards from Barclays Bank Delaware (aka Barclaycard US) customers accumulate points that can be redeemed for air travel hotel stays and other perks. The company a division of Barclays issues Visa and MasterCard credit cards in addition to co-branded credit cards through partnerships with some 60 companies and institutions including Priceline Best Western L.L. Bean and BJ's Wholesale. The company was founded as Juniper Financial in 2000; it became a part of Barclays in 2004.

BARD (CR) INC

NYS: BCR

730 Central Avenue
Murray Hill, NJ 07974
Phone: 908 277-8000
Fax: –
Web: www.crbard.com

CEO: Timothy M. Ring
CFO: Christopher S. (Chris) Holland
HR: Bronwen Kelly
FYE: December 31
Type: Public

C. R. Bard is no upstart in the world of medical devices. The company has been in the business for more than a century and introduced the Foley urological catheter (still one of its top sellers) in 1934. Its products fall into four general therapeutic categories: vascular oncology urology and surgical specialties. Among other things the company makes stents catheters and guidewires used in angioplasties and other vascular procedures; catheters for delivering chemotherapy treatments; and urology catheters and products used to treat urinary incontinence. Its line of specialty surgical tools made by subsidiary Davol includes devices used in laparoscopic and orthopedic procedures and for hernia repair.

	Annual Growth	12/11	12/12	12/13	12/14	12/15
Sales ($ mil.)	4.2%	2,896.4	2,958.1	3,049.5	3,323.6	3,416.0
Net income ($ mil.)	(19.8%)	328.0	530.1	689.8	294.5	135.4
Market value ($ mil.)	22.0%	6,301.1	7,203.2	9,871.0	12,279.5	13,961.2
Employees	5.3%	12,100	12,200	13,000	13,900	14,900

BARD COLLEGE

30 CAMPUS RD
ANNANDALE ON HUDSON, NY 125049800
Phone: 845-758-7518
Fax: –
Web: www.clemente.bard.edu

CEO: –
CFO: –
HR: Dawn Alexander
FYE: June 30
Type: Private

Although Shakespeare might appreciate the curriculum Bard College is not named for the Bard of Avon but for founder John Bard. The institution of higher learning is an independent nonsectarian residential coeducational four-year college of the liberal arts and sciences. Bard's total enrollment of 1900 includes some 600 graduate students. First-year students are required to take a three-week Workshop in Language and Thinking that emphasizes the connection between expression and thought. Students must also complete a year-long senior project that is reviewed by faculty members.

	Annual Growth	06/06	06/07	06/08	06/09	06/10
Sales ($ mil.)	(54.4%)	–	–	873.1	164.5	181.6
Net income ($ mil.)	–	–	–	0.0	0.0	(5.5)
Market value ($ mil.)	–	–	–	–	–	–
Employees	–	–	–	–	–	525

BARE ESCENTUALS INC.

71 Stevenson St. 22nd Fl.
San Francisco CA 94105
Phone: 415-489-5000
Fax: 877-963-3329
Web: www.bareescentuals.com

CEO: Leslie A Blodgett
CFO: Myles B McCormick
HR: –
FYE: December 31
Type: Subsidiary

When it comes to keeping its customers looking naturally pretty Bare Escentuals has a mineral interest. The company which rolled out its bareMinerals makeup brand in 1976 along with its first retail shop develops markets and sells natural cosmetics skin care and body care items. Brand names include bareMinerals Buxom md formulations RareMinerals and its namesake line. Bare Escentuals sells its products in the US through about 120 company-owned shops 880 beauty product retailers and 1500 spas and salons. It also has distributors in Canada Japan and the UK and other European countries. Japanese cosmetics company Shiseido acquired Bare Escentuals for about $1.8 billion in 2010.

BARKLEY INC.

1740 Main St.
Kansas City MO 64108
Phone: 816-842-1500
Fax: 830-788-7279
Web: www.jbfoods.com

CEO: Jeff King
CFO: Greg Trees
HR: –
FYE: December 31
Type: Private

Barkley (formerly known as Barkley Evergreen & Partners) is an employee-owned agency that integrates advertising and marketing services across such disciplines as public relations relationship marketing event marketing and interactive services. It has provided marketing communication services for such clients as Weight Watchers Sonic CITGO NASCAR and the Kansas Lottery. The agency serves national clientele through full-service offices in Kansas City Missouri and Pittsburgh with field offices located across the country. Units within Barkley include Barkley Blacktop and BarkleyREI.

BARNES & THORNBURG LLP

11 S. Meridian St.
Indianapolis IN 46204-3535
Phone: 317-236-1313
Fax: 317-231-7433
Web: www.btlaw.com

CEO: –
CFO: –
HR: –
FYE: December 31
Type: Private - Partnershi

Barnes & Thornburg's more than 550 attorneys counsel clients ranging from individuals to multinational corporations. With particular expertise in serving clients in the technology sector the law firm offers experience in more than 50 practice areas and industry specializations including health care intellectual property global logistics and taxation. Deeply seeded in the Midwest it also owns offices in Delaware and Washington DC. To increase its international footprint the firm is a part of TerraLex a global network of more than 150 law firms in about 100 jurisdictions. Barnes & Thornburg was founded in 1940 as Barnes Hickam Pantzer & Boyd.

BARNES & NOBLE COLLEGE BOOKSELLERS LLC

120 Mountain View Blvd.
Basking Ridge NJ 07920
Phone: 908-991-2665
Fax: 908-991-2846
Web: www.bncollege.com/

CEO: Max J Roberts
CFO: –
HR: –
FYE: April 30
Type: Subsidiary

Barnes & Noble College Booksellers is the scholastic subsidiary of Barnes & Noble (B&N) the nation's #1 bookstore chain. Established in 1965 the company operates some 645 bookstores serving more than 4 million students on college campuses nationwide selling textbooks (new used rental and electronic) trade books school supplies collegiate clothing and emblematic merchandise. It also offers merchandise through campus bookstores' websites. Universities medical and law schools and community colleges hire B&N College to replace traditional campus cooperatives. Some of its well-known campus bookstores include Boston University and Yale. B&N College accounts for nearly 25% of its parent company's sales.

BARNES GROUP INC.   NYS: B

123 Main Street
Bristol, CT 06010
Phone: 860 583-7070
Fax: –
Web: www.bginc.com

CEO: –
CFO: Christopher J. (Chris) Stephens
HR: Dawn N. Edwards
FYE: December 31
Type: Public

Barnes Group keeps a spring in its step. The aerospace and industrial components manufacturer produces precision engineered springs for electronics and machinery nitrogen gas products used to control stamping presses as well as fabricated components and assemblies for turbine engines and airframes. The group also offers commercial and military aviation customers logistical support and repair services primarily on aerospace spare parts. Its customers include original equipment manufacturers (OEMs) of aircraft engines consumer electronics farm equipment home appliances and medical devices located worldwide but primarily in the US. General Electric is Barnes' largest customer (19% of revenues).

	Annual Growth	12/10	12/11	12/12	12/13	12/14
Sales ($ mil.)	2.7%	1,133.2	1,169.4	1,230.0	1,091.6	1,262.0
Net income ($ mil.)	22.1%	53.3	64.7	95.2	270.5	118.4
Market value ($ mil.)	15.7%	1,126.5	1,314.0	1,224.1	2,087.9	2,017.1
Employees	(2.1%)	4,906	4,387	5,110	4,300	4,515

BARNES & NOBLE INC   NYS: BKS

122 Fifth Avenue
New York, NY 10011
Phone: 212 633-3300
Fax: –
Web: www.barnesandnoble.com

CEO: Ronald D. (Ron) Boire
CFO: Allen W. Lindstrom
HR: –
FYE: May 02
Type: Public

Barnes & Noble does business by the book and the NOOK. As the #1 bookstore chain in the US it operates 650 Barnes & Noble superstores in all 50 states and Washington DC. Stores range in size from 3000 sq. ft. to 60000 sq. ft. and stock between 22000 and 163000 book titles. It also sells books and other media online. The company's digital subsidiary NOOK Media develops supports and creates digital content and products for the digital reading and digital education markets. Heavy losses have led the company to restructure its operations. In 2015 it spun off its education division (which oversees the college bookstores unit Barnes & Noble College Booksellers) as Barnes & Noble Education.

BARNES-JEWISH HOSPITAL

1 Barnes-Jewish Hospital Plaza
St. Louis MO 63110-1094
Phone: 314-747-3000
Fax: 314-362-0468
Web: www.barnesjewish.org

CEO: –
CFO: –
HR: Alex Berger
FYE: December 31
Type: Subsidiary

Barnes-Jewish Hospital has a lot to show residents of the Show-Me State. As the largest hospital in Missouri and the top hospital in the St. Louis area it serves the residents of St. Louis and surrounding communities with some 1260 inpatient beds and a medical staff of 1820. The flagship facility of BJC HealthCare the facility is the primary teaching hospital of Washington University School of Medicine and it offers care in a number of medical specialties including organ transplantation pulmonary disease oncology cardiovascular disease and orthopedics. The health center was created in 1996 through the merger of two St. Louis hospitals with roots reaching back to the early 1900s.

	Annual Growth	04/11	04/12	04/13*	05/14	05/15
Sales ($ mil.)	(3.5%)	6,998.6	7,129.2	6,839.0	6,381.4	6,069.5
Net income ($ mil.)	–	(73.9)	(68.9)	(157.8)	(47.3)	36.6
Market value ($ mil.)	19.9%	695.4	865.6	1,148.4	1,055.4	1,436.3
Employees	4.0%	35,000	30,000	33,850	41,000	41,000

*Fiscal year change

BARNESANDNOBLE.COM LLC

76 9th Ave. 9th Fl.
New York NY 10011
Phone: 212-414-6000
Fax: 212-414-6140
Web: www.barnesandnoble.com

CEO: -
CFO: Kevin M Frain
HR: David Willen
FYE: January 31
Type: Subsidiary

barnesandnoble.com (BN.com) wants to be the Internet bookshelf's best seller. A subsidiary of the nation's #1 bookstore chain Barnes & Noble the online retailer sells books textbooks magazines music software videos toys and games and more. BN.com also features author interviews as well as book reviews from in-house editors customers and contributors to such sources as The Boston Globe The Wall Street Journal and The New Yorker. Other offerings include rare and out-of-print books and online book clubs. BN.com attracts bookworms from more than 230 countries. Under pressure from shareholders parent Barnes & Noble put itself up for sale in mid-2010.

BARNEYS NEW YORK INC.

575 5th Ave. 11th Fl.
New York NY 10017
Phone: 212-339-7300
Fax: 212-450-8489
Web: www.barneys.com

CEO: -
CFO: Steven Feldman
HR: Diane Romano
FYE: December 31
Type: Subsidiary

Barneys New York is no purple dinosaur even if it did have a brush with extinction. The luxury department store chain sells designer apparel for men women and children; shoes; accessories; and home furnishings. It operates more than 40 locations including 10 full-size Barneys New York flagship stores in New York City Beverly Hills Boston Chicago Dallas and other major cities; more than 15 smaller Barneys Co-Op shops; and about a dozen outlet stores. Founded in 1923 by Barney Pressman Barneys New York is owned by an affiliate of Istithmar PJSC an investment firm owned by the Dubai government. After a tough couple of years for luxury retailers Barneys has a new leader and is looking to recover.

BARNHILL CONTRACTING COMPANY

2311 N. Main St.
Tarboro NC 27886
Phone: 252-823-1021
Fax: 252-823-0137
Web: www.barnhillcontracting.com

CEO: Robert E Barnhill Jr
CFO: William F Davis
HR: -
FYE: March 31
Type: Private

Barnhill Contracting Company provides general construction site development and heavy highway construction services throughout the Carolinas and Virginia. Barnhill's building division provides construction services in the industrial biotech office retail mixed-use hospitality correctional and institutional markets. The unit offers general construction construction management design/build and fast-track services. Barnhill Contracting also operates asphalt plants and has one of the largest construction equipment divisions in the US Southeast. The family-owned firm was founded in 1949 by Robert E. Barnhill Sr; it is headed by his son Robert Barnhill Jr.

BARNWELL INDUSTRIES, INC.   ASE: BRN

1100 Alakea Street, Suite 2900
Honolulu, HI 96813-2833
Phone: 808 531-8400
Fax: -
Web: www.brninc.com

CEO: Morton H Kinzler
CFO: Russell M Gifford
HR: -
FYE: September 30
Type: Public

Barnwell Industries has more than a barnful of assets which range from oil and gas production contract well drilling and Hawaiian land and housing investments. Barnwell Industries explores for and produces oil and natural gas primarily in Alberta. In 2009 it reported proved reserves of 1.3 million barrels of oil and 20.6 billion cu. ft. of gas. Subsidiary Water Resources International drills water and geothermal wells and installs and repairs water pump systems in Hawaii. The company also owns a 78% interest in Kaupulehu Developments which owns leasehold rights to more than 1000 acres in Hawaii and is engaged in other real estate activities.

	Annual Growth	09/11	09/12	09/13	09/14	09/15
Sales ($ mil.)	(17.8%)	38.5	34.1	24.6	31.4	17.5
Net income ($ mil.)	-	(0.1)	(10.1)	(8.6)	0.7	1.3
Market value ($ mil.)	(14.6%)	28.9	26.7	28.6	21.7	15.4
Employees	(4.0%)	40	37	43	38	34

BARRACUDA NETWORKS INC   NYS: CUDA

3175 S. Winchester Blvd.
Campbell, CA 95008
Phone: 408 342-5400
Fax: -
Web: www.barracuda.com

CEO: William (B. J.) Jenkins
CFO: David Faugno
HR: -
FYE: February 28
Type: Public

Barracuda Networks hunts down network threats. The company provides firewalls that combine computer network hardware and software to protect enterprises from e-mail spam viruses and spyware. Other products include appliances for e-mail archiving Web filtering and load balancing. It serves businesses in industries such as consumer goods financial services manufacturing retail technology and utilities. Barracuda also provides professional services such as support consulting and implementation. Its extensive customer list has included Coca-Cola FedEx IBM and Toshiba. The company went public in 2013.

	Annual Growth	02/11	02/12	02/13	02/14	02/15
Sales ($ mil.)	18.2%	142.1	160.9	198.9	233.8	277.4
Net income ($ mil.)	-	3.0	0.6	(7.4)	(3.6)	(67.5)
Market value ($ mil.)	5.9%	-	-	-	1,901.1	2,014.2
Employees	11.0%	-	-	1,108	1,122	1,365

BARRETT (BILL) CORP   NYS: BBG

1099 18th Street, Suite 2300
Denver, CO 80202
Phone: 303 293-9100
Fax: -

CEO: R. Scot Woodall
CFO: Robert W. Howard
HR: -
FYE: December 31
Type: Public

Bill Barrett Corp. (named after a veteran oil industry wildcatter) is hoping for a Rocky Mountain high as it digs down deep for oil and gas. The company focuses its exploration and development activities in the Wind River Uinta Piceance Big Horn Denver-Julesburg and Paradox Basins and the Montana Overthrusts. Bill Barrett holds almost 1.1 million net undeveloped leasehold acres. The bulk of its properties are unconventional resources such as shale gas. In 2012 the company had net working interests in more than 1360 wells and had estimated net proved reserves of more than 1 trillion cu. ft. of natural gas equivalent. Natural gas accounts for the bulk of its reserves.

	Annual Growth	12/10	12/11	12/12	12/13	12/14
Sales ($ mil.)	(9.3%)	698.5	771.4	700.2	568.1	472.3
Net income ($ mil.)	(34.2%)	80.5	30.7	0.6	(192.7)	15.1
Market value ($ mil.)	(27.5%)	2,037.0	1,687.4	881.1	1,326.3	564.1
Employees	(7.8%)	280	313	344	258	202

BARRETT BUSINESS SERVICES, INC.　　　　　NMS: BBSI

8100 NE Parkway Drive, Suite 200　　　　　CEO: Michael L. (Mike) Elich
Vancouver, WA 98662　　　　　　　　　　　　CFO: James D Miller
Phone: 360 828-0700　　　　　　　　　　　　HR: Brenda Nelson
Fax: 360 828-0701　　　　　　　　　　　　　　FYE: December 31
Web: www.barrettbusiness.com　　　　　　　Type: Public

Barrett Business Services likes to put people to work. The company offers both temporary and long-term staffing to some 1750 small and midsized businesses. Its staffing services focus on light industrial clerical and technical businesses. Barrett also does business as a professional employment organization (PEO) providing outsourced human resource services such as payroll management benefits administration risk management recruiting and placement for more than 1500 clients. Established in 1965 Barrett operates through about 45 branch offices across 10 US states. Each year about 90% of its PEO revenue comes from customers residing in the states of California and Oregon.

	Annual Growth	12/10	12/11	12/12	12/13	12/14
Sales ($ mil.)	23.5%	273.1	314.9	402.7	532.8	636.2
Net income ($ mil.)	–	7.4	14.3	13.1	17.9	(27.1)
Market value ($ mil.)	15.2%	110.8	142.2	271.4	660.9	195.3
Employees	22.8%	40,935	49,355	64,315	79,315	93,040

BARRY (R.G.) CORP.　　　　　　　　　　　NMS: DFZ

13405 Yarmouth Road N.W.　　　　　　　　CEO: Greg A Tunney
Pickerington, OH 43147　　　　　　　　　　CFO: Jose G Ibarra
Phone: 614 864-6400　　　　　　　　　　　　HR: Yvonne E Kalucis
Fax: –　　　　　　　　　　　　　　　　　　　　FYE: June 29
Web: www.rgbarry.com　　　　　　　　　　　Type: Public

R.G. Barry would be perfectly happy if women and men would scuff around everywhere in their slippers. As the world's leading maker and marketer of comfort footwear and slippers the company specializes in manufacturing soft slippers and casual footwear for men women and children. They're sold under such brands as Angel Treads Dearfoams EZfeet My College Footwear Terrasoles Soluna and Snug Treds as well as licensed names which account for most of its revenue. R.G. Barry sells its footwear through department stores nationwide. In 2011 the company added insoles and handbags to its lineup by acquiring a pair of non-shoe makers: Foot Petals and Baggallini.

	Annual Growth	06/09*	07/10	07/11*	06/12	06/13
Sales ($ mil.)	6.6%	113.8	123.8	129.6	155.9	147.0
Net income ($ mil.)	17.3%	7.0	9.4	7.5	14.5	13.3
Market value ($ mil.)	20.8%	86.2	127.6	129.2	153.4	183.4
Employees	(1.0%)	160	154	163	138	154

*Fiscal year change

BARRY UNIVERSITY INC.

11300 NE 2ND AVE　　　　　　　　　　　　　CEO: –
MIAMI SHORES, FL 331616695　　　　　　　CFO: –
Phone: 305-899-3050　　　　　　　　　　　　HR: Jennifer (Jen) Boyd-Pugh
Fax: –　　　　　　　　　　　　　　　　　　　　FYE: June 30
Web: www.barry.edu　　　　　　　　　　　　Type: Private

Barry University is a Catholic institution of Dominican heritage based in South Florida. With a student-faculty ratio of about 14:1 the liberal arts university annually enrolls about 3000 undergraduate students and some 4000 graduate students. The university's academic division includes two colleges (the College of Arts and Sciences and the College of Health Sciences) and seven schools. It offers more than 100 specializations and programs for undergraduate graduate and doctoral studies. Barry University also offers about 35 non-degree and certificate programs. Barry University was founded by the Adrian Dominican Sisters in 1940.

	Annual Growth	06/07	06/08	06/09	06/10	06/13
Sales ($ mil.)	–	–	0.0	147.4	151.3	223.0
Net income ($ mil.)	(4.9%)	–	–	8.3	12.3	6.8
Market value ($ mil.)	–	–	–	–	–	–
Employees	–	–	–	–	–	1,407

BARRY-WEHMILLER GROUP INC.

8020 FORSYTH BLVD　　　　　　　　　　　　CEO: Robert H Chapman
SAINT LOUIS, MO 631051707　　　　　　　　CFO: James W Lawson
Phone: 314-862-8000　　　　　　　　　　　　HR: Akilandeswari Natarajan
Fax: –　　　　　　　　　　　　　　　　　　　　FYE: September 30
Web: www.bwdesigngroup.com　　　　　　　Type: Private

With Barry-Wehmiller you get the whole package. The company manufactures and supplies packaging corrugating paper converting filling and labeling automation equipment for a broad range of industries. It conducts business around the world through a group of 60 companies including Accraply (labeling machinery) Barry-Wehmiller Company (bottle washers and pasteurizers); HayssenSandiacre and Thiele Technologies (packaging systems); Pneumatic-ScaleAngelus (bottle fillers and cappers); and FleetwoodGoldcoWyard (conveyor systems). Other divisions manufacture paper converting machinery and offer engineering/design consulting services.

	Annual Growth	09/08	09/09	09/10	09/11	09/12
Sales ($ mil.)	10.9%	–	976.9	1,097.5	1,241.0	1,332.6
Net income ($ mil.)	–	–	–	–	–	–
Market value ($ mil.)	–	–	–	0.0	0.0	69.8
Employees	–	–	–	–	–	4,500

BARTON MALOW COMPANY

26500 AMERICAN DR　　　　　　　　　　　　CEO: –
SOUTHFIELD, MI 480342252　　　　　　　　CFO: –
Phone: 248-436-5000　　　　　　　　　　　　HR: Jim Nahrgang
Fax: –　　　　　　　　　　　　　　　　　　　　FYE: March 31
Web: www.bartonmalow.com　　　　　　　　Type: Private

Barton Malow scores by building end zones and home plates. The construction management and general contracting firm which has built its share of sporting facilities also focuses on projects such as schools hospitals offices and plants. Across the US and Mexico the company offers design/build and program management services ranging from the pre-planning stage to completion. Projects have included the Detroit Institute of Arts and Cultural Center and the Baltimore Orioles stadium. Affiliate Barton Malow Design provides architecture and engineering services while Barton Malow Rigging installs process equipment and machinery. Carl Osborn Barton founded the employee-owned firm as C.O. Barton Company in 1924.

	Annual Growth	03/10	03/11	03/12	03/13	03/14
Sales ($ mil.)	7.3%	–	–	–	1,005.9	1,078.9
Net income ($ mil.)	(20.9%)	–	–	–	3.5	2.7
Market value ($ mil.)	–	–	–	–	–	–
Employees	–	–	–	–	–	1,200

BASF CATALYSTS LLC

25 Middlesex/Essex Tpke.　　　　　　　　　CEO: –
Iselin NJ 08830-0770　　　　　　　　　　　　CFO: –
Phone: 732-205-5000　　　　　　　　　　　　HR: –
Fax: 732-321-1161　　　　　　　　　　　　　　FYE: December 31
Web: www.catalysts.basf.com　　　　　　　Type: Subsidiary

BASF Catalysts converts base materials into wealth — but no alchemy is involved. Part of chemicals giant BASF it makes chemical catalysts and adsorbents used in pharmaceutical steel and packaging products as well as other chemicals at some 30 sites worldwide. BASF Catalysts produces catalysts used in emission-control systems such as catalytic converters for automobiles. The unit holds leading global positions in making mobile emission catalysts process catalysts for the chemicals industry and fluid catalytic cracking catalysts for refineries. It also sources precious and base metals as raw materials for manufacturers. Its battery materials unit serves cell and battery manufacturers worldwide.

BASHAS' INC.

22402 S. Basha Rd.
Chandler AZ 85248
Phone: 480-895-9350
Fax: 480-895-5371
Web: www.bashas.com

CEO: Edward N Basha III
CFO: –
HR: –
FYE: December 31
Type: Private

Bashas' is working up a sweat standing its ground in the Southwest. The regional grocery chain operates about 130 stores (down from more than 160 in 2008) all but two of which are located in Arizona. (The other locations are in California and New Mexico.) Its holdings include Bashas' traditional supermarkets AJ's Fine Foods (gourmet-style supermarkets) and about a dozen Food City supermarkets (which cater to Hispanics in southern Arizona). It also runs a handful of Dine Markets in the Navajo Nation ("dine" means "the people" in Navajo) and Phoenix wine retailer Sportsman's Fine Wine and Spirits. Founded in 1932 family-owned Bashas' emerged from Chapter 11 bankruptcy in mid-2010 after closing stores.

BASIN ELECTRIC POWER COOPERATIVE

1717 E. Interstate Ave.
Bismarck ND 58503-0564
Phone: 701-223-0441
Fax: 701-557-5336
Web: www.basinelectric.com

CEO: Paul M Sukut
CFO: Steve Johnson
HR: –
FYE: December 31
Type: Private - Cooperativ

Ranges at home on the range depend on Basin Electric Power Cooperative as do other electric-powered items in nine states from Montana to Iowa to New Mexico. The consumer-owned power generation and transmission co-op provides power to 134 rural electric member systems which serve about 2.8 million people. It had generating capacity of 4715 MW (mostly coal-fired) in 2011. Basin Electric's subsidiaries include Dakota Gasification (which produces natural gas from coal) Dakota Coal (markets lignite and limestone) Basin Telecommunications (Internet access) Basin Cooperative Services (property management) Prairie Winds (wind power) and Souris Valley Pipeline (CO2 pipeline).

BASIC AMERICAN INC.

2121 North California Blvd. Ste. 400
Walnut Creek CA 94596
Phone: 925-472-4000
Fax: 925-472-4360
Web: www.baf.com

CEO: Bryan Reese
CFO: Jim Collins
HR: –
FYE: December 31
Type: Private

Basic American Foods caters to your basic meat-and-potatoes kind of person. The company makes dehydrated potato products under such brands as Hungry Jack Nana's Own Potato Pearls Nature's Own Redi-Shred and WHIPP. Its portfolio includes a variety of potato products such as au gratin hash brown mashed and scalloped. It also produces Santiago brand refried and black beans as well as Quick-Start chili mixes. Basic American Foods has processing plants across the US and international operations in Mexico City and Hong Kong. The company's customers include foodservice distributors and operators industrial food manufacturers wholesale clubs and supermarkets.

BASIS TECHNOLOGY CORPORATION

150 CambridgePark Dr.
Cambridge MA 02140
Phone: 617-386-2000
Fax: 617-386-2020
Web: www.basistech.com

CEO: –
CFO: –
HR: –
FYE: December 31
Type: Private

Speaking only one language isn't a good basis for global growth. Basis Technology provides software for companies that want to establish multilingual Web sites products and sales channels. The company's Rosette Linguistics Platform includes text analysis tools for Arabic Asian European and other languages as well as data extraction tools that searches unstructured e-mail Web and other documents. Rosette allows developers to add Unicode (an international standard for software code) compliance to their products. Service offerings include project management engineering and globalization services. Customers have included Cisco L.L. Bean and US defense and intelligence agencies.

BASIC ENERGY SERVICES INC

NYS: BAS

801 Cherry Street, Suite 2100
Fort Worth, TX 76102
Phone: 817 334-4100
Fax: –
Web: www.basicenergyservices.com

CEO: Kenneth V. (Ken) Huseman
CFO: Alan Krenek
HR: Martha Preston
FYE: December 31
Type: Public

Oil and gas producers turn to Basic Energy Services for the fundamentals. The company provides well site services with its fleet of well-servicing rigs (425 the third-largest in the US behind Key Energy Services and Nabors Industries) 955 fluid service trucks and related equipment. These services include acidizing cementing fluid handling fracturing well construction well maintenance and workover. Basic Energy Services serves more than 2000 producers primarily in Texas Louisiana and Oklahoma as well as in Arkansas Kansas New Mexico and the Rocky Mountain and Appalachian regions (where there are more than 600000 active wells). The company also provides contract drilling operations.

BASS PRO INC.

2500 E. Kearney
Springfield MO 65898
Phone: 417-873-5000
Fax: 308-254-4800
Web: www.cabelas.com

CEO: James Hagale
CFO: –
HR: –
FYE: December 31
Type: Private

Bass Pro knows how to reel in shoppers. The company operates about 60 Bass Pro Shops Outdoor World stores in the US and Canada that sell boats firearms equipment and apparel for most outdoor activities. Stores feature archery ranges fish tanks bowling lanes billiards tables and dining areas. Bass Pro also lures shoppers at home with its catalogs online store and TV and radio programs. Its first Outdoor World store (in Missouri) has been one of the state's biggest tourist attractions since it opened in 1981. Bass Pro owns Tracker Marine (boat manufacturing) and American Rod & Gun (sporting goods wholesale) and runs an 850-acre resort in the Ozark Mountains. Founder John Morris owns Bass Pro.

	Annual Growth	12/10	12/11	12/12	12/13	12/14
Sales ($ mil.)	19.6%	728.2	1,243.3	1,374.9	1,262.9	1,491.3
Net income ($ mil.)	–	(43.6)	47.2	20.9	(35.9)	(8.3)
Market value ($ mil.)	(19.2%)	696.1	832.2	482.0	666.6	296.1
Employees	6.1%	4,500	5,600	5,600	5,400	5,700

BASSETT FURNITURE INDUSTRIES, INC
NMS: BSET

3525 Fairystone Park Highway
Bassett, VA 24055
Phone: 276-629-6000
Fax: 276-629-6332
Web: www.bassettfurniture.com

CEO: Robert H. (Rob) Spilman
CFO: J. Michael Daniel
HR: –
FYE: November 28
Type: Public

Bassett Furniture Industries is busy building a better furniture business. The company founded in 1902 makes wooden and upholstered furniture for home use featuring bedroom and dining suites sofas chairs love seats and home office furniture. Bassett sells its products primarily through some 94 Bassett Furniture Direct stores (more than half of which are licensed) and Bassett Home Furnishings locations. Bassett boasts about 55 company-owned stores located mostly in the southern and northeastern US. Operating in more than 20 states nationwide Texas is Bassett's largest market by store count.

	Annual Growth	11/11	11/12	11/13	11/14	11/15
Sales ($ mil.)	14.2%	253.2	269.7	321.3	340.7	430.9
Net income ($ mil.)	(22.0%)	55.3	26.7	5.1	9.3	20.4
Market value ($ mil.)	41.5%	86.6	122.8	172.1	214.0	346.7
Employees	14.0%	1,325	1,412	1,501	1,568	2,237

BATESVILLE TOOL & DIE INC.

177 Six Pine Ranch Rd.
Batesville IN 47006
Phone: 812-934-5616
Fax: 812-934-5828
Web: www.btdinc.com

CEO: Jody Fledderman
CFO: –
HR: –
FYE: November 30
Type: Private

Carving its own niche in the metal stampings industry Batesville Tool & Die manufactures deep drawn stamping and motor housings using cutting edge design and stamping equipment and systems such as CAD systems Wire EDM CNC vertical machining centers and CNC horizontal lathes. Batesville primarily serves the automotive industry; customers include Ford General Motors and Honda. At its two facilities in Batesville Indiana and Queretaro Mexico the company makes a range of 500 metal stampings and assemblies. It also offers prototyping resistance welding and drilling. Batesville Tool & Die operates 40 presses at its US plant and four at its facility in Mexico.

BATH & BODY WORKS LLC

7 Limited Pkwy.
Reynoldsburg OH 43068
Phone: 614-856-6000
Fax: 614-856-6013
Web: www.bathandbodyworks.com

CEO: Nicholas Coe
CFO: Tom Fitzgerald
HR: –
FYE: January 31
Type: Subsidiary

Women turn to Bath & Body Works (BBW) to help wash away the daily stresses of life. A subsidiary of Limited Brands BBW operates more than 1650 stores throughout North America and an online shop. The company sells shower gels lotions antibacterial soaps home fragrance and accessories under its own BBW brand as well as the C.O. Bigelow and White Barn Candle Co. brands. Customers in need of rejuvenation can also find a line of aromatherapy and at-home spa treatments and in some stores extra indulgences such as massages and pedicures. The BBW brand has had an image makeover from country-inspired to a modern-day apothecary of beauty. BBW accounts for about a quarter of Limited Brands' sales.

BATH IRON WORKS CORPORATION

700 Washington St.
Bath ME 04530
Phone: 207-442-3311
Fax: 207-442-1567
Web: www.gdbiw.com

CEO: –
CFO: –
HR: –
FYE: December 31
Type: Subsidiary

Rub-a-dub-dub Bath Iron Works builds some really high-tech tubs. The company which is part of the Marine Systems group of parent company General Dynamics constructs surface ships for the US Navy. BIW is the lead designer and builder for the Arleigh Burke class AEGIS guided-missile destroyer and is building the next-generation Zumwalt class DDG-1000 land attack destroyer and the LPD-17 amphibious assault ship. BIW's Surface Ship Support Center offers design and engineering upgrades logistics manpower management fleet services and other support services. Among the largest private-sector employers in the state of Maine BIW built its first ship for the US Navy the gunboat "USS Machias" in the 1890s.

BATON ROUGE GENERAL MEDICAL CENTER

3600 FLORIDA BLVD
BATON ROUGE, LA 708063842
Phone: 225-387-7000
Fax: –
Web: www.brgeneral.org

CEO: Milton Sietman
CFO: –
HR: –
FYE: September 30
Type: Private

The first hospital founded in Louisiana's capital Baton Rouge General Medical Center is a not-for-profit full-service community hospital offering patients general medical and surgical care. Through the hospital's two locations Bluebonnet and Mid City Baton Rouge General also provides specialty services for cancer heart and neonatal care. In addition the nearly 530-bed health care facility provides services in areas such as burn treatment diabetes sleep disorders and behavioral health. Baton Rouge General Medical Center is the flagship facility of General Health System.

	Annual Growth	12/04	12/05*	09/08	09/09	09/13
Sales ($ mil.)	–	–	0.0	281.9	304.6	382.9
Net income ($ mil.)	21.7%	–	–	2.5	0.8	6.7
Market value ($ mil.)	–	–	–	–	–	–
Employees	–	–	–	–	–	394

*Fiscal year change

BATSON-COOK COMPANY

817 4th Ave.
West Point GA 31833
Phone: 706-643-2500
Fax: 706-643-2199
Web: www.batson-cook.com

CEO: Raymond L Moody Jr
CFO: –
HR: –
FYE: October 31
Type: Subsidiary

Batson-Cook is well prepped in commercial construction. The firm offers general contracting construction management program management and design/build services throughout the Southeastern US. It has worked on a wide variety of projects including aerospace facilities courtrooms hospitals hotels industrial plants offices parking structures places of worship retail stores and schools. Clients have included Lockheed Martin Target and the University of Tampa. Batson-Cook began in West Point Georgia in 1915. It operates from a handful of regional offices in Georgia and Florida. Construction and development firm Kajima U.S.A. acquired Batson-Cook in 2008.

BATTALIA WINSTON INTERNATIONAL

555 Madison Ave.
New York NY 10022
Phone: 212-308-8080
Fax: 212-308-1309
Web: www.battaliawinston.com

CEO: Dale Winston
CFO: –
HR: –
FYE: December 31
Type: Private

Battalia Winston International provides senior-level executive searches in a variety of industries including the technology industrial products professional services consumer health care financial services and not-for-profit sectors. Founded in 1963 the company has locations in Boston; Chicago; Edison New Jersey; Los Angeles; and New York City. It has international capabilities through partnerships with search firms overseas that allow Battalia Winston to service clients in Asia Canada Europe and Latin America.

BATTELLE MEMORIAL INSTITUTE INC

505 KING AVE
COLUMBUS, OH 432012681
Phone: 614-424-6424
Fax: –
Web: www.battelle.org

CEO: Jeffrey (Jeff) Wadsworth
CFO: Dave Evans
HR: Thomas Snowberger
FYE: September 30
Type: Private

When you use a copier hit a golf ball or listen to a CD you're using technologies developed by Battelle Memorial Institute. The not-for-profit is one of the world's largest research enterprises with more than 22000 scientists engineers and staff serving corporate and government clients. Research areas include national security energy and health and life sciences. Battelle owns facilities in the US Asia and Europe and manages six Department of Energy-sponsored labs: Brookhaven National Laboratory Oak Ridge National Laboratory Idaho National Laboratory and Pacific Northwest National Laboratory. The institute was established by the family of steel industry pioneer Gordon Battelle in 1929.

	Annual Growth	09/10	09/11	09/12	09/13	09/14
Sales ($ mil.)	(4.6%)	–	5,499.0	5,228.6	4,796.0	4,769.9
Net income ($ mil.)	–	–	–	(24.5)	(7.3)	(111.9)
Market value ($ mil.)	–	–	–	–	–	–
Employees	–	–	–	–	–	7,457

BATTLE CREEK FARMERS COOPERATIVE NON-STOCK

400 W FRONT ST
BATTLE CREEK, NE 687154402
Phone: 402-675-2375
Fax: –
Web: www.bccoop.com

CEO: Dean Thernes
CFO: –
HR: –
FYE: November 30
Type: Private

From crop aggregation to fuel supply Battle Creek Farmers Cooperative provides its members with an arsenal of farm supplies and services. The co-op serves some 900 northeastern Nebraskan farmers. Its offerings include grain marketing soil nutrient inputs pest-control products seed animal feed transportation and energy (gasoline ethanol diesel kerosene propane and lubricants). The co-op processes soybeans and offers soybean meal and oil under the NewMaSoy brand. In addition to its administrative offices in Battle Creek Nebraska it operates 10 service centers. Battle Creek Farmers Cooperative was established in 1929.

	Annual Growth	11/09	11/10	11/11	11/12	11/13
Sales ($ mil.)	6.6%	–	120.6	188.5	200.8	146.1
Net income ($ mil.)	(9.7%)	–	–	7.5	6.5	6.1
Market value ($ mil.)	–	–	–	–	–	–
Employees	–	–	–	–	–	90

BAUER BUILT INC.

1111 W PROSPECT ST
DURAND, WI 547361061
Phone: 715-672-8300
Fax: –
Web: www.bauerbuilt.com

CEO: –
CFO: –
HR: –
FYE: December 31
Type: Private

Bauer Built ensures its customers are well-treaded. The company owns about 30 automotive tire and service centers throughout the Midwest more than 10 wholesale distribution centers seven tire retread plants and three rim and wheel reconditioning centers. It delivers petroleum products (including gasoline ethanol biodiesel and kerosene) throughout eastern Minnesota and western Wisconsin as well as operates a car wash in Durand Wisconsin. Bauer Built was founded in 1944 by Sam Bauer the father of president Jerome "Jerry" Bauer as Bauer Oil Co. It got into the retread business in 1950. Employees own about 30% of the company; the Bauer family holds the remainder.

	Annual Growth	12/03	12/04	12/05	12/06	12/08
Sales ($ mil.)	4.3%	–	161.7	182.1	171.8	191.0
Net income ($ mil.)	6.1%	–	–	2.9	2.6	3.5
Market value ($ mil.)	–	–	–	–	–	–
Employees	–	–	–	–	–	450

BAUER PUBLISHING USA

270 Sylvan Ave.
Englewood Cliffs NJ 07632-2521
Phone: 201-569-6699
Fax: 201-510-3297
Web: www.bauerpublishing.com/

CEO: Hubert Boehle
CFO: –
HR: –
FYE: December 31
Type: Subsidiary

Feeling out of touch? Turn to Bauer Publishing USA publisher of celebrity and style magazines In Touch Weekly and Life & Style Weekly women's magazines "First" and "Woman's World" soap magazine Soaps in Depth and teen magazines "TWIST" M and "J-14". Bauer Publishing USA uses a European approach to publishing which includes a focus on newsstand not subscription sales. The company is owned by German parent company Bauer Verlagsgruppe (also known as The Bauer Publishing Group). The Bauer Publishing Group operates in the UK through Bauer Publishing USA sister companies H. Bauer Publishing and Bauer Consumer Media.

BAUSCH & LOMB INCORPORATED

1 Bausch & Lomb Place
Rochester NY 14604-2701
Phone: 585-338-6000
Fax: 585-338-6007
Web: www.bausch.com

CEO: –
CFO: Robert Bertolini
HR: –
FYE: December 31
Type: Private

The eyes are the windows to profit for Bausch & Lomb. Operating as Bausch + Lomb the eye care company is best known as a leading maker of contact lenses and lens care solutions (including the PureVision and ReNu brands). Along with its contact lens products Bausch + Lomb makes prescription ophthalmic drugs Alrex Lotemax and Zylet. It also makes over-the-counter vitamins and drops through its pharmaceuticals division. Its surgical unit makes instruments and equipment for cataract vitreoretinal and other ophthalmic surgeries. Bausch + Lomb markets its products in more than 100 countries worldwide. The company is owned by private equity firm Warburg Pincus.

BAXANO SURGICAL INC
NMS: BAXS

110 Horizon Drive, Suite 230
Raleigh, NC 27615
Phone: 919 800-0020
Fax: –

CEO: Ken Reali
CFO: Timothy M Shannon
HR: –
FYE: December 31
Type: Public

Baxano Surgical (formerly TranS1) wants to keep your lower lumbar limber. The medical device company designs develops and sells products that treat degenerative disc disease of the spine's lower lumbar region. Its AxiaLIF products allow spine surgeons to perform procedures on discs in the lower lumbar through an incision by the tailbone; doctors perform a fusion procedure through a tube that provides direct access to the degenerative disc. Baxano Surgical added the iO-Flex system which is used in spinal decompression procedures through the acquisition of Baxano Inc. in 2013; the company changed its name from TranS1 to Baxano Surgical following the purchase.

	Annual Growth	12/09	12/10	12/11	12/12	12/13
Sales ($ mil.)	(11.1%)	29.8	26.2	19.2	14.6	18.6
Net income ($ mil.)	–	(23.2)	(19.5)	(18.3)	(29.9)	(32.0)
Market value ($ mil.)	(28.9%)	182.3	96.0	85.9	114.5	46.6
Employees	(1.4%)	148	129	86	89	140

BAXTER COUNTY REGIONAL HOSPITAL INC.

624 HOSPITAL DR
MOUNTAIN HOME, AR 726532955
Phone: 870-508-1000
Fax: –
Web: www.baxterregional.org

CEO: –
CFO: Ivan Holleman
HR: Charla Foster
FYE: December 31
Type: Private

Hark! If you trip in the Ozarks rest assured that Baxter Regional Medical Center (BRMC) will be there to help. The not-for-profit acute care hospital provides services to residents of north central Arkansas and south central Missouri and has about 270 all-private rooms. BRMC provides general and advanced medical-surgical care in more than 30 medical specialties including cardiology oncology orthopedics women's health and physical rehabilitation. BRMC also runs several primary care and specialty clinics and a home health and hospice agency. The hospital started in 1963 with about 40 beds and four doctors.

	Annual Growth	12/06	12/07	12/08	12/12	12/13
Sales ($ mil.)	1.2%	–	–	142.0	148.5	157.6	152.2
Net income ($ mil.)	–	–	–	–	(6.3)	2.0	1.9
Market value ($ mil.)	–	–	–	–	–	–	–
Employees	–	–	–	–	–	–	1,358

BAXTER INTERNATIONAL INC.
NYS: BAX

One Baxter Parkway
Deerfield, IL 60015-4625
Phone: 224 948-2000
Fax: 847 948-2964
Web: www.baxter.com

CEO: Jos © E. (Joe) Almeida
CFO: James K. Saccaro
HR: Jeanne K. Mason
FYE: December 31
Type: Public

Baxter International makes a wide variety of medical products. The company is a leading manufacturer of intravenous (IV) fluids and systems; it also makes infusion pumps pre-filled syringes biological sealants and inhaled anesthetics as well as dialyzers and other products for the treatment of end-stage renal disease (ESRD). Baxter's former BioScience division makes protein and plasma therapies to treat hemophilia and immune disorders. In 2015 Baxter split its operations into two companies — one focused on biopharmaceuticals (Baxalta) and the other on medical products (Baxter).

	Annual Growth	12/10	12/11	12/12	12/13	12/14
Sales ($ mil.)	6.7%	12,843.0	13,893.0	14,190.0	15,259.0	16,671.0
Net income ($ mil.)	15.2%	1,420.0	2,224.0	2,326.0	2,012.0	2,497.0
Market value ($ mil.)	9.7%	27,455.2	26,836.9	36,154.9	37,722.4	39,750.9
Employees	8.3%	48,000	48,500	51,000	61,000	66,000

BAY BANCORP INC
NAS: BYBK

7151 Columbia Gateway Drive, Suite A
Columbia, MD 21046
Phone: 410 494-2580
Fax: –
Web: www.baybankmd.com

CEO: Joseph Thomas
CFO: Larry D Pickett
HR: –
FYE: December 31
Type: Public

Carrollton Bancorp can babysit your money from Babe Ruth's hometown. It is the holding company for commercial banks serving Baltimore and surrounding areas from about two dozen branches operating under the Bay Bank and Carrollton Bank banners. It offers standard retail services such as checking and savings accounts money market accounts and IRAs. Commercial real estate and residential mortgages account for about 45% and 20% respectively of its loan portfolio. Subsidiary Carrollton Financial Services sells stocks bonds mutual funds and annuities; Carrollton Mortgage Services originates and sells residential mortgages. In 2013 Carrollton Bancorp merged with Jefferson Bancorp holding company of Bay Bank.

	Annual Growth	12/10	12/11	12/12	12/13	12/14
Assets ($ mil.)	5.6%	386.5	365.4	365.2	419.1	479.9
Net income ($ mil.)	–	(0.9)	0.5	(0.1)	3.2	3.0
Market value ($ mil.)	0.5%	47.5	30.8	60.2	54.2	48.4
Employees	3.8%	143	135	137	49	166

BAY CITIES PAVING & GRADING INC.

1450 CIVIC CT BLDG B
CONCORD, CA 945205295
Phone: 925-687-6666
Fax: –
Web: www.baycities.us

CEO: Ben L Rodriguez
CFO: –
HR: –
FYE: September 30
Type: Private

Up among the tall trees or down by the bay Bay Cities Paving & Grading is on the job. The company provides highway and street construction services for private and public projects primarily in Northern California. Bay Cities Paving also performs road improvements renovations and extensions on existing roads. The company has provided work for such clients as the cities of Elk Grove Brentwood and Pleasant Hill and the school district of West Contra Costa. Bay Cities Paving & Grading is one of the largest Hispanic-owned firms in the US.

	Annual Growth	09/05	09/06	09/07	09/08	09/09
Sales ($ mil.)	17.3%	–	73.9	100.3	96.2	119.1
Net income ($ mil.)	(19.8%)	–	–	7.7	9.4	4.9
Market value ($ mil.)	–	–	–	–	–	–
Employees	–	–	–	–	–	250

BAY MEDICAL CENTER

615 N BONITA AVE
PANAMA CITY, FL 324013623
Phone: 850-769-1511
Fax: –
Web: www.baymedical.org

CEO: –
CFO: Chris Brooks
HR: Donna Baird
FYE: September 30
Type: Private

Bay Medical Center is a 320-bed regional hospital located in the Florida panhandle. the center provides general medical and surgical services. The hospital's specialized services and programs include an open-heart surgery program a cancer center women's and children's health and emergency care. It also operates centers for sleep disorder and childhood communication disorders. Bay Medical Center has a staff of more than 300 physicians. The hospital also operates outpatient facilities for primary care and diagnostics. Bay Medical Center is operated by a joint venture between Sacred Heart Health System and LHP Hospital Group.

	Annual Growth	09/06	09/07	09/08	09/09	09/10
Sales ($ mil.)	(52.3%)	–	–	966.2	231.6	219.7
Net income ($ mil.)	–	–	–	0.0	4.4	(5.9)
Market value ($ mil.)	–	–	–	–	–	–
Employees	–	–	–	–	–	2,000

BAY REGIONAL MEDICAL CENTER

1900 COLUMBUS AVE
BAY CITY, MI 487086831
Phone: 989-894-3000
Fax: –
Web: www.bayregional.org

CEO: –
CFO: –
HR: –
FYE: September 30
Type: Private

McLaren Bay Region provides a full range of medical services for the residents at the tip of Saginaw Bay in eastern Michigan. A part of McLaren Health Care the hospital's main campus has more than 400 beds and provides general medical and surgical care as well as specialty care in areas such as cardiovascular disease neuroscience oncology rehabilitation orthopedics and women's health. It also features an emergency room and Level II trauma center and provides home health and hospice care. A second campus McLaren Bay Special Care Hospital is a long-term acute care hospital serving patients requiring hospital stays of longer than 25 days. The regional provider also provides outpatient and home health services.

	Annual Growth	09/10	09/11	09/12	09/13	09/14
Sales ($ mil.)	0.8%	–	271.9	278.1	251.6	278.5
Net income ($ mil.)	(7.7%)	–	–	22.4	31.8	19.1
Market value ($ mil.)	–	–	–	–	–	–
Employees	–	–	–	–	–	2,000

BAYER CORPORATION

100 Bayer Rd.
Pittsburgh PA 15205-9741
Phone: 412-777-2000
Fax: 412-777-3883
Web: www.bayerus.com

CEO: –
CFO: –
HR: –
FYE: December 31
Type: Subsidiary

For when you can't "bayer" the pain Bayer Corporation makes your medicine. The US headquarters of pharmaceuticals and materials giant Bayer AG (or Bayer Group) the company oversees the US subsidiaries of Bayer's three global divisions: Bayer HealthCare (pharmaceuticals animal health and over-the-counter medicines) MaterialScience (plastics coatings and polyurethanes) and Bayer CropScience (herbicides fungicides and insecticides). Bayer Corp.'s internal services unit Bayer Business and Technology Services handles administrative technology human resources legal and procurement functions for the Bayer Group's US operations. Bayer Corp. has around 50 sales and manufacturing locations in the US.

BAYER HEALTHCARE PHARMACEUTICALS INC.

6 W. Belt
Wayne NJ 07470-6806
Phone: 973-694-4100
Fax: 973-487-2003
Web: pharma.bayer.com

CEO: –
CFO: –
HR: –
FYE: December 31
Type: Subsidiary

Bayer HealthCare Pharmaceuticals Inc. brings the Bayer recipe for health to the US market. The company develops and markets prescription medicines for sale in the US and is part of the global Bayer HealthCare Pharmaceuticals (formerly Bayer Schering Pharma) division which is based in Germany. In addition to being a leading provider of women's health products including birth control and hormone therapies (YAZ and Mirena) Bayer HealthCare Pharmaceuticals sells specialty therapeutics in areas including diagnostic imaging hematology neurology and cancer. It makes products that target serious chronic diseases such as multiple sclerosis (Betaseron) and general health ailments such as infections (Avelox).

BAYLAKE CORP. (WI)

217 North Fourth Avenue
Sturgeon Bay, WI 54235
Phone: 920 743-5551
Fax: –
Web: www.baylake.com

NAS: BYLK
CEO: –
CFO: Kevin L Laluzerne
HR: Sharon Haines
FYE: December 31
Type: Public

Baylake Corp. is the holding company for Baylake Bank which provides financial services from about 25 offices in northeastern Wisconsin. Serving individuals and local businesses the bank provides standard products and services such as checking and savings accounts IRAs CDs credit cards mortgages and personal and business loans. It also offers trust financial planning asset management and brokerage services. Additionally Baylake Bank owns an insurance agency and holds a 49.8% stake in United Financial Services which performs electronic banking and data processing services for Baylake and other banks. Nicolet Bankshares agreed to acquire Baylake in September 2015.

	Annual Growth	12/10	12/11	12/12	12/13	12/14
Assets ($ mil.)	(0.7%)	1,052.5	1,086.9	1,024.0	996.8	1,021.6
Net income ($ mil.)	67.4%	1.1	4.5	7.6	8.0	8.9
Market value ($ mil.)	32.1%	37.1	38.0	68.8	117.9	113.1
Employees	(5.2%)	323	310	274	267	261

BAYLOR HEALTH CARE SYSTEM

3500 Gaston Ave.
Dallas TX 75246
Phone: 214-820-0111
Fax: 214-820-4697
Web: www.bhcs.com

CEO: Joel T Allison
CFO: Fredrick Savelsberg
HR: –
FYE: June 30
Type: Private - Not-for-Pr

The Baylor Health Care System (BHCS) offers an array of health care services throughout the Dallas-Fort Worth metroplex. BHCS owns or operates about two dozen acute care and specialty hospitals including the Baylor University Medical Center complex one of the state's major teaching and referral facilities. Other facilities include about 25 surgery centers and more than 250 physician and outpatient care centers as well as senior health clinics pharmacies and research labs. The faith-based (with Baptist roots) non-for-profit system also provides home health care and specialized pediatric services. BHCS is exploring a merger with Scott & White Healthcare.

BAYLOR UNIVERSITY

700 S UNIVERSITY PARKS DR
WACO, TX 76706-1003
Phone: 254-710-3731
Fax: –
Web: www.baylor.edu

CEO: Robert Sloan PHD
CFO: –
HR: –
FYE: May 31
Type: Private

Don't mess with Texas and don't mess around at Baylor University. The world's largest Baptist institution of higher learning requires its more than 15000 students to follow a strict code of conduct. The university has approximately 150 undergraduate degree programs as well as about 75 masters and more than 30 doctoral programs. With a student-to-faculty ratio of 15:1 the private co-educational university also offers degrees from its law school (juris doctor) and theological seminary (master of divinity and doctor of ministry) as well as extensive research programs. Founded in 1845 the college is affiliated with the Baptist General Convention of Texas.

	Annual Growth	05/05	05/06	05/09	05/11	05/12
Sales ($ mil.)	6.9%	–	376.8	577.9	474.8	561.0
Net income ($ mil.)	–	–	170.3	0.0	139.0	(1.8)
Market value ($ mil.)	–	–	–	–	–	–
Employees	–	–	–	–	–	1,550

BAYLOR UNIVERSITY MEDICAL CENTER

2001 BRYAN ST STE 2200
DALLAS, TX 752013024
Phone: 214-820-0111
Fax: –
Web: www.baylorhealth.edu

CEO: –
CFO: –
HR: Wendie Carlson
FYE: June 30
Type: Private

Baylor University Medical Center at Dallas is the flagship institution of the Baylor Health Care System. The medical center (known as Baylor Dallas) serves more than 300000 patients annually with more than 1000 inpatient beds and some 1200 physicians. It offers general medical and surgical services to specialty care in a wide range of fields including oncology cardiovascular disease and neuroscience. The hospital also features a Level I trauma center neonatal ICU and organ transplantation center. Founded in 1903 the Baylor Dallas campus includes the Charles A. Sammons Cancer Center and the Baylor Research Institute which conducts basic and clinical research across numerous medical specialties.

	Annual Growth	06/04	06/05	06/06	06/08	06/09
Sales ($ mil.)	4.3%	–	906.3	937.2	155.9	1,072.7
Net income ($ mil.)	–	–	–	114.1	16.1	0.0
Market value ($ mil.)	–	–	–	–	–	–
Employees	–	–	–	–	–	5,003

BAYOU CITY EXPLORATION INC

NBB: BYCX

632 Adams Street, Suite 700
Bowling Green, KY 42101
Phone: 270 282-8544
Fax: –
Web: www.bcexploration.com

CEO: Stephen C Larkin
CFO: Stephen C Larkin
HR: –
FYE: December 31
Type: Public

An affiliate of the Blue Ridge Group Bayou City Exploration is engaged in oil and gas exploration primarily in Texas and Louisiana. It conducts its activities through partnerships and the acquisition of direct stakes in oil and gas properties and in exploratory and development wells. In 2008 the company reported proved reserves of about 1.1 billion cu. ft. of natural gas equivalent. The Blue Ridge Group owns 14% of Bayou City Exploration. Shifting its exploration focus from Appalachia to the Gulf Coast in 2005 Blue Ridge Energy the exploration and production unit of Blue Ridge Group renamed itself Bayou City Exploration. To raise cash in 2010 the company sold its stakes in two wells in Texas.

	Annual Growth	12/08	12/09	12/10	12/11	12/12
Sales ($ mil.)	84.2%	0.3	1.0	1.4	1.4	3.3
Net income ($ mil.)	–	(0.2)	0.8	0.5	0.3	0.8
Market value ($ mil.)	–	0.0	0.1	0.0	0.0	0.4
Employees	0.0%	1	–	2	2	1

BAYSIDE FUEL OIL DEPOT CORP

1776 SHORE PKWY
BROOKLYN, NY 112146546
Phone: 718-372-9800
Fax: –

CEO: –
CFO: –
HR: –
FYE: December 31
Type: Private

A tree isn't the only thing that has grown in Brooklyn. So has Bayside Fuel Oil Depot which provides heating oil to customers in New York through its own four Brooklyn terminals and from two other locations the 149th Street terminal in the Bronx and the Western Nassau terminal in Nassau County. The company was founded in 1937 as a retail distributor of heating oil by Sergio Allegretti In 1965 Bayside Fuel became a wholesale oil terminal operator. It sold its retail business in 2001. Vincent Allegretti the grandson of the company's founder runs the business.

	Annual Growth	12/02	12/03	12/04	12/05	12/12
Sales ($ mil.)	7.4%	–	146.0	152.8	195.5	276.5
Net income ($ mil.)	–	–	–	1.1	1.2	(3.3)
Market value ($ mil.)	–	–	–	–	–	–
Employees	–	–	–	–	–	36

BAYSTATE HEALTH SYSTEM HEALTH SERVICES INC.

280 CHESTNUT ST
SPRINGFIELD, MA 011991000
Phone: 413-794-9939
Fax: –
Web: www.baystatehealth.org

CEO: Maura C. McCaffrey
CFO: Dennis W. Chalke
HR: –
FYE: September 30
Type: Private

Patients in need of medical care can dock at this bay. Not-for-profit Baystate Health is the largest health care services provider in western Massachusetts. The system operates five acute-care and specialty hospitals with a total of approximately 1000 beds including the flagship Baystate Medical Center which operates a Level 1 Trauma Center and a specialized children's hospital. Baystate Health also offers ancillary medical services such as cancer care respiratory care infusion therapy visiting nurse and hospice services through its regional clinics and agencies. The system controls for-profit health plan provider Health New England as well as clinical pathology firm Baystate Reference Laboratories.

	Annual Growth	09/03	09/04	09/05	09/06	09/07
Sales ($ mil.)	–	–	0.0	0.0	1,209.9	1,286.3
Net income ($ mil.)	–	–	–	0.0	83.7	125.0
Market value ($ mil.)	–	–	–	–	–	–
Employees	–	–	–	–	–	5,000

BAYSTATE MEDICAL CENTER INC.

759 CHESTNUT ST
SPRINGFIELD, MA 01199-0001
Phone: 413-784-0000
Fax: –
Web: www.baystatehealth.org

CEO: Mark R Tolosky
CFO: Dennis W Chalke
HR: –
FYE: September 30
Type: Private

Baystate Medical Center is the flagship facility of the Baystate Health System. It is a tertiary care facility and Level 1 trauma center that provides comprehensive acute care services to residents of Springfield Massachusetts and the surrounding region. The more than 650-bed medical center is also a teaching hospital serving as a secondary campus for Tufts University School of Medicine. The Baystate Medical Center campus includes Baystate Children's Hospital a 110-bed unit that boasts neonatal and pediatric ICUs. Other Baystate Medical Center operations include specialty programs in radiology cardiac care cancer and behavioral health.

	Annual Growth	09/04	09/05	09/06	09/07	09/10
Sales ($ mil.)	4.8%	–	699.0	699.0	797.2	884.9
Net income ($ mil.)	49.4%	–	8.7	0.0	80.0	64.7
Market value ($ mil.)	–	–	–	–	–	–
Employees	–	–	–	–	–	4,691

BAZAARVOICE INC.

NMS: BV

3900 N. Capital of Texas Highway, Suite 300
Austin, TX 78746-3211
Phone: 512 551-6000
Fax: –
Web: www.bazaarvoice.com

CEO: Gene Austin
CFO: James R. (Jim) Offerdahl
HR: –
FYE: April 30
Type: Public

Bazaarvoice considers itself the voice of the marketplace. Its e-commerce software helps retailers and other companies collect socially-generated online consumer feedback about their brands in order to tailor their sales marketing and customer service initiatives. Clients use its flagship Bazaarvoice Conversations platform to offer features such as rate and review Q&A and syncing to Facebook profiles. The Bazaarvoice Connections platform provides a brand interaction network to share captured information. Its Media Solutions creates advertising from word-of-mouth content. Bazaarvoice also offers search engine optimization (SEO) services. Altogether it counts more than 1000 retailers as customers.

	Annual Growth	04/11	04/12	04/13	04/14	04/15
Sales ($ mil.)	31.2%	64.5	106.1	160.3	168.1	191.2
Net income ($ mil.)	–	(20.1)	(24.3)	(63.8)	(63.2)	(34.4)
Market value ($ mil.)	(35.2%)	–	1,587.7	581.1	538.6	431.2
Employees	1.4%	780	840	783	799	826

BB&T CORP.

		NYS: BBT
200 West Second Street		CEO: Kelly S. King
Winston-Salem, NC 27101		CFO: Daryl N. Bible
Phone: 336 733-2000		HR: Betty Putney
Fax: 336 671-2399		FYE: December 31
Web: www.bbt.com		Type: Public

BB&T Corporation provides traditional banking insurance investment banking and wealth management services through more than 1800 bank branches across the South and Southeastern US. The holding company's flagship subsidiary Branch Banking and Trust (BB&T) is one of North Carolina's oldest banks and a leading originator of residential mortgages in the Southeast. The company also operates investment bank Scott & Stringfellow. Boasting assets of nearly $190 billion BB&T is one of the largest financial services holding companies in the US.

	Annual Growth	12/10	12/11	12/12	12/13	12/14
Assets ($ mil.)	4.4%	157,081.0	174,579.0	183,872.0	183,010.0	186,814.0
Net income ($ mil.)	27.1%	854.0	1,332.0	2,028.0	1,729.0	2,226.0
Market value ($ mil.)	10.3%	18,947.2	18,140.0	20,979.5	26,896.4	28,027.9
Employees	1.6%	31,400	31,800	34,000	33,700	33,400

BBDO WORLDWIDE INC.

1285 Avenue of the Americas	CEO: John B Osborn
New York NY 10019	CFO: James Cannon
Phone: 212-459-5000	HR: Ron Mason
Fax: 212-459-6645	FYE: December 31
Web: www.bbdo.com	Type: Subsidiary

This alphabet soup of advertising begins here. As the flagship agency of media conglomerate Omnicom Group BBDO Worldwide offers creative development services for some of the world's top brands using television print and other media. BBDO Worldwide also provides campaign planning and management services as well as other brand promotion services. The firm's Atmosphere BBDO unit offers interactive marketing services in North America. BBDO's clients have included such heavy hitters as Chrysler FedEx and PepsiCo (including the famous "Pepsi Generation" campaign). It operates through some 290 offices in about 80 countries featuring outposts like Abbott Mead Vickers Barefoot Proximity and Proximity London.

BBX CAPITAL CORP

		NYS: BBX
401 East Las Olas Boulevard, Suite 800		CEO: Alan B. Levan
Fort Lauderdale, FL 33301		CFO: Raymond S. Lopez
Phone: 954 940-4000		HR: –
Fax: –		FYE: December 31
Web: www.bbxcapital.com		Type: Public

BBX Capital is a diversified holding company that invests in real estate and development projects confectioneries manufacturers and other businesses. Its BBX Asset Management subsidiary manages the commercial loan portfolio and real estate properties. Renin Holdings manufacturers building supplies and home improvement products. Florida Asset Resolution (FAR) provides asset liquidation services for tax certificates loans and real estate properties. BBX Sweet Holdings owns confectioneries including Hoffman's Chocolates Boca Bons S&F Good Fortunes Williams & Bennett Jer's Helen Grace and Anastasia. Formerly the owner of BankAtlantic BBX sold the struggling bank to BB&T in 2012.

	Annual Growth	12/10	12/11	12/12	12/13	12/14
Assets ($ mil.)	(45.7%)	4,509.4	3,678.1	470.7	431.1	392.9
Net income ($ mil.)	–	(144.2)	(29.1)	235.8	47.8	4.7
Market value ($ mil.)	94.5%	18.6	54.7	108.4	252.3	266.0
Employees	(22.1%)	1,372	1,036	34	366	506

BCB BANCORP INC

		NMS: BCBP
104-110 Avenue C		CEO: Thomas M Coughlin
Bayonne, NJ 07002		CFO: Thomas P Keating
Phone: 201 823-0700		HR: –
Fax: –		FYE: December 31
		Type: Public

BCB Bancorp be the holding company for BCB Community Bank which opened its doors in late 2000. The independent bank serves Hudson County and the surrounding area from about 15 offices in New Jersey's Bayonne Hoboken Jersey City and Monroe. The bank offers traditional deposit products and services including savings accounts money market accounts CDs and IRAs. Funds from deposits are used to originate mortgages and loans primarily commercial real estate and multi-family property loans (which together account for more than half of the bank's loan portfolio). BCB Bancorp's branch network tripled in size when it added 10 locations through its 2010 acquisition of Pamrapo Bancorp.

	Annual Growth	12/10	12/11	12/12	12/13	12/14
Assets ($ mil.)	4.1%	1,106.9	1,216.9	1,171.4	1,208.0	1,301.9
Net income ($ mil.)	(14.7%)	14.3	6.1	(2.1)	9.4	7.6
Market value ($ mil.)	4.6%	82.3	84.7	79.3	112.9	98.5
Employees	17.1%	174	263	269	249	327

BCT INTERNATIONAL INC.

3000 NE 30th Place 5th Fl.	CEO: William Wilkerson
Fort Lauderdale FL 33306	CFO: Andyara Mata
Phone: 954-563-1224	HR: –
Fax: 954-565-0742	FYE: February 28
Web: www.bct-net.com	Type: Private

BCT International focuses on TCB (takin' care of business). The company operates a commercial printing chain of about 70 shops in the US and Canada most of which are franchised. BCT shops specialize in thermographed (a raised printing effect) and offset printed products such as business cards and forms envelopes letterhead rubber stamps and labels. Customers include retail printers superstores mailing centers and advertising and design professionals. The company's Pelican Paper Products unit supplies paper and printing equipment to franchisees. It also operates orderprinting.com and printdesigner.com which provide stationery products to retailers and corporate clients.

BDO USA LLP

130 E. Randolph Ste. 2800 1 Prudential Plaza	CEO: Wayne Berson
Chicago IL 60601	CFO: Howard Allenberg
Phone: 312-240-1236	HR: Kimberly Walsh
Fax: 312-240-3311	FYE: June 30
Web: www.bdo.com	Type: Private - Partnershi

BDO knows accounting. BDO USA is the US member of BDO International one of the largest accounting firms outside of the Big Four (Deloitte Touche Tohmatsu Ernst & Young KPMG and PricewaterhouseCoopers). BDO USA offers midsized companies a broad range of accounting and consulting services such as auditing tax planning litigation consulting and appraisals and valuations. The company has almost 2200 staff members and about 270 partners. It has more than 40 offices in the US. More than 400 additional offices are operated by independent US firms that are members of the BDO Seidman Alliance.

BDP INTERNATIONAL INC.

510 Walnut St.
Philadelphia PA 19106
Phone: 215-629-8900
Fax: 215-629-8940
Web: www.bdpinternational.com

CEO: –
CFO: –
HR: –
FYE: December 31
Type: Private

Be it by air ground or ocean BDP International is in the business of moving raw materials and finished products around the globe. The company provides logistics services such as customs brokerage freight forwarding and warehousing and distribution for customers in a variety of industries including chemicals and retail. It serves more than 4000 customers worldwide including DuPont Panasonic Revlon and Johnson & Johnson. BDP International and its subsidiaries have about 25 offices in the US; internationally it operates through subsidiaries joint ventures and agents in some 120 countries. President and CEO Richard Bolte Jr. and his family own the company which was founded by his father in 1966.

BEACON CAPITAL PARTNERS LLC

200 State St. 5th Fl.
Boston MA 02109
Phone: 617-457-0400
Fax: 617-457-0499
Web: www.beaconcapital.com

CEO: –
CFO: –
HR: –
FYE: December 31
Type: Private

Beacon earns its bacon by collecting offices. A private real estate investment trust (REIT) Beacon Capital Partners invests in renovates and operates commercial and mixed-use properties in major metropolitan markets throughout the US. Beacon also has properties in London and Paris. It buys properties that can be improved through redevelopment repositioning or through managing the capital markets after which it sells its holdings at a profit. The company manages investment funds on behalf of institutional corporate and government investors. Beacon Capital Partners was formed in 1998 after predecessor public REIT Beacon Properties merged with Equity Office Properties Trust in a $4 billion transaction.

BEACON POWER CORPORATION

NASDAQ: BCON

65 Middlesex Rd.
Tyngsboro MA 01879
Phone: 978-694-9121
Fax: 978-694-9127
Web: www.beaconpower.com

CEO: F William Capp
CFO: –
HR: –
FYE: December 31
Type: Private

Beacon Power beckons companies seeking backup power. The development-stage company's flywheel energy storage systems provide uninterruptible electric power for communications networks computers industrial manufacturing and other power generation applications. Beacon Power's flywheel systems draw electrical energy from a power source such as an electric power grid or a fuel cell and then store it. The power can then be delivered as needed when a primary energy source either fails or is disrupted. The company also makes photovoltaic power conversion systems (solar inverters). Beacon Power entered Chapter 11 bankruptcy protection in late 2011 and was acquired by private equity firm Rockland Capital in 2012.

BEACON ROOFING SUPPLY INC

NMS: BECN

505 Huntmar Park Drive, Suite 300
Herndon, VA 20170
Phone: 571 323-3939
Fax: –
Web: www.beaconroofingsupply.com

CEO: Paul M. Isabella
CFO: Joseph M. Nowicki
HR: Christopher Harrison
FYE: September 30
Type: Public

Not all products from Beacon Roofing Supply (BRS) are over your head. One of North America's largest roofing materials distributors the company operates some 13 regional companies with more than 360 branches in 45 US states and six Canadian provinces. BRS distributes some 11000 stock keeping units (SKUs) to about 53000 customers. Along with roofing products Beacon distributes complementary building materials such as siding windows and waterproofing systems. The company's customers include contractors home builders building owners and other resellers.

	Annual Growth	09/11	09/12	09/13	09/14	09/15
Sales ($ mil.)	8.5%	1,817.4	2,043.7	2,240.7	2,326.9	2,515.2
Net income ($ mil.)	1.3%	59.2	75.6	72.6	53.8	62.3
Market value ($ mil.)	19.4%	796.2	1,418.1	1,835.8	1,268.7	1,617.7
Employees	10.1%	2,294	2,712	2,999	3,179	3,366

BEAD INDUSTRIES INC.

11 Cascade Blvd.
Milford CT 06460
Phone: 203-301-0270
Fax: 203-301-0280
Web: www.beadindustries.com

CEO: Kenneth E Bryant
CFO: Jerry Pellegrino
HR: –
FYE: December 31
Type: Private

For nearly 100 years Bead Industries has had its chain yanked. The company makes the beaded chains used to flush toilets and operate ceiling fans and window blinds. The ubiquitous metal swag (branded Bead Chain) has a number of other uses including securing gas tanks attaching commercial shower curtains and leashing bank pens as well as key chains dog tags and neck chains. The company's Bead Electronics division makes various pins and connectors found in PC boards cars and telecom devices. Bead Industries also owns UK-based chain manufacturer Sturge Industries and McGuire Manufacturing a US maker of plumbing products. Founded by Waldo D. Bryant the company is still led by members of his family.

BEAL BANK S.S.B.

6000 Legacy Dr.
Plano TX 75024
Phone: 469-467-5000
Fax: 469-241-9564
Web: www.bealbank.com

CEO: –
CFO: Nancy Richardson
HR: –
FYE: December 31
Type: Private

Everything's bigger in Texas and Beal Bank is no exception. One of the largest private financial services firms based in the state Beal is a wholesale bank that buys and sells pools of loans and debt securities on the secondary market. It also engages in more traditional banking activities offering certificates of deposit money market accounts IRAs and savings accounts to businesses and consumers nationwide. However it does not originate commercial or residential loans. The company has offices in Texas New York California Florida and other states. Beal Bank was founded in 1988 by chairman primary owner and famed poker player Andy Beal.

BEALL'S INC.

1806 38TH AVE E
BRADENTON, FL 342084700
Phone: 941-747-2355
Fax: -
Web: www.beallsinc.com

CEO: Stephen M Knopik
CFO: Brian Crowley
HR: -
FYE: August 03
Type: Private

Residents of the Sun Belt have been known to leave their homes with Beall's on. The retail holding company operates through subsidiaries Beall's Department Stores Beall's Outlet and Burke's Outlet Stores in a dozen states. The multi-brand retailer has more than 530 department and outlet stores (about 200 are in Florida) located throughout states in the southern and western US including Arizona California Georgia Louisiana and Texas. Products range from off-price clothing and footwear for men and women to cosmetics gifts and housewares. Each chain has its own online shopping destination. The family-owned company was founded in 1915 by the grandfather of chairman Robert Beall (pronounced "bell").

	Annual Growth	07/09	07/10	07/11	07/12*	08/13
Sales ($ mil.)	4.2%	-	1,124.0	1,166.8	1,232.2	1,273.3
Net income ($ mil.)	(19.3%)	-	-	15.5	14.2	10.1
Market value ($ mil.)	-	-	-	-	-	-
Employees	-	-	-	-	-	10,100

*Fiscal year change

BEAM INC
NYS: BEAM

510 Lake Cook Road
Deerfield, IL 60015
Phone: 847 948-8888
Fax: -
Web: www.beamglobal.com

CEO: Matthew J Shattock
CFO: -
HR: -
FYE: December 31
Type: Public

Beam Inc. is one spirited company! Beam is a big producer and distributor of premium-branded distilled spirits. Its lineup ranges from bourbon whiskey to Scotch and tequila rum and ready-to-drink cocktails. Beam's portfolio of best-selling brands includes Jim Beam Bourbon Sauza Tequila Canadian Club Whisky Teacher's Scotch and Courvoisier Cognac among many. The company which operates distilleries and other sites worldwide sells primarily through direct sales forces to distributors. The US is Beam's #1 market. Once a cocktail of businesses known as Fortune Brands Beam became a stand-alone company in 2011 after spinning off its home products and hardware business Fortune Brands Home & Security.

	Annual Growth	12/08	12/09	12/10	12/11	12/12
Sales ($ mil.)	(24.5%)	7,608.9	6,694.7	7,141.5	2,311.1	2,465.9
Net income ($ mil.)	5.3%	311.1	242.8	487.6	911.4	382.4
Market value ($ mil.)	10.3%	6,609.8	6,917.2	9,647.3	8,203.0	9,781.8
Employees	(40.5%)	27,100	24,248	24,600	3,200	3,400

BEAR STATE FINANCIAL INC
NMS: BSF

900 South Shackleford Rd, Suite 401
Little Rock, AR 72211
Phone: 501 320-4904
Fax: -
Web: www.ffbh.com

CEO: Mark McFatridge
CFO: Sherri R. Billings
HR: -
FYE: December 31
Type: Public

Bear State Financial (formerly First Federal Bancshares of Arkansas) operates through subsidiary First Federal Bank of Arkansas which serves businesses and individuals through about 45 branches in Arkansas and southeastern Oklahoma. Founded in 1934 the thrift offers standard retail services such as checking and savings accounts money markets and CDs. Funds from deposits are largely used to write residential and commercial mortgages and construction and business loans. Bear State Financial also owns First National Bank in Hot Springs and Heritage Bank in Jonesboro.

	Annual Growth	12/10	12/11	12/12	12/13	12/14
Assets ($ mil.)	26.0%	600.0	579.0	530.4	548.9	1,514.6
Net income ($ mil.)	-	(4.0)	(19.0)	0.8	0.7	24.3
Market value ($ mil.)	64.6%	49.9	144.1	325.3	290.3	366.7
Employees	15.1%	241	221	192	190	423

BEARING DISTRIBUTORS INC.

8000 HUB PKWY
CLEVELAND, OH 441255788
Phone: 216-642-9100
Fax: -
Web: www.bdi-usa.com

CEO: -
CFO: Dan Maisonville
HR: Bob Patyk
FYE: December 31
Type: Private

Bearing Distributors Inc. (BDI) began as a regional Midwestern distributor of replacement parts to OEMs. Among the world's largest industrial suppliers today the company also provides maintenance and repair services as well as training and inventory management. Its offerings include bearings electrical power products material handling systems and motion control products hydraulic and pneumatic systems and fluid power components. BDI serves customers in automotive to power generation industries and from mining to food and beverage paper processing and package handling operations. Founded in 1935 the company a unit of Forge Industries has locations dotting North America Europe and Asia.

	Annual Growth	12/04	12/05	12/06	12/07	12/08
Sales ($ mil.)	-	-	-	(2,099.7)	502.7	528.9
Net income ($ mil.)	44021.8%	-	-	0.0	13.0	5.6
Market value ($ mil.)	-	-	-	-	-	-
Employees	-	-	-	-	-	850

BEASLEY BROADCAST GROUP INC
NMS: BBGI

3033 Riviera Drive, Suite 200
Naples, FL 34103
Phone: 239 263-5000
Fax: 239 263-8191
Web: www.bbgi.com

CEO: George G Beasley
CFO: Caroline Beasley
HR: -
FYE: December 31
Type: Public

Beasley Broadcast Group is a leading radio broadcaster with some 45 stations (about 60% FM) operating in about a dozen large and midsized markets in seven states primarily Florida Georgia and North Carolina. The company's stations broadcast a variety of formats including news sports and talk radio as well as Top 40 Urban Oldies and other music formats. Most of its stations operate as part of a cluster within a specific market allowing the company to combine certain business functions between those stations and achieve greater operating efficiencies.

	Annual Growth	12/10	12/11	12/12	12/13	12/14
Sales ($ mil.)	(12.0%)	98.0	97.7	100.2	104.9	58.7
Net income ($ mil.)	49.6%	8.0	10.1	11.0	11.5	40.0
Market value ($ mil.)	(3.9%)	138.4	72.8	113.0	201.7	118.1
Employees	6.1%	638	642	647	660	807

BEAUTICONTROL INC.

2121 Midway Rd.
Carrollton TX 75006-5039
Phone: 972-458-0601
Fax: 972-341-3071
Web: www.beauticontrol.com

CEO: -
CFO: -
HR: -
FYE: December 31
Type: Subsidiary

BeautiControl is looking to be ageless in the business of aesthetics and enjoys calling the Lone Star State home alongside rival Mary Kay. A unit of household products maker Tupperware BeautiControl sells its personal care items through more than 140000 independent sales consultants who in turn sell to consumers in the US Puerto Rico and Canada. Consultants provide computer-assisted head-to-toe makeup advice through in-home demos. Its products include skin and nail care fragrances cosmetics toiletries nutritional and weight-management food supplements and in-home spa retreats. Tupperware purchased BeautiControl in 2000 in a bid to expand its direct-selling reach to beauty and personal care items.

BEAUTY SYSTEMS GROUP LLC

3001 Colorado Blvd.
Denton TX 76210
Phone: 940-898-7500
Fax: 940-383-8143
Web: www.sallybeautyholdings.com/holdings/bsg.asp

CEO: –
CFO: –
HR: –
FYE: September 30
Type: Subsidiary

Hair stylists and colorists manicurists and cosmetologists stock up at stores operated by Beauty Systems Group (BSG). The beauty supplies distributor operates about 995 company-owned CosmoProf stores open only to the beauty trade. The company also supplies more than 150 franchised Armstrong McCall shops and distributes products directly to salons through a sales force of more than 1100 professional consultants. Customers primarily include salons spas licensed beauticians and nail technicians. Its 10000 products include brands such as Paul Mitchell Wella and more. BSG which covers all 50 US states Puerto Rico and parts of Canada Mexico and Europe is a subsidiary of Sally Beauty Holdings (SBH).

BEAVER DAM COMMUNITY HOSPITALS INC.

803 S UNIVERSITY AVE
BEAVER DAM, WI 539163029
Phone: 920-887-7181
Fax: –
Web: www.bdch.com

CEO: –
CFO: Donna Hutchinson
HR: Bridget Sheridan
FYE: June 30
Type: Private

Beaver Dam Community Hospitals (BDCH) provides medical services for the residents of south central Wisconsin. The non-profit medical center includes the 60-bed Beaver Dam Community Hospital as well as its Hillside Manor skilled nursing facility. Other facilities include an assisted living retirement center community-based residential facilities home health care services and a wellness center. BDCH also operates FastCare clinics in two towns and a dialysis center. BDCH has invested in an electronic medical records system and upgrades to its dialysis services.

	Annual Growth	06/09	06/10	06/11	06/12	06/13
Sales ($ mil.)	5.6%	–	88.2	97.5	103.2	104.0
Net income ($ mil.)	(2.4%)	–	–	2.1	5.3	2.0
Market value ($ mil.)	–	–	–	–	–	–
Employees	–	–	–	–	–	830

BEAVER STREET FISHERIES INC.

1741 W ST BEAVER
JACKSONVILLE, FL 32209
Phone: 904-354-5661
Fax: –
Web: www.beaverstreetfisheries.com

CEO: –
CFO: –
HR: Liz Segura
FYE: May 28
Type: Private

After more than 60 years of fishing Beaver Street Fisheries can tell a tale or two of the one that got away. It's a top supplier of fish and other seafood products to wholesalers retailers and food service operators. Sourcing its products from more than 50 countries family-owned Beaver Street Fisheries offers one of the largest selections of seafood in the US. It boasts a variety of fresh and frozen seafood — including octopus shrimp and turtle — sold under its flagship Sea Best brand as well as the HF's and Island Queen names. Beaver Street Fisheries also imports lamb from New Zealand and sells Silver Fern-brand pork and beef via its Florida-New Zealand Lamb & Meat unit.

	Annual Growth	05/07	05/08	05/09	05/10	05/11
Sales ($ mil.)	(22.0%)	–	–	741.6	442.9	450.7
Net income ($ mil.)	41071.0%	–	–	0.0	19.6	13.4
Market value ($ mil.)	–	–	–	–	–	–
Employees	–	–	–	–	–	200

BEAZER HOMES USA, INC.

NYS: BZH

1000 Abernathy Road, Suite 260
Atlanta, GA 30328
Phone: 770 829-3700
Fax: 770 481-2808
Web: www.beazer.com

CEO: Allan P. Merrill
CFO: Robert L. Salomon
HR: –
FYE: September 30
Type: Public

Beazer Homes USA builds for the middle-class buyer who's ready to make the move into the white-picket-fence scene. Building homes with an average price of about $253000 the company courts the entry-level move-up and active adult markets. Beazer Homes focuses on high-growth regions in the East Southeast and West; it closed on more than 5000 homes in 2013. (For comparison's sake it sold more than 7500 homes in 2006.) Company design centers offer homebuyers limited customization for such features as appliances cabinetry flooring fixtures and wall coverings. Like most large homebuilders Beazer subcontracts to build its homes. Founded in 1985 Beazer is banking on a recovery in new home construction.

	Annual Growth	09/11	09/12	09/13	09/14	09/15
Sales ($ mil.)	21.7%	742.4	1,005.7	1,287.6	1,463.8	1,627.4
Net income ($ mil.)	–	(204.9)	(145.3)	(33.9)	34.4	344.1
Market value ($ mil.)	72.4%	49.3	115.9	587.9	548.0	435.4
Employees	8.0%	781	804	878	1,027	1,063

BEBE STORES INC

NMS: BEBE

400 Valley Drive
Brisbane, CA 94005
Phone: 415 715-3900
Fax: –
Web: www.bebe.com

CEO: James Wiggett
CFO: Liyuan Woo
HR: –
FYE: July 04
Type: Public

Retailer bebe stores offers apparel in two main sizes: slim and none. bebe (pronounced "beebee") designs and sells contemporary women's career evening and casual clothing and accessories under the bebe banner through more than 200 stores in the US Canada and Puerto Rico; abroad through licensees; and online. The company targets hip "body-conscious" (some say skinny) 21- to 34-year-olds. bebe also licenses its name for items such as eyewear and swimwear. The majority of bebe's products are designed in-house and produced by contract manufacturers. Chairman and former CEO Manny Mashouf who founded bebe in 1976 controls the company.

	Annual Growth	07/11*	06/12*	07/13	07/14	07/15
Sales ($ mil.)	(3.5%)	493.3	530.8	484.7	425.1	428.0
Net income ($ mil.)	–	(1.8)	11.7	(77.4)	(73.4)	(27.7)
Market value ($ mil.)	(24.8%)	495.5	467.6	467.6	250.9	158.5
Employees	(3.9%)	3,422	3,294	3,107	3,254	2,924

*Fiscal year change

BECHTEL GROUP INC.

50 Beale St.
San Francisco CA 94105-1895
Phone: 415-768-1234
Fax: 415-768-9038
Web: www.bechtel.com

CEO: Bill Dudley
CFO: Mike Adams
HR: –
FYE: December 31
Type: Private

Whether the job is raising an entire city or razing a nuclear power plant you can bet the Bechtel Group will be there to bid on the business. The engineering construction and project management company serves the oil and gas energy transportation communications mining and government services sectors. It operates worldwide and has participated in such historic projects as the construction of Hoover Dam and the cleanup of the Chernobyl nuclear plant. Bechtel's Oil Gas & Chemical business unit (particularly liquefied natural gas) and its Mining & Metals group are its leading revenue producers. The group is in its fourth generation of Bechtel family leaders with chairman and CEO Riley Bechtel at the helm.

BECK SUPPLIERS INC.

1000 N FRONT ST
FREMONT, OH 434201921
Phone: 419-332-5527
Fax: –
Web: www.friendshipfoodstores.com

CEO: Daryl Becker
CFO: Loren Owens
HR: –
FYE: December 31
Type: Private

More than willing to be at the beck and call of its customers Beck Suppliers provides its clients in Ohio with fuel oil diesel gasoline kerosene and propane. The company annually delivers more than 70 million gallons of fuel at its 58 Sunoco and 28 Marathon gas stations in northwestern Ohio. Beck Suppliers also operates 25 Friendship Food Stores. The company's truck fleet delivers diesel fuel oil gasoline kerosene and propane for farm construction and industrial purposes as well as home heating oil and propane for residential use. Beck Suppliers also operates car washes under the Oasis brand and has a construction division that builds convenience stores gas stations and car washes.

	Annual Growth	12/05	12/06	12/07	12/08	12/09
Sales ($ mil.)	–	–	–	(1,300.0)	316.6	252.3
Net income ($ mil.)	7165.1%	–	–	0.0	0.8	1.4
Market value ($ mil.)	–	–	–	–	–	–
Employees	–	–	–	–	–	250

BECTON, DICKINSON AND CO.

NYS: BDX

1 Becton Drive
Franklin Lakes, NJ 07417-1880
Phone: 201 847-6800
Fax: –
Web: www.bd.com

CEO: Vincent A. (Vince) Forlenza
CFO: Christopher R. (Chris) Reidy
HR: Jerome V. Hurwitz
FYE: September 30
Type: Public

Don't worry you'll only feel a slight prick if Becton Dickinson (BD) is at work. The company's BD Medical segment is one of the top global manufacturers of syringes and other injection and infusion devices. BD Medical also makes IV catheters and syringes prefillable drug delivery systems self-injection devices for diabetes patients and related supplies such as anesthesia trays and sharps disposal systems. The BD Diagnostics segment offers tools for collecting specimens and the equipment and reagents to detect diseases in them. Finally BD caters to researchers through its BD Biosciences unit which makes reagents antibodies and cell imaging systems used in basic and clinical research.

	Annual Growth	09/11	09/12	09/13	09/14	09/15
Sales ($ mil.)	7.1%	7,828.9	7,708.4	8,054.0	8,446.0	10,282.0
Net income ($ mil.)	(14.0%)	1,271.0	1,169.9	1,293.0	1,185.0	695.0
Market value ($ mil.)	16.0%	15,448.2	16,552.2	21,073.8	23,979.3	27,950.9
Employees	14.0%	29,369	29,555	29,979	30,619	49,517

BED, BATH & BEYOND, INC.

NMS: BBBY

650 Liberty Avenue
Union, NJ 07083
Phone: 908 688-0888
Fax: 908 810-8813
Web: www.bedbathandbeyond.com

CEO: Steven H. (Steve) Temares
CFO: Eugene A. (Gene) Castagna
HR: –
FYE: February 28
Type: Public

Bed Bath & Beyond (BBB) has everything you need to play "house" for real. It's the nation's #1 superstore domestics retailer with more than 1000 BBB stores throughout the US Puerto Rico and Canada. The stores' floor-to-ceiling shelves stock better-quality (brand-name and private-label) goods in two main categories: domestics (bed linens bathroom and kitchen items) and home furnishings (cookware and cutlery small household appliances picture frames and more). BBB also operates 270 Cost Plus and World Market stores and three smaller specialty chains: about 80 Christmas Tree Shops; almost 100 buybuy BABY stores; and 50 Harmon discount health and beauty shops.

	Annual Growth	02/11	02/12*	03/13	03/14*	02/15
Sales ($ mil.)	7.9%	8,758.5	9,499.9	10,914.6	11,504.0	11,881.2
Net income ($ mil.)	4.9%	791.3	989.5	1,037.8	1,022.3	957.5
Market value ($ mil.)	11.8%	8,334.4	10,511.6	9,916.0	11,812.8	13,004.1
Employees	7.5%	45,000	48,000	57,000	58,000	60,000

*Fiscal year change

BEEBE MEDICAL CENTER INC.

424 SAVANNAH RD
LEWES, DE 199581462
Phone: 302-645-3300
Fax: –

CEO: –
CFO: –
HR: –
FYE: June 30
Type: Private

Sea shells on the sea shore can be found near Beebe Medical Center. The health care provider offers emergency inpatient long-term care women's health and other medical services to residents of Sussex County Delaware. The hospital is located in the town of Lewes near Rehoboth Beach. It has approximately 210 beds and offers specialized services including cardiology orthopedic rehabilitation and oncology treatments. Beebe Medical Center offers outpatient services including wound care diabetes management surgery radiology and sleep disorder diagnosis. It also operates senior care centers home health agencies medical laboratories and a nursing school.

	Annual Growth	04/08	04/09*	06/09	06/10	06/13
Sales ($ mil.)	–	–	0.0	234.5	259.6	275.5
Net income ($ mil.)	–	–	–	0.0	15.3	16.3
Market value ($ mil.)	–	–	–	–	–	–
Employees	–	–	–	–	–	1,600

*Fiscal year change

BEECH-NUT NUTRITION CORPORATION

100 Hero Dr.
Amsterdam NY 12010
Phone: 518-595-6600
Fax: 910-814-3899
Web: www.boonedam.us/inc/

CEO: –
CFO: –
HR: Diane Yost
FYE: June 30
Type: Private

Peas and applesauce — Beech-Nut Nutrition puts them in jars for baby's lunch or baby's finger-painting. As one of the top branded baby food makers (along with Gerber and Heinz) Beech-Nut Nutrition hopes baby will open up wider for their airplane. In addition to jars of pureed fruits vegetables meats and meals the company makes instant and jarred cereals meals plus juices and water for the youngest palates. It offers more than 150 baby and toddler food products; it was the first baby food manufacturer to offer products (beginning in 2002) containing DHA an essential fatty acid found in human breast milk. Beech-Nut is owned by Swiss branded-food manufacturer Hero.

BEHLEN MFG. CO.

4025 E. 23rd St.
Columbus NE 68602-0569
Phone: 402-564-3111
Fax: 402-563-7405
Web: www.behlenmfg.com

CEO: Phil Raimondo
CFO: –
HR: Roy Ketler
FYE: April 30
Type: Private

Behlen has the metal to grain and bear it.. Behlen makes metal livestock equipment pallets grain storage bins and silos as well as metal buildings and trailers. Over the past 20 years Behlen Country the company's livestock equipment unit has acquired farm gate maker Farmaster cattle handling equipment makers Big Valley and Universal Mfg. and storage tank provider Agri-Engineering to become the industry's largest livestock equipment manufacturer. Behlen Building Systems focuses on making products for the agricultural building market while Behlen's International Ag Systems unit makes silos and other grain storage structures. BMC Transportation maker truck trailers.

BEHRMAN CAPITAL L.P.

126 E. 56th St. 27th Fl.
New York NY 10022
Phone: 212-980-6500
Fax: 212-980-7024
Web: www.behrmancap.com

CEO: –
CFO: –
HR: Laura North
FYE: December 31
Type: Private

Private equity firm Behrman Capital engages in management buyouts recapitalizations acquisitions and consolidations within fragmented industries. Targeting established firms with annual revenues from $50 million to $500 million the company typically makes equity investments from $25 million to $100 million per transaction. It prefers to be the lead investor and assists its portfolio companies in formulating business and financial strategies. Behrman Capital focuses on the defense health care information technology specialty manufacturing and telecommunications sectors. It has stakes in about a dozen companies and more than $2 billion of assets under management.

BEKAERT CORPORATION

3200 W. Market St. Ste. 303
Akron OH 44333-3326
Phone: 330-867-3325
Fax: 330-867-3424
Web: www.bekaert.com

CEO: Matthew Taylor
CFO: Bruno Humblet
HR: –
FYE: December 31
Type: Subsidiary

Bekaert Corporation goes right down to the wire on a daily basis. The company the US subsidiary of Belgium-based NV Bekaert SA manufactures a variety of wire and wire and film coatings. For automobiles Bekaert makes tire cord control cables spring wire and clips. It also produces high carbon low carbon and stainless steel wire for industrial applications. Other Bekaert products include telecom and power cables agricultural fencing material and sawing cable. North America represents approximately 20% of its parent company's revenues.

BEKINS HOLDING CORP.

330 S. Mannheim Rd.
Hillside IL 60162
Phone: 708-547-2000
Fax: 708-547-3228
Web: www.bekins.com

CEO: Michael Petersen
CFO: William Kelly
HR: –
FYE: December 31
Type: Private

Bekins would like to be a beacon of help to families and businesses on the move. Through its Bekins Van Lines subsidiary and its 300 US locations the company provides household and corporate relocation services in North America as well as tradeshow logistics services and transportation of high-value items. In addition Bekins handles international moves through a network of partners around the world; specialties include service to government and military clients. The company is owned by its agents who bought it from former parent GeoLogistics in 2002. Bekins was founded by the Bekins brothers — John and Martin — in 1891.

BEL FUSE, INC.

NMS: BELF B

206 Van Vorst Street
Jersey City, NJ 07302
Phone: 201 432-0463
Fax: –
Web: www.belfuse.com

CEO: Daniel (Dan) Bernstein
CFO: –
HR: –
FYE: December 31
Type: Public

Bel Fuse manufactures electronic components for networking telecommunications high-speed data transmission and automotive and consumer electronics. Its magnetic products include discrete components power transformers and MagJack connector modules. It also offers power conversion modules for a variety of applications. Bel Fuse's miniature micro and surface-mounted fuses create supplementary circuit protection for consumer electronics. The company also makes passive jacks plugs and cable assemblies. Top customers include Hon Hai (14% of sales) and Flextronics (10% of sales).

	Annual Growth	12/10	12/11	12/12	12/13	12/14
Sales ($ mil.)	12.6%	302.5	295.1	286.6	349.2	487.1
Net income ($ mil.)	(9.7%)	13.6	3.8	2.4	15.9	9.1
Market value ($ mil.)	3.4%	283.5	222.4	231.9	252.8	324.3
Employees	18.5%	4,161	3,451	4,166	6,370	8,210

BELCAN CORPORATION

10200 ANDERSON WAY
BLUE ASH, OH 45242-4718
Phone: 513-891-0972
Fax: –
Web: www.belcan.com

CEO: Lance Kwasneiwski
CFO: Michael Wirth
HR: –
FYE: December 31
Type: Private

Belcan provides engineering technical recruiting and staffing services to clients in the aviation consumer products and manufacturing industries among others. Its Belcan Engineering division offers design engineering engineering analysis and computer modeling to customers such as Lockheed Martin and UTC. The company also offers recruiting services — including interviewing screening and workforce management — to fill openings for highly skilled technical personnel through Belcan TechServices. BelFlex Staffing Network supplies light industrial and clerical employees to clients. Family-owned Belcan founded in 1958 by Ralph Anderson operates some 70 offices primarily in the US.

	Annual Growth	12/08	12/09	12/10	12/11	12/12
Sales ($ mil.)	15.0%	–	452.8	538.7	623.5	688.7
Net income ($ mil.)	117.6%	–	1.9	13.5	22.9	19.3
Market value ($ mil.)	–	–	–	–	–	–
Employees	–	–	–	–	–	10,000

BELDEN & BLAKE CORPORATION

1001 Fannin St. Ste. 800
Houston TX 77002
Phone: 713-659-3500
Fax: 310-826-6139
Web: www.cytrx.com

CEO: Mark A Houser
CFO: James M Vanderhider
HR: –
FYE: December 31
Type: Private

It may sound like a law firm but Belden & Blake is in fact an energy company that obeys the laws of supply and demand in the oil and gas market. It acquires properties explores for and develops oil and gas reserves and gathers and markets natural gas in the Appalachian and Michigan basins. In 2010 Belden & Blake reported interests in 1216 gross wells and leases on more than 1.1 million gross acres and it owned and operated 1600 miles of gas gathering lines. That year the company reported estimated proved reserves of 202.4 billion cu. ft. of gas equivalent. Belden & Blake is controlled by Capital C Energy Operations itself controlled by EnerVest Ltd.

BELDEN INC

NYS: BDC

1 North Brentwood Boulevard, 15th Floor
St. Louis, MO 63105
Phone: 314 854-8000
Fax: 314 854-8001
Web: www.belden.com

CEO: John S. Stroup
CFO: Henk Derksen
HR: Ralf Stuerzel
FYE: December 31
Type: Public

Can you hear me now? If not Belden can help. The company designs and manufactures cable connectivity and networking products that make possible the transmission of data sound and video signals. Offerings include copper cables (shielded/unshielded twisted coaxial and stranded) and fiber optic and composite cables (multiconductor coaxial and fiber optic). It also makes fiber and copper connectors and networking products such as Ethernet switches. Products are used in industrial (robotics) enterprise broadcast and consumer electronics applications. The majority of customers are from outside of the US.

	Annual Growth	12/10	12/11	12/12	12/13	12/14
Sales ($ mil.)	9.3%	1,617.1	1,982.0	1,840.7	2,069.2	2,308.3
Net income ($ mil.)	(9.0%)	108.5	114.3	194.5	103.3	74.4
Market value ($ mil.)	21.0%	1,563.5	1,413.2	1,910.5	2,991.6	3,346.6
Employees	3.7%	7,450	7,500	7,000	7,600	8,600

BELFOR USA GROUP INC.

185 Oakland Ave. Ste. 300
Birmingham MI 48009
Phone: 248-594-1144
Fax: 248-594-3190
Web: www.us.belfor.com

CEO: Sheldon Yellen
CFO: Joe Ciolino
HR: –
FYE: December 31
Type: Subsidiary

When bad things happen BELFOR USA steps in to clean up and repair the damage. The company provides disaster recovery and property restoration services to businesses and residences through some 80 offices across the US. Services include reconstruction drying fire storm and water damage restoration emergency power mold remediation semiconductor services and data recovery. Subsidiary DUCTZ International provides air duct cleaning and HVAC restoration services. Additionally BELFOR USA provides consulting and pre-planning services to help minimize potential problems its clients might encounter. Founded in 1995 BELFOR USA is part of global group Belfor International.

BELK INC (DE)

OTC: BLKI B

2801 West Tyvola Road
Charlotte, NC 28217-4500
Phone: 704 357-1000
Fax: –
Web: www.belk.com

CEO: Thomas M Belk Jr
CFO: Adam M Orvos
HR: –
FYE: February 01
Type: Public

Belk is busy bulking up. Already the nation's largest family owned and operated department store chain Belk operates about 300 stores in more than 15 states following its purchase of the Parisian chain from Saks. Previously Belk acquired Saks' McRae's and Proffitt's divisions. Belk stores are located primarily in the southeastern US and offer mid-priced brand-name and private-label apparel shoes jewelry cosmetics gifts and home furnishings. Its stores usually anchor malls or shopping centers in small to midsized markets and target 35- to 54-year-old middle- and upper-income women. Founded in 1888 by William Henry Belk the chain is run by chairman and CEO Thomas Belk.

	Annual Growth	01/10	01/11	01/12*	02/13	02/14
Sales ($ mil.)	4.8%	3,346.3	3,513.3	3,699.6	3,956.9	4,038.1
Net income ($ mil.)	24.0%	67.1	127.6	183.1	188.4	158.5
Market value ($ mil.)	36.1%	656.3	1,004.3	1,242.0	1,602.7	2,253.7
Employees	0.8%	23,880	24,000	23,000	23,800	24,700

*Fiscal year change

BELKIN INTERNATIONAL INC.

12045 E. Waterfront Dr.
Playa Vista CA 90094
Phone: 310-751-5100
Fax: 281-933-0044
Web: www.rose.com

CEO: Chester J Pipkin
CFO: –
HR: –
FYE: December 31
Type: Private

Got a gadget? There's a good chance it's attached to an accessory from Belkin. The company makes a variety of products for Apple's iPod iPhone and iPad as well as eReaders laptops netbooks and TVs. A leading manufacturer of Universal Serial Bus (USB) devices such as networking hubs Belkin also provides media player accessories surge protectors and battery backups. Other products include fiber optic cables router pickers and home theater networking gear. For commercial and government customers Belkin provides security infrastructure and server-room products that include Keyboard-Video-Mouse (KVM) switches rackmount consoles and converters and adaptors. Founder and CEO Chet Pipkin owns Belkin.

BELL HELICOPTER TEXTRON INC.

600 E. Hurst Blvd.
Hurst TX 76053
Phone: 817-280-2011
Fax: 817-280-2321
Web: www.bellhelicopter.com

CEO: John L Garrison Jr
CFO: –
HR: –
FYE: December 31
Type: Subsidiary

Bell Helicopter a Textron company prefers a light lift and a heavy payload. It is a leading manufacturer of commercial helicopters manned and unmanned vertical lift aircraft and military tiltrotor aircraft which lift like a helicopter but fly like an airplane with twice the speed and triple the payload as a traditional helicopter. Different models are suited for transporting troops emergency medical provisioning search and rescue and warfighting. With partner Boeing Bell produces the V-22 Osprey tiltrotor aircraft for the US Department of Defense. Bell also provides training and maintenance repair and overhaul (MRO) services. It maintains operations in North America Europe and Asia.

BELL PARTNERS INC.

300 N. Greene St. Ste. 1000
Greensboro NC 27401
Phone: 336-232-1999
Fax: 336-232-1901
Web: www.bellpartnersinc.com

CEO: Steven D Bell
CFO: John E Tomlinson
HR: –
FYE: December 31
Type: Private

If someone's ringing you up about a real estate deal it might be Bell Partners. The privately-held firm buys sells and manages multi-family residential and commercial real estate. It invests on behalf of individuals and institutional investors. Bell Partners' $5 billion portfolio includes about 200 apartment communities with nearly 60000 individual units; 30 commercial properties with more than 4 million sq. ft. of space; and more than 25 senior housing communities. Bell Partners targets markets in nearly 110 cities throughout the Northeast Southeast and Southwest. The company also offers property management services. CEO Steven D. Bell founded the company in 1976.

BELOIT COLLEGE

700 COLLEGE ST
BELOIT, WI 535115595
Phone: 608-363-2000
Fax: –
Web: www.campus.beloit.edu

CEO: –
CFO: –
HR: –
FYE: May 31
Type: Private

Beloit College home of the famed Beloit Poetry Journal is a liberal arts and sciences college with an enrollment of about 1300 students. The school offers more than 50 majors in nearly 30 departments and has some 100 full-time faculty members. Academic fields include anthropology health and society and philosophy. Beloit College also offers pre-professional programs in medicine law engineering and environmental management. The town of Beloit (population 36500) is home to a Frito-Lay cheese powder plant and incoming freshman are warned about the "cheese breeze" prevalent in winter months.

	Annual Growth	05/08	05/09	05/10	05/11	05/13
Sales ($ mil.)	3.5%	–	59.4	69.6	68.9	68.2
Net income ($ mil.)	–	–	–	1.8	0.9	(3.8)
Market value ($ mil.)	–	–	–	–	–	–
Employees	–	–	–	–	–	450

BELOIT HEALTH SYSTEM INC.

1969 W HART RD
BELOIT, WI 535112298
Phone: 608-364-5011
Fax: –
Web: www.beloithealthsystem.org

CEO: Gregory Britton
CFO: –
HR: –
FYE: December 31
Type: Private

Beloit Wisconsin: Home of the world's largest can of chili the Beloit Snappers and... Beloit Health System. Its Beloit Memorial Hospital acute care facility provides medical care to the city's residents and surrounding areas. Specialty services include emergency medicine cardiology home care and occupational health. Its NorthPointe integrative medicine campus provides traditional and alternative medical approaches including massage Tai Chi and yoga. Beloit Health also provides primary care and specialized services through numerous outreach medical centers and operates an assisted living complex called Riverside Terrace. Beloit Health is affiliated with the University of Wisconsin Hospital and Clinics.

	Annual Growth	12/08	12/09	12/10	12/11	12/12
Sales ($ mil.)	3.3%	–	–	–	187.1	193.3
Net income ($ mil.)	–	–	–	–	(1.6)	7.6
Market value ($ mil.)	–	–	–	–	–	–
Employees	–	–	–	–	–	1,400

BEMIS CO INC

One Neenah Center, 4th Floor, P.O. Box 669
Neenah, WI 54957-0669
Phone: 920 527-5000
Fax: –
Web: www.bemis.com

NYS: BMS
CEO: William F. Austen
CFO: Michael B. Clauer
HR: Timothy S. Fliss
FYE: December 31
Type: Public

Thanks to companies like Bemis delicacies such as potato chips and snack cakes have a longer shelf life than most marriages. Bemis makes a broad line of flexible packaging materials including polymer films barrier laminates and paper-bag packaging used by the food industry to bundle a diversity of edibles. Flexible packaging accounts for about 90% of sales. In addition to the food industry the company sells to the agricultural chemical medical personal care and printing industries. Bemis has sales offices and plants spanning North America Latin America Europe and the Asia/Pacific to serve its 30000 customers.

	Annual Growth	12/10	12/11	12/12	12/13	12/14
Sales ($ mil.)	(2.6%)	4,835.0	5,322.7	5,139.2	5,029.8	4,343.5
Net income ($ mil.)	(1.8%)	205.1	184.1	173.8	212.6	191.1
Market value ($ mil.)	8.5%	3,207.2	2,953.9	3,285.8	4,022.3	4,439.6
Employees	(3.7%)	19,796	20,000	19,600	19,106	17,000

BENCHMARK ELECTRONICS, INC.

3000 Technology Drive
Angleton, TX 77515
Phone: 979 849-6550
Fax: –
Web: www.bench.com

NYS: BHE
CEO: Gayla J. Delly
CFO: Donald F. (Don) Adam
HR: Daniel (Dan) Shane
FYE: December 31
Type: Public

Benchmark Electronics is setting a benchmark for electronics manufacturing services (EMS) in the US. The company which provides contract manufacturing services to electronics makers produces complex printed circuit boards and related electronics systems and subsystems. Customers include manufacturers of computers industrial control equipment medical devices telecommunications systems and test and measurement instruments. Benchmark also offers design direct order fulfillment distribution engineering materials management and testing services. The company has operations in eight countries but derives almost three-quarters of its sales from customers in the Americas.

	Annual Growth	12/10	12/11	12/12	12/13	12/14
Sales ($ mil.)	3.9%	2,402.1	2,253.0	2,468.2	2,506.5	2,797.1
Net income ($ mil.)	0.4%	81.0	52.0	56.6	111.2	82.4
Market value ($ mil.)	8.8%	962.4	713.8	880.8	1,223.1	1,348.2
Employees	2.3%	9,990	9,985	9,949	11,023	10,940

BENCO DENTAL SUPPLY CO.

295 CENTERPOINT BLVD
PITTSTON, PA 186406136
Phone: 800-462-3626
Fax: –
Web: www.benco.com

CEO: –
CFO: –
HR: –
FYE: January 04
Type: Private

Benco Dental Supply is a one-stop shop for the tooth doc. Through regional showrooms and distribution centers Benco provides dental and dentistry supplies to more than 30000 dental professionals throughout the US. Its offerings include dental hand pieces furniture and disposable supplies. Its BencoNET division develops and distributes custom computers and proprietary programming and networking systems for dentists. Other services include dental office design practice consulting financing and real estate planning wealth management and equipment repairs.

	Annual Growth	12/05	12/06	12/07	12/12*	01/14
Sales ($ mil.)	7.6%	–	344.1	389.2	600.8	620.4
Net income ($ mil.)	8.5%	–	–	5.0	7.4	8.9
Market value ($ mil.)	–	–	–	–	–	–
Employees	–	–	–	–	–	1,120

*Fiscal year change

BENDERSON DEVELOPMENT COMPANY LLC

8441 Cooper Creek Blvd.
University Park FL 34201
Phone: 941-359-8303
Fax: 941-359-1836
Web: www.benderson.com

CEO: –
CFO: –
HR: –
FYE: March 31
Type: Private

Benderson Development could probably bend your ear about its real estate portfolio. It develops manages and leases more than 250 properties including shopping centers residential communities industrial properties hotels office buildings self-storage facilities and mixed-use projects throughout the US. About a quarter of its portfolio is in Florida. The company which has more than 25 million sq. ft. of leasable space and more than 4 million sq. ft. of space under development also does business through subsidiaries Buffalo Lodging Associates and Kings Gate Homes. Its construction division designs and manages projects. CEO Nate Benderson founded the firm which he and his family control.

BENEDICT COLLEGE

1600 HARDEN ST
COLUMBIA, SC 292041086
Phone: 803-256-4220
Fax: –
Web: www.benedict.edu

CEO: –
CFO: –
HR: –
FYE: June 30
Type: Private

Benedict College is a private Baptist-affiliated liberal arts college in an urban environment. It has an annual enrollment of about 3140 students from across the US and abroad and its student-faculty ratio is 18:1. Students may choose from 29 majors offered through a dozen academic departments including business education social sciences technology and more. Benedict College is also part of the NCAA II athletic conference. The historically black school began in 1870 when the American Baptist Home Mission Society created Benedict Institute setting as its goal to train emancipated slaves to teach and preach. The school name was changed to Benedict College in 1894.

	Annual Growth	06/09	06/10	06/11	06/12	06/13
Sales ($ mil.)	0.6%	–	61.4	83.2	69.6	62.6
Net income ($ mil.)	–	–	–	7.2	2.6	(0.3)
Market value ($ mil.)	–	–	–	–	–	–
Employees	–	–	–	–	–	600

BENEDICTINE COLLEGE

1020 N 2ND ST
ATCHISON, KS 660021499
Phone: 913-367-5340
Fax: –
Web: www.benedictine-college.learnhub.com

CEO: –
CFO: –
HR: –
FYE: June 30
Type: Private

Benedictine College is a Roman Catholic liberal arts school that provides instruction to nearly 1200 students. It offers bachelor's degrees in nearly 40 major fields as well as three graduate degree programs. The school's Atchison Kansas campus overlooks the Missouri River. The college which opened its doors in 1859 is sponsored by brothers and sisters of the Benedictine monastic order.

	Annual Growth	06/08	06/09	06/10	06/11	06/13
Sales ($ mil.)	–	–	0.0	50.4	53.0	57.3
Net income ($ mil.)	–	–	–	9.4	8.4	(0.3)
Market value ($ mil.)	–	–	–	–	–	–
Employees	–	–	–	–	–	184

BENEDICTINE HEALTH SYSTEM

503 E. 3rd St. Ste. 400
Duluth MN 55805
Phone: 218-786-2370
Fax: 218-786-2373
Web: www.bhshealth.org

CEO: Dale Thompson
CFO: –
HR: –
FYE: June 30
Type: Private

You don't have to be a postulant to enter this Benedictine organization. The Benedictine Health System (BHS) is a provider of senior care services across the Midwest. The health system mostly serves rural and smaller communities in seven states. It owns or operates about 40 long-term care facilities including nursing homes assisted-living centers and independent senior housing developments. Other offerings include adult day-care transitional care and outpatient rehabilitation. Many of its facilities are integrated campuses that provide a spectrum of services. BHS was founded in 1892 and took its present form in 1985. It is sponsored by the Benedictine Sisters of St. Scholastica Monastery.

BENEFICIAL LIFE INSURANCE COMPANY

36 S. State St.
Salt Lake City UT 84136
Phone: 801-933-1100
Fax: 801-521-0903
Web: www.beneficialfinancialgroup.com/

CEO: Kent Cannon
CFO: –
HR: –
FYE: December 31
Type: Subsidiary

Beneficial Life Insurance (doing business as Beneficial Financial Group) provides a variety of insurance and financial products and services primarily to customers in the western US. Its financial division Beneficial Investment Services offers brokerage and investment advisory services. Previously the company offered universal and whole life disability insurance employee benefits and annuities. However in 2009 the company quit selling new insurance and annuities and placed its existing business in run-off. Beneficial Financial was founded in 1905 and is owned by Mormon Church-affiliated Deseret Management Corporation.

BENEFICIAL MUTUAL BANCORP INC

NMS: BNCL

510 Walnut Street
Philadelphia, PA 19106
Phone: 215 864-6000
Fax: 215 864-1770
Web: www.thebeneficial.com

CEO: Gerard P Cuddy
CFO: Thomas D Cestare
HR: –
FYE: December 31
Type: Public

You would expect something beneficial from the city of brotherly love. Beneficial Mutual Bancorp is the holding company for Beneficial Bank which serves the greater Philadelphia area and southern New Jersey through about 65 branches. Founded in 1853 as Beneficial Mutual Savings Bank the bank provides traditional deposit products such as checking savings and money market accounts; IRAs; and CDs. Commercial real estate business and construction loans together account for nearly half of the company's loan portfolio; consumer loans (nearly 30%) and residential mortgages (almost 25%) round out its lending activities. The bank is looking to grow its commercial loan portfolio.

	Annual Growth	12/08	12/09	12/10	12/11	12/12
Assets ($ mil.)	5.8%	4,002.1	4,673.7	4,929.8	4,596.1	5,006.4
Net income ($ mil.)	(3.8%)	16.5	17.1	(9.0)	11.0	14.2
Market value ($ mil.)	(4.1%)	892.1	780.3	700.2	662.9	753.3
Employees	(2.6%)	970	965	965	842	874

BENEFIT COSMETICS LLC

685 Market St. 7th Fl.
San Francisco CA 94105
Phone: 415-781-8153
Fax: 415-781-3930
Web: www.benefitcosmetics.com

CEO: Jean Andre Rougeot
CFO: Lori Smolinski
HR: –
FYE: December 31
Type: Subsidiary

BeneFit Cosmetics will make you look lovely and for a good cause. The company which donates a portion of proceeds to charity boasts products that have clever names and pin-up lasses on nearly every package. BeneFit sells its lines and offers facial services through more than 2000 counters (called "Beauty Bars") in department stores and beauty specialty shops in nearly 40 countries worldwide. It also has more than a dozen dedicated boutiques. BeneFit Cosmetics whose celebrity-endorsed Benetint product brought the fledgling company into the mainstream was founded in 1976 in San Francisco by sisters Jean Ann and Jane Ann Ford as The Face Place. Glamour leviathan LVMH holds a 70% stake.

BENEFIT SOFTWARE INC.

212 Cottage Grove Ave. Ste. A
Santa Barbara CA 93101
Phone: 805-568-0240
Fax: 805-568-0239
Web: www.bsiweb.com

CEO: -
CFO: -
HR: -
FYE: December 31
Type: Private

The benefits of Benefit Software's products are clear to human resources managers. Founded in 1978 Benefit Software provides employee benefit communications and workers' compensation case management software for businesses. The company's Fringe Facts Communicator software enables human resources departments to produce personalized employee benefits statements that summarize and explain employer-paid benefits. Its CompWatch software helps employers lower their workers' compensation costs by more efficiently managing their claims and cases. Benefit Software also offers Fringe Facts Online a hosted application for Internet-based employee benefits program communications.

BENEFITMALL INC.

4851 LBJ Fwy. Ste. 100
Dallas TX 75244
Phone: 469-791-3300
Fax: 469-791-3313
Web: www.benefitmall.com

CEO: -
CFO: -
HR: -
FYE: December 31
Type: Private

Only in insurance would you find a middle man poised to serve the middle men. Such is the business of BenefitMall an online exchange for insurance brokers who sell employee benefits to small businesses. As one of the largest general agencies in the US the company offers access to thousands of employee benefits plans from more than 125 insurance carriers. Its services are free to brokers as carriers pay to be represented. Insurance brokers use the nationwide service to get real-time quotes online and from sales and support offices in about a dozen states. Management bought the company from investors in 2006 and in 2012 privately held payroll company CompuPay Inc. merged with BenefitMall.

BENIHANA INC.

8685 NW 53rd Terrace
Miami FL 33166
Phone: 305-593-0770
Fax: 305-592-6371
Web: www.benihana.com

NASDAQ: BNHN
CEO: Steve Shlemon
CFO: J David Flanery
HR: Maria Gutierrez
FYE: March 31
Type: Public

The main course at Benihana comes with an appetizer of culinary entertainment. A leader in full-service restaurants the company's flagship chain of teppanyaki-style Asian restaurants offers a dining experience that features wisecracking fast-chopping chefs who prepare the meals on a grill that is part of the table. Benihana owns and operates about 60 Benihana and Benihana Grill locations in more than 20 states and it has around 20 franchised restaurants in a dozen other countries. The company also operates more than 30 other restaurants doing business under the names Haru and RA Sushi. In mid-2012 Benihana was acquired by private equity group Angelo Gordon & Co. for about $296 million.

BENJAMIN MOORE & CO.

101 Paragon Dr.
Montvale NJ 07645
Phone: 201-573-9600
Fax: 201-573-0046
Web: www.benjaminmoore.com

CEO: Michael Searles
CFO: -
HR: Sylvie Drouin
FYE: December 31
Type: Subsidiary

Not only can you paint the town red (or any other color) with Benjamin Moore paints you can stain and finish it as well. The company is a leading formulator manufacturer and retailer of a broad range of architectural coatings. In addition to ready-mixed colors — sold under such brands as Benjamin Moore Paints Moorcraft and Coronado Paint — the company can match almost any shade with roughly 3300 colors. Benjamin Moore (a subsidiary of Warren Buffett's Berkshire Hathaway) also makes industrial coatings and coatings for manufacturers of furniture and roof decking.

BENTLEY SYSTEMS INCORPORATED

685 Stockton Dr.
Exton PA 19341-0678
Phone: 610-458-5000
Fax: +886-3-579-2668
Web: www.winbond.com

CEO: Gregory Bentley
CFO: Paul Lamparski
HR: -
FYE: May 31
Type: Private

Bentley Systems wants to be the premier ride for infrastructure engineers. The company's computer-aided design (CAD) software is used to design and build large-scale infrastructure projects such as airports transit and utilities systems manufacturing plants and buildings. Available on both a subscription basis (nearly three quarters of revenue) and as a perpetual license Bentley's software lets architects engineers builders and property owners collaborate over the Web to develop and maintain projects. The company also offers content management applications as well as consulting integration and training. It largely serves the architecture construction engineering and utilities industries.

BENTLEY UNIVERSITY

175 FOREST ST
WALTHAM, MA 024524713
Phone: 781-891-2000
Fax: -

CEO: -
CFO: Paul Clemente
HR: -
FYE: June 30
Type: Private

Bentley University is not the Rolls-Royce of universities but is fairly prestigious nevertheless. It offers undergraduate graduate and doctoral degree programs to its nearly 5670 enrolled students from 82 countries. The university also offers professional development and certificate programs for executives and corporations. The focus at Bentley is on business; the school was a pioneer in integrating information technology into the business curriculum. In the belief that businesspeople need a broad education Bentley requires a liberal arts core of classes in behavioral and social sciences English and other subjects in the humanities as well as math and natural sciences.

	Annual Growth	06/10	06/11	06/12	06/13	06/14
Sales ($ mil.)	3.3%	-	183.4	185.3	192.7	202.4
Net income ($ mil.)	-	-	-	(21.0)	40.5	48.0
Market value ($ mil.)	-	-	-	-	-	-
Employees	-	-	-	-	-	911

BEREA COLLEGE

101 CHESTNUT ST STE 220
BEREA, KY 40403-1516
Phone: 859-985-3000
Fax: -
Web: www.berea.edu

CEO: -
CFO: -
HR: -
FYE: June 30
Type: Private

Berea College is a Christian school that provides a private tuition-free liberal arts education to about 1600 students each year most of whom come from Kentucky and the Appalachian region. In lieu of tuition Berea has a work program that requires its students to work in on-campus jobs for at least 10 hours each week in their choice of some 130 different departments. Berea offers about 30 majors leading to Bachelor of Arts and Bachelor of Science degrees and each student is required to attend seven convocations (guest lectures concerts or other cultural events) each term. It also offers 15 teacher education programs.

	Annual Growth	06/09	06/10	06/10	06/12	06/13
Sales ($ mil.)	8.8%	-	77.5	79.1	81.8	99.9
Net income ($ mil.)	10.3%	-	65.7	148.7	(30.2)	88.1
Market value ($ mil.)	-	-	-	-	-	-
Employees	-	-	-	-	-	550

BERGELECTRIC CORP.

5650 W CENTINELA AVE
LOS ANGELES, CA 900451501
Phone: 310-337-1377
Fax: -
Web: www.bergelectric.com

CEO: William Wingrning
CFO: -
HR: -
FYE: January 31
Type: Private

One of the nation's top electrical contractors Bergelectric provides design/build and design/assist services on projects that include office buildings public-sector facilities bioscience labs entertainment complexes hotels data centers and hospitals. Its projects also consist of parking garages water treatment plants residential towers and correctional facilities. The company boasts expertise in building information modeling fire alarms and security and telecommunications and data infrastructure. Bergelectric operates mainly in the western and southeastern US from about a dozen offices.

	Annual Growth	01/10	01/11	01/12	01/13	01/14
Sales ($ mil.)	9.2%	-	403.5	394.4	478.6	525.2
Net income ($ mil.)	(54.2%)	-	-	23.8	3.0	5.0
Market value ($ mil.)	-	-	-	-	-	-
Employees	-	-	-	-	-	2,100

BERGEN REGIONAL MEDICAL CENTER L.P.

230 E RIDGEWOOD AVE
PARAMUS, NJ 076524142
Phone: 201-967-4000
Fax: -
Web: www.bergenregional.com

CEO: -
CFO: Connie Magdangal
HR: Laruen Scutari
FYE: December 31
Type: Private

Bergen Regional Medical Center (BRMC) is not just the biggest hospital in Paramus New Jersey — it's one of the biggest in the state. BRMC provides acute care long-term care and behavioral health care services to the residents of northeastern New Jersey. The not-for-profit medical center with approximately 1190 beds also offers specialized services including orthopedics cardiology neurology emergency medicine and surgery as well as substance abuse treatment and hospice services. About half of the facility is devoted to long-term nursing care; and about 325 beds serve behavioral health patients.

	Annual Growth	12/05	12/06	12/07	12/08	12/12
Sales ($ mil.)	7.8%	-	-	-	146.2	197.8
Net income ($ mil.)	-	-	-	-	(78.9)	(1.2)
Market value ($ mil.)	-	-	-	-	-	-
Employees	-	-	-	-	-	1,856

BERKELEY FARMS LLC

25500 Clawiter Rd.
Hayward CA 94545
Phone: 510-265-8600
Fax: 510-265-8754
Web: www.berkeleyfarms.com

CEO: -
CFO: -
HR: Marcy Davis
FYE: December 31
Type: Subsidiary

Founded in 1910 California's oldest continuously operating milk processor Berkeley Farms "mooved" right in. The company produces milk ice cream and other dairy products that are sold in northern and central California. Berkeley Farms is one of the largest producers of bovine growth hormone (BGH)-free milk on the West Coast. Its other products include butter buttermilk eggnog cottage cheese eggs juice and sour and whipping cream. The dairy's foodservice division that along with dairy other products offers a full line of cheeses including mozzarella ricotta Parmesan Cheddar Jack Swiss and American varieties. Berkeley Farms is a subsidiary of US dairy giant Dean Foods.

BERKLEE COLLEGE OF MUSIC INC.

1140 BOYLSTON ST
BOSTON, MA 022153693
Phone: 617-266-1400
Fax: -
Web: www.berklee.edu

CEO: -
CFO: Richard M. Hisey
HR: -
FYE: May 31
Type: Private

If you get accepted to this school you've no doubt hit a high note in your musical career. Berklee College of Music the largest independent music college in the world offers bachelor's degrees in a dozen majors including film scoring jazz composition music education music production and engineering performance and songwriting. Located in Boston the school has some 4000 students and 522 faculty members. Notable alumni include Branford Marsalis Quincy Jones Melissa Etheridge and Steely Dan vocalist Donald Fagen. Pianist Lawrence Berk founded the college in 1945. The school was named after his son Lee Berk who served as Berklee president from 1979 to 2004.

	Annual Growth	05/06	05/07	05/09	05/11	05/13
Sales ($ mil.)	10.0%	-	127.7	171.2	220.8	226.0
Net income ($ mil.)	-	-	-	0.0	21.1	11.9
Market value ($ mil.)	-	-	-	-	-	-
Employees	-	-	-	-	-	-

BERKLEY (W. R.) CORP.

NYS: WRB

475 Steamboat Road
Greenwich, CT 06830
Phone: 203 629-3000
Fax: 203 629-3492
Web: www.wrberkley.com

CEO: W. Robert (Rob) Berkley
CFO: Eugene G. Ballard
HR: Jan Whiting
FYE: December 31
Type: Public

W. R. Berkley is a holding company with a full basket. The firm offers an assortment of commercial property/casualty insurance across three segments. Its domestic insurance segment underwrites complex third-party liability risks professional liability and commercial transportation insurance for small to midsized business customers and state and local governments. It also develops self-insuring programs aimed at employers and employer groups. International insurance offers the same services to customers in 60 countries in Europe the Americas Scandinavia and Australia. Its reinsurance unit allows insurance companies in the US Europe and Asia/Pacific region to pool their risks in order to reduce their liability.

	Annual Growth	12/10	12/11	12/12	12/13	12/14
Assets ($ mil.)	5.5%	17,528.5	18,487.7	20,155.9	20,551.8	21,716.7
Net income ($ mil.)	9.6%	449.6	394.7	510.6	505.3	649.6
Market value ($ mil.)	17.0%	3,470.4	4,358.9	4,783.5	5,499.6	6,497.1
Employees	4.7%	6,253	6,642	7,412	7,247	7,521

BERKLEY INSURANCE COMPANY

475 Steamboat Rd.
Greenwich CT 06830
Phone: 203-542-3800
Fax: 203-542-3839
Web: www.wrbc.com/index.shtml

CEO: –
CFO: Andrea Kanefsky
HR: –
FYE: December 31
Type: Subsidiary

Berkley Insurance is the principal reinsurance subsidiary of property/casualty insurance firm W. R. Berkley. Its seven affiliated operating companies provide underwriting for specialty lines including professional liability workers' compensation and commercial automobile and trucking; treaty (automatic) and facultative (individual) reinsurance products; and provide specialty insurance through program administrators and managing general underwriters. Underwriting affiliates include BF Re Underwriters Berkley Risk Solutions Facultative ReSources and Signet Star Re. Chairman William Berkley founded parent firm W. R. Berkley in 1967.

BERKSHIRE HEALTH SYSTEMS INC.

725 North St.
Pittsfield MA 01201
Phone: 413-447-2000
Fax: 413-447-2066
Web: www.berkshirehealthsystems.org

CEO: David E Phelps
CFO: Darlene Rodowicz
HR: –
FYE: December 31
Type: Private - Not-for-Pr

Berkshire Health Systems serves the residents of Massachusetts and surrounding regions. The system operates two acute-care hospitals: Berkshire Medical Center with 300 beds and Fairview Hospital with 25 beds. Berkshire Medical Center is a teaching hospital affiliated with the University of Massachusetts' medical school. It also operates the Berkshire Visiting Nurse Association (home health care) a family health center (BMC Hillcrest) and several outpatient clinics and physician practices. In addition affiliate Berkshire Healthcare runs about 20 long-term care facilities in Massachusetts Ohio and Pennsylvania. Not-for-profit Berkshire Health Systems was founded in 1983.

BERKSHIRE BANCORP INC (DE)

NBB: BERK

160 Broadway
New York, NY 10038
Phone: 212 791-5362
Fax: –
Web: www.berkbank.com

CEO: Joseph Fink
CFO: David W Lukens
HR: –
FYE: December 31
Type: Public

While the company is not looking to win a Tony Award for its work it is on Broadway. Headquartered on this famous Manhattan street Berkshire Bancorp is the holding company for The Berkshire Bank which operates about a dozen branches mostly in New York but also in New Jersey. The bank's products and services include individual and business checking and savings accounts money market accounts and CDs. Lending activities consist mostly of non-residential mortgages (about half of the company's total loan portfolio) and one- to four-family real estate loans (about 30%). Through subsidiaries the bank offers title insurance and property investment services.

	Annual Growth	12/10	12/11	12/12	12/13	12/14
Assets ($ mil.)	(1.9%)	829.9	862.1	828.0	773.0	767.2
Net income ($ mil.)	–	(13.5)	49.8	12.4	(2.5)	6.8
Market value ($ mil.)	11.8%	78.4	102.2	118.2	104.8	122.5
Employees	(2.1%)	120	113	115	–	–

BERKSHIRE HILLS BANCORP, INC.

NYS: BHLB

24 North Street
Pittsfield, MA 01201
Phone: 413 443-5601
Fax: –
Web: www.berkshirebank.com

CEO: Michael P. Daly
CFO: Josephine Iannelli
HR: Linda A. Johnston
FYE: December 31
Type: Public

Berkshire Hills Bancorp is the holding company for Berkshire Bank which serves individuals and small businesses through some 60 branches in Massachusetts New York Connecticut and Vermont. Established in 1846 the bank provides standard deposit products such as savings checking and money market accounts CDs and IRAs in addition to credit cards investments private banking wealth management and lending services. Real estate mortgages make up nearly three-quarters of Berkshire Hills Bancorp's loan portfolio which also includes business and consumer loans. In addition to its banking activities the company also owns insurance agency Berkshire Insurance Group.

	Annual Growth	12/10	12/11	12/12	12/13	12/14
Assets ($ mil.)	22.6%	2,880.7	3,991.2	5,296.8	5,672.8	6,502.0
Net income ($ mil.)	25.2%	13.7	17.6	33.2	41.1	33.7
Market value ($ mil.)	4.8%	556.8	558.8	600.9	686.7	671.4
Employees	16.2%	599	760	1,012	939	1,091

BERKSHIRE HATHAWAY INC.

NYS: BRK B

3555 Farnam Street
Omaha, NE 68131
Phone: 402 346-1400
Fax: –
Web: www.berkshirehathaway.com

CEO: Warren E. Buffett
CFO: Marc D. Hamburg
HR: Jerry Clark
FYE: December 31
Type: Public

Berkshire Hathaway is the holding company where Warren Buffett one of the world's richest men (along with his good friend Bill Gates) spreads his risk by investing in a variety of industries from insurance and utilities to apparel and food and building materials to jewelry and furniture retailers. Its core insurance subsidiaries include GEICO National Indemnity and reinsurance giant General Re. The company's other large holdings include Marmon Group McLane Company MidAmerican Energy and Shaw Industries. Buffett holds more than 20% of Berkshire Hathaway which owns a majority of more than 50 firms in all and has equity stakes in about a dozen others.

	Annual Growth	12/10	12/11	12/12	12/13	12/14
Assets ($ mil.)	9.0%	372,229.0	392,647.0	427,452.0	484,931.0	526,186.0
Net income ($ mil.)	11.3%	12,967.0	10,254.0	14,824.0	19,476.0	19,872.0
Market value ($ mil.)	17.0%	131.6	125.4	147.4	194.8	246.7
Employees	5.0%	260,000	271,000	288,500	32,000	316,000

BERKSHIRE INCOME REALTY INC

ASE: BIR PRA

One Beacon Street
Boston, MA 02108
Phone: 617 523-7722
Fax: –
Web: www.berkshireincomerealty.com

CEO: –
CFO: David E Doherty
HR: –
FYE: December 31
Type: Public

If you enjoy attractive landscaping and swimming pools but can't stand the upkeep and maintenance Berkshire Income Realty might have just the spot for you. The real estate investment trust (REIT) invests and operates apartment communities. It owns more than 25 properties in major cities in Texas Georgia Florida California Oregon North Carolina and Pennsylvania as well as the Washington D.C. metropolitan area. The company (which is controlled by chairman Donald Krupp and his family) often acquires neglected properties and then rehabilitates them. Affiliate Berkshire Property Advisors provides day-to-day management and business operations services to the company.

	Annual Growth	12/09	12/10	12/11	12/12	12/13
Sales ($ mil.)	0.2%	79.5	81.7	84.7	79.0	80.0
Net income ($ mil.)	3.4%	5.9	5.9	6.4	7.0	6.7
Market value ($ mil.)	4.8%	30.9	35.9	36.2	37.1	37.3
Employees		–	–	–	–	–

BERKSHIRE PARTNERS LLC

200 Clarendon St. 35th Fl.　　　　　　　　　　　　CEO: –
Boston MA 02116　　　　　　　　　　　　CFO: Julia Selvig
Phone: 617-227-0050　　　　　　　　　　　　　　　HR: –
Fax: 617-227-6105　　　　　　　　　　　　FYE: December 31
Web: www.berkshirepartners.com　　　　　　　　Type: Private

No not that Berkshire — the other one. Berkshire Partners is a private equity firm that targets established North American and European companies worth $200 million to $2 billion. It targets varied industries including industrial manufacturing consumer products transportation communications business services energy and retailing. An active investor the company usually puts up between $50 million to $500 million per transaction in leveraged buyouts recapitalizations privatizations growth capital investments and special situations. Its Stockbridge affiliate invests in marketable securities to compliment Berkshire Partners' core private equity activities.

BERLIN PACKAGING L.L.C.

525 W. Monroe 14th Fl.　　　　　　　　　　CEO: Andrew T Berlin
Chicago IL 60661　　　　　　　　　　　　CFO: Neil Schwab
Phone: 312-876-9292　　　　　　　　　　　　　　HR: –
Fax: 312-876-9290　　　　　　　　　　　　FYE: December 31
Web: www.berlinpackaging.com　　　　　　　　　Type: Private

Berlin is rigid and closed off but only when it comes to its plastics and lids. Chicago-based Berlin Packaging is a US distributor of rigid packaging such as glass metal and plastic stock bottles and closures dispensing systems and other components used in the personal care chemical food and beverage and pharmaceutical industries. It also offers packaging design inventory management delivery and financing services. Berlin markets and sells its more than 24000 products through its 80 or so sales offices and warehouses in the US and Puerto Rico. Equity group Investcorp owns a majority stake in the company.

BERLITZ LANGUAGES INC.

400 Alexander Park　　　　　　　　　　CEO: Yukako Uchinaga
Princeton NJ 08540-6306　　　　　　　　　　　CFO: –
Phone: 609-514-3400　　　　　　　　　　　　　　HR: –
Fax: 609-514-3405　　　　　　　　　　　　　FYE: March 31
Web: www.berlitz.com　　　　　　　　　　　Type: Subsidiary

Want to speak Dansk Deutsch Espa?ol or Portugues? If so Berlitz can help. Berlitz owns or franchises more than 550 language centers in 70 countries. Founded in 1878 to teach languages through a conversational approach to pleasure travelers Berlitz now serves schools military and government clientele and such corporate clients as Johnson & Johnson Procter & Gamble and ABC News. Besides small-group and one-on-one language courses Berlitz offers study-abroad and cultural-awareness training and online programs for all ages. Japanese education group Benesse Corporation owns parent Berlitz Corporation which it purchased in 2001.

BERNARD CHAUS INC.　　　　　　　　　　　OTC: CHBD

530 7th Ave.　　　　　　　　　　　　CEO: Josephine Chaus
New York NY 10018　　　　　　　　　　CFO: William P Runge
Phone: 212-354-1280　　　　　　　　　　　HR: Courtney Hahn
Fax: 201-863-6307　　　　　　　　　　　　　FYE: June 30
Web: www.bernardchaus.com　　　　　　　　　Type: Private

Bernard Chaus' clothes are made for the days when a woman "has nothing to wear." The company designs and sells upscale women's career and casual sportswear primarily under the Josephine Chaus Chaus Vince Camuto and Cynthia Steffe trademarks. Its jackets skirts pants blouses sweaters dresses and accessories are designed to coordinate by style color and fabric to make dressing for work easier. Manufactured mostly in Asia its apparel is sold in about 4000 US department and specialty stores. The company also makes private-label apparel for others. Widow of founder Bernard Chaus Josephine Chaus is chairwoman and CEO. She owned about 45% of the company before it was taken private in mid-2012.

BERNARD HODES GROUP INC.

220 E. 42nd St.　　　　　　　　　　　　　　　　CEO: –
New York NY 10017-5806　　　　　　　　　　　　CFO: –
Phone: 212-999-9000　　　　　　　　　　　　　　HR: –
Fax: 646-658-0445　　　　　　　　　　　　FYE: December 31
Web: www.hodes.com　　　　　　　　　　　Type: Subsidiary

Bernard Hodes Group helps companies send the right message to potential employees. The marketing communications company provides recruitment marketing response management consulting services and technology to streamline the hiring process. It also assists clients building minority recruitment programs and creating online recruiting strategies. Services include expertise in website design resume mining database creation and job posting strategies. Bernard Hodes has more than 90 offices in the Americas Asia Australasia and Europe. Founded in 1970 by Bernard Hodes the company is a subsidiary of media conglomerate Omnicom.

BERNATELLO"S PIZZA INC

200 CONGRESS ST W　　　　　　　　　　　CEO: William Ramsay
MAPLE LAKE, MN 553583525　　　　　　　　　　　CFO: –
Phone: 320-963-6191　　　　　　　　　　　　　　HR: –
Fax: –　　　　　　　　　　　　　　　　　　　FYE: June 30
Web: www.bernatellos.com　　　　　　　　　　　Type: Private

This company feeds your frozen pizza amore. Bernatello's Pizza is a leading frozen-pizza maker in the US's Northeast Midwest and Rocky Mountain regions marketing its pies under the Bernatello's and Roma brands. Its product line (pumping out 100000 pizzas every day) offers a variety of different pizzas such as pan-style sausage and pepperoni Mexican-style four-cheese half-pounder and thin-and-crispy. The company also produces pizza-related frozen items such as garlic cheese bread mozzarella sticks and jalape?o snappers (Bernie's Bites). In addition Bernatello's provides manufacturing services for private-label customers. The family-owned company is controlled by food-industry veteran Bill Ramsay.

	Annual Growth	06/02	06/03	06/04	06/05	06/07
Sales ($ mil.)	2.7%	–	42.4	40.2	45.7	47.1
Net income ($ mil.)	–	–	–	(0.7)	0.1	(0.0)
Market value ($ mil.)	–	–	–	–	–	–
Employees	–	–	–	–	–	220

BERNER FOOD & BEVERAGE INC.

2034 E FACTORY RD
DAKOTA, IL 610189736
Phone: 815-563-4222
Fax: –
Web: www.bernerfoods.com

CEO: Stephen A Kneubuehl
CFO: Bill Marchido
HR: –
FYE: September 30
Type: Private

Berner Food & Beverage is burning up with dairy fever. The company is a producer of natural cheese (Swiss cheddar American) processed cheese (shelf-stable dips spreads aerosols and jars) and salsa con queso sauce well as energy coffee and specialty beverages. Berner contract-manufactures products for private-label customers including supermarkets drug stores club membership and dollar stores food distributors and foodservice companies. It also sells products under its own Berner labels. The company was founded in 1943 by the Kneubuehl family. It is still owned and operated by the family.

	Annual Growth	12/06	12/07	12/08*	09/12	09/14
Sales ($ mil.)	12.9%	–	–	65.4	74.8	135.5
Net income ($ mil.)	–	–	–	(1.3)	3.2	6.0
Market value ($ mil.)	–	–	–	–	–	–
Employees	–	–	–	–	–	300

*Fiscal year change

BERRY COMPANIES INC.

3223 N HYDRAULIC ST
WICHITA, KS 672193893
Phone: 316-838-3321
Fax: –
Web: www.berrycompaniesinc.com

CEO: –
CFO: –
HR: –
FYE: March 31
Type: Private

Savoring the fruit of its labor Berry Companies makes a living bulldozing big jobs. The employee-owned business runs eight divisions; each independently sells and rents new and used construction and material handling equipment. Berry Cos. specialize in graders tractors loaders excavators cranes rollers construction and woodworking supplies concrete equipment and small tools. The company's five distribution dealerships include White Star Machinery (Kansas); Bobcat of Dallas and Houston (Texas); K.C. Bobcat (Missouri); and Bobcat of the Rockies (Colorado). Berry Cos. also operates Berry Tractor and Equipment Berry Material Handling and Superior Broom (makes self-propelled road construction brooms).

	Annual Growth	03/06	03/07	03/08	03/09	03/13
Sales ($ mil.)	–	–	–	(1,240.6)	203.6	178.6	229.4
Net income ($ mil.)	6.4%	–	–	–	2.6	0.6	3.5
Market value ($ mil.)	–	–	–	–	–	–
Employees	–	–	–	–	–	520

BERRY PLASTICS GROUP INC

101 Oakley Street
Evansville, IN 47710
Phone: 812 424-2904
Fax: –
Web: www.berryplastics.com

NYS: BERY
CEO: Jonathan D. (Jon) Rich
CFO: Mark W. Miles
HR: Ed Stratton
FYE: September 26
Type: Public

When it comes to selling plastic products Berry Plastics practically buries the competition. The company is a leading maker of injection-molded plastic products. Its lineup includes drink cups bottles closures tubes and prescription containers stretch films plastic sheeting tapes and housewares. Customers include the health care personal care food and beverage agricultural industrial construction aerospace and automotive industries. The company has about 70 manufacturing facilities in North America Europe the Middle East and Asia as well as extensive distribution capabilities.

	Annual Growth	10/11*	09/12	09/13	09/14	09/15
Sales ($ mil.)	1.7%	4,561.0	4,766.0	4,647.0	4,958.0	4,881.0
Net income ($ mil.)	–	(299.0)	2.0	57.0	62.0	86.0
Market value ($ mil.)	21.6%	–	–	2,455.6	2,962.7	3,631.8
Employees	1.6%	15,000	15,000	15,000	16,000	16,000

*Fiscal year change

BERTUCCI'S CORPORATION

155 Otis St.
Northborough MA 01532
Phone: 508-351-2500
Fax: 508-393-8046
Web: www.bertuccis.com

CEO: David Lloyd
CFO: Brian P Connell
HR: –
FYE: December 31
Type: Private

New Englanders in need of a taste of Italy can turn to Bertucci's. The company owns and operates more than 90 casual-dining establishments operating under the Bertucci's Italian Restaurant banner. The restaurants located in about 10 states primarily in the Northeast feature a wide array of Tuscan-style dishes including pasta chicken and seafood dishes as well as appetizers and desserts. Bertucci's also offers a variety of premium brick oven pizzas available with a number of different topping combinations. Chairman Benjamin Jacobson controls the company through his Jacobson Partners holding company. The first Bertucci's opened in 1981.

BEST BRANDS CORP.

111 Cheshire Ln. Ste. 100
Minnetonka MN 55305
Phone: 952-404-7500
Fax: 952-404-7501
Web: www.bestbrandscorp.com

CEO: Scott Humphrey
CFO: Michael Skillingstad
HR: –
FYE: December 31
Type: Subsidiary

Best Brands believes it can be the best in the baking industry. The company makes an oven full of fillings frozen doughs and batters icings and baked goods such as cakes cookies muffins croissants puff pastry and baking ingredients — more than 1000 different products. Under the Multifoods Bakery Products brand it produces muffins and baking mixes; the Telco Food Products brand offers retail-ready brownies and Bundt and loaf cakes; and its Fantasia brands makes chocolate desserts. Best Brands has customers in the retail food foodservice and wholesale food and baking industries across North America. The company was acquired by baking-ingredient giant Netherlands-based CSM in early 2010

BEST BUY INC

7601 Penn Avenue South
Richfield, MN 55423
Phone: 612 291-1000
Fax: –
Web: www.bestbuy.com

NYS: BBY
CEO: Hubert Joly
CFO: Sharon L. McCollam
HR: Shari L. Ballard
FYE: January 31
Type: Public

Best Buy wants to be the best consumer electronics outlet in the US and beyond. The multinational retailer sells both products and services through three primary channels: about 1700 retail stores online and call centers. Its branded store banners include Best Buy Best Buy Express Best Buy Mobile Five Star Future Shop Geek Squad Magnolia Audio Video and Pacific Sales. Its stores sell a variety of electronic gadgets movies music computers mobile phones and appliances. On the services side it offers installation and maintenance technical support and subscriptions for mobile phone and Internet services.

	Annual Growth	02/11*	03/12*	02/13	02/14*	01/15
Sales ($ mil.)	(5.4%)	50,272.0	50,705.0	45,085.0	42,410.0	40,339.0
Net income ($ mil.)	(0.9%)	1,277.0	(1,231.0)	(441.0)	532.0	1,233.0
Market value ($ mil.)	2.1%	11,377.0	8,544.2	5,662.1	8,273.6	12,371.7
Employees	(8.7%)	180,000	167,000	165,000	140,000	125,000

*Fiscal year change

BEST FRIENDS PET CARE INC.

520 Main Ave.
Norwalk CT 06851
Phone: 203-846-3360
Fax: 203-849-1092
Web: www.bestfriendspetcare.com

CEO: John A Heyder
CFO: John Hyder
HR: –
FYE: December 31
Type: Private

Best Friends Pet Care takes care of man's best friend. The company provides pet boarding grooming and day care services through more than 40 locations in about 20 states including California Illinois and Florida. It offers dog and cat grooming and boarding as well as dog training through its Canine College. Doggy Day Camp (daytime dog sitting services) is available at some locations. Best Friends also sells a wide range of pet products (such as dishes carriers collars and treats) and apparel cards and accessories adorned with animal images. The company was founded as Windsor Pet Care in 1991.

BEST MEDICAL INTERNATIONAL INC.

7643 Fullerton Rd.
Springfield VA 22153
Phone: 703-451-2378
Fax: 703-451-0922
Web: www.teambest.com

CEO: –
CFO: –
HR: Helene Brock
FYE: December 31
Type: Private

Best Medical International has set a high standard for the medical equipment it manufactures. The vertically-integrated company has rolled up a collection of businesses in the US and Canada that manufacture and distribute radio-therapy systems and supplies. Its product lines include brachytherapy systems (radioactive seeds implanted to zap tumors) external beam therapy systems blood irradiators and other supporting equipment used to deliver and monitor radiation therapy. Its subsidiaries include Best Cyclotron Systems Best NOMOS Best Theratronics CNMC Huestis Medical and Novoste. The company was founded by its president Krishnan Suthanthiran in 1977.

BEST WESTERN INTERNATIONAL INC.

6201 N 24TH PKWY
PHOENIX, AZ 850162023
Phone: 602-957-4200
Fax: –
Web: www.bestwestern.com

CEO: David T. Kong
CFO: Mark Straszynski
HR: Barbara (Barb) Bras
FYE: November 30
Type: Private

Western hospitality has really spread. Begun in 1946 by hotelier M. K. Guertin and named for its California origins Best Western has more than 4000 independently owned and operated hotels throughout the globe (including nearly 2200 in North America) making it the world's largest hotel brand (by number of rooms). Hotels sport its flag in about 100 countries and territories; Australia and the UK have the most outside the US. The company has more than 80 Best Western Premier luxury branded hotels which offer upscale amenities and services in North America Asia and Europe. Best Western is organized as a not-for-profit membership association with most of its sales coming from monthly fees and annual dues.

	Annual Growth	11/03	11/04	11/05	11/06	11/07
Sales ($ mil.)	–	–	–	(1,260.2)	205.5	220.9
Net income ($ mil.)	–	–	–	0.0	2.5	(3.0)
Market value ($ mil.)	–	–	–	–	–	–
Employees	–	–	–	–	–	1,015

BEST WINGS USA INC.

101 Chestnut St.
Sharon PA 16146
Phone: 724-981-3123
Fax: 724-981-5946
Web: www.lubewings.com

CEO: Greg Lippert
CFO: –
HR: –
FYE: December 31
Type: Private

Get in touch with your inner chicken-lovin' grease monkey at one of this company's restaurants. Best Wings USA operates and franchises the Quaker Steak & Lube full-service dining chain with more than 35 locations found in a dozen states mostly in Ohio and Pennsylvania. The auto-themed eateries are best known for chicken wings that can be ordered in a wide range of flavors. The menu also features burgers and other sandwiches ribs and steaks as well as a selection of appetizers. In addition to dining most of the restaurants offer full bar service. Vice chairmen George Warren and Gary Meszaros opened the first Quaker Steak outlet in 1974.

BET INTERACTIVE LLC

BET Plaza 1235 W St. NE
Washington DC 20018
Phone: 202-608-2000
Fax: 202-608-2988
Web: www.bet.com

CEO: –
CFO: –
HR: Shelley Johnson
FYE: July 31
Type: Subsidiary

This company is hoping to create a cultural connection online. BET Interactive operates the BET.com portal a leading provider of Internet content and services targeted to African-Americans. Other digital assets include BET on Blast (broadband media player) BET on Demand (video on demand) and BET Mobile (a mobile content subscription service). BET.com offers information on such topics as news health music and careers to an audience of more than 3 million registered users. It generates revenue from advertisements and sponsorships. BET Interactive is a unit of Viacom subsidiary Black Entertainment Television.

BETH ISRAEL DEACONESS MEDICAL CENTER INC.

330 BROOKLINE AVE
BOSTON, MA 022155400
Phone: 617-667-7000
Fax: –
Web: www.bidmc.org

CEO: John Christoforo
CFO: Steven Fischer
HR: –
FYE: September 30
Type: Private

When a Boston Red Sox player gets slugged he may very well end up at Beth Israel Deaconess Medical Center (BIDMC). Though it's the official hospital for this Major League Baseball team it's perhaps better known for being a teaching hospital of Harvard Medical School. BIDMC has about 650 beds and provides general medical and surgical care as well as outpatient services at its facilities. In addition to a Level I trauma center BIDMC offers specialized care in such areas as organ transplantation breast cancer care and cardiac surgery. Beth Israel Deaconess Medical Center traces its roots to Deaconess Hospital founded in 1896 and Beth Israel Hospital established in 1916.

	Annual Growth	09/09	09/10	09/11	09/12	09/13
Sales ($ mil.)	(2.7%)	–	–	–	1,081.1	1,051.5
Net income ($ mil.)	13.0%	–	–	–	49.8	56.3
Market value ($ mil.)	–	–	–	–	–	–
Employees	–	–	–	–	–	6,500

BETH ISRAEL MEDICAL CENTER

10 NATHAN D PERLMAN PL
NEW YORK, NY 100033881
Phone: 212-420-2000
Fax: –
Web: www.bethisraelny.org

CEO: –
CFO: –
HR: –
FYE: December 31
Type: Private

Residents of New York City's Lower East Side look to Beth Israel Medical Center to keep them healthy. A member of Continuum Health Partners the tertiary care medical facility has more than 1100 inpatient beds at two facilities in the New York area — its main location in Manhattan and another in Brooklyn. It also operates outpatient care centers and physician offices. Along with its patient care operations Beth Israel Medical Center maintains medical residency programs through its affiliation with Yeshiva University's Albert Einstein College of Medicine. The hospital also conducts institutional medical research with Rockefeller University and offers a nursing degree through its Phillips Beth Israel School of Nursing.

	Annual Growth	12/05	12/06	12/07	12/08	12/09
Sales ($ mil.)	34.8%	–	–	–	932.4	1,256.6
Net income ($ mil.)		–	–	–	(59.7)	15.2
Market value ($ mil.)		–	–	–	–	–
Employees		–	–	–	–	8,100

BETHUNE-COOKMAN UNIVERSITY INC.

640 DR MARY MCLEOD BETHUN
DAYTONA BEACH, FL 321143012
Phone: 386-481-2000
Fax: –
Web: www.cookman.edu

CEO: –
CFO: –
HR: –
FYE: June 30
Type: Private

Founded by educator Dr. Mary McLeod Bethune as a school for African-American women Bethune-Cookman University (B-CU) is in the top tier of Historically Black Colleges & Universities (HBCUs) in the US. The Daytona Florida-based university has about 3600 students enrolled in undergraduate and graduate programs in some 40 majors. Approximately 54% of the school's students live in on-campus residential housing. B-CU has about 200 full-time faculty members and faculty/student ratio of 1:17. The university also offers a NCAA Division One athletic program. B-CU charges some $14410 in annual tuition and fees.

	Annual Growth	06/06	06/07	06/09	06/11	06/13
Sales ($ mil.)	1.3%	–	66.0	58.8	76.1	71.4
Net income ($ mil.)		–	–	(4.6)	11.2	2.1
Market value ($ mil.)		–	–	–	–	–
Employees		–	–	–	–	600

BETSEY JOHNSON LLC

498 7th Ave. 21st Fl.
New York NY 10018
Phone: 212-244-0843
Fax: 212-244-0855
Web: www.betseyjohnson.com/

CEO: –
CFO: John Friedman
HR: –
FYE: December 31
Type: Private

Betsey Johnson the person and the brand is a favorite for women with a funky fashion sense. The apparel label named after its eclectic designer is sewn into dresses and other merchandise shoes handbags and accessories (sunglasses legwear and perfume). Private equity firm Castanea Partners and Steven Madden have owned Betsey Johnson's trademark and intellectual property since the company recapitalized in 2010. Betsey Johnson filed for Chapter 11 bankruptcy liquidation in 2012. Subsequently The Levy Group which licenses Betsey Johnson outerwear and other labels picked up the license to make and sell her dresses to boutique retailers and department stores including Bloomingdale's Saks and Nordstrom.

BFC FINANCIAL CORP.

NBB: BFCF

401 East Las Olas Boulevard, Suite 800
Fort Lauderdale, FL 33301
Phone: 954 940-4900
Fax: –
Web: www.bfcfinancial.com

CEO: Jarett Levan
CFO: Raymond S Lopez
HR: –
FYE: December 31
Type: Public

Holding company BFC Financial controls Florida-based BankAtlantic and investment firm Woodbridge Holdings (formerly Levitt Corporation) which has holdings in real estate companies Core Communities and Bluegreen Corporation and restaurant franchise Pizza Fusion. (Famous for constructing Levittown New York — widely regarded as the first planned community in the US — Levitt filed for Chapter 11 bankruptcy protection in 2007 and re-emerged the following year as Woodbridge.) BFC also owns a minority stake in Asian-themed restaurant chain Benihana. Chairman president and CEO Alan Levan and vice chairman Jack Abdo control BFC Financial.

	Annual Growth	12/10	12/11	12/12	12/13	12/14
Sales ($ mil.)	(0.4%)	682.7	674.4	486.0	563.8	672.2
Net income ($ mil.)		(103.8)	(11.3)	166.0	29.1	13.9
Market value ($ mil.)	71.5%	30.9	29.2	105.2	241.2	267.1
Employees	1.3%	5,084	5,119	4,445	5,050	5,364

BG MEDICINE INC

NBB: BGMD

303 Wyman Street, Suite 300
Waltham, MA 02451
Phone: 781 890-1199
Fax: –
Web: www.bg-medicine.com

CEO: Paul R Sohmer
CFO: Stephen P Hall
HR: –
FYE: December 31
Type: Public

BG Medicine wants to fill big gaps in diagnostic medicine. The biosciences researcher specializes in developing biomarkers (substances used to detect disease at a molecular level) that enable research into the causes of disease and the effectiveness of drugs used to treat them. Products in commercialization development and discovery stages include molecular diagnostic tests for heart disease neurological disorders and immune-system ailments. BG Medicine also provides drug research and development services to global pharmaceutical makers US government agencies and other health care organizations. The company built through venture capital backing held its IPO in 2011.

	Annual Growth	12/10	12/11	12/12	12/13	12/14
Sales ($ mil.)	35.8%	0.8	1.6	2.8	4.1	2.8
Net income ($ mil.)	–	(17.2)	(17.6)	(23.8)	(15.8)	(8.1)
Market value ($ mil.)	(53.9%)	–	40.7	19.9	9.0	4.0
Employees	(34.9%)	39	39	30	23	7

BGC PARTNERS, INC.

NMS: BGCP

499 Park Avenue
New York, NY 10022
Phone: 212 610-2200
Fax: –
Web: www.bgcpartners.com

CEO: Howard W. Lutnick
CFO: A. Graham Sadler
HR: Lori Pennay
FYE: December 31
Type: Public

BGC Partners provides inter-dealer brokerage services for banks investment firms and other institutional traders around the world through about 115 offices. Through its eSpeed and BGC Trader-branded platform it offers voice electronic and hybrid trade brokerage for a broad range of financial products including government and corporate bonds interest rate swaps foreign exchange derivatives and futures. The company also provides processing clearing and settlement services as well as market data and analytics products. BGC Partners was established by Cantor Fitzgerald which controls nearly half of the company. (BGC is named after Cantor Fitzgerald founder B. Gerald Cantor.)

	Annual Growth	12/10	12/11	12/12	12/13	12/14
Sales ($ mil.)	7.6%	1,331.1	1,464.7	1,767.0	2,498.1	1,787.5
Net income ($ mil.)	–	45.4	38.4	35.5	173.8	(3.8)
Market value ($ mil.)	2.4%	1,827.8	1,306.5	761.0	1,330.7	2,012.6
Employees	24.8%	2,743	4,129	6,547	6,386	6,656

BHE ENVIRONMENTAL INC.

11733 Chesterdale Rd.
Cincinnati OH 45246
Phone: 513-326-1500
Fax: 513-326-1550
Web: www.bheenv.com

CEO: –
CFO: –
HR: Llyod Carrie
FYE: December 31
Type: Private

Engineering and consulting firm BHE Environmental provides services related to remediation resource management and brownfield restoration to industrial commercial and government clients. The company's specialties include industrial hygiene and safety land reuse management of cultural and natural resources site assessment and wind energy support services. It uses Ultimap technology to provide an online means to collect store and communicate geospatial information and to display it on aerial photographs and maps. BHE Environmental operates from offices in Ohio Missouri Tennessee and West Virginia. The company was founded in 1988.

BI-LO HOLDING LLC

208 BI-LO Blvd.
Greenville SC 29607
Phone: 864-213-2500
Fax: 312-602-8099
Web: www.grantthornton.com

CEO: –
CFO: Brian P Carney
HR: –
FYE: December 31
Type: Private

"Combine and conquer" is the motto at BI-LO Holding. The newly-formed parent company for the BI-LO and Winn-Dixie supermarket chains boasts about 690 stores across eight southeastern states. The BI-LO supermarket chain operates more than 200 BI-LO and Super BI-LO grocery stores in the Carolinas Georgia and Tennessee. Winn-Dixie operates about 480 combination food and drug stores in Alabama Florida Georgia Louisiana and Mississippi under the Winn-Dixie and Winn-Dixie Marketplace banners. BI-LO Holding was formed in 2012 when BI-LO's owner Dallas-based investment firm Lone Star Funds acquired Winn-Dixie for about $560 million and merged the two companies.

BI-RITE RESTAURANT SUPPLY CO. INC.

123 S HILL DR
BRISBANE, CA 940051203
Phone: 415-656-0187
Fax: –
Web: www.birite.com

CEO: –
CFO: Zachary Barulich
HR: Natasha Eltringham
FYE: December 31
Type: Private

Bi-Rite Restaurant Supply which does business as BiRite Foodservice Distributors is a leading food service supplier serving the San Francisco Bay area and Northern California. The company distributes a full line of food equipment and supplies including meat and dairy items seafood frozen foods dry groceries cleaning supplies china kitchen equipment and disposables. Its customers include restaurant operators hotels universities and hospitals. The company's international arm supplied food to the Middle East and Asia. A member of the UniPro Foodservice cooperative the family-owned company was founded in 1966 by cousins Victor and John Barulich.

	Annual Growth	12/09	12/10	12/11	12/12	12/13
Sales ($ mil.)	0.9%	–	271.6	255.0	258.9	279.0
Net income ($ mil.)	21.6%	–	–	4.7	4.6	6.9
Market value ($ mil.)	–	–	–	–	–	–
Employees	–	–	–	–	–	230

BIDZ.COM INC.

2400 Marine Ave.
Redondo Beach CA 90278
Phone: 310-280-7373
Fax: 310-280-7375
Web: www.bidz.com

NASDAQ: BIDZ
CEO: David Zinberg
CFO: Lawrence Y Kong
HR: –
FYE: December 31
Type: Private

Bidz.com combines the discounts of a dollar store the format of an auction house and the convenience of the Internet to bring sparkling deals to shoppers. The firm buys closeout merchandise and sells it using a live-auction format with $1 opening bids. It mostly sells jewelry including gold platinum and silver items set with diamonds as well as precious and semi-precious stones. Visitors can also find deals on electronics apparel and a range of collectibles (such as fine art antiques coins and sports cards). The company's Buyz.com is a fixed-price e-commerce site that offers similar items listed for auction. In a deal that took the company private Bidz.com was acquired by Glendon Group in 2012.

BIG 5 SPORTING GOODS CORP

2525 East El Segundo Boulevard
El Segundo, CA 90245
Phone: 310 536-0611
Fax: –
Web: www.big5sportinggoods.com

NMS: BGFV
CEO: Steven G. Miller
CFO: Barry D. Emerson
HR: –
FYE: December 28
Type: Public

Big 5 Sporting Goods has outgrown its name. The company which started out with five army surplus shops in California in 1955 is a leading sporting goods retailer with some 415 stores in a dozen mostly western states including California Washington and Arizona. The company sells brand-name (adidas Coleman Easton) and private-label equipment apparel and footwear for indoor and outdoor activities such as camping hunting fishing tennis golf and snowboarding. Big 5 has stuck with a neighborhood-store format (averaging approximately 11000 sq. ft.) instead of opening massive superstores. Big 5 Sporting Goods is run by its chairman and CEO Steven Miller the son of company co-founder Robert Miller.

	Annual Growth	01/11	01/12*	12/12	12/13	12/14
Sales ($ mil.)	2.9%	896.8	902.1	940.5	993.3	977.9
Net income ($ mil.)	(10.2%)	20.6	11.7	14.9	27.9	14.9
Market value ($ mil.)	(2.0%)	338.7	231.6	278.8	425.6	318.3
Employees	0.4%	8,900	8,800	9,000	9,000	9,000

*Fiscal year change

BIG LOTS, INC.

300 Phillipi Road, P.O. Box 28512
Columbus, OH 43228-5311
Phone: 614 278-6800
Fax: 614 278-6666
Web: www.biglots.com

NYS: BIG
CEO: David J. (Dave) Campisi
CFO: Timothy A Johnson
HR: Michael A. (Mike) Schlonsky
FYE: January 31
Type: Public

Big Lots believes that a product's shelf life depends solely on which shelf it's on. The company is North America's #1 broadline closeout retailer with about 1570 Big Lots stores in 48 US states and seven provinces in Canada. It sells a variety of brand-name products including food and other consumables furniture housewares seasonal items and toys that have been overproduced returned discontinued or result from liquidations typically at 20%-40% below discounters' prices. Its wholesale division sells its discounted merchandise to a variety of retailers manufacturers distributors and other wholesalers.

	Annual Growth	01/11	01/12*	02/13	02/14*	01/15
Sales ($ mil.)	1.1%	4,952.2	5,202.3	5,400.1	5,301.9	5,177.1
Net income ($ mil.)	(15.3%)	222.5	207.1	177.1	125.3	114.3
Market value ($ mil.)	9.6%	1,683.7	2,116.5	1,711.2	1,417.5	2,429.2
Employees	0.3%	35,600	37,400	37,300	38,100	36,100

*Fiscal year change

BIG WEST OIL LLC

1104 Country Hills Dr.
Ogden UT 84403
Phone: 801-624-1000
Fax: 801-624-1624
Web: www.bigwestoil.com

CEO: –
CFO: –
HR: –
FYE: January 31
Type: Private

Big West Oil keeps the wagon trains rolling across the big West — at least the station wagons. The company is in the oil processing and products business centered around its 35000 barrels-a-day refinery in North Salt Lake Utah to its fleet of tanker trucks that gather crude oil from the refinery and other purchases and deliver to wholesale customers and gas station/convenience stores in seven Western states including Colorado Idaho Nevada Utah and Wyoming. The company's refinery processes crude oil produced in Utah Wyoming and Canada. Big West Oil is a subsidiary of FJ Management.

BIG Y FOODS INC.

2145 Roosevelt Ave.
Springfield MA 01102-7840
Phone: 413-784-0600
Fax: 908-673-9920
Web: authentidate.com

CEO: William Mahoney
CFO: Bill White
HR: –
FYE: December 31
Type: Private

Why call it Big Y? Big Y Foods began as a 900-sq.-ft. grocery at a Y intersection in Chicopee Massachusetts. It now operates some 60 supermarkets throughout Massachusetts and Connecticut. Most of its stores are Big Y World Class Markets offering specialty areas such as bakeries and floral shops as well as banking. The rest consist of Big Y Supermarkets and a single gourmet food and liquor store called Table & Vine in Springfield Massachusetts. Some Big Y stores provide child care dry cleaning photo processing and even propane sales and their delis and food courts offer to-go foods. Big Y is owned and run by the D'Amour family and is one of New England's largest independent supermarket chains.

BIG-D CONSTRUCTION CORP.

404 W 400 S
SALT LAKE CITY, UT 841011108
Phone: 801-415-6000
Fax: –
Web: www.big-d.com

CEO: Jack Livingood
CFO: Larry Worrell
HR: Lori Odell
FYE: December 31
Type: Private

Big-D builds big things. With offices in Utah Arizona California and Wyoming the construction firm offers design/build services to customers in about 20 states. Big-D focuses on projects for clients in such industries as manufacturing health care hospitality food processing and distribution manufacturing and retail. The company's Signature Group builds high-end luxury homes as well as and condominiums spas and other special projects in resort communities. Clients have included SYSCO and Marriott. The company also operates a concrete division devoted to architectural structural and parking garage projects. Big-D was founded in 1967 by Dee Livingood. His family continues to lead the company.

	Annual Growth	12/09	12/10	12/11	12/12	12/13
Sales ($ mil.)	35.1%	–	259.8	554.8	541.6	640.8
Net income ($ mil.)	–	–	–	0.0	0.0	0.0
Market value ($ mil.)	–	–	–	–	–	–
Employees	–	–	–	–	–	433

BIGLARI HOLDINGS INC. NYS: BH

17802 IH 10 West, Suite 400
San Antonio, TX 78257
Phone: 210 344-3400
Fax: 317 633-4105
Web: www.biglariholdings.com

CEO: Sardar Biglari
CFO: –
HR: –
FYE: December 31
Type: Public

Beef and ice cream is an unbeatable combination for this restaurant company. Formerly The Steak n Shake Company Biglari Holdings is a multi-concept dining operator with two chains operating under the names Steak n Shake and WesterN SizzliN. Its flagship concept encompasses more than 590 company-owned and franchised family dining spots in more than 25 states mostly in the Midwest and Southeast. The diners open 24-hours a day are popular for their Steakburger sandwiches and milkshakes as well as breakfast items and other dishes. About 420 of the units are company-owned while the rest are franchised. WesterN SizzliN meanwhile oversees 90 franchised steak buffet restaurants in about 15 states.

	Annual Growth	09/11	09/12	09/13	09/14*	12/14
Sales ($ mil.)	(31.9%)	709.2	740.2	755.8	793.8	224.5
Net income ($ mil.)	38.1%	34.6	21.6	140.3	28.8	91.1
Market value ($ mil.)	8.9%	639.1	771.7	857.5	720.9	825.2
Employees	4.3%	21,000	22,000	21,686	23,130	23,851

*Fiscal year change

BILL & MELINDA GATES FOUNDATION

500 5th Ave. North
Seattle WA 98102
Phone: 206-709-3100
Fax: 206-709-3180
Web: www.gatesfoundation.org

CEO: Bill Gates Sr
CFO: –
HR: –
FYE: December 31
Type: Private - Foundation

You don't have to be one of the world's richest men or know one to make a difference with your charitable gifts — but it helps. Established by the chairman of Microsoft Corporation and his wife the Bill & Melinda Gates Foundation works in developing countries to improve health and reduce poverty and in the US to support education and libraries nationwide and children and families in the Pacific Northwest. With an endowment of about $33.5 billion the foundation is the largest in the US distributing more than $26 billion in total grants since 1994. Investor Warren Buffett plans to give the Bill & Melinda Gates Foundation about $30 billion worth of Berkshire Hathaway stock in installments.

BILLINGS CLINIC

2800 10TH AVE N
BILLINGS, MT 591010703
Phone: 406-657-4000
Fax: –
Web: www.billingsclinic.com

CEO: Nicholas J. Wolter
CFO: Connie F. Prewitt
HR: –
FYE: June 30
Type: Private

Billings Clinic is an integrated health care system that serves the residents of Big Sky Country. Through a group of more than 320 doctors and other providers the clinic caters to some 570000 people in Billings Montana and in surrounding communities. It offers 50-plus specialties such as emergency and trauma cancer orthopedics birthing cardiovascular neurosciences dialysis and pediatrics. Its operations include a more than 285-bed hospital and the organization's main clinic. Additionally Billings Clinic operates the 90-bed Aspen Meadows Retirement Community and provides support services to several regional community hospitals. The not-for-profit health care system is owned by the community.

	Annual Growth	06/08	06/09	06/10	06/11	06/13
Sales ($ mil.)	(4.0%)	–	658.6	494.5	533.3	560.2
Net income ($ mil.)	(17.6%)	–	–	25.9	28.5	14.5
Market value ($ mil.)	–	–	–	–	–	–
Employees	–	–	–	–	–	3,300

BIMINI CAPITAL MANAGEMENT INC   NBB: BMNM

3305 Flamingo Drive
Vero Beach, FL 32963
Phone: 772 231-1400
Fax: –
Web: www.biminicapital.com

CEO: Robert E Cauley
CFO: G Hunter Haas IV
HR: –
FYE: December 31
Type: Public

Bimini Capital Management (formerly Opteum) invests in residential mortgage-backed securities and related securities issued by the likes of Fannie Mae Freddie Mac and Ginnie Mae. The real estate investment trust (REIT) manages a portfolio worth more than $100 million mainly consisting of mortgage-related securities backed by adjustable-rate mortgages. Bimini Capital also invests in fixed-rate mortgage-backed securities and inverse interest-only securities. The company sold its residential mortgage origination business which consisted of about 25 offices in five states to Prospect Mortgage in 2007. It also ceased conduit and wholesale lending.

	Annual Growth	12/10	12/11	12/12	12/13	12/14
Sales ($ mil.)	58.8%	5.6	3.1	1.2	0.5	35.6
Net income ($ mil.)	–	(1.7)	(2.6)	(2.0)	(2.3)	7.7
Market value ($ mil.)	24.8%	9.7	4.5	1.5	3.4	23.5
Employees	(14.3%)	–	–	–	7	6

BIND THERAPEUTICS INC   NMS: BIND

325 Vassar Street
Cambridge, MA 02139
Phone: 617 491-3400
Fax: –
Web: www.bindtherapeutics.com

CEO: Andrew J Hirsch
CFO: –
HR: –
FYE: December 31
Type: Public

BIND Therapeutics believes it's bound on a path and to products that will lead to a breakthrough in the treatment of certain cancers. The company designs nanoparticles with a prolonged circulation in the bloodstream called Accurins that target tumors at the the tissue cellular and molecular levels. Its lead candidate BIND-1014 which seeks out prostate tumors and lung cancers is in Phase 2 clinical trials. The company also aims to produce Accurins to treat non-oncological ailments such as cardiovascular disease and autoimmune disorders and is collaborating with Amgen AstraZeneca and Pfizer to develop such products. BIND founded in 2006 went public in September 2013 raising more than $70 million.

	Annual Growth	12/10	12/11	12/12	12/13	12/14
Sales ($ mil.)	–	0.0	0.9	1.0	10.9	10.4
Net income ($ mil.)	–	0.0	(16.9)	(19.2)	(27.7)	(32.5)
Market value ($ mil.)	–	0.0	–	–	249.7	89.4
Employees	33.4%	–	–	50	59	89

BINGHAM MCCUTCHEN LLP

1 Federal St.
Boston MA 02110-1726
Phone: 617-951-8000
Fax: 617-951-8736
Web: www.bingham.com

CEO: –
CFO: –
HR: –
FYE: December 31
Type: Private - Partnershi

Big and getting bigger Bingham McCutchen has about 1000 lawyers overall. Bingham has grown over the years by absorbing other law firms — adding 10 firms since 1997. It maintains 15 offices in the US Europe and the Asia/Pacific region with concentrations in California and New England. Bingham's wide range of practice areas is divided into major groups such as corporate finance litigation and securities. Along with its law practices the firm offers consulting services through subsidiaries such as Bingham Consulting Group and Bingham Strategic Advisors. Clients have included Guantanamo Bay detainees and ESPN reporter Erin Andrews. The firm was founded in 1891.

BIO-KEY INTERNATIONAL INC   NBB: BKYI

3349 Highway 138, Building A, Suite E
Wall, NJ 07719
Phone: 732 359-1100
Fax: –
Web: www.bio-key.com

CEO: Michael W Depasquale
CFO: Cecilia Welch
HR: –
FYE: December 31
Type: Public

BIO-key International has its finger securely on the pulse of biometrics. The company develops biometric security software and technology designed to secure access to enterprise applications and mobile devices. Its products incorporate biometric technology to scan and analyze fingerprints in order to grant or deny user access to wireless and enterprise data. BIO-key licenses its technology to original equipment manufacturers systems integrators and application developers. End users of its technology include corporations government agencies and other organizations concerned about the theft or misuse of sensitive data.

	Annual Growth	12/10	12/11	12/12	12/13	12/14
Sales ($ mil.)	3.3%	3.5	3.5	3.8	2.0	4.0
Net income ($ mil.)	–	(0.3)	(1.9)	0.0	(2.6)	(1.9)
Market value ($ mil.)	(5.6%)	9.2	4.6	5.7	10.7	7.3
Employees	6.3%	18	18	18	23	23

BIO-RAD LABORATORIES, INC.   NYS: BIO

1000 Alfred Nobel Drive
Hercules, CA 94547
Phone: 510 724-7000
Fax: –
Web: www.bio-rad.com

CEO: Norman Schwartz
CFO: Christine A. Tsingos
HR: –
FYE: December 31
Type: Public

Bio-Rad Laboratories makes a most excellent array of research laboratory and medical testing equipment. The company manufactures and supplies more than 8000 products through two segments. Its clinical diagnostics segment makes products used in blood fluid and tissue testing to detect diseases such as diabetes. Its life science unit offers instruments apparatus reagents and software used in lab settings to study life processes potential drugs and food pathogens. Bio-Rad has a sales force that sells directly to such end users as clinical labs pharmaceutical firms hospitals government agencies and universities. More than two-thirds of sales come from outside the US.

	Annual Growth	12/10	12/11	12/12	12/13	12/14
Sales ($ mil.)	3.1%	1,927.1	2,073.5	2,069.2	2,132.7	2,175.0
Net income ($ mil.)	(16.8%)	185.5	178.2	163.8	77.8	88.8
Market value ($ mil.)	3.8%	3,018.9	2,791.8	3,053.8	3,593.3	3,504.6
Employees	2.5%	6,880	7,030	7,380	7,750	7,600

BIO-REFERENCE LABORATORIES, INC.   NMS: BRLI

481 Edward H. Ross Drive
Elmwood Park, NJ 07407
Phone: 201 791-2600
Fax: 201 791-1941
Web: www.bioreference.com

CEO: Marc D Grodman
CFO: Nicholas Papazicos
HR: –
FYE: October 31
Type: Public

Bio-Reference Laboratories tests positive as the lab of choice for many in the Northeast. Primarily serving the greater New York Metropolitan Area the company offers routine clinical tests including Pap smears pregnancy tests cholesterol checks and blood cell counts. Through its GenPath business unit it also performs more sophisticated esoteric testing such as cancer pathology and molecular diagnostics. It gets most of its orders (close to 8 million per year) from doctors' offices collecting specimens at draw stations scattered throughout its primary service area in the New York area. Bio-Reference Laboratories also provides services in Connecticut Delaware Maryland New Jersey and Pennsylvania.

	Annual Growth	10/10	10/11	10/12	10/13	10/14
Sales ($ mil.)	16.1%	458.0	558.6	661.7	715.4	832.3
Net income ($ mil.)	15.4%	26.4	36.4	42.2	45.8	46.8
Market value ($ mil.)	8.6%	597.8	555.7	769.7	898.7	832.9
Employees	15.7%	2,424	3,155	3,564	4,427	4,347

BIO-SOLUTIONS MANUFACTURING INC. OTC: BSOM

4440 Arville St. Ste. 6
Las Vegas NV 89103-3813
Phone: 702-222-9532
Fax: 702-222-9126
Web: www.todaysalternativeenergy.net

CEO: –
CFO: –
HR: –
FYE: October 31
Type: Public

Clogged drains? Nothing at all! Backed up pipes? P'shaw! Diesel tank empty? No problem for the guys at Bio-Solutions Manufacturing (BSM). The company has two divisions: a Cleaning Division and a Bio Diesel Division. The Cleaning Division's products make use of microbes and enzymes that can be used to treat sites contaminated by such pollutants as hydrocarbons grease hydrogen sulfide and ammonia. In addition Bio-Solutions' micro-organisms can clean up oil spills and contaminated groundwater by literally eating the contaminants. The Bio Diesel Division turns many of the waste products the company collects into biodiesel fuel. BSM distributes its products through subsidiary Bio-Solutions Franchise.

BIOANALYTICAL SYSTEMS, INC. NAS: BASI

2701 Kent Avenue
West Lafayette, IN 47906
Phone: 765 463-4527
Fax: –
Web: www.basinc.com

CEO: Jacqueline M. Lemke
CFO: Jeffrey Potrzebowksi
HR: Lina Reeves-Kerner
FYE: September 30
Type: Public

Analyze this! Bioanalytical Systems Inc. (BASi) provides contract research and development services for the pharmaceutical medical device and biotechnology industries. In addition to providing support functions for preclinical research and clinical drug trials the firm's research services include product purity tests safety evaluations characterization analysis of compounds in vivo (in the body) testing to measure how drugs are metabolized in living systems and pathological laboratory testing. BASi also sells analytical instruments and other products including bioanalytical separation instrumentation patient monitoring and diagnostic equipment and miniaturized in vivo sampling devices.

	Annual Growth	09/11	09/12	09/13	09/14	09/15
Sales ($ mil.)	(9.0%)	33.1	28.2	22.1	24.6	22.7
Net income ($ mil.)	19.3%	0.5	(6.4)	0.8	(1.1)	1.1
Market value ($ mil.)	9.3%	9.6	10.5	10.9	18.7	13.7
Employees	(12.4%)	267	170	159	159	157

BIO-TECHNE CORP NMS: TECH

614 McKinley Place N.E.
Minneapolis, MN 55413
Phone: 612 379-8854
Fax: –
Web: www.bio-techne.com

CEO: Charles R. (Chuck) Kummeth
CFO: Gregory J. (Greg) Melsen
HR: –
FYE: June 30
Type: Public

Bio-Techne (formerly TECHNE Corporation) has biotechnology research down to an art form. Through subsidiaries including Research and Diagnostic Systems (R&D Systems) Boston Biochem BiosPacific and Tocris the firm makes and distributes biological research supplies used by researchers around the globe to study cellular and immune system responses. Bio-Techne's products include cytokines (purified proteins that affect cell behavior) and diagnostic reagents (including antibodies and enzymes) as well as its Quantikine assay kits that determine the amount of cytokine in a given sample. R&D Systems also makes hematology controls and calibrators for blood analysis systems and sells them to equipment makers.

	Annual Growth	06/11	06/12	06/13	06/14	06/15
Sales ($ mil.)	11.8%	290.0	314.6	310.6	357.8	452.2
Net income ($ mil.)	(1.0%)	112.3	112.3	112.6	110.9	107.7
Market value ($ mil.)	4.3%	3,097.4	2,756.8	2,566.5	3,439.3	3,658.5
Employees	12.9%	834	847	854	1,021	1,356

BIOCEPT, INC NAS: BIOC

5810 Nancy Ridge Drive
San Diego, CA 92121
Phone: 858 320-8200
Fax: –
Web: www.biocept.com

CEO: Michael W Nall
CFO: Jennifer (Jen) Crittenden
HR: –
FYE: December 31
Type: Public

The concept at Biocept is to make cancer tumor identification quicker and more accurate. The company's products detect circulating tumor cells (CTCs) in a standard blood sample. Only one test is in production OncoCEE-BR for breast cancer. Its pipeline contains tests for lung gastric colorectal prostate and skin cancers; it plans to launch five new tests by 2017. Biocept collaborates with doctors and researchers at The University of Texas M.D. Anderson Cancer Center and the Dana-Farber Cancer Institute. The company was formed in 1997 and went public in 2014. It raised $18.8 million that it plans to use for sales and marketing R&D and development of tests and scaling up its production capabilities.

	Annual Growth	12/10	12/11	12/12	12/13	12/14
Sales ($ mil.)	–	0.0	0.0	0.1	0.1	0.1
Net income ($ mil.)	–	0.0	(13.6)	(12.3)	(9.2)	(15.9)
Market value ($ mil.)	–	–	0.0	–	–	11.0
Employees	23.9%	–	–	28	28	43

BIOAMBER INC NYS: BIOA

1250 Rene Levesque West, Suite 4310
Montreal, Quebec 55447
Phone: 514 844-8000
Fax: –
Web: www.bio-amber.com

CEO: –
CFO: –
HR: –
FYE: December 31
Type: Public

BioAmber has discovered quite a few new uses for those waves of grain that can help reduce US dependence on oil. The development-stage company uses the sugars found in wheat and corn to create biosuccinic acid a chemical building block used as an alternative to petroleum-derived succinic acid. Biosuccinic acid can be used in polyurethane food additives lubricants cosmetics and personal care products among other products. Formed in 2008 BioAmber has one contract manufacturing plant in France that has produced almost 500000 pounds of biosuccinic acid for about a dozen customers. Seeking further growth the company went public in the US in mid-2013.

BIOCRYST PHARMACEUTICALS, INC. NMS: BCRX

4505 Emperor Blvd., Suite 200
Durham, NC 27703
Phone: 919 859-1302
Fax: 919 859-1314
Web: www.biocryst.com

CEO: Jon P. Stonehouse
CFO: Thomas R. (Tom) Staab
HR: –
FYE: December 31
Type: Public

BioCryst Pharmaceuticals is tackling the bad enzymes that spread disease. The firm creates small molecule compounds that inhibit enzymes associated with viral diseases autoimmune conditions and cancer. BioCryst's most advanced candidate is peramivir a potential treatment for acute influenza that is being developed with funding from the Department of Health and Human Services (HHS). Peramivir is sold as a seasonal flu drug in Asia through licensees. BioCryst's forodesine candidate is licensed to UK-based Mundipharma as a potential treatment for various cancers. Other candidates include enzyme inhibitors for the treatment of gout hepatitis C and inflammatory conditions.

	Annual Growth	12/10	12/11	12/12	12/13	12/14
Sales ($ mil.)	113.0%	0.1	0.6	2.3	2.7	1.5
Net income ($ mil.)	–	(2.0)	(30.6)	(39.4)	(33.2)	(46.4)
Market value ($ mil.)	12.2%	–	–	–	163.3	183.2
Employees	37.0%	–	–	–	54	74

	Annual Growth	12/10	12/11	12/12	12/13	12/14
Sales ($ mil.)	(31.7%)	62.4	19.6	26.3	17.3	13.6
Net income ($ mil.)	–	(33.9)	(56.9)	(39.1)	(30.1)	(45.2)
Market value ($ mil.)	23.8%	372.0	177.7	102.2	546.9	875.0
Employees	(9.9%)	76	77	40	40	50

BIODEL INC.

NASDAQ: BIOD

100 Saw Mill Rd.
Danbury CT 06810
Phone: 203-796-5000
Fax: 203-796-5001
Web: www.biodel.com

CEO: Errol B De Souza
CFO: Gary G Gemignani
HR: –
FYE: September 30
Type: Public

Biodel delves into the development of viable treatments for diabetes. The company uses its VIAdel biological technology to reformulate and administer existing peptide hormones (such as insulin) for the treatment of diabetes and its complications including hyper- and hypoglycemia cardiovascular problems and weight control. Its two lead product candidates are VIAject an injectable insulin formulation designed to be rapidly absorbed into the bloodstream and VIAtab tablets which are administered sublingually (under the tongue). Both candidates are in clinical trials; VIAject is closest to commercialization. Biodel has three other diabetes-related candidates in its pipeline at varying stages of development.

BIODELIVERY SCIENCES INTERNATIONAL INC

NAS: BDSI

4131 ParkLake Avenue, Suite #225
Raleigh, NC 27612
Phone: 919 582-9050
Fax: –
Web: www.bdsi.com

CEO: Mark A. Sirgo
CFO: Ernest R. De Paolantonio
HR: –
FYE: December 31
Type: Public

BioDelivery Sciences International (BDSI) isn't inventing new drugs but it is looking for better ways to administer them. The development-stage firm takes already approved drugs that are normally delivered intravenously and reformulates them into buccal (absorbed by the inner cheek) and oral treatments. Drugs delivered via its BEMA (BioErodible MucoAdhesive) and Bioral systems focus on the areas of pain management and addiction management. Its BEMA fentanyl product ONSOLIS is a buccally delivered polymer film used for the treatment of cancer pain. Recent FDA-approved candidates include BUNAVAIL for the treatment of opioid dependence (2014) and BELBUCA for chronic severe pain management (2015).

	Annual Growth	12/10	12/11	12/12	12/13	12/14
Sales ($ mil.)	83.9%	3.4	3.3	54.5	11.4	38.9
Net income ($ mil.)	–	(13.0)	(23.3)	1.7	(57.4)	(54.2)
Market value ($ mil.)	35.7%	183.1	41.5	222.3	303.9	620.1
Employees	8.4%	21	18	21	24	29

BIOFUEL ENERGY CORP

NAS: BIOF

1600 Broadway, Suite 2200
Denver, CO 80202
Phone: 303 640-6500
Fax: –

CEO: James R Brickman
CFO: Richard A Costello
HR: –
FYE: December 31
Type: Public

BioFuel Energy has climbed aboard the ethanol bandwagon. Now that bandwagon seems to be on an uncertain course. The company's two plants have the combined capacity to produce 220 million gallons of ethanol annually as well as 720000 tons of distillers grains. The company sells all of its production to agribusiness giant Cargill which in turn gives it reliable corn supplies an established logistics/transportation network and marketing expertise. BioFuel Energy went public in 2007 using the proceeds to repay outstanding debts as well as to fund construction of its ethanol facilities. Hedge fund firms Greenlight Capital and Third Point control more than 50% of the company. Cargill owns another 10%.

	Annual Growth	12/08	12/09	12/10	12/11	12/12
Sales ($ mil.)	26.7%	179.9	415.5	453.4	653.1	463.3
Net income ($ mil.)	–	(40.9)	(13.6)	(20.0)	(8.7)	(39.8)
Market value ($ mil.)	79.8%	2.2	16.9	10.9	4.2	23.0
Employees	(12.4%)	151	150	151	149	89

BIOGEN INC

NMS: BIIB

225 Binney Street
Cambridge, MA 02142
Phone: 617 679-2000
Fax: –
Web: www.biogenidec.com

CEO: George A. Scangos
CFO: Paul J. Clancy
HR: Kenneth A. (Ken) DiPietro
FYE: December 31
Type: Public

With its pipeline full of biotech drugs Biogen (formerly Biogen Idec) aims to meet the unmet needs of patients around the world. The biotech giant is focused on developing treatments in the areas of immunology and neurology. Its product roster includes best-selling Avonex a popular drug for the treatment of relapsing multiple sclerosis (MS); Tysabri a drug treatment for MS and Crohn's disease; Rituxan a monoclonal antibody developed jointly with Genentech that treats non-Hodgkin's lymphoma and rheumatoid arthritis; and Fumaderm a psoriasis drug marketed in Germany. Other products include Plegridy for MS and Alprolix for hemophilia B. Founded in 1978 Biogen serves customers in more than 90 countries.

	Annual Growth	12/11	12/12	12/13	12/14	12/15
Sales ($ mil.)	20.8%	5,048.6	5,516.5	6,932.2	9,703.3	10,763.8
Net income ($ mil.)	30.2%	1,234.4	1,380.0	1,862.3	2,934.8	3,547.0
Market value ($ mil.)	29.2%	24,056.9	31,996.5	61,114.4	74,203.8	66,968.1
Employees	10.1%	5,000	5,950	6,850	7,550	7,350

BIOHORIZONS INC.

2300 Riverchase Center
Birmingham AL 35244
Phone: 205-967-7880
Fax: 205-870-0304
Web: www.biohorizons.com

CEO: R Steve Boggan
CFO: David Wall
HR: –
FYE: December 31
Type: Private

BioHorizons offers its customers a beautiful set of choppers with its tools. The company manufactures and sells dental implants — or individual screw-in teeth — as an alternative to conventional dentures. It also sells soft tissue regeneration products called biologics to help patients' gums grow back around the implant. Targeted to oral surgeons BioHorizons offers tools and specialty instruments (including those by Hu-Friedy) as well as a software program under the Virtual Implant Placement (VIP) name to map treatment procedures. BioHorizons sells its products in more than 80 countries and online. The company is owned by private equity firm HealthpointCapital.

BIOJECT MEDICAL TECHNOLOGIES INC.

OTC: BJCT

20245 SW 95th Ave.
Tualatin OR 97062
Phone: 503-692-8001
Fax: 503-692-6698
Web: www.bioject.com

CEO: Tony K Chow
CFO: –
HR: –
FYE: December 31
Type: Public

Bioject Medical Technologies wants to give the medical community a shot in the arm. Its Biojector 2000 jet injection system delivers injectable medication without a needle (and thus without needle-associated risks) by using a fine high-pressure stream that goes through the skin; the injector is powered by CO2 disposable cartridges or tanks. The accompanying vial adapter device allows the Biojector system to be filled without a needle. The company also markets Vitajet a spring-powered needle-free self-injection device that has been cleared for administering injections of insulin and Merck Serono's human growth hormones. Investment firm Signet Healthcare Partners and affiliates own one-third of Bioject.

BIOLA UNIVERSITY INC.

13800 BIOLA AVE
LA MIRADA, CA 906390001
Phone: 562-903-6000
Fax: –
Web: www.offices.biola.edu

CEO: –
CFO: –
HR: Judith Rood
FYE: June 30
Type: Private

The bio of Biola University is that it is a faith-based institution. The university is a private evangelical Christian instituion of higher learning that provides 145 academic programs through seven schools. The nondenominational school offers bachelor's master's first professional and doctoral degrees and has an enrollment of more than 6300. Biola students and faculty donate some 200000 hours of volunteer work annually participating in off-campus activities such as leading Bible studies in nearby churches and evangelizing on the streets of inner cities.

	Annual Growth	06/09	06/10	06/11	06/12	06/13
Sales ($ mil.)	2.6%	–	138.9	170.3	149.7	149.9
Net income ($ mil.)	21.6%	–	–	12.2	10.6	18.1
Market value ($ mil.)	–	–	–	–	–	–
Employees	–	–	–	–	–	1,000

BIOLARGO INC

3500 W. Garry Avenue
Santa Ana, CA 92704
Phone: 949 643-9540
Fax: –
Web: www.biolargo.com

NBB: BLGO
CEO: Dennis P Calvert
CFO: Charles K Dargan II
HR: –
FYE: December 31
Type: Public

After morphing identities several times over the past few years BioLargo (formerly NuWay Medical) hopes that it has found its way. The company went from car dealership and casino ownership to being a medical device maker and application service provider (ASP). It believes it has found its future in designing sanitizing chemicals for specialty packaging (such as pads protective liners and surgical drapes) used for shipping blood biohazardous materials meat and poultry and other items requiring sanitary containment. Consultant Kenneth Code controls 56% of BioLargo.

	Annual Growth	12/10	12/11	12/12	12/13	12/14
Sales ($ mil.)	(8.2%)	0.2	0.2	0.1	0.2	0.1
Net income ($ mil.)	–	(5.7)	(4.0)	(5.3)	(2.5)	(3.7)
Market value ($ mil.)	(30.0%)	107.0	107.0	19.9	20.7	25.7
Employees	31.6%	3	3	6	6	9

BIOLASE, INC

4 Cromwell
Irvine, CA 92618
Phone: 949 361-1200
Fax: –
Web: www.biolase.com

NAS: BIOL
CEO: Jeffrey M Nugent
CFO: –
HR: –
FYE: December 31
Type: Public

BioLase is causing dentists to drop the knife and pick up the laser. The company develops manufactures and sells laser-based systems for use primarily in dental applications. BioLase's surgical cutting system Waterlase uses laser pulses to turn water droplets into high-speed particles that can cut both hard and soft tissues and bones in the mouth. Waterlase is used in procedures traditionally performed with dental drills and scalpels. The company's Diode laser systems are used to perform soft tissue and cosmetic dental procedures as well as non-dental procedures. BioLase markets its products in more than 60 countries.

	Annual Growth	12/10	12/11	12/12	12/13	12/14
Sales ($ mil.)	16.1%	26.2	48.9	57.4	56.4	47.7
Net income ($ mil.)	–	(12.0)	(4.5)	(3.1)	(11.5)	(18.9)
Market value ($ mil.)	10.7%	101.7	149.4	107.5	164.5	152.8
Employees	9.7%	145	184	219	220	210

BIOLIFE SOLUTIONS INC

3303 Monte Villa Parkway, Suite 310
Bothell, WA 98021
Phone: 425 402-1400
Fax: –
Web: www.biolifesolutions.com

NAS: BLFS
CEO: Michael Rice
CFO: Daphne Taylor
HR: –
FYE: December 31
Type: Public

BioLife Solutions makes sure your tissues and organs don't get freezer burn. The company has designed liquid media technologies for frozen (cryogenic) storage and cold (hypothermic) storage of biological products including cells tissues and organs. Its HypoThermosol and CryoStor products minimize the damage done to these biological products during refrigeration and freezing making them viable for transplant or experimentation for longer periods. The company sells its products directly to academic institutions companies and laboratories conducting clinical research.

	Annual Growth	12/10	12/11	12/12	12/13	12/14
Sales ($ mil.)	31.3%	2.1	2.8	5.7	8.9	6.2
Net income ($ mil.)	–	(2.0)	(2.0)	(1.7)	(1.1)	(3.2)
Market value ($ mil.)	130.6%	0.7	0.6	4.1	7.3	19.8
Employees	36.3%	11	16	28	23	38

BIOMED REALTY TRUST INC

17190 Bernardo Center Drive
San Diego, CA 92128
Phone: 858 485-9840
Fax: 858 485-9843
Web: www.biomedrealty.com

NYS: BMR
CEO: Alan D Gold
CFO: Greg N Lubushkin
HR: –
FYE: December 31
Type: Public

BioMed Realty knows its niche. A self-administered real estate investment trust (REIT) the firm acquires develops leases and manages laboratory and office space for biotechnology and pharmaceutical companies scientific research institutions government agencies and other life science tenants. BioMed owns more than 80 properties with around 185 buildings and more than 16 million sq. ft. of rentable space. The REIT's properties which span about a dozen states are often located near universities; its preferred markets include research and development hubs such as Boston New York San Diego San Francisco and Seattle. In 2013 BioMed acquired Wexford Science & Technology.

	Annual Growth	12/09	12/10	12/11	12/12	12/13
Sales ($ mil.)	15.3%	361.2	386.4	439.7	518.2	637.3
Net income ($ mil.)	(5.6%)	58.7	38.8	42.2	11.8	46.6
Market value ($ mil.)	3.5%	3,031.6	3,582.9	3,473.4	3,713.6	3,481.1
Employees	15.5%	132	159	166	175	235

BIOMERICA, INC.

17571 Von Karman Avenue
Irvine, CA 92614
Phone: 949 645-2111
Fax: –
Web: www.bioamerica-inc.com/splash.html

NBB: BMRA
CEO: Zackary Irani
CFO: Janet Moore
HR: MAI Khuu
FYE: May 31
Type: Public

God bless Biomerica. The firm makes diagnostic tests for use worldwide in hospitals and other clinical laboratories as well as in doctors' offices and homes. Its clinical laboratory products are immunoassay tests for conditions such as food allergies diabetes infectious diseases and hyperthyroidism. Its point-of-care product portfolio which includes products that produce rapid results provides tests for prostate cancer pregnancy cat allergies and drugs of abuse. Biomerica has manufacturing facilities in the US and in Mexico. It once owned a minority interest in Lancer Orthodontics a maker of orthodontic products such as arch wires lingual attachments and buccal tubes but it sold its stake in 2008.

	Annual Growth	05/11	05/12	05/13	05/14	05/15
Sales ($ mil.)	0.3%	4.9	6.1	6.5	5.1	5.0
Net income ($ mil.)	–	0.2	0.5	0.5	(0.2)	(0.3)
Market value ($ mil.)	19.8%	3.4	5.2	6.7	6.4	7.0
Employees	6.5%	28	33	46	36	36

BIOMET INC.

56 E. Bell Dr.
Warsaw IN 46582-0587
Phone: 574-267-6639
Fax: 574-267-8137
Web: www.biomet.com

CEO: –
CFO: Daniel P Florin
HR: Darlene K Whaley
FYE: May 31
Type: Private

When the leg bone and the knee bone don't connect so well anymore Biomet may have a solution. Orthopedic specialists use the medical devices made by Biomet whose wares include reconstructive products (hips knees and shoulders) dental implants bone cement systems orthopedic support devices and operating-room supplies. Through Biomet Trauma and other units the firm also sells fixation devices (bone screws and pins) electrical bone-growth stimulators and bone grafting materials. Subsidiary Biomet Microfixation markets implants and bone substitute material for craniomaxillofacial (head and face) surgeries. Biomet is controlled by LVB Acquisition which is owned by a group of private equity firms.

BIOPHAN TECHNOLOGIES INC. OTC: BIPH

15 Schoen Place
Pittsford NY 14534
Phone: 585-267-4800
Fax: 585-267-4819
Web: www.biophan.com

CEO: –
CFO: –
HR: –
FYE: February 28
Type: Public

Biophan Technologies appreciates high visibility and smooth circulation. The company develops blood circulation support systems and technologies to help make medical devices compatible with MRI (magnetic resonance imaging) equipment. Its majority-owned Myotech unit is developing a system to restore and sustain blood flow in patients with acute heart failure. The system is based on a device that even a general surgeon can fit directly on a patient's heart to restart its pumping. Biophan's other technologies improve the visibility of coronary stents and vena cava filters in MRIs.

BIOMIMETIC THERAPEUTICS INC. NASDAQ: BMTI

389-A Nichol Mill Ln.
Franklin TN 37067
Phone: 615-844-1280
Fax: 615-844-1281
Web: www.biomimetics.com

CEO: –
CFO: –
HR: –
FYE: December 31
Type: Public

BioMimetic Therapeutics' GEM might not sparkle but it does attract cells that promote tissue and bone growth when applied to damaged tissue or a bone fracture. The company's products and candidates are based on the GEM (Growth-factor Enhanced Matrix) technology a combination drug and medical device platform that includes a human tissue growth factor with a synthetic bone matrix. BioMimetic Therapeutics develops the GEM technology as a treatment for various fractures where its bone matrix can be used to repair reinforce or fuse broken bones as well as repair tendons ligaments and cartilage. BioMimetic was acquired by Wright Medical Group for $380 million in 2013.

BIORELIANCE CORPORATION

14920 Broschart Rd.
Rockville MD 20850-3349
Phone: 301-738-1000
Fax: 301-610-2590
Web: www.bioreliance.com

CEO: David A Dodd
CFO: David S Walker
HR: Donna Klein
FYE: December 31
Type: Subsidiary

BioReliance is one lab rat whose testing and manufacturing wheels are turning. Founded in 1947 the company is a contract testing and manufacturing services provider hired by drug developers to enhance their products' safety. With laboratories and other operations in the US the UK India and Japan BioReliance conducts biologics safety testing animal diagnostics toxicology and clinical trial assay services. It also manufactures vaccines gene therapies and other biologics for use in clinical trials. Clients include biotech pharmaceutical and chemical companies medical device makers academic institutions and government agencies. Laboratory chemicals supplier Sigma-Aldrich acquired BioReliance in 2012.

BION ENVIRONMENTAL TECHNOLOGIES, INC. NBB: BNET

Box 566 / 1774 Summitview Way
Crestone, CO 81131
Phone: 212 758-6622
Fax: –
Web: www.biontech.com

CEO: Dominic Bassani
CFO: Mark A Smith
HR: –
FYE: June 30
Type: Public

A "moo moo" here and an "oink oink" there are music to the ears of Bion Environmental Technologies. The company provides waste stream remediation for animal operations primarily for large dairy and hog farms. To reduce pollution caused by animal waste Bion Environmental uses organic nutrients bacteria and other microbes to treat the waste before disposal. The treatment creates organic soil and fertilizer products which the company markets for use on athletic fields gardens and golf courses. The company is working closely with government bodies and universities in Pennsylvania to address the major problem of animal waste run-off from farms into the Chesapeake Bay.

	Annual Growth	06/11	06/12	06/13	06/14	06/15
Sales ($ mil.)	(44.5%)	–	–	0.0	0.0	0.0
Net income ($ mil.)	–	(7.0)	(6.4)	(8.2)	(5.8)	(5.6)
Market value ($ mil.)	(17.4%)	52.4	46.6	39.6	23.5	24.4
Employees	(15.9%)	12	12	8	6	6

BIOSCRIP INC NMS: BIOS

100 Clearbrook Road
Elmsford, NY 10523
Phone: 914 460-1600
Fax: –
Web: www.bioscrip.com

CEO: Richard M. (Rick) Smith
CFO: Jeffrey M. Kreger
HR: Lisa Nadler
FYE: December 31
Type: Public

BioScrip gets specialty medications and home health services to the people who need them. The company provides infusion services so that chronic care patients can skip a visit to the hospital and instead receive their medicine at specialty pharmacies in physicians' offices or at home. BioScrip's nurses administer the medicines to treat hemophilia cancer pain management or even simply hydration. The company also offers pharmacy benefit management (PBM) services for customers such as managed care organizations government agencies and self-funded employer groups.

	Annual Growth	12/10	12/11	12/12	12/13	12/14
Sales ($ mil.)	(12.0%)	1,638.6	1,818.0	662.6	842.2	984.1
Net income ($ mil.)	–	(69.1)	7.9	64.7	(69.7)	(147.5)
Market value ($ mil.)	7.5%	359.0	374.8	739.2	507.9	479.8
Employees	(8.0%)	3,475	3,409	2,939	3,909	2,490

BIOSPECIFICS TECHNOLOGIES CORP.   NMS: BSTC

35 Wilbur Street
Lynbrook, NY 11563
Phone: 516 593-7000
Fax: –
Web: www.biospecifics.com

CEO: –
CFO: –
HR: –
FYE: December 31
Type: Public

BioSpecifics Technologies specifically uses collagenase (an enzyme that breaks the bonds of collagen) to treat a variety of skin-thickening diseases and conditions. Its current product named Xiaflex is an injectable collagenase that treats Dupuytren's disease (marketed) and is being tested for Peyronie's disease frozen shoulder and cellulite. The company is working with Auxilium Pharmaceuticals on these indications. On its own BioSpecifics is also testing a collagenase treatment for human and canine lipoma (benign fatty tumor). The company was formed in 1990 to make a topical collagenase for burns and skin ulcers; it sold that business in 2006 but still received payments until 2013.

	Annual Growth	12/10	12/11	12/12	12/13	12/14
Sales ($ mil.)	25.6%	5.7	11.4	11.1	14.5	14.1
Net income ($ mil.)	–	(1.5)	6.6	3.0	5.3	4.6
Market value ($ mil.)	10.8%	172.3	111.9	100.6	145.9	259.9
Employees	0.0%	5	5	5	5	5

BIOSYNERGY, INC.   NBB: BSYN

1940 East Devon Avenue
Elk Grove Village, IL 60007
Phone: 847 956-0471
Fax: 847 956-6050
Web: www.biosynergyinc.com

CEO: Fred K Suzuki
CFO: Laurence Mead
HR: –
FYE: April 30
Type: Public

Biosynergy does its part to keep the good blood good. Biosynergy makes blood monitoring devices most of which are used in blood banks to keep blood healthy and at the right temperature. Its products are disposable cholesteric (asymmetrical) liquid crystal devices that cool heat and monitor blood and other lab materials or samples. The company also distributes some third-party products. In addition Biosynergy is developing antibacterial compounds for use in food and other products. The company sells its products to hospitals laboratories product dealers and clinical end-users. Chairman president and CEO Fred Suzuki controls about 35% of the company which was founded in 1976.

	Annual Growth	04/11	04/12	04/13	04/14	04/15
Sales ($ mil.)	4.9%	1.1	1.2	1.3	1.3	1.4
Net income ($ mil.)	4.1%	0.1	0.1	0.1	0.0	0.1
Market value ($ mil.)	–	0.0	0.0	0.0	0.0	0.0
Employees	4.7%	5	5	6	6	6

BIOTA PHARMACEUTICALS INC   NMS: BOTA

2500 Northwinds Parkway, Suite 100
Alpharetta, GA 30009
Phone: 678 221-3343
Fax: –
Web: www.biotapharma.com

CEO: Russell H Plumb
CFO: Mark P Colonnese
HR: Vivienne Green
FYE: June 30
Type: Public

Biota Biopharmaceuticals would like to wave bye-bye to a host of viral and bacterial infections plaguing mankind. It has two drugs in production and another three in the pipeline. The company licenses its Relenza to GlaxoSmithKline (GSK) which markets it worldwide to prevent and treat the flu. It has a similar agreement allowing DAIICHI SANKYO to market Inavir a long-acting flu drug in Japan. A version of Inavir is in trials in the US. Biota is also working on treatments for respiratory diseases the human rhinovirus (the common cold) and other hard-to-treat ailments. The company was formed in 2012 when Biota Holdings purchased Nabi Pharmaceuticals in an all-stock transaction that left Biota shareholders with 83%.

	Annual Growth	12/11*	06/12	06/13	06/14	06/15
Sales ($ mil.)	13.5%	14.8	20.4	33.6	68.7	24.6
Net income ($ mil.)	–	(4.5)	(19.2)	(8.7)	(11.0)	(19.1)
Market value ($ mil.)	2.4%	72.6	61.0	133.2	110.0	79.9
Employees	4.4%	16	–	89	66	19

*Fiscal year change

BIOTELEMETRY, INC.   NMS: BEAT

1000 Cedar Hollow Road
Malvern, PA 19355
Phone: 610 729-7000
Fax: –

CEO: Joseph H. (Joe) Capper
CFO: Heather C. Getz
HR: –
FYE: December 31
Type: Public

BioTelemetry knows how to keep a beat. The company provides real-time outpatient cardiac rhythm monitoring and telemetry services for patients throughout the US. Its core product Mobile Cardiac Outpatient Telemetry (MCOT) helps physicians diagnose and monitor heart arrhythmia in patients by providing continuous heartbeat monitoring and transmitting a complete picture of the heart's functions to physicians. The system which uses real-time two-way wireless communication accommodates patient mobility and remote physician adjustment. BioTelemetry also manufactures and sells traditional cardiac event and Holter monitors that record patient heart rhythm data but cannot transmit the data in real time.

	Annual Growth	12/10	12/11	12/12	12/13	12/14
Sales ($ mil.)	8.6%	119.9	119.0	111.5	129.5	166.6
Net income ($ mil.)	–	(19.9)	(61.4)	(12.2)	(7.3)	(9.8)
Market value ($ mil.)	21.0%	124.9	63.3	60.9	211.9	267.7
Employees	5.2%	754	665	728	622	922

BIOTIME INC   ASE: BTX

1301 Harbor Bay Parkway, Suite 100
Alameda, CA 94502
Phone: 510 521-3390
Fax: –
Web: www.biotimeinc.com

CEO: Michael D. West
CFO: Russell L. Skibsted
HR: –
FYE: December 31
Type: Public

BioTime helps surgeons face down a long day in surgery. BioTime makes water-based solutions to prevent massive blood loss after traumatic injury preserve organs for transplant and replace blood during such procedures as cardiac bypass. BioTime's Hextend product is approved to maintain blood volume during surgery and is sold in the US and overseas via third parties. The firm is also developing PentaLyte a version of the blood volume replacement product that metabolizes more quickly. BioTime has also expanded into the field of regenerative medicine; it sells a line of therapeutic stem cell research supplies. It is also working to develop its own line of biotech therapeutic candidates for degenerative diseases.

	Annual Growth	12/10	12/11	12/12	12/13	12/14
Sales ($ mil.)	9.3%	3.7	4.4	3.9	4.4	5.2
Net income ($ mil.)	–	(11.2)	(16.5)	(21.4)	(43.9)	(36.4)
Market value ($ mil.)	(18.2%)	651.6	454.5	245.6	281.6	291.8
Employees	35.1%	36	63	76	109	120

BIRDS EYE FOODS LLC

90 Linden Oaks
Rochester NY 14625
Phone: 585-383-1850
Fax: 585-385-2857
Web: www.birdseyefoods.com

CEO: Neil Harrison
CFO: Chris Puma
HR: –
FYE: June 30
Type: Subsidiary

Whether from a bird's eye or with an eye on the bottom line the view is sure to inspire health at Birds Eye Foods. Its namesake packaged frozen vegetables (boxed and bagged) are the #1 brand in the US frozen vegetable industry a more than $2 billion market in terms of retail sales. The company is also the #2 producer of frozen complete bagged meals providing a protein starch and vegetable. Birds Eye also makes such staples as canned pie fillings and chili and bottled salad dressings. It supplies US retail food retailers as well as foodservice and industrial food customers. Birds Eye operates as a division of diversified foods producer Pinnacle Foods itself owned by investment giant The Blackstone Group.

BIRKENSTOCK USA GP LLC

6 Hamilton Landing
Novato CA 94949
Phone: 415-884-3200
Fax: 888-937-2475
Web: www.birkenstockusa.com

CEO: –
CFO: –
HR: –
FYE: September 30
Type: Private

From Woodstock to the stock market Birkenstock wants you to put your best foot forward. Birkenstock USA is the exclusive US importer and distributor of the German-made footwear that was transformed from cult status to mainstream hip as the look of the 1970s re-emerged. The company's high-comfort products include hundreds of styles of shoes sandals clogs and arch supports for men women and children. Birkenstock's footwear is designed around the concept that the shape of the shoe should follow the shape of the foot. Birkenstock sells shoes through more than 1800 retailers and more than 200 licensed specialty shops. Birkenstock employees own 100% of the company.

BIRMINGHAM-SOUTHERN COLLEGE INC

900 ARKADELPHIA RD
BIRMINGHAM, AL 352540002
Phone: 205-226-4600
Fax: –
Web: www.bsc.edu

CEO: –
CFO: –
HR: Jennifer Herring
FYE: May 31
Type: Private

Birmingham-Southern College is a private liberal arts college affiliated with the United Methodist Church. The school offers bachelor's degrees in more than 50 fields of study including art history math physics and religion. It has an enrollment of approximately 1300 students. In addition to core curriculum in areas of arts fine arts music and science the college has study abroad independent study research honors interdisciplinary study and internship programs. Birmingham-Southern College is the result of the 1918 merger between Southern University (founded in 1856) and Birmingham College (founded in 1898).

	Annual Growth	05/08	05/09	05/10	05/11	05/13
Sales ($ mil.)	–	–	0.0	60.3	75.5	73.9
Net income ($ mil.)	–	–	–	(19.0)	0.2	7.9
Market value ($ mil.)	–	–	–	–	–	–
Employees	–	–	–	–	–	299

BIRNER DENTAL MANAGEMENT SERVICES, INC.

NAS: BDMS

1777 S. Harrison Street, Suite 1400
Denver, CO 80210
Phone: 303 691-0680
Fax: –
Web: www.perfectteeth.com

CEO: Frederic W J Birner
CFO: Dennis N Genty
HR: Carl Budke
FYE: December 31
Type: Public

Birner Dental Management Services hopes to leave its customers smiling. The company acquires develops and manages dental practice networks freeing dentists of their administrative duties by providing management services such as billing accounting and marketing. Birner Dental manages about 60 offices under the Perfect Teeth brand name; more than 40 of the practices are located in Colorado and the rest are in Arizona and New Mexico. Some locations offer special services such as orthodontics oral surgery and periodontics. Brothers and co-founders Frederic (chairman and CEO) and Mark Birner (president) together own more than one-quarter of the company.

	Annual Growth	12/10	12/11	12/12	12/13	12/14
Sales ($ mil.)	0.4%	64.0	63.1	62.4	64.1	65.1
Net income ($ mil.)	–	1.4	1.6	0.8	0.1	(0.9)
Market value ($ mil.)	(5.7%)	35.3	29.8	31.8	32.5	27.9
Employees	(7.2%)	708	515	588	594	526

BISCOM INC.

321 Billerica Rd.
Chelmsford MA 01824
Phone: 978-250-1800
Fax: 978-250-4449
Web: www.biscom.com

CEO: Bill Ho
CFO: –
HR: –
FYE: June 30
Type: Private

Biscom can help you get right down to seemingly mundane business details such as faxing and e-mailing. The company provides enterprise fax server and fax software products including products to make various messaging formats and data such as voicemail fax and e-mail accessible and integrated into various applications. Biscom also provides tools for securly tranferring files throughout enterprises as well as document capture and routing products. Biscom's customers come from a variety of industries such as financial services manufacturing retail and health care.

BISON BUILDING MATERIALS LTD.

1445 W. Sam Houston Pkwy. North
Houston TX 77043-3110
Phone: 713-467-6700
Fax: 713-935-1223
Web: www.bisonbuilding.com

CEO: –
CFO: –
HR: –
FYE: April 30
Type: Private

Bison Building Materials provides lumber and building materials to primarily residential contractors and remodelers through about five locations in the Houston area and Central Texas. Besides lumber and plywood Bison Building Materials specializes in engineered wood products such as flooring structural beams fiberglass insulation and millwork. Founded in 1962 by Roy Bierschwale as a small retail store and lumber shed Bison Building Materials filed for Chapter 11 bankruptcy protection in 2009 following the crash in the housing market. Rival Stock Building Supply (SBS) acquired the company in July 2010.

BISSELL HOMECARE INC.

2345 Walker St. NW
Grand Rapids MI 49544
Phone: 616-453-4451
Fax: 616-453-1383
Web: www.bissell.com

CEO: Mark J Bissell
CFO: –
HR: –
FYE: December 31
Type: Private

BISSELL's in the business of seeing spots and taking care of dust bunnies. A pioneer in the carpet-cleaning industry BISSELL Homecare makes a full line of vacuum cleaners sweepers steam cleaners deep cleaners and cleaning chemicals for home use. Its models include the Powersteamer Big Green and Spotlifter machines. The firm sells its products worldwide under the BISSELL and Woolite brand names through mass merchandisers (Best Buy Target Wal-Mart) home centers (Lowe's Home Depot) hardware stores (Ace Hardware) and through BISSELL.com. It entered the deep-cleaning rental business in 2010. Founded in 1876 by Melville and Anna Bissell the company is still owned and operated by the Bissell family.

BITCO CORPORATION

320 18th St.
Rock Island IL 61201
Phone: 309-786-5401
Fax: 309-786-3847
Web: www.bituminousinsurance.com

CEO: Greg Ator
CFO: –
HR: –
FYE: December 31
Type: Subsidiary

Bitco which operates as the Bituminous Insurance Companies provides insurance services with industry specialization in construction construction materials forest products oil and gas and structural moving. The group consists of Bituminous Casualty and Bituminous Fire and Marine Insurance and underwrites primarily commercial automobile commercial property general liability and workers' compensation insurance lines. Bitco also sells insurance through Great West Casualty Company which specializes in coverage primarily for the motor carrier industry. Its products are marketed through independent insurance agents. Bitco and the Bituminous Insurance Companies are subsidiaries of Old Republic International.

BITSTREAM INC.

NASDAQ: BITS

500 Nickerson Rd.
Marlborough MA 01752
Phone: 617-497-6222
Fax: 617-868-0784
Web: www.bitstream.com

CEO: Amos Kaminski
CFO: James P Dore
HR: –
FYE: December 31
Type: Public

Bitstream counts on its fonts to keep business flowing. The company's Font Fusion and Bitstream Panorama technologies help deliver typographic capabilities to hardware software and Web applications. Font Fusion is the company's base text rendering technology designed specifically for small form factors such as mobile phones and set-top boxes. Bitstream Panorama specializes in complex language printing needs such as for Arabic Hebrew and Thai. Bitstream also offers some 62000 fonts to consumers through MyFonts.com. In 2011 Bitstream spun off its mobile browsing and data publishing businesses to facilitate the company's acquisition by Monotype Imaging in 2012.

BJ'S RESTAURANTS INC

NMS: BJRI

7755 Center Avenue, Suite 300
Huntington Beach, CA 92647
Phone: 714 500-2400
Fax: –
Web: www.bjsrestaurants.com

CEO: Gregory A. (Greg) Trojan
CFO: Gregory S. (Greg) Levin
HR: –
FYE: December 30
Type: Public

The Windy City inspires the food and drink at BJ's. BJ's Restaurants owns and operates 130 restaurants in California and 14 other mostly western states under the names BJ's Restaurant & Brewhouse BJ's Restaurant & Brewery and BJ's Pizza & Grill. The casual-dining eateries offer Chicago-style pizza salads sandwiches pasta and the company's own hand-crafted beers. Its Restaurant & Brewery locations which feature an onsite microbrewery help supply beer to the rest of the chain. The Brewhouse locations sell beer from company breweries and from third-parties using the company's recipes. The smaller Pizza & Grill shops have limited menus. The first BJ's opened in California in 1978.

	Annual Growth	12/10*	01/12	01/13*	12/13	12/14
Sales ($ mil.)	13.3%	513.9	620.9	708.3	775.1	845.6
Net income ($ mil.)	4.3%	23.2	31.6	31.4	21.0	27.4
Market value ($ mil.)	8.6%	949.0	1,154.9	862.9	814.7	1,319.3
Employees	11.2%	12,230	14,360	16,430	18,695	18,700

*Fiscal year change

BJ'S WHOLESALE CLUB INC.

25 Research Dr.
Westborough MA 01581
Phone: 508-651-7400
Fax: 508-651-6114
Web: www.bjs.com

CEO: Laura Sen
CFO: Robert Eddy
HR: –
FYE: January 31
Type: Private

"Exclusive membership" has never been as common as it is at BJ's Wholesale Club. The firm is the nation's #3 membership warehouse club (far behind leaders Costco and SAM'S CLUB) and #1 in New England with more than nine million members and about 195 locations in 15 states mostly along the Eastern Seaboard. Food including canned fresh and frozen items accounts for about two-thirds of sales at BJ's. The remainder comes from general merchandise including apparel housewares office equipment small appliances and gas. Unlike its major rivals BJ's targets individual retail customers rather than small businesses. BJ's was taken private in 2011.

BJT INC.

2233 CAPITAL BLVD
RALEIGH, NC 276041421
Phone: 919-828-3842
Fax: –
Web: www.mutualdistributing.com

CEO: –
CFO: –
HR: Hussain B Abbas
FYE: December 31
Type: Private

A wholesaler of Southern comfort Mutual Distributing distributes alcoholic and nonalcoholic beverages in North Carolina. The company started in 1946 operates from seven locations across the state. Alcoholic beverage brands handled by Mutual Distributing include domestic and imported wine labels by Wyndham Estate Robert Mondavi Moet & Chandon and Folie a Deux and beers by Anchor Tecate Heineken and Sapporo. The company distributes bottled waters too such as Evian Perrier San Pellegrino and Fiji. Mutual Distributing caters to retail customers (supermarkets convenience stores and specialty package outlets restaurants and hotels) in every county in North Carolina.

	Annual Growth	12/04	12/05	12/06	12/08	12/09
Sales ($ mil.)	6.1%	–	158.3	172.7	192.0	200.4
Net income ($ mil.)	13.9%	–	–	4.2	7.8	6.2
Market value ($ mil.)	–	–	–	–	–	–
Employees	–	–	–	–	–	650

BKF CAPITAL GROUP INC

NBB: BKFG

3990 - B Heritage Oak Court
Simi Valley, CA 93063
Phone: 805 416-7100
Fax: –
Web: www.bkfcapital.com

CEO: Steven N Bronson
CFO: –
HR: –
FYE: December 31
Type: Public

Wanted: business opportunity for former investment firm. Contact BKF Capital Group. BKF is evaluating strategic alternatives including a possible merger acquisition or other business combination. The company has no operations and only a small revenue stream (more like a trickle) from its days as an asset manager and broker dealer; it is no longer a registered investment advisor and has also surrendered its broker license. Its primary subsidiary is BKF Asset Management but as the company itself points out it has no operations either. BKF Capital's search for a new raison d'etre was put on hold when it was named in a class action shareholder lawsuit but the suit was dropped in 2007 and the search resumed.

	Annual Growth	12/09	12/10	12/11	12/12	12/13
Assets ($ mil.)	(16.9%)	14.5	12.9	11.7	9.8	6.9
Net income ($ mil.)	–	(0.2)	0.6	(0.2)	(0.8)	(2.3)
Market value ($ mil.)	3.4%	6.9	9.3	8.3	7.8	7.9
Employees	0.0%	1	–	–	3	1

BLACK & VEATCH CORPORATION

11401 LAMAR AVE
OVERLAND PARK, KS 662111598
Phone: 913-458-2000
Fax: –
Web: www.bv.com

CEO: O. H. (Dean) Oskvig
CFO: Karen L. Daniel
HR: Craig Anderson
FYE: December 31
Type: Private

One of the US's largest private companies Black & Veatch (BV) is a leading global engineering consulting and construction firm specializing in infrastructure development for the energy water environmental federal and telecommunications markets. BV offers environmental consulting operations and maintenance security design and consulting management consulting and IT services. With offices worldwide it has worked on coal nuclear and combustion turbine plants; drinking water and coastal water operations; and wireless and broadband installation. Clients include Sumitomo Corp. and Southern Water. The company was founded in 1915 in Kansas City Missouri by engineers E. B. Black and Tom Veatch.

	Annual Growth	12/05	12/06	12/07	12/08	12/09
Sales ($ mil.)	2.6%	–	1,075.4	1,287.3	1,267.3	1,163.0
Net income ($ mil.)	31.7%	–	–	33.5	16.9	58.2
Market value ($ mil.)	–	–	–	–	–	–
Employees	–	–	–	–	–	4,065

BLACK BOX CORP. (DE) NMS: BBOX

1000 Park Drive
Lawrence, PA 15055
Phone: 724 746-5500
Fax: –
Web: www.blackbox.com

CEO: E. C. Sykes
CFO: Timothy C. (Tim) Huffmyer
HR: –
FYE: March 31
Type: Public

Black Box packs a lot of equipment in its box of networking products. The company distributes and supports voice and data networking infrastructure offering more than 118000 products including modems routers switches and testing equipment. It also sells cabinets cables and training materials. Black Box primarily distributes and services third-party equipment some of which carries its brand but it also manufactures some products. Most of the company's sales come from its on-site services such as design installation technical support and maintenance. Black Box sells to corporations schools and government agencies primarily in North America and Europe. Key industries served include business services manufacturing banking retail and health care.

	Annual Growth	03/11	03/12	03/13	03/14	03/15
Sales ($ mil.)	(1.8%)	1,068.2	1,087.5	997.8	971.7	992.4
Net income ($ mil.)	(26.6%)	52.9	(247.7)	28.8	(115.9)	15.3
Market value ($ mil.)	(12.2%)	540.1	392.0	335.1	374.0	321.6
Employees	(3.7%)	4,413	4,302	3,900	3,959	3,803

BLACK DIAMOND INC. NMS: BDE

2084 East 3900 South
Salt Lake City, UT 84124
Phone: 801 278-5552
Fax: –

CEO: Peter R. Metcalf
CFO: Robert Peay
HR: –
FYE: December 31
Type: Public

Black Diamond (formerly Clarus Corp.) caters to expert skiers snowboarders rock and ice climbers and other hardy-outdoor types. The company makes and distributes climbing and mountaineering equipment (carabiners harnesses helmets) backpacks tents trekking poles headlamps and lanterns gloves and mittens skis bindings boots avalanche safety equipment mountain biking gear and more under the Black Diamond Gregory PIEPS and POC brands. Predecessor company Clarus which provided procurement and sourcing software liquidated its assets and purchased outdoor products firm Black Diamond Equipment in 2010 and adopted the Black Diamond name the following year.

	Annual Growth	12/10	12/11	12/12	12/13	12/14
Sales ($ mil.)	26.3%	75.9	145.8	175.9	203.0	193.1
Net income ($ mil.)	(27.7%)	51.2	4.9	2.0	(5.9)	14.0
Market value ($ mil.)	2.6%	258.7	244.3	268.2	435.9	286.2
Employees	10.2%	475	560	696	746	700

BLACK ENTERTAINMENT TELEVISION LLC

1 BET Plaza 1235 W St. NE
Washington DC 20018
Phone: 202-608-2000
Fax: 202-608-2589
Web: www.bet.com

CEO: Debra L Lee
CFO: Scott Mills
HR: –
FYE: December 31
Type: Subsidiary

You might say this network gives cable TV some street cred. Black Entertainment Television operates BET the leading cable channel targeting young African-American audiences with a mix of entertainment music and news programming. Reaching about 91 million US homes BET boasts a lineup that includes 106 & Park (music videos); BET Awards and Soul Train Awards (award shows); Harlem Heights (reality shows); The Game (scripted series) and Sunday Best (gospel music). The network is the flagship property of BET Networks which includes sister outlets BET Gospel BET Hip Hop and Centric (targeting multicultural viewers). Launched in 1980 BET is owned by media conglomerate Viacom.

BLACK HILLS CORPORATION NYS: BKH

625 Ninth Street
Rapid City, SD 57701
Phone: 605 721-1700
Fax: –
Web: www.blackhillscorp.com

CEO: David R. Emery
CFO: Richard W. Kinzley
HR: Robert (Bob) Myers
FYE: December 31
Type: Public

The Black Hills (and neighboring states) are alive with the sound of energy generation distribution and exploration activities. Black Hills distributes power to 205400 customers in Colorado Montana South Dakota and Wyoming; its Cheyenne Light Fuel and Power unit serves 40970 electric customers and 36000 natural gas customers in the Cheyenne area. Black Hills' energy segment serves 543200 natural gas customers in Colorado Iowa Kansas Nebraska and Wyoming and 94400 electricity customers in Colorado. The company's unregulated segment is engaged in coal mining power generation oil and gas production and appliance repair services.

	Annual Growth	12/10	12/11	12/12	12/13	12/14
Sales ($ mil.)	1.6%	1,307.3	1,272.2	1,173.9	1,275.9	1,393.6
Net income ($ mil.)	17.0%	68.7	49.7	81.5	115.0	128.8
Market value ($ mil.)	15.3%	1,340.2	1,500.1	1,623.4	2,345.7	2,369.4
Employees	(1.2%)	2,124	2,030	1,925	1,948	2,021

BLACK HILLS POWER INC.

625 Ninth Street
Rapid City, SD 57701
Phone: 605 721-1700
Fax: –
Web: www.blackhillspower.com

CEO: David R Emery
CFO: Richard (Dick) Kinzley
HR: –
FYE: December 31
Type: Public

Mount Rushmore is a monument to the powerful in the Black Hills of South Dakota. Black Hills Power formed in 1941 the same year the Mount Rushmore was completed gets power to the people. It generates transmits and distributes electricity to 66000 customers. Its 9300 sq.ml. service area encompasses western South Dakota northeastern Wyoming and southeastern Montana. The utility became a subsidiary of Black Hills Corporation in 2000. Its five electric power plants are fueled by low-sulphur Wyoming coal mined by Black Hills Corp.'s unit Wyodak Resource Development Corp.

	Annual Growth	12/10	12/11	12/12	12/13	12/14
Sales ($ mil.)	4.0%	229.8	245.6	243.3	254.0	268.5
Net income ($ mil.)	1.8%	31.3	27.1	27.1	30.2	33.6
Market value ($ mil.)	–	–	–	–	–	–
Employees	–	–	–	–	–	–

BLACK RAVEN ENERGY INC.

1875 Lawrence St. Ste. 450
Denver CO 80202
Phone: 303-308-1330
Fax: 303-308-1590
Web: www.blackravenenergy.com

CEO: Thomas E Riley
CFO: Patrick A Quinn
HR: –
FYE: December 31
Type: Private

Black Raven Energy (formerly PRB Energy) is engaged in coal-bed methane production in the Rocky Mountains. The company focuses on natural gas gathering and exploration and production. Its exploration and gathering and processing operations are primarily located in the Powder River Basin. In 2007 PRB Energy was targeting reserves of about 100 billion cu. ft. of natural gas equivalent before deteriorating finances hurt its expansion plans. The company filed for Chapter 11 bankruptcy protection in 2008. In preparation to emerge from bankruptcy it reorganized as Black Raven Energy in 2009.

BLACKBAUD, INC.

NMS: BLKB

2000 Daniel Island Drive
Charleston, SC 29492
Phone: 843 216-6200
Fax: 843 216-6100
Web: www.blackbaud.com

CEO: Michael P. (Mike) Gianoni
CFO: Anthony W. (Tony) Boor
HR: John J. Mistretta
FYE: December 31
Type: Public

Blackbaud provides financial fundraising and administrative software for not-for-profit organizations and educational institutions. Software offerings include The Raiser's Edge for fundraising management Blackbaud Enterprise CRM for customer relationship management The Financial Edge for accounting and The Education Edge for managing school admissions registration and billing. Blackbaud has about 30000 customers in 60 countries including colleges environmental groups health and human services providers churches and animal welfare groups. The company generates most of its sales in the US.

	Annual Growth	12/10	12/11	12/12	12/13	12/14
Sales ($ mil.)	14.6%	327.1	370.9	447.4	503.8	564.4
Net income ($ mil.)	(1.3%)	29.8	33.2	6.6	30.5	28.3
Market value ($ mil.)	13.7%	1,199.4	1,282.7	1,057.2	1,743.5	2,003.3
Employees	10.1%	2,065	2,256	2,705	2,666	3,033

BLACKBOARD INC.

650 Massachusetts Ave. NW 6th Fl.
Washington DC 20001-3796
Phone: 202-463-4860
Fax: 202-463-4863
Web: www.blackboard.com

CEO: William L Ballhaus
CFO: Bill Davis
HR: –
FYE: December 31
Type: Private

Chalk up Blackboard's success to the Internet. Blackboard develops software that lets schools create Internet-based learning programs and communities. Its applications connect teachers students parents and administrators via the Web enabling Internet-based assignments class websites and online collaboration with classmates. The software also includes a content management system for creating and managing digital course content. Other modules include transaction community and payment management tools that enable students to use their college IDs for meal plans events and tuition payments. In 2011 Blackboard was acquired by Providence Equity for about $1.64 billion.

BLACKFOOT TELEPHONE COOPERATIVE INC.

1221 N RUSSELL ST
MISSOULA, MT 598081898
Phone: 406-541-2121
Fax: –
Web: www.blackfoot.com

CEO: Bill Squires
CFO: Theodore Otis
HR: –
FYE: December 31
Type: Private

Blackfoot Telecommunications Cooperative provides phone services to rural communities along the Blackfoot River in western Montana and central Idaho. Founded in 1954 it is the first of the Blackfoot Communications Group of companies which includes competitive local-exchange carrier (CLEC) Blackfoot Communications Blackfoot.net Internet services provider and telecom software maker TeleSphere. The company's services include local and long-distance phone service dial-up and DSL Internet access and PCS wireless. It also owns a stake in video conferencing specialist Vision Net.

	Annual Growth	12/05	12/06	12/07	12/08	12/09
Sales ($ mil.)	0.6%	–	31.6	33.1	33.9	32.1
Net income ($ mil.)	15.5%	–	–	2.9	3.7	3.9
Market value ($ mil.)	–	–	–	–	–	–
Employees	–	–	–	–	–	214

BLACKHAWK NETWORK HOLDINGS INC

NMS: HAWK

6220 Stoneridge Mall Road
Pleasanton, CA 94588
Phone: 925 226-9990
Fax: –
Web: www.blackhawknetwork.com

CEO: William Y. Tauscher
CFO: Jerry N. Ulrich
HR: –
FYE: January 03
Type: Public

When choosing a gift green always fits. But how about plastic? Blackhawk Network sells gift phone sports ticket prepaid debit and prepaid wireless phone cards through a network of more than 195000 retailers around the world. The cards can be found in convenience drug grocery and specialty stores including Chevron Food Lion Kroger and Safeway (Blackhawk's founder). Blackhawk offers more than 600 brands of cards from companies such as Apple Barnes & Noble iTunes Starbucks Visa and the NBA. The cards can be found online or at Gift Card Mall racks which display hundreds of cards that can be redeemed online or on-site at retail locations. Grocer Safeway took Blackhawk public in 2013.

	Annual Growth	01/11*	12/11	12/12	12/13*	01/15
Sales ($ mil.)	25.8%	577.7	751.8	959.1	1,138.1	1,445.0
Net income ($ mil.)	24.1%	19.2	36.5	48.2	54.1	45.5
Market value ($ mil.)	20.1%	–	–	–	1,372.9	1,980.2
Employees	36.9%	–	–	725	1,316	1,860

*Fiscal year change

BLACKROCK, INC.

NYS: BLK

55 East 52nd Street
New York, NY 10055
Phone: 212 810-5300
Fax: –
Web: www.blackrock.com

CEO: Laurence D. (Larry) Fink
CFO: Gary S. Shedlin
HR: Jeffrey A. Smith
FYE: December 31
Type: Public

Now this is the kind of rock you want in your stocking. With some $4.65 trillion in assets under management BlackRock is the world's largest public investment management firm. It specializes in equity and fixed income products as well as alternative and multi-class instruments which it invests in on behalf of institutional and retail investors worldwide; it does not engage in proprietary trading. Clients include pension plans governments insurance companies mutual funds endowments foundations and charities. BlackRock also provides risk management services through BlackRock Solutions and is a leading provider of exchange-traded funds (ETFs) through iShares. The firm has offices in 30 countries.

	Annual Growth	12/10	12/11	12/12	12/13	12/14
Sales ($ mil.)	6.5%	8,612.0	9,081.0	9,337.0	10,180.0	11,081.0
Net income ($ mil.)	12.4%	2,063.0	2,337.0	2,458.0	2,932.0	3,294.0
Market value ($ mil.)	17.0%	31,405.1	29,371.6	34,063.1	52,150.1	58,921.2
Employees	7.5%	9,127	10,100	10,500	11,400	12,200

BLACKSTONE GROUP LP (THE)   NYS: BX

345 Park Avenue
New York, NY 10154
Phone: 212 583-5000
Fax: -
Web: www.blackstone.com

CEO: Stephen A. Schwarzman
CFO: Michael S. Chae
HR: Padraic McGovern
FYE: December 31
Type: Public

Throw a rock and you're bound to hit a Blackstone investment. The Blackstone Group is one of the world's largest real estate private equity and alternative asset managers in the world with over $330 billion in assets under management and such notable holdings as Michaels Stores SeaWorld and Crocs. The firm manages investment vehicles including private equity funds funds of hedge funds and real estate funds. It also provides advisory services on mergers and acquisitions restructuring and other transactions for corporations. Clients include public and corporate pensions financial institutions and individuals. About 60% of its revenue comes from performance fees while one-third comes from management and advisory fees.

	Annual Growth	12/10	12/11	12/12	12/13	12/14
Sales ($ mil.)	24.5%	3,119.3	3,252.6	4,019.4	6,613.2	7,484.7
Net income ($ mil.)	-	(370.0)	(168.3)	218.6	1,171.2	1,584.6
Market value ($ mil.)	24.3%	8,428.1	8,344.7	9,285.8	18,762.2	20,150.0
Employees	11.1%	1,440	1,585	1,780	2,010	2,190

BLACKSTONE MORTGAGE TRUST INC   NYS: BXMT

345 Park Avenue, 42nd Floor
New York, NY 10154
Phone: 212 655-0220
Fax: -
Web: www.blackstonemortgagetrust.com

CEO: Stephen D Plavin
CFO: Paul D Quinlan
HR: -
FYE: December 31
Type: Public

Capital Trust thinks investing in commercial mortgages is a capital idea. The self-managed real estate investment trust (REIT) originates underwrites and invests in commercial real estate assets on its own behalf and for other investors. Its portfolio includes first mortgage and bridge loans mezzanine loans and collateralized mortgage-backed securities. Subsidiary CT Investment Management which the company is selling manages five private equity funds and a separate account for third parties. Most Capital Trust's assets are related to US properties but the REIT does make occasional investments in international instruments.

	Annual Growth	12/10	12/11	12/12	12/13	12/14
Sales ($ mil.)	1.6%	173.7	132.3	34.9	53.2	184.8
Net income ($ mil.)	-	(185.3)	258.1	181.0	15.0	90.0
Market value ($ mil.)	108.2%	90.3	131.1	122.4	1,580.9	1,698.0
Employees	-	-	29	29	-	-

BLAIR CORPORATION

220 Hickory St.
Warren PA 16366
Phone: 814-723-3600
Fax: 814-726-6376
Web: www.blair.com

CEO: -
CFO: Larry Pitorak
HR: Richard Zimmerman
FYE: December 31
Type: Subsidiary

Before its customers pick up the phone to arrange a game of pinochle with their peeps Blair hopes they'll give some attention to its latest mailing. Through its catalogs letter pitches and website Blair sells men's and women's clothing (its biggest sales generators) to middle-aged and senior low- to middle-income customers. The company also sells home decor bedspreads bath accessories drapes kitchenware rugs and vacuums. Most of Blair's merchandise is made to specifications by independent suppliers. Established in 1910 it operates a retail store and a factory outlet in Pennsylvania. Apparel marketer Orchard Brands (formerly Appleseed's Topco) owns Blair.

BLANCHARD VALLEY FARMERS COOPERATIVE INC.

6566 COUNTY ROAD 236
FINDLAY, OH 458409769
Phone: 419-423-2611
Fax: -
Web: www.bvfcoop.com

CEO: -
CFO: -
HR: -
FYE: December 31
Type: Private

Supporting local farmers gives Blanchard Valley Farmers Cooperative (BVFC) roots and reach. Founded in 1989 BVFC has about 1700 area members. The co-op owns more than a dozen locations including four agronomy stations two seasonal grain facilities a farm and garden store and two petroleum sites. Member-farmers benefit from the co-op's array of products and services including seed feed fertilizer grain crop storage crop applications and farming equipment sales and rental. The feed store also sells mulch birdseed and pet supplies as well as conducts soil testing and arranges seeding and fertilizer programs. BVFC's petroleum locations offer gasoline and home-heating oil among several products.

	Annual Growth	12/09	12/10	12/11	12/12	12/13
Sales ($ mil.)	17.9%	-	196.5	292.5	335.8	321.9
Net income ($ mil.)	5.4%	-	-	7.4	5.4	8.2
Market value ($ mil.)	-	-	-	-	-	-
Employees	-	-	-	-	-	122

BLANK ROME LLP

1 Logan Sq.
Philadelphia PA 19103-6998
Phone: 215-569-5500
Fax: 215-569-5555
Web: www.blankrome.com

CEO: -
CFO: -
HR: -
FYE: December 31
Type: Private - Partnershi

Blank Rome has more than 500 lawyers in about 10 offices located mostly in the eastern US with one office in Hong Kong and one in Shanghai. The firm practices in such areas as bankruptcy corporate governance employment government relations intellectual property litigation maritime real estate and tax. Through its Blank Rome Government Relations affiliate the firm provides advocacy and communications services. Blank Rome caters to a wide array of industries such as life sciences chemical private equity real estate and financial institutions. Blank Rome opened a Houston office in 2011 the firm's first Texas office.

BLARNEY CASTLE OIL CO.

12218 WEST ST
BEAR LAKE, MI 496149432
Phone: 231-864-3111
Fax: -
Web: www.blarneycastleoil.com

CEO: -
CFO: Joe Taraskavage
HR: Karen Tetsworth
FYE: March 31
Type: Private

While kissing the Blarney stone has a reputation for reliably making people loquacious Blarney Castle Oil and Propane has a reputation for reliably supplying its customers with fuels. The family-owned company transports petroleum products to customers through about 10 office locations in Michigan. Its products include agricultural and commercial fuels (diesel and gasoline) commercial and industrial lubricants and coolants home heating oil fuel oil and propane. Blarney Castle Oil and Propane also operates 90 convenience stores under the EZ Mart brand name.

	Annual Growth	03/10	03/11	03/12	03/13	03/14
Sales ($ mil.)	8.2%	-	415.3	501.5	513.6	526.0
Net income ($ mil.)	18.4%	-	-	4.0	6.0	5.7
Market value ($ mil.)	-	-	-	-	-	-
Employees	-	-	-	-	-	700

BLESSING HOSPITAL

BROADWAY AT 11TH ST
QUINCY, IL 62301
Phone: 217-223-1200
Fax: –
Web: www.blessinghealthsystem.org

CEO: –
CFO: –
HR: Joellen Randall
FYE: September 30
Type: Private

Blessing Hospital is a not-for-profit acute care medical center that provides a wide range of health services to residents in areas of western Illinois northeast Missouri and southeast Iowa. Through its main campus location it provides primary and emergency care as well as specialty services including diagnostics and surgery. The hospital is home to centers of excellence in the treatment of cancer heart and cardiovascular ailments wound care and women's health issues. Blessing Hospital provides outpatient and behavioral health services at a nearby campus. It also operates family practice centers and provides home and hospice care services. It is part of the Blessing Health System.

	Annual Growth	09/06	09/07	09/08	09/12	09/13
Sales ($ mil.)	4.7%	–	230.0	238.4	289.1	303.3
Net income ($ mil.)	–	–	–	(2.2)	14.8	31.9
Market value ($ mil.)	–	–	–	–	–	–
Employees	–	–	–	–	–	2,500

BLISH-MIZE CO.

223 S 5TH ST
ATCHISON, KS 660022801
Phone: 913-367-1250
Fax: –
Web: www.blishmize.com

CEO: –
CFO: Tom Hottovy
HR: Amy Hendon
FYE: December 31
Type: Private

Hardware supplier Blish-Mize distributes more than 52000 products to hardware stores home centers lumberyards and paint stores in a dozen states in the heartland of the US. Its catalog includes hand and power tools lawn equipment hardware paint heating and cooling products housewares plumbing and electrical supplies and sporting goods. The company has distribution centers in Colorado and Kansas. Aside from its wholesaling business Blish-Mize operates toolmaker Hardware House with House-Hasson. Brothers-in-law David Blish Edward Mize and Jack Silliman founded the firm in 1871 to outfit wagon trains. President and CEO John Mize Jr. represents the fourth generation of the family-owned company.

	Annual Growth	12/05	12/06	12/07	12/08	12/09
Sales ($ mil.)	–	–	–	(1,647.8)	64.0	60.5
Net income ($ mil.)	12586.3%	–	–	0.0	1.8	0.7
Market value ($ mil.)	–	–	–	–	–	–
Employees	–	–	–	–	–	175

BLIZZARD ENTERTAINMENT INC.

16215 Alton Pkwy.
Irvine CA 92623
Phone: 949-955-1380
Fax: +44-20-7802-5600
Web: www.capreg.com

CEO: Mike Morhaime
CFO: –
HR: –
FYE: December 31
Type: Subsidiary

Blizzard Entertainment hopes to continue to produce a flurry of hit games. A unit of Activision Blizzard the company is the leading video game maker in the massively multiplayer online role-playing games (MMORPG) niche. It develops and publishes software titles such as the genre-dominating World of Warcraft (about 10 million subscribers) Starcraft and Diablo series available for play on PCs. Blizzard offers its Battle.net online gaming service that enables the worldwide social gaming experience for its titles. The games are sold through retailers and online download. The company has also leveraged its popular games into related products such as action figures board games graphic novels and comic books.

BLOCK (H & R), INC.

One H&R Block Way
Kansas City, MO 64105
Phone: 816 854-3000
Fax: –
Web: www.hrblock.com

NYS: HRB
CEO: William C. (Bill) Cobb
CFO: Gregory J. (Greg) Macfarlane
HR: Sarah Shahan
FYE: April 30
Type: Public

Only two things are certain in this life and H&R Block has a leg up on one of them. The company is one of the largest tax return preparers in the US where it boasts more than 12000 company-owned and franchised retail locations. It also has almost 1600 locations in Canada and Australia. It serves more than 24 million tax customers in all. The firm also publishes do-it-yourself tax-preparation software and provides retail banking through H&R Block Bank; Though in mid-2015 it was in the process of selling H&R Block Bank to BofI Federal Bank to exit the banking business reflecting H&R Block's ongoing efforts to refocus on its core tax preparation services.

	Annual Growth	04/11	04/12	04/13	04/14	04/15
Sales ($ mil.)	(5.0%)	3,774.3	2,893.8	2,905.9	3,024.3	3,078.7
Net income ($ mil.)	3.9%	406.1	265.9	433.9	475.2	473.7
Market value ($ mil.)	15.0%	4,759.5	4,046.5	7,636.1	7,823.3	8,324.3
Employees	(27.4%)	7,900	2,500	2,200	2,200	2,200

BLOCKBUSTER L.L.C.

9601 S. Meridian Blvd
Englewood CO 80112
Phone: 303-723-1000
Fax: 414-259-5773
Web: www.briggsandstratton.com

CEO: James W Keyes
CFO: –
HR: –
FYE: December 31
Type: Subsidiary

With video stores going the way of the dinosaurs (and record stores) movie rental chain Blockbuster has seen its business take a Hollywood-sized hit. With a library of more than 125000 movie and video game titles Blockbuster has struggled to transform its store-based distribution system to a multichannel content delivery model. The company's customers can either download movies to their home or mobile devices order them by mail or visit one of a dwindling number of Blockbuster stores. Amid rapid technological change and competition from Netflix and Redbox Blockbuster filed for Chapter 11 bankruptcy protection in 2010 and was sold to satellite TV service provider DISH Network.

BLONDER TONGUE LABORATORIES, INC.

One Jake Brown Road
Old Bridge, NJ 08857
Phone: 732 679-4000
Fax: –

ASE: BDR
CEO: Robert J Palle Jr
CFO: Eric S Skolnik
HR: –
FYE: December 31
Type: Public

Blonder Tongue Laboratories isn't involved in genetic modification — it makes equipment for acquiring and distributing cable TV signals. Founded by Isaac Blonder and Ben Tongue the company's offerings center on analog and digital video products for headend facilities (television signal-receiving centers) such as encoders receivers and modulators as well as hybrid fiber-coax (HFC) distribution products which deliver the signal to the viewer. Blonder Tongue mainly serves cable operators TV broadcasters the lodging and hospitality sector and institutional facilities such as schools hospitals stadiums airports and prisons.

	Annual Growth	12/10	12/11	12/12	12/13	12/14
Sales ($ mil.)	(1.1%)	30.5	26.7	30.6	27.9	29.1
Net income ($ mil.)	–	1.8	(0.4)	(5.2)	(2.8)	(0.9)
Market value ($ mil.)	6.2%	13.2	7.6	7.2	6.3	16.8
Employees	0.0%	162	205	161	163	162

BLOOD SYSTEMS INC.

6210 E OAK ST
SCOTTSDALE, AZ 852571101
Phone: 480-946-4201
Fax: –
Web: www.bloodsystems.org

CEO: J Daniel Connor
CFO: Susan L Barnes
HR: Bailey Pell
FYE: December 31
Type: Private

As one might assume from its name Blood Systems collects and provides blood to hospitals. The not-for-profit Blood Systems collects blood and provides blood products and services to more than 500 hospitals in about 20 states. Its network of blood bank facilities are operated through its United Blood Services and Blood Centers of the Pacific subsidiaries. Blood Systems also provides blood donor testing services through its Creative Testing Solutions (CTS) facilities. Its BioCARE division distributes plasma derivative products used in medical procedures.

	Annual Growth	12/09	12/10	12/11	12/12	12/13
Sales ($ mil.)	15.9%	–	476.7	67.2	488.8	743.0
Net income ($ mil.)	812.5%	–	–	0.8	21.5	65.3
Market value ($ mil.)	–	–	–	–	–	–
Employees	–	–	–	–	–	3,900

BLOOMBERG L.P.

731 Lexington Ave.
New York NY 10022
Phone: 212-318-2000
Fax: 917-369-5000
Web: www.bloomberg.com

CEO: Andrew R Lack
CFO: –
HR: –
FYE: December 31
Type: Private

What do you do when you've conquered Wall Street? You become mayor of the city the famous financial district calls home. After leading his financial news and information company to success Michael Bloomberg left to run the Big Apple. His namesake company remains a leader in the market for business media. Its core Bloomberg Professional Service offering is accessed through terminals that provides real-time financial news market data and analysis. The firm also has a syndicated news service publishes magazines (including Bloomberg Businessweek) and disseminates business information via Bloomberg Television radio and the Web. Michael Bloomberg founded the company in 1981; he owns a majority of the firm.

BLOOMIN' BRANDS INC.

NMS: BLMN

2202 North West Shore Boulevard, Suite 500
Tampa, FL 33607
Phone: 813 282-1225
Fax: –
Web: www.bloominbrands.com

CEO: Elizabeth A. (Liz) Smith
CFO: David J. Deno
HR: Grant Jacobs
FYE: December 28
Type: Public

Bloomin' Brands does hope you think of Bloomin' Onions when you see its name. And steaks Italian food and seafood. The company which operates through the US's #2 casual dining company OSI Restaurant Partners owns some 1350 restaurants. It also franchises about 165 restaurants. The portfolio includes Outback Steakhouse Carrabba's Italian Grill Bonefish Grill and Fleming's Prime Steakhouse and Wine Bar. About 975 of the company's restaurants are Outback Steakhouses and all except Fleming's and Roy's are casual full-service restaurants. Bloomin' Brands was formed in 1988 and went public in 2012.

	Annual Growth	12/10	12/11	12/12	12/13	12/14
Sales ($ mil.)	5.2%	3,628.3	3,841.3	3,987.8	4,129.2	4,442.7
Net income ($ mil.)	14.5%	53.0	100.0	50.0	208.4	91.1
Market value ($ mil.)	23.2%	–	–	1,969.9	3,024.1	2,991.3
Employees	5.2%	–	86,000	93,000	101,000	100,000

BLOUNT INTERNATIONAL INC

NYS: BLT

4909 SE International Way
Portland, OR 97222-4679
Phone: 503 653-8881
Fax: –

CEO: Joshua L. (Josh) Collins
CFO: Calvin E. Jenness
HR: –
FYE: December 31
Type: Public

Folks at Blount International have their work cut out for them. The manufacturer produces cutting chain guide bars sprockets and accessories for chainsaws concrete-cutting equipment and lawnmower blades. Blount's lineup is sold under brands Oregon Carlton Tiger and Windsor to outdoor equipment OEMs including Husqvarna and the replacement and retail markets. Other subsidiaries supply log splitters post-hole diggers and other agriculture add-ons. End users are professionals and consumers engaged in forestry lawn and garden farming and construction activities. The company's manufacturing facilities dot the US Canada Brazil and China. About two-thirds of Blount's sales are made outside of the US.

	Annual Growth	12/10	12/11	12/12	12/13	12/14
Sales ($ mil.)	11.5%	611.5	831.6	927.7	900.6	944.8
Net income ($ mil.)	(6.2%)	47.2	49.7	39.6	4.8	36.6
Market value ($ mil.)	2.8%	782.2	720.6	785.1	718.1	872.0
Employees	5.1%	3,600	4,500	4,700	4,200	4,400

BLUCORA, INC.

NMS: BCOR

10900 N.E. 8th Street, Suite 800
Bellevue, WA 98004
Phone: 425 201-6100
Fax: 425 201-6150
Web: www.blucora.com

CEO: William J. (Bill) Ruckelshaus
CFO: Eric M. Emans
HR: Brett Clark-Bolt
FYE: December 31
Type: Public

Why crawl the Web when others can do it for you? Blucora (formerly InfoSpace) operates through two businesses. Its InfoSpace unit consists of online search services that rely on its metasearch search technology. Owned and operated consumer websites include Dogpile.com WebFetch.com and MetaCrawler.com which query such leading search providers as Google and Yahoo! and then collate and rank those search results. InfoSpace also offers a private-label search product for businesses (which it calls distribution partners); it develops hosts and delivers search results for more than 100 distribution partners. Blucora acquired its other primary business online tax solutions provider TaxACT in 2012.

	Annual Growth	12/10	12/11	12/12	12/13	12/14
Sales ($ mil.)	23.8%	246.8	228.8	406.9	574.0	580.7
Net income ($ mil.)	–	13.7	21.6	22.5	24.4	(35.5)
Market value ($ mil.)	13.7%	339.3	449.3	642.3	1,192.1	566.2
Employees	29.9%	174	198	225	450	496

BLUE BIRD CORPORATION

402 Blue Bird Blvd.
Fort Valley GA 31030
Phone: 478-825-2021
Fax: 478-822-2457
Web: www.blue-bird.com

CEO: Phil Horlock
CFO: Wayne Hunnell
HR: –
FYE: December 31
Type: Private

Blue Bird is from the "old school" of bus manufacturers. The largest school bus maker in the US Blue Bird also produces commercial and specialty/activity buses such as security buses shell buses and buses for export. School buses vary in size engine location and fuel used. Independent distributors sell the buses to school districts churches businesses government agencies and non-profit organizations. It also provides financing services through its Blue Bird Financial Services affiliate. The company's buses are globally exported to 60 countries throughout the Middle East Asia/Pacific Europe Africa and Latin America. Parent company Traxis Group is a subsidiary of Cerberus Capital Management L.P.

BLUE CARE NETWORK OF MICHIGAN

20500 Civic Center Dr.
Southfield MI 48076
Phone: 248-799-6400
Fax: 248-799-6327
Web: www.mibcn.com

CEO: –
CFO: Susan Kluge
HR: –
FYE: December 31
Type: Subsidiary

Blue Care Network of Michigan (BCN) keeps its state residents healthy. The health maintenance organization (HMO) provides health insurance products and related services to some 700000 Michigan members. The company's health insurance plans include HMO traditional indemnity and supplemental Medicare. The network also provides wellness and disease management services to its members. Parent company Blue Cross Blue Shield of Michigan (BCBSM) formed BCN one of the largest HMOs in Michigan in 1998 to create a statewide coverage organization. Its network includes about 130 hospitals and 19000 primary and specialty physicians throughout the state.

BLUE CROSS & BLUE SHIELD ASSOCIATION

225 N MICHIGAN AVE FL 5
CHICAGO, IL 60601-7658
Phone: 312-297-6000
Fax: –
Web: www.bcbs.com

CEO: Scott Serota
CFO: –
HR: –
FYE: December 31
Type: Private

Blue insurers prefer to sing a happy healthy tune. Health plan providers affiliated with the Blue Cross and Blue Shield Association (BCBSA) — known as "the Blues" — serve some 100 million members nationwide. The association is a federation of about 40 independent health insurance companies who license the Blue Cross and Blue Shield brand names. Member companies own the rights to sell Blue-branded health plans within defined regions. BCBSA coordinates some national programs such as BlueCard which allows members of one franchisee to have coverage in other service areas and the Federal Employee Program (FEP) which covers more than half of federal government employees retirees and their families.

	Annual Growth	12/03	12/04	12/05	12/06	12/11
Sales ($ mil.)	5.4%	–	270.9	275.4	320.5	392.2
Net income ($ mil.)	–	–	11.7	8.2	14.5	(13.3)
Market value ($ mil.)	–	–	–	–	–	–
Employees	–	–	–	–	–	1,880

BLUE CROSS & BLUE SHIELD OF MISSISSIPPI

3545 Lakeland Dr.
Flowood MS 39232
Phone: 601-932-3704
Fax: 601-939-7035
Web: www.bcbsms.com

CEO: Rick Hale
CFO: Douglas Garrett
HR: –
FYE: December 31
Type: Private - Mutual Com

Like the river that gives the state its name Blue Cross & Blue Shield of Mississippi (BCBSMS) is big and broad. The mutual insurance company which provides health care coverage and related services to members is the state's largest health plan provider. It is an independent licensee of the Blue Cross and Blue Shield Association with managed care offerings that include group (Network Blue) individual (Blue Care) and supplemental Medicare (Blue 65) health plans. Policies are marketed through a statewide network of agents. BCBSMS members have access to a contracted network of some 7500 family care and specialty doctors as well as about 100 hospitals across the state.

BLUE CROSS & BLUE SHIELD OF RHODE ISLAND

500 Exchange St
Providence RI 02903
Phone: 401-459-1000
Fax: 312-943-5316
Web: www.flairpromo.com

CEO: –
CFO: –
HR: –
FYE: December 31
Type: Private - Not-for-Pr

As the state's largest health insurer Blue Cross & Blue Shield of Rhode Island (BCBSRI) has the Ocean State's citizens covered. In fact BCBSRI provides health insurance products and related services to more than 600000 members or more than half of the state's residents primarily through their employers. The company offers a variety of plan types including PPO (HealthMate Coast-to-Coast) HMO (BlueCHiP) and traditional indemnity (Classic Blue). It also sells Medicare Advantage and Medicare supplemental coverage as well as dental coverage plans. A not-for-profit licensee of the Blue Cross and Blue Shield Association

BLUE CROSS AND BLUE SHIELD OF ALABAMA

450 Riverchase Pkwy. East
Birmingham AL 35244
Phone: 205-220-2100
Fax: 205-220-6477
Web: www.bcbsal.com

CEO: G Phillip Pope
CFO: Cynthia Mizell
HR: –
FYE: December 31
Type: Private - Not-for-Pr

Folks who hang their hats in Tuscaloosa or Birmingham (or any other Alabama city) may depend on Blue Cross and Blue Shield of Alabama when they need medical coverage. The state's largest health benefits provider Blue Cross and Blue Shield of Alabama administers individual corporate and federal employer-sponsored and Medicare health plans to more than 3 million members representing about 30000 companies. Its insurance products include PPO and high-deductible health plans as well as dental policies. The company also sells long-term care insurance (dubbed Preferred LTC) and it provides disease management services and wellness programs. It is a licensee of the Blue Cross and Blue Shield Association.

BLUE CROSS AND BLUE SHIELD OF ARIZONA INC.

2444 W LAS PALMARITAS DR
PHOENIX, AZ 850214860
Phone: 602-864-4100
Fax: –
Web: www.azblue.com

CEO: Richard L. (Rich) Boals
CFO: Karen Abraham
HR: –
FYE: December 31
Type: Private

Blue Cross Blue Shield of Arizona (BCBSAZ) provides health insurance products and services to more than 1.3 million Arizonans. The not-for-profit company offers a variety of managed care plans to small and large employer groups individuals and families including PPO HMO and high-deductible health plans. It also provides dental vision and prescription drug coverage as well as supplemental health plans for Medicare beneficiaries. Additionally BCBSAZ's HealthyBlue wellness and disease management programs give members information and services that encourage healthy lifestyles. Founded in 1939 the company is an independent licensee of the Blue Cross and Blue Shield Association.

	Annual Growth	12/05	12/06	12/07	12/08	12/09
Assets ($ mil.)	8.6%	–	–	–	975.9	1,059.5
Net income ($ mil.)	(9.9%)	–	–	–	71.7	64.6
Market value ($ mil.)	–	–	–	–	–	–
Employees	–	–	–	–	–	1,278

BLUE CROSS AND BLUE SHIELD OF MASSACHUSETTS INC.

Landmark Center 401 Park Dr.
Boston MA 02215-3326
Phone: 617-246-5000
Fax: 617-246-4832
Web: www.bluecrossma.com
CEO: Andrew Dreyfus
CFO: –
HR: –
FYE: December 31
Type: Private - Not-for-Pr

The dominant health insurer in the Bay State Blue Cross and Blue Shield of Massachusetts (BCBSMA) covers some 3 million members. The company an independent licensee of the Blue Cross and Blue Shield Association offers a variety of individual and employer-sponsored health care plans including HMO (HMO Blue) PPO (Blue Options) and point-of-service (Blue Choice) plans as well as various hybrid options and personal spending accounts to cover out-of-pocket costs. BCBSMA also provides Medicare options and dental vision and prescription drug coverage. Its provider network includes more than 20000 physicians and about 75 hospitals across the state. The health care firm was founded in 1937.

BLUE CROSS AND BLUE SHIELD OF NORTH CAROLINA

5901 Chapel Hill Rd.
Durham NC 27707
Phone: 919-489-7431
Fax: 919-765-7818
Web: www.bcbsnc.com
CEO: Robert J Greczyn Jr
CFO: Daniel E Glaser
HR: –
FYE: December 31
Type: Private - Not-for-Pr

Blue Cross and Blue Shield of North Carolina (BCBSNC) provides health care insurance products and related services to about 3.7 million members in North Carolina. Founded in 1933 the company's individual and group health plans include Blue Care (HMO) and Blue Options (PPO) as well as consumer-directed plans that couple high-deductible policies with a health savings account. BCBSNC also provides dental life disability long-term care and Medicare supplemental insurance as well as prescription drug coverage. The company's Partners National Health Plans subsidiary offers Medicare Advantage health plans. BCBSNC is a licensee of the Blue Cross and Blue Shield Association.

BLUE CROSS AND BLUE SHIELD OF MINNESOTA

3535 Blue Cross Rd.
Eagan MN 55122-1154
Phone: 651-662-8000
Fax: 651-662-2777
Web: www.bluecrossmn.com
CEO: Scott B Lynch
CFO: Pamela Sedmak
HR: –
FYE: December 31
Type: Private - Not-for-Pr

Blue Cross and Blue Shield of Minnesota is the state's oldest and largest not-for-profit health insurer serving some 2.7 million members including employees for General Mills and Northwest Airlines. The company's insurance plans include traditional indemnity coverage HMOs (Blue Plus and Preferred Gold) PPOs (Aware) and major medical plans. Blue Cross Blue Shield of Minnesota also offers Medicare Advantage PPOs and other products aimed at seniors. Dental coverage is provided through a partnership with Delta Dental. Additionally its health support programs offer disease management assistance for those with chronic conditions as well as health improvement programs such as fitness center discounts.

BLUE CROSS AND BLUE SHIELD OF TEXAS

901 S. Central Expwy.
Richardson TX 75080
Phone: 972-766-6900
Fax: 972-766-6234
Web: www.bcbstx.com
CEO: –
CFO: Denise Bujak
HR: Kathryn Cole
FYE: December 31
Type: Subsidiary

If an apple a day could keep the doctor away Blue Cross and Blue Shield of Texas (BCBSTX) would stock up for its 4.8 million customers. Instead the not-for-profit insurer strives to keep Texans healthy by providing HMO PPO point-of-service (POS) and indemnity insurance health care plans for large to small employer groups. It also provides coverage for individuals families seniors and low-income customers. The company's provider network has about 40000 doctors and 400 hospitals throughout the state. A division of Chicago-based mutual insurance firm Health Care Service Corporation BCBSTX counts among its customers American Airlines the University of Texas System H.E. Butt Grocery and Halliburton.

BLUE CROSS AND BLUE SHIELD OF MONTANA

560 N. Park Ave.
Helena MT 59604
Phone: 406-444-8200
Fax: 406-447-3454
Web: www.bcbsmt.com
CEO: –
CFO: –
HR: –
FYE: December 31
Type: Private - Not-for-Pr

Nearly a quarter of a million residents of Big Sky Country depend on Blue Cross and Blue Shield of Montana for health insurance. The state's largest private health insurer the company provides a variety of coverage types including traditional indemnity policies HMOs POS plans and supplemental Medicare plans to about 240000 customers. It also administers the state-sponsored children's Medicaid and low-income health insurance plans (dubbed Healthy Montana Kids) and participates in InsureMontana a state-sponsored subsidized program designed to encourage small businesses to cover their employees. The not-for-profit company's provider network includes about 1900 physicians and all of the state's hospitals.

BLUE CROSS AND BLUE SHIELD OF VERMONT

445 Industrial Ln.
Berlin VT 05602-4415
Phone: 802-223-6131
Fax: 802-223-4229
Web: www.bcbsvt.com
CEO: –
CFO: Ruth K Greene
HR: Robert Opel
FYE: December 31
Type: Private - Not-for-Pr

Blue Cross and Blue Shield of Vermont (BCBSVT) lauds on healthy Vermont hikers. The company a licensee of the Blue Cross and Blue Shield Association stakes its claim as the largest and oldest health insurance company in Vermont and serves about 150000 members. The company's group and individual health insurance plans include Vermont Freedom Plan (PPO) Vermont Health Partnership Plan (POS) and BlueCare (HMO) as well as high-deductable plans and state-supplemented coverage for low-income members. BCBSVT also offers supplemental Medicare life dental and vision coverage. The company founded in 1944 also provides third-party administrative (TPA) services for medical dental COBRA and other employee benefits.

BLUE CROSS BLUE SHIELD OF GEORGIA INC

3350 Peachtree Rd. NE
Atlanta GA 30326
Phone: 404-842-8000
Fax: 404-842-8100
Web: www.bcbsga.com

CEO: John Watts
CFO: Randall A Edwards
HR: –
FYE: December 31
Type: Subsidiary

Blue Cross Blue Shield of Georgia (BCBSGA) is the Empire State of the South's #1 provider of health insurance and related services. With more than 3 million members the company offers a variety of insurance plans including HMO PPO indemnity and point-of-service (POS) programs to groups and individuals throughout the state. BCBSGA also provides disease management services and supplemental insurance products such as dental vision life and disability coverage as well as Medicare plans. BCBSGA an independent licensee of Blue Cross and Blue Shield Association is a subsidiary of WellPoint.

BLUE CROSS BLUE SHIELD OF MICHIGAN

600 E. Lafayette Blvd.
Detroit MI 48226-2998
Phone: 313-225-9000
Fax: 312-819-1220
Web: www.hcsc.com

CEO: Daniel J Loepp
CFO: Mark Bartlett
HR: –
FYE: December 31
Type: Private - Not-for-Pr

Blue Cross Blue Shield of Michigan (BCBSM) covers Michigan residents from one great lake to another. The company is the state's leading health benefits organization serving some 4.4 million members residing in the state or employed by companies headquartered there and 1.1 million more members in other states. The not-for-profit company's insurance offerings include traditional indemnity PPO and POS plans in addition to its Blue Care Network HMO plans. It also provides consumer-directed Flexible Blue plans paired with health savings accounts (HSAs) as well as options for individual buyers and Medicare beneficiaries. The organization is an independent licensee of the Blue Cross and Blue Shield Association.

BLUE CROSS OF CALIFORNIA

One WellPoint Way
Thousand Oaks CA 91362-5035
Phone: 805-557-6655
Fax: 805-557-6872
Web: www.anthem.com/ca

CEO: –
CFO: Kenneth C Zurek
HR: –
FYE: December 31
Type: Subsidiary

Blue Cross of California which does business as Anthem Blue Cross provides health insurance and related services to more than 8 million residents of the Golden State. Along with its Anthem Blue Cross Life and Health Insurance affiliate it offers HMO PPO and point-of-service health plans for individuals employer groups and public entities. It also sells Medicare supplemental and Medicare Advantage plans to seniors and manages the health care of participants in state-funded programs such as Medi-Cal (Medicaid) and Healthy Families. Blue Cross of California is a licensee of the Blue Cross and Blue Shield Association and a subsidiary of WellPoint.

BLUE CROSS OF IDAHO HEALTH SERVICE INC.

3000 E. Pine Ave.
Meridian ID 83642
Phone: 208-345-4550
Fax: 208-331-7311
Web: www.bcidaho.com

CEO: Zelda Geyer-Sylvia
CFO: –
HR: –
FYE: December 31
Type: Private - Not-for-Pr

Blue Cross of Idaho Health Service shine's like a diamond in the Gem State's health market. The organization is a leading provider of health insurance products and related services to about 650000 Idaho members including individuals corporate groups and government institutions. The company's health insurance products include traditional indemnity HMO PPO and supplemental Medicare plans. It also offers high-deductable plans paired with a health savings accounts. Blue Cross of Idaho a licensee of the Blue Cross and Blue Shield Association also provides dental coverage behavioral health and disease management and access to hearing vision and fitness discount programs.

BLUE DOLPHIN ENERGY CO.

NBB: BDCO

801 Travis Street, Suite 2100
Houston, TX 77002
Phone: 713 568-4725
Fax: –
Web: www.blue-dolphin-energy.com

CEO: Jonathan P Carroll
CFO: Tommy Byrd
HR: –
FYE: December 31
Type: Public

Blue Dolphin Energy is trying to stay afloat in the waters of the Gulf of Mexico. The company's primary asset is its 40-mile-long Blue Dolphin Pipeline System which includes an offshore platform for separation metering and compression; the onshore Buccaneer oil pipeline; onshore facilities including 85000 barrels of surface tankage separation and dehydration facilities; 360 acres of land; and a barge-loading terminal. Blue Dolphin Energy owns interests in three producing blocks in the High Island area in the Gulf of Mexico and has two exploratory prospects for sale. In 2010 the company reported estimated proved reserves of 155.5 cu. ft. of natural gas and 134122 barrels of oil.

	Annual Growth	12/10	12/11	12/12	12/13	12/14
Sales ($ mil.)	244.8%	2.7	2.3	352.1	409.5	387.5
Net income ($ mil.)	–	(1.0)	0.6	(18.3)	(3.8)	15.8
Market value ($ mil.)	19.0%	25.0	43.8	52.5	49.6	50.1
Employees	(14.3%)	7	6	–	–	–

BLUE NILE INC

NMS: NILE

411 First Avenue South, Suite 700
Seattle, WA 98104
Phone: 206 336-6700
Fax: –
Web: www.bluenile.com

CEO: Harvey S. Kanter
CFO: David B. Binder
HR: Derek Mullens
FYE: January 04
Type: Public

Blue Nile helps tech-savvy Marc Antonys bejewel their Cleopatras. The leader in online jewelry sales through its bluenile.com the company offers luxury-grade jewelry loose diamonds settings and engagement rings as well as non-bridal jewelry made of gold platinum and silver set with diamonds pearls emeralds rubies and sapphires. While engagement rings account for about 70% of its sales the e-tailer also sells watches and provides custom jewelry design services. Blue Nile's web sites serve customers in the US Canada Europe and the Asia-Pacific region — more than 40 countries in all. Chairman Mark Vadon and Ben Elowitz formerly of Fatbrain.com founded the site in 1999.

	Annual Growth	01/11	01/12*	12/12	12/13*	01/15
Sales ($ mil.)	9.2%	332.9	348.0	400.0	450.0	473.5
Net income ($ mil.)	(8.9%)	14.1	11.4	8.4	10.9	9.7
Market value ($ mil.)	(11.5%)	676.7	484.8	447.1	566.6	415.5
Employees	11.8%	193	212	253	291	301

*Fiscal year change

BLUE SHIELD OF CALIFORNIA LIFE & HEALTH INSURANCE COM

50 Beale St.
San Francisco CA 94105-1808
Phone: 415-229-5000
Fax: 800-329-2742
Web: www.blueshieldca.com

CEO: Paul Markovich
CFO: –
HR: –
FYE: December 31
Type: Subsidiary

As the name implies Blue Shield of California Life & Health Insurance Company (Blue Shield Life) offers a variety of life and health insurance policies to residents of sunny California. Its primary offerings are group and individual term life insurance policies offered to the existing health plan members of its parent organization California Physicians' Service (aka Blue Shield of California). It also offers disability and accidental death and dismemberment policies and it underwrites some health and vision policies issued by its parent. The company is a member of the Blue Cross Blue Shield Association.

BLUE SKY STUDIOS INC.

One American Ln.
Greenwich CT 06831
Phone: 203-992-6000
Fax: 203-992-6001
Web: www.blueskystudios.com

CEO: –
CFO: Brian Keane
HR: –
FYE: June 30
Type: Subsidiary

Fox Filmed Entertainment hopes its animation sees nothing but blue skies. Its Blue Sky Entertainment division develops and produces animation for feature films and television shows and the studio's CGI Studio proprietary software integrates animation and live action as it did for such Fox films as Fight Club and Alien Resurrection. Blue Sky has produced full-length feature films including Ice Age: Dawn of the Dinosaurs and Horton Hears A Who!. Founded in 1987 the company originally served the advertising industry until its purchase by Fox ten years later. All total Blue Sky has produced about a dozen movies since its first release Bunny which won the Academy Award for Best Animated Short Film in 1999.

BLUE TEE CORP.

250 PARK AVE S RM 203
NEW YORK, NY 100031495
Phone: 212-598-0880
Fax: –
Web: www.bluetee.com

CEO: William M Kelly
CFO: David P Alldian
HR: –
FYE: December 31
Type: Private

Handling a variety of steel products and scrap materials suits Blue Tee to a tee. The holding company which operates through two primary subsidiaries distributes steel building materials and scrap metal. Blue Tee's Brown-Strauss Steel subsidiary is one of the largest distributors of wide flange beam and structural steel products (beams pipe and tubing) in North America. The metal distributor's other primary business is Azcon a leading scrap processor broker and mill services management company which handles scrap metal sales rail cars and other steel parts.

	Annual Growth	12/06	12/07	12/08	12/09	12/10
Sales ($ mil.)	43.4%	–	–	–	564.6	809.8
Net income ($ mil.)	–	–	–	–	(10.1)	14.3
Market value ($ mil.)	–	–	–	–	–	–
Employees	–	–	–	–	–	900

BLUE VALLEY BAN CORP (KS)

NBB: BVBC

11935 Riley St, PO Box 26128
Overland Park, KS 66225-6128
Phone: 913 338-1000
Fax: 913 234-7145
Web: www.bankbv.com

CEO: Robert D Regnier
CFO: Mark A Fortino
HR: Bob Regniers
FYE: December 31
Type: Public

Protect your green at Blue Valley Ban Corp the holding company of Bank of Blue Valley. Founded in 1989 the bank targets closely-held small to midsized businesses and their owners plus professionals and residents in Johnson County Kansas. Through about a half dozen branches located within the Kansas City metropolitan area the bank provides traditional deposit products cash management services investment brokerage and trust services. Its lending activities are focused on construction loans which account for about 30% of its portfolio as well as business and commercial real estate loans which each account for about a quarter.

	Annual Growth	12/10	12/11	12/12	12/13	12/14
Assets ($ mil.)	(3.1%)	723.1	654.5	657.0	609.1	638.4
Net income ($ mil.)	–	(2.7)	(15.8)	0.3	1.0	12.8
Market value ($ mil.)	0.0%	30.2	19.1	20.9	27.9	30.2
Employees	(4.6%)	199	173	–	173	–

BLUEARC CORPORATION

50 Rio Robles
San Jose CA 95134
Phone: 408-576-6600
Fax: 408-576-6601
Web: www.bluearc.com

CEO: –
CFO: –
HR: –
FYE: March 31
Type: Subsidiary

BlueArc is redefining the network storage performance curve. The company provides high-end and mid-range data storage systems used in network-attached storage (NAS) and storage area network (SAN) configurations. Companies involved in drug discovery oil and gas exploration legal electronic discovery high-performance computing media and entertainment Internet services and other data-intensive industries use its scalable Titan servers. BlueArc's servers which are manufactured by Sanmina-SCI utilize programmable chips designed by Altera. Customers in North America account for nearly three-quarters of the company's sales. In 2011 BlueArc filed for an IPO and was then acquired by Hitachi Data Systems (HDS).

BLUEBIRD BIO INC

NMS: BLUE

150 Second Street
Cambridge, MA 02141
Phone: 339 499-9300
Fax: –
Web: www.bluebirdbio.com

CEO: –
CFO: Jeffrey T Walsh
HR: Kathy Wilkinson
FYE: December 31
Type: Public

bluebird bio is ready to fly in the faces of rare genetic diseases. The company is using gene therapy to develop orphan drugs for two rare diseases. Its lead drug candidate Lenti-D is being developed to treat childhood cerebral adrenoleukodystrophy (CCALD) a rare neurological disorder that affects boys. Its second drug candidate LentiGlobin is being developed to treat the blood disorders beta-thalassemia major and sickle cell disease. Both drugs will begin studies by 2014. In addition bluebird bio partnered with Celgene to develop gene therapies for cancer. Founded in 1992 as Genetix Pharmaceuticals the company changed its name to bluebird bio in 2010 and filed an IPO in 2013.

	Annual Growth	12/10	12/11	12/12	12/13	12/14
Sales ($ mil.)	–	0.0	0.9	0.3	20.2	25.4
Net income ($ mil.)	–	0.0	(15.6)	(23.7)	(25.3)	(48.7)
Market value ($ mil.)	–	–	0.0	–	678.5	2,966.2
Employees	69.1%	–	–	50	87	143

BLUEBONNET ELECTRIC COOPERATIVE INC.

155 ELECTRIC AVE
BASTROP, TX 78602
Phone: 800-842-7708
Fax: –

CEO: Mark Rose
CFO: Elizabeth Kana
HR: –
FYE: December 31
Type: Private

Bluebonnet Electric Cooperative's mission has echoes of the late Lady Bird Johnson's quest to spread bluebonnets and other wildflower seeds along Texas' highways. In this case the cooperative spreads power to homes and businesses in rural central and southeast Texas. One of the largest power distribution cooperatives in the state Bluebonnet Electric serves more than 81000 customers in 14 counties (a service area of more than 3800 square miles). The member-owned company which was formed in 1939 operates approximately 11000 miles of transmission and distribution lines and 19 substations. It purchases its wholesale power supply at 21 Lower Colorado River Authority-owned substations.

	Annual Growth	12/09	12/10	12/11	12/12	12/13
Sales ($ mil.)	1.7%	–	191.8	200.0	188.4	201.6
Net income ($ mil.)	6.7%	–	–	5.8	5.5	6.7
Market value ($ mil.)	–	–	–	–	–	–
Employees	–	–	–	–	–	265

BLUECHOICE HEALTHPLAN OF SOUTH CAROLINA INC.

4101 Percival Rd.
Columbia SC 29229
Phone: 803-786-8466
Fax: 803-754-6386
Web: www.bluechoicesc.com

CEO: M Edward Sellers
CFO: Robert A Leichtle
HR: Barbara Kelly
FYE: December 31
Type: Subsidiary

BlueChoice HealthPlan of South Carolina wants Palmetto State residents to get the health care Blues. The company is a health maintenance organization (HMO) offering managed health care products to some 200000 members in South Carolina. The company's group health plans include a basic HMO plan (Primary Choice) open access HMOs (BlueChoice Advantage) and point-of-service and high-deductable options. Its CarolinaADVANTAGE offering is aimed at small businesses with fewer than 50 employees. The company also offers individual health plans for adults families and children. The company is a subsidiary of Blue Cross & Blue Shield of South Carolina.

BLUECROSS BLUESHIELD OF TENNESSEE INC.

1 Cameron Hill Cir. Sheila Clemons 1 5
Chattanooga TN 37402-9815
Phone: 423-535-5600
Fax: 423-535-6255
Web: www.bcbst.com

CEO: Vicky Gregg
CFO: –
HR: –
FYE: December 31
Type: Private - Not-for-Pr

BlueCross BlueShield of Tennessee (BCBST) is the oldest and largest not-for-profit managed care provider in the state of Tennessee. Serving around 3 million people through group and individual policies the company offers HMO PPO and high-deductable health plans. Founded in 1945 BCBST also provides Medicare plans to another 1 million customers and its Group Insurance Services unit brokers vision dental life accident and disability plans. Its Volunteer State Health Plan unit provides coverage for low-income members and children through state-sponsored programs. BCBST is a member of the Blue Cross and Blue Shield Association.

BLUEKNIGHT ENERGY PARTNERS L P

NMS: BKEP

201 NW 10th, Suite 200
Oklahoma City, OK 73103
Phone: 405 278-6400
Fax: –
Web: www.bkep.com

CEO: Mark A Hurley
CFO: Alex G Stallings
HR: Andrew Williams
FYE: December 31
Type: Public

Blueknight Energy Partners (formerly SemGroup Energy Partners) provides gathering transporting terminalling and storage of crude oil in Oklahoma Kansas and Texas. It operates two pipeline systems (1285 miles of pipeline) delivering crude oil to refineries and provides storage services with a capacity of about 8.1 million barrels. It also provides asphalt services. Blueknight Energy Partners has about 7.4 million barrels of asphalt and residual fuel storage in 45 terminals located in 22 states. Blueknight Energy Partners' top customer is Netherlands-based natural resources group Vitol (54% of total revenues in 2010). Vitol and investment firm Charlesbank Capital Partners indirectly own the company.

	Annual Growth	12/10	12/11	12/12	12/13	12/14
Sales ($ mil.)	5.2%	152.6	176.7	182.4	194.7	186.6
Net income ($ mil.)	–	(23.8)	33.5	31.6	28.0	27.6
Market value ($ mil.)	(3.8%)	262.7	221.4	223.1	288.5	225.4
Employees	2.9%	470	500	535	530	526

BLUELINX HOLDINGS INC

NYS: BXC

4300 Wildwood Parkway
Atlanta, GA 30339
Phone: 770 953-7000
Fax: –

CEO: Mitchell B Lewis
CFO: Susan C O'Farrell
HR: –
FYE: January 03
Type: Public

You won't find many building products missing at BlueLinx. Through 49 distribution centers across the US the company distributes some 10000 building products from more than 750 suppliers to some 11500 customers. Specialty products such as roofing insulation molding and engineered wood products account for more than half of BlueLinx's sales. It also distributes structural products including plywood oriented strand board and lumber. BlueLinx serves building material dealers home improvement retailers manufactured housing builders and industrial users of building products. The company is majority-owned by private equity firm Cerberus Capital Management.

	Annual Growth	01/11*	12/11	12/12*	01/14	01/15
Sales ($ mil.)	2.3%	1,804.4	1,755.4	1,907.8	2,152.0	1,979.4
Net income ($ mil.)	–	(53.2)	(38.6)	(23.0)	(40.6)	(13,9)
Market value ($ mil.)	(25.3%)	324.8	133.1	249.4	172.2	101.2
Employees	(3.2%)	1,940	1,860	1,868	1,700	1,700

*Fiscal year change

BLUEPOINT SOLUTIONS INC.

1221 Liberty Way
Vista CA 92081
Phone: 760-410-9000
Fax: 760-410-9010
Web: www.bluepointsolutions.com

CEO: –
CFO: Alfred Riedler
HR: –
FYE: December 31
Type: Private

You have to give Bluepoint credit for its document management skills. Bluepoint Solutions develops sofware used by companies in the financial services industry credit unions in particular to process checks and digitally manage forms. The company's products help credit unions organize information into a single database (Receipt Manager) create loan applications and other electronic forms and enable customers to view an electronic image of member signatures for check verification purposes. Other products are used to import check images (Remote Deposit Capture) enable Internet-based account access (WebShare) and manage branch operations. Bluepoint was founded in 2000 by chairman and CEO Hal Tilbury.

BLUESTAR ENERGY SERVICES INC.

363 W. Erie St. Ste. 700
Chicago IL 60610
Phone: 312-327-0900
Fax: 866-996-3782
Web: www.bluestarenergy.com

CEO: Guy H Morgan
CFO: Steven J Strobel
HR: –
FYE: December 31
Type: Subsidiary

BlueStar Energy intends to burn bright in the firmament of independent electricity providers. Serving more than 23000 customers in the deregulated markets of Delaware Maryland New Jersey Ohio Illinois Pennsylvania and Washington DC it offers variable- and fixed-rate and custom plans along with green energy to industrial commercial and residential customers. Its energy efficiency program examines customers' energy usage and offers services to decrease costs including reworking lighting fixtures monitoring power use rewiring fixtures and performing exterior maintenance. To harness the financial heft of a major company for future growth in 2012 BlueStar Energy was bought by American Electric Power.

BLUESTEM BRANDS INC.

6509 Flying Cloud
Eden Prairie MN 55344-3307
Phone: 952-656-3700
Fax: 952-830-3293
Web: www.jostens.com

CEO: Steven Nave
CFO: Mark Wagener
HR: –
FYE: January 31
Type: Private

You might say this company lets your fingers do the shopping. Bluestem Brands (formerly Fingerhut Direct Marketing) offers an array of private-label and brand-name merchandise including apparel appliances electronics furniture health and beauty products jewelry kitchenware luggage sporting goods tools and toys through its Fingerhut catalog and e-commerce site and via the Gettington.com site. It also offers credit in partnership with MetaBank and WebBank. In addition it also owns PayCheck Direct an employee purchase plan whereby employers can offer high-ticket items to employees who pay for them interest-free via payroll deductions. The company filed an IPO in 2011 but withdrew it a year later.

BLYTH, INC.

NYS: BTH

One East Weaver Street
Greenwich, CT 06831
Phone: 203 661-1926
Fax: 203 661-1969
Web: www.blyth.com

CEO: Harry Slatkin
CFO: –
HR: –
FYE: December 31
Type: Public

Blyth lights up the party with its wicked products. As the largest candle maker in the US Blyth's PartyLite Worldwide subsidiary sells its scented and unscented candles flameless products and reed diffusers all under the PartyLite brand. Blyth's portfolio extends beyond the candle business with ViSalus nutritional supplements as well as a variety of catalog and online businesses that market household goods and gifts under the Silver Star Brands umbrella. Blyth's products are sold through home parties online and by retailers worldwide. The company also supplies institutional customers such as restaurants and hotels. Blyth which is focused on the direct to consumer market was founded in 1977.

	Annual Growth	01/10	01/11*	12/11	12/12	12/13
Sales ($ mil.)	(2.6%)	958.1	900.9	888.3	1,179.5	885.5
Net income ($ mil.)	(48.4%)	17.7	25.5	16.2	44.0	2.4
Market value ($ mil.)	(27.1%)	449.9	538.5	909.7	249.1	174.3
Employees	(9.6%)	2,300	2,300	1,800	1,700	1,700

*Fiscal year change

BMO FINANCIAL CORP.

111 W. Monroe St.
Chicago IL 60603
Phone: 312-461-2121
Fax: 973-245-6714
Web: www.basf.us

CEO: Matthew W Barrett
CFO: –
HR: –
FYE: October 31
Type: Subsidiary

BMO Bankcorp (formerly Harris Bankcorp) represents the US retail banking operations of Canada's Bank of Montreal. It is the holding company for BMO Harris Bank (Harris) which offers personal and commercial banking and other financial services through about 700 bank branches in the Chicago area and the Midwest as well as Arizona Florida and a handful of other states. In addition to BMO Harris Bank the company's operations include financial planner Harris Private Bank and its Harris SBSB division and wealth manager Harris myCFO. BMO Bankcorp is growing Harris through such acquisitions as Milwaukee-based Marshall & Ilsley (M&I) in 2011 and the FDIC-assisted purchase of the failed AMCORE Bank in 2010.

BMW OF NORTH AMERICA LLC

300 Chestnut Ridge Rd.
Woodcliff Lake NJ 07677
Phone: 201-307-4000
Fax: 201-307-0880
Web: www.bmwgroupna.com

CEO: Ludwig Willisch
CFO: Dr Gunter Niedernhuber
HR: –
FYE: December 31
Type: Subsidiary

A key subsidiary of BMW BMW of North America provides marketing sales and financial services through almost 900 dealerships and motorcycle retailers. The company imports and manufactures BMW brands such as the 1 3 5 6 7 Series; the X5 X6 and M Series models; and the MINI and Rolls-Royce brands. Styles include coupes convertibles sedans roadsters sports activity and luxury vehicles. Divisions include BMW Manufacturing (South Carolina) industrial-design firm DesignworksUSA a parts distribution center a technology office a technical training center and other operations in the US. Charged to oversee the group's largest single market — the US — BMW of North America was established in 1975.

BNC BANCORP

NAS: BNCN

3980 Premier Drive, Suite 210
High Point, NC 27265
Phone: 336 476-9200
Fax: –
Web: www.bankofnc.com

CEO: W. Swope Montgomery
CFO: David B. Spencer
HR: –
FYE: December 31
Type: Public

BNC Bancorp knows the ABCs of the financial world. The firm is the holding company for Bank of North Carolina which boasts more than 55 branches mostly across North and South Carolina but also in Virginia. In addition to offering traditional loan and deposit products (including checking savings and money market accounts credit cards and certificates of deposits) for local business and retail customers BNC also offers wealth management retirement planning and brokerage services and insurance products. Nearly 40% of its loans are commercial real estate loans while residential mortgages make up another 15%. Founded in 1991 the bank now has more than $5 billion in total assets.

	Annual Growth	12/10	12/11	12/12	12/13	12/14
Assets ($ mil.)	17.3%	2,149.9	2,454.9	3,083.8	3,229.6	4,072.5
Net income ($ mil.)	39.7%	7.7	6.9	10.5	17.2	29.4
Market value ($ mil.)	17.6%	293.4	236.3	261.1	558.7	561.0
Employees	22.0%	372	455	564	620	823

BNCCORP INC
NBB: BNCC

322 East Main
Bismarck, ND 58501
Phone: 701 250-3040
Fax: 701 222-3653
Web: www.bnccorp.com

CEO: –
CFO: –
HR: Connie Froelich
FYE: December 31
Type: Public

BNCCORP is the holding company for BNC National Bank which has about 20 branches in Arizona North Dakota and Minnesota. Serving individuals and small and midsized businesses the bank offers deposit accounts credit cards and wealth management services. It also has residential mortgage banking operations in Iowa Kansas and Missouri. Real estate loans account for nearly half of the company's portfolio; commercial industrial construction agricultural and consumer loans make up most of the remainder. BNCCORP sold BNC Insurance Services to Hub International in 2007 for more than $37 million. It arranged to sell some of its operations in Arizona and Minnesota to Alerus Financial in 2010.

	Annual Growth	12/10	12/11	12/12	12/13	12/14
Assets ($ mil.)	5.8%	747.1	665.2	770.8	843.1	934.4
Net income ($ mil.)	–	(22.1)	4.2	26.6	8.6	8.5
Market value ($ mil.)	86.8%	4.8	9.4	34.3	41.6	58.4
Employees	–	–	–	–	–	–

BNS HOLDING INC.
PINK SHEETS: BNSSA

61 E. Main St. Ste. B
Los Gatos CA 95031
Phone: 401-848-6300
Fax: 314-854-4274
Web: www.brownshoe.com

CEO: Michael Warren
CFO: Michael Warren
HR: –
FYE: October 31
Type: Public

After trying out a variety of businesses and settling on one that serves the energy market BNS is shutting down. The company is selling North Dakota Sun Well Services a work-over rig service for oil and gas exploration companies to Steel Excel for about $85 million. BNS had acquired Sun Well Services for some $51 million in 2011 after selling its 80% stake in bus maker Collins Industries (purchased in 2006). Once BNS sells Sun Well Services its operating subsidiary it will liquidate and distribute its assets pro rata to its stockholders. Affiliates of private equity firm Steel Partners own about 85% of BNS and 40% of Steel Excel.

BOARD OF TRUSTEES OF COMMUNITY COLLEGE DISTRICT 508 (INC)

226 W JACKSON BLVD # 103
CHICAGO, IL 606066959
Phone: 312-553-2752
Fax: –
Web: www.ccc.edu

CEO: –
CFO: Abe Eshkenazi
HR: –
FYE: June 30
Type: Private

City Colleges of Chicago (CCC) is one of the largest urban community college systems in the US. It includes seven separately accredited schools — Daley College Kennedy-King College Malcolm X College Olive-Harvey College Truman College Washington College and Wright College. CCC offers associate degrees continuing education IT certifications industry training GED and ESL classes and other programs to some 120000 students each year. Other institutions under the CCC umbrella include the French Pastry School the Washburne Culinary Institute three learning centers and the public television station WYCC-TV. City Colleges of Chicago was founded in 1911 as Crane Junior College.

	Annual Growth	06/06	06/07	06/08	06/09	06/11
Sales ($ mil.)	832.8%	–	–	–	0.6	54.5
Net income ($ mil.)	–	–	–	–	0.0	30.3
Market value ($ mil.)	–	–	–	–	–	–
Employees	–	–	–	–	–	3,500

BOARDWALK PIPELINE PARTNERS LP
NYS: BWP

9 Greenway Plaza, Suite 2800
Houston, TX 77046
Phone: 866 913-2122
Fax: –

CEO: –
CFO: –
HR: Stephen (Steve) Bienvenu
FYE: December 31
Type: Public

Boardwalk Pipeline Partners walks a fine (pipe) line. The limited partnership owns and operates three US interstate natural gas pipeline systems — totaling 14450 miles — that originate in the Gulf Coast region Arkansas and Oklahoma and extend to the Midwest. It provides transportation and storage to customers that include gas producers marketers local distribution companies and interstate and intrastate pipelines. It operates through Boardwalk Pipelines LP and its subsidiaries Gulf Crossing Pipeline Company Gulf South Pipeline Company and Texas Gas Transmission. The company's systems carry 11% of the daily US consumption of natural gas. Boardwalk Pipeline Partners is controlled by Loews Corporation.

	Annual Growth	12/10	12/11	12/12	12/13	12/14
Sales ($ mil.)	2.5%	1,116.8	1,138.8	1,185.0	1,205.6	1,233.8
Net income ($ mil.)	(5.2%)	289.4	220.0	306.0	253.7	233.6
Market value ($ mil.)	(13.1%)	7,573.9	6,732.1	6,058.2	6,209.0	4,323.4
Employees	2.8%	1,100	1,170	1,200	1,200	1,230

BOB EVANS FARMS, INC.
NMS: BOBE

8111 Smith's Mill Road
New Albany, OH 43054
Phone: 614 491-2225
Fax: –
Web: www.bobevans.com

CEO: Saed Mohseni
CFO: Mark E. Hood
HR: Joseph R. (Joe) Eulberg
FYE: April 24
Type: Public

This farm is focused on cooks in the kitchen rather than seeds in the ground. Bob Evans Farms is a leading full-service restaurant company with more than 650 locations operating under the names Bob Evans and Mimi's Café. Its namesake chain includes about 565 family-style restaurants in 20 states that are best known for breakfast items such as bacon eggs hotcakes and sausage products. Its Mimi's Café casual dining chain operated through subsidiary SWH Corporation serves American-style dishes at about 150 locations. In addition to its restaurants Bob Evans Farms markets its own sausage and bacon products under the Bob Evans and Owens brands at supermarkets and other grocery retailers.

	Annual Growth	04/11	04/12	04/13	04/14	04/15
Sales ($ mil.)	(5.3%)	1,676.9	1,654.4	1,608.9	1,328.6	1,349.2
Net income ($ mil.)	(25.6%)	54.2	72.9	(2.9)	33.7	16.6
Market value ($ mil.)	9.6%	734.0	905.1	995.3	1,095.4	1,060.1
Employees	(7.8%)	44,819	46,818	34,023	34,470	32,341

BOB ROSS BUICK INC.

85 LOOP RD
DAYTON, OH 454592199
Phone: 937-433-0990
Fax: –
Web: www.bobrossbuickgmc.com

CEO: –
CFO: –
HR: –
FYE: December 31
Type: Private

The Bob Ross Dealerships sells new and used cars made by Buick GMC and Mercedes Benz at in Centerville Ohio. Bob Ross also provides financing parts service and collision repair. The company's bobrossauto.com Web site allows customers to search new and used inventory as well as schedule service order parts and apply for financing. Bob Ross ranks near the top of many categories (Buick sales customer satisfaction GMC truck sales) for Buick dealerships in Ohio. The company was founded in 1979 by the late Bob Ross Sr. and his wife president and CEO Norma Ross (daughter Jenell is owner). It was the first African-American owned Mercedes-Benz dealership in the world.

	Annual Growth	12/09	12/10	12/11	12/12	12/13
Sales ($ mil.)	10.4%	–	49.6	48.5	59.0	66.8
Net income ($ mil.)	(1.1%)	–	–	0.5	0.2	0.5
Market value ($ mil.)	–	–	–	–	–	–
Employees	–	–	–	–	–	100

BODDIE-NOELL ENTERPRISES INC.

1021 NOELL LN
ROCKY MOUNT, NC 278041761
Phone: 252-937-2000
Fax: –
Web: www.bneinc.com

CEO: Bill Boddie
CFO: W Craig Worthy
HR: Ranendra Danging
FYE: December 30
Type: Private

Boddie-Noell Enterprises (BNE) is a hearty competitor in the fast-food business. The company is one of the largest franchise operators of Hardee's a fast-food chain owned by CKE Restaurants with about 330 locations the four southeastern states of Kentucky North Carolina South Carolina and Virginia. In addition the company owns The Highway Diner restaurant concept. BNE is also involved in real estate development through BNE Land & Development. The family owned company was started in 1962 by Carleton Noell and his nephews Nick and Mayo Boddie.

	Annual Growth	12/09	12/10	12/11	12/12	12/13
Sales ($ mil.)	(1.7%)	–	389.9	395.3	395.3	369.9
Net income ($ mil.)	–	–	–	(9.6)	14.0	16.6
Market value ($ mil.)	–	–	–	–	–	–
Employees	–	–	–	–	–	13,000

BODY CENTRAL CORP.

NBB: BODY

6225 Powers Avenue
Jacksonville, FL 32217
Phone: 904 737-0811
Fax: 904 730-0638
Web: www.bodycentral.com

CEO: –
CFO: –
HR: –
FYE: December 28
Type: Public

Body Central likely has something in store for young women who feel that image is everything. The company offers trendy apparel shoes and accessories to women in their late teens and early 20s through about 290 Body Central and Body Shop retail stores. Located primarily in malls in more than 25 states in the South Midwest and Mid-Atlantic the shops carry dresses tops jewelry and shoes sold under its Body Central and Lipstick brands. It also sells its merchandise through catalogs and its e-commerce site. A holding company Body Central operates primarily through its Body Shop of America (not affiliated with The Body Shop) and Catalogue Ventures subsidiaries. Body Central went public in 2010.

	Annual Growth	01/10	01/11*	12/11	12/12	12/13
Sales ($ mil.)	12.6%	198.8	243.4	296.5	311.0	283.6
Net income ($ mil.)	–	2.8	9.8	19.7	11.9	(42.3)
Market value ($ mil.)	(46.8%)	–	23.7	41.5	15.8	6.7
Employees	19.3%	2,300	2,410	2,869	3,305	3,901

*Fiscal year change

BOEING CAPITAL CORP

500 Naches Ave. S.W., 3rd Floor
Renton, WA 98057
Phone: 425 965-4000
Fax: –
Web: www.boeing.com

CEO: –
CFO: Kelvin E Council
HR: Greg Lim
FYE: December 31
Type: Public

Need financing for that 747? Boeing Capital a major subsidiary of Boeing provides asset-backed leasing and lending services through two divisions: Aircraft Financial Services offers financing and leasing services for airlines and governmental customers interested in Boeing aircraft; Space & Defense Financial Services offers similar services for Boeing's Integrated Defense Systems customers. AirTran is Boeing Capital's biggest customer followed by American Airlines Hawaiian Airlines and Continental Airlines. Boeing Capital was founded in 1968 as McDonnell Douglas Finance and changed its name when Boeing acquired McDonnell Douglas in 1997.

	Annual Growth	12/08	12/09	12/10	12/11	12/12
Sales ($ mil.)	(11.3%)	703.0	660.0	639.0	532.0	436.0
Net income ($ mil.)	(20.5%)	120.0	57.0	92.0	83.0	48.0
Market value ($ mil.)	–	–	–	–	–	–
Employees	(2.3%)	160	161	150	146	146

BOEING CO. (THE)

NYS: BA

100 North Riverside Plaza
Chicago, IL 60606-1596
Phone: 312 544-2000
Fax: –
Web: www.boeing.com

CEO: Raymond L. (Ray) Conner
CFO: Gregory D. (Greg) Smith
HR: Grace Miller
FYE: December 31
Type: Public

Boeing has built a big name for itself as one of the world's largest aerospace companies. In addition to commercial jet aircraft like the much anticipated 787 Dreamliner the company manufactures military aircraft including the Apache the Chinook and the Osprey. It also produces satellites missile defense systems and launch systems. These products are rounded out by a portfolio of services. Major customers include the US Department of Defense and NASA. Additionally Boeing provides airplane financing and leasing services to both commercial and military customers.

	Annual Growth	12/11	12/12	12/13	12/14	12/15
Sales ($ mil.)	8.7%	68,735.0	81,698.0	86,623.0	90,762.0	96,114.0
Net income ($ mil.)	6.5%	4,018.0	3,900.0	4,585.0	5,446.0	5,176.0
Market value ($ mil.)	18.5%	48,896.9	50,236.8	90,987.5	86,647.8	96,387.1
Employees	(1.5%)	171,700	174,400	168,400	165,500	161,400

BOEING EMPLOYEES' CREDIT UNION

12770 Gateway Dr.
Tukwila WA 98168
Phone: 206-439-5700
Fax: 206-439-5804
Web: www.becu.org

CEO: Gary J Oakland
CFO: Brad Canfield
HR: –
FYE: December 31
Type: Private - Not-for-Pr

Boeing Employees' Credit Union (BECU) was founded in 1935 to serve the employees of Boeing (naturally) which called Seattle home until 2001. Today membership in the credit union is open to all who live work go to school or belong to a church in Washington State. BECU has about 45 locations in the state's Puget Sound region many of them in Safeway supermarkets. The credit union offers standard retail financial services such as checking and savings accounts credit cards home mortgages and other loans. The credit union also participates in a shared-branch system giving its members access to financial services at more than 4000 locations worldwide. BECU boasts some 800000 members.

BOEING SATELLITE SYSTEMS INTERNATIONAL INC.

2260 E. Imperial Hwy.
El Segundo CA 90245
Phone: 310-364-4000
Fax: 604-681-8240

CEO: Craig R Cooning
CFO: –
HR: –
FYE: December 31
Type: Subsidiary

Boeing Satellite Systems International is happiest when its products are far far away. The company is a contracting unit for commercial and military spacecraft within the Boeing Space & Intelligence Systems division. It manufactures communications meteorological and research satellites. Boeing Satellite Systems International built the world's first geosynchronous communications satellite (Syncom) and estimates that it has manufactured about 40% of all the communications satellites in commercial service today (since its inception in 1961). Other satellite applications include cover radar mapping satellite television and national security. Contracts with the DoD constitute the majority of its revenues.

BOFI HOLDING, INC.

NMS: BOFI

4350 La Jolla Village Drive, Suite 140
San Diego, CA 92122
Phone: 858 350-6200
Fax: –
Web: www.bofiholding.com

CEO: Gregory Garrabrants
CFO: Andrew J. Micheletti
HR: –
FYE: June 30
Type: Public

BofI Holding owns Bank of Internet USA a savings bank that operates online in all 50 states. The bank offers checking savings and money market accounts CDs and ATM and check cards. Multifamily real estate loans account for nearly two-thirds of the company's loan portfolio although the bank only offers them in selected states; it also acquires them on the secondary market. Offered nationwide single-family residential mortgages make up nearly 30% of its loan portfolio. Bank of Internet USA also issues home equity automobile and recreational vehicle loans. Officers and directors own more than 30% of BofI Holding's stock.

	Annual Growth	06/11	06/12	06/13	06/14	06/15
Assets ($ mil.)	31.6%	1,940.1	2,386.8	3,090.8	4,403.0	5,823.7
Net income ($ mil.)	41.6%	20.6	29.5	40.3	56.0	82.7
Market value ($ mil.)	64.6%	894.5	1,226.6	2,844.3	4,560.7	6,561.9
Employees	28.2%	173	230	312	366	467

BOGEN COMMUNICATIONS INTERNATIONAL INC.

PINK SHEETS: BOGN

50 Spring St.
Ramsey NJ 07446
Phone: 201-934-8500
Fax: 201-934-9832
Web: www.bogen.com

CEO: Jonathan Guss
CFO: Maureen Flotard
HR: –
FYE: December 31
Type: Public

Bogen Communications knows how the soothing sounds of smooth jazz can make time fly while holding on the telephone. Through subsidiaries Bogen Communications and Speech Design the company makes telecommunications peripherals and sound equipment. Bogen Communications sells telecom equipment including music-on-hold devices unified messaging systems call distributors and voice mail systems. Speech Design sells call processing and PBX products primarily in Germany. Bogen also makes audio amplifiers and speaker systems. Schools restaurants and stores use the company's line of intercom and paging systems for public address and background music. Executives and directors together own a majority of Bogen.

BOINGO WIRELESS INC

NMS: WIFI

10960 Wilshire Blvd., 23rd Floor
Los Angeles, CA 90024
Phone: 310 586-5180
Fax: –
Web: www.boingo.com

CEO: David (Dave) Hagan
CFO: Peter (Pete) Hovenier
HR: –
FYE: December 31
Type: Public

Boingo keeps travelers connected as they bounce through often unfamiliar locales. The company sells access to a global Wi-Fi network of about 600000 hot spots to about 200000 subscribers through wholesale agreements with wireless network and hot spot operators. Access is offered mainly in such venues as hotels convention centers airports and restaurants including McDonald's and Krispy Kreme. Additionally Boingo offers its roaming network and software to ISPs and managed network service providers. Fiberlink and Verizon Business are among the company's corporate customers. The company was established in 2001 by chairman and Earthlink founder Sky Dayton.

	Annual Growth	12/10	12/11	12/12	12/13	12/14
Sales ($ mil.)	10.4%	80.4	94.6	102.5	106.7	119.5
Net income ($ mil.)	–	15.7	6.3	7.3	(3.8)	(19.5)
Market value ($ mil.)	(3.7%)	–	311.9	273.8	232.5	278.2
Employees	18.4%	135	149	160	239	265

BOISE CASCADE CO. (DE)

NYS: BCC

1111 West Jefferson Street, Suite 300
Boise, ID 83702-5389
Phone: 208 384-6161
Fax: –
Web: www.bc.com

CEO: Thomas K. Corrick
CFO: Wayne M. Rancourt
HR: Claudia Brush
FYE: December 31
Type: Public

Boise Cascade has more than a trickle of building materials. The company is North America's #2 manufacturer of laminated wood I-joists and plywood. Other wood products include lumber and particle board. Boise Cascade is also one of the largest building materials distributors offering its own and third-party products from about 50 locations across the US. Customers include lumberyards home improvement centers and industrial converters (makers of windows doors and other assembled products) in North America and China. Boise Cascade was formed in 2004 and went public in 2013 with an offering attuned to the upturn in the US housing market.

	Annual Growth	12/10	12/11	12/12	12/13	12/14
Sales ($ mil.)	12.4%	2,240.6	2,248.1	2,779.1	3,273.5	3,573.7
Net income ($ mil.)	–	(33.3)	(46.4)	41.5	116.9	80.0
Market value ($ mil.)	26.0%	–	–	–	1,162.0	1,464.4
Employees	10.8%	–	–	4,620	5,290	5,670

BOJANGLES' RESTAURANTS INC.

9432 Southern Pines Blvd.
Charlotte NC 28273
Phone: 704-527-2675
Fax: 704-523-6803
Web: www.bojangles.com/

CEO: Randy Kibler
CFO: John Jordan
HR: –
FYE: December 31
Type: Private

This Bojangles doesn't dance in worn-out shoes but it will cook some chicken for you. Bojangles' Holdings operates and franchises more than 520 quick-service eateries in North Carolina and about a dozen other states. Operating under the name Bojangles' Famous Chicken & Biscuits the restaurants specialize in Cajun-style chicken and biscuits. The menu also includes sandwiches chicken wings and breakfast items. The chain includes more than 150 company-owned locations; the rest are operated by franchisees. Bojangles was founded in 1977 by former KFC president Richard Thomas and partner Jack Fulk. Private equity firm Advent International agreed to buy the chain from Falfurrias Capital Partners in 2011.

BOK FINANCIAL CORP.

NMS: BOKF

Bank of Oklahoma Tower, Boston Avenue at Second Street
Tulsa, OK 74172
Phone: 918 588-6000
Fax: –
Web: www.bokf.com

CEO: Steven G Bradshaw
CFO: Steven E Nell
HR: –
FYE: December 31
Type: Public

Will your money BOK? Multibank holding company BOK Financial tries to make sure it is. With seven principal banking divisions in eight midwestern and southwestern states BOK offers a range of financial services to consumers and regional businesses. In addition to traditional deposit lending and trust services the banks provide investment management wealth advisory and mineral and real estate management services through a network of about 200 branches in Arizona Arkansas Colorado Kansas Missouri New Mexico Oklahoma and Texas. Brokerage subsidiary BOSC underwrites public private and municipal securities. BOK also owns electronic funds network TransFund and institutional asset manager Cavanal Hill.

	Annual Growth	12/10	12/11	12/12	12/13	12/14
Assets ($ mil.)	5.0%	23,941.6	25,493.9	28,148.6	27,015.4	29,089.7
Net income ($ mil.)	4.3%	246.8	285.9	351.2	316.6	292.4
Market value ($ mil.)	3.0%	3,690.7	3,796.4	3,763.9	4,583.6	4,149.6
Employees	1.7%	4,432	4,511	4,704	4,632	4,743

BOLLINGER SHIPYARDS INC.

8365 Hwy. 308 South
Lockport LA 70374
Phone: 985-532-2554
Fax: 985-532-7225
Web: www.bollingershipyards.com

CEO: Ben Bordelon
CFO: Andrew Fc Germain
HR: –
FYE: September 30
Type: Private

Bollinger Shipyards is a leading provider of shipbuilding and ship repair services for both the military and commercial marine industry on the US Gulf Coast. The company specializes in the construction repair and conversion of US Navy and Coast Guard patrol boats oil tankers and supply and utility vessels such as barges and tugboats. It operates from some 13 shipyards primarily in Louisiana but also in Texas and has access to the Mississippi River. Its more than 30 dry docks have the capability to accommodate ships ranging in size from 100 tons to 22000 tons. It also has a more than 460000-sq.-ft. facility for constructing vessels indoors. Bollinger Shipyards was founded in 1946 by Donald Bollinger.

BOLT TECHNOLOGY CORP.   NMS: BOLT

Four Duke Place
Norwalk, CT 06854
Phone: 203 853-0700
Fax: 203 854-9601
Web: www.bolt-technology.com

CEO: Raymond M Soto
CFO: –
HR: –
FYE: June 30
Type: Public

Bolt Technology's action is technology the kind used to map out oil and gas discoveries. Its product suite consists of the key components needed by seismic exploration vessels to acquire seismic data: an energy source (air guns); synchronization (controllers); and communication (cables) linking the guns and the controllers. Its marine air guns help produce 3-D seismic maps for oil and gas exploration by firing high-pressure air into the water producing elastic waves that penetrate deep into the earth. These waves create a "map" of the subsurface geography. The company also operates a fleet of remotely operated vehicles (ROVs). Bolt Technology's major customers include CGG-Veritas and Schlumberger.

	Annual Growth	06/09	06/10	06/11	06/12	06/13
Sales ($ mil.)	4.3%	48.9	31.5	38.9	52.6	57.8
Net income ($ mil.)	(10.6%)	10.5	5.0	5.5	2.0	6.7
Market value ($ mil.)	11.0%	97.0	75.5	107.0	129.5	147.3
Employees	7.3%	139	123	165	176	184

BON SECOURS HEALTH SYSTEM INC

1505 MARRIOTTSVILLE RD
MARRIOTTSVILLE, MD 211041301
Phone: 410-442-5511
Fax: –
Web: www.bshsi.com

CEO: Richard J. (Rich) Statuto
CFO: Katherine A Arbuckle
HR: Mary Howe
FYE: August 31
Type: Private

Bon Secours Health System provides succor to the sick and injured. The Roman Catholic health care organization sponsored by the Bon Secours Ministries is home to about 20 hospitals with some 4400 licensed acute care beds. First founded in 1919 the organization's facilities are in six states in the eastern US from New York to Florida. In addition to its acute care hospitals the not-for-profit health care system operates a psychiatric hospital numerous nursing homes and assisted-living facilities as well as hospices and home health care agencies. Its Global Ministry Initiative provides outreach for health care and social services in developing countries particularly Haiti Peru and South Africa.

	Annual Growth	08/06	08/07	08/08	08/09	08/10
Sales ($ mil.)	6.6%	–	–	–	2,895.2	3,084.9
Net income ($ mil.)	–	–	–	–	(291.9)	(41.4)
Market value ($ mil.)	–	–	–	–	–	–
Employees	–	–	–	–	–	19,000

BON-TON STORES INC   NMS: BONT

2801 East Market Street
York, PA 17402
Phone: 717 757-7660
Fax: –
Web: www.bonton.com

CEO: Kathryn (Kathy) Bufano
CFO: Nancy A. Walsh
HR: –
FYE: January 31
Type: Public

Fashion hounds lost in the wilds of Vermont to Montana can take refuge in The Bon-Ton Stores. The company operates some 270 department stores under seven nameplates including the Bon-Ton Elder-Beerman and Carson Pirie Scott banners in more than two dozen states. The stores sell branded (Calvin Klein Coach Estée Lauder and Michael Kors) and private-label women's children's and men's clothing; accessories; cosmetics; and home furnishings. Women's apparel is its top merchandise category accounting for about a quarter of total sales. The Bon-Ton Stores was founded in 1898 by the Grumbacher family.

	Annual Growth	01/11	01/12*	02/13	02/14*	01/15
Sales ($ mil.)	(1.9%)	3,046.5	2,953.5	2,978.8	2,834.1	2,822.9
Net income ($ mil.)	–	21.5	(12.1)	(21.6)	(3.6)	(7.0)
Market value ($ mil.)	(16.2%)	227.6	83.4	267.7	219.6	112.0
Employees	(1.2%)	26,500	27,100	26,900	25,800	25,200

*Fiscal year change

BONANZA CREEK ENERGY, INC.   NYS: BCEI

410 17th Street, Suite 1400
Denver, CO 80202
Phone: 720 440-6100
Fax: 720 305-0804
Web: www.bonanzacrk.com

CEO: Richard J. Carty
CFO: Bill Cassidy
HR: –
FYE: December 31
Type: Public

Bonanza Creek Energy searches for a treasure of black gold. The independent oil and natural gas company has exploration and production assets in Arkansas California Colorado and Texas. Unlike many in the industry it operates nearly all of its projects and has an 89% working interest in its holdings. The company reported a 32% increase in proved reserves in 2013 to 69.8 million barrels of oil equivalent resulting primarily from the development of the Wattenberg Field in Colorado. Most of the company's proved reserves are in its Rocky Mountains (Niobara oil shale) and Arkansas (Cotton Valley sands) holdings.

	Annual Growth	12/10	12/11	12/12	12/13	12/14
Sales ($ mil.)	323.0%	1.7	112.5	231.2	421.9	558.6
Net income ($ mil.)	–	(0.2)	12.7	46.5	69.2	20.3
Market value ($ mil.)	24.3%	–	516.1	1,147.4	1,794.8	990.9
Employees	51.5%	–	96	155	236	334

BONITZ INC.

645 ROSEWOOD DR
COLUMBIA, SC 292014699
Phone: 803-799-0181
Fax: –
Web: www.bonitz.us

CEO: Thomas B Banks
CFO: Stephen E Lee
HR: –
FYE: December 31
Type: Private

Bonitz is a veteran US acoustical ceiling and drywall contractor. Founded by chairman Bill Rogers in 1954 the company got a humble start in South Carolina and has grown to operate in more than a dozen US locations primarily in the Southeast including Alabama Colorado Georgia Tennessee Virginia and the Carolinas. Through its operating divisions Bonitz also offers commercial and residential flooring contracting roofing contracting and manufacturing of prefabricated light gage metal wall panels and trusses for educational institutional and commercial buildings. Its clients include architects interior designers general contractors and building owners. Bonitz is employee owned.

	Annual Growth	12/09	12/10	12/11	12/12	12/13
Sales ($ mil.)	1.1%	–	139.3	126.5	129.0	143.9
Net income ($ mil.)	(1.1%)	–	–	6.9	3.9	6.7
Market value ($ mil.)	–	–	–	–	–	–
Employees	–	–	–	–	–	850

BONNEVILLE POWER ADMINISTRATION

905 NE 11th Ave.
Portland OR 97232
Phone: 503-230-3000
Fax: 256-350-1770
Web: www.alafarm.com

CEO: –
CFO: –
HR: –
FYE: September 30
Type: Government-owned

Bonneville Power Administration (BPA) keeps the lights on in the Pacific Northwest. The US Department of Energy power marketing agency operates a transmission grid (with more than 15200 miles of high-voltage lines) that delivers about 30% of the electrical power consumed in the region. The electricity that BPA wholesales is generated primarily by 31 federal hydroelectric plants (operated by the US Army Corp of Engineers) and one private nuclear facility. BPA also purchases power from other hydroelectric gas-fired and wind and solar generation facilities in North America. Founded in 1937 BPA sells power to more than 140 primary customers mainly public and investor-owned utilities in the Pacific Northwest.

BONNIER CORPORATION

460 N. Orlando Ave. Ste. 200
Winter Park FL 32789
Phone: 407-628-4802
Fax: 407-628-7061
Web: www.bonniercorp.com

CEO: Terry Snow
CFO: Randy Koubek
HR: –
FYE: December 31
Type: Subsidiary

Packing Salade Nicoise for a typical afternoon cruising the bay on your yacht? If so you would be a target reader of Bonnier Corporation publisher of magazine titles such as such as "Saveur" (an award-winning gourmet foods magazine) Cruising World and "Boating Life". Additional titles include Popular Science Field & Stream and Outdoor Life. Its Garden Design and Florida Travel & Life titles make up the company's Lifestyle & Shelter Group with other groups devoted to Travel Luxury and Parenting. All total Bonnier Corporation publishes about 50 special-interest magazines and produces related multimedia projects and events. The company is owned by 200-year-old Swedish media firm Bonnier AB.

BOOKS-A-MILLION, INC.   NMS: BAMM

402 Industrial Lane
Birmingham, AL 35211
Phone: 205 942-3737
Fax: –
Web: www.booksamillioninc.com

CEO: Terrance G Finley
CFO: R Todd Noden
HR: Mary Jane Karwoski
FYE: February 01
Type: Public

Books-A-Million (BAM) caters to readers who aren't millionaires. One of the nation's largest booksellers (behind Amazon and Barnes & Noble) the company operates some 260 stores in 30-plus states and Washington DC and sells books online. BAM operates superstores under the Books-A-Million Books & Co. and 2nd & Charles banners and traditional smaller stores under the Bookland title. All the stores sell discounted hardcover and paperback books magazines toys music DVDs and general merchandise. Many stores include Joe Muggs cafés and sell frozen yogurt. Other activities comprise online unit booksamillion.com gift card issuer BAM Card Services and book wholesaler American Wholesale Book.

	Annual Growth	01/10	01/11	01/12*	02/13	02/14
Sales ($ mil.)	(1.9%)	508.7	495.0	468.5	503.8	470.3
Net income ($ mil.)	–	13.8	8.9	(2.8)	2.5	(7.6)
Market value ($ mil.)	(22.4%)	97.7	85.7	38.5	38.5	35.4
Employees	(0.5%)	5,500	5,300	6,000	5,500	5,400

*Fiscal year change

BOOKSPAN

501 Franklin Ave.
Garden City NY 11530-5945
Phone: 516-490-4561
Fax: 516-490-4714
Web: www.booksonline.com

CEO: Deborah I Fine
CFO: –
HR: –
FYE: December 31
Type: Private

Spanning the globe to bring you … books. Bookspan is a direct marketer of books operating book clubs under such familiar names as the Book-of-the-Month Club Doubleday Book Club and The Literary Guild. The company operates about 20 clubs that offer bestsellers and feature titles from specific genres including history military mystery and science fiction. Book selections are chosen by editors in various areas. The company was created through a partnership between Bertelsmann and Time Warner which sold its stake to Bertelsmann in 2007. Bertelsmann sold Bookspan Columbia House and its other direct marketing operations in the US to Phoenix-based private investment firm Najafi Cos. in 2008.

BOOZ ALLEN HAMILTON HOLDING CORP.   NYS: BAH

8283 Greensboro Drive
McLean, VA 22102
Phone: 703 902-5000
Fax: –
Web: www.boozallen.com

CEO: Horacio D. Rozanski
CFO: Kevin Cook
HR: Marianne Malizia
FYE: March 31
Type: Public

For almost a century consultants at Booz Allen Hamilton have been helping US government agencies operate more efficiently at home and abroad. The firm provides a wide range of management consulting and technology integration services; its specialties include information technology operations organization and change program management strategy training programs and systems engineering. Booz Allen has long-established relationships with such agencies as the Department of Defense the Federal Aviation Administration and the Internal Revenue Service. Investment firm The Carlyle Group owns a majority interest in the consulting firm which was founded in 1914.

	Annual Growth	03/11	03/12	03/13	03/14	03/15
Sales ($ mil.)	(1.4%)	5,591.3	5,859.2	5,758.1	5,478.7	5,274.8
Net income ($ mil.)	28.7%	84.7	240.0	219.1	232.2	232.6
Market value ($ mil.)	12.6%	2,685.1	2,539.0	2,003.8	3,280.0	4,314.7
Employees	(2.6%)	25,000	25,000	24,500	22,700	22,500

BORGESS MEDICAL CENTER

1521 GULL RD
KALAMAZOO, MI 490481666
Phone: 269-226-7000
Fax: –
Web: www.borgess.com

CEO: –
CFO: –
HR: Laura Lentenbrink
FYE: June 30
Type: Private

Borgess Medical Center is part of the Borgess Health Alliance which is a member of the Ascension Health network. The general acute care facility which serves residents of southwestern Michigan houses more than 420 beds. It has a comprehensive offering of medical and surgical services including specialty care in areas such as cancer heart disease neuroscience and orthopedics. Borgess Medical Center also serves as a Level II trauma center and features a research institute a sleep disorders clinic a weight loss surgery center no-wait emergency room and outpatient facilities. The hospital was founded in 1889 by a local priest.

	Annual Growth	06/06	06/07	06/08	06/09	06/10
Sales ($ mil.)	–	–	–	(1,203.3)	414.9	455.5
Net income ($ mil.)	–	–	–	0.0	(5.3)	(6.4)
Market value ($ mil.)	–	–	–	–	–	–
Employees	–	–	–	–	–	2,200

BORGHESE INC.

10 E. 34th St. 3rd Fl.
New York NY 10016
Phone: 212-659-5300
Fax: 212-659-5301
Web: www.borghese.com

CEO: Georgette Mosbacher
CFO: Frank Palladino
HR: –
FYE: December 31
Type: Private

You can ring up Borghese when you need to be made beautiful. Borghese makes and markets its namesake Italian cosmetics skin care fragrances and hair care products and sells its collections through high-end department stores nationwide including Bloomingdale's Lord & Taylor and Nordstrom. Its products are also marketed internationally in such countries as China Germany Ireland and Mexico. President and CEO Georgette Mosbacher (also a well-known New York City Republican) holds a substantial equity stake in the company while the rest is retained by the original group of Saudi investors who purchased it upon Revlon's divestiture of the firm in 1992.

BORGWARNER INC   NYS: BWA

3850 Hamlin Road
Auburn Hills, MI 48326
Phone: 248 754-9200
Fax: –
Web: www.borgwarner.com

CEO: James R. Verrier
CFO: Ronald T. (Ron) Hundzinski
HR: Monica Rottman
FYE: December 31
Type: Public

If suburbanites need four-wheel-drive vehicles to turbocharge their urban drive that's OK with BorgWarner. The company is a leading maker of engine and drivetrain products for the world's major automotive manufacturers. Products include turbochargers air pumps timing chain systems four-wheel-drive and all-wheel-drive transfer cases (primarily for light trucks and SUVs) and transmission components. Its largest customers include Volkswagen Ford and Daimler. The company nets around 75% of sales from outside the US; more than half come from its European operations.

	Annual Growth	12/11	12/12	12/13	12/14	12/15
Sales ($ mil.)	3.0%	7,114.7	7,183.2	7,436.6	8,305.1	8,023.2
Net income ($ mil.)	2.6%	550.1	500.9	624.3	655.8	609.7
Market value ($ mil.)	(9.3%)	13,979.8	15,708.0	12,262.5	12,051.9	9,481.4
Employees	11.7%	19,250	19,100	19,700	22,000	30,000

BOSCH COMMUNICATIONS SYSTEMS

12000 Portland Ave. South
Burnsville MN 55337
Phone: 952-884-4051
Fax: 916-928-6404
Web: www.daegis.com

CEO: –
CFO: –
HR: –
FYE: December 31
Type: Business Segment

Bosch Communications Systems (formerly Telex Communications) makes sure its customers' voices are heard. The company makes audio and communications equipment for commercial professional and industrial use. Its sound systems can be heard in venues from the Metropolitan Opera to Wrigley Field. A large portion of commercial airline pilots use Telex headsets. Other brand names include Electro-Voice Dynacord Klark Teknik Midas and RTS. Telex Communications was founded in 1936 as a hearing aid manufacturer; Robert Bosch GmbH acquired the company in 2006 and renamed it Bosch Communications Systems.

BOSCH SECURITY SYSTEMS INC.

130 Perinton Pkwy.
Fairport NY 14450-9199
Phone: 585-223-4060
Fax: 585-223-9180
Web: www.boschsecurity.com

CEO: Christopher P Gerace
CFO: –
HR: –
FYE: December 31
Type: Subsidiary

Bosch Security Systems has a sixth sense for finding business. The company makes electronic detection and communications equipment for use in government banking education and gaming sectors as well as at airports and train stations. Products include cameras fire and intrusion alarm systems conference communications and access control. Some of the products send alarm signals over telephone lines or wireless networks. Its personal safety systems transmit the user's identity and location to a monitoring station when activated. The company has sales offices and distribution centers worldwide. Bosch Security Systems is a subsidiary of German manufacturing giant Robert Bosch GmbH.

BOSS HOLDINGS INC.   OTC: BSHI

221 W. 1st St.
Kewanee IL 61443
Phone: 309-852-2131
Fax: 309-852-0848
Web: www.bossgloves.com

CEO: G Louis Graziadio III
CFO: –
HR: –
FYE: December 31
Type: Public

Boss Holdings would rather take orders (for its gloves boots and rainwear) than give them. Its primary subsidiary Boss Manufacturing Company (BMC) imports and markets gloves and protective wear that it sells through mass merchandisers hardware stores and other retailers in North America. The company also sells its products directly to commercial users in industries such as agriculture and automotive. The holding company's Boss Pet Products markets pet supplies to US retailers while its Galaxy Balloons subsidiary sells latex balloons. Boss Holdings was founded in 1893 as a manufacturer of work gloves. Today gloves and protective gear account for a majority of annual sales.

BOSSELMAN INC.

3123 W. Stolley Park Rd.
Grand Island NE 68801
Phone: 308-381-2800
Fax: 308-381-2801
Web: www.bosselman.com

CEO: –
CFO: Brian Larson
HR: –
FYE: December 31
Type: Private

Bosselman depends on truckers needing a pit stop to pump it up and pack it in. The diversified family-owned-and-operated firm runs about 45 Pump & Pantry convenience stores across Nebraska. Other ventures include a full-service Bosselman Travel Center in Grand Island Nebraska as well as 30-plus Boss Truck Shops in 20 states that offer truck repair services. Bosselman also operates restaurants (mostly Grandma Max's) and motels under the Motel 6 Hampton Inn and Pump & Pantry brands. Other operations include Bosselman Energy (wholesale oil fuel and propane delivery) and a sport team. Founder Frederick H. Bosselman — a farmer and part-time truck driver — opened his first truck stop in 1948.

BOSTON ACOUSTICS INC.

300 Jubilee Dr.
Peabody MA 01960
Phone: 978-538-5000
Fax: 978-538-5199
Web: www.bostonacoustics.com

CEO: Yvonne Hao
CFO: Debbie Rickirosato
HR: –
FYE: March 31
Type: Subsidiary

Play Dark Side of the Moon on a set of Boston Acoustics' speakers and you'll see the light. The company designs and makes moderately priced and high-end loudspeaker systems for the home and automotive markets. It also makes home entertainment systems amplifiers and ancillary speaker equipment including selectors and volume controls. Boston Acoustics mostly tunes out mass retailers selling its products through a select group of specialty dealers. Its products are manufactured by third parties in the Asia/Pacific region Europe and North America. Former chairman Andrew Kotsatos and ex-CEO Frank Reed founded the company in 1979. D&M Holdings acquired Boston Acoustics in 2005.

BOSTON MUTUAL LIFE INSURANCE COMPANY

120 Royall St.
Canton MA 02021
Phone: 781-828-7000
Fax: 781-770-0490
Web: www.bostonmutual.com

CEO: –
CFO: Clifford Lange
HR: Kim Brosnan
FYE: December 31
Type: Private - Mutual Com

If life insurance gives you a good feeling at Boston Mutual Life Insurance the feeling is mutual. The company sells traditional group and individual life insurance as well as disability and supplemental accident and illness coverage. The company distributes its products to individuals through its in-house General Agencies division while its Group and Worksite Divisions distribute through employers. Additional products include employee assistance programs and voluntary supplemental insurance products. The company reaches customers in New York through its subsidiary The Life Insurance Company of Boston & New York. Boston Mutual has remained a mutual company since it was founded in 1891.

BOSTON BEER CO., INC   NYS: SAM

One Design Center Place, Suite 850
Boston, MA 02210
Phone: 617 368-5000
Fax: 617 368-5500
Web: www.bostonbeer.com

CEO: Martin F. Roper
CFO: Frank H. Smalla
HR: –
FYE: December 27
Type: Public

A half-pint compared to megabrewers like the world's #1 beer maker Anheuser-Bush InBev The Boston Beer Company holds a distinction all its own — it is the US's largest craft brewer. The company produces more than 50 seasonal and year-round varieties of craft beers at breweries in Boston and four other states. Annually it sells around 2.7 million barrels of lagers and ales (including its flagship Samuel Adams Boston Lager and other Sam Adams brand beers) and Twisted Tea malt beverages. it also brews beer for third parties. Founded in 1984 by its chairman James Koch The Boston Beer Company has grown along with America's increasing thirst for better beer.

	Annual Growth	12/10	12/11	12/12	12/13	12/14
Sales ($ mil.)	18.1%	463.8	513.0	580.2	739.1	903.0
Net income ($ mil.)	16.0%	50.1	66.1	59.5	70.4	90.7
Market value ($ mil.)	31.8%	1,279.7	1,418.8	1,738.0	3,164.2	3,865.2
Employees	14.2%	780	840	950	1,120	1,325

BOSTON PRIVATE FINANCIAL HOLDINGS, INC.   NMS: BPFH

Ten Post Office Square
Boston, MA 02109
Phone: 617 912-1900
Fax: –
Web: www.bostonprivate.com

CEO: Mark D. Thompson
CFO: David J. Kaye
HR: –
FYE: December 31
Type: Public

Boston Private Financial Holdings (BPFH) is a holding company for firms engaged in wealth management and private banking including Boston Private Bank & Trust which operates branches in New England New York Los Angeles and the San Francisco Bay Area. (The bank sold its branches in the Pacific Northwest in 2013.) BPFH also owns four other wealth advisory and investment management firms. The company offers private banking wealth advisory investment management deposits and lending and trust services to wealthy individuals corporations and institutional clients. All told BPFH and its affiliates have more than $30 billion in managed or advised assets.

	Annual Growth	12/10	12/11	12/12	12/13	12/14
Assets ($ mil.)	2.5%	6,152.9	6,048.4	6,465.0	6,437.1	6,797.9
Net income ($ mil.)	–	(11.0)	39.1	53.3	70.5	68.8
Market value ($ mil.)	19.8%	543.4	658.7	747.5	1,047.0	1,117.5
Employees	(0.4%)	890	878	827	781	875

BOSTON MEDICAL CENTER CORPORATION

1 BOSTON MEDICAL CTR PL # 1
BOSTON, MA 021182908
Phone: 617-414-5000
Fax: –
Web: www.bmc.org

CEO: Kate E. Walsh
CFO: Richard Silveria
HR: Manuel Monteiro
FYE: September 30
Type: Private

Located in Boston's South End neighborhood Boston Medical Center (BMC) offers a full spectrum of health care services from prenatal care and obstetrics to surgery and rehabilitation. BMC is also the city's largest provider of indigent care spending millions of dollars annually on care for uninsured patients and offering free screenings and other community outreach programs. The not-for-profit hospital boasts nearly 500 licensed beds more than 700 physicians and includes a Level 1 trauma center acute rehabilitation facilities and neonatal and pediatric intensive care units. The center is the primary teaching hospital of Boston University's School of Medicine.

	Annual Growth	09/07	09/08	09/09	09/12	09/13
Sales ($ mil.)	(4.1%)	–	1,103.2	1,004.4	886.3	893.6
Net income ($ mil.)	–	–	–	(12.2)	2.6	7.0
Market value ($ mil.)	–	–	–	–	–	–
Employees	–	–	–	–	–	4,200

BOSTON PROPERTIES, INC.   NYS: BXP

Prudential Center, 800 Boylston Street, Suite 1900
Boston, MA 02199-8103
Phone: 617 236-3300
Fax: –
Web: www.bostonproperties.com

CEO: Owen D. Thomas
CFO: Michael E Labelle
HR: –
FYE: December 31
Type: Public

Boston Properties knows more than beans about real estate. The firm invests in develops and manages primarily Class-A office buildings in large US cities. Its core markets include Boston New York San Francisco and Washington DC. A self-administered real estate investment trust (REIT) Boston Properties owns about 170 office and office/technical properties including projects under construction. Its largest tenants include the US government Bank of America and Citibank. The REIT also owns a handful of retail hotel residential properties as well as land sites for development. Media czar Mort Zuckerman (U.S. News & World Report and Daily News) is Boston Properties' chairman.

	Annual Growth	12/10	12/11	12/12	12/13	12/14
Sales ($ mil.)	11.5%	1,550.8	1,759.5	1,876.3	2,135.5	2,397.0
Net income ($ mil.)	29.2%	159.1	272.7	289.7	749.8	443.6
Market value ($ mil.)	10.6%	13,183.1	15,250.1	16,201.0	15,368.0	19,704.2
Employees	2.5%	680	700	730	760	750

BOSTON RED SOX BASEBALL CLUB LIMITED PARTNERSHIP

4 Yawkey Way
Boston MA 02215-3496
Phone: 617-267-9440
Fax: 617-375-0944
Web: boston.redsox.mlb.com

CEO: Larry Lucchino
CFO: –
HR: –
FYE: December 31
Type: Private

You might say this team is now a curse on the other clubs in Major League Baseball. Boston Red Sox Baseball Club operates one of the oldest and most storied sports franchises. Founded as a charter member of the American League in 1901 the team owns seven World Series titles but at one time suffered through an 86-year championship drought popularly attributed to "The Curse of the Bambino." Boston broke The Curse in 2004 and then won its seventh championship three years later. Red Sox fans root for their home team at venerable Fenway Park the oldest pro baseball stadium in the country. Businessman John Henry leads a group that has owned the Red Sox franchise since 2002.

BOSTON SYMPHONY ORCHESTRA INC.

301 MASSACHUSETTS AVE
BOSTON, MA 021154557
Phone: 617-266-1492
Fax:
Web: www.bso.org

CEO: –
CFO: –
HR: –
FYE: August 31
Type: Private

If you want to venture out for some live music but are not in the mood for rock or pop then a performance by The Boston Symphony Orchestra (BSO) might strike the right chord with you. Featuring compositions by composers like Beethoven Mozart and Stravinsky the BSO performs more than 100 concerts during the regular season at Symphony Hall. The BSO also performs during the summer at the Tanglewood music center; other BSO-related performances are given by the smaller and lighter Boston Pops orchestra. One of the more prominent orchestras in the US the BSO was founded in 1881 by businessman Henry Lee Higginson. Current music director James Levine is the BSO's first America-born conductor.

	Annual Growth	08/07	08/08	08/09	08/10	08/11
Sales ($ mil.)	–	–	–	(1,675.6)	39.7	38.3
Net income ($ mil.)	4947.6%	–	–	0.0	12.7	41.7
Market value ($ mil.)	–	–	–	–	–	–
Employees	–	–	–	–	–	350

BOSTON RESTAURANT ASSOCIATES INC.

6 Kimball Ln. Ste. 210
Lynnfield MA 01940
Phone: 339-219-0466
Fax: 781-231-5225
Web: www.reginapizza.com

CEO: –
CFO: Fran V Ross
HR: Donna Devlin
FYE: April 30
Type: Private

Boston Restaurant Associates (BRA) is rolling in New England dough. The company operates more than 15 Pizzeria Regina pizza parlors located in shopping mall food courts and other high-traffic areas in Massachusetts and three other states. The restaurants specialize in brick-oven style thin crust Neapolitan pizzas that are available with a variety of toppings (and by the slice). In addition to its food court kiosk units BRA operates the original Regina Pizzeria (built in 1926) in Boston's North End as well as three full-service family-style Polcari's Italian Restaurant locations in the Boston area. The company is controlled by private equity firm Dolphin Asset Management.

BOSTONCOACH

69 Norman St.
Everett MA 02149
Phone: 617-394-3900
Fax: 617-381-8725
Web: www.bostoncoach.com

CEO: –
CFO: Hilary Simons
HR: Mary Aceto
FYE: December 31
Type: Subsidiary

We don't know whether any Celtics coaches call on BostonCoach but the company does provide car and bus transportation for business and leisure travelers as well as shuttle and charter services for groups. Its fleet includes more than 25000 sedans along with limousines vans SUVs minibuses and buses. Through its network of affiliates the company serves more than 450 cities in some 35 countries including North America Asia and Europe. BostonCoach is a subsidiary of investment powerhouse FMR (Fidelity Investments) which founded the company in 1985 with three vehicles to serve its own employees.

BOSTON SCIENTIFIC CORP.   NYS: BSX

300 Boston Scientific Way
Marlborough, MA 01752-1234
Phone: 508 683-4000
Fax: –
Web: www.bostonscientific.com

CEO: Michael F. (Mike) Mahoney
CFO: Daniel J. (Dan) Brennan
HR: Mat Johnson
FYE: December 31
Type: Public

Boston Scientific knows that nothing is simple in matters of the heart. The company makes medical supplies and devices used to diagnose and treat conditions in a variety of medical fields with an emphasis on cardiovascular products and cardiac rhythm management (CRM). It also makes devices used for electrophysiology endoscopy pain management (neuromodulation) urology and women's health. Its 13000 products — made in about a dozen factories worldwide — include biopsy forceps catheters coronary and urethral stents defibrillators needles and pacemakers. Boston Scientific markets its products in more than 100 countries.

	Annual Growth	12/10	12/11	12/12	12/13	12/14
Sales ($ mil.)	(1.4%)	7,806.0	7,622.0	7,249.0	7,143.0	7,380.0
Net income ($ mil.)	–	–	(1,065.0)	441.0	(4,068.0)	(121.0)	(119.0)
Market value ($ mil.)	15.0%	10,048.8	7,088.6	7,606.3	15,956.0	17,588.7
Employees	(1.0%)	25,000	24,000	24,000	23,000	24,000

BOTTOMLINE TECHNOLOGIES (DELAWARE) INC   NMS: EPAY

325 Corporate Drive
Portsmouth, NH 03801-6808
Phone: 603 436-0700
Fax: 603 436-0300
Web: www.bottomline.com

CEO: Robert A. (Rob) Eberle
CFO: Richard D. (Rick) Booth
HR: Karen Brieger
FYE: June 30
Type: Public

Bottomline Technologies wants to help you get more money on the top line and then more of it to your bottom line. The company provides enterprise software for payment and transactional document management and banking functions such as electronic payments automating accounts payable risk mitigation and more. It also operates the Paymode-X Internet-based payment and invoice exchange network for buyers and suppliers. Bottomline counts more than 10000 customers which come from sectors such as financial services health care insurance technology education media retail communications manufacturing and government.

	Annual Growth	06/11	06/12	06/13	06/14	06/15
Sales ($ mil.)	15.0%	189.4	224.3	254.8	300.6	330.9
Net income ($ mil.)	–	–	35.9	1.7	(14.4)	(19.1)	(34.7)
Market value ($ mil.)	3.0%	941.6	687.8	963.7	1,140.1	1,059.7
Employees	14.3%	880	1,000	1,100	1,300	1,500

BOULDER BRANDS INC
NMS: BDBD

1600 Pearl Street, Suite 300
Boulder, CO 80302
Phone: 303 652-0521
Fax: –
Web: www.boulderbrands.com

CEO: Stephen B Hughes
CFO: Christine Sacco
HR: –
FYE: December 31
Type: Public

Walking a nutrition tightrope? Boulder Brands (formerly Smart Balance) may help; its growing portfolio of food brands target the health conscious and those with health problems such as diabetes and glutin allergies. The company makes Smart Balance buttery spreads and other alternative food products including peanut butter popcorn and cooking oils. As the company has grown its Smart Balance business has been outweighed by its Natural foods segment including the Glutino and Gluten-Free Pantry Udi's Earth Balance and the EVOL brands of shelf-stable and frozen products. Boulder Brands' products are sold by food retailers throughout North America. Founded in 2005 the company became Boulder Brands in 2013.

	Annual Growth	12/09	12/10	12/11	12/12	12/13
Sales ($ mil.)	17.8%	239.5	242.0	274.3	369.6	461.3
Net income ($ mil.)	31.7%	3.5	(128.2)	9.7	4.2	10.4
Market value ($ mil.)	27.5%	361.3	260.8	322.8	776.9	955.1
Employees	77.2%	73	69	203	613	720

BOVIE MEDICAL CORP
ASE: BVX

4 Manhattanville Road, Suite 106
Purchase, NY 10577
Phone: 914 468-4009
Fax: –
Web: www.boviemedical.com

CEO: Robert Gershon
CFO: Peter L Donato
HR: –
FYE: December 31
Type: Public

Surgeons don't think about Bovie Medical during surgery but Bovie thinks about them. Bovie makes electrosurgical generators and disposable electrosurgical products (including desiccators electrodes electrosurgical pencils and other devices) for cutting and cauterizing tissue. These are mainly used for outpatient surgical procedures in doctors' offices surgery centers and hospitals. Bovie also makes battery-operated cauteries (to stop bleeding) physician penlights and other medical lighting instruments and nerve locator simulators (used in hand and facial reconstruction) to identify motor nerves. Bovie markets and distributes worldwide under its own Aaron ICON and IDS brands and under private labels.

	Annual Growth	12/10	12/11	12/12	12/13	12/14
Sales ($ mil.)	3.4%	24.2	25.4	27.7	23.7	27.7
Net income ($ mil.)	–	(1.5)	0.1	0.6	(4.3)	(17.3)
Market value ($ mil.)	2.9%	58.6	37.8	43.2	38.4	65.7
Employees	1.5%	143	139	147	136	152

BOWEN ENGINEERING CORPORATION

8802 N MERIDIAN ST
INDIANAPOLIS, IN 462605380
Phone: 219-661-9770
Fax: –
Web: www.bowenengineering.com

CEO: A Douglas Bowen III
CFO: Scot Evans Sr
HR: –
FYE: September 30
Type: Private

Bowen Engineering understands the elements of earth wind and water. The company provides engineering and construction services for water wastewater earthwork concrete industrial power and underground utility projects. It operates through three divisions: Power and industrial; private water; and public works. The company which has offices in Indiana Tennessee and Ohio offers design/build general contracting and construction management services to public and private clients. Bowen Engineering was founded in 1967 by Robert Bowen. The Bowen family continues to lead the company.

	Annual Growth	09/05	09/06	09/07	09/08	09/09
Sales ($ mil.)	–	–	–	(60.9)	288.9	365.2
Net income ($ mil.)	42515.9%	–	–	0.0	17.5	16.2
Market value ($ mil.)	–	–	–	–	–	–
Employees	–	–	–	–	–	700

BOWL AMERICA INC.
ASE: BWL A

6446 Edsall Road
Alexandria, VA 22312
Phone: 703 941-6300
Fax: –
Web: www.bowlamericainc.com

CEO: Leslie H Goldberg
CFO: Cheryl A Dragoo
HR: –
FYE: June 28
Type: Public

This company is looking to make a strike in the recreation business. Bowl America owns and operates about 20 bowling centers in four markets including the Baltimore-Washington DC area; Jacksonville and Orlando Florida; and Richmond Virginia. The bowling centers offer a total of more than 750 lanes for both league and non-league bowling as well as Cosmic Bowling (with glow-in-the-dark balls and laser light shows) for younger patrons. The centers also feature game rooms food and beverage services and other amenities. President Leslie Goldberg and his sister Merle Fabian together own more than 50% of Bowl America.

	Annual Growth	07/11	07/12*	06/13	06/14	06/15
Sales ($ mil.)	(3.4%)	26.5	24.7	23.9	22.8	23.1
Net income ($ mil.)	1.3%	1.6	1.4	3.2	1.4	1.6
Market value ($ mil.)	1.8%	69.7	64.8	67.1	80.0	74.8
Employees	(4.5%)	600	600	500	500	500

*Fiscal year change

BOWLIN TRAVEL CENTERS INC.
OTC: BWTL

150 Louisiana NE
Albuquerque NM 87108
Phone: 505-266-5985
Fax: 504-539-5427
Web: www.luzianne.com

CEO: Michael L Bowlin
CFO: Nina Pratz
HR: Johnny Riley
FYE: January 31
Type: Public

Dotting the desert with gas pumps and gifts Bowlin Travel Centers (BTC) operates about 10 full-service southwestern-themed travel centers along desolate stretches of interstates I-10 and I-40 in arid Arizona and New Mexico. Its travel centers offer snacks souvenirs provided by Native American tribes or imported from Mexico gas (Shell and ExxonMobil brands) and restaurants (Dairy Queen at five locations). It also sells gasoline wholesale. BTC traces its roots to 1912 when founder Claude Bowlin started trading goods and services with Native Americans in New Mexico. Today BTC is controlled by its chairman president and CEO Michael Bowlin and his family.

BOY SCOUTS OF AMERICA

1325 W WALNUT HILL LN
IRVING, TX 750383096
Phone: 972-580-2000
Fax: –
Web: www.scouting.org

CEO: Robert Mazzuca
CFO: Michael Ashline
HR: –
FYE: December 31
Type: Private

Scouts enter dens as Tigers and eventually take flight as Eagles. Boy Scouts of America (BSA) one of the nation's largest youth organizations has about 2.6 million youth members and more than 1 million adult leaders in its ranks. BSA offers educational and character-building programs emphasizing leadership citizenship personal development and physical fitness. In addition to traditional scouting programs (Tiger Cub Webelos and Boy Scouts ranging up to Eagle rank) it offers the Venturing program for boys and girls ages 14-21. BSA generates revenue through membership and council fees food and magazine sales and contributions. The organization was founded by Chicago publisher William Boyce in 1910.

	Annual Growth	12/06	12/07	12/08	12/09	12/10
Sales ($ mil.)	8.0%	–	–	–	287.4	310.5
Net income ($ mil.)	(37.9%)	–	–	–	145.1	90.1
Market value ($ mil.)	–	–	–	–	–	–
Employees	–	–	–	–	–	2,800

BOYD COFFEE COMPANY

19730 NE Sandy Blvd.
Portland OR 97230
Phone: 503-666-4545
Fax: 503-669-2223
Web: www.boyds.com

CEO: –
CFO: –
HR: –
FYE: October 31
Type: Private

Boy oh Boyd! Boyd Coffee Company sells coffees teas and other beverage products (such as flavoring syrups drink mixes) under the names Boyds Coffee Italia D'Oro Coffee House Roasters Coffee House Freezers and Island Mist. The company also markets brewing equipment through its Techni-Brew International division and it offers the Today Foods brand of soups and soup bases. Boyd Coffee supplies retail food outlets and restaurants hotels hospitals and other foodservice venues in about 25 states as well as US military commissaries worldwide. Products are also available to consumers via Boyd's online store. In addition the firm operates three coffee shops in the Portland Oregon area.

BOYD GAMING CORP.   NYS: BYD

3883 Howard Hughes Parkway, Ninth Floor
Las Vegas, NV 89169
Phone: 702 792-7200
Fax: –
Web: www.boydgaming.com

CEO: Keith E. Smith
CFO: Josh Hirsberg
HR: –
FYE: December 31
Type: Public

Boyd Gaming's business model is buoyed by the US public's insatiable appetite for gaming. One of the country's leading casino operators Boyd operates more than 20 gaming entertainment properties located in Nevada and several other US states. Besides Nevada the company has casinos in Illinois Indiana Iowa Kansas Louisiana Mississippi and New Jersey including 50% of Atlantic City's Borgata Hotel Casino & Spa. Most of the company's properties are sprawling resort hotels that feature pools full casinos restaurants shops and on-site entertainment options for guests.

	Annual Growth	12/10	12/11	12/12	12/13	12/14
Sales ($ mil.)	6.0%	2,140.9	2,336.2	2,487.4	2,894.4	2,701.3
Net income ($ mil.)	–	10.3	(3.9)	(908.9)	(80.3)	(53.0)
Market value ($ mil.)	4.8%	1,158.3	815.2	725.6	1,230.5	1,396.6
Employees	(3.7%)	21,300	22,960	25,247	24,207	18,290

BOYS & GIRLS CLUBS OF AMERICA

1275 PEACHTREE ST NE # 500
ATLANTA, GA 303093580
Phone: 404-487-5700
Fax: –
Web: www.bgca.org

CEO: James (Jim) Clark
CFO: Paul Sansone
HR: –
FYE: December 31
Type: Private

There's no secret handshake — or specific gender — required to get into this club only the desire to have fun. The Boys & Girls Clubs of America (BGCA) runs after-school programs nationwide to give children and teenagers a safe and supervised environment. Operating through local affiliates BGCA boasts some 4075 locations that serve nearly 4 million youth. Members engage in sports recreation and fitness activities as well as in programs centered on character development leadership and life skills. BGCA alumni include Bill Clinton Bill Cosby Jackie Joyner-Kersee Martin Sheen Michael Jordan and Queen Latifah. Founded in 1906 the organization traces its roots to 1860.

	Annual Growth	12/04	12/05	12/06	12/08	12/10
Sales ($ mil.)	(2.0%)	–	133.2	126.3	3.5	120.6
Net income ($ mil.)	(78.6%)	–	–	46.0	(84.5)	0.1
Market value ($ mil.)	–	–	–	–	–	–
Employees	–	–	–	–	–	360

BOZZUTO'S INC.

275 Schoolhouse Rd.
Cheshire CT 06410-1241
Phone: 203-272-3511
Fax: 203-250-2954
Web: www.bozzutos.com

CEO: Michael A Bozzuto
CFO: –
HR: –
FYE: September 30
Type: Private

Bozzuto's is a leading wholesale grocery distribution company that supplies food and non-food products to independent supermarkets belonging to the IGA network in New Jersey New York Pennsylvania and in New England. The company distributes a full line of grocery items including meat products produce and frozen food as well as household goods and other general merchandise. It carries goods sold under both the IGA and Hy-Top labels in addition to national brands. Bozzuto's also owns about half a dozen supermarkets in Connecticut and Massachusetts operating under the Adams Super Food Stores banner. The company founded in 1945 is owned and operated by the Bozzuto family.

BPZ RESOURCES, INC.   NYS: BPZ

580 Westlake Park Blvd., Suite 525
Houston, TX 77079
Phone: 281 556-6200
Fax: 281 556-6377
Web: www.bpzenergy.com

CEO: Manuel Pablo Zuniga-Pflucker
CFO: Richard S Menniti
HR: –
FYE: December 31
Type: Public

BPZ Resources is committed to exploring for oil and gas resources in South America. The company is focusing on oil and gas exploration and production in recent years. It operates through its BPZ Energy subsidiary and that unit's BPZ Energy International Holdings subsidiary. BPZ Resources owns 2.2 million acres of oil and gas properties in northwest Peru. It also holds acreage in Ecuador where it holds a 10% stake in producing block. In 2012 the company reported proved reserves of 16.4 million barrels of oil equivalent (of which 13.4 million barrels was in the Corvina field and 3 million barrels in the Albacora field both of which are located offshore of northwest Peru in the Block Z-1 field).

	Annual Growth	12/09	12/10	12/11	12/12	12/13
Sales ($ mil.)	(0.8%)	52.5	110.5	143.7	123.0	50.7
Net income ($ mil.)	–	(35.8)	(59.8)	(33.8)	(39.1)	(57.7)
Market value ($ mil.)	(33.8%)	1,116.5	559.4	333.8	370.2	213.9
Employees	(15.5%)	182	262	270	245	93

BRADFORD SOAP WORKS INC.

200 Providence St.
West Warwick RI 02893-2508
Phone: 401-821-2141
Fax: 401-821-1660
Web: www.bradfordsoap.com

CEO: John H Howland
CFO: Stuart Benton
HR: –
FYE: December 31
Type: Private

Bradford Soap Works is far from being a dud with suds. As a top manufacturer of private-label bath soaps the company makes soap and personal care formulations specifically for consumer products firms. Products which include bar soaps gels powders and mousses are manufactured under names AngelSkin Eco-Ex OrganicChoices Chakra Body Buffing Grain and Watercolors among others. Bradford Soap also makes certified organic ingredients as well as detergent lubricants and foam stabilizers for industrial use. Bradford which has operations in the US and Mexico was founded in 1876 to make soaps for the textile industry. The company grows its operations chiefly through acquisitions of smaller soap makers.

BRADFORD WHITE CORPORATION

725 Talamore Dr.
Ambler PA 19002
Phone: 215-641-9400
Fax: 215-641-1670
Web: www.bradfordwhite.com

CEO: Nicholas J Giuffre
CFO: –
HR: –
FYE: December 31
Type: Private

Bradford White Corporation helps folks get in (and stay in) hot water. The company manufactures water heaters for residential commercial and industrial heating applications. It makes oil-fired products gas power burners and indirect-fired units. Through subsidiaries Bradford White-Canada and LAARS Heating Systems it also manufactures products such as pool heaters oil burners and air handlers. The company wholesales its products through a network of plumbing and heating professionals. Subsidiary Niles Steel Tank produces custom steel tanks for companies in the automotive petrol-chemical pharmaceutical and refrigeration industries. Bradford White Corporation was founded in 1881.

BRAKE PARTS INC.

4400 Prime Pkwy.
McHenry IL 60050-7003
Phone: 815-363-9000
Fax: 815-363-9030
Web: www.raybestos.com

CEO: –
CFO: –
HR: –
FYE: December 31
Type: Private

Brake Parts Inc. knows how to pull out all of the stops. The company doing business under the Raybestos brand manufactures aftermarket motor vehicle brake systems and parts. Products include brake pads and shoes rotors drums calipers wheel cylinders master cylinders and hardware. Brake Parts operates as part of the Affinia Under Vehicle Group which includes AIMCO (brake parts) Spicer (chassis and steering components) and Wix (air fuel and oil filters). The automotive collection is held by investment firm The Cypress Group.

BRADLEY UNIVERSITY

1501 W BRADLEY AVE
PEORIA, IL 616250003
Phone: 309-677-3150
Fax: –
Web: www.cec.bradley.edu

CEO: –
CFO: –
HR: –
FYE: May 31
Type: Private

Bradley University is a private university offering a wide breadth of higher education opportunitites. The school provides 100 undergraduate programs in fields ranging from art science and education to business media and health. Bradley also confers graduate degrees in more than 30 academic fields including a Doctorate of Physical Therapy. With a student-to-teacher ratio of 12:1 the university has an enrollment of approximately 6000 students — more than 5000 of whom are undergraduates — that receive instruction from some 350 full-time faculty members.

	Annual Growth	05/08	05/09	05/10	05/11	05/13
Sales ($ mil.)	–	–	0.0	141.8	151.8	153.2
Net income ($ mil.)	(2.8%)	–	–	30.8	36.2	28.3
Market value ($ mil.)	–	–	–	–	–	–
Employees	–	–	–	–	–	1,000

BRANCH & ASSOCIATES INC.

5732 AIRPORT RD NW
ROANOKE, VA 240121122
Phone: 540-989-5215
Fax: –
Web: www.branchgroup.com

CEO: –
CFO: –
HR: –
FYE: December 31
Type: Private

Branch & Associates is no twig in the Branch Group family tree. The employee-owned subsidiary offers general contracting design/build and construction management services for commercial and industrial construction projects in the Carolinas Tennessee Virginia and West Virginia. The company builds retail health care educational multi-unit residential government hospitality and industrial facilities. Billy Branch founded the company in 1963. It was reorganized and became Branch Associates under the Branch Group in 1985. Other Branch Group subsidiaries include Branch Highways E.V. Williams and G.J. Hopkins.

	Annual Growth	12/09	12/10	12/11	12/12	12/13
Sales ($ mil.)	12.8%	–	90.5	108.0	130.9	129.8
Net income ($ mil.)	–	–	–	0.0	0.0	0.0
Market value ($ mil.)	–	–	–	–	–	–
Employees	–	–	–	–	–	90

BRADY CORP.

6555 West Good Hope Road
Milwaukee, WI 53223
Phone: 414 358-6600
Fax: –
Web: www.bradycorp.com

NYS: BRC
CEO: –
CFO: Aaron J Pearce
HR: Helena Nelligan
FYE: July 31
Type: Public

It's the story of a manufacturing firm named Brady. Brady Corporation makes a diversified array of industrial identification and specialty coated material products. These include industrial and facility ID products such as printable labels and wire markers; safety and regulatory compliance offerings including lockout/tagout products safety signs and traffic control products; and other products such as specialty tapes photo ID card systems and software. Through Accidental Health & Safety and its Trafalgar First Aid unit it supplies safety and first aid products in Australia.

	Annual Growth	07/11	07/12	07/13	07/14	07/15
Sales ($ mil.)	(3.3%)	1,339.6	1,324.3	1,152.1	1,225.0	1,171.7
Net income ($ mil.)	(59.3%)	108.7	(17.9)	(154.5)	(46.0)	3.0
Market value ($ mil.)	(5.6%)	1,519.1	1,361.5	1,707.4	1,342.0	1,207.0
Employees	0.2%	6,500	6,900	7,400	7,200	6,560

BRANDEIS UNIVERSITY

415 SOUTH ST MS110
WALTHAM, MA 024532700
Phone: 781-736-8317
Fax: –
Web: www.cyc.brandeis.edu

CEO: –
CFO: Marianne Cwalina
HR: –
FYE: June 30
Type: Private

Brandeis University offers more than 40 undergraduate majors and more than 30 master's and doctoral degree programs. Located just west of Boston it comprises the College of Arts and Sciences the Graduate School of Arts and Sciences the International Business School the Heller School for Social Policy and Management the Lown School for Near Eastern and Judaic Studies and the Rabb School of Continuing Studies. The university has an enrollment of more than 5000 students; the student/faculty ratio is 9-to-1. A non-sectarian Jewish community-sponsored institution Brandeis University was founded in 1948 and is named after the late Justice Louis Brandeis of the US Supreme Court.

	Annual Growth	06/07	06/08	06/09	06/10	06/13
Sales ($ mil.)	5.3%	–	–	248.6	323.3	305.5
Net income ($ mil.)	–	–	–	(174.0)	(24.1)	77.9
Market value ($ mil.)	–	–	–	–	–	–
Employees	–	–	–	–	–	1,200

BRANDYWINE REALTY TRUST NYS: BDN

555 East Lancaster Avenue
Radnor, PA 19087
Phone: 610-325-5600
Fax: —
Web: www.brandywinerealty.com

CEO: Gerard H Sweeney
CFO: Thomas E Wirth
HR: —
FYE: December 31
Type: Public

If the thought of making it big in real estate intoxicates you look into Brandywine. A self-managed real estate investment trust (REIT) Brandywine buys leases sells and manages commercial properties. It owns more than 200 office properties about 20 industrial properties a handful of mixed-use properties and some 500 acres of undeveloped land. Its portfolio comprises more than 25 million sq. ft. of rentable space located mainly in urban and suburban areas of the mid-Atlantic region as well as California and Texas. Jerry Sweeney who founded Brandywine in 1986 remains president and CEO of the company.

	Annual Growth	12/10	12/11	12/12	12/13	12/14
Sales ($ mil.)	1.3%	566.9	581.8	559.8	562.2	597.0
Net income ($ mil.)	—	(17.1)	(4.5)	6.6	42.8	7.0
Market value ($ mil.)	8.2%	2,088.8	1,703.3	2,185.6	2,526.2	2,865.1
Employees	(0.9%)	439	402	391	406	424

BRANT INDUSTRIES INC.

80 Field Point Rd.
Greenwich CT 06830
Phone: 203-661-3344
Fax: 203-661-3349
Web: www.whitebirchpaper.com

CEO: —
CFO: Tim Butler
HR: Patricia Nowell
FYE: December 31
Type: Private

Brant Industries does its part to keep newspaper delivery boys busy. Operating through White Birch Paper and its subsidiaries the company produces about 1.3 million tons of newsprint and directory paper annually. It also manufactures uncoated specialty paper and paperboard with recycled content. Brant operates four pulp and paper mills three in Canada and one in the US; its lineup is distributed in North America and to some overseas markets. Brant has a saw mill which produces lumber and wood chips and 30000 acres of forestland. The family-run company is owned by CEO Peter Brant and COO Christopher Brant. In early 2010 White Birch filed for bankruptcy in the US and Canada and subsequently sought a buyer.

BRASFIELD & GORRIE L.L.C.

3021 7th Ave. South
Birmingham AL 35233-3502
Phone: 205-328-4000
Fax: 205-251-1304
Web: www.brasfieldgorrie.com

CEO: M James Gorrie
CFO: Randall J Freeman
HR: —
FYE: December 31
Type: Private

Brasfield & Gorrie works alongside clients to build up the South one project at a time. The company provides construction management general contracting and design/build services for commercial industrial governmental health care and institutional projects primarily in the Southeast. Besides LEED-certified buildings its portfolio of projects ranges from high-rise offices and health care facilities to freeway bridges and wastewater treatment plans. The company boasts about a dozen offices as well as locations focused on renting or selling equipment. Originally founded by Thomas C. Brasfield in 1922 the company was acquired by chairman and CEO Miller Gorrie in 1964.

BRAVO BRIO RESTAURANT GROUP INC NMS: BBRG

777 Goodale Boulevard, Suite 100
Columbus, OH 43212
Phone: 614-326-7944
Fax: 614-326-7943
Web: www.bbrg.com

CEO: Brian T. O'Malley
CFO: James J. O'Connor
HR: Demessa Gates
FYE: December 28
Type: Public

Standing ovations are welcomed but not required at these restaurants. Bravo Brio Restaurant Group owns and operates more than 100 upscale casual-dining locations in more than 30 states. The restaurants operate under the names BRAVO! Cucina Italiana and BRIO Tuscan Grille. The company's flagship BRAVO! Cucina Italiana restaurants offer pasta pizza and other affordable Italian-inspired cuisine. The group's BRIO Tuscan Grille concept meanwhile specializes in upscale Tuscan-style ambiance and entrees such as steaks chops and fresh seafood. Bravo Brio Restaurant Group went public in 2010.

	Annual Growth	12/10	12/11	12/12	12/13	12/14
Sales ($ mil.)	4.5%	343.0	369.2	409.1	411.1	408.3
Net income ($ mil.)	—	(1.2)	76.4	16.1	7.5	11.8
Market value ($ mil.)	(8.7%)	282.4	240.4	198.9	252.2	196.5
Employees	8.3%	8,000	8,700	9,500	9,500	11,000

BRAVO MEDIA LLC

30 Rockefeller Plaza 8th Fl. East
New York NY 10112
Phone: 212-664-4444
Fax: 845-424-8286
Web: www.outwardbound.org

CEO: —
CFO: —
HR: —
FYE: December 31
Type: Subsidiary

Fans of this TV channel give a standing ovation to reality programming. Bravo Media operates the popular cable channel Bravo which reaches 90 million homes with a heavy dose of competition shows celebrity reality series and other reality-based programming. The channel's schedule includes such hit shows as Millionaire Matchmaker The Fashion Show Top Chef and the Real Housewives franchise. Bravo also broadcasts movies and reruns as well as such specialty programming as the Inside the Actors Studio interview program. Launched in 1980 by Rainbow Media Holdings (now known as AMC Networks) Bravo is a unit of NBCUniversal one of the largest media and entertainment companies in the world.

BRAZOS ELECTRIC POWER COOPERATIVE INC.

2404 LA SALLE AVE
WACO, TX 767063928
Phone: 254-750-6500
Fax: —
Web: www.brazoselectric.com

CEO: —
CFO: —
HR: —
FYE: December 31
Type: Private

Brazos means "arms" in Spanish and the generation and transmission arms of Brazos Electric Power Cooperative reach across 68 Texas counties. It serves 16 member/owner distribution cooperatives and one municipality in Northern and Central Texas. Brazos Electric Power annually generates (through its four power stations) and/or accesses from other power marketers some 3655 MW of electric power. The cooperative's members include Comanche Electric Cooperative Association Heart of Texas Electric Co-op (McGregor) Mid-South Synergy (Navasota) United Coop Services (Cleburne) and Wise Electric (Decatur).

	Annual Growth	12/96	12/97	12/98	12/99	12/09
Sales ($ mil.)	10.9%	—	278.3	286.7	307.4	963.4
Net income ($ mil.)	46.0%	—	—	0.9	6.9	56.6
Market value ($ mil.)	—	—	—	—	—	—
Employees	—	—	—	—	—	366

BRE PROPERTIES, INC.

NYS: BRE

525 Market Street, 4th Floor
San Francisco, CA 94105-2712
Phone: 415 445-6530
Fax: –
Web: www.breproperties.com

CEO: –
CFO: –
HR: –
FYE: December 31
Type: Public

The huddled masses that yearn to live and breathe California life turn to BRE Properties. The real estate investment trust (REIT) acquires develops and manages multifamily properties in the western US. It owns more than 75 apartment communities with nearly 22000 units in Northern and Southern California and Seattle. Most properties offer amenities including clubhouses exercise facilities business centers and swimming pools. The REIT also has several properties under development and owns stakes in about a dozen more. BRE Properties has shed its holdings in Colorado and Nevada to focus on markets in California where high housing costs and a stable occupancy rate make for an attractive environment.

	Annual Growth	12/08	12/09	12/10	12/11	12/12
Sales ($ mil.)	2.7%	350.9	344.6	342.0	371.4	390.1
Net income ($ mil.)	(0.7%)	140.8	62.5	53.4	77.9	137.1
Market value ($ mil.)	16.1%	2,152.4	2,544.7	3,346.3	3,883.2	3,910.1
Employees	(4.1%)	793	737	628	690	670

BREEZE-EASTERN CORP

ASE: BZC

35 Melanie Lane
Whippany, NJ 07981
Phone: 973 602-1001
Fax: –
Web: www.breeze-eastern.com

CEO: Brad Pedersen
CFO: Serge Dupuis
HR: –
FYE: March 31
Type: Public

Does your cargo need a lift? Breeze-Eastern makes electric and hydraulic rescue hoist systems for helicopters as well as cargo winches and tie-downs hook systems and weapons handling systems. Its external helicopter cargo hook systems range in capacity from 1500 pounds to 36000 pounds. The company's weapons-handling systems include hoists for missiles and gearboxes for specialty weapons applications. It also offers overhaul/repair and engineering sales services. Breeze-Eastern caters mainly to the US government in addition to major aerospace manufacturers and airlines.

	Annual Growth	03/10	03/11	03/12	03/13	03/14
Sales ($ mil.)	5.6%	69.0	78.2	84.9	80.0	85.9
Net income ($ mil.)	–	(6.0)	5.0	3.8	4.1	5.6
Market value ($ mil.)	9.3%	67.1	83.3	81.5	80.1	95.9
Employees	1.3%	172	164	182	187	181

BREITBURN ENERGY PARTNERS LP

NMS: BBEP

515 South Flower Street, Suite 4800
Los Angeles, CA 90071
Phone: 213 225-5900
Fax: –
Web: www.breitburn.com

CEO: Halbert S Washburn
CFO: –
HR: –
FYE: December 31
Type: Public

Oil and gas futures burn brightly for BreitBurn Energy Partners one of California's largest independent exploration and production companies. With assets in Antrim Shale (Michigan) the Los Angeles Basin the Wind River and Big Horn Basins (both in Wyoming) the Sunniland Trend (Florida) the New Albany Shale (Indiana and Kentucky) and the Permian Basin (West Texas) in 2011 the company reported estimated proved reserves of 151.1 million barrels of oil equivalent (65% of which was natural gas). That year 49% of its reserves were in Michigan 29% in Wyoming 14% in California 7% in Florida and 1% in Indiana and Kentucky.

	Annual Growth	12/10	12/11	12/12	12/13	12/14
Sales ($ mil.)	41.6%	355.3	480.4	423.0	634.7	1,430.0
Net income ($ mil.)	86.6%	34.8	110.5	(40.8)	(43.7)	421.3
Market value ($ mil.)	(23.2%)	4,247.4	4,021.7	3,895.2	4,289.6	1,476.3
Employees	24.2%	379	395	450	563	901

BRENTWOOD INDUSTRIES INC.

610 MORGANTOWN RD
READING, PA 196112012
Phone: 610-374-5109
Fax: –
Web: www.brentwood-ind.com

CEO: –
CFO: –
HR: Linette Miller
FYE: September 30
Type: Private

Brentwood Industries can help you wheel it around flush it mold it and cool it among other things. The company manufactures a variety of plastic products including wheelbarrows cooling towers wastewater treatment systems and specialty plastic forming and molding services. Brentwood has expanded its product line with the additions of Polychem Systems (non-metallic chain and flight sludge collectors) NRG Products (non-metallic clarifier systems for municipal and industrial markets) and medical thermoform packaging. It is the world's largest manufacturer of plastic media supplying more than 100 million cubic feet of material for cooling tower and wastewater applications.

	Annual Growth	09/09	09/10	09/11	09/12	09/13
Sales ($ mil.)	–	–	0.0	103.1	110.2	110.2
Net income ($ mil.)	(14.8%)	–	–	6.2	6.4	4.5
Market value ($ mil.)	–	–	–	–	–	–
Employees	–	–	–	–	–	700

BRIDGE BANCORP, INC. (BRIDGEHAMPTON, NY)

NMS: BDGE

2200 Montauk Highway
Bridgehampton, NY 11932
Phone: 631 537-1000
Fax: –
Web: www.bridgenb.com

CEO: Kevin M. O'Connor
CFO: Adam Hall
HR: –
FYE: December 31
Type: Public

Bridge Bancorp wants you to cross over to its subsidiary The Bridgehampton National Bank which operates about 25 branches on eastern Long Island New York. Founded in 1910 the bank offers traditional deposit services to area individuals small businesses and municipalities including checking savings and money market accounts and CDs. Deposits are invested primarily in mortgages which account for some 80% of the bank's loan portfolio. Title insurance services are available through bank subsidiary Bridge Abstract; wealth management services include financial planning estate administration and trustee services. Bridge Bancorp bought Hamptons State Bank in 2011 to fortify its presence on Long Island.

	Annual Growth	12/10	12/11	12/12	12/13	12/14
Assets ($ mil.)	22.1%	1,028.5	1,337.5	1,624.7	1,896.7	2,288.7
Net income ($ mil.)	10.7%	9.2	10.4	12.8	13.1	13.8
Market value ($ mil.)	2.1%	287.2	231.8	237.0	302.9	311.6
Employees	14.0%	206	227	257	271	348

BRIDGE CAPITAL HOLDINGS

NMS: BBNK

55 Almaden Boulevard
San Jose, CA 95113
Phone: 408 423-8500
Fax: –
Web: www.bridgebank.com

CEO: –
CFO: –
HR: –
FYE: December 31
Type: Public

Bridge Capital Holdings helps its business clients get from here to there. It is the holding company of Bridge Bank which caters to small midsized and emerging businesses in California's Silicon Valley and San Francisco Bay area. The bank has regional branches in Palo Alto and San Jose; it also has Small Business Administration (SBA) loan production offices in Pleasanton and San Francisco. Additional SBA offices are located in Irvine California; Dallas; Boston; and Reston Virginia. The bank also has groups devoted to technology banking IPO services and international banking. Its Bridge Capital Finance unit provides factoring and asset-based lending services.

	Annual Growth	12/09	12/10	12/11	12/12	12/13
Assets ($ mil.)	17.4%	844.1	1,029.7	1,161.0	1,343.6	1,604.1
Net income ($ mil.)	78.9%	1.4	2.6	7.8	13.8	14.7
Market value ($ mil.)	29.7%	115.0	138.0	164.9	246.8	325.7
Employees	9.4%	164	170	193	207	235

BRIDGELINE DIGITAL, INC.
NAS: BLIN

80 Blanchard Road
Burlington, MA 01803
Phone: 781 376-5555
Fax: –
Web: www.bridgelinedigital.com

CEO: Michael D. Prinn
CFO: Michael D Prinn
HR: Carl Pizzi
FYE: September 30
Type: Public

Bridgeline Digital believes the Web is the causeway to the customer. The company develops and sells Web application creation and management software. Its iAPPS product suite offers tools for content and relationship management e-commerce website creation and analytics. Bridgeline also offers usability engineering search engine optimization and rich media development services. Bridgeline's target markets are financial services technology health services and life sciences retailers transportation and storage foundations and associations and the US government. Its customers have included Honeywell John Hancock AARP Budget Rent A Car and the Washington Redskins. Bridgeline operates in the US and India.

	Annual Growth	09/11	09/12	09/13	09/14	09/15
Sales ($ mil.)	(7.5%)	26.3	26.3	24.5	23.7	19.2
Net income ($ mil.)	–	(0.8)	(0.9)	(3.6)	(6.2)	(16.8)
Market value ($ mil.)	22.9%	2.5	5.6	5.1	3.0	5.7
Employees	(11.4%)	148	164	165	135	91

BRIDGEPOINT EDUCATION, INC.
NYS: BPI

13500 Evening Creek Drive North
San Diego, CA 92128
Phone: 858 668-2586
Fax: –
Web: www.bridgepointeducation.com

CEO: Andrew S. Clark
CFO: Daniel J. Devine
HR: Charlene Dackerman
FYE: December 31
Type: Public

Bridgepoint Education invites students from all walks of life to cross on over to the higher-education side. The for-profit company offers some 1400 courses and about 85 graduate and undergraduate degree programs online and at its bricks-and-mortar campuses: Ashford University in Iowa and University of the Rockies in Colorado. Academic disciplines include education business psychology and health and social sciences. Most of the company's campus-based revenues are derived from federal financial aid. About 99% of Bridgepoint Education's more than 90000 students are enrolled exclusively online.

	Annual Growth	12/10	12/11	12/12	12/13	12/14
Sales ($ mil.)	(2.7%)	713.2	933.3	968.2	768.6	638.7
Net income ($ mil.)	(47.5%)	127.6	172.8	128.0	41.0	9.7
Market value ($ mil.)	(12.1%)	862.6	1,044.2	467.6	804.0	513.9
Employees	2.6%	6,900	8,900	9,520	8,020	7,660

BRIDGEPORT HOSPITAL & HEALTHCARE SERVICES INC

267 GRANT ST
BRIDGEPORT, CT 06610-2805
Phone: 203-384-3000
Fax: –
Web: www.bridgeporthospital.org

CEO: Robert J Trefry
CFO: –
HR: –
FYE: September 30
Type: Private

Serving as a bridge to wellness and a port in the stormy waters of health care is the 425-bed Bridgeport Hospital. Part of the Yale New Haven Health System the facility offers acute care and specialized services to residents of Bridgeport Connecticut and surrounding counties. The hospital operates a cancer center a burn treatment center a heart center and a rehabilitation therapy center. Its medical staff includes nearly 600 physicians representing more than 60 specialties. Founded in 1878 as Fairfield County's first hospital Bridgeport Hospital has grown into a nearly $350 million regional health care organization.

	Annual Growth	09/06	09/07	09/08	09/09	09/10
Sales ($ mil.)	151445.7%	–	–	–	0.3	380.0
Net income ($ mil.)	7585.1%	–	–	–	0.2	13.9
Market value ($ mil.)	–	–	–	–	–	–
Employees	–	–	–	–	–	150

BRIDGESTONE AMERICAS INC.

535 Marriott Dr.
Nashville TN 37214
Phone: 615-937-1000
Fax: 973-537-8926
Web: www.casio.com

CEO: Gary Garfield
CFO: Bill Thompson
HR: –
FYE: December 31
Type: Subsidiary

The marks that Bridgestone Americas leave have everything to do with tires. The US subsidiary of Japan's Bridgestone Bridgestone Americas operates through a family of companies that run more than 50 production facilities throughout the Americas. Perhaps best known for its Bridgestone and Firestone brands its main tire operations consist of manufacturing and selling tires for passenger cars commercial trucks motorcycles and agricultural and off-road equipment in the US Canada and Latin America. Its retail operations consist of vehicle service and tire centers in the US. Additionally Bridgestone Americas offers natural rubber and latex fibers and textiles and industrial and building products.

BRIDGESTONE RETAIL OPERATIONS LLC

333 E. Lake St.
Bloomingdale IL 60108
Phone: 630-259-9000
Fax: 630-259-9158
Web: www.bsro.com/

CEO: Larry Magee
CFO: Thomas Studer
HR: Ashley Wiepert
FYE: December 31
Type: Subsidiary

You'll find plenty of rolling stock at Bridgestone Retail Operations' (BSRO) stores. BSRO is the US retail division of Japan-based tire giant Bridgestone and it owns and operates more than 2140 service centers in about 45 states under the Firestone Complete Auto Care Expert Tire Tires Plus and Wheel Works banners. BSRO's stores offer a variety of automotive repair services including drive train engine heating and cooling steering and suspension maintenance as well as tire sales. The business serves both consumers and commercial clients. BSRO which was named BFS Retail & Commercial until 2009 also maintains its own credit card operation Credit First National Association.

BRIDGFORD FOODS CORP.
NMS: BRID

1308 N. Patt Street
Anaheim, CA 92801
Phone: 714 526-5533
Fax: –
Web: www.bridgford.com

CEO: William L Bridgford
CFO: Raymond F. Lancy
HR: –
FYE: October 30
Type: Public

Too many cooks might spoil Bridgford Foods' business. The company manufactures markets and distributes a slew of frozen refrigerated and snack foods. Its lineup ranges from biscuits and bread dough to deli meats dry sausage and beef jerky. (It's one of the nation's largest sellers of jerky and other meat snacks). Bridgford adds to its offerings by buying for resale some snack and refrigerated foods made by other processors. The company sells to food service (restaurants and institutions) and retailers (supermarkets mass merchandise and convenience stores) in the US and Canada largely through distributors brokers and a direct store delivery network. Wal-Mart generates about 20% of Bridgford's sales.

	Annual Growth	10/11*	11/12	11/13*	10/14	10/15
Sales ($ mil.)	2.5%	118.3	127.4	129.0	133.4	130.4
Net income ($ mil.)	–	(0.4)	3.7	2.9	(4.3)	15.4
Market value ($ mil.)	(0.6%)	84.7	62.3	86.6	74.9	82.6
Employees	(0.5%)	517	519	539	487	507

*Fiscal year change

BRIGGS & STRATTON CORP.   NYS: BGG

12301 West Wirth Street
Wauwatosa, WI 53222
Phone: 414-259-5333
Fax: 414 259-9594
Web: www.basco.com

CEO: Todd J. Teske
CFO: Mark A. Schwertfeger
HR: Carol Butler
FYE: June 28
Type: Public

The power of Briggs & Stratton's is in its equipment. The company is one of the world's largest manufacturers of gasoline engines for lawn mowers. It designs makes markets and services these engines primarily for lawn and garden OEMs worldwide including Husqvarna MTD Products and Deere & Company. Subsidiary Briggs & Stratton Power Products is a top North American manufacturer of portable generators and pressure washers. It is also a leading maker of lawn mowers garden tillers and related service parts and accessories that are sold through retailers and independent dealers. Briggs & Stratton has offices and manufacturing facilities in North America Europe Asia and Australia.

	Annual Growth	07/11	07/12*	06/13	06/14	06/15
Sales ($ mil.)	(2.7%)	2,110.0	2,066.5	1,862.5	1,859.1	1,894.8
Net income ($ mil.)	17.0%	24.4	29.0	(33.7)	28.3	45.7
Market value ($ mil.)	(1.1%)	906.1	776.1	878.6	914.1	866.2
Employees	(5.0%)	6,716	6,321	5,980	5,695	5,480

*Fiscal year change

BRIGGS & STRATTON POWER PRODUCTS GROUP LLC

12301 W. Wirth St.
Wauwatosa WI 53222
Phone: 414-259-5333
Fax: 863-965-2222
Web: www.coloradoboxedbeef.com

CEO: –
CFO: –
HR: –
FYE: June 30
Type: Subsidiary

Briggs & Stratton Power Products Group (BSPPG) — the power equipment manufacturing subsidiary of Briggs & Stratton designs manufacturers and sells pressure washers pumps portable and home generators powered lawn equipment snow throwers and other related products. BSPPG sells its products through multiple distribution channels including home centers warehouse clubs independent dealers and mass merchants. Customers include Lowe's The Home Depot Sears Wal-Mart Deere & Company and Tractor Supply Company. The Power Products Group accounts for about 40% of its parent company's sales.

BRIGHAM EXPLORATION COMPANY   NASDAQ: BEXP

6300 Bridge Point Pkwy. Building 2 Ste. 500
Austin TX 78730
Phone: 512-427-3300
Fax: 512-427-3400
Web: www.bexp3d.com/

CEO: –
CFO: Eugene B Shepherd Jr
HR: –
FYE: December 31
Type: Subsidiary

Still a young company Brigham Exploration was one of the first small independent exploration and production firms to use 3-D seismic imaging. The company continues to rely on 3-D and other advanced technologies for onshore exploration. It traditionally explored in the Anadarko Basin the onshore Texas/Louisiana Gulf Coast and West Texas but has shifted its focus in recent years to the lucrative oil shale plays in the Rockies. In 2010 Brigham Exploration reported proved reserves of 66.8 million barrels of oil equivalent. Since its founding in 1990 Brigham Exploration has drilled more than 1070 gross wells. In 2011 the company was acquired by Norway's Statoil in a $4.4 billion deal.

BRIGHT HORIZONS FAMILY SOLUTIONS INC.   NYSE: BFAM

200 Talcott Ave. South
Watertown MA 02472
Phone: 617-673-8000
Fax: 617-673-8001
Web: www.brighthorizons.com

CEO: David Lissy
CFO: Elizabeth J Boland
HR: –
FYE: December 31
Type: Private

With Bright Horizons Family Solutions kids learn while parents earn. The company offers full-service child care and early education services to employer clients through more than 700 child care and early education centers with a capacity to serve more than 87000 children in the US Canada India Ireland the Netherlands and the UK. Some of its centers also provide back-up elder and dependent care services. Under multiyear contracts it provides these services to companies hospitals universities and government agencies as part of their employee benefits packages. After being taken private by Bain Capital in 2008 Bright Horizons went public in early 2013 in an IPO worth $222.2 million.

BRIGHT HOUSE NETWORKS LLC

5000 Campuswood Dr.
E. Syracuse NY 13057-1254
Phone: 315-463-7675
Fax: 760-929-8072
Web: www.socogroup.com

CEO: –
CFO: –
HR: –
FYE: December 31
Type: Private

Bright House Networks lights up living rooms — more than 2.5 million of them in fact. The company offers digital cable television video-on-demand (VOD) digital phone service and broadband Internet connections to both residential and business customers in select metropolitan markets in Florida Alabama Indiana Michigan and California. Its Florida systems offer about 300 cable channels. Bright House Networks also owns and operates two 24-hour local news TV stations: Central Florida News 13 in the Orlando area and Bay News 9 for the Tampa Bay area. Bright House Networks is owned by the Advance/Newhouse Partnership (part of Advance Publications).

BRIGHTCOVE INC   NMS: BCOV

290 Congress Street
Boston, MA 02210
Phone: 888 882-1880
Fax: –
Web: www.brightcove.com

CEO: David Mendels
CFO: Kevin R. Rhodes
HR: Katie Kulikoski
FYE: December 31
Type: Public

Putting out loads of video over the Internet? Call on Brightcove. The company offers a cloud-based platform for publishing and distributing digital videos over the Internet. Some 6300 companies in more than 60 countries including broadcasters such as A&E Lifetime and Starz as well as other video-happy firms such as Honda The New York Times and the Army use its flagship Brightcove Video Cloud post videos to share videos with customers. The company has offices in 10 countries and generates about a third of sales outside the US. Founded in 2005 Brightcove went public in 2012.

	Annual Growth	12/10	12/11	12/12	12/13	12/14
Sales ($ mil.)	30.0%	43.7	63.6	88.0	109.9	125.0
Net income ($ mil.)	–	(17.5)	(17.6)	(13.2)	(10.3)	(16.9)
Market value ($ mil.)	(7.2%)	–	–	293.1	458.5	252.3
Employees	12.6%	255	312	335	347	410

BRIGHTPOINT INC.
NASDAQ: CELL

7635 Interactive Way Ste. 200
Indianapolis IN 46278
Phone: 317-707-2355
Fax: 317-707-2512
Web: www.brightpoint.com

CEO: Shailendra Gupta
CFO: Vincent Donargo
HR: –
FYE: December 31
Type: Public

Brightpoint makes money moving mobiles. The company is a top global distributor of mobile phones and other wireless products acting as a middleman between manufacturers and wireless service providers. It ships the equipment to companies that sell mobile phones and accessories including wireless carriers dealers and retailers; customers include Vodafone RadioShack and Sprint Nextel. Brightpoint also offers logistics services such as warehousing product fulfillment purchasing contract manufacturing call center outsourcing customized packaging and activation through subsidiaries the likes of Brightpoint North America. In late 2012 it was acquired by world-leading IT products distributor Ingram Micro.

BRIGHTSTAR CORP.

9725 NW 117th Ave. Ste. 300
Miami FL 33178
Phone: 305-421-6000
Fax: 630-472-7817
Web: www.bcsf.com

CEO: Jaymin Patel
CFO: Thomas J Seifert
HR: –
FYE: December 31
Type: Private

Brightstar hopes to outshine its rivals with service. The company distributes wireless products such as cell phones and prepaid wireless products. It also offers value-added services including merchandising channel sales inventory management logistics packaging and assembly services as well as supply chain and reverse logistics services. It distributes cell phones made by Nokia Samsung Electronics LG Motorola Mobility and RIM among others. Brightstar was founded in 1997 by its Bolivia-born CEO Marcelo Claure who owns more than 40% of the company.

BRILLSTEIN ENTERTAINMENT PARTNERS LLC

9150 Wilshire Blvd. Ste. 350
Beverly Hills CA 90212
Phone: 310-275-6135
Fax: 310-275-6180

CEO: –
CFO: Brian Taylor
HR: –
FYE: December 31
Type: Private

Brillstein Entertainment Partners (formerly Brillstein-Grey Entertainment) has its eyes on the talent. The agency is a powerful Hollywood management firm with a roster of some 200 clients including such stars as Brad Pitt Jennifer Aniston Adam Sandler and Lorne Michaels. It also produces TV shows and films that showcase the talents of its clients. Producer Bernie Brillstein founded the agency in 1969 and later partnered with his protege Brad Grey. Following Grey's departure the company changed its name to Brillstein Entertainment Partners in 2007.

BRINKER INTERNATIONAL, INC.
NYS: EAT

6820 LBJ Freeway
Dallas, TX 75240
Phone: 972 980-9917
Fax: –
Web: www.brinker.com

CEO: Wyman T. Roberts
CFO: Thomas J. Edwards
HR: Tony Birdwell
FYE: June 24
Type: Public

More than a few Chili's heat up this restaurant business. One of the world's largest casual dining companies Brinker International operates and franchises about 1630 Chili's Grill & Bar locations in more than 50 countries. Trailing only Applebee's as the largest full-service restaurant chain Chili's specializes in southwestern-style dishes with a menu featuring fajitas margarita grilled chicken and its popular baby back ribs. About 740 of the eateries are operated by franchisees including more than 250 international locations. In addition to its flagship chain Brinker operates Maggiano's Little Italy a casual Italian chain with around 50 units and it owns a stake in Romano's Macaroni Grill.

	Annual Growth	06/11	06/12	06/13	06/14	06/15
Sales ($ mil.)	2.1%	2,761.4	2,820.7	2,846.1	2,905.5	3,002.3
Net income ($ mil.)	8.7%	141.1	151.2	163.4	154.0	196.7
Market value ($ mil.)	23.8%	1,485.6	1,846.6	2,340.4	3,083.2	3,486.7
Employees	(3.2%)	60,322	58,068	54,653	55,586	53,000

BRINKS CO (THE)
NYS: BCO

1801 Bayberry Court
Richmond, VA 23226-8100
Phone: 804 289-9600
Fax: 804 289-9770
Web: www.brinks.com

CEO: Thomas C. (Tom) Schievelbein
CFO: Joseph W. (Joe) Dziedzic
HR: Holly R. Tyson
FYE: December 31
Type: Public

Teetering on the brink of a security disaster? The Brink's Company can help. It is the largest and oldest operator and logistics supplier of armored cars used in transporting cash. Core services such as cash-in-transit (CIT) and ATM replenishment and maintenance services as well as high-value services including secure long-distance transportation of valuables supply chain management of cash payment and guarding services (including airport security used quite often by government agencies) generate about 90% of revenues. The company serves customers in more than 100 countries. Its operations include approximately 1100 facilities and some 12300 vehicles.

	Annual Growth	12/10	12/11	12/12	12/13	12/14
Sales ($ mil.)	3.4%	3,121.5	3,885.5	3,842.1	3,942.2	3,562.3
Net income ($ mil.)	–	57.1	74.5	88.9	56.8	(83.9)
Market value ($ mil.)	(2.4%)	1,306.4	1,306.4	1,386.6	1,659.2	1,186.3
Employees	(2.5%)	71,000	71,000	70,000	65,100	64,100

BRISTOL HOSPITAL INCORPORATED

41 BREWSTER RD
BRISTOL, CT 060105141
Phone: 860-585-3000
Fax: –
Web: www.bristolhospital.org

CEO: –
CFO: –
HR: Jeanine Reckdenwald
FYE: September 30
Type: Private

Bristol Hospital bristles with health care services for central Connecticut residents. The health care facility has more than 130 beds and offers a range of services including counseling diagnostic imaging inpatient and outpatient care surgery home health and physical therapy. Specialty services include oncology obstetrics neurology pediatrics and orthopedic care. Its wellness center is dedicated to cardiac and pulmonary rehabilitation diabetes care health education health screenings nutrition fitness and pain management. Bristol Hospital also operates Ingraham Manor a skilled nursing residence for seniors.

	Annual Growth	09/02	09/03	09/05	09/08	09/09
Sales ($ mil.)	3.7%	–	104.5	0.1	127.5	130.0
Net income ($ mil.)	–	–	–	(0.0)	1.7	0.4
Market value ($ mil.)	–	–	–	–	–	–
Employees	–	–	–	–	–	1,600

BRISTOL-MYERS SQUIBB CO.   NYS: BMY

345 Park Avenue
New York, NY 10154
Phone: 212 546-4000
Fax: 212 546-4020
Web: www.bms.com

CEO: Giovanni Caforio
CFO: Charles A. Bancroft
HR: –
FYE: December 31
Type: Public

Bristol-Myers Squibb (BMS) makes drugs for the brain heart and other body parts. The biopharmaceutical's blockbuster cardiovascular lineup includes heart disease drug Plavix and Avapro for hypertension. BMS also makes antipsychotic medication Abilify and HIV treatments Reyataz and Sustiva. Most of its sales come from products in the therapeutic areas of cardiovascular care hepatitis B immunology metabolics neuroscience oncology and virology. BMS has global research facilities and manufacturing plants mainly in the US and Europe and its products are marketed to health care practitioners hospitals and managed care providers in 100 countries.

	Annual Growth	12/11	12/12	12/13	12/14	12/15
Sales ($ mil.)	(6.0%)	21,244.0	17,621.0	16,385.0	15,879.0	16,560.0
Net income ($ mil.)	(19.4%)	3,709.0	1,960.0	2,563.0	2,004.0	1,565.0
Market value ($ mil.)	18.2%	58,815.6	54,392.7	88,707.4	98,521.1	114,810.5
Employees	(1.9%)	27,000	28,000	28,000	25,000	25,000

BRISTOW GROUP INC   NYS: BRS

2103 City West Blvd., 4th Floor
Houston, TX 77042
Phone: 713 267-7600
Fax: –

CEO: Jonathan E. Baliff
CFO: Don Miller
HR: –
FYE: March 31
Type: Public

Bristow Group takes its customers for a ride. The company offers helicopter transportation services for offshore petroleum workers and equipment. Offshore Logistics and Bristow Helicopters units and several international affiliates serve oil and gas exploration and production companies in the world's major offshore oil production zones; 85% of its sales come from international operations. Its main operating areas are the North Sea and the Gulf of Mexico. Bristow operates a fleet of almost 370 aircraft which consists primarily of helicopters and also includes some fixed-wing aircraft. Affiliates operate another 150 or so aircraft.

	Annual Growth	03/11	03/12	03/13	03/14	03/15
Sales ($ mil.)	10.8%	1,232.8	1,341.8	1,508.5	1,669.6	1,858.7
Net income ($ mil.)	(10.7%)	132.3	63.5	130.1	186.7	84.3
Market value ($ mil.)	3.6%	1,647.9	1,662.8	2,297.2	2,631.0	1,896.9
Employees	12.3%	3,289	3,281	3,465	4,486	5,232

BRITTON & KOONTZ CAPITAL CORP.   NBB: BKBK

500 Main Street
Natchez, MS 39120
Phone: 601 445-5576
Fax: –
Web: www.bkbank.com

CEO: W Page Ogden
CFO: William M Salters
HR: –
FYE: December 31
Type: Public

You'll find this bank along the banks of the Mississippi. Britton & Koontz Capital is the holding company for Britton & Koontz Bank which has about a half-dozen branches in Natchez and Vicksburg Mississippi and Baton Rouge Louisiana where the company plans to expand. Targeting individual and local business customers the bank offers such standard deposit products as checking savings and money market accounts; CDs; and trust services. A majority of the bank's loan portfolio consists of real estate loans however Britton & Koontz Capital also makes agricultural business and consumer loans. Brothers William and Audley Britton along with George Koontz established the bank in 1836.

	Annual Growth	12/08	12/09	12/10	12/11	12/12
Assets ($ mil.)	(7.3%)	413.1	393.1	375.4	366.1	305.0
Net income ($ mil.)	(55.6%)	3.5	1.6	1.9	0.4	0.1
Market value ($ mil.)	(8.9%)	25.8	24.8	24.3	16.1	17.8
Employees	(1.9%)	110	113	112	104	–

BRIXMOR PROPERTY GROUP INC   NYS: BRX

450 Lexington Avenue
New York, NY 10017
Phone: 212 869-3000
Fax: –
Web: www.brixmor.com

CEO: Daniel B. Hurwitz
CFO: Michael V Pappagallo
HR: Carolyn Carter
FYE: December 31
Type: Public

Brixmor Property Group hopes you swing by the grocery store more than once a week. The internally-managed real estate investment trust (REIT) owns a portfolio of about 520 strip mall-style shopping centers across 38 states. Its properties are situated in high-traffic commercial areas anchored by grocery store chains such as Ahold Kroger Publix Safeway and Wal-Mart. Besides the main grocery store tenant its shopping centers offer a mix of smaller retailers such as Dollar Tree or other big box stores such as Best Buy Kmart and TJX Cos. Altogether Brixmor Property Group owns some 87 million sq. ft. of leasable space; each shopping center averages about 166100 sq. ft. The trust went public in 2013.

	Annual Growth	06/11*	12/11	12/12	12/13	12/14
Sales ($ mil.)	30.7%	553.9	565.6	1,125.8	1,174.7	1,236.6
Net income ($ mil.)	–	(47.8)	115.4	(122.6)	(93.5)	89.0
Market value ($ mil.)	22.2%	–	–	–	6,028.9	7,366.4
Employees	(3.4%)	–	–	475	456	443

*Fiscal year change

BROADCAST INTERNATIONAL INC   NBB: BCST

6952 S. High Tech Drive Suite C
Salt Lake City, UT 84047
Phone: 801 562-2252
Fax: –
Web: www.brin.com

CEO: –
CFO: –
HR: –
FYE: December 31
Type: Public

Broadcast International (BI) provides communication network integration services for large retailers and other geographically dispersed businesses. The company utilizes satellite Internet video streaming and Wi-Fi technologies to connect businesses with employees and customers. Clients use its networks to deliver training programs and make product announcements. BI primarily uses third-party equipment but it also supplies some proprietary technologies. BI also offers hosting of video streaming as well as audio and video production services. Its customers have included Caterpillar Safeway and Chevron.

	Annual Growth	12/08	12/09	12/10	12/11	12/12
Sales ($ mil.)	21.9%	3.4	3.6	7.3	8.4	7.5
Net income ($ mil.)	–	(12.5)	(13.4)	(18.7)	1.3	1.6
Market value ($ mil.)	(56.3%)	236.4	126.8	129.0	58.0	8.6
Employees	(10.9%)	38	49	45	51	24

BROADCAST MUSIC INC.

7 World Trade Center 250 Greenwich St.
New York NY 10007
Phone: 212-220-3000
Fax: 212-621-8453
Web: www.ascap.com

CEO: –
CFO: –
HR: –
FYE: June 30
Type: Private - Not-for-Pr

If you are a composer or musician Broadcast Music Inc. (BMI) is here to see that your royalties are paid. The not-for-profit organization collects licensing fees from a host of outlets and venues (such as radio stations TV programs websites restaurants and nightclubs) and distributes them to the more than 550000 songwriters composers and music publishers it represents. Its catalog of compositions includes more than 7.5 million works by a diverse range of artists including Adele Elton John Eric Clapton Gotye Merle Haggard Natalie Cole Herbie Hancock Kanye West and Sting. BMI was founded in 1939.

BROADCOM CORP.
NMS: BRCM

5300 California Avenue
Irvine, CA 92617-3038
Phone: 949 926-5000
Fax: –
Web: www.broadcom.com

CEO: Scott A McGregor
CFO: Eric K Brandt
HR: –
FYE: December 31
Type: Public

As a semiconductor supplier for the global wired and wireless communications industry Broadcom's reach is far and wide. With locations around the globe Broadcom manufactures billions of chips annually and is one of the world's leading semiconductor companies. Its system-on-a-chip (SoC) technologies and software products deliver voice video data and multimedia in several major market segments: home and office (cable modems DSL and set-top boxes) mobile (Bluetooth and GPS) and infrastructure (controllers embedded processors and security). Broadcom's customer roster includes such elite technology names as Apple Cisco and ZTE. It generates most of its sales from Asia.

	Annual Growth	12/10	12/11	12/12	12/13	12/14
Sales ($ mil.)	5.4%	6,818.3	7,389.0	8,006.0	8,305.0	8,428.0
Net income ($ mil.)	(11.9%)	1,081.8	927.0	719.0	424.0	652.0
Market value ($ mil.)	(0.1%)	26,086.5	17,586.6	19,892.8	17,757.4	25,954.7
Employees	4.4%	8,950	9,590	11,300	12,550	10,650

BROADRIDGE FINANCIAL SOLUTIONS INC
NYS: BR

5 Dakota Drive
Lake Success, NY 11042
Phone: 516 472-5400
Fax: –
Web: www.broadridge.com

CEO: Richard J. Daly
CFO: James M. Young
HR: –
FYE: June 30
Type: Public

Broadridge Financial Solutions does business by proxy. The company provides technology-based investor communications trade processing and related services to financial services companies around the world. Clients include banks broker-dealers mutual funds and institutional investors. Through its proprietary ProxyEdge system Broadridge processes and distributes proxy materials voting instructions and other information to investors processing more than 2 billion investor communications per year. It also offers related services such as marketing communications and online shareholder meetings. Broadridge operates offices in more than a dozen countries in Asia Australia Europe and North America.

	Annual Growth	06/11	06/12	06/13	06/14	06/15
Sales ($ mil.)	5.6%	2,166.9	2,303.5	2,430.8	2,558.0	2,694.2
Net income ($ mil.)	14.1%	169.6	123.6	212.1	263.0	287.1
Market value ($ mil.)	20.1%	2,845.1	2,514.1	3,141.8	4,921.8	5,911.2
Employees	5.8%	5,900	6,200	6,400	6,700	7,400

BROADSOFT INC
NMS: BSFT

9737 Washingtonian Boulevard, Suite 350
Gaithersburg, MD 20878
Phone: 301 977-9440
Fax: –
Web: www.broadsoft.com

CEO: Michael (Mike) Tessler
CFO: James A. (Jim) Tholen
HR: Anne Scotto-Lowery
FYE: December 31
Type: Public

BroadSoft hopes to remove some of the hard work from the process of supplying voice and data services. The company develops software that more than 500 fixed-line mobile and cable telecommunications service providers use to deliver voice and data services. Its BroadWorks software enables carriers to offer their subscribers unified communications services such as video calling hosted multimedia communications business telephone systems and collaboration tools. A hosted program is sold under the BroadCloud platform while its BroadTouch applications facilitate communications services for mobile devices. Customers include Rogers Swisscom Telstra and Verizon.

	Annual Growth	12/10	12/11	12/12	12/13	12/14
Sales ($ mil.)	22.7%	95.6	138.1	164.8	178.5	216.9
Net income ($ mil.)	(40.3%)	8.0	32.3	12.1	(8.9)	1.0
Market value ($ mil.)	5.0%	691.2	874.1	1,051.5	790.7	839.9
Employees	23.6%	372	487	611	725	867

BROADVIEW INSTITUTE INC
NBB: BVII

8147 Globe Drive
Woodbury, MN 55125
Phone: 651 332-8000
Fax: –
Web: www.broadviewmedia.com

CEO: Terry Myhre
CFO: Kenneth J McCarthy
HR: –
FYE: March 31
Type: Public

Broadview Institute isn't narrow-minded about education. The company owns and operates C Square Educational Enterprises dba Utah Career College or UCC which offers career vocational training programs in the Salt Lake City area to about 1000 students. Its degree programs span four growing industries: business and accounting health sciences (including veterinary studies) information technology and legal science. Classes are offered at three campuses in Utah and through online and accelerated programs. Chairman Terry Myhre owns about 65% of Broadview. Additionally Myhre has controlling interest in two other post-secondary career colleges Globe University and Minnesota School of Business.

	Annual Growth	03/10	03/11	03/12	03/13	03/14
Sales ($ mil.)	(8.3%)	19.0	20.5	17.8	14.6	13.4
Net income ($ mil.)	–	2.0	(0.1)	(4.2)	(5.1)	(4.9)
Market value ($ mil.)	(66.4%)	242.2	83.5	25.1	13.4	3.1
Employees	(2.6%)	233	246	214	236	210

BROADVIEW NETWORKS HOLDINGS INC.

800 Westchester Ave. Ste. N501
Rye Brook NY 10573
Phone: 914-922-7000
Fax: +65-67933-8156
Web: www.parkwayholdings.com

CEO: Michael K Robinson
CFO: Corey Rinker
HR: –
FYE: December 31
Type: Private

Broadview Networks seeks to expand its customers' horizons along with its own. The company provides such telecommunications services as local and long-distance computer telephony broadband Internet access and Web hosting. Enterprise data services include hosted business networks and hosted computer telephony services (sold under the OfficeSuite brand). It caters primarily to small and midsized businesses serving 10 states in the northeastern and mid-Atlantic US. Key markets include Baltimore Boston New York Philadelphia and Washington DC. Most of Broadview's sales are made to retail customers but it also serves wholesalers and other telecom carriers. Its majority shareholder is MCG Capital.

BROADVISION INC.
NMS: BVSN

1700 Seaport Blvd., Suite 210
Redwood City, CA 94063
Phone: 650 331-1000
Fax: –

CEO: Pehong Chen
CFO: Peter Chu
HR: –
FYE: December 31
Type: Public

BroadVision gives companies a peek into the world of customer self-service. The company develops software that enables businesses to offer their customers personalized self-service via the Internet. Its software suite includes tools for integrating business processes with self-service operations; managing the sales process including lead generation execution and customer service; connecting customers to personalized online views of content; and managing content from creation through distribution. BroadVision serves such industries as travel retail health care and entertainment. Clients have included Canon Oreck PETCO Vodafone and the US Air Force. Founder and CEO Pehong Chen owns 37% of BroadVision.

	Annual Growth	12/10	12/11	12/12	12/13	12/14
Sales ($ mil.)	(11.2%)	21.8	17.6	15.1	15.6	13.6
Net income ($ mil.)	–	(2.9)	(5.4)	(5.1)	(5.4)	(9.5)
Market value ($ mil.)	(16.7%)	60.4	52.9	43.2	46.7	29.1
Employees	(0.9%)	169	165	175	186	163

BROADWAY BANCSHARES INC.

1177 NE Loop 410
San Antonio TX 78209
Phone: 210-283-6500
Fax: 210-283-5623
Web: www.broadwaybank.com

CEO: –
CFO: Chris Bannwolf
HR: Marilyn Resendez
FYE: December 31
Type: Private

Broadway Bancshares is the holding company for Broadway National Bank (dba Broadway Bank) and its Eisenhower Bank division. The former is a community-oriented financial institution with about 30 branches in San Antonio and Central Texas; the latter has seven offices on military bases throughout the Lone Star State and serves military personnel worldwide. The banks offer traditional deposit products such as checking and savings accounts IRAs and CDs. Both originate various personal consumer construction and commercial loans as well as commercial and residential mortgages. The banks also provide private banking trust investment management and wealth advisory services.

BROADWAY FINANCIAL CORP. (DE)   NAS: BYFC

5055 Wilshire Boulevard, Suite 500
Los Angeles, CA 90036
Phone: 323 634-1700
Fax: –
Web: www.broadwayfederalbank.com

CEO: Wayne-Kent A Bradshaw
CFO: Brenda Battey
HR: –
FYE: December 31
Type: Public

This company won't quit 'til it's a star! Broadway Financial is the holding company for Broadway Federal Bank a savings and loan that serves the low- and moderate-income minority neighborhoods of central and south central Los Angeles and nearby Inglewood. Through about a half-dozen branches and loan offices the bank primarily originates multi-family (about 40% of its loan portfolio) and commercial real estate loans (another 40%). These loans are secured primarily by multi-family dwellings and properties used for business and religious purposes. Deposit products include CDs and savings checking money market and NOW accounts.

	Annual Growth	12/10	12/11	12/12	12/13	12/14
Assets ($ mil.)	(7.7%)	483.9	418.5	373.7	332.5	350.9
Net income ($ mil.)	7.2%	1.9	(9.5)	0.6	(0.3)	2.5
Market value ($ mil.)	(14.3%)	70.7	45.4	19.2	27.0	38.1
Employees	(3.2%)	81	76	73	68	71

BROADWIND ENERGY, INC.   NAS: BWEN

3240 S. Central Avenue
Cicero, IL 60804
Phone: 708 780-4800
Fax: –
Web: www.bwen.com

CEO: Stephanie K. Kushner
CFO: Steve Huntington
HR: –
FYE: December 31
Type: Public

If you're a wind energy producer Broadwind Energy wants to be the wind beneath your wings. The company serves the wind power generation industry with wind turbine towers and gear systems along with engineering repair and logistics services. Its gear systems are also used by other energy and mining companies. Broadwind's logistics segment specializes in transporting the oversize and overweight components used in constructing wind power generation facilities. The company's locations are spread across North America in areas where wind energy production is heavy.

	Annual Growth	12/10	12/11	12/12	12/13	12/14
Sales ($ mil.)	15.2%	136.9	185.9	210.7	215.7	241.3
Net income ($ mil.)	–	(85.2)	(21.9)	(17.9)	(10.5)	(6.2)
Market value ($ mil.)	23.5%	33.7	9.9	31.5	137.5	78.5
Employees	0.2%	850	833	753	775	857

BROAN-NUTONE LLC

926 W. State St.
Hartford WI 53027-1066
Phone: 262-673-4340
Fax: 262-673-8638
Web: www.broan-nutone.com

CEO: David L Pringle
CFO: John Pendergrass
HR: –
FYE: December 31
Type: Subsidiary

Customers are big fans of Broan-NuTone products. Henry Broan started the company in 1932 with the Motordor kitchen fan; today Broan-NuTone a subsidiary of Nortek is a leading maker of residential ventilation products. Offerings include ventilation and ceiling fans heaters indoor air quality products and trash compactors. Central vacuums intercom systems medicine cabinets speakers and doorbells are marketed under the NuTone name. Range hoods are sold under the Best and Broan brands. The company's products are available at retail stores such as Lowe's and The Home Depot and also sold by distributors. Broan-NuTone also makes private label products for GE Sears Whirlpool and others.

BROCADE COMMUNICATIONS SYSTEMS, INC.   NMS: BRCD

130 Holger Way
San Jose, CA 95134-1376
Phone: 408 333-8000
Fax: 408 333-8101
Web: www.brocade.com

CEO: Lloyd A. Carney
CFO: Daniel W. (Dan) Fairfax
HR: Carol Goode
FYE: October 31
Type: Public

Brocade Communications Systems maintains silky smooth computer network operations. A leading supplier of data center networking products Brocade makes Fibre Channel switches and related software for connecting corporate storage systems and servers. Its products are used in storage area networks (SANs) which pool storage resources across enterprises for easier management and more efficient asset utilization. The company's switches reroute data upon path failure and reconfigure the SAN when new devices are added. Brocade's products support Internet connectivity and enterprise mobility as well as key technologies such as software defined networking (SDN) network function virtualization (NFV) and cloud computing. It generates 57% of its sales from the US.

	Annual Growth	10/11	10/12	10/13*	11/14*	10/15
Sales ($ mil.)	1.3%	2,147.4	2,237.8	2,222.9	2,211.3	2,263.5
Net income ($ mil.)	61.0%	50.6	195.2	208.6	238.0	340.4
Market value ($ mil.)	23.3%	1,866.8	2,193.8	3,241.0	4,441.4	4,313.1
Employees	0.5%	4,546	4,536	4,143	4,161	4,640

*Fiscal year change

BROCKTON HOSPITAL INC.

680 CENTRE ST
BROCKTON, MA 023023395
Phone: 508-941-7000
Fax: –
Web: www.signature-healthcare.org

CEO: Kim Hollon
CFO: –
HR: Don Anderson
FYE: September 30
Type: Private

Signature Healthcare Brockton Hospital is a not-for-profit acute medical facility that serves southeastern Massachusetts. The hospital has 245 beds including about 30 beds in its skilled nursing unit. Its emergency department sees more than 62000 patients per year. Specialized services include radiation oncology cardiac care pediatrics orthopedics and joint replacement and inpatient and outpatient psychiatry. It is a community-based teaching hospital and part of the Signature Healthcare network. Brockton Hospital also formed a clinical affiliation with Beth Israel Deaconess Medical Center in 2013.

	Annual Growth	09/08	09/09	09/12	09/13	09/14
Sales ($ mil.)	3.3%	–	200.8	222.2	211.8	236.3
Net income ($ mil.)	–	–	–	19.8	19.6	(15.6)
Market value ($ mil.)	–	–	–	–	–	–
Employees	–	–	–	–	–	1,500

BRODER BROS. CO.

6 Neshaminy Interplex 6th Fl.
Trevose PA 19053
Phone: 215-291-6140
Fax: 800-521-1251
Web: www.broderbrosco.com

CEO: Norman Hullinger
CFO: –
HR: –
FYE: December 31
Type: Private

Selling clothes had been in the genes of sportswear distributor Broder Bros. for years. Begun as a haberdashery in 1919 the company evolved from making hats and gloves into a leading distributor of imprintable sportswear distributing about 1100 products under 40 retail brands including adidas Golf Champion alternative and Dickies and private labels; it operates under the Broder Alpha and NES divisions. Its private labels include Devon & Jones Chestnut Hill and others. Customers mostly small US retailers order merchandise through seasonal catalogs or online. Private investment firm Bain Capital has held a majority interest in the company since 2000 when the Broder family sold the company.

BROMLEY COMMUNICATIONS

401 E. Houston St.
San Antonio TX 78205
Phone: 210-244-2000
Fax: 210-244-2442
Web: www.bromleyville.com

CEO: –
CFO: –
HR: –
FYE: December 31
Type: Subsidiary

Marketers looking to put a multicultural spin on their brand can turn to this company. Bromley Communications is the #1 advertising agency offering communications services targeting the Hispanic population in the US. The firm provides creative ad development and strategic planning services as well as media buying and allied marketing and promotional services. It also offers public relations services through a partnership with PR firm Manning Selvage & Lee. Bromley has served such clients as Burger King Procter & Gamble and Western Union. Founded as Sosa Bromley & Aguilar Associates in 1981 the agency is part of Publicis Worldwide's regional operating unit Publicis USA.

BRONSON HEALTH CARE GROUP INC.

1 HEALTHCARE PLZ
KALAMAZOO, MI 490075339
Phone: 269-341-6000
Fax: –
Web: www.bronsonhealth.com

CEO: –
CFO: –
HR: –
FYE: December 31
Type: Private

Bronson Health Care Group has a strong presence as a provider of a wide range of medical services in southern Michigan and northern Indiana. The company operates several regional hospitals and health clinics including Bronson Methodist Hospital (some 400 beds) Bronson Battle Creek (220 beds) and Bronson Lakeview Hospital (35 beds). The not-for-profit health care system's facilities provide general and specialty services including trauma stroke burn cancer and cardiac care as well as emergency medicine pediatrics obstetrics rehabilitation and home health care.

	Annual Growth	12/04	12/05	12/06	12/08	12/09
Sales ($ mil.)	(32.5%)	–	575.7	476.3	588.9	119.6
Net income ($ mil.)	(27.7%)	–	–	43.7	(62.3)	16.5
Market value ($ mil.)	–	–	–	–	–	–
Employees	–	–	–	–	–	4,180

BRONSON METHODIST HOSPITAL INC

601 JOHN ST STE E-012
KALAMAZOO, MI 490075346
Phone: 269-341-7654
Fax: –
Web: www.bronsonhealth.com

CEO: Frank J Sardone
CFO: Mary Meitz
HR: Chris Cook
FYE: December 31
Type: Private

From your leg bone to your knee bone; your neck bone to your head bone Bronson Methodist Hospital has the specialists to cure what ails you. The 435-bed hospital is the flagship facility of the Bronson Healthcare Group a not-for-profit health care system. Bronson Methodist provides care in just about every specialty including orthopedics surgery and oncology. The hospital also contains specialist units for critical care (level I trauma center) neurology (primary stroke center) cardiology (Chest pain emergency center) women's health (BirthPlace) and pediatrics (children's hospital).

	Annual Growth	12/06	12/07	12/08	12/09	12/12
Sales ($ mil.)	(2.8%)	–	487.2	491.7	524.0	422.5
Net income ($ mil.)	–	–	–	(1.1)	41.3	39.9
Market value ($ mil.)	–	–	–	–	–	–
Employees	–	–	–	–	–	2,861

BRONX LEBANON HOSPITAL CENTER (INC)

1276 FULTON AVE
BRONX, NY 104563499
Phone: 718-590-1800
Fax: –
Web: www.bronx-leb.org

CEO: Miguel Fuentes
CFO: –
HR: Selena Griffin-Mahon
FYE: December 31
Type: Private

Bronx-Lebanon Hospital Center cares for patients in the central and south Bronx no doubt while rooting for the Yankees a few blocks away. The health care provider maintains more than 970 beds across its two campuses as well as psychiatric and nursing home facilities. Hospital specialty units include chest pain orthopedic cancer and women's health centers. Bronx-Lebanon also manages a network of about 70 owned and affiliated medical practices (under the BronxCare brand). This network includes primary care doctors and specialty clinics as well as rehabilitation facilities. The hospital is also a primary teaching hospital for the Albert Einstein College of Medicine.

	Annual Growth	12/05	12/06	12/07	12/08	12/09
Sales ($ mil.)	11.4%	–	513.4	634.2	489.3	710.0
Net income ($ mil.)	1.7%	–	–	21.4	(46.0)	22.1
Market value ($ mil.)	–	–	–	–	–	–
Employees	–	–	–	–	–	4,000

BROOKDALE SENIOR LIVING INC

NYS: BKD

111 Westwood Place, Suite 400
Brentwood, TN 37027
Phone: 615 221-2250
Fax: –
Web: www.brookdale.com

CEO: T. Andrew (Andy) Smith
CFO: Lucinda M. (Cindy) Baier
HR: Angela Ward
FYE: December 31
Type: Public

Over the brook and through the dale to grandmother's house we go! Brookdale Senior Living operates assisted and independent living centers and retirement communities for middle- and upper-income elderly clients. Brookdale has approximately 1000 facilities offering more than 331000 studio one-bedroom and two-bedroom units in 46 states. Services for its residents include meals 24-hour emergency response housekeeping concierge services transportation and recreational activities. Brookdale's continuing care retirement centers include skilled nursing units that serve Alzheimer's patients and others who require ongoing care. The company also owns eldercare company Emeritus Corporation.

	Annual Growth	12/11	12/12	12/13	12/14	12/15
Sales ($ mil.)	19.2%	2,457.9	2,770.1	2,892.0	3,831.7	4,960.6
Net income ($ mil.)	–	(68.2)	(65.6)	(3.6)	(149.4)	(458.2)
Market value ($ mil.)	1.5%	3,275.2	4,768.7	5,119.0	6,906.4	3,476.7
Employees	15.1%	46,400	47,900	49,000	82,000	81,300

BROOKHAVEN MEMORIAL HOSPITAL MEDICAL CENTER INC.

101 HOSPITAL RD
EAST PATCHOGUE, NY 117724870
Phone: 631-654-7100
Fax: –
Web: www.brookhavenhospital.org

CEO: Richard T Margulis
CFO: –
HR: –
FYE: December 31
Type: Private

Brookhaven Memorial Hospital Medical Center is an acute-care facility with more than 300 beds that serves patients primarily in Suffolk County on Long Island New York. The not-for-profit community hospital's Emergency Trauma and Chest Pain Pavilion is one of the largest emergency rooms on Long Island. Founded in 1956 Brookhaven Memorial also offers behavioral health services including inpatient and outpatient mental health and alcohol treatment services. In addition to hospital services the medical center operates two community health clinics and a specialty center that provides hemodialysis women's imaging and home health and hospice services.

	Annual Growth	12/03	12/04	12/05	12/06	12/09
Sales ($ mil.)	5.3%	–	230.9	230.9	269.7	298.6
Net income ($ mil.)	–	–	–	1.3	6.9	(2.3)
Market value ($ mil.)	–	–	–	–	–	–
Employees	–	–	–	–	–	2,100

BROOKLINE BANCORP INC (DE)

NMS: BRKL

131 Clarendon Street
Boston, MA 02116
Phone: 617 425-4600
Fax: –
Web: www.brooklinebancorp.com

CEO: Paul A. Perrault
CFO: Carl M. Carlson
HR: –
FYE: December 31
Type: Public

Brookline Bancorp is the holding company for Brookline Bank Bank Rhode Island (BankRI) and First Ipswich Bank (formerly The First National Bank of Ipswich) which together operate more than 45 full-service branches in eastern Massachusetts and Rhode Island. Commercial and multifamily mortgages backed by real estate such as apartments condominiums and office buildings account for the largest portion of the company's loan portfolio followed by indirect auto loans commercial loans and consumer loans. Established in 1997 as Brookline Savings Bank the bank went public five years later and changed its name to Brookline Bank in 2003. Brookline Bancorp. has expanded by acquiring other regional banks.

	Annual Growth	12/10	12/11	12/12	12/13	12/14
Assets ($ mil.)	20.8%	2,720.5	3,299.0	5,147.5	5,325.1	5,799.9
Net income ($ mil.)	12.3%	26.9	27.6	37.1	35.4	42.8
Market value ($ mil.)	(1.9%)	767.1	596.7	601.0	675.2	709.2
Employees	28.5%	266	358	662	720	725

BROOKLYN ACADEMY OF MUSIC INC

30 LAFAYETTE AVE
BROOKLYN, NY 112171430
Phone: 718-636-4100
Fax: –
Web: www.bam.org

CEO: –
CFO: –
HR: –
FYE: June 30
Type: Private

The Brooklyn Academy of Music (better known as BAM) is famous for its progressive nature. The urban arts center is America's oldest operating performing arts center and brings international performing arts media and film to Brooklyn New York. In addition the academy annually hosts the Next Wave Festival (featuring avant-garde music dance theater and opera) and houses a four-screen cineplex to draw young audiences. BAM's resident orchestra produces an annual season of concerts. BAM was founded in Brooklyn Heights in 1861.

	Annual Growth	06/09	06/10	06/11	06/12	06/13
Sales ($ mil.)	14.0%	–	38.9	50.2	75.3	57.7
Net income ($ mil.)	(26.4%)	–	–	12.2	23.2	6.6
Market value ($ mil.)	–	–	–	–	–	–
Employees	–	–	–	–	–	150

BROOKLYN HOSPITAL CENTER

121 DEKALB AVE
BROOKLYN, NY 112015493
Phone: 718-250-8000
Fax: –
Web: www.tbh.org

CEO: –
CFO: Joseph J Guarracino
HR: –
FYE: December 31
Type: Private

The Brooklyn Hospital Center has been taking care of ailing Kings County residents since before Brooklyn was a borough. Established in 1845 (before Brooklyn became part of New York City) the hospital houses some 460 beds and is a member of the NewYork-Presbyterian Healthcare System. It provides general medical and surgical care as well as a wide variety of specialty medical services including dialysis pediatrics obstetrics and cardiovascular care. The Brooklyn Hospital Center is affiliated with Weill Medical College of Cornell University. The hospital also operates a network of outpatient clinics providing primary and specialty care throughout the borough.

	Annual Growth	12/08	12/09	12/10	12/11	12/12
Sales ($ mil.)	7201.2%	–	0.0	388.3	379.3	384.1
Net income ($ mil.)	(5.0%)	–	–	5.9	10.0	5.3
Market value ($ mil.)	–	–	–	–	–	–
Employees	–	–	–	–	–	3,300

BROOKLYN NAVY YARD DEVELOPMENT CORPORATION

63 FLUSHING AVE UNIT 300
BROOKLYN, NY 112051080
Phone: 718-237-6740
Fax: –

CEO: David Ehrenberg
CFO: Dan Conlon
HR: –
FYE: June 30
Type: Private

After the federal government closed the military facilities at Brooklyn Navy Yard in 1966 the property on the East River was taken over and converted into commercial real estate by The City of New York. Brooklyn Navy Yard Development Corporation is in charge of the management and development of the old Navy Yard which contains about 4 million sq. ft. of leasable office and industrial space. Located near the Brooklyn Bridge the Navy Yard is home to about 250 tenants including small businesses high-tech startups and film and television studios. Since 2006 the company has been managing a Mayor Bloomberg-sanctioned expansion of the yard including some 1.7 million sq. ft. of new industrial space.

	Annual Growth	06/04	06/05	06/06	06/12	06/13
Assets ($ mil.)	14.6%	–	135.5	142.8	329.4	403.7
Net income ($ mil.)	2.7%	–	–	10.7	20.1	12.9
Market value ($ mil.)	–	–	–	–	–	–
Employees	–	–	–	–	–	165

BROOKMOUNT EXPLORATIONS INC.

OTC: BMXI

1465 Slater Rd.
Ferndale WA 98248-9754
Phone: 206-497-2138
Fax: 703-866-2423
Web: www.gaits.com

CEO: –
CFO: –
HR: –
FYE: November 30
Type: Public

Brookmount Explorations hopes it has the Midas touch. Formed in 1999 the exploration-stage mining company is engaged in the exploration of precious metal resource properties located Peru and Canada. Its primary project is the Mercedes 100 gold/silver/lead/zinc property in Peru. The company is also on the lookout for potential acquisitions in Canada and elsewhere in South America. President Peter Flueck controls approximately 40% of Brookmount Explorations having joined the company when he sold his ownership interests in the Mercedes property to Brookmount in 2005.

BROOKS AUTOMATION INC

NMS: BRKS

15 Elizabeth Drive
Chelmsford, MA 01824
Phone: 978-262-2400
Fax: -
Web: www.brooks.com

CEO: Stephen S. Schwartz
CFO: Lindon G. Robertson
HR: -
FYE: September 30
Type: Public

Brooks Automation supplies a steady stream of production tools and factory automation products for the semiconductor industry. It makes tool automation products such as vacuum robots and cluster assemblies used by semiconductor manufacturers. Brooks' wafer handling systems include vacuum cassette elevator loadlocks transfer robots and thermal conditioning modules and aligners. It also makes vacuum equipment for makers of flat-panel displays and data storage devices. Brooks serves top customers such as Applied Materials and Lam Research.

	Annual Growth	09/11	09/12	09/13	09/14	09/15
Sales ($ mil.)	(5.3%)	688.1	519.5	451.0	482.8	552.7
Net income ($ mil.)	(42.3%)	128.4	136.8	(2.2)	31.4	14.2
Market value ($ mil.)	9.5%	551.2	543.4	629.6	710.8	792.0
Employees	(3.6%)	1,650	1,547	1,656	1,455	1,426

BROOKS TROPICALS HOLDING INC.

18400 SW 256TH ST
HOMESTEAD, FL 33031-1892
Phone: 305-247-3544
Fax: -
Web: www.brookstropicals.com

CEO: Greg Smith
CFO: Janice Kolar
HR: Brittany Morrow
FYE: December 31
Type: Private

Brooks Tropicals offers exotic tastes with every bite. The company is a producer importer and supplier of tropical fruits and vegetables. Brooks product line consists of about 25 fruits and vegetables — some familiar some virtually unknown to American palates. They include avocados boniato calabaza chayote coconut ginger key lime kumquat lime malanga mamey sapote mango papaya Scotch bonnet pepper star fruit sugar cane and yuca. Brooks' produce is grown on its more than 6000 acres located in Florida as well as growing operations in Belize. The company was founded in 1928 by J.R. Brooks and is still owned and managed by his son and company president Neal (Pal) Brooks.

	Annual Growth	12/07	12/08	12/09	12/10	12/11
Sales ($ mil.)	5.0%	-	44.8	42.1	48.3	51.8
Net income ($ mil.)	-	-	(1.7)	(2.0)	2.9	3.8
Market value ($ mil.)	-	-	-	-	-	-
Employees	-	-	-	-	-	200

BROOKSTONE INC.

1 Innovation Way
Merrimack NH 03054
Phone: 603-880-9500
Fax: 405-270-1089
Web: www.bancfirst.com

CEO: Tom Via
CFO: Philip Roizin
HR: -
FYE: December 31
Type: Private

Need a putting green for the office? How about an alarm clock that responds to your spoken commands? Then Brookstone is the place for you. It sells gifts gadgets and other doodads targeted primarily at men through about 295 stores in 40-plus states and Puerto Rico. The company's products fall into categories such as technology travel time and weather outdoor living fitness and automotive. Brookstone also sells its wares online and through its eponymous catalog. Because gifts contribute to most of its sales the company operates temporary kiosks during Father's day and busy holiday seasons. Brookstone is owned by a consortium led by Osim International J.W. Childs and Temasek Holdings.

BROTHER INTERNATIONAL CORPORATION

100 Somerset Corporate Blvd.
Bridgewater NJ 08807-0911
Phone: 908-704-1700
Fax: 908-704-8235
Web: www.brother-usa.com

CEO: -
CFO: Anthony Melfi
HR: -
FYE: March 31
Type: Subsidiary

Brother International is part of one big global family. A subsidiary of Japan-based Brother Industries Brother International sells inkjet and laser printers fax machines scanners typewriters stamp-making systems laminators electronic label printers sewing machines garment printers gear motors and machine tools manufactured by its parent company. Its products are marketed to consumers and businesses in North America and across Latin America. Through its subsidiaries Brother International operates production and sales facilities in the US Canada Mexico Argentina Brazil Chile and Peru. The business which accounts for more than 25% of its parent's sales was formed in 1954.

BROWN & BIGELOW INC.

345 PLATO BLVD E
SAINT PAUL, MN 551071269
Phone: 651-293-7000
Fax: -
Web: www.brownandbigelow.com

CEO: William D. (Bill) Smith
CFO: Garry Hoden
HR: -
FYE: December 31
Type: Private

Brown & Bigelow can help keep your company's name on the minds (and walls) of all of your customers. The company distributes corporate promotional products including calendars pens USB flash drives apparel and related items. Brown & Bigelow sells its wares through a network of 250 sales executives located throughout the country supported by more than 15 full-service offices. Brown & Bigelow was founded in 1896 by calendar salesman Herbert Bigelow and financier Hiram Brown. The firm is known for having commissioned works by renowned artists such as Norman Rockwell and Cassius Coolidge (who created the paintings of those famous poker-playing cigar-smoking dogs).

	Annual Growth	12/09	12/10	12/11	12/12	12/13
Sales ($ mil.)	3.3%	-	55.7	59.9	60.5	61.3
Net income ($ mil.)	182.8%	-	-	0.0	0.0	0.0
Market value ($ mil.)	-	-	-	-	-	-
Employees	-	-	-	-	-	475

BROWN & BROWN, INC.

NYS: BRO

220 South Ridgewood Avenue
Daytona Beach, FL 32114
Phone: 386-252-9601
Fax: -
Web: www.bbinsurance.com

CEO: J. Powell Brown
CFO: R. Andrew Watts
HR: -
FYE: December 31
Type: Public

Brown & Brown (B&B) is looking for repeat insurance clients. The independent insurance agency and brokerage firm provides property/casualty life and health insurance and risk management services through its retail division mainly to commercial clients. Its national programs division designs customized programs for such niche clients as dentists lawyers optometrists and towing operators. Its wholesale brokerage unit distributes excess and surplus commercial insurance as well as reinsurance to retail agents. B&B's services segment provides self-insured and third-party administrator services. The company has 230 offices in about 40 states as well as offices in London and Bermuda.

	Annual Growth	12/10	12/11	12/12	12/13	12/14
Sales ($ mil.)	12.8%	973.5	1,013.5	1,200.0	1,363.3	1,575.8
Net income ($ mil.)	6.3%	161.8	164.0	184.0	217.1	206.9
Market value ($ mil.)	8.3%	3,435.1	3,247.1	3,653.2	4,504.0	4,722.1
Employees	9.5%	5,286	5,557	6,438	6,992	7,591

BROWN BROTHERS HARRIMAN & CO.

140 Broadway
New York NY 10005-1101
Phone: 212-483-1818
Fax: 916-327-0489
Web: www.calottery.com

CEO: –
CFO: –
HR: –
FYE: December 31
Type: Private

Brown Brothers Harriman (BBH) is one of the oldest largest and most prestigious private banks in the US. Founded in 1818 and known for its conservative investment approach the company specializes in asset management for wealthy families and institutional investors and corporate banking finance and mergers and acquisitions advisory for closely held middle-market companies. It has expertise in wealth planning and investment advisory banking public and private equity fixed-income strategies commodities and fiduciary services. It also manages four mutual funds. BBH has more than 15 offices in North America Europe and Asia.

BROWN JORDAN INTERNATIONAL INC.

475 W. Town Place Ste. 201
St. Augustine FL 32092
Phone: 904-495-0717
Fax: 408-325-6444
Web: www.ultratech.com

CEO: Gene J Moriarty
CFO: Vincent A Tortorici
HR: –
FYE: December 31
Type: Private

Brown Jordan International (BJI) prefers that its customers take a seat — inside or out. The firm designs and makes upscale indoor and outdoor furniture including chairs tables sofas and loveseats for home and commercial use. Its brands include Brown Jordan Casual Living Charter La-Z-Boy (under license) Lodging by Liberty Wabash and Winston. Residential products are sold by mass merchants (Home Depot and SAM'S CLUB); commercial lines are sold to hotels restaurants health care facilities and schools. BJI is controlled by a trio of hedge funds: TCW Group Stonehill Capital Management and Litespeed Capital.

BROWN PRINTING COMPANY

2300 Brown Ave.
Waseca MN 56093-0517
Phone: 507-835-2410
Fax: 507-835-0420
Web: www.bpc.com

CEO: –
CFO: –
HR: –
FYE: June 30
Type: Subsidiary

Brown doesn't mind getting its hands dirty — with four-color or black and white — with plenty of printer ink. Founded by Wayne "Bumps" Brown in 1949 Brown Printing Company is one of the largest publication printers in the US. The company prints magazines (more than 700 of them) catalogs and inserts for some 400 customers such as catalog retailer Hanover Direct and marketing company Valassis. Brown also provides direct-mail production and distribution through its Alliance List Services division while its Specialty Printing segment concentrates on digital print services. The company is a unit of large European magazine publisher Gruner + Jahr (G+J).

BROWN-FORMAN CORP.

NYS: BF B

850 Dixie Highway
Louisville, KY 40210
Phone: 502 585-1100
Fax: 502 774-7876
Web: www.brown-forman.com

CEO: Paul C. Varga
CFO: Jane C. Morreau
HR: Lisa Steiner
FYE: April 30
Type: Public

Brown-Forman (B-F) leads a spirited existence and spreads its spirits led by Jack Daniel's whiskey around the world. The company's portfolio of mid-priced to super-premium brands includes such well-known spirits as Jack Daniel's Canadian Mist Finlandia Southern Comfort and Woodford Reserve. Its wine labels include Sonoma-Cutrer and Korbel champagnes. Jack Daniel's is the company's signature brand and is the largest-selling American whiskey in the world (by volume). Offering some 30 brands the company's beverages are sold in more than 160 countries throughout the world; sales outside the US account for about 60% of revenue.

	Annual Growth	04/11	04/12	04/13	04/14	04/15
Sales ($ mil.)	4.9%	2,586.0	2,723.0	2,849.0	2,991.0	3,134.0
Net income ($ mil.)	4.6%	572.0	513.0	591.0	659.0	684.0
Market value ($ mil.)	5.9%	14,997.2	18,021.2	14,713.4	18,724.6	18,831.0
Employees	3.1%	3,900	4,000	4,000	4,200	4,400

BROWNING ARMS COMPANY

1 Browning Place
Morgan UT 84050-9326
Phone: 801-876-2711
Fax: 801-876-3331
Web: www.browning.com

CEO: Travis Hall
CFO: Kraig Walker
HR: –
FYE: December 31
Type: Subsidiary

Browning Arms Company has drawn a bead on the firearms market for more than 125 years. The company traces its roots to the late 19th Century when John Moses Browning established his firearms factory in Utah. Mr. Browning who earned many patents for his gunsmithing inventions developed designs that were manufactured by Winchester Colt and Fabrique Nationale. The arms firm which also has operated as the J. M. & M. S. Browning Company and as Browning Industries has built a business making rifles shotguns pistols and accessories along with archery and fishing equipment knives flashlights outdoor apparel footwear and security safes.

BROYHILL FURNITURE INDUSTRIES INC.

1 Broyhill Park
Lenoir NC 28633
Phone: 828-758-3111
Fax: 828-758-3538

CEO: –
CFO: –
HR: –
FYE: December 31
Type: Subsidiary

A century after its inception Broyhill Furniture Industries continues to fill homes and offices with its wares. The company is one of the leading furniture manufacturers in the US. Broyhill's product lines include such items as mid-priced bedroom living room dining room and home office furniture as well as occasional tables and home entertainment systems. The furniture company specializes in making and marketing upholstered goods and serves both residential and contract markets. Founded by Thomas H. (T.H.) Broyhill the company once belonged to Interco but today it operates as a wholly-owned subsidiary of industry behemoth Furniture Brands International.

BRT REALTY TRUST
NYS: BRT

60 Cutter Mill Road
Great Neck, NY 11021
Phone: 516 466-3100
Fax: –
Web: www.brtrealty.com

CEO: Jeffrey A Gould
CFO: George E Zweier
HR: –
FYE: September 30
Type: Public

BRT Realty is a real estate investment trust (REIT) that originates and holds senior and junior mortgage loans for income-producing commercial property. Most are high-yield short-term mortgages or bridge loans secured by shopping centers office buildings hotels and apartments that are being converted into condominiums and other multifamily residential properties. The REIT also invests in real estate joint ventures and in stock of other real estate companies. BRT Realty's loan portfolio consists of approximately 40 mortgages on properties in about a dozen states mainly New York New Jersey and Florida. Chairman Fredric Gould and his family control about a quarter of BRT Realty.

	Annual Growth	09/09	09/10	09/11	09/12	09/13
Assets ($ mil.)	29.8%	193.3	186.3	191.0	386.0	549.5
Net income ($ mil.)	–	(47.8)	(8.0)	6.4	4.4	5.0
Market value ($ mil.)	5.9%	77.1	86.5	84.2	88.0	97.0
Employees						

BRUCE FOODS CORPORATION

1653 Old Spanish Trail
St. Martinville LA 70582
Phone: 337-365-8101
Fax: 337-364-3742
Web: www.brucefoods.com

CEO: –
CFO: –
HR: –
FYE: December 31
Type: Private

Bruce Foods was Cajun long before Cajun was well hot. The company's Original Louisiana Hot Sauce is a top-selling hot sauce nationwide (alongside rival McIlhenny's Tabasco brand hot-pepper sauce). Louisiana-brand hot peppers — for brave souls — are available too. The company makes and markets less incendiary offerings including Tex-Mex products and traditional Southern favorites — canned yams and sweet potato pancake muffin bread-pudding and biscuit mixes. Cajun King seasonings Casa Fiesta Mexican foods Cajun Injector marinades and Mexene chili seasonings round out the company's portfolio of products. Bruce Foods was founded in 1928; the Bruce family still owns and manages the company.

BRUCE OAKLEY INC.

3700 LINCOLN AVE
NORTH LITTLE ROCK, AR 721146448
Phone: 501-945-0875
Fax: –
Web: www.bruceoakley.com

CEO: –
CFO: Tim Cummins
HR: –
FYE: September 25
Type: Private

From little acorns mighty Oakleys grow. Bruce Oakley provides road and river (barge) transportation of dry bulk commodities as well as grain storage and bulk fertilizer sales. The company's trucking division which uses both end-dump and pneumatic tank trailers serves the continental US and Canada. Overall Bruce Oakley operates some 450 trailers. It maintains about half a dozen ports in Arkansas Louisiana and Missouri on the Arkansas Mississippi and Red rivers and the company's river barge transportation unit operates on those and other inland and intracoastal waterways. Grain storage services are available in five ports in Arkansas. Bruce Oakley was founded in 1968.

	Annual Growth	09/04	09/05	09/06	09/07	09/08
Sales ($ mil.)	120.2%	–	–	–	526.8	1,160.1
Net income ($ mil.)	170.9%	–	–	–	11.8	32.0
Market value ($ mil.)	–	–	–	–	–	–
Employees						670

BRUKER AXS INC.

5465 E. Cheryl Pkwy.
Madison WI 53711-5373
Phone: 608-276-3000
Fax: 608-276-3006
Web: www.bruker-axs.com

CEO: Frank Laukien
CFO: –
HR: Lisa Neuenfeldt
FYE: December 31
Type: Subsidiary

Bruker AXS helps companies X-ray their way to the next hot drug. The firm makes X-ray systems that can analyze the structure of small molecules and aid in drug discovery and materials research. Bruker's products assist pharmaceutical firms and life science research entities in studying protein structure abnormalities the cause of many diseases. Chemical and raw material manufacturers use Bruker's systems in their research of materials for making such products as steel semiconductors and plastics. The company is a subsidiary of the Bruker MAT division of Bruker Corporation. Sister subsidiary Bruker Daltonics manufactures mass spectrometers.

BRUKER CORP
NMS: BRKR

40 Manning Road
Billerica, MA 01821
Phone: 978 663-3660
Fax: –
Web: www.bruker.com

CEO: –
CFO: –
HR: Justin Fossbender
FYE: December 31
Type: Public

The life sciences research field likes to put Bruker's equipment to the test. The company makes an array of scientific analysis instruments for pharmaceutical biotech industrial academic and government customers through four business units. Its Bruker MAT unit manufactures a portfolio of X-ray analysis products while Bruker CALID makes mass spectrometry equipment and chromatography instruments used for chemical testing and CBRNE detection. Bruker Energy & Supercon Technologies (BEST) offers superconducting systems and magnetic devices used in medical imaging and energy research. The company also makes magnetic resonance equipment through Bruker BioSpin.

	Annual Growth	12/10	12/11	12/12	12/13	12/14
Sales ($ mil.)	8.5%	1,304.9	1,651.7	1,791.4	1,839.4	1,808.9
Net income ($ mil.)	(12.2%)	95.4	92.3	77.5	80.1	56.7
Market value ($ mil.)	4.3%	2,797.6	2,093.1	2,568.0	3,331.8	3,306.5
Employees	3.1%	5,400	6,000	6,400	6,200	6,100

BRUKER DALTONICS INC.

40 Manning Rd.
Billerica MA 01821
Phone: 978-663-3660
Fax: 978-667-5993
Web: www.daltonics.bruker.com

CEO: –
CFO: John J Hulburt CPA
HR: Linda Deciccio
FYE: December 31
Type: Subsidiary

This company makes masses of spectrometers. Bruker Daltonics makes mass spectrometers along with related software and sample preparation systems that are used in drug development and clinical research applications. It also makes detection systems for nuclear biological and chemical agents. Bruker Daltonics has production facilities in the US and Germany. It sells its products directly and through distribution deals with such firms as Agilent Technologies to pharmaceutical makers biotechnology companies chemical firms and academic and government entities. The company is a subsidiary of Bruker Corporation. Sister subsidiary Bruker AXS manufactures X-ray systems used in drug development.

BRUKER ENERGY & SUPERCON TECHNOLOGIES INC.

15 Fortune Dr.
Billerica MA 01821
Phone: 978-901-7550
Fax: 978-901-7551
Web: www.bruker-est.com

CEO: Burkhard Prause
CFO: Thomas Rosa
HR: –
FYE: December 31
Type: Subsidiary

Bruker Energy and Supercon Technologies (BEST) is definitely wired. BEST makes low-temperature superconducting (LTS) wire used in MRIs and nuclear magnetic resonance (NMR) instruments made by GE Healthcare Siemens Medical and Agilent Technologies. BEST also makes high-temperature superconductors (HTS) used in fusion energy research and scientific research applications. Its cuponal wire is used by the energy infrastructure and transportation industries as an alternative to copper wire. The company is breaking into the renewable energy market by developing superconductors for solar cells and wind turbines. BEST a subsidiary of Bruker Corporation filed to go public in 2010 but withdrew the IPO in 2012.

BRUNO INDEPENDENT LIVING AIDS INC.

1780 Executive Dr.
Oconomowoc WI 53066
Phone: 262-567-4990
Fax: 262-953-5501
Web: www.bruno.com

CEO: –
CFO: –
HR: –
FYE: December 31
Type: Private

Bruno Independent Living Aids supplies the get-up-and-go for people who can't get around like they used to. The company makes accessibility and mobility products notably motorized lifts for getting up the stairs and into cars and vans. It also makes platform lifts for accessing a porch and vehicle lifts that transfer a scooter or wheelchair into the car. The company sells its products through independent dealers throughout the US and globally; it operates in Europe through its Sweden-based affiliate Autoadapt. Bruno Independent Living Aids was founded in 1984; it is owned and operated by the Bruno family.

BRUNSWICK CORP.

NYS: BC

1 N. Field Court
Lake Forest, IL 60045-4811
Phone: 847 735-4700
Fax: –
Web: www.brunswick.com

CEO: Mark D. Schwabero
CFO: William L. Metzger
HR: B. Russell (Russ) Lockridge
FYE: December 31
Type: Public

Brunswick's business is everyone else's free time. The company is a global manufacturer of marine recreation and fitness products. Its largest business segment marine engines comprises outboard inboard and stern drive engines propellers and control systems. The company also makes pleasure craft sports fishing convertibles offshore fishing boats and pontoons. Its fitness segment includes treadmills cross trainers stair climbers and stationary bicycles sold under brands Life Fitness and Hammer Strength. To focus exclusively on its marine engine and boat business Brunswick divested its bowling operations in 2014 and 2015.

	Annual Growth	12/10	12/11	12/12	12/13	12/14
Sales ($ mil.)	3.1%	3,403.3	3,748.0	3,717.6	3,887.5	3,838.7
Net income ($ mil.)	–	(110.6)	71.9	50.0	769.2	245.7
Market value ($ mil.)	28.6%	1,737.1	1,674.1	2,696.5	4,269.5	4,751.5
Employees	(5.6%)	15,290	15,356	16,177	15,701	12,165

BRYAN CAVE LLP

1 Metropolitan Sq. 211 N. Broadway Ste. 3600
St. Louis MO 63102-2750
Phone: 314-259-2000
Fax: 314-259-2020
Web: www.bryancave.com

CEO: –
CFO: –
HR: –
FYE: December 31
Type: Private - Partnershi

With offices in regions ranging from the Midwest to the Middle East law firm Bryan Cave is able to represent its clients' interests worldwide. The firm focuses on corporate transactions and litigation; specialties include agribusiness entertainment environmental health care intellectual property real estate and tax law. Bryan Cave has more than 1100 lawyers working out of about 30 offices around the world. Two affiliates — Bryan Cave International Trade and Bryan Cave Strategies — offer consulting services. Bryan Cave was founded in St. Louis in 1873.

BRYAN MEDICAL CENTER

1600 S 48TH ST
LINCOLN, NE 685061283
Phone: 402-481-3190
Fax: –
Web: www.bryanhealth.com

CEO: Kim Russel
CFO: Russell Gronewold
HR: –
FYE: December 31
Type: Private

Bryan Medical Center is the centerpiece of a not-for-profit health care system serving residents of Lincoln Nebraska and surrounding communities. The medical center which operates as part of Bryan Health features two acute-care hospitals (Bryan East and Bryan West) housing a combined 670 beds. In addition to providing general medical and surgical care it serves as a regional trauma center and provides specialty care in areas such as cancer orthopedics and cardiology. The Bryan Health organization also includes a rural hospital and several outpatient clinics and it provides medical training home health care services and wellness programs.

	Annual Growth	05/10	05/11	05/12	05/13*	12/13
Sales ($ mil.)	(24.4%)	–	479.0	481.5	462.8	273.6
Net income ($ mil.)	–	–	–	(4.3)	77.1	48.4
Market value ($ mil.)	–	–	–	–	–	–
Employees	–	–	–	–	–	3,970

*Fiscal year change

BRYCE CORPORATION

4505 Old Lamar Ave.
Memphis TN 38118
Phone: 901-369-4400
Fax: 901-369-4419
Web: www.brycecorp.com

CEO: Thomas J Bryce
CFO: –
HR: –
FYE: December 31
Type: Private

Sweet! Bryce Corporation produces plastic-film (using polypropylene polyethylene and polyester laminations) packaging for markets including candy snack pet food and other consumer products from its five production facilities in the US. Its Bryce Company business is a pro in film conversion and flexible packaging while its Cyber Graphics business provides package design; product photography; flexographic printing in up to 10 colors; a range of laminations such as solvent adhesives multilayer barrier extrusions and tandem laminations; and barrier coextrusion emulsion and wax coatings. Chairman and CEO Thomas J. Bryce preserves the family's stake in the company which was founded in 1969.

BRYN MAWR BANK CORP.

NMS: BMTC

801 Lancaster Avenue
Bryn Mawr, PA 19010
Phone: 610 525-1700
Fax: –
Web: www.bmtc.com

CEO: Francis J. Leto
CFO: Michael W. (Mike) Harrington
HR: Paul Kistler Jr
FYE: December 31
Type: Public

Bryn Mawr Bank Corporation stands atop a "big hill" in Pennsylvania. Bryn Mawr (which in Welsh translates as "big hill") is the bank holding company for Bryn Mawr Trust operates some 20 offices in Pennsylvania and Delaware. The bank offers traditional services as checking and savings accounts CDs mortgages and business and consumer loans in addition to insurance products equipment leasing investment management retirement planning tax planning and preparation and trust services. Founded in 1889 Bryn Mawr boasts more than $5 billion of assets under administration and management.

	Annual Growth	12/10	12/11	12/12	12/13	12/14
Assets ($ mil.)	6.7%	1,731.8	1,774.9	2,035.9	2,061.7	2,246.5
Net income ($ mil.)	32.0%	9.2	19.7	21.1	24.4	27.8
Market value ($ mil.)	15.7%	240.3	268.4	306.6	415.6	431.0
Employees	5.5%	359	391	432	432	444

BRYN MAWR COLLEGE

101 N MERION AVE
BRYN MAWR, PA 190102899
Phone: 610-526-5000
Fax: –
Web: www.brynmawr.edu

CEO: Hannah Holborn Gray
CFO: –
HR: –
FYE: May 31
Type: Private

These Mawrters aren't sacrificing anything especially when it comes to their education. Bryn Mawr is a college for women often referred to as Mawrters who hail from 60 countries. Its undergraduate programs including biology English math political science and psychology enroll 1300 students. Bryn Mawr also offers degrees through its co-educational Graduate School of Arts and Sciences and Graduate School of Social Work and Social Research which enrolls some 425 students. The college pools resources with Haverford Swarthmore and The University of Pennsylvania. Founded in 1885 Bryn Mawr is one of the nation's oldest women's colleges and the first to offer women an education through the Ph.D. level.

	Annual Growth	05/09	05/10	05/11	05/12	05/13
Sales ($ mil.)	(4.6%)	–	131.9	163.7	108.3	114.4
Net income ($ mil.)	79.8%	–	–	23.5	(42.2)	75.9
Market value ($ mil.)	–	–	–	–	–	–
Employees	–	–	–	–	–	777

BSB BANCORP INC. (MD)

NAS: BLMT

2 Leonard Street
Belmont, MA 02478
Phone: 617 484-6700
Fax: –
Web: www.belmontsavings.com

CEO: Robert M. (Bob) Mahoney
CFO: John A. Citrano
HR: –
FYE: December 31
Type: Public

BSB Bancorp is the holding company for Belmont Savings Bank a community back with about half a dozen branches in southeastern Middlesex County in the suburbs of Boston. The bank offers checking savings money market and retirement accounts to individuals; for local businesses it offers checking accounts. Its loan portfolio is made up primarily of commercial real estate loans. It also offers one-to four-family residential mortgages auto loans home equity lines of credit and construction loans. While Belmont Savings Bank traces its roots back to 1885 BSB Bancorp was formed in 2011 to take the company public.

	Annual Growth	12/10	12/11	12/12	12/13	12/14
Assets ($ mil.)	29.9%	500.3	669.0	838.1	1,054.6	1,425.6
Net income ($ mil.)	23.8%	1.8	0.3	1.4	2.0	4.3
Market value ($ mil.)	20.9%	–	95.6	110.9	136.8	168.9
Employees	10.5%	86	101	119	127	128

BSH HOME APPLIANCES CORPORATION

5551 McFadden Ave.
Huntington Beach CA 92649
Phone: 714-901-6600
Fax: 714-901-5980
Web: www.bsh-group.us/

CEO: Michael Traub
CFO: Stefan Koss
HR: –
FYE: December 31
Type: Subsidiary

BSH can help make an HSH — a home sweet home that is. The company makes and distributes a variety of high-end home appliances under the Gaggenau Bosch and Thermador brands including dishwashers ovens cooktops ranges washing machines and dryers. BSH serves the US and Canadian markets selling products directly to new homebuilders as well as through retailers such as Home Depot Lowe's and Sears. Most BSH appliances which are locally manufactured at plants in North Carolina and Tennessee are made from recyclable materials. Founded in 1997 BSH Home Appliances is a subsidiary of German manufacturer BSH Bosch und Siemens Hausgerate.

BSQUARE CORP

NMS: BSQR

110 110th Avenue NE, Suite 300
Bellevue, WA 98004
Phone: 425 519-5900
Fax: –

CEO: Jerry D Chase
CFO: Marty Heimbigner
HR: –
FYE: December 31
Type: Public

Bsquare hips its clients on how to integrate Microsoft applications with their own products. The company primarily resells software from Microsoft. Domestically its sales center around the Microsoft General Embedded operating system (OS) while international customers look to Bsquare for Microsoft's Windows Mobile OS. Makers of consumer electronics (cell phones) and automobiles in particular power portions of their goods with Microsoft's applications. Bsquare sells software from such other vendors as Adobe and McAfee. Additionally it provides engineering and development services to clients who require help integrating Windows products. The company also sells its own electronics testing software.

	Annual Growth	12/10	12/11	12/12	12/13	12/14
Sales ($ mil.)	(0.2%)	96.8	96.8	101.4	92.1	95.9
Net income ($ mil.)	(21.5%)	6.2	(0.5)	0.9	(5.3)	2.3
Market value ($ mil.)	(15.1%)	103.0	40.2	34.5	42.1	53.5
Employees	(3.9%)	215	315	241	187	183

BT CONFERENCING

150 Newport Avenue Extension Ste. 400
North Quincy MA 02171
Phone: 617-801-6600
Fax: 617-845-1058
Web: www.btconferencing.com

CEO: Aaron McCormack
CFO: Bernard Barlow
HR: –
FYE: December 31
Type: Subsidiary

BT Conferencing wants to connect people wherever they may be. The company provides audio video and Web conferencing and scheduling services and it resells and integrates conferencing systems. Businesses schools and government agencies worldwide use hardware software and services supplied by BT Conferencing to enable meetings and training sessions between participants in far-flung locations. The company offers products from such vendors as Avaya Cisco Polycom and TANDBERG. It also offers consulting installation project management and support. Clients have included food products giant Nestle and clothing maker Tommy Hilfiger. BT Conferencing is a subsidiary of UK-based telecom service provider BT Group.

BTU INTERNATIONAL, INC.   NMS: BTUI

23 Esquire Road   CEO: Paul J Van Der Wansem
North Billerica, MA 01862-2596   CFO: –
Phone: 978 667-4111   HR: Beth Teixeria
Fax: 978 667-9068   FYE: December 31
Web: www.btu.com   Type: Public

Things are heating up at BTU International. BTU makes sells and services thermal processing equipment and controls for the manufacture of printed circuit boards and for semiconductor packaging. The company provides its PYRAMAX branded systems for solder reflow (for printed circuit boards) as well as technical ceramic sintering electrical component brazing and the deposition of film coatings. BTU equipment is also used to make photovoltaic solar cells and solid oxide fuel cells and for sintering nuclear fuel. The company sells its products to the alternative energy and electronics assembly markets mostly manufacturers of computers printed circuit board assemblies and consumer electronics products.

	Annual Growth	12/08	12/09	12/10	12/11	12/12
Sales ($ mil.)	(5.3%)	72.3	45.1	81.6	76.1	58.1
Net income ($ mil.)	–	(1.1)	(14.6)	2.2	(2.7)	(11.0)
Market value ($ mil.)	(16.4%)	38.1	60.5	84.7	24.8	18.6
Employees	(5.6%)	381	352	383	356	302

BUBBA GUMP SHRIMP CO. RESTAURANTS INC.

209 Avenida Fabricante Ste. 200   CEO: –
San Clemente CA 92672-6270   CFO: Dan Bylund
Phone: 949-366-6260   HR: –
Fax: 949-366-6261   FYE: December 31
Web: www.bubbagump.com   Type: Subsidiary

Maybe for this company the restaurant business is like a box of chocolates. Bubba Gump Shrimp Co. Restaurants operates and franchises about 30 themed eateries. Inspired by the 1994 film Forrest Gump the casual dining restaurants offer a menu of seafood appetizers entrees and sandwiches. The chain has about 20 restaurants in 10 states along with another dozen international locations; most Bubba Gump units are found at tourist destinations such as the Mall of America and the Universal Orlando theme park. The chain started after cutting a licensing deal with Paramount Pictures in 1996 and was acquired by multi-concept dining operator Landry's Restaurants in 2010.

BUCKEYE PARTNERS, L.P.   NYS: BPL

One Greenway Plaza, Suite 600   CEO: Clark C. Smith
Houston, TX 77046   CFO: Keith E. St.Clair
Phone: 832 615-8600   HR: Mark Esselman
Fax: –   FYE: December 31
Web: www.buckeye.com   Type: Public

Buckeye Partners serves the Buckeye State and then some. Its main subsidiary Buckeye Pipe Line stretches about 1800 miles from Massachusetts to Illinois. Other pipelines include Laurel Pipe Line (Pennsylvania) Everglades Pipe Line (Florida) and Wood River Pipe Lines (Illinois Indiana Missouri and Ohio). It markets refined petroleum products in a number of the geographic areas served by its pipeline and terminal operations. In the US Buckeye Partners operates about 6000 miles of pipeline and more than 120 storage terminals capable of holding more than 110 million barrels of refined petroleum. It also has storage assets in the Bahamas.

	Annual Growth	12/10	12/11	12/12	12/13	12/14
Sales ($ mil.)	20.4%	3,151.3	4,759.6	4,357.2	5,054.1	6,620.2
Net income ($ mil.)	58.7%	43.1	108.5	226.4	160.3	273.0
Market value ($ mil.)	3.2%	8,490.3	8,128.2	5,769.0	9,021.3	9,612.1
Employees	13.6%	859	1,029	1,020	1,270	1,430

BUCKEYE POWER INC.

6677 BUSCH BLVD   CEO: Anthony J Ahern
COLUMBUS, OH 432291101   CFO: –
Phone: 614-781-0573   HR: –
Fax: –   FYE: June 30
Web: www.buckeyepower.com   Type: Private

It has cost a few bucks to generate power but the effort has been well worth it for Buckeye Power an electricity generation and transmission cooperative that provides electricity to 24 distribution companies in Ohio and one in Michigan. Together they serve about 400000 homes and businesses in 77 of Ohio's 88 counties. The company was established by Ohio's rural electric co-ops to produce and transmit electric power for member systems throughout the state. Buckeye Power contracts with other Ohio electric companies to use their transmission systems to transmit power to its member electric distribution cooperatives.

	Annual Growth	06/09	06/10	06/11	06/12	06/13
Sales ($ mil.)	5.9%	–	538.3	580.7	626.9	639.9
Net income ($ mil.)	(10.7%)	–	–	32.9	31.2	26.3
Market value ($ mil.)	–	–	–	–	–	–
Employees	–	–	–	–	–	300

BUCKHEAD LIFE RESTAURANT GROUP INC.

265 Pharr Rd.   CEO: –
Atlanta GA 30305-2241   CFO: Christe Marridot
Phone: 404-237-2060   HR: –
Fax: 404-237-2160   FYE: December 31
Web: www.buckheadrestaurants.com   Type: Private

Buckhead Life Restaurant Group is a leading multi-concept dining operator in Atlanta with about a dozen upscale and casual-dining restaurants. Its portfolio includes Pricci and Veni Vidi Vici (Italian cuisine) Kyma (Greek food) and Nava (Southwestern) along with Atlanta Fish Market Chops Lobster Bar and the Buckhead Diner. The company also operates private dining and party destination 103 West. In addition to its locations in Atlanta Buckhead Life has a small number of restaurants in Boca Raton Florida. Owner Pano Karatassos started the restaurant business in 1979.

BUCKLE, INC. (THE)   NYS: BKE

2407 West 24th Street   CEO: Dennis H. Nelson
Kearney, NE 68845-4915   CFO: Karen B. Rhoads
Phone: 308 236-8491   HR: –
Fax: –   FYE: January 31
Web: www.buckle.com   Type: Public

The Buckle has done away with the notion that Midwestern kids' fashion sense favors overalls. With some 450 mostly mall-based stores in 40-plus states The Buckle sells fashion-conscious 15- to 30-year-olds the clothes they've just got to have. The company retails a variety of clothing items including mid- to higher-priced casual apparel (pants tops and outerwear) shoes and accessories. Its products portfolio boasts such brands as Lucky Brand Dungarees Hurley Roxy Silver Billabong Fossil and Ed Hardy. The Buckle operates under the names Buckle and The Buckle; it also has an online store. Born in Nebraska in 1948 under the name Mills Clothing the chain has expanded into the South and West.

	Annual Growth	01/11	01/12*	02/13	02/14*	01/15
Sales ($ mil.)	5.0%	949.8	1,062.9	1,124.0	1,128.0	1,153.1
Net income ($ mil.)	4.8%	134.7	151.5	164.3	162.6	162.6
Market value ($ mil.)	9.3%	1,721.8	2,097.3	2,275.3	2,144.2	2,457.2
Employees	4.0%	7,600	8,600	8,600	8,800	8,900

*Fiscal year change

BUCKNELL UNIVERSITY

1 DENT DR
LEWISBURG, PA 178372029
Phone: 570-577-2000
Fax: –
Web: www.bucknell.edu

CEO: –
CFO: –
HR: –
FYE: June 30
Type: Private

Just getting into Bucknell University is an accomplishment. The highly selective private liberal arts school accepts only about 10% of applicants each year. Students who do get in some 3600 of them from around the world have the option to specialize in more than 50 majors and 60 minors. Bucknell confers both undergraduate and master's degrees in the liberal arts sciences engineering and music. It also offers programs in pre-law and pre-med. Bucknell tuition and fees total more than $58000; more than half of the student body typically receives financial aid. The school's student-to-faculty ratio is 10-to-1.

	Annual Growth	06/10	06/11	06/12	06/13	06/14
Sales ($ mil.)	3.8%	–	184.5	189.2	196.7	206.4
Net income ($ mil.)	–	–	–	(28.9)	74.3	93.0
Market value ($ mil.)	–	–	–	–	–	–
Employees	–	–	–	–	–	1,500

BUDGET RENT A CAR SYSTEM INC.

6 Sylvan Way
Parsippany NJ 07054
Phone: 973-496-3500
Fax: 888-304-2315
Web: www.budget.com

CEO: –
CFO: David B Wyshner
HR: –
FYE: December 31
Type: Subsidiary

When your budget won't allow for the fanciest rental car on the lot Budget Rent A Car System might very well have your ride. Budget rents cars through a network of about 1800 locations some 770 of which are company-owned in the Americas and the Asia/Pacific region. The Budget car rental brand is pitched mainly to leisure travelers and the cost-conscious. Together with sister company Avis Rent A Car System the company operates a fleet of more than 400000 rental cars. Affiliate Budget Truck Rental rents some 29000 trucks from about 2550 franchised and company-owned locations in the US. Founded in 1958 Budget Rent A Car System is a unit of Avis Budget Group and accounts for about a third of its sales.

BUFFALO BILLS INC.

1 Bills Dr.
Orchard Park NY 14127
Phone: 716-648-1800
Fax: 716-649-6446
Web: www.buffalobills.com

CEO: Ralph C Wilson Jr
CFO: Jeffrey C Littman
HR: –
FYE: December 31
Type: Private

It doesn't involve horses or gunplay but these Buffalo Bills can put on a wild show for football fans. Buffalo Bills Inc. operates the Buffalo Bills professional football team one of the more storied franchises in the National Football League. A founding member of the American Football League the team made four straight trips to the Super Bowl in the early 1990s but has yet to claim an NFL title. Buffalo has fielded teams with such Hall of Fame talent as OJ Simpson and Jim Kelly. Team owner and Detroit businessman Ralph Wilson founded the franchise in 1960; the Bills joined the NFL in 1970 when the AFL and NFL merged.

BUFFALO WILD WINGS INC   NMS: BWLD

5500 Wayzata Boulevard, Suite 1600
Minneapolis, MN 55416
Phone: 952 593-9943
Fax: –
Web: www.buffalowildwings.com

CEO: Sally J. Smith
CFO: Mary J. Twinem
HR: –
FYE: December 28
Type: Public

Hot sauce fuels the flight of this restaurateur. Buffalo Wild Wings (BWW) operates a chain of more than 1120 Buffalo Wild Wings Grill & Bar quick-casual dining spots that specialize in serving Buffalo-style chicken wings. The eateries found throughout North America the Philippines and the UAE offer more than a dozen unique dipping sauces to go with the spicy wings as well as a complement of other items such as chicken tenders and legs. BWW's menu also features appetizers burgers tacos salads and desserts along with beer wine and other beverages. The company owns and operates about 515 of the restaurants while the rest are operated by franchisees.

	Annual Growth	12/10	12/11	12/12	12/13	12/14
Sales ($ mil.)	25.4%	613.3	784.5	1,040.5	1,266.7	1,516.2
Net income ($ mil.)	25.1%	38.4	50.4	57.3	71.6	94.1
Market value ($ mil.)	42.0%	851.6	1,292.3	1,362.3	2,766.3	3,467.0
Employees	23.7%	15,900	21,000	25,500	31,700	37,200

BUILD-A-BEAR WORKSHOP INC   NYS: BBW

1954 Innerbelt Business Center Drive
St. Louis, MO 63114
Phone: 314 423-8000
Fax: 314 423-8188
Web: www.buildabear.com

CEO: Sharon P. John
CFO: Voin Todorovic
HR: –
FYE: January 03
Type: Public

The Build-A-Bear Workshop (BBW) covers the "bear" necessities and much more. Located mainly in malls the company's stores allow kids to design their own teddy bears and other stuffed animals complete with clothing (formal wear to western wear) shoes (including Skechers) and a barrage of accessories (eyewear cell phones and the like). Customers can build bears online too. The chain offers an in-store Build-A-Party and an interactive online community as well as online games and e-cards. Build-A-Bear founded by Maxine Clark in 1997 boasts more than 400 stores in the US Puerto Rico Canada the UK and Ireland as well as about 70 franchised locations across Europe Asia Australia and Africa.

	Annual Growth	01/11*	12/11	12/12	12/13*	01/15
Sales ($ mil.)	(0.6%)	401.5	394.4	380.9	379.1	392.4
Net income ($ mil.)	242.8%	0.1	(17.1)	(49.3)	(2.1)	14.4
Market value ($ mil.)	25.8%	132.6	146.9	67.9	134.4	331.8
Employees	(6.0%)	5,500	4,800	4,400	4,200	4,300

*Fiscal year change

BUILDERS FIRSTSOURCE INC.   NMS: BLDR

2001 Bryan Street, Suite 1600
Dallas, TX 75201
Phone: 214 880-3500
Fax: 214 880-3599
Web: www.bldr.com

CEO: Floyd F. Sherman
CFO: M. Chad Crow
HR: –
FYE: December 31
Type: Public

If you're a new homebuilder Builders FirstSource wants you to look no further. The company makes and sells hardware and doors windows lumber and other structural building products to construction professionals. Customers have included D.R. Horton and Hovnanian Enterprises. Builders FirstSource has grown through acquisitions to operate about 55 distribution centers and some 55 manufacturing plants in about 10 southern and eastern US states. Its plants make roof and floor trusses wall panels windows and doors and millwork among other products. The company was founded in 1998 as BSL Holdings by a management team headed by former CEO John Roach and private investment firm JLL Partners.

	Annual Growth	12/10	12/11	12/12	12/13	12/14
Sales ($ mil.)	23.0%	700.3	779.1	1,070.7	1,489.9	1,604.1
Net income ($ mil.)	–	(95.5)	(65.0)	(56.9)	(42.7)	18.2
Market value ($ mil.)	36.7%	193.5	200.4	548.1	700.4	674.8
Employees	11.0%	2,500	2,450	2,750	3,300	3,800

BUILDERS FIRSTSOURCE-SOUTHEAST GROUP LLC

2001 Bryan St. Ste. 1600
Dallas TX 75201
Phone: 214-880-3500
Fax: 214-880-3599
Web: www.buildersfirstsource.com
CEO: –
CFO: –
HR: –
FYE: December 31
Type: Subsidiary

Builders FirstSource-Southeast Group knows the true meaning of bricks and mortar. A subsidiary of Builders FirstSource the regional group manufactures roof and floor trusses wall panels stair parts doors and windows and it distributes these products along with lumber and other building supplies (such as concrete paint and power tools) to new home builders. The company's operations include about 50 manufacturing centers and more than 50 distribution facilities in Alabama Florida Georgia Maryland Tennessee Texas Virginia and the Carolinas. Owned by Builders FirstSource since 1998 the business was originally named Pelican Companies when it was founded in 1947.

BULLDOG SOLUTIONS INC.

7600 N. Capital of Texas Hwy. Bldg. C Ste. 250
Austin TX 78731
Phone: +65-6216-0244
Fax: +65-6223-6635
Web: www.wilmar-international.com
CEO: Darin Hicks
CFO: –
HR: –
FYE: December 31
Type: Private

If dog is man's best friend then Bulldog Solutions is a marketer's best friend. The company helps companies looking to generate revenue by creating custom marketing campaigns including Webinars podcasts white papers e-mail blasts and Web site ads. Bulldog tracks analyzes and breaks down benchmarking data into easy-to-read language and graphs for clients in the financial services health care insurance publishing and telecom industries. Among its major clients are Motorola Solutions Avaya and NetIQ. The firm was founded by CEO Rob Solomon and President Todd Davison.

BULOVA CORPORATION

1 Bulova Ave.
Woodside NY 11377-7874
Phone: 718-204-3300
Fax: 718-204-3546
Web: www.bulova.com
CEO: –
CFO: –
HR: –
FYE: December 31
Type: Subsidiary

Bulova is working to keep perfect time in the watch industry. It sells watches clocks and timepiece parts under brands such as Accutron and Wittnauer (luxury) Bulova and Caravelle (lower-priced) as well as licensed Harley-Davidson and Frank Lloyd Wright styles. Its watches range in price from about $150 to $4495. The firm also sells miniature collectible clocks mostly under the Bulova name and has expanded its licensing efforts to include items such as eyewear. Bulova sells its products primarily through department and jewelry stores mostly in North America (about 90% of sales). Founded in 1875 Bulova is a wholly-owned subsidiary of Japan's Citizen Holdings.

BULOVA TECHNOLOGIES GROUP, INC

NBB: BTGI

12645 49th Street North
Clearwater, FL 33762
Phone: 727 536-6666
Fax: –
Web: www.bulovatechgroup.com
CEO: Stephen L Gurba
CFO: Michael J Perfetti
HR: –
FYE: September 30
Type: Public

Bulova Technologies Group believes defense manufacturing and technology is a recipe for business success. Bulova operates in three primary segments: defense contract manufacturing and technologies. Its defense operations provide the DoD with explosive simulators ammunition and pyrotechnic devices as well as integration services. Bulova's contract manufacturing division assembles printed circuit boards and cable assemblies. It sold its BulovaTech Labs which developed and licensed applications for the defense energy and health care markets to Growth Technologies International in 2010. Bulova completed a reverse merger with 3Si Holdings in late 2009 in order to become a publicly traded company.

	Annual Growth	09/11	09/12	09/13	09/14	09/15
Sales ($ mil.)	(22.7%)	4.9	3.1	6.4	3.2	1.8
Net income ($ mil.)	–	(8.1)	(9.1)	11.2	(3.8)	(5.3)
Market value ($ mil.)	46.1%	0.9	0.0	0.0	1.6	4.1
Employees	–	–	–	–	–	–

BUNGE LIMITED

NYSE: BG

50 Main St.
White Plains NY 10606
Phone: 914-684-2800
Fax: 914-684-3497
Web: www.bunge.com
CEO: Alberto Weisser
CFO: Andrew J Burke
HR: –
FYE: December 31
Type: Public

Bunge Limited grinds on in more than 40 countries. It operates through four business segments: An agribusiness segment processes stores and sells agricultural products. Processed agricultural products include oilseeds and grains which are turned into vegetable oils and protein meals. Customers are animal feed poultry and aquaculture producers. The agribusiness markets vegetable oils used in the biodiesel industry. The edible oil products segment sells packaged oils like shortenings and margarines under brands Bunge Pro Floriol and Olek. A sugar and bioenergy unit makes sugar and ethanol which are sold primarily in Brazil. Bunge also mixes and distributes crop fertilizers to farmers in South America.

BUNGE MILLING INC.

11720 Borman Dr.
St. Louis MO 63146-1000
Phone: 314-292-2000
Fax: 314-292-2533
Web: www.bungemilling.com
CEO: Carl L Hausmann
CFO: –
HR: –
FYE: December 31
Type: Subsidiary

Talk about America's breadbasket. Bunge Milling is definitely in the running as a contender for the title and then some. The company is the largest dry corn miller in the world. It processes wheat corn and soybeans for domestic and import sales. Bunge's products include grits corn flour corn oil bulgar wheat hominy feed soy oil soybean hull pellets and soybean meal and pellets all of which are sold as ingredients to feed manufacturers food processors and the foodservice and bakery industries. The company's five mills are located in Mexico and the US. Bunge Milling is a division of Bunge North America a subsidiary of Bunge Limited.

BURGER KING WORLDWIDE INC.   NYSE: BKW

5505 Blue Lagoon Dr.
Miami FL 33126
Phone: 305-378-3000
Fax: 503-472-1048
Web: www.evergreenaviation.com
CEO: Bernardo Hees
CFO: Daniel S Schwartz
HR: –
FYE: June 30
Type: Private

This king rules one whopper of a fast-food empire. Burger King Worldwide operates the world's #3 hamburger chain by sales (behind McDonald's and Wendy's) with more than 12500 restaurants in the US and more than 80 other countries. In addition to its popular Whopper sandwich the chain offers a selection of burgers chicken sandwiches salads and breakfast items along with beverages desserts and sides. Many of the eateries are stand-alone locations offering dine-in seating and drive-through services; the chain also includes units in high-traffic locations such as airports and shopping malls. Investment firm 3G Capital took the company in private in 2010 before taking it public again in mid-2012.

BURGETT INC.

4111 N. Freeway Blvd.
Sacramento CA 95834
Phone: 916-567-9999
Fax: 916-567-1941
Web: www.pianodisc.com
CEO: Gary Burgett
CFO: –
HR: –
FYE: December 31
Type: Private

"Program it again Hal" says Burgett maker of player pianos for the 21st century. Doing business as PianoDisc the company makes electronic reproduction systems that enable acoustic pianos to automatically play music ranging from Mozart to Broadway show tunes to Billy Joel. The company's SilentDrive technology controls the piano keys precisely enough to create whisper-soft notes. Its Opus7 wireless playback device stores hours of uninterrupted piano music and can be used from any room in the house. The firm's products are sold through more than 600 distributors in 45 countries. Burgett was founded in 1979 by two brothers co-CEOs Gary and Kirk Burgett who made their first PianoDisc player in 1989.

BURKHART DENTAL SUPPLY CO.

2502 S 78TH ST
TACOMA, WA 984099053
Phone: 253-474-7761
Fax: –
Web: www.burkhartdental.com
CEO: –
CFO: –
HR: Anne Kerker
FYE: December 31
Type: Private

Burkhart Dental Supply is dedicated to supplying dentists with the tools they need. The family-owned company provides dental equipment and supplies to more than 5000 dentists throughout the midwestern southwestern and western US. The company also offers a variety of technical services equipment repairs office management software continuing education financing and consulting services such as office design and equipment planning. It distributes products made by some 100 manufacturers including DENTSPLY Kimberly Clark and Sirona. Its operating subsidiaries include ADC Group Financial Services Burkhart Consulting and Summit Dental Study Group.

	Annual Growth	12/05	12/06	12/07	12/08	12/09
Sales ($ mil.)	(45.0%)	–	–	471.7	157.1	142.8
Net income ($ mil.)	36328.3%	–	–	0.0	2.1	1.7
Market value ($ mil.)	–	–	–	–	–	–
Employees		–	–	–	–	360

BURLINGTON NORTHERN & SANTA FE RAILWAY CO. (THE)

2650 Lou Menk Drive
Fort Worth, TX 76131-2830
Phone: 800 795-2673
Fax: –
Web: www.bnsf.com
CEO: Carl R. Ice
CFO: Julie A. Piggott
HR: –
FYE: December 31
Type: Public

BNSF Railway operates one of the largest railroad networks in North America. A wholly-owned subsidiary of Burlington Northern Santa Fe itself a unit of Berkshire Hathaway the company provides freight transportation over a network of about 32500 route miles of track across two-thirds of the western US and two provinces in Canada. BNSF Railway owns or leases a fleet of about 8000 locomotives. It also has some 30 intermodal facilities that help to transport agricultural consumer and industrial products as well as coal. In addition to major cities and ports BNSF Railway serves smaller markets in alliance with short-line partners.

	Annual Growth	12/10	12/11	12/12	12/13	12/14
Sales ($ mil.)	11.2%	14,835.0	19,229.0	20,478.0	21,552.0	22,714.0
Net income ($ mil.)	16.6%	2,382.0	3,273.0	3,720.0	4,271.0	4,397.0
Market value ($ mil.)	–	–	–	–	–	–
Employees	6.0%	38,000	39,000	41,000	43,000	48,000

BURLINGTON NORTHERN SANTA FE LLC

2650 Lou Menk Dr.
Fort Worth TX 76131-2830
Phone: 817-352-1000
Fax: 817-352-7171
Web: www.bnsf.com
CEO: Matthew K Rose
CFO: Julie A Piggott
HR: –
FYE: December 31
Type: Subsidiary

Over the years the number of major US railroads has dwindled but Burlington Northern Santa Fe (BNSF) thrives as one of the survivors. Through its primary subsidiary BNSF Railway the company is one of the largest railroad operators in the US along with rival Union Pacific. BNSF makes tracks through 28 states in the West Midwest and SunBelt regions of the US and in two Canadian provinces. The company operates its trains over a system of about 32000 route miles. Along with its rail operations BNSF generates revenue from its BNSF Logistics unit a provider of transportation management services. Already owning 23% of BNSF Warren Buffett's Berkshire Hathaway bought the remaining 77% stake in February 2010.

BURLINGTON STORES INC   NYS: BURL

2006 Route 130 North
Burlington, NJ 08016
Phone: 609 387-7800
Fax: –
Web: www.burlingtonstores.com
CEO: Thomas A. (Tom) Kingsbury
CFO: Marc D. Katz
HR: –
FYE: January 31
Type: Public

Burlington Stores (dba Burlington Coat Factory) has two de facto mottos: "not affiliated with Burlington Industries" (thanks to a 1981 trademark-infringement lawsuit settlement) and "We sell more than coats." The company operates about 550 no-frills retail stores (averaging 80000 square feet) offering off-price current brand-name clothing in about 45 states and Puerto Rico. Although it is one of the nation's largest coat sellers the stores also offer children's apparel bath items furniture gifts jewelry linens and shoes. Sister chains include a pair of higher-priced Cohoes Fashions shops and about a dozen MJM Designer Shoe stores. Founded in 1972 Burlington Coat Factory went public in 2013.

	Annual Growth	01/11	01/12*	02/13	02/14*	01/15
Sales ($ mil.)	7.0%	3,701.1	3,887.5	4,165.5	4,462.0	4,849.6
Net income ($ mil.)	20.8%	31.0	(6.3)	25.3	16.2	66.0
Market value ($ mil.)	95.0%	–	–	–	1,925.0	3,754.5
Employees	7.3%	–	–	29,556	30,095	34,000

*Fiscal year change

BURRELL COMMUNICATIONS GROUP LLC

233 N. Michigan Ave.
Chicago IL 60601
Phone: 312-297-9600
Fax: 312-297-9601
Web: www.burrell.com

CEO: Fay Ferguson
CFO: –
HR: –
FYE: December 31
Type: Private

Corporate America comes to Burrell to get some street cred. Burrell Communications Group specializes in developing advertising and marketing campaigns targeted to African-American consumers and the urban market. It also offers expertise in reaching consumers in the general and youth marketplaces. The advertising agency provides services such as brand consulting account planning public relations event marketing and research in addition to its creative work. Burrell's clients have included McDonald's Procter & Gamble Toyota General Mills Verizon Marriott International Nielsen Media Research and Bacardi. French ad giant Publicis Groupe owns 49% of the shop which was founded by Thomas Burrell in 1971.

BURRILL & COMPANY LLC

1 Embarcadero Center Ste. 2700
San Francisco CA 94111
Phone: 415-591-5400
Fax: 415-591-5401
Web: www.burrillandco.com

CEO: Stephen A Hurly
CFO: –
HR: –
FYE: December 31
Type: Private

Burrill & Company is banking on biotech. The merchant bank serves only life sciences companies involved in such sectors as biotechnology pharmaceuticals diagnostics drug discovery medical devices and nutraceuticals. The firm works with life sciences companies seeking strategic partners mergers acquisitions or financing. It also helps larger companies spin off divisions or technology. Burrill helps steer the industry's growth through its venture capital funds which have more than $1 billion under management. The company also makes private equity investments. Its international arm seeks investments and merchant banking business in developing economies such as China India and Russia.

BURROUGHS & CHAPIN COMPANY INC.

2411 N. Oak St.
Myrtle Beach SC 29577
Phone: 843-448-5123
Fax: 843-448-9838
Web: burroughschapin.com

CEO: James W Apple Jr
CFO: J Bratton Fennell
HR: –
FYE: December 31
Type: Private

Burroughs & Chapin believes in family values and property values. A top land developer in the Myrtle Beach South Carolina area the company owns more than 40 commercial resort recreational and hospitality developments. Its portfolio includes malls strip centers hotels both championship and miniature golf courses land and family-friendly developments such as shopping and recreation venue Broadway at the Beach and Myrtle Waves Water Park. Subsidiary Prudential Burroughs & Chapin Realty a partnership with Prudential Real Estate provides real estate brokerage sales relocation and residential development services in coastal portions of North and South Carolina.

BURSON-MARSTELLER INC.

230 Park Ave. South
New York NY 10003-1556
Phone: 212-614-4000
Fax: 212-598-5407
Web: www.bm.com

CEO: Santiago Hinojaso
CFO: Ignacio Cabez N
HR: –
FYE: December 31
Type: Subsidiary

Burson-Marsteller is a one-stop shop for public relations services. It offers a range of related services including advertising brand building investor and media relations crisis management and Internet strategy and Web development. Serving such clients as SmithKline Beecham American Airlines and Champion Enterprises in the past the company operates through more than 130 offices (including affiliates) in almost 100 countries. Burson-Marsteller was established in 1953 by Harold Burson and Bill Marsteller and joined the Young & Rubicam group of companies in 1979. Young & Rubicam is a subsidiary of media services conglomerate WPP Group.

BURST MEDIA CORPORATION

8 New England Executive Park
Burlington MA 01803
Phone: 781-272-5544
Fax: 434-817-1010
Web: www.crutchfield.com

CEO: –
CFO: –
HR: –
FYE: March 31
Type: Subsidiary

Burst Media helps advertisers reach nearly one in five Web surfers with interests ranging from art to real estate. It sells advertising based on its network of more than 130 million unique users. It offers advertising packages that cover the whole network and smaller packages focusing on a specific category or a few selected sites. Burst Media's AdConductor software automates a variety of services including inventory management ad performance reporting and ad delivery. The company also operates a targeted e-mail delivery service. In May 2011 Burst Media was acquired by blinkx a provider of video search engine services that searches the Web for video clips.

BURTON LUMBER & HARDWARE CO.

1170 S 4400 W
SALT LAKE CITY, UT 841044413
Phone: 801-952-3700
Fax: –
Web: www.burtonlumber.com

CEO: –
CFO: –
HR: –
FYE: December 31
Type: Private

Family-owned-and-run Burton Lumber & Hardware designs makes and installs truss and floor packages wall panels and doors (interior and exterior) from its facility in Salt Lake City. It also sells and installs Heatilator-brand fireplaces and building materials made by Trex James Hardie and other companies. Burton Lumber & Hardware operates half a dozen locations in Utah and offers delivery services throughout the state. Its customers have included contractors home builders and government agencies. The company was founded in 1911 by Willard C. Burton.

	Annual Growth	12/08	12/09	12/11	12/12	12/13
Sales ($ mil.)	17.1%	–	63.8	70.6	93.5	120.0
Net income ($ mil.)	113.5%	–	–	1.2	4.5	5.6
Market value ($ mil.)	–	–	–	–	–	–
Employees	–	–	–	–	–	250

BUSH INDUSTRIES INC.

1 Mason Dr.
Jamestown NY 14702-0460
Phone: 716-665-2000
Fax: 716-665-2510
Web: www.bushindustries.com

CEO: –
CFO: Neil A Frederick
HR: –
FYE: December 31
Type: Private

Bush Industries is jockeying for a permanent seat in the ready-to-assemble (RTA) furniture industry. A leading maker of furniture for homes and offices the company sells its products worldwide with the help of about 10000 retail outlets including furniture and department stores electronics and office product retailers and mass merchandisers. It boasts two operating divisions: Bush Furniture (which sells through retail and ecommerce channels) and BBF (named Bush Business Furniture until 2010). The company's European business operates under the Rohr banner. Founded by the Bush family in 1959 the furniture maker is owned by a group led by DDJ Capital Management and JPMorgan Chase Bank.

BUSHNELL INC.

9200 Cody St.
Overland Park KS 66214
Phone: 913-752-3400
Fax: 913-752-6112
Web: www.bushnell.com/

CEO: –
CFO: Charles Gessler
HR: –
FYE: December 31
Type: Private

Bushnell is one highly focused firm. Also known as Bushnell Outdoor Products the company makes binoculars riflescopes laser-guided rangefinders night vision items trail cameras and other high-end optical equipment. It also produces performance eyewear and has a licensing agreement with Bausch & Lomb (which sold Bushnell in the mid-'90s). The firm's brand portfolio includes Bushnell Bolle Butler Creek Cebe Hoppe's Serengeti Stoney Point Tasco and Uncle Mike's. Bushnell operates offices in the US Canada France Hong Kong and Australia and its products are distributed to more than 25 countries. Established in 1948 the company today is owned by private equity firm MidOcean Partners.

BUSKEN BAKERY INC.

650 WALNUT ST DOWNTOWN
CINCINNATI, OH 45202
Phone: 513-871-2114
Fax: –
Web: www.busken.com

CEO: D Page Busken
CFO: –
HR: –
FYE: December 26
Type: Private

Fans of schnecken can make a connection at these bakery stores. Busken Bakery operates a dozen bakery stores in the Cincinnati area known for schnecken a kind of cinnamon roll that is a regional favorite. The bakeries also make cookies coffee cakes and pies as well as donuts muffins several varieties of bread and custom-made cakes. Its products are also sold through Remke Markets a regional supermarket chain. In addition Busken Bakery offers catering services and provides baked goods for fundraising efforts. Joe Busken Sr. started the family-owned company in 1928.

	Annual Growth	12/04	12/05	12/06	12/08	12/09
Sales ($ mil.)	(82.8%)	–	–	2,057.5	10.7	10.4
Net income ($ mil.)	635.5%	–	–	0.0	0.1	0.1
Market value ($ mil.)	–	–	–	–	–	–
Employees	–	–	–	–	–	175

BUSY BEAVER BUILDING CENTERS INC.

3130 WILLIAM PITT WAY
PITTSBURGH, PA 152381360
Phone: 412-828-2323
Fax: –
Web: www.busybeaver.com

CEO: Frank Filmelk
CFO: –
HR: –
FYE: December 29
Type: Private

|They're busy as well you know what kind of animals at Busy Beaver Building Centers. The company has 15 stores in Ohio Pennsylvania and West Virginia selling ceilings flooring lumber plumbing fixtures and other building materials along with garden supplies hardware power equipment and tools. Busy Beaver serves the professional contractor as well as the do-it-yourselfer. The regional home improvement center chain was founded in 1962. A management group led by chairman and former CEO Charles Bender acquired the company in 1988 and now owns about one-quarter of Busy Beaver which is facing heavyweight competition from big-box chains such as Home Depot and Lowe's.

	Annual Growth	12/09	12/10	12/11	12/12	12/13
Sales ($ mil.)	(1.0%)	–	41.5	40.8	40.4	40.2
Net income ($ mil.)	(86.0%)	–	–	0.4	0.3	0.0
Market value ($ mil.)	–	–	–	–	–	–
Employees	–	–	–	–	–	350

BUTLER MANUFACTURING COMPANY

1540 Genessee St.
Kansas City MO 64102
Phone: 816-968-3000
Fax: 816-968-3279
Web: www.butlermfg.com

CEO: –
CFO: –
HR: –
FYE: December 31
Type: Subsidiary

Need an eight-story building fast? Not a problem for Butler Manufacturing maker of pre-engineered buildings structural systems and roof and wall systems for nonresidential construction. A subsidiary of Australia-based BlueScope Steel Butler produces pre-engineered and custom-designed steel structures used in a range of projects from offices to schools to shopping centers. Through its BUCON and Butler Heavy Structures units the company provides general contracting services for large-scale projects. Butler also offers real estate development services. It distributes its products throughout North America.

BUTLER NATIONAL CORP.

19920 West 161st Street
Olathe, KS 66062
Phone: 913 780-9595
Fax: –
Web: www.butlernational.com

NBB: BUKS
CEO: Clark D Stewart
CFO: Craig D Stewart
HR: –
FYE: April 30
Type: Public

This Butler is at the service of aircraft operators. Butler National's Avcon subsidiary (over half of sales) provides aircraft modification services including the conversion of passenger planes to freighters. The company works mainly on Learjet models; it also modifies Beechcraft Cessna and Dassault Falcon aircraft. It adds aerial photography capability to aircraft and offers stability enhancements. The company's avionics unit makes airborne electronic switching components. Other Butler National businesses provide remote water and wastewater monitoring (SCADA Systems) and architectural services (BCS Design) as well as gaming management services to Indian tribes (Butler National Service Corporation; BNSC).

	Annual Growth	04/11	04/12	04/13	04/14	04/15
Sales ($ mil.)	0.4%	46.3	54.4	50.8	47.3	47.1
Net income ($ mil.)	(61.7%)	1.3	1.9	(0.1)	0.1	0.0
Market value ($ mil.)	(25.3%)	38.3	21.4	11.3	12.5	11.9
Employees	(6.4%)	433	413	377	314	332

BUZZI UNICEM USA INC.

100 Brodhead Rd.
Bethlehem PA 18017-8989
Phone: 610-882-5000
Fax: 610-866-9430
Web: www.buzziunicemusa.com

CEO: Dave Nepereny
CFO: –
HR: Daniel Pilgreen
FYE: December 31
Type: Subsidiary

Buzzi Unicem USA has a concrete goal — to secure a top market spot in US cement manufacturing. The company produces portland and masonry cement and ready-mix concrete used in highway and airport paving and concrete block manufacturing. It runs more than half a dozen cement plants with an annual production capacity of about 8.5 million metric tons and about 30 terminals from which it distributes its products mainly throughout the Midwest Northeast and Southeast. Formed out of the merger of RC Cement and Dyckerhoff's Lone Star Industries Buzzi Unicem USA is a subsidiary of Italy-based BUZZI UNICEM.

BWAY HOLDING COMPANY

8607 Roberts Dr. Ste. 250
Atlanta GA 30350
Phone: 770-645-4800
Fax: 770-645-4810
Web: www.bwaycorp.com

CEO: Kenneth M Roessler
CFO: Michael Clauer
HR: –
FYE: September 30
Type: Private

Trouble containing yourself? BWAY Holding may be of some help. The company manufactures and distributes metal containers from aerosol cans to paint cans steel pails and specialty boxes. It also makes rigid plastic pails drums and other blow-molded containers. BWAY products are used to pack industrial and consumer goods including ammunition deck sealants personal care items and food. Core subsidiaries are BWAY Packaging (metal containers) ICL Industrial Containers (pails) and NAMPAC Packaging (plastic containers). In late 2012 its parent company was acquired by an affiliate of Platinum Equity for approximately $1.24 billion.

BWX TECHNOLOGIES INC

NYS: BWXT

800 Main Street, 4th Floor
Lynchburg, VA 24504
Phone: 980 365-4300
Fax: –
Web: www.babcock.com

CEO: Peyton S. (Sandy) Baker
CFO: David S. Black
HR: –
FYE: December 31
Type: Public

The nuclear option is the only option for BWX Technologies. Formerly Babcock & Wilcox the company makes nuclear reactors for submarines and aircraft carriers and provides nuclear fuel to the US government. It also provides precision manufactured components to the commercial nuclear industry and offers technical management site support and environmental remediation services to both governmental and commercial facilities. Operating through subsidiaries such as Nuclear Fuel Services BWX has locations across North America; US government agencies are its largest customers. In 2015 the former Babcock & Wilcox spun off its power generation business and renamed itself BWX.

	Annual Growth	12/10	12/11	12/12	12/13	12/14
Sales ($ mil.)	2.1%	2,688.8	2,952.0	3,291.4	3,269.2	2,923.0
Net income ($ mil.)	(33.8%)	153.3	169.7	227.7	346.1	29.4
Market value ($ mil.)	4.3%	2,730.2	2,575.5	2,795.2	3,647.7	3,232.7
Employees	(2.2%)	12,000	12,700	14,000	11,000	11,000

BYCOR GENERAL CONTRACTORS INC.

6490 MARINDUSTRY DR STE A
SAN DIEGO, CA 921215297
Phone: 858-587-1901
Fax: –
Web: www.bycor.com

CEO: Scott Kaats
CFO: –
HR: –
FYE: December 31
Type: Private

Bycor General Contractors provides construction services for a variety of commercial retail institutional civic and leisure facilities in the San Diego area. Its offerings include tenant improvements shell construction build-to-suit and LEED-certified services and projects range from church sanctuaries to auto dealerships. The company has served clients including Western University of Health Sciences Northrop Grumman and San Diego National Bank. President Rich Byer CEO Scott Kaats and Van Smith founded co-founded Bycor General Contractors in 1981.

	Annual Growth	12/09	12/10	12/11	12/12	12/13
Sales ($ mil.)	10.3%	–	46.9	58.3	71.8	63.0
Net income ($ mil.)	(5.5%)	–	–	2.2	2.5	1.9
Market value ($ mil.)	–	–	–	–	–	–
Employees	–	–	–	–	–	90

C & F FINANCIAL CORP.

NMS: CFFI

802 Main Street
West Point, VA 23181
Phone: 804 843-2360
Fax: 804 843-3017
Web: www.cffc.com

CEO: Larry G Dillon
CFO: –
HR: Laura Shreves
FYE: December 31
Type: Public

C&F Financial Corporation is the holding company for C&F Bank (aka Citizens and Farmers Bank) which operates about 20 branches in eastern Virginia. The bank targets individuals and local businesses offering such products and services as checking and savings accounts CDs credit cards and trust services. Commercial industrial and agricultural loans account for the largest portion of the company's loan portfolio (about 40%) which also includes residential mortgages consumer auto loans and consumer and construction loans.

	Annual Growth	12/10	12/11	12/12	12/13	12/14
Assets ($ mil.)	10.2%	904.1	928.1	977.0	1,312.3	1,333.3
Net income ($ mil.)	11.1%	8.1	13.0	16.4	14.4	12.3
Market value ($ mil.)	15.5%	76.3	90.9	133.1	156.1	135.9
Employees	3.2%	544	512	528	643	616

C & K MARKET INC.

615 5TH ST
BROOKINGS, OR 974159199
Phone: 541-469-3113
Fax: –
Web: www.ckmarket.com

CEO: Karl Wissmann
CFO: David D Doty
HR: –
FYE: December 31
Type: Private

Family-owned C&K Market operates about 45 supermarkets in southern Oregon and northern California mostly under the name Ray's Food Place but also under Shop Smart and C&K banners. The Shop Smart warehouse-style stores focus on value-priced groceries and household goods. Most of C&K's stores are situated in small rural communities. C&K Market was founded in 1957 by Raymond "Ray" Nidiffer. Stung by competition from large national discounters including Wal-Mart and Costco the regional chain filed for bankruptcy in late 2013 and closed 15 supermarkets and sold 15 pharmacies.

	Annual Growth	12/05	12/06	12/07	12/09	12/10
Sales ($ mil.)	(32.9%)	–	–	1,513.2	467.0	457.1
Net income ($ mil.)	1737.3%	–	–	0.0	5.2	3.5
Market value ($ mil.)	–	–	–	–	–	–
Employees	–	–	–	–	–	2,322

C&A INDUSTRIES INC.

C & A Plaza 13609 California St. Ste. 500
Omaha NE 68154
Phone: 402-891-0009
Fax: 402-891-9461
Web: www.ca-industries.com

CEO: –
CFO: –
HR: –
FYE: December 31
Type: Private

C&A Industries provides staffing services in areas such as finance medicine engineering and administration to clients in the Midwest and elsewhere in the US. The company is made up of Aureus Group (specialty divisions offering staffing services in health care executive recruiting finance IT and travel) AurStaff (industrial and technical staffing) and Celebrity Staffing (administrative managerial and office support staffing). In addition the company has several community outreach units aimed at serving the Nebraska area.

C&S WHOLESALE GROCERS INC.

7 Corporate Dr.
Keene NH 03431
Phone: 603-354-7000
Fax: 661-861-9870
Web: www.calcot.com

CEO: Rick Cohen
CFO: –
HR: –
FYE: September 30
Type: Private

C&S Wholesale Grocers is at the bottom of the food chain — and likes it that way. The company is the second-largest wholesale grocery distributor in the US (after SUPERVALU) supplying goods to some 3900 independent and major supermarkets (including A&P and Safeway) mass marketers and wholesale clubs. C&S Wholesale which serves about a dozen states (from Vermont to Hawaii) distributes more than 95000 food and nonfood items. Its ES3 logistics unit provides warehousing and supply-chain management services. The grocery distributor is exiting the food retail business with the sale of its Grand Union and Southern Family Markets chains in 2012. Israel Cohen started the company with Abraham Siegel in 1918.

C&D ZODIAC INC.

5701 Bolsa Ave.
Huntington Beach CA 92647
Phone: 714-934-0000
Fax: 714-934-0088
Web: zodiac.com/

CEO: Jude F Dozor
CFO: John Maglione
HR: –
FYE: December 31
Type: Subsidiary

Without companies like C&D Zodiac air passengers would tumble around in cavernous flying tubes. The company makes the storage bins that people insist on levering trunk-sized objects into the seats from which your invariably large and bathroom-visiting seatmates invade your space the overhead panels that pinlight your book and keep you cool(ish) the phone-booth-sized lavatories the oft-maligned (and now seldom-used) galleys the ceiling panels you pray to in rough weather and the sidewalls you lean your head against when weary. Thank goodness C&D also makes upgrade and retrofit security kits for cockpit doors. The company is part of the cabin interiors business of France-based Zodiac.

C. B. FLEET COMPANY INCORPORATED

4615 MURRAY PL
LYNCHBURG, VA 24502-2235
Phone: 434-528-4000
Fax: –
Web: www.fleetlabs.com

CEO: Jeffrey R Rowan
CFO: Robert Lemon
HR: –
FYE: December 31
Type: Private

Some of C.B. Fleet's products are tucked away in medicine cabinets worldwide for those times of need. Established as a small family-run pharmacy in 1869 by Dr. Charles Browne Fleet today the company makes about 100 personal health and beauty care products that are distributed to more than 100 countries globally. C.B. Fleet's products include feminine care laxatives oral care skin care and oral rehydration product lines sold under brand names Summer's Eve Vera by CCS Norforms Clinomyn Oliva by CCS BioralSuero and Casen-Fleet among others. It also operates several subsidiaries such as CSS (Europe) DeWitt Personal Care (the UK) and Fleet Laboratories (Asia and Latin America).

	Annual Growth	12/04	12/05	12/06	12/07	12/08
Sales ($ mil.)	2.9%	–	213.7	223.9	235.4	232.6
Net income ($ mil.)	–	–	9.9	21.3	13.6	(2.1)
Market value ($ mil.)	–	–	–	–	–	–
Employees	–	–	–	–	–	696

C&J ENERGY SERVICES INC.

3990 Rogerdale Rd
Houston, TX 77042
Phone: 713 325-6000
Fax: –
Web: www.cjenergy.com

NYS: CJES
CEO: Josh Comstock
CFO: Randall C. McMullen
HR: Marty Kunz
FYE: December 31
Type: Public

Fracturing normally carries negative implications unless of course you're in the oil and gas industry. Serving oil and gas companies C&J Energy Services (C&J) provides hydraulic fracturing (fracking) services in geologically challenging areas in Texas Louisiana and Oklahoma. The company also provides coiled tubing and pressure pumping services which are used during well completion maintenance and other projects and it makes and repairs fraking pumping and other oilfield equipment. Major customers have included EOG Resources EXCO Resources Anadarko Petroleum Penn Virginia Apache Plains Exploration and Chesapeake.

	Annual Growth	12/09	12/10	12/11	12/12	12/13
Sales ($ mil.)	99.9%	67.0	244.2	758.5	1,111.5	1,070.3
Net income ($ mil.)	–	–	(2.4)	32.3	162.0	182.4	66.4
Market value ($ mil.)	5.1%	–	–	1,142.9	1,170.7	1,261.4
Employees	46.4%	–	831	1,127	1,989	2,609

C.D. SMITH CONSTRUCTION INC.

889 E JOHNSON ST
FOND DU LAC, WI 549352933
Phone: 920-924-2900
Fax: –
Web: www.cdsmith.com

CEO: –
CFO: –
HR: –
FYE: September 30
Type: Private

One of the Midwest's top contractors C.D. Smith Construction works on commercial institutional and industrial projects. It builds manufacturing retail correctional health care and education facilities as well as water treatment plants. The company offers general contracting and design/build services and also provides specialty contracting services such as steel erection masonry and concrete work carpentry and demolition. Charles D. Smith grandfather of president Gary Smith founded the company in 1936.

	Annual Growth	09/09	09/10	09/11	09/12	09/13
Sales ($ mil.)	–	–	0.0	0.0	252.1	252.1
Net income ($ mil.)	–	–	–	0.0	0.0	0.0
Market value ($ mil.)	–	–	–	–	–	–
Employees	–	–	–	–	–	440

C.H. GUENTHER & SON INC.

129 E. Guenther St.
San Antonio TX 78204
Phone: 210-227-1401
Fax: 210-227-1409
Web: www.chguenther.com

CEO: Dale Tremblay
CFO: Janelle Sykes
HR: –
FYE: April 30
Type: Private

Business is a grind for C.H. Guenther & Son; the flourmill produces the Pioneer brand of pancake biscuit and gravy mixes as well as the White Wings Peter Pan and Morrison brand name fours tortilla mixes and ready-to-eat tortillas used in homes restaurants and commercial kitchens across the US. Guenther also makes frozen bakery products to supply McDonalds Burger King and other customers in the foodservice industry. In addition the family-owned company operates The Guenther House home of founder Carl Hilmar Guenther restored as a restaurant museum and gift shop located in San Antonio Texas. C.H. Guenther & Son was started in Fredericksburg Texas in 1951.

C.R. ENGLAND INC.

4701 W 2100 S
SALT LAKE CITY, UT 841201223
Phone: 801-974-2712
Fax: –
Web: www.crengland.com

CEO: Chad England
CFO: TJ McGeean
HR: Wayne Cederholm
FYE: December 31
Type: Private

The world's top refrigerated trucking company and one of North America's largest transportation firms C.R. England hauls refrigerated and dry cargo throughout the US. The family-owned company also serves parts of Canada and through alliances points in Mexico. C.R. England's fleet includes more than 3500 Freightliner Peterbilt Volvo and International tractors and 5500 trailers. Besides for-hire freight hauling C.R. England offers dedicated contract carriage in which drivers and equipment are assigned to a customer long-term; logistics services including freight brokerage; and intermodal railroad service.

	Annual Growth	12/06	12/07	12/11	12/12	12/13
Sales ($ mil.)	11.9%	–	829.8	1,315.3	1,579.3	1,628.5
Net income ($ mil.)	(17.6%)	–	–	55.9	56.5	38.0
Market value ($ mil.)	–	–	–	–	–	–
Employees	–	–	–	–	–	6,500

CA INC

520 Madison Avenue
New York, NY 10022
Phone: 631 342-3550
Fax: 631 342-6800
Web: www.ca.com

NMS: CA
CEO: Michael P. (Mike) Gregoire
CFO: Richard J. Beckert
HR: –
FYE: March 31
Type: Public

Once known as Computer Associates CA Technologies is moving toward becoming known as Computer Apps. One of the world's largest software companies CA provides tools for managing networks databases applications storage security and other systems. Primarily serving large enterprises its applications work across both mainframes and cloud computing environments. It current focus is on developing applications for cloud and mobile computing and DevOps (development operations). Most of its software license sales come from subscriptions (primarily 3- to 5-year terms). The company also offers consulting implementation and training services. It sells worldwide to businesses government agencies and schools directly and through various resale channels.

	Annual Growth	03/11	03/12	03/13	03/14	03/15
Sales ($ mil.)	(1.0%)	4,429.0	4,814.0	4,643.0	4,515.0	4,262.0
Net income ($ mil.)	0.6%	827.0	951.0	955.0	914.0	846.0
Market value ($ mil.)	7.8%	10,530.5	12,002.5	10,966.0	13,491.9	14,201.7
Employees	(3.5%)	13,400	13,600	13,600	12,700	11,600

CABELAS INC

One Cabela Drive
Sidney, NE 69160
Phone: 308 254-5505
Fax: –
Web: www.cabelas.com

NYS: CAB
CEO: Thomas L. (Tommy) Millner
CFO: Ralph W. Castner
HR: David (Dave) Homolka
FYE: December 27
Type: Public

Cabela's is a hunter's and fisherman's Disneyland. The seller of outdoor sporting goods operates nearly 60 stores in more than 30 US states plus seven stores in Canada. Located mainly in the Midwest the stores are as big as 247000 sq. ft. and include such features as waterfalls mountain replicas aquariums in-store shooting galleries and banquet and meeting facilities. Cabela's sells footwear clothing and gear for fishing hunting camping and other outdoor activities. Cabela's also mails more than 132 million catalogs each year sells magazines and merchandise online and has an outdoors show on television. Cabela's was founded in 1961 by chairman Dick Cabela and his younger brother Jim.

	Annual Growth	01/11*	12/11	12/12	12/13	12/14
Sales ($ mil.)	11.1%	2,663.2	2,811.2	3,112.7	3,599.6	3,647.7
Net income ($ mil.)	21.6%	112.2	142.6	173.5	224.4	201.7
Market value ($ mil.)	33.2%	1,546.3	1,807.2	2,896.3	4,666.6	3,657.7
Employees	12.1%	13,700	14,800	15,200	16,400	19,300

*Fiscal year change

CABLE MANUFACTURING AND ASSEMBLY CO. INC.

10896 Industrial Pkwy. NW
Bolivar OH 44612
Phone: 330-874-2900
Fax: 330-874-2373
Web: www.cmacable.com

CEO: Robert Clegg
CFO: –
HR: –
FYE: June 30
Type: Private

Cable Manufacturing and Assembly — the name says it all. The company designs and manufactures cable (metal polymer and carbon fiber) for industrial and commercial uses. Its products include mechanical cable assemblies in a wide range of galvanized stainless steel and its proprietary PlastiCable in diameters of 1/32 inches to 3/8 inches and miniature stainless steel mechanical cable assemblies in diameters from .006 inches to .045 inches. Cable Manufacturing and Assembly also offers a wide range of actuators custom cable controls and operators for the remote operation of latches catches mechanisms and locking gas springs. The company has facilities in the US and Mexico.

CABLE NEWS NETWORK INC.

1 CNN Center
Atlanta GA 30348
Phone: 404-827-1700
Fax: 404-827-1099
Web: www.cnn.com

CEO: Tom Johnson
CFO: Wayne H Pace
HR: –
FYE: December 31
Type: Subsidiary

Whether it's reporting on the news or just talking about it this network does both all day long. Cable News Network (CNN) operates one of the top 24-hour news channels reaching more than 100 million US homes. In addition to its flagship channel the company offers HLN (formerly CNN Headline News) and it has an international division that keeps viewers informed in nearly 200 other countries. CNN has about 45 news bureaus around the world including 15 in the US. Away from the television CNN operates the top-ranked CNN.com news website and it offers syndicated news services. Founded in 1980 by cable broadcasting pioneer Ted Turner CNN operates as part of Time Warner's Turner Broadcasting division.

CABLE ONE INC.

1314 N. 3rd St.
Phoenix AZ 85004
Phone: 602-364-6000
Fax: 602-364-6010
Web: www.cableone.net

CEO: Thomas O Might
CFO: Kevin P Coyle
HR: Mary Lee
FYE: December 31
Type: Subsidiary

Its parent company may feed award-winning journalism to Beltway insiders but Cable ONE gives small-town folk CNN "and" The Cartoon Network. A subsidiary of The Washington Post Company the company provides cable television service primarily to small non-urban communities in 19 states throughout the midwestern southern and western US. Its core service areas are the Gulf Coast region and western Idaho. More than 700000 subscribers receive cable television service from Cable ONE and about half of those are also signed up for broadband Internet access sold under the CableONE.net brand. The company also offers voice-over-Internet-protocol (VoIP) computer telephony and digital video services.

CABLEVISION SYSTEMS CORP.   NYS: CVC

1111 Stewart Avenue
Bethpage, NY 11714
Phone: 516 803-2300
Fax: –
Web: www.cablevision.com

CEO: James L. Dolan
CFO: Gregg G. Seibert
HR: Sandra P. Kapell
FYE: December 31
Type: Public

Cablevision Systems is a leading provider of digital television phone and Internet services in the New York City metropolitan area. Through its Optimum brand the company serves nearly 3 million subscribers who receive at least one of the services. It also provides voice data and managed technology services to commercial customers through Cablevision Lightpath. Other operations include newspaper publishing (NYC's Newsday and community papers) regional news and sports networks and cable television advertising. Cablevision agreed to be bought by Altice a telecommunications company based in France. The $17.7 billion deal reached in 2015 was expected to face regulatory scrutiny.

	Annual Growth	12/10	12/11	12/12	12/13	12/14
Sales ($ mil.)	(2.8%)	7,231.2	6,700.8	6,705.5	6,232.2	6,460.9
Net income ($ mil.)	(3.6%)	360.9	291.9	233.5	465.7	311.4
Market value ($ mil.)	(11.6%)	9,284.3	3,901.4	4,098.9	4,919.2	5,662.7
Employees	(5.9%)	19,065	17,815	18,889	15,369	14,968

CABLEXPRESS CORPORATION

5404 S BAY RD
SYRACUSE, NY 132123885
Phone: 315-476-3000
Fax: –
Web: www.cxtec.com

CEO: William G Pomeroy
CFO: Barb Ashkin
HR: –
FYE: December 31
Type: Private

CABLExpress (dba CXtec) is hard wired for hardware. The company sells new and refurbished computer and communications equipment such as networking hardware phone systems and accessories storage products cables and media converters. It also provides such services as asset recovery consulting project management systems integration and technical support. CXtec distributes its products primarily in North America and serves various sectors including education financial services government and health care. The company sells products made by the likes of 3Com and Hewlett-Packard. CEO William Pomeroy founded the company from his home in 1978 as a distributor of used IBM mainframe cables and computer parts.

	Annual Growth	12/08	12/09	12/10	12/12	12/13
Sales ($ mil.)	–	–	0.0	61.7	68.2	73.7
Net income ($ mil.)	–	–	–	0.0	0.0	0.0
Market value ($ mil.)	–	–	–	–	–	–
Employees	–	–	–	–	–	340

CABOT CORP.   NYS: CBT

Two Seaport Lane
Boston, MA 02210-2019
Phone: 617 345-0100
Fax: –
Web: www.cabotcorp.com

CEO: Patrick M. Prevost
CFO: Eduardo E. (Eddie) Cordeiro
HR: Robby Sisco
FYE: September 30
Type: Public

Cabot may be an investor's dream — it's always in the black. The global specialty chemicals and performance materials company ranks among the world's top producers of carbon black a reinforcing and pigmenting agent used in tires inks cables and coatings. Cabot also holds its own as a maker of fumed metal oxides such as fumed silica and fumed alumina used as anti-caking thickening and reinforcing agents in adhesives and coatings. Other products include inkjet colorants aerogels (a synthetic material derived from a gel) and a specialty fluid (cesium formate) for oil and gas drilling. It also makes thermoplastic concentrates and compounds (masterbatch products) used by the plastics industry.

	Annual Growth	09/11	09/12	09/13	09/14	09/15
Sales ($ mil.)	(1.9%)	3,102.0	3,300.0	3,463.0	3,647.0	2,871.0
Net income ($ mil.)	–	236.0	388.0	153.0	199.0	(334.0)
Market value ($ mil.)	6.2%	1,547.7	2,284.1	2,667.6	3,171.0	1,971.2
Employees	2.9%	4,100	4,826	4,638	4,737	4,600

CABOT MICROELECTRONICS CORP   NMS: CCMP

870 North Commons Drive
Aurora, IL 60504
Phone: 630 375-6631
Fax: –
Web: www.cabotcmp.com

CEO: David H. Li
CFO: William S. (Bill) Johnson
HR: –
FYE: September 30
Type: Public

Cabot Microelectronics sits atop a mountain of slurry. The company is a top maker of slurries (consumables) used in chemical mechanical planarization (CMP). CMP is a wafer polishing process that enables semiconductor manufacturers to produce smaller faster and more complex devices. Cabot Micro's CMP slurries consist of liquids containing abrasives and chemicals that aid in the CMP process. The company is also a leading provider of polishing pads for CMP and it makes slurries used to polish the substrates and magnetic heads of hard-disk drives. TSMC United Microelectronics Samsung and Intel are among its largest customers.

	Annual Growth	09/11	09/12	09/13	09/14	09/15
Sales ($ mil.)	(1.8%)	445.4	427.7	433.1	424.7	414.1
Net income ($ mil.)	2.1%	51.7	40.8	51.4	50.8	56.1
Market value ($ mil.)	3.0%	840.7	859.1	941.5	1,013.3	947.1
Employees	2.0%	1,025	1,042	1,053	1,054	1,111

CABOT OIL & GAS CORP.   NYS: COG

Three Memorial City Plaza, 840 Gessner Road, Suite 1400
Houston, TX 77024
Phone: 281 589-4600
Fax: 281 589-4653
Web: www.cabotog.com

CEO: Dan O. Dinges
CFO: Scott C. Schroeder
HR: –
FYE: December 31
Type: Public

Like a cog on a gear in a well-oiled machine Cabot Oil & Gas (ticker symbol: COG) is very efficiently engaged in the oil and gas industry. It explores for and produces primarily natural gas (and some oil) and it sells gas to industrial customers local utilities and gas marketers. In 2014 Cabot Oil & Gas reported estimated proved reserves of 6.6 trillion cu. ft. of natural gas equivalent. About 96% of the company's reserves is in the form of natural gas. Its major areas of operation include gas shale plays in Pennsylvania Oklahoma Louisiana and Texas.

	Annual Growth	12/10	12/11	12/12	12/13	12/14
Sales ($ mil.)	26.7%	844.0	979.9	1,204.5	1,746.3	2,173.0
Net income ($ mil.)	0.3%	103.4	122.4	131.7	279.8	104.5
Market value ($ mil.)	(6.0%)	15,632.9	31,348.4	20,543.7	16,008.8	12,229.6
Employees	14.0%	409	529	589	684	691

CACHE INC

NMS: CACH

256 West 38th Street
New York, NY 10018
Phone: 212 575-3200
Fax: –
Web: www.cache.com

CEO: Jay Margolis
CFO: Anthony F Dipippa
HR: –
FYE: December 28
Type: Public

Caché sells fashions — from ball gowns to blue jeans — that bring cachet to the soirée. The upscale women's apparel retailer owns and operates about 280 specialty stores in shopping malls in 40-plus US states Puerto Rico and the US Virgin Islands under the Caché and Caché Luxe banners as well as an online shopping site. Sportswear including casual wear collections and separates accounts for more than 55% of apparel sales. The retailer courts women ages 25 to 45 with its own brand of apparel and accessories in a boutique-like atmosphere. (Stores average about 2000 square feet.) The firm buys its merchandise primarily from domestic suppliers but it has begun to source more overseas.

	Annual Growth	01/10	01/11*	12/11	12/12	12/13
Sales ($ mil.)	(0.5%)	219.8	206.5	223.9	224.2	216.7
Net income ($ mil.)	–	(8.7)	(22.4)	2.1	(12.1)	(34.4)
Market value ($ mil.)	5.8%	98.4	95.6	133.3	52.1	116.5
Employees	5.6%	2,250	2,204	3,156	2,735	2,652

*Fiscal year change

CACI INTERNATIONAL INC.

NYS: CACI

1100 North Glebe Road
Arlington, VA 22201
Phone: 703 841-7800
Fax: 703 841-7882
Web: www.caci.com

CEO: Kenneth D. Asbury
CFO: Thomas A. (Tom) Mutryn
HR: Marjorie R. Bailey
FYE: June 30
Type: Public

CACI International doesn't need a lot of clients just a few with deep pockets. As one of the largest government IT contractors CACI derives most of its revenue from the US government (including about three-quarters from the US Department of Defense). CACI provides a wide range of technology services including systems integration network management knowledge management engineering and simulation. It helps federal agencies provide national security secure information systems and networks and enhance data collection and analysis. CACI also serves state and local governments as well as commercial customers. It operates internationally through subsidiary CACI Limited and CACI BV.

	Annual Growth	06/11	06/12	06/13	06/14	06/15
Sales ($ mil.)	(1.9%)	3,577.8	3,774.5	3,682.0	3,564.6	3,313.5
Net income ($ mil.)	(3.3%)	144.2	167.5	151.7	135.3	126.2
Market value ($ mil.)	6.4%	1,525.5	1,330.6	1,535.4	1,698.0	1,956.2
Employees	4.9%	13,700	14,500	14,900	15,300	16,600

CACTUS FEEDERS INC.

2209 W. 7th St.
Amarillo TX 79106
Phone: 806-373-2333
Fax: 806-371-4767
Web: www.cactusfeeders.com

CEO: –
CFO: Matt Forrester
HR: Andy Etheredge
FYE: October 31
Type: Private

Cactus Feeders founder and chairman Paul Engler may operate one of the world's largest cattle feedlot businesses but he was no match for Oprah Winfrey. Cactus Feeders operates 10 feedlots with a capacity of some 520000 head of cattle which it beefs up and sells to meat packers. The company's feedyards are located in Texas and Kansas. It also provides market analysis marketing services Cactus Feeders offers financing for its rancher/suppliers. Oh and about Oprah Engler and other cattle ranchers unsuccessfully sued Winfrey and a guest after a 1996 broadcast of Winfrey's TV program The Oprah Show disparaged the beef industry.

CADENCE DESIGN SYSTEMS INC

NMS: CDNS

2655 Seely Avenue, Building 5
San Jose, CA 95134
Phone: 408 943-1234
Fax: –
Web: www.cadence.com

CEO: Lip-Bu Tan
CFO: Geoffrey (Geoff) Ribar
HR: –
FYE: January 03
Type: Public

Cadence Design Systems helps engineers pick up the development tempo. A leader in the market for electronic design automation (EDA) software Cadence sells and leases software and hardware products used to design integrated circuits (ICs) printed circuit boards (PCBs) and other electronic systems. Semiconductor and electronics systems manufacturers use its products to build components for wireless devices networking equipment and other applications. The company also provides maintenance and support and offers design and methodology consulting services. Customers have included Pegatron Silicon Labs and Texas Instruments. Cadence gets more than half of its sales from customers outside the US.

	Annual Growth	01/11*	12/11	12/12	12/13*	01/15
Sales ($ mil.)	14.0%	936.0	1,149.8	1,326.4	1,460.1	1,580.9
Net income ($ mil.)	5.9%	126.5	72.2	439.9	164.2	158.9
Market value ($ mil.)	22.9%	2,408.5	3,032.5	3,918.9	4,061.8	5,490.5
Employees	7.3%	4,600	4,700	5,200	5,700	6,100

*Fiscal year change

CADENCE MCSHANE CONSTRUCTION COMPANY LLC

14860 MONTFORT DR STE 270
DALLAS, TX 752546719
Phone: 972-239-2336
Fax: –
Web: www.cadencemcshane.com

CEO: James A McShane P E
CFO: –
HR: –
FYE: September 30
Type: Private

With a certain cadence Cadence McShane Construction has been right in step with the top contractors in the US. A part of development and construction group The McShane Companies it provides general construction construction management and design/build services for commercial institutional and industrial projects in Texas and the central US. The firm is known for its school and community projects throughout Texas. It also provides services to the manufacturing office multi-family residential government hospitality and retail markets. Recent projects include a 730000 sq. ft Port of Houston distribution center for First Industrial Realty. Cadence McShane was founded in 1995.

	Annual Growth	09/05	09/06	09/07	09/09	09/10
Sales ($ mil.)	–	–	–	(724.4)	259.2	158.2
Net income ($ mil.)	322.0%	–	–	0.0	4.9	1.2
Market value ($ mil.)	–	–	–	–	–	–
Employees	–	–	–	–	–	120

CADENCE PHARMACEUTICALS INC

NMS: CADX

12481 High Bluff Drive, Suite 200
San Diego, CA 92130
Phone: 858 436-1400
Fax: 858 436-1401
Web: www.cadencepharm.com

CEO: –
CFO: –
HR: Christine Aland
FYE: December 31
Type: Public

Cadence Pharmaceuticals figures that if a drug had success in one area it might do well in others. The company licenses rights to compounds and develops them for sale in untapped markets or for new indications. Cadence's sole marketed product is Ofirmev an injectable form of acetaminophen. Cadence licensed the drug from Bristol-Myers Squibb which markets it in Europe under the name Perfalgan. Cadence markets Ofirmev in the US for the treatment of acute pain and fever in children and adults in hospital settings. With one drug on the market Cadence is also on the lookout for other new drugs for its sales force to carry into hospitals.

	Annual Growth	12/08	12/09	12/10	12/11	12/12
Sales ($ mil.)	200.6%	–	–	–	16.7	50.2
Net income ($ mil.)	–	(57.1)	(45.5)	(56.6)	(93.0)	(81.0)
Market value ($ mil.)	(9.8%)	619.4	828.4	646.8	338.4	410.4
Employees	39.1%	55	90	247	220	206

CADIZ INC

550 South Hope Street, Suite 2850
Los Angeles, CA 90071
Phone: 213 271-1600
Fax: –
Web: www.cadizinc.com

NMS: CDZI
CEO: Scott S Slater
CFO: Timothy J Shaheen
HR: –
FYE: December 31
Type: Public

Cadiz hopes to strike gold with water. The land and water resource development firm owns some 45000 acres of land — and the groundwater underneath it — in eastern San Bernardino County California near the Colorado River Aqueduct and in the eastern Mojave Desert. Cadiz is betting on its groundwater storage and distribution project as water supplies become increasingly scarce in Southern California and as the state aims to increase its renewable energy production levels. Cadiz is also looking into commercial and residential development of its land. It has some agricultural assets that are leased as lemon groves and grape vineyards.

	Annual Growth	12/10	12/11	12/12	12/13	12/14
Sales ($ mil.)	(24.3%)	1.0	1.0	0.4	0.3	0.3
Net income ($ mil.)	–	(15.9)	(16.8)	(19.6)	(22.7)	(18.9)
Market value ($ mil.)	(2.6%)	220.0	170.3	140.0	123.1	198.0
Employees	0.0%	10	11	10	10	10

CADUS CORPORATION

767 5th Ave. 47th Fl.
New York NY 10153
Phone: 212-702-4351
Fax: 212-750-5815

OTC: KDUS
CEO: Hunter C Gary
CFO: –
HR: –
FYE: December 31
Type: Public

Cadus had hoped to make some dough from yeast but now is barely more than a hollow crust. Previously the company's drug discovery technologies used genetically engineered yeast cells but the firm sold its discovery programs to OSI Pharmaceuticals years ago and halted all research efforts. Its subsidiary Cadus Technologies still holds some assets related to its yeast cell technology and is seeking interested parties to license the intellectual properties. Its revenues consist of the payments on a sale of technology discoveries it made years ago. Investor Carl Icahn a director and former chairman of the company owns almost 40% of Cadus and effectively controls the company.

CADWALADER WICKERSHAM & TAFT LLP

1 World Financial Center
New York NY 10281
Phone: 212-504-6000
Fax: 212-504-6666
Web: www.cadwalader.com

CEO: –
CFO: –
HR: –
FYE: December 31
Type: Private - Partnershi

Founded during the presidency of George Washington Cadwalader Wickersham & Taft is one of the oldest law firms in the US. Since 1792 the firm has grown to include about 450 lawyers and to encompass offices not only in the US but also in Europe and the Asia/Pacific region. Among the areas of practice for which the firm is regularly recognized are capital markets financial restructuring and mergers and acquisitions. Banks and other financial institutions have been prominently represented on Cadwalader's client list; in addition the firm undertakes work for other large businesses and for government entities health care organizations nonprofits and individuals.

CAESARS ENTERTAINMENT CORP

One Caesars Palace Drive
Las Vegas, NV 89109
Phone: 702 407-6000
Fax: –
Web: www.caesars.com

NMS: CZR
CEO: Mark P. Frissora
CFO: Eric Hession
HR: Mary H. Thomas
FYE: December 31
Type: Public

Caesars Entertainment Corporation (formerly Harrah's Entertainment) likes to spread its bets. The firm owns and/or operates more than 50 casinos (under such names as Harrah's Horseshoe and Rio) in 14 US states and five countries. Altogether its facilities — including hotels dockside and riverboat casinos and Native American gaming establishments — boast more than 3 million sq. ft. of casino space and some 43000 hotel rooms. Among its many locations on the Vegas Strip are Caesars Palace Paris Las Vegas and Planet Hollywood. The company went public in 2012 more than a year after it cancelled a previous IPO.

	Annual Growth	12/10	12/11	12/12	12/13	12/14
Sales ($ mil.)	(0.9%)	8,818.6	8,834.5	8,586.7	8,559.7	8,516.0
Net income ($ mil.)	–	(831.1)	(687.6)	(1,497.5)	(2,948.2)	(2,783.0)
Market value ($ mil.)	50.6%	–	–	1,003.4	3,123.3	2,275.1
Employees	(0.4%)	69,000	70,000	68,000	68,000	68,000

CAFE ENTERPRISES INC.

4324 Wade Hampton Blvd. Ste. B
Taylors SC 29687
Phone: 864-322-1331
Fax: 864-322-1332
Web: www.cafeent.com

CEO: Jim Balis
CFO: Fred Grant Jr
HR: Mark Honeycutt
FYE: December 31
Type: Private

You might say this company wantz to feed you lotz. Cafe Enterprises owns and operates almost 50 FATZ Eatz & Drinkz casual-dining establishments in Georgia North Carolina South Carolina Tennessee and Virginia. The restaurants known for their down-home atmosphere and large portions offer standard American fare such as burgers chicken pasta steaks and seafood. In 2012 the company launched two new concepts — Tavern 24 a casual pub-style restaurant that serves burgers sandwiches and pizza and Tablefields a farm-to-table restaurant that serves fresh locally sourced menu items with a focus on southern comfort fare. Both are in South Carolina.

CAFEPRESS INC

6901 Riverport Drive
Louisville, KY 40258
Phone: 502 995-2258
Fax: –
Web: www.cafepressinc.com

NMS: PRSS
CEO: Fred E Durham III
CFO: Garett Jackson
HR: –
FYE: December 31
Type: Public

Call it a craft fair that meets Amazon.com. CafePress operates an online service that connects millions of buyers and sellers of print-on-demand products. If you've dreamed up a catchy slogan or an arresting image the company's flagship website CafePress.com will print it for you on a T-shirt hat mug poster or other product; post it on cafepress.com for sale; and then ship it off and collect payments keeping a nominal base fee for itself. The company's growing portfolio of websites includes ezprints.com GreatBigCanvas.com CanvasOnDemand.com Imagekind.com. and InvitationBox.com and boasts more than 19 million members across all of its properties. Founded in 1999 CafePress went public in 2012.

	Annual Growth	12/10	12/11	12/12	12/13	12/14
Sales ($ mil.)	4.6%	127.9	175.5	217.8	245.9	153.2
Net income ($ mil.)	–	2.7	3.6	(0.1)	(13.5)	(15.9)
Market value ($ mil.)	(36.2%)	–	–	100.5	110.2	40.9
Employees	(4.7%)	–	523	742	775	452

CAHILL GORDON & REINDEL LLP

80 Pine St.
New York NY 10005-1702
Phone: 212-701-3000
Fax: 212-269-5420
Web: www.cahill.com

CEO: –
CFO: –
HR: –
FYE: December 31
Type: Private - Partnershi

Here's a name plenty of high-profile clients have banked on: Cahill Gordon & Reindel. The firm's roster of clients has included investment banks such as Goldman Sachs J.P. Morgan Chase and Merrill Lynch as well as commercial banks and big companies from a variety of other industries. The firm maintains a broad range of practice areas; among its specialties are corporate transactions intellectual property litigation media law and tax. Cahill which has about 300 lawyers has offices in New York; Washington DC; and London. The firm was founded in 1919.

CAI INTERNATIONAL INC NYS: CAI

Steuart Tower, 1 Market Plaza, Suite 900
San Francisco, CA 94105
Phone: 415 788-0100
Fax: –
Web: www.capps.com

CEO: Victor M. Garcia
CFO: Timothy Page
HR: –
FYE: December 31
Type: Public

Is it bigger than a breadbox? CAI International can pack it. The company leases large steel boxes to ship freight by plane train or truck around the world. More than 65% of its container fleet is owned by CAI and the balance owned by container investors is managed by CAI. The leasing segment offers 280-plus shipping companies short-term and long-term leases with some leases giving the lessees the option to purchase the container. The container management segment provides container investors with the ability to lease release and dispose of their container portfolio; services also include container repair relocation and storage.

	Annual Growth	12/10	12/11	12/12	12/13	12/14
Sales ($ mil.)	30.7%	77.9	125.7	173.9	212.4	227.6
Net income ($ mil.)	20.7%	28.4	50.2	63.5	63.9	60.3
Market value ($ mil.)	4.3%	407.5	321.4	456.3	490.0	482.3
Employees	3.2%	89	83	91	85	101

CAITHNESS CORPORATION

565 5th Ave. 29th Fl.
New York NY 10017
Phone: 212-921-9099
Fax: 212-921-9239
Web: www.caithnessenergy.com

CEO: James D Bishop Jr
CFO: –
HR: –
FYE: December 31
Type: Private

Scotland's windswept Caithness region might well serve as an inspiration for Caithness Corp. which develops wind and other renewable power plants in the US under the Caithness Energy brand. Although the firm has focused on the development acquisition operation and management of geothermal hydroelectric wind and solar energy power projects it also develops environmentally friendly fossil-fueled plants. Caithness is one of the largest producers of renewable energy in the US and has developed more than 350 MW of geothermal projects 160 MW of solar plants and 440 MW produced by wind turbines. On the cleaner fossil fuel plant side it has also developed more than 2000 MW of gas-turbine powered capacity.

CAJUN INDUSTRIES LLC

15635 AIRLINE HWY
BATON ROUGE, LA 708177318
Phone: 225-753-5857
Fax: –
Web: www.cajunusa.com

CEO: Todd Grigsby
CFO: –
HR: –
FYE: September 30
Type: Private

Offering a mixed gumbo of services Cajun Industries builds oil refineries power plants process plants water-treatment plants and other industrial and infrastructure projects primarily in Louisiana and Texas. Subsidiary Cajun Constructors provides a full range of services from design/build to maintenance; Cajun Deep Foundations offers drilling piles installation and related services. Cajun Maritime focuses on marine coastal and oilfield services including construction repair and power distribution. Cajun Equipment Services manages a fleet of trucks and trailers that transport heavy and specialized loads. Chairman and owner Lane Grigsby founded the company as Cajun Contractors and Engineers in 1973.

	Annual Growth	09/10	09/11	09/12	09/13	09/14
Sales ($ mil.)	(1.4%)	–	497.4	246.9	317.1	476.4
Net income ($ mil.)	(20.2%)	–	–	18.4	9.7	11.7
Market value ($ mil.)	–	–	–	–	–	–
Employees	–	–	–	–	–	1,500

CAL DIVE INTERNATIONAL INC NBB: CDVI

2500 CityWest Boulevard, Suite 2200
Houston, TX 77042
Phone: 713 361-2600
Fax: –
Web: www.caldive.com

CEO: Quinn J Hebert
CFO: Quinn J Hebert
HR: –
FYE: December 31
Type: Public

Cal Dive International may or may not be California dreaming but its waking hours are spent beneath the waters of the world's oceans. The subsea contractor operates a fleet of 18 surface and saturation diving support vessels and a handful of shallow water pipelay vessels dedicated pipebury barges combination pipelay/derrick barges and derrick barges. It installs and maintains offshore platforms pipelines and production systems on the Outer Continental Shelf of the Gulf of Mexico as well as in the Middle East Southeast Asia Europe and elsewhere. Cal Dive also provides shallow water diving services and performs salvage operations on abandoned fields.

	Annual Growth	12/09	12/10	12/11	12/12	12/13
Sales ($ mil.)	(11.1%)	829.4	536.5	479.8	464.8	517.0
Net income ($ mil.)	–	76.6	(315.8)	(66.9)	(65.0)	(36.6)
Market value ($ mil.)	(28.2%)	736.6	552.5	219.2	168.6	195.8
Employees	(6.8%)	2,050	1,900	1,700	1,200	1,550

CAL-MAINE FOODS, INC. NMS: CALM

3320 Woodrow Wilson Avenue
Jackson, MS 39209
Phone: 601 948-6813
Fax: 601 969-0905
Web: www.calmainefoods.com

CEO: Adolphus B. (Dolph) Baker
CFO: Timothy A. Dawson
HR: Connie Smith
FYE: May 30
Type: Public

Cal-Maine Foods' more than 26 million laying hens are some of its top performers. The nation's largest shell egg producer and marketer the company sells more than 880 million dozen eggs a year. It is also one of the top suppliers of specialty shell eggs (which are Omega-3 enhanced organic and cage free) that are marketed under the Egg-Land's Best Farmhouse and 4Grain brands. Cal-Maine's operations span all phases of shell egg production: hatching chicks making feed housing hens and distributing eggs. Customers include US grocery stores (such as Publix) superstores the likes of Wal-Mart and warehouse clubs (Sam's Club) as well as foodservice distributors and makers of egg products dotting 29 states.

	Annual Growth	05/11*	06/12	06/13*	05/14	05/15
Sales ($ mil.)	13.7%	942.0	1,113.1	1,288.1	1,440.9	1,576.1
Net income ($ mil.)	27.6%	60.8	89.7	50.4	109.2	161.3
Market value ($ mil.)	18.3%	1,403.0	1,689.7	2,169.8	3,383.2	2,749.4
Employees	8.1%	2,100	2,175	2,479	2,645	2,872

*Fiscal year change

CALADRIUS BIOSCIENCES INC   NAS: CLBS

106 Allen Road, Fourth Floor
Basking Ridge, NJ 07920
Phone: 908 842-0100
Fax: –

CEO: –
CFO: Robert S Vaters
HR: David Schloss
FYE: December 31
Type: Public

Caladrius Biosciences (formerly NeoStem) has a vision and it stems from life's building blocks. Operating in the US and China the development company is working with stem cell-based therapies. Its Progenitor Cell Therapy subsidiary has facilities to collect and store stem cells manufacture cell therapy products and support clinical trials of cell-based therapies for other drug developers. The company's Amorcyte subsidiary has actual product candidates in development to repair cardiac tissues damaged during heart attack. Caladrius also enjoyed revenue from its 51% interest in Suzhou Erye a Chinese generic drug manufacturer until 2012 when it divested those operations.

	Annual Growth	12/10	12/11	12/12	12/13	12/14
Sales ($ mil.)	(28.8%)	69.8	73.7	14.3	14.7	17.9
Net income ($ mil.)	–	(23.3)	(47.1)	(53.8)	(39.0)	(54.9)
Market value ($ mil.)	27.9%	51.9	18.6	21.9	250.9	138.7
Employees	(33.4%)	924	786	97	108	182

CALATLANTIC GROUP INC   NYS: CAA

15360 Barranca Parkway
Irvine, CA 92618-2215
Phone: 949 789-1600
Fax: –

CEO: Scott D. Stowell
CFO: Jeffrey J. (Jeff) McCall
HR: –
FYE: December 31
Type: Public

CalAtlantic's foundation is built on single-family homes. Active in Arizona California the Carolinas Colorado Florida and Texas the company (formerly Standard Pacific) constructs homes that typically range in size from 1100 sq. ft. to more than 6000 sq. ft. with prices ranging from $165000 to more than $1 million. The company also builds townhomes and condominiums and buys and develops tracts of land (both alone and through joint ventures). It offers home loans to its customers in all of its markets through subsidiary Standard Pacific Mortgage and title services in Texas through SPH Title. Standard Pacific acquired The Ryland Group in mid-2015 to form the fourth-largest builder in the US then changed its name to CalAtlantic.

	Annual Growth	12/10	12/11	12/12	12/13	12/14
Sales ($ mil.)	27.4%	924.9	893.9	1,258.3	1,939.5	2,435.3
Net income ($ mil.)	–	(11.7)	(16.4)	531.4	188.7	215.9
Market value ($ mil.)	12.2%	253.1	175.0	404.5	498.0	401.2
Employees	12.7%	775	750	820	1,115	1,250

CALAMOS ASSET MANAGEMENT INC   NMS: CLMS

2020 Calamos Court
Naperville, IL 60563
Phone: 630 245-7200
Fax: –
Web: www.calamos.com

CEO: John P. Calamos
CFO: Nimish S. Bhatt
HR: –
FYE: December 31
Type: Public

Calamos Asset Management wants to make the most of your assets. Through its subsidiaries the company provides money management and investment advice to institutional and individual investors. The firm manages more than 30 mutual funds closed-end funds separately managed portfolios private funds exchange-traded funds and UCITS funds representing a range of investment strategies and risk levels. Calamos has nearly $25 billion of assets under management with most of it invested in US and global equities though it also employs fixed income convertible and alternative investment strategies. The firm mainly distributes its products through large broker-dealers.

	Annual Growth	12/10	12/11	12/12	12/13	12/14
Sales ($ mil.)	(6.3%)	326.0	352.3	326.7	269.1	251.0
Net income ($ mil.)	(9.2%)	19.9	15.9	18.2	18.6	13.5
Market value ($ mil.)	(1.2%)	250.9	224.2	189.4	212.2	238.7
Employees	3.4%	318	341	360	361	363

CALAVO GROWERS, INC.   NMS: CVGW

1141-A Cummings Road
Santa Paula, CA 93060
Phone: 805 525-1245
Fax: 805 921-3223
Web: www.calavo.com

CEO: Lecil E. (Lee) Cole
CFO: B. John Lindeman
HR: –
FYE: October 31
Type: Public

Calavo (a combination of "California" and "avocado") began as a growers' marketing cooperative founded in 1924 in order to transform the exotic hobby crop avocados into a culinary staple. Mission accomplished. Since the avocado has become if not a staple a regular in US supermarket shopping carts. Calavo procures and processes avocados papaya pineapple tomatoes and other fresh fruits grown mainly in California but the company also uses fruit from Chile Peru and Mexico. The products are then distributed to retail food outlets food service operators and produce wholesalers throughout the world.

	Annual Growth	10/11	10/12	10/13	10/14	10/15
Sales ($ mil.)	13.2%	522.5	551.1	691.5	782.5	856.8
Net income ($ mil.)	25.2%	11.1	17.1	17.3	0.1	27.2
Market value ($ mil.)	22.8%	392.4	410.4	516.1	843.8	893.7
Employees	8.1%	1,509	1,531	1,848	1,987	2,064

CALAMP CORP   NMS: CAMP

1401 N. Rice Avenue
Oxnard, CA 93030
Phone: 805 987-9000
Fax: –
Web: www.calamp.com

CEO: Michael J. Burdiek
CFO: Richard K. (Rick) Vitelle
HR: –
FYE: February 28
Type: Public

CalAmp adds a little boost even to the weakest of TV programs. The former military supplier makes microwave amplification and conversion components that improve reception in satellite television wireless cable and wireless broadband access systems. Its products include antennas amplifiers and transceivers and receivers for broadband wireless transmission. CalAmp's wireless datacom segment provides wireless network and mobile resource management products for state and local governments and industrial utility and transportation companies. The company's largest customer EchoStar accounted for 21% of consolidated annual sales in fiscal 2014.

	Annual Growth	02/11	02/12	02/13	02/14	02/15
Sales ($ mil.)	21.7%	114.3	138.7	180.6	235.9	250.6
Net income ($ mil.)	–	(3.3)	5.2	44.6	11.8	16.5
Market value ($ mil.)	58.3%	110.5	155.8	396.7	1,160.6	693.7
Employees	4.8%	440	370	380	490	530

CALCOT LTD.

1900 E BRUNDAGE LN
BAKERSFIELD, CA 933072789
Phone: 661-327-5961
Fax: –
Web: www.calcot.com

CEO: Jarral T Neeper
CFO: Roxanne F. Wang
HR: –
FYE: August 31
Type: Private

With a crop of nearly 1400 members in Arizona California New Mexico and Texas Calcot is one of the top cotton-marketing cooperatives in the US. Members of the co-op which started in 1927 primarily grow premium-grade Far Western cottons including California Upland Pima and San Joaquin Acala varieties. The company operates six warehousing locations and sells between 1 million and 2 million bales of cotton per year. Approximately 85% of Calcot's annual harvest is exported to textile mills worldwide mostly in Pacific Rim countries. Calcot and three other major US co-ops together comprise Amcot a worldwide cotton marketer.

	Annual Growth	08/10	08/11	08/12	08/13	08/14
Sales ($ mil.)	(24.4%)	–	399.6	306.2	195.7	172.7
Net income ($ mil.)	(21.9%)	–	–	5.3	1.6	3.2
Market value ($ mil.)	–	–	–	–	–	–
Employees	–	–	–	–	–	150

CALENDAR HOLDINGS LLC

6411 Burleson Rd.
Austin TX 78744
Phone: 512-386-7220
Fax: 512-369-6192
Web: www.calendarholdings.com

CEO: Marc Winkelman
CFO: Jim Hull
HR: –
FYE: January 31
Type: Private

During the holiday season Calendar Holdings (aka Calendar Club) transforms empty retail space into shops under the banners Go! Calendar Go! Games and Go! Toys. The company's temporary stores range in size from kiosks to some 6000 sq. ft. Founded in 1993 with about 60 stores Calendar Club now operates more than 1200 locations in the US. The company also sells merchandise year-round on its websites including Calendars.com and DogBreedStore.com. Bookseller Barnes & Noble sold its majority stake in Calendar Club to CEO Marc Winkelman and the firm's management in 2009 for $7 million.

CALIBRE SYSTEMS INC.

6354 WALKER LN STE 300
ALEXANDRIA, VA 223103252
Phone: 703-797-8500
Fax: –
Web: www.calibresys.com

CEO: –
CFO: John C Mutarelli
HR: Laura Weil
FYE: February 28
Type: Private

When it comes to information technology CALIBRE aims to please. The employee-owned company provides information technology and management services to government and commercial clients in the US. It specializes in data analytics modeling and simulation financial and cost management land management logistics and strategic planning among other areas. To expand its capabilities the company partners with a host of technology firms consulting firms educational institutions and other enterprises including AT&T IBM KPMG and George Mason University. CALIBRE operates from a handful of US offices as well as on-site at customer facilities.

	Annual Growth	02/06	02/07	02/08	02/09	02/11
Sales ($ mil.)	(46.6%)	–	–	1,037.6	109.0	157.9
Net income ($ mil.)	757.3%	–	–	0.0	6.2	10.3
Market value ($ mil.)	–	–	–	–	–	–
Employees	–	–	–	–	–	682

CALERES INC
NYS: CAL

8300 Maryland Avenue
St. Louis, MO 63105
Phone: 314 854-4000
Fax: –
Web: www.brownshoe.com

CEO: Diane M. Sullivan
CFO: Kenneth H. (Ken) Hannah
HR: –
FYE: January 31
Type: Public

There's no business like shoe business for Caleres (formerly Brown Shoe Company). Caleres operates 1038 value-priced family footwear stores under the Famous Footwear banner in the US and Guam 169 Naturalizer stores in the US and Canada and a growing number of shoe stores in China. The company also sells shoes online and licenses Dr. Scholl's and Disney brand footwear. It distributes footwear worldwide through more than 2500 retailers including independent chain (DSW) department stores (Nordstrom) catalogs and online retailers. Caleres is opening new stores closing underperforming ones and updating styles to appeal to younger bipeds. The company has a growing footprint in China.

	Annual Growth	01/11	01/12*	02/13	02/14*	01/15
Sales ($ mil.)	0.7%	2,504.1	2,582.8	2,598.1	2,513.1	2,571.7
Net income ($ mil.)	22.1%	37.2	24.6	27.5	38.1	82.9
Market value ($ mil.)	22.2%	557.0	424.4	750.8	1,036.0	1,242.1
Employees	(4.8%)	13,400	15,300	14,100	11,200	11,000

*Fiscal year change

CALIENT NETWORKS INC.

2665 N. 1st St. Ste. 204
San Jose CA 95134
Phone: 408-232-6400
Fax: 408-232-6422
Web: www.calient.net

CEO: Atiq Raza
CFO: Jag Setlur
HR: –
FYE: December 31
Type: Private

All light's all right with Calient Networks. The company designs switches used to direct signals in fiber-optic communications networks. Unlike conventional switches that convert light to electrical impulses and back again Calient's DiamondWave switches use MEMS (micro-electromechanical system) technology that redirects optical transmissions using tiny movable mirrors. Its fiber cross-connect systems are used to manage and troubleshoot fiber networks. The company targets telecom service carriers and ISPs. Founded in 1999 Calient has attracted investments from venture capital firms including Enterprise Partners and TeleSoft Partners as well as networking companies such as Juniper Networks and Tellabs.

CALGON CARBON CORP.
NYS: CCC

3000 GSK Drive, Moon Township
Pittsburgh, PA 15108
Phone: 412 787-6700
Fax: 412 787-6676
Web: www.calgoncarbon.com

CEO: Randall S. (Randy) Dearth
CFO: Stevan R. Schott
HR: –
FYE: December 31
Type: Public

Calgon wants impurities in water and air to be gone. Calgon Carbon makes activated carbons and purification systems and offers purification separation and concentration services to industrial process and environmental markets. It is a global leader in activated carbon ballast water treatment ultraviolet light disinfection and advanced ion-exchange technologies used in the treatment of drinking water wastewater ballast water air emissions and manufacturing processes. Calgon Carbon offers carbon technologies used in more than 700 discrete market applications including air drinking water foods and pharmaceuticals purification and the removal of mercury emissions from coal-powered electrical plants.

	Annual Growth	12/10	12/11	12/12	12/13	12/14
Sales ($ mil.)	3.6%	482.3	541.5	562.3	547.9	555.1
Net income ($ mil.)	9.1%	34.9	39.2	23.3	45.7	49.4
Market value ($ mil.)	8.3%	745.0	774.1	698.7	1,013.5	1,023.9
Employees	0.6%	1,070	1,145	1,231	1,112	1,096

CALIFORNIA BANK & TRUST

11622 El Camino Real Ste. 200
San Diego CA 92130
Phone: 858-793-7400
Fax: 858-793-7438
Web: www.calbanktrust.com

CEO: –
CFO: –
HR: –
FYE: December 31
Type: Subsidiary

California Bank & Trust (CB&T) is the second-largest subsidiary of mulitbank holding company Zions Bancorporation (behind flagship affiliate Zions Bank). CB&T operates more than 100 branches in greater Los Angeles Orange County San Diego Northern California and the Inland Empire. It serves business and consumer clients offering standard services such as checking and savings accounts investments and wealth management residential and commercial mortgages credit cards personal loans and business loans including Small Business Administration loans. Specialized services for businesses include cash management lines of credit merchant services and international banking.

CALIFORNIA COASTAL COMMUNITIES INC.

6 Executive Circle Ste. 250
Irvine CA 92614
Phone: 949-250-7700
Fax: 949-250-7705
Web: www.californiacoastalcommunities.com

CEO: Raymond J Pacini
CFO: Sandra G Sciutto
HR: –
FYE: December 31
Type: Private

The tide is turning for California Coastal Communities. Through operating subsidiaries Hearthside Homes and Signal Landmark the company builds homes and develops residential communities in Southern California. Long wrapped up in a battle over land development rights California Coastal Communities has begun development of its Brightwater project some 215 acres (about half of which is undevelopable land) situated near important wetlands in Bolsa Chica the last undeveloped strip of coastal property in Orange County. Besides the controversial parcels the company has homebuilding operations in Los Angeles County. California Coastal Communities emerged from Chapter 11 bankruptcy in March 2011.

CALIFORNIA COMMUNITY FOUNDATION

221 S FIGUEROA ST STE 400
LOS ANGELES, CA 900123760
Phone: 213-413-4130
Fax: –
Web: www.calfund.org

CEO: Antonia Hernandez
CFO: Steve Cobb
HR: –
FYE: June 30
Type: Private

California Community Foundation supports not-for-profit organizations and public institutions in the Los Angeles area. The organization performs its function by offering funding for health and human services affordable housing early childhood education and community arts and culture. The 24th Street Theatre Antelope Valley Hospital and Community Arts Partnership are among the organizations to have received the foundation's grant funding. In times of emergency it has also pitched in to help groups in other areas. California Community Foundation was founded in 1915.

	Annual Growth	06/09	06/10	06/11	06/12	06/13
Assets ($ mil.)	5.5%	–	1,120.5	1,242.4	1,092.0	1,315.9
Net income ($ mil.)	(7.5%)	–	–	139.6	70.7	119.5
Market value ($ mil.)	–	–	–	–	–	–
Employees	–	–	–	–	–	60

CALIFORNIA DAIRIES INC.

2000 N. Plaza Dr.
Visalia CA 93291
Phone: 559-625-2200
Fax: 559-625-5433
Web: www.californiadairies.com

CEO: Andrei Mikhalevsky
CFO: David Camp
HR: Lowell Richardson
FYE: April 30
Type: Private - Cooperativ

Herding dairies together to gain "ag"-gregate strength makes California Dairies the largest dairy processing cooperative in the US. Its 470 member/farmers provide the co-op with more than 17 billion pounds of milk a year. Its plants process milk into mainly butter but also cheese and powdered milk for commercial and consumer use. The co-op's subsidiaries are Challenge Dairy Products (retail food service and ingredient products) and Los Banos Foods (cheddar cheese for food manufacturers). California Dairies also owns majority control of DairyAmerica which markets about 50% of all the milk powder produced in the US as well as other dairy products. The co-op exports to 50-plus countries worldwide.

CALIFORNIA FIRST NATIONAL BANCORP

NMS: CFNB

28 Executive Park
Irvine, CA 92614
Phone: 949 255-0500
Fax: –
Web: www.calfirstbancorp.com

CEO: Patrick E. Paddon
CFO: S Leslie Jewett
HR: Barbara Bumbil
FYE: June 30
Type: Public

California First National Bancorp (CFNB) can't decide if it wants to be a leasing company or a bank. Traditionally it's been mostly a leasing company. Its California First Leasing (CalFirst Leasing) subsidiary leases equipment for a wide variety of industries with nearly 60% of leases for oil and gas production equipment computers and software. Other leases include retail point-of-sale systems office furniture and manufacturing telecommunications and medical equipment. The bank holding company also operates California First National Bank (CalFirst Bank) a branchless FDIC-insured retail bank that conducts business mainly over the Internet but also by mail and phone. CEO Patrick Paddon owns 63% of CFNB.

	Annual Growth	06/11	06/12	06/13	06/14	06/15
Assets ($ mil.)	8.7%	524.4	486.2	558.9	579.6	731.1
Net income ($ mil.)	(4.5%)	10.9	8.9	7.4	7.1	9.1
Market value ($ mil.)	(3.1%)	160.2	164.1	172.6	153.6	141.1
Employees	(8.7%)	154	149	102	113	107

CALIFORNIA INDEPENDENT SYSTEM OPERATOR CORPORATION

250 OUTCROPPING WAY
FOLSOM, CA 956308773
Phone: 916-351-4400
Fax: –
Web: www.caiso.com

CEO: Stephen Berberich
CFO: William J Regan
HR: –
FYE: December 31
Type: Private

The California Independent System Operator (California ISO) manages a 25627-mile power transmission system (about 80% of California's power grid) balancing wholesale supply to meet retail demand. The enterprise directs the flow of electricity along long-distance high-voltage power lines that connect California with neighboring states as well as with Mexico and Canada. It manages the transmission lines and supervises maintenance but the transmission systems are owned and maintained by individual utilities. The not-for-profit public benefit corporation also acts as a transmission planner.

	Annual Growth	12/03	12/04	12/05	12/06	12/07
Sales ($ mil.)	23.5%	–	–	131.6	189.9	200.6
Net income ($ mil.)	34621.9%	–	–	0.0	41.3	46.2
Market value ($ mil.)	–	–	–	–	–	–
Employees	–	–	–	–	–	530

CALIFORNIA PHYSICIANS' SERVICE

50 Beale St.
San Francisco CA 94105-1808
Phone: 415-229-5000
Fax: 415-229-5070
Web: www.blueshieldca.com

CEO: Bruce Bodoken
CFO: Heidi Kunz
HR: –
FYE: December 31
Type: Private - Not-for-Pr

California Physicians' Service which operates as Blue Shield of California provides health insurance products and related services to some 3.4 million members in the state of California. The not-for-profit mutual organization's health plans include HMO PPO dental and Medicaid or Medicare supplemental plans for individuals families and employer groups. Accidental death and dismemberment executive medical reimbursement life insurance vision and short-term health plans are provided by the company's Blue Shield of California Life & Health Insurance subsidiary. Blue Shield of California was established in 1939 and is an independent Blue Cross and Blue Shield Association member.

CALIFORNIA PIZZA KITCHEN INC.

6053 W. Century Blvd. 11th Fl.
Los Angeles CA 90045-6438
Phone: 310-342-5000
Fax: 310-342-4640
Web: www.cpk.com

CEO: Gerard Johan Hart
CFO: Susan M Collyns
HR: Julie Carruthers
FYE: December 31
Type: Private

This company's cookeries are putting a West Coast twist on an old favorite. California Pizza Kitchen (CPK) operates a chain of about 265 casual-dining restaurants that specialize in gourmet pizzas featuring unique topping combinations including duck barbecued chicken and grilled shrimp. The chain also serves Neapolitan pizzas from Italy as well as American-style pies. CPK rounds out its menu with pastas soups salads and desserts. The restaurants are found in more than 30 states and about a dozen other countries; more than 200 of the locations are company-owned. Private equity firm Golden Gate Capital acquired CPK in 2011.

CALIFORNIA PRODUCTS CORPORATION

150 Dascomb Rd.
Andover MA 01810
Phone: 978-623-9980
Fax: 978-623-9960
Web: www.calprocorp.com

CEO: Peter Longo
CFO: Steven McMenamin
HR: Larry Tegtmeyer
FYE: November 30
Type: Private

Don't expect nominal consistency from California Products; no matter its name the company is based in New England. Through its California Paints division the company makes paints and coatings for home and office uses ceiling whites and enamels for hard wall interiors and finishes and primers. Its Plexipave Sport Surfacing Systems and DecoSystems divisions make tennis track and other sport surfaces and subsidiary Fiberlock Technologies manufactures environmental containment products. Employees are majority shareholders in the company whose name dates back to its founding as a subsidiary of a West Coast stucco manufacturer. In 2007 private equity behemoth Apollo Management took a stake in the company.

CALIFORNIA PUBLIC EMPLOYEES' RETIREMENT SYSTEM

Lincoln Plaza 400 Q St.
Sacramento CA 95811
Phone: 916-795-3829
Fax: 916-795-4001
Web: www.calpers.ca.gov

CEO: Anne Stausboll
CFO: –
HR: –
FYE: June 30
Type: Government-owned

California's public-sector retirees already have a place in the sun; CalPERS gives them the money to enjoy it. CalPERS is the California Public Employees' Retirement System the largest public pension system in the US. It manages retirement and health plans for some 1.6 million beneficiaries (employees retirees and their dependents) from more than 3000 public state employers. Most of CalPERS' revenue comes from its enormous investment program: It has interests in US and foreign securities oil and energy real estate and even hedge funds and venture capital. Even though its beneficiaries are current or former employees of the Golden State CalPERS brings its influence to bear in all 50 states and beyond.

CALIFORNIA STEEL INDUSTRIES INC.

14000 San Bernardino Ave.
Fontana CA 92335
Phone: 909-350-6300
Fax: 909-350-6398
Web: www.californiasteel.com

CEO: Toshiyuki Tamai
CFO: –
HR: –
FYE: December 31
Type: Joint Venture

California Steel Industries (CSI) doesn't use forensic evidence but its work does involve a steel slab. The company uses steel slab produced by third parties to manufacture steel products such as hot-rolled and cold-rolled steel galvanized coils and sheets and electric resistance weld (ERW) pipe. Its customers include aftermarket automotive manufacturers oil and gas producers roofing makers tubing manufacturers and building suppliers. CSI serves the western region of the US. The company operates slitting shearing coating and single-billing services for third parties. Japan's JFE Holdings and Brazilian iron ore miner Vale SA each own 50% of CSI.

CALIFORNIA WATER SERVICE GROUP (DE)

NYS: CWT

1720 North First Street
San Jose, CA 95112
Phone: 408 367-8200
Fax: –
Web: www.calwatergroup.com

CEO: Martin A Kropelnicki
CFO: Thomas F Smegal III
HR: Ronald D Webb
FYE: December 31
Type: Public

A big fish in California's water industry pond California Water Service Group is in the swim in three other states as well. The company's main subsidiary regulated utility California Water Service Company (Cal Water) keeps water flowing for 473100 customers in California. California Water Service Group's other water utility subsidiaries include Washington Water (15800 customers) New Mexico Water (7600 water and wastewater customers) and Hawaii Water (4200 customers). The company's CWS Utility Services unit contracts to provide water system operation meter reading and billing services. All told California Water Service Group provides services to about 2 million people in 100 communities.

	Annual Growth	12/10	12/11	12/12	12/13	12/14
Sales ($ mil.)	6.7%	460.4	501.8	560.0	584.1	597.5
Net income ($ mil.)	10.8%	37.7	37.7	48.8	47.3	56.7
Market value ($ mil.)	(9.9%)	1,781.7	872.9	877.2	1,102.9	1,176.5
Employees	(0.5%)	1,127	1,132	1,131	1,125	1,105

CALIFORNIA WELLNESS FOUNDATION

6320 CANOGA AVE STE 1700
WOODLAND HILLS, CA 913672565
Phone: 818-702-1900
Fax: –
Web: www.calwellness.org

CEO: Judy Belk
CFO: Margaret W Minnich
HR: –
FYE: December 31
Type: Private

Health is wealth for The California Wellness Foundation. Its primary mission is to improve the health of the people of California. The foundation extends grants for health promotion wellness education and disease prevention. It focuses on underserved populations including such groups as the poor minority groups and rural residents. On average the foundation grants about $40 million a year toward programs in such areas as environmental health healthy aging mental health teen pregnancy prevention violence prevention and women's health. The California Wellness Foundation was established in 1992 when Health Net (a health maintenance organization) converted to for-profit status.

	Annual Growth	12/08	12/09	12/10	12/11	12/12
Assets ($ mil.)	0.8%	–	828.1	882.1	794.3	848.0
Net income ($ mil.)	2.6%	–	–	51.2	(1.0)	53.8
Market value ($ mil.)	–	–	–	–	–	–
Employees	–	–	–	–	–	41

CALIPER LIFE SCIENCES INC.

68 Elm St.
Hopkinton MA 01748
Phone: 508-435-9500
Fax: 508-435-3439
Web: www.caliperls.com

CEO: E Kevin Hrusovsky
CFO: Peter F McAree
HR: –
FYE: December 31
Type: Subsidiary

Caliper Life Sciences helps pharmaceutical and biotech researchers avoid teeny-tiny spills with its microscopic sample-analysis technologies. Operating as Caliper a PerkinElmer company the firm's research products include miniaturized automation systems for extracting and analyzing biological samples and a line of liquid handling systems which measure and filter liquids robotically. The company also makes IVIS imaging systems which allow researchers to examine molecular interactions in vivo (or inside an organism) as well as related software and accessories. In addition Caliper Life Sciences provides contract research and drug development services. The company is a subsidiary of scientific equipment maker PerkinElmer.

CALIX INC
NYS: CALX

1035 N. McDowell Blvd.
Petaluma, CA 94954
Phone: 707 766-3000
Fax: –
Web: www.calix.com

CEO: Carl Russo
CFO: William Atkins
HR: –
FYE: December 31
Type: Public

With Calix's access equipment your bandwidth runneth over. Calix (Latin for "cup") markets broadband access equipment for communications service providers (CSPs). Its products increase the capacity of fiber-optic and copper lines to deliver next-generation telecommunications services such as Internet protocol television (IPTV) and VoIP as well as mobile broadband and high-speed DSL Internet. The company also supplies Web-based network management software that handles provisioning testing and troubleshooting. In 2014 more than 19 million ports of its Unified Access portfolio have been deployed at a growing number of CSPs worldwide whose networks serve more than 100 million subscriber lines.

	Annual Growth	12/10	12/11	12/12	12/13	12/14
Sales ($ mil.)	8.7%	287.0	344.7	330.2	382.6	401.2
Net income ($ mil.)	–	(18.6)	(52.6)	(28.3)	(17.3)	(20.8)
Market value ($ mil.)	(12.3%)	872.5	334.0	397.0	497.7	517.3
Employees	13.0%	479	625	714	738	782

CALL NOW INC.
OTC: CLNWE

1 Retama Pkwy.
Selma TX 78154
Phone: 210-651-7145
Fax: 781-255-7209
Web: www.gryphonnetworks.com

CEO: Thomas R Johnson
CFO: –
HR: –
FYE: December 31
Type: Public

Call Now operates the Retama Park horse racing facility in Selma Texas through its 80%-owned subsidiary Retama Entertainment Group. The track which opened in 1995 offers both live and simulcast thoroughbred racing. Call Now purchased rights to operate the racetrack a year later (the actual land and facility are owned by Retama Development Corporation which is a division of the city of Selma). Retama Park's grandstand features a dining room and sports bar. Private club facilities also are on site.

CALLAWAY GOLF CO. (DE)
NYS: ELY

2180 Rutherford Road
Carlsbad, CA 92008
Phone: 760 931-1771
Fax: –
Web: www.callawaygolf.com

CEO: Oliver G. (Chip) Brewer
CFO: Robert K. Julian
HR: –
FYE: December 31
Type: Public

Big Bertha keeps Callaway Golf swinging. With its flagship driver named after a WWI cannon Callaway makes premium-priced golf clubs that are popular with amateurs and professionals alike. The company's other drivers as well as its fairway woods irons wedges hybrids and putters are sold under the Callaway and Odyssey names. It also makes Callaway golf balls golf bags and uPro-branded GPS range finders. At the top of the golf market Callaway designs apparel and shoes and licenses its name for travel gear eyewear and other golf accessories. Its products are sold through its websites and in more than 100 countries by golf pro shops sporting goods retailers and mass merchants.

	Annual Growth	12/10	12/11	12/12	12/13	12/14
Sales ($ mil.)	(2.2%)	967.7	886.5	834.1	842.8	886.9
Net income ($ mil.)	–	(18.8)	(171.8)	(122.9)	(18.9)	16.0
Market value ($ mil.)	(1.2%)	626.2	429.1	504.4	654.1	597.5
Employees	(5.1%)	2,100	2,100	1,500	1,700	1,700

CALLIDUS SOFTWARE INC
NMS: CALD

4140 Dublin Boulevard, Suite 400
Dublin, CA 94568
Phone: 925 251-2200
Fax: 925 251-0525
Web: www.calliduscloud.com

CEO: Leslie J. Stretch
CFO: Bob L. Corey
HR: –
FYE: December 31
Type: Public

Callidus takes good care of office overachievers. The company provides enterprise incentive management software for managing employee compensation programs including salaries options bonuses and sales commissions. Its applications grouped under the sobriquet Lead to Money also help businesses align incentive programs with strategy and profit goals. The company's products are sold primarily under the CallidusCloud brand and include additional tools for managing sales hiring coaching training marketing data analysis social network marketing search engine optimization and Web-based compensation reporting. Callidus primarily serves the financial services insurance telecom pharmaceutical and IT industries in the US.

	Annual Growth	12/10	12/11	12/12	12/13	12/14
Sales ($ mil.)	17.8%	70.9	83.8	95.0	112.3	136.6
Net income ($ mil.)	–	(12.7)	(16.1)	(27.7)	(21.4)	(11.6)
Market value ($ mil.)	34.1%	247.2	314.2	222.2	672.0	799.3
Employees	29.9%	260	379	613	612	741

CALLON PETROLEUM CO. (DE)
NYS: CPE

200 North Canal Street
Natchez, MS 39120
Phone: 601 442-1601
Fax: –
Web: www.callon.com

CEO: Fred L. Callon
CFO: Joseph Gatto
HR: –
FYE: December 31
Type: Public

Callon Petroleum can call on new technologies to find old petroleum resources employing computer-aided techniques such as enhanced 3-D surveys and horizontal drilling to explore and develop oil and gas properties. It also focuses on acquiring properties. Once a major offshore player the firm's holdings are now primarily onshore in Texas. In 2012 Callon's estimated proved reserves stood at 14.1 million barrels of oil equivalent. About 68% of Callon's oil and gas reserves are located onshore in the Permian Basin; 77% of its proved reserve volumes are in the form of crude oil which also accounts for the bulk of its the company's revenues.

	Annual Growth	12/10	12/11	12/12	12/13	12/14
Sales ($ mil.)	14.0%	89.9	127.6	110.7	102.6	151.9
Net income ($ mil.)	45.7%	8.4	104.1	2.7	4.3	37.8
Market value ($ mil.)	(2.0%)	326.9	274.5	259.6	360.6	301.0
Employees	8.4%	79	88	87	94	109

CALLOWAY'S NURSERY INC.
PINK SHEETS: CLWY

4200 Airport Fwy. Ste. 200
Fort Worth TX 76117-6200
Phone: 817-222-1122
Fax: 817-302-0031
Web: www.calloways.com

CEO: James C Estill
CFO: Dan Reynolds
HR: –
FYE: December 31
Type: Public

Calloway's Nursery babies its customers with green-thumb know-how — about half of its employees are certified nursery professionals. The company owns and operates about 20 nurseries under the Calloway's name in the Dallas/Fort Worth area and San Antonio and under the Cornelius Nurseries banner in Houston. The company also sells plants online. Offerings include trees shrubs flowers landscaping materials soil fertilizer and Christmas goods. Christmas merchandise includes trees poinsettias wreaths and garlands.

CALMARE THERAPEUTICS INC
NBB: CTTC

1375 Kings Highway East, Suite 400
Fairfield, CT 06824
Phone: 203 368-6044
Fax: –
Web: www.calmaretherapeutics.com

CEO: Conrad F. Mir
CFO: Thomas P. Richtarich
HR: –
FYE: December 31
Type: Public

It doesn't matter how great your invention is if you can't get it to market — that's where Competitive Technologies (CTT) comes in. The company helps individuals corporations government agencies and universities commercialize their inventions. Clients such as Sony and the University of Illinois have used CTT's services which include feasibility and marketability evaluations as well as application for and enforcement of patents. CTT focuses on inventions in life and physical sciences as well as digital technologies. The company established in 1971 also represents companies seeking to license technologies for commercial purposes.

	Annual Growth	12/10	12/11	12/12	12/13	12/14
Sales ($ mil.)	57.8%	0.2	3.4	1.1	0.8	1.2
Net income ($ mil.)	–	(2.4)	(3.6)	(3.0)	(2.7)	(3.4)
Market value ($ mil.)	(41.3%)	33.7	32.6	16.6	8.3	4.0
Employees	6.3%	–	5	5	5	6

CALNET INC.

12359 SUNRISE VALLEY DR # 270
RESTON, VA 20191-3462
Phone: 703-547-6800
Fax: –
Web: www.calnet.com

CEO: –
CFO: –
HR: –
FYE: December 31
Type: Private

CALNET provides information technology (IT) consulting and services for businesses and public sector agencies. The company's IT services include application development and testing; e-commerce consulting; network management and security; and technical staffing. Industries served include technology telecommunications and financial services. In addition CALNET provides intelligence analysis including linguist services in a variety of languages for the US military. Customers have included the Food and Drug Administration Cisco Systems and Intel. The company has offices in Reston Virginia and San Diego. CALNET was founded in 1989 by president Kaleem Shah.

	Annual Growth	12/07	12/08	12/10	12/11	12/12
Sales ($ mil.)	(7.3%)	–	83.7	0.0	82.7	61.7
Net income ($ mil.)	–	–	(0.4)	0.0	14.4	11.7
Market value ($ mil.)	–	–	–	–	–	–
Employees	–	–	–	–	–	362

CALPINE CORP
NYS: CPN

717 Texas Avenue, Suite 1000
Houston, TX 77002
Phone: 713 830-2000
Fax: –
Web: www.calpine.com

CEO: John B. (Thad) Hill
CFO: Zamir Rauf
HR: Annie Tighe
FYE: December 31
Type: Public

Calpine may get hot but it also knows how to blow off some steam. In 2014 the independent power producer and marketer controlled 27000 MW of generating capacity (and 309 MW under construction) through interests in 88 primarily natural gas-fired power plants in 18 US states and Canada. This fleet also includes 15 geothermal power plants in California. Calpine the leading geothermal power producer in North America owns 725 MW of capacity at the largest geothermal facility in the US (the Geysers in northern California) and which accounts for 40% of the country's geothermal energy. The company has major presence in the wholesale power markets in California the Mid-Atlantic and Texas.

	Annual Growth	12/11	12/12	12/13	12/14	12/15
Sales ($ mil.)	(1.2%)	6,800.0	5,478.0	6,301.0	8,030.0	6,472.0
Net income ($ mil.)	–	(190.0)	199.0	14.0	946.0	235.0
Market value ($ mil.)	(3.0%)	5,824.3	6,466.3	6,958.5	7,892.9	5,160.9
Employees	1.3%	2,101	2,151	2,157	2,052	2,209

CALPORTLAND COMPANY

2025 E. Financial Way Ste. 200
Glendora CA 91741-4692
Phone: 626-852-6200
Fax: 317-295-9434
Web: www.graindealers.com

CEO: Allen Hamblen
CFO: James A Wendoll
HR: –
FYE: March 31
Type: Subsidiary

CalPortland supplies building materials such as ready-mix concrete aggregates (sand gravel and rock products) asphalt and cement. It also offers precast building materials and performs road construction and earth moving services for clients such as CalTrans. CalPortland is active in western US and Canada; its operations include more than 60 ready-mix concrete plants in addition to about 25 aggregate yards and plants more than a dozen cement plants and transfer terminals three asphalt plants and five building materials distribution facilities in Alaska Arizona California Idaho Nevada Oregon and Washington as well as Alberta and British Columbia. CalPortland is owned by Taiheiyo Cement.

CALUMET SPECIALTY PRODUCT PARTNERS LP
NMS: CLMT

2780 Waterfront Parkway East Drive, Suite 200
Indianapolis, IN 46214
Phone: 317 328-5660
Fax: –
Web: www.calumetspecialty.com

CEO: Timothy Go
CFO: R. Patrick Murray
HR: David Burford
FYE: December 31
Type: Public

Specialty hydrocarbon producer Calumet Specialty Products Partners operates in three business segments: specialty products fuel products and oilfield services. The specialty products unit the company's largest processes crude oil into lubricating oils solvents waxes and other petroleum products. It sells these items to industrial customers who use them in the manufacture of basic automotive consumer and industrial goods. The fuel products unit processes oil into unleaded gasoline diesel fuel and jet fuel. Calumet also produces asphalt. In terms of its customer base in 2014 the company had 5400 specialty products accounts and 700 fuel products accounts.

	Annual Growth	12/10	12/11	12/12	12/13	12/14
Sales ($ mil.)	27.5%	2,190.8	3,134.9	4,657.3	5,421.4	5,791.1
Net income ($ mil.)	–	16.7	43.0	205.7	3.5	(112.2)
Market value ($ mil.)	1.3%	1,509.5	1,428.7	2,153.7	1,844.6	1,588.2
Employees	35.6%	650	920	1,250	1,420	2,200

CALVARY HOSPITAL INC.

1740 EASTCHESTER RD
BRONX, NY 104612392
Phone: 718-518-2000
Fax: –
Web: www.calvaryhospital.org

CEO: Frank A Calamari
CFO: –
HR: –
FYE: December 31
Type: Private

Calvary Hospital rallies its doctors and nurses around advanced cancer patients hoping to keep them as comfortable as possible. The facility specializes in palliative care the practice of relieving the pain and symptoms associated with an illness (not curing the illness itself). Calvary Hospital offers both inpatient and outpatient services to adult patients in the advanced stages of cancer through two campuses; the main hospital has about 200 beds and a satellite location in Brooklyn has about 25 beds. In addition the hospital operates home health and hospice agencies and provides case management and family support services. The not-for-profit organization is sponsored by the Archdiocese of New York.

	Annual Growth	12/09	12/10	12/11	12/12	12/13
Sales ($ mil.)	(0.4%)	–	–	103.2	103.9	102.3
Net income ($ mil.)	–	–	–	(2.5)	(22.0)	13.1
Market value ($ mil.)	–	–	–	–	–	–
Employees	–	–	–	–	–	900

CALVERT COMPANY INC.

218 N V ST
VANCOUVER, WA 986617701
Phone: 360-693-0971
Fax: –
Web: www.calvert.com

CEO: –
CFO: –
HR: –
FYE: December 31
Type: Private

Strange as it may sound this company makes glulams in Washougal. Calvert manufactures and supplies glulams or pre-shaped glued-laminated lumber products for use in decorative construction work including arches beams bridges domes trusses s-curves columns and even playground equipment. It uses species such as Douglas fir Alaska yellow cedar redwood western red cedar spruce pine fir and more. The company manufactures glulams for export to Asia Canada and the Middle East and provides container loading at its plants in Vancouver and Washougal Washington. Calvert Company was founded by Ray Calvert and others in 1947.

	Annual Growth	12/04	12/05	12/06	12/07	12/08
Sales ($ mil.)	–	–	–	0.0	18.8	12.5
Net income ($ mil.)	–	–	–	0.0	0.9	0.2
Market value ($ mil.)	–	–	–	–	–	–
Employees	–	–	–	–	–	60

CALVERT MEMORIAL HOSPITAL OF CALVERT COUNTY

100 HOSPITAL RD
PRINCE FREDERICK, MD 206784017
Phone: 410-535-4000
Fax: –
Web: www.calvertmemorialhospital.net

CEO: –
CFO: Kirk Blandford
HR: Carrie Forrest
FYE: June 30
Type: Private

Calvert Memorial Hospital provides health care to Chesapeake Bay area residents in Southern Maryland. The medical facility along with Dunkirk Medical Center Solomons Medical Center and a handful of specialty centers and clinics comprise Calvert Health System. In addition to acute care Calvert Memorial Hospital and its affiliates offer same-day surgery outpatient behavioral health care and diagnostic imaging. They also provide such alternative therapies as acupuncture massage and hypnotherapy. For long-term and critical care Calvert Memorial Hospital partners with area facilities including Washington Hospital Center Children's National Medical Center Johns Hopkins and University of Maryland.

	Annual Growth	06/07	06/08	06/09	06/10	06/11
Sales ($ mil.)	–	–	–	0.0	116.8	125.6
Net income ($ mil.)	958.2%	–	–	0.0	(0.1)	1.8
Market value ($ mil.)	–	–	–	–	–	–
Employees	–	–	–	–	–	850

CALYPSO TECHNOLOGY INC.

595 Market St. Ste. 1800
San Francisco CA 94105
Phone: 415-817-2400
Fax: 415-284-1222
Web: www.calypso.com

CEO: Charles Marston
CFO: Kirk Inglis
HR: –
FYE: December 31
Type: Private

Calypso Technology moves not to the tropical rhythms of the Caribbean but to the insistent beat of Wall Street and world financial markets. The company markets an integrated software system used to trade bonds currencies derivatives stocks and other financial instruments. It also provides related services such as consulting implementation support and training. Calypso primarily targets global financial services firms; the company claims more than 125 clients including eight of the world's ten largest global banks. Other customers include local and regional banks asset managers hedge funds and stock exchanges. Founded in 1997 the employee-owned company operates from 16 locations worldwide.

CALYPTE BIOMEDICAL CORPORATION

OTC: CBMC

16290 SW Upper Boones Ferry Rd.
Portland OR 97224
Phone: 503-726-2227
Fax: 503-601-6299
Web: www.calypte.com

CEO: Adel Karas
CFO: Kartlos Edilashvili
HR: –
FYE: December 31
Type: Public

Fear of needles need not stop you from getting tested for HIV infection. Calypte Biomedical's line of HIV testing products includes several tests that use saliva rather than blood. These rapid-detection tests (sold under the Aware brand name) don't require sophisticated laboratory equipment and Calypte hopes that such products will appeal to markets in developing countries where the incidence of HIV is high but health care infrastructure is lacking. The company has obtained regulatory approval for its Aware Rapid HIV tests in several foreign markets including South Africa India and Russia. The company has also developed an Aware HIV blood test and an over-the-counter version of its oral test.

CAMBIUM LEARNING GROUP, INC.

NAS: ABCD

17855 Dallas Parkway, Suite 400
Dallas, TX 75287
Phone: 888 399-1995
Fax: –
Web: www.cambiumlearning.com

CEO: John Campbell
CFO: Barbara Benson
HR: –
FYE: December 31
Type: Public

Cambium cells carry nutrients and form the bark and wood of a tree and Cambium Learning Group carries educational materials to schools to help students succeed. Operating through its Voyager Learning Sopris Learning Learning A-Z and Cambium Learning Technologies business units the company provides comprehensive reading and math programs as well as academic support services for pre-K through 12th grade students particularly those who are at risk or have special learning needs. Its products include instructional software print materials and interactive online tools. Cambium Learning Group offers these products and services to school districts across the US.

	Annual Growth	12/10	12/11	12/12	12/13	12/14
Sales ($ mil.)	(6.0%)	181.3	172.3	148.6	150.5	141.7
Net income ($ mil.)	–	(16.0)	(49.4)	(133.8)	(14.3)	(10.0)
Market value ($ mil.)	(16.6%)	156.4	137.3	50.5	75.5	75.5
Employees	(1.6%)	564	628	526	517	528

CAMBREX CORP
NYS: CBM

One Meadowlands Plaza
East Rutherford, NJ 07073
Phone: 201-804-3000
Fax: 201-804-9852
Web: www.cambrex.com

CEO: Steven M. (Steve) Klosk
CFO: Gregory P. (Greg) Sargen
HR: –
FYE: December 31
Type: Public

Cambrex focuses on health. Providing products services and technologies which help to accelerate the development and commercialization of small molecule therapeutics the company develops products for the human health care market that include active pharmaceutical ingredients (APIs) and intermediates for over-the-counter and prescription branded and generic pharmaceuticals. It also makes intermediates used in cosmetics and food additives. Cambrex focuses on developing drug delivery technologies and the manufacture of high-potency compounds and controlled substances.

	Annual Growth	12/11	12/12	12/13	12/14	12/15
Sales ($ mil.)	14.1%	255.7	276.5	318.2	374.6	433.3
Net income ($ mil.)	51.1%	11.0	62.3	25.9	57.3	57.2
Market value ($ mil.)	60.0%	228.3	361.9	567.0	687.5	1,497.4
Employees	10.2%	833	891	936	1,117	1,228

CAMBRIDGE BANCORP
NBB: CATC

1336 Massachusetts Avenue
Cambridge, MA 02138
Phone: 617 876-5500
Fax: –
Web: www.cambridgetrust.com

CEO: Joseph V. (Joe) Roller
CFO: Albert R. (Al) Rietheimer
HR: Noreen Briand
FYE: December 31
Type: Public

Cambridge Bancorp is the holding company for Cambridge Trust Company a community bank serving Cambridge Massachusetts and the Greater Boston area from about ten locations. It offers standard retail products and services including checking and savings accounts CDs IRAs and credit cards. Residential mortgages including home equity loans account for more than half of the company's loan portfolio; commercial real estate loans make up approximately one-third. The company also offers commercial industrial and consumer loans. Cambridge Trust Company was established in 1892.

	Annual Growth	12/10	12/11	12/12	12/13	12/14
Assets ($ mil.)	8.6%	1,131.0	1,275.9	1,418.0	1,533.7	1,573.7
Net income ($ mil.)	3.0%	13.3	12.5	13.4	14.1	14.9
Market value ($ mil.)	7.9%	135.0	134.0	144.2	157.7	183.2
Employees	(15.0%)	200	200	123	123	–

CAMBRIDGE HEART INC.
OTC: CAMH

1 Oak Park Dr.
Bedford MA 01730
Phone: 781-271-1200
Fax: 781-275-8431
Web: www.cambridgeheart.com

CEO: Ali Haghighi-Mood
CFO: Vincenzo Licausi
HR: –
FYE: December 31
Type: Public

It's not just a heart — it's a "Cambridge" heart. Cambridge Heart makes noninvasive tools for diagnosing cardiac arrest and ventricular arrhythmia. Its CH 2000 system conducts cardiac stress tests and measures extremely low levels of T-wave alternans an irregularity in an electrocardiogram indicating the risk of sudden cardiac death. Another product the Heartwave II System allows T-wave alternans screenings to be performed with any stress test system. The company's Microvolt T-Wave Alternans technology can detect the smallest heartbeat variation measuring from one-millionth of a volt. The company markets its products in the US through direct sales and representatives; it also has international distributors.

CAMBRIDGE PUBLIC HEALTH COMMISSION

1493 CAMBRIDGE ST
CAMBRIDGE, MA 021391047
Phone: 617-665-1000
Fax: –
Web: www.cambridgema.gov

CEO: Patrick Wardell
CFO: Jill Batty
HR: –
FYE: June 30
Type: Private

Because not everyone in the college town of Cambridge Massachusetts can walk into student health centers there is the Cambridge Public Health Commission (doing business as Cambridge Health Alliance or CHA). The health care system operates the Cambridge Public Health Department and three hospitals — Cambridge Hospital Somerville Hospital and Whidden Hospital — with a combined total of more than 490 beds. It also operates 20 primary care and specialty practices specializing in such areas as pediatrics gerontology family medicine psychiatry and dentistry. CHA is a teaching affiliate of Harvard's Medical School and School of Public Health as well as Tufts University's School of Medicine.

	Annual Growth	06/01	06/02	06/03	06/05	06/09
Sales ($ mil.)	(20.9%)	–	384.3	466.1	644.2	74.2
Net income ($ mil.)	–	–	–	(17.0)	6.1	0.0
Market value ($ mil.)	–	–	–	–	–	–
Employees	–	–	–	–	–	2,700

CAMBRIDGE SOUNDWORKS INC.

120 Water St.
Andover MA 01845
Phone: 978-623-4400
Fax: 978-794-2903
Web: www.cambridgesoundworks.com

CEO: –
CFO: Robert Cardin
HR: –
FYE: June 30
Type: Subsidiary

Cambridge SoundWorks wants to be speaker of the house the car and the computer. The company is a leading manufacturer of speaker systems for consumer use including floor speakers and bookshelf models. It also makes home theater speaker systems outdoor speakers and surround sound units. In addition to its own brand Cambridge SoundWorks markets audio and video items from such manufacturers as Samsung Sony and Toshiba as well as products made by its parent company Creative Technology. Steep discounting of consumer electronics contributed to its decision to shut down its 30-store chain to focus on online and catalog sales in 2008.

CAMCO FINANCIAL CORP
NMS: CAFI

814 Wheeling Avenue
Cambridge, OH 43725-9757
Phone: 740 435-2020
Fax: –
Web: www.camcofinancial.com

CEO: –
CFO: –
HR: –
FYE: December 31
Type: Public

Camco Financial tries to give customers a financial edge through its Advantage Bank subsidiary. The company operates about 20 branches loan offices and Camco Title Agency offices in Ohio northern Kentucky and western West Virginia. The bank primarily uses funds from deposits (checking savings and money market accounts; CDs; and IRAs) to originate residential mortgages which make up about 60% of its loan portfolio; the bank also issues nonresidential real estate consumer and construction loans. In 2013 Ohio-based Huntington Bancshares agreed to buy Camco Financial.

	Annual Growth	12/08	12/09	12/10	12/11	12/12
Assets ($ mil.)	(6.5%)	1,000.4	842.7	815.0	767.0	764.3
Net income ($ mil.)	–	(15.3)	(11.2)	(14.6)	0.2	4.2
Market value ($ mil.)	(10.5%)	42.1	26.2	19.3	16.5	27.0
Employees	(5.5%)	276	252	254	222	220

CAMDEN NATIONAL CORP. (ME)   NMS: CAC

2 Elm Street
Camden, ME 04843
Phone: 207 236-8821
Fax: 207 236-6256
Web: www.camdennational.com

CEO: Gregory A. (Greg) Dufour
CFO: Deborah A. Jordan
HR: June B. Parent
FYE: December 31
Type: Public

Camden National Corporation is the holding company for Camden National Bank which boasts nearly 45 branches in about a dozen Maine counties and provides standard deposit products such as checking and savings accounts CDs and IRAs. Commercial mortgages and loans make up 50% of its loan portfolio while residential mortgages make up another 40% and consumer loans constitute the remainder. Subsidiary Acadia Trust provides trust fiduciary investment management and retirement plan administration services while Camden Financial Consultants offers brokerage and insurance services. The largest bank headquartered in Maine Camden National Bank was founded in 1875 and once issued its own US currency.

	Annual Growth	12/10	12/11	12/12	12/13	12/14
Assets ($ mil.)	4.9%	2,306.0	2,302.7	2,564.8	2,603.8	2,789.9
Net income ($ mil.)	(0.2%)	24.8	26.2	23.4	22.8	24.6
Market value ($ mil.)	2.4%	269.1	242.1	252.3	310.7	295.9
Employees	2.8%	421	425	550	481	471

CAMDEN PROPERTY TRUST   NYS: CPT

11 Greenway Plaza, Suite 2400
Houston, TX 77046
Phone: 713 354-2500
Fax: –
Web: www.camdenliving.com

CEO: Richard J. Campo
CFO: Alexander J. (Alex) Jessett
HR: –
FYE: December 31
Type: Public

Camden Property Trust hums along by investing in developing and operating middle-market and luxury apartment complexes in about a dozen states. The real estate investment trust (REIT) which sports a hummingbird logo has about 190 urban and suburban properties with some 62000 apartment units. Its portfolio is made up of both wholly owned and joint-venture holdings; most communities carry the Camden name. Around a quarter of the REIT's properties are in Texas but the company also has a presence in other top markets such as Atlanta Denver Florida Las Vegas North Carolina Phoenix Southern California and Washington DC.

	Annual Growth	12/10	12/11	12/12	12/13	12/14
Sales ($ mil.)	7.7%	638.7	677.3	744.3	810.0	858.6
Net income ($ mil.)	76.4%	31.1	60.0	293.9	346.3	301.3
Market value ($ mil.)	8.1%	5,268.7	6,074.9	6,657.6	5,551.7	7,207.1
Employees	0.4%	1,750	1,885	1,825	1,780	1,780

CAMELOT ENTERTAINMENT GROUP INC.   OTC: CMLT

8001 Irvine Center Dr. Ste. 400
Irvine CA 92618
Phone: 949-754-3030
Fax: 949-754-4309
Web: www.camelotfilms.com

CEO: Robert P Atwell
CFO: Steven Istock
HR: –
FYE: December 31
Type: Public

Camelot Entertainment Group is participating in the quest for the holy grail of movie studios: making low-budget films that sell mountains of tickets. The company plans to produce and distribute low-budget motion pictures with a business model focusing on pre-production digital photography profit participation and stock incentives for its directors and writers. Previously a development stage company Camelot has exited that phase; it got the ball rolling in 2010 with the purchase of the assets of Liberation Entertainment. Included in the deal is 750 titles from Liberation's film library.

CAMERON INTERNATIONAL CORP   NYS: CAM

1333 West Loop South, Suite 1700
Houston, TX 77027
Phone: 713 513-3300
Fax: 713 513-3220
Web: www.c-a-m.com

CEO: Jack B. Moore
CFO: Charles M. Sledge
HR: –
FYE: December 31
Type: Public

Cameron International knows how to work under pressure. A leading manufacturer provider and servicer of oil and gas industry equipment the company makes products that control pressure at oil and gas wells including blowout preventers chokes controls wellheads and valves. Cameron sells its products which are used for offshore onshore and subsea applications under more than 60 brand names including Ajax Cameron Cooper-Bessemer Demco LeTourneau Natco Petreco and Willis. In 2015 Cameron agreed to be acquired rival Schlumberger in a transaction valued at $14.8 billion.

	Annual Growth	12/11	12/12	12/13	12/14	12/15
Sales ($ mil.)	6.0%	6,959.0	8,502.1	9,838.4	10,381.0	8,782.0
Net income ($ mil.)	(1.0%)	521.9	750.5	699.2	811.0	501.0
Market value ($ mil.)	6.5%	9,404.1	10,794.0	11,380.9	9,549.4	12,082.6
Employees	0.6%	22,500	27,000	29,000	28,000	23,000

CAMERON MITCHELL RESTAURANTS LLC

515 Park St.
Columbus OH 43215
Phone: 614-621-3663
Fax: 614-621-1020
Web: www.cameronmitchell.com

CEO: –
CFO: –
HR: –
FYE: December 31
Type: Private

Cameron Mitchell Restaurants lays out the white tablecloth in Columbus Ohio and beyond. The company operates about 20 upscale establishments encompassing more than half a dozen dining concepts including Cameron's American Bistro Cap City Fine Diner & Bar Marcella's Martini Modern Italia Martini Italian Bistro Molly Woo's Asian Bistro and Ocean Prime. Many of the company's restaurants are found in and around Columbus but it also has dining operations in about half a dozen other states. In addition Cameron Mitchell offers catering services. Founder chef and president Cameron Mitchell left cross-town rival Fifty-Five Restaurant Group in 1992 to open his first restaurant Cameron's American Bistro.

CAMPAGNA-TURANO BAKERY INC.

6501 ROOSEVELT RD
BERWYN, IL 604021100
Phone: 708-788-9220
Fax: –
Web: www.turano.com

CEO: –
CFO: –
HR: Monica Scurry
FYE: December 31
Type: Private

The Campagna - Turano Bakery which does does business as the Turano Bakery manufactures fully and partially baked European-style artisan breads. The company's more than 400 varieties include French baguettes ciabatta bread focaccia and kaiser rolls as well as sweet baked goods including cannoli biscotti cakes and cookies. Operating three commercial bakeries Turano serves restaurant in-store bakery and retail grocery customers throughout the US. Its foodservice operation supplies customers in Illinois Wisconsin and northwestern Indiana with parbaked and fully baked goods.

	Annual Growth	12/06	12/07	12/08	12/09	12/12
Sales ($ mil.)	9.8%	–	–	–	5.3	7.0
Net income ($ mil.)		–	–	–	(0.7)	0.3
Market value ($ mil.)		–	–	–	–	–
Employees		–	–	–	–	470

CAMPBELL MITHUN INC.

222 S. 9th St.
Minneapolis MN 55402
Phone: 612-347-1000
Fax: 612-347-1515
Web: www.campbellmithun.com

CEO: Rob Buchner
CFO: Steve Arndt
HR: –
FYE: December 31
Type: Subsidiary

This company brings a little Madison Avenue savvy to the Midwest. Campbell Mithun is one of the leading advertising agencies in the US offering creative development and campaign services for both print and broadcast marketing efforts especially for clients in such industries as food health care and consumer products. It also provides insight into youth marketing through its Boing consultancy as well as general brand marketing services. In addition its Compass Point Media unit offers media planning and buying for spot TV print and radio time. Campbell Mithun is part of global advertising and marketing services conglomerate Interpublic Group.

CAMPBELL SOUP CO.   NYS: CPB

1 Campbell Place
Camden, NJ 08103-1799
Phone: 856 342-4800
Fax: 856 342-3878
Web: www.campbellsoupcompany.com

CEO: Denise M. Morrison
CFO: Anthony P Disilvestro
HR: –
FYE: August 02
Type: Public

Soup boils down to M'm! M'm! Money! at the world's #1 soup maker Campbell Soup. The company's most popular selections among its 90-variety soup portfolio in the US include chicken noodle tomato and cream of mushroom. Campbell also makes many other simple foods snacks and beverages including SpaghettiOs canned pasta Pace picante sauce V8 beverages Aussie favorite Arnott's biscuits and Pepperidge Farm baked goods (including those popular tiny Goldfish crackers). Newer products for the soup company include Garden Fresh Gourmet salsas and dips and Bolthouse Farms carrots and organic baby foods. All told Campbell sells its products in 100-plus countries from facilities across the globe.

	Annual Growth	07/11	07/12	07/13*	08/14	08/15
Sales ($ mil.)	1.2%	7,719.0	7,707.0	8,052.0	8,268.0	8,082.0
Net income ($ mil.)	(3.7%)	805.0	774.0	458.0	818.0	691.0
Market value ($ mil.)	10.5%	10,245.5	10,267.2	14,591.7	13,007.6	15,286.1
Employees	1.5%	17,500	17,700	20,000	19,400	18,600

*Fiscal year change

CAMPBELL-EWALD COMPANY

30400 Van Dyke Ave.
Warren MI 48093
Phone: 586-574-3400
Fax: 586-575-9925
Web: www.campbell-ewald.com

CEO: Anthony J Hopp
CFO: Suzanne H Gilbert
HR: –
FYE: December 31
Type: Subsidiary

This agency knows it takes more than a good name to make a great brand. Campbell-Ewald is one of the Midwest's leading advertising agencies offering creative development and campaign management services for broadcast print and interactive media. In addition to traditional advertising the firm provides services for direct response marketing event marketing and business-to-business selling. Major clients have included Carrier Michelin and the United States Postal Service. Its Campbell-Ewald Publishing unit offers custom publishing services for creating branded content. The agency is part of global marketing services conglomerate Interpublic Group and has a half dozen offices in major cities in the US.

CAMPUS CREST COMMUNITIES INC   NYS: CCG

2100 Rexford Road, Suite 414
Charlotte, NC 28211
Phone: 704 496-2500
Fax: 704 496-2599
Web: www.campuscrest.com

CEO: David Coles
CFO: John Makuch
HR: –
FYE: December 31
Type: Public

College dorms have moved beyond cinder block walls and Murphy beds thanks to Campus Crest Communities. The real estate investment trust (REIT) develops builds and manages on- and off-campus student housing apartment communities at medium-sized colleges and universities. Campus Crest owns interests in more than 25 communities which are branded as The Grove located mostly in the South. Its properties feature furnished apartments with such amenities as a pool library volleyball and basketball courts fitness center tanning beds and gated entry with keyed bedroom locks. The student-friendly rental rates include utilities.

	Annual Growth	12/10	12/11	12/12	12/13	12/14
Sales ($ mil.)	77.1%	10.9	94.8	137.4	142.3	106.7
Net income ($ mil.)	–	(1.6)	3.8	10.8	1.6	(164.0)
Market value ($ mil.)	(15.0%)	907.7	651.3	793.7	609.2	473.3
Employees	4.7%	525	527	650	522	632

CAMSTAR SYSTEMS INC.

13024 Ballantyne Corporate Place Ste. 300
Charlotte NC 28277
Phone: 704-227-6600
Fax: 704-227-6783
Web: www.camstar.com

CEO: Scott Toney
CFO: Darioush Mardan
HR: –
FYE: December 31
Type: Private

Camstar wants your manufacturing operations to play a starring role. The company makes manufacturing execution systems (MES) software for such industries as semiconductors biotechnology electronics medical devices and outsourced operations. Its InSite application helps manufacturers to quickly change production lines and synchronize plant output to meet demand. Other applications include LiveConnect (integration with ERP and CRM applications) LiveSync (replication of processes in other plants) and LiveView (reporting). Customers have included Agilent Technologies Corning JDS Uniphase IBM and Kodak. The company also offers services such as consulting training and support.

CAN-CAL RESOURCES LTD.   OTC: CCRE

2500 Vista Mar Dr.
Las Vegas NV 89128
Phone: 702-243-1849
Fax: 702-243-1869
Web: www.can-cal.com

CEO: –
CFO: –
HR: –
FYE: December 31
Type: Public

Can Can-Cal strike it rich? The question hasn't been answered. Can-Cal Resources is an exploration-stage mining company that owns exploration-stage precious mineral and metal properties in the southwestern US. Its focus is currently on the Pisgah and Wikieup properties in California and Arizona respectively. It also owns the Owl Canyon in California but is holding that property in reserve for exploration at a later date.

CANAAN MANAGEMENT INC.

285 Riverside Ave. Ste. 250
Westport CT 06880
Phone: 203-855-0400
Fax: 203-854-9117
Web: www.canaan.com

CEO: –
CFO: –
HR: –
FYE: December 31
Type: Private

It's the land of milk and honey for start-up companies. Canaan Management (also known as Canaan Partners) is a venture capital firm that invests primarily in early-stage technology and health care companies in the US and abroad. It focuses on digital media mobile communications enterprise software clean technology biopharmaceuticals medical devices and diagnostics. The company typically invests $1 million to $20 million per transaction and has approximately $3 billion in capital under management. Founded in 1987 Canaan has raised eight funds (its most recent in 2008). Notable past investments include Acme Packet Amicus Therapeutics DoubleClick and Match.com.

CANACCORD GENUITY INC.

99 High St. Ste. 1200
Boston MA 02110
Phone: 617-371-3900
Fax: 801-476-9138
Web: www.ut.regence.com

CEO: –
CFO: –
HR: –
FYE: March 31
Type: Subsidiary

Canaccord Genuity (formerly Canaccord Adams) provides equities research sales and trading services and investment banking services such as securities underwriting sales trading mergers and acquisitions advice and industry research. Formed in 1969 through the merger of Weston W. Adams & Company and Harkness & Hill the company specializes in the technology metals mining life sciences real estate and financial services sectors. Canaccord Genuity also acts as a market maker for small- and mid-cap stocks in the US. The company is part of Canaccord Financial.

CANANDAIGUA NATIONAL CORP.
NBB: CNND

72 South Main Street
Canandaigua, NY 14424
Phone: 585 394-4260
Fax: 585 394-4001
Web: www.cnbank.com

CEO: George W Hamlin IV
CFO: Lawrence A Heilbronner
HR: –
FYE: December 31
Type: Public

Canandaigua National can undoubtedly stake its claim as the holding company for Canandaigua National Bank and Trust which operates more than two dozen branches in the Finger Lakes region of upstate New York. In addition to traditional deposits and loans the bank also offers online brokerage insurance and wealth management services including corporate retirement plan management and individual financial planning. The company also owns Genesee Valley Trust Company and the recently formed Canandaigua National Trust Company of Florida. Canandaigua National's loan portfolio is composed largely of commercial mortgages other business loans and residential mortgages.

	Annual Growth	12/10	12/11	12/12	12/13	12/14
Assets ($ mil.)	6.3%	1,661.5	1,761.5	1,887.0	1,963.0	2,117.5
Net income ($ mil.)	4.1%	17.7	16.3	18.8	19.4	20.7
Market value ($ mil.)	(20.5%)	639.8	168.9	243.9	240.2	255.2
Employees	3.1%	481	501	537	526	544

CANCER GENETICS, INC.
NAS: CGIX

201 Route 17 North 2nd Floor
Rutherford, NJ 07070
Phone: 201 528-9200
Fax: –
Web: www.cancergenetics.com

CEO: Panna L Sharma
CFO: Edward J Sitar
HR: –
FYE: December 31
Type: Public

Cancer Genetics Inc. (CGI) takes a personalized approach to diagnosing leukemia. The company developed a DNA-based genomic test to identify chronic lymphocytic leukemia in patients. Called MatBA-CLL the microarray test can improve the diagnosis prognosis and response to treatment. CGI's lab in New Jersey caters to area hospitals cancer centers reference laboratories and doctors' offices. It also has a pipeline of other genomic tests for hematological urogenital (kidney prostate and bladder cancer) and HPV-associated cancers that are complicated to predict. CGI was founded in 1999 by Chairman Dr. Raju Chaganti.

	Annual Growth	12/10	12/11	12/12	12/13	12/14
Sales ($ mil.)	41.8%	2.5	3.0	4.3	6.6	10.2
Net income ($ mil.)	–	(8.4)	(19.9)	(6.7)	(12.4)	(16.6)
Market value ($ mil.)	(51.5%)	–	–	–	135.3	65.6
Employees	74.4%	–	–	49	67	149

CANDELA CORPORATION

530 Boston Post Rd.
Wayland MA 01778
Phone: 508-358-7400
Fax: 508-358-5602
Web: www.candelalaser.com

CEO: –
CFO: –
HR: –
FYE: December 31
Type: Subsidiary

Tattoo regrets? Candela's medical laser technology can remove them and other cosmetic skin issues as well. The company makes light-based (laser) systems including Alex TriVantage for birthmarks lesions sun spots and tattoos; GentleLASE for permanent hair removal facial veins and wrinkles; Vbeam for acne skin rejuvenation scars and warts. Candela sells to cosmetic and surgical markets through a direct sales force and distributors in the US and abroad. Its patent portfolio consists of roughly 25 issued US patents (with some 20 patents applications pending) and 35 international patents. Candela is a wholly-owned subsidiary of aesthetic laser-maker Syneron Medical

CANDLEWICK PRESS INC.

99 Dover St.
Somerville MA 02144
Phone: 617-661-3330
Fax: 617-661-0565
Web: www.candlewick.com

CEO: –
CFO: –
HR: –
FYE: December 31
Type: Private

Candlewick Press shines a light in the children's book world. The company has published more than 3000 children's books. Its catalog is comprised of picture books easy readers middle grade and young adult fiction nonfiction poetry collections and novelty and activity books. Candlewick titles include Can't You Sleep Little Bear? Guess How Much I Love You My Very First Mother Goose and It's Perfectly Normal. Its books are distributed in the US by Random House. The company is 100%-owned by its employees.

CANNONDALE BICYCLE CORPORATION

16 Trowbridge Dr.
Bethel CT 06801
Phone: 203-749-7000
Fax: 203-748-4012
Web: www.cannondale.com

CEO: –
CFO: Ron Lombardi
HR: –
FYE: June 30
Type: Subsidiary

Cannondale's lightweight products are heavyweights in the high-performance bicycle market. The company is a leading maker of mountain road racing multisport recreational and specialty bicycles — most of them with aluminum frames. Cannondale also peddles bicycle-related apparel accessories and gear. The bicycle-maker offers some 80 bike models through specialty bike retailers in about 70 countries. It also co-sponsors bike-racing teams to promote its products. The company boasts major facilities in Japan and Taiwan. Cannondale is owned by juvenile products and bicycle company Dorel Industries and operates as part of its recreational/leisure business generating about one-third of total corporate sales.

CANON U.S.A. INC.

1 Canon Plaza
Lake Success NY 11042
Phone: 516-328-5000
Fax: 718-260-4375
Web: www.trackdata.com

CEO: Yoroku Adachi
CFO: Kunihiko Tedo
HR: Nelson C Remetz
FYE: December 31
Type: Subsidiary

Canon U.S.A. expanded its canon beyond cameras. The US arm of Tokyo-based printer and peripherals giant Canon sells and services office and consumer imaging equipment including copiers printers fax machines and scanners. Its focus on cameras hasn't softened though offering still and video digital cameras for both consumers and professionals in photography broadcast and motion pictures. Industrial and other products include semiconductor and LCD lithography equipment small motors and medical equipment such as eye care cameras and radiography systems. Canon U.S.A. oversees subsidiaries Canon Canada Canon Latin America and Canon Mexicana; the Americas account for more than one-fourth of Canon's global sales.

CANON VIRGINIA INC.

12000 Canon Blvd.
Newport News VA 23606-4299
Phone: 757-881-6000
Fax: 312-565-5823
Web: www.fhlbc.com

CEO: –
CFO: –
HR: –
FYE: December 31
Type: Subsidiary

Canon Virginia provides contract manufacturing and parts fabrication services. The company assembles new and remanufactured office equipment including copiers toner and toner cartridges and laser printers. Its manufacturing capabilities include plastic injection molding metal fabrication and metal stamping. In addition to assembly it offers painting and packaging services as well as reverse-logistics contracts. The unit also provides return product repair services. Canon Virginia is a subsidiary of Canon U.S.A. the US arm of Japanese imaging giant Canon. Canon Virginia was founded in 1985.

CANTEL MEDICAL CORP

150 Clove Road
Little Falls, NJ 07424
Phone: 973 890-7220
Fax: 973 890-7270
Web: www.cantelmedical.com

NYS: CMN
CEO: Andrew A. Krakauer
CFO: Peter G. Clifford
HR: –
FYE: July 31
Type: Public

Cantel Medical can tell you that cleanliness is second to nothing when it comes to medical and scientific equipment. Through its subsidiaries the firm sells infection prevention and control products to hospitals dentists drugmakers researchers and others in the US and abroad in the field of health care. Its diverse offerings include medical device reprocessing systems and disinfectants for dialyzers and endoscopes water purification equipment masks and bibs used in dental offices specialty packaging of biological and pharmaceutical products and therapeutic filtration systems. Fast-growing Cantel Medical employs an active acquisition strategy.

	Annual Growth	07/11	07/12	07/13	07/14	07/15
Sales ($ mil.)	15.1%	321.7	386.5	425.0	488.7	565.0
Net income ($ mil.)	23.8%	20.4	31.3	39.2	43.3	48.0
Market value ($ mil.)	21.8%	1,037.2	1,086.7	1,104.2	1,395.0	2,283.2
Employees	10.7%	1,117	1,198	1,292	1,534	1,680

CANTERBURY PARK HOLDING CORP.

1100 Canterbury Road
Shakopee, MN 55379
Phone: 952 445-7223
Fax: –
Web: www.canterburypark.com

NMS: CPHC
CEO: Randall D Sampson
CFO: David C Hansen
HR: –
FYE: December 31
Type: Public

The tails of this Canterbury are connected to horses running around a track. The operator of the Canterbury Park racetrack in Shakopee Minnesota Canterbury Park Holding offers live pari-mutuel horse racing from May through September. The racetrack also offers year-round betting on simulcast races from racetracks such as Churchill Downs Hollywood Park and Belmont Park. When horses aren't dashing down the track the company stages other events (snowmobile races concerts crafts shows private parties) at Canterbury Park. It also offers gambling for card sharks at its on-site Card Club. Chairman Curtis Sampson owns more than 20% of the company.

	Annual Growth	12/10	12/11	12/12	12/13	12/14
Sales ($ mil.)	5.0%	39.9	40.6	45.5	46.7	48.5
Net income ($ mil.)	–	(1.0)	0.4	1.0	1.0	2.4
Market value ($ mil.)	(5.3%)	48.8	55.7	40.4	43.3	39.2
Employees	10.9%	523	559	565	564	790

CANTOR ENTERTAINMENT TECHNOLOGY INC.

2575 S. Highland Dr.
Las Vegas NV 89109
Phone: 702-677-3800
Fax: 201-528-9201
Web: cancergenetics.com

CEO: Lee M Amaitis
CFO: Douglas R Barnard
HR: Nicole Lanzalaco
FYE: December 31
Type: Private

Cantor Entertainment Technology is willing to bet that high-rollers wouldn't mind replacing that slot machine with a tablet computer. Doing business as Cantor Gaming the company is the only provider of mobile gaming and mobile wagering systems in Nevada. (Mobile betting in casino hotel rooms was legalized in 2011.) Cantor Gaming supplies a handful of Las Vegas resorts with handheld touchscreen computers that offer race and sports books and other mobile casino games; players rent the computers from the casino. In addition it launched a sports wagering app for Android phones that can be used anywhere in Nevada and is developing apps for Apple and Windows phones. The company filed an IPO in 2011 but withdrew it in 2012.

CANTOR FITZGERALD L.P.

110 E. 59th St.
New York NY 10022
Phone: 212-938-5000
Fax: 212-829-5280
Web: www.cantor.com

CEO: –
CFO: –
HR: –
FYE: December 31
Type: Private

Neither a choir leader nor a Jazz Age novelist this Cantor Fitzgerald probably does sing the praises of strong returns. Cantor Fitzgerald provides a variety of investment services including trading and brokerage asset management investment banking and market research. One of the largest traders of US Treasury securities it also deals in global equities bonds and derivatives. Niche operations include UK spread specialist Cantor Index the Cantor FX (foreign exchange trading) and Cantor Gaming (technology services for the gaming industry). Cantor Fitzgerald serves more than 5000 institutional clients around the world. B. Gerald Cantor and John Fitzerald co-founded the company in 1945.

CAPCOM U.S.A. INC.

800 Concar Dr. Ste. 300
San Mateo CA 94402-2649
Phone: 650-350-6500
Fax: +49-1805252587
Web: www.sony.de

CEO: –
CFO: Koko Ishikawa
HR: –
FYE: March 31
Type: Subsidiary

Capcom USA sets its cap at the US video game market. The subsidiary of Japan's Capcom Co. Ltd. was established as the administrative arm for Capcom's US operations in 1985. It is best known for blockbuster video game franchises such as Devil May Cry Mega Man Resident Evil and Street Fighter made for Sony Nintendo and Microsoft game consoles as well as for PCs. Recent hit franchises include Dead Rising and Monster Hunter. Mobile and social games such as Smurf's Village and Shrek's Fairytale Kingdom are developed through the Beeline brand. Beeline avoids established Capcom brands to focus strictly on family-friendly games. The US accounts for about 20% of parent Capcom's overall revenues.

CAPE BANCORP, INC.

225 North Main Street
Cape May Court House, NJ 08210
Phone: 609 465-5600
Fax: –
Web: www.capebanknj.com

NMS: CBNJ
CEO: –
CFO: Guy Hackney
HR: Michelle Perna
FYE: December 31
Type: Public

Cape Bank is a permanent fixture serving the ebb and flow of New Jersey's touristy coastal and inland towns. Serving both commercial and residential customers the community bank provides traditional deposit options such as checking and savings accounts as well as loan services like home equity lines of credit and commercial mortgages (which represents more than half its loan portfolio). The company operates about 15 locations and serves customers in Atlantic and Cape May counties. It was formed in 2007 to be the holding company for Cape Bank and went public the following year; the bank's roots go back to the 1920s. OceanFirst Financial agreed to buy Cape Bancorp for $208.1 million in early 2016.

	Annual Growth	12/10	12/11	12/12	12/13	12/14
Assets ($ mil.)	0.4%	1,061.0	1,071.1	1,040.8	1,092.9	1,079.9
Net income ($ mil.)	13.8%	4.0	8.0	4.6	5.6	6.8
Market value ($ mil.)	2.6%	97.5	90.1	99.7	116.6	108.0
Employees	(1.7%)	213	202	212	203	199

CAPE COD HEALTHCARE INC.

27 PARK ST
HYANNIS, MA 026015230
Phone: 508-862-5030
Fax: –
Web: www.capecodhealthcare.com

CEO: –
CFO: Michael Connors
HR: Emily Schorer
FYE: September 30
Type: Private

There once was a man from Nantucket who broke his leg when he stepped in a bucket. Falmouth Hospital took care of the man and helped him devise a get-well plan and in the end he was hooked on Cape Cod Healthcare. Cape Cod Healthcare is a not-for-profit healthcare organization that includes two acute-care hospitals (Cape Cod Hospital and Falmouth Hospital) with a total of some 350 beds. It also operates a home health services agency (Visiting Nurse Association) primary and specialized care clinics medical labs a 130-bed skilled nursing and rehabilitation facility and a 60-unit assisted living facility. The health care system has a staff of more than 450 physicians.

	Annual Growth	09/08	09/09	09/11	09/12	09/13
Sales ($ mil.)	5.4%	–	587.0	648.3	680.2	724.6
Net income ($ mil.)	10.2%	–	–	37.2	81.0	45.3
Market value ($ mil.)	–	–	–	–	–	–
Employees	–	–	–	–	–	1,850

CAPE COD HOSPITAL

27 PARK ST
HYANNIS, MA 026015203
Phone: 508-862-7575
Fax: –
Web: www.capecodortho.com

CEO: Michael K Lauf
CFO: –
HR: –
FYE: September 30
Type: Private

Get too much sun or eat too much lobster while visiting Cape Cod? Never fear Cape Cod Hospital can treat whatever ails you. Cape Cod Hospital a subsidiary of Cape Cod Healthcare is a 260-bed acute care hospital that serves the Cape Cod Massachusetts area. Its specialty services include pediatrics maternity care cancer treatment and infectious disease therapeutics. The not-for-profit Cape Cod Hospital also includes a specialty cardiovascular center a psychiatry unit a surgical pavilion and a diagnostic imaging facility as well as outpatient medical offices.

	Annual Growth	09/07	09/08	09/11	09/12	09/13
Sales ($ mil.)	3.0%	–	352.1	409.6	427.0	407.7
Net income ($ mil.)	(17.9%)	–	–	29.2	52.4	19.7
Market value ($ mil.)	–	–	–	–	–	–
Employees	–	–	–	–	–	1,700

CAPE ENVIRONMENTAL MANAGEMENT INC.

500 PINNACLE CT STE 100
NORCROSS, GA 300713630
Phone: 770-908-7200
Fax: –
Web: www.capeenv.com

CEO: Fernando J. Rios
CFO: Les Flynn
HR: –
FYE: December 27
Type: Private

Cape Environmental Management offers a number of engineering and environmental services including facility construction and demolition remediation and water and wastewater utility-related services. Clients include government agencies such as the US Air Force and the US Army Corps of Engineers and industrial clients in the petroleum chemical telecommunications and transportation sectors. Specialty areas include engineering scientific construction and industrial hygiene/safety. The company operates from more than a dozen offices located across the US. It also has two offices in Iraq. Cape Environmental Management was founded in 1965 and acquired by its executive team in 1991.

	Annual Growth	12/02	12/03	12/04	12/06	12/08
Sales ($ mil.)	–	–	–	(1,001.6)	117.7	92.9
Net income ($ mil.)	294.8%	–	–	0.0	20.3	4.0
Market value ($ mil.)	–	–	–	–	–	–
Employees	–	–	–	–	–	315

CAPELLA EDUCATION COMPANY
NMS: CPLA

Capella Tower, 225 South Sixth Street, 9th Floor
Minneapolis, MN 55402
Phone: 888 227-3552
Fax: –
Web: www.capellaeducation.com

CEO: J. Kevin Gilligan
CFO: Steven L. (Steve) Polacek
HR: –
FYE: December 31
Type: Public

Capella Education is all about the digital age. The fast-growing company operates Capella University an online school that offers more than 45 undergraduate and graduate degree programs with some 150 specializations. Its 35000 students from the US and abroad are primarily composed of working adults 75% of which are pursuing master's or doctoral degrees. Capella Education's faculty members are mostly part-time employees typically teaching one to three courses per semester. The firm's programs range across a variety of subjects including business health human resources information technology and psychology.

	Annual Growth	12/10	12/11	12/12	12/13	12/14
Sales ($ mil.)	(0.2%)	426.1	430.0	421.9	415.6	422.0
Net income ($ mil.)	(11.3%)	61.3	52.1	36.5	35.2	37.9
Market value ($ mil.)	3.7%	815.1	441.4	345.6	813.4	942.2
Employees	(0.2%)	2,968	2,883	2,829	2,804	2,944

CAPGEMINI NORTH AMERICA INC.

623 5th Ave. 33rd Fl.
New York NY 10022
Phone: 212-314-8000
Fax: 212-314-8001
Web: www.us.capgemini.com

CEO: Paul Hermelin
CFO: –
HR: –
FYE: December 31
Type: Subsidiary

Vive la technologie! Capgemini North America oversees the US Canadian and Mexican operations of Paris-based consulting giant Cap Gemini. Like its parent the subsidiary offers management and IT consulting services systems integration technology development design and outsourcing services through nearly 30 offices in about a dozen US states Puerto Rico and Canada. Its consultants serve clients in a variety of industries including automotive energy and utilities financial services high-tech manufacturing and transportation. The unit was formed in 2000 after Capgemini acquired the consulting arm of accounting giant Ernst & Young. Capgemini North America represents almost 20% of its parent's annual sales.

CAPITAL BANK CORPORATION
NASDAQ: CBKN

333 Fayetteville Ste. 700
Raleigh NC 27601-2950
Phone: 919-645-6400
Fax: 919-645-6435
Web: www.capitalbank-nc.com

CEO: R Eugene Taylor
CFO: Christopher G Marshall
HR: –
FYE: December 31
Type: Public

Capital Bank Corporation owns about a quarter of Capital Bank NA which has more than 140 offices in the Carolinas Florida Tennessee and Virginia. The bank provides consumer and commercial banking services such as savings checking and health savings accounts as well as CDs IRAs and credit cards. Real estate loans including commercial and residential mortgages as well as construction land development and farmland loans make up about 85% of the bank's loan portfolio. Business and consumer loans help to round out its lending activities. The bank offers private banking trust and investment services through affiliate Naples Capital Advisors.

CAPITAL BANK FINANCIAL CORP
NMS: CBF

121 Alhambra Plaza Suite 1601
Coral Gables, FL 33134
Phone: 305 670-0200
Fax: –
Web: www.capitalbank-us.com

CEO: R Eugene Taylor
CFO: Christopher G Marshall
HR: –
FYE: December 31
Type: Public

Capital Bank Financial Corporation (formerly North American Financial Holdings) owns nearly 20% of Capital Bank NA which operates more than branches in Florida North Carolina South Carolina Tennessee and Virginia. The bank offers standard savings and checking accounts as well as mortgages consumer and commercial loans and other financial products and services. Formed in 2009 Capital Bank Financial went public in 2012. The company plans to use the proceeds from the offering (about $180 million) to fund future acquisitions and for general corporate purposes and working capital. To that end it acquired Southern Community Financial Corp. for about $47 million in cash in late 2012.

	Annual Growth	12/10	12/11	12/12	12/13	12/14
Assets ($ mil.)	18.2%	3,497.0	6,587.2	7,295.7	6,617.6	6,831.4
Net income ($ mil.)	43.4%	12.0	6.2	51.2	38.8	50.9
Market value ($ mil.)	25.3%	–	–	812.4	1,082.7	1,275.5
Employees	0.8%	–	1,480	1,588	1,610	1,515

CAPITAL BLUECROSS

2500 Elmerton Ave.
Harrisburg PA 17177
Phone: 717-541-7000
Fax: 717-541-6915
Web: https://www.capbluecross.com

CEO: William Lehr Jr
CFO: Michael Cleary
HR: –
FYE: December 31
Type: Private - Not-for-Pr

If you dwell in the Lehigh Valley Capital BlueCross could be your direct link to health care coverage. A licensee of the Blue Cross and Blue Shield Association the company provides health insurance products to individuals and employer groups with a total of about 1 million members in central and eastern Pennsylvania. It offers traditional PPO HMO and POS health care plans as well as dental and vision coverage and Medicare Advantage plans. Capital BlueCross' network includes more than 11000 health care providers and some 40 hospitals. The company also provides benefits administration services to self-funded customers through for-profit subsidiary Capital Administrative Services (dba NCAS Pennsylvania).

CAPITAL CITY BANK GROUP, INC.
NMS: CCBG

217 North Monroe Street
Tallahassee, FL 32301
Phone: 850 402-7000
Fax: –
Web: www.ccbg.com

CEO: William G. (Bill) Smith
CFO: J. Kimbrough (Kim) Davis
HR: Sharon Martin
FYE: December 31
Type: Public

Capital City Bank Group is the holding company for Capital City Bank (CCB) which serves individuals businesses and institutions from some 70 branches in Florida Georgia and Alabama. CCB offers checking savings and money market accounts; CDs; IRAs; Internet banking; and debit and credit cards. Commercial real estate mortgages account for about 40% of its loan portfolio; residential real estate loans also hover near 40%. The bank also originates business loans and consumer loans including credit cards. Capital City also performs data processing services for other financial institutions in its market area.

	Annual Growth	12/10	12/11	12/12	12/13	12/14
Assets ($ mil.)	0.0%	2,622.1	2,641.3	2,634.0	2,611.9	2,627.2
Net income ($ mil.)	–	(0.4)	4.9	0.1	6.0	9.3
Market value ($ mil.)	5.4%	219.8	166.6	198.4	205.4	271.1
Employees	(1.0%)	975	959	913	927	937

CAPITAL DISTRICT PHYSICIANS' HEALTH PLAN INC.

500 PATROON CREEK BLVD
ALBANY, NY 122065006
Phone: 518-641-3700
Fax: –
Web: www.cdphp.com

CEO: –
CFO: –
HR: –
FYE: December 31
Type: Private

Capital District Physicians' Health Plan (CDPHP) is an independent not-for-profit health plan serving some 448000 members in two dozen New York counties. It offers employer-sponsored and individual managed care plans (including HMO PPO and consumer-directed plans) as well as a Medicare Advantage plan for seniors. The company's coverage include full coverage for some preventative medical services as well as options for covering prescription drugs dental work and vision services. CDPHP also provides wellness programs that help members with weight loss smoking cessation and chronic disease management.

	Annual Growth	12/01	12/02	12/03	12/09	12/13
Sales ($ mil.)	5.6%	–	719.4	818.3	1,037.4	1,314.7
Net income ($ mil.)	–	–	–	(1.8)	33.5	23.0
Market value ($ mil.)	–	–	–	–	–	–
Employees	–	–	–	–	–	700

CAPITAL HEALTH SYSTEM INC.

750 BRUNSWICK AVE
TRENTON, NJ 086384143
Phone: 609-394-6000
Fax: –
Web: www.capitalhealth.org

CEO: Al Maghazehe
CFO: Shane Fleming
HR: –
FYE: December 31
Type: Private

Capital Health System (CHS) serves the residents of New Jersey's capital city through two hospitals. Together they have about 430 beds. The not-for-profit organization offers emergency surgical and acute health care and it serves as a hands-on teaching facility to nursing and medical students. It also operates outpatient care facilities. CHS primarily serves residents of Mercer County and parts of Bucks County in central New Jersey. Capital Health System offers centers for maternal and pediatric health neurology emergency and trauma services oncology orthopedics mental health surgery and sleep diagnostics.

	Annual Growth	12/04	12/05	12/06	12/08	12/12
Sales ($ mil.)	–	–	(1,096.7)	419.3	0.3	538.8
Net income ($ mil.)	–	–	–	28.7	0.0	(58.1)
Market value ($ mil.)	–	–	–	–	–	–
Employees	–	–	–	–	–	3,000

CAPITAL ONE FINANCIAL CORP   NYS: COF

1680 Capital One Drive
McLean, VA 22102
Phone: 703 720-1000
Fax: –
Web: www.capitalone.com

CEO: Richard D. (Rich) Fairbank
CFO: Stephen S. (Steve) Crawford
HR: Sammy Duff
FYE: December 31
Type: Public

Capital One isn't just concerned with what's in your wallet; it's interested in your bank account as well. The company is best known as one of the largest issuers of Visa and MasterCard credit cards in the US but it also boasts a banking network of 900-plus branches in about half a dozen states (including New York and Texas) and the District of Columbia. Bolstered by its 2012 acquisition of ING Direct the bank also offers online and direct banking. Capital One which serves more than 50 million customers in the US Canada and the UK also has units that offer auto financing write home loans sell insurance and manage assets for institutional and high-net-worth clients.

	Annual Growth	12/10	12/11	12/12	12/13	12/14
Assets ($ mil.)	11.8%	197,503.0	206,019.0	312,918.0	297,048.0	308,854.0
Net income ($ mil.)	12.7%	2,743.0	3,147.0	3,517.0	4,159.0	4,428.0
Market value ($ mil.)	18.0%	23,552.3	23,402.9	32,058.0	42,395.3	45,682.5
Employees	13.4%	27,826	31,542	39,593	41,951	46,000

CAPITAL PROPERTIES, INC.   NBB: CPTP

100 Dexter Road
East Providence, RI 02914
Phone: 401 435-7171
Fax: 401 435-7179
Web: www.capitalproperties.com

CEO: –
CFO: –
HR: –
FYE: December 31
Type: Public

Was it providence or clear foresight that led Capital Properties to buy land in what is now Capital Center a downtown revitalization project in Providence Rhode Island? The company owns and leases out about a dozen parcels of land totaling some 18 acres in the area making it Capital Center's largest landowner. It leases parcels for the long term (at least 99 years) and leaves development and improvement to its tenants. Subsidiaries own and operate a petroleum storage facility in East Providence used by Global Partners and lease land to Lamar Advertising for roadside billboards in Rhode Island and Massachusetts. Chairman and CEO Robert Eder and his wife Linda together own a majority of Capital Properties.

	Annual Growth	12/10	12/11	12/12	12/13	12/14
Sales ($ mil.)	2.8%	6.9	8.2	8.2	6.7	7.8
Net income ($ mil.)	(1.2%)	1.5	2.0	2.0	0.7	1.4
Market value ($ mil.)	4.1%	66.0	57.4	44.2	52.8	77.5
Employees	0.0%	10	10	10	10	10

CAPITAL SENIOR LIVING CORP.   NYS: CSU

14160 Dallas Parkway, Suite 300
Dallas, TX 75254
Phone: 972 770-5600
Fax: 972 770-5666
Web: www.capitalsenior.com

CEO: Lawrence A. Cohen
CFO: Carey P. Hendrickson
HR: –
FYE: December 31
Type: Public

Capital Senior Living sets its standards on providing high-class digs to meet the housing needs of the growing number of affluent seniors in the US. The company owns or manages about 100 senior residential properties with a total of more than 13000 beds in some two dozen states scattered across the country. Capital Senior Living provides independent living assisted living and skilled nursing to moderate- and upper-income seniors. Specialized care units for treatment of Alzheimer's patients are available and the company also operates a home health care agency at one of its communities. Private pay sources comprise about 95% of the company's revenue.

	Annual Growth	12/10	12/11	12/12	12/13	12/14
Sales ($ mil.)	16.0%	211.9	263.5	310.5	350.4	383.9
Net income ($ mil.)	–	4.3	3.0	(3.1)	(16.5)	(24.1)
Market value ($ mil.)	38.9%	194.9	231.0	543.8	698.0	724.8
Employees	10.1%	4,188	4,895	4,937	5,623	6,147

CAPITAL SOUTHWEST CORP.   NMS: CSWC

5400 Lyndon B Johnson Freeway, Suite 1300
Dallas, TX 75240
Phone: 972 233-8242
Fax: –
Web: www.capitalsouthwest.com

CEO: Joseph B Armes
CFO: Kelly Tacke
HR: –
FYE: March 31
Type: Public

A private equity firm Capital Southwest owns significant minority stakes in around 30 companies many of them in Texas. The business development company (BDC) offers growth capital recapitalization and acquisition financing and funding for management buyouts to companies in a variety of industries. It typically invests between $5 million to $15 million per transaction in target firms which do not include troubled companies startups real estate developments or other less-than-stable ventures. The company is also focused on investments in the US especially firms located in the Southwest Southeast Midwest and Mountain regions.

	Annual Growth	03/11	03/12	03/13	03/14	03/15
Assets ($ mil.)	9.4%	543.2	633.0	667.7	778.7	776.9
Net income ($ mil.)	–	1.8	2.5	1.9	4.9	(2.4)
Market value ($ mil.)	(15.6%)	1,424.7	1,471.7	1,790.0	540.4	722.5
Employees	11.5%	11	15	15	14	17

CAPITALSOURCE INC.

NYSE: CSE

633 W. 5th St. 33rd Fl.
Los Angeles CA 90071
Phone: 213-443-7700
Fax: 800-543-2095
Web: www.wrighttool.com

CEO: –
CFO: –
HR: –
FYE: December 31
Type: Public

CapitalSource is a capital source of capital for small- and middle-market businesses. Its CapitalSource Bank subsidiary formed in 2008 provides commercial and multifamily mortgages operating loans equipment leases and other finance options to small and midsized companies from about 10 offices throughout the US. It also has about 20 bank branches in central and southern California that offer retail deposit products such as savings and money market accounts CDs and IRAs to help fund its lending activities. Target sectors include health care security technology consumer lending and professional practices such as dentist and physician offices.

CAPITOL FEDERAL FINANCIAL INC

NMS: CFFN

700 Kansas Avenue
Topeka, KS 66603
Phone: 785 235-1341
Fax: –
Web: www.ir.capfed.com

CEO: John B. Dicus
CFO: Kent G Townsend
HR: –
FYE: September 30
Type: Public

Dorothy and Toto may not be in Kansas anymore but Capitol Federal Financial is. The holding company owns Capitol Federal Savings Bank the largest bank headquarted there. The savings bank serves metropolitan areas of the Sunflower State as well as Kansas City Missouri through about 45 branches including nearly a dozen inside retail stores such as Target Price Chopper and Dillons. Serving consumers and commercial customers the thrift offers standard services such as mortgages and loans deposits and retail investments. Its Capitol Agency affiliate sells life liability homeowners renters and vehicle insurance.

	Annual Growth	09/10	09/11	09/12	09/13	09/14
Assets ($ mil.)	3.8%	8,487.1	9,450.8	9,378.3	9,186.4	9,865.0
Net income ($ mil.)	3.4%	67.8	38.4	74.5	69.3	77.7
Market value ($ mil.)	3.8%	–	1,488.4	1,685.8	1,752.0	1,666.0
Employees	(1.3%)	753	734	738	724	716

CAPRI CAPITAL PARTNERS LLC

875 N. Michigan Ave. Ste. 3430
Chicago IL 60611
Phone: 312-573-5300
Fax: 312-573-5273
Web: www.capricapital.com

CEO: Quintin E Primo III
CFO: Brian Fargo
HR: –
FYE: December 31
Type: Private

Capri Capital wants its investors to experience the Mediterranean isle's legendary spirit of "la dolce vita" "the sweet life." The company provides capital in the lending and equity investments arenas to public and private real estate companies. Its Capri Capital Advisors is a real estate investment management firm specializing in multifamily (more than two-thirds of its investments) industrial retail and office projects in major US markets. Capri Capital named after founders Daryl Carter and Quintin Primo was created in 1992 and manages nearly $5 billion in loans and investments related to real estate.

CAPRICOR THERAPEUTICS INC

NAS: CAPR

8840 Wilshire Blvd., 2nd Floor
Beverly Hills, CA 90211
Phone: 310 358-3200
Fax: –
Web: www.capricor.com

CEO: Linda Marban
CFO: Anthony Bergmann
HR: –
FYE: December 31
Type: Public

While its operations are far from the Nile river Nile Therapeutics makes products aimed at getting cardiovascular systems moving like a river. A biopharmaceutical company Nile Therapeutics has a handful of candidates in development in its pipeline that are designed to treat acute heart failure. Its primary candidate CD-NP is a peptide (short specialized amino acid chain) engineered to treat acute decompensated heart failure (ADHF) or the rapid degeneration of the heart resulting from a heart attack or other medical conditions. Nile's other prominent candidate is an early-stage peptide also designed to treat similar cardiovascular conditions.

	Annual Growth	12/10	12/11	12/12	12/13	12/14
Sales ($ mil.)	52.3%	–	1.4	0.2	0.5	4.8
Net income ($ mil.)	–	(6.0)	(4.9)	(1.9)	(8.9)	(6.2)
Market value ($ mil.)	56.6%	7.3	6.4	0.6	38.0	43.9
Employees	80.7%	3	4	2	19	32

CAPRIUS INC.

PINK SHEETS: CAPI

10 Forest Ave. Ste. 220
Paramus NJ 07652
Phone: 201-342-0900
Fax: 913-647-0132
Web: www.elecsyscorp.com

CEO: Dwight Morgan
CFO: Jonathan Joels
HR: –
FYE: September 30
Type: Public

Caprius helps doctors take out the trash. The company owns a majority interest in MCM Environmental Technologies which provides systems for disposal of medical waste. Its SteriMed system can crush grind shred and mix all types of medical waste including metal sharps and needles plastic tubing and IV bags and glass items. Once this process is complete MCM's Steri-Cid chemical process disinfects the waste which can then be discarded as regular waste at as little as 10% of the original volume. MCM manufactures the SteriMed system in Israel; the company distributes parts and supplies from facilities in Israel. In 2011 the company was acquired by Vintage Capital Group LLC.

CAPROCK COMMUNICATIONS INC.

4400 S. Sam Houston Pkwy. East
Houston TX 77048
Phone: 832-668-2300
Fax: 832-668-2388
Web: www.caprock.com

CEO: Peter Shaper
CFO: –
HR: –
FYE: December 31
Type: Subsidiary

CapRock Communications provides satellite communications services where others fear to tread. The company's network enables the secure transmission of voice data and video primarily for customers operating in remote locations or harsh environments such as offshore drilling platforms. Clients come from the construction maritime military mining and energy exploration industries. CapRock also provides systems integration and project management services including engineering design equipment installation and testing. CapRock operates a global communications network in cooperation with other satellite fleet operators. The company was acquired by Harris Corporation in 2010 for about $525 million in cash.

CAPSONIC GROUP LLC

460 2nd St.
Elgin IL 60123-7008
Phone: 847-888-7300
Fax: 847-888-7543
Web: www.capsonic.com

CEO: Greg Liautaud
CFO: Thomas Gillespie
HR: –
FYE: December 31
Type: Private

Following the belief that specialization makes money Capsonic Group specializes in high-volume production of custom molded plastic inserts and composites. Its products include connectors for electronics and vehicles; sensors for telecommunication devices; switch bases for power tools; and brush holders for office machines and appliances. About half of its sales are from automakers and component makers such as GM Ford and Hewlett-Packard. The company operates a plant housing 50 30-ton to 300-ton presses that bind multiple plastic and metal materials to create one part. Its services include product design and prototyping. Sister company Capsonic Automotive produces solenoid switches and lighting components.

CAPSTONE TURBINE CORP. NAS: CPST

21211 Nordhoff Street
Chatsworth, CA 91311
Phone: 818-734-5300
Fax: –
Web: www.capstoneturbine.com

CEO: Darren R. Jamison
CFO: Richard K. (Rich) Atkinson
HR: Larry Colson
FYE: March 31
Type: Public

Capstone Turbine's products are here when the lights go out. The company makes the Capstone MicroTurbine a power-generating system that produces environmentally friendly electricity and heat. The microturbines which can operate on a stand-alone basis or be connected to the utility grid run on a variety of liquid and gaseous fuels such as natural gas diesel kerosene propane and flare gases from landfills and sewage plants. In the event of a power outage customers can use microturbines to produce their own secure power for extended periods of time; microturbines can also be used as onboard battery chargers for hybrid electric vehicles.

	Annual Growth	03/11	03/12	03/13	03/14	03/15
Sales ($ mil.)	9.0%	81.9	109.4	127.6	133.1	115.5
Net income ($ mil.)	–	(38.5)	(18.8)	(22.6)	(16.3)	(31.5)
Market value ($ mil.)	(22.7%)	29.9	16.8	14.9	35.2	10.7
Employees	4.9%	195	215	217	225	236

CAPTAIN D'S LLC

1717 Elm Hill Pike Ste. A-1
Nashville TN 37210
Phone: 615-391-5461
Fax: 615-231-2309
Web: www.captainds.com

CEO: Phil Greifeld
CFO: –
HR: –
FYE: October 31
Type: Private

This Captain sails the fast food seas. Captain D's operates Captain D's Seafood Kitchen a leading quick-service seafood chain with more than 525 company-owned and franchised locations in about 25 states. The eateries feature a menu of fried and broiled fish shrimp and chicken as well as french fries hush puppies and corn on the cob. Captain D's also serves fish and chicken sandwiches salads and menu items for kids. Most of the restaurants are located in such southern states as Georgia Tennessee and Alabama. Ray Danner started the business as Mr. D's in 1969. Private equity firm Sun Capital Partners acquired the chain in 2010.

CAPTECH VENTURES INC.

7100 FOREST AVE STE 204
RICHMOND, VA 232263742
Phone: 804-355-0511
Fax: –
Web: www.captechconsulting.com

CEO: Sandy Williamson
CFO: –
HR: –
FYE: December 31
Type: Private

CapTech Ventures provides management and IT consulting and related services to business and public sector clients primarily in the Mid-Atlantic region. The company specializes in providing technology services and products (covering big data agile methodology mobile app development and digital strategies for top companies and government agencies). Areas of specialty include data warehousing network design systems integration software interface design training and network security. CapTech serves retailers health care providers and financial services companies among others. Clients have included Campbell Soup Company the Richmond Virginia Chamber of Commerce and the US Navy.

	Annual Growth	12/01	12/02	12/04	12/11	12/12
Sales ($ mil.)	23.0%	–	8.7	14.4	49.8	69.1
Net income ($ mil.)	66.4%	–	–	0.1	2.3	5.7
Market value ($ mil.)	–	–	–	–	–	–
Employees	–	–	–	–	–	415

CARA THERAPEUTICS INC NMS: CARA

1 Parrott Drive
Shelton, CT 06484
Phone: 203 567-1500
Fax: –
Web: www.caratherapeutics.com

CEO: Derek Chalmers
CFO: Josef C. Schoell
HR: –
FYE: December 31
Type: Public

Cara Therapeutics cares about pain therapy. The clinical-stage biopharmaceutical company focuses on developing and commercializing new chemical products designed to alleviate pain by selectively targeting kappa opioid receptors. Its proprietary class of product candidates target the body's peripheral nervous system. In test with patients with moderate-to-severe pain they have have demonstrated efficacy without inducing many of the undesirable side effects often associated with pain therapeutics. Cara's most advanced product candidate is intravenous CR845. The company filed to go public in 2014.

	Annual Growth	12/10	12/11	12/12	12/13	12/14
Sales ($ mil.)	–	0.0	–	1.2	12.0	3.2
Net income ($ mil.)	–	0.0	(9.8)	(6.3)	(4.0)	(17.7)
Market value ($ mil.)	–	0.0	–	–	–	227.3
Employees	16.8%	–	–	11	11	15

CARACO PHARMACEUTICAL LABORATORIES LTD. NYSE AMEX: CPD

1150 Elijah McCoy Dr.
Detroit MI 48202
Phone: 313-871-8400
Fax: 313-871-8314
Web: www.caraco.com

CEO: Subramanian Kalyanasundaram
CFO: Mukul Rathi
HR: Annmarie Ryan
FYE: March 31
Type: Public

Caraco Pharmaceutical Laboratories peddles cheaper versions of prescription drugs. The drug company sells generic knock-offs of a wide variety of pharmaceuticals including about 40 prescription products in various strengths and dosages. Its product lineup includes treatments for high blood pressure cancer nervous system conditions diabetes allergies and pain. Indian drugmaker Sun Pharmaceutical Industries owns a majority stake in the firm and licenses US marketing rights to Caraco for a number of generic drugs. Caraco markets its products throughout the US and Puerto Rico selling primarily to pharmaceutical wholesalers. However it has halted manufacturing operations due to regulatory concerns.

CARAHSOFT TECHNOLOGY CORP.

12369 Sunrise Valley Dr. Ste. D2
Reston VA 20191
Phone: 703-871-8500
Fax: 703-871-8505
Web: www.carahsoft.com

CEO: –
CFO: John Bukman
HR: –
FYE: December 31
Type: Private

Carahsoft loves it when the government spends money (on technology that is.) It is a B2G (business to government) contractor that distributes software products by Adobe Red Hat SAP Symantec and VMware to local state and federal agencies especially through the General Services Administration. Carahsoft's technology partners offer data storage cloud computing resources encryption and open-source software and intelligence and human resources technologies among others. Founded in 2004 the company was named after CEO Craig Abod's daughter Carah.

CARAUSTAR RECOVERED FIBER GROUP INC.

5000 Austell-Powder Springs Rd. Ste. 300
Austell GA 30106-3227
Phone: 770-948-3101
Fax: 718-292-6348
Web: www.manhattanbeer.com

CEO: –
CFO: –
HR: –
FYE: December 31
Type: Subsidiary

Caraustar Recovered Fiber Group (RFG) a division of Caraustar Industries provides recovered fiber for use as paperboard through its processing plants and recycling centers located across the US. Recovered paper is processed into paperboard which in turn is converted into products such as tubes cores composite containers cartons and custom packaging. Through its own facilities and through brokerage operations Caraustar RFG distributes over a million tons of paper stock annually. Caraustar Industries filed Chapter 11 in May 2009; it reorganized and emerged as a private company in August 2009 after eliminating approximately $135 million in debt. Wayzata Investment Partners is the controlling stakeholder.

CARBO CERAMICS INC.

NYS: CRR

575 North Dairy Ashford, Suite 300
Houston, TX 77079
Phone: 281 921-6400
Fax: –
Web: www.carboceramics.com

CEO: Gary A. Kolstad
CFO: Ernesto Bautista
HR: Ellen Smith
FYE: December 31
Type: Public

CARBO Ceramics' proppants (tiny alumina-based ceramic beads) are a welcome release for natural gas and oil well operators. To increase well production operators often pump fluids down wells at high pressure to create fractures in the hydrocarbon-bearing rock formation (hydraulic fracturing). Proppants are suspended in the fluid to fill the channels and "prop" up the fissures so that natural gas and oil may flow to the surface. The company's products compete against guar bean and sand-based proppants. CARBO Ceramics also offers related software consulting services and specialty polymers.

	Annual Growth	12/10	12/11	12/12	12/13	12/14
Sales ($ mil.)	8.2%	473.1	625.7	645.5	667.4	648.3
Net income ($ mil.)	(8.3%)	78.7	130.1	105.9	84.9	55.6
Market value ($ mil.)	(21.1%)	2,391.0	2,848.0	1,809.1	2,691.0	924.9
Employees	6.8%	806	961	992	1,025	1,048

CARBONITE INC

NMS: CARB

Two Avenue de Lafayette
Boston, MA 02111
Phone: 617 587-1100
Fax: –
Web: www.carbonite.com

CEO: Mohamad S. Ali
CFO: Anthony Folger
HR: –
FYE: December 31
Type: Public

Carbonite's cloud-based backup service preserves your files just like it did Han Solo but without the hibernation sickness. The company's software backs up documents emails music photos and settings for PCs (Windows or Mac) and mobile devices such as Apple's iPhone RIM's BlackBerry and Google OS Android phones. Carbonite's software is used by more than 1.5 million consumers and small to mid-sized businesses customers in more than 100 countries but mostly in the US (94%); it charges flat rates for varying levels of one year of unlimited online backup. Its backup software saves customers' files on servers at the company's data centers in Massachusetts and Arizona.

	Annual Growth	12/10	12/11	12/12	12/13	12/14
Sales ($ mil.)	33.5%	38.6	60.5	84.0	107.2	122.6
Net income ($ mil.)	–	(25.8)	(23.5)	(18.9)	(10.6)	(9.4)
Market value ($ mil.)	8.7%	–	302.0	251.7	321.9	388.3
Employees	30.0%	206	364	378	434	589

CARDEAN LEARNING GROUP LLC

111 N. Canal St. Ste. 455
Chicago IL 60606-7204
Phone: 312-669-5222
Fax: 954-360-7081
Web: www.valveresearch.com

CEO: J Theodore Sanders
CFO: –
HR: –
FYE: December 31
Type: Private

A maker of Masters of the Universe? Well not quite but Cardean Learning which operates Cardean University can make you a Master of Business. The company offers more than 60 online graduate and undergraduate degrees certificates and specializations including a fully accredited MBA program. Cardean Learning created its MBA courses in collaboration with Carnegie Mellon University Columbia Business School the London School of Economics and Political Science Stanford University and the University of Chicago Graduate School of Business. The institution is accredited by the Accrediting Commission of the Distance Education Training Council (DETC).

CARDIAC SCIENCE CORPORATION

3303 Monte Villa Pkwy.
Bothell WA 98021
Phone: 425-402-2000
Fax: 909-357-2020
Web: www.maisto.com

CEO: Neal K Long
CFO: Doug Pepper
HR: –
FYE: December 31
Type: Subsidiary

The heart can't lie to Cardiac Science. The medical device company makes cardiovascular monitoring and therapeutic equipment including automated external defibrillators (AEDs) and electrocardiograms (ECGs/EKGs) as well as systems that analyze the heart's performance under stress. Its monitoring systems are used for extended surveillance and include telemetry devices for evaluation of the heart during rehabilitation exercise. Cardiac Science sells accessories such as lead wires and electrodes and provides product repair and technical support services. The company which has direct and indirect sales channels in more than 100 countries is a subsidiary of India-based health equipment manufacturer Opto Circuits.

CARDICA INC
NAS: CRDC

900 Saginaw Drive
Redwood City, CA 94063
Phone: 650 364-9975
Fax: –
Web: www.cardica.com

CEO: Julian Nikolchev
CFO: Robert Y. Newell
HR: –
FYE: June 30
Type: Public

Cardica wants to help surgeons treat patients with coronary heart disease. The company makes products including the C-Port and PAS-Port systems that are used in coronary artery bypass surgery. The automated systems connect blood vessels that restore blood flow beyond the closed sections of coronary arteries. Its products offer a less time-consuming and simpler alternative to hand-sewn suturing. Cardica markets its C-Port and PAS-Port systems in the US via direct sales and in the EU through distributors. Century Medical is the exclusive distributor of PAS-Port systems in Japan. The company has a co-development agreement with Cook for a vascular access closure device.

	Annual Growth	06/11	06/12	06/13	06/14	06/15
Sales ($ mil.)	(31.1%)	13.2	3.7	3.5	3.6	3.0
Net income ($ mil.)	–	(3.5)	(13.6)	(16.1)	(17.0)	(19.2)
Market value ($ mil.)	(34.8%)	24.3	16.7	9.9	10.1	4.4
Employees	(2.2%)	48	55	63	69	44

CARDINAL BANKSHARES CORP.
NBB: CDBK

101 Jacksonville Circle, P.O. Box 215
Floyd, VA 24091
Phone: 540 745-4191
Fax: 540 745-4133
Web: www.bankoffloyd.com

CEO: Mark A. Smith
CFO: J. Alan Dickerson
HR: –
FYE: December 31
Type: Public

Cardinal Bankshares may not answer to the Pope but it does pay attention to what its shareholders have to say. It is the holding company for The Bank of Floyd which serves southwest Virginia's Floyd County and surrounding areas from about 10 locations. The bank offers standard retail products and services including checking and savings accounts CDs IRAs and credit cards. It uses funds from deposits to write loans primarily real estate mortgages and loans. Bank subsidiary FBC has interests in two Virginia title insurance firms and an investment services company.

	Annual Growth	12/10	12/11	12/12	12/13	12/14
Assets ($ mil.)	2.7%	249.1	266.2	282.1	268.8	276.8
Net income ($ mil.)	(26.3%)	1.0	1.1	(4.2)	(7.2)	0.3
Market value ($ mil.)	1.4%	12.7	20.3	20.7	17.7	13.4
Employees	(2.5%)	40	39	–	–	–

CARDINAL FINANCIAL CORP
NMS: CFNL

8270 Greensboro Drive, Suite 500
McLean, VA 22102
Phone: 703 584-3400
Fax: –
Web: www.cardinalbank.com

CEO: Christopher W. Bergstrom
CFO: Mark A. Wendel
HR: Eleanor D. Schmidt
FYE: December 31
Type: Public

Cardinal Financial can help you keep out of the red. The holding company owns Cardinal Bank which operates nearly 30 branches in northern Virginia and the Washington DC metropolitan area. Serving commercial and retail customers it offers such deposit options as checking savings and money market accounts; IRAs; and CDs as well as trust services. Commercial real estate loans make up more than 40% of Cardinal Financial's loan portfolio; residential mortgages construction loans business loans and home equity and consumer loans round out the bank's lending activities. Subsidiary Cardinal Wealth Services provides brokerage and investment services through an alliance with Raymond James Financial.

	Annual Growth	12/10	12/11	12/12	12/13	12/14
Assets ($ mil.)	13.2%	2,072.0	2,602.7	3,039.2	2,894.2	3,399.1
Net income ($ mil.)	15.4%	18.4	28.0	45.3	25.5	32.7
Market value ($ mil.)	14.3%	373.1	344.5	522.9	577.1	636.1
Employees	15.1%	417	510	706	809	733

CARDINAL HEALTH PHARMACY SOLUTIONS

1330 Enclave Pkwy.
Houston TX 77077
Phone: 281-749-4000
Fax: 281-749-2068
Web: www.cardinal.com/us/en/pharmacysolutions/overv

CEO: Mike Riddle
CFO: Jeff Henderson
HR: Andy Brinckerhoff
FYE: June 30
Type: Business Segment

Cardinal Health Pharmacy Solutions soars above the playing field as a leading pharmacy management provider for hospitals in the US. The company provides services for all aspects of its institutional clients' pharmacy operations including full-service outsourcing staffing purchasing cost control regulatory compliance consulting finance and efficiency consulting quality and safety control and information technology. Its inventory control products include the Rxe-source remote order entry software (online prescription processing by remote pharmacists) and the Rxe-view medication order management system (for prescription use tracking and metrics). The company is a division of drug distributor Cardinal Health.

CARDINAL HEALTH, INC.
NYS: CAH

7000 Cardinal Place
Dublin, OH 43017
Phone: 614 757-5000
Fax: –
Web: www.cardinalhealth.com

CEO: George S. Barrett
CFO: Michael C. (Mike) Kaufmann
HR: Mindy Stobart
FYE: June 30
Type: Public

When your local pharmacy runs low on drugs or supplies it probably calls Cardinal Health. The company is a top distributor of pharmaceuticals and other medical supplies and equipment in the US. Its pharmaceutical division provides supply chain services including branded and generic prescription and OTC drug distribution. It also franchises Medicine Shoppe retail pharmacies. Its medical division parcels out medical laboratory and surgical supplies and provides logistics consulting and data management. Customers include retail pharmacies hospitals nursing homes doctor's offices and other health care businesses. International markets for Cardinal Health include China.

	Annual Growth	06/11	06/12	06/13	06/14	06/15
Sales ($ mil.)	(0.0%)	102,644.2	107,552.0	101,093.0	91,084.0	102,531.0
Net income ($ mil.)	6.1%	959.0	1,069.0	334.0	1,166.0	1,215.0
Market value ($ mil.)	16.5%	14,897.8	13,776.0	15,481.6	22,487.7	27,437.2
Employees	2.0%	31,900	32,500	33,600	34,000	34,500

CARDINAL LOGISTICS MANAGEMENT CORPORATION

5333 Davidson Hwy.
Concord NC 28027
Phone: 704-786-6125
Fax: 704-788-6618
Web: www.cardlog.com

CEO: –
CFO: Michael Roberts
HR: –
FYE: December 31
Type: Private

Cardinal Logistics Management sings a sweet song when it comes to freight transportation. The company is a leading North American logistics provider with one of the largest dedicated fleet operations in the US. Its services include less-than-truckload (LTL) transportation in which freight from multiple shippers is combined into a single trailer; dedicated contract carriage in which drivers and equipment are assigned to customers long term; bulk transport; supply chain consulting; and warehousing and distribution. Cardinal Logistics which is owned by New York private equity firm Centerbridge Partners merged with another Centerbridge owned company Greatwide Logistics Services in early 2013.

CARDINGTON YUTAKA TECHNOLOGIES INC.

575 W. Main St.
Cardington OH 43315
Phone: 419-864-8777
Fax: 419-864-7771
Web: www.yutakatech.com

CEO: –
CFO: –
HR: –
FYE: March 31
Type: Subsidiary

Cardington Yutaka Technologies (CYT) and its parent company Honda Motor Co. possess a certain synergy; subsidiary CYT supplies its parent with automotive parts and never wishes to appear exhausted. Primary parts manufactured by the company include exhaust systems and torque and catalytic converters. It also manufactures an assortment of other parts for manufacturers of both automobiles and all-terrain vehicles. CYT operates three manufacturing plants in the US — Alabama Ohio and South Carolina. The company's main customers are the various manufacturing plants of Honda of America Mfg. Inc.

CARDONE INDUSTRIES INC.

5501 Whitaker Ave.
Philadelphia PA 19124-1799
Phone: 215-912-3000
Fax: 215-912-3700
Web: www.cardone.com

CEO: Terry McCormack
CFO: Kevin Bagby
HR: Sal Lo Dico
FYE: December 31
Type: Private

Old car parts are the new cool thanks to Cardone Industries. The company is one of the largest remanufacturers of auto parts for the aftermarket. Cardone offers seven lines under the A1 Cardone brand: brakes (master cylinders) drivetrain parts (constant-velocity axles) electronics (ignition distributors mass air flow sensors) fuel/air systems (intake manifolds) motors (window-lift and wiper) pumps (water and vacuum) and steering (power-steering pumps). New parts are also sold under the Cardone Select name. Cardone's eco-friendly benefits include material and energy conservation and landfill reduction.

CARDIOGENESIS CORPORATION

11 Musick
Irvine CA 92618-1638
Phone: 949-420-1800
Fax: 949-420-1888
Web: www.cardiogenesis.com

CEO: –
CFO: William R Abbott
HR: –
FYE: December 31
Type: Subsidiary

Cardiogenesis will leave a hole in your heart and not feel a pang of guilt. The company's laser and fiber-optic systems are used for transmyocardial revascularization (TMR) and percutaneous myocardial channeling (PMC) procedures that use a laser to cut channels through the heart muscle into the heart chamber to help circulation in cardiac patients. Its SolarGen 2100 system is FDA-approved and is marketed through Cardiogenesis' sales force in the US and through international distributors. The company's PMC system is available outside the US. It also sells catheters and other related equipment to operate its laser systems. Tissue preservation firm CryoLife bought Cardiogenesis in 2010 for about $22 million.

CARDTRONICS INC

NMS: CATM

3250 Briarpark Drive, Suite 400
Houston, TX 77042
Phone: 832 308-4000
Fax: –
Web: www.cardtronics.com

CEO: Steven A. (Steve) Rathgaber
CFO: Edward H. (Ed) West
HR: Debra Bronder
FYE: December 31
Type: Public

Cardtronics is the largest non-bank owner and operator of automated teller machines (ATMs) and related financial services equipment in the world. It maintains more than 111000 cash machines in Europe and North America including 93350 locations in the US many of which are branded by banks such as Chase SunTrust and Citibank. The company also leases and sells machines to airports convenience stores supermarkets malls and drug stores including Walgreen and Rite-Aid stores. Most clients pay the company to handle some or all of the maintenance services or operational services of their ATMs. Cardtronics also operates Allpoint which is the largest surcharge-free ATM network in the US with 55000 machines.

	Annual Growth	12/10	12/11	12/12	12/13	12/14
Sales ($ mil.)	18.7%	532.1	624.6	780.4	876.5	1,054.8
Net income ($ mil.)	(3.8%)	41.1	70.1	43.3	23.8	35.2
Market value ($ mil.)	21.5%	788.7	1,205.9	1,057.9	1,936.2	1,719.2
Employees	49.6%	535	643	740	1,070	2,683

CARDIOVASCULAR SYSTEMS, INC

NMS: CSII

1225 Old Highway 8 Northwest
St. Paul, MN 55112-6416
Phone: 651 259-1600
Fax: –
Web: www.csi360.com

CEO: David L. (Dave) Martin
CFO: Laurence L. (Larry) Betterley
HR: –
FYE: June 30
Type: Public

While Cardiovascular Systems Inc. (CSI) deals with blood there's no crime scene investigation here. Its Orbital Atherectomy Systems (OAS) treat calcified and fibrotic plaque in arterial vessels throughout the leg and heart in a few minutes of treatment time and address many of the limitations associated with existing surgical catheter and pharmacological treatment alternatives. CSI's Diamondback 360° Predator 360° and Stealth 360° products are minimally invasive catheter systems that help restore blood flow to the legs of patients with peripheral arterial disease (PAD) a condition that occurs when plaque builds up on limb arteries; and address the effects of coronary arterial disease (CAD).

	Annual Growth	06/11	06/12	06/13	06/14	06/15
Sales ($ mil.)	23.2%	78.8	82.5	103.9	136.6	181.5
Net income ($ mil.)	–	(11.1)	(16.8)	(24.0)	(35.3)	(32.8)
Market value ($ mil.)	16.1%	464.4	312.3	676.2	993.9	843.7
Employees	20.2%	286	290	345	479	597

CARE NEW ENGLAND HEALTH SYSTEM INC

45 WILLARD AVE
PROVIDENCE, RI 029053218
Phone: 401-453-7900
Fax: –
Web: www.carenewengland.org

CEO: Dennis D. Keefe
CFO: Joseph Iannoni
HR: –
FYE: September 30
Type: Private

Care New England Health System take pains to ease its patients' pain. The system operates four hospitals: Kent Hospital a general acute care facility with about 360 beds; the 290-bed Memorial Hospital of Rhode Island; psychiatric facility Butler Hospital; and Women & Infants Hospital of Rhode Island which specializes in obstetrics gynecology and newborn pediatrics. All told the system has more than 963 licensed beds. Care New England formed in 1996 by three member hospitals also operates a home health agency and outpatient care facilities. The system plans to merge with Massachusetts-based Southcoast Health thereby establishing an eight-hospital health system.

	Annual Growth	09/02	09/03	09/04	09/12	09/13
Assets ($ mil.)	(10.7%)	–	435.2	472.5	783.8	139.7
Net income ($ mil.)	(13.3%)	–	–	7.1	24.0	2.0
Market value ($ mil.)	–	–	–	–	–	–
Employees	–	–	–	–	–	6,500

CARE.COM INC
NYS: CRCM

77 Fourth Avenue, Fifth Floor
Waltham, MA 02451
Phone: 781 642-5900
Fax: –
Web: www.care.com

CEO: Sheila Lirio Marcelo
CFO: Steve Boulanger
HR: Joanne Derr
FYE: December 27
Type: Public

Care.com lets families shop for child care senior care special needs care pet care tutoring and housekeeping services via web and mobile platforms. The site has more than 14 million members including more than 7.5 million families and more than 6 million caregivers who use Care.com to market their services and find employment. The service which is actively used in more than 15 countries (primarily the US but also Canada the UK and other parts of Western Europe) averages about 6.5 million unique visitors each month including about 4 million visitors per month from mobile devices. Care.com also offers household payroll management (HomePay) and other services. In early 2014 Care.com went public.

	Annual Growth	12/10	12/11	12/12	12/13	12/14
Sales ($ mil.)	–	0.0	26.0	48.5	81.5	116.7
Net income ($ mil.)	–	0.0	(12.2)	(20.4)	(28.3)	(80.3)
Market value ($ mil.)	–	–	0.0	–	–	263.4
Employees	3.7%	–	–	793	835	853

CAREALLIANCE HEALTH SERVICES

315 CALHOUN ST STE 107
CHARLESTON, SC 294011115
Phone: 843-724-2000
Fax: –

CEO: David L. Dunlap
CFO: Bret Johnson
HR: Melanie Stith
FYE: December 31
Type: Private

CareAlliance Health Services (doing business as Roper St. Francis Healthcare) knows that St. Francis may be the patron saint of animals but its medical centers are more concerned with humans. The company operates four hospitals — the 370-bed Roper Hospital the 200-bed Bon Secours St. Francis Hospital the 85-bed Mount Pleasant Hospital and the Roper Rehabilitation Hospital. Besides providing home health services it also operates outpatient emergency primary care and diagnostic facilities. Roper St. Francis Healthcare serves Charleston South Carolina and surrounding communities. Its Roper St. Francis Physician Partners is one of the region's largest physician practices.

	Annual Growth	12/05	12/06	12/08	12/09	12/12
Sales ($ mil.)	(12.8%)	–	1,658.8	618.0	682.8	729.8
Net income ($ mil.)	–	–	–	(51.9)	56.4	18.3
Market value ($ mil.)	–	–	–	–	–	–
Employees	–	–	–	–	–	5,000

CARECENTRIC INC.

Overlook II 2839 Paces Ferry Rd. Ste. 900
Atlanta GA 30339
Phone: 678-264-4400
Fax: 770-384-1650
Web: www.carecentric.com

CEO: John Driscoll
CFO: Lyle Newkirk
HR: –
FYE: December 31
Type: Subsidiary

CareCentric helps health care providers spend less time managing their business operations and more time paying attention to patients. Formerly Simione Central Holdings the company offers software and services to help manage billing collections back office human resource development and process improvement systems for post-acute and long-term care providers. In addition to its software offerings CareCentric also provides outsourced scheduling patient intake marketing and quality assurance services. In early 2011 Mediware acquired CareCentric.

CAREER EDUCATION CORP
NMS: CECO

231 N. Martingale Road
Schaumburg, IL 60173
Phone: 847 781-3600
Fax: –
Web: www.careered.com

CEO: Todd S. Nelson
CFO: David A. (Dave) Rawden
HR: Maureen Cahill
FYE: December 31
Type: Public

Career Education Corporation (CEC) has made a career of handing out diplomas. The for-profit company owns and operates almost 90 US campuses (a third of which are slated for closure) and online programs that offer post-secondary education to about 53700 enrolled students. CEC offers certificate and degree programs in areas including information technology health education business studies culinary arts and visual communication and design. The group's operating names include Colorado Technical University (CTU) Sanford-Brown Institutes Le Cordon Bleu and American InterContinental University (AIU). CEC schools offers non-degree certificates as well as associate bachelor's master's and doctoral degrees.

	Annual Growth	12/10	12/11	12/12	12/13	12/14
Sales ($ mil.)	(23.1%)	2,124.2	1,884.5	1,489.3	1,057.4	741.4
Net income ($ mil.)	–	157.8	18.6	(142.8)	(164.3)	(178.2)
Market value ($ mil.)	(23.9%)	1,399.7	538.1	237.2	384.9	469.9
Employees	(15.0%)	15,598	14,602	12,435	9,075	8,127

CAREFIRST INC.

10455 Mill Run Circle
Owings Mills MD 21117-5559
Phone: 410-528-7000
Fax: 513-381-0149
Web: www.firststudentinc.com

CEO: Chuck Burrell
CFO: –
HR: –
FYE: December 31
Type: Private - Not-for-Pr

CareFirst makes health care coverage its No.1 priority. The firm is a not-for-profit non-stock holding company with subsidiaries providing managed health care plans to about 3.4 million members in Maryland and Washington DC. The company's main subsidiaries CareFirst of Maryland and Group Hospitalization and Medical Services are licensees of the Blue Cross and Blue Shield Association. Together the subsidiaries do business as CareFirst BlueCross BlueShield and offer Blue-branded HMO and PPO plans as well as consumer-driven coverage to individuals and employers throughout their service areas. Non-Blue subsidiaries and affiliates provide third-party benefits administration and claims processing services.

CAREFUSION CORP
NYS: CFN

3750 Torrey View Court
San Diego, CA 92130
Phone: 858 617-2000
Fax: –
Web: www.carefusion.com

CEO: Kieran T Gallahue
CFO: James F Hinrichs
HR: –
FYE: June 30
Type: Public

CareFusion cares about eliminating confusion and infection in hospital settings. It sells medical equipment - infusion and respiratory ventilation systems - and accompanying disposables for infection prevention. The company's Pyxis automated medication dispensing units cut down on clinician error when dealing with patients in critical care settings. Its Alaris infusion products include software to reduce IV medication errors. The company also makes AVEA respiratory ventilation devices SensorMedics pulmonary care products and V. Mueller surgical instruments. Other products and software help prevent the spread of hospital-acquired infections. Medical equipment maker Becton Dickenson is buying CareFusion.

	Annual Growth	06/10	06/11	06/12	06/13	06/14
Sales ($ mil.)	(0.6%)	3,929.0	3,528.0	3,598.0	3,550.0	3,842.0
Net income ($ mil.)	21.1%	194.0	244.0	293.0	385.0	417.0
Market value ($ mil.)	18.2%	4,639.9	5,553.5	5,249.0	7,532.1	9,065.1
Employees	1.6%	15,000	14,000	15,000	15,000	16,000

CAREGROUP INC.

375 LONGWOOD AVE FL 7
BOSTON, MA 022155395
Phone: 617-667-1715
Fax: -
Web: www.caregroup.org

CEO: -
CFO: -
HR: -
FYE: September 30
Type: Private

Thanks to CareGroup there's well-bein' in Beantown. CareGroup serves Massachusetts residents through its flagship facility the 672-bed Beth Israel Deaconess Medical Center (BIDMC) and five other hospital campuses. With more than 1100 beds total the system provides a comprehensive range of general acute care as well as specialty care in a number of areas including orthopedics obstetrics diabetes and cardiovascular disease. In addition to its hospitals CareGroup operates a network of outpatient clinics and physician practices in the Boston area. It is also heavily involved in biomedical research and medical education.

	Annual Growth	09/08	09/09	09/10	09/11	09/12
Sales ($ mil.)	2.9%	-	-	-	2,380.1	2,448.8
Net income ($ mil.)	179.5%	-	-	-	47.0	131.3
Market value ($ mil.)	-	-	-	-	-	-
Employees	-	-	-	-	-	12,000

CAREY INTERNATIONAL INC.

4530 Wisconsin Ave. NW
Washington DC 20016
Phone: 202-895-1200
Fax: 202-895-1269
Web: www.carey.com

CEO: Gary L Kessler
CFO: -
HR: -
FYE: November 30
Type: Private

Carey International carries passengers in about 550 major cities in some 60 countries. The company provides chauffeured car services primarily to business travelers as well as ground transportation logistics management through a global network of franchisees operated by the Carey family of subsidiaries licensees and affiliates. Services include airport pick-ups and drop-offs hourly charters special events and leisure travel. The company's fleet consists of sedans limousines vans minibuses and buses. Carey links its centralized reservation system to terminals at travel agencies corporate travel departments and government offices. It also offers online reservations. Carey was founded in 1921.

CARHARTT INC.

5750 Mercury Dr.
Dearborn MI 48126
Phone: 313-271-8460
Fax: 313-271-3455
Web: www.carhartt.com

CEO: -
CFO: Linda P Hubbard
HR: Tom Harvey
FYE: December 31
Type: Private

Real workers don't leave home without first donning their Carhartts. The clothing maker produces rugged overalls flame-resistant workwear outerwear sweatshirts sportswear and pants favored by farmers and other hard-working people. Its products have even appeared in such films as "The Perfect Storm" and "The Horse Whisperer". Most of Carhartt's items sold to men women and children are made in US factories; the rest are produced in Mexico and Europe. Besides its own shops Carhartt's apparel is carried by major chains including Bass Pro Shops and Cabela's and international retailers in North America Europe Japan and Australia. The family of founder Hamilton Carhartt owns the firm which was founded in 1889.

CARILION CLINIC

1906 Bellevue Ave.
Roanoke VA 24014
Phone: 540-981-7000
Fax: 540-344-5716
Web: www.carilion.com

CEO: Nancy Howell Agee
CFO: Don Lorton
HR: -
FYE: September 30
Type: Private - Not-for-Pr

Carilion Clinic cares for the citizens of southwestern Virginia. Founded in 1899 as the Roanoke Hospital Association the system today includes eight not-for-profit hospitals and one it co-owns one with Centra Health a network of 600 physicians and a research partnership with Virginia Tech. The system (including affiliates) has more than 1215 beds and 60 neonatal ICU beds available. Along with providing treatments for just about every medical ailment one can imagine Carilion Clinic provides continuing medical education through its affiliation with medical schools including Virginia Tech Carilion School of Medicine and Research Institute (VTC) and the Jefferson College of Health Science.

CARITAS NORWOOD HOSPITAL INC.

800 WASHINGTON ST STE 1
NORWOOD, MA 020623487
Phone: 781-769-4000
Fax: -

CEO: -
CFO: -
HR: -
FYE: September 30
Type: Private

Caritas Norwood Hospital cares for hearts (and other body parts) of people in the greater Boston area. Operating as Norwood Hospital the facility is a community hospital with some 265 beds that serves patients in Norwood Massachusetts and surrounding towns. Founded in 1902 the acute care hospital has a medical staff of more than 460 that provides area residents with emergency and general health care and medical transport services. Norwood Hospital is also home to specialized programs including behavioral health services cancer treatment cardiology obstetrics/gynecology orthopedic medicine pediatrics rehabilitation sleep disorder treatment and surgery. Norwood Hospital is part of the Steward Health Care System.

	Annual Growth	09/04	09/05	09/06	09/08	09/09
Sales ($ mil.)	1.6%	-	150.0	153.4	151.5	159.6
Net income ($ mil.)	(34.3%)	-	-	15.1	(3.7)	4.3
Market value ($ mil.)	-	-	-	-	-	-
Employees	-	-	-	-	-	1,800

CARL BUDDIG & COMPANY

950 W. 175 St.
Homewood IL 60430
Phone: 708-798-0900
Fax: 708-798-1284
Web: www.buddig.com

CEO: Thomas Buddig
CFO: -
HR: Dawn Krzystofiak
FYE: December 31
Type: Private

Less is more at the Carl Buddig & Company which manufactures and markets some of the thinnest lunch meats available. The company's most popular brand Original Buddig is a svelte 10-15 calories per slice and comes in choices such as beef chicken turkey ham pastrami and corned beef. It also offers Old Wisconsin brand smoked beef jerky sticks and snack bites along with wieners bratwurst Polish sausage summer sausage and ring bologna. Carl Buddig's meat products are available in the US Puerto Rico and Canada and are sold at retail food outlets including Kroger Albertson's Safeway Food Lion Giant Roundy's and others.

CARLE FOUNDATION HOSPITAL

611 W PARK ST
URBANA, IL 618012529
Phone: 217-326-2900
Fax: –
Web: www.carle.org

CEO: James C. Leonard
CFO: –
HR: Phil Kubow
FYE: December 31
Type: Private

Carle Foundation Hospital is a 393-bed acute-care facility that serves the residents of east central Illinois. The hospital includes the region's only Level I trauma center as well as a Level III perinatal center a neonatal ICU and centers devoted to cardiac and cancer care. It also runs a handful of specialty centers in the region. Carle Foundation Hospital is the primary teaching hospital for the University of Illinois College of Medicine at Urbana-Champaign. It is controlled by the not-for-profit Carle Foundation; sister company Carle Physician Group which boasts more than 400 physicians representing 80 specialties is one of the nation's largest private physician groups.

	Annual Growth	06/06	06/07	06/08	06/09*	12/12
Sales ($ mil.)	4.8%	–	–	383.0	365.9	462.6
Net income ($ mil.)	30.5%	–	–	36.7	30.6	106.4
Market value ($ mil.)	–	–	–	–	–	–
Employees	–	–	–	–	–	2,500

*Fiscal year change

CARLE PHYSICIAN GROUP

602 W. University Ave.
Urbana IL 61801
Phone: 217-383-3311
Fax: 217-383-6818
Web: www.carle-clinic.com

CEO: –
CFO: –
HR: –
FYE: December 31
Type: Private - Not-for-Pr

Carle Physician Group takes care of patients in east central Illinois. The company formerly named Carle Clinic Association is a not-for-profit physician-owned group made up of some 300 physicians practicing in more than 50 medical specialties at about a dozen locations. The organization's facilities which are spread out over seven different towns are linked by a network of electronic medical records allowing Carle Physician Group's medical providers to access a patient's medical information at any of its locations. The company also has its own managed care company Health Alliance Medical Plans. Carle Physician Group was acquired by Carle Foundation parent of Carle Foundation Hospital in 2010.

CARLETON COLLEGE

1 N COLLEGE ST
NORTHFIELD, MN 550574044
Phone: 507-222-4000
Fax: –
Web: www.apps.carleton.edu

CEO: –
CFO: –
HR: –
FYE: June 30
Type: Private

Curiosity is key at Carleton College. In addition to providing a traditional undergraduate liberal arts education the school encourages critical thinking and creativity at its campus in southern Minnesota. It has an enrollment of some 2000 students and a student-to-teacher ratio of 9:1. The college confers Bachelor of Arts degrees in more than 35 academic majors with a focus on fields including biology chemistry physics mathematics and computer science. The school offers education and foreign language certification and pre-professional programs as well. Carleton College was founded in 1866 by the Minnesota Conference of Congregational Churches under the name of Northfield College.

	Annual Growth	06/10	06/11	06/12	06/13	06/14
Sales ($ mil.)	0.1%	–	232.4	110.2	188.9	233.0
Net income ($ mil.)	–	–	–	(8.1)	66.7	108.2
Market value ($ mil.)	–	–	–	–	–	–
Employees	–	–	–	–	–	650

CARLISLE BRAKE & FRICTION INC.

6180 Cochran Rd.
Solon OH 44139
Phone: 440-528-4000
Fax: 440-528-4098
Web: www.carlislecbf.com

CEO: –
CFO: –
HR: –
FYE: December 31
Type: Subsidiary

Whether race car or dump truck Carlisle Brake & Friction (CBF) enables smoother starts and stops. The company provides high-performance brake clutch and transmission products to the off-highway aerospace agricultural construction industrial military and motorsports markets. Geared at OEMs and the aftermarket products include parking brakes wind turbine brakes brake pads transmission discs insulators and carbon-based friction materials. It has 10 manufacturing facilities in North America Europe and Asia/Pacific with additional R&D centers in the US and Wales and satellite sales offices in India and the Netherlands. CBF was formed in 2011 as a business segment of Carlisle Companies.

CARLISLE COMPANIES INC.

NYS: CSL

11605 North Community House Road, Suite 600
Charlotte, NC 28277
Phone: 704 501-1100
Fax: 704 501-1190
Web: www.carlisle.com

CEO: D. Christian (Chris) Koch
CFO: Steven J. (Steve) Ford
HR: –
FYE: December 31
Type: Public

Commercial manufacturing group Carlisle Companies is nothing if not diverse. Through dozens of subsidiaries and five business segments the multinational company manufactures and distributes an array of products including construction materials automotive products brake and friction products interconnect technologies and foodservice products. Its largest segments are Construction Materials (rubber and plastic roofing systems rigid foam insulation and waterproofing and protective coatings) and Interconnect Technologies (high-performance wire cable connectors contacts and cable assemblies for the aerospace and defense electronics). Carlisle strives to be a market leader in various niche markets.

	Annual Growth	12/11	12/12	12/13	12/14	12/15
Sales ($ mil.)	2.4%	3,224.5	3,629.4	2,943.0	3,204.0	3,543.2
Net income ($ mil.)	15.4%	180.3	270.2	209.7	251.3	319.7
Market value ($ mil.)	19.0%	2,837.5	3,763.7	5,085.7	5,780.0	5,680.7
Employees	2.2%	11,000	11,600	8,000	11,000	12,000

CARLISLE FOODSERVICE PRODUCTS INCORPORATED

4711 E. Hefner Rd.
Oklahoma City OK 73131
Phone: 405-475-5600
Fax: 405-475-5607
Web: www.carlislefsp.com

CEO: –
CFO: –
HR: –
FYE: December 31
Type: Subsidiary

Carlisle FoodService doesn't play tennis but the company does know something about serving. A subsidiary of Carlisle Companies Carlisle FoodService (CFSP) manufactures food service products that range from dinnerware and salad bar display cases to serving spoons and service carts. It also makes janitorial/sanitation products (brooms and brushes). CFSP caters to both commercial and institutional markets including restaurants schools and hospitals. It has manufacturing plants in the US China and Mexico. North America and Europe generate most of CFSP's business which represents about 10% of its parent's sales. Founded in 1955 as Continental Plastics CFSP joined the Carlisle group of companies in 1978.

CARLISLE TIRE & WHEEL COMPANY

23 Windham Blvd.
Aiken SC 29805-9320
Phone: 803-643-2900
Fax: 803-643-2919
Web: www.carlisletire.com

CEO: John Salvatore
CFO: –
HR: –
FYE: December 31
Type: Subsidiary

Big biters golf gliders and turf handlers are the wheels that keep business in motion at Carlisle Tire & Wheel. The company produces bias-ply steel-belted radial trailer tires rubber tires for non-automotive use as well as roll-formed and stamped steel wheels and tire and wheel assemblies. It sells to OEMs mass retailers and replacement markets for outdoor power equipment and power sports construction agricultural and recreational vehicles and home appliances. Manufacturing facilities in the US and China serve its diverse customer base in the US and Canada and less so Europe and Asia. Carlisle Tire & Wheel operates as a subsidiary within Carlisle Companies' family of transportation products.

CARLSON COMPANIES INC.

701 Carlson Pkwy.
Minnetonka MN 55305
Phone: 763-212-5000
Fax: 763-212-2219
Web: www.carlson.com

CEO: Trudy A Rautio
CFO: –
HR: –
FYE: December 31
Type: Private

Carlson Companies began in 1938 as the Gold Bond Stamp Company but has evolved into a leisure services juggernaut. The company owns a majority (55%) of travel giant Carlson Wagonlit. Its Carlson Hotels Worldwide owns and operates approximately 1075 hotels in more than 70 countries under brands such as Radisson Country Inns & Suites By Carlson and Park Plaza. In addition its Carlson Restaurants Worldwide includes the T.G.I. Friday's and Pick Up Stix chains. Chairman Marilyn Carlson Nelson and director Barbara Carlson Gage daughters of founder Curtis Carlson each own half of Carlson Companies.

CARLSON HOTELS WORLDWIDE INC.

701 Carlson Pkwy.
Minnetonka MN 55305
Phone: 763-212-5000
Fax: 763-212-3400
Web: www.carlsonhotels.com

CEO: –
CFO: –
HR: Stephanie Beyer
FYE: December 31
Type: Subsidiary

Carlson Hotels Worldwide has a little R&R on its mind. One of the world's leading hotel franchisors Carlson operates four lodging chains with more than 1000 properties in more than 75 countries including the upscale Radisson Hotel brand. The Radisson chain offers upscale amenities at more than 420 locations in about 70 countries. Carlson also owns the Park Plaza Hotels & Resorts (mid-market) Park Inn (economy) and Radisson Blu (upscale) brands. In addition its Country Inn & Suites chain provides extended-stay service at more than 480 locations. And with a 50.1% stake Carlson is the largest shareholder in The Rezidor Hotel Group. Carlson Hotels is a division of leisure conglomerate Carlson Companies.

CARLSON RESTAURANTS WORLDWIDE INC.

4201 Marsh Ln.
Carrollton TX 75007
Phone: 972-662-5400
Fax: 972-307-2822
Web: www.fridays.com

CEO: Nicholas P Shepherd
CFO: –
HR: Anne Varano
FYE: December 31
Type: Subsidiary

Carlson Restaurants Worldwide (CRW) has a lot of Friday's for which to be thankful. A leader in full-service restaurants the company operates and franchises more than 900 T.G.I. Friday's casual dining locations across the US and in about 60 other countries. The restaurant chain offers a menu featuring beef chicken and seafood entrees along with a selection of popular appetizers. About 300 T.G.I. Friday's units are company-owned while the rest are franchised. The company also operates Pick Up Stix an Asian-themed fast-casual chain with more than 90 locations in California Nevada and Arizona. CRW is a subsidiary of travel and leisure conglomerate Carlson Companies.

CARLTON FIELDS P.A.

Corporate Center 3 Intl Plaza Ste. 1000 4221 W. Boy Scout Blvd.
Tampa FL 33607
Phone: 813-223-7000
Fax: 813-229-4133
Web: www.carltonfields.com

CEO: Thomas A Snow
CFO: –
HR: –
FYE: January 31
Type: Private - Partnershi

Fielding complex questions of law is no monumental task for the firm Carlton Fields. The full service law firm offers expertise in such practice areas as intellectual property business litigation real estate health care and taxation. The firm employs about 300 attorneys in eight offices (six in Florida) serving clients throughout the Southeastern US and Latin America. In Florida its offices are located in Miami Orlando St. Petersburg Tallahassee Tampa and West Palm Beach. The firm also has offices in Atlanta and New York City. Carlton Fields was founded in 1901 by Milton and Giddings Mabry.

CARLYLE GROUP LP (THE)

NMS: CG

1001 Pennsylvania Avenue, N.W.
Washington, DC 20004-2505
Phone: 202 729-5626
Fax: –
Web: www.carlyle.com

CEO: David M. Rubenstein
CFO: Curtis L. (Curt) Buser
HR: Lori R. Sabet
FYE: December 31
Type: Public

One of the world's largest private investment firms The Carlyle Group owns 200-plus companies and boasts more than $190 billion in assets under management. Activities include management-led buyouts minority equity investments real estate venture capital and leveraged finance opportunities in the energy and power consumer and retail defense and aerospace and technology and business services industries. Other target sectors include financial services health care infrastructure aerospace and defense transportation telecommunications and media. Since its founding in 1987 Carlyle has made more than 1100 investments. Just a few years since going public in 2012 the firm has 35 offices across six continents.

	Annual Growth	12/10	12/11	12/12	12/13	12/14
Sales ($ mil.)	8.5%	2,798.9	2,845.3	2,973.1	4,441.2	3,880.3
Net income ($ mil.)	(51.3%)	1,525.6	1,356.9	20.3	104.1	85.8
Market value ($ mil.)	2.8%	–	–	1,763.8	2,413.6	1,863.4
Employees	8.3%	–	1,300	1,400	1,500	1,650

CARMA LABORATORIES INC.

9750 S FRANKLIN DR
FRANKLIN, WI 531328848
Phone: 414-421-7707
Fax: –
Web: www.mycarmex.com

CEO: Eric Woelbing
CFO: –
HR: –
FYE: December 31
Type: Private

Carma Laboratories wants to make it easier for you to smile and sit. The family-owned-and-operated company is most famous for its retro yellow-lidded vials of Carmex lip balm. The company also makes Am-Ren a zinc-oxide based diaper rash ointment and LANEX hemorrhoid ointment to soothe cracked and painful tissues elsewhere. Once sold mostly in the Midwest and the ski areas of the Rockies Carmex (now also in cherry and strawberry flavors) soothes lips in all 50 states Canada Australia and Europe. The company was founded by Alfred Woelbing who developed the formula for Carmex in 1937 as a treatment for his own cold sores.

	Annual Growth	12/03	12/04	12/05	12/07	12/09
Sales ($ mil.)	(38.0%)	–	–	272.7	42.7	40.2
Net income ($ mil.)	433.4%	–	–	0.0	14.9	13.3
Market value ($ mil.)	–	–	–	–	–	–
Employees	–	–	–	–	–	70

CARMAX INC.

NYS: KMX

12800 Tuckahoe Creek Parkway
Richmond, VA 23238
Phone: 804 747-0422
Fax: –
Web: www.carmax.com

CEO: Thomas J. (Tom) Folliard
CFO: Thomas W. (Tom) Reedy
HR: William D. (Bill) Nash
FYE: February 28
Type: Public

To the greatest extent possible CarMax helps drivers find late-model used autos. Typically selling vehicles that are less than six years old with less than 60000 miles the US's largest specialty used-car retailer buys reconditions and sells cars and light trucks through more than 140 superstores in 70-plus metropolitan markets mainly in the Southeast and Midwest. CarMax also operates seven new-car franchises and sells older vehicles through more than 350000 in-store auctions each year at some 50 stores. Additionally it sells older cars and trucks with higher mileage via its ValuMax program and offers vehicle financing through its CarMax Auto Finance unit.

	Annual Growth	02/11	02/12	02/13	02/14	02/15
Sales ($ mil.)	12.3%	8,975.6	10,003.6	10,962.8	12,574.3	14,268.7
Net income ($ mil.)	11.9%	380.9	413.8	434.3	492.6	597.4
Market value ($ mil.)	17.4%	7,387.7	6,410.2	8,022.7	10,115.6	14,017.2
Employees	9.1%	15,565	16,460	18,111	20,171	22,064

CARMIKE CINEMAS, INC.

NMS: CKEC

1301 First Avenue
Columbus, GA 31901-2109
Phone: 706 576-3400
Fax: –
Web: www.carmike.com

CEO: S. David Passman
CFO: Richard B. Hare
HR: –
FYE: December 31
Type: Public

At Carmike Cinemas the show must go on. The movie exhibitor owns operates or has stakes in about 250 theaters with more than 2500 screens in 35 states across the US. The company's theaters are located mostly in small to midsized communities where the chain hosts the only theater in town. Revenues come from the sale of admission tickets and concessions. Carmike also owns two Hollywood Connection family entertainment centers (one in Georgia and one in Utah) which feature multiplex theaters along with skating rinks miniature golf and arcades.

	Annual Growth	12/10	12/11	12/12	12/13	12/14
Sales ($ mil.)	8.9%	491.3	482.2	539.3	634.8	689.9
Net income ($ mil.)	–	(12.6)	(7.7)	96.3	5.8	(8.9)
Market value ($ mil.)	35.8%	188.5	168.0	366.3	679.9	641.5
Employees	6.1%	6,165	6,276	7,119	7,800	7,800

CARNEGIE INSTITUTION OF WASHINGTON

1530 P ST NW
WASHINGTON, DC 200051910
Phone: 202-387-6400
Fax: –
Web: www.rentals.carnegiescience.edu

CEO: –
CFO: –
HR: Yulonda White
FYE: June 30
Type: Private

The folks that work at the Carnegie Institution of Washington aren't exactly melon heads. The organization known to the public as the Carnegie Institution for Science supports scientific research in areas such as plant biology developmental biology Earth and planetary sciences astronomy and global ecology. It operates via six scientific departments on the East and West Coasts. The institution funded primarily by an endowment of more than $530 million was established in 1902 by steel magnate Andrew Carnegie (whose other philanthropic endeavors included the Carnegie Corporation of New York and Carnegie Mellon University).

	Annual Growth	06/07	06/08	06/09	06/10	06/13
Sales ($ mil.)	–	–	–	0.0	92.3	115.7
Net income ($ mil.)	–	–	–	0.0	1.2	17.5
Market value ($ mil.)	–	–	–	–	–	–
Employees	–	–	–	–	–	500

CARNEGIE MELLON UNIVERSITY

5000 FORBES AVE
PITTSBURGH, PA 152133890
Phone: 412-268-8746
Fax: –
Web: www.cmu.edu

CEO: –
CFO: Mark S. Kamlet
HR: Barbara (Barb) Smith
FYE: June 30
Type: Private

If you can't act maybe Carnegie Mellon University can help. The university is known around the world for churning out award-winning actors from its highly regarded drama school. Drama isn't all Carnegie teaches though the school has seven colleges and schools that offer academic programs in areas such as psychology computer science engineering biology and public policy. It has more than 12000 students and 5000 faculty and staff and it has a relatively small student-teacher ratio of 10:1. Carnegie Mellon was founded by philanthropist and industrialist Andrew Carnegie who established the Carnegie Technical Schools in 1900 for the sons and daughters of Pittsburgh's blue-collar workers.

	Annual Growth	06/09	06/10	06/11	06/12	06/13
Sales ($ mil.)	7.1%	–	899.8	956.6	1,061.9	1,106.7
Net income ($ mil.)	(19.0%)	–	–	278.6	44.6	182.7
Market value ($ mil.)	–	–	–	–	–	–
Employees	–	–	–	–	–	4,913

CARNIVAL CORPORATION

NYSE: CCL

3655 NW 87th Ave.
Miami FL 33178-2428
Phone: 305-599-2600
Fax: 305-406-4700
Web: www.carnivalcorp.com

CEO: Ann C. Sherry
CFO: David Bernstein
HR: –
FYE: November 30
Type: Public

Carnival offers a boatload of fun. The company is the world's #1 cruise operator boasting about a dozen cruise lines and about 100 ships with a total passenger capacity of more than 190000. Carnival operates in North America primarily through its Princess Cruise Line Holland America and Seabourn luxury cruise brand as well as its flagship Carnival Cruise Lines unit. Brands such as AIDA P&O Cruises and Costa Cruises offer services to passengers in Europe and the Cunard Line runs luxury trans-Atlantic liners. Carnival operates as a dual-listed company with UK-based Carnival plc forming a single enterprise under a unified executive team.

CAROLINA POWER & LIGHT COMPANY

410 S. Wilmington St.
Raleigh NC 27601-1748
Phone: 919-546-6111
Fax: 919-546-2920
Web: www.progress-energy.com

CEO: Lynn J Good
CFO: Steven K Young
HR: –
FYE: December 31
Type: Subsidiary

The Palmetto state and Tarheels both have Carolina Power & Light on their minds when they need some power. The company which operates as Progress Energy Carolinas transmits and distributes electricity to some 1.5 million homes and businesses in the Carolinas. The utility generates almost 12600 MW of capacity from its fossil-fueled nuclear and hydroelectric power plants. Carolina Power & Light purchases about 5% of the power it distributes. The Duke Energy subsidiary also sells power to wholesale customers primarily other utilities and energy marketers including North Carolina Eastern Municipal Power Agency and North Carolina Electric Membership Corporation.

CAROLINA BANK HOLDINGS INC   NMS: CLBH

101 North Spring Street
Greensboro, NC 27401
Phone: 336 288-1898
Fax: –

CEO: Robert T Braswell
CFO: –
HR: –
FYE: December 31
Type: Public

Carolina Bank Holdings owns Carolina Bank which serves individuals and small to midsized businesses through some 10 branches in northern portions of North Carolina. The community-oriented financial institution offers standard services such as checking and savings accounts money market and individual retirement accounts CDs ATM and debit cards and online banking and bill payment. Loans secured by commercial properties account for about 40% of the company's portfolio followed by residential mortgages construction and land development loans commercial and industrial loans and consumer loans.

	Annual Growth	12/10	12/11	12/12	12/13	12/14
Assets ($ mil.)	0.1%	676.7	673.3	691.9	661.8	679.3
Net income ($ mil.)	–	(2.4)	2.4	7.5	4.0	3.3
Market value ($ mil.)	32.4%	10.8	8.4	25.2	34.8	33.2
Employees	5.1%	155	174	208	191	189

CAROLINA CARE PLAN INC.

201 Executive Center Dr.
Columbia SC 29210-8438
Phone: 803-750-7400
Fax: 803-750-7480
Web: www.carolinacareplan.com

CEO: Richard Chiricosta
CFO: –
HR: –
FYE: December 31
Type: Subsidiary

From Charleston to Greenville Carolina Care Plan has the health costs of South Carolina on its mind. The managed health care company provides coverage to about 50000 members in the state some individually and many through employer groups. Its products include a direct-access HMO that allows users to see any doctor within the network without a referral. The organization also offers a point-of-service plan that covers out-of-network costs and a high-deductible plan paired with a health savings account. Additionally Medicare beneficiaries can buy prescription drug coverage or Medicare Advantage plans. The company is a subsidiary of Medical Mutual of Ohio.

CAROLINA HANDLING LLC

3101 PIPER LN
CHARLOTTE, NC 282086499
Phone: 704-357-6273
Fax: –
Web: www.carolinahandling.com

CEO: Tim Hilton
CFO: –
HR: –
FYE: December 31
Type: Private

Carolina Handling wants to be in the minds of businesses throughout the southeastern US when material-handling equipment is called for. The company distributes a full line of material-handling products made by Raymond. Carolina Handling specializes in lift trucks; it also offers pallet trucks reach trucks stackers and tow tractors. In addition to new and used equipment sales the company provides service parts rentals and training. The company operates from about a half dozen facilities in Alabama Georgia North Carolina Florida and South Carolina. CEO Tim Hilton continues to run the company that was founded in 1966.

	Annual Growth	12/04	12/05	12/06	12/07	12/08
Sales ($ mil.)	(66.7%)	–	–	1,045.5	107.5	116.2
Net income ($ mil.)	33722.9%	–	–	0.0	4.3	4.1
Market value ($ mil.)	–	–	–	–	–	–
Employees	–	–	–	–	–	356

CAROLINA TRUST BANK   NAS: CART

901 East Main Street
Lincolnton, NC 28092
Phone: 704 735-1104
Fax: –
Web: www.carolinatrust.com

CEO: Jay M Cline
CFO: –
HR: –
FYE: December 31
Type: Public

Carolina Trust Bank serves southwestern North Carolina through about a half-dozen locations. It provides a variety of commercial and personal financial services including checking and savings accounts IRAs CDs and credit cards. The bank is mainly a real estate lender with one- to four-family residential mortgage commercial real estate construction and land development loans comprising most of its portfolio. The company acquired the single-branch Carolina Commerce Bank in 2009. Carolina Trust was founded in 2000.

	Annual Growth	12/10	12/11	12/12	12/13	12/14
Assets ($ mil.)	2.3%	267.9	266.2	271.1	266.4	293.0
Net income ($ mil.)	136.0%	0.2	(2.1)	0.2	(1.4)	6.9
Market value ($ mil.)	10.0%	16.0	10.8	10.8	15.3	23.4
Employees	7.7%	55	57	60	61	74

CAROMONT HEALTH INC.

2525 COURT DR
GASTONIA, NC 28054-2140
Phone: 704-834-2000
Fax: –
Web: www.caromonthealth.org

CEO: Douglas Luckett
CFO: David O'Connor
HR: –
FYE: June 30
Type: Private

CaroMont Health is an independent not-for-profit health care system serving residents of North Carolina's Piedmont region. Anchoring CaroMont Health is Gaston Memorial Hospital a 435-bed medical and surgical facility that features a birthing center an inpatient psychiatric ward and specialized facilities for heart disease cancer sleep disorders diabetes and wound care. Other operations include a nearly 100-bed nursing home outpatient surgery and urgent care centers and a network of primary and specialty medical practices. CaroMont Health also provides home health and hospice care services. CaroMont Health is governed by the North Carolina Medical Care Commission.

	Annual Growth	06/06	06/07	06/08	06/10	06/11
Sales ($ mil.)	255.6%	–	–	10.5	6.1	471.7
Net income ($ mil.)	374.2%	–	–	0.9	5.1	94.8
Market value ($ mil.)	–	–	–	–	–	–
Employees	–	–	–	–	–	2,400

CARPENTER CONTRACTORS OF AMERICA INC.

3900 AVE D NW
WINTER HAVEN, FL 33880
Phone: 863-294-6449
Fax: –
Web: www.rdthiel.com

CEO: –
CFO: –
HR: –
FYE: February 03
Type: Private

Carpenter Contractors of America has been working with wood for more than half of a century. The company manufactures roof trusses and wall panels and supplies building materials through its manufacturing facilities in Florida. The company also has offices in North Carolina and Illinois where it operates under the name R&D Thiel. The company's products and services are used in both residential and commercial construction. In 1955 brothers Robert and Donald Thiel founded the company as R&D Thiel in Belvidere Illinois. Carpenter Contractors of America filed for Chapter 11 bankruptcy in 2010.

	Annual Growth	01/0-1	01/00*	02/01	02/02	02/07
Sales ($ mil.)	12.1%	–	159.0	174.2	183.8	353.6
Net income ($ mil.)	7.4%	–	–	8.0	8.1	12.3
Market value ($ mil.)	–	–	–	–	–	–
Employees	–	–	–	–	–	1,000

*Fiscal year change

CARPENTER TECHNOLOGY CORP.   NYS: CRS

P.O. Box 14662
Reading, PA 19610
Phone: 610 208-2000
Fax: –
Web: www.cartech.com

CEO: Tony R. Thene
CFO: Damon J. Audia
HR: John Rice
FYE: June 30
Type: Public

The Tin Man never would have rusted had he been built with metal from Carpenter Technology. It processes basic raw materials such as cobalt nickel manganese and titanium to make various corrosion-resistant materials. Most sales come from stainless steel products and alloys that provide special heat- or wear-resistance or special magnetic or conductive properties. Finished products come in billet bar rod wire and other forms. Carpenter also produces certain metal powders. Markets include aerospace automotive medical and industrial companies. Aerospace and defense accounted for 44% of its total sales in fiscal 2015.

	Annual Growth	06/11	06/12	06/13	06/14	06/15
Sales ($ mil.)	7.4%	1,675.1	2,028.7	2,271.7	2,173.0	2,226.7
Net income ($ mil.)	(4.6%)	71.0	121.2	146.1	132.8	58.7
Market value ($ mil.)	(9.5%)	2,902.4	2,407.2	2,267.8	3,182.6	1,946.3
Employees	8.8%	3,500	4,800	4,800	4,900	4,900

CARQUEST CORPORATION

2635 E. Millbrook Rd.
Raleigh NC 27604
Phone: 919-573-3000
Fax: 610-725-0570
Web: www.dfyoung.com

CEO: –
CFO: –
HR: –
FYE: December 31
Type: Business Segment

Searching for a sensor solenoid or switches? CARQUEST can steer you in the right direction. The replacement auto parts distribution group boasts more than 3400 member-owned locations in the US Canada and Mexico and it runs about 40 distribution centers. CARQUEST sells its own line of auto parts (made by Moog Automotive Dana and Gates) to independent jobbers and wholesalers for eventual resale to professional repair centers service stations dealerships and do-it-yourselfers. CARQUEST was rolled out by General Parts in 1974 as a national marketing program for independent distributors. General Parts is the largest single member-owner in CARQUEST's network with about 1400 locations.

CARR-GOTTSTEIN FOODS CO.

6401 A St.
Anchorage AK 99518
Phone: 907-561-1944
Fax: 412-788-8353
Web: www.indsci.com

CEO: Lawrence H Hayward
CFO: Donald J Anderson
HR: –
FYE: December 31
Type: Subsidiary

Carr-Gottstein Foods could sell ice to the Eskimos ... and it does. Alaska's largest grocery retailer operates more than 30 stores primarily in Anchorage as well as in Fairbanks Kenai and other locations throughout the state. Banners include Carrs Quality Centers which sell food general and drugstore merchandise as well as its smaller food stores in more rural areas under the Eagle Quality Centers banner and other trade names. Carr-Gottstein also runs Oaken Keg Spirit Shops (wine and liquor stores) mostly adjacent to Carrs stores and The Great Alaska Tobacco Company stores. Carr-Gottstein is a wholly owned subsidiary of Safeway one of North America's largest food retailers.

CARRIAGE SERVICES, INC.   NYS: CSV

3040 Post Oak Boulevard, Suite 300
Houston, TX 77056
Phone: 713 332-8400
Fax: –
Web: www.carriageservices.com

CEO: Melvin C. (Mel) Payne
CFO: Terry E. Sanford
HR: –
FYE: December 31
Type: Public

Though it buries its customers Carriage Services hasn't come close to burying its competition. The company is a large US death care company but it trails far behind Service Corporation International and that company's smaller rivals Stewart Enterprises and StoneMor Partners. Carriage Services established in 1993 runs nearly 170 funeral homes (owned and leased) in some 25 states and more than 30 cemeteries (owned and leased) operating in nearly a dozen states mostly in California Massachusetts and Texas. The company removes and prepares remains sells caskets and memorials provides transportation services performs ceremonies and burials and maintains cemeteries.

	Annual Growth	12/10	12/11	12/12	12/13	12/14
Sales ($ mil.)	5.2%	184.9	190.6	204.1	214.0	226.1
Net income ($ mil.)	18.3%	8.1	7.0	11.4	19.3	15.8
Market value ($ mil.)	44.2%	89.8	103.7	219.7	361.5	387.8
Employees	3.0%	1,943	1,856	2,080	2,072	2,187

CARRIZO OIL & GAS, INC.   NMS: CRZO

500 Dallas Street, Suite 2300
Houston, TX 77002
Phone: 713 328-1000
Fax: 281 496-1035
Web: www.carrizo.com

CEO: S. P. (Chip) Johnson
CFO: David L. Pitts
HR: –
FYE: December 31
Type: Public

Carrizo Oil & Gas sees its future in 3-D. An independent exploration and production company that explores for oil and gas in a handful of shale plays across the US and in proven onshore fields along the Gulf Coast of Texas and Louisiana Carrizo aggressively acquires 3-D seismic data and arranges land lease options in conjunction with conducting seismic surveys. As part of its shale strategy the company is exploiting the Marcellus play in Appalachia and the Eagle Ford and Barnett plays in Texas. Carrizo has additional properties in the Rockies Arkansas Kentucky Mississippi New Mexico and in the UK North Sea. In 2011 the firm reported proved reserves of 935.6 billion cu. ft. of natural gas equivalent.

	Annual Growth	12/10	12/11	12/12	12/13	12/14
Sales ($ mil.)	50.2%	139.5	202.2	368.2	520.2	710.2
Net income ($ mil.)	118.4%	10.0	36.6	55.5	43.7	226.3
Market value ($ mil.)	4.8%	1,591.0	1,215.5	965.0	2,065.1	1,918.9
Employees	17.0%	132	169	208	229	247

CARROLS RESTAURANT GROUP INC
NMS: TAST

968 James Street
Syracuse, NY 13203
Phone: 315 424-0513
Fax: –
Web: www.carrols.com

CEO: Daniel T. Accordino
CFO: Paul R. Flanders
HR: –
FYE: December 28
Type: Public

This company has some fast food royalty in its blood. Carrols Restaurant Group is a leading quick-service restaurant operator and the world's #1 Burger King franchisee with about 660 locations in the US. Like other franchise operators Carrols pays Burger King Worldwide royalties in order to use the BK banner and other intellectual property for its restaurants. Prior to the July 2012 spin-off of wholly-owned subsidiary Fiesta Restaurant Group Carrols also operated quick-service chains Taco Cabana and Pollo Tropical. The company has Burger King locations in 15 states.

	Annual Growth	12/10	12/11	12/12	12/13	12/14
Sales ($ mil.)	(3.4%)	796.1	822.5	539.6	663.5	692.8
Net income ($ mil.)	–	11.9	11.2	(18.9)	(13.5)	(38.1)
Market value ($ mil.)	1.0%	258.4	403.0	206.2	231.9	268.5
Employees	5.8%	16,300	15,550	17,050	17,500	20,400

CARSON TAHOE REGIONAL HEALTHCARE

1600 MEDICAL PKWY
CARSON CITY, NV 897034625
Phone: 775-445-8000
Fax: –
Web: www.carsontahoe.com

CEO: Ed Epperson
CFO: Ann Beck
HR: Carie Wilkins
FYE: December 31
Type: Private

Carson Tahoe Regional Healthcare which includes the Carson Tahoe Regional Medical Center (CTRMC) serves Nevada's Carson Valley and its surrounding areas. The not-for-profit CTRMC boasts about 220 beds and provides a wide range of services such as acute general surgical specialty and outpatient care. The medical center also includes a rehabilitation center cardiovascular center surgical unit free-standing cancer center emergency room and women and children's center. Carson Tahoe Regional Healthcare also operates smaller urgent care behavioral health physical therapy and outpatient care centers in Carson City and nearby communities.

	Annual Growth	12/05	12/06	12/08	12/09	12/12
Sales ($ mil.)	2.1%	–	164.1	163.5	195.1	186.4
Net income ($ mil.)	–	–	–	(8.9)	18.4	4.4
Market value ($ mil.)	–	–	–	–	–	–
Employees	–	–	–	–	–	1,500

CARTER & ASSOCIATES ENTERPRISES INC.

171 17th St. NW Ste. 1200
Atlanta GA 30363-1032
Phone: 404-888-3000
Fax: 404-888-3006
Web: www.carterusa.com

CEO: Robert E Peterson
CFO: –
HR: –
FYE: December 31
Type: Private

Carter knows more than just peanuts about real estate. The company provides commercial real estate development project management investment and consulting services. It has more than $2.5 billion in assets under management. Carter also has developed several projects including Atlantic Station a 800000 sq. ft. mixed use property in Atlanta. Carter has offices in Atlanta; Birmingham Alabama; Raleigh North Carolina; and Tampa Florida. A member of the ONCOR International consortium the privately held company was founded in 1958. Carter sold its property management and brokerage business to commercial real estate company Cassidy Turley in 2011.

CARTER'S INC
NYS: CRI

Phipps Tower, 3438 Peachtree Road N.E., Suite 1800
Atlanta, GA 30326
Phone: 678 791-1000
Fax: –
Web: www.carters.com

CEO: Michael D. (Mike) Casey
CFO: Richard F. Westenberger
HR: Jill A Wilson
FYE: January 03
Type: Public

Carter's has built a big business catering to little ones. Operating through its William Carter Company it's the largest US branded marketer of apparel exclusively for babies and young children. Primary products include newborn layette clothing sleepwear and playwear. It markets its items under the Carter's and OshKosh B'Gosh brands as well as private labels Child of Mine Just One You Genuine Kids and Precious Firsts. While Carter's sells products online and as a wholesaler via 18000 department and specialty stores it also operates some 731 Carter's and OshKosh stores nationwide and more than 120 stores in Canada.

	Annual Growth	01/11*	12/11	12/12	12/13*	01/15
Sales ($ mil.)	13.4%	1,749.3	2,109.7	2,381.7	2,638.7	2,893.9
Net income ($ mil.)	7.4%	146.5	114.0	161.2	160.4	194.7
Market value ($ mil.)	30.7%	1,555.5	2,098.5	2,859.1	3,746.3	4,533.2
Employees	7.5%	8,673	8,684	11,786	11,222	11,565

*Fiscal year change

CARTESIAN INC
NMS: CRTN

7300 College Blvd., Suite 302
Overland Park, KS 66210
Phone: 913 345-9315
Fax: –

CEO: Peter H Woodward
CFO: –
HR: –
FYE: January 03
Type: Public

The Management Network Group which does business as TMNG Global helps its clients answer the call in the ever-changing communications industry. The company provides management strategic and operational consulting services to communications service providers technology companies and financial services firms. Its TMNG Marketing unit offers a full range of marketing and customer relationship management services including product development market research and customer retention programs. The company's Ascertain suite of software products allows customers to manage billing services analyze customer data and monitor trends. Founded in 1990 TMNG Global serves clients primarily in the US and the UK.

	Annual Growth	01/11*	12/11	12/12	12/13*	01/15
Sales ($ mil.)	1.6%	67.2	63.1	53.0	55.4	71.7
Net income ($ mil.)	–	(2.2)	(4.4)	(1.2)	(2.1)	(1.4)
Market value ($ mil.)	13.1%	22.8	13.4	20.1	24.7	37.3
Employees	(3.9%)	350	315	298	283	299

*Fiscal year change

CARUS PUBLISHING COMPANY

140 S. Dearborn Ste. 1450
Chicago IL 60603
Phone: 312-701-1720
Fax: 312-701-1728
Web: www.cricketmag.com

CEO: –
CFO: –
HR: –
FYE: December 31
Type: Private

Carus Publishing Company weaves a literary web aimed at capturing kids' imaginations. With a focus on high quality stories and illustrations the company's "Cricket" magazine targets young teens. Other publications include "Babybug" for the youngest tots "Ladybug" for toddlers and preschoolers "Spider" for elementary school kids and "Cicada" magazine for teens. Carus Publishing also publishes a variety of books through its Cricket Books and Open Court divisions. Carus launched in 1887. Its flagship magazine "Cricket" debuted in 1973. Marianne Carus formed the publishing company to bring quality literature to children. Today ePals Corporation operater of an educational digital platform owns Carus Publishing.

CARVEL CORPORATION

200 Glenridge Point Pkwy. Ste. 200
Atlanta GA 30342
Phone: 404-255-3250
Fax: 404-255-4978
Web: www.carvel.com

CEO: Gary Bales
CFO: Lenore Krentz
HR: –
FYE: December 31
Type: Subsidiary

If Fudgie the Whale and Cookie Puss conjure up childhood memories of ice cream you're probably a true fan of Carvel's. The company operates a chain of more than 500 franchised ice cream outlets known for their soft serve ice cream and other frozen treats including character-shaped frozen ice cream cakes. Typically found in high-traffic areas such as airports malls and sports arenas Carvel has locations in 25 mostly Northeastern states Puerto Rico and some Middle Eastern countries. In addition the company sells ice cream cakes through more than 8500 supermarkets. Tom Carvel a traveling salesman founded the chain in 1934. It is owned by FOCUS Brands an affiliate of Atlanta-based Roark Capital Group.

CARVER BANCORP INC.   NAS: CARV

75 West 125th Street
New York, NY 10027
Phone: 718 230-2900
Fax: –
Web: www.carverbank.com

CEO: Michael T. Pugh
CFO: David Toner
HR: –
FYE: March 31
Type: Public

Carver Bancorp one of the largest minority-led financial institutions in the US is the holding company for Carver Federal Savings Bank. The bank was founded in 1948 to provide community banking services to New York City's African-American and Caribbean-American population. From about 10 branches in mostly low- to moderate-income neighborhoods in Harlem Brooklyn and Queens the thrift offers deposit accounts insurance and investment products. Carver Federal's lending activities are focused on housing (residential mortgages and multifamily real estate loans) and non-residential real estate (churches and commercial properties.) The latter makes up about 40% of Carver's loan portfolio.

	Annual Growth	03/11	03/12	03/13	03/14	03/15
Assets ($ mil.)	(1.2%)	709.2	641.2	638.3	639.8	676.4
Net income ($ mil.)	–	(39.5)	(23.4)	0.7	(0.8)	0.4
Market value ($ mil.)	50.9%	3.3	27.7	17.0	47.0	17.1
Employees	1.8%	120	136	133	132	129

CAS MEDICAL SYSTEMS INC   NAS: CASM

44 East Industrial Road
Branford, CT 06405
Phone: 203 488-6056
Fax: –

CEO: Thomas M Patton
CFO: Jeffery A Baird
HR: –
FYE: December 31
Type: Public

It's not a doctor or a nurse but CAS Medical Systems (CASMED) is standing bedside keeping a watchful eye on patients. CASMED makes non-invasive monitoring devices used in critical care settings. Its leading products include its FORE-SIGHT oximeters which monitor oxygen levels in brain and muscle tissue. Other products include its MAXNIBP blood pressure technology bedside monitors and neonatal vital sign supplies (electrodes skin surface probes). CASMED sells its products in North America Europe Latin America Africa and the Pacific Rim to hospitals and other health care professionals through sales representatives and specialty distributors.

	Annual Growth	12/10	12/11	12/12	12/13	12/14
Sales ($ mil.)	(1.2%)	24.1	22.5	22.7	21.9	22.9
Net income ($ mil.)	–	(1.3)	(6.1)	(7.3)	(10.4)	(7.6)
Market value ($ mil.)	(15.3%)	62.3	34.0	41.9	33.1	32.1
Employees	(1.2%)	102	109	106	97	97

CASCADE BANCORP   NAS: CACB

1100 N.W. Wall Street
Bend, OR 97701
Phone: 877 617-3400
Fax: –
Web: www.botc.com

CEO: Terry E. Zink
CFO: Gregory D. Newton
HR: –
FYE: December 31
Type: Public

Forget the dirty dishes. Cascade Bancorp wants to provide sparkling customer service. It's the holding company for Bank of the Cascades which operates some 40 branches serving the Oregon and Boise Idaho markets. Catering to individuals and small to midsized businesses the banks offer traditional deposit services like checking and savings accounts CDs and IRAs as well as credit cards and trust services. Commercial real estate loans make up more than half of the company's loan portfolio; business loans comprise nearly a quarter. To a far lesser extent the bank also originates consumer loans and mortgages. Cascade Bancorp acquired Home Federal Bancorp in 2014 boosting assets to more than $2.3 billion.

	Annual Growth	12/10	12/11	12/12	12/13	12/14
Assets ($ mil.)	8.1%	1,716.5	1,303.5	1,301.4	1,406.2	2,341.1
Net income ($ mil.)	–	(13.7)	(47.3)	6.0	50.8	3.7
Market value ($ mil.)	(11.5%)	612.6	317.5	453.8	379.1	376.2
Employees	4.4%	432	436	432	399	513

CASCADE ENGINEERING INC.

3400 INNOVATION CT SE
GRAND RAPIDS, MI 495122085
Phone: 616-975-4800
Fax: –
Web: www.cascadeng.com

CEO: –
CFO: –
HR: –
FYE: August 30
Type: Private

Ideas about plastic parts cascade down from Cascade Engineering's collection of companies ending up as practical components for many applications. The company manufactures and markets under the Cascade and other brands plastic injection molded products as well as parts for OEMs in the automotive truck material handling waste and recycling and home and office industries. Its auto lineup includes interior and exterior trim HVAC cases and ducts and acoustical parts along with heavy truck fairings fenders and grills. Catering to resource conservation markets Cascade also makes and services an eco-lineup comprising building-mountable wind turbines waste collection bins and water filtration systems.

	Annual Growth	08/10	08/11*	09/12*	08/13	08/14
Sales ($ mil.)	14.7%	–	238.0	238.0	238.0	358.8
Net income ($ mil.)	–	–	–	0.0	0.0	0.0
Market value ($ mil.)	–	–	–	–	–	–
Employees	–	–	–	–	–	1,200

*Fiscal year change

CASCADE MICROTECH INC   NMS: CSCD

9100 S.W. Gemini Drive
Beaverton, OR 97008
Phone: 503 601-1000
Fax: –
Web: www.cascademicrotech.com

CEO: Michael D. (Mike) Burger
CFO: Jeff A. Killian
HR: Ellen Raim
FYE: December 31
Type: Public

In the foothills of the Cascade Range Cascade Microtech makes test systems for microelectronics. Semiconductor makers such as Broadcom Fujitsu Semiconductor IBM Intel Samsung and Toshiba use the company's probe cards probe stations and analytical probes to ensure the quality of their integrated circuits (ICs). Many of Cascade's customers use its tools to test their wireless broadband or other communications ICs at the wafer level before the wafers are cut into individual chips. The company has a development alliance with test equipment giant Agilent Technologies.

	Annual Growth	12/10	12/11	12/12	12/13	12/14
Sales ($ mil.)	9.2%	95.8	104.6	113.0	120.0	136.0
Net income ($ mil.)	–	(10.3)	(5.8)	6.1	13.4	9.9
Market value ($ mil.)	35.4%	71.6	56.1	92.2	153.5	240.6
Employees	2.9%	401	365	383	426	449

CASCADE NATURAL GAS CORPORATION

222 Fairview Ave. North
Seattle WA 98109-5312
Phone: 206-624-3900
Fax: 206-624-7215
Web: www.cngc.com

CEO: David W Stevens
CFO: -
HR: -
FYE: December 31
Type: Subsidiary

To approximately 100 small communities in Washington and Oregon Cascade Natural Gas is the main man. The gas utility transmits and distributes natural gas to more than 250000 residential commercial and industrial customers. It also distributes gas to approximately 200 noncore customers mostly large industrial users buying their supplies from third parties. Cascade Natural Gas' service territory covers more than 3000 sq. miles and 700 highway miles. The utility obtains its gas mainly from Canadian suppliers and producers in the Rocky Mountains. Cascade Natural Gas is a subsidiary of energy giant MDU Resources.

CASE FINANCIAL INC.
OTC: CSEF

7720 El Camino Real Ste. 2E
Carlsbad CA 92009
Phone: 760-804-1449
Fax: 760-804-1566

CEO: Michael A Schaffer
CFO: Lawrence C Schaffer
HR: -
FYE: September 30
Type: Public

Case Financial went from the courtroom to the goldmine. The former business litigation financing business shifted its focus away from loaning money to lawyers in 2005 and now wants to invest in mine exploration. Setbacks have prevented the company from operating since 2004. However in 2008 Case Financial announced that it would provide $4 million in funding to Canada-based Trio Gold Corp for a gold mine exploration project in Nevada.

CASE WESTERN RESERVE UNIVERSITY

10900 EUCLID AVE
CLEVELAND, OH 44106-4901
Phone: 216-368-2000
Fax: -
Web: www.msass.case.edu

CEO: -
CFO: Hossein Sadid
HR: -
FYE: June 30
Type: Private

Looking for a research-oriented university? Case Western Reserve University (CWRU) is a private research school with an enrollment of about 10000 students more than half of whom are graduate and professional students. CWRU offers about 200 undergraduate and graduate degree programs from its eight colleges and schools — business engineering law arts and sciences dentistry social work nursing and medicine — as well as a graduate school at its campus in Cleveland. The university has some 3000 faculty members and a student-to-teacher ratio of 10:1.

	Annual Growth	06/07	06/08	06/09	06/10	06/11
Sales ($ mil.)	3.0%	-	964.3	774.7	932.0	1,052.9
Net income ($ mil.)	5.7%	-	63.9	0.0	(15.9)	75.6
Market value ($ mil.)	-	-	-	-	-	-
Employees	-	-	-	-	-	5,500

CASELLA WASTE SYSTEMS, INC.
NMS: CWST

25 Greens Hill Lane
Rutland, VT 05701
Phone: 802 775-0325
Fax: -
Web: www.casella.com

CEO: John W. Casella
CFO: Edmond R Coletta
HR: -
FYE: December 31
Type: Public

The wasteful habits of Americans are big business for Casella Waste Systems which operates regional waste-hauling businesses mainly in the northeastern US. The company serves residential commercial industrial and municipal customers. In 2012 it owned and/or operated 32 solid waste collection businesses nine disposal facilities 17 recycling facilities 31 transfer stations four landfill gas-to-energy facilities one construction materials landfill and one waste-to-energy plant. Casella Waste Systems holds a 50% stake in GreenFiber a joint venture with Louisiana-Pacific that manufactures cellulose insulation from recycled fiber.

	Annual Growth	04/11	04/12	04/13	04/14*	12/14
Sales ($ mil.)	(7.5%)	466.1	480.8	455.3	497.6	368.4
Net income ($ mil.)	-	38.4	(77.6)	(54.5)	(27.4)	(5.8)
Market value ($ mil.)	(15.8%)	274.3	244.7	176.9	206.9	163.9
Employees	1.8%	1,800	1,800	1,800	1,800	1,900

*Fiscal year change

CASEY'S GENERAL STORES, INC.
NMS: CASY

One Convenience Boulevard
Ankeny, IA 50021
Phone: 515 965-6100
Fax: -
Web: www.caseys.com

CEO: Robert J. (Bob) Myers
CFO: William J. (Bill) Walljasper
HR: Julie L. Jackowski
FYE: April 30
Type: Public

Casey's General Stores makes sure that small towns in the Midwest get their fill of convenient shopping. It operates about 1850 company-owned convenience stores in more than a dozen states primarily in the Midwest and all within about 500 miles of its Iowa headquarters and distribution center. Towns with 5000 people or fewer where rent is low are home to about 60% of the chain's stores. Casey's sells lots of gasoline (some 70% of total sales) as well as beverages groceries and fresh prepared foods including from-scratch pizza donuts and hot sandwiches. It also sells tobacco products automotive goods and other nonfood items such as ammunition and photo supplies.

	Annual Growth	04/11	04/12	04/13	04/14	04/15
Sales ($ mil.)	8.4%	5,635.2	6,987.8	7,250.8	7,840.3	7,767.2
Net income ($ mil.)	17.5%	94.6	116.8	110.6	134.5	180.6
Market value ($ mil.)	20.5%	1,517.7	2,191.2	2,251.9	2,669.9	3,195.7
Employees	9.4%	22,157	24,726	27,079	29,749	31,766

CASH AMERICA INTERNATIONAL, INC.
NYS: CSH

1600 West 7th Street
Fort Worth, TX 76102
Phone: 817 335-1100
Fax: -

CEO: T. Brent Stuart
CFO: Thomas A. Bessant
HR: Clint Jaynes
FYE: December 31
Type: Public

If cash is king then Cash America International is king of pawns. Cash America operates more than 960 stores under the banners Cash America Pawn SuperPawn and Pawn X-Change in the US and Cash America casa de empeño in Mexico. The company is one of the largest providers of secured non-recourse loans (also known as pawn loans). As part of its business Cash America also provides cash advances in half a dozen states through shops operating under the Cashland and Cash America Payday Advance banners. The company offers check cashing money orders and money transfers through about 90 owned and franchised Mr. Payroll stores in about 15 states.

	Annual Growth	12/10	12/11	12/12	12/13	12/14
Sales ($ mil.)	(4.1%)	1,293.3	1,540.6	1,800.4	1,797.2	1,094.7
Net income ($ mil.)	(3.9%)	115.5	136.0	107.5	142.5	98.6
Market value ($ mil.)	(11.5%)	1,063.8	1,343.3	1,142.8	1,103.3	651.6
Employees	1.7%	6,017	6,619	7,035	7,637	6,426

CASH-WA DISTRIBUTING CO. OF KEARNEY INC.

401 W 4TH ST
KEARNEY, NE 688457825
Phone: 308-237-3151
Fax: –
Web: www.cashwa.com

CEO: –
CFO: Edward Bloomfield
HR: –
FYE: November 30
Type: Private

This company keeps the Quik-E Marts in merchandise. Cash-Wa Distributing supplies food produce beverages equipment cleaning supplies and more to foodservice operators and convenience stores throughout Nebraska and in all or parts of 10 surrounding states. It operates three distribution centers and serves more than 6500 customers with an inventory of some 20000 items. The family-owned and -operated company was formed in 1934 as a candy and tobacco wholesaler and was purchased by the Henning family in 1957. Cash-Wa Distributing is a member of the UniPro distribution cooperative.

	Annual Growth	12/09	12/10	12/11	12/12*	11/13
Sales ($ mil.)	10.9%	–	–	306.8	398.8	377.6
Net income ($ mil.)	8.1%	–	–	5.7	11.9	6.6
Market value ($ mil.)	–	–	–	–	–	–
Employees	–	–	–	–	–	539

*Fiscal year change

CASIO AMERICA INC.

570 Mt. Pleasant Ave.
Dover NJ 07801
Phone: 973-361-5400
Fax: 973-537-8926
Web: www.casio.com

CEO: Shigenori ITOH
CFO: –
HR: Amy Hulbert
FYE: March 31
Type: Subsidiary

You might be (G-)shocked to learn how many products Casio America sells. As the US subsidiary of Japanese electronics giant CASIO COMPUTER the firm markets products ranging from handheld computers and calculators to electronic keyboards and its popular G-Shock and high-end Oceanus watch lines. Established in 1957 Casio also makes and markets cell phones digital cameras electronic dictionaries label printers clocks portable TVs and other items. Going beyond the consumer market Casio targets the retail hospitality and industrial markets (cash registers and industrial handheld PDAs). And to make sure that young consumers remember its name the company also sells to the education market.

CASPIAN SERVICES INC

2319 Foothill Drive, Suite 160
Salt Lake City, UT 84109
Phone: 801 746-3700
Fax: –
Web: www.caspianservicesinc.com

OTC: CSSV
CEO: Alexey Kotov
CFO: Indira Kaliyeva
HR: –
FYE: September 30
Type: Public

Caspian Services (formerly EMPS Corporation) provides geophysical and seismic data acquisition and interpretation services to the oil and gas industry operating in the Caspian Sea region. It also owns or leases a fleet of 15 shallow draft vessels that provide offshore marine services including transportation housing and supplies for production personnel. Caspian Services' ships are chartered primarily to Agip KCO a consortium of oil companies operating in the Caspian Sea and CMOC/Shell joint venture. The company owns 56% of a joint venture that operates a desalinization plant and sells purified drinking water.

	Annual Growth	09/11	09/12	09/13	09/14	09/15
Sales ($ mil.)	(23.9%)	49.1	24.9	33.1	29.9	16.4
Net income ($ mil.)	–	(9.7)	(14.0)	(11.5)	(16.6)	(28.0)
Market value ($ mil.)	(41.1%)	5.8	1.5	2.5	1.6	0.7
Employees	(14.7%)	757	516	574	509	400

CASS INFORMATION SYSTEMS INC.

12444 Powerscourt Drive, Suite 550
St. Louis, MO 63131
Phone: 314 506-5500
Fax: –
Web: www.cassinfo.com

NMS: CASS
CEO: Eric H. Brunngraber
CFO: P. Stephen (Steve) Appelbaum
HR: –
FYE: December 31
Type: Public

Cass Information Systems wants to pay your company's bills. The information services firm provides freight payment and information processing services to large manufacturing distribution and retail companies across the US. Its offerings include freight bill payment audit and rating services as well as outsourcing of utility bill processing and payments. Its telecommunications division manages telecom expenses for large companies. Cass grew out of Cass Commercial Bank (now a subsidiary) which provides banking services to private companies and churches as well as to consumers in the St. Louis area and Orange County California. Other major customer bases include Massachusetts Ohio and South Carolina.

	Annual Growth	12/10	12/11	12/12	12/13	12/14
Assets ($ mil.)	6.0%	1,188.0	1,319.3	1,287.4	1,326.0	1,500.7
Net income ($ mil.)	4.3%	20.3	23.0	23.3	23.5	24.0
Market value ($ mil.)	8.8%	436.4	418.6	485.4	774.7	612.5
Employees	4.1%	918	1,037	1,047	1,087	1,077

CASTLE (A.M.) & CO.

1420 Kensington Road, Suite 220
Oak Brook, IL 60523
Phone: 847 455-7111
Fax: –
Web: www.amcastle.com

NYS: CAS
CEO: Scott J. Dolan
CFO: Patrick R. Anderson
HR: –
FYE: December 31
Type: Public

Providing alloys for its allies metals service company A. M. Castle distributes highly engineered metals and metal alloys to a broad range of industrial manufacturers. It sells steel (alloy carbon and stainless) nickel alloys aluminum copper brass cast iron and titanium in bar sheet plate and tube form. Its Transtar Metals unit distributes high-performance metals to the aerospace and defense markets. Through its Total Plastics unit it distributes plastics in forms (such as plate rod and tube). A. M. Castle operates 47 steel service centers throughout North America Europe and Asia. It also holds 50% of steel distributor Kreher Steel. Investor Patrick Herbert controls about 25% of A. M. Castle.

	Annual Growth	12/10	12/11	12/12	12/13	12/14
Sales ($ mil.)	0.9%	943.7	1,132.4	1,270.4	1,053.1	979.8
Net income ($ mil.)	–	(5.6)	(1.8)	(9.7)	(34.0)	(134.7)
Market value ($ mil.)	(18.9%)	433.7	222.9	348.0	348.0	188.0
Employees	0.7%	1,619	1,781	1,701	1,624	1,667

CASTLE BRANDS INC.

122 East 42nd Street, Suite 4700
New York, NY 10168
Phone: 646 356-0200
Fax: –
Web: www.castlebrandsinc.com

ASE: ROX
CEO: Richard J. (Dick) Lampen
CFO: Alfred J. Small
HR: –
FYE: March 31
Type: Public

Castle Brands hopes to earn a king's ransom selling imported distilled spirits. Among its brands are Tierras tequila Pallini liqueur Jefferson's bourbon Brady's Irish cream liqueur Betts & Scholl wine and Knappogue Castle Whiskey. As part of its business the company also owns 60% of Celtic Crossing Irish liqueur. Castle Brands distributes its products nationwide and in a dozen international markets as well as in duty-free markets. Castle Brands boasts marketing and distribution rights for other brands such as Gosling's Rum and Travis Hasse's Original Apple Pie Liqueur. Castle Brands formed in 2003 mainly contracts with other firms to distill and bottle its products.

	Annual Growth	03/11	03/12	03/13	03/14	03/15
Sales ($ mil.)	15.8%	32.0	35.5	41.4	48.1	57.5
Net income ($ mil.)	–	(6.3)	(5.2)	(5.4)	(8.9)	(3.8)
Market value ($ mil.)	43.5%	51.9	42.4	48.7	188.6	220.1
Employees	6.3%	40	39	41	45	51

CASTLE ROCK ENTERTAINMENT INC.

335 N. Maple Dr. Ste. 135
Beverly Hills CA 90210-3879
Phone: 310-285-2300
Fax: 310-285-2345

CEO: Martin Shafer
CFO: –
HR: –
FYE: December 31
Type: Subsidiary

This castle is looking for a few good movies. Castle Rock Entertainment producer of acclaimed films such as "When Harry Met Sally" "A Few Good Men" and The Shawshank Redemption is also responsible for duds such as Miss Congeniality 2: Armed and Fabulous. The company's TV credits include the hit show "Seinfeld". Castle Rock was formed in 1987 by five media moguls including director Rob Reiner Warner Bros. president and COO Alan Horn and Castle Rock CEO Martin Shafer. The company has produced seven movies based on Stephen King novels and takes its name from the fictional Maine town that serves as the setting for many King stories. Castle Rock's films and TV shows are distributed by parent Warner Bros.

CASTLEROCK SECURITY HOLDINGS INC.

2101 S. Arlington Heights Rd. Ste. 150
Arlington Heights IL 60005
Phone: 847-768-6300
Fax: 858-334-2199
Web: www.ambitbio.com

CEO: Brian Johnson
CFO: –
HR: –
FYE: December 31
Type: Private

CastleRock Security Holdings wants to be the moat around your castle. Through its subsidiaries CastleRock provides security system monitoring services and maintenance to residential and light commercial customers. The company which operates in 46 states and select markets in Canada and Puerto Rico monitors a variety of systems including burglary fire environmental and medical alarm systems. CastleRock serves its own retail customer accounts but also offers wholesale monitoring services to third-party alarm system companies. Formed in 2008 CastleRock Security filed to go public in late 2010.

CATALENT PHARMA SOLUTIONS INC.

14 Schoolhouse Rd.
Somerset NJ 08873
Phone: 732-537-6200
Fax: 732-537-6480
Web: www.catalent.com

CEO: John R Chiminski
CFO: Matthew Walsh
HR: Eric Norman
FYE: June 30
Type: Private

Catalyst + talent = Catalent. At least that's the brand Catalent Pharma Solutions is using to try to ensure its customers' success. The company provides contract development and manufacturing of oral (soft and hardshell capsules) topical (ointment applicators) sterile (syringes) and inhaled (nasal sprays) drug delivery products to pharmaceutical and biotechnology companies in some 100 countries. Catalent also provides packaging services using bottles pouches and strips used to hold tablet powder and liquid medicines. Catalent operates 30 facilities worldwide. The company is owned by The Blackstone Group.

CATALINA MARKETING CORPORATION

200 Carillon Pkwy.
St. Petersburg FL 33716
Phone: 727-579-5000
Fax: 727-556-2700
Web: www.catalinamarketing.com

CEO: Jamie Egasti
CFO: –
HR: –
FYE: December 31
Type: Private

To reach shoppers when they are shopping consumer packaged-goods manufacturers call on Catalina Marketing. The company's network installed at the cash registers of more than 26000 supermarkets and drugstores throughout the US prints out coupons and other marketing communications for consumers based on the products they have just purchased. A similar system installed at more than 18300 pharmacies delivers health-related information to consumers based on the prescriptions they pick up. Outside the US Catalina has installed its networks at about 8000 retail locations in Europe and Japan.

CATALINA RESTAURANT GROUP INC.

2200 Faraday Ave. Ste. 250
Carlsbad CA 92008
Phone: 760-804-5750
Fax: 760-476-5141
Web: www.catalinarestaurantgroup.com

CEO: –
CFO: –
HR: –
FYE: December 31
Type: Subsidiary

Catalina Restaurant Group is pretty casual about dining. The company operates and franchises more than 175 casual-dining restaurants under the Carrows and Coco's names. Its Carrows Restaurant chain offers family dining fare for breakfast lunch and dinner at about 65 locations. Several of the eateries are open 24 hours a day. Coco's Bakery Restaurants feature fresh-baked goods burgers sandwiches and breakfast items at more than 110 locations. Most of Catalina Restaurant Group's properties are found in California with additional locations in Arizona Colorado and Nevada. Formed in 2002 the company is a subsidiary of Tokyo-based Zensho Co.

CATALYST BIOSCIENCES INC

NAS: CBIO

260 Littlefield Ave.
South San Francisco, NC 94080
Phone: 650 266-8674
Fax: –
Web: www.targacept.com

CEO: –
CFO: Mauri K. Hodges
HR: Amanda Hill
FYE: December 31
Type: Public

Catalyst Biosciences (formerly Targacept) is a clinical-stage biopharmaceutical focused on developing products in the fields of hemostasis and inflammation. Its candidates treat such ailments as hemophilia and surgical bleeding delayed graft function in kidney transplants and dry age-related macular degeneration. The company's lead candidate is a next-generation coagulation Factor VIIa variant — CB 813d — which has completed Phase 1 clinical trials in severe hemophilia patients. The company was formed in 1997 and went public in 2006. Targacept was acquired by Catalyst Biosciences in a reverse merger mid-2015 after which the firm adopted the Catalyst moniker.

	Annual Growth	12/10	12/11	12/12	12/13	12/14
Sales ($ mil.)	(76.2%)	85.7	97.6	57.9	3.6	0.3
Net income ($ mil.)	–	10.9	(8.5)	(7.0)	(46.7)	(32.6)
Market value ($ mil.)	(43.9%)	127.9	26.9	21.1	20.0	12.7
Employees	(38.4%)	132	142	41	40	19

CATALYST HEALTH SOLUTIONS INC. NASDAQ: CHSI

800 King Farm Blvd.
Rockville MD 20850
Phone: 301-548-2900
Fax: 301-548-2991
Web: www.catalysthealthsolutions.com

CEO: Mark Thierer
CFO: Jeff Park
HR: –
FYE: December 31
Type: Public

Catalyst Health Solutions cooks up efficiencies in the prescription benefits market. The company provides pharmacy benefit management (PBM) services to clients including managed care organizations (MCOs) self-insured employers third-party benefit administrators and hospices. Its Catalyst Rx business helps clients design drug benefit plans that encourage the use of preferred prescriptions bought from one of about 65000 pharmacies (including contracted mail order pharmacies) in the company's nationwide network. It also provides customized reporting and data analysis services. In 2012 Catalyst Health Solutions agreed to be acquired by PBM software firm SXC Health Solutions in a deal worth some $4.4 billion.

CATALYST PHARMACEUTICAL PARTNERS INC. NASDAQ: CPRX

355 Alhambra Circle Ste. 1370
Coral Gables FL 33134
Phone: 305-529-2522
Fax: 305-529-0933
Web: www.catalystpharma.com

CEO: Patrick J McEnany
CFO: Alicia Grande
HR: –
FYE: December 31
Type: Public

Catalyst Pharmaceutical Partners may help certain addicts kick the habit. The development-stage company's lead candidate CPP-109 (based on the chemical compound vigabatrin) is in clinical studies for the treatment of cocaine and methamphetamine addiction. The drug is designed to be readily absorbed into the central nervous system preventing the perception of pleasure that results from dramatic increases in dopamine caused by cocaine and meth use. Contract manufacturer Pharmaceutics International is supplying CPP-109 for use in upcoming clinical trials and may also be contracted for future commercial supplies should the drug become approved in the US.

CATAMOUNT CONSTRUCTORS INC.

1527 COLE BLVD STE 100
LAKEWOOD, CO 804013411
Phone: 303-679-0087
Fax: –

CEO: Geoffrey G Wormer
CFO: –
HR: –
FYE: December 31
Type: Private

A solid foundation is tantamount to Catamount's success. The company provides general contracting services for the construction of commercial industrial health care institutional and residential developments around the US. It offers services from conceptualization and design-build to construction management. Subsidiary CC Residential specializes in midrise multifamily residences including condominiums apartments and mixed-use developments. Catamount Constructors boasts a high customer return rate; it has provided services for such return clients as CarMax Walgreen and Chase Bank. CEO Geoff Wormer and other executives Kurt Kenchel Jeff Sidwell and Jeff Cochran founded the company in 1997.

	Annual Growth	12/05	12/06	12/07	12/08	12/13
Sales ($ mil.)	–	–	(156.4)	183.4	226.2	319.7
Net income ($ mil.)	–	–	–	–	7.5	4.2	(0.8)
Market value ($ mil.)	–	–	–	–	–	–
Employees	–	–	–	–	–	142

CATASYS INC NBB: CATS

11601 Wilshire Boulevard, Suite 1100
Los Angeles, CA 90025
Phone: 310 444-4300
Fax: –
Web: www.catasys.com

CEO: Terren S Peizer
CFO: Susan Etzel
HR: –
FYE: December 31
Type: Public

Catasys (formerly known as Hythiam) specializes in researching developing and licensing medical protocols for the treatment of alcohol and drug addiction. The company's PROMETA treatment programs utilize a combination of medication nutritional supplements and counseling to treat drug and alcohol addiction. Catasys' PROMETA Centers are operated through management or licensing agreements with health care providers in the US. PROMETA also provides maintenance support by offering individualized care programs following medically supervised treatment. Namesake program Catasys offers disease management services. The company changed its name in 2011 to reflect its focus on comprehensive behavioral management.

	Annual Growth	12/10	12/11	12/12	12/13	12/14
Sales ($ mil.)	45.9%	0.4	0.3	0.5	0.9	2.0
Net income ($ mil.)	–	(20.0)	(8.1)	(11.6)	(4.7)	(27.3)
Market value ($ mil.)	110.5%	2.7	6.2	3.4	25.5	53.0
Employees	8.1%	33	32	33	32	45

CATCHMARK TIMBER TRUST INC NYS: CTT

5 Concourse Parkway, Suite 2325
Atlanta, GA 30328
Phone: 855 858-9794
Fax: –
Web: www.catchmark.com

CEO: Jerry Barag
CFO: Brian M Davis
HR: –
FYE: December 31
Type: Public

Wood you be interested in investing in CatchMark Timber Trust? The real estate investment trust (REIT) owns interests in about 282000 acres of timberland – mostly pine forest – across Alabama and Georgia. (As a REIT CatchMark is exempt from paying federal income tax as long as it makes quarterly distributions to shareholders.) Unlike other landowning REITs CatchMark only owns the land; it doesn't have logging operations or make wood products. While the REIT is self-managed CatchMark is affiliated with Wells Real Estate Funds. It went public in 2013 and raised $142 million in its IPO. It plans to use the proceeds to pay down debt and buy more shares from Wells Real Estate Funds.

	Annual Growth	12/10	12/11	12/12	12/13	12/14
Sales ($ mil.)	3.4%	47.6	40.0	44.2	32.0	54.3
Net income ($ mil.)	–	(15.8)	(11.9)	(8.9)	(13.2)	0.7
Market value ($ mil.)	(18.9%)	–	–	–	549.0	445.5
Employees	27.5%	–	–	8	9	13

CATERPILLAR FINANCIAL SERVICES CORP MEDIUM TERM NOTES BOOK ENTRY

2120 West End Ave.
Nashville, TN 37203-0001
Phone: 615 341-1000
Fax: –
Web: www.caterpillar.com

CEO: –
CFO: –
HR: –
FYE: December 31
Type: Public

There's only one way to lease a Cat: Caterpillar Financial Services. Cat Financial provides loans and leases to corporate customers to buy or rent equipment and machinery manufactured by its parent company industry giant Caterpillar. That equipment includes construction equipment; forklifts; generators; mining logging and agricultural machines; gas turbines and engines and off-road trucks. Affiliate Cat Insurance provides extended service contracts property/casualty coverage and other insurance products to customers and dealers. The company has offices in more than 50 countries in North and South America Europe the Middle East and the Asia/Pacific region.

	Annual Growth	12/10	12/11	12/12	12/13	12/14
Sales ($ mil.)	3.1%	2,552.0	2,645.0	2,693.0	2,783.0	2,885.0
Net income ($ mil.)	17.8%	278.0	378.0	432.0	530.0	535.0
Market value ($ mil.)	–	–	–	–	–	–
Employees	3.5%	1,572	1,670	1,745	1,767	1,802

CATERPILLAR INC.
NYS: CAT

100 N.E. Adams Street
Peoria, IL 61629
Phone: 309-675-1000
Fax: 309-675-4332
Web: www.caterpillar.com

CEO: Douglas R. (Doug) Oberhelman
CFO: Bradley M. (Brad) Halverson
HR: Kimberly S Hauer
FYE: December 31
Type: Public

Whether digging loading paving or moving Caterpillar does it all. The company is the world's #1 manufacturer of construction and mining equipment which includes excavators loaders and tractors as well as forestry paving and tunneling machinery. It also manufactures diesel and natural gas engines industrial gas turbines and diesel-electric locomotives. Subsidiary Caterpillar Financial Services offers a slew of financing leasing insurance and warranty products and services for dealers and customers. Among Caterpillar's other services are remanufacturing through Caterpillar Remanufacturing Services and rail-related upgrade repair and maintenance services through Progress Rail Services.

	Annual Growth	12/11	12/12	12/13	12/14	12/15
Sales ($ mil.)	(6.0%)	60,138.0	65,875.0	55,656.0	55,184.0	47,011.0
Net income ($ mil.)	(19.2%)	4,928.0	5,681.0	3,789.0	3,695.0	2,102.0
Market value ($ mil.)	(6.9%)	52,758.4	52,181.0	52,880.7	53,299.9	39,574.6
Employees	(4.1%)	125,099	125,341	118,501	114,233	105,700

CATHAY GENERAL BANCORP
NMS: CATY

777 North Broadway
Los Angeles, CA 90012
Phone: 213-625-4700
Fax: -
Web: www.cathaybank.com

CEO: Dunson K. Cheng
CFO: Heng W. Chen
HR: Geri Santoro
FYE: December 31
Type: Public

Cathay General Bancorp is the holding company for Cathay Bank which mainly serves Chinese and Vietnamese communities from some 30 branches in California and about 20 more in Illinois New Jersey New York Massachusetts Washington and Texas. It also has a branch in Hong Kong and offices in Shanghai and Taipei. Catering to small to medium-sized businesses and individual consumers the bank offers standard deposit services and loans. Commercial mortgage loans account for more than half of the bank's portfolio; business loans comprise nearly 25%. The bank's Cathay Wealth Management unit offers online stock trading mutual funds and other investment products and services through an agreement with PrimeVest.

	Annual Growth	12/10	12/11	12/12	12/13	12/14
Assets ($ mil.)	1.6%	10,802.0	10,644.9	10,694.1	10,989.3	11,516.8
Net income ($ mil.)	85.8%	11.6	100.2	117.4	123.1	137.8
Market value ($ mil.)	11.3%	1,332.9	1,191.6	1,558.8	2,133.4	2,042.5
Employees	1.5%	1,010	1,018	1,092	1,132	1,074

CATHOLIC HEALTH EAST

3805 WEST CHESTER PIKE # 100
NEWTOWN SQUARE, PA 19073-2329
Phone: 610-355-2000
Fax: -
Web: www.che.org

CEO: -
CFO: -
HR: -
FYE: December 31
Type: Private

Catholic Health East (CHE) marries the physical and the spiritual in its vast network of not-for-profit health care facilities. As one of the largest religious health systems in the country CHE carries out its mission of healing the sick through more than 35 acute-care hospitals (7300 beds) four long-term acute care (LTAC) hospitals and 25 freestanding and hospital-based long-term care facilities as well as assisted living behavioral health and rehabilitation centers. Operating in 11 states along the East Coast from Maine to Florida CHE is also one of the country's largest providers of home health care services. The health care organization is sponsored by 10 religious congregations and ministries.

	Annual Growth	12/05	12/06	12/07	12/09	12/10
Sales ($ mil.)	(0.7%)	-	4,175.9	4,364.5	106.6	4,057.5
Net income ($ mil.)	(8.1%)	-	199.2	199.9	(3.3)	142.3
Market value ($ mil.)	-	-	-	-	-	-
Employees	-	-	-	-	-	50,000

CATHOLIC HEALTH SERVICES OF LONG ISLAND

992 N. Village Ave.
Rockville Centre NY 11570
Phone: 516-705-3700
Fax: 516-705-3730
Web: www.chsli.org

CEO: Alan D Guerci
CFO: Terence G Daly
HR: -
FYE: December 31
Type: Private - Not-for-Pr

The long and the short of it is that Catholic Health Services of Long Island (CHS) provides health care to the residents of Long Island. Founded in 1997 and sponsored by the Diocese of Rockville Centre CHS's operations consist of six hospitals and three nursing homes as well as regional home care and hospice services. Within the CHS system member organizations offer virtually any medical specialty or clinical service. The system's hospitals which include Good Samaritan Hospital Medical Center Mercy Medical Center and St. Francis Hospital house some 1725 beds more than 15000 employees and a medical staff of 3300. CHS's MaryHaven Center provides services to people of all ages with disabilities.

CATHOLIC HEALTH SYSTEM

2121 Main St. Ste. 300
Buffalo NY 14214
Phone: 716-862-2400
Fax: 716-862-2468
Web: www.chsbuffalo.org

CEO: -
CFO: -
HR: -
FYE: December 31
Type: Private

The Catholic Health System gives residents of its home state even more reason to proclaim "I heart New York." The health care system recognized for its cardiac services serves residents of western New York through its network of four hospitals and over a dozen primary care centers as well as long-term care facilities diagnostic and treatment centers and assorted other health care sites. Catholic Health is also well-known for its women's health cancer treatment and rehabilitation services and is a leading provider of elderly care in the region. Founded in 1998 its hospitals (including Kenmore Mercy Sisters of Charity Mercy Hospital of Buffalo and St. Joseph's) have a capacity of about 800 beds.

CATHOLIC MEDICAL CENTER

100 MCGREGOR ST
MANCHESTER, NH 031023770
Phone: 603-663-6888
Fax: -
Web: www.catholicmedicalcenter.org

CEO: Alyson Pitman Giles
CFO: -
HR: Margo Campagna
FYE: June 30
Type: Private

Catholic Medical Center is a 330-bed hospital serving southern New Hampshire. Services include cancer treatment surgery rehabilitation treatments for sleep disorders and emergency medical services. Catholic Medical Center (CMC) offers about 40 medical specialties through divisions including The Mom's Place (a birthing facility) and the New England Heart Institute. CMC has partnered with its community to extend health care and dental care to the uninsured and the homeless and has established a health clinic geared to help refugees being resettled in the area.

	Annual Growth	06/07	06/08	06/09	06/10	06/13
Sales ($ mil.)	29.6%	-	88.0	242.0	277.7	322.1
Net income ($ mil.)	-	-	-	(1.3)	11.6	29.5
Market value ($ mil.)	-	-	-	-	-	-
Employees	-	-	-	-	-	1,500

CATO CORP.

NYS: CATO

8100 Denmark Road
Charlotte, NC 28273-5975
Phone: 704 554-8510
Fax: –
Web: www.catocorp.com

CEO: John P. D. Cato
CFO: John R. Howe
HR: Bob Brummer
FYE: January 31
Type: Public

The Cato Corporation caters to fashion-minded Southerners on a budget. The retailer operates more than 1300 apparel stores in 30-plus states (primarily in the Southeast) under the names Cato Cato Plus Versona It's Fashion and It's Fashion Metro. Its mostly private-label merchandise includes misses' juniors' girls' and plus-sized casualwear career clothing coats shoes and accessories geared to low- and middle-income customers mostly females aged 18 to 50. Cato's stores are typically located in shopping centers anchored by a Wal-Mart store or another major discounter or supermarket. Founded in 1946 the company is led by chairman John Cato the third generation of Catos in the family business.

	Annual Growth	01/11	01/12*	02/13	02/14*	01/15
Sales ($ mil.)	1.6%	925.5	931.5	944.0	920.0	986.9
Net income ($ mil.)	1.2%	57.7	64.8	61.7	54.3	60.5
Market value ($ mil.)	15.0%	676.5	752.4	765.0	780.6	1,183.7
Employees	1.0%	9,600	9,500	9,600	10,000	10,000

*Fiscal year change

CAVALIER TELEPHONE LLC

2134 W. Laburnum Ave.
Richmond VA 23227
Phone: 804-422-4100
Fax: 804-422-4392
Web: www.cavtel.com

CEO: –
CFO: –
HR: –
FYE: December 31
Type: Subsidiary

Despite its name Cavalier Telephone takes a serious approach to residential and business telecommunications. The facilities-based telephone and data services company offers local and long-distance voice broadband Internet and computer telephony services in 15 states in the eastern southeastern and midwestern US. It provides commercial communications services such as private networks and broadband Internet connections largely through its Intellifiber Networks division. Digital television programming is offered through an agreement with direct broadcast satellite provider DIRECTV. Key residential markets include Baltimore Philadelphia and Pittsburgh. The company was acquired by PAETEC Holding in late 2010.

CAVCO INDUSTRIES INC (DE)

NMS: CVCO

1001 North Central Avenue, Suite 800
Phoenix, AZ 85004
Phone: 602 256-6263
Fax: –
Web: www.cavco.com

CEO: Joseph H. (Joe) Stegmayer
CFO: Daniel L. Urness
HR: –
FYE: March 28
Type: Public

Cavco's constructions keep customers covered whether they're at home work or vacation. Cavco Industries designs makes and sells manufactured homes (retail prices range from $26000 to more than $190000) under brands including Cavco Palm Harbor and Fleetwood. Its products include full-sized homes (about 500 sq. ft. to 3300 sq. ft.); park model homes (less than 400 sq. ft.) for use as recreational and retirement units; camping cabins; and commercial structures for use as portable classrooms showrooms and offices. Cavco operates about 15 factories in the West and Midwest; its homes are sold by more than 1000 independent retailers and company-owned outlets in the US Canada Mexico and Japan.

	Annual Growth	03/11	03/12	03/13	03/14	03/15
Sales ($ mil.)	34.8%	171.8	443.1	452.3	533.3	566.7
Net income ($ mil.)	70.3%	2.8	15.2	5.0	16.2	23.8
Market value ($ mil.)	13.5%	400.1	412.7	421.4	696.7	664.7
Employees	31.2%	1,250	2,600	2,600	3,000	3,700

CAVIUM INC

NMS: CAVM

2315 N. First Street
San Jose, CA 95131
Phone: 408 943-7100
Fax: –
Web: www.caviumnetworks.com

CEO: Syed B. Ali
CFO: Arthur D Chadwick
HR: –
FYE: December 31
Type: Public

Cavium provides integrated circuits for use in networking equipment such as routers switches security appliances gateway devices and storage networking equipment. The company designs specialized microprocessors used in secure network transmissions based on ARM and MIPS architecture technologies. Manufacturing is contracted out to Taiwan Semiconductor Manufacturing and United Microelectronics among others. Cavium also provides related software and services. Customers outside the US account for more than two-thirds of the company's sales.

	Annual Growth	12/10	12/11	12/12	12/13	12/14
Sales ($ mil.)	15.9%	206.5	259.2	235.5	304.0	373.0
Net income ($ mil.)	–	37.1	0.0	(112.6)	(3.0)	(15.3)
Market value ($ mil.)	13.2%	2,052.0	1,548.2	1,699.6	1,879.4	3,366.6
Employees	10.3%	633	864	831	830	936

CAZENOVIA COLLEGE

22 SULLIVAN ST
CAZENOVIA, NY 130351085
Phone: 315-655-7000
Fax: –
Web: www.cazenovia.edu

CEO: –
CFO: Mark Edwards
HR: Janice A Romagnoli
FYE: June 30
Type: Private

Students wanting individualized attention and a well-rounded education can apply to Cazenovia College. With a a student-faculty ratio of 15 to 1 the school, focuses on liberal arts offering bachelor's and associate degrees in more than 20 fields of study. The school, has, about 1000 students and some 140 full- and part-time faculty members. Cazenovia College opened in 1824 in what had been the Madison County (New York) Courthouse. The school, was founded as the Seminary of the Genesee Conference the second Methodist seminary to be established in the US. Among its early notable alumni is Leland Stanford who founded and endowed Stanford University.

	Annual Growth	06/07	06/08	06/09	06/10	06/11
Sales ($ mil.)	–	–	–	(115.7)	25.8	24.7
Net income ($ mil.)	1765.4%	–	–	0.0	3.6	5.7
Market value ($ mil.)	–	–	–	–	–	–
Employees	–	–	–	–	–	369

CBEYOND INC

NMS: CBEY

320 Interstate North Parkway, Suite 500
Atlanta, GA 30339
Phone: 678 424-2400
Fax: –
Web: www.cbeyond.com

CEO: Vincent Oddo
CFO: Edward James III
HR: –
FYE: December 31
Type: Public

Cbeyond isn't looking past the millions of small businesses in the US to find customers. The company offers local long-distance and cellular telephone and broadband Internet services as well as a host of network and cloud-based services (data center Web hosting security application migration administration management) to more than 60000 small and midsized businesses with fewer than 250 employees. It targets businesses in more than a dozen large metropolitan areas divided between established (Atlanta Dallas Denver) and emerging (Boston Seattle Washington DC) markets. Typical customers include law firms physicians' offices real estate companies and accounting firms.

	Annual Growth	12/08	12/09	12/10	12/11	12/12
Sales ($ mil.)	8.7%	349.7	413.8	452.0	485.4	488.0
Net income ($ mil.)	–	3.7	(2.2)	(1.7)	(8.0)	(2.3)
Market value ($ mil.)	(13.3%)	478.2	471.3	457.2	239.7	270.5
Employees	2.8%	1,493	1,677	1,944	1,928	1,667

CBIZ INC
NYS: CBZ

6050 Oak Tree Boulevard South, Suite 500
Cleveland, OH 44131
Phone: 216 447-9000
Fax: 216 447-4809
Web: www.cbiz.com

CEO: Steven L. Gerard
CFO: Ware H. Grove
HR: Teresa Bur
FYE: December 31
Type: Public

This company helps its clients cut through red tape. CBIZ wants its customers to see the stress reduction and business advantages of farming out some of their financial tasks and other operations. The company provides its clients with outsourced business services including accounting and tax preparation valuation insurance and benefits administration and IT consulting. Overall the company has more than 90000 customers mainly small and midsized businesses but also government agencies individuals and not-for-profits organizations.

	Annual Growth	12/10	12/11	12/12	12/13	12/14
Sales ($ mil.)	(0.4%)	732.5	733.8	766.1	692.0	719.5
Net income ($ mil.)	5.0%	24.5	28.0	31.1	85.9	29.8
Market value ($ mil.)	8.2%	308.8	302.4	292.5	451.3	423.6
Employees	(5.4%)	5,250	5,100	5,200	4,100	4,200

CBL & ASSOCIATES PROPERTIES, INC.
NYS: CBL

2030 Hamilton Place Blvd., Suite 500
Chattanooga, TN 37421-6000
Phone: 423 855-0001
Fax: –
Web: www.cblproperties.com

CEO: Stephen D Lebovitz
CFO: Farzana K Mitchell
HR: –
FYE: December 31
Type: Public

CBL & Associates Properties tenant list is a Who's Who of American retail. The self-managed real estate investment trust (REIT) owns develops manages and finances shopping malls and other retail properties primarily in the Southeast and Midwest. Its largest tenants include The Limited The Gap Foot Locker and Abercrombie & Fitch. The REIT wholly owns or has interests in 152 properties 92 of which are regional malls and open-air shopping centers. Strip malls (typically anchored by grocery or discount stores) associated centers (retail properties adjacent to enclosed malls usually anchored by big-box stores) office buildings and commercial mortgages round out its portfolio.

	Annual Growth	12/10	12/11	12/12	12/13	12/14
Sales ($ mil.)	(0.3%)	1,071.8	1,067.3	1,034.6	1,053.6	1,060.7
Net income ($ mil.)	37.0%	62.2	133.9	131.6	85.2	219.2
Market value ($ mil.)	2.6%	2,979.6	2,673.1	3,611.2	3,057.9	3,306.5
Employees	(2.5%)	905	908	926	861	819

CBOE HOLDINGS INC.
NMS: CBOE

400 South LaSalle Street
Chicago, IL 60605
Phone: 312 786-5600
Fax: –
Web: www.cboe.com

CEO: Edward T. Tilly
CFO: Alan J. Dean
HR: –
FYE: December 31
Type: Public

CBOE (or Chicago Board Options Exchange) may no longer be the only options exchange but it's still the US leader in overall volume. CBOE lists options on more than 3300 stocks as well as on interest rates broad-based stock indexes (such as Standard & Poor's S&P 500 Index) and industry indexes. CBOE operates the fully electronic CBOE Futures Exchange and the CBOE Stock Exchange which goes head-to-head with the NYSE and NASDAQ. CBOE also runs the C2 all-electronic options market and the National Stock Exchange (which it operates as a separate unit). It also operates the Options Institute which provides training for brokers and investors.

	Annual Growth	12/10	12/11	12/12	12/13	12/14
Sales ($ mil.)	9.0%	437.1	508.1	512.3	572.1	617.2
Net income ($ mil.)	17.5%	99.4	139.4	157.4	176.0	189.7
Market value ($ mil.)	29.1%	1,922.9	2,175.2	2,478.0	4,370.6	5,334.5
Employees	(2.7%)	581	596	605	650	520

CBRE GROUP INC
NYS: CBG

400 South Hope Street, 25th Floor
Los Angeles, CA 90071
Phone: 213 613-3333
Fax: –
Web: www.cbre.com

CEO: Robert E. (Bob) Sulentic
CFO: James R. (Jim) Groch
HR: Jean Reynolds
FYE: December 31
Type: Public

CBRE (formerly CB Richard Ellis Group) is all about location location location — not to mention ubicación l'emplacement posizione and Standort. One of the world's largest commercial real estate services companies CBRE provides property and facilities management leasing brokerage appraisal and valuation asset management financing and market research services from around 370 offices worldwide and manages 1.5 billion sq. ft. of commercial space for third-party owners and occupants. Subsidiary Trammell Crow provides property development services for corporate and institutional clients primarily in the US. CBRE Global Investors manages real estate investments for institutional clients.

	Annual Growth	12/10	12/11	12/12	12/13	12/14
Sales ($ mil.)	15.3%	5,115.3	5,905.4	6,514.1	7,184.8	9,049.9
Net income ($ mil.)	24.7%	200.3	239.2	315.6	316.5	484.5
Market value ($ mil.)	13.7%	6,819.7	5,068.1	6,626.5	8,757.7	11,404.9
Employees	13.8%	31,000	34,000	37,000	44,000	52,000

CBS BROADCASTING INC.

51 W. 52nd St.
New York NY 10019
Phone: 212-975-4321
Fax: 212-975-4516
Web: www.cbs.com

CEO: Leslie Moonves
CFO: –
HR: –
FYE: December 31
Type: Subsidiary

The forensic evidence shows this company is tops in the TV ratings. CBS Broadcasting owns and operates the CBS Television Network the #1 watched broadcast network in the US. Its top shows include CSI: Crime Scene Investigation and its two spinoffs as well as The Mentalist NCIS and a host of prime-time comedies. It boasts more than 200 affiliate stations around the country including about 15 stations that are company-owned and -operated. In addition CBS Broadcasting oversees The CW Network a 50%-owned joint venture with Time Warner's Warner Bros. Entertainment. The company is a unit of media conglomerate CBS Corporation.

CBS CORP
NYS: CBS

51 W. 52nd Street
New York, NY 10019
Phone: 212 975-4321
Fax: –
Web: www.cbscorporation.com

CEO: Leslie (Les) Moonves
CFO: Joseph R Ianniello
HR: Anthony G. Ambrosio
FYE: December 31
Type: Public

You might say this company has a real eye for broadcasting. CBS Corporation is a leading mass media conglomerate with television radio online content and publishing operations. Its portfolio is anchored by CBS Broadcasting which operates the #1 rated CBS television network along with a group of local TV stations. CBS also owns cable network Showtime and produces and distributes TV programming through CBS Television Studios and CBS Television Distribution. Other operations include CBS Radio CBS Interactive and book publisher Simon & Schuster. Chairman Sumner Redstone controls CBS Corporation through National Amusements.

	Annual Growth	12/11	12/12	12/13	12/14	12/15
Sales ($ mil.)	(0.6%)	14,245.0	14,089.0	15,284.0	13,806.0	13,886.0
Net income ($ mil.)	2.0%	1,305.0	1,574.0	1,879.0	2,959.0	1,413.0
Market value ($ mil.)	14.8%	12,565.8	17,617.2	29,511.6	25,622.4	21,821.2
Employees	(6.1%)	20,915	20,930	19,490	17,310	16,260

CBS RADIO INC.

40 W. 57th St. 14th Fl.
New York NY 10019
Phone: 212-649-9600
Fax: 212-315-2162
Web: www.cbsradio.com

CEO: Dan Mason
CFO: Jacques Tortoroli
HR: –
FYE: December 31
Type: Subsidiary

This company keeps its eye on radio listeners. CBS Radio is one of the country's leading radio broadcasters with about 130 stations serving about 30 major markets over the airwaves. Its stations offer a variety of programming from news talk and sports to a wide range of music styles; many of the stations are affiliates of the Westwood One radio network. (CBS Radio owns nearly 10% of the radio programming syndicator.) In addition to traditional broadcasting many CBS stations broadcast digital over-the-air signals along with online streaming and on-demand content. CBS Radio is a subsidiary of media giant CBS Corporation.

CC INDUSTRIES INC.

222 N. LaSalle St. Ste. 1000
Chicago IL 60601
Phone: 312-855-4000
Fax: 919-573-3551

CEO: William H Crown
CFO: –
HR: –
FYE: December 31
Type: Subsidiary

A few of the Crown family's affairs are handled by CC Industries. The private equity firm which is controlled by Chicago's Henry Crown and Company manages several investments for its parent including Great Dane which is one of the largest manufacturers of truck trailers in North America. CC Industries also oversees Provisur Technologies a manufacturer of meat processing equipment sold under the Formax Beehive and Weiler brands. CC Industries which was founded in 1986 mostly invests in manufacturing companies in North America and Latin America.

CCA GLOBAL PARTNERS INC.

4301 Earth City Expwy.
St. Louis MO 63045
Phone: 314-506-0000
Fax: 314-493-9671
Web: www.ccaglobalpartners.com

CEO: Howard Brodsky
CFO: Jim Acker
HR: William Smith
FYE: September 30
Type: Private - Cooperativ

Business is "floor"ishing at CCA Global Partners. Formerly named Carpet Co-op the company operates about a dozen independent businesses and more than 2700 locations in North America and abroad. Its largest units are flooring retailers Carpet One with more than 1000 locations in Australia Canada New Zealand and the US and Flooring America with about 550 stores in the US and Canada. CCA Global's other specialty retail operations include The Bike Cooperative with some 300 memeber stores and lighting products seller Lighting One. In addition to its retail lines the company provides mortgage banking and business services. Chairman Howard Brodsky and Alan Greenberg founded the co-op in 1984.

CCA INDUSTRIES, INC.

ASE: CAW

65 Challenger Road, Suite 340
Ridgefield Park, NJ 07660
Phone: 201 935-3232
Fax: 201 935-6784
Web: www.ccaindustries.com

CEO: Lance T. Funston
CFO: Stephen A. (Steve) Heit
HR: –
FYE: November 30
Type: Public

Consumers count on CCA Industries for health and beauty care. The company makes and markets health and beauty aids each under its own brand name including Plus+White (oral care) Bikini Zone (shave gels) Sudden Change (skin care) Solar Sense (sun protection) and Nutra Nail and Gel Perfect (nail care) among many. It also sells dietary supplements (tea and chewing gum) under the Mega-T label. CCA items are made under contract and several such as Hair-Off Mega-T and Kids Sense are made and marketed under licensing agreements. The firm caters to food and drug retailers such as Walgreens and CVS mass merchandisers Wal-Mart and Target warehouse club Sam's and wholesale distributors mainly in the US.

	Annual Growth	11/10	11/11	11/12	11/13	11/14
Sales ($ mil.)	(11.9%)	50.8	49.5	53.8	38.9	30.6
Net income ($ mil.)	–	(1.7)	0.5	0.5	(6.2)	(8.8)
Market value ($ mil.)	(10.3%)	37.1	35.4	30.8	22.1	24.0
Employees	(27.6%)	135	140	148	98	37

CCC GROUP INC.

5797 Dietrich Rd.
San Antonio TX 78219
Phone: 210-661-4251
Fax: 210-661-6060
Web: www.cccgroupinc.com

CEO: Arthur D Huebner
CFO: Nita B Mc Bride
HR: –
FYE: December 31
Type: Private

Construction is at the core of CCC Group. The general contractor founded in 1947 specializes in industrial construction manufacturing and specialty engineering and design services. It performs a laundry list of construction services including site development civil engineering construction management marine construction mining equipment erection and dismantling and plant expansions. CCC Group also installs specialized equipment. The company serves utilities and municipalities as well as the oil and gas and metals and chemicals industries. It operates mostly out of its home state of Texas but maintains offices throughout the South Southwestern and Southeastern US and three international offices.

CCC INFORMATION SERVICES GROUP INC.

222 Merchandise Mart Ste. 900
Chicago IL 60654-1005
Phone: 312-222-4636
Fax: 312-527-2298
Web: www.cccis.com

CEO: Githesh Ramamurthy
CFO: Andrew G Balbirer
HR: –
FYE: December 31
Type: Subsidiary

CCC Information Services Group helps smooth the dents in auto claims processing. The company's software and services help insurance agencies independent appraisers and collision repair shops process auto claims. CCC's offerings include its Pathways application for estimating collision and repair cost and its Valuescope claim settlement services application for estimating the worth of totaled vehicles. Its claims management software is linked to about 21000 auto body collision repair shops and 350 insurance companies. CCC Information Services was founded in 1980 and taken private by Investcorp for about $496 million in 2006.

CCF HOLDING CO.

NBB: CCFH

101 North Main Street
Jonesboro, GA 30236
Phone: 770 478-8881
Fax: 770 478-8929
Web: www.heritagebank.com

CEO: David B Turner
CFO: Mary Jo Rogers
HR: –
FYE: December 31
Type: Public

CCF Holding Company sees green in the Peach State. The institution is the parent of Heritage Bank which operates about a half-dozen branches in Clayton Fayette and Henry counties in greater metropolitan Atlanta. Centered in the fast-growing Hartsfield International Airport region the bank targets individuals and local businesses offering such standard services as checking and savings accounts money market accounts CDs IRAs and credit cards. Real estate loans including construction and land development loan commercial and residential mortgages and farmland loans account for about 95% of the bank's lending portfolio. Heritage Bank also writes consumer and business loans.

	Annual Growth	12/10	12/11	12/12	12/13	12/14
Assets ($ mil.)	(2.0%)	395.5	364.6	358.6	370.2	365.3
Net income ($ mil.)	–	(6.7)	(4.9)	2.0	(0.2)	5.2
Market value ($ mil.)	(2.9%)	3.6	3.6	0.4	3.6	3.2
Employees	–	–	–	–	–	–

CCFNB BANCORP INC.

NBB: CCFN

232 East Street
Bloomsburg, PA 17815
Phone: 570 784-1660
Fax: –
Web: www.firstcolumbiabank.com

CEO: Lance O Diehl
CFO: Jeffrey T Arnold
HR: –
FYE: December 31
Type: Public

CCFNB Bancorp knows the ABCs of banking. It is the holding company for First Columbia Bank & Trust a community institution serving Pennsylvania's Columbia Montour Northumberland and Luzerne counties from some 15 locations. The bank offers standard products and services as well as wealth management and trust services. It uses funds from deposits to write a variety of loans; real estate loans account for more than 80% of its loan portfolio. The bank also offers consumer and construction loans. CCFNB Bancorp owns a 50% stake in Neighborhood Group (dba Neighborhood Advisors) an insurance and financial products agency. CCFNB Bancorp merged with Columbia Financial Corporation in 2008.

	Annual Growth	12/10	12/11	12/12	12/13	12/14
Assets ($ mil.)	1.0%	614.3	624.7	607.7	624.0	639.1
Net income ($ mil.)	2.0%	6.3	6.8	7.2	6.8	6.8
Market value ($ mil.)	6.4%	64.9	79.0	79.2	80.1	83.2
Employees	(6.9%)	185	175	176	172	139

CCH INCORPORATED

2700 Lake Cook Rd.
Riverwoods IL 60015-3888
Phone: 847-267-7000
Fax: 773-866-3095
Web: www.cch.com

CEO: Teresa Mackintosh
CFO: Douglas Winterrose
HR: –
FYE: December 31
Type: Subsidiary

Tax season must be CCH's favorite time of year. Also known as Wolters Kluwer Tax and Accounting CCH publishes more than 700 publications in print and electronic form primarily concerning the subjects of tax and business law. Publications are available in a variety of print and electronic formats that reach a target audience of accountants attorneys and compliance professionals. The company's flagship product is "The Standard Federal Tax Reporter". Its Tax and Accounting unit produces software used for tax preparation audits and office productivity. The company was founded in 1913 the same year the US federal income tax was created. CCH is a subsidiary of Dutch publisher Wolters Kluwer.

CCOM GROUP INC

NBB: CCOM P

275 Wagaraw Road
Hawthorne, NJ 07506
Phone: 973 427-8224
Fax: –
Web: www.colonialcomm.com

CEO: Pete Gasiewicz
CFO: William Salek
HR: –
FYE: December 31
Type: Public

Colonial Commercial through subsidiaries Universal Supply Group The RAL Supply Group and S&A Supply provides HVAC products climate-control systems and plumbing fixtures to mostly builders and contractors in New York and New Jersey. It supplies control-system design custom fabrication technical support training and consultation services (but not installation) for engineers and installers. RAL Supply Group offers plumbing fixtures water systems and water-treatment products and heating and cooling equipment. More than 80% of Colonial's sales come from the replacement market while the balance is generated by new construction. Chairman Michael Goldman owns about 30% of the company.

	Annual Growth	12/10	12/11	12/12	12/13	12/14
Sales ($ mil.)	0.3%	80.1	79.6	86.1	88.5	81.0
Net income ($ mil.)	63.5%	0.1	0.2	0.6	3.0	0.8
Market value ($ mil.)	12.1%	3.8	3.7	1.8	4.7	6.0
Employees	(1.0%)	157	155	154	–	–

CD INTERNATIONAL ENTERPRISES INC

NBB: CDII

431 Fairway Drive, Suite 200
Deerfield Beach, FL 33441
Phone: 954 363-7333
Fax: –
Web: www.cdii.net

CEO: Yuejian Wang
CFO: –
HR: –
FYE: September 30
Type: Public

China Direct Industries cuts out the middleman and goes directly to the source. The company invests in and manages Chinese companies that sell industrial metals and related products. Its portfolio includes controlling stakes in companies that produce and/or distribute magnesium synthetic chemicals steel and other commodities. The company is increasingly focused on the production and distribution of pure magnesium a high-demand commodity. China Direct provides its subsidiaries with management advisory services and strategic planning; its consulting segment specializes in providing services for US companies that primarily do business in China.

	Annual Growth	09/11	09/12	09/13	09/14	09/15
Sales ($ mil.)	(79.1%)	187.8	114.1	2.0	1.7	0.4
Net income ($ mil.)	–	9.3	(41.7)	(24.7)	16.5	(3.1)
Market value ($ mil.)	(60.8%)	101.2	24.1	4.8	6.0	2.4
Employees	(72.5%)	1,578	610	25	10	9

CDC SUPPLY CHAIN

8989 N. Deerwood Dr.
Milwaukee WI 53223
Phone: 414-362-6800
Fax: 414-362-6794
Web: www.cdcsupplychain.com

CEO: Michael Eleftheriou
CFO: David H Jacobson
HR: –
FYE: December 31
Type: Subsidiary

CDC Supply Chain serves as an agent of change in supply chains. The company's supply chain execution performance and process management software helps clients manage inventory and fulfillment monitor their supply chain activities and automate a range of warehouse functions including receiving loading and storage. The company targets clients in the transportation retail consumer packaged goods and processed goods industries. CDC Supply Chain counts multinational companies such as AstraZeneca Boeing Saks and Smucker among its customers. CDC Supply Chain is a unit of CDC Software.

CDW CORPORATION

200 N. Milwaukee Ave.
Vernon Hills IL 60061
Phone: 847-465-6000
Fax: 336-852-2096
Web: www.tangeroutlet.com

CEO: Thomas E Richards
CFO: Ann E Ziegler
HR: –
FYE: December 31
Type: Private

People who get IT shop for it at CDW. The company offers about 100000 information technology products including notebook and desktop computers software printers servers storage devices networking tools and accessories under more than 1000 brands. Top brands include Adobe Apple Cisco Hewlett-Packard Microsoft VMware among others. CDW operates a retail store at its corporate headquarters and manages an e-commerce site. Almost all of the company's sales come from public-sector clients and private businesses. Founded in 1984 as Computer Discount Warehouse today CDW is owned by private equity firms Madison Dearborn Partners and Providence Equity Partners.

CEB INC

NYS: CEB

1919 North Lynn Street
Arlington, VA 22209
Phone: 571 303-3000
Fax: –
Web: www.cebglobal.com

CEO: Thomas L. (Tom) Monahan
CFO: Richard S. Lindahl
HR: –
FYE: December 31
Type: Public

Don't fear the competition; learn from it. So says CEB (formerly The Corporate Executive Board Company) a provider of business research and analysis services to more than 5700 companies worldwide. Its program areas cover "best practices" in such topics as finance human resources information technology operations and sales and marketing. Unlike consulting firms which engage with one client at a time CEB operates on a membership-based business model. Members subscribe to one or more of the company's programs and participate in the research and analysis thus sharing expertise with others. Besides reports on best practices CEB offers seminars customized research briefs and decision-support tools.

	Annual Growth	12/10	12/11	12/12	12/13	12/14
Sales ($ mil.)	20.0%	438.9	484.7	622.7	820.1	909.0
Net income ($ mil.)	6.1%	40.4	52.7	37.1	32.0	51.2
Market value ($ mil.)	17.9%	1,255.9	1,274.3	1,587.3	2,589.7	2,425.8
Employees	23.0%	1,879	2,093	3,400	3,900	4,300

CECIL BANCORP, INC.

NBB: CECB

127 North Street, P.O. Box 568
Elkton, MD 21921
Phone: 410 398-1650
Fax: –
Web: www.cecilbank.com

CEO: –
CFO: R Lee Whitehead
HR: –
FYE: December 31
Type: Public

Cecil Bancorp is the holding company for Cecil Federal Bank which serves northeastern Maryland's Cecil and Harford counties through about a dozen branches. The bank offers standard deposit products such as checking and savings accounts NOW and money market accounts CDs and IRAs. The bank focuses on real estate lending; commercial mortgages make up the largest portion of the bank's loan portfolio followed by one- to four-family residential mortgages and construction loans. It offers investment and insurance services through an agreement with third-party provider Community Bankers Securities. First Mariner Bancorp acquired nearly 25% of Cecil Bancorp in 2012 through the collection of a defaulted loan.

	Annual Growth	12/08	12/09	12/10	12/11	12/12
Assets ($ mil.)	(2.8%)	492.4	509.8	487.2	463.7	439.8
Net income ($ mil.)	–	1.9	(2.5)	1.1	(4.7)	(20.3)
Market value ($ mil.)	(46.2%)	50.1	26.0	23.8	4.1	4.2
Employees	(0.5%)	92	91	93	92	90

CECO ENVIRONMENTAL CORP.

NMS: CECE

4625 Red Bank Road
Cincinnati, OH 45227
Phone: 513 458-2600
Fax: –
Web: www.cecoenviro.com

CEO: Jeff Lang
CFO: Edward J. (Ed) Prajzner
HR: –
FYE: December 31
Type: Public

CECO Environmental wants to clear the air. Through its subsidiaries CECO Environmental makes industrial ventilation and pollution control systems including air filters to remove airborne solid and liquid pollutants. The company serves customers in the automotive chemical electronics refining pharmaceutical and textile industries among others. Customers have included General Motors Honda and Procter & Gamble. CECO Environmental also provides custom metal fabrication services making components for its own ventilation systems. Chairman Phillip DeZwirek and his family control CECO Environmental.

	Annual Growth	12/10	12/11	12/12	12/13	12/14
Sales ($ mil.)	17.0%	140.6	139.2	135.1	197.3	263.2
Net income ($ mil.)	57.9%	2.1	8.3	10.9	6.6	13.1
Market value ($ mil.)	27.1%	156.6	145.8	261.4	424.3	408.2
Employees	11.3%	556	524	452	783	853

CEDAR FAIR LP

NYS: FUN

One Cedar Point Drive
Sandusky, OH 44870-5259
Phone: 419 626-0830
Fax: –
Web: www.cedarfair.com

CEO: Matthew A. (Matt) Ouimet
CFO: Brian C. Witherow
HR: Billy Clark
FYE: December 31
Type: Public

Cedar Fair wants to take you for the ride of your life. The firm owns and manages 11 amusement parks three outdoor water parks one indoor water park and five hotels. Properties include Knott's Berry Farm in Buena Park California (outside of Los Angeles); Michigan's Adventure near Muskegon Michigan; and Cedar Point located on Lake Erie in Sandusky Ohio. The company also has a contract to manage Gilroy Gardens in California. Knott's Berry Farm and Castaway Bay Indoor Waterpark Resort (also in Sandusky) operate year-round while other parks are open daily from Memorial Day through Labor Day plus additional seasonal weekends. Cedar Fair parks together draw some 23 million visitors each year.

	Annual Growth	12/10	12/11	12/12	12/13	12/14
Sales ($ mil.)	4.4%	977.6	1,028.5	1,068.5	1,134.6	1,159.6
Net income ($ mil.)	–	(31.6)	72.2	101.2	108.2	104.2
Market value ($ mil.)	33.3%	846.3	1,200.3	1,867.4	2,767.9	2,670.2
Employees	(5.5%)	55,334	1,700	42,700	44,700	44,100

CEDAR REALTY TRUST, INC.

NYS: CDR

44 South Bayles Avenue
Port Washington, NY 11050-3765
Phone: 516 767-6492
Fax: –
Web: www.cedarrealtytrust.com

CEO: Bruce J. Schanzer
CFO: Philip R. Mays
HR: –
FYE: December 31
Type: Public

Cedar Realty Trust (formerly Cedar Shopping Centers) has tended its portfolio from a sapling to a full-grown evergreen. The self-managed real estate investment trust (REIT) owns develops and manages retail space mainly supermarket-anchored strip centers in the Northeast and mid-Atlantic region. It owns about 65 properties totaling nearly 10 million sq. ft. of leasable space. Its portfolio spans seven states with the heaviest concentration of shopping centers in Pennsylvania and Virginia. Major tenants include Giant Foods LA Fitness and Farm Fresh. The REIT usually redevelops or expands existing properties after it buys them.

	Annual Growth	12/10	12/11	12/12	12/13	12/14
Sales ($ mil.)	(1.5%)	157.2	135.4	140.6	138.8	148.2
Net income ($ mil.)	–	(41.3)	(103.6)	29.7	14.4	29.0
Market value ($ mil.)	3.9%	477.2	327.0	400.6	474.9	556.9
Employees	(10.2%)	109	115	88	71	71

CEDARBURG HAUSER PHARMACEUTICALS INC.

870 Badger Circle
Grafton WI 53024-9436
Phone: 262-376-1467
Fax: 262-376-1068
Web: www.cedarburgpharma.com

CEO: Tony Laughray
CFO: –
HR: –
FYE: December 31
Type: Private

Cedarburg Hauser formerly Cedarburg Pharmaceuticals makes drugs components of drugs and ingredients for drugs. The contract manufacturer does everything from project management to manufacturing to validating study results. It produces custom chemicals natural and synthetic active pharmaceutical ingredients dietary supplements and cosmetics. And because Cedarburg Hauser also holds Drug Enforcement Agency permits it makes controlled substances including pain killers and other narcotics. Other services include process development and a whole host of analytical services including quality control and stability studies.

CEDARS-SINAI MEDICAL CENTER

8700 BEVERLY BLVD
WEST HOLLYWOOD, CA 900481804
Phone: 310-423-3277
Fax: –
Web: www.cedars-sinai.edu

CEO: Thomas M. (Tom) Priselac
CFO: Edward M. Prunchunas
HR: –
FYE: June 30
Type: Private

Many a star has been born literally at Cedars-Sinai Medical Center. The 886-bed teaching and research hospital is located right where Los Angeles meets Beverly Hills and West Hollywood and has tended to the medical needs of a number of celebrities since its founding in 1902. However the center is also a major teaching hospital for UCLA's David Geffen School of Medicine and is engaged in hundreds of research programs in areas such as cancer neuroscience and genetics. It also includes two multi-specialty physician associations Cedars-Sinai Medical Group and Ceders-Sinai Health Associates and operates a number of community health centers and outreach programs (such as mobile health clinics).

	Annual Growth	06/07	06/08	06/09	06/10	06/11
Sales ($ mil.)	15.1%	–	–	–	2,309.3	2,658.1
Net income ($ mil.)	37.7%	–	–	–	152.8	210.4
Market value ($ mil.)	–	–	–	–	–	–
Employees	–	–	–	–	–	8,000

CEGEDIM RELATIONSHIP MANAGEMENT

1425 Rt. 26 S.
Bedminster NJ 07921
Phone: 908-443-2000
Fax: 908-470-9900
Web: crm.cegedim.com/pages/default.aspx

CEO: –
CFO: –
HR: Page Stiger
FYE: December 31
Type: Subsidiary

Cegedim Relationship Management helps pharmaceutical companies conduct business. A subsidiary of Cegedim the company offers services and software that manage and analyze sales efforts for pharmaceutical and other life sciences companies. Its products include applications that can access product information and physician databases evaluate competitors and catalog client and prospect data. The company does business in more than 80 countries and serves small to large companies and government agencies. It routinely partners with consulting and technology companies looking to develop and cross-promote products for the life sciences market. Capgemini Informatica Microsoft TAKE and TIBCO are among its partners.

CEL-SCI CORP.

ASE: CVM

8229 Boone Boulevard, Suite 802
Vienna, VA 22182
Phone: 703 506-9460
Fax: 703 506-9471
Web: www.cel-sci.com

CEO: Geert R Kersten
CFO: –
HR: –
FYE: September 30
Type: Public

CEL-SCI hopes to make L.E.A.P.S. and bounds in preventing and treating deadly diseases. Its L.E.A.P.S. (Ligand Epitope Antigen Presentation System) technology modulates T-cells and may lead to synthetic vaccines for herpes viral encephalitis smallpox and other diseases; the National Institutes of Health is testing CEL-1000 (a compound developed using L.E.A.P.S. technology) as a potential avian flu vaccine. The firm's lead drug candidate however is Multikine which might make tumors more susceptible to radiation therapy and help a patient's body produce tumor-fighting antibodies. Multikine is undergoing clinical trials for the treatment of head and neck tumors.

	Annual Growth	09/11	09/12	09/13	09/14	09/15
Sales ($ mil.)	(8.9%)	1.0	0.3	0.2	0.3	0.7
Net income ($ mil.)	–	(25.7)	(15.5)	(9.2)	(27.4)	(34.7)
Market value ($ mil.)	13.2%	41.0	38.8	191.0	102.4	67.4
Employees	–	44	–	–	–	–

CELADON GROUP, INC.

NYS: CGI

9503 East 33rd Street, One Celadon Drive
Indianapolis, IN 46235-4207
Phone: 317 972-7000
Fax: –
Web: www.celadontrucking.com

CEO: Paul A. Will
CFO: Bobby Peavler
HR: Andy De La Cruz
FYE: June 30
Type: Public

Celadon Group provides long-haul dry van truckload service throughout North America via subsidiaries Celadon Trucking Services Celadon Canada and Mexico-based Jaguar. The group maintains a fleet of about 3300 tractors and 8700 trailers. Celadon also offers dedicated contract carriage in which drivers and equipment are assigned to a customer long-term as well as freight brokerage and warehousing services. Its clients have included large shippers with strict time-delivery requirements such as Alcoa Procter & Gamble Philip Morris and Wal-Mart. An e-commerce unit TruckersB2B serves as a purchasing cooperative for smaller trucking fleets and provides discounts on fuel tires and satellite systems.

	Annual Growth	06/11	06/12	06/13	06/14	06/15
Sales ($ mil.)	12.8%	556.7	599.0	613.6	759.3	900.8
Net income ($ mil.)	26.1%	14.7	25.5	27.3	30.7	37.2
Market value ($ mil.)	10.3%	395.7	464.2	517.2	604.3	586.1
Employees	18.2%	3,901	3,982	4,351	4,876	7,606

CELANESE CORP (DE)

NYS: CE

222 W. Las Colinas Blvd., Suite 900N
Irving, TX 75039-5421
Phone: 972 443-4000
Fax: –
Web: www.celanese.com

CEO: Mark C. Rohr
CFO: Christopher W. (Chris) Jensen
HR: Lori Johnston
FYE: December 31
Type: Public

Celanese Corporation gets a lot of good ink about its acetates. The global technology and specialty materials company's primary operations include the manufacture of building block chemicals like acetic acid and vinyl acetate monomers. Those chemicals are used in everything from inks and paints to agricultural products and chewing gum. Canadian subsidiary Acetex the majority of whose sales come from Europe is the world's largest acetyls manufacturer. Other products include acetate tow (in cigarette filters) which accounted for 16% of the company's total sales in 2013; industrial specialties like ethylene vinyl acetate; and engineered plastics.

	Annual Growth	12/11	12/12	12/13	12/14	12/15
Sales ($ mil.)	(4.3%)	6,763.0	6,418.0	6,510.0	6,802.0	5,674.0
Net income ($ mil.)	(15.9%)	607.0	605.0	1,101.0	624.0	304.0
Market value ($ mil.)	11.1%	6,498.1	6,536.2	8,118.5	8,801.1	9,882.9
Employees	(1.8%)	7,600	7,550	7,430	7,468	7,081

CELEBRATE INTERACTIVE HOLDINGS INC.

11220 120th Ave. NE
Kirkland WA 98033
Phone: 425-250-1064
Fax: 425-828-6252
Web: www.celebrateexpress.com

CEO: –
CFO: –
HR: –
FYE: December 31
Type: Subsidiary

Celebrate Interactive Holdings seeks to provide everything for a birthday party except the birthday suit (although it does sell costumes). The online (and catalog) retailer operates four e-commerce sites: the online party store Celebrate Express; Birthday Express offering more than 150 themed party packages targeting families with young children; 1st Wishes (launched in 2006) specializing in those all-important first birthdays; and Costume Express an online Halloween superstore. Founded in 1994 as Celebrate Express Celebrate Interactive Holdings was formed in 2010 to provide one-stop online party planning and shopping. It is a subsidiary of video and e-commerce conglomerate Liberty Interactive Corp.

CELERA CORPORATION

1401 Harbor Bay Pkwy.
Alameda CA 94502
Phone: 510-749-4200
Fax: 650-854-1515
Web: www.baypartners.com

CEO: Kathy Ordoez
CFO: –
HR: Lidya Tesfaye
FYE: December 31
Type: Subsidiary

Celera spent years mapping the human genome and has put that knowledge to use. Formerly a researcher the firm is now focused on developing diagnostics and providing clinical services. Its genotyping products are used to track genetic mutations that indicate drug resistance in HIV screen for cystic fibrosis and identify the best matches for organ transplants. The company's Berkeley HeartLab (BHL) and 4myheart businesses provide cardiology testing and disease management services respectively. Abbott Laboratories distributes the company's diagnostics. Celera is wholly owned subsidiary of Quest Diagnostics.

CELGENE CORP.   NMS: CELG

86 Morris Avenue
Summit, NJ 07901
Phone: 908 673-9000
Fax: –
Web: www.celgene.com

CEO: Perry A. Karsen
CFO: Peter N. Kellogg
HR: –
FYE: December 31
Type: Public

Celgene lines up cells and genes to create good health. The biopharmaceutical company's lead product is Revlimid which is approved in the US Europe and other select markets as a treatment for multiple myeloma (bone marrow cancer). Revlimid also is used to treat a blood disorder called myelodysplastic syndrome (MDS). The company's second-biggest seller is another treatment for MDS called Vidaza; the drug is also approved to treat leukemia in Europe. Other products include Thalomid used to treat patients newly diagnosed with multiple myeloma as well as breast cancer treatment Abraxane and lymphoma drug Istodax. The firm has other drugs in development that combat inflammatory diseases and cancer.

	Annual Growth	12/11	12/12	12/13	12/14	12/15
Sales ($ mil.)	17.6%	4,842.1	5,506.7	6,493.9	7,670.4	9,256.0
Net income ($ mil.)	5.0%	1,318.2	1,456.2	1,449.9	1,999.9	1,602.0
Market value ($ mil.)	15.4%	53,174.2	61,724.5	132,910.2	87,989.1	94,203.2
Employees	11.8%	4,460	4,700	5,100	6,012	6,971

CELLCO PARTNERSHIP

1 Verizon Way
Basking Ridge NJ 07920
Phone: 908-559-5490
Fax: 919-379-3600
Web: www.xsinc.com

CEO: Daniel Mead
CFO: Andrew Davies
HR: –
FYE: December 31
Type: Joint Venture

Cellco Partnership is the #1 US wireless phone operator in terms of sales and subscribers (ahead of top rival AT&T Mobility). Serving nearly 110 million consumer business and government customers nationwide under the Verizon Wireless brand the joint venture is controlled with a 55% stake by Verizon Communications; UK-based global communications giant Vodafone owns the remainder. Offering both standard post-paid (about 95% of its customers) and prepaid subscriptions it distributes phones from manufacturers including Samsung Electronics Research in Motion LG and Apple. The company also offers mobile data services including text messaging multimedia content (V CAST) and Web access.

CELLDEX THERAPEUTICS, INC.   NMS: CLDX

Perryville III Building,, 53 Frontage Road, Suite 200
Hampton, NJ 08827
Phone: 908 200-7500
Fax: –
Web: www.celldex.com

CEO: Anthony S. Marucci
CFO: Avery W. (Chip) Catlin
HR: –
FYE: December 31
Type: Public

Celldex Therapeutics develops cellular therapies to treat specific forms of cancer autoimmune diseases and infections. The biopharmaceutical company's development technologies use cloned proteins antibody-targeted vaccines and other biologic substances to create disease-specific drugs. It has candidates in clinical development for the treatment of brain cancer breast cancer and other oncology-related ailments. Celldex takes candidates through earlier stages of development then typically seeks partners to usher them through late stages. Its first commercial product rotavirus vaccine Rotarix was marketed worldwide by GlaxoSmithKline but that agreement and the company's rights to any profits ended in 2013.

	Annual Growth	12/10	12/11	12/12	12/13	12/14
Sales ($ mil.)	(47.4%)	46.8	9.3	11.2	4.1	3.6
Net income ($ mil.)	–	(2.5)	(44.8)	(59.1)	(81.6)	(118.1)
Market value ($ mil.)	45.1%	369.1	232.9	601.2	2,169.0	1,635.1
Employees	12.6%	100	103	112	129	161

CELSION CORP   NAS: CLSN

997 Lenox Drive, Suite 100
Lawrenceville, NJ 08648
Phone: 609 896-9100
Fax: –
Web: www.celsion.com

CEO: Michael H Tardugno
CFO: Jeffrey W Church
HR: –
FYE: December 31
Type: Public

Celsion is trying to turn up the heat on cancer. The company is developing a heat-activated cancer therapy in the form of its lead drug ThermoDox. ThermoDox combines a common oncology drug doxorubicin with a heat-activated liposome that may help deliver and release the drug more accurately. The drug is being studied as a treatment for liver cancer and breast cancer. Celsion was previously a device maker and developed the Prolieve Thermodilatation system an FDA-approved device used to treat benign prostatic hyperplasia (prostate enlargement). Celsion sold the product line to Boston Scientific in 2007.

	Annual Growth	12/10	12/11	12/12	12/13	12/14
Sales ($ mil.)	(37.0%)	–	2.0	–	0.5	0.5
Net income ($ mil.)	–	(18.8)	(23.2)	(26.6)	(8.3)	(25.5)
Market value ($ mil.)	3.3%	41.0	34.0	163.7	77.7	46.6
Employees	15.0%	16	19	19	13	28

CELSIUS HOLDINGS INC

NBB: CELH

2424 N. Federal Highway, Suite 208
Boca Raton, FL 33431
Phone: 561 276-2239
Fax: –
Web: www.celsius.com

CEO: Gerry David
CFO: John Fieldly
HR: –
FYE: December 31
Type: Public

Celsius Holdings wants consumers to enjoy the taste of burning calories. The company develops markets and distributes nutritional drinks that claim to burn calories raise metabolism and boost energy. Its first product Celsius is a canned sparkling beverage that comes in a variety of flavors and is marketed as an alternative to soda coffee and traditional energy drinks. Although it has undergone independent clinical studies results have not been US FDA approved. Its products which also include non-carbonated Celsius green tea drinks and single-serving powder mix packets that can be added to water are manufactured by third-party co-packers. Celsius Holdings was founded in 2004 under the name Elite FX.

	Annual Growth	12/09	12/10	12/12	12/13	12/14
Sales ($ mil.)	20.0%	5.9	8.3	7.7	10.6	14.6
Net income ($ mil.)	–	(7.8)	(19.5)	(2.8)	(1.8)	(2.0)
Market value ($ mil.)	(37.1%)	103.5	8.6	4.1	7.0	10.2
Employees	–	–	–	–	–	26

CEM HOLDINGS CORPORATION

3100 Smith Farm Rd.
Matthews NC 28106
Phone: 704-821-7015
Fax: 704-821-7894
Web: www.cem.com

CEO: Michael J Collins
CFO: –
HR: –
FYE: September 30
Type: Private

Scientists mad or otherwise probably love to browse CEM's product catalog. CEM — short for chemistry electronics and mechanics — makes microwave-based instruments that perform testing analysis and process control in laboratory and industrial environments. The company's MARS heating system analyzes samples by dissolving them in acid. CEM's other products include moisture/solids analysis systems and fat analyzers. CEM sells directly in the US and worldwide through subsidiaries and distributors in about 50 countries. It serves such industries as food tobacco to plastics chemicals and textiles. Established in 1978 CEM was taken private in 2000 by founder and CEO Michael J. Collins.

CEMPRA INC

NMS: CEMP

6320 Quadrangle Drive, Suite 360
Chapel Hill, NC 27517
Phone: 919 313-6601
Fax: –
Web: www.cempra.com

CEO: Prabhavathi Fernandes
CFO: Mark W. Hahn
HR: –
FYE: December 31
Type: Public

Cempra isn't afraid of a little staph or pneumonia for that matter. The company is in the clinical stages of developing antibiotics that treat bacterial infectious diseases especially ones that affect the skin and respiratory tract. One of its lead candidates Taksta is an oral treatment that is being tested against linezolid (sold by Pfizer as Zyvox) the only oral antibiotic currently FDA approved for the treatment of a drug-resistant form of staph known as MRSA. Its other main candidate CEM-101 is being developed in IV and oral formulations for the treatment of community-acquired bacterial pneumonia. Cempra completed an IPO in 2012.

	Annual Growth	12/10	12/11	12/12	12/13	12/14
Sales ($ mil.)	94.8%	–	–	–	7.8	15.2
Net income ($ mil.)	–	(19.7)	(21.2)	(24.2)	(45.0)	(61.6)
Market value ($ mil.)	91.7%	–	–	239.8	464.3	881.0
Employees	38.4%	15	14	25	38	55

CENAMA INC.

1410 Commonwealth Dr. Ste. #202
Wilmington NC 28403
Phone: 910-395-5300
Fax: 910-395-6691
Web: www.vpsstores.com/

CEO: –
CFO: Jeff W Turpin
HR: –
FYE: December 31
Type: Private

Cenama which does business as VPS Convenience Store Group can help road hogs to top off their tanks and their tummies. The company operates about 420 convenience stores in the Southeast and Midwest under the Scotchman Young's Li'l Cricket Village Pantry Next Door Stores and Everyday Shop banners. VPS's stores sell name-brand fuels (including BP Exxon and Shell) in addition to its proprietary Carolina Petro brand. Many stores offer Subway Quiznos and Noble Roman's fast food as well as ready-made breakfast and lunch items. The company also runs two truck stops and provides fleet fueling services. VPS is owned by private investment firm Sun Capital Partners.

CENTAUR TECHNOLOGY INC.

7600-C N. Capital of Texas Hwy. Ste. 300
Austin TX 78731
Phone: 512-418-5700
Fax: 512-794-0717
Web: www.centtech.com/

CEO: –
CFO: –
HR: Christy Connelly
FYE: December 31
Type: Subsidiary

The horsepower provided by Centaur Technology's processors is a breed apart. An independent subsidiary and design house of chipset stalwart VIA Technologies Centaur makes low-cost microprocessors for use in mobile PCs and other portable electronics. The company designed VIA's C7-M processor one of the world's smallest lowest-power and most secure x86-architecture processors. Centaur was established in Austin Texas 1995 and prides itself on its employee-friendly work environment with free breakfasts and lunches and an onsite fitness facility. VIA purchased Centaur in 1999. The company has no management hierarchy save for founder and president Glenn Henry.

CENTEGRA HEALTH SYSTEM

385 MILLENNIUM DR STE A
CRYSTAL LAKE, IL 600123761
Phone: 815-788-5800
Fax: –
Web: www.centegra.org

CEO: Michael Eesley
CFO: Robert Rosenberger
HR: –
FYE: June 30
Type: Private

Centegra Health System seeks integrity in the health care services realm. The health network serves residents of the greater McHenry County region in northern Illinois and southern Wisconsin. The company operates two main medical centers Centegra Hospital-McHenry and Centegra Hospital-Woodstock with a total of some 325 beds. They offer emergency and trauma care as well as general medicine surgery and obstetrics services. Centegra has dedicated cancer diabetes and heart centers and also offers rehabilitation behavioral health and fitness services. In addition the community-based health system operates a network of primary care and specialty outpatient clinics.

	Annual Growth	06/09	06/10	06/11	06/12	06/13
Sales ($ mil.)	18.3%	–	80.8	0.0	428.0	133.7
Net income ($ mil.)	–	–	–	0.0	(13.1)	(13.2)
Market value ($ mil.)	–	–	–	–	–	–
Employees	–	–	–	–	–	3,700

CENTENE CORP

NYS: CNC

7700 Forsyth Boulevard
St. Louis, MO 63105
Phone: 314 725-4477
Fax: 314 725-5180
Web: www.centene.com

CEO: Michael F. Neidorff
CFO: William N. Scheffel
HR: Jalie Cohen
FYE: December 31
Type: Public

Centene is sensitive to the needs of those enrolled in government-assisted health programs. The company provides managed care and related services in more than a dozen states under names such as Managed Health Services (Wisconsin and Indiana) Superior HealthPlan (Texas) and Buckeye Community Health Plan (Ohio). Centene provides services to some 2.7 million low-income elderly and disabled people receiving benefits from programs including Medicaid Supplemental Security Income (SSI) and state Children's Health Insurance Program (CHIP). Centene also offers specialty services in areas such as behavioral health (through Cenpatico) vision benefits (OptiCare) and pharmacy benefits management (US Script).

	Annual Growth	12/10	12/11	12/12	12/13	12/14
Sales ($ mil.)	38.9%	4,448.3	5,340.6	8,667.6	10,863.3	16,560.0
Net income ($ mil.)	30.0%	94.8	111.2	1.9	165.1	271.0
Market value ($ mil.)	42.3%	3,001.1	4,688.8	4,855.8	6,981.6	12,299.3
Employees	33.6%	4,200	5,300	6,800	8,800	13,400

CENTER FOR CREATIVE LEADERSHIP INC

1 LEADERSHIP PL
GREENSBORO, NC 274109427
Phone: 336-288-7210
Fax: –
Web: www.ccl.org

CEO: John R. Ryan
CFO: Bradley E. Shumaker
HR: –
FYE: March 31
Type: Private

The Center for Creative Leadership (CCL) is a not-for-profit organization that provides coaching in management training to public private nonprofit government and education sectors worldwide. The center is headquartered in Greensboro North Carolina and offers its programs through open enrollment courses and customized training at its campuses and affiliates across North America Europe Africa and Asia. Virtual learning through webinars podcasts and eBooks also is available. CCL serves some 20000 individuals and 2000 organizations each year with clients such as Wells Fargo Time Warner Cable and the US Army.

	Annual Growth	03/08	03/09	03/10	03/11	03/14
Sales ($ mil.)	(43.3%)	–	1,943.9	86.1	92.6	113.7
Net income ($ mil.)	(49.2%)	–	–	8.0	3.8	0.5
Market value ($ mil.)	–	–	–	–	–	–
Employees	–	–	–	–	–	600

CENTERBEAM INC.

30 Rio Robles Dr.
San Jose CA 95134
Phone: 408-750-0500
Fax: 408-750-0555
Web: www.centerbeam.com

CEO: –
CFO: –
HR: –
FYE: December 31
Type: Private

CenterBeam takes on the day-to-day management and support of everything IT. The company provides outsourced computing and communications infrastructure management services primarily to midsized businesses in North America. Areas of specialty include desktop management (virus protection software patches and data back-up) server and network management (performance and fault management virus protection updates asset tracking and network monitoring) and other support services. Its customers come from a range of industries including construction financial services and health care. Founded in 1999 CenterBeam has received funding from such investors as Intel Apax Partners and New Enterprise Associates.

CENTERLINE CAPITAL GROUP INC.

625 Madison Ave.
New York NY 10022
Phone: 212-317-5700
Fax: 212-751-3550
Web: www.centerline.com

CEO: –
CFO: –
HR: –
FYE: December 31
Type: Subsidiary

Centerline Capital finds its center in real estate financing and asset management for affordable and multifamily housing developments. The subsidiary of Centerline Holding Company has raised about $10 billion used to finance and develop more than 15000 affordable housing properties throughout the US and Puerto Rico. Centerline Capital provides equity and debt financing through low-income housing tax credits. It also underwrites and services mortgages on behalf of Fannie Mae and Freddie Mac. Clients include developers owners and investors. Centerline Capital currently provides asset management for 1300 affordable housing properties in the US.

CENTERPLATE INC.

201 E. Broad St.
Spartanburg SC 29306
Phone: 864-598-8600
Fax: 864-598-8693
Web: www.centerplate.com

CEO: Chris Verros
CFO: Kevin F McNamara
HR: –
FYE: December 31
Type: Private

Wherever there's a sporting event this concessions operator likes to be front and center. Centerplate is a leading provider of catering concessions and merchandise services in the US to about 250 sports stadiums convention centers and other entertainment venues. The company's clients include professional baseball and football stadiums minor league parks and college sports stadiums. It provides catering and other services at convention centers including the Jacob K. Javits Center in Manhattan as well as at airports parks performing arts centers and ski resorts. It also handles a number of special events such as the Kentucky Derby Festival.

CENTERPOINT ENERGY HOUSTON ELECTRIC LLC

1111 Louisiana St.
Houston TX 77002
Phone: 713-207-1111
Fax: 414-383-4339
Web: www.badgermutual.com

CEO: Scott M Prochazka
CFO: William D Rogers
HR: –
FYE: December 31
Type: Subsidiary

Houston we don't have a problem. CenterPoint Energy Houston Electric's glow spreads across the fourth-largest US city and surrounding areas of the Texas Gulf Coast. The utility operates the regulated power transmission and distribution systems in the Houston metropolitan area. CenterPoint Energy Houston Electric a subsidiary of utility holding company CenterPoint Energy serves more than 2 million metered customers over its more than 48230 miles of electric distribution lines and more than 230 substations; the utility's 3780 miles of transmission lines are managed by the Electric Reliability Council of Texas (ERCOT).

CENTERPOINT ENERGY, INC
NYS: CNP

1111 Louisiana
Houston, TX 77002
Phone: 713 207-1111
Fax: –
Web: www.centerpointenergy.com

CEO: Scott M. Prochazka
CFO: William D. (Bill) Rogers
HR: Susan (Sue) Ortenstone
FYE: December 31
Type: Public

CenterPoint Energy pivots around its core operations which include power and gas distribution utilities and natural gas pipeline gathering and marketing operations. CenterPoint Energy's regulated utilities distribute natural gas to 3.4 million customers in six US states and electricity to more than 2.1 million customers on the Texas Gulf Coast. The company's main stomping ground is Texas where it has regulated power distribution operations through subsidiary CenterPoint Energy Houston Electric. CenterPoint Energy operates more than 50717 miles of power distribution lines 20000 miles of interstate gas pipeline and 3700 miles of gas gathering pipeline. It also provides natural gas field services.

	Annual Growth	12/10	12/11	12/12	12/13	12/14
Sales ($ mil.)	1.2%	8,785.0	8,450.0	7,452.0	8,106.0	9,226.0
Net income ($ mil.)	8.4%	442.0	1,357.0	417.0	311.0	611.0
Market value ($ mil.)	10.5%	6,759.6	8,638.7	8,277.5	9,967.4	10,074.9
Employees	(0.9%)	8,843	8,827	8,720	8,591	8,540

CENTERPOINT PROPERTIES TRUST

1808 Swift Dr.
Oak Brook IL 60523
Phone: 630-586-8000
Fax: 630-586-8010
Web: www.centerpoint-prop.com

CEO: –
CFO: Michael J Kraft
HR: –
FYE: December 31
Type: Private

CenterPoint Properties invests in develops and manages industrial and infrastructure projects in transportation hubs throughout the US primarily in Chicago and the Midwest where it is the largest industrial owner. It owns some 28 million sq. ft. of space including warehouses light manufacturing centers distribution facilities and container yards. CenterPoint also provides renovation services for ports and rail terminals and develops industrial and commercial properties for other owners. Subsidiary CenterPoint Capital helps secure project financing. Founded in 1984 the company is owned by CalEast Global Logistics a group which includes Jones Lang LaSalle and CalPERS.

CENTERS FOR DISEASE CONTROL AND PREVENTION

1600 Clifton Rd.
Atlanta GA 30333
Phone: 404-639-3311
Fax: 404-498-1177
Web: www.cdc.gov

CEO: –
CFO: Barbara Michalson
HR: –
FYE: December 31
Type: Business Segment

The name really says it all for the Centers for Disease Control and Prevention (CDC). The lead federal agency for protecting the health and safety of US citizens the CDC investigates health problems performs research and develops public health policies as well as developing and applying disease prevention and control. It is one of the major operating components of the Department of Health and Human Services and comprises seven coordinating centers and the National Institute for Occupational Safety and Health. The CDC which has nine US locations and workers in more than 50 countries partners with public and private entities to improve the flow of information throughout the health care community.

CENTERS FOR MEDICARE & MEDICAID SERVICES

7500 Security Blvd.
Baltimore MD 21244-1850
Phone: 410-786-3000
Fax: 410-786-8060
Web: cms.gov

CEO: –
CFO: –
HR: –
FYE: September 30
Type: Government Agency

The Centers for Medicare & Medicaid Services (CMS) was created in 1977 to administer the Medicare and Medicaid programs which together provide health care coverage to millions of Americans. Medicare provides hospital medical and prescription coverage for people over age 65 and for people with certain disabilities; Medicaid provides health care for people with low incomes (as defined by the government). CMS also runs the Children's Health Insurance Program (CHIP) which in partnership with state legislations provides health care for children and pregnant women that don't qualify for Medicaid. CMS is part of the Department of Health and Human Services; its annual budget was more than $486 billion in 2011.

CENTERSTATE BANKS, INC.
NMS: CSFL

42745 U.S. Highway 27
Davenport, FL 33837
Phone: 863 419-7750
Fax: –
Web: www.centerstatebanks.com

CEO: John Corbett
CFO: James J. Antal
HR: –
FYE: December 31
Type: Public

CenterState Banks is the holding company for CenterState Bank of Florida which serves the Sunshine State through about 60 branches. The bank offers standard deposit products such as checking and savings accounts money market accounts and CDs. Real estate loans primarily residential and commercial mortgages make up 85% of the company's loan portfolio while the rest is made up of business loans and consumer loans. The bank's correspondent division provides bond securities accounting and loans to small and mid-sized banks across the Southeast and Texas. It also sells mutual funds annuities and other investment products.

	Annual Growth	12/10	12/11	12/12	12/13	12/14
Assets ($ mil.)	16.3%	2,063.3	2,284.5	2,363.2	2,415.6	3,776.9
Net income ($ mil.)	–	(5.5)	7.9	9.9	12.2	13.0
Market value ($ mil.)	10.7%	359.0	300.0	386.6	460.0	539.8
Employees	6.9%	600	655	689	693	785

CENTIMARK CORPORATION

12 GRANDVIEW CIR
CANONSBURG, PA 153178533
Phone: 724-743-7777
Fax: –
Web: www.centimarkltd.com

CEO: Edward B. Dunlap
CFO: John L. Heisey
HR: Landon Connolly
FYE: April 30
Type: Private

Shout it from the rooftops Centimark is one of the largest commercial and industrial roofing contractors in North America. The company provides roof installation inspection repair and emergency leak service. Centimark typically works on flat roofs using EPDM rubber thermoplastic bitumen metal and coatings. Top customers have included NASA and the US Army Corps of Engineers. Its QuestMark division offers commercial industrial and retail flooring do-it-yourself (DIY) products and floor maintenance and cleaning products. The company which has about 80 offices throughout North America.

	Annual Growth	04/10	04/11	04/12	04/13	04/14
Sales ($ mil.)	7.9%	–	404.4	474.3	484.7	508.2
Net income ($ mil.)	5.0%	–	–	38.2	38.7	42.1
Market value ($ mil.)	–	–	–	–	–	–
Employees	–	–	–	–	–	2,400

CENTRA HEALTH INC.

1920 ATHERHOLT RD
LYNCHBURG, VA 245011120
Phone: 434-200-4700
Fax: –
Web: www.centrahealth.com

CEO: E. W. Tibbs
CFO: –
HR: –
FYE: December 31
Type: Private

Centra Health is a constellation of hospitals and medical practices targeting the health care needs of residents in central and southern Virginia. At the not-for-profit entity's core are two acute care facilities in Lynchburg: the 358-bed Lynchburg General which is the region's main emergency center and specializes in orthopedic pediatric and cardiac care; and Virginia Baptist a 161-bed facility focused on surgery women's health infant care mental health and rehabilitation. Centra also operates a nearby community hospital and an array of primary care physician practices home health agencies retirement centers and other physical and behavioral health businesses.

	Annual Growth	12/02	12/03	12/04	12/08	12/09
Sales ($ mil.)	9.3%	–	313.8	331.7	419.7	535.0
Net income ($ mil.)	9.1%	–	–	10.9	33.3	16.8
Market value ($ mil.)	–	–	–	–	–	–
Employees	–	–	–	–	–	6,000

CENTRA INC.

12225 Stephen Rd.
Warren MI 48089-2010
Phone: 586-939-7000
Fax: 586-755-5607
Web: www.centraltransportint.com

CEO: –
CFO: –
HR: –
FYE: December 31
Type: Private

At the center of CenTra is Central Transport International a less-than-truckload (LTL) carrier that hauls across North America. (LTL carriers combine freight from multiple shippers into a single truckload.) Central Transport and its affiliates operate via some 200 terminals mainly in the eastern US. CenTra's interests include expedited freight transporter CTX freight forwarder Central Global Express broker/warehouser Custom Services International and supply chain manager Logistics Insight (LINC). CenTra also owns the Ambassador Bridge connecting Detroit with Windsor Ontario. CEO Manuel Moroun and his son Matthew control freight hauler Universal Truckload as well as CenTra (founded by Manuel's father).

CENTRAL DUPAGE HOSPITAL ASSOCIATION

25 N WINFIELD RD
WINFIELD, IL 601901295
Phone: 630-933-1600
Fax: –
Web: www.cdh.org

CEO: –
CFO: James T Spear
HR: –
FYE: June 30
Type: Private

Central DuPage Hospital attends to the health needs of Windy City suburbanites. Located in DuPage County just west of Chicago the hospital has more than 310 beds and provides general medical and surgical care including specialty care in areas such as oncology cardiovascular disease neuroscience and orthopedics. The hospital is the focal point of a network of health services that include a physician medical group home health care services occupational care and about half a dozen urgent care centers. Central DuPage Hospital opened its doors in 1964.

	Annual Growth	06/09	06/10	06/11	06/12	06/13
Sales ($ mil.)	10.2%	–	633.6	667.7	773.2	849.1
Net income ($ mil.)	166.5%	–	–	26.0	112.2	184.4
Market value ($ mil.)	–	–	–	–	–	–
Employees	–	–	–	–	–	1,600

CENTRAL FEDERAL CORP

NAS: CFBK

7000 North High St.
Worthington, OH 43085
Phone: 614 334-7979
Fax: 614 334-7980
Web: www.cfbankonline.com

CEO: Timothy T O'Dell
CFO: John W Helmsdoerfer
HR: –
FYE: December 31
Type: Public

Central Federal Corporation is the holding company for CFBank. Traditionally a retail-focused savings and loan CFBank has added business banking commercial real estate and business lending to its foundation. It now serves not only local individuals but also businesses through five branches in eastern Ohio and the state capital Columbus. Its deposit products include checking savings NOW and money market accounts as well as CDs. Commercial commercial real estate and multifamily residential mortgages represent nearly 80% of the company's loan portfolio. Single-family mortgages make up about 13% of loans. CFBank traces its roots to 1892.

	Annual Growth	12/10	12/11	12/12	12/13	12/14
Assets ($ mil.)	3.5%	275.2	250.9	215.0	255.7	315.6
Net income ($ mil.)	–	(6.9)	(5.4)	(3.8)	(0.9)	0.5
Market value ($ mil.)	24.2%	8.1	9.8	22.9	21.0	19.3
Employees	(4.3%)	74	68	68	66	62

CENTRAL FREIGHT LINES INC.

5601 W. Waco Dr.
Waco TX 76710
Phone: 254-772-2120
Fax: 254-741-5370
Web: www.centralfreight.com

CEO: Vicky Obrien
CFO: –
HR: –
FYE: December 31
Type: Private

The Southwest the Midwest and the Northwest are all central to the business of Central Freight Lines a leading regional less-than-truckload (LTL) carrier. (LTL carriers consolidate freight from multiple shippers into a single truckload.) The company focuses on next-day and second-day services within each of its regions. It operates a fleet of more than 1950 tractors and nearly 8500 trailers from a network of about 50 terminals and provides service to 49 US states. Central Freight Lines serves the rest of the US through alliances with other carriers. Trucking magnate Jerry Moyes owns the company.

CENTRAL GARDEN & PET CO.

NMS: CENT A

1340 Treat Boulevard, Suite 600
Walnut Creek, CA 94597
Phone: 925 948-4000
Fax: –
Web: www.central.com

CEO: John R. Ranelli
CFO: David N. Chichester
HR: Andy Rich
FYE: September 26
Type: Public

Central Garden & Pet is happy to help with both pets and pests. The company is among the largest US producers and distributors of lawn garden and pet supplies providing its products to pet supplies retailers home improvement centers nurseries and mass merchandisers (Wal-Mart is its largest customer). It operates about 30 manufacturing plants and more than 25 distribution centers throughout the US; it also has sales offices in the UK. Central Garden & Pet's proprietary brand lines include AMDRO fire ant bait Four Paws animal products Kaytee bird seed Nylabone dog chews Norcal pottery Pennington grass seed and bird seed products and TFH pet books. Chairman William Brown controls the company.

	Annual Growth	09/11	09/12	09/13	09/14	09/15
Sales ($ mil.)	0.3%	1,628.7	1,700.0	1,653.6	1,604.4	1,650.7
Net income ($ mil.)	3.1%	28.3	21.2	(1.9)	8.8	32.0
Market value ($ mil.)	25.1%	334.7	594.8	351.7	384.7	819.9
Employees	(6.4%)	4,300	3,600	3,300	3,300	3,300

CENTRAL GROCERS INC.

2600 HAVEN AVE
JOLIET, IL 604338467
Phone: 815-553-8800
Fax: -
Web: www.central-grocers.com

CEO: -
CFO: Tim Kubis
HR: -
FYE: July 28
Type: Private

In a city of big stores Central Grocers helps neighborhood markets stay afloat. Founded in 1917 the cooperative wholesale food distributor is owned by some 225 members. It supplies 40000 food items and general merchandise to more than 400 independent grocery stores serving several states such as Illinois Indiana Iowa Michigan and Wisconsin. Central Grocers distributes products under both national brands and its own Centrella brand which is marketed exclusively to its member stores. The co-op also operates about 30 stores under a handful of banner names including Strack & Van Til Town & Country Key Market and the low-cost Ultra Foods chain.

	Annual Growth	07/03	07/04	07/05	07/06	07/07
Sales ($ mil.)	4.5%	-	1,047.9	1,103.2	1,108.9	1,197.2
Net income ($ mil.)	-	-	-	4.8	5.5	(10.3)
Market value ($ mil.)	-	-	-	-	-	-
Employees	-	-	-	-	-	2,300

CENTRAL IOWA POWER COOPERATIVE

1400 HIGHWAY 13
CEDAR RAPIDS, IA 524039060
Phone: 319-366-8011
Fax: -
Web: www.cipco.net

CEO: Dennis Murdock
CFO: -
HR: -
FYE: December 31
Type: Private

Keeping a sharp eye out for the well-being of Iowa's citizens Central Iowa Power Cooperative provides electricity transmission and generation services to 13 member distribution cooperatives (12 rural electric cooperatives and one municipal cooperative) which in turn serve about 320000 residential and 7000 industrial and commercial customers. Central Iowa Power's member distribution cooperatives deliver power to commercial businesses farmsteads industrial parks manufacturers urban residences and other customers in a service area that stretches 300 miles diagonally across the state from Shenandoah in the southwest to the Mississippi River in the east.

	Annual Growth	12/05	12/06	12/08	12/09	12/13
Sales ($ mil.)	4.6%	-	140.6	164.9	185.4	193.1
Net income ($ mil.)	13.0%	-	-	6.6	23.9	12.1
Market value ($ mil.)	-	-	-	-	-	-
Employees	-	-	-	-	-	117

CENTRAL MICHIGAN UNIVERSITY

1200 S FRANKLIN ST
MOUNT PLEASANT, MI 488592001
Phone: 989-774-4000
Fax: -
Web: www.media.cmich.edu

CEO: -
CFO: -
HR: -
FYE: June 30
Type: Private

Academic advancement is central at Central Michigan University (CMU). The university offers more than 200 academic programs for undergraduate graduate and professional coursework through eight colleges including business communication and fine arts medicine and education and human services. The university enrolls more than 20000 students at the main campus in Mt. Pleasant. The institution also enrolls another 7000 students online and at 50 locations throughout North America. In addition CMU offers study abroad programs in 40 countries.

	Annual Growth	06/10	06/11	06/12	06/13	06/14
Sales ($ mil.)	1.9%	-	329.3	321.5	319.5	348.7
Net income ($ mil.)	79.8%	-	-	6.1	32.3	19.8
Market value ($ mil.)	-	-	-	-	-	-
Employees	-	-	-	-	-	2,388

CENTRAL MUTUAL INSURANCE COMPANY

800 S. Washington St.
Van Wert OH 45891-2357
Phone: 419-238-1010
Fax: 800-736-7026
Web: www.central-insurance.com

CEO: -
CFO: Thad Eikenbary
HR: -
FYE: December 31
Type: Private - Mutual Com

Central Mutual Insurance Company is aptly if modestly named: The company is centrally located is mutually held and by golly it does sell insurance. Along with its affiliates All America Insurance and CMI Lloyds Central Mutual operates as Central Insurance Companies. The group offers personal auto and homeowners insurance as well as commercial property/casualty policies. It also provides equipment protection workers' compensation professional liability and other specialty coverage. Central Insurance Companies sells its products through independent agents in almost 20 states. Chairman and president Francis Purmort III is the fifth generation of his family to lead the firm which was founded in 1876.

CENTRAL PACIFIC FINANCIAL CORP NYS: CPF

220 South King Street
Honolulu, HI 96813
Phone: 808 544-0500
Fax: 808 531-2875
Web: www.centralpacificbank.com

CEO: A. Catherine Ngo
CFO: David S. Morimoto
HR: -
FYE: December 31
Type: Public

When in the Central Pacific do as the islanders do. This may include doing business with Central Pacific Financial the holding company for Central Pacific Bank which operates more than 35 branch locations and 110 ATMs across the Hawaiian Islands. Targeting individuals and local businesses the $5 billion bank provides such standard retail banking products as checking and savings accounts money market accounts and CDs. About 70% of the bank's loan portfolio is made up of commercial real estate loans residential mortgages and construction loans though it also provides business and consumer loans.

	Annual Growth	12/10	12/11	12/12	12/13	12/14
Assets ($ mil.)	5.4%	3,938.1	4,132.9	4,370.4	4,741.2	4,853.0
Net income ($ mil.)	-	(251.0)	36.6	47.4	172.1	40.5
Market value ($ mil.)	93.6%	53.9	455.2	549.3	707.5	757.5
Employees	(2.2%)	921	935	948	903	841

CENTRAL REFRIGERATED SERVICE INC.

5175 W 2100 S
SALT LAKE CITY, UT 841201252
Phone: 801-924-7000
Fax: -
Web: www.centralrefrigerated.com

CEO: Jon Isaacson
CFO: Robert Baer
HR: Vickie Bird
FYE: December 31
Type: Private

No matter the weather conditions trucking company Central Refrigerated Service stays cool when it's on the move. The carrier provides temperature-controlled transportation and dry cargo services for major food suppliers and retailers across the US. It specializes in providing a wide array of offerings from private fleet conversion to inner city and solo driver deliveries to long haul truckload transportation services. Central Refrigerated operates a fleet of about 1800 tractors and 2700 refrigerated trailers or reefers. The company was acquired by truckload carrier Swift Transportation in mid-2013.

	Annual Growth	12/04	12/05	12/06	12/07	12/08
Sales ($ mil.)	-	-	-	0.0	361.9	406.9
Net income ($ mil.)	-	-	-	0.0	6.7	9.6
Market value ($ mil.)	-	-	-	-	-	-
Employees	-	-	-	-	-	1,650

CENTRAL SUFFOLK HOSPITAL

1300 ROANOKE AVE
RIVERHEAD, NY 119012058
Phone: 631-548-6000
Fax: -
Web: www.pbmchealth.org

CEO: -
CFO: -
HR: Monica Rauls
FYE: December 31
Type: Private

Central Suffolk Hospital (CSH—doing business as PBMC Health System) provides a sea of medical care services to residents of Long Island. The not-for-profit hospital covers a broad range of general and specialty care services including oncology emergency medicine general surgery neurosurgery orthopedics and women's health care. With a medical staff of more than 200 the medical center has roughly 200 beds. PBMC also operates a 60-bed skilled nursing and rehabilitation center a certified home health agency a palliative care center and a network of primary care centers. PBMC is affiliated with Stony Brook University Medical Center.

	Annual Growth	12/04	12/05	12/06	12/08	12/11
Sales ($ mil.)	-	-	(357.6)	96.3	91.3	149.6
Net income ($ mil.)	32.1%	-	-	0.7	0.7	2.7
Market value ($ mil.)	-	-	-	-	-	-
Employees	-	-	-	-	-	610

CENTRAL VALLEY COMMUNITY BANCORP

NAS: CVCY

7100 N. Financial Drive, Suite 101
Fresno, CA 93720
Phone: 559 298-1775
Fax: -
Web: www.cvcb.com

CEO: James M Ford
CFO: David A Kinross
HR: -
FYE: December 31
Type: Public

Central Valley Community Bancorp is the holding company for Central Valley Community Bank which offers individuals and businesses traditional banking services through about 15 offices in California's San Joaquin Valley. Deposit products include checking savings and money market accounts; IRAs; and CDs. The bank founded in 1979 offers credit card services and originates a variety of loans including residential and commercial mortgage Small Business Administration and agricultural loans. Through Central Valley Community Insurance Services it markets health property and casualty insurance products primarily to business customers.

	Annual Growth	12/10	12/11	12/12	12/13	12/14
Assets ($ mil.)	11.3%	777.6	849.0	890.2	1,145.6	1,192.2
Net income ($ mil.)	12.7%	3.3	6.5	7.5	8.3	5.3
Market value ($ mil.)	18.5%	61.8	59.6	85.2	123.5	121.7
Employees	7.8%	215	231	232	290	290

CENTRAL VERMONT PUBLIC SERVICE CORPORATION

NYSE: CV

77 Grove St.
Rutland VT 05701
Phone: 800-649-2877
Fax: 802-747-2199
Web: www.cvps.com

CEO: -
CFO: Pamela J Keefe
HR: -
FYE: December 31
Type: Public

Moonlight in Vermont may be beautiful but it doesn't provide any power. Vermont's largest electric utility Central Vermont Public Service (CVPS) provides power to more than 159000 customers in 163 communities across the state. It generates approximately 110 MW of nuclear hydroelectric and fossil-fueled capacity; it purchases most of its energy supply of 516 MW. CVPS owns 59% of Vermont Yankee Nuclear Power Corporation and 47% of state transmission firm Vermont Electric Power Company (VELCO). Nonregulated businesses include investments (Catamount Resources) home maintenance contracting real estate (C.V. Realty) and energy-related services. In 2012 CVPS was acquired by Canada-based GazMetro.

CENTRASTATE HEALTHCARE SYSTEM INC

901 W MAIN ST
FREEHOLD, NJ 07728-2537
Phone: 732-431-2000
Fax: -
Web: www.centrastate.com

CEO: John T Gribbin
CFO: John A Dellocono
HR: -
FYE: December 31
Type: Private

CentraState Healthcare System makes healing its central mission while serving residents of central New Jersey. The health system operates CentraState Medical Center an acute-care teaching hospital with more than 280 beds that offers emergency surgical and diagnostic imaging services as well as specialty services including cardiovascular care and women's health. Other CentraState Healthcare facilities include nursing homes wellness centers and outpatient clinics. CentraState Healthcare is an affiliate of the Robert Wood Johnson Health System and Network.

	Annual Growth	12/07	12/08	12/09	12/10	12/11
Sales ($ mil.)	2.1%	-	260.8	254.5	259.2	277.9
Net income ($ mil.)	-	-	(11.4)	17.9	15.4	15.1
Market value ($ mil.)	-	-	-	-	-	-
Employees	-	-	-	-	-	2,527

CENTRE COLLEGE OF KENTUCKY

600 W WALNUT ST
DANVILLE, KY 404221394
Phone: 859-238-5200
Fax: -
Web: www.centre.edu

CEO: -
CFO: Robert Keasler
HR: -
FYE: June 30
Type: Private

Centre College's name reflects its location in the geographic center of Kentucky (near Lexington) as well as its founders' preponderance for British spellings. The private liberal arts school enrolls some 1200 students majoring in about 30 academic areas. Some 85% of students participate in study-abroad opportunities which cost little more than regular tuition. Centre boasts a fraternity that carries an oil portrait of alum former Supreme Court Chief Justice Fred Vinson (Dead Fred) to all home football games. Living alums seem to like the place too: The school is ranked #1 in the nation in terms of percentage of alumni making annual contributions. Centre College was founded in 1819 by Presbyterian leaders.

	Annual Growth	06/07	06/08	06/09	06/10	06/13
Sales ($ mil.)	-	-	0.0	57.0	58.8	89.2
Net income ($ mil.)	(40.3%)	-	-	53.5	(6.8)	6.8
Market value ($ mil.)	-	-	-	-	-	-
Employees	-	-	-	-	-	325

CENTRIA INC.

1005 Beaver Grade Rd.
Moon Township PA 15108
Phone: 800-759-7474
Fax: 412-299-8317
Web: www.centria.com

CEO: -
CFO: -
HR: Bob Burik
FYE: December 31
Type: Private

The metal panel is central to the business of CENTRIA which manufactures architectural industrial nonresidential and institutional metal buildings. The company is the world leader in custom-engineered architectural metal enclosure systems. CENTRIA also provides extensive coil-coating capabilities for a range of industries including automotive and residential building products. Through its H. H. Robertson Floor Systems unit the company offers electrified cellular decking and related products. CENTRIA Worldwide sells factory foamed metal panel systems and profiled panel systems for both walls and roofs worldwide.

CENTRIC GROUP L.L.C.

1260 Andes Blvd.
St. Louis MO 63132
Phone: 314-214-2700
Fax: 314-214-2766
Web: www.centricgp.com

CEO: -
CFO: Russ Willey
HR: -
FYE: December 31
Type: Private

Coffee baggage and commissary essentials are the focal points of Centric Group's business. The holding company operates three manufacturing and distribution divisions. Its Courtesy Products unit distributes coffee irons hair dryers and other guestroom supplies for the hospitality industry. The company's TRG Group manufactures luggage and other travel bags under such brands as Callaway Golf Soren and Victorinox Swiss Army. In addition Centric provides toiletries clothing electronics snacks and beverages to commissaries at correctional facilities through its Keefe Group. The company which is controlled by the Taylor family was formed in 1974 as part of Enterprise Rent-A-Car and spun off in 1999.

CENTRUS ENERGY CORP
ASE: LEU

Two Democracy Center, 6903 Rockledge Drive
Bethesda, MD 20817
Phone: 301 564-3200
Fax: -
Web: www.centrusenergy.com

CEO: -
CFO: Stephen S Greene
HR: Richard (Dick) Rowland
FYE: December 31
Type: Public

USEC beats radioactive swords into enriched uranium plowshares. The company processes used uranium — about half of which comes from old Russian atomic warheads — into enriched uranium which it then supplies for commercial nuclear power plants. USEC is the radioactive recycler of choice for the "Megatons-to-Megawatts" program a US-Russian agreement to convert uranium from warheads into nuclear fuel. In addition USEC develops low-enriched uranium for the nuclear materials industry and also processes uranium for the US Department of Energy (DOE). The company filed for Chapter 11 bankruptcy protection in 2014 and emerged later the same year.

	Annual Growth	12/11	12/12	12/13*	09/14*	12/14
Sales ($ mil.)	(58.0%)	1,671.8	1,918.1	1,307.5	390.5	123.6
Net income ($ mil.)	-	(540.7)	(1,200.6)	(158.9)	340.1	(42.3)
Market value ($ mil.)	55.5%	10.3	4.8	59.6	91.9	38.7
Employees	(35.4%)	1,885	1,770	1,432	-	507

*Fiscal year change

CENTURY 21 REAL ESTATE LLC

1 Campus Dr.
Parsippany NJ 07054
Phone: 877-221-2765
Fax: +44-118-923-1001
Web: www.adeptra.com

CEO: -
CFO: -
HR: -
FYE: December 31
Type: Subsidiary

Home is where the money is for Century 21. A subsidiary of Realogy Corporation Century 21 provides franchises for one of the world's largest residential real-estate sales networks with about 7600 independently owned offices in more than 70 countries and territories worldwide. While homes are its core focus the company also helps customers buy and sell commercial and vacation properties and provides relocation services for individuals corporations and members of the military. Century 21 Fine Homes & Estates offers services for luxury home buyers. Realogy Corporation licenses the Century 21 name among several other major real estate brands. In 2012 Realogy parent Domus filed to go public.

CENTURY ALUMINUM CO.
NMS: CENX

One South Wacker Drive, Suite 1000
Chicago, IL 60606
Phone: 312 696-3101
Fax: -
Web: www.centuryaluminum.com

CEO: Michael A. (Mike) Bless
CFO: Rick T. Dillon
HR: Dave Louis
FYE: December 31
Type: Public

When the aluminum century rolls around this company feels that it has already shown its mettle and will be more than ready. Century Aluminum makes primary molten and ingot aluminum at facilities in Kentucky and West Virginia as well as in Iceland; that last facility is operated by subsidiary Nordural. Century Aluminum also owns an aluminum production plant in South Carolina. In addition the company owns 40% of a joint venture facility in China. Two customers — commodities trader Glencore and wire and cable maker Southwire — account for the bulk of Century Aluminum's sales.

	Annual Growth	12/10	12/11	12/12	12/13	12/14
Sales ($ mil.)	13.4%	1,169.3	1,356.4	1,272.1	1,454.3	1,931.0
Net income ($ mil.)	17.0%	60.0	11.3	(35.6)	(40.3)	112.5
Market value ($ mil.)	12.0%	1,452.0	795.7	819.2	978.0	2,281.3
Employees	16.6%	1,300	1,300	1,300	1,800	2,400

CENTURY BANCORP, INC.
NMS: CNBK A

400 Mystic Avenue
Medford, MA 021255
Phone: 781 391-4000
Fax: -
Web: www.centurybank.com

CEO: Barry R. Sloane
CFO: William P. Hornby
HR: -
FYE: December 31
Type: Public

Century Bancorp is the holding company for Century Bank and Trust which serves Boston and surrounding parts of northeastern Massachusetts from more than 25 branches. Boasting some $3.6 billion in total assets the bank offers standard deposit products including checking savings and money market accounts; CDs; and IRAs. Nearly two-thirds of its loan portfolio is comprised of commercial and commercial real estate loans. while residential mortgages and home equity loans make up around 30%. The bank also writes construction and land development loans business loans and personal loans. It offers brokerage services through an agreement with third-party provider LPL Financial.

	Annual Growth	12/10	12/11	12/12	12/13	12/14
Assets ($ mil.)	10.4%	2,441.7	2,743.2	3,086.2	3,431.2	3,624.0
Net income ($ mil.)	12.7%	13.6	16.7	19.0	20.0	21.9
Market value ($ mil.)	10.6%	149.2	157.2	183.5	185.1	223.1
Employees	3.7%	380	405	418	428	440

CENTURY CASINOS INC.
NAS: CNTY

455 E. Pikes Peak Ave., Suite 210
Colorado Springs, CO 80903
Phone: 719 527-8300
Fax: -
Web: www.cnty.com

CEO: Erwin Haitzmann
CFO: Margaret Stapleton
HR: -
FYE: December 31
Type: Public

In the 19th century people rushed to Cripple Creek Colorado seeking their fortune in gold. Today thanks to Century Casinos they can do basically the same thing (but via midsized regional casinos rather than through prospecting). The company's Womacks Casino & Hotel in Cripple Creek offers some 440 slot machines and video devices as well as a handful of gaming tables. It also owns the Century Casino & Hotel in Central City Colorado and another Century Casino & Hotel in Edmonton Canada. In addition it operate four cruise ship casinos and is the casino concessionaire for cruise lines run by TUI Cruises a joint venture between German travel operator TUI and #2 cruise ship operator Royal Caribbean.

	Annual Growth	12/10	12/11	12/12	12/13	12/14
Sales ($ mil.)	18.6%	60.7	70.9	71.8	104.6	120.0
Net income ($ mil.)	4.8%	1.0	3.0	4.1	6.2	1.2
Market value ($ mil.)	19.9%	59.5	61.7	69.2	127.0	123.1
Employees	16.6%	876	1,000	1,000	1,600	1,620

CENTURY ENERGY LTD.   PINK SHEETS: CEYFF

4605 Post Oak Place Dr. Ste. 250 — CEO: –
Houston TX 77027 — CFO: –
Phone: 713-658-0161 — HR: –
Fax: 713-222-7158 — FYE: August 31
Web: www.centuryenergyltd.com — Type: Public

What can top Topper Resources? How about Century Energy. The junior natural resources company (formerly Topper Resources) buys interests in gas and oil exploration sites in Canada and the US. It owns the petroleum and natural gas rights to 1100 acres in the Bakken oil formation in southern Saskatchewan. In conjunction with TriAxon Resources Ltd. (its joint venture partner with extensive experience in the Bakken Shale play) the company has succeeded in producing oil from its first exploratory Bakken well and plans to develop several others.

CENTURY FOODS INTERNATIONAL LLC

400 Century Ct. — CEO: –
Sparta WI 54656 — CFO: –
Phone: 800-269-1901 — HR: Tim Sawyer
Fax: 608-269-1910 — FYE: October 31
Web: www.centuryfoods.com — Type: Subsidiary

Century Foods International knows where there's swill there's a whey. The company provides dairy and vegetable proteins and nutraceuticals used for muscle-building and weight-loss powders bars and beverages. Clients include food manufacturers and heath nutritional supplement and sports companies. The company serves customers in more than 45 countries. Century Foods provides services such as development manufacturing testing and packaging from its four plants in central Wisconsin. The company is a division of Hormel Foods.

CENTURYLINK, INC.   NYS: CTL

100 CenturyLink Drive — CEO: Glen F. Post
Monroe, LA 71203 — CFO: R. Stewart Ewing
Phone: 318 388-9000 — HR: Scott A. Trezise
Fax: 318 789-8656 — FYE: December 31
Web: www.centurylink.com — Type: Public

CenturyLink would like to be your communications hook-up for more than the next 100 years. Historically a regional wireline local and long-distance telephone provider it's connecting with the times by transforming into a broadband and network services provider for residential business and government clients. The company is the third-largest US wireline telecom company by total access lines and is the incumbent local carrier in 37 states though three-quarters of its lines are in just a dozen mostly in the West and Midwest. Additionally CenturyLink provides wireless service through Verizon and paid television service through its own Prism TV (in selected markets) with satellite provider DIRECTV.

	Annual Growth	12/10	12/11	12/12	12/13	12/14
Sales ($ mil.)	26.5%	7,041.5	15,351.0	18,376.0	18,095.0	18,031.0
Net income ($ mil.)	(5.0%)	947.7	573.0	777.0	(239.0)	772.0
Market value ($ mil.)	(3.8%)	26,248.4	21,148.8	22,240.4	18,107.3	22,501.9
Employees	22.0%	20,300	49,200	47,000	47,000	45,000

CENVEO INC   NYS: CVO

200 First Stamford Place — CEO: –
Stamford, CT 06902 — CFO: Scott J. Goodwin
Phone: 203 595-3000 — HR: Gina Genuario
Fax: – — FYE: December 27
Web: www.cenveo.com — Type: Public

Commercial printer Cenveo knows that when you send mail it's important to consider the envelope. The company provides direct mail and customized envelopes for advertising billing and remittance. It also sells labels and specialty packaging. In addition Cenveo has a commercial printing operations devoted to the production of scientific technical and medical (STM) journals. Included in its services are design content management fulfillment and distribution solutions. Cenveo encompasses about two dozen entities operating more than 50 facilities worldwide.

	Annual Growth	01/11*	12/11	12/12	12/13	12/14
Sales ($ mil.)	2.4%	1,814.7	1,909.2	1,797.6	1,777.8	1,949.0
Net income ($ mil.)	–	(186.4)	(8.6)	(79.9)	(68.8)	(83.9)
Market value ($ mil.)	(25.8%)	361.4	230.1	182.7	238.9	147.5
Employees	(2.4%)	8,700	8,400	7,600	8,700	8,100

*Fiscal year change

CEPHALON INC.

41 Moores Rd. — CEO: J Kevin Buchi
Malvern PA 19355 — CFO: Wilco Groenhuysen
Phone: 610-344-0200 — HR: –
Fax: 561-438-4001 — FYE: December 31
Web: www.officedepot.com — Type: Subsidiary

Cephalon has a handful of powerful specialty drugs. The company's research development manufacturing and marketing activities focus on therapies for central nervous system (CNS) disorders cancer pain and inflammatory disease. Its NUVIGIL and PROVIGIL drugs treat the sleep disorder narcolepsy. The company's other top sellers are cancer drug TREANDA cancer pain medications ACTIQ and FENTORA epilepsy treatment GABITRIL and muscle relaxant AMRIX. Its eight major products are primarily sold in the US and Europe. Cephalon was acquired by top generic drugmaker Teva Pharmaceutical Industries in 2011.

CEPHAS HOLDING CORP   NBB: CEHC

215 Dino Dr. — CEO: Peter Klamka
Ann Arbor, MI 48103 — CFO: –
Phone: 623 738-5792 — HR: –
Fax: – — FYE: December 31
 — Type: Public

Cephas Holding (formerly Legend Mobile) would like you to see its face when you pick up the phone. The company designs and markets accessories for wireless phones such as personalized faceplate covers. It also offers text-messaging services and mobile software. Several of Cephas's products feature branded themes representing such organizations as NASCAR. The company's 50%-owned Legend Credit unit markets promotional stored-value gift cards. Neither of the company's business lines has generated significant revenue however and its auditor has questioned the financial viability of the company. CEO Peter Klamka controls a majority of voting stock of Cephas which changed its name from Legend Mobile in 2009.

	Annual Growth	12/08	12/09	12/10	12/11	12/12
Sales ($ mil.)	(22.9%)	–	0.0	0.0	0.0	0.0
Net income ($ mil.)	–	(0.6)	(0.5)	(0.5)	(0.8)	(4.6)
Market value ($ mil.)	49.5%	0.3	0.3	0.5	0.1	1.5
Employees	0.0%	1	1	1	1	1

CEPHEID
NMS: CPHD

904 Caribbean Drive
Sunnyvale, CA 94089-1189
Phone: 408 541-4191
Fax: -
Web: www.cepheid.com

CEO: John L. Bishop
CFO: Ilan Daskal
HR: Mike Fitzgerald
FYE: December 31
Type: Public

Cepheid helps doctors and scientists see DNA faster. The molecular diagnostics firm develops and manufactures systems that automate the process of preparing and amplifying DNA in order to quickly detect diseases and harmful agents. Its two instrument platforms — GeneXpert and SmartCycler — can perform rapid molecular testing for a number of purposes including diagnosing infectious diseases and cancer as well as detecting biothreats such as anthrax. Cepheid also makes reagents (testing chemicals) and other disposable testing components for use with its systems.

	Annual Growth	12/10	12/11	12/12	12/13	12/14
Sales ($ mil.)	22.0%	212.5	277.6	331.2	401.3	470.1
Net income ($ mil.)	-	(5.9)	2.6	(20.0)	(18.0)	(50.1)
Market value ($ mil.)	24.2%	1,613.1	2,439.8	2,400.8	3,309.2	3,838.8
Employees	24.9%	576	717	945	1,200	1,400

CEQUEL COMMUNICATIONS HOLDINGS I LLC

12444 Powerscourt Dr. Ste. 450
St. Louis MO 63131
Phone: 314-315-9400
Fax: 949-486-3995
Web: www.clickerinc.com

CEO: Jerald L Kent
CFO: Mary Meduski
HR: Amanda Zessinger
FYE: December 31
Type: Private

Cequel Communications which operates through subsidiary Suddenlink provides cable TV high-speed Internet access and phone services to about 1.4 million business and residential customers. The company primarily serves rural markets in Arkansas Louisiana North Carolina Oklahoma Texas and West Virginia among other states. It also offers home security system installation and monitoring services. Suddenlink's services for business clients include high-capacity networking and Web hosting. The company's CoStreet division provides fiber optic networking and backhaul services to other carriers. A group of investors and company executives are acquiring Cequel for $6.6 billion including $4.1 billion in debt.

CERADYNE INC.
NASDAQ: CRDN

3169 Red Hill Ave.
Costa Mesa CA 92626
Phone: 714-549-0421
Fax: 714-549-5787
Web: www.ceradyne.com

CEO: Joel P Moskowitz
CFO: Jerrold J Pellizzon
HR: -
FYE: December 31
Type: Public

A bull in a china shop wouldn't stand a chance against Ceradyne's ceramics. The company's advanced technical ceramics products combine hardness with light weight and the ability to withstand high temperatures resist corrosion and insulate against electricity. Some uses of Ceradyne's materials include armor for military helicopters missile nose cones body armor and helmets for soldiers diesel engine components ceramic industrial products solar glass products and orthodontic brackets. The company sells to contractors and OEMs and the US government and government agencies represent more than 37% of sales. In late 2012 3M Company acquired Ceradyne.

CEREPLAST INC
NBB: CERP

2213 Killion Avenue
Seymour, IN 47274
Phone: 812 200-5400
Fax: -
Web: www.cereplast.com

CEO: -
CFO: -
HR: -
FYE: December 31
Type: Public

Cereplast aims to make plastics greener. The company develops and manufactures bio-based plastic resins that are designed to be eco-friendly alternatives to petroleum-based plastics often used in converting processes such as extrusion coating injection molding and thermoforming. Its family of products include: US- and Europe-certified compostable and biodegradable resins made from corn potato tapioca and wheat starches; hybrid resins that combine bio-based plant starches with traditional plastic; and a technology still in development to convert algae into bioplastics. Cereplast primarily markets to the automotive construction consumer goods electronics and medical packaging industries.

	Annual Growth	12/08	12/09	12/10	12/11	12/12
Sales ($ mil.)	(33.3%)	4.5	2.7	6.3	20.3	0.9
Net income ($ mil.)	-	(12.7)	(6.1)	(7.5)	(14.0)	(30.2)
Market value ($ mil.)	(33.8%)	7.3	6.1	262.7	60.9	1.4
Employees	(14.9%)	-	26	53	46	16

CERES INC
NAS: CERE

1535 Rancho Conejo Boulevard
Thousand Oaks, CA 91320
Phone: 805 376-6500
Fax: -
Web: www.ceres.net

CEO: Richard Hamilton
CFO: Paul Kuc
HR: -
FYE: August 31
Type: Public

Imbued with the spirit of Ceres the Roman goddess of agricultural fertility Ceres Inc. is an agricultural biotechnology firm that specializes in developing plant seeds used for bioenergy feedstock production. Its products which include seeds to grow switchgrass sweet and high-biomass sorghum and miscanthus have the potential as biomass feedstock to generate electric power and produce fuels like celluosic ethanol butanol and jet fuel. Ceres boasts that its grasses can be used with existing agricultural technologies and are suitable for cultivation on marginal crop land. (It claims its crops consume water and nitrogen more efficiently than corn and soybean crops.) Founded in 1996 Ceres went public in 2012.

	Annual Growth	08/11	08/12	08/13	08/14	08/15
Sales ($ mil.)	(19.9%)	6.6	5.4	5.2	2.4	2.7
Net income ($ mil.)	-	(36.3)	(29.4)	(32.5)	(29.3)	(28.2)
Market value ($ mil.)	(44.3%)	-	60.3	10.5	4.8	10.4
Employees	(18.1%)	98	96	85	81	44

CERES SOLUTIONS LLP

2112 INDIANAPOLIS RD
CRAWFORDSVILLE, IN 479333137
Phone: 765-362-6108
Fax: -
Web: www.cereslp.com

CEO: Jeff Troike
CFO: -
HR: -
FYE: July 31
Type: Private

Ceres Solutions is a growth business. The agricultural partnership provides farmers in about a dozen Indiana counties with crop farming support services and supplies. It sells stores and distributes such goods as fertilizers and fuel (gasoline propane home-heating). The company's agronomy services include field mapping crop and pest management soil sampling and yield analysis. Ceres Solutions also offers crop-financing programs sells crop insurance and provides marketing services. Its Green Notes newsletter offers the state's farmers market and technical advice and analysis.

	Annual Growth	07/10	07/11	07/12	07/13	07/14
Sales ($ mil.)	7.8%	-	329.1	399.2	402.5	412.2
Net income ($ mil.)	0.0%	-	-	22.2	25.8	22.2
Market value ($ mil.)	-	-	-	-	-	-
Employees	-	-	-	-	-	125

CERNER CORP.   NMS: CERN

2800 Rockcreek Parkway
North Kansas City, MO 64117
Phone: 816 201-1024
Fax: –
Web: www.cerner.com

CEO: Neal L. Patterson
CFO: Marc G. Naughton
HR: –
FYE: January 03
Type: Public

Cerner serves health care organizations with health care IT (HCIT). The company develops and sells software systems designed to help improve processes and eliminate errors and waste for organizations ranging from single-doctor practices to the pharmaceutical and medical device industries. Its software combines clinical financial and administrative information management applications including tools for managing electronic health records (EHRs). Complementary services include support and maintenance implementation and training remote hosting data analytics and transaction processing. The company's products are licensed by some 18000 facilities across the globe although the US is by far its largest market.

	Annual Growth	01/11*	12/11	12/12	12/13*	01/15
Sales ($ mil.)	16.5%	1,850.2	2,203.2	2,665.4	2,910.7	3,402.7
Net income ($ mil.)	22.0%	237.3	306.6	397.2	398.4	525.4
Market value ($ mil.)	(9.0%)	32,432.7	20,967.9	26,044.7	19,026.9	22,261.9
Employees	17.8%	8,200	9,900	11,900	14,200	15,800

*Fiscal year change

CERTAINTEED CORPORATION

750 E. Swedesford Rd.
Valley Forge PA 19482
Phone: 610-341-7000
Fax: 610-341-7777
Web: www.certainteed.com

CEO: John Crowe
CFO: Robert J Panaro
HR: –
FYE: December 31
Type: Subsidiary

There's no uncertainty about CertainTeed's business. A subsidiary of French industrial giant Compagnie de Saint-Gobain CertainTeed manufactures building products for both commercial and residential construction. CertainTeed's products include fiberglass insulation asphalt roofing shingles gypsum wallboard windows fiber cement siding foundations fencing pipes PVC trim and composite decking and railing. The company sells its products under the Bufftech CertainTeed Form-A-Drain Prestige and Wolverine brands. CertainTeed operates some 65 manufacturing plants in the US and Canada.

CERTCO INC.

5321 VERONA RD
FITCHBURG, WI 537116050
Phone: 608-278-2246
Fax: –
Web: www.certcoinc.com

CEO: Randy Simon
CFO: Steve Baus
HR: –
FYE: April 26
Type: Private

Certco has built a business serving about 200 independent grocers in Minnesota Wisconsin Iowa and Illinois. The food distribution cooperative offers customers an inventory of more than 57000 items including bakery goods frozen foods meat products produce and general merchandise. It distributes products under the Shurfine Shurfresh and Top Care labels. Additionally Certco offers its member-operators such services as advertising accounting client data services warehousing merchandising store planning and design and other business support services. The cooperative was founded in 1930 as Central Wisconsin Cooperative Food Stores.

	Annual Growth	04/10	04/11	04/12	04/13	04/14
Sales ($ mil.)	6.8%	–	525.6	569.7	607.3	640.5
Net income ($ mil.)	5.6%	–	–	5.0	5.5	5.6
Market value ($ mil.)	–	–	–	–	–	–
Employees	–	–	–	–	–	325

CERUS CORP.   NMS: CERS

2550 Stanwell Dr.
Concord, CA 94520
Phone: 925 288-6000
Fax: –
Web: www.cerus.com

CEO: William M. (Obi) Greenman
CFO: Kevin D. Green
HR: –
FYE: December 31
Type: Public

Cerus preaches the power of purity. The company develops blood purification systems under the name INTERCEPT that kill bacteria viruses and other pathogens in donated blood in an effort to improve the safety of blood transfusions. Its INTERCEPT Blood Systems for platelets and plasma are approved for sale in some European and Middle Eastern countries where they are marketed directly to customers through subsidiary Cerus Europe. It also sells to the Commonwealth of Independent States. The company is pursuing regulatory approval to sell its its INTERCEPT plasma and platelets products in the US and in other countries. Cerus also has a system for red blood cell purification in clinical development.

	Annual Growth	12/10	12/11	12/12	12/13	12/14
Sales ($ mil.)	12.0%	23.1	33.0	36.8	39.7	36.4
Net income ($ mil.)	–	(16.9)	(17.0)	(15.9)	(43.3)	(38.8)
Market value ($ mil.)	26.2%	197.8	225.1	254.1	518.6	501.7
Employees	16.2%	79	82	85	115	144

CESCA THERAPEUTICS INC   NAS: KOOL

2711 Citrus Road
Rancho Cordova, CA 95742
Phone: 916 858-5100
Fax: –
Web: www.cescatherapeutics.com

CEO: Robin C Stracey
CFO: Michael (Mike) Bruch
HR: –
FYE: June 30
Type: Public

ThermoGenesis makes blood run cold...really cold. The firm makes equipment that harvests freezes and thaws stem cells and other blood components taken from adult sources like umbilical cord blood placentas and bone marrow. Its core products include the AutoXpress System (AXP) a medical device that retrieves stem cells from cord blood; and the BioArchive System which freezes and stores stem cells harvested from such blood. Other products include Res-Q which processes stems cells from bone marrow. Founded in 1986 the company sells its products to cord blood banks stem cell researchers and clinical laboratories around the world.

	Annual Growth	06/11	06/12	06/13	06/14	06/15
Sales ($ mil.)	(9.0%)	23.4	19.0	18.0	16.0	16.0
Net income ($ mil.)	–	(2.6)	(5.0)	(3.1)	(8.6)	(14.9)
Market value ($ mil.)	(19.4%)	81.4	38.5	54.7	56.3	34.4
Employees	12.2%	70	68	66	95	111

CESSNA AIRCRAFT COMPANY

1 Cessna Blvd.
Wichita KS 67215
Phone: 316-517-6000
Fax: 610-341-7797
Web: www.saint-gobain-corporation.com

CEO: Scott Ernest
CFO: Eric Salander
HR: –
FYE: December 31
Type: Subsidiary

Blue-sky thinking is encouraged at Cessna Aircraft one of the most famous names in small planes. A subsidiary of Textron the company designs and manufactures light and midsize Citation business jets Caravan utility turboprops (primarily used in the US for overnight express package shipments) and single-engine piston and light lift aircraft. It has delivered more than 190000 aircraft over the course of more than eight decades in business making it the world's leading general aviation company by unit sales. In addition to aircraft sales Cessna's other principal line of business is aftermarket services including parts maintenance inspection and repair.

CEVA INC

NMS: CEVA

1174 Castro Street, Suite 210
Mountain View, CA 94040
Phone: 650 417-7900
Fax: –
Web: www.ceva-dsp.com

CEO: Gideon Wertheizer
CFO: Yaniv Arieli
HR: Sandy Grman
FYE: December 31
Type: Public

CEVA has a fever for semiconductor design. CEVA specializes in technology — both integrated circuit and software designs — used in cell phones handheld computers MP3 players and other wireless devices as well as smart TVs and set-top boxes. It licenses its semiconductor intellectual property (SIP) designs to such industry heavyweights as LG Samsung and Sony. CEVA's SIP is shipped in more than 1 billion devices a year including 40% of handsets shipped worldwide. As such CEVA generates most of its revenues outside the US.

	Annual Growth	12/10	12/11	12/12	12/13	12/14
Sales ($ mil.)	3.1%	44.9	60.2	53.7	48.9	50.8
Net income ($ mil.)	–	11.4	18.6	13.7	6.7	(0.8)
Market value ($ mil.)	(3.0%)	415.2	612.8	319.0	308.2	367.4
Employees	7.5%	181	193	193	207	242

CF INDUSTRIES HOLDINGS INC

NYS: CF

4 Parkway North, Suite 400
Deerfield, IL 60015
Phone: 847 405-2400
Fax: –
Web: www.cfindustries.com

CEO: W. Anthony (Tony) Will
CFO: Dennis P. Kelleher
HR: Wendy J Spertus
FYE: December 31
Type: Public

The folks at CF Industries make a lot of fertilizer and they like to spread it around. The international agricultural firm manufactures and markets nitrogen and nitrogen fertilizers. It is North America's top producer of nitrogen-based fertilizers and #2 in the world. The company's ownership of fertilizer producer Terra Industries helps it keep its dominant position. CF Industries' nitrogen products include ammonia granular urea and UAN (urea ammonium nitrate) solutions. In a mjor move in 2014 it exited the phospate business. Its phosphate-based fertilizers included diammonium phosphate (or DAP) and monoammonium phosphate (MAP). The company supplies approximately 20% of the nitrogen used by US farmers.

	Annual Growth	12/10	12/11	12/12	12/13	12/14
Sales ($ mil.)	4.6%	3,965.0	6,097.9	6,104.0	5,474.7	4,743.2
Net income ($ mil.)	41.3%	349.2	1,539.2	1,848.7	1,464.6	1,390.3
Market value ($ mil.)	19.2%	32,662.1	35,037.8	49,098.3	56,319.5	65,865.6
Employees	(2.1%)	2,500	2,500	2,600	2,900	2,300

CFC INTERNATIONAL INC.

500 State St.
Chicago Heights IL 60411
Phone: 708-891-3456
Fax: 708-758-5989
Web: www.cfcintl.com

CEO: –
CFO: Dennis W Lakomy
HR: Susan Contri
FYE: December 31
Type: Subsidiary

At CFC International beauty by design is only skin deep. The company makes transferable chemical coatings to beautify protect and add other kinds of functionality to consumer products. It makes complex functional coatings such as simulated metal used on cosmetic containers and simulated wood grain for ready-to-assemble furniture. CFC also makes holographic authentication seals (popular on tickets and software) heat transfer labels for pharmaceuticals and magnetic strips for security and credit card uses. The company is a part multi-industry conglomerate Illinois Tool Works (ITW).

CGB ENTERPRISES INC.

1127 HWY 190 E SERVICE RD
COVINGTON, LA 704334929
Phone: 985-867-3500
Fax: –
Web: www.cgb.com

CEO: Kevin D. Adams
CFO: Richard S Pemberton
HR: Mark Berry
FYE: May 31
Type: Private

The farmer in the delta relies on CGB Enterprises. Located in Louisiana near the shores of Lake Pontchartrain and the mouth of the Mississippi River the agricultural company provides US farmers with a range of services including grain handling storage and merchandising. It offers inland grain transportation by barge rail and truck and also markets and sells seeds agricultural chemicals and insurance. CGB's Consolidated Terminals and Logistics Co. (CTLC) subsidiary provides transportation logistics and bulk commodity services for both agricultural and non-agricultural customers. The company operates more than 95 locations across the US. Japanese trading conglomerates ITOCHU and ZEN-NOH own CGB.

	Annual Growth	05/10	05/11	05/12	05/13	05/14
Sales ($ mil.)	11.6%	–	5,202.6	6,108.1	6,212.9	7,227.8
Net income ($ mil.)	0.2%	–	–	53.1	30.1	53.3
Market value ($ mil.)	–	–	–	–	–	–
Employees	–	–	–	–	–	1,250

CH2M HILL COMPANIES LTD.

9191 S JAMAICA ST
ENGLEWOOD, CO 801125946
Phone: 303-771-0900
Fax: –
Web: www.ch2m.com

CEO: Jacqueline C. Hinman
CFO: Gary L. McArthur
HR: John A. Madia
FYE: December 31
Type: Private

CH2M HILL's name is a bit tricky but the engineering and construction firm is all up front. The firm (named for its founders Cornell Howland Hayes and Merryfield) operates five main market-oriented divisions: Environment and Nuclear Water Transportation Energy and Industrial and Urban Environments. CH2M Hill's top client is the US Government which contributes more than one-fifth of the company's annual revenue. Public sector clients include the US Department of Energy and the Department of Defense. CH2M HILL also works for state and local governments building water and wastewater systems airports highways and other transportation projects. Founded in 1946 the firm is owned by its employees.

	Annual Growth	12/10	12/11	12/12	12/13	12/14
Sales ($ mil.)	(0.5%)	–	5,555.2	6,224.2	5,931.8	5,468.4
Net income ($ mil.)	–	–	–	98.3	131.2	(318.6)
Market value ($ mil.)	–	–	–	–	–	–
Employees	–	–	–	–	–	26,000

CHADBOURNE & PARKE LLP

30 Rockefeller Plaza
New York NY 10112
Phone: 212-408-5100
Fax: 212-541-5369
Web: www.chadbourne.com

CEO: –
CFO: –
HR: –
FYE: December 31
Type: Private - Partnershi

International law firm Chadbourne & Parke doesn't shy away from controversy. Representing Brown & Williamson Tobacco put the firm on the frontlines in the war between state governments and big tobacco. Its clients also have included liquor producers and a nuclear bomb manufacturer. Chadbourne & Parke is a leader in mergers and acquisitions and project finance; about 420 attorneys also work in areas such as bankruptcy environmental litigation product liability and tax. The firm has about a dozen offices with international locations in Brazil China Kazakhstan Mexico Poland Russia the UK the Ukraine and the United Arab Emirates. The late Thomas Chadbourne founded the firm in 1902.

CHAMPION INDUSTRIES, INC. (WV)   NBB: CHMP

2450 First Avenue, P.O. Box 2968
Huntington, WV 25728
Phone: 304 528-2700
Fax: –

CEO: Marshall T. Reynolds
CFO: Justin T. Evans
HR: –
FYE: October 31
Type: Public

This Champion hopes to win business in the printing and office supply fields. Through more than a dozen operating units Champion Industries prints books brochures business cards business forms posters and tags including complex four- to six-color products. Printing accounts for the majority of sales. The company also sells a wide range of office products and office furniture that it orders from manufacturers and provides office design services. Champion Industries operates primarily in regional markets east of the Mississippi and publishes The Herald-Dispatch the daily newspaper of its hometown in Huntington West Virginia.

	Annual Growth	10/11	10/12	10/13	10/14	10/15
Sales ($ mil.)	(16.9%)	128.5	104.4	72.3	63.5	61.3
Net income ($ mil.)	–	(4.0)	(22.9)	5.7	(1.1)	(1.2)
Market value ($ mil.)	(28.3%)	12.5	2.3	5.1	3.4	3.3
Employees	(16.8%)	660	550	330	330	316

CHAMPION LABORATORIES INC.

200 S. Fourth St.
Albion IL 62806
Phone: 618-445-6011
Fax: 618-445-5489
Web: www.champlabs.com

CEO: –
CFO: Michael Gibbons
HR: –
FYE: December 31
Type: Subsidiary

Champion Laboratories wants to keep your machine cool and clean. It manufactures oil fuel and air filters for motor vehicle OEMs and aftermarket. Other products include breather filters cabin air filters and transmission filters. It also makes engine management systems driveline components and lighting systems for the marine mining construction industrial and agricultural markets. Its primary brand names include Champ Luber-Finer and Kleener. Champion Laboratories has 10 manufacturing and distribution locations in North and South America Europe and Asia. The company is owned by UCI International (formerly United Components) which is owned by New Zealand investment firm Rank Group Limited.

CHAMPIONS ONCOLOGY, INC.   NAS: CSBR

One University Plaza, Suite 307
Hackensack, NJ 07601
Phone: 201 808-8400
Fax: –
Web: www.championsoncology.com

CEO: Joel Ackerman
CFO: –
HR: –
FYE: April 30
Type: Public

Champions Oncology (formerly Champions Biotechnology) is hoping to win big in the field of cancer research. Its Champions Tumorgraft platform allows the company to implant human tumors of various cancer types into mice allowing scientists to study the effects of investigational drugs on human cancers. The company uses the platform in its own research and also provides tumor-specific research to doctors as well as the Tumorgraft platform to other drug developers. The company has licensed the rights to explore Irinophore a nanoparticle in preclinical development.

	Annual Growth	04/11	04/12	04/13	04/14	04/15
Sales ($ mil.)	6.5%	6.9	7.1	8.3	11.6	8.9
Net income ($ mil.)	–	(3.8)	(8.7)	(6.3)	(7.4)	(13.1)
Market value ($ mil.)	(11.7%)	8.7	5.8	4.4	7.9	5.3
Employees	40.9%	18	36	38	60	71

CHANNELADVISOR CORP   NYS: ECOM

2701 Aerial Center Parkway
Morrisville, NC 27560
Phone: 919 228-4700
Fax: –
Web: www.channeladvisor.com

CEO: David J. Spitz
CFO: Mark E. Cook
HR: Judith (Judi) Barnett
FYE: December 31
Type: Public

ChannelAdvisor isn't in the business of doling out spiritual advice; it's in the business of helping online retailers maximize their profits. The company offers software and support services for large midsized and small e-commerce retailers looking for greater product visibility and brand management in marketplaces (such as eBay Amazon.com and Buy.com) comparison shopping sites (Shopping.com Shopzilla and PriceGrabber.com) search engines (Google and Bing) and their own Web stores. ChannelAdvisor counts some 1900 clients including Dell Staples Bed Bath & Beyond and Urban Outfitters. Founded in 2001 the company went public in mid-2013.

	Annual Growth	12/10	12/11	12/12	12/13	12/14
Sales ($ mil.)	23.3%	36.7	43.6	53.6	68.0	84.9
Net income ($ mil.)	–	(4.7)	(3.9)	(4.9)	(20.6)	(34.5)
Market value ($ mil.)	(48.3%)	–	–	–	1,039.2	537.7
Employees	25.7%	–	–	432	594	683

CHAPARRAL ENERGY L.L.C.

701 Cedar Lake Blvd.
Oklahoma City OK 73114
Phone: 405-478-8770
Fax: 405-478-1947
Web: www.chaparralenergy.com

CEO: Mark Fischer
CFO: Joseph O Evans
HR: –
FYE: December 31
Type: Private

Chaparral Energy searches the scrublands of America's Mid-Continent and Permian Basin looking for oil and natural gas. The exploration and production company also drills in North Texas the Gulf Coast the Ark-La-Tex region and the Rocky Mountains. In 2010 the company reported estimated proved reserves of some 149.3 million barrels of oil equivalent. About 30% of the its reserves are in enhanced oil recovery project areas primarily in Oklahoma and Texas where the company uses carbon dioxide (CO_2) to flood wells to release trapped oil in mature and well-worked fields. Securing CO_2 supply from third party plants is key to its enhanced oil recovery an area of expertise the company has pursued since 2000.

CHAPMAN UNIVERSITY

1 UNIVERSITY DR
ORANGE, CA 928661005
Phone: 714-744-7099
Fax: –
Web: www.chapman.edu

CEO: –
CFO: –
HR: –
FYE: May 31
Type: Private

Chapman University enrolls 7000 students at campuses throughout California as well as in Washington State. From its main campus in Orange California the university offers traditional undergraduate graduate and professional programs at seven colleges and schools. It also confers bachelor and master's degrees and teaching credentials to non-traditional students at its two-dozen satellite campuses. The university offers some 50 undergraduate majors and 40 graduate programs. It has 650 faculty members and a student-to-teacher ratio of 15:1. Chapman University includes Brandman University a distance learning program for some 10000 working adults that operates two dozen locations and offers online courses.

	Annual Growth	05/10	05/11	05/12	05/13	05/14
Sales ($ mil.)	7.8%	–	303.8	369.5	356.9	380.4
Net income ($ mil.)	2.1%	–	–	75.1	78.7	78.4
Market value ($ mil.)	–	–	–	–	–	–
Employees	–	–	–	–	–	3,300

CHARGERS FOOTBALL COMPANY LLC

4020 Murphy Canyon Rd.
San Diego CA 92123
Phone: 858-874-4500
Fax: 858-292-2760
Web: www.chargers.com

CEO: –
CFO: Jeanne Bonk
HR: –
FYE: December 31
Type: Private

This company energizes football fans in Southern California. Chargers Football owns and operates the San Diego Chargers professional football team a charter member of the American Football League (AFL) and current member of the National Football League (NFL). Barron Hilton (the son of hotelier Conrad Hilton) founded the team in 1959 as the Los Angeles Chargers; it moved to San Diego in 1961 and won the AFL championship two years later. The AFL and NFL merged in 1970. Despite its lengthy history the franchise has made just one trip to the Super Bowl (a loss to the San Francisco 49ers following the 1994 season). Alex Spanos who owns construction firm A. G. Spanos Companies has owned the Bolts since 1984.

CHARLES INDUSTRIES LTD.

5600 Apollo Dr.
Rolling Meadows IL 60008-4049
Phone: 847-806-6300
Fax: 847-806-6231
Web: www.charlesindustries.com

CEO: –
CFO: –
HR: –
FYE: December 31
Type: Private

Charles Industries goes for cash "and" charge. Charles Industries manufactures telecommunications products industrial chargers and charger components such as transformers and capacitors. It also has a joint venture with Telmax Communications to develop high-speed digital subscriber line access systems and maintains alliances with Corning Cable Systems among other manufacturers. Although Charles Industries has sold its dockside marina products division the company still makes marine battery chargers power cables and related products. Founder president and CEO Joseph Charles owns the company.

CHARLES & COLVARD LTD

170 Southport Drive
Morrisville, NC 27560
Phone: 919 468-0399
Fax: –
Web: www.charlesandcolvard.com

NMS: CTHR
CEO: Suzanne T. Miglucci
CFO: Kyle S Macemore
HR: Amy Wagner
FYE: December 31
Type: Public

Charles & Colvard hopes that it isn't just some shooting star. The company makes gemstones made from moissanite a diamond substitute created in laboratories. Composed of silicon and carbon moissanite (aka silicon carbide or SiC) is typically found in meteorites. Charles & Colvard makes its gemstones from SiC crystals purchased primarily from Cree Inc. and Swedish company Norstel. Charles & Colvard markets its gemstones through two distributors (Stuller and Rio Grande) and jewelry manufacturers such as K&G Creations Reeves Park and Samuel Aaron International.

	Annual Growth	12/10	12/11	12/12	12/13	12/14
Sales ($ mil.)	19.2%	12.7	16.0	22.5	28.5	25.6
Net income ($ mil.)	–	1.6	1.6	4.4	(1.3)	(13.1)
Market value ($ mil.)	(11.7%)	61.6	52.4	79.9	102.9	37.5
Employees	28.5%	26	46	55	71	71

CHARLES PANKOW BUILDERS LTD.

199 S.Los Robles Ave. Ste. 300
Pasadena CA 91101
Phone: 626-304-1190
Fax: 626-696-1782
Web: www.pankow.com

CEO: –
CFO: Kim Petersen
HR: –
FYE: December 31
Type: Private

Charles Pankow Builders has some pretty concrete ideas on how to build high-rises. The design/build general contractor specializes in quake-resistant concrete frames for structures including department stores hotels condominiums medical facilities and office buildings. The firm is primarily active in California and Hawaii. Affiliate Pankow Special Projects focuses on small-scale projects including renovations interior build-outs and seismic upgrades. Unit Mid-State Precast provides structural and architectural precast concrete components for Pankow-managed projects. Employee-owned Charles Pankow Builders was founded in 1963 by the late Charles Pankow who helped pioneer the design/build delivery system.

CHARLES C PARKS CO INC

500 N BELVEDERE DR
GALLATIN, TN 370665408
Phone: 615-452-2406
Fax: –
Web: www.charlescparks.com

CEO: –
CFO: Tom Cripps
HR: –
FYE: April 30
Type: Private

The Charles C. Parks Company is a grocery distributor that primarily supplies convenience stores in more than half a dozen Southern states. It distributes a variety of food items and dry goods as well as beverages cigarettes candy and general merchandise. The company also offers support programs for in-store delis and other quick-service food operations. Carl C. Parks Jr. started the family-run business in 1934.

CHARLES REGIONAL MEDICAL CENTER FOUNDATION INC.

5 GARRETT AVE
LA PLATA, MD 206465960
Phone: 301-609-4000
Fax: –
Web: www.charlesregional.org

CEO: –
CFO: –
HR: –
FYE: June 30
Type: Private

Civista Health sees a civic vista wherever it looks. The organization brings medical care to the residents of Charles County and surrounding areas in southern Maryland. The regional not-for-profit hospital system includes acute care facility Civista Medical Center Civista Women's Health Center Civista Surgery Center (an outpatient facility) and Civista OB/GYN Associates. Civista Health's services include emergency care rehabilitation surgery and cancer treatment offered by more than 230 physicians. The system also offers a chronic pain program radiology and laboratory services. Nearly half the system's revenue comes from Medicare payments.

	Annual Growth	04/09	04/10	04/11	04/12	04/13
Sales ($ mil.)	(2.0%)	–	292.3	264.3	268.3	275.5
Net income ($ mil.)	17.1%	–	–	0.3	(0.7)	0.4
Market value ($ mil.)	–	–	–	–	–	–
Employees	–	–	–	–	–	145

	Annual Growth	06/04	06/05	06/06	06/09	06/10
Sales ($ mil.)	(24.6%)	–	–	318.4	0.1	102.7
Net income ($ mil.)	626.4%	–	–	0.0	0.0	1.8
Market value ($ mil.)	–	–	–	–	–	–
Employees	–	–	–	–	–	668

CHARLES RIVER LABORATORIES INTERNATIONAL INC.   NYS: CRL

251 Ballardvale Street
Wilmington, MA 01887
Phone: 781 222-6000
Fax: –
Web: www.criver.com

CEO: James C. Foster
CFO: David R. Smith
HR: David P. Johst
FYE: December 26
Type: Public

Chickens and rats have an important part to play in Charles River Laboratories International's specialty portfolio of medical products. The company produces lab rats and mice bred specifically for use in medical testing through its Research Models and Services (RMS) segment. It also provides contract drug discovery and development services including toxicology and pathology through its RMS Discovery and Safety Assessment and Manufacturing Support segments. To a smaller degree the company also supplies pathogen-free fertilized chicken eggs used in vaccine production. Charles River Laboratories which traces its roots back to 1947 has operations in 17 countries around the world.

	Annual Growth	12/11	12/12	12/13	12/14	12/15
Sales ($ mil.)	4.5%	1,142.6	1,129.5	1,165.5	1,297.7	1,363.3
Net income ($ mil.)	8.0%	109.6	97.3	102.8	126.7	149.3
Market value ($ mil.)	30.8%	1,276.3	1,722.2	2,490.4	3,002.2	3,739.6
Employees	4.9%	7,100	7,200	7,700	7,900	8,600

CHARLES RIVER SYSTEMS INC.

7 New England Executive Park
Burlington MA 01803-5010
Phone: 781-238-0099
Fax: 781-238-0088
Web: www.crd.com

CEO: –
CFO: David Weber
HR: –
FYE: December 31
Type: Private

The streams of global finance come flowing together in Charles River Systems' software and services. The company (which does business as Charles River Development) provides investment software that performs front- and middle-office functions for clients in the financial services industry. Among its customers are banks hedge funds insurance firms mutual funds and wealth managers. Its offerings include software applications for portfolio management investment management decision support compliance monitoring trading and post-trade order management and performance measurement and risk. Charles River also offers professional services such as remote and hosted application management and consulting.

CHARLESTON AREA MEDICAL CENTER INC.

501 MORRIS ST
CHARLESTON, WV 253011326
Phone: 304-348-5432
Fax: –
Web: www.camc.org

CEO: David L Ramsey
CFO: –
HR: –
FYE: December 31
Type: Private

CAMC Health System is a catalyst for care in Charleston. The health network includes flagship facility Charleston Area Medical Center (CAMC) which is the largest hospital in West Virginia and consists of three campuses with some 840 beds total. The system also includes the CAMC Health Education and Research Institute which coordinates education programs for medical students from West Virginia University. In addition the health system operates smaller rural hospital CAMC Teays Valley and several urgent care and family practice clinics. CAMC Health System operates an online medical information system and physician services company Integrated Health Care Providers.

	Annual Growth	12/04	12/05	12/06	12/07	12/13
Sales ($ mil.)	–	–	(406.3)	703.8	703.8	861.3
Net income ($ mil.)	4.9%	–	–	38.7	9.0	54.0
Market value ($ mil.)	–	–	–	–	–	–
Employees	–	–	–	–	–	4,000

CHARLESTON HOSPITAL INC.

333 LAIDLEY ST
CHARLESTON, WV 253011614
Phone: 304-347-6500
Fax: –
Web: www.thomaswv.stfrancishospital.com

CEO: –
CFO: Brad Owens
HR: –
FYE: September 30
Type: Private

If you get a little overzealous doing the Charleston while you're in Charleston West Virginia head to Charleston Hospital! Doing business as Saint Francis Hospital the 155-bed facility provides a range of services that include the patching up of twisted ankles inpatient surgery nuclear medicine and skilled nursing. Founded in 1913 Saint Francis Hospital is one-half of Thomas Health System (Thomas Memorial Hospital in South Charleston comprises the other half). Since acquiring Saint Francis Hospital a couple of years ago Thomas Health System has invested about $8 million in St. Francis to provide it with updated equipment and a new pain management center.

	Annual Growth	09/08	09/09	09/12	09/13	09/14
Sales ($ mil.)	0.8%	–	102.0	95.1	105.0	106.3
Net income ($ mil.)	(8.7%)	–	–	2.1	1.7	1.8
Market value ($ mil.)	–	–	–	–	–	–
Employees	–	–	–	–	–	570

CHARMING SHOPPES INC.   NASDAQ: CHRS

3750 State Road
Bensalem PA 19020
Phone: 215-245-9100
Fax: 215-633-4640
Web: www.charmingshoppes.com

CEO: Anthony M Romano
CFO: Eric M Specter
HR: Maryann Heatherby
FYE: January 31
Type: Public

Charming Shoppes is big in women's plus-size clothing. The apparel retailer runs more than 1800 stores (and related websites) in 48 US states through three fashion chains that cater to the amply proportioned: about 800 Lane Bryant and Lane Bryant Outlet stores in about 45 states; some 600 Fashion Bug stores that sell moderately priced apparel and accessories in girls juniors misses and plus sizes; and about 425 Catherines Plus Sizes stores. The stores are primarily located in suburban areas and small towns across the US and court low- to middle-income women and teens who follow fashion styles rather than set them. The company was acquired by Ascena Retail Group in June 2012.

CHART INDUSTRIES INC   NMS: GTLS

One Infinity Corporate Centre Drive, Suite 300
Garfield Heights, OH 44125
Phone: 440 753-1490
Fax: –
Web: www.chartindustries.com

CEO: Samuel F. Thomas
CFO: Michael F. Biehl
HR: –
FYE: December 31
Type: Public

Chart Industries is charting its own miracle on ice campaign. The company designs equipment for low-temperature hydrocarbon and industrial gas production and storage including cryogenic systems that can operate near absolute zero. Chart vessels can process liquefy store and transport gases which are marketed to petrochemical and natural gas processors industrial gas producers satellite testing companies and restaurants and convenience stores. The company also offers engineered bulk gas installations and makes specialty liquid nitrogen end-use equipment used in the hydrocarbon processing and industrial gas industries.

	Annual Growth	12/10	12/11	12/12	12/13	12/14
Sales ($ mil.)	21.1%	555.5	794.6	1,014.2	1,177.4	1,193.0
Net income ($ mil.)	42.0%	20.2	44.1	71.3	83.2	81.9
Market value ($ mil.)	0.3%	1,029.7	1,648.2	2,032.8	2,915.3	1,042.5
Employees	15.7%	3,013	3,831	4,842	5,086	5,407

CHARTER COMMUNICATIONS INC
NMS: CHTR

400 Atlantic Street
Stamford, CT 06901
Phone: 203 905-7801
Fax: –
Web: www.charter.com

CEO: Thomas M. (Tom) Rutledge
CFO: Christopher L. (Chris) Winfrey
HR: –
FYE: December 31
Type: Public

The cable system operator has almost 6 million mostly-residential subscribers in more than two dozen states making it one of the top national cable companies behind Comcast Time Warner Cable and Cox Communications. In addition to 4.2 million video customers (92% opting for digital service) Charter also boasts 4.4 million broadband Internet subscribers and 2.3 million digital phone users. Its Business provides Internet access to about 500000 commercial clients. In addition Charter sells local advertising on such cable networks as MTV CNN and ESPN. In 2015 Charter agreed to buy Bright House Networks for $10.4 billion. But wait there's more: in May 2015 Charter agreed to buy Time Warner Cable for $55 billion creating the second biggest cable company.

	Annual Growth	12/11	12/12	12/13	12/14	12/15
Sales ($ mil.)	7.9%	7,204.0	7,504.0	8,155.0	9,108.0	9,754.0
Net income ($ mil.)	–	(369.0)	(304.0)	(169.0)	(183.0)	(271.0)
Market value ($ mil.)	33.9%	6,402.3	8,572.3	15,377.1	18,734.6	20,587.5
Employees	10.4%	16,000	17,800	21,600	23,200	23,800

CHARTER MANUFACTURING COMPANY INC.

1212 W GLEN OAKS LN
MEQUON, WI 530923357
Phone: 262-243-4700
Fax: –
Web: www.chartermfg.com

CEO: –
CFO: Todd Endres
HR: Samantha Inks
FYE: December 31
Type: Private

Charter Manufacturing's magna carta calls for it to make steel products. The family-owned company manufactures such steel products as special bar quality (SBQ) bar rod wire and stainless steel rod. The company also supplies precision cold-rolled custom profiles and engineered components including driveline engine and transmission parts for the automotive industry. It operates primarily in the US but also in Europe and Asia through subsidiaries Charter Steel (general steel products) Charter Wire (precision cold-rolled custom profiles flat wire and standard shapes) Charter Dura-Bar (cast iron bar and bronze alloys) and Charter Automotive (engineered components for automotive applications).

	Annual Growth	12/06	12/07	12/08	12/09	12/10
Sales ($ mil.)	74.4%	–	–	–	517.8	903.3
Net income ($ mil.)	3354.5%	–	–	–	2.2	74.6
Market value ($ mil.)	–	–	–	–	–	–
Employees	–	–	–	–	–	2,000

CHARTIS INC.

175 Water St.
New York NY 10038
Phone: 212-770-7000
Fax: 512-441-9222
Web: www.texasfolklife.org

CEO: Peter Douglas Hancock
CFO: –
HR: Tatiana Frana
FYE: December 31
Type: Private

Chartis has mapped out a new course for its slimmed down parent AIG. The company operating as AIG Property Casualty handles all of AIG's property/casualty operations and serves more than 70 million clients in the US and abroad. The company's commercial offerings include general liability workers' compensation specialty insurance and risk management services for businesses. Consumer lines account for 40% of the company's business including home auto travel and health and accident insurance. AIG Property Casualty is comprised of the operations of many subsidiary companies and affiliates that offer industry-specific insurance coverage to international aerospace marine and energy companies.

CHASE CORP.
ASE: CCF

26 Summer Street
Bridgewater, MA 02324
Phone: 508 819-4200
Fax: –
Web: www.chasecorp.com

CEO: Adam P Chase
CFO: Kenneth J Feroldi
HR: –
FYE: August 31
Type: Public

Duct tape is great but when the job calls for higher-tech stuff Chase has it. The company has made and sold Chase & Sons branded protective tape and coatings including conducting and insulating products for cable and wire makers for more than 50 years. Chase processes almost any flexible material produced on a roll — films to fabrics. It makes laminates sealants and coatings for pipeline construction electronics as well as printing markets. Chase pipe coating tapes Tapecoat and Royston are sold to oil companies and gas utilities. The company also offers expansion/control joint systems and asphalt additives for roads bridges and stadiums. US customers represent about 84% of revenues.

	Annual Growth	08/11	08/12	08/13	08/14	08/15
Sales ($ mil.)	17.9%	123.0	148.9	216.1	224.0	238.0
Net income ($ mil.)	24.6%	10.9	9.3	17.2	26.6	26.3
Market value ($ mil.)	32.6%	117.4	149.6	273.2	326.3	363.1
Employees	20.0%	324	719	666	667	671

CHASE GENERAL CORPORATION
PINK SHEETS: CSGN

1307 S. 59th St.
St. Joseph MO 64507
Phone: 816-279-1625
Fax: 816-279-1997
Web: www.cherrymash.com

CEO: –
CFO: –
HR: –
FYE: June 30
Type: Public

They not only chase but catch the sweet life at Chase General Corporation. Its subsidiary Dye Candy Company makes and distributes candy and confections. Combining chocolate and chopped peanuts and using crushed maraschino cherries for a smooth fondant center the company's Dye Candy division produces its flagship "Cherry Mash" candy bars. Its Seasonal Candy division makes Chase brand coconut haystacks fudge jelly candies peanut brittle and peanut clusters. Chase General's products are distributed mainly in the Midwest. Associated Wholesale Grocers accounted for 26% of the company's 2008 sales; Wal-Mart accounted for 15%.

CHATHAM LODGING TRUST
NYS: CLDT

222 Lakeview Avenue, Suite 200
West Palm Beach, FL 33401
Phone: 561 802-4477
Fax: –
Web: www.chathamlodgingtrust.com

CEO: Jeffrey H. Fisher
CFO: Jeremy Wegner
HR: –
FYE: December 31
Type: Public

In hotels it trusts. A self-advised real estate investment trust (REIT) Chatham Lodging was formed in 2009 to acquire upscale extended-stay hotels including Residence Inn by Marriott Homewood Suites by Hilton and Hyatt House locations To a lesser extent the firm will also buy select-service and full-service hotels such as Courtyard by Marriott and Hampton Inn. Chatham Lodging owns 25 hotels outright and has an interest in about 50 others totaling 10686 rooms/suites in some 15 US states and the District of Columbia. When assembling its portfolio the REIT seeks properties being sold at a discount particularly in large US metropolitan markets including Dallas Denver and Pittsburgh.

	Annual Growth	12/10	12/11	12/12	12/13	12/14
Sales ($ mil.)	66.8%	25.5	73.1	100.5	126.2	197.2
Net income ($ mil.)	–	(1.2)	(9.1)	(1.5)	3.0	66.9
Market value ($ mil.)	13.8%	589.5	368.4	525.6	698.9	990.0
Employees	73.2%	5	6	25	27	45

CHATHAM SEARCH INTERNATIONAL INC.

3 Lion Gardiner
Cromwell CT 06416
Phone: 860-635-5538
Fax: 216-929-0042
Web: www.diseco.com

CEO: –
CFO: –
HR: –
FYE: December 31
Type: Private

In need of an executive? Chatham Search International can help. The company is a generalist executive search firm recruiting senior-level and mid-level management personnel for companies in a variety of industries and across the full spectrum of functional disciplines. The firm operates a division dedicated to recruiting executives from diverse social and cultural backgrounds. Additionally Chatham provides strategic human resources coaching and consulting.

CHATHAM UNIVERSITY

WOODLAND RD
PITTSBURGH, PA 15232
Phone: 412-365-1100
Fax: –
Web: www.chatham.edu

CEO: –
CFO: –
HR: –
FYE: June 30
Type: Private

Men need not apply to Chatham University at least not for its undergraduate program. The university consists of Chatham College for Women which offers bachelor's degrees to women only; Chatham College for Graduate Studies which offers graduate degrees and teaching certificates to both men and women; and Chatham College for Continuing and Professional Studies its co-educational online school. Undergraduate students can choose from more than 30 majors in such areas as the sciences humanities arts environmental studies and pre-professional studies. Chatham has an enrollment of more than 2000 students. The private liberal arts school was founded in 1869 as Pennsylvania Female College.

	Annual Growth	06/07	06/08	06/09	06/11	06/13
Sales ($ mil.)	10.8%	–	–	41.0	26.9	59.6	68.5
Net income ($ mil.)	–	–	–	(16.9)	4.8	18.9
Market value ($ mil.)	–	–	–	–	–	–
Employees	–	–	–	–	–	300

CHATTANOOGA BAKERY INC.

900 Manufacturers Rd.
Chattanooga TN 37405
Phone: 423-267-3351
Fax: 423-266-2169
Web: www.moonpie.com

CEO: –
CFO: –
HR: H Sam
FYE: December 31
Type: Private

Despite the name of its best-selling product Chattanooga Bakery is no pie-in-the-sky outfit. It is the one and only maker of the MoonPie a four-inch-round sandwich cookie made of marshmallow fluff layered between graham crackers and coated with chocolate. In addition to the original iteration MoonPies are available in double-decker and mini versions — and with banana or vanilla coating. Its most recent variation is the crispy-shelled MoonPie Crunch which comes with mint or peanut butter filling. The company also makes pecan and coconut pie snacks under the LookOut! name. Chattanooga's treats are sold nationwide at food retailers mass merchandisers convenience stores and through vending machines.

CHATTEM INC.

1715 W. 38th St.
Chattanooga TN 37409
Phone: 423-821-4571
Fax: 423-821-0395
Web: www.chattem.com

CEO: Zan Guerry
CFO: Robert B Long
HR: –
FYE: November 30
Type: Subsidiary

If it's a well known cream oil paste pill or powder it's likely that Chattem owns that brand name. The Sanofi subsidiary markets some two-dozen over-the-counter branded personal care products and dietary supplements including skin care and pain treatments such as Aspercreme Cortizone-10 Icy Hot muscle pain reliever and Pamprin menstrual symptom reliever. The company also makes the Unisom sleep aid medicated powder Gold Bond Bullfrog sunscreen Mudd clay-based facial masks and Selsun Blue dandruff shampoo. Chattem sells its products to wholesalers and retail merchandisers.

CHECKPOINT SYSTEMS INC   NYS: CKP

101 Wolf Drive, P.O. Box 188
Thorofare, NJ 08086
Phone: 856 848-1800
Fax: –
Web: www.checkpointsystems.com

CEO: George Babich
CFO: James M. Lucania
HR: –
FYE: December 28
Type: Public

Checkpoint Systems wants to keep shoplifters in check. The company makes electronic article surveillance systems (EAS) radio frequency identification (RFID) tags and electronic security devices (using electromagnetic technology) such as intrusion alarms digital video recorders and electronic access control systems used by retailers that have included Barnes & Noble Sears Target and Walgreen. Its EAS units employ paper-thin disposable circuit tags attached to merchandise that are disarmed at checkout; if not disarmed the tags trigger electronic sensors when the customer tries to leave. The company operates in some 30 countries worldwide; about 60% of its sales come from outside the Western Hemisphere.

	Annual Growth	12/10	12/11	12/12	12/13	12/14
Sales ($ mil.)	(5.6%)	834.5	865.3	690.8	689.7	662.0
Net income ($ mil.)	(20.5%)	27.4	(66.6)	(145.9)	(18.9)	11.0
Market value ($ mil.)	(9.4%)	869.5	469.9	436.4	637.9	586.5
Employees	(4.2%)	5,814	6,565	5,132	4,710	4,894

CHEESECAKE FACTORY INC. (THE)   NMS: CAKE

26901 Malibu Hills Road
Calabasas Hills, CA 91301
Phone: 818 871-3000
Fax: –
Web: www.thecheesecakefactory.com

CEO: David Overton
CFO: W. Douglas Benn
HR: Dina Barmasse
FYE: December 30
Type: Public

These restaurants have industrial-strength menus for foodies. The Cheesecake Factory owns and operates about 190 casual-dining restaurants in 37 states that offer more than 200 menu items ranging from sandwiches and salads to steaks and seafood. The highlight of the menu of course is cheesecake which comes in about 70 varieties. Each Cheesecake Factory restaurant has a unique design but all of them feature over-the-top opulence and Las Vegas-style glitz. In addition to the more than 175 locations of its flagship concept the company operates about a dozen upscale Grand Lux Cafes and one RockSugar Pan Asian Kitchen. The Cheesecake Factory also sells desserts to grocery stores and foodservice operators.

	Annual Growth	12/10*	01/12	01/13*	12/13	12/14
Sales ($ mil.)	4.5%	1,659.4	1,757.6	1,809.0	1,877.9	1,976.6
Net income ($ mil.)	5.5%	81.7	95.7	98.4	114.4	101.3
Market value ($ mil.)	13.1%	1,541.0	1,464.2	1,631.3	2,407.3	2,521.0
Employees	3.2%	31,500	32,200	33,900	35,500	35,700

*Fiscal year change

CHEFS INTERNATIONAL INC.

62 Broadway
Point Pleasant Beach NJ 08742
Phone: 732-295-0350
Fax: 732-295-4514

CEO: –
CFO: Martin W Fletcher
HR: –
FYE: January 31
Type: Private

These chefs are busy boiling seafood. Chefs International operates about a dozen casual dining restaurants in New Jersey and Florida mostly doing business under the Lobster Shanty name such as Point Pleasant Lobster Shanty Toms River Lobster Shanty and its flagship Jack Baker's Lobster Shanty. Other locations include Jack Baker's Wharfside & Patio Bar and The Sunset Ballroom event and banquet hall. The restaurants serve a variety of seafood dishes in a casual setting. Jack Baker a New Jersey fisherman opened his first Jack Baker's Lobster Shanty in 1979. Chairman Robert Lombardi and his family control the company.

CHEFS' WAREHOUSE INC (THE)

NMS: CHEF

100 East Ridge Road
Ridgefield, CT 06877
Phone: 203 894-1345
Fax: –
Web: www.chefswarehouse.com

CEO: –
CFO: John D. Austin
HR: Patricia (Pat) Lecouras
FYE: December 26
Type: Public

Before a gourmet chef can say "bon appétit" he must first procure his ingredients. A distributor of specialty food products Chefs' Warehouse sells such gourmet food items as artisan charcuterie specialty cheeses hormone-free protein truffles caviar and chocolates as well as basic food ingredients like cooking oils flour butter milk and eggs. The company's core customers include chefs from independent restaurants fine dining establishments culinary schools hotels and country clubs. It is a leading gourmet ingredient distributor in culinary centers like New York City San Francisco Los Angeles and Washington DC. Tracing its roots back to 1985 Chefs' Warehouse went public in 2011.

	Annual Growth	12/10	12/11	12/12	12/13	12/14
Sales ($ mil.)	26.2%	330.1	400.6	480.3	673.5	836.6
Net income ($ mil.)	(2.7%)	15.9	7.7	14.5	17.0	14.2
Market value ($ mil.)	7.2%	–	447.1	385.5	729.4	551.4
Employees	22.4%	571	600	780	1,160	1,281

CHEGG INC

NYS: CHGG

3990 Freedom Circle
Santa Clara, CA 95054
Phone: 408 855-5700
Fax: –
Web: www.chegg.com

CEO: Daniel L. (Dan) Rosensweig
CFO: Andrew J. (Andy) Brown
HR: –
FYE: December 31
Type: Public

If college students can check out books at the library why can't they check out textbooks for the semester? With Chegg they finally can. Chegg operates an online library that rents out textbooks to cash-strapped students; it has 180000 titles in its library and another 100000 e-textbook titles from major publishers such as Cengage Learning Elsevier McGraw Hill and Pearson. In addition the company's Student Hub offers educational support services such as homework help and a central database to find scholarship opportunities. Chegg also offers enrollment marketing services to about 800 universities including Duke Princeton Rutgers and UCLA. Formed in 2005 Chegg went public in 2013.

	Annual Growth	12/10	12/11	12/12	12/13	12/14
Sales ($ mil.)	19.6%	148.9	172.0	213.3	255.6	304.8
Net income ($ mil.)	–	(26.0)	(37.6)	(49.0)	(55.9)	(64.8)
Market value ($ mil.)	(18.8%)	–	–	–	714.9	580.5
Employees	7.5%	–	–	613	639	709

CHELSEA & SCOTT LTD.

75 Albrecht Dr.
Lake Bluff IL 60044
Phone: 847-615-2110
Fax: 847-615-2290
Web: www.onestepahead.com

CEO: –
CFO: –
HR: –
FYE: December 31
Type: Private

Chelsea & Scott wants children to grow up with its products. Through its One Step Ahead catalog and website the company sells apparel home furnishings feeding and safety products toys and travel accessories for newborns to children under 3. It also provides educational toys and developmental products for children ages 3 to 8 through its Leaps and Bounds catalog and website. Chelsea & Scott offers such brands as ALEX Infantino Lamaze and Manhattan Group as well as its own One Step Ahead branded lines. The company started doing business in 1989 when founders Karen and Ian Scott decided they wanted to offer an easier way for parents to find quality children's products.

CHELSEA PROPERTY GROUP INC.

105 Eisenhower Pkwy.
Roseland NJ 07068
Phone: 973-228-6111
Fax: 973-228-3891
Web: www.premiumoutlets.com

CEO: –
CFO: –
HR: –
FYE: December 31
Type: Subsidiary

Chelsea Property Group (also known as Premium Outlets) a subsidiary of retail giant Simon Property Group owns develops leases and manages some 50 factory outlet shopping centers in the US and abroad. The properties typically are located near metropolitan areas and tourist destinations such as Disney World in Orlando Florida Branson Missouri and California's Monterey Peninsula. The shopping centers feature some 750 tenants including such high-end fashion names as Gucci Versace Coach and Michael Kors. Most of its centers operate under the Premium Outlet name. Through joint ventures Chelsea Property also operates seven outlet malls in Japan one in Korea and one in Mexico.

CHEMED CORP

NYS: CHE

255 East Fifth Street, Suite 2600
Cincinnati, OH 45202
Phone: 513 762-6690
Fax: –
Web: www.chemed.com

CEO: Kevin J. McNamara
CFO: David P. Williams
HR: Jim Taylor
FYE: December 31
Type: Public

Chemed Corporation brings a professional dignity to times of transition and sewer line clogs. Operating through two major subsidiaries Chemed offers hospice care to terminally ill patients through its VITAS Healthcare subsidiary which operates in more than 15 US states. VITAS employs doctors nurses and other professionals to provide at-home and inpatient services in care facilities. Chemed's better-known Roto-Rooter subsidiary offers plumbing and drain-cleaning services for residential and commercial customers through company-owned contractor-operated and franchised locations some 500 total. A stalwart of the industry Roto-Rooter offers services throughout the US and in parts of Canada.

	Annual Growth	12/10	12/11	12/12	12/13	12/14
Sales ($ mil.)	3.3%	1,280.5	1,356.0	1,430.0	1,413.3	1,456.3
Net income ($ mil.)	5.0%	81.8	86.0	89.3	77.2	99.3
Market value ($ mil.)	13.6%	1,072.7	865.0	1,158.5	1,294.2	1,784.8
Employees	2.1%	13,058	13,733	14,096	13,952	14,190

CHEMICAL FINANCIAL CORP   NMS: CHFC

235 E. Main Street
Midland, MI 48640
Phone: 989 839-5350
Fax: –
Web: www.chemicalbankmi.com

CEO: David B. Ramaker
CFO: Lori A. Gwizdala
HR: Joseph (Jo) Torrence
FYE: December 31
Type: Public

Chemical Financial has banking down to a science. It's the holding company for Chemical Bank which provides standard services such as checking and savings accounts CDs and IRAs credit and debit cards and loans and mortgages to individuals and businesses through nearly 190 branches in the lower peninsula of Michigan. The majority of the bank's loan portfolio is made up of commercial loans while consumer loans make up the remainder. Boasting assets of $9 billion Chemical is the second largest bank in Michigan. The company also offers trust investment management brokerage and title insurance services through subsidiaries.

	Annual Growth	12/10	12/11	12/12	12/13	12/14
Assets ($ mil.)	8.7%	5,246.2	5,339.5	5,917.3	6,184.7	7,322.1
Net income ($ mil.)	28.1%	23.1	43.1	51.0	56.8	62.1
Market value ($ mil.)	8.4%	726.0	698.8	778.7	1,038.0	1,004.2
Employees	5.6%	1,608	1,700	1,859	1,700	2,000

CHEMOCENTRYX, INC.   NMS: CCXI

850 Maude Avenue
Mountain View, CA 94043
Phone: 650 210-2900
Fax: 650 210-2910
Web: www.chemocentryx.com

CEO: Thomas J Schall
CFO: Susan M Kanaya
HR: –
FYE: December 31
Type: Public

The nucleus of ChemoCentryx's research is molecular cell secretions. The drug developer focuses on orally administered drugs targeting the body's chemokine system a molecular network that regulates inflammatory and immune responses. Its lead candidate in clinical development is Vercirnon (formerly Traficet-EN) a potential treatment for Crohn's disease. ChemoCentryx's other pipeline candidates include possible treatments for type 2 diabetes several kidney diseases and inflammatory bowel disease (IBD). Early stage candidates target immune system disorders like rheumatoid arthritis. ChemoCentryx was founded in 1997 and went public in 2012.

	Annual Growth	12/09	12/10	12/11	12/12	12/13
Sales ($ mil.)	(40.9%)	49.7	34.9	31.7	5.4	6.1
Net income ($ mil.)	–	15.6	(3.1)	(4.6)	(39.9)	(38.7)
Market value ($ mil.)	(47.1%)	–	–	–	469.2	248.3
Employees	(2.1%)	–	64	64	61	60

CHEMTURA CORP   NYS: CHMT

1818 Market Street, Suite 3700
Philadelphia, PA 19103
Phone: 203 573-2000
Fax: –
Web: www.chemtura.com

CEO: Craig A. Rogerson
CFO: Stephen C. Forsyth
HR: Christine Peterson
FYE: December 31
Type: Public

Chemtura aspires to be the future of chemicals-making. The company ranks among the top specialty chemical companies in the US along with the likes of Ecolab and Hexion and among the leading plastics additives maker globally. It makes chemical products that makes other products more durable safer cleaner and more efficient. Major industries served include transportation energy electronics and agriculture. Aside from plastic additives Chemtura holds niche-leading positions in petroleum additives flame retardants and swimming pool chemicals. Its other products include urethanes.

	Annual Growth	12/10	12/11	12/12	12/13	12/14
Sales ($ mil.)	(5.6%)	2,760.0	3,025.0	2,629.0	2,231.0	2,190.0
Net income ($ mil.)	–	(586.0)	119.0	101.0	(177.0)	763.0
Market value ($ mil.)	11.5%	1,145.8	813.1	1,524.3	2,001.9	1,773.1
Employees	(10.5%)	4,200	4,500	4,600	3,300	2,700

CHEMUNG FINANCIAL CORP.   NMS: CHMG

One Chemung Canal Plaza, P.O. Box 1522
Elmira, NY 14902
Phone: 607 737-3711
Fax: –
Web: www.chemungcanal.com

CEO: Ronald M Bentley
CFO: Karl F Krebs
HR: –
FYE: December 31
Type: Public

Everybody Chemung Financial Tonight probably wouldn't make much of a pop record. The firm is parent to Chemung Canal Trust Company which provides bank and trust services from about 30 offices in upstate New York. The trust company offers such deposit services as savings checking and money market accounts; IRAs; and CDs. It also offers credit cards and originates a variety of loans including personal small business and residential mortgage loans. Other services include retirement and estate planning and tax services. Another Chemung Financial subsidiary CFS Group offers mutual funds discount brokerage and other financial services.

	Annual Growth	12/10	12/11	12/12	12/13	12/14
Assets ($ mil.)	12.3%	958.3	1,216.3	1,248.2	1,476.1	1,524.5
Net income ($ mil.)	(5.2%)	10.1	10.5	11.0	8.7	8.2
Market value ($ mil.)	5.3%	104.2	105.1	138.4	158.2	128.0
Employees	5.5%	317	349	356	390	393

CHENEGA CORPORATION

3000 C ST STE 301
ANCHORAGE, AK 995033975
Phone: 907-277-5706
Fax: –
Web: www.chenega.jobs

CEO: –
CFO: –
HR: Peggy O'Keefe
FYE: September 30
Type: Private

An Alaska Native Corporation Chenega Corporation has gone from landowner to business titan. Representing the Chenega people residing in the central Alaskan Prince William Sound region it operates mostly through its subsidiaries. Chenega Integrated Systems and Chenega Technology Services offer information technology security training manufacturing research and development network engineering and military operation support services. Chenega Corporation's clients have included the Department of Defense Department of Homeland Security and EPA.

	Annual Growth	09/08	09/09	09/10	09/11	09/12
Sales ($ mil.)	0.7%	–	1,077.4	1,115.6	1,108.7	1,099.9
Net income ($ mil.)	(45.1%)	–	–	28.6	28.4	8.6
Market value ($ mil.)	–	–	–	–	–	–
Employees	–	–	–	–	–	4,500

CHENIERE ENERGY INC.   ASE: LNG

700 Milam Street, Suite 1900
Houston, TX 77002
Phone: 713 375-5000
Fax: –
Web: www.cheniere.com

CEO: Neal A. Shear
CFO: Michael J. Wortley
HR: –
FYE: December 31
Type: Public

Gaseous form or liquid state are both OK with Cheniere Energy which is engaged in the development of a liquefied natural gas (LNG) receiving-terminal business. It owns and operates Sabine Pass LNG terminal in Louisiana (with a capacity of 16.9 billion cu. ft.) and the Creole Trail Pipeline which interconnects the Sabine Pass LNG terminal with North American natural gas markets. Cheniere Energy also operates an LNG and natural gas marketing business and has minor exploration and production assets. Its Cheniere Energy Partners unit operates the 59.5%-owned Sabine Pass LNG terminal. The company is building an gas export plant (Sabine Pass Liquefaction) to take advantage of the glut of natural gas in the US.

	Annual Growth	12/10	12/11	12/12	12/13	12/14
Sales ($ mil.)	(2.1%)	291.5	290.4	266.2	267.2	268.0
Net income ($ mil.)	–	(76.2)	(198.8)	(332.8)	(507.9)	(547.9)
Market value ($ mil.)	89.0%	1,306.6	2,056.9	4,445.2	10,206.5	16,663.7
Employees	34.5%	196	232	306	423	642

CHENIERE ENERGY PARTNERS L P
ASE: CQP

700 Milam Street, Suite 1900
Houston, TX 77002
Phone: 713-375-5000
Fax: –
Web: www.cheniereenergypartners.com

CEO: –
CFO: –
HR: –
FYE: December 31
Type: Public

Cheniere Energy Partners a subsidiary of Cheniere Energy Inc. plans to be North America's biggest gas station — natural gas that is. Construction began on the Sabine Pass LNG (liquefied natural gas) receiving terminal in 2005 and was completed in 2008. The terminal is one of the largest in North America: It boasts 4 billion cu. ft. per day of regasification capacity as well as 16.9 billion cu. ft. of LNG storage capacity. All of the Sabine Pass LNG receiving terminal's capacity has already been contracted to Total Gas and Power North America Chevron and Cheniere Energy Inc. subsidiary Cheniere Marketing. In 2012 Blackstone agreed to invest $2 billion in the terminal's Sabine Pass liquefaction project.

	Annual Growth	12/10	12/11	12/12	12/13	12/14
Sales ($ mil.)	(9.4%)	399.3	283.8	264.3	268.2	268.7
Net income ($ mil.)	–	107.6	(31.0)	(150.1)	(258.1)	(410.0)
Market value ($ mil.)	10.7%	7,345.4	6,211.3	7,328.1	9,875.4	11,030.1
Employees	–	–	–	–	–	–

CHEP INTERNATIONAL INC.

8517 S. Park Cir.
Orlando FL 32819-9040
Phone: 407-370-2437
Fax: 407-363-5354
Web: www.chep.com

CEO: Kim Rumph
CFO: Scott Spivey
HR: –
FYE: June 30
Type: Subsidiary

CHEP knows it's sink or swim in the pallet and plastic container pooling services business. The company a unit of Australia-based Brambles manages the movement of more than 300 million pallets and containers used by companies in the automotive consumer goods food and beverage home improvement petrochemical and raw materials industries. It collects cleans and refurbishes the pallets and containers which are used throughout the supply chain. The company's 500000-plus customers have included industry leaders such as General Motors Kraft and Procter & Gamble. CHEP operates from a network of more than 500 service facilities in about 45 countries worldwide.

CHEROKEE INC. (DE)
NMS: CHKE

5990 Sepulveda Boulevard
Sherman Oaks, CA 91411
Phone: 818-908-9868
Fax: –
Web: www.cherokeeglobalbrands.com

CEO: Henry Stupp
CFO: Mark DiSiena
HR: –
FYE: January 31
Type: Public

Cherokee has a license to make money from apparel and accessories. The company owns several trademarks including Cherokee Liz Lange Sideout Tony Hawk and Everyday California and licenses them to retailers and wholesalers of apparel footwear and accessories. The main idea behind Cherokee's business is that large retailers can source merchandise more efficiently than individual brand owners and that licensed brands can sell better for retailers than private labels. In addition to licensing its own brands Cherokee helps other brand owners gain licensing contracts. Target the company's largest customer accounts for more than half of Cherokee's revenue; other licensees include Tesco (in Europe) and TJ Maxx.

	Annual Growth	01/11	01/12*	02/13	02/14*	01/15
Sales ($ mil.)	3.2%	30.8	25.6	26.6	28.6	35.0
Net income ($ mil.)	6.2%	7.7	7.5	6.8	6.1	9.8
Market value ($ mil.)	0.0%	155.3	88.0	119.4	117.2	155.6
Employees	18.2%	21	21	23	39	41

*Fiscal year change

CHERRY BEKAERT LLP

200 S 10TH ST STE 900
RICHMOND, VA 232194064
Phone: 804-673-4224
Fax: –
Web: www.cbh.com

CEO: –
CFO: Ray Christopher
HR: –
FYE: April 30
Type: Private

Life's a bowl of accounting and consulting services at Cherry Bekaert (formerly Cherry Bekaert & Holland). The firm provides financial and management consulting services in the southeastern US. It specializes in serving such sectors as government financial services not-for-profit higher education healthcare retail and manufacturing. In addition to tax and accounting services Cherry Bekaert provides business valuations litigation support M&A advisory and other services. It also has a wealth management arm for well-to-do families. The firm enjoys an international reach through its affiliation with Baker Tilly International.

	Annual Growth	04/06	04/07	04/10	04/11	04/13
Sales ($ mil.)	8.1%	–	77.4	98.4	111.2	123.7
Net income ($ mil.)	0.9%	–	–	24.0	25.8	24.7
Market value ($ mil.)	–	–	–	–	–	–
Employees	–	–	–	–	–	850

CHERRY CENTRAL COOPERATIVE INC.

1771 N US 31 S
TRAVERSE CITY, MI 496858748
Phone: 231-946-1860
Fax: –
Web: www.cherrycentral.com

CEO: –
CFO: –
HR: –
FYE: April 30
Type: Private

Serving as a central hub for cherry pickers' crops Cherry Central Cooperative is a fruit marketing co-operative that consists of more than a dozen member cooperatives representing hundreds of growers in Michigan New York Utah Washington Wisconsin and Ontario. It processes cherries cranberries apples and other fruit products including the Indian Summer brand of apple and cherry juices and ciders. Its Oceana Foods unit makes dried fruit sold under the Traverse Bay label while its Dunkley International subsidiary makes fruit-processing equipment. Cherry Central's products are sold to retail foodservice and ingredient customers. The cooperative was formed in 1973.

	Annual Growth	04/10	04/11	04/12	04/13	04/14
Sales ($ mil.)	5.5%	–	144.5	154.3	185.5	169.7
Net income ($ mil.)	18.0%	–	–	0.7	1.2	1.0
Market value ($ mil.)	–	–	–	–	–	–
Employees	–	–	–	–	–	115

CHERRY HILL MORTGAGE INVESTMENT CORP
NYS: CHMI

301 Harper Drive, Suite 110
Moorestown, NJ 08057
Phone: 877-870-7005
Fax: –
Web: www.chmireit.com

CEO: –
CFO: Martin J Levine
HR: –
FYE: December 31
Type: Public

Cherry Hill Mortgage Investment is interested in real estate assets that lie far beyond Cherry Hill New Jersey. Formed in 2012 Cherry Hill is a real estate investment trust or REIT that looks to acquire invest in and manage real estate assets across the US. It plans to build a portfolio that comprises excess mortgage servicing rights (excess MSRs are servicing fees that exceed basic MSR servicing fees) agency residential mortgage-backed securities (secured by the government agencies like Fannie Mae and Freddie Mac) and other residential mortgage assets. The REIT is externally managed by Cherry Hill Mortgage Management an affiliate of Freedom Mortgage. It went public in 2013.

	Annual Growth	12/10	12/11	12/12	12/13	12/14
Sales ($ mil.)	–	0.0	0.0	–	22.5	7.8
Net income ($ mil.)	–	0.0	0.0	(0.0)	21.2	2.4
Market value ($ mil.)	–	0.0	0.0	–	133.7	138.9
Employees	–	–	–	–	–	–

CHESAPEAKE ENERGY CORP.

NYS: CHK

6100 North Western Avenue
Oklahoma City, OK 73118
Phone: 405 848-8000
Fax: –
Web: www.chk.com

CEO: Robert D. (Doug) Lawler
CFO: Domenic J. (Nick) Dell'Osso
HR: James Hawkins
FYE: December 31
Type: Public

Chesapeake Energy (named after the childhood Chesapeake Bay haunts of a company founder) builds oil and natural gas reserves through the acquisition and development of oil and gas assets across the US. In 2014 the company had estimated proved reserves of 10.7 trillion cu. ft. of natural gas equivalent. Chesapeake has exploration and production assets in Appalachia the Mid-Continent the Barnett Bossier and Haynesville shale plays the Permian Basin and the Rockies. In 2014 Chesapeake had 45100 producing oil and natural gas wells that produced 729000 barrels of oil equivalent per day the bulk of which was natural gas.

	Annual Growth	12/10	12/11	12/12	12/13	12/14
Sales ($ mil.)	22.3%	9,366.0	11,635.0	12,316.0	17,506.0	20,951.0
Net income ($ mil.)	2.0%	1,774.0	1,742.0	(769.0)	724.0	1,917.0
Market value ($ mil.)	(6.8%)	17,186.9	14,785.6	11,024.5	18,002.8	12,981.4
Employees	(13.9%)	10,000	12,600	12,000	10,800	5,500

CHESAPEAKE LODGING TRUST

NYS: CHSP

1997 Annapolis Exchange Parkway, Suite 410
Annapolis, MD 21401
Phone: 410 972-4140
Fax: –
Web: www.chesapeakelodgingtrust.com

CEO: James L. Francis
CFO: Douglas W. Vicari
HR: –
FYE: December 31
Type: Public

As a real estate investment trust (REIT) focused on the hospitality industry Chesapeake Lodging Trust targets upper-upscale hotels located in major US business centers and popular convention markets. The company owns 22 hotels with a total of nearly 6700 rooms in nine US states and Washington DC. Southern California is a major market for the company. Chesapeake Lodging's properties operate under several major brands including Hyatt Marriott and W Hotels. In evaluating properties for purchase the company considers rebranding and renovation options. Formed in mid-2009 Chesapeake Lodging Trust went public in 2010.

	Annual Growth	12/10	12/11	12/12	12/13	12/14
Sales ($ mil.)	72.3%	54.2	172.2	278.3	420.2	478.0
Net income ($ mil.)	–	(0.7)	9.0	27.2	45.3	61.0
Market value ($ mil.)	18.6%	1,031.1	847.5	1,144.6	1,386.3	2,039.8
Employees	16.7%	7	9	10	13	13

CHESAPEAKE OILFIELD SERVICES INC.

6100 N. Western Ave.
Oklahoma City OK 73118
Phone: 405-848-8000
Fax: 732-393-6025
Web: www.blackstratus.com

CEO: –
CFO: –
HR: –
FYE: December 31
Type: Private

"Divide and conquer" might be the strategy behind Chesapeake Oilfield Services a company spun off from Chesapeake Energy one of the top onshore energy companies in the US. Chesapeake Energy reorganized six of its oilfield services subsidiaries into Chesapeake Oilfield Services to create a new publicly traded entity that offers drilling hydraulic fracturing and trucking services as well as renting tools and manufacturing natural gas compressor equipment. With about 110 land drilling rigs Chesapeake Oilfield Services has the fourth-largest rig fleet in the US. The company was formed in October 2011 and filed to go public in April 2012 in an initial public offering seeking up to $862.5 million.

CHESAPEAKE UTILITIES CORP.

NYS: CPK

909 Silver Lake Boulevard
Dover, DE 19904
Phone: 302 734-6799
Fax: –
Web: www.chpk.com

CEO: Michael P. (Mike) McMasters
CFO: Beth W. Cooper
HR: –
FYE: December 31
Type: Public

Chesapeake Utilities gasses up the Chesapeake Bay and then some. Chesapeake's regulated natural gas distribution divisions serve more than 1138000 customers in the Northeast and Florida. Another unit distributes electricity to about 31000 customers in Florida. On the unregulated side the company also serves more than 52000 retail propane customers in Delaware Florida Maryland and Virginia. Another subsidiary Xeron sells propane at wholesale to distributors industrial users and resellers throughout the US. In addition Chesapeake has interstate gas pipeline and gas marketing operations. Through BravePoint the company also offers data services consulting and software development.

	Annual Growth	12/10	12/11	12/12	12/13	12/14
Sales ($ mil.)	3.9%	427.5	418.0	392.5	444.3	498.8
Net income ($ mil.)	8.5%	26.1	27.6	28.9	32.8	36.1
Market value ($ mil.)	4.6%	605.7	632.4	662.3	875.6	724.5
Employees	0.6%	734	711	738	842	753

CHESHIRE OIL COMPANY INC.

678 MARLBORO ST
KEENE, NH 034314008
Phone: 603-352-0001
Fax: –
Web: www.cheshireoil.com

CEO: –
CFO: –
HR: –
FYE: October 31
Type: Private

Cheshire Oil is confident that the smile it has put on customers' faces in Southern New Hampshire and Vermont won't suddenly disappear. The company's services (under the Cheshire Oil and T-Bird Fuel brands) to residential and commercial clients include heating oil delivery oil and propane furnace and boiler installation service and repair fleet fueling and central air-conditioning installation and repair. Cheshire Oil also operates gas stations and convenience stores under the T-Bird Mini-Marts moniker. It also offers storage rental services through Keene Mini Storage. Cheshire Oil is owned and managed by members of the founding Robertson family.

	Annual Growth	10/08	10/09	10/10	10/11	10/12
Sales ($ mil.)	7.2%	–	70.0	77.4	92.7	86.1
Net income ($ mil.)	147.6%	–	–	0.2	0.7	1.2
Market value ($ mil.)	–	–	–	–	–	–
Employees	–	–	–	–	–	175

CHEVIOT FINANCIAL CORP

NAS: CHEV

3723 Glenmore Avenue
Cincinnati, OH 45211
Phone: 513 661-0457
Fax: –
Web: www.cheviotsavings.com

CEO: Mark Reitzes
CFO: Scott T Smith
HR: –
FYE: December 31
Type: Public

Cheviot Financial happily puts the "buck" in "Buckeye State." It is the holding company for Cheviot Savings Bank which operates about a dozen branches in and around Cincinnati. The community-oriented thrift offers traditional products such as checking and savings accounts CDs IRAs and credit cards. Its lending activities primarily consist of residential mortgages; construction consumer and commercial loans round out its loan book. Investment services are offered through through third-party Souders Financial. The bank nearly doubled in size when it acquired First Franklin Corporation in 2011. Formerly 61%-owned by Cheviot Mutual Cheviot Financial converted to a 100% publicly traded stock company in 2012.

	Annual Growth	12/10	12/11	12/12	12/13	12/14
Assets ($ mil.)	12.4%	358.1	616.3	632.0	587.1	571.2
Net income ($ mil.)	11.7%	2.0	3.4	3.4	1.4	3.1
Market value ($ mil.)	12.4%	59.8	50.0	62.5	69.2	95.5
Employees	(2.6%)	–	120	124	111	111

CHEVRON CORPORATION
NYS: CVX

6001 Bollinger Canyon Road
San Ramon, CA 94583-2324
Phone: 925 842-1000
Fax: 925 894-6017
Web: www.chevron.com

CEO: John S. Watson
CFO: Patricia E. (Pat) Yarrington
HR: Juan Garcia
FYE: December 31
Type: Public

Chevron has earned its stripes as the #2 integrated oil company in the US behind Exxon Mobil. In 2014 it reported proved reserves of 11.1 billion barrels of oil equivalent and a daily production of 2.6 million barrels of oil equivalent 5550 miles of oil and gas pipeline and a refining capacity of 2 million barrels of oil per day. Chevron also owns interests in chemicals mining and power production businesses. The company owns or has stakes in 8060 gas stations in the US (and 8600 outside the US) that operate mainly under the Chevron and Texaco brands. Chevron also owns 50% of chemicals concern Chevron Phillips Chemical.

	Annual Growth	12/10	12/11	12/12	12/13	12/14
Sales ($ mil.)	0.8%	204,928.0	253,706.0	241,909.0	228,848.0	211,970.0
Net income ($ mil.)	0.3%	19,024.0	26,895.0	26,179.0	21,423.0	19,241.0
Market value ($ mil.)	5.3%	171,518.0	199,994.6	203,265.2	234,786.9	210,859.0
Employees	1.1%	62,000	61,000	62,000	64,600	64,700

CHEVRON PHILLIPS CHEMICAL COMPANY LP

10001 Six Pines Dr.
The Woodlands TX 77380
Phone: 832-813-4100
Fax: 616-787-7102
Web: www.amway.com/en

CEO: Peter Cella
CFO: Greg G Maxwell
HR: –
FYE: December 31
Type: Joint Venture

A coin toss determined whose name would go first when Chevron and Phillips Petroleum (now Phillips 66) formed 50-50 joint venture Chevron Phillips Chemical Company in 2000. Among the largest US petrochemical firms the company produces ethylene propylene polyethylene and polypropylene — sometimes used as building blocks for the company's other products such as pipe. Chevron Phillips Chemical also produces aromatics such as benzene and styrene specialty chemicals such as acetylene black (a form of carbon black) and mining chemicals. The company has several petrochemical joint ventures in the Middle East including Saudi Chevron Phillips Company (50%) and Qatar Chemical Company (not quite 50%).

CHEVYS RESTAURANTS LLC

5660 Katella Ave.
Cypress CA 90630
Phone: 510-475-5236
Fax: 510-475-9828
Web: www.chevys.com

CEO: –
CFO: Terrie Robinson
HR: –
FYE: December 31
Type: Subsidiary

Fresh Mexican food is the driving force behind this chain. Chevys Restaurants operates and franchises nearly 100 full-service Mexican eateries in about 15 states under the Chevys Fresh Mex banner. The restaurants feature mesquite-grilled beef chicken and vegetarian fajitas as well as such traditional favorites as enchiladas tacos and burritos. The chain also serves a selection of margaritas and tequilas for happy hour celebrations. Nearly 70 locations are company-owned while the rest are franchised. Chevys was formed in 1986 by Warren Simmons Sr. and his son. It is owned by leading Mexican restaurant operator Real Mex Restaurants.

CHICAGO AIRPORT SYSTEM

Chicago Department of Aviation 10510 W. Zemke Rd.
Chicago IL 60666
Phone: 773-686-3700
Fax: 773-686-3573
Web: www.flychicago.com

CEO: –
CFO: –
HR: –
FYE: December 31
Type: Government-owned

Chicago Airport System manages airports in the Windy City including one of the busiest on the planet — O'Hare International. Handling more than 76 million travelers a year O'Hare serves as a hub for such airlines as United and American. The Chicago Airport System also operates Midway Airport which was the world's busiest before the introduction of large jets that needed longer runways; it still serves about 20 million passengers a year who use carriers such as Southwest Airlines. Gary-Chicago International Airport in Indiana also is managed by Chicago Airport System. The system is overseen by the City of Chicago's Department of Aviation.

CHICAGO BEARS FOOTBALL CLUB INC.

1000 Football Dr.
Lake Forest IL 60045
Phone: 847-295-6600
Fax: 847-295-8986
Web: www.chicagobears.com

CEO: –
CFO: –
HR: –
FYE: February 28
Type: Private

These Monsters of the Midway have been scaring opponents since the very beginning. Chicago Bears Football Club operates the storied Chicago Bears professional football team which lays claim to nine National Football League titles (its last in Super Bowl XX at the end of the 1985 season). More than 25 Hall of Fame players have graced the roster of "Da Bears" including Red Grange Dick Butkus Gale Sayers and Walter Payton. Loyal Chicago fans root on their team at venerable Soldier Field. The franchise originally known as the Decatur Staleys was a charter member of the NFL in 1920. Chairman Michael McCaskey (grandson of founder George "Papa Bear" Halas) and his family control the club.

CHICAGO BLACKHAWK HOCKEY TEAM INC.

1901 W. Madison St.
Chicago IL 60612
Phone: 312-455-7000
Fax: 312-455-7041
Web: www.chicagoblackhawks.com

CEO: –
CFO: –
HR: –
FYE: June 30
Type: Subsidiary

When the Windy City turns cold these Hawks start flying on the ice. One of the Original Six professional hockey franchises of the National Hockey League the Chicago Blackhawks boast a long history that includes four Stanley Cup championships and a roster that has featured such Hall of Fame players as Phil and Tony Esposito Bobby Hull and Stan Mikita. The club won its most recent NHL championship title in 2010 breaking a drought that lasted 49 years the longest in league history. Loyal fans support the team at Chicago's United Center. The Wirtz family has owned the Blackhawks franchise through their Wirtz Corporation since 1954.

CHICAGO MEAT AUTHORITY INC.

1120 W. 47th Place
Chicago IL 60609
Phone: 773-254-3811
Fax: 773-254-5851
Web: www.chicagomeat.com

CEO: Jordan Dorfman
CFO: -
HR: Daniel Wang
FYE: December 31
Type: Private

When Chicago needs meat it turns to an authority. Chicago Meat Authority (CMA) processes beef and pork into a variety of sizes and cuts and sells its products not only in Chicago but worldwide. The company's fresh and frozen meats are specially cut for a range of customers including food retailers ethnic markets further processors (such as sausage makers) healthcare providers restaurants and broadline distributors. It also offers services such as aging custom cutting and trimming marinating and precooking as well as a variety of packaging options. Headquartered in the historic Chicago Stockyards Chicago Meat Authority was founded in 1990.

CHICAGO TRANSIT AUTHORITY

567 W. Lake St.
Chicago IL 60661
Phone: 312-664-7200
Fax: 214-871-8357
Web: www.haaswheat.com

CEO: -
CFO: -
HR: Anita Brooks
FYE: December 31
Type: Government-owned

The CTA is focused on making its ETA. The Chicago Transit Authority operates the second-largest public transportation system in the US behind the New York City Transit Authority. On a typical weekday CTA passengers take about 1.6 million rides on the agency's buses and trains which travel in and around Chicago and about 40 suburbs. The CTA operates a fleet of nearly 1800 buses on 140 routes. Its rail system includes some 1200 rail cars operating on 225 miles of track at more than 140 stations. The agency created by the Illinois legislature in 1947 is part of the state's Regional Transportation Authority which also oversees Metra (commuter rail system) and Pace (suburban bus system).

CHICAGO NATIONAL LEAGUE BALL CLUB INC.

Wrigley Field 1060 W. Addison St.
Chicago IL 60613-4397
Phone: 773-404-2827
Fax: 773-404-4129
Web: www.cubs.com

CEO: Tom Ricketts
CFO: -
HR: Jenny Surma
FYE: December 31
Type: Private

This company has thrilled and (mostly) disappointed baseball fans for a long time. Chicago National League Ball Club operates the Chicago Cubs franchise of Major League Baseball which has gone without a World Series title since 1908. The team was formed as the Chicago White Stockings in 1876 and became the Cubs in 1907. Despite the lack of championships Chicagoans still flock to the charming and famed Wrigley Field (the second-oldest ballpark in MLB after Boston's Fenway Park) to see their Cubbies play. A group led by billionaire Tom Ricketts acquired a majority of the Cubs in 2009.

CHICAGO WHITE SOX LTD.

333 W. 35th St.
Chicago IL 60616
Phone: 312-674-1000
Fax: 312-924-3296
Web: chicago.whitesox.mlb.com

CEO: -
CFO: -
HR: -
FYE: October 31
Type: Private

In the summer in Chicago you can either "root root root for the Cubbies" or you can cheer on these southsiders. The venerable Chicago White Sox franchise is one of the oldest clubs in Major League Baseball having joined the American League in 1900. The team boasts just three World Series championships two from the early 1900s and it latest in 2005. (A World Series appearance in 1919 was marred by the "Black Sox" scandal that saw eight teammates banned from baseball for throwing the championship.) Playing host at US Cellular Field the White Sox franchise is owned by real estate developer and chairman Jerry Reinsdorf who also owns the Chicago Bulls basketball team.

CHICAGO RIVET & MACHINE CO.

901 Frontenac Road
Naperville, IL 60563
Phone: 630 357-8500
Fax: -
Web: www.chicagorivet.com

ASE: CVR
CEO: John A Morrissey
CFO: -
HR: Larry Koch
FYE: December 31
Type: Public

Rosie the Riveter might have used rivets made by Chicago Rivet & Machine. The company's main business is making fasteners including rivets screw machine products and cold-formed fasteners. In addition to manufacturing assembly equipment such as automatic rivet-setting equipment and rivet-working tools it leases rivet-setting machines. Chicago Rivet sells its products through internal and independent sales representatives to US automotive and auto parts manufacturers. Major customers include Fisher & Company (accounting for about 20% of the company's sales) and TI Automotive (16% of sales).

	Annual Growth	12/10	12/11	12/12	12/13	12/14
Sales ($ mil.)	6.8%	28.5	30.9	34.2	37.1	37.1
Net income ($ mil.)	34.0%	0.6	1.3	1.7	2.5	2.0
Market value ($ mil.)	15.1%	16.9	16.5	18.8	32.0	29.7
Employees	1.9%	219	221	228	235	236

CHICKASAW HOLDING COMPANY

124 W VINITA AVE
SULPHUR, OK 730863821
Phone: 580-622-2111
Fax: -
Web: www.chickasawholding.com

CEO: RE Gauntt
CFO: -
HR: -
FYE: December 31
Type: Private

Chickasaw Holding's family of businesses keeps south central Oklahoma connected. The company's original business Chickasaw Telephone Company was founded in 1909 and offers local phone service to about 9000 business and residential customers. Its other subsidiaries provide such services as long-distance (Chickasaw Long Distance) Internet access (BrightNet Oklahoma) wireless service (Chickasaw Cellular) and wholesale fiber-optic networking for business customers and other communications carriers (Indian Nations Fiber Optics). The group also installs telecommunications equipment including private branch exchange (PBX) and voice mail systems through its Telco Supply Company subsidiary.

	Annual Growth	12/09	12/10	12/11	12/12	12/13
Sales ($ mil.)	3.2%	-	93.8	81.4	92.0	103.0
Net income ($ mil.)	31.8%	-	-	14.1	20.6	24.6
Market value ($ mil.)	-	-	-	-	-	-
Employees	-	-	-	-	-	600

CHICO'S FAS INC

NYS: CHS

11215 Metro Parkway
Fort Myers, FL 33966
Phone: 239 277-6200
Fax: -
Web: www.chicosfas.com

CEO: Shelley G. Broader
CFO: Todd E. Vogensen
HR: Sara K. Stensrud
FYE: January 31
Type: Public

Chico's FAS wants to color coordinate its customers with its own brands of chic clothes. Once a Mexican folk art shop Chico's owns and operates more than 1550 specialty stores nationwide in Canada and now Mexico (through a franchise agreement). Its stores are mostly located in enclosed malls and shopping centers under the banners Chico's White House/Black Market (WH/BM) Soma and Boston Proper. The boutiques target middle-to-high-income women ages 30 and up with clothes made primarily from natural fabrics (cotton linen silk). Its casual wear includes tops pants shorts skirts and dresses as well as jewelry and accessories.

	Annual Growth	01/11	01/12*	02/13	02/14*	01/15
Sales ($ mil.)	8.9%	1,905.0	2,196.4	2,581.1	2,586.0	2,675.2
Net income ($ mil.)	(13.5%)	115.4	140.9	180.2	65.9	64.6
Market value ($ mil.)	10.9%	1,688.2	1,746.3	2,746.4	2,538.4	2,550.6
Employees	5.9%	18,900	19,800	22,100	23,700	23,800

*Fiscal year change

CHICOPEE BANCORP INC

NMS: CBNK

70 Center Street
Chicopee, MA 01013
Phone: 413 594-6692
Fax: -

CEO: William J Wagner
CFO: Guida R Sajdak
HR: -
FYE: December 31
Type: Public

Chicopee Bancorp is the holding company for Chicopee Savings Bank a community bank which serves the residents and businesses of Hampden and Hampshire counties in western Massachusetts. Through a handful of branches the bank offers deposit services such as savings and checking accounts as well as a variety of lending services. Its loan portfolio consists of one-to-four-family residential real estate loans (its largest loan segment) and commercial real estate loans. Other lending services include multi-family construction home equity commercial business and consumer loans. Chicopee Bank was founded in 1854.

	Annual Growth	12/10	12/11	12/12	12/13	12/14
Assets ($ mil.)	2.7%	573.7	616.3	600.0	587.7	639.2
Net income ($ mil.)	-	0.5	1.1	2.5	2.6	(0.6)
Market value ($ mil.)	7.3%	66.7	74.3	83.8	91.8	88.3
Employees	0.2%	129	130	138	139	130

CHIEF INDUSTRIES INC.

3942 W OLD HIGHWAY 30
GRAND ISLAND, NE 688035051
Phone: 308-389-7200
Fax: -
Web: www.agri.chiefind.com

CEO: D J Eihusen
CFO: David Ostdiek
HR: -
FYE: June 30
Type: Private

When it comes serving the agriculture and transportation industries through its eclectic range of businesses Chief Industries is the head honcho. Chief makes ethanol fuel and manufactures a host of supplies for agricultural industrial correctional building transportation and wastewater treatment applications. Its agri/industrial unit makes grain-drying and storage bins crop-drying fans and aeration systems. Its transportation business makes rail car products while division Chief Custom Homes makes modular homes and RVs. Chief offers services including metal fabrication powder coating design/build general contracting electrical/lighting design and for-hire freight hauling.

	Annual Growth	06/98	06/99	06/00	06/01	06/08
Sales ($ mil.)	(30.0%)	-	256.2	325.2	294.7	10.4
Net income ($ mil.)	-	-	-	6.0	1.6	(0.1)
Market value ($ mil.)	-	-	-	-	-	-
Employees	-	-	-	-	-	1,645

CHILDFUND INTERNATIONAL USA

2821 EMERYWOOD PKWY
RICHMOND, VA 232943726
Phone: 804-756-2700
Fax: -
Web: www.childfund.org

CEO: -
CFO: James Tuite
HR: -
FYE: June 30
Type: Private

ChildFund International (CFI) serves the little ones. The worldwide non-profit organization provides education medical care food and safe water to more than 13 million children — of all faiths — in about 30 countries in Africa Asia the Caribbean Eastern Europe Latin America and the US. It works in areas of early childhood development education family income generation nutrition and sanitation. The group also tries to get child soldiers away from the military and reintegrated into daily life. Founded in 1938 as China's Children Fund the group changed its name to Christian Children's Fund in 1951. In 2009 it again renamed itself ChildFund International.

	Annual Growth	06/08	06/09	06/10	06/11	06/12
Sales ($ mil.)	1.9%	-	217.4	216.0	228.2	230.0
Net income ($ mil.)	(12.8%)	-	-	4.7	12.1	3.5
Market value ($ mil.)	-	-	-	-	-	-
Employees	-	-	-	-	-	160

CHILDREN'S HEALTH SYSTEM

1600 7th Ave. S.
Birmingham AL 35233
Phone: 205-939-9100
Fax: 205-939-9064
Web: www.chsys.org

CEO: -
CFO: -
HR: Douglas Dean
FYE: December 31
Type: Private - Not-for-Pr

Children's Health System is an integrated health network that operates Birmingham's Children's Hospital and a group of medical offices clinics and outpatient facilities located primarily in the Greater Birmingham area. Not-for-profit Children's Hospital is licensed for about 275 beds and provides treatment for pediatric cancers blood disorders sickle cell disease and many other childhood illnesses. It serves as a Level 1 trauma center and houses a regional burn center a poison control center and a pediatric dialysis facility. Founded in 1911 Children's Hospital is also a teaching hospital for the University of Alabama at Birmingham.

CHILDREN'S HEALTH SYSTEM INC.

601 Children's Ln.
Norfolk VA 23507
Phone: 757-668-7500
Fax: 757-668-7745
Web: www.chkd.org

CEO: -
CFO: -
HR: -
FYE: June 30
Type: Private - Not-for-Pr

You don't have to be royalty to be a patient at Children's Hospital of The King's Daughters (CHKD). CHKD is Virginia's only free-standing full-service pediatric facility and as such provides medical dental and therapeutic services to children and adolescents through the age of 21 years old. The 210-bed hospital has a staff of more than 500 physicians and has the state's only dedicated pediatric emergency center which gets more than 47000 patient visits each year. CHKD also operates several outpatient pediatric centers throughout the state. The not-for-profit system was formed in 1961.

CHILDREN'S HOSPITAL & MEDICAL CENTER

8200 Dodge St.
Omaha NE 68114
Phone: 402-955-5400
Fax: 608-873-2355
Web: www.stoughtonhospital.com

CEO: –
CFO: –
HR: –
FYE: December 31
Type: Private - Not-for-Pr

Junior Cornhuskers can have their medical needs met at Children's Hospital & Medical Center. The not-for-profit center Nebraska's only pediatric hospital (and a top US children's hospital) is a 150-bed facility offering pediatric inpatient services. It also operates two urgent care centers in Omaha and outreach clinics in Lincoln Nebraska and Sioux City Iowa. The main hospital facilities in Omaha have neonatal and pediatric intensive care units along with units dedicated surgery child development eating disorders and conditions including asthma allergies cardiac care diabetes nephrology and respiratory care. Children's serves as the teaching hospital for the University of Nebraska and Creighton University.

CHILDREN'S HOSPITAL AND HEALTH SYSTEM

9000 W. Wisconsin Ave.
Wauwatosa WI 53266
Phone: 414-266-2000
Fax: 414-266-6377
Web: www.chw.org

CEO: –
CFO: Tim Birkenstock
HR: Brigitte Hodges
FYE: December 31
Type: Private - Not-for-Pr

The Children's Hospital and Health System serves children and their families in Milwaukee and throughout the Great Lakes region. Its dozen entities dedicated to pediatric health care include the flagship 300-bed Children's Hospital of Wisconsin which is also an affiliate of the Medical College of Wisconsin. Satellite facilities include the Fox Valley hospital as well as a surgical center specialty care clinics in Wisconsin and Illinois and research facilities. The organization also has a network of affiliated primary care pediatricians and manages an HMO that covers Medicaid recipients (children and adults) in several Wisconsin counties.

CHILDREN'S HOSPITAL COLORADO

Anschutz Medical Campus 13123 E. 16th Ave.
Aurora CO 80045
Phone: 720-777-1234
Fax: 607-779-3440
Web: www.crowleyfoods.com

CEO: James Shmerling
CFO: –
HR: –
FYE: December 31
Type: Private - Not-for-Pr

Rocky Mountain rugrats can count on Children's Hospital Colorado (formerly The Children's Hospital Association). The not-for-profit organization runs a network of health facilities in Colorado anchored by its nearly 50-acre main campus in Aurora. The campus includes a 320-bed inpatient hospital and numerous outpatient clinics. Children's Hospital Colorado also operates more than a dozen satellite locations in and around Denver that specialize in providing children with emergency and specialty care. Affiliated with the University of Colorado Denver School of Medicine the hospital provides medical training and performs a wide range of research into pediatric illnesses including cancer and HIV/AIDS.

CHILDREN'S HOSPITAL MEDICAL CENTER

3333 BURNET AVE
CINCINNATI, OH 45229-3039
Phone: 513-636-4200
Fax: –
Web: www.cincinnatichildrens.org

CEO: James M Anderson
CFO: Teresa Bowling
HR: –
FYE: June 30
Type: Private

Cincinnati Children's Hospital Medical Center has a special place in its heart for kids — and vice versa. The pediatric health care facility offers specialty treatments for children and adolescents suffering from just about any malady including ailments of the heart and liver as well as blood diseases and cancer. Cincinnati Children's Hospital has some 590 beds and operates about a dozen outpatient care centers. Founded in 1883 the not-for-profit hospital runs the only Level 1 pediatric trauma center in the region and serves as a teaching and research facility for the University of Cincinnati College of Medicine.

	Annual Growth	06/04	06/05	06/09	06/10	06/11
Sales ($ mil.)	10.9%	–	912.5	1,487.9	1,590.4	1,693.4
Net income ($ mil.)	18.0%	–	19.7	(281.6)	78.3	53.4
Market value ($ mil.)	–	–	–	–	–	–
Employees	–	–	–	–	–	7,700

CHILDREN'S HOSPITAL OF ORANGE COUNTY

455 S. Main St.
Orange CA 92868-3874
Phone: 714-997-3000
Fax: 714-532-8434
Web: www.choc.org

CEO: Kimberly C Cripe
CFO: Kerri Ruppert
HR: –
FYE: June 30
Type: Private - Not-for-Pr

Children's Hospital of Orange County (aka CHOC) fights kid-sized ailments in southern California. The not-for-profit hospital's main campus in Orange has about 240 beds and provides a comprehensive range of care to young patients including pediatric and neonatal intensive care. Its CHOC Mission facility (located within the Mission Hospital in Mission Viejo) has nearly 50 beds for pediatric patients as well as neonatal and pediatric ICUs. CHOC also runs a handful of primary care community clinics and several mobile clinics. It also conducts research and educational programs. The hospital was founded in 1964.

CHILDREN'S HOSPITAL OF PITTSBURGH OF UPMC HEALTH SYSTEM

3705 5th Ave.
Pittsburgh PA 15213
Phone: 412-692-5325
Fax: 412-692-6920
Web: www.chp.edu

CEO: –
CFO: –
HR: –
FYE: June 30
Type: Subsidiary

From polio to poison control Children's Hospital of Pittsburgh has long been at the forefront of children's health care. Jonas Salk developed the polio vaccine there in the 1950s and the ubiquitous Mr. Yuk poison label also got its start there. Founded in 1890 the hospital cares for thousands of sick kids each year — both those who stay in one of its 300 inpatient beds and those who visit its outpatient ambulatory surgery and primary care centers. The hospital's doctors handle everything from flu to organ transplantation and they engage in wide-ranging pediatric medical research as well much of it funded by grants from the National Institutes of Health.

CHILDREN'S PLACE, INC. (THE) NMS: PLCE

500 Plaza Drive
Secaucus, NJ 07094
Phone: 201-558-2400
Fax: –
Web: www.childrensplace.com

CEO: –
CFO: Michael (Mel) Scarpa
HR: Lawrence McClure
FYE: January 31
Type: Public

The Children's Place is the largest pure-play children's specialty apparel retail in North America (ahead of Gymboree). It operates some 960 Children's Place stores primarily in malls and outlet centers throughout the US and Puerto Rico as well as nearly 135 stores in Canada. It has more than 70 international stores operated by franchise partners. It also sells apparel online. The Children's Place outfits children from newborn to 12 years old in its own brand of value-priced apparel shoes and accessories most of which is produced by manufacturers. About 85% of its sales come from stores in the US.

	Annual Growth	01/11	01/12*	02/13	02/14*	01/15
Sales ($ mil.)	1.3%	1,674.0	1,715.9	1,809.5	1,765.8	1,761.3
Net income ($ mil.)	(9.0%)	83.1	77.2	63.2	53.0	56.9
Market value ($ mil.)	9.1%	889.4	1,053.1	1,042.1	1,108.2	1,261.3
Employees	(4.5%)	19,200	18,900	18,300	16,500	16,000

*Fiscal year change

CHILDRENS HOSPITAL MEDICAL CENTER OF AKRON

1 PERKINS SQ
AKRON, OH 443081063
Phone: 330-543-1000
Fax: –
Web: www.akronchildrens.org

CEO: William H. (Bill) Considine
CFO: Michael Trainer
HR: Walt Schwoeble
FYE: December 31
Type: Private

What started as a nursery more than 100 years ago but has since turned into the largest pediatric health care system in northeast Ohio? If you guessed Akron Children's Hospital you'd be right on the money. The health system operates through more than 80 locations scattered around the state including its flagship 253-bed hospital in Akron. Among Children's specialized services are cardiology orthopedics rehabilitation and home care. It also has a second 50-bed inpatient hospital called the Akron Children's Beeghly Campus. The main hospital's emergency department treats nearly 70000 patients each year. Its regional burn center sees about 3700 visits per year.

	Annual Growth	12/07	12/08	12/09	12/12	12/13
Sales ($ mil.)	10.0%	–	387.7	438.4	579.6	623.3
Net income ($ mil.)	15.1%	–	–	46.1	46.9	80.9
Market value ($ mil.)	–	–	–	–	–	–
Employees	–	–	–	–	–	4,763

CHILDREN'S MEDICAL CENTER OF DALLAS

1935 MEDICAL DISTRICT DR
DALLAS, TX 752357701
Phone: 214-456-7000
Fax: –
Web: www.childrens.com

CEO: Christopher J. Share
CFO: Ray Dziesinski
HR: Kimberly Besse
FYE: December 31
Type: Private

Sick kiddos in North Texas who need specialized care don't have to travel far to find it. Children's Medical Center of Dallas (operating as Children's Health) treats children with various medical needs from birth to age 18. Specialties include craniofacial deformities cystic fibrosis gastroenterology cancer and heart disease. Children's is also a major pediatric center for heart kidney bone marrow and other transplant procedures. The not-for-profit hospital has about 600 beds and is the pediatric teaching facility for UT Southwestern Medical. Children's also operates a network of about 20 primary care and specialty clinics in and around Dallas in addition to its two full-service campuses.

	Annual Growth	12/03	12/04	12/05	12/06	12/08
Sales ($ mil.)	13.3%	–	–	–	579.9	744.9
Net income ($ mil.)	–	–	–	–	130.2	(4.1)
Market value ($ mil.)	–	–	–	–	–	–
Employees	–	–	–	–	–	5,318

CHILDREN'S NATIONAL MEDICAL CENTER

111 MICHIGAN AVE NW
WASHINGTON, DC 200102916
Phone: 202-476-5000
Fax: –
Web: www.childrensnational.org

CEO: Kurt D. Newman
CFO: Douglas T. Myers
HR: Christine Porto
FYE: June 30
Type: Private

Along with the National Archives and the National Mall Children's National Medical Center is a US capital city gem. Its flagship Children's Hospital which was founded in 1870 is an acute care facility with some 310 beds. It serves as a regional referral center for pediatric trauma cancer and other kinds of complex pediatric cases. Additionally it operates eight outpatient centers in DC and the Delmarva peninsula that provide specialized medical services (such as chemotherapy and outpatient surgery) and community health clinics that offer primary care to children and adolescents. Children's National Health Network links more than 900 community-based pediatricians with the specialists and services of the center.

	Annual Growth	06/04	06/05	06/06	06/07	06/09
Sales ($ mil.)	(13.8%)	–	–	–	694.6	516.6
Net income ($ mil.)	(53.6%)	–	–	–	76.3	16.4
Market value ($ mil.)	–	–	–	–	–	–
Employees	–	–	–	–	–	6,000

CHILDRESS KLEIN PROPERTIES INC.

301 S. College St. Ste. 2800
Charlotte NC 28202
Phone: 704-342-9000
Fax: 704-342-9039
Web: www.childressklein.com

CEO: J Donald Childress
CFO: Harry Clements
HR: –
FYE: December 31
Type: Private

Childress Klein develops owns leases and manages commercial real estate in the southeastern US. It owns some 20 million sq. ft. of office industrial retail and mixed-use space mostly in the Atlanta and Charlotte North Carolina metropolitan areas. (Nearly 60% of its portfolio is office buildings and business centers.) The company's projects include Atlanta Galleria and LakePointe Corporate Center as well as the Wachovia Center a two-block office residential and hospitality complex in downtown Charlotte. Childress Klein also develops retail properties ranging from strip centers to big box-anchored shopping centers.

CHILTON HOSPITAL

97 W PARKWAY
POMPTON PLAINS, NJ 074441647
Phone: 973-831-5000
Fax: –
Web: www.chiltonhealth.org

CEO: Deborah K Zastocki
CFO: –
HR: –
FYE: December 31
Type: Private

Chilton Medical Center (formerly Chilton Memorial Hospital) serves the residents of northern New Jersey's Morris and Passaic counties. The acute-care facility has some 260 beds and provides emergency diagnostic inpatient surgical and outpatient care. The hospital operates with a staff of about 650 physicians who practice in 60 fields of health care. Chilton Medical Center offers such specialties as a cancer center surgical weight-loss programs occupational health orthopedics stroke care pediatrics and dialysis. Chilton Medical Center merged with Atlantic Health System in 2014.

	Annual Growth	12/03	12/04	12/05	12/08	12/12
Sales ($ mil.)	3.1%	–	130.0	128.8	0.0	165.5
Net income ($ mil.)	21.5%	–	–	2.5	0.0	9.7
Market value ($ mil.)	–	–	–	–	–	–
Employees	–	–	–	–	–	1,188

CHIMERA INVESTMENT CORP — NYS: CIM

520 Madison Avenue, 32nd Floor
New York, NY 10022
Phone: 212 626-2300
Fax: –
Web: www.chimerareit.com
CEO: Matthew Lambiase
CFO: Robert Colligan
HR: –
FYE: December 31
Type: Public

This Chimera has the body of a mortgage real estate investment trust (REIT) but its head is that of its external manager FIDAC (Fixed Income Discount Advisory Company) a fixed-income investment management firm wholly-owned by Annaly Capital Management. Formed in 2007 Chimera invests in residential mortgage loans; residential mortgage-backed securities (RMBS) such as those guaranteed by government agencies Fannie Mae and Freddie Mac; real estate-related securities; and other assets including collateralized debt obligations or CDOs. The REIT went public in 2007 shortly after it was formed.

	Annual Growth	12/10	12/11	12/12	12/13	12/14
Sales ($ mil.)	1.1%	735.5	337.3	513.5	498.8	768.4
Net income ($ mil.)	2.5%	532.9	137.3	327.8	362.7	589.2
Market value ($ mil.)	(6.2%)	844.8	515.9	536.5	637.2	653.6
Employees		–	–	–	–	–

CHIMERIX INC. — NMS: CMRX

2505 Meridian Parkway, Suite 340
Durham, NC 27713
Phone: 919 806-1074
Fax: –
Web: www.chimerix.com
CEO: M. Michelle Berrey
CFO: Timothy W. Trost
HR: –
FYE: December 31
Type: Public

All that shimmers isn't . . . enhanced by lipid conjugate technology. Chimerix has developed technology to make molecules with therapeutic potential into oral drugs. Its lipid conjugate technology can modify drug compounds to mimic a particular lipid metabolite that is absorbed by the small intestine thus protecting the compounds from being broken down in the stomach. Chimerix is using its technology to develop lead drug candidate CMX001 to fight smallpox infections or bad reactions to smallpox vaccinations. The development-stage firm is also targeting drug-resistant HIV and hepatitis. The company went public in 2013.

	Annual Growth	12/10	12/11	12/12	12/13	12/14
Sales ($ mil.)	23.9%	1.7	12.1	33.7	4.4	4.0
Net income ($ mil.)	–	(25.5)	(25.6)	(4.4)	(36.4)	(59.3)
Market value ($ mil.)	166.4%	–	–	–	620.0	1,651.9
Employees	28.5%	–	–	46	52	76

CHINA EDUCATION ALLIANCE INC — NBB: CEAI

58 Heng Shan Road, Kun Lun Shopping Mall
Harbin, Heilongjiang 150090
Phone: (86) 451 8233 5794
Fax: –
Web: www.edu-chn.com
CEO: –
CFO: –
HR: –
FYE: December 31
Type: Public

As long as its students have Internet access China Education Alliance can do its part to educate the masses in China. Through its edu-chn.com site China Education offers online test preparation and tutoring to K-12 students and it provides a database of some 350000 exams and courseware to college secondary and elementary school teachers and instructors. The company also offers on-site tutoring through its Heilongjiang Province-based facility as well as vocational and managerial training services through 360ve.com. China Education which operates primarily through subsidiaries was formed as a shell company in 2004 to acquire education businesses; it became a publicly-traded company later that year.

	Annual Growth	12/10	12/11	12/12	12/13	12/14
Sales ($ mil.)	(50.7%)	46.3	34.8	11.7	6.7	2.7
Net income ($ mil.)		15.3	6.1	(14.1)	(24.7)	(37.4)
Market value ($ mil.)	(61.2%)	26.4	6.4	4.4	2.7	0.6
Employees	27.2%	409	509	615	914	1,071

CHINA RECYCLING ENERGY CORP — NAS: CREG

12/F, Tower A, Chang An International Building, No. 88 Nan Guan Zheng Jie
Xi An City, Shaan Xi Province 710068
Phone: (86) 29 8765 1097
Fax: –
Web: www.creg-cn.com
CEO: –
CFO: –
HR: –
FYE: December 31
Type: Public

Pressure heat and gas may be unpleasant to some but it's all part of the cycle at China Recycling Energy (CREG). The company through subsidiary Shanghai TCH Energy sells and leases equipment that captures waste from large industrial operations and converts it into energy to be used by the company that created the waste. CREG has installed its units which mostly use turbines to generate electricity at steel mills petrochemical and chemical refineries cement manufacturers and mining operations. The company offers turn-key installations as well as engineering design financing procurement installation and testing services. It was formed in 1980 but took its current name and focus in 2007.

	Annual Growth	12/10	12/11	12/12	12/13	12/14
Sales ($ mil.)	(28.6%)	75.6	31.3	1.2	63.2	19.7
Net income ($ mil.)	5.4%	16.0	21.4	3.4	15.6	19.8
Market value ($ mil.)	(29.5%)	253.2	99.6	82.3	285.6	62.5
Employees	(4.2%)	214	170	166	166	180

CHINDEX INTERNATIONAL INC — NMS: CHDX

4340 East West Highway, Suite 1100
Bethesda, MD 20814
Phone: 301 215-7777
Fax: 301 215-7719
Web: www.chindex.com
CEO: Roberta Lipson
CFO: –
HR: –
FYE: December 31
Type: Public

Chindex International provides health care services through its United Family Healthcare (UFH) network of private hospitals and satellite medical clinics in Beijing Shanghai Tianjin and Guangzhou. The growing network's hospitals have a combined licensed bed count of about 200 and cater primarily to the expatriate community and to affluent Chinese patients. Chindex also operates a joint venture — Chindex Medical Limited (CML) — with Shanghai Fosun Pharmaceutical to distribute medical equipment and supplies including diagnostic imaging and robotic surgery systems to hospitals in China and Hong Kong. Western manufacturers including Siemens Hologic and Candela supply these medical products.

	Annual Growth	03/09	03/10*	12/10	12/11	12/12
Sales ($ mil.)	(3.8%)	171.4	171.2	136.7	114.4	152.4
Net income ($ mil.)	(6.2%)	5.0	8.2	5.8	3.2	4.1
Market value ($ mil.)	28.3%	84.8	201.6	281.4	145.4	179.2
Employees	11.1%	1,276	1,328	1,090	1,448	1,749

*Fiscal year change

CHIPOTLE MEXICAN GRILL INC — NYS: CMG

1401 Wynkoop Street, Suite 500
Denver, CO 80202
Phone: 303 595-4000
Fax: –
Web: www.chipotle.com
CEO: M. Steven (Steve) Ells
CFO: John R. (Jack) Hartung
HR: –
FYE: December 31
Type: Public

You might say this company is spicing up the restaurant business. Chipotle Mexican Grill owns and operates more than 1900 quick-casual eateries popular for their burritos and other Mexican food items. Customers can build a 1-1/4 pound burrito from a lineup that includes chicken steak barbecue or free-range pork as well as beans rice guacamole and various other veggies and salsas. The company claims that with extras its menu offers more than 65000 choices. Chipotle restaurants also serve soft tacos crispy tacos chips and salsa beer and margaritas.

	Annual Growth	12/11	12/12	12/13	12/14	12/15
Sales ($ mil.)	18.7%	2,269.5	2,731.2	3,214.6	4,108.3	4,501.2
Net income ($ mil.)	22.0%	214.9	278.0	327.4	445.4	475.6
Market value ($ mil.)	9.2%	10,329.4	9,097.5	16,294.5	20,935.1	14,675.7
Employees	17.7%	30,940	37,310	45,340	53,090	59,330

CHIPPEWA VALLEY BEAN COMPANY INC.

N2960 730TH ST
MENOMONIE, WI 547516615
Phone: 715-664-8342
Fax: –
Web: www.cvbean.com

CEO: –
CFO: –
HR: –
FYE: November 30
Type: Private

Chippewa Valley Bean has found its niche in the world through kidney beans. The company processes and wholesales dried light and dark red kidney beans. It grows and purchases beans grown on irrigated land in Wisconsin and three adjacent states. Chippewa Valley Bean's processing facility handles 40 million pounds of kidney beans every year. It exports its products to European and developing countries. The company also deals in pinto beans and dried green peas and sells prepackaged bean soups. Chippewa Valley Bean is a family-owned and -operated business.

	Annual Growth	11/08	11/09	11/10	11/11	11/12
Sales ($ mil.)	2.4%	–	22.4	19.8	17.2	24.0
Net income ($ mil.)	(14.2%)	–	–	0.8	0.1	0.6
Market value ($ mil.)	–	–	–	–	–	–
Employees	–	–	–	–	–	15

CHIQUITA BRANDS INTERNATIONAL, INC.   NYS: CQB

550 South Caldwell Street
Charlotte, NC 28202
Phone: 980 636-5000
Fax: –
Web: www.chiquita.com

CEO: Brian Kocher
CFO: –
HR: –
FYE: December 31
Type: Public

As one of the world's top banana producers Chiquita Brands deals in big bunches. The company grows procures markets and sells bananas and other fresh fruits and vegetables under the Chiquita name and several others. Bananas account for about 65% of Chiquita's sales. Its other offerings include whole citrus fruits melons grapes apples and tomatoes as well as packaged fresh-cut items processed fruit ingredients and juices. The company's Fresh Express unit generates about a third of sales and is the leading US seller of packaged ready-to-eat salads. Chiquita's products are sold in nearly 70 countries mainly in North America and Europe. Lesser markets include the Middle East Japan and South Korea.

	Annual Growth	12/08	12/09	12/10	12/11	12/12
Sales ($ mil.)	(3.9%)	3,609.4	3,470.4	3,227.4	3,139.3	3,078.3
Net income ($ mil.)	–	–	(323.7)	90.5	57.4	56.8	(405.0)
Market value ($ mil.)	(13.6%)	684.6	835.6	649.4	386.3	382.1
Employees	(3.4%)	23,000	21,000	21,000	21,000	20,000

CHOICE HOTELS INTERNATIONAL, INC.   NYS: CHH

1 Choice Hotels Circle, Suite 400
Rockville, MD 20850
Phone: 301 592-5000
Fax: –
Web: www.choicehotels.com

CEO: Stephen P. Joyce
CFO: David L. White
HR: Patrick (Paddy) Cimerola
FYE: December 31
Type: Public

This company offers a lot of hospitality choices. Choice Hotels is a leading hotel franchisor with more than 6500 locations throughout the US and more than 35 other countries. Its flagship brands include Comfort Inn one of the largest limited-service brands with about 3000 properties (including Comfort Suites) along with Quality Inn which serves the midscale hotel segment. Its Econo Lodge chain offers lodging primarily for budget-minded travelers. Other Choice Hotels brands include the full-service Clarion chain Rodeway Inn budget hotels and Sleep Inn.

	Annual Growth	12/10	12/11	12/12	12/13	12/14
Sales ($ mil.)	6.2%	596.1	638.8	691.5	724.3	758.0
Net income ($ mil.)	3.5%	107.4	110.4	120.7	112.6	123.2
Market value ($ mil.)	10.0%	2,194.3	2,181.7	1,927.7	2,815.9	3,212.1
Employees	(3.3%)	1,524	1,431	1,095	1,088	1,331

CHOICEONE FINANCIAL SERVICES, INC.   NBB: COFS

109 East Division
Sparta, MI 49345
Phone: 616 887-7366
Fax: –
Web: www.choiceone.com

CEO: James A Bosserd
CFO: –
HR: –
FYE: December 31
Type: Public

One choice for a place to park your money is ChoiceOne Financial Services. The institution is the holding company for ChoiceOne Bank which has more than a dozen offices in the western part of Michigan's Lower Peninsula. The bank serves consumers and area businesses offering checking and savings accounts CDs investment planning and other services. Real estate loans including residential and commercial mortgages constitute more than two-thirds of the company's loan portfolio. Agricultural consumer and business loans help to round out the bank's lending activities. ChoiceOne Financial Services sells life health and disability coverage through its ChoiceOne Insurance Agencies subsidiaries.

	Annual Growth	12/10	12/11	12/12	12/13	12/14
Assets ($ mil.)	3.4%	480.5	495.9	508.9	514.6	549.6
Net income ($ mil.)	20.4%	2.7	3.5	4.3	5.1	5.7
Market value ($ mil.)	17.6%	39.6	40.4	47.6	56.3	75.8
Employees	(1.3%)	159	146	147	153	151

CHRISTIAN CASEY LLC

1710 Broadway
New York NY 10019-5254
Phone: 212-500-2200
Fax: 216-581-4970
Web: www.gebauer.com

CEO: –
CFO: –
HR: –
FYE: December 31
Type: Subsidiary

While Diddy is considered a bad boy in the music industry he's busy making a name for his bad boys in fashion circles. Founded by Sean "Diddy" Combs in 1998 and named for his second son Christian Casey designs produces and distributes high-end urban fashion and accessories targeted to trendy males and females. Diddy's Bad Boy Entertainment owns Christian Casey which operates as Sean John Clothing. The apparel firm opened several stores in recent years and formed a joint venture called Outspoke with Zac Posen. Christian Casey has signed numerous licensing agreements for apparel related to its clothing a Sean John fragrance with Estee Lauder and Ciroc Vodka through a partnership with Diageo.

CHRISTIAN FOUNDATION FOR CHILDREN AND AGING

1 ELMWOOD AVE
KANSAS CITY, KS 661033719
Phone: 913-384-6500
Fax: –
Web: www.cfcausa.org

CEO: Scott Wasserman
CFO: –
HR: –
FYE: December 31
Type: Private

The Christian Foundation for Children and Aging (CFCA) may seem at cross purposes but it helps the poor on both ends of the age spectrum. The lay Catholic not-for-profit organization works in about two dozen countries in Africa Asia The Americas and Caribbean. CFCA provides services for children and the elderly in areas such as education medical care clothing and nutrition. It sets up relationships between more than 270000 sponsors in the US and about 310000 who need assistance in countries like Bolivia El Salvador Guatemala India Tanzania and Uganda. CFCA was founded in 1981 by a group of missionaries including its president Bob Hentzen.

	Annual Growth	12/08	12/09	12/10	12/11	12/12
Sales ($ mil.)	2.6%	–	107.4	109.4	110.1	115.8
Net income ($ mil.)	(3.3%)	–	–	2.1	0.8	2.0
Market value ($ mil.)	–	–	–	–	–	–
Employees	–	–	–	–	–	130

CHRISTIAN HOSPITAL NORTHEAST - NORTHWEST

11133 DUNN RD
SAINT LOUIS, MO 631366119
Phone: 314-355-2300
Fax: –
Web: www.christianhospital.org

CEO: –
CFO: –
HR: –
FYE: December 31
Type: Private

Christian or heathen if you're in the St. Louis area and need medical care Christian Hospital wants to help. The not-for-profit hospital which has some 485 beds is part of BJC HealthCare. Established in 1903 it specializes in a range of treatment areas including diabetes and cancer care and cardiothoracic surgery. Its more than 430 physicians also offer services in 40 other specialties from primary care to pulmonology. Christian Hospital offers a comprehensive mental health and substance abuse program that includes an inpatient option as well as specialization in geriatric mental wellness. The hospital is headed by president Ron McMullen a long-time health care administrator.

	Annual Growth	12/95	12/96	12/97	12/00	12/08
Sales ($ mil.)	0.3%	–	–	206.6	207.3	213.6
Net income ($ mil.)	–	–	–	5.4	(20.6)	(24.9)
Market value ($ mil.)	–	–	–	–	–	–
Employees	–	–	–	–	–	2,493

CHRISTIANA CARE HEALTH SYSTEM

501 W. 14th St.
Wilmington DE 19801
Phone: 302-733-1900
Fax: 302-428-5770
Web: www.christianacare.org

CEO: –
CFO: –
HR: –
FYE: June 30
Type: Private - Not-for-Pr

Christiana Care Health System cares for the Brandywine Valley. The not-for-profit health care network serves patients in northern Delaware and surrounding areas of Pennsylvania Maryland and New Jersey. The company operates Christiana Hospital and Wilmington Hospital which together have some 1100 beds. The hospitals provide cardiac care cancer treatment women's health pediatrics rehabilitation general medicine and surgery. Other specialties include urology and gastroenterology. The system also operates area physician clinics and offers home health and adult day care services. In addition Christiana Care conducts education training and research programs.

CHRISTOPHER & BANKS CORP.

NYS: CBK

2400 Xenium Lane North
Plymouth, MN 55441
Phone: 763 551-5000
Fax: –
Web: www.christopherandbanks.com

CEO: Larry C. Barenbaum
CFO: Peter G. Michielutti
HR: –
FYE: January 31
Type: Public

Women's specialty apparel retailer Christopher & Banks has been slimming down. The largely mall-based chain sells moderately priced private-label women's casual fashions through more than 550 locations (down from 830). Its portfolio of stores span some 45 states operating under the Christopher & Banks and C.J. Banks banners. It also operates outlet and MPW dual-concept stores which offer merchandise from both Christopher & Banks and C.J. Banks and sells items online. Christopher & Banks targets women ages 45 to 55 with missy petite and women's fashions. While Aria Partners had offered to buy the company for $1.75 per share Christopher & Banks rejected the offer.

	Annual Growth	02/11*	01/12*	02/13	02/14*	01/15
Sales ($ mil.)	(1.7%)	448.1	412.8	430.3	435.8	418.6
Net income ($ mil.)	–	(22.2)	(71.1)	(16.1)	8.7	47.1
Market value ($ mil.)	(4.0%)	226.7	76.8	236.0	263.7	192.4
Employees	(7.9%)	6,400	6,400	5,500	5,050	4,605

*Fiscal year change

CHRISTOPHER RANCH LLC

305 BLOOMFIELD AVE
GILROY, CA 950209565
Phone: 408-847-1100
Fax: –
Web: www.christopherranch.com

CEO: –
CFO: –
HR: –
FYE: December 31
Type: Private

There are probably a lot of breath mints available at Christopher Ranch the largest garlic producer in the US. Christopher Ranch sells dozens of types of fresh and jarred garlic as well as specialty onions sun-dried tomatoes broccoli dried chilies herbs and spices. Christopher Ranch nestled in California's Santa Clara Valley ships more than 60 million pounds of garlic every year to foodservice companies and grocery stores such as Kroger Safeway and Whole Foods. Its garlic is also exclusively used in Michael Angelo's frozen foods. Christopher Ranch was founded in 1953 by brothers Don and Art Christopher. Don's son Bill now runs the company.

	Annual Growth	12/05	12/06	12/07	12/08	12/09
Sales ($ mil.)	–	–	–	(1,847.1)	111.3	108.5
Net income ($ mil.)	2707.7%	–	–	0.0	7.0	12.9
Market value ($ mil.)	–	–	–	–	–	–
Employees	–	–	–	–	–	200

CHRISTUS HEALTH

919 HIDDEN RDG
IRVING, TX 750383813
Phone: 469-282-2000
Fax: –

CEO: Ernie W. Sadau
CFO: Randolph W. Safady
HR: –
FYE: June 30
Type: Private

In CHRISTUS there is no east or west but plenty of care nonetheless. The not-for-profit Catholic health care system operates about 350 medical facilities from its more than 60 hospitals including general hospitals and long-term acute care facilities to clinics and outpatient centers. It operates mostly in Louisiana and Texas where its hospitals are but also has facilities in Arkansas Georgia Iowa Missouri and New Mexico and in six states in Mexico and one in Chile. In addition to its acute care facilities CHRISTUS runs medical groups home health and hospice agencies and senior living facilities. Specialized services include oncology pediatrics rehabilitation and women's and children's health care.

	Annual Growth	06/07	06/08	06/09	06/10	06/13
Sales ($ mil.)	(34.3%)	–	–	3,466.3	3,653.6	646.8
Net income ($ mil.)	–	–	–	(411.3)	55.7	124.5
Market value ($ mil.)	–	–	–	–	–	–
Employees	–	–	–	–	–	25,000

CHRISTUS HEALTH CENTRAL LOUISIANA

3330 MASONIC DR
ALEXANDRIA, LA 713013841
Phone: 318-487-1122
Fax: –
Web: www.christushealth.org

CEO: Stephen Wright
CFO: –
HR: –
FYE: June 30
Type: Private

CHRISTUS St. Frances Cabrini Hospital provides a wide range of medical services to the denizens of Alexandria Louisiana. If you're ailing down south there's not much the hospital can't do to help especially in the area of cancer. Founded in 1950 the 240-bed St. Frances Cabrini Hospital has a staff of more than 320 physicians providing services that include emergency care women's health surgery and cardiology. For the insomniacs among us the hospital provides specialized care through its sleep center. St. Francis Cabrini's parent company is one of the nation's major hospital operators — with about 50 facilities located around the country.

	Annual Growth	06/07	06/08	06/09	06/10	06/13
Sales ($ mil.)	–	–	(1,027.0)	217.4	219.5	222.3
Net income ($ mil.)	33.3%	–	–	1.6	(0.6)	5.0
Market value ($ mil.)	–	–	–	–	–	–
Employees	–	–	–	–	–	1,287

CHRISTUS ST. CATHERINE HOSPITAL

701 S. Fry Rd.
Katy TX 77450
Phone: 281-599-5700
Fax: 281-398-2265
Web: www.christusstcatherine.org

CEO: Jack McCabe
CFO: –
HR: –
FYE: June 30
Type: Subsidiary

CHRISTUS St. Catherine Hospital serves the Houston-area community of Katy Texas with acute health care services. The hospital which has about 100 beds offers a variety of adult pediatric and surgical medical care services to patients in Katy and surrounding areas. Specialized services include emergency medicine cardiac and orthopedic care rehabilitation women's health home health care and medical imaging and sleep centers. It also offers cancer care through a partnership with the University of Texas MD Anderson Cancer Center. The hospital is part of the not-for-profit CHRISTUS Health system which includes more than 40 hospitals and other facilities in the US and Mexico.

CHRYSLER GROUP LLC

1000 Chrysler Dr.
Auburn Hills MI 48326-2766
Phone: 248-599-5741
Fax: 908-903-2027
Web: www.chubb.com

CEO: Fred Diaz
CFO: Richard K Palmer
HR: –
FYE: December 31
Type: Private

Chrysler hopes its crisis remains in its rearview mirror. After engineering an automotive resurrection by choosing a back-to-basics alliance with Fiat in 2009 the carmaker continues to manufacture its Chrysler brands including its Dodge Dart Fiat 500 Jeep Grand Cherokee SRT8 Jeep Wrangler Town & Country and Ram 1500 vehicles. Chrysler's trademarked MOPAR (MOtor PARts) automobile parts and service division carries almost 300000 parts options and accessories for vehicle customization. Chrysler Group LLC emerged from a US government backed Chapter 11 bankruptcy in mid-2009. It was first founded by Walter Chrysler and organized as Chrysler Corporation in 1925.

CHRISTY SPORTS L.L.C.

875 PARFET ST
LAKEWOOD, CO 802155507
Phone: 303-237-6321
Fax: –
Web: www.patio.christysports.com

CEO: Patrick O'Winter
CFO: Liz Avery
HR: –
FYE: April 30
Type: Private

Christy Sports isn't some girly group of ponytailed cheerleaders. It's the largest specialty ski and snowboard retailer in the Rocky Mountains. With more than 40 retail stores in skiing hot spots like Snowmass Crested Butte Steamboat Springs and Vail the company sells skiing snowboarding snowshoeing mountain biking and golf equipment along with shoes shirts gloves and bags to carry it all. Stores also carry patio furniture grills hammocks and other accessories for the outdoor life and rent skiing and snowboarding gear. Christy's staff are all serious skiers and snowboarders who use the equipment they sell. The company was founded in 1958 by avid skiers Ed and Gale Crist.

	Annual Growth	04/09	04/10	04/11	04/12	04/13
Sales ($ mil.)	5.3%	–	50.4	56.5	56.0	59.0
Net income ($ mil.)	20.0%	–	–	2.4	1.5	3.5
Market value ($ mil.)	–	–	–	–	–	–
Employees	–	–	–	–	–	450

CHS INC

5500 Cenex Drive
Inver Grove Heights, MN 55077
Phone: 651 355-6000
Fax: –
Web: www.chsinc.com

NMS: CHSC M
CEO: Carl M. Casale
CFO: Timothy Skidmore
HR: –
FYE: August 31
Type: Public

CHS goes with the grain. The company is a leading publicly traded cooperative marketer of grain oilseed and energy resources in the US. It represents farmers ranchers and co-ops from the Great Lakes to Texas. CHS trades grain and sells farm supplies through its stores to members. The group processes soybeans for use in food and animal feeds and grinds wheat into flour. Through joint ventures and a variety of business segments it sells soybean oil and crop nutrient products and markets grain. CHS also provides insurance financial and risk-management services and operates petroleum refineries to sell Cenex-brand fuels lubricants and other energy products.

	Annual Growth	08/11	08/12	08/13	08/14	08/15
Sales ($ mil.)	(1.6%)	36,915.8	40,599.3	44,479.9	42,664.0	34,582.4
Net income ($ mil.)	(5.1%)	961.4	1,260.6	992.4	1,081.4	781.0
Market value ($ mil.)	–	–	–	–	–	0.0
Employees	7.0%	9,562	10,216	10,716	11,824	12,511

CHROMADEX CORP

10005 Muirlands Blvd., Suite G
Irvine, CA 92618
Phone: 949 419-0288
Fax: –

NBB: CDXC
CEO: Frank Jaksch Jr
CFO: Thomas Varvaro
HR: –
FYE: January 03
Type: Public

ChromaDex can talk a blue streak about the health benefits of blueberries. The company markets pterostilbene a plant-based chemical found in blueberries that is said to lower cholesterol and reduce the risk of cancer. Sold under the brand pTeroPure the phytochemical is used in about 20 different nutritional supplements including Nutraceutical's Solaray Super Resveratrol with Pterostilbene. ChromaDex also launched its own line of supplements in 2011 called BluScience that are sold at GNC and Walgreens. Biotech investor Philip Frost the chairman of Teva Pharmaceuticals owns almost 20% of ChromaDex.

	Annual Growth	01/11*	12/11	12/12	12/13*	01/15
Sales ($ mil.)	19.3%	7.6	8.1	11.6	10.2	15.3
Net income ($ mil.)	–	(2.1)	(7.9)	(11.7)	(4.4)	(5.4)
Market value ($ mil.)	(9.8%)	143.2	57.9	58.5	168.4	94.7
Employees	5.4%	60	64	73	69	74

*Fiscal year change

CHUBB CORP.

15 Mountain View Road
Warren, NJ 07059
Phone: 908 903-2000
Fax: 908 903-2003
Web: www.chubb.com

NYS: CB
CEO: –
CFO: –
HR: –
FYE: December 31
Type: Public

Here's the skinny on Chubb: The insurer is best known for comprehensive personal homeowners insurance for the demographic that owns yachts (the company insures those too). Chubb also offers commercial property/casualty insurance including multiple peril property and marine and workers' compensation. Its specialty insurance arm offers professional liability policies for executives across a spectrum of industries and also provides construction and commercial surety bonds. Chubb distributes its products through 8500 independent agents and brokers in 120 offices across the US and in more than 25 countries. The company began in 1882 when Thomas Chubb and his son began writing marine insurance in New York City.

	Annual Growth	12/09	12/10	12/11	12/12	12/13
Assets ($ mil.)	(0.0%)	50,449.0	50,249.0	50,865.0	52,184.0	50,433.0
Net income ($ mil.)	1.8%	2,183.0	2,174.0	1,678.0	1,545.0	2,345.0
Market value ($ mil.)	18.4%	12,211.7	14,809.0	17,187.8	18,702.4	23,993.9
Employees	0.0%	10,200	10,100	10,100	10,200	10,200

CHUGACH ALASKA CORPORATION

3800 CENTERPOINT DR # 700
ANCHORAGE, AK 995035825
Phone: 907-563-8866
Fax: –
Web: www.chugach-ak.com

CEO: Gabriel Kompkoff
CFO: –
HR: –
FYE: December 31
Type: Private

At the heart of Chugach Alaska Corporation is a vision of indigenous people running their own businesses on their own land. Chugach Alaska was formed following the activation of the Alaska Native Claims Settlement Act (which was passed by the US Congress in 1971) to provide land management services for the 928000-acre Chugach region of Alaska. The company derives the bulk of its sales from oil and gas production mining commercial timber and tourist activities that occur in the region and from its engagement in military base construction projects at more than 30 locations in Alaska the US Pacific Northwest and the Western Pacific. Chugach Alaska's shareholders consist of Aleut Eskimo and Indian natives.

	Annual Growth	12/09	12/10	12/11	12/12	12/13
Sales ($ mil.)	(13.4%)	–	937.0	765.8	708.8	609.0
Net income ($ mil.)	(9.6%)	–	–	24.1	20.3	19.7
Market value ($ mil.)	–	–	–	–	–	–
Employees	–	–	–	–	–	4,822

CHUGACH ELECTRIC ASSOCIATION, INC.

5601 Electron Drive
Anchorage, AK 99518
Phone: 907 563-7494
Fax: –
Web: www.chugachelectric.com

CEO: Bradley W Evans
CFO: Sherri McKay-Highers
HR: Tyler E Andrews
FYE: December 31
Type: Public

Deriving its name from an old Eskimo tribal word Chugach Electric Association generates transmits distributes and sells electricity in Alaska's railbelt region. This area extends from the coastal Chugach Mountains into central Alaska and includes the state's two largest cities (Anchorage and Fairbanks). The member-owned cooperative utility has 530 MW of generating capacity from its natural gas-fired and hydroelectric power plants. Serving 80300 metered retail locations Chugach Electric the largest electric utility in Alaska also sells wholesale power to other municipal and cooperative utilities in the region.

	Annual Growth	12/10	12/11	12/12	12/13	12/14
Sales ($ mil.)	2.2%	258.3	283.6	267.0	305.3	281.3
Net income ($ mil.)	4.8%	5.4	5.6	5.5	10.5	6.5
Market value ($ mil.)	–	–	–	–	–	–
Employees	(0.8%)	311	318	318	319	301

CHURCH & DWIGHT CO., INC.   NYS: CHD

500 Charles Ewing Boulevard
Ewing, NJ 08628
Phone: 609 806-1200
Fax: 609 497-7269
Web: www.churchdwight.com

CEO: Matthew T. Farrell
CFO: Matthew T Farrell
HR: Jacquelin J. (Jackie) Brova
FYE: December 31
Type: Public

Whether you call it saleratus (aerated salt) sodium bicarbonate or plain old baking soda Church & Dwight is a top maker worldwide of the powder under the ARM & HAMMER name. The consumer products company has expanded the key brand into a products portfolio powerhouse with laundry detergent (the company's top consumer business by sales) bathroom cleaners carpet deodorizer air fresheners toothpaste antiperspirants industrial-grade carbonates cat litter and animal nutrition. The company's other brand names include XTRA Oxiclean Nair First Response Orajel and SpinBrush. Church & Dwight which operates globally also makes Trojan-brand condoms.

	Annual Growth	12/10	12/11	12/12	12/13	12/14
Sales ($ mil.)	6.2%	2,589.2	2,749.3	2,921.9	3,194.3	3,297.6
Net income ($ mil.)	11.2%	270.7	309.6	349.8	394.4	413.9
Market value ($ mil.)	3.4%	9,203.9	6,102.2	7,143.6	8,838.5	10,509.4
Employees	3.9%	3,600	3,500	4,400	4,200	4,200

CHURCH MUTUAL INSURANCE COMPANY

3000 Schuster Ln.
Merrill WI 54452
Phone: 715-536-5577
Fax: 715-539-4650
Web: www.churchmutual.com

CEO: Michael E Ravn
CFO: Daniel T Vander Heiden
HR: –
FYE: December 31
Type: Private - Mutual Com

A reverend a deacon and an insurance salesman walk into a bar... Perhaps not but they do have business together. Church Mutual is the largest provider of property/casualty insurance including liability commercial auto and workers' compensation coverage to the religious market. The company insures more than 100000 religious organizations including churches offices schools senior living facilities conference centers and camps. It also provides homeowners insurance to clergy members. Licensed throughout the US Church Mutual also offers a variety of risk management resources including seminars and safety videos. Church Mutual was founded in 1897.

CHURCH PENSION GROUP SERVICES CORPORATION

445 Fifth Ave.
New York NY 10016
Phone: 212-592-1800
Fax: 801-250-6099
Web: www.cobblestones.com

CEO: T Period D Sullivan
CFO: Daniel Kasle
HR: –
FYE: March 31
Type: Private - Not-for-Pr

Broken stained glass window? Fractured clerical clavicle? Church Pension Group can help. Its Church Pension Fund Church Medical Trust and Church Life Insurance divisions provide pensions health plans life insurance disability coverage and other benefits for clergy and workers of the Protestant Episcopal Church in the US. Church Pension Group also maintains the Episcopal Church Clergy and Employees' Benefit Trust (the "Medical Trust") which was created in 1978 to provide benefits for the Church's employees and their families. The group's Church Insurance Companies division provides specialty property/casualty insurance plans tailored specifically for churches.

CHURCHILL DOWNS, INC.   NMS: CHDN

600 North Hurstbourne Parkway, Suite 400
Louisville, KY 40222
Phone: 502 636-4400
Fax: –
Web: www.churchilldownsincorporated.com

CEO: William C. (Bill) Carstanjen
CFO: Marcia A. Dall
HR: Chuck Kenyon
FYE: December 31
Type: Public

You might say this company has put its money on the sport of champions to win. Churchill Downs is a leading operator of horse racing tracks in the US with four major race courses including its namesake track that hosts the world-famous Kentucky Derby. Other tracks include Arlington Park (Illinois) Calder Race Course (Florida) and Fair Grounds Race Course (Louisiana). In addition to horse racing Churchill Downs has gaming assets. It operates a number of simulcast networks and off-track betting facilities as well as a Twin-Spires wagering deposit service that allows punters to place bets online. Richard Duchossois who controls diversified holding company Duchossois Group owns about 20% of Churchill Downs.

	Annual Growth	12/10	12/11	12/12	12/13	12/14
Sales ($ mil.)	8.6%	585.3	696.9	732.4	779.3	812.9
Net income ($ mil.)	29.8%	16.4	64.4	58.3	54.9	46.4
Market value ($ mil.)	21.7%	758.3	910.8	1,161.0	1,566.4	1,665.1
Employees	24.6%	2,000	2,000	2,300	2,600	4,825

CHUY'S HOLDINGS INC

NMS: CHUY

1623 Toomey Road
Austin, TX 78704
Phone: 512 473-2783
Fax: –
Web: www.chuys.com

CEO: Steve Hislop
CFO: Jon W. Howie
HR: –
FYE: December 28
Type: Public

Where can Tex-Mex connoisseurs and Elvis fans dine under one roof? Chuy's Holdings operates the Chuy's Tex-Mex casual dining restaurant chain which serves up a menu of enchiladas fajitas tacos and "big as yo' face" burritos as well as signature drinks like fresh-squeezed lime margaritas and Texas Martinis. Each of its nearly 50 restaurants offer patrons a funky vibrant and eclectic atmosphere decked out with Mexican folk art vintage hubcap-coated ceilings and a shrine to the "King of Rock and Roll" himself. Originally founded in Austin Texas in 1982 the company went public in mid-2012.

	Annual Growth	12/10	12/11	12/12	12/13	12/14
Sales ($ mil.)	26.8%	94.9	130.6	172.6	204.4	245.1
Net income ($ mil.)	36.7%	3.3	3.5	5.5	11.1	11.5
Market value ($ mil.)	(6.8%)	–	–	368.8	602.2	320.4
Employees	18.4%	–	3,954	4,770	5,712	6,567

CHYRONHEGO CORP

NMS: CHYR

5 Hub Drive
Melville, NY 11747
Phone: 631 845-2000
Fax: –
Web: www.chyron.com

CEO: Johan Apel
CFO: Carl Blandino
HR: –
FYE: December 31
Type: Public

ChyronHego (formerly Chyron) wants customers to stay tuned. The company develops makes and sells software hardware and cloud-based services providing graphics creation and management for live and pre-recorded television broadcasts. Its Windows-based products are used to create logos text and other images that can be superimposed over existing images to display information such as sports scores stock tickers and weather data. The firm's clients include ABC ESPN FOX News CNN and the BBC. In addition to broadcasters Chyron-Hego markets to post-production facilities government agencies schools health care providers and telecom service providers. In 2013 Chyron merged with Hego AB to form ChyronHego.

	Annual Growth	12/09	12/10	12/11	12/12	12/13
Sales ($ mil.)	16.6%	25.6	27.7	31.6	30.2	47.4
Net income ($ mil.)	–	(3.1)	(2.4)	(4.2)	(22.3)	(7.8)
Market value ($ mil.)	0.5%	64.0	67.7	42.8	21.9	65.3
Employees	16.3%	104	114	126	111	190

CIB MARINE BANCSHARES INC

NBB: CIBH

1930 W. Bluemound Road, Suite D
Waukesha, WI 53186
Phone: 262 695-6010
Fax: –
Web: www.cibmarine.com

CEO: J Brian Chaffin
CFO: Patrick J Straka
HR: –
FYE: December 31
Type: Public

CIB Marine Bancshares is semper fi to its banking strategy. The company owns CIBM Bank which operates in the Indianapolis Milwaukee and Phoenix markets. Through some 20 branches the bank caters to individuals and small- and midsized-business customers offering checking and savings accounts ATM and debit cards CDs and IRAs. The company's loan portfolio mainly consists of commercial mortgages business loans and commercial real estate construction loans. CIB Marine Bancshares emerged from Chapter 11 bankruptcy protection in early 2010.

	Annual Growth	12/10	12/11	12/12	12/13	12/14
Assets ($ mil.)	(3.9%)	589.0	504.0	475.1	460.2	501.9
Net income ($ mil.)	–	(17.3)	(5.4)	1.4	(1.4)	0.3
Market value ($ mil.)	54.3%	1.5	3.3	3.6	8.9	8.5
Employees	0.2%	153	146	137	154	154

CIBER, INC.

NYS: CBR

6363 South Fiddleras Green Circle, Suite 1400
Greenwood Village, CO 80111
Phone: 303 220-0100
Fax: 303 220-7100
Web: www.ciber.com

CEO: Michael Boustridge
CFO: Christian Mezger
HR: –
FYE: December 31
Type: Public

CIBER (Consultants in Business Engineering and Research) is a global IT consultancy that provides enterprise systems integration through consulting practices specializing in such software systems as Lawson Microsoft Oracle SAP and Salesforce.com as well as custom software development. It serves corporate customers in such industries as communications financial services manufacturing health care and education as well as not-for-profits. Its diverse client list includes Boeing The University of Texas System Duke Energy and Disney. Founded in 1974 CIBER earns just over half of its sales overseas; international offices in Europe operate through CIBER (UK) Ltd.

	Annual Growth	12/10	12/11	12/12	12/13	12/14
Sales ($ mil.)	(5.2%)	1,071.3	976.9	884.4	877.3	863.6
Net income ($ mil.)	–	(77.2)	(67.3)	(14.6)	(14.5)	(19.6)
Market value ($ mil.)	(6.7%)	368.3	303.8	262.8	325.8	279.4
Employees	(6.8%)	8,600	6,500	6,700	6,500	6,500

CIC GROUP INC.

530 MARYVILLE CENTRE DR
SAINT LOUIS, MO 631415825
Phone: 314-682-2900
Fax: –
Web: www.cicgroup.com

CEO: Donald H Lange
CFO: –
HR: –
FYE: November 30
Type: Private

CIC Group can see clearly that its future (like its present) is in heavy manufacturing and construction. Its group of commercial and industrial subsidiaries specialize in the manufacture maintenance and repair of equipment for the crude oil natural gas coal and other energy industries. Its largest subsidiary is Nooter/Eriksen which supplies heat recovery steam generators for combustion gas turbines worldwide. CIC's Nooter Construction is a construction contractor serving the refining petrochemical pulp and paper and power industries among others. The employee-owned holding company was formed in 2002.

	Annual Growth	11/07	11/08	11/10	11/11	11/12
Sales ($ mil.)	0.6%	–	1,120.6	758.0	838.9	1,149.5
Net income ($ mil.)	–	–	–	0.0	0.0	0.0
Market value ($ mil.)	–	–	–	–	–	–
Employees	–	–	–	–	–	1,500

CICERO INC

NBB: CICN

8000 Regency Parkway, Suite 542
Cary, NC 27518
Phone: 919 380-5000
Fax: –
Web: www.ciceroinc.com

CEO: John P Broderick
CFO: John P Broderick
HR: –
FYE: December 31
Type: Public

Cicero takes a philosophical approach to integrating computer applications. The company provides application integration software used to link a variety of enterprise applications (including mainframe client/server and Web-based environments) primarily for financial service firms' contact centers. It also provides consulting project management and training services which account for more than a third of revenue. Customers include Affiliated Computer Services Deutsche Bank and Merrill Lynch. Cicero's roster of strategic partners includes resellers such as BluePhoenix MphasiS and Tata Consultancy. The company gets all of its sales in the US.

	Annual Growth	12/10	12/11	12/12	12/13	12/14
Sales ($ mil.)	(10.6%)	3.0	3.3	6.0	2.2	1.9
Net income ($ mil.)	–	(0.5)	(3.0)	(0.2)	(3.2)	(3.9)
Market value ($ mil.)	(26.7%)	5.2	4.3	4.1	1.5	1.5
Employees	(6.2%)	31	33	33	25	24

CICI ENTERPRISES LP

1080 W. Bethel Rd.
Coppell TX 75019
Phone: 972-745-4200
Fax: 972-745-4203
Web: www.cicispizza.com

CEO: Darin Harris
CFO: –
HR: –
FYE: December 31
Type: Private

CiCi's pleases penny pinchers and pizzaholics alike. CiCi Enterprises operates and franchises about 650 CiCi's Pizza restaurants in more than 30 states that offer several types of pizza along with salad desserts and pasta at an all-you-can-eat price. Concentrated in Texas Florida and other southern states many of the eateries are located in shopping malls and other suburban retail areas. About 15 of the restaurants are company-owned while the rest are franchised. CiCi Enterprises supplies its franchisees through its JMC Restaurant Distribution unit. Joe Croce opened the first CiCi's Pizza in Plano Texas in 1985. A group including current and former management controls the company.

CIENA CORP

NYS: CIEN

7035 Ridge Road
Hanover, MD 21076
Phone: 410 694-5700
Fax: 410 694-5750
Web: www.ciena.com

CEO: Gary B. Smith
CFO: James E. (Jim) Moylan
HR: Rebecca K Seidman
FYE: October 31
Type: Public

Ciena takes a thousand points of light and puts them in motion at the same time. The company makes transport and switching equipment that increases the capacity of long-distance fiber-optic networks by transmitting multiple light signals simultaneously over the same circuit. It also sells optical transport systems for metro and enterprise wide-area networks as well as broadband access products that enable communications companies to deliver Internet protocol (IP) services such as VoIP IP video and DSL. Ciena serves telecommunications service providers cable companies large enterprises and government entities.

	Annual Growth	10/11	10/12	10/13	10/14	10/15
Sales ($ mil.)	8.9%	1,742.0	1,833.9	2,082.5	2,288.3	2,445.7
Net income ($ mil.)	–	(195.5)	(144.0)	(85.4)	(40.6)	11.7
Market value ($ mil.)	16.3%	1,787.4	1,684.3	3,155.7	2,272.9	3,273.7
Employees	5.4%	4,339	4,481	4,754	5,161	5,345

CIFC CORP

NAS: CIFC

250 Park Avenue, 4th Floor
New York, NY 10177
Phone: 212 624-1200
Fax: –
Web: www.cifc.com

CEO: –
CFO: Rahul Agarwal
HR: –
FYE: December 31
Type: Public

CIFC (a subsidiary of Columbus Nova) is searching for a new world of investments. Through subsidiaries the specialty finance company invests in and manages client assets such as asset-backed securities bank loans and government securities. It offers some 30 investment products including separately managed accounts and a private investment fund. CIFC has more than $12.3 billion of assets under management. Nearly 90% of its portfolio was once devoted to residential mortgage-backed securities (RMBS) but CIFC broadened its investment mix in the wake of the mortgage meltdown.

	Annual Growth	12/09	12/10	12/11	12/12	12/13
Sales ($ mil.)	(39.9%)	66.7	179.2	14.8	10.9	8.7
Net income ($ mil.)	(23.1%)	66.9	85.9	(32.6)	(9.6)	23.4
Market value ($ mil.)	14.1%	95.6	135.1	112.3	166.3	161.8
Employees	2.9%	67	64	71	59	75

CIGNA CORP

NYS: CI

900 Cottage Grove Road
Bloomfield, CT 06002
Phone: 860 226-6000
Fax: 860 226-6741
Web: www.cigna.com

CEO: David M. Cordani
CFO: Thomas A. (Tom) McCarthy
HR: John M. Murabito
FYE: December 31
Type: Public

With a significant position in the US health insurance market CIGNA covers some 14.5 million Americans with its various medical plans. The firm's offerings include PPO HMO point-of-service (POS) indemnity and consumer-directed products as well as specialty coverage in the form of dental vision pharmacy and behavioral health plans. It also sells group accident life and disability insurance. Customers include employers government entities unions Medicare recipients and other groups and individuals in North America. Internationally CIGNA sells life accident and health insurance in parts of Europe and Asia and provides health coverage to expatriate employees of multinational companies. It is being acquired by rival Anthem.

	Annual Growth	12/10	12/11	12/12	12/13	12/14
Assets ($ mil.)	5.2%	45,682.0	51,047.0	53,734.0	54,336.0	55,896.0
Net income ($ mil.)	11.8%	1,345.0	1,327.0	1,623.0	1,476.0	2,102.0
Market value ($ mil.)	29.4%	9,505.1	10,889.6	13,860.9	22,681.5	26,682.1
Employees	5.0%	30,600	31,400	35,800	36,500	37,200

CIM COMMERCIAL TRUST CORP

NMS: CMCT

17950 Preston Road, Suite 600
Dallas, TX 75252
Phone: 972 349-3200
Fax: –
Web: www.cimcommercial.com

CEO: Charles E Garner II
CFO: David Thompson
HR: –
FYE: December 31
Type: Public

PMC Commercial Trust likes lending to little businesses. The real estate investment trust (REIT) makes small business loans primarily to limited-service hotel franchisees. The loans ranging from $100000 to $4 million are secured by first liens on real estate and written for hotel owner/operators of national franchises such as Comfort Inn and Holiday Inn Express. PMC Commercial Trust also lends to owners of convenience stores restaurants and other small businesses. About 20% of its loan portfolio is concentrated in Texas. Subsidiaries are active in Small Business Administration (SBA) lending and in investing (as small business investment companies or SBICs). The company was founded in 1993.

	Annual Growth	12/10	12/11	12/12	12/13	12/14
Assets ($ mil.)	69.8%	252.1	251.2	247.7	253.4	2,094.7
Net income ($ mil.)	54.3%	4.3	3.6	(2.2)	19.6	24.4
Market value ($ mil.)	15.3%	827.5	683.1	692.8	839.2	1,464.7
Employees	0.8%	32	33	32	32	33

CIMAREX ENERGY CO

NYS: XEC

1700 Lincoln Street, Suite 3700
Denver, CO 80203-4518
Phone: 303 295-3995
Fax: 303 295-3494
Web: www.cimarex.com

CEO: Thomas E. Jorden
CFO: Mark Burford
HR: Richard Dinkin
FYE: December 31
Type: Public

Cimarex Energy's energy is devoted to oil and natural gas exploration and production. The independent is focusing its operations developing assets in two regions — the Mid-Continent and the Permian Basin. The company reported proved reserves in 2012 of about 1.3 trillion cu. ft. of natural gas and 168 million barrels of oil and natural gas liquids (NGLs). Cimarex Energy's 2012 production averaged 626.5 million cu. ft. of natural gas equivalent per day. That year company-operated wells accounted for 68% of Cimarex Energy's total proved reserves and some 80% of its total production.

	Annual Growth	12/10	12/11	12/12	12/13	12/14
Sales ($ mil.)	10.7%	1,613.7	1,757.9	1,623.9	1,998.1	2,424.2
Net income ($ mil.)	(3.1%)	574.8	529.9	353.8	564.7	507.2
Market value ($ mil.)	4.6%	7,754.6	5,422.0	5,056.7	9,189.3	9,284.8
Employees	6.3%	775	824	851	908	991

CINCINNATI BELL INC NYS: CBB

221 East Fourth Street
Cincinnati, OH 45202
Phone: 513 397-9900
Fax: –
Web: www.cincinnatibell.com

CEO: Theodore H. (Ted) Torbeck
CFO: Kurt A. Freyberger
HR: –
FYE: December 31
Type: Public

Cincinnati Bell rings for Bengals and Bearcats Musketeers and even the Reds. The company provides local phone service to residential and business customers in southwestern Ohio northern Kentucky and eastern Indiana. It has been the incumbent local-exchange carrier (ILEC) for greater Cincinnati since the 1870s and it operates in other areas as a competitive local-exchange carrier (CLEC) providing voice and Internet service over its networks and through agreements with other network operators. Cincinnati Bell counts almost 575000 wireline customers almost 400000 wireless customers 200000 Internet customers and 55000 digital cable customers. It spun off its data center services for businesses as CyrusOne in 2013.

	Annual Growth	12/10	12/11	12/12	12/13	12/14
Sales ($ mil.)	(1.8%)	1,377.0	1,462.4	1,473.9	1,256.9	1,278.2
Net income ($ mil.)	27.8%	28.3	18.6	11.2	(54.7)	75.6
Market value ($ mil.)	3.3%	586.0	634.2	1,146.9	745.1	667.7
Employees	0.8%	3,000	3,100	3,100	2,900	3,100

CINCINNATI BENGALS INC.

1 Paul Brown Stadium
Cincinnati OH 45202
Phone: 513-621-3550
Fax: 513-621-3570
Web: www.bengals.com

CEO: Michael Brown
CFO: William Scanlon
HR: –
FYE: February 28
Type: Private

These Bengals prowl the jungle of the NFL. The Cincinnati Bengals professional football franchise traces an elite heritage having been formed by Hall of Fame coach Paul Brown in 1968 as part of the American Football League (AFL). Cincinnati joined the National Football League in 1970 when the AFL and NFL merged and went on to make two trips to the Super Bowl (losing both times to the San Francisco 49ers). The team plays host at Paul Brown Stadium which opened in 2000. Brown's family led by his son Mike Brown continues to control the Bengals.

CINCINNATI FINANCIAL CORP. NMS: CINF

6200 S. Gilmore Road
Fairfield, OH 45014-5141
Phone: 513 870-2000
Fax: –
Web: www.cinfin.com

CEO: Steven J. Johnston
CFO: Michael J. (Mike) Sewell
HR: –
FYE: December 31
Type: Public

Cincinnati Financial Corporation (CFC) serves up a whole menu of insurance — plain and simple or with extras if you like. The company's flagship Cincinnati Insurance (operating through four property/casualty subsidiaries) sells commercial property liability excess and surplus auto bond and fire insurance; personal lines include homeowners auto and liability products. Subsidiary Cincinnati Life sells life disability income and annuities. The company's CFC Investment subsidiary provides commercial financing leasing and real estate services to its independent insurance agents. Its CSU Producers Resources offers insurance brokerage services to independent agencies. The Schiff family formed CFC in 1968.

	Annual Growth	12/10	12/11	12/12	12/13	12/14
Assets ($ mil.)	5.6%	15,095.0	15,668.0	16,548.0	17,662.0	18,753.0
Net income ($ mil.)	8.6%	377.0	166.0	421.0	517.0	525.0
Market value ($ mil.)	13.1%	5,187.7	4,986.3	6,410.5	8,573.0	8,484.6
Employees	1.5%	4,060	4,067	4,057	4,163	4,305

CINEDIGM CORP NMS: CIDM

902 Broadway, 9th Floor
New York, NY 10010
Phone: 212 206-8600
Fax: –

CEO: Christopher J McGurk
CFO: Jeffrey S Edell
HR: –
FYE: March 31
Type: Public

Cinedigm Digital Cinema (formerly known as Access Integrated Technologies or AccessIT) hopes to make digital the new cinema paradigm. The company provides software and services for the managed storage and electronic delivery of digital content to movie theaters for major film studios. It also provides alternative digital content to customers such as museums and educational venues. Major customers include Warner Bros. and Universal Pictures. Cinedigm in 2011 sold its digital delivery assets to Technicolor. It kept assets in key areas related to alternative content and digital cinema operational software.

	Annual Growth	03/11	03/12	03/13	03/14	03/15
Sales ($ mil.)	7.2%	79.9	76.6	88.1	104.3	105.5
Net income ($ mil.)	–	(29.2)	(23.0)	(21.1)	(25.9)	(31.3)
Market value ($ mil.)	(2.2%)	136.5	130.3	120.3	197.4	124.9
Employees	(7.5%)	193	90	160	179	141

CINEMARK HOLDINGS INC NYS: CNK

3900 Dallas Parkway, Suite 500
Plano, TX 75093
Phone: 972 665-1000
Fax: –
Web: www.cinemark.com

CEO: Mark Zoradi
CFO: Sean Gamble
HR: –
FYE: December 31
Type: Public

Showing films is where Cinemark Holdings really makes its mark. The third-largest movie exhibitor in the US (following Regal Entertainment and AMC) has more than 5200 screens in some 495 theaters in the US and Latin America. Cinemark operates its multiplex theaters in smaller cities and suburban areas of major metropolitan markets. Some larger theaters operate under the Tinseltown name; others are "discount" theaters showing no first-run films. Nearly 100% of its first-run auditoriums feature stadium seating. The company prefers to build new theaters in midsized markets or in suburbs of major cities where the Cinemark theater is the only game in town.

	Annual Growth	12/10	12/11	12/12	12/13	12/14
Sales ($ mil.)	5.2%	2,141.1	2,279.6	2,473.5	2,682.9	2,627.0
Net income ($ mil.)	7.2%	146.1	130.6	168.9	148.5	192.6
Market value ($ mil.)	19.9%	1,994.7	2,139.3	3,005.9	3,856.3	4,116.6
Employees	13.8%	14,600	14,000	22,500	17,200	24,500

CINER RESOURCES LP NYS: CINR

Five Concourse Parkway, Suite 2500
Atlanta, GA 30328
Phone: 770 375-2300
Fax: –
Web: www.ociresources.com

CEO: Kirk H Milling
CFO: Kevin L Kremke
HR: –
FYE: December 31
Type: Public

They say baking soda has plenty of household uses but soda ash provides even more. OCI Resources operates a soda ash mining and production plant in Wyoming that annually produces about 2.5 million short tons of the raw material used in flat glass container glass detergents chemicals paper and other consumer and industrial products. OCI Resources sells most of its soda ash to export firm American Natural Soda Ash Corporation (ANSAC). Organized as a limited partnership OCI Resources is exempt from paying federal income tax. The company is a subsidiary of OCI Chemical which actually owns the plant. It went public in 2013 raising $95 million which it returned to OCI Chemical.

	Annual Growth	05/11	05/12	05/13*	12/13	12/14
Sales ($ mil.)	–	0.0	0.0	–	442.1	465.0
Net income ($ mil.)	–	0.0	0.0	–	26.3	44.5
Market value ($ mil.)	–	0.0	0.0	–	409.8	514.0
Employees	1.2%	–	–	–	415	420

*Fiscal year change

CINNABON INC.

200 Glenridge Point Pkwy. Ste. 200
Atlanta GA 30342
Phone: 404-255-3250
Fax: 404-255-4978
Web: www.cinnabon.com

CEO: –
CFO: Gregg Kaplan
HR: –
FYE: December 31
Type: Subsidiary

You might say this company is baking up some sweet sales in malls across the country. Cinnabon operates a chain of more than 770 franchised baked goods outlets popular for their cinnamon rolls. The eateries located mostly in shopping areas airports and other high-traffic locations also serve pecan rolls finger-friendly Cinnabon Stix and smaller rolls called Cinnabon Bites along with a variety of flavored coffee drinks and other beverages. The Cinnabon chain has outposts throughout the US and in more than 40 other countries. It is part of FOCUS Brands a multi-concept restaurant franchisor and affiliate of private equity firm Roark Capital Group.

CIRRUS DESIGN CORPORATION

4515 Taylor Circle
Duluth MN 55811
Phone: 218-727-2737
Fax: 218-727-2148
Web: www.cirrusdesign.com

CEO: –
CFO: –
HR: –
FYE: December 31
Type: Private

Cirrus Design asks customers to reach for the clouds — cirrus ones. The company also known as Cirrus Aircraft manufactures the SR20 and the SR22 single-engine four-seater piston-powered aircraft. Cirrus planes are made primarily of composite materials rather than aluminum; the company asserts that composites allow for an aerodynamically superior design. All models come with the trademark Cirrus Airframe Parachute System (CAPS) that will lower the aircraft to the ground in an emergency. The company was founded in 1984 by former chairman Alan Klapmeier and his brother Dale. China Aviation Industry General Aircraft Company (CAIGA) acquired the company in mid-2011.

CINTAS CORPORATION

NMS: CTAS

6800 Cintas Boulevard, P.O. Box 625737
Cincinnati, OH 45262-5737
Phone: 513 459-1200
Fax: 513 573-4030
Web: www.cintas.com

CEO: Scott D. Farmer
CFO: J. Michael (Mike) Hansen
HR: Mark Greiner
FYE: May 31
Type: Public

If Cintas had its way you'd never agonize over what to wear to work. The #1 uniform supplier in the US boasts 900000 clients (McDonald's MGM Resorts) and some 5 million people wear its garb each day. Cintas — which sells leases and rents uniforms — operates 377 facilities in 286 cities across the US and Canada; it leases about half of them. Besides offering shirts jackets slacks and footwear the company provides clean-room apparel and flame-resistant clothing. Other products offered by Cintas include uniform cleaning first-aid and safety products and clean-room supplies. Richard Farmer founded the company in 1968. Cintas is run by his son CEO Scott Farmer.

	Annual Growth	05/11	05/12	05/13	05/14	05/15
Sales ($ mil.)	4.1%	3,810.4	4,102.0	4,316.5	4,551.8	4,476.9
Net income ($ mil.)	14.9%	247.0	297.6	315.4	374.4	430.6
Market value ($ mil.)	27.2%	3,669.4	4,121.8	5,099.8	6,939.0	9,616.5
Employees	1.6%	30,000	30,000	32,000	33,000	32,000

CIRRUS LOGIC, INC.

NMS: CRUS

800 W. 6th Street
Austin, TX 78701
Phone: 512 851-4000
Fax: –
Web: www.cirrus.com

CEO: Jason P. Rhode
CFO: Thurman Case
HR: Jo- Dee Benson
FYE: March 28
Type: Public

Cirrus Logic's approach to computing is hardly wispy. The fabless semiconductor company long a leader in audio chips of all kinds develops integrated circuits (ICs) for specialized applications in consumer electronics energy and industrial equipment. Its more than 700 products include audio encoder/decoders (codecs) digital amplifiers digital audio converters and energy management devices. Cirrus Logic's audio chips are used in smartphones tablet and laptop computers Blu-ray Disc players gaming devices and digital TVs. Energy management products include LED driver ICs ADCs and DACs used to make LEDs digital utility meters and power supplies. The company gets most of its sales from customers in China.

	Annual Growth	03/11	03/12	03/13	03/14	03/15
Sales ($ mil.)	25.5%	369.6	426.8	809.8	714.3	916.6
Net income ($ mil.)	(27.8%)	203.5	88.0	136.6	108.1	55.2
Market value ($ mil.)	12.0%	1,334.9	1,501.4	1,435.2	1,231.4	2,100.1
Employees	18.0%	570	676	652	751	1,104

CIRCOR INTERNATIONAL INC

NYS: CIR

c/o Circor International, Inc., 30 Corporate Drive, Suite 200
Burlington, MA 01803-4238
Phone: 781 270-1200
Fax: –
Web: www.circor.com

CEO: Scott A. Buckhout
CFO: Rajeev Bhalla
HR: Susan M (Sue) McCuaig
FYE: December 31
Type: Public

CIRCOR International is overflowing with valves and other highly engineered products used in the energy industrial and aerospace markets. The global diversified company designs manufactures and markets more than 10000 products namely a wide variety of valves used in flow control applications by the oil and gas petrochemical power generation and processing industries. It also makes landing gear sensors and controls for military and commercial aircraft. Products are sold directly and through about 1000 distributors in some 100 countries around the world.

	Annual Growth	12/10	12/11	12/12	12/13	12/14
Sales ($ mil.)	5.2%	685.9	822.3	845.6	857.8	841.4
Net income ($ mil.)	41.3%	12.6	36.6	30.8	47.1	50.4
Market value ($ mil.)	9.3%	747.6	624.3	700.0	1,428.3	1,065.9
Employees	(1.3%)	2,950	3,390	3,000	2,800	2,800

CIRTRAN CORP.

NBB: CIRC

4125 South 6000 West
West Valley City, UT 84128
Phone: 801 963-5112
Fax: –
Web: www.cirtran.com

CEO: Iehab Hawatmeh
CFO: Iehab Hawatmeh
HR: –
FYE: December 31
Type: Public

CirTran provides contract electronics manufacturing services through which it makes printed circuit boards and cables for customers in consumer electronics networking equipment the automotive industry and other markets. The company has established an Asian subsidiary in Shenzhen China that undertakes manufacturing services for a wider variety of products including cooking appliances fitness equipment and hair products. CirTran's Racore Technology subsidiary makes Ethernet adapter cards for PCs. Racore's customers include the Fire Department of New York City Lear Siegler Lockheed Martin the US Air Force and Walt Disney World.

	Annual Growth	12/09	12/10	12/11	12/12	12/13
Sales ($ mil.)	(22.7%)	9.7	9.0	3.1	4.3	3.5
Net income ($ mil.)	–	(5.8)	(2.6)	(6.3)	(0.2)	0.9
Market value ($ mil.)	–	0.0	0.0	0.0	0.0	0.0
Employees	40.8%	15	88	11	3	59

CISCO SYSTEMS, INC.   NMS: CSCO

170 West Tasman Drive
San Jose, CA 95134-1706
Phone: 408 526-4000
Fax: –
Web: www.cisco.com

CEO: Charles H. (Chuck) Robbins
CFO: Kelly A. Kramer
HR: Kathleen A Weslock
FYE: July 25
Type: Public

Cisco Systems routes packets and routs competitors with equal efficiency. Dominating the market for Internet Protocol-based networking equipment the company makes and sells routers servers security devices Internet conferencing systems set-top boxes and other networking equipment to businesses and government agencies. The company also provides consulting services and offers products for a growing array of household industrial medical and other gadgets that connect to the Internet. Cisco sells its products primarily to large enterprises and telecommunications service providers but it also markets products designed for small businesses. Cisco Systems was founded in 1984 by Stanford University graduates.

	Annual Growth	07/11	07/12	07/13	07/14	07/15
Sales ($ mil.)	3.3%	43,218.0	46,061.0	48,607.0	47,142.0	49,161.0
Net income ($ mil.)	8.5%	6,490.0	8,041.0	9,983.0	7,853.0	8,981.0
Market value ($ mil.)	–	0.0	0.0	0.0	0.0	0.0
Employees	0.0%	71,825	66,639	75,049	74,042	71,833

CISCO WEBEX LLC

3979 Freedom Cir.
Santa Clara CA 95054
Phone: 408-435-7000
Fax: 408-496-4353
Web: www.webex.com

CEO: –
CFO: –
HR: –
FYE: December 31
Type: Subsidiary

Cisco WebEx helps its business customers take the shortest route to their meetings. The company's core subscription-based Web-conferencing software and service is known as Meeting Center. Featuring video and audio transmission functions WebEx is used by businesses to convene with employees clients and partners to make presentations conduct training and share documents and multimedia content online. The company's customers come from such industries as financial services health care telecom and manufacturing. Clients have included community association management specialist Associa. Founded in 1996 Cisco WebEx is a subsidiary of networking equipment maker Cisco which acquired the company in 2007.

CISION US INC.

332 S. Michigan Ave.
Chicago IL 60604
Phone: 312-922-2400
Fax: 312-922-3126
Web: us.cision.com

CEO: Peter Granat
CFO: –
HR: Karin Persson
FYE: December 31
Type: Subsidiary

Cision US doesn't underestimate the value of a precise message. The subsidiary of Sweden-based research firm Cision AB provides software and services for public relations and marketing professionals. Its flagship CisionPoint product is an integrated software application for managing PR campaigns. The company also monitors plans and analyzes news and information from print and electronic media sources; maintains a database of media contacts clippings and reports; and distributes press releases. Cision US has about a dozen offices throughout the US. The company began as a news clipping service (Bacon's Information) in 1932. Cision AB acquired Bacon's in 2001; it was rebranded as Cision US in 2007.

CIT GROUP, INC.   NYS: CIT

11 West 42nd Street
New York, NY 10036
Phone: 212 461-5200
Fax: –
Web: www.cit.com

CEO: John A. Thain
CFO: Carol Hayles
HR: Bryan Allen
FYE: December 31
Type: Public

If you haven't heard of CIT Group then you're O-U-T of the proverbial loop. On the big-business landscape for about a century CIT is a financial holding company that offers lending leasing debt restructuring equipment financing and advisory services to small- and mid-sized businesses in such industries as energy healthcare retail communications manufacturing IT services and sports. The company also operates CIT Bank in Utah which offers commercial financing and leasing as well as online deposit products such as CDs. CIT has some $35 billion in assets and serves clients in more than 20 countries.

	Annual Growth	12/10	12/11	12/12	12/13	12/14
Assets ($ mil.)	(1.5%)	50,958.2	45,235.4	44,012.0	47,139.0	47,880.0
Net income ($ mil.)	21.3%	521.2	31.7	(588.6)	675.7	1,130.0
Market value ($ mil.)	0.4%	8,521.4	6,308.7	6,990.8	9,431.4	8,653.4
Employees	(2.9%)	3,778	3,526	3,560	3,240	3,360

CIT SMALL BUSINESS LENDING CORPORATION

1 CIT Dr.
Livingston NJ 07039
Phone: 973-740-5000
Fax: +66-2399-4877
Web: www.pranda.co.th

CEO: –
CFO: –
HR: –
FYE: December 31
Type: Subsidiary

Small is relative. CIT Small Business Lending is one of the biggest Small Business Administration (SBA) lenders in the nation. Part of the Consumer & Small Business Lending unit of CIT Group the company offers business acquisition and succession loans franchise financing and commercial real estate and construction loans ranging from $350000 to $3 million. CIT Small Business Lending targets primarily US businesses such as day care centers; retailers convenience stores; hotels and motels; woman- veteran- and minority-owned firms; and medical practice startups. The SBA-designated preferred lender operates from offices coast to coast. It also offers an online application process.

CITADEL LLC

131 S. Dearborn St.
Chicago IL 60603
Phone: 312-395-2100
Fax: 312-267-7100
Web: www.citadelgroup.com

CEO: Kenneth Cordele Griffin
CFO: –
HR: –
FYE: December 31
Type: Private

This Citadel aspires not to turn boys into men but to turn cash into well more cash. The Citadel investment group whose seeds were planted in super-trader Ken Griffin's Harvard dorm room in 1987 includes Citadel Asset Management one of the world's largest hedge funds accounting for around 8% of daily trading activity at the NYSE and NASDAQ. Because of this high volume the company also acts as a market maker for equity options and for some blue-chip stocks on smaller exchanges. It manages some $12 billion of assets for institutional and high-net-worth investors as well as on its own account. Citadel also provides investment banking and institutional trading.

CITATION OIL & GAS CORP.

14077 CUTTEN RD
HOUSTON, TX 770692212
Phone: 281-891-1000
Fax: –
Web: www.cogc.com

CEO: –
CFO: Chris Phelps
HR: Laurie Gallaway
FYE: December 31
Type: Private

Citation Oil & Gas is writing its own ticket to prosperity in the petroleum industry. The oil and gas development and production company has interests in about 15000 wells (in more than 480 separately designated fields) and reported 210 million barrels of proved oil equivalent reserves (91% oil) in 2012. Its oil fields are in the Mid-Continent Illinois Basin Permian Basin and Rocky Mountain regions. Citation seeks out properties with high levels of crude oil declining production with long reserve life and low risk. The company uses a variety of techniques to recover oil and gas including waterflood and infill drilling. Subsidiary Citation Crude Marketing sells the company's products to refiners.

	Annual Growth	12/08	12/09	12/11	12/12	12/13
Sales ($ mil.)	18.7%	–	233.1	449.3	424.3	462.9
Net income ($ mil.)	(0.7%)	–	–	251.4	224.9	248.0
Market value ($ mil.)	–	–	–	–	–	–
Employees	–	–	–	–	–	507

CITGO PETROLEUM CORPORATION

1293 Eldridge Pkwy.
Houston TX 77077-1670
Phone: 832-486-4000
Fax: 832-486-1814
Web: www.citgo.com

CEO: Nelson P Martinez
CFO: –
HR: –
FYE: December 31
Type: Subsidiary

From the get-go CITGO Petroleum has been refining and marketing petroleum products including jet fuel diesel fuel heating oils and lubricants. It markets CITGO branded gasoline through about 6000 independent retail outlets in 27 US states mainly east of the Rockies. CITGO Petroleum owns oil refineries in Illinois Louisiana and Texas. The company has the refining capacity to process more than 749000 barrels per day. Its refineries collectively produce about 17 million gallons of gasoline per day. CITGO Petroleum is the operating subsidiary of PDV America itself a subsidiary of Venezuela's national oil company PDVSA.

CITI TRENDS INC

NMS: CTRN

104 Coleman Boulevard
Savannah, GA 31408
Phone: 912 236-1561
Fax: –
Web: www.cititrends.com

CEO: –
CFO: Bruce D Smith
HR: Ivy Council
FYE: January 31
Type: Public

Citi Trends hopes to transport its customers to Trend City as quickly as possible. The fast-growing urban fashion apparel and accessory chain focuses primarily on the African-American market. Its brand-name (Baby Phat Dickies Rocawear) and private-label offerings (Diva Blue Vintage Harlem) — which include men's women's and children's clothing; shoes; fashion accessories; and housewares — sell for 30%-60% lower than department and specialty stores' regular prices. Citi Trends operates more than 500 stores in about 30 states. The company was founded in 1946 as Allied Department Stores.

	Annual Growth	01/11	01/12*	02/13	02/14*	01/15
Sales ($ mil.)	1.9%	622.5	640.8	654.7	622.2	670.8
Net income ($ mil.)	(19.0%)	20.9	(10.0)	(2.2)	0.5	9.0
Market value ($ mil.)	(0.4%)	362.5	144.4	200.8	249.2	356.6
Employees	1.0%	5,000	5,300	5,200	5,000	5,200

*Fiscal year change

CITIGROUP GLOBAL MARKETS INC.

388 Greenwich St.
New York NY 10013
Phone: 212-816-6000
Fax: 817-735-0936
Web: www.sjbrt.com

CEO: –
CFO: –
HR: –
FYE: December 31
Type: Subsidiary

Citigroup Global Markets Inc. (CGMI) is the US-based brokerage and securities arm of banking behemoth Citigroup. The company provides investment banking services to corporate institutional government and retail clients. As a broker-dealer CGMI offers clients access to the global markets in more than 100 countries. Services include underwriting structuring sales and trading across such asset classes as equities corporate government and agency bonds and mortgage-backed securities. Through Citi Futures it offers execution and clearing services.

CITIGROUP INC

NYS: C

399 Park Avenue
New York, NY 10022
Phone: 212 559-1000
Fax: –
Web: www.citigroup.com

CEO: Barbara J. Desoer
CFO: John C. Gerspach
HR: Noreen Chin
FYE: December 31
Type: Public

This is the Citi that never sleeps. One of the largest financial services firms known to man Citigroup (also known as Citi) has some 200 million customer accounts and serves clients around the globe. It offers deposits and loans (mainly through Citibank) investment banking brokerage wealth management and other financial services. Few other banks can equal Citigroup's global reach: In addition to Citibank it owns stakes in several international regional banks and has more than 100 million Citi-branded credit cards in circulation. However Citi has been selling dozens of underperforming and non-core businesses in the aftermath of the financial crisis in order to refocus on its original mission — traditional banking.

	Annual Growth	12/10	12/11	12/12	12/13	12/14
Assets ($ mil.)	(0.9%)	1,913,902.0	1,873,878.0	1,864,660.0	1,880,382.0	1,842,530.0
Net income ($ mil.)	(8.9%)	10,602.0	11,067.0	7,541.0	13,673.0	7,313.0
Market value ($ mil.)	–	0.0	0.0	0.0	0.0	0.0
Employees	(1.9%)	260,000	266,000	259,000	251,000	241,000

CITIMORTGAGE INC.

1000 Technology Dr.
O'Fallon MO 63368
Phone: 636-261-2484
Fax: 636-256-4340
Web: www.citimortgage.com

CEO: –
CFO: –
HR: –
FYE: December 31
Type: Subsidiary

Whether your potential home is in the city or the country CitiMortgage wants to help you buy it. Or fix it up. The mortgage lending unit of Citigroup CitiMortgage originates and services residential mortgages throughout the US. It manages most of its parent's $170 billion mortgage portfolio. CitiMortgage also offers refinancing and investment products. The company sells through retail online and correspondent channels. In 2009 Citigroup separated CitiMortgage and other money-losing units such as CitiFinancial into a new business called Citi Holdings. The reorganization allows Citigroup to spin off or sell struggling assets if it needs to raise money.

CITIZENS & NORTHERN CORP

NAS: CZNC

90-92 Main Street
Wellsboro, PA 16901
Phone: 570 724-3411
Fax: –
Web: www.cnbankpa.com

CEO: J. Bradley (Brad) Scovill
CFO: Mark A. Hughes
HR: –
FYE: December 31
Type: Public

Citizens & Northern Corp. is the holding company for Citizens & Northern (C&N) Bank Citizens & Northern Investment Corp. and Bucktail Life Insurance Company. Its primary business and largest subsidiary is C&N Bank a community bank that serves individuals and commercial customers in north-central Pennsylvania and southern New York. The bank operates 26 branches and offers online and telebanking services. The firm's other subsidiaries are Citizens & Northern Investment Corp. which provides investment services and Bucktail Life Insurance a provider of credit life and property/casualty reinsurance. The bank holding company has assets of more than $1.2 billion.

	Annual Growth	12/10	12/11	12/12	12/13	12/14
Assets ($ mil.)	(1.4%)	1,316.6	1,323.7	1,286.9	1,237.7	1,242.0
Net income ($ mil.)	(2.7%)	19.1	23.4	22.7	18.6	17.1
Market value ($ mil.)	8.6%	182.5	226.8	232.1	253.3	253.8
Employees	(0.3%)	281	290	292	287	278

CITIZENS BANCSHARES CORP. (GA)

NBB: CZBS

75 Piedmont Avenue, N.E.
Atlanta, GA 30303
Phone: 404 659-5959
Fax: –
Web: www.ctbconnect.com

CEO: Cynthia N Day
CFO: Samuel J Cox
HR: –
FYE: December 31
Type: Public

One of the largest minority-led financial institutions in the US Citizens Bancshares is the holding company for Citizens Trust Bank which serves the Atlanta and Columbus Georgia and Birmingham and Eutaw Alabama communities from about 10 branch offices. The bank provides standard services such as checking and savings accounts CDs IRAs credit cards financial planning and investments. Its lending portfolio mainly consists of loans secured by one- to four-family residences multifamily dwellings or commercial or industrial real estate. Former chairman and Atlanta-area entrepreneur and philanthropist Herman J. Russell owns about 30% of Citizens Bancshares' stock.

	Annual Growth	12/10	12/11	12/12	12/13	12/14
Assets ($ mil.)	0.5%	387.8	397.2	395.6	387.7	395.6
Net income ($ mil.)	30.2%	0.6	0.3	0.8	1.3	1.8
Market value ($ mil.)	21.4%	8.8	7.6	9.7	13.3	19.1
Employees	(2.5%)	115	108	105	102	104

CITIZENS COMMUNITY BANCORP INC (MD)

NMS: CZWI

2174 EastRidge Center
Eau Claire, WI 54701
Phone: 715 836-9994
Fax: –

CEO: Edward H Schaefer
CFO: Mark C Oldenberg
HR: –
FYE: September 30
Type: Public

Citizens Community Bancorp is the holding company for Citizens Community Federal a community bank with about two dozen branches in Wisconsin southern Minnesota and northern Michigan. Serving consumers and businesses the bank offers standard deposit services such as savings checking money market and retirement accounts as well as a variety of loan products. The bank focuses its lending activities on one- to four-family mortgages which represent more than half of its loan portfolio. The bank also offers consumer loans such as auto and personal loans; it does not routinely make commercial loans. Founded in 1938 Citizens Community was a state-chartered credit union until 2001.

	Annual Growth	09/10	09/11	09/12	09/13	09/14
Assets ($ mil.)	(1.0%)	594.4	536.6	530.2	554.5	569.8
Net income ($ mil.)	–	–	(7.1)	0.2	0.2	1.0	1.8
Market value ($ mil.)	18.9%	22.9	25.8	30.5	37.5	45.7
Employees	(0.5%)	193	185	269	229	189

CITIZENS ENERGY GROUP

2020 N MERIDIAN ST
INDIANAPOLIS, IN 462021306
Phone: 317-924-3341
Fax: –
Web: www.citizensenergygroup.com

CEO: Carey B Lykins
CFO: –
HR: –
FYE: September 30
Type: Private

Hoosiers are happy to have their homes provided with gas and water services by Public Utilities of the City of Indianapolis (dba Citizens Energy and CWA Authority public charitable trusts). Its Citizens Water unit provides water and wastewater services to 300000 customers in Indianapolis; Citizens Gas serves more than 266000 gas customers. Citizens Energy also provides steam heating and chilled water cooling services to about 250 customers through Citizens Thermal Energy. The regional utility also has a small oil production unit (Citizens Oil Division). Its Citizens Resources unit has joint venture stakes in some companies not regulated by the Indiana Utility Regulatory Commission such as ProLiance Energy.

	Annual Growth	09/09	09/10	09/11	09/12	09/13
Sales ($ mil.)	17.3%	–	440.7	463.6	696.4	711.5
Net income ($ mil.)	–	–	–	32.4	(11.8)	(81.3)
Market value ($ mil.)	–	–	–	–	–	–
Employees	–	–	–	–	–	1,100

CITIZENS EQUITY FIRST CREDIT UNION

5401 W. Dirksen Pkwy.
Peoria IL 61607
Phone: 309-633-7000
Fax: 309-633-3926
Web: www.cefcu.com

CEO: –
CFO: Charles E Walker
HR: –
FYE: December 31
Type: Private - Not-for-Pr

Citizens Equity First Credit Union (CEFCU) first gained traction in 1937 as the credit union of mammoth equipment manufacturer Caterpillar. Through some 20 branches CEFCU now serves employees of more than 550 companies and people who live and work in about a dozen counties in central Illinois and portions of northern California. It boasts more than 275000 members who have access to financial services such as checking and savings accounts CDs home auto and education loans credit cards investments and life and auto insurance. The credit union offers estate retirement and tax planning services through subsidiary CEFCU Financial Services and its partnership with MEMBERS Trust Company.

CITIZENS FINANCIAL CORP. (WV)

NBB: CIWV

213 Third Street
Elkins, WV 26241
Phone: 304 636-4095
Fax: 304 636-6924
Web: www.cnbelkins.com

CEO: Robert J Schoonover
CFO: –
HR: –
FYE: December 31
Type: Public

The proletariat should not confuse Citizens Financial with Citizens Financial Corporation (in Kentucky) Citizens Financial Group (Rhode Island) or Citizens Financial Services (Pennsylvania). This Citizens Financial is the holding company of Citizens National Bank which has about a half-dozen offices in central and eastern West Virginia. Citizens National Bank offers savings and checking accounts consumer and commercial loans trust services and other financial services and products. Real estate loans — including mortgages home equity loans and construction loans — account for some 80% of the bank's lending portfolio.

	Annual Growth	12/06	12/07	12/08	12/13	12/14
Assets ($ mil.)	(1.2%)	243.0	246.6	282.5	208.7	220.8
Net income ($ mil.)	-0.1%	2.1	1.0	0.9	1.5	2.1
Market value ($ mil.)	(10.5%)	35.3	20.4	12.7	12.2	14.5
Employees	(3.9%)	91	88	84	–	–

CITIZENS FINANCIAL GROUP INC (NEW)   NYS: CFG

One Citizens Plaza
Providence, RI 02903
Phone: 401 456-7000
Fax: 401 455-5927
Web: www.citizensbank.com

CEO: Bruce Van Saun
CFO: Eric Aboaf
HR: Joanna Robbins
FYE: December 31
Type: Public

Paper plastic or coin? No matter — Citizens Financial Group can handle it all. The company formerly known as RBS Citizens Financial Group is the parent of Citizens Bank which boasts some 1370 branches — many of which are located in supermarkets — across a dozen US states in the Northeast and the Midwest. The banks offer standard retail and commercial services as well as investment services insurance and employer-sponsored retirement plans. Citizens Financial also operates a network of non-branch banking offices in more than 30 states. Formerly owned by Royal Bank of Scotland RBS sold its remaining stake in Citizens in late 2015.

	Annual Growth	12/09	12/11	12/12	12/13	12/14
Assets ($ mil.)	(2.1%)	147,681.0	–	127,053.0	122,154.0	132,857.0
Net income ($ mil.)	–	(740.0)	0.5	643.0	(3,426.0)	865.0
Market value ($ mil.)	–	–	–	–	–	13,570.7
Employees	0.8%	–	–	–	18,160	18,310

CITIZENS FINANCIAL SERVICES, INC   OTC: CZFS

15 South Main Street
Mansfield, PA 16933
Phone: 570 662-2121
Fax: –
Web: www.firstcitizensbank.com

CEO: Randall E Black
CFO: Mickey L Jones
HR: –
FYE: December 31
Type: Public

Citizens Financial Services is an upstanding resident of the financial community. The holding company for First Citizens National Bank serves north-central Pennsylvania's Tioga Potter and Bradford counties and southern New York. Through some 15 branches the bank offers checking savings time and deposit accounts as well as real estate commercial industrial residential and consumer loans. Residential mortgage loans account for more than half of the bank's total loan portfolio. The Trust and Investment division offers investment advice and employee benefits coordination as well as estate and retirement planning services. Insurance is offered through the First Citizen's Insurance Agency subsidiary.

	Annual Growth	12/10	12/11	12/12	12/13	12/14
Assets ($ mil.)	3.3%	812.5	878.6	882.4	914.9	925.0
Net income ($ mil.)	3.9%	11.5	12.8	14.2	13.4	13.4
Market value ($ mil.)	9.7%	112.4	104.8	130.7	164.1	163.0
Employees	2.6%	186	192	197	200	206

CITIZENS FIRST CORP.   NMS: CZFC

1065 Ashley Street
Bowling Green, KY 42103
Phone: 270 393-0700
Fax: –
Web: www.citizensfirstbank.com

CEO: M Todd Kanipe
CFO: J Steven Marcum
HR: –
FYE: December 31
Type: Public

Citizens First puts the folks of southwestern Kentucky before all else. Founded in 1975 as a small private-investment club Citizens First is the holding company for Citizens First Bank which serves consumers and area businesses through about a dozen locations and 20 ATMs. The company's loan portfolio includes primarily commercial and residential mortgages and business loans. The company also provides title insurance services. Through alliances with other firms it offers its customers trust and investment services as well as insurance products. Fellow Kentucky bank Porter Bancorp withdrew its offer to acquire a controlling stake in Citizens First in late 2009.

	Annual Growth	12/10	12/11	12/12	12/13	12/14
Assets ($ mil.)	4.2%	349.7	403.8	406.6	410.2	412.8
Net income ($ mil.)	6.3%	2.5	2.6	3.2	1.8	3.2
Market value ($ mil.)	11.8%	15.0	13.8	17.3	19.4	23.4
Employees	2.2%	89	100	102	100	97

CITIZENS HOLDING CO   NMS: CIZN

521 Main Street
Philadelphia, MS 39350
Phone: 601 656-4692
Fax: –

CEO: Greg L McKee
CFO: Robert T Smith
HR: –
FYE: December 31
Type: Public

Citizens Holding Company has taken the proletariat approach to banking. The firm is the holding company for The Citizens Bank of Philadelphia Mississippi which operates some 20 locations in the eastern part of the state. Founded in 1908 the bank targets individuals and local businesses offering products such as checking and savings accounts money market accounts CDs IRAs and trust services. Lending activities consist mostly of real estate loans (about 70% of the loan portfolio) and commercial industrial and agricultural loans (more than 10%). Citizens Holding offers discount brokerage services through an agreement with First Tennessee Bank. Subsidiary Title Services offers title insurance.

	Annual Growth	12/10	12/11	12/12	12/13	12/14
Assets ($ mil.)	3.0%	818.2	853.9	880.8	873.1	921.1
Net income ($ mil.)	1.0%	7.2	7.2	6.8	7.1	7.4
Market value ($ mil.)	(2.1%)	103.1	85.5	94.9	90.7	94.8
Employees	(2.0%)	286	277	267	264	264

CITIZENS PROPERTY INSURANCE CORPORATION

101 N. Monroe St. Ste. 1000
Tallahassee FL 32301
Phone: 850-513-3700
Fax: +27-11-502-1301
Web: www.avi.co.za

CEO: –
CFO: Sharon Binnun
HR: –
FYE: December 31
Type: Government Agency

Being known as "The Sunshine State" doesn't stop hurricanes from invading Florida's shores. This fact drives property insurance rates up; so in 2002 Florida's legislature established Citizens Property Insurance Corporation (Citizens) a non-profit state-managed insurance company. It provides last-resort personal and commercial property/casualty insurance to Floridians who are unable to afford coverage from private sector companies. Citizens writes wind damage and hurricane-only wind damage policies as well as multi-peril policies. Over 90% of the company's policies in force are for personal residential coverage.

CITIZENS, INC. (AUSTIN, TX)   NYS: CIA

400 East Anderson Lane
Austin, TX 78752
Phone: 512 837-7100
Fax: –
Web: www.citizensinc.com

CEO: Rick D. Riley
CFO: David S. Jorgensen
HR: –
FYE: December 31
Type: Public

Citizens aims to prepare its customers for two of life's certainties: living and dying. A holding company Citizens provides ordinary life insurance in niche markets through its various operating subsidiaries. Through its CICA Life Insurance Company it issues life insurance in US dollars to wealthy individuals in Latin America and Taiwan. On the other end of the economic and life spectrum its Home Service segment sells life insurance to lower-income individuals in the a few Midwest and southern states primarily to cover final expenses and burial costs. The company has $1.4 billion of assets and $4.7 billion of insurance in force.

	Annual Growth	12/10	12/11	12/12	12/13	12/14
Assets ($ mil.)	9.5%	986.5	1,091.3	1,174.9	1,216.3	1,417.6
Net income ($ mil.)	–	15.5	8.4	4.5	4.8	(6.5)
Market value ($ mil.)	0.5%	373.1	485.3	553.4	438.2	380.6
Employees	(8.4%)	435	416	550	350	306

CITRIX SYSTEMS, INC.

NMS: CTXS

851 West Cypress Creek Road
Fort Lauderdale, FL 33309
Phone: 954 267-3000
Fax: 954 267-9319
Web: www.citrix.com

CEO: Kirill Tatarinov
CFO: David J. Henshall
HR: –
FYE: December 31
Type: Public

Citrix Systems takes connectivity to the next level. The company makes network access devices and software designed to enable PCs IP phones smartphones and other devices to remotely and securely access applications across wired and wireless networks freeing customers from the difficult and costly task of installing and updating software on each piece of hardware. Its product line includes application virtualization software (XenDesktop) network access devices (NetScaler) cloud computing connectivity and aggregation applications (CloudPlatform) and online meeting software (GoToMeeting). Citrix also offers managed online services for meetings and presentations technical support and remote desktop access.

	Annual Growth	12/10	12/11	12/12	12/13	12/14
Sales ($ mil.)	13.8%	1,874.7	2,206.4	2,586.1	2,918.4	3,142.9
Net income ($ mil.)	(2.4%)	277.1	356.3	352.5	339.5	251.7
Market value ($ mil.)	(1.7%)	10,998.7	9,762.3	10,550.1	10,169.1	10,257.5
Employees	15.6%	5,637	6,936	8,212	9,166	10,081

CITRUS VALLEY HEALTH PARTNERS INC.

210 W SAN BERNARDINO RD
COVINA, CA 917231515
Phone: 626-331-7331
Fax: –
Web: www.cvhp.org

CEO: Robert Curry
CFO: Lois Conyers
HR: Lisa Faust
FYE: December 31
Type: Private

Citrus Valley Health Partners is a 660-bed hospital system that serves the residents of California's San Gabriel Valley region located between Los Angeles and San Bernardino. It operates through four health care facilities: Citrus Valley Medical Center (CVMC) Queen of the Valley Campus CVMC Inter-Community Campus Foothill Presbyterian Hospital and Citrus Valley Hospice. Citrus Valley Health Partners also operates a home health care provider that offers nursing and rehabilitation care. The hospital system boasts several areas of specialty including diabetes care cancer treatment palliative care wound care and cardiac therapy.

	Annual Growth	12/00	12/01	12/02	12/03	12/13
Sales ($ mil.)	5.1%	–	256.7	278.3	280.0	467.5
Net income ($ mil.)	–	–	–	(9.1)	(2.5)	34.5
Market value ($ mil.)	–	–	–	–	–	–
Employees	–	–	–	–	–	2,800

CITY HARVEST INC.

6 E 32ND ST FL 5
NEW YORK, NY 100165422
Phone: 917-351-8700
Fax: –
Web: www.cityharvest.org

CEO: –
CFO: –
HR: –
FYE: June 30
Type: Private

The folks at City Harvest have found a way to harvest food straight from the asphalt of New York City streets. City Harvest is a not-for-profit organization that delivers food to about 600 soup kitchens food pantries shelters and community food programs in New York. The organization distributes more than 25 million pounds of excess food each year feeding some 260000 men women and children each week. Founded by Helen verDuin Palit in 1982 City Harvest works with more than 1900 food donors such as Tropicana Dannon Whole Foods D'Agostino Supermarkets and Au Bon Pain as well as roughly 28000 financial supporters to bring food to the city streets.

	Annual Growth	06/07	06/08	06/12	06/13	06/14
Sales ($ mil.)	17.0%	–	40.1	90.9	112.5	102.8
Net income ($ mil.)	–	–	–	4.9	3.7	(1.1)
Market value ($ mil.)	–	–	–	–	–	–
Employees	–	–	–	–	–	100

CITY HOLDING CO.

NMS: CHCO

25 Gatewater Road
Charleston, WV 25313
Phone: 304 769-1100
Fax: –
Web: www.bankatcity.com

CEO: Charles R. (Skip) Hageboeck
CFO: David L. Bumgarner
HR: Craig G. Stilwell
FYE: December 31
Type: Public

Take Me Home Country Roads may be the (unofficial) state song of West Virginia but City Holding hopes all roads lead to its City National Bank of West Virginia subsidiary which operates more than 80 branches in the Mountaineer State and in neighboring areas of southern Ohio eastern Kentucky and northern Virginia. Serving consumers and regional businesses the nearly $4 billion bank offers standard deposit products loans credit cards insurance trust and investment services. Residential mortgages and home equity loans constitute more than half of City Holding's $2.5 billion loan portfolio though the bank also writes commercial industrial commercial mortgage and installment consumer loans.

	Annual Growth	12/10	12/11	12/12	12/13	12/14
Assets ($ mil.)	7.0%	2,637.3	2,777.1	2,917.5	3,368.2	3,461.6
Net income ($ mil.)	8.0%	39.0	40.7	38.9	48.2	53.0
Market value ($ mil.)	6.5%	549.0	513.6	528.1	702.1	705.1
Employees	2.5%	805	795	843	923	889

CITY NATIONAL CORP. (BEVERLY HILLS, CA)

NYS: CYN

City National Plaza, 555 South Flower Street
Los Angeles, CA 90071
Phone: 213 673-7700
Fax: –
Web: www.cnb.com

CEO: –
CFO: –
HR: –
FYE: December 31
Type: Public

For celebrity sightings forget the Hollywood Homes Tour and camp out at City National Bank. The flagship subsidiary of City National Corporation has been known as "Bank to the Stars" since opening in Beverly Hills in 1954. The bank has since grown to some 80 branches in Southern California the San Francisco Bay area and Nevada as well as New York City Nashville and Atlanta. It focuses on personal and business banking investment management and trust services. The bank provides customized service tailoring its offerings to meet the needs of its high-powered clientele. Its target market includes small to midsized businesses entrepreneurs professionals and affluent individuals in urban markets.

	Annual Growth	12/09	12/10	12/11	12/12	12/13
Assets ($ mil.)	9.0%	21,078.8	21,353.1	23,666.3	28,618.5	29,718.0
Net income ($ mil.)	45.5%	51.3	131.2	172.4	208.0	230.0
Market value ($ mil.)	14.8%	2,470.8	3,324.7	2,393.8	2,683.2	4,292.4
Employees	4.3%	3,017	3,178	3,256	3,472	3,566

CITY OF HOUSTON TEXAS

901 Bagby St.
Houston TX 77002
Phone: 713-837-0311
Fax: 210-207-4217
Web: www.sanantonio.gov

CEO: –
CFO: –
HR: –
FYE: June 30
Type: Government Agency

It is bigger in Texas when you consider the City of Houston. As the largest city in the state and one of the largest cities nationwide Houston is more than an oil town. Founded in 1836 and home to Rice University and the Astros it also has a noteworthy museum district and operates the Texas Medical Center one of the world's largest health care facilities. While a mayor oversees Houston's management 14 council members (elected for two-year terms) have the power to enact and enforce city ordinances. With a population of more than 2 million Houston operates through some 20 departments including health and human services police and parks and recreation. It has an annual budget of about $2 billion.

CITY OF SALINAS

200 LINCOLN AVE
SALINAS, CA 939012639
Phone: 831-758-7256
Fax: –
Web: www.cityofsalinas.com

CEO: –
CFO: –
HR: –
FYE: June 30
Type: Private

It isn't known as the "Salad Bowl of America" for nothing; Salinas Valley is responsible for more than 80% of the lettuce grown in the US. With a population of more than 140000 the City of Salinas' economy is primarily based on agriculture. Many major vegetable producers are headquartered in the city and the area is well known for fruits and vegetables including broccoli carrots lettuce spinach strawberries and watermelons. The city's government consists of the mayor (two-year term) and six city council members (four-year terms). Salinas is also the hometown of famed writer and Nobel price laureate John Steinbeck.

	Annual Growth	06/09	06/10	06/11	06/12	06/13
Sales ($ mil.)	(0.5%)	–	111.7	110.9	108.0	109.9
Net income ($ mil.)	–	–	–	(1.9)	(4.9)	(7.5)
Market value ($ mil.)	–	–	–	–	–	–
Employees	–	–	–	–	–	735

CITY OF SEATTLE - CITY LIGHT DEPARTMENT

700 5th Ave. Ste. 3200
Seattle WA 98104-5031
Phone: 206-684-3000
Fax: 206-684-3347
Web: www.cityofseattle.net/light

CEO: Jorge Carrasco
CFO: Brian Brunfield
HR: –
FYE: December 31
Type: Government-owned

City of Seattle - City Light Department (Seattle City Light) keeps guitars humming and coffee grinders running in the Seattle metropolitan area. The US's 10th largest municipally owned power company Seattle City Light transmits and distributes electricity to almost 1 million residential commercial industrial and government customers and owns hydroelectric power plants with more than 1800 MW of generation capacity. The utility also purchases power from the Bonneville Power Administration and other generators and it sells power to wholesale customers.

CITY OF TACOMA DEPARTMENT OF PUBLIC UTILITIES

3628 S. 35th St.
Tacoma WA 98409
Phone: 253-502-8000
Fax: 253-502-8380
Web: www.mytpu.org/

CEO: Bill Gaines
CFO: –
HR: –
FYE: December 31
Type: Government-owned

City of Tacoma Department of Public Utilities (Tacoma Public Utilities) is fated to fulfill the electric and water desires of the City of Destiny's dwellers. The municipal utility's Tacoma Power unit generates transmits and distributes electricity to more than 169100 homes and businesses in Tacoma Washington. Tacoma Water serves more than 96730 customers; the division's water supply comes from wells and the Green River Watershed. Tacoma Public Utilities also oversees Tacoma Rail a freight-switching railroad with 75 customers and more than 200 miles of track and the Click! Network a high-speed data network that serves 23790 cable TV customers via 1460 miles of fiber-optic and coaxial cable.

CITY PUBLIC SERVICES OF SAN ANTONIO

145 NAVARRO ST
SAN ANTONIO, TX 782052986
Phone: 210-353-2222
Fax: –
Web: www.cpsenergy.com

CEO: Doyle N. Beneby
CFO: Richard Williamson
HR: –
FYE: January 31
Type: Private

And the award for being the energy distributor for the seventh-largest city in the US goes to City Public Service of San Antonio (also known as CPS Energy). Serving 728000 electricity customers and 328000 natural gas customers the utility operates in a 1514-sq.-mi. service territory. CPS Energy also has a generating capacity of more than 6570 MW from its 16 fossil-fueled power plants and its ownership interests in STP's South Texas Nuclear Project and wind power and solar power projects. As a municipally owned utility CPS Energy is exempt from retail competition in Texas.

	Annual Growth	01/09	01/10	01/11	01/12	01/13
Sales ($ mil.)	4.7%	–	1,930.9	2,068.7	2,258.4	2,213.5
Net income ($ mil.)	(83.2%)	–	–	78.8	21.3	2.2
Market value ($ mil.)	–	–	–	–	–	–
Employees	–	–	–	–	–	3,743

CITY UTILITIES OF SPRINGFIELD MO

301 E CENTRAL ST
SPRINGFIELD, MO 658023858
Phone: 417-863-9000
Fax: –
Web: www.cityutil.com

CEO: –
CFO: –
HR: –
FYE: September 30
Type: Private

City Utilities of Springfield Missouri springs to action with multiple services and products. The multi-utility supplies electricity natural gas and water for residents and businesses in the southwestern Missouri town. It has about 1870 miles of power lines and 1260 miles of natural gas mains serves about 110000 electric customers 82000 natural gas customers and 81000 water customers. It also operates the municipal bus system which has 25 regular street buses and five demand/response buses and serves about 790 broadband contracts through SpringNet Telecommunications. City Utilities of Springfield has a service region of 320 sq. ml. and serves a base population of 229000.

	Annual Growth	09/09	09/10	09/11	09/12	09/13
Assets ($ mil.)	(0.6%)	–	1,790.3	1,776.3	1,765.3	1,760.3
Net income ($ mil.)	(11.9%)	–	–	18.2	16.2	14.1
Market value ($ mil.)	–	–	–	–	–	–
Employees	–	–	–	–	–	980

CITYSERVICEVALCON LLC

640 W MONTANA ST
KALISPELL, MT 599013834
Phone: 406-755-4321
Fax: –
Web: www.cityservicevalcon.com

CEO: –
CFO: –
HR: –
FYE: September 30
Type: Private

You don't have to live in the city to get the services of CityServiceValcon which markets and distributes petroleum products throughout the Inland Northwest and Rocky Mountain regions of the US as well as in the adjacent Plains states. Its products include gasoline diesel aviation fuels lubricants propane and heating oil. The company has diesel gasoline and heating oils for delivery through its network of bulk plants. CityServiceValcon also operates cardlock fueling facilities under the Pacific Pride brand name. Regional independent petroleum marketers City Service and Valcon merged their operations in 2003 to form CityServiceValcon.

	Annual Growth	09/04	09/05	09/06	09/07	09/08
Sales ($ mil.)	16.6%	–	–	459.5	490.1	625.1
Net income ($ mil.)	(8.0%)	–	–	4.7	3.0	4.0
Market value ($ mil.)	–	–	–	–	–	–
Employees	–	–	–	–	–	150

CIVISTA BANCSHARES INC
NAS: CIVB

100 East Water Street
Sandusky, OH 44870
Phone: 419 625-4121
Fax: -
Web: www.fcza.com

CEO: James O Miller
CFO: -
HR: -
FYE: December 31
Type: Public

First Citizens Banc Corp. is the holding company for The Citizens Banking Company and its Citizens Bank and Champaign Bank divisions which together operate more than 30 branches in northern Ohio. The banks offer such deposit products as checking and savings accounts and CDs in addition to trust services. They concentrate on real estate lending with residential mortgages and commercial mortgages each comprising approximately 40% of the company's loan portfolio. The Citizens Banking Company's Citizens Wealth Management division provides financial planning brokerage insurance and investments through an agreement with third-party provider UVEST (part of LPL Financial).

	Annual Growth	12/10	12/11	12/12	12/13	12/14
Assets ($ mil.)	2.5%	1,100.6	1,113.0	1,137.0	1,167.5	1,213.2
Net income ($ mil.)	-	(1.3)	4.0	5.6	6.2	9.5
Market value ($ mil.)	26.7%	30.7	31.0	40.5	50.3	79.2
Employees	1.1%	290	300	-	313	303

CKX INC.

650 Madison Ave.
New York NY 10022
Phone: 212-838-3100
Fax: 212-872-1473
Web: ir.ckx.com

CEO: Michael G Ferrel
CFO: Thomas P Benson
HR: Kate Duffy
FYE: December 31
Type: Private

CKX is ready to sing "Viva Las Vegas" but any performance will be critiqued by the judges of American Idol. The company controls 85% of Elvis Presley Enterprises which manages the King's estate and licenses his likeness songs and name and operates tours of Graceland. CKX also owns 19 Entertainment the firm responsible for TV shows such as American Idol and So You Think You Can Dance. It owns the rights to the IDOLS brand which appears in more than 100 countries around the world. Additionally CKX has an 80% stake in the name image likeness and intellectual property of Muhammad Ali. Private equity firm Apollo Global Management owns CKX.

CKX LANDS INC
ASE: CKX

1508 Hodges Street
Lake Charles, LA 70601
Phone: 337 493-2399
Fax: -

CEO: -
CFO: -
HR: -
FYE: December 31
Type: Public

Revenues come naturally to CKX Lands. The company owns or has stakes in about 14000 acres in Louisiana that contain oil and gas wells mines timber and agricultural operations. Formed in 1930 the company does not perform any of these operations and is not involved in oil and gas exploration. Instead it generates revenues through royalties from the natural resources produced on its land. Originally set up to receive mineral royalties spun off by a bank to its shareholders CKX Lands' growth strategy is built around acquiring land in southwestern Louisiana. Its largest customers Mayne and Mertz and Cox & Perkins account for nearly 40% of sales.

	Annual Growth	12/10	12/11	12/12	12/13	12/14
Sales ($ mil.)	11.9%	1.7	2.0	3.3	2.1	2.6
Net income ($ mil.)	8.8%	0.9	1.0	2.2	1.0	1.3
Market value ($ mil.)	7.8%	23.4	22.0	26.7	29.1	31.6
Employees	(6.9%)	4	4	4	3	3

CLAFLIN UNIVERSITY

400 MAGNOLIA ST
ORANGEBURG, SC 291156815
Phone: 803-535-5724
Fax: -
Web: www.claflin.edu

CEO: -
CFO: -
HR: Shirley Biggs
FYE: June 30
Type: Private

Independent liberal arts institution Claflin University offers higher education in South Carolina. It provides 40 undergraduate graduate programs internships and other career-focused and continuing education programs for about 2000 in-state and out-of-state students. The university offers more than 30 undergraduate degree programs in fields including education humanities natural science math and music. Masters programs include biotechnology and business administration programs. Claflin University is affiliated with the United Methodist Church.

	Annual Growth	06/10	06/11	06/12	06/13	06/14
Sales ($ mil.)	(1.2%)	-	46.0	53.4	44.5	44.4
Net income ($ mil.)	(0.9%)	-	-	3.2	2.8	3.2
Market value ($ mil.)	-	-	-	-	-	-
Employees	-	-	-	-	-	340

CLAIRE'S STORES INC.

2400 West Central Rd.
Hoffman Estates IL 60195
Phone: 847-765-1100
Fax: 865-380-3742
Web: www.claytonhomes.com

CEO: Beatrice Lafon
CFO: J Per Brodin
HR: -
FYE: January 31
Type: Private

If the difference between men and boys is the price of their toys for young women and girls it may be the price of their accessories. For thrifty fashion-conscious females ages 3 to 27 Claire's Stores is the queen of costume jewelry handbags and hair bows as well as free ear piercing. The company operates more than 3000 shops primarily in malls under the Claire's and Icing banners. (Icing targets twenty-something females.) Its stores are present in all 50 US states Puerto Rico the US Virgin Islands and Canada as well as about a dozen European countries. Founded by Rowland Schaefer and later run by his daughters Claire's Stores is owned by the New York-based private equity firm Apollo Management.

CLARCOR INC.
NYS: CLC

840 Crescent Centre Drive, Suite 600
Franklin, TN 37067
Phone: 615 771-3100
Fax: 615 771-5603
Web: www.clarcor.com

CEO: Christopher L. Conway
CFO: David J. Fallon
HR: Doug Griffin
FYE: November 28
Type: Public

CLARCOR cleans up with filters. The company's industrial and environmental filtration unit makes air and antimicrobial filters for commercial industrial and residential buildings along with filters used in industrial processes. Brands include Airguard Facet ATI Transweb UAS Keddeg MKI TFSand Purolator. Companies in CLARCOR's engine and mobile filtration business make products under brands such as Baldwin Hastings Filters and Clark that filter the air oil fuel coolant and hydraulic fluids used in car truck heavy equipment and marine engines. CLARCOR's consumer packaging group makes custom-designed metal plastic and composite containers for food drug toiletry and chemical products.

	Annual Growth	12/11*	11/12	11/13	11/14	11/15
Sales ($ mil.)	7.1%	1,126.6	1,121.8	1,130.8	1,512.9	1,481.0
Net income ($ mil.)	2.1%	124.0	123.0	118.1	144.1	134.7
Market value ($ mil.)	1.9%	2,395.6	2,277.8	2,972.7	3,235.9	2,581.3
Employees	2.8%	5,447	5,417	5,267	6,015	6,093

*Fiscal year change

CLARE ROSE INC.

100 ROSE EXECUTIVE BLVD
SHIRLEY, NY 119671524
Phone: 631-475-2337
Fax: –
Web: www.clarerose.com

CEO: –
CFO: Monica Ray
HR: –
FYE: December 31
Type: Private

Clare Rose has risen to the top with help from The King of Beers. The company a top beer wholesaler in the US primarily markets Anheuser-Busch products including Budweiser Michelob Bacardi and Busch branded products. Clare Rose dominates distribution of the US beer maker's brands on New York's Long Island and Staten Island. The firm also carries other products including those of Heineken Redhook Ale and Widmer Brothers (both owned by Craft Brewers Alliance) Kona Brewing China's Harbin and Japan's Kirin. Founded in 1936 by Clare Rose the company is still owned and operated by the Rose family.

	Annual Growth	12/09	12/10	12/11	12/12	12/13
Sales ($ mil.)	0.2%	–	200.6	199.8	209.9	202.0
Net income ($ mil.)	(11.4%)	–	–	8.4	9.5	6.6
Market value ($ mil.)	–	–	–	–	–	–
Employees	–	–	–	–	–	267

CLAREMONT GRADUATE UNIVERSITY

150 E 10TH ST
CLAREMONT, CA 917115909
Phone: 909-607-8632
Fax: –
Web: www.cgu.edu

CEO: Deborah Freund
CFO: –
HR: –
FYE: June 30
Type: Private

Claremont Graduate University (CGU) offers sunshine as well as strong academics to students. About 35 miles from Los Angeles the university provides master's and doctoral degrees in 22 disciplines including education mathematics and psychology. A member of the Claremont University Consortium the university is made up of nine academic schools including arts and humanities educational studies and politics and economics. The Peter F. Drucker Graduate School of Management also is housed on the Claremont Graduate University campus. The relatively small university with an enrollment of about 2000 focuses on giving its students individualized attention. CGU was founded in 1925.

	Annual Growth	06/07	06/08	06/09	06/10	06/13
Sales ($ mil.)	–	–	0.0	57.7	59.1	62.6
Net income ($ mil.)	–	–	–	(15.2)	(16.1)	10.6
Market value ($ mil.)	–	–	–	–	–	–
Employees	–	–	–	–	–	250

CLAREMONT MCKENNA COLLEGE FOUNDATION

500 E 9TH ST
CLAREMONT, CA 917115929
Phone: 909-621-8088
Fax: –
Web: www.claremontmckenna.edu

CEO: –
CFO: –
HR: –
FYE: June 30
Type: Private

Claremont McKenna College (CMC) is an coeducational undergraduate liberal arts college with an annual enrollment of some 1250 students. It offers 33 majors and 8 sequences (programs of related courses). Double dual individualized off campus majors and more than 2000 courses available for cross registration across a network of CMC and six affiliated schools. CMC is also home to nearly a dozen research centers including The Keck Center for International and Strategic Studies and The Center for Human Rights Leadership. The college is managed by the Claremont University Consortium which supports seven independent Claremont colleges and is modeled after the University of Oxford.

	Annual Growth	06/09	06/10	06/11	06/12	06/13
Sales ($ mil.)	2.0%	–	109.6	159.1	154.6	116.1
Net income ($ mil.)	25.0%	–	–	53.6	22.9	83.7
Market value ($ mil.)	–	–	–	–	–	–
Employees	–	–	–	–	–	370

CLARIENT INC.

31 Columbia
Aliso Viejo CA 92656-1460
Phone: 949-425-5700
Fax: 949-425-5701
Web: www.clarientinc.com

CEO: Cynthia Collins
CFO: Michael R Rodriguez
HR: –
FYE: December 31
Type: Subsidiary

Clarient can help provide clarity for cancer patients and their physicians. The firm is a specialized diagnostic services provider offering a collection of advanced tests that detect and monitor the progression of various types of cancer. In addition to testing materials Clarient provides pathology lab services and delivers the test results via its PATHSiTE Web portal. The company's primcipal customers include pathologists oncologists hospitals and biopharmaceutical companies that outsource all or most of their specialized testing functions. Founded in 1993 Clarient is owned by GE Healthcare.

CLARION PARTNERS LLC

230 Park Ave.
New York NY 10169
Phone: 212-883-2500
Fax: 212-883-2700
Web: www.clarionpartners.com

CEO: Daniel Simon Heflin
CFO: Patrick J Tully Jr
HR: –
FYE: December 31
Type: Private

Clarion Partners values properties and property values. Formerly ING Clarion Partners the firm assembles and manages commercial real estate asset portfolios for about 250 individual and institutional investors. The company invests in a variety of asset types including real property stakes in real estate companies and trusts and real estate-related debt. It manages assets within separate accounts as well as for pooled funds. Clarion oversees more than $23 billion of commercial real estate assets including office retail industrial multifamily and hospitality properties in the Americas. Company management and Lightyear Capital bought Clarion from ING Groep in 2011.

CLARK CONSTRUCTION GROUP LLC

7500 Old Georgetown Rd.
Bethesda MD 20814
Phone: 301-272-8100
Fax: 301-272-1928
Web: www.clarkconstruction.com

CEO: Robert D Moser Jr
CFO: –
HR: –
FYE: December 31
Type: Subsidiary

Clark Construction Group specializes in building landmarks. The general contractor has constructed iconic structures such as the Boston Convention and Exhibition Center Dulles International Airport and FedEx Field the home of the Washington Redskins. Clark Construction serves commercial institutional and heavy construction customers around the US and is part of Clark Enterprises. It offers construction management design/build and general contracting services. Projects include convention centers sports facilities office complexes hotels airports correctional facilities manufacturing facilities water treatment plants highways and bridges and high-rise apartments.

CLARK ENTERPRISES INC.

7500 Old Georgetown Rd. 15th Fl.
Bethesda MD 20814-6195
Phone: 301-657-7100
Fax: 301-657-7263
Web: www.clarkenterprisesinc.com

CEO: -
CFO: James J Brinkman
HR: -
FYE: December 31
Type: Private

Like Clark Kent this firm holds some super powers. Clark Enterprises Inc. (CEI) is a holding company with diverse investments in real estate construction financial markets and venture capital. Its flagship subsidiary Clark Construction Group is one of the largest private general contractors in the US and provides construction management design/build and consulting services. Other CEI units develop manage and lease residential and office real estate. Private equity and venture capital arm CNF Investments is an active investor in the technology life sciences telecom and energy sectors. Chairman and CEO James Clark owns CEI which was founded in 1972.

CLARK MATERIAL HANDLING COMPANY

700 Enterprise Dr.
Lexington KY 40510
Phone: 859-422-6400
Fax: 859-422-7408
Web: www.clarktheforklift.com/

CEO: Dennis J Lawrence
CFO: Farruk Ghani
HR: -
FYE: December 31
Type: Private

Dealing with CLARK Material Handling can be an uplifting experience. Founded in 1917 to make material handling trucks CLARK has produced more than 1 million forklifts. Selling through its global network of more than 550 dealers the company's line of forklifts includes internal combustion trucks electric riders narrow-aisle stackers and powered hand trucks. CLARK also supplies aftermarket parts as well as Totalift-brand parts to fit other manufacturers' forklifts. The company has more than 250000 lift trucks operating in North America and more than 350000 units globally. Young An Hat Company a South Korean industrial conglomerate controls CLARK.

CLARKSON UNIVERSITY

8 CLARKSON AVE
POTSDAM, NY 136761402
Phone: 315-268-6400
Fax: -
Web: www.libguides.library.clarkson.edu

CEO: -
CFO: James Fish
HR: -
FYE: June 30
Type: Private

Clarkson University knows that quality research never sleeps in The Empire State. The research institution confers bachelor's master's and doctoral degrees in more than 50 fields of study including engineering business science liberal arts and health sciences. It also has well-regarded programs in advanced materials biotech environment and energy entrepreneurship and global supply chain management. The university employs more than 220 full time teachers and scholars catering to more than 4300 students. Clarkson University was founded in 1896 as a memorial to Thomas Clarkson a businessman from Potsdam New York where the primary campus is located. Its Capital Region satellite is located in Schenectady.

	Annual Growth	06/07	06/08	06/09	06/13	06/14
Sales ($ mil.)	(3.9%)	-	151.1	135.8	110.9	118.8
Net income ($ mil.)	-	-	-	0.0	8.0	39.0
Market value ($ mil.)	-	-	-	-	-	-
Employees	-	-	-	-	-	700

CLARUS THERAPEUTICS INC.

555 Skokie Blvd. Ste. 340
Northbrook IL 60062
Phone: 847-562-4300
Fax: 847-562-4306
Web: www.clarustherapeutics.com

CEO: Robert E Dudley
CFO: -
HR: -
FYE: December 31
Type: Private

If low testosterone's got you down Clarus Therapeutics may have your drug. The company is developing CLR-610 (formerly OriTex) an oral therapy to treat testosterone deficiency (hypogonadism) in men. It is a proprietary formulation of the prodrug T undecanoate (TU) and if approved Clarus intends to market it as a safer alternative to existing testosterone replacement products some of which are associated with liver toxicity inconsistent absorption inconvenient dosing and potentially unsafe transference of testosterone to children. The company believes CLR-610 could eventually be developed as a low-dose testosterone supplement for women. Clarus Therapeutics filed an IPO in late 2010 but withdrew it in mid-2011.

CLASSIFIED VENTURES LLC

175 W. Jackson Blvd. Ste. 800
Chicago IL 60604
Phone: 312-601-5000
Fax: +65-6532-6816
Web: www.hwahongcorp.com

CEO: Alex Vetter
CFO: Bob Gallagher
HR: -
FYE: December 31
Type: Joint Venture

You don't need top secret clearance to work with Classified Ventures. It operates a network of websites offering classified advertising space primarily for real estate and automobile sales. Its sites including Apartments.com (rental listings) Cars.com (new and used autos) and HomeGain.com (home sales) also distribute their content to a network of 170 Web sites owned and operated by newspapers and television stations around the country as well as top portal operators such as Yahoo! and MSN. Classified Ventures is a partnership of five leading media companies: A. H. Belo Gannett McClatchy Washington Post and Tribune Company.

CLAY ELECTRIC COOPERATIVE INC.

225 W WALKER DR
KEYSTONE HEIGHTS, FL 326567617
Phone: 352-473-4917
Fax: -
Web: www.clayelectric.com

CEO: Richard K Davis
CFO: -
HR: -
FYE: December 31
Type: Private

Clay Electric Cooperative covers a lot of ground in Florida. The utility distributes electricity to 14 counties in the northeastern part of the state including the suburbs of Jacksonville and Gainesville. It delivers power to about 165000 residential commercial and industrial members over more than 12900 miles of distribution and transmission lines. The consumer-owned utility offers electronic funds transfer average billing and a seniors' payment plan to residential customers and backup diesel power generation and special rate plans to businesses. The consumer-owned utility has a stake in Seminole Electric Cooperative which provides generation services to Clay Electric and nine other cooperatives.

	Annual Growth	12/09	12/10	12/11	12/12	12/13
Sales ($ mil.)	(3.4%)	-	376.5	356.6	337.2	339.7
Net income ($ mil.)	(24.3%)	-	-	20.2	8.2	11.5
Market value ($ mil.)	-	-	-	-	-	-
Employees	-	-	-	-	-	444

CLAYCO INC.

35 E WACKER DR STE 1300
CHICAGO, IL 606012110
Phone: 312-658-0747
Fax: -
Web: www.claycorp.com

CEO: Robert G. (Bob) Clark
CFO: Tony Schofield
HR: -
FYE: December 31
Type: Private

Clayco is a top US general building contractor that offers real estate architecture design engineering and construction services. The privately owned company serves a range of industries with a focus on industrial corporate government residential institutional and financial facilities. Projects include distribution and logistics centers industrial facilities and food and beverage industry warehouses and plants. Clayco also has constructed headquarters and operation centers call and data centers sports and education facilities and retail centers. Its Clayco Realty Group provides land development site selection and project financing.

	Annual Growth	12/09	12/10	12/11	12/12	12/13
Sales ($ mil.)	1.7%	-	443.2	511.3	391.3	466.1
Net income ($ mil.)	55.2%	-	-	2.4	2.4	5.9
Market value ($ mil.)	-	-	-	-	-	-
Employees	-	-	-	-	-	500

CLEAN DIESEL TECHNOLOGIES INC. NAS: CDTI

1621 Fiske Place
Oxnard, CA 93033
Phone: 805 639-9458
Fax: -
Web: www.cdti.com

CEO: Matthew Beale
CFO: David E Shea
HR: -
FYE: December 31
Type: Public

Clean Diesel Technologies (which operates as CDTi) has developed a few cool technologies to counteract global warming. The company is starting to commercialize its chemical fuel additives and other products for reducing diesel engine emissions and improving fuel economy. These include its platinum fuel catalysts which are marketed in Europe and the US under the Platinum Plus brand. CDTi also manufactures and licenses nitrogen oxide reduction systems (under the brand name ARIS) and chemical fuel additives to help control diesel engine emissions. The company has a licensing deal with Mitsui to use the ARIS technology.

	Annual Growth	12/10	12/11	12/12	12/13	12/14
Sales ($ mil.)	(3.8%)	48.1	61.6	60.5	55.3	41.2
Net income ($ mil.)	-	(8.4)	(7.3)	(9.7)	(7.1)	(9.3)
Market value ($ mil.)	(33.9%)	134.3	39.6	30.7	21.2	25.6
Employees	(6.9%)	156	181	164	151	117

CLEAN ENERGY FUELS CORP NMS: CLNE

4675 MacArthur Court, Suite 800
Newport Beach, CA 92660
Phone: 949 437-1000
Fax: -
Web: www.cleanenergyfuels.com

CEO: Andrew J. Littlefair
CFO: Robert M. Vreeland
HR: -
FYE: December 31
Type: Public

Forget cooking with gas — Clean Energy Fuels is driving with gas. Natural gas that is. The company owns and/or supplies more than 500 natural gas fueling stations across the US and Canada. These enable Clean Energy's 650 fleet customers to tank up their more than 35000 fleet vehicles with compressed natural gas (CNG) or liquefied natural gas (LNG). Clean Energy also helps customers buy natural gas vehicles and obtain government incentives. The alternative fuel company has CNG production plants in Canton (Michigan) and in Dallas and produces LNG at its two plants in California and Texas.

	Annual Growth	12/10	12/11	12/12	12/13	12/14
Sales ($ mil.)	19.3%	211.8	292.7	334.0	352.5	428.9
Net income ($ mil.)	-	(2.5)	(47.6)	(101.3)	(67.0)	(89.7)
Market value ($ mil.)	(22.5%)	1,248.4	1,123.9	1,123.0	1,161.8	450.6
Employees	12.3%	710	1,036	1,038	1,084	1,128

CLEAN HARBORS, INC NYS: CLH

42 Longwater Drive
Norwell, MA 02061-9149
Phone: 781 792-5000
Fax: -
Web: www.cleanharbors.com

CEO: Alan S. McKim
CFO: Michael L. Battles
HR: Deirdre J. Evens
FYE: December 31
Type: Public

Hazardous-waste management company Clean Harbors does more than its name suggests. Its major business lines are its technical services and industrial services units. Its technical services group which accounts for 35% of sales provides for the collection transportation treatment and disposal of hazardous waste including chemical and laboratory waste (but not nuclear waste). Its industrial services unit provides high-pressure and chemical cleaning catalyst handling decoking material processing and industrial lodging services. Clean Harbors also has a field services segment and an exploration services unit and recycles used motor oil through its Safety-Kleen unit.

	Annual Growth	12/10	12/11	12/12	12/13	12/14
Sales ($ mil.)	18.4%	1,731.2	1,984.1	2,187.9	3,509.7	3,401.6
Net income ($ mil.)	-	130.5	127.3	129.7	95.6	(28.3)
Market value ($ mil.)	(13.1%)	4,952.6	3,753.9	3,240.3	3,531.9	2,830.3
Employees	17.4%	6,840	8,320	13,180	13,000	13,000

CLEANNET U.S.A. INC.

9861 BROKEN LAND PKWY # 208
COLUMBIA, MD 210461185
Phone: 301-621-8838
Fax: -
Web: www.cleannetusa.com

CEO: -
CFO: -
HR: -
FYE: December 31
Type: Private

If Mr. Clean himself can't make a personal appearance at your office building CleanNet USA will happily come to your rescue. The company provides commercial building cleaning services to clients nationwide through franchises in more than 115 cities across the US. Its clients' properties include commercial buildings and facilities as well as retail properties such as Wachovia. CleanNet USA was founded in 1987 by president Mark Salek.

	Annual Growth	12/09	12/10	12/11	12/12	12/13
Sales ($ mil.)	8.1%	-	61.6	64.6	71.8	77.9
Net income ($ mil.)	-	-	-	5.4	4.6	(2.1)
Market value ($ mil.)	-	-	-	-	-	-
Employees	-	-	-	-	-	150

CLEAR CHANNEL COMMUNICATIONS INC.

200 E. Basse Rd.
San Antonio TX 78209
Phone: 210-822-2828
Fax: 210-822-2299
Web: www.clearchannel.com

CEO: Robert W Pittman
CFO: Richard J Bressler
HR: -
FYE: December 31
Type: Private

This company leaves few open channels on the radio dial. Clear Channel Communications is the #1 radio company in the US with about 860 stations that reach more than 239 million people. Its Premier Radio Networks produces syndicated radio content for more than 5000 stations. Clear Channel also sells spot advertising for about 4000 radio stations and 600 TV stations through Katz Media. (Meanwhile sister company Clear Channel Outdoor Holdings is one of the world's largest outdoor advertising companies with about 840000 display locations worldwide.) Clear Channel Communications a part of CC Media Holdings which is in turn owned by Thomas H. Lee Partners and Bain Capital.

CLEAR CHANNEL OUTDOOR HOLDINGS INC   NYS: CCO

200 East Basse Road, Suite 100
San Antonio, TX 78209
Phone: 210 832-3700
Fax: –
Web: www.clearchanneloutdoor.com

CEO: C William Eccleshare
CFO: Richard J Bressler
HR: –
FYE: December 31
Type: Public

In the great outdoors billboards in clear view mean money for Clear Channel Outdoor Holdings. The company is a leading display advertising operator with about 820000 properties in some 45 countries. Besides billboards Clear Channel Outdoor Holdings sells advertising on buses and trains and on "street furniture" such as bus stops and information kiosks in metropolitan markets. The company sells advertising space in airports and malls and on the sides of high-profile buildings and also creates displays that feature video and moving parts. CC Media which also owns #1 radio broadcaster Clear Channel Communications controls the company.

	Annual Growth	12/10	12/11	12/12	12/13	12/14
Sales ($ mil.)	1.4%	2,798.0	3,003.9	2,946.9	2,946.2	2,961.3
Net income ($ mil.)	–	(87.5)	42.9	(183.1)	(48.5)	(9.6)
Market value ($ mil.)	(6.8%)	5,055.7	4,519.1	2,527.8	3,651.3	3,813.4
Employees	(3.1%)	7,270	7,800	7,700	7,600	6,400

CLEARFIELD HOSPITAL

809 TURNPIKE AVE
CLEARFIELD, PA 16830-1243
Phone: 814-765-2950
Fax: –
Web: www.clearfieldhosp.org

CEO: Robert Murray
CFO: Dave Mc Connell
HR: –
FYE: June 30
Type: Private

Clearly if you are looking for health care in Clearfield Pennsylvania the place to go is Clearfield Hospital. Operated by Clearfield Area Health Services the rural acute care hospital has about 100 beds and provides emergency surgical diagnostic and general inpatient services. Specialized care centers focus on pediatrics obstetrics cardiac care wound healing cancer treatment rehabilitation and home care. Clearfield Hospital — which operates a number of rural primary and specialty care clinics — also provides educational programs classes and community outreach testing and screening services.

	Annual Growth	06/07	06/08	06/09	06/09	06/10
Sales ($ mil.)	(87.8%)	–	–	575.9	69.6	70.2
Net income ($ mil.)	–	–	–	0.0	(0.7)	(0.6)
Market value ($ mil.)	–	–	–	–	–	–
Employees	–	–	–	–	–	700

CLEARFIELD INC   NMS: CLFD

7050 Winnetka Avenue North, Suite 100
Brooklyn Park, MN 55428
Phone: 763 476-6866
Fax: –
Web: www.clearfieldconnection.com

CEO: Cheri P. Beranek
CFO: Dan Herzog
HR: Catherine Loye
FYE: September 30
Type: Public

Clearfield provides fiber optic cable and related optical networking equipment. Products include fiber distribution panels and cable management systems optical components (couplers multiplexers and splitters) and copper and fiber optic cable assemblies. It sells directly to telecom service providers and OEMs. Formerly called APA Enterprises the company merged its operations with those of its primary subsidiary APA Cables & Networks (APACN) and changed its name to Clearfield in 2008. Previously the company also operated an optronics unit but it exited that business in 2007.

	Annual Growth	09/11	09/12	09/13	09/14	09/15
Sales ($ mil.)	14.4%	35.2	37.5	53.4	58.0	60.3
Net income ($ mil.)	(6.7%)	6.2	7.7	4.7	5.4	4.7
Market value ($ mil.)	22.8%	80.9	70.0	184.1	174.5	184.1
Employees	2.5%	165	159	179	185	182

CLEARONE INC   NAS: CLRO

5225 Wiley Post Way, Suite 500
Salt Lake City, UT 84116
Phone: 801 975-7200
Fax: –
Web: www.clearone.com

CEO: Zeynep (Zee) Hakimoglu
CFO: –
HR: –
FYE: December 31
Type: Public

ClearOne Communications wants voices to carry loud and clear. The company provides audio conferencing systems to small and large enterprises educational institutions churches and government agencies largely in the US. It also sells related products including microphones and equipment carts. ClearOne's conferencing systems connect large venues such as auditoriums and board rooms as well as desktops and small conference rooms. Its products are made by contract electronics manufacturer Flextronics. The company markets its products worldwide selling primarily through distributors who in turn sell to systems integrators and resellers.

	Annual Growth	12/10	12/11	12/12	12/13	12/14
Sales ($ mil.)	8.8%	41.3	46.1	46.4	49.6	57.9
Net income ($ mil.)	23.9%	2.4	6.9	26.6	5.2	5.6
Market value ($ mil.)	26.4%	34.8	39.3	36.5	79.8	88.9
Employees	7.6%	123	139	145	141	165

CLEARVIEW HOTEL CAPITAL LLC

180 Newport Center Dr. Ste. 178
Newport Beach CA 92660
Phone: 949-706-9191
Fax: 949-706-3444
Web: www.clearviewhotelcapital.com

CEO: –
CFO: –
HR: –
FYE: December 31
Type: Private

Clearview Hotel Captial believes it can see profit on the horizon. The self-administered REIT (real estate investment trust) invests in upper-echelon hotel properties and hotel-backed securities in the US. It typically targets underperforming hotels in high-demand locations for investment. Formed in 2010 the REIT does not own currently own hotel property but intends to acquire 14 Marriott and Hilton-branded hotels from affiliates of property management company Columbia Sussex Management which will continue to manage the hotel properties. Though a self-managed REIT Clearview is operated by Clearview Hotel Operating Partnership for tax purposes. The company filed an initial public offering in 2010.

CLEARWATER PAPER CORP   NYS: CLW

601 West Riverside Avenue, Suite 1100
Spokane, WA 99201
Phone: 509 344-5900
Fax: –
Web: www.clearwaterpaper.com

CEO: Linda K. Massman
CFO: John D. Hertz
HR: –
FYE: December 31
Type: Public

No pulp fiction here — the story of Clearwater Paper is clearly fact. The company produces solid bleach sulfate paperboard consumer tissue products lumber and hardwood and softwood pulp. Business is divided into two primary divisions: Its Pulp and Paperboard segment manufactures paperboard (used to make packaging for foods liquids pharmaceuticals and toiletries) and pulp (consumed internally to make paperboard and tissues). A Consumer Products arm produces a private label tissue largely for grocery chains. Most of Clearwater sales are made in the US.

	Annual Growth	12/10	12/11	12/12	12/13	12/14
Sales ($ mil.)	9.4%	1,373.0	1,928.0	1,874.3	1,889.8	1,967.1
Net income ($ mil.)	–	73.8	39.7	64.1	107.0	(2.3)
Market value ($ mil.)	(3.3%)	1,531.4	696.4	765.9	1,026.8	1,340.7
Employees	(3.7%)	3,830	3,710	3,860	3,860	3,290

CLEARY GOTTLIEB STEEN & HAMILTON LLP

1 Liberty Plaza
New York NY 10006
Phone: 212-225-2000
Fax: 212-225-3999
Web: www.cgsh.com

CEO: –
CFO: Renee M Lercher
HR: –
FYE: December 31
Type: Private - Partnershi

Cleary Gottlieb Steen & Hamilton may be a big cheese in the Big Apple but the law firm also has made a name for itself in the international arena. Cleary Gottlieb's attorneys work from nearly 15 offices scattered across the globe and are known for their work in such practice areas as corporate finance mergers and acquisitions litigation and intellectual property. The firm boasts about 1200 attorneys with almost half of those based outside the US. Representative clients have included British Airways Deutsche Telekom Nortel and other international corporations. The firm was founded in 1946 by former Root Clark Buckner partners George Cleary Leo Gottlieb Fowler Hamilton and Mel Steen.

CLEARY UNIVERSITY

3601 PLYMOUTH RD
ANN ARBOR, MI 481052659
Phone: 734-332-4477
Fax: –
Web: www.cleary.edu

CEO: –
CFO: –
HR: –
FYE: June 30
Type: Private

Cleary University helps students navigate the murky waters of business education. The school offers associate bachelor's and master's degrees in business administration. Cleary University focuses on adult undergraduate students first-time college students wanting to begin a business career and senior managers seeking to advance their careers through a graduate degree. It has two campuses (Howell and Ann Arbor) and three extension sites (Flint Garden City and Warren) in Michigan. The school also offers distance learning courses online through its eCleary program. Patrick Roger Cleary founded the school as The Cleary School of Penmanship in 1883.

	Annual Growth	06/10	06/11	06/12	06/13	06/14
Sales ($ mil.)	(5.4%)	–	8.8	7.8	7.6	7.5
Net income ($ mil.)	–	–	–	(0.4)	(0.4)	0.1
Market value ($ mil.)	–	–	–	–	–	–
Employees	–	–	–	–	–	200

CLEAVER-BROOKS INC.

221 Law St.
Thomasville GA 31792
Phone: 229-226-3024
Fax: 918-560-3060
Web: www.bcbsok.com

CEO: Bart A Aitken
CFO: John C Oakley
HR: –
FYE: March 31
Type: Private

The Super comes out the basement boiler room thanks to Cleaver-Brooks. The company (C-B) designs and builds a slew of hot water and steam generation equipment is used in boiler burner control and stack exhaust systems. The short list includes watertube and firetube boilers heat recovery systems oil and gas burners breeching and stacks. Applications range from building heat to sterilization and humidification dry cleaning industrial processes and utilities. C-B also offers aftermarket parts engineering services retrofitting and training for its roster of industrial commercial and institutional customers. In 2011 the company expanded by acquiring Canadian exhaust gas stack maker Cheminee Lining.

CLECO CORP.   NYS: CNL

2030 Donahue Ferry Road
Pineville, LA 71360-5226
Phone: 318 484-7400
Fax: –
Web: www.cleco.com

CEO: Bruce A. Williamson
CFO: Thomas R. (Tom) Miller
HR: –
FYE: December 31
Type: Public

Down in the Louisiana bayous Cleco comes alive with the click of a light switch. The holding company's utility unit Cleco Power generates transmits and distributes electricity to approximately 283000 residential and business customers in 108 communities in Louisiana. Cleco Power has a net generating capacity of about 2565 MW from its interests in nine fossil-fueled power plants. It also purchases power from other utilities and energy marketers and it sells some excess power to wholesale customers. Subsidiary Cleco Midstream Resources owns and operates two gas-fired wholesale power plants a gas interconnection link to access the natural gas supply market and offers energy management services. Macquarie is buying Cleco.

	Annual Growth	12/10	12/11	12/12	12/13	12/14
Sales ($ mil.)	2.5%	1,148.7	1,117.3	993.7	1,096.7	1,269.5
Net income ($ mil.)	(11.8%)	255.4	195.8	163.6	160.7	154.7
Market value ($ mil.)	15.4%	1,858.6	2,302.1	2,417.5	2,816.8	3,295.4
Employees	(1.4%)	1,277	1,234	1,259	1,205	1,206

CLEMENT PAPPAS & COMPANY INC.

1 Collins Dr. Ste. 200
Carneys Point NJ 08069
Phone: 856-455-1000
Fax: 856-455-8746
Web: www.clementpappas.com

CEO: Mark A McNeil
CFO: Marc Friedant
HR: Dimitri Pappas
FYE: March 31
Type: Subsidiary

The Clement Pappas company makes canned and bottled apple cranberry and other fruit juices as well as mixers and canned cranberry sauce. The firm markets its products in the US and Canada under its Ruby Kist brand. It also makes the organic Grown Right store brand as well as private-label and foodservice products. Customers include retail food and foodservice companies; mass merchandisers; and drug discount and dollar stores. It sources its fruit from growers throughout the US as well as overseas. The company was founded in 1914 by Clement Dimitri Pappas and continues to be owned and operated by the Pappas family. Canada's Lassonde Industries acquired Clement Pappas for $400 million in mid-2011.

CLEVELAND BIOLABS INC   NAS: CBLI

73 High Street
Buffalo, NY 14203
Phone: 716 849-6810
Fax: –
Web: www.cbiolabs.com

CEO: Yakov Kogan
CFO: C Neil Lyons
HR: –
FYE: December 31
Type: Public

Cleveland BioLabs' scientists are working hard to develop drugs that help healthy cells stay that way as well as drugs that promote cell death in cancerous tumors. The company has based its research on the suppression and stimulation of the process known as apoptosis a form of cell-death that occurs after exposure to radiation toxic chemicals or internal stresses. In development are two product lines: protectans (suppressing apoptosis in healthy cells after radiation exposure) and curaxins (stimulating apoptosis in some forms of cancer). Protectans have applications in reducing side effects from cancer treatment and terrorist or nuclear events while curaxins are being developed as anticancer therapies.

	Annual Growth	12/10	12/11	12/12	12/13	12/14
Sales ($ mil.)	(29.9%)	15.3	8.8	3.6	8.5	3.7
Net income ($ mil.)	–	(26.4)	(4.0)	(18.2)	(17.3)	1.6
Market value ($ mil.)	(55.6%)	20.6	8.2	3.8	3.3	0.8
Employees	(12.0%)	55	60	85	44	33

CLEVELAND BROWNS FOOTBALL COMPANY LLC

76 Lou Groza Blvd.
Berea OH 44017
Phone: 440-891-5000
Fax: 440-891-5009
Web: www.clevelandbrowns.com

CEO: Joe Banner
CFO: David A Jenkins
HR: –
FYE: March 31
Type: Private

The Dawg Pound is the place to be for football fans in Cleveland. The Cleveland Browns Football Company owns and operates the Cleveland Browns one of the more storied franchises in the National Football League. Started in 1944 by Arthur McBride as part of the All-American Football Conference the club joined the NFL in 1949 and boasts four championship titles its last in 1964. The present team was awarded to the late Alfred Lerner and former 49ers president Carmen Policy after Art Modell relocated the original Browns to Baltimore in 1996. (A deal struck with the NFL allowed Cleveland to retain the team name colors and history.) Lerner's family led by son Randy continues to control the team.

CLEVELAND CONSTRUCTION INC.

8620 TYLER BLVD
MENTOR, OH 440604348
Phone: 513-398-8900
Fax: –
Web: www.clevelandconstruction.com

CEO: Richard G. Small
CFO: Mark T. Small
HR: –
FYE: December 31
Type: Private

Cleveland Construction Inc. (CCI) has ventured beyond Cleveland to offer its services nationwide. Beyond general contractor work CCI provides design build construction management and interior trades services for commercial and institutional projects. Also a top interior contractor in the US the contractor installs finishes such as drywall acoustic wall panels and specialty ceilings. Its projects have included hospitals universities correctional facilities hotels convention centers sports complexes retail outlets (including Wal-Mart stores) and public projects such as the Ohio State Stadium and the George Bush Intercontinental Airport in Houston. Founded in 1980 the company remains family-owned.

	Annual Growth	12/05	12/06	12/07	12/08	12/09
Sales ($ mil.)	–	–	–	(2,003.1)	186.5	217.0
Net income ($ mil.)	191622.6%	–	–	0.0	24.0	25.7
Market value ($ mil.)	–	–	–	–	–	–
Employees	–	–	–	–	–	800

CLEVELAND INDIANS BASEBALL COMPANY INC.

Jacobs Field 2401 Ontario St.
Cleveland OH 44115-4003
Phone: 216-420-4636
Fax: 216-420-4430
Web: cleveland.indians.mlb.com

CEO: Paul J Dolan
CFO: –
HR: –
FYE: December 31
Type: Private

Baseball fans in Ohio can cheer for this tribe. The Cleveland Indians Baseball Company owns and operates that city's storied baseball franchise a charter member of the American League dating back to 1901. Originally known as the Bluebirds the franchise adopted the Indians nickname in 1915 and went on to win five league pennants and two World Series championships its last in 1948. The team plays host at Progressive Field. Ohio lawyer Lawrence Dolan whose family controls Madison Square Garden and cable TV giant Cablevision has owned the Indians franchise since 2000.

CLICK COMMERCE INC.

1925 NW Amberglen Pkwy. Ste. 400
Beaverton OR 97006
Phone: 503-601-4000
Fax: 617-425-9201
Web: www.mpmcapital.com

CEO: –
CFO: –
HR: –
FYE: December 31
Type: Private

Click Commerce helped companies change the channel. The company developed software used to automate functions related to sales channel management collaborative commerce and compliance automation. Its applications were used by medical centers and research institutions for example to manage clinical trials automate administration processes such as grant preparation and oversee compliance issues. Click Commerce also targeted clients in the aerospace and defense financial services logistics manufacturing and retail industries among others. Customers included FedEx Lockheed Martin Jabil Circuit Nissan and Wal-Mart. Click Commerce was sold by Marlin Equity Partners to Huron Consulting Group in late 2010.

CLICKER, INC.

1111 Kane Concourse, Suite 304
Bay Harbor Islands, FL 33154
Phone: 786 309-5190
Fax: –
Web: www.clickercorporate.com

NBB: CLKZ
CEO: Willis Arndt Jr
CFO: Mark Noffke
HR: –
FYE: August 31
Type: Public

This company is much more interested in the mouse than the remote control. Clicker operates a network of websites focused around such topics as celebrity news classified advertising investing and sports. Its online properties include the ForWant (classified ads) Sippin' It (celebrity news and gossip) and Wall Street Network (investment community). Most of its sites include social networking functions to help foster interactivity and generate revenue through advertising and rewards programs. Chairman and CEO Albert Aimers owns nearly 45% of Clicker.

	Annual Growth	08/08	08/09	08/10	08/11	08/12
Sales ($ mil.)	(86.4%)	7.8	1.3	0.8	0.0	0.0
Net income ($ mil.)	–	(2.9)	(3.3)	(7.5)	(4.1)	(1.8)
Market value ($ mil.)	(24.0%)	0.3	0.0	0.2	0.0	0.1
Employees	(53.8%)	22	9	6	1	1

CLIENT NETWORK SERVICES INC.

15800 GAITHER DR STE 100
GAITHERSBURG, MD 208771431
Phone: 301-634-4600
Fax: –

CEO: Biswajeet Chatterjee
CFO: Lawrence Sinnott
HR: –
FYE: December 31
Type: Private

Client Network Services Inc. (CNSI) provides IT and business process outsourcing services to corporate and government clients in the US. Its offerings include consulting systems integration project management application development legacy migration and software architecture. The company is particularly active in the health care industry and worked as a subcontractor to support the Federal Health Exchange. It also supports the defense transportation energy and financial industries. CNSI takes an agnostic approach to technology and partners with a range of vendors including IBM Microsoft and Oracle. The company counts Best Buy Health and Human Services and the National Institutes of Health among its clients.

	Annual Growth	12/08	12/09	12/11	12/12	12/13
Sales ($ mil.)	(2.8%)	–	166.6	104.7	109.1	148.6
Net income ($ mil.)	141.2%	–	–	2.1	8.9	12.1
Market value ($ mil.)	–	–	–	–	–	–
Employees	–	–	–	–	–	1,200

CLIENT SERVICES INC.

3451 HARRY S TRUMAN BLVD
SAINT CHARLES, MO 63301-4047
Phone: 636-947-2321
Fax: –
Web: www.clientservices.com

CEO: Brad Franta
CFO: –
HR: –
FYE: October 31
Type: Private

This CSI investigates debt. Client Services Inc. (CSI) is a collections agency that provides accounts receivable management and customer care services nationwide. CSI markets its services to banks and credit card companies utilities and other government and commercial clients. It performs a range of services from pre-collection consultation to skiptracing debt purchasing and recovery consulting. Debtors can also make payments on the company's website. However call centers are the heart of its daily operations. CSI has four call centers that are staffed 24/7 and can handle 10000 calls per day. The company was founded in 1987.

	Annual Growth	10/08	10/09	10/10	10/11	10/12
Sales ($ mil.)	4.5%	–	48.5	68.2	64.3	55.3
Net income ($ mil.)	(7.8%)	–	3.5	8.3	5.7	2.7
Market value ($ mil.)	–	–	–	–	–	–
Employees	–	–	–	–	–	955

CLIFFS NATURAL RESOURCES, INC.

NYS: CLF

200 Public Square
Cleveland, OH 44114-2315
Phone: 216 694-5700
Fax: –
Web: www.cliffsnaturalresources.com

CEO: Lourenco Goncalves
CFO: P. Kelly Tompkins
HR: Maurice D. Harapiak
FYE: December 31
Type: Public

Iron ore fuel Cliffs Natural Resources' business engine. The company produces iron ore pellets a key component of steel making and owns or holds stakes in five iron ore properties that represent more than half of the US' iron ore production capacity. Cliffs' operations including Northshore Mining and Empire Iron produce 32.9 million tons of iron ore pellets annually. The company sells its ore primarily in North America but also in Europe and Asia. It also has a growing number of iron ore interests in the Asia/Pacific region and in Latin America. Cliffs had coal mining operations in North America but was exiting this business in 2015.

	Annual Growth	12/10	12/11	12/12	12/13	12/14
Sales ($ mil.)	(0.3%)	4,682.2	6,794.3	5,872.7	5,691.4	4,623.7
Net income ($ mil.)	–	1,019.9	1,619.1	(899.4)	413.5	(7,224.2)
Market value ($ mil.)	(45.0%)	11,954.8	9,554.9	5,910.7	4,016.6	1,094.2
Employees	(4.8%)	6,567	7,404	7,589	7,138	5,386

CLIFTON SAVINGS BANCORP INC

NMS: CSBK

1433 Van Houten Avenue
Clifton, NJ 07015
Phone: 973 473-2200
Fax: –
Web: www.cliftonsavings.com

CEO: Paul Aguggia
CFO: Christine R Piano
HR: –
FYE: March 31
Type: Public

You don't need CliffsNotes to figure out that Clifton Savings Bancorp is the holding company of Clifton Savings Bank which operates about a dozen branches in northeastern New Jersey's Bergen and Passaic counties. Founded in 1928 the bank serves consumer and business clients offering checking and savings accounts IRAs CDs and mortgages and other loans. Its lending portfolio is dominated by real estate loans primarily one- to four-family residential mortgages; the bank also issues multifamily and commercial real estate construction and consumer loans. Bank subsidiary Botany manages investments and securities. Clifton's majority stockholder is Clifton MHC a mutual holding company.

	Annual Growth	03/09	03/10	03/11	03/12	03/13
Assets ($ mil.)	1.4%	959.8	1,067.7	1,122.6	1,101.4	1,016.1
Net income ($ mil.)	6.5%	5.1	6.3	8.8	7.9	6.6
Market value ($ mil.)	5.6%	261.7	242.6	310.6	272.9	326.0
Employees	(0.2%)	101	110	100	102	100

CLIFTONLARSONALLEN LLP

220 S 6TH ST STE 300
MINNEAPOLIS, MN 554021418
Phone: 612-376-4500
Fax: –
Web: www.cliftonlarsonallen.com

CEO: Tony Hallada
CFO: Sharon Ten Clay
HR: –
FYE: December 31
Type: Private

CliftonLarsonAllen (CLA) is all about the numbers. The major accounting firm serves privately-owned firms and their principals along with not-for-profits and government agencies. It is organized as a holding company with three main segments: public accounting wealth management and outsourcing services. With more than $3 billion in client assets under management and 500 partners CLA is a top 10 US accounting firm. It primarily serves clients in the agribusiness financial employee benefit plan healthcare and manufacturing industries along with various levels of government.

	Annual Growth	12/09	12/10	12/11	12/12	12/13
Sales ($ mil.)	(1.1%)	–	–	–	569.2	563.0
Net income ($ mil.)	(24.4%)	–	–	–	204.7	154.8
Market value ($ mil.)	–	–	–	–	–	–
Employees	–	–	–	–	–	3,600

CLINTON GROUP INC.

9 W. 57th St. 26th Fl.
New York NY 10019
Phone: 212-825-0400
Fax: 212-825-0079
Web: www.clinton.com

CEO: –
CFO: –
HR: –
FYE: December 31
Type: Private

This group doesn't feature space-suit wearing funkmeisters or former presidents. But hedge fund manager Clinton Group does administer more than $1 billion in assets for banks insurance firms pension funds and wealthy individuals in the US and abroad. The firm specializes in alternative investments. Its strategy includes taking simultaneous long and short positions on mortgage-backed securities convertible bonds sovereign debt and equities. It also utilizes a variety of arbitrage techniques to take advantage of price spreads on securities trading on multiple markets. CEO and majority-owner George Hall co-founded Clinton Group in 1991.

CLOCKWORK HOME SERVICES INC.

Plaza Five Points 50 Central Ave. Ste. 920
Sarasota FL 34236
Phone: 941-366-9692
Fax: 941-366-9592
Web: www.clockworkhomeservices.com

CEO: Peter C Grabowski
CFO: –
HR: –
FYE: December 31
Type: Subsidiary

Timeliness is next to godliness at franchiser Clockwork Home Services. The company's 400-plus branded franchises which operate as contractors in the residential plumbing HVAC and electrical services industries emphasize punctuality and offer compensation if workers are late for appointments. Besides its franchised businesses (Benjamin Franklin the Punctual Plumber One Hour Heating & Air Conditioning and Mister Sparky) Clockwork Home Services operates companies that provide supplies services and group memberships to franchisees and other contractors. In mid-2010 the company was acquired by Direct Energy a subsidiary of Centrica (the UK's largest supplier of gas) for $183 million.

CLOPAY CORPORATION

8585 Duke Blvd.
Mason OH 45040-3101
Phone: 513-770-4800
Fax: 513-770-3984
Web: www.clopay.com

CEO: –
CFO: Franklin Smith Jr
HR: Cathy Schwarz
FYE: September 30
Type: Subsidiary

Just like Aldous Huxley and Jim Morrison Clopay knows something about doors. Subsidiary Clopay Building Products makes residential and commercial garage doors for the remodel and new-build markets. Brands include Avante Canyon Ridge Reserve and Coachman and its products are distributed nationwide by independent contractors home improvement stores and wholesalers. The Home Depot and Menard are among its largest customers. Another subsidiary Clopay Plastic Products makes specialty plastic films for hygienic medical and industrial applications. (Procter & Gamble uses the film for its disposable diapers.) Clopay Corp. is owned by holding company Griffon which also owns Telephonics and Ames True Temper.

CLOROX CO (THE) NYS: CLX

1221 Broadway
Oakland, CA 94612-1888
Phone: 510 271-7000
Fax: –
Web: www.thecloroxcompany.com

CEO: Benno Dorer
CFO: Stephen M. (Steve) Robb
HR: Jacqueline P. (Jackie) Kane
FYE: June 30
Type: Public

Bleach is the cornerstone of Clorox. The company's namesake household cleaning products are world leaders but the Clorox business reaches far beyond bleach. While it makes laundry and cleaning items (Formula 409 Pine-Sol Green Works) its vast products portfolio extends into dressings/sauces (Hidden Valley KC Masterpiece) plastic wrap and containers (Glad) cat litters (Fresh Step Scoop Away) and infection control items (HealthLink Aplicare Soy Vay). Other items include filtration systems (Brita in the Americas) charcoal briquettes (Kingsford Match Light) and natural personal care items (Burt's Bees). Clorox makes and sells its products worldwide.

	Annual Growth	06/11	06/12	06/13	06/14	06/15
Sales ($ mil.)	2.0%	5,231.0	5,468.0	5,623.0	5,591.0	5,655.0
Net income ($ mil.)	1.0%	557.0	541.0	572.0	558.0	580.0
Market value ($ mil.)	11.4%	8,673.7	9,319.4	10,693.0	11,755.3	13,378.5
Employees	(1.3%)	8,100	8,400	8,400	8,200	7,700

CLOUD PEAK ENERGY INC NYS: CLD

505 S. Gillette Ave.
Gillette, WY 82716
Phone: 307 687-6000
Fax: –
Web: www.cloudpeakenergy.com

CEO: Colin Marshall
CFO: Heath A. Hill
HR: Cary W Martin
FYE: December 31
Type: Public

Apparently there's also coal in them there hills. Cloud Peak Energy owns and operates three surface coal mines in the Powder River Basin of Montana and Wyoming and has a 50% stake in a mine in Montana. One of the largest producers of coal in the US it sells mainly to utilities and industrial customers and accounts for 4% of the electricity generated in the US. Formerly part of Rio Tinto it produces about 89 million tons of coal annually and controls almost 1.2 billion tons in proved and probable reserves. The company was formed in 1993 as Kennecott Coal.

	Annual Growth	12/10	12/11	12/12	12/13	12/14
Sales ($ mil.)	(0.9%)	1,370.8	1,553.7	1,516.8	1,396.1	1,324.0
Net income ($ mil.)	23.7%	33.7	189.8	173.7	52.0	79.0
Market value ($ mil.)	(20.7%)	1,417.5	1,178.9	1,179.6	1,098.4	560.2
Employees	0.6%	1,774	1,923	1,926	1,959	1,815

CLOUDCOMMERCE INC NBB: CLWD

1933 Cliff Drive, Suite 11
Santa Barbara, CA 93109
Phone: 805 964-3313
Fax: –

CEO: Andrew Van Noy
CFO: Gregory Boden
HR: –
FYE: June 30
Type: Public

Warp 9 (formerly Roaming Messenger) hopes to get all sorts of messages across. The company provides software used for e-commerce applications such as product presentation online catalogs and store management. Warp 9 also offers a Web-based e-mail and list management system that can be used for marketing and customer loyalty campaigns. Former chairman president and CFO Jonathan Lei owns about 48% of the company.

	Annual Growth	06/11	06/12	06/13	06/14	06/15
Sales ($ mil.)	(10.6%)	0.9	0.9	1.0	1.0	0.6
Net income ($ mil.)	–	(2.4)	(0.6)	(0.3)	(2.4)	(0.4)
Market value ($ mil.)	82.1%	0.1	1.0	1.7	2.8	1.1
Employees	9.3%	7	12	8	9	10

CLOVER TECHNOLOGIES GROUP LLC

2700 W. Higgins Rd. Ste. 100
Hoffman Estates IL 60169
Phone: 815-431-8100
Fax: 847-885-6400
Web: www.clovertech.com

CEO: Jim Cerkleski
CFO: William Saracco
HR: –
FYE: December 31
Type: Private

Clover Technologies makes its mark inside many a printer. The company makes toner cartridges for laser and inkjet printers and copiers and sells refurbished printers. Its supplies work with devices made by such vendors as Brother Canon Dell and HP. Clover's products are sold under its own Dataproducts and Genuine Recycled Cartridge brands as well as its private label brand CTG. It also makes ink and ribbon for postage meters and magnetically charged ink and toner cartridges for check printers. It recycles printer cartridges cell phones and other small electronics through its Clover Environmental unit. Golden Gate Capital and company management bought Clover from Key Principal Partners in 2010.

CLOVIS ONCOLOGY INC. NASDAQ: CLVS

2525 28th St. Ste. 100
Boulder CO 80301
Phone: 303-625-5000
Fax: 303-245-0360
Web: www.clovisoncology.com

CEO: Patrick J Mahaffy
CFO: Erle T Mast
HR: –
FYE: December 31
Type: Public

Clovis Oncology isn't trying to treat all cancers just a few that are very hard to treat. A biopharmaceutical company Clovis is seeking to acquire and develop therapies that treat pancreatic lung and other cancers that are traditionally difficult to treat with existing commercial drugs. The company has three candidates in its pipeline including a pancreatic cancer treatment in late-stage clinical development; an orally-available treatment for non-small cell lung cancer in preclinical development; and an orally-available treatment in clinical development for certain breast and ovarian solid tumors. Founded in 2009 Clovis became a publicly traded company in late 2011.

CLUBCORP HOLDINGS INC
NYS: MYCC

3030 LBJ Freeway, Suite 600　　　　　　　　　　　CEO: Eric L. Affeldt
Dallas, TX 75234　　　　　　　　　　　　　　　　CFO: Curt McClellan
Phone: 972-243-6191　　　　　　　　　　　　　　HR: –
Fax: –　　　　　　　　　　　　　　　　　　　　FYE: December 31
Web: www.clubcorp.com　　　　　　　　　　　　Type: Public

This company makes its green from the green — the golf green that is. Club-Corp is one of the world's largest operators of golf courses and private clubs with about 100 facilities in almost 25 states (mostly in the fair weather states of California Florida and Texas) and three in Cozumel Mexico. In addition the company operates about 50 private business sports and alumni clubs across the US as well as one in Beijing China. Its golf courses include such well known venues as Country Club of Hilton Head (Hilton Head South Carolina) Mission Hills Country Club (Palm Springs California) and Woodside Plantation Country Club (Augusta Georgia). Founded in 1957 ClubCorp went public in 2013.

	Annual Growth	12/10	12/11	12/12	12/13	12/14
Sales ($ mil.)	6.5%	687.7	720.0	754.9	815.1	884.2
Net income ($ mil.)	(52.2%)	254.3	(36.2)	(27.3)	(40.9)	13.2
Market value ($ mil.)	1.1%	–	–	–	1,143.2	1,155.5
Employees	6.9%	–	–	14,800	13,300	16,900

CLYDE COMPANIES INC.

730 N. 1500 W.　　　　　　　　　　　　　　　CEO: Wilford W Clyde
Orem UT 84057　　　　　　　　　　　　　　　CFO: –
Phone: 801-802-6900　　　　　　　　　　　　HR: Daniel C Walker
Fax: 305-460-1422　　　　　　　　　　　　　FYE: December 31
Web: www.adorno.com　　　　　　　　　　　　Type: Private

This Clyde is on the "most wanted" list for road construction. Clyde Companies operates through its subsidiaries including heavy civil construction firm W. W. Clyde & Co. which builds highways bridges power plants dams and other projects through the Intermountain West. Other subsidiaries include aggregate producers Geneva Rock Products and Gorge Rock; construction products manufacturer Sunroc; and Beehive Insurance which provides insurance products geared to the construction industry. Its Clements Concrete arm provides ready-mix concrete and sand and gravel products. Family-owned Clyde Companies traces its roots to 1927 when the construction company was established by Wilford W. Clyde.

CME GROUP INC
NMS: CME

20 South Wacker Drive　　　　　　　　　　　　CEO: Phupinder S. Gill
Chicago, IL 60606　　　　　　　　　　　　　　CFO: John W. Pietrowicz
Phone: 312-930-1000　　　　　　　　　　　　　HR: –
Fax: –　　　　　　　　　　　　　　　　　　　FYE: December 31
Web: www.cmegroup.com　　　　　　　　　　　Type: Public

CME Group doesn't predict futures but it does sell them. The company owns the Chicago Mercantile Exchange (or CME launched in 1898 as The Chicago Butter and Egg Board) the Chicago Board of Trade (CBOT) the New York Mercantile Exchange (NYMEX) and the Commodity Exchange (COMEX). The exchanges provide marketplaces for agricultural commodities as well as for interest rate equity government paper and foreign exchange futures. Products are traded on CME's Globex electronic trading system on its floors via an open outcry system using elaborate hand signals and through privately negotiated transactions. CME owns 27% of Dow Jones' index business including the Dow Jones Industrial Average.

	Annual Growth	12/10	12/11	12/12	12/13	12/14
Sales ($ mil.)	0.9%	3,003.7	3,280.6	2,914.6	2,936.3	3,112.5
Net income ($ mil.)	4.3%	951.4	1,812.3	896.3	976.8	1,127.1
Market value ($ mil.)	(27.5%)	107,932.7	81,740.3	16,997.5	26,319.8	29,738.1
Employees	1.1%	2,570	2,740	2,600	2,730	2,680

CMFG LIFE INSURANCE COMPANY

5910 Mineral Point Rd.　　　　　　　　　　　　CEO: Jeff Post
Madison WI 53705　　　　　　　　　　　　　　CFO: Jeffrey Holley
Phone: 608-238-5851　　　　　　　　　　　　　HR: –
Fax: 404-233-4930　　　　　　　　　　　　　　FYE: December 31
Web: www.northhighland.com　　　　　　　　　Type: Private - Mutual Com

CMFG Life Insurance doing business as CUNA Mutual knows a thing or two about credit unions having served them and their members since 1935. The company provides specialized insurance — such as credit insurance bond coverage business auto professional liability and health benefit packages — for the credit unions themselves as well as consumer products like life accident and homeowners insurance that the institutions can offer to their members. CUNA also provides credit unions with software marketing support and investment advice and it has select operations in non-credit union related insurance markets.

CMI TEREX CORPORATION

140 S. Morgan Rd.　　　　　　　　　　　　　　CEO: –
Moore OK 73160　　　　　　　　　　　　　　　CFO: –
Phone: 405-787-6020　　　　　　　　　　　　　HR: –
Fax: 405-491-2417　　　　　　　　　　　　　　FYE: December 31
Web: www.terexrb.com　　　　　　　　　　　　Type: Subsidiary

Whenever a "Men at Work" sign appears look around for CMI Terex's (doing business as Terex Roadbuilding) road building and heavy construction equipment. A unit of Terex Corporation's road building and utility products segment Terex Roadbuilding produces reclaimers/stabilizers pavement profilers asphalt mixing plants asphalt pavers concrete pavers and concrete production plants used to build roads bridges airport runways and parking lots. It also offers used equipment and builds trailers for industrial material hauling landfill compactors and machines for removing medical waste and contaminants from soil. The company has four US production facilities as well as plants in Brazil and Belgium.

CMS BANCORP INC
NAS: CMSB

123 Main Street　　　　　　　　　　　　　　　CEO: –
White Plains, NY 10601　　　　　　　　　　　CFO: –
Phone: 914-422-2700　　　　　　　　　　　　　HR: –
Fax: –　　　　　　　　　　　　　　　　　　　FYE: September 30
Web: www.cmsbk.com　　　　　　　　　　　　　Type: Public

CMS Bancorp was formed in 2007 to be the holding company for Community Mutual Savings Bank which serves the northern suburbs of New York City. Operating through five branches in Westchester County (one of the richest counties in the country) the bank collects deposits from area consumers and small businesses and uses the funds mainly to originate residential mortgages which account for more than 85% of its loan portfolio. It also issues commercial mortgages consumer loans and business loans and lines of credit. Deposit products include checking savings and money market accounts; CDs; and IRAs. Community Mutual Savings Bank was founded in 1887. Pennsylvania-based Customers Bancorp is buying CMS Bancorp.

	Annual Growth	09/10	09/11	09/12	09/13	09/14
Assets ($ mil.)	2.5%	247.4	253.8	264.7	258.3	273.3
Net income ($ mil.)	41.0%	0.2	0.2	(0.6)	0.9	0.7
Market value ($ mil.)	6.6%	18.6	15.1	14.9	16.0	24.0
Employees	(1.2%)	44	50	46	43	42

CMS ENERGY CORP

NYS: CMS

One Energy Plaza
Jackson, MI 49201
Phone: 517 788-0550
Fax: –
Web: www.cmsenergy.com

CEO: John G. Russell
CFO: Thomas J. (Tom) Webb
HR: –
FYE: December 31
Type: Public

Michigan consumers rely on CMS Energy. The energy holding company's utility Consumers Energy has a generating capacity of 8766 MW (primarily fossil-fueled) and distributes electricity and natural gas to more than 6.6 million of Michigan's 10 million residents. CMS Enterprises operates the non-utility businesses of CMS Energy and is an operator of independent power generating plants; its independent power plants (coal- gas- and biomass-fired) have a capacity of 2619 MW and are primarily located in Michigan but also in North Carolina. Subsidiary EnerBank USA provides unsecured home improvement payment option programs for homeowners.

	Annual Growth	12/11	12/12	12/13	12/14	12/15
Sales ($ mil.)	(0.2%)	6,503.0	6,253.0	6,566.0	7,179.0	6,456.0
Net income ($ mil.)	6.1%	415.0	382.0	454.0	479.0	525.0
Market value ($ mil.)	13.1%	6,120.6	6,758.1	7,420.6	9,632.7	10,001.4
Employees	(1.1%)	7,727	7,514	7,781	7,388	7,394

CNA FINANCIAL CORP.

NYS: CNA

333 South Wabash
Chicago, IL 60604
Phone: 312 822-5000
Fax: 312 822-6419
Web: www.cna.com

CEO: Thomas F. (Tom) Motamed
CFO: D. Craig Mense
HR: Liz Aguinaga
FYE: December 31
Type: Public

CNA Financial provides cross-continental coverage. The company is an umbrella organization for a wide range of insurance providers including Continental Casualty and Continental Insurance. It primarily provides commercial policies such as workers' compensation auto and general liability. CNA also sells specialty insurance including professional liability (doctors lawyers and architects) and vehicle warranty service contracts. The firm offers commercial surety bonds (through CNA Surety) risk management claims administration and information services. Its products are sold by independent agents and brokers in the US and through partners abroad. Holding company Loews owns 90% of CNA which was formed in 1897.

	Annual Growth	12/10	12/11	12/12	12/13	12/14
Assets ($ mil.)	0.1%	55,331.0	55,179.0	58,522.0	57,194.0	55,566.0
Net income ($ mil.)	0.0%	690.0	614.0	628.0	937.0	691.0
Market value ($ mil.)	9.4%	7,303.0	7,222.0	7,562.1	11,579.5	10,450.9
Employees	(3.6%)	8,000	7,600	7,500	7,035	6,900

CNA SURETY CORPORATION

333 S. Wabash Ave.
Chicago IL 60604
Phone: 312-822-5000
Fax: 312-822-7517
Web: www.cnasurety.com

CEO: –
CFO: John F Corcoran
HR: –
FYE: December 31
Type: Subsidiary

If the job doesn't get done CNA Surety pays the price. One of the largest surety companies in the US CNA Surety offers contract and commercial surety bonds which guarantee fulfillment of contracts. The company's Western Surety and Universal Surety of America units handle fidelity commercial and contract bonds and international surety and credit insurance; Surety Bonding another subsidiary specializes in commercial and contract bonds to small businesses. Contract surety (for construction contractors) accounts for a majority of CNA Surety's premiums. CNA Surety sells its products throughout the US via a network of independent agents and brokers. CNA Surety is a subsidiary of CNA Financial.

CNB CORP (MI)

NBB: CNBZ

303 North Main Street
Cheboygan, MI 49721
Phone: 231 627-7111
Fax: –
Web: www.cnbismybank.com

CEO: Susan A Eno
CFO: –
HR: –
FYE: December 31
Type: Public

CNB Corporation is the holding company for Citizens National Bank of Cheboygan which serves individuals and local businesses through more than five branches in the northern reaches of Michigan's Lower Peninsula. Serving the counties of Cheboygan Emmet and Presque Isle the bank offers standard fare such as checking savings and money market accounts CDs and IRAs. CNB Mortgage a subsidiary of the bank handles residential mortgage lending activities which account for approximately half of the company's loan portfolio; commercial mortgages make up most of the remainder. Bank affiliate CNB Financial Services provides insurance and financial planning. Citizens National Bank was founded in 1931.

	Annual Growth	12/10	12/11	12/12	12/13	12/14
Assets ($ mil.)	(0.1%)	255.1	250.1	260.9	247.7	253.9
Net income ($ mil.)	56.0%	0.3	(2.7)	1.4	2.7	1.9
Market value ($ mil.)	10.3%	11.5	7.9	12.4	13.3	17.0
Employees	1.3%	78	79	–	–	–

CNB FINANCIAL CORP. (CLEARFIELD, PA)

NMS: CCNE

1 South Second Street, P.O. Box 42
Clearfield, PA 16830
Phone: 814 765-9621
Fax: 814 765-8294
Web: www.bankcnb.com

CEO: Joseph B. Bower
CFO: Brian W. Wingard
HR: –
FYE: December 31
Type: Public

CNB Financial is the holding company for CNB Bank which provides traditional deposit and loan services. The financial institution's network of branches includes nearly 30 full-service CNB Bank and ERIEBANK offices in Pennsylvania and eight full-service offices in central Ohio operating under the FCBank banner. It also operates a loan production office. Commercial financial and agricultural loans make up more than 35% of CNB Financial's loan portfolio which also includes residential mortgages (about 30%) and commercial mortgages (more than 25%). Other offerings include credit cards investments life insurance wealth management and merchant credit card processing.

	Annual Growth	12/10	12/11	12/12	12/13	12/14
Assets ($ mil.)	11.6%	1,413.5	1,602.2	1,773.1	2,131.3	2,189.2
Net income ($ mil.)	19.5%	11.3	15.1	17.1	16.7	23.1
Market value ($ mil.)	5.7%	213.3	227.3	235.9	273.7	266.5
Employees	8.8%	304	314	337	395	426

CNL FINANCIAL GROUP INC.

CNL Center at City Commons 450 S. Orange Ave.
Orlando FL 32801-3336
Phone: 407-650-1000
Fax: 407-650-1011
Web: www.cnl.com

CEO: Thomas K Sittema
CFO: Tracy G Schmidt
HR: Lisa Shultz
FYE: December 31
Type: Private

CNL Financial Group looks to real estate when it wants to invest. Over the years the private investment management firm has created or acquired companies with more than $24 billion in real estate assets including hotel retail restaurant and senior housing. Founded in 1973 by chairman James Seneff the firm's lineup of companies includes CNL Lifestyle Properties a non-traded real estate investment trust (REIT) that invests in golf courses ski resorts theme parks senior housing and other properties. Its CNL Securities arm provides funding for CNL Financial Group and its joint venture partners. Other ventures include banking commerical and residential property development and private equity.

CNO FINANCIAL GROUP INC
NYS: CNO

11825 N. Pennsylvania Street
Carmel, IN 46032
Phone: 317 817-6100
Fax: -
Web: www.cnoinc.com

CEO: Edward J. (Ed) Bonach
CFO: John R. Kline
HR: Susan L. (Sue) Menzel
FYE: December 31
Type: Public

Have a modest but stable income? Graying at the temples? CNO Financial Group finds that especially attractive and has life insurance and related products targeted at you and 4 million other customers. With a focus on middle-income working families and seniors the holding company's primary units include Bankers Life & Casualty which provides Medicare supplement life annuities and long-term care insurance; Washington National which offers specified disease insurance accident insurance life insurance and annuities; and Colonial Penn which offers life insurance to consumers. CNO Financial operates nationwide.

	Annual Growth	12/10	12/11	12/12	12/13	12/14
Assets ($ mil.)	(0.6%)	31,899.6	33,332.7	34,131.4	34,780.6	31,184.2
Net income ($ mil.)	(34.8%)	284.6	382.5	221.0	478.0	51.4
Market value ($ mil.)	26.2%	1,378.5	1,283.0	1,897.0	3,596.8	3,501.2
Employees	3.4%	3,680	3,800	4,200	4,250	4,200

CNX GAS CORPORATION

CNX Center 1000 Consol Energy Dr.
Canonsburg PA 15317-6506
Phone: 724-485-4000
Fax: +351-21-012-9210
Web: www.clix.pt

CEO: -
CFO: William J Lyons
HR: -
FYE: December 31
Type: Subsidiary

CNX Gas may sound like a product for riot control but it is in fact a company that produces a more innocuous but valuable commodity. A subsidiary of CONSOL Energy CNX Gas is one of the most productive coalbed methane gas (CBM) producers in the US. Through its properties in the Appalachian Basin (primarily in Pennsylvania Tennessee Virginia and West Virginia) CNX Gas produced 153.5 net billion cu. ft. of gas in 2011. A significant amount of its gas production is derived in conjunction with CONSOL Energy's coal mining activity although it also produces gas from shale and other unconventional sources. In 2011 the company had proved reserves of 3.5 trillion cu. ft. of natural gas equivalent.

COACH, INC.
NYS: COH

516 West 34th Street
New York, NY 10001
Phone: 212 594-1850
Fax: 212 594-1682
Web: www.coach.com

CEO: Ian Bickley
CFO: Jane H. Nielsen
HR: Sarah Dunn
FYE: June 27
Type: Public

Coach is riding in style thanks to the company's leather items and some savvy licensing deals. The company designs and makes (mostly through third parties) high-end leather goods and accessories including handbags wallets and luggage. Founded in 1941 Coach also licenses its name for watches eyewear fragrances scarves and footwear. The luxury brand sells its wares through more than 1000 department and outlet stores (in the US and more than 45 other countries) catalogs and its website. Macy's Nordstrom Saks and others carry Coach items. It also runs more than 1000 retail and factory outlet stores in North America Japan and China. The company acquired luxury shoe maker Stuart Weitzman Holdings in 2015.

	Annual Growth	07/11*	06/12	06/13	06/14	06/15
Sales ($ mil.)	0.2%	4,158.5	4,763.2	5,075.4	4,806.2	4,191.6
Net income ($ mil.)	(17.8%)	880.8	1,038.9	1,034.4	781.3	402.4
Market value ($ mil.)	(14.0%)	18,252.8	16,175.6	15,791.1	9,534.4	9,990.8
Employees	1.3%	15,000	18,000	17,200	17,200	15,800

*Fiscal year change

COAST CITRUS DISTRIBUTORS

7597 BRISTOW CT
SAN DIEGO, CA 921547419
Phone: 619-661-7950
Fax: -
Web: www.coastcitrus.com

CEO: James M Alvarez
CFO: -
HR: -
FYE: December 29
Type: Private

Coast Citrus Distributors is a leading wholesale distributor of fresh fruits and vegetables in Mexico and the US. The company supplies a variety of produce including bananas lettuce limes and potatoes to retail grocers and other food customers. It distributes under the names Coast Citrus Coast Tropical Olympic Fruit and Vegetable and Importadora y Exportadora. Coast Citrus Distributors operates half a dozen distribution facilities in California Texas and Florida. It also has about five locations in Mexico. The late Roberto Alvarez founded the family-owned business in 1950.

	Annual Growth	06/09	06/10*	01/11*	12/11	12/12
Sales ($ mil.)	(2.2%)	-	293.7	294.0	297.8	281.2
Net income ($ mil.)	(34.2%)	-	-	4.1	3.0	2.7
Market value ($ mil.)	-	-	-	-	-	-
Employees	-	-	-	-	-	389

*Fiscal year change

COAST DISTRIBUTION SYSTEM
ASE: CRV

350 Woodview Avenue
Morgan Hill, CA 95037
Phone: 408 782-6686
Fax: -
Web: www.coastdistribution.com

CEO: James Musbach
CFO: Sandra A Knell
HR: David Smeltzer
FYE: December 31
Type: Public

Be it on wheels or on the water there's no place like home with accessories from The Coast. The Coast Distribution System wholesales accessories replacement parts and supplies for recreational vehicles (RVs). Tapping outdoor recreational markets with much in common the company also distributes boating and marine accessories and parts. Its lineup includes close to 11000 products many of them Coast branded from various appliances to awnings boat covers life jackets and trailer hitches. Products are channeled from 17 distribution centers in the US and Canada to more than 15000 customers primarily RV and boat dealerships supply stores and service centers.

	Annual Growth	12/09	12/10	12/11	12/12	12/13
Sales ($ mil.)	2.5%	103.2	108.6	108.2	113.5	113.9
Net income ($ mil.)	-	0.1	0.2	(0.9)	(2.0)	(0.6)
Market value ($ mil.)	(4.3%)	19.7	19.5	11.4	10.1	16.5
Employees	0.9%	265	265	275	275	275

COAST ELECTRIC POWER ASSOCIATION

18020 HIGHWAY 603
KILN, MS 395568487
Phone: 228-363-7000
Fax: -
Web: www.coastepa.com

CEO: -
CFO: John C Holston
HR: -
FYE: December 31
Type: Private

There's no coasting for the Coast Electric Power Association when it comes to providing residents in three southern Mississippi counties with electricity. The utility uses a 6400-mile distribution network to serve its more than 76000 members (the great majority or which are residential customers) in Hancock Pearl River and Harrison counties. Coast offers electronic fund transfer and average monthly payment plans and rebates on energy efficient home improvements. The utility's power is generated by South Mississippi Electric Power an association of Coast and 10 other cooperatives. It partners with Touchstone Energy Cooperatives.

	Annual Growth	12/09	12/10	12/11	12/12	12/13
Sales ($ mil.)	(1.6%)	-	196.7	185.5	184.8	187.1
Net income ($ mil.)	(3.2%)	-	-	13.5	13.3	12.6
Market value ($ mil.)	-	-	-	-	-	-
Employees	-	-	-	-	-	238

COASTAL BANKING CO INC
NBB: CBCO

36 Sea Island Parkway
Beaufort, SC 29907
Phone: 843 522-1228
Fax: 843 524-4510
Web: www.coastalbanking.com

CEO: Michael G Sanchez
CFO: Paul R Garrigues
HR: –
FYE: December 31
Type: Public

Hoping to provide traditional small-town banking amid rapid growth in the Southeast a group of area banking veterans formed Coastal Banking Company in 2000. The holding company owns CBC National Bank which does business as Lowcountry National Bank from around five branches in southern South Carolina and First National Bank of Nassau County which operates loan offices in Atlanta and Savannah Georgia and Jacksonville Florida in addition to one bank branch in Meigs Georgia under The Georgia Bank name. The banks offer standard products and services including business and consumer loans checking and savings accounts and CDs.

	Annual Growth	12/10	12/11	12/12	12/13	12/14
Assets ($ mil.)	(0.3%)	427.1	477.6	475.0	375.6	421.9
Net income ($ mil.)	–	(3.8)	0.4	1.9	1.6	3.1
Market value ($ mil.)	40.0%	6.4	6.0	13.3	0.2	24.6
Employees	25.2%	142	356	362	333	349

COASTAL CAROLINA UNIVERSITY

642 CENTURY CIR
CONWAY, SC 295268279
Phone: 843-347-3161
Fax: –
Web: www.support.coastal.edu

CEO: –
CFO: –
HR: Pat West
FYE: June 30
Type: Private

It's hard for students at Coastal Carolina University not to be cocky. The university (whose rooster mascot Chanticleer appears in Chaucer's Canterbury Tales) offers bachelor's degrees in about 60 fields of study through schools of science humanities education and business. It also offers about 10 master's degrees in fields including business administration education and coastal marine and wetland studies. Coastal Carolina University has an enrollment of more than 9000 students and about 1000 faculty members. Its student-to-teacher ratio is 17:1.

	Annual Growth	06/10	06/11	06/12	06/13	06/14
Sales ($ mil.)	8.0%	–	117.0	128.8	141.6	147.3
Net income ($ mil.)	186.2%	–	–	29.8	27.7	244.1
Market value ($ mil.)	–	–	–	–	–	–
Employees	–	–	–	–	–	900

COASTAL PACIFIC FOOD DISTRIBUTORS INC.

1015 PERFORMANCE DR
STOCKTON, CA 952064925
Phone: 909-947-2066
Fax: –
Web: www.cpfd.com

CEO: –
CFO: –
HR: –
FYE: December 28
Type: Private

Coastal Pacific Food Distributors (CPF) fuels the military forces from facility to fork. The company is one of the top wholesale food distributors that primarily serves the US armed forces across the Western US and in the Far East. As part of its business CPF provides a full line of groceries to military bases run by the US Army Navy Air Force and Marines. It delivers a variety of products from distribution centers located in California Washington and Hawaii. CPF also offers information system programming services for its customers to track sales and shipping as well as procurement and logistics through partnerships in Iraq Kuwait and Saudi Arabia. The company was founded in 1986.

	Annual Growth	01/10	01/11*	12/11	12/12	12/13
Sales ($ mil.)	6.4%	–	1,113.6	1,162.7	1,213.0	1,260.4
Net income ($ mil.)	(16.0%)	–	–	25.2	15.1	17.8
Market value ($ mil.)	–	–	–	–	–	–
Employees	–	–	–	–	–	459

*Fiscal year change

COATES INTERNATIONAL, LTD.
NBB: COTE

2100 Highway 34
Wall Township, NJ 07719
Phone: 732 449-7717
Fax: –
Web: www.coatesengine.com

CEO: George J Coates
CFO: Barry C Kaye
HR: –
FYE: December 31
Type: Public

Coates International Ltd. (CIL) may be sparking the next industrial revolution. CEO George J. Coates founded CIL to develop his many patents the most noteworthy being the Coates Spherical Rotary Valve (CSRV). The CSRV is designed to replace the century-old technology of the internal combustion engine's camshaft and poppet valve system. An engine equipped with the CSRV can run on different fuels while reducing emissions and increasing efficiency; the need for maintenance is also reduced. CIL licenses its CSRV engine technology to makers of heavy-duty vehicles automobiles and industrial engines. Major customer Almont Energy (Canada) took first delivery of CSRV engines in 2010.

	Annual Growth	12/10	12/11	12/12	12/13	12/14
Sales ($ mil.)	(62.9%)	1.0	0.3	0.0	0.0	0.0
Net income ($ mil.)	–	(1.1)	(3.0)	(4.5)	(2.8)	(12.8)
Market value ($ mil.)	(54.9%)	84.3	59.9	7.8	14.6	3.5
Employees	(3.8%)	7	7	7	7	6

COATING PLACE INC.

200 Paoli St.
Verona WI 53593
Phone: 608-845-9521
Fax: 608-845-9526
Web: www.encap.com

CEO: Timothy Breunig
CFO: –
HR: –
FYE: October 31
Type: Private

At Coating Place any pills that lie down in a Wurster fluid bed get up smooth and dry. The drug delivery development and manufacturer specializes in coating surfaces for pharmaceuticals to improve shelf life and stability allow for controlled or sustained release and eliminate odor or taste. The company specializes in Wurster fluid bed (a process used to coat a variety of substances including pills and tablets) coating services for encapsulation of powders granules and crystals. It also provides research and contract manufacturing services. Privately-held Coating Place is capable of processing controlled substances and its laboratory standards meet GMP (Good Manufacturing Practice) standards.

COBALT INTERNATIONAL ENERGY L.P.
NYSE: CIE

2 Post Oak Central 1980 Post Oak Blvd. Ste. 1200
Houston TX 77056
Phone: 713-579-9100
Fax: 713-579-9196
Web: www.cobaltintl.com

CEO: –
CFO: Shannon E Young III
HR: –
FYE: December 31
Type: Public

Cobalt International Energy scours the deep blue seas in search of oil. An exploration and development company Cobalt International owns interests in offshore properties located in the Gulf of Mexico and West Africa. The company's assets include majority and minority stakes in more than 600000 net acres in almost 50 blocks in the Gulf and more than 2 million acres in more than 100 prospects located off the coast of Gabon and Angola. It focuses primarily on searching for oil pockets encased beneath salt layers which until recently was traditionally untapped geological territory in the oil industry. Cobalt International Energy contracts two drilling rigs one from Ensco and one from Diamond Offshore.

COBB ELECTRIC MEMBERSHIP CORPORATION

1000 EMC PKWY NE
MARIETTA, GA 300607908
Phone: 770-429-2222
Fax: -
Web: www.cobbemc.com

CEO: -
CFO: Robert Steele
HR: Angie Jones
FYE: December 31
Type: Private

Cobb Electric Membership Corporation (Cobb EMC) makes sure that Cobb County Georgia residents can cook corn on the cob (and anything else) using either electric power or natural gas. The utility distributes electricity to more than 200000 meters (more than 177000 residential commercial and industrial members) in Cobb County and four other north metro Atlanta counties. Cobb EMC operates about 10000 miles of power lines. The company's Gas South unit markets natural gas to customers who receive their service on Atlanta Gas & Light's natural gas distribution pipelines in Georgia.

	Annual Growth	12/06	12/07	12/08*	04/09*	12/13
Sales ($ mil.)	2.1%	-	367.4	381.5	641.0	416.3
Net income ($ mil.)	-	-	-	(0.1)	3.6	(8.1)
Market value ($ mil.)	-	-	-	-	-	-
Employees	-	-	-	-	-	548

*Fiscal year change

COBIZ FINANCIAL INC

NMS: COBZ

821 17th Street
Denver, CO 80202
Phone: 303 312-3400
Fax: -
Web: www.cobizbank.com

CEO: Steven Bangert
CFO: Lyne B. Andrich
HR: -
FYE: December 31
Type: Public

CoBiz Financial is reaching new heights in the Rockies and in the Valley of the Sun. It's the holding company for CoBiz Bank which operates as Colorado Business Bank and Arizona Business Bank. The former operates more than 10 branches in the Denver Boulder and Vail areas; the latter has about a half-dozen branches in and around Phoenix. CoBiz's locations operate as separate community banks each with a local president who has decision-making authority. The company offers investment banking services through subsidiary Green Manning & Bunch insurance through CoBiz Insurance and wealth management through CoBiz Investment Management CoBiz Trust and Financial Designs.

	Annual Growth	12/11	12/12	12/13	12/14	12/15
Assets ($ mil.)	8.4%	2,423.5	2,653.6	2,800.7	3,062.2	3,351.8
Net income ($ mil.)	(6.1%)	33.5	24.6	27.6	29.0	26.1
Market value ($ mil.)	23.5%	237.3	307.2	491.8	539.9	551.9
Employees	(0.6%)	546	512	513	534	532

COBORN'S INCORPORATED

1445 HIGHWAY 23 E BLDG A
SAINT CLOUD, MN 563040952
Phone: 763-389-1350
Fax: -
Web: www.coborns.lifepics.com

CEO: Daniel Coborn
CFO: Tom Velin
HR: -
FYE: December 28
Type: Private

Coborn's hopes you'll shop at your convenience. The company operates 52 stores across Minnesota North Dakota South Dakota Iowa Illinois and Wisconsin under the Coborn's Cash Wise Foods and Save-A-Lot banners. To support its more than 100 retail locations Coborn's operates its own central bakery dry cleaning facility and grocery distribution center. It supplies its stores with baked goods deli items and meat from its own central bakery and manufacturing plant. Along with its grocery stores the firm owns and operates pharmacies and convenience liquor and video stores.

	Annual Growth	12/09	12/10	12/11	12/12	12/13
Sales ($ mil.)	4.1%	-	1,103.8	1,191.8	1,220.5	1,246.7
Net income ($ mil.)	2.7%	-	-	29.2	32.4	30.8
Market value ($ mil.)	-	-	-	-	-	-
Employees	-	-	-	-	-	7,000

COBRA ELECTRONICS CORP.

NMS: COBR

6500 West Cortland Street
Chicago, IL 60707
Phone: 773 889-8870
Fax: -
Web: www.cobra.com

CEO: -
CFO: Robert J Ben
HR: Laures Chris
FYE: December 31
Type: Public

Cobra Electronics' citizens band radios and radar detectors are good buddies when you're on the road. Its principal Cobra division markets CB and marine radios two-way radios radar detectors power inverters jump-starters and GPS navigation systems for professional drivers under the Cobra brand. The firm's PPL unit peddles personal navigation systems and speed camera location detectors under the Snooper name. Cobra Electronics also manages the AURA database of photo-enforcement locations (including speed camera and red-light detector positions) in North America and Europe. Cobra's products are sold in the US Canada and Europe through consumer electronics stores discount retailers and truck stops.

	Annual Growth	12/08	12/09	12/10	12/11	12/12
Sales ($ mil.)	(1.2%)	124.7	105.2	110.5	123.3	118.9
Net income ($ mil.)	-	(18.8)	(10.3)	1.6	3.1	3.2
Market value ($ mil.)	38.1%	6.9	11.0	21.2	29.3	25.1
Employees	(2.7%)	174	150	152	150	156

COCA-COLA BOTTLING CO. CONSOLIDATED

NMS: COKE

4100 Coca-Cola Plaza
Charlotte, NC 28211
Phone: 704 557-4400
Fax: -
Web: www.cokeconsolidated.com

CEO: J. Frank Harrison
CFO: James E. (Jamie) Harris
HR: -
FYE: December 28
Type: Public

Southerners like their drinks sweet and for Coca-Cola Bottling Co. Consolidated (CCBCC) there's nothing sweeter than a Coke. CCBCC produces bottles and distributes beverages principally the products of The Coca-Cola Company. Its distribution territory is mainly in the southeastern US. The company is the largest independent coke bottler in the US serving areas in 11 states — home to about 20 million prospective and hopefully thirsty consumers. Coca-Cola products account for about 88% of CCBCC's sales. The company does however handle other manufacturers' beverages and actually owns some brands including the flavored and vitamin-enhanced Tum-E Yummies drink and Country Breeze bottled tea.

	Annual Growth	01/11	01/12*	12/12	12/13	12/14
Sales ($ mil.)	4.9%	1,514.6	1,561.2	1,614.4	1,641.3	1,746.4
Net income ($ mil.)	(4.6%)	36.1	28.6	27.2	27.7	31.4
Market value ($ mil.)	16.8%	515.3	542.8	608.0	676.6	821.0
Employees	6.8%	6,000	6,100	6,500	6,700	7,300

*Fiscal year change

COCA-COLA CO (THE)

NYS: KO

One Coca-Cola Plaza
Atlanta, GA 30313
Phone: 404 676-2121
Fax: 404 676-6792
Web: www.coca-colacompany.com

CEO: Muhtar Kent
CFO: Kathy N. Waller
HR: Stevens Sainte-rose
FYE: December 31
Type: Public

Coke is it — it being the #1 nonalcoholic beverage company as well as one of the world's most recognizable brands. The Coca-Cola Company is home to 20 billion-dollar-brands including four of the top five soft drinks: Coca-Cola Diet Coke Fanta and Sprite. Other top brands include Minute Maid Powerade and vitaminwater. All told the company owns or licenses and markets more than 500 beverage brands mainly sparkling drinks but also waters juice drinks energy and sports drinks and ready-to-drink teas and coffees. With the world's largest beverage distribution system The Coca-Cola Company reaches thirsty consumers in more than 200 countries.

	Annual Growth	12/10	12/11	12/12	12/13	12/14
Sales ($ mil.)	7.0%	35,119.0	46,542.0	48,017.0	46,854.0	45,998.0
Net income ($ mil.)	(11.9%)	11,809.0	8,572.0	9,019.0	8,584.0	7,098.0
Market value ($ mil.)	-	0.0	0.0	0.0	0.0	0.0
Employees	(1.9%)	139,600	146,200	150,900	130,600	129,200

COCA-COLA ENTERPRISES INC   NYS: CCE

2500 Windy Ridge Parkway   CEO: John F. Brock
Atlanta, GA 30339   CFO: Manik H. (Nik) Jhangiani
Phone: 678 260-3000   HR: Brian Wynne
Fax: -   FYE: December 31
Web: www.cokecce.com   Type: Public

Scientists at The Coca-Cola Company concoct the secret syrup but it's up to Coca-Cola Enterprises (CCE) to do the heavy lifting. CCE buys it combines it with other ingredients then bottles and distributes Coke products in Western Europe. One of the world's largest Coca-Cola bottlers by volume CCE bottles and distributes energy drinks sports drinks still and sparkling waters (Dr Pepper Snapple's Schweppes Abbey Well) juices and coffees and teas. The company's European reach includes distribution in Belgium France the Netherlands Norway Sweden and the UK. All told CCE operates more than 15 production and about 50 distribution facilities in Europe.

	Annual Growth	12/11	12/12	12/13	12/14	12/15
Sales ($ mil.)	(4.1%)	8,284.0	8,062.0	8,212.0	8,264.0	7,011.0
Net income ($ mil.)	(5.6%)	749.0	677.0	667.0	663.0	596.0
Market value ($ mil.)	17.6%	5,860.7	7,213.4	10,032.3	10,052.8	11,194.0
Employees	(3.5%)	13,250	13,000	11,750	11,650	11,492

CODALE ELECTRIC SUPPLY INC.

5225 W 2400 S   CEO: -
SALT LAKE CITY, UT 84120-1264   CFO: -
Phone: 801-975-7300   HR: Bud Bonnett
Fax: -   FYE: December 25
Web: www.codale.com   Type: Private

Codale Electric Supply distributes lighting fixtures electrical supplies and datacomm products to wholesale customers through 11 locations in Nevada Utah Idaho and Wyoming. It stocks products from such manufacturers as Brad Harrison Chromalox Greenlee Philips Lighting Southwire and Western Tube & Conduit. The company sells to the aerospace construction mining healthcare schools government and utility markets. Codale Electric also offers consulting and training energy and safety audits and inventory management services. The company was founded in 1975 by CEO Dale Holt who owns nearly all of Codale Electric's equity.

	Annual Growth	12/07	12/08	12/09	12/10	12/11
Sales ($ mil.)	(2.2%)	-	235.5	175.8	175.1	220.4
Net income ($ mil.)	(9.8%)	-	16.3	6.3	6.0	12.0
Market value ($ mil.)	-	-	-	-	-	-
Employees	-	-	-	-	-	230

CODEXIS INC   NMS: CDXS

200 Penobscot Drive   CEO: -
Redwood City, CA 94063   CFO: Robert (Bob) Breuil
Phone: 650 421-8100   HR: Anna Peluffo
Fax: -   FYE: December 31
Web: www.codexis.com   Type: Public

The pharmaceutical and the biodiesel industries don't seem like they have much in common but they both use the chemicals produced by Codexis. The company develops biocatalysts — chemicals used to manufacture other chemicals in a way that's easy on the environment. Its technology is used to make the active ingredients in pharmaceuticals and produce biofuel from plant material. Codexis has a research agreement with Shell to develop new ways of converting biomass to biofuel; Shell accounts for more than half of Codexis' sales. The company is also working within other markets to use its technology to manage carbon emissions from coal-fired power plants and treat wastewater.

	Annual Growth	12/10	12/11	12/12	12/13	12/14
Sales ($ mil.)	(24.2%)	107.1	123.9	88.3	31.9	35.3
Net income ($ mil.)	-	(8.5)	(16.6)	(30.9)	(41.3)	(19.1)
Market value ($ mil.)	(30.2%)	419.4	209.7	87.4	55.4	99.7
Employees	(25.2%)	291	347	154	125	91

CODMAN & SHURTLEFF INC.

325 Paramount Dr.   CEO: -
Raynham MA 02767-0350   CFO: -
Phone: 508-880-8100   HR: -
Fax: 508-880-8122   FYE: December 31
Web: www.codman.com   Type: Subsidiary

Employees of Codman & Shurtleff have brains on their minds. The Johnson & Johnson subsidiary develops and markets thousands of products for use in neurosurgery neurovascular surgery and neuromodulation procedures. Its products include cranial access kits coils for aneurysm treatment fixation systems for the spine and cranium intraspinal catheters and hydrocephalic valve systems (which help drain excess cerebrospinal fluid). Its brands include Isocool Malis and Trufill. The company also distributes neurosurgical and electrosurgical systems for medical device-maker Synergetics under the Malis brand. It is held within J&J subsidiary DePuy.

CODORUS VALLEY BANCORP, INC.   NMS: CVLY

105 Leader Heights Road   CEO: Larry J Miller
York, PA 17405   CFO: -
Phone: 717 747-1519   HR: -
Fax: -   FYE: December 31
Web: www.peoplesbanknet.com   Type: Public

Codorus Valley Bancorp is a people-oriented business. The firm is the holding company for PeoplesBank which operates about 20 branches in southeastern Pennsylvania's York County and Hunt Valley and Bel Air Maryland. The bank offers the standard fare including checking and savings accounts and CDs. It uses funds from deposits to write a variety of loans primarily commercial loans and commercial real estate loans but also residential mortgages and consumer installment loans. Bank subsidiary Codorus Valley Financial Advisors offers investment products while SYC Settlement Services provides real estate settlement services.

	Annual Growth	12/10	12/11	12/12	12/13	12/14
Assets ($ mil.)	6.1%	957.3	1,012.1	1,059.7	1,150.6	1,213.8
Net income ($ mil.)	17.3%	6.2	6.8	9.4	10.6	11.8
Market value ($ mil.)	20.0%	58.2	50.8	92.1	119.6	120.5
Employees	4.1%	220	229	236	248	258

COE COLLEGE

1220 1ST AVE NE   CEO: -
CEDAR RAPIDS, IA 524025092   CFO: -
Phone: 319-399-8000   HR: -
Fax: -   FYE: June 30
Web: www.coe.edu   Type: Private

Coe College is a private liberal arts college with a residential campus in Cedar Rapids Iowa. The school offers more than 40 academic majors and grants undergraduate degrees (Bachelor of Arts Bachelor of Music and Bachelor of Science in Nursing) as well as a Master of Arts in Teaching. It has an annual enrollment of more than 1200 students who are required to participate in an internship student research project practicum or study abroad program as they matriculate. Approximately half of the school's students go on to postgraduate studies. Coe College was founded in 1851.

	Annual Growth	06/10	06/11	06/12	06/13	06/14
Sales ($ mil.)	3.6%	-	37.9	42.0	44.8	42.2
Net income ($ mil.)	(37.0%)	-	-	8.7	7.5	3.5
Market value ($ mil.)	-	-	-	-	-	-
Employees	-	-	-	-	-	272

COEUR MINING, INC.
NYS: CDE

104 S. Michigan Ave., Suite 900
Chicago, IL 60603
Phone: 312 489-5800
Fax: –
Web: www.coeur.com

CEO: Mitchell J. Krebs
CFO: Peter C. Mitchell
HR: Keagan J. Kerr
FYE: December 31
Type: Public

Coeur Mining (formerly Coeur d'Alene Mines) gets to the heart of the matter when it comes to precious metals. A leading primary silver producer the company holds interests in silver and gold properties in Australia North America and South America. It produces 18 million ounces of silver and more than 226490 ounces of gold annually. Coeur has proved and probable reserves of about 220.4 million ounces of silver and almost 2 million ounces of gold. It produces most of its revenue from the San Bartolomé mine in Bolivia and Palmarejo mine in Mexico. Sales of silver account for about three-fourths of the company's revenue. Most of the minerals are sold to bullion-trading banks and to smelters.

	Annual Growth	12/11	12/12	12/13	12/14	12/15
Sales ($ mil.)	(10.8%)	1,021.2	895.5	746.0	635.7	646.1
Net income ($ mil.)	–	93.5	48.7	(650.6)	(1,155.9)	(367.2)
Market value ($ mil.)	(43.4%)	3,653.3	3,722.9	1,642.0	773.3	375.3
Employees	1.3%	1,903	1,898	1,967	1,868	2,005

COFFEE HOLDING CO INC
NAS: JVA

3475 Victory Boulevard
Staten Island, NY 10314
Phone: 718 832-0800
Fax: –
Web: www.coffeeholding.com

CEO: Andrew Gordon
CFO: Andrew Gordon
HR: –
FYE: October 31
Type: Public

Coffee Holding Co. brewed up the idea of selling a wide spectrum of raw and roasted Arabica coffee beans to coffee purveyors such as Green Mountain Roasters as well as private-label coffees to food service suppliers. Coffee Holding imports its green coffee beans from Colombia Brazil Mexico Kenya and Uganda. In addition to producing private-label coffees for stores the company also sells name brands including IL CLASSICO and S&W. Its Cafe Caribe espresso coffee targets the Hispanic market. The company has expanded its offerings through partnerships. The founding Gordon family including CEO Andrew Gordon owns about 60% of the company.

	Annual Growth	10/11	10/12	10/13	10/14	10/15
Sales ($ mil.)	(5.3%)	146.8	173.7	134.0	108.9	118.2
Net income ($ mil.)	–	0.8	2.5	(1.5)	5.0	(1.4)
Market value ($ mil.)	(20.1%)	64.3	39.6	32.9	35.2	26.2
Employees	0.0%	69	71	69	57	69

COGENT COMMUNICATIONS HOLDINGS, INC.
NMS: CCOI

2450 N Street N.W.
Washington, DC 20037
Phone: 202 295-4200
Fax: –
Web: www.cogentco.com

CEO: David (Dave) Schaeffer
CFO: Thaddeus G Weed
HR: –
FYE: December 31
Type: Public

Cogent Communications offers a compelling sales pitch: data at the speed of light. The company operates a fiber-optic data network that serves customers in North America Europe and Japan. It offers dedicated Internet access and data transport services to businesses through Ethernet connections that link its 44 data center facilities directly to customer office buildings. Clients include financial services companies law firms ad agencies and other professional services businesses. Cogent also sells access to its network and provides colocation and modem management services to ISPs hosting companies and other high-volume bandwidth users.

	Annual Growth	12/10	12/11	12/12	12/13	12/14
Sales ($ mil.)	9.6%	263.4	305.5	317.0	348.0	380.0
Net income ($ mil.)	4.5%	0.7	7.5	(4.3)	56.7	0.8
Market value ($ mil.)	25.8%	656.1	783.7	1,050.5	1,875.0	1,642.1
Employees	8.0%	568	623	605	707	772

COGENTIX MEDICAL INC
NAS: CGNT

5420 Feltl Road
Minnetonka, MN 55343
Phone: 952 426-6140
Fax: –
Web: www.visionsciences.com

CEO: Robert C. (Rob) Kill
CFO: Brett A Reynolds
HR: –
FYE: March 31
Type: Public

Even those outside California know Cogentix Medical's products are totally tubular. The firm (formerly named Vision-Sciences) makes endoscopic tools — tubular instruments that let doctors see into the body and perform procedures without invasive surgery. It makes traditional endoscopes and the EndoSheath System which consists of a disposable sterile sheath covering the reusable endoscope. The system allows health care providers to save money by avoiding costly cleaning and repairs and reduces the risk of cross-contamination. Subsidiary Machida makes flexible borescopes endoscope-like tools used in industrial applications. In 2015 Vison-Sciences merged with Uroplasty to create Cogentix Medical.

	Annual Growth	03/11	03/12	03/13	03/14	03/15
Sales ($ mil.)	24.9%	10.9	16.7	15.3	17.1	26.5
Net income ($ mil.)	–	(11.8)	(11.0)	(10.6)	(7.7)	(7.7)
Market value ($ mil.)	(37.8%)	60.1	44.2	27.5	30.8	9.0
Employees	17.6%	112	107	108	105	214

COGNEX CORP.
NMS: CGNX

One Vision Drive
Natick, MA 01760-2059
Phone: 508 650-3000
Fax: –
Web: www.cognex.com

CEO: Robert Willett
CFO: Richard A. Morin
HR: –
FYE: December 31
Type: Public

Machines might not possess big picture vision but Cognex machines have excellent vision when it comes to detail. The company is one of the world's largest producers of systems that linked to a video camera serve as eyes where human vision is insufficient. Semiconductor consumer goods health care and automotive companies among others use the company's machine vision and industrial identification systems to position and identify products gauge sizes and locate defects. Cognex serves three primary markets: factory automation semiconductor and electronics capital equipment and surface inspection. It also offers consulting and educational services as well as tech support for its products. Sales to customers based outside the US account for about two-thirds of sales.

	Annual Growth	12/11	12/12	12/13	12/14	12/15
Sales ($ mil.)	8.8%	321.9	324.3	353.9	486.3	450.6
Net income ($ mil.)	27.9%	69.9	68.1	73.6	121.5	187.1
Market value ($ mil.)	(1.4%)	3,037.0	3,121.9	3,239.8	3,507.1	2,865.6
Employees	9.2%	919	984	1,077	1,322	1,305

COGNIZANT TECHNOLOGY SOLUTIONS CORP.
NMS: CTSH

Glenpointe Centre West, 500 Frank W. Burr Blvd.
Teaneck, NJ 07666
Phone: 201 801-0233
Fax: 201 801-0243
Web: www.cognizant.com

CEO: Rajeev (Raj) Mehta
CFO: Karen McLoughlin
HR: –
FYE: December 31
Type: Public

Cognizant Technology Solutions is aware of the state of your technology and where it should be in becoming digital. The information technology services provider helps customers digitize operations and provides application maintenance services business intelligence data warehousing software and systems development and integration and re-engineering services for legacy systems. Its customers are primarily corporations from the Forbes Global 2000 and it targets customers in the financial services health care manufacturing retail and logistics sectors. Most of Cognizant's software development centers and employees are located in India although it has other development and delivery facilities around the world.

	Annual Growth	12/10	12/11	12/12	12/13	12/14
Sales ($ mil.)	22.3%	4,592.4	6,121.2	7,346.5	8,843.2	10,262.7
Net income ($ mil.)	18.4%	733.5	883.6	1,051.3	1,228.6	1,439.3
Market value ($ mil.)	(7.9%)	44,662.8	39,190.4	45,023.7	61,537.0	32,090.9
Employees	19.4%	104,000	137,700	156,700	171,400	211,500

COHEN & STEERS INC

NYS: CNS

280 Park Avenue
New York, NY 10017
Phone: 212 832-3232
Fax: 212 832-3622
Web: www.cohenandsteers.com

CEO: Martin Cohen
CFO: Matthew S. (Matt) Stadler
HR: –
FYE: December 31
Type: Public

One of the nation's largest managers of real estate funds Cohen & Steers administers about two dozen mutual funds closed-end funds and exchange-traded funds that are invested in real estate securities global infrastructure utilities and large-cap value stocks. It also manages about 95 separate account portfolios for institutional investors and offers alternative investments such as hedged real estate securities portfolios. The company's real estate investment banking practice Cohen & Steers Capital Advisors (now CSCA Capital Advisors) was sold off in 2009 to former managing directors of the unit. Cohen & Steers has nearly $46 billion of assets under management.

	Annual Growth	12/10	12/11	12/12	12/13	12/14
Sales ($ mil.)	14.3%	183.7	237.2	273.6	297.7	313.9
Net income ($ mil.)	12.9%	46.4	54.3	66.1	68.1	75.5
Market value ($ mil.)	12.7%	1,169.1	1,294.5	1,364.8	1,794.4	1,884.9
Employees	4.6%	220	239	240	247	263

COHEN FINANCIAL L.P.

2 N. LaSalle St. Ste. 800
Chicago IL 60602
Phone: 312-346-5680
Fax: 312-346-6669
Web: www.cohenfinancial.com

CEO: Jack M Cohen
CFO: Vincent Beckett
HR: –
FYE: December 31
Type: Subsidiary

Cohen Financial is an investment bank that provides capital and other financial services to those in the commercial real estate industry. Cohen funds loans both directly and indirectly through a cadre of capital sources. Borrowers typically use loans to acquire construct or renovate industrial multifamily office and retail properties. The firm spun off its investment management unit into a joint venture Wrightwood Capital which manages commercial real estate investments on behalf of foundations and endowments institutions private investors and private and public pension funds. Founded in 1960 the company has nearly 10 offices in major US markets.

COHERENT, INC.

NMS: COHR

5100 Patrick Henry Drive
Santa Clara, CA 95054
Phone: 408 764-4000
Fax: –
Web: www.coherent.com

CEO: John R. Ambroseo
CFO: Kevin S. Palatnik
HR: –
FYE: October 03
Type: Public

Coherent's lasers make a lot of sense. The company uses light wave manipulation called photonics to manufacture and market a diverse array of lasers. Its products are used in a host of areas: microelectronics (semiconductor fabrication packaging flat-panel display and solar cell manufacturing) scientific and government research in physical and chemical processes OEM components and instrumentation and materials processing. Its specialty lasers and systems segment (70% of sales) makes configurable laser products while its commercial lasers and components unit (30% of sales) specializes in high-volume products sold in set configurations.

	Annual Growth	10/11*	09/12	09/13	09/14*	10/15
Sales ($ mil.)	(0.0%)	802.8	769.1	810.1	794.6	802.5
Net income ($ mil.)	(4.9%)	93.2	63.0	66.4	59.1	76.4
Market value ($ mil.)	6.2%	1,029.8	1,099.3	1,469.8	1,508.7	1,310.7
Employees	2.9%	2,309	2,328	2,514	2,519	2,586

*Fiscal year change

COHESANT INC.

23400 Commerce Park
Beachwood OH 44122
Phone: 216-910-1700
Fax: 845-512-6070
Web: www.hudsontech.com

CEO: Morris H Wheeler
CFO: Robert W Pawlak
HR: Steve Hurd
FYE: November 30
Type: Private

Cohesant which forms one coherent water-protection company from four subsidiaries believes in repair over replacement. Cohesant Materials produces specialty coatings used in protecting renewing and repairing pipes and other infrastructure. CuraFlo Franchising operates about a dozen North American CuraFlo franchises selling proprietary equipment and coatings for repairing water pipes. CuraFlo Services owns two of the franchises and provides training and support for the franchisees. RLS Solutions offers Cohesant's Raven Engineered System of coatings and epoxies used in municipal water and waste water systems. The company has manufacturing facilities in Ohio and Oklahoma as well as in Vancouver Canada.

COHN & WOLFE

200 5th Ave.
New York NY 10010
Phone: 212-798-9700
Fax: 212-329-9900
Web: www.cohnwolfe.com

CEO: Donna Imperato
CFO: Tom Petrosini
HR: –
FYE: December 31
Type: Business Segment

Public relations firm Cohn & Wolfe an operating unit of ad giant WPP Group's Young & Rubicam serves clients from more than 50 offices in Asia Europe and North America. Its services include crisis management investor relations media relations and public affairs. It also helps clients take the plunge into digital and social media like Facebook and Twitter. The company's specialty divisions provide expertise in the health care consumer corporate energy entertainment sports marketing and technology sectors. Clients have included such notable brands as Taco Bell LG Electronics and The Medicines Company. The firm was founded by Bob Cohn and Norm Wolfe in Atlanta in 1970.

COHU, INC.

NMS: COHU

12367 Crosthwaite Circle
Poway, CA 92064-6817
Phone: 858 848-8100
Fax: –
Web: www.cohu.com

CEO: Luis A. M ller
CFO: Jeffrey D. Jones
HR: Anna Aguirre
FYE: December 27
Type: Public

Cohu tries to blend various technologies into one coherent business. Of the company's three segments the largest is semiconductor equipment (via subsidiaries Delta Design and Rasco) which makes handling equipment used to protect semiconductors during testing procedures. Top customers include Intel (36% of sales) and Texas Instruments (11%). The other segments are video cameras (closed-circuit television systems for surveillance medical and industrial applications) and microwave communications systems (microwave radios antennas and support equipment). Cohu gets three-quarters of sales from customers located outside the US.

	Annual Growth	12/10	12/11	12/12	12/13	12/14
Sales ($ mil.)	0.8%	322.7	309.0	221.2	247.3	333.3
Net income ($ mil.)	(22.9%)	24.6	15.7	(12.2)	(33.4)	8.7
Market value ($ mil.)	(7.0%)	410.6	291.6	266.4	259.0	307.8
Employees	9.8%	1,100	1,200	1,500	1,400	1,600

COLAVITA USA L.L.C.

1 RUNYONS LN
EDISON, NJ 088172219
Phone: 732-404-8300
Fax: –
Web: www.colavita.com

CEO: Giovanni Colavita
CFO: Simon Boltuch
HR: –
FYE: December 31
Type: Private

This company helps bring Italian flavors to American palates. Colavita USA is a leading importer and distributor of Italian foods notably olive oil pastas sauces and vinegars sold under the Colavita label. It supplies products to retail grocery store chains specialty food stores and wholesale distributors as well as restaurants caterers and other foodservice operators. The company was started by John J. Profaci who struck a distribution agreement with Italy's Colavita family in 1978. Rome-based Colavita S.p.A owns 80% of the US importer.

	Annual Growth	12/08	12/09	12/10	12/11	12/12
Sales ($ mil.)	7.5%	–	–	–	85.3	91.7
Net income ($ mil.)	(1.6%)	–	–	–	1.2	1.2
Market value ($ mil.)	–	–	–	–	–	–
Employees	–	–	–	–	–	80

COLBY COLLEGE

4000 MAYFLOWER HL
WATERVILLE, ME 04901-8840
Phone: 207-859-4000
Fax: –
Web: www.colby.edu

CEO: –
CFO: –
HR: –
FYE: June 30
Type: Private

Colby College is one of the nation's oldest liberal arts colleges. The school was founded in 1813 as the Maine Literary and Theological Institution and in 1871 it became the first previously all-male college in New England to admit women. Colby College offers 500 courses 55 majors 30-plus minors and independent major options. Its two dozen academic departments and nearly 10 interdisciplinary programs serve an enrollment of approximately 1800 students. Popular majors are biology economics English government history and international studies. Besides being one of the nation's oldest Colby College is one of the most pricey: Annual tuition room and board and fees total more than $46000.

	Annual Growth	06/09	06/10	06/10	06/12	06/13
Sales ($ mil.)	3.6%	–	108.9	112.0	115.0	121.1
Net income ($ mil.)	(0.9%)	–	68.2	124.3	(13.7)	66.3
Market value ($ mil.)	–	–	–	–	–	–
Employees	–	–	–	–	–	580

COLD STONE CREAMERY INC.

9311 E. Via de Ventura
Scottsdale AZ 85258
Phone: 480-362-4800
Fax: 480-362-4812
Web: www.coldstonecreamery.com

CEO: Kevin Blackwell
CFO: –
HR: –
FYE: December 31
Type: Subsidiary

This chain of ice cream shops is known for using mineral assets. Cold Stone Creamery is a leading franchisor of premium ice cream parlors with a chain of more than 1500 locations in about 15 countries. The parlors offer a menu of premium ice cream treats but patrons can create their own flavors by choosing from a variety of other ingredients including candy fruit and cookie dough. And true to the chain's name the ice cream is blended with those ingredients on a cold stone slab. The shops also offer yogurt sorbet and other frozen treats. A small number of locations are operated by the company. The Cold Stone chain was in 1988 and is owned by multi-concept franchisor Kahala Corp.

COLDWATER CREEK INC.

NMS: CWTR

One Coldwater Creek Drive
Sandpoint, ID 83864
Phone: 208 263-2266
Fax: 208 263-1582
Web: www.coldwatercreek.com

CEO: Jill Brown Dean
CFO: James A Bell
HR: –
FYE: February 02
Type: Public

Women quench their thirst for classic casual clothing and accessories from Coldwater Creek's stores catalog and Web site. The upscale multi-channel retailer sells mostly traditional apparel through some 360 full-line stores and about 35 retail outlets targeting middle- and upper-income women 35 years of age and older. It also sells directly to consumers via its Coldwater Creek catalog and online store and operates about 10 namesake day spas that typically span 5400 sq. ft. While it got its start as a catalog operator today the company's retail presence is felt more at the mall than the mailbox with stores accounting for more than 75% of sales. Coldwater Creek was founded in 1984 by Dennis and Ann Pence.

	Annual Growth	01/09	01/10	01/11	01/12*	02/13
Sales ($ mil.)	(7.7%)	1,024.2	1,038.6	981.1	773.0	742.5
Net income ($ mil.)	–	(26.0)	(56.1)	(44.1)	(99.7)	(81.8)
Market value ($ mil.)	7.0%	86.1	136.2	89.5	27.5	112.7
Employees	(12.4%)	11,200	9,531	9,198	6,900	6,600

*Fiscal year change

COLE HAAN

1 Cole Haan Dr.
Yarmouth ME 04096-6670
Phone: 207-846-2500
Fax: 207-846-6374
Web: www.colehaan.com

CEO: Jack A Boys
CFO: Lisa Kempa
HR: –
FYE: May 31
Type: Subsidiary

Cole Haan caters to the well-heeled. It designs and sells upscale footwear and accessories and was once the fashion-footed subsidiary of athletic products firm NIKE. The shoe maker peddles its products through about 110 Cole Haan stores in the US as well as nearly 70 stores in Japan. It also sells its shoes belts hosiery handbags small leather goods fine outerwear and watches online and in stores run by other retailers. Cole Haan has reached into high-end accessories (encroaching on Coach) in recent years. Most of Cole Haan's products are distributed from New Hampshire; its outerwear is made in Italian factories by G-III Apparel. Cole Haan was founded in Chicago in 1928 by Trafton Cole and Eddie Haan.

COLEMAN TECHNOLOGIES INC.

5337 Millenia Lakes Blvd. Ste. 300
Orlando FL 32839
Phone: 407-481-8600
Fax: 407-481-8618
Web: www.ctiusa.com

CEO: –
CFO: –
HR: –
FYE: December 31
Type: Subsidiary

Coleman Technologies (CTI) offers computer networking systems engineering and other services to US federal state and local government clients as well as commercial firms in such industries as health care transportation and utilities. It specializes in customizing and installing data communications products from networking giant Cisco in particular but it also builds software models for military customers designs and supports voice-over-Internet protocol telephony systems for government agencies and designs electronic surveillance gear for law enforcement agencies. Founded in 1995 CTI was acquired by Maryland-based information technology services provider Presidio in late 2009.

COLFAX CORP
NYS: CFX

420 National Business Parkway, 5th Floor
Annapolis Junction, MD 20701
Phone: 301 323-9000
Fax: –
Web: www.colfaxcorp.com

CEO: Clay H Kiefaber
CFO: C. Scott Brannan
HR: –
FYE: December 31
Type: Public

The cold hard facts are that Colfax works hard to get customers pumped up. The company makes fluid handling products including centrifugal gear progressive cavity and rotary screw pumps under such brands as Allweiler Imo and Total Lubrication Management. Colfax also makes valves and lubrication systems and products and equipment used in the cutting and joinging of steels and metals. Its products are used in cargo handling oil transport firefighting chemical processing and pipeline applications. Colfax has counted such big names as Northrop Grumman Alfa Laval General Dynamics GE Siemens Rolls-Royce and the US Navy among its customers.

	Annual Growth	12/10	12/11	12/12	12/13	12/14
Sales ($ mil.)	70.9%	542.0	693.4	3,913.9	4,207.2	4,624.5
Net income ($ mil.)	121.8%	16.2	4.6	(64.4)	178.6	392.1
Market value ($ mil.)	29.4%	2,277.9	3,523.8	4,992.5	7,880.4	6,380.8
Employees	77.7%	1,524	1,500	13,500	15,200	15,200

COLGATE-PALMOLIVE CO.
NYS: CL

300 Park Avenue
New York, NY 10022
Phone: 212 310-2000
Fax: 212 310-3284
Web: www.colgatepalmolive.com

CEO: Ian M. Cook
CFO: Dennis J Hickey
HR: Martin Collins
FYE: December 31
Type: Public

Colgate-Palmolive takes a bite out of grime. The company is a top global maker and marketer of toothpaste and soap and cleaning products. Colgate-Palmolive also offers pet nutrition products through subsidiary Hill's Pet Nutrition which makes Science Diet and Prescription Diet pet foods. Many of its oral care products fall under the Colgate brand and include toothbrushes mouthwash and dental floss. Its Tom's of Maine unit covers the natural toothpaste niche. Personal and home care items include Ajax brand household cleaner Palmolive dishwashing liquid Softsoap shower gel and Sanex and Speed Stick deodorants. The company has operations in 70-plus countries and sells its products in more than 200 countries.

	Annual Growth	12/10	12/11	12/12	12/13	12/14
Sales ($ mil.)	2.6%	15,564.0	16,734.0	17,085.0	17,420.0	17,277.0
Net income ($ mil.)	(0.3%)	2,203.0	2,431.0	2,472.0	2,241.0	2,180.0
Market value ($ mil.)	(3.7%)	72,872.5	83,771.1	94,787.7	59,126.7	62,735.4
Employees	(1.0%)	39,200	38,600	37,700	37,400	37,700

COLLABERA INC.

25 Airport Rd.
Morristown NJ 07960
Phone: 973-889-5200
Fax: 973-292-1643
Web: www.collabera.com

CEO: Hiten Patel
CFO: Sham Patel
HR: –
FYE: December 31
Type: Private

Collabera knows the value of enabling people to work together effectively. The company provides outsourced IT management consulting and related services such as software development to companies in such industries as inancial services manufacturing media utilities and retail. It specializes in such areas as consulting enterprise resource planning software implementation and data migration. The company also offers IT staffing services. Collabera operates from about 20 US offices a London office seven offices and software development facilities in India and locations in Manila and Singapore. The company was founded in 1991 by chairman Hiten Patel CFO Sham Patel CIO Dhar Patadia and EVP Hemin Shah.

COLLECTIVE BRANDS INC.
NYSE: PSS

3231 SE 6th Ave.
Topeka KS 66607-2207
Phone: 785-233-5171
Fax: 785-368-7510
Web: www.collectivebrands.com

CEO: W Paul Jones
CFO: Douglas G Boessen
HR: –
FYE: January 31
Type: Public

Collective Brands is banking on its collective efforts in shoe making and retailing. The holding company boasts a portfolio of premium and moderate footwear and accessories through its Performance + Lifestyle Group (PLG) a wide reach of some 4455 Payless ShoeSource outlets in about 25 countries and an established licensing and brand management unit in Collective Licensing. Collective Brands was formed in 2007 when powerhouse Payless ShoeSource acquired Stride Rite which is primarily a wholesaler to department stores and operates leased departments at Macy's stores. With brands such as Keds and Saucony the company operates in the US Canada the Caribbean Central and South America and Puerto Rico.

COLLECTORS UNIVERSE INC
NMS: CLCT

1921 E. Alton Avenue
Santa Ana, CA 92705
Phone: 949 567-1234
Fax: –
Web: www.collectors.com

CEO: Robert G. (Bob) Deuster
CFO: Joseph J. (Joe) Wallace
HR: –
FYE: June 30
Type: Public

Before you sell that silver dollar or those baseball cards you might want to check with Collectors Universe. The company provides authentication grading and information services for sellers and buyers of trading cards event tickets vintage autographs and other memorabilia. The company charges a fee — usually between $2 and $10000 per item — to determine the authenticity quality and worth of the collectible. Coins and sports cards account for most of the company's business; notable offerings include its Professional Coin Grading Service (PCGS). Collectors Universe also publishes price guides market reports rarity reports and other information in print form as well as on its website.

	Annual Growth	06/11	06/12	06/13	06/14	06/15
Sales ($ mil.)	8.5%	44.4	48.4	49.1	60.6	61.7
Net income ($ mil.)	9.7%	5.1	6.7	5.7	7.4	7.4
Market value ($ mil.)	7.7%	131.6	130.4	117.7	174.0	177.1
Employees	4.7%	241	249	256	283	290

COLLEGE ENTRANCE EXAMINATION BOARD

45 COLUMBUS AVE
NEW YORK, NY 100236917
Phone: 212-713-8000
Fax: –
Web: www.collegeboard.org

CEO: David Coleman
CFO: Tho Higgins
HR: –
FYE: June 30
Type: Private

There are three letters every high school student must learn: S A and T. Who is responsible for making those letters so infamous? Why The College Board of course. The not-for-profit association owns and administers the Scholastic Assessment Test (SAT) College-Level Examination Program (CLEP) and the Advanced Placement Program (AP) at high schools nationwide. It also offers guidance counseling financial aid student assessment standardized testing and professional development courses. The College Board was founded in 1900; its members include nearly 6000 schools colleges universities and other educational institutions.

	Annual Growth	06/09	06/10	06/11	06/12	06/13
Sales ($ mil.)	5.3%	–	668.0	705.1	746.0	779.5
Net income ($ mil.)	(4.4%)	–	–	102.3	26.9	93.6
Market value ($ mil.)	–	–	–	–	–	–
Employees	–	–	–	–	–	1,259

COLLEGE OF SAINT BENEDICT

37 COLLEGE AVE S
SAINT JOSEPH, MN 563742099
Phone: 320-363-5011
Fax: –
Web: www.csbsju.edu

CEO: –
CFO: –
HR: –
FYE: June 30
Type: Private

The College of Saint Benedict (CSB) is an all-female Catholic liberal arts college with an enrollment of more than 2000 students about 70% of which are Catholic (though students of all faith are welcome). Saint John's University (SJU) located six miles from from CSB in central Minnesota is the school's male counterpart. SJU and CSB share a common curriculum and students from both institutions attend classes together. The schools offer some 60 areas of study with more than 35 majors. CSB was incorporated when it separated from the Saint Benedict's Monastery in 1961.

	Annual Growth	06/10	06/11	06/12	06/13	06/14
Sales ($ mil.)	4.9%	–	60.6	62.3	66.8	70.0
Net income ($ mil.)	155.9%	–	–	1.9	11.2	12.5
Market value ($ mil.)	–	–	–	–	–	–
Employees	–	–	–	–	–	431

COLLEGE OF THE HOLY CROSS

1 COLLEGE ST
WORCESTER, MA 016102395
Phone: 508-793-2011
Fax: –
Web: www.holycross.edu

CEO: –
CFO: –
HR: –
FYE: June 30
Type: Private

College of The Holy Cross has some real Crusaders. The Jesuit-founded college with sports teams nicknamed the Crusaders is a liberal arts undergraduate institution in central Massachusetts with more than 2900 students. Some of the school's more popular areas of study include liberal arts' favorites such as English history and political science but also multidisciplinary concentrations and specialty programs including biochemistry Latin American studies and women's studies. The co-educational school has more than 300 full- and part-time faculty with a 10:1 student-to-faculty ratio. Holy Cross is the oldest Catholic college in New England.

	Annual Growth	06/10	06/11	06/12	06/13	06/14
Sales ($ mil.)	2.6%	–	151.7	154.4	160.7	163.7
Net income ($ mil.)	–	–	–	(16.4)	67.8	112.0
Market value ($ mil.)	–	–	–	–	–	–
Employees	–	–	–	–	–	949

COLLINS INDUSTRIES INC.

15 Compound Dr.
Hutchinson KS 67501
Phone: 620-663-5551
Fax: 620-663-1630
Web: www.collinsind.com

CEO: –
CFO: Hans Heinsen
HR: –
FYE: October 31
Type: Private

Ambulance chasers are no bother for Collins Industries. Founded in 1971 the company is a US manufacturer of ambulances and specialty vehicles such as small school buses shuttle and midsized vans and terminal trucks (used to move trailers and containers in warehouses). Collins also makes commercial bus chassis industrial sweepers and road construction equipment. It has a distribution network of about 70 dealers in the US and Canada. Collins markets its products under brand names including Capacity Collins Bus Wheeled Coach and World Trans. It is part of Allied Specialty Vehicles (ASV) the largest maker of ambulances in North America which is owned by private-equity firm American Industrial Partners.

COLLINS STEWART LLC

350 Madison Ave.
New York NY 10017
Phone: 212-402-8000
Fax: 212-402-5030
Web: www.collinsstewart.com/geographies/usbusiness/

CEO: –
CFO: David Barret
HR: –
FYE: December 31
Type: Subsidiary

Boutique investment banking firm Collins Stewart LLC (formerly C.E. Unterberg Towbin) is the US arm of UK brokerage Collins Stewart plc. Serving more than 700 financial institutions and hedge funds the company trades in and conducts research on US equities and derivatives. It also manages IPOs for technology and health care companies makes markets in American Depositary Receipts and trades foreign stocks and currency. Its research division focuses on the technology health care defense and energy sectors. Collins Stewart has offices in New York City and San Francisco.

COLONIAL FINANCIAL SERVICES, INC.

NMS: COBK

2745 S. Delsea Drive
Vineland, NJ 08360
Phone: 856 205-0058
Fax: –
Web: www.colonialbankfsb.com

CEO: –
CFO: –
HR: –
FYE: December 31
Type: Public

Community banking is a revolutionary idea for Colonial Financial Services. The holding company owns Colonial Bank a regional thrift serving southern New Jersey from about 10 locations. The bank offers products and services including checking and savings accounts bank cards loans and brokerage. It originates primarily real estate loans with one- to four-family home mortgages accounting for nearly 50% of its loan portfolio. Colonial Bank also writes construction business home equity and consumer loans. Colonial Financial Services converted from a mutual holding structure to a stock holding company in 2010.

	Annual Growth	12/09	12/10	12/11	12/12	12/13
Sales ($ mil.)	(6.8%)	27.6	27.9	25.9	23.3	20.9
Net income ($ mil.)	–	1.4	3.9	3.3	(1.7)	(1.8)
Market value ($ mil.)	16.3%	28.0	47.0	48.0	50.5	51.2
Employees	2.8%	104	106	108	116	116

COLONIAL LIFE & ACCIDENT INSURANCE COMPANY

1200 Colonial Life Blvd.
Columbia SC 29210
Phone: 803-798-7000
Fax: 202-785-8576
Web: www.now.org

CEO: Randall C Horn
CFO: –
HR: –
FYE: December 31
Type: Subsidiary

Colonial Life & Accident Insurance steps in where traditional life and health insurance companies leave off. Marketed under the Colonial Life brand the company targets its supplemental insurance products to employees of companies that provide employer-sponsored benefits. Colonial Life's products include disability accident life critical illness hospital confinement and cancer insurance. Operating across the US except in New York and in Puerto Rico the company has some 3 million policies in force with more than 75000 business and organizational clients. Founded in 1939 Colonial Life was acquired in 1993 by Unum Corporation and is now a subsidiary of Unum Group.

COLONIAL PIPELINE COMPANY

1185 Sanctuary Pkwy. Ste. 100
Alpharetta GA 30004-4738
Phone: 678-762-2200
Fax: 678-762-2813
Web: www.colpipe.com

CEO: Tim Felt
CFO: –
HR: –
FYE: December 31
Type: Private

With a reach that extends far beyond the original English colonies Colonial Pipeline delivers about 100 million gallons of gasoline diesel home heating oil aviation and military fuels per day to cities and businesses across the eastern and southern US. The more than 5500-mile Colonial system transports these fuels from Alabama Louisiana Mississippi and Texas to more than 260 marketing terminals near major urban centers in the Southeast and along the Eastern Seaboard. It has shipper terminals in 13 states and the District of Columbia.

COLONY BANKCORP, INC.

NMS: CBAN

115 South Grant Street
Fitzgerald, GA 31750
Phone: 229 426-6000
Fax: –
Web: www.colonybank.com

CEO: Edward P Loomis Jr
CFO: Terry L Hester
HR: –
FYE: December 31
Type: Public

Colony Bankcorp seems to be colonizing Georgia. The multibank holding company owns seven financial institutions doing business under variations of the Colony Bank name throughout central and southern portions of the state. The banks operate more than 25 branches in all. They offer traditional fare such as checking and savings accounts NOW and IRA accounts and CDs. Real estate loans including residential and commercial mortgages and construction and farmland loans make up the largest portion of the company's loan portfolio at more than 80%. The banks also issue business and consumer loans.

	Annual Growth	12/10	12/11	12/12	12/13	12/14
Assets ($ mil.)	(2.6%)	1,275.7	1,195.4	1,139.4	1,148.6	1,146.9
Net income ($ mil.)	99.6%	0.5	2.5	2.6	4.6	7.5
Market value ($ mil.)	18.3%	34.0	18.9	30.4	51.5	66.5
Employees	1.0%	308	313	327	328	320

COLONY CAPITAL INC

NYS: CLNY

515 South Flower Street, 44th Floor
Los Angeles, CA 90071
Phone: 310 282-8820
Fax: –
Web: www.colonyfinancial.com

CEO: Richard B. Saltzman
CFO: Darren J. Tangen
HR: –
FYE: December 31
Type: Public

When most real estate investors are heading for the nearest exit Colony Capital (formerly Colony Financial) is knocking on the doors of opportunity. The real estate investment and finance company which formed in 2009 and immediately filed for an initial public offering was established to acquire originate and manage commercial mortgage loans and other commercial real estate related debts. The firm's portfolio also includes real estate equity including single- and multifamily homes. It also has an interest in about 100 hotels acquired through foreclosure. In 2015 Colony Financial acquired affiliate Colony Capital LLC and changed its name to Colony Capital Inc.

	Annual Growth	12/10	12/11	12/12	12/13	12/14
Sales ($ mil.)	82.0%	27.4	65.5	107.2	180.2	300.6
Net income ($ mil.)	62.3%	17.8	43.4	62.0	101.8	123.1
Market value ($ mil.)	4.4%	2,194.9	1,722.4	2,137.9	2,224.5	2,611.5
Employees	–	–	–	–	–	–

COLONY CAPITAL LLC

2450 Broadway 6th Fl.
Santa Monica CA 90404
Phone: 310-282-8820
Fax: 310-282-8808
Web: www.colonyinc.com

CEO: –
CFO: –
HR: –
FYE: December 31
Type: Private

Colony Capital is one of the largest private equity real estate investors in the world. Although it focuses on real estate (hospitality office residential and retail properties) Colony also looks for other opportunities in the market by investing in non-performing loans and distressed assets. Colony's holdings include stakes in France-based retailer Carrefour hotel operator Accor tropical resort and casino developer Kerzner International and Canada-based luxury hotel chain Fairmont Raffles. The company is controlled by chairman and CEO Tom Barrack a renowned dealmaker who originally formed the firm in 1991 to invest in debt from the savings and loan crisis.

COLOR ART INTEGRATED INTERIORS LLC

1325 N. Warson Rd.
St. Louis MO 63132
Phone: 314-432-3000
Fax: 314-993-2752
Web: www.color-art.com

CEO: Gary Mindel
CFO: –
HR: –
FYE: December 31
Type: Private

Color Art Integrated Interiors believes in combining architecture furniture and technology to add a little color to patient rooms libraries and conference rooms. The company which has been in operation since 1946 is the exclusive distributor of Steelcase office furniture in the St. Louis and Kansas City Missouri areas. It also carries such brands as Hon and Nemschoff. In addition the firm provides planning interior construction long-term facilities management and furniture leasing services to its clients. Color Art purchased former rival Scott Rice Office Works in 2004 and changed its name from Color Art Office Interiors to Color Art Integrated Interiors.

COLORADO COLLEGE

14 E CACHE LA POUDRE ST
COLORADO SPRINGS, CO 809033243
Phone: 719-389-6000
Fax: –
Web: www.coloradocollege.edu

CEO: –
CFO: –
HR: –
FYE: June 30
Type: Private

Colorado College does things a little differently but it shares its mission with other institutions of higher learning. The private liberal arts and sciences college in 1970 adopted the Block Plan which divides the school year into eight three-and-a-half week blocks. Students take one course per three-and-a-half week block allowing them to focus on a single subject at a time. Its class size averages about 15 students with most classes capped at 25. Colorado College's 12000 students can choose from more than 40 majors and 30-plus minors. They are required to live on campus the first three years. Established in 1874 the Colorado Springs school boasts a 10:1 student-faculty ratio.

	Annual Growth	06/10	06/11	06/12	06/13	06/14
Sales ($ mil.)	1.8%	–	119.4	115.5	117.1	125.8
Net income ($ mil.)	332.5%	–	–	4.9	57.4	91.0
Market value ($ mil.)	–	–	–	–	–	–
Employees	–	–	–	–	–	800

COLORADO INTERSTATE GAS CO.

1001 Louisiana Street, Suite 1000
Houston, TX 77002
Phone: 713 369-9000
Fax: –

CEO: –
CFO: David P Michels
HR: –
FYE: December 31
Type: Public

Colorado Interstate Gas knows that there is no fuel like an old fuel — natural gas. The company an indirect subsidiary of Kinder Morgan ransports natural gas from fields in the Rocky Mountains and the Anadarko Basin to customers in the Rocky Mountains Midwest Southwest Pacific Northwest and California. All told Colorado Interstate Gas has some 4300 miles of pipeline that can carry more than 4.6 billion cu. ft. per day. It has 38 billion cu. ft. of storage capacity in facilities in Colorado and Kansas. It also has a 50% stake in WYCO Development LLC a joint venture with an affiliate of Xcel Energy which owns and operates an intrastate gas pipeline.

	Annual Growth	12/10	12/11	12/12	12/13	12/14
Sales ($ mil.)	(0.4%)	410.0	415.0	398.0	397.0	404.0
Net income ($ mil.)	5.5%	143.0	144.0	156.0	170.0	177.0
Market value ($ mil.)	–	–	–	–	–	–
Employees	–	–	–	–	–	–

COLORADO SEMINARY

2199 S UNIVERSITY BLVD
DENVER, CO 802104711
Phone: 303-871-2000
Fax: –
Web: www.du.edu

CEO: –
CFO: –
HR: –
FYE: June 30
Type: Private

Want a mile-high education? Colorado Seminary which does business as University of Denver (DU) offers graduate and undergraduate degrees in more than 100 fields of study including law government humanities education engineering and psychology. About 12000 undergraduate and graduate students from across the US and more than 90 countries are enrolled at the school. Former Secretary of State Condoleezza Rice former Interior Secretary Gale Norton and former Coors Brewing CEO Peter Coors attended DU. Founded in 1864 the university has a staff of some 650 faculty members; its student-to-faculty ratio is 10:1. DU is located on a 125-acre campus.

	Annual Growth	06/09	06/10	06/11	06/12	06/14
Sales ($ mil.)	(4.2%)	–	469.5	398.3	367.0	396.3
Net income ($ mil.)	8.3%	–	–	96.5	57.0	122.7
Market value ($ mil.)	–	–	–	–	–	–
Employees	–	–	–	–	–	2,770

COLORADO SPRINGS UTILITIES

121 S. Tejon St.
Colorado Springs CO 80903
Phone: 719-448-4800
Fax: 719-668-7288
Web: www.csu.org

CEO: Phillip H Tollefson
CFO: –
HR: –
FYE: December 31
Type: Government-owned

Even one of the country's most scenic areas needs creature comforts and that's where utilities come in. Community-owned Colorado Springs Utilities is a mulit-utility company that provides natural gas electric water and wastewater services in the Pikes Peak region. Colorado Springs Utilities' service territories include Colorado Springs Manitou Springs and several of the suburban residential areas surrounding the city. The military installations of Fort Carson Peterson Air Force Base and the US Air Force Academy are also serviced by the multi-utility.

COLORADO STATE UNIVERSITY

6003 CAMPUS DELIVERY
FORT COLLINS, CO 80523-6003
Phone: 970-491-1101
Fax: –
Web: www.co.adams.co.us

CEO: –
CFO: –
HR: –
FYE: June 30
Type: Private

Colorado State University (CSU) got its start as an agricultural college in 1870 six years before Colorado was even a state. The school still has agricultural and forestry programs as well as a veterinary medicine school but it also offers degrees in liberal arts business engineering and the sciences. True to its roots as a land-grant college CSU engages the larger community in research and outreach through statewide Cooperative Extension programs and centers like the Colorado Agricultural Experiment Station. More than 30000 students are enrolled at CSU about 80% of whom are Colorado residents. It employs about 1500 faculty members and has a student-to-teacher ratio of 19:1.

	Annual Growth	06/03	06/04	06/05	06/06	06/08
Sales ($ mil.)	(76.5%)	–	–	56,847.4	562.9	740.3
Net income ($ mil.)	–	–	–	0.2	26.4	(44.5)
Market value ($ mil.)	–	–	–	–	–	–
Employees	–	–	–	–	–	1,306

COLQUITT ELECTRIC MEMBERSHIP CORPORATION

15 ROWLAND DR
MOULTRIE, GA 317684169
Phone: 229-985-3620
Fax: –
Web: www.colquittemc.com

CEO: –
CFO: –
HR: Delores Hancock
FYE: December 31
Type: Private

There's no quit in the electric service to Colquitt and surrounding counties in Georgia thanks to Colquitt Electric Membership Corporation (Colquitt EMC). The consumer-owned non-profit utility distributes electricity to more than 41000 members in Berrien Brooks Colquitt Cook Lowndes Tift and Worth counties. Colquitt EMC distributes electricity via more than 8020 miles of power line. In 1976 the cooperative changed its name from Colquitt County Rural Electric Company to Colquitt EMC. The utility is the largest EMC in south Georgia with some of the lowest electric rates in the state.

	Annual Growth	12/06	12/07	12/08	12/09	12/13
Sales ($ mil.)	3.2%	–	106.1	107.1	110.0	127.8
Net income ($ mil.)	–	–	–	2.5	2.9	0.0
Market value ($ mil.)	–	–	–	–	–	–
Employees	–	–	–	–	–	164

COLSA CORPORATION

6728 ODYSSEY DR NW
HUNTSVILLE, AL 358063305
Phone: 256-964-5555
Fax: –
Web: www.colsa.com

CEO: Francisco J Collazo
CFO: –
HR: –
FYE: December 31
Type: Private

COLSA doesn't mind being called a little defensive. The company provides advanced technology systems and services to US government agencies such as the Missile Defense Agency and NASA. COLSA which specializes in radar and guidance system technology offers services including engineering and testing developing war games simulations analyzing radar technology and virtual prototyping. Its information systems services include integration maintenance and administration for large computer centers. COLSA also offers a software system for nuclear power plants and a gateway for sending simulation data to remote systems. COLSA was founded in 1980.

	Annual Growth	12/09	12/10	12/11	12/12	12/13
Sales ($ mil.)	8.9%	–	155.7	152.2	186.8	201.2
Net income ($ mil.)	15.4%	–	–	11.9	11.0	15.8
Market value ($ mil.)	–	–	–	–	–	–
Employees	–	–	–	–	–	890

COLT'S MANUFACTURING COMPANY LLC

545 New Park Ave.
West Hartford CT 06110
Phone: 860-236-6311
Fax: 860-244-1442
Web: www.coltsmfg.com

CEO: Dennis Veilleux
CFO: Joyce Rubino
HR: Cornelia Menz
FYE: December 31
Type: Private

The Colt .45 may have won the West but it took a New York investment firm stepping in with some cash to keep the company from waving the white flag (during a post-Cold War decline in weapons sales and tough foreign competition). Through the company's subsidiaries Colt's Manufacturing makes handguns (Cowboy Pocket Nine Defender) and semiautomatic rifles (M-4). Colt's Manufacturing boasts more than a dozen distributors throughout Europe Asia and Australia. Founded in 1836 by Samuel Colt the company is about 85%-owned by investment firm Zilkha & Co. which has been breathing new life into the company since 1994 when it bought the firm out of bankruptcy.

COLUMBIA GAS OF MASSACHUSETTS

300 Friberg Pkwy.
Westborough MA 01581-5039
Phone: 508-836-7000
Fax: 508-836-7070
Web: www.columbiagasma.com

CEO: –
CFO: –
HR: –
FYE: December 31
Type: Subsidiary

New England is really pretty and luckily for gas utility Columbia Gas of Massachusetts (formerly Bay State Gas) it can also be pretty chilly. Bay State Gas distributes natural gas to about 300000 customers in 60 communities throughout Massachusetts. Columbia Gas of Massachusetts also provides energy products and services including heating system installation and maintenance and water heater and conversion burner rentals. In response to Massachusetts' deregulation measures the company also offers a customer choice program. Columbia Gas of Massachusetts is a wholly owned subsidiary of energy power player NiSource. The company changed its name in 2010 to be consistent NiSource's other regional utilities.

COLUMBIA BANKING SYSTEM, INC.

NMS: COLB

1301 A Street
Tacoma, WA 98402-2156
Phone: 253 305-1900
Fax: –
Web: www.columbiabank.com

CEO: Melanie J. Dressel
CFO: Clint E. Stein
HR: –
FYE: December 31
Type: Public

Columbia Banking System (CBS) is the holding company for Columbia State Bank (also known as Columbia Bank). The regional community bank has about 155 branches in Washington from Puget Sound to the timber country in the southwestern part of the state as well as in northern Oregon where it also operates as Bank of Astoria. Targeting retail and small and medium-sized business customers the bank offers standard retail services such as checking and savings accounts CDs IRAs credit cards loans and mortgages. Commercial business and real estate loans make up more than 75% of the company's loan portfolio. CBS is increasing its presence in the Pacific Northwest through acquisitions of other community banks.

	Annual Growth	12/10	12/11	12/12	12/13	12/14
Assets ($ mil.)	19.2%	4,256.4	4,785.9	4,906.3	7,161.6	8,578.8
Net income ($ mil.)	27.6%	30.8	48.0	46.1	60.0	81.6
Market value ($ mil.)	7.0%	1,209.6	1,106.8	1,030.4	1,578.9	1,585.8
Employees	14.0%	1,092	1,256	1,198	1,695	1,844

COLUMBIA MANAGEMENT INVESTMENT ADVISERS LLC

100 Federal St. 19th Fl.
Boston MA 02110
Phone: 617-426-3750
Fax: 601-933-3350
Web: www.ergon.com

CEO: –
CFO: –
HR: –
FYE: December 31
Type: Subsidiary

Columbia Management Advisers is an investment management division of Ameriprise Financial. Serving retail clients and high-net-worth investors the company offers more than 125 equity fixed-income cash management asset allocation and balanced mutual funds in addition to closed-end funds offshore funds variable portfolios and 529 college savings plans. Columbia also administers investment portfolios for institutional investors such as corporations foundations pension and benefit plans and endowments. The company distributes its products through Ameriprise financial adivsors and 401(k) plans and third-party financial institutions. It has some $350 billion of assets under management.

COLUMBIA COLLEGE CHICAGO

600 S MICHIGAN AVE FL 5
CHICAGO, IL 606051996
Phone: 312-663-1600
Fax: –
Web: www.colum.edu

CEO: –
CFO: –
HR: Ellen Ryan
FYE: August 31
Type: Private

Columbia College Chicago revels in its creative reputation. Specializing in arts and media the private not-for-profit school offers undergraduate and graduate degrees in the visual performing media and communication arts. The college offers more than 120 academic programs including architecture and interior design photography dance television theater film music composition journalism and marketing communications. Comedian Andy Richter and Wheel of Fortune host Pat Sajak are among the school's notable alumni. Founded in 1890 as the Columbia School of Oratory the college is located in several buildings in downtown Chicago and has about 12000 students. Average teacher to student ratio is 20:1.

	Annual Growth	08/06	08/07	08/08	08/09	08/10
Sales ($ mil.)	–	–	–	0.0	246.7	244.1
Net income ($ mil.)	3259.5%	–	–	0.0	23.8	18.5
Market value ($ mil.)	–	–	–	–	–	–
Employees	–	–	–	–	–	1,000

COLUMBIA PICTURES

10202 W. Washington Blvd.
Culver City CA 90232
Phone: 310-244-4000
Fax: 310-244-2626
Web: www.sonypictures.com/movies/index.html

CEO: Michael Lynton
CFO: Edgar Howells
HR: –
FYE: March 31
Type: Business Segment

The toga lady holds her torch high for film audiences everywhere by representing Columbia Pictures the studio through which Sony Pictures Entertainment produces its big budget movies. The studio was founded in 1924 and in 1982 it was purchased by Coca-Cola. Sony purchased Columbia from Coke in 1989 for $3.4 billion. The deal was the largest acquisition by a Japanese firm up to that time and initially caused headaches for Sony due to losses from elaborate spending budgets and box office duds (Ishtar). In recent years Columbia Pictures has scored hits with its Spider-Man franchise as well as comedies such as Superbad and Hancock. It operates as part of Sony Picture's Columbia TriStar Motion Picture Group.

COLUMBIA SPORTSWEAR CO.

NMS: COLM

14375 Northwest Science Park Drive
Portland, OR 97229
Phone: 503 985-4000
Fax: –
Web: www.columbia.com

CEO: Timothy P. (Tim) Boyle
CFO: Thomas B. Cusick
HR: –
FYE: December 31
Type: Public

Gertrude Boyle is called chairman and occasionally one tough mother. The nonagenarian and face of Columbia Sportswear's "tough mother" and "tested tough" ads heads one of the global powerhouses in the development marketing and distribution of active outerwear. Columbia's trademark Bugaboo parka with weatherproof shell put the company on the map in upscale outdoor wear. Columbia offers performance apparel for a variety of activities as well as sportswear accessories boots and rugged footwear sold under brands Columbia Mountain Hardwear Sorel and Montrail. Founded as a hat company in 1938 Columbia Sportswear is controlled by the Boyle family and run by president and CEO Tim Boyle son of Gert.

	Annual Growth	12/10	12/11	12/12	12/13	12/14
Sales ($ mil.)	9.1%	1,483.5	1,694.0	1,669.6	1,685.0	2,100.6
Net income ($ mil.)	15.5%	77.0	103.5	99.9	94.3	137.2
Market value ($ mil.)	(7.3%)	4,210.6	3,250.5	3,726.0	5,499.0	3,110.1
Employees	10.1%	3,626	4,161	4,166	4,320	5,326

COLUMBIA ST. MARY'S INC.

2025 E. Newport Ave.
Milwaukee WI 53211
Phone: 414-961-3300
Fax: 414-961-8712
Web: www.columbia-stmarys.com

CEO: –
CFO: –
HR: –
FYE: June 30
Type: Subsidiary

Columbia St. Mary's mission is to provide medical care to residents of southeastern Wisconsin. The company operates a health care network that includes two acute care hospitals — Columbia St. Mary's Milwaukee Campus and Columbia St. Mary's Ozaukee Campus — and two specialty hospital the Sacred Heart Rehabilitation Institute and the Columbia St. Mary's Women's Hospital. Altogether the medical centers have some 660 patient beds. The health system also includes about 60 community urgent care and specialist clinics as well as the Columbia College of Nursing. The company which was founded by the Catholic Sisters of Charity in Milwaukee in 1848 is sponsored by Ascension Health and Columbia Health System.

COLUMBIAN CHEMICALS COMPANY

1800 W Oak Commons Ct.
Marietta GA 30062-2253
Phone: 770-792-9400
Fax: 770-792-9623
Web: www.columbianchemicals.com

CEO: –
CFO: Mark Breen
HR: –
FYE: December 31
Type: Subsidiary

Columbian Chemicals likes to be in the black — carbon black that is. The company manufactures carbon black a material used in the production of inks and coatings rubber goods (especially tires) and plastics. Columbian's carbon blacks come in two grades: industrial (sold under the brand names Raven Conductex and Copeblack) and rubber (Statex and Furnex). Carbon black can also be used as an ingredient in fuel cells. Columbian Chemicals operates 11 carbon black manufacturing facilities in nine countries and has a production capacity of 1.1 million metric tons. Expanding its global market share India's Aditya Birla Management Corporation acquired Columbian Chemicals for about $875 million in 2011.

COLUMBUS McKINNON CORP. (NY)

NMS: CMCO

140 John James Audubon Parkway
Amherst, NY 14228-1197
Phone: 716 689-5400
Fax: –
Web: www.cmworks.com

CEO: Timothy T. (Tim) Tevens
CFO: Gregory P. Rustowicz
HR: Randy Biggs
FYE: March 31
Type: Public

Columbus McKinnon's machinery products can be extremely uplifting — literally. Founded in 1875 the company is one of North America's largest producers of equipment for lifting positioning or securing all kinds of large materials. Columbus McKinnon's hoists cranes actuators and steel lifting and rigging tools are used in construction general manufacturing and industrial machinery forestry mining and even wind energy. Well known in the marketplace its brand names include Coffing Duff-Norton Shaw-Box and Yale (made by NACCO). Hoists are the company's biggest seller generating more than two-thirds of sales. In addition to OEMs the company sells to hardware distributors and rental outlets.

	Annual Growth	03/11	03/12	03/13	03/14	03/15
Sales ($ mil.)	2.6%	524.1	591.9	597.3	583.3	579.6
Net income ($ mil.)	–	(36.0)	27.0	78.3	30.4	27.2
Market value ($ mil.)	9.9%	369.0	325.6	384.8	535.5	538.5
Employees	2.1%	2,531	2,549	2,578	2,626	2,747

COLUMBUS SOUTHERN POWER COMPANY

1 Riverside Plaza
Columbus OH 43215-2372
Phone: 614-716-1000
Fax: 614-716-1823
Web: https://www.aepohio.com/

CEO: Michael G Morris
CFO: Brian X Tierney
HR: –
FYE: December 31
Type: Subsidiary

Columbus Southern Power may not have discovered that people in southern Ohio have a need for electricity but it is obligated to provide it. The utility founded in 1937 transmits and distributes electricity to 749000 customers in central and southern Ohio including the capital city of Columbus. The utility a subsidiary of American Electric Power and part of the AEP Ohio unit operates almost 5570 miles of electric transmission and distribution lines and has interests in seven power plants that give it about 3740 MW of coal- and natural gas-fired generating capacity. It also sells bulk power to wholesale customers such as municipal utilities and energy marketers.

COMARCO INC.

NBB: CMRO

25541 Commercentre Drive, Suite 250
Lake Forest, CA 92630
Phone: 949 599-7400
Fax: 800 792-0250
Web: www.comarco.com

CEO: Thomas W Lanni
CFO: –
HR: –
FYE: January 31
Type: Public

Comarco develops universal power supplies that charge various portable devices. Operating solely through wholly owned subsidiary Comarco Wireless Technologies the company's flagship product is its ChargeSource line of adapters that recharge consumer electronic devices such as notebooks mobile phones and music players. Comarco sells directly to consumers through its chargesource.com retail website and to notebook OEMs such as Lenovo who brand the accessories and sell them in conjunction with their notebooks. Comarco was spun off from Genge Industries in 1971. Elkhorn Partners Limited Partnership holds a 49% stake in Comarco.

	Annual Growth	01/10	01/11	01/12	01/13	01/14
Sales ($ mil.)	(36.0%)	26.4	28.9	8.1	6.3	4.4
Net income ($ mil.)	–	(7.4)	(6.0)	(5.3)	(5.6)	(2.1)
Market value ($ mil.)	(49.2%)	38.9	5.0	2.3	2.3	2.6
Employees	(59.2%)	36	24	15	10	1

COMBE INCORPORATED

1101 Westchester Ave.
White Plains NY 10604
Phone: 914-694-5454
Fax: 914-461-4402
Web: www.combe.com

CEO: Christopher B Combe
CFO: Joseph P Gusmano
HR: –
FYE: June 30
Type: Private

Combe comes to the rescue when a touch of grey or other personal indignity appears. The company's health and beauty aids nix the itch with below-the-belt Vagisil as well as color the head turned salt and pepper (Grecian Formula and Just For Men). Combe also combats loose dentures (sold under the Sea-Bond brand) and tough beards (Lectric Shave). Combe's acquisition of J.B. Williams in 2002 added popular personal care brands Aqua Velva after-shave and Brylcreem hair styling cream among others. Founded in 1949 by Ivan Combe and his wife Mary Elizabeth Deming the family-owned company created Clearasil in 1950 the #1 acne medication (later sold) and other familiar brands. Combe's products are sold worldwide.

COMBIMATRIX CORP

NAS: CBMX

310 Goddard, Suite 150
Irvine, CA 92618
Phone: 949 753-0624
Fax: –
Web: www.combimatrix.com

CEO: Mark McDonough
CFO: Scott R Burell
HR: –
FYE: December 31
Type: Public

CombiMatrix works to untangle the complicated matrix of genetic profiles. The company develops and sells diagnostic testing supplies and provides related laboratory services. Through its CombiMatrix Molecular Diagnostics subsidiary it provides molecular diagnostic testing assays and other genetic analysis products. The tests evaluate a patient's DNA to find genetic irregularities which can then help to diagnose health conditions or predict disease susceptibility. CombiMatrix markets its products and services to physician practices hospitals and other health care centers.

	Annual Growth	12/10	12/11	12/12	12/13	12/14
Sales ($ mil.)	22.6%	3.6	4.6	5.4	6.4	8.0
Net income ($ mil.)	–	(13.1)	(7.6)	(9.5)	(3.9)	(8.7)
Market value ($ mil.)	(11.1%)	1.6	1.5	3.9	1.7	1.0
Employees	8.8%	40	45	41	43	56

COMCAST CABLE COMMUNICATIONS LLC

1701 John F. Kennedy Blvd.
Philadelphia PA 19103
Phone: 215-665-1700
Fax: 215-981-7790
Web: www.comcast.com

CEO: Neil Smit
CFO: –
HR: –
FYE: December 31
Type: Subsidiary

Capturing couch potatoes and corporate clients in 39 states from Connecticut to California Comcast Cable Communications is the cable services component of parent Comcast Corporation. The company has more than 22 million video subscribers making it the largest US cable company (ahead of #2 Time Warner Cable) and about 18 million broadband Internet customers. More than 9 million subscribers use its digital phone service to make calls over the Internet. More than 85% of revenues comes from residential customers. Comcast Cable also oversees the advertising business and accounts for more than 90% of sales for parent Comcast Corporation while new sibling NBCUniversal makes up much of the rest.

COMCAST CORP

NMS: CMCS A

One Comcast Center
Philadelphia, PA 19103-2838
Phone: 215 286-1700
Fax:
Web: www.comcastcorporation.com

CEO: Stephen B. (Steve) Burke
CFO: Michael J. (Mike) Cavanagh
HR: Tina Simmons
FYE: December 31
Type: Public

Comcast is the biggest pay-TV provider in the US with about 22 million video subscribers for its core cable division. The company downloads the bulk of its revenue from its cable services offered in 39 states and the District of Columbia. Its broadband Internet service has about 21 million subscribers and its XFINITY computer telephony service has about 11 million customers. Comcast also owns NBCUniversal which includes the NBC TV network Universal Studios and the Universal theme parks. Comcast ended its $45 billion bid to acquire Time Warner Cable in the face of regulatory opposition.

	Annual Growth	12/11	12/12	12/13	12/14	12/15
Sales ($ mil.)	7.5%	55,842.0	62,570.0	64,657.0	68,775.0	74,510.0
Net income ($ mil.)	18.4%	4,160.0	6,203.0	6,816.0	8,380.0	8,163.0
Market value ($ mil.)	–	0.0	0.0	0.0	0.0	0.0
Employees	2.9%	126,000	129,000	136,000	139,000	141,000

COMCAST SPECTACOR L.P.

Wachovia Center Complex 3601 S. Broad St.
Philadelphia PA 19148
Phone: 215-336-3600
Fax: +44-1932-268-756

CEO: –
CFO: –
HR: –
FYE: December 31
Type: Subsidiary

Comcast Spectacor keeps the testosterone flowing in the City of Brotherly Love. The sports and entertainment company owns and operates both the Philadelphia 76ers basketball team and the Philadelphia Flyers hockey team along with the city's Wells Fargo Center arena (formerly the Wachovia Center). Comcast Spectacor also owns event and facility management firm Global Spectrum and Ovations Food Services a contract foodservices provider and concessions operator. Other operations include New Era Tickets and figure skating promoter Disson Skating. Cable giant Comcast owns 66% of the company; chairman and founder Ed Snider leads the minority owners.

COMEDY PARTNERS

345 Hudson St. 9th Fl.
New York NY 10014
Phone: 212-767-8600
Fax: 407-352-8935
Web: www.westgateresorts.com

CEO: Doug Herzog
CFO: –
HR: –
FYE: December 31
Type: Subsidiary

Making television audiences laugh is deadly serious to Comedy Partners. The subsidiary of MTV Networks operates cable network Comedy Central the home of such hits as The Daily Show with Jon Stewart The Colbert Report RENO 911! and South Park. The channel which reaches approximately 98 million US homes also broadcasts feature film comedies stand-up comedy specials and syndicated sitcoms (such as Scrubs). In addition to its TV network Comedy Partners releases its shows on DVD through a distribution deal with Paramount and broadcasts multimedia content through its various websites that are anchored by flagship site ComedyCentral.com. MTV Networks is the cable entertainment arm of media giant Viacom.

COMERICA, INC.   NYS: CMA

Comerica Bank Tower, 1717 Main Street, MC 6404 — CEO: Ralph W. Babb
Dallas, TX 75201 — CFO: Karen L. Parkhill
Phone: 214 462-6831 — HR: Megan D. Burkhart
Fax: - — FYE: December 31
Web: www.comerica.com — Type: Public

If you have a cosigner Comerica will be your copilot. The holding company owns Comerica Bank which has around 480 branches in about a dozen states across the US. The company is organized into three main segments. The Business Bank division is the largest offering loans deposits and capital markets products to middle-market large corporate and government clients. The Retail Bank serves small businesses and consumers while the Wealth Management arm provides private banking investment management financial advisory investment banking brokerage insurance and retirement services. Comerica has total assets of nearly $70 billion.

	Annual Growth	12/10	12/11	12/12	12/13	12/14
Assets ($ mil.)	6.6%	53,667.0	61,008.0	65,359.0	65,227.0	69,190.0
Net income ($ mil.)	21.0%	277.0	393.0	521.0	541.0	593.0
Market value ($ mil.)	2.6%	7,561.7	4,618.7	5,431.4	8,510.5	8,385.2
Employees	(0.7%)	9,365	9,757	9,306	9,207	9,115

COMFORCE CORPORATION

999 Stewart Ave. Ste. 100 — CEO: Andrew Schultz
Bethpage NY 11714-3551 — CFO: Harry V Maccarrone
Phone: 516-437-3300 — HR: Janet Youngstrom
Fax: 516-437-3392 — FYE: December 31
Web: www.comforce.com — Type: Subsidiary

COMFORCE isn't the latest Chuck Norris movie. It's a staffing consulting and outsourcing company that provides clients with temporary employees for high-skills jobs in the information technology telecommunications and health care industries and the tools to manage such contingent workforces. The company also operates subsidiaries COMFORCE Staffing Services (New York-area staffing) and PrO Unlimited (temporary workforce management). COMFORCE also provides payroll funding and outsourcing services to independent consulting and staffing firms through its financial outsourcing services division. The company has about 20 offices in more than a dozen US states. It is is owned by American CyberSystems.

COMFORT SYSTEMS USA, INC.   NYS: FIX

675 Bering Drive, Suite 400 — CEO: Brian E. Lane
Houston, TX 77057 — CFO: William George
Phone: 713 830-9600 — HR: -
Fax: 713 830-9696 — FYE: December 31
Web: www.comfortsystemsusa.com — Type: Public

Comfort Systems USA alters ambient air automatically. The company sells and services commercial HVAC (heating ventilation and air conditioning) systems in apartments health care facilities office buildings manufacturing plants retail centers and schools. In addition to HVAC services Comfort Systems designs building automation control systems that integrate monitor and operate HVAC lighting and access control systems. Some company locations also offer fire protection plumbing and electrical services. Comfort Systems was established in 1997.

	Annual Growth	12/10	12/11	12/12	12/13	12/14
Sales ($ mil.)	6.2%	1,108.3	1,240.0	1,331.2	1,357.3	1,410.8
Net income ($ mil.)	11.8%	14.7	(36.8)	13.5	27.3	23.1
Market value ($ mil.)	6.8%	490.8	399.5	453.2	722.7	638.1
Employees	1.9%	6,569	7,061	6,681	6,698	7,077

COMM-WORKS HOLDINGS LLC

1405 Xenium Lane N. Ste. 120 — CEO: -
Minneapolis MN 55441 — CFO: Mike Kasner
Phone: 763-258-5800 — HR: -
Fax: 763-475-6656 — FYE: December 31
Web: www.comm-works.com — Type: Private

Comm-Works makes even far-flung locations work for enterprising customers. The company specializes in the installation of communications systems security equipment and energy management system for large customers with multiple sites in industries such as retail financial services health care and federal government agencies. Other areas of expertise include cabling infrastructure wireless and data network point-of-sale digital media and conferencing systems. Comm-Works also provides services such as consulting network planning product integration and maintenance. Clients have included Allstate Insurance Qwest and the State of Massachusetts. President and CEO Alan Lampe founded Comm-Works in 1995.

COMMAND CENTER, INC.   NBB: CCNI

3901 N.Schreiber Way — CEO: Frederick J Sandford
Coeur d'Alene, ID 83815 — CFO: Jeff Wilson
Phone: 866 464-5844 — HR: -
Fax: - — FYE: December 26
Web: www.commandonline.com — Type: Public

Command Center wouldn't mind being regarded as the George Patton of the temporary staffing market. The company operates about 50 temporary staffing stores across 20 US states. It specializes in the placement of workers in the event services hospitality construction manufacturing janitorial telemarketing administrative clerical and accounting fields. Command Center was formed in 2005 when Temporary Financial Services acquired Command Staffing and Harborview Software then changed its name. Command Center's top executives own about 34% of the company.

	Annual Growth	12/10	12/11	12/12	12/13	12/14
Sales ($ mil.)	7.2%	69.4	81.9	98.4	93.7	91.8
Net income ($ mil.)	-	(1.6)	0.9	1.6	2.9	9.1
Market value ($ mil.)	17.1%	25.6	18.4	13.5	26.9	48.2
Employees	2.5%	29,171	33,177	35,210	33,210	32,210

COMMAND SECURITY CORP   ASE: MOC

512 Herndon Parkway, Suite A — CEO: Craig P Coy
Herndon, VA 20170 — CFO: N Paul Brost
Phone: 703 464-4735 — HR: -
Fax: - — FYE: March 31
Web: www.commandsecurity.com — Type: Public

Somebody's watching me is a song but also a service thanks to Command Security. The company provides security guards for commercial governmental financial and industrial clients. About half of Command Security's business comes from its aviation services. Although passenger screening services have been taken over by the US government Command Security manages support services such as aircraft and baggage-related security duties and skycap and wheelchair escort services. In addition to general security tasks the company offers recruiting hiring training and supervisory assistance of operating personnel. Federal Express the company's most significant customer accounts for over 20% of total sales.

	Annual Growth	03/11	03/12	03/13	03/14	03/15
Sales ($ mil.)	(1.3%)	146.5	141.6	150.2	156.7	139.2
Net income ($ mil.)	(6.1%)	1.6	0.1	0.5	1.1	1.3
Market value ($ mil.)	1.2%	17.9	13.4	18.0	17.2	18.8
Employees	(3.0%)	5,375	5,100	5,500	5,300	4,750

COMMERCE BANCSHARES, INC. NMS: CBSH

1000 Walnut
Kansas City, MO 64106
Phone: 816 234-2000
Fax: 816 234-2369
Web: www.commercebank.com

CEO: David W. Kemper
CFO: Charles G. (Chuck) Kim
HR: Sara E. Foster
FYE: December 31
Type: Public

Commerce Bancshares owns bank branch operator Commerce Bank. The financial institution boasts a network of more than 360 locations across several US states including Missouri Kansas Illinois Oklahoma and Colorado. The bank focuses on retail and commercial banking services such as deposit accounts mortgages loans and credit cards. Commerce Bank also runs a wealth management division that offers asset management trust private banking brokerage and estate planning services and also manages proprietary mutual funds. As part of its operations Commerce Bank has subsidiaries devoted to insurance leasing and private equity investments.

	Annual Growth	12/10	12/11	12/12	12/13	12/14
Assets ($ mil.)	6.7%	18,502.3	20,649.4	22,159.6	23,072.0	23,994.3
Net income ($ mil.)	4.2%	221.7	256.3	269.3	261.0	261.8
Market value ($ mil.)	2.3%	4,024.1	3,861.0	3,551.1	4,548.8	4,405.0
Employees	(0.7%)	5,005	4,860	4,878	4,889	4,866

COMMERCE GROUP CORP. OTC: CGCO

6001 N. 91st St.
Milwaukee WI 53225-1795
Phone: 414-462-5310
Fax: 414-462-5312
Web: www.commercegroupcorp.com

CEO: -
CFO: -
HR: -
FYE: March 31
Type: Public

Commerce Group owns El Salvador's San Sebastian Gold Mine which contains some 1.5 million ounces of gold reserves. Production at the mine has been suspended since 1999 however while the company works to raise money to upgrade the facility's gold-processing equipment. Commerce Group also explores for other gold and silver mining opportunities in El Salvador. In 2009 the Commerce Group filed a motion for arbitration hearings with the government of El Salvador which revoked the company's permits to explore the San Sebastian Gold Mine in 2006. The company has postponed all business activity pending the outcome of the arbitration.

COMMERCIAL BANCSHARES, INC. (OH) NBB: CMOH

118 S. Sandusky Avenue
Upper Sandusky, OH 43351
Phone: 419 294-5781
Fax: -
Web: www.csbanking.com

CEO: Robert E Beach
CFO: Scott A Oboy
HR: Amy Smalley
FYE: December 31
Type: Public

If Commercial Bancshares were planning to produce a commercial it's quite probable the subject would be Commercial Savings Bank. The holding company owns the community bank which serves northwestern Ohio from about 10 branches. The bank offers standard retail and business services including checking and savings accounts certificates of deposit and loans. Commercial loans make up the largest portion of the bank's loan portfolio (more than two-thirds); other offerings include consumer finance loans home equity loans credit card loans and residential mortgages.

	Annual Growth	12/10	12/11	12/12	12/13	12/14
Assets ($ mil.)	2.5%	304.4	287.8	301.6	318.0	336.5
Net income ($ mil.)	9.1%	2.3	2.8	2.9	3.1	3.3
Market value ($ mil.)	17.3%	17.3	21.7	22.5	27.1	32.8
Employees	(1.2%)	105	104	102	103	100

COMMERCIAL FURNITURE GROUP INC.

810 W. Hwy. 25/70
Newport TN 37821
Phone: 423-623-0031
Fax: 866-319-9371
Web: www.commercialfurnituregroup.com

CEO: Seamus Bateson
CFO: -
HR: Charles A Pineau
FYE: October 31
Type: Private

Thank the Commercial Furniture Group (CF Group) for making you a place at the table. The company designs and manufactures tables and seating for the foodservice and hospitality industries. It also produces furniture on contract for the office health care and education markets as well as for the federal government. The CF Group's stable of well-established brands most of them gained through acquisitions include Falcon Howe Shelby Williams and Thonet. Founded in 1959 as Falcon Manufacturing the company has operations in the US China Denmark and Mexico.

COMMERCIAL METALS CO. NYS: CMC

6565 North MacArthur Blvd
Irving, TX 75039
Phone: 214 689-4300
Fax: 214 689-5886
Web: www.cmc.com

CEO: Joseph (Joe) Alvarado
CFO: Mary A. Lindsey
HR: Terry P. Hatten
FYE: August 31
Type: Public

Man of Steel wanted: Commercial Metals (CMC) manufactures recycles and sells enough steel and metal to test even Superman. CMC operates via five segments: Americas Recycling its metal processing plants in the US Southwest shreds and pulverizes scrap for sale to steel mills. Americas Mills turn out reinforcing bar flats rounds fence post and other shapes. A fabrication arm shapes produces and treats steel bar and angles. International business (rolling and finishing mills recycling and fabrication plants) churn out reinforcing bar and mesh. CMC's marketing and distributing segment sells products in 200 locations in more than 20 countries to the construction energy and transportation markets.

	Annual Growth	08/11	08/12	08/13	08/14	08/15
Sales ($ mil.)	(6.7%)	7,918.4	7,828.4	6,889.6	7,040.0	5,988.6
Net income ($ mil.)	-	(129.6)	207.5	77.3	115.6	141.6
Market value ($ mil.)	7.5%	1,358.7	1,473.2	1,720.7	1,998.2	1,815.5
Employees	(5.5%)	11,422	9,860	9,411	9,293	9,126

COMMERCIAL NATIONAL FINANCIAL CORP. (PA) NBB: CNAF

900 Ligonier Street
Latrobe, PA 15650
Phone: 724 539-3501
Fax: 724 539-1137
Web: www.cnbthebank.com

CEO: Gregg E Hunter
CFO: Thomas D Watters
HR: -
FYE: December 31
Type: Public

Commercial National Financial is the holding company for Commercial Bank & Trust of PA which serves individuals and local businesses through more than five branches in western Pennsylvania's Westmoreland County. Founded in 1934 the bank offers standard deposit services like checking and savings accounts money market investments CDs and IRAs as well as trust and asset management services. Commercial Bank & Trust of PA's loan portfolio consists mostly of residential mortgages (more than 55%) and commercial mortgages (about 30%) in addition to business construction consumer and municipal loans. Executive officers and board members own more than 20% of Commercial National Financial.

	Annual Growth	12/10	12/11	12/12	12/13	12/14
Assets ($ mil.)	2.2%	355.5	401.0	373.1	394.3	387.5
Net income ($ mil.)	3.1%	5.5	6.7	7.3	5.4	6.2
Market value ($ mil.)	3.5%	54.3	67.2	55.8	58.2	62.2
Employees	0.2%	108	108	111	110	109

COMMERCIAL VEHICLE GROUP INC
NMS: CVGI

7800 Walton Parkway
New Albany, OH 43054
Phone: 614-289-5360
Fax: –

CEO: Patrick E. (Pat) Miller
CFO: C. Timothy (Tim) Trenary
HR: –
FYE: December 31
Type: Public

CB radio lingo might have gone the way of mood rings but Commercial Vehicle Group (CVG) is still a trucker's good buddy. The company makes components for the cabs of heavy-duty trucks that help keep drivers comfortable and safe. Products include static and suspension seat systems interior trim (instrument panels door panels headliners) mirrors wiper systems and controls and switches. Its customers include heavy-duty truck manufacturers such as AB Volvo and PACCAR (each about 15% of sales). Besides truck manufacturers CVG sells its products to the fleet maintenance aftermarket and makers of buses military vehicles and agricultural mining and construction equipment among others.

	Annual Growth	12/10	12/11	12/12	12/13	12/14
Sales ($ mil.)	8.9%	597.8	832.0	857.9	747.7	839.7
Net income ($ mil.)	4.1%	6.5	18.6	50.1	(12.4)	7.6
Market value ($ mil.)	(20.0%)	473.7	263.5	239.3	211.9	194.1
Employees	6.0%	5,430	6,356	6,480	6,480	6,850

COMMONWEALTH EDISON COMPANY

440 S. LaSalle St.
Chicago IL 60605-1028
Phone: 312-394-4321
Fax: 312-394-2231
Web: www.comed.com

CEO: Anne R Pramaggiore
CFO: Joseph R Trpik Jr
HR: Michael T Latino
FYE: December 31
Type: Subsidiary

Commonwealth Edison (ComEd) faces the not-so-common task of powering up Chicago. ComEd a subsidiary of utility holding company Exelon distributes electricity to 3.8 million homes and businesses in Chicago and surrounding areas of Northern Illinois representing 70% of population of the the state. The utility owns manages more than 90000 circuit miles of transmission and distribution lines; it receives most of its power supply from sister company Exelon Generation. ComEd works with regional operator PJM Interconnection which manages wholesale activities on the utility's transmission grid.

COMMONWEALTH EQUITY SERVICES LLP

29 Sawyer Rd.
Waltham MA 02453-3483
Phone: 781-736-0700
Fax: 781-529-9297
Web: www.commonwealth.com

CEO: Wayne Bloom
CFO: –
HR: –
FYE: December 31
Type: Private

If it were up to Commonwealth Equity Services we'd all have wealth in common. Operating as Commonwealth Financial Network the independent broker-dealer and investment advisor provides investment products and services to a network of about 1400 independent financial advisors throughout the US. It has about $65 billion in client account assets. Commonwealth Financial Network provides access to such financial products as stocks bonds mutual funds annuities investment trusts life and long-term care insurance retirement plans CDs and money market accounts and alternative investments to its advisors who in turn offer these products to their retail clientele.

COMMONWEALTH HEALTH CORPORATION INC.

800 PARK ST
BOWLING GREEN, KY 421012356
Phone: 270-745-1500
Fax: –
Web: www.chc.net

CEO: Connie D Smith
CFO: –
HR: –
FYE: March 31
Type: Private

For care in Kentucky Bluegrass Staters can turn to Commonwealth Health Corporation. The holding company houses a full spectrum of health care facilities and services including The Medical Center a 415-bed regional health care system comprised of four hospitals long-term health care providers and senior care among other services. Commonwealth's outpatient offerings include nutrition therapy a women's center diabetes programs and adult day care. The corporation's Center Care Health Benefits Program supplies employers with products and services to support the distribution and administration of employee benefits and healthcare services.

	Annual Growth	03/09	03/10	03/11	03/12	03/13
Sales ($ mil.)	1.4%	–	61.6	59.9	60.5	64.3
Net income ($ mil.)	(12.6%)	–	–	6.1	4.5	4.7
Market value ($ mil.)	–	–	–	–	–	–
Employees	–	–	–	–	–	2,700

COMMUNICATIONS SUPPLY CORPORATION

200 E. Lies Rd.
Carol Stream IL 60188
Phone: 630-221-6400
Fax: 630-221-6420
Web: www.gocsc.com

CEO: David Bemoras
CFO: –
HR: –
FYE: December 31
Type: Subsidiary

Communications Supply Corporation (CSC) carries a heavy download. The company is a distributor of equipment and supplies for data communication networks and security systems. It operates from about 50 locations in the US. CSC sells a wide range of products including cable systems (cabling and related components) network and wireless components (transmitters and fiber-optic switches) security products (electronic locks and video gear) data center gear (equipment racks) and low-voltage wiring (coaxial and control cable). It also provides logistics materials management and integration services. Founded in 1972 the company is a subsidiary of electrical and construction products distributor WESCO.

COMMUNICATIONS SYSTEMS, INC.
NMS: JCS

10900 Red Circle Drive
Minnetonka, MN 55343
Phone: 952-996-1674
Fax: –
Web: www.commsystems.com

CEO: Roger H D Lacey
CFO: Edwin Freeman
HR: Jessica Docken
FYE: December 31
Type: Public

Aptly named Communications Systems makes connectors and wiring systems for telecommunications networks. The company operates through subsidiaries. Its Suttle and Austin Taylor units make connectors adapters and other devices for voice data and video communications. Transition Networks makes converters that move data between copper wire and fiber-optic networks LAN switches and print servers. JDL Technologies provides schools and businesses with telecom network development services and software. Communications Systems sells directly and through distributors. Major customers include AT&T and Verizon.

	Annual Growth	12/10	12/11	12/12	12/13	12/14
Sales ($ mil.)	(0.2%)	120.1	143.8	104.2	131.3	119.1
Net income ($ mil.)	(33.0%)	9.7	9.8	2.2	(1.0)	2.0
Market value ($ mil.)	(7.0%)	121.6	121.7	90.0	96.4	90.9
Employees	6.0%	458	410	492	596	578

COMMUNICATIONS TEST DESIGN INC.

1373 Enterprise Dr.
West Chester PA 19380
Phone: 610-436-5203
Fax: 604-684-3451

CEO: Jerry Parsons
CFO: Lawrence E Morgan
HR: –
FYE: December 31
Type: Private

Communications Test Design (CTDI) repairs installs tests and manufactures telecommunications equipment. The company's main business is providing repair and maintenance services to wireless and wireline carriers and cable companies as well as equipment makers such as Alcatel Lucent and Cisco. It offers warehousing and distribution services product testing and equipment installation — from laying cable to integrating customer premise equipment. CTDI also makes a line of broadband switching and access equipment and provides contract manufacturing services. The company was founded in 1975 by chairman and CEO Jerry Parsons his father Donald and brother Dick. CTDI is owned and led by the Parsons family.

COMMUNICATIONS WORKERS OF AMERICA AFL-CIO CLC

501 3RD ST NW
WASHINGTON, DC 200012760
Phone: 202-434-1100
Fax: –
Web: www.cwa-union.org

CEO: –
CFO: –
HR: –
FYE: May 31
Type: Private

CWA knows how to get its message across. Communications Workers of America is a labor union representing more than 700000 employees in the communications and media industries. Members work in a variety of sectors including telecommunications journalism publishing manufacturing and customer service. With about 1200 locals across the US Canada and Puerto Rico CWA is one of the most geographically diverse unions. It holds more than 2000 collective bargaining agreements guaranteeing wages benefits and good working conditions for members. The group is affiliated with the AFL-CIO the Canadian Labour Congress and Union Network International.

	Annual Growth	12/07	12/08*	05/10	05/11	05/13
Sales ($ mil.)	(3.8%)	–	176.9	156.7	155.3	146.0
Net income ($ mil.)	–	–	–	9.2	2.0	(4.2)
Market value ($ mil.)	–	–	–	–	–	–
Employees	–	–	–	–	–	510

*Fiscal year change

COMMUNITY ASPHALT CORP.

9675 NW 117TH AVE STE 108
MEDLEY, FL 331781244
Phone: 305-884-9444
Fax: –
Web: www.cacorp.net

CEO: Jose L Fernandez
CFO: Agustin Arellano Jr
HR: –
FYE: December 31
Type: Private

Community Asphalt provides paving services for the road more traveled. The company's services include grading and paving pavement milling surveying excavation on- and off-road hauling drainage utilities base finishing and highway sweeping. It also provides engineering contracting and design/build services; projects include parking lots industrial and retail complexes auto race tracks and airport runways. Formed in 1980 Community Asphalt has three asphalt plants in southeastern Florida. It also operates a limestone quarry and a fleet of dump trucks. In 2006 Community Asphalt and Spain's Obrascón Huarte Lain (OHL) made a stock purchase agreement which gave OHL a controlling interest in the company.

	Annual Growth	12/09	12/10	12/11	12/12	12/13
Sales ($ mil.)	(14.2%)	–	330.7	260.8	243.9	208.8
Net income ($ mil.)	–	–	–	3.1	2.4	(4.5)
Market value ($ mil.)	–	–	–	–	–	–
Employees	–	–	–	–	–	640

COMMUNITY BANCORP. (DERBY, VT)

NBB: CMTV

4811 US Route 5
Derby, VT 05829
Phone: 802 334-7915
Fax: –

CEO: Stephen P Marsh
CFO: –
HR: –
FYE: December 31
Type: Public

Winters may be cold in Vermont but Community Bancorp. hopes to warm the hearts of its customers with its hometown banking services. It is the holding company for Community National Bank which has been serving Vermont since 1851. Through nearly 20 branches the bank offers such products and services as checking and savings accounts CDs IRAs residential and commercial mortgages and business consumer and other loans. In conjunction with two other regional banks the company is part of Community Financial Services Group which offers trust and investment planning services. At the end of 2007 Community Bancorp. acquired LyndonBank which added about a half-dozen branches to its network.

	Annual Growth	12/10	12/11	12/12	12/13	12/14
Assets ($ mil.)	1.8%	545.9	552.9	575.7	573.7	586.7
Net income ($ mil.)	6.8%	3.9	3.6	4.4	5.1	5.1
Market value ($ mil.)	14.6%	40.9	46.9	54.0	65.4	70.5
Employees	2.8%	156	157	154	151	174

COMMUNITY BANK

790 E. Colorado Blvd.
Pasadena CA 91101
Phone: 626-577-1700
Fax: 626-568-2299
Web: www.cbank.com

CEO: David R Misch
CFO: Nancy L Karlson
HR: –
FYE: December 31
Type: Private

Community Bank serves communities in Southern California. Focusing on small and middle-market businesses the bank mainly offers commercial real estate loans (about two-thirds of its loan portfolio) as well as business loans letters of credit equipment loans foreign receivables financing and funding for employee stock option plans. To a lesser extent it issues residential mortgages home equity loans and personal loans for cars RVs and boats. The bank's deposit products include checking and savings accounts money market accounts CDs and IRAs. Brothers Charlie and Howard Cook founded Community Bank as Huntington Park Bank in 1945; it changed its name in 1950. The bank has more than a dozen branches.

COMMUNITY BANK SYSTEM, INC.

NYS: CBU

5790 Widewaters Parkway
DeWitt, NY 13214-1883
Phone: 315 445-2282
Fax: –
Web: www.communitybankna.com

CEO: Mark E. Tryniski
CFO: Scott A. Kingsley
HR: Michelle Bishop
FYE: December 31
Type: Public

Community Bank System is right up front about what it is. The holding company owns Community Bank which operates about 180 branches across nearly 30 counties in upstate New York and five counties in northeastern Pennsylvania where it operates as First Liberty Bank and Trust. Focusing on small underserved towns the bank offers standard products and services such as checking and savings accounts certificates of deposit and loans and mortgages to consumer business and government clients. The bank's loan portfolio is divided more or less equally among business loans residential mortgages and consumer loans.

	Annual Growth	12/10	12/11	12/12	12/13	12/14
Assets ($ mil.)	8.3%	5,444.5	6,488.3	7,496.8	7,095.9	7,489.4
Net income ($ mil.)	9.6%	63.3	73.1	77.1	78.8	91.4
Market value ($ mil.)	8.2%	1,131.6	1,132.8	1,114.9	1,616.9	1,553.7
Employees	7.6%	1,627	2,030	2,188	2,215	2,182

COMMUNITY BANKERS TRUST CORP
NAS: ESXB

9954 Mayland Drive, Suite 2100
Richmond, VA 23233
Phone: 804 934-9999
Fax: –
Web: www.cbtrustcorp.com

CEO: Rex L Smith III
CFO: Bruce E Thomas
HR: Walter Burlington
FYE: December 31
Type: Public

Community Bankers Trust Corporation formerly Community Bankers Acquisition is the holding company for the Bank of Essex and TransCommunity Bank. Additional divisions of TransCommunity operate as Bank of Goochland Bank of Powhatan Bank of Louisa and Bank of Rockbridge. The company grew in 2008 when it merged with former bank holding companies TransCommunity Financial and BOE Financial Services of Virginia. The company now includes about a dozen bank branches west and north of Richmond Virginia. Subsidiaries offer securities and insurance products. Community Bankers Trust expanded into Georgia when it acquired the branches and deposits of The Community Bank which was the 20th bank to fail in 2008.

	Annual Growth	12/10	12/11	12/12	12/13	12/14
Assets ($ mil.)	0.9%	1,115.6	1,092.5	1,153.3	1,089.5	1,155.7
Net income ($ mil.)	–	(21.0)	1.4	5.6	5.9	7.5
Market value ($ mil.)	43.2%	22.9	25.1	57.7	81.9	96.3
Employees	(5.7%)	287	266	273	234	227

COMMUNITY CAPITAL BANCSHARES, INC.
NBB: ALBY

2815 Meredyth Drive
Albany, GA 31707
Phone: 229 446-2265
Fax: –
Web: www.comcapbancshares.com

CEO: Luke Flatt
CFO: David J Baranko
HR: Ladonna Urick
FYE: December 31
Type: Public

Community Capital Bancshares has taken hometown to heart. The bank holding company owns Albany Bank & Trust a community bank serving southwestern Georgia through three branches. It also includes AB&T National Bank which operates two branches in Alabama. The banks offer standard deposit products and services including checking and savings accounts money market accounts CDs and IRAs. The company mainly uses these deposits to fund residential and commercial construction loans and mortgages as well as business and consumer loans. Real estate loans comprise about 80% of the company's loan book. The company plans to combine all of its banks under the AB&T National Bank name.

	Annual Growth	12/06	12/11	12/12	12/13	12/14
Assets ($ mil.)	(8.5%)	296.9	148.7	131.9	136.0	145.9
Net income ($ mil.)	44.2%	0.4	(0.8)	(0.6)	0.4	7.9
Market value ($ mil.)	(28.4%)	78.5	3.4	3.8	2.5	5.4
Employees	–	84	–	–	–	–

COMMUNITY CHOICE FINANCIAL INC
NL:

6785 Bobcat Way, Suite 200
Dublin, OH 43016
Phone: 614 798-5900
Fax: –
Web: www.ccfi.com

CEO: William E Saunders Jr
CFO: –
HR: –
FYE: December 31
Type: Public

Dire Straits may have gotten their money for nothing but the rest of us sometimes need to hit up payday lenders like Community Choice Financial. Formed in 2011 the company issues unsecured short-term consumer loans of up to $1000 charging fees from $8 to $15 per $100 borrowed in addition to interest rates which vary by state but typically exceed a 395% APR. Its stores operated under the CheckSmart and California Check Cashing Stores brands also issue title loans prepaid MasterCard debit cards and offer check cashing money transfers bill payments and money orders at more than 430 stores in 14 states. Community Choice Financial filed an IPO in 2011 but withdrew it in 2012.

	Annual Growth	12/10	12/11	12/12	12/13	12/14
Sales ($ mil.)	23.3%	224.3	306.9	373.0	439.2	518.3
Net income ($ mil.)	–	31.5	17.0	13.2	8.2	(51.8)
Market value ($ mil.)	–	–	–	–	–	–
Employees	11.7%	–	–	3,071	3,523	3,831

COMMUNITY FINANCIAL CORP (THE)
NAS: TCFC

3035 Leonardtown Road
Waldorf, MD 20601
Phone: 301 645-5601
Fax: –
Web: www.cbtc.com

CEO: –
CFO: William J Pasenelli
HR: –
FYE: December 31
Type: Public

Tri-County Financial is trying to create some interest in the Old Line State. The financial institution is the holding company for Community Bank of Tri-County which operates about 10 branches in Calvert Charles and St. Mary's counties in southern Maryland. The bank which was first organized as a savings and loan association in 1950 offers standard retail products and services including checking and savings accounts IRAs and CDs. It uses funds from deposits to write a variety of loans including commercial mortgages (about 40% of its loan book) residential mortgages and business loans. Home equity construction equipment and consumer loans round out its loan portfolio.

	Annual Growth	12/10	12/11	12/12	12/13	12/14
Assets ($ mil.)	5.1%	885.9	983.5	981.6	1,023.8	1,082.9
Net income ($ mil.)	8.0%	4.8	3.2	5.0	6.7	6.5
Market value ($ mil.)	5.7%	75.7	70.5	75.1	97.4	94.4
Employees	4.9%	142	154	167	165	172

COMMUNITY FIRST BANCORPORATION
OTC: CFOK

449 Hwy. 123 Bypass
Seneca SC 29678
Phone: 864-886-0206
Fax: 864-886-0912
Web: www.c1stbank.com

CEO: –
CFO: –
HR: –
FYE: December 31
Type: Public

Community First Bancorporation puts financial matters first in the northwestern corner of South Carolina. The holding company owns Community First Bank which operates more than five branches in Oconee and Anderson counties. The commercial bank offers traditional deposit products such as checking and savings accounts CDs and IRAs. Deposit funds are primarily used to originate single- to four-family mortgages and commercial mortgages. The bank also writes construction consumer and business loans. In late 2011 Community First Bancorporation bought the single-branch Bank of Westminster which was merged with Community First Bank's existing location in Westminster South Carolina.

COMMUNITY HEALTH GROUP

2420 FENTON ST 200
CHULA VISTA, CA 919143516
Phone: 619-422-0422
Fax: –
Web: www.chgsd.com

CEO: Norma A Diaz
CFO: William Rice
HR: –
FYE: December 31
Type: Private

Community Health Group is the oldest and one of the largest locally based HMOs in San Diego. Founded in 1982 the not-for-profit HMO provides health insurance products and related services to more than 100000 members. Community Health Group's product offerings include its California's Healthy Families program which provides low-cost health dental and vision coverage to children. The company also provides other managed care services to California communities such as Medi-Cal low-income coverage and Medicare Advantage Special Needs plans as well as third-party administration services.

	Annual Growth	12/02	12/03	12/05	12/09	12/12
Sales ($ mil.)	(8.0%)	–	110.2	79.3	40.0	52.2
Net income ($ mil.)	19.5%	–	–	1.2	2.2	4.3
Market value ($ mil.)	–	–	–	–	–	–
Employees	–	–	–	–	–	140

COMMUNITY HEALTH NETWORK INC.

7330 SHADELAND STA # 200
INDIANAPOLIS, IN 462563957
Phone: 317-621-1085
Fax: –
Web: www.ecommunity.com

CEO: William E. (Bill) Corley
CFO: Joe Kessler
HR: Jeffrey (Jeff) Purkey
FYE: December 31
Type: Private

Community Hospitals of Indiana (aka Community Health Network) has Indianapolis surrounded. The health care system includes about a half a dozen acute-care hospitals all operating under the Community Hospital moniker. One Community Hospital Anderson is located outside the state capital. It also runs the Community Heart and Vascular Hospital. Community Health Network whose origin reaches back to the 1950s has a total of about 1080 staffed beds and 1400-plus physicians. The network also includes more than 100 community care sites including physician practices community clinics surgery centers occupational health facilities a rehabilitation center and home health practices.

	Annual Growth	12/07	12/08	12/09	12/12	12/13
Sales ($ mil.)	39.2%	–	337.1	679.8	384.5	1,763.4
Net income ($ mil.)	49.7%	–	–	35.6	44.8	179.1
Market value ($ mil.)	–	–	–	–	–	–
Employees	–	–	–	–	–	5,000

COMMUNITY HEALTH SYSTEM

1500 SW 1ST AVE
OCALA, FL 344716504
Phone: 352-351-7200
Fax: –
Web: www.munroeregional.com

CEO: Richard D Mutarelli
CFO: –
HR: Dan O' Conner
FYE: September 30
Type: Private

Munroe Regional Health System operates the Munroe Regional Medical Center and affiliated facilities serving residents of north central Florida's Marion County and surrounding areas. Munroe Regional Medical Center is a 500-bed acute care hospital that offers comprehensive medical surgical and emergency care along with programs devoted to cardiovascular care stroke prevention and care orthopedics and women's health. The hospital is operated under a lease agreement with the Marion County Hospital District. Munroe Regional Health System also provides home health services and operates outpatient clinics providing primary care diagnostic and rehabilitation therapy services.

	Annual Growth	09/04	09/05	09/06	09/08	09/09
Sales ($ mil.)	4.0%	–	267.8	263.0	312.1	313.6
Net income ($ mil.)	–	–	–	4.1	(3.3)	(7.4)
Market value ($ mil.)	–	–	–	–	–	–
Employees	–	–	–	–	–	2,179

COMMUNITY HEALTH SYSTEMS, INC.

NYS: CYH

4000 Meridian Boulevard
Franklin, TN 37067
Phone: 615 465-7000
Fax: –
Web: www.chs.net

CEO: Wayne T. Smith
CFO: W. Larry Cash
HR: Mike Meeks
FYE: December 31
Type: Public

Community Health Systems (CHS) isn't much of a city dweller. The hospital operator prefers small-town America owning or leasing more than 200 hospitals mostly in rural areas or small cities in 29 states. Its hospitals (which house roughly 31000 beds) typically act as the sole or primary acute health care provider in a service area and offer a variety of medical surgical and emergency services (though a handful are specialty centers). The hospitals generally have ancillary facilities including doctors' offices surgery centers and diagnostic imaging facilities as well as home health and hospice agencies. CHS' Quorum Health Resources subsidiary provides management services to around 150 non-affiliated hospitals.

	Annual Growth	12/10	12/11	12/12	12/13	12/14
Sales ($ mil.)	9.5%	12,986.5	13,626.2	13,029.0	12,997.7	18,639.0
Net income ($ mil.)	(24.3%)	280.0	201.9	265.6	141.2	92.0
Market value ($ mil.)	9.6%	4,362.0	2,036.9	3,588.1	4,583.8	6,293.8
Employees	17.7%	87,000	88,000	96,000	87,000	167,000

COMMUNITY HOSPITAL OF ANDERSON AND MADISON COUNTY INCORPORATED

1515 N MADISON AVE
ANDERSON, IN 460113453
Phone: 765-298-4242
Fax: –
Web: www.communityanderson.com

CEO: Beth Tharp
CFO: –
HR: –
FYE: December 31
Type: Private

The folks of Madison County Indiana needn't race south to Indianapolis to find medical care. Community Hospital Anderson is an acute care facility with some 200 beds. Departments and services include a sleep analysis lab ECG (electrocardiogram) tests for cardiopulmonary conditions and specialized treatment for cancer and diabetes among other conditions. Community Hospital Anderson operates four intermediate and supervised care facilities in the area. The hospital is part of Community Hospitals of Indiana (also known as Community Health Network) a not-for-profit health care system that serves the health care needs of patients in Indiana.

	Annual Growth	12/05	12/06*	05/09*	12/09	12/12
Sales ($ mil.)	4.4%	–	117.5	58.6	120.8	152.0
Net income ($ mil.)	212.4%	–	–	1.2	4.0	35.4
Market value ($ mil.)	–	–	–	–	–	–
Employees	–	–	–	–	–	1,250

*Fiscal year change

COMMUNITY HOSPITAL OF THE MONTEREY PENINSULA

23625 HOLMAN HWY
MONTEREY, CA 939405902
Phone: 831-624-5311
Fax: –
Web: www.chomp.org

CEO: Steven J Packer
CFO: Laura Zehm
HR: –
FYE: December 31
Type: Private

Community Hospital of the Monterey Peninsula has a sunny disposition when it comes to medical care. The not-for-profit health care facility provides general medical and surgical services to residents of Monterey California. It has about 235 acute care and skilled nursing beds and offers specialty services including cardiac and cancer care obstetrics orthopedics and rehabilitation. In addition to its main facility the hospital operates several ancillary centers including a mental health clinic an inpatient hospice medical laboratory branches and several outpatient centers offering diagnostic imaging diabetes care and other services.

	Annual Growth	12/05	12/06	12/08	12/09	12/12
Sales ($ mil.)	2.9%	–	373.8	406.9	475.7	442.9
Net income ($ mil.)	25.8%	–	–	32.5	26.6	81.4
Market value ($ mil.)	–	–	–	–	–	–
Employees	–	–	–	–	–	1,947

COMMUNITY MEDICAL CENTER

99 Hwy. 37 West
Toms River NJ 08755
Phone: 732-557-8000
Fax: 732-557-8087
Web: www.sbhcs.com/hospitals/community_medical/inde

CEO: –
CFO: Mark Ostrander
HR: –
FYE: December 31
Type: Subsidiary

When Garden Staters in Ocean County get sick they look to the community for help. Community Medical Center (CMC) that is. Part of the Saint Barnabas Health Care System CMC is a full-service 590-bed acute care hospital that provides a range of health services including primary and emergency care obstetrics and maternity care pediatrics diabetes and cancer treatment surgery senior care and rehabilitative care. CMC's community wellness centers provide ambulatory health services diagnostic services and primary care as well as prevention and wellness education to the communities they serve. Founded in 1961 CMC is one of New Jersey's largest non-teaching hospitals.

COMMUNITY SHORES BANK CORP
NBB: CSHB

1030 W. Norton Avenue
Muskegon, MI 49441
Phone: 231 780-1800
Fax: –
Web: www.communityshores.com

CEO: Heather D Brolick
CFO: Tracey A Welsh
HR: –
FYE: December 31
Type: Public

Community Shores Bank Corporation is the holding company for Community Shores Bank which has about five branches that serve western Michigan's Muskegon and Ottawa counties. The bank provides deposit services such as checking and savings accounts money market accounts health savings accounts CDs and IRAs. Commercial operating and real estate loans to area businesses make up approximately three-quarters of the company's loan portfolio which also includes residential real estate consumer and construction loans. The bank also offers investment products and services through an agreement with a third-party provider. The bank was founded in 1999.

	Annual Growth	12/10	12/11	12/12	12/13	12/14
Assets ($ mil.)	(6.1%)	237.9	208.7	204.2	190.8	184.7
Net income ($ mil.)	–	(8.9)	(2.5)	0.3	5.5	4.3
Market value ($ mil.)	21.8%	1.0	0.1	0.3	4.8	2.2
Employees	(1.6%)	82	78	74	74	77

COMMUNITY TRUST BANCORP, INC.
NMS: CTBI

346 North Mayo Trail
Pikeville, KY 41501
Phone: 606 432-1414
Fax: –
Web: www.ctbi.com

CEO: Jean R. Hale
CFO: Kevin J. Stumbo
HR: Kevin Burford
FYE: December 31
Type: Public

Community Trust Bancorp is the holding company for Community Trust Bank one of the largest Kentucky-based banks. It operates 70-plus branches throughout the state as well as in northeastern Tennessee and southern West Virginia. The bank offers standard services to area businesses and individuals including checking and savings accounts credit cards and CDs. Loans secured by commercial properties and other real estate account for nearly 70% of the bank's portfolio which also includes business consumer and construction loans. Subsidiary Community Trust and Investment Company provides trust estate retirement brokerage and insurance services through a handful of offices in Kentucky and Tennessee.

	Annual Growth	12/10	12/11	12/12	12/13	12/14
Assets ($ mil.)	2.6%	3,355.9	3,591.2	3,635.7	3,581.7	3,723.8
Net income ($ mil.)	7.0%	33.0	38.8	44.9	45.2	43.3
Market value ($ mil.)	6.0%	505.8	513.9	572.5	788.8	639.4
Employees	(0.7%)	1,041	1,015	1,035	1,022	1,012

COMMUNITY WEST BANCSHARES
NMS: CWBC

445 Pine Avenue
Goleta, CA 93117
Phone: 805 692-5821
Fax: 805 692-5835
Web: www.communitywest.com

CEO: Martin E Plourd
CFO: Charles G Baltuskonis
HR: –
FYE: December 31
Type: Public

Community West Bancshares is the holding company for Community West Bank which serves individuals and small to midsized businesses through five branches along California's Central Coast. Services include checking and savings accounts and CDs as well as health savings accounts. Approximately 40% of the bank's loan portfolio is secured by manufactured housing loans; real estate mortgages account for more than 30%. A preferred Small Business Administration lender Community West also writes SBA loans through offices in about a dozen other states.

	Annual Growth	12/10	12/11	12/12	12/13	12/14
Assets ($ mil.)	(4.4%)	667.6	633.3	532.1	539.0	557.3
Net income ($ mil.)	35.5%	2.1	(10.5)	3.2	9.0	7.0
Market value ($ mil.)	16.2%	29.5	12.2	27.5	53.8	53.8
Employees	(3.0%)	131	134	130	122	116

COMMUNITYONE BANCORP
NAS: COB

1017 E. Morehead Street
Charlotte, NC 28204
Phone: 336 626-8300
Fax: –
Web: www.community1.com

CEO: Robert L. (Bob) Reid
CFO: David Nielsen
HR: –
FYE: December 31
Type: Public

CommunityOne Bancorp (formerly FNB United) is the holding company for CommunityOne Bank (formerly First National Bank and Trust) which has about 50 branches in North Carolina. The bank's offerings include checking savings and money market accounts CDs IRAs credit cards and trust services. It concentrates on real estate lending: Commercial mortgages account for more than 35% of the company's loan portfolio while residential mortgages and construction loans are about 25% apiece. The bank also makes business and consumer loans. Subsidiary Dover Mortgage Company originates mortgages for sale into the secondary market through about five loan production offices in its home state.

	Annual Growth	12/10	12/11	12/12	12/13	12/14
Assets ($ mil.)	3.6%	1,921.3	2,409.1	2,151.6	1,985.0	2,215.5
Net income ($ mil.)	–	(112.9)	(137.3)	(40.0)	(1.5)	150.5
Market value ($ mil.)	143.3%	7.9	309.6	280.6	308.4	276.9
Employees	2.1%	526	609	629	581	571

COMMVAULT SYSTEMS INC
NMS: CVLT

1 Commvault Way
Tinton Falls, NJ 07724
Phone: 732 870-4000
Fax: –
Web: www.commvault.com

CEO: N. Robert (Bob) Hammer
CFO: Brian Carolan
HR: –
FYE: March 31
Type: Public

CommVault Systems wants to have a lock on data management. The company provides software that customers use to store and manage enterprise data. Its Simpana software suite handles resource management backup archiving data replication disaster recovery and search. Altogether CommVault counts some 20000 customers that come from industries such as financial services health care manufacturing and utilities as well as from the public sector. CommVault's strategic partners include systems integrators and professional services firms distributors and resellers and technology providers. About 40% of its revenues are generated outside the US.

	Annual Growth	03/11	03/12	03/13	03/14	03/15
Sales ($ mil.)	17.9%	314.8	406.6	495.9	586.3	607.5
Net income ($ mil.)	5.1%	21.0	31.9	53.2	64.1	25.7
Market value ($ mil.)	2.3%	1,799.5	2,239.9	3,700.0	2,930.7	1,971.8
Employees	15.9%	1,268	1,437	1,740	1,973	2,287

COMP-VIEW INC.

10035 SW ARCTIC DR
BEAVERTON, OR 97005-4181
Phone: 503-641-8439
Fax: –
Web: www.compviewmedical.com

CEO: –
CFO: –
HR: –
FYE: December 31
Type: Private

CompView rents and sells audio-visual computer peripherals (primarily projectors and conferencing systems) to corporations educational organizations and government agencies; it also provides system installation and integration services. Its CompView Medical subsidiary specializes in providing audio-visual equipment for medical applications such as projectors for surgical operating rooms. CompView has facilities in California Minnesota Oregon Utah and Washington state. The company was started in 1987 by Paul White who is the majority owner.

	Annual Growth	12/98	12/99	12/00	12/01	12/11
Sales ($ mil.)	5.9%	–	28.2	38.9	36.3	56.0
Net income ($ mil.)	2.7%	–	0.6	(0.1)	0.1	0.9
Market value ($ mil.)	–	–	–	–	–	–
Employees	–	–	–	–	–	129

COMPANION LIFE INSURANCE COMPANY

7909 Parklane Rd. Ste. 200
Columbia SC 29223-5666
Phone: 803-735-1251
Fax: 803-735-0736
Web: www.companionlife.com

CEO: Jane Ann Morrison-Craig
CFO: Karl Kemmerlin
HR: –
FYE: December 31
Type: Private

Companion Life Insurance makes sure no one has to face death disability or the dentist all alone. The company one of several subsidiaries of Blue Cross & Blue Shield of South Carolina specializes in employee benefits including life disability dental vision and accidental-death coverage. It has packages for small and large employers and a complete line of voluntary products and plans. Independent and affiliated brokers agents and managing general underwriters (MGUs) sell the company's products. Companion Life operates in most US states and the District of Columbia. The company was founded in 1971.

COMPASS GROUP USA INC.

2400 Yorkmont Rd.
Charlotte NC 28217
Phone: 704-329-4000
Fax: 704-329-4010
Web: compass-usa.com

CEO: Gary Green
CFO: Tom Ondrof
HR: –
FYE: September 30
Type: Subsidiary

This company points the way to managed foodservices. Compass Group USA provides catering and dining services to corporate clients educational and healthcare facilities and sports and entertainment venues in Canada Mexico and the US. Its operating units include Bon Appetit Management Co. (corporate dining) Chartwells (school dining services) and Morrison Management Specialists (healthcare dining). The company's Levy Restaurants unit also operates fine dining locations as well as concessions at sports and entertainment venues. In addition the company offers vending services and on-site dining. It is a division of UK-based Compass Group.

COMPASS BANCSHARES INC.

15 S. 20th St.
Birmingham AL 35233
Phone: 205-297-3000
Fax: 205-297-7363
Web: www.bbvacompass.com

CEO: D Paul Jones Jr
CFO: Garrett R Hegel
HR: Arti Rajak
FYE: December 31
Type: Subsidiary

The needle of this Compass points south. Compass Bancshares is the holding company for Compass Bank which does business as BBVA Compass. The bank operates more than 700 branches in Alabama Arizona California Colorado Florida New Mexico and Texas. It provides standard corporate and retail banking services such as deposit accounts credit cards business and personal loans and mortgages. BBVA Compass also offers wealth management services such as securities brokerage mutual funds insurance annuities pension fund management and investment advisory. Compass Bancshares is a subsidiary of Spain-based banking giant Banco Bilbao Vizcaya Argentaria (BBVA).

COMPASS MINERALS INTERNATIONAL INC — NYS: CMP

9900 West 109th Street, Suite 100
Overland Park, KS 66210
Phone: 913 344-9200
Fax: –
Web: www.compassminerals.com

CEO: Francis J. (Fran) Malecha
CFO: Matthew J. Foulston
HR: Victoria Heider
FYE: December 31
Type: Public

Salt is Compass Minerals' true north. The company is one of the largest salt producers in North America. Its salt products include rock evaporated and solar salt and are used for applications such as water softening road deicing and food preparation. Highway deicing salt — generally sold to state province or municipal governments — accounts for almost half of its annual sales. Compass Minerals operates through subsidiaries North American Salt Great Salt Lake Minerals (a top producer of the crop nutrient sulfate of potash) Sifto Canada and Salt Union (based in the UK). It has 11 production and packaging facilities and operates a number of salt mines in Canada the UK and the US.

	Annual Growth	12/10	12/11	12/12	12/13	12/14
Sales ($ mil.)	4.7%	1,068.9	1,105.7	941.9	1,129.6	1,282.5
Net income ($ mil.)	9.7%	150.6	149.0	88.9	130.8	217.9
Market value ($ mil.)	(0.7%)	3,000.3	2,314.0	2,510.9	2,690.4	2,918.3
Employees	2.5%	1,776	1,761	1,778	1,855	1,963

COMPASS DIVERSIFIED HOLDINGS — NYS: CODI

Sixty One Wilton Road, Second Floor
Westport, CT 06880
Phone: 203 221-1703
Fax: –
Web: www.compassdiversifiedholdings.com

CEO: Alan B Offenberg
CFO: Ryan J Faulkingham
HR: –
FYE: December 31
Type: Public

Compass Diversified Holdings helps niche companies navigate their way toward profitability. The holding company owns controlling stakes in and manages promising middle-market businesses throughout North America. Its strategy is two-fold: help its portfolio firms grow and increase their profits and increase the size of its own portfolio. Compass invests in niche businesses across a variety of industries including suspension products maker Fox Factory furniture maker AFM Holdings (sold in 2015) and home and gun safes maker Liberty Safe and Security Products. Its arsenal includes helping its holdings make strategic acquisitions enter new business arenas or improve operations to increase profitability.

	Annual Growth	12/10	12/11	12/12	12/13	12/14
Sales ($ mil.)	(12.3%)	1,657.6	777.5	884.7	985.5	982.3
Net income ($ mil.)	–	(48.8)	65.0	(3.9)	68.1	278.8
Market value ($ mil.)	(2.1%)	960.6	672.8	798.8	1,065.9	882.4
Employees	(46.6%)	45,395	3,483	3,484	3,731	3,701

COMPELLENT TECHNOLOGIES INC.

7625 Smetana Ln.
Eden Prairie MN 55344
Phone: 952-294-3300
Fax: 952-294-3333
Web: www.compellent.com

CEO: Michael S Dell
CFO: John R Judd
HR: –
FYE: December 31
Type: Subsidiary

Compellent Technologies takes a byte out of data storage woes. Storage Center the company's main product is a storage area network (SAN) system that enables users to deposit recover and manage large amounts of data. It is used by customers worldwide in such industries as education financial services government health care insurance retail and transportation. Third-party hardware maintenance provider Anacomp offers storage equipment network device and peripheral repair services to Compellent's end users. Most of the company's sales are made in the US. Compellent was acquired in 2011 by PC and server maker Dell for about $940 million.

COMPLETE PRODUCTION SERVICES INC. — NYSE: CPX

11700 Katy Fwy. Ste. 300
Houston TX 77079
Phone: 281-372-2300
Fax: 281-372-2301
Web: www.completeproduction.com

CEO: –
CFO: Jose A Bayardo
HR: Joni Stoner
FYE: December 31
Type: Subsidiary

Complete Production Services tries to live up to its name as it serves customers in the Rocky Mountains Arkansas Louisiana Oklahoma Pennsylvania and Texas. It is a major provider of services and products that help oil and gas companies develop reserves enhance production and reduce costs. Focusing on basins in North America that have long-term growth potential the company offers a range of oil field services including drilling completion and production services and product sales. In 2012 the company was acquired by Superior Energy Services in a $2.7 billion deal.

COMPRESSOR SYSTEMS INC.

3809 S. FM Rd. 1788
Midland TX 79706
Phone: 432-563-1170
Fax: 432-563-0820
Web: www.compressor-systems.com

CEO: Richard Folger
CFO: –
HR: –
FYE: December 31
Type: Private

Keeping systematic pressure on the competition Compressor Systems (CSI) manufactures sells and services compression equipment used by international oil and gas customers for well head compression gas gathering and storage liquid recovery gas transmission and pressure maintenance. Compressor Systems sells equipment primarily in the Great Plains Intermountain West and Southwest and has sales and service offices in Alabama Arkansas Colorado Kansas Louisiana New Mexico Oklahoma Texas Utah and Wyoming. The company is owned by founder Johnny Warren's Warren Equipment Company.

COMPOSITES ONE LLC

85 W. Algonquin Rd.
Arlington Heights IL 60005-442
Phone: 847-437-0200
Fax: 847-437-0664
Web: www.compositesone.com

CEO: Steve Dehmlow
CFO: –
HR: –
FYE: December 31
Type: Private

Composites One (C1) helps composites fabricators compose their products. The company distributes a variety of fiberglass and composite materials such as additives adhesives gel coats pigments putties polyester and vinyl ester resins. The composite materials that C1 focuses on are fibers impregnated with plastic resins to add strength and corrosion-resistance and at the same time keep the material lightweight. A joint venture formed in 1999 by GLS and Cook Composites and Polymers it maintains more than 30 distribution centers and serves more than 8000 customers throughout North America. Among the chemical makers whose products C1 distributes are Hexcel Owens Corning Georgia Pacific and DuPont.

COMPSYCH CORPORATION

NBC Tower 455 N. Cityfront Plaza Dr.
Chicago IL 60611-5322
Phone: 312-595-4000
Fax: 716-627-3999
Web: goldenhire.com

CEO: Richard A Chaifetz
CFO: –
HR: –
FYE: December 31
Type: Private

ComPsych provides employee assistance programs such as behavioral health work-life wellness and crisis intervention services. The company's services offered under the GuidanceResources brand are designed to help clients' employees improve behavioral and physical health and address personal family and life issues. Clients employ GuidanceResources in order to retain workers and improve employee productivity and performance. ComPsych serves more than 45 million individuals at 17000 organizations across the US and about 100 other countries. Clients consist of FORTUNE 500 companies small businesses and government organizations among other firms. ComPsych was founded in 1984 by Dr. Richard Chaifetz.

COMPREHENSIVE CARE CORP. — NBB: CHCR

3405 W. Dr. Martin Luther King Jr. Blvd., Suite 101
Tampa, FL 33607
Phone: 813 288-4808
Fax: –
Web: www.compcare.com

CEO: Clark Marcus
CFO: –
HR: –
FYE: December 31
Type: Public

It's not comprehensive health care if doesn't cover body and mind. That's why Comprehensive Care helps commercial and government-run health plans nationwide offer behavioral health care services. Through its Comprehensive Behavioral Care subsidiary (CompCare for short) the company manages behavioral health care including psychiatric and substance abuse services through a network of about 21000 health care providers in 39 states and Puerto Rico. For the most part it operates under capitation agreements in which the plans pay CompCare a fixed monthly fee for each member.

COMPUCOM SYSTEMS INC.

7171 Forest Ln.
Dallas TX 75230
Phone: 972-856-3600
Fax: 972-856-5395
Web: www.compucom.com

CEO: Anthony Doye
CFO: Michael Simpson
HR: Kelli Springfield
FYE: December 31
Type: Private

CompuCom Systems urges clients to leave IT management to them. The company provides outsourced information technology infrastructure services that range from planning and purchasing to systems integration and life-cycle support. Its application services include consulting and staffing custom software development and quality assurance. CompuCom also offers third-party hardware and software management services acting as a value-added reseller of products from such providers as Cisco Hewlett-Packard IBM Microsoft and Sony. The company markets primarily to midsized and large enterprises in North America and Mexico. CompuCom is owned by private equity firm Court Square Capital Partners.

	Annual Growth	12/08	12/09	12/10	12/11	12/12
Sales ($ mil.)	18.3%	35.2	14.2	35.2	71.2	68.9
Net income ($ mil.)	–	(5.4)	(18.9)	(10.4)	(14.1)	(7.0)
Market value ($ mil.)	(31.2%)	30.3	26.8	13.5	12.8	6.8
Employees	(11.2%)	74	82	145	135	46

COMPUMED INC
NBB: CMPD

5777 West Century Blvd., Suite 360
Los Angeles, CA 90045
Phone: 310 258-5000
Fax: 310 645-5880
Web: www.compumed.net

CEO: Lee Keddie
CFO: Laura Carroll
HR: –
FYE: September 30
Type: Public

CompuMed won't comp your meds but it might interpret your ECG. Through its CardioGram software the telemedicine company provides online analyses of ECGs (electrocardiograms) for more than 1000 hospitals clinics and other health care facilities throughout the US. The firm's ECG services are available 24 hours a day. CompuMed also rents and to a lesser extent sells ECG equipment. The company's additional product OsteoGram monitors osteoporosis by analyzing bone density; the test involves taking a hand X-ray and can be performed using standard X-ray equipment.

	Annual Growth	09/11	09/12	09/13	09/14	09/15
Sales ($ mil.)	7.7%	1.7	1.7	1.9	1.8	2.3
Net income ($ mil.)	–	(0.2)	(0.1)	(0.1)	(0.1)	0.1
Market value ($ mil.)	15.8%	1.5	1.2	4.6	4.5	2.7
Employees	22.2%	9	11	–	–	–

COMPUNET CLINICAL LABORATORIES LLC

2308 Sandridge Dr.
Dayton OH 45439-1847
Phone: 937-296-0844
Fax: 937-296-1924
Web: www.compunetlab.com

CEO: Kate Langevin
CFO: John Manier
HR: –
FYE: December 31
Type: Joint Venture

If you're a Daytonian in need of a cholesterol check CompuNet Clinical Laboratories has a vial with your name on it. The company provides comprehensive laboratory testing services to physicians patients hospitals and managed care companies in and around Dayton Ohio. It draws blood (and takes other patient samples) at some 30 specimen collection centers throughout its service area and processes them at one of its various laboratory locations including at its headquarters in Dayton and at Miami Valley Hospital. Founded in 1986 the company is a joint venture owned by Miami Valley Hospital Quest Diagnostics and a local pathology group.

COMPUTER GENERATED SOLUTIONS INC.

3 World Financial Center 200 Vesey St. 27th Fl.
New York NY 10281-1017
Phone: 212-408-3800
Fax: 212-977-7474
Web: www.cgsinc.com

CEO: Phil Friedman
CFO: Edward Galati
HR: Paul Joseph
FYE: December 31
Type: Private

Computer Generated Solutions (CGS) fixes computer generated problems. The company resells customizes and supports computer software from such vendors as IBM Microsoft and Avaya. CGS also develops proprietary software including BlueCherry used by the apparel and footwear industries to manage customer service and resource planning among other functions. Its Unlimited Mailbox application is used in the government and education sectors to archive e-mail messages. The company's services include training and vendor management. CGS also serves the manufacturing and professional services markets. Founded in 1984 by CEO Philip Friedman the company operates from about 20 offices in North America Europe and Asia.

COMPUTER PROGRAMS & SYSTEMS INC
NMS: CPSI

6600 Wall Street
Mobile, AL 36695
Phone: 251 639-8100
Fax: –
Web: www.cpsi.com

CEO: J. Boyd Douglas
CFO: David A. Dye
HR: –
FYE: December 31
Type: Public

Computer Programs and Systems sounds like an intro to computers. But what you get at Computer Programs and Systems Inc. (CPSI) is administrative software and hardware systems and outsourcing services for acute care community hospitals. CPSI develops and supports electronic health records (EHR) as well as financial and clinical information management software and IT systems for small and midsized hospitals in the US. The company boasts a client base of more than 1000 healthcare facilities hospitals across 49 states. CPSI's software enables users to manage their patients staff finances and facilities. Subsidiary TruBridge offers managed IT services and business office outsourcing services.

	Annual Growth	12/10	12/11	12/12	12/13	12/14
Sales ($ mil.)	7.5%	153.2	173.5	183.3	200.9	204.7
Net income ($ mil.)	15.1%	18.7	25.8	30.0	32.7	32.9
Market value ($ mil.)	6.7%	525.0	572.9	564.3	692.8	680.9
Employees	3.7%	1,194	1,341	1,420	1,378	1,379

COMPUTER SCIENCES CORP.
NYS: CSC

3170 Fairview Park Drive
Falls Church, VA 22042
Phone: 703 876-1000
Fax: –
Web: www.csc.com

CEO: J. Michael (Mike) Lawrie
CFO: Paul N. Saleh
HR: Dennis McCabe
FYE: April 03
Type: Public

Computer Sciences Corporation (CSC) is one of the world's leading providers of systems integration and other information technology services. It offers application development data center management communications and networking development IT systems management and business consulting. It also provides business process outsourcing (BPO) services in such areas as billing and payment processing customer relationship management (CRM) and human resources. CSC boasts 2500 clients in more than 70 countries. CSC generated about a third of its revenue from US federal agencies through its public sector division which was spun off as CSRA in late 2015.

	Annual Growth	04/11*	03/12	03/13	03/14*	04/15
Sales ($ mil.)	(6.7%)	16,042.0	15,877.0	14,993.0	12,998.0	12,173.0
Net income ($ mil.)	–	740.0	(4,242.0)	961.0	674.0	(8.0)
Market value ($ mil.)	7.3%	6,852.6	4,154.9	6,831.8	8,366.6	9,073.0
Employees	(6.3%)	91,000	98,000	90,000	79,000	70,000

*Fiscal year change

COMPUTER TASK GROUP, INC.
NMS: CTG

800 Delaware Avenue
Buffalo, NY 14209
Phone: 716 882-8000
Fax: –
Web: www.ctg.com

CEO: Cliff Bleustein
CFO: Brendan M. Harrington
HR: David Dummel
FYE: December 31
Type: Public

Computer Task Group (CTG) does exactly what the name says and more. Serving primarily technology service providers health care manufacturing and financial services clients the company offers a wide range of professional technology services including IT staffing custom application development and systems integration. It is placing more emphasis on its strategic consulting services that clients' technology needs as well as project management and application outsourcing management services. It counts about 475 clients in North America and Western Europe; its largest client IBM accounts for more than 23% of revenue. The company was founded in 1966.

	Annual Growth	12/10	12/11	12/12	12/13	12/14
Sales ($ mil.)	4.4%	331.4	396.3	424.4	419.0	393.3
Net income ($ mil.)	5.4%	8.4	11.9	16.2	15.7	10.4
Market value ($ mil.)	(3.2%)	165.0	213.6	276.5	285.6	144.6
Employees	2.8%	3,400	3,700	3,900	3,700	3,800

COMPUTER WORLD SERVICES CORP.

666 11th St. NW Ste. 625
Washington DC 20001
Phone: 202-637-9699
Fax: 202-637-0446
Web: www.cwsc.com

CEO: Farrukh Hameed
CFO: –
HR: –
FYE: December 31
Type: Private

Computer World Services Corp (CWS) wants to be the IT supplier of your world. The company resells technology products including computers networking products software and data storage equipment. Through its Resource Networks unit the company provides information technology services in partnership with Cisco Systems. CWS has four offices in the US mostly on the east coast one in Germany and one in Bahrain. Its customers include NASA and several other components of the US federal state and local government as well as AT&T Sun Microsystems and Northrup Gruman. President and CEO Frank Hameed started CWS in 1990.

COMPUWARE CORP.   NMS: CPWR

One Campus Martius
Detroit, MI 48226-5099
Phone: 313 227-7300
Fax: –
Web: www.compuware.com

CEO: Chris O'Malley
CFO: Joe Aho
HR: –
FYE: March 31
Type: Public

Compuware is more than aware of the power of diversity. The company's software includes testing development and management tools for programs running on traditional mainframe computer systems distributed computer networks and newer Web-based systems. It also makes application development implementation and support software for programmers as well as file data and systems management tools. The company's Gomez platform is a Web-based software testing and monitoring tool sold on a subscription basis. Compuware's services include consulting systems integration custom programming maintenance and support. It sells directly and through distributors to such clients as the BBC the NI IL Google and Facebook.

	Annual Growth	03/09	03/10	03/11	03/12	03/13
Sales ($ mil.)	(3.5%)	1,090.5	892.2	928.9	1,009.8	944.5
Net income ($ mil.)	–	139.6	140.8	107.4	88.4	(17.3)
Market value ($ mil.)	17.3%	1,405.1	1,791.0	2,462.7	1,959.5	2,663.1
Employees	(2.7%)	5,006	4,336	4,396	4,564	4,491

COMPX INTERNATIONAL, INC.   ASE: CIX

5430 LBJ Freeway, Suite 1700, Three Lincoln Centre
Dallas, TX 75240-2697
Phone: 972 448-1400
Fax: –
Web: www.compx.com

CEO: David A Bowers
CFO: James W Brown
HR: Sharon Abernathy
FYE: December 31
Type: Public

CompX International tries to keep the workday smooth theft-free and painless. Through CompX's three operating divisions — security products furniture components and marine components — the company makes ball bearing slides cabinet locks and ergonomic computer support systems. The company's primary customers are office furniture makers but its components are used in recreational marine vehicles ignition systems vending equipment mailboxes appliances and computer equipment. CompX International believes that it is a North American market leader in the manufacture and sale of cabinet locks and other locking mechanisms. The company is majority-owned by NL Industries.

	Annual Growth	12/10	12/11	12/12	12/13	12/14
Sales ($ mil.)	(6.4%)	135.3	138.8	83.2	92.0	103.8
Net income ($ mil.)	29.8%	3.1	7.7	35.0	6.0	8.7
Market value ($ mil.)	1.3%	142.6	182.7	177.4	174.6	150.0
Employees	(10.5%)	828	794	466	506	532

COMSCORE INC   NMS: SCOR

11950 Democracy Drive, Suite 600
Reston, VA 20190
Phone: 703 483-2000
Fax: –
Web: www.comscore.com

CEO: Serge Matta
CFO: Mel Wesley
HR: –
FYE: December 31
Type: Public

comScore knows the score when it comes to measuring online audience behavior. The company provides data analysis and consultancy to some 1200 clients looking to fortify their marketing sales and trading initiatives. Its global panel of more than 2 million Internet users measures and tracks consumer behaviors demographics and advertising responsiveness for clients in such industries as travel pharmaceuticals finance and telecommunications. Branded products include comScore's Media Metrix suite of website and online advertising network measurement tools and comScore's Marketing Solutions products which provide custom research and analysis from its panel. The company was established in 1999.

	Annual Growth	12/10	12/11	12/12	12/13	12/14
Sales ($ mil.)	17.1%	175.0	232.4	255.2	286.9	329.2
Net income ($ mil.)	–	(1.6)	(15.8)	(11.8)	(2.3)	(9.9)
Market value ($ mil.)	20.1%	763.5	724.5	470.9	977.7	1,586.7
Employees	8.9%	920	1,012	1,137	1,180	1,292

COMSTOCK HOLDING COMPANIES, INC   NAS: CHCI

1886 Metro Center Drive, 4th Floor
Reston, VA 20190
Phone: 703 883-1700
Fax: –
Web: www.comstockhomes.com

CEO: Christopher Clemente
CFO: Joseph M Squeri
HR: Rebecca Gehley
FYE: December 31
Type: Public

While people take stock of their lives Comstock takes stock of its portfolio. The homebuilder develops land and builds single-family homes townhouses and mid- and high-rise condominiums in and around Washington DC. The company annually delivers some 200 homes with an average price of approximately $289000. Its customer base includes first-time homebuyers buyers looking to move up empty nesters and active retirees. The company also rents residential properties under the Comstock Communities name. Average rent is appoximately $1500 a month..

	Annual Growth	12/10	12/11	12/12	12/13	12/14
Sales ($ mil.)	19.1%	23.9	22.2	14.3	54.6	48.0
Net income ($ mil.)	–	(7.7)	1.1	(5.7)	(2.0)	(6.8)
Market value ($ mil.)	(3.0%)	3.5	3.3	3.5	6.1	3.1
Employees	22.1%	27	36	38	50	60

COMSTOCK RESOURCES, INC.   NYS: CRK

5300 Town and Country Blvd., Suite 500
Frisco, TX 75034
Phone: 972 668-8800
Fax: –
Web: www.comstockresources.com

CEO: M Jay Allison
CFO: Roland O Burns
HR: –
FYE: December 31
Type: Public

Comstock Resources' stock in trade is exploring for and producing natural gas and oil. In 2012 the midsized independent oil and gas company reported proved reserves of 711.9 trillion cu. ft. of natural gas equivalent (67% natural gas 33% oil) on its properties primarily located in three major areas — East Texas/North Louisiana South Texas and West Texas. Comstock Resources operates more than 960 of the 1640 producing wells in which it holds an interest. The company has grown through the drill bit (by exploiting existing reserves) and through complementary acquisitions.

	Annual Growth	12/10	12/11	12/12	12/13	12/14
Sales ($ mil.)	12.3%	349.1	434.4	456.2	420.3	555.2
Net income ($ mil.)	–	(19.6)	(33.5)	(100.1)	41.0	(57.1)
Market value ($ mil.)	(27.4%)	1,150.8	716.9	708.5	857.0	319.1
Employees	2.3%	127	124	116	131	139

COMTECH TELECOMMUNICATIONS CORP.　　　　NMS: CMTL

68 South Service Road, Suite 230　　　　CEO: Stanton D. (Stan) Sloane
Melville, NY 11747　　　　CFO: Michael D. Porcelain
Phone: 631-962-7000　　　　HR: –
Fax: 631-962-7001　　　　FYE: July 31
Web: www.comtechtel.com　　　　Type: Public

Comtech means contact. Through its subsidiaries Comtech Telecommunications operates in three divisions: mobile data communications telecommunications transmission and radio-frequency (RF) microwave amplifiers. The company makes equipment used largely by the US government and related defense contractors. Other customers include satellite systems integrators communications service providers and oil companies. Its transmission equipment includes modems frequency converters very-small-aperture terminal (VSAT) satellite transceivers and antennas and microwave radios. Comtech's RF amplifiers enable wireless instrumentation and medical systems and provide satellite-based messaging services and location tracking.

	Annual Growth	07/11	07/12	07/13	07/14	07/15
Sales ($ mil.)	(15.8%)	612.4	425.1	319.8	347.2	307.3
Net income ($ mil.)	(23.5%)	67.9	32.4	17.8	25.2	23.2
Market value ($ mil.)	1.7%	434.8	440.7	436.9	545.3	464.8
Employees	(6.3%)	1,268	1,244	1,035	1,069	978

COMTEX NEWS NETWORK INC.　　　　OTC: CMTX

625 N. Washington St. Ste. 301　　　　CEO: Kan Devnani
Alexandria VA 22314　　　　CFO: –
Phone: 703-820-2000　　　　HR: –
Fax: 703-820-2005　　　　FYE: June 30
Web: www.comtexnews.net　　　　Type: Public

Comtex News Network is a leading distributor of electronic news and alerts that specializes in the business and financial markets. The company gathers news and content from more than 10000 national and international news agencies and publications including PR Newswire United Press International and The Associated Press and packages those feeds into several different product offerings. In addition to individual and institutional customers Comtex supplies news to such information distributors as MarketWatch Dow Jones' Factiva and Thomson Financial.

COMVERGE INC.　　　　NASDAQ: COMV

5390 Trianlge Pkwy. Ste. 300　　　　CEO: Gregory J Dukat
Norcross GA 30092　　　　CFO: –
Phone: 888-565-5525　　　　HR: Angelina Pericola
Fax: 770-696-7665　　　　FYE: December 31
Web: www.comverge.com　　　　Type: Private

Comverge seeks a convergence of communications enabling the lights to stay on. The company provides demand management software and systems to electric utilities and other energy suppliers and sells automated meters and related equipment with communications links. The company's products are used by more than 500 utilities and energy providers including PEPCO as well as some 2100 commercial and industrial customers such as Barnes and Noble and Foot Locker. Its products include software and hardware that help control energy load read meters remotely manage billing and detect theft and outages. Comverge was acquired in 2012 by H.I.G. Capital for about $49 million.

CON-WAY FREIGHT INC.

2211 Old Earhart Rd. Ste. 100　　　　CEO: –
Ann Arbor MI 48105-2751　　　　CFO: –
Phone: 734-994-6600　　　　HR: –
Fax: 734-757-1153　　　　FYE: December 31
Web: www.con-way.com/en/freight　　　　Type: Subsidiary

A shipper picks a day then Con-way hits the highway. Con-way Freight specializes in next-day and second-day less-than-truckload (LTL) freight transportation. (LTL carriers consolidate loads from multiple shippers into a single truckload.) The company operates throughout the US with an extended network in North America via Con-way Freight Canada and Con-way Mexico. Transborder services extend to Canada Mexico Asia Europe and the Caribbean. Overall Con-way Freight operates a fleet of about 9100 tractors and 26300 trailers from some 290 owned or leased terminals. Con-way Freight is the main subsidiary of Con-way which also owns supply chain management and truckload freight transportation businesses.

CON-WAY INC　　　　NYS: CNW

2211 Old Earhart Road, Suite 100　　　　CEO: Douglas W Stotlar
Ann Arbor, MI 48105　　　　CFO: Stephen L Bruffett
Phone: 734-994-6600　　　　HR: –
Fax: 734-757-1153　　　　FYE: December 31
Web: www.con-way.com　　　　Type: Public

Providing trucking and logistics services Con-way is at home on the high-way. Con-way Freight the company's less-than-truckload (LTL) unit provides regional inter-regional and transcontinental service throughout North America. (LTL carriers consolidate loads from multiple shippers into a single truckload.) Con-way Freight operates a fleet of about 9300 tractors and some 25000 trailers. Con-way offers full truckload transportation services through its Con-way Truckload subsidiary which maintains a fleet of about 2700 tractors and more than 8000 trailers. Con-way's Menlo Worldwide unit provides contract logistics freight brokerage warehousing and supply chain management services.

	Annual Growth	12/09	12/10	12/11	12/12	12/13
Sales ($ mil.)	6.4%	4,269.2	4,952.0	5,290.0	5,580.2	5,473.4
Net income ($ mil.)	–	(107.7)	4.0	88.4	104.5	99.2
Market value ($ mil.)	3.3%	1,987.2	2,081.7	1,659.9	1,583.6	2,260.4
Employees	1.9%	27,400	27,900	27,800	29,100	29,500

CONAGRA FOODS, INC.　　　　NYS: CAG

One ConAgra Drive　　　　CEO: Sean M. Connolly
Omaha, NE 68102-5001　　　　CFO: John F. Gehring
Phone: 402 240-4000　　　　HR: Nicole B. Theophilus
Fax: –　　　　FYE: May 31
Web: www.conagrafoods.com　　　　Type: Public

ConAgra Foods fills the refrigerators freezers and pantries of most households. The company makes and markets name-brand packaged and frozen foods that are sold in most retail outlets. ConAgra's cornucopia of America's best-known brands includes Banquet Chef Boyardee Egg Beaters Healthy Choice Hunt's Marie Callender Orville Redenbacher's PAM Peter Pan Reddi-Wip Slim Jim Snack Pack and Van Camp's. It is also one of the biggest producers of seasoning and grain ingredients for the US food service food manufacturing and industrial markets. ConAgra Foods sold its private-label food business to TreeHouse Foods for $2.7 billion in February 2016.

	Annual Growth	05/11	05/12	05/13	05/14	05/15
Sales ($ mil.)	6.5%	12,303.1	13,262.6	15,491.4	17,702.6	15,832.4
Net income ($ mil.)	–	817.0	467.9	773.9	303.1	(252.6)
Market value ($ mil.)	11.4%	10,722.2	10,812.2	14,888.7	13,535.5	16,533.0
Employees	9.1%	23,200	26,100	34,840	32,800	32,900

CONAIR CORPORATION

1 Cummings Point Rd.
Stamford CT 06902
Phone: 203-351-9000
Fax: 205-841-9168

CEO: –
CFO: –
HR: –
FYE: December 31
Type: Private

Conair has a place in many bathrooms and kitchens. The company operates through several divisions including personal care and hair goods. Its personal care products consist of grooming and health and wellness appliances made under brands Interplak Travel Smart and Allegro. Conair's hair goods division makes brushes mirrors and Scunci hair accessories. A professional products arm offers BaBylssPRO dryers and ConairPRO pet grooming aids. Conair also makes Cuisinart and Waring kitchen tools and sells its products through the likes of Bed Bath & Beyond Target and Wal-Mart in the US and online overseas. The global appliance maker has offices in Canada Mexico Hong Kong Europe and other countries.

CONCERT PHARMACEUTICALS INC

NMS: CNCE

99 Hayden Avenue, Suite 500
Lexington, MA 02421
Phone: 781 860-0045
Fax: –
Web: www.concertpharma.com

CEO: Roger D Tung
CFO: Ryan Daws
HR: –
FYE: December 31
Type: Public

Concert Pharmaceuticals wants to use deuterium chemistry to conduct a symphony of drugs. The company's process lets it substitute deuterium (also called heavy hydrogen) for hydrogen in a chemical compound thereby making the compound more stable without changing its other properties. It also believes this process will lead to shorter time from discovery to trial for certain drugs. Concert has a handful of clinical-stage candidates in various stages of the approval process including treatments for spasticity kidney disease and neurologic disorders. It collaborates with Avanir Celgene and Jazz Pharmaceuticals on development. Concert began its song in 2006 and took the show public in 2014.

	Annual Growth	12/10	12/11	12/12	12/13	12/14
Sales ($ mil.)	–	0.0	19.5	12.8	25.4	8.6
Net income ($ mil.)	–	0.0	(11.3)	(20.4)	(6.1)	(31.7)
Market value ($ mil.)	–	0.0	–	–	–	242.9
Employees	13.1%	–	–	43	45	55

CONCHO RESOURCES INC

NYS: CXO

One Concho Center, 600 West Illinois Avenue
Midland, TX 79701
Phone: 432 683-7443
Fax: 432 683-7441
Web: www.conchoresources.com

CEO: Timothy A. (Tim) Leach
CFO: Darin G. Holderness
HR: Tammy Compton
FYE: December 31
Type: Public

Concho Resources has more than a hunch that a lucrative resource lies under its feet in Southeastern New Mexico and West Texas. The company explores and develops properties (more than 89012 net acres) located primarily in the Permian Basin region in which it produces oil and natural gas. The bulk of the company's reported 637.2 million barrels of proved reserves in 2014 was crude oil while the rest was natural gas. Concho Resources gets more than 80% its revenues from crude oil which is priced much higher than natural gas. The company drilled 329 net wells in 2014.

	Annual Growth	12/10	12/11	12/12	12/13	12/14
Sales ($ mil.)	28.6%	972.6	1,740.0	1,819.8	2,319.9	2,660.1
Net income ($ mil.)	27.4%	204.4	548.1	431.7	251.0	538.2
Market value ($ mil.)	3.3%	9,907.1	10,594.2	9,103.7	12,204.5	11,272.2
Employees	23.2%	443	592	745	868	1,022

CONCORD HOSPITAL INC.

250 PLEASANT ST
CONCORD, NH 033012598
Phone: 603-227-7000
Fax: –
Web: www.concordhospital.org

CEO: Robert Steigmeyer
CFO: Bruce R Burns
HR: –
FYE: September 30
Type: Private

Concord Hospital is agreeably an acute care regional hospital serving central New Hampshire. The hospital has some 300 licensed beds and provides general inpatient and outpatient medical care as well as specialist centers for cardiology orthopedics cancer care urology and women's health. Concord Hospital operates other medical facilities either on its main campus or nearby including surgery imaging diagnostic hospice and rehabilitation facilities as well as physician practice locations. With roots reaching back to 1884 Concord Hospital is part of the Capital Region Health Care system which also offers mental health and home health care services.

	Annual Growth	09/07	09/08	09/09	09/10	09/13
Sales ($ mil.)	–	–	(1,823.0)	349.1	369.4	371.7
Net income ($ mil.)	–	–	–	0.0	18.9	11.2
Market value ($ mil.)	–	–	–	–	–	–
Employees	–	–	–	–	–	2,000

CONCORD LITHO GROUP

92 OLD TURNPIKE RD
CONCORD, NH 033017305
Phone: 603-224-1202
Fax: –
Web: www.concordlitho.com

CEO: Peter Cook
CFO: Marlin Kaufman
HR: –
FYE: December 31
Type: Private

Concord Litho Group is all about the commercially printed word. The company specializes in producing promotional and marketing materials of all sizes for retailers publishers ad agencies and consumer products brands. It prints catalogs brochures calendars greeting cards and maps as well as point-of-purchase displays art prints and other large-format items. Concord Litho Group also offers product and program development services. Clients have included Macy's Rodale Dunkin' Donuts Publishers Clearing House Prudential Financial and TV Guide. Concord Litho Group was founded in 1958.

	Annual Growth	12/09	12/10	12/11	12/12	12/13
Sales ($ mil.)	9.9%	–	39.0	44.7	50.3	51.8
Net income ($ mil.)	(27.6%)	–	–	1.1	1.9	0.6
Market value ($ mil.)	–	–	–	–	–	–
Employees	–	–	–	–	–	200

CONCORDE CAREER COLLEGES INC.

5800 Foxridge Dr. Ste. 500
Mission KS 66202
Phone: 913-831-9977
Fax: 913-831-6556
Web: www.concorde.edu

CEO: Patrick H Albert
CFO: Paul R Gardner
HR: Diana Hawkins
FYE: December 31
Type: Private

Concorde Career Colleges (CCC) gives students a healthy dose of education. The company provides vocational training in the allied health field including courses in medical and dental assisting (its most popular programs) nursing insurance coding respiratory therapy and radiology. Taught in a classroom format CCC's programs last nine to 24 months and offer clinical and laboratory experience as well as externships. CCC also provides short-term courses in areas such as test preparation and home health aide. The company operates 15 campuses in seven states. Liberty Partners a New York-based private equity firm that invests in manufacturing business services and education-related companies owns CCC.

CONCUR TECHNOLOGIES INC
NMS: CNQR

601 108th Avenue N.E., Suite 1000
Bellevue, WA 98004
Phone: 425 702-8808
Fax: –
Web: www.concur.com

CEO: S Steven Singh
CFO: Francis J Pelzer
HR: –
FYE: September 30
Type: Public

Concur Technologies can ensure that all of your expense reports are in perfect harmony with budgeting and accounting. The company offers expense and spend management cloud computing software that enables businesses to automate and streamline the process for submitting and approving employee expense reports. Concur's software features modules for tracking submitting and processing reports for travel and entertainment costs as well as applications to track employee requests for vendor payments. Other applications include business process management travel booking invoicing auditing and business intelligence. Concur licenses its software to clients primarily on a subscription basis.

	Annual Growth	09/09	09/10	09/11	09/12	09/13
Sales ($ mil.)	21.8%	247.6	292.9	349.5	439.8	545.8
Net income ($ mil.)	–	25.7	20.6	(10.7)	(7.0)	(24.4)
Market value ($ mil.)	29.1%	2,228.3	2,770.8	2,086.5	4,132.1	6,192.9
Employees	36.3%	1,100	1,200	1,600	2,400	3,800

CONCURRENT COMPUTER CORP.
NMS: CCUR

4375 River Green Parkway, Suite 100
Duluth, GA 30096
Phone: 678 258-4000
Fax: –
Web: www.concurrent.com

CEO: Derek Elder
CFO: Emory O Berry
HR: –
FYE: June 30
Type: Public

Watch a video on multiple devices? Simulate the performance of a car or aircraft part in real time? Such processes might be courtesy of Concurrent Computer. The company's video segment is mainly geared toward broadband and content providers worldwide to allow streaming collecting viewer data. The company also develops real-time products that allow manufacturers such as those in the aerospace and automotive industries to run their products through advanced computer simulations. The real-time computing products combine Linux and similar operating systems and software development tools with off-the-shelf hardware for time-critical applications. Besides simulations applications include image generation testing industrial process control and data acquisition and processing.

	Annual Growth	06/11	06/12	06/13	06/14	06/15
Sales ($ mil.)	(0.9%)	66.8	60.3	63.4	71.2	64.5
Net income ($ mil.)	–	(3.3)	(2.9)	4.2	18.5	(0.3)
Market value ($ mil.)	(0.3%)	57.2	38.5	69.9	68.2	56.6
Employees	(3.4%)	298	233	229	236	260

CONCURRENT TECHNOLOGIES CORPORATION

100 CTC Dr.
Johnstown PA 15904-1935
Phone: 814-269-2592
Fax: 814-269-6500
Web: www.ctc.com

CEO: Edward J Sheehan Jr
CFO: –
HR: –
FYE: June 30
Type: Private - Not-for-Pr

Concurrent Technologies Corporation (CTC) helps customers keep pace with all the current technologies. The not-for-profit research and development organization provides IT services to public and private sectors although it primarily serves the needs of the Department of Defense and about 20 other federal departments. CTC provides training rapid prototyping studies and analysis network design project management design and development and systems integration. It serves clients in advanced materials and manufacturing IT healthcare energy environmental sustainability training and intelligence among others. CTC has about 50 locations across the US and one in Canada.

CONDOR HOSPITALITY TRUST INC
NMS: CDOR

1800 W. Pasewalk Ave., Ste. 200
Norfolk, NE 68701
Phone: 402 371-2520
Fax: –
Web: www.supertelinc.com

CEO: J William Blackham
CFO: Corrine L Scarpello
HR: –
FYE: December 31
Type: Public

Condor Hospitality (formerly Supertel Hospitality) wants to help business and leisure travelers have a super overnight stay. The self-administered real estate investment trust (REIT) owns some 39 limited-service and midscale hotels operated by third parties. The hotels are located in 18 primarily midwestern and eastern states and operate under such franchised brand names as Super 8 Comfort Inn Holiday Inn Express Days Inn Hampton Inn and Sleep Inn. The hotels are leased to the REIT's taxable subsidiaries. Condor Hospitality also develops hotel properties on a limited basis.

	Annual Growth	12/10	12/11	12/12	12/13	12/14
Sales ($ mil.)	(9.1%)	84.1	75.8	70.6	56.2	57.4
Net income ($ mil.)	–	(10.6)	(17.4)	(10.2)	(1.4)	(16.2)
Market value ($ mil.)	9.9%	7.4	3.1	4.8	11.5	10.8
Employees	(1.6%)	16	19	18	18	15

CONERGY INC.

2480 W. 26th Ave. Ste. 2B
Denver CO 87507-8021
Phone: 720-305-0700
Fax: 505-216-3008
Web: www.conergy.us

CEO: Anthony Fotopoulos
CFO: –
HR: –
FYE: December 31
Type: Subsidiary

Conergy makes and distributes solar water pumps installs small wind turbines and distributes solar electric power components including solar panels batteries and related electronics. The company also helps arrange financing for residential installations since solar panels can be an expensive proposition to purchase. Conergy uses photovoltaic modules made by its German parent company and by Canadian Solar SANYO Electric and Suntech Power. Customers include Exelon the South San Joaquin Irrigation District in California and the US Army's Fort Carson in Colorado. The company is a subsidiary of Conergy AG.

CONGOLEUM CORPORATION

3500 Quakerbridge Rd.
Mercerville NJ 08619-0127
Phone: 609-584-3000
Fax: 609-584-3522
Web: www.congoleum.com

CEO: Robert Moran
CFO: Howard N Feist III
HR: Barry Criner
FYE: December 31
Type: Private

For more than a century Congoleum has taken a pounding. The company has four manufacturing facilities where it makes hard-surface flooring products for residential and commercial use including resilient sheet flooring (linoleum or vinyl flooring) do-it-yourself vinyl tile and commercial-grade flooring. Its lineup is used in new construction as well as remodeling manufactured housing and commercial applications. Congoleum markets its products via a distributor network and directly to mass market retailers in North America. Distributors Mohawk Industries and LaSalle-Bristol together represent more than 60% of Congoleum sales. The company filed for Chapter 11 reorganization in 2003 and emerged in mid-2010.

CONMED CORP.

NMS: CNMD

525 French Road
Utica, NY 13502
Phone: 315-797-8375
Fax: 315-797-0321
Web: www.conmed.com

CEO: Joseph J. Corasanti
CFO: Robert D. Shallish
HR: Dawn Cavaliere
FYE: December 31
Type: Public

Doctors and their patients get a charge out of CONMED's surgical equipment. The medical technology company develops and manufactures a wide range of electronic instruments such as electrosurgical systems powered surgical instruments and endoscopic devices. Its arthroscopic (joint surgery) products include reconstruction tools scopes implants and fluid management systems. CONMED also manufactures patient monitoring products and handheld medical accessories such as scissors sutures and staplers. Brands include Hall CONMED Linvatec Concept and Shutt. The company sells its products in more than 100 countries.

	Annual Growth	12/10	12/11	12/12	12/13	12/14
Sales ($ mil.)	0.9%	713.7	725.1	767.1	762.7	740.1
Net income ($ mil.)	1.5%	30.3	0.8	40.5	35.9	32.2
Market value ($ mil.)	14.2%	728.3	707.3	770.2	1,171.1	1,238.9
Employees	1.5%	3,300	3,400	3,600	3,600	3,500

CONNECTICARE INC.

175 Scott Swamp Rd.
Farmington CT 06032
Phone: 860-674-5700
Fax: 860-674-2030
Web: www.connecticare.com

CEO: -
CFO: -
HR: -
FYE: December 31
Type: Subsidiary

ConnectiCare is one of the largest HMOs in Connecticut. In 1979 a group of doctors at Hartford Hospital planted the seeds for what would become ConnectiCare; today the company's 240000 members in Connecticut and western Massachusetts choose from HMO PPO or point-of-service options. It also provides supplemental dental and Medicare plans as well as health savings accounts (HSAs) and disease management programs. ConnectiCare has a network of some 125 acute-care hospitals and about 22000 care providers. The company is a subsidiary of Health Insurance Plan of Greater New York (HIP) which is itself a unit of EmblemHealth.

CONNECTICUT CHILDREN'S MEDICAL CENTER

282 WASHINGTON ST
HARTFORD, CT 061063322
Phone: 860-545-9000
Fax: -
Web: www.connecticutchildrensfoundation.org

CEO: -
CFO: Gerald J Boisvert
HR: -
FYE: September 30
Type: Private

When their tiny tykes need some TLC Nutmeg Staters turn to Connecticut Children's Medical Center (CCMC). The 190-bed children's hospital is located on two campuses and provides a variety of pediatric services including surgery behavioral care and emergency medicine. Its facilities house pediatric trauma and intensive care units that receives referral patients from hospitals throughout the region. The medical center also conducts clinical research and provides pediatric training to health professionals. In addition CCMC operates outpatient facilities throughout Connecticut and a school for children with physical and behavioral challenges.

	Annual Growth	09/07	09/08	09/09	09/10	09/13
Sales ($ mil.)	-	-	(1,415.2)	192.8	210.1	264.5
Net income ($ mil.)	-	-	-	7.0	10.1	(2.8)
Market value ($ mil.)	-	-	-	-	-	-
Employees	-	-	-	-	-	1,117

CONNECTICUT COLLEGE

270 MOHEGAN AVE
NEW LONDON, CT 063204150
Phone: 860-447-1911
Fax: -
Web: www.conncoll.edu

CEO: -
CFO: -
HR: -
FYE: June 30
Type: Private

With its picturesque campus overlooking Long Island Sound Connecticut College (CC) strives to be the quintessential New England college. It is a private co-educational liberal arts college in New London which is close to Providence Hartford and New Haven. The college offers approximately 55 majors has an enrollment of 1900 and a reputation as one of the most selective schools in the nation. Top majors include biology English government international relations and psychology. CC is known for its interdisciplinary studies. The school has a 9-to-1 student-faculty ratio. The comprehensive fee (tuition room board and fees) for the 2009-10 academic year is just over $51000. CC was founded in 1911.

	Annual Growth	06/07	06/08	06/09	06/10	06/13
Sales ($ mil.)	-	-	0.0	109.6	123.4	149.4
Net income ($ mil.)	-	-	-	0.0	4.0	14.2
Market value ($ mil.)	-	-	-	-	-	-
Employees	-	-	-	-	-	-

CONNECTICUT LIGHT & POWER CO

NBB: CNTH O

107 Selden Street
Berlin, CT 06037-1616
Phone: 860-665-5000
Fax: -
Web: www.eversource.com

CEO: -
CFO: James J (Jamie) Judge
HR: Christine Carmody
FYE: December 31
Type: Public

Northeast utility Connecticut Light and Power Company (CL&P) keeps the folks in the Constitution State connected. CL&P provides electric utility services to 1.2 million customers in nearly 150 Connecticut communities. The electric utility a subsidiary of Eversource Energy has 225 substations and more than 288400 transformers and owns and operates regulated transmission and distribution assets in its 4400-sq.-mile service territory. It has more than 22800 miles of distribution lines and more than 1770 miles of transmission lines. CL&P's transmission assets are monitored by ISO New England.

	Annual Growth	12/10	12/11	12/12	12/13	12/14
Sales ($ mil.)	(2.7%)	2,999.1	2,548.4	2,407.4	2,442.3	2,692.6
Net income ($ mil.)	4.2%	244.1	250.2	209.7	279.4	287.8
Market value ($ mil.)	1.2%	316.5	338.0	313.8	309.3	331.9
Employees	(4.3%)	1,847	1,828	1,787	1,566	1,548

CONNECTICUT STATE UNIVERSITY SYSTEM

39 WOODLAND ST
HARTFORD, CT 061052337
Phone: 860-493-0000
Fax: -
Web: www.ct.edu

CEO: -
CFO: Pamela J Kedderis
HR: Steve Weinberger
FYE: June 30
Type: Private

The Connecticut State University System (CSUS) is the largest public university system in Connecticut and consists of four universities — Central Connecticut State University Eastern Connecticut State University Southern Connecticut State University and Western Connecticut State University. CSUS has an enrollment of more than 36000 students and its schools offer undergraduate and graduate degrees in some 180 subjects. Programs include courses in liberal arts sciences (including meteorology) business nursing education and technology. CSUS traces its roots to 1849 when Central Connecticut State University was founded. It is part of the broader Connecticut State Colleges & Universities (ConnSCU) system.

	Annual Growth	06/07	06/08	06/09	06/10	06/11
Sales ($ mil.)	3.6%	-	-	-	413.0	428.0
Net income ($ mil.)	143.9%	-	-	-	22.7	55.5
Market value ($ mil.)	-	-	-	-	-	-
Employees	-	-	-	-	-	2,800

CONNECTICUT WATER SERVICE, INC.   NMS: CTWS

93 West Main Street
Clinton, CT 06413
Phone: 860 669-8636
Fax: –
Web: www.ctwater.com

CEO: Eric W. Thornburg
CFO: David C. Benoit
HR: Fred Deluca
FYE: December 31
Type: Public

The operations of Connecticut Water Service (CWS) consist of managing a lot of water in its namesake state and more recently in Maine as well. CWS's regulated subsidiaries — Connecticut Water Company Maine Water and Biddeford & Saco Water — provide water supply and services to 120000 customers in 76 municipalities in Connecticut and Maine. The non-operating holding company's subsidiaries gather water from yield from its 235 active wells and 25 surface water supplies and produce 72 million gallons daily. Other subsidiaries offer fire protection other water-related services and real estate services.

	Annual Growth	12/10	12/11	12/12	12/13	12/14
Sales ($ mil.)	9.1%	66.4	69.4	83.8	91.5	94.0
Net income ($ mil.)	21.5%	9.8	11.3	13.6	18.3	21.3
Market value ($ mil.)	6.8%	310.2	301.8	331.3	395.0	403.7
Employees	6.8%	204	198	259	259	265

CONNECTONE BANCORP INC (NEW)   NMS: CNOB

301 Sylvan Avenue
Englewood Cliffs, NJ 07632
Phone: 201 816-8900
Fax: –
Web: www.centerbancorp.com

CEO: –
CFO: William S Burns
HR: –
FYE: December 31
Type: Public

ConnectOne Bancorp (formerly Center Bancorp) is the holding company for ConnectOne Bank which operates some two dozen branches across New Jersey. Serving individuals and local businesses the bank offers such deposit products as checking savings and money market accounts; CDs; and IRAs. It also performs trust services. Commercial loans account for about 60% of the bank's loan portfolio; residential mortgages account for most of the remainder. It also has a subsidiary that sells annuities and property/casualty life and health coverage. The former Center Bancorp acquired rival community bank ConnectOne Bancorp in 2014 and took that name.

	Annual Growth	12/10	12/11	12/12	12/13	12/14
Assets ($ mil.)	30.0%	1,207.4	1,432.7	1,629.8	1,673.1	3,448.6
Net income ($ mil.)	27.6%	7.0	13.9	17.5	19.9	18.6
Market value ($ mil.)	23.6%	242.0	290.1	343.9	557.1	564.2
Employees	1.4%	159	163	178	166	–

CONNECTRIA CORPORATION

10845 OLIVE BLVD STE 300
SAINT LOUIS, MO 631417760
Phone: 314-395-7787
Fax: –
Web: www.connectria.com

CEO: –
CFO: Robert Strobing
HR: –
FYE: December 31
Type: Private

Businesses around the world hook up with Connectria for their information technology needs. The company provides outsourced IT services such as onsite and offsite management of clients' applications databases and networks. It specializes in products from such vendors as IBM and Oracle among others. Connectria also provides managed data hosting disaster recovery and consulting services. The company operates primary data center facilities in St. Louis and Philadelphia with more than 20 additional data centers scattered across the US. Clients have included 3M Anheuser-Busch and Charter Communications. Connectria was founded in 1996 by Richard Waidmann.

	Annual Growth	12/06	12/07	12/08	12/09	12/10
Sales ($ mil.)	(70.3%)	–	–	273.0	21.1	24.0
Net income ($ mil.)	891.4%	–	–	0.0	1.3	1.6
Market value ($ mil.)	–	–	–	–	–	–
Employees	–	–	–	–	–	167

CONNELL LIMITED PARTNERSHIP

1 International Place Fl. 31
Boston MA 02110
Phone: 617-391-5577
Fax: 617-737-1617
Web: www.connell-lp.com

CEO: –
CFO: –
HR: –
FYE: December 31
Type: Private - Partnershi

Limited partnership unlimited appetite for growth; since 1987 Connell Limited Partnership (Connell) has had a mind for acquisition. It keeps mega funds available for investment in and operation of manufacturing companies principally engaged in the automotive housing appliance and electronics industries. Connell's primary businesses — Anchor Danly (die sets and die makers' supplies) and Dayton Progress (metal stamping tools) — serve customers in these areas. In 2009 Connell shifted its interest away from power and process industries; late that year it sold its heat transfer equipment business Yuba Heat Transfer to a subsidiary of SPX for about $125 million.

CONNEXTIONS INC.

3600 eCommerce Place
Orlando FL 32808
Phone: 407-926-2411
Fax: 407-926-2402
Web: www.connextions.net

CEO: Jack Lefort
CFO: Michael Cooper
HR: –
FYE: December 31
Type: Private

Connextions wants its clients to be connected. The firm helps mostly health insurance and health care providers (but also businesses and the public sector) attract transact with and retain consumers through its call centers software and fulfillment and supply chain management services. The firm has call centers in Florida Indiana and North Carolina that provide customer service sales tech support and licensed personnel such as insurance agents and registered nurses. It manages more than 54 million consumer interactions each year. Connextions was founded in 1992. The company agreed to be acquired by health insurance provider OptumHealth in mid-2011.

CONNEXUS ENERGY

14601 RAMSEY BLVD NW
RAMSEY, MN 553036775
Phone: 763-323-2600
Fax: –
Web: www.connexusenergy.com

CEO: Mike Rajala
CFO: Michael Bash
HR: –
FYE: December 31
Type: Private

Connexus Energy connects more Minnesotans to electricity than any other cooperative. The member-owned organization distributes power to more than 127000 customers in the northern suburbs of Minneapolis-St. Paul. Connexus buys its power from generation and transmission cooperative Great River Energy and distributes it through more than 8880 miles of overhead and underground power lines. It also operates 47 electrical substations. Residential customers account for the bulk of sales. The cooperative is governed by a board of directors elected by its members.

	Annual Growth	12/07	12/08	12/09	12/10	12/13
Sales ($ mil.)	(30.1%)	–	1,544.9	213.3	211.0	258.7
Net income ($ mil.)	–	–	–	11.5	8.6	0.0
Market value ($ mil.)	–	–	–	–	–	–
Employees	–	–	–	–	–	250

CONNOR CO.

2800 NE ADAMS ST
PEORIA, IL 616032806
Phone: 309-693-7229
Fax: –
Web: www.connorco.com

CEO: –
CFO: –
HR: –
FYE: December 31
Type: Private

Goldilocks would like Connor Co. If it's too hot or too cold the heating and A/C company can make it just right. Through about 20 locations in Illinois and one in St. Louis the company distributes heating and air conditioning equipment along with boilers fittings furnaces pipes pumps valves wells and other industrial equipment. The company also conducts its business online. Connor Co. boasts sheet metal fabrication and valve automation facilities and peddles Kohler products within its showrooms in many locations. The company was founded as Kinsey & Mahler a brass valve manufacturer in 1850. It became Connor Co. in 1936.

	Annual Growth	12/03	12/04	12/05	12/06	12/07
Sales ($ mil.)	6.2%	–	91.5	100.6	106.0	109.5
Net income ($ mil.)	15.4%	–	–	4.8	6.9	6.4
Market value ($ mil.)	–	–	–	–	–	–
Employees	–	–	–	–	–	230

CONNS INC

4055 Technology Forest Blvd., Suite 210
The Woodlands, TX 77381
Phone: 936 230-5899
Fax: –
Web: www.conns.com

NMS: CONN
CEO: Norman Miller
CFO: Michael J. Poppe
HR: –
FYE: January 31
Type: Public

Conn's has managed to outlive human life expectancy. Begun as a plumbing and heating business the regional retailer has more than 120 years under its belt. It sells primarily consumer electronics and appliances through about 80 mostly leased stores located in Arizona Colorado New Mexico Tennessee Texas Oklahoma and Louisiana as well as via its website. Conn's markets about 2300 brand-name products such as refrigerators freezers washers dryers air conditioners vacuums TVs and home theater systems. The retailer which offers customers financing also sells lawn mowers furniture bedding and track items including DVD players digital cameras video game equipment camcorders and speakers.

	Annual Growth	01/11	01/12	01/13	01/14	01/15
Sales ($ mil.)	17.1%	790.5	792.3	865.0	1,193.8	1,485.2
Net income ($ mil.)	–	–	(1.0)	(3.7)	52.6	93.4	58.5
Market value ($ mil.)	37.4%	160.7	421.7	1,033.5	2,206.9	572.2
Employees	12.3%	2,700	2,550	2,700	3,600	4,300

CONOCOPHILLIPS ALASKA INC.

700 G St.
Anchorage AK 99501
Phone: 907-276-1215
Fax: 907-263-4731
Web: www.conocophillipsalaska.com

CEO: –
CFO: –
HR: –
FYE: December 31
Type: Subsidiary

ConocoPhillips Alaska is willing to don its long johns to bring oil and natural gas to the lower 48. The company a subsidiary of ConocoPhillips owns stakes in two of Alaska's largest oil fields Prudhoe Bay and Kuparuk in the remote region of Alaska's North Slope as well as in the Western North Slope and Cook Inlet and is the state's largest oil producer. The region has more than 35 trillion cu. ft. of known gas resources. It is projected that Prudhoe Bay can provide more than 3 billion cu. ft. of natural gas per day. ConocoPhillips Alaska produces about 230000 barrels of oil per day and 82 million cu. ft. of natural gas per day.

CONOLOG CORP.

5 Columbia Road
Somerville, NJ 08876
Phone: 908 722-8081
Fax: 908 722-5461
Web: www.conolog.com

NBB: CNLG
CEO: Michael Horn
CFO: Donna Stark
HR: –
FYE: July 31
Type: Public

Conolog makes small electronic and electromagnetic components that military industrial and utilities customers use for microwave radio and telephone transmission. Its products include transducers receivers electromagnetic-wave filters and signal-processing equipment. Its products for commercial customers electrical and industrial utilities in particular are carried under the INIVEN brand name taken from a company Conolog acquired in 1981. Leading customers include the US military and power utilities Bonneville Power Administration NSTAR and Tucson Electric Power.

	Annual Growth	07/08	07/09	07/10	07/11	07/12
Sales ($ mil.)	(9.2%)	1.2	1.5	1.2	1.7	0.8
Net income ($ mil.)	–	(7.0)	(2.4)	(24.9)	(4.3)	(1.8)
Market value ($ mil.)	(45.5%)	19.2	23.1	18.4	1.7	1.7
Employees	(1.7%)	15	16	15	15	14

CONRAD INDUSTRIES, INC.

1100 Brashear Avenue, Suite 200, P.O. Box 790
Morgan City, LA 70381
Phone: 985 702-0195
Fax: 985 702-1126
Web: www.conradindustries.com

NBB: CNRD
CEO: John P Conrad Jr
CFO: Cecil Hernandez
HR: –
FYE: December 31
Type: Public

Like the story of Noah's Ark Conrad Industries starts anew by rescuing the things its likes. Conrad Industries builds converts and repairs small to mid-sized vessels for commercial and government customers. More than half of the company's work is in constructing barges liftboats towboats and tugboats. Its boat-conversion projects mainly involve lengthening vessel mid-bodies or modifying vessels to perform different functions. Conrad Industries operates shipyards along the Gulf Coast in Louisiana and Texas. Conrad also offers fabrication of modular components used on offshore drilling rigs as well as storage and offloading of vessels. Established in 1948 the company is led by the founding Conrad family.

	Annual Growth	12/10	12/11	12/12	12/13	12/14
Sales ($ mil.)	22.1%	138.8	246.5	233.6	303.3	309.0
Net income ($ mil.)	22.0%	10.3	19.2	20.8	28.6	22.8
Market value ($ mil.)	37.6%	57.2	87.3	108.5	216.4	205.2
Employees	7.6%	442	492	549	616	593

CONRAIL INC.

1717 Arch St. 30th Fl.
Philadelphia PA 19103
Phone: 215-209-2000
Fax: 215-209-4819
Web: www.conrail.com

CEO: –
CFO: –
HR: –
FYE: December 31
Type: Holding Company

Conrail whose primary subsidiary is Consolidated Rail Corporation is a switching and terminal agent for its railroad owners CSX and Norfolk Southern. It maintains a total of about 1200 miles of track in heavily industrialized regions of the US including Detroit Philadelphia and parts of northern New Jersey collectively known as its shared asset areas. CSX and Norfolk Southern each pay Conrail fees for maintaining trackage and for access to serve all shippers in these areas. Also used as a switching and terminal agent Conrail ensures that customers' freight is moved safely and swiftly among trains operated by CSX and Norfolk Southern.

CONSOL ENERGY INC
NYS: CNX

1000 Consol Energy Drive
Canonsburg, PA 15317-6506
Phone: 724 485-4000
Fax: –
Web: www.consolenergy.com

CEO: Nicholas J. Deluliis
CFO: David M. Khani
HR: –
FYE: December 31
Type: Public

CONSOL Energy consoles its customers with the warming benefits of coal and natural gas. CONSOL is one of the US's largest coal mining companies along with Peabody Energy and Arch Coal. In 2014 the company had more than 3 billion tons of proved and probable reserves mainly in northern and central Appalachia. CONSOL primarily mines high BTU coal which burns cleaner than lower grades. Customers include electric utilities and steel mills. CONSOL delivers coal using its own railroad cars terminals and barges. The company also engages in natural gas exploration and production through CNX Gas.

	Annual Growth	12/11	12/12	12/13	12/14	12/15
Sales ($ mil.)	(15.5%)	6,117.2	5,430.3	3,299.7	3,726.8	3,114.4
Net income ($ mil.)	–	632.5	388.5	660.4	163.1	(374.9)
Market value ($ mil.)	(31.9%)	8,406.3	7,352.6	8,713.2	7,744.3	1,809.5
Employees	(23.6%)	9,157	8,896	4,633	3,834	3,114

CONSOLIDATED COMMUNICATIONS HOLDINGS INC
NMS: CNSL

121 South 17th Street
Mattoon, IL 61938-3987
Phone: 217 235-3311
Fax: –
Web: www.consolidated.com

CEO: C. Robert (Bob) Udell
CFO: Steven L. (Steve) Childers
HR: Curtis Powell
FYE: December 31
Type: Public

Consolidated Communications is just what its name implies. The rural local exchange carrier (RLEC) operates systems in Illinois Kansas Missouri Pennsylvania Texas and California providing voice and data telecommunications to business and residential customers. It operates RLECs that offer local access and long-distance Internet and TV business phone systems and related services through about 270000 local access lines 167000 voice connections and about 290000 data and Internet connections. The company also offers directory publishing and carrier services. Operating subsidiaries include Illinois Consolidated Telephone Company (ICTC) Consolidated Communications of Fort Bend Company and Consolidated Communications of Texas Company.

	Annual Growth	12/10	12/11	12/12	12/13	12/14
Sales ($ mil.)	13.5%	383.4	374.3	503.5	601.6	635.7
Net income ($ mil.)	(17.5%)	32.6	26.4	5.6	30.8	15.1
Market value ($ mil.)	9.6%	972.0	959.4	801.3	988.7	1,401.6
Employees	18.6%	991	963	1,632	1,521	1,960

CONSOLIDATED CONTAINER COMPANY LLC

3101 Towercreek Pkwy. Ste. 300
Atlanta GA 30339
Phone: 678-742-4600
Fax: 678-742-4750
Web: www.ccclle.com

CEO: Sean Fallmann
CFO: Richard P Sehring
HR: –
FYE: December 31
Type: Private

Sometimes rigid is good. Consolidated Container Company (CCC) is one of the largest manufacturers of rigid plastic packaging in the US. The company markets a myriad of containers (used for milk water fertilizer salsa antifreeze and more) to industries from dairy to water agricultural food and industrial chemical. Custom packaging project management lab work product integration and logistics support are part of CCC's service lineup. CCC operates more than 60 blow-molded manufacturing plants in North America which produce about 7 billion pieces annually. CCC was acquired by private investment firm Bain Capital Partners in mid-2012 for $800 million.

CONSOLIDATED EDISON CO. OF NEW YORK, INC.

4 Irving Place
New York, NY 10003
Phone: 212 460-4600
Fax: –
Web: www.coned.com

CEO: Kevin Burke
CFO: Robert N Hoglund
HR: –
FYE: December 31
Type: Public

Consolidated Edison Company of New York (Con Edison of New York) keeps the nightlife pulsing in The Big Apple. The utility a subsidiary of Consolidated Edison distributes electricity throughout most of New York City and Westchester County. The company distributes electricity to 3.4 million residential and business customers in New York City; it also delivers natural gas to about 1.1 million customers. The utility also provides steam services to 1703 customers in portions of the New York metropolitan area. Con Edison of New York owns and operates more than 133900 miles of overhead and underground power distribution lines.

	Annual Growth	12/10	12/11	12/12	12/13	12/14
Sales ($ mil.)	0.5%	10,573.0	10,484.0	10,187.0	10,430.0	10,786.0
Net income ($ mil.)	4.0%	904.0	989.0	1,017.0	1,020.0	1,058.0
Market value ($ mil.)	–	–	–	–	–	–
Employees	(1.0%)	–	13,605	13,130	13,235	13,200

CONSOLIDATED EDISON SOLUTIONS INC.

100 Summit Lake Dr. Ste. 410
Valhalla NY 10595
Phone: 914-286-7000
Fax: 914-448-0057
Web: www.conedisonsolutions.com

CEO: Jorge Lopez
CFO: –
HR: –
FYE: December 31
Type: Subsidiary

Consolidated Edison Solutions (ConEdison Solutions) works to solve the energy supply needs of retail residential business and government customers in the US Northeast. The company markets electricity and natural gas as an alternative supplier for homes and businesses in deregulated utility markets. It also provides energy procurement and management services and efficiency program consulting. ConEdison Solutions a subsidiary of utility giant Consolidated Edison has offices in Kansas New York Massachusetts New Jersey North Carolina Virginia Texas and Florida. It also partners with government entities to help them meet national efficiency and security goals.

CONSOLIDATED EDISON, INC.
NYS: ED

4 Irving Place
New York, NY 10003
Phone: 212 460-4600
Fax: –
Web: www.conedison.com

CEO: John T. McAvoy
CFO: Robert N. Hoglund
HR: Claude Trahan
FYE: December 31
Type: Public

Utility holding company Consolidated Edison (Con Edison) is the night light for the city that never sleeps. Con Edison's main subsidiary Consolidated Edison Company of New York distributes electricity to 3.4 million residential and business customers in New York City; it also delivers natural gas to about 1.1 million customers and steam service in parts of Manhattan. Subsidiary Orange and Rockland Utilities serves more than 400000 electric and gas customers in three Northeast states. Con Edison's nonutility operations include retail and wholesale energy marketing independent power production and infrastructure project development.

	Annual Growth	12/10	12/11	12/12	12/13	12/14
Sales ($ mil.)	(0.8%)	13,325.0	12,938.0	12,188.0	12,354.0	12,919.0
Net income ($ mil.)	2.1%	1,003.0	1,062.0	1,141.0	1,062.0	1,092.0
Market value ($ mil.)	7.4%	14,517.9	18,167.1	16,266.3	16,190.2	19,332.8
Employees	(1.0%)	15,180	13,605	14,529	14,648	14,601

CONSOLIDATED PIPE & SUPPLY COMPANY INC.

1205 HILLTOP PKWY
BIRMINGHAM, AL 35204-5002
Phone: 205-323-7261
Fax: –
Web: www.consolidatedpipe.com

CEO: –
CFO: –
HR: –
FYE: December 31
Type: Private

Consolidated Pipe and Supply lives up to its name: Its nine divisions supply pipe and pipeline materials to a swath of industries from energy to water and waste treatment chemical mining nuclear oil and gas and pulp and paper. Its industrial unit specializes in carbon and stainless alloy pipe valves and fittings. Vulcan makes all types of PVC. Corrosion resistant coatings are offered by a Line Pipe and Tubular unit and liquid applied coatings by Specialty Coatings. Its Consolidated Power Supply is the largest in the business of safety related metallic materials for commercial nuclear generation. Another unit caters to utilities. Consolidated also provides engineering services and inventory systems.

	Annual Growth	12/03	12/04	12/05	12/05	12/08
Sales ($ mil.)	–	–	–	0.0	387.4	607.3
Net income ($ mil.)	–	–	–	0.0	20.5	53.0
Market value ($ mil.)	–	–	–	–	–	–
Employees	–	–	–	–	–	700

CONSOLIDATED RESTAURANT OPERATIONS INC.

12200 Stemmons Fwy. Ste. 100
Dallas TX 75234
Phone: 972-241-5500
Fax: 972-888-8198
Web: www.croinc.com

CEO: –
CFO: –
HR: –
FYE: December 31
Type: Private

Consolidated Restaurant Operations (CRO) offers several dining concepts on its menu. The company is a full-service restaurant company with more than 85 locations encompassing several different dining concepts. Offering a range of Mexican favorites its flagship El Chico chain operates in a about a dozen states and the United Arab Emirates. CRO also owns the upscale casual Cantina Laredo chain with about 30 locations. Other dining concepts include Cool River Cafe Good Eats and the upscale III Forks. The company also has more than 25 franchised restaurant locations. CRO is controlled by John Harkey who started the restaurant business in 1998 with partners Gene Street and John Cracken.

CONSOLIDATED-TOMOKA LAND CO.

1530 Cornerstone Boulevard, Suite 100
Daytona Beach, FL 32117
Phone: 386 274-2202
Fax: 386 274-1223
Web: www.ctlc.com

ASE: CTO
CEO: John Albright
CFO: Mark Patten
HR: –
FYE: December 31
Type: Public

From golf courses and retail centers to timber and hay farms land developer Consolidated-Tomoka owns a chunk of the Southeast. The company focuses on Florida but also has holdings in other neighboring states. Its portfolio includes retail properties (tenants include Bank of America CVS Walgreens a couple of golf courses (including the national headquarters of the LPGA) and some 10000 acres of agricultural land that the company is converting into other income properties. Through its subsidiaries it also holds subsurface oil gas and mineral interests on land throughout Florida and properties in North Carolina and Georgia. Consolidated-Tomoka was founded in 1902.

	Annual Growth	12/10	12/11	12/12	12/13	12/14
Sales ($ mil.)	27.6%	13.4	14.7	17.3	25.8	35.5
Net income ($ mil.)	–	(0.6)	(4.7)	0.6	3.7	6.4
Market value ($ mil.)	17.9%	170.0	159.2	182.4	213.4	328.2
Employees	(11.7%)	23	18	13	13	14

CONSONA CORPORATION

450 E. 96th St. Ste. 300
Indianapolis IN 46240
Phone: 317-249-1700
Fax: +61-2-9233-6605
Web: www.boral.com.au

CEO: –
CFO: –
HR: –
FYE: December 31
Type: Private

Consona has built a business on helping its customers help their customers as well as themselves. The company's software products include customer relationship management (overseen by Consona CRM) enterprise resource planning (ERP) knowledge management and product configuration management tools for managing supply chains. Its ERP products include comprehensive applications for use in a number of manufacturing scenarios (Intuitive) by plastics makers (DTR) and other specialists. Consona also offers such services as product implementation support and training. Clients have included Amphenol and Ulbrich. The company was bought in 2012 by Vista Equity Partners and merged with CDC Software to form Aptean.

CONSONA CRM INC.

450 E. 96th St. Ste. 300
Indianapolis IN 46240
Phone: 317-249-1700
Fax: 216-692-5293
Web: www.argo-tech.com

CEO: Janice P Anderson
CFO: Robert J Chamberlain
HR: –
FYE: December 31
Type: Subsidiary

Consona CRM helps those who help their clients. The company provides customer relationship management (CRM) software that links marketing sales service technical support and other customer-facing functions providing a central repository for all customer information. With its applications employees can market and sell products and service customers; customers can access information order products and obtain service; and businesses can collaborate with partners. Consona also offers services such as training consulting maintenance and technical support. The company is a subsidiary of Consona Corporation.

CONSTANT CONTACT INC

1601 Trapelo Road, Third Floor
Waltham, MA 02451
Phone: 781 472-8100
Fax: –
Web: www.constantcontact.com

NMS: CTCT
CEO: Gail F Goodman
CFO: Harpreet S Grewal
HR: –
FYE: December 31
Type: Public

Constant Contact makes sure businesses never lose touch with their prospects and customers. The company provides small businesses with Web-based marketing software and services for managing e-mail and social media campaigns as well as offering local deals managing digital storefronts and creating online surveys. Its offerings include tools for creating implementing tracking managing and analyzing marketing materials. Customers include retailers restaurants and other businesses as well as non-profit organizations alumni associations and churches; two-thirds of its clients have fewer than 10 employees. It claims more than 555000 customers for its products.

	Annual Growth	12/09	12/10	12/11	12/12	12/13
Sales ($ mil.)	21.9%	129.1	174.2	214.4	252.2	285.4
Net income ($ mil.)	–	(1.3)	2.9	23.7	12.8	7.2
Market value ($ mil.)	18.0%	499.3	967.0	724.2	443.4	969.5
Employees	18.6%	625	734	367	1,162	1,235

CONSTAR INTERNATIONAL LLC

1 Crown Way
Philadelphia PA 19154-4599
Phone: 215-552-3700
Fax: 215-552-3707
Web: www.constar.net

CEO: Grant H Beard
CFO: J Mark Borseth
HR: –
FYE: December 31
Type: Private

Constar International's PET won't fetch your paper but it will hold your soft drink. With manufacturing and technology centers in the US and Europe the company designs makes and supplies food and beverage containers made from polyethylene terephthalate (PET) a recyclable plastic. Its PET products hold everything from sodas and energy drinks to food and household cleaners. Constar also offers custom development services including packaging design engineering and prototyping. Customers include large branded consumer product companies. However citing a drop in orders from a certain key customer PepsiCo Constar filed for Chapter 11 bankruptcy protection in early 2011 and emerged in mid-2011.

CONSTELLATION BRANDS INC   NYS: STZ

207 High Point Drive, Building 100
Victor, NY 14564
Phone: 585 678-7100
Fax: –
Web: www.cbrands.com

CEO: Robert S. (Rob) Sands
CFO: David Klein
HR: Thomas M. (Tom) Kane
FYE: February 28
Type: Public

Thinking about alcohol makes this company starry-eyed. Constellation Brands is the world's largest premium wine producer. It offers more than 100 brands including Robert Mondavi Clos du Bois and Manischewitz. The company is also the nation's third largest beer distributor and the sole US distributor for Mexican beer giant Grupo Modelo the brewer of Corona Modelo Especial Negra Modelo and other beers. Constellation Brands also markets premium spirits including Black Velvet whiskey and SVEDKA vodka. Constellation Brands' wine beer and spirits are sold in some 100 countries. Brothers Richard and Robert Sands control the company which was founded by the late Marvin Sands.

	Annual Growth	02/11	02/12	02/13	02/14	02/15
Sales ($ mil.)	16.0%	3,332.0	2,654.3	2,796.1	4,867.7	6,028.0
Net income ($ mil.)	10.7%	559.5	445.0	387.8	1,943.1	839.3
Market value ($ mil.)	54.1%	3,953.1	4,248.8	8,606.5	15,763.7	22,317.8
Employees	13.8%	4,300	4,400	4,500	6,300	7,200

CONSTELLATION ENERGY GROUP INC.   NYSE: CEG

100 Constellation Way
Baltimore MD 21202
Phone: 410-470-2800
Fax: 563-262-1069
Web: www.bandag.com

CEO: –
CFO: –
HR: –
FYE: December 31
Type: Subsidiary

Constellation Energy Group's leading light Baltimore Gas and Electric (BGE) distributes electricity and natural gas in Maryland. Constellation Energy operates a number of independent power plants with 11750 MW of generating capacity through its Constellation Generation unit and it competes in retail energy supply through Constellation NewEnergy. Other operations include HVAC services appliance sales nuclear plant development and energy consulting services. In 2012 the company was acquired by Exelon in a $7.9 billion industry-consolidation deal. (Constellation Energy's recent losses made it a prime takeover target).

CONSUMER PORTFOLIO SERVICE, INC.   NMS: CPSS

3800 Howard Hughes Parkway, Suite 1400
Las Vegas, NV 89169
Phone: 949 753-6800
Fax: 949 753-6805
Web: www.consumerportfolio.com

CEO: –
CFO: Jeffrey P Fritz
HR: –
FYE: December 31
Type: Public

Consumer Portfolio Services (CPS) buys sells and services auto loans made to consumers who probably don't have portfolios. The company finances vehicles for subprime borrowers who can't get traditional financing due to poor or limited credit; these loans typically carry a higher interest rate than prime loans. CPS purchases contracts from both new car and independent used car dealers in more than 45 states; the company then securitizes (bundles and sells) them on the secondary market. Its total managed portfolio comprises some $900 million in contracts. The bulk of the contracts CPS acquires finance used vehicles. The company has servicing operations in California Florida Illinois and Virginia.

	Annual Growth	12/10	12/11	12/12	12/13	12/14
Sales ($ mil.)	17.9%	155.2	143.1	187.2	255.8	300.3
Net income ($ mil.)	–	(33.8)	(14.5)	69.4	21.0	29.5
Market value ($ mil.)	57.7%	30.4	22.7	136.9	239.8	188.0
Employees	18.9%	435	530	574	705	869

CONSUMER PRODUCT DISTRIBUTORS INC.

705 MEADOW ST
CHICOPEE, MA 010134820
Phone: 413-592-4141
Fax: –
Web: www.jpolep.com

CEO: –
CFO: Bill Fitzsimmons
HR: –
FYE: September 27
Type: Private

Consumer Product Distributors helps convenience stores provide convenient services to their customers. The company which operates as J. Polep Distribution Services is a leading wholesale supplier serving more than 4000 convenience retailers in New York Pennsylvania and the New England states. J. Polep distributes a variety of products including cigarettes and other tobacco items candy dairy products frozen foods snack items and general merchandise as well as alcohol and other beverages. As part of its business J. Polep provides merchandising sales and marketing and technology services. The family-owned company was founded as Polep Tobacco in 1898 by Charles Polep.

	Annual Growth	10/10	10/11*	09/12	09/13	09/14
Sales ($ mil.)	4.9%	–	778.2	804.9	855.6	898.9
Net income ($ mil.)	(6.6%)	–	–	3.3	2.9	2.9
Market value ($ mil.)	–	–	–	–	–	–
Employees	–	–	–	–	–	400

*Fiscal year change

CONSUMERS BANCORP, INC. (MINERVA, OH)   NBB: CBKM

614 East Lincoln Way, P.O. Box 256
Minerva, OH 44657
Phone: 330 868-7701
Fax: –

CEO: Ralph J Lober II
CFO: Renee K Wood
HR: –
FYE: June 30
Type: Public

You don't have to be a consumer to do business with Consumers — it's happy to serve businesses as well. Consumers Bancorp is the holding company for Consumers National Bank which has about 10 branches in eastern Ohio. The bank offers standard services such as savings and checking accounts CDs and NOW accounts. Business loans make up more than half of the bank's loan portfolio; real estate consumer and construction loans round out its lending activities. CNB Investment Services a division of the bank offers insurance brokerage financial planning and wealth management services through a third-party provider UVEST. Chairman Laurie McClellan owns more than 20% of Consumers Bancorp.

	Annual Growth	06/11	06/12	06/13	06/14	06/15
Assets ($ mil.)	7.7%	300.1	334.8	343.5	382.5	404.0
Net income ($ mil.)	7.1%	2.2	2.8	2.7	2.8	3.0
Market value ($ mil.)	10.3%	33.8	40.9	43.6	52.4	50.1
Employees	3.1%	114	127	124	128	129

CONSUMERS ENERGY CO.

NYS: CMS PRB

One Energy Plaza
Jackson, MI 49201
Phone: 517 788-0550
Fax: –
Web: www.consumersenergy.com

CEO: John G Russell
CFO: Thomas J. (Tom) Webb
HR: –
FYE: December 31
Type: Public

Consumers Energy Company makes sure that the energy consumers in Michigan have the power to crank up their heaters and the gas to fire up their stoves. The company's operating area includes all 68 counties of Michigan's lower peninsula. All told Consumers Energy (the primary operating unit of CMS Energy) has a generating capacity of 6130 MW (primarily fossil-fueled) and distributes electricity to 1.8 million customers and natural gas to 1.7 million customers. Included in the utility's arsenal of power production is electricity generated from fossil-fueled nuclear wind and hydroelectric power plants. Utility customers are a mix of residential commercial and diversified industrial clients.

	Annual Growth	12/11	12/12	12/13	12/14	12/15
Sales ($ mil.)	(0.4%)	6,253.0	6,013.0	6,321.0	6,800.0	6,165.0
Net income ($ mil.)	6.2%	467.0	439.0	534.0	567.0	594.0
Market value ($ mil.)	1.5%	7,690.9	7,883.5	8,100.5	8,789.3	8,158.1
Employees	(0.1%)	7,435	7,205	7,435	7,388	7,394

CONSUMERS UNION OF UNITED STATES INC

101 TRUMAN AVE
YONKERS, NY 107031057
Phone: 914-378-2000
Fax: –
Web: www.consumersunion.org

CEO: –
CFO: Richard Gannon
HR: Lisa Cribari
FYE: May 31
Type: Private

Consumers Union of United States (CU) inspires both trust and fear. Best known for publishing Consumer Reports magazine the independent not-for-profit organization also serves as a consumer watchdog through other print publications and the Web (ConsumerReports.org). Its subscription site rates products ranging from candy bars to cars. CU tests and rates thousands of products annually through its National Testing and Research Center. CU accepts no advertising and derives income from the sale of Consumer Reports and other services and from non-commercial contributions grants and fees. CU traces its roots to 1926 when engineer Frederick Schlink organized a "consumer club" to rate products.

	Annual Growth	05/08	05/09	05/10	05/11	05/13
Sales ($ mil.)	(37.5%)	–	1,700.1	243.0	252.4	259.3
Net income ($ mil.)	(25.6%)	–	–	9.1	32.6	3.7
Market value ($ mil.)	–	–	–	–	–	–
Employees	–	–	–	–	–	480

CONTAINER STORE GROUP, INC

NYS: TCS

500 Freeport Parkway
Coppell, TX 75019
Phone: 972 538-6000
Fax: –
Web: www.containerstore.com

CEO: William A. (Kip) Tindell
CFO: Jodi L. Taylor
HR: –
FYE: February 28
Type: Public

With its packets pockets and boxes The Container Store (TCS) has the storage products niche well-contained. Its merchandise ranges from backpacks to recipe holders. The home-organization pioneer operates about 60 stores in more than 20 states mostly in major cities in Texas California Florida Illinois and New York as well as the District of Columbia. It also runs an e-commerce site. The company offers shipping across the US and to Canada as well as same-day delivery in New York City. Stores carry more than 10000 items; the company's Elfa brand of wire shelving (made in Sweden) accounts for more than 10% of its sales. Founded in 1978 TCS went public in 2013.

	Annual Growth	02/11	02/12*	03/13	03/14	02/15
Sales ($ mil.)	8.3%	568.8	633.6	706.8	748.5	781.9
Net income ($ mil.)	–	(45.1)	(30.7)	(0.1)	8.2	22.7
Market value ($ mil.)	(48.6%)	–	–	–	1,718.3	883.9
Employees	(4.5%)	–	–	5,375	5,300	4,900

*Fiscal year change

CONTANGO OIL & GAS CO. (DE)

ASE: MCF

717 Texas Avenue, Suite 2900
Houston, TX 77002
Phone: 713 236-7400
Fax: –
Web: www.contango.com

CEO: Allan D. Keel
CFO: Sergio Castro
HR: Candace Day-Butler
FYE: December 31
Type: Public

It takes two to tango but a lot more people to make Contango a successful independent oil and natural gas company. Contango Oil & Gas (named after a term used by oil and gas traders to describe anticipated rising prices in the futures market) explores for and acquires oil and gas properties in primarily in the Gulf of Mexico. In 2012 the company reported offshore production of 83.5 million cubic feet equivalent per day which consists primarily of seven federal and five state of Louisiana wells in the shallow waters of the Gulf of Mexico. It also has assets in Wyoming. To expand its Gulf Coast assets in 2013 the company acquired Crimson Exploration for $390 million.

	Annual Growth	06/11	06/12	06/13*	12/13	12/14
Sales ($ mil.)	10.7%	203.8	179.3	127.2	164.1	276.5
Net income ($ mil.)	–	65.0	58.4	(9.7)	41.4	(21.9)
Market value ($ mil.)	(20.6%)	1,119.0	1,133.6	646.2	904.9	559.9
Employees	125.7%	8	10	10	79	92

*Fiscal year change

CONTI ENTERPRISES INC.

2045 LINCOLN HWY
EDISON, NJ 088173334
Phone: 908-561-9025
Fax: –
Web: www.conticorp.com

CEO: Kurt G. Conti
CFO: Dominic Mustillo
HR: –
FYE: December 31
Type: Private

Conti Enterprises is continuing its tour of duty as a civil and heavy construction firm. Active primarily in the Northeast the company provides construction management general contracting and design/build services for a range of projects including commercial and industrial buildings power plants environmental remediation physical security upgrades and infrastructure such as dams roads bridges and rail systems. The company often participates in public-private partnerships. Clients have included the Army Corps of Engineers the EPA the FAA the Department of Energy Con Edison and Dominion Resources.

	Annual Growth	12/03	12/04	12/05	12/08	12/09
Sales ($ mil.)	11.4%	–	115.4	123.4	198.2	198.2
Net income ($ mil.)	–	–	–	0.0	0.0	0.0
Market value ($ mil.)	–	–	–	–	–	–
Employees	–	–	–	–	–	250

CONTINENTAL AIRLINES INC.

1600 Smith St. Dept. HQSEO
Houston TX 77002
Phone: 713-324-2950
Fax: 973-357-3065
Web: www.cytec.com

CEO: Oscar Munoz
CFO: John D Rainey
HR: –
FYE: December 31
Type: Subsidiary

If it's a continent chances are it's accessible via Continental Airlines. The carrier serves about 140 US destinations and another 135 abroad from hubs in Cleveland Houston Newark and Guam (hub of Continental Micronesia). Its network includes regional flights by subsidiary lines. Continental has about 350 jets and more than 250 regional aircraft. It extends its offerings through code-sharing with fellow members of the Star Alliance led by United Continental's United Air Lines Lufthansa and Air Canada. (Code-sharing allows airlines to sell tickets on one another's flights.) In fall 2010 Continental was acquired by United parent UAL Corp. in a $3 billion stock swap to create United Continental Holdings.

CONTINENTAL BUILDING PRODUCTS INC
NYS: CBPX

12950 Worldgate Drive, Suite 700
Herndon, VA 20170
Phone: 703 480-3800
Fax: –
Web: www.continental-bp.com

CEO: Jay Bachmann
CFO: Dennis Schemm
HR: –
FYE: December 31
Type: Public

Continental Building Products (CBP) has got homeowners surrounded. The company is a leading manufacturer of gypsum wallboard (aka drywall) and complementary finishing products used in new residential and commercial construction and for repairs and remodels. CBP manufactures its products at plants in Florida Kentucky and New York for sale east of the Mississippi River and in eastern Canada. The company claims to be the only US producer of gypsum wallboard to use only 100% synthetic gypsum. Product lines include LiftLite a lightweight product Mold Defense which protects against mildew and Weather Defense exterior sheeting. The wallboard producer went public in 2014 in an offering valued at $185 million.

	Annual Growth	12/11	12/12*	08/13*	12/13	12/14
Sales ($ mil.)	19.0%	252.1	311.4	252.2	150.1	424.5
Net income ($ mil.)	–	(60.5)	(12.8)	32.2	2.1	15.9
Market value ($ mil.)	–	–	–	–	–	781.3
Employees	7.0%	–	470	–	480	538

*Fiscal year change

CONTINENTAL MATERIALS CORP.
ASE: CUO

200 South Wacker Drive, Suite 4000
Chicago, IL 60606
Phone: 312 541-7200
Fax: –
Web: www.continental-materials.com

CEO: James G Gidwitz
CFO: Joseph J Sum
HR: –
FYE: January 03
Type: Public

Continental Materials provides construction and heating ventilation and air conditioning (HVAC) services. Its HVAC segment which sccounts for a majority of sales makes wall furnaces console heaters and fan coils through Williams Furnace and evaporative air coolers through Phoenix Manufacturing. Customers include wholesale distributors and retail home centers in the Southwest. The construction products segment produces ready-mix concrete and aggregates through three subsidiaries and metal doors from McKinney Door and Hardware. Contractors government entities and consumers in Colorado are the segment's primary customers. CEO James Gidwitz and family own more than 60% of Continental Materials.

	Annual Growth	01/11*	12/11	12/12	12/13*	01/15
Sales ($ mil.)	3.6%	114.3	107.2	113.2	121.5	131.9
Net income ($ mil.)	–	(0.4)	(1.9)	3.4	(0.9)	(5.5)
Market value ($ mil.)	(7.3%)	36.9	19.7	25.3	32.6	27.2
Employees	(2.3%)	623	568	550	556	568

*Fiscal year change

CONTINENTAL PLASTICS CO.

33525 Groesbeck Hwy.
Fraser MI 48026
Phone: 586-294-4600
Fax: 586-294-1096
Web: www.contplastics.com

CEO: –
CFO: –
HR: Lisa Kmeic
FYE: December 31
Type: Private

Continental Plastics makes thermoplastic injection molded interior and exterior decorative components for the automotive industry. It supplies parts directly to auto OEMs such as General Motors and also to larger parts suppliers such as Lear. Continental Plastics operates five facilities located in Michigan and Georgia comprising in total more than 600000 square feet. The company founded by Patrick Luckino in 1951 is family owned. Continental Plastics began with two employees and two injection molding machines. Growing its production capacity reaches 1 million full center consoles and over half-a-million door and panel assemblies annually. The company ships to Canada Europe Mexico and South America.

CONTINENTAL RESOURCES INC.
NYS: CLR

20 N. Broadway
Oklahoma City, OK 73102
Phone: 405 234-9000
Fax: –
Web: www.clr.com

CEO: Harold G. Hamm
CFO: John D. Hart
HR: –
FYE: December 31
Type: Public

The continental resources that Continental Resources searches for are oil and natural gas assets beneath the North American continent in the Rocky Mountain Mid-Continent and Gulf Coast regions. The independent oil and gas exploration and production company added reserves of 649 million barrels of oil equivalent through internal growth (aka "growing through the drill bit") between early 2008 and the end of 2013. It holds 1.5 million net acres of undeveloped leasehold properties. In 2014 Continental Resources reported estimated proved reserves of 1.3 billion barrels of oil equivalent (about 37% of which were developed and 74% located in the North region); and 2100 net producing wells.

	Annual Growth	12/10	12/11	12/12	12/13	12/14
Sales ($ mil.)	54.7%	839.1	1,649.8	2,572.5	3,455.2	4,801.6
Net income ($ mil.)	55.2%	168.3	429.1	739.4	764.2	977.3
Market value ($ mil.)	(10.1%)	21,892.5	24,816.5	27,338.7	41,858.1	14,270.1
Employees	24.6%	493	609	753	929	1,188

CONTINENTAL TIRE THE AMERICAS LLC

1830 MacMillan Park Dr.
Fort Mill SC 29707
Phone: 704-583-4882
Fax: 604-688-6482
Web: www.sierrasystems.com

CEO: Jochen Etzel
CFO: Narendra M Pathipati
HR: –
FYE: December 31
Type: Subsidiary

Continental Tire the Americas (CTA formerly Continental Tire North America) rounds out tire production for its German parent. The North American subsidiary of Germany-based tire and automotive component manufacturer Continental AG makes tires for cars light- and heavy-duty trucks motorhomes commercial vehicles SUVs and agricultural and industrial vehicles. Its brands include a variety of Conti names (ContiExtreme ContiTrac ContiSport etc.) as well as the General and Euzkadi brands and private labels. CTA's customers include BMW Ford Toyota John Deere Mack and Volvo. The company has tire plants in Ecuador Brazil Mexico and Canada as well as US locations in South Carolina and Illinois.

CONTINUCARE CORPORATION

7200 Corporate Center Dr. Ste. 600
Miami FL 33126
Phone: 305-500-2000
Fax: 305-500-2080
Web: www.continucare.com

CEO: Gemma Rosello
CFO: –
HR: –
FYE: June 30
Type: Subsidiary

Continucare continues to care for South and Central Florida's Medicare recipients. The company provides primary care medical services through a network of some 20 centers in Broward Miami-Dade Hillsborough and Palm Beach counties. It also provides practice management services to independent doctors' offices affiliated with Humana and other insurers. A majority of patients who seek medical assistance at Continucare clinics and practices are members of Medicare Advantage health plans. The company has branched out and also operates a growing number of sleep diagnostic centers. Continucare has been part of neighboring Metropolitan Health Networks (MetCare) since it was acquired in 2011.

CONTRACTORS STEEL COMPANY

36555 AMRHEIN RD
LIVONIA, MI 481501182
Phone: 734-464-4000
Fax: –
Web: www.contractorssteel.com

CEO: Donald R. (Don) Simon
CFO: –
HR: –
FYE: October 31
Type: Private

Steel service center operator Contractors Steel provides products such as bars (cold-rolled and hot-rolled) pipe plate sheet structural members (angles beams and channels) and tubing. The company's fabricating and processing services include burning grinding plasma cutting sawing and shearing. Contractors Steel operates from facilities in Michigan and Ohio. The company maintains its own fleet of delivery trucks. Chairman president and CEO Donald Simon founded Contractors Steel in 1960.

	Annual Growth	10/06	10/07	10/08	10/09	10/10
Sales ($ mil.)	(46.0%)	–	–	632.4	153.1	184.4
Net income ($ mil.)	1889.7%	–	–	0.0	(24.1)	6.5
Market value ($ mil.)	–	–	–	–	–	–
Employees	–	–	–	–	–	250

CONTRAN CORPORATION

Three Lincoln Centre 5430 LBJ Fwy. Ste. 1700
Dallas TX 75240
Phone: 972-233-1700
Fax: 972-448-1444

CEO: Harold C Simmons
CFO: Bobby D Obrien
HR: –
FYE: December 31
Type: Private

Contran is a holding company that owns stakes of varying sizes in subsidiaries including the largest Valhi Inc. (a publicly traded company about 95% controlled by Contran). Primarily through Valhi the company has stakes in diversified operations in chemicals (NL Industries and Kronos Worldwide); metals (Titanium Metals Corporation); waste management (Waste Control Specialists); and computer support systems precision ball bearing slides and security products (CompX International). Contran also holds a controlling interest in Keystone Consolidated Industries a maker of fencing and wire products. Trusts benefiting chairman Harold Simmons' family (with Simmons as the sole trustee) own 95% of Contran.

CONTROL4 CORP

NMS: CTRL

11734 South Election Road
Salt Lake City, UT 84020
Phone: 801 523-3100
Fax: –
Web: www.control4.com

CEO: Martin Plaehn
CFO: Mark Novakovich
HR: –
FYE: December 31
Type: Public

Control4 gives homes a personal touch far beyond throw pillows and new paint. The company makes and sells home automation systems that allow users to control music video lighting temperature and security systems with the touch of a button on a wall panel or mobile device. For example homeowners may program their system to lock the doors close the blinds and turn on the alarm when they leave for work and open the garage door and adjust the thermostat to a particular temperature upon arrival. Control4 systems are only sold through authorized dealers and distributors who design a custom solution for each home (and to a smaller extent businesses).

	Annual Growth	12/11	12/12	12/13	12/14	12/15
Sales ($ mil.)	15.0%	93.4	109.5	128.5	148.8	163.2
Net income ($ mil.)	–	(3.9)	(3.7)	3.5	8.2	(1.7)
Market value ($ mil.)	(35.9%)	–	–	414.8	360.2	170.4
Employees	10.5%	–	333	386	417	449

CONVAID PRODUCTS INC.

2830 CALIFORNIA ST
TORRANCE, CA 905033908
Phone: 310-618-0111
Fax: –
Web: www.convaid.com

CEO: Mervyn M Watkins
CFO: –
HR: Lauri Jackson
FYE: December 31
Type: Private

Convaid makes lightweight compact-folding wheelchairs that are made for clients with orthopedic conditions and limited upper body control. The company also offers accessories such as travel bags canopies footplates incontinence liners and torso support vests. Convaid sells the wheelchairs to the pediatric adult and geriatric markets. The company was founded in 1976.

	Annual Growth	12/03	12/04	12/05	12/06	12/07
Sales ($ mil.)	–	–	–	0.0	9.4	9.2
Net income ($ mil.)	–	–	–	0.0	0.9	0.3
Market value ($ mil.)	–	–	–	–	–	–
Employees	–	–	–	–	–	89

CONVERGENT OUTSOURCING INC.

800 SW 39TH ST
RENTON, WA 980574975
Phone: 206-322-4500
Fax: –
Web: www.convergentusa.com

CEO: –
CFO: –
HR: –
FYE: September 30
Type: Private

Companies send their ailing accounts receivable to Convergent Outsourcing. A subsidiary of Convergent Resources (CRI) one of the largest collections companies in the US Convergent Outsourcing (formerly ER Solutions) provides receivables collections services to creditors in the retail telecommunications utilities and financial services industries. Utilizing a mixture of state-of-the-art technology and old-fashioned diplomacy the company tracks down delinquent customers and encourages voluntary repayment of debt. It also provides customer service both for outbound communications (contacting customers to remind them of their debt and payment options) and inbound customer relations.

	Annual Growth	12/07	12/08	12/10	12/11*	09/13
Sales ($ mil.)	(0.5%)	–	81.2	86.2	95.0	79.3
Net income ($ mil.)	(0.9%)	–	–	8.7	10.4	8.5
Market value ($ mil.)	–	–	–	–	–	–
Employees	–	–	–	–	–	730

*Fiscal year change

CONVERGINT TECHNOLOGIES LLC

1651 WILKENING RD
SCHAUMBURG, IL 60173-5323
Phone: 847-620-5000
Fax: –
Web: www.convergint.com

CEO: Ken Lochiatto
CFO: –
HR: –
FYE: December 31
Type: Private

It's IP for IT at Convergint Technologies. Convergint integrates IT (information technology) and physical security systems at both single- and multi-site facilities. Its security systems include IP (internet protocol) video and cameras biometrics card access and perimeter protection. The company designs installs as well as repairs electronic security fire alarm and life safety and building automation systems for a diverse group of commercial industrial and government customers. Clients have included Boeing and the Oregon Department of Transportation. As a value-added reseller (VAR) and partner Convergint installs products from such major OEMs as Honeywell Lenel and S2 Security.

	Annual Growth	12/06	12/07	12/08	12/08	12/09
Sales ($ mil.)	–	–	–	(1,818.2)	151.5	164.8
Net income ($ mil.)	5181649.0%	–	–	0.0	6.5	13.6
Market value ($ mil.)	–	–	–	–	–	–
Employees	–	–	–	–	–	1,000

CONVERGYS CORP.

NYS: CVG

201 East Fourth Street
Cincinnati, OH 45202
Phone: 513 723-7000
Fax: –
Web: www.convergys.com

CEO: Andrea J Ayers
CFO: Andre S. Valentine
HR: –
FYE: December 31
Type: Public

Convergys is conversant in the languages of customer satisfaction. The company provides business services designed to maximize customer service acquisition and retention. Convergys' call center agents handle customer service interactions such as account service billing inquiries and technical support. The company targets customers in industries such as communications financial services technology retail healthcare and government. All total it has about 70 customer contact centers. Convergys was formed as a division of Cincinnati Bell and spun off in 1998.

	Annual Growth	12/10	12/11	12/12	12/13	12/14
Sales ($ mil.)	6.7%	2,203.4	2,262.0	2,005.0	2,046.1	2,855.5
Net income ($ mil.)	–	(53.2)	334.8	100.6	60.9	120.0
Market value ($ mil.)	11.5%	1,309.1	1,269.3	1,631.2	2,092.4	2,024.8
Employees	15.6%	70,000	77,000	77,000	84,000	125,000

CONVERSANT INC

NMS: CNVR

30699 Russell Ranch Road, Suite 250
Westlake Village, CA 91362
Phone: 818 575-4500
Fax: 818 575-4501
Web: www.valueclick.com

CEO: John Giuliani
CFO: John Pitstick
HR: –
FYE: December 31
Type: Public

If you think that banner ad is worth a look ValueClick will put a price on it. The company brings Web publishers together with advertisers providing the technology necessary for each side to manage online advertising. ValueClick's media services segment offers e-mail marketing search marketing and ad placement services. The company's affiliate marketing tools track and analyze online marketing programs through its Commission Junction subsidiary while its Mediaplex unit provides online ad serving and management tools. Pricerunner Shopping.net and Smarter.com allow consumers to compare and research products online.

	Annual Growth	12/08	12/09	12/10	12/11	12/12
Sales ($ mil.)	1.4%	625.8	422.7	430.8	560.2	660.9
Net income ($ mil.)	–	(214.1)	68.6	90.5	101.1	101.7
Market value ($ mil.)	29.8%	515.1	762.1	1,207.1	1,226.7	1,461.6
Employees	(1.7%)	1,189	686	1,062	1,331	1,111

CONVERSE INC.

1 High St.
North Andover MA 01845-2601
Phone: 978-983-3300
Fax: 978-983-3502
Web: www.converse.com

CEO: Jack A Boys
CFO: Lisa Kempa
HR: –
FYE: May 31
Type: Subsidiary

With its roots as a popular basketball shoe worn by professionals Converse has morphed under NIKE into a fashionable footwear maker for those off the court too. It has sold some 750 million pairs of its classic Chuck Taylor All Star canvas basketball shoes which appeal to consumers ranging from kids to clothing designers. It also licenses its name to sports apparel makers. Converse produces products under the One Star Star Chevron and Jack Purcell names. It sells them through about 60 of its own stores and through retailers the likes of Target and even DSW. Converse operates as a separate unit from NIKE's competing sports brands reining in the kitsch value of Converse's vintage Chuck Taylor brand.

CONVIO INC.

NASDAQ: CNVO

11501 Domain Dr. Ste. 200
Austin TX 78758
Phone: 512-652-2600
Fax: 512-652-2699
Web: www.convio.com

CEO: Gene Austin
CFO: James R Offerdahl
HR: –
FYE: December 31
Type: Subsidiary

Convio takes a community approach to helping not-for-profit organizations institutions of higher education and associations raise money organize volunteer efforts manage online content and get their message out. The company's online Common Ground customer relationship management (CRM) software and services connect potential donors and volunteers to groups they may support and vice versa. Convio's more than 1600 clients include The American Red Cross Meals on Wheels Susan G. Komen and the World Wildlife Fund. Nearly all sales come from customers in North America. Founded in 1999 the company went public in 2010. It was acquired by not-for-profit software maker Blackbaud in 2012.

CONWAY HOSPITAL INC.

300 SINGLETON RIDGE RD
CONWAY, SC 295269142
Phone: 843-347-7111
Fax: –
Web: www.conwaymedicalcenter.com

CEO: Philip A Clayton
CFO: Bret Barr
HR: –
FYE: September 30
Type: Private

Conway Medical Center (CMC) finds a way to provide a wide range of health care services to residents of eastern South Carolina. The private not-for-profit 210-bed hospital (served by a medical staff of 200) provides services including primary diagnostic emergency surgical maternal and pediatric and rehabilitative care. CMC specializes in heart health hospice care and occupational health. Additionally CMC operates the Kingston Nursing Center an about 90-bed long-term nursing and rehabilitative care facility and the Conway Physicians Group which is home to about 10 physician practices offering a range of specialties.

	Annual Growth	09/10	09/11	09/12	09/13	09/14
Sales ($ mil.)	6.2%	–	149.7	158.5	162.4	179.2
Net income ($ mil.)	32.1%	–	–	16.2	21.6	28.2
Market value ($ mil.)	–	–	–	–	–	–
Employees	–	–	–	–	–	1,200

CONWAY REGIONAL MEDICAL CENTER INC.

2302 COLLEGE AVE
CONWAY, AR 720346297
Phone: 501-329-3831
Fax: –
Web: www.conwayregional.org

CEO: –
CFO: Steven Rose
HR: –
FYE: December 31
Type: Private

Ailing Arkansans have a health services provider in Conway Regional Health System. The health system is composed of not-for-profit 154-bed acute care hospital Conway Regional Medical Center as well as four health clinics a home health agency a health and fitness center and an inpatient rehabilitation hospital. Conway Regional provides specialized cardiovascular neurology oncology orthopedics physical therapy and women's services (including obstetrics and gynecology). Its facilities serve the health needs of residents of several central Arkansas counties including Cleburne Conway Faulkner Perry and Van Buren.

	Annual Growth	12/07	12/08	12/09	12/12	12/13
Sales ($ mil.)	1.7%	–	126.2	133.0	135.5	137.1
Net income ($ mil.)	0.1%	–	–	5.8	1.7	5.8
Market value ($ mil.)	–	–	–	–	–	–
Employees	–	–	–	–	–	900

COOK CHILDREN''S HEALTH CARE SYSTEM

801 7TH AVE
FORT WORTH, TX 761042733
Phone: 682-885-4555
Fax: –
Web: www.cookchildrens.org

CEO: Rick W. Merrill
CFO: Stephen W Kimmel
HR: Frank Rossi
FYE: September 30
Type: Private

From the tiniest babies to the gangliest teens Cook Children's Health Care System takes care of children of all ages through more than 60 pediatric medical and specialty clinics in Texas. It encompasses the Cook Children's Medical Center (with roughly 430 beds) Cook Children's Home Health and Cook Children's Health Plan. In addition its physician network has offices at dozens of locations in Denton Hood Johnson Parker Tarrant and Wise counties. Specialties include behavioral health services bone marrow transplants craniofacial reconstruction oncology and dialysis. Cook's Life After Cancer Program is funded by the LIVESTRONG Foundation and helps people manage and survive cancer.

	Annual Growth	09/04	09/05	09/07	09/09	09/13
Sales ($ mil.)	15.2%	–	42.9	500.8	75.8	133.0
Net income ($ mil.)	(23.8%)	–	–	59.9	(1.5)	11.8
Market value ($ mil.)	–	–	–	–	–	–
Employees	–	–	–	–	–	2,000

COOK COMPOSITES AND POLYMERS

820 E. 14th Ave.
Kansas City MO 64116
Phone: 816-391-6000
Fax: 816-391-6122
Web: www.ccponline.com

CEO: –
CFO: –
HR: –
FYE: December 31
Type: Joint Venture

The gel coats are cookin' at Cook Composites and Polymers (CCP) which is the North American resins division of TOTAL's chemicals division. CCP is the world's #1 supplier of gel coats and also manufactures powder coating and composite resins in addition to industrial cleaners and maintenance products. Its products are used for marine construction and transportation applications. They go into such diverse products as furniture cookware showers and tubs and in RV and truck panels. CCP has its headquarters in Kansas City Missouri. In 2010 French chemicals company Arkema acquired CCP and other assets of TOTAL's chemicals business in a $730 million deal.

COOKTEK LLC

156 N. Jefferson St. Ste. 300
Chicago IL 60661-1436
Phone: 312-563-9600
Fax: 312-432-6220
Web: www.cooktek.com

CEO: –
CFO: –
HR: –
FYE: December 31
Type: Subsidiary

Innovation is what's cooking at CookTek. The company manufactures and markets portable appliances for cooking and warming used by the commercial foodservice industry. Its lineup includes cookware cooktops woks FlashPaks (pizza delivery containers) and FaIIeaters (cooktops that convert to fajita platters). Popular with major restaurant chains CookTek products are based on induction heating technology; when a magnetic pan is placed on top an induction cooktop it generates a magnetic field exciting heat-producing molecules in the pan! The result offers precise controllable heat and a faster cooking medium than traditional gas or electric ranges. CookTek is part of the Middleby family of foodservice brands.

COOLEY LLP

5 Palo Alto Sq. 3000 El Camino Real
Palo Alto CA 94306-2155
Phone: 650-843-5000
Fax: 650-857-0663
Web: www.cooley.com

CEO: –
CFO: –
HR: –
FYE: December 31
Type: Private - Partnershi

Clients across 20 different industries rely on Cooley for the legal know-how. Cooley specializes in business law particularly venture capital and private equity corporate securities mergers and acquisitions life sciences and technology transactions and tax and real estate. The firm also has strength in litigation with almost half of its 650 lawyers working in that area. Cooley has about 10 offices throughout the US including four in its home state of California. Other offices are located in Boston; Broomfield Colorado; New York; Reston Virginia; Seattle; and Washington DC. The firm was founded in 1920 as a law partnership by Arthur Cooley and Louis Crowley.

COOPER COMMUNITIES INC.

903 N 47TH ST
ROGERS, AR 727569622
Phone: 479-246-6500
Fax: –
Web: www.ccias.com

CEO: –
CFO: M Kent Burger
HR: –
FYE: December 31
Type: Private

Feeling cooped up in your cookie-cutter house with its bare minimum of surrounding green space? Cooper Communities develops master-planned communities and resorts in the southeastern US. Some properties feature golf courses and lakes with 20-30% of their land set aside for natural landscape. Subsidiaries include custom builder Cooper Homes Cooper Land Development and Escapes! which sells timeshare options for Cooper's resorts. Cooper Realty Investments acquires and manages commercial properties. The largest homebuilder in Arkansas Cooper Communities also has developments in eight other states. Cooper Communities was founded by John Cooper in 1954 and builds about 1300 new homes each year.

	Annual Growth	12/05	12/06	12/07	12/08	12/10
Assets ($ mil.)	10.2%	–	–	170.6	398.6	228.2
Net income ($ mil.)		–	–	0.0	(29.5)	(65.4)
Market value ($ mil.)		–	–	–	–	–
Employees		–	–	–	–	400

COOPER COMPANIES, INC. (THE)

6140 Stoneridge Mall Road, Suite 590
Pleasanton, CA 94588
Phone: 925 460-3600
Fax: 925 460-3648
Web: www.coopercos.com

NYS: COO
CEO: Robert S. Weiss
CFO: Gregory W. Matz
HR: –
FYE: October 31
Type: Public

From eye care to lady care The Cooper Companies has its customers covered. The global company makes specialty medical devices in two niche markets: vision care and gynecology. Its CooperVision subsidiary makes specialty contact lenses including toric lenses for astigmatism multifocal lenses for presbyopia and cosmetic lenses. The company also offers spherical lenses for more common vision problems such as nearsightedness and farsightedness. Subsidiary CooperSurgical specializes in women's health care; its wide range of products includes bone densitometers (for diagnosing osteoporosis) contraceptive devices surgery instruments and fetal monitors. Cooper's products are sold in more than 100 countries.

	Annual Growth	10/11	10/12	10/13	10/14	10/15
Sales ($ mil.)	7.8%	1,330.8	1,445.1	1,587.7	1,717.8	1,797.1
Net income ($ mil.)	3.8%	175.4	248.3	296.2	269.9	203.5
Market value ($ mil.)	21.8%	3,345.0	4,632.8	6,236.7	7,911.1	7,354.1
Employees	8.4%	7,400	7,800	8,000	9,460	10,200

COOPER LIGHTING LLC

1121 Hwy. 74 South
Peachtree City GA 30269
Phone: 770-486-4800
Fax: 770-486-4801
Web: www.cooperlighting.com

CEO: Alexander M Cutler
CFO: Heather Robinson
HR: –
FYE: December 31
Type: Subsidiary

Cooper Lighting a subsidiary of Cooper Industries designs lighting and fixtures for commercial residential and utility applications. The company's products are primarily used in commercial buildings homes landscapes shopping centers high-security areas and industrial plants. Cooper Lighting's brand names include AtLite Fail-Safe Halo IRiS Lumark Streetworks and Sure-Lites among others. The Cooper Lighting SOURCE facilities offer continuing education lighting classes which cover lighting fundamentals and lighting basics to landscape lighting for the lighting professional. Cooper Lighting's origins date back to 1958 when the manufacturer was founded as Halo Lighting Company.

COOPER TIRE & RUBBER CO. NYS: CTB

701 Lima Avenue
Findlay, OH 45840
Phone: 419 423-1321
Fax: 419 424-4305
Web: www.coopertire.com

CEO: Roy V. Armes
CFO: Ginger M. Jones
HR: Brenda S. Harmon
FYE: December 31
Type: Public

Cooper Tire & Rubber is a real wheeler dealer. The company is the fourth-largest tire manufacturer in North America (behind the likes of Bridgestone Michelin and Goodyear). It makes and sells replacement tires mainly for passenger cars and light trucks but also for motorcycles race cars commercial and off-road vehicles for North American and international markets. Cooper operates eight manufacturing facilities and over 20 distribution centers worldwide. Unlike some of its rivals Cooper does not typically sell to automotive OEMs; instead it markets its tires to customers including independent tire dealers wholesale distributors and regional and national tire chains.

	Annual Growth	12/10	12/11	12/12	12/13	12/14
Sales ($ mil.)	0.5%	3,361.0	3,927.2	4,200.8	3,439.2	3,424.8
Net income ($ mil.)	11.0%	140.4	253.5	220.4	111.0	213.6
Market value ($ mil.)	10.1%	1,371.2	814.7	1,474.7	1,398.0	2,014.9
Employees	(8.9%)	12,898	12,890	13,550	13,280	8,881

COOPER-STANDARD HOLDINGS, INC. NYS: CPS

39550 Orchard Hill Place Drive
Novi, MI 48375
Phone: 248 596-5900
Fax: –
Web: www.cooperstandard.com

CEO: Jeffrey S. Edwards
CFO: Matthew W. Hardt
HR: –
FYE: December 31
Type: Public

Nothing standard about Cooper-Standard Automotive (CSA); it is the world's largest maker of auto body sealing systems as well as one of the largest of anti-vibration system (AVS) and fluid handling products. Its body and chassis lines which protect interiors from noise dust and weather include brackets mounts and seals sold under brands StanPro Tecalemit and Metzeler. CSA fluid handling products (sensors tubes and hoses) are used in heating/cooling braking fuel and emissions systems. CSA sells to such major OEMs as Ford GM Fiat Chrysler PSA Peugeot Citroen and some suppliers.

	Annual Growth	12/10	12/11	12/12	12/13	12/14
Sales ($ mil.)	23.3%	1,405.0	2,853.5	2,880.9	3,090.5	3,244.0
Net income ($ mil.)	1.3%	40.6	102.8	102.8	47.9	42.8
Market value ($ mil.)	6.5%	766.8	587.9	647.5	836.8	986.2
Employees	9.2%	19,000	21,500	22,400	25,300	27,000

COOPERATIVE ELEVATOR CO.

7211 E MICHIGAN AVE
PIGEON, MI 48755
Phone: 989-453-4500
Fax: –
Web: www.coopelev.com

CEO: Kurt Ewald
CFO: –
HR: –
FYE: January 31
Type: Private

Cooperative Elevator represents and serves northern Michigan bean and grain farmers. The agricultural cooperative is made up of approximately 900 member/owners. It operates storage facilities and processing plants offers crop marketing and agronomy services and provides farm supplies to its members including seed feed fertilizer herbicides fuel and agricultural chemicals. The co-op's bean farmers grow black red pinto and navy beans which are distributed in bulk throughout the US as well as in Africa and the Caribbean. Cooperative Elevator's grain farmers produce wheat soy corn barley and oats and the co-op provides storage and market services such as price updates for these commodities.

	Annual Growth	01/10	01/11	01/12	01/13	01/14
Sales ($ mil.)	18.4%	–	166.9	242.2	293.3	277.1
Net income ($ mil.)	(12.8%)	–	–	13.1	12.9	10.0
Market value ($ mil.)	–	–	–	–	–	–
Employees	–	–	–	–	–	136

COOPERATIVE FOR ASSISTANCE AND RELIEF EVERYWHERE INC.

151 ELLIS ST NE FL 1
ATLANTA, GA 303032437
Phone: 404-681-2552
Fax: –
Web: www.care.org

CEO: Helene Gayle
CFO: Vickie J Barrow-Klien
HR: Derek Lindars
FYE: June 30
Type: Private

The Cooperative for Assistance and Relief Everywhere (CARE) strives to be the beginning of the end of poverty. The organization works to reduce poverty in about 85 countries by helping communities in areas such as health education economic development emergency relief and agriculture. CARE supports more than 1100 projects to combat poverty. It also operates a small economic activity development (SEAD) unit that supports moneymaking activities. Through SEAD CARE provides technical training and savings and loans programs to help people — particularly women — open or expand small businesses. CARE was founded in 1945 to give aid to WWII survivors.

	Annual Growth	06/04	06/05	06/08	06/11	06/13
Sales ($ mil.)	–	–	(1,545.6)	713.6	589.7	492.0
Net income ($ mil.)	–	–	–	40.1	10.2	(18.8)
Market value ($ mil.)	–	–	–	–	–	–
Employees	–	–	–	–	–	10,000

COOPERATIVE REGIONS OF ORGANIC PRODUCER POOLS

1 ORGANIC WAY
LA FARGE, WI 546396604
Phone: 608-625-2602
Fax: –
Web: www.organicvalley.coop

CEO: George Siemon
CFO: Mike Bedessem
HR: –
FYE: December 31
Type: Private

Cooperative Regions of Organic Producers Pool (CROPP) is the largest organic farming cooperative in North America. The group's 1840-plus farmer/members produce the co-op's Organic Valley Family of Farms and Organic Prairie brands of fluid and shelf-stable milk along with cheese butter and soy milk. Beyond the dairy barn the cooperative also offers organic citrus juices produce eggs meats and poultry. Its Organic Valley products are sold by food retailers and its ingredients are marketed to other organic food processors. Wisconsin-headquartered CROPP's farmer/members are located throughout North America and Australia. The co-op was founded in 1988.

	Annual Growth	12/05	12/06	12/07	12/08	12/10
Sales ($ mil.)	(19.1%)	–	–	1,171.4	527.8	619.7
Net income ($ mil.)	4341.1%	–	–	0.0	3.8	12.1
Market value ($ mil.)	–	–	–	–	–	–
Employees	–	–	–	–	–	764

COORSTEK INC.

16000 Table Mountain Pkwy.
Golden CO 80403
Phone: 303-271-7000
Fax: 303-271-7009
Web: www.coorstek.com

CEO: John K Coors
CFO: –
HR: –
FYE: December 31
Type: Private

CoorsTek is not your next-generation brewery. It might have the same lineage but the company gets its buzz instead from producing advanced technical ceramics precision-machined metals and engineered plastics. Its materials are used in automotive components energy equipment medical devices and high-performance machinery among other products. CoorsTek also offers materials testing analytical chemistry custom manufacturing and precision machining among other services. The company operates more than 40 facilities across the globe (primarily in North America and Europe). Once a part of the Adolph Coors Company (now MillerCoors) it is owned by CEO John Coors and his family.

COPART, INC.

14185 Dallas Parkway, Suite 300
Dallas, TX 75154
Phone: 972 391-5000
Fax: –
Web: www.copart.com

NMS: CPRT
CEO: A Jayson Adair
CFO: Jeffrey Liaw
HR: –
FYE: July 31
Type: Public

What happens after cars are totaled in wrecks or natural disasters? How about stolen cars recovered after the insurance settlement? Perhaps Copart happens; it takes junked cars and auctions them for insurers auto dealers and car rental agencies. The buyers are mostly rebuilders licensed dismantlers and used-car dealers and exporters. It's replaced live auctions with Internet auctions using a platform known as Virtual Bidding Third Generation (VB3 for short). Copart also provides services such as towing and storage to buyers and other salvage companies as well as an online database and search engine for used parts. Copart serves customers throughout North America Europe the Middle East and Brazil.

	Annual Growth	07/11	07/12	07/13	07/14	07/15
Sales ($ mil.)	7.1%	872.2	924.2	1,046.4	1,163.5	1,146.1
Net income ($ mil.)	7.2%	166.4	182.1	180.0	178.7	219.8
Market value ($ mil.)	(4.6%)	5,220.8	2,854.9	3,906.3	4,010.8	4,329.2
Employees	10.9%	2,825	2,981	3,875	4,179	4,267

CORAM LLC

555 17th St. Ste. 1500
Denver CO 80202
Phone: 303-292-4973
Fax: 303-298-0043
Web: www.coramhc.com

CEO: –
CFO: –
HR: Dawn Foley
FYE: December 31
Type: Subsidiary

Coram infuses healing for its patients. The company also known as Coram Specialty Infusion Services provides intravenous administration of drugs as well as specialty pharmaceuticals distribution through CoramRx. With more than 85 branches nationwide Coram administers infusion therapies such as parenteral nutrition antibiotics pain medications and hemophilia treatments. It serves patients in their homes and through more than 70 ambulatory infusion sites (located inside some Coram branches). The company also supplies patients with home respiratory equipment. Its CoramRx unit distributes to patients the high-cost drugs needed for serious diseases. The company is a subsidiary of Apria Healthcare.

CORBIS CORPORATION

710 2nd Ave. Ste. 200
Seattle WA 98104
Phone: 206-373-6000
Fax: 206-373-6100
Web: www.corbis.com

CEO: Gary Shenk
CFO: Joe Schick
HR: –
FYE: December 31
Type: Private

If a picture is worth a thousand words then Corbis has lots to say. The firm's archive of more than 100 million images is one of the largest in the world. Corbis licenses its images — contemporary and archival photography art illustrations and footage — for commercial and editorial use in print and electronic media. Customers can find and license images via the company's branded websites which include Corbis.com CorbisMotion.com and Veer.com. Corbis also offers artist representation (matching photographers with assignments) and rights services (securing rights to images controlled by third parties) through its GreenLight unit. Microsoft co-founder Bill Gates owns Corbis which he founded in 1989.

CORCEPT THERAPEUTICS INC

149 Commonwealth Drive
Menlo Park, CA 94025
Phone: 650 327-3270
Fax: –
Web: www.corcept.com

NAS: CORT
CEO: Joseph K. Belanoff
CFO: Charles Robb
HR: –
FYE: December 31
Type: Public

Corcept Therapeutics wants to help people who are beyond blue. The biotechnology firm is exploring treatments that regulate the presence of cortisol a steroid hormone associated with some psychiatric and metabolic disorders. Its sole commercial product Korlym is a version of the compound mifepristone (commonly known as RU-486 or the "abortion pill") used to regulate release patterns of cortisol. The drug is approved for use in patients with Cushing's Syndrome a metabolic disorder caused by high levels of cortisol in the blood. The company is also developing mifepristone for treatment of patients with psychotic depression.

	Annual Growth	12/10	12/11	12/12	12/13	12/14
Sales ($ mil.)	183.4%	–	–	3.3	10.4	26.6
Net income ($ mil.)	–	(26.0)	(32.4)	(38.0)	(46.0)	(31.4)
Market value ($ mil.)	(6.1%)	391.4	346.8	145.0	325.5	304.2
Employees	27.3%	35	36	69	77	92

CORDIS CORPORATION

430 Route 22 East
Bridgewater NJ 08807
Phone: 908-541-4100
Fax: 800-997-1122
Web: www.cordis.com

CEO: –
CFO: –
HR: –
FYE: December 31
Type: Subsidiary

Cordis is a hearty subsidiary of Johnson & Johnson. The company develops products to treat circulatory system diseases including congestive heart failure and cerebral aneurysms. Cordis is divided into five units: Cordis Cardiology focuses on cardiovascular disease diagnosis and treatment; Cordis Endovascular develops devices for endovascular and liver diseases; Biosense Webster develops medical sensor and electrophysiology technology for cardiovascular use; Conor Medsystems provides vascular drug delivery technologies; and the Biologics Delivery Systems division makes cardiac mapping equipment used to improve the delivery of biological therapies. Cordis was founded in 1959 and bought by Johnson & Johnson in 1996.

CORE CONSTRUCTION INC.

3036 E GREENWAY RD
PHOENIX, AZ 850324414
Phone: 602-494-0800
Fax: –
Web: www.coreconstruct.com

CEO: –
CFO: –
HR: –
FYE: December 31
Type: Private

CORE Construction fits into the core clique of contractors in the southwestern US. The company formerly Targent General is one of the top contractors in the region; it also has offices in Florida and Illinois. CORE offers construction management general contracting and design/build services for municipal educational health care office residential retail sports institutional and industrial projects. It has worked on projects as diverse as Phoenix's Chase Field Ballpark Dodge Theatre and Lower Buckeye Jail. German immigrant Otto Baum founded the company in 1937.

	Annual Growth	12/09	12/10	12/11	12/12	12/13
Sales ($ mil.)	(3.5%)	–	244.3	206.4	162.3	219.3
Net income ($ mil.)	–	–	–	–	–	–
Market value ($ mil.)	–	–	–	0.0	0.0	0.0
Employees	–	–	–	–	–	60

CORE MARK HOLDING CO INC   NMS: CORE

395 Oyster Point Boulevard, Suite 415
South San Francisco, CA 94080
Phone: 650 589-9445
Fax: –
Web: www.core-mark.com

CEO: Thomas B. Perkins
CFO: Stacy Loretz-Congdon
HR: –
FYE: December 31
Type: Public

Smokes and snacks are at the center of Core-Mark Holding's cosmos. The company distributes packaged consumables (including cigarettes and other tobacco products candy snacks grocery items perishables nonalcoholic beverages and health and beauty aids) to about 31000 convenience stores; mass merchandisers; supermarkets; and drug liquor and specialty retailers. Cigarettes and other tobacco products are its top sellers generating about three-quarters of net sales. Through nearly 30 distribution facilities Core-Mark serves customers in all 50 US states and five Canadian provinces. Its 10 biggest clients (which include Couche-Tard and CST Brands) contribute about 35% of sales.

	Annual Growth	12/10	12/11	12/12	12/13	12/14
Sales ($ mil.)	9.1%	7,266.8	8,114.9	8,892.4	9,767.6	10,280.1
Net income ($ mil.)	24.6%	17.7	26.2	33.9	41.6	42.7
Market value ($ mil.)	14.9%	821.4	914.0	1,092.8	1,752.5	1,429.4
Employees	7.8%	4,399	4,852	5,225	5,617	5,933

CORE MOLDING TECHNOLOGIES INC   ASE: CMT

800 Manor Park Drive
Columbus, OH 43228-0183
Phone: 614 870-5000
Fax: –
Web: www.coremt.com

CEO: Kevin L. Barnett
CFO: John P. Zimmer
HR: Dorothy Roush
FYE: December 31
Type: Public

The core business of Core Molding Technologies is fiberglass reinforced plastic and sheet molding composite materials. Through compression molding sprayup hand layup and vacuum-assisted resin infusion molding the company makes truck components (air deflectors fenders hoods) and personal watercraft parts (decks hulls and engine hatches). It divides its operations into two segments: Products and Tooling. Navistar International accounts for one-third sales and other major customers include heavy-duty truck manufacturers Volvo and PACCAR. The company's sales are confined to North America.

	Annual Growth	12/10	12/11	12/12	12/13	12/14
Sales ($ mil.)	15.0%	100.3	143.4	162.5	144.1	175.2
Net income ($ mil.)	41.1%	2.4	10.5	8.2	6.9	9.6
Market value ($ mil.)	24.9%	43.5	61.2	50.0	103.6	105.8
Employees	10.1%	1,014	1,596	1,373	1,458	1,490

CORESITE REALTY CORP.   NYS: COR

1001 17th Street, Suite 500
Denver, CO 80202
Phone: 866 777-2673
Fax: –
Web: www.coresite.com

CEO: Thomas M. (Tom) Ray
CFO: Jeffrey S. (Jeff) Finnin
HR: –
FYE: December 31
Type: Public

CoreSite Realty leases data center space to those with data center needs. The real estate investment trust (REIT) owns develops and operates these specialized facilities which require enough power security and network interconnection to handle often complex IT operations. Its property portfolio includes about 15 operating data center facilities with more space under development. These properties comprise more than 2.7 million rentable sq. ft. and are located in major US tech hubs including Silicon Valley. Tenants include enterprise organizations communications service providers media and content companies government agencies and schools. The REIT has grown along with demand for data center space.

	Annual Growth	12/10	12/11	12/12	12/13	12/14
Sales ($ mil.)	63.3%	38.4	172.8	206.9	234.8	272.4
Net income ($ mil.)	–	(10.7)	(10.8)	5.0	18.8	22.8
Market value ($ mil.)	30.1%	296.8	387.7	601.8	700.4	849.6
Employees	18.6%	179	224	316	363	354

CORESOURCE INC.

400 Field Dr.
Lake Forest IL 60045
Phone: 847-604-9200
Fax: 847-615-3900
Web: www.coresource.com

CEO: –
CFO: Clare Smith
HR: Richard A Btten
FYE: December 31
Type: Subsidiary

CoreSource is a third-party administrator (TPA) of employee benefits programs. As a TPA it manages the health insurance benefits of self-insured employers and their workers throughout the US. Among other services the company handles claims provides access to nationwide and specialty provider networks and manages a variety of ancillary programs such pharmacy benefits flexible spending accounts and COBRA administration. It serves more than 900 clients mostly midsized and large corporations representing about 1.4 million employee members. Other clients include public retiree plans and state high-risk pools. CoreSource is a subsidiary of insurance provider Trustmark Mutual.

CORGENIX MEDICAL CORP.   NBB: CONX

11575 Main Street
Broomfield, CO 80020
Phone: 303 457-4345
Fax: –
Web: www.corgenix.com

CEO: Jim Widergren
CFO: –
HR: –
FYE: June 30
Type: Public

Corgenix Medical wants to take a peek inside you. The company makes in vitro diagnostics to detect autoimmune liver and vascular diseases. Its line of more than 50 diagnostics are used by reference labs hospitals and clinics researchers and other medical facilities around the world. It sells directly to customers in the US and the UK and through independent distributors elsewhere. To expand its product line Corgenix Medical has released an aspirin resistance diagnostic and it is developing new tests to diagnose fibromyalgia (pain disorder) and cardiovascular disease. It is also developing tests that detect potential bioterrorism agents using grant funding from the National Institutes of Health.

	Annual Growth	06/10	06/11	06/12	06/13	06/14
Sales ($ mil.)	7.5%	8.3	7.9	9.3	10.2	11.0
Net income ($ mil.)	253.0%	0.0	(0.4)	(0.6)	0.3	0.4
Market value ($ mil.)	30.7%	5.8	5.3	5.5	9.5	16.9
Employees	3.6%	40	40	48	46	46

CORINTHIAN COLLEGES, INC. NMS: COCO

6 Hutton Centre Drive, Suite 400
Santa Ana, CA 92707
Phone: 714 427-3000
Fax: –
Web: www.cci.edu

CEO: Jack D Massimino
CFO: Robert C Owen
HR: –
FYE: June 30
Type: Public

Corinthian Colleges believes more in marketable skills than in ivory towers. It was one of the largest for-profit post-secondary education companies in North America focused on career-oriented students. It had more than 80000 students enrolled in about 110 schools in some 25 US states as well as in Canada. Corinthian's institutions operate under the Everest College WyoTech (for automotive training) and Heald College brand names. Under pressure from state and federal government investigations into its practices and finances the company is winding down operations by selling off campuses. It has identified buyers for most of its schools.

	Annual Growth	06/09	06/10	06/11	06/12	06/13
Sales ($ mil.)	5.2%	1,307.8	1,763.8	1,868.8	1,605.5	1,600.2
Net income ($ mil.)	–	68.8	146.0	(111.2)	(10.2)	(1.7)
Market value ($ mil.)	(39.7%)	1,459.1	848.9	367.1	249.1	193.0
Employees	8.2%	11,100	15,900	16,600	15,200	15,200

CORMEDIX INC ASE: CRMD

1430 U.S. Highway 206, Suite 200
Bedminster, NJ 07921
Phone: 908 517-9500
Fax: 908 429-4307
Web: www.cormedix.com

CEO: Randy D. Milby
CFO: Harry O'Grady
HR: –
FYE: December 31
Type: Public

CorMedix believes the way to a healthy heart is through the kidney — and vice versa. The biopharmaceutical company develops medications for the treatment and prevention of cardiorenal disease (kidney and related cardiac dysfunctions) including a liquid and gel used to prevent infection and clotting that can occur during intravenous treatments such as dialysis and chemotherapy. Also in an agreement with Shiva Biomedical the company is developing a new formulation of the drug deferipone to be used in the prevention of kidney damage in high-risk patients. The company expects to market its products worldwide. CorMedix controlled by a group of its officers went public in early 2010.

	Annual Growth	12/10	12/11	12/12	12/13	12/14
Sales ($ mil.)	9359.0%	–	–	–	0.0	0.2
Net income ($ mil.)	–	(10.9)	(6.7)	(3.4)	(9.1)	(20.5)
Market value ($ mil.)	1.2%	40.9	6.3	16.2	27.9	42.9
Employees	(4.5%)	6	5	–	2	5

CORNERSTONE BANCORP OTC: CTOT

1670 E. Main St.
Easley SC 29640
Phone: 864-306-1444
Fax: 864-306-1473
Web: www.cornerstonenatlbank.com

CEO: –
CFO: Jennifer M Champagne
HR: –
FYE: December 31
Type: Public

Cornerstone Bancorp has laid the groundwork for three banking branches in northwestern South Carolina. The institution is the holding company for Cornerstone National Bank which offers traditional products and services including checking and savings accounts money market accounts CDs and credit cards. Commercial real estate loans comprise the largest portion of its lending portfolio; other offerings include residential mortgages business and industrial loans real estate construction and consumer loans. Cornerstone National Bank has three offices in Easley Greenville and Powdersville South Carolina. Cornerstone Bancorp also has an insurance agency that operates as Crescent Financial Services.

CORNERSTONE ONDEMAND, INC. NMS: CSOD

1601 Cloverfield Blvd., Suite 620 South
Santa Monica, CA 90404
Phone: 310 752-0200
Fax: –
Web: www.cornerstoneondemand.com

CEO: Adam L. Miller
CFO: Perry A. Wallack
HR: –
FYE: December 31
Type: Public

In the demanding world of developing workers' skills Cornerstone OnDemand stands ready. The company provides on-demand workplace learning tools in a variety of subjects including enterprise social networking performance management and succession planning. Its training programs are meant to improve employee performance communication and collaboration as well as foster professional development and assess employee skills. Its cloud-based software suite includes the Recruiting Cloud the Learning Cloud Performance Cloud and Extended Enterprise Cloud. The company also offers tools for analytics and reporting and e-learning content aggregation as well as its specialty programs Cornerstone Small Business and Cornerstone for salesforce.

	Annual Growth	12/10	12/11	12/12	12/13	12/14
Sales ($ mil.)	56.7%	43.7	73.0	117.9	185.1	263.6
Net income ($ mil.)	–	(48.4)	(63.9)	(31.4)	(40.4)	(64.9)
Market value ($ mil.)	24.5%	–	981.8	1,589.5	2,869.6	1,894.7
Employees	42.8%	327	507	750	987	1,361

CORNING, INC. NYS: GLW

One Riverfront Plaza
Corning, NY 14831
Phone: 607 974-9000
Fax: –
Web: www.corning.com

CEO: –
CFO: R. Tony Tripeny
HR: Christine Pambianchi
FYE: December 31
Type: Public

The source of Corning's revenue and profits transparently obvious: it's glass. Once known for its kitchenware and lab products the company manufactures glass ceramic and other components for a variety of products in the consumer electronics telecommunications automotive and life sciences industries among others. Its products include substrates for flat-panel displays and computer monitors optical fiber and cable substrates and filters for automotive emissions control products labware and scientific equipment and glass and optical materials for a wide range of industries. Corning has about 90 manufacturing and processing facilities across more than a dozen countries. About 60% of its sales come from the Asia/Pacific region.

	Annual Growth	12/11	12/12	12/13	12/14	12/15
Sales ($ mil.)	3.7%	7,890.0	8,012.0	7,819.0	9,715.0	9,111.0
Net income ($ mil.)	(16.9%)	2,805.0	1,728.0	1,961.0	2,472.0	1,339.0
Market value ($ mil.)	8.9%	14,667.4	14,260.6	20,136.6	25,910.9	20,656.4
Employees	5.5%	28,800	28,700	30,400	34,600	35,700

CORPORATE OFFICE PROPERTIES TRUST NYS: OFC

6711 Columbia Gateway Drive, Suite 300
Columbia, MD 21046
Phone: 443 285-5400
Fax: –
Web: www.copt.com

CEO: Roger A. Waesche
CFO: Anthony Mifsud
HR: Holly Edington
FYE: December 31
Type: Public

The name says "corporate" but it's really about the government. A real estate investment trust (REIT) Corporate Office Properties Trust owns and manages some 175 properties totaling some 17 million sq. ft. of leasable space. The REIT focuses on large suburban business parks near federal government hubs and military installations. More than 85% of its office space is located in in the Greater DC/Baltimore regions; other major markets include Northern Virginia San Antonio and Hunstville Alabama. Subsidiaries provide property management construction and development and HVAC services. Founded in 1998 the REIT's largest tenants are the US Government and defense information technology concerns.

	Annual Growth	12/10	12/11	12/12	12/13	12/14
Sales ($ mil.)	1.0%	564.5	556.8	528.0	523.4	586.5
Net income ($ mil.)	(1.5%)	42.8	(117.7)	21.0	93.7	40.3
Market value ($ mil.)	(5.1%)	3,259.3	1,982.6	2,329.5	2,209.2	2,645.7
Employees	(2.1%)	411	428	384	380	378

CORPORATE TRAVEL CONSULTANTS INC

450 E 22ND ST STE 100
LOMBARD, IL 601486175
Phone: 630-691-9100
Fax: –
Web: www.corptrav.com

CEO: –
CFO: –
HR: Angel Wagner
FYE: December 31
Type: Private

Corporate Travel Consultants (CorpTrav) brings order to the chaos of globe-trotting go-getters and far-flung meetings on foreign soil. The company offers Internet-based booking reporting compliance and management tools through CorpTrav On-line as well as meeting and incentive travel arrangements. Its online tools allow customers to check health advisories travel alerts and strike updates for planned destinations. CorpTrav has offices in Chicago Dallas New York and San Francisco. The agency partners with GlobalStar to provide global support and service to travelers. CEO Bonnie Lorefice founded CorpTrav in 1976.

	Annual Growth	12/08	12/09	12/10	12/12	12/14
Sales ($ mil.)	13.7%	–	116.9	135.8	209.4	222.4
Net income ($ mil.)	31.8%	–	–	0.5	1.9	1.6
Market value ($ mil.)	–	–	–	–	–	–
Employees	–	–	–	–	–	120

CORPORATION FOR PUBLIC BROADCASTING

401 9TH ST NW STE 200
WASHINGTON, DC 200042129
Phone: 202-879-9600
Fax: –
Web: www.cpb.org

CEO: –
CFO: William P Tayman
HR: Deborah Carr
FYE: September 30
Type: Private

This organization is made possible by a grant from the federal government and by support from viewers like you. The Corporation for Public Broadcasting (CPB) is a private not-for-profit corporation created by the federal government that receives appropriations from Congress to help fund programming for more than 1000 locally-owned public TV and radio stations. CPB-funded programs are distributed by the Public Broadcasting Service (PBS) National Public Radio (NPR) and Public Radio International (PRI). Funds are also used for research on media and education. CPB was created by Congress in 1967.

	Annual Growth	09/06	09/07	09/08	09/09	09/13
Sales ($ mil.)	(1.9%)	–	–	–	482.5	446.3
Net income ($ mil.)	–	–	–	–	0.0	(18.8)
Market value ($ mil.)	–	–	–	–	–	–
Employees	–	–	–	–	–	99

CORRECTIONS CORPORATION OF AMERICA

NYS: CXW

10 Burton Hills Blvd.
Nashville, TN 37215
Phone: 615 263-3000
Fax: –
Web: www.cca.com

CEO: Damon T. Hininger
CFO: David M. (Dave) Garfinkle
HR: Brian D. Collins
FYE: December 31
Type: Public

Corrections Corporation of America (CCA) has locked up a big share of the private prison market. The company operates about 65 correctional detention and juvenile facilities with a capacity of some 85000 beds in about 20 states (including Washington DC). CCA contracts with federal state and local authorities to manage the facilities 50 of which are company-owned. CCA also owns two facilities that are managed by other companies. Federal correctional and detention authorities account for about 45% of CCA's sales. The company also provides rehabilitation education programs health care food services recreational programs and religious services for inmates of its facilities.

	Annual Growth	12/10	12/11	12/12	12/13	12/14
Sales ($ mil.)	(0.4%)	1,675.0	1,735.6	1,759.9	1,694.3	1,646.9
Net income ($ mil.)	5.5%	157.2	162.5	156.8	300.8	195.0
Market value ($ mil.)	9.7%	2,926.1	2,378.5	4,141.6	3,744.6	4,243.2
Employees	(4.7%)	17,000	16,750	17,000	15,400	14,040

CORSAIR COMPONENTS INC.

46221 Landing Pkwy.
Fremont CA 94538
Phone: 510-657-8747
Fax: 510-657-8748
Web: www.corsair.com

CEO: –
CFO: –
HR: –
FYE: December 31
Type: Private

Hardcore gaming requires hardcore hardware and that's where Corsair Components comes into play. Through subsidiaries Corsair Components is a designer and supplier of high-performance components and peripherals for the PC gaming market. Its two product segments which each generate about half of sales include high-performance memory components (DRAM modules USB flash drives) and gaming components and peripherals (power supply units computer cooling units gaming keyboards and mice headsets and cases). Corsair distributes its products in about 60 countries across the globe under its own name as well as under the Dominator and XMS brands among others. It generates more than half its sales from Europe.

CORT BUSINESS SERVICES CORPORATION

15000 Conference Center Dr. Ste. 440
Chantilly VA 20151
Phone: 703-968-8500
Fax: 703-968-8502
Web: www.cort.com

CEO: –
CFO: –
HR: –
FYE: December 31
Type: Subsidiary

If you need to furnish an office or temporary residence CORT Business Services will come a-courtin'. A subsidiary of Wesco Financial (which is owned by Berkshire Hathaway) CORT is a major renter of office and residential furniture along with trade show and special event furnishings. Small businesses professionals and owners and operators of apartment communities rent the furniture and equipment from about 80 US locations. CORT which offers such well-known brands as HON Lane Bassett Chromcraft United Chair and National Office Furniture also offers space planning and design services and sells previously rented furniture.

CORTLAND BANCORP (OH)

NBB: CLDB

194 West Main Street
Cortland, OH 44410
Phone: 330 637-8040
Fax: –
Web: www.cortland-banks.com

CEO: James M Gasior
CFO: David J Lucido
HR: –
FYE: December 31
Type: Public

Cortland Bancorp is the place to keep your bucks in the Buckeye State. Cortland Bancorp is the holding company for Cortland Savings and Banking Company (aka Cortland Banks) a community-oriented institution serving northeastern Ohio from about 15 banking locations. Cortland Banks offers standard banking services including checking and savings accounts debit cards and business and consumer loans. More than half of Cortland's loan portfolio is composed of commercial mortgages. Other offerings include discount brokerage and trust services.

	Annual Growth	12/10	12/11	12/12	12/13	12/14
Assets ($ mil.)	3.3%	500.3	519.8	582.2	556.9	568.9
Net income ($ mil.)	4.3%	3.3	4.1	2.9	1.8	3.9
Market value ($ mil.)	31.3%	24.0	30.8	43.9	46.4	71.3
Employees	0.6%	156	166	179	157	160

CORVEL CORP.

NMS: CRVL

2010 Main Street, Suite 600
Irvine, CA 92614
Phone: 949-851-1473
Fax: –
Web: www.corvel.com

CEO: V. Gordon Clemons
CFO: Scott R. McCloud
HR: –
FYE: March 31
Type: Public

CorVel has carved out a niche providing medical cost containment for US workers' compensation programs auto insurers and group health plans. CorVel helps insurers third-party administrators and self-insured employers keep down costs associated with workers' compensation and other medical claims and to get employees back on the job as soon as is practicable. Among other things CorVel reviews medical bills to make sure they are in line with state fee schedules using its automated online MedCheck software. It also maintains a health provider network and provides case management and vocational rehabilitation services. Clients access CorVel's range of services through its CareMC web portal.

	Annual Growth	03/11	03/12	03/13	03/14	03/15
Sales ($ mil.)	6.7%	380.7	412.7	429.3	478.8	492.6
Net income ($ mil.)	3.8%	24.7	26.6	26.7	34.4	28.6
Market value ($ mil.)	(10.3%)	1,076.9	807.8	1,002.2	1,007.7	696.8
Employees	4.4%	2,986	3,145	3,172	33,800	3,548

COSCO FIRE PROTECTION INC.

29222 RANCHO VIEJO RD # 205
SAN JUAN CAPISTRANO, CA 926767041
Phone: 714-974-8770
Fax: –
Web: www.coscofire.com

CEO: Keith R Fielding
CFO: –
HR: –
FYE: December 31
Type: Private

COSCO Fire Protection designs installs and inspects automatic fire sprinkler systems as well as fire alarm and detection systems. The company also designs and installs fire suppression systems. Its target customers include owners of office buildings and manufacturing facilities; hospitals and extended-care facilities; schools and universities; retail shopping malls; and government complexes and military facilities. COSCO operates in the western US (from offices in Alaska California Nevada Oregon and Washington). The company was founded in 1959 and is owned by Consolidated Fire Protection which is itself a subsidiary of German fire protection firm Minimax.

	Annual Growth	12/09	12/10	12/11	12/12	12/13
Sales ($ mil.)	4.0%	–	106.4	111.4	115.7	119.7
Net income ($ mil.)	29.4%	–	–	3.7	5.0	6.2
Market value ($ mil.)	–	–	–	–	–	–
Employees	–	–	–	–	–	601

COSI INC

NAS: COSI

294 Washington Street, Suite 510
Boston, MA 02108
Phone: 857-415-5000
Fax: –
Web: www.getcosi.com

CEO: Rj Dourney
CFO: Scott Carlock
HR: –
FYE: December 29
Type: Public

Cosi's recipe calls for one part coffee house one part sandwich shop and one part cocktail bar. The company operates and franchises about 125 eclectic Così cafés in roughly 20 states offering premium and specialty coffees and made-to-order sandwiches. Its menu also features breakfast items (including its bagel-inspired Squagels) salads soups and desserts. Most of the company's restaurants also offer dinner and drinks after 5 p.m. while its Così Downtown units (primarily located in non-residential business districts) close in the evening. Cosi also offers delivery and catering services. About 70 of the locations are company-owned while the rest are franchised.

	Annual Growth	12/10*	01/12*	12/12	12/13	12/14
Sales ($ mil.)	(8.2%)	109.7	102.1	98.0	86.3	77.8
Net income ($ mil.)	–	(3.1)	(6.5)	(4.4)	(11.4)	(16.6)
Market value ($ mil.)	7.2%	45.2	27.0	29.8	66.0	59.8
Employees	(4.1%)	2,038	1,953	1,820	1,674	1,725

*Fiscal year change

COSINE COMMUNICATIONS INC.

PINK SHEETS: COSN

61 E. Main
Los Gatos CA 95030
Phone: 408-399-6494
Fax: 201-767-1903
Web: www.crestron.com

CEO: Terry Gibson
CFO: –
HR: –
FYE: December 31
Type: Public

CoSine Communications is trying to switch businesses. The company was a manufacturer of switches and software that telecom service providers used to manage their Internet protocol networks but the company shuttered its operations and ceased its support services in 2004. CoSine had agreed to be acquired by telecom equipment maker Tut Systems but the deal fell through in 2005. CoSine is seeking to acquire an operating business.

COSKATA INC.

4575 Weaver Pkwy. Ste. 100
Warrenville IL 60555
Phone: 630-657-5800
Fax: 630-657-5801
Web: www.coskata.com

CEO: William Roe
CFO: David Blair
HR: –
FYE: December 31
Type: Private

Coskata is looking to turn biowaste into biotreasure. Through a proprietary process Coskata produces cellulosic ethanol from plant-derived biomass agricultural residues municipal wastes and other feedstock. The company which is currently developing and refining its production technology operates a semi-commercial facility in Pennsylvania and intends to begin producing fuel-grade ethanol on a fully commercial scale at a future plant in Alabama. In an effort to secure funding for its new plant Coskata filed a $100 million IPO in late 2011. It has also received financing from the USDA for the construction of the facility.

COSMOCOM INC.

121 Broad Hollow Rd.
Melville NY 11747
Phone: 631-940-4200
Fax: 631-940-4500
Web: www.cosmocom.com

CEO: ARI Sonesh
CFO: –
HR: –
FYE: December 31
Type: Subsidiary

This company has universal designs for its call center software. CosmoCom develops applications that let businesses interact with their customers worldwide through a variety of media channels. The company's CosmoCall Universe program tracks and manages customers' phone calls voice mails faxes chat room sessions and e-mails and ties the various media together through the Internet. The company also provides related services such as consulting support training maintenance and installation. In 2011 Enghouse acquired CosmoCom for about $20 million in cash.

COSTA DEL MAR SUNGLASSES INC.

2361 Mason Ave. Ste. 100
Daytona FL 32117
Phone: 386-274-4000
Fax: 386-274-4001
Web: www.costadelmar.com

CEO: –
CFO: –
HR: –
FYE: December 31
Type: Subsidiary

Costa Del Mar Sunglasses helps its customers keep their eyes on the prize. The company develops makes and markets upscale polarized sunglasses designed to reduce glare for fisherman and enhance vision during water sports such as kayaking skiing and sailing. Costa Del Mar sells its namesake eyewear to about 3000 US retailers including department stores sporting goods shops and optical and sunglass specialty outlets. It also sells its products online. Its eyewear which comes in some three-dozen styles is backed with a lifetime warranty. The sunglass maker is a subsidiary of the A.T. Cross Company which acquired Costa Del Mar Sunglasses in 2003 and made it part of its Cross Optical Group.

COSTAR GROUP, INC.

NMS: CSGP

1331 L Street, NW
Washington, DC 20005
Phone: 202 346-6500
Fax: 877 739-0486
Web: www.costar.com

CEO: Andrew C. Florance
CFO: Scott Wheeler
HR: Donna Tanenbaumv
FYE: December 31
Type: Public

CoStar has all the dirt on the commercial real estate industry. A provider of commercial real estate information CoStar has a proprietary database of some 4 million properties in the US the UK and France. The database contains information on more than 10 billion square feet of sale and lease listings. It also has more than 12 million digital images of buildings floor plans and maps. Its hundreds of data fields include location ownership and tenant names. CoStar additionally offers marketing and analytic services. Clients include government agencies real estate brokerages real estate investment trusts (REITs) and property owners and managers. Most of CoStar's sales come from subscription fees.

	Annual Growth	12/10	12/11	12/12	12/13	12/14
Sales ($ mil.)	26.3%	226.3	251.7	349.9	440.9	575.9
Net income ($ mil.)	35.6%	13.3	14.7	9.9	29.7	44.9
Market value ($ mil.)	33.6%	1,860.2	2,156.6	2,888.3	5,965.3	5,934.6
Employees	15.2%	1,389	1,514	1,965	2,046	2,444

COSTCO WHOLESALE CORP

NMS: COST

999 Lake Drive
Issaquah, WA 98027
Phone: 425 313-8100
Fax: –
Web: www.costco.com

CEO: W. Craig Jelinek
CFO: Richard A. Galanti
HR: Franz E. Lazarus
FYE: August 30
Type: Public

Wal-Mart isn't a behemoth in every business. Operating more than 680 membership warehouse stores Costco is the nation's largest wholesale club operator (ahead of Wal-Mart's SAM'S CLUB). Primarily under the Costco Wholesale banner it serves more than 71 million members in 40-plus US states and Puerto Rico as well as in Canada Mexico the UK Japan South Korea Taiwan and Spain. Stores offer discount prices on an average of about 4000 products (many in bulk packaging) ranging from alcoholic beverages and appliances to fresh food pharmaceuticals and tires. Certain club memberships also offer products and services such as car and home insurance mortgage and real estate services and travel packages.

	Annual Growth	08/11*	09/12	09/13*	08/14	08/15
Sales ($ mil.)	6.9%	88,915.0	99,137.0	105,156.0	112,640.0	116,199.0
Net income ($ mil.)	12.9%	1,462.0	1,709.0	2,039.0	2,058.0	2,377.0
Market value ($ mil.)	16.0%	33,814.3	42,862.4	48,993.7	53,027.2	61,291.4
Employees	5.7%	164,000	174,000	184,000	195,000	205,000

*Fiscal year change

COTTMAN TRANSMISSION SYSTEMS LLC.

201 Gibraltar Ste. 150
Horsham PA 19044
Phone: 215-643-5885
Fax: 404-321-5483
Web: www.marineproductscorp.com

CEO: –
CFO: Jim Gregory
HR: –
FYE: December 31
Type: Private

Cottman Transmission Systems wants to make sure you have a choice of forward and backward gears in your car or truck. The company franchises about 120 transmission repair outlets throughout the US as well as two locations in Canada. Besides transmission work Cottman provides cooling and electrical system repairs as well as other maintenance services. Cottman is being combined with sister company AAMCO Transmissions which provides similar services at more than 900 franchised locations under the AAMCO name. Cottman and AAMCO are units of American Driveline Systems a holding company controlled by investment firm American Capital.

COTTON INCORPORATED

6399 WESTON PKWY
CARY, NC 275132314
Phone: 919-677-9228
Fax: –
Web: www.cms-cottoninc.cottontest.com

CEO: J Berrye Worsham III
CFO: David N Byrd
HR: –
FYE: December 31
Type: Private

Cotton Incorporated battles both boll weevils and synthetic fibers. The organization bolsters the demand and profitability of the US cotton industry through its research and marketing efforts. To the public Cotton Incorporated is known for its white-on-brown "Seal of Cotton" logo and its advertising slogan "The fabric of our lives." Founded in 1970 Cotton Incorporated is funded by US growers of upland cotton cotton importers and cotton-product makers. Its board consists of representatives from each cotton-growing state — all of whom are cotton producers — and is overseen by the US Department of Agriculture.

	Annual Growth	12/02	12/03	12/04	12/05	12/13
Sales ($ mil.)	–	–	0.0	68.2	72.6	81.1
Net income ($ mil.)	41.1%	–	–	0.2	0.5	5.5
Market value ($ mil.)	–	–	–	–	–	–
Employees	–	–	–	–	–	157

COTY, INC.

NYS: COTY

350 Fifth Avenue
New York, NY 10118
Phone: 212 389-7300
Fax: –
Web: www.coty.com

CEO: Lambertus J. H. (Bart) Becht
CFO: Patrice de Talhouet
HR: Gtraudmarie Lacassagne
FYE: June 30
Type: Public

Sarah Jessica Parker Beyoncé and Lady Gaga are just a few of the celebs to promote Coty one of the world's leading makers of fragrances and beauty products for men and women. Coty has turned heads since François Coty created his first perfume La Rose Jacqueminot in 1904. Its lineup ranges from moderately priced scents sold globally by mass retailers to prestige fragrances and nail polishes found in department stores. Coty's brands include adidas philosophy Rimmel and Sally Hansen. Its prestige perfume labels are led by Calvin Klein. The German investment firm Joh. A. Benckiser SE bought Coty from Pfizer in 1992 to steer its fragrance and cosmetics business. Coty went public in 2013.

	Annual Growth	06/11	06/12	06/13	06/14	06/15
Sales ($ mil.)	1.8%	4,086.1	4,611.3	4,649.1	4,551.6	4,395.2
Net income ($ mil.)	39.3%	61.7	(324.4)	168.0	(97.4)	232.5
Market value ($ mil.)	36.4%	–	–	6,198.5	6,180.5	11,534.8
Employees	(10.0%)	–	–	10,000	9,000	8,100

COUGAR MOUNTAIN INC.

7180 Potomac Dr.
Boise ID 83704
Phone: 208-375-4455
Fax: 208-375-4460
Web: www.cougarmtn.com

CEO: Robert M Gossett
CFO: –
HR: –
FYE: December 31
Type: Private

Cougar Mountain has been counting on accountants for years. The company specializes in the development of accounting software used to automate accounts receivable and payable inventory general ledger order entry and reporting functions for businesses primarily in the Western US. It also offers software for retail point-of-sale (Denali) payroll (CMS Professional) and e-commerce applications. Cougar Mountain also provides accounting and point-of-sale software designed specifically for not-for-profit and government organizations the construction industry and tobacco and liquor stores. The family-owned business was founded by chairman Robert Gossett in 1982 and is led by his son CEO Chuck Gossett.

COUNCIL OF BETTER BUSINESS BUREAUS INC.

3033 WILSON BLVD STE 600
ARLINGTON, VA 222013863
Phone: 703-276-0100
Fax: –

CEO: Stephen A Cox
CFO: Joseph E Dillon
HR: –
FYE: December 31
Type: Private

The Council of Better Business Bureaus (BBB) helps North American consumers and businesses know who's on the up-and-up. The non-profit organization comprises independent BBBs and branches in about 125 locations throughout North America as well as some 240 national companies that have shown a commitment to business ethics. More than 300000 companies that have demonstrated a similar commitment belong to local BBBs. The companies can promote their adherence to BBB standards; in return they are subject to "reliability reports" that consist of any complaints clients or partners have had about them. BBBs work to resolve disputes between consumers and businesses and review companies' advertising.

	Annual Growth	12/06	12/07	12/08	12/09	12/11
Sales ($ mil.)	(70.3%)	–	2,010.8	17.8	18.5	15.7
Net income ($ mil.)	–	–	–	(0.6)	(0.1)	(1.0)
Market value ($ mil.)	–	–	–	–	–	–
Employees	–	–	–	–	–	119

COUNCIL ON FOREIGN RELATIONS INC.

58 E 68TH ST
NEW YORK, NY 100655953
Phone: 212-434-9400
Fax: –
Web: www.cfr.org

CEO: Carla Hills
CFO: –
HR: –
FYE: June 30
Type: Private

The Council on Foreign Relations (CFR) was established in 1921 with support from the Rockefeller family to provide a forum for government officials corporate executives journalists students and other interested parties to study and discuss world issues and the related impact on American foreign policy. The independent nonpartisan council publishes Foreign Affairs a magazine that comes out six times a year along with books and studies by its own scholars. It also sponsors task forces and hosts meetings attended by world leaders government officials and diplomats. Prospective members must be US citizens (native-born or naturalized) and are nominated by an existing member. CFR currently has about 4700 members.

	Annual Growth	06/09	06/10	06/11	06/12	06/13
Sales ($ mil.)	9.4%	–	42.7	59.6	75.4	56.0
Net income ($ mil.)	88.6%	–	–	6.9	19.6	24.5
Market value ($ mil.)	–	–	–	–	–	–
Employees	–	–	–	–	–	200

COUNTERPART INTERNATIONAL INC

2345 CRYSTAL DR STE 301
ARLINGTON, VA 222024810
Phone: 703-236-1200
Fax: –
Web: www.counterpart.org

CEO: Jeffrey T Lariche
CFO: –
HR: –
FYE: September 30
Type: Private

Counterpart International finds perfect partners to work together in improving the quality of life for communities worldwide. The not-for-profit humanitarian relief organization provides food medical supplies disaster relief technical and economic assistance and training to countries in the former Soviet Union Central Asian republics Southeast Asia Eastern Europe and Africa. It helps to form coalitions of companies governments and grass roots organizations to build schools and hospitals foster micro-businesses and develop tourism in war-torn or disaster-affected areas. Counterpart was founded in 1965 as the Foundation for the Peoples of the South Pacific.

	Annual Growth	09/04	09/05	09/06	09/08	09/09
Sales ($ mil.)	(7.0%)	–	116.6	121.8	107.6	87.2
Net income ($ mil.)	–	–	–	(0.5)	(0.2)	(0.6)
Market value ($ mil.)	–	–	–	–	–	–
Employees	–	–	–	–	–	45

COUNTRY MUTUAL INSURANCE COMPANY INC.

1705 N. Towanda Ave.
Bloomington IL 61701-2057
Phone: 309-821-3000
Fax: 309-821-5160
Web: www.countryfinancial.com

CEO: John D Blackburn
CFO: –
HR: –
FYE: December 31
Type: Subsidiary

COUNTRY Mutual Insurance sells property/casualty insurance in both rural and urban settings. A member of CC Services (known as COUNTRY Financial) the company sells homeowners renters farm automobile and commercial insurance to individuals and businesses. The company provides policies in about 30 states in the midwestern western northeastern and southeastern US. Founded in 1925 COUNTRY Mutual's subsidiaries include COUNTRY Preferred Insurance Company COUNTRY Casualty Insurance Company and Modern Service Insurance Company.

COUNTRY PRIDE COOPERATIVE INC.

648 W 2ND ST
WINNER, SD 575801230
Phone: 605-842-2711
Fax: –
Web: www.countrypridecoop.com

CEO: Mike Trosen
CFO: Marsha Whetham
HR: –
FYE: June 30
Type: Private

The Country Pride Cooperative has provided assistance to farmers in south central South Dakota since 1935. Country Pride offers it members an agronomy center seed sales grain storage and merchandising a feed mill and an equipment-rental center as well as finance programs and farm supply stores an auto-service center and bulk refined fuel delivery. It also operates five convenience stores under the Cenex name. The co-op was created through the 2000 merger of two area cooperatives Freeman Oil Cooperative (formed in 1935) and Dakota Pride Cooperative.

	Annual Growth	06/09	06/10	06/11	06/12	06/13
Sales ($ mil.)	5.6%	–	109.4	139.6	170.8	128.7
Net income ($ mil.)	9.7%	–	–	2.3	3.4	2.7
Market value ($ mil.)	–	–	–	–	–	–
Employees	–	–	–	–	–	200

COUNTY BANK CORP. (LAPEER, MI)   NBB: CBNC

83 West Nepessing St.
Lapeer, MI 48446
Phone: 810 664-2977
Fax: -
Web: www.lcbt.com

CEO: -
CFO: Joseph Black
HR: -
FYE: December 31
Type: Public

County Bank Corp is the holding company for Lapeer County Bank & Trust (LCBT) which operates about 10 branches in southeastern Michigan's Lapeer County north of Detroit. Founded in 1902 the bank offers traditional services such as checking and savings accounts CDs IRAs and and trust services. LCBT focuses on real estate lending: Commercial and single-family residential mortgages together make up approximately three-quarters of its loan portfolio. The bank also originates business construction municipal land and consumer loans. Its CBC Financial Services subsidiary offers insurance investment and financial planning services.

	Annual Growth	12/10	12/11	12/12	12/13	12/14
Assets ($ mil.)	2.7%	289.3	300.9	301.8	311.9	321.5
Net income ($ mil.)	48.8%	0.7	2.1	1.9	3.5	3.6
Market value ($ mil.)	15.6%	13.5	15.6	16.7	20.3	24.1
Employees	-	-	-	-	-	-

COURIER CORP.   NMS: CRRC

15 Wellman Avenue
North Chelmsford, MA 01863
Phone: 978 251-6000
Fax: -
Web: www.courier.com

CEO: -
CFO: -
HR: -
FYE: September 27
Type: Public

Courier dispatches books for playing praying and puzzling over. One of the largest book printers in the US Courier manufactures a variety of books for educational religious and specialty trade publishers and organizations. Most of its business comes from book printing operations which produce more than 175 million books per year and serve more than 500 customers; clients include Bible distributor The Gideons International and publishing giant Pearson. A book publisher itself Courier offers books for niche markets through subsidiaries Creative Homeowner (home and garden topics) Dover Publications (fiction and non-fiction) and Research & Education Association (education materials).

	Annual Growth	09/10	09/11	09/12	09/13	09/14
Sales ($ mil.)	2.5%	257.1	259.4	261.3	274.9	283.3
Net income ($ mil.)	2.3%	7.1	0.1	9.2	11.2	7.8
Market value ($ mil.)	(3.2%)	167.6	79.7	139.6	181.0	147.3
Employees	(1.3%)	1,662	1,568	1,501	1,560	1,576

COURT SQUARE CAPITAL PARTNERS

Park Avenue Plaza 55 E. 52nd St. 34th Fl.
New York NY 10055
Phone: 212-752-6110
Fax: 212-752-6184
Web: www.courtsquare.com

CEO: -
CFO: -
HR: -
FYE: December 31
Type: Private

Court Square Capital Partners is courting technology health care industrial and media companies. Spun off from Citigroup in 2006 the private equity and venture capital firm (formerly Citicorp Venture Capital) specializes in buyouts of middle-market companies. A long-term investor Court Square Capital manages approximately $6 billion of capital commitments and takes an active role with its investments helping to improve operational efficiency and often making add-on acquisitions. In order to avoid potential conflicts of interest with its customers or its other investment funds Citigroup no longer has equity in Court Square Capital.

COUSINS PROPERTIES INC.   NYS: CUZ

191 Peachtree Street, Suite 500
Atlanta, GA 30303-1740
Phone: 404 407-1000
Fax: -
Web: www.cousinsproperties.com

CEO: Lillian C. Giornelli
CFO: Gregg D. Adzema
HR: -
FYE: December 31
Type: Public

Cousins Properties owns a brood of office and retail holdings. The real estate investment trust (REIT) invests in develops and manages commercial properties mainly in the Southeast. Its portfolio (some of which is owned through joint ventures) includes nearly 40 office properties and retail shopping centers totaling more than 12 million sq. ft. of space. Other holdings include residential development projects and about 5000 acres of undeveloped land. The company also manages office and retail properties and provides construction management and development services for third parties. Cousins Properties is reshuffling its holdings to focus prime office and retail assets.

	Annual Growth	12/11	12/12	12/13	12/14	12/15
Sales ($ mil.)	20.9%	178.5	148.3	210.7	361.4	381.6
Net income ($ mil.)	-	(128.4)	45.7	121.8	52.0	125.5
Market value ($ mil.)	10.1%	1,355.8	1,766.1	2,178.6	2,415.5	1,994.6
Employees	(5.3%)	320	159	237	257	257

COVAD COMMUNICATIONS GROUP INC.

2220 O'Toole Ave.
San Jose CA 95131-1326
Phone: 408-952-6400
Fax: 408-952-7687
Web: www.covad.com

CEO: D Craig Young
CFO: Jeffrey Bailey
HR: -
FYE: December 31
Type: Subsidiary

Covad Communications converts conventional copper wires for quick connectivity. The company uses digital subscriber line (DSL) Ethernet and T-1 networking technologies to provide broadband Internet access largely on a wholesale basis to business customers in 240 metropolitan markets spanning 45 US states. Covad's main clients are Internet service providers (ISPs) — such as EarthLink AT&T and AOL — as well as smaller communications service resellers. In addition to its wholesale business the company offers wired and wireless broadband access and Voice over Internet Protocol (VoIP) telephony service directly to small and mid-sized businesses. Covad is a subsidiary of MegaPath.

COVANCE INC.   NYS: CVD

210 Carnegie Center
Princeton, NJ 08540
Phone: 609 452-4440
Fax: 609 452-9375
Web: www.covance.com

CEO: Joseph L Herring
CFO: Alison A Cornell
HR: -
FYE: December 31
Type: Public

Behind every great big drug company stands a great big contract research organization (CRO) and Covance is one of the biggest. Covance helps pharmaceutical and biotech companies worldwide develop new drugs by providing the fullest range of testing services from preclinical investigations all the way through designing and carrying out human clinical trials and conducting post-marketing studies to determine if drugs are safe and/or effective. Services include toxicology studies and biostatistical analysis. Among the company's customers are pharmaceutical biotech and medical device companies. Covance also offers laboratory testing services to companies in the chemical agrochemical and food industries.

	Annual Growth	12/08	12/09	12/10	12/11	12/12
Sales ($ mil.)	6.7%	1,827.1	1,962.6	2,038.5	2,236.4	2,365.8
Net income ($ mil.)	(16.7%)	196.8	175.9	68.3	132.2	94.7
Market value ($ mil.)	5.8%	2,531.0	3,000.6	2,826.8	2,513.9	3,176.5
Employees	7.0%	9,000	10,320	10,528	11,292	11,790

COVANTA ENERGY CORPORATION

445 South St.
Morristown NJ 07960
Phone: 862-345-5000
Fax: 330-384-3866
Web: www.firstenergycorp.com

CEO: Anthony J Orlando
CFO: Sanjiv Khattri
HR: Amy Welsh
FYE: December 31
Type: Subsidiary

Generating power from recycled waste is Covanta Energy's forte. A major operating unit of Covanta Holding the alternative energy power producer has interests in more than 40 specialized power plants primarily in the US. Its plants use a variety of waste fuels including municipal solid waste and wood waste (biomass). Covanta Energy's specialized plants can convert 20 million tons of waste into more than 9 million MW hours of electricity annually and create 9 billion pounds of steam that are sold to a range of industries. The company also provides waste management and recycling services.

COVANTA HOLDING CORP

NYS: CVA

445 South Street
Morristown, NJ 07960
Phone: 862 345-5000
Fax: –
Web: www.covanta.com

CEO: Stephen J Jones
CFO: Bradford J Helgeson
HR: –
FYE: December 31
Type: Public

Covanta Holding has seen the light: Waste can be converted into power. Led by Covanta Energy the company is a leader in the waste-to-energy market. Covanta Holding owns or operates more than 60 energy generation facilities (primarily in the US) that use municipal solid waste and biomass as well as fossil fuels and hydroelectric sources to generate power. It processes about 20 million tons of solid waste per year and provides electricity to some 1 million homes. Related businesses include landfills ashfills transfer stations and metals recycling. The company recycles 430000 tons of metal a year.

	Annual Growth	12/10	12/11	12/12	12/13	12/14
Sales ($ mil.)	1.5%	1,582.3	1,650.0	1,644.0	1,630.0	1,682.0
Net income ($ mil.)	–	61.7	219.0	114.0	(7.0)	(2.0)
Market value ($ mil.)	6.4%	2,286.3	1,820.8	2,449.9	2,360.8	2,927.3
Employees	(3.9%)	4,100	3,700	3,500	3,500	3,500

COVENANT HEALTH SYSTEM

3615 19TH ST
LUBBOCK, TX 794101209
Phone: 806-725-1011
Fax: –
Web: www.covenanthealth.org

CEO: Richard Parks
CFO: Denise Saenz
HR: –
FYE: June 30
Type: Private

Covenant Health System ties West Texas and Eastern New Mexico together with quality health care. The health services provider offers some 1100 beds in its five primary acute-care and specialty hospitals; it also manages about a dozen affiliated community hospitals. Covenant Health System part of the St. Joseph Health System also maintains a network of family health care and medical clinics. Covenant Health System's major facilities are Covenant Medical Center Covenant Specialty Hospital and Covenant Women's and Children's Hospital. The health system also includes some 20 clinics and 50 physician practices and its extensive outreach programs target isolated rural communities with mobile services.

	Annual Growth	06/06	06/07	06/08	06/09	06/13
Sales ($ mil.)	(0.7%)	–	–	572.0	1,185.2	552.9
Net income ($ mil.)	33.8%	–	–	8.3	(38.3)	35.7
Market value ($ mil.)	–	–	–	–	–	–
Employees	–	–	–	–	–	5,700

COVENANT HOUSE

5 PENN PLZ STE 201
NEW YORK, NY 100011841
Phone: 212-727-4000
Fax: –
Web: www.covenanthouse.org

CEO: Kevin Ryan
CFO: –
HR: –
FYE: June 30
Type: Private

Young people rely on Covenant House to keep its promises. The not-for-profit group offers outreach and crisis centers for homeless and runaway youths. Its centers offer food shelter clothing and medical and counseling services as well as job skills and substance abuse and parenting programs. There are about 15 centers in the US two in Canada and one each in Mexico Honduras and Nicaragua. Its Rights of Passage Programs and Covenant House Crisis Shelters served more than 15000 people and the entire organization reaches some 71000 homeless kids annually. The group also operates the Nineline (1-800-999-9999) for runaways. Covenant House was founded in 1972 by Franciscan priest Father Bruce Ritter.

	Annual Growth	06/08	06/09	06/10	06/11	06/13
Sales ($ mil.)	–	–	0.0	54.3	56.7	58.7
Net income ($ mil.)	–	–	–	(10.2)	(5.5)	(7.4)
Market value ($ mil.)	–	–	–	–	–	–
Employees	–	–	–	–	–	1,860

COVENANT MEDICAL CENTER INC

1447 N HARRISON ST
SAGINAW, MI 486024727
Phone: 989-583-0000
Fax: –
Web: www.covenanthealthcare.com

CEO: Edward Bruff
CFO: Mark Gronda
HR: Becca Sovansky
FYE: June 30
Type: Private

Covenant Medical Center (operating as Covenant HealthCare) has made a pact with Wolverine Staters to try to keep them in good health. The not-for-profit health care provider operates more than 20 inpatient and outpatient care facilities including its two main Covenant Medical Center campuses. It serves residents in a 20-county area of east-central Michigan with additional facilities in Bay City Frankenmuth and Midland. Specialized care services include cardiovascular health cancer treatment and obstetrics. The regional health care system has more about 650 beds.

	Annual Growth	06/07	06/08	06/09	06/10	06/13
Sales ($ mil.)	–	–	(1,608.4)	467.7	508.5	513.0
Net income ($ mil.)	–	–	–	(15.0)	28.1	31.6
Market value ($ mil.)	–	–	–	–	–	–
Employees	–	–	–	–	–	3,900

COVENANT TRANSPORTATION GROUP INC

NMS: CVTI

400 Birmingham Highway
Chattanooga, TN 37419
Phone: 423 821-1212
Fax: 423 821-5442
Web: www.covenanttransport.com

CEO: David R. Parker
CFO: Richard B. Cribbs
HR: –
FYE: December 31
Type: Public

Truckload freight carrier Covenant Transportation Group promises its customers speedy service on long-haul and regional routes. The company operates a fleet of about 3100 tractors and 7300 trailers including both dry vans and temperature-controlled units (through its Southern Refrigerated Transport subsidiary). In addition to for-hire transportation Covenant offers dedicated contract carriage in which drivers and equipment are assigned long-term to a customer or route and freight brokerage services. The company gets business from manufacturers retailers and other transportation companies; among its top customers are Georgia-Pacific Wal-Mart and UPS.

	Annual Growth	12/10	12/11	12/12	12/13	12/14
Sales ($ mil.)	2.6%	649.7	652.6	674.3	684.5	719.0
Net income ($ mil.)	52.5%	3.3	(14.3)	6.1	5.2	17.8
Market value ($ mil.)	29.4%	175.2	53.7	100.1	148.6	490.6
Employees	(0.8%)	4,740	5,023	4,541	4,434	4,595

COVER-ALL TECHNOLOGIES, INC.

ASE: COVR

412 Mt. Kemble Avenue, Suite 110C
Morristown, NJ 07960
Phone: 973 461-5200
Fax: –
Web: www.cover-all.com

CEO: Manish D Shah
CFO: Ann F Massey
HR: –
FYE: December 31
Type: Public

Cover-All Technologies keeps insurers covered. The company offers software and services for carriers agents and brokers in the property/casualty insurance industry. Cover-All's software which the company licenses and offers as a hosted application automates insurance rating and policy issuance. Its My Insurance Center site an Internet-based portal for insurance professionals helps agents with policy quoting rating issuance and billing; provides quick access to policy information; and offers applications for managing insurance agencies. The company also provides product customization data integration and other support services that keep the software up-to-date on industry information and regulations.

	Annual Growth	12/09	12/10	12/11	12/12	12/13
Sales ($ mil.)	9.0%	14.5	17.5	17.6	16.2	20.5
Net income ($ mil.)	–	3.9	3.0	1.2	(5.0)	(2.9)
Market value ($ mil.)	5.7%	29.6	42.8	47.5	32.7	37.0
Employees	5.7%	48	82	71	76	60

COVERALL NORTH AMERICA INC.

350 SW 12TH AVE
DEERFIELD BEACH, FL 334423106
Phone: 561-922-2500
Fax: –
Web: www.coverall.com

CEO: Laura J Hendricks
CFO: Marilyn Felos
HR: –
FYE: December 31
Type: Private

Coverall North America operating as Coverall Health-Based Cleaning System has commercial cleaning covered. Through more than 90 support centers and 9000 franchisees worldwide (including branches in Asia Australia the Middle East and the Americas) the company offers franchises that provides janitorial services to retail locations office buildings health care facilities manufacturing plants government facilities schools and airports. Services include routine cleaning decontamination cleaning carpet cleaning restroom sanitation and floor restoration. Prominent customers have included Fed Ex the United States Postal Service Orkin and Schenker. The company was founded in 1985.

	Annual Growth	12/03	12/04	12/05	12/06	12/07
Sales ($ mil.)	47.6%	–	–	103.3	205.9	225.1
Net income ($ mil.)	13164.3%	–	–	0.0	6.7	13.2
Market value ($ mil.)	–	–	–	–	–	–
Employees	–	–	–	–	–	476

COVISINT CORP

NMS: COVS

26533 Evergreen Road, Suite 500
Southfield, MI 48076
Phone: 248 483-2000
Fax: –
Web: www.covisint.com

CEO: Sam Inman
CFO: Enrico Digirolamo
HR: –
FYE: March 31
Type: Public

Covisint keeps things copacetic between buyers and suppliers partners and customers with its enterprise and supply chain software. The company provides cloud-based systems for integrating business information and processes between links in the supply chain. The Compuware subsidiary offers industry-tailored products and services to customers in the automotive energy financial services and health care sectors. Customers which include a number of major car manufacturers use its products to share applications with registered users automate partner lifecycle administration and management and create partner portals for information exchange and data messaging. Covisint went public in 2013.

	Annual Growth	03/11	03/12	03/13	03/14	03/15
Sales ($ mil.)	13.1%	54.2	74.7	90.7	97.1	88.5
Net income ($ mil.)	–	(1.3)	(3.3)	(5.6)	(35.7)	(38.6)
Market value ($ mil.)	(72.3%)	–	–	–	286.1	79.2
Employees	(17.8%)	–	–	565	631	382

COWAN SYSTEMS LLC

4555 Hollins Ferry Rd.
Baltimore MD 21227
Phone: 410-247-0800
Fax: 847-676-5136
Web: www.surepayroll.com

CEO: Dennis Morgan
CFO: –
HR: –
FYE: December 31
Type: Private

Not cowed by competition from bigger transportation companies Cowan Systems provides truckload freight transportation primarily in the eastern half of the US. The company's coverage area includes the mid-Atlantic states the Midwest New England and the southeastern US. Cowan has about 1400 tractors and 2600 trailers and its largest customer is Coca-Cola Enterprises. The company arranges the transportation of freight through its logistics unit. Other offerings include ground transportation of airfreight between airports and dedicated contract carriage in which drivers and equipment are assigned to a customer long-term. Cowan Systems has its roots in a trucking company that was founded in 1924.

COWEN GROUP INC

NMS: COWN

599 Lexington Avenue
New York, NY 10022
Phone: 212 845-7900
Fax: –
Web: www.cowen.com

CEO: Peter A. Cohen
CFO: Stephen A. Lasota
HR: –
FYE: December 31
Type: Public

The Cowen Group aims to herd its clients' investments in the right direction. The firm along with its subsidiaries offers alternative investment management research investment banking and sales and trading services. Its Ramius arm with some $12.5 billion of assets under management handles alternative investments while another subsidiary Cowen and Company represents the firm's investment banking and brokerage practice which mainly entails strategic advisory and corporate finance services for small to midsized companies. Cowen Group offers expanded trading operations through LaBranche & Co. a market maker for options exchange-traded funds and futures.

	Annual Growth	12/10	12/11	12/12	12/13	12/14
Sales ($ mil.)	16.3%	233.8	235.3	240.5	327.2	427.8
Net income ($ mil.)	–	(45.4)	(108.0)	(23.9)	4.6	167.2
Market value ($ mil.)	0.6%	523.8	289.3	273.6	436.7	536.1
Employees	4.7%	553	589	571	633	664

COX COMMUNICATIONS INC.

1400 Lake Hearn Dr.
Atlanta GA 30319
Phone: 404-843-5000
Fax: 949-595-7913
Web: www.charismabrands.com

CEO: Patrick J Esser
CFO: Mark F Bowser
HR: –
FYE: December 31
Type: Subsidiary

Cox Communications carries the full complement of cable capacity. The company provides basic cable service to more than 6 million customers including about 3 million digital cable subscribers and 3.5 million Internet access subscribers in 15 states making it the third-largest US cable company behind Comcast and Time Warner Cable. Cox also provides telephone service as a competitive local-exchange carrier (CLEC). In addition Cox offers voice and data communications services to businesses and has investments in television programming and broadband technology companies. Cox Communications is a subsidiary of media conglomerate Cox Enterprises.

COX NEWSPAPERS LLC

6205 Peachtree Dunwoody Rd.
Atlanta GA 30328
Phone: 678-645-0000
Fax: 512-342-2449
Web: www.accruent.com

CEO: –
CFO: –
HR: Robert Bass
FYE: December 31
Type: Subsidiary

Cox Newspapers keeps its nose to the news grindstone. One of the nation's top newspaper businesses the company publishes about 10 dailies including the Austin American-Statesman (Texas) Dayton Daily News (Ohio) and the Atlanta Journal-Constitution. Its portfolio also includes several non-daily newspapers mostly in Texas and Ohio. Its Cox News Service is a leading news syndication network serving more than 650 customers around the world. In addition the company operates more than 100 online properties including websites for its papers. Cox Newspapers is part of Cox Media Group a unit of conglomerate Cox Enterprises.

CP KELCO

1000 Parkwood Circle Ste. 1000
Atlanta GA 30339
Phone: 678-247-7300
Fax: 678-247-2797
Web: www.cpkelco.com

CEO: –
CFO: Phillip Patterson
HR: –
FYE: December 31
Type: Subsidiary

Don't worry teachers: CP Kelco brought enough gum for the entire class. The company's products derived from renewable natural raw materials include carrageenan gellan gum xanthan gum and microparticulated whey protein. A subsidiary of J. M. Huber the company manufactures specialty hydrocolloids (which produce gels). The additives are used in food industrial personal care and pharmaceutical products — everything from jam and ketchup to paint and cosmetics — to give the desired texture viscosity and stability. Other markets include pulp and paper (which uses cellulose derivatives) and oilfield drilling (additives for drilling fluids). CP Kelco operates manufacturing facilities worldwide.

CPA2BIZ INC.

100 Broadway 6th Fl.
New York NY 10005
Phone: 646-233-5000
Fax: 646-233-5090
Web: www.cpa2biz.com

CEO: –
CFO: –
HR: –
FYE: July 31
Type: Subsidiary

CPA2Biz wants to help certified public accountants make their practices perfect. As the for-profit marketing arm of the American Institute of Certified Public Accountants (AICPA) the company offers resources to accounting professionals that include continuing professional education career resources online literature and other products and services. CPA2Biz markets its offerings nationwide through catalogs direct mail conferences specialty brochures e-newsletters e-mail Webcasts and industry tradeshows. It also offers member clients special programs such as small business banking throughJPMorgan Chase payroll through Paychex and bill pay services through Bill.com.

CPAC INC.

2364 Leicester Rd.
Leicester NY 14481
Phone: 585-382-3223
Fax: 585-382-3031
Web: www.cpac-fuller.com

CEO: Thomas N Hendrickson
CFO: Thomas J Weldgen
HR: –
FYE: March 31
Type: Private

CPAC can make your face and floor shine. The company's Fuller Brands segment (more than half of sales) boasts some 2700 consumer and industrial products including brushes cleaning chemicals brooms and personal care products. The segment also licenses the Stanley Home Products brand and makes Stanley cleaning and personal care products for sale at home parties. CPAC's Imaging segment manufactures and markets a line of branded and private-label chemicals and equipment for photographic graphic arts and health care applications. Products include photographic chemical silver-recovery equipment; the shift to digital imaging has hurt this segment. Private equity group Buckingham Capital Partners owns CPAC.

CPG INTERNATIONAL INC.

888 N. Keyser Ave.
Scranton PA 18504
Phone: 570-558-8000
Fax: 570-346-4122
Web: www.cpgint.com

CEO: Eric K Jungbluth
CFO: –
HR: Sandra Mistysyn
FYE: December 31
Type: Private

When it comes to CPG's building products appearance is key. Through its AZEK Scranton and Vycom operating segments CPG is a leading manufacturer of synthetic building products and other materials used in residential remodeling and construction as well as by commercial and industrial clients in the US and Canada. Its core AZEK unit manufactures PVC-based residential products such as trim deck rail moulding and porch materials made to look like wood and other natural materials. CPG's Scranton unit makes polyurethane bathroom partitions and lockers for commercial and institutional end-users while Vycom makes PVC plastic sheeting for industrial uses. CPG filed to go public in 2011.

CPI AEROSTRUCTURES, INC.

91 Heartland Blvd.
Edgewood, NY 11717
Phone: 631 586-5200
Fax: –
Web: www.cpiaero.com

ASE: CVU
CEO: Douglas McCrosson
CFO: Vincent Palazzolo
HR: Carol Morga
FYE: December 31
Type: Public

To build an aircraft some assembly is required and CPI Aerostructures is ready. CPI Aero delivers contract production of structural aircraft subassemblies chiefly for the US Air Force and other US military customers. Military products include skin panels flight control surfaces leading edges wing tips engine components cowl doors and nacelle and inlet assemblies. The lineup is used on military aircraft such as the C-5A Galaxy and C-130 Hercules cargo jets E-3 Sentry AWACs jet and T-38 Talon jet trainer. As a subcontractor to OEMs CPI Aero also makes aprons and engine mounts for commercial aircraft such as business jets. Government prime and subcontracts represent a majority of CPI Aero's sales

	Annual Growth	12/10	12/11	12/12	12/13	12/14
Sales ($ mil.)	(2.5%)	44.0	74.1	89.3	83.0	39.7
Net income ($ mil.)	–	0.5	7.4	11.0	7.7	(25.2)
Market value ($ mil.)	(7.7%)	119.7	100.9	85.1	127.8	86.8
Employees	22.0%	127	157	201	268	281

CPI INTERNATIONAL INC.

5580 Skylane Blvd.
Santa Rosa CA 95403
Phone: 707-525-5788
Fax: 707-545-7901
Web: www.cpii.com

CEO: O Joe Caldarelli
CFO: Joel A Littman
HR: –
FYE: September 30
Type: Private

CPI International makes broadcast and wireless components such as satellite communications transmitters amplifiers sensors X-ray equipment power supplies transmitters and microwave components. Its radio-frequency (RF) and microwave components go into a great deal of military hardware including Aegis-class cruisers and destroyers Patriot missile systems and fighter aircraft. The company serves clients in about 90 countries from sales and service offices across the US Europe Canada and Japan. In 2011 investment firm Veritas Capital took the company private in a transaction valued at around $525 million.

CPS TECHNOLOGIES CORP
NAS: CPSH

111 South Worcester Street
Norton, MA 02766-2102
Phone: 508 222-0614
Fax: –
Web: www.alsic.com

CEO: Grant C Bennett
CFO: Ralph Norwood
HR: –
FYE: December 27
Type: Public

CPS Technologies makes thermal management components for electronics using aluminum silicon carbide (ALSiC) metal matrix composites. Products include substrates baseplates and heat spreaders that are used by customers in motor controller and wireless communications component applications. CPS is working with the US Army on using its composite technology in armor for military vehicles. The company also licenses its technology to other manufacturers; revenue from licenses and royalties however has dwindled away to virtually nothing. CPS Technologies makes more than two-thirds of its sales to locations outside the US although the majority of its customers are actually based in the US.

	Annual Growth	12/10	12/11	12/12	12/13	12/14
Sales ($ mil.)	2.0%	21.4	19.8	14.1	21.4	23.1
Net income ($ mil.)	9.0%	0.7	(0.0)	(1.5)	1.0	1.0
Market value ($ mil.)	15.6%	21.7	24.3	19.6	31.4	38.8
Employees	(5.3%)	194	194	139	151	156

CR BRANDS INC.

9100 Centre Pointe Dr. Ste. 200
West Chester OH 45069
Phone: 513-860-5039
Fax: 513-860-1164
Web: www.crbrandsinc.com

CEO: Richard Owen
CFO: John Samoya
HR: –
FYE: December 31
Type: Private

CR Brands keeps cleaning brands fresh by acquiring and reviving them. Banking on the idea that one company's trash is another's treasure CR Brands bought Oxydol and BIZ detergents from Procter & Gamble (P&G) in 2000. Co-founded by former P&G managers and chemical engineers CR Brands believes that with fresh marketing it can jump-start sales of the 70-year-old Oxydol detergent that put the "soap" in soap opera with its sponsorship of radio programs in the 1930s. BIZ was introduced nationally in 1968. CR Brands makes and markets branded and private label heavy-duty cleaning products through grocery discount and dollar stores. Business development firm Allied Capital owns the company.

CRA INTERNATIONAL INC
NMS: CRAI

200 Clarendon Street
Boston, MA 02116-5092
Phone: 617 425-3000
Fax: 617 425-3132
Web: www.crai.com

CEO: Paul A. Maleh
CFO: Wayne D. Mackie
HR: –
FYE: January 03
Type: Public

Whether you need an expert to help you run your business testify for you in court or evaluate the finances of an acquisition candidate CRA International wants to help. The company which operates under the Charles River Associates trade name employs about 520 consultants offering economic and business counsel from more than 20 offices mainly in North America but also in Europe the Middle East and Asia. Its practices are organized into three areas: finance (valuation and accounting insurance and risk management); litigation and applied economics (competition intellectual property trade and transfer pricing); and business consulting. Clients include government agencies and law firms among others.

	Annual Growth	01/11*	12/11	12/12	12/13*	01/15
Sales ($ mil.)	92.6%	22.3	305.2	270.4	278.4	306.4
Net income ($ mil.)	–	(0.6)	16.9	(53.0)	11.4	13.6
Market value ($ mil.)	6.6%	217.0	183.1	173.5	191.1	280.2
Employees	(10.7%)	710	710	464	597	451

*Fiscal year change

CRACKER BARREL OLD COUNTRY STORE, INC.
NMS: CBRL

305 Hartmann Drive
Lebanon, TN 37087-4779
Phone: 615 444-5533
Fax: –
Web: www.cbrlgroup.com

CEO: Sandra B. (Sandy) Cochran
CFO: Lawrence E. (Larry) Hyatt
HR: Lisa Smith
FYE: July 31
Type: Public

This company has gotten ahead in the restaurant business by holding onto a bit of the past. Cracker Barrel Old Country Store owns and operates about 635 of its flagship restaurants known for their country kitsch rustic decor and down-home cooking. The eateries located in more than 40 states offer mostly standard American fare such as chicken ham and roast beef dishes but they are most popular as breakfast spots. Each Cracker Barrel location features a retail area where patrons can buy hand-blown glassware cast iron cookware and woodcrafts as well as jellies and old-fashioned candies. Most of the restaurants are found along interstate highways and target hungry travelers.

	Annual Growth	07/11*	08/12	08/13	08/14*	07/15
Sales ($ mil.)	3.9%	2,434.4	2,580.2	2,644.6	2,683.7	2,842.3
Net income ($ mil.)	17.8%	85.2	103.1	117.3	132.1	163.9
Market value ($ mil.)	35.5%	1,081.5	1,509.5	2,420.4	2,317.5	3,641.7
Employees	1.8%	67,000	70,000	71,000	72,000	72,000

*Fiscal year change

CRAFT BREW ALLIANCE INC
NMS: BREW

929 North Russell Street
Portland, OR 97227
Phone: 503 331-7270
Fax: –
Web: www.craftbrew.com

CEO: Andrew J. (Andy) Thomas
CFO: Joseph K. (Joe) Vanderstelt
HR: –
FYE: December 31
Type: Public

Elevating beer to a craft takes an alliance; Craft Brew Alliance brews markets and sells the beers of Redhook Ale Brewery (Seattle) Widmer Brothers Brewing (Portland Oregon) and Kona Brewing (Kona Hawaii). The Alliance divides its business between beer comprising brewing and selling craft beers and pubs and other operations including five pubs four of which neighbor its breweries. Its lineup offers year-round and flagship brands (Pilsner Hefeweizen Longboard Island) as well as seasonal and limited releases (Citra Blonde OKTO Winterhook) that are available regionally and nationally in the US. Beers are distributed through an agreement with Anheuser-Busch which owns about 32% of the Alliance.

	Annual Growth	12/10	12/11	12/12	12/13	12/14
Sales ($ mil.)	11.0%	131.7	149.2	169.3	179.2	200.0
Net income ($ mil.)	16.2%	1.7	9.7	2.5	2.0	3.1
Market value ($ mil.)	15.9%	141.3	115.1	123.9	313.9	255.0
Employees	6.9%	600	675	740	745	785

CRAFTMADE INTERNATIONAL INC.

PINK SHEETS: CRFT

650 S. Royal Ln. Ste. 100
Coppell TX 75019-3810
Phone: 972-393-3800
Fax: 972-304-3754
Web: www.craftmade.com

CEO: Jean Liu
CFO: –
HR: Jack Grandel
FYE: June 30
Type: Public

Craftmade International is no celebrity but it is accustomed to fans and bright lights. The company designs manufactures and distributes Craftmade brand ceiling fans as well as lights for home use. Through its subsidiaries — Woodard Prime/Home Impressions and Trade Source International — it sells more than 80 fan models separate light kits doorbells and accessories. It also offers bathstrip and outdoor lighting lamps and Woodard brand outdoor furniture. Asian manufacturers produce most Craftmade lines sold to specialty retailers and mass merchandisers including Lowe's (31% of revenues) and Costco (7%). Craftmade also owns a 50% stake in Design Trends a Chinese distributor of lamps and shades.

CRAIN COMMUNICATIONS INC

1155 Gratiot Ave.
Detroit MI 48207-2997
Phone: 313-446-6000
Fax: 313-446-1616
Web: www.crain.com

CEO: Keith E Crain
CFO: –
HR: Margee Kaczmarek
FYE: December 31
Type: Private

These Crains have been whooping it up in the publishing business for a long time. Crain Communications is a leading publisher of trade journals and weekly business newspapers with about 30 titles serving audiences mostly in North America Europe and Asia. Its portfolio covers such areas as the automotive industry (Automotive News AutoWeek) the financial sector (Business Insurance InvestmentNews) and media (Advertising Age). Crain also publishes business journals in four major US cities (Chicago Cleveland Detroit and New York City) and its publications host events such as the AutoWeek Virtual Green Car Show. The family-owned company was started by G. D. Crain in 1916.

CRANE & CO. INC.

30 South St.
Dalton MA 01226
Phone: 413-684-2600
Fax: 413-684-4278
Web: www.crane.com

CEO: Stephen P Defalco
CFO: Doug Prince
HR: Chad Jzyk
FYE: December 31
Type: Private

Crane & Co.'s early claim to fame was Paul Revere engraving banknotes on its paper during the American Revolution. Today the company manufactures US currency paper and fine cotton papers used for business and personalized stationery such as wedding invitations and thank you notes. Its nonwovens division makes paper-like materials under brand names Craneglas and Cranemat which are used in products ranging from automobiles to satellites. Crane & Co. has manufacturing operations in Massachusetts New Hampshire and internationally in Sweden. The company is owned and managed by the eighth generation of the Crane family. Private equity firm Goldberg Lindsay & Co. also holds a minority stake.

CRANE CO.

NYS: CR

100 First Stamford Place
Stamford, CT 06902
Phone: 203 363-7300
Fax: –
Web: www.craneco.com

CEO: Max H. Mitchell
CFO: Richard A. (Rich) Maue
HR: Linda Wood
FYE: December 31
Type: Public

In many cultures the crane is a symbol of longevity; this Crane claims such endurance. Founded in 1855 the company makes a slew of engineered industrial products through four business segments: its largest Fluid Handling (valves and pumps); Aerospace & Electronics (sensing and control systems); Engineered Materials (plastic composites substrates); and Payment and Merchandising Technologies (vending and coin dispensing machines). Its products are used in the aerospace military and defense recreational vehicle construction transportation automated merchandising petrochemical chemical and power generation industries.

	Annual Growth	12/10	12/11	12/12	12/13	12/14
Sales ($ mil.)	7.2%	2,217.8	2,545.9	2,579.1	2,595.3	2,925.0
Net income ($ mil.)	5.9%	154.2	26.5	217.8	221.0	193.6
Market value ($ mil.)	9.3%	2,387.1	2,714.9	2,689.9	3,908.7	3,411.7
Employees	1.9%	10,500	11,000	10,500	11,500	11,300

CRAVATH SWAINE & MOORE LLP

Worldwide Plaza 825 8th Ave.
New York NY 10019-7475
Phone: 212-474-1000
Fax: 212-474-3700
Web: www.cravath.com

CEO: –
CFO: –
HR: Lina Maglara
FYE: December 31
Type: Private - Partnershi

With almost 500 attorneys working from offices in New York and London Cravath Swaine & Moore is a leading corporate law firm. It is well known for advising companies in such areas as banking and finance capital markets domestic and international law matters and mergers and acquisitions; other practice areas include executive compensation and benefits litigation tax and trusts and estates. The firm which traces its roots to 1819 owes its present structure to Paul Cravath who led it early in the 20th century and is credited by many with developing the configuration of the modern-day law firm.

CRAWFORD & CO.

NYS: CRD B

1001 Summit Boulevard
Atlanta, GA 30319
Phone: 404 300-1000
Fax: –
Web: www.crawfordandcompany.com

CEO: Jeffrey T. (Jeff) Bowman
CFO: W. Bruce Swain
HR: –
FYE: December 31
Type: Public

Crawford & Company is an international insurance services firm that provides claims adjustment and risk management services to insurers and self-insured companies. As the world's largest independent provider of such services to the risk management and insurance industries the firm offers workers' compensation and property/casualty claims investigation evaluation and resolution; statistical and financial reporting; and medical case management. Its subsidiaries provide class-action settlement services property damage repairs and computer-based risk management information services. Founded in 1941 Crawford & Company boasts more than 700 offices in more than 70 countries.

	Annual Growth	12/10	12/11	12/12	12/13	12/14
Sales ($ mil.)	2.3%	1,110.8	1,211.4	1,266.1	1,253.4	1,217.0
Net income ($ mil.)	2.0%	28.3	45.4	48.9	51.0	30.6
Market value ($ mil.)	31.9%	187.6	340.0	440.4	509.9	567.3
Employees	0.5%	8,678	8,691	8,478	8,551	8,841

CRAY INC

NMS: CRAY

901 Fifth Avenue, Suite 1000
Seattle, WA 98164
Phone: 206 701-2000
Fax: –
Web: www.cray.com

CEO: Peter J. Ungaro
CFO: Brian C. Henry
HR: –
FYE: December 31
Type: Public

Cray makes computers that aren't just good — they're super. Its massively parallel and vector supercomputers provide the firepower behind research ranging from weather forecasting and scientific research to design engineering and classified government projects. The company also provides maintenance and support services and it sells its own and third-party data storage products primarily from NetApp and DataDirect Networks. Cray's largest customer is the US government which accounts for about two-thirds of sales. Cray also targets academic institutions and industrial companies. Around 58% of sales come from customers in the US.

	Annual Growth	12/10	12/11	12/12	12/13	12/14
Sales ($ mil.)	15.2%	319.4	236.0	421.1	525.7	561.6
Net income ($ mil.)	42.6%	15.1	14.3	161.2	32.2	62.3
Market value ($ mil.)	48.1%	292.7	264.1	651.1	1,121.0	1,407.6
Employees	6.5%	885	860	929	1,042	1,138

CRAYOLA LLC

1100 Church Ln.
Easton PA 18044-0431
Phone: 610-253-6271
Fax: 610-250-5768
Web: www.crayola.com

CEO: Smith Holland
CFO: Dona Fisher
HR: –
FYE: December 31
Type: Subsidiary

Crayola has cornered the market on colors. The crayon maker's 10 most popular colors include blue red violet green carnation pink black turquoise blue blue green periwinkle and magenta. It produces about 3 billion crayons a year as well as other Crayola art products for children such as markers and craft and activity kits. Crayola also makes Silly Putty the iconic silicone putty with utility; and inkTank pens and markers for adults. The firm's products are packaged in many languages and sold worldwide. Edwin Binney and C. Harold Smith sold their first Crayola crayons in 1903 when a box of eight cost a nickel. Crayola is a subsidiary of Hallmark Cards.

CREATIVE GROUP INC.

619 N LYNNDALE DR
APPLETON, WI 54914-3087
Phone: 920-739-8850
Fax: –
Web: www.creativegroupinc.com

CEO: Ronald Officer
CFO: Martin Van Stippen
HR: Paul Miller
FYE: September 30
Type: Private

Creative Group Inc. has devoted its energy towards business improvement. The company provides a variety of marketing services specializing in building and managing incentive programs and planning corporate meetings and events. The company's incentive programs target sales reseller and employees offering travel merchandise and gift certificates as rewards for good performance. Creative Group also offers personal travel services including travel planning and emergency services that benefit from the company's large corporate travel business.

	Annual Growth	09/08	09/09	09/10	09/11	09/12
Sales ($ mil.)	0.0%	–	80.0	80.0	80.0	80.0
Net income ($ mil.)		–	0.0	0.0	0.0	0.0
Market value ($ mil.)		–	–	–	–	–
Employees		–	–	–	–	173

CREATIVE REALITIES INC

NBB: CREX

22 Audrey Place
Fairfield, NJ 07004
Phone: 973 244-9911
Fax: –
Web: www.wirelessronin.com

CEO: Richard Mills
CFO: John Walpuck
HR: –
FYE: December 31
Type: Public

Wireless Ronin Technologies makes the signs of the time. The company's RoninCast electronic display products combine digital media players video monitors and wireless networking systems to enable the remote distribution of video marketing materials. Its digital signage is used for corporate logos and branding promotional displays interactive touchscreens movie theater schedules and restaurant menus. Wireless Ronin serves the automotive financial services gaming restaurant and retail industries among others. Customers include Chrysler Canada Carnival Ford KFC Thomson Reuters and Travelocity.

	Annual Growth	12/10	12/11	12/12	12/13	12/14
Sales ($ mil.)	11.9%	8.6	9.3	6.7	6.8	13.4
Net income ($ mil.)	–	(7.9)	(6.7)	(5.4)	(3.6)	(3.8)
Market value ($ mil.)	(27.5%)	67.0	55.5	92.4	27.7	18.5
Employees	(5.0%)	81	65	62	47	66

CREDIT ACCEPTANCE CORP. (MI)

NMS: CACC

25505 West Twelve Mile Road
Southfield, MI 48034-8339
Phone: 248 353-2700
Fax: –

CEO: Brett A. Roberts
CFO: Kenneth S. Booth
HR: –
FYE: December 31
Type: Public

In the world of Credit Acceptance Corporation (CAC) to purchase a car is not an impossible dream for problem borrowers. CAC makes the effort a reality. Working with more than 55000 independent and franchised automobile dealers in the US CAC provides capital for auto loans to people with substandard credit. The company also provides other services to dealers including payment servicing receivables management marketing and service contracts. CAC which concentrates its operations in a handful of US states typically funds about 1.5 million auto loans per year.

	Annual Growth	12/10	12/11	12/12	12/13	12/14
Sales ($ mil.)	13.1%	442.1	525.2	609.2	682.1	723.5
Net income ($ mil.)	11.9%	170.1	188.0	219.7	253.1	266.2
Market value ($ mil.)	21.4%	1,292.9	1,694.8	2,094.4	2,677.5	2,809.7
Employees	10.9%	862	1,037	1,264	1,317	1,303

CREDIT SUISSE (USA) INC

Eleven Madison Avenue
New York, NY 10010
Phone: 212 325-2000
Fax: –

CEO: Brady W Dougan
CFO: David C Fisher
HR: –
FYE: December 31
Type: Public

Credit Suisse (USA) is one of the top US investment banks offering advisory services on mergers and acquisitions raising capital securities underwriting and trading research and analytics and risk management products. Clients include corporations governments institutional investors such as hedge funds and private individuals. The company provides asset management services through Credit Suisse Private Equity; while Credit Suisse Private Banking USA offers wealth services to the rich throughout the country. Credit Suisse (USA) is a wholly owned subsidiary of Swiss banking powerhouse Credit Suisse Group and part of Credit Suisse Americas which includes North and South America and the Caribbean.

	Annual Growth	12/03	12/04	12/05	12/11	12/12
Sales ($ mil.)	8.3%	4,993.0	6,341.0	7,025.0	6,738.0	10,232.0
Net income ($ mil.)	5.0%	1,329.0	787.0	127.0	(272.0)	2,063.0
Market value ($ mil.)	0.0%	0.1	0.1	0.1	–	–
Employees	11.9%	8,706	9,344	10,899	–	–

CREDITORS INTERCHANGE RECEIVABLE MANAGEMENT LLC

80 Holtz Dr.
Buffalo NY 14225
Phone: 716-614-7500
Fax: 716-614-7546
Web: www.creditorsinterchange.com

CEO: –
CFO: Brian Berkman
HR: –
FYE: December 31
Type: Private

Collecting on delinquent debt requires a mixture of tenacity tact and — in this day and age — technology. Creditors Interchange provides receivables management and customized collections services to financial institutions in the US and Canada. The company's services include online skip-tracing collections services and recovery assistance advisory services; Creditors Interchange also works through a nationwide network of attorneys and has a bankruptcy and probate division to help clients navigate probate and legal remedy collections. The company was founded as a collection agency for doctors in 1960.

CREDITRISKMONITOR.COM, INC.

704 Executive Boulevard, Suite A
Valley Cottage, NY 10989
Phone: 845 230-3000
Fax: –
Web: www.crmz.com

NBB: CRMZ

CEO: Jerome S. (Jerry) Flum
CFO: Lawrence (Larry) Fensterstock
HR: –
FYE: December 31
Type: Public

Need to monitor credit risk? CreditRiskMonitor.com (also called CRMZ) provides online financial information and news about some 40000 public companies worldwide marketing the service to corporate credit managers who use the data to make credit decisions. Subscribers get access to such information as company background financial statements trend reports and comparative analysis in addition to proprietary credit scores. The firm also provides access to information on more than 6 million public and private US companies through affiliations with third-party providers. CreditRiskMonitor.com was formed in 1999 after buying Market Guide's credit information database.

	Annual Growth	12/10	12/11	12/12	12/13	12/14
Sales ($ mil.)	6.9%	9.3	10.2	11.1	11.8	12.2
Net income ($ mil.)	(22.2%)	1.0	0.9	0.5	0.3	0.4
Market value ($ mil.)	(22.7%)	73.3	30.9	35.6	36.7	26.2
Employees	5.4%	64	78	81	88	79

CREDO PETROLEUM CORPORATION

1801 Broadway Ste. 900
Denver CO 80202-3837
Phone: 303-297-2200
Fax: 303-297-2204
Web: www.credopetroleum.com

NASDAQ: CRED

CEO: Michael D Davis
CFO: Chris Nines
HR: –
FYE: October 31
Type: Public

CREDO Petroleum believes strongly in fossil fuels: It explores for produces and markets natural gas and crude oil in the US Gulf Coast Midcontinent and Rocky Mountain regions. The company has traditionally concentrated on shallow and medium-depth properties (7000-9000 ft.) but in recent years it has launched projects in Kansas and South Texas (where it is drilling to well depths ranging from 10000 to 17000 ft.). Subsidiary United Oil operates the company's properties in Oklahoma and CREDO Petroleum's other subsidiary SECO Energy owns royalty interests in the Rocky Mountains. In 2012 the company was acquired by the Forestar Group for about $146 million.

CREE, INC.

4600 Silicon Drive
Durham, NC 27703
Phone: 919 407-5300
Fax: 919 313-5615
Web: www.cree.com

NMS: CREE

CEO: Charles M. Swoboda
CFO: Michael E. McDevitt
HR: –
FYE: June 28
Type: Public

Cree has its name in lights. Its blue green and near-ultraviolet light-emitting diodes (LEDs) — made from silicon carbide (SiC) and gallium nitride (GaN) — are used in dashboard lights architectural light fixtures market tickers and video screens. Cree also sells SiC wafers which work better at higher temperatures and voltages than other silicon devices and SiC and GaN materials. In addition it offers lighting systems (both LED and traditional) as well as power and radio-frequency (RF) products such as Schottky diodes and transistors. The company makes most of its products at plants in the US (North Carolina Wisconsin) and China. More than 50% of sales come from outside the US.

	Annual Growth	06/11	06/12	06/13	06/14	06/15
Sales ($ mil.)	13.4%	987.6	1,164.7	1,386.0	1,647.6	1,632.5
Net income ($ mil.)	–	146.5	44.4	86.9	124.2	(64.1)
Market value ($ mil.)	(5.6%)	3,583.0	2,579.6	6,734.5	5,115.0	2,848.7
Employees	7.7%	4,753	5,555	6,120	7,130	6,387

CREIGHTON ALEGENT HEALTH

12809 W DODGE RD
OMAHA, NE 68154-2155
Phone: 402-343-4300
Fax: –
Web: www.alegent.com

CEO: Cliff Robertson
CFO: Jeanette Wojtalewicz
HR: –
FYE: June 30
Type: Private

Alegent Creighton Health (formerly Alegent Health) pledges allegiance to medical wellbeing in its corner of the Midwest. The not-for-profit health care system operates 11 hospitals with about 2000 beds in Omaha and surrounding communities in eastern Nebraska and southwestern Iowa including Bergan Mercy Medical Center and Immanuel Medical Center. Alegent Creighton Health's hospitals provide specialty services including cardiovascular orthopedic and cancer care; it also operates psychiatric long-term care home health and outpatient centers. The health system is sponsored by Catholic Health Initiatives and is affiliated with Creighton University.

	Annual Growth	06/07	06/08	06/09	06/10	06/11
Sales ($ mil.)	268.7%	–	5.2	3.2	285.1	262.9
Net income ($ mil.)	–	–	(0.6)	0.0	23.9	26.7
Market value ($ mil.)	–	–	–	–	–	–
Employees	–	–	–	–	–	8,600

CREIGHTON UNIVERSITY

2500 CALIFORNIA PLZ
OMAHA, NE 681780002
Phone: 402-280-2900
Fax: –
Web: www.creighton.edu

CEO: –
CFO: Robert Glow
HR: –
FYE: June 30
Type: Private

Consistently ranked among the top universities in the Midwest Creighton University is a Jesuit Catholic university with an enrollment of approximately 8000 undergraduate graduate and professional students. With a student-to-faculty ratio of 11:1 it offers more than 70 majors through nine schools and colleges including institutions focused on arts and sciences business law medicine dentistry pharmacy and nursing. Its 130-acre campus is adjacent to the downtown business district of Omaha Nebraska. Creighton University was founded in 1878 and named after Omaha businessman Edward Creighton.

	Annual Growth	06/09	06/10	06/11	06/12	06/13
Sales ($ mil.)	0.2%	–	405.9	414.8	419.7	407.9
Net income ($ mil.)	3.0%	–	–	79.7	(28.6)	84.5
Market value ($ mil.)	–	–	–	–	–	–
Employees	–	–	–	–	–	5,000

CRESCENT ELECTRIC SUPPLY COMPANY

7750 Dunleith Dr.
East Dubuque IL 61025
Phone: 815-747-3145
Fax: 815-747-7720
Web: www.cesco.com

CEO: –
CFO: Jim Etheredge
HR: –
FYE: December 31
Type: Private

It's certainly no surprise what business Crescent Electric Supply Company is in. The company distributes electrical supplies from 600 leading vendors including GE Lighting Hubbell Siemens and Thomas & Betts. Main products include lamps light fixtures switchgear door bells and power distribution controls. Customers include Caterpillar Deere and clients in the agriculture construction data communications energy government health care hospitality and industrial sectors. Crescent Electric has more than 120 locations in some 25 states. The company was founded in 1919 by Titus Schmid and later became a lamp agent for General Electric. Members of the Schmid family continue to own the company.

CRESCENT FINANCIAL BANCSHARES INC.   NASDAQ: CRFN

3600 Glenwood Ave. Ste. 300
Raleigh NC 27612
Phone: 919-659-9000
Fax: 919-460-2512
Web: www.crescentstatebank.com

CEO: –
CFO: –
HR: –
FYE: December 31
Type: Public

This Crescent helps your financial health take shape. Crescent Financial Bancshares is the holding company for Crescent State Bank which operates some 15 branches in central North Carolina. The bank focuses on serving businesses business owners and professionals. It offers standard products and services including checking and savings accounts CDs and credit cards. Commercial mortgages make up more than half of the company's loan portfolio; the bank also writes construction loans commercial and industrial loans home equity loans and residential mortgages. Through Crescent Investment Services it offers financial planning products and services.

CRESCENT REAL ESTATE EQUITIES LIMITED PARTNERSHIP

777 Main St. Ste. 2000
Fort Worth TX 76102-5325
Phone: 817-321-2100
Fax: 817-321-2000
Web: www.crescent.com

CEO: –
CFO: –
HR: –
FYE: December 31
Type: Subsidiary

Commercial properties are the butter to Crescent's bread. Property investment firm Crescent Real Estate Equities owns or has interests in some 35 Class-A office buildings totaling more than 17 million sq. ft. of space. Its property portfolio is concentrated in the Dallas Houston Denver and Las Vegas markets. In addition to its office holdings the company owns a handful of upscale spa resorts as well as interests in several residential developments in the Southwest. CEO John Goff founded the company in 1994. He sold Crescent to Morgan Stanley's real estate division in 2007 and reacquired the firm with Barclays Capital in 2009.

CREST OPERATIONS LLC

4725 HIGHWAY 28 E
PINEVILLE, LA 713604730
Phone: 318-448-0274
Fax: –
Web: www.crestoperations.com

CEO: –
CFO: –
HR: Jane Walker
FYE: December 31
Type: Private

Crest Operations part of Crest Industries distributes and installs electrical substations and transmission products for electric power generation and utility customers worldwide through its DIS-TRAN and Beta Engineering subsidiaries. Other subsidiaries grow pine and hardwood trees in Louisiana and Texas (Crest Natural Resources) and make wooden utility poles and cross arms. Crest's Mid-State Supply Company subsidiary is a Louisiana-based distributor of electrical products that has showrooms for appliances and lighting. Crest Operations was founded in 1958.

	Annual Growth	12/07	12/08	12/11	12/12	12/13
Sales ($ mil.)	12.9%	–	178.2	196.5	240.0	326.8
Net income ($ mil.)	46.8%	–	–	16.2	29.0	34.8
Market value ($ mil.)	–	–	–	–	–	–
Employees	–	–	–	–	–	300

CRESTED BUTTE LLC

12 Snowmass Rd.
Mt. Crested Butte CO 81225
Phone: 970-349-2333
Fax: 970-349-2250
Web: www.skicb.com

CEO: –
CFO: –
HR: –
FYE: April 30
Type: Private

Whether it's cross country or downhill this butte is made for skiing. Crested Butte is a leading Colorado ski operator that owns the Crested Butte Mountain Resort within the Gunnison National Forest and the Elk Mountain Range. The ski resort offers more than 1100 acres of skiable terrain 16 lifts and a full range of accommodations and amenities. Crested Butte has hosted such events as Colorado's first X Games the US Extreme Freeskiing Championships and the Elk Mountain Grand Traverse. CNL Lifestyle Properties a real estate investment trust affiliated with CNL Financial Group owns the resort property and leases it to Triple Peaks a ski operator controlled by husband and wife team Tim and Diane Mueller.

CRESTWOOD MIDSTREAM PARTNERS LP (NEW)   NYS: CMLP

700 Louisiana Street, Suite 2060
Houston, TX 77002
Phone: 832 519-2200
Fax: –
Web: www.crestwoodlp.com

CEO: Robert G Phillips
CFO: Michael J Campbell
HR: –
FYE: December 31
Type: Public

The middle of the oil and gas stream is best for Crestwood Midstream Partners (formerly Quicksilver Gas Services). The company gathers and processes natural gas and natural gas liquids from the Barnett Shale formation near Fort Worth Texas. Crestwood Midstream Partners' assets include a pipeline and a processing plant with 200 million cu. ft. a day capacity a processing unit at the existing plant extensions to the existing pipeline and pipelines in other drilling areas in Texas. In 2013 it merged with Inergy Midstream to become an $8 billion midstream entity.

	Annual Growth	09/09	09/10	09/11	09/12*	12/13
Sales ($ mil.)	65.6%	87.5	94.7	110.9	189.8	658.6
Net income ($ mil.)	–	28.3	30.6	41.6	65.7	(20.0)
Market value ($ mil.)	6.6%	–	–	–	4,370.3	4,660.5
Employees	(10.0%)	–	–	–	140	126

*Fiscal year change

CREXENDO INC
NBB: CXDO

1615 South 52nd Street
Tempe, AZ 85281
Phone: 602 714-8500
Fax: -
Web: www.crexendo.com

CEO: Steven G Mihaylo
CFO: Ron Vincent
HR: -
FYE: December 31
Type: Public

Crexendo (formerly iMergent) would like to help increase the volume on your e-commerce business. Catering to home-based small and medium-sized businesses the company's cloud-based software helps merchants create manage and promote their e-commerce website and process orders. Premium services include site and logo design supplier integration and search engine optimization. The company has primarily used training seminars around the country to sell its products to aspiring e-commerce mavens but hopes to open more sales channels. More than 90% of sales come from customers in North America (US and Canada). Chairman and CEO Steven Mihaylo founder and former CEO of Inter-Tel owns more than a third of Crexendo.

	Annual Growth	12/10	12/11	12/12	12/13	12/14
Sales ($ mil.)	(41.7%)	65.8	48.0	17.2	10.3	7.6
Net income ($ mil.)	-	(2.3)	(6.2)	(3.9)	(5.0)	(6.4)
Market value ($ mil.)	(20.1%)	57.1	35.7	35.9	38.8	23.3
Employees	(38.6%)	395	162	123	84	56

CRIDER INC.

1 Plant Ave.
Stillmore GA 30464
Phone: 912-562-4435
Fax: 912-562-4168

CEO: W A Crider Jr
CFO: -
HR: -
FYE: December 31
Type: Private

They may not know why the chicken crossed the road but the folks at Crider apparently have figured out how to get them to climb inside its cans. The company is a leading chicken canner in the US and makes a number of fresh and fully-cooked chicken offerings. It also cans turkey beef and ham. Crider's products are supplied to food retailers including club stores nationwide under branded and private-labels. The Georgia company was founded in 1944 by Ahtee and Emma Lou Crider and is still owned and operated by the founders' descendants.

CRISTA MINISTRIES

19303 FREMONT AVE N
SHORELINE, WA 981333800
Phone: 206-546-7200
Fax: -
Web: www.crista.org

CEO: Robert Lonac
CFO: Brian Kirkpatrick
HR: -
FYE: June 30
Type: Private

World Concern is concerned with the poorest of the poor around the world. The Christian not-for-profit helps about 4 million people a year in more than 30 nations. The group uses its own index of nine factors like economy health issues conflict and food availability along with prayer to determine which nations most need assistance. World Concern provides emergency relief and community development including small business loans agriculture starter kits prenatal education Christian literature village sanitation kits and donated goods (clothing plant seeds bedding). Founded in 1973 the group uses about 1300 volunteers throughout the world working from offices in the US Bolivia Kenya and Thailand.

	Annual Growth	06/08	06/09	06/12	06/13	06/14
Sales ($ mil.)	(5.2%)	-	133.0	96.4	102.8	101.7
Net income ($ mil.)	94.9%	-	-	1.6	1.5	6.0
Market value ($ mil.)	-	-	-	-	-	-
Employees	-	-	-	-	-	1,200

CRITICAL CARE SYSTEMS INTERNATIONAL INC.

c/o Accredo Health 1640 Century Center Pkwy.
Memphis TN 38134
Phone: 901-385-3688
Fax: 818-367-5379
Web: www.tutorperini.com

CEO: -
CFO: -
HR: -
FYE: December 31
Type: Subsidiary

When you need critical infusion services sometimes the last place you want to be is a hospital. That's where Critical Care Systems International steps in. The health care services company offers specialized infusion therapy at patients' homes and its own ambulatory infusion sites. Critical Care Systems administers its services to pediatric and adult patients who suffer from a range of ailments including autoimmune disorders cancer infectious diseases and rheumatoid arthritis. It also provides pre- and post-transplant support. Critical Care Systems is a wholly owned subsidiary of Accredo Health — the specialty pharmacy division of Express Scripts.

CRITTENTON HOSPITAL MEDICAL CENTER

261 E MAPLE RD
BIRMINGHAM, MI 48009-6324
Phone: 248-652-5000
Fax: -
Web: www.crittenton.com

CEO: Roy Powell
CFO: Donna Kopinski
HR: -
FYE: December 31
Type: Private

Crittenton Hospital Medical Center treats patients in the western counties of the suburban Detroit area. The not-for-profit hospital has 290 beds for acute care but also provides primary and specialist care. Crittenton offers such services as urgent pediatric care rehabilitative therapy inpatient psychiatric care joint replacement and sleep analysis. It is a fully accredited teaching campus and partners with area universities and medical providers. It also operates outpatient facilities including surgery imaging and therapy centers. With a heritage that reaches back to the early 1900s Crittenton Hospital Medical Center opened its doors in 1967.

	Annual Growth	12/05	12/06	12/07	12/08	12/09
Sales ($ mil.)	11.7%	-	-	-	200.4	223.7
Net income ($ mil.)	-	-	-	-	(39.9)	(4.2)
Market value ($ mil.)	-	-	-	-	-	-
Employees	-	-	-	-	-	1,515

CROCS INC
NMS: CROX

7477 East Dry Creek Parkway
Niwot, CO 80503
Phone: 303 848-7000
Fax: -
Web: www.crocs.com

CEO: Gregg Ribatt
CFO: Carrie W. Teffner
HR: -
FYE: December 31
Type: Public

Crocs has taken a bite out of the footwear industry. The company's shoe collection has grown by leaps and bounds from its ubiquitous colorful slip-on shoe to mainstream fashion. Branded as Crocs its shoes are made of proprietary closed-cell resin and designed for men women and children; its collection includes 300-plus four-season footwear styles. Jibbitz are their decorative add-on charms. The company sells its products in more than 90 countries operating distribution centers worldwide and manufacturing plants in Mexico and Italy. Crocs sells through retailers such as Dillard's Nordstrom and Dick's Sporting Goods as well as through about 250 of its own stores and kiosks worldwide.

	Annual Growth	12/10	12/11	12/12	12/13	12/14
Sales ($ mil.)	11.0%	789.7	1,000.9	1,123.3	1,192.7	1,198.2
Net income ($ mil.)	-	67.7	112.8	131.3	10.4	(4.9)
Market value ($ mil.)	(7.6%)	1,344.2	1,159.7	1,129.9	1,250.0	980.7
Employees	5.2%	4,000	4,157	4,900	5,000	4,900

CROGHAN BANCSHARES, INC.   NBB: CHBH

323 Croghan Street   CEO: Rick M Robertson
Fremont, OH 43420   CFO: -
Phone: 419 332-7301   HR: -
Fax: -   FYE: December 31
Web: www.croghan.com   Type: Public

Croghan Bancshares is helping to share the wealth in the Buckeye state. The firm is the holding company for Croghan Colonial Bank which has about 10 branches in northern Ohio. Founded in 1888 the bank provides standard products and services including checking and savings accounts money market accounts certificates of deposit and credit cards Its lending activities primarily consist of residential and commercial mortgages and to a lesser extent agricultural business construction and consumer loans. In addition the bank offers wealth management investments estate planning private banking and trust services.

	Annual Growth	12/10	12/11	12/12	12/13	12/14
Assets ($ mil.)	12.3%	489.7	629.7	631.0	817.9	779.4
Net income ($ mil.)	21.0%	4.0	4.8	4.8	4.4	8.6
Market value ($ mil.)	10.0%	54.9	66.2	69.1	78.2	80.3
Employees	5.2%	166	161	167	209	203

CROPKING INCORPORATED

134 West Dr.   CEO: Paul Brentlinger
Lodi OH 44254   CFO: -
Phone: 330-302-4203   HR: -
Fax: 330-302-4204   FYE: July 31
Web: www.cropking.com   Type: Private

Marketing controlled environment agriculture for fun and profit CropKing makes and sells greenhouses equipment and supplies for growing hydroponic crops (that is growing crops without soil in a controlled environment). CropKing's hydroponic greenhouse systems protect crops from environmental elements allowing year-round production of such plants as tomatoes lettuce and herbs. The company sells to hobbyists as well as to commercial customers. It offers grower workshops videos and literature through its Web site. Other products include aquaculture (fish farming) systems and mushroom production units. CropKing sells to customers throughout the US Canada Mexico Europe and the Caribbean.

CROSBY TRUCKING SERVICE INC.

270 Keezletown Rd.   CEO: -
Mt. Sidney VA 24467   CFO: -
Phone: 540-234-9268   HR: -
Fax: 540-234-9269   FYE: December 31
Web: www.crosbytrucking.com   Type: Private

Trucking company Crosby Trucking Service hauls truckload containers of general commodities primarily along the east coast and between the coast and Ohio Indiana and the city of Chicago. The company operates from terminals in Indiana Ohio Tennessee Massachusetts North Carolina and Virginia. It maintains a fleet of about 130 tractors and more than 600 trailers. In addition to freight transportation Crosby Trucking subsidiaries Crosby Leasing Crosby Brokerage and Crosco provide truck leasing and freight brokerage services and manage the company's real estate holdings respectively. Crosby Trucking Service was founded in 1947 to haul milk to a local creamery.

CROSCILL HOME LLC

295 5th Ave. 6th Fl.   CEO: Douglas Kahn
New York NY 10016   CFO: Clifford F Campbell
Phone: 212-689-7222   HR: Jill Ridding
Fax: 212-481-8656   FYE: December 31
Web: www.croscill.com   Type: Private

Croscill Home has made its bed in the textile industry. The company makes coordinated home furnishings including linens for bedrooms bathrooms and windows. It also makes pillows pet beds table lamps and accent furniture. Croscill Home's products are sold by major retailers such as JC Penney and Bed Bath & Beyond throughout North America and by mail order in Australia Canada Japan the UK and the US. Croscill claims credit for producing the first decorative comforter and originating the concept of coordinated merchandise. Founded in 1946 by George Kahn the Kahn family sold the company in 2008 to funds managed by private equity firm Patriarch Partners.

CROSMAN CORPORATION

7629 Routes 5 and 20   CEO: -
East Bloomfield NY 14443   CFO: Robert Beckwith
Phone: 585-657-6161   HR: -
Fax: 585-657-5405   FYE: December 31
Web: www.crosman.com   Type: Private

There's more than air in the cross hairs at Crosman. A leading air gun maker the company has more than 50 models of pellet and BB rifles and pistols as well as crossbows ammunition and optical products (such as riflescopes and crossbow sights). Its guns are offered under the Benjamin Sheridan and Remington names. Crosman markets its products worldwide through select retailers and sporting goods chains such as Wal-Mart and Dick's Sporting Goods as well as through its website. Founded in 1923 the air gun maker is owned by Wellspring Capital Management LLC.

CROSS BORDER RESOURCES INC.   NBB: XBOR

2515 McKinney Avenue, Suite 900   CEO: -
Dallas, TX 75201   CFO: P Stark
Phone: 210 226-6700   HR: -
Fax: -   FYE: December 31
Web: www.xbres.com   Type: Public

Cross Border Resources is focusing its oil and gas exploration and development efforts on New Mexico and Texas. The company owns some 300000 net acres primarily in New Mexico with more than 30000 of those acres located in the prolific Permian Basin in West Texas. Its properties consist of working mineral and royalty interests in various oil and gas wells and lease acreage located in the counties of Chaves Eddy Lea and Roosevelt in New Mexico and the counties of Borden and Dawson in Texas. They produce more than 200 barrels of oil equivalent per day. Cross Border Resources formed in early 2011 following the business combination of Doral Energy and Pure Energy.

	Annual Growth	07/10*	12/11	12/12	12/13	12/14
Sales ($ mil.)	65.1%	1.7	7.3	14.8	13.1	12.4
Net income ($ mil.)	-	(13.8)	(1.2)	(2.4)	3.4	(2.5)
Market value ($ mil.)	128.0%	0.5	28.8	15.6	6.4	13.5
Employees		2	5	-	-	-

*Fiscal year change

CROSS COMPANY

4400 Piedmont Pkwy.
Greensboro NC 27410
Phone: 336-856-6985
Fax: 336-856-6999
Web: www.crossco.com

CEO: Steve Earley
CFO: Jerry Bohnsack
HR: –
FYE: November 30
Type: Private

Cross selling is no problem for Cross Company an industrial distributor of products and solutions for fluid-power motion-control factory-automation fluid-handling and measurement applications. Employee-owned since 1979 the Southeastern US-based automation technology company operates four divisions: Cross Automation Cross Fluid Power Cross Hose & Fittings and Cross Instrumentation. It has operations in seven US states. Division Cross Automation provides industrial plant and machine automation products including controls sensors and drives. Cross Fluid Power is a distributor of hydraulic and pneumatic components and engineered systems.

CROSS COUNTRY HEALTHCARE INC
NMS: CCRN

6551 Park of Commerce Boulevard, N.W.
Boca Raton, FL 33487
Phone: 561 998-2232
Fax: –
Web: www.crosscountryhealthcare.com

CEO: William J. Grubbs
CFO: William J. Burns
HR: Angela Blackledge
FYE: December 31
Type: Public

Cross Country Healthcare is one of the largest health care staffing firms in the US. Under several brands the company places traveling nurses and other health care professionals through about 4300 contracts with acute care hospitals pharmaceutical companies nursing homes schools and other related facilities across the nation. The firm coordinates travel and housing arrangements for its nurses whose assignments usually last about three months at a time. Cross Country also provides health care education training and recruiting services for doctors and health care executives. Subsidiaries and brands include Assignment America Allied Health Group NovaPro Med-Staff Trav-Corps and Cejka Search.

	Annual Growth	12/10	12/11	12/12	12/13	12/14
Sales ($ mil.)	7.2%	468.6	504.0	442.6	438.3	617.8
Net income ($ mil.)	–	(2.8)	4.1	(42.2)	(52.0)	(31.8)
Market value ($ mil.)	10.2%	265.0	173.7	150.2	312.3	390.5
Employees	10.3%	1,100	1,200	1,150	1,100	1,630

CROSS MATCH TECHNOLOGIES INC.

3950 RCA Blvd. Ste. 5001
Palm Beach Gardens FL 33410
Phone: 561-622-1650
Fax: 561-622-9938
Web: www.crossmatch.net

CEO: Richard Agostinelli
CFO: Martin K Weinbaum
HR: –
FYE: December 31
Type: Private

If you dust the fingerprint-recognition technology sector you'll find the prints of Cross Match Technologies all over the scene. The company makes forensic-quality fingerprint recognition and identification systems for law enforcement agencies and corporate customers. Among Cross Match's biometric products are fingerprint scanning facial recognition systems iris capture and other identification systems. The company also offers identification systems for airports national borders nuclear power plants and sea ports. Founded in 1996 Cross Match was acquired by investment firm Francisco Partners Management in mid-2012.

CROSS TIMBERS ROYALTY TRUST
NYS: CRT

Southwest Bank Trustee, P.O. Box 962020
Fort Worth, TX 76162-2020
Phone: 855 588-7839
Fax: –
Web: www.crt-crosstimbers.com

CEO: –
CFO: –
HR: –
FYE: December 31
Type: Public

Cross Timbers Royalty Trust distributes royalties from more than 2900 oil and natural gas producing properties in Texas Oklahoma and New Mexico. The trust which was formed in 1991 does not operate or control any of its properties. Instead it owns stakes in wells located primarily in gas properties in the San Juan Basin of northwestern New Mexico. The trust's estimated proved reserves are 856000 barrels of oil and 25.6 billion cu. ft. of gas. XTO Energy which markets the trust's oil and gas owns the underlying propeties and distributed all of its trust units as a dividend to its stockholders in 2003.

	Annual Growth	12/10	12/11	12/12	12/13	12/14
Sales ($ mil.)	(1.0%)	17.1	18.4	15.3	14.3	16.4
Net income ($ mil.)	(1.2%)	16.7	18.0	14.9	13.9	15.9
Market value ($ mil.)	(18.8%)	239.3	293.2	161.5	176.4	103.9
Employees	–					

CROSSAMERICA PARTNERS LP
NYS: CAPL

645 West Hamilton Street, Suite 500
Allentown, PA 18101
Phone: 610 625-8000
Fax: –
Web: www.crossamericapartners.com

CEO: Joseph V Topper Jr
CFO: Clay Killinger
HR: –
FYE: December 31
Type: Public

CrossAmerica Partners (formerly Lehigh Gas Partners) won't leave motorists running on empty as they drive across America. The company distributes gasoline and diesel fuel to 1174 gas stations in 16 US states mostly along the East Coast. CrossAmerica owns or leases about 660 gas stations franchised under various brands including BP ExxonMobil Shell and Valero; it also distributes branded motor fuel to Gulf and Sunoco gas stations. About 95% of the more than 906.2 million gallons of motor fuels distributed yearly by CrossAmerica is branded (including the Chevron Sunoco Valero Gulf and CITGO brands).

	Annual Growth	12/10	12/11	12/12	12/13	12/14
Sales ($ mil.)	–	0.0	0.0	311.7	1,934.4	2,669.3
Net income ($ mil.)	–	0.0	0.0	(1.4)	18.1	(6.2)
Market value ($ mil.)	–	0.0	0.0	426.6	656.7	925.2
Employees	–	–	–	–	–	–

CROSSBEAM SYSTEMS INC.

80 Central St.
Boxborough MA 01719
Phone: 978-318-7500
Fax: 978-287-4210
Web: www.crossbeam.com

CEO: Michael A Ruffolo
CFO: Tom Sheehan
HR: –
FYE: December 31
Type: Private

Crossbeam Systems lays the foundation for application network security. The company's X-Series software and hardware platform enables customers to manage different security applications from a single unit by consolidating firewall virtual private network (VPN) intrusion detection network gateways and other functions. The platform is certified for applications from vendors such as IBM Check Point and Sourcefire. The X-Series is capable of security application processing speeds of up to 140 Gbps. Its customers have included AT&T GlaxoSmithKline Volkswagen and H&R Block. Blue Coat Systems acquired Crossbeam in late 2012.

CROSSLAND CONSTRUCTION COMPANY INC.

833 S EAST AVE
COLUMBUS, KS 667252307
Phone: 479-464-7077
Fax: –
Web: www.crosslandconstruction.com

CEO: Ivan E Crossland Jr
CFO: –
HR: –
FYE: July 31
Type: Private

Crossland Construction has crossed the prairie transitioning from a local player in Columbus Kansas to a firm with a strong regional presence. The company designs builds and manages construction of government education healthcare retail and other buildings from a handful of offices in Kansas Missouri Arkansas Oklahoma Colorado and Texas. Customers have included Harley-Davidson SAM'S CLUB McCune Brooks Hospital Embassy Suites and a variety of school districts and municipalities. Crossland builds everything from office buildings and warehouses to veteran's memorials and airports. The company which often works in partnership with PBA Architects was founded by Ivan Crossland Sr. in 1978.

	Annual Growth	07/02	07/03	07/04	07/07	07/08
Sales ($ mil.)	–	–	–	(1,316.0)	336.1	434.2
Net income ($ mil.)	2209.5%	–	–	0.0	11.4	10.2
Market value ($ mil.)	–	–	–	–	–	–
Employees	–	–	–	–	–	715

CROSSMARK INC.

5100 Legacy Dr.
Plano TX 75024-3104
Phone: 469-814-1000
Fax: 469-814-1355
Web: www.crossmark.com

CEO: Steve Schuckenbrock
CFO: Don Martin
HR: –
FYE: December 31
Type: Private

CROSSMARK helps clients in the consumer packaged goods industry get products in and out of stores. The company provides headquarter sales (securing distribution in retail outlets) in-store merchandising sales support and supply chain optimization services. Clients include supermarkets convenience stores drug stores and other specialty trade channels. CROSSMARK also helps customers plan promotional events while its CROSSMARK Retail Technologies provides technology solutions for clients. Its expertise spans the grocery mass club drug convenience store and home improvement channels among others. In 2012 the company agreed to be acquired by Warburg Pincus.

CROSSROADS SYSTEMS INC

NAS: CRDS

11000 North Mopac Expressway, Suite 150
Austin, TX 78759
Phone: 512 349-0300
Fax: –
Web: www.crossroads.com

CEO: Richard K Coleman Jr
CFO: Jennifer Ray Crane
HR: –
FYE: October 31
Type: Public

Crossroads Systems sets up shop where business and information intersect. The company provides storage networking equipment and data archiving systems used to manage and protect critical data. Its products include StrongBox (network attached storage appliance that uses linear tape file system technology) RVA (monitoring tape media and the condition of disk drives) and SPHiNX (protecting data by working as a network attached storage device or virtual tape library). Crossroads Systems sells directly to manufacturers such as HP (45% of sales) and EMC and through distributors. The company was founded in 1996.

	Annual Growth	10/11	10/12	10/13	10/14	10/15
Sales ($ mil.)	(15.0%)	15.0	14.0	12.6	11.1	7.8
Net income ($ mil.)	–	(7.5)	(10.7)	(12.1)	(9.2)	(9.0)
Market value ($ mil.)	(27.8%)	122.8	82.9	24.9	67.0	33.4
Employees	(17.4%)	99	139	48	48	46

CROSSTEX ENERGY INC

NMS: XTXI

2501 Cedar Springs
Dallas, TX 75201
Phone: 214 953-9500
Fax: –

CEO: Barry E Davis
CFO: Michael J Garberding
HR: –
FYE: December 31
Type: Public

Crosstex Energy Inc. owns and controls the general partner of and has a 17% limited partnership stake in major operating unit Crosstex Energy L.P. Crosstex Energy's energy sources (the Barnett and Haynesville shale plays) and markets are found in East Texas North Texas and the Louisiana Gulf Coast. It is engaged in natural gas gathering processing transmission and marketing. The company buys natural gas from independent producers. Crosstex Energy's assets include 3500 miles of natural gas gathering and transmission pipeline 10 processing plants and four fractionators. It also operates barge and rail terminals product storage facilities brine disposal wells and an major fleet of trucks.

	Annual Growth	12/08	12/09	12/10	12/11	12/12
Sales ($ mil.)	(23.8%)	4,907.0	1,459.1	1,792.7	2,013.9	1,655.9
Net income ($ mil.)	–	–	24.2	15.6	(11.7)	(6.0)	(12.5)
Market value ($ mil.)	38.5%	184.9	286.9	420.1	599.3	679.9
Employees	(1.4%)	780	456	469	494	736

CROWDER CONSTRUCTION COMPANY INC

6425 BROOKSHIRE BLVD
CHARLOTTE, NC 282160301
Phone: 704-372-3541
Fax: –
Web: www.crowdercc.com

CEO: Otis A. Crowder
CFO: James Baldwin
HR: –
FYE: March 31
Type: Private

Two may be company but a firm located in the Southeast US specializing in bridge and highway civil environmental and industrial construction is a Crowd(er) as in Crowder Construction. The company's projects include parking decks highway and bridge water and sewer treatment plant construction. Projects completed by its Crowder Electrical unit range from power substations to light rail facilities. The now employee-owned company was founded in Charlotte North Carolina in 1947 by Bill and O. P. Crowder; it continues to be led by the Crowder family.

	Annual Growth	03/10	03/11	03/12	03/13	03/14
Sales ($ mil.)	7.8%	–	186.0	222.0	233.0	233.0
Net income ($ mil.)	–	–	–	0.0	0.0	0.0
Market value ($ mil.)	–	–	–	–	–	–
Employees	–	–	–	–	–	900

CROWE HORWATH LLP

320 E. Jefferson Blvd.
South Bend IN 46601-2314
Phone: 574-232-3992
Fax: 574-236-8692
Web: www.crowehorwath.com

CEO: –
CFO: –
HR: Linda Scripter
FYE: March 31
Type: Private - Partnershi

If your organization has something to crow about Crowe Horwath is sure to find out. Crowe Horwath is one of the largest accounting firms in the US with about 30 offices in 13 states (largely in the Midwest Southeast and Mid-Atlantic). The firm provides services including auditing and assurance financial advisory litigation support tax consultation and risk management. It serves clients in sectors including dealerships construction agribusiness and financial services as well as universities not-for-profits and government agencies. Subsidiaries offer wealth management staffing and investment banking. Crowe Horwath is the largest member of global accounting network Crowe Horwath International.

CROWLEY MARITIME CORPORATION

9487 Regency Square Blvd.
Jacksonville FL 32225
Phone: 904-727-2200
Fax: 904-727-2501
Web: www.crowley.com

CEO: Thomas Crowley Jr
CFO: –
HR: –
FYE: December 31
Type: Private

Crowley Maritime has pushed and pulled its way into prominence as a tug and barge operator. The company's Liner Services unit provides scheduled transportation of containers trailers and other cargo mainly among ports in Latin and North America Puerto Rico and the Caribbean Basin. Other units transport oil and chemical products and oil field equipment and provide ship assist/escort marine salvage and emergency towing logistics ship management and fuel distribution services. Overall the company's fleet includes more than 200 vessels. Founded in 1892 Crowley Maritime is owned by members of the founding Crowley family including chairman/CEO Thomas Crowley and company employees.

CROWN BATTERY MANUFACTURING COMPANY

1445 MAJESTIC DR
FREMONT, OH 434209190
Phone: 419-332-0563
Fax: –
Web: www.c-linebattery.com

CEO: –
CFO: –
HR: Scott Macina
FYE: September 30
Type: Private

Crown Battery Manufacturing doesn't let its power go to its head. The company manufactures and sells industrial batteries and chargers automotive batteries and commercial battery products to clients across North America. Products serve clients in the marine railroad mining and automotive industries; the company also offers products with deep-cycle and other heavy-duty applications. Other products include battery chargers and battery cleaners for industrial applications. The company was founded in 1926 by German immigrant William J. Koenig.

	Annual Growth	09/10	09/11	09/12	09/13	09/14
Sales ($ mil.)	(0.2%)	–	215.2	191.1	196.2	214.2
Net income ($ mil.)	40.1%	–	–	6.1	10.8	12.0
Market value ($ mil.)	–	–	–	–	–	–
Employees	–	–	–	–	–	550

CROWN CRAFTS, INC.

916 South Burnside Avenue
Gonzales, LA 70737
Phone: 225 647-9100
Fax: –
Web: www.crowncrafts.com

NAS: CRWS
CEO: E Randall Chestnut
CFO: Olivia W Elliott
HR: –
FYE: March 29
Type: Public

Prospects for new business opportunities keep Crown Crafts drooling. Operating through its subsidiaries Hamco and Crown Crafts Infant Products the company designs and sells textile products for infants and juveniles. Crown Crafts designs makes and markets baby bibs burp cloths bathing accessories and bedding. The childcare products firm founded in 1957 has worked to regain profitability by selling or shuttering its US manufacturing operations and relying on foreign contractors mainly in China to make its goods. Crown Crafts' products are sold in department and specialty stores mass retailers catalog houses and outlet stores.

	Annual Growth	04/11	04/12*	03/13	03/14	03/15
Sales ($ mil.)	(1.1%)	90.0	85.3	78.4	81.3	86.0
Net income ($ mil.)	7.3%	4.3	5.0	5.1	5.8	5.7
Market value ($ mil.)	12.5%	48.4	53.9	60.4	78.8	77.5
Employees	(2.7%)	157	153	145	140	141

*Fiscal year change

CROWN GOLD CORPORATION

970 Caughlin Crossing Ste 100
Reno NV 89509
Phone: 775-284-7200
Fax: 775-284-7202
Web: www.goldsummitcorp.com

TSX VENTURE: CWM
CEO: Anthony P Taylor
CFO: –
HR: –
FYE: April 30
Type: Public

The top of the gold heap is where Crown Gold (formerly Gold Summit) aims to be. The company explores for and develops gold and silver prospect properties in the eastern and western US. Crown Gold focuses on explorations at several properties across Nevada including Monte Cristo Gold Basin and Blue Sphinx. The company with partner Astral Mining is also developing properties in North and South Carolina (Saluda and Bear Creek) where miners have not explored underground since the mid-1800s. It also plans to buy Pasofino Gold Corp. which holds assets in Colombia. The former Gold Summit merged with Crown Minerals in 2010 to form Crown Gold.

CROWN HOLDING COMPANY

Pasquerilla Plaza
Johnstown PA 15901
Phone: 814-536-4441
Fax: 814-535-9388
Web: www.crownamericanhotels.com

CEO: –
CFO: –
HR: –
FYE: January 31
Type: Private

Crown Holding's jewels are in the form of a couple of midscale hotels a restaurant and convention center. Formed as a masonry company in 1950 Crown Holding now focuses on managing a handful of properties in its hometown. Through privately held Crown American Hotels the company owns and manages four hotel restaurant and convention center properties in downtown Johnstown Pennsylvania. Its Holiday Inn and Holiday Inn Express there are both franchised through InterContinental Hotels. The company also owns Harrigan's Cafe and Wine Deck (attached to the Holiday Inn) and the Pasquerilla Conference Center named after company cofounder Frank Pasquerilla.

CROWN HOLDINGS INC

One Crown Way
Philadelphia, PA 19154-4599
Phone: 215 698-5100
Fax: –
Web: www.crowncork.com

NYS: CCK
CEO: Timothy J. Donahue
CFO: Thomas A. Kelly
HR: –
FYE: December 31
Type: Public

Crown Holdings wants to pop a top on profits. The company is a leading global manufacturer of consumer packaging; steel and aluminum food and beverage cans and related packaging are Crown's primary lines. Its portfolio includes aerosol cans and various metal vacuum closures marketed under brands Liftoff SuperEnd and Easylift as well as specialty packaging such as novelty containers and industrial cans. Crown also supplies can-making equipment and parts. Its roster of customers has included Coca-Cola Cadberry Schweppes Heinz Nestl&e SC Johnson Unilever and Procter & Gamble which owns Gillette another customer.

	Annual Growth	12/10	12/11	12/12	12/13	12/14
Sales ($ mil.)	3.5%	7,941.0	8,644.0	8,470.0	8,656.0	9,097.0
Net income ($ mil.)	4.5%	324.0	282.0	557.0	324.0	387.0
Market value ($ mil.)	11.1%	4,639.8	4,667.6	5,116.6	6,195.3	7,075.1
Employees	2.9%	20,500	20,700	21,900	21,300	23,000

CROWN MEDIA HOLDINGS INC   NMS: CRWN

12700 Ventura Boulevard, Suite 200
Studio City, CA 91604
Phone: 818 755-2400
Fax: –
Web: www.hallmarkchannel.com

CEO: William J. (Bill) Abbott
CFO: Andrew (Andy) Rooke
HR: –
FYE: December 31
Type: Public

All for the Family would be the name of a TV series about family-friendly Crown Media Holdings. It owns and operates the Hallmark Channel a cable network that specializes in family-oriented TV fare. It features mostly third-party programming including such TV series as Golden Girls Little House on the Prairie and Matlock as well as made-for-TV movies feature films and miniseries which includes original programming. The channel reaches about 87 million US homes through cable providers such as Comcast and Cox. Crown Media also operates the Hallmark Movies & Mysteries channel a 24-hour channel that primarily offers feature films miniseries and lighter mysteries; it reaches nearly 30 million homes. Hallmark Cards controls more than 90% of the company.

	Annual Growth	12/10	12/11	12/12	12/13	12/14
Sales ($ mil.)	9.7%	287.3	323.4	349.9	377.8	415.6
Net income ($ mil.)	40.7%	24.1	319.0	107.4	67.7	94.5
Market value ($ mil.)	7.8%	942.4	435.2	665.4	1,269.7	1,273.3
Employees	5.2%	170	173	175	187	208

CROZER-KEYSTONE HEALTH SYSTEM

100 W SPROUL RD
SPRINGFIELD, PA 190642033
Phone: 610-338-8200
Fax: –

CEO: Joan Richards
CFO: –
HR: –
FYE: June 30
Type: Private

Crozer-Keystone Health System provides a full range of health care in the Philadelphia metropolitan area. The health system's facilities include five acute care hospitals four outpatient care centers and a sports science and technology center. Combined its not-for-profit member hospitals have about 840 beds. The hospitals' specialty units include trauma cardiac cancer orthopedic wound healing obesity sleep disorder and women's and children's health centers. The system also operates family occupational and diagnostic health clinics as well as home health and hospice agencies. In early the company agreed to be acquired by for-profit hospital operator Prospect Medical Holdings.

	Annual Growth	06/07	06/08	06/09	06/10	06/13
Sales ($ mil.)	–	–	(170.9)	49.0	50.8	807.5
Net income ($ mil.)	–	–	–	(1.1)	0.8	102.4
Market value ($ mil.)	–	–	–	–	–	–
Employees	–	–	–	–	–	7,100

CRST INTERNATIONAL INC.

3930 16th Ave. SW
Cedar Rapids IA 52406
Phone: 319-396-4400
Fax: 319-390-2649
Web: www.crst.com

CEO: David Rusch
CFO: Wesley Brackey
HR: Barnes Joins
FYE: December 31
Type: Private

CRST International promises f-a-s-t freight transportation through its operating units. CRST Expedited provides standard dry van truckload transportation primarily on long-haul routes along with dedicated and expedited transportation services. CRST Malone hauls steel and other freight requiring flatbed trailers or trailers with removable sides and CRST Logistics arranges freight transportation and provides other third-party logistics services. Other operations include CRST Dedicated Services and Specialized Transportation. Overall the companies operate a fleet of about 1200 tractors and 3000 van trailers. Family-owned CRST International was founded in 1955 by Herald Smith father of CEO John Smith.

CRUCIBLE INDUSTRIES LLC

575 State Fair Blvd.
Syracuse NY 13209
Phone: 315-487-0800
Fax: 315-487-4028
Web: www.crucible.com

CEO: –
CFO: William Lester
HR: –
FYE: December 31
Type: Private

Crucible Industries (formerly Crucible Materials) is forging a new path. The reconstituted company makes high speed steel stainless tool steel and tool steel for a variety of industries. The company operates a steel mill in upstate New York with units that manufacture its metal products which are distributed by contract affiliates. The problems of the US auto industry caused Crucible Industries' predecessor to file for Chapter 11 bankruptcy in 2009. Through the court its Research and Compaction Metals divisions were sold to Allegheny Technologies Incorporated while the rest of the company's assets were bought for $8 million by private equity group JP Industries and renamed Crucible Industries.

CRUM & FORSTER HOLDINGS CORP.

305 Madison Ave.
Morristown NJ 07962
Phone: 973-490-6600
Fax: 973-490-6940
Web: www.cfins.com

CEO: Douglas M Libby
CFO: Paul Bassaline
HR: –
FYE: December 31
Type: Subsidiary

Crum & Forster looks out for the best interests of employers. Through its subsidiaries the company offers an array of property/casualty insurance products to businesses including general liability automobile property and workers' compensation coverage. Crum & Forster also offers The Defender a broad commercial umbrella policy. The company's specialty policies include management protection crime insurance; it also offers personal auto and homeowners policies. In addition Crum & Forster provides risk management services. The company's products are sold through some 1500 independent brokers across the US. Crum & Forster is a subsidiary of Fairfax Financial Holdings.

CRYO-CELL INTERNATIONAL, INC.   NBB: CCEL

700 Brooker Creek Blvd.
Oldsmar, FL 34677
Phone: 813 749-2100
Fax: 813 723-0444
Web: www.cryo-cell.com

CEO: David I Portnoy
CFO: Jill Taymans
HR: –
FYE: November 30
Type: Public

Cryo-Cell International freezes the ties that bind. The company collects and cryogenically stores umbilical cord blood stem cells giving expectant parents some insurance in case disease (such as diabetes heart disease or stroke) should strike in the future. Specimens collected in the US are processed and stored at Cryo-Cell's facility in Oldsmar Florida. The company also offers services through subsidiaries in certain countries in Asia Europe Latin America and the Middle East. Cryo-Cell markets its services directly to consumers online through its website and by providing information and education to obstetricians pediatricians childbirth educators and other health care providers.

	Annual Growth	11/10	11/11	11/12	11/13	11/14
Sales ($ mil.)	3.4%	17.6	17.9	18.0	19.0	20.1
Net income ($ mil.)	(36.5%)	3.4	(2.1)	(6.3)	0.0	0.6
Market value ($ mil.)	6.0%	21.4	16.1	24.7	18.0	27.0
Employees	5.6%	57	59	80	80	71

CRYOLIFE, INC.
NYS: CRY

1655 Roberts Boulevard, N.W.
Kennesaw, GA 30144
Phone: 770 419-3355
Fax: 770 426-0031
Web: www.cryolife.com

CEO: James Patrick (Pat) Mackin
CFO: D. Ashley Lee
HR: Marian Fraley
FYE: December 31
Type: Public

CryoLife preserves lives by conserving the tissues that sustain them. The company takes human heart valves and blood vessels from deceased volunteer donors processes them and stores them in liquid nitrogen freezers (a process called cryopreservation). It then ships them to US surgeons who implant them during surgical procedures. For some preserved tissue the company uses its proprietary SynerGraft technology which reduces the presence of donor cells and makes the tissue more compatible with the recipient. CryoLife also develops implantable biomaterials including BioGlue an adhesive used to seal internal surgical wounds.

	Annual Growth	12/11	12/12	12/13	12/14	12/15
Sales ($ mil.)	5.1%	119.6	131.7	140.8	144.6	145.9
Net income ($ mil.)	(14.1%)	7.4	7.9	16.2	7.3	4.0
Market value ($ mil.)	22.4%	136.8	177.6	316.1	322.9	307.2
Employees	5.9%	430	488	510	535	540

CRYSTAL ROCK HOLDINGS INC
ASE: CRVP

1050 Buckingham St.
Watertown, CT 06795
Phone: 860 945-0661
Fax: –
Web: www.crystalrock.com

CEO: –
CFO: David Jurasek
HR: Cheryl Gustafsom
FYE: October 31
Type: Public

When co-workers gather around the water cooler or the coffeepot to discuss the Celtics the Patriots or the Red Sox (or even the Yankees) Crystal Rock wants to be there. The company delivers water and coffee to offices and homes throughout New England and in New York and New Jersey. Non-sparkling water which the company bottles at facilities in Connecticut Vermont and New York is offered under the Vermont Pure Hidden Springs and Crystal Rock brands and private labels. Vermont Pure Holdings' coffee brands include Baronet Coffee and Green Mountain Coffee Roasters. Company president Peter Baker and his family own a majority of Crystal Rock.

	Annual Growth	10/11	10/12	10/13	10/14	10/15
Sales ($ mil.)	0.8%	71.6	71.1	71.0	75.2	73.9
Net income ($ mil.)	–	1.5	(18.5)	0.6	0.2	(0.6)
Market value ($ mil.)	(9.1%)	16.0	22.5	18.6	16.7	10.9
Employees	(1.6%)	355	373	390	374	333

CSG SYSTEMS INTERNATIONAL INC.
NMS: CSGS

9555 Maroon Circle
Englewood, CO 80112
Phone: 303 200-2000
Fax: –
Web: www.csgi.com

CEO: Bret C. Griess
CFO: Randy R. Wiese
HR: –
FYE: December 31
Type: Public

For CSRs CSG Systems International could be a good friend. The company tries to make life a little easier for customer service representatives with its customer care and billing software and services designed for clients handling a high volume of transactions. The company offers outsourced transaction processing and customer service systems that are used to establish customer accounts process orders manage and mail monthly statements and perform marketing analysis among other functions. The company serves primarily North American cable TV direct broadcast satellite online services and telecom companies such as AT&T Time Warner Comcast and Verizon.

	Annual Growth	12/10	12/11	12/12	12/13	12/14
Sales ($ mil.)	8.1%	549.4	734.7	756.9	747.5	751.3
Net income ($ mil.)	13.3%	22.4	42.3	48.9	51.4	37.0
Market value ($ mil.)	7.3%	642.9	499.3	617.1	998.0	851.0
Employees	(0.5%)	3,512	3,352	3,542	3,398	3,448

CSI COMPRESSCO LP
NMS: CCLP

3809 S. FM 1788
Midland, TX 79706
Phone: 432 563-1170
Fax: –
Web: www.compressco.com

CEO: –
CFO: Elijio V Serrano
HR: –
FYE: December 31
Type: Public

Compressco Partners puts the pressure on before the natural gas and oil wells run dry. The company specializes in providing services to more than 400 natural gas and oil companies across 14 states to increase production and total recoverable reserves. The company offers compression liquids separation and gas metering services as well as the GasJack units that perform these operations. It applies its services primarily to mature wells but also on newer wells which have declined in production. Compressco Partners which was spun-off from TETRA Technologies in 2011 also provides well evaluations and well testing and monitoring services in Mexico.

	Annual Growth	12/10	12/11	12/12	12/13	12/14
Sales ($ mil.)	–	0.0	95.2	108.6	121.3	282.6
Net income ($ mil.)	–	0.0	7.3	16.3	17.6	11.3
Market value ($ mil.)	–	0.0	497.1	553.8	667.5	435.2
Employees	31.3%	–	420	286	290	950

CSI LEASING INC.

9990 OLD OLIVE STREET RD # 101
SAINT LOUIS, MO 631415930
Phone: 314-997-4934
Fax: –
Web: www.csileasing.com

CEO: E. William (Bill) Gillula
CFO: Fred O'Neal
HR: –
FYE: June 30
Type: Private

CSI Leasing provides computer products leasing for customers in the Americas Europe and Asia. The company targets businesses looking to lower operational costs by avoiding expenses related to ownership and upkeep of computer and communications network gear. It provides off-lease services through its EPC subsidiary which remarkets recycles and disposes of information technology equipment — and securely wipes and/or destroys the data on the equipment when it is returned. CSI serves clients in such industries as software financial services government and education. Majority-owned by employees and led by co-founder and chairman Ken Steinback the company was founded in 1972 as Computer Sales International.

	Annual Growth	06/00	06/01	06/02	06/03	06/09
Sales ($ mil.)	(5.6%)	–	576.5	502.4	531.3	362.1
Net income ($ mil.)	2.7%	–	–	13.7	14.4	16.4
Market value ($ mil.)	–	–	–	–	–	–
Employees	–	–	–	–	–	540

CSK AUTO CORPORATION

645 E. Missouri Ave. Ste. 400
Phoenix AZ 85012
Phone: 602-265-9200
Fax: 602-631-7321
Web: www.cskauto.com

CEO: Lawrence Mondry
CFO: Steven L Korby
HR: –
FYE: December 31
Type: Subsidiary

For CSK Auto the magic is under the hood. The retailer of auto parts sells to do-it-yourself car owners and increasingly auto professionals and commercial installers. CSK Auto once had 1300-plus stores in about a dozen states including California Oregon Washington and other markets mostly in the West under banners Checker Auto Parts Schuck's Auto Supply Kragen Auto Parts and Murray's Discount Auto Parts. CSK Auto is a subsidiary of O'Reilly which acquired it in 2008. The deal created the third-largest auto parts retailer in the US behind AutoZone and Advance Auto Parts. All CSK stores converted to the O'Reilly brand information systems and inventory offerings a process largely concluded in 2011.

CSL BEHRING LLC

1020 1st Ave.
King of Prussia PA 19406-0901
Phone: 610-878-4000
Fax: 610-878-4009
Web: www.cslbehring.com

CEO: –
CFO: Perry Premdas
HR: –
FYE: June 30
Type: Subsidiary

Take away the red and white blood cells from blood and you get plasma a protein-rich fluid. CSL Behring is among the world's largest fully integrated plasma collection companies. Through subsidiary CSL Plasma (formerly ZLB Plasma) the company collects plasma through dozens of facilities in the US and Germany. CSL Behring then develops plasma-based protein biotherapeutics to treat a range of health ailments including bleeding disorders (such as hemophilia) immune system deficiencies and respiratory disease (including emphysema). Biotherapeutics are also used in critical care settings for surgical and wound healing applications. CSL Behring is a subsidiary of Australian biopharmaceutical firm CSL Limited.

CSP INC

175 Cabot Street, Suite 210
Lowell, MA 01854
Phone: 978 663-7598
Fax: –
Web: www.cspi.com

NMS: CSPI

CEO: Victor Dellovo
CFO: Gary W Levine
HR: –
FYE: September 30
Type: Public

CSP knows IT. The company provides information technology services including the resale and integration of computer hardware and software through its Modcomp subsidiary. Modcomp serves clients in Germany the UK and the US. CSP's MultiComputer systems segment which accounts for about 10% of sales develops and builds computer signal processing systems for aerospace and defense markets. Its MultiComputer product line includes systems used for radar sonar and surveillance; sales are made directly in the US and through distributors and resellers to customers in Asia.

	Annual Growth	09/11	09/12	09/13	09/14	09/15
Sales ($ mil.)	4.9%	73.6	84.8	87.6	84.6	89.3
Net income ($ mil.)	–	0.4	6.6	0.4	1.3	(0.2)
Market value ($ mil.)	11.9%	12.9	16.5	26.1	29.4	20.2
Employees	5.7%	138	147	167	176	172

CSS INDUSTRIES, INC.

1845 Walnut Street
Philadelphia, PA 19103
Phone: 215 569-9900
Fax: –
Web: www.cssindustries.com

NYS: CSS

CEO: Christopher J. Munyan
CFO: Vincent A. Paccapaniccia
HR: –
FYE: March 31
Type: Public

Every day is cause for celebration at CSS Industries a designer maker and distributor of seasonal and everyday decorative products such as ribbons and bows gifts and gift tags boxes and wrap tissue paper and boxed Christmas cards. The company also makes dye for Easter eggs (Dudley's) and valentines for classroom exchange. Customers include mass-merchandise retailers warehouse clubs and retail drug and food stores primarily in the US and Canada. Wal-Mart and Target are CSS's largest customers. Originally founded as a furniture and department store retailer in 1923 the company operates through subsidiaries The Paper Magic Group Berwick Offray and C.R. Gibson.

	Annual Growth	03/11	03/12	03/13	03/14	03/15
Sales ($ mil.)	(8.7%)	450.7	384.7	364.2	320.5	313.0
Net income ($ mil.)	31.8%	5.6	15.7	15.2	18.8	17.0
Market value ($ mil.)	12.5%	176.1	181.8	242.7	252.3	281.7
Employees	(13.2%)	2,550	2,000	1,200	1,500	1,450

CSSI INC.

400 VRGNIA AVE SW STE 710
WASHINGTON, DC 20024
Phone: 202-863-2175
Fax: –
Web: www.cssiinc.com

CEO: Cynthia Castillo
CFO: Christopher Giusti
HR: Denise Wattersvice
FYE: December 31
Type: Private

CSSI turns an eye toward R&D. A technology and engineering services company the company specializes in air traffic management. Areas of expertise include decision support systems safety management and cost-benefit analysis. Its services include information management and custom software development operational analysis and implementation investment strategy and analysis and systems engineering. CSSI's clients have included NASA the US Department of Defense the Federal Aviation Administration and the airline industry. The company has satellite offices in Charleston South Carolina; Landover Maryland; and Northfield New Jersey.

	Annual Growth	12/04	12/05	12/06	12/08	12/12
Sales ($ mil.)	16.6%	–	22.4	21.4	31.2	65.5
Net income ($ mil.)	(25.9%)	–	–	20.1	1.9	3.3
Market value ($ mil.)	–	–	–	–	–	–
Employees	–	–	–	–	–	265

CST BRANDS INC

One Valero Way, Building D, Suite 200
San Antonio, TX 78249
Phone: 210 692-5000
Fax: –
Web: www.cstbrands.com

NYS: CST

CEO: Kimberly S. (Kim) Lubel
CFO: Clay E. (Clay) Killinger
HR: Henry Martinez
FYE: December 31
Type: Public

CST Brands is hoping to corner the market on convenience stores. The holding company spun off from energy giant Valero in 2013 operates more than 1000 gas stations/convenience stores in the US under the Corner Store moniker. Its gasoline is sold under the Valero and Diamond Shamrock brands while its stores are located in 10 US states and sell the usual — snacks drinks tobacco products health and beauty products automotive products and other convenience items. CST Brands has another 850 Dépanneur du Coin stores in eastern Canada (mostly in French-speaking Quebec); however the majority of its Canadian stores are operated by independent dealers.

	Annual Growth	12/10	12/11	12/12	12/13	12/14
Sales ($ mil.)	5.3%	10,371.0	12,863.0	13,135.0	12,777.0	12,758.0
Net income ($ mil.)	0.9%	193.0	214.0	210.0	139.0	200.0
Market value ($ mil.)	18.8%	–	–	2,833.4	3,365.0	–
Employees	7.7%	–	–	11,640	12,321	13,496

CSU FULLERTON AUXILIARY SERVICES CORPORATION

2600 NUTWOOD AVE STE 275
FULLERTON, CA 928313137
Phone: 657-278-4140
Fax: –
Web: www.csufasc.org

CEO: –
CFO: –
HR: –
FYE: June 30
Type: Private

CSU Fullerton Auxiliary Services (formerly California State University Fullerton Foundation) keeps an eye on auxiliary operations at Cal State. The organization administers research and education grants and oversees commercial operations such as the Titan Shops (which stock textbooks computers gifts and clothing) and franchise foodservices. It is also involved in real estate providing affordable housing for sale and lease to the university's faculty and staff. A 25-member board governs CSU Fullerton Auxiliary Services Corporation which was established in 1959.

	Annual Growth	06/07	06/08	06/09	06/10	06/12
Sales ($ mil.)	(50.4%)	–	1,035.7	54.0	55.2	62.9
Net income ($ mil.)	–	–	–	(0.5)	2.3	(2.8)
Market value ($ mil.)	–	–	–	–	–	–
Employees	–	–	–	–	–	1,400

CSX CORP
NMS: CSX

500 Water Street, 15th Floor
Jacksonville, FL 32202
Phone: 904-359-3200
Fax: –
Web: www.csx.com

CEO: Michael J. Ward
CFO: Frank A. Lonegro
HR: Diana Sorfleet
FYE: December 25
Type: Public

CSX banks on the railway as the right way to make money. Its main subsidiary CSX Transportation (CSXT) operates a major rail system of some 21000 route miles in the eastern US. The freight carrier links 23 states 70 ports 240 short-line railroads the District of Columbia and two Canadian provinces (Ontario and Quebec). Freight hauled by the company includes a wide variety of merchandise (food chemicals and consumer goods) coal and automotive products. CSX also transports via intermodal containers and trailers (Intermodal freight hauling uses multiple modes of transportation). CSX's rail segment also includes units that operate motor vehicle distribution centers and bulk cargo terminals.

	Annual Growth	12/11	12/12	12/13	12/14	12/15
Sales ($ mil.)	0.1%	11,743.0	11,756.0	12,026.0	12,669.0	11,811.0
Net income ($ mil.)	1.9%	1,822.0	1,859.0	1,864.0	1,927.0	1,968.0
Market value ($ mil.)	5.5%	20,333.7	18,759.9	27,314.4	35,415.1	25,228.9
Employees	(1.9%)	31,344	32,120	31,254	31,511	29,000

CSX TRANSPORTATION INC.

500 Water St. 15th Fl.
Jacksonville FL 32202
Phone: 904-359-3200
Fax: 904-359-2459
Web: www.csxt.com

CEO: Michael J Ward
CFO: Oscar Munoz
HR: –
FYE: December 31
Type: Subsidiary

Unlike other major railroads CSX Transportation elects not to go west. The company the primary subsidiary of CSX provides rail freight transportation over a network of about 21000 route miles of track in 23 states in the eastern half of the US the District of Columbia and two Canadian provinces that serves about 70 ports. It also has track connections to more than 240 short-line and regional railroads. Freight carried by the railroad includes coal aggregates (sand and gravel) agricultural products chemicals food consumer products forest products fertilizer motor vehicles and intermodal containers. Sister company CSX Intermodal arranges transportation of containerized freight by road and rail.

CTA ACOUSTICS INC.

25211 Dequindre Rd.
Madison Heights MI 48071
Phone: 248-544-2580
Fax: 248-544-2666
Web: www.ctaacoustics.com

CEO: James J Pike
CFO: –
HR: –
FYE: December 31
Type: Private

Life may be full of sound and fury but for CTA Acoustics the din signifies everything. CTA manufactures and supplies an acoustic and thermal insulation lineup used to make vehicles ventilation systems appliances and other equipment quieter cooler and more energy-efficient. Its glass fiber-based sound-absorbing blend for automotive under-hood and exterior use is sold under the QuietBlend brand. Made from textile fiberglass and anti-flame fibers CTA's ThermaBlend line offers an insulating blanket for an array of building products. CTA's customers include carmakers Ford GM and Nissan and material makers John Manville and Owens Corning. Started in 1971 CTA is an affiliated company of Cerberus Capital.

CTI BIOPHARMA CORP
NAS: CTIC

3101 Western Avenue, Suite 600
Seattle, WA 98121
Phone: 206-282-7100
Fax: –
Web: www.celltherapeutics.com

CEO: James A. Bianco
CFO: –
HR: Carol Tharp
FYE: December 31
Type: Public

CTI Biopharma (formerly Cell Therapeutics) is a toxic avenger. The firm creates more effective and less toxic treatments for various forms of cancer. CTI is developing a number of cancer-fighting compounds including Pixuvri (pixantrone) a treatment for non-Hodgkin's lymphoma and other tumorous cancers and Opaxio (paclitaxel poliglumex) for ovarian and brain cancers. CTI also focuses on research and development projects including a Phase 3 clinical trial of Pacritinib a myelofibrosis treatment. The company's Systems Medicine subsidiary is working on a potential sarcoma-fighter called brostallicin. Other subsidiaries include Aequus Biopharma and CTI Life Sciences.

	Annual Growth	12/10	12/11	12/12	12/13	12/14
Sales ($ mil.)	270.4%	0.3	–	–	34.7	60.1
Net income ($ mil.)	–	(82.6)	(62.4)	(101.4)	(42.7)	(93.4)
Market value ($ mil.)	59.5%	64.5	205.0	229.8	337.6	417.2
Employees	9.2%	88	96	114	106	125

CTI GROUP HOLDINGS INC.
NBB: CTIG

333 North Alabama Street, Suite 240
Indianapolis, IN 46204
Phone: 317-262-4666
Fax: –

CEO: Manfred Hanuschek
CFO: Nathan Habegger
HR: –
FYE: December 31
Type: Public

CTI Group (Holdings) helps companies act on their transactions. The company provides software and services for billing customer care and telemanagement. Targeting service providers in the telecom information technology financial cable and health care industries CTI offers software that analyzes billing data (SmartBill) automates telecommunications spending manages electronic invoicing and handles call accounting. The company also offers professional services and outsourced call center management output processing training support and marketing services.

	Annual Growth	12/09	12/10	12/11	12/12	12/13
Sales ($ mil.)	(0.4%)	15.7	15.2	17.0	16.8	15.5
Net income ($ mil.)	–	(1.3)	(3.3)	(0.6)	0.6	(1.1)
Market value ($ mil.)	55.4%	1.8	3.1	2.8	6.7	10.5
Employees	(4.5%)	137	124	111	113	114

CTI INDUSTRIES CORP
NAS: CTIB

22160 N. Pepper Road
Lake Barrington, IL 60010
Phone: 847-382-1000
Fax: 847-382-1219
Web: www.ctiindustries.com

CEO: John H Schwan
CFO: Timothy Patterson
HR: –
FYE: December 31
Type: Public

CTI Industries is full of hot air and that's just fine considering its best-selling product is usually filled with helium. The company designs produces and distributes foil balloons and latex balloons for parties fairs amusement parks and other entertainment-related venues. In addition to its novelty products CTI makes flexible containers primarily zippered bags and pouches for food and household use and film products including specialty film for medical applications and laminated coated and printed films that are sold to industrial and commercial customers who generally convert them into flexible packaging for liquid food products. CTI's largest market is the US followed by Mexico and the UK.

	Annual Growth	12/10	12/11	12/12	12/13	12/14
Sales ($ mil.)	4.9%	47.7	47.2	49.5	56.1	57.8
Net income ($ mil.)	(27.2%)	1.8	0.5	0.1	0.4	0.5
Market value ($ mil.)	(11.0%)	19.8	14.5	17.0	19.3	12.4
Employees	2.2%	370	152	400	105	404

CTPARTNERS EXECUTIVE SEARCH INC NBB: CTPR

1166 Avenue of the Americas, 3rd Fl.
New York, NY 10036
Phone: 212 588-3500
Fax: –
Web: www.ctnet.com
CEO: David C Nocifora
CFO: William J Keneally
HR: –
FYE: December 31
Type: Public

CTPartners finds the hidden treasures of senior management. The company performs CEO board member and senior-level executive management searches for both large and emerging companies worldwide. Operating through more than 20 global offices it has special expertise in filling top-level technology positions but also operates a number of other industry practices including financial services human resources life sciences media and telecommunications. The company delivers talent within an average of about 100 days; it has placed executives with such companies as Sony American Express and RELX Group. CTPartners was founded in 1980.

	Annual Growth	12/10	12/11	12/12	12/13	12/14
Sales ($ mil.)	108.3%	9.4	126.1	132.9	134.3	176.8
Net income ($ mil.)	–	(5.8)	(3.2)	(3.6)	(1.6)	3.3
Market value ($ mil.)	(0.9%)	114.5	38.6	33.2	40.7	110.4
Employees	17.1%	336	369	453	460	631

CTS CORP. NYS: CTS

1142 West Beardsley Avenue
Elkhart, IN 46514
Phone: 574 523-3800
Fax: 574 293-6146
Web: www.ctscorp.com
CEO: Kieran O'Sullivan
CFO: Ashish Agrawal
HR: –
FYE: December 31
Type: Public

CTS is all about electronics. The company makes components and sensors such as actuators switches and resistor networks. The biggest user by far of its products is the automotive market in powertrain safety fuel and emissions control systems. CTS-made products also are used in the aerospace communications computer medical equipment and military contracting industries. Customers have included industry leaders such as Hewlett-Packard and Toyota. The Americas account for nearly 70% of sales with Asia/Pacific bringing in 20% and Europe representing 15%. The company was founded in 1896.

	Annual Growth	12/10	12/11	12/12	12/13	12/14
Sales ($ mil.)	(7.5%)	552.6	588.5	576.9	409.5	404.0
Net income ($ mil.)	4.7%	22.0	21.0	20.3	(3.9)	26.5
Market value ($ mil.)	12.7%	369.3	307.2	355.0	664.8	595.4
Employees	(9.4%)	4,369	4,234	4,234	2,918	2,948

CTS VALPEY CORPORATION NASDAQ: VPF

75 South St.
Hopkinton MA 01748-2204
Phone: 508-435-6831
Fax: 508-497-6377
Web: www.valpeyfisher.com
CEO: –
CFO: Michael J Kroll
HR: –
FYE: December 31
Type: Subsidiary

CTS Valpey (formerly Valpey-Fisher) is all about time and control. The company makes quartz crystals and crystal-based products such as oscillators used for timing and frequency control in telecom computer and aerospace equipment. It also makes ultrasonic transducers which are used in non-destructive testing research and medical applications. Customers include contract electronics manufacturers Celestica and Flextronics. Valpey-Fisher has divested other operations including its AcoustoSizer optical components and piezoelectric product lines. More than two-thirds of sales are to customers in the US. In 2012 the company was acquired by electronic component manufacturer CTS Corporation for about $18 million.

CTSC LLC

10505 FURNACE RD STE 205
LORTON, VA 220792636
Phone: 703-493-9880
Fax: –
Web: www.chenega.jobs
CEO: Ken Ogden
CFO: –
HR: –
FYE: September 30
Type: Private

CTSC (Chenega Technology Services Corporation) is a certified Alaska Native Corporation (ANC) that provides support services to federal agencies. Its core competencies include base operations and facilities management engineering information technology intelligence support logistics and training. Partnering with prime government contractors and sub-contractors CTSC offers information systems development system integration support to military operations network engineering and technical analysis. As an ANC the company enjoys no-bid contracts with the government. CTSC is a subsidiary of Chenega Corporation.

	Annual Growth	09/05	09/06	09/07	09/08	09/09
Sales ($ mil.)	–	–	–	–	0.0	582.7	181.3
Net income ($ mil.)	–	–	–	–	0.0	14.0	15.9
Market value ($ mil.)	–	–	–	–	–	–	–
Employees	–	–	–	–	–	–	620

CUBESMART NYS: CUBE

5 Old Lancaster Road
Malvern, PA 19355
Phone: 610 535-5000
Fax: –
Web: www.cubesmart.com
CEO: Christopher P. (Chris) Marr
CFO: Timothy M. (Tim) Martin
HR: Shelly Azen
FYE: December 31
Type: Public

CubeSmart (formerly U-Store-It Trust) is a real estate investment trust (REIT) that owns more than 420 self-storage facilities with nearly 30 million sq. ft. of rentable space in about 25 states and Washington DC. The company also manages more than 100 self-storage facilities for third parties. Amenities at its properties include security systems and wider aisles for larger vehicles as well as climate-controlled units and outdoor storage for vehicles and boats at selected sites. The REIT also sells storage-related items such as packing supplies and locks to tenants who typically rent units on a month-to-month basis.

	Annual Growth	12/10	12/11	12/12	12/13	12/14
Sales ($ mil.)	14.8%	216.8	237.6	283.1	318.4	377.0
Net income ($ mil.)	–	(7.4)	(0.4)	1.8	41.4	26.4
Market value ($ mil.)	23.4%	1,562.5	1,744.5	2,388.8	2,613.5	3,618.5
Employees	8.8%	1,172	1,276	1,409	1,442	1,640

CUBIC CORP NYS: CUB

9333 Balboa Avenue
San Diego, CA 92123
Phone: 858 277-6780
Fax: –
Web: www.cubic.com
CEO: Bradley H. Feldmann
CFO: John D. (Jay) Thomas
HR: Darryl Albertson
FYE: September 30
Type: Public

Cubic's products and services fit in squarely with the global defense and transportation industries. With business divided into three main segments it provides mission support services which include actual combat rehearsal exercises prior to deployment to national militaries and US security forces and their allies. It manufactures air and ground combat instrumentation systems for live and virtual training as well as communications global asset tracking and cyber security equipment for the defense market. Thirdly it provides automated fare collection (AFC) management systems and services for mass transit (including bus light rail ferry and parking) worldwide.

	Annual Growth	09/11	09/12	09/13	09/14	09/15
Sales ($ mil.)	2.7%	1,285.2	1,381.5	1,360.7	1,398.4	1,431.0
Net income ($ mil.)	(27.9%)	84.8	91.9	19.8	69.5	22.9
Market value ($ mil.)	1.8%	1,050.3	1,345.8	1,443.1	1,258.1	1,127.5
Employees	1.6%	7,800	8,200	8,200	7,900	8,300

CUBIC SIMULATION SYSTEMS INC.

2001 W. Oak Ridge Rd.
Orlando FL 32809-3803
Phone: 407-859-7410
Fax: 407-855-4840
Web: cubic.com/ecc

CEO: Robert L Collins
CFO: Melissa A Van Valkenburgh
HR: –
FYE: September 30
Type: Subsidiary

Ready aim simulate fire and repair! Cubic Simulation Systems Division (SSD) provides a full range of virtual training devices to military and commercial customers worldwide. It develops simulation-based training systems for armor missile small arms and aircraft applications so that military personnel can gain weapons and maintenance experience in a realistic but safe environment before the bits hit the fan. Major products include the Close Combat Tactical Trainer which trains tank crews; the Engagement Skills Trainer 2000 a small arms trainer; Javelin trainers which teach personnel how to use the Javelin missile; and F-16 and F/A-18 Maintenance Trainers which provide aircraft maintenance training.

CUBIST PHARMACEUTICALS INC.   NMS: CBST

65 Hayden Avenue
Lexington, MA 02421
Phone: 781 860-8660
Fax: 781 240-0256
Web: www.cubist.com

CEO: Michael W Bonney
CFO: Michael J Tomsicek
HR: –
FYE: December 31
Type: Public

Fighting infection is a modern art at Cubist Pharmaceuticals. The company develops antimicrobial agents to treat drug-resistant bacterial strains including methicillin-resistant Staphylococcus aureus (MRSA) typically found in hospitals and other health care institutions. Its flagship product Cubicin (daptomycin for injection) is an FDA-approved intravenous antibiotic to fight MRSA infections of the skin and blood. Cubist also markets Entereg a drug to speed patient recovery following bowel resection surgery in the US. Cubist's pipeline includes candidates in various stages of clinical and pre-clinical development.

	Annual Growth	12/08	12/09	12/10	12/11	12/12
Sales ($ mil.)	20.9%	433.6	562.1	636.5	754.0	926.4
Net income ($ mil.)	(2.4%)	169.8	79.6	94.3	33.0	154.1
Market value ($ mil.)	14.9%	1,563.5	1,227.6	1,384.9	2,564.0	2,721.2
Employees	8.3%	554	600	638	669	762

CUI GLOBAL INC   NAS: CUI

20050 SW 112th Avenue
Tualatin, OR 97062
Phone: 503 612-2300
Fax: –
Web: www.cuiglobal.com

CEO: –
CFO: Daniel N Ford
HR: –
FYE: December 31
Type: Public

CUI Global (formerly Waytronx) makes and sells equipment that helps power up and test electrical components and natural gas plants. It makes power supplies transformers converters connectors and industrial controls for OEMs through its CUI Inc. and CUI Japan subsidiaries. Products include the Novum Digital Power modules and Solus Power Topology. The company's Orbital-UK subsidiary is the largest natural gas systems integrator in the UK. Its product are for the gas utility power generation emissions manufacturing and automotive industries. The Vergence GasPT2 device provides energy metering systems for natural gas operators. Most of the company's sales are in the US and UK.

	Annual Growth	12/10	12/11	12/12	12/13	12/14
Sales ($ mil.)	16.7%	40.9	38.9	41.1	60.7	76.0
Net income ($ mil.)	–	(7.0)	0.0	(2.5)	(1.8)	(2.8)
Market value ($ mil.)	133.5%	5.2	3.9	113.9	131.1	154.6
Employees	23.5%	86	61	69	170	200

CUIVRE RIVER ELECTRIC COOPERATIVE INC.

1112 E CHERRY ST
TROY, MO 633791518
Phone: 636-528-8261
Fax: –
Web: www.cuivreriverelectriccooperative.com

CEO: –
CFO: –
HR: –
FYE: December 31
Type: Private

Show me the power. Cuivre River Electric Cooperative provides power to four eastern counties in the "Show Me" state: Lincoln Pike St. Charles and Warren. The membership utility which is one of Missouri's largest cooperatives with more than 58000 residential commercial and industrial customers gets its wholesale power supply from the Associated Electric Cooperative and the Central Electric Power Cooperative. Cuivre River Propane jointly owned and operated by Cuivre River Electric Cooperative and MFA Oil Company supplies propane to co-op members from four locations Bowling Green Elsberry Troy and Wright City.

	Annual Growth	12/07	12/08	12/09	12/11	12/12
Sales ($ mil.)	344.1%	–	0.3	101.5	102.6	107.0
Net income ($ mil.)	(14.6%)	–	–	8.5	10.0	5.3
Market value ($ mil.)	–	–	–	–	–	–
Employees	–	–	–	–	–	134

CULLEN/FROST BANKERS, INC.   NYS: CFR

100 W. Houston Street
San Antonio, TX 78205
Phone: 210 220-4011
Fax: 210 220-5578
Web: www.frostbank.com

CEO: Richard W. (Dick) Evans
CFO: Jerry Salinas
HR: Emily A. Skillman
FYE: December 31
Type: Public

One of the largest independent bank holding companies in Texas Cullen/Frost Bankers owns Frost Bank and other financial subsidiaries through a second-tier holding company The New Galveston Company. The community-oriented bank serves individuals and local businesses as well as clients in neighboring parts of Mexico through 120-plus branches in Texas metropolitan areas. It offers commercial and consumer deposit products and loans trust and investment management services mutual funds insurance brokerage and leasing. Subsidiaries include Frost Insurance Agency Frost Brokerage Services Frost Investment Advisors and investment banking arm Frost Securities. Cullen/Frost has total assets of $26.5 billion.

	Annual Growth	12/11	12/12	12/13	12/14	12/15
Assets ($ mil.)	8.9%	20,317.2	23,124.1	24,312.9	28,277.8	28,567.1
Net income ($ mil.)	6.5%	217.5	238.0	237.9	278.0	279.3
Market value ($ mil.)	3.2%	3,279.5	3,363.8	4,613.3	4,378.4	3,718.9
Employees	2.3%	3,848	3,878	3,979	4,154	4,211

CULP INC.   NYS: CFI

1823 Eastchester Drive
High Point, NC 27265-1402
Phone: 336 889-5161
Fax: –
Web: www.culp.com

CEO: Franklin N. Saxon
CFO: Kenneth R. Bowling
HR: –
FYE: May 03
Type: Public

Culp just wants to keep on ticking. The company is one of the world's largest makers of furniture upholstery fabrics and mattress fabrics (known as ticking). Culp delivers fashion-conscious stylish fabrics with broad appeal to some of the largest home furnishing retailers and manufacturers. Its upholstery fabrics include wovens (jacquards and dobbies) knits screen-prints and velvets (woven and tufted). Its fabrics are used in upholstering residential and commercial furniture such as recliners sofas and love seats. Culp's ticking is used for covering mattresses and box springs.

	Annual Growth	05/11*	04/12	04/13	04/14*	05/15
Sales ($ mil.)	9.4%	216.8	254.4	268.8	287.2	310.2
Net income ($ mil.)	(1.7%)	16.2	13.3	18.3	17.4	15.1
Market value ($ mil.)	26.7%	123.2	135.0	198.6	227.4	317.9
Employees	1.0%	1,143	1,114	1,205	1,167	1,188

*Fiscal year change

CULVER FRANCHISING SYSTEM INC.

1240 WATER ST
PRAIRIE DU SAC, WI 535781091
Phone: 608-643-7980
Fax: –
Web: www.culvers.com

CEO: –
CFO: Joseph Koss
HR: Bruce Anderson
FYE: December 31
Type: Private

If you think ButterBurgers are better burgers then you're probably a fan of Culver's. Culver Franchising System operates a chain of about 500 Culver's quick-service restaurants popular for their signature ButterBurgers (hamburgers served on a grilled buttered bun) and frozen custard. The chain's menu also includes chicken fish and pork sandwiches; salads; and dinner items such as shrimp and Norwegian cod. Nearly all of the restaurants are operated by franchisees. Chairman and CEO Craig Culver started the restaurant as a family business back in 1984.

	Annual Growth	12/07	12/08	12/11	12/12	12/13
Assets ($ mil.)	435.7%	–	0.0	57.6	54.8	65.0
Net income ($ mil.)	18.5%	–	–	14.5	17.3	20.4
Market value ($ mil.)	–	–	–	–	–	–
Employees	–	–	–	–	–	290

CUMBERLAND COUNTY HOSPITAL SYSTEM INC.

1638 OWEN DR
FAYETTEVILLE, NC 283043424
Phone: 910-609-4000
Fax: –
Web: www.capefearvalley.com

CEO: –
CFO: Sandra Williams
HR: William Pryor
FYE: September 30
Type: Private

Don't fear for a lack of medical services at Cumberland County Hospital System (doing business as Cape Fear Valley Health System). The medical provider comprises five acute-care and specialty hospitals with about 765 total beds and more than a dozen primary-care physician practices scattered throughout the region in North Carolina. The hospital system serves residents of coastal North Carolina providing general and specialized medical services such as cancer treatment open-heart surgery psychiatric care and rehabilitation. It also operates the HealthPlex fitness and wellness facility and provides home health and hospice services.

	Annual Growth	09/03	09/04	09/05	09/06	09/07
Sales ($ mil.)	(46.4%)	–	–	1,753.2	492.7	504.6
Net income ($ mil.)	28202.0%	–	–	0.0	29.7	23.1
Market value ($ mil.)	–	–	–	–	–	–
Employees	–	–	–	–	–	5,000

CUMBERLAND FARMS INC.

100 Crossing Blvd.
Framingham MA 01702
Phone: 508-270-1400
Fax: 206-722-2569
Web: www.darigold.com

CEO: –
CFO: –
HR: Foster Macrides
FYE: September 30
Type: Private

Once a one-cow dairy Cumberland Farms now operates a network of 900-plus convenience stores and gas stations in about a dozen eastern seaboard states from Maine to Florida. The company operates its own grocery distribution and bakery operations to supply its stores as well. Cumberland owns a two-thirds limited partnership in petroleum wholesaler Gulf Oil LP giving it the right to use and license Gulf trademarks in Delaware New Jersey New York most of Ohio Pennsylvania and the New England states. The first convenience-store operator in New England Cumberland Farms was founded in 1939 by Vasilios and Aphrodite Haseotes. Their descendants including chairman Lily Haseotes Bentas own the company.

CUMBERLAND PACKING CORP.

2 Cumberland St.
Brooklyn NY 11205
Phone: 718-858-4200
Fax: 718-260-9017
Web: www.cpack.com

CEO: Steven Eisenstadt
CFO: Peter Marshall
HR: Isabel Siegel
FYE: December 31
Type: Private

There's no shame in being artificial at Cumberland Packing; sugar substitutes equal real cash. The company makes Sweet'N Low the pink-packaged saccharin-based sugar substitute. It also makes NatraTaste (an aspartame sugar substitute) Nu-Salt (a sodium-free salt substitute) and Sweet One (an acesulfame potassium sweetener). Cumberland's other brands include Butter Buds (butter-flavored granules) and Sugar In The Raw (turbinado sugar). In addition to the ubiquitous pink presence of Sweet'N Low on restaurant tables (i.e. in the foodservice sector) Cumberland's products are sold to food retailers and food manufacturers worldwide. The company is owned by CEO and president Jeff Eisenstadt and his family.

CUMBERLAND PHARMACEUTICALS INC   NMS: CPIX

2525 West End Avenue, Suite 950
Nashville, TN 37203
Phone: 615 255-0068
Fax: –
Web: www.cumberlandpharma.com

CEO: A. J. Kazimi
CFO: Michael Bonner
HR: –
FYE: December 31
Type: Public

Cumberland Pharmaceuticals wants to make your search for the right drugs less cumbersome. The specialty pharmaceutical company focuses on acquiring developing and commercializing branded prescription drugs. Targeting the hospital acute care and gastroenterology segments Cumberland's FDA-approved drugs include Acetadote for the treatment of acetaminophen poisoning; Kristalose a prescription strength laxative; Vaprisol for low sodium levels; and Caldolor (neé Amelior) the first injectable dosage form of ibuprofen. The company also has several projects in development. Acetadote and Kristalose are marketed through Cumberland's own hospital and gastroenterology sales forces. The company went public in a mid-2009 IPO.

	Annual Growth	12/10	12/11	12/12	12/13	12/14
Sales ($ mil.)	(5.3%)	45.9	51.1	48.9	32.0	36.9
Net income ($ mil.)	(0.3%)	2.5	5.7	5.8	(2.1)	2.4
Market value ($ mil.)	(0.0%)	102.5	92.1	71.9	87.5	102.4
Employees	(10.2%)	131	138	106	96	85

CUMMINS FILTRATION INC.

2931 Elm Hill Pike
Nashville TN 37214
Phone: 615-367-0040
Fax: 615-399-3650
Web: www.cumminsfiltration.com

CEO: –
CFO: –
HR: Maria Bailey
FYE: December 31
Type: Subsidiary

Cummins Filtration gets frustrated when it encounters an unclean machine. The subsidiary of engine manufacturer Cummins is among the world's largest makers of engine-related component products. Cummins Filtration's 7000-plus offerings include filtration coolant and fuel additive products filters for air fuel lube and hydraulics and other filtration systems. Marketed under the Fleetguard brand the lineup is used primarily on heavy- and medium-duty diesel trucks in addition to construction mining agricultural marine and power generation equipment. The company operates more than 20 manufacturing plants (in nine countries) and three joint ventures.

CUMMINS, INC.

NYS: CMI

500 Jackson Street, P.O. Box 3005
Columbus, IN 47202-3005
Phone: 812 377-5000
Fax: 812 377-4937
Web: www.cummins.com

CEO: N. Thomas (Tom) Linebarger
CFO: Patrick J. (Pat) Ward
HR: Jill Cook
FYE: December 31
Type: Public

If it's comin' around the mountain it could have a Cummins' engine powering it. The company makes about half of its revenues from its Engine segment which makes diesel and natural gas powered engines for the heavy and mid-duty truck RV automotive and industrial markets along with marine rail mining and construction. Its other complementary business segments include Components (filtration products and fuel systems); Power Generation (vehicle and residential generators); and Distribution (product distributors and servicing). Major customers include OEMs Chrysler Daimler Ford Komatsu PACCAR and Volvo. More than half of Cummins' sales are from outside the US.

	Annual Growth	12/11	12/12	12/13	12/14	12/15
Sales ($ mil.)	1.4%	18,048.0	17,334.0	17,301.0	19,221.0	19,110.0
Net income ($ mil.)	(6.7%)	1,848.0	1,645.0	1,483.0	1,651.0	1,399.0
Market value ($ mil.)	(0.0%)	15,421.1	18,982.9	24,697.9	25,258.6	15,419.4
Employees	5.9%	43,900	46,000	47,900	54,600	55,200

CUMMINS-ALLISON CORP.

852 Feehanville Dr.
Mt. Prospect IL 60056
Phone: 847-299-9550
Fax: 847-299-4940
Web: www.cumminsallison.com

CEO: William J Jones
CFO: Robert Jordan
HR: –
FYE: December 31
Type: Subsidiary

Cummins-Allison knows how to bring the money in and sort it out. A subsidiary of Cummins-American the company makes a variety of coin and currency sorters counters wrappers and scanners; check signers imprinters and endorsers; and paper shredders and perforators. It also produces cash management software. These products are sold around the world to banks government agencies and the retail casino and gaming and vending industries. Cummins-Allison has R&D centers in the US and a network of 50 sales and service centers across North America. It also has operations in the UK Ireland Germany and France. The family of chairman and CEO John Jones controls Cummins-Allison which was founded 1887.

CUMULUS MEDIA INC.

NMS: CMLS

3280 Peachtree Road, N.W., Suite 2300
Atlanta, GA 30305
Phone: 404 949-0700
Fax: –
Web: www.cumulus.com

CEO: Mary G. Berner
CFO: Joseph P. (J.P.) Hannan
HR: –
FYE: December 31
Type: Public

Cumulus Media reigns over an empire of radio stations. The company is the #2 radio station ownership group in the US (behind Clear Channel) with more than 460 owned or operated stations in about 90 markets throughout the country. In many of its markets Cumulus has built clusters of stations that realize cost savings through shared administrative and sales operations. In addition to its core mid-market stations Cumulus through a partnership with a private equity firm Crestview Partners owns about 30 stations in large markets including Atlanta Dallas and San Francisco. Crestview Partners controls about 40% of Cumulus.

	Annual Growth	12/10	12/11	12/12	12/13	12/14
Sales ($ mil.)	48.0%	263.3	549.5	1,076.6	1,026.1	1,263.4
Net income ($ mil.)	(20.5%)	29.4	63.9	(32.7)	176.1	11.8
Market value ($ mil.)	(0.5%)	1,004.3	778.3	622.2	1,801.3	985.7
Employees	27.5%	2,318	6,323	6,483	6,002	6,132

CUNARD LINE

24303 Town Center Dr. Ste. 200
Valencia CA 91355
Phone: 661-753-1000
Fax: 661-284-4748
Web: www.cunard.com

CEO: –
CFO: –
HR: –
FYE: November 30
Type: Subsidiary

You don't have to be king of the world to travel on these queens of the seas. A venerable name in ocean travel Cunard Line is the last surviving operator of scheduled luxury ocean liner service. Its fleet consists of Queen Victoria (1980 berths) and the recently added Queen Elizabeth (2068 berths) which took its maiden voyage in October 2010. The Cunard vessels offer transatlantic service between the UK and the US as well as cruises in the Asia/Pacific region the Caribbean Europe and around the world. Most of its passengers come from Australia Germany North America and the UK. Founded in 1839 Cunard is part of #1 cruise ship operator Carnival.

CUPERTINO ELECTRIC INC.

1132 N. 7th St.
San Jose CA 95112
Phone: 408-808-8000
Fax: 408-275-8575
Web: www.cei.com

CEO: John Boncher
CFO: Marjorie Goss
HR: –
FYE: December 31
Type: Private

Cupertino Electric Inc. (CEI) likes to get its customers wired. The electrical contractor builds and maintains electrical power and data infrastructure systems for commercial industrial and institutional facilities including semiconductor plants biotech installations data centers network systems and schools. It provides generation facilities for companies that are not on a grid or need additional power. CEI works mostly for companies and schools in the western US. The company's energy alternatives division also offers design and installation of photovoltaics (solar cells) as well as fuel cells. Customers include Apple Google Hyatt Microsoft Oracle and Safeway.

CURASCRIPT INC.

6272 Lee Vista Blvd.
Orlando FL 32822
Phone: 407-852-4903
Fax: 888-773-7386
Web: www.curascript.com

CEO: Dom Meffe
CFO: Claudia Griffith
HR: –
FYE: December 31
Type: Subsidiary

CuraScript offers home delivery of specialty pharmaceuticals across the US. Through its primary CuraScript Specialty Pharmacy (Curascript SP) division the company is one of the top distributors of specialty drugs in the US. It distributes medications and medical supplies to patients with chronic diseases and other conditions that require costly biotech drugs that most pharmacies don't carry. Its smaller CuraScript Specialty Distribution (CuraScript SD) unit distributes specialty drugs to doctors' offices and clinics and provides group purchasing services for its clients. CuraScript is a subsidiary of pharmacy benefit manager (PBM) Express Scripts.

CURIS INC

NMS: CRIS

4 Maguire Road
Lexington, MA 02421
Phone: 617 503-6500
Fax: –
Web: www.curis.com

CEO: Ali Fattaey
CFO: Michael P. Gray
HR: Rachael Blasbalg
FYE: December 31
Type: Public

Curis's cancer patients and Sega's gamers might one day have an unlikely hero in common: Sonic the Hedgehog. Drug development firm Curis is studying hedgehog signaling pathways (including the sonic hedgehog pathway named after the Sega mascot) to find treatments for oncology ailments and other conditions. Such signaling pathways regulate tissue growth and repair and the company is looking for ways to either stimulate them or slow them down as a means of treating disease. Curis is collaborating with Genentech to develop cancer drugs using hedgehog pathways. The company also has internal development programs for cancer treatments using other signaling pathways.

	Annual Growth	12/10	12/11	12/12	12/13	12/14
Sales ($ mil.)	(11.4%)	16.0	14.8	17.0	15.0	9.8
Net income ($ mil.)	—	(4.4)	(9.9)	(16.4)	(12.3)	(18.7)
Market value ($ mil.)	(6.7%)	170.3	402.6	295.1	242.6	129.0
Employees	2.3%	32	35	33	33	35

CURRENT USA INC.

1025 E. Woodmen Rd.
Colorado Springs CO 80920
Phone: 719-594-4100
Fax: 719-531-2283
Web: www.currentinc.com

CEO: Wendy L Huxta
CFO: Kirby Heck
HR: –
FYE: December 31
Type: Subsidiary

Current USA is a leading direct marketer of greeting cards and gift wrap scrapbooking supplies stationery and home decorating items. It sells its products under brands Times to Cherish (scrapbooking supplies) Colorful Images (personalized address labels and other paper products) Lillian Vernon (gifts and home decor) and Current. The company also operates an outlet store in Colorado and a fundraising business that lets not-for-profit groups sell its products and share the proceeds. Founded in the 1950s Current USA was initially run out of the basement of founders Orin and Miriam Loo. The company which was family owned and operated until 1986 is a subsidiary of printing giant Taylor.

CURTCO MEDIA LABS LLC

29160 Heathercliff Rd. Ste. 200
Malibu CA 90265
Phone: 310-589-7700
Fax: 310-589-7701
Web: www.curtco.com

CEO: –
CFO: –
HR: –
FYE: December 31
Type: Private

The wealthy turn to CurtCo Media Labs for ideas on how to spend their riches. CurtCo Media publishes the Robb Report a monthly publication devoted to affluent readers and their luxurious lifestyles. The company also publishes niche titles such as Robb Report Home Entertainment and Robb Report Collection which features houses cars boats and other items for sale. Other titles include Robb Report Vacation Homes San Diego Magazine and ShowBoats International Magazine. The company has offices in Boston and New York as well as California (Malibu San Diego) and throughout Florida (Ft. Lauderdale Jacksonville Naples Orlando and Sarasota). It was founded in 1987.

CURTISS-WRIGHT CORP.

NYS: CW

13925 Ballantyne Corporate Place, Suite 400
Charlotte, NC 28277
Phone: 704 869-4600
Fax: –
Web: www.curtisswright.com

CEO: David C. (Dave) Adams
CFO: Glenn E. Tynan
HR: Larry Berman
FYE: December 31
Type: Public

Once an aeronautical pioneer — its engines powered the B-17 bomber and The Spirit of St. Louis — Curtiss-Wright makes lower-visibility products these days. Curtiss-Wright comprises three business segments. The Commercial/Industrial segment provides ducts and services supporting critical applications across the aerospace automotive and general industrial markets. The Defense segment provides embedded computing board level modules integrated subsystems turret aiming and weapons handling systems to defense markets. The Power segment manufactures and services main coolant pumps power-dense compact motors generators and secondary propulsion systems.

	Annual Growth	12/10	12/11	12/12	12/13	12/14
Sales ($ mil.)	4.3%	1,893.1	2,054.1	2,097.7	2,510.8	2,243.1
Net income ($ mil.)	1.5%	106.6	130.4	113.8	138.0	113.3
Market value ($ mil.)	20.8%	1,590.4	1,692.5	1,572.7	2,981.1	3,381.6
Employees	4.3%	7,600	8,900	9,300	10,000	9,000

CUSHMAN & WAKEFIELD INC.

1290 Avenue of the Americas
New York NY 10104-6178
Phone: 212-841-7500
Fax: 212-359-3601
Web: www.trufoods.com

CEO: Edward Frost
CFO: Michael Bartolotta
HR: –
FYE: December 31
Type: Subsidiary

Cushman & Wakefield heeds the maxim: "Buy land — they aren't making any more." With more than 240 offices in about 60 countries it serves the real estate needs of corporations and financial institutions globally. It specializes in office industrial and retail real estate. In addition to property management and brokerage services Cushman & Wakefield also provides research and analysis on markets while also helping owners and investors optimize their portfolios and manage their supply chains. Worldwide the company has more than $4 billion in assets under management. Cushman & Wakefield is owned by EXOR which is controlled by Italy's Agnelli family which boast the largest holdings on the Italian exchange.

CUSHMAN & WAKEFIELD SONNENBLICK-GOLDMAN LLC

1290 Avenue of the Americas 8th Fl.
New York NY 10104
Phone: 212-841-9220
Fax: 212-479-1875
Web: www2.cushwake.com/sonngold/

CEO: Glenn Rufrano
CFO: Robert Rozek
HR: Joyce Phillips
FYE: December 31
Type: Private

Investment bank Sonnenblick-Goldman knows there's more to a good real estate deal than "just" location location location. Founded in 1893 the firm provides debt and equity placements property sales joint ventures and financial advisory services to the real estate industry. It specializes in a range of industry sectors including office properties; malls and other retail properties; multifamily residential buildings; and upscale hotels and resorts. It provides its services around the globe from offices in Boston Hong Kong New York San Francisco Shanghai Sydney and Tokyo. The company began doing business as Cushman & Wakefield Sonnenblick Goldman in 2007 after it was acquired by Cushman & Wakefield.

CUSO FINANCIAL SERVICES L.P.

10150 MEANLEY DR FL 1
SAN DIEGO, CA 921313008
Phone: 858-530-4400
Fax: –
Web: www.cusonet.com

CEO: –
CFO: Daniel J Kilroy
HR: Janine Holmes
FYE: December 31
Type: Private

For credit unions looking to expand their investment offerings CUSO can do so. CUSO Financial Services (CFS) provides credit unions with online securities trading retirement planning wealth management insurance and other investment services from more than 300 providers that the credit unions can in turn offer to their members. Founded in 1996 by Valorie Seyfert and Amy Beattie (company president and COO respectively) CFS serves about 100 credit unions throughout the US; more than 40 of them are limited partners that hold ownership stakes in the company.

	Annual Growth	12/04	12/05	12/06	12/07	12/08
Sales ($ mil.)	2.4%	–	70.8	79.2	81.3	76.0
Net income ($ mil.)	(24.9%)	–	–	6.0	6.0	3.4
Market value ($ mil.)	–	–	–	–	–	–
Employees	–	–	–	–	–	95

CUSTOM BUILDING PRODUCTS INC.

13001 Seal Beach Blvd.
Seal Beach CA 90740
Phone: 562-598-8808
Fax: 562-598-4008
Web: www.custombuildingproducts.com

CEO: Don Devine
CFO: Bill Klein
HR: –
FYE: December 31
Type: Private

Custom Building Products (CPB) likes to hold things together. The producer of tile-setting grout and adhesives makes such products as epoxies cement household and industrial glues sealants acrylic resins clay mortars putties and latex as well as gypsum products and concrete repair products. The company also offers installation tools cleaning and maintenance equipment and a library of how-to-do-it and other resource materials. CPB manufactures and distributes its wares from about a dozen locations in North America. Its customers include architects contractors dealers distributors and do-it-yourselfers.

CUSTOM SENSORS & TECHNOLOGIES INC.

14401 Princeton Ave.
Moorpark CA 93021
Phone: 805-552-3599
Fax: 805-552-3577
Web: cst.schneider-electric.com

CEO: –
CFO: –
HR: –
FYE: December 31
Type: Subsidiary

Custom Sensors & Technologies (CST) takes a custom approach to the sensor business. The company makes electronic sensors controls and actuators used in factory and industrial process automation aerospace and defense equipment and a wide range of transportation applications. CST's products which include DC motors optical encoders servo systems and trackballs help determine exact positions and link the actions of precision mechanisms such as automotive stability-enhancement systems. The global company has operations across Europe Asia Latin America Mexico and the US. CST is a business unit of Schneider Electric.

CUSTOMERS BANCORP INC

NYS: CUBI

1015 Penn Avenue, Suite 103
Wyomissing, PA 19610
Phone: 610 933-2000
Fax: –
Web: www.customersbank.com

CEO: Jay S. Sidhu
CFO: James D. Hogan
HR: –
FYE: December 31
Type: Public

Customers Bancorp makes it pretty clear who they want to serve. The bank holding company operates about 15 locations in Pennsylvania New York and New Jersey. It offers personal and business checking savings and money market accounts as well as loans certificates of deposit credit cards and concierge or appointment banking (they come to you seven days a week). Customers has about $2 billion in assets; its loan portfolio is about a third commercial and half warehouse lending (short-term loans to mortgage lenders) with consumer loans making up the balance. It was formed in 2010 as a holding company for Customers Bank which was created in 1994 as New Century Bank.

	Annual Growth	12/10	12/11	12/12	12/13	12/14
Assets ($ mil.)	48.7%	–	2,077.5	3,201.2	4,153.2	6,825.4
Net income ($ mil.)	16.2%	23.7	4.0	23.8	32.7	43.2
Market value ($ mil.)	15.9%	–	–	387.8	547.2	520.5
Employees	29.3%	–	–	255	388	426

CUSTOMINK LLC

2910 DISTRICT AVE STE 100
FAIRFAX, VA 220312283
Phone: 703-891-2273
Fax: –
Web: www.customink.com

CEO: –
CFO: –
HR: –
FYE: December 31
Type: Private

CustomInk knows a T-shirt is not just a T-shirt. (It can also be an advertisement a form of self-expression or a fashion statement.) The firm provides screen printing and embroidery services for customers across the US through its online storefront. Customers pick the clothing type (short and long sleeve Ts tank tops sweats) and color and then add text and graphics (picking from available graphics or designing their own). CustomInk team members — or Inkers as they call themselves — then print and ship orders. The firm also offers anout 200 other customized products (pens hats drinkware). CustomInk was founded in 1999 by president Marc Katz and former classmates Mike Driscoll and Dave Christensen.

	Annual Growth	12/03	12/04	12/05	12/06	12/08
Sales ($ mil.)	44.5%	–	13.7	0.0	34.0	59.6
Net income ($ mil.)	–	–	–	0.0	3.8	4.6
Market value ($ mil.)	–	–	–	–	–	–
Employees	–	–	–	–	–	500

CUTERA INC

NMS: CUTR

3240 Bayshore Blvd.
Brisbane, CA 94005
Phone: 415 657-5500
Fax: –

CEO: Kevin P. Connors
CFO: Ronald J. (Ron) Santilli
HR: Amanda Austin
FYE: December 31
Type: Public

Cutera has a handle on hairy situations and a firm plan for flabby faces. The company makes lasers for medical and aesthetic use in doctors' offices and spas. Cutera markets its FDA-approved devices for hair removal and treatments to reduce pigmented lesions (age and sun spots) wrinkles and veins. Products are sold under the names CoolGlide Solera and Xeo. Its Titan line of products use deep tissue heating to firm up saggy skin. In the US the company markets its products through a direct sales force and through distributor PSS World Medical); in 35 other countries it relies on a small sales group and distributors. Cutera also sells a limited number of products online.

	Annual Growth	12/10	12/11	12/12	12/13	12/14
Sales ($ mil.)	10.0%	53.3	60.3	77.3	74.6	78.1
Net income ($ mil.)	–	(10.5)	(10.1)	(6.5)	(4.7)	(10.6)
Market value ($ mil.)	6.5%	119.8	107.6	130.0	147.1	154.3
Employees	9.2%	187	200	227	238	266

CUTTER & BUCK INC.

701 N. 34th St. Ste. 400
Seattle WA 98103
Phone: 206-830-6812
Fax: 206-448-0589
Web: www.cutterbuck.com

CEO: Joel Freet
CFO: –
HR: Chris Nguyen
FYE: April 30
Type: Private

Relatively unknown less than a decade ago Cutter & Buck has climbed onto the leader board of the nation's top makers of golf apparel. Cutter & Buck sells men's and women's golf apparel and other sportswear through golf pro shops resorts and specialty stores throughout North America as well as to corporate accounts. It sells its products in other countries through distributors. Most of its sales come from men's apparel. Cutter & Buck divides its apparel into two lines: the ephemeral fashion line with brighter colors and the seasonless and less-expensive classics line. Its corporate marketing division puts company logos on products for corporate golf events and programs. New Wave Group AB owns the company.

CVB FINANCIAL CORP.

701 North Haven Ave., Suite 350
Ontario, CA 91764
Phone: 909 980-4030
Fax: –
Web: www.cbbank.com

NMS: CVBF
CEO: Christopher D. (Chris) Myers
CFO: Richard C. Thomas
HR: –
FYE: December 31
Type: Public

CVB Financial is into the California Vibe Baby. The holding company's Citizens Business Bank offers community banking services to primarily small and midsized businesses but also to consumers through nearly 50 branch and office locations across central and southern California. Boasting more than $7 billion in assets the bank offers checking money market CDs and savings accounts trust and investment services and a variety of loans. Commercial real estate loans account for about two-thirds of the bank's loan portfolio which is rounded out by business consumer and construction loans; residential mortgages; dairy and livestock loans; and municipal lease financing.

	Annual Growth	12/10	12/11	12/12	12/13	12/14
Assets ($ mil.)	3.5%	6,436.7	6,482.9	6,363.4	6,665.0	7,377.9
Net income ($ mil.)	13.4%	62.9	81.7	77.3	95.6	104.0
Market value ($ mil.)	16.6%	918.1	1,062.1	1,101.3	1,807.6	1,696.4
Employees	(1.4%)	819	811	810	784	–

CVD EQUIPMENT CORP.

355 South Technology Drive
Central Islip, NY 11722
Phone: 631 981-7081
Fax: –

NAS: CVV
CEO: –
CFO: Glen R Charles
HR: –
FYE: December 31
Type: Public

CVD Equipment has expanded well beyond the chemical vapor deposition (CVD) equipment that gave it its name. (During CVD precise layers of chemicals are deposited onto semiconductor wafers during chip manufacturing.) The company's specialized equipment is also used in the development of nanotechnology — namely solar cells smart glass carbon nanotubes nanowires LEDs and micro-electromechanical systems (MEMS). CVD Equipment still makes custom-designed products for major semiconductor companies but its newer technologies are used by universities research labs and startup companies. Its largest shareholder is Chairman and CEO Leonard A. Rosenbaum who founded the company in 1982 and owns 29%.

	Annual Growth	12/10	12/11	12/12	12/13	12/14
Sales ($ mil.)	14.5%	16.3	31.0	22.2	17.9	28.0
Net income ($ mil.)	–	0.5	3.8	0.4	(0.6)	(2.5)
Market value ($ mil.)	18.9%	44.4	74.1	59.2	89.6	88.7
Employees	9.7%	131	161	173	171	190

CVENT, INC

1765 Greensboro Station Place, 7th Floor
Tysons Corner, VA 22102
Phone: 703 226-3500
Fax: –
Web: www.cvent.com

NYS: CVT
CEO: Rajeev K. (Reggie) Aggarwal
CFO: Cynthia A. Russo
HR: –
FYE: December 31
Type: Public

Cvent does everything for event planners except set up the chairs. The company's software automates the event planning process for conferences trade shows and industry events. Its database of more than 200000 hotels and convention centers in more than 175 countries helps event planners in selecting a venue. Its software manages the budget registrations marketing (including social media and event-specific apps) logistics such as travel and lodging and post-event surveys. Customers include more than 6000 event marketing firms (such as Aimia and Maritz) and almost 5000 hotel groups (such as Marriott and Starwood). Founded in 1999 Cvent went public in 2013 raising $117.6 million in its IPO.

	Annual Growth	12/10	12/11	12/12	12/13	12/14
Sales ($ mil.)	–	0.0	60.9	83.5	111.1	142.2
Net income ($ mil.)	–	0.0	(0.2)	4.3	(3.2)	1.8
Market value ($ mil.)	–	0.0	–	–	1,498.0	1,146.0
Employees	15.7%	–	–	1,300	1,450	1,740

CVR ENERGY INC

2277 Plaza Drive, Suite 500
Sugar Land, TX 77479
Phone: 281 207-3200
Fax: –
Web: www.cvrenergy.com

NYS: CVI
CEO: –
CFO: Susan M Ball
HR: Jerry Reed
FYE: December 31
Type: Public

CVR Energy's CV says that it puts its energy into oil refining and ammonia production. It operates a 115000 barrels-per-day-throughput-capacity oil refinery in Coffeyville Kansas and a 70000 barrels-per day refinery in Oklahoma and a crude oil gathering system in Kansas and Oklahoma. CVR Energy's Coffeyville refinery has 1.4 million barrels of storage tanks and it also has 2.8 million barrels of leased storage capacity in Cushing Oklahoma. It has asphalt and refined fuels storage and terminalling plants in Phillipsburg Kansas. The company controls public traded CVR Refining (refining assets) and CVR Partners LP (a producer of ammonia and urea ammonium nitrate fertilizers).

	Annual Growth	12/10	12/11	12/12	12/13	12/14
Sales ($ mil.)	22.2%	4,079.8	5,029.1	8,567.3	8,985.8	9,109.5
Net income ($ mil.)	86.8%	14.3	345.8	378.6	370.7	173.9
Market value ($ mil.)	26.4%	1,318.1	1,626.3	4,236.5	3,771.1	3,361.2
Employees	16.9%	695	764	1,091	1,192	1,298

CVR PARTNERS LP

2277 Plaza Drive, Suite 500
Sugar Land, TX 77479
Phone: 281 207-3200
Fax: –

NYS: UAN
CEO: Mark A Pytosh
CFO: Susan M Ball
HR: –
FYE: December 31
Type: Public

Farmers dreaming of fertile fields can turn to CVR Partners. The company makes nitrogen fertilizers. From its fertilizer manufacturing facility in Kansas CVR Partners produces ammonia and urea ammonia nitrate (UAN). The company sells ammonia to agricultural and industrial customers such as Brandt Consolidated Interchem and National Cooperative Refinery Association and provides UAN products to retailers and distributors. To lower production costs CVR Partners uses petroleum coke instead of the more expensive natural gas. It obtains the majority of its petroleum coke from parent company CVR Energy which founded CVR Partners in 2007. CVR Partners went public in April 2011 raising $307 million.

	Annual Growth	12/10	12/11	12/12	12/13	12/14
Sales ($ mil.)	13.4%	180.5	302.9	302.3	323.7	298.7
Net income ($ mil.)	23.0%	33.3	132.4	112.2	118.6	76.1
Market value ($ mil.)	(26.8%)	–	1,814.9	1,845.6	1,203.6	712.2
Employees	4.2%	122	124	134	133	144

CVR REFINING LP
NYSE: CVRR

2277 Plaza Dr. Ste. 500
Sugar Land TX 77479
Phone: 281-207-3200
Fax: 650-638-1029
Web: www.solarcity.com

CEO: –
CFO: –
HR: –
FYE: December 31
Type: Public

Oil refinery Coffeyville Resources may be located in Coffeyville Kansas but new parent CVR Refining is thinking "We're not just in Kansas anymore." CVR Refining was formed by CVR Energy in September 2012 as an indirect wholly owned subsidiary to take over its downstream operations. CVR Refining is taking ownership of the 115000 barrels-per-day (bpd) Coffeyville refinery and a 70000 bpd refinery in Wynnewood Oklahoma both of which are not too far from a crude oil hub at Cushing Oklahoma. In addition CVR Refining will control 350 miles of pipeline 125 oil tanker trucks tank farms and 6 million barrels of storage capacity. CVR Refining went public in 2013 with an offering worth $600 million.

CVR REFINING, LP
NYS: CVRR

2277 Plaza Drive, Suite 500
Sugar Land, TX 77479
Phone: 281 207-3200
Fax: –
Web: www.cvrrefining.com

CEO: John J Lipinski
CFO: Susan M Ball
HR: –
FYE: December 31
Type: Public

Oil refinery Coffeyville Resources may be located in Coffeyville Kansas but new parent CVR Refining is thinking "We're not just in Kansas anymore." CVR Refining was formed by CVR Energy in September 2012 as an indirect wholly owned subsidiary to take over its downstream operations. CVR Refining is taking ownership of the 115000 barrels-per-day Coffeyville refinery and a 70000 barrels-per-day refinery in Wynnewood Oklahoma both of which are not too far from a crude oil hub at Cushing Oklahoma. In addition CVR Refining will control 350 miles of pipeline 125 oil tanker trucks tank farms and 6 million barrels of storage capacity. CVR Refining went public in 2013 with an offering worth $600 million.

	Annual Growth	12/11*	09/12*	12/12	12/13	12/14
Sales ($ mil.)	22.9%	4,752.8	–	8,281.7	8,683.5	8,829.7
Net income ($ mil.)	(9.3%)	480.3	–	595.3	590.4	358.7
Market value ($ mil.)	(25.7%)	–	–	–	3,338.7	2,479.7
Employees	10.8%	–	800	832	891	982

*Fiscal year change

CVS HEALTH CORPORATION
NYS: CVS

One CVS Drive
Woonsocket, RI 02895
Phone: 401 765-1500
Fax: 401 762-2137
Web: www.cvshealth.com

CEO: Larry J. Merlo
CFO: David M. (Dave) Denton
HR: Lisa Bisaccia
FYE: December 31
Type: Public

Size matters to CVS Health Corp. (formerly CVS Caremark) the nation's #2 drugstore chain and a leading pharmacy benefits manager with nearly 65 million plan members. With more than 7800 retail and specialty drugstores under the CVS Navarro and Longs Drug banners it trails rival Walgreen (8300) in store count. In addition to its stand alone pharmacy operations the company operates CVS locations inside Target stores and runs a prescription management company Caremark Pharmacy Services. The growing company also offers walk-in health services through its retail network of MinuteClinics that are located in more than 900 CVS stores. In mid-2015 it acquired Omnicare in a $12.7 billion mega deal.

	Annual Growth	12/11	12/12	12/13	12/14	12/15
Sales ($ mil.)	9.4%	107,100.0	123,133.0	126,761.0	139,367.0	153,290.0
Net income ($ mil.)	10.9%	3,461.0	3,877.0	4,592.0	4,644.0	5,237.0
Market value ($ mil.)	24.4%	44,898.8	53,233.4	78,798.6	106,037.3	107,644.8
Employees	(3.5%)	280,000	280,000	286,000	297,800	243,000

CYALUME TECHNOLOGIES HOLDINGS, INC
NBB: CYLU

910 S.E. 17th Street, Suite 300
Fort Lauderdale, FL 33316
Phone: 413 858-2500
Fax: –
Web: www.cyalume.com

CEO: Zivi Nedivi
CFO: Michael Bielonko
HR: –
FYE: December 31
Type: Public

Cyalume Technologies Holdings believes in walking softly and carrying a big chemstick. Through two main subsidiaries the company provides an array of tactical gear and training services to militaries and law enforcement agencies. Subsidiary Cyalume Technologies Inc. makes chemical light sticks and other reflective items as well as explosion simulation products. It also offers combat training. Customers include NATO and US militaries and Canadian and German defense procurement agencies. Subsidiary Cyalume Specialty Products makes specialty chemical products for military pharmaceutical and other markets. Cyalume which has manufacturing plants in the US and France filed a $5.8 million IPO in April 2012.

	Annual Growth	12/10	12/11	12/12	12/13	12/14
Sales ($ mil.)	(3.2%)	38.0	34.7	38.6	31.8	33.3
Net income ($ mil.)	–	2.6	0.3	(50.2)	(15.7)	(7.7)
Market value ($ mil.)	(67.2%)	86.7	80.3	44.9	14.8	1.0
Employees	1.9%	166	236	271	190	179

CYANOTECH CORP.
NAS: CYAN

73-4460 Queen Kaahumanu Highway Suite 102
Kailua-Kona, HI 96740
Phone: 808 326-1353
Fax: –
Web: www.cyanotech.com

CEO: Brent D Bailey
CFO: Jole Deal
HR: Andrew Jacobson
FYE: March 31
Type: Public

Cyanotech transforms the scum of the earth into health products. The majority of the company's sales come from Spirulina Pacifica a nutritional supplement made from tiny blue-green vegetable algae and sold as powder flakes and tablets. The firm also produces BioAstin an astaxanthin-based dietary supplement full of antioxidants. Cyanotech produces the microalgae used in its product lines at a 90-acre production facility on the Kona Coast of Hawaii. It sells them primarily to health food and dietary supplement makers. In order to focus on its nutritional supplement business the company has discontinued some other product lines including NatuRose an algae-based pigmentation used to color farm-raised fish.

	Annual Growth	03/11	03/12	03/13	03/14	03/15
Sales ($ mil.)	19.1%	16.8	24.6	27.6	28.9	33.8
Net income ($ mil.)	–	1.7	3.6	4.2	(0.2)	(0.0)
Market value ($ mil.)	25.3%	19.0	56.4	24.9	29.2	46.9
Employees	11.9%	72	80	89	94	113

CYBERDEFENDER CORPORATION
NASDAQ: CYDE

617 W. 7th St. 10th Fl.
Los Angeles CA 90017
Phone: 213-689-8631
Fax: 213-689-8639
Web: www.cyberdefendercorp.com

CEO: –
CFO: –
HR: –
FYE: December 31
Type: Public

If the best defense is a good offense then CyberDefender's got your lineup. Its CyberDefender line of Internet security software protects Windows-based PCs against identity theft viruses malware and spyware. The company boasts about 600000 active subscribers who renew its products on a monthly or yearly basis. CyberDefender markets its applications to consumers and small businesses through e-mails banners and search ads; it also runs a direct marketing campaign with Guthy-Renker. In addition CyberDefender operates a tech-support call center called LiveTech where its 500 help desk agents handle about 160000 calls a month. Co-founder and CEO Gary Guseinov owns almost a quarter of the company's stock.

CYBERNET SOFTWARE SYSTEMS INC.

3031 Tisch Way Ste. 1002
San Jose CA 95128
Phone: 408-615-5700
Fax: 408-615-5707
Web: www.csscorp.com

CEO: Suranjan Pramanik
CFO: Sivaramakrishnan Sundaram
HR: –
FYE: March 31
Type: Private

Cybernet Software Systems (which does business as CSS) helps large corporations consumers and technology vendors worldwide improve software quality and the operations of their IT systems. Among the services the company offers are software testing and development remote infrastructure management application lifecycle management cloud enablement and enterprise and consumer technical support. It serves customers in a wide range of industries including technology (NETGEAR) financial services (Deutsche Bank) and healthcare (Purdue Pharma). The company partners with such tech firms as Blackberry Microsoft and VMware. Privately held CSS has received investments from Goldman Sachs SAIF and Sierra Ventures.

CYBERONICS, INC.
NMS: CYBX

100 Cyberonics Boulevard
Houston, TX 77058
Phone: 281 228-7200
Fax: –
Web: www.cyberonics.com

CEO: Daniel J Moore
CFO: Gregory H Browne
HR: –
FYE: April 25
Type: Public

It may sound futuristic but Cyberonics is all about treating an age-old neurological disorder. The company is the maker of the first medical device to gain clearance by the FDA for treating epilepsy. Its Vagus Nerve Stimulation Therapy system (VNS Therapy) is a pacemaker-like device that is implanted under the collarbone with a lead that connects it to the vagus nerve in the neck. The device delivers intermittent signals to the brain to control epileptic seizures. Physicians can program the signals by computer and patients can start or stop signals with hand-held magnets. VNS Therapy is also used for treating depression that has been treatment-resistant. Cyberonics sells its systems worldwide.

	Annual Growth	04/10	04/11	04/12	04/13	04/14
Sales ($ mil.)	13.9%	167.8	190.5	218.5	254.3	282.0
Net income ($ mil.)	(8.5%)	78.4	46.7	36.1	46.4	54.9
Market value ($ mil.)	32.4%	522.3	951.9	1,031.8	1,149.8	1,605.3
Employees	8.3%	465	484	536	581	639

CYBEROPTICS CORP.
NMS: CYBE

5900 Golden Hills Drive
Minneapolis, MN 55416
Phone: 763 542-5000
Fax: –
Web: www.cyberoptics.com

CEO: Subodh Kulkarni
CFO: Jeffrey A. Bertelsen
HR: Lynee Koester
FYE: December 31
Type: Public

CyberOptics keeps a close eye on the printed circuit board market. The company makes non-contact sensors and integrated systems used during and after the assembly of printed circuit boards and solar cells. Incorporating proprietary laser and optics three-dimensional sensing technology most of the company's products are used in surface mount technology (SMT) assembly and solar cell manufacturing as components used by assembly system manufacturers and as stand-alone products sold directly to end users. It also offers products used for yield improvement in semiconductor fabrication.

	Annual Growth	12/10	12/11	12/12	12/13	12/14
Sales ($ mil.)	(5.0%)	57.0	61.1	41.6	33.3	46.5
Net income ($ mil.)	–		3.1	4.4	(6.7)	(6.2)	(1.5)
Market value ($ mil.)	3.0%	56.7	51.8	49.3	42.5	63.8
Employees	(1.7%)	181	193	168	144	169

CYCLACEL PHARMACEUTICALS, INC
NAS: CYCC

200 Connell Drive, Suite 1500
Berkeley Heights, NJ 07922
Phone: 908 517-7330
Fax: 866 271-3466
Web: www.cyclacel.com

CEO: Spiro Rombotis
CFO: Paul McBarron
HR: –
FYE: December 31
Type: Public

Cyclacel Pharmaceuticals wants to stop the cycle of disease. The company's main focus is on cancer but it is also working on treatments for inflammation type II diabetes and HIV/AIDS. Its cancer programs which seek to halt cell cycles related to disease progression target such ailments as leukemia and non-small cell lung cancer. Cyclacel's R&D operations are supported by commercial products sold through subsidiary ALIGN Pharmaceuticals including Xclair cream for radiation-induced skin conditions and Numoisyn lozenge and liquid formulas for xerostomia (dry mouth often related to chemotherapy).

	Annual Growth	12/10	12/11	12/12	12/13	12/14
Sales ($ mil.)	26.1%	0.7	0.7	0.1	1.1	1.7
Net income ($ mil.)	–	(16.0)	(15.2)	(13.2)	(10.2)	(19.4)
Market value ($ mil.)	(17.0%)	34.1	13.7	140.6	93.3	16.2
Employees	0.0%	18	18	17	18	18

CYCLE COUNTRY ACCESSORIES CORP.
NYSE AMEX: ATC

1701 38th Ave. West
Spencer IA 51301
Phone: 712-262-4191
Fax: 712-262-0248
Web: www.cyclecountry.com

CEO: Robert Davis
CFO: Robert Davis
HR: –
FYE: September 30
Type: Public

Cycle Country Accessories turns ATVs into beasts of burden. The company makes all-terrain vehicle (ATV) accessories such as snowplow blades lawnmowers spreaders sprayers tillage equipment winch mounts utility boxes and wheel covers for Honda Yamaha Kawasaki Suzuki Polaris Arctic Cat and other ATV models. Cycle Country also makes hubcaps for golf carts riding lawnmowers and light-duty trailers. Its products are sold through 20 distributors in the US and more than 30 other countries. The company also makes pull-behind implements and other accessories for riding mowers under the Weekend Warrior brand and offers contract manufacturing services. Cycle Country makes most of its sales in the US.

CYIOS CORPORATION
OTC: CYIO

1300 Pennsylvania Ave. NW Ste. 700
Washington DC 20004
Phone: 202-204-3006
Fax: 202-315-3458
Web: www.cyios.com

CEO: –
CFO: –
HR: –
FYE: December 31
Type: Public

CYIOS is a holding company for two operating subsidiaries. The first which has the same name as the parent company and is referred to as CYIOS DC is a provider of information technology (IT) systems integration services for agencies within the Department of Defense. The second subsidiary CKO offers an online office management software product called XO Office software. The company had previously provided telecommunications services as WorldTeq but has ceased those operations. CEO Tim Carnahan owns 67% of the company.

CYNERGY DATA LLC

30-30 47th Ave. 9th Fl.
New York NY 11101
Phone: 866-906-4040
Fax: 416-850-9828
Web: www.kingproducts.com

CEO: Afshin Yazdian
CFO: Nancy J Disman
HR: Trish Newman
FYE: December 31
Type: Private

Cynergy Data helps merchants generate Cyber cash. The company provides electronic credit debit gift card and check transaction processing services to retailers restaurants e-businesses and catalog firms. The company's proprietary VIMAS software provides instant merchant application approvals; the firm also offers cash advances to merchants. Cynergy Data deploys and supports payment-processing equipment from such market leaders as Hypercom and VeriFone. The company processes more than $13 billion in electronic payment transactions annually. Cynergy Data filed for Chapter 11 bankruptcy protection in 2009.

CYNOSURE INC
NMS: CYNO

5 Carlisle Road
Westford, MA 01886
Phone: 978 256-4200
Fax: –
Web: www.cynosure.com

CEO: Michael R. Davin
CFO: Timothy W. Baker
HR: –
FYE: December 31
Type: Public

If beauty is only skin deep then Cynosure can surely enhance it. The company develops makes and markets aesthetic laser and pulsed light systems used by dermatologists and doctors to remove hair reduce pigmentation rejuvenate the skin and treat vascular lesions. For patients who want to go deeper its Smartlipo workstation allows cosmetic surgeons to perform a less-invasive procedure than conventional liposuction to target and reduce fat. Cynosure's laser systems consist of a control console and one or more handpieces. The company's direct sales force and international distributors market and sell its products worldwide under such names as Accolade Affirm Cynergy Elite and PicoSure.

	Annual Growth	12/10	12/11	12/12	12/13	12/14
Sales ($ mil.)	37.5%	81.8	110.6	153.5	226.0	292.4
Net income ($ mil.)	–	(5.5)	(2.9)	11.0	(1.6)	31.3
Market value ($ mil.)	28.0%	221.2	254.3	521.4	576.1	593.0
Employees	30.7%	259	346	378	576	755

CYOPTICS INC.

9999 Hamilton Blvd.
Breinigsville PA 18031
Phone: 484-397-2000
Fax: 484-397-2014
Web: www.cyoptics.com

CEO: Ed J Coringrato Jr
CFO: Warren Barratt
HR: –
FYE: December 31
Type: Private

CyOptics sees its way clear to optical networks. The company makes optical components based on indium phosphide (InP) a compound semiconductor that runs faster than silicon the material in most microchips. Its chips lasers and receivers are integrated telecommunications network equipment. CyOptics also offers contract design and manufacturing services from facilities in Mexico and the US. Customers include telecom equipment makers module suppliers and defense contractors. Founded in 1999 CyOptics has received funding from equity investors Jerusalem Venture Partners (which owns 54% of the company) Sprout Group Birchmere Ventures and Eurofund. The company filed an IPO in 2011 but withdrew it in 2012.

CYPRESS BIOSCIENCE INC.

4350 Executive Dr. Ste. 325
San Diego CA 92121
Phone: 858-452-2323
Fax: 858-452-1222
Web: www.cypressbio.com

CEO: Jay D Kranzler PHD
CFO: Sabrina Martucci Johnson
HR: –
FYE: December 31
Type: Private

Cypress Bioscience searches for cures in the swampy waters surrounding neurological conditions. The biotech company is focused on researching and developing therapeutic candidates for central nervous system conditions such as schizophrenia and autism. Cypress Bioscience collaborated on the development of Savella (milnacipran) for fibromyalgia a chronic functional condition marked by pain stiffness and fatigue that tends to affect adult women; the drug was approved by the FDA in 2009 and is marketed by former development partner Forest Laboratories. In early 2011 Cypress Bioscience was acquired by investors Ramius Capital and Royalty Pharma for roughly $255 million.

CYPRESS SEMICONDUCTOR CORP.
NMS: CY

198 Champion Court
San Jose, CA 95134
Phone: 408 943-2600
Fax: –
Web: www.cypress.com

CEO: T. J. Rodgers
CFO: Thad Trent
HR: –
FYE: December 28
Type: Public

In Silicon Valley it's perfectly logical for a giant Cypress to put its roots down in pure silicon. Cypress Semiconductor makes a wide array of integrated circuits; its nonmemory products include programmable logic devices touch-screen and touch-sensing controllers Universal Serial Bus (USB) controllers and specialty products for the computer and data communications markets. It also makes memory chips especially static random-access memories (SRAMs). Customers include computer and telecommunications equipment makers such as Samsung Electronics Acer and HTC as well as distributors including Avnet and Tokyo Electron. Customers outside the US account for more than 85% of sales.

	Annual Growth	01/11	01/12*	12/12	12/13	12/14
Sales ($ mil.)	(6.1%)	877.5	995.2	769.7	722.7	725.5
Net income ($ mil.)	(38.1%)	75.7	167.8	(22.4)	(46.4)	17.9
Market value ($ mil.)	(7.7%)	3,028.8	2,753.3	1,711.6	1,677.4	2,380.0
Employees	(95.0%)	3,600	3,400	3,600	3,400	0

*Fiscal year change

CYS INVESTMENTS, INC.
NYS: CYS

890 Winter Street, Suite 200
Waltham, MA 02451
Phone: 617 639-0440
Fax: –
Web: www.cysinv.com

CEO: Kevin E. Grant
CFO: Frances Spark
HR: –
FYE: December 31
Type: Public

CYS Investments (formerly Cypress Sharpridge Investments) is a real estate investment trust (REIT) that invests in residential mortgage-backed securities (RMBS) primarily collateralized by adjustable-rate mortgage loans and guaranteed by government agencies Fannie Mae Freddie Mac and Ginnie Mae. (As a REIT CYS is exempt from paying federal income tax so long as it distributes dividends back to shareholders.) More than three-quarters of its portfolio is backed by hybrid adjustable-rate mortgages (ARMs) and 15-year fixed-rate single-family mortgages. The REIT's investment activities are usually financed through major commercial and investment banks.

	Annual Growth	12/10	12/11	12/12	12/13	12/14
Sales ($ mil.)	43.1%	75.5	232.9	293.3	332.0	317.1
Net income ($ mil.)	108.8%	22.4	291.9	372.8	(475.8)	425.6
Market value ($ mil.)	(9.3%)	2,089.5	2,126.7	1,911.4	1,199.3	1,411.3
Employees	–	–	–	16	16	16

CYSTIC FIBROSIS FOUNDATION

6931 ARLINGTON RD STE 200
BETHESDA, MD 208145269
Phone: 301-951-4422
Fax: –
Web: www.cff.org

CEO: Preston W Campbell III
CFO: –
HR: –
FYE: December 31
Type: Private

The Cystic Fibrosis Foundation funds cystic fibrosis (CF) research and medical programs. Founded in 1955 the organization supports clinical trials and specialized health-care centers provides grants for independent research operates university research centers encourages drug development through matching funds and offers CF-related information and educational materials. Its Cystic Fibrosis Foundation Therapeutics (CFFT) subsidiary partners with pharmaceutical companies and research facilities to develop CF drugs. The foundation provides funding training and accreditation for about 110 treatment centers in the US. It has about 75 chapters and branch offices nationwide.

	Annual Growth	12/06	12/07	12/08	12/12	12/13
Sales ($ mil.)	8.6%	–	246.6	138.5	297.7	405.5
Net income ($ mil.)	–	–	–	(2.1)	175.2	247.1
Market value ($ mil.)	–	–	–	–	–	–
Employees	–	–	–	–	–	550

CYTEC ENGINEERED MATERIALS INC.

2085 E. Technology Cir. Ste. 300
Tempe AZ 85284
Phone: 480-730-2000
Fax: 480-730-2088
Web: www.cytec.com/engineered-materials/index.htm

CEO: David Drillock
CFO: –
HR: –
FYE: December 31
Type: Subsidiary

Because nobody wants parts flying off airplanes cruising at 35000 feet Cytec Engineered Materials or CEM makes a variety of adhesives composites epoxies sealants and ablatives for demanding applications. Typical applications include military and commercial airplanes high-performance automobiles helicopters boats missiles and launch vehicles and composite tooling. As a unit of global chemical company Cytec Industries CEM has 13 manufacturing plants four technology centers and several sales offices throughout North America Europe and Asia. Its headquarters is in Tempe Arizona with European headquarters in Wrexham UK.

CYTEC INDUSTRIES, INC.

NYS: CYT

Five Garret Mountain Plaza
Woodland Park, NJ 07424
Phone: 973 357-3100
Fax: –
Web: www.cytec.com

CEO: Shane D Fleming
CFO: Daniel G Darazsdi
HR: –
FYE: December 31
Type: Public

Cytec Industries makes products that help companies do everything from lifting off driving fast and mining ores. Its Aerospace Materials segment makes advanced composites carbon fiber and structural film adhesives for aerospace markets. The Industrial Materials segment makes structural composite materials (for automotive motorsports and recreation markets) and process materials (for aerospace wind energy and other process materials markets). The In Process Separation segment makes mining chemicals and phosphines primarily used in applications to separate targeted minerals from host ores. The Additive Technologies segment makes polymer additives specialty additives and formulated resins.

	Annual Growth	12/09	12/10	12/11	12/12	12/13
Sales ($ mil.)	(8.7%)	2,789.5	2,748.3	3,073.1	1,708.1	1,935.0
Net income ($ mil.)	–	(2.5)	172.3	207.8	188.0	173.5
Market value ($ mil.)	26.5%	2,586.1	3,767.7	3,170.5	4,887.5	6,615.2
Employees	(6.7%)	5,800	6,000	5,500	6,600	4,400

CYTOKINETICS INC

NMS: CYTK

280 East Grand Avenue
South San Francisco, CA 94080
Phone: 650 624-3000
Fax: –
Web: www.cytokinetics.com

CEO: Robert I. Blum
CFO: Sharon A. Barbari
HR: David (Dave) Cragg
FYE: December 31
Type: Public

Cytokinetics studies the cytoskeleton to get to the heart of the problem. The biopharmaceutical firm's drug development technologies aim to treat disease by modulating muscle function through manipulation of the cytoskeleton (biological infrastructure of cells). Its pipeline includes lead candidate omecamtiv mecarbil which is designed for the treatment of heart failure based on a cytoskeletal protein in the heart muscle. It is being developed in collaboration with Amgen. Its other lead candidate tirasemtiv is in clinical studies for use by patients with ALS. In collaboration with Astellas Cykokinetics is also studying developing CK-2127107 for the treatment of spinal muscular atrophy (SMA).

	Annual Growth	12/10	12/11	12/12	12/13	12/14
Sales ($ mil.)	106.6%	2.6	4.0	7.6	30.6	46.9
Net income ($ mil.)	–	(49.3)	(47.9)	(40.4)	(33.7)	(14.6)
Market value ($ mil.)	39.9%	80.8	37.1	25.5	251.3	309.7
Employees	(3.3%)	105	79	70	85	92

CYTORI THERAPEUTICS INC

NAS: CYTX

3020 Callan Road
San Diego, CA 92121
Phone: 858 458-0900
Fax: –
Web: www.cytori.com

CEO: Marc H. Hedrick
CFO: Tiago M. Gir Ło
HR: –
FYE: December 31
Type: Public

Attention lovers of liposuction: Cytori Therapeutics wants your fat. The firm is developing therapies using regenerative adult stem cells derived from adipose otherwise known as fat tissue. Cytori's Celution is an adipose tissue extraction system that is marketed in Europe and Asia for reconstructive and cosmetic surgery purposes. The company is developing therapies based on the Celution system intended to treat cardiovascular disease (specifically ischemic heart disease) spine and orthopedic injuries and thermal burns. In addition the company sells its StemSource cell banking system which collects and preserves stem and regenerative cells for research purposes to customers around the globe.

	Annual Growth	12/10	12/11	12/12	12/13	12/14
Sales ($ mil.)	(12.0%)	8.3	8.0	8.7	7.1	5.0
Net income ($ mil.)	–	(27.5)	(32.5)	(32.3)	(26.2)	(37.4)
Market value ($ mil.)	(44.6%)	515.6	218.6	278.2	255.3	48.6
Employees	(10.9%)	124	128	127	115	78

CYTOSORBENTS CORPORATION

OTC: CTSO

7 Deer Park Dr. Ste. K
Monmouth Junction NJ 08852
Phone: 732-329-8885
Fax: 732-329-8650
Web: www.cytosorbents.com

CEO: –
CFO: –
HR: –
FYE: December 31
Type: Public

CytoSorbents (formerly Medasorb Technologies) gets the gunk out of blood. The medical device firm is developing blood purification systems for treating patients with infections and kidney disease. Its top priority is its clinical-stage CytoSorb device which draws a patient's blood pumps it through a cartridge with cleansing polymers and returns it to the patient in a closed loop; the company is developing the device as a treatment for sepsis (or blood infection) in collaboration with UPMC. CytoSorbents is also working on BetaSorb a similar system for treating chronic kidney failure in combination with dialysis; Fresenius Medical Care has agreed to help market the device if approved.

CYTRX CORP
NAS: CYTR

11726 San Vicente Blvd., Suite 650
Los Angeles, CA 90049
Phone: 310 826-5648
Fax: 310 826-6139
Web: www.cytrx.com

CEO: Steven A. Kriegsman
CFO: John Y. Caloz
HR: –
FYE: December 31
Type: Public

CytRx keeps an eye on the suspicious activities of cancers. The drug developer is researching and developing several drug candidates to treat conditions such as chronic and acute forms of leukemia pancreatic cancer stomach cancer and soft-tissue sarcomas (malignant tumors). Its pipeline drugs include enhanced chemotherapy agents and proprietary cancer cell inhibiting drugs. The company has sold off all of its non-oncology assets to focus on its drugs in late stage clinical trials.

	Annual Growth	12/10	12/11	12/12	12/13	12/14
Sales ($ mil.)	0.0%	0.1	0.3	0.1	0.3	0.1
Net income ($ mil.)	–	0.4	(14.4)	(18.0)	(47.5)	(30.1)
Market value ($ mil.)	28.3%	56.3	15.6	104.2	349.4	152.7
Employees	14.7%	15	15	15	17	26

D W W CO. INC.

1400 N TUSTIN ST
ORANGE, CA 928673902
Phone: 714-639-6750
Fax: –
Web: www.toyotaoforange.com

CEO: –
CFO: –
HR: Michelle Chauvin
FYE: December 31
Type: Private

First Orange County then the world — or at least as far as Arizona and Mexico. Megadealer David Wilson Automotive Group has its roots in Orange County California with 16 branches that stretch to east to Scottsdale and now south to Puerto Vallarta Mexico. David Wilson's Automotive locations sell new and used Acura Ford Honda and Mazda cars as well as Toyota and Lexus brand vehicles. The group's dealerships also operate parts and service departments; some offer fleet services. Dealership Web sites allow customers to search inventory schedule service appointments and request quotes. David Wilson owns the company that bears his name

	Annual Growth	12/04	12/05	12/06	12/07	12/08
Sales ($ mil.)	(8.8%)	–	214.6	229.9	199.9	162.8
Net income ($ mil.)	(21.0%)	–	–	12.0	7.6	7.5
Market value ($ mil.)	–	–	–	–	–	–
Employees	–	–	–	–	–	135

D'AGOSTINO SUPERMARKETS INC.

1385 Boston Post Rd.
Larchmont NY 10538-3904
Phone: 914-833-4000
Fax: 914-833-4060
Web: www.dagnyc.com

CEO: –
CFO: Ron Munkittrick
HR: Frank Argento
FYE: July 31
Type: Private

D'Agostino Supermarkets sells food for the body and soul to New York City residents. The company operates more than a dozen grocery stores mostly in Manhattan but also in Westchester County New York that feature deli and floral departments seafood and meat counters and an ample supply of fresh and organic produce. In addition to name-brand items the grocer sells everything from ice cream to chips and chickens under its D'Agostino label; it also has developed the Earth Goods product line for environment- and health-conscious shoppers. Founded in 1932 by Nicola and Pasquale D'Agostino the regional supermarket chain in still owned and operated by the D'Agostino family.

D. C. TAYLOR CO.

312 29TH ST NE
CEDAR RAPIDS, IA 524024816
Phone: 319-363-2073
Fax: –
Web: www.dctaylorco.com

CEO: William W Taylor
CFO: –
HR: –
FYE: December 31
Type: Private

D. C. Taylor is one of the largest commercial and industrial roofing contractors in the US providing roof installation repair and maintenance services. It has some 60 service and roofing crews that operate from offices in Arizona California Georgia Illinois and Iowa. Dudley C. Taylor started Taylor Tuckpointing a tuckpointing (cosmetic brick finishing commonly found on Federation houses and Californian bungalows) and masonry repair company in Chicago in 1949; the company's name was changed to D. C. Taylor in 1954 and the firm was formally incorporated in 1960. Chairman and CEO Bill Taylor is the company's majority shareholder.

	Annual Growth	12/06	12/07	12/08	12/09	12/10
Sales ($ mil.)	–	–	–	(1,140.6)	8.4	40.4
Net income ($ mil.)	18944.5%	–	–	0.0	1.2	1.9
Market value ($ mil.)	–	–	–	–	–	–
Employees	–	–	–	–	–	350

D/L COOPERATIVE INC.

5001 BRITTONFIELD PKWY
EAST SYRACUSE, NY 130579201
Phone: 315-233-1000
Fax: –
Web: www.dairylea.com

CEO: –
CFO: –
HR: –
FYE: March 31
Type: Private

Yes the farmer takes a wife then hi-ho the dairy-o the farmer takes membership in milk-marketing organizations such as Dairylea Cooperative. Owned by some 2000 dairy farmers in the northeastern US Dairylea processes and markets 6.3 billion pounds of milk for its farmers annually to dairy-product customers including food manufacturers. Its Agri-Services holding company provides members with a full range of financial and farm-management services as well as insurance. Its Empire Livestock Marketing unit operates regional livestock auction locations. Dairylea which was established in 1907 by New York dairy farmers merged with the US's largest milk marketing coop Dairy Farmers of America in 2014.

	Annual Growth	03/07	03/08	03/09	03/10	03/11
Sales ($ mil.)	25.1%	–	–	–	1,066.4	1,333.9
Net income ($ mil.)	7.6%	–	–	–	1.5	1.7
Market value ($ mil.)	–	–	–	–	–	–
Employees	–	–	–	–	–	107

DAC TECHNOLOGIES GROUP INTERNATIONAL INC.
OTC: DAAT

12120 Colonial Glenn Rd. Ste. 6200
Little Rock AR 72210
Phone: 501-661-9100
Fax: 501-661-9108
Web: www.dactec.com

CEO: David A Collins
CFO: Robert C Goodwin
HR: –
FYE: December 31
Type: Public

This company's aim is to give gun owners a clean shot. DAC Technologies Group International manufactures more than 50 different GunMaster brand gun cleaning kits as well as gun maintenance and safety products such as trigger locks and gun safes. Its gun-related business rings up more than two-thirds of DAC's sales. The company also makes game processing equipment aluminum camping tables and other items for the hunting and camping markets as well as a line of household cleaning dusters. DAC also has a licensing agreement with Olin Corp. to market some of its gun cleaning items under the Winchester brand name for sale at Wal-Mart. (The retail giant accounts for about 55% of DAC's sales.)

DAEGIS INC — NAS: DAEG

600 E. Las Colinas Blvd., Suite 1500
Irving, TX 75039
Phone: 214 584-6400
Fax: –
Web: www.daegis.com

CEO: Timothy P Bacci
CFO: Susan K Conner
HR: –
FYE: April 30
Type: Public

Daegis formerly Unify Corporation has a firm business plan. The company targets corporate law departments and law firms with products and services for the legal discovery process including search analysis review and production. Legal clients also use Daegis's archiving software to manage electronically stored information. The company additionally serves software value-added resellers systems integrators and independent software vendors among others with products that aid in the development and management of business applications and data. Services provided by Daegis include project management maintenance and consulting.

	Annual Growth	04/10	04/11	04/12	04/13	04/14
Sales ($ mil.)	2.0%	28.6	47.0	43.5	40.2	31.0
Net income ($ mil.)	–	(1.8)	(16.7)	(16.7)	0.5	(1.6)
Market value ($ mil.)	(22.8%)	59.0	47.5	22.9	18.7	21.0
Employees	(0.8%)	127	204	213	160	123

DAILY JOURNAL CORPORATION — NAS: DJCO

915 East First Street
Los Angeles, CA 90012
Phone: 213 229-5300
Fax: 213 229-5481
Web: www.dailyjournal.com

CEO: Gerald L. Salzman
CFO: –
HR: –
FYE: September 30
Type: Public

Legal matters dominate in these papers. Daily Journal Corporation is a leading newspaper publisher with about a dozen papers serving markets primarily in California. Its flagship papers include the Los Angeles Daily Journal and the San Francisco Daily Journal which offer in-depth coverage of legal cases and court matters in addition to general interest news. The company also publishes legal affairs magazine California Lawyer operates subscription-based access to court case and real estate information and publishes a legal directory for California. Board members Charles Munger (who also serves as vice chairman of Berkshire Hathaway) and J.P. Guerin together control about 40% of Daily Journal Corporation.

	Annual Growth	09/11	09/12	09/13	09/14	09/15
Sales ($ mil.)	6.2%	34.5	31.9	37.7	43.4	44.0
Net income ($ mil.)	(43.3%)	7.8	5.5	3.8	0.6	0.8
Market value ($ mil.)	30.0%	90.1	129.5	203.0	249.2	257.1
Employees	13.6%	210	205	320	320	350

DAILY NEWS L.P.

450 W. 33rd St.
New York NY 10001
Phone: 212-210-2100
Fax: 212-643-7831
Web: www.nydailynews.com

CEO: –
CFO: Tom Peck
HR: –
FYE: December 31
Type: Private

This daily news might not always be fit to print but it at least keeps New Yorkers entertained. Daily News L.P. publishes New York City's Daily News the big city tabloid that goes toe-to-toe with the New York Post (owned by Rupert Murdoch's News Corporation) by penning over-the-top headlines and sensational stories. The paper founded in 1919 is distributed primarily in the Five Boroughs and boasts a circulation of more than 550000. It also distributes news and features online through its website. The Daily News is owned by real estate magnate Mortimer Zuckerman who also owns news magazine U.S. News & World Report.

DAIRY FARMERS OF AMERICA INC.

10220 N. Ambassador Dr.
Kansas City MO 64153
Phone: 816-801-6455
Fax: 816-801-6456
Web: www.dfamilk.com

CEO: Rick Smith
CFO: –
HR: –
FYE: December 31
Type: Private - Cooperativ

The members of Dairy Farmers of America (DFA) are partners in cream. DFA is one of the world's largest dairy cooperatives with some 15000 member/farmers in 48 states. About 1.7 million cows belonging to member/farmers produce 63 billion pounds of milk a year (roughly 30% of milk production in the US) which DFA markets. Along with fresh and shelf-stable fluid milk the co-op produces cheese butter dried milk powder and other dairy products for industrial wholesale and retail customers. It also offers contract manufacturing services. The co-op owns 20-plus manufacturing plants nationwide. DFA whose profits are shared based on member contribution is a major supplier to dairy king Dean Foods.

DAIRYLAND POWER COOPERATIVE

3200 East Ave. South
La Crosse WI 54601
Phone: 608-788-4000
Fax: 608-787-1420
Web: www.dairynet.com

CEO: William L Berg
CFO: Phillip M Moilien
HR: –
FYE: December 31
Type: Private - Cooperativ

Dairyland Power Cooperative provides its customers with lots of juice in the land of lactose. The firm provides electricity generation (about 1420 MW of generating capacity) and transmission services for 25 member distribution cooperatives and 16 municipal utilities in five states (including Wisconsin). The member cooperatives and municipal utilities in turn distribute electricity to almost 253660 consumers. Dairyland Power generates 1030 MW of capacity from its coal-fired power plants; it also operates more than 3170 miles of transmission lines and 285 substations. The power cooperative also markets electricity and offers energy management services.

DAIS ANALYTIC CORP — NBB: DLYT

11552 Prosperous Drive
Odessa, FL 33556
Phone: 727 375-8484
Fax: –
Web: www.daisanalytic.com

CEO: Timothy N Tangredi
CFO: Peter Dichiara
HR: –
FYE: December 31
Type: Public

Dais Analytic doesn't stand on a dais or do analytics. But it does develop nano polymers it hopes can be used to solve tough global problems like cleaning air and water and reducing harmful emissions. Its only current product is ConsERV an energy recovery ventilator that uses nano technology to improve the efficiency of existing heating and cooling systems. Other Dais products in the development stage including NanoAir NanoClear and NanoCap use the same technology to cleaning air and water and storing energy more efficiently. Formed in 1993 as fuel cell developer Dais the company bought fellow fuel cell firm Analytic in 1999 and changed its name. In 2002 it shifted focus to nano polymers.

	Annual Growth	12/10	12/11	12/12	12/13	12/14
Sales ($ mil.)	(13.2%)	3.3	3.5	3.7	1.7	1.9
Net income ($ mil.)	–	(1.4)	(2.3)	0.0	(2.1)	(1.8)
Market value ($ mil.)	1.7%	29.3	25.3	11.7	4.0	31.3
Employees	2.1%	23	27	34	25	25

DAISY MANUFACTURING COMPANY

400 W. Stribing
Rogers AR 72756
Phone: 479-636-1200
Fax: 479-636-1601
Web: www.daisy.com

CEO: Ray Hobbs
CFO: Bruce Wolf
HR: –
FYE: December 31
Type: Private

Daisy Manufacturing the world's oldest and largest maker of pellet and air-powered guns ammunition and accessories aims to please. The company produces the Red Ryder BB gun (more than 9 million sold since its debut in 1938) plus air rifles pistols CO2 pistols slingshots and branded apparel. Its products are sold at online retailers gun dealers and sporting goods stores such as Bass Pro Shops and Dick's Sporting Goods. Founded in 1882 as the Plymouth Iron Windmill Company Daisy's first air gun was introduced in 1886 as a premium for farmers who purchased windmills. Charter Oak Partners owns a majority interest in the company.

DAKOTA GASIFICATION COMPANY

1600 E. Interstate Ave.
Bismarck ND 58503
Phone: 701-221-4411
Fax: 701-221-4450
Web: www.dakotagas.com

CEO: Paul M Sukut
CFO: Steve Johnson
HR: Erica Petrowitz
FYE: December 31
Type: Subsidiary

A miracle on the prairie? A subsidiary of Basin Electric Power Cooperative Dakota Gasification does not turn water into wine but it does something pretty neat anyway: It turns coal into natural gas. The Great Plains Synfuels Plant harnesses the abundant coal resources underlying the North Dakota prairie. The gasification process transforms more than 6 million tons of coal into more than 57 billion cu. ft. of natural gas annually which is then used to supply the eastern US. In addition to natural gas the company's Synfuels plant produces carbon dioxide fertilizers solvents phenol and other chemicals.

DAK AMERICAS LLC

5925 Carnegie Blvd. Ste. 500
Charlotte NC 28209
Phone: 704-940-7500
Fax: 704-940-7501
Web: www.dakamericas.com/

CEO: –
CFO: –
HR: Betty Sowa
FYE: December 31
Type: Subsidiary

DAK Americas manufactures products that are high in fiber but have nothing to do with your breakfast cereal. The company built its business on producing polyester staple fibers (PSF) used in textiles and home furnishings. DAK Americas is one of the largest producers of polyethylene terephthalate (PET) resins used in carbonated soft drink and water bottles. It also makes terephthalic acid (TPA) monomers used in PSF and PET products and specialty polymers sold in markets such as film and packaging and nonwovens. DAK Americas maintains manufacturing facilities in the Carolinas and Mississippi in the US as well as in Mexico. Alpek a subsidiary of Mexican industrial giant Alfa S.A. de C.V. owns DAK Americas.

DAKOTA SUPPLY GROUP INC.

2601 3RD AVE N
FARGO, ND 581024016
Phone: 701-237-9440
Fax: –
Web: www.dakotasupplygroup.com

CEO: Todd Kumm
CFO: Ross Westby
HR: –
FYE: December 28
Type: Private

Dakota Supply Group (DSG) distributes electrical communications and mechanical equipment to customers through more than a dozen branch locations in Minnesota North Dakota and South Dakota. The company stocks approximately 25000 products. DSG carries products from 3Com 3M A. O. Smith Buckingham Manufacturing Corning Emerson Electric Ferraz Shawmut General Electric Honeywell Hubbell Moen Schneider Electric and Zurn Industries among other manufacturers. The company was founded in 1898. An employee stock ownership plan holds nearly all of Dakota Supply.

	Annual Growth	12/08	12/09	12/11	12/12	12/13
Sales ($ mil.)	22.9%	–	162.2	211.2	297.4	369.6
Net income ($ mil.)	8.5%	–	–	14.0	15.9	16.5
Market value ($ mil.)	–	–	–	–	–	–
Employees	–	–	–	–	–	620

DAKOTA ELECTRIC ASSOCIATION

4300 220TH ST W
FARMINGTON, MN 550249583
Phone: 651-463-6212
Fax: –
Web: www.dakotaelectric.com

CEO: Greg Miller
CFO: –
HR: Chris Dodgeratzlaff
FYE: December 31
Type: Private

The Dakota Electric Association delivers electricity to residents of southeastern Minnesota the Gopher State so they don't have to burrow underground to outlast those long cold winters. The member-owned utility serves more than 103000 customers in portions of Dakota Goodhue Rice and Scott counties south of Minneapolis-St. Paul. The co-op gets its power wholesale from transmission cooperative Great River Energy and distributes it more than 4010 miles of power lines nearly two-thirds of which are buried. Dakota Electric is pushing energy efficiency programs and products to help save its customers money.

	Annual Growth	12/05	12/06	12/08	12/09	12/13
Sales ($ mil.)	6.4%	–	132.4	185.1	178.8	205.0
Net income ($ mil.)	4.3%	–	–	7.0	7.0	8.6
Market value ($ mil.)	–	–	–	–	–	–
Employees	–	–	–	–	–	100,000

DAKTRONICS INC.

NMS: DAKT

201 Daktronics Drive
Brookings, SD 57006
Phone: 605 692-0200
Fax: –
Web: www.daktronics.com

CEO: Reece A. Kurtenbach
CFO: Sheila M. Anderson
HR: Carla Gatzke
FYE: May 02
Type: Public

Daktronics always knows the score. The company is a leading manufacturer of electronic displays audio systems and timing products. Its products include scoreboards game timers shot clocks and animation displays for sports facilities; billboards and price displays for businesses; and displays used by transportation agencies. Other applications include airport information securities trading and outdoor advertising. Daktronics products are used in major sports arenas including venues such as the Olympic Games. Two-thirds of the company's business is made up of live events and commercial clients. While most sales come from the US Daktronics has about a dozen offices worldwide.

	Annual Growth	04/11	04/12	04/13	04/14*	05/15
Sales ($ mil.)	8.7%	441.7	489.5	518.3	552.0	615.9
Net income ($ mil.)	10.0%	14.2	8.5	22.8	22.2	20.9
Market value ($ mil.)	0.1%	467.7	369.1	417.5	569.7	469.0
Employees	1.4%	2,600	2,820	2,620	2,670	2,750

*Fiscal year change

DALE CARNEGIE & ASSOCIATES INC.

290 Motor Pkwy.
Hauppauge NY 11788-5102
Phone: 800-231-5800
Fax: 212-644-5532
Web: www.dale-carnegie.com

CEO: Peter Handal
CFO: Chris Noonan
HR: -
FYE: August 31
Type: Private

Be a good listener remember names and network and you might find success the Dale Carnegie way. Dale Carnegie & Associates started by the author of the 1936 bestseller "How to Win Friends and Influence People" teaches sales teamwork and public-speaking skills. The company founded in 1912 runs courses and franchisees operate offices in more than 85 countries. Dale Carnegie's enduring self-improvement and job skills message has reached some 8 million people who have completed training courses and seminars over the years. The company which boasts a training staff of more than 2700 offers multilingual courses for individuals and custom-made programs for corporations such as AT&T Coca-Cola and BASF.

DALLAS/FORT WORTH INTERNATIONAL AIRPORT

3200 E. Airfield Dr.
DFW Airport TX 75261
Phone: 972-973-8888
Fax: 610-964-9524
Web: www.argosycapital.com

CEO: Jeff P Fegan
CFO: -
HR: -
FYE: September 30
Type: Government-owned

Many things are bigger in Texas and Dallas/Fort Worth International Airport (DFW) is no exception. Covering some 30 square miles DFW is one of the world's largest airports by land mass. The facility includes seven runways two active control towers five terminals and 155 gates. Some 60 million passengers pass through DFW annually to destinations domestic and international. Aside from airport fare DFW provides private warehouse and distribution centers to tenants and features Grand Hyatt and Hyatt Regency hotels. Opened in 1974 DFW is owned by the cities of Dallas and Fort Worth; it is situated halfway between them and within about a four-hour flight time of most US destinations.

DALE JARRETT RACING ADVENTURE INC

NBB: DJRT

116 3rd Street N.W., Suite 302
Hickory, NC 28601
Phone: 888 467-2231
Fax: -
Web: www.racingadventure.com

CEO: Timothy B Shannon
CFO: Timothy B Shannon
HR: -
FYE: December 31
Type: Public

Gentlemen start your engines! Dale Jarrett Racing Adventure brings the thrills (but hopefully not the spills) of NASCAR racing to doctors lawyers Indian chiefs — and even average joes assuming they have enough "fuel" to foot the bill. The company gives racing fans the opportunity to race on a major track. Packages range from riding three laps in the passenger seat with a professional driver to 60 laps of actual driving at speeds of up to 165 mph (after instruction). Events are held at racetracks around the country (including Talladega Superspeedway and Atlanta Motor Speedway). The Dale Jarrett Racing Adventure was founded in 1998 when CEO Tim Shannon approached NASCAR driver Dale Jarrett with the concept.

	Annual Growth	12/10	12/11	12/12	12/13	12/14
Sales ($ mil.)	(6.2%)	3.1	2.9	3.5	2.7	2.4
Net income ($ mil.)	-	0.1	(0.3)	(0.2)	(0.2)	(0.4)
Market value ($ mil.)	(12.0%)	1.5	0.8	2.1	0.5	0.9
Employees	40.1%	7	3	3	2	27

DANA HOLDING CORP

NYS: DAN

3939 Technology Drive
Maumee, OH 43537
Phone: 419 887-3000
Fax: 419 887-5200
Web: www.dana.com

CEO: James K. (Jim) Kamsickas
CFO: William G. (Bill) Quigley
HR: Ari Papadakos
FYE: December 31
Type: Public

When it comes to building cars it starts with the parts and Dana makes the parts that carmakers use to piece together new vehicles. In addition to its core offerings which include driveline products (axles driveshafts transmissions) it provides power technologies (sealing thermal-management products) and service parts. It makes products for vehicles in the light medium/heavy (commercial) and off-highway markets. The company's products carry brand names that include Spicer Victor Reinz and Long. Dana also supplies companies that make commercial and off-highway vehicles such as Deere Navistar Ford and PACCAR.

	Annual Growth	12/10	12/11	12/12	12/13	12/14
Sales ($ mil.)	2.0%	6,109.0	7,592.0	7,224.0	6,769.0	6,617.0
Net income ($ mil.)	137.7%	10.0	219.0	300.0	244.0	319.0
Market value ($ mil.)	6.0%	2,830.7	1,998.4	2,567.5	3,227.1	3,575.8
Employees	0.1%	22,500	24,500	23,300	23,000	22,600

DALLAS COWBOYS FOOTBALL CLUB LTD.

1 Cowboys Pkwy.
Irving TX 75063
Phone: 972-556-9900
Fax: 972-556-9304
Web: www.dallascowboys.com

CEO: -
CFO: George Mitchell
HR: -
FYE: February 28
Type: Private

Proclaiming itself "America's Team" this football franchise certainly has the loyalty of many Texans. Dallas Cowboys Football Club operates the famed Dallas Cowboys professional football franchise one of the most popular teams in the National Football League and the winner of five Super Bowl titles (a mark it shares with the San Francisco 49ers). Dallas has been home to such Hall of Fame players as Troy Aikman Michael Irvin and Roger Staubach as well as famed head coach Tom Landry. The team was founded in 1960 by Clint Murchison Jr. and Bedford Wynne. Oilman Jerry Jones has owned the team since 1989.

DANA-FARBER CANCER INSTITUTE INC.

450 BROOKLINE AVE
BOSTON, MA 022155450
Phone: 617-632-3000
Fax: -
Web: www.dana-farber.org

CEO: Edward J. Benz
CFO: Michael L. Reney
HR: Deborah (Deb) Hicks
FYE: September 30
Type: Private

The Dana-Farber Cancer Institute fights cancer on two fronts: It provides treatment to cancer patients young and old and researches new cancer diagnostics treatments and preventions. The organization's scientists also research AIDS treatments and cures for a host of other deadly diseases. Patients receive treatment from Dana-Farber through its cancer centers operated in conjunction with Brigham and Women's Hospital Children's Hospital Boston and Massachusetts General Hospital. The institute is also a principal teaching affiliate of Harvard Medical School. Dana-Farber is funded by the National Cancer Institute the National Institute of Allergy and Infectious Diseases and private contributions.

	Annual Growth	09/07	09/08	09/09	09/10	09/13
Sales ($ mil.)	(6.1%)	-	-	816.5	894.2	635.5
Net income ($ mil.)	18.4%	-	-	28.6	16.8	56.2
Market value ($ mil.)	-	-	-	-	-	-
Employees	-	-	-	-	-	3,000

DANAHER CORP.

2200 Pennsylvania Avenue, N.W., Suite 800W
Washington, DC 20037-1701
Phone: 202 828-0850
Fax: 202 828-0860
Web: www.danaher.com

NYS: DHR
CEO: Thomas P. Joyce
CFO: Daniel L. Comas
HR: Rich King
FYE: December 31
Type: Public

Danaher is a well-diversified industrial and medical conglomerate whose products test analyze and diagnose. Its subsidiaries design manufacture and market products and offer services geared at worldwide professional medical industrial and commercial markets. Danaher operates through five segments: Life Sciences & Diagnostics (research and clinical tools) Test & Measurement (electronic measurement instruments) Industrial Technologies (product identification motion control equipment and sensors) Environmental (turbine pumps and air/water analysis and treatment equipment) and Dental (orthodontic bracket systems and lab products).

	Annual Growth	12/10	12/11	12/12	12/13	12/14
Sales ($ mil.)	10.8%	13,202.6	16,090.5	18,260.4	19,118.0	19,913.8
Net income ($ mil.)	9.7%	1,793.0	2,172.3	2,392.2	2,695.0	2,598.4
Market value ($ mil.)	16.1%	33,221.8	33,130.3	39,370.4	54,372.0	60,365.6
Employees	10.2%	48,200	59,000	63,000	66,000	71,000

DANCKER SELLEW & DOUGLAS INC.

291 EVANS WAY
BRANCHBURG, NJ 088763766
Phone: 908-429-1200
Fax: –
Web: www.dancker.com

CEO: Steven Lang
CFO: Bill Hendry
HR: –
FYE: March 31
Type: Private

Dancker Sellew & Douglas (DS&D) is a furniture dealership serving the New York City metropolitan area upstate New York and New Jersey. It specializes in providing furniture to businesses with clients including AT&T and Coldwell Banker. DS&D offers chairs desks lighting and storage from a variety of manufacturers including Peter Pepper Products Steelcase and Teknion. The company also offers furniture rental and warehousing along with design consulting inventory management and refurbishment services. DS&D also caters to hospitals and universities and provides lab furniture and equipment to pharmaceutical companies. The firm was founded in 1829 as the T.G. Seller Company making roll-top desks.

	Annual Growth	03/02	03/03	03/04	03/06	03/07
Sales ($ mil.)	(10.2%)	–	111.8	97.9	135.8	72.8
Net income ($ mil.)	–	–	–	(0.8)	0.5	(0.4)
Market value ($ mil.)	–	–	–	–	–	–
Employees	–	–	–	–	–	150

DANIS BUILDING CONSTRUCTION COMPANY

3233 NEWMARK DR
MIAMISBURG, OH 453425422
Phone: 937-228-1225
Fax: –
Web: www.danis.com

CEO: John Danis
CFO: Tim Carlson
HR: –
FYE: December 31
Type: Private

Danis Building Construction can reach from the Buckeye state to the Sunshine state. The company provides commercial and industrial construction services in Ohio Indiana Kentucky Tennessee North Carolina Georgia and Florida. The third-generation family-owned company offers construction management design/build general construction and build-to-suit lease-back services. It specializes in public and private building and industrial projects such as offices health care facilities retail complexes hotels cultural facilities schools and industrial plants. Its projects have included the Cincinnati Children's Hospital and a federal courthouse in Kentucky. B.G. Danis established the company in 1916.

	Annual Growth	12/03	12/04	12/06	12/07	12/08
Sales ($ mil.)	–	–	0.0	0.0	208.6	217.4
Net income ($ mil.)	–	–	–	0.0	0.0	0.0
Market value ($ mil.)	–	–	–	–	–	–
Employees	–	–	–	–	–	475

DANTEL INC.

2991 N. Argyle Ave.
Fresno CA 93727-1388
Phone: 559-292-1111
Fax: 559-292-9355
Web: www.dantel.com

CEO: Alan G Hutcheson
CFO: Mary Papadopoulus
HR: –
FYE: December 31
Type: Private

Dantel's products and services act as security blankets for operators of telecommunications and data networks by monitoring network equipment and facilities. Dantel's services include battery monitoring and facility intrusion detection. Dantel's products include network management and reporting devices (PointMaster Eagle) alarm and control systems (Legacy RemoteMaster) remote monitoring (VisionMaster) and surveillance/heat/motion detection (DREN WebMon). Established in 1971 the company markets its products and services to telecom service providers of all sizes as well as to cable operators military/government agencies railroads utilities and other entities that operate communications networks.

DARA BIOSCIENCES, INC.

8601 Six Forks Road, Suite 160
Raleigh, NC 27615
Phone: 919 872-5578
Fax: –
Web: www.darabiosciences.com

NAS: DARA
CEO: Christopher G Clement
CFO: David L Tousley
HR: –
FYE: December 31
Type: Public

Metabolism out of whack? DARA BioSciences is working on it. The drug development company is testing drugs for metabolic diseases such as diabetes. However it was not always thus for the company. Formerly called Point Therapeutics the firm failed in its previous efforts to advance lead cancer drug talabostat and was forced to regroup and consider its options. The company turned to its preclinical pipeline which included a potential diabetes drug and then in 2008 executed a reverse merger with privately held DARA BioSciences which brought along a complementary set of metabolic compounds as well as programs focused on neuropathic pain and psoriasis.

	Annual Growth	12/09	12/10	12/11	12/12	12/13
Sales ($ mil.)	681.9%	–	–	–	0.1	0.4
Net income ($ mil.)	–	(3.3)	(5.7)	(6.2)	(7.3)	(10.0)
Market value ($ mil.)	5.1%	2.7	20.4	7.7	4.8	3.3
Employees	29.4%	5	6	9	18	14

DARCARS AUTOMOTIVE GROUP

12210 Cherry Hill Rd.
Silver Spring MD 20904
Phone: 301-622-0300
Fax: 301-622-4915
Web: www.darcars.com

CEO: –
CFO: –
HR: –
FYE: December 31
Type: Private

Buying a new vehicle in the Washington DC area can expose you to the Darcars side of human nature. Darcars Automotive Group an automobile dealership holding company has about 25 automobile dealerships in Maryland and Virginia. They sell new and used automobiles including cars made by Ford General Motors Kia Nissan Toyota Volkswagen and Volvo. Darcars also offers a full range of automotive services including collision repair through nearly 10 locations parts and service departments and rental cars. Darcars was founded in 1977 by chairman and CEO John Darvish whose family still owns and runs the company.

DARDEN RESTAURANTS, INC.   NYS: DRI

1000 Darden Center Drive
Orlando, FL 32837
Phone: 407 245-4000
Fax: –
Web: www.darden.com

CEO: Eugene I. (Gene) Lee
CFO: Jeffrey (Jeff) Davis
HR: Ronald (Ron) Bojalad
FYE: May 31
Type: Public

Darden Restaurants is the #1 casual-dining operator (in terms of revenue) with about 1535 restaurants in the US and Canada. Its flagship chain is Italian-themed concept Olive Garden. Olive Garden caters to families by offering mid-priced menu items themed interiors and primarily suburban locations. Darden also operates the LongHorn Steakhouse chain with about 430 outlets. Other dining concepts include The Capital Grille (upscale steakhouse) Bahama Breeze (Caribbean food and drinks) and Seasons 52 (casual grill and wine bar). In 2015 it spun off a chunk of its real estate portfolio as Four Corners Property Trust; the portfolio includes about 425 US restaurants that are all leased to Darden subsidiaries.

	Annual Growth	05/11	05/12	05/13	05/14	05/15
Sales ($ mil.)	(2.5%)	7,500.2	7,998.7	8,551.9	6,285.6	6,764.0
Net income ($ mil.)	10.5%	476.3	475.5	411.9	286.2	709.5
Market value ($ mil.)	6.5%	6,451.6	6,722.7	6,693.6	6,278.0	8,303.9
Employees	(4.2%)	178,380	180,000	206,000	206,489	150,000

DARLING INGREDIENTS INC   NYS: DAR

251 O'Connor Ridge Blvd., Suite 300
Irving, TX 75038
Phone: 972 717-0300
Fax: –

CEO: Randall C. Stuewe
CFO: John O. Muse
HR: Nancy Cooper
FYE: January 03
Type: Public

A rather dainty name for a messy business Darling Ingredients is the largest publicly traded rendering operation in the US; it collects and recycles animal by-products used cooking grease and bakery waste and offers grease-trap cleaning services. It counts restaurants butcher shops grocery stores and independent meat and poultry processors among its customers. Darling also produces yellow grease tallow and meat bone and blood meal. The company sells its products nationwide and overseas to makers of soap rubber oils pet and livestock feed and chemicals.

	Annual Growth	01/11*	12/11	12/12	12/13*	01/15
Sales ($ mil.)	52.8%	724.9	1,797.2	1,701.4	1,723.6	3,956.4
Net income ($ mil.)	9.8%	44.2	169.4	130.8	109.0	64.2
Market value ($ mil.)	8.1%	2,187.4	2,189.0	2,559.6	3,421.1	2,991.2
Employees	31.6%	3,330	3,320	3,400	10,000	10,000

*Fiscal year change

DART TRANSIT COMPANY

800 Lone Oak Rd.
Eagan MN 55121
Phone: 651-688-2000
Fax: 651-683-1650
Web: www.dartadvantage.com

CEO: Donald G Oren
CFO: –
HR: Karen Wamack
FYE: December 31
Type: Private

Dart Transit aims to land its customers' freight on the bull's-eye. The company provides truckload freight transportation intermodal service (arrangement of freight transportation by multiple methods such as truck and train) and logistics services including freight brokerage and warehousing. It also offers dedicated transportation in which drivers and equipment are assigned to a customer long-term. The company operates from its headquarters in Minnesota and operating centers in Texas and Indiana as well as regional facilities located across the US.

DARTMOUTH-HITCHCOCK CLINIC

1 MEDICAL CENTER DR
LEBANON, NH 037560001
Phone: 603-650-5000
Fax: –
Web: www.patients.dartmouth-hitchcock.org

CEO: –
CFO: Robin Mackey
HR: John (Jack) Malanowski
FYE: June 30
Type: Private

The New England Alliance for Health (NEAH) brings together health care facilities and professionals looking to improve health in the New England region. Members of the alliance include about 20 community hospitals home health care agencies and mental health centers in New Hampshire Vermont and Massachusetts. While the members collaborate on wellness quality and communication initiatives each member of the alliance is an independently owned and operated not-for-profit organization with its own board of directors. Collaborative services provided by NEAH include procurement staff training information technology quality control and finance as well as the coordination of facility policies and planning.

	Annual Growth	09/04	09/05	09/06	09/08*	06/13
Sales ($ mil.)	138.9%	–	–	0.9	5.7	406.2
Net income ($ mil.)	307.7%	–	–	0.0	0.0	18.7
Market value ($ mil.)	–	–	–	–	–	–
Employees	–	–	–	–	–	9,300

*Fiscal year change

DASSAULT SYSTEMES SIMULIA CORP.

Rising Sun Mills 166 Valley St.
Providence RI 02909-2499
Phone: 401-276-4400
Fax: 401-276-4408
Web: www.simulia.com

CEO: Bernard Charls
CFO: James Lambert
HR: –
FYE: December 31
Type: Subsidiary

Dassault Systemes Simulia Corp. (doing business as SIMULIA) helps mechanical engineers simulate product design tests to save time and money in the lab. Its engineering analysis software simulates the physical response of structures and solid bodies to load temperature contact impact and other stresses before a physical prototype is built. Abaqus its finite element analysis (FEA) software suite is used in the aerospace automotive consumer goods and manufacturing industries among others. The company also provides engineering legal technical consulting and training services. Clients have included paper and plastic manufacturer AMCOR and automaker Renault. Simulia is a subsidiary of Dassault Systemes.

DASSAULT SYSTEMES SOLIDWORKS CORP.

300 Baker Ave.
Concord MA 01742-2131
Phone: 978-371-5011
Fax: 978-371-7303
Web: www.solidworks.com

CEO: Bertrand Sicot
CFO: –
HR: –
FYE: December 31
Type: Subsidiary

Dassault Systemes SolidWorks wants to beef up your designs. A subsidiary of France's Dassault Systemes SolidWorks develops 3-D design software that helps mechanical engineers speed up product development translate designs into 3-D models and communicate product ideas to customers and collaborators. The company's solid modeling suite includes features for animation analyzing designs and publishing 3-D designs on the Web. Its global client base includes customers from such industries as consumer products automotive and aerospace. Clients have included InFocus Leatherman and Konica Minolta. The company is also entrenched in the global education market with installations in thousands of institutions.

DATA I/O CORP.   NAS: DAIO

6464 185th Ave. N.E., Suite 101
Redmond, WA 98052
Phone: 425 881-6444
Fax: –
Web: www.dataio.com

CEO: Anthony Ambrose
CFO: Joel S Hatlen
HR: John Vicklund
FYE: December 31
Type: Public

Data I/O knows the chip-programming business inside and out. The company makes programming systems used by electronics manufacturers to tailor their integrated circuits (ICs) to suit a broad range of products. Data I/O manufactures both manual and automated programming systems used to manufacture semiconductor components for wireless consumer electronics automotive electronics and flash memory cards. Data I/O sells its devices to manufacturers such as LG Delphi and Foxconn. The company does most of its business outside the US; in fact Singapore-based Flextronics is its largest customer. Data I/O has locations in Brazil Canada China Germany Guam and Hong Kong.

	Annual Growth	12/10	12/11	12/12	12/13	12/14
Sales ($ mil.)	(4.5%)	26.4	26.7	17.1	18.7	21.9
Net income ($ mil.)	(22.3%)	3.0	1.1	(6.4)	(2.6)	1.1
Market value ($ mil.)	(12.4%)	45.1	29.4	13.0	20.2	26.6
Employees	(3.0%)	95	100	94	82	84

DATACOLOR INC.

5 Princess Rd.
Lawrence NJ 08648
Phone: 609-924-2189
Fax: 609-895-7414
Web: www.datacolor.com

CEO: Albert Busch
CFO: Hans Ita
HR: Helen Donovan
FYE: September 30
Type: Business Segment

Datacolor takes its cue from hue. The company makes instruments and software that control color measuring matching and quality control for use in textile paint automotive printing photography and home theater applications. Its Spyder brand targets the consumer market. Datacolor also offers a variety of services including calibration of spectrophotometers on-site consulting product training and education in color theory. The company sells directly to consumers online and through resellers. It also integrates its products with those of partners such as Lectra Fongs and Lawer. Established in 1970 Datacolor is a subsidiary of Datacolor AG (formerly Eichhof Holdings) a Swiss firm.

DATALINK CORP   NMS: DTLK

10050 Crosstown Circle, Suite 500
Eden Prairie, MN 55344
Phone: 952 944-3462
Fax: –
Web: www.datalink.com

CEO: Paul F. Lidsky
CFO: Gregory T. Barnum
HR: Patricia A. (Patty) Hamm
FYE: December 31
Type: Public

Datalink builds and implements high-end custom-designed data storage systems for large corporations. Its storage systems include disk- and tape-based storage devices storage networking components and data management software. The company employs an open-system standard building networks from products made by leading manufacturers such as Brocade EMC and Hitachi Data Systems. Datalink also provides ongoing support and maintenance services. The company markets its products directly to customers in the US. It has designed systems for clients including AT&T Harris Corporation NAVTEQ and St. Jude Medical. It has about 35 locations across the US.

	Annual Growth	12/10	12/11	12/12	12/13	12/14
Sales ($ mil.)	21.0%	293.7	380.0	491.2	594.2	630.2
Net income ($ mil.)	48.1%	2.3	9.8	10.5	10.0	11.1
Market value ($ mil.)	28.9%	106.8	189.0	195.6	249.4	295.1
Employees	22.5%	299	389	459	510	674

DATARAM CORP.   NAS: DRAM

P.O. Box 7528
Princeton, NJ 08543
Phone: 609 799-0071
Fax: 609 799-6734
Web: www.dataram.com

CEO: David A Moylan
CFO: Anthony M Lougee
HR: –
FYE: April 30
Type: Public

Dataram wants you to remember your DRAMs. The company makes add-in memory boards and modules that expand the capacity of computer servers and workstations running under UNIX and Windows operating systems. Its products which use DRAM memory chips are compatible with systems from scores of companies such as HP IBM and Dell and with microprocessors made by AMD and Intel. The company sells its products to OEMs distributors value-added resellers and end-users. The company has a plant in the US & sales offices in the US Japan and Europe. Most sales come from customers in the US.

	Annual Growth	04/11	04/12	04/13	04/14	04/15
Sales ($ mil.)	(11.9%)	46.8	36.1	27.6	30.4	28.3
Net income ($ mil.)	–	(4.6)	(3.3)	(4.6)	(2.6)	(3.8)
Market value ($ mil.)	3.1%	5.3	2.9	5.8	7.5	6.0
Employees	(17.6%)	91	73	71	54	42

DATATRAK INTERNATIONAL INC.   NBB: DTRK

5900 Landerbrook Dr., Suite 170
Mayfield Heights, OH 44124
Phone: 440 443-0082
Fax: 440 442-3482
Web: www.datatrak.net

CEO: Laurence P Birch
CFO: Jennifer Mabe Fox
HR: –
FYE: December 31
Type: Public

Researchers rely on DATATRAK to keep tabs on their clinical data. The company develops online hosted electronic data capture (EDC) software for the biotechnology medical device contract research and pharmaceutical industries. Its software speeds up the process of gathering data during clinical trials by collecting and electronically transmitting trial data from remote research sites to sponsors. DATATRAK also offers project management site assessment training and hosting services. Its products have been used to support hundreds of clinical trials involving patients in more than 50 countries.

	Annual Growth	12/10	12/11	12/12	12/13	12/14
Sales ($ mil.)	10.5%	7.4	7.9	9.7	10.9	11.0
Net income ($ mil.)	–	0.1	(1.0)	(1.5)	(0.1)	(1.3)
Market value ($ mil.)	67.7%	1.2	0.6	0.5	9.7	9.5
Employees	13.6%	42	48	64	68	70

DATAWATCH CORP.   NAS: DWCH

4 Crosby Drive
Bedford, MA 01730
Phone: 978 441-2200
Fax: –
Web: www.datawatch.com

CEO: Michael A. Morrison
CFO: James Eliason
HR: Brigid MacDonald
FYE: September 30
Type: Public

Datawatch want its customers do more than watch data. It wants to help them see the information available in data through visualizations. The company makes enterprise information management software that includes data mining business intelligence and help desk management. Its products include Datawatch Modeler for extracting and manipulating data from ASCII PDF or HTML files; Datawatch Automator a data replication and migration tool used to populate and refresh data marts and data warehouses; Datawatch RMS Web-based report mining and analysis; and Datawatch Report Mining Server. The company serves more than 40000 customers across a broad range of industries worldwide although it generates most of its sales in the US.

	Annual Growth	09/11	09/12	09/13	09/14	09/15
Sales ($ mil.)	14.0%	17.9	26.0	30.3	35.1	30.2
Net income ($ mil.)	–	0.1	1.0	(4.2)	(22.4)	(49.8)
Market value ($ mil.)	2.4%	62.2	235.7	324.4	119.2	68.4
Employees	10.0%	112	130	192	199	164

DATS TRUCKING INC.

321 N OLD HIGHWAY 91
HURRICANE, UT 847373194
Phone: 435-673-1886
Fax: –
Web: www.datstrucking.com

CEO: –
CFO: –
HR: –
FYE: December 31
Type: Private

DATS Trucking specializes in less-than-truckload (LTL) freight transportation in the western US but that's not all there is to the company's operations. In addition to its LTL operations in which freight from multiple shippers is combined into a single trailer DATS Trucking provides truckload transportation. The company's tanker division Overland Petroleum transports gasoline diesel fuel and other petroleum products. Overall DATS Trucking operates a fleet of about 500 tractors and 2500 trailers. It offers LTL service outside its home territory via The Reliance Network a group of regional carriers that covers the US and Canada. President and CEO Don Ipson founded DATS Trucking in 1988.

	Annual Growth	12/03	12/04	12/05	12/06	12/07
Sales ($ mil.)	22.3%	–	391.7	600.1	658.9	717.3
Net income ($ mil.)	22.6%	–	–	1.2	7.8	1.8
Market value ($ mil.)	–	–	–	–	–	–
Employees		–	–	–	–	475

DAVE & BUSTER?S ENTERTAINMENT INC.

2481 Ma?ana Dr.
Dallas TX 75220
Phone: 214-357-9588
Fax: 214-350-0941
Web: www.daveandbusters.com

CEO: Stephen M King
CFO: Brian A Jenkins
HR: Jennifer Yarbrough
FYE: January 31
Type: Private

Fun and games collide with food and drink at these nightspots. Dave & Buster's Entertainment owns and operates about 55 entertainment complexes in 25 states and Canada that offer casual dining full bar service and a cavernous game room. The adult fun centers feature the latest in video games and motion simulators as well as games of skill played for prizes. For dining Dave & Buster's offers a menu that features traditional American fare such as burgers seafood and steak. Partners David Corriveau and James "Buster" Corley opened the first Dave & Buster's in 1982. Private-equity firm Oak Hill Capital Partners acquired the company in 2010. Dave & Buster's cancelled plans for an IPO in 2012.

DAVE'S SUPERMARKETS INC.

5300 Richmond Rd.
Bedford Heights OH 44146
Phone: 216-763-3200
Fax: 216-763-3205
Web: www.davesmarkets.com

CEO: Dan Saltzman
CFO: Tom Thiry
HR: Bonnie Stobierski
FYE: December 31
Type: Private

Dave's Supermarkets operates more than a dozen grocery stores primarily serving the various neighborhoods of Cleveland. Different locations cater to the different needs of the locals — the university location for instance sells fresh doughnuts every morning. The regional supermarket operator acquired four stores in Ohio from Tops Markets in late 2006 and converted them to the Dave's Supermarkets banner in 2007. The acquired stores all house Giant Eagle pharmacies. Founded in 1928 by Alex Saltzman — who named the business for his son Dave — the family-owned company is run by his grandsons Dan and Steve. Their father company chairman Burton Saltzman retired in 2005 but is still active in the business.

DAVENPORT UNIVERSITY

6191 KRAFT AVE SE
GRAND RAPIDS, MI 495129396
Phone: 616-698-7111
Fax: –
Web: www.davenport.edu

CEO: –
CFO: –
HR: –
FYE: June 30
Type: Private

Couch potatoes need not apply to Davenport. A private not-for-profit school Davenport University offers its 11000 students — many of whom are working adults — associate's bachelor's and master's degrees as well as certification and diploma programs. Founded in 1866 Davenport offers some 50 undergraduate majors in fields including business health and technology plus an MBA and several other master's programs. With campuses across Michigan online offerings and a study abroad program Davenport is a top independent university system in Michigan.

	Annual Growth	06/04	06/05	06/10	06/11	06/13
Sales ($ mil.)	(27.7%)	–	1,705.1	132.7	137.2	126.8
Net income ($ mil.)	–	–	–	12.7	9.4	(7.5)
Market value ($ mil.)	–	–	–	–	–	–
Employees		–	–	–	–	927

DAVEY TREE EXPERT CO. (THE)   NBB: DVTX

1500 North Mantua Street, P.O. Box 5193
Kent, OH 44240
Phone: 330 673-9511
Fax: –
Web: www.davey.com

CEO: Karl J Warnke
CFO: David (Dave) Adante
HR: –
FYE: December 31
Type: Public

Business at The Davey Tree Expert Company is as strong as an oak. The company's roots extend back to 1880 when John Davey founded the horticultural services firm which branched into residential commercial utility and other natural resource management services. With offices in the US and Canada Davey's services include treatment planting and removal of trees shrubs and other plants; landscaping; tree surgery; and the application of fertilizers herbicides and insecticides. It also provides line clearing for public utilities forestry research and development and environmental planning. Davey has been employee-owned since 1979.

	Annual Growth	12/10	12/11	12/12	12/13	12/14
Sales ($ mil.)	7.5%	591.7	646.0	680.2	713.8	789.9
Net income ($ mil.)	13.3%	14.1	14.1	24.6	22.9	23.2
Market value ($ mil.)	–	–	–	–	–	–
Employees	2.8%	6,800	7,000	7,000	7,000	7,600

DAVID E. HARVEY BUILDERS INC.

3630 Westchase
Houston TX 77042
Phone: 713-783-8710
Fax: 713-783-5313
Web: www.harveybuilders.com

CEO: –
CFO: Rodney Finke
HR: –
FYE: December 31
Type: Private

David E. Harvey Builders hammers out commercial construction services. The company provides design/build general contracting and construction management services for mid- and high-rise office buildings; it also works on some light industrial facilities and provides interior remodeling services. Projects include office buildings condos hotels and convention centers retail stores parking garages hospitals and research facilities. Harvey's customers have included Exxon Mobil Igloo Hewlett Packard and Marriott. The company was founded by David Harvey Jr. and Joseph Cleary Jr. In addition to its Houston office the company also does business as Harvey-Cleary Builders in Austin and Washington DC.

DAVID'S BRIDAL INC.

1001 Washington St.
Conshohocken PA 19428
Phone: 610-943-5000
Fax: 610-943-5048
Web: www.davidsbridal.com

CEO: Pamela Wallack
CFO: –
HR: –
FYE: January 31
Type: Private

From prom night to the big day itself David's Bridal begs to make an entrance. The largest retail chain specializing in bridal gowns numbers more than 300 stores in 45 US states Canada and Puerto Rico. All gowns are available off the rack and priced from $300 to $1500 to meet most consumers' budgets. David's Bridal also sells invitations and gifts veils and other bridal accessories and apparel for formal occasions such as church communions and Quincea?eras. Besides its brick-and-mortar locations David's Bridal operates an online catalog and spotlights the latest trends through Style Council blogs and podcasts. In 2012 the retailer agreed to be acquired by private equity firm Clayton Dubilier & Rice.

DAVIDSON COMPANIES

Davidson Bldg. 8 3rd St. North
Great Falls MT 59401
Phone: 406-727-4200
Fax: 406-791-7238
Web: www.davidsoncompanies.com

CEO: William Johnstone
CFO: Thomas Nelson
HR: –
FYE: September 30
Type: Private

Employee-owned Davidson Companies offers investment banking asset management brokerage and trust services through its operating subsidiaries. The company's flagship firm D.A. Davidson & Co. was founded in 1935 and offers investment banking services such as mergers and acquisitions advisory capital raising institutional sales and trading and fundamental research. The group provides brokerage trust wealth management and financial planning services for private clients through Davidson Trust Co. and Davidson Investment Advisors. Altogether Davidson has some $30 billion of assets under management. Davidson has more than 60 offices in some 15 states though it is mainly active in the Northwest.

DAVIDSON HOTELS & RESORTS LLC

3340 Players Club Pkwy. Ste. 200
Memphis TN 38125
Phone: 901-761-4664
Fax: 901-821-4104
Web: www.davidsonhotels.com

CEO: John Belden
CFO: –
HR: Lori Bruce
FYE: December 31
Type: Private

Davidson Hotels & Resorts probably has room for you at the inn. The independent hotel management company invests in develops renovates and manages hospitality real estate throughout the US. It owns and operates about 50 upscale hotel and resort properties (containing approximately 14000 rooms) under such brand names as Carlson InterContinental Hilton Hyatt Marriott and Starwood. Davidson also provides consulting and accounting support to the hospitality industry. The company is focused on growth and has been expanding its portfolio through acquisitions and third-party management deals.

DAVIS POLK & WARDWELL LLP

450 Lexington Ave.
New York NY 10017
Phone: 212-450-4000
Fax: 212-701-5800
Web: www.davispolk.com

CEO: –
CFO: Robin Griffiths
HR: Jacqueline Nu EZ
FYE: December 31
Type: Private - Partnershi

Founded in 1849 Davis Polk & Wardwell is one of the oldest law firms in the US. Having built a notable corporate practice early on it helped J. P. Morgan (now JPMorgan Chase) form General Electric. With about 750 lawyers the firm is known for its skill in litigation securities and mergers and acquisitions; other practice areas include real estate tax technology and trusts and estates. Davis Polk has served such high-profile clients as AT&T Comcast General Motors and Philip Morris. In addition more than one-third of the firm's clients are non-US companies or governments. Davis Polk has 10 offices in seven countries.

DAVIS WRIGHT TREMAINE LLP

1201 Third Ave. Ste. 2200
Seattle WA 98101-3045
Phone: 206-622-3150
Fax: 206-757-7700
Web: www.dwt.com

CEO: –
CFO: L Keith Gorder
HR: –
FYE: December 31
Type: Private - Partnershi

Davis Wright Tremaine has expanded beyond its roots in the Pacific Northwest to establish presences in California the eastern US and China. The firm's more than 500 lawyers practice from about 10 offices overall. Among a wide array of practice areas Davis Wright Tremaine's specialties include broadcasting corporate finance employment health care and litigation. Clients have included Boeing Microsoft and Starbucks. Davis Wright Tremaine is a member of Lex Mundi a global organization of law firms that spans the US and in 100 other countries.

DAVIS-STANDARD LLC

1 Extrusion Dr.
Pawcatuck CT 06379-2313
Phone: 860-599-1010
Fax: 860-599-6258
Web: www.davis-standard.com

CEO: James Murphy
CFO: Kevin Coghlan
HR: –
FYE: December 31
Type: Private

Davis-Standard designs and manufactures extrusion systems and process controls for the wire cable plastic and rubber industries. Extrusion products include foam fiber pipe and sheet extruders; its conversion products provide liquid coating and laminating blow molding and industrial films. It operates through subsidiaries which are part of Extrusion Systems or Converting Systems groups. Manufacturing facilities are in Germany the UK and the US with R&D centers in the US and Germany. Davis-Standard was founded in 1848 as a manufacturer of cotton gin machinery but began manufacturing extruders a century later. It is owned by management and an investor group led by equity firm Hamilton Robinson.

DAVITA HEALTHCARE PARTNERS INC NYS: DVA

2000 16th Street
Denver, CO 80202
Phone: 303 405-2100
Fax: –
Web: www.davita.com

CEO: Kent J. Thiry
CFO: James K. (Jim) Hilger
HR: –
FYE: December 31
Type: Public

DaVita HealthCare Partners gives life in the form of dialysis treatments to patients suffering from end-stage renal disease (chronic kidney failure). Through its Kidney Care division the firm is one of the US' largest providers of dialysis providing administrative services to 2200 outpatient centers across the US; it serves some 170000 patients. The company also offers home-based dialysis services as well as inpatient dialysis in about 1000 hospitals. It operates two clinical laboratories that specialize in routine testing of dialysis patients and serve the company's network of clinics. Subsidiary HealthCare Partners (HCP) operates primary care clinics and physician practices in several states.

	Annual Growth	12/10	12/11	12/12	12/13	12/14
Sales ($ mil.)	18.7%	6,447.4	6,731.8	8,186.3	11,764.1	12,795.1
Net income ($ mil.)	15.5%	405.7	478.0	536.0	633.4	723.1
Market value ($ mil.)	2.2%	14,984.9	16,347.7	23,834.8	13,665.2	16,332.6
Employees	12.2%	36,500	41,000	53,400	57,400	57,900

DAWSON GEOPHYSICAL CO (NEW) NMS: DWSN

508 West Wall, Suite 800
Midland, TX 79701
Phone: 432 684-3000
Fax: –

CEO: Stephen C Jumper
CFO: James K Brata
HR: –
FYE: December 31
Type: Public

3-D technology has made TGC Industries one of the movers and shakers in the North American oil patch. From its inception TGC Industries has conducted seismic surveys for oil exploration companies. The company principally employs land surveys using Geospace Technologies and ARAM ARIES seismic systems which obtain 3-D seismic data related to subsurface geological features. Employing radio-frequency telemetry and multichannel recorders the system enables the exploration of rivers swamps and inaccessible terrain. TGC Industries also sells gravity information from its data bank to oil and gas exploration companies. In 2014 it agreed to be acquired by Dawson Geophysical.

	Annual Growth	12/10	12/11	12/12	12/13	12/14
Sales ($ mil.)	2.3%	108.3	151.0	196.3	134.5	118.8
Net income ($ mil.)	–	(1.2)	10.8	15.7	(6.3)	(9.5)
Market value ($ mil.)	(13.3%)	27.9	52.4	60.1	53.5	15.8
Employees	(1.9%)	804	935	1,052	653	745

DAWSON GEOPHYSICAL CO. NMS: DWSN

508 West Wall, Suite 800
Midland, TX 79701
Phone: 432 684-3000
Fax: –
Web: www.dawson3d.com

CEO: Stephen C Jumper
CFO: James K Brata
HR: –
FYE: September 30
Type: Public

The oil industry can be shaky at times but Dawson Geophysical always looks for good vibrations. The company provides data acquisition and data processing services including the analysis of 2-D and 3-D seismic data to assess potential underground oil and gas deposits. Dawson Geophysical's customers both major and independent oil and gas operators use the data in exploration and development activities. The company's 3-D seismic data acquisition crews work in the lower 48 states; data processing is performed by geophysicists at the firm's computer center in Midland Texas.

	Annual Growth	09/09	09/10	09/11	09/12	09/13
Sales ($ mil.)	5.8%	244.0	205.3	333.3	319.3	305.3
Net income ($ mil.)	0.6%	10.2	(9.4)	(3.2)	11.1	10.5
Market value ($ mil.)	4.4%	220.6	214.7	190.0	203.5	261.6
Employees	7.4%	942	1,170	1,507	1,452	1,252

DAWSON METAL COMPANY INC.

825 ALLEN ST
JAMESTOWN, NY 147013998
Phone: 716-664-3811
Fax: –
Web: www.dawsondoors.com

CEO: David G Dawson
CFO: Guy F Lombardo
HR: –
FYE: December 31
Type: Private

Don't knock Dawson Metal's open-door policy. Dawson Metal (which does business as Dawson Doors) manufactures custom-made stainless steel aluminum and bronze doors for businesses and storefronts. The company also manufactures balanced doors which open in an elliptical arch. It mainly serves US corporations and the construction industry and makes doors for private residences as well. Dawson Metal was established in Jamestown New York in 1946 as an industrial and architectural metal fabrication business by Axel Dawson and his son George. The Dawson family continues to own the company.

	Annual Growth	12/09	12/10	12/11	12/12	12/13
Sales ($ mil.)	(0.6%)	–	15.0	14.6	12.9	14.8
Net income ($ mil.)	(22.1%)	–	–	0.5	0.2	0.3
Market value ($ mil.)	–	–	–	–	–	–
Employees	–	–	–	–	–	110

DAXOR CORPORATION NYSE AMEX: DXR

350 5th Ave. Ste. 7120
New York NY 10118
Phone: 212-330-8500
Fax: 212-244-0806
Web: www.daxor.com

CEO: Michael Feldschuh
CFO: David Frankel
HR: –
FYE: December 31
Type: Public

They might not give you a toaster with that new account but Daxor's blood and sperm banks are open to attract new uh deposits. The company offers blood banking through subsidiary Scientific Medical Systems and operates sperm banks through its Idant division. Its main business however has been the development and commercialization of a blood volume analyzer the BVA-100 which hospitals and other health care providers use to diagnose and treat heart and kidney failure anemia and other conditions as well as to manage blood transfusions. The BVA-100 measures a patient's blood volume within 90 minutes.

DAY KIMBALL HEALTHCARE INC.

320 POMFRET ST
PUTNAM, CT 062601836
Phone: 860-928-6541
Fax: –
Web: www.daykimball.org

CEO: Robert Smanik
CFO: –
HR: Monique Richoz
FYE: September 30
Type: Private

With more than 100 beds Day Kimball Hospital is a non-profit acute-care facility that caters primarily to Connecticut with an extended reach into parts of Massachusetts and Rhode Island. The health care provider founded in 1894 offers general medical and surgical care along with the option of home care services. Logging an average of nearly 29000 emergency department visits and 550 births Day Kimball offers specialized services such as pediatrics gynecology emergency medicine and psychiatric health care. It also provides hospice and palliative care for terminally ill patients. Outpatient surgery and other medical services are provided through the facility's Ambulatory Care Unit.

	Annual Growth	09/07	09/08	09/10	09/11	09/13
Sales ($ mil.)	(7.9%)	–	158.6	110.5	119.7	105.0
Net income ($ mil.)	–	–	–	(3.5)	(0.9)	0.9
Market value ($ mil.)	–	–	–	–	–	–
Employees	–	–	–	–	–	900

DAY PITNEY LLP

242 Trumbull St.
Hartford CT 06103
Phone: 860-275-0100
Fax: 860-275-0343
Web: www.daypitney.com

CEO: –
CFO: –
HR: –
FYE: December 31
Type: Private - Partnershi

Day Pitney has about 300 lawyers at nine offices located mostly in the Northeast region of the US. The firm serves regional national and international clients in a variety of practice areas including business transactions intellectual property labor and employment and litigation. It has represented such clients as Centerpoint Energy Prudential Financial and Southern Connecticut Bancorp. Day Pitney was formed in 2007 when Connecticut-based Day Berry & Howard combined with New Jersey firm Pitney Hardin which also had an office in New York.

DAYLIGHT DONUT FLOUR COMPANY LLC

11707 E 11TH ST
TULSA, OK 741284401
Phone: 918-438-0800
Fax: –
Web: www.daylightdonuts.com

CEO: John Bond
CFO: Jimmy Keeter
HR: –
FYE: December 31
Type: Private

|Daylight Donut wants to tempt you whether it's day or night. The company sells a variety of sweet and savory pastries from nearly 1000 Daylight Donuts locations in all 50 states plus single shops in Australia China Mexico and Romania. It offers licenses instead of franchises allowing owners to avoid franchise fees by agreeing to use company products in exchange for the use of the name and trademark. The products licensees agree to use include company-made dry mixes for the stores' signature donuts bear claws cinnamon rolls sausage wraps and other pastries as well as private-label coffee for use in-store and for resale. Formed in 1954 Daylight Donut is owned by John and Sheila Bond husband and wife.

	Annual Growth	12/09	12/10	12/11	12/12	12/13
Sales ($ mil.)	2.9%	–	14.2	15.6	15.2	15.4
Net income ($ mil.)	11.9%	–	–	1.7	1.8	2.1
Market value ($ mil.)	–	–	–	–	–	–
Employees		–	–	–	–	30

DAYS INNS WORLDWIDE INC.

1 Sylvan Way
Parsippany NJ 07054
Phone: 973-753-6000
Fax: 973-496-7658
Web: www.ramada.com

CEO: –
CFO: –
HR: –
FYE: December 31
Type: Subsidiary

Here's a chain that won't charge you an arm and a leg to put your head on a pillow for a day or two. Days Inns Worldwide is a leading franchiser of economy hotels with about 1850 locations in more than a dozen countries including Canada China the UK and the US (all 50 states). The properties which attract budget-minded families and business travelers typically offer affordable rooms with such amenities as cable television complimentary newspaper service and swimming pools. Some locations also provide continental breakfast and pet-friendly rooms. Days Inns is owned by hospitality firm Wyndham Worldwide.

DAYSTAR TECHNOLOGIES INC.

NASDAQ: DSTI

2972 Stender Way
Santa Clara CA 95054
Phone: 408-907-4600
Fax: 408-907-4637
Web: www.daystartech.com

CEO: L Mark Roseborough
CFO: –
HR: –
FYE: December 31
Type: Public

Old Sol otherwise known as the sun is the "day star" providing energy through the solar cells of this company. DayStar Technologies makes energy-generating and storing devices out of copper indium gallium and selenium dubbed CIGS solar cells. The company is developing manufacturing processes for its thin-film photovoltaic foil CIGS solar cells that will be cheaper to produce than conventional polycrystalline silicon solar cells which currently dominate the market. DayStar got out of the business of installing and maintaining solar panels for residences. Running out of cash in 2009 the company warned that it may have to seek Chapter 11 protection from creditors if it is unable to raise capital.

DC PARTNERS INC.

6849 Woodley Ave.
Van Nuys CA 91406
Phone: 818-285-0692
Fax: 818-285-0974
Web: www.soligen2006.com

CEO: –
CFO: –
HR: Dave Shafer
FYE: March 31
Type: Private

DC Partners helps automakers — not film makers — with their casting. DC Partners which does business as Soligen 2006 is a manufacturer of metal cast components for the automotive (engine blocks cylinder heads manifolds) and aerospace (engines) industries. Using direct shell production casting (DSPC) the company generates its casting molds automatically from 3-D CAD data. In addition to offering high quality short- and medium-sized production runs the company also offers prototyping services. Customers have included Ford Visteon Eaton and Boeing to name a few. DC Partners has an engineering and sales facility in Van Nuys California and a manufacturing plant in Santa Ana California.

DCB FINANCIAL CORP.

OTC: DCBF

110 Riverbend Avenue
Lewis Center, OH 43035
Phone: 740 657-7000
Fax: –
Web: www.dcbfinancialcorp.com

CEO: Ronald Seiffert
CFO: J Daniel Mohr
HR: Rebecca Dinovo
FYE: December 31
Type: Public

DCB Financial is the holding company for The Delaware County Bank and Trust which serves individual and commercial customers through some 20 branches in central Ohio. The bank offers traditional products and services such as checking and savings accounts CDs IRAs credit and debit cards and safe deposit facilities. Its loan portfolio primarily consists of commercial mortgages residential mortgages and home equity loans. The bank also writes construction land development industrial and consumer loans. The Delaware County Bank and Trust provides insurance investments wealth management and trust services as well.

	Annual Growth	12/10	12/11	12/12	12/13	12/14
Assets ($ mil.)	(2.3%)	565.1	522.9	506.5	502.4	515.4
Net income ($ mil.)	–	(12.3)	(2.7)	0.6	(2.9)	0.4
Market value ($ mil.)	22.6%	22.4	20.3	33.3	44.5	50.6
Employees	(3.5%)	187	166	181	171	162

DCH HEALTHCARE AUTHORITY

809 University Blvd. East
Tuscaloosa AL 35401-2029
Phone: 205-759-7111
Fax: 205-750-5331
Web: www.dchsystem.com

CEO: Bryan Kindred
CFO: John W Winfrey
HR: –
FYE: September 30
Type: Government-owned

The DCH Healthcare Authority is concerned with the Druid City's health. The company which does business as DCH Health System provides health services to residents of Tuscaloosa and several other communities in Western Alabama. Its flagship facility is the 580-bed DCH Regional Medical Center a full-service teaching hospital located near the University of Alabama campus. DCH Health System also includes the Northport Pickens County and Fayette medical centers which together house 320 acute-care beds. The hospitals offer a full range of inpatient and outpatient services including primary diagnostic emergency surgical rehabilitative and home health care.

DDB WORLDWIDE COMMUNICATIONS GROUP INC.

437 Madison Ave.
New York NY 10022
Phone: 212-415-2000
Fax: 212-415-3414
Web: www.ddb.com

CEO: Chuck Brymer
CFO: –
HR: –
FYE: December 31
Type: Subsidiary

Advertising is whassup at DDB Worldwide Communications Group. One of the world's top creative ad agencies the company has produced memorable spots for such brands as McDonald's ("I'm lovin' it") Avis ("We Try Harder") Budweiser ("Whassup") and Life Cereal ("Hey Mikey"). It offers such services as brand building and consulting campaign planning and management and effectiveness measurement services in addition to creative ad development. The firm operates through more than 200 offices in about 90 countries. Founded in 1949 by Ned Doyle Maxwell Dane and William Bernbach DDB Worldwide Communications is one of the flagship agencies of global media conglomerate Omnicom Group.

DCP MIDSTREAM PARTNERS LP NYS: DPM

370 17th Street, Suite 2500
Denver, CO 80202
Phone: 303 633-2900
Fax: –
Web: www.dcppartners.com

CEO: Wouter van Kempen
CFO: Sean O'Brien
HR: –
FYE: December 31
Type: Public

DCP Midstream Partners is the publicly traded entity of DCP Midstream LLC one of the largest natural gas gatherers in North America and also the top producer and a primary marketer of natural gas liquids (NGLs). It also engages in natural gas compressing treating processing transporting and selling. DCP Midstream LLC also transports and sells NGLs and distributes propane wholesale. The company operates natural gas gathering systems (11435 miles of pipe) in eight states (including Arkansas Louisiana Oklahoma and Texas) seven processing plants four NGL pipelines and nine propane storage terminals. Spectra Energy holds a 50% holding in DCP Midstream Partners (ConocoPhillips holds the other 50%).

	Annual Growth	12/10	12/11	12/12	12/13	12/14
Sales ($ mil.)	30.1%	1,269.5	1,569.8	1,720.7	2,980.0	3,642.0
Net income ($ mil.)	72.3%	48.0	100.4	168.0	181.0	423.0
Market value ($ mil.)	5.0%	4,261.7	5,409.2	4,757.4	5,737.4	5,176.7
Employees	0.0%	7	6	7	7	7

DDI CORP. NASDAQ: DDIC

1220 N. Simon Circle
Anaheim CA 92806
Phone: 714-688-7200
Fax: 714-688-7400
Web: www.ddiglobal.com

CEO: –
CFO: –
HR: –
FYE: December 31
Type: Public

DDi takes a dynamic approach to manufacturing. DDi provides time-critical customized printed circuit board (PCB) design fabrication and assembly services for makers of communications and networking gear computers medical instruments and military equipment. The company produces PCBs backpanels and wire harnesses. Its more than 1000 customers include electronics manufacturers and contract manufacturers worldwide. DDi gets the majority of its business from customers in North America. In 2012 the company was acquired by rival Viasystems in a transaction valued at about $283 million including debt.

DCT INDUSTRIAL TRUST INC NYS: DCT

518 Seventeenth Street, Suite 800
Denver, CO 80202
Phone: 303 597-2400
Fax: –
Web: www.dctindustrial.com

CEO: Philip L. Hawkins
CFO: Matthew T Murphy
HR: –
FYE: December 31
Type: Public

In industry DCT trusts. DCT Industrial Trust is a real estate investment trust (REIT) that owns develops and manages bulk distribution warehouses light industrial properties and service centers located in high-density high-volume markets in the US. It owns interests in or manages some 400 buildings spanning more than 73 million sq. ft. of leasable space in about 15 US states and Mexico. Bulk distribution warehouses account for a majority of the company's rentable space. Companies in the manufacturing wholesale and retail trade and transportation and warehousing sectors make up most of DCT's clients. Major tenants include Clorox Kellogg and DHL.

	Annual Growth	12/10	12/11	12/12	12/13	12/14
Sales ($ mil.)	8.9%	239.4	253.4	260.8	289.0	336.5
Net income ($ mil.)	–	(37.8)	(25.3)	(15.1)	15.9	49.2
Market value ($ mil.)	61.0%	467.3	450.6	571.2	627.5	3,138.5
Employees	7.6%	108	117	131	136	145

DDR CORP. NYS: DDR

3300 Enterprise Parkway
Beachwood, OH 44122
Phone: 216 755-5500
Fax: 216 755-1500
Web: www.ddr.com

CEO: David J. Oakes
CFO: Luke J. Petherbridge
HR: Nan Zieleniec
FYE: December 31
Type: Public

DDR (formerly Developers Diversified Realty) is a self-administered real estate investment trust (REIT) that acquires develops renovates leases and manages retail and office properties. Its portfolio includes some 500 community shopping centers malls and other retail properties in the US Brazil and Puerto Rico. All together DDR owns more than 120 million sq. ft of space and more than 1800 acres of undeveloped land. Almost half of its shopping centers are owned through joint ventures. DDR's largest tenants include Wal-Mart PetSmart TJX and Kohl's. No longer primarily a development firm the REIT changed its name to DDR in 2011.

	Annual Growth	12/10	12/11	12/12	12/13	12/14
Sales ($ mil.)	5.3%	803.1	771.0	800.4	888.8	985.7
Net income ($ mil.)	–	(209.4)	(15.9)	(25.8)	(10.2)	117.3
Market value ($ mil.)	6.8%	5,068.9	4,378.2	5,633.8	5,529.4	6,605.1
Employees	(3.6%)	682	615	607	601	589

DE PAUL UNIVERSITY

1 E JACKSON BLVD
CHICAGO, IL 606042287
Phone: 312-362-6714
Fax: –
Web: www.itunes.depaul.edu

CEO: –
CFO: Bonnie Frankel
HR: Carole S Schor
FYE: June 30
Type: Private

In the land of da Bulls and da Bears there's DePaul. One of the largest private not-for-profit universities in the US DePaul has a total of about 24000 students attending classes at its five Chicago-area campuses. Also one of the country's largest Catholic institutions of higher learning the university offers more than 300 undergraduate and graduate programs through 10 colleges and schools including the Kellstadt Graduate School of Business and the College of Communication. It has a student teacher ratio of 17 to 1. DePaul was founded in 1898 by the Vincentian religious community and is named after 17th century French priest St. Vincent de Paul.

	Annual Growth	06/10	06/11	06/12	06/13	06/14
Sales ($ mil.)	1.8%	–	535.6	546.4	558.9	564.2
Net income ($ mil.)	22.5%	–	–	39.5	76.2	59.2
Market value ($ mil.)	–	–	–	–	–	–
Employees	–	–	–	–	–	3,895

DEACON INDUSTRIAL SUPPLY CO. INC.

1510 GEHMAN RD
HARLEYSVILLE, PA 19438-2929
Phone: 215-256-1715
Fax: –
Web: www.deaconind.com

CEO: –
CFO: Bill Hardie
HR: –
FYE: March 31
Type: Private

In the cold dark night who will be a beacon when the pipes burst? Deacon Industrial Supply will. Through four locations in Delaware New Jersey and Pennsylvania the company distributes pipes valves fittings and other products for plumbing HVAC and waterworks projects. It stocks more than 35000 items from manufacturers such as Cornerstone Valves NIBCO Sure Seal and Victaulic. The company also offers pipe fabrication specialized gasket cutting and emergency services. Deacon serves commercial contractors and professionals in a range of industries including automotive food processing petrochemical steel and pharmaceutical. It was founded in 1963 by Ben Deacon and Les Vail.

	Annual Growth	03/05	03/06	03/07	03/08	03/09
Sales ($ mil.)	11.2%	–	46.4	47.8	55.8	63.9
Net income ($ mil.)	40.1%	–	1.6	1.5	2.3	4.4
Market value ($ mil.)	–	–	–	–	–	–
Employees	–	–	–	–	–	80

DEACONESS HEALTH SYSTEM INC.

600 MARY ST
EVANSVILLE, IN 477101658
Phone: 812-450-5000
Fax: –
Web: www.deaconess.com

CEO: –
CFO: Cheryl Wathen
HR: –
FYE: September 30
Type: Private

While it primarily presides over numerous health care facilities in the southwestern corner of Indiana Deaconess Health System also serves residents in parts of southeastern Illinois and western Kentucky. The system consists of two general acute-care hospitals as well as specialty hospitals for women's health mental health and medical rehabilitation. Its flagship Deaconess Hospital boasts 365 beds and serves as a regional referral center. Deaconess Health also operates a standalone cancer treatment center medical group practice Deaconess Clinic and about 20 outpatient and urgent care clinics. Its Deaconess Health Plans unit is a PPO network that contracts with various health insurers.

	Annual Growth	09/09	09/10	09/11	09/12	09/13
Sales ($ mil.)	3.9%	–	619.8	3.3	3.5	695.6
Net income ($ mil.)	–	–	–	(19.4)	(18.4)	83.8
Market value ($ mil.)	–	–	–	–	–	–
Employees	–	–	–	–	–	6,086

DEACONESS HOSPITAL INC

600 MARY ST
EVANSVILLE, IN 477101674
Phone: 812-450-5000
Fax: –
Web: www.deaconess.com

CEO: –
CFO: Richard Stivers
HR: –
FYE: September 30
Type: Private

Deaconess Hospital provides benevolent medical assistance to residents of southern Indiana western Kentucky and southeastern Illinois. The not-for-profit hospital is a 365-bed acute care medical facility that is the flagship hospital of the Deaconess Health System. Specialized services include cardiovascular surgery cancer treatment orthopedics neurological and trauma care. The hospital also offers home health care hospice services and medical equipment rental and it operates outpatient family practice surgery wellness and community outreach centers. Founded in 1892 Deaconess Hospital is a teaching and research facility affiliated with the Indiana University School of Medicine.

	Annual Growth	09/09	09/10	09/11	09/12	09/13
Sales ($ mil.)	1.3%	–	524.3	550.8	577.1	544.7
Net income ($ mil.)	(39.9%)	–	–	49.7	58.4	18.0
Market value ($ mil.)	–	–	–	–	–	–
Employees	–	–	–	–	–	4,357

DEALERS SUPPLY COMPANY INC.

82 KENNEDY DR
FOREST PARK, GA 302972536
Phone: 404-361-6800
Fax: –
Web: www.dealerssupply.net

CEO: Richard E Laurens
CFO: Earl C Hunter
HR: –
FYE: December 31
Type: Private

Dealers Supply Company (DSC) strives to keep cool during those long Southern summers. Through about 15 locations in Georgia and North Carolina the company distributes air conditioning and heating products to residential customers contractors and small businesses. Products include air conditioners heaters motors insulation lifts sealants and other items from such brands as Airgas, Honeywell RUUD Trion, and WeatherKing. DSC sells the tools needed to install and maintain all the heating and cooling equipment it sells and it offers classes and reference guides. The company's Web site includes an online catalog and searchable database of licensed conditioned air contractors.

	Annual Growth	03/09	03/10	03/11	03/12*	12/12
Sales ($ mil.)	(9.4%)	–	38.5	41.0	40.8	31.6
Net income ($ mil.)	(7.4%)	–	–	0.7	0.5	0.6
Market value ($ mil.)	–	–	–	–	–	–
Employees	–	–	–	–	–	126

*Fiscal year change

DEALERTRACK TECHNOLOGIES, INC.

NMS: TRAK

1111 Marcus Avenue, Suite M04
Lake Success, NY 11042
Phone: 516 734-3600
Fax: –
Web: www.dealertrack.com

CEO: Mark F O'Neil
CFO: Eric D Jacobs
HR: Ana M Herrera
FYE: December 31
Type: Public

DealerTrack keeps auto dealers lenders OEMs and car buyers on track with its Web-based software and services. Using a Software-as-a-Service (SaaS) model the company offers a suite of dealer management system (DMS) vehicle inventory management and merchandising sales and financing compliance and processing (including e-registration and titling application) tools that provide real-time on-demand data for auto dealers to operate more efficiently and cost effectively. DealerTrack also operates the largest online credit application network in the US and Canada.

	Annual Growth	12/09	12/10	12/11	12/12	12/13
Sales ($ mil.)	20.9%	225.6	243.8	353.3	388.9	481.5
Net income ($ mil.)	–	(4.3)	(27.8)	65.1	20.5	5.9
Market value ($ mil.)	26.5%	826.7	883.0	1,199.3	1,263.6	2,115.3
Employees	20.1%	1,200	1,200	1,900	2,000	2,500

DEAN & DELUCA INCORPORATED

2402 E. 37th St. North
Wichita KS 67219-3538
Phone: 316-821-3200
Fax: 800-781-4050
Web: www.deandeluca.com

CEO: Mark Daley
CFO: Rob Driskell
HR: –
FYE: January 31
Type: Private

You could go to Manhattan's tony SoHo neighborhood for a taste of Dean & DeLuca but increasingly you don't have to. The purveyor of pricey gourmet foods fine wines cheeses baked goods coffees and teas and high-end kitchenware operates about 15 specialty markets and cafes in select US cities and is growing rapidly in Japan. The company opened its first cafe in the Middle East located in Dubai in 2008 and now has a store in Kuwait. Dean & DeLuca also offers its goods through consumer and corporate gift catalogs as well as online. It has operated in Japan since 2003 through a distribution agreement with ITOCHU there. Joel Dean and Giorgio DeLuca opened their first market in SoHo in 1977.

DEAN FOODS CO.

NYS: DF

2711 North Haskell Avenue, Suite 3400
Dallas, TX 75204
Phone: 214 303-3400
Fax: –
Web: www.deanfoods.com

CEO: Gregg A. Tanner
CFO: Chris Bellairs
HR: Kimberly (Kim) Warmbier
FYE: December 31
Type: Public

Dean Foods is the nation's largest milk bottler. The company's Fresh Dairy Direct business markets fluid milk ice cream cultured dairy products and beverages (juices teas and bottled water) under more than 50 local regional and private-label brands including Borden Pet Country FreshMeadow Gold and TruMoo a leading national flavored milk brand. Following the spinoff of most of its WhiteWave Foods business Dean Foods still holds about 20% of WhiteWave which makes coffee creamers (International Delight) dips ice cream butter cottage cheese and specialty dairy products. Dean Foods owns and operates a number of smaller dairy companies including Berkeley Farms and Garelick Farms.

	Annual Growth	12/10	12/11	12/12	12/13	12/14
Sales ($ mil.)	(5.9%)	12,122.9	13,055.5	11,462.3	9,016.3	9,503.2
Net income ($ mil.)	–	–	91.5	(1,575.6)	158.6	813.2	(20.3)
Market value ($ mil.)	21.7%	831.7	1,053.7	1,553.3	1,617.2	1,823.3
Employees	(9.6%)	25,780	24,066	21,915	18,040	17,246

DEAN HEALTH PLAN

1277 Deming Way
Madison WI 53717
Phone: 608-828-1301
Fax: 608-827-4212
Web: www.deancare.com/healthplan

CEO: Frank L Lucia
CFO: –
HR: –
FYE: December 31
Type: Subsidiary

Cheeseheads may find themselves going to the Dean for health insurance. Dean Health Plan operating as DeanCare is part of Dean Health Systems. Formed in 1983 the company offers PPO HMO and POS insurance plans as well as public health insurance programs for clients throughout south central Wisconsin. Its provider network includes about 1900 physicians more than 25 hospitals some 50 clinics and roughly 200 pharmacies. The Dean Health Plan also provides a 24-hour nurse line and offers a variety of wellness programs and resources to help its members stay healthy. The company serves members in about 20 counties in Wisconsin.

DEBEVOISE & PLIMPTON LLP

919 3rd Ave.
New York NY 10022
Phone: 212-909-6000
Fax: 212-909-6836
Web: www.debevoise.com

CEO: –
CFO: –
HR: –
FYE: December 31
Type: Private - Partnershi

As an advocate for the interests of businesses Debevoise & Plimpton has more than 700 lawyers in eight offices in the US Europe and the Asia/Pacific region. Corporate law represents the firm's largest practice area but its expertise also spans litigation tax and trusts and estates. High-profile clients have included Sun Life Financial AIG Yahoo Sony and Deutsche Bank. Eli Debevoise (a descendant of Eli Whitney) helped found the firm in 1931; after Francis Plimpton (father of author George Plimpton) joined in 1933 the firm's name was changed to Debevoise & Plimpton.

DEBT RESOLVE INC

NBB: DRSV

1133 Westchester Ave., Suite S-223
White Plains, NY 10604
Phone: 914 949-5500
Fax: –
Web: www.debtresolve.com

CEO: Stanley E. Freimuth
CFO: –
HR: –
FYE: December 31
Type: Public

Debt Resolve isn't intimidated by mountains of debt. The company provides a hosted software service that allows credit card companies and collection agencies to collect money from consumers who are past due on their credit card bills. The online service branded as DebtResolve uses an Internet-based bidding system that allows debtors and creditors to agree on acceptable repayment schedules. Customers include banks and other credit originators credit card issuers and third-party collection agencies as well as assignees and buyers of consumer debt.

	Annual Growth	12/10	12/11	12/12	12/13	12/14
Sales ($ mil.)	5.2%	0.1	0.1	0.2	0.1	0.2
Net income ($ mil.)	–	(0.6)	(2.1)	(1.6)	(0.5)	(0.8)
Market value ($ mil.)	(41.1%)	5.8	10.3	2.9	2.1	0.7
Employees	(15.9%)	8	6	4	4	4

DECARE DENTAL LLC

3560 Delta Dental Dr.
Eagan MN 55122-3166
Phone: 651-406-5994
Fax: 651-406-5932
Web: www.decare.com

CEO: –
CFO: –
HR: –
FYE: December 31
Type: Subsidiary

You take DeCare of your teeth and gums and DeCare will take DeCare of your dental benefits. DeCare Dental provides dental benefits and oral health care insurance plans. The company manages PPO and indemnity dental plans for about 25000 employer groups or some 4.6 million individuals in the US and Europe. It offers third-party administrative support and claims processing among other services. The company's subsidiary DeCare Dental Networks manages 10 direct dental networks in the US and abroad and administers the dental plans of several US leading benefit providers. DeCare is a subsidiary of health insurance giant WellPoint.

DECATUR MEMORIAL HOSPITAL

2300 N EDWARD ST
DECATUR, IL 625264192
Phone: 217-877-8121
Fax: -
Web: www.decaturmemorialhospital.org

CEO: Ken Smithmier
CFO: -
HR: Phil Kubow
FYE: September 30
Type: Private

Not-for-profit Decatur Memorial Hospital (DMH) serves residents of Macon and neighboring counties in central Illinois. The 300-bed regional medical facility has a staff of 300 physicians who provide acute and tertiary care. DMH operates about a dozen Centers of Excellence in areas including cancer heart and lung women's health birthing allergy orthopedic and stroke care. Other health care services include preventive care through its DMH Wellness Center; home health and hospice programs and local urgent care and primary care through centers in the surrounding area.

	Annual Growth	09/04	09/05	09/11	09/12	09/13
Sales ($ mil.)	(0.5%)	-	258.6	-	272.5	249.3
Net income ($ mil.)	-	-	-	-	10.3	(8.9)
Market value ($ mil.)	-	-	-	-	-	-
Employees	-	-	-	-	-	1,311

DECHERT LLP

Cira Centre 2929 Arch St.
Philadelphia PA 19104-2808
Phone: 215-994-4000
Fax: 215-994-2222
Web: www.dechert.com

CEO: -
CFO: -
HR: -
FYE: December 31
Type: Private - Partnershi

The Dechert law firm might have a single name on its shingle but it's no solo practice. The firm's 1000-plus lawyers practice from more than 20 offices in the US (mainly in eastern states) and Europe. Dechert focuses on work related to business transactions government relations (involving both the US and the European Union) litigation and tax. Within those broad areas the firm's specialties include asset management corporate and securities intellectual property product liability and real estate finance. Dechert draws clients from industries such as energy financial services media retail and technology. The firm was founded in 1875.

DECISION DIAGNOSTICS CORP

NBB: DECN

2660 Townsgate Road, Suite 300
Westlake Village, CA 91361
Phone: 805 446-1973
Fax: 805 446-1983
Web: www.decisiondiagnostics.com

CEO: -
CFO: Keith Berman
HR: -
FYE: December 31
Type: Public

Decision Diagnostics Corp. (DDC) hopes IT plus pharmaceuticals will equal success. Previously focused on wireless systems for the health care and lodging markets in 2005 the company added a pharmaceuticals distribution unit through its purchases of CareGeneration and the Pharmaceutical Solutions unit of Kelly Company. DDC drives customers to its pharmaceuticals business by providing wireless computing devices to doctors in clinics for the poor and uninsured; in return doctors direct their patients to the company's discount mail-order prescription service. The company continues to sell its wireless PDA devices for the health care and lodging industries. Clearing company Cede & Co. owns 40% of DDC.

	Annual Growth	12/10	12/11	12/12	12/13	12/14
Sales ($ mil.)	(61.2%)	18.9	12.1	6.2	1.4	0.4
Net income ($ mil.)	-	(0.5)	(2.1)	(3.1)	(8.0)	(1.8)
Market value ($ mil.)	55.0%	2.2	11.0	7.5	27.7	12.7
Employees	(15.5%)	14	14	10	-	-

DECISION RESOURCES INC.

8 New England Executive Park
Burlington MA 01803
Phone: 781-993-2500
Fax: 781-993-2550
Web: www.decisionresourcesinc.com

CEO: James Lang
CFO: Anup Gupta
HR: -
FYE: December 31
Type: Private

Need to know about pharmaceuticals in China or how physicians prescribe certain drugs? Decision Resources Group has that information. The company provides research reports consulting services and other resources to assist drug makers biotech firms health care businesses industry journalists and investment firms get informed. It has primary expertise in providing analysis of the biotech and pharmaceutical industries. Other businesses include HealthLeaders-Inter Study which analyzes health plans and managed care providers and Millennium Research Group which offers insight and analysis of the medical device pharmaceutical and biotech industries. Providence Equity Partners controls the company.

DECISIONONE CORPORATION

426 W. Lancaster Ave.
Devon PA 19333
Phone: 610-296-6000
Fax: 610-296-2910
Web: www.decisionone.com

CEO: William F Comfort
CFO: Thomas Darling
HR: -
FYE: March 31
Type: Private

DecisionOne provides multi-vendor technology services including outsourced computer maintenance equipment installation and repair desktop management and help-desk support. Other services include consulting call center support asset recovery and logistics management. The company serves more than 5000 customers across the US and Canada directly or via partners. In addition to working with electronics manufacturers and technology distributors and resellers DecisionOne targets customers in such industries as retail health care and education. Sony FUJIFILM and Epson are among its clients. The company is owned by Indian IT services firm Glodyne Technoserve.

DECKERS OUTDOOR CORP.

NYS: DECK

250 Coromar Drive
Goleta, CA 93117
Phone: 805 967-7611
Fax: -
Web: www.deckers.com

CEO: Angel R. Martinez
CFO: Thomas A. George
HR: -
FYE: March 31
Type: Public

There's no business like the specialty shoe business for Deckers Outdoor. It designs and markets the iconic UGG brand of luxury sheepskin footwear (58% of sales) and Teva sports sandals — a cross between a hiking boot and a flip-flop used for walking hiking and rafting among other pursuits. Other product lines include Simple TSUBO MOZO and Ahnu. While imitations flood the market the company distinguishes UGG and Teva from its competitors by avoiding distribution in off-price outlets. Deckers Outdoor's products are made by independent contractors in Asia Australia and New Zealand. The company sells its footwear through about 105 retail stores worldwide independent distributors catalogs and online.

	Annual Growth	12/11	12/12	12/13*	03/14	03/15
Sales ($ mil.)	7.2%	1,377.3	1,414.4	1,556.6	294.7	1,817.1
Net income ($ mil.)	(5.1%)	199.1	128.9	145.7	(2.7)	161.8
Market value ($ mil.)	(0.9%)	2,515.9	1,340.7	2,811.8	2,654.4	2,426.0
Employees	15.7%	1,900	2,300	3,200	-	3,400

*Fiscal year change

DECO INC.

11140 ZEALAND AVE N
CHAMPLIN, MN 553163594
Phone: 763-576-9572
Fax: –
Web: www.deco-inc.com

CEO: Robert A Dorr
CFO: Tom Buckingham
HR: –
FYE: December 31
Type: Private

This DECO has nothing to do with art and everything to do with security. The private Native American-owned firm provides professional security services including anti-terrorism training armed and unarmed guards escorts and patrols security system monitoring security consulting and administrative staffing support to federal corporate and tribal clients. Security services account for about 90% of the firm's revenue. The remainder comes from its contracting division which offers construction services for large-scale remodeling projects and electrical and security system installations. DECO counts the US Department of Homeland Security FAA and US Environmental Protection Agency among its clients.

	Annual Growth	12/09	12/10	12/11	12/12	12/13
Sales ($ mil.)	15.2%	–	82.9	94.9	100.0	126.7
Net income ($ mil.)	(19.8%)	–	–	1.2	0.1	0.8
Market value ($ mil.)	–	–	–	–	–	–
Employees	–	–	–	–	–	1,600

DEEP DOWN INC

NBB: DPDW

8827 W. Sam Houston Pkwy. N., Suite 100
Houston, TX 77040
Phone: 281 517-5000
Fax: 281 517-5001
Web: www.deepdowninc.com

CEO: Ronald E Smith
CFO: Eugene L Butler
HR: –
FYE: December 31
Type: Public

Deep down Deep Down understands itself to be in the subsea sector. The company (formerly medical equipment provider Mediquip Holdings) acquired Deep Down in a reverse merger taking on that company's subsea service business as well as its name. An umbilical and flexible pipe installation engineering and installation management company Deep Down also fabricates component parts for subsea distribution systems and assemblies that specialize in the development of offshore subsea fields. The company's product include umbilicals flowlines distribution systems pipeline terminations controls winches and launch and retrieval systems. It serves clients in the Gulf of Mexico and internationally.

	Annual Growth	12/10	12/11	12/12	12/13	12/14
Sales ($ mil.)	(9.4%)	42.5	27.4	29.0	29.6	28.6
Net income ($ mil.)	–	(17.4)	2.1	(2.5)	(0.6)	(5.8)
Market value ($ mil.)	(21.6%)	–	–	19.7	31.2	12.1
Employees	4.7%	75	72	79	84	90

DEERE & CO.

NYS: DE

One John Deere Place
Moline, IL 61265
Phone: 309 765-8000
Fax: 309 765-9929
Web: www.johndeere.com

CEO: Samuel R. (Sam) Allen
CFO: Rajesh (Raj) Kalathur
HR: Johnathan Lawson
FYE: October 31
Type: Public

Deere & Co. is interested in seeing its customers go to seed and grow. The company one of the world's largest makers of farm equipment is also a major producer of construction forestry and commercial and residential lawn care equipment. Deere operates through three business segments: the agriculture and turf and construction and forestry segments make up its equipment operations; a credit segment provides financial services. Deere famous for its "Nothing Runs Like A Deere" marketing sells John Deere and other brands through retail dealer networks and also makes products for outlets Home Depot and Lowes.

	Annual Growth	10/11	10/12	10/13	10/14	10/15
Sales ($ mil.)	(2.6%)	32,012.5	36,157.1	37,795.4	36,066.9	28,862.8
Net income ($ mil.)	(8.8%)	2,799.9	3,064.7	3,537.3	3,161.7	1,940.0
Market value ($ mil.)	0.7%	24,036.6	27,057.8	25,917.7	27,089.4	24,701.6
Employees	(1.7%)	61,300	66,900	67,044	59,623	57,200

DEERE CREDIT SERVICES INC.

6400 NW 86th St.
Johnston IA 50131-6600
Phone: 515-267-3000
Fax: 515-267-4855
Web: www.deere.com/en_us/jdc/index.html

CEO: –
CFO: –
HR: –
FYE: October 31
Type: Subsidiary

Whether you're a farmer buying a combine a golf course owner purchasing a riding bunker rake or a forester leasing a knuckleboom loader Deere Credit Services can help. Operating as John Deere Credit the lender finances sales and leases offered by John Deere dealers on new and used agricultural commercial residential golf and turf construction and forestry equipment. It also provides wholesale financing operating loans and retail revolving charge accounts to dealers. In addition the company sells crop insurance and invests in wind energy. With operations in the Americas Australia and Europe John Deere Credit is part of parent Deere & Company's profitable Worldwide Credit Operations.

DEFENDER SECURITY COMPANY

3750 Priority Way South Dr. Ste. 200
Indianapolis IN 46240
Phone: 317-810-4720
Fax: 317-810-4723
Web: www.defenderdirect.com/

CEO: Jim Boyce
CFO: Bart Shroyer
HR: –
FYE: December 31
Type: Private

Defender Security Company (dba Defender Direct) is the little dealer that could. From its humble homegrown beginnings the former local security systems distributor has blossomed into the #1 authorized dealer of ADT Security Services and one of the top five DISH Network and General Electric Security dealers in the US. The company markets sells and installs new home security systems and satellite TV services in 40 US states as well as in Canada. It plans to add more home technology offerings such as DSL and Internet to its distributorship. Defender Direct was founded by former president and CEO Dave Lindsey in 1998.

DEFFENBAUGH INDUSTRIES INC.

2601 Midwest Dr.
Kansas City KS 66111
Phone: 913-631-3300
Fax: 954-447-7979
Web: www.spiritair.com

CEO: –
CFO: Ron Anderson
HR: –
FYE: April 30
Type: Private

Deffenbaugh Industries doesn't turn a deaf ear to its customers' waste management needs in the Plains and the Midwest. The company collects transports and disposes of commercial and residential waste in Kansas Iowa Missouri and Nebraska. It also provides industrial waste services quarrying services the disposal of construction waste and commercial and residential recycling. Deffenbaugh Industries' more than 700-acre Johnson County Landfill is the largest disposal facility in Kansas. The company's Johnny on the Spot division rents portable toilets.

DEFIANCE METAL PRODUCTS CO.

21 Seneca St.
Defiance OH 43512
Phone: 419-784-5332
Fax: 419-782-0148
Web: www.defiancemetal.com

CEO: Stephen Mance
CFO: Ken Daiss
HR: –
FYE: December 31
Type: Private

Defiance Metal — which takes its name from its headquarters in Defiance Ohio — is a precision fabricator of metal parts and assemblies. Its line runs from brackets and cases to chassis framing housings panels and racks. In addition to fabricating and finishing sheet metal the company manufactures sheet metal forms. Defiance Metal's parts and assembly process begins with design and engineering and moves on to CNC (computer numerical control) laser cutting robotic welding heavy stamping and painting. Products cater to commercial and military vehicle heavy-duty truck and HVAC markets. DMP has been in operation since 1931. It started as a tool and die shop and expanded to a stamping facility.

DEFOE CORP.

800 S COLUMBUS AVE
MOUNT VERNON, NY 105505019
Phone: 914-699-7440
Fax: –
Web: www.defoecorp.com

CEO: –
CFO: Joseph W Giardino
HR: –
FYE: December 31
Type: Private

DeFoe makes sure you can safely cross those proverbial bridges when you get to them. The heavy construction firm specializes in the design and construction of bridges highways airport terminals railroads and other transit projects throughout the New York Metropolitan and Tri-State area. Other areas of expertise include rehabilitation and reconstruction foundations and architectural concrete work. DeFoe which was founded in 1946 often works for the New York State Department of Transportation as well as the The Port Authority of New York and New Jersey. President John Amicucci Sr. who is the son-in-law of former president Dario Cioti owns the company.

	Annual Growth	12/09	12/10	12/11	12/12	12/13
Sales ($ mil.)	10.4%	–	33.9	59.4	54.6	45.7
Net income ($ mil.)	–	–	–	1.3	(1.4)	(7.3)
Market value ($ mil.)	–	–	–	–	–	–
Employees	–	–	–	–	–	130

DEKALB MEDICAL CENTER INC.

2701 N DECATUR RD
DECATUR, GA 300335918
Phone: 404-501-1000
Fax: –
Web: www.dekalbmedical.org

CEO: John A Shelton Jr
CFO: Susan Sciullo
HR: –
FYE: June 30
Type: Private

As far as DeKalb is concerned da healthier da better! Beginning as a rural hospital DeKalb Regional Health System now serves all of the Atlanta metropolitan area. The health system operating as DeKalb Medical is home to two acute care hospitals - DeKalb Medical at North Decatur and DeKalb Medical at Hillandale (with a combined total of about 550 beds). It also operates a 75-bed long-term rehabilitation hospital — DeKalb Medical at Downtown Decatur. Specialty hospital services include oncology cardiology orthopedics and diabetes care. The health system which was founded in 1961 also operates primary specialty and mobile health care clinics partly through the DeKalb Medical Physicians Group.

	Annual Growth	06/07	06/08	06/09	06/10	06/11
Sales ($ mil.)	4.5%	–	370.4	390.8	397.1	422.9
Net income ($ mil.)	–	–	–	0.0	(15.0)	0.9
Market value ($ mil.)	–	–	–	–	–	–
Employees	–	–	–	–	–	2,700

DEL FRISCO'S RESTAURANT GROUP INC

NMS: DFRG

920 S. Kimball Ave., Suite 100
Southlake, TX 76092
Phone: 817 601-3421
Fax: –
Web: www.dfrg.com

CEO: Mark S. Mednansky
CFO: Thomas J. (Tom) Pennison
HR: –
FYE: December 30
Type: Public

Del Frisco's Restaurant Group operates two upscale steakhouse chains Del Frisco's Double Eagle Steak House and Sullivan's with about 30 locations in more than 15 states. The group also runs two more casual Del Frisco's Grille restaurants. Del Frisco's Double Eagle Steak House has about 10 locations and offer upscale dining in a contemporary surrounding. The somewhat less pricey version of the 20-unit Sullivan's chain features an atmosphere reminiscent of a Chicago-style steakhouse. Both concepts serve premium cuts of beef along with seafood lamb and pork dishes and both offer an extensive wine list. The company controlled by Dallas-based private equity firm Lone Star Funds went public in 2012.

	Annual Growth	12/10	12/11	12/12	12/13	12/14
Sales ($ mil.)	16.2%	165.6	201.6	232.4	271.8	301.8
Net income ($ mil.)	17.4%	8.7	9.0	13.8	12.2	16.6
Market value ($ mil.)	23.7%	–	–	359.4	552.6	549.7
Employees	15.3%	–	3,094	3,796	4,222	4,745

DEL GLOBAL TECHNOLOGIES CORP.

OTC: DGTC

11550 W. King St.
Franklin Park IL 60131
Phone: 847-288-7000
Fax: 847-288-7011
Web: www.delglobal.com

CEO: John J Quicke
CFO: Terry Gibson
HR: –
FYE: July 28
Type: Public

Del Global Technologies can see the beauty of the inner you. And your pet. The firm's Medical Systems group makes medical and dental X-ray systems used by hospitals and doctors dentists and veterinarians. It sells its products through distributors worldwide under the Villa brand name; it also provides some of its products to OEMs under private-label agreements. Through its RFI subsidiary Del Global Technologies' Power Conversion Group makes precision electronic components and sub-assemblies for makers of everything from weapons systems to satellites to MRI machines; brands include RFI Filtron Sprague and Stanley. The company was formed in 1954.

DEL MONACO SPECIALTY FOODS INC.

18675 MADRONE PKWY # 150
MORGAN HILL, CA 950372868
Phone: 408-500-4100
Fax: –
Web: www.delmonacofoods.com

CEO: Vic Del Monaco
CFO: –
HR: Mike D Monaco
FYE: December 31
Type: Private

Del Monaco Specialty Foods makes products that any Tuscan Roman or Venetian mama would give her blessing to. The company cooks up and freezes Italian-style food items for the foodservice industry. Del Monaco's certified-organic food products include pastas sauces ravioli tortellini gnocchi polenta pestos and desserts. It offers American-style foods as well including barbecue sauce pot pies and New England clam chowder. It makes its own Del Monaco products and also offers services such as recipe creation duplication and enhancement plus the manufacture of custom products. The company was founded in 1964 by its namesakes the late Mike Del Monaco and his wife Ernestine.

	Annual Growth	12/08	12/09	12/10	12/11	12/12
Sales ($ mil.)	22.2%	–	–	–	21.1	25.8
Net income ($ mil.)	52.4%	–	–	–	2.2	3.3
Market value ($ mil.)	–	–	–	–	–	–
Employees	–	–	–	–	–	88

DEL MONTE CORPORATION

1 Maritime Plaza
San Francisco CA 94111
Phone: 415-247-3000
Fax: 415-247-3565
Web: www.delmonte.com

CEO: -
CFO: Larry E Bodner
HR: -
FYE: April 30
Type: Private

How does Del Monte's garden grow? Quite well. The company is one of the largest makers of branded canned fruit vegetables and broths in the US. Del Monte Foods manufactures tomato-based items such as ketchup and tomato sauce under brands College Inn Del Monte and Contadina. It owns no farms but instead purchases fruits and vegetables from growers. The company helps pets grow too with a stable of popular brands: 9Lives Gravy Train Milk-Bone and Meow Mix. Del Monte Foods makes private-label products as well as ingredients for other food makers and supplies products to foodservice operators. A trio of private equity firms led by Kohlberg Kravis Roberts (KKR) took Del Monte Foods private in 2011.

DEL TACO HOLDINGS INC.

25521 Commercentre Dr.
Lake Forest CA 92630
Phone: 949-462-9300
Fax: 949-462-7444
Web: www.deltaco.com

CEO: Paul J B Murphy III
CFO: Michael Payne
HR: Kevin Pope
FYE: December 31
Type: Private

This taco stand caters to the burger and fries crowd as well as the burrito fans. Formerly known as Sagittarius Brands Del Taco Holdings operates the Del Taco chain the #2 quick-service Mexican brand in the US (behind YUM! Brand's Taco Bell division). The restaurants offer tacos burritos and quesadillas along with such traditional fast-food fare as hamburgers french fries and shakes. The chain was founded in 1964 and has more than 525 locations found mostly in California and about 15 other western states. About 290 of the eateries are company-owned while the rest are franchised. Formed in 2004 Del Taco Holdings is backed by investors led by Charlesbank Capital Partners and Leonard Green & Partners.

DELAWARE NORTH COMPANIES INC.

40 Fountain Plaza
Buffalo NY 14202
Phone: 716-858-5000
Fax: 716-858-5479
Web: www.delawarenorth.com

CEO: Louis Jacobs
CFO: Christopher J Feeney
HR: -
FYE: December 31
Type: Private

This company makes few concessions when it comes to selling hot dogs and sodas at the ball game. Delaware North is a leading provider of food services and hospitality at airports sports stadiums and tourist destinations throughout the US and in a handful of other countries. The company oversees concessions at more than 50 major and minor league sporting arenas and it owns Boston's TD Garden arena. Delaware North also manages concessions and retail operations at more than 25 airports provides hospitality services at several tourist destinations and runs racing and gaming operations in half a dozen states. In all family-owned Delaware North operates at 200 locations and serves 500 million guests a year.

DELAWARE STATE UNIVERSITY

1200 N DUPONT HWY
DOVER, DE 199012202
Phone: 302-857-6060
Fax: -
Web: www.desu.edu

CEO: -
CFO: -
HR: Amal Juracka
FYE: June 30
Type: Private

One of the top historically black colleges and universities in the US Delaware State University (DSU) offers more than 50 bachelor's degree programs 25 graduate degree programs and five doctoral degree programs through more than 20 academic departments and five colleges. In addition to its main 400-acre campus in Dover the university has satellite locations in Georgetown and Wilmington. The school began as a land-grant educational institution founded in 1891 as the State College for Colored Students. It became known as Delaware State College in 1947 and gained university status in 1993. The university has a student-teacher ratio of 14:1 and enrolls more than 3800 students each year.

	Annual Growth	06/08	06/09	06/10	06/11	06/13
Sales ($ mil.)	(44.3%)	-	854.2	67.6	75.2	82.4
Net income ($ mil.)	24.3%	-	-	1.1	9.8	2.1
Market value ($ mil.)	-	-	-	-	-	-
Employees	-	-	-	-	-	600

DELAWARE VALLEY COLLEGE

700 E BUTLER AVE
DOYLESTOWN, PA 189012698
Phone: 215-345-1500
Fax: -
Web: www.delval.edu

CEO: -
CFO: James Schneider
HR: Barbara Hladik
FYE: June 30
Type: Private

Delaware Valley College (DelVal) serves about 2000 undergraduate and graduate students and boasts a student/faculty ratio of 15:1. The school offers associate's bachelor's and master's degrees in fields such as agriculture biology business administration chemistry environmental science media and secondary education; overall it offers about two dozen undergraduate majors. DelVal's campus is located on 570 acres 30 miles north of Philadelphia. The college was founded in 1896 by activist rabbi Joseph Krauskopf.

	Annual Growth	06/09	06/10	06/11	06/12	06/13
Sales ($ mil.)	4.5%	-	47.7	72.2	52.0	54.4
Net income ($ mil.)	(90.0%)	-	-	37.2	(0.6)	0.4
Market value ($ mil.)	-	-	-	-	-	-
Employees	-	-	-	-	-	405

DELCATH SYSTEMS INC.

NAS: DCTH

1301 Avenue of the Americas, 43rd Floor
New York, NY 10019
Phone: 212 489-2100
Fax: -
Web: www.delcath.com

CEO: Jennifer Simpson
CFO: Barbra C Keck
HR: -
FYE: December 31
Type: Public

A cancer-stricken liver might be a lonely little organ thanks to Delcath Systems. The company's technology allows blood infused with chemotherapy drugs to be pumped directly to the liver and then filtered before being returned into the circulation system. By isolating the liver Delcath's proprietary Hepatic CHEMOSATÂ® Delivery System is designed to protect other parts of the body from side effects and allow stronger doses of drugs to be used to treat liver cancer and malignant melanoma that has spread to the liver. The system approved and available in Europe is undergoing clinical trials to gain FDA approval. Delcath is also developing the system for use in treating other cancers and viral hepatitis.

	Annual Growth	12/10	12/11	12/12	12/13	12/14
Sales ($ mil.)	75.8%	-	-	0.3	0.8	1.1
Net income ($ mil.)	-	(46.7)	(30.9)	(51.9)	(30.3)	(17.4)
Market value ($ mil.)	(40.8%)	95.1	29.6	11.9	2.5	11.7
Employees	(14.6%)	47	80	92	37	25

DELEK LOGISTICS PARTNERS LP   NYS: DKL

7102 Commerce Way   CEO: Ezra Uzi Yemin
Brentwood, TN 37027   CFO: Assaf Ginzburg
Phone: 615 771-6701   HR: –
Fax: –   FYE: December 31
Web: www.deleklogistics.com   Type: Public

Oil is on the move at Delek Logistics Partners. An oil transportation and storage company Delek Logistics owns and operates crude oil pipelines storage and distribution facilities and other assets in West Texas and the southeastern US. Core assets include 400 miles of crude oil transportation pipelines and a 600-mile crude oil gathering system. The company also offers wholesale marketing of refined petroleum products. The majority of Delek Logistics' operations serve oil company Delek US Holdings and the holding company's Texas and Arkansas-based refineries. The company was formed in 2012 when Delek US Holdings spun off its pipeline assets; Delek Logistics Partners subsequently went public.

	Annual Growth	12/10	12/11	12/12	12/13	12/14
Sales ($ mil.)	13.6%	504.4	744.1	1,022.6	907.3	841.2
Net income ($ mil.)	63.5%	10.1	12.6	34.1	47.8	72.0
Market value ($ mil.)	24.2%	–	–	568.3	782.1	876.5
Employees	–	–	–	–	–	–

DELEK US HOLDINGS INC   NYS: DK

7102 Commerce Way   CEO: Ezra Uzi Yemin
Brentwood, TN 37027   CFO: Assaf (Assi) Ginzburg
Phone: 615 771-6701   HR: Donald Holmes
Fax: –   FYE: December 31
Web: www.delekus.com   Type: Public

Delek US Holdings' US petroleum business is a delectable mix of refining fuel marketing and retail operations. The company a subsidiary of Israeli-based conglomerate Delek Group operates refineries in Tyler Texas and El Dorado Arkansas with a total production capacity of 140000 barrels per day. Delek US Holdings' marketing segment sells refined products on a wholesale basis in west Texas through company-owned and third-party operated terminals. On the retail side its MAPCO Express unit manages almost 380 convenience store/gas stations (156 company operated) under MAPCO Express East Coast Discount Food Mart and other names in several southern US states.

	Annual Growth	12/10	12/11	12/12	12/13	12/14
Sales ($ mil.)	22.0%	3,755.6	7,198.2	8,726.7	8,706.8	8,324.3
Net income ($ mil.)	–	(79.9)	158.3	272.8	117.7	198.6
Market value ($ mil.)	39.1%	416.9	653.5	1,450.1	1,970.7	1,562.4
Employees	6.5%	3,395	3,801	4,033	4,366	4,361

DELHAIZE AMERICA LLC

2110 Executive Dr.   CEO: Frans W H Muller
Salisbury NC 28145-1330   CFO: –
Phone: 704-633-8250   HR: –
Fax: 704-645-4499   FYE: December 31
Web: www.delhaizegroup.com   Type: Subsidiary

Belgian food retailer Delhaize "Le Lion" has one big cub — Delhaize America. With some 1625 supermarkets and discount grocery stores in 17 states from Maine to Florida the holding company is the third-largest supermarket operator on the East Coast. Banners include: Food Lion (some 1075 stores located mainly in the Carolinas and Virginia but also in eight other eastern seaboard states); the Hannaford Bros. supermarket chain (about 180 stores in New England and New York); and 70 Harveys supermarkets. The grocery operator's Sweetbay chain does business along the west coast of Florida. Delhaize America provides shared services for all of its banners. Delhaize Group established its US subsidiary in 1999.

DELI MANAGEMENT INC.

2400 BROADWAY ST   CEO: –
BEAUMONT, TX 777021904   CFO: Troy Cormier
Phone: 409-838-1976   HR: Michele Ervin
Fax: –   FYE: December 31
Web: www.jasonsdeli.com   Type: Private

This company knows a good sandwich when serves one. Deli Management operates Jason's Deli a chain of sandwich shops with more than 240 company-owned and franchised locations. The quick casual eateries specialize in deli-style sandwiches including such signature varieties as Bird to the Wise The New York Yankee and Rueben THE Great. The chain also serves panini and po'boy sandwiches pasta dishes soups and salads. Many Jason's outposts provide delivery and catering services as well as online ordering. President Joe Tortorice and partner Rusty Coco started the company in 1976.

	Annual Growth	12/03	12/04	12/05	12/06	12/08
Sales ($ mil.)	(37.4%)	–	–	1,402.1	344.2	344.2
Net income ($ mil.)	3425.2%	–	–	0.0	5.8	5.8
Market value ($ mil.)	–	–	–	–	–	–
Employees	–	–	–	–	–	6,000

DELMARVA POWER & LIGHT CO.

500 North Wakefield Drive   CEO: David M Velazquez
Newark, DE 19702   CFO: Frederick J Boyle
Phone: 202 872-2000   HR: –
Fax: –   FYE: December 31
Web: www.delmarva.com   Type: Public

Delmarva Power & Light (DPL) has a delmarvellous proposition — connecting people to an extensive energy supply network. The company is engaged in the transmission and distribution of electricity in Delaware and a portion of Maryland (the Eastern Shore); it delivers electricity to about 501000 customers. DPL also provides natural gas (in northern Delaware) to more than 124000 customers. DPL is an indirect subsidiary of Pepco Holdings which owns two other utilities (Potomac Electric Power and Atlantic City Electric) as well as competitive energy generation marketing and supply businesses.

	Annual Growth	12/10	12/11	12/12	12/13	12/14
Sales ($ mil.)	(2.0%)	1,400.0	1,304.0	1,233.0	1,244.0	1,293.0
Net income ($ mil.)	23.3%	45.0	71.0	73.0	89.0	104.0
Market value ($ mil.)	–	–	–	–	–	–
Employees	(0.6%)	905	916	919	880	883

DELOITTE & TOUCHE LLP

Paramount Bldg. 1633 Broadway   CEO: Joseph Ucuzoglu
New York NY 10019-6754   CFO: –
Phone: 212-489-1600   HR: –
Fax: 212-489-1687   FYE: May 31
Web: www.deloitte.com/view/en_us/us/services/audit-   Type: Subsidiary

Deloitte & Touche LLP touches on all aspects of accounting in the US. The firm is the accounting arm of Deloitte LLP the US affiliate of international Big Four accounting firm Deloitte Touche Tohmatsu. Deloitte & Touche LLP offers audit and enterprise risk services. As part of its business the firm provides clients with audits and financial statement reviews. Other services include financial reporting regulatory updates employee benefit audits and venture capital services. Deloitte & Touche LLP has operations in about 90 US cities. Deloitte LLP also manages other US subsidiaries that offer tax consulting and financial advisory services.

DELOITTE CONSULTING LLP

1633 Broadway
New York NY 10019-6754
Phone: 212-489-1600
Fax: 212-489-1687
Web: www.deloitte.com/view/en_us/us/services/consul

CEO: Jim Moffatt
CFO: -
HR: Jeff Roar
FYE: May 31
Type: Subsidiary

One of the world's largest consulting firms Deloitte Consulting serves customers in industries such as aviation consumer products and services energy financial services health care manufacturing and technology as well as government agencies. The firm's areas of expertise include human resources information technology services outsourcing and strategy and operations. Along with accounting firm Deloitte & Touche Deloitte Consulting is a unit of Deloitte LLP which in turn is an affiliate of global accounting powerhouse Deloitte Touche Tohmatsu. Other Deloitte LLP units offer financial advisory and tax services.

DELOITTE LLP

Paramount Bldg. 1633 Broadway
New York NY 10019-6754
Phone: 212-489-1600
Fax: 212-489-1687
Web: www.deloitte.com/view/en_us/us/index.htm

CEO: Cathy Engelbert
CFO: -
HR: -
FYE: May 31
Type: Private

Deloitte LLP is a US-based member firm of Deloitte Touche Tohmatsu one of the big four global accounting firms. Deloitte LLP does not provide services to clients itself. Rather it does so through its operating subsidiaries primarily Deloitte & Touche LLP Deloitte Consulting LLP Deloitte Financial Advisory Services LLP and Deloitte Tax LLP. Those companies offer audit and enterprise risk consulting financial advisory and tax preparation services. Industry specializations include automotive banking consumer products life sciences oil and gas technology and government. Deloitte LLP and its subsidiaries operate from more than 100 offices across the US employing some 9300 accountants.

DELOITTE TOUCHE TOHMATSU SERVICES INC.

1633 Broadway
New York NY 10019-6754
Phone: 212-489-1600
Fax: 212-489-1687
Web: www.deloitte.com

CEO: James Copeland Jr
CFO: -
HR: -
FYE: May 31
Type: Private

This company is "deloitted" to make your acquaintance particularly if you're a big business in need of accounting services. Deloitte Touche Tohmatsu (or Deloitte) is one of accounting's Big Four along with Ernst & Young KPMG and PricewaterhouseCoopers. Deloitte operates through more than 50 independent firms in some 150 locations around the world including US-based Deloitte LLP and its accounting arm Deloitte & Touche LLP. Each member firm works in a specific geographic area offering audit tax consulting risk management and financial advisory services in addition to human resources and technology services. Deloitte coordinates its member firms but does not provide services directly to clients.

DELPHI FINANCIAL GROUP INC.

NYSE: DFG

1105 N. Market St. Ste. 1230
Wilmington DE 19899
Phone: 302-478-5142
Fax: 302-427-7663
Web: www.delphifin.com

CEO: Robert Rosenkranz
CFO: -
HR: -
FYE: December 31
Type: Public

One doesn't need an oracle to see that Delphi Financial Group knows a thing or two about employee benefits and insurance. Through Reliance Standard Life and Safety National Casualty Delphi sells disability excess workers' compensation group life and personal accident insurance to small and midsized businesses. Its Matrix Absence Management subsidiary provides disability and absence management services to larger employers. The company also offers asset accumulation products mainly annuities to individuals and groups. Delphi Financial's products are sold through independent brokers and agents in the US. In 2012 the insurance group was acquired by leading Japanese insurer Tokio Marine Holdings.

DELTA AIR LINES, INC. (DE)

NYS: DAL

Post Office Box 20706
Atlanta, GA 30320-6001
Phone: 404 715-2600
Fax: -
Web: ir.delta.com

CEO: -
CFO: Paul A. Jacobson
HR: Michael Campbell
FYE: December 31
Type: Public

Delta Air Lines is one of the world's largest airlines by traffic. Through its regional carriers (including subsidiary Comair) the company serves about 330 destinations in about 60 countries and it operates a mainline fleet of 770-plus aircraft as well as maintenance repair and overhaul (MRO) and cargo operations. The airline serves nearly 170 million customers each year and offers more than 15000 daily flights. Delta is a founding member of the SkyTeam marketing and code-sharing alliance (airlines extend their networks by selling tickets on one another's flights) which includes carriers Air France KLM and Alitalia.

	Annual Growth	12/11	12/12	12/13	12/14	12/15
Sales ($ mil.)	3.8%	35,115.0	36,670.0	37,773.0	40,362.0	40,704.0
Net income ($ mil.)	51.7%	854.0	1,009.0	10,540.0	659.0	4,526.0
Market value ($ mil.)	58.2%	6,300.4	9,244.2	21,393.2	38,308.4	39,476.6
Employees	1.4%	78,392	74,000	78,000	80,000	83,000

DELTA AIRELITE BUSINESS JETS INC.

Cincinnati/Northern Kentucky International Airport
Cincinnati OH 45275
Phone: 859-767-3500
Fax: 859-767-1660
Web: www.airelite.com

CEO: -
CFO: Rexford Bevis
HR: Stacy Windows
FYE: December 31
Type: Subsidiary

Delta AirElite Business Jets provides passenger transportation services for those who don't mind paying a little more — or a lot more — to bypass standard scheduled airline services. The company's offerings include membership programs in which customers buy blocks of flying time on a particular type of aircraft; charter services; and aircraft management. On its own through management agreements and through an alliance with fractional jet ownership company Bombardier Flexjet Delta AirElite offers customers access to more than 400 business jets including Bombardier Learjet Cessna Gulfstream and Hawker models. Delta Air Lines owns Delta AirElite.

DELTA APPAREL INC.

ASE: DLA

322 South Main Street
Greenville, SC 29601
Phone: 864 232-5200
Fax: –
Web: www.deltaapparelinc.com

CEO: Robert W. (Bob) Humphreys
CFO: Deborah H. (Deb) Merrill
HR: Martha M. (Sam) Watson
FYE: October 03
Type: Public

Delta Apparel's wares are a wardrobe basic: the t-shirt. The company manufactures knitted cotton and polyester/cotton t-shirts tank tops sweatshirts and caps for screen printers. Through subsidiary M.J. Soffe Delta Apparel also designs makes and sells branded and private-label activewear apparel to mainly to US distributors sporting goods and specialty stores mass merchants traditional and upscale department stores the US military college bookstores and online. The company's garments are finished at plants in North Carolina and abroad in Mexico El Salvador and Honduras. Delta entered the business of custom apparel design by acquiring Art Gun Technologies and hats by taking over Gekko Brands.

	Annual Growth	06/12	06/13*	09/13	09/14*	10/15
Sales ($ mil.)	(2.9%)	489.9	490.5	122.6	452.9	449.1
Net income ($ mil.)	–	(2.4)	9.2	0.6	(1.0)	8.1
Market value ($ mil.)	9.5%	106.5	109.9	127.9	68.6	140.0
Employees	0.9%	7,200	7,000	–	6,800	7,400

*Fiscal year change

DELTA COMMUNITY CREDIT UNION

1025 Virginia Ave.
Atlanta GA 30354
Phone: 404-715-4725
Fax: 404-677-4773
Web: www.deltacommunitycu.com

CEO: Hank Halter
CFO: Jay Gratwick
HR: –
FYE: December 31
Type: Private - Not-for-Pr

Delta Community Credit Union serves employees of Delta Air Lines and its affiliates and group members as well as residents of the Atlanta metro region. It offers traditional banking products such as deposit accounts credit cards home mortgages and consumer loans. The credit union also provides financial planning services and insurance. Delta Community has about a dozen offices in and around Atlanta (where Delta Air Lines is headquartered) and locations near Delta's hub airports including Cincinnati Dallas/Fort Worth and Salt Lake City. Established in 1940 Delta Community is a member-owned and operated institution; it has more than 250000 members and exceeds $4 billion in assets.

DELTA DENTAL OF CALIFORNIA

100 1st St.
San Francisco CA 94105
Phone: 415-972-8300
Fax: 415-972-8466
Web: www.deltadentalins.com

CEO: Gary D Radine
CFO: Mike Castro
HR: –
FYE: December 31
Type: Private - Not-for-Pr

Delta Dental of California doesn't just help keep the mouths of movie stars clean. The not-for-profit company is a member of the Delta Dental Plans Association (DDPA) and has affiliates nationwide. Delta Dental of California provides dental coverage for individuals and groups through HMOs preferred provider plans (PPOs) and such government programs as the TRICARE Retiree Dental Program and California's Denti-Cal (Medicaid) program. The company serves more than 18 million enrollees in California; its programs cover more than one-third of California residents. It also provides dental benefits administration support to employers.

DELTA DENTAL OF RHODE ISLAND

10 Charles St.
Providence RI 02904-2208
Phone: 401-752-6000
Fax: 401-752-6060
Web: www.deltadentalri.com

CEO: Joseph A Nagle
CFO: Richard A Fritz
HR: –
FYE: December 31
Type: Private - Not-for-Pr

Delta Dental of Rhode Island provides dental plans to some 700000 members in Rhode Island. One of the largest dental insurers in the state the company was formed in 1959 and became a Delta Dental plan in 1973. Subsidiary Altus Dental Insurance provides dental benefits to 80000 members in Massachusetts. Delta Dental of Rhode Island also provides access to a national dental network through its membership in the Delta Dental Plans Association. The company also offers health care consulting and benefits administration services to employers through subsidiary Park Row Associates.

DELTA DENTAL PLAN OF MICHIGAN INC.

4100 Okemos Rd.
Okemos MI 48864-3215
Phone: 517-349-6000
Fax: 517-347-5499
Web: www.deltadentalmi.com

CEO: –
CFO: –
HR: –
FYE: December 31
Type: Private - Not-for-Pr

Delta Dental Plan of Michigan knows the drill. The not-for-profit company provides dental benefits and related administrative services for dental patients in Michigan and other states. The company provides HMO PPO and fee-for-service dental plans to customers including employer groups trade associations and unions. Delta Dental Plan of Michigan also provides vision plans and vision plan administration services. It is a member of the Delta Dental Plans Association. In 2011 Delta Dental Plan of Michigan and its affiliates in half a dozen other states paid out $2.2 billion for dental care for its 8.6 million enrollees.

DELTA MUTUAL INC.

OTC: DLTM

14301 N. 87th St. Ste.310
Scottsdale AZ 85260
Phone: 480-221-1989
Fax: 480-584-6138
Web: www.deltamutual.com

CEO: Santiago Peralta
CFO: –
HR: –
FYE: December 31
Type: Public

Delta Mutual tried to clean up during the Internet boom by providing online mortgage services. Today it really does clean up. Literally. This development stage company has shifted its direction to being an environmental services provider. Delta Mutual offers waste processing and reclamation technology and equipment as well as energy-efficient construction technologies to low-cost housing development projects. Its operations are concentrated in the US the Asia/Pacific region the Middle East and Puerto Rico. In 2008 the company acquired American Hedge Fund LLC a limited liability company that intends to make investments in South America.

DELTA NATURAL GAS CO., INC.

NMS: DGAS

3617 Lexington Road
Winchester, KY 40391
Phone: 859 744-6171
Fax: –
Web: www.deltagas.com

CEO: Glenn R Jennings
CFO: John B Brown
HR: –
FYE: June 30
Type: Public

Delta digs blue grass and natural gas. Delta Natural Gas provides gas to some 36000 retail customers in central and southeastern Kentucky and has 2500 miles of gathering transmission and distribution lines. It also provides transportation services to wholesale customers and operates an underground gas storage field. The regulated utility buys almost all of its gas supply from interstate gas marketers. Delta Natural Gas's production subsidiary Enpro has interests in 35 producing gas wells and it has proved developed reserves of 3 billion cu. ft. of natural gas. Other subsidiaries include Delta Resources and Delgasco which purchase gas from marketers and resell it to utilities and large customers.

	Annual Growth	06/11	06/12	06/13	06/14	06/15
Sales ($ mil.)	0.9%	83.0	74.1	80.7	95.8	86.2
Net income ($ mil.)	0.5%	6.4	5.8	7.2	8.3	6.5
Market value ($ mil.)	(10.7%)	222.4	152.7	149.3	154.3	141.2
Employees	(1.8%)	153	151	150	150	142

DELTA REGIONAL MEDICAL CENTER

1400 E UNION ST
GREENVILLE, MS 387033246
Phone: 662-378-3783
Fax: –
Web: www.deltaregional.com

CEO: J Stansel Harvey
CFO: –
HR: –
FYE: September 30
Type: Private

If you're feeling bad down in the Lower Delta Delta Regional Medical Center (DRMC) can help perk you up. The only full service hospital and Level III trauma center in northwest Mississippi DRMC also serves as the tri-state Delta's safety-net hospital. The four medical centers provide heart and vascular care a full service emergency room diagnostics center outpatient rehab a sleep center a wound healing center maternal child center and inpatient psychiatric care. Delta Medical Group includes about 15 clinics specializing in everything from gastroenterology to women's health. Founded as the Washington County General Hospital in 1953 the 358-bed DRMC serves more than 35000 patients each year.

	Annual Growth	09/04	09/05	09/06	09/12	09/13
Sales ($ mil.)	1.5%	–	109.6	116.7	153.1	123.2
Net income ($ mil.)	12.4%	–	–	0.4	2.9	0.9
Market value ($ mil.)	–	–	–	–	–	–
Employees	–	–	–	–	–	800

DELTA TAU DATA SYSTEMS INC.

21314 Lassen St.
Chatsworth CA 91311
Phone: 818-998-2095
Fax: 818-998-7807
Web: www.deltatau.com

CEO: –
CFO: –
HR: –
FYE: March 31
Type: Private

Unlike the Greek frathouse in Animal House that its name evokes everything is in motion and under control at Delta Tau Data Systems. The company makes motion and machine-control products including board and system level motion controllers amplifiers converters control panels and machine tool controllers. It also offers software tools used to develop applications for the hardware. Delta Tau Data Systems serves a wide range of industries including general automation robotics machine tools medical and packaging equipment and semiconductor manufacturing. Founded in 1976 by Dimitri S. Dimitri Delta Tau Data has offices in China Japan South Korea Switzerland the UK and the US.

DELTATHREE INC

NBB: DDDC

1 Bridge Plaza, Fort Lee
West New York, NJ 07024
Phone: 212 500-4850
Fax: –

CEO: Efraim Baruch
CFO:
HR: –
FYE: December 31
Type: Public

Deltathree supplies the pipes that make phone calls via the Internet possible. The company manages an international voice over Internet Protocol (VoIP) network that offers distribution through both service provider and reseller channels. Deltathree sells consumer phone service over the Web under the iConnectHere (or ICH) and joip brands. Using the company's software and network connection customers can place calls from their computers to traditional telephones. Deltathree also provides operational management services such as account provisioning billing and payment processing. The company's network connects points in New Jersey and Georgia plus Frankfurt Germany. It makes more than half of its sales overseas.

	Annual Growth	12/09	12/10	12/11	12/12	12/13
Sales ($ mil.)	(4.1%)	19.0	14.2	10.5	13.7	16.1
Net income ($ mil.)	–	(3.2)	(2.5)	(3.1)	(1.6)	(1.8)
Market value ($ mil.)	(44.7%)	26.7	12.3	2.2	1.4	2.5
Employees	(9.4%)	43	48	32	30	29

DELTEK INC.

NASDAQ: PROJ

2291 Wood Oak Dr.
Herndon VA 20171
Phone: 703-734-8606
Fax: 703-734-1146
Web: www.deltek.com

CEO: Mike Corkery
CFO: Michael Krone
HR: Jennifer Bayat
FYE: December 31
Type: Private

Deltek provides project management software designed to meet the needs of professional services firms and project-based businesses. Its applications handle expense reporting HR administration materials management customer management and sales force automation. Deltek integrates tools from partners such as Microsoft with its own software and provides consulting and other services. Deltek targets the aerospace construction engineering and information technology sectors. It also serves government agencies and contractors an area of strength for Deltek where it holds a large market share. The company which operates primarily in the US is owned by Thoma Bravo.

DELTIC TIMBER CORP.

NYS: DEL

210 East Elm Street, P.O. Box 7200
El Dorado, AR 71731-7200
Phone: 870 881-9400
Fax: –
Web: www.deltic.com

CEO: Ray C. Dillon
CFO: Kenneth D. Mann
HR: Sandy Alley
FYE: December 31
Type: Public

Money doesn't grow on trees? Deltic Timber might beg to differ. The company annually grows and harvests some 605000 tons of timber from the more than 450000 acres of timberland that it owns primarily in Arkansas and northern Louisiana. The company's two sawmills convert the timber (mainly Southern Pine) into softwood lumber products; this is then sold to wholesale distributors lumber treaters and truss manufacturers for use in residential construction to make roof trusses laminated beams and decking. In addition to its timber and lumber businesses Deltic Timber develops real estate in central Arkansas and manufactures medium density fiberboard (MDF) through Del-Tin Fiber.

	Annual Growth	12/10	12/11	12/12	12/13	12/14
Sales ($ mil.)	12.6%	141.6	121.8	140.9	199.7	227.4
Net income ($ mil.)	12.2%	12.4	2.7	9.2	26.2	19.7
Market value ($ mil.)	5.0%	708.9	759.8	888.5	854.8	860.6
Employees	4.5%	454	438	438	537	541

DELUXE CORP.
NYS: DLX

3680 Victoria Street North
Shoreview, MN 55126-2966
Phone: 651 483-7111
Fax: 651 483-7337
Web: www.deluxe.com

CEO: Lee J. Schram
CFO: Terry D. Peterson
HR: Julie Loosbrock
FYE: December 31
Type: Public

When money can move at the speed of a mouse click Deluxe wants to do more than keep its revenues in check. The company is a leading printer of checks in the US. Its Small Business Services segment provides business checks other personalized printed products (business forms marketing materials address labels) and Web design services (through Hostopia.com) to small businesses. Deluxe also operates a Financial Services unit that provides fraud prevention customer acquisition and related services to banks credit unions and financial services firms. In addition its Direct Checks division is the nation's #1 direct-to-consumer seller of checks under the brands Checks Unlimited and Designer Checks.

	Annual Growth	12/10	12/11	12/12	12/13	12/14
Sales ($ mil.)	4.5%	1,402.2	1,417.6	1,514.9	1,584.8	1,674.1
Net income ($ mil.)	7.0%	152.6	144.6	170.5	186.7	199.8
Market value ($ mil.)	28.2%	1,145.1	1,132.1	1,603.7	2,596.0	3,096.4
Employees	0.3%	5,765	5,565	5,476	5,575	5,830

DELUXE ENTERTAINMENT SERVICES GROUP INC.

5433 Fernwood Ave.
Hollywood CA 90027
Phone: 323-960-3600
Fax: 323-960-7016
Web: www.bydeluxe.com

CEO: Cyril Drabinsky
CFO: Mike Gunter
HR: –
FYE: June 30
Type: Subsidiary

There's nothing standard about this company's movie production and distribution services. Deluxe Entertainment Services Group provides a plethora of services to the motion picture industry including film processing and distribution and post-production and visual effects work. It has offices throughout Australia Canada Europe India and the US. Clients include all major Hollywood studios. Since 1943 Deluxe has received 10 Academy Awards for technical achievement. The firm can trace its history back to 1919 when Fox Film Corporation built Deluxe Laboratory on its lot for film processing and printing. Deluxe is part of MacAndrews & Forbes Holdings (the holding company of billionaire Ronald Perelman).

DEMAND MEDIA INC
NYS: DMD

1655 26th Street
Santa Monica, CA 90404
Phone: 310 394-6400
Fax: –
Web: www.demandmedia.com

CEO: Sean Moriarty
CFO: Rachel Glaser
HR: –
FYE: December 31
Type: Public

Demand Media knows that Web branding is in demand. Attracting some 125 million unique visitors each month the company operates through a variety of Web-related enterprises that exist to help drive Web traffic to its clients' sites. Subsidiaries include domain-name wholesaler eNom and Pluck a blog syndicator and provider of social media tools used for integrating websites. Other Demand Media websites include online how-to tutorials provider eHow humor site Cracked.com and Trails.com for outdoor enthusiasts. It also produces online video and written articles through its Demand Studios business which employs freelancers to provide content for its websites. Demand Media launched an IPO in early 2011.

	Annual Growth	12/10	12/11	12/12	12/13	12/14
Sales ($ mil.)	(9.1%)	252.9	324.9	380.6	394.6	172.4
Net income ($ mil.)	–	(5.3)	(18.5)	6.2	(20.2)	(267.4)
Market value ($ mil.)	(2.7%)	–	131.3	183.4	113.9	120.8
Employees	(9.6%)	600	600	700	750	400

DEMANDWARE INC
NYS: DWRE

5 Wall Street
Burlington, MA 01803
Phone: 888 553-9216
Fax: –
Web: www.demandware.com

CEO: Thomas D. Ebling
CFO: Timothy M. (Tim) Adams
HR: –
FYE: December 31
Type: Public

Consumers make a lot of demands on retailers and Demandware is there to provide demand satisfaction. The company's Demandware Commerce is an on-demand software-as-a-service (SaaS) platform that connects users to up-to-date tools for designing and maintaining websites mobile apps and other digital shopping avenues. It uses data centers to monitor customers' websites worldwide. Major customers include retailers Barneys New York Crocs Jones Group and Columbia Sportswear. Demandware receives a share of the revenue its customers generate using the SaaS; it also collects subscription fees for platform use.

	Annual Growth	12/10	12/11	12/12	12/13	12/14
Sales ($ mil.)	44.6%	36.7	56.5	79.5	103.7	160.6
Net income ($ mil.)	–	0.3	(1.4)	(8.1)	(20.9)	(27.1)
Market value ($ mil.)	45.1%	–	–	963.8	2,262.1	2,030.0
Employees	40.0%	–	215	298	383	590

DEMOULAS SUPER MARKETS INC.

875 East St.
Tewksbury MA 01876
Phone: 978-851-8000
Fax: 978-640-8390
Web: www.mydemoulas.net

CEO: Felicia Thornton
CFO: Donald T Mulligan
HR: –
FYE: December 31
Type: Private

The Demoulas supermarket chain is ripe with family history all rolled up into numerous Market Baskets. Demoulas Super Markets runs 60-plus grocery stores under the Market Basket banner in Massachusetts and New Hampshire. One store still operates under the DeMoulas banner. The grocery retailer also manages real estate interests. Market Basket supermarkets are typically located in shopping centers with other retail outlets including properties owned by the company through its real estate arm Retail Management and Development (RMD) Inc. Begun as a mom-and-pop grocery store the chain has since transformed into a traditional yet modern concept. The business is run by CEO Arthur Demoulas.

DENALI INCORPORATED

2400 Augusta Dr. Ste. 340
Houston TX 77057
Phone: 713-627-0933
Fax: 713-627-0937
Web: www.denaliincorporated.com

CEO: –
CFO: –
HR: –
FYE: December 31
Type: Private

Without Denali's holding tanks the world might be a bit more toxic. The company specializes in fiberglass-reinforced composite products used to handle hazardous or valuable fluids. The company's Containment Solutions (CSI) unit makes underground fiberglass storage tanks for the petroleum and water and wastewater industries and above-ground steel storage tanks for the petroleum and automotive industries. Denali's Fabricated Plastics unit makes thermoplastic assemblies for corrosion applications such as in tanks piping and ductwork.

DENBURY RESOURCES, INC. (DE)

NYS: DNR

5320 Legacy Drive
Plano, TX 75024
Phone: 972 673-2000
Fax: 972 673-2150
Web: www.denbury.com

CEO: Phil Rykhoek
CFO: Mark C. Allen
HR: Whitney Shelley
FYE: December 31
Type: Public

Denbury Resources is the largest combined oil and natural gas producer in Mississippi and Montana. In 2014 it reported estimated proved reserves of 437.7 million barrels of oil equivalent of which 83% was oil. It owns the largest reserves of carbon dioxide (CO_2) used in enhanced (also called tertiary) oil recovery east of the Mississippi River and it holds operating acreage in its two core regions Gulf Coast and Rocky Mountains. Using CO_2 in enhanced oil recovery is one of the most efficient tertiary recovery methods for producing crude oil. Denbury Resources generates substantially all of its revenue from sales of oil natural gas and related products.

	Annual Growth	12/10	12/11	12/12	12/13	12/14
Sales ($ mil.)	6.1%	1,921.8	2,309.3	2,456.5	2,517.1	2,435.2
Net income ($ mil.)	23.7%	271.7	573.3	525.4	409.6	635.5
Market value ($ mil.)	(19.2%)	6,745.7	5,335.8	5,724.5	5,805.8	2,872.9
Employees	6.3%	1,195	1,308	1,432	1,501	1,523

DENDREON CORP

NMS: DNDN

1301 2nd Avenue
Seattle, WA 98101
Phone: 206 256-4545
Fax: –
Web: www.dendreon.com

CEO: –
CFO: –
HR: –
FYE: December 31
Type: Public

Dendreon wants to boost your immunity from the start. It is developing therapeutic vaccines that help the body's immune system fight cancer by targeting dendritic cells which initiate an immune response to disease-causing antigens. Its sole commercial product Provenge is a therapeutic vaccine that targets prostate cancer. In 2010 Provenge gained the status of being the first therapeutic cancer vaccine to receive FDA approval. Dendreon is working to expand use of Provenge; it is also working on therapeutic vaccines to treat other types of cancer and it has research programs investigating other cancer-fighting biotech and small molecule drugs. In late 2014 Dendreon filed for Chapter 11 bankruptcy protection.

	Annual Growth	12/09	12/10	12/11	12/12	12/13
Sales ($ mil.)	628.0%	0.1	48.1	341.6	325.5	283.7
Net income ($ mil.)	–	(220.2)	(439.5)	(337.8)	(393.6)	(296.8)
Market value ($ mil.)	(41.9%)	4,133.2	5,492.0	1,195.3	832.0	470.3
Employees	11.8%	484	1,497	1,475	1,050	755

DENISON UNIVERSITY

100 W COLLEGE ST
GRANVILLE, OH 430231100
Phone: 740-587-0810
Fax: –
Web: www.denison.edu

CEO: –
CFO: David English
HR: –
FYE: June 30
Type: Private

Denizens of Denison University have a desire to dedicate themselves to higher learning. The small-town college is a private undergraduate school with an enrollment of about 2200. It has some 220 faculty members and a low student-to-teacher ratio of about 10:1. Denison University offers some 60 majors concentrations and pre-professional programs. Its degrees range across a number of liberal arts and science fields including a pre-medical program and an athletic training program as well as social science and humanities programs.

	Annual Growth	06/09	06/10	06/11	06/12	06/13
Sales ($ mil.)	(1.9%)	–	122.6	110.2	112.2	115.8
Net income ($ mil.)	(29.5%)	–	–	111.0	(14.4)	55.2
Market value ($ mil.)	–	–	–	–	–	–
Employees	–	–	–	–	–	757

DENMARK BANCSHARES, INC.

NBB: DMKB A

103 East Main Street, P.O. Box 130
Denmark, WI 54208-0130
Phone: 920 863-2161
Fax: –
Web: www.denmarkstate.com

CEO: John P Olsen
CFO: Dennis J Heim
HR: –
FYE: December 31
Type: Public

Hold the Shakespeare jokes: Denmark Bancshares is the holding company for Denmark State Bank which serves the Green Bay Wisconsin area through more than five branches. The bank offers a variety of deposit products such as checking and savings accounts CDs individual retirement accounts and health savings accounts in addition to credit cards. Real estate loans including residential and commercial mortgages and agricultural and construction loans comprise the bulk of the bank's lending activities; it also originates consumer and business loans.

	Annual Growth	12/08	12/09	12/10	12/11	12/12
Assets ($ mil.)	1.1%	414.1	408.4	420.3	426.0	432.1
Net income ($ mil.)	(0.2%)	3.8	0.9	3.4	3.6	3.8
Market value ($ mil.)	36.1%	–	28.8	69.2	76.1	72.6
Employees	(1.3%)	97	94	96	93	92

DENNY'S CORP

NAS: DENN

203 East Main Street
Spartanburg, SC 29319-0001
Phone: 864 597-8000
Fax: 864 597-8135
Web: www.dennys.com

CEO: John C. Miller
CFO: F. Mark Wolfinger
HR: Jill Van Pelt
FYE: December 31
Type: Public

Feel like getting slammed for breakfast? The home of the Grand Slam Breakfast Denny's is one of the leading full-service family-style restaurant chains in the US with more than 1680 of its signature eateries located across the country. Typically open 24 hours a day the chain is best known for its menu of breakfast items including eggs pancakes and combination plates carrying such names as All-American Slam Lumberjack Slam and the aforementioned Grand Slam Breakfast. Denny's also serves standard American fare (burgers sandwiches steak) for lunch and dinner. The company owns and operates about 160 of its restaurants while the rest are franchised or operate under licensing agreements.

	Annual Growth	12/10	12/11	12/12	12/13	12/14
Sales ($ mil.)	(3.7%)	548.5	538.5	488.4	462.6	472.3
Net income ($ mil.)	9.6%	22.7	112.3	22.3	24.6	32.7
Market value ($ mil.)	30.9%	297.3	323.6	407.4	626.8	873.3
Employees	(7.8%)	11,500	10,000	8,000	8,250	8,300

DENSO INTERNATIONAL AMERICA INC.

24777 Denso Dr.
Southfield MI 48033-5244
Phone: 248-350-7500
Fax: 248-213-2337
Web: www.densocorp-na.com

CEO: Hikaru Sugi
CFO: –
HR: –
FYE: March 31
Type: Subsidiary

No spherical measurement DIAM (DENSO International America) does encompass the North American operations of Japanese auto parts maker DENSO. The company oversees more than 30 joint ventures and affiliate businesses — mostly in the US but also in Mexico and Canada. In addition to manufacturing everything from automotive radiators and fuel injectors to alternators and air conditioners DIAM manages research and development of electronic components that improve vehicle fuel efficiency emissions reduction safety and comfort. The company's customers include Toyota General Motors Ford Motor Honda of America Cummins Deere & Company Volvo Trucks Mercedes-Benz U.S. International and Harley-Davidson.

DENTSPLY INTERNATIONAL, INC.

NMS: XRAY

221 West Philadelphia Street
York, PA 17405-2558
Phone: 717-845-7511
Fax: –
Web: www.dentsply.com

CEO: Bret W. Wise
CFO: Christopher T. (Chris) Clark
HR: –
FYE: December 31
Type: Public

Open wider please so that DENTSPLY International can fit more of its products in your mouth. The company manufactures a range of dental goods from anesthetics pastes and tooth whiteners to artificial teeth crown and bridge materials and implants. DENTSPLY also makes dental equipment including root canal instruments ultrasonic polishers X-ray viewers and orthodontic appliances. The company manufactures its various products under more than 100 brand names; it also sells products made by third parties. More than half of its products are sold through domestic and international distributors but DENTSPLY also sells directly to dentists dental labs and dental schools in more than 120 countries.

	Annual Growth	12/11	12/12	12/13	12/14	12/15
Sales ($ mil.)	1.3%	2,537.7	2,928.4	2,950.8	2,922.6	2,674.3
Net income ($ mil.)	0.7%	244.5	314.2	313.2	322.9	251.2
Market value ($ mil.)	14.8%	4,902.1	5,549.4	6,792.0	7,463.1	8,525.1
Employees	(0.9%)	11,800	11,900	11,800	11,600	11,400

DENVER HEALTH AND HOSPITAL AUTHORITY

777 Bannock St.
Denver CO 80204-4507
Phone: 303-436-6000
Fax: 303-436-5131
Web: www.denverhealth.org

CEO: Arthur Gonzalez
CFO: Lorraine Montoya
HR: –
FYE: December 31
Type: Private - Not-for-Pr

When you live a mile high you sometimes need a safety net; that's where Denver Health and Hospital Authority comes in. Though it serves all the people of Colorado's capital annually attending to a fourth of the city's population and a third of its children Denver Health is also the "safety net" care provider for the city's indigent uninsured mentally ill and other high-risk patients. The medical system's primary facility is the Denver Health Medical Center a 400-bed hospital that also houses a regional trauma center. It also includes a network of family health and dental clinics; a poison and drug center; and a 911 response system for Denver County.

DEPAUW UNIVERSITY

313 S LOCUST ST
GREENCASTLE, IN 461351736
Phone: 765-658-4800
Fax: –
Web: www.depauw.edu

CEO: –
CFO: –
HR: –
FYE: June 30
Type: Private

DePauw University is a private co-educational liberal arts university with an approximate enrollment of 2300 students. Its campus boasts some 36 major buildings across nearly 700 acres including a 520-acre nature preserve located 45 miles west of Indianapolis. The university offers undergraduate degrees from more than 30 academic departments and programs as well as fellowships in media management and science. Prominent alumni include former US Vice President Dan Quayle former US Rep. Lee Hamilton and best-selling author Barbara Kinsolver. DePauw was founded in 1837 by the Methodist Church. The university's School of Music founded in 1884 is one of the oldest in the US.

	Annual Growth	06/09	06/10	06/11	06/12	06/13
Sales ($ mil.)	26.4%	–	121.9	147.0	154.8	246.2
Net income ($ mil.)	516.7%	–	–	2.5	5.8	94.5
Market value ($ mil.)	–	–	–	–	–	–
Employees	–	–	–	–	–	652

DEPOMED INC

NMS: DEPO

7999 Gateway Boulevard, Suite 300
Newark, CA 94560
Phone: 510-744-8000
Fax: –
Web: www.depomed.com

CEO: James A. Schoeneck
CFO: August J. Moretti
HR: –
FYE: December 31
Type: Public

For comedians and Depomed it's all about the delivery. The drug company makes proprietary drug therapies using its patented delivery technology Acu-Form an extended-release technology that stretches out the time a pill stays in the stomach thus reducing the number of necessary doses and potential side effects. Depomed's internal development efforts have yielded FDA-approved and marketed products: Gralise which is used to treat nerve pain; CAMBIA a non-steroidal anti-inflammatory drug for acute treatment of migraine attacks in adults; Zipsor Liquid Filled Capsules for pain relief in adults; and Lazanda Nasal Spray to manage breakthrough pain in adults.

	Annual Growth	12/10	12/11	12/12	12/13	12/14
Sales ($ mil.)	48.3%	80.8	133.0	90.8	134.2	390.4
Net income ($ mil.)	141.2%	3.9	70.7	(29.8)	43.3	131.8
Market value ($ mil.)	26.2%	377.1	307.1	367.0	627.3	955.2
Employees	47.2%	69	110	267	308	324

DEPUY INC.

325 Paramount Dr.
Raynham MA 02767
Phone: 508-880-8100
Fax: 508-880-8122
Web: www.depuy.com

CEO: –
CFO: –
HR: –
FYE: December 31
Type: Subsidiary

DePuy makes it possible for orthopedic patients to stand up straight and take a step in the right direction. Part of Johnson & Johnson's DePuy Synthes organization the DePuy businesses develop and market orthopedic joint reconstruction spinal care products and neurosurgical devices. As one of the world's largest suppliers of orthopedics DePuy's offerings include hip replacements; knee shoulder and spinal implants; internal and external fixator products for bone fractures; and operating room equipment and supplies. The company's products are used primarily by orthopedic specialists and neurosurgeons to treat patients with musculoskeletal defects resulting from diseases deformities trauma or accidents.

DEPUY ORTHOPAEDICS INC.

700 Orthopaedic Dr.
Warsaw IN 46581
Phone: 574-267-8143
Fax: 518-489-2112
Web: www.liacars.com

CEO: –
CFO: –
HR: Elke Strathmann
FYE: December 31
Type: Subsidiary

The knees have it — and the shoulders elbows hips wrists and ankles too. DePuy Orthopaedics a subsidiary of DePuy (itself part of Johnson & Johnson or J&J) is one of the largest designers manufacturers and distributors of orthopedic devices and supplies. In addition to replacement joints its product line includes the Ci system which includes computer hardware and software needed to assist surgeons in procedures such as full knee replacement surgery and ligament balancing. DePuy Orthopaedics was founded in 1895 by Revra DePuy. One of J&J's fastest growing businesses the company continues to innovate and expand through research and development efforts as well as through acquisitions.

DERMA SCIENCES INC.   NAS: DSCI

214 Carnegie Center, Suite 300
Princeton, NJ 08540
Phone: 609-514-4744
Fax: -
Web: www.dermasciences.com

CEO: -
CFO: John E Yetter
HR: -
FYE: December 31
Type: Public

Time may eventually heal all wounds but in the meantime there's Derma Sciences. The company operates in three segments: advanced wound care traditional wound care and pharmaceutical wound care products. Advanced wound care products include dressings bandages and ointments designed to promote wound healing and/or prevent infection. Traditional wound care products consist of commodity related dressings ointments gauze bandages adhesive bandages wound closer strips catheter fasteners and skin care products. Pharmaceutical wound care products include DSC127 a novel product for the treatment of diabetic foot ulcers which is presently under development having completed its Phase 2 trial..

	Annual Growth	12/10	12/11	12/12	12/13	12/14
Sales ($ mil.)	10.4%	56.5	62.6	72.6	79.7	83.7
Net income ($ mil.)	-	(2.4)	(4.3)	(12.1)	(24.0)	(39.8)
Market value ($ mil.)	18.6%	119.0	191.9	281.3	274.0	235.7
Employees	11.6%	195	214	244	262	303

DESALES UNIVERSITY

2755 STATION AVE
CENTER VALLEY, PA 180349568
Phone: 610-282-1100
Fax: -
Web: www.desales.edu

CEO: -
CFO: Willard Cressman
HR: -
FYE: June 30
Type: Private

Named after scholar writer and Doctor of the Church St. Francis de Sales DeSales University prides itself on providing its students an education based on the philosophy of Christian humanism. The private four-year Catholic university offers bachelor of arts (BA) and bachelor of science (BS) degrees in about 30 major fields of studies. It also administers graduate degrees in education business nursing criminal justice information systems physical therapy and physician assistant studies. Total enrollment is about 3300 students taught by more than 100 faculty members. DeSales University was founded in 1964.

	Annual Growth	06/09	06/10	06/11	06/12	06/13
Sales ($ mil.)	9.6%	-	74.0	83.1	87.7	97.5
Net income ($ mil.)	29.4%	-	-	8.0	7.9	13.3
Market value ($ mil.)	-	-	-	-	-	-
Employees	-	-	-	-	-	580

DESERET GENERATION AND TRANSMISSION CO-OPERATIVE

10714 S JORDAN GTWY # 300
SOUTH JORDAN, UT 840953922
Phone: 435-781-5737
Fax: -
Web: www.wyomingrea.org

CEO: Kimball Rasmussen
CFO: -
HR: -
FYE: December 31
Type: Private

Its service area may be dry but it is not a power desert thanks to Deseret Generation and Transmission Cooperative (aka Deseret Power) which supplies wholesale electricity to its members (six retail distribution cooperatives) and other bulk energy customers in Arizona Colorado Nevada Utah and Wyoming. The member-owned utility operates 223 miles of transmission lines and it has interests in two power generation facilities in Utah that give it 550 MW of capacity. Deseret Power also operates its own coal mine which fuels its main power plant through subsidiary Blue Mountain Energy; other operations include the transportation of coal by railroad and the development of a limestone extraction facility.

	Annual Growth	12/03	12/04	12/05	12/06	12/07
Sales ($ mil.)	(62.6%)	-	-	1,732.6	218.8	242.7
Net income ($ mil.)	-	-	-	0.0	10.8	(9.7)
Market value ($ mil.)	-	-	-	-	-	-
Employees	-	-	-	-	-	250

DESERT SCHOOLS FEDERAL CREDIT UNION

148 N. 48th St.
Phoenix AZ 85034
Phone: 602-433-7000
Fax: 604-608-6717
Web: www.amica.ca

CEO: Susan Frank
CFO: David Dick
HR: -
FYE: December 31
Type: Private - Not-for-Pr

Arizona's largest not-for-profit credit union with $3 billion in assets Desert Schools Federal Credit Union operates more than 50 locations in the Phoenix area and serves some 370000 members. Established by a group of 15 teachers in 1939 the credit union offers traditional banking products and services including checking savings and money market accounts certificates of deposit and credit cards. Its lending activities include home mortgage vehicle personal and student loans as well as business loans and lines of credit. Subsidiary Desert Schools Financial Services provides investment advisory retirement insurance and tax planning services.

DESTINATION MATERNITY CORP   NMS: DEST

232 Strawbridge Drive
Moorestown, NJ 08057
Phone: 856 291-9700
Fax: -
Web: www.destinationmaternity.com; www.motherhoodcanada.ca

CEO: Anthony M. (Tony) Romano
CFO: Judd P Tirnauer
HR: -
FYE: September 30
Type: Public

The destination for moms-to-be may be a store operated by Destination Maternity a designer and seller of mid-priced to high-end maternity apparel. Its three chains (A Pea in the Pod Destination Maternity and Motherhood Maternity) occupy more than 2000 retail locations including more than 650 company-owned sites and about 1400 leased spaces in department and specialty stores (Boscov's Macys) in the US Canada and Puerto Rico. The company is also the exclusive supplier of maternity apparel to more than 1100 Kohl's stores nationwide. Most of its merchandise is designed by the company and made by third-party contractors. The company was founded in 1982 as Mothers Work.

	Annual Growth	09/10	09/11	09/12	09/13	09/14
Sales ($ mil.)	(0.7%)	531.2	545.4	541.5	540.3	517.0
Net income ($ mil.)	(11.1%)	16.8	23.0	19.4	23.9	10.5
Market value ($ mil.)	(17.2%)	451.2	176.4	256.3	435.9	211.6
Employees	(0.4%)	4,367	4,500	4,700	4,300	4,300

DESTINATION XL GROUP INC   NMS: DXLG

555 Turnpike Street
Canton, MA 02021
Phone: 781 828-9300
Fax: -
Web: www.destinationxl.com

CEO: David A. Levin
CFO: Peter H. Stratton
HR: Renee Germain
FYE: January 31
Type: Public

When you've gained enough weight you've arrived at Destination XL. Destination XL Group (formerly Casual Male Retail Group) sells moderately-priced private-label and name-brand casual wear dresswear and suits for big-and-tall men at about 420 Casual MaleXL and Outlet stores in some 45 US states as well as online and through catalogs. It also operates about 40 stores across two smallers chain: upscale Rochester Clothing and its newest concept DestinationXL which houses all the company's brands under one roof. It also sells shoes and home goods under the ShoesXL and LivingXL brands online. Founded in 1976 as Designs Inc. the company has changed its name twice most recentlty to Destination XL Group.

	Annual Growth	01/11	01/12*	02/13	02/14*	01/15
Sales ($ mil.)	1.3%	393.6	397.7	399.6	388.0	414.0
Net income ($ mil.)	-	15.4	42.7	6.1	(59.8)	(12.3)
Market value ($ mil.)	5.3%	209.8	169.8	233.1	272.7	257.5
Employees	(0.3%)	2,464	2,446	2,446	2,374	2,435

*Fiscal year change

DESTINY MEDIA TECHNOLOGIES INC
TVX: DSY

1110 - 885 West Georgia Street
Vancouver, British Columbia V6C 3E8
Phone: 604 609-7736
Fax: 604 609-0611
Web: www.dsny.com

CEO: -
CFO: -
HR: -
FYE: August 31
Type: Public

Destiny Media Technologies develops and markets digital media management software. Operating through through two subsidiaries — Destiny Software Productions and MPE Distribution — the company provides software suites designed to securely distribute streaming (Clipstream) and downloadable (MPE) content including digital music. It also provides software for broadcasting Internet radio from home computers (Radio Destiny). Destiny Media Technologies markets its products primarily to customers in Canada and the US. The company was founded in 1991.

	Annual Growth	08/10	08/11	08/12	08/13	08/14
Sales ($ mil.)	(1.3%)	3.8	4.0	4.0	3.7	3.6
Net income ($ mil.)	-	1.7	0.6	0.6	0.2	(0.3)
Market value ($ mil.)	18.2%	21.7	22.3	49.0	115.6	42.4
Employees	4.1%	23	26	26	25	27

DETECTOR ELECTRONICS CORPORATION

6901 W. 110th St.
Bloomington MN 55438-2356
Phone: 952-941-5665
Fax: 952-829-8750
Web: www.detronics.com

CEO: Gerald F Slocum
CFO: Randy Ruegg
HR: -
FYE: December 31
Type: Business Segment

When the pipes are about to blow Detector Electronics sounds the alarm. The company also called Det-Tronics makes electrical detection products used to monitor industrial facilities for fire and gas leaks. Using UV MIR and fiber optics technology sensors are designed to detect hazardous heat variations radiation and combustible and toxic gases. Its products sold through more than 70 offices worldwide are used to protect applications including offshore oil platforms gas pipelines subway systems and aerospace and defense projects. Det-Tronics is part of UTC Climate Controls & Security a division of United Technologies.

DETERMINE INC
NAS: DTRM

2121 South El Camino Real, 10th Floor
San Mateo, CA 94403
Phone: 650 532-1500
Fax: -
Web: www.selectica.com

CEO: Patrick Stakenas
CFO: -
HR: -
FYE: March 31
Type: Public

Selectica's offerings are choice. Clients use Selectica's applications to sell complex goods and services over intranets extranets and the Internet. Selectica's software helps clients develop and deploy online sales channels that guide their customers through the selection configuration pricing and fulfillment process for consumer goods loans and insurance. The cloud-based software also suggests optimum product configurations (based on sales objectives marketing information and product constraints). Selectica primarily serves clients from the manufacturing retail and consumer goods sectors.

	Annual Growth	03/11	03/12	03/13	03/14	03/15
Sales ($ mil.)	9.5%	14.5	13.8	17.6	15.8	20.9
Net income ($ mil.)	-	(1.5)	(6.3)	(4.7)	(8.2)	(13.7)
Market value ($ mil.)	2.9%	46.0	30.3	71.7	52.8	51.5
Employees	23.1%	51	53	70	75	117

DETREX CORP.
NBB: DTRX

24901 Northwestern Highway, Suite 410
Southfield, MI 48075
Phone: 248 358-5800
Fax: 248 799-7192
Web: www.detrex.com

CEO: Thomas E Mark
CFO: -
HR: -
FYE: December 31
Type: Public

Detrex Corporation has one word for you: plastics. OK three words: plastics and specialty chemicals. Detrex's subsidiary Harvel Plastics which accounts for more than two-thirds of Detrex's sales makes PVC and CPVC pipe and custom extrusions. Detrex's other division The Elco Corporation makes lubricant additives (such as hydraulic fluid additives) fine chemicals and semiconductor-grade hydrochloric acid. The company has operations throughout the US and customers in 50 countries though a clear majority of Detrex's sales are in the US. Those customers include manufacturers of appliances automobiles and farm implements. Summit Capital Partners owns 37% of Detrex.

	Annual Growth	12/10	12/11	12/12	12/13	12/14
Sales ($ mil.)	(18.8%)	93.7	48.9	43.4	41.0	40.8
Net income ($ mil.)	(17.2%)	2.1	4.3	7.7	2.6	1.0
Market value ($ mil.)	51.0%	10.3	23.5	28.5	54.0	53.6
Employees	(24.5%)	203	219	65	68	66

DETROIT DIESEL CORPORATION

13400 Outer Dr. West
Detroit MI 48239
Phone: 313-592-5000
Fax: 313-592-7323
Web: www.detroitdiesel.com

CEO: -
CFO: -
HR: -
FYE: December 31
Type: Subsidiary

Detroit Diesel Corporation (DDC) says "keep on truckin'" as it continues to make a full lineup of engines. DDC sells its heavy-duty diesel engines and hybrid line to the commercial truck market. It offers 190 to 560 horsepower engines for vocational and on-highway customers. The Series 60 a heavy-duty diesel engine with electronic controls is its #1 seller. DDC also remanufactures two- and four-cycle engines. It services its engines through a network of some 800 outlets in North America. Most sales are made directly to truck makers in the US. Detroit Diesel is a brand affiliate of Daimler Trucks North America which makes vehicles under the Freightliner Western Star and Thomas Built Buses nameplates.

DETROIT MEDICAL CENTER

3990 John R. St.
Detroit MI 48201
Phone: 313-745-5111
Fax: 313-578-3225
Web: www.dmc.org

CEO: Joseph Mullany
CFO: Jay B Rising
HR: -
FYE: December 31
Type: Subsidiary

Running this DMC takes more than 3000 physicians and a staff of thousands. With more than 2000 beds the Detroit Medical Center serves patients in southeastern Michigan through eight hospitals and numerous outpatient facilities as well as DMC University Laboratories which provides clinical laboratory services to the medical system. DMC is a teaching and clinical research site for Wayne State University. The medical center's specialized services include cardiology orthopedics rehabilitation and organ transplants. DMC was acquired by Vanguard Health Systems in a deal worth about $1.3 billion. Vanguard's investment in DMC was a shot in the arm for the struggling hospital and the City of Detroit.

DETROIT PISTONS BASKETBALL COMPANY

6 Championship Dr.
Auburn Hills MI 48326
Phone: 248-377-0100
Fax: 248-377-3260
Web: www.nba.com/pistons

CEO: –
CFO: –
HR: –
FYE: June 30
Type: Private

Basketball fans get revved up thanks to these Pistons. Detroit Pistons Basketball Company owns and operates the Detroit Pistons professional basketball team which boasts three National Basketball Association championships its last coming in 2004. The team was formed in 1941 as the Fort Wayne (Indiana) Zollner Pistons by auto piston maker Fred Zollner who moved the team to Detroit in 1957. The Pistons roster has included such stars as Joe Dumars Bill Laimbeer and Isiah Thomas. Karen Davidson widow of the late William Davidson controls the team. The family also owns Palace Sports & Entertainment a holding company that owns Detroit's Palace of Auburn Hills arena.

DETROIT TIGERS INC.

Comerica Park 2100 Woodward Ave.
Detroit MI 48201-3470
Phone: 313-471-2000
Fax: 206-346-4100
Web: seattle.mariners.mlb.com

CEO: –
CFO: Steve Quinn
HR: –
FYE: December 31
Type: Subsidiary

These Tigers prowl in the jungle of Major League Baseball. The Detroit Tigers franchise was a charter member of the American League in 1901 and has won 10 league pennants and four World Series championships (the last in 1984). For all its past success however the team struggled to finish with a winning record for more than a decade until the 2006 season when the club won its first AL pennant since 1984. (Detroit lost the World Series though to the St. Louis Cardinals.) The baseball franchise is part of Ilitch Holdings owned by Mike and Marian Ilitch. The Ilitches who bought the Tigers in 1992 also own the Detroit Red Wings hockey team part of MotorCity Casino and Little Caesar Enterprises.

DEUBLIN COMPANY

2050 Norman Dr. West
Waukegan IL 60085-6747
Phone: 847-689-8600
Fax: 847-689-8690
Web: www.deublin.com

CEO: Donald L Deubler
CFO: Ed Lerner
HR: –
FYE: December 31
Type: Private

Doubling profits would turn some non-union heads at Deublin a leading manufacturer of rotating unions (a specialty mechanical device that allows the transmission of pressurized fluid from a stationary source into rotating machinery for heating cooling or the transfer of fluid power). Rotating unions are used in equipment such as air clutches gearboxes machine tool spindles and rubber and plastic manufacturing machinery. The company also makes turbulence bars siphons and steam joints which are sold to the automotive machine tool and printing industries. Luke Deubler and Dick Linn founded the company in 1945. The name "Deublin" is a combination of the founders' surnames.

DEUTSCH INC.

111 8th Ave.
New York NY 10011
Phone: 212-981-7600
Fax: 212-981-7525
Web: www.deutschinc.com

CEO: –
CFO: Nina Werner
HR: –
FYE: December 31
Type: Subsidiary

Advertising is the big idea at Deutsch. The firm led by advertising-guru-turned-television-personality Donny Deutsch offers creative development and brand marketing services through offices in New York and Los Angeles. Clients have included such notable brands as DIRECTV GM Novartis Worldwide and Johnson & Johnson. Deutsch also does interactive and direct marketing work as well as event marketing. The agency creates branded entertainment through its media unit. Founded in 1969 Deutsch is a subsidiary of global advertising conglomerate Interpublic Group. It enhances its geographical presence by working closely with Lowe & Partners Worldwide another Interpublic agency.

DEUTSCHE BANK SECURITIES INC.

60 Wall St.
New York NY 10005-2858
Phone: 212-250-2500
Fax: 212-797-4664
Web: www.db.com/us

CEO: –
CFO: Doug Barnard
HR: –
FYE: December 31
Type: Subsidiary

Deutsche Bank Securities is the US arm of German banking colossus Deutsche Bank. Its Deutsche Bank USA is the only investment bank physically located on Wall Street; it offers securities brokerage and investment advisory services to both domestic and international private clients and institutions and correspondent clearing services to broker-dealers. Deutsche Bank Securities also provides investment products brokerage and financial advice to wealthy individual investors through its Deutsche Bank Alex. Brown division. Deutsche Bank opened its first branch in New York in 1979 and now has offices in some 90 cities in nearly 30 US states.

DEVCON CONSTRUCTION INCORPORATED

690 GIBRALTAR DR
MILPITAS, CA 950356317
Phone: 408-942-8200
Fax: –
Web: www.devcon-const.com

CEO: Gary Filizetti
CFO: Brett Sisney
HR: Jennifer Cooke
FYE: December 31
Type: Private

Devcon Construction has built a sturdy business from building in the Bay Area. One of the area's top general building contractors Devcon has constructed more than 30 million sq. ft. of office industrial and commercial space. Its focus is on Northern California mainly in the San Francisco Bay Area and Silicon Valley. The company provides engineering design/build and interior design services. It specializes in high-tech projects including data centers and industrial research and development facilities. In addition to building company facilities and offices Devcon works on such projects as hotels restaurants parking structures retail stores sports facilities and schools.

	Annual Growth	12/09	12/10	12/11	12/12	12/13
Sales ($ mil.)	29.2%	–	469.9	434.4	779.0	1,012.4
Net income ($ mil.)	228.0%	–	–	1.2	3.5	12.5
Market value ($ mil.)	–	–	–	–	–	–
Employees	–	–	–	–	–	350

DEVEREUX FOUNDATION

444 DEVEREUX DR
VILLANOVA, PA 190851932
Phone: 610-520-3000
Fax: –
Web: www.devereux.org

CEO: –
CFO: –
HR: Timothy (Tim) Dillon
FYE: June 30
Type: Private

Devereux Foundation endeavors to make a difference in the lives of people with behavioral psychological intellectual or neurological problems. A not-for-profit organization Devereux serves children adolescents and adults and their families through about 15 centers in about a dozen states. Its offerings include hospitalization group homes respite care family counseling and vocational training. Devereux also conducts behavioral health research and provides consulting services for other organizations with similar concerns. The group's work began in 1912 when Philadelphia educator Helena Devereux began working with three special education students in her parents' home.

	Annual Growth	06/07	06/08	06/11	06/12	06/13
Sales ($ mil.)	0.3%	–	384.9	395.2	395.7	391.6
Net income ($ mil.)	(56.2%)	–	–	17.9	(5.4)	3.4
Market value ($ mil.)	–	–	–	–	–	–
Employees	–	–	–	–	–	6,000

DEVON ENERGY CORP.   NYS: DVN

333 West Sheridan Avenue
Oklahoma City, OK 73102-5015
Phone: 405 235-3611
Fax: –
Web: www.devonenergy.com

CEO: David A. (Dave) Hager
CFO: Thomas L. Mitchell
HR: Frank W. Rudolph
FYE: December 31
Type: Public

Despite its name independent oil and gas producer Devon Energy puts its energy into oil and gas fields far from England's southwestern coast. It focuses on exploration and production assets in Oklahoma Texas Wyoming and western Canada. In 2014 Devon Energy reported proved reserves of almost 3 billion barrels of oil equivalent. Devon Energy produces about 2.4 billion cu. ft. of of gas equivalent a day (3% of all the gas consumed in North America). It also has midstream and marketing assets. The company is the largest producer and lease holder in the Barnett Shale (Texas) and is looking to replicate its success there in other unconventional plays.

	Annual Growth	12/10	12/11	12/12	12/13	12/14
Sales ($ mil.)	18.4%	9,940.0	11,454.0	9,502.0	10,397.0	19,566.0
Net income ($ mil.)	(22.9%)	4,550.0	4,704.0	(206.0)	(20.0)	1,607.0
Market value ($ mil.)	(6.0%)	32,110.6	25,358.0	21,284.4	25,304.8	25,034.9
Employees	7.2%	5,000	5,200	5,700	5,900	6,600

DEVRY EDUCATION GROUP INC   NYS: DV

3005 Highland Parkway
Downers Grove, IL 60515
Phone: 630 515-7700
Fax: –
Web: www.devryeducationgroup.com

CEO: Daniel M. Hamburger
CFO: Timothy J. Wiggins
HR: –
FYE: June 30
Type: Public

It isn't exactly Ivy League but DeVry Education Group is in the big leagues of technical health care and business schools. The for-profit educational company offers professional undergraduate and graduate degrees through subsidiary schools. Flagship DeVry University with about 80 locations in roughly 25 states and Canada specializes in business and technology education. Its Keller Graduate School of Management unit offers MBA and other graduate programs while its Ross University offers medical and veterinary school training. The company also offers health care education through Chamberlain College of Nursing and Carrington College. In all DeVry has 49000 students through campus and online enrollment.

	Annual Growth	06/11	06/12	06/13	06/14	06/15
Sales ($ mil.)	(3.3%)	2,182.4	2,089.8	1,964.4	1,923.4	1,909.9
Net income ($ mil.)	(19.3%)	330.4	141.6	106.8	134.0	139.9
Market value ($ mil.)	(15.6%)	3,762.0	1,970.4	1,973.6	2,693.8	1,907.4
Employees	11.4%	12,599	13,521	12,668	12,517	19,404

DEWEY & LEBOEUF LLP

1301 Avenue of the Americas
New York NY 10019-6092
Phone: 212-259-8000
Fax: 212-259-6333
Web: www.deweyleboeuf.com

CEO: –
CFO: –
HR: –
FYE: September 30
Type: Private - Partnershi

International law firm Dewey & LeBoeuf has 1100 lawyers in about 25 offices worldwide in 15 countries. Dewey & LeBoeuf's areas of expertise include antitrust bankruptcy government investigations real estate tax and trade law as well as mergers and acquisitions. The firm is the result of the October 2007 merger between law firms Dewey Ballantine and LeBoeuf Lamb Greene & MacRae. Dewey Ballantine was initially founded in 1909; the Dewey in the name refers to former partner Thomas Dewey a three-term New York governor and two-time Republican presidential nominee in the 1940s. LeBoeuf Lamb was established in 1929. Dewey & LeBoeuf filed for Chapter 11 bankruptcy protection in 2012.

DEWEY ELECTRONICS CORP.   NBB: DEWY

27 Muller Road
Oakland, NJ 07436
Phone: 201 337-4700
Fax: –
Web: www.deweyelectronics.com

CEO: John H D Dewey
CFO: –
HR: –
FYE: June 30
Type: Public

The Dewey Electronics Corporation powers the military and powders the slopes. The company's electronics segment which accounts for nearly all of Dewey's sales provides the US Army with diesel-operated tactical generator sets and produces underwater speed and distance measuring instrumentation for the US Navy. The US Department of Defense and its various agencies provide around 72% of sales. Dewey's HEDCO division designs manufactures and services the Snow Cub brand of snowmaking equipment which it has sold to more than 300 ski resorts around the world. The family of late CEO Gordon Dewey owns about 37% of the company.

	Annual Growth	06/11	06/12	06/13	06/14	06/15
Sales ($ mil.)	(3.1%)	7.5	9.1	8.3	6.5	6.6
Net income ($ mil.)	–	(0.4)	0.3	0.1	(0.1)	(0.1)
Market value ($ mil.)	(3.2%)	3.3	2.5	2.1	3.0	2.9
Employees	0.0%	31	34	30	29	31

DEXCOM INC   NMS: DXCM

6340 Sequence Drive
San Diego, CA 92121
Phone: 858 200-0200
Fax: 858 200-0201
Web: www.dexcom.com

CEO: Kevin Sayer
CFO: Jess Roper
HR: –
FYE: December 31
Type: Public

DexCom wants to bring dexterity and communication to diabetes patients. The company develops and manufactures a glucose monitoring system called G4 PLATINUM that measures and wirelessly transmits blood sugar levels from a sensor on the patient to the company's receiver. Real-time data is processed and displayed so patients can assess blood glucose trends. Patients are also alerted when levels are too high or too low. The company's other product GlucoClear is used in hospitals to monitor blood glucose levels in critical care patients. DexCom's products are marketed to physicians endocrinologists and diabetes educators in the US and select international markets.

	Annual Growth	12/10	12/11	12/12	12/13	12/14
Sales ($ mil.)	51.9%	48.6	76.3	99.9	160.0	259.2
Net income ($ mil.)	–	(55.2)	(44.7)	(54.5)	(29.8)	(22.4)
Market value ($ mil.)	41.7%	1,055.1	719.7	1,050.5	2,737.2	4,255.4
Employees	19.5%	520	620	698	765	1,061

DFB PHARMACEUTICALS INC.

3909 HULEN ST
FORT WORTH, TX 761077253
Phone: 817-900-4050
Fax: –
Web: www.dfb.com

CEO: H Paul Dorman
CFO: –
HR: –
FYE: December 31
Type: Private

DFB Pharmaceuticals contributes to drug development and manufacturing processes by providing essential ingredients. The company produces various pharmaceutical ingredients for its own use and for other drug makers through its Phyton Biotech operating subsidiary. Phyton Biotech uses its plant cell culture technology to make APIs (active pharmaceutical ingredients). Phyton Biotech is a global provider of chemotherapeutic agents including paclitaxel and docetaxel APIs and taxane intermediates. Affiliate Phyton LTD. operates Phyton Biotech LLC and Phyton Biotech GmbH.

	Annual Growth	12/05	12/06	12/07	12/08	12/10
Sales ($ mil.)	(44.8%)	–	–	1,916.0	318.7	322.4
Net income ($ mil.)	–	–	–	0.0	0.0	0.0
Market value ($ mil.)	–	–	–	–	–	–
Employees	–	–	–	–	–	700

DFC GLOBAL CORP.

NMS: DLLR

1436 Lancaster Avenue
Berwyn, PA 19312
Phone: 610 296-3400
Fax: –
Web: www.dfcglobalcorp.com

CEO: Jeffrey A Weiss
CFO: Randy Underwood
HR: –
FYE: June 30
Type: Public

If your wallet is flat and payday is far away DFC Global can tide you over. The company owns some 1350 check-cashing and payday loan stores (and franchises about 50 additional locations) in North America and Europe. The stores operate under such names as Money Mart Money Shop Insta-Cheques Sefina Suttons and Robertsons and The Check Cashing Store. In addition to check cashing and short-term loans the stores offer money transfer services money orders tax filing services gold purchasing foreign exchange and reloadable Visa and MasterCard debit cards to customers who choose not to use or don't have access to traditional banks or financial institutions.

	Annual Growth	06/09	06/10	06/11	06/12	06/13
Sales ($ mil.)	20.8%	527.9	610.9	788.4	1,061.7	1,122.3
Net income ($ mil.)	–	1.8	(4.9)	65.8	52.4	(0.7)
Market value ($ mil.)	0.0%	553.1	793.8	868.4	739.3	554.0
Employees	9.9%	4,522	4,966	5,375	6,528	6,600

DGSE COMPANIES, INC.

ASE: DGSE

15850 Dallas Parkway, Suite 140
Dallas, TX 75248
Phone: 972 587-4049
Fax: 972 674-2596
Web: www.dgsecompanies.com

CEO: Matthew M Peakes
CFO: C Brett Burford
HR: –
FYE: December 31
Type: Public

Attracted to things gold and shiny? If so DGSE is for you. The company buys and sells jewelry bullion rare coins fine watches and collectibles to retail and wholesale customers across the US through its various websites and 30-plus retail stores in California Texas and South Carolina. The company's eight e-commerce sites let customers buy and sell jewelry and bullion interactively and obtain current precious-metal prices. In all more than 7500 items are available for sale on DGSE websites including $2 million in diamonds. DGSE also owns Fairchild Watches a leading vintage watch wholesaler and the rare coin dealer Superior Galleries. The company sold its pair of pawn shops in Dallas in 2009.

	Annual Growth	12/10	12/11	12/12	12/13	12/14
Sales ($ mil.)	(3.8%)	82.6	149.6	127.9	108.5	70.7
Net income ($ mil.)	–	5.7	1.0	(2.3)	(2.7)	(4.5)
Market value ($ mil.)	(27.0%)	52.4	91.4	66.5	27.3	14.9
Employees	4.0%	70	173	173	192	82

DHG MANAGEMENT COMPANY LLC

551 Fifth Ave.
New York NY 10176
Phone: 212-465-3700
Fax: 212-465-3511
Web: www.denihan.com

CEO: Patrick Denihan
CFO: Bob Smitt
HR: –
FYE: December 31
Type: Private

DHG Management Company (doing business as Denihan Hospitality Group) has an affinity for luxury accommodations. The company develops and manages boutique luxury hotels in urban markets. DHG properties operate under brands such as Affinia Hotels and The James. Its portfolio includes about a dozen properties located in New York (throughout Manhattan) Chicago (near the Magnificent Mile) and Washington DC (on Capitol Hill). DHG Management also owns independent New York hotels The Benjamin (in Midtown) and The Surrey Hotel (Upper East Side). Benjamin "Bud" Denihan Sr. founded the company's first hotel Lyden Gardens in 1962 and members of the Denihan family still own and operate a majority of the company.

DHI GROUP INC

NYS: DHX

1040 Avenue of the Americas, 8th Floor
New York, NY 10018
Phone: 212 725-6550
Fax: –
Web: www.diceholdingsinc.com

CEO: Michael P. Durney
CFO: John J. Roberts
HR: –
FYE: December 31
Type: Public

DHI Group (formerly Dice Holdings) doesn't think recruiting and hiring or job-seeking should be left to a roll of the dice – unless that means using the company's websites devoted to employee recruiting and career development. Through its flagship website Dice.com it provides job postings and career-related resources for technology professionals. DHI also operates ClearanceJobs.com for people with US government security clearances; eFinancialCareers.com aimed at financial workers; AllHealthcareJobs.com targeting health care workers; and WorldwideWorker.com and Rigzone.com for professionals in the energy sector. It also puts on job fairs. Most of the company's revenue comes from employers who pay to post job listings and view resumes.

	Annual Growth	12/11	12/12	12/13	12/14	12/15
Sales ($ mil.)	9.7%	179.1	195.4	213.5	262.6	259.8
Net income ($ mil.)	–	34.1	38.1	16.2	27.6	(11.0)
Market value ($ mil.)	2.6%	436.2	483.1	381.5	526.7	482.5
Employees	21.4%	396	534	755	831	861

DI LLC

PINK SHEETS: DINI

1400 E. Ash St.
Abbotsford WI 54405
Phone: 715-223-2384
Fax: 715-223-3689
Web: www.decoratorindustries.com

CEO: –
CFO: –
HR: –
FYE: December 31
Type: Public

Travelers can sleep easier thanks to Decorator Industries. The company manufactures and sells window coverings that keep the light out and bedspreads and comforters that keep the warmth in. The firm's products include draperies curtains blinds valance boards pillows cushions and other products. Decorator Industries sells its merchandise to manufactured home builders makers of recreational vehicles (RVs) and to hotels motels and other customers across the US. CMH Manufacturing accounted for more than 15% of the company's sales in 2009. Decorator Industries was established in 1953. William Bassett owns about 11% of Decorator Industries.

DIADEXUS INC.
NBB: DDXS

349 Oyster Point Boulevard
South San Francisco, CA 94080
Phone: 650 246-6400
Fax: –
Web: www.diadexus.com

CEO: Lori F. Rafield
CFO: Leone D. Patterson
HR: Roberto A Macina
FYE: December 31
Type: Public

diaDexus wants to help you protect your heart. The diagnostic company's products test for heart disease and other cardiovascular conditions. Its flagship product the PLAC test ELISA Kit is FDA-approved to detect a specific enzyme linked to coronary heart disease and ischemic stroke and helps predict risk in patients with otherwise low to moderate cholesterol levels. It licenses the test-associated intellectual property from GlaxoSmithKline. diaDexus is testing its PLAC Activity Test in the US as a risk assessment tool for cardiovascular disease; the test is already commercialized in Europe. The company changed its name from VaxGen after acquiring fellow drug development firm diaDexus in 2010.

	Annual Growth	12/10	12/11	12/12	12/13	12/14
Sales ($ mil.)	22.5%	11.8	16.4	20.8	24.9	26.4
Net income ($ mil.)	–	(8.4)	(7.5)	(2.8)	(2.2)	(8.5)
Market value ($ mil.)	14.6%	1.1	0.7	1.3	3.4	1.9
Employees	(7.5%)	56	51	57	67	41

DIALOGIC INC
NBB: DLGC

1504 McCarthy Boulevard
Milpitas, CA 95035-7405
Phone: 408 750-9400
Fax: 408 750-9450
Web: www.dialogic.com

CEO: –
CFO: –
HR: –
FYE: December 31
Type: Public

Dialogic serves as a gateway to Internet protocol (IP)-based communications. The company provides hardware and software systems used to build and integrate computer telephony networks over IP connections. Its products include software (PowerMedia) computer signaling boards that handle multimedia and message processing and media gateways (I-Gate) for delivering voice calls over digital lines with a level of quality comparable to analog landline phone systems. Dialogic sells its products worldwide to enterprises and service providers through resellers distributors and systems integrators including Advantech and Syntellect. The company merged with Veraz Networks in 2010.

	Annual Growth	12/08	12/09	12/10	12/11	12/12
Sales ($ mil.)	–	0.0	176.3	178.8	198.1	160.0
Net income ($ mil.)	–	0.0	(37.6)	(46.7)	(54.8)	(37.8)
Market value ($ mil.)	–	0.0	–	56.9	17.3	19.7
Employees	(14.5%)	–	–	935	808	684

DIALYSIS CLINIC INC.

1633 CHURCH ST STE 500
NASHVILLE, TN 372032948
Phone: 615-327-3061
Fax: –
Web: www.dciinc.org

CEO: –
CFO: –
HR: Audrey Semke
FYE: September 30
Type: Private

Dialysis Clinic Inc. or DCI is dedicated to caring for patients with end-stage renal disease (ESRD). The not-for-profit company which operates a network of more than 210 dialysis centers serving more than 14000 patients in 27 states also provides kidney transplant assistance services. Affiliate DCI Donor Services is an organ and tissue procurement agency. DCI also funds kidney-related research and educational programs and is affiliated with various universities and teaching hospitals throughout the US including Tufts University the University of Arizona and Tulane University.

	Annual Growth	09/10	09/11	09/12	09/13	09/14
Sales ($ mil.)	1.1%	–	642.9	664.7	650.8	663.4
Net income ($ mil.)	(11.5%)	–	–	45.5	51.0	35.7
Market value ($ mil.)	–	–	–	–	–	–
Employees	–	–	–	–	–	5,000

DIAMOND DISCOVERIES INTERNATIONAL CORP.
PINK SHEETS: DMDD

45 Rockefeller Plaza Ste. 2000
New York NY 10111
Phone: 212-332-8016
Fax: 212-332-3401
Web: www.diamonddiscoveries.com

CEO: –
CFO: –
HR: –
FYE: December 31
Type: Public

Diamond Discoveries International: The name says it all. The company is a minerals exploration company that leases property in the Torngat fields in northern Quebec. The company is firmly in the exploration and development phase of the project which will last at least through 2008. Former chairman and CEO Teodosia Pangia holds nearly 25% of Diamond Discoveries.

DIAMOND FOODS INC
NMS: DMND

600 Montgomery Street, 13th Floor
San Francisco, CA 94111-2702
Phone: 415 445-7444
Fax: –
Web: www.diamondfoods.com

CEO: Brian J Driscoll
CFO: Raymond P Silcock
HR: –
FYE: July 31
Type: Public

Diamond Foods has come out of its shell. While the company still sells plenty of walnuts peanuts almonds and other varieties of nuts primarily under the Diamond and Emerald brands snacks are a growing part of its business. Diamond Foods sells microwave popcorn under the Pop Secret brand and Kettle brand potato chips. The snack food maker sells its products to food retailers; Wal-Mart and Costco combined account for about 25% of sales. Non-retail customers include food processors restaurants bakeries and food service operators. Snack maker Synder's-Lance the maker of Cape Cod chips Lance crackers and Synder's of Hanover pretzels agreed to buy Diamond Foods for nearly $1.3 billion in late 2015.

	Annual Growth	07/11	07/12	07/13	07/14	07/15
Sales ($ mil.)	(2.7%)	965.9	981.4	864.0	865.2	864.2
Net income ($ mil.)	(9.9%)	50.2	(86.3)	(163.2)	(164.7)	33.0
Market value ($ mil.)	(18.0%)	2,254.4	512.4	642.1	845.8	1,017.5
Employees	(1.4%)	1,797	1,407	1,266	1,731	1,696

DIAMOND HILL INVESTMENT GROUP INC.
NMS: DHIL

325 John H. McConnell Blvd., Suite 200
Columbus, OH 43215
Phone: 614 255-3333
Fax: –
Web: www.diamond-hill.com

CEO: Christopher (Chris) Bingaman
CFO: Thomas E. (Tom) Line
HR: –
FYE: December 31
Type: Public

Diamond Hill Investment Group takes a shine to investment management. Operating through flagship subsidiary Diamond Hill Capital Management the firm oversees some $11.5 billion in assets most of it invested in mutual funds. Serving institutional and individual clients the company administers several mutual funds and sells them mainly through independent investment advisers broker-dealers financial planners investment consultants and third-party marketing firms. The firm hews to a value-based investment philosophy and takes a long-term perspective to investing. Formed in 1990 Diamond Hill Investment Group also manages separate accounts and hedge funds.

	Annual Growth	12/10	12/11	12/12	12/13	12/14
Sales ($ mil.)	16.5%	56.7	63.8	66.6	81.4	104.6
Net income ($ mil.)	26.3%	12.4	14.4	16.9	22.2	31.6
Market value ($ mil.)	17.5%	240.0	245.4	225.1	392.6	458.0
Employees	8.6%	77	73	79	98	107

DIAMOND OFFSHORE DRILLING, INC. NYS: DO

15415 Katy Freeway
Houston, TX 77094
Phone: 281 492-5300
Fax: 281 492-5316
Web: www.diamondoffshore.com

CEO: Marc Edwards
CFO: Gary T. Krenek
HR: –
FYE: December 31
Type: Public

This Diamond is an oiler's best friend. Diamond Offshore Drilling is a contract offshore oil and gas driller capable of descending in the deep blue to depths of 10000 feet and deeper. A leading US drilling contractor Diamond Offshore has 44 offshore drilling rigs including 32 semisubmersibles seven jack-up rigs (mobile drilling platforms) and five drillships. Operating in waters off six of the world's continents Diamond Offshore contracts with almost 50 oil and gas companies; Brazil's PETROBRAS is its major customer. The company which also provides project management and other drilling-related services is a subsidiary of Loews Corp.

	Annual Growth	12/10	12/11	12/12	12/13	12/14
Sales ($ mil.)	(4.1%)	3,323.0	3,322.4	2,986.5	2,920.4	2,814.7
Net income ($ mil.)	(20.2%)	955.5	962.5	720.5	548.7	387.0
Market value ($ mil.)	(13.9%)	9,171.1	7,578.8	9,320.6	7,806.5	5,034.7
Employees	(0.5%)	5,300	5,300	5,300	5,500	5,200

DIAMOND RESORTS HOLDINGS LLC

3745 Las Vegas Blvd South
Las Vegas NV 89109
Phone: 702-261-1010
Fax: 602-852-6686
Web: www.drivetime.com

CEO: Stephen J Cloobeck
CFO: –
HR: Charlene Gehrig
FYE: December 31
Type: Private

Diamond Resorts Holdings formerly Sunterra Corporation can help you shine on in all your crazy vacation adventures. The time-share vacation company doing business as Diamond Resorts International owns or manages more than 220 resorts across the globe including 70 managed resorts and some 130 affiliated resorts. About 495000 owners and members vacation at the resorts through the purchase of either vacation intervals (generally a one-week stay) or vacation points (redeemable for varying lengths of stay). The company's holdings also include four cruise ships. Stephen Cloobeck a real estate developer and time share industry executive owns Diamond Resorts.

DIAMONDBACK ENERGY INC. NASDAQ: FANG

500 West Texas Ste. 1225
Midland TX 79701
Phone: 432-617-0511
Fax: 432-689-5299
Web: www.legacylp.com

CEO: Raty Straehla
CFO: –
HR: –
FYE: December 31
Type: Private

Diamondback Energy is not selling snake oil. It is selling crude oil. The company is engaged in the exploration and production of unconventional oil and natural gas reserves in the Permian Basin in West Texas. In particular it is focusing on the oil-rich Wolfberry play which has a long production history long-lived reserves and proven drilling success rates. In 2011 Diamondback Energy reported estimated proved oil and natural gas reserves of 24.8 billion barrels of oil equivalent and more than 28140 net acres of leasehold properties. It operates more than 140 wells. The company raised $218 million in an initial public offering (IPO) in 2012.

DIAMONDROCK HOSPITALITY CO. NYS: DRH

3 Bethesda Metro Center, Suite 1500
Bethesda, MD 20814
Phone: 240 744-1150
Fax: –
Web: www.drhc.com

CEO: Mark W. Brugger
CFO: Sean M. Mahoney
HR: –
FYE: December 31
Type: Public

If diamonds are a girl's best friend then DiamondRock Hospitality might be an investor's best friend. Operating as an umbrella partnership real estate investment trust (UPREIT) it owns (but does not operate) nearly 30 upper-upscale hotels with about 11000 rooms in the North America and the US Virgin Islands with an emphasis on major urban markets such as New York Los Angeles Chicago and Boston as well as destination resorts. Its hotels are operated under the banners of Hilton Worldwide Marriott International Starwood Hotels & Resorts Worldwide and Westin. DiamondRock mostly operates through its taxable REIT subsidiary Bloodstone TRS.

	Annual Growth	12/10	12/11	12/12	12/13	12/14
Sales ($ mil.)	8.7%	624.4	638.2	749.6	799.7	872.9
Net income ($ mil.)	–	(9.2)	(7.7)	(16.6)	49.1	163.4
Market value ($ mil.)	5.5%	2,399.6	1,927.7	1,799.7	2,309.6	2,973.5
Employees	2.4%	20	22	22	22	22

DICK CLARK PRODUCTIONS INC.

9200 Sunset Blvd. 10th Fl.
Los Angeles CA 90069
Phone: 310-786-8900
Fax: 310-777-2187
Web: www.dickclarkproductions.com

CEO: Allen Shapiro
CFO: –
HR: –
FYE: June 30
Type: Private

From the Bandstand to the red carpet this company is anywhere there is celebrity entertainment. dick clark productions is best-known for producing televised awards shows ceremonies such as The American Music Awards and the Golden Globes. In addition to awards shows dick clark productions produces ABC's Bloopers and current FOX hit So You Think You Can Dance. It also owns the rights to the iconic music and dance program American Bandstand licensing TV clips as well as the Bandstand brand for use by restaurants and theatres. The company was founded by legend Dick Clark in 1957. A consortium of private equity firms including Guggenheim Partners and Mandalay Entertainment acquired the company in 2012.

DICK'S SPORTING GOODS, INC NYS: DKS

345 Court Street
Coraopolis, PA 15108
Phone: 724 273-3400
Fax: –
Web: www.dicks.com

CEO: Edward W. (Ed) Stack
CFO: Teri L. List-Stoll
HR: Deborah M. Victorelli
FYE: January 31
Type: Public

See Dick's shoppers run putt dunk dribble — and buy. Dick's Sporting Goods operates about 690 stores in 45-plus states. The stores usually contain five smaller shops ("stores within a store") that feature sporting goods apparel and footwear for leisure pursuits ranging from football golf and cycling to hunting and camping. In addition to brands including NIKE and adidas Dick's carries Ativa Walter Hagen Top-Flite and others exclusive to the firm. The company also operates more than 75 Golf Galaxy stores in 30 states as well as 10 Field & Stream and three True Runner stores. Dick's was founded in 1948 when Dick Stack father of company chairman and CEO Edward Stack opened a bait and tackle shop.

	Annual Growth	01/11	01/12*	02/13	02/14*	01/15
Sales ($ mil.)	8.8%	4,871.5	5,211.8	5,836.1	6,213.2	6,814.5
Net income ($ mil.)	17.3%	182.1	263.9	290.7	337.6	344.2
Market value ($ mil.)	9.6%	4,228.2	4,861.3	5,657.3	6,200.6	6,100.2
Employees	8.9%	26,700	28,400	29,800	34,300	37,600

*Fiscal year change

DICKINSON COLLEGE

COLLEGE & LOUTHER ST | CEO: –
CARLISLE, PA 17013 | CFO: –
Phone: 717-245-1010 | HR: –
Fax: – | FYE: June 30
Web: www.dickinsonathletics.com | Type: Private

Located in Carlisle Pennsylvania Dickinson College is a private liberal arts college with a penchant for international study. The small but selective college has an annual enrollment of some 2400 students half of which study abroad in programs that span 24 countries on six continents. The college offers more than 40 programs in arts and humanities (including a significant foreign language program) social sciences and natural sciences. It also offers minors in fields including astronomy creative writing and film studies. Dickinson College traces its roots back to 1773; it is named for John Dickinson who signed the US Constitution and was known as "The Penman of the [American] Revolution."

	Annual Growth	06/10	06/11	06/12	06/13	06/14
Sales ($ mil.)	2.8%	–	159.8	115.4	159.6	173.8
Net income ($ mil.)	–	–	–	(0.6)	37.6	51.0
Market value ($ mil.)	–	–	–	–	–	–
Employees	–	–	–	–	–	632

DICKINSON FINANCIAL CORPORATION II

1100 Main St. Ste. 350 | CEO: Paul P Holewinski
Kansas City MO 64105 | CFO: –
Phone: 816-471-9800 | HR: Janet Anderson
Fax: 816-412-0022 | FYE: December 31
Web: https://www.sunbankaz.com | Type: Private

Drop and give me a twenty. Dickinson Financial is the holding company for SunBank Southern Commerce Bank and three military banks: Armed Forces Bank Armed Forces Bank of California and Academy Bank. SunBank and Southern Commerce Bank have about a dozen branches apiece in Arizona and Florida respectively. Academy Bank has more than 50 locations in Colorado; the other two military banks have about 60 locations on or around military bases in nearly 20 states. Many of Dickinson's banks are located within Wal-Mart stores. The banks offer traditional deposit and lending products such as savings checking money market and retirement accounts loans mortgages and CDs.

DICON FIBEROPTICS INC.

1689 Regatta Blvd. | CEO: –
Richmond CA 94804 | CFO: –
Phone: 510-620-5000 | HR: –
Fax: 510-620-4100 | FYE: March 31
Web: www.diconfiberoptics.com | Type: Private

DiCon aims to be an icon when it comes to micro-electromechanical systems (MEMS) for the fiber optics industry. At its facility in the San Francisco Bay area the company manufactures passive optical components integrated modules and test instruments. Products include optical switches attenuators optical filters and channel monitors splitters detectors and rackmount systems. The company sells its products to customers in the optical communications test and measurement military and defense biomedical sensing and lighting sectors. Customers have included Alcatel-Lucent Cisco Systems Nortel Networks and Tellabs.

DIEBOLD, INC.   NYS: DBD

5995 Mayfair Road, P.O. Box 3077 | CEO: Andy W. Mattes
North Canton, OH 44720-8077 | CFO: Christopher A. Chapman
Phone: 330 490-4000 | HR: Sheila M. Rutt
Fax: – | FYE: December 31
Web: www.diebold.com | Type: Public

Cash is king at Diebold. The company is one of the leading global producers of automated teller machines (ATMs). In addition it offers remote teller systems cash dispensers and check cashing machines. Originally a manufacturer of safes the company is still active in its original market offering products that include vaults and security systems for financial institutions. It also provides electronic voting machines in Brazil. The company's related services range from traditional maintenance to remote monitoring transaction processing and currency management. Diebold which has operations in more than 90 countries gets half of sales outside North America.

	Annual Growth	12/10	12/11	12/12	12/13	12/14
Sales ($ mil.)	2.0%	2,823.8	2,835.8	2,991.7	2,857.5	3,051.1
Net income ($ mil.)	–	(20.3)	144.8	78.5	(181.6)	114.4
Market value ($ mil.)	2.0%	2,071.5	1,943.5	1,978.4	2,133.5	2,238.5
Employees	(0.2%)	16,124	16,515	16,751	16,000	16,000

DIEDRICH COFFEE INC.

28 Executive Park Ste. 200 | CEO: Carl Diedrich
Irvine CA 92614 | CFO: Sean M McCarthy
Phone: 949-260-1600 | HR: –
Fax: 949-260-1610 | FYE: June 30
Web: www.diedrich.com | Type: Subsidiary

This company keeps caffeine lovers buzzing. Diedrich Coffee is a leading coffee producer and wholesale supplier that distributes coffee products to retailers and foodservice customers. The company produces a variety of specialty coffee blends and flavors under the brands Coffee People Diedrich Coffee and Gloria Jean's. Its primary product is K-Cup single-serving portion packs produced under license for Keurig's single-service coffee machines. Diedrich Coffee produces and distributes fresh roasted coffee from its facility in California. In 2010 the company was acquired by Green Mountain Coffee Roasters.

DIERBERGS MARKETS INC.

16690 Swingley Ridge Rd. | CEO: –
Chesterfield MO 63017 | CFO: –
Phone: 636-532-8884 | HR: –
Fax: 636-812-1603 | FYE: December 31
Web: www.dierbergs.com | Type: Private

Dierbergs Markets has a taste of what folks in St. Louis like to eat. Dierbergs operates about two dozen upscale supermarkets in the St. Louis area where rival Schnuck Markets is the market leader. Dierbergs' stores offer food drugs photo processing and video centers as well as cooking schools banks self-service checkout Krispy Kreme donuts and made-to-order Chinese food at some locations. The company also offers online grocery shopping. Dierbergs Florist and Gifts affiliated with FTD offers gift baskets and floral services at its stores and over the Internet for local and international delivery. Founded as a trading outpost in 1854 the Dierberg family has owned and operated Dierbergs since 1914.

DIFFERENTIAL BRANDS GROUP INC

NAS: DFBG

2340 South Eastern Avenue
Commerce, CA 90040
Phone: 323 837-3700
Fax: –
Web: www.joesjeans.com

CEO: Samuel J Furrow
CFO: Hamish Sandhu
HR: Anita Besharat
FYE: November 30
Type: Public

A pair of jeans that fit just right; Joe's Jeans gets us. The company designs develops and markets premium designer denim jeans under the Joe's Hudson and Else brands. Its Joe's line also includes men's jeans and pants as well as shirts sweaters jackets and accessories for both sexes. Newly-acquired Hudson targets a more fashion forward customers looking for a great fit. Joe's Jeans sells its lineup to US retailers such as Saks Nordstrom and Macy's boutiques and through its namesake stores and website. It operates about 35 full-price retail and outlet stores in the US and now Canada. Founded in 1987 Joe's Jeans nearly doubled in size with the purchase of Hudson in 2013.

	Annual Growth	11/10	11/11	11/12	11/13	11/14
Sales ($ mil.)	17.8%	98.2	95.4	118.6	140.2	188.8
Net income ($ mil.)	–	2.6	(1.4)	5.6	(7.3)	(27.7)
Market value ($ mil.)	(21.6%)	3.7	1.2	2.1	2.8	1.4
Employees	9.2%	281	320	384	561	400

DIGERATI TECHNOLOGIES INC

NBB: DTGI

3463 Magic Drive, Suite 355
San Antonio, TX 78229
Phone: 210 775-0888
Fax: –
Web: www.digerati-inc.com

CEO: Arthur L Smith
CFO: Antonio Estrada
HR: –
FYE: July 31
Type: Public

Digerati Technologies (formerly ATSI Communications) has its head in the clouds and its feet in the oil wells. Digerati is a diversified holding company with operating subsidiaries that specialize in cloud-based technology services most notably Shift8 Technologies. Shift8 provides telecommunications solutions to commercial consumers. Digerati is also actively pursuing possible investments in the fossil fuels sector.

	Annual Growth	07/11	07/12	07/13	07/14	07/15
Sales ($ mil.)	(62.7%)	15.2	4.1	0.9	0.4	0.3
Net income ($ mil.)	–	(1.6)	(1.2)	(2.9)	4.2	(1.0)
Market value ($ mil.)	41.4%	0.2	0.0	0.8	0.7	0.8
Employees	(12.0%)	10	6	6	6	6

DIGI INTERNATIONAL, INC.

NMS: DGII

11001 Bren Road East
Minnetonka, MN 55343
Phone: 952 912-3444
Fax: –
Web: www.digi.com

CEO: Ronald E. Konezny
CFO: Mike Goergen
HR: Tracy L. Roberts
FYE: September 30
Type: Public

Digi serves up peripherals on a serial platter. Digi International makes serial cards and ports for connecting peripherals to networks as well as networking devices that utilize the USB (Universal Serial Bus) interface. The company makes machine-to-machine (M2M) networking systems and software that connect electronic devices to networks allowing for monitoring and control of local or remote physical assets. Digi's products are used in point-of-sale (POS) systems as well as industrial automation medical hospitality and building automation applications. It also provides deployment and support services. The company sells directly and through resellers and distributors.

	Annual Growth	09/11	09/12	09/13	09/14	09/15
Sales ($ mil.)	1.0%	204.2	190.6	195.4	192.7	212.9
Net income ($ mil.)	(12.1%)	11.0	7.6	5.8	1.8	6.6
Market value ($ mil.)	1.8%	275.5	254.5	250.2	187.9	295.3
Employees	(4.9%)	691	643	686	649	565

DIGI-KEY CORPORATION

701 Brooks Ave. South
Thief River Falls MN 56701-067
Phone: 218-681-6674
Fax: 218-681-3380
Web: www.digikey.com

CEO: Ronald A Stordahl
CFO: –
HR: –
FYE: December 31
Type: Private

Digi-Key holds more than one key to electronics distribution. One of the top distributors of electronic components in North America it supplies some 2 million products to customers in 170 countries. The company sells products from A to Z — analog integrated circuits to zener diodes — and every letter in between. It prides itself on same-day service for 99.9% of its orders all from one facility in the US. Digi-Key uses an entirely in-house sales force and does most of its business by means of the Internet in addition to catalogs. Founded in 1971 by CEO and owner Ronald Stordahl Digi-Key takes its name from the ham radio digital electronic keyer kit he developed and sold in college.

DIGIMARC CORP

NMS: DMRC

9405 SW Gemini Drive
Beaverton, OR 97008
Phone: 503 469-4800
Fax: –
Web: www.digimarc.com

CEO: Bruce Davis
CFO: Michael E. McConnell
HR: –
FYE: December 31
Type: Public

Digimarc makes its mark on media. The company provides digital watermarking software that embeds code in printed and digital content including photographs music movies and television content as well as currency documents and packages. Customers - which include movie studios record labels broadcasters creative professionals and government agencies — use Digimarc's software to control copyrights deter piracy license online content and manage digital assets. The company generates revenue from software development consulting services and technology licensing and subscription fees. Its licensees include Microsoft Adobe Systems The Nielsen Company and Open Text.

	Annual Growth	12/10	12/11	12/12	12/13	12/14
Sales ($ mil.)	(4.7%)	31.2	36.0	44.4	35.0	25.7
Net income ($ mil.)	–	4.2	5.7	8.3	(0.5)	(15.8)
Market value ($ mil.)	(2.5%)	252.9	201.3	174.4	162.3	228.8
Employees	11.2%	98	109	124	149	150

DIGIRAD CORP

NMS: DRAD

1048 Industrial Court
Suwanee, GA 30024
Phone: 858 726-1600
Fax: –

CEO: Matthew (Matt) Molchan
CFO: Jeffry R. (Jeff) Keyes
HR: –
FYE: December 31
Type: Public

What's radical in the world in the nuclear imaging? Digirad. The company makes and sells nuclear imaging equipment and provides mobile imaging services. Nuclear imaging uses low-level radioactive drugs introduced into a patient's bloodstream to detect heart disease cancer and neurological disorders. The company leases its equipment and provides staffing through the Digirad Imaging Solutions (DIS) unit which allows doctors to offer imaging in their offices with less capital investment. DIS also provides mobile cardiovascular ultrasound services. Digirad sells larger solid state cameras through its Product segment using a direct sales force and distributors in the US.

	Annual Growth	12/10	12/11	12/12	12/13	12/14
Sales ($ mil.)	(0.3%)	56.2	53.7	50.5	49.4	55.6
Net income ($ mil.)	–	(6.2)	(3.3)	(4.9)	0.3	2.5
Market value ($ mil.)	20.0%	39.1	36.5	38.2	68.9	81.2
Employees	(4.0%)	349	261	248	253	297

DIGITAL ALLY INC
NAS: DGLY

9705 Loiret Blvd.
Lenexa, KS 66219
Phone: 913-814-7774
Fax: –
Web: www.digitalally.com

CEO: Stanton E Ross
CFO: Thomas J Heckman
HR: –
FYE: December 31
Type: Public

Digital video systems manufacturer Digital Ally is an ally to police and other law enforcement that want more than a paper record of their traffic stops. Targeted to city state and commercial law enforcement agencies the company designs and manufactures specialized digital video cameras including a rearview mirror with a built-in digital video camera (used to capture video from inside police vehicles) as well as a portable digital video flashlight which can be used to record routine traffic stops sobriety tests and other law enforcement/civilian interactions. The company also offers a version of their video camera that can be worn on law enforcement officers' uniforms. Digital Ally was formed in 2004.

	Annual Growth	12/10	12/11	12/12	12/13	12/14
Sales ($ mil.)	(8.8%)	25.2	19.6	17.6	17.8	17.4
Net income ($ mil.)	–	(6.5)	(4.0)	(2.0)	(2.5)	(9.2)
Market value ($ mil.)	72.0%	5.3	1.8	10.5	27.8	46.4
Employees	1.7%	99	87	91	119	106

DIGITAL CINEMA DESTINATIONS CORP.

250 East Broad St.
Westfield NJ 07090
Phone: 908-396-1360
Fax: 908-396-1361
Web: www.digiplexdest.com

CEO: Bud Mayo
CFO: –
HR: –
FYE: June 30
Type: Private

It's out with the celluloid and in with the megapixels at Digital Cinema Destinations (DCDC). Operating under the Digiplex Destinations brand DCDC owns a small but growing chain of movie theaters that show first-run movies in an entirely digital format. Its theaters located in New Jersey and Connecticut also show non-movie recorded and broadcasted events such as concerts operas and ballets and live sporting events. DCDC's theaters offer an interactive element as well allowing patrons to text comments and questions sing along and host tailgate parties. Founded in 2010 the company filed to go public in late 2011.

DIGITAL ENVOY INC.

250 Scientific Dr. Ste. 800
Norcross GA 30092
Phone: 678-258-6300
Fax: 678-258-6363
Web: www.digitalenvoy.net

CEO: William J Calpin
CFO: –
HR: –
FYE: December 31
Type: Private

George Orwell would be proud of Digital Envoy. The company's big brother-like software figures out the connection speed and location of people visiting Web sites so content can be accurately targeted and served up for different demographics and potential customer bases. Digital Envoy's DigitalElement its IP Intelligence product is used by some of the world's largest networks Web sites and enterprises including Google Microsoft Disney Siemens and Time Warner.

DIGITAL FEDERAL CREDIT UNION

220 Donald Lynch Blvd.
Marlborough MA 01752
Phone: 508-263-6700
Fax: 508-263-6430
Web: www.dcu.org

CEO: James Regan
CFO: –
HR: –
FYE: December 31
Type: Private - Not-for-Pr

Digital Federal Credit Union (DCU) provides old-fashioned financial services with modern technology. Its more than 370000 members can conduct business online at about 20 branch locations in Massachusetts and New Hampshire or at some 6400 credit unions that accept transactions on behalf of DCU. The credit union offers a range of commercial and retail products and services including savings and checking accounts; Visa credit cards; residential and commercial mortgages; and auto business construction and home equity loans. Founded in 1979 the credit union also operates DCU Insurance residential real estate brokerage DCU Realty DCU Financial which offers investments and financial planning services.

DIGITAL FUSION INC.

5030 Bradford Dr. NW Ste. 210
Huntsville AL 35805
Phone: 256-327-0000
Fax: 256-327-8120
Web: www.digitalfusion.com

CEO: Eric M Demarco
CFO: Deanna H Lund
HR: –
FYE: December 31
Type: Subsidiary

Digital Fusion is always on the search for critical IT mass. The company offers a variety of information technology services including technical consulting research and engineering systems integration and support and software development. It also provides services in the areas of project management business support and data management. Digital Fusion primarily serves state and federal government agencies particular in the defense sector but it also has higher education and commercial clients. Customers have included NASA and the US Army. Digital Fusion is a subsidiary of of San Diego-based defense contractor Kratos Defense and Security Solutions.

DIGITAL POWER CORP.
ASE: DPW

48430 Lakeview Blvd.
Fremont, CA 94538-3158
Phone: 510-657-2635
Fax: –
Web: www.digipwr.com

CEO: Amos Kohn
CFO: –
HR: –
FYE: December 31
Type: Public

Digital Power is a real switch hitter. The company makes power supplies such as AC/DC switchers and DC/DC converters for OEMs in the industrial medical military and telecommunications markets. Its products protect electronic components and circuits from power surges while converting a single input voltage into different output voltages. Most of Digital Power's products which can be easily modified to meet the specific needs of its 400 customers are made by subcontractors in China and Mexico. UK-based subsidiary Digital Power Limited doing business as Gresham Power Electronics makes AC/DC power supplies uninterruptible power supplies and power inverters; it accounts for more than half of sales.

	Annual Growth	12/10	12/11	12/12	12/13	12/14
Sales ($ mil.)	(3.5%)	10.4	11.2	8.6	8.8	9.0
Net income ($ mil.)	–	0.5	1.1	(0.3)	(0.6)	(0.7)
Market value ($ mil.)	(5.6%)	11.2	12.5	4.7	4.5	8.9
Employees	(4.3%)	31	30	29	28	26

DIGITAL REALTY TRUST, INC. NYS: DLR

Four Embarcadero Center, Suite 3200
San Francisco, CA 94111
Phone: 415 738-6500
Fax: 415 738-6501
Web: www.digitalrealty.com

CEO: A. William (Bill) Stein
CFO: Andrew P. Power
HR: Rita da Luz
FYE: December 31
Type: Public

Technically Digital Realty Trust puts its chips in real estate. The real estate investment trust (REIT) owns properties that are leased to firms in the technology sector. Its portfolio includes more than 100 properties in the US Europe and Asia including data communications hubs electronic storage and processing centers tech manufacturing facilities and offices of tech companies. All told the REIT owns more than 18 million sq. ft. of rentable space including space held for redevelopment. Digital Realty Trust focuses on hot tech markets such as Chicago Dallas Phoenix New Jersey New York northern Virginia and California's San Francisco Bay area and Silicon Valley (its largest market).

	Annual Growth	12/10	12/11	12/12	12/13	12/14
Sales ($ mil.)	16.9%	865.4	1,062.7	1,279.1	1,482.3	1,616.4
Net income ($ mil.)	18.3%	102.3	156.3	210.3	314.5	200.2
Market value ($ mil.)	6.5%	6,990.2	9,042.2	9,207.7	6,662.0	8,992.0
Employees	17.3%	454	532	702	784	860

DIGITAL RIVER, INC. NMS: DRIV

10380 Bren Road West
Minnetonka, MN 55343
Phone: 952 253-1234
Fax: –
Web: www.digitalriver.com

CEO: David C Dobson
CFO: Stefan Shulz
HR: Bonnie Murkowski
FYE: December 31
Type: Public

Digital River helps keep the e-commerce flowing. The company provides technology and services that enable its clients to sell their products on the Web without building an e-commerce platform from the ground up. Using its own proprietary server technology Digital River offers Web development and hosting transaction processing fulfillment and fraud screening services to tens of thousands of customers operating online retail and distribution businesses. It also provides its customers with Web traffic data that allows them to better market their online presence. Digital River was established in 1994 and began offering online stores for its clients in 1996.

	Annual Growth	12/08	12/09	12/10	12/11	12/12
Sales ($ mil.)	(0.5%)	394.2	403.8	363.2	398.1	386.2
Net income ($ mil.)	–	63.6	49.8	15.7	17.2	(195.9)
Market value ($ mil.)	(12.7%)	876.9	954.4	1,217.1	531.1	508.5
Employees	2.5%	1,335	1,239	1,280	1,419	1,473

DIGITAL TURBINE INC NAS: APPS

1300 Guadalupe Street, Suite #302
Austin, TX 78701
Phone: 512 387-7717
Fax: –
Web: www.digitalturbine.com

CEO: William Stone III
CFO: Lisa Higgins-Lucero
HR: –
FYE: March 31
Type: Public

When it comes to mobile digital content Digital Turbine (formerly Mandalay Digital) doesn't play games (but it does make them). Through its Twistbox and AMV subsidiaries the company develops content for 3G mobile phones including games images chat services and other products. Its content is targeted to users aged 18 to 40 and covers a variety of themes including mature entertainment. The company distributes its products in 40 European North American Latin American and Asian countries through agreements with major mobile phone operators including Verizon Virgin Mobile T-Mobile and Vodafone.

	Annual Growth	03/11	03/12	03/13	03/14	03/15
Sales ($ mil.)	32.4%	9.2	7.2	6.0	24.4	28.3
Net income ($ mil.)	–	(9.4)	(30.7)	(14.2)	(18.7)	(24.6)
Market value ($ mil.)	90.0%	14.3	53.4	53.2	225.8	186.4
Employees	40.8%	40	33	89	101	157

DIGITALGLOBE INC NYS: DGI

1300 West 120th Avenue
Westminster, CO 80234
Phone: 303 684-4000
Fax: –
Web: www.digitalglobe.com

CEO: Jeffrey R. (Jeff) Tarr
CFO: Gary W. Ferrara
HR: –
FYE: December 31
Type: Public

Look up and smile. DigitalGlobe might be capturing an image of you — and the rest of the planet. From its array of satellites the company captures imagery used for a variety of applications including mapping urban planning oil exploration land management disaster assessment and humanitarian relief. DigitalGlobe's products include standard images panchromatic images multispectral images and color infrared images as well as mosaics and digital elevation models. About 60% of its revenues come from the US government; commercial customers include oil and gas exploration companies and GPS navigation system makers. DigitalGlobe's images are incorporated into popular mapping apps such as Google Maps and Microsoft Virtual Earth as well as into GPS systems from DeLorme and Garmin.

	Annual Growth	12/10	12/11	12/12	12/13	12/14
Sales ($ mil.)	19.4%	322.2	339.5	421.4	612.7	654.6
Net income ($ mil.)	45.7%	4.1	(28.1)	39.0	(68.3)	18.5
Market value ($ mil.)	(0.6%)	2,321.2	1,252.5	1,789.0	3,012.2	2,267.0
Employees	20.8%	629	708	749	1,235	1,339

DIGITAS INC.

33 Arch St.
Boston MA 02110
Phone: 617-867-1000
Fax: 617-867-1111
Web: www.digitasinc.com

CEO: David W Kenny
CFO: Joseph Tomasulu
HR: –
FYE: December 31
Type: Subsidiary

This company knows the important bits (and bytes) about interactive marketing. Digitas provides digital communications and direct marketing services through several operating agencies: Digitas Health Prodigious Solutions Digitas and Publicis Modem (formerly Modem Media). Operating from about 30 offices spanning 16 countries the agency offers website design e-mail management and demand generation services which enable clients to build marketing campaigns across a plethora of media channels. It has worked with such big clients as American Express Kraft General Motors and MillerCoors. Digitas is a part of VivaKi an advertising and marketing communications division of Publicis.

DIGNITY HEALTH

185 Berry St. Ste. 300
San Francisco CA 94107-1739
Phone: 415-438-5500
Fax: 415-438-5724
Web: www.dignityhealth.org

CEO: Lloyd Dean
CFO: Michael Blaszyk
HR: –
FYE: June 30
Type: Private - Not-for-Pr

Dignity Health (formerly Catholic Healthcare West) has steadily grown to become the largest private not-for-profit health care provider in the state of California. Dignity Health operates a network of 40 acute-care facilities located in the Golden State and to a lesser extent in Arizona and Nevada. Those facilities house 8400 acute care beds as well as 800 skilled nursing beds. Dignity Health provides home health and hospice services through agencies in California and Nevada. It also operates more than 300 emergency and specialty clinics imaging centers and medical labs as well as managed care and wellness programs. Dignity Health is the official health care provider of the San Francisco Giants.

DILLARD UNIVERSITY

2601 GENTILLY BLVD
NEW ORLEANS, LA 701223097
Phone: 504-283-8822
Fax: –
Web: www.dillard.edu

CEO: –
CFO: –
HR: Nick L Harris
FYE: June 30
Type: Private

Dillard University is diligent about providing a quality liberal arts education for its students. The historically black institution is named after James Hardy Dillard the former president of Tulane University who played a role in the education of African Americans in the South. The New Orleans-based university enrolls some 850 students. Enrollment fell in the wake of Hurricane Katrina which flooded the university in 2005. The damage forced Dillard to suspend operations for a semester and lay off staff and faculty. The university resumed operations at a temporary campus in Spring 2006. Classes resumed on campus later that same year. Dillard has been busy rebuilding facilities and recruiting new students.

	Annual Growth	06/06	06/07	06/08	06/09	06/10
Sales ($ mil.)	–	–	–	0.0	51.5	59.9
Net income ($ mil.)	37167.5%	–	–	0.0	(10.7)	4.2
Market value ($ mil.)	–	–	–	–	–	–
Employees	–	–	–	–	–	338

DILLARD'S INC.

1600 Cantrell Road
Little Rock, AR 72201
Phone: 501 376-5200
Fax: –
Web: www.dillards.com

NYS: DDS
CEO: William (Bill) Dillard
CFO: James I. Freeman
HR: –
FYE: January 31
Type: Public

Tradition is trying to catch up with the times at Dillard's. Sandwiched between retail giant Macy's and discount chains such as Kohl's Dillard's is rethinking its strategy and trimming its store count. The department store chain operates about 270 locations (down from 330 in 2005) in some 30 US states covering the Sunbelt and the central US. Its stores cater to middle- and upper-middle-income women selling name-brand and private-label merchandise with a focus on apparel and home furnishings. Women's apparel and accessories account for nearly 40% of its sales. Founded in 1938 by William Dillard family members through the W. D. Company control the company.

	Annual Growth	01/11	01/12*	02/13	02/14*	01/15
Sales ($ mil.)	2.0%	6,253.5	6,399.8	6,751.6	6,691.8	6,780.1
Net income ($ mil.)	16.6%	179.6	463.9	336.0	323.7	331.9
Market value ($ mil.)	29.6%	1,656.3	1,900.6	3,518.2	3,596.1	4,679.4
Employees	0.7%	38,900	38,900	38,000	40,000	40,000

*Fiscal year change

DILLON COMPANIES INC.

2700 E. 4th Ave.
Hutchinson KS 67504-1608
Phone: 620-665-5511
Fax: 620-669-3160
Web: www.dillons.com

CEO: –
CFO: –
HR: Frank J Remar
FYE: January 31
Type: Subsidiary

Dillon Companies which began as J.S. Dillon and Sons Stores has been selling bread to America's breadbasket bread since 1921. The regional supermarket operator has more than 200 combination food and drug stores under several banners; Dillons and Dillons Marketplace stores in Kansas; Baker's Supermarkets and Food-4-Less in Nebraska; Gerbes in Missouri; and City Market and King Soopers in Colorado. In addition to traditional supermarket fare Dillon's supermarkets have in-store pharmacies and many sell gas in the parking lot. Dillon Companies is losing market share to discounters including Wal-Mart Supercenters which has surpassed Dillon's parent company Kroger to become the #1 seller of groceries in the US.

DILLON SUPPLY CO.

216 S. West St.
Raleigh NC 27601
Phone: 919-838-4200
Fax: 919-838-4251
Web: www.dillonsupply.com

CEO: Dean Wagoner
CFO: Jeff Bell
HR: –
FYE: December 31
Type: Subsidiary

If opportunity knocks only once Dillon Supply has the equipment to take advantage of it. A one-stop source the company distributes all kinds of industrial construction and materials handling equipment. To do so its work is divided between eight divisions: industrial and maintenance equipment repair and overhaul machines; safety and janitorial supplies; storage and handling hardware; cutting tools abrasives and lubricants; industrial coatings; pipe valve and fittings; steel products (beams angles flats tubing); and forklift trucks. Customers include the Army Corps of Engineers and industries large and small. Founded in 1914 Dillon Supply operates as a subsidiary of supply giant Descours Et Cabaud.

DIME COMMUNITY BANCSHARES, INC

209 Havemeyer Street
Brooklyn, NY 11211
Phone: 718 782-6200
Fax: –
Web: www.dime.com

NMS: DCOM
CEO: Vincent F. Palagiano
CFO: Michael Pucella
HR: –
FYE: December 31
Type: Public

Dime Community Bancshares is in a New York state of mind. It is the holding company for The Dime Savings Bank of Williamsburgh which boasts $4.5 billion in assets and operates more than 25 branches in Brooklyn Queens and the Bronx as well as Nassau County on Long Island. Founded in 1864 the bank provides standard products and services including checking savings retirement money market and club accounts accounts. Multifamily residential and commercial real estate loans comprise the vast majority of the bank's loan portfolio. Subsidiary Dime Insurance Agency (formerly Havemeyer Investments) offers life policies fixed annuities and wealth management services.

	Annual Growth	12/10	12/11	12/12	12/13	12/14
Assets ($ mil.)	2.7%	4,040.3	4,021.2	3,905.4	4,028.2	4,497.1
Net income ($ mil.)	1.7%	41.4	47.3	40.3	43.5	44.2
Market value ($ mil.)	2.8%	537.7	464.4	511.9	623.6	600.0
Employees	(1.9%)	442	435	421	413	409

DIMENSIONS HEALTH CORPORATION

7582 ANNAPOLIS RD
HYATTSVILLE, MD 207841744
Phone: 301-322-2326
Fax: –
Web: www.princegeorgescountymd.gov

CEO: –
CFO: –
HR: –
FYE: June 30
Type: Private

Dimensions Healthcare System takes care of the many many facets of a human's dimensions. Dimensions Healthcare System operates a handful of medical facilities serving the residents in Prince George's County Maryland and the surrounding area. Acute care centers include Prince George's Hospital Center and Laurel Regional Hospital. Specialty services include rehabilitation behavioral health cardiology emergency medicine senior care pediatrics and a sleep disorders center. The not-for-profit health care system was established in 1982.

	Annual Growth	06/03	06/04	06/05	06/06	06/13
Sales ($ mil.)	0.6%	–	345.5	338.3	367.0	365.9
Net income ($ mil.)	–	–	–	3.9	17.7	(1.2)
Market value ($ mil.)	–	–	–	–	–	–
Employees	–	–	–	–	–	2,800

DIMEO CONSTRUCTION COMPANY

75 CHAPMAN ST
PROVIDENCE, RI 029055496
Phone: 401-781-9800
Fax: –
Web: www.dimeo.com

CEO: –
CFO: Steven B. Avery
HR: R L Blackwell
FYE: June 30
Type: Private

Dimeo Construction has built a reputation in New England. The company provides general contracting design/build and construction management services ranging from pre-planning to post-construction commissioning. It focuses on commercial education health care residential and public projects such as schools hospitals corporate headquarters research and development facilities and shopping centers. It also has worked on renovation projects such as The Mark Twain House & Museum and the Ocean House. The family-owned company was established in 1930 by Joseph Dimeo. Current CEO Brad Dimeo represents the third generation to lead the firm.

	Annual Growth	06/08	06/09	06/10	06/11	06/12
Sales ($ mil.)	(13.0%)	–	567.8	356.1	300.9	373.3
Net income ($ mil.)	(20.1%)	–	–	9.6	9.3	6.2
Market value ($ mil.)	–	–	–	–	–	–
Employees	–	–	–	–	–	300

DINEEQUITY INC

NYS: DIN

450 North Brand Boulevard
Glendale, CA 91203-1903
Phone: 818-240-6055
Fax: –
Web: www.dineequity.com

CEO: Julia A. Stewart
CFO: Thomas W. (Tom) Emrey
HR: –
FYE: December 31
Type: Public

This company shows an equal bias for breakfast lunch and dinner. DineEquity is one of the leading chain restaurant companies in the US with two flagship concepts IHOP (the International House of Pancakes) and Applebee's Neighborhood Grill and Bar (operated through subsidiary Applebee's Services). The #3 family-style diner chain behind Denny's and Waffle House IHOP has about 1500 mostly franchised restaurants that are open 24 hours a day. The chain is best known for its breakfast menu but it also offers standard family fare for lunch and dinner. Applebee's is the #1 casual-dining chain with about 2000 locations in the US and about 20 other countries offering a wide variety of appetizers and entrees.

	Annual Growth	12/10	12/11	12/12	12/13	12/14
Sales ($ mil.)	(16.3%)	1,333.1	1,075.2	849.9	640.5	655.0
Net income ($ mil.)	–	(2.8)	75.2	127.7	72.0	36.5
Market value ($ mil.)	20.4%	935.9	800.0	1,269.9	1,583.6	1,964.3
Employees	(39.8%)	17,700	10,900	2,450	2,530	2,325

DIODES, INC.

NMS: DIOD

4949 Hedgcoxe Road, Suite 200
Plano, TX 75024
Phone: 972 987-3900
Fax: –
Web: www.diodes.com

CEO: Keh-Shew Lu
CFO: Richard D. White
HR: –
FYE: December 31
Type: Public

Diodes Incorporated knows how important it is to be discrete in business. The company makes discrete semiconductors — fixed-function devices that are much less complex than integrated circuits. Diodes' products include diodes transistors and rectifiers; they are used by computer and consumer electronics manufacturers in products such as notebooks LCD monitors smartphones and game consoles. Other applications include power supplies climate control systems GPS devices and networking gear. Cisco LG Electronics Samsung Flextronics and Hon Hai are among its 150 OEM and contract manufacturing customers. The company's products are sold throughout Asia Europe and North America.

	Annual Growth	12/10	12/11	12/12	12/13	12/14
Sales ($ mil.)	9.8%	612.9	635.3	633.8	826.8	890.7
Net income ($ mil.)	(4.6%)	76.7	50.7	24.2	26.5	63.7
Market value ($ mil.)	0.5%	1,284.5	1,013.7	825.7	1,121.2	1,312.1
Employees	14.3%	3,986	4,499	4,605	6,151	6,794

DIONEX CORPORATION

1228 Titan Way
Sunnyvale CA 94085-3603
Phone: 408-737-0700
Fax: 408-730-9403
Web: www.dionex.com

CEO: Mark Casper
CFO: Craig A McCollam
HR: Michael Mallory
FYE: June 30
Type: Subsidiary

Dionex's instruments keep the contaminants away while scientists play. The company makes instruments used for substance analysis including identifying contaminants in everything from drinking water to industrial chemicals. Dionex is a leading maker of ion chromatography instruments devices used by chemists to isolate and quantify charged molecules in complex chemical mixtures. It also makes high-performance liquid chromatography (used to separate and identify biological molecules such as amino acids carbohydrates and proteins) sample extraction and sample handling equipment. It gets about 70% of its sales outside the US. In 2011 rival Thermo Fisher bought Dionex for $2.1 billion.

DIRECT INSITE CORP

NBB: DIRI

500 East Broward Boulevard, Suite 1550
Fort Lauderdale, FL 33394
Phone: 631 873-2900
Fax: 954 846-8841
Web: www.directinsite.com

CEO: Matthew E Oakes
CFO: Lowell Rush
HR: –
FYE: December 31
Type: Public

Direct Insite helps give its customers insight into their customers. The company's hosted software and services provide data mining and analysis reporting electronic invoice management and electronic bill presentment and payment functions. Its products are used to manage such functions as customer service workflows order processing dispute resolution and accounts payable and receivable. Direct Insite serves clients in more than 60 countries with its applications available in 15 languages and all major currencies. IBM is responsible for 51% of the company's sales while EDS accounts for 46%.

	Annual Growth	12/10	12/11	12/12	12/13	12/14
Sales ($ mil.)	(2.2%)	9.1	8.6	8.8	9.0	8.3
Net income ($ mil.)	(43.4%)	1.0	(2.7)	0.5	0.2	0.1
Market value ($ mil.)	(1.3%)	10.0	8.9	10.4	16.0	9.5
Employees	0.0%	38	43	45	46	38

DIRECT MEDIA MILLARD INC.

200 Pemberwick Rd.
Greenwich CT 06830
Phone: 203-532-1000
Fax: 203-532-3766
Web: www.dmminfo.com

CEO: Larry May
CFO: –
HR: –
FYE: December 31
Type: Private

Direct Media Millard offers mailing list management and brokerage services which generate direct marketing leads for clients. The company's other services include media buying (for insert marketing programs) interactive marketing (including search engine marketing e-mail marketing and promotion) and market research. Clients include catalogers publishers fundraisers and financial institutions. The company owns almost 10 offices across the US. Direct Media was bought by Infogroup (formerly infoUSA) in 2008. Infogroup combined Direct Media with Millard another direct marketing unit it owned in mid-2009 to form Direct Media Millard.

DIRECT RELIEF

27 S LA PATERA LN
GOLETA, CA 931173214
Phone: 805-964-4767
Fax: –
Web: www.directrelief.org

CEO: Thomas Tighe
CFO: Bhupi Singh
HR: Jenna Cox
FYE: June 30
Type: Private

Direct Relief International wants to relieve the health problems of people around the world. The not-for-profit organization is dedicated to providing health care support and emergency relief to people in developing countries as well as victims of disasters and war. Active in 50 US states and 70 countries it gives medicine supplies and equipment through partnerships with local groups that make specific requests and coordinates distribution. The group also has partnered with nonprofit clinics and community health centers to provide medical care and medicine for homeless and low-income people in California. Direct Relief was founded in 1948 by Estonian immigrant William Zimdin.

	Annual Growth	06/08	06/09	06/11	06/12	06/13
Sales ($ mil.)	23.9%	–	164.9	405.0	299.7	388.3
Net income ($ mil.)	–	–	–	95.6	(17.9)	(0.4)
Market value ($ mil.)	–	–	–	–	–	–
Employees	–	–	–	–	–	2

DIRECTV

2260 East Imperial Highway
El Segundo, CA 90245
Phone: 310 964-5000
Fax: –
Web: www.directv.com

NMS: DTV
CEO: Michael White
CFO: Patrick Doyle
HR: –
FYE: December 31
Type: Public

DIRECTV takes television straight to the masses. The company operates the largest direct-to-home (DTH) digital TV service in the US ahead of #3 DISH Network and in direct competition with cable providers Comcast (#1 overall in the pay-TV market) and Time Warner. In addition to its roughly 20 million US customers the company counts about another 18 million subscribers in Latin America under the DIRECTV and SKY brands. Services include HD 3D and video-on-demand (VOD) programming. Phone companies such as Verizon and AT&T bundle the company's video services with traditional voice digital telephone and Internet packages. In 2014 DIRECTV and AT&T agreed to take their relationship a big step further. A deal for AT&T to buy DIRECTV is awaiting approval.

	Annual Growth	12/09	12/10	12/11	12/12	12/13
Sales ($ mil.)	10.2%	21,565.0	24,102.0	27,226.0	29,740.0	31,754.0
Net income ($ mil.)	32.0%	942.0	2,198.0	2,609.0	2,949.0	2,859.0
Market value ($ mil.)	20.0%	17,318.9	20,735.9	22,205.5	26,048.4	35,863.3
Employees	8.0%	23,300	25,100	26,800	29,700	31,700

DISABLED AMERICAN VETERANS

3725 ALEXANDRIA PIKE
COLD SPRING, KY 410761712
Phone: 859-441-7300
Fax: –
Web: www.auxiliary.dav.org

CEO: –
CFO: –
HR: –
FYE: December 31
Type: Private

Disabled American Veterans (DAV) helps ex-military men and women fight personal battles. The nonprofit group strives to improve the quality of life for some 200000 wounded veterans and their families by helping them navigate the US Department of Veterans Affairs system to obtain benefits. DAV also represents the political interests of veterans and provides various outreach and volunteer programs. The group which generates most of its revenue from tax-exempt contributions has about 1.2 million members and boasts some 110 offices in the US and Puerto Rico. DAV was formed in 1920 and chartered by Congress in 1932. The organization has partnered with large corporations to help veterans get assistance.

	Annual Growth	12/05	12/06	12/07	12/08	12/09
Sales ($ mil.)	(3.1%)	–	169.9	185.1	152.0	154.6
Net income ($ mil.)	35.5%	–	–	24.0	(102.2)	44.1
Market value ($ mil.)	–	–	–	–	–	–
Employees	–	–	–	–	–	615

DISCOUNT DRUG MART INC.

211 Commerce Dr.
Medina OH 44256
Phone: 330-725-2340
Fax: 330-722-2990
Web: www.discount-drugmart.com

CEO: Donald Boodjeh
CFO: Thomas McConnell
HR: –
FYE: March 31
Type: Private

Drugs are merely part of the story at Discount Drug Mart. One of the largest drugstore chains in Ohio the company offers pharmacy services medical and home health care supplies and over-the-counter medications. Stocking some 40000 items it also sells groceries beauty aids pet supplies housewares and hardware. As part of its business Discount Drug Mart offers its customers video rentals and photo-developing services. Its 70-plus stores measure 25000 sq. ft. on average — about twice the size of its rivals' locations but smaller and more convenient than its national big-box competitors Wal-Mart and Target. Chairman and CEO Parviz Boodjeh owns the company which he founded in 1969.

DISCOUNT TIRE CO. INC.

20225 N. Scottsdale Rd.
Scottsdale AZ 85255
Phone: 480-606-6000
Fax: 480-951-8619
Web: www.discounttire.com

CEO: –
CFO: Christian Roe
HR: –
FYE: December 31
Type: Private

Concerned about that upcoming "re-tire-ment"? Discount Tire one of the largest independent tire dealers in the US can provide several options. With more than 830 company-owned stores in 20-plus states the company sells such leading tire brands as Michelin Goodyear and Uniroyal as well as wheels from Enkei Konig and TSW. Discount Tire operates mostly in the West Midwest Southwest and Southeast. Some of its stores in California and Washington operate as America's Tire Co. because of a naming conflict. Customers can search for tires by make and model on the company's website. Chairman and owner Bruce Halle founded Discount Tire in 1960 with six tires — four of them retreads.

DISCOVER FINANCIAL SERVICES

2500 Lake Cook Road
Riverwoods, IL 60015
Phone: 224 405-0900
Fax: –
Web: www.discover.com

NYS: DFS
CEO: David W. Nelms
CFO: R. Mark Graf
HR: –
FYE: December 31
Type: Public

Seems cardholders aren't the only ones getting paid to discover. Discover Financial Services is best known for issuing Discover-brand credit cards which are used by more than 25 million members. The company's cards which include several levels of business and consumer accounts repay cardholders a percentage of the purchase price each time they use their cards. Discover also licenses Diners Club credit cards which are accepted in more than 185 countries. But there's more to this business than just plastic. The company also offers direct banking services makes student and personal loans including mortgages and runs the PULSE Network ATM system. Morgan Stanley spun off Discover Financial Services in 2007.

	Annual Growth	11/10	11/11	11/12*	12/13	12/14
Assets ($ mil.)	8.1%	60,785.0	68,783.9	75,283.0	79,340.0	83,126.0
Net income ($ mil.)	32.0%	764.8	2,226.7	2,345.0	2,470.0	2,323.0
Market value ($ mil.)	37.6%	8,211.2	10,699.7	18,690.7	25,132.1	29,417.3
Employees	9.3%	10,300	11,650	13,009	14,128	14,676

*Fiscal year change

DISCOVERY COMMUNICATIONS, INC.
NMS: DISC A

One Discovery Place
Silver Spring, MD 20910
Phone: 240 662-2000
Fax: –
Web: www.corporate.discovery.com

CEO: David M. Zaslav
CFO: Andrew C. (Andy) Warren
HR: Carrie Storer
FYE: December 31
Type: Public

Discovery Communications allows viewers to go on safari without ever having to leave their couch. It is the world's #1 non-fiction media company with more than 150 worldwide cable TV networks including Discovery Channel Animal Planet and The Learning Channel (TLC). Among its US joint venture networks are The Oprah Winfrey Network (OWN) The Hub and 3net (the first 24-hour 3D network). Discovery Communications reaches more than 2.2 billion subscribers in more than 220 countries. In addition the company offers educational products and services to school; a diverse set of digital media services; and online content through Discovery.com and AnimalPlanet.com.

	Annual Growth	12/10	12/11	12/12	12/13	12/14
Sales ($ mil.)	13.5%	3,773.0	4,235.0	4,487.0	5,535.0	6,265.0
Net income ($ mil.)	14.9%	653.0	1,132.0	943.0	1,075.0	1,139.0
Market value ($ mil.)	(4.7%)	18,316.8	17,996.2	27,883.7	39,717.2	15,132.2
Employees	12.8%	4,200	4,600	4,500	5,700	6,800

DISCOVERY LABORATORIES, INC.
NAS: DSCO

2600 Kelly Road, Suite 100
Warrington, PA 18976-3622
Phone: 215 488-9300
Fax: –
Web: www.discoverylabs.com

CEO: Craig Fraser
CFO: John Tattory
HR: –
FYE: December 31
Type: Public

If you're waiting to exhale Discovery Laboratories may be able to help. The biotechnology company focuses on treatments for respiratory disorders. The company bases its therapies on surfactants which are naturally produced by the lungs and essential for breathing. Its only product Surfaxin gained FDA approval in 2012 for the prevention of respiratory distress syndrome (RDS) in premature infants. Another candidate Aerosurf (licensed from Philip Morris) will allow for the delivery of RDS surfactant medicine in aerosol form and is being developed as an alternative to endotracheal intubation and conventional mechanical ventilation. The firm also makes respiratory drug delivery devices.

	Annual Growth	12/10	12/11	12/12	12/13	12/14
Sales ($ mil.)	69.5%	–	0.6	0.2	0.4	2.8
Net income ($ mil.)	–	(19.2)	(21.0)	(37.3)	(45.2)	(44.1)
Market value ($ mil.)	(23.2%)	20.4	10.3	12.9	13.8	7.1
Employees	12.4%	69	73	121	126	110

DISH NETWORK CORP
NMS: DISH

9601 South Meridian Boulevard
Englewood, CO 80112
Phone: 303 723-1000
Fax: 303 723-1499
Web: www.dishnetwork.com.

CEO: James (Jim) DeFranco
CFO: Steve Swain
HR: Stephen Wood
FYE: December 31
Type: Public

DISH Network serves up fare intended to whet everyone's appetite for televised entertainment. The #2 provider of satellite-based pay-TV in the US (behind DIRECTV) the company serves more than 14 million subscribers which include business clients in such industries as hospitality restaurant and retail. Programming includes premium movies SIRIUS radio on-demand video service regional and specialty sports local and international channels and pay-per-view in addition to basic video programming. It offers bundled voice and Internet services through partnerships with voice and data communications providers. DISH generates all of its sales in the US.

	Annual Growth	12/10	12/11	12/12	12/13	12/14
Sales ($ mil.)	3.7%	12,640.7	14,048.4	14,266.5	13,904.9	14,643.4
Net income ($ mil.)	(1.0%)	984.7	1,515.9	636.7	807.5	944.7
Market value ($ mil.)	38.8%	9,077.5	13,149.9	16,806.7	26,743.0	33,655.0
Employees	(3.6%)	22,000	34,000	35,000	25,000	19,000

DISNEY (WALT) CO. (THE)
NYS: DIS

500 South Buena Vista Street
Burbank, CA 91521
Phone: 818 560-1000
Fax: –
Web: www.disney.com

CEO: Robert A. (Bob) Iger
CFO: James A Rasulo
HR: Mary Jayne Parker
FYE: October 03
Type: Public

The monarch of this magic kingdom is no man but a mouse: Mickey Mouse. The Walt Disney Company is the world's largest media conglomerate with assets encompassing movies television publishing and theme parks. Its Disney/ABC Television Group includes the ABC television network and 10 broadcast stations as well as a portfolio of cable networks including ABC Family Disney Channel and ESPN (80%-owned). Walt Disney Studios produces films through imprints Walt Disney Pictures Disney Animation and Pixar. It also owns Marvel Entertainment and Lucasfilm two extremely successful film producers. In addition Walt Disney Parks and Resorts runs its popular theme parks including Walt Disney World and Disneyland.

	Annual Growth	10/11*	09/12	09/13	09/14*	10/15
Sales ($ mil.)	6.4%	40,893.0	42,278.0	45,041.0	48,813.0	52,465.0
Net income ($ mil.)	14.9%	4,807.0	5,682.0	6,136.0	7,501.0	8,382.0
Market value ($ mil.)	35.9%	48,256.0	83,648.0	104,304.0	141,984.0	164,800.0
Employees	4.4%	156,000	166,000	175,000	180,000	185,000

*Fiscal year change

DIVERSEY INC.

8310 16th St.
Sturtevant WI 53177-0902
Phone: 262-631-4001
Fax: 262-631-4282
Web: www.diversey.com

CEO: Edward F Lonergan
CFO: Norman Clubb
HR: Evelyne Rasugu
FYE: December 31
Type: Subsidiary

In the war on germs Diversey serves as a first line of defense. The company is one of world's largest manufacturers of industrial and institutional cleaning hygiene and sanitation products trailing only Ecolab. Diversey also tackles the job of floor care housekeeping and room care and laundry and hand care. It provides safety and hygiene training and consulting too. Customers include food service operators and food and beverage processing plants as well as retailers building service contractors and lodging and healthcare facilities in some 175 countries. Europe accounts for more than half of the company's sales. Diversey was sold to Sealed Air Corporation (SAC) for about $2.6 billion in October 2011.

DIVERSIFIED CHEMICAL TECHNOLOGIES INC.

15477 WOODROW WILSON ST
DETROIT, MI 482381586
Phone: 313-867-5444
Fax: –
Web: www.diversifiedchemicalinc.com

CEO: –
CFO: –
HR: Patricia Clark
FYE: February 01
Type: Private

True to its name Diversified Chemical Technologies manufactures a diverse range of specialty chemical products for a diverse range of customers. It serves a number of industries but is best known for its process and maintenance chemicals for metalworking and cleaning and sanitation chemicals for the food and beverage markets. Working through subsidiaries it produces various adhesives (hot melt pressure sensitive and water-based adhesives) polymeric materials (including PVC seals epoxies acrylics polyesters and polyurethanes) custom-formulated specialty products and recycled polymeric materials to make polyurethane foam for autos. It also offers office supplies through Detroit-based Paperworks.

	Annual Growth	01/08	01/09	01/10	01/11*	02/13
Sales ($ mil.)	0.6%	–	69.1	59.8	70.3	70.7
Net income ($ mil.)	(23.7%)	–	–	1.0	7.1	0.4
Market value ($ mil.)	–	–	–	–	–	–
Employees	–	–	–	–	–	225

*Fiscal year change

DIVERSIFIED RESTAURANT HOLDINGS INC.   NAS: SAUC

27680 Franklin Road
Southfield, MI 48034
Phone: 248 223-9160
Fax: 248 223-9165
Web: www.diversifiedrestaurantholdings.com

CEO: T Michael Ansley
CFO: David G Burke
HR: –
FYE: December 28
Type: Public

Diversified Restaurant Holdings owns and operates about 25 Buffalo Wild Wings Grill & Bar locations in Florida Illinois Indiana and Michigan. Franchised from Buffalo Wild Wings (BWW) the quick-casual eateries are popular for their Buffalo-style chicken wings served with a variety of dipping sauces. The restaurants also serve burgers sandwiches and tacos along with beer and other beverages. Many of the eateries are located near large suburban shopping and entertainment areas. Diversified Restaurant Holdings also operates its own dining concept Bagger Dave's Legendary Burgers and Fries an upscale hamburger joint with two locations in Michigan.

	Annual Growth	12/10	12/11	12/12	12/13	12/14
Sales ($ mil.)	29.8%	45.2	60.7	77.4	108.9	128.4
Net income ($ mil.)	–	0.5	1.8	0.2	0.1	(1.3)
Market value ($ mil.)	(1.3%)	137.3	128.1	104.6	129.4	130.5
Employees	38.7%	1,143	1,519	2,200	–	–

DIXIE GAS AND OIL CORPORATION

229 LEE HWY
VERONA, VA 244822500
Phone: 540-438-9811
Fax: –
Web: www.dixiegas.com

CEO: –
CFO: –
HR: –
FYE: June 30
Type: Private

Far from looking away local petroleum retailers look to Dixie Gas & Oil a distributor of propane heating oil industrial lubricants and other petroleum products to customers in Virginia and West Virginia. The company also operates gas stations and convenience stores and provides fleeting fueling services. In addition to propane and petroleum Dixie Gas & Oil supplies CITGO- and Castrol-branded commercial and food grade lubricants; it also supplies some retailers with BP and Pure petroleum products. The company was founded as Dixie Bottled Gas Company in 1946. Dixie Gas & Oil's five gas stations/convenience stores offer BP fuels Subway sandwiches and salads as well as convenience food items.

	Annual Growth	06/10	06/11	06/12	06/13	06/14
Sales ($ mil.)	7.6%	–	56.0	62.1	70.6	69.8
Net income ($ mil.)	16.5%	–	–	0.3	0.5	0.4
Market value ($ mil.)	–	–	–	–	–	–
Employees	–	–	–	–	–	115

DIXIE GROUP INC.   NMS: DXYN

104 Nowlin Lane, Suite 101
Chattanooga, TN 37421
Phone: 423 510-7000
Fax: –
Web: www.thedixiegroup.com

CEO: Daniel K Frierson
CFO: Jon A Faulkner
HR: –
FYE: December 27
Type: Public

The Dixie Group takes its business to the rug. Once a textile concern the company has evolved into a maker of tufted broadloom carpets and custom rugs and proprietary yarns used in manufacturing the soft floorcoverings. Its brands Dixie Home Masland Carpets Fabrica International and Candlewick Yarn are differentiated by product price and styling. Dixie markets and sells carpets to high-end residential customers including interior decorators retailers home builders and motorhome and yacht OEMs. Less so it supplies carpet for the specified (contract) market such as architectural and commercial customers as well as consumers through specialty floorcovering retailers.

	Annual Growth	12/10	12/11	12/12	12/13	12/14
Sales ($ mil.)	15.1%	231.3	270.1	266.4	345.1	406.6
Net income ($ mil.)	–	(4.7)	1.0	(0.9)	5.3	(1.4)
Market value ($ mil.)	26.0%	56.1	46.4	50.8	190.7	141.5
Employees	10.9%	1,150	1,171	1,200	1,423	1,740

DLH HOLDINGS CORP   NAS: DLHC

3565 Piedmont Road, NE, Bldg. 3, Suite 700
Atlanta, GA 30305
Phone: 866 952-1647
Fax: –
Web: www.dlhcorp.com

CEO: Zachary C Parker
CFO: Kathryn M Johnbull
HR: –
FYE: September 30
Type: Public

If you run a government facility TeamStaff wants its workers to be on your team. The company provides temporary and permanent medical office administration and technical staffing services to US government facilities nationwide through TeamStaff Government Solutions its core subsidiary. TeamStaff's strategic lines of business include Logistics and Technical Services (expertise in supply chain and inventory management) Healthcare Delivery Solutions (medical and pharmaceutical staff augmentation) and Contingency/Staff Augmentation (disaster and emergency response staffing). The company has contracts with the Department of Defense and Department of Veterans Affairs. It was originally founded in 1969.

	Annual Growth	09/11	09/12	09/13	09/14	09/15
Sales ($ mil.)	11.7%	41.9	49.2	53.5	60.5	65.3
Net income ($ mil.)	–	(4.3)	(2.0)	(0.2)	5.4	8.7
Market value ($ mil.)	14.8%	15.6	10.1	12.2	18.5	27.1
Employees	8.3%	910	1,100	1,100	1,200	1,250

DLT SOLUTIONS LLC

13861 SUNRISE VALLEY DR # 400
HERNDON, VA 20171-6124
Phone: 703-709-7172
Fax: –
Web: www.dlt.com

CEO: –
CFO: Craig Adler
HR: –
FYE: December 31
Type: Private

DLT Solutions is a middleman for G-men. The company resells IT products and services primarily to local state and federal government clients in the US. The company sells and integrates hardware and software from such vendors as Autodesk Oracle NetApp Red Hat and Symantec. DLT's contracts are primarily with the US Department of Defense's Enterprise Software Initiative (ESI) and the US Navy. It also has more than a dozen other contracts with state and city governments. To a smaller extent it offers consulting network design application development training and other professional services. The company's areas of expertise include cloud computing data center consolidation cybersecurity and computer-aided design.

	Annual Growth	12/07	12/08	12/09	12/10	12/11
Sales ($ mil.)	9.3%	–	271.7	–	447.7	354.5
Net income ($ mil.)	18.8%	–	8.7	–	13.0	14.5
Market value ($ mil.)	–	–	–	–	–	–
Employees	–	–	–	–	–	253

DMC OPERATING L.P.

2100 Stemmons Fwy.
Dallas TX 75207
Phone: 214-655-6100
Fax: 214-743-5511
Web: www.brierley.com

CEO: Bill Winsor
CFO: –
HR: –
FYE: December 31
Type: Private

Dallas Market Center (DMC) is where shop owners go to shop. The largest wholesale merchandise market in the world DMC hosts some 50 tradeshow events each year with leading manufacturers showing more than 37000 product lines of apparel garden accessories gifts gourmet food home furnishings and lighting to 200000 retail buyers from all across the globe. DMC operates four buildings that house 2000 permanent custom showrooms as well as temporary exhibit show space. There it hosts fashion shows product displays educational programs and seminars and industry award galas. DMC was founded in 1957 by Trammell Crow and is majority owned by CNL Financial affiliate CNL Lifestyle Properties.

DMX INC.

600 Congress Ave. Fl. 14
Austin TX 78701
Phone: 512-380-8500
Fax: +81-72-753-6880
Web: www.daihatsu.co.jp

CEO: Steve Richards
CFO: Randal Rudniski
HR: –
FYE: December 31
Type: Private

DMX gives the sights sounds and scents of your business a twist. The company provides what it calls "sensory branding" through the distribution of commercial-free music video on-air and on-hold messages and environmental fragrances to companies around the globe. Clients include retailers restaurants hotels health clubs resorts and casinos such as Gold's Gym McDonald's Burberry and Whole Foods. DMX has license agreements with Sony Music Entertainment Universal Music EMI and Warner Music as well as more than 2500 independent record labels. The company also provides music for cable television networks. Founded in 1971 DMX is owned by Mood Media Corporation.

DNB FINANCIAL CORP.

NAS: DNBF

4 Brandywine Avenue
Downingtown, PA 19335
Phone: 610 269-1040
Fax: –
Web: www.dnbfirst.com

CEO: William J. Hieb
CFO: Gerald F. Sopp
HR: –
FYE: December 31
Type: Public

DNB Financial Corporation is the holding company for DNB First a bank with about a dozen branches in Chester and Delaware counties in southeastern Pennsylvania. Founded in 1861 the bank serves area consumers but mainly lends to small and midsized businesses with mortgages secured by commercial property (approximately 35% of its loan portfolio) commercial operating loans (more than 25%) and equipment leases representing most of its financing activity. The bank also writes residential mortgages and consumer loans. Deposit products include checking savings and money market accounts.

	Annual Growth	12/10	12/11	12/12	12/13	12/14
Assets ($ mil.)	4.7%	602.3	607.1	639.6	661.5	723.3
Net income ($ mil.)	7.0%	3.7	4.9	5.2	3.9	4.8
Market value ($ mil.)	24.5%	25.0	29.7	43.1	57.7	60.0
Employees	0.8%	129	130	134	139	133

DO IT BEST CORP.

6502 Nelson Rd.
Fort Wayne IN 46803-1920
Phone: 260-748-5300
Fax: 201-271-0164
Web: www.hartz.com

CEO: Robert N Taylor
CFO: –
HR: –
FYE: June 30
Type: Private - Cooperativ

For home builders and Mr. Fix-its hardware cooperative Do it Best wants you to make the best even better. One of the industry's largest hardware cooperatives it boasts more than 4000 member-owned stores in 50-plus countries but primarily the US. Besides the usual tools and building materials merchandise includes automotive items bicycles camping gear housewares office supplies and small appliances. Customers also can have products specially shipped to their local stores through Do it Best's e-commerce site. The co-op's buying power enables members to offer items at competitive prices. Formerly named Hardware Wholesalers Do it Best was founded in 1945 by Arnold Gerberding.

DOALL COMPANY

1480 S. Wolf Rd.
Wheeling IL 60090
Phone: 847-495-6800
Fax: 203-595-3070
Web: www.cenveo.com

CEO: –
CFO: –
HR: –
FYE: May 31
Type: Private

DoALL wants to be the end-all and be-all of metal cutting. For more than eight decades it has engineered and manufactured saw machinery and accessories and distributed industrial products. Its four businesses include DoALL Sawing which makes saw blades sawing machines and cutting oils; Greenlee Diamond Tool makes diamond and superabrasive products; Continental Hydraulics makes hydraulic pumps valves and power units; and DGI Supply distributes 1500 industrial brands through a national network of more than 40 supply centers. DoALL is owned by the Wilkie family who founded it in 1927.

DOC"S DRUGS LTD.

455 E REED ST
BRAIDWOOD, IL 604082090
Phone: 815-458-6104
Fax: –
Web: www.docsdrugs.com

CEO: –
CFO: –
HR: –
FYE: October 31
Type: Private

After visiting the doc customers in northeastern Illinois can fill their prescriptions at Doc's Drugs. The regional drugstore chain operates more than15 pharmacies under the Doc's Discount Drugs banner. In addition to dispensing prescription medications Doc's Drugs sells medical equipment collectibles electronics and toys as well as offering in-store photo processing. Doc's Drugs also sells more than 100 products online. The company is remodeling many of its stores to focus on its pharmacy operation which accounts for 80% of sales. To that end it is eliminating hardware liquor and groceries from its shelves. Doc's Drugs was founded by Dave Sartoris who runs the company with his son Tony.

	Annual Growth	10/10	10/11	10/12	10/13	10/14
Sales ($ mil.)	3.3%	–	59.6	60.1	60.8	65.7
Net income ($ mil.)	49.2%	–	–	0.3	0.8	0.8
Market value ($ mil.)	–	–	–	–	–	–
Employees	–	–	–	–	–	210

DOCTORS' HOSPITAL INC.

8118 GOOD LUCK RD
LANHAM, MD 207063574
Phone: 301-552-8118
Fax: –
Web: www.dchweb.org

CEO: Philip B Down
CFO: –
HR: –
FYE: June 30
Type: Private

Doctors Community Hospital is an acute care and surgical hospital serving the Washington DC area. The not-for-profit medical center admits 12000 patients each year and has some 220 beds and offers standard and specialty services such as diagnostics emergency and cardiac care diagnostics rehabilitation wound care and neurology. The hospital which has some 600 doctors on staff also includes a women's health center a sleep therapy division and the Joslin Diabetes Center. Established in 1975 Doctors Community Hospital provides community health services such as educational programs and support groups for specific medical conditions.

	Annual Growth	06/08	06/09	06/10	06/11	06/13
Sales ($ mil.)	–	–	0.0	198.4	211.1	181.6
Net income ($ mil.)	–	–	–	(1.6)	16.6	1.3
Market value ($ mil.)	–	–	–	–	–	–
Employees	–	–	–	–	–	1,200

DOCTOR'S ASSOCIATES INC.

325 BIC DR
MILFORD, CT 064613072
Phone: 203-877-4281
Fax: –
Web: www.subway.com

CEO: –
CFO: –
HR: Cathy Savoie
FYE: December 31
Type: Private

You're more likely to catch a sub than a train at these Subway stations. Doctor's Associates owns the Subway chain of sandwich shops the world's largest quick-service restaurant chain by number of locations having surpassed burger giant McDonald's. It boasts about 41500 locations in more than 100 countries. Virtually all Subway restaurants are franchised and offer such fare as hot and cold sub sandwiches turkey wraps and salads. The eateries are located in freestanding buildings as well as in airports convenience stores sports facilities and other locations.

	Annual Growth	12/05	12/06	12/07	12/08	12/10
Assets ($ mil.)	9.3%	–	–	–	95.5	114.1
Net income ($ mil.)	8.4%	–	–	–	6.3	7.5
Market value ($ mil.)	–	–	–	–	–	–
Employees	–	–	–	–	–	650

DOCUMENT CAPTURE TECHNOLOGIES INC   NBB: DCMT

4255 Burton Drive
San Jose, CA 95054
Phone: 408 436-9888
Fax: –
Web: www.docucap.com

CEO: Michael J Campbell
CFO: M Carolyn Ellis
HR: –
FYE: December 31
Type: Public

Like The Lorax Document Capture Technologies speaks for the trees. The company makes digital scanners used to upload paper documents into electronic data. Its line of USB-powered portable image scanners sold under the TravelScan and DocketPORT brand names are used in bank note and check verification devices ID card and passport scanners barcode scanners and business card readers. A handful of customers including Brother Industries NCR and Newell Rubbermaid account for more than half of sales. Subsidiary Syscan Inc. develops contact image sensor (CIS) modules used in fax machines and scanners. Investor Richard Dietl owns more than 35% of the company; Hong Kong-based Syscan Imaging Ltd. holds around 15%.

	Annual Growth	12/08	12/09	12/10	12/11	12/12
Sales ($ mil.)	10.5%	11.6	11.5	14.8	17.7	17.3
Net income ($ mil.)	–	(0.1)	(0.3)	0.3	(0.4)	(0.7)
Market value ($ mil.)	(22.3%)	10.4	7.1	11.9	8.6	3.8
Employees	16.9%	15	22	25	30	28

DOCUMENT SECURITY SYSTEMS INC   ASE: DSS

28 Main Street East, Suite 1525
Rochester, NY 14614
Phone: 585 325-3610
Fax: 585 325-2977
Web: www.dsssecure.com

CEO: Jeffrey Ronaldi
CFO: Philip Jones
HR: –
FYE: December 31
Type: Public

Document Security Systems (DSS) caters to those who are insecure about their security particularly on paper. The company develops anti-counterfeiting products. Its offerings include technology that prevents documents from being accurately scanned or copied and authentication coding that can be used in conjunction with a handheld reader to verify that a document is genuine. DSS also sells paper that displays words such as "void" or "unauthorized copy" if it goes through a copier fax machine or scanner. Customers include corporations governments and financial institutions. DSS is slated to merge with Lexington Technology Group (LTG) in 2013.

	Annual Growth	12/10	12/11	12/12	12/13	12/14
Sales ($ mil.)	8.1%	13.4	13.4	17.1	17.5	18.3
Net income ($ mil.)	–	(4.6)	(3.2)	(4.3)	2.6	(45.9)
Market value ($ mil.)	(46.2%)	248.9	117.7	100.2	95.6	20.8
Employees	1.6%	104	105	107	108	111

DOKA USA LTD.

214 Gates Rd.
Little Ferry NJ 07643
Phone: 201-641-6500
Fax: 201-641-6254
Web: www.doka.com

CEO: Andrew Mair
CFO: Alan Pearson
HR: –
FYE: December 31
Type: Private

Doka USA part of Germany-based Doka Group manufactures sells and rents frameworks for concrete construction projects. Its products include formwork beams panels floor props and supporting frames for walls floors platforms and load-bearing towers. They are used in major public structures such as bridges roadways tunnels airports and dams. The company also offers tie rods and anchors climbing cones and suspension accessories all used to ensure safety when installing formworks. Formerly known as Conesco Doka Doka USA has sales and branch offices in California Florida Georgia Illinois Maryland New Jersey and Texas.

DOLAN COMPANY (THE)   NBB: DOLN

222 South Ninth Street, Suite 2300
Minneapolis, MN 55402
Phone: 612 317-9420
Fax: –
Web: www.thedolancompany.com

CEO: Mark McEachen
CFO: Vicki J Duncomb
HR: –
FYE: December 31
Type: Public

Helping law firms is a big part of the process for this publisher. Formerly Dolan Media Company The Dolan Company is a diversified professional services provider with a significant interest in local business news publishing. Through subsidiary National Default Exchange (NDeX) the company offers mortgage default processing services to lenders loan servicers and law firms around the country. Dolan's Counsel Press and DiscoverReady units provide services for law firms including outsourced document management to support litigation discovery. The company changed its name in 2010 to reflect its focus on providing diversified professional services.

	Annual Growth	12/08	12/09	12/10	12/11	12/12
Sales ($ mil.)	7.6%	189.9	262.9	311.3	285.6	254.3
Net income ($ mil.)	–	14.3	30.8	32.4	19.5	(101.8)
Market value ($ mil.)	(12.4%)	204.0	316.1	430.9	263.7	120.4
Employees	(1.5%)	1,812	1,903	2,034	2,006	1,708

DOLBY LABORATORIES INC   NYS: DLB

1275 Market Street
San Francisco, CA 94103-1410
Phone: 415 558-0200
Fax: –
Web: www.dolby.com

CEO: Kevin J. Yeaman
CFO: Lewis Chew
HR: Andrew (Andy) Dahlkemper
FYE: September 25
Type: Public

Talk about having a sound business model. Dolby Laboratories is the market leader in developing sound processing and noise reduction systems for use in professional and consumer audio and video equipment. Though it does make some of its own products Dolby mostly licenses its technology to other manufacturers. (Licensing accounts for more than 90% of revenue.) The firm has about 4300 patents and more than 900 trademarks worldwide. In film the Dolby Digital format has become the de facto audio standard; its systems equip movie screens around the globe. The company has expanded into digital audio compression. American engineer and physicist Ray Dolby and his family own the more than 40-year-old company.

	Annual Growth	09/11	09/12	09/13	09/14	09/15
Sales ($ mil.)	0.4%	955.5	926.3	909.7	960.2	970.6
Net income ($ mil.)	(12.5%)	309.3	264.3	189.3	206.1	181.4
Market value ($ mil.)	3.4%	2,772.4	3,308.9	3,474.6	4,168.7	3,172.5
Employees	8.1%	1,369	1,480	1,597	1,667	1,867

DOLLAR BANK FSB

3 Gateway Center
Pittsburgh PA 15222
Phone: 412-261-4900
Fax: 412-261-7567
Web: www.dollarbank.com

CEO: Robert Oeler
CFO: Thomas A Kobus
HR: –
FYE: December 31
Type: Private

Founded in 1855 Dollar Bank serves business and retail customers from more than 60 branches and loan offices in the Pittsburgh and Cleveland metropolitan areas. Serving consumers and small business clients the bank offers standard products such as checking and savings accounts CDs mortgages and loans. Dollar Bank also performs private banking corporate banking and correspondent banking services. In addition it offers payment protection insurance and mortgage life/disability coverage; subsidiary Dollar Bank Insurance Agency sells term life insurance.

DOLLAR GENERAL CORP   NYS: DG

100 Mission Ridge
Goodlettsville, TN 37072
Phone: 615 855-4000
Fax: 615 855-5527
Web: www.dollargeneral.com

CEO: Todd J. Vasos
CFO: John W. Garratt
HR: –
FYE: January 30
Type: Public

Dollar General's at ease with living off the crumbs of Wal-Mart. The fast-growing retailer boasts roughly 12200 discount stores in over 40 US states mostly in the South East the Midwest and the Southwest. It generates about 75% of its sales from consumables (including refrigerated shelf-stable and perishable foods) and another 10% from seasonal items. The stores also offer household products (cleaning supplies and health and beauty aids) and apparel. Pricing its items at $10 or less (and 25% of items at or under $1) Dollar General targets low- middle- and fixed-income shoppers. The no-frills stores typically measure about 7400 sq. ft. and are located in small towns that are off the radar of giant discounters.

	Annual Growth	01/11*	02/12	02/13*	01/14	01/15
Sales ($ mil.)	9.7%	13,035.0	14,807.2	16,022.1	17,504.2	18,909.6
Net income ($ mil.)	14.1%	627.9	766.7	952.7	1,025.1	1,065.3
Market value ($ mil.)	24.0%	8,617.9	12,726.6	14,043.5	17,090.1	20,349.2
Employees	5.3%	85,900	90,000	90,500	100,600	105,500

*Fiscal year change

DOLLAR THRIFTY AUTOMOTIVE GROUP INC.   NYSE: DTG

5330 E. 31st St.
Tulsa OK 74135
Phone: 918-660-7700
Fax: 918-669-2934
Web: www.dtag.com

CEO: –
CFO: Steven B Hildebrand
HR: Stephenb Laurent
FYE: December 31
Type: Public

Thrifty drivers looking to get the most for a buck might try Dollar Thrifty Automotive Group (DTG) which rents cars under the Dollar Rent A Car and Thrifty Car Rental brands. Combined Dollar and Thrifty rent cars from some 280 company-owned locations in the US and Canada as well as about 1300 franchise locations in 80-plus countries. Both brands target the airport market; Thrifty also has off-airport locations. The combined DTG fleet of over 100000 vehicles comprises mainly Chrysler Ford and GM cars. Although the brands retain their separate identities key operations and administrative functions have been consolidated under the company umbrella. DTG is owned by Hertz Global Holdings.

DOLLAR TREE, INC.   NMS: DLTR

500 Volvo Parkway
Chesapeake, VA 23320
Phone: 757 321-5000
Fax: –
Web: www.dollartree.com

CEO: Bob Sasser
CFO: Kevin S. Wampler
HR: –
FYE: January 31
Type: Public

Dollars may not grow on trees but Dollar Tree stores work hard to bring in the green. The company operates more than 13200 Dollar Tree Deal$ Dollar Bills and Family Dollar discount stores in 48 US states and the District of Columbia and in five provinces in Canada. Stores carry a mix of housewares toys seasonal items food health and beauty aids gifts and books. At Dollar Tree shops most priced at $1 or less while Family Dollar merchandise is usually less that $10. The stores are located in high-traffic strip centers and malls often in small towns. It purchased fellow discounter Family Dollar in 2015.

	Annual Growth	01/11	01/12*	02/13	02/14*	01/15
Sales ($ mil.)	10.0%	5,882.4	6,630.5	7,394.5	7,840.3	8,602.2
Net income ($ mil.)	10.8%	397.3	488.3	619.3	596.7	599.2
Market value ($ mil.)	8.7%	10,487.8	17,409.0	8,252.0	10,391.1	14,624.1
Employees	9.0%	63,860	72,770	81,920	87,400	90,000

*Fiscal year change

DOMAIN ASSOCIATES L.L.C.

1 Palmer Sq. Ste. 515
Princeton NJ 08542
Phone: 609-683-5656
Fax: 609-683-9789
Web: www.domainvc.com

CEO: –
CFO: –
HR: –
FYE: December 31
Type: Private

Life science companies are the domain of Domain Associates. The venture capital firm invests in pharmaceutical biotechnology and other health care-related companies preferring to participate in the first round of financing and taking an active role in the management and development of its portfolio companies. Domain Associates which has approximately $2.5 billion in capital under management also invests in small public companies in the health care industry and often forms new companies to in-license health care technologies and products. The firm's portfolio includes interests in Altea Therapeutics Cadence Pharmaceuticals and REVA Medical.

DOMINION HOMES INC.

4900 Tuttle Crossing Blvd.
Dublin OH 43016
Phone: 614-356-5000
Fax: 614-356-6010
Web: www.dominionhomes.com

CEO: Donn Borror
CFO: William G Cornely
HR: –
FYE: December 31
Type: Private

Dominion Homes is the master of its domain — some 60 communities in central Ohio and in and around Jefferson Indiana and Louisville and Lexington Kentucky. The company builds single-family entry-level move-up and luxury homes as well as townhomes that range from about 1000 sq. ft. to 3500 sq. ft. Homes are priced between $90000 to more than $300000. Centennial Home Mortgage an affiliate of Wells Fargo Home Mortgage offers financing and affiliate Alliance Title Agency sells title insurance. In 2008 Dominion Homes was taken private by a group of investors including founder and CEO Donald Borror and his BRC Properties plus Angelo Gordon & Co. and Silver Point Capital.

DOMINION RESOURCES BLACK WARRIOR TRUST   NBB: DOMR

Royalty Trust Management, Southwest Bank, 2911 Turtle Creek Boulevard, Suite 850
Dallas, TX 75219
Phone: 855 588-7839
Fax: –
Web: www.dom-dominionblackwarriortrust.com

CEO: –
CFO: –
HR: –
FYE: December 31
Type: Public

Dominion Resources Black Warrior Trust knows that when the wells get old financial warriors (aka shareholders) don't give up on the economic possibilities. The trust holds royalty interests in 532 natural gas producing wells and is set to terminate when these wells no longer produce enough gas to be profitable. The trust receives then distributes to shareholders 65% of the gross proceeds that Dominion Resources (via its subsidiary Dominion Black Warrior Basin) earns by selling the natural gas from its wells in the Black Warrior Basin of Alabama. In 2008 the trust had proved reserves of 22.6 billion cu. ft. of natural gas equivalent.

	Annual Growth	12/10	12/11	12/12	12/13	12/14
Sales ($ mil.)	(8.8%)	10.2	8.4	5.3	6.4	7.1
Net income ($ mil.)	(10.7%)	9.2	7.4	4.2	5.4	5.8
Market value ($ mil.)	(22.1%)	121.3	62.7	23.2	43.7	44.7
Employees	–	–	–	–	–	–

DOMINION RESOURCES INC   NYS: D

120 Tredegar Street
Richmond, VA 23219
Phone: 804 819-2000
Fax: 804 775-5819
Web: www.dom.com

CEO: Paul D. Koonce
CFO: Mark F. McGettrick
HR: –
FYE: December 31
Type: Public

And darkness shall have no dominion .... as long as Dominion Resources powers lights across the territory it serves. Dominion is one of the top energy players in the US. Dominion Generation (its largest revenue generator) manages regulated and non-regulated power plants Through its Dominion Virginia Power unit the company transmits and distributes electricity across 57100 miles of electric distribution lines to 2.5 million customers and natural gas to 1.7 million customers. Subsidiary Dominion Energy trades and markets energy oversees natural gas transmission pipelines and operates underground gas storage facilities (928 billion cu. ft. of capacity.)

	Annual Growth	12/10	12/11	12/12	12/13	12/14
Sales ($ mil.)	(4.9%)	15,197.0	14,379.0	13,093.0	13,120.0	12,436.0
Net income ($ mil.)	(17.4%)	2,808.0	1,408.0	302.0	1,697.0	1,310.0
Market value ($ mil.)	15.8%	24,991.2	31,051.8	30,303.0	37,843.7	44,986.5
Employees	(2.3%)	15,800	15,800	15,500	14,500	14,400

DOMINOS PIZZA INC.   NYS: DPZ

30 Frank Lloyd Wright Drive
Ann Arbor, MI 48105
Phone: 734 930-3030
Fax: –
Web: www.dominos.com

CEO: James G. Stansik
CFO: Jeffrey D. Lawrence
HR: –
FYE: December 28
Type: Public

This company knows the rules of the pizza delivery game. Domino's Pizza runs the world's #2 pizza chain (behind YUM! Brands' Pizza Hut division) with more than 10300 delivery locations in about 70 countries. (The chain includes almost 5000 stores throughout the US.) Domino's menu features several different styles of pizza with a wide array of topping options as well as additional items such as bread sticks cheese bread and chicken wings. Its stores are principally delivery locations and generally do not have any dine-in seating. The company owns and operates about 385 locations in the US while the rest are franchised.

	Annual Growth	01/11	01/12*	12/12	12/13	12/14
Sales ($ mil.)	8.3%	1,570.9	1,652.2	1,678.4	1,802.2	1,993.8
Net income ($ mil.)	22.7%	87.9	105.4	112.4	143.0	162.6
Market value ($ mil.)	81.6%	886.1	1,886.0	2,368.2	3,899.8	5,302.5
Employees	0.3%	10,900	10,000	10,000	10,000	11,000

*Fiscal year change

DON MIGUEL MEXICAN FOODS INC.

1501 W. Orangewood Ave.
Orange CA 92868
Phone: 714-634-8441
Fax: 714-937-0493
Web: www.donmiguel.com

CEO: Jeff Frank
CFO: Dori Reap
HR: Jenny Ortiz
FYE: November 30
Type: Private

Don Miguel Mexican Foods makes tastebuds say "Ole!" The company manufactures and sells frozen and fresh Mexican meals and snacks for the retail market. Its products include burritos chimichangas empanadas enchiladas tacos taquitos tamales quesadillas party trays and family-style dinner entrees all of which are sold under the Don Miguel brand name. Customers include convenience stores (7-Eleven) as well as wholesale clubs (Sams Club and BJ's) and supermarkets. The company's manufacturing facility is in Dallas. Founded in 1908 Don Miguel is owned by MegaMex Foods a joint venture between Hormel Foods and Herdez Del Fuerte which bought the company from a private equity firm in 2010.

DONAHUE SCHRIBER REALTY GROUP INC.

200 E. Baker St. Ste. 100
Costa Mesa CA 92626
Phone: 714-545-1400
Fax: 714-545-4222
Web: www.donahueschriber.com

CEO: –
CFO: Larry Casey
HR: –
FYE: December 31
Type: Private

Donahue Schriber is its own one-stop shopping center. A private real estate investment trust (REIT) the company invests in develops redevelops owns manages and leases neighborhood and community shopping centers in the western US primarily California. It handles everything from project management to marketing of its property holdings which typically feature grocery stores or other anchor retailers. The REIT owns and operates about 95 shopping centers totaling more than 16 million sq. ft. of leasable space. It also provides third-party management services. Donahue Schriber The late Daniel Donahue (the brother of CEO Patrick Donahue) and chairman Thomas Schriber founded the company in 1969.

DONALDSON CO. INC.   NYS: DCI

1400 West 94th Street
Minneapolis, MN 55431
Phone: 952 887-3131
Fax: –
Web: www.donaldson.com

CEO: Tod E. Carpenter
CFO: Scott J. Robinson
HR: –
FYE: July 31
Type: Public

Grime fighter Donaldson is cleaning up the industrial world. The company makes filtration systems designed to remove contaminants from air and liquids. Donaldson's engine products business makes air intake and exhaust systems liquid-filtration systems and replacement parts; products are sold to manufacturers of construction mining and transportation equipment as well as parts distributors and fleet operators. The company's industrial products include dust fume and mist collectors and air filtration systems used in industrial gas turbines computer disk drives and manufacturers' clean rooms. Donaldson operates in more than 40 countries worldwide and has 39 manufacturing plants.

	Annual Growth	07/11	07/12	07/13	07/14	07/15
Sales ($ mil.)	0.8%	2,294.0	2,493.2	2,436.9	2,473.5	2,371.2
Net income ($ mil.)	(2.0%)	225.3	264.3	247.4	260.2	208.1
Market value ($ mil.)	(11.7%)	7,454.1	4,593.8	4,879.2	5,221.1	4,522.5
Employees	(1.0%)	13,000	13,000	12,400	12,500	12,500

DONATOS PIZZERIA LLC

935 Taylor Station Rd.
Columbus OH 43230
Phone: 614-416-7700
Fax: 614-416-7701
Web: www.donatos.com

CEO: –
CFO: –
HR: –
FYE: December 31
Type: Private

You might say this company knows how to toss around some dough. Donatos Pizzeria operates and franchises more than 175 Donatos Pizza restaurants in about half a dozen states primarily in Ohio and surrounding areas. The chain serves several varieties of specialty pizza along with sub sandwiches salads and desserts. Most Donatos locations offer dine-in seating as well as carry-out delivery and take-and-bake pizzas; some eateries also offer catering services for group events. About two-thirds of the pizza joints are company-owned. CEO Jim Grote and his family own the business that he founded in 1963.

DONEGAL GROUP INC.

NMS: DGIC A

1195 River Road, P.O. Box 302
Marietta, PA 17547
Phone: 717 426-1931
Fax: –
Web: www.donegalgroup.com

CEO: Kevin G. Burke
CFO: Jeffrey D. Miller
HR: Charles Smith
FYE: December 31
Type: Public

Risk is Donegal Group's middle name. Through its subsidiaries including Atlantic States Insurance and Southern Insurance Company of Virginia Donegal Group provides clients in 22 mid-Atlantic Midwestern and Southeastern states with personal farm and commercial property/casualty insurance products. The group's personal insurance offerings range from auto and boat policies to homeowners and fire coverage; its commercial insurance products include business owners multiperil and workers' compensation. Donegal's financial services arm owns Union Community Bank with 13 branches in Pennsylvania. Donegal Mutual Insurance controls two-thirds of the company's voting stock.

	Annual Growth	12/10	12/11	12/12	12/13	12/14
Assets ($ mil.)	5.6%	1,174.6	1,290.8	1,336.9	1,385.4	1,458.7
Net income ($ mil.)	6.1%	11.5	0.5	23.1	26.3	14.5
Market value ($ mil.)	2.5%	391.3	382.7	379.4	429.7	431.9
Employees		–	–	–	–	–

DONNELLEY (R.R.) & SONS CO.

NMS: RRD

35 West Wacker Drive
Chicago, IL 60601
Phone: 312 326-8000
Fax: –
Web: www.rrdonnelley.com

CEO: Thomas J. Quinlan
CFO: Daniel N. Leib
HR: –
FYE: December 31
Type: Public

If you can read it R.R. Donnelley & Sons can print it. A leading full-service printing company R.R. Donnelley produces magazines catalogs and books as well as advertising material business forms financial reports and telephone directories. The company offers graphics and prepress services in conjunction with printing. In addition it provides logistics distribution and business process outsourcing services related to getting printed material to its audience. Along with publishers R.R. Donnelley's customers include companies in the advertising financial services healthcare retail and technology industries.

	Annual Growth	12/10	12/11	12/12	12/13	12/14
Sales ($ mil.)	3.7%	10,018.9	10,611.0	10,221.9	10,480.3	11,603.4
Net income ($ mil.)	(14.7%)	221.7	(122.6)	(651.4)	211.2	117.4
Market value ($ mil.)	(1.0%)	3,490.5	2,883.1	1,796.2	4,051.9	3,357.6
Employees	3.7%	58,700	58,000	57,000	57,000	68,000

DOOLEYMACK CONSTRUCTORS INC.

5800 LAKEWOOD RANCH BLVD
LAKEWOOD RANCH, FL 342408479
Phone: 954-484-9800
Fax: –

CEO: Kenneth D Smith
CFO: Wendy L Mack
HR: –
FYE: December 31
Type: Private

DooleyMack Constructors does the heavy lifting on big construction projects. The company provides design and planning construction management and general contracting services for commercial industrial multifamily residential and institutional projects. DooleyMack has built and renovated everything public schools condos and performance arts centers to waste disposal facilities and laboratories. The company mainly operates in the central and southeastern regions of the US and has several offices in Florida as well as locations in Georgia Texas North Carolina and South Carolina. The privately-owned company was founded in 1977 by executives Bill Dooley and Ken Smith. CFO Wendy Mack later joined the firm.

	Annual Growth	12/04	12/05	12/06	12/07	12/08
Sales ($ mil.)	14.8%	–	72.5	83.5	91.0	109.5
Net income ($ mil.)	24.7%	–	–	0.5	1.2	0.8
Market value ($ mil.)		–	–	–	–	–
Employees		–	–	–	–	93

DOONEY & BOURKE INC.

1 Regent St.
Norwalk CT 06855
Phone: 203-853-7515
Fax: 800-326-1496
Web: www.dooney.com

CEO: –
CFO: –
HR: –
FYE: December 31
Type: Private

With young rocker-types actresses and general trendsetters seen spotted with its products this late 20-something company is hardly showing its age. Dooney & Bourke makes high-end handbags and accessories mostly for women but also for men. They're sold in department stores (such as Macy's and Nordstrom) online and by catalog. The company operates about 10 of its own stores internationally including seven locations in the US and a flagship shop in Manhattan. It boasts about 20 US outlets. Best-known for its distinctive initial-covered purses Dooney & Bourke also makes cell phone and iPod cases as well as jewelry luggage apparel shoes totes wallets and assorted accessories.

DOPACO INC.

100 Arrandale Blvd.
Exton PA 19341
Phone: 610-269-1776
Fax: 610-524-9188
Web: www.dopaco.com

CEO: –
CFO: –
HR: –
FYE: December 31
Type: Subsidiary

If your two favorite words in meal planning are "take-out" invite Dopaco to dinner. Dopaco manufactures take-out containers for customers in the food service industry. Its lineup includes folding cartons hot and cold beverage cups and accompanying lids and carriers as well as cartons for fries and clamshells and food trays for pizza and hot dogs. The company also touts customized packaging design services to meet menu and marketing requirements. Customers have included such notable names as Jack in the Box Burger King McDonald's and Wendy's. In spring 2011 Canadian tissue and packaging paper manufacturer Cascades sold Dopaco to Reynolds Group Holdings.

DORCHESTER MINERALS LP   NMS: DMLP

3838 Oak Lawn Avenue, Suite 300
Dallas, TX 75219
Phone: 214 559-0300
Fax: –
Web: www.dmlp.net

CEO: William Casey McManemin
CFO: Leslie A Moriyama
HR: –
FYE: December 31
Type: Public

The stakeholders of Dorchester Minerals are enjoying the benefits of three natural resource exploitation enterprises which came together as one. The oil and gas exploration company was formed by the 2003 merger of oil trust Dorchester Hugoton with Republic Royalty and Spinnaker Royalty. Dorchester Minerals' holdings include about 141600 net acres in Texas and 62850 net acres in Montana. The company holds assets (producing and nonproducing mineral royalty overriding royalty net profits and leasehold interests) in properties in 574 counties in 25 states. In 2009 Dorchester Minerals reported proved reserves of 60.3 billion cu. ft. of natural gas and 3.3 million barrels of oil and condensate.

	Annual Growth	12/10	12/11	12/12	12/13	12/14
Sales ($ mil.)	1.6%	61.1	69.5	63.2	65.9	65.2
Net income ($ mil.)	6.7%	34.9	42.2	38.0	43.6	45.2
Market value ($ mil.)	(1.8%)	842.7	695.1	623.6	796.9	783.1
Employees	2.4%	20	28	26	21	22

DOREL JUVENILE GROUP INC.

2525 State St.
Columbus IN 47201-7494
Phone: 812-372-0141
Fax: 812-372-0893
Web: www.djgusa.com

CEO: –
CFO: –
HR: –
FYE: December 31
Type: Subsidiary

Getting little ones around town safely is Dorel Juvenile Group's primary push. The global group makes children's car seats strollers high chairs changing tables monitors and toddler beds. Dorel Juvenile's brands include Cosco Juvenile Maxi-Cosi and Safety 1st and in Europe Bebe Confort Maxi-Cosi Quinny Baby Relax Safety 1st HOPPOP and BABY ART. Under license it also makes the name brand infant safety products of Eddie Bauer Playskool and Disney Baby. Dorel Juvenile is part of Canadian Dorel Industries. Formed in 2000 the group which combined the child safety lineup of Safety 1st with parent Dorel's juvenile business Cosco has expanded internationally and generates about 45% of total sales.

DORMAN PRODUCTS INC   NMS: DORM

3400 East Walnut Street
Colmar, PA 18915
Phone: 215 997-1800
Fax: –
Web: www.dormanproducts.com

CEO: Mathias J. Barton
CFO: Matthew S Kohnke
HR: Penny Boyer
FYE: December 27
Type: Public

Got parts? Dorman does. From its stock of more than 140000 products Dorman Products is a leading supplier of automotive replacement parts (including brake parts) fasteners and service line products to the automotive aftermarket. It also provides household hardware and organization items to mass merchants. About 85% of revenue comes from parts sold under Dorman's sub-brands which include AutoGrade FirstStop and OE Solutions. Dorman sells to auto aftermarket retailers and warehouse distributors (such as AutoZone CARQUEST) as well as to parts manufacturers for resale under private labels. Dorman distributes its products in the North America Asia Europe and the Middle East.

	Annual Growth	12/10	12/11	12/12	12/13	12/14
Sales ($ mil.)	13.3%	455.7	529.3	570.4	664.5	751.5
Net income ($ mil.)	18.2%	46.1	53.3	71.0	81.9	90.0
Market value ($ mil.)	7.9%	1,281.6	1,315.1	1,216.1	1,961.8	1,740.0
Employees	10.8%	1,185	1,265	1,321	1,452	1,785

DORSEY & WHITNEY LLP

50 S. 6th St. Ste. 1500
Minneapolis MN 55402-1498
Phone: 612-340-2600
Fax: 612-340-2868
Web: www.dorsey.com

CEO: –
CFO: Roderick N Dolan
HR: –
FYE: December 31
Type: Private - Partnershi

Dorsey & Whitney is more than a big fish in the land of 1000 lakes. Founded in 1912 the law firm has grown into a truly global practice with more than 600 lawyers operating in about 20 offices across the US Canada Europe and Asia. Traditionally strong in matters of mergers and acquisitions corporate finance and litigation the firm is focused on intellectual property patent and trademark issues in the international arena. It has expertise in Canadian cross-border transactions and has conducted US securities work in India China and Hong Kong.

DOT FOODS INC.

1 Dot Way
Mt. Sterling IL 62353
Phone: 217-773-4411
Fax: 217-773-3321
Web: www.dotfoods.com

CEO: –
CFO: William H Metzinger
HR: –
FYE: December 31
Type: Private

You don't have to buy a lot to work with Dot. A leading foodservice redistributor Dot Foods hauls more than 60000 dry frozen and refrigerated products from roughly 700 food industry manufacturers to customers who buy in less-than-truckload quantities. The company also offers foodservice equipment and supplies. Dot's customer base consists of more than 3300 distributors nationwide (including convenience store retail food and vending wholesalers as well as foodservice suppliers). The company also sells food ingredients to dairies bakeries confectioners and meat processors.

DOT HILL SYSTEMS CORP.   NMS: HILL

1351 S. Sunset Street
Longmont, CO 80501
Phone: 303 845-3200
Fax: –
Web: www.dothill.com

CEO: –
CFO: –
HR: –
FYE: December 31
Type: Public

Dot Hill Systems designs and markets RAID (redundant array of independent disks) storage devices that are used in corporate data centers and other network environments by enterprises in data-intensive industries such as financial services and telecommunications. It also makes entry-level and mid-range storage area network (SANs) and fibre channel systems and it provides storage system and data management software. Dot Hill's products are sold under the Assured brand. Most of the company's sales are made to manufacturing partners namely including Hewlett-Packard which accounts for nearly three-quarters of sales. Dot Hill has international offices in Germany Israel Japan and the UK.

	Annual Growth	12/09	12/10	12/11	12/12	12/13
Sales ($ mil.)	(3.1%)	234.4	252.5	197.5	194.5	206.6
Net income ($ mil.)	–	(13.6)	(13.3)	(22.0)	(15.0)	5.1
Market value ($ mil.)	15.4%	112.4	103.5	78.7	55.4	199.3
Employees	3.4%	285	293	322	324	326

DOUGLAS DYNAMICS, INC.   NYS: PLOW

7777 North 73rd Street
Milwaukee, WI 53223
Phone: 414 354-2310
Fax: –
Web: www.douglasdynamics.com

CEO: James L. Janik
CFO: Robert McCormick
HR: –
FYE: December 31
Type: Public

Let it snow Let it snow Let it snow! It's a song made to order for Douglas Dynamics. The company makes snowplows and sand-and-salt spreading equipment for light trucks. One of the biggest manufacturers in its industry the company sells its lineup under brand names Western Fisher Snowex Turfex Sweepex and Blizzard via equipment distributors. It also supplies related parts and accessories. End customers are mainly snowplowers in the business of removing snow and ice for municipalities and commercial and private owners in the Midwest East and Northeast US as well as throughout Canada. Douglas traces its roots back to the 1970s.

	Annual Growth	12/10	12/11	12/12	12/13	12/14
Sales ($ mil.)	14.5%	176.8	208.8	140.0	194.3	303.5
Net income ($ mil.)	121.4%	1.7	19.0	6.0	11.6	40.0
Market value ($ mil.)	9.1%	337.6	325.8	320.6	374.8	477.5
Employees	21.9%	450	525	465	520	993

DOUGLAS EMMETT INC   NYS: DEI

808 Wilshire Boulevard, Suite 200
Santa Monica, CA 90401
Phone: 310 255-7700
Fax: –
Web: www.douglasemmett.com

CEO: Jordan L. Kaplan
CFO: Mona Gisler
HR: –
FYE: December 31
Type: Public

Office Space is more than the name of a cult movie to Douglas Emmett. The self-administered and self-managed real estate investment trust (REIT) invests in commercial real estate in Southern California and Hawaii. It owns about 50 Class A office properties (totaling 13.3 million sq. ft.) mostly in the heart of Hollywood and surrounding areas. Its office holdings account for about 85% of its total revenues. The REIT also owns nearly 2900 apartment units in tony neighborhoods of West Los Angeles and Honolulu. Douglas Emmett's portfolio includes some of the most notable addresses on the West Coast including the famed Sherman Oaks Galleria Burbank's Studio Plaza and office tower 100 Wilshire.

	Annual Growth	12/10	12/11	12/12	12/13	12/14
Sales ($ mil.)	1.2%	570.8	575.3	579.0	591.5	599.5
Net income ($ mil.)	–	(26.4)	1.5	22.9	45.3	44.6
Market value ($ mil.)	14.4%	2,404.8	2,642.4	3,375.5	3,374.0	4,114.3
Employees	0.9%	540	530	520	500	560

DOVER CORP   NYS: DOV

3005 Highland Parkway
Downers Grove, IL 60515
Phone: 630 541-1540
Fax: –
Web: www.dovercorporation.com

CEO: William W. (Bill) Spurgeon
CFO: Brad M. Cerepak
HR: Scott Greenhouse
FYE: December 31
Type: Public

The "D" in Dover could stand for diversity. Dover manages more than 30 companies that make equipment ranging from car wash systems to aerospace components. Dover operates in four segments: engineered systems (products for printing and identification transportation waste handling and industrial markets) energy (extraction and handling of oil and gas); fluids (fluid handling products for oil and gas chemical and hygienic markets); and refrigeration and food equipment (systems and products serving the commercial refrigeration and food service industries). Dover traces its historical roots back to 1955.

	Annual Growth	12/11	12/12	12/13	12/14	12/15
Sales ($ mil.)	(3.3%)	7,950.1	8,104.3	8,729.8	7,752.7	6,956.3
Net income ($ mil.)	(0.7%)	895.2	811.1	1,003.1	775.2	869.8
Market value ($ mil.)	1.4%	8,998.0	10,185.3	14,964.1	11,116.9	9,503.3
Employees	(6.5%)	34,000	35,000	37,000	27,000	26,000

DOVER DOWNS GAMING & ENTERTAINMENT, INC.   NYS: DDE

1131 North DuPont Highway
Dover, DE 19901
Phone: 302 674-4600
Fax: –
Web: www.doverdowns.com

CEO: –
CFO: Timothy R Horne
HR: Janie Libby
FYE: December 31
Type: Public

Dover Downs Gaming & Entertainment is betting on being the first stop for gamblers in the First State. The company operates three facilities all in Dover Delaware adjacent to Dover Motorsports' Dover Downs International Speedway. Dover Downs Casino a 165000 square-foot facility has more than 2700 video slot machines; Dover Downs Hotel and Conference Center is a 500-room luxury hotel featuring ballroom concert hall banquet dining meeting room and spa facilities; and Dover Downs Raceway features harness racing and simulcast horse race betting. Dover Downs' video slot operations are operated and administered by the Delaware State Lottery Office. Dover Downs was spun off from Dover Motorsports in 2002.

	Annual Growth	12/10	12/11	12/12	12/13	12/14
Sales ($ mil.)	(6.1%)	238.1	239.9	225.9	197.2	185.4
Net income ($ mil.)	–	6.7	5.4	4.8	0.0	(0.7)
Market value ($ mil.)	(29.7%)	111.4	70.1	72.1	48.5	27.2
Employees	0.8%	1,346	1,346	1,289	1,465	1,391

DOVER MOTORSPORTS, INC.   NYS: DVD

1131 North DuPont Highway
Dover, DE 19901
Phone: 302 883-6500
Fax: 302 672-0100
Web: www.dovermotorsports.com

CEO: –
CFO: Timothy R Horne
HR: Janie Libby
FYE: December 31
Type: Public

This company makes its money when rubber meets the pavement at its racetrack. Dover Motorsports host more several auto racing events each year at its flagship Dover International Speedway in Delaware. The track hold events sponsored by all the major US racing leagues including NASCAR the Indy Racing League and the National Hot Rod Association though stock car racing accounts for 80% of sales. Dover Motorsports and Dover Downs Gaming & Entertainment were operating as one company before being separated in a spin-off in 2002. In 2014 the company sold off its Nashville area racetrack.

	Annual Growth	12/10	12/11	12/12	12/13	12/14
Sales ($ mil.)	(7.7%)	63.0	51.9	46.7	46.2	45.7
Net income ($ mil.)	–	(8.2)	(9.2)	4.6	2.0	3.1
Market value ($ mil.)	10.0%	65.2	38.1	61.9	91.9	95.6
Employees	(3.9%)	74	58	54	57	63

DOVER SADDLERY INC   NAS: DOVR

525 Great Road
Littleton, MA 01460
Phone: 978 952-8062
Fax: –
Web: www.doversaddlery.com

CEO: Stephen L Day
CFO: David R Pearce
HR: –
FYE: December 31
Type: Public

Dover Saddlery is an upscale specialty retailer and direct marketer of equestrian products. The company's specialty is English-style riding gear and its selection features riding apparel tack and stable supplies as well as horse health care products. Its brand-name products include names such as Ariat Grand Prix Mountain Horse Passier and Prestige. Dover operates more than 20 retail stores mostly on the East Coast and in Texas under the Dover Saddlery and Smith Brothers banners (Western-style gear) and it also markets products on its website and in catalogs. The company was founded in 1975 by US Equestrian Team members including company directors Jim and Dave Powers.

	Annual Growth	12/09	12/10	12/11	12/12	12/13
Sales ($ mil.)	5.3%	76.2	78.2	80.8	86.0	93.8
Net income ($ mil.)	15.2%	0.9	2.0	1.7	1.6	1.6
Market value ($ mil.)	24.2%	12.0	13.9	21.4	17.7	28.6
Employees	8.8%	520	497	565	614	729

DOW AGROSCIENCES LLC

9330 Zionsville Rd.
Indianapolis IN 46268
Phone: 317-337-3000
Fax: 415-364-2695
Web: www.tweisel.com

CEO: –
CFO: –
HR: Jason Kilgore
FYE: December 31
Type: Subsidiary

Dow AgroSciences is all about growth — crop growth to be exact. The Dow Chemical subsidiary operates as part of its parent's Agricultural Sciences operating segment developing crop protection products such as insecticides herbicides fungicides and fumigants for agricultural industrial and commercial pest control. Its seed technology business called Seeds Traits & Oils develops genetically modified (GM) resilient seeds and healthy oils like canola. With a broad and balanced product portfolio other offerings include vegetation management and turf products. Its AgroFresh unit makes products to keep fruits vegetables and flowers fresh.

DOW CHEMICAL CO.   NYS: DOW

2030 Dow Center
Midland, MI 48674
Phone: 989 636-1000
Fax: 989 638 1740
Web: www.dow.com

CEO: Andrew N. Liveris
CFO: Howard I. Ungerleider
HR: Johanna S ¶derstr ¶m
FYE: December 31
Type: Public

The Tao of Dow Chemical is its integrated production of plastics chemicals hydrocarbons and agrochemicals. The largest chemical company in the US and #2 worldwide behind BASF Dow also makes performance plastics (engineering plastics polyurethanes and materials) for Dow Automotive. It uses chlorine-based and hydrocarbon-based raw materials to make more than 6000 finished chemical products at 201 sites in 35 countries. The maker of Styrofoam insulation also is the world's #1 producer of chlorine and caustic soda and a top maker of ethylene dichloride and vinyl chloride monomer. Dow also owns 50% of silicone products maker Dow Corning. In late 2015 Dow agreed to merge with Dupont.

	Annual Growth	12/11	12/12	12/13	12/14	12/15
Sales ($ mil.)	(5.0%)	59,985.0	56,786.0	57,080.0	58,167.0	48,778.0
Net income ($ mil.)	29.4%	2,742.0	1,182.0	4,787.0	3,772.0	7,685.0
Market value ($ mil.)	15.7%	32,123.2	36,110.1	49,592.2	50,943.7	57,500.2
Employees	(1.1%)	51,705	54,000	53,000	53,000	49,500

DOW JONES & COMPANY INC.

1155 Avenue of the Americas 7th Fl.
New York NY 10036
Phone: 212-416-2000
Fax: 413-592-4783
Web: www.dj.com

CEO: William Lewis
CFO: Anna Sedgley
HR: –
FYE: December 31
Type: Subsidiary

This company covers the news from Wall Street to Main Street. Dow Jones & Company is a leading provider of news and information with a portfolio of newspapers and magazines anchored by The Wall Street Journal the #1 daily paper in the US with a circulation of more than 2 million. Dow Jones also publishes international editions of the Journal serving readers in Asia and Europe. Its Dow Jones Local Media Group meanwhile runs a collection of local papers serving smaller communities on the East and West coasts. Beyond newspapers Dow Jones owns business magazine Barron's financial news site MarketWatch SmartMoney magazine and research service Factiva. The company is a subsidiary of News Corporation.

DOWLING COLLEGE

150 IDLE HOUR BLVD
OAKDALE, NY 11769-1999
Phone: 631-244-3000
Fax: –
Web: www.dowling.edu

CEO: –
CFO: –
HR: –
FYE: June 30
Type: Private

Dowling College is private but not exclusive. The college offers undergraduate and graduate educational opportunities from campuses in Oakdale Shirley and Melville New York. Dowling enrolls about 6500 students who can earn bachelors masters and doctoral degrees from four schools: Arts and Sciences the Townsend School of Business Education and Aviation. Popular degrees include business administration psychology elementary education and special education. Dowling's Aviation program includes a fleet of aircraft and offers flight simulation and air traffic control courses. Dowling College has a student/faculty ratio of 17:1.

	Annual Growth	06/07	06/08	06/09	06/09	06/10
Sales ($ mil.)	–	–	–	(1,491.7)	73.6	78.5
Net income ($ mil.)	6824.8%	–	–	0.0	(3.6)	1.1
Market value ($ mil.)	–	–	–	–	–	–
Employees	–	–	–	–	–	1,030

DOYLESTOWN HOSPITAL HEALTH AND WELLNESS CENTER INC.

595 W STATE ST
DOYLESTOWN, PA 189012597
Phone: 215-345-2200
Fax: –
Web: www.doylestown-hospital.net

CEO: –
CFO: Dan Upton
HR: –
FYE: June 30
Type: Private

It takes a village to own a hospital and Doylestown Hospital is owned by the local women's civic organization Village Improvement Association (VIA Health). Founded in 1923 the hospital serves southeastern Pennsylvania and neighboring areas of New Jersey. With some 240 beds Doylestown Hospital provides a variety of acute and tertiary medical services. Specialties include cardiac surgery cancer care (as part of the University of Pennsylvania Cancer Network) and orthopedics. Affiliated with the hospital are two Pine Run nursing and assisted-living centers. Doylestown Hospital the flagship facility of the Doylestown Health system.

	Annual Growth	06/07	06/08	06/09	06/10	06/13
Sales ($ mil.)	–	–	(467.8)	202.6	234.4	265.6
Net income ($ mil.)	26.6%	–	–	6.2	3.5	16.0
Market value ($ mil.)	–	–	–	–	–	–
Employees	–	–	–	–	–	2,853

DPL INC.   NYSE: DPL

1065 Woodman Dr.
Dayton OH 45432
Phone: 937-224-6000
Fax: 937-259-7147
Web: www.dplinc.com

CEO: Phil Herrington
CFO: Craig Jackson
HR: –
FYE: December 31
Type: Public

When it's dark in Dayton DPL turns on the lights. The holding company's main subsidiary regulated utility Dayton Power and Light (DP&L) which was established in 1911 brightens the night for more than 500000 electricity customers in 24 counties in west central Ohio. Nonregulated subsidiary DPL Energy operates DPL's 10 power plants which produce more than 3800 MW of primarily coal-fired generating capacity. It also sells power to energy marketing affiliate DPL Energy Resources to meet the electric requirements of its retail customers. Other activities include street lighting and financial support services. In 2011 DPL was acquired by AES in a $4.7 billion transaction.

DPR CONSTRUCTION INC.

1450 VETERANS BLVD OFC
REDWOOD CITY, CA 940632618
Phone: 650-474-1450
Fax: –
Web: www.dpr.com

CEO: Douglas E Woods
CFO: Michele Leiva
HR: –
FYE: December 31
Type: Private

From bio labs to wafer fabs DPR Construction runs the gamut for its high-tech and health care clients. The employee-owned firm provides general contracting and construction management services for the advanced technology/mission-critical life sciences health care higher education and corporate office markets. The construction firm specializes in developing retail stores hospitals data centers clean rooms laboratories manufacturing facilities and green buildings. Altogether DPR Construction boasts about 20 regional offices nationwide. Company head Doug Woods former CEO Peter Nosler and secretary/treasurer Ron Davidowski (the D P and R in DPR Construction) founded the firm in 1990.

	Annual Growth	12/0-3	12/0-2	12/0-1	12/00	12/08
Sales ($ mil.)	(0.8%)	–	–	–	1,958.1	1,836.1
Net income ($ mil.)	13.0%	–	–	–	25.7	68.5
Market value ($ mil.)	–	–	–	–	–	–
Employees	–	–	–	–	–	2,300

DR PEPPER SNAPPLE GROUP INC   NYS: DPS

5301 Legacy Drive
Plano, TX 75024
Phone: 972 673-7000
Fax: –
Web: www.drpeppersnapplegroup.com

CEO: Larry D. Young
CFO: Martin M. (Marty) Ellen
HR: Lain Hancock
FYE: December 31
Type: Public

For many consumers it's a snap decision about which doctor to choose. Dr Pepper Snapple Group (DPS) is the bottler and distributor of Dr Pepper soda and Snapple drinks. Serving Canada Mexico and the US the company offers a vast portfolio of non-alcoholic beverages including flavored carbonated soft drinks and non-carbonated soft drinks along with ready-to-drink non-carbonated teas juices juice drinks and mixers. Among its brands are Dr Pepper and Snapple of course along with A&W Root Beer Hawaiian Punch Mott's and Schweppes. It has some cult favorites as well including Vernors Squirt and Royal Crown Cola. DPS is the #3 soda business in North America after #1 Coke and #2 Pepsi.

	Annual Growth	12/10	12/11	12/12	12/13	12/14
Sales ($ mil.)	2.1%	5,636.0	5,903.0	5,995.0	5,997.0	6,121.0
Net income ($ mil.)	7.4%	528.0	606.0	629.0	624.0	703.0
Market value ($ mil.)	19.5%	6,784.4	7,618.0	8,524.9	9,400.9	13,831.2
Employees	0.0%	19,000	19,000	19,000	19,000	19,000

DRAKE BEAM MORIN INC.

750 3rd Ave. 28th Fl.
New York NY 10017
Phone: 212-692-7700
Fax: 212-297-0426
Web: www.dbm.com

CEO: Robert Gasparini
CFO: J Todd King
HR: –
FYE: December 31
Type: Subsidiary

Drake Beam Morin (DBM) is always in transition. The company provides strategic human resources services focusing on employee selection development retention and transition. DBM is best known for outplacement and transition services which help corporate clients plan for workforce reductions and assist former employees in finding new positions. It aids clients in improving hiring practices through workshops research studies and online hiring site JobScout. DBM also offers executive coaching and training and offers research analysis and consulting to increase employee retention. In mid-2011 the company was acquired by Adecco the world's largest staffing agency.

DRAKE UNIVERSITY

2507 UNIVERSITY AVE
DES MOINES, IA 503114505
Phone: 515-271-2011
Fax: –
Web: www.artsci.drake.edu

CEO: –
CFO: –
HR: –
FYE: June 30
Type: Private

You won't find duck duck goose as part of the curriculum at Drake University. The Des Moines Iowa school provides undergraduate and graduate education programs for some 5500 students through its six colleges and schools: arts and sciences business and public administration education journalism and mass communications law and pharmacy and health sciences. It has a 15:1 student-to-faculty ratio. A private school Drake University was founded in 1881 with seed money from General Francis Marion Drake a Civil War general and former Iowa governor banker railroad builder and attorney. Drake University also hosts the Drake Relays one of the largest track and field events in the US.

	Annual Growth	05/09	05/10	05/12	05/13*	06/14
Sales ($ mil.)	12.4%	–	123.4	180.6	184.7	196.9
Net income ($ mil.)	29.6%	–	–	5.3	4.6	8.9
Market value ($ mil.)	–	–	–	–	–	–
Employees	–	–	–	–	–	830

*Fiscal year change

DREAMS INC.   NYSE AMEX: DRJ

2 S. University Dr. Ste. 325
Plantation FL 33324
Phone: 954-377-0002
Fax: 954-475-8785
Web: www.fanaticsinc.com/

CEO: –
CFO: –
HR: –
FYE: December 31
Type: Private

Talk about a dream team: Troy Aikman Emmitt Smith Randy Moss and Jerry Rice; these sports heroes mean money to Dreams. It owns and operates about 15 US stores under the Field of Dreams and FansEdge banners as well as about five franchised stores. The stores network sells signed balls jerseys photos plaques and other collectibles which it licenses from the NFL MLB NHL NBA NCAA and NASCAR. It also reaches shoppers via the FansEdge catalog and online at FansEdge.com and ProSportsMemorabilia.com. The company's Mounted Memories makes and distributes sports memorabilia; its Greene Organization handles special appearances endorsements and other off-field activities for athletes. It's owned by Fanatics.

DREAMWORKS ANIMATION SKG INC   NMS: DWA

1000 Flower Street
Glendale, CA 91201
Phone: 818 695-5000
Fax: –
Web: www.dreamworksanimation.com

CEO: Jeffrey Katzenberg
CFO: Fazal Merchant
HR: –
FYE: December 31
Type: Public

While live action isn't a nightmare for DreamWorks Animation SKG this company definitely prefers CGI. DreamWorks Animation has produced more than 30 computer-animated family-friendly features — including high-earning hits such as Shrek the Third Shrek 2 and Madagascar. (Its Shrek 2 is one of the highest grossing films of all time at the domestic box office.) The studio's movies are distributed and marketed by Twentieth Century Fox. DreamWorks Animation earns most of its revenues from distributing its films in theaters and ancillary markets such as home entertainment and cable and broadcast TV. In 2004 former parent DreamWorks spun off DreamWorks Animation as a separate company.

	Annual Growth	12/10	12/11	12/12	12/13	12/14
Sales ($ mil.)	(3.4%)	784.8	706.0	749.8	706.9	684.6
Net income ($ mil.)	–	170.6	86.8	(36.4)	55.1	(309.6)
Market value ($ mil.)	(6.7%)	2,524.8	1,421.7	1,419.6	3,041.4	1,913.1
Employees	6.5%	2,100	2,100	2,400	2,200	2,700

DREAMWORKS STUDIOS

100 Universal City Plaza Dr. Bldg. 5121
Universal City CA 91608
Phone: 818-733-9300
Fax: 610-838-2031
Web: p2ionline.com

CEO: Michael Wright
CFO: Jeff Small
HR: –
FYE: December 31
Type: Private

Steven Spielberg has long since realized his dream. The filmmaker's DreamWorks Studios is a producer of movies and TV shows (I Love You Man; The United States of Tara). The company was founded in 1994 by Spielberg animation guru Jeffrey Katzenberg and recording industry maven David Geffen as a diversified media firm. It struggled with any business beyond films and TV and later shed its arcade business and a music label. Money-maker DreamWorks Animation was spun off to shareholders as a separate company in 2004. DreamWorks Studios operates through a financing partnership with Reliance Big Entertainment which distributes its movies in India. DreamWorks Studios also has a distribution deal with Disney.

DRESSER INC.

15455 Dallas Pkwy. Ste. 1100
Addison TX 75001
Phone: 972-361-9800
Fax: 972-361-9903
Web: www.dresser.com

CEO: Greg Cominos
CFO: –
HR: –
FYE: December 31
Type: Subsidiary

Is your energy business all dressed up with no place to flow? Learn to love Dresser. The company formerly Dresser Industries (and once a part of Halliburton) makes flow control products (relief valves actuators meters fittings and the like for oil and gas exploration) measurement systems (gas pumps and point of sale terminals made by business unit Wayne) power and compression systems (Waukesha engines fuel testing systems) and other infrastructure technologies (Roots blowers and compressors piping and pumps). Dresser serves customers in the oil and gas and power generation industries as well as water and wastewater and others worldwide. In early 2011 GE acquired Dresser for $3 billion.

DRESSER-RAND GROUP INC.   NYSE: DRC

10205 Westheimer Rd. West8 Tower Ste. 1000
Houston TX 77042
Phone: 713-354-6100
Fax: 713-354-6110
Web: www.dresser-rand.com

CEO: –
CFO: Heribert Stumpf
HR: Jennifer Maas
FYE: December 31
Type: Public

Dresser-Rand is going in circles but that's a good thing. The company is a leading maker of industrial rotating equipment that includes steam and gas turbines centrifugal and reciprocating compressors hot gas expanders and control systems. It makes new and replacement units and offers aftermarket repair and upgrades for its own and third-party products. Dresser-Rand serves customers in the oil and gas power and chemical and petrochemical markets through 12 manufacturing and nearly 40 service facilities in about 30 countries. More than 80% of its sales come from energy infrastructure and oilfield projects. Chevron BP Royal Dutch Shell Exxon Mobil and Dow Chemical are among its blue-chip customers.

DREW INDUSTRIES, INC.   NYS: DW

3501 County Road 6 East
Elkhart, IN 46514
Phone: 574 535-1125
Fax: –
Web: www.drewindustries.com

CEO: Jason D. Lippert
CFO: David M. Smith
HR: –
FYE: December 31
Type: Public

Drew Industries makes wanderlust — in comfort and style — a possibility. The company manufactures aluminum and vinyl windows and doors and other products (furniture and slide-out walls) for travel trailers and fifth-wheel recreational vehicles (RVs) (some 85% of sales) and manufactured housing (MH). Drew does business via two subsidiaries: Kinro produces windows doors and screens and Lippert Components churns out axles ramps and chassis parts as well as specialty trailers for hauling boats and snowmobiles. Brands include Equa-Flex Happijac RV Lock Solera Ground Control and Level Up.

	Annual Growth	12/10	12/11	12/12	12/13	12/14
Sales ($ mil.)	20.1%	572.8	681.2	901.1	1,015.6	1,190.8
Net income ($ mil.)	22.1%	28.0	30.1	37.3	50.1	62.3
Market value ($ mil.)	22.4%	541.9	585.0	769.2	1,221.1	1,218.0
Employees	18.0%	3,016	4,130	5,179	5,109	5,845

DREW UNIVERSITY

36 MADISON AVE
MADISON, NJ 079401493
Phone: 973-408-3000
Fax: –
Web: www.home.drew.edu

CEO: –
CFO: Michael Groener
HR: –
FYE: June 30
Type: Private

Drew University draws interest with its seminary. The school is a liberal arts college that offers both graduate school and as many as 30 undergraduate degrees including master's and Ph.D. studies in religion from the Drew Theological School. It's the home of the Caspersen School of Graduate Studies. The educational institution's campus is located in Madison New Jersey on 186 wooded acres in the foothills of northern New Jersey. The school boasts an enrollment of about 2370 students and has NCAA Division III teams playing as the Drew Rangers. With more than 150 faculty members of which 98% hold terminal degrees Drew University boasts a student/faculty ratio of 10:1 and an average class size of 17.

	Annual Growth	06/03	06/04	06/05	06/08	06/09
Sales ($ mil.)	(2.9%)	–	64.4	101.9	86.1	55.5
Net income ($ mil.)	–	–	–	12.2	(21.9)	0.0
Market value ($ mil.)	–	–	–	–	–	–
Employees	–	–	–	–	–	550

DREXEL UNIVERSITY

3141 CHESTNUT ST
PHILADELPHIA, PA 191042875
Phone: 215-895-2000
Fax: –
Web: www.drexel.edu

CEO: George W. Gephart
CFO: Jeff Eberly
HR: –
FYE: June 30
Type: Private

Drexel doesn't want to train its dragons but to educate them in a wide range of disciplines. Drexel University (home of the Drexel Dragons) is a private coeducational institution of higher learning with an enrollment of more than 26000 undergraduate and graduate students and a student-teacher ratio of about 17:1. It operates more than a dozen schools and colleges in the US; the Drexel University College of Medicine is the one of the country's largest private medical schools. Drexel runs a mandatory co-operative education program that helps students gain real-world experience while supplying local employers with trained workers. Philadelphia financier and philanthropist Anthony Drexel founded the university in 1891.

	Annual Growth	12/07	12/08*	06/11	06/12	06/13
Sales ($ mil.)	–	–	0.0	897.0	910.8	965.3
Net income ($ mil.)	(19.6%)	–	–	166.4	34.4	107.5
Market value ($ mil.)	–	–	–	–	–	–
Employees	–	–	–	–	–	2,868

*Fiscal year change

DREYER'S GRAND ICE CREAM HOLDINGS INC.

5929 College Ave.
Oakland CA 94618
Phone: 510-652-8187
Fax: 510-450-4621
Web: www.nestleusa.com/en/brands/ice-cream/dreyers.

CEO: Michael T Mitchell
CFO: Steve Barbour
HR: –
FYE: December 31
Type: Subsidiary

This company gets in its last licks; Dreyer's Grand Ice Cream manufactures premium ice creams and other frozen dairy desserts. Products are marketed to food retailers and foodservice operators under the Dreyer's brand in the western US and Texas and under the Edy's name across the rest of the country. Internationally Dreyer's is distributed in parts of the Far East and the Edy's brand the Caribbean and South America — all told some 25 overseas markets. Dreyer's distributes Nestle's Haagen-Dazs brand ice cream and frozen dairy novelties too along with operating the Haagen-Dazs Shoppe Company which franchises ice cream parlors worldwide. Dreyer's is a division of the Swiss food giant Nestle.

DRI CORPORATION

NASDAQ: TBUS

13760 Noel Rd. Ste. 830
Dallas TX 75240
Phone: 214-378-8992
Fax: 214-378-8437
Web: www.digrec.com

CEO: David L Turney
CFO: –
HR: –
FYE: December 31
Type: Public

DRI drives transportation technology. The company designs automatic voice announcement systems and electronic destination signs for mass transit operators as well as vehicle location systems. Its Talking Bus announcement systems broadcast stops and transfer information for buses subways trains and other private and commercial vehicles. DRI also makes electronic destination signs that display transit information for buses. The company counts vehicle makers transit operators and state and local governments among its customers. It operates through subsidiaries in the US (Digital Recorders TwinVision) and abroad (Mobitec). DRI filed for chapter 11 bankruptcy in 2012 and is looking for a buyer for its assets.

DRIL-QUIP, INC.

NYS: DRQ

6401 N. Eldridge Parkway
Houston, TX 77041
Phone: 713 939-7711
Fax: 713 939-8063
Web: www.dril-quip.com

CEO: Blake DeBerry
CFO: Jerry M. Brooks
HR: –
FYE: December 31
Type: Public

Dril-Quip equips the folks who operate the expensive drills — the global deepwater oil and gas industry. The company specializes in deepwater harsh-environment and/or severe-condition equipment. Its products include drilling and production riser systems subsea and surface wellheads and production trees mudline hanger systems (which support the weight of each casing string at the mudline) and specialty connectors and pipe. Dril-Quip's offshore rig equipment includes drilling and completion riser systems wellhead connectors and diverters. The company also provides reconditioning tool rental and technical advisory services.

	Annual Growth	12/10	12/11	12/12	12/13	12/14
Sales ($ mil.)	13.2%	566.3	601.3	733.0	872.4	931.0
Net income ($ mil.)	19.5%	102.2	95.3	119.2	169.8	208.7
Market value ($ mil.)	(0.3%)	3,025.8	2,562.5	2,844.0	4,279.9	2,987.3
Employees	6.3%	2,127	2,194	2,451	2,637	2,720

DRINKER BIDDLE & REATH LLP

1 Logan Sq. Ste. 2000
Philadelphia PA 19103-6996
Phone: 215-988-2700
Fax: 215-988-2757
Web: www.drinkerbiddle.com

CEO: –
CFO: Rich Ciccotto
HR: –
FYE: December 31
Type: Private - Partnershi

Headquartered in Philadelphia since 1849 law firm Drinker Biddle & Reath has slowly grown beyond the borders of the Keystone State and now employs about 650 attorneys working out of a dozen offices. The firm maintains a broad range of practices including commercial litigation corporate and securities bankruptcy government and regulatory affairs health intellectual property private equity and real estate. Its clients reside chiefly in the communications health care information technology insurance pharmaceutical and transportation industries and have included such notable names as Comcast General Electric The University of Pennsylvania and Pfizer.

DRINKS AMERICAS HOLDINGS LTD.

OTC: DKAM

372 Danbury Rd. Ste. 163
Wilton CT 06897
Phone: 203-762-7000
Fax: 203-762-8992
Web: www.drinksamericas.com

CEO: Leonard Moreno
CFO: –
HR: –
FYE: April 30
Type: Public

Image sells for Drinks Americas Holdings. The company markets and distributes alcoholic and non-alcoholic beverages bearing the face and name of such celebrities as Donald Trump (vodka) Willie Nelson (bourbon whiskey) and Paul Newman (fruit juice). It also makes ready-to-drink tea beer rum tequila and the first US-made ultra-premium sake. Subsidiary Drinks Global Imports offers premium European and Australian wines. Drinks Americas sells via a network of North American distributors for resale to supermarkets and liquor and convenience stores. Southern Wine & Spirits is its largest alcohol distributor. Worldwide Beverage Imports and Drinks America management own 49% and 35% respectively of the company.

DRIVECAM INC.

8911 Balboa Ave.
San Diego CA 92123
Phone: 858-430-4000
Fax: 858-430-4001
Web: www.drivecam.com

CEO: Brandon Nixon
CFO: Paul J Pucino
HR: –
FYE: December 31
Type: Private

DriveCam has its electronic eyes on your driving skills. The company designs manufactures and sells video surveillance equipment used by commercial fleets to improve driver and traffic safety. Video cameras installed in vehicles are used to record accidents and otherwise monitor drivers' actions with an eye toward controlling insurance costs. In addition to video monitoring the company's Driving Behavior Management System incorporates driving performance management software and driver counseling. Customers include utility waste management and transit companies as well as operators of taxi ambulance and bus fleets. The company also has a DriveCam for Families product that monitors teen drivers.

DRIVER-HARRIS COMPANY

200 Madison Ave.
Morristown NJ 07960
Phone: 973-267-8100
Fax: 973-267-4499

CEO: –
CFO: –
HR: –
FYE: December 31
Type: Private

Driver-Harris has walked the business high wire for over a century. An electrical wire and cable maker the firm produces insulated electrical thermocouple and fire resistance wire. Subsidiary Irish Driver-Harris (IDH) specializes in the manufacture of insulated electrical cable. Driver-Harris sells to the construction appliance and electrical equipment industries; its customers include global distributors wholesalers and OEMs. Former jewelry salesman and bicycle shop manager Frank Driver joined his brother Wilbur and wire drawer Francis Harris to form the company in 1900; IDH was founded in 1934. Driver-Harris' 2003 bankruptcy protection plan was approved in 2006.

DRIVETIME AUTOMOTIVE INC.

4020 E. Indian School Rd.
Phoenix AZ 85018
Phone: 602-852-6600
Fax: 602-852-6686
Web: www.drivetime.com

CEO: Raymond C Fidel
CFO: Mark G Sauder
HR: –
FYE: December 31
Type: Private

In this story the ugly duckling changes into DriveTime Automotive. Formerly known as Ugly Duckling the company is a used-car dealership chain that primarily targets low-income customers and those with credit problems. To cater to subprime clients it's a "buy here-pay here" dealer meaning it finances and services car loans rather than using outside lenders. DriveTime operates some 90 dealerships located in 30 metropolitan areas in about 15 mostly southern and western states. It reconditions cars at more than a dozen of its own facilities. The cars undergo a 53-point inspection and are run through Experian AutoCheck. DriveTime owned by chairman Ernest Garcia II filed in 2010 to go public.

DRS TECHNOLOGIES INC.

5 Sylvan Way
Parsippany NJ 07054
Phone: 973-898-1500
Fax: 973-898-4730
Web: www.drs.com

CEO: William J Lynn III
CFO: Thomas Crimmins
HR: –
FYE: December 31
Type: Subsidiary

DRS Technologies has zeroed in on its target — to be the fastest growing defense company in the world. It offers mission-critical products and services that support military forces intelligence agencies and prime contractors with leading market positions in air combat training systems combat display workstations electronic sensors environmental controls flight recorders rugged computers communications systems thermal imaging devices and logistics support services. Most of its revenue is derived from the US government primarily the US Department of Defense but it also serves foreign allies. DRS is a subsidiary of Italy's Finmeccanica and functions as part of its Defense and Security Electronics division.

DRUGSTORE.COM INC.

411 108th Ave. NE Ste. 1400
Bellevue WA 98004
Phone: 425-372-3200
Fax: 425-372-3800
Web: www.drugstore.com

CEO: –
CFO: –
HR: –
FYE: August 31
Type: Subsidiary

drugstore.com hopes it has the right Rx for e-commerce success. The e-tailer sells some 60000 name-brand and private-label health and beauty items personal care products household goods and over-the-counter (OTC) drugs through its website and by telephone. A partnership with GNC Corporation allows drugstore.com to offer the retailer's vitamins and wellness products online. It also sells high-end cosmetics and skin care items through its Beauty.com unit. The company markets contact lenses through its Vision Direct subsidiary and customized nutritional supplement programs through its Custom Nutrition Services subsidiary. In 2011 behemoth retailer Walgreen bought drugstore.com in a deal valued at $410 million.

DRUMMOND COMPANY INC.

1000 Urban Center Dr. Ste. 300
Birmingham AL 35242
Phone: 205-945-6300
Fax: 205-945-6440
Web: www.drummondco.com

CEO: –
CFO: Ken Dortch
HR: Betty Crow
FYE: December 31
Type: Private

Drummond does business from the ground down. The company mines and processes thermal and metallurgical coal. It operates the Shoal Creek underground coal mine in Alabama and the Mina Pribbenow surface coal mine in Colombia. Drummond controls more than 2 billion tons of reserves and sells about 29 million tons of coal annually. Its ABC Coke unit in Alabama (the US' largest merchant coke producer) makes foundry coke used mainly in the automotive construction and sugar industries. Drummond's Perry Supply unit a mining and foundry supply business distributes products for more than 20 different manufacturers. Drummond also develops housing communities and office parks in Alabama California and Florida.

DS WATERS OF AMERICA INC.

5660 New Northside Dr. Ste. 500
Atlanta GA 30328
Phone: 770-933-1400
Fax: 770-956-9495
Web: www.water.com

CEO: Tom Harrington
CFO: Ron Z Frieman
HR: –
FYE: December 31
Type: Private

Whether your glass is half empty or half full DS Waters of America works to fill it up. The nation's largest water-cooler delivery company DS Waters serves both homes and offices through its nearly 30 company-owned manufacturing sites across some 40 US states and through 10 supplier-managed facilities. Its regional brands include Alhambra Belmont Springs Crystal Springs Deep Rock Hinckley Springs Kentwood Springs Nursery Sierra Springs and Sparkletts. The company also operates a national coffee and tea delivery service under the Roast2Coast name and sells water-filtration systems. Founded in 2003 DS Waters is owned by private investment fund Kelso & Co.

DSC LOGISTICS INC.

1750 S. Wolf Rd.
Des Plaines IL 60018
Phone: 800-372-1960
Fax: 847-390-7276
Web: www.dsclogistics.com

CEO: Ann Drake
CFO: Joann Lilek
HR: –
FYE: December 31
Type: Private

DSC Logistics knows the ABCs of supply chain management. The third-party logistics company manages services such as warehousing transportation and packaging for its customers; it also offers logistics consulting services. DSC maintains a network of logistics centers spread throughout the US. Customers have included Georgia-Pacific Heinz Kimberly-Clark and Wal-Mart. DSC founder Jim McIlrath the father of CEO Ann Drake started the company as Dry Storage Corporation in 1960 after a former boss refused to offer dry storage along with refrigerated storage services.

DSL.NET INC.

50 Barnes Park North Ste. 104
Wallingford CT 06492
Phone: 203-284-6100
Fax: 203-284-6102
Web: www.dsl.net

CEO: David F Struwas
CFO: Walter R Keisch
HR: –
FYE: December 31
Type: Subsidiary

DSL.net lets others fight it out for the big fish in the pond. The company provides high-speed Internet access and data communications to small and mid-sized businesses primarily over a digital subscriber line (DSL) network as well as via higher capacity T-1 lines. Other services include integrated voice and data systems using voice over Internet Protocol (VoIP) Web hosting virtual private networks (VPNs) and remote access to corporate networks. In addition to selling directly to customers DSL.net uses third-party resellers such as GRIC Communications. DSL.net is a subsidiary of MegaPath Networks.

DSP GROUP, INC.   NMS: DSPG

2161 S. San Antonio Road, Suite 10
Los Altos, CA 94022
Phone: 408 986-4300
Fax: –
Web: www.dspg.com

CEO: Ofer Elyakim
CFO: Dror Levy
HR: –
FYE: December 31
Type: Public

DSP Group loves the sound of its own voice ... chips. The company's name derives from the digital signal processors (DSPs) and related speech compression software it develops that convert speech and other audio data into digital values for cordless telephones wireless phones answering devices PCs and other consumer electronics. Top customers include landline makers VTech Panasonic Uniden and CCT Telecom. With offices in 10 countries the company gets most of its sales in Asia.

	Annual Growth	12/10	12/11	12/12	12/13	12/14
Sales ($ mil.)	(10.8%)	225.5	193.9	162.8	151.1	143.0
Net income ($ mil.)	–	(7.4)	(16.2)	(8.0)	2.7	3.6
Market value ($ mil.)	7.5%	177.8	113.8	125.8	212.1	237.4
Employees	4.8%	259	395	317	297	312

DST SYSTEMS INC. (DE)   NYS: DST

333 West 11th Street
Kansas City, MO 64105
Phone: 816 435-1000
Fax: –
Web: www.dstsystems.com

CEO: Stephen C. Hooley
CFO: Gregg W. Givens
HR: Lisa Hilliard
FYE: December 31
Type: Public

DST Systems provides information processing software and services to the mutual fund insurance retirement and healthcare industries among others primarily in North America. Its two top segments (customer communications and financial services) together contribute most of sales. Its financial services segment offers software and systems used to handle a wide range of tasks including shareowner recordkeeping investment management and business process management; the customer communications division includes integrated print and electronic billing and statement products. DST generates most of its sales in the US.

	Annual Growth	12/10	12/11	12/12	12/13	12/14
Sales ($ mil.)	4.2%	2,328.5	2,388.7	2,576.6	2,658.6	2,749.3
Net income ($ mil.)	16.8%	318.5	183.1	324.0	352.6	593.3
Market value ($ mil.)	20.7%	1,667.6	1,711.6	2,278.6	3,411.8	3,540.0
Employees	16.4%	11,200	12,300	17,925	19,530	20,525

DSW INC   NYS: DSW

810 DSW Drive
Columbus, OH 43219
Phone: 614 237-7100
Fax: –
Web: www.dswinc.com

CEO: Roger L. Rawlins
CFO: Mary Meixelsperger
HR: Kathleen Maurer
FYE: January 31
Type: Public

While you don't have to watch out for trees in this jungle you may want to watch your back. DSW (short for Designer Shoe Warehouse) sells discounted brand-name footwear for style-conscious men women and kids through some 430 stores in 40-plus US states and Puerto Rico as well as online at dsw.com. DSW stores average 21500 square feet and stock about 22000 pair of dress casual and athletic shoes as well as a complementary array of handbags hosiery and accessories. The company also operates about 370 leased departments inside stores operated by other retailers. The discount footwear giant is dipping its toe in the luxury shoe market. DSW was founded in 1969.

	Annual Growth	01/11	01/12*	02/13	02/14*	01/15
Sales ($ mil.)	8.2%	1,822.4	2,024.3	2,257.8	2,368.7	2,496.1
Net income ($ mil.)	9.2%	107.6	174.8	146.4	151.3	153.3
Market value ($ mil.)	1.7%	2,941.9	4,374.9	5,971.4	3,328.2	3,143.5
Employees	3.0%	10,500	10,800	11,000	11,000	11,800

*Fiscal year change

DTE ELECTRIC COMPANY

One Energy Plaza
Detroit, MI 48226-1279
Phone: 313 235-4000
Fax: –
Web: www.dteenergy.com

CEO: Gerard M Anderson
CFO: Peter B Oleksiak
HR: –
FYE: December 31
Type: Public

Ford Motors is not the only powerhouse operating in Detroit — DTE Electric is another. The utility (formerly known as Detroit Edison) generates and distributes electricity to 2.1 million customers in Michigan. The company a unit of regional power player DTE Energy has almost 11000 MW of generating capacity from its interests in primarily fossil-fueled nuclear and hydroelectric power plants. It operates more than 46000 circuit miles of distribution lines and owns and operates more than 670 distribution substations. DTE Electric also sells excess power to wholesale customers and provides coal transportation services.

	Annual Growth	12/10	12/11	12/12	12/13	12/14
Sales ($ mil.)	1.4%	4,993.0	5,152.0	5,291.0	5,197.0	5,282.0
Net income ($ mil.)	4.8%	441.0	437.0	486.0	487.0	532.0
Market value ($ mil.)	–	–	–	–	–	–
Employees	1.0%	4,700	4,800	4,800	4,800	4,900

DTE ENERGY CO.

NYS: DTE

One Energy Plaza
Detroit, MI 48226-1279
Phone: 313 235-4000
Fax: -
Web: www.dteenergy.com

CEO: Gerard M. Anderson
CFO: Peter B. Oleksiak
HR: -
FYE: December 31
Type: Public

Detroit's economy may be lackluster but DTE Energy still provides a reliable spark. The holding company's main subsidiary DTE Electric (formerly Detroit Edison) distributes electricity to some 2.1 million customers in southeastern Michigan. The utility's power plants (mainly fossil-fueled) have a generating capacity of more than 10418 MW. The company's DTE Gas (formerly Michigan Consolidated Gas) unit distributes natural gas to 1.2 million customers. DTE Energy's nonregulated operations (in more than 20 states) include energy marketing and trading; coal transportation and procurement; energy management services for commercial and industrial customers; and independent and on-site power generation.

	Annual Growth	12/11	12/12	12/13	12/14	12/15
Sales ($ mil.)	3.8%	8,897.0	8,791.0	9,661.0	12,301.0	10,337.0
Net income ($ mil.)	0.6%	711.0	610.0	661.0	905.0	727.0
Market value ($ mil.)	10.2%	9,772.2	10,777.2	11,915.0	15,500.8	14,391.7
Employees	0.5%	9,800	9,900	9,900	10,000	10,000

DTJ HOLDINGS INC.

5034 GRAND RIDGE DR
WEST DES MOINES, IA 502655754
Phone: 515-262-6600
Fax: -
Web: www.robertsdybdahl.com

CEO: -
CFO: -
HR: -
FYE: December 31
Type: Private

Roberts & Dybdahl can't sell you a house but it can sell you some important pieces. The company is a wholesale distributor of lumber lumber products and building materials to customers in Illinois Indiana Iowa Kansas Nebraska and Wisconsin. Products include treated lumber boards shingles siding studs trusses joists and engineered wood products. Roberts & Dybdahl operates about 10 distribution centers and some half a dozen on-site truss manufacturing facilities able to custom build roof and floor trusses to customer specifications. The company was founded as Carroll Wholesale in 1955 by Howard Roberts and Hub Dybdahl.

	Annual Growth	12/08	12/09	12/10	12/11	12/12
Sales ($ mil.)	11.2%	-	160.5	187.8	181.5	220.7
Net income ($ mil.)	7.0%	-	-	1.4	0.8	1.6
Market value ($ mil.)	-	-	-	-	-	-
Employees	-	-	-	-	-	238

DTS INC

NMS: DTSI

5220 Las Virgenes Road
Calabasas, CA 91302
Phone: 818 436-1000
Fax: -
Web: www.dts.com

CEO: Jon E. Kirchner
CFO: Melvin L. (Mel) Flanigan
HR: Kris M. Graves
FYE: December 31
Type: Public

DTS (formerly Digital Theater Systems) surrounds movie lovers with sound. The company's multi-channel audio systems are used in consumer electronic devices such as audio/video receivers DVD and Blu-ray HD players PCs car audio products video game consoles and home theater systems. DTS has licensing agreements with major consumer electronics manufacturers (Sony Samsung and Philips). It also provides DTS-encoded soundtracks in movies TV shows and music content. The firm was founded in 1990 as Digital Theater Systems by scientist Terry Beard. It received initial funding from Universal Pictures in 1993 and used that relationship to debut its audio system in the soundtrack to Universal's Jurassic Park.

	Annual Growth	12/10	12/11	12/12	12/13	12/14
Sales ($ mil.)	13.4%	87.1	96.9	100.6	125.1	143.9
Net income ($ mil.)	14.1%	16.0	18.3	(15.9)	15.8	27.1
Market value ($ mil.)	(11.0%)	852.1	473.2	290.1	415.4	534.2
Employees	13.0%	228	258	369	373	372

DUANE MORRIS LLP

30 S. 17th St.
Philadelphia PA 19103-4196
Phone: 215-979-1000
Fax: 215-979-1020
Web: www.duanemorris.com

CEO: John J Soroko
CFO: -
HR: -
FYE: December 31
Type: Private - Partnershi

The more than 700 lawyers who call Duane Morris home practice in areas ranging from tax to trial and from real estate to intellectual property. Clients are drawn from a variety of industries including automotive construction energy financial services and telecommunications and have included companies such as Exxon Mobil Ford Motor Groupon Sunoco and Stryker. Duane Morris has about 25 offices mainly in the US but also in Europe and the Asia/Pacific region. As part of an international network of independent law firms it can serve clients around the globe through affiliates. The firm was founded in 1904.

DUCOMMUN INC.

NYS: DCO

23301 Wilmington Avenue
Carson, CA 90745-6209
Phone: 310 513-7200
Fax: -
Web: www.ducommun.com

CEO: Anthony J. (Tony) Reardon
CFO: Douglas L. Groves
HR: -
FYE: December 31
Type: Public

Too common? Not at all Ducommun. The company designs and makes aerostructures and electromechanical components for commercial and military aircraft as well as for missile and space programs. Ducommun AeroStructures (DAS) engineers and manufactures structures and assemblies such as aircraft wing spoilers and helicopter blades using aluminum composites and titanium. Ducommun LaBarge Technologies (DLT) makes electromechanical components such as switch assemblies actuators keyboard panels and avionics racks. Its Miltec subsidiary designs missile and aerospace systems. Products for military and space applications accounted for 54% of 2013 sales. Boeing accounted for 18% of 2013 revenues; Raytheon 10%.

	Annual Growth	12/10	12/11	12/12	12/13	12/14
Sales ($ mil.)	16.1%	408.4	580.9	747.0	736.7	742.0
Net income ($ mil.)	0.1%	19.8	(47.6)	16.4	9.3	19.9
Market value ($ mil.)	3.8%	238.5	139.6	177.1	326.5	276.9
Employees	14.8%	1,815	3,541	3,294	3,264	3,150

DUCOMMUN LABARGE TECHNOLOGIES

9900 Clayton Rd.
St. Louis MO 63124
Phone: 314-997-0800
Fax: 314-812-9438
Web: www.ducommun.com/dti

CEO: -
CFO: Joseph Bellino
HR: -
FYE: December 31
Type: Subsidiary

Contract manufacturer Ducommun LaBarge Technologies (formerly LaBarge Inc.) designs and produces complex electronics and interconnect systems able to withstand the physical extremes of combat space sea and inner earth. Its printed circuit boards cables electronic assemblies and other products are used for such applications as military communication systems commercial aircraft satellites medical equipment airport security glass container fabrication systems and oil drilling equipment. Customers have included Owens-Illinois and Raytheon. Ducommun acquired LaBarge for $340 million in 2011 to expand its manufacturing capabilities. LaBarge was combined with Ducommun's technologies subsidiary and renamed.

DUKANE CORPORATION

2900 Dukane Dr.
St. Charles IL 60174
Phone: 630-584-2300
Fax: 630-682-3093
Web: www.berlinindustries.com

CEO: Michael W Ritschdorff
CFO: Bradley J Johnson
HR: –
FYE: December 31
Type: Private

"Death by PowerPoint" isn't pretty but Dukane's advanced technologies offers a remedy. Dukane's Audio Visual division manufactures video projectors cameras screens and flat-panel (LCD) monitors. The lineup is sold to customers looking for visual aids for use in business government school and church venues. Dukane's Intelligent Assembly Solutions supplies ultrasonic microprocessor-controlled joining equipment for plastics metal as well as food processing assembly. This division courts big assembly operations such as automotive aerospace and appliance as well as smaller operations like electronics and toys. Founded in 1922 by J. McWilliams "Mac" Stone Sr. Dukane was acquired in an MBO in 2005.

DUKE ENERGY CORP
NYS: DUK

550 South Tryon Street
Charlotte, NC 28202-1803
Phone: 704 382-3853
Fax: –
Web: www.duke-energy.com

CEO: Lynn J. Good
CFO: Steven K. Young
HR: Jim O'Connor
FYE: December 31
Type: Public

Duke Energy is a John Wayne-sized power business. It serves electric and gas customers in the South and Midwest. Its US Franchised Electric and Gas unit operates through its Duke Energy Carolinas Duke Energy Ohio Progress EnergyDuke Duke Energy Progress Duke Energy Florida Duke Energy Indiana and Duke Energy Kentucky regional businesses. The company has 57500 MW of electric generating capacity from diverse mix of coal nuclear natural gas oil and renewable resources. Duke Energy also has domestic commercial and international power assets. The company serves 7.3 million electric retail customers in the Southeast and Midwest. It also has some limited insurance real estate and telecom assets.

	Annual Growth	12/10	12/11	12/12	12/13	12/14
Sales ($ mil.)	13.8%	14,272.0	14,529.0	19,624.0	24,598.0	23,925.0
Net income ($ mil.)	9.3%	1,320.0	1,706.0	1,768.0	2,665.0	1,883.0
Market value ($ mil.)	47.2%	12,591.7	15,554.0	45,106.6	48,790.1	59,062.8
Employees	11.3%	18,440	18,249	27,885	27,948	28,344

DUKE ENERGY INDIANA, INC.

1000 East Main Street
Plainfield, IN 46168
Phone: 704 382-3853
Fax: –
Web: www.duke-energy.com

CEO: Lynn J Good
CFO: Steven K Young
HR: –
FYE: December 31
Type: Public

Duke Energy Indiana helps to light up the Hoosier state. Indiana's largest utility Duke Energy subsidiary Duke Energy Indiana transmits and distributes electricity to 69 of the state's 92 counties (approximately 790000 customers). The utility also owns power plants (about 7000 MW of primarily fossil-fueled capacity) which are operated by its parent's merchant energy division. Duke Energy Indiana's service area covers about 22000 sq. miles with an estimated population of 2.4 million. The company operates about 31000 miles of distribution lines and a 5400-mile transmission system.

	Annual Growth	12/10	12/11	12/12	12/13	12/14
Sales ($ mil.)	5.9%	2,520.0	2,622.0	2,717.0	2,926.0	3,175.0
Net income ($ mil.)	5.9%	285.0	168.0	(50.0)	358.0	359.0
Market value ($ mil.)	–	–	–	–	–	–
Employees	–	–	–	–	–	–

DUKE REALTY CORP.
NYS: DRE

600 East 96th Street, Suite 100
Indianapolis, IN 46240
Phone: 317 808-6000
Fax: –
Web: www.dukerealty.com

CEO: Dennis D. Oklak
CFO: Mark A Denien
HR: –
FYE: December 31
Type: Public

Duke Realty is royalty in the realm of US commercial real estate. The self-managed and self-administered real estate investment trust (REIT) owns and develops office and industrial properties primarily in major cities in the Midwest and East. In addition to about 750 properties totaling more than 135 million sq. ft. of rentable space the company owns some 4800 acres of undeveloped land with options to acquire more. The REIT is also building its holdings of industrial and medical office properties which account for about three-quarters of its portfolio. Duke's service operations include construction and development asset and property management and leasing. The company was founded in 1972.

	Annual Growth	12/10	12/11	12/12	12/13	12/14
Sales ($ mil.)	(4.4%)	1,393.6	1,274.3	1,109.4	1,081.8	1,164.7
Net income ($ mil.)	39.4%	65.3	96.3	(75.9)	196.5	246.5
Market value ($ mil.)	12.8%	4,287.6	4,146.5	4,772.8	5,175.4	6,951.1
Employees	(6.9%)	1,000	850	840	790	750

DULCICH INC.

16797 SE 130th Ave.
Clackamas OR 97015
Phone: 503-905-4500
Fax: 503-905-2491
Web: www.pacseafood.com

CEO: Frank Dominic Dulcich
CFO: Paul Minter
HR: Brandie Hogg
FYE: December 31
Type: Private

Dulcich Inc. which does business as the Pacific Seafood Group is always fishing for acquisitions. The Oregon-based company has built its business by snapping up competitors giving it a wide array of offerings. Its more than 1800 different products range from shellfish (clams crab lobster mussels oysters scallops) to finfish (catfish cod flounder sable salmon swordfish trout and tuna). In addition to fresh and frozen seafood the company offers value-added products including battered breaded marinated and smoked fish. Pacific Seafood operates distribution and processing centers from Alaska to Mexico and throughout the western US. It exports products to Asia Europe and the Middle East.

DUN & BRADSTREET CORP (DE)
NYS: DNB

103 JFK Parkway
Short Hills, NJ 07078
Phone: 973 921-5500
Fax: –
Web: www.dnb.com

CEO: Jeffrey M. (Jeff) Stibel
CFO: Richard H. (Rich) Veldran
HR: –
FYE: December 31
Type: Public

The Dun & Bradstreet Corporation is one of the world's leading suppliers of business information and research. Its global database contains commercial data on more than 240 million companies. D&B also holds the largest volume of business-credit information in the world. The company mines its data to create software products web-based applications and marketing information and purchasing-support services for its customers. Its data and content can be integrated into clients' systems workflows and apps. The company's operations are split into two main segments: risk management and sales and marketing solutions. Hoover's the publisher of this profile is part of D&B.

	Annual Growth	12/10	12/11	12/12	12/13	12/14
Sales ($ mil.)	0.1%	1,676.6	1,758.5	1,663.0	1,655.2	1,681.8
Net income ($ mil.)	4.0%	252.1	260.3	295.5	258.5	294.4
Market value ($ mil.)	10.2%	2,947.0	2,686.4	2,823.5	4,406.7	4,342.5
Employees	(1.5%)	5,200	5,100	4,600	4,600	4,900

DUNCAN ENERGY PARTNERS L.P.

1100 Louisiana St. 10th Fl.
Houston TX 77002
Phone: 713-381-6500
Fax: 713-381-6668
Web: www.deplp.com

CEO: W Randall Fowler
CFO: Bryan F Bulawa
HR: –
FYE: December 31
Type: Subsidiary

Duncan Energy Partners (DEP) went deep and wide to make its money. The midstream operator a former spinoff from Enterprise Products Partners found stored and transported natural gas and other petrochemicals. Its operations included Mont Belvieu Caverns (with a 100-million-barrel capacity) the 1000-mile-long Acadian Gas pipeline in Louisiana propylene pipelines between Texas and Louisiana and a 297-mile-long intrastate natural gas liquids (NGLs) pipeline. It owned stakes in 9430 miles of natural gas pipelines and more than 1480 miles of NGL pipelines. Reconsolidating to boost its market share in 2011 Enterprise Products Partners bought the 40% of DEP it did not own for $2.4 billion.

DUNCAN EQUIPMENT COMPANY

3450 S MACARTHUR BLVD
OKLAHOMA CITY, OK 73179-7638
Phone: 405-688-2300
Fax: –
Web: www.blackhawkid.com

CEO: –
CFO: –
HR: –
FYE: December 31
Type: Private

Industrial companies run on Dunkin' — Duncan Equipment that is. Doing business as Duncan Industrial Solutions the company supplies its industrial customers with a slew of maintenance repair and overhaul (MRO) tools. Duncan distributes name brand process equipment pumps electronic and cutting tools power transmission equipment safety supplies and material handling supplies. It also offers bar coding supply chain and inventory management services as well as safety compliance and product training. Duncan has offices in Oklahoma Texas and through Atlantic Tool Systems (ATS) New Jersey. Founded in 1948 the company is owned by BlackHawk Industrial Distribution and Brazos Private Equity.

	Annual Growth	12/03	12/04	12/05	12/06	12/07
Sales ($ mil.)	–	–	–	(895.4)	74.6	77.8
Net income ($ mil.)	23676.1%	–	–	0.0	13.9	2.4
Market value ($ mil.)	–	–	–	–	–	–
Employees	–	–	–	–	–	170

DUNCAN-WILLIAMS INC.

6750 POPLAR AVE STE 300
MEMPHIS, TN 381387433
Phone: 901-385-7575
Fax: –
Web: www.duncanwilliams.com

CEO: –
CFO: Frank Reid
HR: –
FYE: December 31
Type: Private

Duncan-Williams raises its capital by helping others raise theirs. An investment banking firm Duncan-Williams offers research sales and trading of fixed income securities, (bonds) and equities (stock), to individual and, institutional investors including banks credit unions corporations and public entities (e.g. municipalities housing authorities school districts). Other services include underwriting financial analysis bond structuring for public entities and equity capital market research of emerging growth companies in the health care and financial technology sectors. Founded in 1969 by the late A. Duncan Williams, the firm, operates 16 offices across the eastern US and in Texas and California.

	Annual Growth	12/08	12/09	12/10	12/11	12/13
Sales ($ mil.)	–	–	0.0	49.5	53.2	36.5
Net income ($ mil.)	–	–	–	2.7	3.0	(3.8)
Market value ($ mil.)	–	–	–	–	–	–
Employees	–	–	–	–	–	65

DUNE ENERGY, INC.

NBB: DUNR

811 Louisiana Street,, Suite 2300
Houston, TX 77002
Phone: 713 229-6300
Fax: –
Web: www.duneenergy.com

CEO: –
CFO: –
HR: –
FYE: December 31
Type: Public

Like sand piling up in a windblown sand dune Dune Energy is looking to pile up profits from its Texas and Louisiana oil and gas properties. The oil and gas exploration and production independent has leases on 100000 gross acres across 23 producing oil and natural gas fields along the Texas and Louisiana Gulf Coast. In 2008 Dune Energy reported proved reserves of 8.2 million barrels of oil and 83.8 billion cu. ft. of natural gas. It has a more than two-year current drilling inventory for its properties along the Gulf Coast. Swiss bank UBS owns 35% of the company; Russian gas company ITERA's Tierra Holdings BV unit 33%.

	Annual Growth	12/09	12/10	12/11	12/12	12/13
Sales ($ mil.)	(3.8%)	64.9	64.2	62.9	52.1	55.5
Net income ($ mil.)	–	(59.1)	(75.5)	(60.4)	(7.9)	(47.0)
Market value ($ mil.)	55.0%	16.3	29.0	2.0	112.4	94.2
Employees	(8.3%)	48	38	34	32	34

DUNHAM'S ATHLEISURE CORPORATION

5000 Dixie Hwy.
Waterford MI 48329
Phone: 248-674-4991
Fax: 248-674-4980
Web: www.dunhamssports.com

CEO: –
CFO: –
HR: –
FYE: December 31
Type: Private

It's all about athletic leisure at Dunham's Athleisure. The company's Dunham's Sports stores sell sporting goods through more than 160 locations in a dozen states in the Midwest and Northeast as well as online. Its stores which average 30000 sq. ft. offer gear for team sports individual endeavors and outdoor pursuits as well as apparel fan merchandise electronics and fitness machines (including ellipticals pilates boards rowers steppers treadmills). Dunham's also carries a full line of casual apparel footwear and eyewear for men women and children. The company began as Dunham's Bait and Tackle in 1937.

DUNKIN' BRANDS GROUP INC.

NASDAQ: DNKN

130 Royall St.
Canton MA 02021
Phone: 781-737-3000
Fax: 781-737-4000
Web: www.dunkinbrands.com

CEO: Nigel Travis
CFO: Cornelius F Moses
HR: –
FYE: December 31
Type: Public

Doughnuts and ice cream make sweet bedfellows at Dunkin' Brands Group. The company is a leading multi-concept quick-service restaurant franchisor that operates both the Dunkin' Donuts and Baskin-Robbins chains. It has more than 16800 franchise locations operating in about 60 countries. With some 10000 units in about 30 countries (including approximately 7000 in the US) Dunkin' Donuts is the world's leading doughnut chain. Baskin-Robbins is a top ice cream and frozen snacks outlet with more than 6700 locations in 45 countries (2450 in the US). The company went public in mid-2011.

DUNKIN' BRANDS GROUP, INC.

NMS: DNKN

130 Royall Street
Canton, MA 02021
Phone: 781 737-3000
Fax: –
Web: www.dunkinbrands.com

CEO: Nigel Travis
CFO: Paul C. Carbone
HR: –
FYE: December 27
Type: Public

Doughnuts and ice cream make sweet bedfellows at Dunkin' Brands Group. The company is a leading multi-concept quick-service restaurant franchisor that operates both the Dunkin' Donuts and Baskin-Robbins chains. It has more than 18000 franchise locations operating in about 60 countries. With nearly 11000 units in about 30 countries (including approximately 7675 in the US) Dunkin' Donuts is the world's leading doughnut chain. Baskin-Robbins is a top ice cream and frozen snacks outlet with more than 7300 locations in 45 countries (roughly 2450 in the US). The company went public in mid-2011.

	Annual Growth	12/10	12/11	12/12	12/13	12/14
Sales ($ mil.)	6.7%	577.1	628.2	658.2	713.8	748.7
Net income ($ mil.)	60.1%	26.9	34.4	108.3	146.9	176.4
Market value ($ mil.)	19.3%	–	2,613.7	3,384.8	4,996.1	4,433.2
Employees	1.3%	1,075	1,128	1,104	1,144	1,134

DUPONT AUTOMOTIVE

950 Stephenson Hwy.
Troy MI 48083
Phone: 248-583-8000
Fax: 248-583-4556
Web: automotive.dupont.com

CEO: –
CFO: –
HR: –
FYE: December 31
Type: Private - Associatio

DuPont Automotive has a hand in building your car from beginning to end. It has been working with the auto industry for nearly a century providing everything from the glass in a sunroof to the rubber in the tires from thermoplastic front end systems to the R&D involved in producing tail lights. The business segment of DuPont operates more than 100 plants and labs in about 70 countries and is the largest provider of automotive coatings. Its plants make coatings and plastics and provide compounding services to the auto industry in North America Asia and Europe. In 2010 it launched a new line of nylon Zytel PLUS to resist heat chemicals and pressure on underhood and engine parts.

DUPONT FABROS TECHNOLOGY INC

NYS: DFT

1212 New York Avenue, NW, Suite 900
Washington, DC 20005
Phone: 202 728-0044
Fax: –
Web: www.dft.com

CEO: Christopher P. (Chris) Eldredge
CFO: Jeffrey H. Foster
HR: –
FYE: December 31
Type: Public

DuPont Fabros Technology's server farms corral a lot of data. The company owns develops operates and manages 10 wholesale data centers — the facilities that house power and cool computer servers for such technology companies as Facebook Rackspace Microsoft and Yahoo! Other tenants come from the media communications health care and financial services industries. Organized as a real estate investment trust (REIT) DuPont Fabros is exempt from paying federal income tax as long as it makes quarterly distributions to shareholders.

	Annual Growth	12/10	12/11	12/12	12/13	12/14
Sales ($ mil.)	14.5%	242.5	287.4	332.4	375.1	417.6
Net income ($ mil.)	36.6%	30.4	65.0	53.0	48.4	105.9
Market value ($ mil.)	11.8%	1,405.1	1,600.0	1,596.1	1,632.4	2,195.9
Employees	4.0%	83	91	93	92	97

DUQUESNE UNIVERSITY OF THE HOLY SPIRIT

600 FORBES AVE
PITTSBURGH, PA 152193016
Phone: 412-396-6000
Fax: –
Web: www.duq.edu

CEO: –
CFO: –
HR: –
FYE: June 30
Type: Private

Duquesne University of The Holy Ghost keeps a keen eye on the spiritual as well as the academic. The school offers more than 100 undergraduate degree programs about 65 graduate and professional degree programs and more than 20 doctoral programs at schools of business education law liberal arts nursing pharmacy health sciences natural and environmental sciences music and leadership and professional advancement. Duquesne was founded in 1878 as the Pittsburgh Catholic College of the Holy Ghost. It has an annual enrollment of more than 10000 undergraduate graduate and law students.

	Annual Growth	06/09	06/10	06/11	06/12	06/13
Sales ($ mil.)	7.2%	–	290.5	333.2	262.7	357.8
Net income ($ mil.)	(3.4%)	–	–	21.9	7.3	20.5
Market value ($ mil.)	–	–	–	–	–	–
Employees	–	–	–	–	–	3,601

DURA AUTOMOTIVE SYSTEMS LLC

1780 Pond Run
Auburn Hills MI 48326
Phone: 248-299-7500
Fax: 248-475-4378
Web: www.duraauto.com

CEO: Lynn Tilton
CFO: Jim Gregory
HR: –
FYE: December 31
Type: Private

You wouldn't be able to keep the pedal to the metal without DURA Automotive Systems' driver control systems. The company is a leading supplier of pedal systems parking brake mechanisms manual and automatic transmission gear shifter systems and auto cables. DURA also designs and makes engineered assemblies such as tailgate latches and seating adjustment controls as well as structural door modules and exterior trim. The company sells to auto OEMs and many suppliers in North America Europe and Asia. Customers include Ford Volkswagen GM Chrysler and BMW. DURA has about 30 facilities in 17 countries. In late 2009 private equity Patriarch Partners bought a majority interest in DURA for about $125 million.

DURA COAT PRODUCTS INC.

5361 VIA RICARDO
RIVERSIDE, CA 925092414
Phone: 951-341-6500
Fax: –
Web: www.duracoatproducts.com

CEO: Mike K Hong
CFO: –
HR: –
FYE: December 31
Type: Private

Durability is fundamental to Dura Coat Products. The company specializes in high-performance coatings for metal surfaces. Dura Coat develops and makes coil-applied coatings to protect metal building exteriors and roofing trim and sidewall rain ware and HVAC components. Coatings are also used on garage doors appliances hardware and vehicles. Spray coatings protect aluminum extrusions such as window frames and storefronts. For galvanized tubing its high-solids exterior and water-based interior coatings are made to meet mechanical and electrical tubing markets. Dura Coat operates manufacturing plants in Huntsville Alabama and Riverside California.

	Annual Growth	12/09	12/10	12/11	12/12	12/13
Sales ($ mil.)	–	–	0.0	0.0	100.0	100.0
Net income ($ mil.)	–	–	–	0.0	0.0	0.0
Market value ($ mil.)	–	–	–	–	–	–
Employees	–	–	–	–	–	120

DURATA THERAPEUTICS INC.

NASDAQ: DRTX

89 Headquarters Plaza North 14th Fl.
Morristown NJ 07960
Phone: 973-993-4865
Fax: 610-930-2042
Web: www.globusmedical.com

CEO: Paul Edick
CFO: Corey N Fishman
HR: –
FYE: December 31
Type: Private

You don't even want to think about the infections Durata Therapeutics is hoping to treat. Its lead candidate dalbavancin is designed for people with acute bacterial skin and skin structure infections (abSSSI) usually caused by Strep and Staph bacteria. Dalbavancin is given once a week by IV as opposed to the current treatment which must be given several times a day. The development stage company is conducting clinical trials in the US and Western Europe and hopes to begin selling dalbavancin to hospitals through its own sales force in late 2013. Durata's other drug candidates include pleuromutalins and lincosamide also high level antibacterials. The company formed in 2009 went public in 2012.

DURECT CORP

NMS: DRRX

10260 Bubb Road
Cupertino, CA 95014
Phone: 408 777-1417
Fax: –
Web: www.durect.com

CEO: James E. Brown
CFO: Matthew J. (Matt) Hogan
HR: –
FYE: December 31
Type: Public

DURECT wants your medicine to go DURECTly where it's needed. The company is developing drug delivery systems to provide long-term therapy for such conditions as chronic pain heart disease cancer and neurological disorders. Drug delivery technologies provided by DURECT include TRANSDUR and ELADUR transdermal patches; ORADUR a sustained release oral gel-cap; SABER and MICRODUR injectable delivery systems; Remoxy an extended release capsule of oxycodone; and the DURIN biodegradable implant. DURECT conducts R&D efforts independently and collaboratively. The firm also sells biodegradable polymers (LACTEL) and osmotic pumps (ALZET) to pharmaceutical and medical research firms.

	Annual Growth	12/10	12/11	12/12	12/13	12/14
Sales ($ mil.)	(11.5%)	31.6	33.5	53.1	15.3	19.4
Net income ($ mil.)	–	(22.9)	(18.8)	16.2	(21.5)	(22.1)
Market value ($ mil.)	(30.8%)	392.4	134.2	104.6	196.8	89.8
Employees	(6.1%)	131	106	102	101	102

DUSA PHARMACEUTICALS INC.

NASDAQ: DUSA

25 Upton Dr.
Wilmington MA 01887
Phone: 978-657-7500
Fax: 978-657-9193
Web: www.dusapharma.com

CEO: Robert F Doman
CFO: –
HR: Marianne Mullin
FYE: December 31
Type: Public

DUSA Pharmaceuticals has seen the light. The company develops photodynamic therapy (PDT) devices and drugs for treating and diagnosing dermatological conditions using a combination of drugs and light. DUSA markets its Levulan Kerastick topical solution and applicator which are used in combination with the BLU-U light to treat actinic keratoses or pre-cancerous skin lesions caused by sun exposure. When used together Levulan Kerastick and BLU-U are known as the Levulan PDT process; on its own BLU-U is also FDA approved to treat moderate acne. While DUSA packages Levulan into its Kerastick applicator products third parties manufacture its drugs and light systems. DUSA is being acquired by Sun Pharmaceutical.

DXP ENTERPRISES, INC.

NMS: DXPE

7272 Pinemont
Houston, TX 77040
Phone: 713 996-4700
Fax: –

CEO: David R Little
CFO: Mac McConnell
HR: –
FYE: December 31
Type: Public

DXP Enterprises (DXP) knows that distribution is the quickest way to a customer's doorstep. The company is a distributor of industrial products and services through its three main segments Service Centers Supply Chain Services and Innovative Pumping Solutions. Generating the majority of sales the company's service centers offer bearing rotating fluid power and power transmission products and safety equipment as well as technical design and logistics services. Industries served include agriculture chemical construction food and beverage mining and municipal government. DXP operates from about 150 locations throughout North America.

	Annual Growth	12/10	12/11	12/12	12/13	12/14
Sales ($ mil.)	23.0%	656.2	807.0	1,097.1	1,241.5	1,499.7
Net income ($ mil.)	–	19.4	31.4	51.0	60.2	(45.2)
Market value ($ mil.)	20.5%	345.0	462.9	705.4	1,656.0	726.4
Employees	8.5%	1,772	2,093	2,817	3,207	2,460

DYADIC INTERNATIONAL INC

NBB: DYAI

140 Intracoastal Pointe Drive, Suite 404
Jupiter, FL 33477
Phone: 561 743-8333
Fax: 561 743-8343
Web: www.dyadic.com

CEO: Mark A Emalfarb
CFO: Thomas Dubinski
HR: –
FYE: December 31
Type: Public

Dyadic International hopes to unlock biotechnology dynasties using its C1 technology. The company uses its C1 Expression System to develop biological and chemical substances for a variety of life sciences and industrial applications. The firm's enzyme business makes enzymes and other products for commercial and industrial uses employing C1 know-how. Industries served include textiles agriculture and paper mills. Dyadic's biopharma division uses the expression system to make therapeutic proteins for drugmakers. The company is also developing its enzymes for bioenergy applications including biofuels.

	Annual Growth	12/10	12/11	12/12	12/13	12/14
Sales ($ mil.)	10.4%	8.4	10.3	15.6	17.1	12.5
Net income ($ mil.)	–	(5.5)	(4.7)	1.3	(0.4)	(6.0)
Market value ($ mil.)	(18.5%)	72.7	33.1	64.5	51.2	32.1
Employees	12.2%	36	36	38	39	57

DYAX CORP

NMS: DYAX

55 Network Drive
Burlington, MA 01803
Phone: 617 225-2500
Fax: –
Web: www.dyax.com

CEO: Gustav Christensen
CFO: George V Migausky
HR: Joan Nickerson
FYE: December 31
Type: Public

Dyax has two ways to make a difference — by developing its own drugs or by licensing its proprietary discovery technology to help others discover and develop drugs. The biopharmaceutical company's phage display technology rapidly identifies proteins peptides and antibodies useful in treating disease. Dyax's first commercial drug Kalbitor (ecallantide) is approved in the US to treat hereditary angioedema (HAE a condition causing tissue swelling) and enjoys orphan drug designation. The company is also investigating the drug for use in treating other types of angioedema and working to obtain regulatory approval for the drug in overseas markets.

	Annual Growth	12/09	12/10	12/11	12/12	12/13
Sales ($ mil.)	25.6%	21.6	51.4	48.7	54.7	53.9
Net income ($ mil.)	–	(62.4)	(24.5)	(34.6)	(29.3)	(27.8)
Market value ($ mil.)	22.1%	412.6	262.9	165.5	423.5	917.0
Employees	(0.2%)	121	137	120	125	120

DYCOM INDUSTRIES, INC.   NYS: DY

11780 US Highway 1, Suite 600
Palm Beach Gardens, FL 33408
Phone: 561 627-7171
Fax: 561 627-7709
Web: www.dycomind.com

CEO: -
CFO: H Andrew Deferrari
HR: Kimberly Dickens
FYE: July 25
Type: Public

The telecommunications industry dials up Dycom Industries for construction and engineering assistance. Operating through more than 30 subsidiaries the company primarily designs builds and maintains coaxial copper and fiber-optic cable systems for local and long-distance phone companies and cable television operators. Dycom also provides wiring services for businesses and government agencies installs and maintains electrical lines for electric and gas utilities and locates underground wires and pipelines for excavators. Dycom operates in the US and Canada.

	Annual Growth	07/11	07/12	07/13	07/14	07/15
Sales ($ mil.)	18.2%	1,035.9	1,201.1	1,608.6	1,811.6	2,022.3
Net income ($ mil.)	51.3%	16.1	39.4	35.2	40.0	84.3
Market value ($ mil.)	39.2%	568.8	590.2	883.9	963.1	2,133.1
Employees	7.6%	8,320	8,111	10,822	10,592	11,159

DYNACQ HEALTHCARE INC   NBB: DYII

4301 Vista Road
Pasadena, TX 77504
Phone: 713 378-2000
Fax: -
Web: www.dynacq.com

CEO: -
CFO: Philip Chan
HR: Mirna Lee
FYE: August 31
Type: Public

Dynacq Healthcare is a holding company that owns and operates acute-care specialty hospitals providing electively scheduled surgeries such as bariatric (weight loss) and orthopedic surgeries and pain management procedures. Dynacq operates Vista Hospital in Garland Texas and Surgery Specialty Hospitals of America in Pasadena Texas (suburbs of Dallas and Houston respectively). Most of the Dynacq's revenues come from workers' compensation insurance and commercial insurers on an out-of-network basis. Chairman and CEO Chiu Moon Chan owns more than half of Dynacq.

	Annual Growth	08/11	08/12	08/13	08/14	08/15
Sales ($ mil.)	-	(2.0)	5.5	6.1	10.2	7.0
Net income ($ mil.)	-	(19.2)	(12.2)	(3.3)	(3.8)	(3.8)
Market value ($ mil.)	(31.3%)	24.3	7.6	0.4	0.1	5.4
Employees	(2.1%)	137	111	127	131	126

DYNAMEX INC.

5429 LBJ Fwy. Ste. 1000
Dallas TX 75240
Phone: 214-560-9000
Fax: 214-560-9349
Web: www.dynamex.com

CEO: -
CFO: -
HR: -
FYE: July 31
Type: Subsidiary

Dynamex knows the dynamics of same-day delivery. The company provides both scheduled and on-demand delivery of time-sensitive items such as medical supplies and financial documents. It operates from more than 60 company-owned (but locally managed) facilities in the US and Canada. A network of ground couriers focuses on intracity deliveries while hird-party air and ground carriers fulfill same-day intercity services. Dynamex also supports clients in outsourcing certain logistics functions including management of dedicated vehicle fleets and facilities such as mailrooms and inventory-tracking call centers. The company has been owned by Canada's TransForce since 2011.

DYNAMIC MATERIALS CORP.   NMS: BOOM

5405 Spine Road
Boulder, CO 80301
Phone: 303 665-5700
Fax: -
Web: www.dmcglobal.com

CEO: Kevin Longe
CFO: Michael Kuta
HR: -
FYE: December 31
Type: Public

Dynamic Materials Corporation (DMC) has an explosive personality when it comes to working with metal. Formerly Explosive Fabricators the company uses explosives to metallurgically bond or "clad" metal plates; the process usually joins a corrosion-resistant alloy with carbon steel — metals that do not bond easily. Its clad metal plates are central to making heavy-duty pressure vessels and heat exchangers used in such industries as alternative energy and shipbuilding. Its Oilfield Products segment (operating as DYNAenergetics) makes explosive devices used to knock open oil and gas wells. Its AMK Welding unit machines and welds parts for commercial and military aircraft engines and power-generation turbines.

	Annual Growth	12/10	12/11	12/12	12/13	12/14
Sales ($ mil.)	7.0%	154.7	208.9	201.6	209.6	202.6
Net income ($ mil.)	(16.4%)	5.3	12.5	11.7	7.5	2.6
Market value ($ mil.)	(8.2%)	315.9	276.9	194.6	304.3	224.2
Employees	3.8%	433	456	511	555	503

DYNAMIC OFFSHORE RESOURCES LLC

1301 McKinney Ste. 900
Houston TX 77010
Phone: 713-728-7840
Fax: 713-728-7860
Web: www.dynamicosr.com

CEO: -
CFO: -
HR: -
FYE: December 31
Type: Private

Dynamic Offshore Resources isn't giving up on the Gulf of Mexico. While other companies are pulling out of the gulf it has amassed offshore oil and natural gas properties stretching from Texas to Alabama. The company has interests in about 200 producing wells mostly located in water depths of less than 300 feet and 200 offshore leases covering 315000 net acres. It also owns a 49% interest in the deepwater Bullwinkle field and platform located at 1350 feet. (Superior Energy owns the other 51%). Dynamic Offshore Resources reported proved reserves of 62.5 million barrels of oil equivalent at the end of 2011. In 2012 the debt-laden company was acquired by SandRidge Energy for about $1.2 billion.

DYNAMIX GROUP INC

1905 WOODSTOCK RD # 4150
ROSWELL, GA 300755616
Phone: 770-643-8877
Fax: -
Web: www.dynamix-group.com

CEO: -
CFO: David A Delong
HR: -
FYE: December 31
Type: Private

Dynamix Group understands that business technology never sits still. The company provides information technology (IT) products and services including the implementation and configuration of software and hardware as well as network systems maintenance and technical support from its offices throughout the southeastern US. The company's core business is centered around IBM products but it also has product partnerships with other business software vendors including Oracle and VMware. Additional data network services include disaster recovery and storage management. Dynamix was founded in 1995 by CEO Chuck Hawkins and COO Dave DeLong both veterans of IBM.

	Annual Growth	12/09	12/10	12/11	12/12	12/13
Sales ($ mil.)	15.4%	-	84.2	120.4	107.1	129.4
Net income ($ mil.)	(3.3%)	-	-	10.4	8.5	9.7
Market value ($ mil.)	-	-	-	-	-	-
Employees	-	-	-	-	-	93

DYNAPAC USA INC.

16435 IH 35 North
Selma TX 78154
Phone: 210-474-5770
Fax: 210-474-5780
Web: www.dynapac.com

CEO: –
CFO: –
HR: –
FYE: December 31
Type: Subsidiary

Dynapac USA is rolling along in the compaction and paving machinery business. A division of Sweden-based Dynapac AB its products primarily include compactors cutters and grinders pavers planers poker vibrators rollers rammers and submersible pumps for use in road building and civil construction. Dynapac also offers service spare parts and training. Formerly a subsidiary of Metso Minerals Industries Dynapac was taken private by Nordic investment firm Altor in 2004. Dynapac has eight production facilities in Brazil China France Germany Sweden and the US and has sales operations in 16 countries worldwide. Dynapac AB was purchased by Atlas Copco in 2007.

DYNASIL CORP OF AMERICA

NAS: DYSL

313 Washington Street, Suite 403
Newton, MA 02458
Phone: 617 668-6855
Fax: –
Web: www.dynasil.com

CEO: Peter Sulick
CFO: Robert J. Bowdring
HR: –
FYE: September 30
Type: Public

Dynasil Corporation of America likes playing with the dynamics of silica. The company manufactures custom synthetic-fused silica and quartz products primarily used in industrial optical materials. Its products include filters lenses prisms reflectors windows and mirrors. Customers use the company's fabricated optical products in lasers aircraft optical equipment analytical instruments semiconductors and electronics. Manufacturers Corning Schott Glass Technologies and General Electric supply the company with some fused silica fused quartz and optical materials. Dynasil sells its products in the US and overseas.

	Annual Growth	09/11	09/12	09/13	09/14	09/15
Sales ($ mil.)	(3.6%)	47.0	47.9	42.8	42.3	40.5
Net income ($ mil.)	–	1.4	(4.3)	(8.7)	2.0	(0.4)
Market value ($ mil.)	(7.5%)	43.9	26.5	14.6	25.7	32.1
Employees	(0.7%)	237	237	233	224	230

DYNATRONICS CORP.

NAS: DYNT

7030 Park Centre Drive
Cottonwood Heights, UT 84121
Phone: 801 568-7000
Fax: 801 568-7711
Web: www.dynatronics.com

CEO: –
CFO: Terry M Atkinson
HR: –
FYE: June 30
Type: Public

Dynatronics makes medical equipment to keep active people on the go. Its physical medicine products include electrotherapy ultrasound and infrared light therapy equipment; medical supplies such as wraps braces bandages walking aids and training equipment; and rehabilitation therapy tables. Dynatronics also sells aesthetic products under the Synergie brand including the Synergie Aesthetic Massage System (AMS) for cosmetic weight loss and the Synergie Elite microdermabrasion device that reduces wrinkles. The company's products are sold directly through its own distributors and catalogs as well as through independent dealers. Customers include physicians surgeons and physical therapists.

	Annual Growth	06/11	06/12	06/13	06/14	06/15
Sales ($ mil.)	(2.9%)	32.7	31.7	29.5	27.4	29.1
Net income ($ mil.)	–	0.3	(0.0)	(0.0)	(0.3)	(2.3)
Market value ($ mil.)	21.5%	3.9	1.3	6.9	9.8	8.5
Employees	(3.9%)	165	146	144	140	141

DYNAVAX TECHNOLOGIES CORP

NAS: DVAX

2929 Seventh Street, Suite 100
Berkeley, CA 94710-2753
Phone: 510 848-5100
Fax: –
Web: www.dynavax.com

CEO: Eddie Gray
CFO: Michael S Ostrach
HR: Cecilia Vitug
FYE: December 31
Type: Public

Dynavax Technologies is trying to reprogram the way the body reacts to disease. The firm focuses on immunostimulatory sequences (ISS) which are short strands of DNA found to strengthen the immune system. The company's lead candidate in clinical trials is HEPLISAV a hepatitis B vaccine. Other candidates in the company's pipeline include a universal flu vaccine that would cover a wider span of flu viruses than traditional flu vaccines as well as potential treatments for asthma hepatitis C and other autoimmune and inflammatory diseases. To share the expense and risk of development Dynavax has partnered with drugmakers including AstraZeneca and GlaxoSmithKline to further the development of some candidates.

	Annual Growth	12/10	12/11	12/12	12/13	12/14
Sales ($ mil.)	(17.6%)	24.0	21.6	9.7	11.3	11.0
Net income ($ mil.)	–	(57.3)	(48.6)	(69.9)	(66.7)	(90.7)
Market value ($ mil.)	51.5%	84.2	87.3	75.0	51.6	443.5
Employees	11.4%	128	150	167	151	197

DYNAVOX INC.

NASDAQ: DVOX

2100 Wharton St. Ste. 400
Pittsburgh PA 15203
Phone: 412-381-4883
Fax: 412-381-5241
Web: www.dynavoxtech.com

CEO: –
CFO: Raymond Merk
HR: –
FYE: June 30
Type: Public

DynaVox gives its customers a voice — literally. The company provides speech generation communication and environment control devices used by persons with speech learning and physical disabilities. Its products which come in various keyboard- and touchscreen-based form factors are used by individuals diagnosed with amyotrophic lateral sclerosis (ALS or Lou Gehrig's disease) autism cerebral palsy stroke traumatic brain injury and similar conditions. Besides the proprietary technology that drives its devices DynaVox also develops and sells the Boardmaker special education and text-to-speech software. The company generates most of its sales from the US.

DYNCORP INTERNATIONAL INC.

3190 Fairview Park Dr. Ste. 700
Falls Church VA 22042
Phone: 571-722-0210
Fax: 571-722-0252
Web: www.dyn-intl.com

CEO: Lewis Von Thaer
CFO: William Kansky
HR: –
FYE: December 31
Type: Private

DynCorp International works behind the scenes to support military and diplomatic efforts on front lines. A US national security contractor DynCorp (DI) supports the US departments of State and Defense by providing linguist services and international police force training especially in Afghanistan and Iraq. It provides turnkey solutions for post-conflict countries to rebuild infrastructure install utilities/telecommunications provide security transport equipment and remove/dismantle weapons. It also constructs barracks hangars and provides aircraft repairs and service.

DYNEGY INC (NEW)　　　　　　　　　　　NYS: DYN

601 Travis, Suite 1400　　　　　　　CEO: Robert C. (Bob) Flexon
Houston, TX 77002　　　　　　　　　CFO: Clint C. Freeland
Phone: 713 507-6400　　　　　　　　HR: –
Fax: –　　　　　　　　　　　　　　FYE: December 31
Web: www.dynegy.com　　　　　　　　Type: Public

Power company Dynegy (a short version of "dynamic energy") has lost some of its dynamism in recent years but is looking to get some of that energy back as a reorganized company. Dynegy provides wholesale power capacity and other services to a broad range of customers (utilities cooperatives municipalities and other energy operations) in six states in the Midwest the Northeast and on the West Coast. The company's power generation portfolio consists of a dozen plants fueled by coal fuel oil and natural gas with a total capacity of more than 6770 MW.

	Annual Growth	12/11*	10/12*	12/12	12/13	12/14
Sales ($ mil.)	23.3%	1,333.0	981.0	312.0	1,466.0	2,497.0
Net income ($ mil.)	–	(940.0)	(32.0)	(107.0)	(356.0)	(273.0)
Market value ($ mil.)	26.0%	–	–	2,380.5	2,677.9	3,776.7
Employees	17.8%	–	–	1,210	1,710	1,679

*Fiscal year change

DYNEON L.L.C.

6744 33rd St. North　　　　　　　　CEO: –
Oakdale MN 55128　　　　　　　　　CFO: –
Phone: 651-733-5353　　　　　　　　HR: –
Fax: 651-737-7686　　　　　　　　　FYE: December 31
Web: www.dyneon.com　　　　　　　　Type: Subsidiary

Dyneon stretches the limits of plastics technology. The company a unit of 3M develops advanced elastomers (an elastomer is a material that returns rapidly to its initial shape). Dyneon's products include fluoroelastomers (FKMs used as seals in high-heat and chemically stressful applications) fluorothermoplastics (used to make industrial components) and polytetrafluoroethylenes (PTFEs used in metal coatings and electronics). The company also produces fluoropolymer-based additives used in thermoplastic resins. Dyneon's products are used by the automotive chemical processing electrical food packaging and semiconductor industries. In 2008 the company acquired thermoplastics maker Hitech Polymers.

DYNEX CAPITAL, INC.　　　　　　　　　　NYS: DX

4991 Lake Brook Drive, Suite 100　　CEO: Byron L. Boston
Glen Allen, VA 23060-9245　　　　　CFO: Stephen J. Benedetti
Phone: 804 217-5800　　　　　　　　HR: Jeffrey Chidress
Fax: –　　　　　　　　　　　　　　FYE: December 31
　　　　　　　　　　　　　　　　　Type: Public

Dynex Capital is a real estate investment trust (REIT) that invests in loans and fixed-income securities backed by single-family residential and commercial mortgage loans. The company isn't too picky investing in both investment-grade and subprime loans and adjustable-rate and fixed-rate loans. However citing competition and a "lack of compelling opportunities" in a volatile marketplace the company makes few new investments and has been slimming down its balance sheet by selling off assets including all of its manufactured home lending and delinquent property-tax receivable portfolios.

	Annual Growth	12/10	12/11	12/12	12/13	12/14
Sales ($ mil.)	21.3%	48.8	83.4	113.5	127.1	105.6
Net income ($ mil.)	(1.4%)	29.5	39.8	74.0	68.1	27.8
Market value ($ mil.)	(6.8%)	597.8	499.8	516.7	437.9	451.6
Employees	3.2%	15	15	17	18	17

DYNTEK INC.　　　　　　　　　　　　PINK SHEETS: DYNE

4440 Von Karman Ste. 200　　　　　CEO: Ron Ben-Yishay
Newport Beach CA 92660　　　　　　CFO: Karen S Rosenberger
Phone: 949-271-6700　　　　　　　　HR: –
Fax: 949-271-6794　　　　　　　　　FYE: June 30
Web: www.dyntek.com　　　　　　　　Type: Public

DynTek sees a bright future in technology services. The company previously a provider of medication and services to diabetes patients now provides a variety of information technology services to local and state governments schools and commercial enterprises. Its services include technology procurement systems integration business process outsourcing network engineering and technical support. While its marketing emphasis focuses on its IT services business the bulk of its of sales are derived from the resale of hardware and software from partners such as Cisco IBM Microsoft and Novell.

E Z LOADER BOAT TRAILERS INC.

717 N HAMILTON ST　　　　　　　　CEO: –
SPOKANE, WA 992022044　　　　　　CFO: –
Phone: 574-266-0092　　　　　　　　HR: Christina Lafleur
Fax: –　　　　　　　　　　　　　　FYE: December 31
Web: www.estore.ezloader.com　　　　Type: Private

Nine years after manufacturing its first boat trailer in 1953 EZ Loader invented the all-roller trailer and made loading boats easier for everyone. Its patented design has rubber rollers in key locations along the top of the trailer to allow boats to avoid damage and slide easily into place. The company's website includes an e-store that sells trailer kits for home assembly and replacement and spare parts. EZ Loader also sells its trailers through independent distributors located in the US Japan the Middle East Asia Australia and Africa. The company has grown to include 10 divisions across the country. It is owned by Dave Thielman and president Randy Johnson.

	Annual Growth	12/02	12/03	12/04	12/06	12/08
Sales ($ mil.)	(2.6%)	–	–	56.3	66.3	50.6
Net income ($ mil.)	–	–	–	0.0	0.5	(0.1)
Market value ($ Mil.)	–	–	–	–	–	–
Employees	–	–	–	–	–	275

E*TRADE BANK

671 N. Glebe Rd. 10th Fl.　　　　　CEO: Mitchell Caplan
Arlington VA 22203　　　　　　　　CFO: –
Phone: 678-624-6210　　　　　　　　HR: –
Fax: 800-664-4641　　　　　　　　　FYE: December 31
Web: https://us.etrade.com/e/t/banking　Type: Subsidiary

If you want to e-void e-nnoying trips to the bank try e-banking with E*TRADE Bank. A subsidiary of online brokerage E*TRADE Financial the bank is one of the largest electronic banks in the US. Its customers can access their accounts via the Internet mail phone and ATMs as well as through more than 25 bricks-and-mortar locations in major metropolitan areas across the US. Like most traditional banks E*TRADE Bank offers deposits loans credit cards and other financial services. Unlike most traditional banks however E*TRADE Bank allows its customers to transfer funds between their banking and E*TRADE brokerage accounts in real time.

E*TRADE FINANCIAL CORP.

NMS: ETFC

1271 Avenue of the Americas, 14th Floor
New York, NY 10020
Phone: 646 521-4300
Fax: –
Web: www.etrade.com

CEO: Paul T. Idzik
CFO: Michael A. Pizzi
HR: –
FYE: December 31
Type: Public

E*TRADE wants you to use its services for nearly E*VERYTHING financial. Known for its brokerage services the firm provides the products tools services and advice to individual investors and stock plan participants wanting to manage their own investments. For corporate clients it offers market making trade clearing and employee stock option plan admin services. Subsidiary E*TRADE Bank offers deposits savings and credit cards online and from 30 financial centers in major US cities. E*TRADE Clearing offers securities clearing and settlement while E*TRADE Securities the bank's broker-dealer arm offers mutual funds options fixed income products exchange-traded funds and portfolio management services.

	Annual Growth	12/10	12/11	12/12	12/13	12/14
Assets ($ mil.)	(0.5%)	46,373.0	47,940.5	47,386.7	46,279.9	45,530.0
Net income ($ mil.)	–	(28.5)	156.7	(112.6)	86.0	293.0
Market value ($ mil.)	11.0%	4,628.4	2,302.6	2,589.0	5,681.3	7,016.3
Employees	2.0%	2,962	3,240	3,000	3,009	3,200

E-DIALOG INC.

65 Network Dr. Ste. 400
Burlington MA 01803
Phone: 781-863-8117
Fax: 781-863-8118
Web: www.e-dialog.com

CEO: John Rizzi
CFO: John E Macphee
HR: –
FYE: December 31
Type: Subsidiary

Permission-based e-mail marketing — now that's what I'm talking about. e-Dialog provides e-mail marketing tools and services to more than 75 large corporate clients. The company provides Web-based software that helps clients implement and manage e-mail marketing campaign functions such as reporting message deployment segmentation and analysis. e-Dialog also offers campaign management services for clients needing a full-service option. It operates from six offices in the US Singapore and the UK. Clients have included such high-profile brands as British Airways the NFL and Reuters. e-Dialog which was founded in 1997 is a subsidiary of GSI Commerce a provider of e-commerce services.

E-LOAN INC.

6230 Stoneridge Mall Rd.
Pleasanton CA 94588
Phone: 925-847-6200
Fax: 925-847-0831
Web: www.eloan.com

CEO: Mark E Lefanowicz
CFO: –
HR: –
FYE: December 31
Type: Subsidiary

E-LOAN has E-LIMINATED its direct-to-consumer lending activities and now only provides access to CDs and savings accounts through its website. The struggling division of Banco Popular North America (BPNA) stopped issuing new auto home and other types of loans in 2008 after it faced significant losses amid illiquid credit markets declining mortgage originations and a spike in foreclosures. E-LOAN attempted to restructure itself in 2007 and it cut 40% of its workforce. But a year later its parent company Puerto Rico's Popular began scaling back its US operations. All of E-LOAN'S functions were transferred to BPNA and Popular's processing unit EVERTEC in mid-2009.

E-Z MART STORES INC.

602 FALVEY AVE
TEXARKANA, TX 755016677
Phone: 903-832-6502
Fax: –

CEO: Sonja Hubbard
CFO: Stacy Yates
HR: –
FYE: December 31
Type: Private

E-Z Mart Stores aims to make filling gas tanks and stomachs EZR for small-town America. The regional convenience store chain operates about 295 stores across four neighboring states including Arkansas Louisiana Oklahoma and Texas. Rather than build its own stores the company usually expands through acquisitions. In addition to the standard hot dogs sodas coffee and cigarettes most E-Z Mart locations also offer Shell Conoco Phillips 66 or CITGO gasoline. E-Z Mart was founded in 1970 by Jim Yates in Nashville Arkansas. Yates died in 1998 when the plane he was piloting crashed leaving his daughter Sonja Hubbard at the company's helm as CEO.

	Annual Growth	12/09	12/10	12/11	12/12	12/13
Sales ($ mil.)	8.2%	–	793.1	961.1	1,018.2	1,003.8
Net income ($ mil.)	5.9%	–	–	13.5	33.8	15.2
Market value ($ mil.)	–	–	–	–	–	–
Employees	–	–	–	–	–	2,100

E. & J. GALLO WINERY

600 Yosemite Blvd.
Modesto CA 95354
Phone: 209-341-3111
Fax: 323-563-5500
Web: www.emjmetals.com

CEO: Joseph E Gallo
CFO: –
HR: –
FYE: December 31
Type: Private

E. & J. Gallo Winery brings merlot to the masses. The company is the world's largest family-owned winemaker thanks in part to such value-jug and -box labels as Carlo Rossi and Peter Vella. The vintner owns seven wineries and some 16000 acres of California vineyards; it also contracts with other growers statewide to meet its supply needs. It is the leading US exporter of California wine selling some 60 brands including table and sparkling wines and imports 14 of its name brands from countries dotting the globe. Gallo Family Vineyards Sonoma Reserve and the Italian wine Ecco Domani are among its premium wines and imports.

E. C. BARTON & COMPANY

2929 BROWNS LN
JONESBORO, AR 724017208
Phone: 870-932-6673
Fax: –
Web: www.ecbarton.com

CEO: Niel Crowson
CFO: Tom Ford
HR: –
FYE: October 30
Type: Private

E. C. Barton & Company sells a variety of homebuilding tools and goods under a handful of banner names. A member of industry cooperative Do It Best the company sells lumber and building materials through more than 120 locations throughout Texas as well as 14 other states in the Southeast and the Northeast. It operates several divisions including Barton's Builders Material Company E.C.B. Brokerage and Surplus Purchasing Surplus Warehouse and Grossman's Bargain Outlet. E. C. Barton also manages an e-commerce site. Professional builders and remodelers generate most of the company's revenue. Founded in 1885 the company is employee-owned.

	Annual Growth	10/10	10/11	10/12	10/13	10/14
Sales ($ mil.)	(2.1%)	–	263.3	265.2	241.1	247.3
Net income ($ mil.)	–	–	–	(2.2)	(1.8)	0.9
Market value ($ mil.)	–	–	–	–	–	–
Employees	–	–	–	–	–	700

E. GLUCK CORPORATION

29-10 Thomson Ave.
Long Island City NY 11101
Phone: 718-784-0700
Fax: 718-482-2702
Web: www.egluck.com

CEO: –
CFO: Renee Jacobs
HR: Robert Nublin
FYE: December 31
Type: Private

E. Gluck wonders "Do you have the time?" The company makes quartz watches that bear monikers such as Anne Klein Nine West and its own Armitron. Its timepieces also feature characters from Disney Mattel and Warner Bros as well as the designer labels of Lucky Brand and JLO by Jennifer Lopez. E. Gluck uses edgy styling microfiber bands and digital colors to attract younger customers as well as interchangeable bracelets and bezels (and even diamonds) for the more sophisticated set. Its watches which carry a lifetime guarantee on working parts are sold through jewelers department stores and specialty retailers. Owner and CEO Eugen Gluck founded the company in 1955.

EA ENGINEERING SCIENCE AND TECHNOLOGY INC.

225 SCHILLING CIR STE 400
HUNT VALLEY, MD 210311124
Phone: 410-584-7000
Fax: –
Web: www.eaest.com

CEO: –
CFO: Peter Ney
HR: –
FYE: June 30
Type: Private

EA Engineering Science and Technology wants to stop pollution before it starts by offering environmental consulting services. The company's specialties include brownfields and urban redevelopment environmental compliance management and natural resources management. Its more than 450 professionals have completed more than 100000 environmental projects worldwide (more than $1 billion of services). Customers include government agencies and industrial manufacturers. EA Engineering operates from more than 25 offices — 23 in the US (including facilities in Alaska and Hawaii) and one in Guam.

	Annual Growth	06/10	06/11	06/12	06/13	06/14
Sales ($ mil.)	2.6%	–	99.3	59.5	105.0	107.1
Net income ($ mil.)	(22.3%)	–	–	3.6	2.8	2.2
Market value ($ mil.)	–	–	–	–	–	–
Employees	–	–	–	–	–	440

E.DIGITAL CORP.   NBB: EDIG

16870 West Bernardo Drive, Suite 120
San Diego, CA 92127
Phone: 858 304-3016
Fax: –
Web: www.edigital.com

CEO: Alfred H Falk
CFO: Mardee Haring-Layton
HR: –
FYE: March 31
Type: Public

e.Digital believes that the future is digital. The company provides engineering services product reference designs and technology platforms to customers focusing on the digital video and audio markets. e.Digital however plans to focus future growth on selling its eVU mobile entertainment device which features a 7-inch LCD screen dual stereo headphone jacks embedded credit card reader and touch screen capabilities. The eVu is geared towards customers in the airline health care military and travel and leisure industries.

	Annual Growth	03/11	03/12	03/13	03/14	03/15
Sales ($ mil.)	14.6%	1.3	4.7	0.4	2.3	2.2
Net income ($ mil.)	–	(1.1)	1.2	(1.5)	0.1	(0.2)
Market value ($ mil.)	2.8%	27.9	11.8	49.5	20.2	31.1
Employees	(11.1%)	8	9	7	7	5

EACO CORP   NBB: EACO

1500 North Lakeview Avenue
Anaheim, CA 92807
Phone: 714 876-2490
Fax: –
Web: www.eacocorp.com

CEO: Glen F Ceiley
CFO: –
HR: –
FYE: August 31
Type: Public

EACO Corporation lost its appetite for the buffet business. For a half-dozen years after selling its restaurant operations to pursue a new line of business the company generated revenues from a handful of rental properties including restaurant and industrial properties. (Tenant NES Rentals accounts for about half of its rental revenues.) In 2010 the company acquired Bisco Industries which distributes electronics components in the US and Canada. EACO was once the sole franchisee of Ryan's Restaurant Group restaurants in Florida; it also owned a chain of 16 Whistle Junction and Florida Buffet locations. CEO Glen Ceiley owns 98.9% of EACO.

	Annual Growth	08/11	08/12	08/13	08/14	08/15
Sales ($ mil.)	7.6%	104.7	114.6	120.4	134.7	140.2
Net income ($ mil.)	15.0%	2.1	2.4	2.6	5.6	3.7
Market value ($ mil.)	23.4%	10.9	14.3	15.6	35.2	25.3
Employees	4.3%	358	400	424	426	424

E.N.M.R. TELEPHONE COOPERATIVE

7111 N PRINCE ST
CLOVIS, NM 881019730
Phone: 575-389-5100
Fax: –
Web: www.plateautel.com

CEO: Tom Phelps
CFO: David Robinson
HR: –
FYE: December 31
Type: Private

ENMR-Plateau Telecommunications is a telephone cooperative providing wireless and wired communications services in about two dozen communities in eastern New Mexico and western Texas. Mobile services are offered through its Plateau Wireless unit while Plateau Internet provides Internet access and other services including Web hosting. ENMR-Plateau has about 75000 wireless users 12000 landline customers and 15000 Internet subscribers. Area farmers ranchers and other residents founded the company in 1949 as Eastern New Mexico Rural Telephone Cooperative. It operates from offices in Roswell and Carlsbad New Mexico as well as in Levelland and Plainview Texas among other cities.

	Annual Growth	12/09	12/10	12/11	12/12	12/13
Sales ($ mil.)	(9.0%)	–	110.8	106.5	98.0	83.4
Net income ($ mil.)	(48.5%)	–	–	30.6	40.9	8.1
Market value ($ mil.)	–	–	–	–	–	–
Employees	–	–	–	–	–	270

EAGLE BANCORP INC (MD)   NAS: EGBN

7830 Old Georgetown Road, Third Floor
Bethesda, MD 20814
Phone: 301 986-1800
Fax: –
Web: www.eaglebankcorp.com

CEO: Ronald D. Paul
CFO: James H. Langmead
HR: –
FYE: December 31
Type: Public

For those nest eggs that need a little help hatching holding company Eagle Bancorp would recommend its community-oriented EagleBank subsidiary. The bank serves businesses and individuals through more than 15 branches in Washington DC and its suburbs. Deposit products include checking savings and money market accounts; certificates of deposit; and IRAs. Commercial real estate and construction real estate loans combined represent about 70% of its loan portfolio. The bank which has significant expertise as a Small Business Administration lender also writes business consumer and home equity loans. EagleBank offers insurance products through an agreement with The Meltzer Group.

	Annual Growth	12/10	12/11	12/12	12/13	12/14
Assets ($ mil.)	25.9%	2,089.4	2,831.3	3,409.4	3,771.5	5,247.9
Net income ($ mil.)	34.3%	16.7	24.6	35.3	47.0	54.3
Market value ($ mil.)	25.3%	434.9	438.2	601.9	923.2	1,070.6
Employees	10.0%	292	338	393	386	427

EAGLE BANCORP MONTANA, INC.
NMS: EBMT

1400 Prospect Avenue
Helena, MT 59601
Phone: 406 442-3080
Fax: –
Web: www.opportunitybank.com

CEO: Peter J Johnson
CFO: Laura F Clark
HR: –
FYE: December 31
Type: Public

Eagle Bancorp Montana hopes to swoop down on every potential account holder in its home state. The holding company owns American Federal Savings Bank a thrift that serves businesses and residents of southwestern Montana through six branches and seven ATMs. American Federal primarily writes mortgages on one- to four-family residences (these comprise almost half of its loan book); the rest of its portfolio consists of commercial mortgages (25%) home equity (about 20%) and consumer business and construction loans. The bank's deposit products include checking money market and savings accounts; CDs; IRAs; and Visa debit cards. Eagle Bancorp Montana is buying seven branches from Sterling Financial.

	Annual Growth	06/11	06/12	06/13	06/14*	12/14
Assets ($ mil.)	19.2%	331.1	327.3	510.5	539.1	560.2
Net income ($ mil.)	(12.0%)	2.4	2.2	2.0	2.1	1.6
Market value ($ mil.)	0.9%	41.5	38.8	41.4	40.7	42.6
Employees	25.8%	88	90	197	177	175

*Fiscal year change

EAGLE BULK SHIPPING INC.
NASDAQ: EGLE

477 Madison Ave. Ste. 1405
New York NY 10022
Phone: 212-785-2500
Fax: 212-785-3311
Web: www.eagleships.com

CEO: Gary Vogel
CFO: Adir Katzav
HR: –
FYE: December 31
Type: Public

Some eagles soar through the skies but Eagle Bulk Shipping rides the waves. The company owns a fleet of 45 Handymax dry bulk carriers that it charters to customers typically on one- to three-year contracts. Most of its vessels are classified as Supramaxes — large Handymaxes essentially. The Supramaxes range in capacity from 50000 to 60000 deadweight tons (DWT) and feature on-board cranes for cargo loading and unloading. Overall the company's fleet has a carrying capacity of more than 1.1 million DWT. Cargo carried by charterers of Eagle Bulk Shipping's vessels includes cement coal fertilizer grain and iron ore.

EAGLE CREEK INC.

3055 Enterprise Ct.
Vista CA 92081
Phone: 760-599-6500
Fax: 760-599-4722
Web: www.eaglecreek.com

CEO: –
CFO: Bert Fenenga
HR: –
FYE: December 31
Type: Subsidiary

Eagle Creek takes the lug out of luggage by making backpacks and other carrying bags that are designed for comfort. The company specializes in making outdoor backpacks but it also makes and markets wheeled switchbacks and trunks duffel bags shoulder bags and even money belts and wallets. Eagle Creek's Pack-It-System helps to organize and pack clothes and other travel items within a suitcase backpack or briefcase. Its products are sold through specialty luggage stores outdoor shops and department stores in the US and Europe. Employee-owned Eagle Creek was acquired by top jeans manufacturer and outdoor enthusiast V.F. Corporation in 2007.

EAGLE MATERIALS INC
NYS: EXP

3811 Turtle Creek Blvd., Suite 1100
Dallas, TX 75219
Phone: 214 432-2000
Fax: 214 432-2100
Web: www.eaglematerials.com

CEO: Steven R. (Steve) Rowley
CFO: D. Craig Kesler
HR: –
FYE: March 31
Type: Public

Eagle Materials is perched near the top of the building materials business. The company manufactures and distributes cement and gypsum wallboard which together account for nearly 75% of its total sales. Eagle Materials also produces ready-mix concrete aggregates and recycled paperboard. Its products are sold to residential commercial and industrial construction customers throughout the US. The company operates about 25 plants and manufacturing facilities. It also has about 100 railcars for shipping its wallboard products to customers across the country. Founded in 1963 Eagle Materials was spun off by homebuilder Centex Corporation in 2004.

	Annual Growth	03/11	03/12	03/13	03/14	03/15
Sales ($ mil.)	23.2%	462.2	495.0	642.6	898.4	1,066.4
Net income ($ mil.)	88.3%	14.8	18.7	57.7	124.2	186.9
Market value ($ mil.)	28.9%	1,520.4	1,746.0	3,347.8	4,454.8	4,198.5
Employees	10.3%	1,350	1,350	1,800	1,800	2,000

EAGLE PHARMACEUTICALS, INC.
NMS: EGRX

50 Tice Boulevard, Suite 315
Woodcliff Lake, NJ 07677
Phone: 201 326-5300
Fax: –
Web: www.eagleus.com

CEO: Scott L. Tarriff
CFO: David E. Riggs
HR: –
FYE: September 30
Type: Public

Eagle Pharmaceuticals wants to build a better (pharmacological) mousetrap. The company focuses its development efforts on addressing the shortcomings of existing drugs for oncology and critical care. It has two approved products and a handful in the pipeline. Eagle plans to sell its products as branded versions once the drug's initial patent expires. Its only commercialized product is EP-1101 (argatroban) a treatment for blood clotting usually associated with heparin use. The company partners with drug manufacturers Sandoz and The Medicines Company to market the drug in the US. Its EP-2101 (topotecan) is approved for small cell lung cancer in the EU but not sold there. Eagle was formed in 2007 and went public in 2014.

	Annual Growth	09/10	09/11	09/12	09/13	09/14
Sales ($ mil.)	–	0.0	0.0	2.5	13.7	19.1
Net income ($ mil.)	–	0.0	0.0	(19.4)	(6.0)	(18.0)
Market value ($ mil.)	–	0.0	0.0	–	–	177.5
Employees	34.8%	–	–	–	23	31

EAGLE ROCK ENERGY PARTNERS LP
NMS: EROC

1415 Louisiana Street, Suite 2700
Houston, TX 77002
Phone: 281 408-1200
Fax: –
Web: www.eaglerockenergy.com

CEO: Scott W Smith
CFO: Richard A Robert
HR: –
FYE: December 31
Type: Public

The Eagles are into soft rock whereas Eagle Rock Energy Partners is into developing and producing hydrocarbons. The company has oil and gas properties that include more than 560 gross operated productive wells and 1200 gross non-operated wells. The company's upstream operations have exploration and production assets in Alabama Louisiana Mississippi and Texas and has proved reserves of 252.5 billion cu. ft. of natural gas of equivalent. Eagle Rock's former midstream business which included 8100 miles of gathering pipeline and over 800 million cu. ft. of processing plants was sold to Regency Energy Partners in mid-2014.

	Annual Growth	12/09	12/10	12/11	12/12	12/13
Sales ($ mil.)	18.3%	610.5	758.4	1,059.9	984.0	1,195.3
Net income ($ mil.)	–	(171.3)	(5.3)	73.1	(150.6)	(278.0)
Market value ($ mil.)	0.7%	907.0	1,381.6	1,824.9	1,354.9	932.0
Employees	13.5%	353	367	462	510	586

EARL G. GRAVES LTD.

130 5th Ave. 10th Fl.
New York NY 10011-4399
Phone: 212-242-8000
Fax: 212-886-9633
Web: www.blackenterprise.com

CEO: -
CFO: Jacques Jiha
HR: -
FYE: December 31
Type: Private

The eponymous Earl G. Graves Ltd. (founded in 1968 by chairman and publisher Earl G. Graves) publishes Black Enterprise a business magazine aimed at African-American executives that reaches some 4 million readers. The company also operates the online companion BlackEnterprise.com and organizes events for black entrepreneurs and professionals such as The Black Enterprise Entrepreneurs Conference + Expo. In addition the company produces two nationally syndicated television shows: Our World with Black Enterprise and the Black Enterprise Business Report.

EARL L HENDERSON TRUCKING COMPANY

206 W MAIN ST
SALEM, IL 628811519
Phone: 618-548-4667
Fax: -
Web: www.hendersontrucking.com

CEO: -
CFO: -
HR: -
FYE: December 31
Type: Private

This Earl aspires to hold a royal rank in the world of refrigerated transportation. Earl L. Henderson Trucking hauls food and other perishable products throughout the US. The company operates a fleet of some 400 tractors and 600 trailers including about 500 refrigerated trailers. It offers long-haul service in the US and parts of Canada and regional service in the eastern half of the US. In addition to perishable products Henderson Trucking transports time-sensitive printed matter. Company president John Kaburick owns Henderson Trucking which was founded by Earl Henderson in 1978.

	Annual Growth	12/04	12/05	12/06	12/07	12/08
Sales ($ mil.)	(73.9%)	-	-	1,465.6	94.9	100.0
Net income ($ mil.)	3340.1%	-	-	0.0	93.0	0.5
Market value ($ mil.)	-	-	-	-	-	-
Employees	-	-	-	-	-	600

EARLHAM COLLEGE

801 NATIONAL RD W
RICHMOND, IN 473744095
Phone: 765-983-1200
Fax: -
Web: www.earlham.edu

CEO: -
CFO: -
HR: -
FYE: June 30
Type: Private

Earlham College is a private liberal arts college located in Richmond Indiana. The venerable school originally founded by Quakers enrolls about 1100 undergraduate students a year and offers 40 courses of study in the fine arts humanities natural sciences and social sciences. Earlham also offers a three-year pre-professional course of study as well as master's degree programs in teaching and education. The college's annual tuition is approximately $34000. The affiliated Earlham School of Religion established in 1960 offers graduate degrees in religion and ministry.

	Annual Growth	06/07	06/08	06/09	06/10	06/13
Sales ($ mil.)	-	-	-	0.0	53.2	76.4	58.9
Net income ($ mil.)	-	-	-	-	(91.0)	6.6	30.5
Market value ($ mil.)	-	-	-	-	-	-
Employees	-	-	-	-	-	365

EARTH FARE INC.

145 Cane Creek Industrial Park Dr. Ste. 150
Fletcher NC 28732
Phone: 828-281-4800
Fax: 828-254-7556
Web: www.earthfare.com

CEO: Jack Murphy
CFO: Gary Jones
HR: -
FYE: December 31
Type: Private

Shoppers looking to fill their carts with products containing high fructose corn syrup trans fats artificial flavors and synthetic growth hormones need not shop at Earth Fare. The organic and natural foods supermarket chain operates more than 20 stores in Alabama Florida the Carolinas Georgia Ohio and Tennessee. Its stores are smaller than those of its conventional supermarket competitors and national natural foods chains like Whole Foods Market. Even so Earth Fare stores offer about 26000 natural and organic products house cafes and juice bars sell vitamins and herbs and offer deli service and cooking classes. Earth Fare was founded in 1975 by Roger Derrough who owns it along with other investors.

EARTH SEARCH SCIENCES INC.   OTC: ESSE

306 Stoner Loop Rd. Ste. 6
Lakeside MT 59922
Phone: 406-751-5200
Fax: 406-752-7433
Web: www.earthsearch.com

CEO: Larry F Vance
CFO: -
HR: -
FYE: March 31
Type: Public

The technology used by Earth Search Sciences (ESSI) is rooted in the stars not the ground. The company has developed remote sensing instruments (using what is called hyperspectral remote sensing technology) based on NASA's Airborne Visible and Infra-Red Imaging Spectrometer (AVIRIS). The instruments designed by ESSI collect and analyze data for use in oil and gas exploration mining hazardous material remediation and ecosystem monitoring among other things. The company has served customers in the private military and government sectors. Chairman and CEO Larry Vance owns 74% of the company.

EARTHSTONE ENERGY INC.   ASE: ESTE

1400 Woodloch Forest Drive, Suite 300
The Woodlands, TX 77380
Phone: 281 298-4246
Fax: -
Web: www.earthstoneenergy.com

CEO: Frank A. Lodzinski
CFO: G Bret Wonson
HR: -
FYE: December 31
Type: Public

Earthstone Energy (formerly Basic Earth Science Systems) taps into some of Planet Earth's basic energy sources — oil and gas. It is involved in exploration production operation and development activities exploiting crude oil and natural gas assets in Colorado's Denver-Julesburg Basin the Williston Basin of Montana North Dakota and along the Gulf Coast. The company drills about 48 net wells a year and has proved reserves of 638000 barrels of oil and 936 million cu. ft. of gas. Most of Earthstone Energy's productive wells are in Montana North Dakota and Texas.

	Annual Growth	03/11	03/12	03/13	03/14*	12/14
Sales ($ mil.)	80.2%	8.2	11.7	11.4	17.5	48.0
Net income ($ mil.)	-	1.6	3.3	1.8	3.9	(28.8)
Market value ($ mil.)	5.4%	277.5	297.3	228.2	294.0	325.1
Employees	63.0%	12	17	23	19	52

*Fiscal year change

EAST BAY MUNICIPAL UTILITY DISTRICT

375 11th St.
Oakland CA 94607
Phone: 866-403-2683
Fax: 510-465-3470
Web: www.ebmud.com

CEO: –
CFO: –
HR: –
FYE: June 30
Type: Government-owned

It is part of the job description of East Bay Municipal Utility District (EBMUD) to keep the mud out of the drinking water. The utility provides potable water to 1.3 million people in a 331-square-mile area (which includes the cities of Alameda Berkeley and Oakland). Its wastewater system serves about 650000 people in an 88-square-mile area of Alameda and Contra Costa counties along San Francisco Bay's east shore. EBMUD operates a wastewater treatment plant that treats wastewater collected by nine East Bay cities and cleans it before discharge to the San Francisco Bay.

EAST KENTUCKY POWER COOPERATIVE INC.

4775 Lexington Rd.
Winchester KY 40391
Phone: 859-744-4864
Fax: 859-744-6008
Web: www.ekpc.com

CEO: Anthony Campbell
CFO: Bennett Hastie
HR: –
FYE: December 31
Type: Private - Cooperativ

When the Blue Moon of Kentucky is not enough to light the way East Kentucky Power Cooperative is there to help. The company generates and transmits electricity to 16 local distribution cooperatives which in turn provide electricity to more than 521150 customers in 87 counties in eastern Kentucky. East Kentucky Power operates more than 2800 miles of transmission lines and generates most of its electricity from primarily fossil-fueled power plants with about 2500 MW of capacity. The company also operates a natural gas/fuel oil plant and a handful of landfill-gas generation plants and purchases hydroelectric power from the Southeastern Power Administration.

EAST ORANGE GENERAL HOSPITAL INC

300 CENTRAL AVE
EAST ORANGE, NJ 070182897
Phone: 973-672-8400
Fax: –
Web: www.evh.org

CEO: –
CFO: Al Aboud
HR: Valarie Butler
FYE: December 31
Type: Private

East Orange General Hospital pairs medical services with community action. Established in 1903 the not-for-profit hospital is the home of the first Candy Striper program in 1944 and continues with a number of community outreach programs. The 210-bed facility provides inpatient acute care in a wide range of specialties including critical care oncology behavioral health surgery and intensive care. East Orange General Hospital also offers cardiology physical rehabilitation dialysis respiratory care diagnostic testing and wound care among other services. The hospital's Family Health Center provides primary and specialty care as well as outpatient surgery. East Orange General Hospital is part of Essex Valley Healthcare.

	Annual Growth	12/08	12/09	12/10	12/11	12/12
Sales ($ mil.)	(7.2%)	–	113.6	112.5	118.2	90.8
Net income ($ mil.)	–	–	–	0.4	1.3	(1.3)
Market value ($ mil.)	–	–	–	–	–	–
Employees	–	–	–	–	–	960

EAST TENNESSEE CHILDREN'S HOSPITAL ASSOCIATION INC.

2018 W CLINCH AVE
KNOXVILLE, TN 379162301
Phone: 865-541-8000
Fax: –
Web: www.etch.com

CEO: –
CFO: Zane Goodrich
HR: –
FYE: June 30
Type: Private

ETCH has made a permanent mark on the lives of countless children over the years. Knoxville-based East Tennessee Children's Hospital (ETCH) with more than 150 beds provides a full range of health care services to children from eastern Tennessee and portions of surrounding states. Among its 30 specialized services are cardiology neonatal care orthopedics and psychiatry as well as cystic fibrosis and hearing impairment services. The hospital also offers support such as for families of children stricken by cancer. The hospital's roots are in the foundation of Knox County Crippled Children's Hospital in 1937 with less than 50 beds.

	Annual Growth	06/10	06/11	06/12	06/13	06/14
Sales ($ mil.)	4.7%	–	183.6	209.4	216.3	210.8
Net income ($ mil.)	(10.4%)	–	–	29.7	37.6	23.8
Market value ($ mil.)	–	–	–	–	–	–
Employees	–	–	–	–	–	1,500

EAST TENNESSEE STATE UNIVERSITY

807 UNIVERSITY PKWY
JOHNSON CITY, TN 376146500
Phone: 423-439-1000
Fax: –
Web: www.etsu.edu

CEO: –
CFO: –
HR: –
FYE: June 30
Type: Private

East Tennessee State University (ETSU) is a public coeducational member of the Tennessee Board of Regents' network of 45 postsecondary educational institutions. The university has 11 colleges and schools representing arts and sciences business and technology clinical and rehabilitative health sciences education medicine nursing pharmacy public health honors as well as continuing and graduate studies. It offers approximately 125 undergraduate programs 95 master's programs and a dozen doctoral programs as well as graduate certificates teacher licensure and specialist programs. Founded as East Tennessee State Normal School in 1911 ETSU has an enrollment of more than 15000 students.

	Annual Growth	06/04	06/05	06/06	06/08	06/13
Sales ($ mil.)	(19.3%)	–	995.9	16.3	14.7	179.7
Net income ($ mil.)	(4.3%)	–	–	8.8	7.6	6.4
Market value ($ mil.)	–	–	–	–	–	–
Employees	–	–	–	–	–	2,400

EAST TEXAS MEDICAL CENTER REGIONAL HEALTHCARE SYST

1000 S BECKHAM AVE
TYLER, TX 757011908
Phone: 903-597-0351
Fax: –
Web: www.etmc.org

CEO: Elmer G Ellis
CFO: –
HR: Anita Hays
FYE: October 31
Type: Private

East Texas Medical Center (ETMC) Regional Healthcare System works to meet the health care needs of residents of the Piney Woods. The not-for-profit health system operates more than a dozen hospitals across eastern Texas along with behavioral rehabilitation and home health care businesses. Its flagship 450-bed Tyler location serves as the hub and referral center for satellite medical centers located in more rural locations. The system also runs numerous primary care and outpatient clinics throughout the region. Serving more than 300000 patients each year ETMC operates an emergency ambulance service subsidiary and a clinical laboratory which provide services to the ETMC Regional Healthcare System.

	Annual Growth	10/04	10/05	10/06	10/07	10/08
Sales ($ mil.)	1.5%	–	837.5	837.5	827.9	877.0
Net income ($ mil.)	–	–	–	0.0	40.0	30.1
Market value ($ mil.)	–	–	–	–	–	–
Employees	–	–	–	–	–	7,600

EAST WEST BANCORP, INC   NMS: EWBC

135 N. Los Robles Ave., 7th Floor
Pasadena, CA 91101
Phone: 626 768-6000
Fax: –
Web: www.eastwestbank.com

CEO: Dominic Ng
CFO: Irene Oh
HR: –
FYE: December 31
Type: Public

East West Bancorp banks in both hemispheres of the world. It's the holding company for East West Bank which provides standard banking services and loans through more than 130 branches in major US metropolitan areas and about 10 offices across in China Hong Kong and Taiwan. Boasting $29 billion in assets East West Bank focuses on making commercial and industrial real estate loans which account for the majority of the company's loan portfolio. Catering to the Asian-American community it also provides international banking and trade financing to importers/exporters doing business in the Asia/Pacific region. East West Bank offers multilingual service in English Cantonese Mandarin Vietnamese and Spanish.

	Annual Growth	12/10	12/11	12/12	12/13	12/14
Assets ($ mil.)	8.5%	20,700.5	21,968.7	22,536.1	24,730.1	28,738.0
Net income ($ mil.)	20.1%	164.6	245.2	281.7	295.0	342.5
Market value ($ mil.)	18.6%	2,807.0	2,835.7	3,085.6	5,021.1	5,558.1
Employees	6.2%	2,131	2,329	2,306	2,542	2,709

EASTER SEALS INC.

233 S WACKER DR STE 2400
CHICAGO, IL 606066410
Phone: 312-726-6200
Fax: –
Web: www.easterseals.com

CEO: –
CFO: Gordon Hauge
HR: Dorothy Moser
FYE: December 31
Type: Private

A year round effort that has nothing to do with Easter seals or flowers the National Easter Seal Society annually helps more than one million children and adults with disabilities through over 550 service centers in the US Puerto Rico Canada and Australia. The organization offers medical rehabilitation job training child care and adult day services. It began in 1907 as the National Society for Crippled Children and launched its first "seal" campaign around Easter in 1934. Supporters placed stickers or seals depicting the lily a symbol of renewal on letters and envelopes. The campaign was so successful and the symbol so associated with the organization that it changed its name in 1967.

	Annual Growth	08/07	08/08*	12/08	12/09	12/13
Assets ($ mil.)	105.0%	–	0.9	–	24.1	34.2
Net income ($ mil.)	(6.7%)	–	–	–	1.1	0.8
Market value ($ mil.)	–	–	–	–	–	–
Employees	–	–	–	–	–	120

*Fiscal year change

EASTERN AMERICAN NATURAL GAS TRUST   NYSE: NGT

919 Congress Ave. Ste. 500
Austin TX 78701
Phone: 800-852-1422
Fax: 512-479-2553

CEO: –
CFO: –
HR: –
FYE: December 31
Type: Public

Shareholders of Eastern American Natural Gas Trust know all about the clean-burning royalty-producing attributes of natural gas. The trust receives royalty interests from 650 producing natural gas wells in West Virginia and Pennsylvania and operated by Eastern American Energy. The trust distributes the royalties to its shareholders quarterly. As a grantor trust Eastern American Natural Gas Trust does not pay federal income taxes and the production on some of its wells qualifies for tax credits because the wells are located on hard-to-drill formations. The trust which in 2008 reported proved reserves of 12.9 billion cu. ft. of natural gas equivalent on its properties will be liquidated no later than 2013.

EASTERN BAG AND PAPER COMPANY INCORPORATED

200 RESEARCH DR
MILFORD, CT 064602880
Phone: 203-878-1814
Fax: –
Web: www.easternbag.com

CEO: Meredith Reuben
CFO: William J O Donnell
HR: Angela D'Arena
FYE: December 31
Type: Private

Eastern Bag and Paper Co. (dba EBP Supply) is a leading distributor of paper products in the northeastern US. In addition to disposable tableware and packaging the company offers foodservice products (including china and glassware) restaurant equipment (can openers refrigerators) personal care items (bath mats roll towels) and cleansers and maintenance supplies (air fresheners vacuums). Its name-brand products are used by the industrial healthcare foodservice and janitorial industries. Founded in 1918 by Samuel Baum the company is owned and run by CEO Meredith Baum Reuben.

	Annual Growth	12/07	12/08	12/11	12/12	12/13
Sales ($ mil.)	–	–	0.0	174.5	178.0	182.5
Net income ($ mil.)	–	–	–	0.0	1.1	2.0
Market value ($ mil.)	–	–	–	–	–	–
Employees	–	–	–	–	–	285

EASTERN BANK CORPORATION

265 Franklin St.
Boston MA 02110-3113
Phone: 617-897-1008
Fax: 617-897-1105
Web: www.easternbank.com

CEO: Richard Holbrook
CFO: Charles M Johnston
HR: –
FYE: December 31
Type: Private - Mutual Com

Eastern Bank wants to help you count your clams. The holding company owns Eastern Bank which operates approximately 100 branch locations in Massachusetts. Eastern Bank offers retail and commercial products including deposit accounts investments and credit cards. Its lending activities are focused on commercial loans and leases residential mortgages and consumer loans. Eastern Bank also provides wealth management services through a third-party provider. Insurance subsidiary Eastern Insurance offers personal and commercial coverage group health and life insurance employee benefit plans and 401(k) administration through some 25 locations. Eastern Bank Corporation is mutually owned.

EASTERN CO.   NMS: EML

112 Bridge Street
Naugatuck, CT 06770
Phone: 203 729-2255
Fax: –
Web: www.easterncompany.com

CEO: August M. Vlak
CFO: John L Sullivan III
HR: –
FYE: January 03
Type: Public

The Eastern Company has latched on to the security industry. The company's security products group makes coin acceptors used in laundry facilities smart card payment systems and keyless locks sold under such brands as Big Tag Duo Warlock Searchalert Sesamee Prestolock and Huski. It also manufactures industrial hardware including latches locks and hinges used by the transportation industry. Eastern owns a foundry that makes metal anchoring devices to support underground mine roofs clamps for construction and railroad brake system components. The company sells mainly to manufacturers distributors and locksmiths through its operations in North America China Mexico and Taiwan.

	Annual Growth	01/11*	12/11	12/12	12/13*	01/15
Sales ($ mil.)	2.0%	130.1	142.9	157.5	142.5	140.8
Net income ($ mil.)	8.4%	5.5	5.5	8.6	6.9	7.7
Market value ($ mil.)	0.9%	111.5	124.9	100.0	100.5	115.5
Employees	10.4%	633	688	729	737	942

*Fiscal year change

EASTERN MAINE HEALTHCARE SYSTEMS

43 Whiting Hill Rd.
Brewer ME 04412
Phone: 207-973-7064
Fax: 905-944-6520
Web: www.connexservice.ca

CEO: Terri Vieira
CFO: Derrick Hollings
HR: –
FYE: December 31
Type: Private - Not-for-Pr

Eastern Maine Healthcare Systems (EMHS) keeps the folks in the Pine Tree State feeling fine. With more than a dozen member hospitals and multiple medical practices and clinics the organization offers patients emergency primary mental-health laboratory and other specialty services. It primarily serves eastern central and northern portions of rural Maine. Some hospitals include Eastern Maine Medical Center (410 beds) Acadia Hospital (100 beds) Aroostook Medical Center (75 beds) and Inland Hospital (50 beds). The system established in 1982 also operates long-term care hospice and home health facilities as well as emergency transportation and administrative services businesses.

EASTERN MICHIGAN UNIVERSITY

202 WELCH HALL
YPSILANTI, MI 481972214
Phone: 734-487-2031
Fax: –
Web: www.emich.edu

CEO: –
CFO: –
HR: –
FYE: June 30
Type: Private

Eastern Michigan University (known affectionately as just plain Eastern) has long been an affordable place to study your way into a better career. The university began as a teachers' college in 1849 and it still graduates one out of every four teachers in Michigan. Eastern has an enrollment of more than 23000 students (90% are Michigan residents) who participate in undergraduate and graduate degree programs on its campus in the southeastern part of the state. Its 200 majors minors and concentrations are offered through colleges of arts and sciences business education technology and health and human services.

	Annual Growth	06/08	06/09	06/10	06/11	06/13
Sales ($ mil.)	1.8%	–	212.0	217.8	221.4	227.2
Net income ($ mil.)	–	–	–	(1.4)	24.7	(3.4)
Market value ($ mil.)	–	–	–	–	–	–
Employees	–	–	–	–	–	2,000

EASTERN MOUNTAIN SPORTS INC.

1 Vose Farm Rd.
Peterborough NH 03458
Phone: 603-924-9571
Fax: 603-924-9138
Web: www.emsonline.com

CEO: –
CFO: –
HR: –
FYE: January 31
Type: Private

Eastern Mountain Sports (EMS) can prepare you for a life of climb. EMS sells a wide range of outdoor gear apparel footwear and accessories from more than 65 stores in a dozen East Coast states from Maine to Virginia and through its website. Outdoor enthusiasts can purchase or rent tents sleeping bags and other equipment — choosing from brands such as Patagonia Columbia The North Face REEF and Teva. The retailer's own EMS-branded products account for about a third of sales. Founded in 1967 by two New England rock climbers EMS offers outdoor skills clinics provides guides for hire arranges day and overnight trips and operates climbing and kayaking schools.

EASTERN VIRGINIA BANKSHARES, INC

NMS: EVBS

330 Hospital Road
Tappahannock, VA 22560
Phone: 804 443-8400
Fax: –
Web: www.evb.org

CEO: Joe A Shearin
CFO: J Adam Sothen
HR: –
FYE: December 31
Type: Public

Founded in 1997 Eastern Virginia Bankshares is the holding company for EVB a community bank that operates more than two dozen branches in — believe it or not — eastern Virginia. Targeting individuals and local business customers the bank offers such standard retail services as checking and savings accounts money market accounts CDs IRAs and credit cards. Residential mortgages make up nearly half of the the company's loan portfolio which also includes commercial real estate construction business and consumer loans. Subsidiary EVB Financial Services owns interests in companies that offer investments and insurance.

	Annual Growth	12/10	12/11	12/12	12/13	12/14
Assets ($ mil.)	1.4%	1,119.3	1,063.0	1,075.6	1,027.1	1,182.0
Net income ($ mil.)	–	(10.8)	1.8	3.5	(2.6)	5.7
Market value ($ mil.)	14.0%	49.7	26.1	70.1	90.9	84.0
Employees	3.0%	314	307	306	315	353

EASTERN VIRGINIA MEDICAL SCHOOL

714 WOODIS AVE
NORFOLK, VA 235101026
Phone: 757-446-6052
Fax: –
Web: www.evms.edu

CEO: –
CFO: –
HR: –
FYE: June 30
Type: Private

Eastern Virginia Medical School (EVMS) sends graduated physicians down the Hampton Roads. The school offers medical and doctoral degrees residencies and specialty programs such as reproductive medicine. The community-oriented school does not have a teaching hospital but rather partners with about a dozen regional hospitals. Its main campus is part of the Eastern Virginia Medical Center which is also home to Sentara Norfolk General Hospital and Children's Hospital of The King's Daughters located in the Hampton Roads region of southeastern Virginia. The south campus hosts pediatric and diabetes research programs. EVMS also has research programs devoted to cancer infectious diseases and heart disease.

	Annual Growth	06/10	06/11	06/12	06/13	06/14
Sales ($ mil.)	(0.6%)	–	238.3	227.0	229.6	234.3
Net income ($ mil.)	(0.9%)	–	–	17.1	21.6	16.7
Market value ($ mil.)	–	–	–	–	–	–
Employees	–	–	–	–	–	1,500

EASTERN WASHINGTON UNIVERSITY INC

307 SHOWALTER HALL
CHENEY, WA 990042445
Phone: 509-359-6200
Fax: –
Web: www.ewu.edu

CEO: –
CFO: Toni Havegger
HR: –
FYE: June 30
Type: Private

Eagles — the mascot kind at any rate — soar around Eastern Washington University (EWU). The university serves about 13000 undergraduate and graduate students in the area around metropolitan Spokane Washington. Most students study at EWU's Cheney campus but the school includes other learning centers around the state. EWU has 23:1 student-to-faculty ratio. About 140 fields of study are offered through four colleges: Arts Letters and Education; Business and Public Administration; Science Health and Engineering; and Social and Behavioral Sciences and Social Work. The school was founded in 1882 as the Benjamin P. Cheney Academy.

	Annual Growth	06/02	06/03	06/04	06/05	06/08
Sales ($ mil.)	–	–	–	0.0	4.1	110.4
Net income ($ mil.)	1574.4%	–	–	0.0	0.3	4.9
Market value ($ mil.)	–	–	–	–	–	–
Employees	–	–	–	–	–	1,550

EASTGROUP PROPERTIES, INC. NYS: EGP

190 East Capitol Street, Suite 400
Jackson, MS 39201
Phone: 601 354-3555
Fax: –
Web: www.eastgroup.net

CEO: David H. Hoster
CFO: N. Keith McKey
HR: –
FYE: December 31
Type: Public

EastGroup Properties points its compass all across the Sunbelt. The self-administered real estate investment trust (REIT) invests in develops and manages industrial properties with a particular emphasis on Florida Texas Arizona and California. EastGroup specializes in operating multitenant distribution and bulk distribution facilities from 5000 to 50000 sq. ft. in size located near major transportation hubs. Its portfolio includes some 300 industrial properties and an office building totaling more than 34 million sq. ft. of leasable space. The REIT has developed build-to-suit projects for clients including United Stationers Supply Company and Dal-Tile Corporation.

	Annual Growth	12/10	12/11	12/12	12/13	12/14
Sales ($ mil.)	6.2%	173.1	174.6	186.2	202.2	219.8
Net income ($ mil.)	27.2%	18.3	22.4	32.4	32.6	47.9
Market value ($ mil.)	10.6%	1,364.1	1,401.5	1,734.4	1,867.2	2,041.0
Employees	2.2%	65	72	68	73	71

EASTMAN CHEMICAL CO. NYS: EMN

200 South Wilcox Drive
Kingsport, TN 37662
Phone: 423 229-2000
Fax: –
Web: www.eastman.com

CEO: Mark J. Costa
CFO: Curtis E. (Curt) Espeland
HR: –
FYE: December 31
Type: Public

Eastman Chemical can recall its past through photos — it was once part of film giant Eastman Kodak. The company is now a major producer of chemicals fibers plastics rubber materials polymers and solvents. The chemicals and materials manufacturer is one of the world's largest suppliers of acetate tow for cigarette filters. Eastman's products include such items as food and medical packaging films and toothbrushes. In 2014 the US accounted for 46% of company's revenues; Asia Pacific 27%; Europe Middle East and Africa 22%; and Latin America 5%.

	Annual Growth	12/10	12/11	12/12	12/13	12/14
Sales ($ mil.)	13.0%	5,842.0	7,178.0	8,102.0	9,350.0	9,527.0
Net income ($ mil.)	14.4%	438.0	696.0	437.0	1,165.0	751.0
Market value ($ mil.)	(2.5%)	12,494.0	5,804.2	10,112.0	11,991.8	11,272.5
Employees	10.7%	10,000	10,000	13,500	14,000	15,000

EASTMAN KODAK CO. NYS: KODK

343 State Street
Rochester, NY 14650
Phone: 585 724-4000
Fax: –
Web: www.kodak.com

CEO: Jeffrey J. (Jeff) Clarke
CFO: John N. McMullen
HR: –
FYE: December 31
Type: Public

When Kodak made Brownies folks said "Cheese!" Now the inventor of the Brownie camera has abandoned consumer photography altogether to focus on imaging for businesses. Kodak which has staked its future on commercial printing makes presses and imprinting systems as well as technology to print documents publications and product packaging for corporate customers. It also serves the motion picture industry with motion imaging products services and technology for studios labs and independent filmmakers. Founded in 1880 by George Eastman Eastman Kodak emerged from bankruptcy in 2013 after restructurings made it a smaller company focused on commercial printing products and services.

	Annual Growth	12/11	12/12*	08/13*	12/13	12/14
Sales ($ mil.)	(29.6%)	6,022.0	4,114.0	1,542.0	805.0	2,102.0
Net income ($ mil.)	–	(764.0)	(1,379.0)	2,066.0	(81.0)	(123.0)
Market value ($ mil.)	(37.5%)	–	–	–	1,454.3	909.6
Employees	(24.7%)	17,100	13,000	–	8,800	7,300

*Fiscal year change

EASTON-BELL SPORTS INC.

7855 Haskell Ave. Ste. 200
Van Nuys CA 91406-1902
Phone: 818-902-5800
Fax: 212-415-3530
Web: www.omnicomgroup.com

CEO: Terry G Lee
CFO: Mark A Tripp
HR: –
FYE: December 31
Type: Private

Afraid your favorite athlete might take a knockin' on the noggin? Easton-Bell Sports (EBS) products can help soften the blow. A leading maker of helmets and other sporting goods used by professional and recreational athletes EBS caters to the baseball softball football and hockey markets as well as to cycling snowsports and powersports enthusiasts. The company's items are sold under the Easton Bell Giro and Riddell names among others. It also owns the licensing rights for the MacGregor golf brand. EBS' products are sold at national chains the likes of Wal-Mart and to local retailers. A subsidiary of RBG Holdings EBS was created by the merger of Riddell Bell and Easton Sports in 2006.

EASYLINK SERVICES INTERNATIONAL CORPORATION NASDAQ: ESIC

6025 The Corners Pkwy. Ste. 100
Norcross GA 30092
Phone: 678-533-8000
Fax: 203-755-5105
Web: www.diasys.com

CEO: Mark J Barrenechea
CFO: Paul McFeeters
HR: –
FYE: July 31
Type: Public

EasyLink Services International made sure that clients got the message. The company provided electronic data interchange (EDI) and telex software and services through its supply chain messaging division. Its data translation systems allowed trading partners with incompatible information systems to exchange invoices purchase orders shipping notices and other documents. EasyLink's on-demand messaging segment provided a document delivery system that handles fax e-mail and messaging communications. The company offered services ranging from consulting and training to outsourced document processing. EasyLink was acquired by Open Text in 2012 for $232 million.

EATERIES INC.

1208 E. Broadway Rd. Ste. 120
Tempe AZ 85282
Phone: 480-347-3800
Fax: 918-665-7919
Web: www.edcpub.com

CEO: Richard Cervera
CFO: Adam Romo
HR: –
FYE: December 31
Type: Private

Eateries is a full-service restaurant company that operates two regional casual dining concepts. It operates and franchises about 30 Garfield's Restaurant & Pub locations in 15 states mostly in Michigan Ohio and Pennsylvania. The chain offers a menu of sandwiches and burgers along with traditional American fare including pasta steak and seafood entrees. The company also operates Garcia's Mexican Restaurants an ethnic chain with a dozen locations mostly in Arizona. Vincent Orza a former candidate for governor in Oklahoma and James Burke founded the company in 1984. Owned by private equity firms Cordova Smart & Williams and Waterview Capital Eateries filed for bankruptcy in 2009.

EATON VANCE CORP
NYS: EV

Two International Place
Boston, MA 02110
Phone: 617 482-8260
Fax: 617 482-2396
Web: www.eatonvance.com

CEO: Thomas E. (Tom) Faust
CFO: Laurie G. Hylton
HR: –
FYE: October 31
Type: Public

Eaton Vance offers a investing supermarket of more than 100 mutual funds and manages $310 billion-plus in assets on behalf of retail high-net-worth and institutional clients. Its investment specialties include tax-managed equity funds municipal bond funds floating-rate bank-loan funds income and value equity funds global and high-yield bonds closed-end funds and alternative investments such as private equity funds commodity-based investments and absolute return strategies. Its Eaton Vance Distributors unit markets and sells its products through sales associates in the US the UK Europe the Asia-Pacific region and Latin America as well as a network of brokers independent financial advisors banks and insurance firms.

	Annual Growth	10/11	10/12	10/13	10/14	10/15
Sales ($ mil.)	2.7%	1,260.0	1,209.0	1,357.5	1,450.3	1,403.6
Net income ($ mil.)	1.7%	214.9	203.5	193.8	304.3	230.3
Market value ($ mil.)	8.3%	3,046.6	3,261.0	4,845.2	4,268.1	4,184.6
Employees	6.3%	1,155	1,197	1,330	1,403	1,473

EAU TECHNOLOGIES INC
NBB: EAUI

1890 Cobb International Blvd., Suite A
Kennesaw, GA 30152
Phone: 678 388-9492
Fax: –
Web: www.eau-x.com

CEO: Doug Kindred
CFO: Brian D Heinhold
HR: –
FYE: December 31
Type: Public

Of all the vowels O is EAU's bread and butter (as in H2O). Using water electrolysis technology EAU Technologies (formerly Electric Aquagenics Unlimited) makes equipment and process systems that clean and disinfect surfaces and foods. Its Empowered Water generators are sold and leased to companies in search of improved cleaning and sanitizing. The firm's water-based nontoxic products reduce bacteria viruses spores and molds in food processing living surfaces and other environments. Director Peter Ullrich individually and through his Water Science firm is EAU Technologies largest shareholder. Water Science is also EAU's biggest customer and it licenses EAU technology in Latin America.

	Annual Growth	12/10	12/11	12/12	12/13	12/14
Sales ($ mil.)	9.2%	0.7	1.9	0.5	2.0	1.0
Net income ($ mil.)	–	2.4	(3.0)	(2.0)	(2.0)	(1.9)
Market value ($ mil.)	(40.8%)	4.9	5.7	0.6	1.1	0.6
Employees	(10.7%)	11	11	11	9	7

EBARA TECHNOLOGIES INC.

51 Main Ave.
Sacramento CA 95838
Phone: 916-920-5451
Fax: 916-830-1900
Web: www.ebaratech.com

CEO: Naoki Ando
CFO: –
HR: –
FYE: March 31
Type: Subsidiary

Ebara Technologies takes it seriously when its parent says "keep your room clean." Ebara manufactures cleanroom equipment necessary in semiconductor production. Through its two divisions Components and Semiconductor Equipment Ebara provides cleaning and ozone systems exhaust systems chemical mechanical polishing systems wafer plating heaters and other equipment used in the electronics industry for silicon wafer processing. It also offers solar exhaust management products. Ebara Technologies has sales offices throughout the US and sales and production facilities in Asia and Europe. Founded in 1990 the company is a part of Ebara Corporation's Precision Machinery Group.

EBAY INC.
NMS: EBAY

2065 Hamilton Avenue
San Jose, CA 95125
Phone: 408 376-7400
Fax: –
Web: www.ebay.com

CEO: Devin N. Wenig
CFO: Scott Schenkel
HR: Kristin Yetto
FYE: December 31
Type: Public

I got it on eBay has barreled its way into the lexicon of the new millennium placing a cyber-grin on the corporate face of this online auctioneer. Trading goods every second of every day eBay offers an online forum for selling merchandise worldwide from fine antiques to the latest video games. eBay generates revenue through listing and selling fees and through advertising and boasts more than 155 million users. Its e-commerce platforms include StubHub and Half.com. eBay also has a mobile version of its service and owns e-commerce services provider GSI Commerce as well as a minority stake in online classifieds service craigslist.

	Annual Growth	12/11	12/12	12/13	12/14	12/15
Sales ($ mil.)	(7.3%)	11,651.7	14,072.0	16,047.0	17,902.0	8,592.0
Net income ($ mil.)	(14.5%)	3,229.4	2,609.0	2,856.0	46.0	1,725.0
Market value ($ mil.)	(2.4%)	35,910.7	60,381.3	64,960.2	66,446.1	32,536.3
Employees	(19.6%)	27,770	31,500	33,500	36,500	11,600

EBIX INC
NMS: EBIX

1 Ebix Way
Johns Creek, GA 30097
Phone: 678 281-2020
Fax: –
Web: www.ebix.com

CEO: Robin Raina
CFO: Robert F. (Bob) Kerris
HR: –
FYE: December 31
Type: Public

Ebix knows a lot about the insurance biz. The company sells insurance industry software products and professional services to property/casualty insurers brokerages and individuals in Asia Australia Europe and North America. The company's EbixExchange service acts as an online auction house where buyers and carriers can exchange bids for auto home health life and other types of insurance while paying Ebix a fee on each transaction. Ebix also provides agency management software that includes workflow and customer relationship management (CRM) capabilities as well as other back-office functions for insurance brokers and insurance carriers. The company generates most of its sales in North America.

	Annual Growth	12/10	12/11	12/12	12/13	12/14
Sales ($ mil.)	12.8%	132.2	169.0	199.4	204.7	214.3
Net income ($ mil.)	1.9%	59.0	71.4	70.6	59.3	63.6
Market value ($ mil.)	(8.0%)	856.7	799.8	583.4	532.4	614.9
Employees	18.7%	1,179	1,426	1,903	1,927	2,343

EBL&S DEVELOPMENT LLC

230 S. Broad St. Mezzanine Level
Philadelphia PA 19102
Phone: 215-790-4700
Fax: 215-790-4732
Web: www.ebl-s.com

CEO: –
CFO: –
HR: –
FYE: December 31
Type: Private

Ever Been Last-minute Shopping? You may have zipped in and out of one of this company's shopping centers. EBL&S Development renovates develops and manages retail real estate in several US markets. It owns more than 35 big-box anchored shopping centers and shopping malls totaling more than 4.2 million sq. ft. of space. The company is renovating and converting some of its older and underutilized properties to create mixed-use residential developments. Major tenants include Kmart Office Depot and Wal-Mart. The firm operates in the Midwest Northeast Pacific and Southeast. President and CEO Ed Lipkin co-founded the company in 1976.

EBSCO INDUSTRIES INC.

5724 Hwy. 280 East
Birmingham AL 35242
Phone: 205-991-6600
Fax: 256-430-4030
Web: www.avocent.com

CEO: Timothy R Collins
CFO: –
HR: –
FYE: June 30
Type: Private

Few portfolios are more diverse than that of EBSCO Industries (short for Elton B. Stephens Company). Among the conglomerate's more than 50 information services manufacturing and sales subsidiaries are magazine subscription and fulfillment firms a fishing lure manufacturer (the world's largest) a rifle manufacturer a specialty office and computer furniture retailer and real estate holdings. Its main businesses revolve around the publishing industry: EBSCO operates a subscription management agency and is one of the largest publishers of digital information. It offers about 375000 articles from more than 95000 publishers worldwide. The family of founder Elton B. Stephens Sr. owns the company.

EBY CORPORATION

610 N MAIN ST STE 500
WICHITA, KS 672033619
Phone: 316-268-3500
Fax: –
Web: www.ebycorp.com

CEO: –
CFO: –
HR: Karman Diehl
FYE: December 31
Type: Private

General contractor Eby Corporation operating primarily through its Martin K. Eby Construction subsidiary provides design-build construction management general contracting and related services on projects such as office buildings medical facilities athletic facilities and historical renovations. Eby serves major corporations universities hospitals and state and local governments. Clients have included Disney The University of Texas Wichita State University and The Salvation Army. Martin K. Eby Construction named after the group's founder and the father of chairman Martin K. Eby Jr. was founded in 1937.

	Annual Growth	12/05	12/06	12/08	12/09	12/13
Sales ($ mil.)	–	–	(1,566.5)	43.5	33.8	93.3
Net income ($ mil.)	30.0%	–	–	0.5	(2.3)	1.7
Market value ($ mil.)	–	–	–	–	–	–
Employees	–	–	–	–	–	135

EBY-BROWN COMPANY LLC

280 SHUMAN BLVD STE 280
NAPERVILLE, IL 60563-8106
Phone: 630-778-2800
Fax: –
Web: www.eby-brown.com

CEO: –
CFO: –
HR: –
FYE: October 01
Type: Private

Eby-Brown makes its money on such vices as munchies and nicotine. The company is a leading convenience store supplier that distributes more than 11000 products to some 13500 retail locations in 30 states mostly east of the Mississippi. Eby-Brown operates about half a dozen distribution centers (with total capacity of about 2 million sq. ft.) that supply such items as beverages candy and snack foods frozen and refrigerated foods tobacco products and general merchandise. The convenience store supplier also offers advertising and promotion services for its customers. Eby-Brown which is still family-owned was founded in 1887 by the Wake family.

	Annual Growth	09/06	09/07	09/08*	10/10	10/11
Sales ($ mil.)	–	–	0.0	0.0	4,730.4	4,730.4
Net income ($ mil.)	–	–	0.0	0.0	0.0	0.0
Market value ($ mil.)	–	–	–	–	–	–
Employees	–	–	–	–	–	2,500

*Fiscal year change

ECHELON CORP.   NMS: ELON

550 Meridian Avenue
San Jose, CA 95126
Phone: 408 938-5200
Fax: –
Web: www.echelon.com

CEO: Ronald Sege
CFO: Bill Slakey
HR: –
FYE: December 31
Type: Public

Echelon Corp. has made the infrastructure that connected industrial devices into networks that morphed into the Internet of Things. The company's combination of computer chips routers and controllers network interfaces and software have enabled connections for about 100 million devices for lighting heating and cooling security manufacturing lighting and building automation around the world. Echelon is moving to develop networking resources for the Industrial Internet of Things (IIoT) providing the capability for things such as sensors inside jet engines to communicate their operating status. The company also develops and sells an array of lighting control systems another portion of the Internet of Things.

	Annual Growth	12/10	12/11	12/12	12/13	12/14
Sales ($ mil.)	(23.1%)	111.0	156.5	134.0	86.2	38.7
Net income ($ mil.)	–	(31.3)	(13.0)	(12.8)	(17.6)	(24.3)
Market value ($ mil.)	(36.0%)	44.8	21.4	10.8	9.5	7.5
Employees	(24.0%)	318	302	223	192	106

ECHO GLOBAL LOGISTICS INC   NMS: ECHO

600 West Chicago Avenue, Suite 725
Chicago, IL 60654
Phone: 800 354-7993
Fax: –
Web: www.echo.com

CEO: Douglas R. (Doug) Waggoner
CFO: Kyle L. Sauers
HR: –
FYE: December 31
Type: Public

By land air or sea Echo Global Logistics can help you deliver the goods. The company provides a wide range of transportation and logistics services such as carrier management rate negotiation freight bill audit and payment routing compliance and shipment execution and tracking. In addition its Evolved Transportation Manager (ETM) software analyzes clients' transportation needs and helps reduce costs as well as manages all procedures in shipping. Established in 2005 Echo Global Logistics customer base are primarily companies in the manufacturing and consumer products industries.

	Annual Growth	12/10	12/11	12/12	12/13	12/14
Sales ($ mil.)	28.8%	426.4	602.8	757.7	884.2	1,173.4
Net income ($ mil.)	18.9%	8.4	12.0	12.3	14.2	16.8
Market value ($ mil.)	24.8%	279.4	374.8	417.0	498.5	677.6
Employees	25.1%	709	913	1,364	1,297	1,734

ECHO THERAPEUTICS INC   NAS: ECTE

99 Wood Avenue South, Suite 302
Iselin, NJ 08830
Phone: 732 549-0128
Fax: –
Web: www.echotx.com

CEO: Scott W Hollander
CFO: Alan W Schoenbart
HR: –
FYE: December 31
Type: Public

Echo Therapeutics tries not to scratch the surface. The company develops instruments for transdermal (through the skin) drug delivery and diagnostics. Its devices use gentle abrasion and ultrasound technologies to painlessly extract analytes or introduce drugs without breaking the skin. The firm's proprietary Prelude SkinPrep technology platform is being developed for use in glucose monitoring under the name Symphony. Echo is also developing a system to provide needle-free drug administration of lidocaine and other pharmaceuticals. Echo is also developing Azone a transdermal technology used for reformulated drugs already on the market.

	Annual Growth	12/10	12/11	12/12	12/13	12/14
Sales ($ mil.)	(39.5%)	0.4	0.4	0.0	0.0	0.1
Net income ($ mil.)	–	(4.1)	(10.0)	(12.3)	(19.1)	(15.0)
Market value ($ mil.)	(4.1%)	20.2	28.5	13.1	39.7	17.1
Employees	13.1%	11	29	44	28	18

ECHOPASS CORPORATION

6601 Koll Center Pkwy. Ste. 180
Pleasanton CA 94566
Phone: 801-258-7000
Fax: 801-258-7101
Web: www.echopass.com

CEO: -
CFO: -
HR: -
FYE: December 31
Type: Private

Echopass provides hosted contact center services. The company's EchoSystem service integration platform incorporates carrier and network services customer relationship management (CRM) software consulting and call routing. Its managed CRM services include Microsoft RightNow Technologies and salesforce.com products. It also has technology partnerships with such companies as Cisco Genesys Telecommunications Intervoice and NICE Systems. Echopass was founded in 1998 as a unit of Sento and spun off as an independent company in 2000. The company counts Coverall Cleaning Concepts Kodak Outrigger Enterprises and Ulta among its customers.

ECHOSTAR CORP
NMS: SATS

100 Inverness Terrace East
Englewood, CO 80112-5308
Phone: 303 706-4000
Fax: -
Web: www.echostar.com

CEO: Michael T. Dugan
CFO: David J. Rayner
HR: Sandra L. Kerentoff
FYE: December 31
Type: Public

EchoStar is thinking inside the box. The company provides TV set-top boxes (STBs) primarily to former parent DISH Network as well as similar satellite service providers. Its STB portfolio includes HD and standard definition devices that incorporate digital video recorders. Other products include satellite dishes remote controls and cable receivers. EchoStar also owns Sling Media which sells STBs that enable customers to view their home TV signal on Internet-connected devices. Subsidiary Hughes Communications provides Internet service to consumers in North America and network services and systems to businesses worldwide. The US accounts for most of sales.

	Annual Growth	12/10	12/11	12/12	12/13	12/14
Sales ($ mil.)	10.0%	2,350.4	2,761.4	3,121.7	3,282.5	3,445.6
Net income ($ mil.)	(7.0%)	204.4	3.6	211.0	2.5	152.9
Market value ($ mil.)	20.4%	2,290.5	1,920.8	3,139.0	4,560.9	4,815.9
Employees	17.6%	2,300	4,200	4,000	4,000	4,400

ECKERD COLLEGE INC.

4200 54TH AVE S
SAINT PETERSBURG, FL 337114700
Phone: 727-867-1166
Fax: -
Web: www.eckerd.edu

CEO: Peter Armacost
CFO: -
HR: -
FYE: June 30
Type: Private

What better place to study marine science than on nearly 200 acres of Florida waterfront? Eckerd College is a private co-educational college located in St. Petersburg. The school has more than 1800 students and 160 faculty members and it offers about 40 majors for students to earn bachelor of arts and bachelor of science degrees. Areas of study include marine science psychology economics biology biochemistry international studies literature and art. The school also operates a Program for Experienced Learners where about 700 adult students can earn a bachelor's degree in about a dozen areas as well as study abroad offerings. Eckerd College is affiliated with the Presbyterian Church (U.S.A.).

	Annual Growth	06/10	06/11	06/12	06/13	06/14
Sales ($ mil.)	(13.0%)	-	110.1	96.7	101.2	72.4
Net income ($ mil.)	51.8%	-	-	4.2	4.3	9.7
Market value ($ mil.)	-	-	-	-	-	-
Employees	-	-	-	-	-	377

ECKERD YOUTH ALTERNATIVES INC.

100 STARCREST DR
CLEARWATER, FL 337653224
Phone: 727-461-2990
Fax: -
Web: www.eckerd.org

CEO: -
CFO: -
HR: -
FYE: June 30
Type: Private

Eckerd Youth Alternatives (EYA) provides early intervention and prevention wilderness education residential and day treatment and re-entry and aftercare programs for at-risk youths. The not-for-profit organization has worked to help more than 80000 kids through its operations in about 10 states located primarily in the eastern US. Many of EYA's some 40 programs are offered under contract with state juvenile justice agencies. EYA was established in 1968 by Jack Eckerd the founder of the Eckerd drugstore chain and his wife Ruth Eckerd. During the past few years the company has been focused on expanding its community-based support programs.

	Annual Growth	06/09	06/10	06/11	06/12	06/13
Sales ($ mil.)	15.0%	-	100.6	99.9	89.9	153.3
Net income ($ mil.)	(10.8%)	-	-	2.0	(2.7)	1.6
Market value ($ mil.)	-	-	-	-	-	-
Employees	-	-	-	-	-	1,400

ECLINICALWORKS LLC

2 TECHNOLOGY DR
WESTBOROUGH, MA 01581-1727
Phone: 508-475-0450
Fax: -

CEO: Girish Navani
CFO: -
HR: Debbie Cellucci
FYE: December 31
Type: Private

eClinicalWorks helps physicians focus on their patients by offering a hand in organizing their administrative records. The company provides medical software that manages medical documents also known as electronic health records. It serves both small and mid-sized health care practitioners and large practice groups such as Houston's Memorial Hermann Healthcare System and Chicago's Rush Health. The eClinicalWorks client roster includes some 85000 physicians and more than 470000 medical professionals operating businesses throughout the US. Owned by its executives and employees the company provides software for primary care practices and most medical specialties.

	Annual Growth	12/05	12/06	12/07	12/08	12/10
Sales ($ mil.)	-	-	-	0.0	64.7	140.4
Net income ($ mil.)	-	-	-	0.0	1.9	34.7
Market value ($ mil.)	-	-	-	-	-	-
Employees	-	-	-	-	-	2,800

ECLIPSE INC.

1665 Elmwood Rd.
Rockford IL 61103
Phone: 815-877-3031
Fax: 815-877-2656
Web: www.eclipsenet.com

CEO: -
CFO: -
HR: Jim Corbett
FYE: March 31
Type: Private

Eclipse has found a hot market: industrial heating and drying systems used by such industries as manufacturing pharmaceuticals food and pollution control. The company makes low-emission gas and oil burners and related combustion system components as well as combustion systems for the ceramics and glass industries. It also offers design installation and service. The company's Algas-SDI subsidiary makes gas vaporizing and mixing equipment while its Exothermic subsidiary produces heat exchangers and recuperators that process dry cure bake or finish products. Eclipse's customers include 3M Dow Chemical General Motors and Owens Corning. Eclipse is owned by the family of former chairman Campbell Perks.

ECLIPSE RESOURCES CORP

2121 Old Gatesburg Road, Suite 110
State College, PA 16803
Phone: 814 308-9754
Fax: –
Web: www.eclipseresources.com

NYS: ECR
CEO: Benjamin W. Hulburt
CFO: Matthew R. DeNezza
HR: –
FYE: December 31
Type: Public

Looking to eclipse its oil and gas rivals Eclipse Resources is an independent exploration and production company active in the Appalachian Basin. It has 227230 net acres in Eastern Ohio including 96240 net acres in the most prolific and economic area of the Utica Shale fairway (Utica Core Area) with 25740 net acres targeted as a highly liquids-rich area in the Marcellus Shale in Eastern Ohio (Marcellus Project Area). Eclipse operates 81% of its net acreage within the Utica Core and Marcellus Project areas. In 2014 the company reported estimated proved reserves of 109.6 billion cu. ft. equivalent and 18.3 million barrels of oil equivalent. It went public in June of that year.

	Annual Growth	12/10	12/11	12/12	12/13	12/14
Sales ($ mil.)	–	0.0	0.0	0.4	12.9	137.8
Net income ($ mil.)	–	0.0	0.0	(8.8)	(43.5)	(183.2)
Market value ($ mil.)	–	0.0	0.0	–	–	1,125.0
Employees	42.8%	–	–	–	159	227

ECOLAB, INC.

370 Wabasha Street North
St. Paul, MN 55102
Phone: 800 232-6522
Fax: –
Web: www.ecolab.com

NYS: ECL
CEO: Douglas M. (Doug) Baker
CFO: Daniel J. (Dan) Schmechel
HR: Laurie M. Marsh
FYE: December 31
Type: Public

Ecolab cleans up by cleaning up. The company offers cleaning sanitation pest-elimination and maintenance products and services to energy healthcare hospitality industrial and other customers. Its cleaning and sanitizing operations serve hotels schools commercial and institutional laundries and quick-service restaurants. Other units focus on products for textile care water care health care food and beverage processing and pest control. It also makes chemicals used in water treatment for industrial processes including in the paper and energy industries. The company is expanding its services to the offshore and international energy market.

	Annual Growth	12/10	12/11	12/12	12/13	12/14
Sales ($ mil.)	23.7%	6,089.7	6,798.5	11,838.7	13,253.4	14,280.5
Net income ($ mil.)	22.7%	530.3	462.5	703.6	967.8	1,202.8
Market value ($ mil.)	20.0%	15,118.6	17,334.5	21,559.4	31,265.6	31,340.6
Employees	15.7%	26,494	40,200	40,860	45,415	47,430

ECOLOGY AND ENVIRONMENT, INC.

368 Pleasant View Drive
Lancaster, NY 14086
Phone: 716 684-8060
Fax: 716 684-0844
Web: www.ene.com

NMS: EEI
CEO: Gerard A Gallagher III
CFO: H John Mye III
HR: –
FYE: July 31
Type: Public

Every day is Earth Day at environmental consulting and testing company Ecology and Environment (E & E). The company which has completed more than 50000 projects in some 120 countries provides engineering permitting and environmental support for all types of energy development including offshore energy power plants pipelines and renewables. Services include environmental impact assessments air pollution control wastewater analyses and site-planning. It also consults on natural resource restoration programs green initiatives emergency planning and hazardous waste projects. E & E which generates most of its sales in the US targets government industrial and engineering clients.

	Annual Growth	07/11	07/12	07/13	07/14	07/15
Sales ($ mil.)	(7.0%)	169.2	155.4	134.9	128.4	126.7
Net income ($ mil.)	(16.4%)	7.0	0.8	(2.1)	(1.4)	3.4
Market value ($ mil.)	(9.7%)	72.9	52.3	45.7	44.5	48.5
Employees	(4.4%)	1,140	1,175	1,130	1,013	952

ECOM ECOM.COM INC.

1016 Clemmons St. Ste. 302
Jupiter FL 33477-3305
Phone: 561-880-0004
Fax: 561-337-9356
Web: www.ecomecom.net

PINK SHEETS: ECEC
CEO: Barney A Richmond
CFO: Richard C Turner
HR: –
FYE: May 31
Type: Public

eCom eCom.com has lightened its load. The company also known simply as eCom developed a diverse lineup of businesses that were spun off as separate entities. The subsidiaries were involved in a variety of diverse operations ranging from file compression software development to paintball gun sales. The company was involved in involuntary Chapter 11 bankruptcy proceedings that resulted in creditor American Capital Holdings taking control and distributing shares in eCom to American Capital Holdings shareholders. eCom has no active businesses nor revenues.

ECONOLITE CONTROL PRODUCTS INC.

3360 E. La Palma Ave.
Anaheim CA 92806-2856
Phone: 714-630-3700
Fax: 714-630-6349
Web: www.econolite.com

CEO: Michael C Doyle
CFO: –
HR: –
FYE: December 31
Type: Private

STOP! That familiar sign that prompts motorists to brake at intersections was Econolite Control Products' first transportation management offering. The company now manufactures and distributes much more sophisticated traffic control equipment. Its products include loop traffic control systems vehicle detection systems traffic control cabinets and signal display equipment. Econolite boasts about 5000 arterial systems in operation controlling 100000-plus intersections and more than 90000 wide-area video vehicle detection systems set at intersections and on freeways. Econolite began in 1933 when company founders developed a stop sign with a built-in flashing red light controlled by a bi-metal sun valve.

ECOTALITY INC

Post Montgomery Center, One Montgomery Street, Suite 2525
San Francisco, CA 94104
Phone: 415 992-3000
Fax: –
Web: www.ecotality.com

NBB: ECTY Q
CEO: –
CFO: –
HR: –
FYE: December 31
Type: Public

ECOtality is all juiced up for the electric car revolution. The company develops power storage technologies including battery chargers and charging stations for electric vehicles. Its Minit-Charger system takes about 15 minutes to charge the batteries for electric forklifts golf carts airport trucks and other off-road electric vehicles; the company has sold about 6000 chargers since 2008. Now that the all-electric Nissan Leaf and the hybrid-electric Chevrolet Volt are in production ECOtality is marketing car charging stations called Blink in select cities. ECOtality is also involved in developing solar modules and distributing fuel cell systems. CEO Jonathan Read owns 10% of the company's stock.

	Annual Growth	12/08	12/09	12/10	12/11	12/12
Sales ($ mil.)	48.7%	11.2	8.6	13.7	28.4	54.7
Net income ($ mil.)	–	(8.1)	(29.5)	(16.4)	(22.5)	(9.6)
Market value ($ mil.)	96.3%	0.7	131.6	76.5	25.7	10.4
Employees	38.2%	45	67	116	179	164

ECOVA INC.

1313 N. Atlantic Ste. 5000
Spokane WA 99201
Phone: 509-329-7600
Fax: 509-329-7287
Web: www.ecova.com

CEO: Jana Schmidt
CFO: -
HR: Julie Kearney
FYE: December 31
Type: Subsidiary

Ecova (formerly Advantage IQ) maintains that intelligence plays a key role in business success. The company helps multi-site commercial customers in the US manage their facilities utilities and telecommunications costs by providing outsourced services for such tasks as estimating and managing facility-related expenses handling billing and managing invoices and vendor contracts. It serves clients in industries including communications retail financial services and health care. The company was founded in 1995 as an affiliate of parent Avista Corporation a provider of utilities services in the northwestern US. Ecova has satellite offices in Colorado Minnesota Ohio and Oregon.

EDELBROCK LLC

2700 California St.
Torrance CA 90503
Phone: 310-781-2222
Fax: 310-3201187-
Web: www.edelbrock.com

CEO: John Colainne
CFO: -
HR: -
FYE: June 30
Type: Private

Speed enthusiast Edelbrock makes performance-enhancing parts for race cars and motorcycles recreational and passenger vehicles light trucks and watercraft. The short list includes carburetors intake manifolds cylinder heads water pumps air cleaners camshafts exhaust systems an array of other aftermarket parts and even some branded sportswear. Specifically for Harley-Davidson motorcycles Edelbrock tailors a line of aftermarket engine parts. The company markets its products mainly through automotive chain stores online dealers mail-order houses and warehouse distributors. The Edelbrock family — led by company chairman president and CEO Vic Edelbrock Jr. — runs the 70-plus year old company.

ECRM INCORPORATED

554 Clark Rd.
Tewksbury MA 01876
Phone: 978-851-0207
Fax: 978-851-7016
Web: www.ecrm.com

CEO: Rick Black
CFO: Michael Hurton
HR: -
FYE: March 31
Type: Private

ECRM can capture the picture "with" the thousand words. The company makes and services high-resolution color imaging systems for the printing publishing and graphic arts markets. ECRM's commercial and newspaper printing products include computer-to-plate (CTP) devices imagesetters and software. Its products use laser-based cameras to convert text and graphics into film images or plates for prepress duplication. ECRM was founded in 1969 by three MIT engineers who developed the first commercial laser-based optical character recognition equipment.

EDEN FOODS INC.

701 TECUMSEH RD
CLINTON, MI 492369599
Phone: 517-456-7424
Fax: -
Web: www.edenfoods.com

CEO: -
CFO: -
HR: -
FYE: December 31
Type: Private

Known for its Edensoy organic soymilk Eden Foods offers more than 300 organic food items. It's North America's oldest natural and organic food company and the largest independent manufacturer of dry grocery organic foods. Products include canned beans and tomatoes condiments dry pasta dried fruit and seeds juices oils vinegars teas and spices. They're made using ingredients from more than 325 certified-organic North American farms. Eden Foods also imports sea salts from Europe and traditional Japanese miso and rice vinegar from Asia. Subsidiaries include American Soy Products Eden Organic Pasta Meridian Foods and Sobaya. Family-owned Eden Foods began in 1968 as a natural foods cooperative.

	Annual Growth	12/09	12/10	12/11	12/12	12/13
Sales ($ mil.)	7.0%	-	44.7	46.4	51.0	54.8
Net income ($ mil.)	79.8%	-	-	2.8	5.8	8.9
Market value ($ mil.)	-	-	-	-	-	-
Employees	-	-	-	-	-	117

ECS FEDERAL INC.

2750 PROSPERITY AVE # 600
FAIRFAX, VA 22031-4312
Phone: 703-270-1540
Fax: -
Web: www.ecs-federal.com

CEO: George Wilson
CFO: -
HR: -
FYE: December 31
Type: Private

Electronic Consulting Services (ECS) provides computer and telecommunications network consulting services primarily in the Eastern US. The company specializes in such areas as systems engineering enterprise communications project management and program support. It also offers information assurance help desk operations and Web development services. ECS primarily serves government agencies and defense contractors. Customers have included Lockheed Martin Titan the US Department of Housing and Urban Development and Advanced Technology Systems. The company has satellite offices in Florida Missouri North Carolina Pennsylvania and Washington D.C. Electronic Consulting Services was founded in 1993.

	Annual Growth	12/05	12/06	12/10	12/11	12/12
Sales ($ mil.)	39.6%	-	28.1	112.4	138.8	208.1
Net income ($ mil.)	40.9%	-	2.1	11.1	8.0	16.4
Market value ($ mil.)	-	-	-	-	-	-
Employees	-	-	-	-	-	1,184

EDGEWATER TECHNOLOGY INC

NMS: EDGW

200 Harvard Mill Square, Suite 210
Wakefield, MA 01880-3209
Phone: 781 246-3343
Fax: 781 246-5903
Web: www.edgewater.com

CEO: Shirley Singleton
CFO: Timothy R Oakes
HR: -
FYE: December 31
Type: Public

Edgewater Technology tries to stay on the cutting edge of technology management consulting. The company provides management consulting designs customized software applications implements third-party software and helps enterprises optimize business processes. Its managed services division allows clients to outsource management and maintenance of IT facilities. Edgewater Technology has expertise in such markets as financial services health care insurance and higher education and targets middle-market clients and divisions of large (Global 2000) firms located mostly in the US. Edgewater counts more than 400 customers and its consultants work onsite at clients' facilities.

	Annual Growth	12/10	12/11	12/12	12/13	12/14
Sales ($ mil.)	6.3%	88.5	102.4	100.9	103.6	113.0
Net income ($ mil.)	-	(23.6)	0.3	1.4	34.7	4.1
Market value ($ mil.)	33.7%	26.9	31.6	43.5	80.0	85.9
Employees	2.2%	380	380	395	407	414

EDGEWELL PERSONAL CARE CO NYS: EPC

1350 Timberlake Manor Parkway
Chesterfield, MO 63017
Phone: 314 594-1900
Fax: –
Web: www.energizer.com

CEO: David P. Hatfield
CFO: Sandy J. Sheldon
HR: –
FYE: September 30
Type: Public

Edgewell Personal Care Company has the edge by offering some of the most popular brands in your household. Its portfolio of personal care products includes razors shaving cream moist wipes pet care products sunscreen and feminine care products sold under brands such as Schick Edge Skintimate Wet Ones o.b. Playtex Carefree Banana Boat Hawaiian Tropic Litter Genie and Stayfree. Edgewell Personal Care was formed in mid-2015 when famous battery maker Energizer Holdings was spun off as a publicly traded company. Edgewell was created to focus solely on its personal care products operations.

	Annual Growth	09/11	09/12	09/13	09/14	09/15
Sales ($ mil.)	(15.0%)	4,645.7	4,567.2	4,466.0	4,447.7	2,421.2
Net income ($ mil.)	–	–	261.2	408.9	407.0	356.1	(275.3)
Market value ($ mil.)	5.3%	3,998.1	4,489.7	5,485.1	7,414.3	4,910.4
Employees	(20.5%)	15,000	14,800	13,000	12,500	6,000

EDISON INTERNATIONAL NYS: EIX

2244 Walnut Grove Avenue, P.O. Box 976
Rosemead, CA 91770
Phone: 626 302-2222
Fax: –
Web: www.edisoninvestor.com

CEO: Theodore F. (Ted) Craver
CFO: William J. (Jim) Scilacci
HR: Patricia (Pat) Miller
FYE: December 31
Type: Public

Edison International has been around the world but its largest subsidiary is Southern California Edison (SCE) which distributes electricity to a population of almost 14 million people in central coastal and southern California; it is also the top purchaser of renewable energy in the US. The utility's system consists of more than 12780 circuit miles of transmission lines and more than 91800 circuit miles of distribution lines. SCE also has 6287 MW of generating capacity from interests in nuclear hydroelectric and fossil-fueled power plants. Through Edison Energy the company owns and operates solar power projects.

	Annual Growth	12/10	12/11	12/12	12/13	12/14
Sales ($ mil.)	2.0%	12,409.0	12,760.0	11,862.0	12,581.0	13,413.0
Net income ($ mil.)	6.4%	1,256.0	(37.0)	(183.0)	915.0	1,612.0
Market value ($ mil.)	14.1%	12,576.3	13,488.6	14,723.4	15,085.1	21,334.1
Employees	(9.2%)	20,117	19,930	16,593	13,677	13,690

EDISON MISSION ENERGY

3 MacArthur Place, Suite 100
Santa Ana, CA 92707
Phone: 714 513-8000
Fax: –
Web: www.edisonmissionenergy.com

CEO: –
CFO: Maria Rigatti
HR: –
FYE: December 31
Type: Public

At one time the mission of Edison Mission Energy (EME) was to conquer the nonregulated energy sector around the world but it has since settled for focusing on a big slice of the US market. An indirect subsidiary of Edison International it has interests in more than 40 coal-fired natural gas-fired and wind power plants in the US and one in Turkey (Doga project) that give it a net physical generating capacity of more than 8900 MW. EME sells power wholesale through contracts with large utilities regional distributors and other energy companies; it also trades and hedges energy on the open power markets through Edison Mission Marketing & Trading.

	Annual Growth	12/08	12/09	12/10	12/11	12/12
Sales ($ mil.)	(17.7%)	2,811.0	2,377.0	2,423.0	2,180.0	1,287.0
Net income ($ mil.)	–	501.0	197.0	164.0	(1,078.0)	(925.0)
Market value ($ mil.)	–	–	–	–	–	–
Employees	(9.2%)	1,889	1,843	1,828	1,783	1,283

EDP RENEWABLES NORTH AMERICA LLC

808 Travis St. Ste. 700
Houston TX 77002
Phone: 713-265-0350
Fax: 713-265-0365
Web: www.edpr.com

CEO: –
CFO: –
HR: Candace Vaughn
FYE: December 31
Type: Subsidiary

EDP Renewables North America (formerly Horizon Wind Energy) is the US subsidiary of Spain-based EDP Renovaveis. The US company owns and operates more than 20 onshore wind farms across nine states that have a generating capacity of 2800 MW. It has another 20000 MW of wind projects in various stages of development around the country. EDP Renewables North America sells its electricity wholesale as Power Purchase Agreements (PPAs) to utility companies such as AmerenUE Direct Energy Great River and the TVA. It has also developed and sold seven farms to Entergy Florida Power & Light and Puget Energy.

EDUCATION MANAGEMENT CORP NBB: EDMC

210 Sixth Avenue, 33rd Floor
Pittsburgh, PA 15222
Phone: 412 562-0900
Fax: 412 562-0598
Web: www.edmc.edu

CEO: Mark A. McEachen
CFO: Mick J. Beekhuizen
HR: Mark E Novad
FYE: June 30
Type: Public

Worried that traditional higher education could leave you enlightened but unemployed? Education Management may have the solution. The company operates five main branches with about 110 locations in more than 30 states and in Canada. The Art Institutes Argosy University South University and Brown Mackie College offer degree programs from associate to postgraduate and Western State University College of Law offers juris doctoral degrees. The company also offers online courses through three of its divisions. Education Management institutions boast a combined enrollment of more than 125500 students and some 21000 faculty and staff. Education Management voluntarily delisted from the NASDAQ in 2014.

	Annual Growth	06/10	06/11	06/12	06/13	06/14
Sales ($ mil.)	(2.4%)	2,508.5	2,887.6	2,761.0	2,498.6	2,272.7
Net income ($ mil.)	–	168.5	229.5	(1,515.7)	(268.0)	(663.9)
Market value ($ mil.)	(42.3%)	1,922.2	3,017.5	876.0	708.4	213.0
Employees	(1.7%)	22,300	16,900	24,700	23,400	20,800

EDUCATION REALTY TRUST INC NYS: EDR

999 South Shady Grove Road, Suite 600
Memphis, TN 38120
Phone: 901 259-2500
Fax: –
Web: www.edrtrust.com

CEO: Randall L. (Randy) Churchey
CFO: Bill Brewer
HR: –
FYE: December 31
Type: Public

This company can give your college student a home away from home. Education Realty Trust a self-administered real estate investment trust (REIT) develops buys owns and operates residential communities for university students. It owns roughly 50 communities in more than 20 US states consisting of almost 28000 beds in nearly 10500 units. Through its Allen & O'Hara Education Services subsidiary the REIT manages another 20-plus student housing properties owned by others. Education Realty Trust communities offer private rooms as well as amenities such as Internet access fitness centers game rooms dining facilities swimming pools — and even study rooms.

	Annual Growth	12/10	12/11	12/12	12/13	12/14
Sales ($ mil.)	17.2%	119.6	125.4	145.0	184.4	225.8
Net income ($ mil.)	–	(42.1)	(11.0)	8.4	4.3	47.1
Market value ($ mil.)	47.3%	373.0	491.0	510.7	423.4	1,756.5
Employees	3.0%	1,138	1,077	1,222	1,288	1,283

EDUCATIONAL & INSTITUTIONAL COOPERATIVE SERVICE INC.

2 JERICHO PLZ STE 309
JERICHO, NY 117531681
Phone: 631-273-7900
Fax: –
Web: www.eandi.org

CEO: Tom Fitzgerald
CFO: John D Orlando
HR: –
FYE: December 31
Type: Private

Educational & Institutional Cooperative Service (E&I) is a not-for-profit buying cooperative that provides goods and services to its members at discounted prices. E&I seeks and enters contracts with athletic equipment furniture computer and electronics maintenance food service office products and transportation and delivery service suppliers. Established in 1934 the cooperative is owned by more than 1600 tax-exempt organizations including colleges universities private schools health care institutions and hospitals.

	Annual Growth	12/03	12/04	12/05	12/06	12/07
Sales ($ mil.)	0.7%	–	10.9	12.5	13.8	11.1
Net income ($ mil.)	–	–	–	1.4	1.9	(0.6)
Market value ($ mil.)	–	–	–	–	–	–
Employees	–	–	–	–	–	55

EDUCATIONAL DEVELOPMENT CORP.

NMS: EDUC

10302 East 55th Place
Tulsa, OK 74146-6515
Phone: 918 622-4522
Fax: –
Web: www.edcpub.com

CEO: –
CFO: Marilyn Pinney
HR: –
FYE: February 28
Type: Public

Educational Development Corporation (EDC) likes being in a bind as long as the cover appeals to youngsters. The company is the exclusive US distributor of a line of about 1500 children's books published by the UK's Usborne Publishing Limited. EDC's Home Business Division markets the books to individuals using independent sales reps who sell through personal websites home parties direct sales and book fairs; this division also distributes books to public and school libraries. EDC's Publishing Division distributes the Usborne line to a network of book toy and other retail stores. EDC bought multi-cultural children's book publisher Kane/Miller in 2008 to complement its product offerings.

	Annual Growth	02/11	02/12	02/13	02/14	02/15
Sales ($ mil.)	4.5%	27.2	26.3	25.5	26.1	32.5
Net income ($ mil.)	(7.4%)	1.2	1.4	0.8	0.4	0.9
Market value ($ mil.)	(9.9%)	26.2	20.0	15.7	15.1	17.3
Employees	3.6%	72	71	76	74	83

EDUCATIONAL SERVICES OF AMERICA INC.

1321 MURFREESBORO PIKE
NASHVILLE, TN 372172626
Phone: 615-361-4000
Fax: –
Web: www.esa-education.com

CEO: –
CFO: Bryan Skelton
HR: Janet Medina
FYE: July 31
Type: Private

Educational Services of America (ESA) knows that public school isn't a one-size-fits-all model for every student. A provider of K-12 and post-secondary alternative and specialized education programs ESA targets and teaches students with special needs learning disabilities and emotional and behavioral difficulties through five divisions. Its Ombudsman division partners with school districts to provide off-campus education to at-risk stiudents while College Living Experience teaches independent living and social skills to those with learning disabilities. It also offers an academic program for exceptional students. Founded in 1999 ESA owns and operates more than 130 accredited schools in 17 states.

	Annual Growth	12/05	12/06	12/07*	07/08	07/09
Sales ($ mil.)	110.9%	–	8.6	74.9	85.1	80.7
Net income ($ mil.)	–	–	–	(8.6)	(10.6)	(12.8)
Market value ($ mil.)	–	–	–	–	–	–
Employees	–	–	–	–	–	2,500

*Fiscal year change

EDUCATIONAL TESTING SERVICE INC

666 ROSEDALE RD STOP 85D
PRINCETON, NJ 08540-2218
Phone: 609-921-9000
Fax: –
Web: www.ets.org

CEO: –
CFO: Jack Hayon
HR: –
FYE: December 31
Type: Private

Please completely fill in each circle on the answer sheet as prepared by Educational Testing Service (ETS). Founded in 1947 ETS develops and administers the Graduate Record Examinations (GRE) and Test of English as a Foreign Language (TOEFL). The not-for-profit group develops and administers more than 50 million achievement admissions academic and professional tests a year at some 9000 locations in more than 180 countries. It also develops assessment programs for corporations professional associations and state entities. ETS' research unit conducts education-focused analysis and policy studies; test-development firm Prometric is a for-profit subsidiary.

	Annual Growth	12/08	12/09	12/10	12/11	12/12
Sales ($ mil.)	5.3%	–	1,225.0	1,272.8	1,357.5	1,431.8
Net income ($ mil.)	25.7%	–	44.5	67.6	70.8	88.5
Market value ($ mil.)	–	–	–	–	–	–
Employees	–	–	–	–	–	2,614

EDW. C. LEVY CO.

8800 Dix Ave.
Dearborn MI 48120
Phone: 313-429-2200
Fax: 313-849-9441
Web: www.edwclevy.com

CEO: –
CFO: –
HR: –
FYE: December 31
Type: Private

When you say "slag off" Edw. C. Levy doesn't take offense it gets to work. Operating as the Levy Group of Companies or Levy Company the firm processes slag an impurity that forms on the surface of molten metal from blast and steel furnaces. The company processes more than 10 million tons of slag each year which is made into aggregates for the construction industry. It has slag operations in about two-dozen steel mills mostly in the Midwest but also in Australia and Thailand. The company also has asphalt cement and concrete products. Founded in 1918 the Levy Group is still controlled by the Levy family.

EDWARD DON & COMPANY

2500 S. Harlem Ave.
North Riverside IL 60546
Phone: 708-442-9400
Fax: 708-442-0436
Web: www.don.com

CEO: Steven R Don
CFO: –
HR: –
FYE: December 31
Type: Private

Edward Don & Company sells just about everything to kitchen managers including the kitchen sink. Among the top 10 dealers of food service equipment nationwide the company provides more than 12000 products to restaurants hospitals schools and other institutional food service operators. It operates half a dozen distribution centers nationwide that deliver such goods as catering and cooking equipment flatware tableware paper goods cleaning products and sanitation supplies through its fleet of 100-plus delivery trucks. Edward Don & Company also designs and builds full-service kitchens for customers through its Foodservice Equipment Division. The family-owned firm was founded in 1921.

EDWARD ROSE BUILDING ENTERPRISES

30057 Orchard Lake Rd.
Farmington Hills MI 48334
Phone: 248-539-2130
Fax: 248-539-2125
Web: www.edwardrose.com

CEO: –
CFO: –
HR: –
FYE: December 31
Type: Private

A rose by any other name probably wouldn't lease as many apartments as Edward Rose Building Enterprises which does business as Edward Rose & Sons. The family-owned company is a residential developer general contractor and property owner and manager with a large presence in the Midwest. Founded in 1921 Edward Rose & Sons has developed and built more than 60000 single- and multi-family apartment communities from Nebraska to the Carolinas. It offers single studios to house-size townhomes as well as one- to three-bedroom furnished corporate suites for businesses looking to relocate or temporarily house employees.

EDWARDS ANGELL PALMER & DODGE LLP

111 Huntington Ave.
Boston MA 02199-7613
Phone: 617-239-0100
Fax: 617-227-4420
Web: www.eapdlaw.com

CEO: –
CFO: –
HR: –
FYE: December 31
Type: Private - Partnershi

Edward Angell Palmer & Dodge (EAPD) goes to bat for corporations in need of legal representation. The firm has 625 attorneys and departments that include Business Law (mergers and acquisitions venture capital public offerings) Insurance (reinsurance arbitration litigation regulatory matters) Intellectual Property Litigation (in pharmaceuticals finance IT and government) Private Client (tax and finance matters for individuals) Public Finance (funding efforts and financial transactions for public entities) Real Estate (financing development permitting) and Restructuring and Insolvency (including bankruptcy).

EDWARDS LIFESCIENCES CORP

One Edwards Way
Irvine, CA 92614
Phone: 949 250-2500
Fax: –
Web: www.edwards.com

NYS: EW
CEO: Michael A. Mussallem
CFO: Scott B. Ullem
HR: Serge Panczuk
FYE: December 31
Type: Public

Edwards Lifesciences has its heart in the right place. Named for the co-inventor of the first artificial heart valve Miles "Lowell" Edwards its main products are still heart valve devices including valves made from animal tissue annuloplasty rings that repair damaged valves and transcatheter heart valves for minimally invasive procedures. The company also makes monitoring systems that measure heart function during surgery; embolectomy catheters that remove blood clots from peripheral arteries; and various types of cannulae (surgical tubes used for delivery drainage or filtration) and other surgical supplies. Edwards Lifesciences markets its products worldwide.

	Annual Growth	12/10	12/11	12/12	12/13	12/14
Sales ($ mil.)	12.6%	1,447.0	1,678.6	1,899.6	2,045.5	2,322.9
Net income ($ mil.)	38.9%	218.0	236.7	293.2	391.7	811.1
Market value ($ mil.)	12.0%	17,429.1	15,242.9	19,440.7	14,177.9	27,463.1
Employees	6.8%	7,000	7,800	8,200	8,600	9,100

EDWIN WATTS GOLF LLC

20 Hill Ave.
Fort Walton Beach FL 32548
Phone: 850-244-2066
Fax: 850-244-5217
Web: www.edwinwatts.com

CEO: –
CFO: –
HR: –
FYE: December 31
Type: Private

Golfers often hit Edwin Watts before hitting the links. Edwin Watts Golf is a leading golf specialty retailer in the US. The company operates a chain of nearly 90 stores across 10 mostly southeastern states and Texas as well as shops inside Sears stores. Edwin Watts Golf stores stock clubs golf balls bags training aids and more. The company also sells golf equipment by catalog and online and it operates a club leasing program for novices and golfers who like to test-drive state-of-the-art gear. Founded in 1968 as a small pro shop at the municipal golf course in Fort Walton Beach Florida Edwin Watts Golf is owned by an affiliate of investment firm Sun Capital Partners.

EEI HOLDING CORPORATION

700 N MACARTHUR BLVD
SPRINGFIELD, IL 627022304
Phone: 217-523-0108
Fax: –
Web: www.eeiholding.com

CEO: Robert Egizii
CFO: John Hinkle
HR: –
FYE: December 31
Type: Private

Electricity comes easy for EEI Holding. The company owns Egizii Electric and other firms that provide electrical and general construction and contracting services throughout the US. It has expertise in utilities medical facilities infrastructure telecommunications data systems and traffic control. The company also assists clients with site selection budget development and property leaseback transactions. EEI Holding began operations in the late 1940s. Chairman and CEO Robert Egizii is the firm's majority shareholder. The company has offices in Illinois and Florida.

	Annual Growth	12/98	12/99	12/00	12/01	12/09
Sales ($ mil.)	(12.0%)	–	71.3	98.4	117.4	19.8
Net income ($ mil.)	–	–	–	(2.4)	1.0	0.2
Market value ($ mil.)	–	–	–	–	–	–
Employees	–	–	–	–	–	500

EF JOHNSON TECHNOLOGIES INC.

1440 Corporate Dr.
Irving TX 75038-2401
Phone: 972-819-0700
Fax: 972-819-0639
Web: www.efjohnsontechnologies.com

CEO: –
CFO: –
HR: –
FYE: December 31
Type: Private

EF Johnson is secure with how it communicates. The company makes radio and radio-security systems for police departments government agencies the military and service providers. Its EF Johnson-branded products include handheld and mobile radios base stations and signal repeaters. Sold as aftermarket add-ons its Transcrypt-branded products include security modules that encrypt and decode radio and wireless phone signals to prevent eavesdropping. EF Johnson sells directly and through dealers and equipment makers. It has counted DRS Technologies Sprint Nextel and theUS Department of Defense among its clients.

EGAIN CORP

NAS: EGAN

1252 Borregas Avenue
Sunnyvale, CA 94089
Phone: 408 636-4500
Fax: 408 636-4400
Web: www.egain.com

CEO: Ashutosh (Ashu) Roy
CFO: Eric Smit
HR: –
FYE: June 30
Type: Public

This company would like those looking for eBusiness help to look to it eGain and again. eGain Corporation offers call center software that integrates online and telephone communications with other data sources. The company's software suite includes applications for routing e-mails giving customers self-service options enabling live Web chat and providing call center agents with customer information. Its products are offered as both cloud-based Software-as-a-Service (SaaS) and as installed in-house applications. In addition eGain provides such services as consulting hosting maintenance implementation and support. Its customers have included AT&T Cox Newspapers and Hewlett-Packard.

	Annual Growth	06/11	06/12	06/13	06/14	06/15
Sales ($ mil.)	14.6%	44.1	43.4	58.9	70.3	75.9
Net income ($ mil.)	–	8.5	(4.9)	0.7	(5.2)	(12.4)
Market value ($ mil.)	17.8%	70.3	147.3	260.0	182.9	135.4
Employees	15.0%	321	454	550	681	562

EGPI FIRECREEK INC

NBB: EFIR

6564 Smoke Tree Lane
Scottsdale, AZ 85253
Phone: 480 948-6581
Fax: –
Web: www.egpifirecreek.com

CEO: –
CFO: Dennis R Alexander
HR: –
FYE: December 31
Type: Public

The fire in EGPI Firecreek's belly is for oil and gas exploration and production and traffic systems. Once dependent on the sale of private leisure and commercial vessels EGPI Firecreek has refocused on US oil and gas activities. The company produces and sells oil and natural gas from wells in Sweetwater County Wyoming and Knox County Texas. In 2009 in a diversification move EGPI Firecreek subsidiary Asian Ventures Corp. acquired M3 Lighting as the company expanded into light and traffic fixture manufacturing. It picked up communications technology firm Terra Telecom in 2010. That year it moved to expand its assets by agreeing to acquire Caddo International and by buying Arctic Solar Engineering in 2011.

	Annual Growth	12/08	12/09	12/10	12/11	12/12
Sales ($ mil.)	(53.2%)	–	1.2	0.0	0.3	0.1
Net income ($ mil.)	–	3.3	(3.4)	(4.5)	(5.0)	(6.1)
Market value ($ mil.)	–	0.0	0.0	0.0	0.0	0.0
Employees	–	–	–	–	–	–

EHEALTH INC

NMS: EHTH

440 East Middlefield Road
Mountain View, CA 94043
Phone: 650 584-2700
Fax: –
Web: www.ehealth.com

CEO: Gary L. Lauer
CFO: Stuart M. Huizinga
HR: Shannon Fallick
FYE: December 31
Type: Public

eHealth brought e-commerce to the insurance business. Through its eHealth-Insurance subsidiary the company sells health insurance online to more than 3 million individual family Medicare and small business members. The company is licensed to sell insurance policies throughout the US. It has partnerships with more than 180 health insurance carriers for which it processes and delivers potential members' applications in return for commission on policy sales. It lets consumers compare some 10000 products online — including health dental and vision insurance products from the likes of Aetna Humana UnitedHealth and Anthem.

	Annual Growth	12/10	12/11	12/12	12/13	12/14
Sales ($ mil.)	2.9%	160.4	151.6	155.5	179.2	179.7
Net income ($ mil.)	–	17.5	6.7	7.1	1.7	(16.2)
Market value ($ mil.)	15.1%	253.0	262.1	490.0	828.9	444.3
Employees	13.3%	641	635	772	972	1,058

EIDE BAILLY LLP

4310 17TH AVE S
FARGO, ND 581033339
Phone: 701-239-8500
Fax: –
Web: www.eidebailly.com

CEO: –
CFO: –
HR: –
FYE: April 30
Type: Private

Eide Bailly is how the West was audited. The company which was founded in 1917 provides clients with audit accounting tax and consulting services from more than 20 offices in nearly a dozen western and central US states. Eide Bailly's target industries include construction agricultural processing oil and gas real estate renewable energy government financial services manufacturing health care and not-for-profit organizations. Additional services are provided by subsidiaries and affiliates including Eide Bailly Technology Consulting. International services are provided through Eide Bailly's affiliation with HLB International. The accounting firm serves some 44000 clients annually.

	Annual Growth	04/10	04/11	04/12	04/13	04/14
Sales ($ mil.)	10.6%	–	142.5	148.1	167.7	192.9
Net income ($ mil.)	13.0%	–	–	51.1	56.9	65.2
Market value ($ mil.)	–	–	–	–	–	–
Employees	–	–	–	–	–	1,282

EILEEN FISHER INC.

2 BRIDGE ST STE 230
IRVINGTON, NY 10533-3500
Phone: 914-591-5700
Fax: –
Web: www.eileenfisher.com

CEO: –
CFO: Kenneth Pollak
HR: Ingrid Turner
FYE: December 31
Type: Private

Eileen Fisher — the woman and the company — has an eye for clothing that's fashionable and comfortable. The company makes and sells upscale women's business and casual clothing (tops jackets pants skirts and dresses) made mostly from organic and natural fabrics. Fisher's unfussy forgivingly tailored block color lineup is sold through nearly 60 of its namesake stores in about 15 states Canada and the UK as well as through upscale department and specialty stores (including Nordstrom Saks Fifth Avenue and Neiman Marcus) nationwide. It also offers personal shopping services for US customers. After working in the fields of graphic arts and interior design Eileen Fisher founded the company in 1984.

	Annual Growth	12/05	12/06	12/07	12/07	12/08
Sales ($ mil.)	(80.0%)	–	–	1,361.8	253.8	272.9
Net income ($ mil.)	306258.7%	–	–	0.0	7.4	2.7
Market value ($ mil.)	–	–	–	–	–	–
Employees	–	–	–	–	–	900

EINSTEIN NOAH RESTAURANT GROUP INC

NMS: BAGL

555 Zang Street, Suite 300
Lakewood, CO 80228
Phone: 303 568-8000
Fax: –
Web: www.einsteinnoah.com

CEO: Frank G Paci
CFO: John A Coletta
HR: –
FYE: January 01
Type: Public

Bagels and coffee are key ingredients for this company. Einstein Noah Restaurant Group is the largest bagel shop operator in the US with more than 815 company-owned and franchised locations. Its flagship chain Einstein Bros. Bagels offers more than a dozen varieties of fresh-made bagels and spreads along with coffee pastries and a menu of sandwiches and salads at its 685 outlets. In addition to Einstein Bros. the company operates the Noah's New York Bagels and Manhattan Bagel chains. Some 460 of the bagel shops are company-owned while the rest are operated by franchisees or licensees. Investment firm Greenlight Capital controls about 65% of Einstein Noah.

	Annual Growth	12/08	12/09	12/10*	01/12	01/13
Sales ($ mil.)	0.6%	413.5	408.6	411.7	423.6	427.0
Net income ($ mil.)	(9.6%)	21.1	72.0	10.6	13.2	12.7
Market value ($ mil.)	18.0%	91.2	166.7	234.8	257.9	208.5
Employees	(2.1%)	7,698	7,054	6,796	6,506	6,912

*Fiscal year change

EISAI INC.

100 Tice Blvd.
Woodcliff Lake NJ 07677
Phone: 201-692-1100
Fax: 201-692-1804
Web: us.eisai.com

CEO: Lonnel Coats
CFO: Barry Lederman
HR: –
FYE: March 31
Type: Subsidiary

Eisai Inc. develops and markets pharmaceuticals to treat a variety of ills. As the US production arm of Eisai Co. its roster includes Alzheimer's treatment Aricept Aciphex for acid reflux anti-seizure medication Banzel anticoagulant Fragmin lymphoma drug Ontak and anti-convulsant Zonegran. In addition to neurology oncology and vascular ailments the firm has drug research development marketing and manufacturing programs in areas including infectious disease inflammation and critical care. The company supplies its products to health care professionals pharmacies and hospitals through wholesale distributors.

EISENHOWER MEDICAL CENTER

39000 BOB HOPE DR
RANCHO MIRAGE, CA 922703221
Phone: 760-340-3911
Fax: –
Web: www.emc.org

CEO: G Aubrey Serfling
CFO: Kimberly Osborne
HR: –
FYE: June 30
Type: Private

The Eisenhower Medical Center is perhaps better known for the name of a first lady than the 34th US president: The not-for-profit medical campus is the home of the Betty Ford Center. In addition to the renowned alcohol and drug rehabilitation center Eisenhower Medical Center comprises the more than 540-bed Eisenhower Memorial Hospital the Barbara Sinatra Children's Center and the Annenberg Center for Health Sciences. In addition to medical surgical and emergency services the hospital offers cancer care neurology orthopedics cardiology and rehabilitation. An accredited teaching hospital it also conducts training and research programs and operates outpatient clinics in surrounding areas.

	Annual Growth	06/07	06/08	06/09	06/10	06/13
Sales ($ mil.)	6.1%	–	–	395.0	411.2	501.4
Net income ($ mil.)	–	–	–	25.3	6.9	(27.3)
Market value ($ mil.)	–	–	–	–	–	–
Employees	–	–	–	–	–	2,200

EISNERAMPER LLP

750 3RD AVE FL 16
NEW YORK, NY 100172716
Phone: 212-949-8700
Fax: –
Web: www.eisneramper.com

CEO: –
CFO: Jeffrey Melnick
HR: –
FYE: January 31
Type: Private

EisnerAmper provides accounting and consulting services for middle-market businesses and Fortune 500 companies. It specializes in industries and sectors including health sciences sports and entertainment not-for-profit financial services and technology. EisnerAmper provides auditing and accounting services tax planning legal support bankruptcy consulting corporate finance employee benefits plan services and IT consulting. Services outside the US are provided through EisnerAmper's Cayman Islands office as well as through its affiliation with PKF International. Founded in 1963 the firm operates out of US offices on the East and West coast.

	Annual Growth	01/10	01/11	01/12	01/13	01/14
Sales ($ mil.)	34.8%	–	173.8	230.7	247.6	425.6
Net income ($ mil.)	(1.0%)	–	–	59.7	55.7	58.5
Market value ($ mil.)	–	–	–	–	–	–
Employees	–	–	–	–	–	1,895

EL DORADO FURNITURE CORP

4200 NW 167TH ST
MIAMI GARDENS, FL 330546112
Phone: 305-624-9700
Fax: –
Web: www.eldoradofurniture.com

CEO: Luis E Capo
CFO: –
HR: –
FYE: December 31
Type: Private

The road to El Dorado Furniture is covered in sand. The company sells home furnishings in South Florida through about a dozen retail showrooms and a pair of outlets located in Broward Miami-Dade Palm Beach and Lee counties. El Dorado Furniture stores offer wood upholstered and leather furniture for every room in the house as well as mattresses bedding and decorative accessories. Its stores are designed to look like small towns with building façades situated along a boulevard; some locations also feature cafés. Founded in 1967 and run by the Capó family El Dorado Furniture has become the nation's largest Hispanic-owned retail enterprises.

	Annual Growth	12/09	12/10	12/11	12/12	12/13
Sales ($ mil.)	8.0%	–	131.5	152.6	153.2	165.4
Net income ($ mil.)	12.4%	–	–	23.6	25.9	29.8
Market value ($ mil.)	–	–	–	–	–	–
Employees	–	–	–	–	–	705

EL PASO CORPORATION

NYSE: EP

El Paso Bldg. 1001 Louisiana St.
Houston TX 77002
Phone: 713-420-2600
Fax: 713-420-4417
Web: www.elpaso.com

CEO: Richard D Kinder
CFO: John R Sult
HR: –
FYE: December 31
Type: Public

Out in the West Texas town of El Paso this company fell in love with the natural gas industry. Founded in 1928 in its namesake city El Paso Corporation is primarily engaged in gas transportation and storage (including liquefied natural gas LNG) oil and gas exploration and production and gas gathering and processing. The operator of the largest gas transportation system in the US El Paso has interests in 44000 miles of interstate pipeline. In 2011 subsidiary El Paso Exploration and Production had estimated proved reserves of about 3.9 trillion cu. ft. of natural gas equivalent in Brazil Egypt and the US. In a major move in 2012 El Paso Corp. was acquired by Kinder Morgan for about $38 billion.

EL PASO ELECTRIC COMPANY

NYS: EE

Stanton Tower, 100 North Stanton
El Paso, TX 79901
Phone: 915 543-5711
Fax: –
Web: www.epelectric.com

CEO: Mary E. Kipp
CFO: Nathan T. Hirschi
HR: –
FYE: December 31
Type: Public

El Paso Electric (EPE) creates currents along the Rio Grande River. The utility transmits and distributes electricity to some 392000 customers in West Texas and southern New Mexico. More than half of the company's sales come from its namesake city and nearby Las Cruces New Mexico. The firm has 1852 MW of nuclear fossil-fuel and wind-based generating capacity. EPE also purchases power from other utilities and marketers and sells wholesale power in Texas and New Mexico as well as in Mexico. Its largest customers include military installations such as Fort Bliss in Texas and White Sands Missile Range and Holloman Air Force Base in New Mexico.

	Annual Growth	12/10	12/11	12/12	12/13	12/14
Sales ($ mil.)	1.1%	877.3	918.0	852.9	890.4	917.5
Net income ($ mil.)	(2.4%)	100.6	103.5	90.8	88.6	91.4
Market value ($ mil.)	9.8%	1,107.6	1,393.6	1,283.8	1,412.6	1,611.7
Employees	0.0%	1,000	1,000	1,000	1,000	1,000

EL PASO PIPELINE PARTNERS LP

NYS: EPB

500 Dallas Street, Suite 1000
Houston, TX 77002
Phone: 713 369-9000
Fax: –
Web: www.eppipelinepartners.com

CEO: Richard D Kinder
CFO: –
HR: –
FYE: December 31
Type: Public

El Paso Pipeline Partners is a natural gas pipeline and storage company with interests that extend far beyond its West Texas roots. The firm which consists primarily of Wyoming Interstate Company (WIC) Cheyenne Plains Gas (CPG) Colorado Interstate Gas Company (CIG) Elba Express and Southern Natural Gas Company (SNG) has 12900 miles of pipeline and storage facilities totaling 97 billion cu. ft. El Paso Pipeline Partners' customers include local distribution companies industrial users electricity generators and natural gas marketing and trading companies. Kinder Morgan controls the company.

	Annual Growth	12/08	12/09	12/10	12/11	12/12
Sales ($ mil.)	81.0%	141.1	537.6	1,344.1	1,425.0	1,515.0
Net income ($ mil.)	50.0%	114.5	213.5	378.5	472.0	579.0
Market value ($ mil.)	24.1%	3,435.0	5,716.2	7,365.5	7,623.1	8,140.5
Employees		–	–	–	–	–

EL POLLO LOCO HOLDINGS INC.

3535 Harbor Blvd. Ste. 100
Costa Mesa CA 92626
Phone: 714-599-5000
Fax: 775-827-5517
Web: www.millerheiman.com

CEO: Stephen J Sather
CFO: Laurance Roberts
HR: –
FYE: December 31
Type: Private

You might say this company is trying to fuel a chicken craze. El Pollo Loco Holdings operates and franchises more than 400 fast-casual restaurants operating under the El Pollo Loco banner. Specializing in Mexican-style chicken dishes the chain's menu includes chicken burritos and tacos as well as complete chicken dinners and sides. Most El Pollo Loco outlets are found in the Los Angeles area and other markets in California. A small number can be found in about 10 other states. About 240 of the restaurants are operated by franchisees. Juan Francisco Ochoa started the chain in Mexico in 1975. El Pollo Loco is owned by private equity firm Trimaran Capital.

ELAVON INC.

1 Concourse Pkwy. Ste. 300
Atlanta GA 30328
Phone: 678-731-5000
Fax: +52-55-5261-2494
Web: www.televisa.com

CEO: Simon Haslam
CFO: James Steawart Walker
HR: –
FYE: December 31
Type: Subsidiary

Nothing makes Elavon more elated than customers who say "Put it on my card." The firm is a major processor of credit and debit card transactions in the US Brazil Canada Mexico and Europe. A subsidiary of U.S. Bancorp it offers point-of-sale (POS) authorization and reporting for all major credit and debit cards as well as gift cards prepaid cardsand checks. Transactions can be authorized in more than 90 currencies and converted in nearly 50 currencies. Working directly with clients or through affiliations with banks Elavon serves more than one million clients in the retail hospitality airline health care education and public sectors. It processes some 5.5 million transactions daily.

ELDORADO ARTESIAN SPRINGS INC

NBB: ELDO

1783 Dogwood Street
Louisville, CO 80027
Phone: 303 499-1316
Fax: –

CEO: –
CFO: Cathleen M Shoenfeld
HR: Jeanne Hohnstein
FYE: March 31
Type: Public

If Cortez had sought a wealth of water instead of streets of gold he might have headed for Eldorado Artesian Springs. The company bottles water from springs it owns in the foothills of the Rocky Mountains. About 70% of its sales come from home and office delivery of three and five gallon bottles of its natural spring water (and water cooler rentals); it also supplies smaller bottles to wholesalers and distributors for retail sale. Eldorado's water is distributed primarily in Colorado but also in regions of bordering states. In addition to its bottled water business the company owns and operates a resort on its property.

	Annual Growth	03/11	03/12	03/13	03/14	03/15
Sales ($ mil.)	9.4%	8.9	9.2	9.9	11.4	12.7
Net income ($ mil.)	–	(0.5)	0.1	0.5	0.5	0.6
Market value ($ mil.)	36.1%	2.1	1.1	3.1	11.4	7.2
Employees	6.3%	76	78	82	89	97

ELECSYS CORP.

NAS: ESYS

846 N. Mart-Way Court
Olathe, KS 66061
Phone: 913 647-0158
Fax: 913 647-0132
Web: www.elecsyscorp.com

CEO: Karl B Gemperli
CFO: Todd A Daniels
HR: –
FYE: April 30
Type: Public

Many companies elect Elecsys to make their electronics. Elecsys is a contract manufacturer of electronic assemblies and displays. The company makes custom electronic assemblies — including printed circuit boards electronic modules LCDs light-emitting diodes (LEDs) and wireless communication interface modules — for OEMs in the aerospace industrial communications safety transportation military and other industries. Elecsys also makes ruggedized handheld computers and printers as well as remote monitoring equipment for customers in the oil and gas exploration and production industries. About 85% of the company's sales come from customers located in the US.

	Annual Growth	04/09	04/10	04/11	04/12	04/13
Sales ($ mil.)	3.8%	21.9	17.0	23.6	23.1	25.4
Net income ($ mil.)	25.6%	0.7	(0.7)	0.9	1.2	1.7
Market value ($ mil.)	10.5%	14.1	15.6	19.8	20.9	21.0
Employees	(1.4%)	132	120	129	127	125

ELECTION SYSTEMS & SOFTWARE INC.

11208 John Galt Blvd.
Omaha NE 68137
Phone: 402-593-0101
Fax: 402-593-8107
Web: www.essvote.com

CEO: Aldo Tesi
CFO: Tom O'Brien
HR: –
FYE: December 31
Type: Private

Election Systems & Software (ES&S) casts its vote in favor of e-lections. The largest voting machine company in the US provides systems used to manage all stages of elections including voter registration ballot creation voting and tabulation. Its products include voting terminals with features such as touchscreens and paper audits as well as ballot counters. Its election management software helps voting officials maintain databases format ballots and program election equipment. ES&S also provides maintenance and support services. Its equipment supports elections in some 45 US states and four countries including Canada. ES&S is jointly owned by McCarthy Capital and company management.

ELECTRIC BOAT CORPORATION

75 Eastern Point Rd.
Groton CT 06340-4989
Phone: 860-433-3000
Fax: 860-433-1400
Web: www.gdeb.com

CEO: –
CFO: –
HR: –
FYE: December 31
Type: Subsidiary

Electric Boat is not a float in the Disney Electric Light Parade. Electric Boat designs builds and maintains nuclear attack and ballistic-missile submarines for the US Navy. A subsidiary of defense giant General Dynamics Electric Boat was established in 1899 and won its first US Navy contract within a year. It has delivered the lead ship of the Virginia class (USS Virginia-SSN774) and its third and final Seawolf-class submarine (Jimmy Carter-SSN23) to the US Navy and is working on several Virginia-class submarines with Northrop Grumman. Electric Boat continues to provide support and maintenance for Seawolf- Ohio- and Los Angeles-class submarines. Electric Boat operates in Connecticut and Rhode Island.

ELECTRIC ENERGY INC.

2100 Portland Rd.
Joppa IL 62953
Phone: 618-543-7531
Fax: 618-543-7420

CEO: –
CFO: –
HR: –
FYE: December 31
Type: Private

It does not take a genius to figure out what business Electric Energy (EEI) is involved in. The company generates 1000 MW of electric capacity at its coal-fired power plant in Joppa Illinois (which began operating in 1953) and 74 MW at it natural gas-fired facility (which commenced operations in 2000) at the same location. The independent producer sells its power output to its shareholders. The Missouri-based utility holding company Ameren holds an 80% stake in EEI; Kentucky Utilities (a subsidiary of LG&E Energy) owns the remaining 20% of the company.

ELECTRIC INSURANCE COMPANY

75 Sam Fonzo Dr.
Beverly MA 01915
Phone: 978-921-2080
Fax: 978-236-5700
Web: www.electricinsurance.com

CEO: Doug Seymour
CFO: –
HR: –
FYE: December 31
Type: Private

Electric Insurance has a certain glow about it. Its long affiliation with General Electric was begun by its predecessor in 1927. Today Electric Insurance provides commercial insurance policies that include compensation general and excess liability insurance for GE in the US and abroad. Outside the GE family the company is licensed throughout the US to underwrite auto homeowner renter and umbrella insurance for all; an affiliate is licensed in Canada. Customers from outside GE make up almost half of its auto and homeowner policyholders. The firm serves more than 130000 policyholders and distributes its products directly via mobile application and the web and through independent agencies.

ELECTRIC POWER BOARD OF THE METROPOLITAN GOVERNMENT OF NASHVILLE

1214 CHURCH ST
NASHVILLE, TN 372460001
Phone: 615-747-3831
Fax: –
Web: www.nespower.com

CEO: –
CFO: Teresa Broyles Aplin
HR: Jack Patel
FYE: June 30
Type: Private

The Electric Power Board of the Metropolitan Government of Nashville and Davidson County is a mouthful. Its operating name Nashville Electric Service (NES) sounds much better. And talking of sound the legendary "Nashville Sound" would be hard to hear without the resources of this power distributor which serves more than 360000 customers in central Tennessee. NES is one of the largest government-owned utilities in the US. The company is required to purchase all its power from another government-owned operator the Tennessee Valley Authority (TVA).

	Annual Growth	06/05	06/06	06/07	06/08	06/09
Sales ($ mil.)	8.3%	–	903.3	962.8	1,030.8	1,146.7
Net income ($ mil.)	(39.7%)	–	–	44.0	33.5	16.0
Market value ($ mil.)	–	–	–	–	–	–
Employees	–	–	–	–	–	990

ELECTRIC POWER RESEARCH INSTITUTE INC.

3420 HILLVIEW AVE
PALO ALTO, CA 943041382
Phone: 650-855-2000
Fax: –
Web: www.epri.com

CEO: Michael Howard
CFO: Pamela (Pam) Keefe
HR: –
FYE: December 31
Type: Private

The Electric Power Research Institute (EPRI) knows there's more to electricity than putting a plug in a socket. From its headquarters in Palo Alto California the institute works to bring together investor-owned and government-owned utility companies as well as other industry representatives. EPRI operates as a not-for-profit research consortium that organizes and funds collaborative research. The organization identifies and works on issues related to electricity generation delivery and use including questions related to environmental protection. More than 10% of the organization's members are located outside the US. EPRI was founded in 1973.

	Annual Growth	12/03	12/04	12/05	12/06	12/13
Sales ($ mil.)	–	–	(504.9)	276.4	285.0	383.0
Net income ($ mil.)	(25.1%)	–	–	265.4	16.9	26.4
Market value ($ mil.)	–	–	–	–	–	–
Employees	–	–	–	–	–	891

ELECTRIC RELIABILITY COUNCIL OF TEXAS INC.

7620 METRO CENTER DR
AUSTIN, TX 787441613
Phone: 512-225-7000
Fax: –
Web: www.ercot.com

CEO: Bill Magness
CFO: –
HR: –
FYE: December 31
Type: Private

ERCOT works to ensure that Texas power grid errors are caught before triggering a massive blackout. The Electric Reliability Council of Texas (ERCOT) is responsible for the reliable operation of 550 generation units (74000 MW capacity) and a 40500-mile power transmission system carrying about 85% of the state's electric load and serving 23 million customers. A member of the North American Electric Reliability Council ERCOT functions as the independent system operator for the region. It also administers financial settlement for the competitive wholesale bulk-power market and oversees customer switching for 6.7 million Texans who live in areas where they have a competitive choice of power supplier.

	Annual Growth	12/07	12/08	12/09	12/10	12/11
Sales ($ mil.)	14.4%	–	187.0	206.9	272.5	279.8
Net income ($ mil.)	–	–	–	28.7	19.1	(2.0)
Market value ($ mil.)	–	–	–	–	–	–
Employees	–	–	–	–	–	625

ELECTRO RENT CORP. NMS: ELRC

6060 Sepulveda Boulevard
Van Nuys, CA 91411-2501
Phone: 818 787-2100
Fax: –
Web: www.electrorent.com

CEO: Daniel Greenberg
CFO: Craig R Jones
HR: –
FYE: May 31
Type: Public

Electro Rent rents leases and resells electronic test and measurement equipment computers servers and related equipment. The company's test instruments come from suppliers that include Agilent Technologies and Tektronix while its computers and workstations are primarily sourced from from such manufacturers as Apple Dell Hewlett-Packard and Toshiba. Electro Rent provides new and used equipment to government agencies and companies in the aerospace and defense electronics semiconductor and telecommunications industries.

	Annual Growth	05/11	05/12	05/13	05/14	05/15
Sales ($ mil.)	1.0%	228.7	248.6	248.7	241.1	238.3
Net income ($ mil.)	(10.2%)	23.8	25.8	22.8	20.4	15.4
Market value ($ mil.)	(9.5%)	369.8	333.7	410.1	389.3	247.6
Employees	2.5%	371	393	417	420	410

ELECTRO SCIENTIFIC INDUSTRIES, INC. NMS: ESIO

13900 N.W. Science Park Drive
Portland, OR 97229
Phone: 503 641-4141
Fax: –
Web: www.esi.com

CEO: Ed Grady
CFO: Paul Oldham
HR: Kristin Buckner
FYE: March 28
Type: Public

Electro Scientific Industries (ESI) has a laser focus locked on lasers. Lasers that help its customers make and test micron- and submicron-sized electronics that go into bigger electronics. The company's laser-based fabrication equipment is used for ultra-fine work in semiconductors interconnect devices and other microtechnology components as well as thin films and glass for touch screens. Its products provide yield improvement optical inspection wafer scribing high-capacity test and inspection and more. ESI's customers include Apple which accounts for about 15% of sales. Most sales come from customers in Asia.

	Annual Growth	04/11*	03/12	03/13	03/14	03/15
Sales ($ mil.)	(11.3%)	256.8	254.2	216.6	181.2	159.1
Net income ($ mil.)	–	7.9	4.9	(54.7)	(38.3)	(43.8)
Market value ($ mil.)	(22.5%)	523.2	460.9	339.3	303.7	189.1
Employees	3.3%	648	627	599	658	739

*Fiscal year change

ELECTRO-MATIC PRODUCTS INC.

23409 INDUSTRIAL PARK CT
FARMINGTON HILLS, MI 483352849
Phone: 248-478-1182
Fax: –
Web: www.electromatic.com

CEO: James C Baker Jr
CFO: –
HR: –
FYE: September 30
Type: Private

Electro-Matic Products are not "as seen on TV." The company distributes industrial automation equipment and electrical supplies to customers in the industrial chemical pharmaceutical utility and automotive industries. Products include cables connectors sensors fuses and control devices along with automation tools indoor and outdoor LED displays and industrial computer hardware. Electro-Matic stocks products from Littelfuse Molex Rittal Corporation Siemens and Woodhead Industries among other vendors. Founded in 1969 the company sells worldwide through sales engineering and support offices in Michigan and Ohio. Electro-Matic established an employee stock ownership plan in 2007.

	Annual Growth	09/06	09/07	09/08	09/10	09/11
Sales ($ mil.)	–	–	–	(729.4)	53.9	81.9
Net income ($ mil.)	2838.3%	–	–	0.0	0.3	2.8
Market value ($ mil.)	–	–	–	–	–	–
Employees	–	–	–	–	–	110

ELECTRO-SENSORS, INC. NAS: ELSE

6111 Blue Circle Drive
Minnetonka, MN 55343-9108
Phone: 952 930-0100
Fax: –
Web: www.electro-sensors.com

CEO: David L Klenk
CFO: David L Klenk
HR: –
FYE: December 31
Type: Public

Electro-Sensors supports the manufacturing process with sensitive loving care. The company's Product Monitoring Division which accounts for the bulk of sales makes computerized systems that monitor and regulate the production speed of industrial machinery. Products are sold worldwide. Electro-Sensors also has an AutoData Systems unit which makes software that reads hand-printed characters check marks and bar code information from scanned or faxed forms. The unit has an exclusive license to use a neural network algorithm developed by PPT Vision. Its software sells mostly in North America and Western Europe. Electro-Sensors director and secretary Peter Peterson and his family own 38% of the company.

	Annual Growth	12/10	12/11	12/12	12/13	12/14
Sales ($ mil.)	3.2%	6.2	6.1	6.5	6.5	7.0
Net income ($ mil.)	20.0%	0.5	0.5	1.1	0.7	1.1
Market value ($ mil.)	(3.3%)	15.2	13.3	12.8	13.6	13.3
Employees	1.6%	31	28	29	31	33

ELECTROMED, INC. ASE: ELMD

500 Sixth Avenue N.W.
New Prague, MN 56071
Phone: 952 758-9299
Fax: –
Web: www.electromed.com

CEO: Kathleen S Skarvan
CFO: Jeremy Brock
HR: –
FYE: June 30
Type: Public

Electromed aims to clear the way for patients suffering from respiratory ailments. A medical device maker the company manufactures respiratory products designed to treat patients with cystic fibrosis chronic obstructive pulmonary disease (COPD) and other ailments that affect respiratory systems. Its FDA-approved SmartVest System is a vest worn by patients that helps loosen lung congestion. A self-administered therapy the vest works by administering high frequency pulsations that compress and release the patient's chest area. Electromed sells its SmartVest and related products primarily in the US to patients home health care professionals and hospitals. Founded in 1992 the company went public in 2010.

	Annual Growth	06/11	06/12	06/13	06/14	06/15
Sales ($ mil.)	0.5%	19.0	19.5	15.1	15.5	19.4
Net income ($ mil.)	0.9%	1.1	0.2	(1.3)	(1.3)	1.1
Market value ($ mil.)	(13.5%)	26.8	17.1	10.3	11.6	15.0
Employees	1.3%	92	91	91	97	97

ELECTRONIC ARTS, INC. NMS: EA

209 Redwood Shores Parkway
Redwood City, CA 94065
Phone: 650 628-1500
Fax: –
Web: www.ea.com

CEO: Andrew Wilson
CFO: Blake J. Jorgensen
HR: Theresa Zember
FYE: March 31
Type: Public

To armchair quarterbacks and couch-potato commandos Electronic Arts (EA) is their Picasso. EA is a leading global interactive entertainment software publisher with popular titles such as Battlefield FIFA Madden NFL The Sims and Bejeweled. The company also distributes third-party titles such as Rock Band and Valve Software's Left 4 Dead and it publishes games based on other media franchises such as Star Wars. EA develops its games for consoles from Sony Nintendo and Microsoft as well as for PCs. EA also serves mobile devices and provides online social games including Hasbro-licensed games such as Monopoly via websites Pogo and Playfish. Electronic Arts was founded in 1982.

	Annual Growth	03/11	03/12	03/13	03/14	03/15
Sales ($ mil.)	5.9%	3,589.0	4,143.0	3,797.0	3,575.0	4,515.0
Net income ($ mil.)	–	(276.0)	76.0	98.0	8.0	875.0
Market value ($ mil.)	31.7%	6,048.1	5,105.1	5,481.4	8,983.8	18,213.9
Employees	2.5%	7,600	9,200	9,300	8,300	8,400

ELECTRONIC CONTROL SECURITY INC.

NBB: EKCS

790 Bloomfield Avenue, Bldg. C-1
Clifton, NJ 07012
Phone: 973 574-8555
Fax: 973 574-8562
Web: www.anti-terrorism.com

CEO: Arthur Barchenko
CFO: Daryl Holcomb
HR: –
FYE: June 30
Type: Public

Electronic Control Security (ECSI) is a leading provider of integrated security systems for government and commercial facilities worldwide. Its products include command and control intrusion detection and sensing and surveillance systems used at airports military bases ports and other sensitive facilities such as embassies and power plants. ECSI also provides risk assessment and other security consulting services. Its customers include a number of government agencies such as the US Department of Energy and the Department of Defense. In addition to offices in the US the company has operations in the Middle East and Latin America.

	Annual Growth	06/10	06/11	06/12	06/13	06/14
Sales ($ mil.)	(38.3%)	4.5	4.0	2.2	1.0	0.7
Net income ($ mil.)	–	0.4	0.5	(1.5)	(1.2)	(0.9)
Market value ($ mil.)	(41.7%)	5.2	2.9	1.3	1.0	0.6
Employees	(10.6%)	21	22	19	15	–

ELECTRONIC SYSTEMS TECHNOLOGY, INC.

NBB: ELST

415 N. Quay St. Bldg B1
Kennewick, WA 99336
Phone: 509 735-9092
Fax: –
Web: www.esteem.com

CEO: T L Kirchner
CFO: –
HR: –
FYE: December 31
Type: Public

Electronic Systems Technology (EST) makes wireless modems that it markets under the ESTeem brand. EST targets the modems for applications in industrial automation the military and public safety. The ESTeem line includes Ethernet radios that can be used for handling video and voice over Internet protocol (VoIP) transmissions. EST buys parts from Hitachi Intersil Integrated Microelectronics Mitsubishi Murata Manufacturing Rakon and Toko America for its products. Assembly of EST's products is farmed out to Manufacturing Services.

	Annual Growth	12/10	12/11	12/12	12/13	12/14
Sales ($ mil.)	(4.3%)	2.2	1.8	2.1	2.2	1.9
Net income ($ mil.)	–	0.1	(0.1)	0.0	0.1	(0.1)
Market value ($ mil.)	(7.5%)	3.0	1.9	1.3	1.9	2.2
Employees	0.0%	15	13	14	14	15

ELECTRONICS FOR IMAGING, INC.

NMS: EFII

6750 Dumbarton Circle
Fremont, CA 94555
Phone: 650 357-3500
Fax: –
Web: www.efi.com

CEO: Guy Gecht
CFO: Marc Olin
HR: –
FYE: December 31
Type: Public

Electronics For Imaging (EFI) wants to take control of your color. The company makes hardware and software systems for commercial and enterprise digital printing and print management. EFI's Fiery line includes print servers as well as print controllers that copier and printer vendors such as Ricoh Xerox Canon Epson and Konica Minolta integrate into their equipment. EFI's Print MIS (management information systems) software provides supply chain and customer relationship management from job submission to fulfillment. Its Inkjet segment products include super-wide format (VUTEk) and industrial printers (Jetrion). It's also the world's largest manufacturer of digital UV ink.

	Annual Growth	12/10	12/11	12/12	12/13	12/14
Sales ($ mil.)	11.9%	504.0	591.6	652.1	727.7	790.4
Net income ($ mil.)	45.7%	7.5	27.5	83.3	109.1	33.7
Market value ($ mil.)	31.5%	671.6	668.8	891.3	1,817.8	2,010.2
Employees	9.1%	1,886	2,142	2,393	2,523	2,672

ELEMENTIS SPECIALTIES INC.

329 Wyckoffs Mill Rd.
Hightstown NJ 08520
Phone: 609-443-2000
Fax: 609-443-2422
Web: www.elementis-specialties.com

CEO: –
CFO: –
HR: –
FYE: December 31
Type: Subsidiary

Elementis Specialties focuses on the elements of specialty chemicals. The company manufactures additives that improve the various properties of products made by the coatings building products and cosmetics industries. A subsidiary of Elementis plc it manufactures rheological additives that affect thinning thickening and flow in products like cosmetics coatings and drilling fluids. The company also makes a line of pigment dispersions and a variety of other specialty additives and polymers. Although its parent is based in the UK Elementis Specialties makes its home in New Jersey and has operations worldwide. It generates more than half of its additives sales by supplying the US paints and coatings market.

ELEVANCE RENEWABLE SCIENCES INC.

2501 W. Davey Rd.
Woodridge IL 60440
Phone: 866-625-7103
Fax: 630-633-7295
Web: www.elevance.com

CEO: K'Lynne Johnson
CFO: David H Kelsey
HR: –
FYE: December 31
Type: Private

If cars can run on vegetable oil why can't palm oil clean clothes? Elevance Renewable Sciences figured it out. The chemical company is developing new applications to use plant-based oils as an eco-friendly alternative to petrochemicals. It plans to make chemicals from palm soy and rapeseed oil to use in household and personal care products as well as lubricants coatings and plastics. The company is building a biorefinery with Wilmar International in Indonesia to manufacture specialty chemicals oleochemicals and olefins. Currently it only makes vegetable wax candles sold under the NatureWax brand through a partnership with Cargill. In mid-2012 Elevance withdrew an initial public offering that was originally filed in 2011.

ELEVEN BIOTHERAPEUTICS INC

NMS: EBIO

215 First Street, Suite 400
Cambridge, MA 02142
Phone: 617 871-9911
Fax: –
Web: www.elevenbio.com

CEO: Abbie C Celniker
CFO: –
HR: –
FYE: December 31
Type: Public

There won't be a dry eye in the house if Eleven Biotherapeutics gets its way. The clinical-stage biopharmaceutical company has a proprietary protein engineering platform (AMP-Rx) which it applies to the discovery and development of protein therapeutics to treat eye diseases. It focuses on the role of cytokines (cell-signaling molecules) in diseases of the eye and designs and develops proteins to modulate the effects of cytokines. The company's most advanced product candidate is EBI-005 a topical treatment for dry eye disease and allergic conjunctivitis. Eleven went public in 2014.

	Annual Growth	12/10	12/11	12/12	12/13	12/14
Sales ($ mil.)	–	0.0	–	–	1.3	2.2
Net income ($ mil.)	–	0.0	(12.8)	(19.7)	(18.0)	(34.2)
Market value ($ mil.)	–	0.0	–	–	–	213.0
Employees	14.6%	–	–	16	15	21

ELGIN NATIONAL INDUSTRIES INC.

2001 Butterfield Rd. Ste. 1020
Downers Grove IL 60515-1050
Phone: 630-434-7200
Fax: 630-434-7272
Web: www.elginindustries.com

CEO: Fred C Schulte
CFO: Wayne J Conner
HR: –
FYE: December 31
Type: Private

Diversity fuels the engine of Elgin National Industries (ENI). ENI manages about a dozen manufacturing and engineering/construction service companies that cater primarily to the coal processing and underground mining oil and gas exploration and electric utility industries. Elgin Equipment group manufactures engineered products including centrifuges rotary breakers mine electrical gear vibrating screens and feeders and rectifiers for power supplies. A fabrication arm produces components used in power plants and other industrial applications. Elgin Fasteners International makes specialty fastener products. ENI majority owned by GFI Energy Ventures markets its products and services worldwide.

ELGIN SWEEPER COMPANY

1300 W. Bartlett Rd.
Elgin IL 60120-7529
Phone: 847-741-5370
Fax: 847-742-3035
Web: www.elginsweeper.com

CEO: Robert Welding
CFO: Charles Avery
HR: –
FYE: December 31
Type: Subsidiary

Elgin Sweeper can sweep you off your street. The company's street sweeping vehicles have been forcing big-city drivers to switch sides of the street since 1914. A subsidiary of Federal Signal Elgin Sweeper makes street sweepers including broom air and specialty sweepers marketed under brands like Road Wizard Broom Bear and Crosswind. Elgin also makes sweepers that run on alternative fuels (compressed natural gas and liquefied natural gas). Besides streets the vehicles are used to clear debris from airport runways industrial plants and construction sites. The company's products are sold through more than 100 dealers worldwide. Elgin Sweeper is a part of Federal Signal's Environmental Products Group.

ELITE PHARMACEUTICALS, INC.

NBB: ELTP

165 Ludlow Avenue
Northvale, NJ 07647
Phone: 201 750-2646
Fax: –
Web: www.elitepharma.com

CEO: Nasrat Hakim
CFO: Carter A. Ward
HR: –
FYE: March 31
Type: Public

Elite Pharmaceuticals isn't above peddling generics. Subsidiary Elite Laboratories develops generic versions of existing controlled-release drugs whose patents are about to expire. Its commercial products include allergy therapeutics Lodrane 24 and Lodrane 24D which are marketed by ECR Pharmaceuticals. Products in various stages of testing and preclinical development include oxycodone pain medications anti-infectives and treatments for gastrointestinal disorders. Elite Laboratories also provides contract research and development services for other drugmakers.

	Annual Growth	03/11	03/12	03/13	03/14	03/15
Sales ($ mil.)	4.1%	4.3	2.4	3.4	4.6	5.0
Net income ($ mil.)	–	(13.6)	(15.1)	1.5	(96.6)	28.9
Market value ($ mil.)	33.1%	49.2	56.2	48.0	258.4	154.6
Employees	20.6%	17	19	26	38	36

ELIXIR INDUSTRIES

24800 CHRISANTA DR # 210
MISSION VIEJO, CA 926914833
Phone: 949-860-5000
Fax: –
Web: www.elixirind.com

CEO: –
CFO: Chris Brown
HR: Johnny Streat
FYE: December 31
Type: Private

Elixir Industries is a diversified manufacturer of aluminum extrusions aluminum fabrication and custom metal fabrication products. Its portfolio of offerings includes doors siding and roofing window guards recreational vehicle products cargo trailers and aluminum painted coil. It also makes a variety of coatings sealants and tapes. The company operates from about a dozen locations in half a dozen states serving clients across the US as well as in selected international markets. Roland Sahm founded what is now Elixir Industries in 1948.

	Annual Growth	12/02	12/03	12/04	12/05	12/11
Sales ($ mil.)	(6.7%)	–	–	–	221.0	146.0
Net income ($ mil.)	–	–	–	–	0.0	14.4
Market value ($ mil.)	–	–	–	–	–	–
Employees	–	–	–	–	–	700

ELIZABETH ARDEN INC.

NMS: RDEN

2400 S.W. 145 Avenue
Miramar, FL 33027
Phone: 954 364-6900
Fax: –
Web: www.elizabetharden.com

CEO: E. Scott Beattie
CFO: Rod R. Little
HR: Lita Cunningham
FYE: June 30
Type: Public

Sweet scents and more are behind Elizabeth Arden's auspicious red door. The firm owns and licenses prestige and mass market celebrity lifestyle and designer fragrances and distributes about 280 prestige fragrance brands. Fragrance generated some 77% of 2014 sales. Established labels include Red Door Elizabeth Arden 5th Avenue and Elizabeth Taylor's White Diamonds. Scents aimed at younger wearers include the Justin Bieber and Nicki Minaj licensed brands. Its fragrances cosmetics and skin care lines (Ceramide PREVAGE Visible Difference) are sold to US department stores and mass retailers as well as international retailers.

	Annual Growth	06/11	06/12	06/13	06/14	06/15
Sales ($ mil.)	(4.7%)	1,175.5	1,238.3	1,344.5	1,164.3	971.1
Net income ($ mil.)	–	41.0	57.4	40.7	(145.7)	(224.0)
Market value ($ mil.)	(16.3%)	865.4	1,157.0	1,342.7	638.6	425.1
Employees	(1.1%)	2,665	2,789	2,990	2,790	2,550

ELKINS CONSTRUCTORS INC.

701 W ADAMS ST STE 1
JACKSONVILLE, FL 322041600
Phone: 904-353-6500
Fax: –
Web: www.elkinsconstructors.com

CEO: Barry L Allred
CFO: –
HR: –
FYE: December 31
Type: Private

Elkins Constructors builds it all. The company one of Florida's largest privately held construction companies works on commercial industrial multifamily residential institutional and retail projects mainly in the Southeast. It offers general contracting design/build and construction management services and its retail market clients have included Lowe's British Airways and Castleton Beverage. Other projects include the America Online call center and headquarters for PGA Tour Productions. Elkins also has been named one of the top green contractors in the US by Engineering News-Record. Founded in 1955 by Martin Elkins the company was acquired in 1984 by CEO Barry Allred and a team of investors.

	Annual Growth	12/05	12/06	12/07	12/08	12/12
Sales ($ mil.)	11.7%	–	60.8	231.7	286.0	117.8
Net income ($ mil.)	(57.9%)	–	–	8.1	10.2	0.1
Market value ($ mil.)	–	–	–	–	–	–
Employees	–	–	–	–	–	126

ELLIE MAE INC
NYS: ELLI

4420 Rosewood Drive, Suite 500
Pleasanton, CA 94588
Phone: 925 227-7000
Fax: 925 227-9030
Web: www.elliemae.com

CEO: Jonathan H. Corr
CFO: Edgar A. (Ed) Luce
HR: –
FYE: December 31
Type: Public

Ellie Mae might sound like Fannie Mae's backwoods cousin but they're just in related industries not bloodlines. The company provides automation software and operates the Ellie Mae Network that facilitates the residential mortgage origination and funding process. Its Encompass software suite combines loan origination with CRM (customer relationship management) to gather review and verify data from a single database. Other programs handle regulatory compliance appraisal and title services underwriting tax transcripts and document preparation and management. More than 90000 mortgage professionals use its software and network to process more than 3 million new mortgages an estimated 20% of its addressable market.

	Annual Growth	12/10	12/11	12/12	12/13	12/14
Sales ($ mil.)	39.0%	43.2	55.5	101.8	128.5	161.5
Net income ($ mil.)	109.0%	0.8	3.6	19.5	12.6	14.8
Market value ($ mil.)	92.5%	–	163.3	802.2	776.7	1,165.5
Employees	35.5%	190	270	308	407	640

ELLINGTON FINANCIAL LLC
NYS: EFC

53 Forest Avenue
Old Greenwich, CT 06870
Phone: 203 698-1200
Fax: –
Web: www.ellingtonfinancial.com

CEO: Laurence Penn
CFO: Lisa Mumford
HR: –
FYE: December 31
Type: Public

Mortgage-related assets are music to Ellington Financial's ears. The specialty finance company manages a portfolio of primarily non-agency residential mortgage-backed securities valued at more than $366 million. It also seeks to acquire other target assets such as residential whole mortgage loans commercial mortgage-backed securities commercial real estate debt and asset-backed securities. Riskier residential whole mortgage loans which are generally not guaranteed by the US government include subprime non-performing and sub-performing mortgage loans. Founded in 2007 Ellington Financial went public in 2010 in hopes of taking advantage of the current credit environment.

	Annual Growth	12/10	12/11	12/12	12/13	12/14
Sales ($ mil.)	19.8%	45.6	63.5	63.9	85.7	93.9
Net income ($ mil.)	24.1%	24.8	44.7	24.2	49.7	58.8
Market value ($ mil.)	(2.7%)	743.9	574.4	751.3	758.3	667.7
Employees	10.7%	100	100	100	130	150

ELLINGTON RESIDENTIAL MORTGAGING REAL ESTATE INVESTMENT TRUST
NYS: EARN

53 Forest Avenue
Old Greenwich, CT 06870
Phone: 203 698-1200
Fax: –

CEO: Laurence Penn
CFO: Lisa Mumford
HR: –
FYE: December 31
Type: Public

Ellington Financial LLC is ready to double its money. The investment firm formed Ellington Residential Mortgage REIT a real estate residential trust (REIT) to invest in agency residential mortgage-backed securities (Agency RMBS) or those guaranteed by federally sponsored entities Fannie Mae Freddie Mac and Ginnie Mae. (Agency RMBS carry less risk than privately issued mortgage securities.) The trust's portfolio is balanced out with about 10% non-Agency RMBS such as residential whole mortgage loans mortgage servicing rights (MSRs) and residential real properties. (Non-Agency RMBS carry more risk but might offer better returns.) The trust went public in 2013.

	Annual Growth	12/10	12/11	12/12	12/13	12/14
Sales ($ mil.)	–	0.0	0.0	0.2	27.9	46.8
Net income ($ mil.)	–	0.0	0.0	(0.5)	(1.9)	16.2
Market value ($ mil.)	–	0.0	0.0	–	140.7	148.9
Employees	15.4%	–	–	–	130	150

ELLIOT HOSPITAL OF THE CITY OF MANCHESTER

1 ELLIOT WAY
MANCHESTER, NH 031033502
Phone: 603-669-5300
Fax: –
Web: www.elliothospital.org

CEO: –
CFO: Richard Elwell
HR: Catherine Bardier
FYE: June 30
Type: Private

Elliot Health System provides medical care to southern New Hampshire. The health care organization operates Elliot Hospital an acute care hospital with nearly 300 beds that is home to a regional cancer center a designated regional trauma center and a level III neonatal intensive care unit (NICU). In addition to general and surgical care the hospital offers rehabilitation behavioral health obstetrics cardiology and lab services. The system also operates the Elliot Physician Network which operates primary care centers specialty clinics and surgery centers in various regional communities. Elliot Hospital was founded in 1890.

	Annual Growth	06/06	06/07	06/08	06/09	06/10
Sales ($ mil.)	(19.6%)	–	–	502.2	288.4	324.6
Net income ($ mil.)	2074.8%	–	–	0.0	0.0	7.7
Market value ($ mil.)	–	–	–	–	–	–
Employees	–	–	–	–	–	2,000

ELLIS (PERRY) INTERNATIONAL INC
NMS: PERY

3000 N.W. 107 Avenue
Miami, FL 33172
Phone: 305 592-2830
Fax: –
Web: www.pery.com

CEO: Oscar Feldenkreis
CFO: Anita D. Britt
HR: –
FYE: January 31
Type: Public

You'll find Perry Ellis International (PEI) apparel worn about town during the workweek and on the links most weekends. It designs distributes and licenses men's and women's sportswear under 30-plus company-owned or licensed brands including Jantzen Laundry Manhattan Munsingwear Original Penguin and namesake Perry Ellis among others. PEI also distributes PGA and Champions Tour golf apparel and NIKE swimwear under licenses. PEI's customers include some of the nation's largest retailers (Wal-Mart Kohl's and Macy's) and it distributes its products to 20000 stores. The apparel maker also operates more than 40 Perry Ellis stores in the US Puerto Rico and the UK and several Original Penguin US shops.

	Annual Growth	01/11	01/12*	02/13	02/14*	01/15
Sales ($ mil.)	3.0%	790.3	980.6	969.6	912.2	890.0
Net income ($ mil.)	–	24.1	25.5	14.8	(22.8)	(37.2)
Market value ($ mil.)	(4.2%)	435.7	237.1	297.3	240.7	367.2
Employees	2.0%	2,400	2,600	2,600	2,700	2,600

*Fiscal year change

ELLIS HOSPITAL

1101 NOTT ST
SCHENECTADY, NY 123082489
Phone: 518-243-4000
Fax: –
Web: www.ellismedicine.org

CEO: James W Connolly
CFO: G E Hoffman
HR: –
FYE: December 31
Type: Private

Schenectady-based Ellis Hospital (dba Ellis Medicine) serves the residents of New York's capital area as part of Ellis Medicine a 438-bed community and teaching health care system. The hospital provides emergency inpatient medical/surgical and psychiatric care including diagnostic primary and rehabilitative care. The hospital is also home to centers of excellence in the treatment of and care for heart and cardiovascular ailments cancer women's health issues stroke-related problems and behavioral health concerns. It also operates the Ellis Center the Bellvue Woman's Center the satellite outpatient clinic Ellis Health Center and recently-constructed Medical Center of Clifton Park.

	Annual Growth	12/07	12/08	12/09	12/12	12/13
Sales ($ mil.)	156.1%	–	3.5	374.0	379.9	380.6
Net income ($ mil.)	26.7%	–	–	15.0	10.8	38.6
Market value ($ mil.)	–	–	–	–	–	–
Employees	–	–	–	–	–	2,000

ELLSWORTH COOPERATIVE CREAMERY

232 N WALLACE ST
ELLSWORTH, WI 54011
Phone: 715-273-4311
Fax: –
Web: www.ellsworthcheesecurds.com

CEO: Paul Bauer
CFO: –
HR: –
FYE: December 31
Type: Private

Ellsworth Cooperative Creamery processes and markets the cream of its members' crops which in this instance are dairy cows. The creamery manufactures and distributes butter cheese whey powder cheese curds and other dairy foods. Founded in 1908 (as the Milton Dairy Company and taking its current name in 1910) the cooperative processes 1.5 million pounds of milk daily. The co-op has more than 500 farmer/members whose dairy operations are located in Minnesota and Wisconsin. It is known for its cheddar cheese curds; the company was officially nicked-named the "Cheese Curd Capital of the World" by (former) Wisconsin's governor Anthony Earl.

	Annual Growth	12/03	12/04	12/05	12/06	12/07
Sales ($ mil.)	11.7%	–	–	116.7	92.2	145.7
Net income ($ mil.)	185726.5%	–	–	0.0	2.8	3.5
Market value ($ mil.)	–	–	–	–	–	–
Employees	–	–	–	–	–	60

ELLUCIAN INC.

4375 Fair Lakes Ct.
Fairfax VA 22033
Phone: 703-968-9000
Fax: 703-968-4573
Web: www.ellucian.com

CEO: Jeff Ray
CFO: Kevin M Boyce
HR: –
FYE: December 31
Type: Private

Ellucian (formerly Datatel+SGHE) doesn't care if you're a Bruin (USC) a Longhorn (University of Texas) or a Hurricane (University of Miami) as long as you've got data that needs managing. The company which serves higher education institutions in North America develops software that integrates administrative and academic computing systems. Its products manage information about students — grading finances financial aid and advancement — and it streamlines such processes as enterprise resource planning IT e-recruitment and alumni communications. The company took its current form when owner Hellman & Friedman combined it with SunGard Higher Education (SGHE) in 2012.

ELMA ELECTRONIC INC.

44350 S GRIMMER BLVD
FREMONT, CA 945386385
Phone: 510-656-3400
Fax: –
Web: www.elma.com

CEO: Fred Ruegg
CFO: –
HR: –
FYE: December 31
Type: Private

Elma Electronic thinks your electronics equipment should be contained not your enthusiasm. The US subsidiary of Elma Electronic AG manufactures and distributes an array of electronic enclosures backplanes and server racks. It also makes passive electronic components from rotary switches to knobs and light-emitting diodes. Elma Electronic's slate of services includes component customization design engineering manufacture systems integration and verification. Subsidiary Elma Bustronic offers custom backplane applications and Optima EPS makes electronic enclosures. The company courts industries worldwide in telecommunications medical electronics industrial control defense and aerospace.

	Annual Growth	12/09	12/10	12/11	12/12	12/13
Sales ($ mil.)	2.4%	–	63.6	70.1	64.6	68.2
Net income ($ mil.)	(10.8%)	–	–	3.3	1.6	2.6
Market value ($ mil.)	–	–	–	–	–	–
Employees	–	–	–	–	–	280

ELMHURST MEMORIAL HOSPITAL INC

155 E BRUSH HILL RD
ELMHURST, IL 601265658
Phone: 331-221-1000
Fax: –
Web: www.emhc.org

CEO: Mary Lou Mastro
CFO: James Doyle
HR: –
FYE: June 30
Type: Private

Elmhurst Memorial Healthcare operates Elmhurst Memorial Hospital an acute care facility located in DuPage County Illinois in the western suburbs of Chicago. Founded in 1926 the hospital provides a comprehensive range of medical services — from emergency care to specialty cancer and orthopedics care to behavioral health services. In addition to the 310-bed main hospital Elmhurst Memorial Healthcare operates several facilities such as doctors' offices outpatient centers occupational health programs and other ancillary health care operations. Elmhurst Memorial Healthcare is part of Edward-Elmhurst Healthcare after it merged with Edward Hospital & Health Services and Linden Oaks.

	Annual Growth	06/04	06/05	06/07	06/08	06/09
Sales ($ mil.)	(1.7%)	–	327.3	341.8	345.8	305.7
Net income ($ mil.)	(31.8%)	–	–	43.3	(22.1)	20.1
Market value ($ mil.)	–	–	–	–	–	–
Employees	–	–	–	–	–	2,444

ELMIRA SAVINGS BANK (NY)

NAS: ESBK

333 East Water Street
Elmira, NY 14901
Phone: 607 735-8660
Fax: 607 732-4007
Web: www.elmirasavingsbank.com

CEO: –
CFO: –
HR: Alan (Al) Garcia
FYE: December 31
Type: Public

The Elmira Savings Bank is a community bank that serves individuals and small to midsized businesses through about a dozen branch offices in upstate New York's Cayuga Chemung Steuben and Tompkins counties. The bank offers traditional deposit products such as checking and savings accounts CDs and IRAs. With these funds it mainly originates residential and commercial mortgages business loans and auto and other consumer loans. The bank offers investments and financial planning through its ESB Advisory Services subsidiary. Elmira Savings Bank was organized in 1869.

	Annual Growth	12/10	12/11	12/12	12/13	12/14
Assets ($ mil.)	2.2%	499.8	523.4	536.9	514.3	546.0
Net income ($ mil.)	(6.7%)	4.8	5.0	5.2	5.1	3.7
Market value ($ mil.)	5.9%	49.4	44.3	61.5	68.2	62.2
Employees	3.1%	113	–	128	124	–

ELOQUA LIMITED

NASDAQ: ELOQ

1921 Gallows Rd. Ste. 250
Vienna VA 22182-3900
Phone: 703-584-2750
Fax: 956-381-5706
Web: www.fronteraproduce.com

CEO: Joseph P Payne
CFO: Donald E Clarke
HR: –
FYE: December 31
Type: Private

Eloqua wants its clients to be fluent in customer data and lead generation. The company makes demand generation software that helps corporate marketing and sales personnel pull data from website tracking and customer relationship management (CRM) applications. Its software captures search terms used by website visitors and translates those into relevant data to improve revenue performance management. Customers have included Ellie Mae Nokia Sybase and Pitney Bowes. The company has sales partnerships with Omniture Microsoft Dynamics and Oracle. Founded in 1999 Eloqua received funding from JMI Equity Fund prior to going public on the NASDAQ exchange in 2012. It is being acquired by Oracle.

ELSTER AMERICAN METER COMPANY LLC

2221 Industrial Rd.   CEO: –
Nebraska City NE 68410   CFO: –
Phone: 402-873-8200   HR: –
Fax: 402-873-7616   FYE: December 31
Web: www.elster-americanmeter.com   Type: Subsidiary

Elster American Meter's products have been ticking for more than 170 years. The specialty manufacturer formerly known as American Meter makes natural gas meters regulators shutoff devices filters test equipment and accessories and provides services including metering data collection and transfer and evaluation. The company is a unit of the Elster Group which has some 70 natural gas measurement and control subsidiaries worldwide. Elster American Meter introduced the synthetic molded convoluted diaphragm that established new industry standards for long-term accuracy and reliability. Founded in 1836 the company pioneered the shift to aluminum-case meters as a replacement for cast iron.

ELVIS PRESLEY ENTERPRISES INC.

3734 Elvis Presley Blvd.   CEO: Jack Soden
Memphis TN 38116-0508   CFO: –
Phone: 901-332-3322   HR: –
Fax: 901-345-8511   FYE: September 30
Web: www.elvis.com   Type: Subsidiary

Elvis may have permanently left the building but his legacy is still taking care of business. Elvis Presley Enterprises (EPE) manages the late singer's estate and licenses his name likeness and songs for a variety of commercial purposes. Revenue mostly comes from operating Presley's Graceland mansion in Memphis. The company runs tours at Graceland and also operates the associated museum visitor's center and the Heartbreak Hotel. EPE was created in 1981 (four years after Presley's death) and was owned by The Elvis Presley Trust. EPE and The Elvis Presley Trust were wholly owned by Elvis' daughter Lisa Marie Presley until 2005 when she sold an 85% stake to entertainment investor Robert Sillerman's CKX.

ELWYN

111 ELWYN RD   CEO: –
MEDIA, PA 190634622   CFO: –
Phone: 610-891-2000   HR: Susan Ladd
Fax: –   FYE: June 30
Web: www.caelwyn.org   Type: Private

Elwyn isn't a character out of Harry Potter or Lord of the Rings. It's a not-for-profit organization that serves more than 13000 disabled and disadvantaged people of all ages at multiple sites through education rehabilitation and vocational counseling. The organization also operates residential communities including more than 80 group homes and apartments and provides a variety of health care services for persons with developmental physical and emotional disabilities. The group also publishes training materials and hosts conferences and seminars for human services professionals. Founded in 1852 as a school for children with mental retardation Elwyn is one of the oldest organizations of its kind in the US.

	Annual Growth	06/08	06/09	06/10	06/11	06/12
Sales ($ mil.)	3.1%	–	192.7	254.0	264.0	211.0
Net income ($ mil.)	(51.4%)	–	–	6.1	14.6	1.4
Market value ($ mil.)	–	–	–	–	–	–
Employees	–	–	–	–	–	2,500

ELXSI CORP   NBB: ELXS

3600 Rio Vista Avenue, Suite A   CEO: Alexander M Milley
Orlando, FL 32805   CFO: –
Phone: 407 849-1090   HR: –
Fax: –   FYE: December 31
  Type: Public

This restaurant operator comes with a side of technology. ELXSI Corporation's hospitality division operates about 15 family-style restaurants in New England while its CUES division manufactures sewer inspection equipment. The eateries operate under the Bickford's Grille brand and offer casual dining with an emphasis on breakfast items served throughout the day. Its equipment manufacturing operation makes remote-control video cameras and robotic cutting devices used by municipalities and contractors. ELXSI is controlled by chairman and CEO Alexander Milley.

	Annual Growth	12/07	12/11	12/12	12/13	12/14
Sales ($ mil.)	0.8%	72.2	60.4	63.9	64.4	76.5
Net income ($ mil.)	–	(0.3)	3.8	4.6	4.5	7.1
Market value ($ mil.)	33.4%	6.4	10.6	38.5	30.9	48.2
Employees	–	–	–	–	–	–

EMAGIN CORP   ASE: EMAN

2070 Route 52, Hopewell Junction   CEO: Andrew G. Scully
New York, NY 12533   CFO: Jeffrey P. Lucas
Phone: 845 838-7900   HR: –
Fax: –   FYE: December 31
Web: www.emagin.com   Type: Public

eMagin is imagining eye-opening technology. The company develops virtual imaging and organic light-emitting diodes (OLEDs) that can be used in applications ranging from wearable PCs and virtual imaging devices to more mundane products such as DVD headset systems video games and high-definition televisions. The technology also extends to military uses. eMagin's products use microcircuits and displays to magnify images of text or video. Subsidiary Virtual Vision develops near-eye and virtual image display products including headset viewer systems. eMagin markets to OEMs and directly to customers in the government industrial and medical sectors.

	Annual Growth	12/10	12/11	12/12	12/13	12/14
Sales ($ mil.)	(4.1%)	30.5	29.2	30.6	28.0	25.7
Net income ($ mil.)	–	14.8	5.0	2.3	(14.1)	(5.3)
Market value ($ mil.)	(21.1%)	151.2	93.2	89.9	71.3	58.5
Employees	5.8%	67	92	101	110	84

EMBARCADERO TECHNOLOGIES INC.

100 California St. 12th Fl.   CEO: Wayne Williams
San Francisco CA 94111   CFO: Robert Levin
Phone: 415-834-3131   HR: –
Fax: 415-434-1721   FYE: December 31
Web: www.embarcadero.com   Type: Private

Thinking of setting out on a database development adventure? Embarcadero wants to be along for the ride. The company makes data lifecycle management software used to build test optimize and manage application infrastructure and databases for large corporations and government agencies. Its applications are used in the food services health care IT financial services education travel utilities industries among others. Embarcadero's software is used for modeling change management performance optimization and administration of database platforms made by Oracle IBM and Microsoft. It has offices in nearly 30 countries. Founded in 1993 the company is owned by private equity group Thoma Cressey Bravo.

EMBLEMHEALTH INC.

55 Water St.
New York NY 10041
Phone: 646-447-5000
Fax: 646-447-3011
Web: www.emblemhealth.com

CEO: Anthony L Watson
CFO: Arthur Byrd
HR: –
FYE: December 31
Type: Private

EmblemHealth is set on being the mark of good health in the Northeast. The not-for-profit company provides health insurance through subsidiaries Group Health Incorporated (GHI) and the Health Insurance Plan of Greater New York (HIP). Collectively the two health insurers cover some 2.8 million New Yorkers primarily state government and New York City employees. The two companies cover upwards of 90% of Big Apple city workers and retirees. Both provide a variety of managed health plans to their members including prescription drug and dental coverage and Medicare plans. GHI and HIP joined together under the EmblemHealth banner in 2006.

EMBREE CONSTRUCTION GROUP INC.

4747 WILLIAMS DR
GEORGETOWN, TX 786333799
Phone: 512-819-4700
Fax: –
Web: www.embreegroup.com

CEO: Jim Embree
CFO: –
HR: –
FYE: December 31
Type: Private

The Embree Construction Group develops designs and builds free-standing buildings for business chains across the US. The group serves as a general contractor or construction manager primarily for major national companies. It is active throughout the US. Ground-up and remodeling projects include retail properties restaurants gas stations convenience stores automotive service centers and correctional facilities. Operating companies include Embree Healthcare Group which develops assisted-living and specialty medical projects and Embree Asset Group which develops build-to-suit single-tenant buildings and leases them back to clients. Owner and chairman Jim Embree founded the firm in 1979 in Kansas City.

	Annual Growth	12/09	12/10	12/11	12/12	12/13
Sales ($ mil.)	29.3%	–	64.8	106.2	128.8	140.0
Net income ($ mil.)	90.8%	–	–	0.8	2.8	3.0
Market value ($ mil.)	–	–	–	–	–	–
Employees	–	–	–	–	–	175

EMBRY-RIDDLE AERONAUTICAL UNIVERSITY INC.

600 S CLYDE MORRIS BLVD
DAYTONA BEACH, FL 321143966
Phone: 386-226-6000
Fax: –
Web: www.erau.edu

CEO: –
CFO: Eric B Weekes
HR: –
FYE: June 30
Type: Private

Embry-Riddle Aeronautical University (ERAU) helps students solve the mysteries of space and flying. The not-for-profit corporation teaches aviation aerospace and engineering to about 30000 students a year (and a student-teacher ratio of about 13:1). ERAU which offers hands-on training through a fleet of 90 instructional aircraft has residential campuses in Daytona Beach Florida and Prescott Arizona. Its Embry-Riddle Worldwide program provides learning through more than 150 teaching centers and online training in the US Canada Europe and Middle East. It offers bachelor's master's and doctoral degrees in 35 areas.

	Annual Growth	06/10	06/11	06/12	06/13	06/14
Sales ($ mil.)	(1.7%)	–	359.4	318.0	384.6	340.9
Net income ($ mil.)	19.2%	–	–	24.3	26.7	34.5
Market value ($ mil.)	–	–	–	–	–	–
Employees	–	–	–	–	–	4,719

EMC CORP. (MA)

NYS: EMC

176 South Street
Hopkinton, MA 01748
Phone: 508 435-1000
Fax: 508 435-5222
Web: www.emc.com

CEO: Joseph M. (Joe) Tucci
CFO: Zane C. Rowe
HR: Aissa Chorki
FYE: December 31
Type: Public

EMC has its head in the cloud ... and rightly so for a company that's helping businesses build Web-based computing systems with its data storage products and services. Its hardware and software platforms enable enterprises to store manage protect and analyze massive volumes of data. EMC also offers data security products through its RSA Security business and virtualization software through majority-owned VMware. The company serves both large FORTUNE 500 organizations and smaller businesses across many industries. Banks government agencies ISPs and manufacturers are among its customers. EMC serves a global client base from facilities and partners worldwide; it generates nearly half its sales outside the US. In October 2015 EMC agreed to be bought by Dell Inc. for $67 billion.

	Annual Growth	12/10	12/11	12/12	12/13	12/14
Sales ($ mil.)	9.5%	17,015.1	20,007.6	21,713.9	23,222.0	24,440.0
Net income ($ mil.)	9.3%	1,900.0	2,461.3	2,732.6	2,889.0	2,714.0
Market value ($ mil.)	6.8%	45,456.5	42,756.9	50,220.5	49,922.8	59,033.9
Employees	9.6%	48,500	53,600	60,000	63,900	70,000

EMC INSURANCE GROUP INC.

NMS: EMCI

717 Mulberry Street
Des Moines, IA 50309
Phone: 515 345-2902
Fax: –
Web: www.emcins.com

CEO: Bruce G. Kelley
CFO: Mark E. Reese
HR: –
FYE: December 31
Type: Public

Holding company EMC Insurance Group may be publicly traded but in its heart it's a mutual insurance company. Subsidiaries EMCASCO Insurance Illinois EMCASCO and Dakota Fire Insurance sell commercial and personal property/casualty insurance including automobile property liability and workers' compensation. Its commercial customers are primarily small and medium-sized businesses. Other group companies include EMC Underwriters which offers excess and surplus lines of insurance and EMC Reinsurance which provides reinsurance for the group and other unaffiliated insurers. Employers Mutual Casualty a multiple-line property/casualty insurance company owns about 60% of EMC Insurance Group.

	Annual Growth	12/10	12/11	12/12	12/13	12/14
Assets ($ mil.)	6.0%	1,187.8	1,230.5	1,290.7	1,378.9	1,497.8
Net income ($ mil.)	(1.1%)	31.3	(2.1)	38.0	43.5	30.0
Market value ($ mil.)	11.9%	460.6	418.5	485.8	622.9	721.4
Employees	–	–	–	–	–	–

EMCLAIRE FINANCIAL CORP.

NAS: EMCF

612 Main Street
Emlenton, PA 16373
Phone: 844 767-2311
Fax: –
Web: www.emclairefinancial.com

CEO: William C Marsh
CFO: Matthew J Lucco
HR: –
FYE: December 31
Type: Public

Emclaire Financial is the holding company for the Farmers National Bank of Emlenton which operates about a dozen branches in northwestern Pennsylvania. Serving area consumers and businesses the bank offers standard deposit products and services including checking and savings accounts money market accounts and CDs. The bank is mainly a real estate lender with commercial mortgages residential first mortgages and home equity loans and lines of credit making up most of its loan portfolio. Emclaire Financial also owns title insurance and real estate settlement services provider Emclaire Settlement Services.

	Annual Growth	12/10	12/11	12/12	12/13	12/14
Assets ($ mil.)	4.8%	481.9	491.9	509.0	525.8	581.9
Net income ($ mil.)	7.0%	3.1	3.8	3.7	3.8	4.0
Market value ($ mil.)	11.2%	29.1	28.4	37.1	44.8	44.5
Employees	1.1%	115	118	115	116	120

EMCOR GROUP, INC.
NYS: EME

301 Merritt Seven
Norwalk, CT 06851-1092
Phone: 203 849-7800
Fax: –
Web: www.emcorgroup.com

CEO: Keith Chanter
CFO: Mark A. Pompa
HR: Carla Woodall
FYE: December 31
Type: Public

Electrical and mechanical construction is at the core of EMCOR Group. One of the world's largest specialty construction firms EMCOR designs installs operates and maintains complex mechanical and electrical systems. These include systems for power generation and distribution lighting water and wastewater treatment voice and data communications fire protection plumbing and heating ventilation and air-conditioning (HVAC). EMCOR also provides facilities services including management and maintenance support. Through some 70 subsidiaries and joint ventures the company serves a range of commercial industrial institutional and utility customers. EMCOR exited the UK market in 2014 to focus on the US.

	Annual Growth	12/04	12/11	12/12	12/13	12/14
Sales ($ mil.)	3.1%	4,747.9	5,613.5	6,346.7	6,417.2	6,425.0
Net income ($ mil.)	17.6%	33.2	130.8	146.6	123.8	168.7
Market value ($ mil.)	(0.2%)	2,845.5	1,688.5	2,179.8	2,672.9	2,802.0
Employees	0.4%	26,000	25,000	26,000	27,000	27,000

EMCORE CORP.
NMS: EMKR

2015 W. Chestnut Street
Alhambra, CA 91803
Phone: 626 293-3400
Fax: –
Web: www.emcore.com

CEO: Jeffrey S. (Jeff) Rittichier
CFO: Mark Weinswig
HR: –
FYE: September 30
Type: Public

EMCORE has gone full fiber. The company makes optical computer chips and systems for fiber optic cable and broadband systems. Its products are components in cable TV fiber-to-the-premise (FTTP) networks telecommunications and data centers satellite communications aerospace and defense wireless networks and broadcast audio/video systems. EMCORE sold its photovoltaic business in 2014 to focus on fiber. The company makes about two-thirds of its revenue from companies based in the US.

	Annual Growth	09/11	09/12	09/13	09/14	09/15
Sales ($ mil.)	(20.1%)	200.9	163.8	168.1	174.8	81.7
Net income ($ mil.)	–	(34.2)	(39.2)	5.0	4.9	63.1
Market value ($ mil.)	61.9%	25.4	145.1	115.0	146.1	174.6
Employees	(14.2%)	1,000	1,060	857	769	543

EMD MILLIPORE CORPORATION

290 Concord Rd.
Billerica MA 01821
Phone: 978-715-4321
Fax: 800-645-5439
Web: www.emdmillipore.com

CEO: –
CFO: Anthony L Mattacchione
HR: –
FYE: December 31
Type: Subsidiary

Life at EMD Millipore is about making life science research development and production faster easier and more effective. The company is a US-based subsidiary and one of four main divisions of Germany's Merck KGaA. Outside of North America it is known as the Merck Millipore division. The company is a top tier supplier of a comprehensive set of products and services primarily to pharma biotech and academic markets worldwide. Its product portfolio includes active pharmaceutical ingredients drug delivery compounds chemicals and reagents and instrumentation. Among EMD Millipore's services are contract manufacturing custom packaging testing consulting and maintenance.

EMDEON INC.
NYSE: EM

3055 Lebanon Pike
Nashville TN 37214
Phone: 615-932-3000
Fax: 615-231-7972
Web: www.emdeon.com

CEO: Neil De Crescenzo
CFO: Bob A Newport Jr
HR: –
FYE: December 31
Type: Private

Emdeon wants to make the servicing of medical accounts a little easier. The company's offerings are designed to simplify and streamline health care billing for insurance companies health care systems and doctors. Emdeon offers discounted office supplies online automated billing and document mailing services and insurance card printing and has products specifically for dental and pharmaceutical offices. It processes more than 5 billion health care-related transactions each year. It also owns Chamberlin Edmonds & Associates a provider of revenue recovery assistance to healthcare clients. Emdeon was acquired by The Blackstone Group in 2011.

EMERALD DAIRY INC.
OTC: EMDY

11990 Market St. Ste. 205
Reston VA 20190
Phone: 703-867-9247
Fax: +61-3-5563-2156
Web: www.wcbf.com.au

CEO: Yang Yong Shan
CFO: Shu Kaneko
HR: –
FYE: December 31
Type: Public

Emerald Dairy's formula for success is turning milk into milk powder. The company produces milk powder (infant formula and enriched milk powders for children and adults) as well as rice and soybean powders. Its product line includes two brands: Xing An Ling which is marketed to low-end customers and Yi Bai which is marketed to middle and high-end customers. Producing more than 9000 tons of milk powder annually the dairy distributes its products to more than 5800 retail stores located in 20 of China's 30 provinces. Emerald Dairy gets its milk supply through contracting with local dairy farmers. Chairman and CEO Yong Shan Yang owns 47% of Emerald John Winfield owns 10% and Farallon Partners owns 9%.

EMERALD OIL, INC
ASE: EOX

200 Columbine Street, Suite 500
Denver, CO 80206
Phone: 303 595-5600
Fax: –
Web: www.voyageroil.com

CEO: McAndrew Rudisill
CFO: Ryan Smith
HR: –
FYE: December 31
Type: Public

Emerald Oil (formerly Voyager Oil & Gas) is involved in energy exploration and production in the northern US. It has oil and gas rights in properties Colorado Montana and North Dakota primarily in the Bakken and Three Forks formations in the Williston Basin. Growing its assets in the Rockies in 2012 Voyager Oil & Gas acquired fellow oil and gas exploration and production company Emerald Oil and assumed that company's name. That year the company reported proved reserves of approximately 5.35 million barrels of oil equivalent all of which were located in the Williston Basin.

	Annual Growth	12/10	12/11	12/12	12/13	12/14
Sales ($ mil.)	230.6%	0.9	8.4	27.9	51.3	112.6
Net income ($ mil.)	–	(4.3)	(1.3)	(62.3)	(10.9)	(52.1)
Market value ($ mil.)	(31.3%)	420.3	200.0	407.8	596.2	93.4
Employees	93.4%	3	5	15	30	42

EMERGE ENERGY SERVICES LP
NYS: EMES

180 State Street, Suite 225
Southlake, TX 76092
Phone: 817 865-5830
Fax: –
Web: www.emergelp.com

CEO: Rick Shearer
CFO: Jody Tusa
HR: –
FYE: December 31
Type: Public

Emerge Energy Services is ready to come into being. The company formed in April 2012 by an investment firm Insight Equity to take over three of its portfolio investments — Allied Energy Company LLC; Direct Fuels Partners L.P.; and Superior Silica Sands LLC. Allied Energy and Direct Fuels distribute petroleum products including ethanol and biodiesel while Superior Silica Sands owns three processing plants that supply sand to natural gas production companies. (Sand is one of the key components in hydraulic fracturing the process in producing natural gas.) When Emerge Energy Services went public in March 2013 it took ownership of the three companies.

	Annual Growth	12/10	12/11	12/12	12/13	12/14
Sales ($ mil.)	–	0.0	0.0	–	873.3	1,111.3
Net income ($ mil.)	–	0.0	0.0	(0.1)	35.2	89.1
Market value ($ mil.)	–	0.0	0.0	–	1,051.5	1,280.8
Employees	–	–	–	–	–	–

EMERGENT BIOSOLUTIONS INC
NYS: EBS

400 Professional Drive, Suite 400
Gaithersburg, MD 20879
Phone: 240 631-3200
Fax: –
Web: www.emergentbiosolutions.com

CEO: Daniel J. Abdun-Nabi
CFO: Robert G Kramer
HR: Paula Lazarich
FYE: December 31
Type: Public

Emergent BioSolutions is preparing for a bioterrorism or pandemic worst-case scenario. The company develops and produces vaccines that treat or protect against infectious diseases and bio-agents. The company supplies BioThrax (the US's only FDA-approved anthrax vaccine) primarily to the US Department of Defense (DOD) Centers for Disease Control (CDC) and the US Department of Health and Human Services (HHS). Its biodefense unit is also developing a post-exposure treatment for anthrax. The company's biosciences division is working on therapies for leukemia and lymphoma and vaccines for such infectious as influenza. In 2015 the firm announced it would spin off its biosciences division as a separate public entity.

	Annual Growth	12/10	12/11	12/12	12/13	12/14
Sales ($ mil.)	12.0%	286.2	273.4	281.9	312.7	450.1
Net income ($ mil.)	(8.2%)	51.7	23.0	23.5	31.1	36.7
Market value ($ mil.)	3.8%	884.7	635.0	604.9	866.9	1,026.8
Employees	13.7%	767	811	877	1,353	1,280

EMERGENT CAPITAL INC
NYS: EMG

5355 Town Center RoadaSuite 701
Boca Raton, FL 33486
Phone: 561 995-4200
Fax: –
Web: www.imperial.com

CEO: Antony Mitchell
CFO: Richard O'Connell Jr
HR: –
FYE: December 31
Type: Public

Specialty finance company Emergent Capital (formerly Imperial Holdings) offers loans allowing policyholders to postpone or consolidate insurance premium payments using the policy as collateral. Emergent Capital has issued loans mostly to senior citizens secured by about $4 billion in insurance policies. The average loan is for $216000 on policies with an average death payout of $4 million. In addition to premium financing the company also purchases structured settlements allowing customers to exchange a long-term settlement plan for an immediate lump sum of lesser value. Formed in 2006 Emergent Capital went public in 2011.

	Annual Growth	12/10	12/11	12/12	12/13	12/14
Sales ($ mil.)	(13.1%)	76.9	44.2	19.1	89.1	43.8
Net income ($ mil.)	–	(15.7)	(39.2)	(44.6)	65.3	(5.5)
Market value ($ mil.)	51.4%	–	40.2	95.2	140.0	139.5
Employees	(26.1%)	131	130	119	107	39

EMERGENT GROUP INC.
NYSE AMEX: LZR

10939 Pendleton St.
Sun Valley CA 91352
Phone: 818-394-2800
Fax: 818-394-2850
Web: www.emergentgroupinc.com

CEO: Bruce J Haber
CFO: William M McKay
HR: –
FYE: December 31
Type: Public

Mobile medical equipment for rent? Emergent Group's got it. Through wholly-owned operating subsidiary PRI Medical Technologies the company rents mobile medical laser and surgical equipment in more than 15 states on a per-procedure basis to hospitals surgical care centers and doctors' offices. The equipment comes with operation and maintenance services from technical support personnel. The company serves both small health care providers that cannot afford to purchase expensive medical equipment for their facilities and larger hospitals that cannot justify buying certain equipment due to infrequent usage. Universal Hospital Services (UHS) acquired Emergent Group in 2011 in a transaction worth about $70 million.

EMERGING VISION INC.
OTC: ISEE

520 8th Ave. 23rd Fl.
New York City NY 10018
Phone: 646-737-1500
Fax: 724-720-1530
Web: www.tollgrade.com

CEO: –
CFO: Brian P Alessi
HR: –
FYE: December 31
Type: Public

Emerging Vision doesn't have to strain to keep its business in focus. The firm owns and franchises about 130 optical outlets under the Sterling Optical Site For Sore Eyes Kindy Optical and Singer Specs names in more than a dozen states the District of Columbia and the US Virgin Islands. It also runs an optical purchasing group offering vendor discounts to independent eyewear retailers in the US under the Combine Optical name and in Canada under The Optical Group name. In addition the company operates VisionCare of California a specialized HMO whose dues-paying members may receive eye care services at Emerging Vision's optical outlets throughout the state.

EMERITUS CORP.
NYS: ESC

3131 Elliott Avenue, Suite 500
Seattle, WA 98121
Phone: 206 298-2909
Fax: 206 378-4205
Web: www.emeritus.com

CEO: Granger Cobb
CFO: Robert C Bateman
HR: –
FYE: December 31
Type: Public

The Emeritus Corporation honors the retirement set. The company operates assisted living communities for senior citizens who need help with daily activities such as feeding bathing housekeeping and managing their medications as well as for those patients suffering from dementia. Emeritus' communities also organize social and recreational activities for residents and most of them provide special services (called Join Their Journey programs) to support residents with Alzheimer's disease or other forms of dementia. Throughout the US Emeritus owns leases or manages about 480 communities. It also manages communties through joint ventures and for third parties.

	Annual Growth	12/08	12/09	12/10	12/11	12/12
Sales ($ mil.)	19.5%	769.4	898.7	1,007.1	1,254.8	1,568.1
Net income ($ mil.)	–	(104.8)	(53.9)	(57.0)	(71.9)	(84.8)
Market value ($ mil.)	25.3%	459.5	859.0	903.0	802.2	1,132.5
Employees	12.8%	18,671	12,577	29,300	28,100	30,236

EMERSON COLLEGE

120 BOYLSTON ST STE 414
BOSTON, MA 021164624
Phone: 617-824-8500
Fax: –
Web: www.emersonlions.com

CEO: –
CFO: –
HR: Richard (Dick) West
FYE: June 30
Type: Private

Emerson College specializes in teaching subjects in the fields of communication and the arts in a liberal arts context. Areas of study include journalism; marketing; organizational and political communication; performing arts; visual and media arts; and writing literature and publishing. Its also has an acclaimed communication sciences and disorders program. The college enrolls about 3200 full-time undergraduates and 1000 full and part-time graduate students on its Boston-based campus. Among its alumni are producer Norman Lear talk show host Jay Leno and journalist Morton Dean. The college has additional facilities in Los Angeles and in the Netherlands. Emerson was founded in 1880 as a school of oratory.

	Annual Growth	06/06	06/07	06/08	06/09	06/10
Sales ($ mil.)	–	–	–	0.0	147.6	154.3
Net income ($ mil.)	3200.1%	–	–	0.0	16.0	17.8
Market value ($ mil.)	–	–	–	–	–	–
Employees	–	–	–	–	–	425

EMERSON ELECTRIC CO.   NYS: EMR

8000 W. Florissant Avenue, P.O. Box 4100
St. Louis, MO 63136
Phone: 314 553-2000
Fax: –
Web: www.emerson.com

CEO: David N. Farr
CFO: Frank J. Dellaquila
HR: Cathy Bevan
FYE: September 30
Type: Public

Ralph Waldo Emerson's adage "Make yourself necessary to somebody" holds true for Emerson Electric. The company makes a slew of electrical electro-mechanical and electronic products many of which are used to control gases liquids and electricity. Its InSinkErator is a maker of food waste disposers and hot water dispensers. Emerson pursues an aggressive acquisition strategy coupled with select divestitures in building up its global presence. The company gathers its business units and divisions under five business segments. It has more than 235 manufacturing locations with about 160 outside of the US. International markets make up 60% of Emerson's sales.

	Annual Growth	09/11	09/12	09/13	09/14	09/15
Sales ($ mil.)	(2.0%)	24,222.0	24,412.0	24,669.0	24,537.0	22,304.0
Net income ($ mil.)	2.2%	2,480.0	1,968.0	2,004.0	2,147.0	2,710.0
Market value ($ mil.)	1.7%	27,041.9	31,598.0	42,353.2	40,965.4	28,914.1
Employees	(4.5%)	133,200	134,900	131,600	115,100	110,800

EMERSON HOSPITAL

133 ORNAC
CONCORD, MA 017424169
Phone: 978-369-1400
Fax: –
Web: www.emersonhospital.org

CEO: Christine C Schuster
CFO: Dana Diggins
HR: –
FYE: September 30
Type: Private

Ralph Waldo Emerson said "the first wealth is health" and Emerson Hospital would agree. The hospital tends to the well-being of patients in and around historic Concord Massachusetts. The 179-bed community hospital is staffed by more than 300 doctors and specialists. Emerson partners with Massachusetts General on several specialty programs including pain management neonatology and radiation oncology which is housed within its Bethke Cancer Center. It also operates outpatient clinics serving residents in nearby communities such as Groton Sudbury and Westford. All told Emerson provides advanced medical services to more than 300000 people.

	Annual Growth	09/05	09/06	09/09	09/12	09/13
Sales ($ mil.)	3.2%	–	146.8	0.0	180.3	183.2
Net income ($ mil.)	–	–	–	0.0	3.4	2.9
Market value ($ mil.)	–	–	–	–	–	–
Employees	–	–	–	–	–	1,450

EMERSON NETWORK POWER-EMBEDDED COMPUTING INC.

2900 S. Diablo Way Ste. 190
Tempe AZ 85282
Phone: 602-438-5720
Fax: 602-438-5825
Web: www.emerson.com/sites/network_power/en-us/page

CEO: Jay L Geldmacher
CFO: Nate Myer
HR: –
FYE: September 30
Type: Subsidiary

Emerson Network Power-Embedded Computing Inc. (dba Emerson Network Power) makes some powerful products for a broad range of applications. The company makes standard and custom power supplies including switches rectifiers breaker interface panels AC/DC and DC/DC power supplies and related accessories. Its products are used in computing medical networking and telecommunications process control and test instrumentation applications. One of the largest manufacturers of power supplies in the world Emerson Network Power also a company brand is a subsidiary of Emerson Electric. It has manufacturing and direct sales force operations in Asia Europe and North America. The US represents about 40% of sales.

EMERSON RADIO CORP.   ASE: MSN

3 University Plaza, Suite 405
Hackensack, NJ 07601
Phone: 973 428-2000
Fax: 973 428-2067
Web: www.emersonradio.com

CEO: Duncan Hon
CFO: Andrew L Davis
HR: –
FYE: March 31
Type: Public

Emerson Radio is tuned to the crowd that thinks a new television or microwave oven shouldn't cost an arm and a leg. The company designs imports sells and licenses housewares and audio and video products under the Emerson H.H. Scott and Olevia brand names. Its products are sold primarily by mass merchants in the US. (Wal-Mart and Target account for more than 85% of the company's sales.) Emerson's products include microwave ovens compact refrigerators wine openers and coolers clock radios televisions and other audio and video products. Its products are sourced from foreign suppliers primarily in China. Emerson Radio was founded in 1948.

	Annual Growth	03/11	03/12	03/13	03/14	03/15
Sales ($ mil.)	(21.5%)	200.8	163.3	128.4	77.8	76.3
Net income ($ mil.)	(41.3%)	15.9	10.6	6.0	1.3	1.9
Market value ($ mil.)	(14.1%)	65.7	54.5	44.8	56.4	35.8
Employees	(16.7%)	85	63	55	42	41

EMI MUSIC PUBLISHING

75 9th Ave.
New York NY 10011
Phone: 212-492-1200
Fax: 703-691-9047
Web: www.trailways.com

CEO: Martin Bandier
CFO: –
HR: –
FYE: March 31
Type: Business Segment

EMI Music Publishing is looking after the business part of the music business. As one of the world's top music publishers (along withUMPG) the firm administers the rights to some 2 million songs. Its collection includes classics and standards such as "Blue Moon" "I Left My Heart in San Francisco" and "Santa Claus Is Comin' to Town" as well as more recent hits like "Genie in a Bottle" and "Smells Like Teen Spirit." The firm collects royalties for including its songs on CDs as well as live performance fees; it also licenses its music for use in movies TV shows and advertising. Formerly a division of UK-based recording giant EMI Group in 2012 EMI Music Publishing was acquired by a consortium led by Sony.

EMISPHERE TECHNOLOGIES INC.   OTC: EMIS

240 Cedar Knolls Rd.
Cedar Knolls NJ 07927
Phone: 973-532-8000
Fax: 914-347-2498
Web: www.emisphere.com

CEO: Alan L Rubino
CFO: Michael R Garone
HR: –
FYE: December 31
Type: Public

Needle prick be gone. Development-stage Emisphere Technologies is offering an alternative to traditional injection of certain drugs with an oral drug delivery technology called eligen which is designed to improve the way certain therapeutic molecules (such as proteins carbohydrates and peptides) are administered to and absorbed by the body. With collaborative partners including Novartis Roche and Genta Emisphere is developing oral formulations that incorporate eligen to deliver drugs that treat such health problems as osteoporosis diabetes growth disorders and cardiovascular disease. Emisphere was formed in 1986.

EMJ CORPORATION

2034 HAMILTON PLACE BLVD # 400
CHATTANOOGA, TN 374216061
Phone: 423-855-1550
Fax: –
Web: www.emjcorp.com

CEO: James Jolley
CFO: David Keller
HR: –
FYE: December 31
Type: Private

EMJ does it all for the mall. Founded in 1968 by namesake Edgar M. Jolley the company specializes in building and renovating retail outlets and shopping centers throughout the US. It is also known for other building projects such as offices warehouses churches hotels multifamily residences hospitals and wind farms. Working from five offices nationwide EMJ provides general construction and construction management. The company's pre-construction services include creating detailed budgets and construction schedules and coordinating permitting utility companies and municipal requirements. To track a project's progress and monitor costs EMJ offers quality control and safety and warranty management.

	Annual Growth	12/06	12/07	12/08	12/11	12/12
Sales ($ mil.)	(14.9%)	–	959.2	821.8	437.5	428.5
Net income ($ mil.)	(29.5%)	–	–	7.9	0.4	2.0
Market value ($ mil.)	–	–	–	–	–	–
Employees	–	–	–	–	–	210

EMKAY INC.

805 W. Thorndale Ave.
Itasca IL 60143
Phone: 630-250-7400
Fax: 630-250-7077
Web: www.emkay.com

CEO: Greg L Tepas
CFO: –
HR: –
FYE: February 28
Type: Private

Emkay is an ehiclevay easerlay. Or for the Pig Latin challenged: Emkay is a vehicle leaser. One of the oldest and largest fleet leasing and management companies in the nation it leases and manages some 75000 cars trucks and electric vehicles to more than 500 corporate clients. The employee-owned company offers open- and closed-end leasing programs as well as assistance with fleet purchase and disposal. Other services include maintenance and fuel management It also operates Emkay Motors a retail used vehicle outlet in Illinois. Founded in 1946 Emkay has 10 US offices and is active in Canada Mexico and the Caribbean. It operates Unico CarLease in Europe.

EMMIS COMMUNICATIONS CORP.   NMS: EMMS

One Emmis Plaza, 40 Monument Circle, Suite 700
Indianapolis, IN 46204
Phone: 317 266-0100
Fax: –
Web: www.emmis.com

CEO: –
CFO: Patrick M Walsh
HR: Traci Thomson
FYE: February 28
Type: Public

Emmis Communications is into communicating — whether it's through the radio or magazines. It owns and operates about 20 radio stations (18 FM and 3 AM) serving more than a half dozen markets in the US including cities such as New York Los Angeles and St. Louis. Emmis also owns Network Indiana which syndicates programming to more than 70 affiliate stations. In addition to broadcasting the company owns a portfolio of regional magazines and specialty publications including Atlanta Los Angeles and Texas Monthly. CEO Jeffrey Smulyan controls about 70% of Emmis.

	Annual Growth	02/11	02/12	02/13	02/14	02/15
Sales ($ mil.)	(1.4%)	251.3	236.0	196.1	205.1	237.9
Net income ($ mil.)	–	(15.6)	26.2	43.8	43.5	(99.3)
Market value ($ mil.)	18.2%	48.0	31.8	70.2	137.0	93.8
Employees	(2.1%)	1,220	1,140	1,020	1,000	1,120

EMPIRE DISTRICT ELECTRIC CO.   NYS: EDE

602 S. Joplin Avenue
Joplin, MO 64801
Phone: 417 625-5100
Fax: –
Web: www.empiredistrict.com

CEO: Bradley P. Beecher
CFO: Laurie A. Delano
HR: –
FYE: December 31
Type: Public

Empire District Electric (EDE) has the sovereign authority to light up its territory. The utility transmits and distributes electricity to a population base of more than 450000 (about 217000 customers in southwestern Missouri and adjacent areas of Arkansas Kansas and Oklahoma. It also supplies water to three Missouri towns and natural gas throughout most of the state. EDE's interests in fossil-fueled and hydroelectric power plants give it a generating capacity of 1377 MW; it also wholesales power. The company also provides fiber-optic services. In 2016 the company agreed to be bought by Algonquin Power & Utilities in a C$3.4 billion (US$2.4 billion) deal.

	Annual Growth	12/10	12/11	12/12	12/13	12/14
Sales ($ mil.)	4.8%	541.3	576.9	557.1	594.3	652.3
Net income ($ mil.)	9.1%	47.4	55.0	55.7	63.4	67.1
Market value ($ mil.)	7.6%	965.2	917.0	886.1	986.5	1,293.1
Employees	0.0%	750	746	756	751	751

EMPIRE RESORTS INC   NMS: NYNY

c/o Monticello Casino and Raceway, 204 State Route 17B, P.O. Box 5013
Monticello, NY 12701
Phone: 845 807-0001
Fax: –
Web: www.empireresorts.com

CEO: Joseph A D'Amato
CFO: Laurette Pitts
HR: –
FYE: December 31
Type: Public

Empire Resorts has taken up permanent residence in New York's playground. The company operates Catskills-area harness horseracing track Monticello Gaming and Raceway which features pari-mutuel wagering and more than 1100 video gaming machines (VGMs). The property located 90 miles northwest of New York City also includes a clubhouse entertainment lounge bar and food court. Its VGMs are owned by the State of New York and are overseen by the state's Division of the Lottery which distributes a percentage of VGM revenue to Empire Resorts. Other company revenues primarily come from wagering fees admission fees program and racing form sales and food and beverages sales.

	Annual Growth	12/10	12/11	12/12	12/13	12/14
Sales ($ mil.)	(1.2%)	68.5	70.2	72.0	71.0	65.2
Net income ($ mil.)	–	(17.6)	(0.0)	(0.7)	(21.5)	(23.9)
Market value ($ mil.)	65.9%	8.1	11.9	17.4	38.2	61.3
Employees	(1.7%)	310	310	310	288	290

EMPIRE RESOURCES INC
NAS: ERS

2115 Linwood Avenue
Fort Lee, NJ 07024
Phone: 201 944-2200
Fax: –

CEO: Nathan Kahn
CFO: Sandra Kahn
HR: –
FYE: December 31
Type: Public

When it comes to aluminum Empire Resources is especially resourceful. The company distributes semi-finished aluminum products including sheet foil wire plate and coil. Products are sold primarily to manufacturers of appliances automobiles packaging and housing materials. Empire Resources provides a variety of related services including sourcing of aluminum products storage and delivery and handling foreign exchange transactions. Company president and CEO Nathan Kahn and CFO Sandra Kahn who are husband and wife own some 40% of Empire Resources.

	Annual Growth	12/10	12/11	12/12	12/13	12/14
Sales ($ mil.)	5.8%	465.0	514.6	538.5	482.7	582.3
Net income ($ mil.)	(20.1%)	9.1	5.0	4.0	2.4	3.7
Market value ($ mil.)	(2.8%)	46.3	24.9	26.6	31.9	41.4
Employees	2.2%	55	55	60	60	60

EMPIRE SOUTHWEST LLC

1725 S COUNTRY CLUB DR
MESA, AZ 852106099
Phone: 480-633-4000
Fax: –
Web: www.empire-cat.com

CEO: Jeffrey S. (Jeff) Whiteman
CFO: –
HR: Cassandra Garcia
FYE: October 31
Type: Private

With CAT-like tread Empire Southwest has created a heavy equipment sales rental and leasing empire in the US Southwest. One of the largest Caterpillar dealerships in the US Empire Southwest operates through five divisions: hydraulic service machinery power systems precision machining and transport. The company's equipment includes backhoes compactors dozers front shovels loaders pipelayers telehandlers and tractors. It also handles equipment used for mining and forestry projects. Empire Southwest also sells ARCO agricultural equipment carries batteries power generators engines and tools and has a service department.

	Annual Growth	10/08	10/09	10/10	10/11	10/12
Sales ($ mil.)	25.3%	–	448.2	528.5	683.9	881.9
Net income ($ mil.)	54.5%	–	–	22.5	38.0	53.8
Market value ($ mil.)	–	–	–	–	–	–
Employees	–	–	–	–	–	1,450

EMPIRE STATE REALTY TRUST INC
NYS: ESRT

One Grand Central Place, 60 East 42nd Street
New York, NY 10165
Phone: 212 687-8700
Fax: –
Web: www.empirestaterealtytrust.com

CEO: Anthony E Malkin
CFO: David A Karp
HR: Donna Olsen
FYE: December 31
Type: Public

If King Kong were around he'd be an executive at Empire State Realty Trust. The self-administered and self-managed real estate investment trust (REIT) formed in mid-2011 to take over a portfolio of high-profile Manhattan properties from its previous owners the Malkin family. Its flagship property is of course the 102-story Empire State Building but the trust also owns more than a dozen other buildings in the greater New York area totaling almost 7.7 million sq. ft. of office and retail space. In addition it plans to build a 340000-sq.-ft. building at the train station in Stamford Connecticut. Empire State Realty Trust went public in 2013 raising $929 million.

	Annual Growth	12/11	12/12*	10/13*	12/13	12/14
Sales ($ mil.)	29.2%	294.8	260.3	206.1	127.6	635.3
Net income ($ mil.)	6.9%	57.4	48.6	(37.2)	193.4	70.2
Market value ($ mil.)	33.7%	–	–	1,409.6	1,640.0	1,884.4
Employees	17.1%	–	629	–	607	862

*Fiscal year change

EMPIRIX INC.

600 TECHNOLOGY PARK DR #1
BILLERICA, MA 01821-4154
Phone: 978-313-7000
Fax: –
Web: www.empirix.com

CEO: John Danna
CFO: Ray Dezenzo
HR: –
FYE: December 31
Type: Private

Empirix elucidates about communications service quality. The company provides testing and monitoring applications that manage and enhance IP communications networks and systems for service providers equipment manufacturers and corporate contact centers. Its systems rely on the Hammer Test Engine a technology that duplicates user behavior to test and validate the performance of voice data video and mobile communications networks under real-world conditions. Empirix's global customer base includes Amtrak Cisco China Mobile Sonus Networks Time Warner Cable and lastminute.com.

	Annual Growth	12/03	12/04	12/05	12/06	12/07
Sales ($ mil.)	7.2%	–	58.8	70.6	73.0	72.4
Net income ($ mil.)	–	–	(3.6)	(2.3)	(3.7)	(7.6)
Market value ($ mil.)	–	–	–	–	–	–
Employees	–	–	–	–	–	380

EMPLOYERS HOLDINGS INC
NYS: EIG

10375 Professional Circle
Reno, NV 89521
Phone: 888 682-6671
Fax: –

CEO: Douglas D. Dirks
CFO: William E. Yocke
HR: –
FYE: December 31
Type: Public

Because workers' compensation is nothing to gamble with small business owners can turn to Employers Holdings. The Reno-based holding company provides workers' compensation services including claims management loss prevention consulting and care management to small businesses in low hazard industries including retailers and restaurants. The company provides workers' compensation through its Employer Insurance Company of Nevada (EICN) and Employers Compensation Insurance Company. Employers Holdings also operates Employers Assurance and Employers Preferred Insurance Company both of which also offer workers' compensation.

	Annual Growth	12/10	12/11	12/12	12/13	12/14
Assets ($ mil.)	2.0%	3,480.1	3,481.7	3,511.3	3,643.4	3,769.7
Net income ($ mil.)	12.5%	62.8	48.3	106.9	63.8	100.7
Market value ($ mil.)	7.7%	550.5	569.7	648.1	996.8	740.4
Employees	0.4%	699	651	667	723	709

EMPORIA STATE UNIVERSITY

1200 COMMERCIAL ST CA
EMPORIA, KS 668015087
Phone: 620-341-1200
Fax: –
Web: www.emporia.edu

CEO: –
CFO: –
HR: –
FYE: June 30
Type: Private

Emporia State University (ESU) offers more than 35 undergraduate and roughly two dozen graduate degrees and programs as well as certification programs specialist degrees and doctoral degrees. It has four schools and colleges: the School of Business School of Library and Information Management College of Liberal Arts and Sciences and The Teachers College. Some 6500 students are enrolled at the school which employs about 260 full-time faculty members. ESU is said to be the first and only university to offer a four-year degree in Engraving Arts. The school offers an additional 35 programs online. ESU was founded as Kansas State Normal School in 1863. It adopted its current name in 1977.

	Annual Growth	06/05	06/06	06/08	06/13	06/14
Sales ($ mil.)	3.3%	–	37.3	10.4	42.3	48.4
Net income ($ mil.)	(15.5%)	–	–	6.1	(0.7)	2.2
Market value ($ mil.)	–	–	–	–	–	–
Employees	–	–	–	–	–	1,700

EMRISE CORP

NBB: EMRI

2530 Meridian Parkway
Durham, NC 27713
Phone: 408 200-3040
Fax: –
Web: www.emrise.com

CEO: –
CFO: –
HR: –
FYE: December 31
Type: Public

The sun doesn't set on EMRISE. Through its worldwide subsidiaries the company makes electronic components and communications equipment for customers in the aerospace military and telecommunications industries. Its CXR Larus units produce network transmission and access equipment and a range of testing gear. EMRISE's EEC Corporation subsidiary manufactures power converters digital and rotary switches and subsystem assemblies. The company counts BAE SYSTEMS EMS Technologies Harris ITT Raytheon Rockwell Collins and Thales Air Defence among its top clients. EMRISE gets more than 80% of sales outside the US principally in the UK.

	Annual Growth	12/09	12/10	12/11	12/12	12/13
Sales ($ mil.)	(12.2%)	53.8	30.6	33.5	34.0	31.9
Net income ($ mil.)	–	1.0	(3.4)	(1.6)	0.1	(0.4)
Market value ($ mil.)	2.7%	8.1	9.2	4.6	5.2	9.0
Employees	(11.8%)	335	213	213	213	203

EMS TECHNOLOGIES INC.

660 Engineering Dr.
Norcross GA 30092
Phone: 770-263-9200
Fax: 770-263-9207
Web: www.ems-t.com

CEO: Darius Adamczyk
CFO: John J Tus
HR: –
FYE: December 31
Type: Subsidiary

EMS Technologies' wireless systems can help you communicate whether you're walking the warehouse floor or floating in space. The company's LXE unit provides rugged mobile computers and wireless networks for logistics and other applications. EMS also makes engineered hardware for civilian and military applications through its Defense & Space (D&S) unit. Its Aviation unit makes data communications equipment that provides Internet video conferencing and other capabilities on aircraft. Global Tracking provides tracking and mapping products and services for transport and emergency operations. Customers in the US account for more than two-thirds of sales. In 2011 Honeywell bought EMS for about $491 million.

EMTEC INC.

NBB: ETEC

11 Diamond Road
Springfield, NJ 07081
Phone: 973 376-4242
Fax: –
Web: www.emtecinc.com

CEO: Dinesh R Desai
CFO: Gregory P Chandler
HR: –
FYE: August 31
Type: Public

Emtec provides information technology services including product procurement and infrastructure design and implementation. The company primarily resells and supports computer hardware and software from leading providers such as Cisco Dell Hewlett-Packard and Oracle but it is building its newer IT consulting and application services business which also includes training technical staffing and network management services. Federal government agencies including the US Department of Defense Department of Justice and Department of Homeland Security account for nearly half of sales; other customers include state governments corporations and educational organizations.

	Annual Growth	08/08	08/09	08/10	08/11	08/12
Sales ($ mil.)	1.6%	211.2	223.8	224.6	212.1	224.6
Net income ($ mil.)	–	1.3	1.7	(0.5)	(4.3)	(12.4)
Market value ($ mil.)	3.9%	17.4	15.9	20.1	14.1	20.3
Employees	6.3%	574	572	649	761	733

EMULEX CORPORATION

NYS: ELX

3333 Susan Street
Costa Mesa, CA 92626
Phone: 714 662-5600
Fax: –
Web: www.emulex.com

CEO: Hock E Tan
CFO: –
HR: –
FYE: June 29
Type: Public

Emulex sets an example in the data storage market. The company is a leading maker of host server products (HSP) and embedded storage products (ESP). Its LightPulse fibre channel host bus adapters (HBA) are used to connect storage devices in direct-attached storage configurations as well as storage area network (SAN) and network-attached storage (NAS) systems. Emulex also develops HBAs based on the fibre channel over Ethernet protocol. The company primarily sells directly to equipment makers who incorporate Emulex components into their own storage platforms; its top customers are IBM (29% of sales) and Hewlett-Packard (16%).

	Annual Growth	06/10*	07/11	07/12*	06/13	06/14
Sales ($ mil.)	2.9%	399.2	452.5	501.8	478.6	447.3
Net income ($ mil.)	–	23.6	(83.6)	(11.1)	(5.2)	(29.5)
Market value ($ mil.)	(13.5%)	687.3	617.1	510.7	462.5	385.2
Employees	9.1%	791	972	1,011	1,264	1,122

*Fiscal year change

EMUSIC.COM INC.

244 Fifth Ave. Ste. 2070
New York NY 10001
Phone: 212-201-9240
Fax: 440-323-3623
Web: www.spitzer.com

CEO: Peter Chapman
CFO: Tom Epergino
HR: Meagan Breen
FYE: December 31
Type: Private

eMusic.com previously wanted the whole world in its hands. Now it's focusing on the corner market. eMusic is one of the oldest digital music subscription services in operation allowing consumers to download music legally. However after business suffered as customers turned to newer services from Apple and RealNetworks eMusic repositioned itself as "the Internet's corner music store" providing music from independent labels as well as editorial content and social networking services geared toward music lovers. Former chairman Bob Kohn and ex-CEO Gene Hoffman founded eMusic in 1998. The company is owned by Dimensional Associates the private equity arm of JDS Capital Management.

ENABLE HOLDINGS INC.

PINK SHEETS: ENAB

1140 W. Thorndale Ave.
Itasca IL 60143-1335
Phone: 773-272-5000
Fax: 773-272-4000
Web: www.enableholdings.com

CEO: –
CFO: Patrick L Neville
HR: –
FYE: December 31
Type: Public

Enable Holdings (formerly uBid.com Holdings) is a multi-channel seller of refurbished and closeout merchandise that hosts both online and live auctions. In addition its RedTag.com site offers merchandise at a fixed price instead of through an auction process. Through its Dibu Trading Company the company helps businesses sell entire inventories in a single transaction. Enable's merchandise includes computers automobiles and other consumer goods from some 200 product categories and comes directly from manufacturers such as Hewlett-Packard IBM and Sony. As a result of the credit markets drying up Enable Holdings was forced to file for Chapter 11 bankruptcy in September 2010.

ENABLE MIDSTREAM PARTNERS L.P.   NYS: ENBL

One Leadership Square, 211 North Robinson Avenue, Suite 150
Oklahoma City, OK 73102
Phone: 405 525-7788
Fax: –
Web: www.enablemidstream.com
CEO: Lynn L. Bourdon
CFO: Rodney J. Sailor
HR: –
FYE: December 31
Type: Public

Enable Midstream Partners is a limited partnership owned by OGE Energy CenterPoint Energy and ArcLight and is one of the largest midstream partnerships in the US. It's energy infrastructure assets include 11000 miles of gathering pipelines; 12 major processing plants (2.1 billion cu. ft. per day of processing capacity); 7900 miles of interstate pipelines; 2300 miles of intrastate pipelines; and eight storage facilities (86.5 billion cu. ft. of storage capacity). It raised $500 million in a 2014 IPO to help it develop new energy infrastructure assets and add complementary services and business lines. Following the offering CenterPoint Energy held a 55% stake; OGE Energy 27%; and ArcLight 11.5%.

	Annual Growth	12/11	12/12	12/13	12/14	12/15
Sales ($ mil.)	26.9%	932.0	952.0	2,489.0	3,367.0	2,418.0
Net income ($ mil.)	–	232.0	316.0	1,615.0	530.0	(752.0)
Market value ($ mil.)	(52.6%)	–	–	–	8,190.3	3,886.1
Employees	54566.7%	–	–	–	3	1,640

ENANTA PHARMACEUTICALS, INC.   NMS: ENTA

500 Arsenal Street
Watertown, MA 02472
Phone: 617 607-0800
Fax: –
Web: www.enanta.com
CEO: Jay R. Luly
CFO: Paul J. Mellett
HR: –
FYE: September 30
Type: Public

Enanta Pharmaceuticals is getting hip to Hep C. The company is developing treatments for hepatitis C (HCV) a virus that can lead to chronic liver diseases such as cirrhosis organ failure and cancer. Enanta has four small molecule drugs under development: ABT-450 an NS3 protease inhibitor; EDP-239 an NS5A inhibitor; EDP-546 a cyclophilin inhibitor; and a nucleotide polymerase inhibitor. Two of the candidates are being developed in collaboration with pharmaceutical bigwigs Abbott Laboratories and Novartis. In addition the company is working on a new class of antibiotics to treat multi-drug resistant bacteria. Enanta Pharmaceuticals went public in 2013.

	Annual Growth	09/11	09/12	09/13	09/14	09/15
Sales ($ mil.)	40.0%	41.9	41.7	32.1	47.7	160.9
Net income ($ mil.)	35.7%	23.3	21.4	9.6	34.4	79.0
Market value ($ mil.)	25.6%	–	–	429.0	740.6	676.4
Employees	20.9%	–	39	44	52	69

ENBRIDGE ENERGY MANAGEMENT LLC   NYS: EEQ

1100 Louisiana Street, Suite 3300
Houston, TX 77002
Phone: 713 821-2000
Fax: 713 821-2230
Web: www.enbridgemanagement.com
CEO: Mark A Maki
CFO: –
HR: –
FYE: December 31
Type: Public

Enbridge Energy Management bridging the gap over a complex structure of pipeline partnerships manages and controls the business of Enbridge Energy Partners (formerly Lakehead Pipe Line Partners). The company's only asset is its 10% limited partner interest and 2% general partner interest in Enbridge Energy Partners which owns the US part of North America's longest liquid petroleum pipeline (Lakehead System) and also has interests in natural gas gathering treating processing and transmission operations in East Texas. Enbridge Energy Company a wholly owned subsidiary of Enbridge Inc. holds a 17% stake in the company and serves as the general partner of Enbridge Energy Partners.

	Annual Growth	12/10	12/11	12/12	12/13	12/14
Sales ($ mil.)	–	(38.2)	72.3	50.5	(26.3)	43.7
Net income ($ mil.)	–	(23.7)	45.5	31.8	(18.1)	27.1
Market value ($ mil.)	(11.7%)	4,361.3	2,374.3	1,973.3	1,959.0	2,649.6
Employees	–	–	–	–	–	–

ENBRIDGE ENERGY PARTNERS, L.P.   NYS: EEP

1100 Louisiana Street, Suite 3300
Houston, TX 77002
Phone: 713 821-2000
Fax: –
Web: www.enbridgepartners.com
CEO: Mark A Maki
CFO: Stephen J Neyland
HR: –
FYE: December 31
Type: Public

Head of the class in transporting petroleum around the Great Lakes is Enbridge Energy Partners which owns the 2211-mile US portion (Lakehead System) of the world's longest liquid petroleum pipeline. When combined with the Canadian segment (owned and operated by Enbridge Inc.) the pipeline system spans some 5100 miles across North America. Other midstream assets include 5300 miles of crude oil gathering and transportation lines and 34 million barrels of crude oil storage and terminaling capacity and 11100 miles of natural gas gathering and transportation pipelines. Enbridge's US unit Enbridge Energy Management owns a 23% stake in the company.

	Annual Growth	12/10	12/11	12/12	12/13	12/14
Sales ($ mil.)	0.7%	7,736.1	9,109.8	6,706.1	7,117.1	7,964.7
Net income ($ mil.)	–	(137.9)	677.2	550.1	160.4	740.0
Market value ($ mil.)	(10.6%)	24,729.9	13,157.8	11,060.7	11,841.7	15,818.0
Employees	–	–	–	–	–	–

ENCISION INC.   NBB: ECIA

6797 Winchester Circle
Boulder, CO 80301
Phone: 303 444-2600
Fax: –
Web: www.encision.com
CEO: Gregory J Trudel
CFO: –
HR: –
FYE: March 31
Type: Public

Encision enables doctors to make the cut during surgery. The company makes instruments for use in laparoscopic surgical procedures including electrodes graspers monitors and scissor inserts. Encision's products sold under the brand name AEM Surgical Instruments work like conventional electrosurgical instruments but incorporate proprietary technology that reduces the risk of accidental damage to surrounding tissues caused by stray electrosurgical energy. The company has been working to expand its marketing and distribution network using independent distributors and sales representatives as well as agreements with group purchasing organizations such as Novation and Premier.

	Annual Growth	03/11	03/12	03/13	03/14	03/15
Sales ($ mil.)	(4.5%)	11.6	13.0	11.8	10.5	9.7
Net income ($ mil.)	–	0.0	(0.5)	(0.6)	(1.8)	(1.4)
Market value ($ mil.)	(12.7%)	14.3	12.3	17.6	10.7	8.3
Employees	(4.6%)	52	61	60	47	43

ENCORE BANCSHARES INC.   NASDAQ: EBTX

9 Greenway Plaza Ste. 1000
Houston TX 77046
Phone: 713-787-3100
Fax: 585-321-1707
Web: www.harperhewes.com
CEO: James S D'Agostino Jr
CFO: Patrick T Oakes
HR: –
FYE: December 31
Type: Public

Encore! Encore! Encore Bancshares is taking its bows as the holding company for Encore Bank. Encore operates a dozen branches in Houston offering traditional retail banking products such as deposits mortgages and loans as well as wealth management and insurance through subsidiaries Town & Country Insurance Agency Encore Trust Company and Linscomb & Williams. The bank mostly caters to wealthy clients investment firms investors and privately owned business. Its staff of private bankers and relationship managers even makes house calls. Bank holding company Cadence Bancorp is buying Encore Bancshares for some $250 million; the acquiring firm was formed in 2010 to invest in community banks in the Southeast.

ENCORE CAPITAL GROUP INC
NMS: ECPG

3111 Camino Del Rio North, Suite 103
San Diego, CA 92108
Phone: 877 445-4581
Fax: –
Web: www.encorecapital.com

CEO: Kenneth A. (Ken) Vecchione
CFO: Jonathan Clark
HR: Marie Burris
FYE: December 31
Type: Public

Credit junkies beware: Encore Capital Group has your number. The firm and its Midland Credit Management subsidiary purchase at a discount defaulted consumer receivables that banks credit unions consumer and auto finance companies credit card issuers telecommunications firms retailers and other lenders have given up on. The group then does its best to collect the money via phone direct mail third-party collection agencies and legal action; it employs skip-tracing to track down stubborn debtors. Subsidiary Ascension Capital Group provides bankruptcy support services to the financial services industry. Encore collects debts in the US the UK and Ireland and now Colombia and Peru.

	Annual Growth	12/10	12/11	12/12	12/13	12/14
Sales ($ mil.)	29.5%	381.3	467.4	555.9	773.4	1,072.8
Net income ($ mil.)	20.6%	49.1	61.0	69.5	75.3	103.7
Market value ($ mil.)	17.3%	604.9	548.4	789.8	1,296.4	1,145.3
Employees	29.8%	1,900	2,200	2,800	5,300	5,400

ENCORE ENERGY PARTNERS LP
NYSE: ENP

777 Main St. Ste. 1400
Fort Worth TX 76102
Phone: 817-877-9955
Fax: +86-790-666-9000
Web: www.ldksolar.com

CEO: –
CFO: –
HR: –
FYE: December 31
Type: Subsidiary

Encore Energy Partners is banking on a second trip to the well. The partnership acquires exploits and develops existing oil and natural gas properties. Encore Energy's primary assets consist of oil and natural gas properties in the Big Horn Basin of Wyoming and Montana the Permian Basin of West Texas and the Williston Basin of North Dakota. In 2009 the company reported proved reserves of 28.9 million barrels of oil and 84.7 billion cu. ft. of natural gas. In a move to expand its property base Denbury Resources acquired Encore Energy's former parent Encore Acquisition in early 2010 for $4.5 billion. Vanguard Natural Resourcesthen acquired Denbury Resources' 46% stake in Encore Energy for $380 million.

ENCORE NATIONWIDE INC.

18150 S FIGUEROA ST STE B
GARDENA, CA 902484215
Phone: 866-438-7823
Fax: –
Web: www.encorenationwide.com

CEO: Larry Hess
CFO: Tom Gowrie
HR: –
FYE: December 31
Type: Private

Encore Nationwide provides event staffing services for marketing and promotional campaigns. With a talent database of more than 12000 people across the US Encore can match the right person with appropriate event to create successful promotional events. The company can supply everything from promotional models and product demonstrators to emcees tour managers and all manner of casual laborers. Events include trade shows bar and nightclub promotions fashion shows and guerilla marketing campaigns.

	Annual Growth	12/09	12/10	12/11	12/12	12/13
Sales ($ mil.)	(0.6%)	–	–	–	11.8	11.7
Net income ($ mil.)	1118.5%	–	–	–	0.0	0.2
Market value ($ mil.)	–	–	–	–	–	–
Employees	–	–	–	–	–	25

ENCORE WIRE CORP.
NMS: WIRE

1329 Millwood Road
McKinney, TX 75069
Phone: 972 562-9473
Fax: 972 562-4744
Web: www.encorewire.com

CEO: Daniel L. Jones
CFO: Frank J. Bilban
HR: Brad Donovan
FYE: December 31
Type: Public

Encore Wire likes to keep customers applauding and calling for more — more wire that is. A low-cost manufacturer of copper electrical building wire and cable Encore produces NM-B cable a sheathed cable used to wire homes apartments and pre-fabricated housing and UF-B cable an underground feeder cable for outside lighting and remote residential building connections. Its inventory of stock-keeping units include THWN-2 cable an insulated feeder circuit and branch wiring for commercial and industrial buildings and other wires like armored cable. The company sells to wholesale electrical distributors and select retail home-improvement centers. It is the only public copper building wire company in the US.

	Annual Growth	12/10	12/11	12/12	12/13	12/14
Sales ($ mil.)	6.4%	910.2	1,180.5	1,072.3	1,158.3	1,167.0
Net income ($ mil.)	24.8%	15.3	50.1	19.8	46.9	37.1
Market value ($ mil.)	10.5%	519.7	536.7	628.1	1,123.2	773.6
Employees	12.5%	737	886	998	1,108	1,182

ENDEAVOUR INTERNATIONAL CORP
NBB: ENDR Q

811 Main Street, Suite 2100
Houston, TX 77002
Phone: 713 307-8700
Fax: –
Web: www.endeavourcorp.com

CEO: Catherine L Stubbs
CFO: –
HR: –
FYE: December 31
Type: Public

Like famous British explorer Captain James Cook and his vessel the Endeavour Endeavour International is looking to make new discoveries of great economic benefit. The exploration and production company has traditionally sought developed new oil assets by buying stakes in mature North Sea fields that the oil majors are moving away from. Endeavour International is also developing a second core area the US and has bought stakes in oil and gas properties particularly shale plays in Louisiana New Mexico and Texas and elsewhere. In 2012 Endeavour International reported proved reserves of 25.7 million barrels of oil equivalent (90% of which is in the North Sea).

	Annual Growth	12/09	12/10	12/11	12/12	12/13
Sales ($ mil.)	52.6%	62.3	71.7	60.1	219.1	337.7
Net income ($ mil.)	–	(41.0)	56.5	(131.0)	(126.2)	(95.5)
Market value ($ mil.)	48.5%	50.7	648.3	408.3	243.4	246.7
Employees	(1.2%)	43	58	102	87	41

ENDO HEALTH SOLUTIONS INC
NMS: ENDP

1400 Atwater Drive
Malvern, PA 19355
Phone: 484 216-0000
Fax: –
Web: www.endo.com

CEO: Rajiv De Silva
CFO: Suketu P Upadhyay
HR: –
FYE: December 31
Type: Public

Endo Health Solutions formerly known as Endo Pharmaceuticals wants the pain to end preferably through the drugs it acquires and markets. The company has a portfolio of both branded and generic prescription products for pain management and other health conditions. Its best-selling drug is Lidoderm a lidocaine patch that treats nerve pain caused by shingles. Endo also sells pain medications Percocet and Opana migraine therapy Frova cancer drug Valstar and urology treatment Sanctura. Its generics include morphine and oxycodone tablets. In addition the firm makes and sells urology and prostate devices and provides related medical services.

	Annual Growth	12/08	12/09	12/10	12/11	12/12
Sales ($ mil.)	24.5%	1,260.5	1,460.8	1,716.2	2,730.1	3,027.4
Net income ($ mil.)	–	261.7	266.3	259.0	187.6	(740.3)
Market value ($ mil.)	0.3%	2,867.3	2,273.5	3,956.4	3,825.7	2,906.1
Employees	39.7%	1,216	1,487	2,947	4,566	4,629

ENDOCYTE INC

NMS: ECYT

3000 Kent Avenue, Suite A1-100
West Lafayette, IN 47906
Phone: 765 463-7175
Fax: –
Web: www.endocyte.com

CEO: P. Ron Ellis
CFO: Michael A. Sherman
HR: –
FYE: December 31
Type: Public

Like "smart bombs" the receptor-targeted therapeutics (or "smart drugs") that Endocyte develops aim to take out bad cells without causing collateral damage. Receptor-targeted therapeutics are a precision alternative to non-targeted cancer drugs that can destroy healthy cells. Founded in 1996 Endocyte uses its drug guidance system to deliver drugs including small molecule cancer drugs and RNA-based therapies directly to cancerous cells while leaving other cells unaffected. Its lead candidate EC145 is in clinical trials to treat ovarian cancer. Endocyte went public in early 2011 in a $75 million IPO. It plans to use the proceeds to fund development of EC145 and other candidates in its pipeline.

	Annual Growth	12/10	12/11	12/12	12/13	12/14
Sales ($ mil.)	616.8%	–	0.2	34.7	64.9	70.4
Net income ($ mil.)	–	(20.1)	(40.5)	(17.3)	(18.0)	5.5
Market value ($ mil.)	18.7%	–	157.1	375.2	446.3	262.8
Employees	10.2%	55	61	71	91	81

ENDOLOGIX INC.

NMS: ELGX

2 Musick
Irvine, CA 92618
Phone: 949 595-7200
Fax: –

CEO: John McDermott
CFO: Vaseem Mahboob
HR: –
FYE: December 31
Type: Public

Medical device maker Endologix strengthens weak arteries. The company makes endovascular systems that use stents graft material and catheter delivery devices to treat abdominal aortic aneurysm (AAA weakening of the aortic wall). Its endovascular aneurysm repair (EVAR) products include the Endologix AFX Endovascular AAA System (AFX) and the Endologix Powerlink with Intuitrak Delivery System. Endologix sells its products in the US and some European countries through its own sales representatives and elsewhere through more than a dozen independent distributors. The firm's products are pitched primarily to vascular surgeons and to a lesser extent interventional cardiologists and radiologists.

	Annual Growth	12/10	12/11	12/12	12/13	12/14
Sales ($ mil.)	21.7%	67.3	83.4	105.9	132.3	147.6
Net income ($ mil.)	–	10.7	(28.7)	(35.8)	(16.1)	(32.4)
Market value ($ mil.)	20.9%	480.2	771.0	956.4	1,171.3	1,026.9
Employees	18.7%	297	370	411	482	590

ENDURANCE INTERNATIONAL GROUP HOLDINGS INC

NMS: EIGI

10 Corporate Drive, Suite 300
Burlington, MA 01803
Phone: 781 852-3200
Fax: –
Web: www.endurance.com

CEO: Hari Ravichandran
CFO: Tivanka Ellawala
HR: –
FYE: December 31
Type: Public

Endurance International helps small businesses thrive on the Internet. The company owns a portfolio of brands that offer website design and hosting domain name registry and web security as well as e-commerce tools online marketing and search engine optimization. Bluehost targets small businesses (fewer than five employees) with technical know-how while HostGator helps those who need to offer more customer support. Altogether the company offers a comprehensive suite of some 150 products and services under the brands A Small Orange Domain.com Dotster FatCow Homestead HostMonster JustHost iPage and iPower. Endurance International counts more than 3 million subscribers. The company went public in 2013.

	Annual Growth	12/11	12/11	12/12	12/13	12/14
Sales ($ mil.)	49.8%	187.3	3.0	292.2	520.3	629.8
Net income ($ mil.)	–	(73.9)	(4.4)	(139.3)	(159.2)	(42.8)
Market value ($ mil.)	30.0%	–	–	–	1,856.4	2,412.8
Employees	(1.5%)	–	–	2,580	2,204	2,503

ENEL GREEN POWER NORTH AMERICA INC.

1 Tech Dr. Ste. 220
Andover MA 01810
Phone: 978-681-1900
Fax: 978-681-7727
Web: www.enelgreenpower.com/en-gb/ena/

CEO: –
CFO: Marco Fossataro
HR: –
FYE: December 31
Type: Subsidiary

You can't spell renewable without Enel. The North American arm of Italy's Enel Green Power S.p.A. owns and operates more than 70 renewable energy plants in 20 states and two Canadian provinces. Enel Green Power North America's plants have a capacity to generate 800 MW of power through wind hydropower biomass and geothermal energy. Its wind farms use Vestas and GE Energy turbines; its largest project the Smoky Hills Wind Farm in Kansas has 155 wind turbines that alone generate 250 MW of power (enough to power 85000 homes for a year). Enel North America's only biomass plant is located in Quebec where it offsets 1 million tons of carbon dioxide by burning wood waste each year.

ENERGEN CORP.

NYS: EGN

605 Richard Arrington Jr. Boulevard North
Birmingham, AL 35203-2707
Phone: 205 326-2700
Fax: –
Web: www.energen.com

CEO: James T. McManus
CFO: Charles W. (Chuck) Porter
HR: William (Bill) Bibb
FYE: December 31
Type: Public

Energen develops acquires explores for and produces oil natural gas and natural gas liquids across the continental US. The oil and gas exploration and production company operates principally through Energen Resources Corporation which in 2014 had proved reserves of 372.7 million barrels of oil equivalent mainly located in the Permian Basin (West Texas) and the San Juan Basin (New Mexico and Colorado). Oil accounted for 49% of the company's proved reserves; natural gas 31%; and natural gas liquids 20%. In 2014 Energen exited the gas utility business selling Alabama Gas Corporation (Alagasco) to the Laclede Group for $1.6 billion.

	Annual Growth	12/11	12/12	12/13	12/14	12/15
Sales ($ mil.)	(12.3%)	1,483.5	1,617.2	1,738.7	1,679.2	878.6
Net income ($ mil.)	–	259.6	253.6	204.6	568.0	(945.7)
Market value ($ mil.)	(4.8%)	3,937.2	3,550.6	5,571.1	5,020.7	3,227.7
Employees	(25.7%)	1,540	1,575	1,434	550	470

ENERGY & EXPLORATION PARTNERS INC.

Two City Place Ste. 1700 100 Throckmorton
Fort Worth TX 76102
Phone: 817-789-6712
Fax: 510-995-9092
Web: www.singulex.com

CEO: Hunt Pettit
CFO: Brian C Nelson
HR: –
FYE: December 31
Type: Private

After exploring for energy Energy & Exploration Partners Inc. (ENEXP) might need a little R&R. The independent exploration and production company formed in July 2012 to begin buying rights to three different oil and natural gas plays across the US. ENEXP has almost 45000 net acres in three areas: the Eagle Ford Shale and Woodbine Sandstone formations in East Texas; the Wolfcamp play in the Permian Basin in West Texas; and the Niobrara Shale in the Denver-Julesburg Basin in Colorado and Wyoming. The company has not yet commenced operations but it did file a $275 million initial public offering in September 2012.

ENERGY ALLOYS L.L.C.

350 Glenborough Ste. 300
Houston TX 77067
Phone: 832-601-5800
Fax: 832-601-5801
Web: www.ealloys.com

CEO: Dave Warren
CFO: Paul F Patek
HR: –
FYE: December 31
Type: Private

A fistful of steel is just another day on the job at Energy Alloys. The company provides oilfield metals and equipment to global oil and gas manufacturers and service companies. Energy Alloys stocks oilfield-specific inventories of carbon alloy stainless steel and nickel bars as well as tubes and engineered steel products. It also offers made-to-order machining capability for finished and semi-finished components and expert materials consulting when clients need help selecting materials material grades or sizes. The company has international sourcing expertise and is a global supplier.

ENERGY AND POWER SOLUTIONS INC.

150 Paularino Ave. Ste. A120
Costa Mesa CA 92626
Phone: 714-586-8002
Fax: 714-957-1093
Web: www.epsway.com

CEO: Jay B Zoellner
CFO: –
HR: –
FYE: December 31
Type: Private

Think your plant isn't as energy efficient as it could be? Energy and Power Solutions (EPS) would like to help. The start up company which promises up to a 25% energy savings using its methods makes most of its money building on-site clean energy power plants. It also sells electrical and thermal power and operates power plants on behalf of its customers. But EPS touts its xChange Point energy monitoring software as the growth engine of the future. The software tracks energy use at the device plant and enterprise level in real time; EPS analysts use the data to recommend energy saving changes. The company which filed to go public in 2010 has four customers using its products at more than 60 locations.

ENERGY BRANDS INC.

17-20 Whitestone Expwy.
Whitestone NY 11357-3000
Phone: 718-746-0087
Fax: 718-747-1748
Web: www.energybrands.com

CEO: J Darius Bikoff
CFO: Michael Venuti
HR: –
FYE: December 31
Type: Subsidiary

What's in the water? Energy Brands has an answer. The company produces bottled water (under the glaceau label) and the #1 enhanced bottled water in the US vitaminwater a beverage fortified with such nutrients as folic acid magnesium vitamin B-12 and zinc. Energy Brands also makes the #1 premium bottled water in the US smartwater a no-calorie vapor-distilled electrolyte-enriched water. Other offerings include vitaminenergy a nutrient-enhanced energy drink and fruitwater a flavored version of smartwater sweetened with fructose. The company's lineup is sold worldwide to retailers or to distributors wholesalers and bottling partners. Energy Brands is a subsidiary of beverage behemoth Coca-Cola.

ENERGY CONVERSION DEVICES INC. NASDAQ: ENER

2956 Waterview Dr.
Rochester Hills MI 48309
Phone: 248-293-0440
Fax: 248-844-1214
Web: www.energyconversiondevices.com

CEO: Julian Hawkins
CFO: William C Andrews
HR: –
FYE: June 30
Type: Public

Energy Conversion Devices (ECD) gets a charge out of its technology. ECD makes storage products that generate and store power or store information electronically. Subsidiary United Solar Ovonic which accounts for more than 90% of sales makes flexible solar panels mainly for roofs but also for telecom lighting and other uses. The Ovonic Materials Division produces materials for use in NiMH and other batteries. ECD's largest customers are Enel Green Power EDF En Developpement Solardis-Soprasolar and Centrosolar AG. Around 85% of sales come from outside the US; customers in France Italy Germany and Spain account for more than two-thirds of sales. In 2012 ECD filed for Chapter 11 bankruptcy.

ENERGY FOCUS INC NAS: EFOI

32000 Aurora Road, Suite B
Solon, OH 44139
Phone: 440 715-1300
Fax: –
Web: www.energyfocusinc.com

CEO: James Tu
CFO: Marcia J Miller
HR: –
FYE: December 31
Type: Public

The Illuminator may be coming to a theater near you but it isn't a movie— its what Energy Focus does. The company makes products such as energy-efficient fiber-optic light-emitting diode ceramic metal halide and high-intensity discharge lighting systems. Serving the commercial/industrial and pool lighting markets Energy Focus' systems illuminate cinemas shopping malls parking garages performing arts centers restaurants pools/spas and homes. Its lighting products include acrylic accent fixtures downlight fixtures spotlights and display-case lighting. The company's Stones River Companies (SRC) unit concentrates on turnkey lighting projects and solar retrofit jobs.

	Annual Growth	12/10	12/11	12/12	12/13	12/14
Sales ($ mil.)	(4.7%)	35.1	25.8	29.8	21.5	29.0
Net income ($ mil.)	–	(8.5)	(6.1)	(5.7)	(2.4)	(5.8)
Market value ($ mil.)	50.8%	9.0	1.9	1.5	4.4	46.5
Employees	3.2%	68	67	71	59	77

ENERGY FUTURE HOLDINGS CORP NYS: TXU 19

1601 Bryan Street
Dallas, TX 75201-3411
Phone: 214 812-4600
Fax: –
Web: www.energyfutureholdings.com

CEO: John F. Young
CFO: Paul M. Keglevic
HR: Carrie Kirby
FYE: December 31
Type: Public

Energy Future Holdings has seen the future and it works — with electricity. It operates the largest nonregulated retail electric provider in Texas (TXU Energy) with more than 1.7 million customers and its Luminant unit has a generating capacity of more than 15400 MW from its interests in nuclear and fossil-fueled power plants in the state. Energy Future Holdings has regulated power transmission and distribution operations through 80%-owned Oncor Electric Delivery which operates the largest regulated distribution and transmission system in Texas providing power to more than 3.2 million electric delivery points over 119000 miles of transmission and distribution lines. The company filed for bankruptcy in 2014.

	Annual Growth	12/10	12/11	12/12	12/13	12/14
Sales ($ mil.)	(7.7%)	8,235.0	7,040.0	5,636.0	5,899.0	5,978.0
Net income ($ mil.)	–	(2,812.0)	(1,913.0)	(3,360.0)	(2,218.0)	(6,406.0)
Market value ($ mil.)	–	–	–	–	–	–
Employees	(0.8%)	9,200	9,300	9,100	9,000	8,920

ENERGY RECOVERY INC   NMS: ERII

1717 Doolittle Drive
San Leandro, CA 94577
Phone: 510 483-7370
Fax: –

CEO: Thomas S. Rooney
CFO: Chris M. Gannon
HR: Andrew (Andy) Stroud
FYE: December 31
Type: Public

Desalination makes seawater potable; Energy Recovery (ERI) makes desalination practical. The company designs develops and manufactures energy recovery devices used in sea water reverse osmosis (SWRO) desalination plants. The SWRO process is energy intensive using high pressure to drive salt water through membranes to produce fresh water. The company's main product the PX Pressure Exchanger helps recapture and recycle up to 98% of the energy available in the high-pressure reject stream a by-product of the SWRO process. The PX can reduce the energy consumption of a desalination plant by up to 60% compared with a plant lacking an energy recovery device. Subsidiary Pump Engineering also makes high pressure pumps.

	Annual Growth	12/10	12/11	12/12	12/13	12/14
Sales ($ mil.)	(9.7%)	45.9	28.0	42.6	43.0	30.4
Net income ($ mil.)	–	(3.6)	(26.4)	(8.3)	(3.1)	(18.7)
Market value ($ mil.)	9.5%	190.0	134.0	176.5	288.2	273.6
Employees	(1.0%)	129	96	116	112	124

ENERGY SERVICES OF AMERICA CORP.   NBB: ESOA

75 West 3rd Ave.
Huntington, WV 25701
Phone: 304 522-3868
Fax: –
Web: www.energyservicesofamerica.com

CEO: Douglas V Reynolds
CFO: Charles P Crimmel
HR: –
FYE: September 30
Type: Public

When energy companies don't want to get their hands dirty they can call on Energy Services of America (ESA). The service company provides installation repair and maintenance work primarily for natural gas and electricity providers. It also installs water and sewer lines for government agencies. ESA operates mostly in the Mid Atlantic region; its customers include Spectra Energy Hitachi Columbia Gas Transmission Toyota MarkWest Energy and American Electric Power. Typically the pipes steel plates wire and fittings used by the company are supplied by their customer keeping costs low. The company operates through subsidiaries ST Pipeline and C.J. Hughes Construction which it purchased in 2008.

	Annual Growth	09/11	09/12	09/13	09/14	09/15
Sales ($ mil.)	(5.0%)	143.4	157.7	108.8	93.3	116.8
Net income ($ mil.)	–	(5.3)	(48.5)	3.6	3.3	1.8
Market value ($ mil.)	(12.5%)	29.2	15.7	15.7	17.7	17.1
Employees	(5.6%)	771	601	610	584	612

ENERGY TRANSFER EQUITY L P   NYS: ETE

3738 Oak Lawn Avenue
Dallas, TX 75219
Phone: 214 981-0700
Fax: –
Web: www.energytransfer.com

CEO: –
CFO: Thomas E. (Tom) Long
HR: Robert (Bob) Kerrigan
FYE: December 31
Type: Public

Energy Transfer Equity transfers natural gas and other energy resources through its massive pipelines running across the country. The company acts as the general partner of Energy Transfer Partners and Regency Energy Partners. Through these operations and through Sunoco and Southern Union the company owns natural gas pipelines all over the country and a crude oil pipeline with the capacity of around 12800 miles. All in all Energy Transfer Equity's family of companies owns more than 71000 miles of natural gas natural gas liquids refined products and crude pipelines. In 2015 Energy Transfer Equity agreed to buy Tulsa-based Williams Companies in a $37.7 billion merger deal.

	Annual Growth	12/10	12/11	12/12	12/13	12/14
Sales ($ mil.)	70.4%	6,598.1	8,240.7	16,964.0	48,335.0	55,691.0
Net income ($ mil.)	34.6%	192.8	309.8	304.0	196.0	633.0
Market value ($ mil.)	10.1%	42,219.6	43,851.3	49,146.3	88,329.4	62,005.6
Employees	45.1%	6,229	2,477	14,433	13,573	27,605

ENERGYUNITED ELECTRIC MEMBERSHIP CORPORATION

567 MOCKSVILLE HWY
STATESVILLE, NC 286258269
Phone: 704-873-5241
Fax: –
Web: www.energyunited.com

CEO: –
CFO: –
HR: Eric McIntire
FYE: December 31
Type: Private

Electrical energy and propane energy come together under the auspices of EnergyUnited Electric Membership. One of North Carolina's largest power utilities EnergyUnited distributes electricity to more than 120000 residential and business customers in 19 counties. The member-owned not-for-profit cooperative also provides propane to 23000 customers in 74 counties in North and South Carolina and it also offers home security bill management and facility monitoring services. The third largest supplier of residential electricity in the state its service territory includes three of the largest cities in North Carolina - Charlotte Greensboro and Winston-Salem.

	Annual Growth	12/10	12/11	12/12	12/13	12/14
Sales ($ mil.)	8.4%	–	215.5	245.5	258.3	274.8
Net income ($ mil.)	(15.9%)	–	–	13.6	7.3	9.6
Market value ($ mil.)	–	–	–	–	–	–
Employees	–	–	–	–	–	175

ENERJEX RESOURCES INC   ASE: ENRJ

4040 Broadway, Suite 508
San Antonio, TX 78209
Phone: 210 451-5545
Fax: –
Web: www.enerjex.com

CEO: Robert G Watson Jr
CFO: Douglas M Wright
HR: –
FYE: December 31
Type: Public

When other oil companies have given up EnerJex Resources steps in and injects some capital. The oil and gas exploration and production company works primarily in Eastern Kansas buying producing properties that it feels are undervalued or that were abandoned by other oil companies when oil prices were below $10 a barrel. The company which has proved reserves of 1.2 million barrels of oil equivalent holds full or partial interest in half a dozen oil gas and oil and gas projects across Kansas. It uses enhanced drilling techniques to recover additional oil and gas from already explored fields.

	Annual Growth	12/10	12/11	12/12	12/13	12/14
Sales ($ mil.)	48.6%	2.9	6.3	8.5	10.9	14.3
Net income ($ mil.)	–	(0.9)	(2.0)	0.7	1.3	4.6
Market value ($ mil.)	–	–	–	–	–	146.7
Employees	12.7%	18	15	20	35	29

ENERLABS INC   NBB: ENLB

800 Northeast 63rd Street
Oklahoma City, OK 73105
Phone: 405 879-1752
Fax: 405 879-0175
Web: www.energasresources.com

CEO: –
CFO: –
HR: –
FYE: January 31
Type: Public

Turning subterranean natural gas into a useful energy is the goal of exploration and development independent Energas Resources. Operating through its A.T. Gas Gathering Systems and TGC subsidiaries the company is primarily focused on exploring and producing in the Arkoma Basin in Oklahoma and the Powder River Basin in Wyoming. Energas Resources has proved reserves of 22143 barrels of oil and 1.9 billion cu. ft. of natural gas. In 2007 the company sold most of its assets in the shallow Devonian Shale natural gas strata in the Appalachian Basin of Kentucky. President George Shaw owns about 24% of the company.

	Annual Growth	01/08	01/09	01/10	01/14	01/15
Sales ($ mil.)	(23.2%)	0.4	0.3	0.2	0.1	0.1
Net income ($ mil.)	–	(1.5)	(2.5)	(1.9)	(0.2)	(0.2)
Market value ($ mil.)	15.5%	0.4	0.6	0.4	6.8	1.1
Employees	(10.6%)	5	4	4	–	–

ENERNOC INC
NMS: ENOC

One Marina Park Drive, Suite 400
Boston, MA 02210
Phone: 617 224-9900
Fax: –
Web: www.enernoc.com

CEO: Timothy G. (Tim) Healy
CFO: Neil Moses
HR: Holly Lynch
FYE: December 31
Type: Public

EnerNOC knocks on the door of large energy customers and kindly asks them to dim the lights. Not literally of course but the company has added its technology to utility companies' traditional demand response model. Rather than manually calling up their largest end users EnerNOC's Network Operations Center (NOC) through its DemandSMART program remotely monitors their customers' energy assets and has the capability to adjust their electrical use. It caters to commercial industrial and technological educational and other institutional organizations as well as electric power grid operators and utilities. EnerNOC has operations around the world.

	Annual Growth	12/10	12/11	12/12	12/13	12/14
Sales ($ mil.)	13.9%	280.2	286.6	278.0	383.5	471.9
Net income ($ mil.)	6.0%	9.6	(13.4)	(22.3)	22.1	12.1
Market value ($ mil.)	(10.3%)	713.3	324.3	350.5	513.4	460.9
Employees	23.5%	484	599	685	716	1,125

ENERSYS
NYS: ENS

2366 Bernville Road
Reading, PA 19605
Phone: 610 208-1991
Fax: –
Web: www.enersys.com

CEO: John D. Craig
CFO: Michael J. Schmidtlein
HR: –
FYE: March 31
Type: Public

EnerSys' batteries are there when industrial-strength power is needed. The company makes stationary industrial batteries that provide uninterruptible power and backup power for electronic systems and motive power batteries for big equipment such as forklifts. Other products include battery chargers and accessories and batteries used for industrial and military applications. The battery manufacturer sells directly and through distributors to more than 10000 customers in more than 100 countries. It serves distributors warehouse operators retailers airports and mine operators as well as customers in the telecom electric utilities emergency lighting security systems and space satellites markets.

	Annual Growth	03/11	03/12	03/13	03/14	03/15
Sales ($ mil.)	6.3%	1,964.5	2,283.4	2,277.6	2,474.4	2,505.5
Net income ($ mil.)	12.4%	113.4	144.0	166.5	150.3	181.2
Market value ($ mil.)	12.8%	1,751.7	1,527.0	2,008.6	3,053.5	2,831.0
Employees	3.1%	8,400	9,200	9,000	9,500	9,500

ENERVEST LTD.

1001 Fannin St. Ste. 800
Houston TX 77002-6707
Phone: 713-659-3500
Fax: +974-4429-3750
Web: www.industriesqatar.com.qa

CEO: John B Walker
CFO: Micheal Mercer
HR: –
FYE: December 31
Type: Private

Want to invest in energy? Call up EnerVest. The investment group manages oil and gas properties on behalf of institutional investors such as pension plans university endowments and family foundations. Investors pool their money into a fund for EnerVest to buy and operate oil and gas wells; the company acts as a general partner and distributes dividends from the proceeds. Its 12th fund closed in December 2010 raising $1.5 billion from about 115 investors. EnerVest owns 19000 onshore wells spanning 4 million acres in a dozen states. It also owns 71% of EV Energy Partners a publicly traded master limited partnership through general partner is EV Energy GP.

ENESCO LLC

225 Windsor Dr.
Itasca IL 60143
Phone: 630-875-5300
Fax: 630-875-5350
Web: www.enesco.com

CEO: Todd Mavis
CFO: Theodore Eischeid
HR: –
FYE: December 31
Type: Private

Enesco collects cash from collectibles. The company founded in 1958 is a global marketer of porcelain and cold-cast collectibles (such as figurines and cottages) giftware (including ornaments music boxes and plush animals) garden accessories and home decor (tableware and sculpture). Enesco's 25000-item products portfolio includes the Cherished Teddies line of figurines and Gregg Gift faith-based items as well as licensed brands such as Boyds Bears Disney Gund and Pooh & Friends. It sells products through some 44000 card and gift retailers home decor chains mass merchants and catalogs in the US Canada Europe Australia and Asia. The company is owned by Tinicum Capital Partners.

ENFORA INC.

251 Renner Pkwy.
Richardson TX 75080
Phone: 972-633-4400
Fax: 972-633-4444
Web: www.enfora.com

CEO: –
CFO: –
HR: –
FYE: December 31
Type: Subsidiary

Enfora's customers are in for a wireless treat. The company makes integrated and modular electronics platforms sold under the N4 brand that are used to power wireless communications devices. For the asset management market it offers gateway software such as its Enabler product that enables clients to access monitor and control a wide range of connected devices. Enfora also develops wireless applications used by telecommunications service providers for deploying and managing wireless networks. Its services include consulting integration implementation and support. The company has international sales offices in Hong Kong Bogota and the UK. Enfora is a subsidiary of Novatel Wireless

ENGILITY HOLDINGS INC (NEW)
NYS: EGL

3750 Centerview Drive
Chantilly, VA 20151
Phone: 703 708-1400
Fax: –
Web: www.engilitycorp.com

CEO: Anthony Smeraglinolo
CFO: Michael J. Alber
HR: –
FYE: December 31
Type: Public

When Uncle Sam says "I want you for the US Army" Engility Holdings strives to answer the call and then some. A government services provider Engility offers government agencies a myriad of support services including systems engineering and software development program management defense-related education training and staffing field management and logistics and language translation services. Its customers have included the US Department of Defense and foreign governments as well as US civilian agencies and commercial entities. Engility was formed in 2012 when L-3 Communications spun off five of its government services businesses which were in turn organized under the Engility Holdings banner.

	Annual Growth	12/10	12/11	12/12	12/13	12/14
Sales ($ mil.)	(14.2%)	2,521.0	2,180.0	1,655.3	1,407.4	1,367.1
Net income ($ mil.)	–	(9.0)	26.0	(350.4)	49.5	35.4
Market value ($ mil.)	49.1%	–	–	338.8	587.6	752.9
Employees	(10.5%)	–	9,200	7,800	6,600	6,600

ENGINEERED MATERIALS SOLUTIONS INC.

39 Perry Ave.
Attleboro MA 02703
Phone: 508-342-2100
Fax: 508-342-2538
Web: www.emsclad.com

CEO: –
CFO: Kevin Folan
HR: Kayla Goff
FYE: December 31
Type: Private

Engineered Materials Solutions (EMS) is so very glad to bring you clad metals and electrical contacts (in button inlay toplay rivet forms). With clad metals EMS bonds two or more alloys (such as aluminum and steel) using a high pressure process to roll a layered metal composite. Offering a cost-effective alternative to a traditional single metal the company manufactures pieces for appliance automotive electrical HVAC and telecommunications markets. The US Mint has used its cladding for coinage. Wickeder Westfalenstahl a Germany-based metal fabrication company owns EMS which traces its roots back to 1916.

ENHERENT CORP.

101 Eisenhower Pkwy. Ste. 300
Roseland NJ 07068
Phone: 973-795-1290
Fax: 973-795-1311
Web: www.enherent.com

OTC: ENHT
CEO: Pamela A Fredette
CFO: Karl Brenza
HR: –
FYE: December 31
Type: Public

Little "e" big on "IT." Information technology (IT) consultancy enherent provides software development and technical staffing. Its software integrates Web-enabled communication and transaction applications with legacy systems as well as other enterprise information systems. Through its staffing business enherent provides technical personnel and project management services. Targeting "FORTUNE" 1000 companies enherent's customers come from industries such as financial services health care and manufacturing and include AIG Bank of America New England Motor Freight GlaxoSmithKline and Wachovia Securities.

ENGLEFIELD OIL COMPANY

447 James Pkwy.
Heath OH 43056
Phone: 740-928-8215
Fax: 740-928-1531
Web: www.englefieldoil.com

CEO: –
CFO: –
HR: –
FYE: June 30
Type: Private

Englefield Oil Company supplies fuel and lubricants and operates about 100 convenience stores under the Duke and Duchess Shoppe banner in Ohio and West Virginia. Many of the company's convenience stores sell BP brand gasoline. In addition Englefield Oil operates several truck stops a pair of Super 8 motels several Taco Bell Express restaurants and other various businesses in Ohio and West Virginia. Englefield also operates more than a dozen Pacific Pride automated commercial fueling sites. Chairman F. W. "Bill" Englefield III founded the company in 1961 with three service stations and an office operating out of his basement.

ENIGMA INC.

200 Wheeler Rd.
Burlington MA 01803
Phone: 781-273-3600
Fax: 781-273-4400
Web: www.enigma.com/

CEO: Jonathon Yaron
CFO: –
HR: –
FYE: December 31
Type: Private

The sum of all parts is no mystery for Enigma. This company makes software that aggregates and updates information from parts catalogs manuals and service bulletins creating a product encyclopedia that improves the processes of installing operating and maintaining complex equipment. Maintenance technicians use Enigma's software to search databases by brand part number or keyword and the software allows clients to establish passwords for various levels of security clearance. The company sells to companies in the aerospace and defense automotive maintenance repair and semiconductor sectors; clients have included Ford Motor Company and Rolls-Royce.

ENGLOBAL CORP.

654 N. Sam Houston Parkway E., Suite 400
Houston, TX 77060-5914
Phone: 281 878-1000
Fax: –
Web: www.englobal.com

NAS: ENG
CEO: William Coskey
CFO: Mark A Hess
HR: –
FYE: December 27
Type: Public

ENGlobal is engineering its way into the hearts of energy companies. A leading provider of engineering and automation services the company provides engineering and systems services procurement construction management inspection and control system automation design fabrication and implementation to the pipeline and process divisions of major oil and gas companies primarily in the US. Following a downturn in its business and heavy losses ENGlobal has repositioned itself as a leaner operation by selling or discontinuing certain lines of business including its Field Solutions and Electrical Services divisions closing offices and shedding about 75% of its workforce. ENGlobal was founded in 1994.

	Annual Growth	12/10	12/11	12/12	12/13	12/14
Sales ($ mil.)	(23.8%)	320.6	312.7	227.9	169.0	107.9
Net income ($ mil.)	–	(11.8)	(7.1)	(33.6)	(3.0)	6.0
Market value ($ mil.)	(16.0%)	103.2	58.5	16.4	40.2	51.3
Employees	(31.0%)	2,030	1,943	1,700	430	459

ENNIS INC

2441 Presidential Pkwy.
Midlothian, TX 76065
Phone: 972 775-9801
Fax: 972 775-9820
Web: www.ennis.com

NYS: EBF
CEO: Keith S. Walters
CFO: Richard L. Travis
HR: –
FYE: February 28
Type: Public

Ennis is in the forms and fashion business. Through its print division the company makes a variety of custom business forms financial and security documents envelopes tags labels and promotional products. Its print units include Northstar Computer Forms Skyline Business Forms and Adams McClure. The company's Alstyle Apparel subsidiary markets activewear basics (such as T-shirts tank tops and fleece) primarily under the AAA and Murina brands among others. About 98% of Alstyle's revenue is from T-shirt sales. Customers include forms distributors printers ad agencies retailers and mass marketers. Founded in 1909 the company operates 55-plus manufacturing plants in the US Mexico and Canada.

	Annual Growth	02/11	02/12	02/13	02/14	02/15
Sales ($ mil.)	1.3%	550.0	517.0	533.5	542.4	580.2
Net income ($ mil.)	–	44.6	31.4	24.7	13.2	(44.5)
Market value ($ mil.)	(3.7%)	415.0	428.0	399.9	403.5	356.3
Employees	0.8%	5,812	5,816	5,818	6,278	6,009

ENOVA SYSTEMS INC
NBB: ENVS

2945 Columbia Street
Torrance, CA 90503
Phone: 650 346-4770
Fax: –
Web: www.enovasystems.com

CEO: –
CFO: John J Micek
HR: –
FYE: December 31
Type: Public

Enova Systems makes commercial digital power management systems for controlling and monitoring electric power in automobiles and stationary power generators. Products include hybrid-electric drive systems electric drive motors electric motor controllers hybrid drive systems battery care units safety disconnect units generator units fuel cell management units and fuel cell power conditioning units. The company counts EDO First Auto Works of China Ford Motor Hyundai Motor Navistar International and Volvo/Mack among its customers. Enova gets more than half of its sales outside the US primarily in China.

	Annual Growth	12/09	12/10	12/11	12/12	12/13
Sales ($ mil.)	(47.5%)	5.6	8.6	6.6	1.1	0.4
Net income ($ mil.)	–	(7.0)	(7.4)	(7.0)	(8.2)	(2.9)
Market value ($ mil.)	(73.6%)	82.4	57.1	7.4	0.7	0.4
Employees	(51.5%)	36	59	30	3	2

ENPHASE ENERGY INC.
NMS: ENPH

1420 N. McDowell Blvd.
Petaluma, CA 94954
Phone: 707 774-7000
Fax: –
Web: www.enphase.com

CEO: Paul B. Nahi
CFO: Kris Sennesael
HR: Steve Lapointe
FYE: December 31
Type: Public

Enphase Energy is ready to usher in a new phase of solar power. The company makes all-in-one solar panel systems for residential and commercial use in the US and Canada. Unlike typical small-scale photovoltaic systems Enphase's solar modules are connected on a microinverter system where each panel has its own inverter that converts the sun's rays into electricity. The company claims its microinverter technology is more energy efficient than having all the panels hooked up to one big inverter. Enphase Energy sells its solar power systems to a network of 2200 distributors including AEE Solar and Conergy. The company went public in 2012 with an offering valued at nearly $54 million.

	Annual Growth	12/10	12/11	12/12	12/13	12/14
Sales ($ mil.)	53.7%	61.7	149.5	216.7	232.8	343.9
Net income ($ mil.)	–	(21.8)	(32.3)	(38.2)	(25.9)	(8.1)
Market value ($ mil.)	97.9%	–	–	159.7	277.4	625.3
Employees	19.9%	–	313	384	398	539

ENPRO INDUSTRIES INC
NYS: NPO

5605 Carnegie Boulevard, Suite 500
Charlotte, NC 28209
Phone: 704 731-1500
Fax: –
Web: www.enproindustries.com

CEO: Stephen E. (Steve) Macadam
CFO: J. Milton Childress
HR: –
FYE: December 31
Type: Public

EnPro is a real professional when it comes to sealing systems engineered products and heavy-duty engines. The company operates from three segments: Sealing Products (comprising product lines including GST Stemco and Plastomer Technologies); Engineered Products (GGB Compressor Products International) and Engine Products & Services (Fairbanks Morse Engine). Products include gaskets hydraulic components self-lubricating bearings air compressors vacuum pumps and heavy/medium-duty diesel and natural gas engines. These serve the automotive aerospace chemical and petrochemical and food processing power generation and semiconductor industries. More than 50% of sales are generated by the US.

	Annual Growth	12/10	12/11	12/12	12/13	12/14
Sales ($ mil.)	9.0%	865.0	1,105.5	1,184.2	1,144.2	1,219.3
Net income ($ mil.)	(38.7%)	155.4	44.2	41.0	27.4	22.0
Market value ($ mil.)	10.9%	996.3	790.6	980.5	1,382.0	1,504.5
Employees	8.0%	3,600	4,500	4,500	4,600	4,900

ENSERVCO CORP
ASE: ENSV

501 South Cherry St., Ste. 320
Denver, CO 80246
Phone: 303 333-3678
Fax: 702 974-3417
Web: www.enservco.com

CEO: Rick Kasch
CFO: Robert J Devers
HR: Kimberly Lona
FYE: December 31
Type: Public

Aspen Exploration (which does business as ENSERVCO) is a leading provider of fluid-related services to the oil and gas production industry in the US. In 2008 Aspen Exploration announced that because of high expenses and rising debt it was pursuing strategic alternatives and subsequently sold its exploration and production oil and gas assets. In 2010 the shell company merged with oilfield services provider Dillco Fluid Service and reorganized under the ENSERVCO brand name. Its two operating subsidiaries (Dillco Fluid Services and Heat Wave Hot Oil) operate a fleet of 200 vehicles. Services include acidizing water hauling and disposal and well-site construction.

	Annual Growth	12/10	12/11	12/12	12/13	12/14
Sales ($ mil.)	32.0%	18.6	24.7	31.5	46.5	56.6
Net income ($ mil.)	–	(1.8)	(2.0)	(0.1)	4.3	4.0
Market value ($ mil.)	42.4%	14.5	37.8	27.4	67.1	59.7
Employees	18.4%	120	125	125	193	236

ENSIGN GROUP INC
NMS: ENSG

27101 Puerta Real, Suite 450
Mission Viejo, CA 92691
Phone: 949 487-9500
Fax: –
Web: www.ensigngroup.net

CEO: Christopher R. Christensen
CFO: Suzanne D. Snapper
HR: –
FYE: December 31
Type: Public

The Ensign Group hangs its insignia at more than 180 senior living facilities. Most of its facilities are skilled nursing homes but it also operates a number of assisted-living and independent-living facilities as well as combination nursing assisted and independent-living centers. Some locations also offer rehabilitation hospice and physical therapy services. Ensign's facilities are either owned by the company or operated under lease agreements. The health care provider operates some 120 long-term care centers with a capacity of some 13200 beds in about a dozen states in the southwestern and western US. Ensign also operates home health and hospice agencies.

	Annual Growth	12/11	12/12	12/13	12/14	12/15
Sales ($ mil.)	15.3%	758.3	824.7	904.6	1,027.4	1,341.8
Net income ($ mil.)	3.8%	47.7	40.6	24.0	36.0	55.4
Market value ($ mil.)	(2.0%)	1,258.6	1,394.7	2,274.1	2,280.3	1,162.5
Employees	15.0%	9,433	10,371	11,372	13,229	16,494

ENSIGN-BICKFORD INDUSTRIES INC.

125 Powder Forest Dr. 3rd fl.
Simsbury CT 06070-0007
Phone: 860-843-2000
Fax: 860-843-2600
Web: www.e-bind.com

CEO: Caleb E White
CFO: Scott Deakin
HR: Michael J Butler
FYE: December 31
Type: Private

Finicky dog? Short fuse? Ensign-Bickford Industries' (EBI) has a solution. Through its subsidiaries — Aerospace & Defense (EBA&D) AFB International EnviroLogix DanChem and Renewable Energies — the company manufactures one-shot systems for military demolition combat explosives and space (flight initiation and termination) applications as well as taste enhancers (Optimizor brand) for pet foods agricultural diagnostic test kits to detect markers for genetically modified organisms (GMO) specialty chemical products biomass wood pellets for energy and animal bedding and real estate services. EBI was incorporated in 1971 but dates back to William Bickford the inventor of the safety fuse in the 1830s.

ENSYNC INC
ASE: ESNC

N93 W14475 Whittaker Way
Menomonee Falls, WI 53051
Phone: 262 253-9800
Fax: –
Web: www.zbbenergy.com

CEO: Bradley L Hansen
CFO: Jim Schott
HR: –
FYE: June 30
Type: Public

ZBB Energy makes and sells energy storage systems designed to store surplus energy for use at times when energy demand is higher than the utility company (or other generator) can provide. Its products — based on the company's zinc-bromine battery technology — also provide a source of power protection from voltage current or frequency deviations that can cause brownouts or power outages. While ZBB Energy markets its products primarily to utility companies and renewable energy generators in Australia China Europe and North America it has had only one customer to date the California Energy Commission. ZBB Energy operates one manufacturing facility in Menomonee Falls Wisconsin.

	Annual Growth	06/11	06/12	06/13	06/14	06/15
Sales ($ mil.)	(0.5%)	1.8	4.8	7.7	7.9	1.8
Net income ($ mil.)	–	(8.4)	(13.9)	(11.9)	(8.9)	(12.9)
Market value ($ mil.)	(1.1%)	36.0	15.7	10.3	63.4	34.4
Employees	2.2%	54	69	69	58	59

ENT FEDERAL CREDIT UNION

7250 Campus Dr.
Colorado Springs CO 80920
Phone: 719-574-1100
Fax: 719-388-0104
Web: www.entfederal.com

CEO: Charles F Emmer
CFO: Mj Coon
HR: –
FYE: December 31
Type: Private - Not-for-Pr

Ent Federal Credit Union (Ent FCU) is named for Uzal Girard Ent a WWII Air Force commander for which Ent Air Force Base in Colorado Springs is also named. Founded in 1957 the credit union provides personal business and corporate financial services including checking and savings accounts credit cards home mortgages business and personal loans and insurance as well as wealth management private banking and trust services. FCU serves more than 200000 members in the Front Range area of Colorado including Denver through about two dozen locations

ENTECH SALES AND SERVICE INC.

3404 GARDEN BROOK DR
DALLAS, TX 752342496
Phone: 972-241-8188
Fax: –
Web: www.entechsales.com

CEO: –
CFO: –
HR: –
FYE: December 31
Type: Private

Entech keeps Texans cool and safe. The company which was founded in 1981 has business units that provide air-conditioning heating and refrigeration equipment and services in about a half-dozen cities across the Lone Star State. Entech also offers integrated-system building automation that syncs HVAC controls access controls security closed-circuit television alarms and other automated systems. The company keeps its systems running by offering design installation maintenance and repair of HVAC and refrigeration. Other products and services include rebuilt cooling towers and HVAC and power equipment rentals.

	Annual Growth	12/03	12/04	12/05	12/06	12/07
Sales ($ mil.)	(79.4%)	–	–	1,342.6	52.4	56.8
Net income ($ mil.)	12787.3%	–	–	0.0	5.1	6.8
Market value ($ mil.)	–	–	–	–	–	–
Employees	–	–	–	–	–	290

ENTECH SOLAR INC.
OTC: ENSL

13301 Park Vista Blvd. Ste. 100
Fort Worth TX 76177
Phone: 817-224-3600
Fax: 817-224-3601
Web: www.entechsolar.com

CEO: David Gelbaum
CFO: Shelley Hollingsworth
HR: –
FYE: December 31
Type: Public

Entech Solar aims to shine brightly in the solar energy market. The company designs makes and markets solar energy systems that provide electricity and thermal energy for commercial industrial and utility applications. Its products include ThermoVolt System (a proprietary concentrating photovoltaic and thermal technology that produces both electricity and thermal energy) and Solar Volt System (which uses a concentrating photovoltaic technology that produces cost-competitive electricity). Entech Solar also makes energy-efficient skylights and provides engineering services. Venture capital firm Quercus Trust owns 54% of Entech Solar.

ENTEGRIS INC
NMS: ENTG

129 Concord Road
Billerica, MA 01821
Phone: 978 436-6500
Fax: 952 556-1880
Web: www.entegris.com

CEO: Bertrand Loy
CFO: Gregory B. (Greg) Graves
HR: John Murphy
FYE: December 31
Type: Public

Entegris makes products integral to the manufacture of semiconductors and computer disk drives. The company makes more than 17000 standard and custom products used to transport and protect semiconductor and disk drive materials during processing. Its semiconductor products include wafer carriers storage boxes and chip trays as well as chemical delivery products such as pipes fittings and valves. Its disk drive offerings include shippers stamper cases and transport trays. Top customers include Applied Materials ASML MEMC Siltronic Tokyo Electron and Taiwan Semiconductor Manufacturing. More than 70% of Entegris' sales come from customers located outside the US primarily in the Asia/Pacific region.

	Annual Growth	12/10	12/11	12/12	12/13	12/14
Sales ($ mil.)	8.7%	688.4	749.3	715.9	693.5	962.1
Net income ($ mil.)	(44.7%)	84.4	123.8	68.8	74.5	7.9
Market value ($ mil.)	15.3%	1,044.3	1,219.7	1,283.3	1,620.2	1,846.7
Employees	4.4%	2,975	2,765	3,050	3,200	3,528

ENTERCOM COMMUNICATIONS CORP
NYS: ETM

401 E. City Avenue, Suite 809
Bala Cynwyd, PA 19004
Phone: 610 660-5610
Fax: –

CEO: David J. Field
CFO: Stephen F. (Steve) Fisher
HR: John C (Jack) Donlevie
FYE: December 31
Type: Public

The signals from Entercom Communications come through loud and clear. The company is among the largest radio broadcasters in the US with about 125 stations clustered in more than 25 markets including Austin Boston Denver Kansas City New Orleans San Francisco and Seattle. Operating a number of stations in one market allows the company to combine such back office functions as finance and accounting as well as advertising sales and marketing. Its stations program a variety of formats including oldies country and adult contemporary as well as talk sports and news. The Field family including founder and chairman Joseph Field controls more than 65% of Entercom.

	Annual Growth	12/10	12/11	12/12	12/13	12/14
Sales ($ mil.)	(0.8%)	391.4	382.7	388.9	377.6	379.8
Net income ($ mil.)	(12.8%)	46.4	68.5	11.3	26.0	26.8
Market value ($ mil.)	1.2%	452.3	240.2	272.6	410.5	475.0
Employees	(0.6%)	2,372	2,008	2,191	2,252	2,315

ENTERGY ARKANSAS, INC.   NYS: EAE

425 West Capitol Avenue
Little Rock, AR 72201
Phone: 501 377-4000
Fax: –
Web: www.entergy.com

CEO: Hugh McDonald
CFO: Andrew S Marsh
HR: –
FYE: December 31
Type: Public

Entergy Arkansas is the largest power provider in the Natural State. The utility serves approximately 700000 residential commercial industrial and government customers in 63 eastern and central Arkansas counties. Residential customers account for about 84% of total clients. The Entergy subsidiary also has interests in fossil-fueled nuclear and hydroelectric power generation facilities with 4736 MW of capacity and it offers energy conservation and management programs. Entergy's utilities (including Entergy Arkansas) deliver power to 2.8 million utility customers in Arkansas Louisiana Mississippi and Texas.

	Annual Growth	12/10	12/11	12/12	12/13	12/14
Sales ($ mil.)	1.1%	2,082.4	2,084.3	2,127.0	2,190.2	2,172.4
Net income ($ mil.)	(8.4%)	172.6	164.9	152.4	161.9	121.4
Market value ($ mil.)	17.0%	–	–	–	897.3	1,049.5
Employees	(4.8%)	1,411	1,357	1,372	1,274	1,160

ENTERGY LOUISIANA LLC (NEW)   NYS: ELU

4809 Jefferson Highway
Jefferson, LA 70121
Phone: 504 576-4000
Fax: –

CEO: Phillip R May Jr
CFO: Leo Denault
HR: –
FYE: December 31
Type: Public

Entergy Louisiana energizes everything from fishing shacks and suburban enclaves to petroleum refineries and city infrastructure for the storm-weary citizens of the Bayou State. The utility serves electric customers in 58 parishes of northeast and south Louisiana. The company holds non-exclusive franchises to provide electric service in 116 incorporated Louisiana municipalities. It also supplies electric service in 45 Louisiana parishes in which it holds non-exclusive franchises. Of the Entergy subsidiary's almost 5670 MW of generating capacity about 4900 MW comes from gas- and oil-fired power plants and almost 1160 MW from nuclear power plants.

	Annual Growth	12/10	12/11	12/12	12/13	12/14
Sales ($ mil.)	2.7%	2,538.8	2,508.9	2,149.4	2,626.9	2,825.9
Net income ($ mil.)	5.2%	231.4	473.9	281.1	252.5	283.5
Market value ($ mil.)	–	–	–	0.0	0.0	0.0
Employees	(2.0%)	964	937	947	923	890

ENTERGY CORP.   NYS: ETR

639 Loyola Avenue
New Orleans, LA 70113
Phone: 504 576-4000
Fax: –
Web: www.entergy.com

CEO: Hugh McDonald
CFO: Andrew S. (Drew) Marsh
HR: Peter Proulx
FYE: December 31
Type: Public

Entergy is into energy. The integrated utility holding company's subsidiaries distribute electricity to 2.8 million customers in four southern states (Arkansas Louisiana Mississippi and Texas) and provide natural gas to 196000 customers in Louisiana. Entergy operates 15500 miles of high-voltage transmission lines and 1500 transmission substations. In addition the company has interests in regulated and nonregulated power plants in North America that have a combined generating capacity of about 30000 MW (including nearly 10000 MW of nuclear power). Entergy is one of the largest nuclear power generators in the US.

	Annual Growth	12/10	12/11	12/12	12/13	12/14
Sales ($ mil.)	2.1%	11,487.6	11,229.1	10,302.1	11,390.9	12,494.9
Net income ($ mil.)	(6.8%)	1,270.3	1,367.4	868.4	730.6	960.3
Market value ($ mil.)	5.4%	12,695.6	13,093.5	11,426.6	11,340.6	15,680.0
Employees	(2.8%)	15,000	14,682	14,625	13,808	13,393

ENTERGY MISSISSIPPI, INC   NYS: EMZ

308 East Pearl Street
Jackson, MS 39201
Phone: 601 368-5000
Fax: –
Web: www.entergy.com

CEO: Haley R Fisackerly
CFO: –
HR: –
FYE: December 31
Type: Public

Much like Old Man River that "just keeps rolling along" Entergy Mississippi keeps electricity flowing across the Magnolia state. With a physical presence in 45 of the state's 82 counties the utility provides electricity to about 440000 residential business and institutional customers (roughly 16% of electric customers in Mississippi) throughout the western half of its namesake state. Residential customers account for more than 90% of the company's client base. Entergy Mississippi is a subsidiary of the Louisiana-based utility holding company Entergy.

	Annual Growth	12/10	12/11	12/12	12/13	12/14
Sales ($ mil.)	5.5%	1,230.2	1,266.5	1,120.4	1,334.5	1,524.2
Net income ($ mil.)	(2.8%)	83.7	108.7	46.8	82.2	74.8
Market value ($ mil.)	(2.6%)	–	242.7	233.0	206.8	224.5
Employees	(3.4%)	773	736	749	724	673

ENTERGY GULF STATES LOUISIANA LLC   OTC: EYGF N

446 North Boulevard
Baton Rouge, LA 70802
Phone: 800 368-3749
Fax: –
Web: www.entergy.com

CEO: Phillip R May Jr
CFO: –
HR: –
FYE: December 31
Type: Public

Entergy Gulf States Louisiana keeps energy flowing in the Bayou State. The utility a subsidiary of Entergy and an affiliate of Entergy Louisiana provides electrical service to about 383900 customers in the state of Louisiana; its customer base is comprised of residential commercial industrial and governmental entities. The company owns or leases about 6660 MW of generating capacity including the River Bend Steam Electric Generation Station a Louisiana-based 978 MW nuclear facility. Together Entergy Louisiana and Entergy Gulf States Louisiana serve about 1 million electric customers in 58 parishes. Entergy Gulf States Louisiana also provides natural gas service to about 92000 customers in Baton Rouge.

	Annual Growth	12/09	12/10	12/11	12/12	12/13
Sales ($ mil.)	1.3%	1,844.4	2,097.0	2,134.4	1,654.9	1,941.1
Net income ($ mil.)	1.4%	153.0	190.7	203.0	159.0	161.7
Market value ($ mil.)	–	–	–	–	–	–
Employees	(2.4%)	840	816	805	798	763

ENTERGY NEW ORLEANS INC.   NYS: ENJ

1600 Perdido Street
New Orleans, LA 70112
Phone: 504 670-3700
Fax: –
Web: www.entergy.com

CEO: Charles L Rice Jr
CFO: Leo Denault
HR: –
FYE: December 31
Type: Public

Entergy New Orleans lights up the path for the unsteady libation-influenced patrons of Bourbon Street and others in the Crescent City. The regulated utility a subsidiary of Entergy distributes electricity to 161000 residential commercial and industrial customers and natural gas to more than 100000 customers in Orleans Parish Louisiana; it also owns two generating stations that give it more than 930 MW of generating capacity.

	Annual Growth	12/10	12/11	12/12	12/13	12/14
Sales ($ mil.)	1.1%	659.3	630.2	569.7	620.2	690.1
Net income ($ mil.)	(1.9%)	31.0	36.0	17.1	11.7	28.7
Market value ($ mil.)	(1.4%)	–	–	211.1	162.5	205.4
Employees	(3.6%)	345	342	341	318	298

ENTERGY NUCLEAR INC.

1340 Echelon Pkwy.
Jackson MS 39213
Phone: 504-576-4238
Fax: 520-434-3719
Web: www.davisfunds.com

CEO: John Herron
CFO: –
HR: –
FYE: December 31
Type: Subsidiary

Despite a difficult political and environmental market Entergy Nuclear has kept its faith in the realm of nuclear possibilities. The company owns and operates 12 nuclear reactors at 10 sites primarily in the northeastern and southern US with a combined maximum output of more than 10000 MW; the unit provides power to parent Entergy's utility and marketing subsidiaries. The unit also provides operations and maintenance services for other utilities' nuclear plants including plant decommissioning and license renewals. In 2007 the company acquired Palisades Nuclear Plant (near South Haven Michigan) from Consumers Energy for $380 million.

ENTEROMEDICS INC.

NASDAQ: ETRM

2800 Patton Rd.
St. Paul MN 55113
Phone: 651-634-3003
Fax: +60-3-9280-7229
Web: rhbbank.com.my

CEO: Mark B Knudson
CFO: Greg S Lea
HR: –
FYE: December 31
Type: Public

EnteroMedics is trying to quiet those grumbling hunger pangs. The development-stage medical device company uses neuroblocking technology called VBLOC therapy to combat obesity. Its initial product in development the Maestro System is a device laparoscopically implanted near the diaphragm that uses electrical impulses to limit the expansion of the stomach thereby producing a feeling of prolonged fullness. The Maestro System is in US and international clinical trials with FDA approval and commercial sales anticipated by 2010. EnteroMedics plans to build a direct sales force to market the product to bariatric surgeons and weight management specialists.

ENTERPRISE BANCORP, INC. (MA)

NMS: EBTC

222 Merrimack Street
Lowell, MA 01852
Phone: 978 459-9000
Fax: –

CEO: John P. (Jack) Clancy
CFO: James A. (Jim) Marcotte
HR: –
FYE: December 31
Type: Public

Enterprising entrepreneurs might consider seeking financial intervention from Enterprise Bancorp. The holding company owns Enterprise Bank and Trust which operates around 20 branches in northeastern Massachusetts and southern New Hampshire. The bank specializes in lending to businesses professionals high-net-worth individuals and not-for-profits. Business loans including commercial mortgage construction and working capital loans; revolving lines of credit; and equipment financing and asset-based lending products account for some 85% of the company's loan portfolio. The bank also offers deposit accounts consumer loans residential mortgages and investment management and trust services.

	Annual Growth	12/10	12/11	12/12	12/13	12/14
Assets ($ mil.)	9.7%	1,397.3	1,489.2	1,665.7	1,849.9	2,022.2
Net income ($ mil.)	8.3%	10.6	10.9	12.4	13.5	14.7
Market value ($ mil.)	16.7%	138.8	146.0	168.6	216.1	257.8
Employees	5.5%	333	347	372	398	412

ENTERPRISE ELECTRIC LLC

1300 FORT NEGLEY BLVD
NASHVILLE, TN 372034854
Phone: 615-350-7270
Fax: –
Web: www.enterprisellc.com

CEO: –
CFO: David Miller
HR: –
FYE: December 31
Type: Private

Enterprise Electric welcomes the power hungry. The full service electrical firms specializes in construction and design of electrical systems for institutional commercial industrial and services projects from planning through construction. The company completes projects large and small and has completed design and installation of wiring and electrical systems for health care correctional commercial and industrial clients. Services include temporary power installations voice data and fiber optic cabling systems emergency generator and substation installations maintenance services. Headquartered in Nashville Tennessee the company serves clients throughout the US.

	Annual Growth	12/09	12/10	12/11	12/12	12/13
Sales ($ mil.)	9.5%	–	69.4	86.6	59.1	91.2
Net income ($ mil.)	(41.0%)	–	–	6.2	(2.9)	2.2
Market value ($ mil.)	–	–	–	–	–	–
Employees	–	–	–	–	–	400

ENTERPRISE FINANCIAL SERVICES CORP

NMS: EFSC

150 North Meramec
Clayton, MO 63105
Phone: 314 725-5500
Fax: –
Web: www.enterprisebank.com

CEO: Peter F. Benoist
CFO: Keene S. Turner
HR: –
FYE: December 31
Type: Public

Enterprise Financial Services wants you to boldly bank where many have banked before. It's the holding company for Enterprise Bank & Trust which mostly targets closely-held businesses and their owners but also serves individuals in the St. Louis Kansas City and Phoenix metropolitan areas. Boasting $3.5 billion in assets and 15 branches Enterprise offers standard products such as checking savings and money market accounts and CDs. Commercial and industrial loans make up over half of the company's lending activities while real estate loans make up another 45%. The bank also writes consumer and residential mortgage loans. Bank subsidiary Enterprise Trust offers wealth management services.

	Annual Growth	12/10	12/11	12/12	12/13	12/14
Assets ($ mil.)	4.0%	2,805.8	3,377.8	3,325.8	3,170.2	3,277.0
Net income ($ mil.)	31.4%	9.1	25.4	28.3	33.1	27.2
Market value ($ mil.)	17.2%	207.5	293.6	259.3	405.1	391.4
Employees	8.1%	331	450	450	455	452

ENTERPRISE PRODUCTS PARTNERS L.P.

NYS: EPD

1100 Louisiana Street, 10th Floor
Houston, TX 77002
Phone: 713 381-6500
Fax: –
Web: www.enterpriseproducts.com

CEO: A. James (Jim) Teague
CFO: Bryan F. Bulawa
HR: –
FYE: December 31
Type: Public

Both enterprising and productive Enterprise Products Partners is a leading player in the North American natural gas natural gas liquids (NGL) and crude oil industries with a range of processing transportation and storage services. Operations include natural gas processing NGL fractionation petrochemical services and crude oil transportation including 51300 miles of pipelines 14 billion cu. ft. of natural gas storage and 225 million barrels of NGL refined products and crude oil storage capacity. It also has about 22 NGL fractionators and some 131 barges and 63 tow boats. The hub of Enterprise Products Partners' business is Houston's Mont Belvieu refinery complex.

	Annual Growth	12/10	12/11	12/12	12/13	12/14
Sales ($ mil.)	9.2%	33,739.3	44,313.0	42,583.1	47,727.0	47,951.2
Net income ($ mil.)	72.4%	320.8	2,088.3	2,428.0	2,607.1	2,833.5
Market value ($ mil.)	(3.5%)	80,612.1	89,853.1	97,021.2	128,444.6	69,976.2
Employees	–	–	–	–	–	–

ENTORIAN TECHNOLOGIES INC.   PINK SHEETS: ENTN

8900 Shoal Creek Blvd. Ste. 125
Austin TX 78757
Phone: 512-454-9531
Fax: 512-454-9409
Web: www.entorian.com

CEO: Stephan B Godevais
CFO: W Kirk Patterson
HR: –
FYE: December 31
Type: Public

Entorian Technologies knows all about the rugged side of computers. Through its Augmentix subsidiary the company re-engineers and ruggedizes Dell notebooks and servers. Its products are used in environments where computers and other electronics are subjected to heavy wear and tear including military applications field service and sales industrial manufacturing and for emergency responders. Entorian sells its ruggedized notebooks directly to Dell which in turn sells and markets them in North America and Europe. The company's ruggedized servers are sold directly to end users and channel partners.

ENTREPRENEUR MEDIA INC.

2445 McCabe Way Ste. 400
Irvine CA 92614
Phone: 949-261-2325
Fax: 949-261-0234
Web: www.entrepreneur.com

CEO: Ryan Shea
CFO: Joe Goodman
HR: –
FYE: December 31
Type: Private

Entrepreneur Media has some reading material for the self-employed. Targeting small-business owners and those thinking about taking the leap Entrepreneur Media publishes "Entrepreneur" magazine a monthly publication with a paid circulation of more than 600000. The company also operates the corresponding Web site Entrepreneur.com. In addition Entrepreneur Media publishes books (titles such as Start Your Own Business and Master of Success) through its Entrepreneur Press unit.

ENTRAVISION COMMUNICATIONS CORP.   NYS: EVC

2425 Olympic Boulevard, Suite 6000 West
Santa Monica, CA 90404
Phone: 310 447-3870
Fax: –

CEO: Walter F. Ulloa
CFO: Christopher T. Young
HR: –
FYE: December 31
Type: Public

This company wants to be the whole enchilada for advertisers trying to reach the US Hispanic market. Entravision Communications is the #2 Spanish-language media company in the country (behind Univision Communications) with about 55 television stations and 50 radio stations located mostly in the Southwest. It is the largest affiliate of Univision's two Spanish-language television networks Univision and TeleFutura; Entravision's TV portfolio also includes a small number of stations affiliated with The CW Network FOX and MyNetworkTV. On the radio the company offers a variety of programming formats including music news sports and talk radio.

	Annual Growth	12/10	12/11	12/12	12/13	12/14
Sales ($ mil.)	4.8%	200.5	194.4	223.3	223.9	242.0
Net income ($ mil.)	–	(18.1)	(8.2)	13.6	133.8	27.1
Market value ($ mil.)	26.0%	224.0	136.0	144.7	530.9	564.9
Employees	3.6%	876	925	957	962	1,010

ENTROPIC COMMUNICATIONS, INC.   NMS: ENTR

6250 Sequence Drive
San Diego, CA 92121
Phone: 858 768-3600
Fax: –
Web: www.entropic.com

CEO: Kishore Seendripu
CFO: –
HR: –
FYE: December 31
Type: Public

Entropic Communications is far from sluggish when it comes to broadband. The fabless semiconductor company designs specialized chipsets for video and broadband multimedia applications. Through the Multimedia over Coax Alliance (MoCA) networking standard Entropic is targeting digital home entertainment networks linked by coaxial cable connections a market being promoted by cable TV services providers and others. The company's c.LINK technology enables broadband networking between an access node and cable outlets. Leading customers include Actiontec Electronics Samsung Motorola Mobility (16% of sales) and Wistron NeWeb (18%). The Asia/Pacific region accounts for most sales.

	Annual Growth	12/09	12/10	12/11	12/12	12/13
Sales ($ mil.)	22.2%	116.3	210.2	240.6	321.7	259.4
Net income ($ mil.)	–	(13.2)	64.7	26.6	4.5	(66.2)
Market value ($ mil.)	11.2%	278.7	1,096.6	463.9	480.2	426.6
Employees	25.0%	262	300	344	693	639

ENTREMED, INC.   NAS: ENMD

9620 Medical Center Drive, Suite 300
Rockville, MD 20850
Phone: 240 864-2600
Fax: 240 864-2601
Web: www.entremed.com

CEO: Ken K Ren
CFO: –
HR: –
FYE: December 31
Type: Public

EntreMed wants to get in between cancer and the blood vessels that feed it. The biotech pharmaceutical company develops drugs that inhibit angiogenesis or the growth of new blood vessels. Its lead candidate ENMD-2076 inhibits aurora kinases which regulate cell division and are linked to several cancers. The company has several other product candidates in its pipeline. EntreMed receives royalties from sales of Thalomid a multiple myeloma therapy marketed by EntreMed's minority shareholder Celgene.

	Annual Growth	12/08	12/09	12/10	12/11	12/12
Sales ($ mil.)	(45.3%)	7.5	5.3	3.7	1.9	0.7
Net income ($ mil.)	–	(23.9)	(8.2)	(8.1)	(4.6)	(14.5)
Market value ($ mil.)	71.4%	3.6	18.0	114.3	21.4	31.1
Employees	(19.1%)	21	14	14	8	9

ENTRUST INC.

One Lincoln Centre 5400 LBJ Freeway Ste. 1340
Dallas TX 75240
Phone: 972-728-0447
Fax: 972-728-0440
Web: www.entrust.com

CEO: –
CFO: –
HR: –
FYE: December 31
Type: Private

Entrust is like a bodyguard for your e-Identity. The company's software and services ensure the privacy of electronic communications and transactions across corporate networks and the Internet. Its applications are used to authenticate users via smart cards passwords and biometric devices to control access to e-mail databases websites and business applications. Services include consulting deployment and security systems management. Entrust serves some 5000 enterprise government and financial customers worldwide from offices in about 10 countries. The company is controlled by private equity firm Thoma Bravo which acquired it in 2009.

ENTRX CORPORATION

PINK SHEETS: ENTX

800 Nicollet Mall Ste. 2690
Minneapolis MN 55402
Phone: 612-333-0614
Fax: 612-338-7332
Web: metalclad.com

CEO: Peter L Hauser
CFO: Brian D Niebur
HR: –
FYE: December 31
Type: Public

The raison d'etre of Entrx as of late has been to insulate and abate. The company provides insulation and asbestos abatement services through subsidiary Metalclad Insulation. Operating primarily in California it installs insulation on pipes ducts furnaces boilers and other industrial equipment. It also maintains and removes insulation and sells specialty insulation products to public utilities oil petrochemical and heavy construction companies. Metalclad's customers have included Jacobs Engineering Group and Southern California Edison .

ENVESTNET INC

NYS: ENV

35 East Wacker Drive, Suite 2400
Chicago, IL 60601
Phone: 312 827-2800
Fax: 312 827-2801
Web: www.envestnet.com

CEO: Judson (Jud) Bergman
CFO: Peter (Pete) D'Arrigo
HR: –
FYE: December 31
Type: Public

Envestnet provides managed account services for some 30000 financial institutions and investment advisers. The company's online financial planning programs assist brokers banks insurance companies and registered investment advisers with portfolio construction and analysis generating proposals and managing client accounts. Subsidiary Portfolio Management Consultants (Envestnet | PMC) provides consulting services to financial advisors and affords them access to managed accounts mutual funds exchange-traded funds and alternative investments. Founded in 1999 Envestnet supports approximately $535 billion of assets in some 2.2 million investor accounts.

	Annual Growth	12/10	12/11	12/12	12/13	12/14
Sales ($ mil.)	37.3%	98.1	123.2	157.3	242.5	348.7
Net income ($ mil.)	–	(0.6)	7.6	0.5	3.7	14.0
Market value ($ mil.)	30.3%	589.3	413.2	481.9	1,392.1	1,697.5
Employees	28.8%	457	524	769	948	1,257

ENVIRO VORAXIAL TECHNOLOGY INC.

NBB: EVTN

821 N.W. 57th Place
Fort Lauderdale, FL 33309
Phone: 954 958-9968
Fax: –
Web: www.evtn.com

CEO: John A Dibella
CFO: John A Dibella
HR: –
FYE: December 31
Type: Public

Enviro Voraxial Technology has a voracious appetite for developing equipment to separate solids and liquids with different specific gravities. The company's Voraxial Separator can be used for wastewater treatment grit and sand separation oil and water separation marine-oil-spill cleanup bilge and ballast treatment stormwater treatment and food-processing-waste treatment. The separator is capable of processing volumes as low as 3 gallons per minute as well as volumes of more than 10000 gallons per minute with only one moving part. Chairman and CEO Alberto DiBella officers and directors control almost 35% of the company.

	Annual Growth	12/10	12/11	12/12	12/13	12/14
Sales ($ mil.)	(3.0%)	0.7	2.1	0.8	1.2	0.6
Net income ($ mil.)	–	(1.7)	(1.0)	(1.5)	(0.4)	(0.7)
Market value ($ mil.)	(52.4%)	11.7	3.3	6.5	4.8	0.6
Employees	0.0%	6	6	6	6	6

ENVIRONMENTAL DEFENSE FUND

257 PARK AVE S FL 17
NEW YORK, NY 100107386
Phone: 212-505-2100
Fax: –
Web: www.edf.org

CEO: –
CFO: –
HR: –
FYE: September 30
Type: Private

Environmental Defense fights for those without a voice. The not-for-profit group works to protect the environment through programs in areas such as ecosystem restoration environmental health ocean protection and global and regional air and energy. The organization which has tripled in size since it was founded in 1967 boasts more than 500000 members and employs some 300 scientists attorneys economists and other professionals. In addition to its New York City headquarters Environmental Defense maintains 10 regional offices nationwide and in Beijing. Environmental Defense initially funded its efforts from a battle won against the DDT pesticide which had been harming wildlife.

	Annual Growth	09/05	09/06	09/08	09/09	09/12
Sales ($ mil.)	(33.7%)	–	1,319.3	122.8	19.6	111.9
Net income ($ mil.)	(21.3%)	–	–	25.8	0.0	9.9
Market value ($ mil.)	–	–	–	–	–	–
Employees	–	–	–	–	–	450

ENVIRONMENTAL TECTONICS CORP.

NBB: ETCC

County Line Industrial Park, 125 James Way
Southampton, PA 18966
Phone: 215 355-9100
Fax: –
Web: www.etcusa.com

CEO: –
CFO: –
HR: –
FYE: February 27
Type: Public

Environmental Tectonics Corporation (ETC) believes virtual environments can teach us a lot about real life. Through its Aerospace Solutions segment (formerly Training Services Group) the company makes software-driven aircrew training systems and disaster simulators. Through its Commercial/Industrial Systems segment (formerly Control Systems Group) it designs manufactures and sells industrial steam and gas sterilizers for the pharmaceutical medical device and animal research industries hyperbaric chambers for the medical industry and environmental testing products for the automotive and HVAC industries.

	Annual Growth	02/11	02/12	02/13	02/14	02/15
Sales ($ mil.)	(9.4%)	55.5	66.3	62.8	48.3	37.3
Net income ($ mil.)	–	14.5	4.9	4.9	0.6	(3.7)
Market value ($ mil.)	(14.5%)	23.9	15.1	18.5	18.4	12.8
Employees	(2.2%)	323	336	336	316	295

ENVIROSTAR INC

ASE: EVI

290 N.E. 68 Street
Miami, FL 33138
Phone: 305 754-4551
Fax: 305 751-4903
Web: www.envirostarinc.com

CEO: Henry M Nahmad
CFO: Venerando J Indelicato
HR: –
FYE: June 30
Type: Public

EnviroStar (formerly DRYCLEAN USA) is anything but hard pressed. The firm franchises and licenses more than 400 retail dry cleaners in three US states the Caribbean and Latin America. However most of its sales are generated by subsidiary Steiner-Atlantic which sells coin-operated laundry machines steam boilers and other laundry equipment; most are sold under the Aero-Tech Green-Jet and Multi-Jet names to some 750 customers and include independent dry cleaners hotels cruise lines and hospitals. Other EnviroStar divisions offer business brokerage and turn-key development of new dry cleaning businesses.

	Annual Growth	06/11	06/12	06/13	06/14	06/15
Sales ($ mil.)	9.6%	21.3	22.5	36.2	33.8	30.8
Net income ($ mil.)	29.0%	0.6	0.5	1.6	1.6	1.7
Market value ($ mil.)	35.2%	9.4	9.1	12.4	17.6	31.4
Employees	0.0%	29	29	28	29	29

ENVISION HEALTHCARE CORP   NYS: EMS

6200 S. Syracuse Way, Suite 200
Greenwood Village, CO 80111
Phone: 303 495-1200
Fax: –
Web: www.evhc.net

CEO: William A Sanger
CFO: Randel G Owen
HR: Janice Gonzales
FYE: December 31
Type: Public

Municipalities and hospitals can't call 911 when they have an emergency — but they can call Envision Healthcare. The holding company (formerly Emergency Medical Services Corporation) is the parent of EmCare Holdings a leading medical management firm that specializes in staffing emergency rooms and AMR Inc. the largest private ambulance service in the US. EmCare holds more than 700 staffing and service contracts with hospitals and physician groups in more than 45 states and the District of Columbia. AMR has more than 3800 contracts with clients (cities government agencies health care providers and insurance firms) in some 40 states for emergency and non-emergency transport services. The company went public in 2013.

	Annual Growth	12/10*	05/11*	12/11	12/12	12/13
Sales ($ mil.)	9.2%	2,859.3	1,221.8	1,885.8	3,300.1	3,728.3
Net income ($ mil.)	(30.9%)	131.7	20.7	13.0	48.5	43.4
Market value ($ mil.)	0.0%	0.1	0.1	–	–	–
Employees	20.1%	17,520	–	9,098	16,547	30,339

*Fiscal year change

ENVISION HEALTHCARE HOLDINGS INC   NYS: EVHC

6200 S. Syracuse Way, Suite 200
Greenwood Village, CO 80111
Phone: 303 495-1200
Fax: –
Web: www.evhc.net

CEO: William A. (Bill) Sanger
CFO: Randel G. (Randy) Owen
HR: –
FYE: December 31
Type: Public

Municipalities and hospitals can't call 911 when they have an emergency — but they can call Envision Healthcare. The holding company (formerly Emergency Medical Services Corporation) is the parent of EmCare Holdings a leading medical management firm that specializes in staffing emergency rooms and AMR Inc. the largest private ambulance service in the US. EmCare holds about 800 staffing and service contracts with hospitals and physician groups in more than 40 states and the District of Columbia. AMR has more than 3800 contracts with clients (cities government agencies health care providers and insurance firms) in some 40 states for emergency and non-emergency transport services. The company went public in 2013.

	Annual Growth	05/11*	12/11	12/12	12/13	12/14
Sales ($ mil.)	53.3%	1,221.8	1,885.8	3,300.1	3,728.3	4,397.6
Net income ($ mil.)	82.4%	20.7	13.0	41.2	6.0	125.5
Market value ($ mil.)	(2.3%)	–	–	–	6,524.3	6,371.8
Employees	12.4%	–	–	26,700	30,339	33,748

*Fiscal year change

ENVIVIO INC.   NASDAQ: ENVI

400 Oyster Point Blvd. Ste. 325
South San Francisco CA 94080
Phone: 650-243-2700
Fax: 650-243-2750
Web: www.envivio.com

CEO: Julien Signes
CFO: Erik E Miller
HR: –
FYE: January 31
Type: Public

You could say Envivio is the middleman between content providers and consumers of video. The company designed and sells an Internet Protocol (IP) video processing and distribution product that helps deliver high-quality content such as broadcast and on-demand video to audiences via multiple screens such as PCs TVs laptops and mobile phones. The software-based system runs on industry-standard hardware and consists of encoders transcoders network media processors and gateways. Envivio sells through a direct sales forces and a global distribution network that includes telecom systems integrators. A smaller portion of revenues is made from support and maintenance services. Envivio went public in 2012.

ENXNET INC.   OTC: EXNT

11333 E. Pine St. Ste. 75
Tulsa OK 74116
Phone: 918-592-0015
Fax: 918-592-0016
Web: www.enxnet.com

CEO: Ryan Corley
CFO: Stephen Hoelscher
HR: –
FYE: March 31
Type: Public

EnXnet licenses and markets emerging multimedia technologies including video compression and content storage. It has acquired the licensing rights to a video compression technology called ClearVideo used for distribution downloading and streaming of video and audio content over the Internet. Other technologies and products include DVDPlus a media storage product that combines a CD and DVD on the same disc gift cards and CD/DVD anti-theft technologies. CEO Ryan Corley owns a majority stake in the company.

ENZO BIOCHEM, INC.   NYS: ENZ

527 Madison Ave.
New York, NY 10022
Phone: 212 583-0100
Fax: –
Web: www.enzo.com

CEO: –
CFO: Barry W Weiner
HR: Paul O'Brien
FYE: July 31
Type: Public

For Enzo Biochem genomic research is the key to both diagnostic and therapeutic care. The biotech company is focused on the development and sale of gene-based tests and pharmaceuticals through its three operating divisions. The Enzo Clinical Labs unit provides diagnostic testing services in the New York City area while Enzo Life Sciences makes reagents used in research by pharmaceutical firms biotech companies academic institutions. The third division Enzo Therapeutics is a development-stage firm working to treat ophthalmic conditions gastrointestinal ailments and other diseases.

	Annual Growth	07/11	07/12	07/13	07/14	07/15
Sales ($ mil.)	(1.1%)	102.0	103.1	93.7	95.9	97.6
Net income ($ mil.)	–	(13.0)	(39.3)	(18.2)	(10.0)	(2.3)
Market value ($ mil.)	(6.0%)	176.9	69.1	100.4	221.1	138.2
Employees	(5.5%)	606	531	484	475	483

ENZON PHARMACEUTICALS INC   NAS: ENZN

20 Kingsbridge Road
Piscataway, NJ 08854
Phone: 732 980-4500
Fax: 908 575-9457
Web: www.enzon.com

CEO: –
CFO: Richard L Feinstein
HR: –
FYE: December 31
Type: Public

Enzon Pharmaceuticals has PEGged its future on researching ways to fight cancer. The company has developed compounds using its PEGylation and Locked Nucleic Acid (LNA) technology platforms to improve the performance and deliverability of existing cancer drugs. PEGylation involves attaching polyethylene glycol (PEG) to a drug compound to make it more effective and less toxic for patients. However in 2012 Enzon suspended clinical efforts and began reviewing strategic options; in 2013 it refocused on minimizing expenses and maximizing royalty revenue returns.

	Annual Growth	12/10	12/11	12/12	12/13	12/14
Sales ($ mil.)	(24.9%)	97.9	48.1	42.6	34.5	31.2
Net income ($ mil.)	(36.5%)	177.2	(20.8)	(2.8)	18.2	28.8
Market value ($ mil.)	(45.3%)	537.2	296.0	195.7	51.2	48.2
Employees	(70.2%)	126	72	43	1	1

EOG RESOURCES, INC.   NYS: EOG

1111 Bagby, Sky Lobby 2
Houston, TX 77002
Phone: 713 651-7000
Fax: -
Web: www.eogresources.com

CEO: William R. Thomas
CFO: Timothy K. Driggers
HR: Bryan Baldwin
FYE: December 31
Type: Public

EOG Resources' geographic focus is determined by where it can locate primary energy resources — natural gas natural gas liquids and oil. In recent years that focus has been on exploiting shale plays in the US. The independent oil and gas company is engaged in exploring for natural gas and crude oil and developing producing and marketing those resources. In 2014 EOG's total estimated net proved reserves was 2.5 billion barrels of oil equivalent of which 1.1 billion barrels was crude oil and condensate reserves and 5 trillion cubic feet was natural gas reserves.

	Annual Growth	12/10	12/11	12/12	12/13	12/14
Sales ($ mil.)	31.1%	6,099.9	10,126.1	11,682.6	14,487.1	18,035.3
Net income ($ mil.)	106.4%	160.7	1,091.1	570.3	2,197.1	2,915.6
Market value ($ mil.)	0.2%	50,119.6	54,012.5	66,228.5	92,025.8	50,481.5
Employees	7.0%	2,290	2,550	2,650	2,800	3,000

EP ENERGY CORP.   NYS: EPE

1001 Louisiana Street
Houston, TX 77002
Phone: 713 997-1000
Fax: -
Web: www.epenergy.com

CEO: Brent J. Smolik
CFO: Dane E. Whitehead
HR: Joan M. Gallagher
FYE: December 31
Type: Public

The old El Paso Corporation may be no longer but EP Energy is alive and well. In 2012 El Paso Corporation sold its exploration and production assets to an investor group led by Apollo Global Management and Riverstone Holdings for $7.2 billion; the new company emerged as EP Energy. (El Paso Corporation was ultimately bought by Kinder Morgan.) EP Energy explores for oil in the Eagle Ford Shale and Wolfcamp Shale in Texas and the Altamont Field in Utah; its natural gas and natural gas liquids (NGLs) assets are located in the Haynesville Shale in Louisiana. The company reported proved reserves of 622.2 million barrels of oil equivalent in 2014 about half of which is oil and NGLs. It went public in 2014.

	Annual Growth	12/10	12/11	12/12	12/13	12/14
Sales ($ mil.)	-	0.0	0.0	727.0	1,640.0	3,084.0
Net income ($ mil.)	-	0.0	0.0	(256.0)	450.0	731.0
Market value ($ mil.)	-	0.0	0.0	-	-	2,566.2
Employees	(1.9%)	-	-	778	770	748

EPAM SYSTEMS, INC.   NYS: EPAM

41 University Drive, Suite 202
Newtown, PA 18940
Phone: 267 759-9000
Fax: -
Web: www.epam.com

CEO: Arkadiy Dobkin
CFO: Anthony J. Conte
HR: -
FYE: December 31
Type: Public

EPAM provides software development and other IT services to US and European customers primarily from development centers in Russia Belarus Hungary Ukraine Kazakhstan and Poland. In addition to software product development the company offers services in such areas as e-commerce support data warehousing customer relationship management and application integration. EPAM also offers its own hosted and stand-alone enterprise software for sales force automation content management order management and other business processes. Half of sales come from North America.

	Annual Growth	12/10	12/11	12/12	12/13	12/14
Sales ($ mil.)	34.7%	221.8	334.5	433.8	555.1	730.0
Net income ($ mil.)	25.2%	28.3	44.4	54.5	62.0	69.6
Market value ($ mil.)	62.4%	-	-	874.3	1,687.7	2,306.5
Employees	23.0%	6,168	8,125	10,043	11,056	14,109

EPIC SYSTEMS CORPORATION

1979 Milky Way
Verona WI 53593-9179
Phone: 608-271-9000
Fax: 608-271-7237
Web: www.epic.com

CEO: -
CFO: -
HR: -
FYE: December 31
Type: Private

Epic Systems tells a grand tale of health care technology. The company provides health care management software that integrates financial and clinical information across inpatient ambulatory and payer technology systems. Epic's products include scheduling and registration tools billing and managed care administration applications inpatient and outpatient core clinical systems electronic health record (EHR) applications and software for managing hospital pharmacy emergency surgery radiology laboratory and intensive care departments. Outside the US it serves European clients from an office in the Netherlands. The employee-owned company was founded in 1979 by CEO Judith Faulkner.

EPICORE BIONETWORKS INC.   PINK SHEETS: EPCBF

4 Lina Ln.
Eastampton NJ 08060
Phone: 609-267-9118
Fax: 609-267-9336
Web: www.epicorebionetworks.com

CEO: -
CFO: Russell Rosenzweig
HR: -
FYE: June 30
Type: Public

Epicore BioNetworks puts the earth at the core of its scientific creations. The company manufactures environmentally sensitive biotechnology products for commercial industrial and consumer applications and specialty animal feeds. It mixes natural bacteria enzymes microbes and other biodegradable nontoxic ingredients to create products for diverse industries like agriculture cleaning and sanitation food processing and nutrition and environmental remediation. Those products include water treatment chemicals agrochemicals and sanitizers and deodorizers. Epicore is a major supplier of products to the aquaculture industry especially to the shrimp industries in Asia and in Latin America.

EPIQ SYSTEMS INC   NMS: EPIQ

501 Kansas Avenue
Kansas City, KS 66105-1300
Phone: 913 621-9500
Fax: -
Web: www.epiqsystems.com

CEO: Tom W. Olofson
CFO: Karin-Joyce S.F. (KJ) Tjon
HR: -
FYE: December 31
Type: Public

Epiq Systems wants to make legal discovery and bankruptcy proceedings as quick and painless as possible (for attorneys that is). The company provides case and document management software for bankruptcy class action mass tort and other legal proceedings. Its software automates tasks including electronic discovery legal notice claims management and government reporting. Epiq's software line includes products for Chapter 7 liquidations as well as Chapter 13 and 11 reorganizations. The company which caters to law firms and bankruptcy trustees also offers consulting and case management services and software for class action mass tort and bankruptcy case administration. Epiq operates primarily in the US.

	Annual Growth	12/10	12/11	12/12	12/13	12/14
Sales ($ mil.)	17.7%	247.2	283.3	373.1	482.1	474.5
Net income ($ mil.)	-	13.9	12.1	22.4	11.1	(1.3)
Market value ($ mil.)	5.6%	503.6	440.9	467.7	593.1	626.5
Employees	18.9%	550	1,000	1,000	1,000	1,100

EPITEC INC.

24800 DENSO DR STE 150
SOUTHFIELD, MI 480337464
Phone: 248-353-6800
Fax: –
Web: www.epitecinc.com

CEO: Jerome Sheppard
CFO: Mark J Ruma
HR: –
FYE: December 31
Type: Private

Epitec supports the idea that surrounding oneself with smart people is the key to a successful business. The company provides information technology staffing services to businesses across the US although its primary market is the Detroit area. It offers contract contract-to-hire and direct hire placement of developers analysts architects engineers and other technical staff to companies in a wide range of industries. Epitec also provides on-site management services and related custom software development. It was founded by CEO Jerry Sheppard in 1978.

	Annual Growth	12/05	12/06	12/07	12/08	12/12
Sales ($ mil.)	21.9%	–	–	–	28.5	63.0
Net income ($ mil.)	(3.2%)	–	–	–	0.8	0.7
Market value ($ mil.)	–	–	–	–	–	–
Employees	–	–	–	–	–	900

EPIZYME INC.

400 Technology Square
Cambridge, MA 02139
Phone: 617 229-5872
Fax: –
Web: www.epizyme.com

NMS: EPZM
CEO: Robert J. Gould
CFO: Andrew Singer
HR: –
FYE: December 31
Type: Public

Epizyme is taking on the epic task of writing the epitaph for genetically derived cancer. A clinical-stage biopharmaceutical company Epizyme targets cancer-causing genes by designing the therapeutics to inhibit them. It uses a highly personalized approach to choose the cancers the company contends with and the patients it selects. Epizyme has made the most progress with treatments for a leukemia and for a non-Hodgkin lymphoma. It is also working with an affiliate of GlaxoSmithKline on the development of three other enzyme inhibitors. Founded in 2007 the company went public in 2013.

	Annual Growth	12/10	12/11	12/12	12/13	12/14
Sales ($ mil.)	–	0.0	6.9	45.2	68.5	41.4
Net income ($ mil.)	–	0.0	(21.0)	(0.7)	(3.5)	(55.0)
Market value ($ mil.)	–	0.0	–	–	716.1	649.6
Employees	15.9%	–	–	64	74	86

EPL OIL & GAS INC

919 Milam Street, Suite 1600
Houston, TX 77002
Phone: 713 228-0711
Fax: –
Web: www.eplweb.com

NYS: EPL
CEO: Antonio De Pinho
CFO: Rick Fox
HR: –
FYE: December 31
Type: Public

It pays for EPL Oil & Gas (formerly Energy Partners) to have friends in the oil and gas business. The independent explorer and producer focuses on the waters of the Gulf of Mexico off the Gulf Coast. It partners with big oil companies to explore for reserves on properties the majors have left behind; EPL Oil & Gas earns an interest in the new reserves and production. The company has grown through a combination of exploration exploitation and development drilling as well as strategic acquisitions of oil and natural gas fields. It changed its corporate name in 2012 to reflect its oil and gas focus.

	Annual Growth	09/09*	12/09	12/10	12/11	12/12
Sales ($ mil.)	46.4%	134.9	56.8	239.9	348.3	423.6
Net income ($ mil.)	–	(36.1)	(21.0)	(8.5)	26.6	58.8
Market value ($ mil.)	44.6%	291.7	334.3	581.1	570.9	881.8
Employees	19.6%	–	101	100	108	173

*Fiscal year change

EPLUS INC

13595 Dulles Technology Drive
Herndon, VA 20171-3413
Phone: 703 984-8400
Fax: –
Web: www.eplus.com

NMS: PLUS
CEO: Phillip G. Norton
CFO: Elaine D. Marion
HR: Jim Solomon
FYE: March 31
Type: Public

ePlus wants to rate an A-plus from its customers by meeting their hardware and software needs. ePlus is a holding company and operates through two business segments that deal in technology sales and financing. Its ePlus Technology subsidiary resells and leases products from top IT infrastructure providers. Offerings include security storage and networking products as well as consulting and systems integration services. It also offers supply chain management software and services; its proprietary applications include procurement asset management spend analytics and document management tools. The company's Leasing and Financial Services arm offers lease financing and leases IT and medical equipment.

	Annual Growth	03/11	03/12	03/13	03/14	03/15
Sales ($ mil.)	7.3%	863.0	825.6	983.1	1,057.5	1,143.3
Net income ($ mil.)	17.9%	23.7	23.4	34.8	35.3	45.8
Market value ($ mil.)	34.4%	196.6	236.2	341.4	412.0	642.5
Employees	8.0%	725	833	904	934	986

EPOLIN INC.

358-364 Adams St.
Newark NJ 07105
Phone: 973-465-9495
Fax: 973-465-5353
Web: www.epolin.com

OTC: EPLN
CEO: Greg Amato
CFO: –
HR: –
FYE: February 28
Type: Private

Welders and army tank drivers alike owe their continued ability to see to Epolin. The company develops near-infrared dyes used to make eyewear for protection against lasers (used in range finders in tanks) and face shields used by welders. Epolin also makes intermediates for the specialty chemical industry. Additionally Epolin sells its dyes as security inks for credit cards drug and food labels and official documents. Products are sold in 20 countries; the US accounts for about 80% of sales. Epolin was acquired by New Jersey-based investment managing firm Polymathes Holdings in 2012.

EPR PROPERTIES

909 Walnut Street, Suite 200
Kansas City, MO 64106
Phone: 816 472-1700
Fax: 816 472-5794
Web: www.eprkc.com

NYS: EPR
CEO: Gregory K. (Greg) Silvers
CFO: Mark A. Peterson
HR: –
FYE: December 31
Type: Public

EPR Properties (formerly Entertainment Properties Trust) invests in places to play. The self-administered real estate investment trust (REIT) owns more than 120 movie megaplex theaters and eight theater-anchored entertainment retail centers around the US and Canada. EPR also owns other recreational properties including ski and golf resorts waterparks and several wineries. In a more recent twist the company began to diversify its holdings by acquiring public charter schools. However movie megaplexes remain the featured attraction at EPR. The REIT buys properties from theater operators and leases them back to the original owners. Many of its theaters are leased to AMC Entertainment.

	Annual Growth	12/10	12/11	12/12	12/13	12/14
Sales ($ mil.)	5.3%	313.1	301.7	321.8	343.1	385.1
Net income ($ mil.)	11.8%	114.9	115.2	121.6	180.2	179.6
Market value ($ mil.)	5.7%	2,642.1	2,497.0	2,634.1	2,808.3	3,292.2
Employees	12.5%	25	27	31	38	40

EPSILON SYSTEMS SOLUTIONS INC.

9242 LIGHTWAVE AVE # 100　　　　　　　　　　　　CEO: –
SAN DIEGO, CA 921236402　　　　　　　　　CFO: Stuart Teshima
Phone: 619-702-1700　　　　　　　　　　　　　　HR: –
Fax: –　　　　　　　　　　　　　　　　FYE: December 31
Web: www.epsilonsystems.com　　　　　　　　　Type: Private

Epsilon Systems Solutions is not afraid of its alpha beta gamma and delta rivals. The diversified engineering services company offers consultation field services and IT support to the applied technology energy environmental industrial and marine markets. It also maintains and repairs ships for the US Navy and Coast Guard. Epsilon Systems caters to federal agencies including the Department of Energy the Department of Defense and the Department of Homeland Security as well as to major contractors such as Boeing Lockheed Martin SPAWAR NAVAIR Lakehurst and Raytheon.

	Annual Growth	12/04	12/05	12/06	12/07	12/08
Sales ($ mil.)	–	–	–	(2,073.1)	94.1	93.8
Net income ($ mil.)	18143.4%	–	–	0.0	1.7	1.7
Market value ($ mil.)	–	–	–	–	–	–
Employees	–	–	–	–	–	875

EPSTEIN

600 W. Fulton St.　　　　　　　　　　　　CEO: Melvin Kupperman
Chicago IL 60661-1199　　　　　　　　　　　CFO: James Jirsa
Phone: 312-454-9100　　　　　　　　　　　　　HR: –
Fax: 312-559-1217　　　　　　　　　　FYE: December 31
Web: www.epsteinglobal.com　　　　　　　　　Type: Private

From the jazz age to the tech age Epstein has made its mark. The company provides architectural engineering and construction management services in the US and Europe. Epstein serves the commercial industrial and public sector markets building and designing projects such as office buildings corporate headquarters manufacturing plants convention centers hospitals and schools. It has worked on O'Hare International Airport and Whirlpool's headquarters as well as projects for Apple Serta and Hyatt. The employee-owned firm was founded in 1921 by Abraham Epstein. The company has offices in the US Poland and Romania.

EQT CORP.　　　　　　　　　　　　　　　　　NYS: EQT

625 Liberty Avenue, Suite 1700　　　　　　　　CEO: David L. Porges
Pittsburgh, PA 15222　　　　　　　　　　CFO: Philip P. (Phil) Conti
Phone: 412 553-5700　　　　　　　　　　HR: Carol Caracciolo
Fax: –　　　　　　　　　　　　　　　　FYE: December 31
Web: www.eqt.com　　　　　　　　　　　　　　Type: Public

Integrated natural gas company EQT Corporation (formerly Equitable Resources) hopes to get its fair share of the natural gas market. EQT Production exploits proved natural gas reserves of 10.7 trillion cu. ft. of natural gas equivalent in the Appalachian region (primarily in the Marcellus shale basin). EQT Production sells its natural gas products to Appalachian-area utilities and industrial customers and to marketers including EQT Energy its own gas marketing affiliate. EQT Midstream Partners operates about 8200 miles of gathering pipeline and 750 miles of transmission lines.

	Annual Growth	12/11	12/12	12/13	12/14	12/15
Sales ($ mil.)	9.3%	1,639.9	1,641.6	1,862.0	2,469.7	2,339.8
Net income ($ mil.)	(35.1%)	479.8	183.4	390.6	387.0	85.2
Market value ($ mil.)	(1.2%)	8,358.4	8,997.6	13,696.3	11,548.3	7,952.6
Employees	1.1%	1,835	1,873	1,621	1,750	1,914

EQUIFAX, INC.　　　　　　　　　　　　　　　NYS: EFX

1550 Peachtree Street, N.W.　　　　　　CEO: Richard F. (Rick) Smith
Atlanta, GA 30309　　　　　　　　　　　　CFO: John W. Gamble
Phone: 404 885-8000　　　　　　　　　　HR: Coretha M. Rushing
Fax: –　　　　　　　　　　　　　　　　FYE: December 31
Web: www.equifax.com　　　　　　　　　　　　Type: Public

Ever get the feeling you're being watched? You could be sensing the gaze of Equifax. One of the top credit bureaus in the US (Experian and TransUnionare the others) Equifax provides consumer credit scores credit histories and risk analysis to lenders and others. The company collects data on more than 600 million consumers and 80 million businesses around the world. Through its Workforce Solutions unit Equifax provides outsourced payroll and human resources services. The company also offers subscription-based credit monitoring for consumers. Clients include financial institutions retailers automotive dealers and mortgage companies. Equifax operates in North America Latin America and Europe.

	Annual Growth	12/10	12/11	12/12	12/13	12/14
Sales ($ mil.)	7.0%	1,859.5	1,959.8	2,160.5	2,303.9	2,436.4
Net income ($ mil.)	8.3%	266.7	232.9	272.1	351.8	367.4
Market value ($ mil.)	22.8%	4,250.6	4,625.6	6,461.9	8,249.3	9,655.9
Employees	3.6%	6,500	6,500	7,000	7,000	7,500

EQUILAR INC.

1100 Marshall St.　　　　　　　　　　　　　　CEO: David Chun
Redwood City CA 94063　　　　　　　　　　　　CFO: –
Phone: 650-286-4512　　　　　　　　　　　　　HR: –
Fax: 650-701-0993　　　　　　　　　　FYE: December 31
Web: www.equilar.com　　　　　　　　　　　Type: Private

Equilar earns its bread and butter by finding out how much everyone else gets paid. The executive compensation research company manages a database compiled with the salary information of more than 20000 executives of public companies registered with the US Securities and Exchange Commission. Equilar reports and analyses are available through a subscription; customers can also buy printed copies of its reports. Fortune 500 corporations use the information to determine executive and board member pay; consulting firms such as Deloitte and media firms such as Bloomberg and the Wall Street Journal also use Equilar's data. The company was founded in 2001 by CEO David Chun.

EQUINIX INC　　　　　　　　　　　　　　　　NMS: EQIX

One Lagoon Drive, Fourth Floor　　　　CEO: Stephen M. (Steve) Smith
Redwood City, CA 94065　　　　　　　　　　CFO: Keith D. Taylor
Phone: 650 598-6000　　　　　　　　　　　HR: Marianne Spring
Fax: –　　　　　　　　　　　　　　　　FYE: December 31
Web: www.equinix.com　　　　　　　　　　　　Type: Public

Equinix provides data and network hosting and colocation facilities (it calls them Internet Business Exchanges or IBXs) where ISPs telecommunications carriers and content providers can locate equipment and interconnect networks and operations. The company also offers colocation-related services to provide clients with cabinets operating space and storage. Customers include network and mobility providers (such as AT&T BT and Comcast); cloud and IT services (Amazon.com Microsoft and Salesforce.com); and content providers (DIRECTV Facebook). Altogether Equinix operates more than 100 data centers around the world and international customers make up about one-third of sales.

	Annual Growth	12/10	12/11	12/12	12/13	12/14
Sales ($ mil.)	19.0%	1,220.3	1,606.8	1,895.7	2,152.8	2,443.8
Net income ($ mil.)	–	36.9	94.0	144.7	94.7	(259.5)
Market value ($ mil.)	29.2%	4,587.2	5,724.2	11,640.2	10,017.3	12,799.2
Employees	19.1%	1,921	2,709	3,153	3,500	3,866

EQUINOX PAYMENTS LLC

8901 E. Raintree Dr. Ste. 400
Scottsdale AZ 85260
Phone: 480-551-7800
Fax: 512-491-8026
Web: www.lso.com

CEO: Philippe Tartavull
CFO: –
HR: –
FYE: December 31
Type: Private

Equinox Payments formerly Hypercom USA provides electronic payment terminals and associated software and services to customers across the US. Businesses use its products to swipe credit debit and smart cards. Its product line also includes printers keypads and networking gear. The company's software encompasses point-of-sale management systems terminal operations and systems monitoring. In addition Equinox provides asset management systems implementation and transaction services. It sells to distributors financial institutions payment processors and retailers. The company is owned by private equity firm The Gores Group.

EQUITY LIFESTYLE PROPERTIES INC   NYS: ELS

Two North Riverside Plaza, Suite 800
Chicago, IL 60606
Phone: 312 279-1400
Fax: –
Web: www.equitylifestyle.com

CEO: –
CFO: Paul Seavey
HR: Barb Itter
FYE: December 31
Type: Public

Snow birds and empty nesters flock to communities developed and owned by Equity LifeStyle Properties. The real estate investment trust (REIT) owns and operates lifestyle-oriented residential properties aimed at retirees vacationers and second home owners. Other properties provide affordable housing for families. Equity LifeStyle Properties leases lots for factory-built homes cottages cabins and recreational vehicles. Available homes range in size and style. The REIT's portfolio includes more than 380 properties containing some 141000 lots in about 30 states and Canada. Properties are similar to site-built residential subdivisions with centralized entrances utilities gutters curbs and paved streets.

	Annual Growth	12/10	12/11	12/12	12/13	12/14
Sales ($ mil.)	11.0%	511.4	580.1	709.9	728.4	776.8
Net income ($ mil.)	23.1%	60.4	42.5	74.5	125.9	138.5
Market value ($ mil.)	(2.0%)	4,691.4	5,593.9	5,644.3	3,039.0	4,324.0
Employees	2.0%	3,600	3,500	3,600	3,700	3,900

EQUISTAR CHEMICALS LP

1221 McKinney St. Ste. 700
Houston TX 77010
Phone: 713-652-7200
Fax: 713-652-4151
Web: www.equistarchem.com

CEO: James L Gallogly
CFO: –
HR: –
FYE: December 31
Type: Subsidiary

Someone's got to build the building blocks too you know? Equistar Chemicals a subsidiary of LyondellBasell does just that. Its primary product is ethylene which is the world's most-used petrochemical and the basis for any number of other chemicals plastics and synthetics. Among the company's other products are propylene butadiene polyethylene polypropylene ethylene oxide ethylene glycol benzene and toluene. Polyethylene is used in plastic bags and bottles; polypropylene is used in plastic caps rigid packaging automotive components and carpet.

EQUITY OFFICE MANAGEMENT L.L.C.

2 N. Riverside Plaza Ste. 2100
Chicago IL 60606
Phone: 312-466-3300
Fax: 312-454-0332
Web: www.equityoffice.com

CEO: Tom August
CFO: Kurt Heister
HR: –
FYE: December 31
Type: Subsidiary

All else being equal Equity Office is one of the largest commercial landlords in the US. The company owns 400 buildings with more than 59 million sq. ft. of premiere Class A office space in the country's top markets including Boston Manhattan Los Angeles and Northern California. Equity Office has experience with major renovations and developments. It also handles large corporate leases. Former chairman Sam "Grave Dancer" Zell founded Equity Office in 1976. The company is now owned by The Blackstone Group.

EQUITY COMMONWEALTH   NYS: EQC

Two North Riverside Plaza, Suite 600
Chicago, IL 60606
Phone: 312 646-2800
Fax: 617 332-2261
Web: www.cwhreit.com

CEO: David Helfand
CFO: Adam S Markman
HR: –
FYE: December 31
Type: Public

Equity CommonWealth (formerly CommonWealth REIT) invests in office and industrial properties primarily in the US mainly located in suburbs of major metropolitan markets. Its portfolio includes about 265 properties about two-thirds of which are offices comprising some 51 million sq. ft. of leasable space. Equity CommonWealth was one of the largest industrial private land owners in Oahu until it spun off those assets in 2012; other markets include Boston Philadelphia Southern California the District of Columbia and Australia. GlaxoSmithKline and Office Depot are among the REIT's largest tenants.

	Annual Growth	12/10	12/11	12/12	12/13	12/14
Sales ($ mil.)	2.1%	793.4	911.9	1,013.1	885.5	861.9
Net income ($ mil.)	(35.1%)	135.4	110.0	(79.8)	(157.0)	24.0
Market value ($ mil.)	0.2%	3,306.3	2,156.7	2,053.0	3,021.1	3,327.0
Employees	—	—	—	—	—	62

EQUITY ONE, INC.   NYS: EQY

410 Park Avenue, Suite 1220
New York, NY 10022
Phone: 212 796-1760
Fax: –
Web: www.equityone.com

CEO: David R. Lukes
CFO: Mark Langer
HR: –
FYE: December 31
Type: Public

Equity One wants to be #1: the number one shopping center owner that is. A real estate investment trust (REIT) Equity One acquires develops and manages shopping centers in urban areas across the US targeting markets in California the northeastern US South Florida Atlanta and Washington DC. Its portfolio consists primarily of more than 120 properties including shopping centers anchored by supermarkets drug stores and other specialty retail chains totaling about 14 million sq. ft. The REIT's top five tenants include Albertsons Publix LA Fitness Food Emporium and TJX Companies. Chairman Chaim Katzman controls the REIT through his Israeli real estate firm Gazit-Globe.

	Annual Growth	12/10	12/11	12/12	12/13	12/14
Sales ($ mil.)	5.5%	285.2	291.9	325.6	332.5	353.2
Net income ($ mil.)	18.1%	25.1	33.6	(3.5)	78.0	48.9
Market value ($ mil.)	8.7%	2,259.4	2,110.3	2,611.1	2,788.9	3,151.8
Employees	(2.0%)	168	185	177	168	155

EQUITY RESIDENTIAL
NYS: EQR

Two North Riverside Plaza
Chicago, IL 60606
Phone: 312 474-1300
Fax: –
Web: www.equityresidential.com

CEO: David J. Neithercut
CFO: Mark J. Parrell
HR: John Powers
FYE: December 31
Type: Public

All things begin equal Equity Residential is one of the largest apartment owners in the US. The company acquires develops and manages multifamily residential properties which includes the generation of rental and other related income through the leasing of apartment units to residents. A real estate investment trust (REIT) the company wholly owns about 400 garden-style high-rise and mid-rise multifamily communities with some 110000 units in large metropolitan areas. Equity Residential also owns two military housing complexes and partially owns about two dozen other apartment properties totaling around an additional 10000 units. Its properties are spread across 12 states and Washington DC.

	Annual Growth	12/10	12/11	12/12	12/13	12/14
Sales ($ mil.)	7.0%	1,995.5	1,989.5	2,123.7	2,387.7	2,614.7
Net income ($ mil.)	22.1%	296.0	935.2	881.2	1,905.4	658.7
Market value ($ mil.)	8.4%	18,850.3	20,693.6	20,563.0	18,821.3	26,067.5
Employees	(3.3%)	4,000	3,800	3,600	3,600	3,500

ERA GROUP INC
NYS: ERA

818 Town & Country Blvd., Suite 200
Houston, TX 77024
Phone: 713 369-4700
Fax: –
Web: www.eragroupinc.com

CEO: Christopher S. Bradshaw
CFO: Andrew (Andy) Puhala
HR: –
FYE: December 31
Type: Public

Some of Era Group's offshore helicopter rides probably take a long long time. Operating a fleet of some 180 light to heavy-duty helicopters Era provides helicopter transportation services primarily to offshore oil and gas personnel working in the Gulf of Mexico and Alaska. The company also caters to offshore oil and gas companies operating in Brazil Asia and Europe but to a lesser extent. Era provides other helicopter-based services as well including search and rescue missions air medical services and aircraft leasing. The company — which traces its roots back to the 1950s — has been a unit of SEACOR Holdings since 2004.

	Annual Growth	12/10	12/11	12/12	12/13	12/14
Sales ($ mil.)	8.9%	235.4	258.1	272.9	299.0	331.2
Net income ($ mil.)	–	(3.6)	2.1	7.8	18.7	17.1
Market value ($ mil.)	(31.5%)	–	–	–	628.7	430.9
Employees	(2.8%)	–	846	837	875	777

ERBA DIAGNOSTICS
ASE: ERB

14100 NW 57th Court
Miami Lakes, FL 33014
Phone: 305 324-2300
Fax: 305 324-2385
Web: www.erbadiagnostics.com

CEO: Mohan Gopalkrishnan
CFO: Ernesina Scala
HR: –
FYE: December 31
Type: Public

Using blood sweat or tears ERBA Diagnostics (formerly IVAX Diagnostics) can tell if something is wrong. The company develops manufactures and distributes in vitro diagnostic products to identify autoimmune and infectious diseases based upon samples of bodily fluids. It operates through three subsidiaries. Delta Biologicals develops and manufactures the MAGO and Aptus instrument systems and distributes products to hospitals and medical laboratories in Italy. Diamedix makes and markets diagnostic test kits in the US. ImmunoVision develops makes and markets autoimmune reagents for use by clinical and research labs and other diagnostic manufacturers. ERBA Diagnostics Mannheim holds 72% of the company.

	Annual Growth	12/10	12/11	12/12	12/13	12/14
Sales ($ mil.)	11.6%	17.0	16.8	19.3	28.3	26.4
Net income ($ mil.)	–	(4.2)	(3.3)	(1.6)	0.7	0.4
Market value ($ mil.)	53.6%	25.1	19.4	39.2	120.4	139.8
Employees	6.0%	106	87	99	135	134

ERESEARCHTECHNOLOGY INC.
NASDAQ: ERT

1818 Market St. Suite 1000
Philadelphia PA 19103
Phone: 215-972-0420
Fax: 215-972-0414
Web: www.ert.com

CEO: Jeffrey S Litwin
CFO: Keith D Schneck
HR: –
FYE: December 31
Type: Private

eResearchTechnology (ERT) e-cares about your e-clinical e-trial by offering support services software and hardware to help streamline the clinical trials process that drugs and medical devices must pass to earn regulatory approval. Its products automate all aspects of the process from setup and data gathering to analysis and FDA application preparation. ERT also provides site support including ECG equipment rentals and sales. Customers include contract research organizations (CROs) drugmakers and medical device firms. Flagship product EXPERT ensures cardiac safety by collecting processing and interpreting electrocardiogram (ECG) data. ERT was taken private by affiliates of Genstar Capital LLC in 2012.

ERHC ENERGY INC.
OTC: ERHE

5444 Westheimer Rd. Ste. 1570
Houston TX 77056
Phone: 713-626-4700
Fax: 713-626-4704
Web: www.erhc.com/

CEO: Peter C Ntephe
CFO: –
HR: –
FYE: September 30
Type: Public

Oil out of Africa is the hope of ERHC Energy (formerly Environmental Remediation Holding Corporation) an independent oil and gas company whose sole assets are two West African oil and gas exploration concessions: in the Joint Development Zone between the Sao Tome and Nigeria; and in the Exclusive Economic Zone in Sao Tome. ERHC is teaming up with larger oil and gas companies (such as Noble Energy and Pioneer Natural Resources) to help it develop its holdings. The company is also hoping to acquire interests in high-potential non-producing international prospects in known oil producing areas. Former chairman and CEO Emeka Offor the owner of Chrome Oil Services and Chrome Energy controls about 40% of ERHC.

ERICKSON INC
NMS: EAC

5550 S.W. Macadam Avenue, Suite 200
Portland, OR 97239
Phone: 503 505-5800
Fax: –
Web: www.ericksonaircrane.com

CEO: Udo Rieder
CFO: Eric K. Struik
HR: Glenn Splieth
FYE: December 31
Type: Public

No light-weight Erickson operates and manufactures S-64 Aircrane helicopters able to lift up to 25000 pounds! Its fleet of 90 rotary-wing and fixed wing aircraft includes 20 S-64s which provide aerial services for such jobs as firefighting and utility logging construction and relief work. Some S-64s are equipped with incident response kits: hose nozzle and holding tank for firefighting rescue basket and aero-medical pod. The company also offers maintenance repair and overhaul services. Customers are fire and forestry agencies construction companies utilities and governments. Founded in 1971 by Jack Erickson the company redeveloped the Sikorsky S-64 and has since expanded internationally.

	Annual Growth	12/10	12/11	12/12	12/13	12/14
Sales ($ mil.)	30.8%	118.2	152.8	180.8	318.2	346.6
Net income ($ mil.)	–	(8.3)	15.9	15.2	9.7	(10.3)
Market value ($ mil.)	(0.5%)	–	–	116.5	287.4	115.3
Employees	12.6%	–	700	700	1,200	1,000

ERICSSON INC.

6300 Legacy Dr.
Plano TX 75024
Phone: 972-583-0000
Fax: 218-327-6212

CEO: Angel Ruiz
CFO: –
HR: –
FYE: December 31
Type: Subsidiary

Ericsson is Swede on North America. The US subsidiary of Sweden-based global wireless network equipment leader Telefonaktiebolaget LM Ericsson oversees the North American business of its parent company. Its core network products are antennas transmitters switching systems and other gear used to build wireless telecommunications networks. Ericsson Inc. primarily serves network operators transportation companies utilities providers and broadcasters in the US. Its growing services business offers consulting network build-out and network management and maintenance services. The company also makes multimedia software and related products that enable such digital media services as Internet television.

ERIE FAMILY LIFE INSURANCE COMPANY

100 Erie Insurance Place
Erie PA 16530
Phone: 814-870-2000
Fax: 814-870-3126
Web: www.erie-insurance.com

CEO: Jeffrey A Ludrof
CFO: –
HR: –
FYE: December 31
Type: Subsidiary

Life is good at Erie Family Life Insurance. The insurer serves as the life insurance division of the Erie Insurance Group by providing individual and group life insurance annuities and disability income policies. Its group insurance products include a voluntary payroll deduction program and its life insurance products include include term whole life and universal coverage. The company's insurance policies are marketed through more than 8000 independent agents in 11 states and Washington DC. In 2006 Erie Insurance Group formally acquired Erie Family Life and now hold nearly 80% of its shares.

ERIE INDEMNITY CO.

NMS: ERIE

100 Erie Insurance Place
Erie, PA 16530
Phone: 814 870-2000
Fax: –
Web: www.erieinsurance.com

CEO: Terrence W. Cavanaugh
CFO: Marcia A Dall
HR: –
FYE: December 31
Type: Public

Erie Indemnity may be near a lake but it prefers pools. Founded in 1925 as an auto insurer it now provides management services that relate to the sales underwriting and issuance of policies of one customer: Erie Insurance Exchange. The Exchange is a reciprocal insurance exchange that pools the underwriting of several property/casualty insurance firms. It offers coverage ranging from homeowners to boat policies through independent representatives with a reach that extends to about a dozen states east of the Mississippi River. Erie Indemnity charges a management fee of 25% of all premiums written or assumed by the Exchange. It is the only publicly traded part of the Erie Insurance Group.

	Annual Growth	12/10	12/11	12/12	12/13	12/14
Assets ($ mil.)	5.5%	14,344.0	14,348.0	15,441.0	16,676.0	17,758.0
Net income ($ mil.)	0.9%	162.0	169.0	160.0	163.0	168.0
Market value ($ mil.)	8.5%	3,024.2	3,610.3	3,197.4	3,377.5	4,192.8
Employees	2.9%	4,200	4,300	4,400	4,450	4,700

ERIN ENERGY CORP

ASE: ERN

1330 Post Oak Blvd., Suite 2250
Houston, TX 77056
Phone: 713 797-2940
Fax: –
Web: www.camacenergy.com

CEO: Kase L. Lawal
CFO: Daniel Ogbonna
HR: –
FYE: December 31
Type: Public

Erin Energy (formerly CAMAC Energy) likes to share the wealth and the work. Rather than owning oil and gas assets outright the company owns interests in production sharing contracts with a focus on West Africa and Asia. It has two producing wells at Oyo Field (75 miles off the coast of Nigeria) with plans for two more. Erin Energy shares the Nigerian oil profits with sister company Nigerian Agip Exploration Limited which runs the operation. The company's total proved reserves of 5.2 billion barrels of oil most of which is undeveloped are all at Oyo. Its Chinese Zijinshan Project an exploration-stage coal bed methane play is shared with PetroChina CBM. Erin Energy was formed in 2005 to focus on energy projects in China.

	Annual Growth	12/10	12/11	12/12	12/13	12/14
Sales ($ mil.)	14.2%	31.6	38.9	16.6	7.9	53.8
Net income ($ mil.)	–	(230.5)	(24.9)	(6.1)	(15.9)	(96.1)
Market value ($ mil.)	(34.3%)	418.5	212.4	124.1	311.3	77.8
Employees	31.2%	29	23	35	47	86

ERNIE BALL INC.

151 Suburban Rd.
San Luis Obispo CA 93401
Phone: 805-544-7726
Fax: 805-544-7275
Web: www.ernieball.com

CEO: –
CFO: –
HR: –
FYE: December 31
Type: Private

Ernie Ball has the music world on a string — a guitar string that is. In addition to making Slinky strings Ernie Ball makes Music Man guitars and basses. The music company also produces cables locks volume pedals picks straps and other guitar accessories such as motorized peg winders. The firm's products are sold in more than 6000 music stores in the US and about 80 countries worldwide. Founder Roland S. "Ernie" Ball (who died in 2004 at age 74) challenged conventional wisdom in 1958 by opening the first music store in the US devoted solely to guitar sales (he sold it in 1967). He also was the first in the industry to offer guitar strings in various gauges an innovation that has improved playability.

EROOM SYSTEM TECHNOLOGIES INC

NBB: ERMS

150 Airport Road, Suite 1200
Lakewood, NJ 08701
Phone: 732 730-0116
Fax: 732 810-0380
Web: www.eroomsystem.com

CEO: –
CFO: –
HR: –
FYE: December 31
Type: Public

eRoomSystem Technologies is keeping tabs for hotels. The company provides computer-based refreshment centers for the hospitality industry. Its eRoomSystem products track beverage and other refreshment purchases and automatically charge lodgers' accounts. The eRoomSystem generates reports on sales statistics inventory control and restocking requirements. The company's other products include room safes that feature reprogrammable electronic combinations. Through revenue-sharing agreements the company installs its systems and takes a cut of the sales they generate.

	Annual Growth	12/10	12/11	12/12	12/13	12/14
Sales ($ mil.)	(8.5%)	1.1	0.8	0.7	0.6	0.8
Net income ($ mil.)	57.5%	0.0	(0.1)	(0.3)	(0.3)	0.1
Market value ($ mil.)	(7.8%)	2.9	3.7	4.1	2.3	2.1
Employees	8.1%	11	15	17	19	15

ESCALADE, INC.

NMS: ESCA

817 Maxwell Ave
Evansville, IN 47711
Phone: 812 467-4449
Fax: –
Web: www.escaladeinc.com

CEO: David L. Fetherman
CFO: Stephen R. Wawrin
HR: –
FYE: December 27
Type: Public

Escalade isn't in the business of making high-end SUVs but rather helping customers get their game on as the world's largest producer of tables for table tennis under the Ping-Pong STIGA Prince and Head brands. Its other sporting goods include pool tables hockey and soccer tables play systems archery darts and fitness equipment. Products are sold under the Goalrilla Silverback Minnesota Fats USWeight and Woodplay names as well as private labels. Escalade also sells office products through its Martin Yale unit which makes and markets data shredders paper trimmers and folding machines that are sold worldwide under several names (Intimus Paper Monster Martin Yale) and private labels.

	Annual Growth	12/10	12/11	12/12	12/13	12/14
Sales ($ mil.)	3.4%	120.7	134.3	147.6	163.7	138.0
Net income ($ mil.)	18.2%	6.1	4.4	(4.9)	9.8	11.8
Market value ($ mil.)	24.1%	85.4	62.0	73.5	167.0	202.6
Employees	(6.4%)	608	618	633	648	466

ESCALERA RESOURCES CO

NBB: ESCS Q

1675 Broadway, Suite 2200
Denver, CO 80202
Phone: 303 794-8445
Fax: 303 794-8451
Web: www.escaleraresources.com

CEO: Charles F Chambers
CFO: Adam Fenster
HR: –
FYE: December 31
Type: Public

It's double or nothing for Double Eagle Petroleum (formerly Double Eagle Petroleum and Mining) which gambles on hitting pay dirt as it explores for and produces oil and gas in the Rocky Mountains of Utah and Wyoming. Double Eagle owns interests in about 900 producing wells; natural gas accounts for more than 95% of the oil and gas independent's production and reserves. The company has proved reserves of more than 413000 barrels of oil and 71.3 billion cu. ft. of natural gas and leases acreage in seven states. Double Eagle sells its oil and gas on the spot market.

	Annual Growth	12/10	12/11	12/12	12/13	12/14
Sales ($ mil.)	(5.4%)	55.0	64.7	38.2	35.3	44.1
Net income ($ mil.)	–	5.5	11.7	(10.3)	(13.1)	(7.6)
Market value ($ mil.)	(16.4%)	370.2	369.8	360.2	329.7	180.8
Employees	3.0%	24	24	24	22	27

ESCALON MEDICAL CORP.

NAS: ESMC

435 Devon Park Drive, Building 100
Wayne, PA 19087
Phone: 610 688-6830
Fax: 610 688-3641
Web: www.escalonmed.com

CEO: Richard J Depiano Jr
CFO: Robert M O'Connor
HR: –
FYE: June 30
Type: Public

Escalon Medical has an eye for ophthalmic instruments. The company develops manufactures markets and distributes diagnostic and surgical devices for use in ophthalmology specifically ultrasound digital photography and image management systems. Its subsidiary companies are branded and operate under the Sonomed Escalon name. Products include the PacScan Plus and Master-Vu ultrasound systems and AXIS image management system. Escalon Medical was founded in 1987. It divested its Escalon Clinical Diagnostics (ECD) business in 2012 to put more focus into growing its ophthalmic business.

	Annual Growth	06/11	06/12	06/13	06/14	06/15
Sales ($ mil.)	(18.6%)	29.9	24.4	11.5	12.4	13.1
Net income ($ mil.)	–	(5.8)	(5.9)	2.6	(0.4)	(0.5)
Market value ($ mil.)	5.0%	8.8	5.3	10.1	12.9	10.7
Employees	(22.5%)	158	118	56	58	57

ESCO CORPORATION

2141 NW 25th Ave.
Portland OR 97210-2578
Phone: 503-228-2141
Fax: 503-226-8071
Web: www.escocorp.com

CEO: Calvin W Collins
CFO: Ray Verlinich
HR: –
FYE: December 31
Type: Private

ESCO is well ensconced as a global manufacturer of metal parts castings and components for industrial machinery. It operates through two segments: engineered products and turbine technologies. Mining customers account for the majority of sales for ESCO's engineered products which include crusher wear-parts and bi-metallic buttons as well as screens blocks tooth systems and other heavy parts that hit the dirt and wear out. Turbine technologies makes cast parts such as blades and vanes used in the aerospace and power generation industries. ESCO was founded in 1913 as Electric Steel Foundry which primarily made trolley car replacement parts. The company filed to go public in 2011.

ESCO TECHNOLOGIES, INC.

NYS: ESE

9900A Clayton Road
St. Louis, MO 63124-1186
Phone: 314 213-7200
Fax: –
Web: www.escotechnologies.com

CEO: –
CFO: Gary E Muenster
HR: Deborah (Deb) Hanlon
FYE: September 30
Type: Public

Diversified manufacturing company ESCO Technologies focuses on three business segments: Utility Solutions (automation and communication devices for utilities) Filtration/Fluid Flow and RF Shielding and Test. ESCO's communications equipment includes meter-reading technology and video surveillance systems used to monitor industrial applications. The company's filters are used in industrial applications fuel systems medical applications and appliances. Test products include electromagnetic compatibility equipment such as antennas probes turntables and calibration equipment as well as radio-frequency shielding products.

	Annual Growth	09/11	09/12	09/13	09/14	09/15
Sales ($ mil.)	(6.2%)	693.7	688.4	490.1	531.1	537.3
Net income ($ mil.)	(5.1%)	52.5	46.9	(25.6)	0.4	42.5
Market value ($ mil.)	8.9%	658.3	1,003.0	857.9	897.9	926.8
Employees	(1.6%)	2,480	2,690	2,620	2,103	2,323

ESCREEN INC.

7500 W. 110th St. Ste. 500
Overland Park KS 66210
Phone: 913-327-5915
Fax: 913-327-8606
Web: www.escreen.com

CEO: –
CFO: Mark Brockelman
HR: Ana Grobe
FYE: December 31
Type: Private

eScreen tests for a full range of drugs and e-delivers the results. The company provides drug testing products and services to occupational health facilities throughout the US. eScreen's products are primarily used for pre-employment drug testing. Sample collection takes place at its nationwide network of about 2600 contracted clinics that are equipped with eScreen's products and technology. Samples are collected in an eCup screening device optically scanned on site by the eReader and negative results are electronically reported directly to employers within minutes. Positive results are sent on for further testing before being reported. eScreen was acquired by diagnostics firm Alere in 2012.

ESILICON CORPORATION

501 Macara Ave.
Sunnyvale CA 94085
Phone: 408-616-4600
Fax: 408-991-9567
Web: www.esilicon.com

CEO: Jack Harding
CFO: Robert Selvi
HR: –
FYE: March 31
Type: Private

eSilicon tries to make it easy for electronics makers to come up with custom silicon. The company offers design engineering and testing services helping customers produce semiconductors for applications in communications consumer electronics networking security storage and wireless devices. eSilicon formed alliances with such companies as Agilent Amkor ARM Rambus Synopsys and TSMC. The company helps small chip startups get better prices from chip foundries by representing dozens of companies at a time. The fabless application-specific integrated circuit (ASIC) design firm was established in 2000. eSilicon is owned by its executives and investors.

ESL FEDERAL CREDIT UNION

225 Chestnut St.
Rochester NY 14604
Phone: 585-336-1000
Fax: +44-20-7691-7745
Web: www.africaneagle.co.uk

CEO: –
CFO: Walter F Rufnak
HR: –
FYE: June 30
Type: Private - Not-for-Pr

Founded in 1920 by George Eastman (also the founder of Eastman Kodak) ESL Federal Credit Union was known as Eastman Savings and Loan until 1996 when it changed its charter from a thrift to a credit union. The company has about 20 branches in upstate New York that offer deposit accounts credit cards insurance and investment products. It originates consumer loans and mortgages including automobile boat and home improvement loans. The credit union has some 310000 members; membership is available to employees and retirees of Eastman Kodak and its subsidiaries as well as a handful of other employer groups and residents of Rochester New York.

ESOTERIX INC.

4509 Freidrich Ln. Bldg. 1 Ste. 100
Austin TX 78744
Phone: 512-225-1100
Fax: 512-225-1250
Web: www.esoterix.com

CEO: –
CFO: –
HR: Kathleen Brown
FYE: December 31
Type: Subsidiary

Esoterix wasn't being ironic when it chose its name. A subsidiary of LabCorp the firm specializes in performing esoteric laboratory tests. Unlike routine tests that detect things like cholesterol levels or pregnancy using blood and urine samples esoteric testing involves highly specialized often gene-based assays that help doctors diagnose and monitor disease. The firm's services include testing for bleeding disorders allergies and diabetes as well as infectious diseases such as HIV and hepatitis C. Esoterix provides its services to hospitals and specialist physicians; it also serves drug companies by performing esoteric testing during clinical trials.

ESPEY MANUFACTURING & ELECTRONICS CORP.

ASE: ESP

233 Ballston Avenue
Saratoga Springs, NY 12866
Phone: 518 245-4400
Fax: –
Web: www.espey.com

CEO: Patrick Enright Jr
CFO: David O'Neil
HR: –
FYE: June 30
Type: Public

Espey is on a power trip. Espey Mfg. & Electronics makes electronic equipment for high-voltage applications including specialized electronic power supplies transformers and electronic system components. Its transformers and electronic systems include high-power radar transmitters antennas and iron-core products such as magnetic amplifiers and audio filters. The company's products are used by industrial and military customers in radar missile guidance and control communications aircraft navigation and nuclear submarine control. Customers include General Electric Lockheed Martin Raytheon and the US government. Exports account for more than 20% of Espey's sales.

	Annual Growth	06/11	06/12	06/13	06/14	06/15
Sales ($ mil.)	(2.3%)	29.5	32.0	34.3	27.1	26.8
Net income ($ mil.)	(4.7%)	3.9	4.4	5.6	1.2	3.2
Market value ($ mil.)	1.3%	58.3	62.4	60.7	59.4	61.4
Employees	(2.5%)	166	162	173	145	150

ESPN INC.

ESPN Plaza 935 Middle St.
Bristol CT 06010
Phone: 860-766-2000
Fax: +60-3-2273-0608
Web: www.aet-tankers.com

CEO: Pittsburgh Penguins
CFO: Christine F Driessen
HR: –
FYE: September 30
Type: Joint Venture

ESPN is a superstar of the sports broadcasting world. The company is the leading cable sports broadcaster reaching about 100 million US viewers per month with its stable of channels including ESPN ESPN2 and ESPN Classic. The 24-hour networks carry a variety of live sporting events as well as programs devoted to news and analysis. ESPN also creates original programming for TV and radio and lends content for ESPN.com one of the most popular sports sites on the Internet. Its international operations extend the ESPN brand to another 200 countries. ESPN is 80% owned by Walt Disney (through ABC); media conglomerate Hearst has a 20% stake.

ESSA BANCORP INC

NMS: ESSA

200 Palmer Street
Stroudsburg, PA 18360
Phone: 570 421-0531
Fax: –
Web: www.essabank.com

CEO: Gary S Olson
CFO: Allan A Muto
HR: –
FYE: September 30
Type: Public

ESSA Bancorp is the holding company for ESSA Bank & Trust. Founded in 1916 the bank offers deposit and lending services to consumers and businesses through more than 25 branches located in eastern Pennsylvania's Lehigh Monroe and Northampton counties. One- to four-family residential mortgages dominate the bank's lending activities representing more than 80% of its loan portfolio. Commercial real estate loans account for 10% while home equity loans and lines of credit make up ESSA's other significant loan segments. The bank also offers financial and investment services through a third-party firm. ESSA Bancorp acquired First Star Bancorp in 2012 adding nine branches in Lehigh County.

	Annual Growth	09/11	09/12	09/13	09/14	09/15
Assets ($ mil.)	10.0%	1,097.5	1,418.8	1,372.3	1,574.8	1,606.5
Net income ($ mil.)	16.8%	5.3	0.2	8.8	8.5	9.8
Market value ($ mil.)	5.4%	119.3	118.0	118.3	128.3	147.1
Employees	9.2%	213	270	282	303	303

ESSENCE COMMUNICATIONS INC.

135 W. 50th St. 4th Floor
New York NY 10020
Phone: 212-522-1212
Fax: 952-897-5173
Web: www.hfit.com

CEO: Ed Lewis
CFO: Harry Dedyo
HR: Elaine Williams
FYE: December 31
Type: Subsidiary

Essence Communications Inc. (ECI) is out to capture the essence of African-American culture through publishing fashion and entertainment. The company publishes ESSENCE a magazine geared toward African-American women which has a monthly circulation of more than 1 million and a readership of 8.5 million. ECI also publishes books and online content (Essence.com) and has licensing operations. In addition the company hosts the Essence Music Festival which is held every Fourth of July weekend and has featured superstars such as Prince Beyonce Mary J. Blige and Lionel Richie. The first issue of ESSENCE hit the newsstands in 1970. ECI is a subsidiary of Time Inc.

ESSENDANT INC

NMS: ESND

One Parkway North Boulevard, Suite 100
Deerfield, IL 60015-2559
Phone: 847 627-7000
Fax: 847 627-7001
Web: www.unitedstationers.com

CEO: Robert B. (Bob) Aiken
CFO: Todd A. Shelton
HR: Julie Rose
FYE: December 31
Type: Public

Don't think that Essendant (formerly United Stationers) is just another paper pusher. The company is a leading pure wholesale distributor of office supplies and equipment in North America offering more than 160000 of its own and national brand products to about 30000 reseller customers. Through subsidiaries Essendant supplies such items as business machines computer products and peripherals janitorial supplies and office products and furniture. It also offers office furniture for such markets as education and health care. The company sells primarily to resellers through catalogs and over the Internet as well as through its direct sales force.

	Annual Growth	12/10	12/11	12/12	12/13	12/14
Sales ($ mil.)	2.5%	4,832.2	5,005.5	5,080.1	5,085.3	5,327.2
Net income ($ mil.)	1.4%	112.8	109.0	111.8	123.2	119.2
Market value ($ mil.)	(9.8%)	2,470.5	1,260.6	1,199.8	1,776.7	1,632.3
Employees	2.2%	5,950	5,950	6,100	6,100	6,500

ESSENTIA HEALTH

502 E 2ND ST
DULUTH, MN 558051913
Phone: 218-786-8376
Fax: –
Web: www.essentiahealth.org

CEO: Peter Person
CFO: Bert Norman
HR: –
FYE: June 30
Type: Private

Access to rural health care is of the essence for Essentia Health. The integrated health system has a network of 17 hospitals about 70 clinics more than a dozen long-term care assisted living or independent living facilities and a research institute. Its service area spans rural communities in the Midwest and part of the western region with locations in Minnesota southeastern North Dakota northeastern Wisconsin and Idaho. Among its hospitals are Clearwater Valley in Orofino Idaho; St. Mary's in Cottonwood Idaho; and Catholic facility Holy Trinity Hospital in Graceville Minnesota. The system also provides ambulance services.

	Annual Growth	06/08	06/09	06/10	06/11	06/13
Sales ($ mil.)	(62.4%)	–	–	1,500.3	1,593.5	79.7
Net income ($ mil.)	(48.4%)	–	–	56.7	153.7	7.8
Market value ($ mil.)	–	–	–	–	–	–
Employees	–	–	–	–	–	18,177

ESSEX PROPERTY TRUST, INC.

NYS: ESS

925 East Meadow Drive
Palo Alto, CA 94303
Phone: 650 494-3700
Fax: –
Web: www.essex.com

CEO: Michael J. (Mike) Schall
CFO: Michael T Dance
HR: –
FYE: December 31
Type: Public

Essex Property Trust acquires develops redevelops and manages apartment communities focusing on the metropolitan areas of Los Angeles San Diego San Francisco and Seattle. The self-managed and self-administered real estate investment trust (REIT) owns more than 230 residential communities — mostly in Southern California — and 15 properties under development. Essex also owns a handful of office buildings in its home state and has partial stakes in several apartment communities through joint ventures. The REIT adds to its portfolio through acquisitions and through the development and renovation of properties. In 2014 Essex acquired BRE Properties in a big deal valued at approximately $4.3 billion.

	Annual Growth	12/10	12/11	12/12	12/13	12/14
Sales ($ mil.)	23.6%	415.7	475.6	543.4	613.7	969.3
Net income ($ mil.)	35.8%	35.9	47.1	125.3	156.3	122.2
Market value ($ mil.)	16.0%	7,273.8	8,948.0	9,339.1	9,139.1	13,156.8
Employees	13.5%	1,039	1,099	1,144	1,173	1,725

ESSEX RENTAL CORP

NBB: ESSX

1110 Lake Cook Road, Suite 220
Buffalo Grove, IL 60089
Phone: 847 215-6500
Fax: –
Web: www.essexrentalcorp.com

CEO: Nicholas J Matthews
CFO: Kory M Glen
HR: –
FYE: December 31
Type: Public

Unless you employ construction workers who moonlight as super heroes you may need to rent one of Essex Rental's cranes to hoist those steel beams and concrete pipes. Specializing in lattice-boom crawler cranes (large heavy-duty cranes with dynamic lifting capabilities) Essex Rental rents a fleet of some 350 Manitowoc and Liebherr brand cranes and attachments to North American construction and industrial companies and municipalities. Its cranes are typically used in the construction of power plants petrochemical plants water treatment and purification facilities as well as in commercial and infrastructure construction. Essex also sells used equipment and offers crane transportation and repair services.

	Annual Growth	12/10	12/11	12/12	12/13	12/14
Sales ($ mil.)	25.6%	41.5	89.6	98.3	95.5	103.4
Net income ($ mil.)	–	(9.6)	(17.1)	(12.7)	(9.6)	(11.2)
Market value ($ mil.)	(30.0%)	136.5	73.2	84.9	81.2	32.8
Employees	(1.5%)	276	273	250	236	260

ESSROC CEMENT CORP.

3251 Bath Pike
Nazareth PA 18064
Phone: 610-837-6725
Fax: 610-837-9614
Web: www.essroc.com

CEO: Jean Paul Meric
CFO: –
HR: Craig Becker
FYE: December 31
Type: Subsidiary

Essroc Cement likes to mix it up. The company operates about a dozen cement plants and other facilities in the US Canada and Puerto Rico and has an annual capacity of more than 6.5 million metric tons of cement. Essroc makes bulk and packaged cement products including portland cement ready mix concrete and masonry cement. Its Axim Concrete Technologies subsidiary creates chemical admixtures used to improve the performance quality of cement. Essroc's brands include BRIXMENT Saylor's PLUS and VELVET masonry. Its BRAVO line includes masonry chemical products. Founded in 1866 by David Saylor as Coplay Cement the company is part of Italian cement and building materials group Italcementi.

ESTEE LAUDER INTERNATIONAL INC.

767 5th Ave.
New York NY 10153-0023
Phone: 212-572-4200
Fax: 212-572-3941
Web: www.esteelauder.com

CEO: –
CFO: Rick Kunes
HR: –
FYE: June 30
Type: Subsidiary

While its parent company is well-established in the US Estee Lauder International enjoys the same prestige worldwide. The company is a subsidiary of Estee Lauder Companies and is the arm of the company that extends outside the US and Canada. The company sells cosmetics fragrances and skin care products under the Flirt! Tom Ford Beauty Bobbi Brown Clinique Prescriptives and Donna Karan Cosmetics names among others. Founded in 1946 the Estee Lauder company is known for its upscale beauty items and dedication to research and product testing. The company develops and markets men's fragrances (such as Sean John Fragrances and Aramis) as well as men's Lab Series Skin Care for Men.

ESTWING MANUFACTURING COMPANY INC.

2647 8th St
Rockford IL 61109-1120
Phone: 815-397-9558
Fax: 815-397-8665
Web: www.estwing.com

CEO: –
CFO: Sharon L Phillips
HR: –
FYE: December 31
Type: Private

Business is quite striking at Estwing Manufacturing. That's because the company makes striking and struck tools including axes chisels claw hammers and pry bars. The company produces a hammer with a shock-reduction gasket and a smooth face-to-claw radius that facilitates nail pulling. Besides the usual hand tools Estwing also specializes in strike tools used by geologists such as rock picks and chipping hammers. For the international market Estwing makes strike tools adapted to other countries' patterns including the schlosserhammer for Germany. Founded in 1923 the company is owned by the Estwing family.

ESTERLINE TECHNOLOGIES CORP

NYS: ESL

500 108th Avenue N.E.
Bellevue, WA 98004
Phone: 425 453-9400
Fax: –
Web: www.esterline.com

CEO: Curtis C. Reusser
CFO: Robert D. George
HR: Marcia Greenberg
FYE: October 02
Type: Public

You couldn't build an entire jet just from Esterline Technologies products but it would hard to fly one without them. The aerospace company's offerings extend from the cockpit to electrical subsystems to materials inside and outside aircraft. It make avionics that control and communicate sensors and power switching devices that monitor conditions and materials necessary for commercial and military aircraft. Esterline with $1.7 billion in sales sells mostly to the US government particularly the Department of Defense and aircraft manufacturers. There can be as much as $1 million worth of Esterline products in jet fighters and airliners. About a fifth of sales come from high-end non-aerospace products.

	Annual Growth	10/11	10/12	10/13	10/14	10/15
Sales ($ mil.)	0.8%	1,718.0	1,992.3	1,969.8	2,051.2	1,774.4
Net income ($ mil.)	(18.2%)	133.0	112.5	164.7	102.4	59.6
Market value ($ mil.)	5.9%	1,685.1	1,667.6	2,387.4	3,460.2	2,116.1
Employees	2.3%	12,114	12,185	12,049	12,874	13,290

ET3 LLC

2500 Northwinds Pkwy. Ste. 600
Alpharetta GA 30004
Phone: 770-521-1964
Fax: 770-521-6084
Web: www.executrain.com

CEO: –
CFO: –
HR: –
FYE: December 31
Type: Private

Need to brush up on skills for the new economy? ET3 which does business as ExecuTrain offers computer training at more than 150 franchise locations in 25 countries. Programs include classroom or online courses in basic business software Web design programming network certification and database development. The company also offers customized courses classroom rentals and professional development programs geared to corporations with employees in numerous locations. Four University of Georgia graduates — David Deutsch Kim Deutsch Mike Addison and Mike Moss — founded the company in 1984. In 2002 Addison and a group of franchise owners bought the assets of ExecuTrain back from International Data Group.

ESTES EXPRESS LINES INC.

3901 W BROAD ST
RICHMOND, VA 232303962
Phone: 804-353-1900
Fax: –
Web: www.estes-express.com

CEO: Rob W. Estes
CFO: –
HR: Tom Donahue
FYE: December 31
Type: Private

Estes Express makes a business out of beating expectations. Founded during the Depression with a Chevy truck the company has grown into a multiregional less-than-truckload (LTL) freight hauler. Its fleet of some 6600 tractors and 24600 trailers operates via a network of 210 terminals dotting the US. Service in Canada is provided by TST Overland Express an ExpressLINK partner and in Mexico through affiliate Almex. Estes Express works with designated carriers to offer door-to-door delivery in the Caribbean and in Mexico. Subsidiary Estes Forwarding Worldwide services ocean/air freight forwarding. The company is owned and run by the family of founder W.W. Estes.

ETELOS INC.

OTC: ETLO

1900 O'Farrell St. Ste. 320
San Mateo CA 94403
Phone: 425-458-4510
Fax: 425-458-4511
Web: www.etelos.com

CEO: –
CFO: –
HR: –
FYE: December 31
Type: Public

Etelos is developing into a provider of Web applications tools with a higher profile. The company completed a reverse merger in 2008 with Tripath Technology a bankrupt chip design firm and became a publicly held venture in the process. Pursuing the software-as-a-service market where companies offer applications as a resource on the Internet rather than as packages that need to be installed and maintained at a customer's facilities Etelos offers what it calls a "platform as a service" for developing Web apps a Web-based service that developers can access. Its Etelos Marketplace service allows developers to distribute license and support Web applications.

	Annual Growth	12/09	12/10	12/11	12/12	12/13
Sales ($ mil.)	9.1%	–	1,506.3	1,738.2	1,864.8	1,958.3
Net income ($ mil.)	16.2%	–	–	52.9	63.5	71.3
Market value ($ mil.)	–	–	–	–	–	–
Employees	–	–	–	–	–	14,000

ETHAN ALLEN INTERIORS, INC.

NYS: ETH

Ethan Allen Drive
Danbury, CT 06811
Phone: 203 743-8000
Fax: –
Web: www.ethanallen.com

CEO: M. Farooq Kathwari
CFO: Corey Whitely
HR: –
FYE: June 30
Type: Public

Furniture maker Ethan Allen Interiors (the holding company for Ethan Allen Inc.) has some revolutionary ideas for your home's living room and other areas. Named after the American patriot the vertically integrated firm boasts about half a dozen US furniture factories including a couple of saw mills. The company's products include casegoods (wood furniture such as beds dressers and tables) upholstery items (sofas recliners) and accessories (wall decor lighting). They're sold through nearly 300 Ethan Allen stores located primarily in the US. About half of its stores are operated by independent dealers who are required to deal exclusively in Ethan Allen products and follow company guidelines.

	Annual Growth	06/11	06/12	06/13	06/14	06/15
Sales ($ mil.)	2.7%	679.0	729.4	729.1	746.7	754.6
Net income ($ mil.)	6.2%	29.3	49.7	32.5	42.9	37.1
Market value ($ mil.)	5.5%	604.8	566.2	818.1	702.8	748.2
Employees	1.6%	4,700	5,000	4,900	5,000	5,000

ETHICON ENDO-SURGERY INC.

4545 Creek Rd.
Cincinnati OH 45242
Phone: 513-337-7000
Fax: 513-337-7912
Web: www.ethiconendo.com

CEO: –
CFO: –
HR: Veronica M Gilbert
FYE: December 31
Type: Subsidiary

When surgeons need to stock up on tools Ethicon Endo-Surgery (EES) has an endless supply on hand. A subsidiary of Johnson & Johnson the company makes surgical devices and equipment for open surgeries and minimally invasive procedures in the areas of bariatrics gastrointestinal health gynecology and surgical oncology. Its products include endoscopic and laparoscopic tools adjustable gastric bands EnSeal bipolar tissue sealing systems and the Harmonic Scalpel which simultaneously cuts and cauterizes tissue using ultrasonic technology to minimize damage during surgery. EES markets its products in more than 50 countries worldwide.

ETHICON INC.

Route 22 West
Somerville NJ 08876
Phone: 800-255-2500
Fax: 818-287-3001
Web: www.unitedonline.net

CEO: –
CFO: David Kurklander
HR: Allan Weisberg
FYE: December 31
Type: Subsidiary

Johnson & Johnson subsidiary Ethicon has the operating room all sewn up. The company's Ethicon Products division is a leading maker of sutures and wound-closure products including sutures Dermabond skin glue Mentor surgical mesh products and wound drains as well as breast implants and plastic surgery devices. Another division Ethicon Biosurgery provides a line of absorbable hemostats and other products that help control bleeding during surgery while its Biopatch product offers infection-resistant wound dressings. Ethicon Women's Health and Urology makes surgical grafts devices and equipment under the Gynecare brand.

ETIENNE AIGNER HOLDINGS INC.

29 W. 35th St. 2nd Fl.
New York City NY 10001
Phone: 212-239-7788
Fax: 212-239-7981
Web: www.etienneaigner.com

CEO: Richard Schaffer
CFO: –
HR: –
FYE: March 31
Type: Private

The big horseshoe-shaped "A" has been a lucky symbol for Etienne Aigner. The company's leather goods are sold in department and specialty stores across the US through catalogs and the Internet as well outlet stores. Etienne Aigner's products include handbags and accessories (such as key chains gloves and wallets). The firm's brand name also is licensed for gloves belts and footwear. Founded in 1950 by Hungarian leather craftsman Etienne Aigner himself the company has been owned by Wooster Investments since 2004. Etienne Aigner is not affiliated with Germany-based Etienne Aigner AG which distributes its products in Europe Africa and Asia.

ETNA DISTRIBUTORS LLC

529 32ND ST SE
GRAND RAPIDS, MI 495482303
Phone: 616-245-4373
Fax: –
Web: www.etnasupply.com

CEO: Russ Visner
CFO: –
HR: Julie Pardoe
FYE: December 31
Type: Private

Unlike the volcano in Sicily that shares its name Etna Supply spews out water not fire. The company distributes equipment and supplies for residential and commercial plumbing hydronic heating waterworks and sewage facilities and fire protection. It operates through about 15 locations in Michigan Indiana and Ohio. The company also offers related services such as custom pipe flaring and threading welding valve and hydrant maintenance and meter reading. Customers include architects engineers contractors and homeowners. Etna Supply was founded in 1965.

	Annual Growth	12/09	12/10	12/11	12/12	12/13
Sales ($ mil.)	4.6%	–	130.2	132.8	141.8	149.3
Net income ($ mil.)	72.2%	–	–	0.8	0.7	2.4
Market value ($ mil.)	–	–	–	–	–	–
Employees	–	–	–	–	–	285

ETS-LINDGREN LP

1301 Arrow Point Dr.
Cedar Park TX 78613
Phone: 512-531-6400
Fax: 512-531-6500
Web: www.ets-lindgren.com

CEO: –
CFO: –
HR: Sandra Lopera
FYE: September 30
Type: Subsidiary

ETS-Lindgren (ETS) makes working with energy emissions A-OK. The company offers products that detect measure and manage electromagnetic magnetic and acoustic energy. Its products are used in the acoustics automotive electronics health and safety medical military and wireless communications markets. ETS also provides supporting services such as consultation custom designs and site surveying. Customers include Apple Cisco GE Healthcare GM IBM Siemens Healthcare Sony Electronics Sun Microsystems and Xerox. Founded in 1951 by Erik Lindgren the company became a subsidiary of ESCO Technologies in 2000. ETS-Lindgren has offices in China Finland France Japan Singapore Taiwan the UK and the US.

EUREKA FINANCIAL CORP (MD) NBB: EKFC

3455 Forbes Avenue
Pittsburgh, PA 15213
Phone: 412 681-8400
Fax: 412 681-6625
Web: www.eurekabancorp.com

CEO: –
CFO: –
HR: –
FYE: September 30
Type: Public

Eureka will help you eke the most out of your income. Eureka Financial is the holding company of the single-branch Eureka Bank a thrift serving Pittsburgh's Oakland neighborhood near the University of Pittsburgh. Originally chartered in 1886 the bank offers standard personal and business deposit products including checking and savings accounts CDs and IRAs. Eureka Bank is focused on real estate lending: Real estate loans — mostly single-family mortgages — account for three-quarters of its total loan portfolio. It also offers commercial and consumer loans. Eureka Bancorp MHC owns a majority of Eureka Financial.

	Annual Growth	09/10	09/11	09/12	09/13	09/14
Sales ($ mil.)	3.7%	6.0	6.8	7.0	6.9	6.9
Net income ($ mil.)	20.8%	0.7	1.3	1.5	1.4	1.5
Market value ($ mil.)	15.2%	–	14.7	19.1	21.0	22.5
Employees	(3.0%)	–	23	22	21	21

EUROMARKET DESIGNS INC.

1250 Techny Rd.
Northbrook IL 60062
Phone: 847-272-2888
Fax: 847-272-5366
Web: www.crateandbarrel.com

CEO: Adrian Mitchell
CFO: Diane Pearce
HR: Lynne Saltzman
FYE: February 28
Type: Private

Think you've never bought anything from Euromarket Designs? Think again. The retailer which does business under the Crate & Barrel name pioneered the fashionable-yet-homey look for contemporary interiors offering furniture housewares and linens in au courant colors and styles. It operates some 160 Crate & Barrel locations (including a dozen outlet stores) in 30 states and also peddles products through its catalogs and website. Euromarket Designs' other retailing ventures include CB2 (modern home furnishings) and The Land of Nod (furniture and toys for kids). Founded by Carole and Gordon Segal in 1962 the company is majority-owned by Germany-based Otto one of the world's leading mail-order merchants.

EURONET WORLDWIDE INC. NMS: EEFT

3500 College Boulevard
Leawood, KS 66211
Phone: 913 327-4200
Fax: 913 327-1921
Web: www.euronetservices.com

CEO: Michael J. (Mike) Brown
CFO: Rick L. Weller
HR: Karyn Clewes Zaborny
FYE: December 31
Type: Public

Euronet Worldwide might soon have the whole world in its net — thanks to the growing electronic payments industry. The company offers money transfer and processing services and manages ATM networks and point-of-sale (POS) terminals for itself and others. It operates in three primary segments: epay (which sells prepaid mobile airtime and related products and services) EFT (electronic financial transaction processing software and ATM/POS management services); and consumer-to-consumer money transfer. Traditionally Euronet is highly acquisitive and has snatched up money transfer processing and similar companies around the world. Founded in 1994 its top markets are in the US Germany and the UK.

	Annual Growth	12/10	12/11	12/12	12/13	12/14
Sales ($ mil.)	12.5%	1,038.3	1,161.3	1,267.6	1,413.2	1,664.2
Net income ($ mil.)	–	(38.4)	37.0	20.5	88.0	101.6
Market value ($ mil.)	33.2%	899.8	953.5	1,217.7	2,468.9	2,832.7
Employees	10.4%	3,100	3,800	3,900	4,100	4,600

EV ENERGY PARTNERS LP NMS: EVEP

1001 Fannin, Suite 800
Houston, TX 77002
Phone: 713 651-1144
Fax: –
Web: www.evenergypartners.com

CEO: Michael E Mercer
CFO: Michael (Mel) Mercer
HR: –
FYE: December 31
Type: Public

EV Energy Partners (the EV is from founding company EnerVest) is a natural gas and oil exploration and production company which operates in the Appalachian Basin primarily in West Virginia and Ohio as well as in Kansas Louisiana Michigan Oklahoma and Texas. In 2011 EV Energy Partners reported estimated proved reserves of 1.14 trillion cu. ft. of natural gas equivalent. The company's base in the Appalachian Basin puts EV Energy Partners in close proximity to the nation's major consuming markets allowing for stronger pricing power. The partnership focuses on acquiring and operating oil and gas properties in the continental US.

	Annual Growth	12/10	12/11	12/12	12/13	12/14
Sales ($ mil.)	18.6%	171.5	261.8	285.5	315.3	339.4
Net income ($ mil.)	5.2%	106.1	102.6	(16.3)	(76.2)	129.7
Market value ($ mil.)	(16.3%)	1,906.5	3,200.9	2,747.2	1,648.0	936.0
Employees	10.0%	707	783	878	938	1,036

EV3 INC.

3033 Campus Dr.
Plymouth MN 55441
Phone: 763-398-7000
Fax: 763-398-7200
Web: www.ev3.net

CEO: Jose E Almeida
CFO: –
HR: –
FYE: December 31
Type: Subsidiary

ev3 offers endovascular doctors everything they need to keep blood moving in the right direction. More specifically it develops manufactures and sells catheter-based medical devices used to treat disorders in the lower extremities (peripheral vascular) and brain (neurovascular). ev3's products include stents microcatheters guidewires embolic coils and stroke reduction devices. The company sells more than 100 products in more than 65 countries through a direct sales team and distributors. Among its customers are radiologists cardiologists neurosurgeons and vascular surgeons. ev3 is part of medical equipment firm Covidien vascular products division.

EVANGELICAL COMMUNITY HOSPITAL

1 HOSPITAL DR
LEWISBURG, PA 178379350
Phone: 570-522-2000
Fax: –
Web: www.evanhospital.com

CEO: –
CFO: Christine Martin
HR: –
FYE: June 30
Type: Private

Evangelical Community Hospital brings the good news of community health to residents in central Pennsylvania. The hospital provides a wide range of medical services to communities in the Susquehanna Valley. Among its specialized services are home health care and hospice maternity oncology rehabilitation and pediatrics. The hospital delivers more than 1000 babies annually and treats more than 30000 patients in its emergency department each year. Its outreach network includes family practice offices and other medical services. Despite its name the hospital has no affiliation with any religious organization.

	Annual Growth	06/09	06/10	06/11	06/12	06/13
Sales ($ mil.)	9.7%	–	122.9	142.8	154.3	162.1
Net income ($ mil.)	(16.9%)	–	–	18.1	9.6	12.5
Market value ($ mil.)	–	–	–	–	–	–
Employees	–	–	–	–	–	1,360

EVANS & SUTHERLAND COMPUTER CORP. NBB: ESCC

770 Komas Drive
Salt Lake City, UT 84108
Phone: 801 588-1000
Fax: –
Web: www.es.com

CEO: –
CFO: Paul L Dailey
HR: Carol Young
FYE: December 31
Type: Public

Evans & Sutherland Computer (E&S) makes products that can impartially be described as stellar. The company provides hardware and software used in digital planetariums and other theaters. Its products include laser projectors domed projection screens and complete planetarium packages. The company also produces planetarium content. E&S sells its visual systems to theaters and schools; its domes are additionally marketed to casinos theme parks and military contractors. The company counts Disney Griffith Observatory IMAX Texas A&M University and Universal Studios among its customers. E&S gets more than half of its sales in the US.

	Annual Growth	12/10	12/11	12/12	12/13	12/14
Sales ($ mil.)	(0.9%)	27.5	28.3	24.9	29.6	26.5
Net income ($ mil.)	–	(4.6)	(2.1)	(2.3)	1.2	(1.3)
Market value ($ mil.)	(20.7%)	11.1	2.5	0.2	1.1	4.4
Employees	(0.7%)	102	99	97	96	99

EVANS BANCORP, INC. ASE: EVBN

One Grimsby Drive
Hamburg, NY 14075
Phone: 716 926-2000
Fax: –

CEO: David J Nasca
CFO: Gary Kajtoch
HR: –
FYE: December 31
Type: Public

Evans National Bank wants to take care of Buffalo's bills. The subsidiary of Evans Bancorp operates about a dozen branches in western New York (including Buffalo). The bank primarily uses funds gathered from deposits to originate commercial and residential real estate loans (more than 70% of its loan portfolio) and to invest in securities. Subsidiaries include ENB Insurance Agency which sells property/casualty insurance; ENB Associates offering mutual funds and annuities to bank customers; and Evans National Leasing which provides financing for business equipment throughout the US. In 2009 Evans Bancorp acquired the assets and single branch of the failed Waterford Village Bank in Clarence New York.

	Annual Growth	12/10	12/11	12/12	12/13	12/14
Assets ($ mil.)	6.0%	671.5	740.9	809.7	833.5	846.8
Net income ($ mil.)	14.0%	4.8	6.1	8.1	7.9	8.2
Market value ($ mil.)	14.3%	59.9	50.1	65.2	88.7	102.2
Employees	2.9%	224	242	238	241	251

EVAPCO INC.

5151 Allendale Ln.
Taneytown MD 21787
Phone: 410-756-2600
Fax: 410-756-6450
Web: www.evapco.com

CEO: –
CFO: –
HR: –
FYE: December 31
Type: Private

Evapco keeps its cool especially under pressure. The company is a manufacturer of evaporative cooling and heat transfer equipment for both the commercial and industrial refrigeration markets. Its products include condensers coolers cooling towers pressure vessels recirculator packages thermal ice coils and water treatment systems. Evapco's products are used by customers engaged in food and beverage and industrial processing. It has sales offices research and development centers and manufacturing facilities in the US Africa Asia/Pacific and Europe. Evapco is an employee-owned firm founded in 1976 by William Kahlert Wilson Bradley and John Luetkemeyer.

EVENFLO COMPANY INC.

225 Byers Rd.
Miamisburg OH 45342
Phone: 937-415-3300
Fax: 937-415-3112
Web: www.evenflo.com

CEO: Scott Weiss
CFO: Peter Banat
HR: Cherry Smith
FYE: December 31
Type: Private

Those having a baby say hello to Evenflo. Named for a nursing device patented in 1935 the longtime company offers hundreds of items for the well-equipped baby and tot including car seats strollers portable cribs bath items baby monitors and feeding and safety products under the names Evenflo ExerSaucer and Snugli among others. Its Web site offers parenting resources with safety recalls and child care information. Evenflo has international sales operations in Canada Mexico and the Philippines. The firm sells its products through specialty retailers and big box stores such as Target and Wal-Mart. Evenflo is owned by an affiliate of private equity firm Weston Presidio.

EVENT NETWORK INC.

9606 AERO DR STE 1000
SAN DIEGO, CA 921231869
Phone: 858-488-7507
Fax: –
Web: www.eventnetwork.com

CEO: –
CFO: Jerry Gilbert
HR: Meredith Demartino
FYE: September 27
Type: Private

Event Network would like you to exit through the gift shop. The company (doing business as e|n) manages the retail gift shops on behalf of museums zoos aquariums gardens and other public cultural attractions. It designs and supplies stores with distinctive merchandise such as apparel toys and games coffee mugs key chains jewelry books and art. e|n's partner network includes more than 70 cultural attractions including the American Museum of Natural History in New York City the Gettysburg National Battlefield Museum the Philadelphia Zoo and the Shedd Aquarium in Chicago. It also operates the e-commerce websites of more than 55 attractions. e|n was founded in 1998 by Larry Gilbert and Helen Sherman.

	Annual Growth	09/05	09/06	09/07	09/08	09/09
Sales ($ mil.)	(55.9%)	–	–	547.6	92.5	106.7
Net income ($ mil.)	41113.7%	–	–	0.0	2.8	5.6
Market value ($ mil.)	–	–	–	–	–	–
Employees	–	–	–	–	–	900

EVERBANK FINANCIAL CORP NYS: EVER

501 Riverside Ave.
Jacksonville, FL 32202
Phone: 904 281-6000
Fax: –
Web: www.everbank.com

CEO: Robert M. Clements
CFO: Steven J. Fischer
HR: Scott Romick
FYE: December 31
Type: Public

EverBank Financial and its subsidiaries provide a range of financial services including banking investment services lending commercial financing and mortgage servicing. Its EverBank subsidiary offers community banking from more than a dozen branches in Florida. The bank's wholesale lending division provides loan products to mortgage brokers nationwide while its Everhome Mortgage subsidiary services a nearly $60 billion home loan portfolio. EverBank Direct provides online banking and brokerage. EverBank's Advisor Services arm allows financial planners and investment professionals to offer banking services to their clients. EverBank Financial also has units devoted to wealth management and commercial finance.

	Annual Growth	12/10	12/11	12/12	12/13	12/14
Sales ($ mil.)	2.5%	970.3	821.3	1,025.3	1,255.1	1,071.0
Net income ($ mil.)	(5.9%)	188.9	52.7	74.0	136.7	148.1
Market value ($ mil.)	13.1%	–	–	1,844.1	2,268.3	2,357.3
Employees	8.9%	–	2,400	3,700	4,000	3,100

EVERCORE PARTNERS INC
NYS: EVR

55 East 52nd Street, 38th Floor
New York, NY 10055
Phone: 212 857-3100
Fax: 212 857-3101
Web: www.evercore.com

CEO: Ralph L. Schlosstein
CFO: Robert B. Walsh
HR: –
FYE: December 31
Type: Public

Evercore Partners makes Investment Banking advisory its core business. It provides advisory services on mergers and acquisitions restructurings divestitures and financing to corporate clients. Boasting some $14 billion in assets under management the firm's investment management business principally manages and invests capital for clients including institutional investors such as corporate and public pension funds endowments insurance companies and high net-worth individuals. Evercore also makes private equity investments. Beyond the US the company operates globally through subsidiaries such as Protego in Mexico and Evercore Europe in London. Evercore also has offices in Brazil Hong Kong and Singapore.

	Annual Growth	12/10	12/11	12/12	12/13	12/14
Sales ($ mil.)	24.7%	378.9	524.3	642.4	765.4	915.9
Net income ($ mil.)	76.5%	9.0	7.0	28.9	53.3	86.9
Market value ($ mil.)	11.4%	1,232.7	965.1	1,094.5	2,167.3	1,898.7
Employees	20.8%	610	800	900	1,000	1,300

EVERGREEN FS INC

402 N HERSHEY RD
BLOOMINGTON, IL 61704-3546
Phone: 309-663-2392
Fax: –
Web: www.home.evergreen-fs.com

CEO: –
CFO: –
HR: –
FYE: August 31
Type: Private

Evergreen FS is an agricultural cooperative serving the needs of northern Illinois farmers. The co-op provides a full range of farm supplies and services including agronomy feed seed fertilizer fuel financing and marketing advice and products. It also operates six grain elevators. The co-op's 13000 member/owners operate farmland in the counties of McLean Woodford and Livingston. Evergreen FS is a member of the GROWMARK system.

	Annual Growth	08/06	08/07	08/09	08/10	08/11
Sales ($ mil.)	10.7%	–	204.9	0.0	246.7	307.9
Net income ($ mil.)	28.4%	–	3.8	0.0	7.8	10.4
Market value ($ mil.)	–	–	–	–	–	–
Employees	–	–	–	–	–	240

EVERGREEN STATE COLLEGE

2700 EVERGREEN PKWY NW
OLYMPIA, WA 985050005
Phone: 360-867-6000
Fax: –
Web: www.evergreen.edu

CEO: –
CFO: –
HR: –
FYE: June 30
Type: Private

Puget Sounders can earn their sheepskins at The Evergreen State College. The public liberal arts and sciences college the largest of its type in Washington state offers a variety of undergraduate degrees as well as graduate-level programs in environmental studies public administration and education. Evergreen is known for its unusual approach to learning; students enroll in comprehensive programs rather than a series of separate classes and courses are taught by teams of two to four professors. Students then receive "narrative" evaluations rather than traditional letter grades. Tuition per year is $5133 (residents) and $16440 (non-residents).

	Annual Growth	06/04	06/05	06/06	06/07	06/08
Sales ($ mil.)	–	–	–	0.0	56.5	56.7
Net income ($ mil.)	–	–	–	0.0	6.6	20.8
Market value ($ mil.)	–	–	–	–	–	–
Employees	–	–	–	–	–	580

EVERI HOLDINGS INC
NYS: EVRI

7250 S. Tenaya Way, Suite 100
Las Vegas, NV 89113
Phone: 800 833-7110
Fax: –
Web: www.gcainc.com

CEO: Ram V. Chary
CFO: Randy L. Taylor
HR: Pamela Picard
FYE: December 31
Type: Public

If you're losing your shirt at the casino tables Global Cash Access can get you more money on the spot. The company provides such services as ATM cash withdrawals credit- and debit-card advances and check guarantee to the gaming industry in the US Canada Europe Central America the Caribbean and Asia. The company provides services to some 1000 casinos such as Foxwoods Resort Casino. Global Cash Access also has developed cashless gaming systems including special ticket vouchers and systems that allow players to access funds without leaving their gaming machines. Other services include casino marketing and patron credit information through its QuikReports and CentralCredit database.

	Annual Growth	12/10	12/11	12/12	12/13	12/14
Sales ($ mil.)	(0.5%)	605.6	544.1	584.5	582.4	593.1
Net income ($ mil.)	(8.7%)	17.5	9.1	25.7	24.4	12.1
Market value ($ mil.)	22.4%	209.2	291.9	514.2	655.2	469.0
Employees	21.1%	419	416	435	427	900

EVERSOURCE ENERGY
NYS: ES

300 Cadwell Drive
Springfield, MA 01104
Phone: 413 785-5871
Fax: –
Web: www.eversource.com

CEO: Thomas J. (Tom) May
CFO: James J. (Jim) Judge
HR: –
FYE: December 31
Type: Public

Eversource Energy (formerly Northeast Utilities) uses Yankee ingenuity power and gas to keep customers happy. The largest utility in New England Eversource operates six electric and gas utilities in Connecticut Massachusetts and New Hampshire and serves more than 3.6 million electric and gas customers. It has 3880 miles of power transmission lines 48486 miles electric distribution lines and 6400 miles of gas distribution lines. Subsidiaries include Connecticut Light and Power Public Service Company of New Hampshire and Western Massachusetts Electric. Eversource's Yankee Gas supplies natural gas to 220000 customers in 71 cities and towns in Connecticut.

	Annual Growth	12/10	12/11	12/12	12/13	12/14
Sales ($ mil.)	12.1%	4,898.2	4,465.7	6,273.8	7,301.2	7,741.9
Net income ($ mil.)	20.6%	387.9	394.7	525.9	786.0	819.5
Market value ($ mil.)	13.8%	10,105.4	11,433.6	12,387.7	13,436.9	16,964.9
Employees	7.5%	6,182	6,063	8,842	8,697	8,248

EVINE LIVE INC
NMS: EVLV

6740 Shady Oak Road
Eden Prairie, MN 55344-3433
Phone: 952 943-6000
Fax: –
Web: www.valuevisionmedia.com

CEO: Robert (Bob) Rosenblatt
CFO: Tim A. Peterman
HR: –
FYE: January 31
Type: Public

Shopaholic insomniacs tune to EVINE Live's 24-hour at-home shopping channel. Its ShopHQ unit which trails industry leaders QVC and HSN sells jewelry and watches (about 40% of sales) home goods and electronics beauty and fitness products and apparel and accessories. The shopping network (formerly named ValueVision Media) reaches more than 87 million homes nationwide via cable and satellite TV. Programming is also streamed live across the Internet and on various mobile devices as well as through social networking sites. Typical viewers are women between the ages of 40 and 69 with household incomes that exceed $70000. E-commerce arm ShopHQ accounts for a growing portion of the company's sales.

	Annual Growth	01/11	01/12*	02/13	02/14*	01/15
Sales ($ mil.)	4.7%	562.3	558.4	586.8	640.5	674.6
Net income ($ mil.)	–	(25.9)	(48.1)	(27.7)	(2.5)	(1.4)
Market value ($ mil.)	(0.7%)	364.1	86.9	156.9	348.3	353.9
Employees	9.5%	905	920	1,000	1,100	1,300

*Fiscal year change

EVITE LLC

8833 Sunset Blvd.
West Hollywood CA 90069
Phone: 310-360-4500
Fax: 215-706-5388
Web: www.nutrisystem.com

CEO: –
CFO: –
HR: –
FYE: December 31
Type: Subsidiary

An invite from Evite gets you in with the cyber in-crowd. The company offers registered users online tools for planning parties activities and other social events both private and public. Services include e-mail invitations calendars photo sharing and address books. Customized Web invitations allow guests to RSVP post comments view the names of other invitees and get additional information (such as a map to the event or items to bring). Revenues primarily come from advertising and sponsorships. The company was launched in 1998 by Adam Lieb and Selina Tobaccowala. Today it is part of John Malone's Internet retail firm Liberty Interactive.

EVOLUTION PETROLEUM CORP   ASE: EPM

2500 City West Blvd., Suite 1300
Houston, TX 77042
Phone: 713 935-0122
Fax: 713 935-0199
Web: www.evolutionpetroleum.com

CEO: Robert S. Herlin
CFO: Randall D. Keys
HR: –
FYE: June 30
Type: Public

Just as petroleum and natural gas evolves from old living forms Evolution Petroleum has evolved by exploring for and producing those ancient hydrocarbons. The company operates oil and gas producing fields in Louisiana Oklahoma and Texas. Its strategy is to acquire already-established properties and redevelop them making the fields more profitable. One method it uses is gas flooding which uses carbon dioxide to free up trapped oil deposits. In 2013 it reported 13.8 million barrels of proved reserves. Its assets include a CO2-project in Louisiana's Delhi Field and a patented artificial lift technology designed to extend the life and ultimate recoveries of wells with oil or associated water production.

	Annual Growth	06/11	06/12	06/13	06/14	06/15
Sales ($ mil.)	38.7%	7.5	18.0	21.3	17.7	27.8
Net income ($ mil.)	–	(0.2)	5.1	6.6	3.6	5.0
Market value ($ mil.)	(1.9%)	233.2	273.9	358.3	359.7	216.4
Employees	(2.4%)	11	10	11	8	10

EVOLVING SYSTEMS, INC.   NAS: EVOL

9777 Pyramid Court, Suite 100
Englewood, CO 80112
Phone: 303 802-1000
Fax: 303 802-1420
Web: www.evolving.com

CEO: Thomas Thekkethala
CFO: Daniel J. (Dan) Moorhead
HR: –
FYE: December 31
Type: Public

Evolving Systems offers software for the ever-evolving telecommunications industry. The company provides applications used by telecom companies to automate and manage parts of their network operations including tools applications that allow users to route calls and messages to various devices. The company also provides local number portability software that allows telephone customers to keep the same phone number when changing to a new carrier. Evolving Systems has expanded its international operations in Africa Asia and Central America and added products for managing SIM cards. The company agreed to sell its number management and monitoring assets to NeuStar in 2011 for $39 million.

	Annual Growth	12/10	12/11	12/12	12/13	12/14
Sales ($ mil.)	(5.6%)	37.3	19.0	26.2	25.1	29.7
Net income ($ mil.)	1.2%	5.4	32.3	5.6	3.8	5.6
Market value ($ mil.)	3.0%	97.1	86.9	69.5	113.6	109.3
Employees	(6.0%)	248	140	160	176	194

EVONIK CORPORATION

299 Jefferson Rd.
Parsippany NJ 07054
Phone: 973-541-8000
Fax: 973-541-8013
Web: north-america.evonik.com

CEO: –
CFO: Burkhard Zoller
HR: –
FYE: December 31
Type: Subsidiary

Evonik Corporation (formerly Evonik Degussa Corp.) is the North American arm of German chemical giant Evonik Degussa GmbH. Like its parent it operates through six divisions the biggest of which are Industrial Chemicals (chlorides and peroxides) and Inorganic Materials (silicon products and carbon black). The other units are Consumer Specialties Health and Nutrition Coatings and Additives and Performance Polymers. Products range from amino acids and building protection coatings to another of its specialties specialty acrylic products including its best known brand Plexiglas. In addition to the automotive industry Evonik serves makers of coatings pharmaceuticals and plastics.

EWING IRRIGATION PRODUCTS INC.

3441 E HARBOUR DR
PHOENIX, AZ 850340908
Phone: 602-437-9530
Fax: –
Web: www.ewing1.com

CEO: –
CFO: –
HR: –
FYE: June 29
Type: Private

You can thank Ewing Irrigation Products for that lush verdant golf course you occasionally call home. The company wholesales more than 13000 types of irrigation products for water management/conservation and erosion control for commercial and residential yards golf courses landscaping hardscape and turf maintenance. Ewing serves customers in the aquaculture food processing industrial process piping plumbing pool/spa construction and water treatment sectors. The family owned company also supplies water features landscape lighting and pumps.

	Annual Growth	06/07	06/08	06/09	06/10	06/12
Sales ($ mil.)	0.7%	–	306.7	278.9	260.8	315.8
Net income ($ mil.)	(3.5%)	–	–	11.2	0.0	10.1
Market value ($ mil.)	–	–	–	–	–	–
Employees	–	–	–	–	–	850

EXA CORP   NMS: EXA

55 Network Drive
Burlington, MA 01803
Phone: 781 564-0200
Fax: –
Web: www.exa.com

CEO: Stephen A Remondi
CFO: Richard F Gilbody
HR: –
FYE: January 31
Type: Public

Exa Corporation strives to be irresistible to its customers. A developer of engineering software for vehicle manufacturers Exa makes digital simulation software used by engineers to enhance the performance of automobiles trucks trains and off-road equipment. Its core product PowerFLOW can simulate structural and heating/cooling system fluid flow problems in vehicles namely aerodynamics thermal management and aeroacoustics. (Aeroacoustics is the generation and transfer of sound by fluid flow.) The company sells PowerFLOW and related products in Japan the US and Europe through its direct sales force; it also sells in China and India through distributors. Exa went public in a 2012 IPO.

	Annual Growth	01/11	01/12	01/13	01/14	01/15
Sales ($ mil.)	12.8%	37.9	45.9	48.9	54.5	61.4
Net income ($ mil.)	–	0.4	14.5	0.8	(0.7)	(19.2)
Market value ($ mil.)	0.7%	–	–	138.6	194.9	140.5
Employees	13.4%	–	203	239	257	296

EXACT SCIENCES CORP.

NAS: EXAS

441 Charmany Drive
Madison, WI 53719
Phone: 608 284-5700
Fax: –
Web: www.exactsciences.com

CEO: Kevin T. Conroy
CFO: John K. Bakewell
HR: –
FYE: December 31
Type: Public

Guesstimates aren't good enough when diagnosing a deadly cancer so Exact Sciences aims for accuracy. The firm develops non-invasive tests for the early detection of colorectal cancer and precancerous lesions. Its Cologuard test isolates DNA in stool samples then identifies genetic mutations associated with cancer. Colorectal cancer is a common (and one of the deadliest) cancers and Exact believes its method is superior to existing diagnostic methods because it may be able to discern colorectal cancer in its early stages when it is most treatable. The company received FDA approval for Cologuard in mid-2014.

	Annual Growth	12/10	12/11	12/12	12/13	12/14
Sales ($ mil.)	(23.8%)	5.3	4.2	4.1	4.1	1.8
Net income ($ mil.)	–	(11.6)	(28.7)	(52.4)	(46.5)	(100.0)
Market value ($ mil.)	46.4%	530.0	719.6	938.5	1,041.4	2,431.9
Employees	61.1%	35	61	87	102	236

EXACT SOFTWARE NORTH AMERICA INC.

35 Village Rd.
Middleton MA 01949
Phone: 978-560-6900
Fax: 978-560-6901
Web: www.exactamerica.com

CEO: –
CFO: –
HR: –
FYE: December 31
Type: Subsidiary

Exact Software North America wants to give North American customers an exact view of their operations and clients. The company which was called Macola before its acquisition by Dutch software maker Exact Holding provides small to medium-sized businesses with enterprise resource planning (ERP) customer relationship management (CRM) and related software. These applications help companies track and manage their interactions with customers — even when both supplier and customer have widely scattered operations — as well as the interactions between various parts of their own operations.

EXACTECH, INC.

NMS: EXAC

2320 NW 66th Court
Gainesville, FL 32653
Phone: 352 377-1141
Fax: 352 378-2617
Web: www.exac.com

CEO: David W. Petty
CFO: Joel C. (Jody) Phillips
HR: Jody Swanson
FYE: December 31
Type: Public

Exactech has joint replacement technologies down to an exact science. Health professionals worldwide use the company's orthopedic devices to replace joints weakened by injury or disease. Its Optetrak knee implants Equinoxe shoulder systems and Novation hip implants either partially or totally replace patients' damaged joints. It also markets Opteform and Optefil bone allograft materials used to correct bone defects and damage. Exactech markets its products through direct sales representatives and independent dealers in the US as well as through affiliated and independent distributors in about 35 other countries. Customers include hospitals clinics surgeons and physicians.

	Annual Growth	12/10	12/11	12/12	12/13	12/14
Sales ($ mil.)	6.9%	190.5	205.4	224.3	237.1	248.4
Net income ($ mil.)	12.0%	10.5	8.8	12.7	15.4	16.5
Market value ($ mil.)	5.8%	261.4	228.8	235.4	330.0	327.4
Employees	3.8%	553	574	590	608	642

EXAMWORKS GROUP INC

NYS: EXAM

3280 Peachtree Road, N.E., Suite 2625
Atlanta, GA 30305
Phone: 404 952-2400
Fax: –
Web: www.examworks.com

CEO: James K. (Jim) Price
CFO: J. Miguel Fernandez de Castro
HR: –
FYE: December 31
Type: Public

ExamWorks Group examines whether people should qualify for certain types of insurance. Through subsidiary ExamWorks Inc. the holding company is a leading North American provider of independent medical examinations (IMEs). IMEs are physical exams conducted by independently contracted physicians to verify illness and injury claims for individuals seeking workers' compensation automotive and personal injury liability and disability insurance coverage. Its network consists of thousands of doctors and medical providers. ExamWorks also offers medical record and medical bill reviews. Clients include insurance companies and law firms in the US and abroad.

	Annual Growth	12/10	12/11	12/12	12/13	12/14
Sales ($ mil.)	47.6%	163.5	397.9	521.2	616.0	775.6
Net income ($ mil.)	–	(6.0)	(8.3)	(14.9)	(10.2)	10.5
Market value ($ mil.)	22.5%	746.1	382.7	564.8	1,205.9	1,679.0
Employees	17.2%	1,485	1,880	2,100	2,400	2,800

EXAR CORP.

NYS: EXAR

48720 Kato Road
Fremont, CA 94538
Phone: 510 668-7000
Fax: –
Web: www.exar.com

CEO: Richard L. Leza
CFO: Ronald W Guire
HR: Jan Henry
FYE: March 29
Type: Public

Exar seeks excellence in the exacting world of integrated circuits. The fabless semiconductor company's digital analog and mixed-signal integrated circuits (ICs) are used in networking equipment — especially telecom infrastructure gear — as well as in video and imaging devices such as handheld electronics set-top boxes and DVRs. It also makes ICs and subsystems for the power management and datacom and storage markets including storage optimization and network security processors. Customers include Alcatel Lucent EMC Huawei Teradata and ZTE. The company gets about 85% of its sales outside the US.

	Annual Growth	03/11*	04/12*	03/13	03/14	03/15
Sales ($ mil.)	2.6%	146.0	130.6	122.0	125.3	162.1
Net income ($ mil.)	–	(35.7)	(28.8)	2.9	5.8	(45.0)
Market value ($ mil.)	14.1%	290.3	401.1	501.3	559.1	491.8
Employees	(9.0%)	477	304	291	312	327

*Fiscal year change

EXCEL TRUST INC.

NYS: EXL

Excel Centre, 17140 Bernardo Center Drive, Suite 300
San Diego, CA 92128
Phone: 858 613-1800
Fax: –
Web: www.exceltrust.com

CEO: –
CFO: –
HR: –
FYE: December 31
Type: Public

Excel Trust likes to buy retail space off the clearance rack. Based in San Diego the self-managed self-administered real estate investment trust (REIT) has a penchant for acquiring high-value retail properties at a reduced cost — including value-oriented community and "power" shopping centers grocery anchored neighborhood centers and freestanding retail properties — located in California Arizona Texas and about a dozen other states. Excel owns about 35 retail and office properties totaling more than 5.8 million sq. ft. of leasable space. Tenants include chain stores Bed Bath & Beyond and PetSmart among many others and health care systems operator Kaiser Permanente.

	Annual Growth	04/10*	12/10	12/11	12/12	12/13
Sales ($ mil.)	315.6%	1.6	15.9	55.2	87.1	112.5
Net income ($ mil.)	–	(0.1)	(3.7)	0.4	1.9	19.5
Market value ($ mil.)	(4.3%)	629.0	585.4	580.6	613.0	551.1
Employees	29.3%	–	31	38	45	67

*Fiscal year change

EXCELLUS HEALTH PLAN INC.

165 Court St.
Rochester NY 14647
Phone: 585-454-1700
Fax: 585-238-4233
Web: www.excellusbcbs.com

CEO: David H Klein
CFO: Emil D Duda
HR: –
FYE: December 31
Type: Subsidiary

Excellus Health Plan better known as Excellus BlueCross BlueShield aims to excel as a provider of health insurance plans. The insurance firm serves some 1.8 million members in more than 30 counties in upstate New York. Its offerings include HMO PPO managed care and low-cost health plans for individuals families and businesses large and small as well as Medicare and supplemental dental plans. Excellus BlueCross BlueShield operates through four regional divisions: Central New York Central New York Southern Tier Rochester and Utica. The company is a subsidiary of the not-for-profit organization The Lifetime Healthcare Companies and is a licensee of the Blue Cross and Blue Shield Association.

EXCHANGE BANK

545 4th St.
Santa Rosa CA 95401
Phone: 707-524-3000
Fax: 707-579-4745
Web: www.exchangebank.com

OTC: EXSR

CEO: Gary T Hartwick
CFO: Greg Jahn
HR: –
FYE: December 31
Type: Public

Exchange Bank serves personal and business customers from some 20 branch offices throughout Sonoma County California. It also has a branch in nearby Placer County. The bank provides standard products including checking and savings accounts Visa credit cards online banking and a variety of real estate business and consumer loans. It also offers investment services such as wealth management personal trust administration employee benefits plans and individual retirement accounts. Exchange Bank has had just seven presidents since its inception in 1890. The Doyle Trust which was established by co-founder Frank Doyle owns a majority of the bank.

EXCO RESOURCES INC.

12377 Merit Drive, Suite 1700, LB 82
Dallas, TX 75251
Phone: 214 368-2084
Fax: –
Web: www.excoresources.com

NYS: XCO

CEO: Harold L Hickey
CFO: Mark F Mulhern
HR: –
FYE: December 31
Type: Public

EXCO Resources puts extra effort into oil and gas exploration and production operations in Colorado Ohio Oklahoma Louisiana Pennsylvania Texas and West Virginia. In 2012 the oil and gas explorer reported proved reserves of 1 trillion cu. ft. of natural gas equivalent. EXCO produced 189.9 billion cubic feet of natural gas equivalent that year. The company pursuing a strategy of growth through the drill bit coupled with selective acquisitions. It is looking to shape its future growth by focusing on developing its shale plays (such as Eagle Ford Haynesville and Marcellus increasingly accessible thanks to new drilling technologies). It also has minority stakes in midstream joint ventures.

	Annual Growth	12/10	12/11	12/12	12/13	12/14
Sales ($ mil.)	6.4%	515.2	754.2	546.6	634.3	660.3
Net income ($ mil.)	(34.9%)	671.9	22.6	(1,393.3)	22.2	120.7
Market value ($ mil.)	(42.2%)	5,316.7	2,860.9	1,853.4	1,453.7	594.1
Employees	(11.9%)	927	1,093	919	755	558

EXEL INC.

570 Polaris Pkwy.
Westerville OH 43082
Phone: 614-865-8500
Fax: 614-865-8875
Web: www.exel.com

CEO: Scott Sureddin
CFO: Scot Hofacker
HR: –
FYE: December 31
Type: Subsidiary

For Exel the goal is to excel at supply chain management. The company arranges for its customers' freight to be hauled in truckload and less-than-truckload (LTL) quantities; in addition it oversees intermodal freight transportation involving the use of both trucks and trains. Exel provides services such as international freight forwarding warehousing supply chain analysis and management in-plant services assembly and packaging and transportation management. It is part of the Supply Chain business unit of DHL the global express delivery and logistics giant. DHL itself is a subsidiary of Germany's Deutsche Post. Exel has about 440 sites in the US and Canada totaling 86 million sq. ft. of warehousing.

EXELIS INC.

1650 Tysons Boulevard, Suite 1700
McLean, VA 22102
Phone: 703 790-6300
Fax: –
Web: www.exelisinc.com

NYS: XLS

CEO: –
CFO: –
HR: –
FYE: December 31
Type: Public

Exelis excels when it comes to high-tech modern weaponry. The company manufactures products for integrated electronic warfare sensing and surveillance air traffic management information and cyber security and networked communications. It also focuses on composite aerostructures logistics and technical services. Exelis generates most of its business from the US government particularly the Department of Defense (about 60% of sales) the FAA and NASA. The company also serves commercial clients with international customers comprising about 10% of sales. Formerly the defense and information solutions unit of ITT Corp. Exelis was spun off in 2011 as a publicly-traded company.

	Annual Growth	12/09	12/10	12/11	12/12	12/13
Sales ($ mil.)	(5.6%)	6,061.0	5,891.0	5,839.0	5,522.0	4,816.0
Net income ($ mil.)	(12.0%)	469.0	587.0	326.0	330.0	281.0
Market value ($ mil.)	45.1%	–	–	1,714.1	2,134.5	3,610.0
Employees	(5.5%)	–	20,400	20,500	19,900	17,200

EXELIXIS INC

210 East Grand Ave.
South San Francisco, CA 94080
Phone: 650 837-7000
Fax: –
Web: www.exelixis.com

NMS: EXEL

CEO: Michael M. Morrissey
CFO: Christopher J. (Chris) Senner
HR: –
FYE: December 31
Type: Public

We've come a long way baby but we still have a lot in common with the fruit fly. Exelixis a pharmaceutical research and development firm got its start analyzing genetic data from fruit flies and other organisms as a means to speed the development of drugs and other products. Its early genomic work has yielded a pipeline of drug candidates primarily in the area of cancer therapies as well as some potential treatments for metabolic and cardiovascular diseases. Lead candidate Cometriq gained FDA approval for treatment of thyroid cancer in late 2012 and was launched in the US in early 2013. Exelixis takes its name from the Greek word for evolution.

	Annual Growth	12/10	12/11	12/12	12/13	12/14
Sales ($ mil.)	(39.3%)	185.0	289.6	47.5	31.3	25.1
Net income ($ mil.)	–	(92.3)	75.7	(147.6)	(244.8)	(268.5)
Market value ($ mil.)	(35.3%)	1,608.3	927.6	895.2	1,200.8	282.1
Employees	(28.9%)	383	200	174	227	98

EXELON CORP.

NYS: EXC

10 South Dearborn Street, P.O. Box 805379
Chicago, IL 60680-5379
Phone: 800 483-3220
Fax: –
Web: www.exeloncorp.com

CEO: Christopher M. (Chris) Crane
CFO: Jonathan W. (Jack) Thayer
HR: –
FYE: December 31
Type: Public

The City of Brotherly Love meets the Windy City and The Greatest City in America in utility and power generating holding company Exelon. It distributes electricity and gas to 7.8 million customers in Illinois Maryland and Pennsylvania through subsidiaries Baltimore Gas and Electric Commonwealth Edison and PECO Energy. Exelon Generation holds power assets of 32265 MW (19316 MW of which is nuclear). Exelon Power Team is a top wholesale energy marketer and Exelon Energy markets retail power and offers other energy-related services. The company's Constellation unit serves 2.5 million retail customers. In a major expansion in 2014 Exelon agreed to buy Pepco for $6.8 billion.

	Annual Growth	12/11	12/12	12/13	12/14	12/15
Sales ($ mil.)	11.7%	18,924.0	23,489.0	24,888.0	27,429.0	29,447.0
Net income ($ mil.)	(2.6%)	2,495.0	1,171.0	1,729.0	1,820.0	2,250.0
Market value ($ mil.)	(10.5%)	39,897.1	27,358.6	25,196.7	34,110.8	25,546.3
Employees	11.5%	19,267	26,057	25,829	28,993	29,762

EXELON ENERGY COMPANY

300 Exelon Way
Kennett Square PA 19348
Phone: 440-449-1000
Fax: 508-862-7919
Web: www.capecodhealth.org

CEO: –
CFO: –
HR: –
FYE: December 31
Type: Subsidiary

You cannot accuse Exelon Energy of lacking energy — it has access to major supplies of both electric power and natural gas. The retail marketing subsidiary of Exelon 's Exelon Generation unit is an unregulated supplier of natural gas and electricity to commercial and industrial users. Exelon Energy markets electricity to customers in Illinois and Pennsylvania and natural gas to customers in Illinois Michigan and Ohio. It has more than 9500 electricity accounts in Illinois and about 11000 natural gas accounts in Illinois Michigan Ohio and Pennsylvania. The company works closely with Exelon's wholesale marketing unit Exelon Power Team to secure the best power prices for their customers.

EXELON GENERATION CO LLC

300 Exelon Way
Kennett Square, PA 19348-2473
Phone: 610 765-5959
Fax: –
Web: www.exeloncorp.com

CEO: Christopher M Crane
CFO: –
HR: –
FYE: December 31
Type: Public

Exelon Generation Company has built an excellent reputation by generating electricity. The company a subsidiary of Exelon Corporation is one of the largest electric wholesale and retail power generation companies in the US. In 2013 Exelon Generation had a generation capacity of more than 44560 MW (primarily nuclear but also fossil-fired and hydroelectric and other renewable energy-based plants). Subsidiary Exelon Nuclear operates the largest fleet of nuclear power plants in the US. Exelon Generation's Exelon Power unit oversees a fleet of more than 100 fossil- and renewable-fueled plants (more than 15875 MW of capacity) in Illinois Maryland Massachusetts Pennsylvania and Texas.

	Annual Growth	12/10	12/11	12/12	12/13	12/14
Sales ($ mil.)	14.8%	10,025.0	10,308.0	14,437.0	15,630.0	17,393.0
Net income ($ mil.)	(19.3%)	1,972.0	1,771.0	562.0	1,070.0	835.0
Market value ($ mil.)	–	–	–	–	–	–
Employees	10.6%	9,595	9,586	12,116	11,973	14,370

EXIDE TECHNOLOGIES

NBB: XIDE Q

13000 Deerfield Parkway, Building 200
Milton, GA 30004
Phone: 678 566-9000
Fax: 678 566-9188
Web: www.exide.com

CEO: Victor M. (Vic) Koelsch
CFO: Anthony L. (Tony) Genito
HR: Leslie W. Joyce
FYE: March 31
Type: Public

Exide Technologies hopes you'll get a charge out of its products. The company makes and recycles automotive and industrial batteries for retailers and transportation manufacturers. It also makes batteries for boats farm equipment golf carts hybrid vehicles and wheelchairs. Industrial applications include computer locomotive power plant and telecommunications systems. Centra DETA Exide NASCAR Select Absolyte and Sonnenschein make up some of the company's brand names. Operations outside the US account for about 60% of sales. In mid-2013 Exide voluntarily filed for Chapter 11 bankruptcy protection and emerged in mid-2015 as a private company.

	Annual Growth	03/10	03/11	03/12	03/13	03/14
Sales ($ mil.)	1.5%	2,685.8	2,887.5	3,084.7	2,971.7	2,855.4
Net income ($ mil.)	–	–	(11.8)	26.4	56.7	(223.4)	(217.8)
Market value ($ mil.)	(55.3%)	455.5	883.4	247.5	213.5	18.2
Employees	(3.5%)	10,349	10,027	9,988	9,628	8,986

EXLSERVICE HOLDINGS INC

NMS: EXLS

280 Park Avenue, 38th Floor
New York, NY 10017
Phone: 212 277-7100
Fax: –
Web: www.exlservice.com

CEO: Rohit Kapoor
CFO: Vishal Chhibbar
HR: Aabha Nanda
FYE: December 31
Type: Public

Have an extra-large task you'd rather not take on? Outsource it to ExlService Holdings. The company known as EXL offers business process outsourcing (BPO) research and analytics and consulting services. EXL's BPO offerings which generate most of its sales include claims processing collections customer support and finance and accounting. Customers come mainly from the banking financial services and insurance industries as well as from the utilities and telecommunications sectors. EXL operates offices around the world including the US and countries in Eastern Europe and Asia. The company was established in 1999.

	Annual Growth	12/10	12/11	12/12	12/13	12/14
Sales ($ mil.)	18.6%	252.8	360.5	442.9	478.5	499.3
Net income ($ mil.)	5.1%	26.6	34.8	41.8	48.1	32.4
Market value ($ mil.)	7.5%	706.8	736.1	872.0	908.8	944.7
Employees	15.8%	12,700	18,900	21,000	22,200	22,800

EXONE CO. (THE)

NMS: XONE

127 Industry Boulevard
North Huntingdon, PA 15642
Phone: 724 863-9663
Fax: –
Web: www.exone.com

CEO: S Kent Rockwell
CFO: Brian W Smith
HR: –
FYE: December 31
Type: Public

ExOne wants to be THE one when it comes to non-traditional manufacturing. The company "prints" three-dimensional (3D) parts and materials — literally creating a prototype or part quickly from a computer model by laying down successive layers of material to form the part. It prints in silica sand ceramic stainless steel bronze and glass. ExOne also sells 3D printing machines and makes casting molds from silica sand and ceramics from five production centers in the US Germany and Japan. The company's key customers Ford BMW Boeing Caterpillar and the KSB Group operate primarily in the aerospace automotive heavy equipment and oil and gas industries. It formed in 2005 and went public in 2013.

	Annual Growth	12/10	12/11	12/12	12/13	12/14
Sales ($ mil.)	34.4%	13.4	15.3	28.7	39.5	43.9
Net income ($ mil.)	–	(5.5)	(8.0)	(10.2)	(6.5)	(21.8)
Market value ($ mil.)	(72.2%)	–	–	–	871.7	242.2
Employees	25.2%	–	155	163	229	304

EXOPACK LLC

2800 W. Higgins Rd. Ste. 435
Hoffman Estates IL 60169
Phone: 847-885-8884
Fax: 847-885-8886
Web: www.exopack.com

CEO: –
CFO: –
HR: –
FYE: December 31
Type: Private

Rover loves Exopack. His dog food often shows up in one of its bags. Exopack manufactures a slew of flexible packaging film and paper products for over 1300 customers that market pet food as well as consumer food and beverages and lawn and garden cement agricultural staples and more. Its core products are plastic films such as laminated rollstock converted plastics (standup pouches and edge seam bags) consumer paper for popcorn coffee and pet food bags and coated products for printing electronic medical or security uses. The company's facilities dot North America and the UK. Exopack and sister subsidiaries Cello-Foil and The Packaging Group are owned by an affiliate of Sun Capital.

EXPEDIA INC

333 108th Avenue N.E.
Bellevue, WA 98004
Phone: 425 679-7200
Fax: –
Web: www.expediainc.com

NMS: EXPE
CEO: Dara Khosrowshahi
CFO: Mark D. Okerstrom
HR: Connie Symes
FYE: December 31
Type: Public

These days expediting your vacation begins online. As the market leader in online travel services (ahead of rival Priceline) Expedia offers online trip-planning tools that allow users to book airline tickets hotel reservations car rentals cruises and vacation packages. Its portfolio of brands includes flagship Expedia.com accommodations manager Hotels.com travel discounter Hotwire travel booker Orbitz luxury package provider Classic Vacations and Chinese travel service eLong among others. Launched in 1996 the company serves travelers in North America Europe and the Asia/Pacific region. In late 2015 Expedia purchased vacation rental site operator HomeAway.

	Annual Growth	12/11	12/12	12/13	12/14	12/15
Sales ($ mil.)	17.9%	3,449.0	4,030.3	4,771.3	5,763.5	6,672.3
Net income ($ mil.)	12.8%	472.3	280.2	232.9	398.1	764.5
Market value ($ mil.)	43.9%	4,360.5	9,231.9	10,467.0	12,826.1	18,677.2
Employees	18.6%	9,480	12,330	14,570	18,210	18,730

EXPEDITORS INTERNATIONAL OF WASHINGTON, INC.

1015 Third Avenue, 12th Floor
Seattle, WA 98104
Phone: 206 674-3400
Fax: 206 674-3459
Web: www.expeditors.com

NMS: EXPD
CEO: Jeffrey S. Musser
CFO: Bradley S. (Brad) Powell
HR: –
FYE: December 31
Type: Public

Need your goods moved expeditiously? Freight forwarder Expeditors International of Washington can help. As a freight forwarder the company purchases air and ocean cargo space on a volume basis and resells that space to its customers at lower rates than they could obtain directly from the carriers. The company also acts as a customs broker for air and ocean freight shipped by its customers and offers supply chain management services. Customers include global businesses engaged in retailing/wholesaling electronics and manufacturing. Founder Peter Rose used $55000 in seed money to establish Expeditors International of Washington in 1979.

	Annual Growth	12/10	12/11	12/12	12/13	12/14
Sales ($ mil.)	2.4%	5,967.6	6,150.5	5,980.9	6,080.3	6,564.7
Net income ($ mil.)	2.3%	344.2	385.7	333.4	348.5	376.9
Market value ($ mil.)	(4.9%)	10,464.4	7,850.2	7,580.0	8,480.8	8,549.8
Employees	3.3%	12,880	13,590	13,700	13,910	14,670

EXPERIAN INFORMATION SOLUTIONS INC.

475 Anton Blvd.
Costa Mesa CA 92626
Phone: 714-830-7000
Fax: 714-830-2449
Web: www.experian.com

CEO: Chris Callero
CFO: –
HR: Heather Rubner
FYE: March 31
Type: Subsidiary

Experian Information Solutions also known as Experian Americas is the US-based arm of global credit reporting agency Experian plc. The unit provides credit reporting and lead generation services by tapping its database of more than 220 million US consumers and some 25 million US businesses. Clients include retailers financial services firms utilities not-for-profits and small businesses among others. The company also provides addresses for more than 20 billion pieces of promotional mail every year. Services include skip tracing and collections direct marketing sales prospecting demographic information and more. Experian Americas boasts about a dozen offices nationwide.

EXPERIENCE WORKS INC.

4401 WILSON BLVD STE 1100
ARLINGTON, VA 222034196
Phone: 703-522-7272
Fax: –
Web: www.experienceworks.org

CEO: –
CFO: –
HR: –
FYE: June 30
Type: Private

Experience Works makes experience pay. The not-for-profit organization helps low-income individuals 55 years of age and older find jobs. It provides training as well as community service and employment opportunities for more than 125000 mature workers in 30 states and Puerto Rico. The group offers annual local state and national awards computer and technology skills services targeted to local markets and Senior Community Service Employment Program funded by the Older Americans Act to help low-income seniors. Experience Works was created in 1965. The company was called Green Thumb before it was renamed in 2002.

	Annual Growth	06/08	06/09	06/10	06/11	06/13
Sales ($ mil.)	(44.3%)	–	1,105.3	166.2	181.0	106.4
Net income ($ mil.)	–	–	–	(1.9)	0.4	(0.3)
Market value ($ mil.)	–	–	–	–	–	–
Employees	–	–	–	–	–	400

EXPERT GLOBAL SOLUTIONS INC.

507 Prudential Rd.
Horsham PA 19044
Phone: 215-441-3000
Fax: 724-867-1614
Web: www.emclairefinancial.com

CEO: –
CFO: –
HR: –
FYE: December 31
Type: Private

Expert Global Solutions (formerly NCO Group) is a holding company engaged in an alphabet soup of businesses such as BPO ARM and CRM. Through subsidiary NCO it specializes in business process outsourcing (BPO) accounts-receivable management (ARM) and customer relationship management (CRM) in an effort to streamline the financial operational and customer service activities of its clients. NCO serves businesses worldwide in such industries as financial services health care technology transportation logistics telecommunications utilities government and education. NCO Group merged with APAC Customer Services in 2012 and the combined company was renamed Expert Global Solutions.

EXPONENT INC.

NMS: EXPO

149 Commonwealth Drive
Menlo Park, CA 94025
Phone: 650 326-9400
Fax: –
Web: www.exponent.com

CEO: Paul R. Johnston
CFO: Richard L. Schlenker
HR: –
FYE: January 02
Type: Public

A risky business is a potential customer for Exponent Inc. If Exponent doesn't get in to assess the risk it's there to figure out what failed. The science and engineering consulting firm specializes in analyzing and solving complex problems and preventing disasters and product failures. The company's cadre of scientists physicians engineers and business consultants assess environmental risks regulatory issues and workplace hazards for government agencies and clients from such industries as transportation construction and manufacturing. Established in 1967 its work has included analyzing such disasters as the Exxon Valdez oil spill and the bombing of the Murrah Federal Building in Oklahoma City.

	Annual Growth	12/10	12/11	12/12*	01/14	01/15
Sales ($ mil.)	4.1%	248.8	272.4	292.7	296.2	304.7
Net income ($ mil.)	8.1%	27.5	32.7	37.2	38.6	40.7
Market value ($ mil.)	16.7%	966.4	1,183.4	1,382.3	1,991.9	2,087.4
Employees	1.7%	901	937	960	984	981

*Fiscal year change

EXPONENTIAL INTERACTIVE INC.

2200 Powell St. Ste. 600
Emeryville CA 94608
Phone: 510-250-5500
Fax: 510-250-5700
Web: www.exponential.com

CEO: Dilip Dasilva
CFO: –
HR: –
FYE: December 31
Type: Private

Exponential Interactive envisions a world where all Internet advertisements will be specifically tailored to individual users. The company's proprietary eX Advertising Intelligence Platform is used by advertising agencies to process massive amounts (2 billion user events per day) of non-personal consumer data (what you click not who you are). Agencies use the data to create custom ad campaigns for relevant demographics. The company has partnered with almost 2000 advertisers such as Coca-Cola and McDonald's to develop ad campaigns for display video and mobile platforms. It also owns a handful of digital advertising services companies including Tribal Fusion. Exponential filed a $75 million IPO in March 2012.

EXPORT-IMPORT BANK OF THE UNITED STATES

811 Vermont Ave. NW
Washington DC 20571
Phone: 202-565-3946
Fax: 202-565-3210
Web: www.exim.gov

CEO: –
CFO: John F Simonson
HR: –
FYE: September 30
Type: Government Agency

Sure the US is running a huge trade deficit but don't blame the Export-Import Bank of the United States for not trying to stem the tide. The government agency (Ex-Im Bank for short) provides financing for the export of American goods and services mainly to developing countries and regions. Ex-Im Bank which assumes credit and country risks that private-sector lenders cannot or will not stomach furnishes US businesses (most of them with fewer than 100 employees) with operating credit and export credit insurance and provides loans and loan guarantees to foreign buyers of US goods. President Franklin D. Roosevelt established Ex-Im Bank as part of the New Deal in 1934.

EXPRESS SCRIPTS HOLDING CO

NMS: ESRX

One Express Way
St. Louis, MO 63121
Phone: 314 996-0900
Fax: –
Web: www.express-scripts.com

CEO: George Paz
CFO: Eric R. Slusser
HR: –
FYE: December 31
Type: Public

Express Scripts Holding knows that its customers like their medicine delivered quickly. The company administers more than a billion prescription drug benefits of tens of millions of health plan members in the US and Canada. Members have access to a network of about 69000 retail pharmacies as well as the company's own mail-order pharmacies. On behalf of its insurer clients Express Scripts processes claims for prescriptions designs drug benefit plans and offers such services as specialty drug delivery disease management programs and consumer drug data analysis. The firm merged with rival Medco Health Solutions in 2012 creating the largest pharmacy benefits management (PBM) company in North America.

	Annual Growth	12/11	12/12	12/13	12/14	12/15
Sales ($ mil.)	21.9%	46,128.3	93,858.1	104,098.8	100,887.1	101,751.8
Net income ($ mil.)	18.0%	1,275.8	1,312.9	1,844.6	2,007.6	2,476.4
Market value ($ mil.)	18.3%	30,250.7	36,552.6	47,545.5	57,313.1	59,167.8
Employees	18.5%	13,120	30,215	29,975	29,500	25,900

EXPRESS, INC.

NYS: EXPR

1 Express Drive
Columbus, OH 43230
Phone: 614 474-4001
Fax: –
Web: www.express.com

CEO: Michael A. Weiss
CFO: Perry Pericleous
HR: Michael C. Keane
FYE: January 31
Type: Public

Right from the runway is the Express way. Express operates nearly 640 stores throughout the US Canada and Puerto Rico that sell trendy private-label apparel and accessories targeted to men and women between the ages of 20 and 30. (The chain's fashions are styled to have an international influence and modern appeal.) The stores are located primarily in malls. Express also sells denim and lingerie and operates a growing online business. The chain's international footprint is growing through franchise agreements in the Middle East and Latin America. Launched by Limited Brands (later renamed L Brands) in 1980 Express was taken public in 2010 by the private equity firm Golden Gate Capital.

	Annual Growth	01/11	01/12*	02/13	02/14*	01/15
Sales ($ mil.)	3.2%	1,905.8	2,073.4	2,148.1	2,219.1	2,165.5
Net income ($ mil.)	(14.4%)	127.4	140.7	139.3	116.5	68.3
Market value ($ mil.)	(6.6%)	1,448.2	1,843.6	1,559.5	1,460.0	1,102.6
Employees	3.0%	16,000	18,000	17,000	19,000	18,000

*Fiscal year change

EXPRESSJET HOLDINGS INC.

700 N. Sam Houston Pkwy. West Ste. 200
Houston TX 77067
Phone: 832-353-1000
Fax: 832-353-1008
Web: www.expressjet.com

CEO: –
CFO: –
HR: Veronica Orso
FYE: December 31
Type: Subsidiary

ExpressJet Holdings' main subsidiary ExpressJet Airlines operates as a regional carrier through capacity purchase agreements as American Eagle Delta Connection and United Express — enabling American Airlines Delta and United to reach markets that would be inefficiently served by their big aircraft. Its corporate aviation division offers charter service and sister company ExpressJet Services provides ground-handling and aircraft MRO services. Its fleet of more than 400 Bombardier and Embraer regional jets flies from about a dozen hubs across the US to some 190 destinations in the US Canada Mexico and the Caribbean. Rival SkyWest acquired ExpressJet Holdings in late 2010.

EXTENDED STAY AMERICA INC
NYS: STAY

11525 N. Community House Road, Suite 100
Charlotte, NC 28277
Phone: 980 345-1600
Fax: –
Web: www.extendedstay.com

CEO: James L Donald
CFO: Jonathan S Halkyard
HR: –
FYE: December 31
Type: Public

Guests at this hotel chain need not worry about wearing out their welcome. The company owns and operates some 680 Extended Stay hotels. Extended Stay brands include Extended Stay America Extended Stay Canada and Crossland Economy Studios. A hybrid between a hotel and an apartment its lodgings offer all-suite accommodations targeting business and leisure travelers looking for a temporary place to call home. The rooms feature separate living and dining areas and fully-equipped kitchens. Extended Stay can charge lower rates than hotels by eliminating room service and daily maid services. In 2013 the company went public.

	Annual Growth	12/10	12/11	12/12	12/13	12/14
Sales ($ mil.)	57.9%	195.4	942.7	1,011.5	1,132.8	1,213.5
Net income ($ mil.)	–	(22.5)	45.6	20.7	86.2	150.6
Market value ($ mil.)	(26.5%)	–	–	–	5,370.6	3,949.2
Employees	(6.5%)	–	–	10,400	10,000	9,100

EXTRA SPACE STORAGE INC
NYS: EXR

2795 East Cottonwood Parkway, Suite 400
Salt Lake City, UT 84121
Phone: 801 365-4600
Fax: –
Web: www.extraspace.com

CEO: Spencer F. Kirk
CFO: Scott Stubbs
HR: –
FYE: December 31
Type: Public

When closets are bursting at the seams and garages are overflowing Extra Space Storage gives its customers room to breathe. One of the largest operators and managers of self-storage properties in the US the self-administered self-managed real estate investment trust (REIT) wholly-owns owns in joint-venture partnerships or operates for third parties about 1030 facilities with some 680000 units totaling nearly 76 million sq. ft. of rentable space. Active in metropolitan areas in nearly 35 states and Washington DC the company also offers business boat and RV storage and leases to nearly 600000 tenants nationwide.

	Annual Growth	12/10	12/11	12/12	12/13	12/14
Sales ($ mil.)	23.1%	281.5	329.9	409.4	520.6	647.2
Net income ($ mil.)	55.7%	33.4	58.4	127.7	185.6	195.9
Market value ($ mil.)	35.5%	2,024.7	2,819.4	4,234.3	4,902.3	6,823.4
Employees	5.6%	2,125	2,239	2,283	2,584	2,643

EXTREME NETWORKS INC
NMS: EXTR

145 Rio Robles
San Jose, CA 95134
Phone: 408 579-2800
Fax: –
Web: www.extremenetworks.com

CEO: Charles W. (Chuck) Berger
CFO: Ken Arola
HR: –
FYE: June 30
Type: Public

Extreme Networks keeps devices connected from data centers to schools and stadiums. The company designs and markets Ethernet switches to address the networking needs of enterprises cloud data centers mobile operators and service providers. Its switches are marketed primarily under the BlackDiamond and Summit brands. The company also offers RidgeLine software for central configuration among other functions the ExtremeXOS operating system and IdentiFi a family of wireless access points. It serves some 12000 customers - including businesses schools and hospitals — across 50 countries. The company acquired Enterasys Networks which added technologies customers and revenue.

	Annual Growth	07/11*	06/12	06/13	06/14	06/15
Sales ($ mil.)	13.4%	334.4	322.7	299.3	519.6	552.9
Net income ($ mil.)	–	2.7	15.9	9.7	(57.3)	(71.6)
Market value ($ mil.)	(4.5%)	324.9	345.0	345.0	445.3	269.8
Employees	16.6%	732	668	625	1,563	1,351

*Fiscal year change

EXX INC

1350 E. Flamingo Rd. Ste. 689
Las Vegas NV 89119-5263
Phone: 702-598-3223
Fax: 216-432-6281
Web: www.sifco.com/

CEO: David A Segal
CFO: –
HR: –
FYE: December 31
Type: Private

With a Las Vegas location it seems fitting that EXX may be a little down on its luck due to the economic downturn and its slow recovery and other setbacks. The company organizes its several subsidiaries into two business segments: Mechanical Equipment including Deco Engineering Blackhawk Rochester Gear Machine Tool & Gear and TX Technology produces precision machined components and assemblies; and Plastics and Rubber (Henry Gordy Handi-Pac Hi-Flier and Sellers & Josephson) churns out rubber and plastic parts used in cars and agricultural vehicles. The US accounts for most of EXX sales. Chairman and CEO David Segal and family members own the company which was taken private in 2010.

EXXON MOBIL CORP.
NYS: XOM

5959 Las Colinas Boulevard
Irving, TX 75039-2298
Phone: 972 444-1000
Fax: 972 444-1505
Web: www.exxonmobil.com

CEO: Rex W. Tillerson
CFO: Andrew P Swiger
HR: –
FYE: December 31
Type: Public

It's not necessarily the oil standard but Exxon Mobil is one of the world's largest integrated oil companies (with Royal Dutch Shell and BP). Exxon Mobil engages in oil and gas exploration production supply transportation and marketing. In 2014 it had proved reserves of 25.2 billion barrels of oil equivalent including major holdings in oil sands through Imperial Oil. Exxon Mobil's 30 refineries in 17 countries have a throughput capacity of 5.2 million barrels per day and lubricant basestock manufacturing capacity of 131000 barrels per day. It supplies refined products to more than 19000 gas stations worldwide (including almost 10000 in the US). Exxon Mobil is also a major petrochemical producer.

	Annual Growth	12/10	12/11	12/12	12/13	12/14
Sales ($ mil.)	1.8%	383,221.0	486,429.0	482,295.0	438,255.0	411,939.0
Net income ($ mil.)	1.6%	30,460.0	41,060.0	44,880.0	32,580.0	32,520.0
Market value ($ mil.)	–	0.0	0.0	0.0	0.0	0.0
Employees	(2.6%)	83,600	82,100	76,900	75,000	75,300

EXXONMOBIL PIPELINE COMPANY

800 Bell St.
Houston TX 77002
Phone: 713-656-3636
Fax: 713-656-9586
Web: www.exxonmobilpipeline.com

CEO: –
CFO: –
HR: –
FYE: December 31
Type: Subsidiary

This company makes its mark by sending its business down the tubes. Each day ExxonMobil Pipeline the oil and gas transportation arm of Exxon Mobil transports about 2.7 million barrels of crude oil refined petroleum products liquefied petroleum gases natural gas liquids and chemicals through 8000 miles of pipeline that runs through 23 US states Canada and the Gulf of Mexico. The company also provides engineering and inspection services. Its joint interest pipelines include Mustang Pipeline Plantation Pipe Line and Wolverine Pipe Line. ExxonMobil Pipeline also owns a minority stake in The Trans-Alaska Pipeline System Alaska's major vehicle for moving crude from Prudhoe Bay to the port of Valdez.

EYEMED VISION CARE LLC

4000 Luxottica Place
Mason OH 45040
Phone: 513-765-4321
Fax: 513-765-6388
Web: www.eyemedvisioncare.com

CEO: –
CFO: –
HR: –
FYE: December 31
Type: Subsidiary

EyeMed Vision Care delivers the visuals. A subsidiary of Italian eyewear maker Luxottica the company administers managed vision care plans to about 160 million members through a nationwide network of providers that includes optometrists ophthalmologists opticians and retailers (including Luxottica subsidiaries LensCrafters and Pearle Vision). EyeMed offers several different plans all of which provide various levels of discounts on exams and vision products such as eyeglass frames and lenses contact lenses and other eye care services. The company has a diverse customer base that includes large corporations (Cintas) government entities (the State of New York) and health insurers (Health Net).

EZCORP, INC.

NMS: EZPW

2500 Bee Cave Road
Rollingwood, TX 78746
Phone: 512 314-3400
Fax: 512 314-3404
Web: www.ezcorp.com

CEO: Stuart I. Grimshaw
CFO: Mark Ashby
HR: Irma Arguijo-Rivera
FYE: September 30
Type: Public

No mere pawn in the game EZCORP is one of the nation's largest operators of pawnshops. The company operates about 500 EZPAWN and Value Pawn locations in the US and almost 250 stores in Mexico under the Empeño Fácil brand. EZCORP also offers customers unsecured loans commonly referred to as payday loans or payroll advances through some of its pawnshops and from almost 500 EZMONEY stores in the US and 40 locations in Canada under the CASHMAX and Cash Converters banners. EZCORP also issues larger longer-term consumer installment loans and loans secured by automobile titles and loans money via the Internet through its 2013 acquisition of online lender Go Cash.

	Annual Growth	09/11	09/12	09/13	09/14	09/15
Sales ($ mil.)	(2.4%)	869.3	992.5	1,010.3	988.5	788.4
Net income ($ mil.)	–	122.2	143.7	34.1	(45.7)	(86.4)
Market value ($ mil.)	(31.8%)	1,565.8	1,258.1	925.6	543.7	338.5
Employees	9.2%	5,600	7,200	7,500	7,300	–

F & M BANK CORP.

NBB: FMBM

P. O. Box 1111
Timberville, VA 22853
Phone: 540 896-8941
Fax: –
Web: www.fmbankva.com

CEO: Dean W Withers
CFO: Carrie A Comer
HR: –
FYE: December 31
Type: Public

F & M Bank has deep roots in Virginia's Shenandoah Valley. Founded in 1908 the holding company operates about 10 Farmers & Merchants Bank branches in the northern Virginia counties of Rockingham and Shenandoah. Farmers & Merchants caters to individuals and businesses. It provides typical deposit products including checking and savings accounts CDs and IRAs. Some 40% of its loans are mortgages; it also writes agricultural business construction and consumer loans. The company offers insurance brokerage and financial services through TEB Life Insurance and Farmers & Merchants Financial Services.

	Annual Growth	12/10	12/11	12/12	12/13	12/14
Assets ($ mil.)	3.0%	538.9	566.7	596.9	552.8	605.3
Net income ($ mil.)	11.6%	3.7	4.7	4.9	4.7	5.8
Market value ($ mil.)	7.5%	48.0	45.1	50.2	60.9	64.2
Employees	2.6%	141	144	142	153	156

F & S PRODUCE CO INC

913 BRIDGETON AVE
ROSENHAYN, NJ 08352
Phone: 856-453-0316
Fax: –
Web: www.freshcutproduce.com

CEO: –
CFO: –
HR: –
FYE: December 31
Type: Private

F&S Produce is into slicing and dicing. The company is a supplier of processed fresh produce including chunked diced and sliced fruits and vegetables and prepared fruit and vegetable salads and trays; it also makes brined and pickled products. Customers include food processors food service distributors and chain account representatives. F&S processes more than 75 million pounds of produce annually. Affiliate Pipco Transportation distributes the company's products through a fleet of approximately 30 trucks and 50 refrigerated trailers. The company is owned by president Sam Pipitone who founded F&S in 1981.

	Annual Growth	12/09	12/10	12/11	12/12	12/13
Sales ($ mil.)	6.1%	–	58.3	61.4	63.0	69.5
Net income ($ mil.)	(23.8%)	–	–	1.5	(0.3)	0.8
Market value ($ mil.)	–	–	–	–	–	–
Employees	–	–	–	–	–	35

F&B MANUFACTURING COMPANY

4316 N. 39th Ave.
Phoenix AZ 85019
Phone: 602-272-3900
Fax: 602-272-4117
Web: www.fbmfg.com

CEO: John Newell
CFO: –
HR: –
FYE: June 30
Type: Private

Don't confuse it with food and beverage production. F&B Manufacturing makes parts and assemblies for the aerospace industry among others. The company's capabilities include hydroforming machining mechanical and hydraulic stamping and spot and laser welding as well as heat treating processes. Hydroforming a company specialty involves the use of pressurized hydraulic fluid to form metal into shapes that would be difficult to achieve by other methods. F&B Manufacturing also is able to design and make the tools necessary to produce the parts requested by its customers. The family-owned company was founded in 1923.

F+W MEDIA INC.

10151 Carver Rd. Ste. 200
Blue Ash OH 45242
Phone: 513-531-2690
Fax: 336-545-0233
Web: www.bgf.com

CEO: –
CFO: Jim Ogle
HR: –
FYE: December 31
Type: Private

When it comes to niche content F+W Media is forward thinking. The company is a special interest content provider and marketer of enthusiast magazines books conferences trade shows and interactive media properties. Publications are organized around some 20 community-based units each of which focuses on a particular special interest category such as writing fine arts design and sports. F+W publishes more than 30 magazines including Antique Trader The Artist's Magazine and Rural Builder. The company also publishes about 600 new book titles annually and has a library of some 4000 titles. In addition F + W owns special interest publisher Adams Media.

F.A. WILHELM CONSTRUCTION COMPANY INC.

3914 Prospect St.
Indianapolis IN 46203
Phone: 317-359-5411
Fax: 317-359-8346
Web: www.fawilhelm.com

CEO: –
CFO: Joseph D Cathcart
HR: –
FYE: December 31
Type: Private

The Indianapolis Museum of Art is a stand-up example of the structures that F.A. Wilhelm Construction Company builds. The general contractor provides construction and construction management in the Midwest particularly in its home state of Indiana. The firm focuses on commercial industrial and institutional buildings for the health care research and education sectors. It also owns fabrication facilties that produce concrete formwork process piping sheet metal and structural steel. F.A. Wilhelm is a subsidiary of Wilhelm Construction which also operates mechanical contractor Freitag-Weinhardt and sheet metal contractor Poynter Sheet Metal. The group began in 1923 as a masonry contractor.

F.N.B. CORP. NYS: FNB

One North Shore Center, 12 Federal Street
Pittsburgh, PA 15212
Phone: 800 555-5455
Fax: –
Web: www.fnbcorporation.com

CEO: Vincent J. (Vince) Delie
CFO: Vincent J. Calabrese
HR: –
FYE: December 31
Type: Public

F.N.B. Corporation is the holding company for First National Bank of Pennsylvania which serves consumers and small to midsized businesses though more than 270 bank branches in Pennsylvania northeastern Ohio and Maryland. The company also has more than 50 consumer finance offices operating as Regency Finance in those states as well as Tennessee and Kentucky. In addition to community banking and consumer finance F.N.B. also has segments devoted to insurance and wealth management. It also offers leasing and merchant banking services. F.N.B. has extended its reach in its target states through acquisitions of banks including Metro Bancorp Annapolis Bancorp and PVF Capital Corp.

	Annual Growth	12/10	12/11	12/12	12/13	12/14
Assets ($ mil.)	15.8%	8,959.9	9,786.5	12,024.0	13,563.4	16,127.1
Net income ($ mil.)	17.9%	74.7	87.0	110.4	117.8	144.1
Market value ($ mil.)	7.9%	1,708.6	1,967.9	1,847.8	2,195.8	2,317.6
Employees	3.7%	2,718	3,015	2,975	3,103	3,145

F.W. WEBB COMPANY

160 Middlesex Tpke.
Bedford MA 01730
Phone: 781-272-6600
Fax: 781-275-3354
Web: www.fwwebb.com

CEO: Jeff Pope
CFO: –
HR: –
FYE: December 31
Type: Private

Since 1866 F.W. Webb has kept people warm in winter and cool in summer. One of the largest wholesale distributors of LP gas industrial fittings and plumbing products in the northeastern US F.W. Webb offers a slew of blue chip lines for plumbers HVAC technicians and institutional buyers. Through some 70 outlets the company sells refrigeration pipe and plumbing products (fountains pumps) and HVAC equipment (air filters furnaces). It also offers gas boilers and automation valves and biotech equipment as well as general industrial items such as adhesives and sealants. F.W. Webb through its subsidiaries offers customized fabrication and inventory programs. John Pope and his family own the company.

F5 NETWORKS, INC. NMS: FFIV

401 Elliott Avenue West
Seattle, WA 98119
Phone: 206 272-5555
Fax: –
Web: www.f5.com

CEO: John McAdam
CFO: Andy Reinland
HR: Kristen R. Dimlow
FYE: September 30
Type: Public

F5 Networks wants to help your network take a load off. The company's products include application delivery controllers (ADC) and software that are used for network load balancing availability assurance and security assessment. The company also provides file virtualization WAN optimization and remote access products. It additionally offers such services as network monitoring performance analysis and training. F5 targets a variety of industries including telecommunications manufacturing and financial services. The company gets more than half of its sales from the Americas.

	Annual Growth	09/11	09/12	09/13	09/14	09/15
Sales ($ mil.)	13.6%	1,151.8	1,377.2	1,481.3	1,732.0	1,919.8
Net income ($ mil.)	10.9%	241.4	275.2	277.3	311.2	365.0
Market value ($ mil.)	13.0%	4,983.3	7,339.2	6,018.4	8,328.2	8,122.0
Employees	13.8%	2,488	3,029	3,356	3,834	4,178

FAB UNIVERSAL CORP NBB: FABU

5001 Baum Boulevard, Suite 770
Pittsburgh, PA 15213
Phone: 412 621-0902
Fax: 412 621-2625
Web: www.fabuniversal.com

CEO: Christopher J Spencer
CFO: John Busshaus
HR: –
FYE: December 31
Type: Public

Wizzard Software has a lot to say. The company provides podcast hosting services and develops computer software products that focus on speech recognition and text-to-speech technology. The company's technology products serve as the basis for computer telephones other devices to to listen to spoken commands and respond with synthetic speech. Wizzard's Voice Tools suite enables programmers to integrate the company's speech technologies in their applications. The company also offers podcast hosting and operates a speech technology consulting services division that offers custom programming training and support services.

	Annual Growth	12/09	12/10	12/11	12/12	12/13
Sales ($ mil.)	115.0%	5.2	5.5	6.5	27.5	110.9
Net income ($ mil.)	–	(6.5)	(4.1)	(10.0)	(4.0)	20.7
Market value ($ mil.)	73.2%	7.1	5.2	2.7	67.0	63.9
Employees	15.1%	110	110	150	215	193

FACEBOOK, INC. NMS: FB

1601 Willow Road
Menlo Park, CA 94025
Phone: 650 543-4800
Fax: –
Web: www.facebook.com

CEO: Mark Zuckerberg
CFO: David M. (Dave) Wehner
HR: –
FYE: December 31
Type: Public

When it comes to social networking it's wise to put your best face forward. Facebook the social networking juggernaut lets users share information post photos and videos play games and otherwise connect with one another through online profiles. The site which allows outside developers to build apps that integrate with Facebook boasts more than a billion total users. The firm was launched in 2004 by Harvard student Mark Zuckerberg as an online version of the Harvard Facebook. (The name comes from books of freshmen's faces majors and hometowns that are distributed to students.) In 2012 Facebook began publicly trading after filing one of the largest IPOs in US history.

	Annual Growth	12/11	12/12	12/13	12/14	12/15
Sales ($ mil.)	48.3%	3,711.0	5,089.0	7,872.0	12,466.0	17,928.0
Net income ($ mil.)	38.6%	1,000.0	53.0	1,500.0	2,940.0	3,688.0
Market value ($ mil.)	–	–	0.0	0.0	0.0	0.0
Employees	37.6%	3,539	4,619	6,337	9,199	12,691

FACILITY SOLUTIONS GROUP INC.

4401 Westgate Blvd. Ste. 310 — CEO: –
Austin TX 78745 — CFO: –
Phone: 512-440-7985 — HR: –
Fax: 512-440-0399 — FYE: December 31
Web: www.fsgi.com — Type: Private

Facility Solutions Group (FSG) distributes electrical products and lighting equipment to customers in the US Canada and Puerto Rico through its FSG Lighting (formerly American Light) subsidiary. The company also provides electrical contracting services through its FSG Electric (formerly Design Electric) subsidiary. Other divisions include those focused on energy management technology (combining voice data video and security) and sign design and installation. The company has some 16 locations across the US. Facility Solutions Group was established in 1982 by CEO William Graham.

FACTORY MUTUAL INSURANCE COMPANY

270 Central Ave. — CEO: Shivan S Subramaniam
Johnston RI 02919 — CFO: Jeffrey A Burchill
Phone: 401-275-3000 — HR: –
Fax: 401-275-3029 — FYE: December 31
Web: www.fmglobal.com — Type: Private - Mutual Com

If you're looking to protect your corporation turn your insurance dial to FM Global. Factory Mutual Insurance (operating as FM Global) provides commercial and industrial property/casualty insurance and a variety of risk management services. It provides specialized products for ocean cargo and machinery equipment as well as property loss prevention engineering and research. FM Global operates through such subsidiaries as Affiliated FM Insurance FM Global Cargo and Mutual Boiler Re. In addition to the Americas the company has offices throughout Europe the Middle East Africa and the Asia/Pacific region.

FACTSET RESEARCH SYSTEMS INC.   NYS: FDS

601 Merritt 7 — CEO: Philip Snow
Norwalk, CT 06851 — CFO: Maurizio Nicolelli
Phone: 203 810-1000 — HR: –
Fax: 203 810-1001 — FYE: August 31
Web: www.factset.com — Type: Public

Analysts portfolio managers and investment bankers know FactSet Research Systems has the facts down pat. The company offers global financial and economic information for investment analysis. FactSet also offers software for use in downloading and manipulating the data. (Its products can be fully integrated with Microsoft applications such as Excel and PowerPoint.) Among the company's applications are tools for presentations data warehousing portfolio analysis and report writing. Revenues are derived from month-to-month subscriptions to services databases and financial applications. More than 80% of revenue comes from investment managers; investment banking clients account for the rest.

	Annual Growth	08/11	08/12	08/13	08/14	08/15
Sales ($ mil.)	8.5%	726.5	805.8	858.1	920.3	1,006.8
Net income ($ mil.)	9.0%	171.0	188.8	198.6	211.5	241.1
Market value ($ mil.)	15.8%	3,631.8	3,812.3	4,228.8	5,263.8	6,524.8
Employees	8.8%	5,251	5,735	6,258	6,639	7,360

FAIR ISAAC CORP   NYS: FICO

181 Metro Drive, Suite 700 — CEO: Wayne Orchowski
San Jose, CA 95110-1346 — CFO: Michael J. (Mike) Pung
Phone: 408 535-1500 — HR: –
Fax: – — FYE: September 30
Web: www.fico.com — Type: Public

Fair or not Fair Isaac has a lot to say about whether you get that loan approval. Also known as FICO the company provides credit scores and risk management tools for businesses worldwide including banks credit card issuers mortgage and auto lenders retailers insurance firms and health care providers. FICO is the creator of the FICO Score one of the most widely-used scoring systems to determine borrowers' creditworthiness. FICO also provides software for managing decisions and for consumers online credit management tools. While the US accounts for nearly 60% of its revenue the company operates globally in more than 100 countries.

	Annual Growth	09/11	09/12	09/13	09/14	09/15
Sales ($ mil.)	7.9%	619.7	676.4	743.4	789.0	838.8
Net income ($ mil.)	4.9%	71.6	92.0	90.1	94.9	86.5
Market value ($ mil.)	40.3%	683.1	1,384.9	1,729.7	1,724.1	2,644.0
Employees	8.5%	2,023	2,315	2,482	2,646	2,803

FAIRCHILD FASHION MEDIA

750 3rd Ave. Floor 7 & 8 — CEO: –
New York NY 10017 — CFO: John Balendo
Phone: 212-630-4000 — HR: –
Fax: +86-10-8261-7072 — FYE: December 31
Web: corp.163.com/ — Type: Business Segment

Fairchild Fashion Media is becoming all the fashion in a brand new kingdom. A unit of Advance Magazine Publishers (doing business as Conde Nast) the publisher produces the bible of the fashion industry trade magazine Women's Wear Daily (WWD) as well as WWD.com. The publication is known as the paper of record for executives in the fashion retail and beauty industries. Other holdings include menswear and Footwear News (FN). Fairchild also produces conferences through Fairchild Summits while its Fairchild Books produces textbooks and educational resources for students of fashion merchandising retail and interior design. The company was founded in Chicago by Louis Fairchild in 1892.

FAIRCHILD SEMICONDUCTOR INTERNATIONAL, INC.   NMS: FCS

3030 Orchard Parkway — CEO: Mark S. Thompson
San Jose, CA 95134 — CFO: Mark S. Frey
Phone: 408 822-2000 — HR: –
Fax: – — FYE: December 28
Web: www.fairchildsemi.com — Type: Public

One of the world's oldest chip makers Fairchild Semiconductor makes semiconductors for tens of thousands of customers in the automotive computer consumer electronics industrial mobile and communications markets. Its diversified product line includes logic chips discrete power and signal components optoelectronics and many types of analog and mixed-signal chips. The company subcontracts a small amount of its fabrication assembly and test operations to companies that include TSMC Amkor and ASE among others. In late 2015 Fairchild agreed to be bought on On Semiconductor for $2.4 billion. The deal is expected to close in 2Q 2016.

	Annual Growth	12/10	12/11	12/12	12/13	12/14
Sales ($ mil.)	(2.7%)	1,599.7	1,588.8	1,405.9	1,405.4	1,433.4
Net income ($ mil.)	–	153.2	145.5	24.6	5.0	(35.2)
Market value ($ mil.)	3.4%	1,793.4	1,435.2	1,655.7	1,551.0	2,047.6
Employees	(2.0%)	8,977	8,817	9,077	8,659	8,272

FAIRFIELD MEDICAL CENTER

401 N EWING ST
LANCASTER, OH 431303371
Phone: 740-687-8000
Fax: –
Web: www.fmchealth.org

CEO: Sky Gettys
CFO: –
HR: –
FYE: December 31
Type: Private

Fairfield Medical Center is a more than 220-bed acute care hospital serving residents in southeastern and central Ohio. In addition to providing comprehensive medical and surgical care Fairfield Medical Center offers specialty services including cancer cardiovascular women's and children's health and rehabilitation services. The not-for-profit hospital also operates offsite facilities for physician practices as well as specialty diagnostic and laboratory services. The Center employs more than 250 physicians and is served by a number of volunteer organizations which help to support and operate it.

	Annual Growth	12/05	12/06	12/07	12/08	12/09
Sales ($ mil.)	–	–	–	(744.9)	187.2	197.2
Net income ($ mil.)	15655.9%	–	–	0.0	(11.9)	7.5
Market value ($ mil.)	–	–	–	–	–	–
Employees	–	–	–	–	–	2,200

FAIRFIELD UNIVERSITY

1073 N BENSON RD
FAIRFIELD, CT 068245195
Phone: 203-254-4000
Fax: –
Web: www.fairfield.edu

CEO: –
CFO: Michael Trafecante
HR: –
FYE: June 30
Type: Private

Fairfield University welcomes students to the fair fields of Connecticut and prepares them for a life of service. The university is a private Jesuit school with an enrollment of more than 5000 undergraduate and graduate students. It offers about 40 undergraduate majors as well as 40 graduate degree programs through six schools and colleges: College of Arts and Sciences; School of Nursing; School of Engineering; Dolan School of Business; Graduate School of Education and Allied Professions; and University College. With a faculty of about 550 professionals Fairfield University has one campus in Fairfield Connecticut and offers about 60 study abroad programs.

	Annual Growth	06/10	06/11	06/12	06/13	06/14
Sales ($ mil.)	2.9%	–	176.5	187.2	191.7	192.4
Net income ($ mil.)	–	–	–	(0.5)	39.8	56.5
Market value ($ mil.)	–	–	–	–	–	–
Employees	–	–	–	–	–	883

FAIRLEIGH DICKINSON UNIVERSITY

1000 RIVER RD
TEANECK, NJ 076661914
Phone: 201-692-2000
Fax: –
Web: www.view.fdu.edu

CEO: –
CFO: –
HR: Sally A Bengasi
FYE: June 30
Type: Private

It's fair to say that Fairleigh Dickinson University (FDU) is the largest private university in New Jersey. It has an enrollment of approximately 12000 students and 260 full-time faculty members. It has a student-teacher ratio of 14:1 and offers more than 100 undergraduate and graduate degree programs as well as doctoral programs in clinical psychology and school psychology. In addition to its main Metropolitan Campus in Teaneck New Jersey; the university also offers degree programs at the College at Florham in Madison New Jersey; at FDU-Vancouver in Canada; and at Wroxton College in Oxfordshire England. Fairleigh Dickinson was founded in 1942.

	Annual Growth	06/09	06/10	06/11	06/12	06/13
Sales ($ mil.)	3.3%	–	192.0	202.3	204.7	211.4
Net income ($ mil.)	(2.6%)	–	–	22.9	8.0	21.7
Market value ($ mil.)	–	–	–	–	–	–
Employees	–	–	–	–	–	1,505

FAIRPOINT COMMUNICATIONS INC

NAS: FRP

521 East Morehead Street, Suite 500
Charlotte, NC 28202
Phone: 704 344-8150
Fax: –
Web: www.fairpoint.com

CEO: Paul H. Sunu
CFO: Ajay Sabherwal
HR: –
FYE: December 31
Type: Public

FairPoint Communications provides local and long-distance phone services as well as broadband Internet access and cable TV to residential and business customers. It serves about 1.3 million subscribers through more than 30 local-exchange carriers in 17 US states. FairPoint concentrates on rural and small urban markets mainly in northern New England but it also serves spots in the Midwest South and Northwest. FairPoint emerged from Chapter 11 bankruptcy in 2011.

	Annual Growth	01/11*	12/11	12/12	12/13	12/14
Sales ($ mil.)	138.6%	66.4	963.1	973.6	939.4	901.4
Net income ($ mil.)	–	586.9	(414.9)	(153.3)	(93.5)	(136.3)
Market value ($ mil.)	48.6%	–	115.7	212.3	302.1	379.6
Employees	(4.8%)	–	3,541	3,369	3,171	3,052

*Fiscal year change

FAIRVIEW HEALTH SERVICES

2450 RIVERSIDE AVE
MINNEAPOLIS, MN 554541450
Phone: 612-672-6300
Fax: –
Web: www.umphysicians.oit.umn.edu

CEO: Rulon F Stacey
CFO: James M Fox
HR: –
FYE: December 31
Type: Private

It's fair to say that when it comes to health care Fairview Health Services takes the long view. The not-for-profit system serves Minnesota's Twin Cities and nearby communities. Fairview Health is affiliated with the medical school of the University of Minnesota and counts among its 10 hospitals the University of Minnesota Medical Center. The hospitals house more than 2500 beds and provide comprehensive medical and surgical services. The system also operates primary and specialty care clinics that provide preventive and wellness care. Additionally it operates retail pharmacies and nursing homes and provides home health care and rehabilitation. Fairview plans to merge with University of Minnesota Physicians.

	Annual Growth	12/08	12/09	12/11	12/12	12/13
Sales ($ mil.)	5.3%	–	2,744.6	2,575.1	3,218.1	3,370.5
Net income ($ mil.)	643.1%	–	–	4.5	168.9	249.3
Market value ($ mil.)	–	–	–	–	–	–
Employees	–	–	–	–	–	18,000

FAIRWAY GROUP HOLDINGS CORP

NMS: FWM

2284 12th Avenue
New York, NY 10027
Phone: 646 616-8000
Fax: –
Web: www.fairwaymarket.com

CEO: Jack Murphy
CFO: Edward C. (Ed) Arditte
HR: –
FYE: March 29
Type: Public

Fairway Group Holdings Corp. keeps a well-stocked grocery cart for discerning Manhattan shoppers. The parent company of Fairway Market operates a growing chain of more than a dozen upscale grocery stores in the greater New York City metropolitan area. Three of those stores (in Connecticut New Jersey and New York) have adjacent liquor stores under the Fairway Wines & Spirits name. Fairway Markets feature fresh produce meat and seafood as well as organic products prepared foods and hard-to-find specialty and gourmet products. Some Fairway Markets have on-site cafes that serve coffee salads and sandwiches while other locations offer delivery. Fairway Group went public in 2013.

	Annual Growth	04/11	04/12*	03/13	03/14	03/15
Sales ($ mil.)	13.2%	485.7	554.9	661.2	776.0	797.6
Net income ($ mil.)	–	(18.6)	(11.9)	(62.9)	(80.3)	(46.5)
Market value ($ mil.)	(22.1%)	–	–	–	333.9	260.2
Employees	0.5%	–	4,230	4,800	4,200	4,300

*Fiscal year change

FAITH TECHNOLOGIES INC.

225 MAIN ST
MENASHA, WI 549523186
Phone: 920-225-6500
Fax: –
Web: www.faithtechnologies.com

CEO: Mike Jansen
CFO: Betty R Johnson
HR: –
FYE: December 31
Type: Private

Keeping the faith in technology is a basic commitment of Faith Technologies one of the largest privately held electrical and specialty systems contractors in the US. The company's specialties include electrical contracting and service automated controls lighting security technology and preconstruction. It primarily serves clients in the commercial government industrial institutional health care manufacturing power residential retail transportation and data center sectors. The company has worked on a range of projects such as airports bridges correctional facilities government agencies hospitals restaurants and shopping centers.

	Annual Growth	12/08	12/09	12/10	12/11	12/12
Sales ($ mil.)	5.9%	–	219.3	228.3	248.6	260.2
Net income ($ mil.)	107.8%	–	–	2.3	4.6	10.0
Market value ($ mil.)	–	–	–	–	–	–
Employees	–	–	–	–	–	1,820

FALCON PHARMACEUTICALS LTD.

6201 South Fwy.
Fort Worth TX 76134-2099
Phone: 817-293-0450
Fax: 800-777-2799
Web: www.falconpharma.com

CEO: Cary Rayment
CFO: Jacqualyn Fouse
HR: –
FYE: December 31
Type: Subsidiary

Falcon Pharmaceuticals has a keen eye for alternatives. The company specializes in making generic equivalents of ophthalmic drugs that treat a range of eye conditions as well as otic (ear) and nasal ailments. Its lead product Timolol GFS is a generic equivalent of Merck's glaucoma treatment Timoptic-XE gel. The company also offers anti-infective steroid anti-viral anti-allergy and anesthetic pharmaceutical products without the markup typically associated with brand names. Falcon Pharmaceuticals is a subsidiary of eye care products company Alcon.

FALCONSTOR SOFTWARE INC. NMS: FALC

2 Huntington Quadrangle
Melville, NY 11747
Phone: 631 777-5188
Fax: –
Web: www.falconstor.com

CEO: James P. (Jim) McNiel
CFO: Louis J. Petrucelly
HR: Bruce Sasson
FYE: December 31
Type: Public

FalconStor Software watches data like a hawk. The company provides hardware and software used in data storage protection and virtualization applications. Its IPStor software is used to manage storage provisioning and virtualization data availability replication and disaster recovery functions in disk-based systems. Ranging from small and midsized businesses to large enterprises the company's customers come from such fields as health care financial services education and information technology. FalconStor sells predominantly through distributors manufacturers and resellers.

	Annual Growth	12/10	12/11	12/12	12/13	12/14
Sales ($ mil.)	(13.5%)	82.8	82.9	75.4	58.6	46.3
Net income ($ mil.)	–	(35.4)	(23.4)	(15.0)	(10.9)	(7.2)
Market value ($ mil.)	(20.5%)	137.1	105.6	95.4	55.2	54.8
Employees	(14.9%)	501	468	427	285	263

FALLBROOK TECHNOLOGIES INC.

9444 Waples St. Ste. 410
San Diego CA 92121
Phone: 858-623-9557
Fax: 858-623-9563
Web: www.fallbrooktech.com

CEO: –
CFO: John K Penver
HR: –
FYE: December 31
Type: Private

Fallbrook Technologies (FT) hopes to ride the green technology wave all the way to the bank. Using its NuVinci Technology the start-up company has developed a continuously variable transmission (CVT) that it calls continuously variable planetary technology or CVP. Rotating spheres replace traditional gears for smoother acceleration and improved engine efficiency. FT's Hodyon subsidiary (acquired in 2011) makes energy efficient products and systems including auxiliary power unit (APU) products. Hodyon aims to use FT's CVT to develop new APUs. FT investors include venture capital firms Macquarie Capital Markets NGEN Partners and Robeco a subsidiary of Rabobank. Fallbrook has scrapped plans to go public.

FALLON GROUP INC.

901 Marquette Ave. Ste. 2400
Minneapolis MN 55402
Phone: 612-758-2345
Fax: 612-758-2346
Web: www.fallon.com

CEO: Patrick R Fallon
CFO: –
HR: Karen Rogers
FYE: December 31
Type: Subsidiary

This agency wants to lend a hand if your brand has "fallen" on hard times. Doing business as Fallon Worldwide Fallon Group is a leading creative ad agency that has served such notable clients as Travelers Insurance General Mills and NBCUniversal and operates through offices in Minneapolis London and Tokyo. The firm offers creative development marketing and branding services brand and corporate identity consulting and campaign planning services. Fallon also provides interactive marketing services and website development. The agency was founded as Fallon McElligott Rice in 1981 by partners Pat Fallon Tom McElligott and Nancy Rice. Fallon is a subsidiary of Paris-based advertising conglomerate Publicis.

FAMILY DOLLAR STORES, INC. NYS: FDO

10401 Monroe Road
Matthews, NC 28105
Phone: 704 847-6961
Fax: –
Web: www.familydollar.com

CEO: –
CFO: Mary A Winston
HR: Bryan E Venberg
FYE: August 30
Type: Public

Penny-pinching single moms are drawn to Family Dollar. The nation's #2 dollar store (behind Dollar General) targets forty-something women shopping for a family earning less than $40000 a year. It operates about 8000 stores across some 45 states and Washington DC. Consumables (food health and beauty aids and household items) account for more than 70% of sales; stores also sell apparel shoes and linens. Family Dollar runs small neighborhood stores near its fixed- low- and middle-income customers in rural and urban areas. Most merchandise costs less than $10. Family Dollar was founded in 1959 by the father of CEO Howard Levine. Family Dollar has agreed to be acquired by rival Dollar Tree.

	Annual Growth	08/10	08/11	08/12	08/13	08/14
Sales ($ mil.)	7.5%	7,867.0	8,547.8	9,331.0	10,391.5	10,489.3
Net income ($ mil.)	(5.6%)	358.1	388.4	422.2	443.6	284.5
Market value ($ mil.)	16.5%	4,940.2	5,420.0	7,107.0	8,114.7	9,099.5
Employees	4.7%	50,000	52,000	55,000	58,000	60,000

FAMILY EXPRESS CORPORATION

213 S STATE ROAD 49
VALPARAISO, IN 463837976
Phone: 219-531-6490
Fax: –
Web: www.familyexpress.com

CEO: –
CFO: –
HR: –
FYE: December 31
Type: Private

Convenience is all in the family at this Indiana chain. Family Express operates about 50 convenience store/gasoline stations in north central and northwestern Indiana (split almost evenly between city and rural locations). The chain's Cravin's Market in-house foodservice features fresh sandwiches fruits vegetables salads and a selection of floral items. Family Express also has launched its own proprietary brands including Java Wave gourmet coffees Squeeze Freeze carbonated beverages natural spring water and bread and milk products. In addition Family Express operates a small fleet of delivery trucks that say "moo." The company was founded in 1975.

	Annual Growth	12/06	12/07	12/09	12/10	12/12
Sales ($ mil.)	6.6%	–	275.6	244.8	277.4	379.2
Net income ($ mil.)	24.2%	–	–	2.8	4.4	5.4
Market value ($ mil.)	–	–	–	–	–	–
Employees	–	–	–	–	–	500

FAMILY HEALTH INTERNATIONAL INC

359 BLACKWELL ST STE 200
DURHAM, NC 277012477
Phone: 919-544-7040
Fax: –
Web: www.fhi360.org

CEO: Albert J Siemens
CFO: Hubert C Graves
HR: –
FYE: September 30
Type: Private

Known as FHI 360 Family Health International believes that health is wealth. From a handful of offices located in the US Asia-Pacific and South Africa FHI 360 funds and manages public health programs research education and other resources in more than 60 countries. Founded in 1971 as the International Fertility Research Program of the University of North Carolina at Chapel Hill FHI 360 primarily focuses on and supports HIV/AIDS prevention research reproductive health services and maternal and neonatal health programs. The organization works with governments private agencies and non-governmental organizations to develop the most appropriate programs for different areas.

	Annual Growth	09/06	09/07	09/08	09/09	09/13
Sales ($ mil.)	–	–	(154.7)	369.9	327.6	664.1
Net income ($ mil.)	25.3%	–	–	3.3	2.9	10.2
Market value ($ mil.)	–	–	–	–	–	–
Employees	–	–	–	–	–	4,000

FAMOUS DAVE'S OF AMERICA INC.   NMS: DAVE

12701 Whitewater Drive, Suite 200
Minnetonka, MN 55343
Phone: 952 294-1300
Fax: –
Web: www.famousdaves.com

CEO: Adam J. Wright
CFO: Richard A Pawlowski
HR: Joleen Flory-Lundgren
FYE: December 28
Type: Public

Barbecue made this Dave famous. Famous Dave's of America operates and franchises about 185 barbecue restaurants in some 35 states primarily Minnesota Illinois California and Wisconsin. The eateries serve St. Louis-style ribs Georgia chopped pork and Texas brisket. Most of the restaurants are designed to resemble 1930s-era roadhouse shacks complete with antique items and Americana touches. Other units try to recreate the feeling of a hunting lodge or a Chicago-style blues club featuring live music. The company also distributes barbecue sauce seasonings and prepared meats through grocery stores and other retail outlets. Famous Dave's owns and operates about 50 of its restaurants and franchises the rest.

	Annual Growth	01/11	01/12*	12/12	12/13	12/14
Sales ($ mil.)	0.2%	148.3	154.8	155.0	155.4	149.4
Net income ($ mil.)	(26.2%)	7.2	5.6	4.4	4.8	2.9
Market value ($ mil.)	36.1%	79.6	73.5	63.7	135.2	200.5
Employees	(8.4%)	3,175	3,315	3,165	3,013	2,438

*Fiscal year change

FANDANGO INC.

12200 W. Olympic Blvd. Ste. 150
Los Angeles CA 90064
Phone: 310-451-7690
Fax: 310-451-7861
Web: www.fandango.com

CEO: Chuck Davis
CFO: Daniel V Murray
HR: –
FYE: January 31
Type: Subsidiary

Better than cutting ahead in line Fandango lets you skip the line. The firm provides advance movie tickets and show time information via the Internet (at Fandango.com) phone (at 1-800-FANDANGO) and wireless mobile (mobile.fandango.com). Customers can use credit cards to guarantee tickets which they pick up at the theater. Fandango also offers print-at-home tickets and is supported by more than 20 movie exhibitors including Cinemark and Regal Entertainment Group providing tickets to some 16000 screens across the US. A group of exhibitors — seven of the 10 largest in the US — formed Fandango in 2000; today the company is part of Comcast Interactive Media a division of cable giant Comcast.

FANNIE MAE   OTC: FNMA

3900 Wisconsin Avenue, N.W.
Washington, DC 20016
Phone: 202 752-7000
Fax: –
Web: www.fanniemae.com

CEO: Timothy J. (Tim) Mayopoulos
CFO: David C Benson
HR: Megan Gaither
FYE: December 31
Type: Public

The Federal National Mortgage Association or Fannie Mae has helped more than 50 million low- to middle-income families realize the American Dream. Like its brother Freddie Mac the government-supported enterprise (GSE) provides liquidity in the mortgage market by buying mortgages from lenders and packaging them for resale transferring risk from lenders and allowing them to offer mortgages to those who may not otherwise qualify. It owns or guarantees about $10.7 trillion in home loans or more than a quarter of all outstanding mortgages in the US. Due to losses caused largely by the subprime mortgage crisis the government seized both Fannie and Freddie in 2008. It plans to wind the GSEs down over time.

	Annual Growth	12/10	12/11	12/12	12/13	12/14
Assets ($ mil.)	0.2%	3,221,972.0	3,211,484.0	3,222,422.0	3,270,108.0	3,248,176.0
Net income ($ mil.)	–	(14,014.0)	(16,855.0)	17,224.0	83,963.0	14,208.0
Market value ($ mil.)	61.8%	347.4	233.0	295.3	3,485.8	2,379.9
Employees	1.0%	7,300	7,000	7,200	7,400	7,600

FAR EAST ENERGY CORP   NBB: FEEC

333 N. Sam Houston Parkway East, Suite 230
Houston, TX 77060
Phone: 832 598-0470
Fax: –
Web: www.fareastenergy.com

CEO: –
CFO: –
HR: –
FYE: December 31
Type: Public

Far East Energy is engaged in coalbed methane gas exploration and production in China and in the development of related technologies. The company works with ConocoPhillips and China United Coalbed Methane Company to acquire and explore assets across China. Far East Energy's Shanxi coalbed methane project when fully developed could sustain more than 3000 horizontal gas wells making it one of the world's largest coalbed methane projects. The company has drilled five coalbed methane gas exploration wells in Shanxi and six in its other major project area in Yunnan Province. It holds more than 1.3 million acres of leasehold properties.

	Annual Growth	12/09	12/10	12/11	12/12	12/13
Sales ($ mil.)	36.0%	–	–	0.9	1.6	1.6
Net income ($ mil.)	–	(13.8)	(16.2)	(21.2)	(27.2)	(34.0)
Market value ($ mil.)	(26.3%)	159.2	242.3	72.7	19.0	46.9
Employees	1.7%	29	28	25	26	31

FAR EAST NATIONAL BANK

2 California Plaza 350 S. Grand Ave. Ste. 4100
Los Angeles CA 90071
Phone: 213-687-1200
Fax: 213-687-8511
Web: www.fareastnationalbank.com

CEO: –
CFO: Cynthia Tseng
HR: –
FYE: December 31
Type: Subsidiary

Far East National Bank serves California's Asian-American community through about a dozen branches in Southern California and the San Francisco Bay area. It also has representative offices in China and Vietnam. The bank offers traditional banking services such as checking savings and investment accounts and business commercial real estate and residential mortgage loans. It also has divisions devoted to treasury services and international banking. Far East Capital Corporation a subsidiary of the bank provides capital raising and advisory services to high-growth companies in California and the Pacific Rim. Founded in 1974 Far East National Bank is owned by Taiwan's SinoPac Financial Holdings.

FAREWAY STORES INC.

2300 E. 8th St.
Boone IA 50036
Phone: 515-432-2623
Fax: 515-433-4416
Web: www.fareway.com/index.cfm

CEO: –
CFO: Craig A Shepley
HR: –
FYE: March 31
Type: Private

Fareway Stores makes the green through groceries. The regional grocery chain operates under the Fareway banner primarily in Iowa but also in Illinois Nebraska and now Minnesota. Fareway's 100 locations average about 25000 sq. ft. Eschewing such amenities as video rentals and dry-cleaning services Fareway Stores sticks to the basics — lots of meat (all cut to order) and groceries only — counts on low prices and customer service to compete with supercenter operators such as Wal-Mart. Former Safeway workers Paul Beckwith and Fred Vitt founded Fareway in 1938; the Beckwith family controls the company. Because of the founders' biblical beliefs the stores are closed on Sundays.

FARM BUREAU PROPERTY & CASUALTY INSURANCE COMPANY

5400 University Ave.
West Des Moines IA 50266-5997
Phone: 515-225-5400
Fax: 515-225-5419
Web: www.fbfs.com

CEO: James E Hohmann
CFO: Jim Brannen
HR: –
FYE: December 31
Type: Private

Farm Bureau Property & Casualty lends an insurance-friendly hand to agricultural businesses and other customers in the Midwest and West. The company primarily offers property/casualty insurance products to farmers and ranchers. Its lines of coverage include farmowners homeowners commercial liability crop auto and disability. A network of exclusive agents distributes the company's products in Arizona Iowa Kansas Minnesota Nebraska New Mexico South Dakota and Utah. The insurance provider and its sister company Western Agricultural Insurance are held by Farm Bureau Mutual Holding Company and managed by life insurance provider FBL Financial Group.

FARM CREDIT BANK OF TEXAS

4801 Plaza on the Lake Dr.
Austin TX 78746
Phone: 512-465-0400
Fax: 512-465-0675
Web: www.farmcreditbank.com

CEO: Larry R Doyle
CFO: Thomas W Hill
HR: –
FYE: December 31
Type: Private - Member-Own

The largest member of the federal Farm Credit System the Farm Credit Bank of Texas provides loans and financial services to about 20 lending cooperatives and financial institutions in Alabama Louisiana Mississippi New Mexico and Texas. These include agricultural credit associations which provide agricultural production loans agribusiness financing and rural mortgage financing; and federal land credit associations which offer real estate loans on farms ranches and other rural property. Farm Credit Bank of Texas is owned by the lending cooperatives it serves.

FARM CREDIT SERVICES OF MID-AMERICA ACA

1601 UPS Dr.
Louisville KY 40223
Phone: 502-420-3700
Fax: 804-225-1725
Web: www.bonsecours.com/hospitals/richmond/index.as

CEO: Bill Johnson
CFO: –
HR: –
FYE: December 31
Type: Private - Cooperativ

If Old McDonald's farm is in Indiana Kentucky Ohio or Tennessee he might have a loan-loan-here and a loan-loan-there from Farm Credit Services of Mid-America. The cooperative association one of the largest in the National Farm Credit System provides lending and other financial services to these states' farmers and rural homeowners. Borrowers use Farm Credit's products to purchase real estate homes livestock and farming equipment to fund capital improvements and to cover operating and living expenses. It has a loan volume of about $12 billion and serves some 85000 customers through nearly 100 offices located throughout its service area.

FARM FAMILY CASUALTY INSURANCE COMPANY

344 Rte. 9 West
Glenmont NY 12077-2910
Phone: 518-431-5000
Fax: 518-431-5992
Web: www.farmfamily.com

CEO: Tim Walsh
CFO: –
HR: –
FYE: December 31
Type: Subsidiary

Farm Family Casualty Insurance one of three insurance carriers owned by Farm Family Holdings offers property/casualty insurance to farming agricultural and related customers. The company offers coverage for farms horses country estates floral and other businesses landscaping contractors homeowners commercial and personal automobiles pollution liability and personal watercraft. Farm Family Casualty Insurance is exclusively endorsed by the American Farm Bureau Federation in several of its markets. Some 600 agents distribute the Farm Family life and property/casualty insurance products in twelve northeastern states.

FARM SERVICE COOPERATIVE

2308 PINE ST
HARLAN, IA 515371884
Phone: 712-755-2207
Fax: –
Web: www.fscoop.com

CEO: –
CFO: –
HR: –
FYE: August 31
Type: Private

Farm Service Cooperative (FSC) offers a big bushel basket full of products and services to farmers in west central Iowa. The agricultural co-op offers its members such farm-management supplies and services as grain elevator operations grain marketing equipment rental tires livestock feed and fertilizer sales soil sampling on-staff crop advisors farm credit and financing agronomy and Cenex energy products (diesel home-heating oil propane ethanol gasoline) from its 10 locations.

	Annual Growth	08/03	08/04	08/05	08/06	08/07
Sales ($ mil.)	(82.5%)	–	–	2,122.1	53.2	65.4
Net income ($ mil.)	34677.7%	–	–	0.0	15.0	14.4
Market value ($ mil.)	–	–	–	–	–	–
Employees	–	–	–	–	–	110

FARMER BROS. CO. NMS: FARM

13601 North Freeway, Suite 200
Fort Worth, TX 76177
Phone: 888 998-2468
Fax: –
Web: www.farmerbros.com

CEO: Michael H. (Mike) Keown
CFO: Isaac Johnston
HR: –
FYE: June 30
Type: Public

Farmer Bros. may know beans about farming but just ask the firm about coffee beans. Farmer Bros. roasts and packages coffee and sells it mainly to institutional foodservice operators such as restaurants fast-food outlets hotels and hospitals. It also distributes related coffee products such as filters sugar and creamers as well as assorted teas and culinary products (spices soup and gelatins). As part of its business it provides private brand coffee programs nationwide to retail customers such as convenience and grocery stores. Founded in 1912 Farmer Bros. distributes more than 3500 stock keeping units (SKUs) from more than 115 branch warehouses located in or near major US cities in five states.

	Annual Growth	06/11	06/12	06/13	06/14	06/15
Sales ($ mil.)	4.1%	463.9	495.4	510.0	528.4	545.9
Net income ($ mil.)	–	(54.3)	(29.3)	(8.5)	12.1	0.7
Market value ($ mil.)	23.4%	168.9	132.6	234.2	360.0	391.5
Employees	(0.5%)	1,820	1,821	1,793	1,846	1,784

FARMERS & MERCHANTS INVESTMENT INC.

4732 Calvert St.
Lincoln NE 68506
Phone: 402-323-1574
Fax: 858-587-0902
Web: www.charlotterusse.com

CEO: –
CFO: –
HR: –
FYE: December 31
Type: Private

Farmers & Merchants Investment is a financial services holding company that owns student loan servicer National Education Loan Network (Nelnet) and financial services technology company Infovisa which provides trust accounting software and performance measurement products and services to trust companies bank trust departments and foundations. It is also the holding company for Union Bank & Trust which operates some 40 branches in Nebraska and Kansas. Other affiliates include property/casualty insurance agency Union Agency title insurer Union Title and Union Investment Advisors which manages the Stratus Family of Mutual Funds. CEO Mike Dunlap and his family own Farmers & Merchants Investment.

FARMERS CAPITAL BANK CORP. NMS: FFKT

P.O. Box 309, 202 West Main St.
Frankfort, KY 40601
Phone: 502 227-1668
Fax: –
Web: www.farmerscapital.com

CEO: Lloyd C. Hillard
CFO: Mark A. Hampton
HR: Carla Miles
FYE: December 31
Type: Public

Farmers Capital has found some green in the Bluegrass State. Its four bank subsidiaries — Citizens Bank of Northern Kentucky Farmers Bank & Capital Trust First Citizens Bank and United Bank & Trust Company — operate more than 35 branches in northern and central Kentucky. Serving individuals and local businesses they offer standard retail services such as checking and savings accounts and CDs as well as trust activities. Real estate loans including (primarily) residential mortgages and commercial real estate loans account for around 90% of the company's loan portfolio. Nonbank subsidiaries of Farmers Capital provide insurance and data processing services.

	Annual Growth	12/10	12/11	12/12	12/13	12/14
Assets ($ mil.)	(2.0%)	1,935.7	1,883.6	1,807.2	1,809.6	1,782.6
Net income ($ mil.)	24.1%	6.9	2.7	12.1	13.4	16.5
Market value ($ mil.)	47.8%	36.5	33.6	91.7	162.9	174.4
Employees	(0.1%)	512	510	518	519	510

FARMERS COOPERATIVE COMPANY

105 GARFIELD AVE
FARNHAMVILLE, IA 505386712
Phone: 515-544-3213
Fax: –
Web: www.fccoop.com

CEO: James Chism
CFO: –
HR: –
FYE: August 31
Type: Private

The importance of cooperation — it's one of life's most important lessons. Dating back to the early 1900s the Farmers Cooperative Company (FCC) learned that lesson early on. The 5500-member-plus co-op offers agronomy and grain marketing services to its members who oversee some 3 million acres of farmland in central and north central Iowa. The largest of its kind in Iowa FCC operates 40 grain elevators and provides soil testing and mapping services. It sells supplies including seed feed and fertilizer to its members. The acquisitive coop was itself acquired by another Iowa coop NEW Cooperative in 2014.

	Annual Growth	08/06	08/07	08/08	08/09	08/10
Sales ($ mil.)	(12.8%)	–	–	–	894.5	779.6
Net income ($ mil.)	(19.9%)	–	–	–	13.0	10.4
Market value ($ mil.)	–	–	–	–	–	–
Employees	–	–	–	–	–	450

FARMERS COOPERATIVE SOCIETY

317 3RD ST NW
SIOUX CENTER, IA 512501897
Phone: 712-722-2671
Fax: –
Web: www.farmerscoopsociety.com

CEO: –
CFO: –
HR: –
FYE: July 31
Type: Private

When farmers cooperate society benefits. Through its seven centers in northwest Iowa Farmers Cooperative Society offers its member/farmers a full range of agricultural growing and marketing products and services including crop-storage facilities and business consulting. Its feedlot with room for some 5500 head of cattle helps members buy and care for feeder cattle and provides discounts on grain for members. The co-op also operates a member-only How-To Building Store in Sioux Center Iowa that sells hardware lawn-care products lumber and paint as well as brand-name home appliances. Farmers Cooperative Society has roots dating back to 1907.

	Annual Growth	12/10	12/11*	07/12	07/13	07/14
Sales ($ mil.)	–	–	0.0	434.6	496.5	418.5
Net income ($ mil.)	(31.0%)	–	–	8.1	5.0	3.9
Market value ($ mil.)	–	–	–	–	–	–
Employees	–	–	–	–	–	160

*Fiscal year change

FARMERS NATIONAL BANC CORP. (CANFIELD, OH)   NAS: FMNB

20 South Broad Street
Canfield, OH 44406
Phone: 330 533-3341
Fax: –
Web: www.farmersbankgroup.com

CEO: Kevin J Helmick
CFO: –
HR: –
FYE: December 31
Type: Public

Farmers National Banc is willing to help even nonfarmers grow their seed income into thriving bounties of wealth. The bank provides commercial and personal banking from nearly 20 branches in Ohio. Founded in 1887 Farmers National Banc offers checking and savings accounts credit cards and loans and mortgages. Farmers' lending portfolio is composed of real estate mortgages consumer loans and commercial loans. The company also includes Farmers National Insurance and Farmers Trust Company a non-depository trust bank that offers wealth management and trust services.

	Annual Growth	12/10	12/11	12/12	12/13	12/14
Assets ($ mil.)	3.7%	982.8	1,067.9	1,139.7	1,137.3	1,137.0
Net income ($ mil.)	(0.1%)	9.0	9.2	9.9	7.8	9.0
Market value ($ mil.)	23.3%	66.6	91.1	114.1	120.6	153.7
Employees	5.1%	268	315	335	328	327

FARMERS TELEPHONE COOPERATIVE INC.

1101 E MAIN ST
KINGSTREE, SC 295564105
Phone: 843-382-2333
Fax: –
Web: www.ftc-i.net

CEO: Bradley Erwin
CFO: Jeffrey Lawrimore
HR: –
FYE: June 30
Type: Private

Farmers Telephone Cooperative (FTC) is the incumbent local-exchange carrier (ILEC) in Williamsburg Lee Sumter Clarendon and Florence counties in eastern South Carolina. Serving more than 60000 customers in a 3000 mile area the company provides traditional phone services including local-exchange access and long-distance as well as dial-up and DSL Internet access. The company also offers wireless phone service through a partnership with AT&T Mobility as well as security services and enterprise communications services. In operation since 1951 FTC claims to be the second-largest co-op in the US and should not be confused with the Farmers Telephone Cooperative serving the Rainsville Alabama area.

	Annual Growth	06/05	06/06	06/07	06/08	06/10
Sales ($ mil.)	(56.5%)	–	–	1,597.6	83.7	131.2
Net income ($ mil.)	2582.1%	–	–	0.0	2.3	8.6
Market value ($ mil.)	–	–	–	–	–	–
Employees	–	–	–	–	–	418

FARMINGTON FOODS INC.

7419 FRANKLIN ST
FOREST PARK, IL 601301016
Phone: 708-771-3600
Fax: –
Web: www.farmingtonfoods.com

CEO: –
CFO: Albert J Lavalle
HR: –
FYE: December 29
Type: Private

Farmington Foods takes food from the farm adds value and sells the results. The company processes markets and distributes Value-added pork products including pork loin chops and ribs. Its Lean N' Juicy product line consists of case-ready enhanced pork such as bone-in or boneless loin chops baby backribs spareribs pork shoulder and tenderloin. Farmington also offers a variety of marinated pork products in flavors like Teriyaki lemon pepper and Italian. In addition to pork products the company also sells pre-packaged kabobs made with beef chicken and pork. Formerly known as the Farmington Meat Company the family-owned company was established in 1972.

	Annual Growth	12/00	12/01	12/02	12/03	12/07
Sales ($ mil.)	(4.6%)	–	90.1	67.5	73.8	68.0
Net income ($ mil.)	–	–	–	0.0	0.0	0.0
Market value ($ mil.)	–	–	–	–	–	–
Employees	–	–	–	–	–	155

FARO TECHNOLOGIES INC.   NMS: FARO

250 Technology Park
Lake Mary, FL 32746
Phone: 407 333-9911
Fax: –
Web: www.faro.com

CEO: Simon Raab
CFO: Laura A. Murphy
HR: Wes Warner
FYE: December 31
Type: Public

FARO Technologies is arming companies with a means to inspect the world around them. With the touch of its mechanical arm FARO's measuring systems can facilitate reverse engineering of an undocumented part or a competitor's product. The portable FaroArm FARO Laser ScanArm and FARO Gage are jointed devices that simulate the human arm's movement. Along with the FARO Laser Scanner LS and Laser Tracker inspections and measurements are integrated with 3-D software. Aerospace automotive consumer goods and heavy equipment companies such as Boeing Honda GM GE and Johnson Controls use FARO Arm units in their factories. Customers located outside the Americas account for about 60% of sales in 2014.

	Annual Growth	12/10	12/11	12/12	12/13	12/14
Sales ($ mil.)	15.5%	191.8	254.2	273.4	291.8	341.8
Net income ($ mil.)	32.0%	11.1	23.4	23.0	21.5	33.6
Market value ($ mil.)	17.5%	568.7	796.6	617.9	1,009.6	1,085.5
Employees	11.9%	781	885	961	1,078	1,223

FARREL CORPORATION

25 Main St.
Ansonia CT 06401
Phone: 203-736-5500
Fax: 203-736-5580
Web: www.farrel.com

CEO: Mark Meulbroek
CFO: Paul M Zepp
HR: Angela Dawley
FYE: December 31
Type: Private

Before the rubber meets the road tire makers meet with Farrel maker of rubber and plastic production machinery. The company's products include batch mixers extruders (used to make hoses and sheathings) mills and pelletizers under brand names Banbury Technolab and Intermix. It also provides related services such as equipment upgrading consulting rebuilding remanufacturing and spare parts. Farrel sells its machinery to petrochemical plastic resins and plastic compounder firms. Rubber-making equipment customers include tire makers automotive parts manufacturers and footwear producers. In late 2009 Germany-based industrial conglomerate L. Possehl & Co. acquired Farrel for about $14 million.

FARSTAD OIL INC.

100 27TH ST NE
MINOT, ND 58703-5164
Phone: 701-852-1194
Fax: –
Web: www.farstadoil.com

CEO: –
CFO: Bruce Hest
HR: –
FYE: December 31
Type: Private

When you are freezing in Fargo fuel is more than a luxury it's a necessity. Farstad Oil makes sure that gas stations lube shops and propane dealers are well stocked for those living through the cold winters in the Upper Midwest and West. Farstad Oil is a regional wholesale petroleum products distributor serving customers in North Dakota Montana Minnesota and Wyoming. The company a subsidiary of holding company SPF Energy wholesales about 250 million gallons of gas and fuel 20 million gallons of propane and 2.5 million gallons of lubricants each year. Its Minot operation is the largest lubricant plant in the region.

	Annual Growth	12/08	12/09	12/10	12/11	12/12
Sales ($ mil.)	28.5%	–	476.6	686.7	1,034.6	1,010.1
Net income ($ mil.)	47.8%	–	1.2	2.1	3.8	4.0
Market value ($ mil.)	–	–	–	–	–	–
Employees	–	–	–	–	–	125

FASHION BUG RETAIL COMPANIES LLC

450 Winks Ln.
Bensalem PA 19020
Phone: 215-245-9100
Fax: 215-633-4640
Web: www.fashionbug.com

CEO: Alan Rosskamm
CFO: Michele Pascoe
HR: Donna D Desilets
FYE: January 31
Type: Subsidiary

When women get the bug to shop they hop on over to Fashion Bug. The chain which operates more than 600 shops (down from more than 1200 a decade ago) in 40-plus US states and an online store sells low- to moderately priced casual and career apparel for women in juniors misses and plus sizes. The stores are located mainly in strip shopping centers and average about 8700 sq. ft. In addition to fashionable clothing Fashion Bug offers intimate apparel footwear and accessories (including jewelry handbags and hair goods). Fashion Bug's parent company Charming Shoppes was acquired by Ascena Retail Group in 2012. Ascena plans to shut down Fashion Bug founded in the 1960s by early 2013.

FASTENAL CO.

NMS: FAST

2001 Theurer Boulevard
Winona, MN 55987-1500
Phone: 507 454-5374
Fax: 507 453-8049
Web: www.fastenal.com

CEO: Daniel L. (Dan) Florness
CFO: Daniel L Florness
HR: Reyne K. Wisecup
FYE: December 31
Type: Public

Some might say it has a screw loose but things are really pretty snug at Fastenal. The industrial and fastener distributor sells almost 1.4 million products in about a dozen categories including threaded fasteners (such as screws nuts and bolts) which represent about 40% of overall sales. Other sales come from fluid-transfer parts for hydraulic and pneumatic power; janitorial electrical and welding supplies; material handling items; metal-cutting tool blades; and power tools. Founded in 1967 as a fastener shop Fastenal now operates about 2700 stores in all 50 US states and in Canada Mexico Asia and Europe. Its customers include construction manufacturing and other industrial professionals.

	Annual Growth	12/11	12/12	12/13	12/14	12/15
Sales ($ mil.)	8.7%	2,766.9	3,133.6	3,326.1	3,733.5	3,869.2
Net income ($ mil.)	9.6%	357.9	420.5	448.6	494.2	516.4
Market value ($ mil.)	(1.6%)	12,628.7	13,509.0	13,758.0	13,772.5	11,820.7
Employees	8.1%	15,168	15,145	17,277	18,417	20,746

FATBURGER CORPORATION

301 Arizona Ave. Ste. 200
Santa Monica CA 90401-1364
Phone: 310-319-1850
Fax: 310-319-1863
Web: www.fatburger.com

CEO: Andrew Wiederhorn
CFO: Harold Fox
HR: –
FYE: June 30
Type: Private

It's a little more expensive than 99 cents but you don't need to be a real fat cat to enjoy one of these burgers. Fatburger operates and franchises more than 90 hamburger stands known for their 1/3 pound signature sandwich. Located primarily in Southern California the 1950s-style restaurants also offer a 1/2 pound Kingburger and 1/8 pound Baby Fat burger as well as a variety of side orders and other sandwiches. Franchisees operate more than 60 of the chain's locations. Lovie Yancey opened the first Fatburger in 1952 when "fat" was used to describe the size not the content of the burger. Fog Cutter Capital Group owns more than 80% of the company.

FATWIRE CORPORATION

330 Old Country Rd. Ste. 303
Mineola NY 11501-4143
Phone: 516-328-9473
Fax: 516-739-5069
Web: www.fatwire.com

CEO: Dorian Daley
CFO: Jim Driscoll
HR: –
FYE: May 31
Type: Subsidiary

FatWire's Web content and experience management software helped organizations build and run online corporate portals with complex features. Its software enabled businesses to create and manage content access it through a variety of channels and deliver and reuse it across multiple applications and websites. FatWire sold to companies in the financial services manufacturing retail media and entertainment telecom health care and travel markets. The company also offered tools for managing social media and user-generated content (UGC) including Community Server and Gadget Server (Web page personalization tools). Key clients included Wal-Mart Best Buy Pfizer and Ford. FatWire was acquired by Oracle in 2011.

FAULKNERUSA INC.

535 E. 5th St.
Austin TX 78701
Phone: 512-652-4000
Fax: 512-652-4001
Web: www.faulknerusa.com

CEO: –
CFO: Don Schulze
HR: Lori Fraser
FYE: December 31
Type: Private

"The Sound and the Fury" for this Faulkner is only the din of nails being pounded into buildings. FaulknerUSA provides design-build construction program management and development services nationwide but primarily focuses its efforts on Texas. The company builds military housing correctional facilities hotels and hospitals and retail and manufacturing sites. Services include preconstruction design construction and furnishings. The company has several high-profile projects to its name including the Grand Hyatt Hotel in San Antonio Gucci on Rodeo Drive in Beverly Hills the Williamson County Jail in Georgetown Texas and Navy housing at the Naval Air Station in Corpus Christi Texas.

FAUQUIER BANKSHARES, INC.

NAS: FBSS

10 Courthouse Square
Warrenton, VA 20186
Phone: 540 347-2700
Fax: –
Web: www.fauquierbank.com

CEO: Randy K Ferrell
CFO: Eric P Graap
HR: –
FYE: December 31
Type: Public

Fauquier Bankshares is the holding company for The Fauquier Bank which operates about 10 branches in Fauquier and Prince William counties in northern Virginia southwest of Washington DC. The bank targets individuals and regional business customers offering standard deposit products such as checking savings and money market accounts CDs and IRAs. Its lending activities consist mostly of residential and commercial mortgages. The bank's wealth management division provides investment management trust estate retirement insurance and brokerage services. Through subsidiary Fauquier Bank Services it has equity ownership stakes in Bankers Insurance Infinex Investments and Bankers Title Shenandoah.

	Annual Growth	12/10	12/11	12/12	12/13	12/14
Assets ($ mil.)	0.3%	598.0	614.2	601.4	615.8	606.3
Net income ($ mil.)	7.0%	3.7	4.1	2.1	4.3	4.8
Market value ($ mil.)	9.2%	48.3	40.5	44.7	51.1	68.8
Employees	(4.6%)	175	167	152	143	145

FAURECIA EXHAUST SYSTEMS INC.

543 Matzinger Rd.
Toledo OH 43612
Phone: 419-727-5000
Fax: 419-727-5025

CEO: –
CFO: Philippe Vienney
HR: –
FYE: December 31
Type: Subsidiary

Faurecia Exhaust Systems once known as AP Automotive Systems ends each day exhausted but rewarded. Reportedly one in five vehicles in the world operates with an exhaust system made by this company. Faurecia Exhaust Systems produces complete automotive exhaust systems including manifolds tailpipes and other exhaust system components for such major carmakers as Volkswagen Peugeot and Ford. Its manufacturing facilities are located in the US as well as Mexico the Netherlands Sweden the Czech Republic South Africa and China. The company operates as part of the emissions control technologies business group of French automotive equipment maker Faurecia which is owned by Peugeot.

FAYETTE COMMUNITY HOSPITAL INC.

1255 HIGHWAY 54 W
FAYETTEVILLE, GA 302144526
Phone: 770-719-7000
Fax: –
Web: www.piedmont.org

CEO: James Michael Burnette
CFO: John Miles
HR: –
FYE: June 30
Type: Private

If you do too much boogying at the Fayetteville Bluegrass Blast or slip in the sleet at the Christmas in Fayetteville festival Piedmont Fayette Hospital (PFH) is there to help. The acute care hospital is home to centers in cardiovascular medicine diabetes treatment sleep disorder therapy women's health fitness and rehabilitative care. With more than 500 physicians on staff the former Fayette Community Hospital has the ability to treat just about whatever comes through its doors — from ear nose throat problems to pediatric dentistry. The about 155-bed hospital opened in 1997 and is part of the not-for-profit Piedmont Healthcare network.

	Annual Growth	06/04	06/05	06/08	06/09	06/13
Sales ($ mil.)	–	–	(1,449.1)	163.8	165.2	283.1
Net income ($ mil.)	13.5%	–	–	12.7	18.2	23.9
Market value ($ mil.)	–	–	–	–	–	–
Employees	–	–	–	–	–	1,045

FAZOLI'S RESTAURANTS LLC

2470 Palumbo Dr.
Lexington KY 40509
Phone: 859-268-1668
Fax: 859-268-2263
Web: www.fazolis.com

CEO: Carl Howard
CFO: –
HR: –
FYE: March 31
Type: Private

The taste of Italy can be as close as your local shopping mall thanks to this company. Fazoli's Restaurants operates a leading quick-service Italian food chain with more than 220 locations in about 25 states. The eateries serve pasta pizzas (whole pies and by the slice) and panini sandwiches as well as soups salads and dessert items. Many Fazoli's locations can be found in shopping centers highway service areas and other high-traffic locations. Most of the chain's locations are operated by franchisees. Fazoli's was launched in 1988 by restaurant operator Jerrico which also started the Long John Silver's chain. The company is owned by private equity firm Sun Capital Partners.

FBL FINANCIAL GROUP, INC.

NYS: FFG

5400 University Avenue
West Des Moines, IA 50266-5997
Phone: 515 225-5400
Fax: –
Web: www.fblfinancial.com

CEO: James P Brannen
CFO: James P. (Jim) Brannen
HR: –
FYE: December 31
Type: Public

Insurance holding company FBL Financial Group (FBL) is the parent of Farm Bureau Life Insurance Company. Through its subsidiary the firm sells life insurance annuities and investment products to farmers ranchers and agricultural businesses. Farm Bureau Life sells insurance and annuities through an exclusive network of about 2000 agents across some 15 states in the Midwest and West. (In Colorado it operates as Greenfields Life Insurance.) The company markets its products through an affiliation with the American Farm Bureau Federation. FBL also manages for a fee two Farm Bureau-affiliated property/casualty insurance companies. The Iowa Farm Bureau Federation owns close to 60% of the company.

	Annual Growth	12/10	12/11	12/12	12/13	12/14
Assets ($ mil.)	(12.3%)	15,334.1	8,225.9	8,417.7	8,461.3	9,064.4
Net income ($ mil.)	(2.3%)	120.7	31.3	79.9	108.6	109.9
Market value ($ mil.)	19.3%	708.6	840.8	845.5	1,107.0	1,434.2
Employees	(0.8%)	1,679	1,570	1,582	1,589	1,628

FBR & CO.

NMS: FBRC

1300 North Seventeenth Street
Arlington, VA 22209
Phone: 703 312-9500
Fax: –
Web: www.fbr.com

CEO: Richard J Hendrix
CFO: Bradley J Wright
HR: –
FYE: December 31
Type: Public

Don't confuse FDR and FBR: One was a beloved US president while the other loves dead presidents. FBR & Co. provides investment banking and institutional brokerage services for institutional and corporate clients and wealthy individuals. It also conducts equities research manages mutual funds and invests its own capital in merchant banking transactions alongside its clients. The company focuses on the consumer industrials energy financial services health care real estate media telecommunications and technology markets Crestview Partners. Its principal operating subsidiaries are FBR Capital Markets & Co. and FBR Fund Advisers.

	Annual Growth	12/10	12/11	12/12	12/13	12/14
Sales ($ mil.)	(7.3%)	246.6	147.2	151.5	259.8	182.1
Net income ($ mil.)	–	(37.6)	(49.6)	29.7	92.9	17.0
Market value ($ mil.)	59.3%	32.0	17.2	32.5	221.3	206.3
Employees	(12.0%)	501	295	256	302	300

FCCI MUTUAL INSURANCE HOLDING COMPANY

6300 University Pkwy.
Sarasota FL 34240
Phone: 941-907-3224
Fax: 800-226-3243
Web: www.fcci-group.com

CEO: G W Jacobs
CFO: Craig Johnson
HR: –
FYE: December 31
Type: Private - Mutual Com

FCCI Mutual Insurance (operating as FCCI Insurance Group) offers a variety of commercial insurance lines in more than a dozen Southeast and Midwest states. Its products include commercial workers' compensation liability auto inland marine farmowners and umbrella coverage. The company's clients span variety of industries including construction manufacturing agriculture and retail. In addition to insurance products FCCI provides bill review claims management services and loss control programs including safety training and online risk management tools. FCCI Insurance Group was founded in 1959 as a Florida workers' compensation insurer.

FCI CONSTRUCTORS INC.

3070 I-70 BUSINESS LOOP
GRAND JUNCTION, CO 81504-4468
Phone: 970-434-9093
Fax: –
Web: www.fciol.com

CEO: –
CFO: Mark Labere
HR: –
FYE: March 31
Type: Private

FCI Constructors focuses on commercial building and renovation projects in the Rocky Mountain and southwestern US. Its projects range from hospitals assisted living facilities municipal projects and recreation centers to office buildings banks churches and educational manufacturing warehouse correctional and postal facilities. The company has offices in Arizona Colorado and Wyoming. Projects include the Mesa County Justice Center in Phoenix Crossroads Urgent Psychiatric Care Hospital in Durango Colorado and the Denver Public Schools Bus Terminal. The company which was founded in 1978 by M. L. Francis is owned by CEO Ed Forsman EVP Ron Choate and its employees.

	Annual Growth	03/07	03/08	03/09	03/10	03/12
Sales ($ mil.)	(13.1%)	–	–	379.1	315.0	248.8
Net income ($ mil.)	(30.1%)	–	–	3.3	1.7	1.1
Market value ($ mil.)	–	–	–	–	–	–
Employees	–	–	–	–	–	275

FEATHERLITE INC.

Hwy. 63 and 9
Cresco IA 52136
Phone: 563-547-6000
Fax: 563-547-6100
Web: www.fthr.com

CEO: –
CFO: –
HR: –
FYE: December 31
Type: Private

Featherlite belongs in the aluminum trailer industry's Haul of Fame. The company offers a line of standard and specialty trailer models. Featherlite's trailers are used to haul horses racecars livestock construction equipment ATVs and motorcycles. The company also makes custom specialty trailers used for vending offices kitchens passenger trams and classrooms. Fellow trailer maker Universal Trailer bought Featherlite for $29 million in cash and the assumption of $109 million in debt late in 2006. Featherlite branded trailers are sold throughout Canada and the US through a network of more than 200 dealers; it also has dealers in Australia and Europe.

FEDERAL AGRICULTURAL MORTGAGE CORP   NYS: AGM

1999 K Street, N.W., 4th Floor
Washington, DC 20006
Phone: 202 872-7700
Fax: 202 872-7713
Web: www.farmermac.com

CEO: Timothy L. (Tim) Buzby
CFO: R. Dale Lynch
HR: –
FYE: December 31
Type: Public

Farmer Mac (Federal Agricultural Mortgage Corporation) is Fannie Mae and Freddie Mac's country cousin. Like its city-slicker kin it provides liquidity in its markets (agricultural real estate and rural housing mortgages) by buying loans from lenders and then securitizing the loans into Farmer Mac Guaranteed Securities. Farmer Mac buys both conventional loans and those guaranteed by the US Department of Agriculture. Farmer Mac was created by Congress in 1987 to establish a secondary market for agricultural mortgage and rural utilities loans. It is a stockholder-owned publicly-traded corporation based in Washington DC with an underwriting office in Iowa.

	Annual Growth	12/10	12/11	12/12	12/13	12/14
Assets ($ mil.)	10.8%	9,479.9	11,883.5	12,622.2	13,361.8	14,287.8
Net income ($ mil.)	10.7%	32.0	16.7	46.8	75.3	48.1
Market value ($ mil.)	16.8%	178.5	197.1	355.5	374.6	331.8
Employees	5.2%	58	62	64	67	71

FEDERAL AVIATION ADMINISTRATION

800 Independence Ave. SW
Washington DC 20591
Phone: 866-835-5322
Fax: 617-568-5079
Web: www.massport.com

CEO: –
CFO: –
HR: –
FYE: September 30
Type: Government Agency

Nobody goes up up and away until the folks at the FAA say it's OK. The Federal Aviation Administration (FAA) is the government agency responsible for overseeing air transportation in the US. An arm of the US Department of Transportation the FAA focuses on air transportation safety including the enforcement of safety standards for aircraft manufacturing operation and maintenance. It also manages air traffic in the US through a network of towers overseeing an average of 50000 flights per day. It maintains radar systems communication equipment and air traffic security systems. The FAA's annual budget is typically around $15 billion.

FEDERAL DEPOSIT INSURANCE CORPORATION

550 17th St. NW
Washington DC 20429-9990
Phone: 202-898-7021
Fax: 202-942-3427
Web: www.fdic.gov

CEO: –
CFO: –
HR: –
FYE: December 31
Type: Government Agency

The FDIC is like money in the bank only better. The Federal Insurance Corporation (FDIC) insures deposits and retirement accounts in member accounts for up to $250000 protecting depositors in the event of bank failure. It also supervises financial institutions and manages failed banks. The FDIC is funded by member bank premiums for deposit insurance coverage and from earnings on investments in US Treasury securities. It insures more than $9 trillion of deposits covering virtually every bank in the country. (It does not cover mutual funds securities or related investments.) An independent federal agency the FDIC was created in 1933 in response to bank runs during the Great Depression.

FEDERAL EXPRESS CORPORATION

3610 Hacks Cross Rd.
Memphis TN 38125
Phone: 901-369-3600
Fax: 212-636-5481
Web: www.dccomics.com/vertigo

CEO: David J Bronczek
CFO: Elise L Jordan
HR: –
FYE: May 31
Type: Subsidiary

You can't spell FedEx without Federal Express Corporation which does business as FedEx Express. The largest subsidiary of FedEx (about 60% of sales) FedEx Express is responsible for its parent's namesake express delivery business the world's largest. FedEx Express delivers some 3.5 million packages per day throughout the US and to some 220 countries and territories worldwide. Packages (from envelopes to boxes weighing up to 150 pounds) account for most of the company's sales; FedEx Express also delivers pallets of freight weighing from 150 pounds to 2200 pounds. The company operates a fleet of about 690 aircraft and about 50000 motor vehicles and trailers.

FEDERAL HOME LOAN BANK BOSTON

800 Boylston Street
Boston, MA 02199
Phone: 617 292-9600
Fax: –
Web: www.fhlbboston.com

CEO: Edward A Hjerpe III
CFO: Frank Nitkiewicz
HR: –
FYE: December 31
Type: Public

Federal Home Loan Bank of Boston (FHLB Boston) is banking on the continued support of other banks. The government-supported enterprise provides funds for residential mortgages and community development loans to its members which consist of more than 440 financial institutions across New England including banks thrifts credit unions and insurance companies. The bank also lends to nonmember institutions the likes of state housing finance agencies primarily to promote the funding of low to moderate income housing in the region. FHLB Boston is one of 12 regional wholesale banks in the Federal Home Loan Bank System. Its region includes Connecticut Maine Massachusetts New Hampshire Rhode Island and Vermont.

	Annual Growth	12/10	12/11	12/12	12/13	12/14
Sales ($ mil.)	(10.5%)	870.5	765.0	730.2	586.8	558.6
Net income ($ mil.)	8.9%	106.6	159.6	207.1	212.3	149.8
Market value ($ mil.)	–	–	–	–	–	–
Employees	1.7%	187	189	188	199	200

FEDERAL HOME LOAN BANK NEW YORK

101 Park Avenue
New York, NY 10178
Phone: 212 681-6000
Fax: –
Web: www.fhlbny.com

CEO: –
CFO: Kevin M Neylan
HR: Mildred Tse-Gonzalez
FYE: December 31
Type: Public

Federal Home Loan Bank of New York (FHLBNY) provides funds for residential mortgages and community development to more than 330 member banks savings and loans credit unions and life insurance companies in New York New Jersey Puerto Rico and the US Virgin Islands. One of a dozen Federal Home Loan Banks in the US it is cooperatively owned by its member institutions and supervised by the Federal Housing Finance Agency. FHLBNY like others in the system is privately capitalized; it receives no taxpayer funding. The bank instead raises funds mainly by issuing debt instruments in the capital markets.

	Annual Growth	12/10	12/11	12/12	12/13	12/14
Assets ($ mil.)	7.3%	100,212.1	97,662.3	102,988.8	128,332.9	132,825.4
Net income ($ mil.)	3.4%	275.5	244.5	360.7	304.6	314.9
Market value ($ mil.)	–	–	–	–	–	–
Employees	(1.2%)	271	276	272	258	258

FEDERAL HOME LOAN BANK OF PITTSBURGH

601 Grant Street
Pittsburgh, PA 15219
Phone: 412 288-3400
Fax: –
Web: www.fhlb-pgh.com

CEO: Winthrop Watson
CFO: David G Paulson
HR: –
FYE: December 31
Type: Public

The Federal Home Loan Bank of Pittsburgh helps revitalize neighborhoods and fund low-income housing in the City of Champions and beyond. One of a dozen banks in the Federal Home Loan Bank System the government-sponsored entity (FHLB Pittsburgh for short) uses private capital and public sponsorships to provide low-cost funding for residential mortgages and community and economic development loans in Delaware Pennsylvania and West Virginia. It is cooperatively owned by about 300 member banks thrifts credit unions and insurance companies in its three-state district. The bank also offers member banks correspondent banking services such as depository funds transfer settlement and safekeeping services.

	Annual Growth	12/10	12/11	12/12	12/13	12/14
Sales ($ mil.)	(3.8%)	818.5	743.4	737.6	644.1	701.8
Net income ($ mil.)	135.6%	8.3	38.0	129.7	147.9	255.8
Market value ($ mil.)	–	–	–	–	–	–
Employees	(1.4%)	232	234	236	210	219

FEDERAL HOME LOAN BANK OF SAN FRANCISCO

600 California Street
San Francisco, CA 94108
Phone: 415 616-1000
Fax: –
Web: www.fhlbsf.com

CEO: –
CFO: Kenneth C Miller
HR: Gregory Fontenot
FYE: December 31
Type: Public

The city by the bay is the home to the Federal Home Loan Bank of San Francisco one of a dozen regional banks in the Federal Home Loan Bank System chartered by Congress in 1932 to provide credit to residential mortgage lenders. The government-sponsored enterprise is privately owned by its members which include some 400 commercial banks credit unions industrial loan companies savings and loans insurance companies and housing associates headquartered in Arizona California and Nevada. The bank links members to worldwide capital markets which provide them with low-cost funding. Members then pass these advances along to their customers in the form of affordable home mortgage and economic development loans.

	Annual Growth	12/10	12/11	12/12	12/13	12/14
Assets ($ mil.)	(16.0%)	152,423.0	113,552.0	86,421.0	85,774.0	75,807.0
Net income ($ mil.)	(15.3%)	399.0	216.0	491.0	308.0	205.0
Market value ($ mil.)	–	–	–	–	–	–
Employees	(4.3%)	304	274	264	262	255

FEDERAL PRISON INDUSTRIES INC.

320 1st St. NW Bldg. 400
Washington DC 20534
Phone: 202-305-3500
Fax: 202-305-7340
Web: www.unicor.gov

CEO: Steve V Schwalb
CFO: –
HR: –
FYE: September 30
Type: Government Agency

Some businesses benefit from captive audiences; this company benefits from captive employees. Federal Prison Industries (FPI) known by its trade name UNICOR uses prisoners to make products and provide services mainly for US government agencies. Nearly 16000 inmates (about 9% of the total eligible inmate population) are employed in 94 FPI factories in prisons across the US. UNICOR which is part of the Justice Department's Bureau of Prisons manufactures products such as office furniture clothing beds and linens and electronics equipment. It also offers services including data entry bulk mailing laundry services recycling and refurbishing of vehicle components.

FEDERAL REALTY INVESTMENT TRUST (MD)   NYS: FRT

1626 East Jefferson Street
Rockville, MD 20852
Phone: 301 998-8100
Fax: –
Web: www.federalrealty.com

CEO: Donald C. (Don) Wood
CFO: James M. (Jim) Taylor
HR: –
FYE: December 31
Type: Public

It's a safe bet that Federal Realty Investment Trust makes a federal case of shopping centers. The real estate investment trust (REIT) owns or has a majority interest in about 85 retail properties with more than 19 million sq. ft. of leasable space including community and neighborhood shopping centers and mixed-use complexes. Its key markets are densely populated affluent areas in the Northeast Mid-Atlantic and California; it also has properties in Florida Illinois Michigan and Texas. The REIT's occupancy rate is around 93%. Principal tenants include Giant Food Barnes & NobleBed Bath & Beyond and T.J. Maxx. One of the oldest publicly traded REITs in the US Federal Realty was founded in 1962.

	Annual Growth	12/11	12/12	12/13	12/14	12/15
Sales ($ mil.)	7.7%	553.1	608.0	637.4	686.1	744.0
Net income ($ mil.)	9.9%	143.9	151.9	162.7	164.5	210.2
Market value ($ mil.)	12.6%	6,306.5	7,228.7	7,047.3	9,274.6	10,153.0
Employees	1.2%	416	421	425	405	436

FEDERAL RESERVE BANK OF ATLANTA, DIST. NO. 6

1000 Peachtree Street, N.E.
Atlanta, GA 30309-4470
Phone: 404 498-8500
Fax: –
Web: www.frbatlanta.org

CEO: –
CFO: –
HR: Clifford (Cliff) Stanford
FYE: December 31
Type: Public

One of 12 regional banks in the Federal Reserve System the Federal Reserve Bank of Atlanta oversees Fed member banks and thrifts and their holding companies throughout the Southeast including Alabama Florida Georgia and parts of Louisiana Mississippi and Tennessee. It conducts examinations and investigations of member institutions distributes cash issues savings bonds and Treasury securities and assists the Fed in setting monetary policy such as interest rates. The bank also processes checks and acts as a clearinghouse for payments between banks. Fed Reserve Banks are independent arms within the government and return earnings (gleaned mostly from investments in government bonds) to the US Treasury.

	Annual Growth	12/10	12/11	12/12	12/13	12/14
Sales ($ mil.)	(4.4%)	8,205.0	7,222.0	6,317.0	6,105.0	6,861.0
Net income ($ mil.)	–	(7,567.0)	(6,450.0)	135.0	89.0	156.0
Market value ($ mil.)	–	–	–	–	–	–
Employees						

FEDERAL RESERVE BANK OF BOSTON, DIST. NO. 1

600 Atlantic Avenue
Boston, MA 02210
Phone: 617 973-3000
Fax: –
Web: www.bostonfed.org

CEO: Eric S Rosengren
CFO: –
HR: –
FYE: December 31
Type: Public

One of 12 regional banks in the Federal Reserve System the Federal Reserve Bank of Boston oversees more than 100 banks and bank holding companies in six New England states including Connecticut (except Fairfield County) Massachusetts Maine New Hampshire Rhode Island and Vermont. It conducts examinations and investigations of member institutions distributes money issues savings bonds and Treasury securities and assists the Fed in setting monetary policy. The bank also processes checks and acts as a clearinghouse for payments between banks. Federal Reserve Banks are not-for-profit and return most of their earnings (primarily from investments in government bonds) to the US Treasury.

	Annual Growth	12/10	12/11	12/12	12/13	12/14
Sales ($ mil.)	7.2%	1,872.0	2,207.0	2,327.0	2,335.0	2,472.0
Net income ($ mil.)	(47.8%)	1,605.0	1,909.0	483.0	(33.0)	119.0
Market value ($ mil.)	–	–	–	–	–	–
Employees						

FEDERAL RESERVE BANK OF CHICAGO, DIST. NO. 7

230 South La Salle Street, P.O. Box 834
Chicago, IL 60690-0834
Phone: 312 322-5322
Fax: –
Web: www.chicagofed.org

CEO: Charles L Evans
CFO: –
HR: –
FYE: December 31
Type: Public

The Federal Reserve Bank of Chicago regulates banks and bank holding companies in northern Illinois northern Indiana southern Wisconsin the Lower Peninsula of Michigan and all of Iowa. It supervises more than 850 bank holding companies and state member banks distributes money issues savings bonds and Treasury securities and assists the Fed in setting monetary policy. The Chicago Fed also processes checks and acts as a clearinghouse for payments between banks. Like the 11 other regional banks in the Federal Reserve System it returns its profits (earned largely from investments in government and federal agency securities) to the US Treasury.

	Annual Growth	12/10	12/11	12/12	12/13	12/14
Sales ($ mil.)	(5.7%)	6,541.0	5,586.0	5,409.0	5,001.0	5,176.0
Net income ($ mil.)	(67.7%)	6,068.0	5,026.0	122.0	(12.0)	66.0
Market value ($ mil.)	–	–	–	–	–	–
Employees						

FEDERAL RESERVE BANK OF CLEVELAND, DIST. NO. 4

P.O. Box 6387
Cleveland, OH 44101-1387
Phone: 216 579-2000
Fax: –
Web: www.clevelandfed.org

CEO: –
CFO: Lori Schumacher
HR: Thomas Sohlberg
FYE: December 31
Type: Public

One of 12 regional banks in the Federal Reserve System the Federal Reserve Bank of Cleveland oversees more than 200 member banks and thrifts and their holding companies in the Fourth Federal Reserve District (Ohio western Pennsylvania eastern Kentucky and northern West Virginia). It conducts examinations and investigations of member institutions distributes money issues savings bonds and Treasury securities and participates in setting monetary policy. The bank also processes checks and acts as a clearinghouse for payments between banks in its region. Federal Reserve Banks are not-for-profit and return earnings (mostly from investments in government bonds) to the US Treasury.

	Annual Growth	12/10	12/11	12/12	12/13	12/14
Sales ($ mil.)	(3.4%)	2,822.0	2,591.0	2,422.0	2,255.0	2,458.0
Net income ($ mil.)	(47.3%)	2,540.0	2,246.0	280.0	160.0	196.0
Market value ($ mil.)	–	–	–	–	–	–
Employees						

FEDERAL RESERVE BANK OF DALLAS, DIST. NO. 11

2200 North Pearl Street
Dallas, TX 75201-2272
Phone: 214 922-6000
Fax: –
Web: www.dallasfed.org

CEO: Robert S. (Rob) Kaplan
CFO: –
HR: –
FYE: December 31
Type: Public

One of 12 regional banks in the Federal Reserve System the Federal Reserve Bank of Dallas oversees system member banks and bank holding companies in southern New Mexico northern Louisiana and all of Texas. It conducts examinations and investigations of member institutions distributes money issues savings bonds and Treasury securities and assists the Federal Reserve in setting monetary policy. The bank also processes checks and acts as a clearinghouse for payments between banks. Federal Reserve Banks are not-for-profit and return earnings (mostly from investments in government bonds) to the US Treasury. The bank has branches in El Paso Houston and San Antonio.

	Annual Growth	12/10	12/11	12/12	12/13	12/14
Sales ($ mil.)	3.0%	3,352.0	3,495.0	3,696.0	3,531.0	3,769.0
Net income ($ mil.)	–	3,060.0	3,134.0	37.0	24.0	(12.0)
Market value ($ mil.)	–	–	–	–	–	–
Employees						

FEDERAL RESERVE BANK OF KANSAS CITY, DIST. NO. 10

1 Memorial Drive
Kansas City, MO 64198
Phone: 816 881-2000
Fax: –
Web: www.kansascityfed.org

CEO: –
CFO: –
HR: Veronica M Sellers
FYE: December 31
Type: Public

One of 12 regional banks in the Federal Reserve System the Federal Reserve Bank of Kansas City oversees system member banks and bank holding companies in Colorado Kansas Nebraska northern New Mexico Oklahoma western Missouri and Wyoming. The bank also has branch offices in Denver Oklahoma and Omaha. Considered the 10th District it conducts examinations and investigations of member institutions distributes money issues savings bonds and Treasury securities and assists the Fed in setting monetary policy. The bank established in 1914 also processes checks and acts as a clearinghouse for payments between banks.

	Annual Growth	12/10	12/11	12/12	12/13	12/14
Sales ($ mil.)	(12.0%)	2,891.0	2,520.0	2,120.0	1,793.0	1,737.0
Net income ($ mil.)	(65.8%)	2,620.0	2,245.0	29.0	18.0	36.0
Market value ($ mil.)	–	–	–	–	–	–
Employees						

FEDERAL RESERVE BANK OF MINNEAPOLIS, DIST. NO. 9

90 Hennepin Avenue, P.O. Box 291
Minneapolis, MN 55408-0291
Phone: 612 204-5000
Fax: –
Web: www.minneapolisfed.org

CEO: Narayana Kocherlakota
CFO: –
HR: –
FYE: December 31
Type: Public

The Federal Reserve Bank of Minneapolis one of the 12 regional banks in the Federal Reserve System regulates banks and bank holding companies in the Ninth District in Minnesota Montana North Dakota South Dakota northern Wisconsin and the Upper Peninsula of Michigan. It conducts investigations of member institutions distributes money issues savings bonds and Treasury securities and assists the Fed in setting monetary policy. The bank also processes checks and acts as a clearinghouse for payments between banks. The Federal Reserve Bank of Minneapolis like its 11 counterparts returns its profits (earned largely from investments in government and federal agency securities) to the US Treasury.

	Annual Growth	12/10	12/11	12/12	12/13	12/14
Sales ($ mil.)	(7.1%)	1,198.0	1,376.0	1,114.0	934.0	894.0
Net income ($ mil.)	(58.9%)	981.0	1,160.0	18.0	(8.0)	28.0
Market value ($ mil.)	–	–	–	–	–	–
Employees						

FEDERAL RESERVE BANK OF NEW YORK, DIST. NO. 2

33 Liberty Street
New York, NY 10045-0001
Phone: 212 720-5000
Fax: –
Web: www.newyorkfed.org

CEO: William C. Dudley
CFO: –
HR: Christina Miller
FYE: December 31
Type: Public

The Federal Reserve Bank of New York is the largest in the Federal Reserve System to oversee US bank activities. It issues currency clears money transfers and lends to banks in its district. In addition to the duties it shares with 11 other regional Federal Reserve Banks the New York Fed trades US government securities to regulate the money supply intervenes on foreign exchange markets and stores monetary gold for foreign central banks and governments. The New York Fed's district is relatively small (made up of New York Puerto Rico the US Virgin Islands northern New Jersey and Fairfield County Connecticut) but the bank is the largest in the Federal Reserve System in assets and volume of transactions.

	Annual Growth	12/10	12/11	12/12	12/13	12/14
Sales ($ mil.)	12.3%	43,290.0	39,655.0	56,361.0	50,355.0	68,824.0
Net income ($ mil.)	(50.4%)	39,761.0	35,026.0	525.0	(1,397.0)	2,398.0
Market value ($ mil.)	–	–	–	–	–	–
Employees						

FEDERAL RESERVE BANK OF PHILADELPHIA, DIST. NO. 3

10 Independence Mall
Philadelphia, PA 19106-1574
Phone: 215 574-6000
Fax: 215 574-6030
Web: www.philadelphiafed.org

CEO: –
CFO: Michael J Angelakis
HR: Brad Bralow
FYE: December 31
Type: Public

One of 12 regional banks in the Federal Reserve System the Federal Reserve Bank of Philadelphia oversees system member banks and bank holding companies in eastern and central Pennsylvania southern New Jersey and Delaware. It conducts examinations and investigations of member institutions distributes money issues savings bonds and Treasury securities and assists the Fed in setting monetary policy. The bank also processes checks and acts as a clearinghouse for payments between banks in its region. Federal Reserve Banks are not-for-profit and return most of their income (primarily earned from investments in US government and federal agency securities) to the US Treasury.

	Annual Growth	12/10	12/11	12/12	12/13	12/14
Sales ($ mil.)	12.6%	1,723.0	2,774.0	3,120.0	2,673.0	2,765.0
Net income ($ mil.)	–	1,399.0	2,382.0	(77.0)	60.0	(342.0)
Market value ($ mil.)	–	–	–	–	–	–
Employees						

FEDERAL RESERVE BANK OF RICHMOND, DIST. NO. 5

Post Office Box 27622
Richmond, VA 23261
Phone: 804 697-8000
Fax: –
Web: www.richmondfed.org

CEO: Jeffrey M. (Jeff) Lacker
CFO: Michael L. (Mike) Wilder
HR: Wendi L Hickman
FYE: December 31
Type: Public

One of 12 regional banks in the Federal Reserve System the Federal Reserve Bank of Richmond oversees the Fifth District's system member banks and bank holding companies in Virginia; Maryland; the Carolinas; Washington DC; and most of West Virginia from branches in Maryland North Carolina and Virginia. It conducts examinations and investigations of member institutions distributes money issues savings bonds and Treasury securities and assists the Federal Reserve System in setting monetary policy. The bank also processes checks and acts as a clearinghouse for payments between banks. Federal Reserve Banks return earnings (mostly from investments in government bonds) to the US Treasury.

	Annual Growth	12/10	12/11	12/12	12/13	12/14
Sales ($ mil.)	(3.8%)	7,178.0	10,043.0	7,799.0	5,666.0	6,148.0
Net income ($ mil.)	(33.8%)	6,241.0	9,222.0	542.0	284.0	1,202.0
Market value ($ mil.)	–	–	–	–	–	–
Employees						

FEDERAL RESERVE BANK OF SAN FRANCISCO, DIST. NO. 12

101 Market Street
San Francisco, CA 94105
Phone: 415 974-2000
Fax: –
Web: www.frbsf.org

CEO: John C. Williams
CFO: –
HR: –
FYE: December 31
Type: Public

One of 12 regional banks in the Federal Reserve System the Federal Reserve Bank of San Francisco through four branch offices oversees hundreds of banks and thrifts in nine western states and American Samoa Guam and the Northern Mariana Islands - the largest of the 12 districts. It conducts examinations and investigations of member institutions distributes money issues savings bonds and Treasury securities and assists the Federal Reserve in setting monetary policy. The bank also processes checks and acts as a clearinghouse for payments between banks. Federal Reserve Banks are not-for-profit and return earnings (mostly from investments in government bonds) to the US Treasury.

	Annual Growth	12/10	12/11	12/12	12/13	12/14
Sales ($ mil.)	7.9%	8,622.0	8,863.0	8,357.0	8,507.0	11,704.0
Net income ($ mil.)	(50.6%)	7,890.0	8,071.0	26.0	323.0	470.0
Market value ($ mil.)	–	–	–	–	–	–
Employees						

FEDERAL RESERVE BANK OF ST. LOUIS, DIST. NO. 8

One Federal Reserve Bank Plaza, Broadway and Locust Street
St. Louis, MO 63102
Phone: 314 444-8444
Fax: –
Web: www.stlouisfed.org

CEO: James B Bullard
CFO: –
HR: –
FYE: December 31
Type: Public

One of 12 regional banks in the Federal Reserve System the Federal Reserve Bank of St. Louis regulates banks and bank holding companies in its region. Its territory encompasses eastern Missouri southern Illinois all of Arkansas and portions of Indiana Kentucky Mississippi and Tennessee. The bank operating from four offices conducts examinations and investigations of member institutions distributes money processes checks and payments between banks issues savings bonds and Treasury securities and assists the Fed in setting monetary policy. Federal Reserve Banks are not-for-profit and return almost all of their earnings (gleaned mostly from investments in government bonds) to the US Treasury.

	Annual Growth	12/10	12/11	12/12	12/13	12/14
Sales ($ mil.)	(8.3%)	2,356.0	1,895.0	1,667.0	1,562.0	1,666.0
Net income ($ mil.)	(61.2%)	2,084.0	1,617.0	29.0	1.0	47.0
Market value ($ mil.)	–	–	–	–	–	–
Employees	–	–	–	–	1,032	–

FEDERAL RESERVE SYSTEM

20th Street and Constitution Avenue N.W.
Washington, DC 20551
Phone: 202 452-3245
Fax: 202 728-5886
Web: www.federalreserve.gov

CEO: James B. Bullard
CFO: –
HR: –
FYE: December 31
Type: Public

Where do banks go when they need a loan? To the Federal Reserve System which sets the discount interest rate the base rate at which its member banks may borrow. Known as the Fed the system oversees a network of 12 Federal Reserve Banks located in major US cities; these in turn regulate banks in their districts and ensure they maintain adequate reserves. The Fed also clears money transfers issues currency and buys or sells government securities to regulate the money supply. Through its powerful New York bank the Fed conducts foreign currency transactions trades on the world market to support the US dollar's value and stores gold for foreign governments and international agencies.

	Annual Growth	12/10	12/11	12/12	12/13	12/14
Sales ($ mil.)	6.2%	89,816.0	88,027.0	100,526.0	90,540.0	114,299.0
Net income ($ mil.)	(51.9%)	81,689.0	78,538.0	2,151.0	(492.0)	4,363.0
Market value ($ mil.)	–	–	–	–	–	–
Employees	–	–	–	–	–	–

FEDERAL SCREW WORKS

NBB: FSCR

34846 Goddard Road
Romulus, MI 48174-3406
Phone: 734 941-4211
Fax: 586 443-4210
Web: www.federalscrew.com

CEO: Thomas Zurschmiede
CFO: –
HR: –
FYE: June 30
Type: Public

Federal Screw Works (FSW) doesn't mind if you think of your car as a bucket of bolts. The Detroit native makes fasteners and related items primarily for the automotive industry. The company produces high-volume lots to the specifications of manufacturers. Nonautomotive sales are mainly to makers of durable goods. FSW's products include locknuts bolts piston pins studs bushings shafts and other machined cold-formed hardened and ground-metal parts. It maintains five manufacturing facilities all of which are located in Michigan.

	Annual Growth	06/11	06/12	06/13	06/14	06/15
Sales ($ mil.)	3.5%	55.8	58.6	57.2	61.1	64.0
Net income ($ mil.)	–	(2.2)	(0.6)	0.1	0.6	1.3
Market value ($ mil.)	(8.2%)	8.3	8.6	3.5	3.5	5.9
Employees	2.7%	181	183	184	201	201

FEDERAL SIGNAL CORP.

NYS: FSS

1415 West 22nd Street
Oak Brook, IL 60523
Phone: 630 954-2000
Fax: 630 954-2030
Web: www.federalsignal.com

CEO: Jennifer L. Sherman
CFO: Brian S. Cooper
HR: –
FYE: December 31
Type: Public

Federal Signal likes to believe it keeps people property and the environment safe. Through segments include environmental solutions safety and security systems fire rescue the company designs and manufactures products for municipal governmental industrial and commercial customers. Offerings include street sweepers vacuum trucks and water blasters for environmental cleanup; emergency communications and public warning systems for public safety; aerial platforms for firefighting and utility maintenance. Federal Signal caters primarily to the US market.

	Annual Growth	12/10	12/11	12/12	12/13	12/14
Sales ($ mil.)	6.0%	726.5	795.6	803.2	851.3	918.5
Net income ($ mil.)	–	(175.7)	(14.2)	(27.5)	160.0	63.7
Market value ($ mil.)	22.5%	428.8	259.4	475.5	915.6	965.0
Employees	(1.0%)	2,812	2,900	2,558	2,550	2,700

FEDERAL-MOGUL HOLDINGS CORP

NMS: FDML

27300 West 11 Mile Road
Southfield, MI 48034
Phone: 248 354-7700
Fax: –
Web: www.federalmogul.com

CEO: Daniel A. (Dan) Ninivaggi
CFO: Jerome Rouquet
HR: –
FYE: December 31
Type: Public

For Federal-Mogul the sum of the parts is greater than the whole. The company makes components used in cars trucks and commercial vehicles as well as in energy industrial and other transportation equipment. Its products include pistons spark plugs ignition coils bearings gaskets seals and brake pads sold under brand names such as Champion Federal-Mogul Fel-Pro Glyco and Moog. Federal-Mogul has manufacturing and distribution facilities in 34 countries worldwide; customers include global automakers BMW Ford General Motors and Volkswagen. Federal-Mogul also distributes its own and other company's auto parts to aftermarket customers. About 60% of sales come from outside the US.

	Annual Growth	12/10	12/11	12/12	12/13	12/14
Sales ($ mil.)	4.1%	6,219.0	6,910.0	6,664.0	6,786.0	7,317.0
Net income ($ mil.)	–	161.0	(90.0)	(117.0)	41.0	(168.0)
Market value ($ mil.)	(6.0%)	3,098.1	2,212.9	1,203.2	2,952.6	2,414.0
Employees	3.3%	42,700	45,000	45,000	44,275	48,600

FEDERATED INSURANCE COMPANIES

121 E. Park Sq.
Owatonna MN 55060
Phone: 507-455-5200
Fax: 507-455-5452
Web: www.federatedinsurance.com

CEO: Jeffrey Fetters
CFO: –
HR: –
FYE: December 31
Type: Private - Mutual Com

Federated Insurance is a mutual firm with a clear focus. The company provides multiple lines of business insurance coverage and risk management to niche businesses including automotive repair and sales building contractors printers funeral homes and jewelers among others. Its products and services include property liability and auto coverage as well as workers' compensation risk management group life and health and retirement planning. Federated Insurance markets its products across the US. Since its founding in 1904 the company has worked closely with trade associations to develop and endorse its insurance programs.

FEDERATED INVESTORS INC (PA)

NYS: FII

Federated Investors Tower
Pittsburgh, PA 15222-3779
Phone: 412 288-1900
Fax: –
Web: www.federatedinvestors.com

CEO: John B. Fisher
CFO: Thomas R. Donahue
HR: Wayne Shipley
FYE: December 31
Type: Public

One of the country's largest investment managers Federated Investors provides investment advisory and administrative services to some 135 mutual funds. Federated Investors offers fixed-income and equity mutual funds separate accounts closed-end funds variable annuity funds and alternative investments though money market funds make up most of the company's approximately $376 billion in assets under management. Its products are sold through banks brokerages wealth managers investment advisors trust companies and other financial intermediaries. Chairman John Donahue and his family including his son president and CEO J. Christopher control Federated Investors.

	Annual Growth	12/10	12/11	12/12	12/13	12/14
Sales ($ mil.)	(2.5%)	951.9	895.1	945.7	878.4	859.3
Net income ($ mil.)	(4.5%)	179.1	150.9	188.1	162.2	149.2
Market value ($ mil.)	5.9%	2,746.0	1,589.7	2,122.7	3,021.9	3,455.3
Employees	1.8%	1,334	1,351	1,402	1,431	1,435

FEDERATED NATIONAL HOLDING CO. NMS: FNHC

14050 N.W. 14th Street, Suite 180 — CEO: Michael H. Braun
Sunrise, FL 33323 — CFO: Peter J. Prygelski
Phone: 954 581-9993 — HR: Tracy Wiggan
Fax: – — FYE: December 31
Web: www.21stcenturyholding.com — Type: Public

Trashed trailer crashed car damaged dwelling? Federated National Holding Company has a policy to cover that. Through Federated National Insurance Company and other subsidiaries it underwrites a variety of personal property/casualty insurance lines in Florida. Products include homeowners flood liability and nonstandard automobile coverage. Recently formed property insurance unit Monarch National (established in 2015) offers a complete homeowners policy special form (HO-3) multi-peril insurance product for Florida homeowners (and plans to introduce a similar product for condominiums). The firm distributes its products through independent agents and its Insure-Link agency.

	Annual Growth	12/10	12/11	12/12	12/13	12/14
Assets ($ mil.)	28.6%	184.0	180.0	185.9	316.7	503.6
Net income ($ mil.)	–	(8.0)	(0.4)	4.3	12.7	37.2
Market value ($ mil.)	66.0%	43.4	40.4	72.9	200.0	329.4
Employees	14.6%	127	112	116	153	219

FEDEX CORP NYS: FDX

942 South Shady Grove Road — CEO: Frederick W. (Fred) Smith
Memphis, TN 38120 — CFO: Alan B. Graf
Phone: 901 818-7500 — HR: Jerry Tims
Fax: – — FYE: May 31
Web: www.fedex.com — Type: Public

Holding company FedEx hopes its package of subsidiaries will keep delivering significant market share. Its FedEx Express unit is the world's #1 express transportation provider delivering about 3.5 million packages daily to more than 220 countries and territories from about 1800 FedEx Office shops. It maintains a fleet of about 650 aircraft and more than 56000 motor vehicles and trailers. To complement the express delivery business FedEx Ground provides small-package ground delivery in North America and less-than-truckload (LTL) carrier FedEx Freight hauls larger shipments. FedEx Office stores offer a variety of document-related and other business services and serve as retail hubs for other FedEx units.

	Annual Growth	05/11	05/12	05/13	05/14	05/15
Sales ($ mil.)	4.8%	39,304.0	42,680.0	44,287.0	45,567.0	47,453.0
Net income ($ mil.)	(7.8%)	1,452.0	2,032.0	1,561.0	2,097.0	1,050.0
Market value ($ mil.)	16.6%	26,446.3	25,175.8	27,209.3	40,715.1	48,922.6
Employees	3.8%	143,000	149,000	160,700	162,000	166,000

FEDEX CUSTOM CRITICAL INC.

1475 Boettler Rd. — CEO: Virginia Albanese
Uniontown OH 44685 — CFO: –
Phone: 234-310-4090 — HR: Christine Middleton
Fax: 234-310-4111 — FYE: May 31
Web: customcritical.fedex.com — Type: Subsidiary

FedEx Custom Critical a subsidiary of FedEx specializes in surface-expedited freight delivery services when time is of the essence. It operates throughout North America. Transportation is provided door-to-door with no intermediate handling by a fleet of about 1400 vehicles owned and operated by independent contractors. FedEx Custom Critical's Air Expedite unit arranges air transportation of customers' goods while Surface Expedite offers exclusive network-based transport for critical shipments and expedited less-than-truckload deliveries. Its White Glove Services division transports sensitive cargo such as electronics medical equipment and trade show exhibits as well as temperature-controlled freight.

FEDEX GROUND PACKAGE SYSTEM INC.

1000 FedEx Dr. — CEO: Henry J Maier
Coraopolis PA 15108 — CFO: –
Phone: 412-269-1000 — HR: –
Fax: 412-747-4290 — FYE: May 31
Web: www.fedex.com/us/ground/main — Type: Subsidiary

When it doesn't absolutely positively have to be there overnight there's FedEx Ground Package System. An operating company of air-express giant FedEx FedEx Ground provides ground delivery of small packages throughout the US and Canada. Deliveries are generally made within one to five business days depending on distance. The company offers both business-to-business and home delivery services via a fleet of more than 30000 motorized vehicles most of which are operated by independent contractors. FedEx Ground handles an average of more than 3.5 million shipments per day from a network of more than 30 hubs.

FEDEX OFFICE AND PRINT SERVICES INC.

3 Galleria Tower 13155 Noel Rd. Ste. 1600 — CEO: –
Dallas TX 75240 — CFO: –
Phone: 214-550-7000 — HR: –
Fax: 214-550-7001 — FYE: May 31
Web: www.fedex.com/us/officeprint/main/index.html — Type: Subsidiary

FedEx Office and Print Services has duplicated its business formula many times. The company operates 1840 stores ("business service centers") in the US and five other countries. Stores provide printing and duplication presentation support and related business assistance and serve as drop-off points for deliveries to be made by sister companies FedEx Express and FedEx Ground. Stores also sell office supplies and rent computers and videoconferencing rooms. FedEx Office has traditionally targeted small business and home offices and individual consumers. Formerly known as Kinko's FedEx Office operates as part of the Services unit of delivery giant FedEx which purchased the business for $2.4 billion in 2004.

FEDFIRST FINANCIAL CORPORATION NASDAQ: FFCO

Donner at 6th St. — CEO: –
Monessen PA 15062 — CFO: –
Phone: 724-684-6800 — HR: –
Fax: 724-684-4851 — FYE: December 31
Web: www.firstfederal-savings.com — Type: Public

FedFirst Financial wants to be first in the hearts of its customers. It is the holding company for First Federal Savings Bank a community-oriented thrift serving southwestern Pennsylvania. From about 10 branches the bank offers traditional products and services including checking and savings accounts money markets accounts and IRAs. Residential mortgages secured by homes in the Pittsburgh metropolitan area make up more than three-fourths of a lending portfolio that also includes multi-family and commercial mortgages and construction business and consumer loans. FedFirst Financial converted from the mutual holding company structure to a stock holding company in 2010.

FEED THE CHILDREN INC.

333 N MERIDIAN AVE
OKLAHOMA CITY, OK 731076507
Phone: 405-942-0228
Fax: –
Web: www.feedthechildren.org

CEO: Vic Diffee
CFO: –
HR: –
FYE: June 30
Type: Private

Tuppence a bag might feed some birds but it takes more to feed growing children. Feed The Children (FTC) is a not-for-profit Christian charity that distributes food medicine clothing and other necessities. In the US FTC accepts bulk contributions of surplus food from businesses packages it in various ways at six main facilities nationwide and distributes it to food banks homeless shelters churches and other organizations that help feed the hungry. In more than 120 countries overseas FTC works with organizations such as schools orphanages and churches to provide food medical supplies clothing and educational support to the needy. Larry and Frances Jones founded FTC in 1979.

	Annual Growth	06/08	06/09	06/10	06/11	06/13
Sales ($ mil.)	(21.4%)	–	1,189.2	520.1	436.5	453.9
Net income ($ mil.)	–	–	–	(368.0)	10.6	42.3
Market value ($ mil.)	–	–	–	–	–	–
Employees	–	–	–	–	–	160

FEI CO.
NMS: FEIC

5350 NE Dawson Creek Drive
Hillsboro, OR 97124-5793
Phone: 503 726-7500
Fax: –
Web: www.fei.com

CEO: Don R. Kania
CFO: Anthony L. Trunzo
HR: –
FYE: December 31
Type: Public

FEI makes instruments to find very small defects. The company makes structural process management systems that use ion beams to analyze and diagnose submicron structures in integrated circuits (ICs) data storage components and biological and industrial compounds. FEI makes focused ion beam and dual beam electron microscopes that analyze ICs. It also makes scanning and transmission electron microscopes that detect defects in ICs and analyze biological specimens and materials. FEI targets applications in nanotechnology R&D but still gets significant sales from the semiconductor and data storage markets.

	Annual Growth	12/10	12/11	12/12	12/13	12/14
Sales ($ mil.)	10.8%	634.2	826.4	891.7	927.5	956.3
Net income ($ mil.)	18.4%	53.5	103.6	114.9	126.7	105.1
Market value ($ mil.)	36.0%	1,103.9	1,704.5	2,318.5	3,735.0	3,776.4
Employees	10.1%	1,813	2,074	2,518	2,611	2,660

FELCOR LODGING TRUST, INC.
NYS: FCH

545 E. John Carpenter Freeway, Suite 1300
Irving, TX 75062
Phone: 972 444-4900
Fax: –
Web: www.felcor.com

CEO: Richard A. (Rick) Smith
CFO: Michael C. Hughes
HR: –
FYE: December 31
Type: Public

FelCor Lodging welcomes weary North American travelers looking for a little luxury. One of the top hotel real estate investment trusts in the US FelCor owns interests in 60 properties with almost 18000 rooms in more than 20 US states and one in Toronto Canada. Most are upscale hotels operating under the Embassy Suites Holiday Inn Doubletree Sheraton Westin Renaissance and Hilton brands. The properties are managed by Hilton Worldwide InterContinental Hotels Marriott International Starwood Hotels & Resorts and Fairmont. It also has several independent hotels in New York. FelCor's portfolio is concentrated in major metropolitan and resort areas of Florida California and Texas.

	Annual Growth	12/10	12/11	12/12	12/13	12/14
Sales ($ mil.)	(0.2%)	928.3	946.0	909.5	893.4	921.6
Net income ($ mil.)	–	(223.0)	(129.9)	(128.0)	(61.5)	92.1
Market value ($ mil.)	11.3%	877.2	380.0	581.9	1,016.8	1,348.2
Employees	(2.7%)	68	66	63	62	61

FELD ENTERTAINMENT INC.

8607 Westwood Center Dr.
Vienna VA 22182
Phone: 703-448-4000
Fax: 703-448-4100
Web: www.feldentertainment.com

CEO: –
CFO: Michael Ruch
HR: –
FYE: January 31
Type: Private

A lot of clowning around has helped Feld Entertainment become one of the largest live entertainment producers in the world. The company entertains people through its centerpiece Ringling Bros. and Barnum & Bailey Circus which visits about 90 cities in North America each year. Through a partnership with Walt Disney Feld also produces touring Disney On Ice shows such as Treasure Trove. In addition its Disney Live! produces live Disney-themed touring stage productions. Chairman and CEO Kenneth Feld whose father Irvin began managing the circus in 1956 owns the company and personally oversees most of its productions. Ringling Bros. and Barnum & Bailey Circus made its first performance in 1871.

FEMALE HEALTH CO. (THE)
NAS: FHCO

515 N. State Street, Suite 2225
Chicago, IL 60654
Phone: 312 595-9123
Fax: –
Web: www.femalehealth.com

CEO: O B Parrish
CFO: Michele Greco
HR: –
FYE: September 30
Type: Public

Move over Trojan Man! Business at The Female Health Company (FHC) maker of condoms for women is gaining momentum. The female condom is the only female contraceptive that is FDA-approved for preventing both pregnancy and sexually transmitted diseases including HIV/AIDS. The firm's condoms are sold in 140-plus countries worldwide (under the FC2 name) mostly in South Africa Brazil and Uganda. Outside the US many of its products bear the Femidom name among others. FHC also provides low-cost female condoms in Africa through an agreement with the Joint United Nations Programme on HIV/AIDS (UNAIDS). It sponsors the Female Health Foundation which provides women with health education.

	Annual Growth	09/11	09/12	09/13	09/14	09/15
Sales ($ mil.)	15.1%	18.6	35.0	31.5	24.5	32.6
Net income ($ mil.)	(5.3%)	5.4	15.3	14.3	2.4	4.3
Market value ($ mil.)	(21.1%)	118.4	207.4	286.0	101.2	45.8
Employees	36.6%	52	144	134	150	181

FENDER MUSICAL INSTRUMENTS CORPORATION

17600 N. Perimeter Dr. Ste. 100
Scottsdale AZ 85250
Phone: 480-596-9690
Fax: 480-596-1384
Web: www.fender.com

CEO: Andrew P Mooney
CFO: Richard Kerley
HR: –
FYE: December 31
Type: Private

Jimi Hendrix's electrified version of "The Star-Spangled Banner" showed what at least one Fender guitar could do. Fender Musical Instruments Corporation (FMIC) is the world's #1 maker of stringed instruments and the nation's #1 manufacturer of solid-body electric guitars including the Stratocaster and Telecaster lines that have made it a favorite of strummers. FMIC makes other instruments and PA equipment such as acoustic guitars electric basses mandolins banjos and violins as well as amplifiers. The company's other notable brands include Guild Tacoma Gretsch Jackson Charvel EVH SWR Groove Tubes and Squier. Fender pulled the plug on its 2012 initial public offering (IPO).

FENTURA FINANCIAL INC

OTC: FETM

175 North Leroy, P.O. Box 725
Fenton, MI 48430-0725
Phone: 810 629-2263
Fax: –
Web: www.fentura.com

CEO: Ronald L Justice
CFO: James W Distelrath
HR: Kristina Premo
FYE: December 31
Type: Public

It just makes cents to say that Fentura Financial has its hands full. Fentura Financial is the holding company for Michigan community banks The State Bank Davison State Bank and West Michigan Community Bank. From about 20 branch locations the banks provide commercial and consumer banking services and products including checking and savings accounts and loans. Commercial loans account for some two-thirds of the bank's combined loan portfolio. The State Bank Fentura's first subsidiary traces its origins to 1898.

	Annual Growth	12/10	12/11	12/12	12/13	12/14
Assets ($ mil.)	(1.9%)	424.2	298.9	310.7	335.2	393.6
Net income ($ mil.)	–	(5.4)	(1.5)	1.3	8.5	3.4
Market value ($ mil.)	54.1%	4.4	5.4	8.8	17.4	24.8
Employees	(26.7%)	176	129	–	–	–

FENWICK & WEST LLP

Silicon Valley Center 801 California St.
Mountain View CA 94041
Phone: 650-988-8500
Fax: 650-938-5200
Web: www.fenwick.com

CEO: –
CFO: Scott Pine
HR: –
FYE: October 31
Type: Private - Partnershi

Go West young lawyer. General practice law firm Fenwick & West offers services to national and international high-tech and life sciences clients with specializations in corporate law (venture capital mergers IPOs) intellectual property domestic and international tax law and litigation and other dispute-resolution methods. Founded in 1972 Fenwick & West has about 300 attorneys working out of offices in Silicon Valley San Francisco Seattle and Boise Idaho. The law firm's clients have included such technology industry giants as Apple Oracle Electronic Arts Symantec and eBay.

FERGUSON ENTERPRISES INC.

12500 Jefferson Ave.
Newport News VA 23602
Phone: 757-874-7795
Fax: 757-989-2501
Web: www.ferguson.com

CEO: Frank W Roach
CFO: –
HR: –
FYE: July 31
Type: Subsidiary

Ferguson Enterprises is part of the pipeline for pipes. It is one of North America's largest wholesale distributors of plumbing supplies pipes valves and fittings. It also is a major distributor of heating and cooling equipment waterworks (water hydrants and meters) kitchen and bath lighting safety equipment fireplaces and appliances and tools and safety equipment. Ferguson has some than 1300 branches and 11 distribution centers in the US Puerto Rico Mexico and the Caribbean. Its customers include plumbing contractors home owners air conditioning dealers the government and irrigation and fire suppression equipment installers. Ferguson which was formed in 1953 is a subsidiary of Wolseley.

FERNDALE PHARMA GROUP INC.

780 W. 8 Mile Rd.
Ferndale MI 48220
Phone: 248-548-0900
Fax: 248-548-0279
Web: www.ferndalepharmagroup.com

CEO: James McMillan
CFO: Mark Diekman
HR: –
FYE: December 31
Type: Private

Ferndale Pharma Group wants to help your skin flourish. Through a handful of operating companies the holding company is responsible for making prescription generic and over-the-counter (OTC) medications. Its products are primarily focused on skin care maladies including acne dry skin eczema psoriasis and inflammation. Ferndale Pharma Group also produces topical pain relief creams surgical adhesives and adhesive removers. The company markets its products internationally to physicians hospitals and consumers. It also offers contract drug manufacturing warehousing and distribution services to third parties. Ferndale Pharma Group was founded in 1897 as the J.F. Hartz Company.

FERRELLGAS PARTNERS, L.P.

NYS: FGP

7500 College Boulevard, Suite 1000
Overland Park, KS 66210
Phone: 913 661-1500
Fax: –
Web: www.ferrellgas.com

CEO: Stephen L. (Steve) Wambold
CFO: Alan C. Heitmann
HR: Cathy Brown
FYE: July 31
Type: Public

Ferrellgas Partners' flame is burning brightly as the second-largest US retail marketer of propane behind AmeriGas. The company sells propane to 1 million industrial commercial and agricultural customers in all 50 states. It operates 49.7 million gallons of propane storage capacity more than 50 service centers and 864 retail distribution locations and its delivery fleet includes more than 2450 trucks and trailers. Its Blue Rhino unit operates a propane cylinder-exchange business across the US. Ferrellgas trades propane and natural gas markets wholesale propane provides liquid natural gas storage and markets chemical feedstock. It also has a small midstream business.

	Annual Growth	07/11	07/12	07/13	07/14	07/15
Sales ($ mil.)	(4.4%)	2,423.2	2,339.1	1,975.5	2,405.9	2,024.4
Net income ($ mil.)	–	(43.6)	(11.0)	56.4	33.2	29.6
Market value ($ mil.)	0.9%	2,044.0	2,019.7	2,239.7	2,575.3	2,115.0
Employees	–	–	–	–	–	–

FERRIS STATE UNIVERSITY

1201 S STATE ST
BIG RAPIDS, MI 493072714
Phone: 231-591-2000
Fax: –
Web: www.osprey.ferris.edu

CEO: –
CFO: –
HR: –
FYE: June 30
Type: Private

Going to college is no carnival but Ferris State University still hopes the experience is enjoyable. The career-oriented public university offers more than 180 degree programs including associate's bachelor's master's and doctoral degrees through the colleges of Allied Health Sciences Arts and Sciences Business Education and Human Services Optometry Pharmacy Technology and Kendall College of Art and Design. The school has some 14500 students on 21 campuses located across Michigan. Ferris State was founded in 1884 by Michigan educator and statesman Woodbridge N. Ferris.

	Annual Growth	06/10	06/11	06/12	06/13	06/14
Sales ($ mil.)	1.9%	–	153.1	158.4	164.1	162.2
Net income ($ mil.)	40.3%	–	–	10.4	15.2	20.4
Market value ($ mil.)	–	–	–	–	–	–
Employees	–	–	–	–	–	1,200

FERRO CORP.   NYS: FOE

6060 Parkland Boulevard, Suite 250
Mayfield Heights, OH 44124
Phone: 216 875-5600
Fax: 216 875-5627
Web: www.ferro.com

CEO: Peter T. Thomas
CFO: Jeffrey L. (Jeff) Rutherford
HR: P Richard
FYE: December 31
Type: Public

Ferro holds a colorful portfolio of products. The specialty materials and chemicals producer makes various colorants including ceramic glazes pigments and porcelain enamels. It also produces electronics color and glass materials (such as conductive metals and pastes used in solar cells) and polymer and ceramic engineered materials. Its products are used in construction and by makers of appliances autos ceramic tile electronics and household furnishings. With 39 manufacturing plants worldwide Ferro is a global leader in producing glass and porcelain enamels ceramic glaze coatings and conductive metal pastes. Billionaire investor Mario Gabelli owns about 12% of Ferro.

	Annual Growth	12/10	12/11	12/12	12/13	12/14
Sales ($ mil.)	(14.7%)	2,101.9	2,155.8	1,768.6	1,635.4	1,111.6
Net income ($ mil.)	97.2%	5.7	31.6	(374.3)	71.9	86.1
Market value ($ mil.)	(3.0%)	1,273.7	425.4	363.7	1,116.2	1,127.5
Employees	(5.7%)	5,034	5,120	4,948	4,364	3,979

FFD FINANCIAL CORP   NBB: FFDF

321 North Wooster Avenue
Dover, OH 44622
Phone: 330 364-7777
Fax: -
Web: www.onlinefirstfed.com

CEO: -
CFO: Robert R Gerber
HR: Stephenie Wilson
FYE: June 30
Type: Public

FFD Financial is the holding company for First Federal Community Bank which serves Tuscarawas County and contiguous portions of eastern Ohio through about five branches. Founded in 1898 the bank offers a full range of retail products including checking and savings accounts CDs IRAs and credit cards. The bank mainly uses these funds to originate one- to four-family residential mortgages nonresidential real estate loans and land loans. First Federal Community Bank also originates business consumer and multifamily residential real estate loans. In 2012 First Federal Community Bank converted its charter from a savings bank to a national commercial bank.

	Annual Growth	06/10	06/11	06/12	06/13	06/14
Assets ($ mil.)	5.3%	206.5	219.5	235.2	245.3	254.1
Net income ($ mil.)	27.4%	1.0	1.4	1.8	2.5	2.5
Market value ($ mil.)	11.2%	14.4	14.7	15.9	20.2	22.0
Employees	23.1%	52	64	-	-	-

FFF ENTERPRISES INC

41093 County Center Dr.
Temecula CA 92591
Phone: 951-296-2500
Fax: 800-418-4333
Web: www.fffenterprises.com

CEO: Patrick M Schmidt
CFO: Brad Cooper
HR: Georgina Hernandez
FYE: December 31
Type: Private

FFF Enterprises really puts the "fff" in pharmaceuticals. The company distributes biopharmaceuticals plasma products and vaccines to medical providers pharmaceutical companies contract research organizations and other medical supply distributors. Already a top distributor of intravenous immune globulin used to bolster weakened immune systems FFF Enterprises is also a leading US distributor of influenza vaccines and medicines including Roche's Tamiflu Sanofi Pasteur's Fluzone and Novartis' Fluvirin. FFF Enterprises supplies more than 80% of the nation's hospitals with biopharmaceuticals.

FFW CORP.   NBB: FFWC

1205 North Cass Street
Wabash, IN 46992-1027
Phone: 260 563-3185
Fax: -
Web: www.crossroadsbanking.com

CEO: Roger K Cromer
CFO: -
HR: -
FYE: June 30
Type: Public

You can find this company at the intersection of Savings and Loans. FFW Corporation is the holding company for Crossroads Bank (formerly First Federal Savings Bank of Wabash) founded in 1920 as Home Loan Savings Association. Today the bank has five branches in Columbia City North Manchester South Whitley Syracuse and Wabash Indiana. Its deposit products include CDs and checking savings and NOW accounts. Lending activities consist mostly of residential mortgages (almost half of the company's loan portfolio) commercial mortgages home equity and improvement loans and auto loans; the bank also offers business construction manufactured home and consumer loans.

	Annual Growth	06/10	06/11	06/12	06/13	06/14
Assets ($ mil.)	0.1%	333.6	323.0	329.0	337.8	335.5
Net income ($ mil.)	24.5%	1.5	2.2	0.1	2.3	3.6
Market value ($ mil.)	0.9%	22.1	22.1	22.1	17.5	22.9
Employees		-	-	-	-	-

FHI SERVICES

500 HOSPITAL DR
WARRENTON, VA 201863027
Phone: 540-347-2550
Fax: -
Web: www.fauquierhealth.org

CEO: -
CFO: -
HR: -
FYE: September 30
Type: Private

Fauquier Hospital takes care of the populace of rural northern Virginia. The multi-location system provides medical surgical outpatient and home health care services to a four county area. With more than 85 beds the facility is the only hospital in Fauquier and also serves Culpeper Prince William and Rappahannock Counties. Specialized services include emergency medicine oncology rehabilitation and cardiac and pulmonary care. The hospital's emergency room has more than 30 private rooms and services about 30000 patients each year. Fauquier Hospital partners with Prince William Hospitalto operate the Cancer Center at Lake Manassas. Fauquier Hospital was founded in 1925.

	Annual Growth	09/03	09/04	09/05*	06/06*	09/09
Sales ($ mil.)		-	-	(1,451.4)	95.3	132.6
Net income ($ mil.)	1183.8%	-	-	0.0	1.9	10.3
Market value ($ mil.)		-	-	-	-	-
Employees		-	-	-	-	700

*Fiscal year change

FHM INSURANCE COMPANY

4601 Touchton Rd. East Bldg. 300 Ste. 3150
Jacksonville FL 32246
Phone: 904-724-9890
Fax: 416-646-1042
Web: www.vixs.com

CEO: -
CFO: -
HR: -
FYE: December 31
Type: Private

If a busboy slips or a concierge trips FHM has hotels resorts and restaurants comfortably covered. FHM Insurance provides workers' compensation coverage loss control and fraud investigation services. It also employs a cost containment team of nurses and others who analyze provider bills explore alternatives to hospitalization and scrutinize treatment plans. From its home base in Florida the company operates in seven southeastern states. Formerly operating as Florida Hotel-Motel Workers' Compensation FHM Insurance was founded in 1954.

FIBERLINK COMMUNICATIONS CORPORATION

1787 SENTRY PKWY W # 200
BLUE BELL, PA 19422-2213
Phone: 215-664-1600
Fax: –
Web: www.maas360.com

CEO: James Sheward
CFO: Mark Parin
HR: –
FYE: December 31
Type: Private

Fiberlink combines mobility with stability. The company's cloud-based offering MaaS360 provides mobile device and mobile application management for employees using mobile devices in the workplace as well as those working remotely and needing access to corporate networks data and applications. Its platform allows employees to securely and stably connect to enterprise networks while guarding against hackers viruses and data theft. The company also provides managed virtual private network (VPN) services to connect companies with branch offices. It manages some 1 million devices for more than 700 large and small clients in the financial services healthcare and government industries among others.

	Annual Growth	12/03	12/04	12/05	12/06	12/07
Sales ($ mil.)	–	–	–	(281.5)	68.9	57.4
Net income ($ mil.)	–	–	–	0.0	2.2	(1.4)
Market value ($ mil.)	–	–	–	–	–	–
Employees	–	–	–	–	–	238

FIBERMARK NORTH AMERICA INC.

70 Front St.
West Springfield MA 01089
Phone: 413-533-0699
Fax: 413-532-4810
Web: www.fibermark.com

CEO: Anthony Pd Maclaurin
CFO: –
HR: –
FYE: December 31
Type: Private

In the material world FiberMark North America makes its mark with flexible fibers. The company manufactures an array of fiber-based textiles and papers. Its capabilities range from papermaking to nonwoven production and converting processes such as saturating and coating. FiberMark products are used in industrial and consumer markets: office and school (pressboards and edge binding tapes); publishing (CD covers and carton stock); luxury packaging (book and box coverings); technical/industrial (jean labels wallpaper vacuum bags); graphic design (book covers); and crafting (textured paper). The company has seven manufacturing sites throughout the northeastern US and the UK.

FIBERTOWER CORPORATION — NASDAQ: FTWR

185 Berry St. Ste. 4800
San Francisco CA 94107
Phone: 415-659-3500
Fax: 415-659-0007
Web: www.fibertower.com

CEO: –
CFO: –
HR: –
FYE: December 31
Type: Public

FiberTower rises to the occasion with wireless backhaul (commercial wholesale bandwidth) and access services. An alternative provider of facilities-based backhaul it offers spectrum leasing mobile phone traffic and broadband connectivity and extensions to fiber-optic networks. Customers include mobile fiber and other high-speed telecommunications carriers large-volume enterprise users and government agencies. Its largest customer AT&T Mobility accounts for nearly half of revenues. FiberTower serves more than a dozen markets across the country and it owns high-frequency band wireless spectrum licenses that cover essentially all of the US. The company filed for Chapter 11 bankruptcy in 2012.

FIBROCELL SCIENCE, INC. — NAS: FCSC

405 Eagleview Boulevard
Exton, PA 19341
Phone: 484 713-6000
Fax: 484 713-6001
Web: www.fibrocellscience.com

CEO: –
CFO: Keith A. Goldan
HR: Laura Campbell
FYE: December 31
Type: Public

No cow collagen here — Fibrocell Science (formerly Isolagen) lets you be your beautiful self using your beautiful cells. The company's autologous cellular therapy process used in its primary LAVIV product offering extracts fibroblasts (collagen-producing cells) from a small tissue sample taken from behind a patient's ear. The cells reproduce over six to eight weeks and are then injected back into the patient giving him or her a "natural" boost. The company gained FDA approval for LAVIV for use on wrinkle correction in 2011. It also hopes to gain approval for indications such as burn and acne scar treatment and to regenerate tissue lost from periodontal disease.

	Annual Growth	12/10	12/11	12/12	12/13	12/14
Sales ($ mil.)	(33.8%)	0.9	0.8	0.2	0.2	0.2
Net income ($ mil.)	–	(12.9)	(31.4)	(23.2)	(30.6)	(25.7)
Market value ($ mil.)	50.2%	20.8	16.3	6.1	165.9	105.8
Employees	22.3%	25	60	71	64	56

FIDELITONE INC.

1260 Karl Ct.
Wauconda IL 60084
Phone: 847-487-3300
Fax: 847-469-6581
Web: www.fidelitone.com

CEO: Craig Hudson
CFO: –
HR: Bonnie Zotos
FYE: December 31
Type: Private

Fidelitone has an ear for the supply chain. The company which does business as Fidelitone Logistics offers a range of key third-party logistics (3PL) services including warehousing inventory management packaging shipping freight forwarding customs brokerage and returns handling. Managing 1 million shipments per month it serves markets such as consumer goods electronics health care medical devices retail and publishing. With more than 30 locations in some 15 states the company which was started as a manufacturer/distributor of phonograph record needles in 1929 by Arthur Olsen is now run by Olsen's in-laws — the Hudson family.

FIDELITY & GUARANTY LIFE INSURANCE COMPANY

1001 Fleet St.
Baltimore MD 21202-1137
Phone: 410-895-0100
Fax: 410-895-0132
Web: https://home.fglife.com/default.aspx

CEO: Lee Launerce
CFO: John M Varvaris
HR: –
FYE: December 31
Type: Subsidiary

Fidelity & Guaranty Life Insurance (FGL Insurance) is faithfully toiling away selling you life insurance and a whole range of annuity products. FGL Insurance sells life insurance in 49 states and Washington DC; it also operates in the Empire State through sister company Fidelity & Guaranty Life Insurance Company of New York (FGL NY Insurance). FGL Insurance's products include everything from universal life insurance and fixed deferred indexed annuities to single premium immediate annuities. The company is a subsidiary of Fidelity & Guaranty Life Holdings (FGL) which is owned by investment firm Harbinger Group.

FIDELITY D&D BANCORP, INC.   NBB: FDBC

Blakely & Drinker Streets   CEO: Daniel J Santaniello
Dunmore, PA 18512   CFO: Salvatore R Defrancesco Jr
Phone: 570 342-8281   HR: –
Fax: –   FYE: December 31
    Type: Public

Fidelity D & D Bancorp has loyal banking customers. The institution is the holding company for The Fidelity Deposit and Discount Bank serving Lackawanna and Luzerne counties in northeastern Pennsylvania through about a dozen locations and about the same number of ATM locations. The bank attracts local individuals and business customers by offering such products and services as checking and savings accounts certificates of deposit investments and trust services. Commercial real estate loans account for the bulk of the company's loan portfolio followed by consumer loans business and industrial loans and residential mortgages. The bank also writes construction loans and direct financing leases.

	Annual Growth	12/10	12/11	12/12	12/13	12/14
Assets ($ mil.)	4.8%	561.7	606.7	601.5	623.8	676.5
Net income ($ mil.)	–	(3.2)	5.0	4.9	7.1	6.4
Market value ($ mil.)	13.0%	49.2	50.4	49.8	64.3	80.1
Employees	0.0%	159	161	159	162	159

FIDELITY NATIONAL FINANCIAL INC   NYS: FNF

601 Riverside Avenue   CEO: Raymond R. (Randy) Quirk
Jacksonville, FL 32204   CFO: Anthony J. (Tony) Park
Phone: 904 854-8100   HR: Kavi Shankar
Fax: –   FYE: December 31
Web: www.fnf.com   Type: Public

To make sure that buying a dream home doesn't become a nightmare Fidelity National Financial (also known as FNF) provides title insurance escrow home warranties and other services related to real estate transactions. It is now the biggest dog in the residential and commercial title insurance sectors (the next largest player is First American) and accounts for 35% of all title insurance policies in the US. The company operates through underwriters including Fidelity National Title Company Chicago Title Commonwealth Land Title Alamo Title and National Title of New York. It sells its products both directly and through independent agents. Fidelity National has also grown its holdings in casual restaurant chains.

	Annual Growth	12/10	12/11	12/12	12/13	12/14
Assets ($ mil.)	15.2%	7,887.5	7,862.1	9,902.6	10,524.0	13,868.0
Net income ($ mil.)	12.0%	370.1	369.5	606.5	402.0	583.0
Market value ($ mil.)	–	–	–	–	–	12,807.8
Employees	33.0%	18,200	17,396	60,451	63,861	56,883

FIDELITY NATIONAL INFORMATION SERVICES INC   NYS: FIS

601 Riverside Avenue   CEO: –
Jacksonville, FL 32204   CFO: Jeffrey (Jeff) Carbiener
Phone: 904 438-6000   HR: Bart Ballew
Fax: –   FYE: December 31
Web: www.fisglobal.com   Type: Public

At Fidelity National Information Services (FIS) the check will never get lost in the mail. FIS provides software outsourcing and IT consulting for the financial services industry. For banks and other financing entities the company's offerings address financial functions such as core processing decision and risk management and retail channel operations as well as payment services such as electronic funds transfer check and ticket processing and credit card production and activation. The company's 14000 customers aren't just the largest private financial institutions but also small businesses and government entities and are in more than 100 countries.

	Annual Growth	12/10	12/11	12/12	12/13	12/14
Sales ($ mil.)	5.0%	5,269.5	5,745.7	5,807.6	6,070.7	6,413.8
Net income ($ mil.)	13.8%	404.5	469.6	461.2	493.1	679.1
Market value ($ mil.)	22.8%	7,803.4	7,575.5	9,917.4	15,293.4	17,720.8
Employees	4.9%	33,000	33,000	35,000	38,000	40,000

FIDELITY SOUTHERN CORP   NMS: LION

3490 Piedmont Road, Suite 1550   CEO: James B. Miller
Atlanta, GA 30305   CFO: Stephen H. Brolly
Phone: 404 639-6500   HR: Jimmy Trimble
Fax: –   FYE: December 31
    Type: Public

Fidelity Southern Corp. is the holding company for Fidelity Bank which boasts over $3 billion in assets and some 45 branches in the Atlanta metro and in northern Florida markets. The bank offers traditional deposit services such as checking and savings accounts CDs and IRAs. Consumer loans primarily indirect auto loans which the company purchases from auto franchises and independent dealers throughout the Southeast make up more than 50% of its loan portfolio. Real estate construction commercial real estate business residential mortgage and other consumer loans round out Fidelity Southern's lending activities. Subsidiary LionMark Insurance Company offers consumer credit-related insurance products.

	Annual Growth	12/10	12/11	12/12	12/13	12/14
Assets ($ mil.)	12.2%	1,945.3	2,234.8	2,477.3	2,564.2	3,085.2
Net income ($ mil.)	31.2%	10.1	11.4	25.3	27.6	30.0
Market value ($ mil.)	23.3%	149.1	129.9	204.0	354.9	344.2
Employees	16.7%	559	174	774	890	1,038

FIDUS INVESTMENT CORPORATION   NASDAQ: FDUS

1603 Orrington Ave. Ste. 820   CEO: Edward H Ross
Evanston IL 60201   CFO: Shelby E Sherard
Phone: 847-859-3940   HR: –
Fax: 847-859-3953   FYE: December 31
Web: www.fdus.com   Type: Public

Fidus Investment Corporation is faithful to earning ROI. The externally managed closed-end business development company (BDC) formed in 2011 to begin investing in low- to mid-market companies that earn between $10 million and $150 million per year. (BDCs are exempt from paying federal income tax as long as they distribute 90% of profits back to shareholders.) Fidus has provided mezzanine debt and equity financing to 25 companies representing a range of industries typically investing between $5 million and $15 million for each transaction. It has financed recapitalizations acquisitions expansions and changes in ownership. Fidus Investment is externally managed by Fidus Investment Advisors LLC.

FIELD MUSEUM OF NATURAL HISTORY

1400 S LAKE SHORE DR   CEO: –
CHICAGO, IL 60605-2429   CFO: –
Phone: 312-922-9410   HR: –
Fax: –   FYE: December 31
Web: www.meteorites.fieldmuseum.org   Type: Private

The Field Museum is one of the world's leading natural history museums. Founded as the Columbian Museum of Chicago in 1893 the institution adopted the Field name in 1905 in honor of major benefactor (and department store mogul) Marshall Field. The museum houses enormous biological and anthropological collections — more than 24 million specimens in all — along with a quarter-million-volume natural history library. It is also home to Sue the largest most complete and best preserved Tyrannosaurus rex fossil discovered to date. The Field Museum conducts basic research in anthropology and biology as well as an extensive program of public education.

	Annual Growth	12/01	12/02	12/03	12/09	12/11
Sales ($ mil.)	0.5%	–	64.6	66.5	47.0	67.4
Net income ($ mil.)	–	–	2.7	38.9	(25.2)	(25.1)
Market value ($ mil.)	–	–	–	–	–	–
Employees	–	–	–	–	–	600

FIELDPOINT PETROLEUM CORP. ASE: FPP

609 Castle Ridge Road, Suite 335
Austin, TX 78746
Phone: 512 579-3560
Fax: –
Web: www.fppcorp.com

CEO: Roger D Bryant
CFO: Philip H Roberson
HR: –
FYE: December 31
Type: Public

Got oil and gas? FieldPoint Petroleum can point to its oil and gas fields and its interests in 480 productive oil and gas wells (96 net) in Louisiana New Mexico Oklahoma Texas and Wyoming. The independent oil and gas exploration company operates some 19 of these wells. About two-thirds of its gross productive oil wells are located in Oklahoma. FieldPoint Petroleum has proved reserves of more than 1.1 million barrels of oil and 1.9 billion cu. ft. of natural gas. Its business strategy is to expand its reserve base as well as its production and cash flow through the acquisition of producing oil and gas properties. However low oil prices have forced the company to hold back on further acquisitions.

	Annual Growth	12/10	12/11	12/12	12/13	12/14
Sales ($ mil.)	7.1%	7.0	7.2	10.4	10.5	9.2
Net income ($ mil.)	–	0.8	0.6	2.1	1.3	(1.9)
Market value ($ mil.)	(48.7%)	–	–	7.6	4.6	2.0
Employees	0.0%	4	4	4	4	4

FIESTA MART INC.

5235 KATY FWY
HOUSTON, TX 77007-2210
Phone: 713-869-5060
Fax: –
Web: www.fiestamart.com

CEO: Michael Byars
CFO: Vicki J Baum
HR: –
FYE: January 03
Type: Private

Fiesta Mart celebrates food every day of the year. The company runs some 60 stores in Texas that sell ethnic and conventional groceries including items popular with its target customers: Mexican- and Asian-Americans. Its stores are located mainly in the Houston area but Fiesta also has been adding stores in the Dallas/Fort Worth area and in Austin. Fiesta purchased three supermarkets from Winn-Dixie Stores when the grocer left Texas. At its supermarkets Fiesta leases kiosks to vendors who offer such items as jewelry and cell phones. The company also runs some 15 Beverage Mart liquor stores. Fiesta Mart founded in 1972 by Donald Bonham and O. C. Mendenhall is owned by grocery wholesaler Grocers Supply Co.

	Annual Growth	12/03	12/04	12/05	12/06*	01/10
Sales ($ mil.)	6.9%	–	–	–	1,137.7	1,483.9
Net income ($ mil.)	9.3%	–	–	–	21.1	30.1
Market value ($ mil.)	–	–	–	–	–	–
Employees	–	–	–	–	–	8,200

*Fiscal year change

FIESTA RESTAURANT GROUP, INC NMS: FRGI

14800 Landmark Boulevard, Suite 500
Addison, TX 75254
Phone: 972 702-9300
Fax: –
Web: www.frgi.com

CEO: Timothy P. (Tim) Taft
CFO: Lynn S. Schweinfurth
HR: –
FYE: December 28
Type: Public

The restaurant business is a party for Fiesta Restaurant Group. The company operates and franchises the Taco Cabana and Pollo Tropical brands. It owns and franchises a total of about 315 locations in the US the Caribbean Central America and South America; most of the restaurants are company operated. Taco Cabana locations found mostly in Texas feature Tex-Mex and traditional Mexican food in a quick service atmosphere. Pollo Tropical found mostly in South Florida and the Caribbean offer Caribbean-inspired dishes in a fast casual setting. Former parent Carrols Restaurant Group Burger King's largest US franchisee spun off Fiesta Restaurant Group in 2012 so each company could focus on its target markets.

	Annual Growth	12/10	12/11	12/12	12/13	12/14
Sales ($ mil.)	8.6%	439.1	475.0	509.7	551.3	611.1
Net income ($ mil.)	50.5%	7.0	9.5	8.3	9.3	36.2
Market value ($ mil.)	96.4%	–	–	398.5	1,350.6	1,537.2
Employees	10.3%	–	7,900	8,170	9,175	10,600

FIFTH STREET FINANCE CORP NMS: FSC

777 West Putnam Avenue, 3rd Floor
Greenwich, CT 06830
Phone: 203 681-3600
Fax: –
Web: www.fifthstreetfinance.com

CEO: Todd G Owens
CFO: Steven M Noreika
HR: –
FYE: September 30
Type: Public

Fifth Street Finance works to put the companies it lends money to on easy street. A business development firm Fifth Street lends capital to and invests in small and midsized firms with annual revenues between $25 million and $250 million. The company typically invests $10 million to $100 million in the form of senior debt or equity per transaction. It favors established firms over start-ups and prefers to participate actively in its investments as advisors. Fifth Street's portfolio comprises more than 85 companies many of which operate in the health care manufacturing IT services and business services sectors. Formed in 2007 the specialty finance company boasts about $2 billion in assets under management.

	Annual Growth	09/11	09/12	09/13	09/14	09/15
Sales ($ mil.)	20.7%	125.2	165.1	221.6	294.0	265.5
Net income ($ mil.)	14.4%	67.1	88.0	115.0	142.6	114.9
Market value ($ mil.)	(9.8%)	1,400.3	1,649.7	1,545.3	1,379.2	927.0
Employees	–	–	–	–	–	–

FIFTH THIRD BANCORP (CINCINNATI, OH) NMS: FITB

Fifth Third Center
Cincinnati, OH 45263
Phone: 800 972-3030
Fax: –
Web: www.53.com

CEO: Greg D. Carmichael
CFO: Tayfun Tuzun
HR: –
FYE: December 31
Type: Public

Fifth Third Bancorp strives to be first in the hearts and minds of its customers (not fifth or third). The holding company of Fifth Third Bank boasts assets of nearly $140 billion and more than 1300 branches across Ohio Michigan Florida and several other states in the Midwest and Southeast. Fifth Third operates through four segments: branch banking (deposit accounts and loans for consumers and small businesses) commercial banking (lending leasing and syndicated and trade finance for corporations) consumer lending (residential mortgages home equity loans and credit cards) and investment advisers (private banking brokerage and asset management).

	Annual Growth	12/10	12/11	12/12	12/13	12/14
Assets ($ mil.)	5.7%	111,007.0	116,967.0	121,894.0	130,443.0	138,706.0
Net income ($ mil.)	18.4%	753.0	1,297.0	1,576.0	1,836.0	1,481.0
Market value ($ mil.)	8.5%	12,097.0	10,481.9	12,525.5	17,329.7	16,790.0
Employees	(3.1%)	20,838	21,334	20,798	19,446	18,351

FILA U.S.A. INC

1 Fila Way
Sparks MD 21152-3000
Phone: 410-773-3000
Fax: 410-773-4989
Web: www.fila.com

CEO: Gene Yoon
CFO: Yung Chan Jo
HR: –
FYE: December 31
Type: Private

Staying fit is always in style at Fila U.S.A. The US subsidiary of Fila Korea markets Fila brand athletic and leisure shoes and sportswear. The lineup is sold through Fila's website and at major and specialty sporting goods stores such as Dick's Foot Locker and Kohl's. In addition to footwear Fila U.S.A. offers apparel for tennis basketball yoga and running as well as sports-inspired streetwear. The company relies largely on athletes and fitness professionals to tout its products. Among the endorsements Fila U.S.A. has inked deals with tennis stars Vera Zvonareva and Jelena Jankovic yoga instructor Kristin McGee and rap artist Nas. Fila Korea chairman Gene Yoon holds a 20% stake in the company.

FILEMAKER INC.

5201 Patrick Henry Dr.
Santa Clara CA 95054-1171
Phone: 408-987-7000
Fax: 408-987-7105
Web: www.filemaker.com

CEO: -
CFO: Bill Epling
HR: -
FYE: September 30
Type: Subsidiary

FileMaker believes data's place is in the database. A subsidiary of Apple File-Maker provides its eponymous database software that is compatible with Mac OS and Microsoft's Windows operating systems. The application makes it possible for multiple users to access and exchange information instantaneously over corporate intranets or the Internet. It also offers an advanced version of FileMaker that includes development tools. The company markets to customers ranging from individual users and small businesses to universities and large corporations. Licensees include AT&T Bank of America Coca-Cola Hitachi Nokia the Smithsonian Institution Time Warner and Wal-Mart Stores.

FINANCIAL EXECUTIVES INTERNATIONAL

1250 Headquarters Plaza West Tower 7th Fl.
Morristown NJ 07960
Phone: 973-765-1000
Fax: 973-765-1018
Web: www.financialexecutives.org

CEO: Jim Abel
CFO: -
HR: -
FYE: June 30
Type: Private - Associatio

Financial Executives International (FEI) knows where the dough is. Or at least its members do. The group is a professional association for CFOs VPs of finance treasurers controllers tax executives and others in finance. It has 15000 members throughout the US and Canada in about 85 branches. The association advocates the views of its members notifies members of current issues and promotes ethical conduct for financial executives. FEI also hosts conferences and networking opportunities for its members and publishes Financial Executive Magazine. The group was founded at the Controllers Institute of America in 1931.

FILETEK INC.

9400 Key West Ave.
Rockville MD 20850
Phone: 301-251-0600
Fax: 301-251-1990
Web: www.filetek.com

CEO: William P Loomis
CFO: -
HR: -
FYE: December 31
Type: Private

FileTek can help corporate packrats keep track of all their enterprise data. The company provides storage software used to manage archive protect and access structured and unstructured data. Customers use its StorHouse software for tasks such as e-mail archiving storing point of sale records and tracking and managing customer statements. FileTek also provides a variety of professional services including consulting maintenance training support and implementation. Clients come from industries such as financial services health care and manufacturing. The company was founded in 1984. Chairman William Thompson and technology VP John Burgess are FileTek's co-founders.

FINANCIAL GUARANTY INSURANCE COMPANY

125 Park Ave.
New York NY 10017
Phone: 212-312-3000
Fax: 212-312-3093
Web: www.fgic.com

CEO: -
CFO: -
HR: -
FYE: December 31
Type: Private

Financial Guaranty Insurance Company (FGIC) like a superhero secured the city ... well secured the city bonds anyway until things got really tough. The company provided credit enhancement on public finance (including transportation state and local leases and municipal electric utility) structured finance (asset-backed securities including mortgage and consumer loans) and global infrastructure and utility securities. FGIC has historically guaranteed the scheduled payments of principal and interest on an issuer's obligation. Founded in 1983 the company is owned by a collection of investors including the Blackstone Group. FGIC is currently not issuing new policies or paying claims.

FINANCIAL ENGINES INC   NMS: FNGN

1050 Enterprise Way, 3rd Floor
Sunnyvale, CA 94089
Phone: 408 498-6000
Fax: 408 498-6010
Web: www.financialengines.com

CEO: Lawrence M. (Larry) Raffone
CFO: Raymond J. (Ray) Sims
HR: Gina M. Cruse
FYE: December 31
Type: Public

Like the little engine that could Financial Engines provides financial advice portfolio management and retirement assessment services. The company serves US retirement-plan participants sponsors and service providers across a wide range of industries that includes more than 100 FORTUNE 500 companies and several of the largest retirement plan operators. It delivers its services online as well as by telephone. Financial Engines boasts more than $88 billion in assets under management and serves some 9 million individual retirement-plan participants. The company went public in 2010 with an offering worth $127.2 million.

	Annual Growth	12/10	12/11	12/12	12/13	12/14
Sales ($ mil.)	26.0%	111.8	144.1	185.8	239.0	281.9
Net income ($ mil.)	(12.7%)	63.6	15.1	18.6	30.0	37.0
Market value ($ mil.)	16.5%	1,030.0	1,159.9	1,440.9	3,609.0	1,898.5
Employees	12.9%	303	355	380	442	493

FINANCIAL INDUSTRY REGULATORY AUTHORITY INC.

1735 K ST NW
WASHINGTON, DC 200061506
Phone: 301-590-6500
Fax: -
Web: www.finra.org

CEO: Richard G Ketchum
CFO: Todd T Diganci
HR: Rosa Reyes
FYE: December 31
Type: Private

FINRA is one of the long arms of the law for the securities industry. A non-governmental regulatory authority FINRA regulates all securities firms (roughly 4250) that conduct business in the US. Its activities include writing and enforcing rules; enforcing federal securities laws; licensing and registering brokerages and private equity firms; and providing educational information and arbitration services to investors. The regulator works with the SEC and the Fed and possesses the authority to issue fines and bar violators among other punitive actions. FINRA was formed in 2007 from the consolidation of the National Association of Securities Dealers and certain regulatory and enforcement elements of the NYSE.

	Annual Growth	12/09	12/10	12/11	12/12	12/13
Sales ($ mil.)	2.0%	-	849.9	880.1	878.6	900.7
Net income ($ mil.)	-	-	-	(84.0)	10.5	1.7
Market value ($ mil.)	-	-	-	-	-	-
Employees	-	-	-	-	-	3,400

FINANCIAL INSTITUTIONS INC. — NMS: FISI

220 Liberty Street
Warsaw, NY 14569
Phone: 585 786-1100
Fax: –
Web: www.fiiwarsaw.com

CEO: Martin K. Birmingham
CFO: Kevin B. Klotzbach
HR: Paula D. Dolan
FYE: December 31
Type: Public

Financial Institutions may not have a luxurious name but they specialize in five star service. The holding company owns Five Star Bank which provides standard deposit products such as checking and savings accounts CDs and IRAs to retail and business customers through some 50 branches across western and central New York. Indirect consumer loans originated through agreements with area franchised car dealers account for the largest percentage of the company's loan portfolio (35%) followed by commercial mortgages. The company also sells insurance while its Five Star Investment Services subsidiary offers brokerage and financial planning services.

	Annual Growth	12/10	12/11	12/12	12/13	12/14
Assets ($ mil.)	8.7%	2,214.3	2,336.4	2,764.0	2,928.6	3,089.5
Net income ($ mil.)	8.4%	21.3	22.8	23.4	25.5	29.4
Market value ($ mil.)	7.3%	267.8	227.9	263.0	348.9	355.1
Employees	1.2%	616	613	662	645	645

FINDEX.COM INC. — OTC: FIND

11204 Davenport St. Ste. 100
Omaha NE 68154
Phone: 402-333-1900
Fax: 402-778-5763
Web: www.quickverse.com/shopfiles/default.asp

CEO: Steven Malone
CFO: Steven Malone
HR: –
FYE: December 31
Type: Public

For churches needing more than divine inspiration FindEx.com answers prayers. The company develops publishes and distributes software for churches ministries and other Christian organizations. Its primary product - making up almost 90% of sales - is QuickVerse which is designed to facilitate biblical research. Other offerings include publishing software for Christian-themed printed materials a program to assist pastors in developing sermons children's Christian entertainment software and language tutorials for Greek and Hebrew. In 2008 the company bought FormTool.com which offers 800 form templates - its first non-Christian product. Director Gordon Landies controls more than 20% of FindEx.com.

FINISAR CORP — NMS: FNSR

1389 Moffett Park Drive
Sunnyvale, CA 94089
Phone: 408 548-1000
Fax: –
Web: www.finisar.com

CEO: Jerry S. Rawls
CFO: Kurt Adzema
HR: –
FYE: May 03
Type: Public

Finisar helps put the "work" in network with optical components and subsystems that enable high-speed data communications over LANs or metro-area and storage-area networks (MANs/SANs). The company's subsystems include transmitters receivers transceivers transponders optical cables and wavelength selective switches. Its components consist primarily of packaged lasers photodetectors and passive devices. The company sells products to manufacturers of storage systems networking equipment and telecom equipment. Customers have included such tech giants as Alcatel-Lucent Brocade Cisco Systems and EMC Ericcson HP Huawei Technologies and IBM.

	Annual Growth	04/11	04/12	04/13	04/14*	05/15
Sales ($ mil.)	7.2%	948.8	952.6	934.3	1,156.8	1,250.9
Net income ($ mil.)	(39.4%)	88.1	43.0	(5.5)	111.8	11.9
Market value ($ mil.)	(7.1%)	2,925.1	1,720.3	1,342.3	2,870.9	2,180.5
Employees	13.5%	8,065	8,910	9,720	13,000	13,400

*Fiscal year change

FINISH LINE, INC. (THE) — NMS: FINL

3308 North Mitthoeffer Road
Indianapolis, IN 46235
Phone: 317 899-1022
Fax: –
Web: www.finishline.com

CEO: Samuel M. (Sam) Sato
CFO: Edward W. (Ed) Wilhelm
HR: Cindy Cook
FYE: February 28
Type: Public

The Finish Line is engaged in a three-legged race for athletic footwear sales. The company sells performance and casual footwear and apparel through about 645 Finish Line stores in more than 45 states about 50 Running Specialty stores and 200-plus branded shops inside department stores (Macy's). Its core Finish Line stores are bigger than competitors' and offer a wider array of clothing accessories and other merchandise including jackets backpacks sunglasses and watches. Finish Line offers big brand names (such as adidas NIKE and Timberland) and also markets its own private-label line of T-shirts socks and other basics. The company also sells athletic shoes and apparel online.

	Annual Growth	02/11*	03/12	03/13	03/14*	02/15
Sales ($ mil.)	10.3%	1,229.0	1,369.3	1,443.4	1,670.4	1,820.6
Net income ($ mil.)	4.5%	68.8	84.8	71.5	76.9	82.0
Market value ($ mil.)	9.0%	798.5	1,087.7	840.9	1,244.3	1,127.4
Employees	1.7%	11,500	11,800	11,900	12,600	12,300

*Fiscal year change

FINJAN HOLDINGS INC — NAS: FNJN

2000 University Avenue, Suite 600
East Palo Alto, CA 94303
Phone: 650 282-3228
Fax: –
Web: www.finjan.com

CEO: Philip Hartstein
CFO: Michael Noonan
HR: –
FYE: December 31
Type: Public

Converted Organics is not a group of new and fervent farmers but a company that is religiously developing a process to turn food into fertilizer. The company uses organic food waste as raw material to make all-natural fertilizers that combine both disease suppression and nutritional characteristics. Its manufacturing process uses heat and bacteria to transform food waste into a high-value natural fertilizer. It sells its environmentally friendly products in the agribusiness turf management and retail markets. The company which acquired vertical farming operation TerraSphere Systems in 2010 also has an industrial wastewater treatment unit. Converted Organics is restructuring to streamline operations.

	Annual Growth	12/10	12/11	12/12	12/13	12/14
Sales ($ mil.)	9.1%	3.5	3.2	1.5	0.7	5.0
Net income ($ mil.)	–	(50.6)	(17.4)	(8.4)	(6.1)	(10.5)
Market value ($ mil.)	63.4%	8.5	0.1	0.0	144.2	60.6
Employees	(14.3%)	26	13	12	20	14

FINNEGAN HENDERSON FARABOW GARRETT & DUNNER LLP

901 New York Ave. NW
Washington DC 20001-4413
Phone: 202-408-4000
Fax: 202-408-4400
Web: www.finnegan.com

CEO: –
CFO: –
HR: –
FYE: December 31
Type: Private - Partnershi

Finnegan Henderson Farabow Garrett & Dunner has its domain well staked out in the legal landscape. Specializing in intellectual property law Finnegan has more than 375 lawyers that practice from five US and four international offices. The firm covers all aspects of patent trademark copyright and trade secret law providing counseling prosecution licensing and litigation services. 80% of its work is patent-related. Clients have included drug maker Eli Lilly hair care products maker Conair and construction equipment manufacturer Caterpillar. The firm traces its roots to when law firm Finnegan & Henderson was founded in 1965.

FIOS INC.

921 SW Washington St. Ste. 850
Portland OR 97205
Phone: 503-265-0700
Fax: 503-265-0001
Web: www.fiosinc.com

CEO: Christopher Junker
CFO: John Hesse
HR: -
FYE: December 31
Type: Private

Fios helps law firms be finders and keepers with their legal discovery processes. The company develops electronic discovery software to help corporate legal departments and law firms reduce costs associated with their discovery processes (Clarify) manage and process the large volumes of information and documents they collect (Relativity) and ensure that their electronic evidence will be admissible in court (Equivio). It also offers related electronic discovery services including evidence collection processing and review. Investors in Fios (which takes its name from the Gaelic word for knowledge pronounced "fee-os") include Banyan Capital Partners Fluke Venture Partners and W Capital.

FIREEYE INC   NMS: FEYE

1440 McCarthy Blvd.
Milpitas, CA 95035
Phone: 408 321-6300
Fax: -
Web: www.fireeye.com

CEO: David G. DeWalt
CFO: Michael J. (Mike) Berry
HR: Barbara (Barb) Massa
FYE: December 31
Type: Public

FireEye stands virtual guard over corporate and government networks detecting attacks and rapidly responding to them. The company's Threat Prevention Platform with the MVX virtualized execution engine provides real-time protection from cyber attacks from detecting threats and rapid response. The company's cloud-based monitoring system covers Web email file endpoint and mobile. FireEye has more than 3100 customers.

	Annual Growth	12/10	12/11	12/12	12/13	12/14
Sales ($ mil.)	145.3%	11.8	33.7	83.3	161.6	425.7
Net income ($ mil.)	-	(9.5)	(16.8)	(35.8)	(120.6)	(443.8)
Market value ($ mil.)	(27.6%)	-	-	-	6,666.2	4,827.3
Employees	63.8%	-	-	932	1,678	2,500

FIRELANDS REGIONAL HEALTH SYSTEM

1111 HAYES AVE
SANDUSKY, OH 448703323
Phone: 419-557-7400
Fax: -
Web: www.firelands.com

CEO: Martin E Tursky
CFO: Daniel Moncher
HR: -
FYE: December 31
Type: Private

Firelands Regional Health System primarily operates through its Firelands Regional Medical Center (FRMC). The center serves eight counties in northern Ohio. It operates two hospital campuses with a total of 400 beds a medical office building and outpatient clinics throughout the region. FRMC's medical staff of 225 represents more than 35 specialties. The center's broad range of services include cardiovascular care home health care mental health services palliative care dialysis oncology care and chemical dependency programs. It also has hospital network and teaching affiliations with several area hospitals medical schools and community colleges. The medical center is supported by a non-profit foundation.

	Annual Growth	12/08	12/09	12/10	12/11	12/12
Sales ($ mil.)	-	-	-	0.0	0.3	230.4	200.4
Net income ($ mil.)	-	-	-	-	(0.2)	11.6	36.2
Market value ($ mil.)	-	-	-	-	-	-	-
Employees	-	-	-	-	-	-	1,635

FIREMAN'S FUND INSURANCE COMPANY

777 San Marin Dr.
Novato CA 94998
Phone: 415-899-2000
Fax: 415-899-3600
Web: www.firemansfund.com

CEO: -
CFO: Kevin Walker
HR: -
FYE: December 31
Type: Subsidiary

Firemen still appreciate Fireman's Fund Insurance. The property/casualty insurer sells commercial insurance for small and midsized businesses and personal lines focused on wealthy individuals. Its commercial products include ordinary specialty insurance such as professional liability insurance as well as truly niche coverage to protect vineyards and wineries from crop damage and shipping mishaps. Founded in 1863 the company is named for a now-defunct arrangement that saw 10% of its profits supporting widows and orphans of firefighters. These days the Fireman's Fund Heritage program provides grants for equipment and training to fire departments. Fireman's Fund is a subsidiary of German insurer Allianz.

FIRST ACCEPTANCE CORP   NYS: FAC

3813 Green Hills Village Drive
Nashville, TN 37215
Phone: 615 844-2800
Fax: -

CEO: Joseph S Borbely
CFO: Brent J Gay
HR: -
FYE: December 31
Type: Public

First Acceptance sells car insurance to customers wanting to stay on the right side of the law. The personal auto insurer operates its business in a dozen states specializing in providing non-standard auto insurance (insurance for drivers who have trouble getting coverage because of poor driving records or payment histories). As part of its business First Acceptance sells its policies under the brand names Acceptance Insurance (in the Chicago area) Yale Insurance and Insurance Plus brand. Altogether the company operates about 350 retail offices staffed by employee agents and through independent agents at more than a dozen retail locations.

	Annual Growth	06/11*	12/11	12/12	12/13	12/14
Assets ($ mil.)	3.5%	296.3	257.3	262.3	273.7	328.6
Net income ($ mil.)	-	(56.8)	(29.4)	(9.0)	9.2	28.1
Market value ($ mil.)	11.3%	75.9	55.8	51.3	93.1	104.6
Employees	1.7%	1,045	1,100	1,100	1,100	1,100

*Fiscal year change

FIRST ADVANTAGE BANCORP   NBB: FABK

1430 Madison Street
Clarksville, TN 37040
Phone: 931 552-6176
Fax: -
Web: www.firstadvantagebanking.com

CEO: Earl O Bradley III
CFO: Patrick Greenwell
HR: -
FYE: December 31
Type: Public

First Advantage Bancorp is the holding company for First Federal Savings Bank which serves northern Tennessee from about a half-dozen branch offices. Founded in 1953 the thrift offers standard retail products and services including deposit accounts and loans. One- to four-family residential and commercial mortgages account for about half of First Federal's loan portfolio; the company also writes construction and land loans and to a lesser extent consumer and business loans. First Advantage was established when the bank converted to a holding company structure in 2007.

	Annual Growth	12/10	12/11	12/12	12/13	12/14
Assets ($ mil.)	6.4%	345.3	366.1	357.7	408.2	442.5
Net income ($ mil.)	17.7%	1.7	1.9	2.4	3.1	3.3
Market value ($ mil.)	3.5%	44.8	47.5	47.5	47.3	51.5
Employees	6.1%	87	95	98	-	-

FIRST AMERICAN FINANCIAL CORP
NYS: FAF

1 First American Way
Santa Ana, CA 92707-5913
Phone: 714 250-3000
Fax: 714 250-3151
Web: www.firstam.com

CEO: Dennis J. Gilmore
CFO: Mark E. Seaton
HR: Mark Rutherford
FYE: December 31
Type: Public

First American Financial knows that when you're buying real estate you'll probably want some insurance to go along with it. In addition to good old title insurance from its First American Title subsidiary the company's financial services arm also provides specialty property/casualty insurance and home warranties through its First American Home Buyers Protection business. Its First American Trust offers banking and trust services to the escrow and real estate industries. Other offerings include settlement title plant management record keeping valuation and investment advisory services.

	Annual Growth	12/10	12/11	12/12	12/13	12/14
Assets ($ mil.)	7.1%	5,821.8	5,370.3	6,050.8	6,520.6	7,666.1
Net income ($ mil.)	16.3%	127.8	78.3	301.0	186.4	233.5
Market value ($ mil.)	22.7%	1,606.7	1,362.5	2,590.7	3,032.7	3,645.6
Employees	0.3%	16,879	16,117	17,312	17,292	17,103

FIRST AVIATION SERVICES INC.
PINK SHEETS: FAVS

15 Riverside Ave.
Westport CT 06880-4214
Phone: 203-291-3300
Fax: 203-291-3330
Web: www.favs.com

CEO: Aaron P Hollander
CFO: James Howell
HR: Gary Taylor
FYE: December 31
Type: Public

The superstore of aerospace First Aviation Services (FAvS) pushes parts and components that keep aircraft flying high. FAvS sells about 200000 new and reconditioned parts from more than 150 manufacturers and OEMs such as General Electric Goodrich and Parker Hannifin. Cornerstone unit Aerospace Products International (API) and subsidiaries worldwide tap 6000-plus manufacturers maintenance providers and operators of commercial corporate and general aviation aircraft. In addition to offering maintenance overhaul and repair (MRO) services for brakes and starters/generators and builds hose assemblies API provides third-party logistics and inventory management services.

FIRST BANCORP
NYS: FBP

1519 Ponce de Leon Avenue, Stop 23
Santurce 00908
Phone: 787 729-8200
Fax: –
Web: www.firstbankpr.com

CEO: Aurelio Aleman-Bermudez
CFO: Orlando Berges-Gonzalez
HR: –
FYE: December 31
Type: Public

Not to be confused with North Carolina's First Bancorp this First BanCorp is the holding company for FirstBank Puerto Rico which provides business and retail banking services through more than 50 branches in Puerto Rico and about two dozen more in Florida and the Virgin Islands. Puerto Rico's second-largest bank gets more than one-third of its business from its Commercial and Corporate Banking loans and services. Residential mortgages make up nearly one-third of FirstBank's $9 billion loan portfolio while commercial mortgages make up another one-fifth. First BanCorp also owns FirstBank Insurance Agency Firstbank Puerto Rico Securities and the consumer loan company Money Express La Financiera.

	Annual Growth	12/10	12/11	12/12	12/13	12/14
Assets ($ mil.)	(4.9%)	15,593.1	13,127.3	13,099.7	12,656.9	12,727.8
Net income ($ mil.)	–	(524.3)	(82.2)	29.8	(164.5)	392.3
Market value ($ mil.)	89.0%	98.0	743.3	975.5	1,318.4	1,250.2
Employees	1.0%	2,518	2,490	2,512	2,458	2,617

FIRST BANCORP (NC)
NMS: FBNC

300 S.W. Broad Street
Southern Pines, NC 28387
Phone: 910 246-2500
Fax: –
Web: www.localfirstbank.com

CEO: Richard T. Moore
CFO: Eric P. Credle
HR: –
FYE: December 31
Type: Public

First things first: Don't confuse this First Bancorp with Virginia's First Bancorp or First BanCorp in Puerto Rico. This one is the holding company for First Bank which operates about 100 branch locations in east-central North Carolina east South Carolina and western Virginia (where it operates under the name First Bank of Virginia). In addition to offering standard commercial banking services such as deposit accounts and lending the bank offers investment products and discount brokerage services. Another subsidiary First Bank Insurance Services offers property/casualty products. First Bank focuses its lending on mortgages which account for more than half of its loan portfolio.

	Annual Growth	12/10	12/11	12/12	12/13	12/14
Assets ($ mil.)	(0.5%)	3,278.9	3,290.5	3,244.9	3,185.1	3,218.4
Net income ($ mil.)	25.8%	10.0	13.6	(23.4)	20.7	25.0
Market value ($ mil.)	4.8%	301.8	219.8	252.7	327.6	364.0
Employees	1.0%	794	849	852	873	825

FIRST BANCORP INC (ME)
NMS: FNLC

Main Street
Damariscotta, ME 04543
Phone: 207 563-3195
Fax: –
Web: www.thefirstbancorp.com

CEO: Tony C. McKim
CFO: F. Stephen Ward
HR: –
FYE: December 31
Type: Public

It may not actually be the first bank but The First Bancorp (formerly First National Lincoln) was founded over 150 years ago. It is the holding company for The First a regional bank serving coastal Maine from more than 15 branches. The bank offers traditional retail products and services including checking and savings accounts CDs IRAs and loans. Residential mortgages make up about 40% of the company's loan portfolio; business loans account for another 40%; and home equity and consumer loans comprise the rest. Bank subsidiary First Advisors offers private banking and investment management services. Founded in 1864 the bank now boasts more than $1.4 billion in assets.

	Annual Growth	12/10	12/11	12/12	12/13	12/14
Assets ($ mil.)	1.5%	1,393.8	1,372.9	1,415.0	1,464.0	1,482.1
Net income ($ mil.)	5.0%	12.1	12.4	12.7	13.0	14.7
Market value ($ mil.)	3.5%	169.3	164.8	176.6	186.8	194.0
Employees	2.6%	212	210	228	233	235

FIRST BANCORP OF INDIANA, INC.
OTC: FBPI

5001 Davis Lant Drive
Evansville, IN 47715
Phone: 812 492-8104
Fax: –
Web: www.firstfedevansville.com

CEO: Michael H Head
CFO: George J Smith
HR: –
FYE: June 30
Type: Public

First Bancorp of Indiana wants to be second to none. It's the holding company for First Federal Savings Bank which serves individuals and local businesses through nine branches in the Evansville Indiana area. The bank offers standard retail products and services like checking savings and money market accounts; certificates of deposit; and retirement savings plans. Its lending activities primarily consist of mortgage and consumer loans (approximately 50% and 40% of the company's loan portfolio respectively). The bank also offers savings account loans and business loans.

	Annual Growth	06/10	06/11	06/12	06/13	06/14
Assets ($ mil.)	2.2%	343.8	356.1	381.2	376.9	375.4
Net income ($ mil.)	0.5%	1.4	0.9	1.1	1.6	1.4
Market value ($ mil.)	8.5%	17.9	18.4	19.0	22.7	24.8
Employees	–	–	–	–	–	–

FIRST BANCSHARES INC
NMS: FBMS

6480 U.S. Highway 98 West
Hattiesburg, MS 39402
Phone: 601 268-8998
Fax: –
Web: www.thefirstbank.com

CEO: M Ray Cole Jr
CFO: Dee Dee Lowery
HR: –
FYE: December 31
Type: Public

Hoping to be first in the hearts of its customers The First Bancshares is the holding company for The First a community bank with some two dozen branch locations in southern Mississippi's Hattiesburg Alabama and Louisiana. The company provides such standard deposit products as checking and savings accounts NOW and money market accounts and IRAs. Real estate loans account for about 80% of the bank's lending portfolio including about equal portions of residential mortgages commercial mortgages and construction loans. The bank also writes business loans and consumer loans. The bank which has expanded beyond Mississippi through several acquisitions has approximately $970 million in assets.

	Annual Growth	12/10	12/11	12/12	12/13	12/14
Assets ($ mil.)	21.4%	503.0	681.4	721.4	940.9	1,093.8
Net income ($ mil.)	26.9%	2.5	2.9	4.0	4.6	6.6
Market value ($ mil.)	14.3%	45.4	40.7	50.4	74.9	77.5
Employees	15.2%	158	212	212	266	278

FIRST BANCSHARES INC. (MO)
NBB: FBSI

142 East First Street, P.O. Box 777
Mountain Grove, MO 65711
Phone: 417 926-5151
Fax: 417 926-4362
Web: www.fhsb.com

CEO: R Bradley Weaver
CFO: Ronald J Walters
HR: –
FYE: December 31
Type: Public

First Bancshares is the holding company for First Home Savings Bank which has about a dozen locations serving south-central Missouri. First Home Savings offers a range of retail banking services including checking and savings as well as NOW accounts and CDs. Residential mortgages account for more than half of First Home Savings' lending portfolio; commercial real estate loans represent another quarter. First Home Savings Bank was founded in 1911 as Mountain Grove Building and Loan Association

	Annual Growth	06/11	06/12	06/13	06/14*	12/14
Assets ($ mil.)	(2.1%)	209.3	193.4	191.7	192.5	196.4
Net income ($ mil.)	–	(4.1)	(1.4)	(0.1)	0.6	0.1
Market value ($ mil.)	(3.3%)	11.6	8.1	12.0	13.2	10.5
Employees	–	96	–	–	–	–

*Fiscal year change

FIRST BANCTRUST CORP
NBB: FIRT

101 South Central Avenue
Paris, IL 61944
Phone: 217 465-6381
Fax: 217 465-0201
Web: www.firstbanktrust.com

CEO: Terry J Howard
CFO: Ellen M Litteral
HR: –
FYE: December 31
Type: Public

You can spend your money along the banks of the Seine in Paris but you can save your money at First BancTrust Corporation in Paris (Illinois that is). It's the holding company for First Bank & Trust which has offices in the rural eastern Illinois towns of Marshall Martinsville Paris Rantoul and Savoy. Founded in 1887 the bank attracts deposits by offering such services as checking and savings accounts CDs and IRAs. Its lending activities primarily consist of residential mortgages commercial mortgages farmland loans commercial and industrial loans and consumer loans. First Bank also offers trust investment and financial planning services.

	Annual Growth	12/10	12/11	12/12	12/13	12/14
Assets ($ mil.)	1.7%	405.4	392.8	389.6	407.3	433.8
Net income ($ mil.)	3.4%	2.8	3.8	3.4	3.1	3.2
Market value ($ mil.)	20.1%	16.5	17.8	24.3	30.9	34.3
Employees	–	–	–	–	–	–

FIRST BANKS, INC. (MO)

135 North Meramec
Clayton, MO 63105
Phone: 314 854-4600
Fax: –
Web: www.firstbanks.com

CEO: Timothy J Lathe
CFO: Lisa K Vansickle
HR: –
FYE: December 31
Type: Public

First Banks keeps it in the family. The holding company for First Bank it is owned by chairman James Dierberg and his family; many of the bank's branches and ATMs are located in Dierbergs Markets a Missouri-based grocery chain owned by relatives of the chairman. First Bank has about 130 branches in California Florida Illinois and Missouri with a concentration in metropolitan markets such as Los Angeles San Diego San Francisco Sacramento and St. Louis. The bank offers standard services like deposits mortgages and business and consumer loans. Additional services include brokerage insurance trust and private banking as well as commercial treasury management and international trade services.

	Annual Growth	12/10	12/11	12/12	12/13	12/14
Assets ($ mil.)	(5.3%)	7,378.1	6,608.9	6,509.1	5,919.0	5,935.5
Net income ($ mil.)	–	(191.7)	(41.2)	26.3	241.7	21.7
Market value ($ mil.)	–	–	–	–	–	–
Employees	(4.1%)	1,380	1,171	1,177	1,147	1,167

FIRST BUSEY CORP
NMS: BUSE

100 West University Avenue
Champaign, IL 61820
Phone: 217 365-4544
Fax: –
Web: www.busey.com

CEO: Van A. Dukeman
CFO: Robin N. Elliott
HR: –
FYE: December 31
Type: Public

First Busey Corporation keeps itself busy taking care of deposits and making loans. It's the holding company for Busey Bank which boasts $4 billion in assets and 40 branches across Illinois Florida and Indiana. The bank offers standard deposit products and services using funds from deposits to originate primarily real estate loans and mortgages. Subsidiary Busey Wealth Management which manages $5 billion in assets provides asset management trust brokerage and related services to individuals businesses and foundations while FirsTech provides retail payment processing services. Most of Busey Bank's branches are located in downstate Illinois.

	Annual Growth	12/10	12/11	12/12	12/13	12/14
Assets ($ mil.)	0.4%	3,605.0	3,402.1	3,618.1	3,539.6	3,665.6
Net income ($ mil.)	9.0%	23.2	29.9	22.4	28.7	32.8
Market value ($ mil.)	8.5%	136.1	144.8	134.6	167.9	188.5
Employees	(1.9%)	866	888	948	849	801

FIRST BUSINESS FINANCIAL SERVICES, INC.
NMS: FBIZ

401 Charmany Drive
Madison, WI 53719
Phone: 608 238-8008
Fax: –
Web: www.firstbusiness.com

CEO: Corey A. Chambas
CFO: Edward G. (Ed) Sloane
HR: –
FYE: December 31
Type: Public

Business comes first at First Business Financial Services which serves small and midsized companies entrepreneurs professionals and high-net-worth individuals through First Business Bank and First Business Bank - Milwaukee. The banks offer deposits loans cash management and trust services from a handful of offices in Wisconsin and Kansas. Over 60% of the company's loan portfolio is made up of commercial real estate loans. Subsidiary First Business Capital specializes in asset-based lending while First Business Equipment Finance provides commercial equipment financing. First Business Trust & Investments offers investment management and retirement services.

	Annual Growth	12/10	12/11	12/12	12/13	12/14
Assets ($ mil.)	10.1%	1,107.1	1,177.2	1,226.1	1,268.7	1,629.4
Net income ($ mil.)	96.9%	0.9	8.4	8.9	13.7	14.1
Market value ($ mil.)	37.5%	116.4	143.1	199.0	326.3	415.5
Employees	13.1%	141	143	155	164	231

FIRST CAPITAL BANCORP INC (VA)   NAS: FCVA

4222 Cox Road
Glen Allen, VA 23060
Phone: 804 273-1160
Fax: –
Web: www.1capitalbank.com

CEO: –
CFO: –
HR: –
FYE: December 31
Type: Public

Moolah scratch bread chedda bucks dough ducats or skrilla — it all means business for First Capital Bank and its holding company First Capital Bancorp. Founded in 1998 the bank provides general commercial banking services through seven branches in the Richmond Virginia area. First Capital Bank offers the usual array of personal and business banking services including credit cards IRAs consumer and commercial loans Internet banking services and deposit accounts. The company terminated its agreement to merge with Eastern Virginia Bankshares in 2009 after regulatory approval for the deal stalled.

	Annual Growth	12/09	12/10	12/11	12/12	12/13
Assets ($ mil.)	0.8%	530.4	536.0	541.7	542.9	547.9
Net income ($ mil.)	88.4%	0.3	(2.2)	(3.1)	(6.0)	3.9
Market value ($ mil.)	(0.8%)	60.2	45.3	30.5	35.6	58.2
Employees	7.2%	78	82	91	101	103

FIRST CAPITAL INC.   NAS: FCAP

220 Federal Drive NW
Corydon, IN 47112
Phone: 812 738-2198
Fax: –
Web: www.firstharrison.com

CEO: William W Harrod
CFO: M Chris Frederick
HR: Kim Banet
FYE: December 31
Type: Public

First Capital is the holding company for First Harrison Bank which operates about a dozen branches in Clark Floyd Harrison and Washington counties in southern Indiana. Targeting area consumers and small to midsized businesses the bank offers standard deposit products such as checking and savings accounts certificates of deposit and individual retirement accounts. Residential mortgages make up nearly half of the company's loan portfolio; consumer loans and commercial mortgages are around 20% apiece. First Harrison Bank also offers access to investments such as stocks bonds and mutual funds.

	Annual Growth	12/10	12/11	12/12	12/13	12/14
Assets ($ mil.)	1.1%	452.4	438.9	459.1	444.4	472.8
Net income ($ mil.)	9.7%	3.9	4.0	3.9	5.1	5.6
Market value ($ mil.)	10.0%	45.6	50.8	53.4	58.3	66.7
Employees	0.2%	149	148	133	145	150

FIRST CASH FINANCIAL SERVICES INC   NMS: FCFS

690 East Lamar Blvd., Suite 400
Arlington, TX 76011
Phone: 817 460-3947
Fax: –
Web: www.firstcash.com

CEO: Rick L. Wessel
CFO: R. Douglas (Doug) Orr
HR: Jan Hartz
FYE: December 31
Type: Public

First Cash Financial Services is the original pawn star. The company operates more than 1000 pawnshops and cash advance stores in about a dozen US states and nearly 30 states in Mexico. First Cash lends money secured by such personal property as jewelry electronics tools sporting goods musical equipment and firearms (in select markets). Its First Cash Pawn and Famous Pawn shops sell merchandise forfeited by borrowers. The company's Fast Cash Advance locations offer short-term and payday loans. The company exited the check cashing business in late 2014 when it discontinued its Cash & Go joint venture. Founded in 1988 fast-growing Fast Cash has acquired about 500 stores over the past five years.

	Annual Growth	12/10	12/11	12/12	12/13	12/14
Sales ($ mil.)	13.4%	431.1	521.3	595.9	660.8	712.9
Net income ($ mil.)	10.2%	57.7	77.8	80.4	83.8	85.2
Market value ($ mil.)	15.8%	883.5	1,000.3	1,414.6	1,762.9	1,587.0
Employees	13.9%	4,700	5,300	6,400	7,100	7,900

FIRST CENTURY BANKSHARES, INC.   OTC: FCBS

500 Federal Street
Bluefield, WV 24701
Phone: 304 325-8181
Fax: 304 325-3727
Web: www.firstcentury.com

CEO: Frank W Wilkinson
CFO: J Ronald Hypes
HR: –
FYE: December 31
Type: Public

First Century Bankshares is the holding company for First Century Bank which serves southern West Virginia and southwestern Virginia from about a dozen branch locations. The bank provides traditional deposit services such as checking accounts statement savings money market accounts CDs and IRAs. It uses funds from deposits to write commercial and consumer loans primarily real estate mortgages which account for some 70% of the company's loan book. First Century Bank also offers real estate construction and development loans agricultural loans and check cards. Bank subsidiary First Century Financial Services provides trust investment and financial planning services.

	Annual Growth	12/10	12/11	12/12	12/13	12/14
Assets ($ mil.)	(0.4%)	408.0	417.8	410.8	412.5	401.2
Net income ($ mil.)	10.4%	2.1	2.2	2.9	3.1	3.2
Market value ($ mil.)	10.1%	22.8	23.3	28.4	32.6	33.5
Employees	(2.5%)	157	153	–	–	–

FIRST CITIZENS BANCORPORATION INC.   OTC: FCBN

1230 Main
Columbia SC 29201
Phone: 803-733-2020
Fax: 803-733-2763
Web: www.firstcitizensonline.com

CEO: –
CFO: –
HR: –
FYE: December 31
Type: Public

First Citizens Bancorporation is the holding company for First Citizens Bank and Trust Company which has nearly 200 branches in South Carolina and Georgia and The Exchange Bank of South Carolina which has four branches. The banks provide standard products and services for individuals and businesses including checking and savings accounts credit cards investments and online banking. Residential and commercial mortgages comprise most of First Citizens Bancorporation's loan portfolio. First Citizens Bank's Wealth Advisory Group provides investment management trust and private banking services. Subsidiary First Citizens Securities offers brokerage retirement planning and insurance services.

FIRST CITIZENS BANCSHARES, INC. (NC)   NMS: FCNC A

4300 Six Forks Road
Raleigh, NC 27609
Phone: 919 716-7000
Fax: –
Web: www.firstcitizens.com

CEO: Frank B. Holding
CFO: Craig L. Nix
HR: Lou J. Davis
FYE: December 31
Type: Public

First Citizens BancShares knows commercial banking. It owns First-Citizens Bank which operates about 400 branches in 17 states mainly in the southeastern and western US and urban areas scattered nationwide. The bank provides standard services such as deposits loans mortgages and trust services in addition to processing and operational support to other banks. Subsidiary First Citizens Investor Services offers investments and discount brokerage services to bank clients. Real estate loans including commercial residential and revolving mortgages and construction and land development loans comprise most of its loan portfolio.

	Annual Growth	12/10	12/11	12/12	12/13	12/14
Assets ($ mil.)	9.6%	20,806.7	20,881.5	21,283.7	21,199.1	30,075.1
Net income ($ mil.)	(8.0%)	193.0	195.0	134.3	167.7	138.6
Market value ($ mil.)	7.5%	2,270.6	2,101.7	1,963.7	2,673.9	3,036.1
Employees	5.8%	5,135	5,077	4,821	4,875	6,440

FIRST CLOVER LEAF FINANCIAL CORP

NAS: FCLF

6814 Goshen Road
Edwardsville, IL 62025
Phone: 618 656-6122
Fax: –

CEO: P David Kuhl
CFO: Darlene F McDonald
HR: –
FYE: December 31
Type: Public

First Clover Leaf Financial counts itself lucky to be in the banking business in the greater St. Louis area. The company (formerly First Federal Financial Services) is the holding company for three-branch First Clover Leaf Bank. Under its former name the company in 2006 acquired Clover Leaf Financial and merged the acquisition's Clover Leaf Bank with First Federal Savings & Loan Association of Edwardsville to form First Clover Leaf Bank. The bank serves individuals and businesses in and around Edwardsville and Glen Carbon offering such standard services as deposit accounts credit cards and loans including real estate (about 85% of its total portfolio) business and consumer loans.

	Annual Growth	12/10	12/11	12/12	12/13	12/14
Assets ($ mil.)	1.4%	575.0	562.7	600.8	622.0	607.6
Net income ($ mil.)	0.1%	3.8	1.9	4.1	3.4	3.8
Market value ($ mil.)	6.6%	47.5	42.7	43.7	68.7	61.4
Employees	4.6%	87	93	103	103	104

FIRST COMMONWEALTH FINANCIAL CORP. (INDIANA, PA)

NYS: FCF

601 Philadelphia Street
Indiana, PA 15701
Phone: 724 349-7220
Fax: –
Web: www.fcbanking.com

CEO: Thomas Michael (Mike) Price
CFO: James R. Reske
HR: Carrie Riggle
FYE: December 31
Type: Public

First Commonwealth Financial is the holding company for First Commonwealth Bank which provides consumer and commercial banking services from nearly 115 branches across 15 central and western Pennsylvania counties as well as in Columbus Ohio. The bank's loan portfolio mostly consists of commercial and industrial loans including real estate operating agricultural and construction loans. It also issues consumer loans such as education automobile and home equity loans and offers wealth management insurance financial planning retail brokerage and trust services. The company has total assets exceeding $6 billion with deposits of roughly $4.5 billion.

	Annual Growth	12/10	12/11	12/12	12/13	12/14
Assets ($ mil.)	2.3%	5,812.8	5,841.1	5,995.4	6,214.9	6,360.3
Net income ($ mil.)	17.9%	23.0	15.3	42.0	41.5	44.5
Market value ($ mil.)	6.8%	649.4	482.5	625.6	809.0	845.7
Employees	(4.3%)	1,622	1,506	1,482	1,437	1,363

FIRST COMMONWEALTH INC.

550 W. Jackson Ste. 800 Ste. 600
Chicago IL 60661
Phone: 312-993-1000
Fax: 312-279-5140
Web: www.guardianlife.com/solutions/product_portfol

CEO: Christopher Multhauf
CFO: –
HR: –
FYE: December 31
Type: Subsidiary

First Commonwealth wants to come in first in the dental plan business. Founded until 1986 the company offers group dental care benefits services. Operating primarily in the Midwest the company maintains affordable managed care (HMO) and indemnity plans as well as out-of-network PPO options. First Commonwealth is a subsidiary of The Guardian Life Insurance Company of America which serves 6.7 million members through its nationwide dental network of more than 90000 health professionals. Dental members also have access to Guardian's vision benefits.

FIRST COMMUNITY BANCSHARES, INC. (NV)

NMS: FCBC

P.O. Box 989
Bluefield, VA 24605-0989
Phone: 276 326-9000
Fax: –
Web: www.fcbinc.com

CEO: William P. Stafford
CFO: David D. Brown
HR: Cassandra Boothe
FYE: December 31
Type: Public

First Community Bancshares doesn't play second fiddle to other area banks. The firm is the holding company for First Community Bank which provides traditional services like checking and savings accounts CDs and credit cards and serves communities through some 55 branches across Virginia West Virginia North Carolina and Tennessee. Commercial real estate loans make up 45% of its loan portfolio while commercial business loans make up another 5%. First Community Bancshares offers insurance through subsidiary Greenpoint Insurance and wealth management and investment advisory services through Trust Services and First Community Wealth Management.

	Annual Growth	12/10	12/11	12/12	12/13	12/14
Assets ($ mil.)	3.8%	2,244.2	2,164.8	2,728.9	2,602.5	2,607.9
Net income ($ mil.)	3.9%	21.8	20.0	28.6	23.3	25.5
Market value ($ mil.)	2.5%	275.0	229.7	293.9	307.4	303.2
Employees	(0.2%)	683	633	760	729	678

FIRST COMMUNITY CORP. (SC)

NAS: FCCO

5455 Sunset Boulevard
Lexington, SC 29072
Phone: 803 951-2265
Fax: –
Web: www.firstcommunitysc.com

CEO: Michael C Crapps
CFO: Joseph G Sawyer
HR: –
FYE: December 31
Type: Public

Putting first things first First Community is the holding company for First Community Bank which serves individuals and smaller businesses in central South Carolina. Through about a dozen offices the bank which was founded in 1995 offers such products and services as checking and savings accounts money market accounts CDs IRAs credit cards insurance and investment services. Commercial mortgages make up about 60% of First Community Bank's loan portfolio which also includes residential mortgages and business consumer and construction loans. The company's First Community Financial Consultants division offers asset management and estate planning.

	Annual Growth	12/10	12/11	12/12	12/13	12/14
Assets ($ mil.)	7.9%	599.0	593.9	602.9	633.3	812.4
Net income ($ mil.)	28.9%	1.9	3.3	4.0	4.1	5.1
Market value ($ mil.)	18.3%	38.5	41.3	55.9	69.3	75.4
Employees	5.9%	147	157	158	171	185

FIRST CONNECTICUT BANCORP INC. (MD)

NMS: FBNK

One Farm Glen Boulevard
Farmington, CT 06032
Phone: 860 676-4600
Fax: –
Web: www.farmingtonbankct.com

CEO: John J. Patrick
CFO: Gregory A. White
HR: –
FYE: December 31
Type: Public

One of the oldest states in the union also has some of the oldest banks in the union. First Connecticut Bancorp (FCB) is the holding company of one such bank. Farmington Bank is a Connecticut-based community bank that traces its roots back to the mid-1800s. The bank offers traditional deposit accounts to consumers businesses and government clients including savings money market and checking accounts. Its lending activity consists primarily of commercial and residential real estate loans. Farmington Bank operates through about 20 branches most of which are located in suburban communities in central Connecticut. In 2011 FCB converted from a mutual holding structure to a public company.

	Annual Growth	12/10	12/11	12/12	12/13	12/14
Assets ($ mil.)	15.1%	1,416.6	1,617.7	1,822.9	2,110.0	2,485.4
Net income ($ mil.)	17.7%	4.9	(4.0)	3.9	3.7	9.3
Market value ($ mil.)	7.8%	–	208.5	220.4	258.3	261.5
Employees	4.2%	278	299	326	337	328

FIRST DATA CORP (NEW) NYS: FDC

225 Liberty Street, 29th Floor
New York, NY 10281
Phone: 800 735-3362
Fax: –
Web: www.firstdata.com

CEO: Frank J. Bisignano
CFO: Himanshu A Patel
HR: Anthony S. (Tony) Marino
FYE: December 31
Type: Public

Paper plastic or digital — in whatever form First Data moves the money. One of the world's largest electronic payments processors First Data serves more than 6 million merchants and some 4000 card issuers in some 35 countries. It provides a variety of secure funds transfer and related services including credit card payment processing fraud protection and authentication check guarantee (through subsidiary TeleCheck) electronic bill payment management and point-of-sale (POS) services. First Data operates through three primary segments: retail and alliance services financial services and international. It owns a majority stake in Bank of America Merchant Services. The company went public in late 2015.

	Annual Growth	12/10	12/11	12/12	12/13	12/14
Sales ($ mil.)	1.8%	10,380.4	10,713.6	10,680.3	10,808.9	11,151.8
Net income ($ mil.)	–	(1,021.8)	(516.1)	(700.9)	(869.1)	(457.8)
Market value ($ mil.)	–	–	–	–	–	–
Employees	(1.6%)	24,500	24,000	24,000	23,000	23,000

FIRST DEFIANCE FINANCIAL CORP. NMS: FDEF

601 Clinton Street
Defiance, OH 43512
Phone: 419 782-5015
Fax: –
Web: www.fdef.com

CEO: James L. Rohrs
CFO: Kent T. Thompson
HR: Diane Beam
FYE: December 31
Type: Public

Named for its hometown not its attitude First Defiance Financial is the holding company for First Federal Bank of the Midwest which operates more than 30 branches serving northwestern Ohio western Indiana and southern Michigan. The thrift offers standard deposit products including checking savings and money market accounts and CDs. Commercial real estate loans account for more than half of the bank's loan portfolio; commercial loans make up another quarter of all loans. The company's insurance agency subsidiary First Insurance Group of the Midwest which accounts for some 7% of the company's revenues provides life insurance property/casualty coverage and investments.

	Annual Growth	12/10	12/11	12/12	12/13	12/14
Assets ($ mil.)	1.7%	2,035.5	2,068.2	2,046.9	2,137.1	2,179.0
Net income ($ mil.)	31.6%	8.1	15.5	18.7	22.2	24.3
Market value ($ mil.)	30.1%	109.9	134.7	177.2	239.8	314.5
Employees	0.9%	536	581	553	549	555

FIRST EAGLE INVESTMENT MANAGEMENT LLC

1345 Avenue of the Americas 44th Fl.
New York NY 10105-4300
Phone: 212-698-3300
Fax: 212-299-4360
Web: www.firsteagleinstitutional.com

CEO: –
CFO: –
HR: –
FYE: December 31
Type: Private

First Eagle wants to fly high in the world of investment management. The firm (formerly Arnhold and S. Bleichroeder Advisers) manages more than $55 million of assets for institutional investors such as corporations pension funds foundations endowments and high net-worth investors. It manages the First Eagle Funds a family of five value-oriented mutual funds geared toward capital preservation. Other products include separate accounts and commingled funds. The company's portfolio management strategies include US equities global value and international value. First Eagle is owned by its employees and the Arnhold family.

FIRST ELECTRIC CO-OPERATIVE CORPORATION

1000 S JP WRIGHT LOOP RD
JACKSONVILLE, AR 720765264
Phone: 501-982-4545
Fax: –
Web: www.firstelectric.coop

CEO: Don Crabbe
CFO: Bruce Andrews
HR: –
FYE: December 31
Type: Private

First Electric Cooperative wasn't the first electric cooperative ever formed but it was the first such entity created in its home state. The member-owned utility distributes power to more than 85000 customers in 17 central and southeastern Arkansas counties. It also offers its members a range of energy products and value-added services including energy efficient Marathon water heaters surge and lightning protection equipment and compact fluorescent light bulbs. Some 72% of the cooperative's revenues come from residential customers; commercial and industrial customers account for another 20% and the rest comes from such sources as irrigation and street lighting.

	Annual Growth	12/04	12/05	12/06	12/07	12/13
Sales ($ mil.)	(20.5%)	–	1,151.0	0.0	154.3	184.1
Net income ($ mil.)	–	–	–	0.0	20.5	0.0
Market value ($ mil.)	–	–	–	–	–	–
Employees	–	–	–	–	–	237

FIRST FEDERAL OF NORTHERN MICHIGAN BANCORP INC NBB: FFNM

100 S. Second Avenue
Alpena, MI 49707
Phone: 989 356-9041
Fax: –
Web: www.first-federal.com

CEO: Michael W Mahler
CFO: –
HR: Joseph W Gentry
FYE: December 31
Type: Public

First Federal of Northern Michigan Bancorp is the holding company for First Federal of Northern Michigan a savings bank serving area residents and businesses from nearly 10 locations in the northern part of the state's Lower Peninsula. Deposit services include checking savings and money market accounts CDs and IRAs. The bank's lending activities mainly consist of residential mortgages (nearly half of its loan portfolio) commercial mortgages business loans and home equity loans. It also offers construction loans consumer loans and credit cards. In 2009 First Federal sold InsuranCenter of Alpena (ICA) which provided life property/casualty and health insurance and investment products.

	Annual Growth	12/10	12/11	12/12	12/13	12/14
Assets ($ mil.)	10.9%	215.7	217.0	213.8	209.7	325.9
Net income ($ mil.)	75.3%	0.2	0.7	(0.2)	0.1	2.2
Market value ($ mil.)	18.5%	10.4	10.7	17.1	20.1	20.5
Employees	1.8%	94	93	92	92	101

FIRST FINANCIAL BANCORP (OH) NMS: FFBC

255 East Fifth Street, Suite 700
Cincinnati, OH 45202
Phone: 877 322-9530
Fax: –
Web: www.bankatfirst.com

CEO: Claude E. Davis
CFO: John Gavigan
HR: –
FYE: December 31
Type: Public

First Financial Bancorp spreads itself thick. The holding company's flagship subsidiary First Financial Bank operates nearly 110 branches in Ohio Indiana and Kentucky. Founded in 1863 the bank offers checking and savings accounts money market accounts CDs credit cards private banking and wealth management services through its First Financial Wealth Management subsidiary. Commercial loans including real estate and construction loans make up more than 50% of First Financial's total loan portfolio; the bank also offers residential mortgage and consumer loans. First Financial Bancorp boasts more than $7 billion in assets including nearly $5 billion in loans.

	Annual Growth	12/10	12/11	12/12	12/13	12/14
Assets ($ mil.)	3.7%	6,250.2	6,671.5	6,497.0	6,417.2	7,217.8
Net income ($ mil.)	2.3%	59.3	66.7	67.3	48.3	65.0
Market value ($ mil.)	0.1%	1,135.7	1,022.6	898.5	1,071.1	1,142.5
Employees	(3.5%)	1,664	1,656	1,547	1,422	1,442

FIRST FINANCIAL BANKSHARES, INC. NMS: FFIN

400 Pine Street
Abilene, TX 79601
Phone: 325 627-7155
Fax: –
Web: www.ffin.com

CEO: F. Scott Dueser
CFO: J. Bruce Hildebrand
HR: Racheal Carter
FYE: December 31
Type: Public

Texas hold 'em? Well sort of. First Financial Bankshares is the holding company for eleven banks consolidated under the First Financial brand all of which are located in small and midsized markets in Texas. Together they have about 50 locations. The company maintains a decentralized management structure with each of the subsidiary banks having their own local leadership and decision-making authority. Its First Financial Trust & Asset Management subsidiary administers retirement and employee benefit plans in addition to providing trust services. First Financial Bankshares also owns an insurance agency.

	Annual Growth	12/10	12/11	12/12	12/13	12/14
Assets ($ mil.)	11.6%	3,776.4	4,120.5	4,502.0	5,222.2	5,848.2
Net income ($ mil.)	10.7%	59.7	68.4	74.2	78.9	89.6
Market value ($ mil.)	(12.6%)	3,257.5	2,124.8	2,479.5	4,202.0	1,899.2
Employees	3.3%	1,000	980	1,000	1,100	1,140

FIRST FINANCIAL CORP. (IN) NMS: THFF

One First Financial Plaza
Terre Haute, IN 47807
Phone: 812 238-6000
Fax: –
Web: www.first-online.com

CEO: Norman D. Lowery
CFO: Rodger A McHargue
HR: Racheal Carter
FYE: December 31
Type: Public

Which came first the First Financial in Indiana Ohio South Carolina or Texas? Regardless this particular First Financial Corporation is the holding company for First Financial Bank which operates more than 60 branches in west-central Indiana and central Illinois. The bank offers traditional services such as checking and savings accounts CDs and credit cards. It also provides trust private banking wealth management and investment services. First Financial sells personal and commercial insurance through regional agency subsidiary Forrest Sherer. Another unit Morris Plan originates indirect auto loans through some 70 dealerships in the bank's market area.

	Annual Growth	12/10	12/11	12/12	12/13	12/14
Assets ($ mil.)	5.2%	2,451.1	2,954.1	2,895.4	3,018.7	3,002.5
Net income ($ mil.)	4.8%	28.0	37.2	32.8	31.5	33.8
Market value ($ mil.)	0.3%	454.8	430.7	391.4	473.2	461.0
Employees	4.0%	813	932	928	954	952

FIRST FINANCIAL NORTHWEST INC NMS: FFNW

201 Wells Avenue South
Renton, WA 98057
Phone: 425 255-4400
Fax: –

CEO: Joseph W Kiley III
CFO: Richard P Jacobson
HR: Janice Clusserath
FYE: December 31
Type: Public

Searching for green in The Evergreen State First Financial Northwest is the holding company for First Financial Northwest Bank (formerly First Savings Bank Northwest). The small community bank offers deposit services like checking and savings accounts and a variety of lending services to customers in western Washington. Almost 40% of First Savings Bank's loan portfolio consists of one- to four-family residential loans while commercial real estate loans made up another 35%. Because the bank focuses almost exclusively on real estate loans it writes very few unsecured consumer and commercial loans.

	Annual Growth	12/10	12/11	12/12	12/13	12/14
Assets ($ mil.)	(5.9%)	1,193.7	1,059.4	942.7	921.0	937.0
Net income ($ mil.)	–	(54.1)	4.2	2.7	24.5	10.7
Market value ($ mil.)	31.7%	60.7	89.5	114.5	157.3	182.6
Employees	(2.6%)	112	108	113	93	101

FIRST FINANCIAL SERVICE CORP NMS: FFKY

2323 Ring Road
Elizabethtown, KY 42701
Phone: 270 765-2131
Fax: 270 769-5811
Web: www.ffsbky.com

CEO: –
CFO: –
HR: –
FYE: December 31
Type: Public

First Financial Service Corporation is the holding company for First Federal Savings Bank of Elizabethtown which has 18 branches in six central Kentucky counties. Founded in 1923 the bank offers CDs IRAs and savings NOW and money market accounts primarily using deposit funds to originate commercial real estate loans (about 60% of its loan portfolio) and residential mortgages (about 20%). Other loans include home equity consumer and business loans. First Service Corporation of Elizabethtown a subsidiary of the bank sells investment products to the bank's customers.

	Annual Growth	12/08	12/09	12/10	12/11	12/12
Assets ($ mil.)	(0.2%)	1,017.0	1,209.5	1,320.5	1,228.8	1,007.1
Net income ($ mil.)	–	4.8	(6.7)	(8.3)	(23.2)	(8.4)
Market value ($ mil.)	(36.1%)	56.4	43.3	19.4	7.3	9.4
Employees	(3.3%)	321	333	335	325	281

FIRST FRANKLIN CORPORATION NASDAQ: FFHS

4750 Ashwood Dr.
Cincinnati OH 45241
Phone: 513-469-8000
Fax: 513-469-5360
Web: www.franklinsavings.com

CEO: –
CFO: –
HR: –
FYE: December 31
Type: Public

First Franklin was the holding company for The Franklin Savings and Loan Company which served individuals and businesses through nearly 10 branches in and around Cincinnati. Established in 1883 Franklin Savings offered standard retail banking services such as savings checking and money market accounts as well as CDs IRAs and credit cards. Residential mortgage loans accounted for more than half of the company's loan portfolio which also included commercial real estate construction and consumer loans. First Franklin also had a 51% interest in DirectTeller Systems a provider of software for the financial industry. Cheviot Financial another Cincinnati-area bank bought First Franklin in 2011.

FIRST HARTFORD CORP NBB: FHRT

149 Colonial Road
Manchester, CT 06042
Phone: 860 646-6555
Fax: 860 646-8572
Web: www.firsthartford.com

CEO: Neil H Ellis
CFO: Eric J Harrington
HR: –
FYE: April 30
Type: Public

First Hartford puts real estate first. The company operating through subsidiary First Hartford Realty invests in and develops commercial and other real estate. Its portfolio is located primarily in the Northeast and includes shopping centers a restaurant and a business and technology school campus. First Hartford has also built single-family homes public housing units government facilities and several industrial properties. It is a preferred developer for CVS Health in areas of Lousiana New Jersey New York and Texas. The company's largest tenants include Stop & Shop Big Y Foods and Kmart. Subsidiary Lead Tech provides lead and asbestos inspection and remediation services.

	Annual Growth	04/11	04/12	04/13	04/14	04/15
Sales ($ mil.)	33.2%	22.1	27.6	39.3	41.1	69.5
Net income ($ mil.)	–	(4.4)	(0.9)	0.2	(4.7)	16.9
Market value ($ mil.)	1.4%	5.1	3.3	5.4	4.2	5.4
Employees	(5.7%)	120	103	77	89	95

FIRST HAWAIIAN BANK

999 Bishop St. 29th Fl.
Honolulu HI 96813
Phone: 808-525-7000
Fax: 808-525-5798
Web: www.fhb.com

CEO: Donald Horner
CFO: Albert M Yamada
HR: –
FYE: December 31
Type: Subsidiary

First Hawaiian Bank is the oldest and largest bank on the archipelago. It is a subsidiary of BancWest which in turn is owned by French bank BNP Paribas. Founded in 1858 to serve the whaling industry First Hawaiian Bank has about 60 branches in Hawaii plus locations in Guam and Saipan. The bank also has operations in the British West Indies and Japan. It offers standard deposit products such as checking and savings accounts CDs and IRAs as well as private banking and wealth management services. The bank mainly originates real estate-related loans such as residential and commercial mortgages and construction and land development loans. It also writes business and consumer loans.

FIRST HORIZON NATIONAL CORP — NYS: FHN

165 Madison Avenue
Memphis, TN 38103
Phone: 901 523-4444
Fax: –
Web: www.firsthorizon.com

CEO: D. Bryan Jordan
CFO: William C. (BJ) Losch
HR: John M. Daniel
FYE: December 31
Type: Public

First Horizon National would like to be on banking consumers' horizons in the Volunteer State and beyond. The bank holding company operates more than 170 First Tennessee Bank branches in its home state and neighboring markets. Boasting roughly $26 billion in total assets it offers traditional banking services like loans deposit accounts and credit cards as well as trust asset management financial advisory and investment services. Subsidiary FTN Financial performs securities sales and trading fixed-income underwriting and other investment banking services through more than 25 offices in more than 15 states as well as in Hong Kong.

	Annual Growth	12/10	12/11	12/12	12/13	12/14
Assets ($ mil.)	1.0%	24,699.0	24,789.4	25,520.1	23,789.8	25,672.9
Net income ($ mil.)	44.6%	50.2	131.2	(27.8)	29.6	219.5
Market value ($ mil.)	3.6%	2,759.1	1,873.8	2,321.1	2,728.7	3,180.7
Employees	(5.9%)	5,487	4,809	4,514	4,340	4,310

FIRST INDEPENDENCE CORPORATION — OTC: FFSL

Myrtle and 6th
Independence KS 67301
Phone: 620-331-1660
Fax: 620-331-1600
Web: www.firstfederalsl.com

CEO: –
CFO: –
HR: –
FYE: September 30
Type: Public

First Independence is the holding company for First Federal Savings and Loan Association of Independence. Founded in 1905 First Federal has branches in Coffeyville Independence Neodesha and Pittsburg Kansas and a loan production office in Lawrence Kansas. Deposit products include checking savings health savings and retirement accounts as well as certificates of deposit. First Federal mainly originates one- to four-family residential mortgages and construction and land loans. Commercial real estate multifamily residential and consumer loans round out the bank's portfolio.

FIRST INDUSTRIAL REALTY TRUST, INC. — NYS: FR

311 South Wacker Drive, Suite 3900
Chicago, IL 60606
Phone: 312 344-4300
Fax: 312 922-6320
Web: www.firstindustrial.com

CEO: Bruce W. Duncan
CFO: Scott A. Musil
HR: Sue Klaus
FYE: December 31
Type: Public

First Industrial Realty Trust wants to be the first and only stop for your industrial property needs. The self-administered real estate investment trust (REIT) owns manages and develops industrial real estate. Its portfolio consists of about 740 properties in some 25 states; Detroit Dallas and Denver are key markets. The REIT's approximately 68 million sq. ft. of space is weighted toward light industrial properties but also includes bulk and regional warehouses research and development buildings and manufacturing facilities. Tenants include manufacturing retail wholesale trade distribution and professional services firms. Founded in 1994 First Industrial also develops customized spaces.

	Annual Growth	12/10	12/11	12/12	12/13	12/14
Sales ($ mil.)	4.5%	288.5	317.8	327.3	328.2	344.6
Net income ($ mil.)	–	(202.8)	(7.4)	(1.3)	40.3	49.1
Market value ($ mil.)	23.8%	968.9	1,131.4	1,557.3	1,930.0	2,274.0
Employees	(1.4%)	183	176	173	169	173

FIRST INTERNET BANCORP — NAS: INBK

8888 Keystone Crossing, Suite 1700
Indianapolis, IN 46240
Phone: 317 532-7900
Fax: –
Web: www.firstinternetbancorp.com

CEO: David B Becker
CFO: Kenneth J Lovik
HR: –
FYE: December 31
Type: Public

First Internet Bancorp was formed in 2006 to be the holding company for First Internet Bank of Indiana (First IB). Launched in 1999 the bank was the first state-chartered FDIC-insured institution to operate solely via the Internet. It now operates two locations in Indianapolis after adding one via its 2007 purchase of Landmark Financial (the parent of Landmark Savings Bank) a deal that also brought aboard residential mortgage brokerage Landmark Mortgage. First IB offers traditional checking and savings accounts in addition to CDs IRAs credit and check cards consumer installment and residential mortgage loans and lines of credit. It serves customers in all 50 states.

	Annual Growth	12/10	12/11	12/12	12/13	12/14
Assets ($ mil.)	–	0.0	585.4	636.4	802.3	970.5
Net income ($ mil.)	–	0.0	3.2	5.6	4.6	4.3
Market value ($ mil.)	–	0.0	41.5	93.2	99.9	74.3
Employees	21.4%	–	–	97	130	143

FIRST INTERSTATE BANCSYSTEM, INC. — NMS: FIBK

401 North 31st Street
Billings, MT 59116-0918
Phone: 406 255-5390
Fax: –
Web: www.fibk.com

CEO: Edward Garding
CFO: Terrill R. Moore
HR: –
FYE: December 31
Type: Public

This Treasure State bank wants to be your treasury. First Interstate BancSystem is the holding company for First Interstate Bank which has about 80 branches in Montana western South Dakota and Wyoming. Serving area consumers businesses and municipalities the bank provides traditional services including deposit accounts wealth management and loans. Commercial loans including mortgages make up more than half of the bank's loan portfolio; residential real estate agricultural and construction loans round out its lending activities. On the wealth management side the bank has more than $8 billion in trust assets held in a fiduciary or agent capacity.

	Annual Growth	12/10	12/11	12/12	12/13	12/14
Assets ($ mil.)	3.5%	7,501.0	7,325.5	7,721.8	7,564.7	8,609.9
Net income ($ mil.)	22.6%	37.4	44.5	58.2	86.1	84.4
Market value ($ mil.)	16.2%	697.8	596.6	706.5	1,299.0	1,273.8
Employees	(0.3%)	1,723	1,677	1,683	1,635	1,705

FIRST KEYSTONE CORP.
OTC: FKYS

111 West Front Street
Berwick, PA 18603
Phone: 570 752-3671
Fax: –
Web: www.firstkeystonecorporation.com

CEO: Matthew P Prosseda
CFO: Diane C A Rosler
HR: –
FYE: December 31
Type: Public

First Keystone Corporation is the holding company for First Keystone Community Bank which serves individuals and businesses from more 18 bank locations in northeastern and central Pennsylvania. The bank provides traditional deposit products including checking and savings accounts debit cards and CDs; it also offers trust and investment advisory services. It also operates 20 ATMs and offers online banking services. Commercial mortgages constitute more than half of the bank's loan portfolio; residential mortgages business loans and consumer installment loans make up the remainder. The bank was founded in 1864.

	Annual Growth	12/10	12/11	12/12	12/13	12/14
Assets ($ mil.)	3.5%	796.6	818.5	820.0	901.6	912.4
Net income ($ mil.)	3.3%	9.0	9.9	10.2	10.3	10.2
Market value ($ mil.)	8.9%	97.4	114.1	135.3	139.2	137.2
Employees	2.6%	197	207	206	224	218

FIRST MARBLEHEAD CORP
NYS: FMD

One Cabot Road, Suite 200
Medford, MA 02155
Phone: 800 895-4283
Fax: –
Web: www.firstmarblehead.com

CEO: Daniel Meyers
CFO: Alan Breitman
HR: –
FYE: June 30
Type: Public

With a Harvard education costing six figures that government student loan just isn't going to cut it anymore. Enter First Marblehead. The firm provides underwriting and risk management services for lenders and schools who offer private student loans for undergraduate graduate and professional education and to a lesser extent continuing education and study abroad programs. First Marblehead also provides marketing and processing services. In response to deteriorating economic conditions and upheaval in the private student loan industry First Marblehead has adapted its business model to focus on providing outsourced fee-based services such as tuition planning portfolio management and asset servicing.

	Annual Growth	06/11	06/12	06/13	06/14	06/15
Sales ($ mil.)	(39.6%)	345.9	40.7	46.0	44.2	46.2
Net income ($ mil.)	–	(221.6)	1,102.2	(50.2)	(37.6)	(47.8)
Market value ($ mil.)	34.3%	20.4	13.5	13.6	60.6	66.4
Employees	(6.2%)	339	306	302	294	262

FIRST MARINER BANCORP.
OTC: FMAR Q

1501 South Clinton Street
Baltimore, MD 21224
Phone: 410 342-2600
Fax: 410 563-1594
Web: www.1stmarinerbank.com

CEO: –
CFO: –
HR: –
FYE: December 31
Type: Public

First Mariner Bancorp helps customers navigate banking seas (and fees). It's the holding company for First Mariner Bank which operates more than 20 branches along the Baltimore/Washington DC corridor. Serving retail and business clients the bank offers standard deposit products such as checking savings and money market accounts. Lending activities consist of commercial mortgages as well as consumer residential construction and mortgage and business loans. More than 95% of First Mariner's loans are secured by real estate. Subsidiary First Mariner Mortgage which has more than a dozen offices in Delaware North Carolina Maryland and Virginia originates mortgages for sale into the secondary market.

	Annual Growth	12/08	12/09	12/10	12/11	12/12
Assets ($ mil.)	1.3%	1,307.5	1,384.6	1,309.6	1,179.0	1,377.5
Net income ($ mil.)	–	(15.1)	(22.3)	(46.6)	(30.2)	16.1
Market value ($ mil.)	8.0%	13.6	17.9	8.3	3.0	18.5
Employees	(14.4%)	1,100	1,100	700	503	590

FIRST MERCHANTS CORP.
NMS: FRME

200 East Jackson Street
Muncie, IN 47305-2814
Phone: 765 747-1500
Fax: –
Web: –

CEO: Michael C. (Mike) Rechin
CFO: Mark K. Hardwick
HR: Leslie Holland
FYE: December 31
Type: Public

First Merchants is the holding company that owns First Merchants Bank which operates more than 100 branches in Indiana Illinois and western Ohio. Along with its Lafayette Bank & Trust and Commerce National Bank divisions the bank provides standard consumer and commercial banking services including checking and savings accounts CDs check cards and loans and mortgages. First Merchants Corporation also owns First Merchants Trust Company which provides trust and asset management services and First Merchants Insurance Group which sells personal property/casualty and employee benefit coverage. Founded in 1982 First Merchants has nearly $6 billion worth of consolidated assets.

	Annual Growth	12/10	12/11	12/12	12/13	12/14
Assets ($ mil.)	8.7%	4,170.8	4,173.1	4,304.8	5,437.3	5,824.1
Net income ($ mil.)	71.8%	6.9	25.3	45.1	44.5	60.2
Market value ($ mil.)	26.6%	333.8	319.1	559.0	855.9	857.0
Employees	4.7%	1,178	1,144	1,149	1,449	1,415

FIRST MID-ILLINOIS BANCSHARES, INC.
NMS: FMBH

1421 Charleston Avenue
Mattoon, IL 61938
Phone: 217 234-7454
Fax: 217 258-0485
Web: www.firstmid.com

CEO: Joseph R Dively
CFO: Michael L Taylor
HR: –
FYE: December 31
Type: Public

Money doesn't grow on trees so when farmers in Illinois need a little cash they turn to First Mid-Illinois Bank & Trust. The primary subsidiary of First Mid-Illinois Bancshares is a major supplier of farm credit (including real estate machinery and production loans; inventory financing; and lines of credit) in its market area. In addition to agricultural loans the bank offers commercial consumer and real estate lending. It also provides deposit products such as savings and checking accounts plus trust and investment services through a partnership with Raymond James. First Mid-Illinois Bank & Trust has about 40 branches. Other subsidiaries provide data processing services and insurance products and services.

	Annual Growth	12/10	12/11	12/12	12/13	12/14
Assets ($ mil.)	2.3%	1,468.2	1,501.0	1,578.0	1,605.5	1,607.1
Net income ($ mil.)	15.3%	8.8	11.4	14.0	14.7	15.5
Market value ($ mil.)	1.8%	121.3	129.8	160.0	154.7	130.5
Employees	(1.2%)	419	402	400	406	400

FIRST MIDWEST BANCORP, INC. (NAPERVILLE, IL)
NMS: FMBI

One Pierce Place, Suite 1500
Itasca, IL 60143-9768
Phone: 630 875-7450
Fax: –
Web: www.firstmidwest.com

CEO: Michael L. Scudder
CFO: Paul F. Clemens
HR: Joe Hoffman
FYE: December 31
Type: Public

There's a lot of cabbage in corn country. Just ask First Midwest Bancorp the holding company for First Midwest Bank. Through nearly 110 branches the bank mainly serves suburban Chicago though its market extends into central and western Illinois and neighboring portions of Iowa and Indiana. Focusing on area small to midsized businesses it offers deposit products loans trust services wealth management insurance and retirement plan services; it has $7.2 billion of client trust and investment assets under management. Commercial real estate loans account for more than half of the company's portfolio.

	Annual Growth	12/10	12/11	12/12	12/13	12/14
Assets ($ mil.)	3.8%	8,147.0	7,973.6	8,099.8	8,253.4	9,445.1
Net income ($ mil.)	–	(9.7)	36.6	(21.1)	79.3	69.3
Market value ($ mil.)	10.4%	895.0	787.1	972.7	1,362.0	1,329.4
Employees	(0.4%)	1,820	1,768	1,707	1,647	1,788

FIRST MORTGAGE CORPORATION

3230 Fallow Field Dr.
Diamond Bar CA 91765
Phone: 909-595-4394
Fax: 909-869-8546
Web: www.firstmortgage.com

CEO: –
CFO: –
HR: –
FYE: March 31
Type: Private

First Mortgage issues and purchases mortgage loans. Founded in 1975 the company originates loans for the purchase or refinancing of single-family residences. The company offers conventional jumbo and nonconforming loans as well as loans backed by the Federal Housing Administration (FHA) and the Veterans Administration (VA). First Mortgage has more than 15 offices in California. The company is also an approved lender of the state's Public Employees' Retirement System its State Teachers' Retirement System and the state Housing Finance Agency.

FIRST NATIONAL BANK ALASKA

NBB: FBAK

101 West 36th Avenue, Post Office Box 100720
Anchorage, AK 99510-0720
Phone: 907 777-4362
Fax: 907 265-3528
Web: www.fnbalaska.com

CEO: –
CFO: –
HR: –
FYE: December 31
Type: Public

First National Bank Alaska is a financial anchor in Anchorage. Founded in 1922 the bank is one of the state's oldest and largest financial institutions. With about 30 branches throughout The Last Frontier (and about 20 ATMs in rural communities) the bank offers traditional deposit products such as checking and savings accounts CDs and IRAs as well as loans and mortgages credit and debit cards and trust and investment management services. The family of longtime president Daniel Cuddy owns a majority of First National Bank Alaska; he took the helm of the bank in 1951.

	Annual Growth	12/10	12/11	12/12	12/13	12/14
Assets ($ mil.)	5.0%	2,725.6	2,870.2	3,015.6	3,102.8	3,312.2
Net income ($ mil.)	(5.2%)	40.4	34.8	40.0	32.3	32.6
Market value ($ mil.)	(3.1%)	576.9	493.6	536.9	561.2	509.0
Employees	–	–	662	–	–	–

FIRST NATIONAL COMMUNITY BANCORP, INC. (DUNMORE, PA)

NBB: FNCB

102 E. Drinker St.
Dunmore, PA 18512
Phone: 570 346-7667
Fax: –
Web: www.fncb.com

CEO: –
CFO: Edward (Ed) Lipkus
HR: Don Ryan
FYE: December 31
Type: Public

First National Community Bancorp is the holding company for First National Community Bank which has about 20 offices in Lackawanna Luzerne Wayne and Monroe counties in northeastern Pennsylvania. The bank provides standard retail services such as checking and savings accounts certificates of deposit credit cards mortgages and other loans. It also offers wealth management services. The bank is mainly a business lender with commercial mortgages accounting for more than 40% of its loan portfolio and operating loans comprising about another quarter. Chairman Louis DeNaples and his brother Dominick who is vice chairman each own around 10% of First National Community Bancorp.

	Annual Growth	12/10	12/11	12/12	12/13	12/14
Assets ($ mil.)	(4.5%)	1,167.3	1,102.6	968.3	1,003.8	970.0
Net income ($ mil.)	–	(31.7)	(0.3)	(13.7)	6.4	13.4
Market value ($ mil.)	18.8%	49.6	41.2	49.9	143.4	98.9
Employees	(8.4%)	–	336	298	285	258

FIRST NATIONAL CORP. (STRASBURG, VA)

NBB: FXNC

112 West King Street
Strasburg, VA 22657
Phone: 540 465-9121
Fax: –
Web: www.fbvirginia.com

CEO: –
CFO: M Shane Bell
HR: Lisa Rutherford
FYE: December 31
Type: Public

First National Corporation knows that being number one is always good. The financial institution is the holding company for First Bank which has about a dozen branches in northern Virginia's Shenandoah Valley. The bank provides community-oriented deposit products and services including checking and savings accounts IRAs money market accounts CDs and NOW accounts. Mortgages account for about 60% of the company's loan portfolio; it also provides business construction and consumer loans. Additionally First Bank provides trust and asset management services.

	Annual Growth	12/10	12/11	12/12	12/13	12/14
Assets ($ mil.)	(1.2%)	544.6	539.1	532.7	522.9	518.2
Net income ($ mil.)	–	(3.6)	(11.0)	2.8	9.9	7.6
Market value ($ mil.)	(9.2%)	62.3	29.4	25.7	27.7	42.4
Employees	0.2%	155	151	151	141	156

FIRST NBC BANK HOLDING CO.

NMS: FNBC

210 Baronne Street
New Orleans, LA 70112
Phone: 504 566-8000
Fax: –

CEO: Ashton J Ryan Jr
CFO: Mary Beth Verdigets
HR: –
FYE: December 31
Type: Public

First NBC Holding Company is a new kid in the Old South. The bank holding company was created in 2006 to help revive New Orleans after Hurricane Katrina. First NBC Holding Company operates through subsidiary First NBC Bank which has about 30 branches in New Orleans neighboring Jefferson Parish and the surrounding suburban parishes north of Lake Ponchartrain. Its retail operation offers standard checking saving and money market accounts to individuals and businesses. In addition the company has a loan production office in Gulfport Mississippi and offers trust and wealth management services. First NBC Holding Company went public in 2013.

	Annual Growth	12/10	12/11	12/12	12/13	12/14
Assets ($ mil.)	19.2%	–	2,216.5	2,670.9	3,286.6	3,750.6
Net income ($ mil.)	53.3%	10.1	19.4	28.9	40.9	55.6
Market value ($ mil.)	9.0%	–	–	–	600.0	653.9
Employees	5.9%	–	–	433	494	486

FIRST NIAGARA FINANCIAL GROUP, INC.

NMS: FNFG

726 Exchange Street, Suite 618
Buffalo, NY 14210
Phone: 716 819-5500
Fax: –
Web: www.firstniagara.com

CEO: –
CFO: Gregory W. Norwood
HR: Patty Swan
FYE: December 31
Type: Public

A lot of water and a few barrels have gone over Niagara Falls since First Niagara Bank was founded. Tracing its roots to 1870 the flagship subsidiary of acquisitive First Niagara Financial operates nearly 400 branches in upstate New York Connecticut Massachusetts and Pennsylvania. Boasting $39 billion in assets the bank offers financial services like deposits loans insurance investments and wealth management. Commercial real estate loans business loans and residential mortgages account for most of the bank's loan portfolio. Subsidiary First Niagara Risk Management offers insurance risk management and claims investigations. KeyCorp agreed to acquire the bank in 2015.

	Annual Growth	12/11	12/12	12/13	12/14	12/15
Assets ($ mil.)	5.0%	32,810.6	36,806.2	37,628.0	38,551.0	39,918.0
Net income ($ mil.)	6.5%	173.9	168.4	295.0	(715.0)	224.0
Market value ($ mil.)	5.9%	3,061.6	2,813.3	3,767.6	2,990.6	3,849.2
Employees	3.0%	4,827	5,927	5,807	5,572	5,428

FIRST NILES FINANCIAL INC.
NBB: FNFI

55 North Main Street
Niles, OH 44446
Phone: 330 652-2539
Fax: 330 652-0911

CEO: –
CFO: –
HR: –
FYE: December 31
Type: Public

First Niles ain't a river in Egypt. It is the holding company for Home Federal Savings and Loan Association of Niles a one-branch thrift serving its namesake town in northeastern Ohio. Founded in 1897 the association offers a variety of deposit products including checking savings money market and NOW accounts and CDs. With these funds Home Federal primarily originates residential mortgages which account for approximately 70% of its loan portfolio. The thrift also originates commercial mortgages construction and development loans and consumer loans.

	Annual Growth	12/07	12/08	12/12	12/13	12/14
Assets ($ mil.)	(0.6%)	100.9	100.9	102.2	96.8	96.4
Net income ($ mil.)	(16.5%)	0.8	0.7	0.2	(0.3)	0.2
Market value ($ mil.)	(3.5%)	13.3	13.3	7.1	6.6	10.4
Employees	–	–	–	–	1	–

FIRST NORTHERN COMMUNITY BANCORP
NBB: FNRN

195 N. First Street
Dixon, CA 95620
Phone: 707 678-3041
Fax: –
Web: www.thatsmybank.com

CEO: –
CFO: Jeremiah Z Smith
HR: Larry Miller
FYE: December 31
Type: Public

First Northern Community Bancorp is the holding company for First Northern Bank which operates about 10 branches in the northern California counties of El Dorado Placer Sacramento Solano and Yolo. Founded in 1910 the bank offers community-oriented services such as checking savings and money market accounts and certificates of deposit. It also offers electronic check depositing. Its loan products include real estate mortgages (which account for about half of the bank's portfolio) commercial and construction loans and agricultural and installment loans. Investment products and services are available to customers via a pact with Raymond James Financial.

	Annual Growth	12/10	12/11	12/12	12/13	12/14
Assets ($ mil.)	6.8%	737.2	781.2	831.5	897.7	957.9
Net income ($ mil.)	21.8%	2.7	2.7	4.6	5.4	5.9
Market value ($ mil.)	15.2%	45.9	47.0	53.1	73.5	80.8
Employees	(0.4%)	212	207	221	209	209

FIRST OF LONG ISLAND CORP.
NAS: FLIC

10 Glen Head Road
Glen Head, NY 11545
Phone: 516 671-4900
Fax: –
Web: www.fnbli.com

CEO: Michael N. Vittorio
CFO: Mark D. Curtis
HR: Sue Hempton
FYE: December 31
Type: Public

When it comes to banking The First of Long Island wants to be the first thing on Long Islanders' minds. The company owns The First National Bank of Long Island which offers a variety of lending investment and deposit services through more than 30 commercial and retail branches on New York's Long Island and in Manhattan. Loans secured by real estate including residential and commercial mortgages and home equity loans make up more than 90% of the bank's loan portfolio. To a lesser extent the bank also writes business and consumer loans. Other services include checking and savings accounts IRAs CDs and credit cards. Subsidiary The First of Long Island Agency sells mutual funds and annuities.

	Annual Growth	12/10	12/11	12/12	12/13	12/14
Assets ($ mil.)	12.3%	1,711.0	2,022.4	2,108.3	2,399.9	2,721.5
Net income ($ mil.)	5.8%	18.4	19.5	20.4	21.3	23.0
Market value ($ mil.)	(0.3%)	399.4	365.5	393.3	595.3	394.0
Employees	3.3%	249	251	255	260	284

FIRST PHYSICIANS CAPITAL GROUP INC
NBB: FPCG D

433 North Camden Drive #810
Beverly Hills, CA 90210
Phone: 310 860-2501
Fax: –
Web: www.firstphysicianscapitalgroup.com

CEO: Sean Kirrane
CFO: Adrian Reeder
HR: –
FYE: September 30
Type: Public

First Physicians Capital Group (formerly Tri-Isthmus Group or TIGroup) is an investment and financing firm with an eye toward the health care industry. The group invests in and manages health care facilities primarily rural critical access hospitals and ambulatory surgical centers. It owns or holds stakes in about a half-dozen medical facilities in Southern California and Oklahoma. In 2009 First Physicians Capital signed a letter of intent to acquire the assets of a hospital in southeastern Texas and to develop a new community hospital in the region. Oklahoma-based investor Carol Schuster owns more than 40% of the company's common stock. Director David Hirschhorn holds about 20%.

	Annual Growth	09/09	09/10	09/11	09/12	09/13
Sales ($ mil.)	(16.1%)	39.1	39.5	6.7	16.2	19.4
Net income ($ mil.)	–	(10.1)	(9.5)	(0.5)	5.6	5.8
Market value ($ mil.)	–	0.0	0.0	0.0	0.0	0.0
Employees	(19.6%)	424	4	174	174	177

FIRST POTOMAC REALTY TRUST
NYS: FPO

7600 Wisconsin Avenue, 11th Floor
Bethesda, MD 20814
Phone: 301 986-9200
Fax: –
Web: www.first-potomac.com

CEO: Robert M. Milkovich
CFO: Andrew P. Blocher
HR: –
FYE: December 31
Type: Public

First Potomac Realty Trust is a self-managed real estate investment trust (REIT) that acquires owns and manages a $1.6 billion portfolio of more than 130 single- and multi-tenant office and business park properties spanning some 8 million square feet of rentable space across the mid-Atlantic region in Washington DC Maryland and Virginia. More than 60% of the REIT's rental income comes from its office properties while the rest comes from its business park and industrial properties. As with many real estate firms located in the region the REIT's largest tenants are the US government and government contractors.

	Annual Growth	12/10	12/11	12/12	12/13	12/14
Sales ($ mil.)	3.7%	140.0	172.3	193.3	156.6	161.7
Net income ($ mil.)	–	(11.4)	(8.1)	(7.4)	11.1	16.8
Market value ($ mil.)	(7.4%)	989.3	767.5	727.0	684.0	727.0
Employees	4.2%	144	176	184	189	170

FIRST REPUBLIC BANK (SAN FRANCISCO, CA)
NYS: FRC

111 Pine Street, 2nd Floor
San Francisco, CA 94111
Phone: 415 392-1400
Fax: –
Web: www.firstrepublic.com

CEO: James H. Herbert
CFO: Michael J. (Mike) Roffler
HR: –
FYE: December 31
Type: Public

No not the original Roman Republic but rather a modern-day haven for the elite. Founded in 1985 First Republic Bank offers private banking wealth management trust and brokerage services for businesses and high-net-worth clients though about 70 branches. Its main geographic focus is on urban markets including San Francisco Los Angeles New York Boston Portland and San Diego. The bank's lending focuses on commercial and residential real estate and personal loans including vacation home mortgages and aircraft and yacht financing. Trust services are offered through the bank's First Republic Trust Company division. First Republic Bank has some $41.6 billion of assets under management.

	Annual Growth	12/10	12/11	12/12	12/13	12/14
Assets ($ mil.)	21.2%	22,377.6	27,791.8	34,387.7	42,112.8	48,353.3
Net income ($ mil.)	36.0%	142.4	352.1	402.5	462.1	487.0
Market value ($ mil.)	15.7%	4,026.4	4,232.4	4,532.5	7,238.4	7,206.6
Employees	13.7%	1,502	1,821	2,110	2,388	2,506

FIRST ROBINSON FINANCIAL CORP.　　　　NBB: FRFC

501 East Main Street　　　　CEO: Rick L Catt
Robinson, IL 62454　　　　CFO: Jamie E McReynolds
Phone: 618 544-8621　　　　HR: –
Fax: 618 544-7506　　　　FYE: March 31
Web: www.frsb.net　　　　Type: Public

If heaven holds a place for those who pay hey hey hey then here's to you First Robinson! First Robinson Financial is the holding company for First Robinson Savings Bank which provides traditional banking services to individuals and businesses through four locations in eastern Illinois' Crawford County. In 2008 the bank opened a division in Vincennes Indiana called First Vincennes Savings Bank. The banks' services include savings checking and NOW accounts; IRAs; and CDs. They use funds from deposits primarily to originate one- to four-family real estate loans (accounting for about half of the company's loan portfolio) and to a lesser extent consumer business agricultural and municipal loans.

	Annual Growth	03/11	03/12	03/13	03/14	03/15
Assets ($ mil.)	7.5%	208.8	215.5	230.5	271.9	279.3
Net income ($ mil.)	10.7%	1.4	1.9	2.4	1.6	2.1
Market value ($ mil.)	1.0%	18.9	19.2	18.7	19.2	19.7
Employees	(0.4%)	69	74	59	66	68

FIRST SAVINGS FINANCIAL GROUP INC　　　　NAS: FSFG

501 East Lewis & Clark Parkway　　　　CEO: Larry W Myers
Clarksville, IN 47129　　　　CFO: Anthony A Schoen
Phone: 812 283-0724　　　　HR: –
Fax: –　　　　FYE: September 30
Web: www.fsbbank.net　　　　Type: Public

First Savings Financial Group was formed in 2008 to be the holding company for First Savings Bank a community bank serving consumers and small businesses in southern Indiana. Through more than a dozen branches the bank offers standard deposit services like savings checking and retirement accounts as well as a variety of lending services. One- to four- family residential loans make up about 60% of First Savings Bank's loan portfolio; other loans in the bank's portfolio include commercial real estate construction consumer and commercial business. In 2012 First Savings Financial expanded its footprint by acquiring the four Indiana branches of First Financial Service Corporation.

	Annual Growth	09/11	09/12	09/13	09/14	09/15
Assets ($ mil.)	8.7%	537.1	638.9	660.5	713.1	749.9
Net income ($ mil.)	13.9%	4.0	4.3	4.7	5.4	6.8
Market value ($ mil.)	21.7%	33.8	42.6	49.1	54.5	74.2
Employees	1.5%	160	179	187	168	170

FIRST SECURITY GROUP INC　　　　NAS: FSGI

531 Broad Street　　　　CEO: –
Chattanooga, TN 37402　　　　CFO: –
Phone: 423 266-2000　　　　HR: –
Fax: –　　　　FYE: December 31
Web: www.fsgbank.com　　　　Type: Public

Pardon me boy as Glenn Miller would say but if you've got your fare and a trifle to spare you might want to turn to First Security Group. The holding company for FSGBank operates about 40 branches in eastern and middle Tennessee (including Chattanooga) and northern Georgia; in addition to the FSGBank brand the company also operates certain locations under the Dalton Whitfield Bank Jackson Bank & Trust and Primer Banco Seguro names. The bank offers standard deposit and lending services including checking and savings accounts and CDs. Real estate loans and mortgages make up about three-quarters of First Security's loan portfolio which also includes business agricultural and consumer loans.

	Annual Growth	12/09	12/10	12/11	12/12	12/13
Assets ($ mil.)	(7.8%)	1,353.8	1,168.5	1,114.9	1,063.6	977.6
Net income ($ mil.)	–	(33.0)	(44.3)	(23.1)	(37.6)	(13.4)
Market value ($ mil.)	(0.8%)	158.5	59.9	156.5	148.5	153.2
Employees	(5.1%)	356	316	306	333	289

FIRST SOLAR INC　　　　NMS: FSLR

350 West Washington Street, Suite 600　　　　CEO: James A. Hughes
Tempe, AZ 85281　　　　CFO: Mark R. Widmar
Phone: 602 414-9300　　　　HR: –
Fax: 602 414-9400　　　　FYE: December 31
Web: www.firstsolar.com　　　　Type: Public

First Solar takes energy from the sun and converts it to electricity to keep your refrigerator running and your smartphone charged. The company's photovoltaic (PV) modules do the conversion using a thin-film semiconductor process. First Solar's manufacturing process converts a piece of glass into a complete solar module in less than three hours. The technology is cheaper and produces more electricity under real-world conditions than conventional solar panels with similar power ratings. First Solar also provides project development services for planning building and operating solar power generating systems. The company makes 90% of sales in the US.

	Annual Growth	12/10	12/11	12/12	12/13	12/14
Sales ($ mil.)	7.3%	2,563.5	2,766.2	3,368.5	3,309.0	3,391.8
Net income ($ mil.)	(12.1%)	664.2	(39.5)	(96.3)	353.0	396.9
Market value ($ mil.)	(23.5%)	13,051.6	3,385.8	3,094.5	5,479.8	4,472.4
Employees	(0.2%)	6,100	7,000	5,600	4,850	6,060

FIRST SOUTH BANCORP INC (VA)　　　　NMS: FSBK

1311 Carolina Avenue　　　　CEO: Bruce W Elder
Washington, NC 27889　　　　CFO: William (Bill) Wall
Phone: 252 946-4178　　　　HR: –
Fax: –　　　　FYE: December 31
Web: www.firstsouthnc.com　　　　Type: Public

First South Bancorp (not to be confused with the South Carolina company of the same name) is the holding company for First South Bank. Founded in 1902 the bank has about 30 offices throughout the eastern half of North Carolina. Its deposit products include checking savings and money market accounts; CDs; and IRAs; funds generated are mainly used to fund a variety of loans. Commercial mortgages comprise more than half of the bank's loan portfolio which is rounded out by construction loans residential mortgages home equity loans and business and consumer loans. Retail investment services are offered through an alliance with UVEST; bank subsidiary First South Leasing provides equipment lease financing.

	Annual Growth	12/10	12/11	12/12	12/13	12/14
Assets ($ mil.)	2.7%	797.2	746.9	707.7	674.7	885.9
Net income ($ mil.)	–	(2.4)	1.6	(11.0)	6.0	3.9
Market value ($ mil.)	5.3%	62.1	30.7	45.9	74.9	76.4
Employees	2.8%	294	267	255	261	328

FIRST TECH FEDERAL CREDIT UNION

3408 Hillview Ave.　　　　CEO: Steve Lumm
Palo Alto CA 94304　　　　CFO: –
Phone: 855-855-8805　　　　HR: –
Fax: 503-672-3801　　　　FYE: December 31
Web: www.firsttechfed.com　　　　Type: Private - Not-for-Pr

First Tech Federal Credit Union provides deposit lending and investment services to some 350000 members through about 40 branches; most are in California Colorado Oregon and Washington with single branches in Georgia Idaho Massachusetts Texas and Puerto Rico. Its products include checking and savings accounts CDs IRAs and credit cards as well as home vehicle and personal loans. The credit union also offers insurance investment accounts and brokerage services. Membership in First Tech is open to employees of hundreds of sponsor companies most of them tech firms as well as those who work for the state of Oregon or live or work in Lane County Oregon.

FIRST UNITED CORPORATION (MD)

NMS: FUNC

19 South Second Street
Oakland, MD 21550-0009
Phone: 800 470-4356
Fax: 301 334-8351
Web: www.mybank4.com

CEO: Carissa L. Rodeheaver
CFO: Tonya K Sturm
HR: –
FYE: December 31
Type: Public

First United is the holding company for First United Bank & Trust and other financial services subsidiaries. Founded in 1900 the bank operates about 25 branches in the panhandles of western Maryland and eastern West Virginia as well as the Morgantown West Virginia area. The bank provides standard services such as checking and savings accounts money market accounts and CDs as well as retirement and trust services. Commercial loans make up the largest portion of the company's loan portfolio (more than 45%) followed by real estate mortgages (more than 35%) consumer installment loans and construction loans.

	Annual Growth	12/10	12/11	12/12	12/13	12/14
Assets ($ mil.)	(5.9%)	1,696.4	1,390.9	1,320.8	1,333.5	1,332.3
Net income ($ mil.)	–	(10.2)	3.6	4.7	6.4	5.6
Market value ($ mil.)	25.6%	21.4	19.7	44.7	47.8	53.2
Employees	(4.7%)	451	429	398	375	372

FIRST WEST VIRGINIA BANCORP INC

NBB: FWVB

1701 Warwood Avenue
Wheeling, WV 26003
Phone: 304 277-1100
Fax: 304 218-2458
Web: www.firstwvbancorp.com

CEO: William G Petroplus
CFO: Francie P Reppy
HR: –
FYE: December 31
Type: Public

First West Virginia and then the world! First West Virginia Bancorp is the holding company for Progressive Bank which operates about ten branches in the upper Ohio River Valley of the Mountaineer State and neighboring parts of eastern Ohio. Targeting individuals and local businesses the bank offers standard retail products like checking and savings accounts certificates of deposit and individual retirement accounts. Lending activities consist primarily of commercial and residential real estate mortgages (which together account for approximately two-thirds of the company's loan portfolio) but Progressive Bank also originates business consumer and municipal loans.

	Annual Growth	12/10	12/11	12/12	12/13	12/14
Assets ($ mil.)	4.6%	278.0	293.3	306.5	342.1	332.4
Net income ($ mil.)	(5.0%)	2.3	2.5	2.5	2.2	1.9
Market value ($ mil.)	6.1%	27.5	25.7	25.4	29.1	34.9
Employees	(2.9%)	108	98	95	91	96

FIRST WIND HOLDINGS INC.

179 Lincoln St. Ste. 500
Newton MA 02111
Phone: 617-960-2888
Fax: 617-960-2889
Web: www.firstwind.com

CEO: –
CFO: –
HR: –
FYE: December 31
Type: Private

At First Wind wind is the first and last item in its business model. The vertically integrated energy company (formerly UPC Wind) develops owns and operates wind energy plants in the Northeastern and Western US and Hawaii. Its six projects in Hawaii Maine Vermont New York and Utah generate more than 500 MW of electricity. First Wind which targets states with high energy prices renewable energy requirements and favorable wind conditions plans to have more than 2000 MW of capacity by the end 2014. The company was formed in 2002 by individuals experienced with building wind power plants in Italy. In 2010 First Wind began construction of its 102 MW Utah-based Milford Wind project.

FIRSTBANK CORP. (MI)

NMS: FBMI

311 Woodworth Avenue
Alma, MI 48801
Phone: 989 463-3131
Fax: 989 466-2042
Web: www.firstbankmi.com

CEO: –
CFO: –
HR: –
FYE: December 31
Type: Public

Firstbank Corporation is the holding company for six separately chartered subsidiary banks offering services under the Firstbank banner; it also owns Keystone Community Bank which it acquired in 2005. Through more than 50 branches in Michigan's Lower Peninsula the banks attract deposits from area residents and businesses by providing standard services such as checking and savings accounts and CDs. The company also owns subsidiaries that provide real estate appraisal services armored car services and title insurance. Firstbank bought another Michigan-based bank holding company ICNB Financial parent of Ionia County Community Bank (now Firstbank - West Michigan) in 2007.

	Annual Growth	12/08	12/09	12/10	12/11	12/12
Assets ($ mil.)	1.3%	1,425.3	1,482.4	1,458.3	1,485.3	1,498.8
Net income ($ mil.)	95.6%	0.7	2.7	3.8	5.6	10.5
Market value ($ mil.)	7.3%	64.5	67.4	46.9	41.0	85.5
Employees	(2.6%)	483	466	435	435	435

FIRSTENERGY CORP.

NYS: FE

76 South Main Street
Akron, OH 44308
Phone: 800 736-3402
Fax: –
Web: www.firstenergycorp.com

CEO: Charles E. (Chuck) Jones
CFO: James F. (Jim) Pearson
HR: –
FYE: December 31
Type: Public

FirstEnergy's first goal is to generate and deliver power but its second goal is to stay profitable in a market undergoing deregulation. Its ten utilities provide electricity to 6 million customers in the Midwest and the Mid-Atlantic. The company's domestic power plants have a total generating capacity of more than 17000 MW most generated by coal-fired plants. Subsidiary FirstEnergy Solutions trades energy commodities in deregulated US markets. FirstEnergy's other nonregulated operations include electrical and mechanical contracting and energy planning and procurement.

	Annual Growth	12/11	12/12	12/13	12/14	12/15
Sales ($ mil.)	(2.0%)	16,258.0	15,303.0	14,917.0	15,049.0	15,026.0
Net income ($ mil.)	(10.1%)	885.0	770.0	392.0	299.0	578.0
Market value ($ mil.)	(8.0%)	18,763.7	17,687.9	13,969.0	16,514.6	13,439.6
Employees	(2.2%)	17,257	16,495	15,754	15,557	15,781

FIRSTENERGY SOLUTIONS CORP.

341 White Pond Dr. Bldg B3
Akron OH 44320
Phone: 888-347-7826
Fax: 303-939-6104
Web: www.ballaerospace.com

CEO: –
CFO: –
HR: –
FYE: December 31
Type: Subsidiary

First things first. FirstEnergy Solutions (formerly Allegheny Energy Supply) serves more than one million residential commercial and industrial customers in the Northeast Midwest and Mid-Atlantic regions. It operates 35 plants with 23000 MW of generating capacity and supplies electricity to customers in Illinois Maryland Michigan New Jersey Ohio and Pennsylvania. It also manages the energy and procurement needs for more than 120000 business clients. Allegheny Energy Supply the former power production subsidiary of utility holding company Allegheny Energy which was acquired by FirstEnergy in 2011 was merged into FirstEnergy Solutions.

FIRSTFLEET INC.

202 HERITAGE PARK DR
MURFREESBORO, TN 371291556
Phone: 615-890-9229
Fax: –
Web: www.firstfleetinc.com

CEO: –
CFO: –
HR: Jim Skaare
FYE: March 31
Type: Private

FirstFleet helps its customers move their freight — not just by the truckload but by providing fleets of trucks. The company offers dedicated contract carriage in which it supplies its customers with tractors and trailers and the drivers to operate them. In addition FirstFleet provides related fleet management logistics and maintenance services. The company operates a fleet of about 1450 trucks and tractors from facilities in some 30 states in the US and it provides transportation services throughout the 48 contiguous states and in Canada and Mexico. FirstFleet began operations in 1986.

	Annual Growth	03/07	03/08	03/09	03/10	03/12
Sales ($ mil.)	0.1%	–	288.1	274.6	259.4	288.7
Net income ($ mil.)	173.0%	–	–	0.1	0.5	2.8
Market value ($ mil.)	–	–	–	–	–	–
Employees	–	–	–	–	–	2,000

FIRSTGROUP AMERICA INC

600 Vine St. Ste. 1400
Cincinnati OH 45202
Phone: 513-241-2200
Fax: 513-419-3242
Web: www.firstgroup.com/north_america/

CEO: –
CFO: –
HR: Renee Farnham
FYE: March 31
Type: Subsidiary

FirstGroup America's business is on a roll in bus form. The company through its First Student unit and sister unit FirstCanada provides school bus services as well as charter services and transit management under contract with public districts throughout the US and Canada. FirstGroup America's First Transit unit manages transit systems and contracting for agencies in North America and First Services a division provides vehicle maintenance and related support services to private fleet operators in the US. Greyhound is North America's leading intercity coach service. FirstGroup America has a fleet of about 60000 vehicles. The company is a subsidiary of FirstGroup plc a leading UK bus and rail operator.

FIRSTHEALTH OF THE CAROLINAS INC.

155 MEMORIAL DR
PINEHURST, NC 28374-8710
Phone: 910-715-1000
Fax: –
Web: www.nccancercare.org

CEO: Charles T Frock
CFO: Lynn De Jaco
HR: Margaret Fountain
FYE: September 30
Type: Private

FirstHealth of the Carolinas maintains a health care network that extends to 15 counties across the mid-Carolinas. The health network includes three hospitals — Moore Regional Richmond Memorial and Montgomery Memorial — that provide emergency surgical acute care and diagnostic services and have a combined capacity of about 580 beds. Moore Regional its largest hospital includes an inpatient rehabilitation center and a heart hospital. FirstHealth of the Carolinas also operates satellite facilities including family practice clinics fitness centers and dental practices. The system's FirstCarolinaCare provides home health and hospice services emergency care medical transportation and health insurance.

	Annual Growth	09/08	09/09	09/11	09/12	09/13
Sales ($ mil.)	5.4%	–	462.4	507.4	565.7	569.7
Net income ($ mil.)	–	–	(9.7)	12.0	69.4	51.5
Market value ($ mil.)	–	–	–	–	–	–
Employees	–	–	–	–	–	3,897

FIRSTMERIT CORP

NMS: FMER

III Cascade Plaza, 7th Floor
Akron, OH 44308
Phone: 330 996-6000
Fax: –
Web: www.firstmerit.com

CEO: Nicholas V. Browning
CFO: Terrence E. Bichsel
HR: –
FYE: December 31
Type: Public

FirstMerit Corporation is the holding company for FirstMerit Bank which provides retail and commercial banking services through more than 360 branches in five US states primarily in the Midwest. Serving local consumers and small to midsized businesses the bank provides standard services such as deposit accounts credit and debit cards and loans as well as wealth management and trust services. Subsidiaries offer investment and brokerage services financial planning commercial lease financing life and title insurance annuities and mortgage servicing. Huntington Bancshares agreed to buy FirstMerit for $3.4 billion in January 2016.

	Annual Growth	12/10	12/11	12/12	12/13	12/14
Assets ($ mil.)	15.2%	14,136.9	14,441.7	14,913.0	23,909.0	24,902.3
Net income ($ mil.)	23.3%	102.9	119.6	134.1	183.7	238.0
Market value ($ mil.)	(1.2%)	3,273.1	2,502.4	2,346.9	3,676.6	3,124.2
Employees	9.6%	3,058	3,177	2,836	4,570	4,419

FISERV, INC.

NMS: FISV

255 Fiserv Drive
Brookfield, WI 53045
Phone: 262 879-5000
Fax: 262 879-5013
Web: www.fiserv.com

CEO: Jeffery W. Yabuki
CFO: Thomas J. Hirsch
HR: Kevin P. Pennington
FYE: December 31
Type: Public

Fiserv gives financial companies the tech services they need to run. The company provides core processing systems electronic billing and payment systems ATM management and loan processing services to banks thrifts credit unions and other financial institutions. It also provides licensed software consulting and other support services to round out its offerings. Fiserv serves customers of all sizes but its bread and butter has traditionally been small to midsized banks without in-house processing units. Other clients include insurance companies merchants leasing firms and government agencies. Founded in 1984 Fiserv serves some 14500 clients in 100-plus countries.

	Annual Growth	12/10	12/11	12/12	12/13	12/14
Sales ($ mil.)	5.2%	4,133.0	4,337.0	4,482.0	4,814.0	5,066.0
Net income ($ mil.)	11.0%	496.0	472.0	611.0	648.0	754.0
Market value ($ mil.)	4.9%	14,072.0	14,115.2	18,990.9	14,189.7	17,054.1
Employees	2.5%	19,000	20,000	20,000	21,000	21,000

FISH & RICHARDSON P.C.

225 Franklin St.
Boston MA 02110-2804
Phone: 617-542-5070
Fax: 617-542-8906
Web: www.fr.com

CEO: –
CFO: Daniel Lasman
HR: –
FYE: December 31
Type: Private - Partnershi

When this fish gets hooked patents are on the line. Fish & Richardson is a national law firm specializing in patent litigation intellectual property trademarks and corporate law. The firm also has divisions devoted to new media and entertainment government affairs and venture and technology groups. It has more than 350 lawyers in 11 offices located throughout the US and in Munich Germany. Fish & Richardson traces its roots all the way back to 1878; some of its most famous clients included the Wright Brothers Thomas Edison and Alexander Graham Bell. In more recent history the firm has represented big names like Harvard University Nokia Ocean Spray Cranberries Microsoft and Target.

FISKARS BRANDS INC.

2537 Daniels St.
Madison WI 53718
Phone: 608-259-1649
Fax: 608-294-4790
Web: www2.fiskars.com

CEO: Kari Kauniskangas
CFO: Teemu Kangas-Karki
HR: –
FYE: December 31
Type: Subsidiary

Fiskars Brands is fairly frisky in its old age. The company is the North American manufacturing and marketing subsidiary of Finland's Fiskars Corporation — the second-oldest incorporated business in the world having celebrated some 360 anniversaries. Orange-handled scissors are a signature item for consumers but Fiskars Brands' namesake line also includes garden tools (such as pruners reel mowers and axes) craft tools (hand drills punches) school and office supplies (child-sized scissors rulers and trimmers). It also makes ergonomic cutting tools for the garden as part of its PowerGear line scissors and shears for sewing and quilting under the Gingher name and outdoor cutting tools by Gerber.

FIVE GUYS ENTERPRISES LLC

10440 Furnace Rd. Ste. 205
Lorton VA 22079
Phone: 703-339-9500
Fax: +86-10-5970-8818
Web: www.youku.com

CEO: –
CFO: –
HR: Sara Wenrich
FYE: December 31
Type: Private

If you're thinking that Five Guys Enterprises is a moving company or a band of enterprise application software engineers think again. The company operates the Five Guys Burgers and Fries quick-service restaurant franchise which offers a simple menu of burgers fries and hot dogs. It prides itself on using fresh ground beef and cooking its fries in peanut oil; in keeping with the peanut theme its restaurants also serve peanuts in bulk. Five Guys takes its name from Jerry Murrell who opened his first restaurant in Arlington Virginia with his wife in 1986 and the couple's five sons — Jim Matt Chad Ben and Tyler. Since its founding Five Guys has grown to more than 900 locations in 40 states and Canada.

FITCH RATINGS INC.

1 State Street Plaza
New York NY 10004
Phone: 212-908-0500
Fax: 212-480-4435
Web: www.fitchratings.com

CEO: Paul Taylor
CFO: Theodore E Niedermayer
HR: –
FYE: December 31
Type: Subsidiary

Because governments can have lousy credit too Fitch Ratings issues ratings for some 17000 banks financial institutions insurance companies corporations and governments. It's one of the top three credit rating agencies in the world (alongside Moody's and Standard & Poor's). Maintaining dual headquarters in New York and London and about 50 offices worldwide Fitch Ratings engages in the politically charged business of rating the debt of nations. It covers companies and governments in more than 90 nations. French holding company Fimalac owns 60% of Fitch Ratings; The Hearst Corporation owns the rest. Financial statistician John Knowles Fitch founded the company in 1913.

FIVE OAKS INVESTMENT CORP.

641 Lexington Ave. Ste. 1432
New York NY 10022
Phone: 212-328-9521
Fax: 877-376-5832
Web: www.hiiquote.com

CEO: David C Carroll
CFO: David Oston
HR: –
FYE: December 31
Type: Private

Five Oaks Investment Corp. is looking to grow some healthy dividends. The real estate investment trust (REIT) primarily invests in residential mortgage-backed securities (RMBS) issued or guaranteed by the government-sponsored entities Fannie Mae Freddie Mac and Ginnie Mae. The REIT also invests in non-agency RMBS and has plans to build out its portfolio with residential mortgage loans and other mortgage-related investments such as prime mortgage loans. As a REIT Five Oaks is exempt from paying corporate income tax as long as it distributes 90% of income back to shareholders. The company launched in May 2012 and filed a $115 million initial public offering later that year.

FIVE BELOW INC NMS: FIVE

1818 Market Street, Suite 2000
Philadelphia, PA 19103
Phone: 215 546-7909
Fax: –
Web: www.fivebelow.com

CEO: Joel D. Anderson
CFO: Kenneth R. Bull
HR: –
FYE: January 31
Type: Public

Five Below may be growing as quickly as its youthful clientele. Operating a fast-growing chain of specialty retail stores Five Below sells a broad range of trend-right products all priced under $5. The retailer which targets teenage and pre-teen girls and boys operates 300-plus stores in shopping centers located across the northeastern US. Core merchandise includes fun but inexpensive items that entice teens such as jewelry and accessories novelty t-shirts casual footwear sports gear decor and crafts and mobile phone accessories. Five Below was founded in 2002 by CEO Thomas Vellios and David Schlessinger. The retailer went public in 2012.

	Annual Growth	01/11	01/12*	02/13	02/14*	01/15
Sales ($ mil.)	36.3%	197.2	297.1	418.8	535.4	680.2
Net income ($ mil.)	61.7%	7.0	16.1	20.0	32.1	48.0
Market value ($ mil.)	(5.2%)	–	–	2,019.0	1,994.5	1,813.3
Employees	31.3%	–	2,960	3,750	5,500	6,700

*Fiscal year change

FIVE PRIME THERAPEUTICS, INC NMS: FPRX

Two Corporate Drive
South San Francisco, CA 94080
Phone: 415 365-5600
Fax: –
Web: www.fiveprime.com

CEO: Lewis T. (Rusty) Williams
CFO: Marc L Belsky
HR: –
FYE: December 31
Type: Public

Five Prime Therapeutics is counting down the ways to fight cancer. The clinical-stage company is developing drugs that use protein therapy to block the disease process in cancer and inflammatory diseases such as rheumatoid arthritis. Through a collaboration with GlaxoSmithKline it is developing a protein therapy that neutralizes fibroblast growth factors to inhibit cancerous tumors such as squamous non-small cell lung cancer. Another collaboration with UCB will develop therapies for fibrosis-related inflammatory diseases and central nervous system disorders. Founded by CEO Rusty Williams in 2001 the company went public in 2013 raising $62 million in its IPO which it will use toward funding clinical trials.

	Annual Growth	12/10	12/11	12/12	12/13	12/14
Sales ($ mil.)	(5.1%)	23.7	64.9	10.0	13.8	19.2
Net income ($ mil.)	–	(13.5)	19.7	(27.6)	(28.9)	(37.4)
Market value ($ mil.)	60.8%	–	–	–	364.0	585.4
Employees	7.2%	–	–	108	106	124

FIVE STAR COOPERATIVE

1949 N LINN AVE
NEW HAMPTON, IA 506599406
Phone: 641-394-3052
Fax: –
Web: www.fivestar.coop

CEO: –
CFO: –
HR: –
FYE: June 30
Type: Private

If Old MacDonald actually had a farm he'd want to be a member of the Five Star Cooperative. Operating in north-central and northeast Iowa Five Star has operations in more than 15 small to midsized towns in the Hawkeye State. The cooperative is divided into five divisions according to the products and services offered — agronomy petroleum (diesel fuel and home heating oil) feed (for beef cattle and swine) grain and hardware — it operates a True Value hardware store in New Hampton that offers all the usual hardware products and services. Established in 1916 Five Star Cooperative provides a full complement for its member/farmers.

	Annual Growth	06/10	06/11	06/12	06/13	06/14
Sales ($ mil.)	(1.1%)	–	376.2	479.1	427.1	364.1
Net income ($ mil.)	(14.6%)	–	–	9.8	8.1	7.1
Market value ($ mil.)	–	–	–	–	–	–
Employees	–	–	–	–	–	140

FIVE STAR QUALITY CARE INC

NYS: FVE

400 Centre Street
Newton, MA 02458
Phone: 617 796-8387
Fax: –

CEO: Bruce J. Mackey
CFO: Richard A. (Rick) Doyle
HR: Janet Mercier
FYE: December 31
Type: Public

Hoping to capitalize on the legacy and reputation of "Five Star" service Five Star Quality Care is out to become the long-term care industry's premier provider. Five Star Quality Care runs more than 260 senior living communities with around 30400 living units across 30 states. More than 85% of its properties are independent- and assisted-living communities that include independent living apartments assisted living suites and nursing homes. The rest of its properties are skilled nursing facilities involving Alzheimer's and memory care healthcare centers with skilled nursing and rehabilitation centers and continuing care retirement communities. In 2013 the company sold its two rehabilitation hospitals as well as more than a dozen affiliated rehabilitation clinics.

	Annual Growth	12/10	12/11	12/12	12/13	12/14
Sales ($ mil.)	1.7%	1,240.7	1,281.8	1,350.9	1,296.8	1,328.1
Net income ($ mil.)	–	23.5	64.2	24.9	(2.3)	(85.4)
Market value ($ mil.)	(12.5%)	346.4	147.0	245.5	269.0	203.3
Employees	2.7%	22,500	25,600	27,144	25,100	25,000

FLAGSTAR BANCORP, INC.

NYS: FBC

5151 Corporate Drive
Troy, MI 48098-2639
Phone: 248 312-2000
Fax: –
Web: www.flagstar.com

CEO: Alessandro P. DiNello
CFO: James K. Ciroli
HR: Cynthia M. Myers
FYE: December 31
Type: Public

Flagstar Bancorp is the holding company for Flagstar Bank which operates about 115 branches (including some in retail stores) in Michigan. Home loans are a major focus for Flagstar. The thrift originates purchases and services residential mortgages in all 50 states through a network of brokers and correspondents as well as nearly 30 of its own loan offices in more than a dozen states. More than three-quarters of the company's revenue (after interest expenses) is linked to residential lending but the reliance on this business hurt Flagstar during the housing bust. Expanding its commercial lending operations the firm in 2011 opened four full-service branches in Massachusetts Connecticut and Rhode Island.

	Annual Growth	12/10	12/11	12/12	12/13	12/14
Assets ($ mil.)	(7.8%)	13,643.5	13,637.5	14,082.0	9,407.3	9,839.9
Net income ($ mil.)	–	(374.8)	(181.8)	68.4	267.0	(69.5)
Market value ($ mil.)	76.3%	91.8	28.4	1,092.8	1,105.2	886.1
Employees	(4.4%)	3,279	3,136	3,328	3,253	2,739

FLANDERS CORPORATION

PINK SHEETS: FLDR

531 Flanders Filters Rd.
Washington NC 27889
Phone: 252-946-8081
Fax: 760-602-1450
Web: www.docscience.com

CEO: Peter Jones
CFO: Scott Brown
HR: Juliette Sykes
FYE: December 31
Type: Public

This Flanders handles flecks fleas flies fluff and other airborne flotsam. The company makes air filters under such brand names as Air Seal Eco-Air and Precisionaire. Its products include high-efficiency particulate air known as HEPA filters used in industrial cleanrooms as well as standard residential and commercial heating ventilation and air-conditioning filters. The company makes most of its sales from aftermarket replacement filters that it sells directly to wholesalers distributors and retail outlets. Flanders' customers include The Home Depot Texas Instruments and Wal-Mart. Robert Amerson owns 24% of the company which has agreed to be acquired by an affiliate of Insight Equity Holdings.

FLANIGAN'S ENTERPRISES, INC.

ASE: BDL

5059 N.E. 18th Avenue
Fort Lauderdale, FL 33334
Phone: 954 377-1961
Fax: –

CEO: James G Flanigan
CFO: Jeffrey D Kastner
HR: –
FYE: October 03
Type: Public

Seafood and sauce are the catch of the day at Flanigan's Enterprises. The company operates and manages about 20 restaurants that do business as Flanigan's Seafood Bar and Grill along with a chain of eight package liquor stores called Big Daddy's Liquors. (Four properties have combination liquor store/restaurant operations.) Six of its restaurants are franchised and owned primarily by family members of company executives. All the company's lounges and liquor stores are located in Florida. In addition Flanigan's owns the Mardi Gras adult entertainment club in Atlanta which is operated by a third party. The family of former chairman and CEO Joseph "Big Daddy" Flanigan owns more than 50% of the company.

	Annual Growth	10/11*	09/12	09/13	09/14*	10/15
Sales ($ mil.)	8.2%	72.3	77.3	82.8	89.8	99.1
Net income ($ mil.)	24.3%	1.4	1.4	2.0	2.8	3.5
Market value ($ mil.)	40.0%	13.5	14.0	19.4	37.4	51.9
Employees	9.6%	1,082	1,109	1,208	1,278	1,561

*Fiscal year change

FLATBUSH FEDERAL BANCORP INC.

OTC: FLTB

2146 Nostrand Ave.
Brooklyn NY 11210
Phone: 718-859-6800
Fax: 718-421-3210
Web: www.flatbush.com

CEO: Jesus R Adia
CFO: John S Lotardo
HR: –
FYE: December 31
Type: Public

Flatbush Federal Bancorp is the holding company for Flatbush Federal Savings and Loan which has been serving the Flatbush neighborhood of Brooklyn New York since 1883. Through three branches the bank offers checking and savings accounts CDs IRAs credit cards and a variety of loans. One- to four-family real estate mortgages account for about three-quarters of the company's loan portfolio. The bank also writes commercial mortgages construction loans consumer loans and Small Business Administration loans. Mutual holding company Flatbush Federal Bancorp MHC owns a majority of Flatbush Federal Bancorp which was acquired by Northfield Bancorp in late 2012.

FLATIRON CONSTRUCTION CORP.

10188 E. I-25 Frontage Rd.
Firestone CO 80504
Phone: 303-485-4050
Fax: 303-485-3922
Web: www.flatironcorp.com

CEO: John Diciurcio
CFO: Paul R Driscoll
HR: –
FYE: December 31
Type: Subsidiary

There's not a Bridge Too Far for Flatiron Construction (as long as it's in North America). The company which has regional offices throughout the US and Canada provides transportation construction and civil engineering services for major bridge highway and rail projects. Flatiron splits its work among divisions: Canadian Intermountain Western and heavy civil. Its E.E. Cruz subsidiary provides heavy civil construction in the Northeast. Flatiron has worked on such projects as California's Carquinez Suspension Bridge the John James Audubon Bridge in Louisiana and the San Francisco/Oakland Bay Bridge. Founded in 1947 the company is a part Germany's HOCHTIEF.

FLEETCOR TECHNOLOGIES INC — NYS: FLT

5445 Triangle Parkway
Norcross, GA 30092
Phone: 770 449-0479
Fax: –
Web: www.fleetcor.com

CEO: Ronald F. (Ron) Clarke
CFO: Eric R. Dey
HR: –
FYE: December 31
Type: Public

Helping companies manage motor fleets is at the core of FleetCor's mission. The company is a leading provider of fleet cards and payment processing services aimed at commercial and government fleets. Its cards carry the names Fuelman CFN Mannatec Keyfuels CCS and Fuelcard. The fleet cards function like typical charge cards and can be used to purchase fuel and lodging. FleetCor tracks purchases in order to help manage employee spending. The company serves more than 500000 accounts and has more than 2 million cards active in Africa Asia Europe and North America. Major customers include oil giants BP Chevron and Shell. FleetCor is expanding rapidly at home and abroad via acquisitions.

	Annual Growth	12/10	12/11	12/12	12/13	12/14
Sales ($ mil.)	28.9%	433.8	519.6	707.5	895.2	1,199.4
Net income ($ mil.)	36.0%	107.9	147.3	216.2	284.5	368.7
Market value ($ mil.)	48.1%	2,834.2	2,737.9	4,917.7	10,740.0	13,631.1
Employees	41.4%	1,197	2,130	2,650	3,500	4,780

FLEETPRIDE INC.

8708 Technology Forest Pl. Ste. 125
The Woodlands TX 77381
Phone: 866-435-3387
Fax: 832-592-9970
Web: www.fleetpride.com

CEO: Don Sturdivant
CFO: Jeff Liaw
HR: –
FYE: December 31
Type: Private

For FleetPride bigger is better. The company is one of the largest independent distributors of heavy-duty truck and trailer parts in the US; it offers hefty parts for buses tractor-trailers waste-disposal trucks and large off-road vehicles as well as repair and maintenance services. FleetPride operates through five regional distributions centers to stock 435 FleetPride parts and FleetCare service outlets in 45 states. FleetCare stores which are company owned carry 400000-plus SKUs including brands by ArvinMeritor Federal Signal Ingersoll-Rand and ZF Group on top of private-label and rebuilt (in-house) parts. FleetPride is owned by TPG Capital one of the world's largest private equity firms.

FLEMING GANNETT INC

207 SENATE AVE
CAMP HILL, PA 170112316
Phone: 717-763-7211
Fax: –
Web: www.gfnet.com

CEO: William M Stout
CFO: –
HR: –
FYE: December 31
Type: Private

Engineering firm Gannett Fleming has waded through water waste and sludge for nearly a century. Gannett Fleming operates through more than a dozen subsidiaries that offer a variety of services that range from design/build construction management ground testing and soil strengthening site remediation structural rehabilitation electrical and mechanical installation geophysical mapping and surveying and 3D visualization. Founded in 1915 Gannett Fleming serves the transportation water and wastewater facilities energy and environmental industries working on projects around the world from more than 60 offices across North America and Middle East.

	Annual Growth	12/08	12/09	12/10	12/11	12/13
Sales ($ mil.)	2.2%	–	283.3	287.7	286.5	309.5
Net income ($ mil.)	46.6%	–	–	2.3	4.5	7.2
Market value ($ mil.)	–	–	–	–	–	–
Employees	–	–	–	–	–	1,743

FLETCHER ALLEN HEALTH CARE INC.

111 COLCHESTER AVE # 75911
BURLINGTON, VT 054011416
Phone: 802-847-0000
Fax: –
Web: www.fletcherallen.org

CEO: John R. Brumsted
CFO: Roger Deshaies
HR: Laurie Gunn
FYE: September 30
Type: Private

The University Of Vermont Medical Center (formerly Fletcher Allen Health Care) provides medical care in the Green Mountain State. The company operates an academic medical center in alliance with the University of Vermont. The not-for-profit health system serves residents of Vermont and northern New York through three primary hospital campuses and more than 130 outpatient clinics patient care sites and outreach programs. Its acute care medical centers have a combined 560-bed capacity and a medical staff of some 800 health care providers representing medical specializations including emergency/trauma care pediatrics and women's health. The health care system is a subsidiary of Fletcher Allen Partners.

	Annual Growth	09/08	09/09	09/12	09/13	09/14
Sales ($ mil.)	–	–	0.0	900.8	1,043.2	1,065.6
Net income ($ mil.)	21.9%	–	–	46.5	88.1	69.1
Market value ($ mil.)	–	–	–	–	–	–
Employees	–	–	–	–	–	6,000

FLETCHER MUSIC CENTERS INC.

3966 AIRWAY CIR
CLEARWATER, FL 337624206
Phone: 727-571-1088
Fax: –
Web: www.fletchermusic.com

CEO: John K Riley
CFO: –
HR: –
FYE: December 31
Type: Private

Yearning to learn to play — and maybe own — a home organ? Fletcher Music Centers would be a company to call. The firm sells a variety of Lowrey-brand organs and teaches aspiring organists to play. The company is one of the world's largest retailers of organs for home use. It boasts about 20 stores located in Arizona and Florida. Most of its locations offer lessons and the company plans special occasions such as student concerts parties and potlucks. Fletcher Music Centers operates OrganFest a three-day event featuring discussions seminars and professional concerts. Founded by Robert Fletcher in 1975 the company is still owned by the Fletcher family.

	Annual Growth	12/06	12/07	12/08	12/09	12/10
Sales ($ mil.)	(5.9%)	–	18.4	19.6	14.4	15.3
Net income ($ mil.)	(49.7%)	–	–	0.8	(0.0)	0.2
Market value ($ mil.)	–	–	–	–	–	–
Employees	–	–	–	–	–	90

FLEXIINTERNATIONAL SOFTWARE INC.

2 Enterprise Dr.
Shelton CT 06484
Phone: 203-925-3040
Fax: 203-925-3044
Web: www.flexi.com

CEO: Stefan R Bothe
CFO: Patrick Malooly
HR: –
FYE: December 31
Type: Private

FlexiInternational Software hopes to provide some flexibility for companies that deal with hard numbers every day. Founded in 1991 the company offers accounting and financial analysis software primarily to midsized banks insurance companies and corporate accounting departments. Its software includes back-office applications for financials payables receivables general ledger asset tracking and reporting. Flexi's applications manage financial information across different tax jurisdictions currencies and languages. The company also offers outsourced back-office accounting services.

FLEXSTEEL INDUSTRIES, INC.

NMS: FLXS

385 Bell Street
Dubuque, IA 52001-0877
Phone: 563 556-7730
Fax: –
Web: www.flexsteel.com

CEO: Karel K. Czanderna
CFO: Timothy E. Hall
HR: –
FYE: June 30
Type: Public

If you're not sitting down for this Flexsteel Industries might ask why not. It's not as if the company hasn't given you plenty of options. Flexsteel incorporated in 1929 makes wood and upholstered furniture for every room in the home as well as for the recreational vehicle and commercial markets. Most of its upholstered products — including recliners rockers and sofas — incorporate a unique drop-in spring for which the company is named. Crafting its goods mostly in the US Flexsteel distributes to furniture retailers department stores catalog companies RV manufacturers hotels and health care facilities. The company's DMI Furniture unit produces furnishings for the home and office.

	Annual Growth	06/11	06/12	06/13	06/14	06/15
Sales ($ mil.)	8.3%	339.4	352.1	386.2	438.5	466.9
Net income ($ mil.)	21.0%	10.4	13.1	13.2	15.0	22.3
Market value ($ mil.)	31.0%	109.4	148.0	182.4	249.5	322.3
Employees	0.8%	1,300	1,300	1,360	1,350	1,340

FLIGHTSAFETY INTERNATIONAL INC.

Marine Air Terminal La Guardia Airport
Flushing NY 11371-1061
Phone: 718-565-4100
Fax: 718-565-4134
Web: www.flightsafety.com

CEO: –
CFO: Ken Motschwiller
HR: Barbara Shea
FYE: December 31
Type: Subsidiary

On-the-job training may work in some industries but FlightSafety International helps train pilots before they ever step into a cockpit. A Berkshire Hathaway subsidiary FlightSafety instructs pilots maintenance personnel and other aviation professionals for airlines and airplane manufacturers. It has more than 300 flight simulators and training devices at about 40 training centers mostly in the US but also in Canada Asia Europe the Pacific Rim and South Africa. FlightSafety provides training on a variety of aircraft (including helicopters) for corporate commercial private and military pilots. The company also offers training for aircraft maintenance technicians dispatchers and flight attendants.

FLINT ELECTRIC MEMBERSHIP CORPORATION

3 S MACON ST
REYNOLDS, GA 310763104
Phone: 478-847-3415
Fax: –
Web: www.flintenergies.com

CEO: Bob Ray
CFO: Anissa Derieux
HR: –
FYE: December 31
Type: Private

The Native American inhabitants of Georgia may have used flint to spark the fires that brought light to their dwellings. Central Georgians today rely on the Flint Electric Membership Corporation which does business as Flint Energies to light their homes. Flint Energies serves 250000 residential commercial and industrial customers (through 82500 meters) in 17 counties Fort Benning and the city of Warner Robins. The customer-owned cooperative operates more than 6250 miles of distribution line and about 50 substations. Flint Energies first flicked the switch in 1937.

	Annual Growth	12/06	12/07	12/08	12/12	12/13
Sales ($ mil.)	4.0%	–	148.6	180.4	175.0	188.5
Net income ($ mil.)	(95.8%)	–	–	7.3	0.0	0.0
Market value ($ mil.)	–	–	–	–	–	–
Employees	–	–	–	–	–	227

FLINT TELECOM GROUP INC

NBB: FLTT

7500 College Blvd, Suite 500
Overland Park, KS 66210
Phone: 913 815-1570
Fax: –
Web: www.flinttelecomgroup.com

CEO: –
CFO: –
HR: –
FYE: June 30
Type: Public

Flint Telecom Group fans the flame of advanced communications. Through eight subsidiaries the holding company provides a host of products and technologies to US and international communications service providers including cable companies ISPs and telcos. It distributes advanced broadband hosted digital phone voice and data and wireless products as well as prepaid cellular and calling card products. The company's Digital Phone Solutions subsidiary offers VoIP services to independent cable companies a niche that is showing strong market growth particularly in the US.

	Annual Growth	03/08*	06/09	06/10	06/11	06/12
Sales ($ mil.)	82.6%	1.0	34.3	34.1	15.8	10.7
Net income ($ mil.)	–	(2.1)	(14.6)	(28.9)	(9.3)	0.4
Market value ($ mil.)	(80.1%)	192.4	423.3	2.9	2.7	0.3
Employees	(38.5%)	14	21	7	–	2

*Fiscal year change

FLIR SYSTEMS, INC.

NMS: FLIR

27700 S.W. Parkway Avenue
Wilsonville, OR 97070
Phone: 503 498-3547
Fax: 503 498-3911
Web: www.flir.com

CEO: Andrew C. Teich
CFO: Anthony L. Trunzo
HR: Detlev Suderow
FYE: December 31
Type: Public

FLIR Systems doesn't sweat it when the heat is on. It finds it. Its thermal imaging and obscurant-proof camera systems detect heat and radiation allowing operators to see objects through fog darkness or smoke. Its sensors and imaging products enhance vision for military and commercial applications such as search and rescue drug interdiction border patrol navigation environmental monitoring and explosives threat detection. Industrial customers use FLIR's thermography products which employ cooled and uncooled infrared technologies to measure temperatures from a distance for equipment monitoring process control product development and other applications. Almost half of FLIR's sales are generated outside the US.

	Annual Growth	12/10	12/11	12/12	12/13	12/14
Sales ($ mil.)	2.5%	1,385.3	1,544.1	1,405.4	1,496.4	1,530.7
Net income ($ mil.)	(5.2%)	248.1	221.5	222.4	177.0	200.3
Market value ($ mil.)	2.1%	4,152.5	3,499.3	3,114.8	4,201.3	4,509.8
Employees	(3.9%)	3,215	3,084	2,962	2,839	2,741

FLORIDA CRYSTALS CORPORATION

1 N. Clematis St. Ste. 200
West Palm Beach FL 33401
Phone: 561-366-5100
Fax: 561-366-5158
Web: www.floridacrystals.com

CEO: Alfonso Fanjul
CFO: -
HR: -
FYE: March 31
Type: Private

Florida Crystals leans heavily on its cane. One of the top US sugar producers the company processes some seven million tons of sugar a year. It farms sugar cane and rice on some 190000 acres and operates two sugar mills a rice mill a sugar refinery a packaging and distribution center as well as a renewable power plant. Its products include certified organic granulated powdered and brown sugars and agave nectar which are sold under the C&H Florida Crystals Jack Frost and Redpath brands. With the Sugar Cane Growers Cooperative of Florida Florida Crystals owns American Sugar Refining the world's largest care sugar refiner and holder of the Domino and Tate & Lyle sugar brands. The company is owned by the Fanjul Corp.

FLORIDA GAMING CORP.

3500 N.W. 37th Avenue
Miami, FL 33142
Phone: 305 633-6400
Fax: -
Web: www.fla-gaming.com

NBB: FGMG Q
CEO: -
CFO: -
HR: -
FYE: December 31
Type: Public

Jai-alai is the high life for this company. Florida Gaming Corporation owns and operates two jai-alai frontons in Miami and Ft. Pierce Florida that feature live jai-alai competition with wagering. The gaming centers offer wagering on simulcast jai-alai from other locations as well as simulcast horse racing and dog racing. In addition its Miami location features a card room for poker. Florida Gaming also owns Tara Club Estates a real estate development project near Atlanta. Chairman W. Bennett Collett owns more than 45% of the company partially through his holding company Freedom Financial.

	Annual Growth	12/08	12/09	12/10	12/11	12/12
Sales ($ mil.)	34.2%	14.0	14.0	9.3	8.1	45.5
Net income ($ mil.)	-	-	(0.1)	(4.9)	(4.8)	(21.8)	(22.7)
Market value ($ mil.)	(53.1%)	8.3	18.2	8.7	12.1	0.4
Employees	5.2%	426	402	310	279	521

FLORIDA HOSPITAL HEARTLAND MEDICAL CENTER

4200 SUN N LAKE BLVD
SEBRING, FL 338721986
Phone: 863-314-4466
Fax: -
Web: www.fhheartland.org

CEO: Bruce Bergherm
CFO: Dima Didenko
HR: -
FYE: December 31
Type: Private

Florida Hospital Heartland Medical Center provides care to residents of central Florida. The not-for-profit 160-bed medical center is the flagship facility of the Florida Hospital Heartland division of Adventist Health System. Other facilities in the Heartland system include Florida Hospital Lake Placid (a 50-bed community hospital) Florida Hospital Wauchula (25 beds) various fitness centers medical clinics and counseling agencies. Together the facilities provide primary and acute care as well as specialty medical services including diagnostics obstetrics cardiac care and cancer treatment. The Florida Hospital Heartland Medical Center opened in 1997.

	Annual Growth	12/04	12/05	12/06	12/07	12/08
Sales ($ mil.)	-	-	0.0	124.7	121.5	126.5
Net income ($ mil.)	(98.1%)	-	-	4.0	4.6	0.0
Market value ($ mil.)	-	-	-	-	-	-
Employees	-	-	-	-	-	1,200

FLORIDA HOSPITAL WATERMAN INC

1000 WATERMAN WAY
TAVARES, FL 327785266
Phone: 352-253-3333
Fax: -

CEO: David Ottati
CFO: Fran Counk
HR: -
FYE: December 31
Type: Private

Florida Hospital Waterman is a 270-bed community hospital serving the residents of Lake County Florida just north of Orlando. The hospital provides a full range of acute care services including cardiac and cancer care emergency services obstetrics pediatrics and rehabilitation. It also offers outpatient surgery diagnostic imaging laboratory and home health services. As part of its portfolio of services Florida Hospital Waterman operates a primary care clinic. Established in 1938 and named after the philanthropic leader of the Waterman Fountain Pen Company Florida Hospital Waterman has been part of the Adventist Health System since 1992.

	Annual Growth	12/07	12/08	12/09	12/12	12/13
Sales ($ mil.)	3.2%	-	174.2	212.0	217.4	204.4
Net income ($ mil.)	(3.9%)	-	-	18.9	19.0	16.1
Market value ($ mil.)	-	-	-	-	-	-
Employees	-	-	-	-	-	1,200

FLORIDA POWER & LIGHT CO.

700 Universe Boulevard
Juno Beach, FL 33408
Phone: 561 694-4000
Fax: -
Web: www.nexteraenergy.com

CEO: Eric E. Silagy
CFO: Moray P. Dewhurst
HR: Shaun J. Francis
FYE: December 31
Type: Public

Florida Power & Light (FPL) sheds extra light onto the Sunshine State. The company a subsidiary of utility holding company NextEra Energy serves some 4.6 million electricity customers in eastern and southern Florida. FPL has more than 74160 miles of transmission and distribution lines as well as interests in fossil-fueled nuclear and solar power plants that give it a generating capacity of about 24100 MW. Its 73 natural gas units and 3 coal plants accounted for 86% of the power it generated in 2012. FPL also purchases and sells energy commodities to wholesale customers.

	Annual Growth	12/10	12/11	12/12	12/13	12/14
Sales ($ mil.)	2.2%	10,485.0	10,613.0	10,114.0	10,445.0	11,421.0
Net income ($ mil.)	12.6%	945.0	1,068.0	1,240.0	1,349.0	1,517.0
Market value ($ mil.)	-	-	-	-	-	-
Employees	(3.4%)	10,000	9,800	9,700	8,900	8,700

FLORIDA POWER CORP.

299 First Avenue North
St. Petersburg, FL 33701
Phone: 704 382-3853
Fax: 727 866-4990

NL:
CEO: Lynn J Good
CFO: Steven K Young
HR: -
FYE: December 31
Type: Public

Sometimes the sunshine state just isn't bright enough and that's when Florida Power (doing business as Progress Energy Florida) really shines. The utility transmits and distributes electricity to 1.6 million customers and oversees 10025 MW of generating capacity from interests in 14 nuclear and coal- oil- and gas-fired power plants. Additionally Florida Power purchases about 20% of the energy it provides. Florida Power operates 5100 miles of transmission lines and 52000 miles of overhead and 18700 miles of underground distribution cable. It also has 500 electric substations. A subsidiary of holding company Duke Energy the company also sells wholesale power to other utilities and marketers.

	Annual Growth	12/10	12/11	12/12	12/13	12/14
Sales ($ mil.)	(1.4%)	5,254.0	4,369.0	4,689.0	4,527.0	4,975.0
Net income ($ mil.)	4.9%	453.0	314.0	266.0	325.0	548.0
Market value ($ mil.)	-	0.0	0.0	0.0	-	-
Employees	0.0%	4,000	4,000	-	-	-

FLORIDA'S NATURAL GROWERS

20205 US Hwy. 27 North
Lake Wales FL 33853
Phone: 863-676-1411
Fax: 817-837-8004
Web: www.americanhealthchoice.com

CEO: Stephen M Caruso
CFO: William Hendry
HR: –
FYE: August 31
Type: Private - Cooperativ

Florida's Natural Growers is known for squeezing out pulpy profits. The cooperative is one of the largest citrus juice sellers in the US ranking right up there with the country's two giant brand names: PepsiCo's Tropicana and Coca-Cola's Minute Maid. Some 1000 farmer/members harvest more than 50000 acres of citrus groves for the co-op's products — frozen concentrated and not-from-concentrate juices (orange grapefruit lemonade apple and fruit blends). The co-op provides juice to customers in the foodservice retail food and vending industries. Its brands include Florida's Natural Growers Pride Bluebird and Donald Duck among others.

FLORSTAR SALES INC.

1075 TAYLOR RD
ROMEOVILLE, IL 604464265
Phone: 815-836-2800
Fax: –
Web: www.florstar.com

CEO: F Wade Cassidy
CFO: Greg Stirrett
HR: Lori Turner
FYE: September 30
Type: Private

At FlorStar Sales the floor is the star. The company distributes floor coverings to retailers throughout the Midwest from four locations in Illinois Iowa Michigan and Minnesota. Florstar's product offerings include hardwoods laminates ceramic porcelain vinyl rugs and carpets from Armstrong Interceramic Milliken Wilsonart and Weyerhaeuser. From its four locations the company serves nearly 5000 customers in six additional Midwest states. In addition it offers floor installation training and certification. FlorStar was part of Carson Pirie Scott & Co. until 1988 when management purchased the flooring division and created a separate company.

	Annual Growth	09/96	09/97	09/98	09/99	09/08
Sales ($ mil.)	1.1%	–	95.2	120.3	130.9	107.9
Net income ($ mil.)	(2.5%)	–	–	0.8	2.6	0.7
Market value ($ mil.)	–	–	–	–	–	–
Employees	–	–	–	–	–	190

FLOTEK INDUSTRIES INC
NYS: FTK

10603 W. Sam Houston Parkway N., Suite 300
Houston, TX 77064
Phone: 713 849-9911
Fax: 713 896-4511
Web: www.flotekind.com

CEO: John W. Chisholm
CFO: Robert M. Schmitz
HR: Jim Kulina
FYE: December 31
Type: Public

Flotek Industries works to keep oil and gas flowing. The company provides the chemicals and logistical services required in the cementing and stimulation of oil and gas wells. (Cementing holds well casings in place; stimulation opens up cracks in the earth to allow for the easier flow of oil.) Flotek also provides drilling equipment used in cementing and stimulation as well as Petrovalve downhole pump valves (used to pump off the liquids in gas wells in a process known as artificial lift) and Spidle Turbeco (drilling tools motors and casing accessories). The company markets its products throughout the US and is expanding into international markets.

	Annual Growth	12/11	12/12	12/13	12/14	12/15
Sales ($ mil.)	6.6%	258.8	312.8	371.1	449.2	334.4
Net income ($ mil.)	–	31.4	49.8	36.2	53.6	(13.5)
Market value ($ mil.)	3.5%	533.2	653.1	1,074.5	1,002.7	612.5
Employees	8.9%	379	405	487	561	534

FLOWERS FOODS, INC.
NYS: FLO

1919 Flowers Circle
Thomasville, GA 31757
Phone: 229 226-9110
Fax: –
Web: www.flowersfoods.com

CEO: Allen L. Shiver
CFO: R. Steve Kinsey
HR: Don Thriffiley
FYE: January 03
Type: Public

Flowers Foods is a bright bloom in baked goods. The company is one of the largest wholesale bakeries in the US. Flowers Foods bakes markets and distributes fresh breads buns rolls corn and flour tortillas and sweet bakery goodies to retail food and foodservice customers in the western southern and northeastern US. The company's brand names include Cobblestone Mill Nature's Own and Tastykake. Flowers Foods makes snack cakes pastries donuts and frozen bread products for retail vending and co-pack customers nationwide. It also rolls out hamburger buns for national fast-food chains. Flowers Foods bought several bread brands including Wonder and about 20 bakeries from Hostess Brands.

	Annual Growth	01/11*	12/11	12/12	12/13*	01/15
Sales ($ mil.)	9.9%	2,573.8	2,773.4	3,046.5	3,751.0	3,749.0
Net income ($ mil.)	6.4%	137.0	123.4	136.1	230.9	175.7
Market value ($ mil.)	(8.2%)	5,633.5	3,973.4	4,802.4	4,465.4	4,006.9
Employees	4.2%	8,800	9,400	9,800	10,500	10,380

*Fiscal year change

FLOWSERVE CORP.
NYS: FLS

5215 North O'Connor Boulevard, Suite 2300
Irving, TX 75039
Phone: 972 443-6500
Fax: 972 443-6800
Web: www.flowserve.com

CEO: Mark A. Blinn
CFO: Karyn F. Ovelmen
HR: Shelly Catalina
FYE: December 31
Type: Public

Flowserve is positively pumped about flow control equipment. Its engineered product division (EPD) makes pumps and mechanical seals while the industrial product division (IPD) makes pre-configured engineered pumps and pump systems. The flow control division (FCD) makes valves and actuators that control the flow of liquids and gases. Flowserve also provides services that include installation diagnostics repair and retrofitting. Flowserve's client base includes customers in the chemical oil and gas power generation and water management industries. The company operates in more than 50 countries.

	Annual Growth	12/10	12/11	12/12	12/13	12/14
Sales ($ mil.)	4.9%	4,032.0	4,510.2	4,751.3	4,954.6	4,877.9
Net income ($ mil.)	7.5%	388.3	428.6	448.3	485.5	518.8
Market value ($ mil.)	(15.8%)	16,017.1	13,343.5	19,722.4	10,590.7	8,038.1
Employees	4.7%	15,000	16,000	17,000	18,000	18,000

FLOYD HEALTHCARE MANAGEMENT INC.

304 TURNER MCCALL BLVD SW
ROME, GA 301655621
Phone: 706-509-5000
Fax: –
Web: www.floyd.org

CEO: Kurt Stuenkel
CFO: Cheryl Lucas
HR: –
FYE: June 30
Type: Private

If you need heart help in the Heart of Dixie Floyd Healthcare Management is there for you. Its main hospital Floyd Medical Center has more than 300 beds and serves northwestern Georgia and northeastern Alabama with more than 40 medical specialties. In addition to medical surgical and emergency care (including a Level II trauma center and Level III neonatal intensive care unit) the hospital offers rehabilitation programs hospice and home health care. It also operates a 25-bed community hospital (Polk Medical Center) and the 53-bed Floyd Behavioral Health Center. Floyd Healthcare also operates outpatient centers including primary care surgery and urgent care locations. The organization was founded in 1942.

	Annual Growth	06/05	06/06	06/08	06/10	06/11
Sales ($ mil.)	9.0%	–	215.9	237.3	288.6	332.8
Net income ($ mil.)	0.4%	–	–	11.3	8.6	11.5
Market value ($ mil.)	–	–	–	–	–	–
Employees	–	–	–	–	–	2,400

FLUIDIGM CORP (DE)
NMS: FLDM

7000 Shoreline Court, Suite 100
South San Francisco, CA 94080
Phone: 650 266-6000
Fax: –
Web: www.fluidigm.com

CEO: Gajus V. Worthington
CFO: Vikram Jog
HR: Bernhard Zimmerman
FYE: December 31
Type: Public

When Fluidigm's microfluidic systems measure volume by the nanoliter they're not using itty bitty Erlenmeyer flasks. Based on the fabrication technology that brought forth semiconductors Fluidigm develops integrated fluidic circuits (IFCs) and strings them together as systems to automate certain tasks in life sciences research. Fluidigm's BioMark HD and EP1 systems enable genetic analyses including genotyping and high-throughput gene expression. Its Access Array system enables automated sample preparation for DNA sequencing. Customers include academic institutions diagnostic laboratories and pharmaceutical biotechnology and agricultural biotechnology (AgBio) companies. Fluidigm completed an IPO in 2011.

	Annual Growth	12/10	12/11	12/12	12/13	12/14
Sales ($ mil.)	36.5%	33.6	42.9	52.3	71.2	116.5
Net income ($ mil.)	–	(16.9)	(22.5)	(19.0)	(16.5)	(52.8)
Market value ($ mil.)	36.8%	–	373.0	405.6	1,085.0	955.9
Employees	23.2%	206	239	278	325	474

FLUOR CORP.
NYS: FLR

6700 Las Colinas Boulevard
Irving, TX 75039
Phone: 469 398-7000
Fax: –
Web: www.fluor.com

CEO: David T. Seaton
CFO: Biggs C. Porter
HR: Glenn C. Gilkey
FYE: December 31
Type: Public

From the ground up Fluor is one of the world's largest international design engineering and contracting firms. Through subsidiaries it provides engineering procurement construction and maintenance (EPCM) as well as project management services for a variety of industrial sectors around the world. Its construction portfolio includes manufacturing plants refineries pharmaceutical facilities health care buildings power plants and telecommunications and transportation infrastructure. Oil and gas projects account for more than 50% of sales. The group also provides operations and maintenance services for its projects as well as administrative and support services to the US government.

	Annual Growth	12/10	12/11	12/12	12/13	12/14
Sales ($ mil.)	0.8%	20,849.3	23,381.4	27,577.1	27,351.6	21,531.6
Net income ($ mil.)	9.3%	357.5	593.7	456.3	667.7	510.9
Market value ($ mil.)	(2.2%)	9,848.5	7,468.8	8,730.7	11,933.8	9,011.7
Employees	(1.2%)	39,329	43,087	41,193	38,129	37,508

FLUSHING FINANCIAL CORP.
NMS: FFIC

220 RXR Plaza
Uniondale, NY 11556
Phone: 718 961-5400
Fax: –

CEO: John R. Buran
CFO: Susan Cullen
HR: –
FYE: December 31
Type: Public

Flush with cash? You could keep it at Flushing Financial Corp. (FFC). The holding company's Flushing Savings Bank operates more than 15 branches in the Brooklyn Manhattan and Queens boroughs of New York City and in nearby Nassau County. The bank offers services catering to the sizable populations of Asians and other ethnic groups in its market. Deposit products include CDs and checking savings passbook money market and NOW accounts. Mortgages secured by multifamily residential commercial and mixed-use real estate account for most of the company's loan portfolio.

	Annual Growth	12/10	12/11	12/12	12/13	12/14
Assets ($ mil.)	4.1%	4,324.7	4,287.9	4,451.4	4,721.5	5,077.0
Net income ($ mil.)	3.3%	38.8	35.3	34.3	37.8	44.2
Market value ($ mil.)	9.7%	411.7	371.4	451.1	608.7	596.0
Employees	2.8%	379	394	385	378	424

FLYING FOOD GROUP LLC

212 N. Sangamon St. Ste. 1-A
Chicago IL 60607
Phone: 312-243-2122
Fax: 847-808-5599
Web: www.ipa-iba.com

CEO: David Cotton
CFO: –
HR: Cherice Gilmore
FYE: December 31
Type: Private

The food is really flying in this company's kitchens. Flying Food Group is a leading US provider of in-flight catering services to the airline industry. It supplies prepared meals to some 70 airline customers (primarily long-haul carriers) from more than 15 kitchen facilities located throughout the US. (The company also has one flight kitchen location in Shanghai.) In addition to in-flight meals its Fresh Food Solutions unit supplies prepared snacks salads sandwiches desserts and meals to other food service companies and specialty food retailers. With six US fresh food operations it serves customers such as HMS Host Aramark and Starbucks. Flying Food Group was founded in 1983 by CEO Sue Ling Gin.

FMC CORP.
NYS: FMC

1735 Market Street
Philadelphia, PA 19103
Phone: 215 299-6000
Fax: 215 299-5998
Web: www.fmc.com

CEO: Pierre R. Brondeau
CFO: Paul Graves
HR: Preston W Brawn
FYE: December 31
Type: Public

E may = mc2 but FMC = chemicals and lots of them. Once in areas as diverse as oil field equipment and food machinery FMC Corporation now focuses on industrial specialty and agricultural chemicals. The company's industrial chemicals include hydrogen peroxide and phosphorus chemicals. The rest of its sales come from agricultural products (insecticides herbicides and fungicides) and specialty chemicals (food and pharmaceutical additives). FMC's equation has improved after a few years' effort to increase its efficiency profitability and credit rating.

	Annual Growth	12/10	12/11	12/12	12/13	12/14
Sales ($ mil.)	6.7%	3,116.3	3,377.9	3,748.3	3,874.8	4,037.7
Net income ($ mil.)	15.5%	172.5	365.9	416.2	293.9	307.5
Market value ($ mil.)	(8.1%)	10,650.7	11,470.7	7,801.8	10,060.2	7,603.1
Employees	5.2%	4,900	5,000	5,700	5,600	6,000

FMC TECHNOLOGIES, INC.
NYS: FTI

5875 N. Sam Houston Parkway West
Houston, TX 77086
Phone: 281 591-4000
Fax: –
Web: www.fmctechnologies.com

CEO: John T. Gremp
CFO: Maryann T. Seaman
HR: Katie Fouch
FYE: December 31
Type: Public

FMC Technologies' name is a vestige of its early years as a food machinery maker but today this company's bread and butter is oil and gas equipment. FMC Technologies offers subsea drilling and production systems for the exploration and production of oil and gas. It also offers similar equipment and services for onshore oil production. In addition the company's energy infrastructure segment makes fluid control measurement marine loading separation material handling blending systems and other equipment. Its offerings are divided into three chief segments: subsea technologies surface technologies and energy infrastructure.

	Annual Growth	12/10	12/11	12/12	12/13	12/14
Sales ($ mil.)	17.8%	4,125.6	5,099.0	6,151.4	7,126.2	7,942.6
Net income ($ mil.)	16.8%	375.5	399.8	430.0	501.4	699.9
Market value ($ mil.)	(14.8%)	20,584.9	20,092.6	9,916.2	12,087.9	10,844.6
Employees	15.3%	11,500	14,200	18,400	19,300	20,300

FNB BANCORP (CA)
NBB: FNBG

975 El Camino Real
South San Francisco, CA 94080
Phone: 650 588-6800
Fax: –
Web: www.fnbnorcal.com

CEO: Thomas C McGraw
CFO: David A Curtis
HR: –
FYE: December 31
Type: Public

To be or not to FNB? If that's your question you might want to look into FNB Bancorp. It's the holding company for First National Bank of Northern California which serves consumers and small to midsized businesses in San Mateo and San Francisco counties. Through about a dozen branches the bank offers traditional products such as checking and savings accounts IRAs CDs and credit cards. Real estate loans including commercial and residential mortgages account for approximately 70% of the company's loan portfolio. The bank also originates business consumer and construction loans. FNB Bancorp has agreed to acquire Oceanic Bank which has two offices in San Francisco and one branch in Guam.

	Annual Growth	12/10	12/11	12/12	12/13	12/14
Assets ($ mil.)	6.4%	714.6	715.6	875.3	891.9	917.2
Net income ($ mil.)	26.6%	3.7	4.3	8.8	7.4	9.4
Market value ($ mil.)	29.0%	41.8	50.5	77.5	117.0	115.9
Employees	1.8%	171	175	214	184	184

FNBH BANCORP, INC.
OTC: FNHM

101 East Grand River
Howell, MI 48843
Phone: 517 546-3150
Fax: –
Web: www.fnbh.com

CEO: Ronald L Long
CFO: Mark Huber
HR: –
FYE: December 31
Type: Public

If Thurston III and Lovey ever did get off that island they might've stashed their fortune here. FNBH Bancorp is the holding company for First National Bank of Howell which serves individuals and local businesses through nearly ten branches in Livingston County Michigan west of Detroit. The bank offers traditional deposit products such as checking and savings accounts in addition to trust investment and wealth management services. Commercial loans including loans for land development new home construction and business leasing comprise about 85% of the company's loan portfolio. Founded in 1934 the bank has traditionally served rural communities but has seen its market become increasingly suburban.

	Annual Growth	12/10	12/11	12/12	12/13	12/14
Assets ($ mil.)	1.4%	305.3	292.1	296.9	312.3	322.8
Net income ($ mil.)	–	(3.9)	(3.6)	0.3	3.0	3.1
Market value ($ mil.)	41.9%	6.9	6.4	23.6	69.4	28.0
Employees	0.3%	85	85	86	92	86

FOCUS FEATURES

65 Bleecker St. 3rd Fl.
New York NY 10012
Phone: 212-539-4000
Fax: 212-539-4099
Web: www.focusfeatures.com

CEO: –
CFO: –
HR: –
FYE: December 31
Type: Subsidiary

This moviemaker is focused on producing sharp films. Focus Features is the specialty film unit of Universal Pictures. The unit which produces films by cutting edge directors like Sophia Coppola has become a frequent industry award winner and nominee in recent years scoring several Oscar nods for The Kids Are All Right Milk Atonement and Brokeback Mountain. Other titles include In Bruges and Burn After Reading. Focus and Universal Pictures together operate as the film holdings of Universal Studios. Focus was formed in 2002 through the merger of USA Films and Good Machine. Today Universal Studios is a part of NBCUniversal (NBCU).

FOILMARK INC.

5 Malcolm Hoyt Dr.
Newburyport MA 01950
Phone: 978-225-8200
Fax: 978-462-0831
Web: www.itwfoils.com/

CEO: –
CFO: –
HR: Bonnie Eichel
FYE: December 31
Type: Subsidiary

Foilmark loves to hear its clients say "Curses! Foiled again!" The company also called ITW Foils makes hot stamping foils and holographic foils films and lamination products that put a shine on everything from cosmetic bottles to paperbacks. Hot foils are stamped on merchandise to create eye-catching designs and logos in pigmented colors metallic shades printed designs diffraction patterns and holograms. Its security product group offers high-security holograms that prevent unauthorized duplication. ITW Foils also makes equipment and supplies for the printing and pharmaceutical industries. The company was acquired by Illinois Tool Works in 2001.

FOLEY & LARDNER LLP

777 E. Wisconsin Ave.
Milwaukee WI 53202-5306
Phone: 414-271-2400
Fax: 414-297-4900
Web: www.foley.com

CEO: Rolf Reinhard Boer
CFO: Tom L Budde
HR: –
FYE: January 31
Type: Private - Partnershi

Though most famous for its cheese Wisconsin has another thing going for it: lawyers. Foley & Lardner the largest and oldest law firm in Wisconsin has nearly 1000 lawyers and has expanded far beyond its Milwaukee base with offices in more than 15 other US cities (including four in Florida and six in California). In addition Foley & Lardner has international offices in Brussels Shanghai and Tokyo. The firm founded in 1842 has one of the nation's leading health law practices and an increased focus on its intellectual property practice; other areas of expertise include business law litigation regulatory issues and tax planning.

FOLEY HOAG LLP

Seaport World Trade Center West 155 Seaport Blvd.
Boston MA 02210-2600
Phone: 617-832-1000
Fax: 617-832-7000
Web: www.foleyhoag.com

CEO: –
CFO: –
HR: Dorothy Piazza
FYE: December 31
Type: Private - Partnershi

Founded in 1943 Foley Hoag employs more than 225 attorneys. With two offices in the Boston metro area one in Washington DC and one in Paris the business law firm practices in a wide range of areas including banking and finance bankruptcy environmental and land use intellectual property litigation and mergers and acquisitions. Clients come primarily from industries such as technology energy life sciences and health care. The partners of the law firm established The Foley Hoag Foundation in 1980 to tackle racism in Boston. (The Foundation gives grants to organizations working to improve race relations within the community.)

FOLLETT HIGHER EDUCATION GROUP

1818 Swift Dr.
Oak Brook IL 60523
Phone: 630-279-2330
Fax: 630-279-2569
Web: www.fheg.follett.com

CEO: -
CFO: Robert Parrish
HR: -
FYE: March 31
Type: Subsidiary

Follett Higher Education Group (FHEG) hopes that you're not too cool for school. The company in existence for well over a century is the leading operator of campus bookstores in North America supplying students and faculty with textbooks and other course materials through 850-plus bookstores. FHEG also provides about 1800 individually managed stores with wholesale books and related services such as point of sale management systems buyback services and store design and consulting services. FHEG offers apparel software textbooks and more through its websites including efollett.com follett-books.com and cafescribe.com. The company is a subsidiary of educational materials wholesaler Follett Corp..

FONAR CORP. NAS: FONR

110 Marcus Drive
Melville, NY 11747
Phone: 631 694-2929
Fax: -
Web: www.fonar.com

CEO: Timothy Damadian
CFO: Lou Bonanni
HR: -
FYE: June 30
Type: Public

SONAR finds objects hidden under the water using sound waves; FONAR uses magnetic resonance imaging (MRI) to find disease or injury hidden inside the body. The company was the first to market a commercial MRI scanner in 1980 and it is trying to stay at the forefront of the field. Its primary products include the Upright MRI which scans patients in sitting standing or bending positions and the FONAR 360 a room-sized MRI. Both systems do away with the claustrophobia-producing enclosed tubes of traditional machines. Additionally FONAR's Health Management Corporation of America (HMCA) subsidiary provides management services to more than 20 diagnostic imaging centers primarily in Florida and New York.

	Annual Growth	06/11	06/12	06/13	06/14	06/15
Sales ($ mil.)	20.1%	33.1	39.4	49.1	68.5	69.1
Net income ($ mil.)	42.2%	3.2	5.8	8.7	10.4	12.9
Market value ($ mil.)	52.4%	12.6	26.4	42.2	78.5	68.0
Employees	21.4%	214	244	411	430	465

FONTAINE TRAILER COMPANY INC.

430 Letson Rd.
Haleyville AL 35565
Phone: 205-486-5251
Fax: 205-486-8985
Web: www.fontainetrailer.com

CEO: -
CFO: -
HR: -
FYE: December 31
Type: Subsidiary

Fontaine Trailer Company has found its fortune on the highways of North America. The company manufactures a line of flatbed extendable dropdeck and lowbed trailers for the trucking industry and for the military as well. The latest addition to the company's lineup of products is its branded Revolution lightweight all-aluminum and hybrid trailers (steel and aluminum). Fontaine Trailers are sold by independent dealers throughout the US and Canada. Brand names include Infinity Magnitude Phantom Renegade Velocity and Ventura. The company a part of The Marmon Group's Marmon Highway Technologies division and Berkshire Hathaway was founded in 1945 by John P. K. Fontaine.

FOOD FOR THE POOR INC.

6401 LYONS RD
COCONUT CREEK, FL 330733602
Phone: 954-427-2222
Fax: -
Web: www.foodforthepoor.org

CEO: -
CFO: Robin G Mahfood
HR: -
FYE: December 31
Type: Private

Food For The Poor feeds spiritual and physical hunger. The Christian charity provides health social economic and religious services for impoverished people in 17 countries in Latin America and the Caribbean. Food For The Poor believes its organization serves God by helping those most in need distributing requested goods through local churches and charities. The group works through Caritas the American-Nicaraguan Foundation and others to provide vocational training clinic and school construction educational materials feeding programs and medical supplies. Food For The Poor has distributed more than $3 billion in goods since its 1982 inception; the group uses 96% of its funds on programs.

	Annual Growth	12/09	12/10	12/11	12/12	12/13
Sales ($ mil.)	14.4%	-	-	-	900.1	1,030.2
Net income ($ mil.)	(57.1%)	-	-	-	4.0	1.7
Market value ($ mil.)	-	-	-	-	-	-
Employees	-	-	-	-	-	335

FOOD LION LLC

2110 Executive Dr.
Salisbury NC 28145-1330
Phone: 704-633-8250
Fax: 704-636-5024
Web: www.foodlion.com

CEO: Rick Anicetti
CFO: -
HR: -
FYE: December 31
Type: Subsidiary

Food Lion is a king among grocery chains in the Southeast and Mid-Atlantic regions where it operates about 1200 supermarkets under the Food Lion Bottom Dollar and Harveys banners. About half of the company's stores are in the Carolinas but it also has outlets in 10 other states including Virginia Georgia and Tennessee. Food Lion which prides itself on low prices has taken a beating from low-cost competitors most notably Wal-Mart Supercenters and a weak economy. The company's private-label Food Lion brand products accounts for about 20% of sales. Founded in 1957 as Food Town Food Lion is the largest US subsidiary of Delhaize America a subsidiary of Brussels-based grocer Delhaize.

FOOD TECHNOLOGY SERVICE INC. NAS: VIFL

502 Prairie Mine Road
Mulberry, FL 33860
Phone: 863 425-0039
Fax: -

CEO: Richard G Hunter
CFO: Richard G Hunter
HR: -
FYE: December 31
Type: Public

Food Technology Service operates a facility in Mulberry Florida that irradiates foods using gamma irradiation to kill insects and pathogens and to extend the shelf-life of foods by retarding spoilage. The company provides contract sterilization services to the food medical-device and consumer-goods industries and also irradiates packaging cosmetic ingredients and horticultural items. Given that only three customers account for 67% of its sales Food Technology has sought to diversify its customer base mainly by emphasizing its medical sterilization services which now account for 80% of its sales. Canada-based MDS Inc. a life-science services company owns about 31% of Food Technology Service.

	Annual Growth	12/08	12/09	12/10	12/11	12/12
Sales ($ mil.)	12.1%	2.5	2.5	3.0	3.7	4.0
Net income ($ mil.)	(2.6%)	1.0	0.7	1.1	0.9	0.9
Market value ($ mil.)	51.4%	2.7	4.9	10.9	14.7	14.2
Employees	3.6%	13	13	15	15	15

FOOT LOCKER, INC.
NYS: FL

112 West 34th Street
New York, NY 10120
Phone: 212 720-3700
Fax: –
Web: www.footlocker-inc.com

CEO: Richard A. (Dick) Johnson
CFO: Lauren B. Peters
HR: Paulette R. Alviti
FYE: January 31
Type: Public

Foot Locker leads the pack in the race to capture the biggest share of the global athletic footwear market. The company is a leading retailer of athletic shoes and apparel with more than 3400 specialty stores mostly in US malls but also in 20-plus countries in North America and Europe as well as in Australia and New Zealand. Its 1830-store namesake Foot Locker chain is the #1 seller of name-brand (NIKE) athletic footwear in the US. The company also operates stores under the Lady Foot Locker Kids Foot Locker Footaction Champs Sports and CCS banners. Beyond its bricks-and-mortar business Foot Locker markets sports gear through its direct-to-customer unit which consists of catalog retailer Eastbay and Footlocker.com.

	Annual Growth	01/11	01/12*	02/13	02/14*	01/15
Sales ($ mil.)	9.1%	5,049.0	5,623.0	6,182.0	6,505.0	7,151.0
Net income ($ mil.)	32.4%	169.0	278.0	397.0	429.0	520.0
Market value ($ mil.)	31.6%	2,503.2	3,724.4	4,868.3	5,437.4	7,496.8
Employees	4.1%	38,007	39,077	40,639	43,518	44,568

*Fiscal year change

FOOTBALL NORTHWEST LLC

12 Seahawks Way
Renton WA 98056-1572
Phone: 425-203-8000
Fax: 703-726-7086
Web: www.redskins.com

CEO: –
CFO: –
HR: –
FYE: January 31
Type: Private

The Northwest is a prime nesting spot for this football team. Football Northwest owns and operates the Seattle Seahawks professional football franchise. The team joined the National Football League during the league expansion of 1976 (the same year as the Tampa Bay Buccaneers) but suffered through mostly disappointing seasons until a resurgence beginning in the late 1990s. Fans were finally treated to a Super Bowl appearance following the 2005 season; however Seattle fell to the Pittsburgh Steelers in that game. Founded by department store magnate Lloyd Nordstrom the Seahawks franchise has been owned by Microsoft co-founder Paul Allen since 1997.

FORBES ENERGY SERVICES LTD.
NMS: FES

3000 South Business Highway 281
Alice, TX 78332
Phone: 361 664-0549
Fax: –
Web: www.forbesenergyservices.com

CEO: John E Crisp
CFO: L Melvin Cooper
HR: Dawn Wittner
FYE: December 31
Type: Public

This Forbes wants to be a titan in its own right. Forbes Energy Services (FES) an independent oilfield services company offers well servicing and fluid management to onshore oil and gas drilling and production companies in Texas Mississippi and Pennsylvania. Its Fluid Logistics segment handles pumping transport and storage of fracking liquid salt water and other fluids used in drilling and extraction. FES's well-servicing segment provides well maintenance repairs cleanup and plugging; the unit also offers pressure testing. Major customers have included Apache Chesapeake Energy ConocoPhillips and EOG Resources.

	Annual Growth	12/10	12/11	12/12	12/13	12/14
Sales ($ mil.)	7.7%	334.1	445.8	472.6	419.9	449.3
Net income ($ mil.)	–	(11.3)	(12.3)	1.6	(13.1)	(8.3)
Market value ($ mil.)	(3.9%)	31.0	139.2	55.3	71.4	26.4
Employees	4.2%	1,893	2,124	2,272	2,230	2,232

FORBES INC.

60 5th Ave.
New York NY 10011
Phone: 212-620-2200
Fax: 212-398-1678
Web: www.brand-matter.com

CEO: –
CFO: –
HR: –
FYE: December 31
Type: Private

Repeat after Forbes: Capitalism is good! The family-owned company publishes the biweekly business magazine Forbes long promoted as the "Capitalist Tool." It also publishes a handful of other magazines including ForbesWoman and ForbesLife a lifestyle magazine for business leaders. Forbes Web properties include sites such as Forbes.com Investopedia.com and RealClearPolitics.com. In addition the company produces business-related conferences and publishes newsletters and custom magazines. Scottish immigrant and journalist B.C. Forbes launched "Forbes" in 1917. Chairman and former CEO Malcolm "Steve" Forbes is B.C.'s grandson. Forbes is majority-owned by private equity firm Elevation Partners.

FORCE 3 INC.

2151 PRIEST BRIDGE DR # 7
CROFTON, MD 211142466
Phone: 301-261-0204
Fax: –
Web: www.force3.com

CEO: Les Trachtman
CFO: Steve Scribner
HR: Dee Taylor
FYE: December 31
Type: Private

In the world of federal IT contractors Force 3 aims to be a force to be reckoned with. The company provides integrated computer network systems for government agencies and to a smaller extent private industry customers. Force 3's services include consulting network design system integration training and support. The company also provides network security assessment services as well as business continuity and disaster recovery. The company specializes in military hospital network systems and has done work for more than 150 military medical facilities. Force 3 was founded in 1991 by Chairman Rocky Cintron.

	Annual Growth	12/05	12/06	12/07	12/08	12/09
Sales ($ mil.)	(63.5%)	–	–	1,934.5	325.5	257.2
Net income ($ mil.)	28133.2%	–	–	0.0	5.7	7.0
Market value ($ mil.)	–	–	–	–	–	–
Employees	–	–	–	–	–	300

FORCE PROTECTION INC.
NASDAQ: FRPT

1520 Old Trolley Rd.
Summerville SC 29485
Phone: 843-574-7000
Fax: 843-329-0380
Web: www.forceprotectioninc.com

CEO: Michael Moody
CFO: Charles A Mathis
HR: –
FYE: December 31
Type: Subsidiary

Force Protection's vehicles protect military forces from deadly blasts. The company makes armored land vehicles designed to protect troops from landmines roadside bombs and hostile fire. It is a key provider of the US military's Mine Resistant Ambush Protected (MRAP) vehicle program. It also provides its large Buffalo and medium-sized Cougar mine-protected vehicles to foreign customers such as the UK Ministry of Defence. The Cougar family includes such variants as the Mastiff Ridgback and Wolfhound. Its other main products include the lighter-weight Cheetah Ocelot and JAMMA (joint all-terrain modular mobility asset) vehicles. In late 2011 Force Protection was bought by General Dynamics for $360 million.

FORD MOTOR CO. (DE)   NYS: F

One American Road
Dearborn, MI 48126
Phone: 313 322-3000
Fax: –
Web: www.corporate.ford.com

CEO: Mark Fields
CFO: Robert L. (Bob) Shanks
HR: Felicia J Fields
FYE: December 31
Type: Public

Ford Motor began a manufacturing revolution with mass production assembly lines in the early 20th century but today it is one of the world's largest automakers. The carmaker's staple of brands and models includes the Ford Mustang the F-Series pickup Focus Lincoln Fiesta and Taurus. In addition finance unit Ford Motor Credit is one of the US's leading auto finance companies and accounted for 6% of Ford's sales in 2014. Ford owns a small stake in Mazda and operates about 65 plants worldwide. The company generated 65% of its sales from North America in 2014.

	Annual Growth	12/11	12/12	12/13	12/14	12/15
Sales ($ mil.)	2.4%	136,264.0	134,252.0	146,917.0	144,077.0	149,558.0
Net income ($ mil.)	(22.3%)	20,213.0	5,665.0	7,155.0	3,187.0	7,373.0
Market value ($ mil.)	–	0.0	0.0	0.0	0.0	0.0
Employees	5.0%	164,000	171,000	181,000	187,000	199,000

FORD MOTOR CREDIT COMPANY LLC   NYS: F 12A

One American Road
Dearborn, MI 48126
Phone: 313 322-3000
Fax: –
Web: www.fordcredit.com

CEO: Alan Mulally
CFO: Kenneth R. Kent
HR: –
FYE: December 31
Type: Public

Seems its trucks aren't the only things built Ford tough. The automaker's subsidiary Ford Motor Credit is proving to be pretty resilient too. One of the world's largest auto financing companies it funds autos for and through Ford and Lincoln dealerships in some 70 countries. It finances new used and leased vehicles and provides wholesale financing mortgages and capital loans for dealers. The company also offers business fleet financing and insurance. Founded in 1959 Ford Motor Credit generates more than half of its revenue from operating leases and more than 70% of revenue from the US.

	Annual Growth	12/11	12/12	12/13	12/14	12/15
Sales ($ mil.)	1.4%	3,442.0	2,778.0	3,055.0	3,252.0	3,641.0
Net income ($ mil.)	(6.7%)	1,795.0	1,214.0	1,479.0	1,705.0	1,363.0
Market value ($ mil.)	–	–	–	–	–	–
Employees	1.1%	6,500	6,300	6,200	6,500	6,800

FORDHAM UNIVERSITY

441 E FORDHAM RD
BRONX, NY 104589993
Phone: 718-817-1000
Fax: –
Web: www.bnet.fordham.edu

CEO: –
CFO: –
HR: –
FYE: June 30
Type: Private

A private Catholic university Fordham offers its 15100 students — hailing from 48 US states and some 65 other countries — degree programs through 10 graduate and undergraduate schools. Called the Jesuit University of New York Fordham has four locations including the original Rose Hill campus in the Bronx (often the scene of location shooting for movies TV shows and commercials) the Westchester campus the Lincoln Center campus in Manhattan as well as a biological field station in Armonk New York and international centers in China and the UK.

	Annual Growth	06/09	06/10	06/11	06/12	06/14
Sales ($ mil.)	(0.1%)	–	568.7	494.9	518.1	566.1
Net income ($ mil.)	(29.3%)	–	–	284.0	60.2	100.2
Market value ($ mil.)	–	–	–	–	–	–
Employees	–	–	–	–	–	4,070

FOREMOST INSURANCE COMPANY

5600 Beech Tree Ln.
Caledonia MI 49316
Phone: 616-942-3000
Fax: 616-956-3990
Web: www.foremost.com

CEO: –
CFO: F Robert Woudstra
HR: –
FYE: December 31
Type: Subsidiary

Home Sweet Motorhome? Vintage Ford Fairlane? Summer cottage at Coldwater Lake? Foremost Insurance Company will insure them all. Foremost Insurance is a holding company for six insurance companies that underwrite property/casualty insurance primarily for assets on wheels ranging from luxury motor coaches and motorcycles to golf carts and collectible autos. No wheels? Foremost has coverage for boats and snowmobiles as well. Foremost also provides specialty homeowners insurance for rental seasonal and vacant homes. Insurance products are sold direct nationwide and through company agencies as well as by independent agents. Founded in 1952 Foremost Insurance became part of the Farmers Group in 2000.

FOREST ANTHONY PRODUCTS COMPANY

309 N WASHINGTON AVE
EL DORADO, AR 717305614
Phone: 870-862-3414
Fax: –
Web: www.anthonyforest.com

CEO: Aubra H Anthony Jr
CFO: –
HR: –
FYE: April 24
Type: Private

Anthony Forest Products first logged on well before the computer age. The company which began in 1916 obtains its timber from more than 90000 acres maintained according to Sustainable Forestry Initiative policy in Arkansas Louisiana and Texas. Anthony Forest Products then processes the timber into lumber and wood chips at mills located in the same three states. The company operates engineered wood laminating plants in Arkansas and Georgia and through a joint venture with Domtar it produces I-joists under the Power Joist name at a plant in Canada. Anthony's Power Log products are used for log-home construction. Anthony Forest Products is owned by the fourth generation of the Anthony family.

	Annual Growth	04/06	04/07	04/08	04/09	04/10
Sales ($ mil.)	–	–	–	(1,423.0)	91.4	98.3
Net income ($ mil.)	31511.1%	–	–	0.0	(5.8)	49.3
Market value ($ mil.)	–	–	–	–	–	–
Employees	–	–	–	–	–	470

FOREST CITY ENTERPRISES, INC.   NYS: FCE A

Terminal Tower, Suite 1100, 50 Public Square
Cleveland, OH 44113
Phone: 216 621-6060
Fax: –
Web: www.forestcity.net

CEO: David J Larue
CFO: Robert G O'Brien
HR: –
FYE: December 31
Type: Public

Forest City Enterprises has grown from treeline to skyline. Founded in 1920 as a lumber dealer the company now focuses on commercial and residential real estate development in metropolitan areas across the US. Forest City which has more than $10.7 billion in assets owns and develops commercial properties including 44 retail centers and shopping malls 47 office buildings two hotels and Brooklyn's Barclays Center in 15 states. The company's residential group owns and manages 115 upscale and middle-market apartments condominiums and senior housing properties as well as more than 14000 military housing units in two dozen states. Forest City also owns about 290 acres of undeveloped land.

	Annual Growth	01/10	01/11	01/12	01/13*	12/13
Sales ($ mil.)	(6.7%)	1,257.2	1,177.7	1,090.0	1,134.7	1,020.1
Net income ($ mil.)	–	(30.7)	58.7	(86.5)	36.4	(5.3)
Market value ($ mil.)	19.1%	2,236.3	3,343.6	2,596.2	3,343.6	3,776.7
Employees	(2.2%)	3,019	2,917	2,870	2,914	2,822

*Fiscal year change

FOREST LABORATORIES, INC. NYS: FRX

909 Third Avenue
New York, NY 10022-4731
Phone: 212 421-7850
Fax: 212 750-9152
Web: www.frx.com

CEO: -
CFO: -
HR: Bernard McGovern
FYE: March 31
Type: Public

Forest Laboratories doesn't just blend in with the trees. The company develops and manufactures prescription drugs to address a wide field of ailments. Its central nervous system (CNS) drugs include Namenda which treats Alzheimer's disease; Savella for fibromyalgia; and antidepressants Celexa Lexapro and Viibryd. Other products include treatments for hypertension (Bystolic) thyroid disease respiratory ailments gastrointestinal conditions and pain. In addition to its branded prescription drugs Forest has limited operations in generic and over-the-counter (OTC) drug manufacturing. Forest Laboratories largely serves customers in the US.

	Annual Growth	03/09	03/10	03/11	03/12	03/13
Sales ($ mil.)	(5.5%)	3,922.8	4,192.9	4,419.7	4,586.0	3,126.1
Net income ($ mil.)	-	767.7	682.4	1,046.8	979.1	(32.1)
Market value ($ mil.)	14.7%	5,852.3	8,357.4	8,607.9	9,244.9	10,137.6
Employees	2.6%	5,225	5,200	5,600	5,700	5,800

FOREST RIVER INC.

55470 County Rd. 1
Elkhart IN 46514
Phone: 574-389-4600
Fax: 574-296-7558
Web: www.forestriverinc.com

CEO: Peter J Liegl
CFO: -
HR: -
FYE: December 31
Type: Subsidiary

Over the river and through the woods with Forest River products you go. The company makes recreational vehicles (RVs) cargo trailers buses boats and modular homes/offices. Forest River's RVs include fifth wheels motor homes tent campers and travel trailers. The company's Bus division offers wheelchair-accessible vehicles and customizes vehicles for use as personal and commercial shuttle vans. Its Housing unit constructs manufactured homes branded Sterling Homes and Hart Housing. Forest River also makes pontoon boats and truck bodies. CEO Peter Liegl who founded Forest River in 1996 sold the company in 2005 to Berkshire Hathaway the diversified holding company controlled by investor Warren Buffett.

FOREST SNAVELY PRODUCTS INC

600 DELWAR RD
PITTSBURGH, PA 152361351
Phone: 412-885-4000
Fax: -
Web: www.snavelyforest.com

CEO: Stephen V. Snavely
CFO: John A. Stockhausen
HR: -
FYE: December 31
Type: Private

Snavely Forest Products hopes it's never out of the woods. The company wholesales appearance-grade lumber and other wood products through some 10 sales and distribution centers. Snavely Forest Products' operations span Arizona California Colorado Florida Maryland North Carolina Pennsylvania and Texas. Its products include doors engineered wood millwork molding and softwood as well as composite factory fire-retardant structural and treated lumber. The company sources much of its product from sustainable-yield forests. Founded in 1902 Snavely Forest Products is still owned by the Snavely family and is run by Chris Snavely its chairman.

	Annual Growth	12/09	12/10	12/11	12/12	12/13
Sales ($ mil.)	(0.4%)	-	128.1	116.2	114.6	126.7
Net income ($ mil.)	-	-	-	(0.3)	1.3	1.5
Market value ($ mil.)	-	-	-	-	-	-
Employees	-	-	-	-	-	145

FORESTAR GROUP INC NYS: FOR

6300 Bee Cave Road, Building Two, Suite 500
Austin, TX 78746
Phone: 512 433-5200
Fax: -
Web: www.forestargroup.com

CEO: Phillip J. (Phil) Weber
CFO: Charles D. (Chuck) Jehl
HR: -
FYE: December 31
Type: Public

Forestar Group aims to make five-star investments in real estate mineral resources and wood fiber resources. Through ventures or directly the company owns over 110000 acres of mostly undeveloped real estate mostly in high-growth markets across about 10 (mostly southern) US states. While it sometimes develops land for multifamily commercial properties Forestar primarily sells lots to home builders and developers for mid-priced single-family homes and mixed-use properties. Beyond real estate Forestar also owns or leases nearly one million net acres of oil & gas mineral interests 1.5 million acres of groundwater interests and 100000 acres of timberland.

	Annual Growth	12/10	12/11	12/12	12/13	12/14
Sales ($ mil.)	31.9%	101.4	135.6	172.6	331.0	306.8
Net income ($ mil.)	34.1%	5.1	7.2	12.9	29.3	16.6
Market value ($ mil.)	(5.5%)	645.8	506.3	579.9	711.7	515.3
Employees	13.0%	92	101	130	145	150

FOREVER 21 INC.

2001 S. Alameda St.
Los Angeles CA 90058
Phone: 213-741-5100
Fax: 213-741-5161
Web: www.forever21.com

CEO: Do Won Chang
CFO: Ann Cadier Kim
HR: -
FYE: February 28
Type: Private

You don't have to be 21 or older to shop at Forever 21 stores — you just need your wallet. The fast-growing retailer operates about 500 stores under the Forever 21 XXI Forever Love 21 and Heritage 1981 banners throughout North America Asia the Middle East and the UK as well as an e-commerce site. The chain which helped to pioneer fast fashion offers cheap and chic apparel and accessories for women men teens and kids. It also carries women's footwear lingerie plus sizes and cosmetics — all at bargain basement prices. Most of Forever 21's trendy wares are private label. About 60% of its apparel is manufactured in China. CEO Don Chang and his wife founded the company as Fashion 21 in 1984.

FOREVERGREEN WORLDWIDE CORP NBB: FVRG

644 North 2000 West
Lindon, UT 84042
Phone: 801 655-5500
Fax: -
Web: www.forevergreen.org

CEO: Ronald K Williams
CFO: Jack B Eldridge Jr
HR: -
FYE: December 31
Type: Public

ForeverGreen Worldwide wants to give customers a piece of its mind naturally. The holding company through its ForeverGreen International subsidiary offers a menu of whole foods nutritional supplements personal care products and essential oils al sold via a network of independent distributors in the US and abroad. Company brands include LegaSea O3World Smart Food and TRUessence Oils. Its products which include energy bars drinks and snacks body oils creams lotions cleansers and shampoos claim to boost energy and mental acuity shed pounds ward off disease and help forestall biological aging with ingredients such as marine phytoplankton and organic chocolate.

	Annual Growth	12/10	12/11	12/12	12/13	12/14
Sales ($ mil.)	53.1%	10.6	13.7	12.5	17.8	58.3
Net income ($ mil.)	-	-	(0.4)	(1.5)	(0.9)	0.1	1.0
Market value ($ mil.)	60.5%	2.8	2.9	3.0	19.8	18.6
Employees	27.2%	37	38	35	69	97

FORGE INDUSTRIES INC.

4450 MARKET ST
YOUNGSTOWN, OH 445121512
Phone: 330-782-8301
Fax: –

CEO: –
CFO: Dan Maisonville
HR: –
FYE: December 31
Type: Private

Forge Industries connects a diverse group of businesses. Operating via several subsidiaries the family-owned private holding company distributes thousands of products from industrial gears and bearings to asphalt and concrete construction equipment. Businesses include construction/landscape equipment maker Miller Spreader and sister companies Akron Gear & Engineering and Bearing Distributors (BDI) Forge's global product and service distributor. Forge's lineup includes curb builders and hand tools as well as rebuild and repair gearboxes redesign customer equipment customize gear reducers and machining services. Customers work in the automotive package handling food processing and landscape industries.

	Annual Growth	12/04	12/05	12/06	12/07	12/08
Sales ($ mil.)	9.9%	–	404.6	0.0	605.8	537.6
Net income ($ mil.)	–	–	–	0.0	0.0	6.2
Market value ($ mil.)	–	–	–	–	–	–
Employees	–	–	–	–	–	2,000

FORMFACTOR INC

NMS: FORM

7005 Southfront Road
Livermore, CA 94551
Phone: 925 290-4000
Fax: –
Web: www.formfactor.com

CEO: Michael (Mikie) Slessor
CFO: Michael M. Ludwig
HR: –
FYE: December 27
Type: Public

Why test each microchip one by one when you can test them all in one place? That's the question FormFactor answers with its interconnect technology called MicroSpring. The companyy makes wafer probe cards that test semiconductor circuits (especially memory chips) while they are still part of semiconductor wafers — before the wafers are cut into individual chips. FormFactor touts the process for its cost-effectiveness since it allows testing of many chips at once across a range of scales and temperatures. While the most of the company's products are made in the US the majority of sales are to customers in the Asia/Pacific region.

	Annual Growth	12/10	12/11	12/12	12/13	12/14
Sales ($ mil.)	9.2%	188.6	169.3	178.5	231.5	268.5
Net income ($ mil.)	–	(188.3)	(66.0)	(35.5)	(57.7)	(19.2)
Market value ($ mil.)	(0.4%)	497.6	286.0	257.2	347.0	488.9
Employees	5.6%	729	709	1,021	961	907

FORMICA CORPORATION

10155 Reading Rd.
Cincinnati OH 45241
Phone: 513-786-3400
Fax: 513-786-3566
Web: www.formica.com

CEO: –
CFO: –
HR: –
FYE: December 31
Type: Subsidiary

Formica Corporation knows a thing or two about counter-culture. The company designs manufactures and distributes its eponymous high-pressure laminate used for countertops tables floors and other surfaces. Other products include fire-rated wall panels sinks doors and toilet partitions. It also makes metal stone and wood veneer surface materials. In addition to residential kitchens Formica's products are used in commercial buildings including restaurants stores offices and hospitals. The company manufactures its products in Spain and sells them worldwide. Founded in 1913 Formica was acquired by New Zealand materials company Fletcher Building in 2007.

FORMS & SUPPLY INC.

6410 ORR RD
CHARLOTTE, NC 28213-6332
Phone: 704-598-8971
Fax: –
Web: www.fsioffice.net

CEO: Jimmy D Godwin Sr
CFO:
HR: –
FYE: May 31
Type: Private

Whether your boss needs a new mini-fridge for the office or you are just running low on staples Forms & Supply (FSI) can help out. The company carries 8500 products including office supplies furniture and equipment. It equips offices from nearly ten locations in five states a fleet of some 75 distribution trucks and national accounts service capabilities through its partnership with American Office Products Distributor. Customers can also place orders online. FSI was founded in 1962 by Jimmy Godwin.

	Annual Growth	05/08	05/09	05/09	05/11	05/13
Sales ($ mil.)	(0.6%)	–	76.3	79.9	76.1	74.5
Net income ($ mil.)	–	–	(0.1)	0.4	0.3	0.7
Market value ($ mil.)	–	–	–	–	–	–
Employees	–	–	–	–	–	300

FORREST COUNTY GENERAL HOSPITAL (INC)

6051 U S HIGHWAY 49
HATTIESBURG, MS 39401-7200
Phone: 601-288-7000
Fax: –
Web: www.forrestgeneral.com

CEO: Evan Dillard
CFO: Andy Woodard
HR: –
FYE: September 30
Type: Private

Forrest General Hospital is the hub of health care in Hattiesburg Mississippi. Founded in 1952 the regional medical center serves southern Mississippi and its "Hub City" so named for its importance to early rail and lumber interests in the Pine Belt area. With some 400 acute care beds Forrest General offers general medical and surgical care as well as specialty care in heart disease cancer and women's health. Other facilities include the 90-bed Pine Grove behavioral health center for psychiatric and substance abuse treatment a 25-bed inpatient rehabilitation facility and an outpatient surgery center. The hospital system also operates a home health care agency and two nearby community hospitals.

	Annual Growth	09/03	09/04	09/05	09/06	09/12
Sales ($ mil.)	(5.0%)	–	586.8	291.6	346.1	388.7
Net income ($ mil.)	6.2%	–	20.2	0.0	31.3	32.6
Market value ($ mil.)	–	–	–	–	–	–
Employees	–	–	–	–	–	4,030

FORRESTER RESEARCH INC.

NMS: FORR

60 Acorn Park Drive
Cambridge, MA 02140
Phone: 617 613-6000
Fax: –
Web: www.forrester.com

CEO: George F. Colony
CFO: Michael A. Doyle
HR: –
FYE: December 31
Type: Public

Can't see the tech forest for the trees? Maybe a Forrester ranger can guide you through the technological timber. One of the leading market research firms focused on the Internet and technology Forrester Research supplies reports and briefs to more than 2400 corporate clients providing insight into market forces industry trends and consumer behavior. Forrester also offers custom research and consulting services to give its clients additional understanding of the technology market. In addition the company produces a number of events where its clients can network with each other as well as with players in the technology industry.

	Annual Growth	12/10	12/11	12/12	12/13	12/14
Sales ($ mil.)	5.6%	250.7	283.6	292.9	297.7	312.1
Net income ($ mil.)	(14.7%)	20.5	23.0	25.6	13.0	10.9
Market value ($ mil.)	2.8%	640.6	616.1	486.5	694.5	714.5
Employees	5.8%	1,078	1,208	1,236	1,288	1,351

FORSYTHE TECHNOLOGY INC.

7770 Frontage Rd.
Skokie IL 60077
Phone: 847-213-7000
Fax: 847-213-7922
Web: www.forsythe.com

CEO: –
CFO: Albert L Weiss
HR: –
FYE: December 31
Type: Private

Forsythe Technology has the foresight to provide its clients with valuable business and information technology consulting services. The company helps businesses and government agencies manage their IT infrastructure providing services ranging from strategic planning to implementation and support. It also provides leasing and other financial services. Serving clients primarily located in the US and Canada the company works with IT product vendors such as Cisco and Oracle. Customers have included Alegent and Ricoh Canada. Chairman Richard Forsythe founded the company in 1971 as Forsythe McArthur Associates. Today the employee-owned company operates from offices in North America Singapore and the UK.

FORTITECH INC.

Riverside Technology Park 2105 Technology Dr.
Schenectady NY 12308
Phone: 518-372-5155
Fax: 518-372-5599
Web: www.fortitech.com

CEO: –
CFO: –
HR: –
FYE: December 31
Type: Private

Spinach might make you strong but Fortitech can make you stronger. The company makes nutrient-rich premixes — chock full of vitamins minerals and other ingredients — that food and beverage makers add to their products to improve their nutritional content. Companies use Fortitech's custom-made nutrient premixes to fortify a variety of foods and other products including baby formula cereals sports drinks nutrition bars supplements snack foods noodles and rice. The firm works with its customers to develop blends that target various health conditions or demographic groups; it then makes and distributes the premixes which come in both liquid and powder form from facilities located around the world.

FORTEGRA FINANCIAL CORP   NYS: FRF

10151 Deerwood Park Boulevard, Building 100, Suite 330
Jacksonville, FL 32256
Phone: 866 961-9529
Fax: –
Web: www.fortegra.com

CEO: Richard S Kahlbaugh
CFO: Walter P Mascherin
HR: Della Boyea
FYE: December 31
Type: Public

Fortegra Financial foresees a fortuitous future in specialty insurance. The company's payment protection division offers credit insurance debt protection and warranties under the Life of the South brand to consumer finance firms banks retailers and other lenders; it also operates several car club membership groups. Fortegra Financial's brokerage units (including Bliss & Glennon eReinsure and South Bay Acceptance) provide wholesale placement of insurance and reinsurance policies while its business process outsourcing (BPO) subsidiaries provide billing collections underwriting and call center management services for insurers.

	Annual Growth	12/08	12/09	12/10	12/11	12/12
Sales ($ mil.)	14.9%	167.1	186.1	204.3	225.3	291.6
Net income ($ mil.)	17.2%	8.0	11.6	16.2	14.5	15.2
Market value ($ mil.)	(10.3%)	–	–	217.5	131.5	175.0
Employees	16.1%	–	447	460	545	700

FORTRESS INVESTMENT GROUP LLC   NYS: FIG

1345 Avenue of the Americas
New York, NY 10105
Phone: 212 798-6100
Fax: –

CEO: Randal A Nardone
CFO: Daniel N. Bass
HR: –
FYE: December 31
Type: Public

Fortress Investment Group protects its investors' money. The global investment firm manages private equity and hedge funds for institutional investors wealthy individuals and on its own behalf. Its private equity arm buys long-term controlling stakes in undervalued or distressed companies and credit assets; it also manages real estate investors Newcastle Investment and Eurocastle Investment. The hedge fund arm invests in liquid markets. Fortress offers traditional asset management through Logan Circle Partners. Fortress earns fees performance-based incentive revenues and investment income on its own investments. The firm has more than $67 billion in assets under management.

	Annual Growth	12/10	12/11	12/12	12/13	12/14
Assets ($ mil.)	30.0%	2,076.7	2,220.7	2,161.5	2,674.4	5,934.9
Net income ($ mil.)	–	(284.6)	(431.5)	78.3	200.4	100.0
Market value ($ mil.)	8.9%	2,478.7	1,469.8	1,909.1	3,722.5	3,487.6
Employees	33.5%	900	979	1,996	2,324	2,860

FORTINET INC   NMS: FTNT

899 Kifer Road
Sunnyvale, CA 94086
Phone: 408 235-7700
Fax: 408 235-7737
Web: www.fortinet.com

CEO: Ken Xie
CFO: Andrew Matto
HR: –
FYE: December 31
Type: Public

Fortinet secures the fortress against Internet marauders. The company makes network security appliances (sold under its FortiGate line) and software that integrate antivirus firewall content filtering intrusion prevention systems (IPS) and anti-spam functions to protect against computer viruses worms and inappropriate Web content. Its FortiGuard subscription services offer continuous updates on all new threats to provide real-time network protection. The company also offers complementary products that include its FortiManager security management and FortiAnalyzer event analysis systems.

	Annual Growth	12/10	12/11	12/12	12/13	12/14
Sales ($ mil.)	24.1%	324.7	433.6	533.6	615.3	770.4
Net income ($ mil.)	(11.5%)	41.2	62.5	66.8	44.3	25.3
Market value ($ mil.)	(1.3%)	5,384.4	3,630.1	3,498.6	3,184.1	5,103.1
Employees	20.9%	1,336	1,583	1,954	2,308	2,854

FORTUNE BRANDS HOME & SECURITY, INC.   NYS: FBHS

520 Lake Cook Road
Deerfield, IL 60015-5611
Phone: 847 484-4400
Fax: –
Web: www.fbhs.com

CEO: Christopher J. (Chris) Klein
CFO: E. Lee Wyatt
HR: Sheri Grissom
FYE: December 31
Type: Public

Fortunately for you this company has some stellar brands to offer. Formerly a unit of Fortune Brands (now Beam Suntory) Fortune Brands Home & Security (FBHS) holds the keys to the kitchen and the garden shed. With more than 35 plants the consumer products manufacturer makes and sells kitchen and bathroom cabinets faucets entry doors trim and padlocks. Its well-known brands include Moen faucets MasterBrand Cabinets SentrySafe and Therma-Tru entry doors along with Master Lock American Lock and Waterloo Industries padlocks and other security products. Most of the company's products are the top sellers in their respective markets.

	Annual Growth	12/10	12/11	12/12	12/13	12/14
Sales ($ mil.)	5.6%	3,233.5	3,328.6	3,591.1	4,157.4	4,013.6
Net income ($ mil.)	28.9%	57.2	(35.6)	118.7	229.7	158.1
Market value ($ mil.)	38.5%	–	2,693.1	4,620.9	7,227.0	7,159.0
Employees	2.8%	16,100	16,100	16,100	19,500	18,000

FORUM ENERGY TECHNOLOGIES INC
NYS: FET

920 Memorial City Way, Suite 1000
Houston, TX 77024
Phone: 281 949-2500
Fax: 281 949-2554
Web: www.f-e-t.com

CEO: C. Christopher ("Cris") Gaut
CFO: James W. Harris
HR: –
FYE: December 31
Type: Public

There is a proper forum for everything; for oil and natural gas drilling and control equipment it would be Forum Energy Technologies. The company designs makes and sells equipment for global customers including drilling contractors oilfield service businesses equipment rental companies and assemblers of drilling and well servicing equipment. Drilling products include tubular handling equipment and drilling data-management systems. Flow control products include expendable fluid end-components for mud and centrifugal pumps valves choke and kill manifolds and pressure control equipment. It also makes remote operating vehicles (ROVs) for subsea work.

	Annual Growth	12/10	12/11	12/12	12/13	12/14
Sales ($ mil.)	23.5%	747.3	1,128.1	1,414.9	1,524.8	1,739.7
Net income ($ mil.)	64.3%	23.9	93.3	151.5	129.5	174.4
Market value ($ mil.)	(8.5%)	–	–	2,221.5	2,536.5	1,860.6
Employees	7.4%	–	3,150	3,400	3,500	3,900

FORWARD AIR CORP
NMS: FWRD

430 Airport Road
Greeneville, TN 37745
Phone: 423 636-7000
Fax: –
Web: www.forwardair.com

CEO: Bruce A. Campbell
CFO: Rodney L. Bell
HR: –
FYE: December 31
Type: Public

When it's time to haul freight Forward Air never looks back. The company transports deferred airfreight by truck — cargo that requires specific-time delivery but is less time-sensitive than airfreight. Forward Air typically receives freight that has been transported by plane sends it to a sorting facility then dispatches it by truck to a terminal near its destination. The company has nearly 3777 trailers and more than 570 owned and 100 leased tractors and straight trucks in its fleet. It operates from about 85 terminals at or near airports in the US and Canada including about a dozen regional hubs. It also provides services such as warehousing and local pick-up and delivery.

	Annual Growth	12/10	12/11	12/12	12/13	12/14
Sales ($ mil.)	12.7%	483.9	536.4	584.4	652.5	781.0
Net income ($ mil.)	17.6%	32.0	47.2	52.7	54.5	61.2
Market value ($ mil.)	15.4%	858.6	969.7	1,059.2	1,328.5	1,524.0
Employees	9.5%	2,717	3,136	2,128	3,537	3,902

FORWARD INDUSTRIES, INC.
NAS: FORD

477 Rosemary Ave., Suite 219
West Palm Beach, FL 33401
Phone: 561 465-0030
Fax: –

CEO: Terence Wise
CFO: Michael Matte
HR: –
FYE: September 30
Type: Public

Forward Industries knows how to make a good case. The company designs and markets carrying cases bags clips hand straps and related items for medical monitoring kits bar code scanners and a range of consumer products (such as cell phones MP3 players cameras and firearms). Contractors in China manufacture most of the company's products which are made of leather nylon vinyl plastic PVC and other synthetic fibers. The products are primarily sold to original equipment manufacturers (OEMs). Forward's top three customers are makers of diabetic testing kits and generate more than 70% of revenues.

	Annual Growth	09/11	09/12	09/13	09/14	09/15
Sales ($ mil.)	7.1%	22.8	29.4	30.9	33.4	30.0
Net income ($ mil.)	–	(2.9)	(9.6)	(0.2)	(0.8)	(1.4)
Market value ($ mil.)	(11.9%)	19.4	10.1	16.2	11.5	11.7
Employees	(24.0%)	45	18	19	20	15

FOSSIL GROUP INC
NMS: FOSL

901 S. Central Expressway
Richardson, TX 75080
Phone: 972 234-2525
Fax: –
Web: www.fossil.com

CEO: Kosta N. Kartsotis
CFO: Dennis R. Secor
HR: Darren E. Hart
FYE: January 03
Type: Public

Fossil mines the watch business while digging a niche in accessory and apparel sales. A leading seller of mid-priced fashion watches in the US its brands include company-owned Fossil and Relic watches as well as licensed names Armani Michael Kors adidas Burberry and Marc Jacobs and private-label watches for Target and Wal-Mart. Fossil also distributes fashion accessories such as leather goods handbags sunglasses and apparel. The company peddles its products through department stores mass merchandisers and specialty shops in some 150 countries as well as online and at more than 600 company-owned stores in the US and abroad. Its products are also sold on cruise ships and in airports.

	Annual Growth	01/11*	12/11	12/12	12/13*	01/15
Sales ($ mil.)	14.7%	2,030.7	2,567.3	2,857.5	3,260.0	3,509.7
Net income ($ mil.)	10.2%	255.2	294.7	343.4	378.2	376.7
Market value ($ mil.)	11.9%	3,578.3	4,029.2	4,534.4	6,098.6	5,601.6
Employees	9.7%	10,500	13,100	14,000	14,600	15,200

*Fiscal year change

FOSTER (L.B.) CO.
NMS: FSTR

415 Holiday Drive
Pittsburgh, PA 15220
Phone: 412 928-3400
Fax: –

CEO: Robert P. Bauer
CFO: David J. Russo
HR: –
FYE: December 31
Type: Public

L. B. Foster can help keep you on track whether you're riding the rails or cruising the open road. The company manufactures new and relay rail and trackwork used in railroad and mass transit systems as well as in industrial markets such as mining. L. B. Foster also supplies pipe coatings for oil and natural gas industries and pipe products for industrial utility and agricultural water wells. It taps federal state and local infrastructure markets too selling and renting steel sheet piling and earth wall systems necessary in highway and levee construction and repair. Foster's products have been used for the construction and rehabilitation of such projects as the Brooklyn Bridge and Panama Canal.

	Annual Growth	12/10	12/11	12/12	12/13	12/14
Sales ($ mil.)	6.3%	475.1	590.9	588.5	598.0	607.2
Net income ($ mil.)	5.8%	20.5	22.9	16.2	29.3	25.7
Market value ($ mil.)	4.4%	419.3	289.8	444.9	484.4	497.5
Employees	6.5%	866	845	820	830	1,113

FOSTER DAIRY FARMS OF CALIFORNIA

1707 McHenry Ave.
Modesto CA 95350
Phone: 209-576-3400
Fax: 209-576-3437
Web: www.fosterfarmsdairy.com

CEO: Frank Otis
CFO: Mark Shaw
HR: Ron Foster
FYE: December 31
Type: Private

The folks at Foster Farms know better than to try to milk a rooster so they keep their dairy and meat businesses separate. While Foster Poultry Farms tends its chickens its sister company family-owned Foster Dairy Farms of California is one of the state's largest private dairy operations milking more than 5000 cows a week. It processes some 2.5 million gallons of milk a week at its processing plants. Along with retail fluid and cultured dairy products (milk yogurt ice cream butter cottage cheese fruit juice and more) the company produces powdered milk and bulk dairy products for foodservice operators and food manufacturers including candy makers. Its principal brands are Crystal and Humboldt.

FOUNDATION HEALTHCARE, INC
NBB: FDNH

14000 N. Portland Avenue, Suite 200
Oklahoma City, OK 73134
Phone: 405 608-1700
Fax: –
Web: www.fdnh.com

CEO: Stanton Nelson
CFO: Hubert King
HR: –
FYE: December 31
Type: Public

Graymark Healthcare wants its businesses to help remedy the ills of small-town Americans. Through its operating subsidiaries Graymark Healthcare acquires and operates independent pharmacies and sleep diagnostic centers many of which are located in smaller US markets. Its ApothecaryRx subsidiary manages pharmacies doing business in a handful of central US states and the company's Sleep Disorder Centers (SDC) subsidiary manages sleep diagnostics businesses in the South and Midwest. Formerly Graymark Productions (a film production firm) Graymark changed its name in 2008 following the acquisitions of ApothecaryRx and SDC. The company sold sell its ApothecaryRx stores to Walgreen in late 2010.

	Annual Growth	12/10	12/11	12/12	12/13	12/14
Sales ($ mil.)	46.5%	22.8	17.5	17.0	93.1	104.8
Net income ($ mil.)	–	(19.1)	(5.9)	(22.4)	(19.4)	(1.3)
Market value ($ mil.)	(19.1%)	12.6	7.9	3.9	5.9	5.4
Employees	47.3%	206	217	155	1,012	971

FOUNDATION MEDICINE INC
NMS: FMI

150 Second Street
Cambridge, MA 02141
Phone: 617 418-2200
Fax: –
Web: www.foundationmedicine.com

CEO: Michael J. (Mike) Pellini
CFO: –
HR: Sarah Larson
FYE: December 31
Type: Public

The right course of cancer treatment starts with a good foundation — at the molecular level. Foundation Medicine's personalized medicine test kit named FoundationOne analyzes a patient's genetic profile to determine a treatment strategy. The company processes the tests for solid tumor cancers and provides doctors and oncologists with a written report that matches detected molecular alterations with relevant treatment options and clinical trials. Foundation Medicine which has received investment funding from Bill Gates went public in 2013. In 2015 Roche acquired a controlling interest in the company for just over $1 billion.

	Annual Growth	12/10	12/11	12/12	12/13	12/14
Sales ($ mil.)	–	0.0	2.1	10.6	29.0	61.1
Net income ($ mil.)	–	0.0	(17.0)	(22.4)	(42.9)	(52.2)
Market value ($ mil.)	–	0.0	–	–	672.3	627.1
Employees	43.6%	–	–	142	186	293

FOUR OAKS FINCORP, INC.
NBB: FOFN

6114 U.S. 301 South
Four Oaks, NC 27524
Phone: 919 963-2177
Fax: –
Web: www.fouroaksbank.com

CEO: –
CFO: Deanna W Hart
HR: Wanda J Blow
FYE: December 31
Type: Public

There's no need to knock on wood when trusting your money to Four Oaks Fincorp. It's the holding company for Four Oaks Bank & Trust which (with the 2008 acquisition of LongLeaf Community Bank) operates about 20 branches in central and eastern North Carolina. The bank offers standard retail products and services including checking and savings accounts CDs IRAs and money market accounts. It originates mostly real estate loans which account for nearly 90% of loans. It also writes business consumer and farm loans. Four Oaks Bank also offers insurance and investment services. The company in 2009 acquired Nuestro Banco a single-branch bank serving Hispanic customers in Raleigh.

	Annual Growth	12/10	12/11	12/12	12/13	12/14
Assets ($ mil.)	(3.5%)	947.6	916.6	865.5	821.5	820.8
Net income ($ mil.)	–	(28.3)	(9.1)	(7.0)	(0.4)	(4.2)
Market value ($ mil.)	(15.5%)	95.5	30.4	28.8	51.3	48.7
Employees	(2.8%)	205	194	192	177	183

FOX & HOUND RESTAURANT GROUP

1551 N. Waterfront Pkwy. Ste. 310
Wichita KS 67206
Phone: 316-634-0505
Fax: 316-634-6060
Web: www.foxandhound.com

CEO: –
CFO: –
HR: –
FYE: December 31
Type: Private

Sports fans can really dig in at this bar and grill chain. Fox & Hound Restaurant Group operates about 85 sports bars and pubs in 25 states under the banners Fox & Hound Pub & Grille and Bailey's Pub & Grille. Popular for watching sports on TV while enjoying a menu heavy on burgers the locations also offer a wide selection of beer billiards darts and other entertainment. Most of the pubs are found in Texas North Carolina and Tennessee. Restaurateur Jamie Coulter started the Fox & Hound chain in 1997. The company is owned by F & H Acquisition Corp. an investment group led by Dallas-based Newcastle Partners that also owns the Champps family entertainment chain.

FOX BROADCASTING COMPANY

10201 W. Pico Blvd.
Los Angeles CA 90035
Phone: 310-369-1000
Fax: 310-969-0468
Web: www.foxmovies.com

CEO: David F Devoe Jr
CFO: –
HR: –
FYE: June 30
Type: Subsidiary

TV viewers worshiping the Idol have helped make FOX a ratings superstar. FOX Broadcasting operates the #2 broadcast television network in the US (behind CBS). It has more than 200 affiliate stations including 17 company-owned TV outlets that reach 99% of all US television households. The network offers such hit primetime shows as New Girl Raising Hope Bones Glee Fringe So You Think You Can Dance and House as well as its Sunday night lineup of comedy animation programs The Simpsons Family Guy The Cleveland Show and American Dad. Launched with only six stations in 1986 FOX is a major subsidiary of Rupert Murdoch's News Corporation.

FOX CHASE BANCORP, INC.
NMS: FXCB

4390 Davisville Road
Hatboro, PA 19040
Phone: 215 283-2900
Fax: –
Web: www.foxchasebank.com

CEO: Thomas M. Petro
CFO: Roger Deacon
HR: –
FYE: December 31
Type: Public

Fox Chase Bancorp is the holding company for Fox Chase Bank which has served individuals and businesses in the Philadelphia area since 1867. The bank operates about a dozen offices in southeastern Pennsylvania and southern New Jersey; it offers standard products and services including checking and savings accounts CDs and money market accounts. Multifamily and commercial real estate loans make up the largest part of Fox Chase Bank's loan portfolio; commercial and industrial loans are the second-largest loan type. Other offerings include consumer residential and construction loans. Local-peer Univest Corporation of Pennsylvania agreed to buy Fox Chase for $244 million in late 2015.

	Annual Growth	12/10	12/11	12/12	12/13	12/14
Assets ($ mil.)	(0.0%)	1,095.5	1,015.9	1,088.3	1,116.6	1,094.6
Net income ($ mil.)	31.5%	2.7	4.8	5.1	5.5	8.2
Market value ($ mil.)	8.9%	139.9	149.1	196.5	203.9	196.8
Employees	0.2%	148	146	152	153	149

FOX FACTORY HOLDING CORP

NMS: FOXF

915 Disc Drive
Scotts Valley, CA 95066
Phone: 831-274-6500
Fax: –
Web: www.ridefox.com

CEO: Larry L. Enterline
CFO: Zvi Glasman
HR: –
FYE: December 31
Type: Public

Talk about shock value. Fox Factory makes suspension products — i.e. shocks — for high-performance mountain bikes and other powered vehicles that give riders a smooth ride over rough terrain. Some two-thirds of sales are for shocks for bicycles but the other third of revenue comes from shocks for ATVs motorcycles snowmobiles and off-road vehicles and trucks. Fox Factory sells its shocks to original equipment manufacturers (OEMs) such as Specialized and Trek (bikes) and Ford and Polaris (powered vehicles). It also sells branded apparel such as T-shirts sweatshirts and hats. Majority-owned by Compass Diversified Holdings Fox Factory went public in 2013.

	Annual Growth	12/10	12/11	12/12	12/13	12/14
Sales ($ mil.)	15.7%	171.0	197.7	235.9	272.7	306.7
Net income ($ mil.)	26.6%	10.8	13.5	14.2	24.1	27.7
Market value ($ mil.)	(7.9%)	–	–	–	653.3	601.8
Employees	35.5%	–	–	545	670	1,000

FOX HEAD INC.

18400 SUTTER BLVD
MORGAN HILL, CA 950372819
Phone: 408-776-8633
Fax: –
Web: www.foxhead.com

CEO: Paul E Harrington
CFO: –
HR: –
FYE: December 31
Type: Private

Got a need for speed and big jumps? Fox Racing makes and distributes motocross and other extreme sport apparel accessories and protective gear such as racewear pants jerseys gloves boots and helmets emblazoned with its fox head graphic logo. The company also offers bicycle motocross (BMX) and mountain bike apparel T-shirts hats jeans hoodies and pullovers and jackets. Line extensions include eyewear footwear and surf and wakeboard wear. Fox Racing sells its apparel through retail sporting goods and cycle and surf shops nationwide. International offices are located in Canada and the UK. Founded in 1974 by Geoff Fox the company is family-owned and run by its second generation.

	Annual Growth	12/05	12/06	12/07	12/08	12/09
Sales ($ mil.)	–	–	–	(444.5)	244.0	216.3
Net income ($ mil.)	3430.2%	–	–	0.0	24.4	20.4
Market value ($ mil.)	–	–	–	–	–	–
Employees	–	–	–	–	–	462

FOX NEWS NETWORK LLC

1211 Avenue of the Americas
New York NY 10036
Phone: 212-301-3000
Fax: 212-301-8588
Web: www.foxnews.com

CEO: Roger Ailes
CFO: Jack Abernethy
HR: –
FYE: June 30
Type: Subsidiary

This news channel reports and people have decided to watch … a lot of people. FOX News Network operates the FOX News Channel the leading 24-hour cable news station reaching more than 90 million US homes. It provides round-the-clock news coverage and commentary including programs such as The O'Reilly Factor featuring commentator Bill O'Reilly and Hannity with Sean Hannity. FOX News also produces content distributed to TV affiliates of the FOX network and publishes news online; its FOX News Radio Network syndicates news to radio stations around the country. Launched by Rupert Murdoch's News Corp. in 1996 the channel's less than tacit support of conservative politics has stirred both passion and criticism.

FOX SEARCHLIGHT PICTURES INC.

10201 W. Pico Blvd. Bldg. 769
Los Angeles CA 90035
Phone: 310-369-4402
Fax: 310-369-1491
Web: www.foxsearchlight.com

CEO: –
CFO: –
HR: –
FYE: June 30
Type: Subsidiary

The light shines brightly on this specialty film division of Fox Filmed Entertainment. Rather than produce big-budget blockbusters Fox Searchlight Pictures produces smaller specialized films in genres such as drama comedy horror and science fiction. Notable titles in the Fox Searchlight canon include successful indie films such as Little Miss Sunshine Napoleon Dynamite and "Boys Don't Cry". More recent movies include Cyrus and Crazy Heart. Fox Searchlight was founded in 1994 by Fox Filmed Entertainment Co-Chairman Tom Rothman as the independent arm of Twentieth Century Fox. It has its own marketing and distribution operations. International distribution is handled by Twentieth Century Fox.

FOXWORTH GALBRAITH LUMBER COMPANY

4965 PRESTON PARK BLVD # 400
PLANO, TX 750935180
Phone: 972-665-2400
Fax: –
Web: www.foxgal.com

CEO: Walter L Foxworth
CFO: Rich Perkins
HR: –
FYE: December 31
Type: Private

Foxworth-Galbraith Lumber Company is helping to build out the Southwest. The company sells hardware lumber paint plumbing equipment tools and other building supplies through more than 20 locations across Texas New Mexico Arizona and Colorado (versus about 70 stores in 2006). Foxworth-Galbraith's main customers are residential and commercial builders; other clients include do-it-yourselfers specialty contractors and federal and state agencies. Foxworth-Galbraith is still owned and operated by the families of W.L. Foxworth and H.W. Galbraith who founded the company in Dalhart Texas in 1901 to take advantage of railroad construction.

	Annual Growth	12/09	12/10	12/11	12/12	12/13
Sales ($ mil.)	13.9%	–	154.7	164.4	197.6	228.3
Net income ($ mil.)	–	–	–	(3.9)	0.8	1.7
Market value ($ mil.)	–	–	–	–	–	–
Employees	–	–	–	–	–	2,500

FPB BANCORP INC.

NASDAQ: FPBI

1301 SE Port St. Lucie Blvd.
Port St. Lucie FL 34952
Phone: 772-398-1388
Fax: 772-398-1399
Web: www.1stpeoplesbank.com

CEO: David W Skiles
CFO: –
HR: –
FYE: December 31
Type: Public

FPB Bancorp is for the birds. Snow birds that is. It's the holding company for First Peoples Bank which targets retired winter visitors as well as year-round residents and small to midsized businesses in southeastern Florida. The six-branch bank operates in Fort Pierce Palm City Port St. Lucie Stuart and Vero Beach offering such standard deposit products as CDs and checking savings and money market accounts. Commercial real estate and business loans together account for about 85% of its loan portfolio; consumer loans make up most of the rest. The bank sells into the secondary market all of the fixed-rate residential mortgages that it writes. First Peoples Bank opened two new branches in 2008.

FPIC INSURANCE GROUP INC.

NASDAQ: FPIC

1000 Riverside Ave. Ste. 800
Jacksonville FL 32204
Phone: 904-354-2482
Fax: 904-475-1159
Web: www.fpic.com

CEO: John R Byers
CFO: Charles Divita III
HR: –
FYE: December 31
Type: Public

Pulled the wrong tooth or read an X-ray backwards? FPIC Insurance Group knows that these things happen. Through its First Professionals Insurance subsidiary the company sells medical professional liability insurance (including medical error and malpractice) to more than 18000 physicians and dentists. Its Anesthesiologists Professional Assurance subsidiary serves that specialty market. Although FPIC operates in more than a dozen states Florida accounts for more than 70% of its premiums written. Its subsidiaries sell policies through independent agents and First Professionals Insurance is an endorsed carrier for several regional medical associations. FPIC was acquired by The Doctors Company in 2011.

FRANCESCA'S HOLDINGS CORPORATION

NASDAQ: FRAN

3480 W. 12th St.
Houston TX 77008
Phone: 713-864-1358
Fax: +90-532-215-4846
Web: www.unio.com.tr

CEO: William J McCabe
CFO: Kyong Gill
HR: –
FYE: January 31
Type: Public

Customers of Francesca's Holdings are left holding the bag - one full of trendy wares. The company sells apparel and accessories to 18- to 35-year old women at some 280 Francesca's Collections shops in 41 states. It opens more than 70 new stores a year yet promotes an independent upscale boutique image by allowing store managers to personalize shops. Francesca's Collections also deliberately carries limited quantities of certain items to create a "treasure hunt" ambiance. It relies on a mix of half apparel and half jewelry and accessories along with rapid product turnover to encourage customers to return often. Formed in 1999 the company entered the stock market in 2011.

FRANCIS SAINT MEDICAL CENTER

211 SAINT FRANCIS DR
CAPE GIRARDEAU, MO 637035049
Phone: 573-331-3000
Fax: –
Web: www.sfmc.net

CEO: –
CFO: –
HR: –
FYE: June 30
Type: Private

It may be guided by Catholic principles but you don't have to be a saint to get medical care at Saint Francis Medical Center. The hospital serves a five-state region from Missouri (its home base) to Arkansas with about 285 beds. Services include emergency medicine orthopedics cancer rehabilitation and women's health care. It also offers heart and neurosciences institutes as well as diabetes education and wound healing centers. The health care provider which was established in 1875 partners with Poplar Bluff Medical Partners to provide outpatient care at Poplar Bluff Medical Complex. Services include family practice OB-GYN and pain management.

	Annual Growth	06/07	06/08	06/09	06/10	06/11
Sales ($ mil.)	(24.5%)	–	–	743.0	369.5	423.1
Net income ($ mil.)	39185.7%	–	–	0.0	34.4	48.2
Market value ($ mil.)	–	–	–	–	–	–
Employees	–	–	–	–	–	1,500

FRANCISCAN ALLIANCE INC.

1515 W DRAGOON TRL
MISHAWAKA, IN 465444710
Phone: 574-256-3935
Fax: –
Web: www.franciscanalliance.org

CEO: –
CFO: –
HR: Tom Creevey
FYE: December 31
Type: Private

The Franciscan Alliance keeps watch over a family of hospitals. The not-for-profit organization operates more than a dozen hospitals in Indiana and south suburban Chicago. The hospitals house about 3500 beds and include specialist centers for cancer care heart and vascular care weight loss pediatrics and women's health. In addition to inpatient acute care services they operate numerous outpatient facilities and medical practices within their local service areas. Other subsidiaries and affiliates perform clinical laboratory tests offer home health services and provide support services to the system. Franciscan Alliance was founded and is sponsored by the Sisters of St. Francis of Perpetual Adoration.

	Annual Growth	12/04	12/05	12/06	12/07	12/12
Sales ($ mil.)	4.8%	–	–	1,983.1	2,065.5	2,625.3
Net income ($ mil.)	(5.1%)	–	–	187.0	204.7	136.8
Market value ($ mil.)	–	–	–	–	–	–
Employees	–	–	–	–	–	9,000

FRANCISCAN HEALTH SYSTEM

1717 S. J St.
Tacoma WA 98405
Phone: 253-426-4100
Fax: 253-426-6589
Web: https://www.fhshealth.org

CEO: Joseph W Wilczek
CFO: Mike Fitzgerald
HR: David Lawson
FYE: June 30
Type: Private - Not-for-Pr

St. Francis himself may have hailed from Italy but his followers look after the health of the residents of the South Puget Sound area through the Franciscan Health System. The not-for-profit system includes five full-service hospitals. The oldest and largest hospital is St. Joseph Medical Center in Tacoma Washington a 320-bed facility. Its facilities include community hospitals St. Clare Hospital (in Lakewood) and St. Francis Hospital (in Federal Way) as well as a hospice program and numerous primary and specialty care clinics. Its St. Anthony Hospital is an 80-bed full service pharmacy and home medical equipment retail location at Gig Harbor.

FRANCISCAN SKEMP HEALTHCARE INC.

700 West Ave. South
LaCrosse WI 54601
Phone: 608-785-0940
Fax: 608-791-7808
Web: www.franciscanskemp.org

CEO: Timothy Johnson
CFO: Tom Tiggelaar
HR: Dick Berendes
FYE: December 31
Type: Subsidiary

St. Francis friend to all living things was also a caretaker of body mind and spirit a philosophy still espoused at Franciscan Skemp. Franciscan Skemp Healthcare (FSH) is a community health system serving residents of northeastern Iowa southeastern Minnesota and western Wisconsin. Three hospitals in Wisconsin comprise the main facilities of the healthcare network — the La Crosse campus Sparta campus and Arcadia campus hospitals. It also operates primary care clinics. Services include home healthcare nursing homes and tertiary care. FSH is an affiliate of the Mayo Foundation for Medical Education and Research.

FRANCISCAN UNIVERSITY OF STEUBENVILLE

1235 UNIVERSITY BLVD
STEUBENVILLE, OH 439521792
Phone: 740-283-3771
Fax: -
Web: www.bookstore.franciscan.edu

CEO: -
CFO: -
HR: -
FYE: May 31
Type: Private

Franciscan University of Steubenville is a Roman Catholic school that provides instruction to more than 2300 students. It offers more than 30 undergraduate majors as well as master's degrees in six separate fields. The college was established in 1946 when Steubenville Ohio's first bishop John King Mussio invited Franciscan friars to establish a college to serve the needs of local students especially veterans of WWII.

	Annual Growth	05/05	05/06	05/09	05/10	05/13
Sales ($ mil.)	-	-	(3.9)	56.9	63.5	73.7
Net income ($ mil.)	-	-	-	0.0	1.9	7.6
Market value ($ mil.)	-	-	-	-	-	-
Employees	-	-	-	-	-	375

FRANK CONSOLIDATED ENTERPRISES INC.

666 Garland Place
Des Plaines IL 60016
Phone: 847-699-7000
Fax: 847-699-6494
Web: www.wheels.com

CEO: -
CFO: -
HR: -
FYE: August 31
Type: Private

Frank Consolidated Enterprises works to keep the wheels turning. Frank Consolidated is a holding company for Wheels which pioneered the auto leasing concept and provides fleet management services (including administrative management and financing assistance) to help clients maintain their vehicle fleets. The company operates in the US as Wheels and does business in other countries through Fleet Synergy International an alliance of fleet management and leasing firms. Wheels manages more than 295000 vehicles in North America. It also purchases and remarkets some 100000 vehicles annually. Wheels was established in 1939 and is owned and led by the family of founder Zollie Frank.

FRANK'S INTERNATIONAL INC.

10260 Westheimer Rd.
Houston TX 77042
Phone: 281-966-7300
Fax: 281-966-0948
Web: www.franksinternational.com

CEO: Donald Keith Mosing
CFO: Mark Margavio
HR: -
FYE: December 31
Type: Private

If you are building an oil well drilling platform or offshore rig you probably know Frank. Frank's International supplies tools equipment and specialty services to oil exploration and production companies worldwide. Its products include pipes tools connectors casings and specialty hammers. Frank's also offers engineering design installation testing and custom fabrication services. With five affiliated companies including Antelope Oil Tools and Pilot Drilling Control operating in 11 US cities and about 40 countries on every continent it goes where the oil is. Frank's was formed in 1938 by Frank Mosing as Frank's Casing and Tool Rental. The Mosing family continues to own and run the company.

FRANKENMUTH MUTUAL INSURANCE COMPANY

1 Mutual Ave.
Frankenmuth MI 48787-0001
Phone: 989-652-6121
Fax: 989-652-3588
Web: www.fmins.com

CEO: John S Benson
CFO: Brian S McLeod
HR: -
FYE: December 31
Type: Private - Mutual Com

Frankenmuth Mutual Insurance provides property/casualty products including personal automobile umbrella and homeowners coverage as well as commercial liability workers' compensation and other business products. Other offerings include identity theft coverage and yacht and collector car policies. The company also offers life insurance protection through subsidiary Patriot Life Insurance and its network of some 4000 independent agents. More than 500 independent agencies market the firm's products. Frankenmuth Mutual is licensed in 47 states and does business in 15 states east of the Mississippi. Founded by Bavarian settlers in 1868 the company limited its service to Michigan policyholders until the 1970s.

FRANKLIN AMERICAN MORTGAGE CO INC

501 CORP CNTRE DR STE 400
FRANKLIN, TN 37067
Phone: 615-778-1000
Fax: -
Web: www.franklinamerican.com

CEO: -
CFO: Scott J Tansil
HR: -
FYE: December 31
Type: Private

Franklin American Mortgage Company (FAMC) is flying as high as a kite. The private mortgage bank is one of the country's largest and fastest-growing mortgage brokers. Franklin American Mortgage operates through three loan production channels. The correspondent lending division services lenders nationwide while the wholesale division funds and underwrites loans for mortgage brokers. The firm's retail division offers mortgages directly to individuals from about 20 offices (mostly located in the East and South). Founded in 1994 Franklin American Mortgage CEO Dan Crockett owns the company.

	Annual Growth	12/03	12/04	12/05	12/07	12/08
Assets ($ mil.)	416.4%	-	-	2.2	206.8	298.1
Net income ($ mil.)	29429.6%	-	-	0.0	5.5	25.7
Market value ($ mil.)	-	-	-	-	-	-
Employees	-	-	-	-	-	700

FRANKLIN AND MARSHALL COLLEGE

415 HARRISBURG AVE
LANCASTER, PA 176032827
Phone: 717-291-3911
Fax: -
Web: www.fandm.edu

CEO: -
CFO: Eileen Austin
HR: -
FYE: June 30
Type: Private

Franklin & Marshall College named after Benjamin Franklin and John Marshall is a private liberal arts institution serving about 2400 students. It offers academic and research programs in about 60 fields including biology chemistry English history mathematics political science art sociology and environmental studies. It offers programs in 11 languages including Arabic and Greek. Franklin & Marshall College was created in 1853 through the merger of Franklin College (founded in 1787 with a contribution from Ben Franklin) and Marshall College (opened in 1836 and named after Chief Justice John Marshall).

	Annual Growth	06/07	06/08	06/10	06/11	06/13
Sales ($ mil.)	8.4%	-	110.1	141.6	114.7	165.0
Net income ($ mil.)	(3.9%)	-	-	10.3	46.6	9.2
Market value ($ mil.)	-	-	-	-	-	-
Employees	-	-	-	-	-	722

FRANKLIN COMMUNITY HEALTH NETWORK

111 FRANKLIN HEALTH CMNS
FARMINGTON, ME 049386144
Phone: 207-779-2265
Fax: –
Web: www.doctorinmaine.com

CEO: Rebecca Ryder
CFO: –
HR: –
FYE: June 30
Type: Private

Frankly when it comes to providing health care Franklin Community Health Network would rather rough it. The not-for-profit health care system serves mountainous rural areas in western Maine. Franklin Community Health Network consists of a 70 bed acute care hospital a behavioral health facility and several physician management groups. Its Franklin Memorial Hospital offers specialized services such as cardiology orthopedics emergency medicine and occupational health care. The health network's unique Contract for Care program allows former patients to volunteer at the hospital if they do not have the means to pay all of their bill.

	Annual Growth	06/10	06/11	06/12	06/13	06/14
Sales ($ mil.)	172.3%	–	3.7	1.0	0.7	75.6
Net income ($ mil.)	50.6%	–	–	0.1	(1.2)	0.2
Market value ($ mil.)	–	–	–	–	–	–
Employees	–	–	–	–	–	900

FRANKLIN COVEY CO
NYS: FC

2200 West Parkway Boulevard
Salt Lake City, UT 84119-2099
Phone: 801 817-1776
Fax: –
Web: www.franklincovey.com

CEO: Robert A. (Bob) Whitman
CFO: Stephen D. (Steve) Young
HR: Clifton Davis
FYE: August 31
Type: Public

Franklin Covey publisher of the popular book The 7 Habits of Highly Effective People knows a thing or two about performance improvement. Targeted at individuals teams and organizations the company is a global provider of training programs consulting services books and planning products designed around seven practice areas: leadership productivity trust execution sales performance education and customer loyalty. Franklin Covey's more than 4200 clients include about 90% of the FORTUNE 100 75% of the FORTUNE 500 and thousands of small and midsized businesses. In addition to companies it serves government entities and educational institutions mostly in the US.

	Annual Growth	08/11	08/12	08/13	08/14	08/15
Sales ($ mil.)	6.9%	160.8	170.5	190.9	205.2	209.9
Net income ($ mil.)	23.3%	4.8	7.8	14.3	18.1	11.1
Market value ($ mil.)	15.1%	153.7	167.1	253.7	307.9	270.1
Employees	8.2%	590	630	660	825	810

FRANKLIN CREDIT HOLDING CORPORATION
PINK SHEETS: FCMC

101 Hudson St.
Jersey City NJ 07302
Phone: 201-604-1800
Fax: 201-604-4400
Web: www.franklincredit.com

CEO: –
CFO: Paul D Colasono
HR: –
FYE: December 31
Type: Public

Franklin Credit Holding is the holding company of mortgage servicer Franklin Credit Management. In 2009 the company entered into a restructuring agreement with The Huntington National Bank in which a large number (about 83%) of Franklin's subprime mortgages were transferred to the bank's real estate investment trust (REIT); in exchange Franklin received a capital infusion of more than $13 million and services the mortgages transferred to the bank's books in order to generate fee income. Chairman and president Thomas Axon owns some 45% of Franklin Credit Holdings. Director Frank Evans more than 10%.

FRANKLIN ELECTRIC CO., INC.
NMS: FELE

9255 Coverdale Road
Fort Wayne, IN 46809
Phone: 260 824-2900
Fax: –
Web: www.franklin-electric.com

CEO: R. Scott Trumbull
CFO: John J. Haines
HR: Claudia Fallon
FYE: January 03
Type: Public

When it comes to making pumps and motors Franklin Electric would make Old Ben proud. The company keeps things flowing by making and distributing submersible and specialty electric motors electronic drives and controls and related items. Its fueling system products include electronic tank monitoring equipment fittings flexible piping nozzles and vapor recovery systems. Franklin Electric's products are used by OEMs that incorporate them in underground petroleum pumping systems sewage pumps vacuum pumping systems and freshwater pumping systems. Some customers such as independent distributors and repair shops buy the company's products as replacement motors. Franklin Electric was founded in 1944.

	Annual Growth	01/11*	12/11	12/12	12/13*	01/15
Sales ($ mil.)	10.1%	713.8	821.1	891.3	965.5	1,047.8
Net income ($ mil.)	15.7%	39.0	63.1	82.9	82.0	69.8
Market value ($ mil.)	(1.0%)	1,852.4	2,073.2	2,858.0	2,166.0	1,776.2
Employees	9.0%	3,470	3,800	4,200	4,400	4,900

*Fiscal year change

FRANKLIN ELECTRONIC PUBLISHERS INCORPORATED

1 Franklin Plaza
Burlington NJ 08016-4907
Phone: 609-386-2500
Fax: 609-387-1787
Web: www.franklin.com

CEO: Barry J Lipsky
CFO: Frank A Musto
HR: –
FYE: March 31
Type: Private

Like to read but hate turning those pesky pages? Franklin Electronic Publishers may have a solution for you. The company markets handheld electronic devices (which are made by third parties) that display the text of reference and educational publications in four areas: Language Expansion Language Learning Reading Enhancement and Writing Enhancement. It owns or licenses more than 110000 electronic titles including Merriam-Webster's Collegiate Dictionary Bartlett's Familiar Quotations and the Holy Bible which can be downloaded to Franklin's handheld devices and those of other manufacturers. Products are available in 16 languages at nearly 50000 retail outlets worldwide. The company was founded in 1981.

FRANKLIN FINANCIAL SERVICES CORP
NBB: FRAF

20 South Main Street
Chambersburg, PA 17201-0819
Phone: 717 264-6116
Fax: 717 264-7129
Web: www.franklinfin.com

CEO: William E Snell Jr
CFO: Mark R Hollar
HR: –
FYE: December 31
Type: Public

Ben Franklin said "A penny saved is a penny earned" but Franklin Financial might be able to convert those pennies into dollars. It's the holding company for Farmers and Merchants Trust Company (F&M Trust) a community bank serving south-central Pennsylvania from more than 20 locations. Established in 1906 F&M Trust offers standard deposit products including checking and savings accounts IRAs and CDs. It also provides discount brokerage insurance retirement planning and other investment services. More than half of the company's lending portfolio is devoted to commercial industrial and agricultural loans; the bank also makes consumer construction and residential mortgage loans.

	Annual Growth	12/10	12/11	12/12	12/13	12/14
Assets ($ mil.)	1.3%	951.9	990.2	1,027.4	984.6	1,001.4
Net income ($ mil.)	2.5%	7.6	6.6	5.4	6.2	8.4
Market value ($ mil.)	4.8%	77.0	52.1	59.1	72.1	92.8
Employees	0.3%	263	274	283	275	266

FRANKLIN HOSPITAL

900 FRANKLIN AVE
VALLEY STREAM, NY 115802190
Phone: 516-256-6000
Fax: –
Web: www.concordhospital.org

CEO: Michael J Dowling
CFO: –
HR: –
FYE: December 31
Type: Private

Franklin Hospital is part of the North Shore-Long Island Jewish Health System. The medical center has more than 300 beds and provides emergency and specialty care services. Franklin Hospital includes the 120-bed Orzac Center a long-term care rehabilitation unit as well as a 21-bed psychiatric unit and an adult day care center. Franklin Hospital also provides outpatient care — including pediatrics and women's health — and home health services. Established in 1963 as a small community hospital Franklin offers services and programs to the residents of Nassau and southeastern Queens Counties.

	Annual Growth	12/00	12/01*	04/05*	12/08	12/12
Sales ($ mil.)	5.0%	–	103.0	0.1	169.5	175.3
Net income ($ mil.)	–	–	–	(0.0)	(3.8)	5.6
Market value ($ mil.)	–	–	–	–	–	–
Employees	–	–	–	–	–	1,300

*Fiscal year change

FRANKLIN RESOURCES, INC. NYS: BEN

One Franklin Parkway
San Mateo, CA 94403
Phone: 650 312-2000
Fax: 650 312-3655
Web: www.franklinresources.com

CEO: Gregory E. Johnson
CFO: Kenneth A. Lewis
HR: Allison Katz
FYE: September 30
Type: Public

Franklin Resources believes a penny saved is a penny lost — if it's not wisely invested. Operating as Franklin Templeton Investments the firm manages more than 100 mutual funds that invest in international and domestic stocks; taxable and tax-exempt money market instruments; and corporate municipal and US government bonds. Franklin Resources also offers separately managed accounts closed-end funds insurance product funds and retirement and college savings plans. Its investment products are sold through more than 1600 banks securities firms and financial advisors under the Franklin Templeton Mutual Series Bissett Darby and Fiduciary Trust banners.

	Annual Growth	09/11	09/12	09/13	09/14	09/15
Sales ($ mil.)	2.7%	7,140.0	7,101.0	7,985.0	8,491.4	7,948.7
Net income ($ mil.)	1.4%	1,923.6	1,931.4	2,150.2	2,384.3	2,035.3
Market value ($ mil.)	(21.0%)	57,720.4	75,481.9	30,507.8	32,958.1	22,487.1
Employees	2.8%	8,500	8,600	9,000	9,300	9,500

FRANKLIN SQUARE HOSPITAL CENTER INC.

9000 FRANKLIN SQUARE DR
BALTIMORE, MD 21237-3901
Phone: 443-777-7000
Fax: –
Web: www.franklinsquare.org

CEO: –
CFO: Robert P Lally Jr
HR: –
FYE: June 30
Type: Private

Franklin Square Hospital Center has made a declaration to care for the residents of eastern Baltimore County Maryland. The facility offers a wide range of specialties through some 700 doctors and about 375 beds. Since 1998 the hospital has been part of MedStar Health the region's largest integrated health system. As a teaching hospital Franklin Square offers a number of residency programs including internal and family medicine OB-GYN and surgery. The not-for-profit hospital's medical services are provided via six primary service lines: Medicine Surgery Women's and Children's Care Oncology Behavioral Health and Community Health and Wellness.

	Annual Growth	04/08	04/09*	06/10	06/11	06/12
Sales ($ mil.)	1028.5%	–	–	0.3	439.4	452.9	471.5
Net income ($ mil.)	–	–	–	0.0	31.2	18.1	(5.7)
Market value ($ mil.)	–	–	–	–	–	–	–
Employees	–	–	–	–	–	–	3,019

*Fiscal year change

FRANKLIN STREET PROPERTIES CORP ASE: FSP

401 Edgewater Place, Suite 200
Wakefield, MA 01880
Phone: 781 557-1300
Fax: –
Web: www.franklinstreetproperties.com

CEO: George J. Carter
CFO: John G. Demeritt
HR: –
FYE: December 31
Type: Public

A real estate investment trust (REIT) Franklin Street Properties acquires finances leases and manages office properties in about 15 states throughout the US. It owns some 40 properties located mainly in suburban areas and manages about 15 others; Dallas Denver Houston and Washington DC are its largest markets. The company's FSP Investment unit is an investment bank and brokerage that organizes REITs that invest in single properties and raises equity for them through private placements. Another subsidiary FSP Property Management manages properties for Franklin Street as well as for some of the REITs sponsored by FSP Investments.

	Annual Growth	12/10	12/11	12/12	12/13	12/14
Sales ($ mil.)	19.3%	123.1	139.5	162.8	213.6	249.7
Net income ($ mil.)	(12.2%)	22.1	43.5	7.6	19.8	13.1
Market value ($ mil.)	(3.7%)	1,427.7	996.9	1,233.3	1,197.2	1,229.3
Employees	(1.8%)	42	32	35	37	39

FRANKLIN WIRELESS CORP NBB: FKWL

9707 Waples Street, Suite 150
San Diego, CA 92121
Phone: 858 623-0000
Fax: 858 623-0050
Web: www.franklinwireless.com

CEO: –
CFO: Richard Walker
HR: –
FYE: June 30
Type: Public

Franklin Wireless hopes lightning strikes with its wireless data products. The company makes high speed connectivity products for wireless devices. Its products include USB embedded and standalone modems as well as modules PC cards and Wi-Fi hotspot routers. Customers use its products to connect their mobile computers to wireless broadband networks. Franklin Wireless primarily sells directly to wireless operators but also through partners and distributors. The US is its largest market but the Caribbean and South America have collectively grown to nearly 25% of sales. The company uses contract manufacturers such as South Korea-based shareholder (about 13%) C-Motech and Samsung Electro-Mechanics.

	Annual Growth	06/11	06/12	06/13	06/14	06/15
Sales ($ mil.)	(0.1%)	46.5	24.3	32.8	31.0	46.3
Net income ($ mil.)	(36.1%)	4.5	(0.1)	0.2	(1.0)	0.8
Market value ($ mil.)	(10.0%)	25.8	14.5	17.9	19.0	16.9
Employees	(0.7%)	68	74	67	65	66

FRASER/WHITE INC.

1631 PONTIUS AVE
LOS ANGELES, CA 900253307
Phone: 310-319-3737
Fax: –
Web: www.frasercommunications.com

CEO: Renee Fraser
CFO: –
HR: –
FYE: December 31
Type: Private

Fraser/White speaks the languages of advertising and marketing. The agency — which does business as Fraser Communications — offers market research media planning and buying interactive (Web design) and public relations services. The company takes an approach it calls 360 Communications — surrounding consumers with a client's message. Clients which tend to come from such industries as automotive consumer goods financial services and health care have included Cedars-Sinai Frederick's of Hollywood and Toyota. President and CEO Renee Fraser founded Fraser Communications in 1992.

	Annual Growth	11/03	11/04	11/05*	12/06	12/08
Sales ($ mil.)	–	–	–	(1,239.4)	32.7	42.0
Net income ($ mil.)	1631.7%	–	–	0.0	3.6	0.1
Market value ($ mil.)	–	–	–	–	–	–
Employees	–	–	–	–	–	35

*Fiscal year change

FRAZIER INDUSTRIAL COMPANY (INC)

91 FAIRVIEW AVE
LONG VALLEY, NJ 078533381
Phone: 908-876-3001
Fax: –
Web: www.frazier.com

CEO: William L. Mascharka
CFO: Peter Acerra
HR: –
FYE: December 31
Type: Private

This company's racket is structural steel storage systems. Frazier Industrial Co. is a leading manufacturer of structural as opposed to roll-formed steel storage racks at nearly a dozen production centers located across the US Canada and Mexico. These facilities can adapt production to demand and receive just-in-time delivery of raw materials. Customers use Frazier Industrial's storage racks in warehouses factories farms and other industrial and commercial facilities. Among the company's storage products is the Glide 'N Pick pallet cart that automatically rolls out for greater ease in retrieving items. Frazier Industrial is owned by CEO William Mascharka.

	Annual Growth	12/09	12/10	12/11	12/12	12/13
Sales ($ mil.)	19.8%	–	133.8	178.1	183.3	230.1
Net income ($ mil.)	(16.9%)	–	–	4.8	2.9	3.3
Market value ($ mil.)	–	–	–	–	–	–
Employees	–	–	–	–	–	750

FRED MEYER STORES INC.

3800 SE 22nd Ave.
Portland OR 97202
Phone: 503-232-8844
Fax: 503-797-5609
Web: www.fredmeyer.com

CEO: –
CFO: David Deatherage
HR: –
FYE: January 31
Type: Subsidiary

Fred Meyer Stores went out for groceries and wound up in Kroger's cart. Freddy's — as the chain is known — is a supercenter pioneer providing food and general merchandise to cost-conscious consumers in the Pacific Northwest and Alaska. One of the largest supercenter operators in the US (along with Wal-Mart and Costco Wholesale) Fred Meyer's 130 multidepartment stores (averaging more than 165000 sq. ft.) offer everything from apparel and home goods to groceries consumer electronics fuel and jewelry. Its Web store delivers to the Alaska Bush. Kroger has leveraged Fred Meyer's general merchandising expertise as defense against Wal-Mart which has overtaken Kroger as the #1 seller of groceries in the US.

FRED'S INC.

NMS: FRED

4300 New Getwell Road
Memphis, TN 38118
Phone: 901 365-8880
Fax: –
Web: www.fredsinc.com

CEO: Jerry A. Shore
CFO: –
HR: –
FYE: January 31
Type: Public

Those whose greenbacks feature George and Abe rather than Andrew and Ulysses may very well shop at Fred's. Generally serving customers with modest or fixed incomes Fred's operates more than 650 discount stores in some 15 states primarily in small- to medium-sized towns in the Southeast. The stores carry more than 12000 brand-name off-brand and private-label products including pharmaceuticals household goods clothing and linens food and tobacco items health and beauty aids and paper and cleaning supplies. Nearly 60% of its stores have full-service pharmacies. The company also provides goods and services to some 20 franchised Fred's stores. Founded in 1947 Fred's is exploring strategic alternatives.

	Annual Growth	01/11	01/12*	02/13	02/14*	01/15
Sales ($ mil.)	1.7%	1,841.8	1,879.1	1,955.3	1,939.2	1,970.0
Net income ($ mil.)	–	29.6	33.4	29.6	26.0	(28.9)
Market value ($ mil.)	5.5%	495.0	557.1	490.6	646.2	613.7
Employees	(1.8%)	9,852	10,568	9,505	9,122	9,148

*Fiscal year change

FREDDIE MAC

OTC: FMCC

8200 Jones Branch Drive
McLean, VA 22102-3110
Phone: 703 903-2000
Fax: –
Web: www.freddiemac.com

CEO: Donald H. (Don) Layton
CFO: James G. Mackey
HR: –
FYE: December 31
Type: Public

These siblings know there's no place like home. Government-sponsored enterprises (GSEs) Freddie Mac (officially Federal Home Loan Mortgage Corporation) and Fannie Mae were established to buy residential mortgages and boost the housing market. They do so by purchasing mortgages from lenders and packaging them for resale thereby mitigating risk and allowing lenders to provide mortgages to those who may not otherwise qualify. The agency also provides assistance for affordable rental housing. Together Fannie and Freddie guarantee some 70% of all new home loans in the US. Due to losses related to the subprime mortgage crisis the government seized Fannie and Freddie in 2008. It now plans to wind the GSEs down.

	Annual Growth	12/10	12/11	12/12	12/13	12/14
Assets ($ mil.)	(3.7%)	2,261,780.0	2,147,216.0	1,989,856.0	1,966,061.0	1,945,539.0
Net income ($ mil.)	–	(14,025.0)	(5,266.0)	10,982.0	48,668.0	7,690.0
Market value ($ mil.)	61.2%	198.1	137.8	171.0	1,885.1	1,339.1
Employees	(1.5%)	5,309	4,921	5,017	5,112	5,007

FREDERICK MEMORIAL HOSPITAL INC.

400 W 7TH ST
FREDERICK, MD 217014593
Phone: 240-566-3300
Fax: –
Web: www.fmh.org

CEO: Thomas A Kleinhanzl
CFO: Michelle Nahan
HR: –
FYE: June 30
Type: Private

Frederick Memorial Healthcare System cares for the sick and unhealthy across The Old Line State. The system operates Frederick Memorial Hospital an acute care facility with some 240 beds and 20 satellite facilities in and around Frederick Maryland. Specialty services include cardiology oncology pediatrics and psychiatry. Other facilities in the system include FMH Immediate Care at Oak Street FMH Crestwood FMH Medical Fitness FMH Rose Hill FMH Wellness FMH Urbana Mt. Airy Health Services and the FMH Regional Cancer Therapy Center. The hospital traces its historical roots all the way back to 1902.

	Annual Growth	06/09	06/10	06/11	06/12	06/13
Sales ($ mil.)	3.9%	–	307.3	348.6	355.1	344.8
Net income ($ mil.)	(47.2%)	–	–	16.0	(13.1)	4.5
Market value ($ mil.)	–	–	–	–	–	–
Employees	–	–	–	–	–	2,600

FREDERICK'S OF HOLLYWOOD GROUP INC

NBB: FOHL

6255 Sunset Boulevard
Hollywood, CA 90028
Phone: 323 466-5151
Fax: 212 684-3400
Web: www.fredericks.com; www.fohgroup.com

CEO: Thomas J Lynch
CFO: Thomas Rende
HR: –
FYE: July 27
Type: Public

Frederick's of Hollywood Group makes big money out of little somethings. Initially formed by the merger of Frederick's of Hollywood and Movie Star it sells intimates wigs hosiery and dresses through its catalog division (which mails more than 13 million) website and about 120 namesake stores in the US. It's also developing a presence in the Middle East. The manufacturer now soley focuses on its retail business. Years after acquiring Movie Star the group shed the wholesaler which made intimate apparel sleepwear leisurewear and loungewear. Additionally Frederick's of Hollywood Group in late 2010 sold off its wholesale unit to Dolce Vita Intimates amid declining revenues.

	Annual Growth	07/09	07/10	07/11	07/12	07/13
Sales ($ mil.)	(16.3%)	176.3	133.9	119.6	111.4	86.5
Net income ($ mil.)	–	(34.0)	(21.2)	(12.1)	(6.4)	(22.5)
Market value ($ mil.)	(32.3%)	33.3	36.0	26.2	15.3	7.0
Employees	(15.6%)	1,779	1,179	1,044	926	902

FREDERICK'S OF HOLLYWOOD INC.

6255 W. Sunset Blvd. Suite 600
Hollywood CA 90028
Phone: 323-466-5151
Fax: 323-464-5149
Web: www.fredericks.com

CEO: William Soncini
CFO: Thomas Rende
HR: –
FYE: July 31
Type: Subsidiary

Even in a town not known for modesty Frederick's of Hollywood is an eye-opener. Operating about 120 women's intimate apparel shops in the US (primarily in malls) it sells lingerie bras panties foundations dresses wigs and hosiery under the Frederick's of Hollywood brand name. The firm pioneered the push-up bra and other dainties designed from a man's point of view but has extended its reach by adding ready-to-wear items jewelry and perfume. It operates a mail-order catalog unit in the US and Canada which produces some 13 million catalogs and an online store. When Frederick's of Hollywood merged with Movie Star the combined entity and new parent became known as Frederick's of Hollywood Group.

FREEDOM COMMUNICATIONS INC.

17666 Fitch Ave.
Irvine CA 92614-6022
Phone: 949-253-2300
Fax: 949-474-7675
Web: www.freedom.com

CEO: Richard E Mirman
CFO: Mark A McEachen
HR: –
FYE: December 31
Type: Private

You might say this company really believes in freedom of the press. Freedom Communications is a leading newspaper publisher with more than 30 daily papers mostly in California North Carolina and Texas. Its portfolio includes The Orange County Register in California which boasts a circulation of about 195000. The company also publishes more than 60 weekly community papers and it owns nearly 10 TV stations mostly affiliated with CBS and ABC serving markets in a half dozen states. Freedom Communications which emerged from bankruptcy in 2010 was founded by R. C. Hoiles. It is controlled by an investment group that includes Angelo Gordon & Co. Alden Global Capital and Luxor Capital Group.

FREEDOM FROM HUNGER

1644 Da Vinci Ct.
Davis CA 95618
Phone: 530-758-6200
Fax: 530-758-6241
Web: www.freefromhunger.org

CEO: –
CFO: –
HR: Holly Bowers
FYE: June 30
Type: Private - Not-for-Pr

Freedom from Hunger wants to give everybody just that. The not-for-profit organization strives to solve the problem of chronic hunger and poverty in 16 countries worldwide. The group provides self-help programs and training for more than 650000 poor women to learn to better feed and tend the health of their families and turn a small enterprise into a sustaining business. Its main program Credit With Education is a microcredit program that provides loans to small groups of women who attend classes on nutrition health family planning and sound business practices. Freedom From Hunger was founded in 1946 as Meals for Millions.

FREEDOM GROUP INC.

870 Remington Dr.
Madison NC 27025-1776
Phone: 336-548-8700
Fax: 717-520-1111
Web: www.hersheytrust.com

CEO: George Kollitide
CFO: –
HR: –
FYE: December 31
Type: Private

Fired up and ready to go? The Freedom Group Inc. (FGI) is one of the largest firearms ammunition and related accessories companies in the world. Its lineup is sold under time-honored brand names including Remington Marlin and Bushmaster. Shotguns and rifles target both outdoor enthusiasts and law enforcement agencies such as the US military. Wal-Mart is the group's largest retail customer. FGI is the only US company to manufacture both firearms and ammunition at its manufacturing plants enabling distribution primarily in the US (the biggest firearms market in the world) but also to some 65 countries. Owner Cerberus Capital is selling its stake in FGI after the shootings at Sandy Hook Elementary School.

FREEDOM RESOURCES ENTERPRISES INC.   OTC: FRDR

901 E. 7800 South
Midvale UT 84047
Phone: 801-566-5931
Fax: 904-280-7794
Web: www.syfobeverages.com

CEO: –
CFO: –
HR: –
FYE: December 31
Type: Public

Freedom Resources Enterprises is a development stage company. It developed a series of eight self-help self-improvement workshops. Each self-taught workshop consisted of an audio tape and a workbook which Freedom Resources marketed over the Internet. The company's workshops did not generated expected revenue and Freedom Resources has announced plans to pursue other business opportunities.

FREEDOMROADS LLC

250 Parkway Dr. Ste. 270
Lincolnshire IL 60069
Phone: 847-808-3000
Fax: 713-621-9545
Web: www.copanoenergy.com

CEO: Marcus A Lemonis
CFO: –
HR: –
FYE: December 31
Type: Private

"Home home on the road where the semis and the SUVs play..." That's how FreedomRoads would sing it. The nation's largest RV retailer FreedomRoads (dba Camping World RV Sales) sells and rents new and used recreational vehicles and accessory products through more than 75 locations in 30-plus states. Its locations feature Camping World stores which offer RV-specific items not usually carried by general merchandise retailers including bedding furniture replacement hardware and sanitation systems. Camping World RV Sales dealers provide maintenance and repair services as well as financing. Chairman and CEO Marcus Lemonis founded the company in 2003.

FREEMAN HEALTH SYSTEM

1102 W 32ND ST
JOPLIN, MO 648043503
Phone: 417-623-2801
Fax: –
Web: www.freemanhealth.com

CEO: Paula Baker
CFO: Steven Graddy
HR: Debbie Bainbridge
FYE: March 31
Type: Private

Freeman Health System (FHS) offers comprehensive health and behavioral health services to the residents of Arkansas Kansas Missouri and Oklahoma through three hospitals with a total of more than 500 beds. Specialty facilities include a full-service cardiothoracic and vascular program at the Freeman Heart Institute and behavioral health services through its Ozark Health Center. Community-owned not-for-profit FHS also operates two urgent care centers a separate sleep center several doctors' office buildings and serves as a teaching hospital with three residency programs (ear nose and throat; emergency medicine; and internal medicine). FHS employs more than 300 physicians in 60 specialties.

	Annual Growth	03/07	03/08	03/09	03/10	03/11
Sales ($ mil.)	(14.5%)	–	–	619.2	474.9	452.5
Net income ($ mil.)	13560.1%	–	–	0.0	30.7	7.5
Market value ($ mil.)	–	–	–	–	–	–
Employees	–	–	–	–	–	3,887

FREEPORT REGIONAL HEALTH CARE FOUNDATION

1045 W STEPHENSON ST
FREEPORT, IL 610324864
Phone: 815-599-6000
Fax: –
Web: www.fhn.org

CEO: –
CFO: –
HR: –
FYE: December 31
Type: Private

FHN is a regional health care system serving residents in northwestern Illinois and southern Wisconsin. At its heart is the nearly 200-bed FHN Memorial Hospital which provides general medical and surgical care emergency services and specialty care in areas such as sleep disorders orthopedics obstetrics and cardiology. The health system also features a cancer center home health care and hospice operations and a network of satellite facilities providing primary medical and dental care as well as occupational health chiropractic and counseling services. Its Northern Illinois Health Plan subsidiary supplies PPO health plans and third-party administrative services to the region's employers.

	Annual Growth	12/05	12/06	12/07	12/08	12/09
Sales ($ mil.)	(29.7%)	–	158.5	164.5	169.5	55.0
Net income ($ mil.)	–	–	–	7.6	(13.2)	(16.1)
Market value ($ mil.)	–	–	–	–	–	–
Employees	–	–	–	–	–	1,500

FREEPORT-MCMORAN INC   NYS: FCX

333 North Central Avenue
Phoenix, AZ 85004-2189
Phone: 602 366-8100
Fax: –
Web: www.fcx.com

CEO: Richard C. Adkerson
CFO: Kathleen L. Quirk
HR: Debra Ricco
FYE: December 31
Type: Public

Freeport-McMoRan (FCX formerly Freeport-McMoRan Copper & Gold) digs its profits from copper and precious metal mines and from oil and gas assets. In 2014 FCX's proven and probable reserves totaled 103.5 billion pounds of copper 28.5 million ounces of gold and 282.9 million ounces of silver. Subsidiary PT Freeport Indonesia (PT-FI) operates the vast Grasberg gold copper and silver mine in Indonesia. FCX is also engaged in smelting and refining via PT-FI's 25% stake in PT Smelting a copper smelter in Indonesia. In 2014 the company reported estimated proved oil and natural gas reserves of 390 million barrels of oil equivalent. In 2016 it agreed to sell 13% of its Morenci (US) copper mine for $1 billion.

	Annual Growth	12/10	12/11	12/12	12/13	12/14
Sales ($ mil.)	3.1%	18,982.0	20,880.0	18,010.0	20,921.0	21,438.0
Net income ($ mil.)	–	5,544.0	5,747.0	3,980.0	3,441.0	(745.0)
Market value ($ mil.)	(33.6%)	124,773.5	38,224.8	35,533.8	39,211.9	24,271.0
Employees	4.2%	29,700	31,800	34,000	36,100	35,000

FREESCALE SEMICONDUCTOR INC.

6501 W. William Cannon Dr.
Austin TX 78735
Phone: 512-895-2000
Fax: 801-222-0977
Web: www.hogiyogi.com

CEO: Rich Beyer
CFO: Alan Campbell
HR: –
FYE: December 31
Type: Subsidiary

Freescale Semiconductor just wants to be free. Once the semiconductor products business of the former Motorola Inc. the company is one of the oldest makers of microchips in the world. It produces a diverse range of chips for use in automobiles computers industrial equipment wireless communications and networking gear and consumer products. The company's global client roster has included such blue-chip companies as Alcatel-Lucent Continental Automotive DENSO Huawei Cisco Systems Fujitsu Nokia Siemens Networks Research in Motion and Valeo. Freescale Semiconductor is a subsidiary of Freescale Semiconductor Holdings I which went public in 2011.

FREESE AND NICHOLS INC.

4055 INTL PLAZA STE 200
FORT WORTH, TX 76109-4814
Phone: 817-735-7300
Fax: –
Web: www.freese.com

CEO: Robert F Pence
CFO: Cynthia P Milrany
HR: –
FYE: December 31
Type: Private

Freese and Nichols (FNI) keeps water in the Lone Star State flowing in the right direction. The consulting firm specializes in water management engineering but also offers architecture environmental science and construction management to clients in the Southwest primarily Texas and the Southeast. The company has designed more than 150 dams and reservoirs and also works on such projects as municipal waterworks water treatment facilities and highways. Freese and Nichols serves the private and public sectors; its clients include all levels of government. The company has offices in about 15 Texas cities and in North Carolina. It traces its roots to a Fort Worth firm founded in 1894 by John B. Hawley.

	Annual Growth	12/08	12/09	12/10	12/11	12/12
Sales ($ mil.)	23.4%	–	–	–	106.0	130.8
Net income ($ mil.)	13.3%	–	–	–	1.5	1.8
Market value ($ mil.)	–	–	–	–	–	–
Employees	–	–	–	–	–	487

FREIGHTCAR AMERICA INC   NMS: RAIL

Two North Riverside Plaza, Suite 1300
Chicago, IL 60606
Phone: 800 458-2235
Fax: –
Web: www.freightcaramerica.com

CEO: Joseph E. McNeely
CFO: Matthew S. (Matt) Kohnke
HR: Tom McCarthy
FYE: December 31
Type: Public

Coal keeps FreightCar America in the black. The company designs and makes aluminum-bodied railroad cars that are used to transport coal. It also manufactures coil steel cars flatcars intermodal cars mill gondola cars and motor vehicle carriers. FreightCar America refurbishes and rebuilds railcars and supplies forged cast and fabricated parts for its railcars and ones made by other companies. Its FreightCar Rail Services subsidiary supplies fleet management software and provides inspections and railcar repair and maintenance services. Customers include leasing companies railroads and shippers. The company has been making railcars since 1901.

	Annual Growth	12/10	12/11	12/12	12/13	12/14
Sales ($ mil.)	43.1%	142.9	487.0	677.4	290.4	598.5
Net income ($ mil.)	–	–	(12.8)	4.9	19.1	(19.3)| 5.9
Market value ($ mil.)	(2.4%)	349.2	252.8	270.5	321.2	317.5
Employees	31.3%	464	941	918	819	1,381

FREIGHTQUOTE.COM INC.

16025 W 113TH ST
LENEXA, KS 66219-5105
Phone: 913-642-4700
Fax: –
Web: www.freightquote.com

CEO: –
CFO: –
HR: –
FYE: December 31
Type: Private

Where should one go on the Web to find quotes for freight carriers? Freightquote.com silly. The company rates schedules and tracks all types of freight comparing numerous carriers in seconds through its free service. Freightquote serves customers across North America who use its services to schedule and track their shipments entirely on the Web. It also offers free online freight shipping quotes. Modes of freight transport include trucks airplanes and ships. The company moves more than one million shipments across North America per year. Freightquote was founded in 1998 by Timothy Barton. It has received funding from investment firms such as Menlo Ventures and Morgan Stanley Venture Partners.

	Annual Growth	12/08	12/09	12/10	12/11	12/12
Sales ($ mil.)	16.8%	–	359.8	0.0	385.9	573.8
Net income ($ mil.)	–	–	0.0	0.0	0.0	0.0
Market value ($ mil.)	–	–	–	–	–	–
Employees	–	–	–	–	–	1,200

FREMONT AREA MEDICAL CENTER

450 E 23RD ST
FREMONT, NE 680252387
Phone: 402-727-3795
Fax: –
Web: www.famc.org

CEO: Patrick Booth
CFO: Mike Sindelar
HR: Harvey Raymond
FYE: June 30
Type: Private

Fremont Area Medical Center's area of expertise is serving patients in Nebraska's Dodge County and surrounding areas. The non-profit healthcare facility has more than 200 beds with about 112 beds dedicated to long-term care patients. Specialized services include cancer care emergency medicine rehabilitation home health and hospice and surgery. Fremont Area Medical Center is owned by Dodge County and its operations are funded by taxpayers. The institution is licensed by the Nebraska State Board of Health and maintains accreditation through the Joint Commission.

	Annual Growth	06/02	06/03	06/04	06/05	06/07
Sales ($ mil.)	–	–	–	(1,279.3)	77.7	91.8
Net income ($ mil.)	5767.2%	–	–	0.0	6.7	12.9
Market value ($ mil.)	–	–	–	–	–	–
Employees	–	–	–	–	–	900

FREMONT BANCORPORATION

39150 Fremont Blvd.
Fremont CA 94538
Phone: 510-505-5226
Fax: 510-795-5758
Web: www.fremontbank.com

CEO: –
CFO: –
HR: –
FYE: December 31
Type: Private

Fremont Bancorporation lets freedom ka-ching! It's the holding company for Fremont Bank which operates more than 20 branches in the San Francisco Bay area. Serving area consumers and businesses the bank provides traditional banking services such as savings checking and money market accounts; check cards; IRAs; and CDs. It uses funds from deposits mainly to originate home mortgages and commercial real estate loans as well as commercial industrial construction and land development loans. The bank which was founded in 1964 provides investments wealth management retirement planning and insurance products through an agreement with UVEST (a division of LPL Financial).

FREMONT CONTRACT CARRIERS INC.

865 BUD BLVD
FREMONT, NE 680256270
Phone: 402-721-3020
Fax: –
Web: www.fcc-inc.com

CEO: Michael F Herre
CFO: –
HR: –
FYE: December 31
Type: Private

Truckload carrier Fremont Contract Carriers (FCC) hauls general and non-hazardous freight throughout the US and Canada. Its fleet consists of some 315 trucks 550 high-cubed dry van trailers and 100 flatbed curtain-side and step-deck trailers. The company's FCC Transportation Services unit provides freight brokerage and logistics services in which customers' freight is matched with carriers' capacity. In addition to offering traditional trucking services the company provides online load tracking and reporting on its Web site. FCC was founded in 1966.

	Annual Growth	12/09	12/10	12/11	12/12	12/13
Sales ($ mil.)	9.9%	–	55.0	61.0	67.6	73.1
Net income ($ mil.)	–	–	–	0.2	0.3	(0.4)
Market value ($ mil.)	–	–	–	–	–	–
Employees	–	–	–	–	–	91

FREQUENCY ELECTRONICS INC

NMS: FEIM

55 Charles Lindbergh Blvd.
Mitchel Field, NY 11553
Phone: 516 794-4500
Fax: 516 794-4340
Web: www.frequencyelectronics.com

CEO: Martin B Bloch
CFO: Alan Miller
HR: –
FYE: April 30
Type: Public

Frequency Electronics Inc. (FEI) lets the good times roll. The company makes quartz- rubidium- and cesium-based time and frequency control products such as oscillators and amplifiers used to synchronize voice data and video transmissions in satellite and wireless communications. The US military uses its products for navigation communications surveillance and timing systems in aircraft satellites radar and missiles. Though FEI has diversified into commercial markets nearly half of its sales still come from the US government. Other top clients include AT&T Lockheed Martin Northrop Grumman and Thales Alenia Space. The company was formed in 1961 as a time and frequency control R&D firm.

	Annual Growth	04/11	04/12	04/13	04/14	04/15
Sales ($ mil.)	9.5%	53.2	63.6	68.9	71.6	76.6
Net income ($ mil.)	(17.2%)	6.0	7.4	3.7	4.0	2.8
Market value ($ mil.)	6.5%	89.4	66.1	87.2	92.2	115.2
Employees	5.3%	350	420	420	430	430

FRESH CHOICE LLC

8371 Central Ave. Ste. A
Newark CA 94560
Phone: 510-857-1230
Fax: 510-857-1269
Web: www.freshchoice.com

CEO: –
CFO: David E Pertl
HR: Joan Miller
FYE: December 31
Type: Private

It's actually good for you to belly-up to this bar. Fresh Choice owns and operates about 30 salad bar eateries mostly located in Northern California featuring tossed and prepared salads along with more than 40 ingredients and toppings. In addition to greens the restaurants offer soup pasta pizza and dessert items as well as breads and muffins. Fresh Choice's restaurants operate primarily under its signature brand; it also has a Zoopa location a small number of units branded with Starbucks and Fresh Choice Express quick-service satellite locations. The management-owned company is backed by Crescent Real Estate Equities and California-based frozen foods maker Cedarlane Natural Foods.

FRESH ENTERPRISES LLC

5900A Katella Ave. Ste. 101
Cypress CA 90630
Phone: 562-391-2400
Fax: 441-295-4605
Web: www.platinumre.com

CEO: -
CFO: -
HR: -
FYE: December 31
Type: Private

This company thinks it has a fresh take on fast food. Fresh Enterprises operates and franchises more than 250 Baja Fresh Mexican Grill fast-casual restaurants mostly in California and about 20 other states. The chain's menu features made-to-order burritos and tacos as well as quesadillas nachos and salads. Founded in 1990 Baja Fresh is known for using fresh ingredients without fillers and eschewing freezers and microwaves. In addition to its flagship chain Fresh Enterprises oversees the La Salsa Fresh Mexican Grill chain and Canyons Burger Company. An investment group led by David Kim owns the company.

FRESH MARK INC.

1888 SOUTHWAY ST SE
MASSILLON, OH 44648
Phone: 330-834-3669
Fax: -
Web: www.freshmark.com

CEO: Neil Genshaft
CFO: David Cochenour
HR: -
FYE: January 01
Type: Private

This company continues to make its mark in the processed meat market. Fresh Mark is a leading producer of smoked and processed meat products for the domestic and international retail and foodservice industries. From its three plants in Ohio the company makes and markets such products as deli meats hot dogs lunch meats hams and bacon sold under the names Superior's Brand and Sugardale. The company also produces private-label processed meat products for others and supplies the foodservice industry through its Sugardale Food Service business. Founded in 1920 Fresh Mark is owned and operated by the Genshaft family.

	Annual Growth	12/04	12/05	12/06	12/07*	01/11
Sales ($ mil.)	8.7%	-	481.7	481.5	534.6	795.7
Net income ($ mil.)	22.3%	-	-	21.7	31.0	59.5
Market value ($ mil.)	-	-	-	-	-	-
Employees	-	-	-	-	-	2,300

*Fiscal year change

FRESH MARKET, INC.

NMS: TFM

628 Green Valley Road, Suite 500
Greensboro, NC 27408
Phone: 336 272-1338
Fax: -
Web: www.thefreshmarket.com

CEO: -
CFO: Jeffrey C Ackerman
HR: Matt Argano
FYE: January 25
Type: Public

When it comes to food fresh is best. The Fresh Market operates about 160 full-service upscale specialty grocery stores in some 25 US states from Florida to Wisconsin. As the name suggests the chain specializes in perishable goods (two-thirds of sales) including fruits and vegetables meat and seafood. The stores average 21000 square feet about a third to half the size of a conventional supermarket. However customers won't find the nonfood items sold in most grocery stores these days such as cleaning and cooking supplies. Founded by husband-and-wife team Ray and Beverly Berry who opened their first store in 1982 The Fresh Market which went public in 2010 is expanding in the Southeast.

	Annual Growth	01/11	01/12	01/13	01/14	01/15
Sales ($ mil.)	117.6%	78.1	1,108.0	1,329.1	1,511.7	1,753.2
Net income ($ mil.)	120.6%	2.7	51.4	64.1	50.8	63.0
Market value ($ mil.)	1.5%	1,756.2	2,165.1	2,305.4	1,748.4	1,864.1
Employees	14.2%	7,300	8,500	10,000	11,700	12,400

FRESHPOINT INC.

1390 Enclave Pkwy.
Houston TX 77077-2025
Phone: 281-584-1390
Fax: 281-584-1188
Web: www.freshpoint.com

CEO: Robert Gordon
CFO: -
HR: -
FYE: June 30
Type: Subsidiary

Fresh produce is the ingredient for success at FreshPoint. The company is one of the largest foodservice distributors of fresh fruits and vegetables in North America. Its operations span more than 30 distribution centers in the US and Canada. In addition to produce the company offers some fresh dairy items as well as value-added and fancy foods. It targets regional and national foodservice customers in such markets as catering healthcare hospitality restaurants and schools. FreshPoint also supplies certain retail grocery stores and other wholesale suppliers. The company is a subsidiary of foodservice titan SYSCO. Although increasing in importance fresh produce generates less than 10% of SYSCO's sales.

FRIED FRANK HARRIS SHRIVER & JACOBSON LLP

1 New York Plaza
New York NY 10004-1980
Phone: 212-859-8000
Fax: 212-859-4000
Web: www.friedfrank.com

CEO: -
CFO: -
HR: -
FYE: February 28
Type: Private - Partnershi

Known for its mergers and acquisitions practice law firm Fried Frank Harris Shriver & Jacobson also offers expertise in such fields as bankruptcy intellectual property litigation real estate and securities regulations. The firm serves as counsel to many of the world's largest companies financial institutions and investment firms. Clients have included such big names as Bank of America Deutsche Bank Dow Jones Thomson Reuters Goldman Sachs and Credit Suisse. Fried Frank has more than 500 lawyers. The modern Fried Frank was formed in 1971 but the firm traces its roots to law practices that began early in the 1900s.

FRIEDMAN INDUSTRIES, INC.

ASE: FRD

19747 Hwy. 59 N., Suite 200
Humble, TX 77338
Phone: 713 672-9433
Fax: -
Web: www.friedmanindustries.com

CEO: William E. (Bill) Crow
CFO: -
HR: -
FYE: March 31
Type: Public

Steel processor Friedman Industries operates in two business segments: coil products and tubular products. The company's Texas Tubular Products unit the larger of Friedman Industries' segments buys pipe and coil material and processes it for use in pipelines oil and gas drilling and piling and structural applications. Friedman Industries' coil products unit purchases hot-rolled steel coils and processes them into sheet and plate products. The company's XSCP unit sells surplus prime secondary and transition steel coils. Friedman Industries' processing facilities are located near mills operated by U.S. Steel and Nucor Corp. and work closely with both facilities.

	Annual Growth	03/11	03/12	03/13	03/14	03/15
Sales ($ mil.)	(4.8%)	131.7	161.5	136.4	116.1	108.3
Net income ($ mil.)	(53.5%)	8.2	8.2	6.1	1.7	0.4
Market value ($ mil.)	(11.7%)	69.3	74.5	67.7	57.3	42.2
Employees	0.0%	100	100	100	100	100

FRIENDFINDER NETWORKS INC
NBB: FFNT Q

6800 Broken Sound Parkway, Suite 200　　　　　CEO: -
Boca Raton, FL 33487　　　　　　　　　　　　　CFO: -
Phone: 561 912-7000　　　　　　　　　　　　　HR: -
Fax: -　　　　　　　　　　　　　　　　　FYE: December 31
Web: www.ffn.com　　　　　　　　　　　　　Type: Public

If you're looking for friendship try knocking on some doors below the penthouse. FriendFinder Networks (publisher of the venerable adult magazine Penthouse and producer of adult video content and images) now owns and operates some 38000 social networking websites including Adult-FriendFinder.com Amigos.com AsiaFriendFinder.com Cams.com FriendFinder.com BigChurch.com and SeniorFriendFinder.com. In total its sites are offered to about 528 million members in more than 200 countries. FriendFinder also distributes original pictorial and video content and engages in brand licensing. It emerged from Chapter 11 bankruptcy protection in late 2013 returning control to company founder Andrew Conru.

	Annual Growth	12/09	12/10	12/11	12/12	12/13
Sales ($ mil.)	(4.6%)	327.7	346.0	331.3	314.4	271.4
Net income ($ mil.)	-	(41.2)	(43.2)	(31.1)	(49.4)	175.2
Market value ($ mil.)	(20.0%)	-	-	0.5	0.4	-
Employees	(8.3%)	-	407	692	342	-

FRIENDLY'S ICE CREAM LLC

1855 Boston Rd.　　　　　　　　　　　　　CEO: John M Maguire
Wilbraham MA 01095　　　　　　　　　CFO: Todd Schwendenmann
Phone: 413-731-4000　　　　　　　　　　　HR: David Weaver
Fax: 413-731-4471　　　　　　　　　　　FYE: December 31
Web: www.friendlys.com　　　　　　　　　　　Type: Private

Screaming ice cream lovers can soothe their pipes at Friendly's. Friendly's Ice Cream operates a chain of some 380 family-style restaurants in 15 states that specialize in frozen dairy treats. In addition to ice cream the restaurants serve breakfast lunch and dinner — mostly traditional American fare such as sandwiches and burgers. More than half of the chain's locations are franchised. Friendly's also distributes ice cream and other frozen desserts through supermarkets and other retail sites. The company filed for Chapter 11 bankruptcy protection in late 2011 and emerged early in 2012 after closing about 20% of its locations.

FRISBIE MEMORIAL HOSPITAL

11 WHITEHALL RD　　　　　　　　　　　　CEO: John Marzinzik
ROCHESTER, NH 038673297　　　　　　　　　　　　CFO: -
Phone: 603-332-3100　　　　　　　　　　　　　HR: -
Fax: -　　　　　　　　　　　　　　　　　FYE: September 30
Web: www.frisbiehospital.com　　　　　　　　　Type: Private

Frisbie Memorial Hospital hopes to maintain a high-flying reputation as it serves southeastern New Hampshire and southern Maine. The acute-care facility has nearly 90 beds and about 250 physicians on staff. The not-for-profit community hospital offers patients a variety of services including emergency radiology cardiology neurology and respiratory and surgical care. Frisbie Memorial also operates outpatient and primary medical care facilities and it provides oncology services through a partnership with the Dartmouth-Hitchcock Medical Center in Lebanon New Hampshire.

	Annual Growth	09/10	09/11	09/12	09/13	09/14
Sales ($ mil.)	(1.0%)	-	130.5	123.3	124.1	126.4
Net income ($ mil.)	-	-	-	(0.3)	4.3	0.5
Market value ($ mil.)	-	-	-	-	-	-
Employees	-	-	-	-	-	900

FRISCH'S RESTAURANTS, INC.
ASE: FRS

2800 Gilbert Avenue　　　　　　　　　　　　CEO: Aziz Hashim
Cincinnati, OH 45206　　　　　　　　　　　　　CFO: -
Phone: 513 961-2660　　　　　　　　　　HR: Barb Duermit
Fax: -　　　　　　　　　　　　　　　　　　FYE: June 03
Web: www.frischs.com　　　　　　　　　　　Type: Public

Buddie Boy Big Boy Super Big Boy Brawny Lad — Frisch's burger menu reads like an arm-wrestling contest marquee. Frisch's Restaurants operates and licenses about 95 Frisch's Big Boy family-style restaurants in Indiana Kentucky and Ohio (25 locations are operated by licensees) targeting the family-dining segment. Famous for its double-decker hamburgers the Big Boy chain also offers chicken roast beef pasta and seafood dinners as well as a breakfast bar that converts to a soup and salad bar at lunch. President and CEO Craig Maier owns about 25% of the company.

	Annual Growth	06/10*	05/11	05/12	05/13*	06/14
Sales ($ mil.)	(8.1%)	292.9	303.5	205.1	203.7	209.2
Net income ($ mil.)	(1.4%)	10.0	9.5	2.1	6.8	9.4
Market value ($ mil.)	3.1%	106.4	110.8	140.7	87.4	120.1
Employees	(7.7%)	8,400	8,400	6,050	5,860	6,100

*Fiscal year change

FRITO-LAY NORTH AMERICA INC.

7701 Legacy Dr.　　　　　　　　　　　　　CEO: Albert P Carey
Plano TX 75024　　　　　　　　　　　　　　　CFO: -
Phone: 972-334-7000　　　　　　　　　　　　　HR: -
Fax: 972-334-2019　　　　　　　　　　　FYE: December 31
Web: www.fritolay.com　　　　　　　　　　　Type: Subsidiary

Frito-Lay is the undisputed chip champ of North America. The company makes some of the best-known and top-selling savory snacks around including Cheetos Doritos Lay's Ruffles SunChips and Tostitos. On the sweet side Frito-Lay also makes Grandma's cookies Funyuns onion-flavored rings Cracker Jack candy-coated popcorn and Smartfood popcorn. It also makes a line of chips made with the fat substitute Olestra under the Light brand name. Owned by PepsiCo Frito-Lay North America's operations span the US and Canada and account for about a quarter of the soda maker's sales. Frito-Lay's Mexican sales are reported within PepsiCo's Latin America Foods segment.

FROEDTERT MEMORIAL LUTHERAN HOSPITAL INC

9200 W WISCONSIN AVE　　　　　　　　　CEO: William Petasnick
MILWAUKEE, WI 532263522　　　　　　　　　　　CFO: -
Phone: 414-805-3000　　　　　　　　　　　　　HR: -
Fax: -　　　　　　　　　　　　　　　　　　FYE: June 30
Web: www.froedtert.com　　　　　　　　　　　Type: Private

Patients in southeastern Wisconsin count on Froedtert Memorial Lutheran Hospital for a full range of health services including trauma transplant sports medicine and senior care. The 500-bed hospital also known as Froedtert & The Medical College of Wisconsin is part of the Froedtert (pronounced "fray-dert") Health system. Specialty units include cancer dermatology neuroscience birthing fertility urology and vein clinics. The hospital also serves as a teaching facility for the Medical College of Wisconsin and it partners with the Children's Hospital of Wisconsin to provide pediatric services. Froedtert Hospital which was founded in 1980 operates the only adult Level I trauma center in the region.

	Annual Growth	06/08	06/09	06/10	06/11	06/12
Sales ($ mil.)	9.3%	-	810.3	894.4	980.4	1,057.4
Net income ($ mil.)	30.7%	-	-	59.7	79.1	101.8
Market value ($ mil.)	-	-	-	-	-	-
Employees	-	-	-	-	-	3,459

FRONTIER AIRLINES INC.

7001 Tower Rd.
Denver CO 80249-7312
Phone: 720-374-4200
Fax: 720-374-4175
Web: www.frontierairlines.com

CEO: David N Siegel
CFO: –
HR: –
FYE: December 31
Type: Subsidiary

Faster than covered wagons Frontier Airlines' planes part the clouds and fly the skies above the Rockies and beyond. The company operates as a scheduled passenger air carrier from hubs at Denver International and Milwaukee's General Mitchell International Airport. The airline maintains a fleet of about 60 Airbus 318/319/320 jets with onboard amenities that include satellite and roughly 20 Embraer E170/190 jet aircraft. Along with subsidiary Lynx Aviation it serves about 80 destinations in the US west of the Mississippi and less so Mexico and Costa Rica. In 2008 Frontier Airlines entered Chapter 11 bankruptcy protection. It emerged in 2009 after it was acquired by Republic Airways for about $109 million.

FRONTIER COMMUNICATIONS CORP   NMS: FTR

401 Merritt 7
Norwalk, CT 06851
Phone: 203 614-5600
Fax: 203 614-4602
Web: www.frontier.com

CEO: Daniel J. McCarthy
CFO: John M. Jureller
HR: Cecilia K. McKenney
FYE: December 31
Type: Public

Serving city dwellers and country folk alike Frontier Communications provides phone Internet and satellite TV (through a partnership with DISH Network) services across 28 US states. The company has some 7.5 million residential and business voice subscribers. It also has 4.5 million broadband Internet customers and about 1.8 million video subscribers. Frontier is active mostly in rural and small to mid-sized markets where it is the incumbent local-exchange carrier (ILEC). The company's top four markets in terms of subscribers are West Virginia Illinois Indiana and New York. The company's 2015 acquisition of Verizon's wireline operations for $10.5 billion substantially expanded Frontier's footprint.

	Annual Growth	12/10	12/11	12/12	12/13	12/14
Sales ($ mil.)	5.9%	3,797.7	5,243.0	5,011.9	4,761.6	4,772.5
Net income ($ mil.)	(3.4%)	152.7	149.6	136.6	112.8	132.9
Market value ($ mil.)	(9.0%)	9,754.0	5,162.7	4,290.6	4,661.5	6,686.5
Employees	4.1%	14,800	15,400	14,700	13,650	17,400

FRONTIER OILFIELD SERVICES INC.   PINK SHEETS: TBXC

3030 LBJ Freeway Ste. 1320
Dallas TX 75234
Phone: 972-243-2613
Fax: 972-243-2066
Web: www.tbxresources.com

CEO: Donald Ray Lawhorne
CFO: –
HR: –
FYE: November 30
Type: Public

Frontier Oilfield Services (formerly TBX Resources) has switched from exploring for and producing natural gas to providing oilfield services to other companies that do. Frontier Oilfield Services now focuses on saltwater and drilling fluid disposal services for oil and gas producers and operators in East Texas. The company is targeting the Haynesville share area where it believes as many as 35000 additional wells will be drilled by 2023. Frontier currently manages the operations of Trinity Disposal and Trucking which owns saltwater disposal wells and a fleet of trucks and trailers and is seeking to buy the service. In 2012 it bought salt water disposal firm Chico Coffman Tank Trucks for $17 million.

FRONTIER TECHNOLOGY LLC

8160 S. Hardy Dr. Ste. 101
Tempe AZ 85284
Phone: 480-366-2000
Fax: 480-366-2224
Web: www.microage.com

CEO: –
CFO: Roger Rouse
HR: –
FYE: October 31
Type: Private

From its pioneering outpost in Arizona Frontier Technology knows no boundaries when it comes to supplying the right technology. Doing business as MicroAge the company sells a wide range of computing products primarily to small and midsized organizations including hospitals schools and local governments. It offers products such as PCs networking equipment software servers storage systems displays printers and copiers and power supply products. MicroAge also offers its customers technical assistance in selecting products and vendors that best suit their needs. The family-led company is controlled by co-founder and chairman Jeff McKeever; his son Mark is also an officer.

FRONTRANGE SOLUTIONS INC.

5675 Gibraltar Dr.
Pleasanton CA 94588
Phone: 925-398-1800
Fax: 719-536-0620
Web: www.frontrange.com

CEO: Jon Temple
CFO: Kevin Thompson
HR: –
FYE: June 30
Type: Private

FrontRange Solutions has a GoldMine for customer relationship management. Customers use its GoldMine software to maintain customer contacts and automate sales marketing scheduling and project management functions. Its HEAT software offers help desk ticket processing reporting and analysis. FrontRange also provides a VoIP telephone system that integrates with its software. Other offerings include hosted versions of its help desk service management and asset management software and a Web-based services catalog that functions like a shopping cart. FrontRange primarily targets small and midsized businesses. It has customers in some 45 countries. Private equity firm Francisco Partners bought FrontRange in 2005.

FROST BROWN TODD LLC

3300 Great American Tower 301 E. 4th St.
Cincinnati OH 45202
Phone: 513-651-6800
Fax: 513-651-6981
Web: www.frostbrowntodd.com

CEO: –
CFO: –
HR: –
FYE: December 31
Type: Private - Partnershi

Middle America deserves a top law firm. Frost Brown Todd's more than 450 attorneys practice business law across nine offices in Ohio Kentucky Indiana Tennessee and West Virginia. Areas of specialty include corporate mergers tax law subprime lending environmental law financial restructuring intellectual property technology issues arbitration and antitrust litigation. It has conducted legal work for such high-profile clients as Ford Motor Company Toyota Motor Manufacturing General Electric and E.W. Scripps Co. The firm was created by the 2000 merger of Kentucky law firm Brown Todd & Heyburn with Ohio's Frost & Jacobs. It traces the roots of its legacy firms back to 1917.

FROZEN SPECIALTIES INC.

8600 S WILKINSON WAY G　　　　　　　　　　　　CEO: Daniel Bender
PERRYSBURG, OH 43551-2598　　　　　　　　　　CFO: Gary Swartzbeck
Phone: 419-445-9015　　　　　　　　　　　　　　HR: -
Fax: -　　　　　　　　　　　　　　　　　　　　　FYE: June 26
Web: www.frozenspecialties.com　　　　　　　　Type: Private

Frozen Specialties' specialty arena lies in frozen pizza pies. The company makes private-label frozen pizzas (in value-priced lean and microwaveable variations) and a frozen pizza-flavored snack called Pizza Bites for the North American convenience and grocery store markets. Its pizzas are primarily sold under store-brand names at major grocery chains. Frozen Specialties Inc. (also known as FSI) is a top player in the frozen pizza industry and produces more than 100 million pizzas every year. Investment firm Swander Pace Capital is the majority owner of Frozen Specialties.

	Annual Growth	06/01	06/02	06/03	06/04	06/11
Sales ($ mil.)	(2.5%)	-	-	-	67.0	56.2
Net income ($ mil.)	-	-	-	-	0.0	(1.1)
Market value ($ mil.)	-	-	-	-	-	-
Employees	-	-	-	-	-	140

FRP HOLDINGS INC　　　　　　　　　　　　NMS: FRPH

200 W. Forsyth St., 7th Floor　　　　　　　　　CEO: -
Jacksonville, FL 32202　　　　　　　　　　　　CFO: John D Milton Jr
Phone: 904 396-5733　　　　　　　　　　　　　HR: Jeffrey (Jeff) Anthony
Fax: -　　　　　　　　　　　　　　　　　　　　FYE: September 30
Web: www.frpholdings.com　　　　　　　　　　Type: Public

Patriot Transportation Holding has plenty of tanks but hasn't fired a shot. The company's Transportation segment comprising Florida Rock & Tank Lines subsidiary transports liquid and dry bulk commodities mainly petroleum (including ethanol) and chemicals in tank trucks. Patriot Transportation's combined fleet of about 435 trucks and 530 trailers operates primarily in the southeastern and mid-Atlantic US. The company's Real Estate unit comprising Florida Rock Properties and FRP Development owns office and warehouse properties as well as sand and gravel deposits on the East Coast that are leased to Vulcan Materials Company.

	Annual Growth	09/11	09/12	09/13	09/14	09/15
Sales ($ mil.)	(26.7%)	120.1	127.5	139.8	160.1	34.6
Net income ($ mil.)	(9.3%)	12.2	7.8	15.4	10.0	8.3
Market value ($ mil.)	10.5%	197.9	273.0	331.3	332.1	295.1
Employees	(61.3%)	802	828	886	957	18

FRU-CON CONSTRUCTION CORPORATION

4310 Prince William Pkwy. Ste. 200　　　　　CEO: -
Woodbridge VA 22192-5199　　　　　　　　　CFO: -
Phone: 703-586-6100　　　　　　　　　　　　HR: -
Fax: 703-586-6101　　　　　　　　　　　　　FYE: December 31
Web: www.frucon.com　　　　　　　　　　　Type: Subsidiary

Fru-Con Construction is an engineering and construction firm that offers services from design through procurement construction start-up and maintenance. It targets the environmental heavy industrial and government and institutional facilities markets. With the search for alternative and cleaner burning fuels in the forefront of energy concerns the company has also been active in building new plants capable of satisfying some of those needs. Founded in 1872 by Jeremiah Fruin Fru-Con Construction was bought by Bilfinger Berger in 1984. Balfour Beatty Infrastructure acquired it from the German company in 2011.

FRUIT GROWERS SUPPLY COMPANY INC

14130 RIVERSIDE DR　　　　　　　　　　　　CEO: Mark H Lindgren
SHERMAN OAKS, CA 914232313　　　　　　　CFO: Charles Boyce
Phone: 805-933-2723　　　　　　　　　　　　HR: Greg Cook
Fax: -　　　　　　　　　　　　　　　　　　　FYE: December 31
Web: www.fruitgrowers.com　　　　　　　　　Type: Private

Shipping cartons are the real fruit of labor for Fruit Growers Supply (FSG). The non-profit cooperative association supplies affiliate Sunkist Growers and other agricultural businesses with packing materials fertilizer and related implements. Offerings include a range of equipment used to grow pick package and transport many commodity cash crops. FSG also provides packing services and custom design and installation of irrigation systems. It owns and operates some 335000 acres of timberland along the West coast (a source of box material and income) a carton manufacturing and supply plant and seven retail operations centers. FGS is owned by 6000-plus citrus growers and shippers in the US.

	Annual Growth	12/09	12/10	12/11	12/12	12/13
Sales ($ mil.)	10.4%	-	151.4	177.2	179.6	203.6
Net income ($ mil.)	(8.0%)	-	-	6.8	6.8	5.8
Market value ($ mil.)	-	-	-	-	-	-
Employees	-	-	-	-	-	240

FRUIT OF THE LOOM INC.

1 Fruit of the Loom Dr.　　　　　　　　　　　CEO: -
Bowling Green KY 42103　　　　　　　　　　CFO: Richard C Price
Phone: 270-781-6400　　　　　　　　　　　　HR: Russell Dewberry
Fax: 270-781-6588　　　　　　　　　　　　　FYE: December 31
Web: www.fruit.com　　　　　　　　　　　　Type: Subsidiary

Fruit of the Loom wants to be in everyone's drawers. Besides the basics — underwear made under the BVD Fruit of the Loom and Lofteez names — its products include activewear casualwear and children's underwear sold under such labels as Russell Funpals Fungals and Underoos (with licensed characters). Its items are sold primarily in North America through discount and mass merchandisers the likes of Wal-Mart and Target as well as to department stores wholesale clubs and screen printers. Fruit of the Loom owned by Berkshire Hathaway enjoys the largest market share for branded men's and boy's underwear and its Russell Athletic unit leads in team uniforms.

FRUTH INC.

4016 OHIO RIVER RD　　　　　　　　　　　　CEO: -
POINT PLEASANT, WV 255503257　　　　　　CFO: Bob Messick
Phone: 304-675-1612　　　　　　　　　　　　HR: -
Fax: -　　　　　　　　　　　　　　　　　　　FYE: June 30
Web: www.fruthpharmacy.com　　　　　　　Type: Private

Fruth Pharmacy operates about 25 drugstores in southern Ohio and West Virginia. While prescriptions account for the majority of sales Fruth pharmacies also sell gift items and computer supplies and have floral departments and digital printing. The regional drugstore chain competes by constantly trying new things such as participating in the Face2Face diabetes program and testing in-store dollar departments. It is countering Wal-Mart Stores's $4 generic offering with a discount generic drug program created by Cardinal Health. Founded in 1952 by its namesake — the late Jack Fruth — the company is family-owned and -operated.

	Annual Growth	06/05	06/06	06/07	06/08	06/09
Sales ($ mil.)	1.3%	-	128.7	136.0	135.7	133.7
Net income ($ mil.)	-	-	-	0.3	0.9	(0.5)
Market value ($ mil.)	-	-	-	-	-	-
Employees	-	-	-	-	-	545

FRY'S ELECTRONICS INC.

600 E. Brokaw Rd.
San Jose CA 95112
Phone: 408-487-4500
Fax: 408-487-4741
Web: www.frys.com

CEO: John Charles Fry
CFO: David Fry
HR: –
FYE: December 31
Type: Private

Trying to catalog all the products this superstore carries could fry your brain. Fry's Electronics is a top big-box retailer of computers consumer electronics and appliances with some 35 stores in about 10 states. The chain's extensive inventory includes computer software and components industry magazines movies and music refrigerators washers and dryers small appliances stereo equipment and televisions. Each store also typically stocks a variety of snacks and other impulse items. The technogeek's dream store began in 1985 as the brainchild of CEO John Fry (with brothers Randy and Dave) and VP Kathy Kolder. The Fry brothers who got their start at Fry's Food and Drug Stores still own the company.

FRY'S FOOD AND DRUG STORES

500 S. 99th Ave.
Tolleson AZ 85353
Phone: 623-936-2100
Fax: 623-907-1910
Web: www.frysfood.com

CEO: Dennis R Hood
CFO: Ron Schuster
HR: –
FYE: January 31
Type: Subsidiary

Fry's Food Stores operates about 100 supermarkets under the Fry's Food Stores and Fry's Mercado banners mostly in Phoenix but also in Tucson and Prescott Arizona. The grocery store chain also also operates about two dozen Fry's Marketplace stores large (up to 120000 sq. ft.) multi-department stores that offer full-service grocery and pharmacy departments as well as expanded general merchandise electronics home goods and toy sections. In addition to traditional supermarket fare many Fry's stores have in-store pharmacies and offer full-service banking through Kroger Personal Finance. Fry's is owned by The Kroger Co. the #1 pure grocery chain in the US.

FS BANCORP INC

NAS: FSBW

6920 220th Street SW
Mountlake Terrace, WA 98043
Phone: 425 771-5299
Fax: –
Web: www.fsbwa.com

CEO: Joseph C Adams
CFO: Matthew D Mullet
HR: –
FYE: December 31
Type: Public

FS Bancorp is the holding company for 1st Security Bank of Washington which operates six branches in the Puget Sound region. The bank provides standard deposit products such as checking and savings accounts CDs and IRAs to area businesses and consumers. Its lending activities are focused on consumer loans (more than half of its portfolio) including home improvement boat and automobile loans. The bank also writes business and construction loans and commercial and residential mortgages. FS Bancorp went public via in initial public offering in 2012.

	Annual Growth	12/10	12/11	12/12	12/13	12/14
Assets ($ mil.)	–	0.0	283.8	359.0	419.2	509.8
Net income ($ mil.)	–	0.0	1.5	5.3	3.9	4.5
Market value ($ mil.)	–	0.0	–	42.0	55.5	59.1
Employees	26.6%	–	–	131	160	210

FTD COMPANIES INC

NMS: FTD

3113 Woodcreek Drive
Downers Grove, IL 60515
Phone: 630 719-7800
Fax: –
Web: www.ftd.com

CEO: Robert S. (Rob) Apatoff
CFO: Becky A. Sheehan
HR: Megan Hayes
FYE: December 31
Type: Public

Mercury the Roman god of speed and commerce with winged feet (and an icon for megaflorist FTD) comes bearing flowers. FTD Group is the holding company for operating subsidiaries FTD.COM and FTD Inc. established in 1910 as the Florists' Telegraph Delivery Association by a group of 15 florists. Besides flowers the company offers plants gourmet foods and gift baskets to a variety of customers including consumers retailers and more than 40000 florist shops in the US Canada and the UK and under the brand Interflora in Ireland. FTD was spun off into a publicly traded company in 2013; it owns online floral and gift company Provide Commerce.

	Annual Growth	12/10	12/11	12/12	12/13	12/14
Sales ($ mil.)	3.7%	554.6	587.2	613.5	627.3	640.5
Net income ($ mil.)	36.3%	6.6	15.7	21.2	12.5	22.8
Market value ($ mil.)	6.9%	–	–	–	951.1	1,016.5
Employees	44.0%	–	–	871	941	1,807

FTI CONSULTING INC.

NYS: FCN

1101 K Street N.W.
Washington, DC 20005
Phone: 202 312-9100
Fax: –
Web: www.fticonsulting.com

CEO: Jack B. Dunn
CFO: Roger D. Carlile
HR: –
FYE: December 31
Type: Public

When someone has been cooking the books FTI Consulting has a recipe for recovery. The company is one of the leading providers of consulting services related to corporate finance and restructuring (through FD International and other units). It also offers forensic accounting litigation support and investigative services to companies confronted with problems fraud in order to assist them in their legal defense or pursuit of recoveries. Other consulting service areas include economics strategic and financial communications and technology. FTI's main clients are large business enterprises and major law firms. The business was established in 1982.

	Annual Growth	12/10	12/11	12/12	12/13	12/14
Sales ($ mil.)	5.8%	1,401.5	1,566.8	1,576.9	1,652.4	1,756.2
Net income ($ mil.)	(4.9%)	71.9	103.9	(37.0)	(10.6)	58.8
Market value ($ mil.)	0.9%	1,535.2	1,746.9	1,359.0	1,694.2	1,590.8
Employees	5.7%	3,527	3,817	3,915	4,207	4,404

FTS INTERNATIONAL INC.

777 Main St. Ste. 3000
Fort Worth TX 76102
Phone: 817-862-2000
Fax: 817-339-3640
Web: www.fractech.net

CEO: Greg A Lanham
CFO: Royce Mitchell
HR: –
FYE: December 31
Type: Private

FTS International (formerly Frac Tech Services) has found a way to mix oil and water. The company helps US oil and gas firms make the most of their older assets by releasing tough-to-recover petroleum through hydraulic fracturing a process which pumps a proprietary solution of sand and water into shale reservoirs to release oil and gas. FTS International runs 33 fracturing units (1.4 million horsepower) in the shale basins of Louisiana Texas Pennsylvania West Virginia and New Mexico. It also owns sand mining and processing operations that supply most of its primary raw material. In 2011 the company was acquired by a Temasek Holdings-led consortium and reorganized as FTS International.

FUBU THE COLLECTION LLC

350 5th Ave. Ste. 6617
New York NY 10118
Phone: 212-273-3300
Fax: 212-273-3333
Web: www.fubu.com

CEO: –
CFO: –
HR: –
FYE: December 31
Type: Private

Urban youth and youthful are down with FUBU's hip-hop inspired sportswear. Besides making sportswear FUBU (an acronym for "for us by us") also licenses its name for men's women's and children's wear as well as footwear and accessories such as watches eyewear caps and bags. The company also offers a line of suits athletic shoes tuxedos and housewares (sheets and pillows in university colors). Its collections are named FUBU and Platinum FUBU which includes the Fat Albert and Harlem Globetrotters clothing lines. The apparel maker which is expanding rapidly in Asia boasts about 100 franchised stores worldwide. Founders Daymond John Alexander Martin Carl Brown and Keith Perrin own FUBU.

FUEL SYSTEMS SOLUTIONS INC   NMS: FSYS

780 Third Avenue, 25th Floor
New York, NY 10017
Phone: 646 502-7170
Fax: –
Web: www.fuelsystemssolutions.com

CEO: Mariano Costamagna
CFO: Pietro Bersani
HR: –
FYE: December 31
Type: Public

Fuel Systems Solutions was going green before green was the way to go. Founded in 1957 the holding company operates through two subsidiaries BRC and IMPCO Technologies as a designer and manufacturer of alternative fuel components that allow engines in vehicles and industrial equipment to operate on cleaner burning gaseous fuels such as propane and compressed natural gas (CNG). BRC's customers include some of the world's largest automotive OEMs and IMPCO's customers include some of the leading engine OEMs. Products include fuel injectors electronic controls compressors and auxiliary power systems. The group also offers services ranging from system integration to environmental certification.

	Annual Growth	12/10	12/11	12/12	12/13	12/14
Sales ($ mil.)	(5.8%)	430.6	418.1	393.9	399.8	339.1
Net income ($ mil.)	–	39.7	5.2	(15.6)	(0.5)	(53.4)
Market value ($ mil.)	(21.9%)	580.8	326.0	290.8	274.2	216.3
Employees	(1.6%)	1,600	1,700	1,700	1,700	1,500

FUEL TECH INC   NMS: FTEK

27601 Bella Vista Parkway
Warrenville, IL 60555-1617
Phone: 630 845-4500
Fax: –
Web: www.ftek.com

CEO: Vincent J Arnone
CFO: David S Collins
HR: –
FYE: December 31
Type: Public

Fuel Tech develops technologies and products so industrial plants and utilities around the world can run cleanly and efficiently. The company's air pollution control systems segment offers nitrogen oxide reduction products (such as NOxOUT and Over-Fire Air Systems) which reduce nitrogen oxide emissions from boilers incinerators furnaces and other combustion sources. Fuel Tech's technologies are used on more than 700 combustion units including utility industrial and municipal solid waste applications. The company's FUEL CHEM segment develops chemical products used to reduce slag formation and corrosion. Each segment accounts for about half of the company's sales.

	Annual Growth	12/10	12/11	12/12	12/13	12/14
Sales ($ mil.)	(0.9%)	81.8	93.7	97.6	109.3	79.0
Net income ($ mil.)	–	1.8	6.1	2.8	5.1	(17.7)
Market value ($ mil.)	(20.7%)	222.0	150.4	96.0	162.1	87.6
Employees	5.3%	161	168	184	198	198

FUELCELL ENERGY INC   NMS: FCEL

3 Great Pasture Road
Danbury, CT 06810
Phone: 203 825-6000
Fax: –
Web: www.fuelcellenergy.com

CEO: Arthur (Chip) Bottone
CFO: Michael Bishop
HR: Ana Venancia
FYE: October 31
Type: Public

FuelCell Energy engages in fuelish pursuits. Founded in 1969 the company develops electrochemical technologies such as carbonate and planar oxide fuel cells and electrochemical engines which generate electricity without combustion. The company's commercial products include Direct FuelCell (DFC) which does not need an external hydrogen supply and can be fed fuel directly without an external reactor; the equipment can be fired up with biogas coal gas coal-mine methane diesel methanol natural gas or propane. FuelCell Energy operates more than 50 branded DFC Power Plants for government industrial and utility customers around the world. It caters primarily to South Korea and the US.

	Annual Growth	10/11	10/12	10/13	10/14	10/15
Sales ($ mil.)	7.4%	122.6	120.6	187.7	180.3	163.1
Net income ($ mil.)	–	(45.7)	(35.5)	(34.4)	(38.1)	(29.4)
Market value ($ mil.)	(4.6%)	27.8	24.2	34.8	52.4	23.0
Employees	7.1%	471	541	644	640	619

FUELSTREAM, INC.   NBB: FLST

11650 South State Street, Suite 240
Draper, UT 84020
Phone: 801 816-2510
Fax: –
Web: www.thefuelstream.com

CEO: John D Thomas
CFO: –
HR: –
FYE: December 31
Type: Public

Nutty about sports? SportsNuts is a sports management and marketing company that helps sports planners organize amateur sporting events and tournaments. The firm offers online event registration merchandising sponsorship and promotion services. The SportsNuts Web site is a resource for events coordinators coaches athletes and fans to post or obtain relevant information such as schedules statistics and pictures. The company spun off its Web hosting and design subsidiary Synerteck and did the same with Secure Networks which sold computer hardware.

	Annual Growth	12/10	12/11	12/12	12/13	12/14
Sales ($ mil.)	(19.2%)	–	–	1.1	0.0	0.7
Net income ($ mil.)	–	(5.6)	(2.5)	(19.7)	(4.1)	(3.2)
Market value ($ mil.)	–	0.0	0.5	2.8	0.0	0.0
Employees	56.5%	1	2	6	6	6

FUJIFILM MEDICAL SYSTEMS USA INC.

419 West Ave.
Stamford CT 06902
Phone: 203-324-2000
Fax: 203-327-6485
Web: www.fujimed.com

CEO: Naohiro Fujitani
CFO: –
HR: –
FYE: March 31
Type: Subsidiary

FUJIFILM Medical Systems USA knows a picture is worth both a thousand words and a better diagnosis. The company is a leading provider of diagnostic imaging and medical informatics products including digital X-ray systems such as computed radiography (CR) advanced mammography systems and Synapse brand software for analyzing archiving and managing digital images for cardiology and radiology. It markets sells and services these products in the US Puerto Rico and the Caribbean. Other products include conventional X-ray equipment imaging printers and film processors. The company is a wholly-owned subsidiary of FUJIFILM Holdings America itself the US holding subsidiary of Japan's FUJIFILM Holdings.

FUJIFILM NORTH AMERICA CORPORATION

200 Summit Lake Dr. 2nd Fl.
Valhalla NY 10595
Phone: 914-789-8100
Fax: 914-789-8295
Web: www.fujifilmusa.com/northamerica/

CEO: Masato Yamamoto
CFO: –
HR: Joe Convery
FYE: March 31
Type: Subsidiary

Smile you've been captured by FUJIFILM North America a sales and marketing subsidiary of Tokyo's FUJIFILM Holdings. Catering to the US and Canada the business offers cameras film printers and other photographic products and services (such as printing and sharing services for digital pictures). Its customer base includes consumers professional photographers cinematographers and retail photofinishers and processing labs. FUJIFILM North America operates through several divisions including photo imaging electronic imaging motion picture products and graphic systems. Its FUJIFILM Canada subsidiary peddles products north of the US border.

FUJITSU COMPUTER PRODUCTS OF AMERICA INC.

1255 E. Arques Ave.
Sunnyvale CA 94085-4701
Phone: 408-746-7000
Fax: 212-645-8437
Web: www.hnabooks.com

CEO: Etsuro Sato
CFO: Motoyasu Matsuzaki
HR: –
FYE: March 31
Type: Subsidiary

Belying its somewhat over-encompassing name Fujitsu Computer Products of America (FCPA) sells scanners and related software and accessories in only part of one of the Americas. The company a subsidiary of Japanese technology titan Fujitsu Limited is the US distribution arm of the group's document imaging scanner business. Besides distribution sales and marketing it also handles finance and administration in the country as well as engineering and technical support and servicing. FCPA's scanners are sold under two main product lines: the ScanSnap series targeted at consumers and small businesses and the enterprise-level Fi-Series. It also offers the Rack2-Filer document management and editing software.

FUJITSU SEMICONDUCTOR AMERICA INC.

1250 E. Arques Ave. M/S 333
Sunnyvale CA 94085-5401
Phone: 408-737-5600
Fax: 408-737-5999
Web: www.fujitsu.com/us/semiconductors

CEO: Shinichi Machida
CFO: –
HR: –
FYE: March 31
Type: Subsidiary

Fujitsu Semiconductor America (FSA) is the US subsidiary of Japanese electronics giant Fujitsu's Fujitsu Semiconductor. Founded in 1979 FSA offers many types of semiconductors which are used in industries such as automotive industrial medical network connectivity and more. It also offers related manufacturing and packaging services. The company markets its products in North and South America. Among the company's strategic partnerships have been Taiwan Semiconductor Manufacturing semiconductor designer ARM and distributors Digi-Key and Symmetry Electronics.

FULCRUM BIOENERGY INC.

4900 Hopyard Rd. Ste. 220
Pleasanton CA 94588
Phone: 925-730-0150
Fax: 925-730-0157
Web: www.fulcrum-bioenergy.com

CEO: –
CFO: Eric N Pryor
HR: –
FYE: December 31
Type: Private

Fulcrum BioEnergy doesn't let anything go to waste. The development-stage company has a plan to make biofuel out of garbage (garbage!) using a proprietary process to convert solid waste into ethanol thus keeping it out of landfills. (The majority of ethanol produced in the US comes from corn which still takes time and resources to grow and is subject to commodity prices). Fulcrum BioEnergy intends to build a plant that can produce 10 million gallons of ethanol per year using solid waste purchased from Waste Management and Waste Connections. Energy marketer Tenaska has already agreed to sell its ethanol. Fulcrum BioEnergy filed a $115 million IPO in 2011 but withdrew it a year later.

FULL CIRCLE CAPITAL CORP

102 Greenwich Avenue, 2nd Floor
Greenwich, CT 06830
Phone: 203 900-2100
Fax: –
Web: www.fccapital.com

NMS: FULL
CEO: John E Stuart
CFO: Michael J Sell
HR: –
FYE: June 30
Type: Public

Full Circle Capital isn't so much about circles as it is about jagged lines that trend upwards. An investment firm Full Circle Capital invests primarily in senior secured loans for small and lower middle-market companies. The firm typically targets companies in the communications business services and media sectors for investment contributing between $3 million and $10 million per transaction. Its investments help fuel growth and fund capital appreciation among its 20 portfolio companies. Full Circle leaders often sit on portfolio companies' boards and advise on business strategy and other matters. Formed in 2010 Full Circle is externally-managed by investment adviser Full Circle Advisors.

	Annual Growth	06/11	06/12	06/13	06/14	06/15
Sales ($ mil.)	22.2%	8.0	9.8	12.0	13.8	17.7
Net income ($ mil.)	18.7%	4.3	4.8	5.4	6.0	8.6
Market value ($ mil.)	(18.0%)	183.6	177.8	183.6	181.5	83.0
Employees	–	–	–	–	–	–

FULL COMPASS SYSTEMS LTD.

9770 Silicon Prairie Pkwy
Madison WI 53593
Phone: 608-831-7330
Fax: 608-831-6330
Web: www.fullcompass.com

CEO: Jonathan B Lipp
CFO: –
HR: –
FYE: December 31
Type: Private

Church got a brand new big sanctuary that you want to fill with sound? Full Compass Systems can point you in the right direction for a righteous sound system. The company sells more than 700 lines of audio video and lighting equipment for audio/video recording special effects lighting and sound reinforcement via its catalogs. It also offers musical instruments (percussion keyboards and drum machines) along with furniture software and computers needed to complete a theatrical show. Retail rental and warehouse inventory is housed in the company's 140000 square foot facility in Madison Wisconsin. Customers include churches theaters hotels schools and sound studios. Full Compass was founded in 1977.

FULL HOUSE RESORTS, INC.   NAS: FLL

4670 S. Fort Apache Road, Suite 190
Las Vegas, NV 89147
Phone: 702 221-7800
Fax: –
Web: www.fullhouseresorts.com

CEO: Daniel R Lee
CFO: Lewis A Fanger
HR: –
FYE: December 31
Type: Public

When it comes to gaming outside Sin City nothing beats a Full House. Full House Resorts owns Stockman's Casino in Fallon Nevada featuring 260 slot and gaming machines four table games and keno. In addition its Rising Star Casino Resort in Rising Son Indiana includes a riverboat casino with 40000 square feet of gaming space a 200-room hotel a theater and several restaurants. The company also operates the Grand Lodge Casino at the Hyatt Regency Lake Tahoe Resort Spa and Casino in Incline Village Nevada through a five-year lease agreement with Hyat Hotels Corporationt.

	Annual Growth	12/10	12/11	12/12	12/13	12/14
Sales ($ mil.)	38.6%	32.9	105.5	128.8	144.7	121.4
Net income ($ mil.)	–	7.7	2.3	27.8	(4.0)	(20.8)
Market value ($ mil.)	(19.9%)	64.0	49.6	65.1	52.9	26.4
Employees	(11.4%)	2,069	2,508	1,985	1,871	1,274

FULLER (H.B.) COMPANY   NYS: FUL

1200 Willow Lake Boulevard
St. Paul, MN 55110-5101
Phone: 651 236-5900
Fax: 651 236-5161
Web: www.hbfuller.com

CEO: James J. (Jim) Owens
CFO: James R. (Jim) Giertz
HR: Judy Favia
FYE: November 28
Type: Public

H.B. Fuller has "stuck to its knitting" which ironically is glue for more than a century. Long known for making adhesives sealants and specialty chemicals the company markets its products in some 40 countries. Industrial adhesives are its core product offering and customers include companies in the assembly packaging automotive woodworking and nonwoven textiles industries. Other products include construction materials principally ceramic tile installation products (such as grouts mortars and sealers) and HVAC insulating coatings (duct sealants fungicidal coatings and weather barriers).

	Annual Growth	12/11	12/12*	11/13	11/14	11/15
Sales ($ mil.)	7.5%	1,557.6	1,886.2	2,047.0	2,104.5	2,083.7
Net income ($ mil.)	(0.7%)	89.1	125.6	96.8	49.8	86.7
Market value ($ mil.)	15.5%	1,120.2	1,644.9	2,565.3	2,162.7	1,991.5
Employees	5.9%	3,500	3,700	3,700	3,700	4,400

*Fiscal year change

FULLER THEOLOGICAL SEMINARY

135 N OAKLAND AVE
PASADENA, CA 911820002
Phone: 626-584-5200
Fax: –
Web: www.stage.fuller.edu

CEO: –
CFO: –
HR: –
FYE: June 30
Type: Private

Looking for a fuller life experience? Fuller Theological Seminary one of the world's largest multidenominational seminaries offers just that through its schools of theology psychology and intercultural studies. It offers about 20 master's and doctoral degree programs and eight certificate programs to more than 4200 students from more than 70 countries. In addition to its main campus in Pasadena California the seminary operates eight campuses as well as online classes. It also offers degree programs in Spanish and Korean. Fuller Theological Seminary was founded in 1947 by radio evangelist Charles E. Fuller and pastor Harold John Ockenga.

	Annual Growth	06/08	06/09	06/10	06/11	06/13
Sales ($ mil.)	(2.7%)	–	66.8	60.8	70.2	59.9
Net income ($ mil.)	10.4%	–	–	4.6	10.9	6.2
Market value ($ mil.)	–	–	–	–	–	–
Employees	–	–	–	–	–	550

FULLNET COMMUNICATIONS INC   NBB: FULO

201 Robert S. Kerr Avenue, Suite 210
Oklahoma City, OK 73102
Phone: 405 236-8200
Fax: –
Web: www.fullnet.net

CEO: Timothy J Kilkenny
CFO: Roger P Baresel
HR: –
FYE: December 31
Type: Public

FullNet Communications is trying to net as many Oklahoma Internet users as possible. Established in 1995 the company provides dial-up Internet access to the state's consumers and small to midsized businesses. It sells connectivity on a retail or wholesale basis allowing other Internet service providers to resell the service under their own brand names. FullNet's wholly-owned Full-Tel subsidiary is a competitive local-exchange carrier (CLEC) that provides the company with the local phone numbers necessary to offer dial-up service.

	Annual Growth	12/10	12/11	12/12	12/13	12/14
Sales ($ mil.)	1.0%	1.7	1.9	1.6	1.6	1.8
Net income ($ mil.)	–	0.8	0.1	(0.2)	0.2	(0.2)
Market value ($ mil.)	25.7%	0.2	0.0	0.3	0.4	0.5
Employees	1.9%	13	14	14	14	14

FULTON FINANCIAL CORP. (PA)   NMS: FULT

One Penn Square, P.O. Box 4887
Lancaster, PA 17604
Phone: 717 291-2411
Fax: –
Web: www.fult.com

CEO: R. Scott Smith
CFO: Charles J. Nugent
HR: Craig H. Hill
FYE: December 31
Type: Public

Fulton Financial is a $17 billion financial holding company that owns six community banks which together operate more than 250 branches in rural and suburban areas of Pennsylvania Maryland Delaware New Jersey and Virginia. The banks offer standard products such as checking and savings accounts CDs IRAs and credit cards. While commercial mortgage and construction loans account for about 45% of the company's loan portfolio home loans are also available through subsidiary Fulton Mortgage Company. Other non-bank units include investment management and trust services provider Fulton Financial Advisors and Fulton Insurance an agency selling life insurance and related products.

	Annual Growth	12/10	12/11	12/12	12/13	12/14
Assets ($ mil.)	1.3%	16,275.3	16,370.5	16,528.2	16,934.6	17,124.8
Net income ($ mil.)	5.3%	128.3	145.6	159.8	161.8	157.9
Market value ($ mil.)	4.6%	1,850.1	1,755.2	1,719.5	2,341.2	2,211.5
Employees	0.2%	3,530	3,530	3,570	3,620	3,560

FURIEX PHARMACEUTICALS INC   NMS: FURX

3900 Paramount Parkway, Suite 150
Morrisville, NC 27560
Phone: 919 456-7800
Fax: –
Web: www.furiex.com

CEO: –
CFO: –
HR: Deena Pierce
FYE: December 31
Type: Public

Furiex Pharmaceuticals knows two heads are better than one. The drug development company partners with pharmaceutical and biotechnology businesses in the early stages of developing new medications to combine R&D know-how. A company can reduce time and cost by teaming up with Furiex to handle safety and efficacy tests for new compounds. (It takes on average more than 10 years and almost $1 billion to bring a new drug to market.) In return Furiex receives a share of the rewards after a drug continues into the late stages of clinical development. The company began in 1998 as a division of PPD; it was named Furiex and spun off into a separate publicly traded company in mid-2010.

	Annual Growth	12/08	12/09	12/10	12/11	12/12
Sales ($ mil.)	21.8%	18.4	6.3	9.0	4.5	40.5
Net income ($ mil.)	–	–	5.8	(8.9)	(54.7)	(49.0)	(42.9)
Market value ($ mil.)	15.5%	–	–	144.7	167.4	192.9
Employees	(18.9%)	–	45	25	24	24

FURMAN FOODS INC.

770 CANNERY RD
NORTHUMBERLAND, PA 178578615
Phone: 570-473-3516
Fax: –
Web: www.furmanosfs.com

CEO: –
CFO: Ted Hancock
HR: Kermit Kohl
FYE: March 28
Type: Private

Furman Foods has firm ideas about tomatoes and other food products. The Pennsylvania company has built a business producing a complete line of canned tomatoes and tomato products. It also offers canned beans; spaghetti pasta and pizza sauces; bean salads; vegetables; and ketchup and other condiments. The company's brand names include Furmano's Conte and Bella Vista. Furman Foods boasts customers in the foodservice (restaurants schools and hospitals) retail (supermarkets and grocery stores) export branded manufacturing and private-label sectors along the US's East Coast. Furman Foods is a family-owned business founded in 1921 by J. W. Furman.

	Annual Growth	04/05	04/06*	03/07	03/08	03/09
Sales ($ mil.)	9.2%	–	73.9	77.2	83.4	96.3
Net income ($ mil.)	(65.2%)	–	–	13.8	1.2	1.7
Market value ($ mil.)	–	–	–	–	–	–
Employees	–	–	–	–	–	250

*Fiscal year change

FURMAN UNIVERSITY FOUNDATION INC.

3300 POINSETT HWY
GREENVILLE, SC 296130002
Phone: 864-294-2000
Fax: –
Web: www.furman.edu

CEO: –
CFO: –
HR: –
FYE: June 30
Type: Private

The school's slogan could be "Go Further than Furman." More than 70% of Furman University's graduates go on to law medical or other graduate schools. The private school offers an undergraduate liberal arts curriculum and a graduate program focused on teaching and education. Furman offers more than 40 majors through more than 25 departments to some 2700 undergraduate and graduate students from US 46 states and 53 foreign countries. It also offers internship and study away programs. The university has 240 faculty members. The student-faculty ratio is 11:1. Its 750-acre campus features a lake bell tower amphitheater and rose and Japanese gardens and is regarded as one of the most beautiful in the US.

	Annual Growth	06/09	06/10	06/11	06/12	06/13
Sales ($ mil.)	(3.0%)	–	158.8	132.8	142.8	145.1
Net income ($ mil.)	(17.5%)	–	–	83.3	(5.6)	56.7
Market value ($ mil.)	–	–	–	–	–	–
Employees	–	–	–	–	–	759

FURMANITE CORP

10370 Richmond Avenue, Suite 600
Houston, TX 77042
Phone: 713 634-7777
Fax: –
Web: www.furmanite.com

NYS: FRM
CEO: Joseph E. (Joe) Milliron
CFO: Robert S. Muff
HR: Mike Dills
FYE: December 31
Type: Public

Furmanite thrives under pressure. The specialty contractor provides a variety of technical services for petroleum refineries chemical plants nuclear power stations and other clients in the power generation manufacturing and processing industries. Furmanite specializes in sealing leaks in valves pipes and other flow-process systems often under emergency conditions involving exposure to high temperatures and pressures potential contact with dangerous materials explosion hazards and environmental contamination. It also provides onsite machining and custom engineering services as well as consulting and support services. Company rival Team Inc agreed to buy Furmanite in late 2015 for $335 million.

	Annual Growth	12/10	12/11	12/12	12/13	12/14
Sales ($ mil.)	16.6%	286.0	316.2	326.5	427.3	529.2
Net income ($ mil.)	4.6%	9.5	24.0	0.8	14.0	11.4
Market value ($ mil.)	3.1%	260.8	238.1	202.7	400.8	295.1
Employees	18.7%	1,521	1,529	1,833	3,110	3,017

FUSION TELECOMMUNICATIONS INTERNATIONAL INC

420 Lexington Avenue, Suite 1718
New York, NY 10170
Phone: 212 201-2400
Fax: –
Web: www.fusionconnect.com

NAS: FSNN
CEO: Matthew D. Rosen
CFO: Gordon Hutchins Jr
HR: –
FYE: December 31
Type: Public

Fusion Telecommunications International understands that modern communications is a blend of old and familiar processes with new technologies. The company provides VoIP (Voice over Internet Protocol) telephone and other Internet-based communications services primarily to larger US carriers. Its other clients include businesses with a need to outsource the hosting and management of their computer-based corporate telephony systems. Fusion offers also such services as call termination and broadband Internet access. The company also provides ISP and hosted PBX services to its enterprise customers. Top clients include Qwest and Verizon. Fusion was founded in 1997.

	Annual Growth	12/10	12/11	12/12	12/13	12/14
Sales ($ mil.)	21.8%	41.8	42.4	44.3	61.5	92.1
Net income ($ mil.)	–	(5.8)	(4.5)	(5.2)	(5.1)	(2.6)
Market value ($ mil.)	149.1%	0.6	0.6	0.6	0.9	23.1
Employees	42.0%	56	53	109	193	228

FUSION-IO INC.

2855 E. Cottonwood Parkway, Suite 100
Salt Lake City, UT 84121
Phone: 801 424-5500
Fax: –
Web: www.fusionio.com

NYS: FIO
CEO: Shane Robison
CFO: Ted Hull
HR: –
FYE: June 30
Type: Public

Fusion-io wants to help businesses access data in a flash. The company's ioMemory hardware modules offer storage and processing using an array of flash memory delivered through its proprietary data-path controller and virtual storage layer (VSL) software. VSL allows ioMemory to function as data storage within a server allowing data access without traditional storage devices. Fusion-io's products are used in sectors such as education energy entertainment financial services government and life sciences among others. The company's three biggest clients are Facebook (30% of sales) Apple (25%) and HP (17%). Fusion-io was formed in 2005 and went public in 2011.

	Annual Growth	06/09	06/10	06/11	06/12	06/13
Sales ($ mil.)	155.5%	10.2	36.2	197.2	359.3	432.4
Net income ($ mil.)	–	(25.6)	(31.7)	4.6	(5.6)	(38.2)
Market value ($ mil.)	(31.2%)	–	–	2,964.6	2,058.1	1,403.0
Employees	33.4%	–	395	441	669	938

FUSIONSTORM

2 Bryant St. Ste. 150
San Francisco CA 94105
Phone: 415-623-2626
Fax: 415-623-2630
Web: www.fusionstorm.com

CEO: John Varel
CFO: Michael Soja
HR: –
FYE: December 31
Type: Private

FusionStorm whips up a combination of IT services. The company provides a variety of information technology and remote support services to businesss in a variety of industries. FusionStorm develops configures implements and hosts data networks; provides IT consultancy and training services; sources hardware and software; and performs security and vulnerability assessments. The company supplies and supports products from key IT vendors such as IBM Oracle Cisco and Hewlett-Packard. Founded in 1995 FusionStorm has offices throughout the US although more than half of its offices are in its home state of California. The firm's officers hold a majority ownership in the company.

FUSIONSTORM GLOBAL INC.

8 Cedar St. Ste. 54A
Woburn MA 01801
Phone: 781-782-1900
Fax: +48-17-888-55-50
Web: www.asseco.pl

CEO: –
CFO: –
HR: –
FYE: December 31
Type: Private

FusionStorm Global has a plan for global domination of the IT services market. The company formed in 2009 with the idea to acquire three companies — FusionStorm Red River Computer and Global Technology Resources Inc. (GTRI) that provide IT consulting and services. FusionStorm works with small businesses and large corporations while Red River sells computer products to government agencies and GTRI is focused on services for corporations and the public sector. FusionStorm Global filed a $175 million IPO in August 2011. If the company successfully goes public it will use the proceeds to buy FusionStorm for $100 million Red River for $26 million and GTRI for $12.5 million and pay off their debt.

FUTUREFUEL CORP

NYS: FF

8235 Forsyth Blvd., Suite 400
St. Louis, MO 63105
Phone: 314 854-8385
Fax: –
Web: www.futurefuelcorporation.com

CEO: Paul A. (Tony) Novelly
CFO: Rose M Sparks
HR: –
FYE: December 31
Type: Public

FutureFuel's future may be in biofuels but for now it still relies on chemicals. The company manufactures biodiesel and other biofuels; however its core business is specialty chemicals which include a bleach activator and detergent additives a proprietary herbicide and chlorinated polyolefin adhesion promoters (used in coatings for the automotive industry). It synthesizes custom chemicals for a variety of industries and applications. Selling its products primarily in North America FutureFuel markets to customers that include industrial and consumer goods manufacturers as well as pharmaceutical companies and agribusinesses. It manufactures its biofuels and chemicals at a single plant in Arkansas.

	Annual Growth	12/10	12/11	12/12	12/13	12/14
Sales ($ mil.)	11.8%	219.2	309.9	351.8	444.9	341.8
Net income ($ mil.)	23.2%	23.1	34.5	34.3	74.0	53.2
Market value ($ mil.)	7.0%	435.0	543.0	517.7	690.8	569.3
Employees	0.0%	500	500	500	500	500

FX ALLIANCE INC.

NYSE: FX

909 Third Ave. 10th Fl.
New York NY 10022
Phone: 646-268-9900
Fax: 646-268-9996
Web: www.fxall.com

CEO: Philip Weisberg
CFO: John Cooley
HR: –
FYE: December 31
Type: Public

It just makes cents to use FX Alliance for foreign exchange trading online. The company operates an electronic platform for foreign exchange (FX) trading whereby market participants buy one currency and sell in another primarily on the over-the-counter (OTC) market. FX Alliance counts more than 1150 institutional clients such as asset managers banks broker-dealers corporate treasurers hedge funds and prime brokers. More than half of its trading volume comes from customers outside the US. FX Alliance has international offices in Australia India Japan Singapore and the UK. Thomson Reuters is buying FX Alliance for $616 million.

FX ENERGY INC.

NMS: FXEN

3006 Highland Drive, Suite 206
Salt Lake City, UT 84106
Phone: 801 486-5555
Fax: 801 486-5575
Web: www.fxenergy.com

CEO: David N Pierce
CFO: –
HR: –
FYE: December 31
Type: Public

FX Energy is not exactly fixated on energy in Poland but it is in western Poland's Permian Basin where it is hoping to make its big breakthrough. In 2012 the independent exploration and production company reported proved reserves of 44.1 billion cu. ft. of natural gas equivalent in Poland and 0.6 million barrels of oil equivalent in the US (from properties in Montana and Nevada). Partners include state-owned Polish Oil and Gas and CalEnergy Gas which have served as operators for exploration wells in Poland. FX Energy holds about 2.7 million gross acres (2 million net) in western Poland.

	Annual Growth	12/09	12/10	12/11	12/12	12/13
Sales ($ mil.)	23.9%	14.7	25.0	35.4	36.6	34.5
Net income ($ mil.)	–	(0.5)	(0.8)	(28.5)	4.1	(11.8)
Market value ($ mil.)	6.5%	153.1	330.5	257.9	220.8	196.7
Employees	3.4%	49	49	48	50	56

FXCM INC

NYS: FXCM

55 Water Street, Floor 50
New York, NY 10041
Phone: 646 432-2986
Fax: –
Web: www.fxcm.com

CEO: Dror Niv
CFO: Robert Lande
HR: –
FYE: December 31
Type: Public

Money talks in more than a dozen different languages at FXCM. The online brokerage specializes in over-the-counter (OTC) foreign exchange (forex) trading for individual investors or transactions that are bought in one currency and sold in another. FXCM operates through FXCM Holdings which processes more than 300000 trades per day for its 163000 account holders. The firm's institutional trading segment FXCM Pro used by banks hedge funds and other financial service companies accounts for less than 10% of revenue. More than three-quarters of the company's trading volume comes from outside the US. FXCM was founded in 1999 and went public in a 2010 initial public offering (IPO).

	Annual Growth	12/10	12/11	12/12	12/13	12/14
Sales ($ mil.)	6.5%	360.3	415.9	417.3	489.6	463.8
Net income ($ mil.)	229.2%	0.1	12.7	9.0	14.8	17.2
Market value ($ mil.)	5.7%	63.5	46.7	48.2	85.4	79.4
Employees	1.8%	844	868	864	934	908

G & J PEPSI-COLA BOTTLERS INC.

9435 Waterstone Blvd. Ste. 390
Cincinnati OH 45249-8205
Phone: 513-785-6060
Fax: 513-683-9467

CEO: –
CFO: –
HR: –
FYE: December 31
Type: Private

G & J Pepsi-Cola Bottlers battles for business from cola consumers. The company has distributed Pepsi products across the Ohio and Kentucky territory for the more than 40 years. Among the larger Pepsi bottlers in the US it ships the PepsiCo name brands including Pepsi-Cola Mountain Dew Gatorade Slice and SoBe (teas juices and energy drinks) to beverage retailers. The bottler through Pepsi joint ventures and licenses offers Aquafina water Dr Pepper products Dole and Tropicana juices Lipton teas and Starbucks' Frappuccino. G&J Pepsi-Cola comprises seven franchises which distribute through centers in Cheshire Chillicothe and Hillsboro Ohio as well as in Winchester and Harrodsburg Kentucky.

G & K SERVICES, INC.
NMS: GK

5995 Opus Parkway
Minnetonka, MN 55343
Phone: 952 912-5500
Fax: –
Web: www.gkservices.com

CEO: Douglas A. (Doug) Milroy
CFO: Jeffrey L. (Jeff) Wright
HR: Kristie Porter
FYE: June 27
Type: Public

G&K Services likes uniformity. The company is the third-largest uniform rental agency (behind #1 Cintas and #2 ARAMARK). G&K makes and supplies uniforms for about 170000 customers in the automotive manufacturing hospitality and technology industries among others from about 165 locations in the US Canada Ireland and the Dominican Republic. Along with rentals and sales the company provides cleaning repair and replacement services for all of its uniforms. G&K also carries clean room garments used by the semiconductor industry. In addition the company offers facility services providing restroom supplies and renting items such as dust mops floor mats and towels. G&K was founded in 1902.

	Annual Growth	07/11*	06/12	06/13	06/14	06/15
Sales ($ mil.)	3.1%	828.9	869.9	907.7	900.9	937.6
Net income ($ mil.)	15.9%	33.2	24.1	46.7	47.7	59.9
Market value ($ mil.)	19.4%	689.6	622.3	949.8	1,032.4	1,403.9
Employees	1.6%	7,500	7,800	7,800	7,800	8,000

*Fiscal year change

G&P TRUCKING COMPANY INC.

126 ACCESS RD
GASTON, SC 290539501
Phone: 803-791-5500
Fax: –
Web: www.gptruck.com

CEO: –
CFO: Billy Lynch
HR: –
FYE: December 31
Type: Private

G&P Trucking provides truckload freight hauling and related logistics services mainly in the southeastern US. The company which specializes in next-day and same-day service operates a fleet of about 520 tractors and 1500 trailers from about a dozen terminals in the Carolinas Georgia Virginia Tennessee and Texas. Some of its business comes from handling cargo coming into and out of ports such as Charlotte North Carolina; Norfolk Virginia; and Savannah Georgia; it also arranges transportation to and from Mexico. G&P Trucking is owned by the Cassels family which also controls less-than-truckload carrier Southeastern Freight Lines.

	Annual Growth	12/03	12/04	12/05	12/06	12/07
Sales ($ mil.)	8.8%	–	76.9	84.7	93.4	99.2
Net income ($ mil.)	–	–	–	1.9	1.1	(5.1)
Market value ($ mil.)	–	–	–	–	–	–
Employees	–	–	–	–	–	700

G-I HOLDINGS INC.

1361 Alps Rd.
Wayne NJ 07470
Phone: 973-628-3000
Fax: 303-744-4443
Web: www.gates.com

CEO: Robert B Tafaro
CFO: Susan Yoss
HR: –
FYE: December 31
Type: Private

G-I Holdings isn't your average Joe in the roofing materials business. The company and its subsidiary Building Materials Corporation of America (which do business as GAF) manufacture flashing vents and complete roofing systems. It is one of North America's leading roofing manufacturers with residential shingles and related products as well as built-up roofing single-ply roofing and modified bitumen products for commercial use. GAF markets its products under such brands as Metalastic Timberline EverGuard GAFGLAS and Ruberoid. Other products include natural stone ornamental ironwork fiber-cement siding and ducting.

G-III APPAREL GROUP LTD.
NMS: GIII

512 Seventh Avenue
New York, NY 10018
Phone: 212 403-0500
Fax: –
Web: www.g-iii.com

CEO: Morris Goldfarb
CFO: Neal S. Nackman
HR: –
FYE: January 31
Type: Public

G-III Apparel Group is into leather but not exclusively. The company is best known for making leather jackets under the G-III Marvin Richards Black Rivet Winlit Siena Studio and other labels (such as Andrew Marc) as well as under licensed names. It also makes pants skirts and sportswear from leather and other materials. More than two-thirds of G-III's sales are generated from licensed apparel it makes for the NFL NBA NHL and MLB teams as well as for Jones New York Nine West and Kenneth Cole. The company's customers include department stores such as Macy's Nordstrom Lord & Taylor and Kohl's.

	Annual Growth	01/11	01/12	01/13	01/14	01/15
Sales ($ mil.)	18.8%	1,063.4	1,231.2	1,399.7	1,718.2	2,116.9
Net income ($ mil.)	18.1%	56.7	49.6	56.9	77.4	110.4
Market value ($ mil.)	29.2%	1,568.6	1,027.7	1,613.5	3,145.7	4,369.8
Employees	32.5%	2,154	2,592	3,109	6,631	6,641

G. L. HOMES OF FLORIDA CORPORATION

1600 Sawgrass Corporate Pkwy. Ste. 400
Sunrise FL 33323
Phone: 954-753-1730
Fax: 954-753-4509
Web: www.glhomes.com

CEO: –
CFO: –
HR: –
FYE: December 31
Type: Private

G.L. Homes calls Florida home and more than 60000 Floridians live in those homes. G.L. Homes of Florida began as a small local builder and is now one of the nation's largest privately held builders of homes and residential communities (some active-adult) It operates in Broward Hillsborough Indian River Lee and Palm Beach counties. The company's homes range from around $160000 to about $1 million. Preferred lender G.L. Financial offers mortgage financing on homes while affiliate G.L. Commercial is a commercial real estate firm that develops and manages retail mixed-use and suburban office space throughout the Southeast. G.L. Homes was established in 1976 by founder and president Itchko Ezratti.

G. P. & W. INC.

600 Mason Ridge Center Dr. 2nd Fl.
St. Louis MO 63141-8557
Phone: 314-682-3500
Fax: 314-682-3599
Web: www.centeroil.com

CEO: –
CFO: –
HR: –
FYE: December 31
Type: Private

G. P. & W.'s core business is peddling petroleum. The company which markets under and is known by the name Center Oil is one of the largest private wholesale distributors of gasoline and other petroleum products to customers primarily in the eastern region of the US. Center Oil owns a dozen storage terminals capable of storing 2.8 million barrels of petroleum products. It also has access to 36 terminals in 10 states as well as access to the Magellan Texas Eastern Kinder Morgan Chicago and Kaneb pipeline systems. Its products are also distributed through a fleet of ships barges and trucks.

G.S.E. CONSTRUCTION COMPANY INC.

6950 PRESTON AVE
LIVERMORE, CA 945519545
Phone: 925-447-0292
Fax: –
Web: www.gseconstruction.com

CEO: Orlando Gutierrez
CFO: –
HR: –
FYE: December 31
Type: Private

GSE Construction Company provides heavy construction for government agencies public utilities and the private sector. The general engineering contractor specializes in building water and wastewater infrastructure. GSE provides services such as new construction renovation work and upgrades and construction labor. Projects range from retrofitting old systems and expanding capacity to constructing storage tanks treatment facilities and pump stations. The company also often teams with fellow engineering firm Applied Technologies to complete waste-to-energy conversion projects. GSE performs most of its work in California and Nevada. President and CEO Orlando Gutierrez founded GSE Construction in 1980.

	Annual Growth	12/06	12/07	12/08	12/09	12/10
Sales ($ mil.)	–	–	–	(1,344.3)	69.8	63.7
Net income ($ mil.)	12635.9%	–	–	0.0	2.1	0.3
Market value ($ mil.)	–	–	–	–	–	–
Employees	–	–	–	–	–	140

G4S SECURE SOLUTIONS (USA) INC.

1395 University Blvd.
Jupiter FL 33458
Phone: 561-622-5656
Fax: 561-691-6423
Web: www.g4s.us

CEO: Grahame Gibson
CFO: Susanne Jorgensen
HR: –
FYE: December 31
Type: Subsidiary

G4S Secure Solutions (G4S) counters the perils of modern life by providing a full slate of security services to corporate industrial and government organizations. The company's offerings include armed guards background investigations program development and security consulting. G4S also provides fire and rescue services as well as specialized security for airports nuclear power plants and US embassies. The company markets security services to federal state and local government agencies via its Wackenhut Services subsidiary. Formerly known as Wackenhut Corporation G4S is the US business unit of UK-based G4S plc one of the world's largest security companies.

GABRIEL BROTHERS INC.

55 Scott Ave.
Morgantown WV 26508
Phone: 304-292-6965
Fax: 304-292-3874
Web: www.gabrielbrothers.com

CEO: –
CFO: –
HR: –
FYE: January 31
Type: Private

Gabriel blow your horn — your magical mystical discount horn that is. Gabriel Brothers sells discounted brand-name clothing through more than 100 stores under the Gabriel Brothers (commonly called "Gabes") and Rugged Wearhouse banners. Its stores are located in about a dozen East Coast and Mid-Atlantic states. The company's offerings include men's women's and children's apparel and footwear as well as housewares. Gabriel Brothers carries such brands as Anne Klein Kenneth Cole and Liz Claiborne and features markdowns as high as 70% off of their original retail prices. The family-run company was established in 1961 by James and Arthur Gabriel.

GAGE MARKETING GROUP LLC

10000 Hwy. 55
Minneapolis MN 55441
Phone: 763-595-3800
Fax: 763-595-3871
Web: www.gage.com

CEO: Edwin C Gage
CFO: Keith Braddeck
HR: Deb McCreight
FYE: December 31
Type: Private

If you're ready to acquire new customers retain the old ones and build your sales then you are ready to get enGaged. Gage Marketing Group specializes in blending strategic services with technological aptitude to implement marketing programs that produce measurable results. The company provides expertise in customer relationship management and design services as well as direct loyalty promotional and interactive marketing disciplines. It has developed online and offline promotions for Best Buy 3M and Coca-Cola. Founder and CEO Edwin "Skip" Gage the former CEO of Carlson Companies owns Gage Marketing Group.

GAIAM INC

NMS: GAIA

833 West South Boulder Road
Louisville, CO 80027
Phone: 303 222-3600
Fax: –
Web: www.gaiam.com

CEO: Lynn Powers
CFO: Stephen J. (Steve) Thomas
HR: –
FYE: December 31
Type: Public

If you're into living a healthy sustainable lifestyle Gaiam is your kind of company. The name Gaiam (pronounced "guy-um") is a combination of Gaia (the Earth goddess) and "I am." Most of the company's sales come from proprietary products and media for consumers interested in yoga fitness and wellness. Other merchandise includes organic cotton apparel bedding and personal care and home care products. Gaiam boasts a library of more than 7000 DVD titles and a TV channel (which the company plans to spin off). It also owns a stake in Real Goods Solar which designs and installs solar energy systems. Gaiam's offerings are sold through catalogs its e-commerce site and major retailers (including Target and Whole Foods).

	Annual Growth	12/10	12/11	12/12	12/13	12/14
Sales ($ mil.)	(11.7%)	274.3	274.8	202.5	155.5	166.7
Net income ($ mil.)	–	4.3	(24.9)	(12.9)	(22.8)	(9.9)
Market value ($ mil.)	(1.9%)	188.5	79.3	77.4	162.1	174.6
Employees	(17.9%)	574	315	345	277	261

GAIN CAPITAL HOLDINGS INC

NYS: GCAP

Bedminster One, 135 Route 202/206
Bedminster, NJ 07921
Phone: 908 731-0700
Fax: –
Web: www.gaincapital.com

CEO: Glenn H. Stevens
CFO: Jason E. Emerson
HR: –
FYE: December 31
Type: Public

There is plenty to lose in the foreign currency exchange market but this company would like you to focus on the potential gains. GAIN Capital Holdings provides over-the-counter foreign exchange (forex) services to retail traders (responsible for about 97% of the company's trading volume) and institutional investors and through financial intermediaries such as broker-dealers banks and futures commission merchants. The company's FOREXTrader platform provides online trading tools and educational resources to help individual investors deal in forex trading online. It has 133000 funded retail accounts.

	Annual Growth	12/10	12/11	12/12	12/13	12/14
Sales ($ mil.)	18.2%	189.1	181.5	151.4	266.4	369.5
Net income ($ mil.)	(4.4%)	37.8	15.7	2.6	31.3	31.6
Market value ($ mil.)	(0.5%)	395.0	287.7	175.6	322.4	387.3
Employees	9.5%	333	364	363	551	479

GAINESVILLE REGIONAL UTILITIES (INC)

301 SE 4TH AVE STE A105
GAINESVILLE, FL 326016857
Phone: 352-334-3400
Fax: –
Web: www.cityofgainesville.org

CEO: –
CFO: Justin M. Locke
HR: –
FYE: September 30
Type: Private

Multi-service utility Gainesville Regional Utilities (GRU) started out small more than a century ago but has been gaining ground ever since. The company (now the fifth largest municipal electric utility in Florida) is the sole utilities provider in Gainesville and surrounding areas in Alachua County. The municipal utility distributes electric water wastewater natural gas and telecommunications services to approximately 93000 retail and wholesale customers. GRU has interests in power generation facilities that give it more than 600 MW of capacity. It also offers internet and other communications services. GRU gets the bulk of its revenues from its electric utility operations.

	Annual Growth	09/05	09/06	09/07	09/08	09/09
Sales ($ mil.)	5.7%	–	–	–	350.0	369.9
Net income ($ mil.)	83.0%	–	–	–	18.3	33.6
Market value ($ mil.)	–	–	–	–	–	–
Employees	–	–	–	–	–	750

GAINSCO INC.   NYSE AMEX: GAN

3333 Lee Pkwy. Ste. 1200
Dallas TX 75219
Phone: 972-629-4301
Fax: 972-629-4302
Web: www.gainsco.com

CEO: Glenn Anderson
CFO: Daniel Coots
HR: –
FYE: December 31
Type: Private

Well you wouldn't call an insurance company LOSSCO would you? Through its MGA Insurance subsidiary GAINSCO sells personal nonstandard auto insurance under the GAINSCO Auto Insurance brand. The company does a majority of its business in Florida but has laid the groundwork for sales growth in other states in the southwestern and southeastern US. Its products are sold through some 4800 independent agencies. GAINSCO aims its marketing efforts at Hispanics its core customer market and most of the company's customer service staff is bilingual. Officers of GAINSCO own a majority of the company.

GALDERMA LABORATORIES L.P.

14501 North Fwy.
Fort Worth TX 76177
Phone: 817-961-5000
Fax: 817-961-0041
Web: www.galdermausa.com

CEO: –
CFO: –
HR: –
FYE: December 31
Type: Private

Galderma Laboratories can't soothe all of the irritations of the world but it can help with itchy spotty and sensitive skin. The company is the North American operation of Swiss firm Galderma Pharma a joint venture between L'Oreal and Nestle founded in 1981. As part of its business Galderma Laboratories focuses exclusively on developing over-the-counter and prescription dermatology products. In addition to such consumer brands as Cetaphil the company offers treatments for a variety of skin conditions. Areas of focus include remedies for acne rosacea atopic dermatitis (eczema) psoriasis and melasma (darkening of the skin due to excessive melanin production).

GALECTIN THERAPEUTICS INC.   OTC: GALT

7 Wells Ave. Ste. 34
Newton MA 02459
Phone: 617-559-0033
Fax: 617-928-3450
Web: www.galectintherapeutics.com

CEO: Peter G Traber
CFO: Jack W Callicutt
HR: –
FYE: December 31
Type: Public

Galectin Therapeutics (formerly known as Pro-Pharmaceuticals) has a knack for inhibiting galectin proteins. The drug developer is targeting galectin proteins as they play a key role in the development of a variety of diseases. It is developing such inhibitors to treat liver fibrosis which is currently untreatable. Its GM-CT-01 drug candidate is being investigated for use targeting certain melanomas and in combination with another drug to improve its effectiveness in treating colorectal cancer.

GALENA BIOPHARMA INC   NAS: GALE

2000 Crow Canyon Place, Suite 380
San Ramon, CA 94583
Phone: 855 855-4253
Fax: –

CEO: Mark W. Schwartz
CFO: Ryan M Dunlap
HR: –
FYE: December 31
Type: Public

While there's no vaccine for breast cancer Galena Biopharma has big plans for NeuVax its drug candidate. NeuVax which is in Phase III clinical trials is being tested for its efficacy in reducing the recurrence of breast cancer in patients who can't take Genentech's Herceptin. Galena Biopharma acquired the rights to NeuVax when it bought the drug's developer Arizona-based Apthera Inc. for about $7 million in April 2011. Galena itself was spun off from RXi Pharmaceuticals in a one-for-one stock split in March 2012. Galena having more potential for success with NeuVax became the public company while RXi Pharmaceuticals became a private company focused on developing RNA interference (RNAi) therapies.

	Annual Growth	12/10	12/11	12/12	12/13	12/14
Sales ($ mil.)	274.7%	–	–	–	2.5	9.3
Net income ($ mil.)	–	(12.0)	(11.5)	(35.0)	(76.7)	(36.6)
Market value ($ mil.)	(12.5%)	334.0	60.7	198.1	642.2	195.5
Employees	15.5%	32	29	12	60	57

GALLAGHER (ARTHUR J.) & CO.   NYS: AJG

Two Pierce Place
Itasca, IL 60143-3141
Phone: 630 773-3800
Fax: –
Web: www.ajg.com

CEO: J. Patrick Gallagher
CFO: Douglas K. (Doug) Howell
HR: Kristin M Sampson
FYE: December 31
Type: Public

Arthur J. Gallagher knows all about risky business. The company provides insurance brokerage and risk management services through a network of subsidiaries and agencies. It places traditional and niche property/casualty lines in addition to offering retirement solutions and managing employee benefits programs. Risk management services include claims management loss control consulting and workers' compensation investigations. Gallagher UK places insurance with the Lloyd's of London exchange. The global company operates 650 sales and service locations in about 30 nations and through correspondent brokers and consultants does business in more than 140 countries.

	Annual Growth	12/11	12/12	12/13	12/14	12/15
Sales ($ mil.)	26.1%	2,134.7	2,520.3	3,179.6	4,626.5	5,392.4
Net income ($ mil.)	25.4%	144.1	195.0	268.6	303.4	356.8
Market value ($ mil.)	5.2%	5,915.5	6,129.6	8,301.9	8,328.5	7,242.3
Employees	14.8%	12,400	13,700	16,400	20,200	21,500

GALLAUDET UNIVERSITY

800 FLORIDA AVE NE
WASHINGTON, DC 200023600
Phone: 202-651-5000
Fax: –
Web: www.gallaudet.edu

CEO: –
CFO: –
HR: –
FYE: September 30
Type: Private

Gallaudet University (GU) gives deaf and hard-of-hearing students the chance to be in the majority. Designed to accommodate hearing-impaired students GU offers undergraduate and graduate degrees in more than 40 majors to about 2000 students annually. The bilingual university which uses both American Sign Language (ASL) and English admits a small number of hearing ASL-proficient students to each incoming freshman class. Through its Laurent Clerc National Deaf Education Center GU provides training and support for teachers and parents of hearing impaired children and operates demonstration schools. Founded in 1864 GU was named for Thomas Hopkins Gallaudet a pioneer in education for the deaf.

	Annual Growth	09/09	09/10	09/11	09/12	09/13
Sales ($ mil.)	(1.4%)	–	179.3	177.4	190.2	171.9
Net income ($ mil.)	–	–	–	4.7	17.5	(0.1)
Market value ($ mil.)	–	–	–	–	–	–
Employees	–	–	–	–	–	1,200

GALLERY MODEL HOMES INC.

6006 NORTH FWY
HOUSTON, TX 770764029
Phone: 713-692-1111
Fax: –
Web: www.galleryfurniture.com

CEO: –
CFO: –
HR: –
FYE: December 31
Type: Private

Gallery Furniture and its founder Jim "Mattress Mac" McIngvale have become something of a Houston institution. McIngvale's animated TV ads promise they "really will save you money." With two locations the firm has evolved into a leading regional furniture retailer accounting for about 20% of Houston's market share. Gallery Furniture also ranks as one of the nation's top sellers in terms of sales per square foot. In addition to mattresses (Simmons Beautyrest and Tempur Sealy brands) it sells bedroom dining room home office and living room furniture. The firm was founded in 1981. A fire in May 2009 destroyed its 100000-sq.-ft. warehouse and damaged its North Freeway showroom.

	Annual Growth	12/03	12/04	12/05	12/06	12/07
Sales ($ mil.)	(1.1%)	–	115.3	130.4	129.5	111.4
Net income ($ mil.)	162.0%	–	–	0.5	1.0	3.6
Market value ($ mil.)	–	–	–	–	–	–
Employees	–	–	–	–	–	400

GALLERY OF HISTORY INC.

3601 W. Sahara Ave. Promenade Ste.
Las Vegas NV 89102-5379
Phone: 702-364-1000
Fax: 702-364-1285
Web: www.galleryofhistory.com

CEO: Todd M Axelrod
CFO: Rod R Lynam
HR: –
FYE: September 30
Type: Private

Those who don't know the Gallery of History are doomed to buy their memorabilia from another auction house. The company auctions autographs memorabilia and manuscripts from artists authors athletes entertainers politicians and scientists among other notable figures. Its inventory of about 190000 items have included baseballs autographed by Hank Aaron letters written by Albert Einstein and signed photos from Cecil B. De Mille. Although the Internet is its primary sales channel the company also offers autographs and manuscripts through a retail gallery located at its headquarters. The Gallery of History was incorporated in 1981. Founder chairman and CEO Todd Axelrod owns about 90% of the company.

GALLUP INC.

901 F ST NW STE 400
WASHINGTON, DC 200041419
Phone: 202-715-3030
Fax: –
Web: www.gallup.com

CEO: Jim Clifton
CFO: James (Jim) Krieger
HR: –
FYE: December 31
Type: Private

More than a pollster Gallup draws from its research and behavioral studies to offer consulting services related to performance management. Other specialties include branding marketing and recruiting. The company delivers its services on the Web through its Gallup University campuses and through about 40 global offices. It draws customers from a variety of industries including automotive business services health care hospitality manufacturing and retail. Despite its diversified business offerings the company is still most famous for its Gallup Poll surveys. It is owned by its employees.

	Annual Growth	12/08	12/09	12/11	12/12	12/13
Sales ($ mil.)	(1.4%)	–	264.1	303.2	275.4	249.2
Net income ($ mil.)	(37.3%)	–	–	34.0	23.0	13.4
Market value ($ mil.)	–	–	–	–	–	–
Employees	–	–	–	–	–	2,000

GALPIN MOTORS INC.

15505 Roscoe Blvd.
North Hills CA 91343
Phone: 818-787-3800
Fax: 818-778-2210
Web: www.gogalpin.com

CEO: Herbert F Boeckman II
CFO: –
HR: –
FYE: December 31
Type: Private

Galpin Motors will do just about anything to get you to buy a car even jolt you with joe at the full-service Starbucks shops attached to its luxury car dealerships. Claiming to have sold the first Saturn and ranking as the top Ford dealer in the world it also sells Aston Martin Jaguar Lincoln Mazda Mercury and Volvo models as well as used cars from four dealerships and a Web site. It also rents and customizes — or "Galpinizes" — vehicles such as the Tailgate Party Truck with a built-in stainless steel barbecue blender DVD/TV combo and refrigerated beer kegs. Founded as Galpin Ford in 1946 Galpin Motors is owned and run by the Boeckmann family.

GAMCO INVESTORS INC

One Corporate Center
Rye, NY 10580-1422
Phone: 914 921-3700
Fax: –
Web: www.gabelli.com

NYS: GBL
CEO: Mario J. Gabelli
CFO: Vince Capurso
HR: –
FYE: December 31
Type: Public

Investing is anything but a game for "Super Mario" Gabelli the self-made billionaire investor and founder and CEO of GAMCO Investors. The firm oversees the mutual fund- and securities-related portion of Gabelli's financial empire. It provides advisory services to some 20 mutual funds and 10 closed-end funds under the Gabelli GAMCO and Comstock brands. Most of the company's approximately $34 billion in assets under management are invested in stocks though company also has a well-performing money-market fund. GAMCO also offers wealth management services for private clients and institutional investors such as pension plans endowments and municipalities. Gabelli controls the firm.

	Annual Growth	12/10	12/11	12/12	12/13	12/14
Sales ($ mil.)	11.9%	280.4	327.1	344.3	397.6	440.4
Net income ($ mil.)	12.3%	68.8	75.5	116.9	109.4	
Market value ($ mil.)	16.7%	1,241.3	1,124.5	1,372.1	2,248.7	2,299.6
Employees	1.1%	222	218	224	228	232

GAME SHOW NETWORK LLC

2150 Colorado Ave. Ste. 100
Santa Monica CA 90404
Phone: 310-255-6800
Fax: 310-255-6810
Web: www.gsn.com

CEO: David Goldhill
CFO: Brent Williams
HR: –
FYE: December 31
Type: Subsidiary

Answer: This company broadcasts game shows on cable TV. Question: What is GSN? Game Show Network (GSN) operates a cable channel that reaches about 75 million US Canadian and Caribbean homes with a programming slate heavy on quiz shows and other game programs. It offers reruns of such classic shows as Are You Smarter Than a Fifth Grader? Family Feud Jeopardy! and Match Game as well as updated and original shows including PYRAMID and Whammy! The All-New Press Your Luck. In addition to its GSN cable network the company offers a variety of games and streaming video on its website. Direct satellite TV provider DIRECTV Group has a 65% stake in GSN; Sony Pictures Entertainment owns the rest.

GAMING PARTNERS INTERNATIONAL CORP

NMS: GPIC

1700 Industrial Road
Las Vegas, NV 89102
Phone: 702 384-2425
Fax: –

CEO: Gregory S Gronau
CFO: Alain Thieffry
HR: –
FYE: December 31
Type: Public

This company doesn't care if gamblers win or crap out as long as they do it using its products. Gaming Partners International is a leading manufacturer of casino gaming products including dealing shoes dice gaming chips playing cards and roulette wheels. It also supplies table furniture and layouts for blackjack poker baccarat craps and other casino games. With manufacturing facilities in the US Mexico and France the company markets its products under the brands Bourgogne et Grasset Bud Jones and Paulson to casino operators around the world. French holding company Holding Wilson owns almost 50% of Gaming Partners International.

	Annual Growth	12/10	12/11	12/12	12/13	12/14
Sales ($ mil.)	0.5%	59.9	61.1	62.9	56.2	61.0
Net income ($ mil.)	(11.8%)	4.4	3.7	6.1	1.2	2.7
Market value ($ mil.)	8.5%	49.2	49.1	54.3	64.7	68.1
Employees	(1.3%)	764	803	1,035	730	726

GAMEFLY INC.

5340 Alla Rd. Ste. 110
Los Angeles CA 90006
Phone: 310-664-6400
Fax: +41-44-248-50-61
Web: www.tamedia.ch

CEO: Dave Hodess
CFO: Stacey M Peterson
HR: –
FYE: March 31
Type: Private

GameFly is to gamers what Netflix is to movie lovers. The video game provider offers more than 8000 titles for rent — both newer releases and classics — for entertainment systems such as Microsoft Xbox Nintendo Wii and Sony PlayStation as well as handheld consoles. Some 334000 members pay a monthly subscription fee to rent games with no due dates or late charges. To support this effort GameFly maintains shipping centers in Austin Los Angeles Pittsburgh Seattle and Tampa. Through its Direct2Drive website gamers can buy video games among 3000 choices to download to PCs or Macs. Founded in 2002 GameFly counts among its backers venture firms Sequoia Capital and Tenaya Capital.

GANDER MOUNTAIN COMPANY

180 E. 5th St. Ste. 1300
St. Paul MN 55101
Phone: 651-325-4300
Fax: 651-325-2003
Web: www.gandermountain.com

CEO: David C Pratt
CFO: –
HR: –
FYE: January 31
Type: Private

Gander Mountain has got the gear to get you out of the office and up the mountain. The company operates nearly 120 outdoor sporting goods stores focused on a variety of outdoor activities such as hunting camping and fishing in some two dozen states. In addition to outdoor equipment and related accessories the stores also sell apparel and footwear. While Gander Mountain has sold fishing and pontoon boats since 2007 through an arrangement with Tracker Marine Group a unit of Bass Pro Shops the retailer exited its all terrain vehicle (ATV) and boat categories by 2010. Founded in 1960 as an outdoor catalog operation Gander Mountain went private in early 2010.

GAMESTOP CORP

NYS: GME

625 Westport Parkway
Grapevine, TX 76051
Phone: 817 424-2000
Fax: –
Web: www.gamestop.com

CEO: J. Paul Raines
CFO: Robert A. (Rob) Lloyd
HR: –
FYE: January 31
Type: Public

GameStop holds the top score in video game retailing. The largest retailer of new and used games hardware entertainment software and accessories boasts over 4100 GameStop EB Games and Micromania branded stores in the US and 1500-plus stores in Europe Australia and Canada. Its stores and e-commerce websites stock more than 5000 video game related items with more than half of its sales coming from new video game hardware and software. GameStop also sells downloadable add-on content from publishers operates nearly 500 smartphone retail locations (under the AT&T Cricket Wireless Simply Mac and Spring Mobile banners) and publishes video game magazine Game Informer.

	Annual Growth	01/11	01/12*	02/13	02/14*	01/15
Sales ($ mil.)	(0.5%)	9,473.7	9,550.5	8,886.7	9,039.5	9,296.0
Net income ($ mil.)	(0.9%)	408.0	339.9	(269.7)	354.2	393.1
Market value ($ mil.)	13.9%	2,259.5	2,619.3	2,659.1	3,777.0	3,796.4
Employees	1.8%	68,000	71,000	65,000	69,000	73,000

*Fiscal year change

GARAN INCORPORATED

350 Fifth Ave.
New York NY 10118
Phone: 212-563-2000
Fax: 212-971-2250
Web: www.garanimals.com

CEO: Seymour Lichtenstein
CFO: David M Fligel
HR: –
FYE: December 31
Type: Subsidiary

If you've ever enlisted the help of a monkey to match your shirt and shorts you're likely to be familiar with Garan. The company designs manufactures and distributes coordinated apparel for infants toddlers and children. Products are sold under its customers' private labels as well as its own brand Garanimals. Characters like Charley Chimp help young children dress themselves with coordinated hang-tags. Most of Garan's products are sold through distribution centers in the US to major national chains such as Wal-Mart department stores and specialty stores. Founded in 1941 Garan is a subsidiary of Warren Buffett's Berkshire Hathaway.

GARDEN CITY HOSPITAL

6245 INKSTER RD
GARDEN CITY, MI 48135-4001
Phone: 734-421-3300
Fax: –
Web: www.gchosp.org

CEO: –
CFO: –
HR: –
FYE: September 30
Type: Private

Garden City Hospital provides health care services and medical education in western Wayne County Michigan. With about 320 licensed beds the community hospital offers emergency inpatient and surgical care in a variety of general and specialist fields including cardiology women's health and sports rehabilitation. Some of its more unusual services include clinical hypnotherapy and a massage clinic. Garden City Hospital also provides residency and internship programs through partnerships with universities and medical schools.

	Annual Growth	09/06	09/07	09/08*	04/09*	09/09
Sales ($ mil.)	(0.9%)	–	150.6	142.5	0.1	148.0
Net income ($ mil.)	(58.4%)	–	9.1	0.1	0.0	1.6
Market value ($ mil.)	–	–	–	–	–	–
Employees	–	–	–	–	–	1,200

*Fiscal year change

GARDEN FRESH RESTAURANT CORP.

15822 Bernardo Ctr. Dr. Ste. A
San Diego CA 92127
Phone: 800-874-1600
Fax: 858-675-1617
Web: www.souplantation.com

CEO: John Morberg
CFO: David A Carr
HR: –
FYE: September 30
Type: Private

Soup or salad is the question to ponder at these eateries. Garden Fresh Restaurant owns and operates more than 100 buffet-style restaurants under the names Souplantation and Sweet Tomatoes. Found mostly in California and more than a dozen other states the diners feature salad bars that include all the usual fixings as well as specialty and prepared salads. The restaurants also feature self-serve bars for pasta soups breads and fresh fruit. The company's Souplantation banner is used mostly in Southern California markets while Sweet Tomatoes is the brand outside that region. Founded in 1983 by CEO Michael Mack and partner Anthony Brooke the company is owned by private equity firm Sun Capital Partners.

GARDEN RIDGE CORPORATION

19411 Atrium Place Ste. 170
Houston TX 77084
Phone: 832-391-7201
Fax: 914-694-2286
Web: www.orthometrix.net

CEO: Bob Demer
CFO: Rich Brown
HR: –
FYE: January 31
Type: Private

Megastore retailer Garden Ridge offers decorating items for more than just the garden. The company owns and operates nearly 50 stores each covering some 3 acres and mostly located off major highways in about 20 states from Florida to Michigan. Its headquarters state of Texas is home to some 15 stores. Considered the "home decor depot" Garden Ridge stores sell about 500000 decorating items such as seasonal decor framed art baskets silk and dried flowers furniture home textiles and pottery as well as crafts and party supplies. Garden Ridge which began as a single store outside of San Antonio in 1979 is owned by an investment group led by the New York-based private equity firm Three Cities Research.

GARTNER, INC.   NYS: IT

56 Top Gallant Road
Stamford, CT 06902-7700
Phone: 203 316-1111
Fax: –
Web: www.gartner.com

CEO: Eugene A. (Gene) Hall
CFO: Craig Safian
HR: Rob Phillips
FYE: December 31
Type: Public

You might not know IT but Gartner does. The company helps clients understand the information technology (IT) industry and make informed decisions about IT products. It provides more than 9950 client organizations with competitive analysis reports industry overviews market trend data and product evaluation reports. Its GartnerG2 Gartner Dataquest and other research services are made available through subscriptions primarily to CIOs and other IT professionals. Gartner also offers technology and management consulting services and it produces a number of conferences seminars and other events aimed at the technology sector.

	Annual Growth	12/10	12/11	12/12	12/13	12/14
Sales ($ mil.)	11.9%	1,288.5	1,468.6	1,615.8	1,784.2	2,021.4
Net income ($ mil.)	17.5%	96.3	136.9	165.9	182.8	183.8
Market value ($ mil.)	26.2%	2,905.7	3,043.1	4,027.7	6,218.3	7,370.1
Employees	10.9%	4,461	4,975	5,468	5,997	6,758

GARY RABINE & SONS INC.

900 National Pkwy. Ste 260
Schaumburg IL 60173
Phone: 815-675-0555
Fax: +358-207-888-333
Web: www.rovio.com

CEO: –
CFO: –
HR: –
FYE: December 31
Type: Private

Gary Rabine & Sons known as The Rabine Group provides the Chicago region with what any US metropolitan area at its latitude needs: paving roofing and snow removal. It specializes in paving roads parking lots driveways and sidewalks. Rabine and its group of about a dozen companies also provide commercial and industrial roofing including solar panel and gardentop installation. When winter arrives it offers snow plowing blowing and rooftop shoveling. In addition the company owns a fuel distribution business hot mix asphalt plants and an operation enabling televised views inside pipelines for maintenance crews. Rabine got its start in 1981 and was founded by Gary Rabine.

GAS DEPOT OIL COMPANY

8700 N. Waukegan Rd. Ste. 200
Morton Grove IL 60053
Phone: 847-581-0303
Fax: 847-581-0309
Web: www.gasdepot.com

CEO: –
CFO: Nick Tanglis
HR: –
FYE: December 31
Type: Private

Gas Depot sits on a pot of oil but doesn't plan to hold on to it. The petroleum marketing company retails and wholesales gas and propane in the Midwest under the Gas Depot Valero CITGO Marathon Shell and Clark names. Gas Depot's nearly 20 retail locations are confined to the Chicago area while the company's wholesale business (about 160 customers) covers Illinois Indiana and Missouri. In addition to gas stations and convenience stores Gas Depot also offers store design real estate construction and financing services. The company began selling gasoline and propane to wholesale accounts in 2000. It bought into retail as many larger oil and gas firms dumped their retail holdings to focus on refining.

GASCO ENERGY INC.

NBB: GSXN

7979 E. Tufts Avenue, Suite 1150
Denver, CO 80237
Phone: 303 483-0044
Fax: 303 483-0011
Web: www.gascoenergy.com

CEO: Richard S Langdon
CFO: -
HR: -
FYE: December 31
Type: Public

Gasco Energy is not your local gas company or energy provider. The exploration and production independent develops and explores for natural gas and crude petroleum primarily in the Rocky Mountains. The company's exploration activities are focused on Utah's Uinta Basin and Wyoming's Green River Basin. At the end of 2008 Gasco Energy's proved reserves stood at 53.1 billion cu. ft. of natural gas equivalent. It had working interests in 330923 gross acres (214483 net acres) located in California Nevada Utah and Wyoming. That year it had stakes in 126 gross producing wells (77 net).

	Annual Growth	12/08	12/09	12/10	12/11	12/12
Sales ($ mil.)	(32.1%)	41.9	21.1	20.3	18.3	8.9
Net income ($ mil.)	-	14.5	(50.2)	10.1	(7.3)	(22.2)
Market value ($ mil.)	(34.9%)	66.2	90.0	59.4	38.2	11.9
Employees	(9.3%)	37	28	25	25	25

GATE GOURMET INC.

11710 Plaza America Dr. Ste. 800
Reston VA 20190
Phone: 703-964-2300
Fax: 703-964-2399
Web: www.gategourmet.com

CEO: Andrew Gibson
CFO: -
HR: -
FYE: December 31
Type: Subsidiary

Dining at 30000 feet is no problem when the plane is loaded with food from Gate Gourmet. The foodservice company is one of the world's largest in-flight caterers alongside rival LSG Sky Chefs. Gate Gourmet prepares more than 200 million meals each year for travelers. It serves customers from its 100 flight kitchens in more than 25 countries. The company boasts contracts with about 250 airlines including American Airlines Delta Air Lines and Thai Airways. Gate Gourmet also offers consulting on menu and service design cost monitoring and logistics. Gate Gourmet began in 1992 as the catering arm of Swissair; it is now part of the publicly traded gategroup.

GATES MCDONALD & COMPANY

215 N. Front St.
Columbus OH 43215
Phone: 614-677-3700
Fax: 614-677-3740
Web: www.nwbetterhealth.com

CEO: -
CFO: John Mier
HR: -
FYE: December 31
Type: Subsidiary

Gates McDonald & Company (GatesMcDonald) helps manage the three A's — absences accidents and ailments. Doing business as Nationwide Better Health the company is a third-party administrator (TPA) providing services including evaluation and management assistance for disability leave management and employee benefits programs. Customers range from small non-profit organizations to Fortune 100 companies. GatesMcDonald offers interactive management of family and medical leave administration of short- and long-term disability plans and management of vacation sick leave and other absences under the Better Health brand. The company is a subsidiary of Nationwide Mutual.

GATEWAY ENERGY CORPORATION

OTC: GNRG

500 Dallas St. Ste. 2615
Houston TX 77002
Phone: 713-336-0844
Fax: 713-336-0855
Web: www.gatewayenergy.com

CEO: -
CFO: -
HR: Skip Paterson
FYE: December 31
Type: Public

The door swings both ways for Gateway Energy which serves as a go-between for natural gas producers and customers. It owns natural gas gathering transportation and distribution systems (totaling 280 miles of pipeline) in Texas and in the Gulf of Mexico. Gateway Offshore Pipeline Company owns pipelines and a related operating platform. Onshore Gateway Energy owns two active onshore pipeline system in Texas. The company gathers gas at the wellhead and transports it to distribution companies or its own processing facilities. It also operates a natural gas processing unit and and a gas marketing company.

GATEWAY HEALTH PLAN INC.

US Steel Tower 600 Grant St. Fl. 41
Pittsburgh PA 15219-2704
Phone: 412-255-4640
Fax: 973-633-0879
Web: www.castrolusa.com

CEO: Patricia J Darnley
CFO: -
HR: Diana Vodzak
FYE: December 31
Type: Private

For many residents Gateway Health Plan is the keystone to health care coverage in Pennsylvania. The company provides managed health care services (as an HMO) to residents in 28 counties. Its Medicaid HMO serves some 220000 eligible recipients. In addition the company serves about 25000 members who qualify for both Medicare and Medicaid assistance through its Medicare Assured HMO special needs program (Medicare Assured?HMO SNP). Gateway's services include primary care dental prescriptions disease management and mental health services. Gateway an affiliate of Highmark was founded in 1992 as an alternative to the Department of Public Welfare's Medical Assistance Program in Pennsylvania.

GATEWAY INC.

7565 Irvine Center Dr.
Irvine CA 92618
Phone: 949-471-7000
Fax: 949-471-7041
Web: www.gateway.com

CEO: Ed Coleman
CFO: John Goldsberry
HR: -
FYE: December 31
Type: Subsidiary

Gateway opens doors to the world of computers. The company a subsidiary of Taiwanese PC maker Acer sells desktop and portable PCs as well as LCD displays and third-party accessories such as speakers and carrying cases. It also provides technical support services for its products as well as for electronics products by other manufacturers. The company sells through retailers including Best Buy Office Depot Wal-Mart Frys Electronics and Newegg and various channel partners. Parent company Acer also markets the eMachines and Packard Bell brands making it among the top PC manufacturers in the world trailing such stalwarts as Hewlett-Packard Lenovo and Dell.

GATEWAY US RETAIL INC.

7565 Irvine Center Dr.
Irvine CA 92618
Phone: 949-471-7000
Fax: 949-471-7041
Web: www.emachines.com
CEO: Wayne R Inouye
CFO: –
HR: –
FYE: December 31
Type: Subsidiary

Gateway US Retail doing business as eMachines cranks out affordable computers. A subsidiary of Gateway eMachines now represents Gateway's value brand. eMachines' products include PCs and desktop displays. Marketed toward budget-conscious consumers its desktop and notebook PCs are sold by a variety of electronics retailers. Former rival Gateway purchased eMachines for approximately $235 million in cash and stock. After the acquisition Gateway closed its retail stores and installed a number of eMachines executives in top management posts. eMachines' products are sold exclusively through retailers.

GATX CORP.
NYS: GMT

222 West Adams Street
Chicago, IL 60606-5314
Phone: 312 621-6200
Fax: –
Web: www.gatx.com
CEO: Brian A. Kenney
CFO: Robert C. Lyons
HR: Mary K. (Katie) Lawler
FYE: December 31
Type: Public

GATX never tried to unite Georgia and Texas but the holding company does bring together some diverse businesses. Short for General American Transportation Corporation GATX operates through three business segments. Rail with about 164000 railcars (mostly tank and freight plus 570 locomotives) is the company's biggest unit handling tank freight car and locomotive leasing in the US and Europe. The American Steamship Company (ASC) business is a shipping company with a fleet of self-unloading ships operating on the Great Lakes. Its third segment portfolio management handles leases affiliate investments and loans for the marine construction and mining and manufacturing equipment industries.

	Annual Growth	12/10	12/11	12/12	12/13	12/14
Sales ($ mil.)	4.8%	1,204.9	1,308.5	1,243.2	1,321.0	1,451.0
Net income ($ mil.)	26.2%	80.8	110.8	137.3	169.3	205.0
Market value ($ mil.)	13.0%	1,559.3	1,929.7	1,913.8	2,305.9	2,543.2
Employees	3.3%	1,947	1,999	2,046	2,139	2,213

GAVIN DE BECKER & ASSOCIATES

11684 Ventura Blvd Ste. 440
Studio City CA 91604
Phone: 818-505-0177
Fax: 818-506-0426
Web: www.gavindebecker.com
CEO: –
CFO: –
HR: Jeanette Tran
FYE: December 31
Type: Private

Need a bodyguard at your beck and call? Gavin de Becker & Associates is a security consulting firm that provides protective services and consultation to high-profile individuals political and cultural leaders federal government agencies institutions and large corporations worldwide. The company's services include personal protection threat assessment violence prevention training and support services. Gavin de Becker has provided its services for events such as the Emmy Awards the Academy Awards and presidential inaugurations. Its clients have included Sony Pictures Michael J. Fox and NBC News.

GC SERVICES LIMITED PARTNERSHIP

6330 Gulfton St.
Houston TX 77081-1108
Phone: 713-777-4441
Fax: 713-777-6619
Web: www.gcserv.com
CEO: Frank A Taylor
CFO: Michael Jones
HR: Richard Gutierrez
FYE: December 31
Type: Private

GC Services considers it a Good Call when it Gets Cash. The company one of the nation's top collection agencies provides a wide range of services including customer relations and receivables management to clients throughout North America from more than 30 call centers. Its teleservices division provides inbound and outbound call center management services including general reception and operator services billing and payment assistance and back-office processing of accounts. Its receivables management division provides debt collection data management and other services. The company has the capacity to take operator-assisted calls in various languages and handles about 20 million calls each month.

GCT SEMICONDUCTOR INC.

2121 Ringwood Ave.
San Jose CA 95131
Phone: 408-434-6040
Fax: 408-434-6050
Web: www.gctsemi.com
CEO: John Schlaefer
CFO: Gene Kulzer
HR: –
FYE: June 30
Type: Private

While not a household name GCT Semiconductor enables activities most people are familiar with. The fabless semiconductor company's wireless communications chips include LTE-based radio-frequency (RF) transceivers for cell phones WiMAX networking chips and RF transceivers for WLAN equipment. Its single-chip LTE product for smartphones is used in mobile devices made by LG and sold by AT&T and Verizon among others. Unlike many chip developers GCT has its semiconductors fabricated with a CMOS silicon process. The company was co-founded in 1998 by CEO Kyeongho Lee. Chairman Paul Kim owns 31% GCT of GCT through Parakletos Ventures. The company filed for an IPO in 2011.

GE AVIATION

1 Neumann Way
Cincinnati OH 45215-6301
Phone: 513-243-2000
Fax: 502-452-0352
Web: www.geappliances.com
CEO: –
CFO: –
HR: –
FYE: December 31
Type: Business Segment

GE Aviation joins the podium — alongside the likes of Pratt & Whitney and Rolls-Royce — as one of the world's largest providers of jet engines and services for commercial and military aircraft. A business segment of GE GE Aviation produces large and small jet turboprop and turbo shaft engines. It also offers replacement parts and maintenance repair and overhaul (MRO) services. Some engines are produced and marketed through CFM International and Engine Alliance (jointly owned by GE and Pratt & Whitney. Newer engines are also being designed and marketed in joint ventures with Rolls-Royce and Honda Aero. GE Aviation operates globally.

GEEKNET INC
NMS: GKNT

11216 Waples Mill Rd., Suite 100
Fairfax, VA 22030
Phone: 877 433-5638
Fax: –
Web: www.geek.net

CEO: Kathryn K McCarthy
CFO: Julie A Pangelinan
HR: –
FYE: December 31
Type: Public

Geeknet is tuned in to what hipster techies crave. The company operates through its wholly-owned subsidiary ThinkGeek an online retailer of goodies for the global geek community. The company (formerly SourceForge) exited the business of producing websites for software developers to focus entirely on its ThinkGeek website which offers a broad range of apparel edibles electronics gadgets and other geek-themed merchandise for fans of movies and TV programs such as Star Wars Star Trek Dr. Who and Game of Thrones. Founded by former chairman Larry Augustin in 1993 Geeknet sold its Media business including the SourceForge Slashdot and Freecode websites in 2012 to focus on online retail.

	Annual Growth	12/09	12/10	12/11	12/12	12/13
Sales ($ mil.)	20.5%	65.6	94.6	119.5	118.9	138.3
Net income ($ mil.)	–	(14.0)	(4.4)	(1.2)	13.9	(0.2)
Market value ($ mil.)	97.5%	7.9	166.2	113.2	106.9	120.1
Employees	(8.0%)	127	122	143	76	91

GEHAN HOMES LTD.

15725 DALLAS PKWY STE 300
ADDISON, TX 750013850
Phone: 972-663-9100
Fax: –
Web: www.gehanhomes.com

CEO: Tim Gehan
CFO: –
HR: –
FYE: December 31
Type: Private

They say everything is bigger in Texas and for Gehan Homes that hopefully applies to the number of homes sold. Gehan Homes builds single-family houses in about 60 communities in and around Austin Dallas Fort Worth Houston and San Antonio. Its houses range in price from the low $100000s to the low $300000s. Gehan Homes owns the land it builds on and provides mortgage brokerage through majority-owned Suburban Mortgage. Through cutting costs and slowing down production the homebuilder is working to stay afloat in a market that has caused several competitors to file for bankruptcy or shut down operations. John Gehan founded the family-owned company in the 1960s.

	Annual Growth	11/0-1	11/00	11/01	11/02*	12/07
Sales ($ mil.)	7.4%	–	–	–	150.5	214.6
Net income ($ mil.)	(21.8%)	–	–	–	13.8	4.0
Market value ($ mil.)	–	–	–	–	–	–
Employees	–	–	–	–	–	175

*Fiscal year change

GEHL COMPANY

143 Water St.
West Bend WI 53095
Phone: 262-334-9461
Fax: 262-338-7517
Web: www.gehl.com

CEO: William D Gehl
CFO: Malcolm F Moore
HR: –
FYE: December 31
Type: Subsidiary

Gehl Company asks the question "Can you dig it?" The company manufactures light-construction equipment bearing the Gehl and Mustang brand names primarily used by building contractors. Products include mini-excavators mini-loaders and skid steer loaders for material handling; telescopic loaders; and asphalt pavers for building sidewalks parking lots trails and driveways. It has about several hundred independent dealers around the globe but most are located in North America. Gehl also offers financing to its dealers and their customers. France-based MANITOU BF previously one of Gehl's largest shareholders acquired the company in 2008.

GEICO CORPORATION

5260 Western Ave.
Chevy Chase MD 20076
Phone: 301-986-3000
Fax: 281-879-3626
Web: www.iongeo.com

CEO: Tony Nicely
CFO: Mike Campbell
HR: –
FYE: December 31
Type: Subsidiary

GEICO (an acronym for Government Employees Insurance Company) has found that driving down costs brings drivers by the droves into its fold. GEICO has traditionally provided auto and other insurance to preferred low-risk demographic groups (such as government and military employees) but has also begun to sell to nonstandard (high-risk) drivers. In addition to auto coverage the company's offerings include motorcycle and RV insurance and emergency road service. GEICO eschews agents in favor of direct marketing through such vehicles as direct mail TV radio and the Internet. Its gecko mascot is one of the most recognized marketing icons. The company is a subsidiary of Warren Buffett's Berkshire Hathaway.

GEISINGER HEALTH SYSTEM FOUNDATION

100 N. Academy Ave.
Danville PA 17822
Phone: 570-271-6211
Fax: 570-271-7498
Web: www.geisinger.org

CEO: Glenn D Steele Jr
CFO: –
HR: –
FYE: June 30
Type: Private - Not-for-Pr

Geisinger Health System provides health care to a large portion of the Keystone State. The health care system serves more than 2.6 million residents of nearly 45 counties spanning central and northeastern Pennsylvania. Founded in 1915 the organization's flagship facility is Geisinger Medical Center a 400-bed medical-surgical hospital located in Danville. It includes the Janet Weis Children's Hospital. With joint venture partner HealthSouth Geisinger also runs a rehabilitation hospital in Danville. As part of its operations the health system runs the 240-bed Geisinger Wyoming Valley Medical Center as well as numerous outpatient facilities and doctors' offices located throughout the region.

GELBER GROUP LLC

350 N ORLEANS ST FL 7
CHICAGO, IL 606541601
Phone: 312-253-0005
Fax: –
Web: www.gelbergroup.com

CEO: –
CFO: Franklin A Gelber
HR: –
FYE: December 31
Type: Private

Gelber Group develops proprietary technology-based trading models for dealing in equities cash currencies commodities sovereign debt futures and related options markets. The company no longer has outside clients or investors; all of its trading activity is undertaken for its own account. Gelber Group which previously provided electronic trading services to individual professional traders was co-founded in 1982 by Brian Gelber (company chairman and president) and Frank Gelber (CFO). In addition to its Chicago Apparel Center headquarters the company also boasts offices in Connecticut New Jersey and New York as well as the UK.

	Annual Growth	12/01	12/02	12/03	12/04	12/07
Assets ($ mil.)	–	–	–	0.0	106.8	338.9
Net income ($ mil.)	811.0%	–	–	0.0	70.2	112.9
Market value ($ mil.)	–	–	–	–	–	–
Employees	–	–	–	–	–	300

GEMMA POWER SYSTEMS

2461 Main St.
Glastonbury CT 06033
Phone: 860-659-0509
Fax: 860-659-0607
Web: www.gemmapower.com

CEO: William F Griffin Jr
CFO: –
HR: Bill Griffin
FYE: December 31
Type: Subsidiary

Gemma Power Systems (GPS) is a top designer and builder of power generation facilities in the New England region of the US. The company a subsidiary of Argan provides a full range of services to the energy market from development consulting engineering and procurement to construction start-up operation and maintenance. Gemma Power Systems has completed more than 70 projects including district heating and cooling systems boiler plant construction and renovations utility maintenance combined-cycle and cogeneration facilities emergency peaking plants and alternative fuel-powered facilities (wood-fired power plants wind plants and more). Argan bought GPS in 2006 for more than $33 million.

GEN-PROBE INCORPORATED

NASDAQ: GPRO

10210 Genetic Center Dr.
San Diego CA 92121-4362
Phone: 858-410-8000
Fax: 858-410-8625
Web: www.gen-probe.com

CEO: Carl W Hull
CFO: Herm Rosenman
HR: –
FYE: December 31
Type: Private

Gen-Probe knows the answer is flowing through your veins. The company is a leading provider of molecular diagnostic tests and instruments to detect a host of infectious disease-causing viruses and bacteria including those behind HIV Chlamydia tuberculosis strep throat and influenza. Gen-Probe's diagnostic tests provide results within hours while traditional cultured tests can take days. In addition the firm has screening products to help identify compatible transplant matches and it also makes instruments and testing assays to screen donated blood for diseases. Customers include clinical and research laboratories and blood banks. Gen-Probe was acquired by medical equipment maker Hologic in 2012.

GENBAND INC.

2801 Network Blvd. Ste. 300
Frisco TX 75034
Phone: 972-521-5800
Fax: 972-265-3599
Web: www.genband.com

CEO: David Walsh
CFO: Daryl Raiford
HR: –
FYE: December 31
Type: Private

GENBAND ensures a smooth migration to next-generation networks. The company provides carrier-class networking gear that some 600 telecommunications providers use to deploy voice and multimedia services. Designed for fixed wireless and cable operators its products include media gateways call controllers and application servers. Communications service providers such as PAETEC and Axtel use GENBAND's products to build and upgrade their networks. The company counts One Equity Partners Sevin Rosen Oak Investment Partners and Venrock Associates among its investors.

GENCO DISTRIBUTION SYSTEM INC.

100 Papercraft Park
Pittsburgh PA 15238
Phone: 412-820-3700
Fax: 412-820-3689
Web: www.genco.com

CEO: Todd R Peters
CFO: –
HR: –
FYE: December 31
Type: Private

Generations of businesses in need of third-party logistics have deferred to GENCO Distribution System. Founded in 1898 the company also doing business as GENCO ATC offers warehousing and distribution services reverse logistics (processing of returned goods) product liquidation supply chain analysis transportation management including parcels and damage research (analyzing the cause of customers' damaged products). Customers include manufacturers retailers and government agencies. The company manages 130 locations in North America providing a combined 38 million square feet of warehouse space. CEO Herb Shear owns the company which was started by his grandfather Hyman Shear.

GENCO SHIPPING & TRADING LIMITED

NYSE: GNK

299 Park Ave. 20th Fl.
New York NY 10171
Phone: 646-443-8550
Fax: 646-443-8551
Web: gencoshipping.com

CEO: John C Wobensmith
CFO: Apostolos Zafolias
HR: –
FYE: December 31
Type: Public

Marine transportation company Genco Shipping & Trading transports dry cargo in a wet environment. The company maintains a fleet of about 50 oceangoing dry bulk carriers which it charters mainly on long-term contracts to shippers of bulk commodities and marine transportation companies. Its fleet has an overall capacity of almost 4 million deadweight tons (DWT). Genco Shipping's vessels transport cargo such as coal grain iron ore and steel products. More than half of its vessels are on time-charter contracts. Customers have included BHP Billiton Lauritzen Bulkers and NYK; clients Cargill and Pacific Basin Shipping make up about 10% of the company's revenues. Genco Shipping & Trading was founded in 2004.

GENCOR INDUSTRIES, INC.

NMS: GENC

5201 North Orange Blossom Trail
Orlando, FL 32810
Phone: 407 290-6000
Fax: –
Web: www.gencor.com

CEO: E J Elliott
CFO: Eric E Mellen
HR: –
FYE: September 30
Type: Public

Gencor Industries is a US manufacturer of heavy machinery used in the production of highway construction materials synthetic fuels and environmental control equipment. Subsidiary Bituma designs and manufactures hot-mix asphalt batch plants used in the production of asphalt paving materials. Subsidiary General Combustion engineers combustion systems namely large burners that can transform almost any fuel into energy or burn multiple fuels simultaneously and fluid heat transfer systems under the Hy-Way and Beverley brands. With two manufacturing facilities in the US it sells products through its own sales force and independent dealers and agents located throughout the world.

	Annual Growth	09/11	09/12	09/13	09/14	09/15
Sales ($ mil.)	(10.0%)	59.7	63.2	48.9	40.0	39.2
Net income ($ mil.)	–	0.2	4.5	6.7	3.5	(1.8)
Market value ($ mil.)	5.6%	69.2	70.6	81.8	93.7	86.2
Employees	(5.9%)	275	263	237	222	216

GENELINK INC

NBB: GNLK

8250 Exchange Drive, Suite 120
Orlando, FL 32809
Phone: 407 680-1150
Fax: –
Web: www.genelink.info

CEO: –
CFO: Michael Smith
HR: –
FYE: December 31
Type: Public

GeneLink has taken the science of molecular genetics and turned it into a way to sell face cream and vitamins. Although the promise of immortality is out of its reach the biosciences company aims to improve one's health beauty and wellness with customized nutritional supplements and anti-aging skin care products based upon proprietary DNA assessments obtained from a cheek swab. Other consumer genomic products in development include products to predict how an individual's skin will age or if an individual has a significant risk of developing cardiovascular disease Alzheimer's ADHD or loss of bone density.

	Annual Growth	12/08	12/09	12/10	12/11	12/12
Sales ($ mil.)	(23.9%)	6.4	8.6	7.8	4.7	2.1
Net income ($ mil.)	–	(2.6)	(2.7)	(2.4)	(3.8)	(3.1)
Market value ($ mil.)	(48.0%)	35.5	30.4	10.4	15.5	2.6
Employees	–	–	–	–	–	–

GENENCOR INTERNATIONAL INC.

925 Page Mill Rd.
Palo Alto CA 94304
Phone: 650-846-7500
Fax: 650-845-6500
Web: www.genencor.com

CEO: James C Collins
CFO: –
HR: –
FYE: December 31
Type: Subsidiary

If you've got the money honey Genencor International's got the 'zyme. Genencor manufactures genetically modified enzymes for the industrial agricultural and consumer products markets. Using its biotechnology know-how the company discovers useful enzymes (naturally occurring protein catalysts) and develops them for mass production; the enzymes are used in myriad ways including as additives in animal feed and detergents as a method of converting starch into ethanol and in the production of textiles and paper. Genencor International is a division of food ingredient company Danisco.

GENENTECH INC.

1 DNA Way
South San Francisco CA 94080-4
Phone: 650-225-1000
Fax: 650-225-6000
Web: www.gene.com

CEO: Ian Clark
CFO: Steve Krognes
HR: –
FYE: December 31
Type: Subsidiary

"The few the proud the profitable" could be Genentech's motto. One of the world's oldest and most successful biotechs (in an industry full of money-losers) the firm has a number of blockbuster cancer therapies based on its antibody (protein) technologies. Its oncology portfolio contains Rituxan (non-Hodgkin's lymphoma) Avastin (colorectal and lung cancers) Herceptin (breast cancer) Tarceva (lung cancer) Xeloda (metastatic colorectal cancer) and Zelboraf (inoperable melanoma). Other marketed drugs include age-related macular degeneration treatment Lucentis human growth hormone Nutropin cystic fibrosis drug Pulmozyme and asthma drug Xolair. Genentech is wholly owned by Swiss drugmaker Roche.

GENERAC HOLDINGS INC

NYS: GNRC

S45 W29290 Hwy. 59
Waukesha, WI 53189
Phone: 262 544-4811
Fax: –
Web: www.generac.com

CEO: Aaron Jagdfeld
CFO: York A. Ragen
HR: –
FYE: December 31
Type: Public

Perfect storms make good business for Generac Power Systems. That's because the company manufactures engine-driven standby and portable generators for homes businesses hospitals and recreational vehicles. The company also makes industrial power generation equipment automatic transfer switches switch gear and controls and remote monitoring software. Brands include Generac Magnum Ottomotores and Tower Light. Generac sells its products through retailers as well as through wholesale distributors. The US and Canada represent nearly 90% of the company sales.

	Annual Growth	12/10	12/11	12/12	12/13	12/14
Sales ($ mil.)	25.3%	592.9	792.0	1,176.3	1,485.8	1,460.9
Net income ($ mil.)	32.3%	56.9	324.6	93.2	174.5	174.6
Market value ($ mil.)	30.4%	1,114.5	1,931.9	2,364.8	3,903.9	3,222.9
Employees	25.5%	1,444	2,223	3,048	3,380	3,587

GENERAL ATLANTIC LLC

Three Pickwick Plaza
Greenwich CT 06830
Phone: 203-629-8600
Fax: 203-622-8818
Web: www.generalatlantic.com

CEO: William E Ford
CFO: Thomas J Murphy
HR: –
FYE: December 31
Type: Private

General Atlantic helps little fish become bigger fish in the big pond called business. The private equity firm provides both capital and strategic support to public and private growth companies. With about $17 billion in capital under management General Atlantic focuses its investments on such sectors as energy financial services health care media and technology. Typical investments range from $50 million to $500 million per transaction and its average investment period lasts from five to seven years. Established in 1980 General Atlantic has stakes in about 40 firms. Portfolio holdings include AKQA Genpact and Facebook.

GENERAL ATOMICS

3550 General Atomics Ct.
San Diego CA 92121-1122
Phone: 858-455-3000
Fax: 858-455-3621
Web: www.ga.com

CEO: J Neal Blue
CFO: Tony Navarra
HR: –
FYE: December 31
Type: Private

General Atomics has more than nuclear energy these days. The company which was founded in 1955 to research atomic energy continues to develop and operate nuclear power reactor systems but may be finding more demand for its research and engineering expertise in areas such as unmanned military aircraft airborne sensors hazardous waste superconducting magnets and information technology. Through several divisions and subsidiaries the company commercializes and develops its technology to customers worldwide. Customers have included the US Department of Defense the US Department of Energy and National Science Foundation. General Atomics was originally a division of defense titan General Dynamics.

GENERAL ATOMICS AERONAUTICAL SYSTEMS INC.

14200 Kirkham Way
Poway CA 92065
Phone: 858-312-2810
Fax: 858-312-4247
Web: www.ga-asi.com

CEO: Neal Blue
CFO: –
HR: –
FYE: December 31
Type: Subsidiary

General Atomics Aeronautical Systems Inc. (GA-ASI) knows that some aircraft are better off without human pilots. The company is a designer and manufacturer of unmanned aircraft systems (UAS) with names like Predator Avenger and Gray Eagle as well as airborne intelligence reconnaissance and surveillance (ISR) sensor systems including the Lynx multi-function radar and the Highlighter sensor for detecting improvised explosive devices. The company also manufactures solid-state digital ground control stations and provides UAS training and field operations support services. Additionally it is developing lasers for rangefinding and marking targets. GA-ASI is an affiliate of privately-held General Atomics.

GENERAL CASUALTY INSURANCE COMPANIES

1 General Dr.
Sun Prairie WI 53596
Phone: 608-837-4440
Fax: 608-837-0583
Web: www.generalcasualty.com

CEO: John R Pollock
CFO: –
HR: –
FYE: December 31
Type: Subsidiary

Despite its name General Casualty Insurance Companies (GCIC) gets very specific about its property/casualty products. The company administers personal and commercial auto homeowners liability and workers' compensation coverage through regional offices. GCIC's products are sold through more than 1000 independent insurance agencies in all 50 states though it focuses on the northeastern and midwestern US. The company specializes in packages for large commercial accounts; it also serves niche and small business clients including golf courses and restaurants (read: niche). Its individual auto insurance segment includes nonstandard policies. GCIC is a subsidiary of QBE Regional Insurance.

GENERAL BEARING CORPORATION

PINK SHEETS: GNRL

44 High St.
West Nyack NY 10994-2702
Phone: 845-358-6000
Fax: 845-358-6277
Web: www.generalbearing.com

CEO: David L Gussack
CFO: Rocky Cambrea
HR: –
FYE: December 31
Type: Public

General Bearing has been on a roll for more than half a century. Founded in 1958 the company sources assembles and distributes roller bearings primarily under the Hyatt brand name. Products include ball bearings tapered roller bearings precision roller bearings spherical roller bearings and other related components. The lineup is sold primarily to OEMs of trains trucks trailers office equipment and appliances as well as to industrial aftermarket distributors. Based in the US General Bearing operates an array of plants and an engineering and technology center through four facilities in China. In mid-2012 General Bearing was acquired by rival bearings manufacturer SKF for about $125 million.

GENERAL CIGAR CO. INC.

7300 Beaufont Springs Dr. Ste. 400
Richmond VA 23225-5551
Phone: 804-302-1700
Fax: 804-302-1760
Web: www.cigarworld.com

CEO: –
CFO: –
HR: –
FYE: December 31
Type: Subsidiary

It may be true that sometimes a cigar is just a cigar but for General Cigar a cigar is money. The company produces Macanudo the #1 premium cigar in the US and other brands such as Cohiba and Bolivar which are distributed for sale through tobacco retailers nationwide. The Macanudo brand consists of Macanudo Macanudo Robust Macanudo Maduro and Macanudo Vintage Cabinet Selection. The firm operates the Club Macanudo cigar bar in New York City and grows cures ages and processes wrapper tobacco in Connecticut through its Culbro Tobacco unit. Swedish Match the world's leading producer of matches acquired the cigar maker in 2005. General Cigar sells about 30% of the cigars consumed in the US.

GENERAL CABLE CORP. (DE)

NYS: BGC

4 Tesseneer Drive
Highland Heights, KY 41076-9753
Phone: 859 572-8000
Fax: 859 572-8458
Web: www.generalcable.com

CEO: Gregory J. Lampert
CFO: Brian J. Robinson
HR: Sonya Reed
FYE: December 31
Type: Public

General Cable keeps power flowing and communication going. The company designs manufactures and distributes copper aluminum and fiber optic wire and cable products that are used in electrical transmission and distribution power generation and voice and data communications. Major brands include BICC (energy cables) Carol (temporary power cables) and NextGen (data communication cables). General Cable's products are sold to commercial industrial electric utility telecom military and government retail and OEM distributor customers worldwide. The company also makes copper and aluminum rod for other wire and cable manufacturers and it integrates and installs high voltage systems on land and under water.

	Annual Growth	12/10	12/11	12/12	12/13	12/14
Sales ($ mil.)	5.3%	4,864.9	5,866.7	6,014.3	6,421.2	5,979.8
Net income ($ mil.)	–	76.9	85.2	9.8	(10.1)	(643.0)
Market value ($ mil.)	(19.3%)	1,708.3	1,217.6	1,480.5	1,431.8	725.4
Employees	2.7%	11,700	12,000	14,000	15,000	13,000

GENERAL COMMUNICATION INC

NMS: GNCM A

2550 Denali Street, Suite 1000
Anchorage, AK 99503
Phone: 907 868-5600
Fax: –
Web: www.gci.com

CEO: Ronald A. (Ron) Duncan
CFO: Peter J. (Pete) Pounds
HR: Kathy Carr
FYE: December 31
Type: Public

A land of long distances needs good long distance service. Through its operating subsidiaries General Communication Inc. (GCI) provides facilities-based phone services to more than 144000 local callers and 97000 long-distance customers in the five largest population areas of Alaska: Anchorage Fairbanks Juneau the Matanuska-Susitna Valley and the Kenai Peninsula. The competitive local-exchange carrier is also one of Alaska's leading cable TV providers with more than 147000 basic cable subscribers; it provides wireless services to 138000-plus customers through a partnership with AT&T Mobility. More than 116000 subscribers receive cable modem service.

	Annual Growth	12/10	12/11	12/12	12/13	12/14
Sales ($ mil.)	8.7%	651.3	679.4	710.2	811.6	910.2
Net income ($ mil.)	(4.2%)	9.0	5.8	9.7	9.4	7.6
Market value ($ mil.)	2.1%	520.7	402.7	394.4	458.6	565.6
Employees	8.0%	1,655	1,702	1,734	1,924	2,255

GENERAL DYNAMICS CORP.
NYS: GD

2941 Fairview Park Drive, Suite 100
Falls Church, VA 22042-4513
Phone: 703 876-3000
Fax: –
Web: www.generaldynamics.com

CEO: Phebe N. Novakovic
CFO: Jason W. Aiken
HR: Jack Picker
FYE: December 31
Type: Public

Generally dynamic General Dynamics is a prime military contractor to the Pentagon (the US government accounts for about 60% of sales). The company's military operations include information systems and technology (information technology and collection as well as command control systems); marine systems (warships commercial tankers and nuclear submarines); and combat systems (battle tanks wheeled combat/tactical vehicles munitions and rockets and gun systems). Its aerospace unit which is composed of Gulfstream Aerospace and Jet Aviation designs makes and refurbishes business jets primarily for civilian customers.

	Annual Growth	12/11	12/12	12/13	12/14	12/15
Sales ($ mil.)	(0.9%)	32,677.0	31,513.0	31,218.0	30,852.0	31,469.0
Net income ($ mil.)	4.1%	2,526.0	(332.0)	2,357.0	2,533.0	2,965.0
Market value ($ mil.)	19.9%	20,785.5	21,680.6	29,905.9	43,073.3	42,991.9
Employees	1.2%	95,100	92,200	96,000	99,500	99,900

GENERAL DYNAMICS LAND SYSTEMS INC.

38500 Mound Rd.
Sterling Heights MI 48310-3200
Phone: 586-825-4000
Fax: 586-825-4013
Web: www.gdls.com

CEO: –
CFO: Evelyn Milan
HR: –
FYE: December 31
Type: Subsidiary

Patton and Rommel would love General Dynamics Land Systems' (GDLS) products. A business unit of General Dynamics' Combat Systems division GDLS makes tracked and wheeled armored and amphibious combat vehicles for the US military and its allies (for personnel transport medical evacuation fire support anti-tank missions combat engineering and reconnaissance). Its big gun is the Abrams main battle tank (MBT). Other products include the Stryker infantry combat vehicle and gun systems its LAV family of combat and reconnaissance vehicles mine resistant ambush protected vehicles (MRAPs) the Marines' Expeditionary Fighting Vehicle (EFV) and the FOX Nuclear Biological Chemical Reconnaissance System.

GENERAL ELECTRIC CAPITAL CORPORATION

901 Main Ave.
Norwalk CT 06851-1168
Phone: 203-840-6300
Fax: +81-3-5606-1502
Web: www.fujikura.co.jp

CEO: Keith S Sherin
CFO: Robert C Green
HR: –
FYE: December 31
Type: Subsidiary

General Electric Capital (GE Capital) encompasses the financing operations of sprawling conglomerate General Electric. The group's five segments provide commercial loans and leases consumer loans and credit cards and real estate financing services around the world. GE Capital's largest segments are commercial lending and leasing and consumer lending which together account for about 80% of revenues. Its GE Commercial Aviation Services specialist segment leases commercial aircraft while its energy financial services segment provides project funding for customers in the energy and water sectors. GE Capital is active in more than 50 countries but does most of its business in the US and Europe.

GENERAL ELECTRIC CO
NYS: GE

3135 Easton Turnpike
Fairfield, CT 06828-0001
Phone: 203 373-2211
Fax: 203 373-3131
Web: www.ge.com

CEO: Keith S. Sherin
CFO: Jeffrey S. (Jeff) Bornstein
HR: Melissa Reinke
FYE: December 31
Type: Public

From turbines and TVs to aircraft engines and power plants General Electric (GE) is plugged in to businesses that shape the modern world. The company produces — take a deep breath — aircraft engines locomotives and other transportation equipment lighting electric control equipment generators and turbines and medical imaging equipment. GE also owns mega-financial company GE Capital which offers commercial finance commercial aircraft leasing real estate and energy financial services. GE's other segments include Aviation Home & Business Solutions and Transportation. GE looks to sell its GE Capital and home appliances businesses to focus on its core industrial business.

	Annual Growth	12/10	12/11	12/12	12/13	12/14
Sales ($ mil.)	(0.3%)	150,211.0	147,300.0	147,359.0	146,045.0	148,589.0
Net income ($ mil.)	6.9%	11,644.0	14,151.0	13,641.0	13,057.0	15,233.0
Market value ($ mil.)	–	0.0	0.0	0.0	0.0	0.0
Employees	1.5%	287,000	301,000	305,000	307,000	305,000

GENERAL EMPLOYMENT ENTERPRISES INC
ASE: JOB

184 Shuman Blvd., Suite 420
Naperville, IL 60563
Phone: 630 954-0400
Fax: 630 954-0447
Web: www.generalemployment.com

CEO: Andrew J. Norstrud
CFO: Frank Elenio
HR: –
FYE: September 30
Type: Public

Who's got jobs for information technology engineering and accounting professionals? General Employment Enterprises specializes in finding this group permanent and temporary employment. Most offices operate under the General Employment name and provide both full-time employee placement and contract staffing (other brand names include Triad Personnel Services Business Management Personnel Generation Technologies and Omni One). The firm places permanent employees for a fee based on a percentage of their salaries. Contract workers remain employees of the company which bills clients hourly for their services. In mid-2009 the company was acquired by PSQ LLC a newly-formed limited liability company.

	Annual Growth	09/11	09/12	09/13	09/14	09/15
Sales ($ mil.)	3.9%	37.2	52.4	46.5	39.8	43.4
Net income ($ mil.)	–	0.4	(1.0)	(1.9)	(1.4)	(4.7)
Market value ($ mil.)	15.0%	2.0	5.7	2.0	1.4	3.5
Employees	(3.4%)	140	140	160	140	122

GENERAL FINANCE CORP
NMS: GFN

39 East Union Street
Pasadena, CA 91103
Phone: 626 584-9722
Fax: –
Web: www.generalfinance.com

CEO: Ronald F Valenta
CFO: Charles E Barrantes
HR: –
FYE: June 30
Type: Public

General Finance Corporation wants to help you get your hands on some equipment. The investment holding company is building up a portfolio of specialty financing and equipment leasing companies in North America Europe and the Asia-Pacific. It made its first acquisition of RWA Holdings and its subsidiaries (collectively known as Royal Wolf) in 2007. Royal Wolf leases and sells portable storage containers portable buildings and freight containers to customers in the defense mining moving and storage and road and rail markets in Australia. General Finance acquired Pac-Van a provider of modular buildings and mobile offices in 2008. CEO Ronald Valenta owns 20% of the company.

	Annual Growth	06/11	06/12	06/13	06/14	06/15
Sales ($ mil.)	13.6%	182.3	212.2	245.5	287.1	303.8
Net income ($ mil.)	–	(8.9)	8.7	11.4	15.1	13.0
Market value ($ mil.)	14.9%	77.8	83.7	120.9	247.1	135.8
Employees	37.2%	229	439	729	902	811

GENERAL GROWTH PROPERTIES INC
NYS: GGP

110 N. Wacker Dr.
Chicago, IL 60606
Phone: 312 960-5000
Fax: –
Web: www.ggp.com

CEO: Sandeep Mathrani
CFO: Michael B. Berman
HR: Kristen Freeland
FYE: December 31
Type: Public

General Growth Properties (GGP) has an idea for an economic stimulus plan: Let's all hang out at the mall! GGP is the country's #2 mall operator behind Simon Property Group. The self-managed and self-administered real estate investment trust (REIT) has a portfolio that includes 128 regional shopping malls (some 127 million sq. ft. of space) in major US markets. GGP owns manages leases and redevelops its malls which generate more than $570 per square foot in sales each year. Some of GGP's shopping locations include Ala Moana Center in Honolulu and Fashion Show in Las Vegas. GGP also has an interest in a mall in Brazil. Top tenants include L Brands Abercrombie & Fitch Foot Locker and The Gap.

	Annual Growth	12/10	12/11	12/12	12/13	12/14
Sales ($ mil.)	57.1%	416.5	2,742.9	2,511.9	2,527.4	2,535.6
Net income ($ mil.)	–	(254.2)	(313.2)	(481.2)	302.5	665.9
Market value ($ mil.)	16.1%	13,698.4	13,291.4	17,565.5	17,760.2	24,892.6
Employees	(10.5%)	2,800	1,750	1,670	1,500	1,800

GENERAL HEALTH SYSTEM

8585 PICARDY AVE
BATON ROUGE, LA 708093679
Phone: 225-237-1500
Fax: –

CEO: Mark F Slyter
CFO: Kendall Johnson
HR: –
FYE: September 30
Type: Private

Injured? We're sending you to the General. General Health System provides a comprehensive range of health services to residents of southern Louisiana. The system's flagship facility is the not-for-profit community-owned Baton Rouge General Medical Center aka "the General". The medical center founded in 1927 houses some 550 beds split between two campuses in Louisiana's capital. It provides general medical and surgical care emergency services and specialty care in a number of areas including burn cancer and heart disease. General Health System is affiliated with Advanced Medical Concepts (a supplier of medical equipment) and First Care Physicians (a network of primary care physicians).

	Annual Growth	09/03	09/04	09/05	09/09	09/13
Sales ($ mil.)	6.0%	–	–	42.9	56.0	68.4
Net income ($ mil.)	(19.2%)	–	–	0.6	(29.9)	0.1
Market value ($ mil.)	–	–	–	–	–	–
Employees	–	–	–	–	–	4,686

GENERAL MAGNAPLATE CORPORATION

1331 Rte. 1 and 9 North
Linden NJ 07036
Phone: 908-862-6200
Fax: 908-862-6110
Web: www.magnaplate.com

CEO: –
CFO: –
HR: –
FYE: June 30
Type: Private

General Magnaplate is one slick out-of-this-world company. Magnaplate makes coatings that increase the performance of metals. Every NASA vehicle sent into space has had parts coated by Magnaplate. The company's products include HI-T-LUBE (a Guinness record holder as the most slippery solid in the world) TUFRAM coating (used to machine aluminum) and other basic metal coatings used by the food processing packaging electronics aerospace and other industries. These coatings significantly increase the durability and lubricity of both ferrous and nonferrous metals. General Magnaplate is controlled by the family of its founder the late Charles Covino including his daughter CEO Candida Aversenti.

GENERAL MARITIME CORPORATION
NYSE: GMR

299 Park Ave.
New York NY 10171
Phone: 212-763-5600
Fax: 212-763-5602
Web: www.generalmaritimecorp.com

CEO: Peter C Georgiopoulos
CFO: Leonard J Vrondissis
HR: Karen Niro
FYE: December 31
Type: Public

Black gold on the deep blue brings in the green for General Maritime. A leading operator of midsized tankers the company transports crude oil and refined petroleum products mainly in the Atlantic Basin but also in the Black Sea. Its fleet of nearly 30 double-hull tankers includes Aframax and Suezmax vessels and Panamax Handymax and Very Large Crude Carriers (VLCCs) with an overall capacity of 5 million deadweight tons (DWT). General Maritime deploys its vessels on the spot market (short term/single voyage) and under long-term charter. Customers have included major oil companies Chevron ConocoPhillips and Exxon Mobil. In 2012 the company completed financial restructuring and emerged from Chapter 11.

GENERAL MICROWAVE CORPORATION

425 Smith St.
Farmingdale NY 11735
Phone: 631-630-2000
Fax: 631-630-2066
Web: www.herley.com/index.cfm?act=companies_farming

CEO: –
CFO: –
HR: –
FYE: July 31
Type: Subsidiary

General Microwave Corporation operating as Herley New York makes microwave components and electronic systems. The company's products include attenuators phase shifters couplers power and radiation meters modulators switch filters and oscillators that are used in military and commercial equipment. The company has a novel place in the wireless industry; it provides telecom companies with radiation hazard meters used to indicate dangerously high levels of microwave radio frequencies. A subsidiary of Herley Industries General Microwave Corp. was founded in 1960 and acquired by Herley in 1999.

GENERAL MILLS, INC.
NYS: GIS

Number One General Mills Boulevard
Minneapolis, MN 55426
Phone: 763 764-7600
Fax: 763 764-8330
Web: www.generalmills.com

CEO: Kendall J. (Ken) Powell
CFO: Donal L Mulligan
HR: Peter (Pete) Mcdonald
FYE: May 31
Type: Public

General Mills gets its Kix vying for the top spot among cereal makers. Every year it jockeys with Kellogg to be #1 in that market with a brand arsenal that includes kid-friendly Kix as well as Chex Cheerios Lucky Charms and Wheaties. Much more than a cereal maker General Mills is one of the world's largest food companies. Some of its #1 and #2 market-leading brands include Betty Crocker dessert mixes Gold Medal flour Green Giant vegetables Pillsbury cookie dough and Yoplait yogurt. While most of the firm's sales come from the US General Mills is working to extend the reach and position of its brands globally. It picked up natural foods maker Annie's in 2014.

	Annual Growth	05/11	05/12	05/13	05/14	05/15
Sales ($ mil.)	4.3%	14,880.2	16,657.9	17,774.1	17,909.6	17,630.3
Net income ($ mil.)	(9.2%)	1,798.3	1,567.3	1,855.2	1,824.4	1,221.3
Market value ($ mil.)	9.3%	23,522.9	23,397.2	29,324.3	32,216.0	33,617.0
Employees	4.7%	35,000	35,000	41,000	43,000	42,000

GENERAL MOLY INC.
NYSE AMEX: GMO

1726 Cole Blvd. Ste 115
Lakewood CO 80401
Phone: 303-928-8599
Fax: 303-928-8598
Web: www.generalmoly.com

CEO: Bruce D Hansen
CFO: David A Chaput
HR: Carri Wright
FYE: December 31
Type: Public

General Moly reporting for molybdenum duty. The mineral development exploration and mining company (formerly Idaho General Mines) finds and exploits molybdenum oxide (moly) a mineral used primarily as an alloy in steel production. Steel makers create moly-enhanced pipes valued by the construction aircraft manufacturing and desalinization industries for their strength and resistance to heat and corrosion. Refiners use the pipes and employ the mineral to remove sulfur from diesel fuel and crude oil. General Moly owns two properties in Nevada one in an 80/20 joint venture with Korean steel company POSCO and one outright. The company's move from development to production was pending in early 2011.

GENERAL MOTORS CO.
NYS: GM

300 Renaissance Center
Detroit, MI 48265-3000
Phone: 313 556-5000
Fax: –
Web: www.gm.com

CEO: Daniel E. (Dan) Berce
CFO: Charles K. (Chuck) Stevens
HR: –
FYE: December 31
Type: Public

General Motors (GM) one of the world's largest auto manufacturers makes cars and trucks with well known brands such as Buick Cadillac Chevrolet and GMC. GM also builds cars through its GM Daewoo Opel Vauxhall and Holden units. The company operates through five business segments: GM North America GM Europe GM International Operations and GM South America. Financing activities are primarily conducted by General Motors Financial Company. The current iteration of GM traces its roots to mid-2009 when the former GM was split into two companies after it emerged from Chapter 11 bankruptcy protection: General Motors and Motors Liquidation (the name for leftover assets).

	Annual Growth	12/11	12/12	12/13	12/14	12/15
Sales ($ mil.)	0.3%	150,276.0	152,256.0	155,427.0	155,929.0	152,356.0
Net income ($ mil.)	1.3%	9,190.0	6,188.0	5,346.0	3,949.0	9,687.0
Market value ($ mil.)	13.8%	31,306.9	44,527.7	63,123.4	53,918.2	52,528.2
Employees	1.0%	207,000	213,000	219,000	216,000	215,000

GENERAL MOTORS FINANCIAL COMPANY INC.

801 Cherry St. Ste. 3500
Fort Worth TX 76102
Phone: 817-302-7000
Fax: 817-302-7897
Web: www.gmfinancial.com

CEO: Daniel E Berce
CFO: Chris A Choate
HR: –
FYE: June 30
Type: Subsidiary

General Motors Financial Company brings motors to the general public. Formerly AmeriCredit and now operating as GM Financial the company is the in-house auto financing arm of General Motors. It works with GM dealers around the US and in Canada to offer new- and used-vehicle financing services. Founded in 1992 the former AmeriCredit traditionally provided credit to customers with less-than-ideal credit histories. Today GM Financial owns a portfolio of some $12 billion in finance receivables and leased vehicles. The company operates about 20 credit and customer service centers ithroughout the US. General Motors acquired AmeriCredit for some $3.5 billion in 2010 in an effort to boost auto sales.

GENERAL STEEL HOLDINGS INC
NYS: GSI

Level 2, Building G, No. 2A Chen Jia Lin, Ba Li Zhuang, Chaoyang District
Beijing 100025
Phone: (86) 10 8572 3073
Fax: –
Web: www.gshi-steel.com

CEO: Zuosheng (Henry) Yu
CFO: –
HR: –
FYE: December 31
Type: Public

True to its name General Steel doesn't limit itself to a specific product. Through its main operating subsidiaries the company produces a variety of steel products including rebar round bar hot-rolled carbon sheets silicon steel sheets spiral-weld pipes and high-speed wire. General Steel's four production facilities which are based in different regions around China and Mongolia are capable of producing a total of 4.8 million tons of steel. The company's primary customers include Chinese construction companies and appliance and machine manufacturers. General Steel was founded in 2004.

	Annual Growth	12/10	12/11	12/12	12/13	12/14
Sales ($ mil.)	4.9%	1,893.6	3,563.9	2,863.6	2,463.7	2,289.4
Net income ($ mil.)	–	(7.7)	(177.2)	(152.7)	(33.0)	(48.7)
Market value ($ mil.)	(30.7%)	35.6	12.3	12.3	11.5	8.2
Employees	0.3%	8,407	9,900	10,300	9,050	8,505

GENERAL SUPPLY & SERVICES INC.

2 Corporate Dr. 10th Fl. Ste. 150
Shelton CT 06484
Phone: 203-944-3000
Fax: 402-593-5366
Web: www.csystems.com

CEO: Mitchell D Williams
CFO: Mark Testa
HR: –
FYE: December 31
Type: Subsidiary

When working with electricity Gexpro feels quite at ohm with watt industry needs. The company once a unit of General Electric is a global distributor of electrical voice and data products. Its inventory of products — from GE and more than 200 other manufacturers — includes such items as cable and wire conduits industrial controls electrical distribution equipment lighting products motors and power conditioning devices. Gexpro also offers supply chain and support services. In 2006 Rexel acquired GE Supply for $725 million in cash; it changed the unit's name to Gexpro the following year. Gexpro continues to operate as a stand-alone organization with more than 150 locations on four continents.

GENESCO INC.
NYS: GCO

Genesco Park, 1415 Murfreesboro Road
Nashville, TN 37217-2895
Phone: 615 367-7000
Fax: –
Web: www.genesco.com

CEO: James C. Estepa
CFO: Mimi E. Vaughn
HR: –
FYE: January 31
Type: Public

Genesco's sole concern is nicely capped off to boot (so to speak). It sells casual and dress footwear headwear and sports apparel through more than 2820 shoe and cap stores in the US Canada Puerto Rico the UK and Ireland. Genesco's shoe operations include Journeys upscale Johnston & Murphy Schuh and Licensed Brands (Levi Strauss' Dockers footwear Keuka). Its fast-growing Lids Sports division operates the Lids Locker Room retail chain and website as well as the Lids Team Sports team dealer business. Founded in 1924 as a shoe retailer Genesco has diversified by adding hats and sports apparel and selling merchandise online. It expanded overseas with the purchase of Scotland's Shuh.

	Annual Growth	01/11	01/12*	02/13	02/14*	01/15
Sales ($ mil.)	12.4%	1,789.8	2,292.0	2,604.8	2,625.0	2,859.8
Net income ($ mil.)	16.4%	53.2	82.0	110.5	92.7	97.7
Market value ($ mil.)	18.5%	871.2	1,480.3	1,509.6	1,687.2	1,716.7
Employees	15.8%	15,200	21,475	22,700	22,250	27,325

*Fiscal year change

GENESEE & WYOMING INC.

NYS: GWR

20 West Avenue
Darien, CT 06820
Phone: 203 202-8900
Fax: –
Web: www.gwrr.com

CEO: John C. Hellmann
CFO: Timothy J. Gallagher
HR: –
FYE: December 31
Type: Public

Genesee & Wyoming (GWI) once relied on the salt of the earth — hauling salt on a 14-mile railroad for one customer. Now however the company owns stakes in more than 115 freight railroads including 103 short-line and regional freight railroads that operate over a total of more than 18000 miles of track including 15600 miles of track owned and leased by the company and another 3300 miles additional miles under contractual track access arrangements to more than 40 ports in North America Europe and Australia. Freight transported by GWI railroads includes coal forest products and pulp and paper.

	Annual Growth	12/10	12/11	12/12	12/13	12/14
Sales ($ mil.)	27.0%	630.2	829.1	874.9	1,569.0	1,639.0
Net income ($ mil.)	33.9%	81.3	119.5	52.4	272.1	261.0
Market value ($ mil.)	14.2%	2,857.1	3,268.8	4,105.2	5,182.7	4,852.0
Employees	20.1%	2,502	2,620	4,600	4,800	5,200

GENESEE VALLEY GROUP HEALTH ASSOCIATION

800 CARTER ST
ROCHESTER, NY 146212604
Phone: 585-338-1400
Fax: –
Web: www.lifetimehealth.org

CEO: –
CFO: Deke Duda
HR: Timothy (Tim) Mcnamara
FYE: December 31
Type: Private

Primary care is the primary concern of Lifetime Health Medical Group. The organization a subsidiary of The Lifetime Healthcare Companies offers up family practitioners as well as internists pediatricians OB/GYNs and specialists to about 100000 patients in Upstate New York. Lifetime Medical operates about 10 family health centers in Buffalo and Rochester that offer diagnostic therapeutic and pharmacy services; the group also includes several affiliated physicians offices a family medicine center for deaf patients and a primary care practice staffed exclusively by female physicians. Lifetime Health Medical Group has been active in the Buffalo and Rochester communities since the 1970s.

	Annual Growth	12/03	12/04*	06/06*	12/09	12/12
Sales ($ mil.)	0.2%	–	106.6	106.6	120.0	107.9
Net income ($ mil.)	(0.5%)	–	–	3.9	(2.1)	3.8
Market value ($ mil.)	–	–	–	–	–	–
Employees	–	–	–	–	–	576

*Fiscal year change

GENESIS CORP.

950 3RD AVE STE 2702
NEW YORK, NY 10022-2874
Phone: 212-688-5522
Fax: –
Web: www.genesis10.com

CEO: Harley Lippman
CFO: Glenn Klein
HR: –
FYE: December 31
Type: Private

Genesis Corp.'s raison d'etre is business and technology consulting. Focused on helping organizations streamline processes manage employees and minimize costs the company (doing business as Genesis10) provides services in areas such as project management application development enterprise systems integration staffing and management support. The company's managed service program assists businesses in managing its workforce as well as outsourced work. Genesis10 founded in 1999 also helps organizations with their hiring compliance and change management issues.

	Annual Growth	12/06	12/07	12/08	12/10	12/11
Sales ($ mil.)	13.7%	–	131.0	123.0	173.6	218.6
Net income ($ mil.)	38.1%	–	3.3	2.7	10.6	12.0
Market value ($ mil.)	–	–	–	–	–	–
Employees	–	–	–	–	–	2,105

GENESIS ENERGY L.P.

NYS: GEL

919 Milam, Suite 2100
Houston, TX 77002
Phone: 713 860-2500
Fax: –
Web: www.genesisenergy.com

CEO: Grant E. Sims
CFO: Robert V. (Bob) Deere
HR: –
FYE: December 31
Type: Public

In the beginning was the oil. And on the third day (or thereabouts) there was oil gathering transportation marketing and related activities. Genesis Energy purchases and aggregates crude oil at the wellhead and makes bulk buys at pipeline and terminal facilities for resale. The company transports crude oil (and CO_2) through 1200 miles of pipeline primarily along the US Gulf Coast. Genesis Energy has a storage capacity of 2.9 million barrels and a fleet of more than 300 trucks 400 trailers and 562 railcars that carry oil from the wellhead to end users. It also provides sulfur-related refinery services to eight refineries and is engaged in wholesale CO_2 and other industrial gas marketing.

	Annual Growth	12/10	12/11	12/12	12/13	12/14
Sales ($ mil.)	16.3%	2,101.3	3,089.7	4,070.1	4,134.8	3,846.2
Net income ($ mil.)	–	(48.5)	51.2	96.3	86.1	106.2
Market value ($ mil.)	12.6%	2,508.8	2,664.6	3,394.4	4,995.7	4,031.1
Employees	14.8%	690	740	950	1,200	1,200

GENESIS HEALTH INC.

3599 UNIVERSITY BLVD S # 1
JACKSONVILLE, FL 322164252
Phone: 904-858-7600
Fax: –
Web: www.brookshealth.org

CEO: Douglas M Baer
CFO: –
HR: –
FYE: December 31
Type: Private

Genesis Health helps people get back on their feet — literally. The company (doing business as Brooks Rehabilitation) operates a 160-bed facility dedicated to helping patients recover from injury and illness. Rehab services include physical occupational speech aquatic and recreational therapy. The hospital also helps patients coping with chronic pain cognitive disorders and other long-term disabilities. Brooks Rehabilitation provides outpatient care through a network of more than two dozen clinics a nursing home and a home health care agency in northern Florida and southeastern Georgia.

	Annual Growth	12/08	12/09	12/10	12/11	12/13
Sales ($ mil.)	9.3%	–	98.4	120.0	123.5	140.3
Net income ($ mil.)	(9.3%)	–	–	27.7	(19.6)	20.6
Market value ($ mil.)	–	–	–	–	–	–
Employees	–	–	–	–	–	1,400

GENESIS HEALTH SYSTEM

1227 E RUSHOLME ST
DAVENPORT, IA 528032459
Phone: 563-421-1000
Fax: –
Web: www.genesishealth.com

CEO: –
CFO: Mark Rogers
HR: Edwin Maxwell
FYE: June 30
Type: Private

Genesis Health System operates three acute care hospitals in Iowa and Illinois that have more than 660 beds total and employ some 700 doctors. Genesis Medical Center in Davenport Iowa with more than 500 beds is the system's flagship facility; the hospital offers a range of general surgical and specialist health services. The system's Illini Campus in Silvis Illinois features an assisted-living center. The Genesis Medical Center Dewitt Campus serves that Iowa town and the surrounding area with its 13-bed hospital nursing home and related care facilities. Genesis Health System also operates physician practices outpatient centers and a home health agency.

	Annual Growth	06/06	06/07	06/08	06/09	06/10
Sales ($ mil.)	(47.0%)	–	–	1,643.1	993.7	461.9
Net income ($ mil.)	3045.0%	–	–	0.0	0.0	16.2
Market value ($ mil.)	–	–	–	–	–	–
Employees	–	–	–	–	–	5,000

GENESIS HEALTHCARE INC

101 East State Street
Kennett Square, PA 19348
Phone: 610 444-6350
Fax: -
Web: www.genesishcc.com

NYS: GEN
CEO: Robert H. Fish
CFO: Christopher N. (Chris) Felfe
HR: -
FYE: December 31
Type: Public

Genesis Healthcare (formerly Skilled Healthcare Group) is adept at helping seniors live their lives comfortably. Genesis is a holding company for more than 500 skilled nursing facilities and assisted-living centers in some 34 states nationwide; its facilities have more than 4900 beds in total. Its subsidiaries also provide rehab and respiratory therapy as well as administrative and consultative services to more than 1800 third-party care providers in 47 states and the District of Columbia. In early 2015 Genesis Healthcare LLC merged with Skilled Healthcare Group to become one of the US' largest post-acute care providers.

	Annual Growth	12/10	12/11	12/12	12/13	12/14
Sales ($ mil.)	0.4%	820.2	869.7	872.6	842.3	833.3
Net income ($ mil.)	-	(1.0)	(203.3)	21.6	(10.5)	(0.9)
Market value ($ mil.)	(1.2%)	359.1	218.4	254.8	192.4	342.7
Employees	7.5%	9,736	9,600	15,000	15,050	13,025

GENESIS HEALTHCARE LLC

101 E. State St.
Kennett Square PA 19348
Phone: 610-444-6350
Fax: 610-925-4000
Web: www.genesishcc.com

CEO: George V Hager Jr
CFO: James V McKeon
HR: -
FYE: September 30
Type: Private

Genesis HealthCare is in the business of caring for the US senior population and those in need of assistance with daily living tasks. The company is one of the largest skilled nursing care providers in the country offering both short-term transitional care and long-term hospice care through more than 400 skilled nursing centers and assisted living residences in 29 states. It also provides rehabilitation therapy to more than 1500 health care providers across the US. Some of its rehabilitation specialties include cardiac management dialysis care orthopedic care and ventilator care. In Maryland Genesis SelectCare is a licensed private duty home care agency that assists people in their own homes.

GENESIS HEALTHCARE SYSTEM

800 FOREST AVE
ZANESVILLE, OH 437012821
Phone: 740-454-5000
Fax: -
Web: www.genesishcs.org

CEO: Matthew Perry
CFO: Paul Masterson
HR: Diana Maple
FYE: December 31
Type: Private

Genesis HealthCare System takes care of the beginning (and the middle and the end) of a patient's medical experience. The not-for-profit system health care system consists of two acute care hospitals (Genesis-Bethesda and Genesis-Good Samaritan Hospital) in Zanesville Ohio. In addition to general medical emergency and surgical care the hospitals' specialty areas include oncology trauma cardiovascular health orthopedics neurology and women's health. Genesis HealthCare also operates facilities for pharmacy child development and home health and hospice services as well as family practice and specialist offices.

	Annual Growth	12/05	12/06	12/07	12/09	12/10
Sales ($ mil.)	-	-	-	(95.8)	353.9	369.4
Net income ($ mil.)	3881.1%	-	-	0.0	23.9	15.6
Market value ($ mil.)	-	-	-	-	-	-
Employees	-	-	-	-	-	3,500

GENETHERA INC.

3930 Youngfield St.
Wheat Ridge CO 80033-3865
Phone: 303-463-6371
Fax: 303-463-6377
Web: www.genethera.net

OTC: GTHA
CEO: Antonio Milici
CFO: -
HR: -
FYE: December 31
Type: Public

GeneThera does its part to protect the world's fauna. GeneThera formerly called Hand Brand Distribution develops genetic diagnostic assays for the agriculture and veterinary industries. The biotech company has developed assays that detect Chronic Wasting Disease in elk and deer and Mad Cow Disease in cattle. The company is working on cancer detection tests for animals as well as similar tests for humans through its partnership with Xpention a biotechnology company focused on oncology diagnostics. GeneThera is also developing vaccines for animal diseases such as E. coli.

GENICA CORPORATION

43195 BUSINESS PARK DR
TEMECULA, CA 925903629
Phone: 855-433-5747
Fax: -
Web: www.genica.com

CEO: -
CFO: Geoffrey Hildebrandt
HR: -
FYE: December 31
Type: Private

Think of Genica as computerdom's bargain basement. The company sells computer components peripherals and accessories — mainly overstocks and closeouts — over the Internet. It operates through two business units: Computer Geeks (which targets consumers through its geeks.com website) and Evertek Computer (which markets to small businesses and FORTUNE 500 firms via evertek.com). The company which offers more than 3000 brand-name products was formed by the merger of online seller Computer Geeks with computer importer/distributor Evertek Computer and its Hong Kong-based sister firm Evertek Trading. Chairman and CEO Frank Segler owns a majority stake in Genica.

	Annual Growth	12/05	12/06	12/07	12/08	12/09
Sales ($ mil.)	(49.4%)	-	-	672.7	164.7	172.5
Net income ($ mil.)	53932.2%	-	-	0.0	3.6	5.5
Market value ($ mil.)	-	-	-	-	-	-
Employees	-	-	-	-	-	334

GENIE ENERGY LTD.

520 Broad Street
Newark, NJ 07102
Phone: 973 438-3500
Fax: -
Web: www.genie.com

NYS: GNE
CEO: Howard S. Jonas
CFO: Avi Goldin
HR: -
FYE: December 31
Type: Public

Electric utilities in the Northeast have been wishing for an energy marketer like Genie Energy to come along. The company operates through two subsidiaries — IDT Energy and Genie Oil and Gas. IDT Energy resells electricity and natural gas bought from BP to residential and small business customers in New Jersey New York and Pennsylvania. In 2012 IDT Energy serviced 502000 meters (331000 electric and 171000 natural gas). Top customers include Con Edison and National Grid and their subsidiaries. Genie Oil and Gas is exploring for oil in unconventional shale plays in Colorado Israel and Mongolia through subsidiaries. Genie Energy is controlled by Chairman and CEO Howard Jonas.

	Annual Growth	12/10	12/11	12/12	12/13	12/14
Sales ($ mil.)	-	0.0	76.8	229.5	279.2	275.0
Net income ($ mil.)	-	0.0	0.8	(3.3)	(5.9)	(26.5)
Market value ($ mil.)	-	0.0	194.7	174.4	250.7	151.8
Employees	26.2%	-	-	98	156	156

GENMARK DIAGNOSTICS, INC. NMS: GNMK

5964 La Place Court, Suite 100
Carlsbad, CA 92008-8829
Phone: 760 448-4300
Fax: –
Web: www.genmarkdx.com

CEO: Hany Massarany
CFO: Scott Mendel
HR: Jennifer Williams
FYE: December 31
Type: Public

GenMark Diagnostics knows the secrets that DNA holds are just as helpful to doctors as they are to CSI detectives. The company makes molecular diagnostic equipment designed to detect diseases and determine the best medications for a person's genotype. Its XT-8 system is FDA-approved to test for cystic fibrosis and sensitivity to the blood thinner warfarin and the company is seeking approval for other diagnostics including tests for viral respiratory infections and thrombosis. The XT-8 is about the size of a microwave can hold 24 blood-sample cartridges and offers results in 30 minutes. GenMark Diagnostics which was formed by Osmetech completed an IPO in 2010.

	Annual Growth	12/10	12/11	12/12	12/13	12/14
Sales ($ mil.)	86.9%	2.5	5.0	20.5	27.4	30.6
Net income ($ mil.)	–	(18.4)	(24.0)	(22.1)	(33.6)	(38.3)
Market value ($ mil.)	35.1%	171.2	172.5	376.7	556.3	569.7
Employees	25.3%	79	82	130	153	195

GENOPTIX INC. NMS:

1811 Aston Ave.
Carlsbad CA 92008
Phone: 760-268-6200
Fax: 760-268-6201
Web: www.genoptix.com

CEO: Tina S Nova PHD
CFO: Douglas A Schuling
HR: Nancy Clodfelter
FYE: December 31
Type: Subsidiary

Genoptix looks deep into blood and tissue to diagnose cancer and other disorders. The specialized laboratory service provider analyzes blood bone marrow tumors and lymph node samples in order to diagnose monitor and track diseases such as leukemia lung cancer and colorectal cancer. Its service offerings include COMPASS for hematology (blood testing for condition diagnosis and condition monitoring) and NexCourse for the evaluation of solid tumors to predict patient response to different treatments. Genoptix which is a subsidiary of Novartis uses a specialized direct sales force to promote its services to community-based hematologists and oncologists across the US.

GENOCEA BIOSCIENCES INC NMS: GNCA

100 Acorn Park Drive
Cambridge, MA 02140
Phone: 617 876-8191
Fax: –
Web: www.genocea.com

CEO: William D. (Chip) Clark
CFO: Jonathan Poole
HR: –
FYE: December 31
Type: Public

Genocea Biosciences seeks a panacea for human infection. It does this using its proprietary ATLAS technology that acts through T cells to target infectious diseases. The company's lead candidates treat herpes and prevent pneumococcus (causes pneumonia sepsis middle ear infection and bacterial meningitis) respectively. Other prophylactics take aim at chlamydia and malaria. Genocea believes its T-cell methodology allows it to develop vaccines more quickly than the traditional method which uses B cells or antibodies. It also thinks certain infections respond better to T cell treatments which operate at the cellular level. The development-stage pharmaceutical company was formed in 2006 and went public in 2014.

	Annual Growth	12/10	12/11	12/12	12/13	12/14
Sales ($ mil.)	–	0.0	1.8	2.0	0.7	0.3
Net income ($ mil.)	–	0.0	(14.7)	(13.4)	(20.8)	(35.3)
Market value ($ mil.)	–	0.0	–	–	–	125.0
Employees	20.9%	–	–	39	44	57

GENTEX CORP. NMS: GNTX

600 N. Centennial
Zeeland, MI 49464
Phone: 616 772-1800
Fax: 616 772-7348
Web: www.gentex.com

CEO: Fred T. Bauer
CFO: Steve Downing
HR: Bruce Los
FYE: December 31
Type: Public

Gentex would agree that competitors never look better than when they are in the rearview. The company focuses on designing making and marketing interior and exterior auto-dimming rearview mirrors and camera-based driver-assist systems for the automotive market. It serves customers worldwide but its largest base includes big carmakers such as Toyota General Motors and Volkswagen. Its products are found as standard or optional features on hundreds of vehicle models. To a lesser degree Gentex also makes dimmable aircraft windows found on commercial aircraft and fire protection products — including smoke detectors fire alarms and signaling devices — primarily for commercial buildings.

	Annual Growth	12/10	12/11	12/12	12/13	12/14
Sales ($ mil.)	13.9%	816.3	1,023.8	1,099.6	1,171.9	1,375.5
Net income ($ mil.)	20.3%	137.7	164.7	168.6	222.9	288.6
Market value ($ mil.)	5.1%	8,727.5	8,736.4	5,565.4	9,737.3	10,667.3
Employees	9.6%	2,908	3,481	3,605	3,801	4,196

GENOMIC HEALTH INC NMS: GHDX

301 Penobscot Drive
Redwood City, CA 94063
Phone: 650 556-9300
Fax: –
Web: www.genomichealth.com

CEO: Kimberly J. (Kim) Popovits
CFO: G. Bradley (Brad) Cole
HR: –
FYE: December 31
Type: Public

Genomic Health believes the genome is key to good health. The company conducts genomic research to develop molecular diagnostics and assays that can predict the likelihood of disease recurrence and response to therapy and treatments. Genomic Health's Oncotype DX breast cancer test predicts the likelihood of chemotherapy effectiveness and cancer recurrence in women with newly diagnosed early stage invasive breast cancer. Genomic Health's research efforts are targeted at providing a wider base of cancer-related tests and in 2010 it launched a new Oncotype DX colon cancer test to predict recurrence rates for stage II colon cancer patients. The company generates more than 85% of sales in the US.

	Annual Growth	12/10	12/11	12/12	12/13	12/14
Sales ($ mil.)	11.5%	178.1	206.1	235.2	261.6	275.7
Net income ($ mil.)	–	4.3	7.8	8.2	(12.8)	(24.6)
Market value ($ mil.)	10.6%	682.6	810.2	869.3	934.1	1,020.2
Employees	12.3%	472	511	612	684	752

GENTHERM INC NMS: THRM

21680 Haggerty Road, Ste. 101
Northville, MI 48167
Phone: 248 504-0500
Fax: –
Web: www.gentherm.com

CEO: Daniel R.Coker
CFO: Barry G. Steele
HR: Erin Ascher
FYE: December 31
Type: Public

Don't worry TED can keep your car seat cool ... or warm. Gentherm develops thermoelectric device (TED) technology and incorporates it into its branded climate-control seat (CCS) which allows year-round temperature control and ventilation of car and truck seats on more than 50 vehicle models available in North America Europe and Asia that are made by Ford General Motors and Nissan. Gentherm also provides heated and cooled cup holder and cable systems in addition to mattress systems. The company has locations around in 11 countries worldwide with the US representing its largest market.

	Annual Growth	12/10	12/11	12/12	12/13	12/14
Sales ($ mil.)	63.9%	112.4	369.6	555.0	662.1	811.3
Net income ($ mil.)	62.9%	10.0	10.3	17.9	33.8	70.1
Market value ($ mil.)	35.4%	388.4	509.0	474.8	957.0	1,307.2
Employees	210.2%	93	110	116	7,403	8,607

GENTIVA HEALTH SERVICES INC

NMS: GTIV

3350 Riverwood Parkway, Suite 1400
Atlanta, GA 30339-3314
Phone: 770 951-6450
Fax: –
Web: www.gentiva.com

CEO: Tony Strange
CFO: Eric R Slusser
HR: –
FYE: December 31
Type: Public

Gentiva Health Services is a gentle giant. As one of the nation's largest home health care and hospice services firms the company provides home nursing care through a network of about 270 agency locations in some 40 states. Gentiva's home care nurses provide services ranging from acute-care treatment to housekeeping for the elderly or disabled. Its hospice services are offered through 150 locations in 30 states. Gentiva also offers consulting services to the home care industry to help with regulatory and reimbursement issues. Gentiva also provides hospice operations through subsidiary Odyssey Health-Care.

	Annual Growth	12/08*	01/10*	12/10	12/11	12/12
Sales ($ mil.)	7.1%	1,300.4	1,152.5	1,447.0	1,798.8	1,712.8
Net income ($ mil.)	(35.4%)	153.5	59.2	52.2	(450.5)	26.8
Market value ($ mil.)	(21.9%)	829.0	830.5	817.9	207.6	309.0
Employees	(1.4%)	15,450	5,200	9,600	14,800	14,600

*Fiscal year change

GENUARDI'S FAMILY MARKETS INC.

805 E. Germantown Pike
Norristown PA 19401
Phone: 610-277-6000
Fax: 610-277-7783
Web: www.genuardis.com

CEO: –
CFO: –
HR: –
FYE: December 31
Type: Subsidiary

Gaspare Genuardi put the horse before the cart in 1920 selling produce from a horse-drawn wagon. He founded Genuardi's Family Markets in Philadelphia which was family owned and operated for three generations before it was acquired by one of the nation's top supermarket chains Safeway. Today Genuardi's Family Market stores located primarily in Pennsylvania but also in nearby Delaware and New Jersey. As part of Safeway's Eastern Division Genuardi's has struggled and lost market share to competitors including Acme Markets and ShopRite. Recently Safeway has been selling Genuardi's supermarkets to other grocery chains leaving it with only three locations all slated for closure by the end of 2012.

GENUINE PARTS CO.

NYS: GPC

2999 Circle 75 Parkway
Atlanta, GA 30339
Phone: 770 953-1700
Fax: 770 956-2211
Web: www.genpt.com

CEO: Thomas C. (Tom) Gallagher
CFO: Carol B. Yancey
HR: James R. (Jim) Neill
FYE: December 31
Type: Public

What do spark plugs hydraulic hoses paper clips and magnet wire have in common? They're all Genuine Parts. The diversified company is the sole member and majority owner of National Automotive Parts Association (NAPA) a voluntary trade association that distributes auto parts nationwide. Genuine Parts Company (GPC) operates about 1100 NAPA Auto Parts stores in more than 45 US states. North of the border NAPA Canada runs some 700 auto parts and TRACTION stores supplied by UAP. GPC's Auto Todo operates eight stores and tire centers in Mexico. Other subsidiaries include auto parts distributor Balkamp industrial parts supplier Motion Industries and office products distributor S.P. Richards.

	Annual Growth	12/10	12/11	12/12	12/13	12/14
Sales ($ mil.)	8.2%	11,207.6	12,458.9	13,013.9	14,077.8	15,341.6
Net income ($ mil.)	10.6%	475.5	565.1	648.0	685.0	711.3
Market value ($ mil.)	20.0%	7,860.8	9,370.5	9,734.9	12,737.5	16,317.3
Employees	7.2%	29,500	29,800	31,900	37,500	39,000

GENVEC INC. (DE)

NAS: GNVC

910 Clopper Road, Suite 220N
Gaithersburg, MD 20878
Phone: 240 632-0740
Fax: –
Web: www.genvec.com

CEO: Douglas J Swirsky
CFO: –
HR: –
FYE: December 31
Type: Public

GenVec is all over the medical map. The clinical-stage biopharmaceutical firm develops gene-based drugs and vaccines for everything from cancer to HIV. GenVec has multiple vaccine candidates for contagious diseases such as HIV malaria and foot-and-mouth through grants and partnerships with several federal agencies including the US departments of Health and Human Services Homeland Security and Agriculture. The company's other drug research and development programs target cancers and hearing and balance disorders mostly through collaborations with other drugmakers.

	Annual Growth	12/10	12/11	12/12	12/13	12/14
Sales ($ mil.)	(22.2%)	16.5	17.7	9.4	3.7	6.0
Net income ($ mil.)	–	(12.3)	(7.4)	(14.1)	(10.0)	(2.5)
Market value ($ mil.)	38.7%	9.7	40.2	23.1	40.1	35.9
Employees	(39.7%)	83	78	45	11	11

GENWORTH FINANCIAL, INC. (HOLDING CO)

NYS: GNW

6620 West Broad Street
Richmond, VA 23230
Phone: 804 281-6000
Fax: –
Web: www.genworth.com

CEO: Thomas J. (Tom) McInerney
CFO: Kelly Groh
HR: Michael S. Laming
FYE: December 31
Type: Public

What's a Genworth? Insurance and investment specialist Genworth Financial might ask what your nest egg is worth. The company specializes in life insurance and retirement investments in the US market. Internationally Genworth offers mortgage insurance and other payment protection products. The firm also provides private residential mortgage insurance in the US. Genworth focuses its retirement investment products including fixed annuities and mutual funds on affluent individuals. Genworth serves over 15 million customers in 25 countries.

	Annual Growth	12/10	12/11	12/12	12/13	12/14
Assets ($ mil.)	(0.2%)	112,395.0	114,302.0	113,312.0	108,045.0	111,358.0
Net income ($ mil.)	–	142.0	122.0	323.0	560.0	(1,244.0)
Market value ($ mil.)	(10.3%)	6,530.6	3,255.4	3,732.5	7,718.4	4,224.5
Employees	(5.0%)	6,500	6,400	6,300	5,000	5,300

GENWORTH MORTGAGE INSURANCE CORPORATION

6601 Six Forks Rd.
Raleigh NC 27615
Phone: 919-846-4100
Fax: 919-846-3188
Web: mortgageinsurance.genworth.com

CEO: Thomas H Mann
CFO: Marcia A Dal
HR: –
FYE: December 31
Type: Subsidiary

Movin' on up but don't want to put too much down? Adding Genworth Mortgage Insurance to your home-buying plans may help you. One of the biggest private mortgage insurers in the US Genworth Mortgage Insurance allows customers to buy homes with a low down payment (less than 20%) and reduces financial risk for lenders and investors by protecting them against borrower default. Committed to doing business on the Internet about 90% of the company's products are now available online. In addition to straight mortgage insurance the company also offers homebuyer education classes and job-loss mortgage insurance. The mortgage insurer is a subsidiary of Genworth Financial.

GENZYME CORPORATION

500 Kendall St.
Cambridge MA 02142
Phone: 617-252-7500
Fax: 617-252-7600
Web: www.genzyme.com

CEO: –
CFO: Marc Esteva
HR: –
FYE: December 31
Type: Subsidiary

Genzyme makes big money off uncommon diseases. The company's product portfolio focuses on treatments for rare genetic disorders as well as kidney disease and cancer. One of its main products Cerezyme is a leading (and pricey) treatment for Gaucher disease a rare enzyme-deficiency condition. Founded in 1981 Genzyme has treatments for other enzyme disorders including Fabry disease and Pompe disease. In addition the company develops gene-based cancer treatment products renal care and immunological therapies organ transplant drugs and orthopedic biosurgery products. The company was acquired by Sanofi for some $20.1 billion in 2011.

GEO GROUP INC (THE) (NEW)
NYS: GEO

One Park Place, 621 NW 53rd Street, Suite 700
Boca Raton, FL 33487
Phone: 561 893-0101
Fax: –
Web: www.geogroup.com

CEO: George C. Zoley
CFO: Brian R. Evans
HR: –
FYE: December 31
Type: Public

The GEO Group sticks to its convictions and it relies on them to generate business. With locations in about 25 states the company one of the largest operators of private correctional facilities in the US (along with Corrections Corporation of America) operates more than 100 correctional detention and mental health facilities with some 85500 beds. Besides incarceration GEO offers educational rehabilitative and vocational training programs at its facilities. The firm offers mental health and residential treatment services through its GEO Care subsidiary.

	Annual Growth	01/11	01/12*	12/12	12/13	12/14
Sales ($ mil.)	10.0%	1,270.0	1,612.9	1,479.1	1,522.1	1,691.6
Net income ($ mil.)	31.4%	63.5	78.6	134.8	115.1	143.9
Market value ($ mil.)	17.8%	1,829.5	1,242.7	2,092.2	2,390.4	2,994.3
Employees	(3.3%)	19,352	18,894	18,733	16,292	17,479

*Fiscal year change

GEOBIO ENERGY INC.
OTC: GBOE

601 Union St. Ste. 4500
Seattle WA 98121
Phone: 206-838-9715
Fax: 760-597-4900
Web: www.aqualung.com

CEO: –
CFO: Clayton Shelver
HR: –
FYE: September 30
Type: Public

GeoBio Energy used to think biodiesel was the way of the future but lately it's decided that the oil and gas industry isn't going anywhere anytime soon. Though it acquired GeoAlgae Technologies which develops low-cost renewable feedstock used for the production of biodiesel in 2008 GeoBio Energy has since switched directions. In 2009 it agreed to buy H&M Precision Products which makes chemicals used in the drilling of oil and gas wells. In 2010 it also agreed to acquire a Colorado-based oil field site preparation and maintenance company.

GEOMET INC (DE)
NBB: GMET

1221 McKinney Street, Suite 3840
Houston, TX 77010
Phone: 713 659-3855
Fax: –
Web: www.geometinc.com

CEO: Michael Y McGovern
CFO: Tony Oviedo
HR: –
FYE: December 31
Type: Public

Hoping for the day when high gas prices will result in geometric financial growth GeoMet is explores for develops and produces natural gas from coalbed methane properties in Alabama Virginia West Virginia and British Columbia. The company is developing the Gurnee field in the Cahaba Basin and the Garden City Chattanooga Shale prospect (in Alabama) as well as the Pond Creek and Lasher fields in the Central Appalachian Basin. It also has holdings in the Peace River field in British Columbia. GeoMet controls a total of 160000 net acres of coalbed methane assets. In 2010 the company had proved reserves of 215.9 billion cu. ft. of coalbed methane. Yorktown Energy Partners IV controls about 40% of GeoMet.

	Annual Growth	12/09	12/10	12/11	12/12	12/13
Sales ($ mil.)	5.4%	31.0	33.4	35.6	39.4	38.2
Net income ($ mil.)	–	(167.1)	5.8	2.8	(150.0)	35.3
Market value ($ mil.)	(49.4%)	59.4	46.8	37.8	5.7	3.9
Employees	(12.4%)	73	–	68	64	43

GEOPETRO RESOURCES CO
NBB: GEOR

150 California Street, Suite 600
San Francisco, CA 94111
Phone: 415 398-8186
Fax: –
Web: www.geopetro.com

CEO: Stuart J Doshi
CFO: –
HR: –
FYE: December 31
Type: Public

You have to drill down deep to figure out exactly what GeoPetro Resources does. It's an oil and natural gas exploration and production company with projects in Canada Indonesia and the US. These sites cover about 1 million gross acres consisting of mineral leases production-sharing contracts and exploration permits. GeoPetro operates one cash-generating property in the Madisonville Project in Texas; almost all of the revenue from this project has been derived from natural gas sales to two clients: Luminant Energy and ETC Katy Pipeline. GeoPetro Resources also has a geographically diverse portfolio of oil and natural gas prospects. In 2013 the company agreed to be bought by fuel distributor MCW Energy Group.

	Annual Growth	12/08	12/09	12/10	12/11	12/12
Sales ($ mil.)	(51.1%)	6.2	4.1	3.1	1.0	0.4
Net income ($ mil.)	–	(0.2)	(25.8)	(4.9)	(1.5)	(3.9)
Market value ($ mil.)	(44.2%)	34.0	34.0	20.5	10.7	3.3
Employees	(26.0%)	20	20	14	14	6

GEORGE E. WARREN CORPORATION

3001 OCEAN DR STE 203
VERO BEACH, FL 329631992
Phone: 772-778-7100
Fax: –
Web: www.gewarren.com

CEO: Thomas L. Corr
CFO: –
HR: –
FYE: December 31
Type: Private

By barge by pipeline by tank truck by George; George E. Warren is a major private wholesale distributor of refined petroleum products. The company which has business activities in about 30 US states distributes product mostly by barge and pipeline though it uses some tank trucks as well. It distributes by pipeline via the Buckeye Colonial Magellan Nester and Explorer pipelines and by barges and vessels from facilities on the Gulf Coast and in the New York Harbor area. It distributes a range of petroleum products including ethylene and heating oil to various industries.

	Annual Growth	12/09	12/10	12/11	12/12	12/13
Sales ($ mil.)	10.6%	–	79.1	91.4	156.3	106.9
Net income ($ mil.)	15.6%	–	–	27.2	56.1	36.3
Market value ($ mil.)	–	–	–	–	–	–
Employees	–	–	–	–	–	35

GEORGE FOREMAN ENTERPRISES INC.

100 N. Wilkes-Barre Blvd. 4th Fl.
Wilkes-Barre PA 18702
Phone: 570-822-6277
Fax: 330-848-4287
Web: www.juice4u.com

CEO: Chuck Gartenhaus
CFO: Jeremy Anderson
HR: –
FYE: December 31
Type: Private

George Foreman Enterprises doesn't sell the boxer's namesake grills (Salton does); however the company actively looks to make acquisitions and licensing deals to keep George Foreman's name in the ring. Through its InStride Ventures George Foreman Enterprises makes and markets therapeutic footwear under the George Foreman name to ShopKo. The company also has partnered with G-Nutritional and Vitaquest International (which later formed Vita Ventures) to market and sell vitamins and nutritional supplements using the Foreman trade name. The company signed on legendary boxing champ George Foreman to a licensing and pitchman deal in 2005 in exchange for 35% of the company and his name on the marquee.

GEORGETOWN MEMORIAL HOSPITAL

606 BLACK RIVER RD
GEORGETOWN, SC 294403368
Phone: 843-626-9040
Fax: –
Web: www.georgetownhospitalsystem.org

CEO: Jeannie Davis
CFO: –
HR: –
FYE: September 30
Type: Private

Georgetown Hospital System may be set amidst the Antebellum grace of the South but its health care services are far from antiquated. The system on the southeast coast of South Carolina operates Georgetown Memorial Hospital an acute-care facility with more than 130 beds and Waccamaw Community Hospital which operates with about 170 beds. Georgetown Memorial Hospital features ICU cardiac and surgical services labor and delivery and a pediatric wing. Waccamaw Community Hospital covering the northern part of the system's service area provides 24-hour emergency services rehabilitation obstetrics and inpatient and outpatient surgery.

	Annual Growth	09/08	09/09	09/11	09/12	09/13
Sales ($ mil.)	(3.5%)	–	125.6	120.4	101.9	108.8
Net income ($ mil.)	4.9%	–	–	8.0	5.0	8.8
Market value ($ mil.)	–	–	–	–	–	–
Employees	–	–	–	–	–	1,300

GEORGIA FARM BUREAU MUTUAL INSURANCE COMPANY

1620 Bass Rd.
Macon GA 31209
Phone: 478-474-8411
Fax: 478-474-8869
Web: www.gfb.org/insurance/default.html

CEO: Vincent M Duvall
CFO: –
HR: –
FYE: December 31
Type: Private - Mutual Com

You don't have to be a farmer to get insurance coverage here but it helps. Georgia Farm Bureau Mutual Insurance Company (GFNMIC) and its subsidiaries offer a variety of commercial and individual property/casualty products to members of the Georgia Farm Bureau. Its products include farmowners automobile homeowners marine business owners and personal liability insurance. The company specializes in writing lower-cost preferred risk policies (policies for customers that are less likely to file claims). A network of nearly 500 agents and representatives market GFNMIC's products. The company which was founded in 1959 is a part of the Georgia Farm Bureau. It is owned by its policyholders.

GEORGIA LOTTERY CORPORATION

250 Williams St. Ste. 3000
Atlanta GA 30303
Phone: 404-215-5000
Fax: 404-215-8983
Web: www.galottery.com

CEO: Debbie Dlugolenski Alford
CFO: –
HR: Doug Parker
FYE: June 30
Type: Government-owned

You might say these games of chance are just peachy. The Georgia Lottery Corporation (GLC) operates a number of instant-win ticket and lotto-style games including Cash 4 Fantasy 5 and Win for Life. It also takes part in the multi-state Mega Millions drawing game. Tickets are sold through more than 8200 retailers throughout the state. The GLC was established in 1992 to enhance the state's education funding. Since its founding the lottery has contributed more than $13 billion in proceeds to state education programs including the HOPE Scholarship Program and the Georgia Prekindergarten Program. The GLC has eight district offices in Atlanta Augusta Columbus Dalton Duluth Macon Savannah and Tifton.

GEORGIA POWER CO.

NYS: GPE PRA

241 Ralph McGill Boulevard, N.E.
Atlanta, GA 30308
Phone: 404 506-6526
Fax: –
Web: www.georgiapower.com

CEO: Paul Bowers
CFO: Ronnie R. Labrato
HR: Sloane Evans
FYE: December 31
Type: Public

Bigger than a giant peach Georgia Power is the largest subsidiary of US utility holding company Southern Company. The regulated utility provides electricity to about 2.4 million residential commercial and industrial customers throughout most of Georgia. It has interests in about 20 fossil-fueled 2 nuclear and 20 hydroelectric power plants that give it about 22000 MW of generating capacity. When necessary the company purchases excess power from nine small power producers. Georgia Power sells wholesale electricity to several cooperatives and municipalities in the region. The utility also offers energy efficiency surge protection and outdoor lighting products and services.

	Annual Growth	12/10	12/11	12/12	12/13	12/14
Sales ($ mil.)	1.9%	8,349.0	8,800.0	7,998.0	8,274.0	8,988.0
Net income ($ mil.)	6.5%	967.0	1,162.0	1,185.0	1,191.0	1,242.0
Market value ($ mil.)	0.3%	972.5	1,015.1	1,037.3	929.9	985.4
Employees	(1.3%)	8,330	8,310	8,094	7,886	7,909

GEORGIA SOUTHERN UNIVERSITY

1582 SOUTHERN DR
STATESBORO, GA 30458
Phone: 912-681-5224
Fax: –
Web: www.gsustore.com

CEO: –
CFO: –
HR: –
FYE: June 30
Type: Private

Georgia Southern University shows students that higher education can be just peachy. Georgia Southern offers its student body more than 125 bachelor master and doctoral programs from eight colleges; academic fields include business education science and public health. One of 35 colleges and universities in the University System of Georgia it enrolls more than 20500 students most of which hail from Georgia. The average class size of lower division courses is about 43 upper division 23 and graduate level 11. The student to faculty ratio is 22:1.

	Annual Growth	06/09	06/10	06/11	06/12	06/13
Sales ($ mil.)	10.8%	–	151.4	177.8	185.6	206.1
Net income ($ mil.)	77.9%	–	–	10.3	0.9	32.7
Market value ($ mil.)	–	–	–	–	–	–
Employees	–	–	–	–	–	1,700

GEORGIA TRANSMISSION CORPORATION

2100 E EXCHANGE PL
TUCKER, GA 300845342
Phone: 770-270-7400
Fax: –
Web: www.gatrans.com

CEO: Jerry Donovan
CFO: Barbara Hampton
HR: Sharon N Williamson
FYE: December 31
Type: Private

With Georgia on its mind Georgia Transmission provides electric transmission services to power producers and distribution utilities. The company primarily transports power for its 39 member distribution cooperatives (out of Georgia's total of 42 coops) and their electricity supplier Oglethorpe Power. Georgia Transmission owns 3060 miles of transmission lines asn more that 640 substations. It jointly owns and plans the state's entire 17500 miles of transmission lines through the Integrated Transmission System in collaboration with Georgia Power MEAG Power and Dalton Utilities.

	Annual Growth	12/06	12/07	12/08	12/09	12/13
Sales ($ mil.)	3.2%	–	–	225.1	229.6	263.2
Net income ($ mil.)	–	–	–	13.5	14.5	0.0
Market value ($ mil.)	–	–	–	–	–	–
Employees	–	–	–	–	–	160

GEORGIA-CAROLINA BANCSHARES, INC.   NBB: GECR

3527 Wheeler Road
Augusta, GA 30909
Phone: 706 731-6600
Fax: –

CEO: –
CFO: –
HR: –
FYE: December 31
Type: Public

Georgia-Carolina Bancshares is holding the line on banking in and around Augusta Georgia. The holding company owns First Bank of Georgia which has about a half-dozen branches along the eastern edge of the Peach State. The company also owns First Bank Mortgage which originates residential loans and other mortgage products through offices in Georgia and Florida. The bank focuses on real estate lending in addition to providing standard deposit products such as checking and savings accounts. Other lending activities include business and consumer loans. The bank's FB Financial Services division offers financial planning and investment services through an agreement with LPL Financial.

	Annual Growth	12/08	12/09	12/10	12/11	12/12
Assets ($ mil.)	2.4%	460.8	484.0	495.3	493.3	506.2
Net income ($ mil.)	24.0%	2.8	3.8	1.5	4.1	6.6
Market value ($ mil.)	5.8%	35.3	25.4	27.2	24.7	44.3
Employees	(1.2%)	167	172	166	147	159

GEORGIA-PACIFIC LLC

133 Peachtree St. NE
Atlanta GA 30303
Phone: 404-652-4000
Fax: 404-749-2454
Web: www.gp.com

CEO: James Hannan
CFO: Tyler Woolson
HR: –
FYE: December 31
Type: Subsidiary

What's on Georgia-Pacific's mind? A whole lotta different products that's what. Georgia-Pacific (GP) is one of the leading tissue products producers and the force behind such household items as Brawny paper towels and Quilted Northern bath tissues. Not one to be pigeonholed it makes a wide variety of other products including cardboard packaging plywood and lumber related chemicals fertilizers recycled paper fibers Dixie-brand paper cups touchless towel dispensers and office paper. GP is one of the largest US forest products manufacturers (up there with rival International Paper). A subsidiary of diversified group Koch Industries GP has around 200 facilities spread across the US.

GEOSPACE TECHNOLOGIES CORP   NMS: GEOS

7007 Pinemont Drive
Houston, TX 77040-6601
Phone: 713 986-4444
Fax: –
Web: www.geospace.com

CEO: Gary D. Owens
CFO: Thomas T McEntire
HR: –
FYE: September 30
Type: Public

Geospace Technologies (formerly OYO Geospace) analyzes the spaces below the earth's surface to help companies find gas and oil. It makes instruments and equipment used by seismic contractors and oil and gas companies to gather and process seismic data to zero in on hydrocarbons. The company's geophones detect energy from the earth's subsurface and its hydrophones detect changes in pressure and gather seismic data in water. Other products include seismic leader wire geophone string connectors seismic telemetry cable and thermal imaging equipment; all are compatible with most seismic data-acquisition systems. Geospace also makes its thermal printers available for the commercial graphics industry.

	Annual Growth	09/11	09/12	09/13	09/14	09/15
Sales ($ mil.)	(16.3%)	173.0	191.7	300.6	236.9	84.9
Net income ($ mil.)	–	29.7	35.1	69.6	36.9	(32.6)
Market value ($ mil.)	(29.6%)	740.1	1,609.4	1,108.2	462.1	181.6
Employees	(0.8%)	1,008	1,164	1,333	1,149	978

GERBER CHILDRENSWEAR LLC

7005 PELHAM RD
GREENVILLE, SC 296155782
Phone: 864-987-5200
Fax: –
Web: www.gerberchildrenswear.com

CEO: –
CFO: –
HR: David Hammer
FYE: January 29
Type: Private

Gerber Childrenswear may be one of the first companies to make kids brand-conscious. The company makes infant and toddler clothing sold under the licensed Gerber and Curity labels as well as its own Onesies brand. Products include sleepwear underwear playwear cloth diapers footwear and bibs. Through a licensing deal with Jockey International Gerber Childrenswear also offers Jockey-branded underwear sleepwear and thermal items for children. The company sells its products primarily through national retailers (such as Wal-Mart Kmart and Toys "R" Us) department stores and specialty shops. Gerber Childrenswear is a unit of Childrenswear LLC a portfolio company of investment firm Sun Capital Partners.

	Annual Growth	01/06	01/07	01/08	01/09	01/11
Sales ($ mil.)	(9.1%)	–	–	–	193.8	160.1
Net income ($ mil.)	(12.0%)	–	–	–	6.6	5.1
Market value ($ mil.)	–	–	–	–	–	–
Employees	–	–	–	–	–	120

GERBER SCIENTIFIC INC.

24 Industrial Park Rd. West
Tolland CT 06084
Phone: 860-644-1551
Fax: 516-478-5476
Web: www.gettyrealty.com

CEO: Michael Elia
CFO: John Capasso
HR: –
FYE: April 30
Type: Private

When it comes to its manufacturing systems Gerber Scientific is no baby. The company - not affiliated with baby food maker Gerber Products Co. — is a giant in the automated manufacturing systems industry. Its systems which include equipment and software are used by graphics apparel industrial and flexible materials companies to manufacture goods. Gerber's signage subsidiary Gerber Scientific Products makes digital imaging systems materials cutting systems and related software. Its Gerber Technology subsidiary provides CAD/CAM pattern-making and cutting systems for apparel furniture aerospace and textile companies. In 2011 Gerber Scientific was acquired by investment firm Vector Capital.

GERMAN AMERICAN BANCORP INC   NMS: GABC

711 Main Street
Jasper, IN 47546
Phone: 812 482-1314
Fax: –
Web: www.germanamerican.com

CEO: Mark A. Schroeder
CFO: Bradley M. Rust
HR: –
FYE: December 31
Type: Public

German American Bancorp is the holding company for German American Bank which operates some 30 branches in 10 southwestern Indiana counties and offers such standard retail products as checking and savings accounts certificates of deposit and IRAs. German American Bank was founded in 1910. Commercial and industrial loans make up about half of the bank's loan portfolio; agricultural loans account for about 20%. Other offerings include residential mortgages and consumer loans. German American Bancorp also operates insurance and trust financial planning and brokerage subsidiaries.

	Annual Growth	12/10	12/11	12/12	12/13	12/14
Assets ($ mil.)	12.9%	1,375.9	1,873.8	2,006.3	2,163.8	2,237.1
Net income ($ mil.)	20.6%	13.4	20.2	24.1	25.4	28.3
Market value ($ mil.)	13.5%	243.4	240.4	287.0	375.6	403.3
Employees	5.1%	396	417	440	480	484

GERON CORP.   NMS: GERN

149 Commonwealth Drive, Suite 2070
Menlo Park, CA 94025
Phone: 650 473-7700
Fax: –
Web: www.geron.com

CEO: John A. Scarlett
CFO: Olivia K. Bloom
HR: –
FYE: December 31
Type: Public

Geron is working to get important things through our thick heads. More specifically it is working to developing compounds able to penetrate the blood-brain barrier that otherwise keeps potentially valuable cancer drugs out of the brain. The company is also developing pharmaceuticals based on protein inhibitor technologies that aim to demolish enzymes that feed cancer cells. The clinical stage biopharmaceutical company is developing a telomerase inhibitor imetelstat in hematologic myeloid malignancies. Geron's research and development efforts are focused on oncology targets including breast and lung cancer though it has also explored treatments for injuries and degenerative diseases.

	Annual Growth	12/10	12/11	12/12	12/13	12/14
Sales ($ mil.)	(24.6%)	3.6	2.4	2.7	1.3	1.2
Net income ($ mil.)	–	(111.4)	(96.9)	(68.9)	(38.4)	(35.7)
Market value ($ mil.)	(11.0%)	816.7	233.0	222.0	746.2	511.6
Employees	(30.0%)	175	178	105	46	42

GERRITY'S SUPER MARKET INC.

950 N SOUTH RD STE 5
SCRANTON, PA 185041430
Phone: 570-342-4144
Fax: –
Web: www.gerritys.com

CEO: –
CFO: Anna Corcoran
HR: –
FYE: December 29
Type: Private

Gerrity's Super Market is not yet part of a matriarchal society but does boast that it's where Mom is "always in charge!" The regional grocery chain operates about 10 supermarkets under the Gerrity's Supermarket banner in Lackawanna and Luzerne counties in northeastern Pennsylvania. The regional chain also operates an online grocery order and home delivery service. Founded in 1895 by William Gerrity the family-owned company is run by mother and son team Joyce ("Mom") and Joseph Fasula. Gerrity's Supermarkets is a member of the Shursave Supermarkets Co-op.

	Annual Growth	12/02	12/03*	01/05	01/06*	12/13
Sales ($ mil.)	(9.4%)	–	425.9	117.0	114.6	158.4
Net income ($ mil.)	(21.4%)	–	–	28.2	1.4	4.1
Market value ($ mil.)	–	–	–	–	–	–
Employees	–	–	–	–	–	900

*Fiscal year change

GETTY REALTY CORP.   NYS: GTY

Two Jericho Plaza, Suite 110
Jericho, NY 11753
Phone: 516 478-5400
Fax: 516 478-5476
Web: www.gettyrealty.com

CEO: Christopher J. Constant
CFO: Danion Fielding
HR: –
FYE: December 31
Type: Public

Some black gold is sold on property owned by Getty Realty. The self-administered real estate investment trust (REIT) owns and leases about 1000 gas service stations adjacent convenience stores and petroleum distribution terminals in about 20 states. Most of the gas station landlord's properties are company-owned and located primarily in the Northeast. However some are found as far away as Hawaii. New York is the company's largest market. More than three-quarters of its properties are leased to one tenant Getty Petroleum Marketing which is responsible for operating and maintaining its properties as well as the remediation of any environmental contamination caused on them. Getty Realty was founded in 1955.

	Annual Growth	12/10	12/11	12/12	12/13	12/14
Sales ($ mil.)	3.1%	88.3	112.9	102.2	102.5	99.9
Net income ($ mil.)	(18.0%)	51.7	12.5	12.4	70.0	23.4
Market value ($ mil.)	(12.7%)	1,045.3	466.2	603.5	613.9	608.5
Employees	12.5%	20	22	37	29	32

GETTYSBURG COLLEGE

300 N WASHINGTON ST
GETTYSBURG, PA 173251483
Phone: 717-337-6000
Fax: –
Web: www.gettysburg.edu

CEO: –
CFO: –
HR: –
FYE: May 31
Type: Private

Four score and many years ago Gettysburg College opened its doors. The private four-year liberal arts and sciences college offers about 65 academic programs and about 40 majors to 2600 students who come from more than 40 states and 35 countries. Gettysburg's student-faculty ratio is 10:1. The campus is adjacent to the Gettysburg National Military Park in Pennsylvania. The college was founded in 1832; its first building Pennsylvania Hall served during and after the Battle of Gettysburg as a hospital for the wounded. In 1863 students and faculty of Gettysburg College walked from Pennsylvania Hall to the national cemetery in Gettysburg to hear President Lincoln deliver his legendary Gettysburg Address.

	Annual Growth	05/10	05/11	05/12	05/13	05/14
Sales ($ mil.)	4.0%	–	115.9	122.1	126.8	130.4
Net income ($ mil.)	–	–	–	(4.5)	38.8	33.3
Market value ($ mil.)	–	–	–	–	–	–
Employees	–	–	–	–	–	–

GEVO INC.   NAS: GEVO

345 Inverness Drive South, Building C, Suite 310
Englewood, CO 80112
Phone: 303 858-8358
Fax: –
Web: www.gevo.com

CEO: Patrick R Gruber
CFO: –
HR: –
FYE: December 31
Type: Public

Putting sugar in a gas tank is generally not a good idea but Gevo has figured out a way to make it beneficial. A renewable chemical and biofuels company Gevo produces isobutanol a multi-purpose chemical derived from glucose and other cellulosic biomass extracted from plant matter. Its isobutanol can be used as a blendstock (additive used during the refining process) for gasoline and jet fuel production and as a chemical used in the production of plastics fibers and rubber. Gevo does not yet produce isobutanol on a commercial scale but it is in the process of building its customer and partnership base in preparation of commencing production.

	Annual Growth	12/10	12/11	12/12	12/13	12/14
Sales ($ mil.)	14.6%	16.4	64.5	24.4	8.2	28.3
Net income ($ mil.)	–	(40.1)	(48.2)	(60.7)	(66.8)	(41.1)
Market value ($ mil.)	(63.1%)	–	41.8	10.2	9.5	2.1
Employees	1.6%	91	114	120	112	97

GFI GROUP INC
NYS: GFIG

55 Water Street
New York, NY 10041
Phone: 212-968-4100
Fax: –
Web: www.gfigroup.com

CEO: Colin Heffron
CFO: James A Peers
HR: –
FYE: December 31
Type: Public

A financial matchmaker GFI Group is an inter-dealer hybrid brokerage that acts as an intermediary for more than 2600 institutional clients such as banks large corporations insurance companies and hedge funds. The firm deals primarily in over-the-counter (OTC) derivatives which tend to be less liquid and thus harder to trade than other assets. It also offers market data and analysis on credit equity commodity and currency derivatives and other financial instruments. Other products include foreign exchange options freight and energy derivatives including electric power coal and carbon emissions options. GFI operates in North and South America Europe Africa the Middle East and Australasia.

	Annual Growth	12/09	12/10	12/11	12/12	12/13
Sales ($ mil.)	2.4%	818.7	862.1	1,015.5	924.6	901.5
Net income ($ mil.)	–	16.3	25.6	(3.2)	(10.0)	(20.0)
Market value ($ mil.)	(3.7%)	561.0	578.2	507.9	399.4	482.1
Employees	4.2%	1,768	1,990	2,176	2,062	2,087

GGNSC HOLDINGS LLC

1000 Fianna Way
Fort Smith AR 72919
Phone: 479-201-2000
Fax: 605-721-2599
Web: www.blackhillscorp.com

CEO: Ronald Silva
CFO: Ruth Ann Harmon
HR: –
FYE: December 31
Type: Private

GGNSC Holdings puts the "Golden" in "Golden Years." The holding company does business as Golden Living and operates more than 300 skilled nursing homes (LivingCenters) and some 16 assisted living facilities nationwide. Golden Living's subsidiaries operate under a range of names including Aegis Therapies for rehabilitation therapy AseraCare hospice and home health care 360 Healthcare Staffing and Ceres a buying cooperative for health care products such as disposable gloves sanitary products and wheelchairs. The company sees patients covered by a range of payors including Medicare and Medicaid the US Department of Veterans Affairs and private insurance.

GHSP INC.

1250 S. Beechtree St.
Grand Haven MI 49417
Phone: 616-842-5500
Fax: 616-850-1247
Web: www.ghsp.com

CEO: Paul Doyle
CFO: –
HR: Wendy Cherry
FYE: December 31
Type: Subsidiary

Stop the stamping presses! GHSP formerly Grand Haven Stamped Products designs manufactures and supplies mechanical as well as mechatronic control systems used in automotive heavy truck and other industries. For over 85 years the company has focused on shift systems for passenger vehicles. Its move to mechatronic systems a marriage of mechanical elements electronics and software expands the GHSP lineup to smart actuators and electronic controls. Products include actuator pumps for hybrid motor generator cooling and electronic shift and adjustable pedal controls. The company's customers include Caterpillar Chrysler Cooper Standard Ford Motor GM SPX and Sub-Zero. GHSP is JSJ Corporation business.

GIANT EAGLE INC.

101 Kappa Dr.
Pittsburgh PA 15238
Phone: 412-963-6200
Fax: 412-968-1617
Web: www.gianteagle.com

CEO: –
CFO: –
HR: –
FYE: June 30
Type: Private

Giant Eagle has its talons firmly wrapped around parts of Pennsylvania and Ohio. The grocery chain a market leader in Pittsburgh and eastern Ohio operates about 175 company-owned stores and 50-plus franchised supermarkets as well as about 160 GetGo convenience stores (which feature fresh foods and sell gas at discounted prices through the fuelperks! program). The regional chain also has stores in Maryland and West Virginia. Many Giant Eagle stores feature video rental banking photo processing dry cleaning services and ready-to-eat meals. Executive chairman David Shapira is the grandson of one of the men who founded the company in 1931. The founders' families own Giant Eagle.

GIANT FOOD INC.

8301 Professional Place Ste. 115
Landover MD 20785-2351
Phone: 301-341-4100
Fax: 301-618-4998
Web: www.giantfood.com

CEO: Richard A Baird
CFO: Paula A Price
HR: –
FYE: December 31
Type: Subsidiary

A monster among mid-Atlantic grocers Giant Food (dba Giant-Landover) operates about 175 Giant Food and Super G supermarkets. It's #1 in the Baltimore and Washington DC markets; it also operates in the most populous areas of Delaware Maryland and Virginia. Most of its supermarkets house full-service pharmacies. Giant Food also operates about a dozen fuel stations as well as its own dairy beverage bottling and ice cream plants. Founded in 1936 Giant is owned by Ahold USA the US arm of Dutch grocer Royal Ahold. Ahold USA owns more than 700 supermarkets in the US including the New England-based Stop & Shop chain Giant Food's sister company.

GIANT FOOD STORES LLC

1149 Harrisburg Pike
Carlisle PA 17013
Phone: 717-249-4000
Fax: 717-960-1327
Web: www.giantpa.com

CEO: Carl Schlicker
CFO: Rick Herring
HR: –
FYE: December 31
Type: Subsidiary

Giant Food Stores (aka Giant-Carlisle) operates nearly 200 supermarkets and superstores under the Giant and Martin's Food Markets banners in Pennsylvania and in Maryland Virginia and West Virginia. Not to be confused with its Landover Maryland-based sister company Giant Food both firms are divisions of Ahold USA which operates some 750 supermarkets along the East Coast. Giant Food Stores was founded in 1923 in Carlisle Pennsylvania and acquired by Amsterdam-based Royal Ahold in 1981. As a result of the latest reorganization of its US operations the grocery company's Dutch parent has positioned Giant Food Stores for growth by separating its support functions from those of its other US chains.

GIBBS DIE CASTING CORPORATION

369 COMMUNITY DR
HENDERSON, KY 42420-4397
Phone: 270-827-1801
Fax: -
Web: www.supplier.gibbsdc.com

CEO: -
CFO: -
HR: -
FYE: December 31
Type: Private

There's plenty to die for at Gibbs Die Casting. The company manufactures aluminum and magnesium die-castings such as air conditioning compressor commercial refrigeration and engine and viscous clutch parts. Its Comac Machining Division provides precision machining and assembly work. The Audubon Tool Division uses fused deposition modeling prototyping equipment and CNC electrical discharge machines to build die-casting tools. Gibbs Engineering offers on-site product design prototype models and production tooling services. Gibbs Die Casting serves industries such as automobile and appliance manufacturing and alternative energy. Gibbs is owned by Koch Enterprises.

	Annual Growth	12/08	12/09	12/10	12/11	12/12
Sales ($ mil.)	3.5%	-	158.4	210.3	187.7	175.5
Net income ($ mil.)	-	-	0.0	0.0	0.0	0.0
Market value ($ mil.)	-	-	-	-	-	-
Employees	-	-	-	-	-	1,299

GIBRALTAR INDUSTRIES INC   NMS: ROCK

3556 Lake Shore Road, P.O. Box 2028
Buffalo, NY 14219-0228
Phone: 716 826-6500
Fax: -
Web: www.gibraltar1.com

CEO: Frank G. Heard
CFO: Kenneth W. (Ken) Smith
HR: Paul M. Murray
FYE: December 31
Type: Public

What rocks Gibraltar's world? A good strong structure. The company makes and distributes products for residential and commercial construction including metal roofing vents rain gutters steel framing and mailboxes. Gibraltar is a leading producer of metal roofing and accessories products as well as metal structural connectors including foundation anchors anchor bolts and foundation straps. The company operates about 45 facilities in the US Canada and Europe. Its building products are sold to builders architects and homeowners. Building materials retailer Home Depot is the company's largest customer accounting for 12% of overall sales.

	Annual Growth	12/10	12/11	12/12	12/13	12/14
Sales ($ mil.)	5.9%	685.1	766.6	790.1	827.6	862.1
Net income ($ mil.)	-	(91.1)	16.5	12.6	(5.6)	(81.8)
Market value ($ mil.)	4.6%	419.5	431.5	493.1	574.7	502.6
Employees	4.1%	2,054	2,221	2,306	2,274	2,416

GIBRALTAR PACKAGING GROUP INC.

2000 Summit Ave.
Hastings NE 68901
Phone: 402-463-1366
Fax: 402-463-2467
Web: www.gibpack.com

CEO: Walter E Rose
CFO: -
HR: Kolleen Peterson
FYE: June 30
Type: Private

Gibraltar Packaging displays rock-solid commitment to the idea that good things come in small packages ... like the ones it makes! The company's folding carton unit makes product packaging and point-of-purchase retail displays for a variety of consumer goods. Customers supply artwork; Gibraltar Packaging prints die cuts folds and glues the cartons. Flexible poly-film packaging specialty laminated cartons and corrugated containers are also made. Gibraltar Packaging's plants in Nebraska and North Carolina market to US customers large and small in industries from textiles to pharmaceuticals office supplies auto parts and food and tobacco goods. The company was acquired by Rosmar Litho in 2008.

GIBSON DUNN & CRUTCHER LLP

333 S. Grand Ave.
Los Angeles CA 90071-3197
Phone: 213-229-7000
Fax: 213-229-7520
Web: www.gibsondunn.com

CEO: -
CFO: -
HR: -
FYE: October 31
Type: Private - Partnershi

One of the top US corporate-transactions law firms Gibson Dunn & Crutcher also practices in such areas as labor and employment crisis management litigation public policy real estate tax and white-collar defense and investigations. The firm has about 1000 lawyers working from more than 15 offices in California Colorado Texas and various financial capitals worldwide. The firm also has a significant presence in Washington DC. Along with multinational companies Gibson Dunn clients include commercial and investment banks government entities individuals and startups. The firm was founded in 1890.

GIBSON GUITAR CORP.

309 Plus Park Blvd.
Nashville TN 37217
Phone: 615-871-4500
Fax: 615-889-5509
Web: www.gibson.com

CEO: Henry E Juszkiewicz
CFO: Dan Krawczyk
HR: Michael L Allen
FYE: December 31
Type: Private

Real pickers put Gibson Guitar on a pedestal. Although it trails top guitar maker Fender Gibson builds instruments that are held in unparalleled esteem by many guitarists including professional musicians. The company's most popular guitar is the legendary Les Paul. Gibson also makes guitars under brands Epiphone Kramer and Steinberger. In addition to guitars the company makes pianos through its Baldwin unit Slingerland drums Tobias bass Cerwin-Vega! pro audio equipment Wurlitzer vending machines and jukeboxes and Echoplex amps as well as accessory items. Company namesake Orville Gibson began making mandolins in the late 1890s. Gibson Guitar is owned by executives Henry Juszkiewicz and David Berryman.

GIGA-TRONICS INC.   NAS: GIGA

4650 Norris Canyon Road
San Ramon, CA 94583
Phone: 925 328-4650
Fax: 925 328-4700
Web: www.gigatronics.com

CEO: John R Regazzi
CFO: Steven D Lance
HR: -
FYE: March 28
Type: Public

Giga-tronics has a cool gig in electronics. Its three units — Giga-tronics Instruments Microsource and ASCOR — make test measurement and control equipment for both commercial and military customers. The units make synthesizers and power measurement instruments used in electronic warfare radar satellite and telecommunications devices; switching systems for aircraft and automated test equipment; and oscillators and filters used in microwave instruments. Top customers include the US Department of Defense and its prime contractors. The majority of the company's business is done the US.

	Annual Growth	03/11	03/12	03/13	03/14	03/15
Sales ($ mil.)	(3.2%)	21.0	13.1	14.2	13.3	18.5
Net income ($ mil.)	-	14.1	(5.9)	(4.2)	(3.7)	(1.7)
Market value ($ mil.)	(11.0%)	16.6	8.0	11.1	7.7	10.4
Employees	(6.8%)	94	89	90	76	71

GIGAMON INC

NYS: GIMO

3300 Olcott Street
Santa Clara, CA 95054
Phone: 408 831-4000
Fax: –
Web: www.gigamon.com

CEO: Paul A. Hooper
CFO: Michael J. (Mike) Burns
HR: Rich Jacquet
FYE: December 27
Type: Public

An invisibility cloak won't fly at Gigamon. A Unified Visibility Fabric on the other hand will definitely fly. The company's visibility fabric is a layer of technology that steers information on networks to the appropriate destination. Gigamon's products such as the GigaVUE platform can handle video voice and data. Gigamon's products which include cloud-based software help IT managers of enterprises data centers and service providers see what's happening with their networks manage risks and maintain network performance. Gigamon has customers in finance health care higher education government technology and telecom as well as other businesses. The company went public in 2013.

	Annual Growth	12/10	12/11	12/12	12/13	12/14
Sales ($ mil.)	35.6%	46.5	68.1	96.7	140.3	157.1
Net income ($ mil.)	–	6.6	16.9	7.5	(9.5)	(40.8)
Market value ($ mil.)	(38.2%)	–	–	–	923.4	570.3
Employees	13.5%	–	–	288	352	371

GIGOPTIX, INC.

ASE: GIG

130 Baytech Drive
San Jose, CA 95134
Phone: 408 522-3100
Fax: –
Web: www.gigoptix.com

CEO: Avi Katz
CFO: –
HR: –
FYE: December 31
Type: Public

GigOptix hopes its light shines bright in an optical universe. The company develops polymer materials and products for use in wireless and optical communications networks. Products include optical and radio-frequency (RF) amplifiers compact panel wireless antennas and electro-optic modulators and optical interconnects for use in telecommunications. Its products are used in fiber-optic communications networks and for connecting to other types of electronic equipment. GigOptix also develops custom electro-optic devices for the US government particularly the Department of Defense which accounts most of sales. Customers have included Multiplex Inc. and ZTE Corporation.

	Annual Growth	12/10	12/11	12/12	12/13	12/14
Sales ($ mil.)	5.2%	26.9	32.3	36.7	28.9	32.9
Net income ($ mil.)	–	(4.4)	(14.1)	(7.0)	(1.9)	(5.8)
Market value ($ mil.)	(18.7%)	89.1	58.3	62.2	49.6	38.9
Employees	(1.9%)	83	80	84	76	77

GILBANE INC.

7 Jackson Walkway
Providence RI 02903
Phone: 401-456-5800
Fax: 401-456-5936
Web: www.gilbaneco.com

CEO: Thomas F Gilbane Jr
CFO: John Ruggieri
HR: –
FYE: December 31
Type: Private

Family-owned Gilbane Inc. has served the construction and real estate industry for five generations. Founded by William Gilbane in 1873 the company operates through chief subsidiaries: Gilbane Building and Gilbane Development Company. Its building arm provides construction management contracting and design and build services to construct office buildings manufacturing plants schools and prisons. Signature projects include the National WWII Memorial and Capitol Visitors Center in Washington DC. Gilbane Development offers real estate development property management financing and asset repositioning services to its clients in Maryland Ohio Pennsylvania Rhode Island Vermont.

GILEAD SCIENCES, INC.

NMS: GILD

333 Lakeside Drive
Foster City, CA 94404
Phone: 650 574-3000
Fax: –
Web: www.gilead.com

CEO: John C. Martin
CFO: Robin L. Washington
HR: Eva Sanchez
FYE: December 31
Type: Public

Gilead Sciences has biotech balms for infectious diseases including hepatitis HIV and infections related to AIDS. The company's HIV franchise includes Truvada a combination of two of its other drugs Viread and Emtriva. It co-promotes another HIV treatment called Atripla in the US and Europe with Bristol-Myers Squibb (BMS). Other products on the market include AmBisome used to treat systemic fungal infections such as those that accompany AIDS or kidney disease; and hepatitis B antiviral Hepsera. Beyond HIV/AIDS Gilead also markets cardiovascular drugs Letairis and Ranexa as well as respiratory and ophthalmic medicines.

	Annual Growth	12/10	12/11	12/12	12/13	12/14
Sales ($ mil.)	33.0%	7,949.4	8,385.4	9,702.5	11,201.7	24,890.0
Net income ($ mil.)	42.9%	2,901.3	2,803.6	2,591.6	3,074.8	12,101.0
Market value ($ mil.)	27.0%	54,323.8	61,354.1	110,101.6	112,574.9	141,295.7
Employees	15.0%	4,000	4,500	5,000	6,100	7,000

GILLETTE CHILDREN'S SPECIALTY HEALTHCARE

200 UNIVERSITY AVE E
SAINT PAUL, MN 551012507
Phone: 651-291-2848
Fax: –
Web: www.gillettechildrens.org

CEO: –
CFO: James Haddican
HR: –
FYE: December 31
Type: Private

Caring for the Twin Cities' tiniest tykes and most truculent teens Gillette Children's Specialty Healthcare provides diagnostic therapeutic and support services to children adolescents and young adults. Gillette Children's consists of a main campus in St. Paul Minnesota and eight clinics in the immediate and outlying areas of the city. The health system also provides adult services at its St. Paul-Phalen clinic. The main campus hospital (with about 345 beds) operates Centers of Excellence for cerebral palsy craniofacial services and pediatric neurosciences among others. The not-for-profit hospital also provides outreach services through its mobile health care unit.

	Annual Growth	12/01	12/02	12/08	12/09	12/13
Sales ($ mil.)	10.4%	–	70.1	133.3	139.9	208.1
Net income ($ mil.)	–	–	–	0.0	7.7	17.4
Market value ($ mil.)	–	–	–	–	–	–
Employees	–	–	–	–	–	623

GILLMAN COMPANIES

10595 W. Sam Houston Pkwy. South
Houston TX 77099
Phone: 713-776-4800
Fax: 713-776-7057
Web: www.gillmanauto.com

CEO: Ramsay H Giliman
CFO: Bart McAndrews
HR: Claire Mullins
FYE: December 31
Type: Private

Views of Texas bluebonnets come as a free accessory with cars sold by Gillman Companies. The firm sells new cars trucks and SUVs made by Acura Buick Chevrolet GMC Honda Mitsubishi Nissan and Subaru at more than a dozen dealerships spanning five Texas cities including Austin and Houston. Gillman Companies also sells used cars and fleet units and offers parts and service. Shoppers can browse for cars and apply for credit on Gillman's Web site. Gillman expanded into the Rio Grande Valley with its purchase of Kellogg Motor Company in 2008. Founded in 1938 family-run Gillman Companies is now owned by Ramsay Gillman who started out working at his father's dealership and opened his first car lot in 1967.

GILSTER-MARY LEE CORPORATION

1037 State St.
Chester IL 62233
Phone: 618-826-2361
Fax: 618-826-2973
Web: www.gilstermarylee.com

CEO: Donald E Welge
CFO: –
HR: –
FYE: December 31
Type: Private

Breakfast is the most important meal of the day especially at Gilster-Mary Lee. One of the largest private-label cereal manufacturers in the US (along with Ralcorp Holdings) Gilster-Mary Lee makes more than 8000 products under 500 private labels including breakfast cereal cake baking mixes cocoa and other drink mixes dinner mixes pasta and more. The company's customers include major US grocery chains and food wholesalers. The company also offers products under its own Hospitality brand name. Gilster-Mary Lee owns about 15 manufacturing operations located in Arkansas Illinois and Missouri. Its products are available worldwide.

GINKGO RESIDENTIAL TRUST INC.

301 S. College St. Ste. 3850
Charlotte NC 28202
Phone: 704-944-0100
Fax: +82-31-387-9321
Web: www.knoc.co.kr

CEO: –
CFO: –
HR: –
FYE: December 31
Type: Private

Ginkgo Residential Trust hopes its tenants make lasting memories at its apartment properties. A self-managed self-administered real estate investment trust (REIT) Ginkgo Residential acquires owns and manages multifamily residential properties in the southern US. Its properties located predominantly in North Carolina South Carolina and Virginia comprise 24 middle-market apartment complexes that together house more than 5760 units. Ginkgo Residential was formed in early 2012 to acquire the portfolio of 24 properties from predecessor company BNP Residential Properties. Shortly after its formation the REIT filed to go public.

GIRL SCOUTS OF THE UNITED STATES OF AMERICA

420 5TH AVE FL 13
NEW YORK, NY 100182729
Phone: 212-852-8000
Fax: –
Web: www.girlscouts.org

CEO: Kathy Cloninger
CFO: Florence Corsello
HR: –
FYE: September 30
Type: Private

For the Girl Scouts of the United States of America the calendar includes one month of cookie sales and 12 months of character-building. One of the largest groups devoted to girls it has more than 2.5 million girl members plus some 800000 adult volunteers. Girl Scouts of the USA founded in 1912 is open to girls between ages 5 and 17. It strives to develop character and leadership skills through projects using technology sports the environment literacy and the arts and sciences. Girl Scouts of the USA operates through 112 chartered regional councils. The US organization is part of the World Association of Girl Guides and Girl Scouts which numbers some 10 million girls and adults in about 145 countries.

	Annual Growth	09/08	09/09	09/10	09/11	09/12
Sales ($ mil.)	16.6%	–	66.4	80.7	129.8	105.2
Net income ($ mil.)	–	–	–	(4.8)	(2.6)	5.9
Market value ($ mil.)	–	–	–	–	–	–
Employees	–	–	–	–	–	500

GIRLING HEALTH CARE INC.

1703 W. 5th St.
Austin TX 78703
Phone: 800-447-5464
Fax: 512-478-0801
Web: www.browndistributing.com/

CEO: –
CFO: –
HR: Brianna Braden
FYE: December 31
Type: Private

Girling Health Care offers home health personal care and homemaker services for grown-up girls and boys who need living assistance. The company serves customers in about a dozen states scattered across the US. Girling provides home health services including skilled nursing rehabilitation therapy condition monitoring and wound care. It also provides personal services including housekeeping living assistance and respite care. Texas is the health care firm's largest market. Girling Healthcare is a subsidiary of another Austin-based health care company privately held Harden Healthcare.

GKN DRIVELINE NORTH AMERICA INC.

3300 University Dr.
Auburn Hills MI 48326-2362
Phone: 248-377-1200
Fax: 248-377-1370
Web: www.gkndriveline.com

CEO: –
CFO: Craig Connop
HR: Andrea Blake
FYE: December 31
Type: Business Segment

GKN Driveline North America is driven; the business oversees the US operations of the GKN Driveline segment of British engineering firm GKN plc. The segment builds and supplies driveline components and systems constant velocity joint (CVJ) side shafts bevel gear differentials prop shafts and power transfer units for automotive applications. GKN's driveline products have been used by just about all of the light vehicle makers worldwide including VW Fiat Chrysler General Motors Ford and Renault/Nissan. GKN Driveline North America has five manufacturing facilities in the US. North America generates about 20% of Driveline revenues.

GKN SINTER METALS LLC

3300 University Dr.
Auburn Hills MI 48326-2362
Phone: 248-371-0800
Fax: 248-371-0809
Web: www.gknsintermetals.com

CEO: –
CFO: –
HR: –
FYE: December 31
Type: Subsidiary

GKN Sinter Metals makes precision pressed-powder metal components for use principally in the automotive lawn and garden power tool and home appliance industries. The company uses a process known as powder metallurgy to make intricate and complex parts with performance attributes comparable with components produced through such processes as forging and casting. Its metal components include gears bearings and pulleys primarily for use in engines transmissions and other drive mechanisms. Customers include Deere Volkswagen and Ford. GKN Sinter Metals which operates about 30 locations on five continents is a subsidiary of UK-based automotive components and aerospace concern GKN plc.

GLACIER BANCORP, INC.
NMS: GBCI

49 Commons Loop
Kalispell, MT 59901
Phone: 406 756-4200
Fax: –
Web: www.glacierbank.com

CEO: Michael J. (Mick) Blodnick
CFO: Ronald J. (Ron) Copher
HR: Robin S Roush
FYE: December 31
Type: Public

Glacier Bancorp is on a Rocky Mountain high. The holding company owns about a dozen community bank divisions with about 100 locations in Montana Idaho Utah Washington Colorado and Wyoming. Serving individuals small to midsized businesses not-for-profits and public entities the banks offer traditional deposit products and credit cards in addition to retail brokerage and investment services through agreements with third-party providers. Its lending activities consist of commercial real estate loans (about half of the company's loan portfolio) as well as residential mortgages business loans and consumer loans.

	Annual Growth	12/10	12/11	12/12	12/13	12/14
Assets ($ mil.)	5.3%	6,759.3	7,187.9	7,747.4	7,884.4	8,306.5
Net income ($ mil.)	27.8%	42.3	17.5	75.5	95.6	112.8
Market value ($ mil.)	16.4%	1,133.6	902.6	1,103.6	2,235.0	2,083.5
Employees	4.9%	1,674	1,653	1,753	1,919	2,030

GLACIER WATER SERVICES INC.
PINK SHEETS: GWSV

1385 Park Center Dr.
Vista CA 92081
Phone: 760-560-1111
Fax: 760-560-3333
Web: www.glacierwater.com

CEO: Brian H McInerney
CFO: Steve Stringer
HR: –
FYE: December 31
Type: Public

Glacier Water Services serves those who shun the tap. The company operates more than 18000 self-service vending machines that dispense filtered drinking water making it a leading brand in vended water. Its machines which are located in more than 40 US states and Canada are connected to municipal water sources and are designed to reduce impurities in the water through processes such as micron filtration reverse osmosis carbon absorption and ultraviolet disinfection. Glacier Water's machines are placed outside supermarkets and other stores. The company conducts business in Canada through subsidiary Gestion Bi-Eau Pure. Glacier Water plans to buy the Aqua Fill water vending business.

GLADSTONE CAPITAL CORPORATION
NASDAQ: GLAD

1521 Westbranch Dr. Ste. 200
McLean VA 22102
Phone: 703-287-5800
Fax: 703-287-5801
Web: www.gladstonecapital.com

CEO: David Gladstone
CFO: Melissa Morrison
HR: –
FYE: September 30
Type: Public

If your fledgling company shows promise Gladstone Capital might be glad to provide some capital. The business development company (BDC) provides loans generally between $5 million and $20 million to small and midsized family-owned US companies or firms backed by leveraged buyout funds or venture capital outfits. Gladstone Capital particularly targets firms undergoing ownership transitions. The firm then shepherds its portfolio companies towards merger or acquisition transactions or initial public offerings. Company affiliate Gladstone Management Corporation provides management services to the firm's portfolio companies. Subsidiary Gladstone Business Loan holds the loan investment portfolio.

GLADSTONE COMMERCIAL CORP
NMS: GOOD

1521 Westbranch Drive, Suite 100
McLean, VA 22102
Phone: 703 287-5800
Fax: 703 287-5801
Web: www.gladstonecommercial.com

CEO: Daniel Birnbaum
CFO: Danielle Jones
HR: –
FYE: December 31
Type: Public

Gladstone Commercial will gladly buy your commercial property or lease you some if you need a business home. A real estate investment trust (REIT) Gladstone invests in and owns commercial and industrial real estate properties and long-term commercial mortgages. The company owns more than 85 properties across the US with assets that include office buildings warehouses retail and manufacturing facilities. Gladstone predominantly leases to small and midsized businesses; most properties carry triple-net leases. Tenants include Corning Cummins and T-Mobile. The firm is closely affiliated with management investment firm Gladstone Capital which is also headed by chairman and CEO David Gladstone.

	Annual Growth	12/10	12/11	12/12	12/13	12/14
Sales ($ mil.)	15.2%	41.9	44.0	51.3	61.3	73.8
Net income ($ mil.)	–	4.9	5.7	3.8	1.5	(5.9)
Market value ($ mil.)	(2.3%)	384.1	358.0	366.2	366.6	350.3
Employees	–	–	–	–	–	–

GLADSTONE INVESTMENT CORP
NMS: GAIN

1521 Westbranch Drive, Suite 200
McLean, VA 22102
Phone: 703 287-5800
Fax: –
Web: www.gladstoneinvestment.com

CEO: David Gladstone
CFO: Julia Ryan
HR: –
FYE: March 31
Type: Public

Gladstone Investment is happy to invest if a business shows potential for growth. The company makes debt and equity investments typically in subordinated loans mezzanine debt and preferred stock to buy out or recapitalize small and medium-sized private US businesses. It generally does so in conjunction with a company's management team or with other buyout funds. Investments usually range from $3 million to $40 million. Gladstone invests in a variety of businesses ranging from industrial product manufacturers to media companies in TV radio and publishing. Sister companies Gladstone Capital and Gladstone Commercial provide business development loans and finance commercial and industrial real estate.

	Annual Growth	03/09	03/10	03/11	03/12	03/13
Assets ($ mil.)	3.8%	326.8	297.2	241.1	325.3	379.8
Net income ($ mil.)	5.3%	13.4	10.6	16.2	13.7	16.5
Market value ($ mil.)	17.6%	101.1	158.3	205.5	200.4	193.5
Employees	–	–	–	–	–	–

GLADSTONE LAND CORP
NMS: LAND

1521 Westbranch Drive, Suite 100
McLean, VA 22102
Phone: 703 287-5800
Fax: –
Web: www.gladstoneland.com

CEO: David Gladstone
CFO: Lewis Parrish
HR: –
FYE: December 31
Type: Public

Gladstone Land buys farm properties in the US and rents them to corporate farming operations and medium-sized independent farmers through triple net leases arrangements in which the tenant is responsible for maintaining the property. Gladstone Land is an externally managed real estate company that owns about a dozen row crop properties in California and Florida which total more than 1600 acres. It leases most of its properties to Dole Fresh Vegetables a subsidiary of Dole Foods which uses the farmland to grow annual fruit and vegetable crops like berries melons and lettuce among others. Gladstone Land went public in early 2013 with an offering worth $50 million.

	Annual Growth	12/10	12/11	12/12	12/13	12/14
Sales ($ mil.)	31.3%	2.4	3.0	3.4	4.0	7.2
Net income ($ mil.)	–	0.6	0.0	0.6	(1.2)	(0.1)
Market value ($ mil.)	(33.9%)	–	–	–	125.6	83.0
Employees	–	–	–	–	–	–

GLASSHOUSE TECHNOLOGIES INC.

200 Crossing Blvd.
Framingham MA 01702
Phone: 508-879-5729
Fax: 508-879-7319
Web: www.glasshouse.com

CEO: –
CFO: –
HR: –
FYE: December 31
Type: Private

GlassHouse wants businesses to put down their stones and pick up its data center IT services. The company provides a range of managed services to improve the way businesses store retrieve and maintain data. Offering consulting cloud services data center management and technology integration the company specializes in such areas as virtualization data center migration and operational support services. It also resells third-party hardware and software. GlassHouse serves customers — about half of the Fortune 100 among them — in the public sector and the energy entertainment and travel industries among others and have included such companies as Biogen Idec and JPMorgan Chase.

GLAZER'S WHOLESALE DRUG COMPANY INC.

14911 Quorum Dr. Ste. 400
Dallas TX 75254
Phone: 972-392-8200
Fax: 972-702-8508
Web: www.glazers.com

CEO: Sheldon Stein
CFO: –
HR: –
FYE: December 31
Type: Private

Glazer's Wholesale Drug Company named during Prohibition when only drugstores and drug wholesalers could deal in liquor is a wholesale distributor of alcoholic beverages. In Texas it is the largest company of its kind and one of the largest wine and spirits distributors in the US. The company distributes Budweiser beer Robert Mondavi wines Brown-Forman and Bacardi spirits and Diageo products. CEO Bennett Glazer and his family own Glazer's. The company's origins date back to the early 1900s when the Glazer family sold flavored soda water which it distributed using horse-drawn wagons. Today Glazer has operations in 12 US states.

GLEACHER & CO, INC. (DE)

NMS: GLCH

1290 Avenue of the Americas
New York, NY 10104
Phone: 212-273-7100
Fax: –
Web: www.gleacher.com

CEO: –
CFO: –
HR: –
FYE: December 31
Type: Public

Gleacher & Co. provides advisory services capital raising research and securities and brokerage services to institutional clients in the US and Europe. The firm's MBS/ABS & Rates arm sells and trades asset and mortgage-backed securities. Gleacher's Corporate Credit unit offers sales and trading on a range of debt securities. Its FA Technology Ventures subsidiary provides growth capital to technology firms. Gleacher is restructuring after exiting its primary business investment banking and selling its ClearPoint Funding subsidiary in 2013. The firm's namesake founder and former chairman Eric Gleacher has resigned.

	Annual Growth	12/08	12/09	12/10	12/11	12/12
Assets ($ mil.)	15.4%	694.3	1,216.2	1,657.9	3,303.6	1,229.6
Net income ($ mil.)	–	(17.4)	54.9	(20.6)	(82.1)	(77.7)
Market value ($ mil.)	(29.0%)	18.5	27.8	14.7	10.5	4.7
Employees	(3.6%)	255	342	368	453	220

GLEN BURNIE BANCORP

NAS: GLBZ

101 Crain Highway, S.E.
Glen Burnie, MD 21061
Phone: 410-766-3300
Fax: –
Web: www.thebankofglenburnie.com

CEO: Michael G Livingston
CFO: John M Wright
HR: –
FYE: December 31
Type: Public

Glen Burnie Bancorp has an interest in the Old Line State. The institution is the holding company for Bank of Glen Burnie which has about 10 branches in central Maryland's Anne Arundel County south of Baltimore. The bank offers such services as checking and savings accounts money market and individual retirement accounts CDs and remote banking services. It focuses on real estate lending with residential and commercial mortgages accounting for the largest portions of its loan portfolio. The bank also writes indirect automobile loans which are originated through a network of about 50 area car dealers. Bank of Glen Burnie was founded in 1949.

	Annual Growth	12/10	12/11	12/12	12/13	12/14
Assets ($ mil.)	3.3%	347.1	365.3	387.4	377.2	394.6
Net income ($ mil.)	(1.9%)	2.1	3.0	2.7	2.6	1.9
Market value ($ mil.)	8.5%	23.8	22.5	31.6	33.4	33.0
Employees	(3.1%)	118	108	103	100	104

GLENDALE ADVENTIST MEDICAL CENTER INC

1509 WILSON TER
GLENDALE, CA 912064007
Phone: 818-409-8000
Fax: –
Web: www.glendaleadventist.com

CEO: Warren L Tetz
CFO: –
HR: –
FYE: December 31
Type: Private

Treating ladies from Pasadena and other patients throughout the suburbs of sunny Southern California Glendale Adventist Medical Center (GAMC) is a stalwart community member. The hospital is part of Adventist Health a not-for-profit group of about 20 hospitals and health care organizations in four western states. GAMC provides a range of specialty services including cancer treatment cardiology emergency medicine neuroscience home care psychiatry rehabilitation and women's healthcare. It also provides medical training and residency programs. The 515-bed hospital was founded in 1905 by the Seventh-Day Adventist Church.

	Annual Growth	06/04	06/05*	12/07	12/09	12/12
Sales ($ mil.)	(12.5%)	–	985.2	273.7	307.8	387.1
Net income ($ mil.)	95.1%	–	–	0.2	12.7	5.5
Market value ($ mil.)	–	–	–	–	–	–
Employees	–	–	–	–	–	2,600

*Fiscal year change

GLENN O. HAWBAKER INC.

1952 WADDLE RD STE 203
STATE COLLEGE, PA 16803-1649
Phone: 814-237-1444
Fax: –
Web: www.goh-inc.com

CEO: –
CFO: –
HR: –
FYE: December 31
Type: Private

For Glenn O. Hawbaker (GOH) it's all about making the grade. Founded as an excavating and grading company GOH provides heavy construction concrete construction utility work asphalt production and heavy equipment rentals and sales. From its home base in Pennsylvania the company serves customers in the north-central portion of the state. As part of its business GOH operates two dozen quarries and eight asphalt production facilities in Pennsylvania New York and eastern Ohio (since 2012). Its Hawbaker Engineering subsidiary provides civil engineering services and site designs. The family-owned company was founded in 1952 by Glenn and Thelma Hawbaker the parents of president and CEO Daniel Hawbaker.

	Annual Growth	12/08	12/09	12/10	12/11	12/12
Sales ($ mil.)	4.4%	–	220.5	337.6	326.1	251.0
Net income ($ mil.)	(50.3%)	–	7.8	25.3	20.8	1.0
Market value ($ mil.)	–	–	–	–	–	–
Employees	–	–	–	–	–	1,300

GLIMCHER REALTY TRUST

NYS: GRT

180 East Broad Street
Columbus, OH 43215
Phone: 614 621-9000
Fax: 614 621-9311
Web: www.glimcher.com

CEO: –
CFO: –
HR: –
FYE: December 31
Type: Public

In Glimcher's ideal world we'd all be shopaholics. A self-administered and self-managed real estate investment trust (REIT) Glimcher acquires develops and manages retail real estate. Its portfolio includes about 25 enclosed and open-air shopping malls (a handful are owned through joint ventures) and three strip shopping centers. Its properties which have more than 21 million sq. ft. of space are scattered across 15 states; Ohio is home to the greatest number of its properties. The company's occupancy rate is around 95%. Major tenants include L Brands The Gap and Foot Locker.

	Annual Growth	12/08	12/09	12/10	12/11	12/12
Sales ($ mil.)	0.5%	319.1	308.4	274.8	267.9	326.0
Net income ($ mil.)	–	16.8	4.6	5.9	19.6	(2.1)
Market value ($ mil.)	40.9%	402.1	386.3	1,202.0	1,316.4	1,586.9
Employees	0.9%	1,054	1,038	1,428	1,088	1,094

GLOBAL AXCESS CORP.

NBB: GAXC Q

7800 Belfort Parkway, Suite 165
Jacksonville, FL 32256
Phone: 904 280-3950
Fax: –
Web: www.globalaxcess.biz

CEO: Kevin L Reager
CFO: Michael J Loiacono
HR: –
FYE: December 31
Type: Public

Global Axcess has no ax to grind just a bunch of kiosks to manage. Through subsidiary Nationwide Money Services the company operates a network of some 4700 ATMs around the US. More than half of the ATMs it manages are owned by merchants but Global Axcess does own around 2000 of the machines. The company provides maintenance cash management and network processing services; it processes some 1.5 million financial transactions per month. Its machine network is concentrated in the South and East. In 2009 Global Axcess formed subsidiary Nationwide Ntertainment to operate self-serve DVD rental kiosks under the InstaFlix brand. It operates more than 500 of the mini video rental stores.

	Annual Growth	12/08	12/09	12/10	12/11	12/12
Sales ($ mil.)	8.9%	22.2	21.5	22.7	31.9	31.2
Net income ($ mil.)	–	1.2	2.8	(0.9)	(1.9)	(12.1)
Market value ($ mil.)	(8.5%)	3.0	20.2	12.7	13.6	2.1
Employees	0.0%	45	48	61	54	45

GLOBAL BRASS & COPPER HOLDINGS INC

NYS: BRSS

475 N. Martingale Road, Suite 1050
Schaumburg, IL 60173
Phone: 847 240-4700
Fax: –
Web: www.gbcholdings.com

CEO: John J. Wasz
CFO: Robert T. Micchelli
HR: –
FYE: December 31
Type: Public

Global Brass and Copper Holdings (GBC) is okay knowing that not all that glitters is gold. Through its subsidiaries GBC is a leading North American manufacturer and distributor of fabricated copper and copper-alloy products. The company's operations are divided into three segments: Olin Brass (fabricator of copper and brass sheet strip foil and tubing) Chase Brass (manufacturer of brass rods used by OEMs to make valves fittings and other machining products) and A.J. Oster (distributor of copper-alloy products). GBC serves customers from a variety of sectors including construction automotive coinage electronics and industrial manufacturing. Formed in 2007 the company went public in 2013.

	Annual Growth	12/10	12/11	12/12	12/13	12/14
Sales ($ mil.)	0.8%	1,658.7	1,779.1	1,650.5	1,758.5	1,711.4
Net income ($ mil.)	(6.6%)	41.6	55.1	12.5	10.4	31.7
Market value ($ mil.)	(20.5%)	–	–	–	353.2	280.8
Employees	(2.3%)	–	–	1,986	2,062	1,896

GLOBAL BRASS AND COPPER HOLDINGS INC.

1901 N. Roselle Rd. Ste. 800
Schaumburg IL 60195
Phone: 847-517-6340
Fax: 610-687-9565
Web: www.jlyonsmarketing.com

CEO: John J Wasz
CFO: –
HR: –
FYE: December 31
Type: Private

Global Brass and Copper Holdings (GBC) is okay knowing that not all that glitters is gold. Through its subsidiaries GBC is a leading North American manufacturer and distributor of fabricated copper and copper-alloy products. The company's operations are divided into three segments: Olin Brass (fabricator of copper and brass sheet strip foil and tubing) Chase Brass (manufacturer of brass rods used by OEMs to make valves fittings and other machining products) and A.J. Oster (distributor of copper-alloy products). GBC serves customers from a variety of sectors including construction automotive coinage electronics and industrial manufacturing. Formed in 2007 the company filed to go public in 2011.

GLOBAL COMMUNICATION SEMICONDUCTORS INC.

23155 Kashiwa Ct.
Torrance CA 90505-4026
Phone: 310-530-7274
Fax: 310-530-7279
Web: www.gcsincorp.com

CEO: Bau-Hsing Ann
CFO: –
HR: –
FYE: June 30
Type: Private

Global Communication Semiconductors (GCS) aspires to be a global force in communications chips. GCS offers contract manufacturing or foundry services to makers of chips used in RF communications devices such as wireless phones and base stations as well as telecommunications and high-speed networking. GCS uses compound semiconductor materials that offer various performance benefits — such as faster operation or lower power consumption — in comparison with standard silicon. Global Communication Semiconductors was founded by former CEO Owen Wu in 1997. The company is owned by several individuals and institutional investors including RF Micro Devices (12% ownership).

GLOBAL CUSTOM COMMERCE L.P.

10555 Richmond Ave. Ste. 200
Houston TX 77042
Phone: 800-505-1905
Fax: 800-810-5919
Web: www.blinds.com

CEO: –
CFO: –
HR: –
FYE: December 31
Type: Private

NoBrainerBlinds.com makes and markets custom window shades shutters and blinds. The company offers popular brand names including Hunter Douglas Bali Levolor and Graber among others. The company sells its window coverings through its Web site which also offers decorating advice on topics ranging from installation and maintenance to child- and pet-proofing customers' homes. Company president and CEO Jay Steinfeld founded NoBrainerBlinds in 1996.

GLOBAL DIVERSIFIED INDUSTRIES INC. OTC: GDIV

1200 Airport Dr.
Chowchilla CA 93610
Phone: 559-665-5800
Fax: 559-665-5700
Web: www.gdvi.net

CEO: –
CFO: –
HR: –
FYE: April 30
Type: Public

Global Diversified Industries is the new mod squad. Through its Global Modular subsidiary the company makes pre-fabricated portable modular buildings mainly for use as classrooms. It also constructs permanent one- and two-story structures. Clients include public and private schools universities child-care facilities and municipalities. The company is active throughout California. Global Diversified divested its MBS Construction subsidiary which provided construction site management services in 2006. Company president Phil Hamilton has voting control of more than 20% of Global Diversified's stock.

GLOBAL EARTH ENERGY INC. OTC: GLER

534 Delaware Ave. Ste. 412
Buffalo NY 14202
Phone: 716-332-7150
Fax: 716-332-7170
Web: www.globalearthenergy.com

CEO: –
CFO: Edmund J Gorman
HR: –
FYE: August 31
Type: Public

Global Earth Energy (formerly Global Wataire) believes strongly that the global earth energy to exploit is biodiesel. The company plans to build on the growing momentum for using biodiesel as way to decrease US dependency on foreign crude oil and limit carbon emissions by establishing a 1 million-gallon-per-year biodiesel production plant in North Carolina. It is also planning to move into the even greener energy sources of solar and wind power generation. The company acquired Kentucky-based Samuel Coal for $7.5 million in 2011. Formerly operating as water purification firm Global Wataire the company changed its name and industry focus in 2008. Chairman Betty-Ann Harland owns 25% of Global Earth Energy.

GLOBAL ENTERTAINMENT CORPORATION OTC: GNTP

1600 N. Desert Dr. Ste. 301
Tempe AZ 85281
Phone: 480-994-0772
Fax: 480-994-0759
Web: www.globalentertainment2000.com

CEO: Richard Kozuback
CFO: –
HR: –
FYE: May 31
Type: Public

Global Entertainment Corporation is helping to bring sports to the hinterlands. The event and entertainment company through its various subsidiaries offers project management services to midsized communities looking to develop event centers and sports facilities. It also offers facilities and venue management and ticketing services as well as sponsorship and marketing consulting. Through its WPHL (Western Professional Hockey League) subsidiary Global Entertainment manages the Central Hockey League a development league affiliated with the National Hockey League. WPHL Holdings which is affiliated with chairman James Treliving controls more than 40% of the company.

GLOBAL GEOPHYSICAL SERVICES INC NYS: GGS

13927 South Gessner Road
Missouri City, TX 77489
Phone: 713 972-9200
Fax: –

CEO: Ross Peebles
CFO: Sean M Gore
HR: –
FYE: December 31
Type: Public

Global Geophysical builds its business from the ground down. It provides seismic data acquisition services to the oil and gas industry for locating potential reservoirs and studying known reserves. Global Geophysical transmits sound waves below the earth's surface to create images of the existing subsurface geology. Its integrated suite of seismic data solutions includes high-resolution RG-3D Reservoir Grade seismic data acquisition microseismic monitoring seismic data processing and interpretation services and Multi Client data products. The firm's seismic crews work in a wide variety of terrains including deserts jungles mountains and swamps and have completed projects in more than 100 countries.

	Annual Growth	12/08	12/09	12/10	12/11	12/12
Sales ($ mil.)	(2.6%)	376.3	312.8	254.7	385.4	339.0
Net income ($ mil.)	–	(8.0)	0.4	(39.7)	5.7	(13.3)
Market value ($ mil.)	(39.1%)	–	–	390.3	252.7	144.8
Employees	13.6%	–	818	1,667	1,300	1,200

GLOBAL HEALTHCARE EXCHANGE LLC

1315 W. Century Dr.
Louisville CO 80027
Phone: 720-887-7000
Fax: 720-887-7200
Web: www.ghx.com

CEO: Bruce Johnson
CFO: Richard Hunt
HR: –
FYE: December 31
Type: Private

Global Healthcare Exchange (GHX) provides an electronic trading exchange designed for health care providers suppliers and manufacturers to buy and sell supplies online. GHX aims to lower supply chain costs for its users by allowing them to perform transactions with multiple parties through one electronic platform as well as by automating the purchasing process and reducing purchase order errors. The firm was founded in 2000 by a group of five health care manufacturers: Abbott Labs Baxter International GE Medical Systems Johnson & Johnson and Medtronic. It is now owned by the original five plus a slew of other distributors hospitals group purchasing organizations and manufacturers.

GLOBAL HEALTHCARE REIT INC NBB: GBCS

3050 Peachtree Road, Suite 355
Atlanta, GA 30305
Phone: 404 549-4293
Fax: –

CEO: Christopher Brogdon
CFO: Philip Scarborough
HR: –
FYE: December 31
Type: Public

Global Casinos owns and operates two casinos in Colorado. Its Bull Durham Saloon & Casino in Black Hawk Colorado boasts more than 180 slot machines and offers limited food services along with other customer amenities. Its customer base consists primarily of day visitors from Denver. The company also owns a second property the Doc Holliday Casino in Central City Colorado with about 200 slot machines. Both casinos offer charter services to bring groups of patrons from Denver. In 2012 the company announced plans to divest of all of its gaming interests and acquire a real estate investment trust (REIT) focused on the healthcare industry. Clifford Neuman owns nearly 10% of Global Casinos.

	Annual Growth	06/11	06/12	06/13*	12/13	12/14
Sales ($ mil.)	(30.5%)	5.5	5.2	3.1	0.4	1.9
Net income ($ mil.)	–	(1.4)	(0.8)	(1.8)	(0.6)	1.4
Market value ($ mil.)	41.6%	8.0	10.0	21.2	21.6	22.7
Employees	(73.7%)	55	55	44	1	1

*Fiscal year change

GLOBAL IMAGING SYSTEMS INC.

3820 Northdale Blvd. Ste. 200A
Tampa FL 33624
Phone: 813-960-5508
Fax: 813-264-7877
Web: www.global-imaging.com

CEO: Thomas Salierno Jr
CFO: R Edward Bass
HR: –
FYE: March 31
Type: Subsidiary

Global Imaging Systems (GIS) is consolidating the fragmented office equipment industry one acquisition at a time. The company sells and services products such as copiers fax machines printers projectors and conferencing equipment under such brands as Canon Hewlett-Packard InFocus Konica and Sharp. It also provides its customers — principally businesses with fewer than 1000 employees — with network integration services and systems (network design software hardware). GIS operates from about 200 locations in more than 35 states and the District of Columbia. In 2007 the acquisitive firm was purchased by Xerox for about $1.5 billion and became a subsidiary of the technology products giant.

GLOBAL KNOWLEDGE TRAINING LLC

9000 Regency Pkwy. Ste. 400
Cary NC 27518
Phone: 919-461-8600
Fax: 919-461-8646
Web: www.globalknowledge.com

CEO: Sean J Dolan
CFO: –
HR: –
FYE: December 31
Type: Private

Companies keep employee skills up-to-date with Global Knowledge. The firm provides technical training services to the employees of clients such as travel reservations firm Sabre ACTS Retirement-Life Communities and the Netherlands Ministry of Defence. Specializing in networking systems and telecommunications Global Knowledge offers more than 1200 vendor-authorized and proprietary courses covering the products of specific manufacturers including Microsoft and Cisco Systems. The company also provides custom integration and training services and outsourced education management services. Global Knowledge operates in about two-dozen countries around the world. It is owned by equity firm MidOcean Partners.

GLOBAL PACIFIC PRODUCE INC.

11500 S EASTRN AVE 120
HENDERSON, NV 89052
Phone: 702-898-8051
Fax: –
Web: www.globalpacificproduce.com

CEO: –
CFO: –
HR: –
FYE: December 31
Type: Private

Global Pacific Produce is a leading exporter of fresh produce serving international retailers. It sources such goods as apples citrus grapes pears and stone fruit mostly from California and Mexico. The company supplies grocery store chains and other retailers in South America and Europe. Chris Kilvington originally from London started the business in 2000.

	Annual Growth	12/08	12/09*	01/11*	12/11	12/12
Sales ($ mil.)	26.0%	–	157.7	192.8	263.0	315.4
Net income ($ mil.)	60.6%	–	2.4	4.5	5.8	9.8
Market value ($ mil.)	–	–	–	–	–	–
Employees	–	–	–	–	–	250

*Fiscal year change

GLOBAL PARTNERS LP   NYS: GLP

P.O. Box 9161, 800 South Street
Waltham, MA 02454-9161
Phone: 781 894-8800
Fax: –
Web: www.globalp.com

CEO: Eric Slifka
CFO: Daphne H. Foster
HR: Barbara (Barb) Rosenbloom
FYE: December 31
Type: Public

Global Partners (formerly Global Companies) imports petroleum products from global sources but its marketing is largely regional. The company wholesales heating oil residual fuel oil diesel oil kerosene distillates and gasoline to commercial retail and wholesale customers in New England and New York. A major player in the regional home heating oil market Global Partners operates storage facilities at 25 bulk terminals each with a storage capacity of more than 50000 barrels and with a collective storage capacity of 11.2 million barrels. It also owns and supplies a network of gasoline stations. Wholesale revenues accounts for the bulk of the company's sales.

	Annual Growth	12/10	12/11	12/12	12/13	12/14
Sales ($ mil.)	22.0%	7,801.6	14,835.7	17,626.0	19,589.6	17,270.0
Net income ($ mil.)	43.5%	27.0	19.4	46.7	42.6	114.7
Market value ($ mil.)	4.8%	844.9	674.4	781.7	1,091.3	1,017.3
Employees	41.7%	286	264	788	943	1,154

GLOBAL PAYMENTS, INC.   NYS: GPN

10 Glenlake Parkway, North Tower
Atlanta, GA 30328
Phone: 770 829-8000
Fax: –
Web: www.globalpaymentsinc.com

CEO: Jeffrey S. Sloan
CFO: Cameron M. Bready
HR: Karen Matterson
FYE: May 31
Type: Public

Go ahead — Chaaaaaarge! And when you do Global Payments will do what it does to ensure a seamless transaction. The company provides credit and debit card processing check authorization and other electronic payment processing services for more than 1 million merchant and business locations worldwide including retailers financial institutions governments gaming locations and multinational corporations. It targets small and midsized merchants who are often overlooked by other payment processors. Subsidiary HSBC Merchant Services provides payment processing services to merchants in the UK. The company operates throughout North America Europe and the Asia/Pacific region.

	Annual Growth	05/11	05/12	05/13	05/14	05/15
Sales ($ mil.)	10.5%	1,859.8	2,203.8	2,375.9	2,554.2	2,773.7
Net income ($ mil.)	7.4%	209.2	188.2	216.1	245.3	278.0
Market value ($ mil.)	19.1%	6,783.8	5,546.1	6,261.5	8,951.0	13,627.6
Employees	4.3%	3,753	3,796	3,954	4,135	4,438

GLOBAL POWER EQUIPMENT GROUP, INC.   NYS: GLPW

400 E. Las Colinas Blvd., Suite 400
Irving, TX 75039
Phone: 214 574-2700
Fax: –
Web: www.globalpower.com

CEO: Terence J Cryan
CFO: Raymond K Guba
HR: –
FYE: December 31
Type: Public

Global Power Equipment Group keeps its customers in power. Through its subsidiaries the company designs and manufactures power generation equipment for OEMs engineering construction and power generation customers. Its products sold under its Braden Manufacturing Consolidated Fabricators TOG and Koontz-Wagner brands include auxiliary parts for steam and gas turbines electric transmission systems and controls and custom components. Additionally subsidiary Williams Industrial Services offers upgrades and maintenance services to industrial and utility companies and nuclear and hydroelectric power plants while its Hetsco unit provides welding and fabrication services. The company was formed in 1998.

	Annual Growth	12/10	12/11	12/12	12/13	12/14
Sales ($ mil.)	0.9%	520.1	456.8	462.8	484.2	538.5
Net income ($ mil.)	(27.6%)	40.6	76.9	17.6	11.8	11.1
Market value ($ mil.)	(12.2%)	397.4	406.8	293.7	335.2	236.6
Employees	16.0%	687	1,493	1,437	1,244	1,244

GLOBAL TELECOM & TECHNOLOGY INC. OTC: GTLT

8484 Westpark Dr. Ste. 720
McLean VA 22102
Phone: 703-442-5500
Fax: 703-442-5501
Web: www.gt-t.net

CEO: Richard D Calder Jr
CFO: Eric A Swank
HR: –
FYE: December 31
Type: Public

Global Telecom & Technology (GTT) gets carried away providing network integration for wide area network (WAN) dedicated Internet access and managed data services to system integrators telecom carriers and government agencies. GTT combines multiple networks and technologies such as traditional OC-x MPLS and Ethernet and has distribution partnerships with more than 800 technology suppliers including iPass for wireless services. Past customers include Avaya Lockheed Martin and Telefonica. GTT counts customers in about 80 countries; it earns almost half of its revenues outside the US. Chairman H. Brian Thompson owns nearly 31% of the company's stock.

GLOBALOPTIONS GROUP INC. NASDAQ: GLOI

75 Rockefeller Plaza 27th Fl.
New York NY 10019
Phone: 212-445-6262
Fax: 212-445-0053
Web: www.globaloptionsgroup.com

CEO: Jonathan Ellenthal
CFO: Kara Jenny
HR: –
FYE: December 31
Type: Public

GlobalOptions likes to think of itself as the secure choice. The firm provides security consulting and investigation services including risk mitigation decision support emergency management litigation support anti-fraud solutions business intelligence and related security services. The company provides services to government entities corporations and high net-worth and high-profile individuals. The company divested its Fraud and Special Investigative Unit (SIU) as well as its Preparedness Services and Forensic DNA Solutions and Products units in 2010. GlobalOptions was founded in 1999.

GLOBAL TRAFFIC NETWORK INC.

880 3rd Ave. 6th Fl.
New York NY 10022
Phone: 212-896-1255
Fax: 312-669-9800
Web: www.emergenow.com

CEO: William L Yde III
CFO: Scott E Cody
HR: –
FYE: June 30
Type: Subsidiary

Great just what we need: more traffic. Global Traffic Network (GTN) provides customized traffic reports to some 70 radio stations in nearly 20 markets in Australia. In exchange for its content GTN receives commercial airtime from the stations which the company sells to advertisers. In addition the firm produces radio and TV news reports in Australia. GTN additionally provides radio traffic reporting services to more than 10 stations in the UK and does business in the US through a deal with Metro Networks. It provides traffic reports in Canada through an agreement with Corus Entertainment and provides news weather sports and business reports in Canada through subsidiary Wise Broadcasting Network.

GLOBALSCAPE INC ASE: GSB

4500 Lockhill-Selma, Suite 150
San Antonio, TX 78249
Phone: 210 308-8267
Fax: –
Web: www.globalscape.com

CEO: James L Bindseil
CFO: James W Albrecht Jr
HR: –
FYE: December 31
Type: Public

GlobalSCAPE is pretty cute for a software company. With packages like CuteFTP and Enhanced File Transfer (EFT) Server GlobalSCAPE provides managed file transfer software for businesses and individuals. The company also offers software used to collaborate share and backup data in real-time across multiple sites. Its software which is also offered in hosted and managed versions is sold primarily to small and midsized businesses and enterprise customers worldwide. GlobalSCAPE has counted Aon Thomas Cook Lone Star Bank and the US Army among its clients. More than two-thirds of sales come from customers in the US.

	Annual Growth	12/10	12/11	12/12	12/13	12/14
Sales ($ mil.)	9.6%	18.6	20.9	23.4	24.3	26.8
Net income ($ mil.)	36.1%	0.9	0.6	(1.8)	3.8	3.0
Market value ($ mil.)	2.9%	40.8	32.7	29.4	48.0	45.7
Employees	5.7%	84	96	96	103	105

GLOBALFLUENCY

4151 Middlefield Rd.
Palo Alto CA 94303
Phone: 650-328-5555
Fax: 650-328-5016
Web: www.globalfluency.com

CEO: –
CFO: –
HR: –
FYE: December 31
Type: Private

GlobalFluency (formerly Neale-May & Partners) offers services with some spin. The independent firm specializes in communications for high-tech companies but doesn't shy away from more traditional companies that need help sending a message. GlobalFluency provides its clients with such services as promotional marketing crisis management corporate and financial communication strategic consulting and event marketing. The company which operates more than 70 offices in 40 nations worldwide serves customers including Google AT&T and IBM. In 1987 Donovan Neale-May left his job at Ogilvy & Mather to establish the PR firm which changed its name in 2008.

GLOBALSPEC INC.

30 Tech Valley Dr. Ste. 102
East Greenbush NY 12061
Phone: 518-880-0200
Fax: 518-880-0250
Web: www.globalspec.com

CEO: Jeffrey M Killeen
CFO: William Hollyer
HR: –
FYE: December 31
Type: Private

Sometimes engineers need more than a good pair of specs to find the right component. Billing itself as "The Engineering Search Engine" GlobalSpec offers engineers scientists and related professionals a searchable online database of supplier catalogs. Its SpecSearch search engine lets registered users search by specifications to find technical products and services such as mechanical electrical and custom manufacturing offerings. Its Engineering Web search engine indexes millions of pages of engineering content. GlobalSpec also offers a suite of more than 70 product and industry specific e-newsletters. The firm was founded in 1996 by engineers John Schneiter and Thomas Brownell. Today it is owned by IHS.

GLOBALSTAR INC
ASE: GSAT

300 Holiday Square Blvd.
Covington, LA 70433
Phone: 985 335-1500
Fax: –
Web: www.globalstar.com

CEO: James (Jay) Monroe
CFO: Rebecca S. Clary
HR: –
FYE: December 31
Type: Public

When you're really working out in the middle of nowhere grab that sat phone and call up Globalstar. The company provides satellite voice and data service to remote areas underserved by traditional phone service. Its network of satellites and ground stations provides service to more than 580000 subscribers worldwide. Customers include the US government as well as companies in the energy maritime and mining industries with job sites underground or out at sea. Half of its ground stations are operated by independent companies that buy Globalstar's services on a wholesale basis. It also sells a handheld GPS navigation system called SPOT for adventure travelers or anyone needing a GPS device.

	Annual Growth	12/10	12/11	12/12	12/13	12/14
Sales ($ mil.)	7.3%	67.9	72.8	76.3	82.7	90.1
Net income ($ mil.)	–	(97.5)	(54.9)	(112.2)	(591.1)	(462.9)
Market value ($ mil.)	17.4%	1,447.7	539.1	304.5	1,747.2	2,745.6
Employees	(3.3%)	322	239	267	267	282

GLOBE SPECIALTY METALS INC
NMS: GSM

600 Brickell Ave, Suite 1500
Miami, FL 33131
Phone: 786 509-6900
Fax: 212 798-8155
Web: www.glbsm.com

CEO: Jeff Bradley
CFO: Joseph Ragan
HR: –
FYE: June 30
Type: Public

Globe Specialty Metals is an apt name for a company that peddles its metals around the world. The specialty metals manufacturer sells silicon metal and silicon-based alloys to customers in the Americas Asia and Europe from facilities in the US Argentina China and Poland. Its silicon metal and alloys are used to make a variety of industrial products from aluminum and automotive parts to steel and semiconductors. It holds about one-fifth of the Western market share for magnesium ferrosilicon. Globe also recycles by-products such as silica fume (a dustlike material known as microsilica that is collected in air filtration systems) which it sells for use as a concrete additive.

	Annual Growth	06/10	06/11	06/12	06/13	06/14
Sales ($ mil.)	12.3%	472.7	641.9	705.5	757.6	752.8
Net income ($ mil.)	(19.4%)	34.1	52.8	54.6	(21.0)	14.4
Market value ($ mil.)	19.1%	761.8	1,653.5	990.5	801.7	1,532.5
Employees	8.4%	1,136	1,213	1,493	1,353	1,569

GLOBEIMMUNE, INC
NAS: GBIM

1450 Infinite Drive
Louisville, CO 80027
Phone: 303 625-2700
Fax: –

CEO: Timothy C Rodell
CFO: –
HR: April Duffey
FYE: December 31
Type: Public

GlobeImmune would like to stop disease around the world. For now it works on its proprietary Tarmogen method of stimulating cell-level immunity to cancer and other diseases. It has five cancer candidates targeting pancreatic lung colorectal and thyroid cancers while the fifth addresses the metastasis mechanism in multiple tumors. GlobeImmune's current infectious disease candidates seek to permanently cure hepatitis B and C. The company which produces its own products works with Celgene and Gilead Sciences to develop and commercialize the cancer and infectious disease drugs respectively. The company was formed in 1995 as Ceres Pharmaceutical and changed its name in 2001. It went public in 2014.

	Annual Growth	12/10	12/11	12/12	12/13	12/14
Sales ($ mil.)	–	0.0	0.0	14.6	22.5	6.0
Net income ($ mil.)	–	0.0	0.0	(2.0)	9.5	(16.3)
Market value ($ mil.)	–	–	–	–	–	43.7
Employees	–	–	–	–	–	22

GLOBUS MEDICAL INC
NYS: GMED

2560 General Armistead Avenue
Audubon, PA 19403
Phone: 610 930-1800
Fax: 302 636-5454
Web: www.globusmedical.com

CEO: David C. Paul
CFO: Daniel T. Scavilla
HR: –
FYE: December 31
Type: Public

If Globus Medical helps you stand up straight then the company's products are working. Globus Medical makes medical devices used during spinal surgery to treat a variety of spinal disorders and assist surgeons with different types of spinal procedures from screws and plates to disc replacement systems and biomaterials for bone grafts. Top sellers include the REVERE screw-and-rod system and the COALITION cervical fusion device. Altogether Globus Medical has more than 100 spinal devices on the market in the US; its products are also sold in about 25 international markets. Globus Medical went public in 2012.

	Annual Growth	12/10	12/11	12/12	12/13	12/14
Sales ($ mil.)	13.3%	288.2	331.5	386.0	434.5	474.4
Net income ($ mil.)	14.2%	54.5	60.8	73.8	68.6	92.5
Market value ($ mil.)	50.5%	–	–	993.5	1,911.2	2,251.2
Employees	7.5%	–	724	810	850	900

GLORI ENERGY INC.

4315 South Dr.
Houston TX 77053
Phone: 713-237-8880
Fax: 860-676-8655
Web: www.horizontechnologyfinancecorp.com

CEO: Stuart Page
CFO: Victor M Perez
HR: –
FYE: December 31
Type: Private

"Like oil and water" may no longer be a cliche if Glori Energy has its way. The company's novel AERO System for oil recovery uses naturally occurring microbes to break down the barrier between oil and water allowing more oil to flow from underground formations. It uses a three-step approach to create custom nutrient formulas for microbes at each well site and estimates that its technology which uses existing pumps and pipelines can increase oil recovery by up to 100%. While it sounds like something from a sci-fi movie Shell Husky Merit Energy and Citation Oil are all customers; it has about 10 projects in various stages. Glori Energy filed to go public in 2011 but withdrew the IPO a year later.

GLOWPOINT INC
ASE: GLOW

1776 Lincoln Street, Suite 1300
Denver, CO 80203
Phone: 303 640-3838
Fax: –
Web: www.glowpoint.com

CEO: –
CFO: David Clark
HR: Jeanne Leasure
FYE: December 31
Type: Public

Glowpoint adds a little light to virtual meeting rooms providing hosted and managed video-conferencing services via subscription that allow businesses government offices educational institutions and other customers to engage in two-way video communications over Internet protocol networks. Its cloud-based technology is compatible with any video-conferencing equipment (e.g. Cisco LifeSize Polycom and Avaya) across any IP network. Glowpoint also offers Webcasting services streaming live and recorded video by standard video-conferencing systems. In addition the company offers wholesale private labeling of its services to third-party companies. Glowpoint serves some 500 customers across the US and abroad.

	Annual Growth	12/10	12/11	12/12	12/13	12/14
Sales ($ mil.)	3.9%	27.6	27.8	29.1	33.5	32.2
Net income ($ mil.)	–	(2.7)	0.4	1.1	(4.2)	(2.8)
Market value ($ mil.)	15.0%	22.6	84.4	71.5	49.6	39.5
Employees	3.7%	109	100	130	117	126

GLU MOBILE INC
NMS: GLUU

500 Howard Street, Suite 300
San Francisco, CA 94105
Phone: 415 800-6100
Fax: –
Web: www.glu.com

CEO: Niccolo M. de Masi
CFO: Eric R. Ludwig
HR: Caroline LI
FYE: December 31
Type: Public

Glu Mobile hopes to get your phone stuck permanently to your hand and your eyes glued to the screen. The company develops and publishes video games for mobile devices targeting both casual and conventional gamers. Glu's portfolio includes original titles such as Blood & Glory: Legend and Contract Killer 2 as well as licensed third-party brands such as Activision Blizzard's Call of Duty. With more than 63 million active monthly users Glu brings its applications to the mobile masses through wireless service providers such as Sprint Nextel T-Mobile USA Verizon Wireless and Vodafone. The company which also develops games for social sites such as Facebook Google+ hi5 and Wild Tangent gets nearly 60% of sales in the US.

	Annual Growth	12/10	12/11	12/12	12/13	12/14
Sales ($ mil.)	36.5%	64.3	66.2	87.5	105.6	223.1
Net income ($ mil.)	–	(13.4)	(21.1)	(20.5)	(19.9)	8.1
Market value ($ mil.)	17.2%	221.9	336.5	244.4	415.9	418.0
Employees	14.2%	384	575	567	545	653

GLYCOMIMETICS INC
NMS: GLYC

401 Professional Drive, Suite 250
Gaithersburg, MD 20879
Phone: 240 243-1201
Fax: –
Web: www.glycomimetics.com

CEO: Rachel K King
CFO: Brian M Hahn
HR: –
FYE: December 31
Type: Public

Carbs are a good thing to GlycoMimetics. The biotechnology company uses carbohydrate chemistry to develop drug candidates for rare diseases. Its lead drug candidate is designed to treat vaso-occlusive crisis (VOC) a painful condition that affects people with sickle cell disease. If approved it would be the first drug to treat the cause of VOC and potentially reduce dependence on narcotics for pain management. Pfizer bought the rights to develop and commercialize the VOC drug. In addition the company is developing a drug to assist people with acute myeloid leukemia (AML) during chemotherapy. GlycoMimetics went public in 2014. It raised $56 million and plans to use the proceeds to further fund clinical trials.

	Annual Growth	12/10	12/11	12/12	12/13	12/14
Sales ($ mil.)	–	0.0	3.8	15.3	4.0	15.0
Net income ($ mil.)	–	0.0	(6.1)	3.7	(10.6)	(11.1)
Market value ($ mil.)	–	0.0	–	–	–	136.4
Employees	10.2%	–	–	28	27	34

GMAC MORTGAGE LLC

1100 Virginia Dr.
Fort Washington PA 19034
Phone: 215-734-8899
Fax: 770-419-6550
Web: www.us.heidelberg.com

CEO: –
CFO: –
HR: –
FYE: December 31
Type: Subsidiary

GMAC Mortgage is one of the largest residential mortgage servicing companies in the US. The company offers consumers purchasing and refinancing FHA loans and flexible down payment options. Its ditech.com arm provides online mortgage brokerage services. GMAC Mortgage is part of the Residential Capital (ResCap) mortgage arm of Ally Financial the financing arm of General Motors. The US government owns a majority of Ally Financial after providing the group with a series of financial bailouts. GMAC Mortgage was created in 1985 when Ally Financial (then GMAC) acquired mortgage operations of Colonial Mortgage Service and Norwest Mortgage.

GMP COMPANIES INC.

1 E. Broward Blvd. Ste. 1701
Fort Lauderdale FL 33301
Phone: 866-324-3888
Fax: 954-745-7654
Web: www.lifesynccorp.com

CEO: –
CFO: –
HR: –
FYE: December 31
Type: Private

GMP Companies has pinned its future on medical device maker LifeSync Corporation its sole commercial operation. LifeSync develops and markets wireless electrocardiogram (ECG) systems for use in hospitals and outpatient settings. Based on Bluetooth technology the LifeSync system can transmit a patient's vital signs to existing monitors. The system uses disposable Lead-Wear sensors which cut down on infection risk and eliminate tangled wires that can hinder care and movement. LifeSync also licenses its technology to other medical equipment makers such as Medtronic for use with implantable or wearable medical devices.

GNC HOLDINGS INC
NYS: GNC

300 Sixth Avenue
Pittsburgh, PA 15222
Phone: 412 288-4600
Fax: –
Web: www.gnc.com

CEO: Michael G. (Mike) Archbold
CFO: Tricia Tolivar
HR: Daisy L. Vanderlinde
FYE: December 31
Type: Public

What's good for the GNC customer is great for the company's bottom line. GNC Holdings operates the world's leading nutritional-supplements retail chain devoted to items such as vitamins supplements minerals and dietary products. The firm manufactures private-label products for Rite Aid Sam's Club and PetSmart and drugstore.com. Altogether GNC boasts more than 8900 stores consisting of almost 3500 company-owned stores in the US Canada and Puerto Rico followed by 3210 franchised stores in 50-plus countries and 2277 store-within-a-store sites in Rite Aid locations. Fast-growing GNC Holdings was founded as a health food store in Pittsburgh in 1935.

	Annual Growth	12/10	12/11	12/12	12/13	12/14
Sales ($ mil.)	9.4%	1,822.2	2,072.2	2,430.0	2,630.3	2,613.2
Net income ($ mil.)	27.6%	96.6	132.3	240.2	265.0	255.9
Market value ($ mil.)	17.5%	–	2,557.3	2,939.8	5,163.2	4,148.2
Employees	6.0%	13,086	13,800	14,500	15,900	16,500

GODFATHER'S PIZZA INC.

2808 N. 108th St.
Omaha NE 68114
Phone: 402-391-1452
Fax: 402-255-2687
Web: www.godfathers.com

CEO: –
CFO: Richard W Ramm
HR: –
FYE: May 31
Type: Private

Maybe the head of this family is named Don Pizzeria. Godfather's Pizza operates a leading quick-service restaurant chain with more than 600 family-oriented pizza joints in more than 40 states mostly in the Upper Midwest. The parlors offer a crew of pizzas and a mob of topping choices as well as appetizers salads and sandwiches. The company's locations typically offer dine-in delivery and carry-out service. More than 100 restaurants are company-owned while the rest are franchised. Founded by Nebraska native Willy Theisen in 1973 the business is owned by a group led by CEO Ron Gartlan.

GOJO INDUSTRIES

1 GOJO Plaza Ste. 500　　　　　　　　　　　　　　　　CEO: -
Akron OH 44311　　　　　　　　　　　　　　　　　　　CFO: -
Phone: 330-255-6000　　　　　　　　　　　　　　　HR: Bob Smith
Fax: 330-255-6119　　　　　　　　　　　　　　　FYE: December 31
Web: www.gojo.com　　　　　　　　　　　　　　　　　Type: Private

GOJO Industries wants to go where other forms of good hygiene haven't. The company makes hand cleaners for professional and consumer use for clients such as automotive foodservice education government and health care facilities. GOJO's product dispensers are seen in many public restrooms as well. The firm also provides a line of health care products under the PROVON brand name. GOJO's waterless hand sanitizer PURELL is sold through retail channels. The company sells its products worldwide and operates offices in Brazil Japan the UK and the US. GOJO is named after its heavy-duty hand cleaner which was formulated by founder Jerome Lippman.

GOLD STAR CHILI INC.

650 Lunken Park Dr.　　　　　　　　　　　　　　　　CEO: -
Cincinnati OH 45226-1800　　　　　　　　　　　　　　CFO: -
Phone: 513-231-4541　　　　　　　　　　　　　　　　HR: -
Fax: 513-624-4415　　　　　　　　　　　　　　　FYE: December 31
Web: www.goldstarchili.com/　　　　　　　　　　　　Type: Private

It's pretty easy to guess what the specialty of the house is at these restaurants. Gold Star Chili operates and franchises about 100 quick-service style eateries in Ohio Indiana and Kentucky that specialize in chili. Customers can have chili over fries hot dogs chips or with garlic bread. The signature "3 Way" includes chili over spaghetti with grated cheese; more toppings can be added to make a four- or five-way. Gold Star the official chili of the Cincinnati Bengals football team also sells products through retail grocers and online. The Daoud family founded the company in 1965.

GOLD RESERVE INC.　　　　　　　　　　　NYSE AMEX: GRZ

926 W. Sprague Ave. Ste. 200　　　　　　　　　　CEO: Rockne J Timm
Spokane WA 99201　　　　　　　　　　　　CFO: Robert A McGuinness
Phone: 509-623-1500　　　　　　　　　　　　　　　　HR: -
Fax: 509-623-1634　　　　　　　　　　　　　　　FYE: December 31
Web: www.goldreserveinc.com　　　　　　　　　　　　Type: Public

Gold Reserve's primary asset was the Brisas project in Venezuela which contains estimated reserves of about 10 million ounces of gold and 1.4 billion pounds of copper. Gold Reserve had been developing Brisas since 1992. However all activity on the mine ceased in late 2009 when the Venezuelan government canceled Gold Reserve's permits and seized the assets of the Brisas project. The company is pursuing an arbitration claim through the World Bank against the Venezuelan government in an effort to recoup its investment in the Brisas project. The company is restructuring its debt while it continues it $2.1 arbitration claim.

GOLD'S GYM INTERNATIONAL INC.

125 E. John Carpenter Fwy Ste. 1300　　　　　　　　　CEO: -
Irving TX 75062　　　　　　　　　　　　　CFO: Randall R Schultz
Phone: 214-574-4653　　　　　　　　　　　　　　　　HR: -
Fax: 214-296-5000　　　　　　　　　　　　　　　FYE: February 28
Web: www.goldsgym.com　　　　　　　　　　　　　　Type: Private

The site of America's most famous muscle beach is the birth place of one of the world's best-known muscle makers. Gold's Gym which first opened in Venice Beach California in 1965 has more than 600 gyms in some 30 countries with franchises accounting for most of its locations. The chain boasts more than 3 million members. In addition to opening franchises the firm buys smaller regional health clubs and converts them to Gold's Gyms. The company also licenses the Gold's Gym name for products such as fitness equipment and accessories luggage t-shirts and men's and women's sportswear. Gold's Gym is owned by TRT Holdings the umbrella company for Dallas-based investor Robert Rowling's holdings.

GOLD RESOURCE CORP　　　　　　　　　　　　ASE: GORO

2886 Carriage Manor Point　　　　　　　　　　　　　CEO: -
Colorado Springs, CO 80906　　　　　　　　　　CFO: Joe Rodriguez
Phone: 303 320-7708　　　　　　　　　　　　　　　　HR: -
Fax: -　　　　　　　　　　　　　　　　　　　　FYE: December 31
Web: www.goldresourcecorp.com　　　　　　　　　　Type: Public

Mining company Gold Resource aims to produce gold and other minerals from projects where operating costs are low. The company focuses on its El Aguila project in the southern Mexican state of Oaxaca. The El Aguila project which began in 2010 at a shallow open-pit mine now includes an underground mine La Arista. The deposit being mined at El Aguila includes not only gold and silver but also copper lead and zinc. In addition to its primary operations the company has interests in exploration properties in Oaxaca. Gold Resource was formed in 1998.

GOLD-EAGLE COOPERATIVE

415 LOCUST ST　　　　　　　　　　　　　　　　　　CEO: -
GOLDFIELD, IA 505425092　　　　　　　　　　　　　CFO: -
Phone: 515-825-3161　　　　　　　　　　　　　　　　HR: -
Fax: -　　　　　　　　　　　　　　　　　　　FYE: September 30
Web: www.goldeaglecoop.com　　　　　　　　　　　Type: Private

For Gold-Eagle Cooperative service to its member/farmers is the golden rule. The firm is a member-owned agricultural co-op located in north central Iowa. It offers its members grain drying custom crop spraying feed seed fertilizer and other bulk and packaged farm chemicals storage and warehousing as well as feed milling and marketing. The co-op runs a transportation fleet of grain-hoppers feed-bottle trucks and specialty trailers that take members' crops to and from its facilities. Gold-Eagle operates nine grain elevator/service center locations.

	Annual Growth	12/10	12/11	12/12	12/13	12/14
Sales ($ mil.)	67.2%	14.8	105.2	131.8	125.8	115.4
Net income ($ mil.)	-	(23.1)	58.4	33.7	0.1	16.2
Market value ($ mil.)	(41.8%)	1,592.9	1,151.3	834.9	245.4	183.1
Employees	18.8%	196	312	363	359	391

	Annual Growth	09/05	09/06	09/07	09/08	09/09
Sales ($ mil.)	31.9%	-	132.0	216.1	304.6	302.7
Net income ($ mil.)	37.2%	-	-	5.3	9.7	10.0
Market value ($ mil.)	-	-	-	-	-	-
Employees	-	-	-	-	-	170

GOLDEN EAGLE INSURANCE CORP.

525 B St.
San Diego CA 92101
Phone: 619-744-6000
Fax: 619-744-3513
Web: www.goldeneagle-ins.com

CEO: J Paul Condrin III
CFO: –
HR: –
FYE: December 31
Type: Subsidiary

Golden Eagle Insurance is keeping watch over California businesses. The company offers a variety of commercial insurance for small and midsized businesses including auto liability property umbrella and equipment breakdown coverages. It also offers claims and litigation management services and loss control programs for businesses. Golden Eagle Insurance is one of several regional carriers in the Agency Markets unit of Boston-based Liberty Mutual. In addition to its headquarters in San Diego the firm has a claims office in Walnut Creek California.

GOLDEN ENTERPRISES, INC.   NMS: GLDC

One Golden Flake Drive
Birmingham, AL 35205
Phone: 205 458-7316
Fax: –
Web: www.goldenflake.com

CEO: Mark W McCutcheon
CFO: Patty Townsend
HR: Linda Gunn
FYE: May 29
Type: Public

Snackers who crave a taste for the South seek Golden Enterprises. Operating through subsidiary Golden Flake Snack Foods the company makes and distributes a barbecue and other Southern flavored-varieties of potato chips fried pork skins corn chips onion rings and baked and fried cheese curls among others. It also markets peanut butter canned dips dried meat snacks pretzels and nuts packed by other manufacturers under the Golden Flake brand. The Golden Flake lineup is sold through the company's sales force to commercial enterprises that sell food products across the Southeastern US as well as through independent distributors. The company was founded in 1946 as Magic City Food Products.

	Annual Growth	06/11	06/12*	05/13	05/14	05/15
Sales ($ mil.)	0.1%	131.0	136.2	137.3	135.9	131.7
Net income ($ mil.)	(12.4%)	3.0	2.2	1.1	0.9	1.8
Market value ($ mil.)	6.4%	35.8	39.3	40.1	50.2	45.8
Employees	(1.6%)	793	795	790	750	744

*Fiscal year change

GOLDEN ENTERTAINMENT INC   NMS: GDEN

6595 S Jones Boulevard
Las Vegas, NE 89118
Phone: 702 893 7777
Fax: –
Web: www.lakesentertainment.com

CEO: Lyle Berman
CFO: Timothy J Cope
HR: –
FYE: December 28
Type: Public

Even though Lakes Entertainment doesn't own a casino it still keeps its eye on the slots. The company manages Indian-owned casinos including the Four Winds Casino Resort in New Buffalo Township Michigan (approximately 75 miles east of Chicago) for the Pokagon Band of Potawatomi Indians; and the Red Hawk Casino in El Dorado County California (some 30 miles east of Sacramento) for the Shingle Springs Band of Miwok Indians. Nearly all of Lakes Entertainment's revenues come from management fees. The company is also exploring other development projects through agreements with tribes for additional casinos in Michigan and California and a possible non-Indian casino project in Mississippi.

	Annual Growth	01/11	01/12*	12/12	12/13	12/14
Sales ($ mil.)	30.9%	24.6	35.6	11.0	38.8	55.2
Net income ($ mil.)	–	(13.8)	(1.8)	3.2	18.7	(24.8)
Market value ($ mil.)	33.8%	38.2	24.8	41.0	53.2	91.4
Employees	184.0%	22	19	134	536	504

*Fiscal year change

GOLDEN GATE PETROLEUM

501 Shell Ave.
Martinez CA 94553
Phone: 925-228-2222
Fax: 925-957-9589
Web: www.ggpetrol.com

CEO: –
CFO: John Bailey
HR: Patti Ricci
FYE: December 31
Type: Private

Based just outside that City by the Bay Golden Gate Petroleum distributes daily about 2 million gallons of petroleum products including BP Chevron ExxonMobil and Shell branded fuels base oils and lubricants to customers located throughout northern California and Nevada. The company transports its products through a system of pipelines bulk terminals railroad cars and trucks. Its customers include agricultural commercial and industrial users. Golden Gate Petroleum also operates 25 gas stations. The company maintains and operate seven plant facilities located in Martinez Hayward San Jose Richmond Salinas Brentwood and Paso Robles encompassing tank farms office space and warehouses.

GOLDEN GRAIN ENERGY LLC

1822 43RD ST SW
MASON CITY, IA 504017071
Phone: 641-423-8525
Fax: –
Web: www.goldengrainenergy.com

CEO: Curtis Strong
CFO: Christine A Marchand
HR: –
FYE: October 31
Type: Private

The fruited plains with their golden grains have yielded Golden Grain Energy an ethanol production company with a plant in Iowa that converts corn into ethanol which is most commonly used as an additive to unleaded gasoline. Other uses include high octane fuel enhancer and a non-petroleum fuel substitute. Golden Grain Energy's plant has a production capacity of 110 million gallons of ethanol and 120000 tons of distillers grains per year. The distillers grains are used to produce animal feed. In 2009 with raw material costs rising and selling prices falling the company cut back production at the plant.

	Annual Growth	10/10	10/11	10/12	10/13	10/14
Sales ($ mil.)	(3.8%)	–	324.9	327.8	350.7	289.2
Net income ($ mil.)	246.9%	–	–	6.6	14.2	79.3
Market value ($ mil.)	–	–	–	–	–	–
Employees	–	–	–	–	–	47

GOLDEN MINERALS CO   ASE: AUMN

350 Indiana Street, Suite 800
Golden, CO 80401
Phone: 303 839-5060
Fax: –
Web: www.goldenminerals.com

CEO: Warren M Rehn
CFO: Robert P Vogels
HR: –
FYE: December 31
Type: Public

Golden Minerals owns and operates a precious metals mine in Mexico an exploration property in Argentina and a portfolio of mining and exploration sites in parts of Mexico and South America. The company has been expanding its production at the Velardeña and Chicago mines in Mexico and is in the advanced evaluation stage at its El Quevar silver project in northwest Argentina. It sold most of its exploration properties in Peru in 2013. The company's strategy is focused on establishing itself as a mid-tier producer and expanding its precious metal operations in Mexico and Argentina. The company also has a joint venture with Golden Tag Resources in the San Diego silver project in Mexico.

	Annual Growth	12/10	12/11	12/12	12/13	12/14
Sales ($ mil.)	(62.0%)	11.2	1.8	26.1	10.7	0.2
Net income ($ mil.)	–	(33.3)	(62.7)	(92.0)	(240.4)	(18.8)
Market value ($ mil.)	(62.3%)	1,419.4	308.9	244.0	25.1	28.7
Employees	9.3%	205	680	492	65	293

GOLDEN STATE FOODS CORP.

18301 Von Karman Ave. Ste. 1100
Irvine CA 92612-1009
Phone: 949-252-2000
Fax: 949-252-2080
Web: www.goldenstatefoods.com

CEO: Mark Wetterau
CFO: Bill Sanderson
HR: –
FYE: December 31
Type: Private

You might say this company helps make the Golden Arches shine. Golden State Foods is a leading US foodservice company that is a primary supplier for McDonald's restaurants with products including beef patties Big Mac sauce (which it helped formulate) buns ketchup and mayonnaise. It distributes goods to more than 20000 quick-service eateries from nearly 30 distribution centers. In addition the company runs the GSF Foundation a not-for-profit organization that supports local charities focused on helping needy children and families. Founded in 1947 by the late William Moore Golden State Foods is controlled by Wetterau Associates an investment group led by the company's chairman and CEO Mark Wetterau.

GOLDFIELD CORP.   ASE: GV

1684 West Hibiscus Boulevard
Melbourne, FL 32901
Phone: 321 724-1700
Fax: 321 724-1703
Web: www.goldfieldcorp.com

CEO: John H Sottile
CFO: Stephen R Wherry
HR: –
FYE: December 31
Type: Public

The Goldfield Corporation earns more laying cable now than it used to digging for mother lodes. Through subsidiary Southeast Power Goldfield builds and maintains electrical facilities in the Southeast West and Mid-Atlantic regions for utilities and industrial customers including Florida Power & Light Company and Duke Energy. The unit also installs transmission lines and fiber-optic cable. Goldfield's Bayswater Development subsidiary maintains real estate operations in Florida specializing in developing waterfront condominiums for retirees. The company which had been in the mining industry since 1906 divested those operations in 2002 after deciding that it had become economically unfeasible.

	Annual Growth	12/10	12/11	12/12	12/13	12/14
Sales ($ mil.)	31.0%	33.4	32.8	81.6	89.2	98.4
Net income ($ mil.)	–	(0.3)	0.9	12.0	3.8	(0.3)
Market value ($ mil.)	67.2%	7.9	6.2	47.8	49.6	61.8
Employees	36.1%	122	163	226	302	418

GOLDMAN SACHS GROUP, INC.   NYS: GS

200 West Street
New York, NY 10282
Phone: 212 902-1000
Fax: 212 902-3000
Web: www.gs.com

CEO: Esta E. Stecher
CFO: Harvey M. Schwartz
HR: Nancy Whalen
FYE: December 31
Type: Public

Goldman Sachs has traditionally possessed the Midas touch in the investment banking world. A global leader in mergers and acquisitions advice and securities underwriting Goldman offers a gamut of investment banking and asset management services to corporate and government clients worldwide as well as institutional and wealth individual investors. It owns Goldman Sachs Execution & Clearing one of the largest market makers on the NYSE and a leading market maker for fixed income products currencies and commodities. Through affiliates Goldman Sachs is also one of the largest private equity investors in the world. Goldman Sachs was founded in 1869.

	Annual Growth	12/10	12/11	12/12	12/13	12/14
Assets ($ mil.)	(1.5%)	911,332.0	923,225.0	938,555.0	911,507.0	856,240.0
Net income ($ mil.)	0.4%	8,354.0	4,442.0	7,475.0	8,040.0	8,477.0
Market value ($ mil.)	3.6%	72,352.4	38,908.3	54,883.9	76,267.7	83,397.1
Employees	(1.2%)	35,700	33,300	32,400	32,900	34,000

GOLF GALAXY LLC

300 Industry Dr. RIDC Park West
Pittsburgh PA 15275
Phone: 724-273-3400
Fax: 724-227-1904
Web: www.golfgalaxy.com

CEO: Edward W Stack
CFO: –
HR: –
FYE: January 31
Type: Subsidiary

Let Golf Galaxy help with your galactic battle to break par. It operates about 80 golf superstores in 30 states. Stores offer "Everything for the Game" including equipment apparel and shoes gifts accessories books and videos. Golf Galaxy also sells pre-owned clubs and boasts a trade-in program. In-store amenities include computer video swing analysis onsite certified club technicians indoor driving bays full-sized putting greens and advice on equipment from a staff that includes PGA and LPGA professionals. Golf Galaxy also operates a namesake website and catalog. Founded in 1997 by former executives Randy Zanatta and Greg Maanum it is owned by Dick's Sporting Goods.

GOLFSMITH INTERNATIONAL HOLDINGS INC.   NASDAQ: GOLF

11000 N. IH-35
Austin TX 78753-3195
Phone: 512-837-8810
Fax: 512-837-1245
Web: www.golfsmith.com

CEO: Martin E Hanaka
CFO: Sue E Gove
HR: –
FYE: December 31
Type: Public

Golfsmith International caters to sports clubs on both sides of the US-Canada border. Formed by the combination of Texas-based Golfsmith and Canada's Golf Town newly-formed Golfsmith International operates about 95 golf stores in the US and another 55 (under the Golf Town banner) in Canada and Boston. It also sells golf and tennis equipment apparel and accessories online. Brands include TaylorMade-adidas Callaway Mizuno and Nike. Golfsmith also teaches golfers to assemble their own clubs and offers custom fitting and repair services for clubs and racquets. Founded in 1967 as a mail-order seller of custom-made golf clubs Golfsmith in 2012 was acquired by Canada's Golf Town.

GOLUB CAPITAL BDC INC.   NASDAQ: GBDC

150 S. Wacker Dr. Ste. 800
Chicago IL 60606
Phone: 312-205-5050
Fax: 607-786-8663
Web: www.mmcweb.com

CEO: David B Golub
CFO: Ross A Teune
HR: –
FYE: September 30
Type: Public

The Golub brothers are at it again. Lawrence and David Golub the investors behind Golub Capital Partners founded Golub Capital BDC to assist small businesses amid the tight credit market. Organized as a business development company (BDC) Golub Capital BDC makes debt and minority investments (between $5 million to $25 million) to smaller companies that earn between $5 million to $40 million a year. Its investment portfolio primarily consists of senior secured loans as well as some unitranche mezzanine and second lien loans. It has investments in more than 90 companies owned by private equity firms. Lawrence (Chairman) and David (CEO) control more than half its stock through various entities.

GONNELLA BAKING CO.

2006 W. Erie St.
Chicago IL 60612
Phone: 312-733-2020
Fax: 312-733-7056
Web: www.gonnella.com

CEO: -
CFO: -
HR: -
FYE: December 31
Type: Private

Alessandro Gonnella made his dough like many Italian-Americans — he baked it. Founded in 1886 Gonnella Baking makes fresh Italian- and French-style specialty breads for grocers and restaurants in the Midwest. The company also makes frozen dough and fresh baked frozen bread for in-store bakeries and restaurants. Gonnella rolls out a variety of bread crumbs rolls and breadsticks for retail sale. From its frozen dough plants in Schaumburg Illinois and Hazle Township Pennsylvania Gonnella ships its in-store bakery and foodservice products throughout the US. The company has six production facilities total. The Gonnella and Marcucci families own the company.

GOOD SAM ENTERPRISES LLC

2575 Vista Del Mar
Ventura CA 93001
Phone: 805-667-4100
Fax: 805-667-4419
Web: www.affinitygroup.com

CEO: Marcus A Lemonis
CFO: Thomas F Wolfe
HR: -
FYE: December 31
Type: Private

Members needn't be good to join the Good Sam Club (formerly Affinity Group). One of several membership clubs operated by Good Sam Enterprises (GSE) the Good Sam Club and President's Club cater to the RV community offering goods and services to some 1.3 million members. GSE is also a direct marketer specialty retailer and publisher for RVers and outdoor enthusiasts. Its retail business Camping World operates 80-plus stores (plus a catalog and website) in more than 30 states that sell aftermarket RV parts and accessories and offer repair and maintenance services. GSE also publishes magazines and travel guides. Founded in 1966 members originally promised to help fellow travelers on the road.

GOOD SAMARITAN HOSPITAL MEDICAL CENTER

1000 Montauk Hwy.
West Islip NY 11795
Phone: 631-376-3000
Fax: 631-376-3392
Web: goodsamaritan.chsli.org

CEO: -
CFO: William E Allison
HR: -
FYE: December 31
Type: Subsidiary

The folks at Good Samaritan Hospital Medical Center have plenty of reasons to feel good about their efforts. The hospital is part of Catholic Health Services of Long Island (CHS) and serves the south shore community of West Islip New York. As a full-service medical center with 440 acute care beds and 900 physicians it offers a complete range of health care counseling and rehabilitation services. Good Samaritan provides emergency medicine and trauma care in addition to oncology cardiology pediatric woman's health diagnostic and surgical care. It also operates the Good Samaritan Nursing Home a 100-bed skilled nursing facility as well as satellite clinics and a home health care agency.

GOOD SOURCE SOLUTIONS INC.

1525 Faraday Ave. Ste. 200
Carlsbad CA 92008
Phone: 760-448-8299
Fax: 858-435-1187
Web: www.goodsource.com

CEO: Richard Friedlen
CFO: Bryon Borgardt
HR: -
FYE: December 31
Type: Private

Good Source Solutions makes organizations' food budgets (even tight ones) easy to digest. The company distributes surplus food products to more than 5000 customers including correctional institutions schools relief and faith-based organizations and nonprofit food groups. Its secondary food products including meats vegetables and fruits come from more than 500 food processors. Good Source also provides menu planning portion control and delivery services from its five warehouses across the US. In addition to foodservice distribution the company offers purchasing and logistics services to food producers. In 2011 private equity firm Evergreen Pacific Partners acquired a majority stake in Good Source.

GOOD TECHNOLOGY INC.

430 N. Mary Ave. Ste. 200
Sunnyvale CA 94085
Phone: 408-212-7500
Fax: 408-212-7505
Web: www.good.com

CEO: Christy Wyatt
CFO: Ronald J Fior
HR: -
FYE: December 31
Type: Private

Good Technology develops mobility software allowing employees to use their cell phones and smartphones for business communication and collaboration. It serves more than 4000 enterprises worldwide in the financial services healthcare retail and manufacturing industries among others. Its offerings (Good for Enterprise Good Connect Good Share) include secure e-mail collaboration and application management tools for use with a Apple's iOS Google's Android and Microsoft's Windows devices. Good Technology has received funding from Blueprint Ventures Draper Fisher Jurvetson Meritech Capital Partners and Oak Investment Partners among others.

GOOD TIMES RESTAURANTS INC.   NAS: GTIM

141 Union Blvd., Suite 400
Lakewood, CO 80228
Phone: 303 384-1400
Fax: -
Web: www.goodtimesburgers.com

CEO: Boyd E Hoback
CFO: James Zielke
HR: -
FYE: September 30
Type: Public

Good Times Restaurants operates and franchises more than 50 Good Times Drive Thru fast-food eateries located primarily in the Denver area. The hamburger chain is made up mostly of double drive-through and walk-up eateries that feature a menu of burgers fries and frozen custard. A limited number of Good Times outlets also offer dine-in seating. More than 20 of the locations are operated by franchisees while the rest are co-owned and co-operated under joint venture agreements. The family of director Geoffrey Bailey owns almost 30% of the company.

	Annual Growth	09/11	09/12	09/13	09/14	09/15
Sales ($ mil.)	20.9%	20.6	19.7	22.9	28.0	44.1
Net income ($ mil.)	-	(0.9)	(0.7)	(0.5)	(0.7)	(0.8)
Market value ($ mil.)	41.7%	19.0	15.7	28.8	73.6	76.6
Employees	36.6%	411	400	435	583	1,431

GOOD360

1330 BRADDOCK PL STE 600
ALEXANDRIA, VA 223149702
Phone: 703-836-2121
Fax: –
Web: www.giftsinkind.org

CEO: Cindy Hallberlin
CFO: Gerald Borenstein
HR: –
FYE: December 31
Type: Private

Gifts in Kind International helps companies find ways to be kind. The not-for-profit organization accepts gifts of products and services from corporate clients and distributes these donations to more than 150000 community charities in the US and globally that directly help communities and people in need. About half of the FORTUNE 100 makes contributions through Gifts in Kind International which has certified more than 200000 charities as potential recipients. Gifts in Kind International began operating in 1983 when 3M donated $12 million in new office equipment. The organization is known for its cost-efficiency as more than 99% of its donations go directly to communities.

	Annual Growth	12/04	12/05	12/06	12/07	12/08
Sales ($ mil.)	–	–	–	(995.1)	388.9	426.6
Net income ($ mil.)	–	–	–	0.0	32.4	0.0
Market value ($ mil.)	–	–	–	–	–	–
Employees	–	–	–	–	–	36

GOODBY SILVERSTEIN & PARTNERS INC.

720 California St.
San Francisco CA 94108
Phone: 415-392-0669
Fax: 415-788-4303
Web: www.goodbysilverstein.com

CEO: Rich Silverstein
CFO: Jerry Barnhart
HR: –
FYE: December 31
Type: Subsidiary

Just making good ads doesn't seem to be enough for this firm. Goodby Silverstein & Partners is one of the premier names in advertising with a long heritage of cutting edge and effective creative work. Perhaps best known for the "Got Milk" campaign (produced for the California Milk Processors) the agency has also worked for blue chip brands such as Haagen-Dazs Hewlett-Packard and Saturn. In addition to traditional ad work Goodby Silverstein offers interactive and brand promotion services. Co-chairmen Rich Silverstein and Jeff Goodby started the company in 1983; it operates today as a subsidiary of advertising services conglomerate Omnicom Group.

GOODFELLOW BROS. INC.

1407 WALLA WALLA AVE
WENATCHEE, WA 988011530
Phone: 509-667-9095
Fax: –
Web: www.goodfellowbros.com

CEO: –
CFO: –
HR: –
FYE: December 31
Type: Private

The good men at Goodfellow Bros. build everything from golf courses to runways to dams and residences. The family-owned company specializes in heavy construction infrastructure transportation systems and housing and recreation facilities in the western continental US and Hawaii. Goodfellow Bros. also offers earth moving and paving services. Its Blasting Technologies subsidiary blasts drills and demolishes rock and other structures. The company was founded in 1921 by brothers Jack Bert and Jim Sr. Their early business included the first excavation work on the Grand Coulee Dam in 1933. Now the company has a number of planned communities public facilities and other projects under its belt.

	Annual Growth	12/06	12/07	12/08	12/09	12/13
Sales ($ mil.)	(14.5%)	–	519.9	0.0	240.2	203.1
Net income ($ mil.)	–	–	–	0.0	19.8	7.3
Market value ($ mil.)	–	–	–	–	–	–
Employees	–	–	–	–	–	1,050

GOODMAN GLOBAL INC.

5151 San Felipe Ste. 500
Houston TX 77056
Phone: 713-861-2500
Fax: 713-861-3207
Web: www.goodmanglobal.com

CEO: David L Swift
CFO: Lawrence M Blackburn
HR: –
FYE: December 31
Type: Private

While a good man may be hard to find "this" Goodman makes it easy to find comfort with its residential and light commercial heating ventilation and air-conditioning (HVAC) products. Goodman Global makes HVAC equipment including split-system air conditioners and heat pumps gas furnaces packaged units air handlers and evaporator coils. The company operates about eight plants in Arizona Florida Pennsylvania Tennessee and Texas. It sells products under the Goodman Amana and Quietflex brands through about 135 company-operated distribution centers and some 700 independent distributor locations throughout North America. Goodman Global is owned by Daikin Industries.

GOODMAN NETWORKS INC.

6400 International Ste. 1000
Plano TX 75093
Phone: 972-406-9692
Fax: 972-406-9291
Web: www.goodmannetworks.com

CEO: Ron B Hill
CFO: Joy L Brawner
HR: –
FYE: December 31
Type: Private

Goodman Networks provides a variety of telecommunications services to the wireless and wireline industries. The company's services include network design engineering deployment integration and maintenance. The company also offers staffing services as well as supply chain management services such as materials management and logistics. Goodman Networks specializes in providing equipment lifecycle services for telecom carriers and equipment manufacturers in the public and private sector. Customers have included big names such as AT&T and Alcatel-Lucent. Goodman Networks was founded in 2000 by the five Goodman brothers: James Jody Jonathan Jason and John.

GOODRICH CORPORATION

NYSE: GR

Four Coliseum Centre 2730 W. Tyvola Rd.
Charlotte NC 28217-4578
Phone: 704-423-7000
Fax: 704-423-7002
Web: www.goodrich.com

CEO: –
CFO: Scott E Kuechle
HR: –
FYE: December 31
Type: Public

Goodrich is a tireless leader in aerospace systems. The company serves regional/business aircraft original equipment and aftermarket helicopters military and space markets through its three aerospace divisions. Goodrich's largest segment actuation and landing systems makes fuel systems aircraft wheels brakes landing gear and flight control systems. Nacelles and interior systems offers maintenance/repair services and makes aerostructures (cowlings and thrust reversers) as well as aircraft seats and cargo and lighting systems. Its electronic systems division makes fuel controls flight management systems and reconnaissance systems. In 2012 Goodrich was acquired by United Technologies (UTC).

GOODRICH PETROLEUM CORP. (HOLDING CO.) — NBB: GDPM

801 Louisiana, Suite 700
Houston, TX 77002
Phone: 713 780-9494
Fax: –
Web: www.goodrichpetroleum.com

CEO: Walter G Goodrich
CFO: Jan L Schott
HR: –
FYE: December 31
Type: Public

From deep in the good rich hydrocarbon-impregnated rocks of ancient Mother Earth Goodrich Petroleum brings forth oil and gas. The independent exploration and production company delves into formations in the Hayneville Shale play in Texas and Louisiana. The company also operates in the Eagle Ford Shale Trend in South Texas the Tuscaloosa Marine Shale in Louisiana and the Cotton Valley trend (in Texas and Louisiana). Goodrich Petroleum owns interests in more than 390 producing oil and gas wells in eight states and reported estimated proved reserves of 333.1 billion cu. ft. of natural gas equivalent at the end of 2012.

	Annual Growth	12/10	12/11	12/12	12/13	12/14
Sales ($ mil.)	8.9%	148.3	201.1	180.8	203.3	208.6
Net income ($ mil.)	–	(262.1)	(31.8)	(84.2)	(95.2)	(353.1)
Market value ($ mil.)	(29.2%)	795.7	619.3	420.4	767.7	200.3
Employees	(2.5%)	116	113	112	103	105

GOODWILL INDUSTRIES INTERNATIONAL INC.

15810 INDIANOLA DR
ROCKVILLE, MD 20855-2674
Phone: 301-530-6500
Fax: –
Web: www.global.goodwill.org

CEO: Jim Gibbions
CFO: –
HR: –
FYE: December 31
Type: Private

Goodwill Industries International supports the operations of about 165 independent Goodwill chapters in the US and Canada. Though most well known for its 2700 thrift stores the group focuses on providing rehabilitation job training placement and employment services for people with disabilities and others. Founded in 1902 Goodwill is one of the world's largest providers of such services as well as one of the world's largest employers of the physically mentally and emotionally disabled. Support for its programs is generated primarily from sales of donated goods both at the retail stores and through an online auction site as well as from contract work and government grants.

	Annual Growth	12/06	12/07	12/08	12/09	12/11
Sales ($ mil.)	–	–	(735.8)	31.7	37.6	52.7
Net income ($ mil.)	–	–	0.0	(1.5)	0.8	(0.4)
Market value ($ mil.)	–	–	–	–	–	–
Employees	–	–	–	–	–	100

GOODWIN PROCTER LLP

Exchange Place 53 State St.
Boston MA 02109
Phone: 617-570-1000
Fax: 617-523-1231
Web: www.goodwinprocter.com

CEO: –
CFO: Michael Barton
HR: Heidi Goldstein Shepherd
FYE: September 30
Type: Private - Partnershi

One of the largest law firms in Beantown Goodwin Procter has branched beyond its Boston roots to establish offices on the East and West Coasts of the US. The firm has about 850 lawyers practicing in a variety of areas including corporate real estate environmental litigation tax and estate planning. It helps emerging multinational companies to achieve growth and advises on everything from critical regulatory and compliance matters to deals transactions and critical litigation issues. Goodwin Procter has offices in Boston Hong Kong London Los Angeles New York City San Diego San Francisco Silicon Valley and Washington DC. Robert Goodwin and Joseph Procter founded the firm in 1912.

GOODY PRODUCTS INC.

3 Glenlake Pkwy.
Atlanta GA 30328
Phone: 770-418-7300
Fax: 770-615-4740
Web: www.goody.com

CEO: –
CFO: –
HR: Amanda Assenza
FYE: December 31
Type: Subsidiary

Goody has the tools to help even the Bride of Frankenstein have a good hair day. Goody Products manufactures hair care accessories brushes combs and travel storage products and sells them through food drug and discount stores such as Target Wal-Mart and Walgreen. The firm makes products under the Goody Ace Stayput Ouchless TherapySolutions Styling Therapy ColourCollection and StylingSolutions trademarks. The Goody brand set root in 1907 when Henry Goodman and his son Abraham began selling rhinestone-studded hair combs off a pushcart in New York City. Since 1993 it has been owned by Newell Rubbermaid. Goody Products is a subsidiary in its parent's home-and-family segment.

GOODYEAR DUNLOP TIRES NORTH AMERICA LTD.

200 John James Audubon Pky.
Amherst NY 14228-1120
Phone: 716-639-5200
Fax: 716-639-5017
Web: www.dunloptire.com

CEO: –
CFO: –
HR: –
FYE: December 31
Type: Subsidiary

You could say that Goodyear Dunlop Tires North America knows its way around the tire industry. The company a part of The Goodyear Tire & Rubber Company makes tires bearing the Dunlop brand name. Other product offerings include tires for all terrain vehicles (ATVs) commercial trucks competition go-carts (karts) and motorcycles. As legend has it the late John Boyd Dunlop patented his design for the modern tire after watching his son ride a tricycle with solid rubber wheels. The Dunlop brand is a sponsor for many racing and other high-performance automotive events.

GOODYEAR TIRE & RUBBER CO. — NMS: GT

200 Innovation Way
Akron, OH 44316-0001
Phone: 330 796-2121
Fax: 330 796-4099
Web: www.goodyear.com

CEO: Richard J. (Rich) Kramer
CFO: Laura K. Thompson
HR: Joe Ruocco
FYE: December 31
Type: Public

When the rubber hits the road most years are good years for Goodyear Tire & Rubber. Through a global alliance with Sumitomo Rubber Industries Goodyear is working to unseat tire industry leaders Bridgestone and Michelin (by total sales). Goodyear sells mainly new tires under the Goodyear Dunlop Kelly Fulda Debica and Sava brand names. With Sumitomo Goodyear makes markets and sells Dunlop tires in North America and Western Europe. In Japan the tire makers own businesses that sell tires separately to OEMs and to aftermarket companies. Goodyear sells some 58% of its products outside the US.

	Annual Growth	12/11	12/12	12/13	12/14	12/15
Sales ($ mil.)	(7.8%)	22,767.0	20,992.0	19,540.0	18,138.0	16,443.0
Net income ($ mil.)	(2.7%)	343.0	212.0	629.0	2,452.0	307.0
Market value ($ mil.)	23.2%	3,783.6	3,687.5	6,368.4	7,628.7	8,723.5
Employees	(2.5%)	73,000	69,000	69,000	67,000	66,000

GORDMANS STORES INC

NMS: GMAN

1926 South 67 Street
Omaha, NE 68106
Phone: 402 691-4000
Fax: 402 691-4269
Web: www.gordmans.com

CEO: Andrew T Hall
CFO: James B Brown
HR: –
FYE: January 31
Type: Public

Midwestern shoppers head to Gordmans Stores for deeply-discounted fashionable apparel and home décor. The department store chain operates 90-plus stores in regional shopping centers in about 20 mostly Midwestern states. The stores specialize in selling women's men's and junior's apparel accessories footwear and home décor items at up to 60% off regular department and specialty store prices (known as off-price). Gordmans competes in the off-price market of the retail industry and also separates itself from discount stores by offering brand-name fashions and a more upscale shopping environment. The discount department store chain is run by CEO Jeff Gordman grandson of founder Dan Gordman.

	Annual Growth	01/11	01/12*	02/13	02/14*	01/15
Sales ($ mil.)	5.3%	523.3	558.1	615.1	627.4	643.2
Net income ($ mil.)	–	15.6	25.2	23.5	8.0	(3.5)
Market value ($ mil.)	(29.1%)	286.0	285.4	239.0	141.3	72.4
Employees	2.4%	5,000	4,900	5,200	5,500	5,500

*Fiscal year change

GORDON & REES LLP

275 Battery St. Ste. 2000
San Francisco CA 94111
Phone: 415-986-5900
Fax: 415-986-8054
Web: www.gordonrees.com

CEO: –
CFO: –
HR: –
FYE: December 31
Type: Private - Partnershi

Law firm Gordon & Rees specializes in handling litigation and business transactions for clients in such industries as construction health care maritime pharmaceutical and real estate. The firm has about 525 attorneys in almost 30 offices primarily in the western US the Midwest and the East Coast. Gordon & Rees boasts expertise in more than 30 different types of practice areas including employment law environmental law franchise law intellectual property international law product liability and white collar criminal defense.

GORDON BROTHERS GROUP LLC

101 Huntington Ave. 10th Fl.
Boston MA 02199
Phone: 617-426-3233
Fax: 617-422-6222
Web: www.gordonbrothers.com

CEO: Gary M Talarico
CFO: Robert Paglia
HR: –
FYE: December 31
Type: Private

Gordon Brothers Group can sell your assets in a flash. The company founded in 1903 organizes the sale of retail inventories equipment real estate accounts receivable intellectual property and other assets. Priding itself on discretion and speed Gordon Brothers also facilitates mergers and acquisitions and manages closings of underperforming stores for top retailers. Its GB Merchant Partners affiliate provides debt financing to and takes equity positions in middle-market retail and consumer products firms for growth acquisitions or turnarounds. The private investment firm holds stakes in Deb Shops Toys R Us and Things Remembered. Gordon Brothers has about 15 offices in the US Japan and Europe.

GORDON COLLEGE

255 GRAPEVINE RD
WENHAM, MA 019841899
Phone: 978-927-2300
Fax: –
Web: www.gordon.edu

CEO: –
CFO: –
HR: –
FYE: June 30
Type: Private

Gordon College a New England non-denominational Christian liberal arts college offers nearly 40 majors and has about 1800 students. A demonstrated Christian commitment is required for admission. Undergraduate tuition is approximately $20000. In 1985 Gordon merged with Barrington College with the combined school retaining Gordon College's name. Gordon College was founded in 1889 by Reverend Dr. A.J. Gordon as a missionary training institute.

	Annual Growth	06/10	06/11	06/12	06/13	06/14
Sales ($ mil.)	5.3%	–	52.2	51.7	54.3	61.0
Net income ($ mil.)	–	–	–	(1.4)	1.9	4.9
Market value ($ mil.)	–	–	–	–	–	–
Employees	–	–	–	–	–	496

GORDON FOOD SERVICE INC.

333 50th St. SW
Grand Rapids MI 49501
Phone: 616-530-7000
Fax: 616-717-7600
Web: www.gfs.com

CEO: James Gordon
CFO: Jeff Maddox
HR: –
FYE: October 31
Type: Private

This company delivers the goods that feed hungry restaurant patrons. Gordon Food Service (GFS) is North America's largest family-owned broadline food service supplier. The company boasts more than 20 distribution centers across the US and Canada. GFS's primary focus is distributing a variety of food items ingredients and beverages to restaurant operators schools healthcare facilities and institutional foodservice operators in parts of 15 states and across Canada. In addition to its distribution operation GFS operates more than 150 wholesale stores under the GFS Marketplace banner; these are open to the public. Isaac Van Westenbrugge started the family-owned business in 1897 to deliver eggs and butter.

GORMAN-RUPP CO.

ASE: GRC

600 South Airport Road
Mansfield, OH 44903
Phone: 419 755-1011
Fax: 419 755-1233
Web: www.gormanrupp.com

CEO: Jeffrey S. Gorman
CFO: Wayne L. Knabel
HR: –
FYE: December 31
Type: Public

Gorman-Rupp keeps pumping out pumps. The company founded in 1933 by engineers J. C. Gorman and H. E. Rupp makes a myriad of pumps and fluid controls used in construction sewage treatment petroleum refining agriculture and fire fighting as well as for HVAC and military applications. Gorman-Rupp's pumps range in size from 1/4-inch (one gallon per minute) to 180-inch and ranging in rated capacity from less than one gallon per minute to nearly one million gallons per minute. Smaller pumps are used for dispensing soft drinks and making ice cubes while large pumps are central to refueling aircraft and boosting low water pressure in municipal fresh-water markets.

	Annual Growth	12/10	12/11	12/12	12/13	12/14
Sales ($ mil.)	10.0%	296.8	359.5	375.7	391.7	434.9
Net income ($ mil.)	8.6%	26.0	28.8	28.2	30.1	36.1
Market value ($ mil.)	(0.2%)	848.7	713.0	783.4	877.9	843.5
Employees	3.6%	1,082	1,123	1,247	1,247	1,247

GOSH ENTERPRISES INC.

2500 Farmers Dr. Ste. 140 — CEO: Charley Shin
Columbus OH 43235 — CFO: Candra Alisiswanto
Phone: 614-923-4700 — HR: Mary Rauchenstein
Fax: 614-923-4701 — FYE: March 31
Web: www.charleys.com — Type: Private

Gosh Enterprises might have cheese steak lovers saying "Oh my!" The company operates and franchises more than 350 Charley's Grilled Subs quick-service restaurants in about 40 states and 10 other countries. Known for its signature Philly Steak Deluxe the chain serves a variety of sub sandwiches and other styles of deli sandwiches as well as a selection of soups and salads. About 90% of Charley's Grilled Subs locations are owned and operated by franchisees. Company president Charley Shin opened his first namesake eatery at Ohio State University in 1986.

GOTTLIEB MEMORIAL HOSPITAL

701 W NORTH AVE — CEO: –
MELROSE PARK, IL 601601699 — CFO: Ellen Chin
Phone: 708-681-3200 — HR: Beverly Lehmann
Fax: – — FYE: June 30
Web: www.gottliebhospital.org — Type: Private

Got health? Out in the western suburbs of Chicago the staff at Gottlieb Memorial Hospital can help you find it. The not-for-profit community general hospital — also known as Loyola Gottlieb — boasts more than 250 beds a staff of more than 300 physicians and dentists 200 volunteers a Level II trauma center with a heliport heart and cancer care clinics and a health and fitness center on site. The healthcare facility also offers rehabilitation services a pharmacy and a kidney dialysis center. Other Gottlieb Memorial Hospital services include outpatient clinics hospice and home health care. Gottlieb is part of Loyola University Health System.

	Annual Growth	06/09	06/10	06/11	06/12	06/13
Sales ($ mil.)	(0.5%)	–	144.2	129.8	132.7	142.2
Net income ($ mil.)	–	–	–	(1.2)	(0.7)	5.6
Market value ($ mil.)	–	–	–	–	–	–
Employees	–	–	–	–	–	900

GOULDS PUMPS INCORPORATED

240 Fall St. — CEO: –
Seneca Falls NY 13148 — CFO: –
Phone: 315-568-2811 — HR: –
Fax: 315-568-2418 — FYE: December 31
Web: www.gouldspumps.com — Type: Subsidiary

When it comes to energy and maintenance issues Goulds Pumps has a fluid answer that folks listen to. The company manufactures water utility irrigation and industrial pumping products. For more than 150 years Goulds Pumps has been producing pumps; it boasts more than a million of its centrifugal and turbine pumps installed worldwide. Goulds Pumps also offers replacement parts and repair services for its lineup. Its products are sold under brands including Goulds A-C Pump PumpSmart and ProServices. The company's industrial pumps cater to the chemical pulp and paper power generation oil refining and mining industries. Goulds Pumps operates as a part of ITT Fluid Technology a subsidiary of ITT.

GOVERNMENT EMPLOYEES HEALTH ASSOCIATION INC

310 NE Mulberry St. — CEO: –
Lees Summit MO 64086 — CFO: Eileen Hutchinson
Phone: 816-257-5500 — HR: Deana Ham II
Fax: 816-257-1944 — FYE: December 31
Web: www.geha.com — Type: Private - Not-for-Pr

Ever wonder what kind of medical coverage your congressman has access to? If he chooses Government Employees Health Association (GEHA) it's a not-for-profit health plan with low overhead. With more than 415000 members GEHA is the second-largest health and dental coverage plan available to federal employees. Established in 1939 GEHA maintains a nationwide network of more than 8750000 healthcare providers some 4000 hospitals and more than 74000 dental providers nationwide. GEHA began as the Railway Mail Hospital Association a group of railway mail clerks that put money together to pay for each others' hospital expenses.

GOVERNMENT PROPERTIES INCOME TRUST

NYS: GOV

Two Newton Place, 255 Washington Street, Suite 300 — CEO: –
Newton, MA 02458-1634 — CFO: Mark L. Kleifges
Phone: 617 219-1440 — HR: –
Fax: – — FYE: December 31
 — Type: Public

If Government Properties Income Trust had one request of Uncle Sam it would be this: "I want you to lease our properties." As a real estate investment trust (REIT) Government Properties Income Trust invests in properties that are leased to government tenants. It owns nearly 11 million sq. ft. of leasing space across more than 70 properties across the US. The company leases mostly to federal agencies (such as the FBI IRS and FDA) but it does lease to some state-run agencies and the United Nations as well. It also makes some equity investments. Government Properties Income Trust went public in 2009.

	Annual Growth	12/10	12/11	12/12	12/13	12/14
Sales ($ mil.)	21.1%	116.8	179.0	211.1	226.9	251.0
Net income ($ mil.)	19.4%	27.8	46.0	50.0	54.6	56.5
Market value ($ mil.)	(3.7%)	1,884.7	1,586.4	1,686.3	1,748.2	1,618.7
Employees	–	–	–	–	–	–

GOYA FOODS INC.

100 Seaview Dr. — CEO: –
Secaucus NJ 07096 — CFO: –
Phone: 201-348-4900 — HR: –
Fax: 201-348-6609 — FYE: December 31
Web: www.goya.com — Type: Private

Whether you call 'em frijoles or habichuelas beans are beans and Goya's got 'em. Goya Foods produces more than 1600 Hispanic and Caribbean grocery items including canned and dried beans canned meats beverages cooking oils and olives. Its products portfolio also offers rice seasonings and sauces plantain and yucca chips ready meals and frozen treats and entrees. Goya sells many rice styles and nearly 40 types of beans and peas under the Goya and Canilla brand names. The company sells such beverages as tropical fruit nectars juices tropical sodas and coffee. Goya is owned and operated by one of the richest Hispanic "familias" in the US — the Unanues — who founded the company in 1936.

GPM INVESTMENTS LLC

8565 MAGELLAN PKWY # 400
RICHMOND, VA 232271167
Phone: 804-266-1363
Fax: –
Web: www.fasmart.com

CEO: Dave McComas
CFO: Mark King
HR: Alan Ritchie
FYE: December 31
Type: Private

GPM Investments is where it's at for convenience store operators Fas Mart and Shore Stop. The investment firm operates more than 465 company-owned stores and some 145 independent convenience stores in 10 states mainly on the East Coast. The company has a high concentration of Fas Mart and Shore Stop stores in Virginia; others are located in nine states from Connecticut to Tennessee. The stores sell BP Exxon Marathon and Valero brand gas. (GPM's petroleum wholesaling business delivers petro to independent dealers.) In addition to the usual beer smokes and snacks the stores sell hot foods for breakfast lunch and dinner including the company's own brand of fried Fas Chicken at cafe sites.

	Annual Growth	12/04	12/05	12/06	12/07	12/08
Sales ($ mil.)	40.2%	–	–	–	891.8	1,249.9
Net income ($ mil.)	–	–	–	–	3.2	(1.3)
Market value ($ mil.)	–	–	–	–	–	–
Employees	–	–	–	–	–	1,300

GRACE (WR) & CO

7500 Grace Drive
Columbia, MD 21044
Phone: 410 531-4000
Fax: –
Web: www.grace.com

CEO: Alfred E. (Fred) Festa
CFO: Thomas E. Blaser
HR: Elizabeth Brown
FYE: December 31
Type: Public

NYS: GRA

W. R. Grace & Co. operates through two major segments. Grace Catalysts Technologies includes catalysts used in refining petrochemical and other chemical manufacturing processes. Grace Materials Technologies makes packaging technologies and engineered materials used in consumer industrial and pharmaceutical applications. In 2016 the company spun off its Grace Construction Products segment (which makes concrete and cement products including specialty construction chemicals and specialty building materials) and its Darex packaging business as GCP Applied Technologies.

	Annual Growth	12/10	12/11	12/12	12/13	12/14
Sales ($ mil.)	4.9%	2,675.0	3,211.9	3,155.5	3,060.7	3,243.0
Net income ($ mil.)	7.5%	207.1	269.4	94.1	256.1	276.3
Market value ($ mil.)	28.4%	2,561.8	3,348.6	4,902.6	7,209.9	6,956.1
Employees	2.1%	5,970	6,300	6,500	6,700	6,500

GRACELAND FRUIT INC.

1123 MAIN ST
FRANKFORT, MI 496359341
Phone: 231-352-7181
Fax: –
Web: www.gracelandfruit.com

CEO: Alan DeVore
CFO: Troy Terwilliger
HR: –
FYE: September 30
Type: Private

It's possible that Elvis would have liked Graceland Fruit's products. The company makes dried refrigerated and frozen fruit and vegetable ingredients for the food-manufacturing industry. Its product lines include infused dried fruit infused dried vegetables Soft-N-Frozen fruit and Fridg-N-Fresh vegetables. Graceland Fruit has also expanded into the fruit juice concentrate industry through a partnership with Milne Fruit Products. The company was founded in 1973 by president and CEO Donald Nugent.

	Annual Growth	09/01	09/02	09/03	09/04	09/07
Sales ($ mil.)	–	–	–	(1,021.2)	33.5	56.1
Net income ($ mil.)	847.6%	–	–	0.0	0.1	0.9
Market value ($ mil.)	–	–	–	–	–	–
Employees	–	–	–	–	–	180

GRACO INC.

88 - 11th Avenue N.E
Minneapolis, MN 55413
Phone: 612 623-6000
Fax: 612 623-6777
Web: www.graco.com

CEO: Patrick J. McHale
CFO: James A. Graner
HR: David (Dave) Ahlers
FYE: December 25
Type: Public

NYS: GGG

Graco has fluid management skills. The company which was founded in 1926 as Gray Company manufactures fluid-handling equipment designed to move measure control dispense and apply fluid materials. Products include pumps applicators spray guns pressure washers filters valves and accessories; these goods are used in industrial and commercial applications to handle paints adhesives sealants and lubricants. In addition to painting contractors Graco's customers include automotive construction equipment and vehicle lubrication companies. Graco sells its products through independent distributors worldwide.

	Annual Growth	12/11	12/12	12/13	12/14	12/15
Sales ($ mil.)	9.5%	895.3	1,012.5	1,104.0	1,221.1	1,286.5
Net income ($ mil.)	24.8%	142.3	149.1	210.8	225.6	345.7
Market value ($ mil.)	15.7%	2,280.3	2,835.7	4,339.7	4,541.0	4,085.4
Employees	8.6%	2,300	2,600	2,700	3,100	3,200

GRADALL INDUSTRIES INC.

406 Mill Ave. SW
New Philadelphia OH 44663
Phone: 330-339-2211
Fax: 330-339-8468
Web: www.gradall.com

CEO: –
CFO: –
HR: –
FYE: July 31
Type: Subsidiary

Gradall Industries is diggin' it up and movin' it out — far out. A subsidiary of Alamo Group Gradall makes non-traditional telescopic boom material handlers traditional conventional knuckle booms rough-terrain wheeled and industrial maintenance machines and mine scalers as well as spare parts for its products. Contractors use Gradall's material handlers for lumber and other materials; its industrial machines tackle tough mining railroad construction and hazardous waste removal jobs. In 2006 parent JLG Industries sold Gradall to maintenance and agricultural equipment maker Alamo Group. Gradall supports Alamo's Vacall subsidiary which makes sewer cleaning equipment hydro-excavators and vacuum loaders.

GRAEBEL COMPANIES INC.

16346 AIRPORT CIR
AURORA, CO 800111558
Phone: 303-214-6683
Fax: –
Web: www.graebelmoving.com

CEO: –
CFO: Brad Siler
HR: Mary Dymond
FYE: December 31
Type: Private

Graebel can move your table ... and just about anything else you need relocated. Offering both domestic and international household and commercial relocation services most of the company's business comes from firms transferring employees but it also provides individual household moving services and storage as well as freight forwarding. Graebel operates from service centers throughout the US and from international forwarding offices at major ports. It provides transportation services in Asia Europe the Middle East and Africa through hubs in Prague and Singapore and elsewhere in the world via a network of partners. Dave Graebel founded the family-run company in 1950.

	Annual Growth	12/05	12/06	12/09	12/11	12/12
Sales ($ mil.)	0.4%	–	334.2	260.8	322.9	341.9
Net income ($ mil.)	–	–	–	(3.3)	3.0	4.5
Market value ($ mil.)	–	–	–	–	–	–
Employees	–	–	–	–	–	1,771

GRAFTECH INTERNATIONAL LTD.   NYS: GTI

12900 Snow Road
Parma, OH 44130
Phone: 216 676-2000
Fax: –
Web: www.graftech.com
CEO: Joel L Hawthorne
CFO: Erick R Asmussen
HR: Lakeisha Brooks
FYE: December 31
Type: Public

If GrafTech International were a bard it could wax poetic in an ode to the electrode. The company is a leading maker in the US of graphite electrodes which are essential to the production of electric arc furnaces. GrafTech also manufactures advanced carbon materials flexible graphite products flow field plates gas diffusion layers and carbon electrodes and refractories for the aeronautics construction energy fire protection marine and transportation industries. Customers have included such notable names as Arcelor Mittal BaoSteel Elkem Griffin Wheel (railroad wheels) Samsung Electronics and ThyssenKrupp Steel.

	Annual Growth	12/09	12/10	12/11	12/12	12/13
Sales ($ mil.)	15.3%	659.0	1,007.0	1,320.2	1,248.3	1,166.7
Net income ($ mil.)	–	–	12.6	175.1	153.2	117.6	(27.3)
Market value ($ mil.)	(7.8%)	2,108.4	2,690.1	1,850.8	1,273.2	1,522.7
Employees	9.0%	2,147	2,915	3,284	2,990	3,034

GRAHAM CORP.   NYS: GHM

20 Florence Avenue
Batavia, NY 14020
Phone: 585 343-2216
Fax: –
Web: www.graham-mfg.com
CEO: James R. Lines
CFO: Jeffrey F. Glajch
HR: –
FYE: March 31
Type: Public

Graham Corporation knows how to take the heat and not crack under pressure. The company through its two subsidiaries manufactures mainly heat-transfer equipment including helical coil heat exchangers plate and frame heat exchangers and vacuums such as pumps and compressors and steam jet ejector vacuum systems. The lineup is used in myriad industrial and energy applications from petroleum refining to chemical and petrochemical processing power generation propulsion systems for nuclear-powered defense vessels and even food and soap making. The company sells its products directly and through independent sales representatives worldwide. More than 35% of Graham's sales are generated outside of the US.

	Annual Growth	03/11	03/12	03/13	03/14	03/15
Sales ($ mil.)	16.2%	74.2	103.2	105.0	102.2	135.2
Net income ($ mil.)	25.9%	5.9	10.6	11.1	10.1	14.7
Market value ($ mil.)	0.0%	242.6	221.8	250.7	322.7	242.9
Employees	4.8%	329	349	378	395	397

GRAHAM HOLDINGS CO.   NYS: GHC

1300 North 17th Street
Arlington, VA 22209
Phone: 703 345-6300
Fax: –
Web: www.ghco.com
CEO: Andrew S. (Andy) Rosen
CFO: Hal S. Jones
HR: Ann McDaniel
FYE: December 31
Type: Public

Best known as the former publisher of The Washington Post newspaper Graham Holdings (formerly the Washington Post Company) is now focused on education broadcasting and print and online news magazines. Its largest segment is education conducted via Kaplan which includes tutoring and test preparation services. Other operations include a portfolio of five TV stations and online and print publications such as Slate and Foreign Policy. It spun off cable TV systems operator Cable One in 2015. Owned by the family of its chairman Donald Graham for 80 years the flagship newspaper was sold to Internet mogul Jeff Bezos in 2013.

	Annual Growth	01/11*	12/11	12/12	12/13	12/14
Sales ($ mil.)	(9.2%)	4,723.6	4,214.8	4,017.7	3,487.9	3,535.2
Net income ($ mil.)	66.9%	278.1	117.2	132.1	236.9	1,293.8
Market value ($ mil.)	25.3%	2,548.6	2,185.0	2,117.8	3,846.5	5,008.5
Employees	(10.2%)	20,000	18,000	17,000	14,000	14,500

*Fiscal year change

GRAHAM PACKAGING COMPANY L.P.

2401 Pleasant Valley Rd.
York PA 17402
Phone: 717-849-8500
Fax: +45-44-85-95-95
Web: www.dako.com
CEO: Philip R Yates
CFO: –
HR: –
FYE: December 31
Type: Subsidiary

People can't keep their hands off Graham Packaging. Graham designs manufactures and sells blow-molded plastic containers for a slew of consumer goods including food and beverages automotive lubricants and household and personal care items. Graham's 90-plus manufacturing plants dot the Americas Europe and Asia to supply such multi-national customers as Clorox Danone and PepsiCo. About one-third of plant operations are set onsite at customers' production facilities; its top 20 customers represent nearly 70% of sales each year. Reynolds Group Holdings an affiliate of New Zealand's Rank Group Limited acquired the packager in 2011 for about $4.5 billion.

GRAINGER (W.W.) INC.   NYS: GWW

100 Grainger Parkway
Lake Forest, IL 60045-5201
Phone: 847 535-1000
Fax: 847 535-0878
Web: www.grainger.com
CEO: James T. (Jim) Ryan
CFO: Ronald L Jadin
HR: Joseph (Jo) High
FYE: December 31
Type: Public

Grainger is no stranger to those in need of a wide variety of industrial products. W.W. Grainger distributes more than 1.2 million industrial products from supplies to equipment and tools. The short list has electrical devices fasteners fleet maintenance equipment hand tools hardware janitorial lighting office supplies power and plumbing tools and safety security and test instruments. Its some two million customers are contractors maintenance and repair shops manufacturers and commercial government and educational facilities. Grainger sells through a network of branches distribution centers catalogs and websites.

	Annual Growth	12/10	12/11	12/12	12/13	12/14
Sales ($ mil.)	8.5%	7,182.2	8,078.2	8,950.0	9,437.8	9,965.0
Net income ($ mil.)	11.9%	510.9	658.4	689.9	797.0	801.7
Market value ($ mil.)	16.6%	9,313.0	12,622.6	13,646.2	17,223.5	17,187.8
Employees	6.3%	18,500	21,400	22,400	23,700	23,600

GRAMERCY PROPERTY TRUST INC   NYS: GPT

521 5th Avenue, 30th Floor
New York, NY 10175
Phone: 212 297-1000
Fax: –
Web: www.gptreit.com
CEO: –
CFO: –
HR: –
FYE: December 31
Type: Public

Gramercy Property Trust (formerly Gramercy Capital) a self-managed real estate investment trust (REIT) invests in commercial properties and real estate loan products secured throughout the US. Its Gramercy Finance arm originates and acquires mezzanine financing bridge loans interests in whole loans preferred equity private equity investments and mortgage-backed securities. Gramercy Real Estate primarily manages commercial properties mostly leased to financial institutions. Its management portfolio is made up of more than 25 million sq. ft of space in some 40 states.

	Annual Growth	12/09	12/10	12/11	12/12	12/13
Sales ($ mil.)	(45.4%)	636.1	607.1	211.2	36.8	56.7
Net income ($ mil.)	–	(519.6)	(973.7)	337.5	(171.5)	384.8
Market value ($ mil.)	22.1%	184.7	164.7	178.3	209.7	410.1
Employees	(10.8%)	131	135	121	93	83

GRAN TIERRA ENERGY INC — ASE: GTE

200, 150 13 Avenue S.W.
Calgary, Alberta T2R 0V2
Phone: 403 265-3221
Fax: 403 265-3242
Web: www.grantierra.com

CEO: Gary S. Guidry
CFO: Ryan Ellson
HR: –
FYE: December 31
Type: Public

Gran Tierra Energy hopes the earth still holds a wealth of oil and gas to be tapped especially in South America. Headquartered in Canada and incorporated and trading in the US this oil and gas exploration and production company holds interests in producing and prospective properties primarily in Argentina Brazil Colombia and Peru and is moving into the next phase which is focused on production growth through drilling. It has estimated proved reserves of about 24 million barrels of oil equivalent thanks in large part to increasing production at Costayaco in the Putumayo Basin in Colombia. Colombian oil and gas sales generate a lion's share of Gran Tierra Energy's revenues.

	Annual Growth	12/10	12/11	12/12	12/13	12/14
Sales ($ mil.)	10.7%	374.5	597.4	585.2	723.6	562.3
Net income ($ mil.)	–	37.2	126.9	99.7	126.3	(171.3)
Market value ($ mil.)	(16.8%)	2,303.8	1,373.7	1,576.9	2,092.1	1,101.8
Employees	11.4%	307	446	485	520	473

GRAND AIRE INC.

11777 W. Airport Service Rd.
Swanton OH 43558
Phone: 419-865-1760
Fax: 419-865-2965
Web: www.grandaire.com

CEO: Zachary Cheema
CFO: –
HR: –
FYE: December 31
Type: Private

If you like Tony Bennett ever leave a body part in San Francisco Grand Aire can get it back to you in a heartbeat. The air charter operator contracts for the transportation of cargo packages executives — and even organ transplant teams. Major customers have included leading automakers and FedEx. Grand Aire operates through affiliates Grand Aire Express (cargo carrier) and Executive Aire Express (passenger carrier). The company also runs AireBuy an online brokerage network that allows other North American charter carriers to bid for business. Grande Aire was founded in 1985 by CEO Katrina Cheema and her late husband Tahir Cheema. The Cheema family still owns Grand Aire.

GRAND CANYON EDUCATION INC — NMS: LOPE

3300 W. Camelback Road
Phoenix, AZ 85017
Phone: 602 639-7500
Fax: –
Web: www.gcu.edu

CEO: Brian E. Mueller
CFO: Daniel E. (Dan) Bachus
HR: –
FYE: December 31
Type: Public

Grand Canyon Education (dba Grand Canyon University) spans a broad educational horizon. The regionally accredited educator offers graduate and undergraduate degrees online at its campus in Phoenix and onsite at corporate facilities. Grand Canyon University offers career-oriented degree programs focused on the core disciplines of business education health care and liberal arts. Working adults make up most of the school's student body. Grand Canyon University enrolls almost 60000 students annually; about 83% are in online programs and about 45% of those pursue advanced degrees. Most classes have a student-teacher ratio of about 20:1. The company was formed in 1949 as a not-for-profit college and in 2004.

	Annual Growth	12/10	12/11	12/12	12/13	12/14
Sales ($ mil.)	15.7%	385.8	426.7	511.3	598.3	691.1
Net income ($ mil.)	25.9%	44.4	50.5	69.4	88.7	111.5
Market value ($ mil.)	24.2%	915.7	746.0	1,097.1	2,038.0	2,181.1
Employees	8.5%	2,600	2,550	2,655	3,100	3,600

GRAND CIRCLE LLC

347 Congress St.
Boston MA 02210
Phone: 617-350-7500
Fax: 617-346-6030
Web: www.gct.com

CEO: Alan E Lewis
CFO: Sean Stover
HR: Kate Creagh
FYE: December 31
Type: Private

Grand Circle wants to take your grandparents there and back again. Offering more than 75 vacations worldwide the company provides travel services via land and its fleet of small ships primarily to customers over 50 years old. Its Grand Circle Travel division offers all-inclusive package tours at a leisurely pace while its Overseas Adventure subsidiary organizes small groups for land canal barge and small ship journeys of the more rugged variety. Grand Circle's roughly 35 offices are located in Africa North and South America Europe and the Asia/Pacific region. It began life in 1958 as part of a plan by AARP founder Ethel Andrus to help older Americans be more active.

GRAND PIANO & FURNITURE CO.

4235 ELECTRIC RD STE 100
ROANOKE, VA 240188445
Phone: 540-774-7004
Fax: –
Web: www.grandhomefurnishings.com

CEO: George B Cartledge Jr
CFO: Randy Lundy
HR: –
FYE: October 31
Type: Private

Grand Home Furnishings formerly Grand Piano & Furniture got its start as a piano and musical instrument store in Roanoke Virginia. Several decades later the company sells mattresses and home furnishings through more than 15 stores in Virginia West Virginia and Tennessee. The company stocks furniture from such manufacturers as Hooker La-Z-Boy Klaussner Vaughan-Bassett Meadowcraft and Thomasville and the mattresses come from Tempur Sealy to name a few. Grand Home Furnishings was founded in 1910 and acquired in 1945 by the current owners the Cartledge family. George Cartledge Jr. is the company's CEO.

	Annual Growth	10/09	10/10	10/11	10/12	10/13
Sales ($ mil.)	0.0%	–	123.0	0.0	123.0	123.0
Net income ($ mil.)	–	–	–	0.0	0.0	0.0
Market value ($ mil.)	–	–	–	–	–	–
Employees	–	–	–	–	–	700

GRAND STRAND REGIONAL MEDICAL CENTER LLC

809 82ND PKWY
MYRTLE BEACH, SC 295724607
Phone: 843-449-4411
Fax: –
Web: www.grandstrandmed.com

CEO: Mark Sims
CFO: –
HR: –
FYE: April 30
Type: Private

Grand Strand Regional Medical Center (GSRMC) is an acute care hospital serving Myrtle Beach South Carolina and surrounding Georgetown and Horry counties. The 220-bed hospital a designated trauma center is home to the only cardiac surgery program in those counties. GSRMC has a staff of more than 250 physicians representing a range of specializations including oncology wound treatment and emergency care women's health pediatrics rehabilitation behavioral health and treatment for sleeping disorders. Grand Strand Regional Medical Center includes the medical center and other satellite diagnostic ambulatory care and senior care facilities throughout the area.

	Annual Growth	04/06	04/07	04/08	04/09	04/13
Sales ($ mil.)	641.9%	–	–	–	0.1	265.2
Net income ($ mil.)	565.8%	–	–	–	0.0	65.3
Market value ($ mil.)	–	–	–	–	–	–
Employees	–	–	–	–	–	1,000

GRAND VIEW HOSPITAL

700 LAWN AVE
SELLERSVILLE, PA 189601548
Phone: 215-453-4000
Fax: –
Web: www.gvh.org

CEO: Stuart Fine
CFO: –
HR: Lauren Maddalo
FYE: June 30
Type: Private

Grand View Health (GVH) formerly Grand View Hospital hopes to give patients a glimpse of great health care. The hospital provide emergency inpatient surgery and specialty services including cardiology orthopedics sleep diagnostic rehabilitation women's and children's care and other medical services to the Bucks County region of Pennsylvania. GVH's oncology program is affiliated with the Fox Chase Cancer Center in Philadelphia. The medical center also operates primary care and outpatient clinics in the region and it provides home health hospice fitness and community outreach programs. The hospital has about 200 beds.

	Annual Growth	06/09	06/10	06/11	06/12	06/13
Sales ($ mil.)	(2.7%)	–	182.8	177.4	169.3	168.2
Net income ($ mil.)	76.1%	–	–	10.1	(26.5)	31.4
Market value ($ mil.)	–	–	–	–	–	–
Employees	–	–	–	–	–	1,600

GRANDE COMMUNICATIONS HOLDINGS INC.

401 Carlson Cir.
San Marcos TX 78666
Phone: 512-878-4000
Fax: 512-878-4010
Web: www.grandecom.com

CEO: Michael Wilfley
CFO: –
HR: –
FYE: December 31
Type: Private

Grande Communications' big idea is to become a bigger player in Texas telecommunications. Through operating subsidiary Grande Communications Networks the company provides bundled telephone services Internet access and cable television to about 140000 residential and business customers over its own fiber-optic network. It also offers wholesale communications services to other telecoms and ISPs through its Grande Networks division. While its core Central Texas service area includes Austin San Marcos and San Antonio it also provides service in Corpus Christi Dallas Midland Odessa and Waco. Grande Communications is controlled by Boston-based private equity firm ABRY Partners.

GRANGE MUTUAL CASUALTY COMPANY

650 S. Front St.
Columbus OH 43206
Phone: 614-445-2900
Fax: 614-445-2337
Web: www.grangeinsurance.com

CEO: Tom Welch
CFO: J Paul McCaffrey
HR: –
FYE: December 31
Type: Private - Mutual Com

Grange Mutual Casualty and its subsidiaries offer many breeds of insurance and financial products to grangers and others mainly in the midwestern US. Founded in 1935 the company (also known as Grange Insurance) offers auto commercial farm homeowners and life insurance coverage to customers in more than a dozen states mostly in the farm belt region. The firm targets small to midsized businesses for its commercial policies; its offerings include workers' compensation commercial auto and umbrella insurance. Grange and its subsidiaries including Grange Life and Grange Property and Casualty sell their products through a network of some 3000 independent agents.

GRANITE BROADCASTING CORPORATION

767 3rd Ave. 34th Fl.
New York NY 10017
Phone: 212-826-2530
Fax: 212-826-2858
Web: www.granitetv.com

CEO: –
CFO: –
HR: –
FYE: December 31
Type: Private

Television really rocks the world of this company. Granite Broadcasting owns jointly operates or provides programming to more than 20 TV stations in about a dozen markets in about half a dozen states. Several of its stations are affiliated with major broadcast networks NBC and CBS while others are affiliated with smaller networks The CW and MyNetworkTV. Granite Broadcasting also operates a number of independent stations as well as online news and information portals serving its stations' viewers. Founded by former CEO W. Don Cornwell in 1988 the company is owned by private equity firm Silver Point Capital.

GRANITE CITY FOOD & BREWERY LTD   NBB: GCFB

701 Xenia Avenue South, Suite 120
Minneapolis, MN 55416
Phone: 952 215-0660
Fax: –
Web: www.gcfb.net

CEO: Robert J Doran
CFO: James G Gilbertson
HR: –
FYE: December 30
Type: Public

Drinking and dining form the bedrock of this small restaurant chain. Granite City Food & Brewery owns and operates more than 25 casual dining brewpubs in about a dozen Midwestern states mostly in Minnesota Kansas Illinois Indiana and Iowa. The restaurants offer a variety of handcrafted beers that are brewed on-site including such varieties as Broad Axe Stout Duke of Wellington (English ale) and Northern Light Lager. Granite City's broad food menu features chicken steak and seafood entrees along with appetizers burgers sandwiches and salads. The company also owns and operates five Cadillac Ranch All American Bar & Grill restaurants.

	Annual Growth	12/10	12/11	12/12	12/13	12/14
Sales ($ mil.)	11.1%	89.3	93.2	120.9	134.2	136.2
Net income ($ mil.)	–	(4.5)	(4.6)	(4.1)	(3.4)	(3.1)
Market value ($ mil.)	(5.0%)	27.4	31.7	32.0	15.1	22.3
Employees	10.7%	2,322	2,800	3,236	3,153	–

GRANITE CONSTRUCTION INC.   NYS: GVA

585 West Beach Street
Watsonville, CA 95076
Phone: 831 724-1011
Fax: –
Web: www.graniteconstruction.com

CEO: James H. Roberts
CFO: Laurel J. Krzeminski
HR: Richard (Dick) Boslow
FYE: December 31
Type: Public

Granite Construction is building its way from coast to coast. The holding company operates through its main subsidiary Granite Construction Company a transportation and heavy construction contractor that works on public infrastructure projects such as airports bridges dams highways mass transit and tunnels. For private-sector firms Granite performs site preparation for residential and commercial development. In addition to construction services the company mines and processes aggregates and has plants that produce construction materials such as asphalt and concrete. Granite has offices from Alaska to Florida. Granite was incorporated in 1922.

	Annual Growth	12/10	12/11	12/12	12/13	12/14
Sales ($ mil.)	6.6%	1,763.0	2,009.5	2,083.0	2,266.9	2,275.3
Net income ($ mil.)	–	(59.0)	51.2	45.3	(36.4)	25.3
Market value ($ mil.)	8.5%	1,074.9	929.5	1,317.4	1,370.7	1,489.9
Employees	6.9%	2,300	3,000	4,100	3,600	3,000

GRANITE TELECOMMUNICATIONS LLC

100 NEWPORT AVENUE EXT # 1
QUINCY, MA 021712126
Phone: 617-933-5500
Fax: -
Web: www.granitenet.com

CEO: Robert T. (Rob) Hale
CFO: Richard Wurman
HR: -
FYE: December 31
Type: Private

Granite Telecommunications is looking for rock solid growth as a reseller of telecommunications services to commercial clients in the US and Canada. The company is a wholesaler of local and long distance telephone service as well as broadband Internet connections over 1.3 million lines provided by network operators. It serves corporate clients many of whom run offices in multiple states offering them no account transfer charges and no term or volume contracts on telephone service. Granite also designs and installs network cabling and security systems and provides loss prevention and risk management services.

	Annual Growth	12/09	12/10	12/11	12/12	12/13
Sales ($ mil.)	18.7%	-	517.2	609.0	736.2	865.8
Net income ($ mil.)	26.5%	-	-	143.0	187.8	228.8
Market value ($ mil.)	-	-	-	-	-	-
Employees	-	-	-	-	-	650

GRAPHIC PACKAGING HOLDING CO   NYS: GPK

1500 Riveredge Parkway, Suite 100
Atlanta, GA 30328
Phone: 770 240-7200
Fax: -
Web: www.graphicpkg.com

CEO: Michael P. Doss
CFO: Stephen R. Scherger
HR: Paul Evans
FYE: December 31
Type: Public

Ever toted a 12-pack home? If so you can appreciate Graphic Packaging Holding Company's (GPHC) work. Operating subsidiary Graphic Packaging International (GPI) is a leading maker of laminated coated and printed packaging such as beverage carriers cereal boxes microwavable food packaging and detergent cartons. Its two business segments include flexible packaging and paperboard packaging. The larger paperboard segment includes strength promotional and barrier packaging technologies. Customers include Kraft Foods MillerCoors Anheuser-Busch General Mills and various Coca-Cola and Pepsi bottlers.

	Annual Growth	12/10	12/11	12/12	12/13	12/14
Sales ($ mil.)	0.9%	4,095.0	4,206.3	4,337.1	4,478.1	4,240.5
Net income ($ mil.)	70.2%	10.7	276.9	122.6	146.6	89.7
Market value ($ mil.)	36.8%	1,272.2	1,393.2	2,112.7	3,139.6	4,454.3
Employees	(1.9%)	12,400	12,300	13,900	12,900	11,500

GRAY TELEVISION INC   NYS: GTN

4370 Peachtree Road, NE
Atlanta, GA 30319
Phone: 404 504-9828
Fax: -
Web: www.gray.tv

CEO: -
CFO: James C. (Jim) Ryan
HR: -
FYE: December 31
Type: Public

Gray Television has The Eye for local television markets. The company is the largest independent operator of TV stations affiliated with the CBS network with 17 stations in more than a dozen states. In total the company operates more than 35 stations in 30 midsized and smaller markets mostly in the Midwest and South. Its other stations are affiliated with ABC NBC and FOX. In addition to traditional analog signals Gray Television broadcasts an additional 40 digital channels mostly carrying programming from The CW and MyNetworkTV. Former CEO J. Mack Robinson and his family control nearly 40% of the company.

	Annual Growth	12/10	12/11	12/12	12/13	12/14
Sales ($ mil.)	10.1%	346.1	307.1	404.8	346.3	508.1
Net income ($ mil.)	20.0%	23.2	9.0	28.1	18.3	48.1
Market value ($ mil.)	56.4%	109.4	94.8	128.7	870.5	655.2
Employees	7.8%	2,171	2,105	2,084	2,248	2,937

GRAYBAR ELECTRIC CO., INC.   NBB: GRBE

34 North Meramec Avenue
St. Louis, MO 63105
Phone: 314 573-9200
Fax: -
Web: www.graybar.com

CEO: Kathleen M. Mazzarella
CFO: Randall R. Harwood
HR: Vicki Hall
FYE: December 31
Type: Public

There's no gray area when it comes to Graybar Electric: it's one of the largest distributors of electrical products in the US. The employee-owned company distributes more than 1 million electrical communications and data networking products through a network of around 260 distribution facilities. Its diversified lineup includes a myriad of wire cable and lighting products from thousands of manufacturers and suppliers. It also offers supply chain management and logistics services. Affiliate Graybar Financial Services provides equipment leasing and financing. Graybar Electric sells to construction contractors industrial plants power utilities and telecommunications providers primarily in the US.

	Annual Growth	12/10	12/11	12/12	12/13	12/14
Sales ($ mil.)	6.7%	4,616.4	5,374.8	5,413.3	5,659.1	5,978.9
Net income ($ mil.)	20.1%	42.0	81.4	86.3	81.1	87.4
Market value ($ mil.)	-	-	-	-	-	-
Employees	4.2%	7,000	7,400	7,500	7,600	8,250

GRAYCOR INC.

2 Mid America Plaza Ste. 400
Oakbrook Terrace IL 60181
Phone: 630-684-7110
Fax: 630-684-7111
Web: www.graycor.com

CEO: -
CFO: Steven Gray
HR: -
FYE: September 30
Type: Private

Graycor translates blueprints into buildings. The company provides contracting construction design/build and facilities management services across the US through four main units. Graycor Industrial has expertise in the steel and energy industries and performs trade services such as concrete and carpentry work. Graycor Blasting offers industrial cleaning blast furnace delining and salamander (heat source) removal services. Graycor Construction has built edifices ranging from retail centers and hotels to manufacturing plants to corporate education health care and distribution facilities. Graycor International is active in Canada and Mexico. Chairman and CEO Melvin Gray and his family control Graycor.

GREAT AMERICAN BANCORP, INC.   OTC: GTPS

1311 S. Neil Street
Champaign, IL 61820
Phone: 217 356-2265
Fax: 217 356-2502
Web: www.greatamericanbancorp.com

CEO: George R Rouse
CFO: Jane F Adams
HR: Ata Zurukan
FYE: December 31
Type: Public

Great American Bancorp is the holding company for First Federal Savings Bank of Champaign-Urbana which operates two branches in Champaign and one in Urbana Illinois. Targeting individuals and local businesses First Federal provides retail banking products such as checking savings and money market accounts credit cards and CDs. Lending activities consist primarily of residential mortgages as well as commercial real estate construction business and consumer loans. The bank was founded in 1908. Through a partnership with UMB Financial Corporation subsidiary UMB Financial Services First Federal Savings Bank also offers investment services.

	Annual Growth	12/10	12/11	12/12	12/13	12/14
Assets ($ mil.)	2.8%	158.1	160.3	170.4	171.7	176.7
Net income ($ mil.)	(13.8%)	1.3	1.1	1.0	0.5	0.7
Market value ($ mil.)	(10.7%)	16.5	17.4	15.1	15.0	10.5
Employees	-	-	-	-	-	-

GREAT AMERICAN FINANCIAL RESOURCES INC.

525 Vine St.
Cincinnati OH 45202
Phone: 513-333-5300
Fax: 513-412-3777
Web: www.gafri.com

CEO: S Craig Lindner
CFO: Christopher P Miliano
HR: –
FYE: December 31
Type: Subsidiary

Great American Financial Resources Inc. (GAFRI) flies the patriotic banners of retirement products and insurance. Its principal subsidiary Great American Life Insurance Company (GALIC) has marketed insurance products since 1959. The company sells retirement products primarily fixed and variable annuities. Independent agents and financial advisors sell GAFRI's products to its core customers: teachers government employees and folks working in the not-for-profit sector. It also services select traditional life and long-term care policies that are not actively marketed. GAFRI is owned by American Financial Group.

GREAT LAKES AVIATION LTD.
NBB: GLUX

1022 Airport Parkway
Cheyenne, WY 82001
Phone: 307 432-7000
Fax: –
Web: www.flygreatlakes.com

CEO: Charles R Howell IV
CFO: Michael O Matthews
HR: –
FYE: December 31
Type: Public

Great Lakes Aviation goes to great lengths to get people where they need to be even if it's far from the big city. Flying as Great Lakes Airlines the regional carrier transports passengers to more than 60 destinations in the western and midwestern US mainly from Denver but also from markets such as Phoenix Kansas City and Ontario California. It maintains code-sharing agreements with Frontier Airlines and United Airlines. (Code-sharing enables carriers to sell tickets on one another's flights and thus extend their networks.) Great Lakes operates a fleet of about 40 turboprop aircraft consisting mostly of 19-passenger Beechcraft 1900Ds but also including 30-passenger Embraer Brasilia 120s.

	Annual Growth	12/10	12/11	12/12	12/13	12/14
Sales ($ mil.)	(17.1%)	125.4	124.4	137.8	117.2	59.2
Net income ($ mil.)	–	5.1	10.7	2.9	(0.4)	(7.4)
Market value ($ mil.)	(29.9%)	15.3	6.7	18.0	10.9	3.7
Employees	(16.4%)	1,122	1,068	1,164	657	548

GREAT LAKES CHEESE COMPANY INC.

17825 Great Lakes Pkwy.
Hiram OH 44234-1806
Phone: 440-834-2500
Fax: 440-834-1002
Web: www.greatlakescheese.com

CEO: Gary Vanic
CFO: –
HR: –
FYE: December 31
Type: Private

Great Lakes Cheese understands the power of provolone the charm of cheddar and the goodness of gruyere. The Ohio-based firm manufactures about 165 million pounds of cheese annually. The cheesemaker distributes natural and processed cheeses and cheese spreads including varieties such as cheddar Colby Swiss mozzarella and provolone. It also makes the premium Adams Reserve New York Cheddar. Great Lakes packages shredded chunked and sliced cheese for deli bulk and foodservice sale under the Great Lakes Adams Reserve and private-label brands. Chairman Hans Epprecht a Swiss immigrant founded the firm in 1958 as a Cleveland bulk-cheese distributor. Epprecht and Great Lakes employees own the company.

GREAT LAKES DREDGE & DOCK CORP
NMS: GLDD

2122 York Road
Oak Brook, IL 60523
Phone: 630 574-3000
Fax: –
Web: www.gldd.com

CEO: Jonathan W. Berger
CFO: Bruce J. Biemeck
HR: –
FYE: December 31
Type: Public

Great Lakes Dredge & Dock is an expert at keeping waterways and shorelines clear. Founded in 1890 this company is a stalwart of dredging services in the US mainly in the East West and Gulf Coast region. It also provides dredging abroad. Dredging involves enhancing or preserving waterways for navigability or protecting shorelines by removing or replenishing soil sand or rock. Great Lakes is involved in three major types of dredging work: capital (primarily port expansion projects) beach nourishment (movement of sand from ocean floor to shoreline to alleviate erosion) and maintenance (removal of silt and sediment from existing waterways and harbors). Great Lakes also provides environmental & remediation clean-up services.

	Annual Growth	12/10	12/11	12/12	12/13	12/14
Sales ($ mil.)	4.1%	686.9	627.3	687.6	731.4	806.8
Net income ($ mil.)	(26.1%)	34.6	16.5	(2.7)	(34.4)	10.3
Market value ($ mil.)	3.8%	443.5	334.5	537.3	553.6	515.1
Employees	2.9%	1,721	1,726	1,598	1,977	1,928

GREAT NORTHERN IRON ORE PROPERTIES
NYS: GNI

W-1290 First National Bank Building, 332 Minnesota Street
Saint Paul, MN 55101-1361
Phone: 651 224-2385
Fax: 651 224-2387
Web: www.gniop.com

CEO: Joseph S Micallef
CFO: Thomas A Janochoski
HR: –
FYE: December 31
Type: Public

Great Northern Iron Ore Properties is the landlord of one big iron formation. The trust gets income from royalties on iron ore minerals (principally taconite) taken from its more than 67000 acres on the Mesabi Iron Formation in Minnesota. The trust was formed in 1906 to own the properties of an affiliate of Burlington Northern Santa Fe (BNSF formerly Great Northern Railway). The trust's beneficiaries were the heirs of railroad founder James Hill; however the last survivor his grandson Louis Hill died in 1995. In 2015 (20 years after Louis Hill's death) the land will be transferred to a unit of ConocoPhillips which acquired the BNSF assets in 2005.

	Annual Growth	12/09	12/10	12/11	12/12	12/13
Sales ($ mil.)	6.3%	14.8	20.9	26.7	24.2	19.0
Net income ($ mil.)	6.6%	11.4	17.5	23.0	20.1	14.8
Market value ($ mil.)	(7.7%)	141.0	214.5	165.4	100.8	102.2
Employees	0.0%	10	10	10	10	10

GREAT PLAINS ENERGY, INC.
NYS: GXP

1200 Main Street
Kansas City, MO 64105
Phone: 816 556-2200
Fax: –
Web: www.greatplainsenergy.com

CEO: Terry Bassham
CFO: James C. (Jim) Shay
HR: –
FYE: December 31
Type: Public

Great Plains Energy is sweeping the fruited plains with electric power. The holding company serves about 838400 electricity customers in Missouri and Kansas through regulated utility Kansas City Power & Light (KCP&L) and KCP&L Greater Missouri Operations Company which both operate under the KCP&L brand. The utility company has more than 6600 MW of primarily coal-fired generating capacity. Great Plains Energy has exited most of its deregulated businesses in order to focus on its utility operations. Electric utility retail revenues account for more than 90% of Great Plains Energy's total operating revenues.

	Annual Growth	12/10	12/11	12/12	12/13	12/14
Sales ($ mil.)	3.3%	2,255.5	2,318.0	2,309.9	2,446.3	2,568.2
Net income ($ mil.)	3.5%	211.7	174.4	199.9	250.2	242.8
Market value ($ mil.)	10.0%	2,989.2	3,357.7	3,131.0	3,736.9	4,379.8
Employees	(2.0%)	3,188	3,053	3,090	2,964	2,935

GREAT PLAINS MANUFACTURING INCORPORATED

1525 E. North St.
Salina KS 67401
Phone: 785-823-3276
Fax: 785-822-5600
Web: www.greatplainsmfg.com

CEO: –
CFO: –
HR: Tammy Rhea
FYE: June 30
Type: Private

Great Plains Manufacturing goes to great pains to help farmers across the fruited plain to sow grow and harvest the fruits of their labor. Through its Great Plains division the company designs manufactures and sells agricultural planting spraying and cultivating equipment. Its Land Pride unit sells landscaping products such as mowers and aerators. Great Plains Acceptance Corporation (GPAC) provides equipment financing and Great Plains Trucking provides related trucking services in the US and Canada. Great Plains Manufacturing distributes its products through a network of about 1000 Great Plains dealers and some 1600 Land Pride dealers. The company also sells equipment to more than 50 countries.

GREAT RIVER ENERGY

12300 Elm Creek Blvd.
Maple Grove MN 55369-4718
Phone: 763-445-5000
Fax: 763-445-5050
Web: www.greatriverenergy.com

CEO: David Saggau
CFO: Larry Schmid
HR: –
FYE: December 31
Type: Private - Cooperativ

Great River Energy powers up cooperatives along the Great River Road. The utility provides wholesale electricity to 1.7 million people (at 650000 homes businesses and farms) through 28 distribution cooperatives in Minnesota and Wisconsin. It operates more than 4600 miles of transmission lines and has more than 3500 MW of capacity from 12 fossil-fueled hydroelectric and renewable power generation facilities. The company also owns or partially owns more than 100 transmission substations. Great River Energy is the #2 electric utility in Minnesota in terms of generating capacity and one of the top five largest generation and transmission cooperatives in the US (based on assets).

GREAT SOUTHERN BANCORP, INC.
NMS: GSBC

1451 E. Battlefield
Springfield, MO 65804
Phone: 417 887-4400
Fax: –
Web: www.greatsouthernbank.com

CEO: Joseph W. (Joe) Turner
CFO: Rex A. Copeland
HR: Matt Snyder
FYE: December 31
Type: Public

Despite its name Great Southern Bancorp is firmly entrenched in the heartland. It is the holding company for Great Southern Bank which operates more than 75 branches in Missouri plus more than two dozen locations in Iowa Kansas Nebraska and Arkansas. Founded in 1923 the bank offers checking and savings accounts CDs IRAs and credit cards. The firm's Great Southern Travel division is one of the largest travel agencies in Missouri. It serves both leisure and corporate travelers through about a dozen offices. Among other units Great Southern Insurance offers property/casualty and life insurance while Great Southern Financial provides investment products and services through an agreement with Ameriprise.

	Annual Growth	12/10	12/11	12/12	12/13	12/14
Assets ($ mil.)	3.7%	3,411.5	3,790.0	3,955.2	3,560.3	3,951.5
Net income ($ mil.)	16.2%	23.9	30.3	48.7	33.7	43.5
Market value ($ mil.)	13.9%	324.5	324.5	350.1	418.3	545.7
Employees	3.6%	1,086	1,256	1,164	1,163	1,252

GREAT WEST CASUALTY COMPANY

1100 W. 29th St.
South Sioux City NE 68776-0277
Phone: 402-494-2411
Fax: 402-494-7480
Web: https://ssl.gwccnet.com

CEO: –
CFO: Gaylen Tenhulzen
HR: –
FYE: December 31
Type: Subsidiary

Great West Casualty Company keeps truckers hauling from the West Coast to the East Coast and back again. The company specializes in providing insurance and various services for the transportation industry. It offers several kinds of niche property/casualty coverage — including auto liability cargo garage-keepers and inland marine — with trucking companies and owner-operators in mind. It also provides general liability umbrella and workers' compensation policies for semi-truck operators. Through its service offices and the agency offices of subsidiary Joe Morten & Son the company serves customers in more than 40 states. Great West Casualty is part of the Old Republic International insurance group.

GREAT WEST LIFE & ANNUITY INSURANCE CO - INSURANCE PRODUCTS

8515 East Orchard Road
Greenwood Village, CO 80111
Phone: 303 737-3000
Fax: –
Web: www.greatwest.com

CEO: Robert L. Reynolds
CFO: Louis J. Mannello
HR: –
FYE: December 31
Type: Public

Great-West Life & Annuity Insurance is the southern arm of a northern parent. The company a subsidiary of Canada's Great-West Lifeco and a member of the Power Financial family represents the Great-West group's primary US operations. It offers life insurance and annuities to individuals and employer groups. Under the Great-West Retirement Services brand it administers employer-sponsored retirement products including defined-benefit pension and 401(k) plans. Additional Great-West services include investment consulting and fund management. Great-West Life & Annuity markets products through its sales representatives and regional offices as well as independent brokers.

	Annual Growth	12/10	12/11	12/12	12/13	12/14
Assets ($ mil.)	5.2%	47,627.4	48,336.0	52,818.6	55,323.5	58,348.2
Net income ($ mil.)	11.9%	202.8	214.1	238.1	128.7	317.4
Market value ($ mil.)	–	–	–	–	–	–
Employees	9.8%	3,100	3,200	3,300	3,300	4,500

GREAT WOLF RESORTS INC.
NASDAQ: WOLF

525 Junction Rd. Ste. 6000 S.
Madison WI 53717
Phone: 608-662-4700
Fax: +44-141-332-2012
Web: www.carnyx.com

CEO: Kimberly K Schaefer
CFO: –
HR: Kim Reese
FYE: December 31
Type: Private

Great Wolf Resorts has its customers muttering "Great Scott!" as they pull up to the company's drive-to family resorts. Great Wolf owns and operates about a dozen resorts. Nearly all of its properties operate under the Great Wolf Lodge name many of which are located in Midwestern US states. The company's properties are open year-round and include lodging indoor water parks themed restaurants and other diversions such as arcades spas and organized children's activities. Great Wolf targets families with children aged 2 to 14 years old who live within a convenient driving distance of its resorts. Private equity firm Apollo Global Management owns the company.

GREATBATCH INC
NYS: GB

2595 Dallas Parkway, Suite 310
Frisco, TX 75034
Phone: 716 759-5600
Fax: –
Web: www.greatbatch.com

CEO: Scott F. Drees
CFO: Michael Dinkins
HR: Kristin E. Trecker
FYE: January 02
Type: Public

Greatbatch likes to keep its business close to the heart. The company is a leading maker of batteries used in implantable medical devices such as pacemakers and implantable cardioverter defibrillators (ICDs). Other medical components include electrodes capacitors engineered components enclosures and feedthroughs (used to deliver electrical signals from an implantable medical device to an electrode). Greatbatch also makes batteries for demanding industrial applications such as oil and gas exploration. Greatbatch gets nearly half of its sales from US clients.

	Annual Growth	12/10	12/11	12/12*	01/14	01/15
Sales ($ mil.)	5.2%	533.4	568.8	646.2	663.9	687.8
Net income ($ mil.)	10.8%	33.1	33.1	(4.8)	36.3	55.5
Market value ($ mil.)	15.0%	605.5	554.1	573.9	1,098.1	1,220.0
Employees	4.4%	2,976	3,271	3,310	3,385	3,690

*Fiscal year change

GREATER BALTIMORE MEDICAL CENTER INC.

6701 N CHARLES ST
BALTIMORE, MD 21204-6808
Phone: 443-849-2000
Fax: –
Web: www.gbmc.org

CEO: John Chessare
CFO: Eric Melchior
HR: –
FYE: June 30
Type: Private

Greater Baltimore Medical Center also known as GBMC operates an integrated health system for residents of Baltimore and surrounding counties. The 280-bed medical center provides surgery women's health oncology cardiology and other specialty and general medical services. In addition to inpatient and outpatient services it provides teaching services through an affiliation with Johns Hopkins University. GBMC also includes area clinics and physician practice locations. The GBMC Foundation coordinates fundraising for the health network.

	Annual Growth	06/07	06/08	06/09	06/10	06/11
Sales ($ mil.)	2.0%	–	393.0	388.9	403.1	416.5
Net income ($ mil.)	45.7%	–	8.3	0.0	20.4	25.6
Market value ($ mil.)	–	–	–	–	–	–
Employees	–	–	–	–	–	–

GREATER LAFAYETTE HEALTH SERVICES INC.

1501 HARTFORD ST
LAFAYETTE, IN 479042134
Phone: 765-423-6011
Fax: –
Web: www.franciscanalliance.org

CEO: Terry Wilson
CFO: Keith Lauter
HR: –
FYE: December 31
Type: Private

Part of Franciscan Alliance St. Elizabeth Regional Health (operating as Franciscan Saint Elizabeth Health) operates three acute care hospitals that provide health services to residents of northwestern Indiana's Tippecanoe County. The facilities are full-service acute care hospitals providing primary rehabilitative and surgery care. Specialty units include centers for diabetes cancer wound pulmonary cardiac and women's and children's care. The Franciscan St. Elizabeth Health-Lafayette East campus is home to a school of nursing. St. Elizabeth Regional Health also provides home health and hospice services and operates area poison control centers.

	Annual Growth	12/0-1	12/00	12/01	12/02	12/08
Sales ($ mil.)	(4.6%)	–	211.1	211.1	231.9	144.7
Net income ($ mil.)	–	–	–	21.3	16.5	(3.9)
Market value ($ mil.)	–	–	–	–	–	–
Employees	–	–	–	–	–	2,660

GREATER WASHINGTON EDUCATIONAL TELECOMMUNICATIONS ASSOCIATION IN

3939 CAMPBELL AVE
ARLINGTON, VA 222063440
Phone: 703-998-2600
Fax: –
Web: www.weta.org

CEO: Sharon Percy Rockefeller
CFO: James Bond
HR: –
FYE: June 30
Type: Private

The Greater Washington Educational Telecommunications Association is a leading public broadcaster serving the Washington DC area with a television station and a radio station operating under the call letters WETA. It is also a leading producer of content for the Public Broadcasting Service including PBS NewsHour (created in partnership with MacNeil/Lehrer Productions) and Washington Week. WETA has also co-produced several documentaries by Ken Burns including The Civil War and Baseball. The not-for-profit organization was formed in 1953 and received a TV broadcast license in 1961.

	Annual Growth	06/09	06/10	06/11	06/12	06/13
Sales ($ mil.)	4.7%	–	65.8	72.1	69.9	75.6
Net income ($ mil.)	–	–	–	16.8	12.9	(7.1)
Market value ($ mil.)	–	–	–	–	–	–
Employees	–	–	–	–	–	236

GREATWIDE LOGISTICS SERVICES LLC

12404 Park Central Dr. Ste. 300S
Dallas TX 75251-1803
Phone: 972-228-7300
Fax: 972-228-7328
Web: www.greatwide.com

CEO: John Tague
CFO: –
HR: Doug Clark
FYE: December 31
Type: Private

Greatwide Logistics Services brings together a world of freight transportation and logistics companies. The third-party logistics provider offers dedicated transportation in which drivers and equipment are assigned to a customer long-term; distribution logistics; truckload freight brokerage; and truckload freight transportation largely via a network of more than 20000 independent owner-operators. Greatwide calls upon a fleet of some 5000 trucks and has 3 million sq. ft. of warehouse space in the US. Clients have included such heavy hitters as Target Wal-Mart and IBM. Greatwide emerged from Chapter 11 bankruptcy protection in 2009 after being acquired by an investor group.

GREEN DOT CORP
NYS: GDOT

3465 E. Foothill Blvd.
Pasadena, CA 91107
Phone: 626 765-2000
Fax: –
Web: www.greendot.com

CEO: Steven W. Streit
CFO: Grace T. Wang
HR: –
FYE: December 31
Type: Public

If you've got the green but not the plastic Green Dot would like to help. The company offers prepaid debit cards through more than 100000 retail locations in the US. The MasterCard- and Visa-branded reloadable cards function like credit cards for purchases and cash withdrawals. Green Dot which has about 4.5 million cards in circulation partners with Wal-Mart Kmart Walgreens Home Depot and other retailers to enable its customers to add funds to their accounts. The company's products are designed for people who aren't able or choose not to utilize traditional credit card and banking services. Green Dot makes most of its money from new card monthly maintenance and ATM fees.

	Annual Growth	12/10	12/11	12/12	12/13	12/14
Sales ($ mil.)	13.4%	363.9	467.4	546.3	573.6	601.6
Net income ($ mil.)	0.3%	42.2	52.1	47.2	34.0	42.7
Market value ($ mil.)	(22.5%)	2,902.0	1,596.8	624.0	1,286.3	1,048.0
Employees	24.9%	352	464	596	562	857

GREEN HILLS SOFTWARE INC.

30 W. Sola St.
Santa Barbara CA 93101-2526
Phone: 805-965-6044
Fax: 805-965-6343
Web: www.ghs.com

CEO: Daniel O Dowd
CFO: Jeffrey Hazarian
HR: –
FYE: December 31
Type: Private

From the seasonally green hills of Santa Barbara comes Green Hills Software an oasis for embedded systems developers. The company provides a variety of software tools for developers of embedded systems (combinations of microprocessors and components used in many different products including disk drives mobile devices video games braking and avionics systems). Green Hills' products include real-time operating systems (INTEGRITY) development environments (MULTI IDE) debugging devices and routing and switching technology as well as custom software development services. Green Hills Software was founded in 1982 by president and CEO Dan O'Dowd who owns the company.

GREENBERG TRAURIG P.A.

333 Avenue of the Americas (333 SE 2nd Ave.) Ste. 4400
Miami FL 33131
Phone: 305-579-0500
Fax: 305-579-0717
Web: www.gtlaw.com

CEO: Richard A Rosenbaum
CFO: –
HR: –
FYE: December 31
Type: Private - Partnershi

Greenberg Traurig is known for its entertainment practice but show business isn't the firm's only legal business. Its 1800-plus lawyers maintain a wide range of practices including corporate and securities intellectual property labor and employment litigation and real estate. The firm has about 30 offices mainly in the US but also in Latin America Europe and Asia. It extends its network in Europe and Asia via strategic alliances. In the U.K. the firm operates as Greenberg Traurig Maher LLP. Greenberg Traurig was founded in 1967 by Mel Greenberg.

GREEN MOUNTAIN POWER CORPORATION

163 Acorn Ln.
Colchester VT 05446
Phone: 802-864-5731
Fax: 651-293-3622
Web: www.gtservicing.com

CEO: –
CFO: Dawn D Bugbee
HR: –
FYE: December 31
Type: Subsidiary

Public utility Green Mountain Power (GMP) lights up the hills of Vermont supplying electricity to more than 250000 customers in the state. The utility also markets wholesale electricity in New England. The company operates several thousand miles of transmission and distribution lines and owns a minority stake in high-voltage transmission operator Vermont Electric Power (VELCO). About half of the generation capacity GMP taps is from hydroelectric and other renewable energy sources. GMP is an indirect subsidiary of Canada's GazMetro. The company absorbed Central Vermont Public Service's assets in 2012.

GREENBRIER COMPANIES INC (THE)   NYS: GBX

One Centerpointe Drive, Suite 200
Lake Oswego, OR 97035
Phone: 503 684-7000
Fax: 503 684-7553
Web: www.gbrx.com

CEO: William A. (Bill) Furman
CFO: Lorie L. Tekorius
HR: –
FYE: August 31
Type: Public

On land and by sea: Greenbrier Companies' recipe for growth involves the manufacturing of freight cars and marine barges. Through its primary Manufacturing segment Greenbrier produces 100-ton-capacity boxcars; intermodal and conventional railcars; center-partition flat and tank cars; and marine vessels. Its Wheels & Parts segment repairs and services wheels and offers railcar refurbishment and parts in nearly 40 locations. Its Leasing & Services unit manages a fleet of about 9300 railcars. Alan James and William Furman founded The Greenbrier Companies in 1981.

	Annual Growth	08/11	08/12	08/13	08/14	08/15
Sales ($ mil.)	20.3%	1,243.3	1,807.7	1,756.4	2,204.0	2,605.3
Net income ($ mil.)	133.7%	6.5	58.7	(11.0)	111.9	192.8
Market value ($ mil.)	24.5%	502.4	417.7	652.4	2,067.4	1,205.4
Employees	15.4%	6,032	7,396	7,959	9,244	10,689

GREEN PLAINS INC.   NMS: GPRE

450 Regency Parkway, Suite 400
Omaha, NE 68114
Phone: 402 884-8700
Fax: –
Web: www.gpreinc.com

CEO: Todd A. Becker
CFO: Jerry L. Peters
HR: Mark Hudak
FYE: December 31
Type: Public

It's plain to Green Plains that with stratospheric oil prices there is green to be made in ethanol production. The company operates a dozen ethanol facilities in Indiana Iowa Nebraska Michigan and Tennessee. The vertically integrated Green Plains has the annual capacity to produce 1 billion gallons of ethanol. It also sells ethanol produced by others. In addition Green Plains' plants when operating at full capacity produce about 2.9 million tons of animal feed known as distillers grains the primary co-product of ethanol production. Another co-product is corn oil sold to biodiesel manufacturers and feed lot markets.

	Annual Growth	12/10	12/11	12/12	12/13	12/14
Sales ($ mil.)	11.0%	2,133.0	3,553.7	3,476.9	3,041.0	3,235.6
Net income ($ mil.)	35.0%	48.0	38.4	11.8	43.4	159.5
Market value ($ mil.)	21.8%	423.5	367.1	297.5	728.9	932.0
Employees	8.6%	605	665	529	710	840

GREENE COUNTY BANCORP INC   NAS: GCBC

302 Main Street
Catskill, NY 12414
Phone: 518 943-2600
Fax: –
Web: www.tbogc.com

CEO: –
CFO: Michelle M Plummer
HR: Jason Meeks
FYE: June 30
Type: Public

This company helps put the "green" in upstate New York. Greene County Bancorp is the holding company for The Bank of Greene County serving New York's Catskill Mountains region from about a dozen branches. Founded in 1889 as a building and loan association the bank offers traditional retail products such as savings NOW checking and money market accounts; IRAs; and CDs. Real estate loans make up about 85% of the bank's lending activities; it also writes business and consumer loans. Through affiliations with Fenimore Asset Management and Essex Corp. Greene County Bancorp offers investment products. Subsidiary Greene County Commercial Bank is a state-chartered limited purpose commercial bank.

	Annual Growth	06/11	06/12	06/13	06/14	06/15
Assets ($ mil.)	7.8%	547.5	590.7	633.6	674.2	738.6
Net income ($ mil.)	8.0%	5.3	5.8	6.4	6.5	7.2
Market value ($ mil.)	12.7%	74.7	78.8	90.8	112.1	120.3
Employees	1.5%	128	130	131	133	136

GREENE TWEED & CO. INC.

2075 Detwiler Rd.
Kulpsville PA 19443-0305
Phone: 215-256-9521
Fax: 215-256-0189
Web: www.gtweed.com

CEO: Felix Paino
CFO: William Maher
HR: Shelita Allen
FYE: December 31
Type: Private

If Ralph Waldo Emerson were writing today he might put to paper "Build a better valve or gasket and the world will beat a path to your door." Greene Tweed & Co. (Greene Tweed) manufactures next generation technology seals gaskets fiber optic connectors and custom engineered plastic components for use in aerospace and defense medical and pharmaceutical nuclear and chemical industries. The company's products are also at the heart of the petrochemical oilfield OEM industrial hydraulics semiconductor and solar markets. Greene Tweed's facilities are located in the Americas Asia and Europe. It answers its door to customers such as Airbus Boeing Bayer and the DoD among others.

GREENHECK FAN CORPORATION

P.O. Box 410
Schofield WI 54476
Phone: 715-359-6171
Fax: 715-355-2444
Web: www.greenheck.com

CEO: James McIntyre
CFO: Gary M Stroyny
HR: Sarah Casey
FYE: March 31
Type: Private

Breathe deep; Greenheck Fan does a heck of a job. The employee-owned company one of Wisconsin's largest manufacturers makes industrial ventilation equipment including fans ventilators and dampers. Precision Coils Valent Accurate and other affiliates supply louvers heating and cooling coils air-handling systems and related offerings. Greenheck Fan operates plants in the US as well as Asia and Mexico and it is supported by a distribution network in the US and a global sales force. Products are used primarily behind walls or on the roofs of offices hotels malls schools and industrial plants. Brothers Bob and Bernie Greenheck founded the company as a small sheet metal shop in 1947.

GREENHILL & CO INC

NYS: GHL

300 Park Avenue
New York, NY 10022
Phone: 212 389-1500
Fax: -
Web: www.greenhill.com

CEO: Scott L. Bok
CFO: Christopher Grubb
HR: -
FYE: December 31
Type: Public

It's no secret what the favorite color is at Greenhill & Co. The investment bank specializes in mergers and acquisitions advisory restructurings and capital raising for corporate clients and governments around the globe. To avoid potential conflicts of interest and focus solely on the client it does not engage in lending or capital markets services such as securities underwriting research and trading unlike many of its rivals. Greenhill mainly advises companies in the industrial consumer & retail healthcare and communications sectors. Its top clients include Alcoa AT&T GlaxoSmithKline London Stock Exchange Tesco Visa and Wells Fargo among others.

	Annual Growth	12/10	12/11	12/12	12/13	12/14
Sales ($ mil.)	(0.3%)	278.3	294.0	285.1	287.2	275.2
Net income ($ mil.)	5.9%	34.5	44.6	42.1	46.7	43.4
Market value ($ mil.)	(14.5%)	2,294.1	1,021.5	1,460.2	1,627.3	1,224.6
Employees	(1.4%)	323	316	324	319	305

GREENHUNTER RESOURCES, INC

ASE: GRH

1048 Texan Trail
Grapevine, TX 76051
Phone: 972 410-1044
Fax: 972 410-1066
Web: www.greenhunterenergy.com

CEO: -
CFO: Ronald McClung
HR: Meredith Hohenberger
FYE: December 31
Type: Public

Searching for its share of the green GreenHunter Energy has renewable energy in its sights. Focusing on wind biomass (plant material and animal waste) and biofuels the company owns generation projects and refineries in California Wyoming and Texas. Its biofuels group the only segment producing revenue refines processes and stores biofuels at the company's Houston plant. It uses purchased methanol to create biodiesel up to 105 million gallons per year. GreenHunter's other operations include a biomass plant in California (currently being refurbished) and three development-stage wind energy projects in Wyoming and Texas. The company began operations in 2007 when it purchased the biofuels plant.

	Annual Growth	12/10	12/11	12/12	12/13	12/14
Sales ($ mil.)	190.6%	–	1.1	17.1	25.7	27.1
Net income ($ mil.)	–	20.6	(4.8)	(17.6)	(9.9)	(6.8)
Market value ($ mil.)	(2.9%)	29.0	31.2	58.1	41.6	25.8
Employees	94.3%	8	–	164	134	114

GREENPAGES INC.

33 Badgers Island West
Kittery ME 03904
Phone: 207-439-7310
Fax: 207-439-7334
Web: www.greenpages.com

CEO: Ron Dupler
CFO: Stephen Manero
HR: -
FYE: December 31
Type: Private

No GreenPages isn't the environmentally conscious version of the Yellow Pages. The company which does business as GreenPages Technology Solutions provides information technology consulting project management and systems integration services in the eastern US. It focuses on cloud computing and virtualization among other areas and installs and supports hardware and software products from such vendors as Hewlett-Packard Cisco and VMware. GreenPages also offers managed network services related to network security server management and technical support. The employee-owned company targets clients in the financial services and health care industries among others as well as public sector agencies.

GREENSHIFT CORP

NBB: GERS

5950 Shiloh Road East, Suite N
Alpharetta, GA 30005
Phone: 770 886-2734
Fax: -
Web: www.greenshift.com

CEO: Kevin Kreisler
CFO: Kevin Kreisler
HR: -
FYE: December 31
Type: Public

In a case of modern alchemy GreenShift (formerly GS CleanTech) is working overtime to turn organic material into biodiesel. The company's proprietary technologies are used to produce biomass-derived end products and at reduced cost and risk by extracting and refining raw materials that other producers cannot access or process. GreenShift owns and operates four proprietary corn oil extraction facilities one biodiesel production facility and one vegetable oilseed crushing plant. GreenShift claims that its technologies have the capability of extracting more than 6.5 million gallons of crude corn oil for every 100 million gallons of corn ethanol produced. The company also produces culinary oil.

	Annual Growth	12/10	12/11	12/12	12/13	12/14
Sales ($ mil.)	13.3%	7.7	20.0	14.5	15.5	12.8
Net income ($ mil.)	–	(12.1)	7.9	2.5	(4.4)	2.0
Market value ($ mil.)	–	0.0	0.7	0.4	0.0	0.0
Employees	(8.1%)	14	15	13	13	10

GREENSTONE FARM CREDIT SERVICES ACA

3515 WEST RD
EAST LANSING, MI 488237312
Phone: 517-324-0213
Fax: –
Web: www.greenstonefcs.com

CEO: –
CFO: –
HR: Bethany Barker
FYE: December 31
Type: Private

One of the largest associations in the Farm Credit System GreenStone offers FARM CREDIT SERVICES (FCS) provides short intermediate and long-term loans; equipment and building leases; appraisal services; and life and crop insurance to farmers in Michigan and Wisconsin. It serves about 15000 members and has nearly 40 locations. Through an alliance with AgriSolutions a farm software and consulting company Greenstone provides income tax planning and preparation services farm business consulting and educational seminars. FCS Mortgage provides residential loans for rural properties as well as loans for home improvement construction and refinancing.

	Annual Growth	12/03	12/04	12/05	12/06	12/07
Assets ($ mil.)	17.0%	–	–	–	3,691.3	4,317.3
Net income ($ mil.)	8.9%	–	–	–	63.9	69.6
Market value ($ mil.)	–	–	–	–	–	–
Employees		–	–	–	–	380

GREENVILLE HOSPITAL SYSTEM

701 Grove Rd.
Greenville SC 29605-5601
Phone: 864-455-7000
Fax: 864-455-6218
Web: www.ghs.org

CEO: Michael C Riordan
CFO: Susan J Bichel
HR: –
FYE: September 30
Type: Private - Not-for-Pr

From education and research to primary care and surgery Greenville Hospital System (GHS) is out to keep residents of the "Golden Strip" (the corridor connecting Charlotte North Carolina and Atlanta) healthy. Founded in 1912 the system encompasses six campuses with some 1300 inpatient beds. Its flagship facility is Greenville Memorial Hospital a tertiary referral and academic medical center with more than 700 beds; other facilities include several smaller community hospitals a nursing home and a long-term acute care hospital. GHS offers a full range of services including a primary care physician network outpatient services and home health care.

GREENWAY MEDICAL TECHNOLOGIES INC.   NYSE: GWAY

121 Greenway Blvd.
Carrollton GA 30117
Phone: 770-836-3100
Fax: 770-836-3200
Web: www.greenwaymedical.com

CEO: Wyche T Green III
CFO: James A Cochran
HR: –
FYE: June 30
Type: Public

Greenway Medical Technologies sees a lot of green in the health care market. The company provides doctor-centered software and services designed to integrate the clinical and business sides of physician practices. Its Web-based PrimeSUITE software is used to automate practice management electronic health records (EHR) and managed care functions as well as to link patient chart records to billing processes. Customers include some 33000 health care providers. Greenway was involved in creating definitions and certification standards related to EHR in the health IT portion of the federal stimulus bill the American Recovery and Reinvestment Act of 2009. It filed an IPO seeking $100 million in 2011.

GREIF INC   NYS: GEF

425 Winter Road
Delaware, OH 43015
Phone: 740 549-6000
Fax: –
Web: www.greif.com

CEO: Peter G. (Pete) Watson
CFO: Lawrence A. (Larry) Hilsheimer
HR: Getitia Matheny
FYE: October 31
Type: Public

Unlike a box of chocolates with Greif (rhymes with "life") you know what you're going to get. The company produces rigid industrial packaging products including steel plastic and fibre drums and related closure systems. Greif also makes flexible intermediate bulk containers (based on polypropylene woven fabric) used to ship an array of bulk industrial and consumer goods. It sells corrugated products and containerboard as well for packaging home appliances and small machinery and grocery and building products. Greif caters to a diverse group of industries from chemical to food and beverage petroleum agricultural and pharmaceutical. It traces its history back to 1877.

	Annual Growth	10/11	10/12	10/13	10/14	10/15
Sales ($ mil.)	(3.9%)	4,248.0	4,269.5	4,353.4	4,239.1	3,616.7
Net income ($ mil.)	(20.1%)	176.0	126.1	147.3	91.5	71.9
Market value ($ mil.)	(7.5%)	2,141.1	2,006.3	2,557.5	2,106.7	1,567.3
Employees	(4.3%)	15,660	13,560	13,085	13,325	13,150

GREY GLOBAL GROUP INC.

200 5th Ave.
New York NY 10010
Phone: 212-546-2000
Fax: 212-546-2001
Web: www.grey.com

CEO: Jim Heekin
CFO: Robert Oates
HR: –
FYE: December 31
Type: Subsidiary

Advertising expertise is certainly no gray area for this company. A unit of UK-based conglomerate WPP Group Grey Global Group provides advertising and marketing services in more than 50 countries in Asia Pacific Europe the Middle East Africa Latin America and North America. Its flagship agency network Grey Worldwide offers creative ad development and campaign management services along with a variety of other marketing disciplines. The firm also offers specialized public relations and communications services through Grey Healthcare. Its G2 Worldwide is a leading brand development agency while G2 Direct & Digital offers direct marketing services. It was originally founded in 1917 as Grey Advertising.

GREY HEALTHCARE GROUP INC.

114 5th Ave.
New York NY 10011
Phone: 212-886-3000
Fax: 212-886-3297
Web: www.ghgroup.com

CEO: –
CFO: –
HR: –
FYE: December 31
Type: Subsidiary

This firm helps get the word out about all the colored little pills. Grey Healthcare Group is a leading advertising and marketing business focused on serving the pharmaceutical and health care industries. Through more than 40 offices spanning 20 countries around the globe it operates through several subsidiary agencies including GHG Advertising Nova Grey Newton Grey Phase Five Communications (medical education and meeting management) Avenue Grey (direct-to-patient marketing) Insight Medical Communications and OnCall (contract sales). Grey Healthcare is a unit of Grey Group which itself is a division of UK-based communications services giant WPP Group.

GREYHAWK NORTH AMERICA LLC

260 Crossways Park Dr.
Woodbury NY 11797
Phone: 516-921-1900
Fax: 516-921-5649
Web: www.greyhawk.com

CEO: –
CFO: Ronald Kerins
HR: –
FYE: December 31
Type: Private

GREYHAWK North America provides construction consulting services including project management cost estimating claims assessment contract administration and IT services. The company also provides expert witnesses for litigation support. GREYHAWK operates from its offices in Manasquan and Moorestown New Jersey; Woodbury and New York City New York; and Houston. The firm also has an office in London. President and CEO Gary Berman and principals Steve Tell and Rick Fennema started the company in 1996. In 2009 consultancy Berger Group Holding (BGHi) acquired a non-controlling interest in GREYHAWK. BGHi became a major shareholder and is represented on the company's board of directors.

GREYLOCK MANAGEMENT CORPORATION

880 Winter St.
Waltham MA 02451
Phone: 781-622-2200
Fax: 781-622-2300
Web: www.greylock.com

CEO: –
CFO: –
HR: –
FYE: December 31
Type: Private

Greylock Management believes it holds the key to venture capital investing. Also doing business as Greylock Partners the firm provides funding to development-stagecompanies involved in such sectors as information technology enterprise software semiconductors the Internet clean technology and consumer services with a focus on the San Francisco Bay area and Boston as well as emerging markets like China India and Israel. Its current portfolio consists of interests in some 50 firms including interests in Digg Facebook LinkedIn Pandora Red Bend Software Zend and Zipcar.

GREYSTONE LOGISTICS INC.   OTC: GLGI

1613 E. 15th St.
Tulsa OK 74120
Phone: 918-583-7441
Fax: 918-583-7442
Web: www.greystonelogistics.com

CEO: Warren F Kruger
CFO: William W Rahhal
HR: –
FYE: May 31
Type: Public

If you need plastic pallets then Greystone Logistics is the logical choice for you. The company manufactures and sells plastic pallets for various commercial applications. Its products include the Greystone Beverage Pallet Hawker Series fire-retardant plastic pallets Tank picture frame pallets and the Granada Series (including nestable and flat-deck plastic pallets). Greystone Logistics also offers multi-station plastic injection molding systems. The company uses a proprietary recycled resin mix and manufacturing process to produce its plastics. It serves customers in the pharmaceutical beverage and other industries primarily in the US.

GRIFFIN INDUSTRIAL REALTY INC   NMS: GRIF

One Rockefeller Plaza
New York, NY 10020
Phone: 212 218-7910
Fax: –
Web: www.grifland.com

CEO: Michael S Gamzon
CFO: Anthony J Galici
HR: –
FYE: November 30
Type: Public

Griffin Land & Nurseries has forsaken plants in favor of the dirt underneath. Following the sale of its Imperial Nurseries subsidiary which grew and distributed container-based plants to garden center operators and the garden departments of retail chain stores the company's sole business is real estate. Subsidiary Griffin Land owns about 30 buildings comprising approximately 2.5 million square feet. The company also owns a small stake in Centaur Media a business information publisher in the UK. Griffin Land & Nurseries was founded in 1970 and is controlled by the Cullman and Ernst families. It is one of the largest private landowners in Connecticut.

	Annual Growth	11/10*	12/11	12/12*	11/13	11/14
Sales ($ mil.)	(9.2%)	35.6	37.2	36.6	25.5	24.2
Net income ($ mil.)	–	(4.5)	(2.5)	1.0	(5.8)	(1.1)
Market value ($ mil.)	(0.5%)	146.6	137.8	130.6	169.9	143.6
Employees	(29.3%)	104	103	99	99	26

*Fiscal year change

GRIFFITH LABORATORIES INC.

1 Griffith Center
Alsip IL 60803
Phone: 708-371-0900
Fax: 708-389-4055
Web: www.griffithlaboratories.com

CEO: D L Griffith
CFO: Joseph R Maslick
HR: Jamie Mathieson
FYE: September 30
Type: Private

A little pinch here a little pinch there pretty soon you have a business. Founded in 1919 Griffith Laboratories is a food-ingredient manufacturer with operations and customers worldwide. The company's clients include food manufacturers; foodservice operators such as restaurants hotels and cruise lines; and food retailers and wholesalers. Its products include seasonings sauce and soup mixes condiments texturizers and bakery blends. Griffith's subsidiaries include Custom Culinary (food bases and mixes) and Innova (meat and savory flavors). The company also offers customized ingredient services.

GRIFFON CORP.   NYS: GFF

712 Fifth Avenue, 18th Floor
New York, NY 10019
Phone: 212 957-5000
Fax: –
Web: www.griffoncorp.com

CEO: Ronald J. Kramer
CFO: Douglas J. Wetmore
HR: –
FYE: September 30
Type: Public

Griffon has its talons in a number of businesses. Its largest Clopay Plastic Products develops and produces thin-gauge embossed and printed films used in infant diapers adult incontinence products medical gowns and surgical drapes. A Home & Building Products segment makes residential and commercial garage doors (Clopay Building) and lawn and garden tools (Ames True Temper). Home Depot is a big customer. Clopay units are part of subsidiary Clopay Corp. Information communication and sensor systems made by Telephonics are sold to the US Department of Defense and Homeland Security other government agencies and defense contractors such as Lockheed Martin and Boeing.

	Annual Growth	09/11	09/12	09/13	09/14	09/15
Sales ($ mil.)	2.4%	1,830.8	1,861.1	1,871.3	1,991.8	2,016.0
Net income ($ mil.)	–	(7.4)	17.0	3.8	(0.2)	34.3
Market value ($ mil.)	17.8%	395.4	497.9	606.2	550.6	762.4
Employees	0.4%	5,900	5,400	5,400	6,100	6,000

GRILL CONCEPTS INC.
PINK SHEETS: GLLC

6300 Canoga Ave. Ste. 600
Woodland Hills CA 91367
Phone: 818-251-7000
Fax: 818-999-4745
Web: www.dailygrill.com

CEO: Bob Spivak
CFO: Wayne Lipschitz
HR: Kevin McAndrews
FYE: December 31
Type: Public

You might say this company is cooking up some classics on a daily basis. Grill Concepts operates a chain of more than 20 Daily Grill restaurants offering upscale casual dining in a setting reminiscent of a classic American grill during the 1930s and 1940s. Located primarily in California the restaurants serve such fare as chicken pot pie meatloaf and cobbler as well as steak seafood and pasta. In addition to its company-owned locations Grill Concepts has a small number of licensed and managed units operating in shopping areas and hotels. The Daily Grill concept is based on the company's half dozen Grill on the Alley fine dining restaurants. CEO Robert Spivak co-founded the Daily Grill chain in 1984.

GROCERYWORKS.COM LLC

5912 Stoneridge Mall Rd. Bldg. C
Pleasanton CA 94588
Phone: 925-467-3000
Fax: 925-467-3321
Web: groceryworks.com

CEO: –
CFO: Thomas Lo
HR: –
FYE: December 31
Type: Subsidiary

Grocery e-tailer GroceryWorks.com hopes shoppers stay home. The company is an online shopping and delivery service for bricks-and-mortar grocer Safeway and its subsidiaries Vons and Genuardis. Safeway.com operates in the San Francisco Bay Area and Sacramento California Portland Oregon Seattle Washington Phoenix Arizona and the District of Columbia. Vons.com does business in the Southern California and Nevada markets while Genuardis.com serves Philadelphia. GroceryWorks is now wholly owned by Safeway which purchased the 38% stake in the company previously held by the UK's leading grocery chain Tesco PLC in 2006. The move anticipated Tesco's entry into the US where it will compete with Safeway.

GRIMMWAY ENTERPRISES INC.

6900 Mountain View Rd.
Bakersfield CA 93307
Phone: 661-845-5200
Fax: 661-845-9585
Web: www.grimmway.com

CEO: Jeff Meger
CFO: Steve Barnes
HR: –
FYE: December 31
Type: Private

If Bugs Bunny were to visit Grimmway he would think he'd died and gone to heaven. The company which does business as Grimmway Farms produces everything carrot — from bagged carrots to carrot coins carrot juice carrot sticks and good ol' carrot bunches. It is in fact the world's largest producer of baby carrots under the Bunny Luv label; it sells organic vegetables under the Cal-Organic Farms name. The company processes the crops grown on some 40000 acres of California farmland. Grimmway's fresh carrots are sold at food retailers and foodservice operators worldwide. As if carrots weren't enough it also offers potatoes and citrus fruits. The family-owned company was formed by Rod and Bob Grimm in 1968.

GROEN BROTHERS AVIATION INC
NBB: GNBA

2640 West California Avenue
Salt Lake City, UT 84104-4593
Phone: 801 973-0177
Fax: –

CEO: David L Groen
CFO: David L Groen
HR: –
FYE: June 30
Type: Public

A centaur is part man part horse; a griffin is part eagle part lion; and a gyroplane is part helicopter part airplane. Through its subsidiaries Groen Brothers Aviation (GBA) develops and manufactures gyroplane and gyrodyne rotor-wing aircraft. Its Hawk series gyroplane is designed to be safer in low and slow flight than either an airplane or a helicopter. Gyroplanes get lift from rotary blades and thrust from a propeller. Potential applications for the Hawk series include commercial surveying fire patrol law enforcement and military surveillance. In 2012 GBA reached an agreement with its creditors to enter a period of financial restructuring and eliminate its debt of more than $170 million.

	Annual Growth	06/08	06/09	06/10	06/11	06/12
Sales ($ mil.)	(78.8%)	5.9	1.1	0.1	0.0	0.0
Net income ($ mil.)	–	(19.8)	(16.1)	(19.4)	(23.3)	(25.8)
Market value ($ mil.)	(15.9%)	8.6	2.7	1.7	2.9	4.3
Employees	16.7%	7	9	11	12	13

GRISTEDE'S FOODS INC.

823 11th Ave.
New York NY 10019
Phone: 212-956-5803
Fax: 212-247-4509
Web: www.gristedes.com

CEO: John Catsimatidis
CFO: Mark Kassner
HR: Renee Flores
FYE: November 30
Type: Private

New York City never sleeps but eating is another matter. Gristede's Foods feeds hungry New Yorkers through about 30 area supermarkets (most are located in Manhattan) including the newer Gristede's Mega Stores. The stores offer fresh meats produce dairy products baked goods frozen foods gourmet foods and nonfood items. Some of Gristede's supermarkets have in-store pharmacies; it offers online shopping through XpressGrocer.com. The firm owns City Produce Operating which supplies the supermarkets with groceries and produce and sells wholesale fresh produce to third parties. Gristede's Foods is 100%-owned by John Catsimatidis through his Red Apple Group.

GROSSMONT HOSPITAL CORPORATION

5555 GROSSMONT CENTER DR
LA MESA, CA 919423077
Phone: 619-740-6000
Fax: –
Web: www.sharp.com

CEO: Dan Gross
CFO: –
HR: –
FYE: September 30
Type: Private

Residents of the eastern San Diego community of La Mesa California depend on Grossmont for medical care. Grossmont Hospital is a 540-bed not-for-profit health care facility. The hospital which opened in 1955 has a staff of about 700 physicians. The full-service acute care facility provides specialty services in the areas of cardiology oncology mental health orthopedics pediatrics physical therapy sleep therapy hospice and women's health care. The Grossmont Hospital Corporation is a subsidiary of Sharp HealthCare; it operates the Grossmont Hospital through a lease agreement with state-owned Grossmont Hospital District.

	Annual Growth	09/03	09/04	09/08	09/09	09/13
Sales ($ mil.)	7.4%	–	327.0	452.4	500.5	621.6
Net income ($ mil.)	13.1%	–	–	37.3	41.5	69.1
Market value ($ mil.)	–	–	–	–	–	–
Employees		–	–	–	–	2,697

GROTE INDUSTRIES INC.

2600 Lanier Dr.
Madison IN 47250
Phone: 812-273-1296
Fax: 812-265-8440
Web: grote.com

CEO: –
CFO: –
HR: –
FYE: December 31
Type: Private

When it comes to vehicle safety Grote Industries provides illumination. The company manufactures a range of vehicle safety systems such as lamps emergency lighting reflectors wiring harnesses and mirrors. Other products include backup alarms flashers and turn signal switches. Grote's products are used on heavy-duty trucks industrial and military vehicles and agricultural machinery as well as passenger cars and pickups. The company counts automotive OEMs and automotive aftermarket retailers among its customers and has operations in Canada Germany Mexico and the US. The company was founded by William Grote in 1901 and is owned by the Grote family.

GROUP 1 AUTOMOTIVE, INC.

NYS: GPI

800 Gessner, Suite 500
Houston, TX 77024
Phone: 713 647-5700
Fax: 713 647-5858
Web: www.group1auto.com

CEO: Earl J. Hesterberg
CFO: John C. Rickel
HR: J. Brooks O'Hara
FYE: December 31
Type: Public

Group 1 Automotive is only one in a group of firms (AutoNation and Penske Automotive Group are the largest) striving to consolidate US auto sales. The company owns and operates more than 145 franchises at about 115 dealerships as well as about 28 collision service centers in about 15 US states. More than half of Group 1's dealerships are located in Texas Oklahoma and California. Group 1 Automotive also has 25 franchises at about 20 dealerships and several collision centers in the UK and 20 franchises at dealerships and five collision centers in Brazil. The company's dealerships offer new (more than 55% of sales) and used cars and light trucks under some 30 different brands. It also offers financing provides maintenance and repair services and sells replacement parts.

	Annual Growth	12/10	12/11	12/12	12/13	12/14
Sales ($ mil.)	15.9%	5,509.2	6,079.8	7,476.1	8,918.6	9,937.9
Net income ($ mil.)	16.6%	50.3	82.4	100.2	114.0	93.0
Market value ($ mil.)	21.0%	1,016.4	1,260.8	1,508.8	1,728.6	2,181.3
Employees	12.6%	7,454	8,267	9,343	11,510	11,978

GROUP HEALTH COOPERATIVE

320 Westlake Ave. North Ste. 100
Seattle WA 98109-5233
Phone: 206-448-5600
Fax: 206-448-4010
Web: www.ghc.org

CEO: Scott Armstrong
CFO: Richard Magnuson
HR: Cindy Johnson
FYE: December 31
Type: Private - Cooperativ

Group Health Cooperative gives new meaning to the term "consumer-driven health care." The organization is a not-for-profit managed health care group serving more than 600000 residents of Washington and Northern Idaho. Founded in 1947 and governed by a member-elected board the co-op offers health insurance through its Group Health Options and KPS Health Plans subsidiaries. It also operates a research institute and offers health care clinical services primarily through its affiliated Group Health Physicians organization. It also maintains partnerships with other health facility operators.

GROUP O INC.

4905 77TH AVE E
MILAN, IL 612643250
Phone: 309-736-8100
Fax: –
Web: www.groupo.com

CEO: Gregg Ontiveros
CFO: Bob Marriott
HR: –
FYE: December 31
Type: Private

The "O" in Group O stands for optimization. It also stands for Ontiveros the family that leads this company. Founded by chairman Robert Ontiveros Group O is one of the largest Hispanic-owned companies in the US. It helps big businesses improve their operations through three divisions: marketing packaging and supply chain. It offers everything from direct mail creation to shrink wrap procurement to warehousing and distribution and business intelligence. It has served clients from various industries including food and beverage (Kerry) consumer goods (P&G) manufacturing (Johnson Controls) pharmaceutical (Bristol-Myers Squibb) and telecommunications (AT&T).

	Annual Growth	12/02	12/03	12/04	12/05	12/13
Sales ($ mil.)	11.4%	–	–	–	240.4	569.5
Net income ($ mil.)	0.9%	–	–	–	5.3	5.6
Market value ($ mil.)	–	–	–	–	–	–
Employees	–	–	–	–	–	1,520

GROUPON INC.

NMS: GRPN

600 West Chicago Avenue, Suite 400
Chicago, IL 60654
Phone: 312 334-1579
Fax: –
Web: www.groupon.com

CEO: Rich Williams
CFO: Brian Kayman
HR: –
FYE: December 31
Type: Public

Savvy consumers get their coupon on with Groupon. Tapping into the power of collective buying the company helps businesses attract customers by offering them a unique way to save on things to eat see and do in almost 50 countries. In each participating city Groupon advertises a daily deal typically a half-off coupon for anything from a local restaurant or retail store to a hotel or spa; if enough consumers buy the coupon online by midnight the deal is on and the featured business can achieve a nice chunk in sales. It also sells merchandise in rotating categories via Groupon Goods. In late 2010 the company rejected a reported $5.3 billion buyout offer from Google. Groupon went public instead in late 2011.

	Annual Growth	12/10	12/11	12/12	12/13	12/14
Sales ($ mil.)	78.7%	312.9	1,610.4	2,334.5	2,573.7	3,191.7
Net income ($ mil.)	–	(389.6)	(279.4)	(54.8)	(95.4)	(73.1)
Market value ($ mil.)	(26.3%)	–	13,908.1	3,276.5	7,931.6	5,568.6
Employees	3.3%	10,418	11,471	11,394	11,283	11,843

GROWMARK INC.

1701 TOWANDA AVE
BLOOMINGTON, IL 617012057
Phone: 309-557-6000
Fax: –
Web: www.growmark.com

CEO: Jeff Solberg
CFO: Marshall Bohbrink
HR: Gary Swango
FYE: August 31
Type: Private

Retail farm-supply and grain-marketing cooperative GROWMARK can mark its growth by the grain. A member-owed agricultural co-op GROWMARK has more than 100000 members. Under the FAST STOP name the co-op runs more than 250 fuel stations and convenience stores in the Midwest. Its Seedway subsidiary sells commercial vegetable seed and farm seed for turf and grains including alfalfa corn wheat and soybeans. GROWMARK also offers fertilizer seeds ethanol biodiesel and farm financing. Its MID-CO COMMODITIES subsidiary trades grain and offers advice regarding futures and options.

	Annual Growth	08/10	08/11	08/12	08/13	08/14
Sales ($ mil.)	6.5%	–	8,597.2	10,057.4	10,171.2	10,372.3
Net income ($ mil.)	(18.3%)	–	–	249.6	189.8	166.6
Market value ($ mil.)	–	–	–	–	–	–
Employees	–	–	–	–	–	1,036

GRUNLEY CONSTRUCTION CO. INC.

15020 SHADY STE 500
ROCKVILLE, MD 20850
Phone: 240-399-2000
Fax: –
Web: www.grunley.com

CEO: Kenneth M Grunley
CFO: –
HR: –
FYE: December 31
Type: Private

Grunley gets it done from the monumental to the mundane. Founded in 1955 Grunley Construction Company provides general contracting engineering architectural and construction management services and specializes in the renovation restoration and modernization of historic buildings in the Washington DC area. Its projects range from prestigious undertakings — the Smithsonian Institution the Washington Monument and the US Treasury building — to more pedestrian endeavors such as office buildings apartment buildings schools and power plants. The company also has lent its services to the construction of embassies airports and military facilities.

	Annual Growth	12/07	12/08	12/09	12/10	12/11
Sales ($ mil.)	(46.5%)	–	–	1,129.8	310.5	324.0
Net income ($ mil.)	–	–	–	0.0	0.0	0.0
Market value ($ mil.)	–	–	–	–	–	–
Employees	–	–	–	–	–	320

GSI COMMERCE INC.

935 1st Ave.
King of Prussia PA 19406
Phone: 610-491-7000
Fax: 617-787-9355
Web: www.newbalance.com

CEO: –
CFO: –
HR: –
FYE: December 31
Type: Subsidiary

If you're not feeling generally secure in your e-commerce initiatives GSI Commerce aims to help. The company provides e-commerce services such as website development and maintenance order fulfillment payment processing and customer service. Its digital advertising offerings include brand development and e-mail marketing services. The company serves hundreds of companies and brands in markets such as retail consumer goods manufacturing and media. In 2011 GSI was acquired by auction powerhouse eBay. Under the terms of the deal eBay divested GSI's RueLaLa unit (online private sales business) and 70% of its ShopRunner operations (provides members-only online shopping and shipping services).

GSE HOLDING INC.
NYSE: GSE

19103 Gundle Rd.
Houston TX 77073
Phone: 281-443-8564
Fax: 281-230-8650
Web: www.gseworld.com

CEO: Robert Preston
CFO: Daniel C Storey
HR: –
FYE: December 31
Type: Public

GSE has a hold on containment. The plastics company makes and sells a variety of geosynthetic materials used for lining landfills water treatment ponds canals tanks and in other infrastructure applications. It produces smooth and textured geomembranes drainage products (geonets and geocomposites) synthetic clay liners and nonwoven textiles. Specialty products include curtain walls concrete embedment strips and aquaculture tank and tunnel liners. GSE's seven manufacturing plants in Thailand Germany the US Chile and Egypt support nearly 20 sales offices in a dozen countries. A subsidiary of containment specialist Gundle/SLT Environmental formed in 2004 GSE went public in early 2012.

GSI GROUP INC.
NASDAQ: GSIG

39 Manning Rd.
Billerica MA 01821
Phone: 978-439-5511
Fax: 978-663-0131
Web: www.gsig.com

CEO: –
CFO: Robert Buckley
HR: Anthony Bellantuoni
FYE: December 31
Type: Public

GSI Group's business is laser focused. The company uses its expertise in laser and motion control technologies to design and manufacture sets of products that are geared at different markets. Laser products are sold primarily to the industrial and scientific markets. GSI's precision motion and technologies unit supplies lasers optics encoders and spindles to the electronics medical and aerospace markets for high-precision cutting drilling marking and measuring. A third segment semiconductor systems designs laser-based systems that process wafers and integrated circuits. After a lengthy reorganization GSI emerged from Chapter 11 protection in 2010.

GSE SYSTEMS, INC.
ASE: GVP

1332 Londontown Blvd., Suite 200
Sykesville, MD 21784
Phone: 410 970-7800
Fax: –

CEO: Kyle J Loudermilk
CFO: Jeffery G Hough
HR: –
FYE: December 31
Type: Public

GSE Systems is into the appearance of power and control. The company provides simulation software to train power plant operators engineers and managers. Its systems used primarily for the nuclear power fossil energy and chemical industries can also be used to test new plant systems before they are installed. GSE Systems also offers training services through a partnership with General Physics. Customers include Slovenske electrarneAmerican Electric Power Emerson Process Management Statoil ASA and Westinghouse Electric. With international offices in China India Sweden and the UK GSE Systems generates about 70% of sales from customers located outside the US.

	Annual Growth	12/10	12/11	12/12	12/13	12/14
Sales ($ mil.)	(5.3%)	47.2	51.1	52.2	47.6	37.9
Net income ($ mil.)	–	(2.2)	2.8	1.2	(10.5)	(6.7)
Market value ($ mil.)	(18.6%)	64.8	34.9	38.6	28.6	28.4
Employees	7.8%	248	262	246	235	335

GSI TECHNOLOGY INC
NMS: GSIT

1213 Elko Drive
Sunnyvale, CA 94089
Phone: 408 331-8800
Fax: 408 331-9795
Web: www.gsitechnology.com

CEO: Lee-Lean Shu
CFO: Douglas Schirle
HR: –
FYE: March 31
Type: Public

GSI Technology makes very fast chips. The company's specialized SRAM (static random-access memory) integrated circuits are used in high-speed networking equipment. Marketed under the Very Fast brand its chips allow routers switches and other gear from the likes of Alcatel-Lucent and Cisco Systems to retrieve data at the speeds needed for broadband transmission. The fabless semiconductor company does most of its business through contract manufacturers such as Jabil Circuit (20% of sales) and Flextronics (9%) and through distributors such as Avnet (20%) and Nexcomm (11%). Other top customers include SMART Modular Technologies (11%) which buys memory chips for products it makes on behalf of Cisco.

	Annual Growth	03/11	03/12	03/13	03/14	03/15
Sales ($ mil.)	(14.0%)	97.8	82.5	66.0	58.6	53.5
Net income ($ mil.)	–	18.9	6.8	3.8	(6.2)	(5.0)
Market value ($ mil.)	(10.2%)	210.2	98.1	152.4	159.8	136.5
Employees	0.9%	133	137	140	138	138

GT ADVANCED TECHNOLOGIES INC.   NBB: GTAT Q

20 Trafalgar Square
Nashua, NH 03063
Phone: 603 883-5200
Fax: –
Web: www.gtsolar.com
CEO: David Keck
CFO: Kenwardev Raja Singh Bal
HR: –
FYE: December 31
Type: Public

GT Advanced Technologies (formerly GT Solar International) is a beacon on the path of the solar power supply chain. The company manufactures the equipment used by other companies to produce silicon wafers and solar cells. Key products include chemical vapor deposition (CVD) reactors used to produce polysilicon the raw material in solar cells; and directional solidification systems (DSS) the furnaces used to transform polysilicon into ingots which are sliced into silicon wafers to become solar cells. GT Advanced Technologies does most of its business in Asia primarily in Malaysia. In 2014 the company filed for Chapter 11 bankruptcy protection.

	Annual Growth	04/10	04/11*	03/12*	12/12	12/13
Sales ($ mil.)	(18.1%)	544.2	899.0	955.7	379.6	299.0
Net income ($ mil.)	–	87.3	174.8	183.4	(142.3)	(82.8)
Market value ($ mil.)	18.7%	700.6	1,399.8	1,112.0	407.4	1,171.8
Employees	12.1%	384	622	663	531	541

*Fiscal year change

GTC BIOTHERAPEUTICS INC.

175 Crossing Blvd. Ste. 410
Framingham MA 01702-9322
Phone: 508-620-9700
Fax: 508-370-3797
Web: www.gtc-bio.com
CEO: William Heiden
CFO: John B Green
HR: Dawn Curry
FYE: December 31
Type: Subsidiary

Transgenic manipulation is the name of the game at GTC Biotherapeutics. The firm makes its products by inserting human DNA into animals who then produce the protein in their milk; the proteins are purified from the milk and used for human treatments. This process of creating what are known as recombinant proteins makes it easier and cheaper to produce large quantities of certain therapeutic proteins. The company's first commercial product ATryn received European regulatory approval in 2006 and FDA approval in 2009; the product is a recombinant human antithrombin designed to help prevent blood clots. GTC is a wholly owned subsidiary of French firm LFB Biotechnologies.

GTCR GOLDER RAUNER LLC

6100 Sears Tower Ste. 5600
Chicago IL 60606
Phone: 312-382-2200
Fax: 312-382-2201
Web: www.gtcr.com
CEO: –
CFO: –
HR: –
FYE: December 31
Type: Private - Partnershi

GTCR Golder Rauner is a privately held investment firm that focuses on such industries as financial services health care technology and information services. Specializing in management-led industry consolidation deals the firm has invested more than $8.5 billion in capital in more than 200 companies and has taken about 40 of them public since its founding in 1980 by private equity guru Stanley Golder. The company also establishes partnerships with veterans of its target industries to launch or acquire companies in those fields. Its current portfolio includes stakes in some two dozen firms including APS Healthcare PrivateBancorp and Sorenson Communications.

GTSI CORP.   NASDAQ: GTSI

2553 Dulles View Dr. Ste. 100
Herndon VA 20171
Phone: 703-502-2000
Fax: 703-463-5101
Web: www.gtsi.com
CEO: Corry S Hong
CFO: Charles Hasper
HR: –
FYE: December 31
Type: Private

When the government goes shopping GTSI supplies the goods. The company resells computers software and networking products to US federal state and local governments. It offers products from vendors including Cisco Hewlett-Packard NetApp and Microsoft. Founded in 1983 GTSI also provides asset management consulting design integration maintenance procurement and support services. It offers financing through affiliate GTSI Financial and logistics services via another unit. Business with the federal government generates close to three-quarters of sales. GTSI also sells to prime government contractors. In 2012 the company was acquired for some $76.7 million by UNICOM Systems part of the UNICOM group.

GTT COMMUNICATIONS, INC   NYS: GTT

7900 Tysons One Place, Suite 1450
McLean, VA 22102
Phone: 703 442-5500
Fax: –
Web: www.gtt.net
CEO: Richard D. (Rick) Calder
CFO: Michael Bauer
HR: Mike Avis
FYE: December 31
Type: Public

GTT Communications (formerly Global Telecom & Technology) provides network integration for wide area network (WAN) dedicated Internet access and managed data services to system integrators telecom carriers and government agencies. GTT combines multiple networks and technologies such as traditional OC-x MPLS and Ethernet and has distribution partnerships with more than 800 technology suppliers including iPass for wireless services. Past customers include Avaya Lockheed Martin and Telefónica. GTT counts customers in about 80 countries; it earns almost half of its revenues outside the US. Chairman Brian Thompson owns nearly 31% of the company's stock.

	Annual Growth	12/10	12/11	12/12	12/13	12/14
Sales ($ mil.)	26.5%	81.1	91.2	107.9	157.4	207.3
Net income ($ mil.)	–	1.4	0.3	(1.6)	(20.8)	(23.0)
Market value ($ mil.)	78.6%	44.0	39.9	94.8	247.1	447.8
Employees	38.0%	81	88	97	189	294

GTX INC.   NASDAQ: GTXI

175 Toyota Plaza 7th Fl.
Memphis TN 38103
Phone: 901-523-9700
Fax: 901-523-9772
Web: www.gtxinc.com
CEO: Marc S Hanover
CFO: Jason T Shackelford
HR: –
FYE: December 31
Type: Public

GTx knows hormones are just as important to men as they are to women. The company develops therapies targeting estrogens and androgens for prostate cancer and other diseases. GTx is developing Capesaris a potential therapy that could cases of metastatic hormone-sensitive prostate cancer and castration resistant prostate cancer with a reduced occurance of side-effects such as osteoporosis and hot flashes. Another candidate Enobosarm aims to treat muscle wasting in patients with non-small cell lung cancer and other conditions.

GUADALUPE VALLEY TELEPHONE COOPERATIVE INC.

36101 FM 3159
NEW BRAUNFELS, TX 781325900
Phone: 830-885-4411
Fax: –
Web: www.gvtc.com

CEO: Ritchie Sorrells
CFO: Mark J Gitter
HR: –
FYE: December 31
Type: Private

Guadalupe Valley Telephone Cooperative (GVTC) offers telecommunications services to residential and business customers in the Hill Country area of south Texas. The cooperative local exchange carrier provides traditional local and long-distance telephone services Internet access digital cable television high speed Fiber-To-The-Business (FTTB) service and high-speed Fiber-To-The-Home (FTTH) converged service packages. GVTC also installs and monitors residential and commercial security systems and provides additional enterprise services such as its ID Vault information security service. Founded in 1951 GVTC also offers Web hosting technical support domain registration and Web scam alert services.

	Annual Growth	12/09	12/10	12/11	12/12	12/13
Sales ($ mil.)	2.6%	–	59.1	60.6	60.8	63.8
Net income ($ mil.)	15.5%	–	–	18.2	18.3	24.3
Market value ($ mil.)	–	–	–	–	–	–
Employees	–	–	–	–	–	229

GUARANTEE ELECTRICAL COMPANY

3405 BENT AVE
SAINT LOUIS, MO 631162601
Phone: 314-772-5400
Fax: –
Web: www.geco.com

CEO: Rick Oertli
CFO: Josh Voegtli
HR: –
FYE: September 30
Type: Private

Guarantee Electrical has been a power in St. Louis since it "guaranteed" to light up the 1904 World's Fair. (It delivered on the guarantee). Now a major US electrical contractor the company offers commercial institutional and industrial services including construction design/build communications/data and maintenance. Guarantee Electrical operates throughout the country and has worked on such varied projects as the MGM Grand in Las Vegas and several post office and prison facilities. Its GECO Systems division installs and services intercom closed-circuit television and other audio-visual systems. The Oertli family owns and operates the firm.

	Annual Growth	09/10	09/11	09/12	09/13	09/14
Sales ($ mil.)	12.1%	–	119.9	136.0	169.6	168.9
Net income ($ mil.)	–	–	–	0.0	0.0	0.0
Market value ($ mil.)	–	–	–	–	–	–
Employees	–	–	–	–	–	700

GUARANTEE TRUST LIFE INSURANCE COMPANY

1275 Milwaukee Ave.
Glenview IL 60025
Phone: 847-699-0600
Fax: 847-298-1215
Web: www.gtlic.com

CEO: –
CFO: –
HR: –
FYE: December 31
Type: Private - Mutual Com

Guarantee Trust Life Insurance (GTL) understands that life holds few guarantees. The mutual insurance company offers life credit life accident and health insurance primarily for senior citizens. Policies available include Medicare supplement insurance credit insurance and special risk policies for students of all ages. Subsidiary Cornerstone Senior Services provides consumers with long-term care and Medicare supplement insurance; VantageAmerica Solutions offers outsourced benefits administration services. GTL is licensed in 49 states the District of Columbia and Puerto Rico. Members of the Holson family have led the insurer since it was founded in 1936.

GUARANTY BANCORP (DE)   NMS: GBNK

1331 Seventeenth St., Suite 200
Denver, CO 80202
Phone: 303 675 1194
Fax: –
Web: www.gbnk.com

CEO: Paul W. Taylor
CFO: Christopher G. Treece
HR: –
FYE: December 31
Type: Public

Guaranty Bancorp knows a thing or two about dollars and cents. After all it's the holding company for Colorado's Guaranty Bank and Trust which operates more than 25 branches primarily in the metropolitan Denver and Northern Front Range areas. It offers traditional retail and commercial banking including deposit accounts loans and trust services. Residential and commercial mortgages and commercial and industrial loans (with a focus on the energy sector) make up most of the bank's portfolio. With $2 billion in assets Guaranty also originates construction consumer and agricultural loans and home equity lines of credit.

	Annual Growth	12/10	12/11	12/12	12/13	12/14
Assets ($ mil.)	3.2%	1,870.1	1,689.7	1,886.9	1,911.0	2,124.8
Net income ($ mil.)	–	(31.3)	6.4	15.1	14.0	13.5
Market value ($ mil.)	78.6%	30.7	31.8	42.2	303.9	312.3
Employees	0.9%	375	379	378	374	389

GUARANTY CHEVROLET INC.

20 Hwy. 99 South
Junction City OR 97448
Phone: 541-998-2333
Fax: 541-465-8061
Web: www.guarantycars.com

CEO: –
CFO: –
HR: –
FYE: December 31
Type: Private

It's a guarantee that you can find new Chevys at Guaranty. The company sells new and used cars and trucks from a handful of locations in Oregon and California. Its six RV showrooms offer new and used RVs as well as repair and maintenance services. With more than 60 brands Guaranty RV is one of the largest motorhome dealers on the West Coast and its boasts some 500 new and used vehicles in stock. It also has operations in Arizona. In addition to motorhomes trailers and vans the company also offers a travelers club for those who enjoy the RV lifestyle. Guaranty was founded in 1966 by GM and owner Shannon Nil's father Herb Nil.

GUARDIAN BUILDING PRODUCTS DISTRIBUTION INC.

979 Batesville Rd.
Greer SC 29651
Phone: 864-297-6101
Fax: 864-281-3498
Web: www.guardianbp.com

CEO: Thomas Highley
CFO: Wayne Feasby
HR: –
FYE: December 31
Type: Subsidiary

With products from Guardian Building Products Distribution (GBPD) some assembly is required. The company supplies building products through 50-plus distribution centers across North America. GBPD sells roofing millwork insulation vinyl siding and other materials for home improvement remodeling and new home and commercial construction. It also partners with other building products OEMs to supply building materials. The company's customers include builders building materials dealers contractors cooperatives and warehouse chains such as The Home Depot and Lowe's. GBPD is part of Guardian Building Products' group of companies owned by Guardian Industries one of the world's largest glassmakers.

GUARDIAN GLASS COMPANY

2300 Harmon Rd
Auburn Hills MI 48326-1714
Phone: 248-340-1800
Fax: 248-340-9988
Web: www.guardian.com/guardianglass/index.htm

CEO: William Davidson
CFO: –
HR: –
FYE: December 31
Type: Private

Guardian Glass is a leading global manufacturer of commercial residential automotive energy/solar and technical glass. The company's glass products include InGlass (interior glass) SunGuard (advanced architectural glass) ClimaGuard (residential glass) EcoGuard (glass for solar energy systems) and technical glass for electronics lighting and commercial refrigeration. Its glass performs a variety of functions for buildings such as insulate reflect heat save energy and beautify. Guardian Glass is a subsidiary and one of three business units operated by privately held Guardian Industries.

GUARDIAN LIFE INSURANCE CO. OF AMERICA (NYC)

7 Hanover Square, H-26-E
New York, NY 10004-2616
Phone: 212 598-8000
Fax: –
Web: www.guardianlife.com

CEO: Deanna Mulligan
CFO: Marc Costantini
HR: –
FYE: December 31
Type: Public

Guardian Life Insurance Company of America keeps a sharp eye on the investments of its policyholders. Guardian and its subsidiaries offer life insurance disability income insurance and retirement programs to individuals business owners and their employees. Its employee health indemnity plans provide HMO PPO and dental and vision plans as well as disability plans. Its Guardian Insurance & Annuity subsidiary offers retirement options that include mutual funds and annuity products which its Guardian Investor Services manages. Guardian also offers estate planning and education savings programs. The firm is a mutual company owned by its policyholders.

	Annual Growth	12/02	12/03	12/04	12/11	12/12
Assets ($ mil.)	1.0%	34,074.0	21,671.0	23,336.0	35,127.0	37,529.0
Net income ($ mil.)	–	(283.0)	218.0	286.0	196.0	253.0
Market value ($ mil.)	–	–	–	–	–	–
Employees	–	–	–	–	–	–

GUARDSMARK LLC

10 Rockefeller Plaza
New York NY 10020-1903
Phone: 212-765-8226
Fax: 212-603-3854
Web: www.guardsmark.com

CEO: Ira A Lipman
CFO: –
HR: –
FYE: June 30
Type: Private

When FBI agents leave Quantico the agency's training academy they go to Guardsmark. The company provides security services to companies in the financial health care transportation utility and other industries. It is also a leading employer of former FBI agents as well as former agents of the Secret Service the DEA state and local police forces and the military. Guardsmark offers security guards private investigation and drug testing services. In addition the company conducts background checks (employment education and criminal history) and consults with architects and builders to design security programs. Chairman and president Ira Lipman owns the company which he founded in 1963.

GUESS ?, INC.

NYS: GES

1444 South Alameda Street
Los Angeles, CA 90021
Phone: 213 765-3100
Fax: –
Web: www.guess.com

CEO: Victor Herrero Amigo
CFO: Sandeep Reddy
HR: David Kosten
FYE: January 31
Type: Public

Guess? wants you to get in its jeans and other attire and accessories. Founded to make flattering designer jeans the company manufactures trendy upscale apparel and accessories for men women and children under brands GUESS GUESS Kids Baby GUESS and GUESS by MARCIANO among others. Its trademark sexy ads featuring the likes of Claudia Schiffer are designed in-house. Guess? operates a noteworthy 1690 stores worldwide. It directly operates more than 830 stores and concessions in the US Canada Europe the Middle East and Asia. Another 800 stores and concessions are run by licensees in the same markets. To get more bang from its brand Guess? licenses its name for eyewear footwear jewelry and watches.

	Annual Growth	01/11	01/12*	02/13	02/14*	01/15
Sales ($ mil.)	(0.7%)	2,487.3	2,688.0	2,658.6	2,569.8	2,417.7
Net income ($ mil.)	(24.4%)	289.5	265.5	178.7	153.4	94.6
Market value ($ mil.)	(18.3%)	3,591.3	2,496.6	2,326.8	2,393.3	1,602.4
Employees	(2.2%)	15,000	14,300	15,200	14,600	13,700

*Fiscal year change

GUEST SERVICES INC.

3055 PROSPERITY AVE
FAIRFAX, VA 220312290
Phone: 703-849-9300
Fax: –
Web: www.guestservices.com

CEO: Gerard T. Gabrys
CFO: Nico Foris
HR: –
FYE: December 31
Type: Private

Guest Services satisfies hungry and sleepy patrons. The company provides contract food services and hospitality-management services nationwide. It operates cafeterias and onsite restaurants and offers catering to businesses hotels hospitals conference centers and government operations including the US Supreme Court the US House of Representatives and the National Park Service. For leisure and resort facilities Guest Services also provides special-event catering and offers management services such as marketing human resources procurement quality-assurance and information technology services. Guest Services was founded in 1917 as a private company to serve governmental agencies.

	Annual Growth	12/09	12/10	12/11	12/12	12/13
Sales ($ mil.)	3.8%	–	346.8	369.3	377.1	387.6
Net income ($ mil.)	1690.0%	–	–	0.0	2.5	2.3
Market value ($ mil.)	–	–	–	–	–	–
Employees	–	–	–	–	–	3,500

GUIDANCE SOFTWARE INC

NMS: GUID

1055 E. Colorado Blvd.
Pasadena, CA 91106
Phone: 626 229-9191
Fax: –
Web: www.guidancesoftware.com

CEO: Patrick Dennis
CFO: Barry J. Plaga
HR: Sandy Gyenes
FYE: December 31
Type: Public

Guidance Software could be the digital version of TV's CSI only in real life. The company provides applications that government authorities police agencies and corporate investigators use for digital forensic investigations information auditing e-discovery and incident response. The company's EnCase software is a forensics platform that helps organizations respond to threats and analyze information including court-validated forensics tools to conduct investigations. Founded in 1997 Guidance serves some two-thirds of FORTUNE 100 companies such as Apple BoeingCoca-Cola Facebook Whole Foods Yahoo! government agencies such as the CIA and NASA and international organizations such as NATO.

	Annual Growth	12/10	12/11	12/12	12/13	12/14
Sales ($ mil.)	4.3%	91.9	104.6	129.5	110.5	108.7
Net income ($ mil.)	–	(4.6)	(1.6)	(2.0)	(21.5)	(14.7)
Market value ($ mil.)	0.2%	211.2	190.4	348.7	296.7	213.0
Employees	1.9%	371	378	475	495	400

GUIDED THERAPEUTICS, INC.

OTC: GTHP

5835 Peachtree Corners East, Suite D
Norcross, GA 30092
Phone: 770 242-8723
Fax: –
Web: www.guidedinc.com

CEO: –
CFO: Gene S Cartwright
HR: –
FYE: December 31
Type: Public

Guided Therapeutics (formerly SpectRx) can shed some light on your condition. The firm is developing diagnostic products including a cervical cancer detection device using its proprietary biophotonic technology known as LightTouch. The technology uses optics and spectroscopy to provide doctors with non-invasive diagnostic methods for finding cancer. In order to zero in on its diagnostic business the company in 2007 sold its SimpleChoice line of insulin pumps which diabetics use to control blood glucose levels to ICU Medical; it changed its name to Guided Therapeutics the following year to reflect its new focus.

	Annual Growth	12/10	12/11	12/12	12/13	12/14
Sales ($ mil.)	(29.7%)	3.4	3.6	3.4	1.2	0.8
Net income ($ mil.)	–	(2.8)	(6.6)	(4.4)	(7.2)	(9.9)
Market value ($ mil.)	(26.8%)	77.5	147.3	65.9	46.5	22.3
Employees	8.9%	27	39	40	34	38

GUIDEONE INSURANCE

1111 Ashworth Rd.
West Des Moines IA 50265-3538
Phone: 515-267-5000
Fax: 515-267-5530
Web: www.guideone.com

CEO: Jim Wallace
CFO: –
HR: Alexandra Cannistra
FYE: December 31
Type: Private - Mutual Com

The spirit has guided this company towards churches across the US and the faithful that attend them. GuideOne provides personal and commercial lines of property/casualty and liability insurance including standard auto and homeowners coverage. The company targets churches of all faiths (it insures nearly 45000 — nearly a fifth of the nation's churches) as well as faith-based private schools and colleges and church-affiliated senior living facilities. GuideOne's FaithGuard products offer coverage for people who actively attend church. A network of more than 1500 independent and company agents sell its products. GuideOne was founded in 1947.

GUIDEWIRE SOFTWARE INC

NYS: GWRE

1001 E. Hillsdale Blvd., Suite 800
Foster City, CA 94404
Phone: 650 357-9100
Fax: 650 357-9101
Web: www.guidewire.com

CEO: Marcus S Ryu
CFO: Richard Hart
HR: –
FYE: July 31
Type: Public

Guidewire Software develops software for the insurance industry. The company's InsuranceSuite offers applications to property and casualty insurers for underwriting policy administration (PolicyCenter) claims management (ClaimsCenter) and billing (BillingCenter). Its software is intended to replace paper-based processes and legacy systems built around outdated programming languages. Its products can run on-premise or from the cloud. Guidewire counts some 210 customers in two dozen countries. It customers include Tokio Marine Nationwide Mutual and Zurich Financial Services.

	Annual Growth	07/11	07/12	07/13	07/14	07/15
Sales ($ mil.)	21.9%	172.5	232.1	300.6	350.2	380.5
Net income ($ mil.)	(27.4%)	35.6	15.2	15.4	14.7	9.9
Market value ($ mil.)	32.0%	–	1,822.0	3,107.2	2,875.7	4,192.9
Employees	18.3%	684	837	1,149	1,183	1,341

GUILFORD MILLS INC.

1001 Military Cutoff Rd. Ste. 300
Wilmington NC 28405
Phone: 910-794-5800
Fax: 816-854-8500
Web: www.hrblock.com

CEO: Matt Simoncini
CFO: –
HR: –
FYE: September 30
Type: Private

Guilford Mills makes fabrics to cover your ride and your hide. The textile maker produces fabrics for car and heavy truck cab interiors from bodycloth to headliners. Its specialty products group makes consumer and industrial fabrics including loop closure fabrics (used in medical braces) window coverings technical stretch pieces for athletic wear and even shoe linings and casket liners. Customers include Johnson Controls. Founded in 1946 Guilford Mills (aka Guilford Performance Textiles) has sales and manufacturing locations in the US Asia and Europe. Lear bought Guilford Mills from private equity firm Cerberus Capital Management its owner since 2005 for about $257 million in 2012.

GUITAR CENTER INC.

5795 Lindero Canyon Rd.
Westlake Village CA 91362
Phone: 818-735-8800
Fax: 818-735-8822
Web: www.guitarcenter.com

CEO: Darrell Webb
CFO: Tim Martin
HR: –
FYE: December 31
Type: Private

What AutoZone is to the garage Guitar Center is to the garage band. The #1 US retailer of guitars amps keyboards percussion and pro-audio equipment operates about 225 stores in more than 40 states. Major brands include Fender Gibson and Martin as well as Ampeg Crate and Vox. Stores also offer used and vintage instruments computer hardware and software and musician services (such as CD duplication and digital distribution). In addition to Guitar Center the firm runs about 100 Music & Arts Center stores that sell and rent band and orchestral instruments. Its Musician's Friend and Music 123 units sell merchandise online and by catalog. Guitar Center is owned by the private equity firm Bain Capital.

GULF ISLAND FABRICATION, INC.

NMS: GIFI

16225 Park Ten Place, Suite 280
Houston, TX 77084
Phone: 713 714-6100
Fax: 985 876-5414
Web: www.gulfisland.com

CEO: Kirk J. Meche
CFO: Jeffrey Favret
HR: –
FYE: December 31
Type: Public

Through its subsidiaries holding company Gulf Island Fabrication makes islands in the stream — the Gulf Stream that is. Its subsidiaries which operate under Gulf Island and Gulf Marine monikers make offshore drilling and production platforms for use mainly in the Gulf of Mexico. Products include jackets and deck sections of fixed production platforms hull and deck sections of floating production platforms piles subsea templates wellhead protectors and various production compressor and utility modules. Gulf Island also produces and repairs pressure vessels and refurbishes existing platforms. Reliant on a few key customers in 2013 94% of its backlog was accounted for by nine customers.

	Annual Growth	12/10	12/11	12/12	12/13	12/14
Sales ($ mil.)	19.5%	248.3	307.8	521.3	608.3	506.6
Net income ($ mil.)	4.0%	13.1	(1.8)	(4.1)	7.2	15.3
Market value ($ mil.)	(8.9%)	409.7	424.7	349.4	337.6	281.9
Employees	8.0%	1,250	1,950	2,200	1,900	1,700

GULF OIL LIMITED PARTNERSHIP

100 Crossing Blvd.
Framingham MA 01702
Phone: 508-270-8300
Fax: 626-440-2630
Web: www.parsons.com

CEO: Joe Petrowski
CFO: –
HR: –
FYE: September 30
Type: Private - Partnershi

Gulf Oil bridges the gap between petroleum producers and retail sales outlets. The petroleum wholesaler distributes gasoline and diesel fuel to more than 2500 Gulf-brand stations in 23 northeastern and southeastern states. Gulf Oil owns 12 storage terminals and operates a network of more than 50 other terminals. It also distributes motor oils lubricants and heating oil to commercial industrial and utility customers. The company has alliances with terminal operators in areas where it does not have a proprietary terminal. Gulf Oil boasts one of the oldest and most recognizable brands in the oil business. Regional convenience store chain and gas retailer Cumberland Farms controls the company.

GULF POWER COMPANY

NYS: GUA

One Energy Place
Pensacola, FL 32520
Phone: 850 444-6111
Fax: –
Web: www.gulfpower.com

CEO: S W Connally Jr
CFO: Richard S Teel
HR: –
FYE: December 31
Type: Public

Pensacola power users patronize Gulf Power. The regulated utility a subsidiary of The Southern Company transmits and distributes electricity to more than 436000 customers in eight counties in northwestern Florida. Gulf Power generates about 2060 MW of capacity from its fossil-fueled power plants and it operates about 1600 miles of transmission lines and more than 7720 miles of distribution lines in its service territory. The utility which serves more than 70 towns and cities also provides wholesale electricity to two distributors in Florida and it offers conservation programs outdoor lighting surge protection and other energy-related products and services.

	Annual Growth	12/10	12/11	12/12	12/13	12/14
Sales ($ mil.)	0.0%	1,590.2	1,519.8	1,439.8	1,440.3	1,590.5
Net income ($ mil.)	4.0%	127.7	111.2	132.1	132.1	149.2
Market value ($ mil.)	(4.4%)	–	159.2	149.7	124.4	139.2
Employees	1.0%	1,330	1,424	1,416	1,410	1,384

GULF STATES TOYOTA INC.

1375 Enclave Pkwy.
Houston TX 77077
Phone: 713-580-3300
Fax: 713-580-3332
Web: www.gstcareers.com

CEO: Thomas H Friedkin
CFO: –
HR: –
FYE: December 31
Type: Private

Even good ol' boys buy foreign cars from Gulf States Toyota (GST). One of only two US Toyota distributors not owned by Toyota Motor Sales (the other is JM Family Enterprises' Southeast Toyota Distributors) GST distributes Toyota Lexus and Scion brand cars trucks and sport utility vehicles in Arkansas Louisiana Mississippi Oklahoma and Texas. GST has expanded its vehicle processing center in Houston to handle Toyota Tundra pickup trucks built in nearby San Antonio. Founded in 1969 by its Chairman and owner Thomas Friedkin GST distributes new Toyotas parts and accessories to more than 150 dealers in Texas and other states in the region. GST accounts for 13% of Toyota sales in the US.

GULF UNITED ENERGY INC.

OTC: GLFE

1222 Barkdull St.
Houston TX 77006
Phone: 713-942-6575
Fax: 604-420-8711
Web: www.tenpeakscoffee.ca

CEO: –
CFO: David C Pomerantz
HR: –
FYE: August 31
Type: Public

The Gulf of Mexico unites this company's headquarters with its operations. Houston-based oil and gas company Gulf United Energy holds oil and gas leases on one project in Colombia and three in Peru. The exploration and development stage company doesn't have any producing wells (or revenue) but it is working with Upland Oil and Gas and SK Energy to look for resources on nearly 44 million acres. Gulf United owns between two and 40 percent working interests on the four projects. The company which was formed in 2003 exited the pipeline and liquefied natural gas business in 2010. John B. Connally III grandson of former Texas governor John B. Connally owns about 16% of Gulf United.

GULFMARK ENERGY INC.

4400 Post Oak Pkwy. Ste. 2700
Houston TX 77027
Phone: 713-881-3603
Fax: 713-881-3491
Web: www.adamsresources.com/index.php?option=com_co

CEO: –
CFO: Richard Abshire
HR: –
FYE: December 31
Type: Subsidiary

Gulfmark Energy a subsidiary of NFL franchise owner Bud Adams' Adams Resources & Energy makes its mark though energy delivery operations on the Gulf Coast. The company purchases crude oil and transports it to refiners and other customers in the US via a fleet of about 150 tractor-trailer rigs. It also maintains more than 50 pipeline inventory locations or injection facilities. The company purchases about 81600 barrels of crude oil per day from 3800 independent oil supply locations and sells more than 2.25 million barrels per month to local and regional refiners.

GULFMARK OFFSHORE, INC.

NYS: GLF

842 West Sam Houston Parkway North, Suite 400
Houston, TX 77024
Phone: 713 963-9522
Fax: 281 664-5057
Web: www.gulfmark.com

CEO: Quintin V. Kneen
CFO: James M. (Jay) Mitchell
HR: David (Dave) Darling
FYE: December 31
Type: Public

GulfMark Offshore makes its mark on the high seas. The company offers support services for the construction positioning and operation of offshore oil and natural gas rigs and platforms. Marine services include anchor handling; cargo supply and crew transportation; towing; and emergency services. Some of its ships conduct seismic data gathering and provide diving support. GulfMark Offshore serves both major oil companies and smaller independents. It owns manages or almost 80 vessels in the North Sea the Americas (Brazil Mexico and Trinidad) and Southeast Asia with occasional operations in the Mediterranean and off the coast of Africa.

	Annual Growth	12/10	12/11	12/12	12/13	12/14
Sales ($ mil.)	8.3%	359.8	381.9	389.2	454.6	495.8
Net income ($ mil.)	–	(34.7)	49.9	19.3	70.6	62.4
Market value ($ mil.)	(5.3%)	763.5	1,055.0	865.2	1,183.6	613.3
Employees	1.4%	1,700	1,700	1,850	2,000	1,800

GULFPORT ENERGY CORP.

NMS: GPOR

14313 North May Avenue, Suite 100
Oklahoma City, OK 73134
Phone: 405 848-8807
Fax: –
Web: www.gulfportenergy.com

CEO: Michael G. (Mike) Moore
CFO: Aaron Gaydosik
HR: –
FYE: December 31
Type: Public

Gulfport Energy put its energy into exploring for hydrocarbons near the Gulf of Mexico and elsewhere. The oil and gas exploration and production company' main producing properties are located along the Louisiana Gulf Coast in the Permian basin in West Texas in the Niobrara Shale Formation in western Colorado and in the Utica Shale in eastern Ohio. Additionally Gulfport Energy holds a sizeable acreage position in the Alberta oil sands in Canada through its interest in Grizzly Oil Sands ULC and it has interests in entities that operate in the Phu Horm gas field in northern Thailand. In 2012 the company reported proved reserves of 8.3 million barrels of oil and 33.8 trillion cu. ft. of natural gas.

	Annual Growth	12/10	12/11	12/12	12/13	12/14
Sales ($ mil.)	51.6%	126.9	229.3	248.9	262.8	671.3
Net income ($ mil.)	51.2%	47.4	108.4	68.4	153.2	247.4
Market value ($ mil.)	17.8%	1,857.0	2,522.6	3,273.8	5,407.4	3,575.3
Employees	45.7%	45	50	128	118	203

GULFSTREAM INTERNATIONAL GROUP INC.

PINK SHEETS: GIGIQ

3201 Griffin Rd. 4th Fl.
Fort Lauderdale FL 33312
Phone: 954-985-1500
Fax: 954-985-5245
Web: www.gulfstreamair.com/default.htm

CEO: –
CFO: –
HR: –
FYE: December 31
Type: Public

Going to the Bahamas on a Gulfstream isn't just for the jet set. Gulfstream International through subsidiary Gulfstream International Airlines provides service between Florida and the Bahamas with a fleet of about 20 turboprop aircraft. It serves about two dozen destinations. The regional airline no relation to business jet manufacturer Gulfstream Aerospace flies primarily under the Continental Connection brand on behalf of United Continental's carriers. It also is a code-sharing partner of Copa Airlines as well as offers charter services. In addition to its airline business Gulfstream International runs a pilot-training school. In late 2010 the company filed for Chapter 11 bankruptcy relief.

GUNDERSEN LUTHERAN INC.

1900 South Ave.
La Crosse WI 54601
Phone: 608-782-7300
Fax: 608-775-3199
Web: www.gundluth.org

CEO: Jeffrey E Thompson
CFO: Michael Allen
HR: –
FYE: December 31
Type: Private - Not-for-Pr

Gundersen Lutheran provides health care services to residents in about 20 counties in western Wisconsin northeastern Iowa and southeastern Minnesota. The medical provider is a regional health care system which includes the 325-bed Gundersen Lutheran Medical Center more than 20 community clinics nursing homes and a group medical practice representing multiple specialties. The health system also provides dental care vision care behavioral medicine home health care and air and ground emergency transportation service. In addition the Gundersen Lutheran Health Plan provide medical insurance coverage.

GUNDERSEN LUTHERAN MEDICAL CENTER INC.

1910 SOUTH AVE
LA CROSSE, WI 54601-5467
Phone: 608-782-7300
Fax: –
Web: www.gundersenhealth.org

CEO: Jeffery Thompson
CFO: Daryl Applebury
HR: –
FYE: December 31
Type: Private

At the heart of the Gundersen Lutheran health system Gundersen Lutheran Medical Center serves residents of nearly 20 counties that stretch across the upper Midwest. The clinical campus for the University of Wisconsin's medical and nursing schools operates a 325-bed teaching hospital with a Level II Trauma and Emergency Center. Focused on caring for patients in western Wisconsin the hospital boasts several specialty services such as bariatrics behavioral health cancer care orthopedics palliative care pediatrics rehabilitation and women's health. The physician-led not-for-profit medical center is affiliated with a group of regional clinics and specialty centers.

	Annual Growth	12/08	12/09	12/10	12/11	12/12
Sales ($ mil.)	(8.2%)	–	–	–	431.9	396.3
Net income ($ mil.)	134.2%	–	–	–	49.6	116.1
Market value ($ mil.)	–	–	–	–	–	–
Employees	–	–	–	–	–	4,500

GUNDLE/SLT ENVIRONMENTAL INC.

19103 Gundle Rd.
Houston TX 77073
Phone: 281-443-8564
Fax: 281-230-2504
Web: www.gseworld.com

CEO: Charles A Sorrentino
CFO: Ernest C English Jr
HR: –
FYE: December 31
Type: Private

Oil and water don't mix and Gundle/SLT Environmental (GSE) plans to keep it that way. GSE through its global subsidiaries manufactures and installs an array of flexible geosynthetic liners used to prevent groundwater contamination. Waste-management firms mining companies water and industrial businesses among many others use these liners at landfills water-containment facilities canals and aquaculture lagoons. GSE makes high-density polyethylene smooth-sheet liners as well as textured sheets and geosynthetic clay liners. The company has manufacturing and sales operations in the Americas Asia/Pacific and EMEA (Europe the Middle East and Africa). GSE is a subsidiary of GEO Holdings.

GUNTHER INTERNATIONAL LTD.

NBB: SORT

One Winnenden Road
Norwich, CT 06360
Phone: 860 823-1427
Fax: 860 886-0135
Web: www.guntherintl.com

CEO: –
CFO: –
HR: –
FYE: March 31
Type: Public

When customers want help with their document processing Gunther tells them to stuff it. Gunther International makes electronic publishing mailing and billing systems that automate the assembly of printed documents. Its equipment is used to staple bind match and insert documents into envelopes for distribution. Gunther targets insurance companies such as Allstate and Metropolitan Life as well as businesses in the government retail and service bureau sectors. Subsidiary inc.jet offers industrial inkjet printers that OEMs incorporate into other devices. Gunther International was established in 1977.

	Annual Growth	03/11	03/12	03/13	03/14	03/15
Sales ($ mil.)	4.6%	23.2	29.6	28.0	26.5	27.8
Net income ($ mil.)	–	(0.3)	(0.1)	0.6	4.1	0.7
Market value ($ mil.)	8.9%	4.2	5.9	2.6	3.0	5.9
Employees	–	–	–	–	–	–

GUSTAVUS ADOLPHUS COLLEGE

800 W COLLEGE AVE
SAINT PETER, MN 560821498
Phone: 507-933-7508
Fax: –
Web: www.gustavus.edu

CEO: –
CFO: –
HR: –
FYE: May 31
Type: Private

You don't have to enter the Pearly Gates to get into this St. Peter Minnesota university. However Gustavus Adolphus College is deeply rooted in its Evangelical Lutheran Church heritage. The private liberal arts coeducational school offers some 70 majors in about two dozen academic departments including education fine arts humanities and social sciences. It has a student population of about 2500 and a student/faculty ratio of 12-to-1. Gustavus Adolphus College was founded in 1862 by Swedish Lutheran immigrant and pastor Eric Norelius. It is named after 17th-century Swedish king Gustav II Adolf.

	Annual Growth	05/09	05/10	05/11	05/12	05/13
Sales ($ mil.)	(1.1%)	–	107.0	97.7	134.3	103.5
Net income ($ mil.)	4.3%	–	–	19.5	9.0	21.3
Market value ($ mil.)	–	–	–	–	–	–
Employees	–	–	–	–	–	700

GUTHRIE HEALTHCARE SYSTEM

GUTHRIE SQ
SAYRE, PA 18840
Phone: 570-888-6666
Fax: –
Web: www.guthrie.org

CEO: –
CFO: –
HR: –
FYE: June 30
Type: Private

Guthrie Healthcare System is a community health care organization serving residents of the Twin Tiers region of northern Pennsylvania and southern New York through a network of hospitals community clinics physicians' practices and specialty care facilities. The flagship facility is Robert Packer Hospital in Sayre Pennsylvania a 238-bed tertiary care teaching hospital (affiliated with Pennsylvania's Mansfield University) that provides a comprehensive range of health services including emergency/trauma care pediatric care orthopedics and rehabilitative care. The system also includes two additional hospitals nursing homes a senior care community a hospice care program and a home health agency.

	Annual Growth	06/06	06/07	06/08	06/10	06/11
Sales ($ mil.)	(1.3%)	–	–	52.7	56.7	50.7
Net income ($ mil.)	(6.1%)	–	–	17.7	24.6	14.7
Market value ($ mil.)	–	–	–	–	–	–
Employees	–	–	–	–	–	2,575

GUY CARPENTER & COMPANY LLC

1166 Avenue of the Americas
New York NY 10036
Phone: 917-937-3000
Fax: 917-937-3500
Web: www.guycarp.com

CEO: Andrew Marcell
CFO: Robert Pietrucha
HR: Catherine Sacks
FYE: December 31
Type: Subsidiary

Formed in 1923 as a cotton harvest reinsurer Guy Carpenter has become a top provider of intermediary services for insurance firms seeking to reinsure their risks. The reinsurance broker helps insurers find coverage for property/casualty life and annuity and accident and health policies. Its GC Analytics unit offers related services including catastrophe modeling reinsurance utilization and regulatory consulting while its GC Securities division provides alternative risk financing options. The company has some 20 offices in the US and about 35 international offices employing thousands of brokers worldwide. Guy Carpenter is a subsidiary of insurance brokerage giant Marsh & McLennan Companies (MMC).

GYRODYNE CO. OF AMERICA, INC.

NAS: GYRO

1 Flowerfield, Suite 24
St. James, NY 11780
Phone: 631 584-5400
Fax: 631 584-7075
Web: www.gyrodyne.com

CEO: –
CFO: –
HR: –
FYE: December 31
Type: Public

This Gyro has the wrap on real estate. Gyrodyne is a self-managed and self-administered real estate investment trust (REIT) that buys owns and manages a variety of property types. Its portfolio includes medical office parks and industrial properties as well as undeveloped land. Gyrodyne began as a helicopter maker working from its 68-acre Flowerfield site on Long Island New York but switched to real estate development as its helicopter business declined in the 1970s. Since then it has been converting its Flowerfield property for commercial industrial and residential use. The REIT has also acquired medical properties in New York and Virginia and owns a minority stake in a planned development in Florida.

	Annual Growth	12/09	12/10	12/11	12/12	12/13
Sales ($ mil.)	1.0%	4.8	5.6	5.5	5.0	5.0
Net income ($ mil.)	134.5%	1.5	(1.1)	(1.1)	99.0	46.1
Market value ($ mil.)	(25.8%)	62.1	119.1	151.2	106.8	18.8
Employees	(12.6%)	12	12	12	11	7

H&E EQUIPMENT SERVICES INC

NMS: HEES

7500 Pecue Lane
Baton Rouge, LA 70809
Phone: 225 298-5200
Fax: –
Web: www.he-equipment.com

CEO: John M. Engquist
CFO: Leslie S. Magee
HR: –
FYE: December 31
Type: Public

Whether you're a he or a she if you have a construction or industrial project that requires heavy lifting H&E Equipment Services can help. The company sells and rents new and used equipment for construction earthmoving and materials handling made by lift crane and truck manufacturers such as JLG Bobcat and Komatsu. H&E Equipment also offers a full slate of services including planned maintenance fleet maintenance on-site and mobile repair parts supply crane manufacturing and operator and safety training. The company serves some 36400 customers across more than 20 states through about 70 service centers.

	Annual Growth	12/10	12/11	12/12	12/13	12/14
Sales ($ mil.)	17.4%	574.2	720.6	837.3	987.8	1,090.4
Net income ($ mil.)	–	(25.5)	8.9	28.8	44.1	55.1
Market value ($ mil.)	24.8%	407.6	472.8	530.9	1,043.9	989.7
Employees	4.1%	1,616	1,646	1,744	1,775	1,900

H. C. SCHMIEDING PRODUCE CO. INC.

2330 N THOMPSON ST
SPRINGDALE, AR 727641709
Phone: 479-751-4517
Fax: –

CEO: –
CFO: Chris Gryskiewicz
HR: –
FYE: December 31
Type: Private

H. C. Schmieding Produce is a leading wholesale distributor of fresh fruits and vegetables. The company supplies primarily grocery store chains and independent retailers from two distribution centers in Arkansas and Florida. President Laurence Schmieding started the family-owned company in 1961 and heads a charitable organization called The Schmieding Foundation. Through their holding company Schmieding Enterprises the family also has interests in real estate.

	Annual Growth	12/07	12/08	12/09	12/12	12/13
Sales ($ mil.)	(2.3%)	–	108.6	108.1	103.4	96.4
Net income ($ mil.)	(30.9%)	–	–	1.4	0.6	0.3
Market value ($ mil.)	–	–	–	–	–	–
Employees	–	–	–	–	–	35

H. E. BUTT GROCERY COMPANY

646 S. Main Ave.
San Antonio TX 78204
Phone: 210-938-8000
Fax: 210-938-8169
Web: www.heb.com

CEO: Charles C Butt
CFO: Martin H Otto
HR: –
FYE: October 31
Type: Private

The Muzak bounces between Tejano and country and the warm tortillas and marinated fajita meat are big sellers at H. E. Butt Grocery (H-E-B). Texas' largest private company and the #1 food retailer in South and Central Texas H-E-B owns more than 335 supermarkets including a growing number of large (70000 sq. ft.) gourmet Central Market stores in major metropolitan areas and 80-plus smaller (24000-30000 sq. ft.) H-E-B-Pantry stores often in more rural areas. H-E-B also has about 40 upscale and discount stores in Northern Mexico. H-E-B processes some of its own bread dairy products meat and tortillas. The 100-year-old company is owned by the Butt family which founded H-E-B in Kerrville Texas in 1905.

H. J. RUSSELL & COMPANY

504 FAIR ST SW
ATLANTA, GA 303131206
Phone: 404-330-1000
Fax: –
Web: www.hjrussell.com

CEO: Michael B Russell
CFO: Ed Bradford
HR: –
FYE: December 31
Type: Private

H.J. Russell & Company one of the nation's largest minority-owned enterprises helps shape southeastern cities. It's a general contractor construction manager property manager and developer that specializes in affordable multi-family housing and mixed-use communities. It also has expertise in building airports hospitals office towers retail stores and schools. Its development arm Russell New Urban Development offers such services as feasibility analysis land development and asset management; it has more than $500 million in development underway. H.J. Russell also manages more than 6000 apartment and public housing units. The family-owned company was founded by chairman Herman J. Russell in 1952.

	Annual Growth	12/05	12/06	12/07	12/08	12/09
Sales ($ mil.)	–	–	–	(322.0)	222.2	170.9
Net income ($ mil.)	64434.9%	–	–	0.0	3.9	2.1
Market value ($ mil.)	–	–	–	–	–	–
Employees	–	–	–	–	–	733

H. LEE MOFFITT CANCER CENTER & RESEARCH INSTITUTE HOSPITAL INC.

12902 USF MAGNOLIA DR
TAMPA, FL 336129416
Phone: 813-745-4673
Fax: –
Web: www.moffitt.org

CEO: Alan F List
CFO: Yvette Tremonti
HR: –
FYE: June 30
Type: Private

The H. Lee Moffitt Cancer Center and Research Institute founded in 1986 is a National Cancer Institute-designated Comprehensive Cancer Center located on the Tampa campus of the University of South Florida. The institute carries it out its stated mission of "contributing to the prevention and cure of cancer" through patient care research and education. It operates a 210-bed medical and surgical facility as well as outpatient treatment programs and a blood and marrow transplant program. Its research programs include study in the areas of molecular oncology immunology risk assessment health outcomes and experimental therapeutics.

	Annual Growth	06/10	06/11	06/12	06/13	06/14
Sales ($ mil.)	4.7%	–	744.4	771.6	779.5	855.2
Net income ($ mil.)	–	–	–	(7.7)	26.2	50.2
Market value ($ mil.)	–	–	–	–	–	–
Employees	–	–	–	–	–	4,200

H.C. BRILL COMPANY INC.

1912 Montreal Rd.
Tucker GA 30084
Phone: 770-938-3823
Fax: 770-939-2934
Web: www.hcbrill.com

CEO: Robert Sharpe
CFO: George Batton
HR: Jo Webster
FYE: December 31
Type: Subsidiary

If you love ooey-gooey-good baked goods H.C. Brill has found your thrill. The company a subsidiary of Netherlands-based global ingredients giant CSM makes a wide variety of commercial bakery products including frozen doughs and batters icings and glazes powdered and liquid fillings whipped toppings and frozen cakes. It also makes consumer products such as prepared mixes for bread brownies cakes and puddings as well as fruit-based glazes and fillings. Brill is part of CSM Bakery Products North America unit which also oversees CSM's Best Brands Multifoods Henry & Henry Fantasia Karp's and Telco products.

H.D. VEST INC.

6333 N. State Hwy. 161 4th Fl.
Irving TX 75038
Phone: 972-870-6000
Fax: 972-870-6128
Web: www.hdvest.com

CEO: –
CFO: Ted Sinclair
HR: –
FYE: December 31
Type: Private

H.D. Vest oversees a network of more than 4800 tax professionals who provide money management services to approximately 2 million individuals and small businesses in every US state. The company provides training technology and operational support to its financial advisors as well as expertise in wealth management estate planning retirement planning and insurance planning. An investment group led by Parthenon Capital Partners and Lovell Minnick Partners acquired H.D. Vest from megabank Wells Fargo in 2011. Founded in 1983 by Herb D. Vest a certified public accountant who recognized his tax clients' need for financial advice the company was initially acquired by Wells Fargo in 2001.

H.D.R. INC.

8404 INDIAN HILLS DR
OMAHA, NE 68114-4098
Phone: 402-399-1000
Fax: –
Web: www.hdrinc.com

CEO: George A Little
CFO: Terrence C Cox
HR: –
FYE: December 29
Type: Private

With projects ranging from restoring the Pentagon and the Everglades to working on the Hoover Dam Bypass project HDR has left its mark on the US. HDR is an architecture engineering and consulting firm that specializes in such projects as bridges water- and wastewater-treatment plants and hospitals. The company also provides mechanical and plumbing services construction and project management and utilities planning. It has completed projects nationwide and in some 60 countries through its more than 200 global locations. The employee-owned company was founded as Henningson Engineering in 1917 to build municipal plants in the rural Midwest.

	Annual Growth	12/08	12/09	12/10	12/11	12/12
Sales ($ mil.)	5.8%	–	1,486.2	1,553.9	1,691.7	1,760.8
Net income ($ mil.)	72.5%	–	17.7	61.3	54.1	90.8
Market value ($ mil.)	–	–	–	–	–	–
Employees	–	–	–	–	–	7,800

H.H. BROWN SHOE COMPANY INC.

124 W. Putnam Ave.
Greenwich CT 06830
Phone: 203-661-2424
Fax: 904-357-1105
Web: www.fisglobal.com

CEO: Francis C Rooney Jr
CFO: –
HR: –
FYE: December 31
Type: Subsidiary

This Brown is no Buster (tap dance star) but it does make shoes. H.H. Brown manufactures and distributes casual work and dress shoes and boots under more than a dozen brands including B?c B?rn Carolina Corcoran Dexter Double-H Kork-Ease Matterhorn Nurse Mates Sofft and Softspots. Founded in 1883 H.H. Brown is named after Massachusetts shoemaker Henry H. Brown and is a subsidiary of Berkshire Hathaway. The company owns and sells through websites (shoeline.com and supershoes.com); more than 40 of its own H.H. Brown SuperShoes stores which span the East Coast; a leather goods flagship shop in Connecticut; and retailers such as Bergdorf Goodman Macy's Neiman Marcus Payless ShoeSource and REI.

HABASIT AMERICA

805 Satellite Blvd.
Suwanee GA 30024
Phone: 678-288-3600
Fax: 678-288-3651
Web: www.habasitamerica.com

CEO: –
CFO: Victor D'Adamio
HR: –
FYE: August 31
Type: Private

Need a belt? Not for your trousers but for your conveyor systems and other industrial machinery? Turn to Habasit America. The company makes power transmission belts and conveyor belts along with related gears and motors for material handling equipment in a variety of industries. Habasit America's products move automotive parts beverages electronic components food packaging paper and tissue pharmaceuticals textiles tires tobacco wood and other commodities. Its conveyor belts also are used in airport baggage handling systems and supermarket check-out stands. Habasit America's Swiss parent company Habasit Group Reinach operates globally.

HABIF AROGETI & WYNNE LLP

5 Concourse Pkwy. Ste. 1000
Atlanta GA 30328
Phone: 404-892-9651
Fax: 404-602-4684
Web: www.hawcpa.com

CEO: –
CFO: –
HR: –
FYE: December 31
Type: Private

HA&W hopes its clients laugh all the way to the bank. One of Georgia's largest independent certified public accounting and business advisory firms Habif Arogeti & Wynne provides traditional accounting and tax services as well as financial planning staffing and management and technology consulting. HA&W specializes in asset management employee benefits financial staffing international tax planning litigation support and mergers and acquisitions consulting. The firm serves clients in industries such as health care insurance manufacturing real estate retail and technology. Isaac Habif and Jimmy Arogeti created the firm in 1952. They were later joined by Merrill Wynne.

HABITAT FOR HUMANITY INTERNATIONAL INC.

121 HABITAT ST
AMERICUS, GA 317093498
Phone: 800-422-4828
Fax: –
Web: www.habitat.org

CEO: Jonathan T. M. Reckford
CFO: Ed Quibell
HR: –
FYE: June 30
Type: Private

Thanks to Habitat for Humanity more than 5 million people worldwide know there's no place like home. The mission of the not-for-profit ecumenical Christian organization is to provide adequate and affordable shelter. It has built or remodeled more than 800000 houses at cost for families who demonstrate a need and are willing to invest "sweat equity" during construction. Homeowners make payments on no-interest mortgages; Habitat for Humanity funnels the funds back into the construction of homes for others. The group operates in all 50 states the District of Columbia Guam and Puerto Rico in addition to affiliates in nearly 80 countries. It was founded in 1976 by Linda Fuller and her late husband Millard.

	Annual Growth	06/09	06/10	06/11	06/12	06/13
Sales ($ mil.)	1418.9%	–	–	1.3	292.8	296.5
Net income ($ mil.)	–	–	–	0.1	(31.6)	(29.7)
Market value ($ mil.)	–	–	–	–	–	–
Employees	–	–	–	–	–	1,500

HACHETTE BOOK GROUP

237 Park Ave.
New York NY 10017
Phone: 212-364-1200
Fax: 212-364-0930
Web: www.hachettebookgroup.com

CEO: David Young
CFO: Thomas A Maciag
HR: –
FYE: December 31
Type: Subsidiary

Hachette Book Group goes by the book. The division of Hachette Livre is home to book publisher Little Brown and hardcover mass market and trade paperback publisher Grand Central Publishing (formerly Warner Books). Other imprints include FaithWords (religious books) and Center Street (for readers in America's heartland). Hachette best sellers have included books by Malcolm Gladwell (The Tipping Point) Stephenie Meyer (Twilight) and Jon Stewart and the Daily Show writers (Earth: The Book). The current iteration of the company was formed in 2006 when French media firm Lagardere acquired Time Warner Book Group from Time Warner's Time Inc. unit. Time Warner Book Group subsequently became Hachette Book Group.

HACKENSACK UNIVERSITY MEDICAL CENTER

30 PROSPECT AVE STE 1
HACKENSACK, NJ 076011912
Phone: 201-996-2000
Fax: –
Web: www.hackensackumc.org

CEO: Robert Charles Garrett
CFO: Robert L (Bob) Glenning
HR: –
FYE: December 31
Type: Private

Hackensack University Medical Center (HUMC) is an acute care teaching and research hospital that serves the residents of northern New Jersey and parts of New York. The hospital has about 775 beds and staffs more than 2200 medical professionals. HUMC administers general medical surgical emergency and diagnostic care. The medical center also includes specialized treatment centers including a children's hospital a women's hospital a cancer center and a heart and vascular hospital. HUMC is part of the Hackensack University Health Network which also includes a physician practice group and a joint venture that operates two community hospitals. Hackensack University Health Network is merging with Meridian Health.

	Annual Growth	12/03	12/04	12/05	12/07	12/08
Sales ($ mil.)	4.4%	–	873.2	1,004.5	1,183.9	1,037.4
Net income ($ mil.)	–	–	–	26.4	48.5	(86.4)
Market value ($ mil.)	–	–	–	–	–	–
Employees	–	–	–	–	–	7,175

HACKETT GROUP INC

NMS: HCKT

1001 Brickell Bay Drive, Suite 3000
Miami, FL 33131
Phone: 305 375-8005
Fax: –
Web: www.thehackettgroup.com

CEO: Ted A. Fernandez
CFO: Robert A. Ramirez
HR: Robert C Greene
FYE: January 02
Type: Public

The Hackett Group a business and technology consultancy provides corporations with advisory programs benchmarking business transformation services and working capital management. It specializes in IT human resources accounting and customer service. The Hackett Group also offers services related to best practice research with a focus on sales general and administrative functions and supply chain services. The company's business applications consulting is performed by its Hackett Technology Solutions (HTS) unit which specializes in software from Oracle and SAP. Its clients have included ABIOMED Exelon and Waste Management.

	Annual Growth	12/10	12/11	12/12	12/13*	01/15
Sales ($ mil.)	3.3%	201.3	225.1	234.1	223.8	236.7
Net income ($ mil.)	(7.4%)	14.2	21.8	16.7	8.7	9.7
Market value ($ mil.)	19.9%	102.5	109.3	116.9	181.4	254.2
Employees	1.1%	854	914	947	848	904

*Fiscal year change

HACKLEY HOSPITAL

1700 CLINTON ST
MUSKEGON, MI 494425591
Phone: 231-728-4950
Fax: –
Web: www.mercyhealthmuskegon.com

CEO: Gordon A Mudler
CFO: –
HR: –
FYE: June 30
Type: Private

Medical professionals at Hackley Hospital aim to heal. Operating as as Mercy Health Partners Hackley Campus the hospital is a 210-bed acute care facility that serves patients living in Muskegon opposite the thumb on Michigan's shoreline. The teaching hospital offers such services as behavioral health care a sleep analysis lab a bariatric treatment center a cancer center stroke care emergency medicine and rehabilitation therapies. Mercy Health Partners Hackley Campus is part Mercy Health Partners Muskegon.

	Annual Growth	06/07	06/08	06/09	06/10	06/13
Sales ($ mil.)	(36.1%)	–	1,673.5	144.4	151.0	177.8
Net income ($ mil.)	–	–	–	(6.8)	(42.2)	5.6
Market value ($ mil.)	–	–	–	–	–	–
Employees	–	–	–	–	–	1,500

HAEMONETICS CORP.

NYS: HAE

400 Wood Road
Braintree, MA 02184
Phone: 781 848-7100
Fax: –

CEO: Ronald G. (Ron) Gelbman
CFO: Christopher J. (Chris) Lindop
HR: –
FYE: March 28
Type: Public

Haemonetics helps health care providers keep track of blood. The company develops and produces automated blood collection systems that collect and process whole blood taking only the components (such as plasma or red blood cells) needed and returning the remainder to the donors. Typically these systems sold under the Cell Saver TEG and OrthoPAT brands are bought and used by plasma centers and blood banks. Haemonetics also makes hospital systems that collect and re-infuse a patient's own blood during surgery; these are sold under the cardioPAT and Cell Saver brand names. Additionally the company sells information management software and provides consulting services to blood banks and hospitals.

	Annual Growth	04/11*	03/12	03/13	03/14	03/15
Sales ($ mil.)	7.7%	676.7	727.8	892.0	938.5	910.4
Net income ($ mil.)	(32.2%)	80.0	66.9	38.8	35.1	16.9
Market value ($ mil.)	(9.7%)	3,439.7	3,600.4	2,152.6	1,659.2	2,284.4
Employees	11.3%	2,201	2,337	3,563	3,782	3,383

*Fiscal year change

HAGEMEYER NORTH AMERICA INC.

1460 Tobias Gadson Blvd.
Charleston SC 29407
Phone: 843-745-2400
Fax: 843-745-6942
Web: www.hagemeyerna.com

CEO: Lisa Mitchell
CFO: –
HR: Jon E May
FYE: December 31
Type: Subsidiary

Hagemeyer North America (HNA) gets a charge out of spreading things around. The company — a subsidiary of French distribution giant Sonepar's US subsidiary Sonepar Management US — distributes electrical industrial safety and other maintenance repair and operations (MRO) products from about 70 locations across North America and over the Web. It also performs instrumentation repair and calibration hydrostatic testing air sampling lighting design and various other services. Companies such as 3M DuPont Philips Cardiac Science and more supply products to electrical contractors and other customers in industries that include government metals transportation pharmaceuticals and utilities.

HAGGAR CLOTHING CO.

11511 Luna Rd.
Dallas TX 75234
Phone: 214-352-8481
Fax: 214-654-5500
Web: www.iphase.com

CEO: Michael B Stitt
CFO: John W Feray
HR: –
FYE: September 30
Type: Private

Haggar is hooked on classics. A leading maker and marketer of men's casual and dress apparel the company's products include pants sport coats suits shirts and shorts. Haggar's clothes (including its "wrinkle-free" shirts and tab-waist expandable pants) are sold through about 10000 stores in the US Canada Mexico and the UK. Its Haggar brand is sold in department stores such as Belk J. C. Penney Kohl's Macys and Sears and at more than 70 Haggar outlet stores. The men's apparel maker invented the word "slacks" and has sold plenty of them in its 80-plus years in business.

HAGGEN INC.

2211 RIMLAND DR STE 300
BELLINGHAM, WA 982265699
Phone: 360-733-8720
Fax: –
Web: www.haggen.com

CEO: –
CFO: Ron Stevens
HR: –
FYE: December 31
Type: Private

Haggen showers shoppers in the Pacific Northwest with salmon coffee and other essentials. One of the area's largest independent grocers Haggen operates some 130 supermarkets in Washington and Oregon as well as California Nevada and Arizona. Most of the stores were acquired from Albertsons in late 2014. After the purchase Haggen sued Albertsons for attempted monopolization and unfair competition. In late 2015 Haggen filed for Chapter 11 bankruptcy protection. The chain was founded in 1933 in Bellingham Washington.

	Annual Growth	12/03	12/04	12/05	12/06	12/07
Sales ($ mil.)	–	–	–	(164.8)	758.7	787.8
Net income ($ mil.)	20237.1%	–	–	0.0	6.5	8.6
Market value ($ mil.)	–	–	–	–	–	–
Employees	–	–	–	–	–	3,900

HAHN AUTOMOTIVE WAREHOUSE INC.

415 W. Main St.
Rochester NY 14608
Phone: 585-235-1595
Fax: 585-235-8615
Web: www.hahnauto.com

CEO: –
CFO: –
HR: Joanne Tucker
FYE: September 30
Type: Private

You rely on your mechanic and your mechanic relies on Hahn Automotive Warehouse. The company distributes aftermarket auto parts to independent jobbers (middlemen who buy from distributors and sell to retailers) and about 80 company-owned Genuine Parts Advantage Auto and Nu-Way Auto stores as well as professional installers. It operates about 30 distribution centers in the Midwest and along the East Coast. The company carries some 200 name-brand and 50 private-label parts. Eli Futerman and his son-in-law Daniel Chessin own and lead the company. Hahn Automotive Warehouse (formerly Hahn Tire and Battery) was purchased in 1958 by Futerman's father Mike and a partner.

HAIN CELESTIAL GROUP INC — NMS: HAIN

1111 Marcus Avenue
Lake Success, NY 11042
Phone: 516 587-5000
Fax: –
Web: www.hain-celestial.com

CEO: Irwin D. Simon
CFO: Pasquale (Pat) Conte
HR: –
FYE: June 30
Type: Public

The Hain Celestial Group serves up guiltless eating and grooming. The company manufactures and distributes natural and organic food snacks beverages and personal care and cleaning products in North America and Europe. Its vast pantry of "better-for-you" brands includes Celestial Seasonings (specialty teas) Terra and Garden of Eatin' (snacks) and Earth's Best (organic baby food). Hain's products are mainstays in natural foods stores and are increasingly available in mainstream supermarkets; club mass-market and drug stores; and grocery wholesalers. Fast-growing Hain is also a supplier of TenderCare disposable diapers; its JÃSÖN Natural Products makes grooming products.

	Annual Growth	06/11	06/12	06/13	06/14	06/15
Sales ($ mil.)	24.2%	1,130.3	1,378.2	1,734.7	2,153.6	2,688.5
Net income ($ mil.)	32.2%	55.0	79.2	114.7	139.9	167.9
Market value ($ mil.)	18.5%	3,423.1	5,647.7	6,670.8	9,105.7	6,758.0
Employees	32.7%	2,031	3,720	3,665	4,400	6,307

HALCON RESOURCES CORP — NYS: HK

1000 Louisiana Street, Suite 6700
Houston, TX 77002
Phone: 832 538-0300
Fax: –
Web: www.halconresources.com

CEO: Floyd C. Wilson
CFO: Mark J. Mize
HR: –
FYE: December 31
Type: Public

Halcón Resources is hoping that its halcyon days are ahead. The independent exploration and production company operates in Louisiana Montana North Dakota Oklahoma and Texas. In 2012 the company reported proved reserves of 108.8 million barrels of oil equivalent. It owned stakes in more than 3320 gross wells and operated more than 1820 of these. In 2012 the company participated in drilling of 192 gross (88 net) wells of which 189 gross (85 net) wells were completed. Halcón Resources' average production was 9404 barrels of oil equivalent per day in 2012.

	Annual Growth	12/10	12/11	12/12	12/13	12/14
Sales ($ mil.)	78.8%	112.3	107.9	247.9	999.5	1,148.3
Net income ($ mil.)	238.1%	2.4	(1.4)	(53.9)	(1,222.7)	316.0
Market value ($ mil.)	(0.8%)	157.4	267.8	592.1	330.3	152.3
Employees	19.4%	206	188	435	420	419

HALLADOR ENERGY CO — NAS: HNRG

1660 Lincoln Street, Suite 2700
Denver, CO 80264-2701
Phone: 303 839-5504
Fax: –
Web: www.halladorenergy.com

CEO: Brent K. Bilsland
CFO: Lawrence D. (Larry) Martin
HR: –
FYE: December 31
Type: Public

Hallador Energy puts most of its energy into selling coal from its Carlisle Mine in Indiana to three utilities in the Midwest and one in Florida. Hallador has recoverable coal reserves of 43.5 million tons (34.2 million tons proven and 9.3 million tons probable). In addition to the Carlisle Mine it get coals from a mine in Clay County Indiana and has two inactive mines in Illinois. The company is exploring the possibility of other contracts with a number of coal purchasers (primarily utilities and distribution cooperatives). Additionally Hallador has a 45% stake in Savoy Energy L.P. an oil and gas company with operations in Michigan and a 50% interest in Sunrise Energy LLC a private oil and gas exploration and production company with assets in Indiana.

	Annual Growth	12/10	12/11	12/12	12/13	12/14
Sales ($ mil.)	16.9%	129.2	157.4	141.3	153.9	241.2
Net income ($ mil.)	(17.8%)	22.4	35.8	23.8	23.2	10.2
Market value ($ mil.)	1.2%	303.8	287.6	239.2	233.4	318.9
Employees	32.6%	332	333	330	376	1,027

HALLIBURTON COMPANY — NYS: HAL

3000 North Sam Houston Parkway East
Houston, TX 77032
Phone: 281 871-2699
Fax: –
Web: www.halliburton.com

CEO: David J. (Dave) Lesar
CFO: Christian A. Garcia
HR: Lawrence J. Pope
FYE: December 31
Type: Public

One of the largest oilfield services companies in the world Halliburton serves the upstream oil and gas industry in 80 countries with a complete range of services from the location of hydrocarbons to the production of oil and gas. It operates in two segments: Drilling and Evaluation and Completion and Production. Services include providing production optimization drilling evaluation fluid services and oilfield drilling software and consulting. It combines tried-and-true well drilling and optimization techniques with high-tech analysis and modeling software and services. In a major expansion in 2014 the company agreed to acquire Baker Hughes for about $35 billion.

	Annual Growth	12/11	12/12	12/13	12/14	12/15
Sales ($ mil.)	(1.2%)	24,829.0	28,503.0	29,402.0	32,870.0	23,633.0
Net income ($ mil.)	–	2,839.0	2,635.0	2,125.0	3,500.0	(671.0)
Market value ($ mil.)	(0.3%)	29,540.6	29,694.6	43,442.0	33,666.5	29,138.2
Employees	(1.1%)	68,000	73,000	77,000	80,000	65,000

HALLMARK FINANCIAL SERVICES INC. — NMS: HALL

777 Main Street, Suite 1000
Fort Worth, TX 76102
Phone: 817 348-1600
Fax: –
Web: www.hallmarkgrp.com

CEO: Naveen Anand
CFO: –
HR: –
FYE: December 31
Type: Public

Personal or commercial on the ground or in the air Hallmark Financial Services sells insurance to cover risks both general and exceptional. Its standard commercial unit markets and underwrites general commercial property/casualty insurance while its excess and surplus unit writes specialty property/casualty coverage to businesses that don't fit into standard coverage. Its general aviation unit provides aviation insurance to both commercial and private pilots and small airports. Other Hallmark Financial units provide personal non-standard auto insurance and specialty commercial auto and umbrella policies.

	Annual Growth	12/10	12/11	12/12	12/13	12/14
Assets ($ mil.)	7.4%	736.6	746.9	790.5	909.0	980.9
Net income ($ mil.)	16.3%	7.3	(10.8)	3.5	8.2	13.4
Market value ($ mil.)	7.4%	174.9	134.3	180.5	170.7	232.3
Employees	2.9%	351	382	360	376	393

HALLWOOD GROUP INC.

ASE: HWG

3710 Rawlins, Suite 1500
Dallas, TX 75219
Phone: 214 528-5588
Fax: –
Web: www.hallwood.com

CEO: Anthony J Gumbiner
CFO: Richard Kelley
HR: Donna Henton
FYE: December 31
Type: Public

The Hallwood Group spawns fabric for everyday life. The group is a holding company of Brookwood Companies a producer of high-tech fabric for the outdoor and sportswear industries and one of the largest suppliers of coated nylon fabric in the US. Brookwood dyes finishes coats and prints woven synthetics used in products such as consumer apparel luggage and sailcloth. A laminating arm processes fabrics for military uniforms and camouflage equipment industrial applications and waterproof gear. Roughly two-thirds of sales are made to makers of military goods such as Tennier Industries and ORC Industries. Hallwood's former interest in Hallwood Energy ended in 2009 following the latter's reorganization.

	Annual Growth	12/08	12/09	12/10	12/11	12/12
Sales ($ mil.)	(5.3%)	162.2	179.6	168.4	139.5	130.5
Net income ($ mil.)	–	1.4	17.1	9.9	(6.3)	(17.9)
Market value ($ mil.)	(27.9%)	50.3	59.2	40.3	13.8	13.6
Employees	(1.0%)	460	478	470	458	441

HALOZYME THERAPEUTICS INC

NMS: HALO

11388 Sorrento Valley Road
San Diego, CA 92121
Phone: 858 794-8889
Fax: –
Web: www.halozyme.com

CEO: Gregory I. Frost
CFO: Laurie Stelzer
HR: –
FYE: December 31
Type: Public

Halozyme Therapeutics is searching for cures through a number of "ologys" by developing treatments for use in endocrinology oncology and dermatology fields. It is also creating products for the drug delivery market. Its Hylenex recombinant is used as an adjuvant for drug and fluid infusions. Most of Halozyme's products and candidates (including Hylenex) are based on rHuPH20 its patented recombinant human hyaluronidase enzyme while its lead cancer program is PEGPH20 which targets solid tumors. Halozyme partners with such pharmaceuticals as Roche Pfizer Janssen Baxalta and AbbVie for its ENHANZE drug delivery platform which enables biologics and small molecule compounds to be delivered subcutaneously.

	Annual Growth	12/10	12/11	12/12	12/13	12/14
Sales ($ mil.)	53.3%	13.6	56.1	42.3	54.8	75.3
Net income ($ mil.)	–	(53.2)	(19.8)	(53.6)	(83.5)	(68.4)
Market value ($ mil.)	5.1%	995.7	1,195.6	843.6	1,884.6	1,213.2
Employees	10.7%	102	135	152	170	153

HAMILTON COLLEGE

198 COLLEGE HILL RD
CLINTON, NY 13323-1295
Phone: 315-859-4011
Fax: –
Web: www.hamilton.edu

CEO: –
CFO: –
HR: –
FYE: June 30
Type: Private

Hamilton College is a private liberal arts school that serves some 1800 students and employs about 180 faculty members. The school offers undergraduate programs in a variety of subjects including economics government psychology computer science education and English. Hamilton College which has a 10-to-1 student/faculty ratio is supported by a more than $500 million endowment. Located in the foothills of the Adirondack Mountains the school is one of the oldest colleges in New York State. Hamilton College was founded in 1793 by Samuel Kirkland missionary to the Oneida Indians; it was named for Alexander Hamilton the first secretary of the US Treasury.

	Annual Growth	06/06	06/07	06/08	06/11	06/12
Sales ($ mil.)	3.5%	–	–	98.6	138.9	112.7
Net income ($ mil.)	–	–	–	1.3	12.0	142.9
Market value ($ mil.)	–	–	–	–	–	–
Employees	–	–	–	–	–	650

HAMMACHER SCHLEMMER & CO. INC.

9307 N. Milwaukee Ave.
Niles IL 60714
Phone: 847-581-8600
Fax: 847-581-8616
Web: www.hammacher.com

CEO: –
CFO: –
HR: Juliete Kracik
FYE: December 31
Type: Private

Its name may not roll off the tongue but Hammacher Schlemmer has been spoken for more than 160 years. Founded as a New York hardware store it's one of the nation's most seasoned retailers producing the longest continually published US catalog (since 1881). Offering a pricey lineup it calls "the Best the Only and the Unexpected" the retailer sells innovative upscale gifts gadgets and housewares. It has been the first to sell a number of cutting-edge products including the pop-up toaster (1930) steam iron (1948) microwave oven (1968) portable DVD player (1998) and robotic lawnmower (2000). It operates a flagship store in New York City and a website. Heirs of J. Roderick MacArthur own the company.

HAMPDEN BANCORP INC

NMS: HBNK

19 Harrison Ave.
Springfield, MA 01102
Phone: 413 736-1812
Fax: –
Web: www.hampdenbank.com

CEO: –
CFO: –
HR: –
FYE: June 30
Type: Public

Despite its name Hampden Bancorp's (the holding company for Hampden Bank) services extend beyond Massachusetts's Hampden County. Serving a handful of cities and towns in western Massachusetts Hampden Bank offers savings and checking deposit services as well as a variety of lending services to its consumer and business customers. The bank's primary loan products include one-to-four-family residential loans and commercial real estate loans each of which make up about a third of the bank's total loan portfolio. Loans for construction businesses and consumers make up the rest. Hampden Bancorp operates through more than a half-dozen branches.

	Annual Growth	06/10	06/11	06/12	06/13	06/14
Assets ($ mil.)	4.7%	584.0	573.3	616.0	653.0	701.5
Net income ($ mil.)	–	(0.4)	1.3	3.0	3.0	4.5
Market value ($ mil.)	15.4%	53.7	75.0	73.1	84.3	95.3
Employees	3.2%	113	115	120	118	128

HAMPSHIRE GROUP, LTD.

NBB: HAMP

114 W. 41st Street
New York, NY 10036
Phone: 212 840-5666
Fax: –
Web: www.hamp.com

CEO: Paul M Buxbaum
CFO: William Drozdowski
HR: –
FYE: December 31
Type: Public

Hampshire Group has cooled on the women's sweater business. After years of declining sales and mounting losses the company in 2011 sold its women's lines to focus exclusively on men's sweaters and woven and knit tops. The firm is licensed to manufacture men's knitwear under the Geoffrey Beene Dockers and Joseph Abboud labels. Hampshire Group's own brands include Spring+Mercer and scott james. The company's apparel is sold by major department store chains and specialty retailers throughout the US. JC Penney Kohl's and Macy's are Hampshire Group's largest customers accounting for more than 50% of total annual sales.

	Annual Growth	12/10	12/11	12/12	12/13	12/14
Sales ($ mil.)	(9.2%)	134.5	86.1	117.6	105.1	91.5
Net income ($ mil.)	–	(9.7)	(10.0)	(11.7)	(16.0)	(28.8)
Market value ($ mil.)	(17.9%)	31.9	20.4	25.7	28.9	14.5
Employees	45.2%	162	1,215	1,073	831	720

HAMPTON ROADS BANKSHARES INC

NMS: HMPR

641 Lynnhaven Parkway
Virginia Beach, VA 23452
Phone: 757 217-1000
Fax: –
Web: www.bankofhamptonroads.com

CEO: W. Thomas Mears
CFO: Thomas B. Dix
HR: Denise D. Hinkle
FYE: December 31
Type: Public

Hampton Roads Bankshares is the holding company for the Bank of Hampton Roads Gateway Bank & Trust and Shore Bank which together have about 35 branches in southeastern Virginia eastern Maryland and northeastern North Carolina. Serving area consumers and businesses the banks offer standard services such as checking and savings accounts CDs retirement accounts and loans. Its Gateway Investment Services subsidiary provides brokerage services through a third-party broker while its Gateway Bank Mortgage originates sells mortgage loans in the secondary market. Hampton Roads Bankshares' commercial real estate and real estate construction loans made up 55% of its loan portfolio in 2014.

	Annual Growth	12/10	12/11	12/12	12/13	12/14
Assets ($ mil.)	(9.0%)	2,900.2	2,166.9	2,054.1	1,950.3	1,988.6
Net income ($ mil.)	–	(211.3)	(98.6)	(25.1)	4.1	9.3
Market value ($ mil.)	34.1%	88.7	467.4	203.0	298.5	286.6
Employees	(8.5%)	767	596	587	536	537

HAMPTON UNIVERSITY

100 E QUEEN ST
HAMPTON, VA 236680108
Phone: 757-727-5000
Fax: –
Web: www.hamptonu.edu

CEO: –
CFO: –
HR: Lottie Hall
FYE: June 30
Type: Private

Hampton University is composed of six undergraduate schools as well as a graduate college and a college of continuing education. It offers some 70 bachelor's degree programs more than 25 master's degree programs and several doctoral or professional degrees in nursing physics atmospheric and planetary science physical therapy and pharmacy. It also includes the Scripps Howard School of Journalism and Communications. The school has an enrollment of about 5000 students. Hampton University has more than 300 full-time faculty members and a student-to-teacher ratio of 16:1.

	Annual Growth	06/07	06/08	06/09	06/10	06/11
Sales ($ mil.)	–	–	–	0.0	140.2	140.2
Net income ($ mil.)	–	–	–	0.0	(1.6)	(1.6)
Market value ($ mil.)	–	–	–	–	–	–
Employees	–	–	–	–	–	1,050

HANCOCK FABRICS, INC.

NBB: HKFI Q

One Fashion Way
Baldwyn, MS 38824
Phone: 662 365-6000
Fax: –
Web: www.hancockfabrics.com

CEO: –
CFO: Rebecca Flick
HR: Michele Chappell
FYE: January 31
Type: Public

Through careful piecing and pinning Hancock Fabrics has become a leading nationwide fabric chain (far behind Jo-Ann Stores). The company caters to customers (mostly women) who sew by offering fabrics crafts sewing machines and accessories through some 260 stores (down from more than 400 five years ago) in more than 35 states. It also sells merchandise online. To compensate for the waning popularity of sewing clothes the company has expanded its selection of craft and home decorating products including drapery and upholstery fabrics and home accent pieces. Founded in 1957 Hancock Fabrics has struggled to grow its sales in recent years. The company filed for Chapter 11 bankruptcy protection in February 2016 to reorganize its business.

	Annual Growth	01/11	01/12	01/13	01/14	01/15
Sales ($ mil.)	0.7%	275.5	272.0	278.0	276.0	283.1
Net income ($ mil.)	–	(10.5)	(11.3)	(8.5)	(1.9)	(3.2)
Market value ($ mil.)	(17.5%)	30.8	20.7	11.0	22.0	14.3
Employees	(7.9%)	4,300	3,700	3,200	3,300	3,100

HANCOCK HOLDING CO.

NMS: HBHC

One Hancock Plaza, P.O. Box 4019
Gulfport, MS 39501
Phone: 228 868-4000
Fax: –
Web: www.hancockbank.com

CEO: John M. Hairston
CFO: Michael M. Achary
HR: –
FYE: December 31
Type: Public

Hancock Holding holds its own as a Gulf Coast financial force. It is the holding company of Mississippi-based Hancock Bank and Louisiana-based Whitney Bank. Together the banks have about 250 branches and 300 ATMs throughout the Gulf South from Florida to Texas. The community-oriented banks offer traditional products and services such as deposit accounts trust services and consumer and business lending. Hancock Holding also has subsidiaries or business units that offer insurance discount brokerage services mutual funds and consumer financing.

	Annual Growth	12/10	12/11	12/12	12/13	12/14
Assets ($ mil.)	26.4%	8,138.3	19,774.1	19,464.5	19,009.3	20,747.3
Net income ($ mil.)	35.4%	52.2	76.8	151.7	163.4	175.7
Market value ($ mil.)	(3.1%)	2,557.8	2,345.7	2,328.1	2,691.3	2,252.6
Employees	13.7%	2,271	4,745	4,235	3,978	3,794

HANCOR INC.

401 Olive St.
Findlay OH 45840
Phone: 419-424-8222
Fax: 419-424-8337
Web: www.hancor.com

CEO: –
CFO: John Maag
HR: –
FYE: December 31
Type: Subsidiary

Hancor has a hankering for plastic drainage and storm management projects. The company's products are used in a swath of markets from sanitary sewer to commercial residential construction and agricultural. Hancor pushes the movement toward environmentally-conscious building with its lineup. Drainage and water conservation products are made of high density polyethylene (HDPE) touted as a green alternative to concrete and steel pipe. The company's products include pipes fittings catch basins detention and retention tanks drains inserts meter pits and wastewater equipment. Since 2005 Hancor has operated as a part of Advanced Drainage Systems creating the world's largest HDPE corrugated-pipe company.

HANDGARDS INC.

901 Hawkins Blvd.
El Paso TX 79915-1202
Phone: 915-779-6606
Fax: 915-779-1312
Web: www.handgards.com

CEO: Robert McLellan
CFO: –
HR: –
FYE: December 31
Type: Private

You've got to hand it to them — Handgards helps foodservice providers get a grip on hygiene and sanitation issues. The largest manufacturer of plastic gloves in the US Handgards produces an array of safety and handling products including disposable gloves adult and children's bibs along with high density polyethylene (HDPE) aprons and food storage and preparation bags and covers. Its 200 different products are sold through independent representatives across the US. About 2000 North American food service providers and other businesses and institutions are catered to from McDonald's to Darden Restaurants' Red Lobster Doctor's Associates' Subway Sandwiches and SYSCO.

HANDY & HARMAN LTD
NAS: HNH

1133 Westchester Avenue, Suite N222
White Plains, NY 10604
Phone: 914 461-1300
Fax: –
Web: www.handyharman.com

CEO: Jeffrey A. Svoboda
CFO: James F. McCabe
HR: –
FYE: December 31
Type: Public

Handy & Harman (HNH) is certainly handy when it comes to producing precious metals tubing and engineered materials in the US and Canada. The company makes 35% of its sales from its Building Materials segment which makes fasteners and systems for building roofs. Other units make and supply brazing alloys steel tubing and meat-room products used in construction electronics telecommunications medical and aviation transportation appliance semiconductor signage and food industries. In addition its Arlon Electronic Material segment produces components for the printed circuit board industry as well as rubber-based insulation materials used by industrial military and aerospace customers.

	Annual Growth	12/10	12/11	12/12	12/13	12/14
Sales ($ mil.)	0.8%	581.5	664.0	629.4	655.2	600.5
Net income ($ mil.)	49.1%	5.1	138.8	26.5	42.0	25.2
Market value ($ mil.)	37.1%	140.3	106.7	162.4	261.0	496.2
Employees	0.5%	1,884	1,621	1,648	1,836	1,925

HANES COMPANIES INC.

600 W. Northwest Blvd.
Winston-Salem NC 27101
Phone: 336-747-1600
Fax: 732-591-0705
Web: www.amboybank.com

CEO: –
CFO: Waller Kim Howard
HR: –
FYE: December 31
Type: Subsidiary

When the job calls for specialty threads look no further than Hanes Companies. Part of Leggett & Platt since 1993 the group makes converts and distributes woven and non-woven textiles and knits under the Hanes brand name. The company's fabrics are used in applications including automotive (headliners acoustic panel materials and seat fabrics) bedding (flame retardant fabrics) filtration furniture (dust covers and skirt linings) geotextiles and landscape (ground cover and filter/drainage fabric). Its label reaches to building products too like roof fabrics insulation and underlayment. Additionally Hanes provides dye and finishing services.

HANESBRANDS INC
NYS: HBI

1000 East Hanes Mill Road
Winston-Salem, NC 27105
Phone: 336 519-8080
Fax: –
Web: www.hanes.com

CEO: Richard A. (Rich) Noll
CFO: Richard D. Moss
HR: Thomas Tom (Thom) Payne
FYE: January 02
Type: Public

Hanesbrands can't wait 'til it gets its Hanes on you. The company designs makes and sells bras hosiery men's boxers socks and other intimate apparel under brand names such as Bali Champion barely there Just My Size Hanes L'eggs Playtex and Wonderbra. Its bras are tops in the US; its underwear legwear and activewear units are market leaders as well. Hanesbrands also makes basic outerwear such as T-shirts and licensed logo apparel for collegiate bookstores legwear for Donna Karan and underwear for Polo Ralph Lauren. The lineup is sold to wholesalers major retail chains (Wal-Mart Target and Kohls) and through Hanesbrands' value outlets and Internet site. It acquired Maidenform in 2013.

	Annual Growth	12/11	12/12	12/13*	01/15	01/16
Sales ($ mil.)	4.3%	4,637.1	4,525.7	4,627.8	5,324.7	5,731.5
Net income ($ mil.)	10.0%	266.7	164.7	330.5	404.5	428.9
Market value ($ mil.)	6.1%	8,561.9	13,700.6	27,162.4	43,322.7	11,526.9
Employees	4.1%	53,300	51,500	49,700	59,500	65,300

*Fiscal year change

HANGER INC
NYS: HGR

10910 Domain Drive, Suite 300
Austin, TX 78758
Phone: 512 777-3800
Fax: –
Web: www.hanger.com

CEO: –
CFO: Thomas E Kiraly
HR: –
FYE: December 31
Type: Public

Hanger gets people back to reaching walking and running. It is one of the leading US operators of orthotic and prosthetic (O&P) patient care centers with more than 770 facilities nationwide. The company's Southern Prosthetic Supply procures and distributes standard and customized braces and prosthetic devices to affiliated and independent O&P centers. Its therapeutic solutions units Accelerated Care Plus (ACP) and Innovative Neurotronics (IN) respectively provide rehabilitation supplies to care centers and make neuromuscular stimulation products for patients with a loss of mobility. The company also manages O&P networks and care programs for health insurers through subsidiary Linkia.

	Annual Growth	12/09	12/10	12/11	12/12	12/13
Sales ($ mil.)	8.3%	760.1	817.4	918.5	985.6	1,046.4
Net income ($ mil.)	15.2%	36.1	21.4	55.0	63.5	63.6
Market value ($ mil.)	29.9%	497.5	762.2	672.3	984.2	1,415.1
Employees	7.2%	3,636	4,273	4,420	4,700	4,800

HANLEY WOOD LLC

1 Thomas Circle NW Ste. 600
Washington DC 20005
Phone: 202-452-0800
Fax: 202-785-1974
Web: www.hanleywood.com

CEO: Peter Goldstone
CFO: Matthew Flynn
HR: –
FYE: December 31
Type: Private

Devotees of the PBS program "This Old House" might like Hanley-Wood. The company operates through four divisions. Its Business Media division publishes about 30 magazines and trade journals for the residential and commercial construction markets including Builder residential architect and EcoHome. The unit also publishes related e-newsletters (BuilderJobs) and websites (Builder Online). Hanley Wood's Exhibition unit produces trade shows conferences and other industry events such as World of Concrete. The company additionally offers marketing communication services through Hanley Wood Marketing and real estate research and information through Hanley Wood Market Intelligence. Hanley Wood was founded in 1976.

HANMI FINANCIAL CORP.
NMS: HAFC

3660 Wilshire Boulevard, Penthouse Suite A
Los Angeles, CA 90010
Phone: 213 382-2200
Fax: –
Web: www.hanmi.com

CEO: Chong Guk (C. G.) Kum
CFO: Michael W. McCall
HR: –
FYE: December 31
Type: Public

No hand-me-down operation Hanmi Financial is headquartered in a penthouse suite along Los Angeles' Wilshire Boulevard. The company owns Hanmi Bank which serves California's Korean-American community and others in the multi-ethnic Los Angeles San Diego San Francisco Bay and Silicon Valley areas. Hanmi Bank offers retail and small business banking with an emphasis on the latter from more than 25 California branches and loan offices throughout the US. Commercial and industrial loans including SBA and international trade finance loans account for about 60% of its loan portfolio; real estate loans make up most of the rest.

	Annual Growth	12/10	12/11	12/12	12/13	12/14
Assets ($ mil.)	9.8%	2,907.1	2,744.8	2,882.5	3,055.5	4,232.4
Net income ($ mil.)	—	(88.0)	28.1	90.4	39.9	49.8
Market value ($ mil.)	108.7%	36.7	236.1	433.7	698.5	696.0
Employees	8.8%	499	483	470	499	699

HANNA ANDERSSON LLC

1010 NW Flanders
Portland OR 97209
Phone: 503-242-0920
Fax: 503-222-0544
Web: www.hannaandersson.com

CEO: –
CFO: Laura A McCue
HR: –
FYE: December 31
Type: Private

Hanna Andersson brings a whole new meaning to the concept of having your own MiniMe. The Swedish-inspired firm makes and sells colorful 100% cotton and organic cotton clothing and sleepwear for the whole family specializing in mother-daughter ensembles. Founded by the husband-and-wife team Tom and Gun Denhart in 1983 it sells its premium apparel — as well as backpacks baby toys and gifts — online by catalog and at more than 30 retail and outlet stores in about 15 US states. Unhappy with the cotton apparel available after their son's birth the Denharts started their own mail-order business and named it after Gun's grandmother: Hanna Andersson. The apparel company is owned by Sun Capital Partners (SCP).

HANNON ARMSTRONG SUSTAINABLE INFRASTRUCTURE CAPITAL INC

NYS: HASI

1906 Towne Centre Blvd., Suite 370
Annapolis, MD 21401
Phone: 410 571-9860
Fax: –
Web: www.hannonarmstrong.com

CEO: Jeffrey W. Eckel
CFO: J. Brendan Herron
HR: –
FYE: December 31
Type: Public

Hannon Armstrong Sustainable Infrastructure Capital has its hands in both kinds of green. The real estate investment trust (REIT) provides securitized funding for environmentally friendly infrastructure projects. It is a key provider of financing for the US government's energy efficiency projects. Hannon Armstrong focuses on energy efficiency clean energy (solar wind geothermal biomass) and other sustainable projects including water and communications that improve energy consumption and the use of natural resources. It works with Honeywell Ingersoll-Rand Johnson Controls and Siemens. Formed in 2012 to be a REIT the company went public in 2013 though it traces its roots to the 1980s.

	Annual Growth	12/10	12/11	12/12	12/13	12/14
Sales ($ mil.)	–	0.0	0.0	–	3.6	28.6
Net income ($ mil.)	–	0.0	0.0	–	(10.5)	9.6
Market value ($ mil.)	–	0.0	0.0	–	368.2	375.3
Employees	18.3%	–	–	20	22	28

HANOVER COLLEGE

484 BALL DR
HANOVER, IN 472439669
Phone: 812-866-7000
Fax: –
Web: www.hanover.edu

CEO: –
CFO: –
HR: –
FYE: June 30
Type: Private

Hanover College is a private coeducational liberal arts college affiliated with the Presbyterian Church. The school offers bachelor's degrees in about 30 areas of study. Students who are required to take four classes each fall and winter term as well as one class during the spring term can design their own majors as well. The school also offers pre-professional programs in areas of study such as medicine law and dentistry. Hanover College has an enrollment of approximately 1000. The oldest private college in Indiana it was founded in 1827 by the Rev. John Finley Crowe.

	Annual Growth	06/03	06/04	06/05	06/08	06/12
Sales ($ mil.)	4.4%	–	–	38.9	47.6	52.7
Net income ($ mil.)	–	–	–	(2.1)	3.7	0.2
Market value ($ mil.)	–	–	–	–	–	–
Employees	–	–	–	–	–	300

HANOVER DIRECT INC.

1500 Harbor Blvd.
Weehawken NJ 07086
Phone: 201-863-7300
Fax: 201-272-3280
Web: www.hanoverdirect.com

CEO: –
CFO: –
HR: –
FYE: December 31
Type: Private

If catalogs are junk mail then Hanover Direct is one big junkyard dog. Mailing more than 180 million catalogs a year the company sells home fashions (The Company Store Company Kids Domestications) as well as men's and women's apparel (International Male Silhouettes and Undergear). Each catalog has a corresponding e-commerce site. The company makes Scandia Down brand comforters and pillows for sale in its catalogs on its websites and several retail outlet stores in Wisconsin. Hanover Direct is owned by the New York-based hedge fund Chelsey Capital.

HANOVER FOODS CORPORATION

1486 York St.
Hanover PA 17331
Phone: 717-632-6000
Fax: 717-637-2890
Web: hanoverfoods.com

CEO: John A Warehime
CFO: –
HR: –
FYE: May 31
Type: Private

Hanover Foods manufactures its foods hand over fist. The company makes more than 40 million cases of prepared food each year and boasts a vast portfolio of products. It makes and markets canned and frozen vegetables canned and fresh soups frozen entrees fresh produce soft pretzels potato chips desserts and fresh deli foods such as pasta and potato salad. Hanover Foods sells its products under the Aunt Kitty's Bickel's Myers Hanover Spring Glen Fresh Foods and Sunsprout brand names. The company caters to several customer types throughout the US including those in the retail food service fresh home meal replacement private label military club store and industrial markets.

HANOVER INSURANCE GROUP INC

NYS: THG

440 Lincoln Street
Worcester, MA 01653
Phone: 508 855-1000
Fax: 508 855-6332
Web: www.hanover.com

CEO: Frederick H. (Fred) Eppinger
CFO: David B Greenfield
HR: Christine Bilotti-Peterson
FYE: December 31
Type: Public

The Hanover Insurance Group is an all-around property/casualty insurance holding company. Through Hanover Insurance Company it provides personal and commercial automobile homeowners and workers' compensation coverage as well as commercial multi-peril insurance and professional liability coverage. The group sells its products through a network of 2000 independent agents throughout the US but Michigan Massachusetts and New York account for about 40% of its business. In Michigan it operates as Citizens Insurance Company. Hanover's Opus Investment Management subsidiary provides institutional investment management services and it operates internationally through UK subsidiary Chaucer Holdings.

	Annual Growth	12/10	12/11	12/12	12/13	12/14
Assets ($ mil.)	12.6%	8,569.9	12,624.4	13,484.5	13,378.7	13,759.7
Net income ($ mil.)	16.2%	154.8	37.1	55.9	251.0	282.0
Market value ($ mil.)	11.2%	2,051.0	1,534.3	1,700.7	2,621.3	3,130.9
Employees	3.8%	4,400	5,100	5,100	5,100	5,100

HANSEN MEDICAL INC
NMS: HNSN

800 East Middlefield Road
Mountain View, CA 94043
Phone: 650 404-5800
Fax: –
Web: www.hansenmedical.com

CEO: Cary Vance
CFO: Christopher P Lowe
HR: –
FYE: December 31
Type: Public

Hansen Medical helps doctors maneuver through matters of the heart. The company develops medical devices designed to diagnose and treat common types of cardiac arrhythmia (irregular heartbeats) such as atrial fibrillation. Its core portable Sensei system (used along with its Artisan and Lynx catheters) incorporates robotics to assist in guiding the movement of flexible catheters in such places as the atria and ventricles. Sensei has received FDA and European regulatory approval for certain uses including manipulation and control of catheters during diagnostic electrophysiology procedures which detect irregular heartbeats by mapping the electrical impulses of the heart.

	Annual Growth	12/10	12/11	12/12	12/13	12/14
Sales ($ mil.)	4.0%	16.6	22.1	17.6	17.0	19.5
Net income ($ mil.)	–	(37.9)	(16.7)	(22.1)	(55.7)	(54.2)
Market value ($ mil.)	(21.9%)	19.9	34.4	27.7	23.1	7.4
Employees	(0.3%)	171	174	160	171	169

HANSON BRICK EAST LLC

15720 John J. Delaney Dr. Ste. 555
Charlotte NC 28277
Phone: 704-341-8750
Fax: 704-341-8735
Web: www.hansonbrick.com

CEO: Michael J Donahue
CFO: Charlie Ward
HR: –
FYE: December 31
Type: Subsidiary

Brick by brick Hanson Brick East has risen up as North America's biggest brick maker. It has capacity to churn out 1.7 billion bricks annually from plants in the US and Canada. Over 1000 styles in five regional brick lines are offered. Its clay brick and concrete roof tiles are touted for their "green" building durability. Hanson Brick and five sister companies operate as divisions of Hanson Building Products North America. Often sold in conjunction with brick Hanson Roof Tile makes concrete roof tile for residential and commercial projects and its Hardscape makes pavers tiles and retaining walls. Hanson companies are part of HeidelbergCement Group a global cement concrete and heavy building products giant.

HARBOR BIOSCIENCES INC.
OTC: HRBR

4435 Eastgate Mall Ste. 400
San Diego CA 92121
Phone: 858-587-9333
Fax: 858-558-6470
Web: www.harborbiosciences.com

CEO: James M Frincke PHD
CFO: Robert W Weber
HR: –
FYE: December 31
Type: Public

Adrenal steroids do the heavy lifting in the body's natural defense and metabolic systems and Harbor Biosciences (formerly Hollis-Eden Pharmaceuticals) hopes to harness their power. The company focuses on developing adrenal steroid hormones and hormone analogs which may reduce inflammation regulate immunity and stimulate cell growth. Natural levels of adrenal steroid hormones can decline as a result of aging or stress leaving the body less able to fend off illnesses. Harbor Biosciences' TRIOLEX candidate is being tested as a possible treatment for type 2 diabetes rheumatoid arthritis and ulcerative colitis. Its APOPTONE candidate is being investigated as a therapy for prostate and breast cancer.

HARBOR HOSPITAL

3001 S. Hanover St.
Baltimore MD 21225
Phone: 410-350-3200
Fax: 410-350-3315
Web: www.harborhospital.org

CEO: L Barney Johnson
CFO: –
HR: Pamela Williams
FYE: June 30
Type: Subsidiary

When you're more than just water-logged when you suffer from more than just salty seasickness Harbor Health Center can pull you back into the swim of things. A subsidiary of MedStar Health Harbor Hospital Center is a 220-bed hospital providing health care to Baltimore area residents. Founded in 1903 the hospital's present location overlooking the Patapsco River was built in 1968. Its specialty care units include the HarborView Cancer Center as well as women's care and community outreach divisions. Harbor Hospital also operates outpatient primary care surgery and orthopedic clinics.

HARBOUR GROUP INDUSTRIES INC.

7701 Forsyth Blvd. Ste. 600
St. Louis MO 63105-1802
Phone: 314-727-5550
Fax: 314-727-9912
Web: www.harbourgroup.com

CEO: Jeff Fox
CFO: Mike Santoni
HR: –
FYE: December 31
Type: Private

Harbour Group sees a sea of possibility in the art of acquisition-making. The investment firm has holdings in the consumer and industrial product manufacturing and distribution industries. It focuses on investing in and building North American companies valued from $30 million to $500 million. The company's portfolio includes both new and mature businesses that make everything from plastic processing equipment (Plastic Automation Exchange) and LED lighting (Watchfire) to music and entertainment systems (Merit Industries) and kitchen and bath hardware (Top Knobs USA). The Fox family controls Harbour Group.

HARD ROCK CAFE INTERNATIONAL INC.

6100 Old Park Ln.
Orlando FL 32835
Phone: 407-445-7625
Fax: 407-445-9709
Web: www.hardrock.com

CEO: Hamish Dodds
CFO: –
HR: Kim Creighton
FYE: December 31
Type: Subsidiary

You can rock hard eat hard buy merchandise hard and even sleep hard with Hard Rock Cafe International. The company operates the Hard Rock Cafe chain of theme restaurants with more than 130 company-owned and franchised locations in about 50 countries. Offering a menu of mostly American fare the eateries attract attention with a collection of rock music memorabilia and Hard Rock-branded merchandise. The company also licenses the Hard Rock name for use by more than a dozen hotels and casino resorts. Its collection of rock n' roll memorabilia boasts more than 70000 items. Peter Morton and Isaac Tigrett opened the first Hard Rock Cafe in London in 1971. Today the Seminole Tribe of Florida owns the chain.

HARD ROCK HOTEL HOLDINGS LLC

4455 Paradise Rd.
Las Vegas NV 89169
Phone: 702-693-5000
Fax: 702-693-5021
Web: www.hardrockhotel.com

CEO: –
CFO: –
HR: –
FYE: December 31
Type: Private

This might be one of the only times in your life that you can find a Rolling Stone pinned to The Wall as you contemplate the glamour of Ziggy Stardust. Hard Rock Hotel Holdings owns and operates the Hard Rock Hotel and Casino in Las Vegas. Using the well-known cafe with the same name as its inspiration the hotel boasts a collection of rock memorabilia as well as the giant outside guitar synonymous with the Hark Rock name. It has more than 72000 square feet of casino space and some 1500 guest rooms as well meeting and convention space a nightclub and concert venue a spa and fitness center and several restaurants and retail shops. Brookfield Asset Management is a major investor.

HARDEE'S FOOD SYSTEMS INC.

100 N. Broadway Ste. 1200
St. Louis MO 63102-2706
Phone: 314-259-6200
Fax: 314-621-1778
Web: www.hardees.com

CEO: Andrew F Puzder
CFO: Theodore Abajian
HR: –
FYE: January 31
Type: Subsidiary

This might be the right place if you have a hearty appetite for burgers. Hardee's Food Systems is a leading fast food chain operator with more than 1900 locations in some 30 states primarily in the Midwest and Southeast. The chain offers a variety of premium-priced Angus beef hamburgers under such names as Thickburger Six Dollar Burger and the Monster Thickburger. Hardee's also serves up chicken sandwiches salads fries and beverages as well as dessert items. About 475 of the restaurants are operated by the company while the rest are franchised. Hardee's is a subsidiary of fast food giant CKE Restaurants.

HARDIN CONSTRUCTION COMPANY LLC

3301 Windy Ridge Pkwy. Ste. 400
Atlanta GA 30339-5618
Phone: 404-264-0404
Fax: 404-264-3514
Web: www.hardinconstruction.com

CEO: –
CFO: –
HR: –
FYE: December 31
Type: Private

Working hard works for Hardin Construction. The private contractor offers design-build services construction management general and interior construction and renovation for commercial projects. It builds shopping malls office complexes convention centers multifamily residences and hotels. The company also manages education government and health care projects. Hardin has completed more than 1400 projects in nearly 30 states as well as in Mexico Puerto Rico and the US Virgin Islands. Repeat clients have included Chelsea Property Group Georgia Institute of Technology Cousins Properties and Simon Property Group. Founded in 1946 by Ira Hardin the firm was acquired by employees in 1993.

HARDINGE INC.

NMS: HDNG

One Hardinge Drive
Elmira, NY 14902
Phone: 607 734-2281
Fax: –
Web: www.hardinge.com

CEO: Richard L Simons
CFO: Douglas J Malone
HR: –
FYE: December 31
Type: Public

Hardinge keeps on turning. The company manufactures precision turning milling and grinding machine tools that shape metals composites and plastics. It makes industrial machine tools for small and midsized shops that create machined parts for the aerospace automotive construction medical equipment and farm equipment industries. Its computer-controlled machines cut horizontally or vertically and can be connected to automatic material feeders for unattended machining. Hardinge also offers a line of work- and tool-holding devices. It gets about 70% of its sales outside of North America predominantly in China and Western Europe.

	Annual Growth	12/10	12/11	12/12	12/13	12/14
Sales ($ mil.)	4.9%	257.0	341.6	334.4	329.5	311.6
Net income ($ mil.)	–	(5.2)	12.0	17.9	9.9	(2.1)
Market value ($ mil.)	5.2%	124.9	103.2	127.4	185.5	152.8
Employees	5.6%	1,189	1,332	1,417	1,445	1,478

HARDWOOD PRODUCTS COMPANY LP

31 SCHOOL ST
GUILFORD, ME 04443
Phone: 207-876-3311
Fax: –
Web: www.foodsticks.com

CEO: –
CFO: –
HR: –
FYE: December 31
Type: Private

Hardwood Products Company manufactures woodenware items for applications in the dairy foodservice and crafts markets as well as for medical and industrial uses. Its food and craft products include skewers sticks spoons and other items produced under the Gold Bond and Trophy brands. The company markets its single-use swabs applicators tongue depressors and specialty products for medical and diagnostic applications under the Puritan brand. It also offers critical-environment cleaning applicators. Hardwood Products Company was founded in 1919.

	Annual Growth	12/09	12/10	12/11	12/12	12/13
Sales ($ mil.)	8.8%	–	35.4	44.4	42.5	45.5
Net income ($ mil.)	(0.9%)	–	–	6.2	5.7	6.1
Market value ($ mil.)	–	–	–	–	–	–
Employees	–	–	–	–	–	382

HARGROVE INC.

1 HARGROVE DR
LANHAM, MD 207061804
Phone: 301-306-9000
Fax: –
Web: www.hargroveinc.com

CEO: Timothy McGill
CFO: –
HR: –
FYE: December 31
Type: Private

Hargrove has been in the background of every Presidential inauguration for more than 50 years. A trade show and special events company Hargrove has a tradition of organizing the inaugural festivities as well as decorating the National Christmas Tree. The firm also organizes more than 1200 trade shows and events annually in the US providing design production installation and management services. Hargrove also exercises its design and production capabilities by crafting parade floats that have appeared in Mardi Gras Thanksgiving and bowl game parades. The family-owned company was founded in 1949 by Earl Hargrove Jr. when he set the stage for Harry S Truman's presidential inaugural.

	Annual Growth	12/02	12/03	12/11	12/12	12/13
Sales ($ mil.)	8.5%	–	30.0	73.2	100.8	67.6
Net income ($ mil.)	(26.6%)	–	–	3.4	3.4	1.8
Market value ($ mil.)	–	–	–	–	–	–
Employees	–	–	–	–	–	185

HARLAN LABORATORIES INC.

8520 Allison Pointe Blvd. Ste. 400
Indianapolis IN 46250
Phone: 317-806-6060
Fax: 317-806-6090
Web: www.harlan.com

CEO: –
CFO: –
HR: –
FYE: December 31
Type: Private

You won't find "research models" from Harlan Laboratories on any fashion runways — that's just the industry term for rodents and other animals bred for scientific research. The company is comprised of two operating groups focused on animal breeding and research services. The Research Models group provides rodents and large animals testing services Teklad-brand animal diets and bedding to pharmaceutical and biotech companies universities and government agencies. The Contract Research Services division provides researchers with analytical chemistry toxicology and agrochemical testing services. Investment firm Genstar Capital controls Harlan Laboratories.

HARLAND CLARKE CORP.

10931 Laureate Dr.
San Antonio TX 78249
Phone: 210-697-8888
Fax: 210-696-1676
Web: www.harlandclarke.com

CEO: Dan Singleton
CFO: Peter A Fera Jr
HR: –
FYE: December 31
Type: Subsidiary

Is your check in the mail? Ask Harland Clarke. The company produces billions of checks and deposit slips annually. In addition to checks and check-related products (such as business cards and stationary) Harland Clarke offers direct marketing services delivery and anti-fraud products and contact center services to financial institutions such as banks credit unions and securities firms. Harland Clarke maintains about 20 manufacturing and administrative facilities throughout the US and Puerto Rico. The company became Harland Clarke in 2007 after holding company M & F Worldwide the owner of Clarke American Checks bought rival printer John H. Harland and combined the two companies' check-related operations.

HARLAND FINANCIAL SOLUTIONS INC.

605 Crescent Executive Ct. Ste. 600
Lake Mary FL 32746
Phone: 407-804-6600
Fax: 407-829-6702
Web: www.harlandfs.com

CEO: –
CFO: Eric Cummins
HR: –
FYE: December 31
Type: Subsidiary

Harland Financial Solutions gives banks answers to their backoffice problems. The company's software products for financial institutions include tools for lending and account origination customer relationship management business intelligence bank and credit union core processing systems teller and call center platforms mortgage lending and servicing risk management and regulatory compliance. Harland also offers a service bureau for outsourced core processing as well as document imaging and electronic statement processing services. The company supplements its financial services software with related applications for content management and business intelligence. Harland is a subsidiary of M & F Worldwide.

HARLAND M. BRAUN & CO. INC.

4010 WHITESIDE ST
LOS ANGELES, CA 900631617
Phone: 323-263-9275
Fax: –
Web: www.braunexp.com

CEO: –
CFO: –
HR: –
FYE: October 31
Type: Private

Hide (the raw material) and seek (find a buyer) are all in a day's work for Harland M. Braun & Co. Operating through its subsidiary Braun Export the company supplies raw hide goods primarily cattle hides and skins and to a lesser extent pigskin and kipskins to tanners. A slate of services is provided for leather (wet blue and crust) hide and skin manufacturing as well as brokering exporting and importing. Dotting the US Braun & Co.'s processing facilities tie in with several suppliers of Holstein steer hides. Partnerships are sealed with such meat packers as JBS Packerland Group Central Valley Meat Creekstone Farms Premium Beef Manning Beef Nebraska Beef and American Beef Packers.

	Annual Growth	10/09	10/10	10/11	10/12	10/13
Sales ($ mil.)	13.1%	–	212.5	290.1	277.3	307.5
Net income ($ mil.)	123.2%	–	–	0.0	0.5	0.1
Market value ($ mil.)	–	–	–	–	–	–
Employees		–	–	–	–	30

HARLEM FURNITURE

1000-46 Rohlwing Rd.
Lombard IL 60148
Phone: 630-261-1600
Fax: 630-261-1080
Web: www.theroomplace.com

CEO: –
CFO: Joe Connolly
HR: –
FYE: December 31
Type: Private

Harlem Furniture is steeped in history. Named Harlem Furniture because of its flagship location on Harlem Avenue the company was founded by Sam Berman in 1912 in downtown Chicago where he sold furniture door-to-door. The retailer sells furniture by the room at a discount and operates nearly 25 retail stores primarily in Illinois under The RoomPlace banner. Private equity firms Pouschine Cook Capital Management Bear Growth Capital Partners and Mercantile Capital bought a controlling stake in Harlem Furniture in 2005. The move eventually spurred a change in the executive suite. In November 2009 founder Berman's grandson Bruce left as president and CEO; he remains on the board and as a shareholder.

HARLEY-DAVIDSON INC   NYS: HOG

3700 West Juneau Avenue
Milwaukee, WI 53208
Phone: 414 342-4680
Fax: 414 343-4621
Web: www.harley-davidson.com

CEO: Matthew S. (Matt) Levatich
CFO: John A. Olin
HR: Tonit M. Calaway
FYE: December 31
Type: Public

Four wheels move the body. Two wheels move the soul. Harley-Davidson is a major US maker of motorcycles and seller of heavyweight cruisers. The company offers touring and custom Harleys through a worldwide network of more than 1400 dealers. The company manufactures and markets six families of motorcycles: Touring Dyna Softail Street Sportster and V-Rod. It also makes three-wheeled motorcycles. Harley-Davidson sells attitude with its brand-name products which include a line of clothing and accessories (MotorClothes). Harley-Davidson Financial Services (HDFS) offers financing to dealers and consumers in the US and Canada.

	Annual Growth	12/10	12/11	12/12	12/13	12/14
Sales ($ mil.)	6.4%	4,859.3	5,311.7	5,580.5	5,899.9	6,228.5
Net income ($ mil.)	54.9%	146.5	599.1	623.9	734.0	844.6
Market value ($ mil.)	17.4%	7,345.8	8,235.7	10,345.9	14,670.4	13,964.8
Employees	(1.5%)	6,900	6,600	5,800	6,400	6,500

HARLEYSVILLE GROUP INC.

NASDAQ: HGIC

355 Maple Ave.
Harleysville PA 19438-2297
Phone: 215-256-5000
Fax: 215-256-5799
Web: www.harleysvillegroup.com

CEO: Michael L Browne
CFO: Arthur E Chandler
HR: –
FYE: December 31
Type: Subsidiary

The reckless the accident-prone or the just plain apprehensive take heed: Harleysville Group hopes to extend a safety net to all of you. An insurance holding company Harleysville Group (also known as Harleysville Insurance) sells a broad line of commercial property/casualty insurance policies including auto commercial multi-peril and workers' compensation policies. It also sells personal auto and homeowners coverage. The company which maintains regional offices in about a dozen states markets its products in more than 30 eastern and midwestern states through some 1300 independent agencies. Harleysville Group was acquired by Nationwide Mutual Insurance in 2012.

HARLEYSVILLE SAVINGS FINANCIAL CORP

NBB: HARL

271 Main Street
Harleysville, PA 19438
Phone: 215 256-8828
Fax: 215 256-0510
Web: www.harleysvillesavings.com

CEO: Ronald B Geib
CFO: M Shane Michalak
HR: –
FYE: September 30
Type: Public

Get your moola runnin'! Harleysville Savings Financial is the holding company of Harleysville Savings Bank which operates about a half-dozen branches in southeastern Pennsylvania's Montgomery County. The bank offers standard deposit products such as checking and savings accounts CDs and IRAs. Its lending activities consist primarily of single-family residential mortgages which account for more than two-thirds of the company's loan portfolio; home equity loans account for nearly 15%. To a lesser extent Harleysville Savings Bank also originates commercial mortgages residential construction loans and consumer lines of credit.

	Annual Growth	09/10	09/11	09/12	09/13	09/14
Assets ($ mil.)	(2.0%)	857.1	835.7	802.6	810.4	791.4
Net income ($ mil.)	(0.5%)	5.0	5.4	5.1	4.8	4.9
Market value ($ mil.)	3.2%	54.9	52.8	61.8	69.7	62.2
Employees	1.2%	125	130	128	–	–

HARMAN INTERNATIONAL INDUSTRIES, INC.

NYS: HAR

400 Atlantic Street, Suite 1500
Stamford, CT 06901
Phone: 203 328-3500
Fax: –
Web: www.harman.com

CEO: Dinesh C. Paliwal
CFO: Sandra E. (Sandy) Rowland
HR: Udo Huels
FYE: June 30
Type: Public

Harman International Industries is loud and clear. It makes high-end stereo and audio equipment for consumer and professional markets. The company makes loudspeakers CD and DVD players CD recorders and amplifiers under such brands as Mark Levinson JBL Harman/Kardon Revel AKG Infinity Logic 7 and others. Harman's auto unit sells branded audio systems through several carmakers including Toyota Lexus and BMW. Its professional unit makes audio equipment such as monitors amplifiers microphones and mixing consoles for recording studios cinemas touring performers and others. Harman also offers computer software and development tools to the automotive energy medical and telecom industries.

	Annual Growth	06/11	06/12	06/13	06/14	06/15
Sales ($ mil.)	13.0%	3,772.3	4,364.1	4,297.8	5,348.5	6,155.3
Net income ($ mil.)	26.0%	135.9	329.5	142.4	234.7	342.7
Market value ($ mil.)	27.1%	3,245.5	2,820.3	3,860.1	7,651.1	8,470.8
Employees	24.4%	10,103	11,366	12,221	14,202	24,197

HARMONIC, INC.

NMS: HLIT

4300 North First Street
San Jose, CA 95134
Phone: 408 542-2500
Fax: –
Web: www.harmonicinc.com

CEO: –
CFO: Harold L. (Hal) Covert
HR: Anne M Lynch
FYE: December 31
Type: Public

Harmonic answers the demand for advanced television features. The company provides fiber-optic and wireless network transmission products used to enable video-on-demand services. Its video transmission equipment includes digital headend systems digital signal encoders and complete provider-to-subscriber delivery systems. Harmonic also supplies multiplexers optical nodes transmitters optical amplifiers and other broadband network access equipment. The company sells directly and through distributors and systems integrators primarily to cable and satellite TV providers. Customers include Swisscom and British Sky in Europe and Comcast and Time Warner Cable in the US.

	Annual Growth	12/10	12/11	12/12	12/13	12/14
Sales ($ mil.)	0.6%	423.3	549.3	530.5	461.9	433.6
Net income ($ mil.)	–	(4.3)	8.8	(10.9)	37.0	(46.2)
Market value ($ mil.)	(4.9%)	751.6	442.0	444.6	647.2	614.8
Employees	(1.8%)	1,106	1,145	1,148	1,032	1,028

HARNISH GROUP INC.

17025 W. Valley Hwy.
Tukwila WA 98188-5519
Phone: 425-251-5800
Fax: 425-251-5886
Web: www.ncmachinery.com

CEO: –
CFO: –
HR: –
FYE: December 31
Type: Private

Harnish Group Inc. (HGI) harnesses the power of the Caterpillar brand in some sparsely populated pieces of real estate. The equipment dealer services rents and sells new and used Caterpillar machines (including bulldozers tractors earthmovers and graders) and parts in Washington and Alaska. It also distributes equipment made by other manufacturers and provides engines and power systems. Harnish operates about 20 equipment branches under the name N C Machinery as well as a dozen rental locations as The Cat Rental Store. Descendants of founder J. J. Niehenke including CEO John J. Harnish own the company.

HARP'S FOOD STORES INC.

918 S. Gutensohn Rd.
Springdale AR 72765
Phone: 479-751-7601
Fax: 479-751-3625
Web: www.harpsfood.com

CEO: Roger Collins
CFO: Jim Natz
HR: –
FYE: August 31
Type: Private

It's tough to survive in the face of Arkansas giant Wal-Mart but Harps Food Stores (founded when Sam Walton was 12 years old) is putting up a fight. The company which got its start when Floy and Harvard Harp put down $500 cash and opened the first Harp's Cash Grocery in 1930 operates more than 65 grocery stores mostly in Arkansas but also in Missouri and Oklahoma. Its stores operating under the Harps Food Stores and Price Cutter Food Warehouse banners range in size from 13000 to 63000 sq. ft. and often feature bakeries pharmacies and meat departments. Harps operated as a family-run chain until 2001 when it became an employee-owned business.

HARRINGTON MEMORIAL HOSPITAL INC.

100 SOUTH ST STE 1
SOUTHBRIDGE, MA 015504047
Phone: 508-765-9771
Fax: –
Web: www.harringtonhospital.org

CEO: –
CFO: –
HR: Donald (Don) Brechner
FYE: September 30
Type: Private

Harrington Memorial Hospital works to ensure that its patients feel less harried about health care. The health care facility founded in 1931 serves south-central Massachusetts and northeastern Connecticut. Harrington Memorial boasts nearly 115 beds and some 180 physicians who provide general and emergency medical care. It offers such specialized services as obstetrics physical therapy pediatrics diagnostic imaging and substance abuse treatment. The hospital also provides patients with home health care services and operates health clinics. Harrington Memorial invests in nearby Hubbard Regional Hospital through a management agreement in an effort to shore up the finances of both facilities.

	Annual Growth	09/05	09/06	09/08	09/09	09/13
Sales ($ mil.)	(3.0%)	–	130.0	76.4	86.7	105.3
Net income ($ mil.)	61.1%	–	–	0.4	2.7	4.6
Market value ($ mil.)	–	–	–	–	–	–
Employees	–	–	–	–	–	900

HARRIS & HARRIS GROUP, INC.   NMS: TINY

1450 Broadway
New York, NY 10018
Phone: 212 582-0900
Fax: –
Web: www.hhvc.com

CEO: Douglas W Jamison
CFO: Patricia N Egan
HR: –
FYE: December 31
Type: Public

Harris & Harris Group likes to think small. The business development company (BDC) invests mostly in startup firms developing so-called "tiny technology" — microsystems microelectromechanical systems and nanotechnology used in applications in such sectors as electronics medical devices pharmaceuticals semiconductors telecommunications and clean technology. The company seeks out small thinly capitalized firms lacking operating history or experienced management. Harris & Harris has made more than 80 venture capital investments since 1983; its current portfolio consists of interests in some 30 firms including Molecular Imprints Nanosys and NeoPhotonics.

	Annual Growth	12/10	12/11	12/12	12/13	12/14
Sales ($ mil.)	3.8%	0.4	0.7	0.7	0.5	0.5
Net income ($ mil.)	–	10.6	(3.5)	(20.0)	(7.8)	(13.6)
Market value ($ mil.)	(9.4%)	137.0	108.2	103.2	93.2	92.3
Employees	6.8%	10	10	13	13	13

HARRIS CONNECT LLC

1400-A Crossways Blvd.
Chesapeake VA 23320
Phone: 757-965-8100
Fax: 845-940-0801
Web: www.harrisconnect.com

CEO: Robert Gluck
CFO: John Harris
HR: –
FYE: December 31
Type: Private

This company would hate for you to miss a class reunion. Harris Connect maintains membership databases for more than 4900 institutions including schools alumni associations and other membership-based organizations. It produces more than 600 directories a year both in print and online. Among its clients are colleges and universities fraternities and sororities and private and public high schools. The company has built more than 500 online communities for alumni groups and professional organizations to network and organize. The information hubs offer message boards online chat and e-mail services. New York-based private equity fund Wicks Communications & Media Partners III owns the company.

HARRIS CORP.   NYS: HRS

1025 West NASA Boulevard
Melbourne, FL 32919
Phone: 321 727-9100
Fax: –
Web: www.harris.com

CEO: William M. (Bill) Brown
CFO: Rahul Ghai
HR: Robert L. Duffy
FYE: July 03
Type: Public

Harris has ways to make its customers communicate. The company which develops communications products for government and commercial customers in more than 125 countries makes radio-frequency (RF) and satellite communications and other wireless network transmission equipment; air traffic control systems; and digital network management systems. Harris also offers specialized IT services. Harris' commercial clients come from the construction energy health care maritime oil transportation and utilities industries.

	Annual Growth	07/11*	06/12	06/13	06/14*	07/15
Sales ($ mil.)	(3.8%)	5,924.6	5,451.3	5,111.7	5,012.0	5,083.0
Net income ($ mil.)	(13.2%)	588.0	30.6	113.0	534.8	334.0
Market value ($ mil.)	14.3%	5,633.4	5,175.8	6,091.0	9,396.9	9,614.6
Employees	7.2%	16,900	15,200	14,000	14,000	22,300

*Fiscal year change

HARRIS TEETER INC.

701 Crestdale Rd.
Matthews NC 28105
Phone: 704-844-3100
Fax: 704-844-3138
Web: www.harristeeter.com

CEO: –
CFO: –
HR: –
FYE: September 30
Type: Subsidiary

Neither teetering nor tottering Harris Teeter operates more than 200 supermarkets in North Carolina and seven other southeastern states and the District of Columbia. Most of the regional chain's grocery stores feature niceties such as sushi bars gourmet delis cafes and wine departments; many also house pharmacies. Harris Teeter which also has a handful of distribution centers is accelerating its growth in Maryland northern Virginia and the competitive Washington D.C. market and nearby suburbs. Formed by the combination of Harris Super Markets and Teeter's Food Marts in 1960 Harris Teeter is owned by holding company Harris Teeter Supermarkets.

HARRY & DAVID HOLDINGS INC.

2500 S. Pacific Hwy.
Medford OR 97501
Phone: 541-864-2362
Fax: 800-648-6640
Web: www.hndcorp.com

CEO: –
CFO: –
HR: –
FYE: June 30
Type: Private

Harry & David Holdings (HDH) wants customers to enjoy the fruits — and flowers — of its labors. Its Harry and David Direct Marketing catalogs and e-commerce unit offers gift baskets filled with gourmet foods most notably its Royal Riviera pears Moose Munch popcorn snacks and Tower of Treats gifts. It also runs the Fruit-of-the-Month Club. Harry and David Stores sell fruits flowers gourmet specialties and wine through about 70 locations in more than 35 states. The company's products are sold under its namesake Harry & David Wolferman's and Cushman brands. HDH emerged from six months in Chapter 11 bankruptcy protection in September 2011 after the court approved its reorganization plan in August.

HARRY WINSTON INC.

1330 Avenue of the Americas
New York NY 10019
Phone: 212-315-7900
Fax: 212-581-2612
Web: www.harrywinston.com

CEO: Frederic De Narp
CFO: Robert Scott
HR: –
FYE: January 31
Type: Subsidiary

Diamonds are Harry Winston's best friend. The diamond jeweler and luxury timepiece retailer is one of the prized assets held by Canadian diamond titan Harry Winston Diamond. Harry Winston buys designs and sells fine diamonds and gems and watches through 20 salons in Beijing Beverly Hills London New York and Paris and other prime locations. Timepieces are also sold in some 190 locations worldwide as well as online. The company draws an affluent clientele including sultans starlets and business moguls who demand the highest quality. The House of Harry Winston was established in 1932 by Harry Winston the son of a New York jeweler. Harry Winston generates more than half of its parent company's sales.

HARSCO CORP.
NYS: HSC

350 Poplar Church Road
Camp Hill, PA 17011
Phone: 717 763-7064
Fax: –
Web: www.harsco.com

CEO: F. Nicholas (Nick) Grasberger
CFO: Peter F. Minan
HR: –
FYE: December 31
Type: Public

If you're a metal producer or a construction company with metal to spare Harsco is at your service. The company's metals and minerals segment provides mill services at steel factories and offers metal reclamation slag processing scrap management and other services for steel and nonferrous metals producers. The manufacturer's Harsco Industrial makes industrial grating air-cooled heat exchangers boilers and water heaters and related products. Another Harsco unit Harco Rail makes railway track and other equipment and provides rail maintenance services.

	Annual Growth	12/10	12/11	12/12	12/13	12/14
Sales ($ mil.)	(9.2%)	3,038.7	3,302.7	3,046.0	2,896.5	2,065.7
Net income ($ mil.)	–	6.8	(11.5)	(254.6)	(227.9)	(24.8)
Market value ($ mil.)	(9.6%)	2,284.3	1,660.0	1,895.5	2,260.9	1,523.7
Employees	(10.8%)	19,300	19,650	18,500	12,300	12,200

HARTE-HANKS INC
NYS: HHS

9601 McAllister Freeway, Suite 610
San Antonio, TX 78216
Phone: 210 829-9000
Fax: –
Web: www.hartehanks.com

CEO: Karen A. Puckett
CFO: Douglas (Doug) Shepard
HR: Gavin Pommernelle
FYE: December 31
Type: Public

Harte-Hanks gives thanks to direct marketing services. One of the largest producers of shoppers (advertising circulars sent by mail) in the country the company provides integrated direct-marketing services in the US and internationally including market research and analytics (with help from its Aberdeen subsidiary). It designs contact databases tracks leads and provides telephone e-mail and printing and mailing services to connect customers with their potential clients. Customers include major retailers and companies from the financial services health care and technology industries.

	Annual Growth	12/10	12/11	12/12	12/13	12/14
Sales ($ mil.)	(10.4%)	860.5	850.8	767.7	559.6	553.7
Net income ($ mil.)	(18.2%)	53.6	44.2	(83.4)	13.4	24.0
Market value ($ mil.)	(11.8%)	788.9	561.5	364.5	483.1	478.1
Employees	1.3%	5,150	6,260	6,410	5,360	5,423

HARTFORD FINANCIAL SERVICES GROUP INC.
NYS: HIG

One Hartford Plaza
Hartford, CT 06155
Phone: 860 547-5000
Fax: –
Web: www.thehartford.com

CEO: Christopher J. Swift
CFO: Beth A. Bombara
HR: Martha (Marty) Gervasi
FYE: December 31
Type: Public

Despite its name at its heart The Hartford Financial Services Group is an insurer with a range of commercial and personal property/casualty insurance and financial products. Its commercial operations include auto liability workers' compensation policies as well as group benefits and specialty commercial coverage for large companies. The Hartford also offers consumer homeowners and auto coverage. It has been the direct auto and home insurance writer for AARP's members for more than 30 years. Through its mutual fund division the company offers wealth management products and services. The Hartford in business since 1810 sells products through a network of independent agents and brokerages.

	Annual Growth	12/10	12/11	12/12	12/13	12/14
Assets ($ mil.)	(6.3%)	318,346.0	304,064.0	298,513.0	277,884.0	245,013.0
Net income ($ mil.)	(17.0%)	1,680.0	662.0	(38.0)	176.0	798.0
Market value ($ mil.)	12.0%	11,242.8	6,896.8	9,523.9	15,376.6	17,693.9
Employees	(10.1%)	26,800	24,400	22,500	18,800	17,500

HARTFORD HEALTH CARE CORPORATION

80 Seymour St.
Hartford CT 06102
Phone: 860-545-5000
Fax: 860-545-5066
Web: hartfordhealthcare.org

CEO: Elliot Joseph
CFO: Thomas Marcoczi
HR: –
FYE: September 30
Type: Private - Not-for-Pr

Hartford Health Care provides a variety of health services to the descendants of our founding fathers. Founded in 1854 the health care system operates a network of hospitals behavioral health centers nursing and rehabilitation facilities medical labs and numerous community programs for residents in northern Connecticut. Medical specialties range from orthopedics and women's health to cancer and heart care. Hartford Health Care's flagship facility is the Hartford Hospital an 870-bed teaching hospital affiliated with the University of Connecticut Medical School. Its network also includes MidState Medical Center (some 140 beds) Windham Hospital (130 beds) and The Hospital of Central Connecticut (410 beds).

HARVARD BIOSCIENCE INC.
NMS: HBIO

84 October Hill Road
Holliston, MA 01746
Phone: 508 893-8999
Fax: –
Web: www.harvardbioscience.com

CEO: Jeffrey A. Duchemin
CFO: Robert E. Gagnon
HR: –
FYE: December 31
Type: Public

Toss an 850-page Harvard Bioscience catalog toward a bioscience researcher and it will keep him or her busy for hours. The company develops manufactures and markets the scientific gizmos and instruments used in pharmaceutical biotechnology academic and government labs worldwide. Its 11000-item product line focuses on molecular biology and ADMET (absorption distribution metabolism elimination and toxicology) testing. ADMET tests are used to screen drug candidates. Other products include spectrophotometers multi-well plate readers and protein calculators. Customers can shop directly online from its printed Harvard Apparatus catalog or through distributors.

	Annual Growth	12/10	12/11	12/12	12/13	12/14
Sales ($ mil.)	0.1%	108.2	108.9	111.2	105.2	108.7
Net income ($ mil.)	(40.7%)	19.0	3.8	2.4	(1.8)	2.4
Market value ($ mil.)	8.6%	132.9	126.0	142.6	153.0	184.6
Employees	3.5%	389	396	422	368	447

HARVARD PILGRIM HEALTH CARE INC.

93 Worcester St.
Wellesley MA 02481
Phone: 617-509-1000
Fax: 617-495-0754
Web: www.harvard.edu

CEO: Charles Baker
CFO: –
HR: –
FYE: December 31
Type: Private - Not-for-Pr

Harvard Pilgrim Health Care takes care of New Englanders. A leading provider of health benefits in Massachusetts the not-for-profit organization also offers plans to residents of New Hampshire and Maine. It has more than 1 million members enrolled in its HMO PPO point-of-service and government plans. Those members have access to regional and national networks of hospitals and doctors. Harvard Pilgrim also targets multi-state employers with its Choice Plus and Options PPO plans offered through a partnership with UnitedHealthcare. Harvard Pilgrim has a network of more than 135 hospitals and 28000 doctors and clinicians.

HARVEST NATURAL RESOURCES INC.

1177 Enclave Pkwy. Ste. 300
Houston TX 77077
Phone: 281-899-5700
Fax: 281-899-5702
Web: www.harvestnr.com

NYSE: HNR
CEO: James A Edmiston
CFO: Stephen C Haynes
HR: –
FYE: December 31
Type: Public

Harvest Natural Resources is keen to harvest the natural resources of oil and gas. The independent's main exploration and production work takes place in Venezuela where operations hit a snag in 2005 due to Venezuela's difficult political climate which has restricted the company's contracts and production activities. Harvest currently operates in Venezuela through a 40% interest in exploration firm Petrodelta. In 2008 it acquired a 50% stake in the Dussafu Marin exploration- and production-sharing contract located offshore Gabon from South African synthetic fuels firm Sasol. It has also begun exploring in the western states and the Gulf Coast in the US as well as in Indonesia the Middle East and China.

HARVEY MUDD COLLEGE

301 PLATT BLVD
CLAREMONT, CA 917115901
Phone: 909-621-8000
Fax: –
Web: www.hmc.edu

CEO: –
CFO: Andrew Dorantes
HR: Alicia Guzman
FYE: June 30
Type: Private

Mudders get down and dirty with math and science. About 800 undergraduate students (called "Mudders") attend Harvey Mudd College (HMC) a private non-profit liberal arts school that specializes in engineering mathematics and the sciences. HMC is a member of The Claremont Colleges a confederation of five independent undergraduate colleges and two graduate schools that is managed by the Claremont University Consortium. The group shares resources and offers dual degree programs. HMC alums include Jonathan Gay creator of Flash software and Unison founder Rick Sontag.

	Annual Growth	06/07	06/08	06/10	06/11	06/13
Sales ($ mil.)	–	–	–	0.0	56.3	65.5	79.8
Net income ($ mil.)	–	–	–	(5.0)	1.6	41.0
Market value ($ mil.)	–	–	–	–	–	–
Employees	–	–	–	–	–	235

HASBRO, INC.

1027 Newport Avenue
Pawtucket, RI 02861
Phone: 401 431-8697
Fax: –
Web: www.hasbro.com

NMS: HAS
CEO: Brian Goldner
CFO: Deborah M. (Deb) Thomas
HR: Dolph Johnson
FYE: December 28
Type: Public

It's all fun and games at Hasbro the #2 toy maker in the US (after Mattel) and the producer of such childhood favorites as G.I. Joe Play-Doh Tonka toys Mr. Potato Head Nerf balls and My Little Pony. Besides toys Hasbro makes board games under its Milton Bradley (Scrabble Candy Land) Cranium and Parker Brothers (Monopoly Trivial Pursuit) brands as well as trading cards including Magic: The Gathering (through its Wizards of the Coast unit) and Dungeons & Dragons. Hasbro is also famous for making Star Wars action figures. In addition to Disney and Disney's Marvel Entertainment Hasbro licenses popular names and characters for other toys and games.

	Annual Growth	12/10	12/11	12/12	12/13	12/14
Sales ($ mil.)	1.7%	4,002.2	4,285.6	4,089.0	4,082.2	4,277.2
Net income ($ mil.)	1.1%	397.8	385.4	336.0	286.2	415.9
Market value ($ mil.)	3.4%	6,042.0	4,038.4	4,397.0	6,774.2	6,916.2
Employees	(2.7%)	5,800	5,900	5,500	5,000	5,200

HASTINGS ENTERTAINMENT, INC.

3601 Plains Boulevard
Amarillo, TX 79102
Phone: 806 351-2300
Fax: 806 351-2424
Web: www.gohastings.com

NAS: HAST
CEO: Joel Weinshanker
CFO: Dan Crow
HR: –
FYE: January 31
Type: Public

Hastings Entertainment has it all for a smaller-town Saturday night. The company operates about 135 superstores in nearly 20 Midwestern and western US states. Hastings' stores and website sell new and used CDs movies books magazines and video games in addition to related electronics such as video game consoles and DVD players. Hastings also rents DVDs and video games. Its store locations average 24000 sq. ft. and offer such amenities as music listening stations reading chairs coffee bars and children's play areas. Hastings' other store concepts include Sun Adventure Sports which offers bicycles skateboards and other sporting goods and Tradesmart a seller of mostly used entertainment products.

	Annual Growth	01/09	01/10	01/11	01/12	01/13
Sales ($ mil.)	(3.7%)	538.7	531.3	521.1	496.4	462.5
Net income ($ mil.)	–	4.1	6.9	1.7	(17.6)	(9.3)
Market value ($ mil.)	(3.7%)	20.6	34.5	45.1	13.2	17.7
Employees	(2.4%)	5,774	5,704	5,848	5,153	5,233

HAT WORLD CORPORATION

7555 Woodland Dr.
Indianapolis IN 46278
Phone: 317-334-9428
Fax: 317-337-1428
Web: www.hatworld.com

CEO: –
CFO: Richard E Cramer
HR: –
FYE: January 31
Type: Subsidiary

Hat World thanks you for putting a lid on it. The mostly mall-based retailer specializes in caps featuring licensed logos of pro sports teams (MLB NBA NFL and NHL) and collegiate athletics. It operates 985 stores under the banners Hat World Lids Head Quarters and several others in the US Puerto Rico and Canada. Its websites which run under about 15 names stock caps with popular regional team logos. The company also holds a licensing agreement with Mainland Headwear. Hat World opened its first store in 1995; six years later it bought out bankrupt rival Lids and tripled in size. Acquired in 2004 by Genesco Hat World is part of the parent's Lids Sports Group which generates about 30% of total sales.

HATCH MOTT MACDONALD GROUP INC.

111 WOOD AVE S STE 5 — CEO: Nicholas DeNichilo
ISELIN, NJ 088302700 — CFO: –
Phone: 973-379-3400 — HR: –
Fax: – — FYE: December 31
Web: www.hatchmott.com — Type: Private

Hatch Mott MacDonald (HMM) is the consulting engineering subsidiary of Mott MacDonald and offers planning project development analysis design construction management facility maintenance and facility management for all types of infrastructure projects to public and private clients across North America. It specializes in tunnels wastewater systems pipelines rail and transit systems buildings and utilities. Customers are both private companies and municipalities. HMM strategically acquires specialized engineering firms in new regions to expand its service offerings and geographic market reach. Formed in 1996 HHM now boasts a staff of 25000 and has more than 75 offices in the US and Canada.

	Annual Growth	12/09	12/10	12/11	12/12	12/13
Sales ($ mil.)	10.7%	–	374.2	440.6	478.0	507.4
Net income ($ mil.)	16.9%	–	–	25.4	27.2	34.7
Market value ($ mil.)	–	–	–	–	–	–
Employees	–	–	–	–	–	2,500

HATTERAS FINANCIAL CORP
NYS: HTS

751 W. Fourth Street, Suite 400 — CEO: Michael R. Hough
Winston Salem, NC 27101 — CFO: Kenneth A. Steele
Phone: 336 760-9347 — HR: –
Fax: – — FYE: December 31
Web: www.hatfin.com — Type: Public

Hatteras Financial hopes for smooth sailing on the sometimes tumultuous seas of mortgage investing. The company is a real estate investment trust (REIT) that invests in adjustable-rate and hybrid adjustable-rate single-family residential mortgages guaranteed by a US government agency or a government-backed company such as Ginnie Mae Fannie Mae or Freddie Mac. Hatteras Financial's investment portfolio valued at some $7 billion consists mostly of hybrid adjustable-rate loans with terms of three to five years. Hatteras Financial is externally managed by Atlantic Capital Advisors.

	Annual Growth	12/10	12/11	12/12	12/13	12/14
Sales ($ mil.)	7.6%	265.0	426.1	506.3	452.3	355.8
Net income ($ mil.)	(24.1%)	169.5	284.4	349.2	(134.1)	56.4
Market value ($ mil.)	(11.7%)	2,929.3	2,551.9	2,400.9	1,581.2	1,783.5
Employees	–	–	–	–	–	13

HAUPPAUGE DIGITAL, INC.
NBB: HAUP

91 Cabot Court — CEO: Kenneth Plotkin
Hauppauge, NY 11788 — CFO: Gerald Tucciarone
Phone: 631 434-1600 — HR: –
Fax: – — FYE: September 30
Web: www.hauppauge.com — Type: Public

Wanna watch TV at work? Hauppauge Digital's WinTV analog and digital video boards let viewers videoconference watch TV and view input from VCRs and camcorders in a resizable window on a PC monitor. Hauppauge (pronounced "HAW-pog") also offers boards that accommodate radio and Internet broadcasts and makes a line of PC video editing boards. The company outsources its manufacturing to companies in Europe and Asia. The company sells its products to contract electronics manufacturers including ASUSTeK Computer and Hon Hai Precision Industry (Foxconn) and partners with companies such as Intel and Microsoft. Customers outside the US make up more than half of sales.

	Annual Growth	09/09	09/10	09/11	09/12	09/13
Sales ($ mil.)	(13.0%)	59.3	56.9	42.3	44.6	34.0
Net income ($ mil.)	–	(7.1)	(1.8)	(5.8)	(2.5)	(4.0)
Market value ($ mil.)	(24.0%)	11.7	26.0	8.7	10.9	3.9
Employees	(12.5%)	169	167	146	132	99

HAWAI I PACIFIC HEALTH

55 MERCHANT ST STE 2500 — CEO: Raymond Vara
HONOLULU, HI 968134306 — CFO: David (Dave) Okabe
Phone: 808-535-7350 — HR: –
Fax: – — FYE: June 30
Web: www.kapiolani.org — Type: Private

Hawaii may be paradise but even in paradise's some residents get sick. That's when Hawai'i Pacific Health (HPH) surfs in to save the day. HPH is a not-for-profit health care system consisting of four hospitals (Kapi'olani Medical Center for Women & Children Pali Momi Medical Center Straub Clinic & Hospital and Wilcox Memorial Hospital) across the islands with a combined capacity of 550 beds. The system offers a full array of tertiary specialty and acute care services through its hospitals which also serve as teaching and research centers as well as about 50 outpatient centers. Specialized services offered by HPH include cardiac care maternity services oncology orthopedics and pediatric care.

	Annual Growth	06/09	06/10	06/11	06/12	06/13
Sales ($ mil.)	5.3%	–	112.3	901.6	119.4	131.0
Net income ($ mil.)	–	–	–	75.7	(1.7)	(3.8)
Market value ($ mil.)	–	–	–	–	–	–
Employees	–	–	–	–	–	5,400

HAWAI I PACIFIC UNIVERSITY

1164 BISHOP ST STE 800 — CEO: –
HONOLULU, HI 968132817 — CFO: Bruce Edwards
Phone: 808-544-0200 — HR: –
Fax: – — FYE: June 30
Web: www.hpu.edu — Type: Private

Hawai'i Pacific University infuses a little aloha spirit into the liberal arts. The state's largest private institution of higher education offers some 50 undergraduate degrees and about a dozen graduate programs to more than 7000 students with majors ranging from journalism to business administration. The university's main campus is located in downtown Honolulu while two others also on the island of Oahu focus on environmental science marine biology oceanography and nursing. Students come from more than 80 countries making it one of the most diverse campuses in the world. Founded in 1965 the not-for-profit university's student/faculty ratio is 15:1.

	Annual Growth	12/04	12/05*	06/06	06/09	06/13
Sales ($ mil.)	–	–	(838.8)	88.3	89.0	99.8
Net income ($ mil.)	–	–	–	5.8	(7.2)	(11.7)
Market value ($ mil.)	–	–	–	–	–	–
Employees	–	–	–	–	–	1,300

*Fiscal year change

HAWAIIAN ELECTRIC INDUSTRIES, INC.
NYS: HE

1001 Bishop Street, Suite 2900 — CEO: Constance H. (Connie) Lau
Honolulu, HI 96813 — CFO: James A. (Jim) Ajello
Phone: 808 543-5662 — HR: –
Fax: 808 543-7966 — FYE: December 31
Web: www.hei.com — Type: Public

When the luau bonfires go out Hawaiian Electric Industries (HEI) keeps the islands lit up. HEI is the holding company for Hawaiian Electric Company (HECO) and some non-utility businesses. HECO (along with its utility subsidiaries Maui Electric and Hawaii Electric Light) serves about 450000 customers (95% of the population) as the sole public electricity provider on the islands of Hawaii Lanai Maui Molokai and Oahu. The utilities account for the bulk of HEI's sales and have a generating capacity of about 2350 MW. On the non-utility side it operates American Savings Bank with 56 retail branches in the state (although company is selling this business).

	Annual Growth	12/10	12/11	12/12	12/13	12/14
Sales ($ mil.)	5.0%	2,665.0	3,242.3	3,375.0	3,238.5	3,239.5
Net income ($ mil.)	10.2%	115.4	140.1	140.5	163.4	170.2
Market value ($ mil.)	10.1%	2,337.5	2,715.9	2,578.5	2,672.9	3,433.9
Employees	3.7%	3,427	3,654	3,870	3,966	3,965

HAWAIIAN HOLDINGS INC
NMS: HA

3375 Koapaka Street, Suite G-350
Honolulu, HI 96819
Phone: 808 835-3700
Fax: –
Web: www.hawaiianairlines.com
CEO: Mark B. Dunkerley
CFO: Shannon L. Okinaka
HR: Barbara D Falvey
FYE: December 31
Type: Public

Luaus leis and laying in the sun — Hawaiian Holdings knows how to get you there. The company's main subsidiary Hawaiian Airlines transports passengers and cargo between Honolulu and about a dozen major cities in the western US. Transpacific routes account for most of the carrier's revenue. Hawaiian Airlines also serves four of the six main Hawaiian Islands and destinations in the South Pacific such as American Samoa Australia the Philippines and Tahiti. It operates a fleet of about 50 aircraft (most are Boeing 717s for flights between the Hawaiian Islands and Boeing 767s for transpacific flights). In addition to its scheduled passenger and cargo operations Hawaiian Airlines provides charter services.

	Annual Growth	12/11	12/12	12/13	12/14	12/15
Sales ($ mil.)	8.9%	1,650.5	1,962.4	2,155.9	2,314.9	2,317.5
Net income ($ mil.)	–	(2.6)	53.2	51.9	68.9	182.6
Market value ($ mil.)	57.1%	309.7	350.8	514.3	1,391.1	1,886.7
Employees	6.5%	4,314	4,906	5,249	5,380	5,548

HAWAIIAN TELCOM HOLDCO, INC.
NMS: HCOM

1177 Bishop Street
Honolulu, HI 96813
Phone: 808 546-4511
Fax: –
Web: www.hawaiiantel.com
CEO: Eric K. Yeaman
CFO: Dan T. Bessey
HR: –
FYE: December 31
Type: Public

No "coconut telegraph" Hawaiian Telcom through its operating subsidiaries provides modern telecommunications services to residential and business customers in the island state. The company has almost 400000 local access lines (aka landlines) in service serving about one-third of the state's 1.3 million people. It also provides long-distance phone service to about 200000 customers and broadband Internet access to about 100000 customers. Hawaiian Telcom resells wireless communications services through an agreement with Sprint Nextel but wireless services only account for 1% of sales. The company has been in operation since 1883.

	Annual Growth	12/10	12/11	12/12	12/13	12/14
Sales ($ mil.)	55.5%	66.8	395.2	385.5	391.2	390.7
Net income ($ mil.)	26.8%	3.1	26.2	110.0	10.5	8.1
Market value ($ mil.)	(0.4%)	298.9	164.4	208.1	313.5	294.3
Employees	0.0%	1,400	1,300	1,400	1,400	1,400

HAWKER PACIFIC AEROSPACE

11240 Sherman Way
Sun Valley CA 91352
Phone: 818-765-6201
Fax: 818-765-5759
Web: www.hawker.com
CEO: Bernd Riggers
CFO: Troy Trower
HR: –
FYE: December 31
Type: Subsidiary

Hawker Pacific Aerospace has made it through the turbulence of the aviation industry on a fixed wing and a repair. A subsidiary of Lufthansa Technik and part of that firm's Landing Gear Division Hawker provides overhaul and repair services for aircraft landing gear hydromechanical components wheels and brake systems from locations in London and California. It has smaller operations in Germany and China operated with Ameco a joint venture controlled by Lufthansa and Air China. Hawker Pacific also sells aftermarket parts for the fixed-wing aircraft and helicopters of about 80 manufacturers. Customers include commercial airlines cargo carriers and the US government.

HAWKINS CONSTRUCTION COMPANY

2516 DEER PARK BLVD
OMAHA, NE 681053771
Phone: 402-342-4455
Fax: –
Web: www.hawkins1.com
CEO: Fred Hawkins Jr
CFO: –
HR: –
FYE: December 31
Type: Private

Hawkins Construction provides both commercial building and heavy/highway contracting services. The diversified contractor has a project portfolio that includes regional banks warehouses schools churches and prisons. It also works on highways bridges site developments and parking structures and is one of the Midwest's largest road builders. Clients include the University of Nebraska Mutual of Omaha and Hewlett-Packard. The family-owned company began with a successful contract bid in 1922 by Kenneth Hawkins and his brother Earl for what is now Lincoln Nebraska's Memorial Stadium; the firm was incorporated in 1960 by Kenneth and his son Fred.

	Annual Growth	12/06	12/07	12/08	12/12	12/13
Sales ($ mil.)	(5.3%)	–	223.4	239.0	0.0	160.6
Net income ($ mil.)	(10.9%)	–	–	16.0	0.0	9.0
Market value ($ mil.)	–	–	–	–	–	–
Employees	–	–	–	–	–	400

HAWKINS INC
NMS: HWKN

2381 Rosegate
Roseville, MN 55113
Phone: 612 331-6910
Fax: –
CEO: Patrick H. Hawkins
CFO: Kathleen P. Pepski
HR: –
FYE: March 29
Type: Public

Hawkins wants its customers to bulk up — on chemicals that is. The company processes and distributes bulk specialty chemicals. Its Industrial Chemicals segment stores and distributes caustic soda phosphoric acid and aqua ammonia among others. The segment also makes bleach (sodium hypochlorite) repackages liquid chlorine and custom blends other chemicals. Hawkins' Water Treatment group distributes products and equipment used to treat drinking water municipal and industrial wastewater and swimming pools. It also distributes laboratory-grade chemicals for the pharmaceutical industry. The company operates 29 facilities and has a fleet of trucks and tankers to serve customers throughout the Midwest US.

	Annual Growth	04/11	04/12*	03/13	03/14	03/15
Sales ($ mil.)	5.2%	297.6	343.8	350.4	348.3	364.0
Net income ($ mil.)	(1.4%)	20.3	22.7	17.1	18.1	19.2
Market value ($ mil.)	(1.9%)	431.8	393.0	422.1	382.0	400.4
Employees	6.9%	321	343	354	361	419

*Fiscal year change

HAWORTH INC.

1 Haworth Center
Holland MI 49423-9576
Phone: 616-393-3000
Fax: 616-393-1570
Web: www.haworth.com
CEO: Franco Bianchi
CFO: –
HR: –
FYE: December 31
Type: Private

Designers at Haworth sit at their cubicles and think about ... more cubicles. The company is one of the top office furniture manufacturers in the US competing with top rivals Steelcase and HNI. Known for innovative design it offers a full range of furniture including partitions desks chairs tables and storage products. Brands include Monaco Patterns PLACES and X99. The company operates 80-plus showrooms worldwide and sells its products through more than 600 dealers. Haworth is the company behind the prewired partitions that make today's cubicled workplace possible. Haworth is owned by the family of Gerrard W. Haworth who founded the company in 1948.

HAWTHORNE MACHINERY CO.

16945 CAMINO SAN BERNARDO
SAN DIEGO, CA 921272499
Phone: 858-674-7000
Fax: -
Web: www.hawthornecat.com

CEO: Tee K Ness
CFO: -
HR: Phil Zamora
FYE: December 31
Type: Private

Leader of the track Hawthorne Machinery a Caterpillar dealership sells and rents more than 300 CAT equipment models including tractors trucks loaders compactors harvesters graders excavators and power systems. It also provides more than 73000 parts and repair services for industrial and construction contractors and other public and private customers around San Diego County. Hawthorne Machinery offers new and used equipment and rentals of brand-name equipment by such blue chip OEMs as Kubota Spartan and Sullair. The company was founded in 1956 by Tom Hawthorne.

	Annual Growth	12/01	12/02	12/03	12/06	12/07
Sales ($ mil.)	13.9%	-	176.2	170.8	377.2	338.1
Net income ($ mil.)	(69.1%)	-	-	44.8	7.6	0.4
Market value ($ mil.)	-	-	-	-	-	-
Employees	-	-	-	-	-	1,000

HAY HOUSE INC.

2776 LOKER AVE W
CARLSBAD, CA 920106611
Phone: 760-431-7695
Fax: -
Web: www.hayhouse.com

CEO: -
CFO: -
HR: -
FYE: December 31
Type: Private

Self-help publisher Hay House publishes books and sells audio and video content covering topics such as self-help sociology philosophy psychology alternative health and environmental issues. It has more than 300 print books and 350 audio programs from some 130 authors including TV psychic John Edward talk show host Montel Williams and radio personality Tavis Smiley. In addition to its eponymous imprint the company publishes under the New Beginnings Press Princess Books and Smiley Books labels; the firm has international divisions in Australia the UK India and South Africa. Hay House was founded in 1984 by Louise Hay to self-publish her first two books Heal Your Body and You Can Heal Your Life.

	Annual Growth	12/03	12/04	12/05	12/06	12/08
Sales ($ mil.)	-	-	-	0.0	57.0	60.5
Net income ($ mil.)	-	-	-	0.0	1.5	0.9
Market value ($ mil.)	-	-	-	-	-	-
Employees	-	-	-	-	-	92

HAYES GREEN BEACH MEMORIAL HOSPITAL

321 E HARRIS ST
CHARLOTTE, MI 48813-1629
Phone: 517-543-1050
Fax: -
Web: www.hgbhealth.com

CEO: Matthew Rush
CFO: Kim Capp
HR: -
FYE: March 31
Type: Private

Hayes Green Beach Memorial Hospital (HGB) provides a variety of medical services for the residents of central Michigan. Specialized services include cardiology emergency medicine home care radiology pain management and rehabilitation. The 25-bed hospital also offers wellness programs a family birthing center and community education services and it operates several community clinics. The hospital was founded in 1933 and is governed by the Eaton County Board of Commissioners.

	Annual Growth	03/05	03/06	03/07	03/09	03/12
Sales ($ mil.)	5.2%	-	38.1	41.5	42.9	51.7
Net income ($ mil.)	10.6%	-	1.4	(0.2)	(1.3)	2.6
Market value ($ mil.)	-	-	-	-	-	-
Employees	-	-	-	-	-	290

HAYES LEMMERZ INTERNATIONAL INC.

15300 Centennial Dr.
Northville MI 48168
Phone: 734-737-5000
Fax: 716-887-7464
Web: www.ctg.com

CEO: Pieter Klinkers
CFO: Oscar Becker
HR: -
FYE: January 31
Type: Private

Steel Wheels is more than a Stones' album — it's a living for Hayes Lemmerz. The company rolls along as the world's #1 manufacturer of fabricated steel and cast aluminum wheels for passenger cars and light trucks and steel wheels primarily for commercial trucks and sport utility vehicles. The company operates through two segments: automotive wheels and other products. It has however eliminated most of its components and intercompany activities comprising automotive brakes suspensions and powertrain parts. Customers are major car and truck OEMs in North America Europe and Japan including GM Ford Honda Nissan and Toyota. Hayes Lemmerz was acquired by Brazil's Iochpe-Maxion in 2012.

HAYNES INTERNATIONAL, INC.

NMS: HAYN

1020 West Park Avenue
Kokomo, IN 46904-9013
Phone: 765 456-6000
Fax: -
Web: www.haynesintl.com

CEO: Mark M. Comerford
CFO: Daniel W. Maudlin
HR: -
FYE: September 30
Type: Public

Haynes International is an ally of companies that use alloys. Haynes develops and manufactures nickel- and cobalt-based alloys. The company specializes in high-temperature alloys (HTAs) able to withstand extreme temperatures and corrosion-resistant alloys (CRAs) that stand up to corrosive substances and processes. HTAs are used in jet engines gas turbines used for power generation and waste incinerators while CRAs have applications in chemical processing power plant emissions control and hazardous waste treatment. HTAs account for about three-quarters of the company's sales. The aerospace industry is the biggest market for Haynes accounting for 43% of its business.

	Annual Growth	09/11	09/12	09/13	09/14	09/15
Sales ($ mil.)	(2.6%)	542.9	579.6	482.7	455.4	487.6
Net income ($ mil.)	(0.5%)	31.1	50.2	21.6	3.8	30.5
Market value ($ mil.)	(3.4%)	540.8	649.1	563.2	572.4	471.0
Employees	2.1%	1,057	1,086	1,043	1,053	1,147

HAYS MEDICAL CENTER INC.

2220 CANTERBURY DR
HAYS, KS 676012370
Phone: 785-623-5000
Fax: -
Web: www.haysmed.com

CEO: John H Jeter
CFO: William Overbey
HR: -
FYE: June 30
Type: Private

Hays Medical Center brings big city health care to rural Kansas. The not-for-profit hospital which has about 210 beds provides both acute and tertiary medical care to the Midwestern plains serving more than 13000 emergency patients each year. In addition to medical surgical and pediatric care Hays Medical Center offers home care hospice skilled nursing rehabilitation and behavioral health services. It operates centers for cardiac care (the DeBakey Heart Institute) fitness and rehabilitation (Center for Health Improvement) orthopedics (Hays Orthopedic Institute) and cancer treatment (the Dreiling/Schmidt Cancer Center). The organization also operates specialty and rural health clinics.

	Annual Growth	06/09	06/10	06/11	06/12	06/13
Sales ($ mil.)	2.6%	-	185.0	189.6	209.2	199.6
Net income ($ mil.)	37.3%	-	-	9.0	17.0	17.0
Market value ($ mil.)	-	-	-	-	-	-
Employees	-	-	-	-	-	1,178

HAYWARD BAKER INC.

1130 Annapolis Rd. Ste. 202
Odenton MD 21113-1635
Phone: 410-551-8200
Fax: 410-551-1900
Web: www.haywardbaker.com

CEO: –
CFO: –
HR: –
FYE: December 31
Type: Subsidiary

Hayward Baker is well grounded. The company provides ground modification services used to prepare soil foundations prior to commercial and infrastructure construction. Its services include soil stabilization underpinning excavation support foundation rehabilitation and groundwater and settlement control. Hayward Baker has worked on projects including the Dalles Lock and Dam spanning the Columbia River in Oregon levee work in New Orleans and improvements to the Queretaro Bus Terminal in Queretaro Mexico. Hayward Baker is a subsidiary of UK-based Keller Group and operates from offices in the US Canada and Latin America.

HAYWARD INDUSTRIES INC.

620 Division St.
Elizabeth NJ 07201
Phone: 908-351-5400
Fax: 908-351-5675
Web: www.haywardnet.com

CEO: Robert Davis
CFO: Andrew Diamond
HR: Bernard Figueroa
FYE: December 31
Type: Private

Hayward Industries encourages folks to take the plunge. The company manufactures pool and spa equipment. Hayward's work is divided between residential pool products; commercial pools; and flow control. The residential arm the industry's largest produces cleaners filters heaters pumps and other pool-related accessories including safety barriers and vacuum release systems. It also distributes fiber-optic lighting designed to illuminate pools and backyards. The commercial division caters to pool professionals and the flow control division makes thermoplastic valves and process controls. Hayward operates in North America Europe and Australia. Founded in 1923 Hayward is owned by chairman Oscar Davis.

HAYWOOD REGIONAL MEDICAL CENTER

262 LEROY GEORGE DR
CLYDE, NC 287217430
Phone: 828-456-7311
Fax: –

CEO: Steve Heatherly
CFO: Gene Winters
HR: –
FYE: September 30
Type: Private

Got a bad case of hay fever? Head to Haywood! Haywood Regional Medical Center (HRMC) provides a wide range of health care services to the residents of western North Carolina. Specialty services include emergency medicine home and hospice care occupational health immediate and prolonged physical rehabilitation and surgery. Founded in 1927 the medical center offers imaging services diabetes education and health and fitness centers. HRMC also houses a state-funded adult psychiatric inpatient program managed by Smoky Mountain Center a local provider of behavioral health care services. The HRMC Foundation provides charitable giving and administration services.

	Annual Growth	09/06	09/07	09/08	09/12	09/13
Sales ($ mil.)	5.3%	–	74.4	0.6	100.1	101.3
Net income ($ mil.)	–	–	–	(0.2)	(4.9)	(2.6)
Market value ($ mil.)	–	–	–	–	–	–
Employees	–	–	–	–	–	1,000

HAZEN AND SAWYER P.C.

498 7TH AVE FL 11
NEW YORK, NY 100186710
Phone: 212-539-7000
Fax: –
Web: www.hazenandsawyer.com

CEO: –
CFO: –
HR: –
FYE: December 31
Type: Private

There is nothing hazy about Hazen and Sawyer's focus on water wastewater and solid waste infrastructure. The environmental engineering firm specializes in planning designing and constructing clean drinking water systems for public and private clients worldwide. Hazen and Sawyer's specific areas of expertise include architectural design aquatic sciences biosolids management buried infrastructure odor control resource economics risk management utility management services and wastewater and stormwater collection. The employee-owned firm operates from about 40 offices throughout the eastern US and several international branch offices in South America.

	Annual Growth	12/03	12/04	12/05	12/07	12/08
Sales ($ mil.)	–	–	–	(868.5)	131.4	147.6
Net income ($ mil.)	–	–	–	0.0	62.8	0.0
Market value ($ mil.)	–	–	–	–	–	–
Employees	–	–	–	–	–	775

HC2 HOLDINGS INC

505 Huntmar Park Drive, Suite 325
Herndon, VA 20170
Phone: 703 865-0700
Fax: –
Web: www.hc2.com

ASE: HCHC
CEO: Rustin Roach
CFO: Mesfin Demise
HR: –
FYE: December 31
Type: Public

Consolidation in the US telecom industry has left HC2 Holdings looking for a new business opportunity. The former Primus Telecommunications sold its legacy telecom business operations in the US and Canada to York Capital Management for $129 million in 2013. It also sold its Canadian data center business Blackiron Data to Rogers Communications for $200 million. HC2 Holdings kept its PTGi International Carrier Services business which provides network access to other telecommunications carriers on a wholesale basis. In 2014 it made its first foray outside the telecom industry when it bought a 60% stake in steel construction company Schuff for $79 million.

	Annual Growth	12/10	12/11	12/12	12/13	12/14
Sales ($ mil.)	(8.2%)	764.9	989.3	260.6	230.7	543.2
Net income ($ mil.)	–	(19.1)	(38.7)	27.9	111.6	(12.1)
Market value ($ mil.)	(9.4%)	297.7	301.5	258.8	67.9	200.7
Employees	3.1%	1,672	1,479	834	89	1,886

HCA HOLDINGS INC

One Park Plaza
Nashville, TN 37203
Phone: 615 344-9551
Fax: –
Web: www.hcahealthcare.com

NYS: HCA
CEO: R. Milton Johnson
CFO: William B. (Bill) Rutherford
HR: Yonnie Chesley
FYE: December 31
Type: Public

HCA dispenses TLC for a profit. HCA Holdings through its HCA Inc. (Hospital Corporation of America) unit operates 166 hospitals comprising 162 acute care centers three psychiatric facilities and one rehabilitation hospital in the US and UK. It also runs more than 110 ambulatory surgery centers — as well as cancer treatment urgent care and outpatient rehab centers — that form health care networks in many of the communities it serves. In total its hospitals are home to some 43000 beds. HCA's facilities are located in 20 states; roughly half of its hospitals are in Florida and Texas. The HCA International unit operates the company's hospitals and clinics in the UK.

	Annual Growth	12/10	12/11	12/12	12/13	12/14
Sales ($ mil.)	4.7%	30,683.0	29,682.0	33,013.0	34,182.0	36,918.0
Net income ($ mil.)	11.6%	1,207.0	2,465.0	1,605.0	1,556.0	1,875.0
Market value ($ mil.)	49.4%	–	9,263.1	12,685.8	20,061.0	30,858.9
Employees	3.8%	194,000	199,000	204,000	215,000	225,000

HCA-HEALTHONE LLC

4900 S. Monaco St. Ste. 380
Denver CO 80237-3487
Phone: 303-788-2500
Fax: 303-779-4993
Web: www.healthonecares.com

CEO: –
CFO: David Housand
HR: Nora Anderson
FYE: December 31
Type: Private

HCA-HealthONE wants to be #1 in the lives of Denverites. The health care network provides residents of Denver and surrounding communities with a range of health care services through seven hospitals with some 2300 beds as well as more than a dozen ambulatory surgery centers and 30 outpatient facilities. HealthONE's hospitals include The Medical Center of Aurora North Suburban Medical Center Presbyterian/St. Luke's Medical Center Rose Medical Center Swedish Medical Center Sky Ridge Medical Center and Spalding Rehabilitation Hospital. Hospital system giant HCA owns HealthOne.

HCBECK LTD.

1807 Ross Ave. Ste. 500
Dallas TX 75201-8006
Phone: 214-303-6200
Fax: 214-303-6300
Web: www.beckgroup.com

CEO: Brad Phillips
CFO: Mark Collins
HR: –
FYE: December 31
Type: Private

HCBeck which does business as The Beck Group is at the beck and call of commercial developers. The company provides design/build general contracting and construction management services in the US and Mexico. It also offers project management and outsourcing of facilities construction. The Beck Group focuses on commercial and institutional building and has built everything from hospitals and hotels to racetracks and retail centers. The company is involved in real estate development and sustainable construction having completed several projects that meet LEED (Leadership in Energy & Environmental Design) standards. The group which was founded in 1912 by Henry Beck is owned by its managing directors.

HCC INSURANCE HOLDINGS, INC.   NYS: HCC

13403 Northwest Freeway
Houston, TX 77040-6094
Phone: 713 690-7300
Fax: –
Web: www.hcc.com

CEO: Christopher J B Williams
CFO: Brad T Irick
HR: –
FYE: December 31
Type: Public

From corporate office to offshore rig HCC Insurance Holdings sells specialized property/casualty insurance for commercial and individual customers. Through Houston Casualty Corporation and other subsidiaries the company provides insurance and reinsurance coverage in specialty markets such as directors' and officers' liability errors and omissions and surety and credit policies. It also provides medical stop-loss coverage and policies for aviation marine and energy industries. HCC's underwriting agency division provides brokerage services for affiliated and unaffiliated insurance firms. The company which underwrites more than 100 classes of specialty insurance does business in some 180 countries.

	Annual Growth	12/09	12/10	12/11	12/12	12/13
Assets ($ mil.)	4.0%	8,834.4	9,064.1	9,625.3	10,267.8	10,344.5
Net income ($ mil.)	3.6%	353.9	345.1	255.2	391.2	407.2
Market value ($ mil.)	13.3%	2,806.4	2,903.7	2,759.2	3,733.5	4,629.5
Employees	0.5%	1,864	1,883	1,874	1,870	1,900

HCI GROUP INC   NYS: HCI

5300 West Cypress Street, Suite 100
Tampa, FL 33607
Phone: 813 849-9500
Fax: –
Web: www.hcigroup.com

CEO: Paresh Patel
CFO: Richard R. Allen
HR: –
FYE: December 31
Type: Public

Floridian homeowners are picking HCI Group for their insurance needs — by default. The company's Homeowners Choice Property and Casualty Insurance (HCPCI) subsidiary provides homeowners' insurance and other property/casualty coverage in the state. HCPCI sells policies through a network of independent agents. Other HCI Group subsidiaries provide real estate reinsurance and information technology products and services. The firm changed its name from Homeowners Choice Inc. to HCI Group in 2013 to reflect its diversified businesses.

	Annual Growth	12/10	12/11	12/12	12/13	12/14
Assets ($ mil.)	43.8%	140.9	214.8	338.3	526.3	602.2
Net income ($ mil.)	84.4%	5.4	10.0	30.2	65.6	62.7
Market value ($ mil.)	52.1%	82.3	81.6	211.8	545.1	440.6
Employees	44.6%	80	190	290	329	350

HCP, INC.   NYS: HCP

1920 Main Street, Suite 1200
Irvine, CA 92614
Phone: 949 407-0700
Fax: 562 733-5200
Web: www.hcpi.com

CEO: Lauralee E. Martin
CFO: Timothy M. (Tim) Schoen
HR: –
FYE: December 31
Type: Public

Old age isn't for sissies but as far as HCP is concerned it's for making money. HCP is a self-administered real estate investment trust (REIT) that invests in develops and manages real estate that it leases to health care facilities. Its diversified real estate portfolio consists of senior living and skilled nursing facilities hospitals medical office buildings and biotech and pharmaceutical laboratories. HCP has interests in more than 1100 properties in 40-plus states and Mexico. California and Texas are its largest markets. The REIT which has nearly $24 billion in assets under management invests in properties through direct ownership mortgage loans and joint ventures.

	Annual Growth	12/11	12/12	12/13	12/14	12/15
Sales ($ mil.)	10.2%	1,725.4	1,900.7	2,099.9	2,266.3	2,544.3
Net income ($ mil.)	–	538.9	832.5	970.8	922.2	(559.2)
Market value ($ mil.)	(2.0%)	19,285.2	21,021.5	16,906.5	20,495.5	17,800.3
Employees	6.2%	147	149	154	170	187

HCR MANORCARE INC.

333 N. Summit St.
Toledo OH 43604-2617
Phone: 419-252-5500
Fax: 419-252-5554
Web: www.hcr-manorcare.com

CEO: Paul A Ormond
CFO: Steven M Cavanaugh
HR: Patricia Sullivan
FYE: December 31
Type: Private

HCR Manor Care is a lord of the manor in the nursing home kingdom. The company operates about 500 nursing homes assisted living centers and rehabilitation facilities in more than 30 states. Its facilities which operate under the names Heartland ManorCare Health Services and Arden Courts provide not only long-term nursing care but also rehabilitation services and short-term post-acute care for patients recovering from serious illness or injury. Many of its facilities house special units for Alzheimer's patients. In addition to its nursing and assisted-living facilities HCR Manor Care offers hospice and home health care through offices across the US. It is owned by private equity firm The Carlyle Group.

HCSB FINANCIAL CORP

NBB: HCFB

5201 Broad Street
Loris, SC 29569
Phone: 843 756-6333
Fax: –
Web: www.hcsbaccess.com

CEO: James R Clarkson
CFO: Edward L Loehr Jr
HR: –
FYE: December 31
Type: Public

HCSB Financial has erased the state lines in the Carolinas. The institution is the holding company for Horry County State Bank which operates more than a dozen branches that serve Horry and Marion counties in South Carolina and Columbus and Brunswick counties in North Carolina. Horry County State Bank offers traditional deposit products such as checking and savings accounts CDs money market accounts and IRAs. The bank originates primarily real estate loans (more than half of its loan portfolio) followed by business loans construction and development loans consumer loans and agricultural loans. The bank also offers investment services.

	Annual Growth	12/10	12/11	12/12	12/13	12/14
Assets ($ mil.)	(14.5%)	787.4	535.7	469.0	434.6	421.6
Net income ($ mil.)	–	(17.3)	(29.0)	(9.5)	1.8	(0.3)
Market value ($ mil.)	(49.2%)	9.0	1.9	0.3	0.7	0.6
Employees	(7.8%)	141	122	106	106	102

HD SUPPLY HOLDINGS INC

NMS: HDS

3100 Cumberland Boulevard, Suite 1480
Atlanta, GA 30339
Phone: 770 852-9000
Fax: –
Web: www.hdsupply.com

CEO: Joseph J. (Joe) DeAngelo
CFO: Evan J. Levitt
HR: –
FYE: February 01
Type: Public

Do-it-yourselfers shop Home Depot or Lowe's but the pros do business at HD Supply. One of the largest industrial distributors in North America (and formerly the professional services division of Home Depot) HD Supply provides building materials and tools and installation services to professionals in the specialty construction; maintenance repair and operations (MRO); and infrastructure and power markets through 500-plus locations across 48 US states and six Canadian provinces. It operates more than a handful of business units including HD Supply Facilities Maintenance Waterworks Construction & Industrial - White Cap Interior Solutions and Home Improvement Solutions. HD Supply went public in 2013.

	Annual Growth	01/11	01/12*	02/13	02/14	02/15
Sales ($ mil.)	8.3%	6,449.0	7,028.0	8,035.0	8,487.0	8,882.0
Net income ($ mil.)	–	(619.0)	(543.0)	(1,179.0)	(218.0)	3.0
Market value ($ mil.)	34.3%	–	–	–	4,209.1	5,652.0
Employees	0.0%	–	–	15,000	15,500	15,000

*Fiscal year change

HEADWATERS INC

NYS: HW

10701 South River Front Parkway, Suite 300
South Jordan, UT 84095
Phone: 801 984-9400
Fax: –
Web: www.headwaters.com

CEO: Kirk A. Benson
CFO: Donald P. Newman
HR: –
FYE: September 30
Type: Public

Headwaters is a modern-day alchemist turning stone and coal into money. Through subsidiaries it provides building materials and coal combustion products (CCP) and reclaims waste coal in North America. Headwaters' light building products segment - its largest — makes stone products and siding accessories under brands including FlexCrete Building Systems and Eldorado Stone. The heavy construction materials segment sells residuals from the coal combustion process (such as fly ash) which can be used as a substitute for Portland cement in building materials. Headwaters' energy technology segment owns and operates coal-cleaning facilities and licenses coal conversion and heavy oil upgrading technology.

	Annual Growth	09/11	09/12	09/13	09/14	09/15
Sales ($ mil.)	10.9%	592.0	632.8	702.6	791.4	895.3
Net income ($ mil.)	–	(229.9)	(62.2)	7.1	15.3	130.8
Market value ($ mil.)	90.1%	106.3	485.7	663.6	925.6	1,387.7
Employees	0.9%	2,735	2,465	2,355	2,665	2,831

HEADWAY CORPORATE RESOURCES INC.

One Bank of America Plaza 421 Fayetteville St. Mall Ste. 1020
Raleigh NC 27601
Phone: 919-376-4929
Fax: 919-376-4936
Web: www.headwaycorp.com

CEO: –
CFO: –
HR: –
FYE: December 31
Type: Private

It's tough to make progress when your business is short on quality workers and that's where Headway Corporate Resources can help. The company provides recruitment and staffing services primarily in the Los Angeles metro area and the Mid-Atlantic region. It specializes in filling administrative accounting legal technology and engineering positions. Headway also offers such business process outsourcing services as payroll and workforce management on-site management and outsourced recruitment to clients nationwide. Owning five offices across the country the company was formed in 1974.

HEADWAY TECHNOLOGIES INC.

678 S. Hillview Dr.
Milpitas CA 95035
Phone: 408-934-5300
Fax: 408-934-5475
Web: www.headway.com

CEO: –
CFO: Thomas Surran
HR: Casey Matthews
FYE: March 31
Type: Subsidiary

Headway Technologies is making progress in the disk drive market. The company designs and manufactures recording heads for computer disk drives including giant magnetoresistive heads the industry's current standard. Headway's products are used in disk drives for PCs portable computers and computer servers. They are sold in the form of sliced wafer rows (sliders) sliders attached to steel suspensions (head gimbal assemblies) and ceramic wafers. Headway's customers include disk drive manufacturers Fujitsu Hitachi Seagate and Toshiba. The company is a subsidiary of TDK.

HEALTH ALLIANCE MEDICAL PLANS INC.

301 S. Vine St.
Urbana IL 61801-2744
Phone: 217-337-8000
Fax: 217-255-4699
Web: https://healthalliance.org

CEO: Jeff Ingrum
CFO: Gordon W Salm
HR: Lauren Schmid
FYE: December 31
Type: Subsidiary

It's good to have allies in the fight for good health care and for folks in Illinois and Iowa Health Alliance Medical Plans is ready to help. The managed health care provider covers more than 335000 health plan members in the two states. Its products include HMO PPO and POS group and individual plans as well as Medicare and state employee plans. Health Alliance Medical Plans also offers a variety of health and wellness resources. The company manages a provider network of more than 3000 physicians. Its HCH Administration subsidiary provides third-party administration services in the Midwest. Health Alliance Medical Plans is a subsidiary of Carle Physician Group.

HEALTH ALLIANCE PLAN OF MICHIGAN

2850 W. Grand Blvd.
Detroit MI 48202
Phone: 313-872-8100
Fax: 630-887-2334
Web: www.cnhcapital.com

CEO: –
CFO: Ronald Berry
HR: –
FYE: December 31
Type: Subsidiary

If you happen to need health insurance in Michigan you might want to visit the HAP. Health Alliance Plan of Michigan (HAP) provides health insurance products and related services to some 650000 members. A subsidiary of the Henry Ford Health System the not-for-profit corporation offers managed care plans (including HMO PPO and consumer-directed plans) to individuals and companies throughout its service area which covers about two dozen Michigan counties. It also offers Medicare Advantage plans and Medicare prescription drug coverage to retirees. In addition HAP offers disease management behavioral health and wellness programs.

HEALTH FIRST INC.

6450 US HIGHWAY 1
ROCKLEDGE, FL 329555747
Phone: 321-434-4300
Fax: –
Web: www.health-first.org

CEO: Steve Johnson
CFO: Robert C Galloway
HR: Paula Just
FYE: September 30
Type: Private

Health First works to keep Florida's Space Coast denizens in tip-top shape. The not-for-profit health system operates four hospitals in Brevard County. Health First's biggest hospital is Holmes Regional Medical Center in Melbourne with more than 500 beds. Its Cape Canaveral Hospital and Palm Bay Community Hospital have 150 and 60 beds respectively. Its Viera Hospital is a 100-bed acute-care hospital. The system also runs outpatient clinics a home health service and a physicians group. Its for-profit subsidiary Health First Health Plans is the county's largest insurer with about 60000 commercial members and 23000 Medicare members.

	Annual Growth	09/07	09/08	09/11	09/13	09/14
Sales ($ mil.)	48.8%	–	104.6	129.4	1,059.4	1,137.0
Net income ($ mil.)	–	–	–	(0.4)	51.1	90.2
Market value ($ mil.)	–	–	–	–	–	–
Employees	–	–	–	–	–	6,900

HEALTH MANAGEMENT SYSTEMS INC.

401 Park Ave. South
New York NY 10016
Phone: 212-725-7965
Fax: 212-857-5973
Web: www.hmsy.com

CEO: –
CFO: Walter Hosp
HR: –
FYE: December 31
Type: Subsidiary

The biggest risk Health Management Systems faces is a simplification of the US health care payment system. The company offers such cost containment services as fraud detection eligibility audits and collection of improperly paid claims. It refers to its services as coordination of benefits (making sure the right party pays) cost avoidance (validating coverage and rejecting invalid claims) and program integrity (clinical reviews and recoupment services). Its clients include government-sponsored and private health plan providers pharmacy benefits managers and self-insured employers. With offices in more than 25 states Health Management Systems is the operating business of HMS Holdings Corp.

HEALTH NET OF CALIFORNIA

21281 Burbank Blvd.
Woodland Hills CA 91367-6607
Phone: 818-676-5000
Fax: 818-676-5382
Web: https://www.healthnet.com/portal/home.do

CEO: –
CFO: Rob Beltch
HR: –
FYE: December 31
Type: Subsidiary

Health Net of California (HNCA) a subsidiary of Health Net has tossed out a safety net for Californians in the form of health care insurance. The company is one of the largest providers in the state offering coverage to more than 2 million members; its network encompasses about 55000 physicians 300 hospitals and 5000 pharmacies. Plans include PPO HMO point of service (POS) Medicare supplement and Medicare Advantage plans. HNCA also provides services for customers enrolled in California's Medi-Cal (Medicaid) and Healthy Families (CHIP program) programs. Its Salud con Health Net plan provides coverage in the US and Mexico.

HEALTH NET, INC.

NYS: HNT

21650 Oxnard Street
Woodland Hills, CA 91367
Phone: 818 676-6000
Fax: –
Web: www.healthnet.com

CEO: Jay M. Gellert
CFO: James E. (Jim) Woys
HR: Debbie Cholea
FYE: December 31
Type: Public

Health Net has woven together a web of health plan services. The company provides managed health care medical coverage to about 6 million members. The company's health plan services unit offers HMO PPO Medicare and Medicaid plans as well as vision dental care and pharmacy benefit programs to customers in Arizona California Oregon and Washington. Health Net's Managed Health Network subsidiary provides behavioral health substance abuse and employee assistance to employer groups and traditional health plan customers. The company also provides administration services for self-funded medical plans. Medicaid insurer Centene plans to buy Health Net for $6.3 billion.

	Annual Growth	12/10	12/11	12/12	12/13	12/14
Sales ($ mil.)	0.7%	13,619.9	11,901.0	11,289.1	11,053.7	14,008.6
Net income ($ mil.)	(8.1%)	204.2	72.1	122.1	170.1	145.6
Market value ($ mil.)	18.3%	2,130.6	2,375.0	1,897.2	2,316.4	4,179.2
Employees	(0.5%)	8,169	7,471	7,378	7,659	8,014

HEALTH PARTNERS PLANS INC.

901 MARKET ST STE 500
PHILADELPHIA, PA 191074496
Phone: 215-849-9606
Fax: –
Web: www.healthpart.com

CEO: –
CFO: Martin J Brill
HR: –
FYE: December 31
Type: Private

Health Partners wants to partner up with Pennsylvanians in need of health care. The company is a not-for-profit health plan that provides health benefits to some 210000 Medicaid recipients in the Philadelphia area. Its HealthChoices plans for Medicaid participants cover medical dental prescription and vision costs. Its KidzPartners program is provided in partnership with the state of Pennsylvania's Children's Health Insurance Program (CHIP). Its provider network includes about 6000 primary and specialty care doctors and 30 hospitals in the region. The company also provides community outreach and wellness programs. Health Partners was founded in 1985 by a group of hospitals in the Philadelphia area.

	Annual Growth	12/07	12/08	12/09	12/12	12/13
Sales ($ mil.)	7.3%	–	702.6	805.5	1,034.9	1,000.3
Net income ($ mil.)	–	–	–	2.9	(1.6)	(0.2)
Market value ($ mil.)	–	–	–	–	–	–
Employees	–	–	–	–	–	620

HEALTH PLAN OF NEVADA INC.

2720 N. Tenaya Way
Las Vegas NV 89128-0424
Phone: 702-242-7300
Fax: 702-242-7960
Web: www.healthplanofnevada.com

CEO: –
CFO: –
HR: –
FYE: December 31
Type: Subsidiary

Health Plan of Nevada a subsidiary of UnitedHealth is a Nevada health maintenance organization (HMO) offering health care coverage to the state's residents. Its offerings include various HMO and point-of-service (POS) plans as well as prescription drug coverage. It also gives members access to its affiliated multi-specialty medical group Southwest Medical Associates and other health care and wellness services. Established in 1982 Health Plan of Nevada offers plans through employer groups as well as to individuals. It sells its Senior Dimensions HMO plans to Medicare beneficiaries.

HEALTH RESEARCH INC.

150 BROADWAY STE 560
MENANDS, NY 122042736
Phone: 518-431-1200
Fax: –
Web: www.healthresearch.org

CEO: –
CFO: –
HR: Dolores Wilson
FYE: March 31
Type: Private

Health Research Inc. (HRI) knows where the money is. The group is a not-for-profit organization that helps the New York State Department of Health and its affiliated Roswell Park Cancer Institute solicit evaluate and administer financial support. Sources of that support come from federal and state government sources other non-profits and businesses. HRI's Technology Transfer office also assists the Department of Health in sharing its research findings with other public and private institutions and finding ways to create biomedical technologies through private sector development. HRI was founded in 1953 and has administered $7 billion over its lifetime.

	Annual Growth	03/10	03/11	03/12	03/13	03/14
Sales ($ mil.)	1.9%	–	665.2	661.6	665.9	703.4
Net income ($ mil.)	–	–	–	(10.7)	26.0	13.5
Market value ($ mil.)	–	–	–	–	–	–
Employees	–	–	–	–	–	1,400

HEALTHCARE DISTRIBUTION MANAGEMENT ASSOCIATION

901 N GLEBE RD STE 1000
ARLINGTON, VA 222031854
Phone: 703-787-0000
Fax: –
Web: www.hdma.net

CEO: John M Gray
CFO: –
HR: –
FYE: December 31
Type: Private

The Healthcare Distribution Management Association (HDMA) helps the medicine get where it's needed. HDMA is a trade association representing healthcare and pharmaceutical products distributors. Its members include hundreds of manufacturers and some 70 distributors as well as numerous service providers that deliver to pharmacies hospitals nursing homes and health clinics. The organization provides opportunities for members to share industry best practices represents member concerns before Congress and regulatory agencies and publishes newsletters and state by state information sheets for members. HDMA was founded in the late 1800s.

	Annual Growth	12/05	12/06	12/08	12/09	12/13
Sales ($ mil.)	4.9%	–	9.2	11.3	9.6	12.9
Net income ($ mil.)	–	–	–	0.0	(2.3)	0.1
Market value ($ mil.)	–	–	–	–	–	–
Employees	–	–	–	–	–	40

HEALTHCARE PARTNERS LLC

19191 Vermont Ave. Ste. 200
Torrance CA 90502
Phone: 310-354-4200
Fax: 310-538-3385
Web: www.healthcarepartners.com

CEO: Robert J Margolis
CFO: –
HR: –
FYE: December 31
Type: Private

A health care management services and accountable care organization HealthCare Partners owns and operates groups of medical practices in California Florida New Mexico and Nevada. The company provides administrative services to subsidiary HealthCare Partners Medical Group which operates more than 65 medical practices in Los Angeles and surrounding areas. Its JSA Healthcare unit provides primary care and pharmacy services at some 40 facilities in central Florida while its HealthCare Partners of Nevada unit operates 45 facilities around Las Vegas. The company also conducts clinical research at its Health Care Partners Institute. HealthCare Partners was acquired by renal care giant DaVita in 2012.

HEALTHCARE REALTY TRUST, INC.   NYS: HR

3310 West End Avenue, Suite 700
Nashville, TN 37203
Phone: 615 269-8175
Fax: –
Web: www.healthcarerealty.com

CEO: David R. Emery
CFO: Scott W. Holmes
HR: Rebecca T Oberlander
FYE: December 31
Type: Public

Healthcare Realty Trust has the prescription for health care providers. The self-managed and self-administered real estate investment trust (REIT) invests in develops and manages medical office buildings physician clinics surgical centers and specialty outpatient and inpatient rehabilitation facilities. It owns about 200 properties with more than 13 million sq. ft. of leasable space in nearly 30 states. Healthcare Realty Trust also invests in mortgages backed by health care properties and provides property management services for about 140 health care facilities. The REIT's largest tenant is HealthSouth which accounts for more than 10% of the company's revenues.

	Annual Growth	12/10	12/11	12/12	12/13	12/14
Sales ($ mil.)	9.5%	258.4	296.6	316.4	336.9	370.9
Net income ($ mil.)	40.4%	8.2	(0.2)	5.5	6.9	31.9
Market value ($ mil.)	6.6%	2,092.2	1,837.2	2,372.9	2,106.0	2,700.0
Employees	(0.1%)	240	260	244	243	239

HEALTHCARE SERVICES GROUP, INC.   NMS: HCSG

3220 Tillman Drive, Suite 300
Bensalem, PA 19020
Phone: 215 639-4274
Fax: 215 639-2152
Web: www.hcsgcorp.com

CEO: Theodore Wahl
CFO: John Shea
HR: –
FYE: December 31
Type: Public

Healthcare Services Group gets swept up in its work every day. The company provides housekeeping laundry and linen food and maintenance services to hospitals nursing homes rehabilitation centers and retirement facilities. It tidies up around 3500 long-term care facilities in Canada and almost every state in the US. Housekeeping and laundry and linen services are the company's top revenue generators. The company's dietary division prepares food for residents and monitors nutritional needs in more than 900 facilities. Healthcare Services Group was established in 1977.

	Annual Growth	12/10	12/11	12/12	12/13	12/14
Sales ($ mil.)	13.7%	774.0	889.1	1,077.4	1,149.9	1,293.2
Net income ($ mil.)	(10.8%)	34.4	38.2	44.2	47.1	21.9
Market value ($ mil.)	17.4%	1,156.1	1,257.0	1,650.7	2,015.9	2,197.8
Employees	12.3%	5,400	6,850	7,000	7,600	8,600

HEALTHEAST ST JOHN'S HOSPITAL

1575 BEAM AVE
SAINT PAUL, MN 55109-1126
Phone: 651-232-7000
Fax: –
Web: www.stjohnshospital-mn.org

CEO: –
CFO: –
HR: Julie Garrison
FYE: August 31
Type: Private

St. John's Hospital provides health care to folks residing the suburbs of the Twin Cities. The hospital has about 185 beds and is an acute-care facility with emergency inpatient and outpatient medicine departments. Its facilities include specialty centers for breast care cancer care heart health maternity services and orthopedics among other offerings. St. John's started in 1910 with a private home that was converted into a 25-bed hospital. St. John's Hospital is part of the HealthEast Care System which includes other hospitals and health centers in the Minneapolis/St. Paul metropolitan area.

	Annual Growth	08/01	08/02	08/05	08/06	08/09
Sales ($ mil.)	6.0%	–	168.1	190.2	204.0	252.1
Net income ($ mil.)	(1.8%)	–	21.1	11.6	14.6	18.6
Market value ($ mil.)	–	–	–	–	–	–
Employees	–	–	–	–	–	713

HEALTHFIRST

25 Broadway
New York NY 10004-1058
Phone: 212-801-6000
Fax: 212-801-3245
Web: www.healthfirstny.com

CEO: Pat Wang
CFO: –
HR: Liz Cook
FYE: December 31
Type: Private - Not-for-Pr

If you want to be first in your field it helps if your owners are first in theirs. Owned by some of the most prestigious hospitals in the region Healthfirst might just have a leg-up on other health care management organizations. The not-for-profit has about 500000 members throughout New York City Long Island and northern New Jersey. It offers government-sponsored health insurance programs including Medicaid Medicare Family Health Plus and Child Health Plus plans to low-income and special needs clients. It also offers commercial HMO and point-of-service plans to individuals and small employer groups. Healthfirst was formed in 1993; its plans are administered by HF Management Services.

HEALTHMARKETS INC.

9151 Boulevard 26
North Richland Hills TX 76180
Phone: 817-255-5200
Fax: 817-255-5390
Web: www.healthmarkets.com

CEO: Kenneth J Fasola
CFO: R Scott Donovan
HR: –
FYE: December 31
Type: Private

HealthMarkets lets the self-employed shop for better insurance. The company offers health insurance through its MEGA Life and Health Insurance Mid-West National Life Insurance Company of Tennessee Chesapeake Life Insurance Company and HealthMarkets Insurance to mostly self-employed individuals in the US. Health care options include PPOs high-deductable plans and health spending accounts (HSAs). HealthMarkets also provides supplemental dental vision accident illness and hospital indemnity insurance. The company manages a network of insurance brokers through its Insphere Insurance Solutions division. A consortium led by the Blackstone Group owns HealthMarkets.

HEALTHPLUS OF MICHIGAN INC.

2050 S. Linden Rd.
Flint MI 48532
Phone: 810-230-2000
Fax: 810-230-2208
Web: www.healthplus.com

CEO: Michael Genord
CFO: Keith Collin CPA
HR: –
FYE: December 31
Type: Private

PPO + HMO +POS + the Great Lakes State = HealthPlus of Michigan. The not-for-profit company provides health care coverage to more than 200000 members in about a dozen Michigan counties. The company offers HMO PPO and point-of-service (POS) health plans. It also manages a Medicaid HMO through its HealthPlus Partners subsidiary as well as a Medicare Advantage program. Its provider network includes more than 2700 primary care and specialist doctors in addition to 30 area hospitals and numerous other health care facilities. HealthPlus of Michigan also offers wellness and disease management programs. Subsidiary HealthPlus Options is a third-party claims administrator.

HEALTHPORT TECHNOLOGIES LLC

925 North Point Pkwy. Ste. 350
Alpharetta GA 30005
Phone: 770-670-2150
Fax: 925-251-0525
Web: www.callidussoftware.com

CEO: Mike Labetz
CFO: Brian Grazzini
HR: Sharon Parham
FYE: December 31
Type: Private

HealthPort offers safe harbor in a choppy sea of medical information. The company develops software used to manage hospitals and medical practice operations electronic medical records and insurance claims. Its auditing health data auditing application is known as AudaPro. HealthPort's software is used to cut operational costs and guard against unauthorized disclosure of confidential data. It also provides release of information services and it offers network design and implementation training consulting and technical support. The company serves health care facilities nationwide including hospitals health systems and independent physician practices. HealthPort is owned private equity firm ABRY Partners.

HEALTHSOUTH CORP

NYS: HLS

3660 Grandview Parkway, Suite 200
Birmingham, AL 35243
Phone: 205 967-7116
Fax: –
Web: www.healthsouth.com

CEO: Jay Grinney
CFO: Douglas E. (Doug) Coltharp
HR: –
FYE: December 31
Type: Public

HealthSouth actually covers all points of the compass as one of the nation's largest providers of rehabilitation services. The company boasts a variety of facilities including inpatient rehabilitation hospitals outpatient centers and home health care agencies that provide nursing and therapy to patients who are recovering from brain and spinal cord injuries cardiac and pulmonary conditions or neurological disorders (stroke aneurysm). HealthSouth operates about 155 inpatient outpatient and home health centers in more than 30 states and in Puerto Rico.

	Annual Growth	12/10	12/11	12/12	12/13	12/14
Sales ($ mil.)	4.4%	1,999.3	2,026.9	2,134.9	2,247.2	2,374.3
Net income ($ mil.)	(29.5%)	899.0	208.7	185.0	323.6	222.0
Market value ($ mil.)	16.7%	1,818.1	1,551.2	1,853.2	2,925.1	3,376.4
Employees	1.2%	23,000	22,000	22,700	23,600	24,100

HEALTHSPRING INC.

NYSE: HS

9009 Carothers Pkwy. Ste. 501
Franklin TN 37067
Phone: 615-291-7000
Fax: 615-401-4566
Web: www.healthspring.com

CEO: Herbert A Fritch
CFO: Karey L Witty
HR: –
FYE: December 31
Type: Subsidiary

Looking to keep a spring in Grandma's step HealthSpring provides Medicare Advantage plans and Medicare Part D prescription drug benefits to members in 11 states and the District of Columbia across some 65000 pharmacies. Its Medicare Advantage plans offer the support of Medicare with additional benefits such as the Medicare Part D prescription benefits vision and hearing benefits and transportation programs. In addition HealthSpring runs a nationwide prescription drug plan (otherwise known as PDPs) and offers management services to independent physician associations in Alabama Tennessee and Texas. HealthSpring was acquired by insurance giant CIGNA in 2012.

HEALTHSTREAM INC

NMS: HSTM

209 10th Avenue South, Suite 450
Nashville, TN 37203
Phone: 615 301-3100
Fax: –
Web: www.healthstream.com

CEO: Robert A. Frist
CFO: Gerard M. (Gerry) Hayden
HR: –
FYE: December 31
Type: Public

HealthStream replenishes the well of knowledge for medical workers. The company supplies Internet-based learning and research content to health care organizations throughout the US to meet their training certification and development needs. HealthStream's core learning product is HealthStream Learning Center (HLC) which offers educational and training courseware to about 4.8 million subscribers (representing some 4000 hospitals) via a software-as-a-service (SaaS) model. The company's research offerings include quality and satisfaction surveys data analysis and other research-based management tools; the Patient Insights survey generates most of the research business' revenues.

	Annual Growth	12/10	12/11	12/12	12/13	12/14
Sales ($ mil.)	26.9%	65.8	82.1	103.7	132.3	170.7
Net income ($ mil.)	25.8%	4.2	6.9	7.6	8.4	10.4
Market value ($ mil.)	38.4%	222.5	510.6	672.8	903.0	815.9
Employees	16.2%	432	504	587	686	787

HEALTHTRONICS INC.

9825 Spectrum Dr. Bldg. 3
Austin TX 78717
Phone: 512-328-2892
Fax: 512-328-8510
Web: www.healthtronics.com

CEO: Richard Rusk
CFO: –
HR: –
FYE: December 31
Type: Subsidiary

HealthTronics trains electronic equipment to zap kidney stones and blast cancer tumors. The company contracts with medical facilities to provide urology treatment services including the provision of equipment scheduling training and clinical technicians. It makes sells and services such equipment as lasers and lithotripters which use shock waves to break up kidney and gall-bladder stones. HealthTronics also offers urological pathology testing and cryosurgical (freezing of tissue) treatments for enlarged prostate and prostate cancer. In addition HealthTronics offers related consumable supplies and maintenance services. The company is owned by drug and device maker Endo Pharmaceuticals.

HEALTHWAREHOUSE.COM, INC.

NBB: HEWA

7107 Industrial Road
Florence, KY 41042
Phone: 800 748-7001
Fax: –
Web: www.healthwarehouse.com

CEO: Lalit P. Dhadphale
CFO: Daniel (Dan) Seliga
HR: –
FYE: December 31
Type: Public

HealthWarehouse.com sells over-the-counter in more than one way. The online pharmacy sells prescription and over-the-counter drugs to more than 160000 customers. It sources its products from suppliers including Masters Pharmaceutical and The Harvard Drug Group. HealthWarehouse went public through a reverse merger with OTC-traded Clacendix in 2009. Clacendix provided products that protected enterprise data and networks from security threats. Faced with declining sales and mounting losses Clacendix sold its assets to API Cryptek for $3.2 million in 2008. Clacendix later merged with HealthWarehouse and changed its name in 2009. HealthWarehouse purchased the online assets of Hocks Pharmacy in 2011.

	Annual Growth	12/10	12/11	12/12	12/13	12/14
Sales ($ mil.)	1.9%	5.7	10.4	11.1	10.2	6.1
Net income ($ mil.)	–	(3.7)	(5.7)	(5.6)	(5.5)	(1.8)
Market value ($ mil.)	(57.4%)	103.3	221.7	159.7	13.1	3.4
Employees	4.9%	33	63	45	40	40

HEALTHWAYS INC

NMS: HWAY

701 Cool Springs Boulevard
Franklin, TN 37067
Phone: 615 614-4929
Fax: –

CEO: Ben R. Leedle
CFO: Alfred Lumsdaine
HR: Jeff Klem
FYE: December 31
Type: Public

For health insurers healthy plan members are cheap plan members; that's where Healthways comes in. The health services company provides disease management and wellness programs to managed care companies self-insured employers governments and hospitals with the ultimate goals of improving members' health and lowering health care costs. Its disease management programs help members manage chronic illnesses like diabetes and emphysema making sure they keep up with treatment plans and maintain healthy behaviors. Healthways' wellness offerings including its SilverSneakers program for seniors encourage fitness and other positive lifestyle choices.

	Annual Growth	12/10	12/11	12/12	12/13	12/14
Sales ($ mil.)	0.7%	720.3	688.8	677.2	663.3	742.2
Net income ($ mil.)	–	47.3	(157.7)	8.0	(8.5)	(5.6)
Market value ($ mil.)	15.5%	396.3	243.6	380.0	545.1	706.0
Employees	(0.9%)	2,800	2,400	2,400	2,500	2,700

HEARTH & HOME TECHNOLOGIES INC.

7571 215th St. W.
Lakeville MN 55044
Phone: 952-985-6000
Fax: 952-985-6001
Web: www.hearthtech.com

CEO: –
CFO: –
HR: –
FYE: December 31
Type: Subsidiary

Hearth & Home Technologies believes home is where the hearth is. A subsidiary of office furniture maker HNI Corporation the company makes and installs wood gas electric and pellet fireplace and stove products under brand names such as Heatilator Heat & Glo and Quadra-Fire. Hearth & Home Technologies also makes indoor hearth products including mantelpieces cabinets shelves and wall systems. Other products range from outdoor fireplaces and barbecue grills to electric fireplaces. The company mainly sells its products in the East and Midwest US. Hearth & Home Technologies accounted for 17% of parent company HNI's revenues in 2011.

HEARTLAND EXPRESS, INC. — NMS: HTLD

901 North Kansas Avenue
North Liberty, IA 52317
Phone: 319 626-3600
Fax: –
Web: www.heartlandexpress.com

CEO: Michael J. Gerdin
CFO: John P. Cosaert
HR: Don McLaughlin
FYE: December 31
Type: Public

Home is where the heart is and Heartland Express stays close to home as a short- to medium-haul truckload carrier — its average trip is just over 500 miles. With the exception of traffic from its Phoenix hub the company mainly operates east of the Rockies; it also offers service in the southwestern US. Although most of its loads go directly from origin to destination Heartland also operates from about 20 regional distribution hubs which are located near major customers. The company regional hubs focus on short-haul freight movements (less than 500 miles). Heartland transports general commodities including appliances auto parts consumer products food and paper products.

	Annual Growth	12/10	12/11	12/12	12/13	12/14
Sales ($ mil.)	14.9%	499.5	528.6	545.7	582.3	871.4
Net income ($ mil.)	8.1%	62.2	69.9	61.5	70.6	84.8
Market value ($ mil.)	13.9%	1,406.3	1,254.4	1,147.3	1,722.3	2,371.0
Employees	10.8%	2,990	2,862	2,993	5,220	4,500

HEARTLAND FINANCIAL USA, INC. (DUBUQUE, IA) — NMS: HTLF

1398 Central Avenue
Dubuque, IA 52001
Phone: 563 2000
Fax: 563 589-2011
Web: www.htlf.com

CEO: Catherine T. (Kate) Kelly
CFO: Bryan McKeag
HR: Mark Murtha
FYE: December 31
Type: Public

Heartland Financial USA brings heart-felt community banking to nation's heartland. The $5.9 billion multi-bank holding company owns flagship subsidiary Dubuque Bank & Trust and nine other banks that together operate more than 75 branches in 55-plus communities in the Midwest and Southwest US. In addition to standard deposit loan and mortgage services the banks also offer retirement wealth management trust insurance and investment services including socially responsible investing. Heartland Financial USA also owns consumer lender Citizens Finance which has about a dozen offices in Illinois Iowa and Wisconsin.

	Annual Growth	12/10	12/11	12/12	12/13	12/14
Assets ($ mil.)	10.9%	3,999.5	4,305.1	4,990.6	5,923.7	6,052.4
Net income ($ mil.)	15.1%	23.9	28.0	49.8	36.8	41.9
Market value ($ mil.)	11.6%	323.2	284.0	484.1	532.9	501.7
Employees	11.2%	1,066	1,195	1,498	1,676	1,631

HEARTLAND HEALTH

5325 FARAON ST
SAINT JOSEPH, MO 645063488
Phone: 816-271-6000
Fax: –
Web: www.mymosaiclifecare.org

CEO: –
CFO: John Wilson
HR: Michael (Mel) Pulido
FYE: June 30
Type: Private

Heartland Health provides medical care in the heart of the Midwest. The integrated health care system serves residents of northwest Missouri as well as bordering areas of Kansas and Nebraska. Its flagship facility is Heartland Regional Medical Center a 350-bed acute-care hospital that features an emergency room and Level II trauma center as well as specialty care programs in heart disease cancer and obstetrics. Heartland Health also provides primary care through a multi-specialty medical practice (Heartland Clinic) and it offers home health hospice and long-term care services from the primary medical center facility. The company's Community Health Improvement Solutions unit is an HMO health insurer.

	Annual Growth	06/10	06/11	06/12	06/13	06/14
Sales ($ mil.)	2.0%	–	528.2	584.8	572.8	560.8
Net income ($ mil.)	143.5%	–	–	10.8	76.6	64.2
Market value ($ mil.)	–	–	–	–	–	–
Employees	–	–	–	–	–	32,000

HEARTLAND PAYMENT SYSTEMS INC — NYS: HPY

90 Nassau Street
Princeton, NJ 08542
Phone: 609 683-3831
Fax: –
Web: www.heartlandpaymentsystems.com

CEO: Robert O. (Bob) Carr
CFO: Samir Zabaneh
HR: Chris Hill
FYE: December 31
Type: Public

If you're using a plastic card to charge throughout the heartland Heartland Payment Systems (HPS) makes sure the transactions don't get lost along the way. The company performs credit debit and prepaid card processing services to more than 300000 business and education locations nationwide. Customers include restaurants retailers convenience stores and professional service providers. Another unit Heartland Payroll Solutions provides payroll processing including check printing and direct deposit for more than 10000 customers. Other markets for the company include K-12 school nutrition programs and payment processing for colleges and universities. Global Payments agreed to buy Heartland for $4.3 billion in late 2015.

	Annual Growth	12/10	12/11	12/12	12/13	12/14
Sales ($ mil.)	5.5%	1,864.3	1,997.0	2,013.4	2,135.4	2,311.4
Net income ($ mil.)	(0.5%)	34.5	43.9	65.9	78.6	33.9
Market value ($ mil.)	36.8%	560.4	885.4	1,072.2	1,811.4	1,960.8
Employees	9.3%	2,612	2,667	3,002	3,184	3,734

HEARTLAND REGIONAL MEDICAL CENTER

5325 FARAON ST
SAINT JOSEPH, MO 645063488
Phone: 816-271-7211
Fax: –

CEO: Mark Laney
CFO: Spencer Klaasen
HR: –
FYE: June 30
Type: Private

Heartland Regional Medical Center strives for healthy hearts minds and bodies in the US heartland. The acute care hospital a subsidiary of Heartland Health provides medical services to residents of St. Joseph Missouri and some 20 surrounding counties in northwest Missouri southeast Nebraska and northeast Kansas. Heartland Regional Medical Center encompasses specialty centers for trauma and long-term care acute rehabilitation cancer heart disease and birthing. As part of the services provided by the medical center Heartland Regional Medical Center offers services such as arthritis pain and wound treatments as well as home health and hospice care.

	Annual Growth	06/09	06/10	06/11	06/12	06/13
Sales ($ mil.)	7.7%	–	484.0	514.4	564.3	605.0
Net income ($ mil.)	(21.2%)	–	–	72.2	11.5	44.8
Market value ($ mil.)	–	–	–	–	–	–
Employees	–	–	–	–	–	2,600

HEARTWARE INTERNATIONAL INC — NMS: HTWR

500 Old Connecticut Path
Framingham, MA 01701
Phone: 508 739-0950
Fax: –
Web: www.heartware.com

CEO: Douglas E. (Doug) Godshall
CFO: Peter F. McAree
HR: –
FYE: December 31
Type: Public

HeartWare International makes hardware for your heart. The company's proprietary heart pump is an implantable device designed for patients suffering from advanced-stage heart failure. The pump branded as HVAD (for HeartWare Ventricular Assist System) is used for people who can't undergo a heart transplant or who are on a waiting list for a heart to become available. The HVAD is small fits above the diaphragm (not the abdomen like other VADs which makes it less invasive) and can generate up to 10 liters of blood flow per minute. HeartWare International is a development-stage company; the HVAD is approved for sale in Europe and Australia.

	Annual Growth	12/10	12/11	12/12	12/13	12/14
Sales ($ mil.)	49.9%	55.2	82.8	110.9	207.9	278.4
Net income ($ mil.)	–	(29.4)	(55.1)	(87.7)	(59.3)	(19.4)
Market value ($ mil.)	(4.3%)	1,502.4	1,183.8	1,440.2	1,611.0	1,259.8
Employees	29.8%	206	330	396	569	585

HEATWURX INC
NBB: HUWX

18001 S. Figueroa, Unit G
Gardena, CA 90248
Phone: 888 817-9879
Fax: -
Web: www.heatwurx.com

CEO: Stephen Garland
CFO: -
HR: -
FYE: December 31
Type: Public

Heatwurx provides a way to fix cracks and potholes in the roadway not by just laying more asphalt but by repairing them through the use of plenty of heat. The company manufactures machinery that recycles broken asphalt at temperatures above 300° F. with infrared heating equipment that is electrically powered. Heatwurx claims it is an environmentally friendly method by virtue of its reuse of distressed pavement and the lack of need to transport material from asphalt plants. It incorporated in early 2011 and is a development-stage company with negligible sales. In late 2012 Heatwurx filed an IPO initially aiming to raise $7.6 million.

	Annual Growth	12/10	12/11	12/12	12/13	12/14
Sales ($ mil.)	-	0.0	0.0	0.2	0.3	0.2
Net income ($ mil.)	-	0.0	(0.9)	(2.4)	(3.1)	(4.5)
Market value ($ mil.)	-	0.0	-	-	36.7	24.1
Employees	13.4%	-	-	7	8	9

HEAVEN HILL DISTILLERIES INC.

1064 Loretto Rd.
Bardstown KY 40004
Phone: 502-348-3921
Fax: 502-348-0162
Web: www.heaven-hill.com/

CEO: -
CFO: Kelvin Haynes
HR: -
FYE: April 30
Type: Private

Angels don't help the Christian Brothers bottle their brandy port and sherry; Heaven Hill does. One of Kentucky's oldest and largest distilling operations Heaven Hill Distilleries makes Evan Williams Bourbon as well as super-premium bourbons under the brand names Elijah Craig and Henry McKenna. The company also owns the Christian Brothers and Old Fitzgerald brand names. Heaven Hill distributes a variety of other spirits including the aperitif Dubonnet Ansac cognac Burnett's gin and Blackheart Premium Spiced Rum among others. Founded in 1934 by five brothers from the Shapira family Heaven Hill is still family owned.

HECLA MINING CO.
NYS: HL

6500 Mineral Drive, Suite 200
Coeur d'Alene, ID 83815-9408
Phone: 208 769-4100
Fax: -
Web: www.hecla-mining.com

CEO: Phillips S. Baker
CFO: James A. (Jim) Sabala
HR: -
FYE: December 31
Type: Public

Not all that glisters at Hecla Mining is gold — in fact a large proportion of the precious ores that it mines is made of silver. Hecla explores for and mines gold silver lead and zinc. In 2014 the mining and natural resource exploration company produced 1.7 million ounces of silver 6702 ounces of gold 10394 tons of zinc and 4542 tons of lead. Hecla operates mines in the Alaska and the Lucky Friday Mine in Idaho and has interests in mines in Colorado Nevada and in Mexico. The company sells to metals buyers around the world primarily to zinc producers in Asia.

	Annual Growth	12/10	12/11	12/12	12/13	12/14
Sales ($ mil.)	4.6%	418.8	477.6	321.1	382.6	500.8
Net income ($ mil.)	(22.3%)	49.0	151.2	15.0	(25.1)	17.8
Market value ($ mil.)	(29.4%)	4,136.7	1,921.4	2,141.8	1,131.5	1,025.0
Employees	18.5%	686	735	735	1,312	1,354

HEERY INTERNATIONAL INC.

999 Peachtree St. NE
Atlanta GA 30309-3953
Phone: 404-881-9880
Fax: 404-946-2398
Web: www.heery.com

CEO: -
CFO: -
HR: -
FYE: December 31
Type: Subsidiary

Engineering and architectural group Heery International is known as much for its program management as for the schools and stadiums it designs. Architect George Heery who helped found the firm in 1952 was an early practitioner of program management which involves consulting and client representation for complex projects at each phase of construction. Heery with its 35 offices also offers facilities and construction management and interior design services. Most of its billings come from government projects; its markets include educational medical correctional and judicial facilities. A subsidiary of UK engineering giant Balfour Beatty Heery operates as the buildings division for Parsons Brinckerhoff.

HEICO CORP.
NYS: HEI A

3000 Taft Street
Hollywood, FL 33021
Phone: 954 987-4000
Fax: -

CEO: Victor H. Mendelson
CFO: Carlos L. Macau
HR: -
FYE: October 31
Type: Public

Here's a HEICO haiku: HEICO companies/ Providing for jet engines/ In flight or on land. Its Flight Support Group consisting of HEICO Aerospace and its subsidiaries makes FAA-approved replacement parts for jet engines that can be substituted for original parts including airfoils bearings and fuel pump gears. Flight Support also repairs overhauls and distributes jet engine parts as well as avionics and instruments for commercial air carriers. HEICO's second segment Electronic Technologies Group makes a variety of electronic equipment for the aerospace/defense electronic medical and telecommunications industries. The company has facilities in the US Canada India Singapore and the UK among other locations.

	Annual Growth	10/11	10/12	10/13	10/14	10/15
Sales ($ mil.)	11.7%	764.9	897.3	1,008.8	1,132.3	1,188.6
Net income ($ mil.)	16.3%	72.8	85.1	102.4	121.3	133.4
Market value ($ mil.)	2.7%	2,628.8	2,038.3	2,605.4	3,059.6	2,921.0
Employees	16.5%	2,500	3,100	3,500	3,500	4,600

HEIDRICK & STRUGGLES INTERNATIONAL, INC.
NMS: HSII

233 South Wacker Drive, Suite 4200
Chicago, IL 60606-6303
Phone: 312 496-1200
Fax: -
Web: www.heidrick.com

CEO: Tracy R. Wolstencroft
CFO: Richard W. (Rich) Pehlke
HR: Kevan Skelton
FYE: December 31
Type: Public

Finding top dogs for clients in many industries Heidrick & Struggles International is one of the largest global recruiting firms. The company has more than 300 headhunters spanning 50 offices in 25 countries filling CEO CFO director and other high-level positions for companies that range from start-up ventures to established FORTUNE 500 firms. It's divided into search groups that specialize by industry such as financial services and industrial which together account for half of sales. The company's fees are generally equal to one-third of a hired executive's first-year compensation. Heidrick & Struggles also provides temporary placement management assessment and professional development services.

	Annual Growth	12/10	12/11	12/12	12/13	12/14
Sales ($ mil.)	0.0%	513.2	554.0	465.1	481.0	513.2
Net income ($ mil.)	(2.4%)	7.5	(33.7)	6.2	6.3	6.8
Market value ($ mil.)	(5.3%)	522.6	392.9	278.5	367.4	420.4
Employees	(0.5%)	1,516	1,506	1,469	1,499	1,483

HEIDTMAN STEEL PRODUCTS INC.

2401 FRONT ST
TOLEDO, OH 43605-1199
Phone: 419-691-4646
Fax: –
Web: www.heidtman.avatarsyn.com

CEO: –
CFO: Mark Ridenour
HR: –
FYE: March 31
Type: Private

Steel life is an art at Heidtman Steel Products a provider of steel processing services such as blanking leveling and pickling. One of the largest privately held flat-rolled steel service networks in the US the company processes more than five million tons of steel annually. Services include hot-rolling cold-rolling and steel coating a full-range of slitting capabilities and galvanizing. Heidtman Steel operates plants in five mainly Midwestern states that serve automotive bus and truck manufacturers as well as furniture and appliance makers. The company is an approved steel supplier to Caterpillar and Ford.

	Annual Growth	03/03	03/04	03/05	03/06	03/07
Sales ($ mil.)	12.8%	–	443.6	679.5	599.2	637.1
Net income ($ mil.)	114.4%	–	1.4	5.2	(0.3)	14.3
Market value ($ mil.)	–	–	–	–	–	–
Employees	–	–	–	–	–	1,000

HEIFER PROJECT INTERNATIONAL INC

1 WORLD AVE
LITTLE ROCK, AR 722023825
Phone: 501-907-2600
Fax: –
Web: www.heifer.org

CEO: Pierre Ferrari
CFO: Robert Bob Bloom
HR: –
FYE: June 30
Type: Private

It's not just a handout; it's a new way of life. Heifer Project International (known as Heifer International) runs more than 925 projects that help millions of impoverished families become self-sufficient. Current recipients are located in more than 50 countries around the world including about 28 US states. The non-profit organization provides more than 25 different kinds of breeding livestock and other animals (bees rabbits ducks) that can be used for food income or plowing power in addition to training in sustainable agriculture techniques. In exchange the family agrees to pass on not only the animals' first female offspring to another needy family but their knowledge too.

	Annual Growth	06/10	06/11	06/12	06/13	06/14
Sales ($ mil.)	3.9%	–	127.6	112.4	114.9	143.0
Net income ($ mil.)	–	–	–	(3.3)	(8.9)	26.3
Market value ($ mil.)	–	–	–	–	–	–
Employees	–	–	–	–	–	304

HEINEKEN USA INC.

360 Hamilton Ave. Ste. 1103
White Plains NY 10601-1841
Phone: 914-681-4100
Fax: 914-681-1900
Web: www.heinekenusa.com

CEO: Frans Van Der Minne
CFO: Dan Sullivan
HR: –
FYE: December 31
Type: Subsidiary

Heineken USA taps a lush market thanks to America's thirst for foreign suds. The US beer-importing unit of Heineken (Netherlands) offers Heineken Amstel Light (one of the US's best-selling imported light beers) Murphy's Irish Stout and Irish Amber. Its parent's joint acquisition with Carlsberg in 2008 of Scottish & Newcastle Britain's largest brewer won Heineken USA the import rights to Newcastle Brown Ale. Heineken USA is also the sole US importer and seller of Mexico's former FEMSA Cerveza's beer brands Tecate Dos Equis Sol Carta Blanca and Bohemia. For drinkers who want the brew without the buzz the company sells Buckler a nonalcoholic beer. Heineken beer was first imported into the US in 1880.

HELEN KELLER INTERNATIONAL

352 PARK AVE S FL 12
NEW YORK, NY 100101723
Phone: 212-532-0544
Fax: –
Web: www.hki.org

CEO: Kathy Spahn
CFO: Elspeth Taylor
HR: –
FYE: June 30
Type: Private

Helen Keller International (HKI) has vision. The organization fights blindness by working with doctors government agencies partner groups and individuals in 22 countries citing that 80% of all blindness is avoidable. Its core areas of focus are eye health overall health and nutrition and poverty reduction. HKI distributes antibiotics performs cataract surgery and provides eye screenings glasses and education. The group works to combat malnutrition by promoting prenatal care supplying Vitamin A and helping others set up sustainable gardens and nutrition programs. It aims to reduce poverty through projects for literacy pre-school and clean water and offers entrepreneurial support for women.

	Annual Growth	06/09	06/10	06/11	06/12	06/13
Sales ($ mil.)	13.2%	–	94.6	162.4	220.2	137.2
Net income ($ mil.)	–	–	–	(0.3)	2.2	6.2
Market value ($ mil.)	–	–	–	–	–	–
Employees	–	–	–	–	–	600

HELICON THERAPEUTICS INC.

7473 Lusk Blvd. Ste. 100
San Diego CA 92121
Phone: 858-246-8120
Fax: 858-246-8130
Web: www.helicontherapeutics.com

CEO: –
CFO: –
HR: –
FYE: December 31
Type: Private

Who knew the humble fruit fly could hold the key to the mysteries of the human mind? Helicon Therapeutics that's who! The development-stage biotechnology firm develops novel therapies for memory loss and other cognition disorders by focusing on the cAMP Response Element Binding Protein (CREB). The CREB controls the signal pathway that is vital to forming long-term memories. Scientists working for Helicon Therapeutics discovered the CREB gene while studying the fruit fly genome. The company is working on drugs to not only maintain memory but also to treat patients who have had suffered brain traumas through injury or stroke.

HELICOS BIOSCIENCES CORPORATION   PINK SHEETS: HLCS

1 Kendall Sq. Bldg. 700
Cambridge MA 02139
Phone: 617-264-1800
Fax: 617-252-6924
Web: www.sirtrispharma.com

CEO: –
CFO: –
HR: –
FYE: December 31
Type: Public

Helicos BioSciences is in the business of developing genetic analysis technologies. Its True Single Molecule Sequencing (tSMS) platform allows for the direct analysis of DNA and RNA samples without amplification cloning or other time-consuming preparation techniques. The company serves the research clinical diagnostic and drug discovery markets and aims to provide customers with the ability to compare thousands of samples. Its HeliScope genetic analysis system can be integrated into existing laboratories and consists of a computer-controlled instrument and related supplies and reagents.

HELIOS & MATHESON ANALYTICS, INC   NAS: HMNY

Empire State Building, 350 5th Avenue
New York, NY 10118
Phone: 212 979-8228
Fax: –

CEO: Divya Ramachandran
CFO: Umesh Ahuja
HR: –
FYE: December 31
Type: Public

Helios & Matheson Analytics Inc. (formerly Helios & Matheson Information Technology Inc.) is a source (or outsource) of IT services. The company provides database management project management network design and implementation application development and Web enablement and related e-business services. The company also markets and distributes third-party software products. HMNA primarily serves global corporations and larger organizations in the financial services banking insurance and pharmaceutical industries. The company is controlled by India-based Helios & Matheson Information Technology Ltd.

	Annual Growth	12/10	12/11	12/12	12/13	12/14
Sales ($ mil.)	(5.4%)	13.3	12.2	12.4	13.3	10.6
Net income ($ mil.)	–	(0.9)	0.2	0.4	0.4	(0.2)
Market value ($ mil.)	33.0%	1.5	4.7	8.6	13.4	4.7
Employees	(3.6%)	37	26	38	44	32

HELIX BIOMEDIX INC.   OTC: HXBM

22122 20th Ave. SE Ste. 204
Bothell WA 98021-4433
Phone: 425-402-8400
Fax: 425-806-2999
Web: www.helixbiomedix.com

CEO: R Stephen Beatty
CFO: –
HR: –
FYE: December 31
Type: Public

Helix BioMedix wants to remove wrinkles and acne without leaving red itchy skin. The company has a library of bioactive peptides with antimicrobial properties it hopes to exploit as it works to formulate wrinkle- and acne-fighting creams along with topical treatments for skin and wound infections. The firm also hopes to use its peptides to develop a treatment that will speed the healing of wounds with minimal scarring as well as to prevent drug resistant staph infections. Helix is looking to partner with large better-funded drugmakers to develop some of its product candidates. The company also licenses its peptides to consumer products makers.

HELIX ENERGY SOLUTIONS GROUP INC   NYS: HLX

3505 West Sam Houston Parkway North, Suite 400
Houston, TX 77043
Phone: 281 618-0400
Fax: 281 618-0500
Web: www.helixesg.com

CEO: Owen E. Kratz
CFO: Anthony (Tony) Tripodo
HR: –
FYE: December 31
Type: Public

Helix Energy Solutions is in the energy services mix as a top marine deepwater contractor. Its Contracting Deepwater unit primarily works in water depths ranging from 200 to 10000 feet using dynamically positioned and remotely operated vehicles (ROVs) that offer a range of engineering repair maintenance and pipe and cable burial services in global offshore markets. Former subsidiary Energy Resource Technology (ERT) bought and operated mature fields primarily in the Gulf of Mexico but in 2013 Helix Energy Solutions sold this business in order to focus on its offshore contracting operations.

	Annual Growth	12/10	12/11	12/12	12/13	12/14
Sales ($ mil.)	(2.0%)	1,199.8	1,398.6	846.1	876.6	1,107.2
Net income ($ mil.)	–	(127.0)	130.0	(46.3)	109.9	195.0
Market value ($ mil.)	15.6%	1,281.8	1,668.3	2,179.3	2,447.5	2,291.2
Employees	3.1%	1,590	1,655	1,695	1,600	1,800

HELLA CORPORATE CENTER USA INC.

43811 Plymouth Oaks Blvd.
Plymouth MI 48170-2539
Phone: 734-414-0900
Fax: 734-414-5098
Web: www.hella.com/produktion/hellausa/website/chan

CEO: Joseph V Borruso
CFO: Edward L Macek
HR: –
FYE: May 31
Type: Subsidiary

As the North American headquarters for Germany-based Hella KGaA Hueck & Co. Hella Corporate Center USA (formerly known as Hella North America) offers a helluva selection when it comes to aftermarket and OEM automotive lighting products. Through its subdivision Product Development Center for Lighting Hella Corporate Center manufactures aftermarket lighting products that include auxiliary lighting such as fog lamps replacement headlamps work lamps LED lighting warning lights and bulbs. Additionally it makes OEM automotive electronics and vehicle modules through its manufacturing facilities in the US and Mexico.

HELM U.S. CORPORATION

1110 Centennial Ave.
Piscataway NJ 08854-4169
Phone: 732-981-1116
Fax: 732-981-0528
Web: www.helmusa.com

CEO: –
CFO: William V Fossen
HR: –
FYE: December 31
Type: Subsidiary

Chemical distributor HELM U.S. (a subsidiary of Germany-based HELM Aktiengesellschaft) distributes specialty and industrial chemicals from chemical producers to industrial customers in the Americas. Founded in 1976 the company specializes in distributing raw materials for producers of thermoset resins and coatings. Typical products include both liquid (acetone acrylates methanol propylenes xylenes) and solid (borax fumaric acid melamine titanium dioxide) chemicals. The company also offers logistics services such as chemical tanker chartering documentation and import and export regulatory assistance.

HELMERICH & PAYNE, INC.   NYS: HP

1437 South Boulder Avenue
Tulsa, OK 74119
Phone: 918 742-5531
Fax: 918 742-0237
Web: www.hpinc.com

CEO: John W. Lindsay
CFO: Juan P. Tardio
HR: –
FYE: September 30
Type: Public

In the oil and gas industry Helmerich & Payne (H&P) knows the drill: The contract driller operates 344 land rigs in the US 38 international land rigs and nine offshore platform rigs for industry giants such as Occidental Petroleum Marathon Oil and Devon Energy. Its US contract land drilling operations in a dozen states accounts for the bulk of its revenues. It also drills offshore in California and the Gulf of Mexico and has drilling units in South America and North and West Africa. H&P operates FlexRigs (drilling rigs equipped with new technologies environmental and safety design). It also has real estate operations including a shopping center and office buildings in Tulsa.

	Annual Growth	09/11	09/12	09/13	09/14	09/15
Sales ($ mil.)	5.6%	2,543.9	3,151.8	3,387.6	3,719.7	3,165.4
Net income ($ mil.)	(0.7%)	434.2	581.0	736.6	708.7	422.2
Market value ($ mil.)	3.9%	4,375.4	5,130.8	7,430.6	10,547.2	5,093.1
Employees	(6.3%)	8,724	9,429	10,333	11,914	6,738

HELMSLEY ENTERPRISES INC.

230 Park Ave.
New York NY 10169-0399
Phone: 212-679-3600
Fax: 212-953-2810
Web: www.helmsleyhotels.com

CEO: –
CFO: Abe Wolf
HR: Jessica Ng
FYE: December 31
Type: Private

"Infamous" doesn't begin to cover Helmsley Enterprises and its former chairman the late Leona Helmsley. The company holds the real estate empire amassed by the late Harry Helmsley over a period of 50 years. Leona who was dubbed the "Queen of Mean" in her heyday served time for tax evasion and had interests in such high-profile properties as the Helmsley Park Lane and the Helmsley Windsor. Other holdings include apartment buildings and millions of square feet of New York real estate as well as a lease on the Empire State Building. The portfolio was valued at $5 billion before Harry Helmsley's death in 1997. Leona Helmsley sold more than $2 billion worth of property between 1997 and her death in 2007.

HEMACARE CORP.   NBB: HEMA

15350 Sherman Way, Suite 350
Van Nuys, CA 91406
Phone: 877 310-0717
Fax: 818 251-5300
Web: www.hemacare.com

CEO: Pete Van Der Wal
CFO: Lisa Bacerra
HR: –
FYE: December 31
Type: Public

HemaCare is not a vampire but it does need your blood to survive. A supplier of blood products and services to hospitals and researchers the company collects whole blood from donors at donor centers and mobile donor vehicles and processes it into plasma and platelets used for blood transfusions. HemaCare has blood collection centers in California and Maine; it operates under the name Coral Blood Services at its East Coast facilities. The company also provides therapeutic apheresis a kind of blood treatment used for patients with autoimmune and other conditions for hospitals in California and some mid-Atlantic states including New York.

	Annual Growth	12/08	12/09	12/10	12/11	12/12
Sales ($ mil.)	(16.9%)	37.6	36.4	30.3	16.2	17.9
Net income ($ mil.)	4.4%	1.0	0.9	(0.8)	(0.8)	1.2
Market value ($ mil.)	(12.6%)	3.6	6.2	5.7	3.1	2.1
Employees	(22.1%)	254	251	214	120	–

HEMAGEN DIAGNOSTICS INC   NBB: HMGN

9033 Red Branch Road
Columbia, MD 21045
Phone: 443 367-5500
Fax: –
Web: www.hemagen.com

CEO: William P Hales
CFO: M Robert Campbell
HR: –
FYE: September 30
Type: Public

Hemagen Diagnostics lets no disease go undetected. The company makes diagnostic kits and related components. Its Virgo product line is used to identify infectious and autoimmune diseases such as rheumatoid arthritis lupus measles and syphilis. Physicians and veterinarians use its Analyst reagent system and related components to test blood for substances like cholesterol glucose and triglycerides. Hemagen sells products internationally primarily through distributors; its Brazilian subsidiary markets its products in South America.

	Annual Growth	09/08	09/09	09/10	09/11	09/12
Sales ($ mil.)	(10.8%)	6.4	5.4	5.2	5.1	4.0
Net income ($ mil.)	–	0.4	(0.8)	(0.2)	(0.9)	(0.9)
Market value ($ mil.)	(28.4%)	1.9	1.2	0.9	0.5	0.5
Employees	(14.7%)	34	25	29	31	18

HEMISPHERX BIOPHARMA, INC.   ASE: HEB

1617 JFK Boulevard, Suite 500
Philadelphia, PA 19103
Phone: 215 988-0080
Fax: –

CEO: William A Carter
CFO: Thomas K Equels
HR: Nancy Schocklin
FYE: December 31
Type: Public

Targeting chronic viral diseases and immune disorders Hemispherx Biopharma hopes to do a world of good with its RNA (ribonucleic acid) and other drugs. The company has acquired the rights to Alferon N an FDA-approved drug for genital warts that the company is developing to fight other viral diseases such as West Nile virus. Hemispherx also is developing Ampligen an intravenously administered RNA drug that is in clinical trials to treat HIV and chronic fatigue syndrome (CFS). Ampligen is also being tested as an adjuvant for vaccines conditions including seasonal flu and bird flu. The compound has received orphan status from the FDA for kidney cancer melanoma CFS and HIV.

	Annual Growth	12/10	12/11	12/12	12/13	12/14
Sales ($ mil.)	9.9%	0.1	0.2	0.2	0.2	0.2
Net income ($ mil.)	–	(13.1)	(9.0)	(17.4)	(16.2)	(17.5)
Market value ($ mil.)	(15.6%)	100.7	39.8	51.2	54.1	51.0
Employees	9.7%	56	59	37	39	81

HEMMINGS MOTOR NEWS

222 W. Main St.
Bennington VT 05201-2103
Phone: 802-442-3101
Fax: 802-447-1561
Web: www.hemmings.com

CEO: –
CFO: –
HR: –
FYE: July 31
Type: Subsidiary

Hemmings Motor News knows how to get a car enthusiast's motor running. The company publishes the monthly "Hemmings Motor News" (at more than 600 pages a month it is considered the bible for car collectors) "Hemmings Classic Car" Hemmings Muscle Machines and "Hemmings Sports and Exotic Car". Hemmings Motor News also publishes collector's guides and almanacs. The company's Web site provides classified listings hosts forums publishes auto blogs and posts notices of upcoming automobile shows and events. The company operates as part of American City Business Journals itself a unit of media giant Advance Publications. The company was founded in 1954 by Ernest Hemmings.

HENKEL CORPORATION

1001 Trout Brook Crossing
Rocky Hill CT 06067-3910
Phone: 860-571-5100
Fax: 860-571-5465
Web: www.henkelna.com

CEO: Kasper Rorsted
CFO: –
HR: –
FYE: December 31
Type: Subsidiary

Henkel Corporation sticks with glue and a slew of other consumer products. The North American unit of German giant Henkel KGaA manufactures branded household and personal care goods in three categories: laundry and home care cosmetics/toiletries and adhesive technologies. Some of consumers' favorite brands are made by Henkle including Dial soap Soft Scrub cleaner Purex laundry detergent Right Guard antiperspirant got2b hair styling products and Loctite and LePage adhesives and sealants. Customers are retail groceries and wholesalers and distributors. Henkel has some 50 manufacturing facilities and accounts for nearly 20% of its parent's worldwide sales. The founding Henkel family controls the business.

HENRICKSEN & COMPANY INC.

1070 ARDMORE AVE
ITASCA, IL 601431366
Phone: 630-250-9090
Fax: –
Web: www.henricksen.com

CEO: –
CFO: Tim Osborn
HR: –
FYE: April 30
Type: Private

Henricksen & Company wants your company to be comfortable. The firm is an office furniture distributor that specializes in selling mid- and high-end office furnishings. Its portfolio consists of desks chairs filing systems and partitions from manufacturers including Allsteel Gunlocke and HON. Henricksen also offers its customers furniture warehousing installation maintenance and cleaning as well as reconfiguration design and space planning services. The company also leases furniture. Customers have included Cray Huron Consulting Restaurant Technologies SXC Health Solutions and Roundy's. The company was founded by the Henricksen family in the 1960s.

	Annual Growth	04/10	04/11	04/12	04/13	04/14
Sales ($ mil.)	5.6%	–	129.6	147.4	153.0	152.4
Net income ($ mil.)	(1.8%)	–	–	0.1	0.1	0.1
Market value ($ mil.)	–	–	–	–	–	–
Employees	–	–	–	–	–	197

HENRY COUNTY MEMORIAL HOSPITAL

1000 N 16TH ST
NEW CASTLE, IN 473624395
Phone: 765-521-0890
Fax: –
Web: www.hcmhcares.org

CEO: Blake Dye
CFO: Paul F Janssen
HR: –
FYE: December 31
Type: Private

Henry County east of Indianapolis is a perfect slice of the Midwest: farms small towns and its own county hospital system. Henry County Memorial Hospital actually serves parts of three counties with a 110-bed general hospital medical offices specialty centers a long-term care unit and an assisted living center. The hospital offers patients emergency care general medical obstetric pediatric hospice and surgical services. The Henry County Hospital Foundation funds a program to train nurses through the local schools and college. The hospital opened its doors in 1930.

	Annual Growth	12/05	12/06	12/08	12/09	12/12
Sales ($ mil.)	1.3%	–	58.7	63.0	0.1	63.4
Net income ($ mil.)	21.0%	–	–	3.1	(0.0)	6.6
Market value ($ mil.)	–	–	–	–	–	–
Employees	–	–	–	–	–	660

HENRY CROWN AND COMPANY

222 N. LaSalle St.
Chicago IL 60601
Phone: 312-236-6300
Fax: 312-899-5039

CEO: –
CFO: –
HR: John Merritt
FYE: December 31
Type: Private

The jewels of Henry Crown and Company shine on like crazy diamonds. Controlled by Chicago's prominent Crown family Henry Crown and Company is an investment firm that owns or has interests in a variety of business assets. These holdings include stakes in sports teams (the Chicago Bulls and the New York Yankees) leisure (Aspen Skiing Company) banking (JPMorgan Chase) and real estate (Rockefeller Center). The company also has a stake in General Dynamics; after once controlling the company outright it still has a seat on the board. Affiliate CC Industries holds and manages some of the Crown family's investments.

HENRY FORD HEALTH SYSTEM

1 FORD PL
DETROIT, MI 482023450
Phone: 313-916-2600
Fax: –
Web: www.henryford.com

CEO: –
CFO: James M Connelly
HR: Kathy Oswald
FYE: December 31
Type: Private

Built around a hospital founded by Detroit's favorite son the not-for-profit Henry Ford Health System (HFHS) is a hospital network that is also involved in medical research and education. The system's half-dozen hospitals — including the flagship Henry Ford Hospital as well as Henry Ford Wyandotte Hospital and mental health facility Kingswood Hospital — are home to roughly 2200 beds. HFHS also operates a 1200-doctor-strong medical group (with more than 40 specialties) as well as nursing homes hospice and a home health care network. The system's Health Alliance Plan of Michigan provides managed care and health insurance to more than half a million members.

	Annual Growth	12/06	12/07	12/08	12/09	12/13
Sales ($ mil.)	16.4%	–	1,820.5	1,083.6	2,118.4	4,517.0
Net income ($ mil.)	–	–	–	(122.9)	26.8	135.3
Market value ($ mil.)	–	–	–	–	–	–
Employees	–	–	–	–	–	23,000

HENRY MAYO NEWHALL MEMORIAL HOSPITAL

23845 MCBEAN PKWY
SANTA CLARITA, CA 913552001
Phone: 661-253-8000
Fax: –
Web: www.henrymayo.com

CEO: Roger E Seaver
CFO: –
HR: Yolanda Davis
FYE: September 30
Type: Private

Had a bit too much mayo? Arteries feeling a bit clogged? Henry Mayo Newhall Memorial Hospital exists for just this reason (among others). The hospital serves the healthcare needs of the Santa Clarita Valley in northern Los Angeles County. The not-for-profit community hospital houses more than 220 beds and provides general medical and surgical care as well as trauma services (it is a Level II trauma center) outpatient services psychiatric care and emergency services among other specialties. In operation since 1975 the hospital was built to serve the needs of the at-the-time unincorporated City of Santa Clara on land donated by The Newhall Land and Farming Company.

	Annual Growth	09/03	09/04	09/05	09/06	09/09
Sales ($ mil.)	(39.4%)	–	–	1,525.4	146.0	205.5
Net income ($ mil.)	1040.7%	–	–	0.0	10.1	11.9
Market value ($ mil.)	–	–	–	–	–	–
Employees	–	–	–	–	–	1,000

HENRY MODELL & COMPANY INC.

498 7TH AVE FL 20
NEW YORK, NY 100186704
Phone: 212-822-1000
Fax: –
Web: www.modells.com

CEO: Mitchell B. (Mitch) Modell
CFO: –
HR: –
FYE: February 01
Type: Private

A model corporate citizen retailer Henry Modell & Company sells sporting goods fitness equipment apparel and brand-name athletic footwear as America's oldest family-owned and -operated sporting goods retailer. Established in 1889 the business also ensures it has local team apparel on hand. Through more than 155 stores that operate under the Modell's Sporting Goods banner the company serves some 10 East Coast states and the District of Columbia. Known for its reasonably priced branded products Modell's locates its stores in malls regional shopping centers and busy urban areas. It also boasts an online presence at Modells.com.

	Annual Growth	01/10	01/11	01/12*	02/13	02/14
Sales ($ mil.)	2.7%	–	558.8	570.3	608.0	604.8
Net income ($ mil.)	–	–	–	(3.3)	0.6	(4.8)
Market value ($ mil.)	–	–	–	–	–	–
Employees	–	–	–	–	–	5,430

*Fiscal year change

HENSEL PHELPS CONSTRUCTION CO.

420 6TH AVE
GREELEY, CO 806312332
Phone: 970-352-6565
Fax: -
Web: www.henselphelps.com

CEO: Jeffrey K. (Jeff) Wenaas
CFO: Stephen J. (Steve) Carrico
HR: -
FYE: December 31
Type: Private

Hensel Phelps Construction builds it all from the courthouse to the big house. The employee-owned general contractor provides a full range of development pre-construction construction and renovation services for commercial institutional and government projects throughout the US and abroad. Its project portfolio includes prisons airports arenas laboratories government complexes offices and more. Major public and private clients have included the US Army Corps of Engineers IBM United Airlines The University of Texas Kodak and Whole Foods. Hensel Phelps founded the eponymous company as a homebuilder in 1937.

	Annual Growth	05/10	05/11	05/12*	12/12	12/13
Sales ($ mil.)	(5.0%)	-	2,494.2	2,178.9	1,220.3	2,248.8
Net income ($ mil.)	6.5%	-	-	54.4	35.7	58.0
Market value ($ mil.)	-	-	-	-	-	-
Employees	-	-	-	-	-	2,000

*Fiscal year change

HERALD NATIONAL BANK

NYSE AMEX: HNB

623 Fifth Ave. 11th Fl.
New York NY 10022
Phone: 212-421-0030
Fax: +86-20-8466-2252
Web: www.subaye.com

CEO: -
CFO: -
HR: -
FYE: December 31
Type: Subsidiary

They say money can't buy happiness but it can buy exceptional customer service from Herald National Bank. The private bank caters to high-net-worth individuals and small and midsize businesses from three branches in Manhattan Brooklyn and Long Island. It offers personal and business checking or money market accounts as well as credit cards and other lending products but the bank prides itself on its wealth management capabilities. Commercial mortgages account for the majority of the bank's loan portfolio followed by commercial and personal loans. Florida-based BankUnited acquired Herald National for $71.4 million in cash and stock in early 2012.

HERBERT MINES ASSOCIATES INC.

600 Lexington Ave. 2nd Fl.
New York NY 10022
Phone: 212-355-0909
Fax: 212-223-2186
Web: www.herbertmines.com

CEO: Hal Reiter
CFO: -
HR: -
FYE: December 31
Type: Private

Herbert Mines Associates mines the workforce to find high-performers for jobs in high fashion. The executive search firm recruits senior-level personnel in the retail food service apparel hospitality e-commerce and consumer products sectors. It has conducted work for such clients as Neiman Marcus Kimberly-Clark and Starbucks. Headquartered in New York the company strengthens its international presence through an affiliation with Globe Search Group an assortment of independently-owned executive search firms. Herbert Mines a former personnel executive with Revlon Neiman Marcus and Macy's founded the firm in 1981.

HERBST GAMING LLC

3440 West Russell Rd.
Las Vegas NV 89118
Phone: 702-889-7695
Fax: 702-889-7691
Web: www.herbstgaming.com

CEO: Michael Silberling
CFO: Walter Bogumil
HR: -
FYE: December 31
Type: Private

You can hope to win big at Herbst Gaming. The firm operates about 15 casinos hotels RV parks and slot routes in Nevada and the Midwest. Its flagship property Terrible's Sands Regency in Reno Nevada has more than 800 hotel rooms and some 600 slot machines as well as table games such as blackjack craps and roulette. It also houses restaurants lounges a gift shop and a video arcade. Other Herbst properties are located in smaller towns throughout Nevada including Henderson Dayton and Primm (where its Primm Casinos subsidiary operates). In addition the firm has a handful of locations in Iowa and Missouri. In 2009 Herbst Gaming filed Chapter 11; it exited bankruptcy at the close of 2010.

HERCULES OFFSHORE INC

NMS: HERO

9 Greenway Plaza, Suite 2200
Houston, TX 77046
Phone: 713 350-5100
Fax: 713 979-9301
Web: www.herculesoffshore.com

CEO: John T Rynd
CFO: Troy L Carson
HR: -
FYE: December 31
Type: Public

As a provider of shallow-water drilling and liftboat services Hercules Offshore supplies the muscle to major integrated energy companies and independent oil and natural gas exploration and production companies. It owns and operates a fleet of 27 jackup rigs two submersible rigs and one platform rig as well as 24 self-propelled self-elevating liftboats. About 78% of its jack up rigs are operating in the Gulf of Mexico although it works in other oil patches around the world. The company also operates a fleet of four conventional and 10 posted barge rigs that operate inland in marshes rivers lakes and shallow bay or coastal waterways along the US Gulf Coast. Hercules Offshore declared bankruptcy in 2015.

	Annual Growth	12/10	12/11	12/12	12/13	12/14
Sales ($ mil.)	8.2%	657.5	655.4	709.8	858.3	900.3
Net income ($ mil.)	-	(134.6)	(76.1)	(127.0)	(68.1)	(216.1)
Market value ($ mil.)	-	-	-	-	-	-
Employees	(4.9%)	2,200	2,300	2,600	2,200	1,800

HERCULES TECHNOLOGY GROWTH CAPITAL INC.

NASDAQ: HTGC

400 Hamilton Ave. Ste. 310
Palo Alto CA 94301
Phone: 650-289-3060
Fax: 650-473-9194
Web: www.herculestech.com

CEO: Manuel A Henriquez
CFO: Jessica Baron
HR: -
FYE: December 31
Type: Public

Hercules Technology Growth Capital (HTGC) performs its feats of strength with money. The closed-end investment firm offers financing vehicles to companies in the technology and life sciences sectors. A business development company (BDC) HTGC provides primarily US-based private firms with such products as mezzanine loans senior secured loans and select private-equity investments. Loans typically range from $1 million to $25 million. HTGC's portfolio includes around 125 companies; about half of its portfolio comprises drug discovery and development Internet consumer and business services and clean tech firms. Holdings include stakes in data network provider IKANO Communications and software firm Daegis.

HERITAGE BANKSHARES, INC. (NORFOLK, VA) — NBB: HBKS

150 Granby Street
Norfolk, VA 23510
Phone: 757 648-1700
Fax: 757 626-3933
Web: www.heritagebankva.com

CEO: –
CFO: –
HR: –
FYE: December 31
Type: Public

Heritage Bankshares comes from a long line of money. Heritage Bankshares is the holding company for Heritage Bank & Trust a community-based institution in Virginia with about half a dozen branches in Chesapeake Norfolk and Virginia Beach. The bank which opened in the mid-1970s offers standard banking products and services including checking and savings accounts debit cards CDs and IRAs. Real estate loans primarily mortgages account for the largest portion of its loan portfolio; the bank also originates loans for businesses individuals and municipalities. The bank offers insurance and investment services through its subsidiary Sentinel Financial.

	Annual Growth	12/09	12/10	12/11	12/12	12/13
Assets ($ mil.)	3.0%	274.6	267.1	294.6	336.6	309.0
Net income ($ mil.)	24.4%	1.1	2.1	2.4	2.3	2.5
Market value ($ mil.)	8.1%	21.6	28.4	25.3	26.7	29.5
Employees	(6.0%)	59	58	54	49	–

HERITAGE COMMERCE CORP. — NMS: HTBK

150 Almaden Boulevard
San Jose, CA 95113
Phone: 408 947-6900
Fax: –
Web: www.heritagecommercecorp.com

CEO: Walter T. (Walt) Kaczmarek
CFO: Lawrence D. McGovern
HR: –
FYE: December 31
Type: Public

If you know the way to San Jose you may also know the way to Heritage Commerce. It is the holding company for Heritage Bank of Commerce which operates 10 branches in the South Bay region of the San Francisco area. Serving consumers and small to midsized businesses and their owners and managers the bank offers savings and checking accounts money market and retirement accounts and CDs as well as cash management services and loans. Commercial construction land and mortgage loans make up most of the company's loan portfolio which is rounded out by home equity and consumer loans. The bank was founded in 1994.

	Annual Growth	12/10	12/11	12/12	12/13	12/14
Assets ($ mil.)	6.7%	1,246.4	1,306.2	1,693.3	1,491.6	1,617.1
Net income ($ mil.)	–	(55.9)	11.4	9.9	11.5	13.4
Market value ($ mil.)	18.3%	119.3	125.6	185.0	218.4	234.0
Employees	7.5%	181	189	190	193	242

HERITAGE FINANCIAL CORP. (WA) — NMS: HFWA

201 Fifth Avenue SW
Olympia, WA 98501
Phone: 360 943-1500
Fax: –
Web: www.hf-wa.com

CEO: Brian L. Vance
CFO: Donald J. Hinson
HR: –
FYE: December 31
Type: Public

Heritage Financial is ready to answer the call of Pacific Northwesterners seeking to preserve their heritage. Heritage Financial is the holding company for Heritage Bank which operates more than 65 branches throughout Washington and Oregon. Boasting nearly $4 billion in assets the bank offers a range of deposit products to consumers and businesses such as CDs IRAs and checking savings NOW and money market accounts. Commercial and industrial loans account for over 50% of Heritage Financial's loan portfolio while mortgages secured by multi-family real estate comprise about 5%. The bank also originates single-family mortgages land development construction loans and consumer loans.

	Annual Growth	12/10	12/11	12/12	12/13	12/14
Assets ($ mil.)	26.1%	1,367.7	1,369.0	1,345.5	1,659.0	3,457.8
Net income ($ mil.)	12.0%	13.4	6.5	13.3	9.6	21.0
Market value ($ mil.)	6.0%	421.2	380.1	444.5	517.4	531.1
Employees	23.6%	321	354	363	373	748

HERITAGE FINANCIAL GROUP INC. — NMS: HBOS

721 N. Westover Blvd.
Albany, GA 31707
Phone: 229 420-0000
Fax: –
Web: www.eheritagebank.com

CEO: –
CFO: –
HR: –
FYE: December 31
Type: Public

Established in the 1950s as a credit union to serve its hometown Marine base HeritageBank of the South (HBOS) has remained always faithful to its local customers. The flagship subsidiary of Heritage Financial Group operates more than 25 branches that provide traditional deposit and loan products and services to individuals and small to midsized businesses in southwestern Georgia Florida and Alabama. Nonresidential commercial real estate loans make up nearly a third of the bank's loan portfolio. HBOS also operates 15 mortgage offices and five investment offices. In late 2014 Heritage Financial Group was acquired by Renasant in a merger agreement totaling $258 million.

	Annual Growth	12/09	12/10	12/11	12/12	12/13
Sales ($ mil.)	28.1%	31.2	40.9	56.9	68.4	84.1
Net income ($ mil.)	–	(1.7)	1.4	3.8	6.8	11.3
Market value ($ mil.)	15.7%	–	97.3	92.4	108.0	150.8
Employees	21.7%	194	217	327	321	426

HERITAGE GLOBAL INC — CNQ: HGP

12625 High Bluff Drive, Suite 305
San Diego, CA 92130
Phone: 858 847-0656
Fax: –
Web: www.heritageglobalinc.com

CEO: –
CFO: –
HR: –
FYE: December 31
Type: Public

Change seems to be the only constant for Counsel RB Capital (which was known as C2 Global Technologies prior to 2011). The asset liquidation and patent licensing company sold its original business — the operation of a communications network — in 2003 and began providing phone and Internet service to residential and business customers. It sold the telecom unit which provided long-distance and business communications services to North Central Equity in 2005 to focus on the licensing of patents including two Voice-over-IP (VoIP) technologies. Counsel RB Capital is also involved in the acquisition and disposition of distressed and surplus assets in North America. Counsel Corporation owns 93% of the company.

	Annual Growth	12/10	12/11	12/12	12/13	12/14
Sales ($ mil.)	44.4%	3.3	17.2	14.1	8.9	14.2
Net income ($ mil.)	–	4.8	30.7	(1.8)	(6.4)	(26.5)
Market value ($ mil.)	27.6%	3.4	50.7	31.0	20.0	9.0
Employees	40.0%	13	16	44	34	50

HERITAGE OAKS BANCORP — NAS: HEOP

1222 Vine Street
Paso Robles, CA 93446
Phone: 805 369-5200
Fax: –
Web: www.heritageoaksbancorp.com

CEO: Simone F. Lagomarsino
CFO: Jason Castle
HR: Malati Shinazy
FYE: December 31
Type: Public

Stash your acorns at Heritage Oaks Bancorp. It's the holding company for Heritage Oaks Bank which serves retail customers farmers and small to midsized businesses in Central California's San Luis Obispo Santa Barbara and Ventura counties. Through about a dozen offices the bank offers standard products such as checking savings and money market accounts CDs IRAs and credit cards. It also has loan production offices in Goleta and Oxnard. In 2014 it took over Mission Community Bancorp and consolidated its five branches into existing locations of Heritage Oaks. Commercial real estate loans account for almost 80% of its loan portfolio; business loans make up the other 20%.

	Annual Growth	12/10	12/11	12/12	12/13	12/14
Assets ($ mil.)	14.9%	982.6	987.1	1,097.5	1,203.7	1,710.1
Net income ($ mil.)	–	(17.6)	7.7	13.0	10.8	9.0
Market value ($ mil.)	26.4%	111.5	120.0	196.6	254.3	284.5
Employees	1.1%	281	256	251	234	294

HERITAGE-CRYSTAL CLEAN INC
NMS: HCCI

2175 Point Boulevard, Suite 375
Elgin, IL 60123
Phone: 847 836-5670
Fax: –
Web: www.crystal-clean.com

CEO: Joseph Chalhoub
CFO: Mark DeVita
HR: –
FYE: January 03
Type: Public

It's a dirty job but somebody's gotta do it ... and Heritage-Crystal Clean wants to be that somebody. The company helps US businesses clean parts and dispose of highly regulated waste materials such as cleaning solvents used oil and paint that can't be discarded through municipal trash systems or standard drains. Customers primarily small to midsize companies include car dealerships auto repair shops trucking firms and manufacturers such as metal fabricators. Heritage-Crystal Clean (#2 in the industry behind Safety-Kleen) serves customers in 42 states in the central and eastern US.

	Annual Growth	01/11*	12/11	12/12	12/13*	01/15
Sales ($ mil.)	31.9%	112.1	152.9	252.5	283.1	339.1
Net income ($ mil.)	–	3.3	1.5	2.3	4.5	(7.0)
Market value ($ mil.)	5.1%	222.4	366.1	329.4	438.7	271.7
Employees	25.5%	581	796	892	958	1,441

*Fiscal year change

HERMES MUSIC

830 N. Cage Blvd.
Pharr TX 78577
Phone: 956-781-8472
Fax: 956-781-8772
Web: www.hermes-music.com

CEO: Alberto Kreimerman
CFO: –
HR: –
FYE: December 31
Type: Private

Hermes Music hears melodies when the cash register rings. The company named for the Greek god of commerce has distribution operations in Mexico Colombia and Argentina as well as in Florida and Texas. It imports and distributes musical instruments and pro-audio and lighting equipment throughout Latin America. The company also installs and repairs laser DJ and lighting systems in dance clubs. Hermes Music company was founded in 1982 by Alberto Kreimerman. In an effort to boost its distribution business the company sold its chain of stores in Texas to Guitar Center in 2006 thereby exiting the retail market in the US.

HERSCHEND FAMILY ENTERTAINMENT CORPORATION

5445 Triangle Pkwy. Ste. 200
Norcross GA 30029
Phone: 770-441-1940
Fax: 630-655-3377
Web: www.silvon.com

CEO: Joel Manby
CFO: Andrew Wexler
HR: –
FYE: April 30
Type: Private

Herschend Family Entertainment (HFE) makes more than a few silver dollars. The company owns and operates (or co-owns) more than 25 amusement parks in about 10 states. Properties include Silver Dollar City in Branson Missouri and Tennessee's Dollywood in partnership with country legend Dolly Parton. HFE also owns aquariums near Philadelphia and Cincinnati and the Ride the Ducks amphibious tours in a handful of cities including Atlanta and Philadelphia. The firm touts that it offers family entertainment "with Christian values and ethics". The family-owned company was founded in 1950 by Hugo and Mary Herschend to manage the Marvel Cave in the Ozarks a tourist attraction that opened in 1894.

HERSHA HOSPITALITY TRUST
NYS: HT

44 Hersha Drive
Harrisburg, PA 17102
Phone: 717 236-4400
Fax: 717 774-7383
Web: www.hersha.com

CEO: –
CFO: Ashish R Parikh
HR: Keith Black
FYE: December 31
Type: Public

Hersha Hospitality Trust's fortune is in hotels not chocolate. The self-advised real estate investment trust (REIT) invests in hotel properties primarily midscale upscale and extended stay properties in metropolitan markets across the US. It owns or co-owns more than 50 hotels containing nearly 8000 rooms most of them in Boston New York and Washington DC as well as in Miami and Los Angeles. The properties are operated under such brand names as Marriott International Hilton Hotels Starwood Hotels and Hyatt. Hersha Hospitality Trust owns a minority stake in Hersha Hospitality Management which manages the REIT's properties. Starwood Capital Group owns the remainder of Hersha Hospitality Management.

	Annual Growth	12/10	12/11	12/12	12/13	12/14
Sales ($ mil.)	10.2%	282.8	286.4	358.2	338.4	417.4
Net income ($ mil.)	–	(17.2)	(27.0)	22.2	49.9	68.3
Market value ($ mil.)	1.6%	328.1	242.6	248.5	276.9	349.5
Employees	14.4%	28	36	46	49	48

HERSHEY COMPANY (THE)
NYS: HSY

100 Crystal A Drive
Hershey, PA 17033
Phone: 717 534-4200
Fax: 717 531-6161
Web: www.hersheys.com

CEO: John P. (J.P.) Bilbrey
CFO: Patricia A. Little
HR: –
FYE: December 31
Type: Public

The Hershey Company works to inspire Almond Joy and lots of Kisses. As a global leader and North America's top chocolate producer the company has built a big business manufacturing such well-known chocolate and candy brands as Hershey's Kisses Reese's peanut butter cups Twizzlers licorice and under license Mounds candy bar York peppermint pattie and Kit Kat wafer bar. Hershey also makes grocery goods including baking chocolate chocolate syrup cocoa mix cookies snack nuts breath mints and bubble gum. Products from the chocolate king are sold to a variety of wholesale distributors and retailers throughout North America and exported overseas.

	Annual Growth	12/10	12/11	12/12	12/13	12/14
Sales ($ mil.)	7.0%	5,671.0	6,080.8	6,644.3	7,146.1	7,421.8
Net income ($ mil.)	13.5%	509.8	629.0	660.9	820.5	846.9
Market value ($ mil.)	21.8%	10,422.3	13,656.2	15,963.9	21,492.2	22,973.2
Employees	13.6%	13,500	13,800	14,200	14,800	22,450

HERSHEY ENTERTAINMENT & RESORTS COMPANY

100 HOTEL RD
HERSHEY, PA 170339507
Phone: 717-534-3131
Fax: –
Web: www.thehotelhershey.com

CEO: –
CFO: –
HR: –
FYE: December 31
Type: Private

Life is sweet for Hershey Entertainment & Resorts. The company owns the many chocolate-related entertainment destinations in Hershey Pennsylvania. Its holdings include Hersheypark one of the nation's top amusement parks with more than 65 rides and attractions; ZooAmerica wildlife park; the Hotel Hershey; and the Hershey Lodge. Hershey Entertainment also owns four golf courses and the Giant Center arena in Hershey. Hershey Entertainment & Resorts is fully owned by the Hershey Trust Company which controls a majority stake in candymaker The Hershey Company. The Hershey Trust Co. also acts as trustee for the Milton Hershey School.

	Annual Growth	12/05	12/06	12/07	12/08	12/09
Sales ($ mil.)	(54.9%)	–	–	1,333.8	274.0	271.0
Net income ($ mil.)	16391.2%	–	–	0.0	13.9	6.9
Market value ($ mil.)	–	–	–	–	–	–
Employees	–	–	–	–	–	7,100

HERTZ GLOBAL HOLDINGS INC
NYS: HTZ

999 Vanderbilt Beach Road - 3rd Floor
Naples, FL 34108
Phone: 239 552-5800
Fax: -
Web: www.hertz.com

CEO: John P Tague
CFO: Thomas C Kennedy
HR: -
FYE: December 31
Type: Public

If you've ever said "Don't worry about it it's just a rental" guess who hurts: Hertz a world leader in car rental. On its own and through agents and licensees Hertz operates about 11555 rental locations in about 150 countries under the Hertz Dollar and Thrifty brands. About 70% of its US revenues come from airport locations. Its fleet includes approximately 524500 cars from Ford General Motors Toyota and other manufacturers. While car rental accounts for about 80% of its sales Hertz also rents a variety of heavy equipment through about 335 locations in North America Europe and China.

	Annual Growth	12/10	12/11	12/12	12/13	12/14
Sales ($ mil.)	9.9%	7,562.5	8,298.4	9,020.8	10,771.9	11,046.0
Net income ($ mil.)	-	(48.0)	176.2	243.1	346.2	(82.0)
Market value ($ mil.)	14.5%	6,650.9	5,379.5	7,467.9	13,136.6	11,447.5
Employees	9.6%	22,900	23,900	30,200	30,400	33,000

HESKA CORP.
NAS: HSKA

3760 Rocky Mountain Avenue
Loveland, CO 80538
Phone: 970 493-7272
Fax: -
Web: www.heska.com

CEO: Kevin S. Wilson
CFO: Jason A. Napolitano
HR: -
FYE: December 31
Type: Public

If you lie down with dogs Heska makes sure you don't get up with fleas. The company makes diagnostic products vaccines and pharmaceuticals for domestic animals primarily cats and dogs. Its products — both on the market and in development — include diagnostics and treatments for allergies arthritis cancer fleas heartworms skin problems thyroid problems and viral infections. As part of its business Heska also operates a diagnostic lab and manufactures veterinary diagnostic and monitoring devices. The company develops vaccines for cattle small mammals and fish as well. Products are sold worldwide through direct sales representatives and independent distributors.

	Annual Growth	12/10	12/11	12/12	12/13	12/14
Sales ($ mil.)	8.2%	65.5	70.1	72.8	78.3	89.8
Net income ($ mil.)	246.8%	0.0	2.1	1.2	(1.2)	2.6
Market value ($ mil.)	38.2%	31.5	46.3	51.4	55.3	115.0
Employees	2.2%	276	277	280	290	301

HESS CORP
NYS: HES

1185 Avenue of the Americas
New York, NY 10036
Phone: 212 997-8500
Fax: -
Web: www.hess.com

CEO: John B. Hess
CFO: John P. Rielly
HR: Helena Deal
FYE: December 31
Type: Public

Oil and gas company Hess has exploration and production operations worldwide. In 2014 Hess reported proved reserves totaling more than 1.4 billion barrels of oil equivalent. In 2014 51% of the company's total proved reserves were located in the US; 61% of its crude oil and natural gas liquids production and 32% of its natural gas production came from US operations. In a major shift in strategy Hess has sold all its its downstream businesses (refining and petroleum product and energy marketing) in order to focus on its higher margin exploration and production activities.

	Annual Growth	12/10	12/11	12/12	12/13	12/14
Sales ($ mil.)	(24.2%)	34,613.0	37,871.0	38,373.0	24,421.0	11,439.0
Net income ($ mil.)	2.2%	2,125.0	1,703.0	2,025.0	5,052.0	2,317.0
Market value ($ mil.)	(0.9%)	21,877.8	16,235.4	15,137.8	23,724.3	21,100.3
Employees	(31.5%)	13,800	14,350	14,775	12,225	3,045

HEXCEL CORP.
NYS: HXL

281 Tresser Boulevard
Stamford, CT 06901
Phone: 203 969-0666
Fax: -
Web: www.hexcel.com

CEO: David E. Berges
CFO: Wayne C. Pensky
HR: Robert G. Hennemuth
FYE: December 31
Type: Public

The first footprints on the moon didn't come from Neil Armstrong but from Hexcel a maker of composite materials. Back then Hexcel made the footpads on the Apollo 11 lunar module; today the company makes advanced structural materials used in everything from aircraft components to wind turbine blades. Its composite materials include structural adhesives and honeycomb panels used in products like satellites auto parts golf clubs and even window blinds. Commercial aerospace companies account for nearly 60% of Hexcel's sales; governmental space and defense sales and industrial sales account for the rest. Markets for Hexcel industrial products include wind energy recreational equipment and transportation.

	Annual Growth	12/11	12/12	12/13	12/14	12/15
Sales ($ mil.)	7.5%	1,392.4	1,578.2	1,678.2	1,855.5	1,861.2
Net income ($ mil.)	15.0%	135.5	164.3	187.9	209.4	237.2
Market value ($ mil.)	17.7%	2,263.6	2,520.8	4,178.5	3,879.3	4,343.1
Employees	6.9%	4,508	4,973	5,274	5,663	5,897

HEXION INC
NL:

180 East Broad St.
Columbus, OH 43215
Phone: 614 225-4000
Fax: -
Web: www.momentive.com

CEO: Craig O. Morrison
CFO: William H. (Bill) Carter
HR: Judith A. (Judy) Sonnett
FYE: December 31
Type: Public

Hexion (formerly Momentive Specialty Chemicals) is the world's largest thermosetting resins (or thermosets) maker ahead of competitor Georgia-Pacific. Thermosets add a desired quality (heat resistance gloss adhesion etc.) to a number of different paints coatings and adhesives. They include an array of resins: phenolic epoxy polyester acrylic and urethane. The company also is a leading producer of adhesive and structural resins and coatings. It serves several markets including paints consumer products and automotive coatings. Hexion (which changed its name in early 2015) is a subsidiary of Momentive Performance Materials Holdings.

	Annual Growth	12/10	12/11	12/12	12/13	12/14
Sales ($ mil.)	1.6%	4,818.0	5,207.0	4,756.0	4,890.0	5,137.0
Net income ($ mil.)	-	214.0	118.0	324.0	(633.0)	(148.0)
Market value ($ mil.)	-	-	-	-	-	-
Employees	(3.5%)	6,000	5,300	5,100	5,000	5,200

HF FINANCIAL CORP.
NMS: HFFC

225 South Main Avenue
Sioux Falls, SD 57104
Phone: 605 333-7556
Fax: -
Web: www.homefederal.com

CEO: Stephen M Bianchi
CFO: Brent R Olthoff
HR: -
FYE: June 30
Type: Public

Those in South Dakota who want their finances to go north might turn to HF Financial. It's the holding company for Home Federal Bank which serves consumers and businesses through more than 30 branches in eastern and central South Dakota and a single branch in southwestern Minnesota. Deposit products include checking and savings accounts and CDs. Commercial mortgages and loans account for about 40% of HF Financial's loan portfolio. Residential multifamily and agricultural real estate loans account for another 30% of loans. Bank subsidiary Hometown Insurors sells insurance and annuities; Mid America Capital provides equipment financing. Home Federal Bank was founded in 1929. Great Western Bancorp agreed to buy HF Financial for $139.5 million in late 2015.

	Annual Growth	06/11	06/12	06/13	06/14	06/15
Assets ($ mil.)	(0.1%)	1,191.3	1,192.6	1,217.5	1,274.7	1,185.4
Net income ($ mil.)	52.0%	0.7	5.2	5.9	6.6	3.6
Market value ($ mil.)	8.5%	77.2	85.6	91.8	98.0	107.0
Employees	(4.5%)	359	311	334	285	299

HFB FINANCIAL CORP.
NBB: HFBA

1602 Cumberland Avenue
Middlesboro, KY 40965
Phone: 606 242-1071
Fax: 606 242-3432
Web: www.homefederalbank.com

CEO: David B Cook
CFO: Stanley Alexander Jr
HR: –
FYE: December 31
Type: Public

HFB Financial Corporation is the holding company for Home Federal Bank which provides community banking services to individuals and small to mid-sized businesses through three offices in southeastern Kentucky and two more in eastern Tennessee. Standard retail services include savings checking and money market accounts as well as certificates of deposit individual retirement accounts and Keogh plans. Home Federal focuses on residential lending but also originates commercial real estate construction business and consumer loans. Home Federal Bank was founded as People's Building and Loan Association in 1920.

	Annual Growth	12/09	12/10	12/11	12/12	12/13
Assets ($ mil.)	(0.6%)	342.4	348.0	347.1	344.3	334.8
Net income ($ mil.)	(10.9%)	3.1	1.9	1.4	2.0	2.0
Market value ($ mil.)	2.5%	20.3	23.3	21.1	21.5	22.4
Employees	–	90	–	–	–	–

HFF INC
NYS: HF

One Oxford Centre, 301 Grant Street, Suite 1100
Pittsburgh, PA 15219
Phone: 412 281-8714
Fax: –
Web: www.hfflp.com

CEO: Mark D. Gibson
CFO: Gregory R. Conley
HR: –
FYE: December 31
Type: Public

Don't huff and puff — HFF will help you finance that high-rise. The company's Holliday Fenoglio Fowler subsidiary is a large commercial real estate capital intermediary. The firm provides capital markets services including structured financing commercial loan servicing investment sales loan sales and debt placement. Real estate investment banking subsidiary HFF Securities provides advisory services seeks private and joint venture equity capital places private listings and provides institutional marketing for property investments. Unlike most commercial property brokerage firms HFF does not provide leasing or property management services. The company operates about 20 offices throughout the US.

	Annual Growth	12/10	12/11	12/12	12/13	12/14
Sales ($ mil.)	32.1%	140.0	254.7	285.0	355.6	425.9
Net income ($ mil.)	54.0%	10.9	40.0	43.9	51.4	61.3
Market value ($ mil.)	38.9%	364.0	389.2	561.4	1,011.7	1,353.4
Employees	14.0%	427	498	574	637	721

HHGREGG INC
NYS: HGG

4151 East 96th Street
Indianapolis, IN 46240
Phone: 317 848-8710
Fax: –
Web: www.hhgregg.com

CEO: Dennis L. May
CFO: Robert J. Riesbeck
HR: Charles B. Young
FYE: March 31
Type: Public

hhgregg has evolved from black-and-white to digital. The appliance and electronics retailer began as a small storefront selling washing machines refrigerators and black-and-white TVs. Today the fast-growing company sells name-brand products at more than 225 stores in about 20 mostly southern states and online. Its offerings include TV and video products (LED TVs Blu-ray disc players) home and car audio gear (CD players home theater systems) appliances (refrigerators washers and dryers) computers gaming consoles digital cameras GPS navigators and mattresses. Founded in 1955 hhgregg has been growing aggressively amid tough economic conditions and a bleak outlook for consumer electronics retailers.

	Annual Growth	03/11	03/12	03/13	03/14	03/15
Sales ($ mil.)	0.6%	2,077.7	2,493.4	2,474.8	2,338.6	2,129.4
Net income ($ mil.)	–	48.2	81.4	25.4	0.2	(132.7)
Market value ($ mil.)	(17.7%)	370.4	314.8	305.7	265.9	169.6
Employees	(0.9%)	5,600	6,700	6,300	6,100	5,400

HI-SHEAR TECHNOLOGY CORPORATION

24225 Garnier St.
Torrance CA 90505
Phone: 310-784-2100
Fax: 310-325-5354
Web: www.hstc.com

CEO: –
CFO: Jan L Hauhe
HR: Richard Crisa
FYE: May 31
Type: Subsidiary

Hi-Shear Technology cuts loose with a slew of electronic pyrotechnic and mechanical devices used by the defense and aerospace industry. Hi-Shear's power cartridges and separation devices provide command-release for structures designed to hold together under rigorous conditions. The devices are used in rockets and satellites such as the Space Shuttle and the Patriot missile and in airplane ejector seats. Major customers include the US Government Boeing and Lockheed Martin. Hi-Shear also makes pyrotechnic-powered LifeShear cutters that slice through steel and other materials to free trapped victims. In late 2009 British defense contractor Chemring Group acquired the company for about $132 million.

HI-TECH PHARMACAL CO., INC.
NMS: HITK

369 Bayview Avenue
Amityville, NY 11701
Phone: 631 789-8228
Fax: –
Web: www.hitechpharm.com

CEO: –
CFO: William Peters
HR: –
FYE: April 30
Type: Public

Hi-Tech Pharmacal combines imitation with innovation making and distributing dozens of liquid and semi-solid prescription over-the-counter (OTC) and vitamin products. The company primarily produces generic forms of prescription drugs including versions of allergy medicine Flonase (from Glaxo-SmithKline). Hi-Tech's ECR Pharmaceuticals business makes branded over-the-counter products including Bupap analgesic tablets and Zolpimist insomnia spray. Its Health Care Products division markets OTC products including nutritional products and devices for people with diabetes and the Zostrix line of pain and arthritis medications. Hi-Tech Pharmacal is being acquired by drugmaker Akorn.

	Annual Growth	04/09	04/10	04/11	04/12	04/13
Sales ($ mil.)	20.9%	108.7	163.7	190.8	230.0	232.4
Net income ($ mil.)	13.4%	9.8	31.1	41.5	48.4	16.3
Market value ($ mil.)	44.7%	102.5	330.3	375.5	442.4	448.8
Employees	4.5%	375	391	408	428	448

HIBBETT SPORTS INC
NMS: HIBB

2700 Milan Court
Birmingham, AL 35211
Phone: 205 942-4292
Fax: –
Web: www.hibbett.com

CEO: Jeffry O. Rosenthal
CFO: Scott Bowman
HR: –
FYE: January 31
Type: Public

Small-town sports fans are the bread and butter for Hibbett Sports. The company sells sports equipment athletic apparel and footwear in small to midsized markets in more than 30 states mainly in the South and Midwest. Its flagship Hibbett Sports chain boasts more than 925 locations; stores are primarily found in malls and strip centers anchored by a Wal-Mart. Hibbett also operates a single Sports & Co. superstore a larger format featuring in-store putting greens basketball hoops and appearances by athletes. On a smaller scale it runs about 20 mall-based Sports Additions shoe shops most of which are situated near Hibbett Sports stores. The company also operates an e-commerce site.

	Annual Growth	01/11	01/12*	02/13	02/14*	01/15
Sales ($ mil.)	8.3%	665.0	732.6	818.7	852.0	913.5
Net income ($ mil.)	12.2%	46.4	59.1	72.6	70.9	73.6
Market value ($ mil.)	9.7%	807.8	1,217.4	1,323.6	1,492.5	1,169.9
Employees	9.5%	6,050	6,700	7,400	8,100	8,700

*Fiscal year change

HICKMAN WILLIAMS & COMPANY

250 E 5TH ST STE 300
CINCINNATI, OH 452024198
Phone: 513-621-1946
Fax: –
Web: www.hicwilco.com

CEO: –
CFO: –
HR: –
FYE: March 31
Type: Private

Hickman Williams makes carbon products (anthracite coal metallurgical coke and reactive char coke) and metals and alloys (chromium manganese and silicon) used by metals producers. The company also manufactures service injection systems and cored wire feeding units for metal production facilities. Hickman Williams operates about 50 warehouse facilities throughout the nation. Founded by Richard Hickman and Harry Williams in 1891 the company is now owned by its employees.

	Annual Growth	03/10	03/11	03/12	03/13	03/14
Sales ($ mil.)	(6.4%)	–	299.0	0.0	287.1	245.2
Net income ($ mil.)	–	–	–	0.0	5.8	0.0
Market value ($ mil.)	–	–	–	–	–	–
Employees	–	–	–	–	–	93

HICKOK INC.

NBB: HICK A

10514 Dupont Avenue
Cleveland, OH 44108
Phone: 216 541-8060
Fax: –
Web: www.hickok-inc.com

CEO: Robert L Bauman
CFO: Gregory M Zoloty
HR: –
FYE: September 30
Type: Public

Like "Wild Bill" of Wild West lore Hickok is quite comfortable shooting it out with competitors on its own measured road to success. The company manufactures testing equipment used by automotive technicians to repair cars. Hickok also makes instruments indicators and gauges for manufacturers of aircraft and locomotives. While Ford and General Motors traditionally were the company's largest customers its biggest customer now is Environmental Systems Products (ESP) at 53% of sales. Hickok sells products primarily in the US. President and CEO Robert Bauman and the three daughters of founder Robert D. Hickok including chairman Janet Slade control the company.

	Annual Growth	09/11	09/12	09/13	09/14	09/15
Sales ($ mil.)	3.7%	5.1	4.8	6.5	6.3	5.9
Net income ($ mil.)	–	(0.7)	(0.8)	0.1	0.0	(0.1)
Market value ($ mil.)	(13.8%)	2.9	2.1	3.3	3.5	1.6
Employees	4.0%	71	76	79	87	83

HICKORY FARMS INC.

1505 Holland Rd.
Maumee OH 43537
Phone: 419-893-7611
Fax: 419-893-0164
Web: www.hickoryfarms.com

CEO: Mark S Rodriguez
CFO: Joe Herman
HR: –
FYE: January 31
Type: Private

Before your relationship goes to hell in a "gift" basket try delighting your honey with a ham from Hickory Farms. The gift-food company sells high-end beef and cheese chocolates desserts fresh fruits and nuts seafood and other delectables in eco-friendly gift boxes. Prices range from about $10 to more than $200. Gift-givers may order through catalogs and the company's website. In addition Hickory Farms sells direct through about 700 shopping-mall kiosks during the holiday season and it retails at discount merchandisers and grocers (such as Target and Safeway). Founded in 1951 Hickory Farms is owned by private investment firm Sun Capital Partners.

HICKORY TECH CORP.

NMS: HTCO

221 East Hickory Street
Mankato, MN 56002-3248
Phone: 800 326-5789
Fax: –
Web: www.hickorytech.com

CEO: Robert J Currey
CFO: Steven L Childers
HR: –
FYE: December 31
Type: Public

Its name may sound like a Division II college but Hickory Tech's field of play is telecommunications. The company operates two business segments: Telecom and Enventis (Internet protocol-based voice and data services). Through its subsidiaries the company provides 55000 residential and business customers with access lines in Iowa and Minnesota. It also offers long-distance services to 36000 customers broadband Internet access services to 19000 customers and digital television service to about 10000 customers. Its National Independent Billing unit which is part of the Telecom segment provides data processing services to other telecommunications companies.

	Annual Growth	12/08	12/09	12/10	12/11	12/12
Sales ($ mil.)	4.6%	153.2	139.1	162.2	163.5	183.2
Net income ($ mil.)	0.8%	8.0	11.3	12.1	9.2	8.3
Market value ($ mil.)	15.7%	73.5	119.4	129.2	149.8	131.5
Employees	4.1%	433	448	463	500	508

HID GLOBAL CORPORATION

15370 Barranca Pkwy.
Irvine CA 92618-3106
Phone: 949-732-2000
Fax: 949-732-2120
Web: www.hidcorp.com

CEO: Denis Hebert
CFO: –
HR: –
FYE: December 31
Type: Subsidiary

HID Global Corporation doesn't have to keep things hidden — it just keeps things under restricted access. The company provides products and services for physical access control authentication and credential management highly secure government ID identification technologies and card printing and personalization. HID uses radio-frequency identification (RFID) technology in electronic locks alarms biometric devices and systems that use encrypted access control. In addition to HID brands include ActivIdentity EasyLobby and FARGO. With locations worldwide the company serves customers across a broad range of industries. HID is a subsidiary of the world's largest lock maker Sweden's ASSA ABLOY.

HIGH CONCRETE GROUP LLC

125 DENVER RD
DENVER, PA 175179315
Phone: 717-336-9300
Fax: –
Web: www.highconcrete.com

CEO: Michael F Shirk
CFO: Michael W Van Belle
HR: –
FYE: December 31
Type: Private

High Concrete Group offers concrete solutions for your building needs. The company produces precast concrete structures including walls architectural facades and floor slabs to create everything from office buildings to sports arenas. It is one of the leading makers of precast parking structures in the US. Its StructureCare service provides preventive maintenance to extend the life of those structures. A subsidiary of High Industries High Concrete Group counts architects contractors and building owners among its customers. It primarily serves the Mid-Atlantic Midwest and New England regions of the country with projects that include the Baltimore Ravens' stadium and a Harrah's casino parking garage.

	Annual Growth	12/05	12/06	12/07	12/08	12/09
Sales ($ mil.)	–	–	–	0.0	255.3	104.5
Net income ($ mil.)	–	–	–	0.0	22.4	0.0
Market value ($ mil.)	–	–	–	–	–	–
Employees	–	–	–	–	–	900

HIGH COUNTRY BANCORP, INC.

NBB: HCBC

7360 West US Highway 50
Salida, CO 81201
Phone: 719-539-2516
Fax: 719-539-6216

CEO: Larry D Smith
CFO: –
HR: –
FYE: June 30
Type: Public

High Country Bancorp is in rarefied air. It is the holding company for High Country Bank which was founded in 1886 as the first savings and loan association chartered in Colorado. Serving the state's tourist-oriented "Fourteener" region (for the number of mountain peaks exceeding 14000 feet) the bank operates four branches in Salida Buena Vista and Canon City. It offers traditional services such as personal and business checking accounts CDs and IRAs as well as financial planning and investment services. The bank's lending activities include residential and commercial mortgages construction and land loans and home equity and personal loans.

	Annual Growth	06/01	06/02	06/03	06/13	06/14
Assets ($ mil.)	1.7%	161.3	176.6	187.4	196.7	201.8
Net income ($ mil.)	2.8%	1.3	1.7	1.9	1.9	1.8
Market value ($ mil.)	5.6%	13.9	17.1	25.5	27.0	28.3
Employees	8.6%	67	70	79	–	–

HIGH INDUSTRIES INC.

1853 WILLIAM PENN WAY
LANCASTER, PA 176016713
Phone: 717-293-4444
Fax: –
Web: www.highindustries.org

CEO: Michael F Shirk
CFO: Michael W Van Belle
HR: –
FYE: December 31
Type: Private

High Industries has ascended to the top of the steel and construction business. Doing business as High Companies its subsidiaries are active in heavy construction and materials mostly along the East Coast. Its High Steel Structures is one of North America's largest steel bridge fabricators. Other group companies include High Steel Service Center (metal processing) High Concrete Group (precast concrete) High Transit (specialty hauler) and High Structural Erectors (field erection services). Affiliates of High Companies such as High Hotels are active in real estate. Tracing its roots to a welding shop founded by Sanford H. High in 1931 the family-owned company is controlled by the High Family Council.

	Annual Growth	12/05	12/06	12/07	12/08	12/09
Assets ($ mil.)	(8.2%)	–	297.7	266.6	272.7	230.3
Net income ($ mil.)	–	–	–	23.1	31.9	0.0
Market value ($ mil.)	–	–	–	–	–	–
Employees	–	–	–	–	–	2,107

HIGH PERFORMANCE TECHNOLOGIES INC.

11955 Freedom Dr. Ste. 1100
Reston VA 20190
Phone: 703-707-2700
Fax: 703-707-0103
Web: www.hpti.com

CEO: James P Regan
CFO: David Keleher
HR: –
FYE: December 31
Type: Subsidiary

High Performance Technologies (HPTi) hopes to take your technological efforts to the max. The company provides information technology services to the US military and other parts of the federal government. Offerings include systems development network security design financial management systems modeling and simulation and information sharing and analysis. HPTi's services are primarily used in advanced and battlefield systems computational technologies and homeland security operations. The US Army and Air Force and the departments of Justice Homeland Security and Energy are among its chief clients. Dynamics Research Corporation (DRC) agreed to buy the company in 2011 for $143 million.

HIGH POINT REGIONAL HEALTH SYSTEM

601 N ELM ST
HIGH POINT, NC 272624398
Phone: 336-878-6000
Fax: –
Web: www.highpointregional.com

CEO: Ernie Bovio
CFO: Kimberly Crews
HR: –
FYE: September 30
Type: Private

Hospital stays are usually not the high point of one's life but High Point Regional Health System aims to make patients comfortable. Its main facility is High Point Regional Hospital a medical/surgical facility with about 380 beds serving the Piedmont Triad region of North Carolina. The private not-for-profit health care system also operates the Carolina Regional Heart Center Neuroscience Center Piedmont Joint Replacement Center Emergency Center Culp Women's Center and Hayworth Cancer Center. Other operations include primary care physician practices mental health wound care and home health care services. The hospital was founded in 1904. It became part of the UNC Health Care System in 2013.

	Annual Growth	09/09	09/10	09/11	09/12	09/13
Sales ($ mil.)	(10.9%)	–	296.9	276.7	274.9	209.9
Net income ($ mil.)	–	–	–	(13.1)	2.0	(21.6)
Market value ($ mil.)	–	–	–	–	–	–
Employees	–	–	–	–	–	2,338

HIGH POINT SOLUTIONS INC.

5 GAIL CT
SPARTA, NJ 078713438
Phone: 973-940-0040
Fax: –
Web: www.highpoint.com

CEO: –
CFO: Sandra Curran
HR: –
FYE: December 31
Type: Private

High Point Solutions can solve your networking needs. The company supplies network hardware — routers switches and access servers — to telecommunications companies and other large enterprises. High Point's procurement specialists provide equipment from leading manufactures such as Cisco Systems and Nortel Networks. The company also provides services in repair network design and installation. Owners Mike and Tom Mendiburu maintain a lean-and-mean corporate philosophy: a small staff dedicated to procurement and focused on speed and service for a short list of large clients. The brothers founded High Point in 1996.

	Annual Growth	12/07	12/08	12/09	12/12	12/13
Sales ($ mil.)	–	–	0.0	9.3	107.0	197.2
Net income ($ mil.)	–	–	–	0.0	0.0	7.9
Market value ($ mil.)	–	–	–	–	–	–
Employees	–	–	–	–	–	75

HIGH STEEL STRUCTURES LLC

1915 OLD PHLADELPHIA PIKE
LANCASTER, PA 176023410
Phone: 717-299-5211
Fax: –
Web: www.highsteel.com

CEO: Michael F Shirk
CFO: Michael W Van Belle
HR: –
FYE: December 31
Type: Private

Steel fabricator High Steel Structures helps to build bridges — literally. The company manufactures structural steel beams and girders used to build bridges and elevated roads in the US. High Steel also makes steel structures for buildings such as manufacturing plants power plants and sports arenas and offers erection services and emergency repair services. Working with contractors such as Balfour Beatty Skanska and Middlesex High Steel has fabricated steel for thousands of bridges mainly along the East Coast. The company has four fabrication plants in Pennsylvania and is a part of High Industries. High Steel traces its roots back to 1931 when it was founded as High Welding Company.

	Annual Growth	12/05	12/06	12/07	12/08	12/09
Sales ($ mil.)	15.4%	–	–	136.0	131.5	181.0
Net income ($ mil.)	–	–	–	5.9	7.1	0.0
Market value ($ mil.)	–	–	–	–	–	–
Employees	–	–	–	–	–	600

HIGHER ONE HOLDINGS INC. NYS: ONE

115 Munson Street
New Haven, CT 06511
Phone: 203 776-7776
Fax: –
Web: www.higherone.com

CEO: –
CFO: Christopher Wolf
HR: Donna Verdisco
FYE: December 31
Type: Public

The higher ambition at Higher One Holdings is to facilitate higher education payments. The company provides payment processing and disbursement services to nearly 2000 colleges and universities and over 13 million enrolled students across the US. To make financial transactions more efficient the firm offers Refund Management disbursement service which schools use to electronically distribute financial aid and other funds to students; CASHNet Payment Solutions which offers online and mobile billing and tuition payment options to students and parents; OneAccount banking deposit and card services for students; and Campus Labs data and analytics tools designed to help schools retain students and develop curriculum.

	Annual Growth	12/10	12/11	12/12	12/13	12/14
Sales ($ mil.)	11.0%	145.0	176.3	197.7	211.1	220.1
Net income ($ mil.)	(12.1%)	25.1	31.9	36.9	14.1	15.0
Market value ($ mil.)	(32.5%)	964.1	878.8	502.3	465.1	200.6
Employees	30.4%	450	700	880	1,000	1,300

HIGHJUMP SOFTWARE INC.

5600 W. 83rd St. Ste. 600 8200 Tower
Minneapolis MN 55437
Phone: 952-947-4088
Fax: 952-947-0440
Web: www.highjumpsoftware.com

CEO: Michael Cornell
CFO: Flint Seaton
HR: –
FYE: December 31
Type: Private

Keeping your warehouse operations running smoothly shouldn't require a leap of faith. HighJump Software provides enterprise information applications designed to monitor and manage fulfillment and distribution channels. Its warehouse management suite includes tools for inventory management logistics analysis and transportation planning. HighJump's software also features supply-chain management applications that allow companies to interact with suppliers. It sells directly and through partners to customers in the aerospace automotive food and beverage consumer packaged goods health care manufacturing and retail industries among others. HighJump was taken private by Battery Ventures in 2008.

HIGHLANDS BANKSHARES INC. NBB: HBSI

P.O. Box 929, 3 North Main Street
Petersburg, WV 26847
Phone: 304 257-4111
Fax: –

CEO: John G Van Meter
CFO: Jeffrey B Reedy
HR: –
FYE: December 31
Type: Public

No matter if you take the high road or the low road Highlands Bankshares will take of your money afore ye. The company (not to be confused with Highlands Bankshares headquartered in Virginia) is the holding company for The Grant County Bank and Capon Valley Bank which together operate about a dozen branches in Virginia and West Virginia. The banks offer standard retail products and services including demand and time deposit accounts and business and consumer loans. Real estate loans account for about 80% of the company's loan book. Highlands Bankshares also offers credit life accident and health insurance through HBI Life.

	Annual Growth	12/09	12/10	12/11	12/13	12/14
Assets ($ mil.)	(1.0%)	407.8	399.9	404.2	382.8	388.1
Net income ($ mil.)	(0.3%)	3.4	1.6	1.4	2.4	3.3
Market value ($ mil.)	4.2%	29.4	25.4	18.4	35.1	36.1
Employees	2.1%	120	128	125	–	–

HIGHLANDS BANKSHARES, INC. (VA) NBB: HBKA

P.O. Box 1128
Abingdon, VA 24212-1128
Phone: 276 628-9181
Fax: –
Web: www.hubank.com

CEO: Samuel L Neese
CFO: Robert M Little Jr
HR: –
FYE: December 31
Type: Public

Highlands Bankshares is the holding company for Highlands Union Bank which operates about a dozen branches in Virginia North Carolina and Tennessee. Unrelated to Highlands Bankshares in West Virginia the company offers checking and savings accounts IRAs and CDs. Residential mortgages and commercial construction and land development loans make up most of its loan portfolio. The bank has two subsidiaries: Highlands Union Insurance Services is part of a consortium of more than 40 other financial institutions that owns Bankers' Insurance which in turn owns nearly 10 insurance agencies in Virginia; Highlands Union Financial Services provides trust investment and retirement services.

	Annual Growth	12/10	12/11	12/12	12/13	12/14
Assets ($ mil.)	(2.0%)	655.5	621.0	592.5	598.3	605.1
Net income ($ mil.)	–	(2.1)	(6.5)	2.0	1.5	2.5
Market value ($ mil.)	1.9%	25.5	9.8	14.3	30.2	27.5
Employees	(0.4%)	214	208	211	213	211

HIGHLANDS FUEL DELIVERY LLC

190 Commerce Way
Portsmouth NH 03801
Phone: 603-559-8739
Fax: 330-491-1471
Web: www.thekag.com

CEO: –
CFO: –
HR: –
FYE: December 31
Type: Private

Highlands Fuel Delivery (dba Irving Oil) the US arm of Irving Oil Limited is engaged in the refining and distribution of oil and natural gas; it serves wholesale commercial and retail customers in eastern Canada Quebec and New England. The Irving Oil Canaport refinery in Saint John New Brunswick is the Western Hemisphere's first deep-water terminal and Canada's largest refinery. It has 800 fueling locations operations at 13 marine terminals and a delivery fleet of tractor-trailers. It serves US retail customers via 300 convenience stores and gas stations and also has home heating and wholesale operations in Maine New Hampshire and Vermont. The company is owned by the founding Irving family.

HIGHMARK BCBSD INC.

800 Delaware Ave.
Wilmington DE 19801
Phone: 302-421-3000
Fax: 302-421-8864
Web: www.highmarkbcbsde.com

CEO: Timothy J Constantine
CFO: Mark G Chaney
HR: Kathie Catanzarite
FYE: December 31
Type: Private

Blue Cross Blue Shield of Delaware (BCBSD) is the first choice for health insurance for First State residents. As one of Delaware's largest health coverage providers the company administers traditional indemnity insurance and managed care plans for some 400000 members. Its coverage options include Blue Choice PPO Blue Care IPA (an HMO plan) Blue Select point-of-service (POS) plan and BlueAdvantage consumer-directed plans. The firm also provides dental vision and supplemental Medicare coverage as well as disease management programs for members with chronic and serious illnesses. Founded in 1935 BCBSD is a licensee of the Blue Cross Blue Shield Association and an affiliate of Highmark.

HIGHWOODS PROPERTIES, INC.
NYS: HIW

3100 Smoketree Court, Suite 600
Raleigh, NC 27604
Phone: 919 872-4924
Fax: 919 431-1439
Web: www.highwoods.com

CEO: Edward J. (Ed) Fritsch
CFO: Mark F. Mulhern
HR: Will Howard
FYE: December 31
Type: Public

When it comes to office space Highwoods Properties takes the road most traveled especially if it runs through the Southeast. A self-administered real estate investment trust (REIT) the company owns or has an interest in more than 300 commercial properties totaling more than 28.5 million sq. ft. of leasable space. The REIT's holdings include mostly office properties (which generate more than 90% of its total revenue in the form of lease income) but also industrial and retail properties in about a dozen metropolitan markets the Southeast and Midwest. Its largest tenants include the federal government MetLife and PPG Industries. Highwoods also owns more than 520 acres of undeveloped land.

	Annual Growth	12/11	12/12	12/13	12/14	12/15
Sales ($ mil.)	5.8%	482.9	516.1	556.8	608.5	604.7
Net income ($ mil.)	20.5%	48.0	84.2	131.1	116.0	101.3
Market value ($ mil.)	10.1%	2,851.0	3,214.3	3,475.6	4,255.0	4,189.6
Employees	1.9%	415	415	426	432	447

HILAND DAIRY FOODS COMPANY. LLC

1133 E KEARNEY ST
SPRINGFIELD, MO 658033435
Phone: 417-862-9311
Fax: -
Web: www.hilanddairy.com

CEO: -
CFO: -
HR: Angela Nunn
FYE: September 30
Type: Private

Reflecting the herd mentality of its industry Hiland Dairy Foods is a joint venture between Prairie Farms Dairy and Dairy Farmers of America. Hiland's cows produce the raw ingredient for churning out butter ice cream fluid milk cheese yogurt and other dairy products free of artificial growth hormones. The milk is distributed through 25 sites dotting the southwest US. Beyond dairy Hiland supplies juices bottled milk and coffee (cravé latté) as well as green tea water and other to-go drinks. It features limited-run specialty items such as peanut butter s'mores ice cream. Founded in 1938 the farmer-owned venture operates manufacturing plants in the Midwest.

	Annual Growth	09/07	09/08	09/09	09/10	09/11
Sales ($ mil.)	(32.6%)	-	-	2,110.0	588.6	958.2
Net income ($ mil.)	35387.7%	-	-	0.0	24.6	8.7
Market value ($ mil.)	-	-	-	-	-	-
Employees	-	-	-	-	-	1,350

HILL & KNOWLTON INC.

825 3rd Ave.
New York NY 10022
Phone: 212-885-0300
Fax: 212-885-0570
Web: www.hillandknowlton.com

CEO: Jack Martin
CFO: Mark Thorne
HR: -
FYE: December 31
Type: Subsidiary

Public relations firm Hill & Knowlton has ridden its reputation as a straight-shooter straight to the top. The company (whose founder John W. Hill emphasized the importance of dealing honestly and openly with the press) is one of the largest PR firms in the US and a part of advertising conglomerate WPP Group. Hill & Knowlton's services range from marketing communications to corporate reputation management to political lobbying. With almost 80 offices spanning some 45 countries it caters to the technology and health industries; Lobbying firm Wexler & Walker Public Policy Associates and Finnish unit Hill and Knowlton Finland Oy act as subsidiaries for Hill & Knowlton.

HILL COUNTRY MEMORIAL HOSPITAL

1020 S STATE HIGHWAY 16
FREDERICKSBURG, TX 786244471
Phone: 830-997-4353
Fax: -
Web: www.hillcountrymemorial.org

CEO: -
CFO: Mark Jones
HR: -
FYE: December 31
Type: Private

Hill Country Memorial takes care of the peaks and valleys in the wellness of area residents. The health system provides medical services to eight counties near Fredericksburg in Central Texas. Its hospital Hill Country Memorial Hospital has about 85 beds and a staff of close to 100 physicians. Specialties include cardiology obstetrics oncology orthopedics and emergency medicine. The health system also operates a wellness center that offers locals yoga stress management weight loss and massage. Other community services include hospice and home care and the administration of state-funded services for low income women infants children (WIC).

	Annual Growth	12/08	12/09	12/10	12/11	12/12
Sales ($ mil.)	11.0%	-	-	-	63.7	70.6
Net income ($ mil.)	-	-	-	-	(9.7)	3.0
Market value ($ mil.)	-	-	-	-	-	-
Employees	-	-	-	-	-	626

HILL HOLLIDAY CONNORS COSMOPULOS INC.

53 State St.
Boston MA 02109
Phone: 617-366-4000
Fax: 617-366-8405
Web: www.hhcc.com

CEO: Mike Sheehan
CFO: Steve Andrews
HR: -
FYE: December 31
Type: Subsidiary

These hills are alive with the sound of advertising. Hill Holliday Connors Cosmopulos — which does business as Hill Holliday — is a full-service advertising agency operating through offices in Boston New York City and Greenville South Carolina. It offers creative development and campaign management services along with media planning brand promotion direct marketing customer relationship management and corporate communications. In addition the firm offers expertise in Hispanic marketing strategies. Clients have included Dunkin' Donuts CVS Chili's Grill & Bar and Liberty Mutual. Founded in 1968 the agency is part of advertising services giant Interpublic Group.

HILL INTERNATIONAL INC
NYS: HIL

One Commerce Square, 2005 Market Street, 17th Floor
Philadelphia, PA 19103
Phone: 215 309-7700
Fax: -

CEO: David L Richter
CFO: John Fanelli
HR: -
FYE: December 31
Type: Public

Hill International a leader in the construction advice business is far from over the hill. The company offers project management and construction claims consulting services worldwide. It manages all aspects of the construction process from pre-design through completion — even troubled project turnaround. Construction claims services include expert witness testimony and litigation support. The company has provided services for such clients as the Arizona Diamondbacks Consolidated Edison Kimpton Hotel & Restaurant Group and Walt Disney. It also counts US government agencies and international governments among its clients. Hill International operates out of around 100 offices in more than 35 countries.

	Annual Growth	12/10	12/11	12/12	12/13	12/14
Sales ($ mil.)	9.1%	451.8	501.5	480.8	576.7	640.3
Net income ($ mil.)	-	14.2	(6.0)	(28.2)	1.6	(10.9)
Market value ($ mil.)	(12.2%)	325.9	258.9	184.4	199.0	193.4
Employees	10.5%	3,060	3,168	3,663	4,111	4,558

HILL PHOENIX INC.

1003 Sigman Rd.
Conyers GA 30013
Phone: 770-285-3264
Fax: 770-285-3224
Web: www.hillphoenix.com

CEO: Bill Johnson
CFO: Al Alden
HR: –
FYE: December 31
Type: Subsidiary

Hill Phoenix has been keepin' it cool since 1887 when a New Jersey grocer developed the first cold case. The company engineers manufactures and sells as well as installs industrial walk-in coolers freezers and refrigerated display cases. It also makes electrical distribution units featuring switchboards load centers and lighting control panels. Aside from the expected supermarkets other customers of Hill Phoenix include big-box retailers commercial and industrial refrigeration companies and convenience stores. The Dover subsidiary has mushroomed through acquisitions including Tyler Refrigeration formerly a unit of Carrier Commercial Refrigeration and expansion of its sales and service network.

HILL PHYSICIANS MEDICAL GROUP INC.

2409 CAMINO RAMON
SAN RAMON, CA 945834285
Phone: 925-820-3536
Fax: –
Web: www.hillphysicians.com

CEO: –
CFO: –
HR: –
FYE: December 31
Type: Private

Hill Physicians Medical Group is the doctors' answer to HMOs. The company is an independent practice association (IPA) serving some 300000 health plan members in northern California. The company contracts with managed care organizations throughout the region — including HMOs belonging to Aetna CIGNA and Health Net — to provide care to health plan members through its provider affiliates. Its network includes about 3800 primary care and specialty physicians 38 hospitals and 24 urgent care centers. The company also provides administrative services for doctors and patients. PriMed a management services organization created Hill Physicians Medical Group in 1984 and still runs the company.

	Annual Growth	12/03	12/04	12/05	12/06	12/10
Sales ($ mil.)	(21.1%)	–	–	1,401.9	427.5	427.5
Net income ($ mil.)	1018.5%	–	–	0.0	5.3	5.3
Market value ($ mil.)	–	–	–	–	–	–
Employees	–	–	–	–	–	488

HILL-ROM HOLDINGS, INC.   NYS: HRC

Two Prudential Plaza, Suite 4100
Chicago, IL 60601
Phone: 312 819-7200
Fax: 812 934-8189
Web: www.hill-rom.com

CEO: John J. Greisch
CFO: Steven J. (Steve) Strobel
HR: –
FYE: September 30
Type: Public

Hill-Rom Holdings holds Hill-Rom Company which in turn holds hospital patients safe and secure. Hill-Rom makes sells and rents hospital beds and other patient-room furniture and equipment along with stretchers surgical table accessories and other equipment for lifting and transporting patients. The company also sells non-invasive therapeutic products and surfaces for the care of pulmonary bariatric and circulatory conditions and wounds. As most of its beds are designed to connect to patient monitoring equipment Hill-Rom also provides information technology products for use in health care settings. Its primary customers include worldwide acute and long-term care facilities.

	Annual Growth	09/11	09/12	09/13	09/14	09/15
Sales ($ mil.)	5.7%	1,591.7	1,634.3	1,716.2	1,686.1	1,988.2
Net income ($ mil.)	(22.7%)	133.3	120.8	105.0	60.6	47.7
Market value ($ mil.)	14.7%	1,956.3	1,893.7	2,334.9	2,699.8	3,388.0
Employees	12.6%	6,230	6,950	6,775	7,325	10,000

HILLENBRAND INC   NYS: HI

One Batesville Boulevard
Batesville, IN 47006
Phone: 812 934-7500
Fax: –
Web: www.hillenbrand.com

CEO: Joe A Raver
CFO: Cynthia L. (Cindy) Lucchese
HR: –
FYE: September 30
Type: Public

Hillenbrand knows a thing or two about life and death. Through its largest subsidiary BatesvilleHillenbrand is a top supplier to the death care industry providing nearly half the caskets used in the US. Batesville makes a variety of caskets in materials ranging from wood to stainless steel. Increasingly it also produces urns and other cremation products to satisfy increasing demand for lower-cost cremation. The company's Process Equipment Group (PEG) designs and makes equipment and systems used by industrial manufacturers. The PEG includes subsidiaries K-Tron Rotex and Coperion and was formed by a trio of acquisitions made in the past several years. Hillenbrand was spun off from Hillenbrand Industries.

	Annual Growth	09/11	09/12	09/13	09/14	09/15
Sales ($ mil.)	16.0%	883.4	983.2	1,553.4	1,667.2	1,596.8
Net income ($ mil.)	1.2%	106.1	104.8	63.4	109.7	111.4
Market value ($ mil.)	9.0%	1,157.4	1,144.2	1,721.6	1,943.0	1,636.0
Employees	9.3%	4,200	3,900	6,000	5,900	6,000

HILLS BANCORPORATION   NBB: HBIA

131 Main Street
Hills, IA 52235
Phone: 319 679-2291
Fax: –
Web: www.hillsbank.com

CEO: –
CFO: Shari J Demaris
HR: –
FYE: December 31
Type: Public

There's gold in them thar hills! Hills Bancorporation is the holding company for Hills Bank and Trust which has about a dozen branches located in the eastern Iowa counties of Johnson Linn and Washington. The bank provides standard commercial services to area individuals businesses government entities and institutional customers. Offerings include deposit accounts loans and debit and credit cards. Hills Bank and Trust also administers estates personal trusts and pension plans and provides farm management and investment advisory and custodial services. The bank traces its roots to 1904.

	Annual Growth	12/10	12/11	12/12	12/13	12/14
Assets ($ mil.)	4.9%	1,931.3	2,018.3	2,099.7	2,167.8	2,334.3
Net income ($ mil.)	3.7%	23.3	26.8	26.8	25.9	27.0
Market value ($ mil.)	6.6%	600.3	591.0	628.5	675.4	773.9
Employees	0.3%	423	415	423	421	428

HILLSHIRE BRANDS CO   NYS: HSH

400 South Jefferson Street
Chicago, IL 60607
Phone: 312 614-6000
Fax: 312 558-4913
Web: www.hillshirebrands.com

CEO: Sean M Connolly
CFO: Maria Henry
HR: –
FYE: June 29
Type: Public

Got meat? Hillshire Brands Company (formerly Sara Lee Corp.) certainly does. Hillshire Brands is the new home of the Hillshire Farm Ball Park Jimmy Dean and State Fair brands of deli meats and other packaged-meat products including hot dogs and sausages as well as the artisanal brands Aidells and Gallo. For dessert the company serves up Sara Lee's line of frozen desserts including cheesecake. Taking its name from its predecessor's most-recognized meat brand Hillshire Brands was formed in 2012 when Sara Lee split to form two publicly-traded companies the other being its European coffee-and-tea business D.E. Master Blenders 1753. The split followed years of divestitures and strategic acquisitions.

	Annual Growth	06/09*	07/10	07/11*	06/12	06/13
Sales ($ mil.)	(25.7%)	12,881.0	10,793.0	8,681.0	4,094.0	3,920.0
Net income ($ mil.)	(8.8%)	364.0	506.0	1,287.0	845.0	252.0
Market value ($ mil.)	36.3%	1,180.7	1,724.2	2,381.1	3,573.0	4,077.0
Employees	(31.4%)	41,000	33,000	21,000	9,500	9,100

*Fiscal year change

HILLTOP HOLDINGS, INC.   NYS: HTH

200 Crescent Court, Suite 1330   CEO: Jeremy B. Ford
Dallas, TX 75201   CFO: –
Phone: 214 855-2177   HR: –
Fax: –   FYE: December 31
Web: www.hilltop-holdings.com   Type: Public

Hilltop Holdings sits on top of a mound of money-related businesses. The company's PlainsCapital subsidiary operates more than 80 branches in Texas and an offshore branch in the Caymans offers residential mortgages through 200 PrimeLending offices in 40-plus and provides securities brokerage and investment banking through HilltopSecurities. Subsidiary National Lloyds Corporation (NLC) offers fire and homeowners' coverage for low-value and manufactured homes and insurance through independent agents in Texas and more than 25 other (mostly) southern states. NLC operates as National Lloyds Insurance and American Summit Insurance. Hilltop has more than $12 billion in assets under management.

	Annual Growth	12/10	12/11	12/12	12/13	12/14
Sales ($ mil.)	73.3%	131.7	152.2	263.3	1,179.2	1,188.1
Net income ($ mil.)	–	(0.5)	(6.5)	(5.6)	125.3	111.7
Market value ($ mil.)	19.1%	894.6	762.0	1,221.1	2,085.9	1,799.1
Employees	139.8%	133	135	3,950	4,550	4,400

HILTI INC.

5400 S. 122nd East Ave.   CEO: Cary Evert
Tulsa OK 74146   CFO: Eugene Hodel
Phone: 918-252-6000   HR: Kate McCulloch
Fax: 800-879-7000   FYE: December 31
Web: www.us.hilti.com   Type: Subsidiary

Hilti makes drills that cut through brick like butta. A subsidiary of Liechtenstein-based Hilti Corporation the company manufactures and markets tools and related items including adhesives blades compressors drills fastening systems foam screws and studs for the construction and building-maintenance industries. It operates throughout North America. For contractors who frequent big-box retailers Hilti runs some 300 Pro Shops inside Home Depot stores. Hilti Tool Fleet Management provides maintenance repair and replacement services for the construction industry. As its parent invests in R&D Hilti has been rolling out new products. In 2010 it acquired Unirac a maker of solar-panel mounting products.

HILTON WORLDWIDE HOLDINGS INC   NYS: HLT

7930 Jones Branch Drive, Suite 1100   CEO: Christopher J. (Chris) Nassetta
McLean, VA 22102   CFO: Kevin J. Jacobs
Phone: 703 883-1000   HR: Matthew W. (Matt) Schuyler
Fax: –   FYE: December 31
Web: www.hiltonworldwide.com   Type: Public

If you need a bed for the night Hilton has a few hundred thousand of them. The company is one of the world's largest hoteliers with a lodging empire that includes more than 4300 hotels and resorts in some 95 countries operating under such names as Doubletree Embassy Suites and Hampton as well as its flagship Hilton brand. Many of its hotels serve the mid-market segment though its Hilton and Conrad hotels offer full-service upscale lodging. In addition its Homewood Suites chain offers extended-stay services. The company franchises many of its hotels; it owns the Waldorf-Astoria brand and the New York Hilton. Hilton became a public company again in 2013.

	Annual Growth	12/10	12/11	12/12	12/13	12/14
Sales ($ mil.)	6.8%	8,068.0	8,783.0	9,276.0	9,735.0	10,502.0
Net income ($ mil.)	51.4%	128.0	253.0	352.0	415.0	673.0
Market value ($ mil.)	17.3%	–	–	–	21,907.9	25,688.8
Employees	2.0%	–	–	151,000	152,000	157,000

HILTON WORLDWIDE INC.

7930 Jones Branch Dr. Ste. 1100   CEO: Christopher J Nassetta
McLean VA 22102   CFO: Thomas C Kennedy
Phone: 703-883-1000   HR: –
Fax: 973-994-3001   FYE: December 31
Web: www.columbialabs.com   Type: Private

If you need a bed for the night Hilton Worldwide (formerly Hilton Hotels) has a few hundred thousand of them. The company is one of the world's largest hoteliers with a lodging empire that includes more than 3900 hotels and resorts in some 90 countries operating under such names as Doubletree Embassy Suites and Hampton as well as its flagship Hilton brand. Many of its hotels serve the mid-market segment though its Hilton and Conrad hotels offer full-service upscale lodging. In addition its Homewood Suites chain offers extended-stay services. The company franchises many of its hotels; it owns the Waldorf-Astoria and the New York Hilton. Hilton is owned by private equity firm The Blackstone Group.

HINES INTERESTS LIMITED PARTNERSHIP

2800 POST OAK BLVD # 4800   CEO: Michael J. G. Topham
HOUSTON, TX 770566118   CFO: Charles M. Baughn
Phone: 713-621-8000   HR: Stephanie Fore
Fax: –   FYE: December 31
Web: www.hines.com   Type: Private

Hines has many interests but none of them involve ketchup. The real estate firm invests in develops renovates manages and finances commercial real estate including high-rise office buildings industrial parks medical facilities mixed-use developments and master-planned residential communities. Its portfolio boasts more than 1280 properties completed under development managed or invested. They span 100-plus cities worldwide and 516 million sq. ft. Hines has collaborated with such world-renowned architects as I. M. Pei Philip Johnson and Frank Gehry. Management services include marketing tenant relations and contract negotiations. Chairman Gerald Hines founded the family-controlled firm in 1957.

	Annual Growth	12/06	12/07	12/08	12/09	12/10
Sales ($ mil.)	–	–	–	(1,216.5)	200.0	234.1
Net income ($ mil.)	–	–	–	0.0	0.0	0.0
Market value ($ mil.)	–	–	–	–	–	–
Employees	–	–	–	–	–	3,200

HINGHAM INSTITUTION FOR SAVINGS   NMS: HIFS

55 Main Street   CEO: –
Hingham, MA 02043   CFO: –
Phone: 781 749-2200   HR: –
Fax: 781 740-4889   FYE: December 31
Web: www.hinghamsavings.com   Type: Public

The Hingham Institution for Savings is a haven for wayward cash. The company boasts about 10 branches in Boston's south shore communities operating in Massachusetts in Boston Cohasset Hingham Hull Norwell Scituate South Hingham and South Weymouth. Founded in 1834 the bank offers traditional deposit products such as checking and savings accounts NOW accounts IRAs and certificates of deposit. Its loan portfolio is roughly split between commercial mortgages and residential mortgages (including home equity loans). To a far lesser extent the bank also originates construction business and consumer loans.

	Annual Growth	12/10	12/11	12/12	12/13	12/14
Assets ($ mil.)	11.1%	1,017.8	1,127.3	1,205.9	1,356.4	1,552.2
Net income ($ mil.)	21.5%	10.2	12.1	13.3	13.4	22.3
Market value ($ mil.)	18.3%	94.7	101.8	133.3	167.1	185.2
Employees	(2.0%)	–	–	126	131	121

HINSHAW & CULBERTSON LLP

222 N LASALLE ST STE 300
CHICAGO, IL 60601
Phone: 312-704-3000
Fax: -
Web: www.hinshawlaw.com

CEO: -
CFO: Robert P. Johnson
HR: -
FYE: December 31
Type: Private

Hinshaw & Culbertson's 500 lawyers offer a wide range of legal services though the firm specializes in commercial and defense litigation and corporate environmental employment and construction law. It represents professionals dealing with corporate health care taxation malpractice white collar crime insurance coverage immigration intellectual property securities and real estate liability and risk management issues. The firm also offers legal advisement services to architects engineers and people residing in the financial services sector. Hinshaw & Culbertson has about 25 offices throughout 12 states in the US. The firm was founded in 1934.

	Annual Growth	12/00	12/01	12/02	12/03	12/10
Sales ($ mil.)	7.2%	-	108.5	116.2	124.6	202.8
Net income ($ mil.)	8.8%	-	-	50.2	53.7	98.4
Market value ($ mil.)	-	-	-	-	-	-
Employees	-	-	-	-	-	1,010

HITACHI GLOBAL STORAGE TECHNOLOGIES INC.

3403 Yerba Buena Rd.
San Jose CA 95135
Phone: 408-717-6000
Fax: 503-843-2450
Web: www.yamhill.com

CEO: John Coyne
CFO: Michael A Murray
HR: -
FYE: December 31
Type: Subsidiary

Hitachi Global Storage Technologies (HGST) makes external and internal hard-disk and solid-state drives for a wide range of IT products from laptops to servers. Its data storage product portfolio ranges from 3.5-inch computer drives to solid-state drives for such applications as database analytics and cloud computing. HGST sells through distributors such as Ingram Micro and Arrow Electronics. The company has development and manufacturing operations in Asia and North America. Hitachi sold HGST to Western Digital in 2012 for about $4.3 billion in cash and stock.

HITACHI METALS AMERICA LTD.

2 Manhattanville Rd. Ste. 301
Purchase NY 10577-2103
Phone: 914-694-9200
Fax: 914-694-9279
Web: www.hitachimetals.com

CEO: Hideaki Takahashi
CFO: Toshiki Aoki
HR: -
FYE: March 31
Type: Subsidiary

Heavy metal — the industrial kind — is hip at Hitachi Metals America (HMA). Founded in 1965 the North American outfit of Hitachi Metals makes and markets a slew of groundbreaking products. Its lineup includes auto castings ceramics cutting tools gas piping components permanent magnets radio frequency components and power inductors sensors and specialty steel. The company manages about a dozen sales offices and plants two of which specialize in auto OEM machining and assembly. HMA primarily serves the automotive consumer products energy industrial information technology semiconductor and telecommunications sectors.

HITCHINER MANUFACTURING CO. INC.

594 Elm St.
Milford NH 03055
Phone: 603-673-1100
Fax: 603-673-7960
Web: www.hitchiner.com

CEO: -
CFO: -
HR: -
FYE: December 31
Type: Private

There's no hitch in Hitchiner Manufacturing's business plan. The family-owned supplier of thin-wall investment castings and subassemblies and components operates via four facilities: Ferrous-USA produces countergravity castings for the auto defense and pump and valve industries; Gas Turbine specializes in hot-section parts utilizing vacuum-melted alloys for the jet engine component market; Hitchiner Manufacturing Company de Mexico makes rocker arms for auto OEMs; and Ferrous Mexico auto rocker arm assemblies. Hitchiner is primarily a tier-two supplier (its parts go to another company that contracts directly with the OEM) for majors such as BorgWarner Goodrich General Motors and General Electric.

HITT CONTRACTING INC.

2900 FAIRVIEW PARK DR # 300
FALLS CHURCH, VA 22042-4513
Phone: 703-846-9000
Fax: -
Web: www.hitt-gc.com

CEO: -
CFO: Michael McGrae
HR: -
FYE: December 31
Type: Private

HITT Contracting hits the nail on the general contracting head. The group provides turnkey construction services for corporate base building aviation legal hospitality technology research medical and institutional and governmental facilities. Projects have included construction and design for the Federal Reserve DirecTV and Greenpeace. In addition to general contracting HITT offers design interior paint preconstruction and construction management services. It handles eco-friendly projects historic renovations and infrastructure refits. HITT which operates in more than 30 states is a family-owned and -operated firm that was founded in 1937 as W.A. Hitt Decorating Co. by Warren and Myrtle Hitt.

	Annual Growth	12/08	12/09	12/10	12/11	12/12
Sales ($ mil.)	2.6%	-	767.1	706.5	976.4	827.4
Net income ($ mil.)	(17.9%)	-	33.6	25.3	30.4	18.6
Market value ($ mil.)	-	-	-	-	-	-
Employees	-	-	-	-	-	600

HITTITE MICROWAVE CORP

NMS: HITT

2 Elizabeth Drive
Chelmsford, MA 01824
Phone: 978 250-3343
Fax: -
Web: www.hittite.com

CEO: Rick D Hess
CFO: William W Boecke
HR: Susan J Dicecco
FYE: December 31
Type: Public

And lo the Hittites did rise up out of their land (the Commonwealth of Massachusetts) and they did conquer Babylon...well semiconductors in any case. Hittite Microwave designs and develops microwave millimeter-wave and radio-frequency integrated circuits (RFICs) for aerospace broadband cellular and military applications. In addition to standard amplifiers frequency multipliers mixers modulators switches and other components the company provides custom RFICs. It gets more than half of its sales from customers in international locations. Boeing (more than 15% of sales) is Hittite Microwave's top customer.

	Annual Growth	12/08	12/09	12/10	12/11	12/12
Sales ($ mil.)	10.1%	180.3	163.0	244.3	264.1	264.4
Net income ($ mil.)	6.2%	53.8	46.2	77.0	84.7	68.6
Market value ($ mil.)	20.5%	929.8	1,286.8	1,926.6	1,558.6	1,958.8
Employees	10.0%	332	349	402	469	486

HKN INC

NBB: HKNI

180 State Street, Suite 200
Southlake, TX 76092
Phone: 817 424-2424
Fax: –
Web: www.hkninc.com

CEO: Mikel D Faulkner
CFO: Kristina M Humphries
HR: –
FYE: December 31
Type: Public

HKN (formerly Harken Energy) harkens back to the days when a certain President George W. Bush was an oil man. HKN which bought Bush's small oil company more than a decade ago explores for and produces oil and gas primarily in the US where it has interests in oil and gas wells in the Gulf Coast region of Texas and Louisiana and holds coalbed methane assets in the Midwest. Internationally it has stakes in exploration and production assets in South America (Global Energy Development 34%) and in Canada (Spitfire Energy 27%). In 2008 HKN reported proved reserves (all in the US) of 4.2 billion cu. ft. of gas and 1.5 million barrels of oil. Lyford Investments Enterprises owns 36% of the voting stock of HKN.

	Annual Growth	12/10	12/11	12/12	12/13	12/14
Sales ($ mil.)	(47.4%)	12.9	–	0.4	1.1	1.0
Net income ($ mil.)	–	0.6	(3.0)	(3.2)	(1.5)	(24.0)
Market value ($ mil.)	98.9%	1.4	0.8	29.1	30.1	21.9
Employees	3.0%	16	16	14	16	18

HMG/COURTLAND PROPERTIES, INC.

ASE: HMG

1870 S. Bayshore Drive
Coconut Grove, FL 33133
Phone: 305 854-6803
Fax: –
Web: www.hmgcourtland.com

CEO: Maurice Wiener
CFO: –
HR: –
FYE: December 31
Type: Public

Sun sea and sand are key parts of the business mix for HMG/Courtland Properties a real estate investment trust (REIT) that owns and manages commercial properties in the Miami area. The company owns the posh Grove Isle — a Coconut Grove-area luxury resort which includes a hotel restaurant spa and marina. The property managed by Grand Heritage Hotel Group accounts for about 70% of HMG/Courtland's rental income. The REIT also holds a 50% interest in a 16000 sq. ft. seafood restaurant at the marina in addition to a 5000 sq. ft. corporate office building. HMG/Courtland has two properties held for development in Rhode Island and Vermont and has equity interests in other commercial real estate operations.

	Annual Growth	12/10	12/11	12/12	12/13	12/14
Sales ($ mil.)	(70.1%)	9.6	9.9	8.0	0.1	0.1
Net income ($ mil.)	–	(1.3)	(0.9)	0.0	15.2	0.2
Market value ($ mil.)	17.5%	6.3	4.1	5.2	19.0	12.0
Employees	–	100	99	103	–	–

HMI INDUSTRIES INC.

13325 Darice Pkwy. Unit A
Strongsville OH 44149
Phone: 440-846-7800
Fax: 440-846-7899
Web: www.filterqueen.com

CEO: Kirk Foley
CFO: Julie A McGraw
HR: –
FYE: September 30
Type: Private

Looking for a product that will really clear the air? HMI Industries is up to the job. Under the Filterqueen brand name the company (aka Health-Mor) sells portable vacuum cleaners and air filtration systems. Using high-efficiency filters and cartridges HMI's systems are designed to rid homes of surface and airborne particles and allergens (dust smoke pollen mold spores pet dander) better than standard vacuum cleaners. Its products are sold through distributors in more than 40 countries. Chairman Kirk Foley acquired HMI for about $3 million in 2006 through 1670255 Ontario Inc. (dba Ace Distribution Ltd.) an entity he controls.

HMN FINANCIAL INC.

NMS: HMNF

1016 Civic Center Drive N.W.
Rochester, MN 55901
Phone: 507 535-1200
Fax: –
Web: www.hmnf.com

CEO: Bradley C Krehbiel
CFO: Jon J Eberle
HR: Lisa Ketterling
FYE: December 31
Type: Public

HMN Financial is the holding company for Home Federal Savings Bank which operates about a dozen branches in southern Minnesota and central Iowa. Serving individuals and local businesses the bank offers such deposit products as checking and savings accounts CDs and IRAs. Its lending activities include commercial mortgages (more than 30% of the company's loan portfolio) business loans (about 25%) residential mortgages and construction development and consumer loans. The bank provides financial planning investment management and investment products through its Osterud Insurance Agency subsidiary and Home Federal Investment Management.

	Annual Growth	12/10	12/11	12/12	12/13	12/14
Assets ($ mil.)	(10.0%)	880.6	790.2	653.3	648.6	577.4
Net income ($ mil.)	–	(29.0)	(11.6)	5.3	26.7	7.4
Market value ($ mil.)	44.8%	12.6	8.7	15.5	47.3	55.4
Employees	(4.3%)	225	219	204	195	189

HMS HOLDINGS CORP

NMS: HMSY

5615 High Point Drive
Irving, TX 75038
Phone: 214 453-3000
Fax: –
Web: www.hms.com

CEO: William C. (Bill) Lucia
CFO: Jeffrey S. (Jeff) Sherman
HR: Sara K Epperlein
FYE: December 31
Type: Public

HMS Holdings makes sure health benefits providers are paying only as much as they have to. Through its Health Management Systems subsidiary the company specializes in helping providers determine participant eligibility coordinate benefits and identify and recover claims that were paid in error or should have been paid by another party. It serves state Medicaid agencies and Children's Health Insurance Programs in some 40 states as well as federal agencies including Centers for Medicare & Medicaid Services and Veterans Health Administration. The company also provides services to commercial insurers employer groups and pharmacy benefits managers.

	Annual Growth	12/10	12/11	12/12	12/13	12/14
Sales ($ mil.)	10.0%	302.9	363.8	473.7	491.8	443.2
Net income ($ mil.)	(23.2%)	40.1	47.8	50.5	40.0	13.9
Market value ($ mil.)	(24.4%)	5,698.8	2,813.8	2,280.6	1,997.3	1,860.0
Employees	7.2%	1,736	2,249	2,702	2,657	2,296

HNI CORP

NYS: HNI

408 East Second Street
Muscatine, IA 52761-0071
Phone: 563 272-7400
Fax: 563 272-7114
Web: www.hnicorp.com

CEO: Stanley A. (Stan) Askren
CFO: Kurt A. Tjaden
HR: Brad Determan
FYE: January 03
Type: Public

HNI Corporation specializes in making office furniture including seating storage modular workspaces and desks. Its products are sold under brands such as HON Allsteel Gunlocke Maxon Paoli and Sagus (among others) to furniture dealers wholesalers and office product distributors as well as retailers such as Office Depot and Staples. Office furniture generates roughly 80% of sales; the remainder is driven through HNI's Hearth & Home Technologies. The unit one of the largest US makers of fireplaces for the home operates under the Fireside Hearth & Home banner. Founded in 1944 HNI has distribution partners in 50-plus countries but most of its products are sold in North America.

	Annual Growth	01/11*	12/11	12/12	12/13*	01/15
Sales ($ mil.)	7.1%	1,686.7	1,833.5	2,004.0	2,060.0	2,222.7
Net income ($ mil.)	22.9%	26.9	46.0	49.0	63.7	61.5
Market value ($ mil.)	12.8%	1,378.0	1,152.7	1,281.2	1,739.2	2,230.4
Employees	6.7%	8,500	9,500	10,400	10,300	11,000

*Fiscal year change

HNTB CORPORATION

715 Kirk Dr.
Kansas City MO 64105
Phone: 816-472-1201
Fax: 816-472-4060
Web: www.hntb.com

CEO: Robert Slimp
CFO: –
HR: –
FYE: December 31
Type: Private

HNTB knows the ABCs of A/E. The company is a pure design firm which derives most of its revenues from architecture engineering or environmental design operations. HNTB specializes in transportation infrastructure projects and government contracts. The firm is best-known for its highway and transit system design (its portfolio includes the New Jersey Turnpike) as well as airports (Chicago's Midway) and sports arenas (Invesco Field in Denver). The company operates some 60 locations across the US. The employee-owned HNTB (its name once stood for Howard Needles Tammen & Berendoff) traces its roots to 1914.

HO-CHUNK INC.

1 MISSION DR
WINNEBAGO, NE 68071
Phone: 402-878-4135
Fax: –
Web: www.hochunkinc.com

CEO: Lance Morgan
CFO: Dennis Johnson
HR: Mary Smith-Feeny
FYE: December 31
Type: Private

Ho-Chunk Inc. (HCI) the economic development corporation run by the Winnebago Tribe of Nebraska manages about 18 subsidiaries in the fields of communications construction distribution gasoline and convenience store retail (under the Heritage Express banner in Iowa and Nebraska) government contracting lodging (The WinnaVegas Inn) marketing used-vehicle sales and more. The profits from these businesses are in turn managed by the Ho-Chunk Community Development Corporation a not-for-profit organization that directs commercial growth and community infrastructure development for the tribe. "Ho-Chunk" is a modernized form of Hochungra the Winnebago tribe's traditional name.

	Annual Growth	12/04	12/05	12/06	12/07	12/09
Sales ($ mil.)	8.5%	–	111.3	113.0	121.4	154.5
Net income ($ mil.)	89.4%	–	–	0.7	1.1	4.5
Market value ($ mil.)	–	–	–	–	–	–
Employees	–	–	–	–	–	310

HOAG HOSPITAL FOUNDATION

500 Superior Ave. Ste. 350
Newport Beach CA 92663-4162
Phone: 949-764-7217
Fax: 212-423-0758
Web: www.mcny.org

CEO: Karen Linden
CFO: –
HR: –
FYE: September 30
Type: Private - Foundation

Hoag Hospital Foundation supports the Hoag Memorial Hospital Presbyterian by raising money for the hospital's operations medical research education and community outreach activities through more than 1400 volunteers. Its volunteers are organized into groups such as the 552 Club and Circle 1000. The groups host events like the Christmas Carol Ball and the Toshiba Senior Classic and encourage donors to make annual gifts raising about $20 million annually. The Hoag Hospital Foundation was formed in 1948.

HOAG MEMORIAL HOSPITAL PRESBYTERIAN

1 HOAG DR
NEWPORT BEACH, CA 926634162
Phone: 949-764-5689
Fax: –
Web: www.hoag.org

CEO: –
CFO: Andrew (Andy) Guarni
HR: Janet Blue
FYE: September 30
Type: Private

Serving California's Orange County population Hoag Memorial Hospital Presbyterian boasts several hospitals and even more clinics to cater to area residents. The not-for-profit health care system is home to two acute care hospitals seven health centers five urgent care centers and a network of more than 1500 physicians. Its hospitals include Hoag Hospital Irvine and Hoag Hospital Newport Beach in Southern California. Combined the two hospitals have 617 beds and provide a comprehensive range of medical and surgical services with specialized expertise in a number of areas such as oncology cardiovascular disease neuroscience and orthopedics. Hoag is an affiliate of St. Joseph Health.

	Annual Growth	09/09	09/10	09/11	09/12	09/13
Sales ($ mil.)	3.6%	–	–	–	757.3	784.6
Net income ($ mil.)	14.3%	–	–	–	136.2	155.7
Market value ($ mil.)	–	–	–	–	–	–
Employees	–	–	–	–	–	3,800

HOB ENTERTAINMENT INC.

6255 Sunset Blvd. 16th Fl.
Hollywood CA 90028
Phone: 323-769-4600
Fax: 323-769-4787
Web: www.hob.com

CEO: Michael Rapino
CFO: –
HR: –
FYE: December 31
Type: Subsidiary

HOB Entertainment has the low-down dirty blues — and that's a good thing. The company owns and operates a dozen House of Blues clubs in cities across the US. The venues offer food drinks and live music from some of the top blues and rock performers in the country. All total HOB Entertainment hosts more than 3500 events for some 400000 attendees each year. Isaac Tigrett an American entrepreneur and co-founder of the first Hard Rock Cafe in London opened the first House of Blues venue in 1992. HOB is a subsidiary of live music conglomerate Live Nation Entertainment.

HOBART AND WILLIAM SMITH COLLEGES

300 PULTENEY ST
GENEVA, NY 144563304
Phone: 315-781-3337
Fax: –
Web: www.hws.edu

CEO: –
CFO: –
HR: –
FYE: May 31
Type: Private

Hobart and William Smith Colleges offer a liberal arts education on the shores of Seneca Lake. The schools operate in conjunction on adjacent campuses making a nearly 200-acre complex in Geneva New York. Male students attend Hobart College and female students go to William Smith College for a total enrollment of about 2400. The colleges have nearly 230 faculty members and offer degrees in arts sciences and teaching. Hobart and William Smith students hail from 41 US states and more than 30 other countries. About 86% of its students receive financial aid.

	Annual Growth	05/08	05/09	05/10	05/11	05/13
Sales ($ mil.)	–	–	0.0	86.4	88.7	146.0
Net income ($ mil.)	(30.4%)	–	–	14.7	18.9	5.0
Market value ($ mil.)	–	–	–	–	–	–
Employees	–	–	–	–	–	337

HOFFER PLASTICS CORPORATION

500 N. Collins St.
South Elgin IL 60177
Phone: 847-741-5740
Fax: 847-741-3086
Web: www.hofferplastics.com

CEO: William A Hoffer
CFO: –
HR: –
FYE: December 31
Type: Private

Like a well-performing ATM machine Hoffer Plastics turns plastic into cash. The major US custom injection-molding company makes plastic products for the automotive communications consumer goods and soft drink industries. Products range from tamper-resistant closures (Drop-Lok) to engine components headlight covers flashlight and beeper casings and even dispensing valves for Coca-Cola's syrup used in soft drink machines worldwide. Hoffer Plastics manufactures small intricate single-cavity molds to molds with more than 200 cavities. Still led by the founding Hoffer family the company also offers engineering design (primarily part and tool design) and support services.

HOLCIM (US) INC.

201 Jones Rd.
Waltham MA 02451
Phone: 781-647-2501
Fax: 781-647-2516
Web: www.holcim.com/usa

CEO: Filiberto Ruiz
CFO: –
HR: GA Tan Jacques
FYE: December 31
Type: Subsidiary

There's nothing abstract about the concrete made by Holcim (US). The American arm of Swiss building products giant Holcim Ltd. it produces imports and sells cement ready-mix concrete asphalt and aggregates to manufacturers builders public works managers and architects around the nation. Holcim (US) operates 15 manufacturing facilities and has an annual production capacity of more than 18 million metric tons; it also imports products from overseas affiliates. The company has about 75 distribution terminals in a dozen sales regions. Top customers include manufacturers of concrete products and building materials dealers. Holcim (US) accounts for about 14% of its Swiss parent company's sales.

HOLIDAY BUILDERS INC.

2293 W EAU GALLIE BLVD
MELBOURNE, FL 329353184
Phone: 321-610-5156
Fax: –
Web: www.holidaybuilders.com

CEO: Bruce Assam
CFO: Richard Fadil
HR: –
FYE: December 31
Type: Private

Holiday Builders is out to make buying a new home a vacation-like experience. The company a 100% employee-owned enterprise since 1999 builds single-family detached homes throughout Florida and in Alabama South Carolina and Texas. Since its inception the company has built more than 30000 homes sold primarily to first-time and value-conscious buyers. The company offers full homebuying services to its clients through HBI Title Company Holiday Builders Real Estate HB Designs and a partnership with Shelter Mortgage. Holiday Builders was founded in 1983.

	Annual Growth	12/03	12/04	12/05	12/06	12/07
Sales ($ mil.)	–	–	–	(1,030.4)	699.2	234.1
Net income ($ mil.)	–	–	–	0.0	40.5	(26.2)
Market value ($ mil.)	–	–	–	–	–	–
Employees	–	–	–	–	–	101

HOLIDAY WHOLESALE INC.

225 PIONEER DR
WISCONSIN DELLS, WI 539658397
Phone: 608-253-0404
Fax: –
Web: www.holidaywholesale.com

CEO: –
CFO: –
HR: –
FYE: February 28
Type: Private

Holiday Wholesale services most of south and central Wisconsin with confections tobacco products paper goods and food products. The company's customers are primarily convenience stores and other small businesses. Holiday Wholesale also offers consultation services including a demographic study of the customer's location estimate of foot traffic and evaluation of proposed floor plans. In addition to its wholesale business the company also sells a number of its products (at wholesale prices) to the general public through its Showroom Store location. The company was founded in 1951 when it began operating out of a one-car garage.

	Annual Growth	02/05	02/06	02/07	02/08	02/09
Sales ($ mil.)	4.3%	–	111.4	113.3	120.2	126.5
Net income ($ mil.)	(9.0%)	–	–	0.8	0.8	0.6
Market value ($ mil.)	–	–	–	–	–	–
Employees	–	–	–	–	–	250

HOLLAND & HART LLP

555 17th St. Ste. 3200
Denver CO 80202
Phone: 303-295-8000
Fax: 303-295-8261
Web: www.hollandhart.com

CEO: –
CFO: –
HR: –
FYE: December 31
Type: Private - Partnershi

Holland & Hart is deeply rooted in the West. The full-service law firm is one of the largest in the Rocky Mountain region with 400 lawyers in 15 offices. Business litigation and natural resources are Holland & Hart's main practice groups. Within those groups the company offers legal services specializing in affordable housing bankruptcy oil and gas real estate securities and capital markets and environmental litigation among others. The firm handles cases for both individual clients and businesses. Holland & Hart was founded in 1947 by Steve Hart and Joe Holland.

HOLLAND & KNIGHT LLP

100 N. Tampa St. Ste. 4100
Tampa FL 33602
Phone: 813-227-8500
Fax: 813-229-0134
Web: www.hklaw.com

CEO: –
CFO: Michael Marget
HR: –
FYE: December 31
Type: Private - Partnershi

Your legal knight in shining armor might be just around the corner. Holland & Knight maintains more than 15 offices throughout the US plus another four in other countries including representative offices. The firm has more than 1000 lawyers overall. Holland & Knight maintains about 100 practice areas and draws clients from a wide range of industries; it has been recognized for its work in such areas as corporate transactions litigation maritime law and real estate. Clients have included companies such as EZCORP Harris Corporation Pearson and Sunovion Pharmaceuticals.

HOLLAND COMMUNITY HOSPITAL INC

602 MICHIGAN AVE
HOLLAND, MI 494234999
Phone: 616-748-9346
Fax: -
Web: www.hollandhospital.org

CEO: -
CFO: -
HR: Michael (Mel) Matthews
FYE: March 31
Type: Private

Holland Hospital (formerly Holland Community Hospital) provides a comprehensive range of health services to residents of western Michigan's Lakeshore region. The 190-bed not-for-profit hospital provides a variety of medical care and health services including primary emergency diagnostic surgical rehabilitative and inpatient behavioral health care. Holland Hospital is home to centers of excellence in the treatment of sleep disorders cancer women's health issues and cardiovascular ailments. The hospital provides community health and wellness education programs and operates a regional community health clinic. Founded in 1917 Holland Hospital employs some 330 physicians across 14 medical specialties.

	Annual Growth	03/05	03/06	03/07*	12/08*	03/10
Sales ($ mil.)	(43.4%)	-	-	938.8	0.3	170.1
Net income ($ mil.)	3607.9%	-	-	0.0	0.0	10.6
Market value ($ mil.)	-	-	-	-	-	-
Employees	-	-	-	-	-	1,500

*Fiscal year change

HOLLEY PERFORMANCE PRODUCTS INC.

1801 Russellville Rd.
Bowling Green KY 42101
Phone: 270-782-2900
Fax: 270-745-9940
Web: www.holley.com

CEO: Tom Tomlinson
CFO: -
HR: Deana Britt
FYE: December 31
Type: Private

Holley Performance Products has the cure for your automotive doldrums. The company specializes in making aftermarket automotive components including carburetors exhaust systems fuel pumps camshafts intake manifolds and superchargers. Its carburetors are designed for everything from racing cars to boats to that 1969 vintage Camaro. The company's brands include Flowtech Holley Hooker NOS and Weiand. Remanufactured carburetors and fuel injection components are part of its line as well. In September 2009 Holley filed for Chapter 11 bankruptcy protection its second in two years. It emerged in mid-2010.

HOLLINGSWORTH & VOSE COMPANY

112 Washington St.
East Walpole MA 02032
Phone: 508-850-2000
Fax: 301-429-5748
Web: www.rlpgbooks.com/

CEO: -
CFO: Joseph Sherer
HR: -
FYE: December 31
Type: Private

It's tough to get past Hollingsworth & Vose Company unless you're squeaky clean — they filter out the riff-raff. The company manufactures products for engine filtration air and liquid filtration and battery separators using nonwoven materials. It also makes advanced composites as well as technical filter and specialty papers. The company's engine and industrial filtration products are made to perform in harsh environments and are used in automotive air automotive lubrication diesel fuel hydraulic oil and other specialty filtration applications. Hollingsworth & Vose's battery separators are made with uniform pore structure chemical stability and high wicking and absorbency.

HOLLINGSWORTH OIL CO. INC.

1503 MEMORIAL BLVD STE B
SPRINGFIELD, TN 371723269
Phone: 615-242-8466
Fax: -
Web: www.hoclubes.com

CEO: -
CFO: -
HR: -
FYE: December 31
Type: Private

The Hollingsworth Companies meets companies' industrial-strength needs. The company develops and builds industrial parks and facilities in the southeastern US. It provides build-to-suit and finish-to-suit structures primarily on its SouthPoint Business Park pad-ready sites located in Alabama North Carolina Tennessee and Virginia. Developments typically range from 50000 sq. ft. to 500000 sq. ft. Hollingsworth also provides facility expansion and funding services. All of the company's SouthPoint properties are located in areas convenient to interstate highways and airport services. CEO and owner Joe Hollingsworth Jr. founded The Hollingsworth Companies in 1986.

	Annual Growth	12/09	12/10	12/11	12/12	12/13
Sales ($ mil.)	4.0%	-	501.9	593.1	584.5	564.5
Net income ($ mil.)	(20.9%)	-	-	0.9	0.1	0.5
Market value ($ mil.)	-	-	-	-	-	-
Employees	-	-	-	-	-	300

HOLLISTER INCORPORATED

2000 Hollister Dr.
Libertyville IL 60048
Phone: 847-680-1000
Fax: 847-680-2123
Web: www.hollister.com

CEO: -
CFO: Sam Brilliant
HR: -
FYE: December 31
Type: Private

The products Hollister makes may not be fun to use but they are necessary. The employee-owned company makes medical devices used for wound continence bowel and ostomy care as well as tube fasteners and various related accessories. Its vast range of products include catheters collection devices and wound dressings. The company has manufacturing centers in Missouri and Virginia in the US and in Denmark Ireland and India. It distributes products worldwide. John Dickinson Schneider founded the company in 1921 as JDS Printer Craftsman. Its first products were birth certificates printed for the Franklin C. Hollister Company. In 1948 Schneider bought the Hollister name and began developing medical products.

HOLLY ENERGY PARTNERS LP

NYS: HEP

2828 N. Harwood, Suite 1300
Dallas, TX 75201
Phone: 214 871-3555
Fax: -
Web: www.hollyenergy.com

CEO: Michael C Jennings
CFO: -
HR: -
FYE: December 31
Type: Public

Holly Energy Partners is having a jolly good time piping petroleum products and crude oil from refineries. It operates petroleum product and crude gathering pipelines (in New Mexico Oklahoma Texas and Utah) distribution terminals (in Arizona Idaho New Mexico Oklahoma Texas Utah and Washington) and refinery tankage in New Mexico and Utah. It operates 1330 miles of refined petroleum pipelines (340 miles leased) 960 miles of crude oil trunk lines 10 refined product terminals one jet fuel terminal and two truck-loading facilities. It also has three 65-mile pipelines that ship feedstocks and crude oil. HollyFrontier holds a 41% stake in Holly Energy Partners.

	Annual Growth	12/10	12/11	12/12	12/13	12/14
Sales ($ mil.)	16.2%	182.1	213.5	292.6	305.2	332.5
Net income ($ mil.)	17.9%	58.9	78.0	91.1	86.1	113.8
Market value ($ mil.)	(12.5%)	2,986.2	3,154.6	3,858.5	1,896.4	1,754.4
Employees	16.5%	148	216	232	257	273

HOLLY HUNT LTD.

801 W. Adams St.
Chicago IL 60607
Phone: 312-329-5999
Fax: 312-993-0331
Web: www.hollyhunt.com

CEO: Holly Hunt
CFO: –
HR: –
FYE: December 31
Type: Private

Holly wants to facilitate your hunt for fancy furniture pieces. Holly Hunt is an upscale design house that makes and markets home and office furnishings lighting fixtures rugs and textiles. The company has about 20 showrooms across North America including locations in Chicago Miami New York Los Angeles Washington DC and Toronto. The retailer showcases such furniture designers as Christian Liaigre Alison Berger John Hutton Studio H and Jean-Michel Wilmotte. Texan Holly Hunt founded the design firm as a single store in 1984.

HOLLYFRONTIER CORP.

NYS: HFC

2828 North Harwood, Suite 1300
Dallas, TX 75201-1507
Phone: 214 871-3555
Fax: –
Web: www.hollyfrontier.com

CEO: Michael C. Jennings
CFO: Douglas S. Aron
HR: –
FYE: December 31
Type: Public

HollyFrontier refines crude oil to produce gasoline diesel and jet fuel and sells it in erstwhile American frontier territories: the Southwest northern Mexico Kansas and the Rockies. Its major assets are a 52000 barrels-per-day refinery in Wyoming; the El Dorado Kansas refinery 135000 barrels; a Utah refinery 31000 barrels; a Tulsa refinery 125000 barrels and subsidiary Navajo Refining (New Mexico) which has a capacity of 100000 barrels a day. The company also has a 39% stake in Holly Energy Partners which operates crude oil and petroleum product pipelines. It also has owns 50% of Sabine Biofuels II LLC.

	Annual Growth	12/10	12/11	12/12	12/13	12/14
Sales ($ mil.)	24.1%	8,322.9	15,439.5	20,090.7	20,160.6	19,764.3
Net income ($ mil.)	28.3%	104.0	1,023.4	1,727.2	735.8	281.3
Market value ($ mil.)	(2.1%)	7,994.4	4,588.4	9,127.8	9,743.5	7,349.3
Employees	12.8%	1,661	2,382	2,534	2,662	2,686

HOLLYWOOD MEDIA CORP

NMS: HOLL

301 East Yamato Road, Suite 2199
Boca Raton, FL 33431
Phone: 561 998-8000
Fax: –
Web: www.hollywoodmedia.com

CEO: Mitchell Rubenstein
CFO: Tammy G Hedge
HR: –
FYE: December 31
Type: Public

This company helps get people to the local multiplex. Hollywood Media Corp. owns more than a quarter of movie ticket seller MovieTickets.com. In addition it owns ad sales firm CinemasOnline which maintains websites for theaters in exchange for the right to sell ads on the sites; it also sells ads on plasma TVs in cinemas hotels car dealerships and other venues in the UK and Ireland. Its growing intellectual property division owns the rights to concepts by authors such as Tom Clancy and Isaac Asimov developing them into books (through 51%-owned Tekno Books) movies and TV shows software and other merchandise. In late 2010 it sold its theater ticketing division which accounted for most of its business.

	Annual Growth	12/08	12/09	12/10	12/11	12/12
Sales ($ mil.)	(73.1%)	117.1	103.4	4.0	3.8	0.6
Net income ($ mil.)	–	(16.9)	(5.6)	4.9	(6.9)	10.4
Market value ($ mil.)	7.8%	23.2	32.4	38.0	29.4	31.3
Employees	(41.7%)	130	122	36	24	15

HOLMES LUMBER & BUILDING CENTER INC.

6139 STATE ROUTE 39
MILLERSBURG, OH 446548830
Phone: 330-674-9060
Fax: –
Web: www.holmeslumber.com

CEO: –
CFO: –
HR: –
FYE: December 31
Type: Private

Try building a home — or any, other structure — without the products that Holmes Lumber supplies. The building, materials retailer, sells, lumber blocks bricks cabinets doors paneling ceiling tiles hardware and other building materials to professional contractors and consumers at three Holmes Lumber and Building Centers, in Hartville Millersburg and Sugarcreek, Ohio. Founded in 1952 as Holmes Door & Lumber Co. the business was acquired by, family-owned Carter Lumber of Kent Ohio, in 2004 adding Holmes' operations to its 200-plus stores in 10 states.

	Annual Growth	12/04	12/05	12/06	12/07	12/08
Sales ($ mil.)	5.1%	–	–	–	47.1	49.5
Net income ($ mil.)	–	–	–	–	0.4	(0.5)
Market value ($ mil.)	–	–	–	–	–	–
Employees	–	–	–	–	–	150

HOLMES REGIONAL MEDICAL CENTER INC.

1350 HICKORY ST
MELBOURNE, FL 329013224
Phone: 321-434-7000
Fax: –
Web: www.holmesregionalmedicalcenter.org

CEO: Steve Johnson
CFO: Robert C Galloway
HR: –
FYE: September 30
Type: Private

If you're a Great Space Coaster you might depend on Holmes Regional Medical Center in times of medical need. The general acute-care hospital which houses about 515 beds and provides comprehensive medical and surgical care serves residents of Brevard County on Florida's Space Coast. A member of not-for-profit health care system Health First Holmes Regional Medical Center offers specialty care in a number of areas including trauma oncology cardiology orthopedics pediatrics and women's health. It also operates an air ambulance service a stroke care center a full-service endoscopy unit and an outpatient diagnostic facility as well as advanced robotic surgery and joint replacement centers.

	Annual Growth	09/04	09/05	09/06	09/12	09/13
Sales ($ mil.)	210.7%	–	0.0	0.5	411.6	391.8
Net income ($ mil.)	140.5%	–	–	0.0	63.1	0.6
Market value ($ mil.)	–	–	–	–	–	–
Employees	–	–	–	–	–	2,778

HOLOGIC, INC.

NMS: HOLX

250 Campus Drive
Marlborough, MA 01752
Phone: 508 263-2900
Fax: 781 280-0669
Web: www.hologic.com

CEO: Stephen P. (Steve) MacMillan
CFO: Robert W. McMahon
HR: –
FYE: September 26
Type: Public

Hologic markets a variety of women's health products focused on four areas: breast health diagnostics surgical health and skeletal health. Lead products include the Selenia digital mammography system the ThinPrep Pap test for cervical cancer screening the NovaSure System to treat excessive bleeding bone densitometry systems and Fluoroscan Mini C-arm Imaging systems used to guide doctors during orthopedic surgery. Hologic sells its products to hospitals and clinical labs worldwide through distributors and a direct sales force.

	Annual Growth	09/11	09/12	09/13	09/14	09/15
Sales ($ mil.)	10.9%	1,789.3	2,002.7	2,492.3	2,530.7	2,705.0
Net income ($ mil.)	(4.3%)	157.2	(73.6)	(1,172.8)	17.3	131.6
Market value ($ mil.)	26.5%	4,406.9	5,712.0	5,907.0	6,881.6	11,299.8
Employees	1.3%	5,019	6,157	5,615	5,351	5,290

HOLOPHANE

Granville Business Park Bldg. A 3825 Columbus Rd. SW
Granville OH 43023
Phone: 740-345-9631
Fax: 866-637-7069
Web: www.holophane.com

CEO: Vernon J Nagel
CFO: -
HR: -
FYE: August 31
Type: Business Segment

Holophane lights things up all around the world. A company and brand of Acuity Brands Holophane makes lighting fixtures and systems for industrial commercial and outdoor markets. Its largest product line industrial fixtures features lighting for vast indoor spaces (retail spaces convention centers factories warehouses etc.). Holophane also makes lighting products for large outdoor areas such as highway interchanges and it offers commercial and institutional lighting for schools and offices. Its ISD SuperGlass prismatic lighting technology allows reflectors to cast more light. Holophane was founded in 1895 in London and its founder helped start the Illuminating Engineering Society of North America.

HOLY CARITAS FAMILY HOSPITAL INC

70 EAST ST
METHUEN, MA 018444597
Phone: 978-687-0156
Fax: -
Web: www.steward.org

CEO: -
CFO: -
HR: -
FYE: September 30
Type: Private

Caritas Holy Family Hospital is part of a large family of hospitals. The acute care medical facility is a more than 260-bed hospital that serves the residents of some 20 communities in northern Massachusetts and southern New Hampshire. Holy Family Hospital offers specialized services in areas including surgery diagnostics pediatrics obstetrics oncology cardiology and psychiatric care. The hospital founded in 1985 also operates an outpatient surgery center and provides community outreach services. It is a member of Steward Health Care System (formerly Caritas Christi) one of the largest health care systems in New England.

	Annual Growth	09/01	09/02	09/03	09/08	09/09
Sales ($ mil.)	2.6%	-	122.0	122.7	149.2	145.7
Net income ($ mil.)	-	-	-	(1.0)	2.0	6.0
Market value ($ mil.)	-	-	-	-	-	-
Employees	-	-	-	-	-	1,700

HOLY CROSS HOSPITAL INC.

4725 N FEDERAL HWY
FORT LAUDERDALE, FL 333084668
Phone: 954-771-8000
Fax: -
Web: www.holy-cross.com

CEO: Patrick Taylor
CFO: Linda Wilford
HR: -
FYE: December 31
Type: Private

Holy Cross Hospital's patients have more than just doctors on their side. Holy Cross is a Catholic community hospital serving the Ft. Lauderdale Florida area. The hospital has about 560 beds and offers inpatient and outpatient medical services along with a cancer treatment center heart and vascular center women's health center orthopedic unit and home health division as well as outpatient imaging centers. It also operates family health and specialist clinics in the region. Sponsored by the Sisters of Mercy Holy Cross Hospital is a part of Trinity Health.

	Annual Growth	04/04	04/05*	12/08	12/09	12/12
Sales ($ mil.)	173.3%	-	0.4	373.9	420.7	426.6
Net income ($ mil.)	-	-	-	(25.4)	7.3	21.1
Market value ($ mil.)	-	-	-	-	-	-
Employees	-	-	-	-	-	2,300

*Fiscal year change

HOLY SPIRIT HOSPITAL OF THE SISTERS OF CHRISTIAN CHARITY

503 N 21ST ST
CAMP HILL, PA 170112288
Phone: 717-763-2100
Fax: -
Web: www.hsh.org

CEO: -
CFO: Donna Hotham
HR: -
FYE: June 30
Type: Private

Holy Spirit Health tends to the health of the incarnate. The Holy Spirit Health System (HSHS) provides cardiology women's health care pediatric care and other acute and emergency medical services to the residents of greater Harrisburg in south-central Pennsylvania. The flagship Holy Spirit Hospital has some 310 beds as well as a level III neonatal intensive care unit. The hospital also operates an adjoining cardiac treatment facility and it has a network of affiliated family practice urgent care surgical and specialty health clinics. HSHS was established in 1963 and is an affiliate of Geisinger Health System.

	Annual Growth	06/06	06/07	06/08	06/09	06/10
Sales ($ mil.)	(59.4%)	-	-	1,650.1	5.6	271.7
Net income ($ mil.)	2533.5%	-	-	0.0	0.0	11.4
Market value ($ mil.)	-	-	-	-	-	-
Employees	-	-	-	-	-	2,698

HOME BANCORP INC

NMS: HBCP

503 Kaliste Saloom Road
Lafayette, LA 70508
Phone: 337 237-1960
Fax: 337 264-9280
Web: www.home24bank.com

CEO: John W Bordelon
CFO: Joseph B Zanco
HR: -
FYE: December 31
Type: Public

Making its home in Cajun Country Home Bancorp is the holding company for Home Bank a community bank which offers deposit and loan services to consumers and small to midsized businesses in southern Louisiana. Through about two dozen branches the bank offers standard savings and checking accounts as well as lending services such as mortgages consumer loans and credit cards. Its loan portfolio includes commercial real estate commercial and industrial loans as well as construction and land loans. Home Bancorp also operates about half a dozen bank branches in west Mississippi which were formerly part of Britton & Koontz Bank.

	Annual Growth	12/10	12/11	12/12	12/13	12/14
Assets ($ mil.)	14.9%	700.4	963.8	962.9	984.2	1,221.4
Net income ($ mil.)	20.5%	4.7	5.1	9.2	7.3	9.9
Market value ($ mil.)	13.5%	98.4	110.4	130.0	134.3	163.4
Employees	-	-	-	-	-	-

HOME BANCSHARES INC

NMS: HOMB

719 Harkrider, Suite 100
Conway, AR 72032
Phone: 501 328-4770
Fax: -
Web: www.homebancshares.com

CEO: C. Randall (Randy) Sims
CFO: Randy E. Mayor
HR: -
FYE: December 31
Type: Public

At this Home you don't have to stash your cash under the mattress. Home BancShares is the holding company for Centennial Bank which operates about 150 branches in Arkansas Alabama and Florida. The bank offers traditional services such as checking savings and money market accounts; IRAs; and CDs. It focuses on commercial real estate lending including construction land development and agricultural loans which make up more than 55% of its lending portfolio. The bank also writes residential mortgage business and consumer loans. Nonbank subsidiaries offer trust and insurance services. Investments are available to customers through an agreement with third-party provider LPL Financial.

	Annual Growth	12/10	12/11	12/12	12/13	12/14
Assets ($ mil.)	18.4%	3,762.6	3,604.1	4,242.1	6,811.9	7,403.3
Net income ($ mil.)	59.2%	17.6	54.7	63.0	66.5	113.1
Market value ($ mil.)	9.9%	1,488.6	1,750.8	2,231.2	2,523.8	2,173.1
Employees	18.5%	698	774	926	1,497	1,376

HOME CITY FINANCIAL CORP

NBB: HCFL

2454 North Limestone Street
Springfield, OH 45503
Phone: 937 390-0470
Fax: -
Web: www.homecityfederal.com

CEO: -
CFO: Charles A Mihal
HR: -
FYE: December 31
Type: Public

Home City Financial is where the heartland is. Home City is the holding company for Home City Federal Savings Bank of Springfield a two-branch thrift serving Clark County in southwestern Ohio. The bank offers standard deposit products including checking and savings accounts NOW accounts individual retirement accounts and certificates of deposit. Residential mortgages (nearly half of the company's loan portfolio) and commercial real estate loans (almost a quarter) are its primary lending focus; the bank also makes business consumer land construction and multifamily real estate loans. The company plans to go private through a reverse stock split.

	Annual Growth	12/10	12/11	12/12	12/13	12/14
Assets ($ mil.)	1.0%	145.9	143.8	142.9	143.6	151.6
Net income ($ mil.)	23.4%	0.6	0.9	1.0	1.1	1.3
Market value ($ mil.)	15.9%	7.2	6.6	8.2	12.8	13.0
Employees	-	-	-	-	-	-

HOME DEPOT INC

NYS: HD

2455 Paces Ferry Road N.W.
Atlanta, GA 30339
Phone: 770 433-8211
Fax: 770 431-2707
Web: www.homedepot.com

CEO: Craig A. Menear
CFO: Carol B. Tom ©
HR: Timothy M. (Tim) Crow
FYE: February 01
Type: Public

When embarking on household projects many start their journey at The Home Depot. As the world's largest home improvement chain and one of the largest US retailers the company operates nearly 2270 stores in the US Canada and Mexico as well as an online business. It targets the do-it-yourself (DIY) and professional markets with its selection of some 40000 items including lumber flooring plumbing supplies garden products tools paint and appliances. Home Depot also offers installation services for carpeting cabinetry and other products. After regaining its footing after the deep recession and housing crisis in the US Home Depot was stung by a massive payment data breach in 2014.

	Annual Growth	01/11	01/12*	02/13	02/14	02/15
Sales ($ mil.)	5.2%	67,997.0	70,395.0	74,754.0	78,812.0	83,176.0
Net income ($ mil.)	17.4%	3,338.0	3,883.0	4,535.0	5,385.0	6,345.0
Market value ($ mil.)	29.9%	47,966.9	58,645.1	87,961.1	100,443.0	136,476.9
Employees	3.7%	321,000	331,000	340,000	365,000	371,000

*Fiscal year change

HOME FEDERAL BANCORP INC.

NASDAQ: HOME

500 12th Ave. South
Nampa ID 83651
Phone: 208-468-5189
Fax: 208-468-5001
Web: www.myhomefed.com

CEO: -
CFO: -
HR: -
FYE: September 30
Type: Public

Home Federal Bancorp's location provides it with a treasure trove of opportunity. Its subsidiary Home Federal Bank (formerly Home Federal Savings and Loan Association of Nampa) serves the Treasure Valley region of southwestern Idaho which includes Ada Canyon Elmore and Gem counties (where nearly 40% of the state's population resides). Home Federal has 15 branches (three in Wal-Mart stores) and a loan center in Idaho as well as seven branches in central Oregon. It also offers banking through an ATM network and on the Internet. Its primary business is attracting deposits and using them to originate loans. In 2007 Home Federal converted from a mutual holding company to a stock ownership company.

HOME FINANCIAL BANCORP

NBB: HWEN

279 East Morgan Street
Spencer, IN 47460
Phone: 812 829-2095
Fax: 812 829-3069
Web: www.owencom.com

CEO: -
CFO: -
HR: -
FYE: June 30
Type: Public

When folks southwest of Indianapolis are ownin' they turn to Owen to help pay their bills. Home Financial Bancorp is the holding company for Owen Community Bank which operates two branches in Cloverdale and Spencer Indiana. Formed in 1911 the bank attracts deposits from Owen and Putnam counties by offering CDs IRAs and checking savings money market and NOW accounts. More than half of Owen Community's loan portfolio is comprised of one- to four-family residential mortgages; the bank also makes mobile home and land loans (nearly 30%) nonresidential mortgages (14%) and industrial commercial and consumer loans.

	Annual Growth	06/11	06/12	06/13	06/14	06/15
Assets ($ mil.)	(3.5%)	74.8	76.0	72.8	67.8	64.9
Net income ($ mil.)	(23.2%)	0.5	0.5	0.5	0.4	0.2
Market value ($ mil.)	13.5%	4.1	4.8	6.0	7.1	6.8
Employees	-	-	-	-	-	-

HOME INSTEAD INC.

13323 California St.
Omaha NE 68154
Phone: 402-498-4466
Fax: 402-498-5757
Web: www.homeinstead.com

CEO: Roger Baumgart
CFO: -
HR: -
FYE: December 31
Type: Private

Home Instead helps keep the elderly at home instead of in assisted living or nursing homes. The company which operates under the name Home Instead Senior Care provides non-medical home care assistance for seniors. Its services are designed for people who may be capable of managing their physical needs but require assistance supervision light housework meals errands or simply companionship in order to remain in their homes. Home Instead has a network of some 900 franchises operating throughout the US and in more than a dozen countries worldwide. Employees known as CAREGivers provide the elderly with one-on-one assistance in the home and at assisted living or nursing care facilities.

HOME LOAN FINANCIAL CORP.

OTC: HLFN

401 Main Street
Coshocton, OH 43812
Phone: 740 622-0444
Fax: 740 623-6000
Web: www.homeloanfinancialcorp.com

CEO: Robert C Hamilton
CFO: Preston W Bair
HR: -
FYE: June 30
Type: Public

Home Loan Financial is the holding company for Home Loan Savings which has about five branches in eastern Ohio's Coshocton and Knox counties. True to its name the bank primarily originates one- to four-family residential mortgages which account for more than two-thirds of its loan portfolio. It also issues commercial loans and mortgages construction loans and consumer loans. Founded in 1882 as The Home Building Savings and Loan the bank offers standard deposit products including checking and savings accounts CDs and money market accounts. Home Loan Financial completed a reverse stock split transaction in August 2005 allowing it to deregister from the Nasdaq.

	Annual Growth	06/10	06/11	06/12	06/13	06/14
Assets ($ mil.)	1.0%	163.5	162.4	166.6	164.6	170.1
Net income ($ mil.)	16.9%	1.5	1.9	2.4	2.8	2.9
Market value ($ mil.)	5.1%	19.9	19.6	18.2	23.4	24.3
Employees	-	-	-	-	-	-

HOME MERIDIAN INTERNATIONAL INC.

3980 Premier Dr. Ste. 310
High Point NC 27265
Phone: 336-819-7200
Fax: 800-835-8009
Web: www.homemeridian.com

CEO: George Revington
CFO: Dough Townsend
HR: –
FYE: October 31
Type: Private

Home Meridian International is the group home for furniture companies Pulaski Furniture and SLF (formerly Samuel Lawrence Furniture). Pulaski Furniture is known for its high-end curio cabinets but both companies sell wood furniture for the bedroom and dining room. They also market occasional pieces including credenzas chests home entertainment centers desks and bookcases. Pulaski and SLF both import furniture from Asia. The companies merged to form Home Meridian which is majority owned by Dymas Capital Management an affiliate of Cerberus Capital Management. Home Meridian's other brands include Creations Baby Prime Resources International and Samuel Lawrence Hospitality.

HOME PRODUCTS INTERNATIONAL INC.

4501 W. 47th St.
Chicago IL 60632
Phone: 773-890-1010
Fax: 773-890-0523
Web: www.hpii.com

CEO: –
CFO: Dennis Doheny
HR: –
FYE: December 31
Type: Private

Home Products International (HPI) helps folks get organized. The company makes an array of plastic storage containers including carts crates bins totes and tubs (some with more than 60 gallons of stowing space). It also produces closet organizers clothing hampers ironing boards shower caddies hangers and hooks. HPI's products are marketed under the HOMZ brand and sold in North and South America through retailers such as Wal-Mart Target Staples and Bed Bath & Beyond as well as online via Amazon.com and other merchants. The company also markets its products to hotels and other clients in the hospitality industry. HPI is majority owned by Third Avenue Management.

HOME PROPERTIES INC

NYS: HME

850 Clinton Square
Rochester, NY 14604
Phone: 585 546-4900
Fax: –
Web: www.homeproperties.com

CEO: Edward J Pettinella
CFO: David P Gardner
HR: Janine M Schue
FYE: December 31
Type: Public

It's balconies and pools for the middle-income set. Home Properties invests in develops renovates and operates multifamily residential properties primarily in growth markets in the Northeast and Mid-Atlantic. The self-administered real estate investment trust (REIT) owns and manages a portfolio of about 125 properties with around 42000 individual units. Home Properties typically invests in communities for which it can provide a little TLC (such as improved landscaping interior upgrades and amenities such as swimming pools) allowing it to benefit from increased property values post-rehabilitation. The REIT also develops new properties usually on raw land adjacent to existing properties in its portfolio.

	Annual Growth	12/09	12/10	12/11	12/12	12/13
Sales ($ mil.)	7.1%	503.6	516.6	580.0	644.3	663.6
Net income ($ mil.)	42.0%	47.1	26.3	47.7	163.6	191.6
Market value ($ mil.)	3.0%	2,717.6	3,160.8	3,279.3	3,492.3	3,054.3
Employees	2.2%	1,100	1,100	1,200	1,200	1,200

HOMEAWAY, INC.

NMS: AWAY

1011 W. Fifth Street, Suite 300
Austin, TX 78703
Phone: 512 684-1100
Fax: –
Web: www.homeaway.com

CEO: –
CFO: –
HR: –
FYE: December 31
Type: Public

There's no place like a home away from home for fun or functionality. HomeAway boasts nearly 1 million paid listings for vacation rental properties across 190 countries worldwide and helps property owners rent out their shack condo or château. Its HomeAway.com website is free to travelers who are typically affluent and is searchable by destination. Its listings include information on weekly rates availability and amenities as well as photographs descriptions and contact information. HomeAway also maintains 30 other travel-related websites. Founded in 2005 as WVR Group the company changed its name in 2006 to HomeAway launched its flagship website that year and went public in mid-2011.

	Annual Growth	12/09	12/10	12/11	12/12	12/13
Sales ($ mil.)	30.3%	120.2	167.9	230.2	280.4	346.5
Net income ($ mil.)	23.2%	7.7	16.9	6.2	15.0	17.7
Market value ($ mil.)	32.6%	–	–	2,147.4	2,031.9	3,775.7
Employees	22.3%	–	842	935	1,228	1,542

HOMEFED CORP.

NBB: HOFD

1903 Wright Place, Suite 220
Carlsbad, CA 92008
Phone: 760 918-8200
Fax: –
Web: www.homefedcorporation.com

CEO: –
CFO: –
HR: –
FYE: December 31
Type: Public

HomeFed won't provide you with room and board but it can help you get a home. The company earns its keep by investing in and developing residential real estate. Through subsidiaries HomeFed is developing a master-planned community in San Diego County called San Elijo Hills which contains approximately 3500 residences as well as commercial space and a town center. In 2014 Leucadia Financial increased its ownership in HomeFed from 31% to 65%. It also enhanced HomeFed's geographic presence by adding land and commercial real estate assets in New York Florida Maine and South Carolina.

	Annual Growth	12/10	12/11	12/12	12/13	12/14
Sales ($ mil.)	13.4%	35.9	34.1	35.7	56.6	59.5
Net income ($ mil.)	2.4%	3.5	4.5	6.0	11.3	3.9
Market value ($ mil.)	19.9%	335.4	298.5	407.8	563.2	692.4
Employees	20.0%	13	13	14	16	27

HOMELAND STORES INC.

28 E. 33rd St.
Edmond OK 73013
Phone: 301-215-8500
Fax: 480-368-4747
Web: www.huntconstructiongroup.com

CEO: Darryl Fitzgerald
CFO: Deborah A Brown
HR: –
FYE: December 31
Type: Subsidiary

Shoppers who call Oklahoma home shop at Homeland Stores' supermarkets. The regional grocery chain a division of grocery distributorAssociated Wholesale Grocers (AWG) operates more than 45 stores throughout Oklahoma and a single store in Kansas. AWG operates Homeland stores through its Associated Retail Grocers subsidiary and supplies the majority of the products sold in Homeland stores. The stores sell groceries and general merchandise; most have delicatessens pharmacies and some have specialty departments (ethnic foods floral services seafood). Homeland still has struggled as a result of stiff competition from Wal-Mart and other rival chains.

HOMESTREET INC
NMS: HMST

601 Union Street, Suite 2000
Seattle, WA 98101
Phone: 206-623-3050
Fax: –
Web: www.homestreet.com

CEO: Mark K. Mason
CFO: –
HR: –
FYE: December 31
Type: Public

HomeStreet brings community banking home to the Pacific Northwest and Hawaii. Its subsidiary HomeStreet Bank operates some 30 branches and 45 loan offices in the Pacific Northwest California and Hawaii. Serving individuals and businesses the bank offers standard services including checking savings and money market accounts CDs credit cards loans and mortgages and investments. The bank originates home loans both directly and through a joint venture Windermere Real Estate which operates about 40 offices in Washington and Oregon. HomeStreet also provides specialty financing for income-producing properties. It operates an insurance agency as well. HomeStreet went public in 2012.

	Annual Growth	12/10	12/11	12/12	12/13	12/14
Assets ($ mil.)	9.2%	2,485.7	2,265.0	2,631.2	3,066.1	3,535.1
Net income ($ mil.)	–	(34.2)	16.1	82.1	23.8	22.3
Market value ($ mil.)	(17.4%)	–	–	379.6	297.1	258.7
Employees	38.0%	–	613	1,099	1,502	1,611

HONDA MANUFACTURING OF ALABAMA LLC

1800 Honda Dr.
Lincoln AL 35096-5105
Phone: 205-355-5000
Fax: 205-355-5020
Web: www.hondaalabama.com

CEO: –
CFO: –
HR: –
FYE: March 31
Type: Subsidiary

If you drive a Honda Odyssey your minivan's Sweet Home is probably in Alabama. Honda Manufacturing of Alabama (HMA) manufactures Honda Odyssey minivans and the Honda Pilot SUV. The company's plant in Lincoln Alabama (near Talladega) expanded its operations and makes up to 300000 vehicles each year. A third vehicle the Ridgeline pickup (previously produced by Honda of Canada) joined the production line at HMA in 2009 and Honda plans to add the V-6 Accord sedan to the HMA portfolio. The plant began production in 2001. In addition to vehicle production Honda Manufacturing of Alabama also makes V-6 Honda engines. Honda Manufacturing of Alabama is part of Honda Motor's Honda of America Mfg. division.

HONDA NORTH AMERICA INC.

700 Van Ness Ave.
Torrance CA 90501-1486
Phone: 310-783-2000
Fax: 212-818-8282
Web: www.itochu.com

CEO: –
CFO: –
HR: –
FYE: March 31
Type: Subsidiary

Its cars might not be as American as apple pie but Honda North America keeps the US appetite for Hondas sated. The subsidiary of Honda Motor coordinates the operations in North America that manufacture market and distribute Accord Civic and Acura cars as well as Gold Wing Shadow and Valkyrie motorcycles. Of the 15 models made Honda North America's best-selling cars include the Odyssey minivan and the CR-V SUV. Honda North America also markets hybrid versions of several of its sedans. New launches have included the Crosstour and Acura ZDX. Honda also makes jet and marine engines and power equipment. North America is Honda Motor's largest market representing 45% of the carmaker's sales.

HONDA OF AMERICA MFG. INC.

24000 Honda Pkwy.
Marysville OH 43040
Phone: 937-642-5000
Fax: 937-644-6575
Web: www.ohio.honda.com

CEO: Tomomi Kosaka
CFO: –
HR: –
FYE: March 31
Type: Subsidiary

Boast build and sell: Honda of America Mfg. makes vehicles said to be as unconventional as their plants. Its four Ohio plants produce Honda automobiles engines and transmissions. The company's Marysville Auto Plant assembles the Acura TL and RDX and the Accord coupe and sedan. Its eco-designed East Liberty plant produces the Honda CR-V and Accord Crosstour. Together Honda of Americas' two assembly plants have annual capacity of 700000 vehicles which are sold primarily in North America. In addition the company's auto engine plant its Anna facility produces four- and six-cylinder engines and related parts. Honda of America also produces automatic transmissions at its Russells Point Ohio plant.

HONEYWELL ELECTRONIC MATERIALS INC.

15128 E Euclid Ave.
Spokane WA 99216
Phone: 509-252-2200
Fax: 508-315-3333
Web: www.vmr.com

CEO: –
CFO: –
HR: –
FYE: December 31
Type: Subsidiary

Microchip makers looking for a honey of a material often turn to Honeywell Electronic Materials (HEM). The Honeywell International unit develops and manufactures chemicals and specialty materials used in the production of semiconductors flat-panel displays and printable electronics as well as in photovoltaic (PV) applications. Its offerings include dielectric and metal thin films interconnect and optoelectronic materials and processing chemicals (such as etchants acids and solvents) used at various points in the chip manufacturing cycle. HEM is part of Honeywell's Specialty Materials segment one of the industrial conglomerate's smaller operating groups.

HONEYWELL INTERNATIONAL INC
NYS: HON

115 Tabor Road
Morris Plains, NJ 07950
Phone: 973-455-2000
Fax: 973-455-4807
Web: www.honeywell.com

CEO: David M. (Dave) Cote
CFO: Tom Szlosek
HR: Jeff Tepperman
FYE: December 31
Type: Public

Thermostats and jet engines seem worlds apart but they're the wind beneath Honeywell International's wings. More than a century old the company is a diverse industrial conglomerate with four segments the largest are Automation and Control Solutions (ACS — making HVAC and manufacturing process products) and Aerospace (turbo engines and flight safety and landing systems). Additional segments include Performance Materials and Technology (PMT formerly Honeywell Specialty Materials thermal switches fibers and chemicals) and Transportation Systems (engine boosting systems and brake materials).

	Annual Growth	12/11	12/12	12/13	12/14	12/15
Sales ($ mil.)	1.4%	36,529.0	37,665.0	39,055.0	40,306.0	38,581.0
Net income ($ mil.)	23.2%	2,067.0	2,926.0	3,924.0	4,239.0	4,768.0
Market value ($ mil.)	17.5%	41,871.9	48,897.3	70,391.4	76,978.4	79,790.3
Employees	(0.6%)	132,000	132,000	131,000	127,000	129,000

HONEYWELL SPECIALTY MATERIALS

101 Columbia Rd.
Morristown NJ 07962-2497
Phone: 973-455-2000
Fax: 973-455-4807
Web: www.honeywellspecialtymaterials.com

CEO: David Cote
CFO: John Gottshall
HR: –
FYE: December 31
Type: Business Segment

Honeywell Specialty Materials handles Honeywell's specialty chemical materials including fluorocarbons specialty films high performance fibers reagents and laboratory chemicals high purity electronic materials luminescent materials fine and special chemicals intermediates and specialty additives. The company makes fluorine chemicals (for refrigerants) electronic materials (acids thin films and interconnects) performance products (specialty fibers and films) and chemical intermediates and polymers (caprolactam ammonium sulfate and nylon resins). Honeywell Specialty Materials' units include UOP (formerly a joint venture with Dow's Union Carbide). UOP licenses chemical process technology.

HONEYWELL TECHNOLOGY SOLUTIONS INC.

7000 Columbia Gateway Dr.
Columbia MD 21046-5555
Phone: 410-964-7000
Fax: 804-354-2578
Web: www.anthem.com

CEO: –
CFO: Robert B Topolski
HR: –
FYE: December 31
Type: Subsidiary

The world is Honeywell Technology Solutions' (HTSI) sweet spot. HTSI a subsidiary of Honeywell International provides a slew of aerospace-related products and services to customers worldwide. Its operations include: space systems and services (satellite flight control and mission support); logistics/sustainment (expeditionary logistics depot-level maintenance sustaining and systems engineering and integration); IT/communication (security and information assurance); technical and engineering (system installation testing maintenance and repair); programs (safety performance tracking quality inspection and auditing risk management); and metrology (lab support). HTSI's largest and oldest customer is NASA.

HONIGMAN MILLER SCHWARTZ AND COHN LLP

660 Woodward Ave. Ste. 2290
Detroit MI 48226-3583
Phone: 313-465-7000
Fax: 313-465-8000
Web: www.honigman.com

CEO: David Foltyn
CFO: –
HR: –
FYE: December 31
Type: Private - Partnershi

Honigman Miller Schwartz and Cohn LLP is a leading Michigan law firm with expertise in a range of practice areas. Through four offices it offers representation in the Midwest and beyond to the energy environmental financial services health care labor and real estate industries. Founded in 1948 by Jason Honigman and Milton "Jack" Miller the firm handles litigation in areas of bankruptcy immigration intellectual property tax and zoning among others. Its regulatory law department has taken cases before state and federal administrative agencies involving the Michigan Department of Labor as well as the state's natural resources and insurance bureaus.

HOOKER FURNITURE CORP

NMS: HOFT

440 East Commonwealth Boulevard
Martinsville, VA 24112
Phone: 276 632-0459
Fax: –
Web: www.hookerfurniture.com

CEO: Paul B. Toms
CFO: Paul A. Huckfeldt
HR: Anne Jacobson
FYE: February 01
Type: Public

Hooker Furniture wants to sell you the pieces that will turn your house into a home. The company offers hardwood and metal furniture including wall units home office items home theater cabinets living and dining room tables bedroom furniture and accent pieces. Its youth furniture is sold under the Opus Designs by Hooker label. Hooker Furniture's popular Bradington-Young line of residential upholstered furniture features leather reclining chairs and sofas. The furniture manufacturer's Sam Moore unit makes high-end chairs. Hooker Furniture's products are sold through specialty shops (Star Furniture Nebraska Furniture Mart) and department stores (Dillard's). Hooker Furniture was founded in 1924.

	Annual Growth	01/11	01/12*	02/13	02/14	02/15
Sales ($ mil.)	3.2%	215.4	222.5	218.4	228.3	244.4
Net income ($ mil.)	40.4%	3.2	5.1	8.6	7.9	12.6
Market value ($ mil.)	6.6%	150.7	131.8	160.6	163.2	194.4
Employees	(0.5%)	688	614	600	670	674

*Fiscal year change

HOOPER HOLMES INC

ASE: HH

560 N. Rogers Road
Olathe, KS 66062
Phone: 913 764-1045
Fax: –
Web: www.hooperholmes.com

CEO: Henry E Dubois
CFO: Steven Balthazor
HR: Khalilah Tillman
FYE: December 31
Type: Public

Hooper Holmes helps companies manage risk. Not financial risk but threats to employees' health. The company's Health and Wellness segment provides on-site health and wellness exams risk assessment and management and wellness coaching for companies that manage healthcare for corporate and government clients. Its Heritage Labs performs lab tests on samples collected by its own and third-party exam providers. The Hooper Holmes Services segment performs phone interviews to collect medical histories retrieves medical records and underwriting services on behalf of insurance companies. In 2014 Hooper Holmes sold its Portamedic on-site testing unit to Piston Acquisition.

	Annual Growth	12/10	12/11	12/12	12/13	12/14
Sales ($ mil.)	(35.7%)	166.4	157.5	146.3	49.2	28.5
Net income ($ mil.)	–	1.5	(3.5)	(17.6)	(11.3)	(8.5)
Market value ($ mil.)	(7.4%)	49.6	42.5	28.1	37.6	36.5
Employees	(46.0%)	1,700	1,725	1,510	300	145

HOOSIER ENERGY RURAL ELECTRIC COOPERATIVE INC

7398 N STATE ROAD 37
BLOOMINGTON, IN 474049424
Phone: 812-356-4291
Fax: –
Web: www.hepn.com

CEO: J Steven Smith
CFO: –
HR: –
FYE: December 31
Type: Private

Who's yer daddy? In terms of providing electricity for many Indianans (and some residents of Illinois) that would be Hoosier Energy Rural Electric Cooperative which provides wholesale electric power to 18 member distribution cooperatives in 59 central and southern Indiana counties and 11 counties in southeastern Illinois. These electric cooperatives serve 300000 consumers (650000 residents businesses industries and farms) in a 18000 sq. ml. service area. Hoosier Energy operates six power plants and a 1720-mile transmission system and maintains the Tuttle Creek Reservoir in Southwest Indiana. Hoosier Energy is part of the Touchstone Energy network of electric cooperatives.

	Annual Growth	12/08	12/09	12/11	12/12	12/13
Sales ($ mil.)	3.8%	–	575.0	649.6	647.9	668.0
Net income ($ mil.)	(3.5%)	–	–	30.3	27.9	28.3
Market value ($ mil.)	–	–	–	–	–	–
Employees	–	–	–	–	–	450

HOOTERS OF AMERICA LLC

1815 The Exchange
Atlanta GA 30339
Phone: 770-951-2040
Fax: 770-618-7032
Web: www.hooters.com

CEO: Coby Brooks
CFO: Rodney Foster
HR: Ali Reardon
FYE: December 31
Type: Private

The chicken wings aren't the only spicy items at Hooters. Hooters of America operates and franchises more than 430 Hooters restaurants in about 40 states and more than 25 other countries. The beach-themed bar-and-grills catering to sports fans are known for their spicy chicken wings and their hostesses who dress in the chain's trademark bright orange short shorts and tight T-shirts. Other menu items include chili burgers sandwiches and beer. The company operates about 160 locations and franchises the rest. The first Hooters opened in 1983 and in 2011 an investment consortium led by Chanticleer Holdings bought the chain.

HOOVER PRECISION PRODUCTS INC.

2200 Pendley Rd.
Cumming GA 30041
Phone: 770-889-9223
Fax: 770-889-0828
Web: www.hooverprecision.com

CEO: Kenji Yamada
CFO: James W Brandon Jr
HR: –
FYE: March 31
Type: Subsidiary

Hoover is having a ball asking "How are balls made?" Its answer: "heading flashing heat treating grinding lapping and polishing." Hoover Precision Products manufactures a range of ball bearings (ceramic metal and plastic) and cylindrical roller bearings (chrome carbon and steel). Its products are used by customers in such industries as automotive bearing medical equipment and furniture manufacturing. Hoover Precision Products was founded in 1913 as Hoover Steel Ball Company. The company operates from eight divisions in the Asia/Pacific region Europe Mexico and the US. Hoover Precision Products was acquired in 1990 by Tsubaki Nakashima of which the company is now a wholly owned subsidiary.

HOOVER'S INC.

5800 Airport Blvd.
Austin TX 78752-3812
Phone: 512-374-4500
Fax: 512-374-4501
Web: www.hoovers.com

CEO: –
CFO: –
HR: –
FYE: December 31
Type: Subsidiary

If you're reading this sentence you know where to go for company data. Hoover's the publisher of this profile offers proprietary business information through the Internet (Hoover's Online) and through integration with clients' existing enterprise infrastructure (Hoover's API). Its database of information includes about 85 million corporations and other entities and 100 million people and its First Research product covers some 900 industries. Most revenues come from selling subscriptions to a target audience of marketing sales and business development professionals. Hoover's also offers mobile apps (Hoover's Connect+) and publishes a business blog (Bizmology). It is a subsidiary of Dun & Bradstreet (D&B).

HOPFED BANCORP, INC.

NMS: HFBC

4155 Lafayette Road
Hopkinsville, KY 42240
Phone: 270 885-1171
Fax: –
Web: www.bankwithheritage.com

CEO: John E Peck
CFO: Billy C Duvall
HR: –
FYE: December 31
Type: Public

HopFed Bancorp is the holding company for Heritage Bank (formerly Hopkinsville Federal Savings Bank) which started operations in 1879 as a building and loan association. The bank has about a dozen branches in southwestern Kentucky with its market area extending into northwestern Tennessee. It offers standard products like checking savings money market and NOW accounts as well as CDs IRAs property/casualty insurance and annuities. One- to four-family residential mortgages account for about 40% of its loan portfolio. To a lesser extent Heritage Bank also writes multifamily residential construction commercial and consumer loans. Directors and executives control 12% of the bank.

	Annual Growth	12/10	12/11	12/12	12/13	12/14
Assets ($ mil.)	(3.6%)	1,082.6	1,040.8	967.7	973.6	935.8
Net income ($ mil.)	(23.8%)	6.5	2.9	4.1	3.8	2.2
Market value ($ mil.)	8.9%	64.8	46.3	61.8	81.7	91.2
Employees	(0.1%)	263	271	281	256	262

HOPTO INC

NBB: HPTO D

1919 S. Bascom Avenue, Suite 600
Campbell, CA 95008
Phone: 408 688-2674
Fax: –
Web: www.hopto.com

CEO: Eldad Eilam
CFO: Jean-Louis Casabonne
HR: –
FYE: December 31
Type: Public

GraphOn keeps its thin clients on a diet. The company provides business connectivity software that delivers applications to PCs and workstations from a host computer. The company's products enable clients to relocate desktop software to centralized servers and deploy and manage applications when needed thus conserving computing resources. GraphOn's software can be used to provide access to applications through Linux UNIX and Windows platforms. The company serves clients in a variety of industries including telecommunications software development manufacturing financial services and electronics.

	Annual Growth	12/10	12/11	12/12	12/13	12/14
Sales ($ mil.)	(7.3%)	7.5	6.6	6.5	5.9	5.6
Net income ($ mil.)	–	(0.8)	(1.8)	(8.2)	(3.7)	(3.6)
Market value ($ mil.)	–	–	–	–	–	–
Employees	(1.6%)	33	34	37	40	31

HORACE MANN EDUCATORS CORP.

NYS: HMN

1 Horace Mann Plaza
Springfield, IL 62715-0001
Phone: 217 789-2500
Fax: –
Web: www.horacemann.com

CEO: –
CFO: Dwayne D Hallman
HR: Kathi Karr
FYE: December 31
Type: Public

Naming itself in honor of Horace Mann considered the father of public education Horace Mann Educators is an insurance holding company that primarily serves K-12 school teachers and other public school employees throughout the US. Through its operating subsidiaries the company offers homeowners auto (majority of revenue) and individual and group life insurance as well as retirement annuities. Horace Mann employs some 800 agents many of whom are former teachers themselves. Writing business in 48 states and Washington DC the company derives about a third of its direct premiums and contract deposits from five states - California North Carolina Texas Minnesota and Illinois.

	Annual Growth	12/10	12/11	12/12	12/13	12/14
Assets ($ mil.)	8.7%	7,005.5	7,483.7	8,167.7	8,826.7	9,768.5
Net income ($ mil.)	6.6%	80.9	70.5	103.9	110.9	104.2
Market value ($ mil.)	16.5%	738.5	561.2	817.1	1,291.1	1,358.3
Employees	(1.4%)	2,121	2,107	2,058	2,095	2,008

HORIZON BANCORP (MICHIGAN CITY, IN)   NMS: HBNC

515 Franklin Square
Michigan City, IN 46360
Phone: 219 879-0211
Fax: –
Web: www.accesshorizon.com

CEO: Craig M. Dwight
CFO: Mark E. Secor
HR: –
FYE: December 31
Type: Public

Despite its name Horizon Bancorp is on the up-and-up. It's the holding company for Horizon Bank (and its Heartland Community Bank division) which provides checking and savings accounts IRAs CDs and credit cards to customers through more than 30 branches in north and central Indiana and southwest and central Michigan. Commercial financial and agricultural loans make up the largest segment of its loan portfolio which also includes mortgage warehouse loans (loans earmarked for sale into the secondary market) consumer loans and residential mortgages. Through subsidiaries the bank offers trust and investment management services; life health and property/casualty insurance; and annuities.

	Annual Growth	12/10	12/11	12/12	12/13	12/14
Assets ($ mil.)	10.3%	1,400.9	1,547.2	1,848.2	1,758.3	2,076.9
Net income ($ mil.)	14.7%	10.5	12.8	19.5	19.9	18.1
Market value ($ mil.)	(0.4%)	245.1	159.7	181.0	233.4	240.8
Employees	9.5%	312	323	419	421	448

HORIZON BAY MANAGEMENT L.L.C

5102 W. Laurel St. Ste. 700
Tampa FL 33607
Phone: 813-287-3900
Fax: 813-287-3914
Web: www.horizonbay.com

CEO: –
CFO: –
HR: –
FYE: December 31
Type: Subsidiary

Horizon Bay Management operates a spread of senior housing communities in the US. Operating as Horizon Bay Retirement Living the company manages independent- and assisted-living residential facilities primarily targeting the higher-end market. It operates more than 90 senior housing communities which are located in about 20 primarily southern and midwestern states and have a total of about 16000 living units. The company's facilities offer wellness lifestyle transportation dining and housekeeping services to residents. Horizon Bay was acquired by Brookdale Senior Living in 2011.

HORIZON DISTRIBUTORS INC.

5214 S 30th St.
Phoenix AZ 85040
Phone: 602-276-7700
Fax: 602-276-7800
Web: www.horizononline.com

CEO: –
CFO: –
HR: –
FYE: December 31
Type: Subsidiary

Horizon doesn't worry about the rain clouds. The company operating through about 60 locations in 11 mostly western US states offers products for landscapers and other professionals in the landscaping industry. The company markets fertilizer landscape lighting turf and irrigation equipment and other related products including mowers pruners blowers and chainsaws. It specializes in helping golf course groundskeepers keep the greens green and the roughs soft with products like Rain Bird Golf nozzles and rotors Seed Research forage and grass seeds and Lasco Fittings swing joints. Pool supply company Pool Corporation (formerly SCP Pool) owns Horizon.

HORIZON GROUP PROPERTIES INC.   PINK SHEETS: HGPI

5000 Hakes Dr. Ste. 500
Muskegon MI 49441
Phone: 231-798-9100
Fax: 231-798-5100
Web: www.horizongroup.com

CEO: Gary J Skoien
CFO: David R Tinkham
HR: –
FYE: December 31
Type: Public

Horizon Group Properties owns develops renovates and operates shopping properties. The company's portfolio includes a handful of factory outlet shopping centers in a number of states throughout the US. Horizon's centers are occupied by tenants such as clothing retailers Polo Ralph Lauren Tommy Hilfiger and The Gap. Horizon Group Properties is also developing a master-planned community in suburban Chicago. The company is the product of a spinoff of properties left over from the 1998 merger of Prime Retail and Horizon Group.

HORIZON HEALTH CORPORATION

2941 S. Lake Vista Dr.
Lewisville TX 75067-6011
Phone: 972-420-8200
Fax: 972-420-8252
Web: www.horizonhealth.com

CEO: –
CFO: Jack E Polson
HR: –
FYE: August 31
Type: Subsidiary

Horizon Health sees hope on the horizon for those in need of psychiatric care and physical rehabilitation. The firm provides contract psychiatric and rehabilitation management services to hospitals across the country running its clients' inpatient and outpatient mental health programs and rehab departments. Horizon also offers contract management to handle licensing and accreditation for its client hospitals' clinical programs; it also develops community awareness programs and hires most non-nursing staff. The group offers some specialty psychiatric services including geropsychiatry for people aged 65-years and older and adolescent psychiatric care. Horizon Health is owned by Universal Health Services (UHS).

HORIZON HEALTHCARE SERVICES INC.

3 Penn Plaza East
Newark NJ 07105-2200
Phone: 973-466-4000
Fax: 973-466-4317
Web: www.horizon-bcbsnj.com

CEO: Robert A Marino
CFO: Robert J Pures
HR: –
FYE: December 31
Type: Private - Not-for-Pr

Horizon Healthcare Services is growing good health for Garden Staters. The company dba Horizon Blue Cross Blue Shield of New Jersey is New Jersey's top health insurance provider serving about 3.6 million members. The not-for-profit company a licensee of the Blue Cross and Blue Shield Association offers traditional indemnity and managed care plans including HMO PPO and POS plans as well as Medicaid and Medicare Advantage coverage options. It also provides dental and behavioral health coverage and manages workers' compensation claims.

HORIZON LINES INC   NBB: HRZL

4064 Colony Road, Suite 200 | CEO: Steven L Rubin
Charlotte, NC 28211 | CFO: Michael T Avara
Phone: 704 973-7000 | HR: –
Fax: – | FYE: December 22
Web: www.horizonlines.com | Type: Public

Horizon Lines rides the waves to connect the mainland US with its far-flung states and territories. The container shipping company transports cargo such as building materials consumer goods and foodstuffs to and from the continental US and Alaska Hawaii and Puerto Rico. Horizon Lines maintains a fleet of about 15 containerships and 30000 cargo containers; it also operates five port terminals. The majority of its revenue comes from operations subject to the Jones Act which restricts marine shipping between US ports to companies with vessels that are US built/owned/crewed.

	Annual Growth	12/09	12/10	12/11	12/12	12/13
Sales ($ mil.)	(2.8%)	1,158.5	1,162.5	1,026.2	1,073.7	1,033.3
Net income ($ mil.)	–	(31.3)	(58.0)	(229.4)	(94.7)	(31.9)
Market value ($ mil.)	(34.5%)	210.8	171.9	182.8	60.3	38.9
Employees	(3.8%)	1,895	1,890	1,635	1,599	1,621

HORIZON MILLING LLC

15407 McGinty Rd. West | CEO: Dan Dye
Wayzata MN 55391 | CFO: –
Phone: 952-742-2373 | HR: –
Fax: 952-742-4050 | FYE: December 31
Web: www.horizonmilling.com | Type: Joint Venture

Horizon Milling is a leading producer of durum and semolina wheat flours with about 20 production facilities throughout the US and in Canada. The company makes bakery flours and other specialty products primarily for food manufacturers and foodservice operators as well as private-label flours for the retail market. In addition to customers in North America Horizon Milling exports flour worldwide. Horizon Milling was formed in 2002 as a joint venture between diversified food and agricultural products giant Cargill and grain marketer CHS (which owns about a quarter of the business). Horizon Milling has been expanding its products portfolio in 2010.

HORIZON PHARMA INC   NMS: HZNP

520 Lake Cook Road, Suite 520 | CEO: Timothy P Walbert
Deerfield, IL 60015 | CFO: Paul W Hoelscher
Phone: 224 383-3000 | HR: –
Fax: – | FYE: December 31
Web: www.horizonpharma.com | Type: Public

Horizon Pharma sees commercial drug success in its future. The biopharmaceutical company develops medicines for arthritis pain and inflammatory diseases through its two operating subsidiaries Horizon Pharma USA and Horizon Pharma AG. Its DUEXIS pill combines two existing drugs to treat mild to moderate pain from rheumatoid arthritis. Its LODOTRA is a low form of prednisone formulated to reduce morning stiffness associated with rheumatoid arthritis. DUEXIS has received approval for sale in the US while LODOTRA is approved for sale and marketed in Europe. Horizon Pharma also has a pipeline of earlier stage candidates to treat pain-related diseases and chronic inflammation. The company went public in 2011.

	Annual Growth	12/08	12/09	12/10	12/11	12/12
Sales ($ mil.)	187.4%	–	–	2.4	6.9	19.6
Net income ($ mil.)	–	(27.9)	(20.5)	(27.1)	(113.3)	(87.8)
Market value ($ mil.)	(41.8%)	–	–	–	246.9	143.8
Employees	151.7%	–	–	39	164	247

HORMEL FOODS CORP.   NYS: HRL

1 Hormel Place | CEO: Jeffrey M. Ettinger
Austin, MN 55912-3680 | CFO: Jody H Feragen
Phone: 507 437-5611 | HR: –
Fax: 507 437-5489 | FYE: October 25
Web: www.hormel.com | Type: Public

The maker of such thrifty pantry staples as SPAM lunch meat and Dinty Moore stew has turned sophisticated. Besides canned meats Hormel Foods produces a slew of refrigerated processed meats and deli items ethnic entrees and frozen foods sold under the Hormel brand as well as Don Miguel and MegaMex Mexican Country Crock (side dishes) and Lloyd's barbeque. Food service offerings include Hormel Natural Choice meats Café H ethnic Austin Blues barbeque and Bread Ready pre-sliced meats. Hormel is also a major US turkey and pork processor churning out Jennie-O turkey Cure 81 hams and Always Tender pork. More than 30 Hormel brands are ranked #1 or #2 in their respective markets.

	Annual Growth	10/11	10/12	10/13	10/14	10/15
Sales ($ mil.)	4.1%	7,895.1	8,230.7	8,751.7	9,316.3	9,263.9
Net income ($ mil.)	9.7%	474.2	500.1	526.2	602.7	686.1
Market value ($ mil.)	22.9%	15,825.9	15,503.6	23,049.3	27,762.7	36,106.4
Employees	1.5%	19,500	19,700	19,800	20,400	20,700

HORNBECK OFFSHORE SERVICES INC   NYS: HOS

103 Northpark Boulevard, Suite 300 | CEO: Todd M. Hornbeck
Covington, LA 70433 | CFO: James O. Harp
Phone: 985 727-2000 | HR: –
Fax: – | FYE: December 31
Web: www.hornbeckoffshore.com | Type: Public

At the beck and call of oil companies Hornbeck Offshore Services provides marine transportation of oil field equipment and supplies and petroleum products. The company operates offshore supply vessels (OSVs) that support offshore oil and gas drilling and production in the deepwater regions of the Gulf of Mexico. Its fleet of about 63 OSVs and five multi-purpose support vessels (MPSVs) transports cargo such as pipe and drilling mud as well as rig crew members. In addition Hornbeck has seven additional ultra high-spec upstream vessels under construction for delivery in 2016.

	Annual Growth	12/10	12/11	12/12	12/13	12/14
Sales ($ mil.)	10.8%	420.8	381.6	512.7	548.1	634.8
Net income ($ mil.)	24.9%	36.4	(2.6)	37.0	111.4	88.5
Market value ($ mil.)	4.6%	742.4	1,103.0	1,221.0	1,750.5	887.9
Employees	13.2%	999	1,036	1,263	1,397	1,641

HORNBLOWER YACHTS INC.

ON THE EMBARCADERO PIER 3 ST PIER | CEO: Terry MacRae
SAN FRANCISCO, CA 94111 | CFO: –
Phone: 415-788-8866 | HR: –
Fax: – | FYE: December 31
Web: www.hornblower.com | Type: Private

Hornblower Cruises and Events is happy to toot its own horn. The company provides sightseeing dining and wedding cruises via its fleet of 35 yachts sailing from about a half dozen California ports including Berkeley San Diego Newport Beach Marina del Rey and San Francisco. Regularly scheduled tours include lunch dinner dance and concert cruises. Hornblower also provides cruises for private events including corporate functions. Subsidiaries Alcatraz Cruises and Statue Cruises run a ferry service to Alcatraz in California and the Statue of Liberty National Monument and Ellis Island in New York through a deal with the National Park Service. CEO Terry MacRae founded Hornblower in 1980 with two yachts.

	Annual Growth	12/02	12/03	12/04	12/06	12/09
Sales ($ mil.)	29.5%	–	–	32.2	35.2	117.6
Net income ($ mil.)	9.9%	–	–	7.5	2.0	11.9
Market value ($ mil.)	–	–	–	–	–	–
Employees	–	–	–	–	–	350

HORNE INTERNATIONAL INC
NBB: HNIN

3975 University Drive, Suite 100
Fairfax, VA 22030
Phone: 703 641-1100
Fax: -
Web: www.horne.com

CEO: Dallas Evans
CFO: John E Donahue
HR: -
FYE: December 31
Type: Public

At the nexus where government agencies national security and environmental sustainability meet you'll find Horne International. Through its primary operating subsidiary Horne Engineering Services the company offers military base and homeland security missile defense ecosystems management and restoration and business process engineering services. It also offers public outreach services including the organization of public meetings and drafting Congressional testimony. Not surprisingly the US government's departments of Homeland Security Defense and Transportation are Horne's primary customers. Horne which has struggled in the recession owes nearly 85% of sales to its three largest customers.

	Annual Growth	12/08	12/09	12/10	12/11	12/12
Sales ($ mil.)	(4.0%)	4.9	4.7	3.4	5.7	4.1
Net income ($ mil.)	-	(6.1)	(0.3)	(1.0)	(0.1)	(1.6)
Market value ($ mil.)	(8.1%)	1.4	4.3	7.1	6.2	1.0
Employees	-	-	-	-	-	-

HORNELL BREWING CO. INC.

644 Linn St. Ste. 318
Cincinnati OH 45203
Phone: 516-812-0300
Fax: 516-326-4988
Web: www.arizonabev.com

CEO: -
CFO: Rick Adonilla
HR: -
FYE: December 31
Type: Private

At Hornell Brewing (which does business as Ferolito Vultaggio & Sons) image is everything. Colorful arty bottle and can designs distinguish the company's beverages including AriZona iced teas energy drinks and fruit drinks from the competition. The company's beverages are top sellers in the ready-to-drink iced tea sector in the US. Flavors include Green Tea with Ginseng Pomegranate Green Tea and Blueberry White Tea. Hornell's other products include energy and sports drinks juice and smoothies. Co-founders John Ferolito and Don Vultaggio own and run the company.

HORRY TELEPHONE COOPERATIVE INC.

3480 HIGHWAY 701 N
CONWAY, SC 295265702
Phone: 843-365-2151
Fax: -
Web: www.htcinc.net

CEO: Mike Hagg
CFO: Duane Carlton Lewis Jr
HR: Robin Ard
FYE: December 31
Type: Private

Horry Telephone Cooperative (HTC) is the incumbent local exchange carrier (ILEC) serving rural Horry County in South Carolina (population: about 270000). HTC offers local and long-distance voice service Internet access cable TV home security service and mobile phone service (through AT&T Mobility). It also offers business services such as remote recovery LAN and WAN design and firewall and network security and provides bundled telecommunications services to residential and business customers via its Bluewave fiber-to-the-home business. Membership in the cooperative is open to any customer who receives at least one of HTC's primary services.

	Annual Growth	12/06	12/07	12/08	12/09	12/13
Sales ($ mil.)	-	-	(1,361.9)	162.9	172.8	177.1
Net income ($ mil.)	42.7%	-	-	3.7	4.3	21.7
Market value ($ mil.)	-	-	-	-	-	-
Employees	-	-	-	-	-	690

HORSEHEAD HOLDING CORP
NBB: ZINC Q

4955 Steubenville Pike, Suite 405
Pittsburgh, PA 15205
Phone: 724 774-1020
Fax: -
Web: www.horsehead.net

CEO: James M. Hensler
CFO: Robert D. (Bob) Scherich
HR: -
FYE: December 31
Type: Public

Bearing out the adage that one person's trash is another's treasure through Horsehead Corporation Horsehead Zinc Powders INMETCO and Zochem Horsehead Holdings turns zinc-containing dust and discarded batteries into value-added zinc and nickel-based products. Key raw materials for the company include dust from the electric-arc furnaces (EAF) used at steel minimills and residue from the galvanizing of metals. Besides zinc metal (used in galvanizing and alloying) Horsehead's products include zinc oxide (used in the agricultural chemical and pharmaceutical industries) zinc dust (used in corrosion-resistant coatings) and nickel-based metals (used as a feedstock to produce stainless and specialty steels).

	Annual Growth	12/10	12/11	12/12	12/13	12/14
Sales ($ mil.)	4.4%	382.4	451.2	435.7	441.9	453.9
Net income ($ mil.)	-	24.8	21.5	(30.4)	(14.0)	(15.5)
Market value ($ mil.)	5.0%	661.4	457.0	517.8	822.2	802.9
Employees	(9.0%)	1,089	1,064	1,062	1,074	747

HORTON (D.R.) INC.
NYS: DHI

301 Commerce Street, Suite 500
Fort Worth, TX 76102
Phone: 817 390-8200
Fax: -
Web: www.drhorton.com

CEO: -
CFO: William W. (Bill) Wheat
HR: Cassie Kropp
FYE: September 30
Type: Public

When this Horton heard a Who it built the little guy a house. One of the largest homebuilding companies in the US D.R. Horton constructs single-family homes that range in size from 1000 sq. ft. to 4000 sq. ft. and sell for an average price of about $285700 under the D.R. Horton Emerald Homes Regent Homes and Express Homes brand names. Texas-based D.R. Horton is active in nearly 80 markets in 27 states and generates more than 75% of its revenue in the Southeast South Central and Western regions of the US. Beyond single-family detached homes which account for some 90% of sales D.R. Horton builds duplexes townhomes and condominiums. It also provides mortgage title and closing services.

	Annual Growth	09/11	09/12	09/13	09/14	09/15
Sales ($ mil.)	31.3%	3,636.8	4,354.0	6,259.3	8,024.9	10,824.0
Net income ($ mil.)	79.8%	71.8	956.3	462.7	533.5	750.7
Market value ($ mil.)	34.2%	3,332.6	7,603.4	7,162.8	7,564.6	10,823.5
Employees	19.9%	3,010	3,477	4,609	5,621	6,230

HORWATH INTERNATIONAL SERVICES LTD.

420 Lexington Ave. Ste. 526
New York NY 10170-0526
Phone: 212-808-2000
Fax: 212-808-2020
Web: www.crowehorwathinternational.com

CEO: J Kevin McGrath
CFO: -
HR: -
FYE: December 31
Type: Private - Associatio

Crowe Horwath International says "accounting" in numerous languages. The accounting and management consulting network is made up of more than 140 independent member firms with more than 560 offices around the globe. Areas of specialty include auditing and accounting tax planning corporate finance risk management and tax and information technology consulting. Crowe Horwath International targets companies in a variety of industries including financial and professional services health care hospitality and leisure entertainment manufacturing technology and telecommunications. Horwath International added "Crowe" to its name in 2009 to align its brand with that of Crowe Horwath its largest member firm.

HOSPICE OF MICHIGAN INC.

400 MACK AVE
DETROIT, MI 482012136
Phone: 313-578-5000
Fax: -
Web: www.hom.org

CEO: Dottie Deremo
CFO: Robert Cahill
HR: Rita Mahon
FYE: December 31
Type: Private

When it comes to hospice care experience counts. As the largest hospice provider in Michigan Hospice of Michigan (HOM) has plenty of it. HOM provides specialized health care to patients with terminal illnesses. The organization's nurses home health aids and volunteers help patients manage pain and other symptoms provide spiritual and emotional support and offer grief counseling to family members. The organization works with about 1000 patients on any given day at some 20 locations throughout Michigan's lower peninsula. Its services are offered in patient homes as well as in hospitals and nursing homes. Hospice of Michigan was created in 1994 when several smaller hospice programs joined forces.

	Annual Growth	12/03	12/04	12/05	12/06	12/13
Sales ($ mil.)	(28.7%)	-	1,393.6	0.0	59.0	66.0
Net income ($ mil.)	-	-	-	0.0	2.5	2.3
Market value ($ mil.)	-	-	-	-	-	-
Employees	-	-	-	-	-	500

HOSPIRA INC

275 North Field Drive
Lake Forest, IL 60045
Phone: 224 212-2000
Fax: -
Web: www.hospira.com

NYS: HSP
CEO: F Michael Ball
CFO: Thomas E Werner
HR: -
FYE: December 31
Type: Public

Hospira helps hospitals heal the hurting. The firm makes specialty injectable pharmaceuticals (primarily generics) including cardiovascular anesthesia oncology and anti-infective therapies as well as the related drug delivery systems such as prefilled syringes. Its more complicated medication delivery systems include electronic drug pumps infusion therapy devices and related medication management software. In addition Hospira makes IV nutritional solutions and provides contract manufacturing services. Key customers include hospitals alternate site facilities (such as nursing and outpatient surgical care facilities) wholesalers and other drug manufacturers. Pfizer plans to buy Hospira for some $17 billion.

	Annual Growth	12/10	12/11	12/12	12/13	12/14
Sales ($ mil.)	3.3%	3,917.2	4,057.1	4,092.1	4,002.8	4,463.7
Net income ($ mil.)	(1.7%)	357.2	(9.4)	44.2	(8.3)	333.2
Market value ($ mil.)	2.4%	9,489.6	5,175.0	5,323.3	7,034.1	10,437.0
Employees	7.9%	14,000	15,000	16,000	17,000	19,000

HOSPITAL OF CENTRAL CONNECTICUT

100 GRAND ST
NEW BRITAIN, CT 060522016
Phone: 860-224-5011
Fax: -
Web: www.thocc.org

CEO: Clarence J Silvia
CFO: Ralph Becker
HR: Elizabeth Lynch
FYE: September 30
Type: Private

The Hospital of Central Connecticut an acute care facility serves the communities of central Connecticut from two campuses. With approximately 415 beds and more than 400 physicians the hospital offers a full range of diagnostic and treatment services as well as education and prevention programs. Its diabetes treatment program is an affiliate of the Boston-based Joslin Diabetes Center; the hospital is also affiliated with the University of Connecticut School of Medicine and other universities. Central Connecticut Health Alliance (CCHA) is the parent company of The Hospital of Central Connecticut and is part of the Hartford Health Care network.

	Annual Growth	09/04	09/05	09/06	09/08	09/09
Sales ($ mil.)	69.1%	-	-	83.0	358.7	401.5
Net income ($ mil.)	-	-	-	0.0	8.9	(71.6)
Market value ($ mil.)	-	-	-	-	-	-
Employees	-	-	-	-	-	2,500

HOSPITAL PHYSICIAN PARTNERS INC.

300 S. Park Rd. Suite 400
Hollywood FL 33021
Phone: 800-815-8377
Fax: 615-771-5603
Web: www.clarcor.com

CEO: -
CFO: -
HR: -
FYE: December 31
Type: Private

They say one is the loneliest number and it looks like Hospital Physician Partners agrees. The company supplies hospitals in 20 states with thousands of physicians and allied health care professionals. Hospital Physician Partners specializes in emergency medicine and hospitalist program management and recruitment. (Hospitalists coordinate the care of hospital patients.) Through its PhyAmerica Government Services subsidiary Hospital Physician Partners supplies medical personnel to military hospitals clinics and urgent-care centers. It also provides staffing for state-run facilities and other government health care entities. Hospital Physician Partners is owned by private-equity firm Beecken Petty O'Keefe.

HOSPITAL SERVICE DISTRICT 1 INC

1101 MEDICAL CENTER BLVD
MARRERO, LA 700723147
Phone: 504-349-1124
Fax: -
Web: www.wjmc.org

CEO: -
CFO: Nancy Bassagne
HR: Frank Martinez
FYE: September 30
Type: Private

West Jefferson Medical Center keeps the suburbs of New Orleans in tune. A full-service community hospital located in Marrero Louisiana the not-for-profit hospital has about 430 beds and provides general medical-surgical care as well as specialty care in a number of areas including cardiovascular disease neurosciences orthopedics women's health and oncology. The medical center also operates several primary care clinics throughout its service area and provides behavioral health and occupational health services. The hospital is also part of The Louisiana Organ Procurement Agency.

	Annual Growth	12/03	12/04	12/05	12/06*	09/13
Sales ($ mil.)	(12.2%)	-	192.3	172.3	234.9	59.5
Net income ($ mil.)	-	-	-	(28.0)	(9.1)	2.3
Market value ($ mil.)	-	-	-	-	-	-
Employees	-	-	-	-	-	2,000

*Fiscal year change

HOSPITAL SISTERS HEALTH SYSTEM

4936 LAVERNA RD
SPRINGFIELD, IL 627079797
Phone: 217-523-4747
Fax: -
Web: www.hshs.org

CEO: Mary Starmann-Perharrison
CFO: -
HR: -
FYE: June 30
Type: Private

These sisters want their big family to benefit everyone in the community. Hospital Sisters Health System (HSHS) a Catholic ministry of the Hospital Sisters of the Third Order of St. Francis operates more than a dozen hospitals located throughout Wisconsin and Illinois. Its facilities have a total of more than 2500 beds and range from large-scale acute care facilities such as St. John's Hospital (Springfield Illinois) St. Elizabeth's Hospital (Bellevue Illinois) and St. Vincent Hospital (Green Bay Wisconsin) to small community hospitals; it also operates regional outpatient clinics. While the organization was incorporated in 1978 the health care ministry of the HSHS goes back to 1875.

	Annual Growth	06/07	06/08	06/09	06/10	06/13
Sales ($ mil.)	24.4%	-	-	60.7	92.9	145.3
Net income ($ mil.)	-	-	-	(7.2)	10.5	4.4
Market value ($ mil.)	-	-	-	-	-	-
Employees	-	-	-	-	-	14,000

HOSPITALITY PROPERTIES TRUST

NYS: HPT

Two Newton Place, 255 Washington Street, Suite 300
Newton, MA 02458
Phone: 617 964-8389
Fax: -
Web: www.hptreit.com

CEO: -
CFO: Mark L. Kleifges
HR: -
FYE: December 31
Type: Public

Hospitality Properties Trust (HPT) rolls out the welcome mat for the road-weary. The real estate investment trust (REIT) owns nearly 300 hotels throughout the US and in Canada and Puerto Rico as well as 185 full-service truck stops operating as TravelCenters of America and Petro Stopping Centers. Unlike some hospitality REITs HPT is not affiliated with any one hotel company. Its properties target different markets from upscale (Crowne Plaza Hotels & Resorts) to business and family travelers on long-term trips (Residence Inn by Marriott). HPT maintains a geographically diverse portfolio with hotels or travel centers (usually both) in nearly 45 states as well as Canada and Puerto Rico.

	Annual Growth	12/10	12/11	12/12	12/13	12/14
Sales ($ mil.)	12.5%	1,085.5	1,210.3	1,297.0	1,563.9	1,736.3
Net income ($ mil.)	74.3%	21.4	190.4	151.9	133.2	197.2
Market value ($ mil.)	7.7%	3,454.2	3,445.2	3,511.1	4,052.3	4,647.5
Employees	-	-	-	-	-	-

HOSS"S STEAK & SEA HOUSE INC.

170 PATCHWAY RD
DUNCANSVILLE, PA 166358431
Phone: 814-695-7600
Fax: -
Web: www.hosspeople.com

CEO: Willard E Campbell
CFO: Carl Raup
HR: Don Imler
FYE: December 30
Type: Private

Don't expect to find any Cartwright memorabilia here just plenty of hearty food. Hoss's Steak and Sea House operates about 40 of its signature family-style restaurants in Pennsylvania. The diners offer standard American fare and seafood for lunch and dinner along with an all-you-can-eat soup and salad bar. Each restaurant sports local memorabilia as part of its d□©cor. The company also operates Hoss's Fresh Xpress its own warehouse and distribution system used to supply the restaurants. CEO Bill Campbell a former WesterN SizzliN franchisee opened the first Hoss's in 1983.

	Annual Growth	12/03	12/04	12/05	12/06	12/07
Sales ($ mil.)	(0.9%)	-	78.0	77.6	81.7	75.9
Net income ($ mil.)	-	-	-	0.7	0.7	(0.8)
Market value ($ mil.)	-	-	-	-	-	-
Employees	-	-	-	-	-	3,000

HOST HOTELS & RESORTS INC

NYS: HST

6903 Rockledge Drive, Suite 1500
Bethesda, MD 20817
Phone: 240 744-1000
Fax: -
Web: www.hosthotels.com

CEO: W. Edward (Ed) Walter
CFO: Gregory J. (Greg) Larson
HR: Joanne G. Hamilton
FYE: December 31
Type: Public

Host Hotels & Resorts will leave the chandelier on for you. It's the nation's largest hospitality real estate investment trust and one of the top owners of luxury and upscale hotels. It owns about 115 luxury and "upper upscale" hotels mostly in the US but also in Canada Australia New Zealand Chile Mexico and Brazil totaling some 60000 rooms. Properties are managed by third parties; most operate under the Marriott brand and are managed by sister firm Marriott International. Other brands include Hyatt Ritz-Carlton Sheraton and Westin. To maintain its status as a real estate investment trust (REIT) which carries tax advantages Host operates through majority-owned Host Hotels & Resorts LP.

	Annual Growth	12/10	12/11	12/12	12/13	12/14
Sales ($ mil.)	4.8%	4,437.0	4,998.0	5,286.0	5,166.0	5,354.0
Net income ($ mil.)	-	(130.0)	(15.0)	61.0	317.0	732.0
Market value ($ mil.)	7.4%	13,506.1	11,163.2	11,843.4	14,692.8	17,965.4
Employees	5.4%	203	219	233	242	251

HOSTMARK HOSPITALITY GROUP

1300 E. Woodfield Rd. Ste. 400
Schaumburg IL 60173
Phone: 847-517-9100
Fax: 847-517-9797
Web: www.hostmark.com

CEO: -
CFO: -
HR: -
FYE: December 31
Type: Private

Hostmark Hospitality plays host to travelers around the world. The company manages more than 40 resort and hotel properties with more than 8500 rooms in more than a dozen US states and Egypt. It handles property sales and marketing assists with personnel develops information systems offers food and beverage services oversees renovations and manages accounting and purchasing. Its portfolio of resorts operate under banners such as Marriott Hilton Starwood InterContinental Hotels Group and Wyndham. Many of its properties are located near vacation destinations airports or convention facilities. Hostmark also operates a handful of stand-alone concept restaurants.

HOTELS.COM L.P.

10440 N. Central Expwy. Ste. 400
Dallas TX 75231
Phone: 214-361-7311
Fax: 214-361-7299
Web: www.hotels.com

CEO: David Litman
CFO: Mel Robinson
HR: -
FYE: December 31
Type: Subsidiary

Hotels.com (formerly Hotel Reservations Network) wants to transform the Internet into the Inn-ternet. The company books rooms at more than 135000 properties in markets throughout North America Europe Asia the Middle East and Africa via its localized websites. It also accepts reservations through its call centers. Hotels.com offers rooms that are discounted by up to 70%. The site includes 360-degree virtual tours property descriptions rate calendars maps and more than 2 million guest reviews. The company has room supply agreements with hotel chains such as Hilton Worldwide Best Western Radisson and Sheraton. Hotels.com is a subsidiary of Expedia.

HOUCHENS INDUSTRIES INC.

700 Church St.
Bowling Green KY 42102
Phone: 270-843-3252
Fax: 270-780-2877
Web: www.houchensindustries.com

CEO: James P Gipson
CFO: James Gordon Minter
HR: -
FYE: September 30
Type: Private

Houchens Industries is a supermarket of businesses as well as an operator of supermarkets. The diversified company runs more than 150 supermarkets under the Houchens Food Giant IGA Piggly Wiggly Buehler Foods White's Fresh Foods and Mad Butcher banners. Its 220 Save-A-Lot discount grocery stores in a dozen states offer limited selections and cover 15000 sq. ft. or less. Houchens also owns convenience stores operates Cohen's Fashion Optical franchise stores and several Sheldon's Express Pharmacy stores. Other businesses include construction financial services real estate and recycling. Founded as BG Wholesale in 1917 by Ervin Houchens the firm is 100%-owned by its employees.

HOUGHTON INTERNATIONAL INC.

945 Madison Ave.
Norristown PA 19482
Phone: 610-666-4000
Fax: 610-666-1376
Web: www.houghtonintl.com

CEO: –
CFO: Keller Arnold
HR: –
FYE: December 31
Type: Private

It might not have been called the Rust Belt if they'd used Houghton International's products more often. The company is the world leader in industrial fluids providing both high-tech fluid products and fluid management services. Houghton manufactures oils and specialty chemicals for lubrication in several major industries: metalworking automotive and steel as well as offshore deepwater oil drilling. Its products range from aluminum and steel rolling lubricants to rust preventatives to fire-resistant hydraulic fluids. Its Fluidcare system helps manufacturers reduce costs through chemical management and recycling.

HOUGHTON MIFFLIN HARCOURT CO.   NMS: HMHC

222 Berkeley Street
Boston, MA 02116
Phone: 617 351-5000
Fax: –

CEO: Linda K. Zecher
CFO: Eric Shuman
HR: Joanne Karimi
FYE: December 31
Type: Public

Houghton Mifflin Harcourt Company (HMH) would like to thank all the professional students out there. The firm is a publisher of educational material covering areas from pre-K through grade 12 as well as adult learners. HMH publishes textbooks and printed materials and provides digital content online to 50 million students and 116000 school districts in more than 150 countries. It additionally publishes fiction (including J.R.R. Tolkien's The Lord of the Rings series and the popular line of Curious George books) as well as nonfiction titles and reference materials and offers professional resources and educational services to teachers.

	Annual Growth	12/10	12/11	12/12	12/13	12/14
Sales ($ mil.)	(0.4%)	1,397.1	1,295.3	1,285.6	1,378.6	1,372.3
Net income ($ mil.)	–	(507.7)	(2,182.4)	(87.1)	(111.2)	(111.5)
Market value ($ mil.)	22.1%	–	–	–	2,406.9	2,939.1
Employees	0.0%	–	–	3,300	3,300	3,300

HOUGHTON MIFFLIN HARCOURT PUBLISHING COMPANY

222 Berkeley St.
Boston MA 02116-3748
Phone: 617-351-5000
Fax: 703-876-3125
Web: www.gendyn.com

CEO: Linda K Zecher
CFO: Eric Shuman
HR: –
FYE: December 31
Type: Private

Houghton Mifflin Harcourt Publishing Company would like to thank all the professional students out there. The firm is a publisher of educational material covering areas from pre-K through grade 12 as well as adult learners. Houghton Mifflin publishes textbooks and printed materials and provides digital content online and via CD-ROM. It additionally publishes fiction (including J.R.R. Tolkien's The Lord of the Rings series) as well as nonfiction titles and reference materials and offers professional resources and educational services to teachers. Houghton Mifflin has origins dating back to 1832 and is owned by private-equity concerns including hedge fund Paulson & Co. It filed for bankruptcy in 2012.

HOULIHAN LOKEY INC.

10250 Constellation Blvd. 5th Fl.
Los Angeles CA 90067
Phone: 310-553-8871
Fax: 310-553-2173
Web: www.hl.com

CEO: Scott L Beiser
CFO: J Lindsey Alley
HR: –
FYE: December 31
Type: Subsidiary

International investment bank Houlihan Lokey soldiers on for mergers on the economic front. The firm provides advisory services for primarily mid-market companies involved in M&A deals and corporate restructurings including the sale of distressed assets and other turnaround situations. Houlihan Lokey also raises private and public equity for midsized private and small-cap public companies. The company is among the top M&A advisors in the US especially for deals valued at less than $1 billion. Houlihan Lokey operates about 15 offices in the US Europe and Asia. Founded in 1972 Houlihan Lokey is majority-owned by Japanese financial services company ORIX; employees own the rest of the firm.

HOUSTON AMERICAN ENERGY CORP.   ASE: HUSA

801 Travis Street, Suite 1425
Houston, TX 77002
Phone: 713 222-6966
Fax: –
Web: www.houstonamericanenergy.com

CEO: John P Boylan
CFO: –
HR: –
FYE: December 31
Type: Public

Houston-based with North and South American properties and energy focused Houston American Energy explores for and produces oil and natural gas primarily in Colombia but also along the US Gulf Coast (Louisiana and Texas although the oil and gas independent also holds some acreage in Oklahoma). In 2011 the company reported proved reserves of 115627 barrels of oil equivalent. President and CEO John Terwilliger owns 27.5% of Houston American Energy; director Orrie Tawes 10%. In 2012 the debt-plagued company was pursuing strategic alternatives.

	Annual Growth	12/10	12/11	12/12	12/13	12/14
Sales ($ mil.)	(63.1%)	19.5	1.2	0.4	0.3	0.4
Net income ($ mil.)	–	21.0	(4.3)	(56.8)	(3.2)	(4.4)
Market value ($ mil.)	(69.3%)	943.8	636.0	11.5	13.0	8.4
Employees	(15.9%)	4	4	4	2	2

HOUSTON SAM STATE UNIVERSITY

1806 AVE J
HUNTSVILLE, TX 77340
Phone: 936-294-1111
Fax: –
Web: www.shsu.edu

CEO: –
CFO: –
HR: –
FYE: August 31
Type: Private

Part of the Texas State University System Sam Houston University has an enrollment of nearly 18500 students. It consists of six schools: Business Administration Criminal Justice Education Fine Arts and Mass Communications Humanities and Social Sciences and Sciences. The university offers some 130 undergraduate and master programs as well as doctoral programs in counselor education criminal justice educational leadership reading and clinical psychology. It offers more than 20 undergraduate and graduate degrees entirely online. Sam Houston State was founded as Sam Houston Normal Institute in 1879 and is named after Texas hero General Sam Houston.

	Annual Growth	08/05	08/06	08/07	08/08	08/13
Sales ($ mil.)	–	–	0.0	128.8	136.5	183.7
Net income ($ mil.)	1.8%	–	–	14.9	63.4	16.7
Market value ($ mil.)	–	–	–	–	–	–
Employees	–	–	–	–	–	2,200

HOUSTON WIRE & CABLE CO
NMS: HWCC

10201 North Loop East
Houston, TX 77029
Phone: 713 609-2100
Fax: 713 609-2101
Web: www.houwire.com

CEO: James L. Pokluda
CFO: Nicol G. (Nic) Graham
HR: –
FYE: December 31
Type: Public

Houston Wire & Cable (HWC) may have a Texas name but it can keep customers wired from Seattle to Tampa. The company is a conduit between cable manufacturers and electrical distributors and their customers. It distributes specialty (electrical and electronic) wire and cable products such as cable terminators fiber-optic cables and bare copper and building wire as well as voice data and premise wire. It also owns the brand LifeGuard a low-smoke zero-halogen cable. HWC operates a network of multiple distribution centers across the US and sells primarily to electrical distributors.

	Annual Growth	12/10	12/11	12/12	12/13	12/14
Sales ($ mil.)	6.0%	308.5	396.4	393.0	383.3	390.0
Net income ($ mil.)	14.8%	8.6	19.7	17.0	7.9	15.0
Market value ($ mil.)	(2.9%)	235.3	242.0	214.8	234.3	209.2
Employees	(1.3%)	380	410	427	403	360

HOVENSA LLC

1 ESTATE HOPE
CHRISTIANSTED, VI 00820
Phone: 340-692-3000
Fax: –
Web: www.hovensallc.com

CEO: –
CFO: –
HR: Jennifer D Aubain
FYE: December 31
Type: Private

HOVENSA brings together US and Latin American know-how and operations to handle oil products in the US Virgin Islands. HOVENSA is a joint venture of Hess and Venezuelan oil giant PDVSA (its major crude oil supplier). Once the largest private employer in the US Virgin Islands the company operated a 500000-barrels-per-day crude oil refinery on St. Croix along with two specialized oil processing complexes a 150000-barrels-per-day fluid catalytic cracking unit and a 58000-barrels-per-day delayed coker unit. However the St. Croix refinery had run up losses for years; it was shut down in 2012 and was put up for sale in 2013.

	Annual Growth	12/05	12/06	12/07	12/08	12/09
Sales ($ mil.)	(42.5%)	–	–	–	17,479.7	10,048.3
Net income ($ mil.)	–	–	–	–	95.0	(451.2)
Market value ($ mil.)	–	–	–	–	–	–
Employees	–	–	–	–	–	1,300

HOVNANIAN ENTERPRISES, INC.
NYS: HOV

110 West Front Street, P.O. Box 500
Red Bank, NJ 07701
Phone: 732 747-7800
Fax: –
Web: www.khov.com

CEO: Ara K. Hovnanian
CFO: J. Larry Sorsby
HR: –
FYE: October 31
Type: Public

You don't have to live in a hovel if you buy a Hovnanian. Hovnanian Enterprises designs builds and markets single-family detached homes condominiums and townhomes for first-time move-up and luxury buyers as well as for empty-nesters and active adults. The builder sells homes in 220 communities across 16 US states under the K. Hovnanian Brighton Matzel and Mumford Oster Parkwood Builders and Town & Country brands. The company's K. Hovnanian American Mortgage unit offers mortgage financing and title services. In FY2015 Hovnanian Enterprises delivered 5776 homes for an average sale price of $382300 each with prices ranging from $116 thousand to $1.67 million per home. Almost 40% of its home sales came from Texas and Arizona.

	Annual Growth	10/11	10/12	10/13	10/14	10/15
Sales ($ mil.)	17.3%	1,134.9	1,485.4	1,851.3	2,063.4	2,148.5
Net income ($ mil.)	–	–	(286.1)	(66.2)	31.3	307.1	(16.1)
Market value ($ mil.)	9.4%	211.0	630.0	741.4	550.9	301.8
Employees	8.5%	1,500	1,565	1,749	2,006	2,078

HOWARD HUGHES CORP
NYS: HHC

13355 Noel Road, 22nd Floor
Dallas, TX 75240
Phone: 214 741-7744
Fax: 214 741-3021
Web: www.howardhughes.com

CEO: David R. Weinreb
CFO: Andrew C. Richardson
HR: –
FYE: December 31
Type: Public

The Howard Hughes Corporation (THHC) is involved in neither planes movies or medical research but one of the 20th century entrepreneur's later interests real estate. The company arose from the bankruptcy restructuring of shopping mall developer General Growth Properties (GGP) to oversee much of GGP's non-retail assets. THHC owns GGP's former portfolio of four master planned communities outside Columbia Maryland; Houston Texas; and Summerlin Nevada; as well as about two dozen other as-yet undeveloped sites and commercial properties in 16 states from New York to Hawaii including GGP's own headquarters building in downtown Chicago. Unlike GGP THHC does not operate as a REIT.

	Annual Growth	12/10	12/11	12/12	12/13	12/14
Sales ($ mil.)	45.2%	142.7	275.7	376.9	474.6	634.6
Net income ($ mil.)	–	(69.2)	148.5	(127.5)	(73.7)	(23.5)
Market value ($ mil.)	24.4%	2,157.1	1,750.8	2,894.4	4,760.5	5,169.6
Employees	63.2%	155	835	842	1,000	1,100

HOWARD MILLER COMPANY

860 E. Main Ave.
Zeeland MI 49464-1300
Phone: 616-772-7277
Fax: 616-772-1670
Web: www.howardmiller.com

CEO: –
CFO: –
HR: –
FYE: December 31
Type: Private

Few things run like clockwork like the nation's largest private clock manufacturer. Howard Miller Company previously Howard Miller Clock Company makes an array of grandfather wall and mantel clocks curio cabinets wine and spirits furnishings rugs and home furniture as well as memorial urns. Products are sold primarily through dealers in the US Canada and Mexico. Since the 1920s Howard Miller has specialized in clock-making as it grew through acquisitions including furniture maker Hekman German clock movement master Kieninger and Pulaski Furniture's Ridgeway Clocks. Howard Miller also markets home storage and console units and other furnishings under celebrity Ty Pennington's brand name.

HP ENTERPRISE SERVICES LLC

5400 Legacy Dr.
Plano TX 75024-3199
Phone: 972-604-6000
Fax: 972-605-6033
Web: h10134.www1.hp.com

CEO: Ronald A Rittenmeyer
CFO: Ronald P Vargo
HR: –
FYE: December 31
Type: Subsidiary

They started it! HP Enterprise Services formerly Electronic Data Systems (EDS) pioneered the computer outsourcing business. The company delivers such services as cloud computing systems integration network and systems operations data center management applications development and outsourcing. It is one of the largest federal government contractors but it also serves commercial customers in a wide range of industries including energy entertainment health care manufacturing and transportation. Top clients have included the US Navy and former parent General Motors. HP Enterprise Services is a subsidiary of Hewlett-Packard and operates as part of the HP Enterprise Business segment.

HP HOOD LLC

6 Kimball Ln.
Lynnfield MA 01940
Phone: 617-887-3000
Fax: 617-887-8484
Web: www.hood.com

CEO: –
CFO: –
HR: –
FYE: December 31
Type: Private

HP Hood tries to cream the competition — with ice cream sour cream and whipping cream. The leading US dairy producer also makes fluid milk cottage cheese and juices. Its home turf is New England where it is one of the few remaining dairies to offer home milk delivery serving some 15000 customers. However Hood's products are distributed throughout the US to chain and independent food retailers and convenience stores and to foodservice purveyors. In addition to its own and subsidiary brands the Massachusetts company makes private-label and licensed dairy products and owns regional dairy producer Crowley Foods. Hood operates about 15 manufacturing plants throughout the US.

HP INC

1501 Page Mill Road
Palo Alto, CA 94304
Phone: 650 857-1501
Fax: –
Web: www.hp.com

NYS: HPQ
CEO: Dion J. Weisler
CFO: Catherine A. (Cathie) Lesjak
HR: Jason Wilkinson
FYE: October 31
Type: Public

Making a hard copy takes a device often a personal computer to create a document or presentation and a printer to transfer words and images to paper. That's pretty much the business of HP Inc. one of two companies created from the breakup of Hewlett-Packard Co. HP makes 60% of its revenue from personal systems (notebook computers and desktops) and 40% from printers and supplies such as ink. It's the No. 1 printer company and No. 1 commercial PC maker in the world (Lenovo is tops overall). About half of revenue comes from customers in the Americas. Even after the breakup HP and sibling HP Enterprise (HPE) would rank in the Fortune 100.

	Annual Growth	10/11	10/12	10/13	10/14	10/15
Sales ($ mil.)	(5.1%)	127,245.0	120,357.0	112,298.0	111,454.0	103,355.0
Net income ($ mil.)	(10.4%)	7,074.0	(12,650.0)	5,113.0	5,013.0	4,554.0
Market value ($ mil.)	0.3%	47,997.0	24,981.5	43,956.6	64,717.4	48,628.3
Employees	(4.8%)	349,600	331,800	317,500	302,000	287,000

HRG GROUP INC

450 Park Avenue, 29th Floor
New York, NY 10022
Phone: 212 906-8555
Fax: –
Web: www.harbingergroupinc.com

NYS: HRG
CEO: Omar M. Asali
CFO: Thomas A. (Tom) Williams
HR: –
FYE: September 30
Type: Public

HRG Group (formerly Harbinger Group) has zapped its former image as an oil and gas company and instead looks to pump up its portfolio. Like an investment firm the holding company acquires businesses across a diverse array of industries. Harbinger Group makes most of its revenue from the sale of branded consumer products such as residential locksets consumer batteries grooming and personal products small household appliances and pest control products. It also deals in life insurance and annuities provides asset-backed loans and owns energy assets. The company was co-founded in 1953 by former US President George H. W. Bush under the name Zapata.

	Annual Growth	09/11	09/12	09/13	09/14	09/15
Sales ($ mil.)	13.7%	3,477.8	4,480.7	5,543.4	5,963.0	5,815.9
Net income ($ mil.)	–	34.8	89.6	(45.8)	(10.3)	(556.8)
Market value ($ mil.)	23.3%	1,021.0	1,697.7	2,088.4	2,642.2	2,362.2
Employees	27.6%	6,009	6,019	13,742	14,427	15,922

HSB GROUP INC.

1 State St.
Hartford CT 06103
Phone: 860-722-1866
Fax: 860-722-5106
Web: www.hsb.com

CEO: Gregory Barats
CFO: –
HR: –
FYE: December 31
Type: Subsidiary

While its company's names might seem quaint HSB Group is fully modernized and up to speed. The holding company for The Hartford Steam Boiler Inspection and Insurance Company HSB Group subsidiaries provide commercial insurance reinsurance (insurance for insurers) and engineering consulting services. The firm specializes in coverage for equipment breakdown with specific policies for boilers pressure vessels computer systems and other machinery. HSB Group also offers engineering services to prevent equipment failure as well as risk management consulting services that help assess potential equipment losses. HSB Group is owned by German reinsurer Munich Re and operates as part of Munich Re America.

HSBC USA, INC.

452 Fifth Avenue
New York, NY 10018
Phone: 212 525-5000
Fax: –

NYS: HUSI PRH
CEO: Irene M. Dorner
CFO: John T. McGinnis
HR: Mary E. Bilbrey
FYE: December 31
Type: Public

HSBC USA a subsidiary of British banking behemoth HSBC Holdings operates HSBC Bank USA one of the biggest foreign-owned banks in the country by assets. With about 240 offices (including 155 in New York City) the bank has one of the largest branch networks in New York State plus more than 100 additional locations in about a dozen other states and Washington DC; California New Jersey and Florida are its next largest markets. The bank offers personal commercial and mortgage banking services. Its personal financial services segment provides mutual funds investments and insurance. HSBC Bank USA also offers investment banking private banking brokerage and trust services.

	Annual Growth	12/10	12/11	12/12	12/13	12/14
Assets ($ mil.)	0.2%	183,813.0	210,280.0	196,567.0	185,487.0	185,539.0
Net income ($ mil.)	(31.0%)	1,564.0	1,018.0	(1,045.0)	(338.0)	354.0
Market value ($ mil.)	–	0.0	0.0	0.0	0.0	0.0
Employees	(14.5%)	12,000	9,000	7,000	6,500	6,400

HSN INC (DE)

1 HSN Drive
St. Petersburg, FL 33729
Phone: 727 872-1000
Fax: –
Web: www.hsni.com

NMS: HSNI
CEO: Mindy Grossman
CFO: Judy A. Schmeling
HR: Lisa Letizio
FYE: December 31
Type: Public

No need to worry about normal business hours when shopping with this retailer. HSN (known to night owls and from-the-couch shoppers as Home Shopping Network) operates a home shopping television network which reaches some 95 million US homes and a fast-growing online business HSN.com. In general HSN sells apparel and accessories jewelry electronics housewares and health beauty and fitness products. Its Cornerstone Brands business is a catalog and Internet retailer whose titles include Garnet Hill Ballard Designs and TravelSmith among others. The segment also operates about 12 retail shops.

	Annual Growth	12/10	12/11	12/12	12/13	12/14
Sales ($ mil.)	4.6%	2,996.8	3,177.2	3,266.7	3,404.0	3,588.0
Net income ($ mil.)	15.1%	98.5	123.1	130.7	178.4	173.0
Market value ($ mil.)	25.5%	1,606.9	1,901.0	2,887.6	3,266.1	3,984.4
Employees	21.2%	3,200	6,400	6,700	6,800	6,900

HTC GLOBAL SERVICES INC.

3270 W. Big Beaver Rd.
Troy MI 48084
Phone: 248-786-2500
Fax: 248-786-2515
Web: www.htcinc.com

CEO: Madhava Reddy
CFO: –
HR: Suresh Subramanian
FYE: December 31
Type: Private

HTC Global Services offers information technology (IT) services to customers in a wide range of industries. The company specializes in such areas as application development integration and reengineering software testing enterprise content management business intelligence and IT infrastructure management. It also sells business process automation software for such functions as content management claims processing and tax accounting. Founded in 1990 HTC serves customers worldwide in industries that include automotive manufacturing education health care financial services insurance publishing and retail.

HUB GROUP, INC.   NMS: HUBG

2000 Clearwater Drive
Oak Brook, IL 60523
Phone: 630 271-3600
Fax: –

CEO: David P. Yeager
CFO: Terri A. Pizzuto
HR: –
FYE: December 31
Type: Public

Hub Group helps its clients by handling the hubbub of freight movement throughout North America. An intermodal marketing company Hub Group specializes in arranging the transportation of freight by a combination of rail and truck. A customer's freight is loaded into a container or trailer and transported by rail from one Hub Group distribution center to another then taken to its destination by a local trucking company which in some cases is a Hub Group unit. The company also provides truck brokerage and logistics services. Hub Group's Mode operations offer complementary services including temperature protected transportation.

	Annual Growth	12/10	12/11	12/12	12/13	12/14
Sales ($ mil.)	18.1%	1,833.7	2,751.5	3,124.1	3,373.9	3,571.1
Net income ($ mil.)	4.4%	43.5	58.2	68.0	69.1	51.6
Market value ($ mil.)	2.0%	1,297.0	1,197.0	1,240.2	1,472.0	1,405.5
Employees	16.5%	1,392	1,616	1,652	1,982	2,568

HUB INTERNATIONAL LIMITED

55 E. Jackson Blvd. Fl. 14A
Chicago IL 60604
Phone: 877-402-6601
Fax: 877-402-6606
Web: www.hubinternational.com

CEO: Martin P Hughes
CFO: Joseph C Hyde
HR: –
FYE: December 31
Type: Private

Hub International is an insurance broker that operates more than 250 offices in a decentralized regional hub-and-satellite-office structure. It provides property/casualty employee benefits risk management life and health reinsurance and investment products and services to clients in North America (the US and Canada) Latin America and the Caribbean. Hub is licensed in every state and all Canadian provinces. The acquisitive firm focuses on midsized commercial clients and affluent individuals. The US accounts for the bulk of its revenues. Hub is also able to facilitate cross-border business between the US and Mexico and operates in Brazil.

HUBBELL INC.   NYS: HUBB

40 Waterview Drive
Shelton, CT 06484
Phone: 475 882-4000
Fax: –
Web: www.hubbell.com

CEO: David G. Nord
CFO: William R. Sperry
HR: Alyssa Flynn
FYE: December 31
Type: Public

You don't have to go into space to check out this Hubbell. The company makes electrical and electronic products for commercial industrial telecommunications and utility applications. Its electrical segment which accounts for more than two-thirds of sales includes wiring connector and grounding products lighting fixtures and controls and other electrical equipment used by electricians and electrical contractors and maintenance personnel. The power segment includes distribution transmission substation and telecommunications products used by electric utilities. The company gets most of its sales in the US.

	Annual Growth	12/10	12/11	12/12	12/13	12/14
Sales ($ mil.)	7.2%	2,541.2	2,871.6	3,044.4	3,183.9	3,359.4
Net income ($ mil.)	10.6%	217.2	267.9	299.7	326.5	325.3
Market value ($ mil.)	–	–	–	–	–	–
Employees	4.3%	13,000	13,500	13,600	14,300	15,400

HUDSON CITY BANCORP INC   NMS: HCBK

West 80 Century Road
Paramus, NJ 07652
Phone: 201 967-1900
Fax: 201 967-0559
Web: www.hcbk.com

CEO: –
CFO: –
HR: –
FYE: December 31
Type: Public

Hudson City Bancorp is the holding company for Hudson City Savings Bank one of the largest thrifts in the US. Founded in 1868 the bank has more than 130 branches in the New York City metropolitan area including northern New Jersey; Long Island; and Fairfield County Connecticut; as well as central New Jersey and that state's Philadelphia suburbs. Serving middle- to high-income consumers it issues and purchases high-quality first residential mortgages which account for about 99% of its loan portfolio. It originates loans at its branches through mortgage bankers and brokers and (to a lesser extent) on a wholesale basis nationwide. Acquisitive M&T Bank is buying Hudson City Bancorp for some $3.7 billion.

	Annual Growth	12/09	12/10	12/11	12/12	12/13
Assets ($ mil.)	(10.5%)	60,267.8	61,166.0	45,355.9	40,596.3	38,607.4
Net income ($ mil.)	(23.0%)	527.2	537.2	(736.0)	249.1	185.2
Market value ($ mil.)	(9.0%)	7,255.2	6,732.1	3,302.6	4,296.0	4,983.0
Employees	0.5%	1,552	1,626	1,645	1,792	1,581

HUDSON GLOBAL INC   NMS: HSON

1325 Avenue of the Americas
New York, NY 10019
Phone: 212 351-7300
Fax: –
Web: www.hhgroup.com

CEO: Stephen Nolan
CFO: Stephen A Nolan
HR: –
FYE: December 31
Type: Public

Hudson Global offers specialty staffing and related consulting services through the regional businesses of Hudson Global Resources which target the Americas the Asia/Pacific region and Europe. Hudson Global Resources provides temporary and contract personnel as well as permanent recruitment services. The company focuses on mid-level professionals in specialized areas such as accounting and finance legal and information technology. Among the company's clients are small and large businesses government agencies and educational institutions.

	Annual Growth	12/10	12/11	12/12	12/13	12/14
Sales ($ mil.)	(7.5%)	794.5	933.7	777.6	660.1	581.2
Net income ($ mil.)	–	(4.7)	10.9	(5.3)	(30.4)	(13.2)
Market value ($ mil.)	(14.6%)	195.5	160.7	150.3	134.8	103.8
Employees	(4.9%)	2,200	2,200	2,000	1,700	1,800

HUDSON GROUP

One Meadowlands Plaza
East Rutherford NJ 07073
Phone: 201-939-5050
Fax: 201-867-0067
Web: www.hudsongroupusa.com

CEO: -
CFO: -
HR: -
FYE: December 31
Type: Private

Hudson Group doesn't care if you're traveling to Pasadena California or Poughkeepsie New York as long as you visit one of its shops. The company operates more than 580 newsstands bookstores cafes and specialty shops in about 70 airports and other transportation terminals throughout the US and Canada. The group's flagship Hudson News format is North America's only national newsstand brand. The shops offer travelers books magazines apparel souvenirs snacks and beverages for their journey. Other formats include Hudson Booksellers Kids Works and Euro Cafe. Private equity firm Advent International has owned Hudson Group since 2008 merging the business with Swiss travel retailer Dufry AG soon after.

HUDSON VALLEY FEDERAL CREDIT UNION

159 Barnegat Rd.
Poughkeepsie NY 12601-5454
Phone: 845-463-3011
Fax: 845-463-3229
Web: www.hvfcu.org

CEO: Mary D Madden
CFO: -
HR: Janet Giannetta
FYE: December 31
Type: Private - Not-for-Pr

Hudson Valley Federal Credit Union (HVFCU) provides financial services to more than 260000 members from about 20 branches in eastern New York's Hudson Valley region. Membership is available to all who reside work volunteer worship or attend school in Dutchess Orange Putnam or Ulster counties. In addition to savings accounts credit cards mortgages and business and personal loans the credit union offers insurance and financial planning services to its individual and small business members. It provides access to investments and asset management services through an agreement with third-party provider LPL Financial. HVFCU was founded in 1963 as the IBM Poughkeepsie Employees Federal Credit Union.

HUDSON PACIFIC PROPERTIES INC

NYS: HPP

11601 Wilshire Blvd., Sixth Floor
Los Angeles, CA 90025
Phone: 310 445-5700
Fax: 310 445-5710
Web: www.hudsonpacificproperties.com

CEO: Victor J. Coleman
CFO: Mark T. Lammas
HR: -
FYE: December 31
Type: Public

Hudson Pacific Properties wants to be the landlord to the stars. One of Hollywood's biggest landlords the real estate investment trust (REIT) buys and manages primarily office buildings but also and media and entertainment properties in Northern and Southern California in cities such as Los Angeles Orange County San Diego San Francisco and Seattle. It owns about 25 properties totaling some more than 6 million sq. ft. including the Technicolor Building and two production studios on Hollywood's Sunset Boulevard. It also owns about 2 million sq. ft. of undeveloped land adjacent to its Hollywood production studios. Tenants include Amazon Warner Bros. Entertainment and Warner Music Group.

	Annual Growth	12/10	12/11	12/12	12/13	12/14
Sales ($ mil.)	43.0%	60.6	142.2	166.2	205.6	253.4
Net income ($ mil.)	-	(3.3)	(10.4)	(17.2)	(2.6)	23.5
Market value ($ mil.)	18.9%	1,005.3	945.9	1,406.8	1,460.9	2,007.9
Employees	23.0%	66	88	106	130	151

HUDSON VALLEY HOLDING CORP.

NYS: HVB

21 Scarsdale Road
Yonkers, NY 10707
Phone: 914 961-6100
Fax: -
Web: www.hudsonvalleybank.com

CEO: -
CFO: -
HR: -
FYE: December 31
Type: Public

Hudson Valley Holding is the parent company of Hudson Valley Bank which serves individuals businesses municipalities and not-for-profit organizations from more than 35 locations throughout metropolitan New York and lower Connecticut. The bank focuses on real estate lending which accounts for more than 80% of the company's loan portfolio. Hudson Valley Holding offers other standard banking products such savings checking and money market accounts commercial and industrial loans consumer loans credit cards CDs and IRAs. Bank subsidiary A.R. Schmeidler & Co. offers investment management services.

	Annual Growth	12/09	12/10	12/11	12/12	12/13
Assets ($ mil.)	3.0%	2,665.6	2,669.0	2,797.7	2,891.2	2,999.2
Net income ($ mil.)	(50.6%)	19.0	5.1	(2.1)	29.2	1.1
Market value ($ mil.)	(4.7%)	491.6	493.6	423.0	310.4	405.7
Employees	(4.2%)	498	478	489	460	419

HUDSON TECHNOLOGIES INC

NAS: HDSN

1 Blue Hill Plaza, P.O. Box 1541
Pearl River, NY 10965
Phone: 845 735-6000
Fax: -
Web: www.hudsontech.com

CEO: Kevin J. Zugibe
CFO: James R. Buscemi
HR: -
FYE: December 31
Type: Public

Hudson Technologies defends the ozone. Using proprietary reclamation technology to remove moisture and impurities from refrigeration systems it recovers and reclaims chlorofluorocarbons (CFCs) used in commercial air-conditioning and refrigeration systems. The company sells both reclaimed and new refrigerants and also buys used refrigerants for reclamation and sale. In addition Hudson Technologies offers on-site decontamination services as well as services designed to improve the efficiency of customers' refrigeration systems. Customers include commercial and industrial enterprises and government entities along with refrigerant contractors distributors and wholesalers and makers of refrigeration equipment.

	Annual Growth	12/10	12/11	12/12	12/13	12/14
Sales ($ mil.)	10.6%	37.3	44.3	56.4	58.6	55.8
Net income ($ mil.)	-	0.7	1.0	12.8	(5.8)	(0.7)
Market value ($ mil.)	23.1%	53.0	46.9	117.6	119.6	121.8
Employees	13.5%	79	88	94	93	131

HUFFY CORPORATION

6551 Centerville Business Pkwy.
Centerville OH 45459
Phone: 937-865-2800
Fax: 937-865-5470
Web: www.huffy.com

CEO: William A Smith
CFO: Steven D Lipton
HR: -
FYE: December 31
Type: Private

Huffy's business isn't as old as the bicycle (invented in 1861) but it's close. The company which has been peddling bikes and other wheeled vehicles for more than a century is best known for its all-purpose bikes although scooters also play a role in its product portfolio. Its Huffy Micro and Royce Union bikes include kids' bikes and tricycles comfort cruisers mountain bikes and BMX racing bikes. Products include licensed names Disney Dora and Thomas & Friends among others. Most of the company's bikes are manufactured in Asia and are sold throughout North America and Australia by mass marketers and specialty retailers such as Wal-Mart The Sports Authority Target and Kmart.

HUGHES COMMUNICATIONS INC.

11717 Exploration Ln.
Germantown MD 20876
Phone: 301-428-5500
Fax: 301-428-1868
Web: www.hughes.com

CEO: Pradman P Kaul
CFO: Grant A Barber
HR: –
FYE: December 31
Type: Subsidiary

Hughes Communications aims even higher than visionary company namesake Howard Hughes did. Through operating subsidiary Hughes Network Systems the company provides broadband satellite equipment and services based largely on very small aperture terminal (VSAT) technology. Over a network of owned and leased satellites it provides consumers businesses and government agencies worldwide with broadband Internet access via the HughesNet service. The network also enables voice calling video transmission and data services such as credit authorization. Hughes also sells network hardware systems used by fixed and mobile communication systems operators. EchoStar bought the company for almost $2 billion in 2011.

HUGHES HUBBARD & REED LLP

1 Battery Park Plaza
New York NY 10004-1482
Phone: 212-837-6000
Fax: 212-422-4726
Web: www.hugheshubbard.com

CEO: –
CFO: –
HR: –
FYE: December 31
Type: Private - Partnershi

Hughes Hubbard & Reed isn't afraid to break new ground — in 1999 it became the first major New York law firm to name a woman Candace Beinecke as its chair. The firm's main practice areas are corporate law and litigation including insurance and product liability. With lawyers working in more than 30 practice areas the firm has served clients such as Goldman Sachs Hasbro and the Boy Scouts of America (in a fight to overturn a court ruling that prohibits excluding gays from membership). Hughes Hubbard has offices in Jersey City New Jersey; Los Angeles; Miami; New York; and Washington DC and internationally in Paris and Tokyo. The law firm traces its historical roots back to 1888.

HUGHES NETWORK SYSTEMS LLC

11717 Exploration Ln.
Germantown MD 20876
Phone: 301-428-5500
Fax: 310-428-1868
Web: www.hughes.com

CEO: –
CFO: Grant A Barber
HR: –
FYE: December 31
Type: Subsidiary

Hughes Network Systems wrote the book on satellite data and Internet access network services. The pioneering company is a leading provider of broadband satellite network equipment and services to the very small aperture terminal (VSAT) business market. It is also a leading provider of satellite Internet access to consumers in North America serving about 575000 subscribers with its HughesNet service. Hughes sells communications equipment for mobile satellite-based voice and data network operators and cellular mobile network operators as well as other users of terrestrial microwave technology. Hughes Network Systems is the primary operating subsidiary of Hughes Communications which was acquired by EchoStar in 2011.

HUGHES TELEMATICS INC.   OTC: HUTC

2002 Summit Blvd. Ste. 1800
Atlanta GA 30319
Phone: 404-573-5800
Fax: 404-573-5827
Web: www.hughestelematics.com

CEO: –
CFO: –
HR: –
FYE: December 31
Type: Public

HUGHES Telematics Inc. (HTI) wants to keep drivers and fleet managers oriented. The company provides vehicle telematics products and services such as GPS navigation emergency support and vehicle diagnostic systems. Through its Networkfleet subsidiary (more than half of sales) HTI offers fleet tracking and reporting services to companies who want to track the location of company vehicles monitor vehicle maintenance needs or track mileage. It also designs systems that allow drivers to access content on the Web and in mobile devices such as phones and digital music players as well as features such as vehicle locating and locking or unlocking the vehicle from a smartphone. It was bought in 2012 by Verizon.

HUGOTON ROYALTY TRUST (TX)   NYS: HGT

Southwest Bank Trustee, P.O. Box 962020
Forth Worth, TX 76162-2020
Phone: 855 588-7839
Fax: –
Web: www.hugotontrust.com

CEO: –
CFO: –
HR: –
FYE: December 31
Type: Public

Hugoton Royalty Trust was formed by Cross Timbers Oil Company (now XTO Energy) to pay royalties to shareholders based on the proceeds of sales from its oil and gas holdings. Payouts depend on oil and gas prices the volume of gas and oil produced and production and other costs. The trust receives 80% of the net proceeds from XTO Energy's properties located in the Hugoton fields of Kansas Oklahoma and Texas; the Anadarko Basin of Oklahoma; and the Green River Basin of Wyoming. In 2008 the trust reported proved reserves of 3.3 million barrels of oil and 366.3 billion cu. ft. of natural gas. XTO Energy controls the trust which is administered through Bank of America and has no officers.

	Annual Growth	12/10	12/11	12/12	12/13	12/14
Sales ($ mil.)	(8.0%)	62.9	56.6	25.1	37.3	45.0
Net income ($ mil.)	(8.3%)	62.0	55.8	23.3	34.5	43.8
Market value ($ mil.)	(19.9%)	820.8	753.6	292.4	300.0	338.4
Employees		–	–	–	–	–

HUHTAMAKI AMERICAS INC.

9201 Packaging Dr.
De Soto KS 66018
Phone: 913-583-3025
Fax: 913-583-8725
Web: www.us.huhtamaki.com

CEO: Jukka Moisio
CFO: –
HR: Aimee Davis
FYE: December 31
Type: Subsidiary

Huhtamaki Americas doesn't have customers eating out of its hands but it does make the packaging to serve up dinner. The company manufactures sturdy disposable tableware and food packaging as well as shaped paperboard plastic and molded fiber plates cups bowls and trays under the Chinet brand for foodservice customers and consumers. Huhtamaki Americas also supplies flexible packaging products for goods such as baking and snack foods detergents personal care electronics and pet foods. Product extensions include dinner napkins and guest towels. The company operates a dozen plus facilities in North America and Mexico and is the regional headquarters for Finland's global packaging giant Huhtamaki Oyj.

HUHTAMAKI INC.

9201 Packaging Dr.
De Soto KS 66018
Phone: 913-583-3025
Fax: 913-583-8781
Web: www.us.huhtamaki.com/apps/fsbu/fsbusite.nsf

CEO: Jukka Moisio
CFO: –
HR: Aimee Davis
FYE: December 31
Type: Subsidiary

Huhtamaki Inc. creates the perfect teacup for your tempest! The company makes and markets dinnerware under the Chinet brand name to consumers as well as an array of disposable foodservice products used by caterers to take-outs. Its offerings include plastic and paperboard cups and containers and molded fiber trays plates and bowls in various shapes and sizes. Instead of virgin wood fiber the company's molded-fiber lines use either post-industrial or post-consumer recycled fiber which are compostable too. Huhtamaki's plants dot the US. Established through the acquisition of Sealright and molded fiber originator Keyes Fibre it is the US business of Huhtamaki Americas part of Finland giant Huhtamaki Oyj.

HULU LLC

12312 W. Olympic Blvd.
Los Angeles CA 90064
Phone: 310-571-4700
Fax: 310-571-4701
Web: www.hulu.com

CEO: Mike Hopkins
CFO: –
HR: –
FYE: December 31
Type: Joint Venture

Hulu is a go-to service for online TV. The company operates an ad-supported website Hulu.com that allows viewers to watch online video content — TV shows clips and movies — for free. Its premium service Hulu Plus allows streaming of full current and past season content on everything from TV sets and PCs to mobile phones and tablets for a monthly subscription fee. Hulu's programming is provided by more than 400 content companies including network TV providers ABC FOX and NBC as well as film studios MGM Paramount and Sony. Those that have advertised on Hulu since its launch in 2008 include McDonald's Microsoft Target and Toyota.

HUMAN GENOME SCIENCES INC.

NASDAQ: HGSI

14200 Shady Grove Rd.
Rockville MD 20850-7464
Phone: 301-309-8504
Fax: 301-309-8512
Web: www.hgsi.com

CEO: H Thomas Watkins
CFO: David P Southwell
HR: –
FYE: December 31
Type: Public

Human Genome Sciences (HGS) starts at the molecular level for good health. Using its expertise in human genetics the biopharmaceutical discovery and development firm is working on therapies for infectious and autoimmune diseases cardiovascular disease and cancer. In 2011 lead candidate Benlysta gained FDA approval to treat systemic lupus and has since been extended into international markets. The company's only other commercial product is raxibacumab an antibody treatment for inhaled anthrax. In addition the company provides contract research and manufacturing services to other biotechs. Benlysta was developed through a partnership with GlaxoSmithKline (GSK). In 2012 HGS was acquired by GSK.

HUMAN PHEROMONE SCIENCES INC.

OTC: EROX

84 W. Santa Clara St. Ste. 720
San Jose CA 95113
Phone: 408-938-3030
Fax: 408-938-3025
Web: www.naturalattraction.com

CEO: William P Horgan
CFO: Gregory S Fredrick
HR: –
FYE: December 31
Type: Public

Human Pheromone Sciences (HPS) hopes its animal magnetism makes consumers hot under the collar. It makes fragrances that contain a patented synthetic version of a pheromone produced by the human body to stimulate the senses. It also licenses its technology to partners in the personal care products industry. The company's products are sold through its website and through direct marketing under the Natural Attraction name. It has granted non-exclusive rights to the Natural Attraction brand in the US Europe and Japan. HPS also partners with makers of consumer products to license its patented technology; CrowdGather is launching a unisex scent EroxA in 2011 with HPS. Renovatio Global Funds owns 16% of the firm.

HUMAN RIGHTS WATCH INC.

350 5TH AVE FL 34
NEW YORK, NY 101183499
Phone: 212-290-4700
Fax: –
Web: www.hrw.org

CEO: –
CFO: –
HR: –
FYE: June 30
Type: Private

Human Rights Watch (HRW) is watching out for everyone. The organization's mission is to prevent discrimination uphold political freedom protect people during wartime and bring offenders to justice. HRW researches human rights violations around the world and publishes its findings to help generate publicity about the atrocities it uncovers. The nongovernmental organization (NGO) also meets with national and international governing officials to help steer policy change. Along with partner organizations HRW won the 1997 Nobel Peace Prize for its International Campaign to Ban Landmines. HRW is an independent organization; all funds come from private contributors. The group was founded in 1978.

	Annual Growth	06/09	06/10	06/11	06/12	06/13
Sales ($ mil.)	11.8%	–	42.5	151.7	70.5	59.3
Net income ($ mil.)	–	–	–	101.0	11.8	(3.7)
Market value ($ mil.)	–	–	–	–	–	–
Employees	–	–	–	–	–	348

HUMANA INC.

NYS: HUM

500 West Main Street
Louisville, KY 40202
Phone: 502 580-1000
Fax: –
Web: www.humana.com

CEO: Bruce D. Broussard
CFO: Brian A. Kane
HR: Timothy S. (Tim) Huval
FYE: December 31
Type: Public

Medicare has made Humana a big-time player in the insurance game. One of the country's largest Medicare providers and a top health insurer Humana provides Medicare Advantage plans and prescription drug coverage to more than 5 million members throughout the US. It also administers managed care plans for other government programs including Medicaid plans in Florida and Puerto Rico and TRICARE (a program for military personnel) in 10 southern states. Additionally Humana offers commercial health plans and specialty (life dental and vision) coverage; it also provides health management services and operates outpatient care clinics. All told it covers about 20 million members in the US. Aetna is buying Humana for $37.1 billion.

	Annual Growth	12/10	12/11	12/12	12/13	12/14
Assets ($ mil.)	9.9%	16,103.3	17,708.0	19,979.0	20,735.0	23,466.0
Net income ($ mil.)	1.1%	1,099.4	1,419.0	1,222.0	1,231.0	1,147.0
Market value ($ mil.)	27.3%	8,189.3	13,106.8	10,267.3	15,442.1	21,487.6
Employees	12.8%	35,200	40,000	43,400	52,000	57,000

HUMAX USA INC.

17501 VON KARMAN AVE
IRVINE, CA 926146207
Phone: 949-251-5200
Fax: –
Web: www.humaxdigital.com

CEO: –
CFO: –
HR: –
FYE: December 31
Type: Private

Humax USA prefers to connect with its customers through its products. The company develops and manufactures flat-panel TV sets and digital set-top boxes for satellite cable and terrestrial connections. Humax USA is the US-based subsidiary of Korean consumer electronics manufacturing firm Humax Co. which was founded in 1989. The brand has become one of the most popular worldwide among set-top boxes. Humax's products are available in more than 90 countries as well as in the US. The company primarily serves customers in Asia and Europe.

	Annual Growth	12/10	12/11	12/12	12/13	12/14
Sales ($ mil.)	8.9%	–	347.5	290.4	317.0	448.9
Net income ($ mil.)	(4.4%)	–	–	0.6	0.3	0.5
Market value ($ mil.)	–	–	–	–	–	–
Employees	–	–	–	–	–	26

HUNT (J.B.) TRANSPORT SERVICES, INC.

NMS: JBHT

615 J.B. Hunt Corporate Drive
Lowell, AR 72745
Phone: 479 820-0000
Fax: –
Web: www.jbhunt.com

CEO: John N. Roberts
CFO: David G. Mee
HR: –
FYE: December 31
Type: Public

When it comes to hauling freight J.B. Hunt Transport Services knows how to deliver. Its intermodal unit the company's largest maintains about 4000 tractors 4750 drivers and more than 73000 pieces of trailing equipment and moves customers' cargo by combinations of truck and train. JBI's dedicated contract services unit supplies customers with drivers and equipment; it operates about 6500 company-owned trucks. The company's truckload transportation unit provides dry freight transportation with a fleet of about 1300 tractors. A fourth business segment integrated capacity solutions (ICS) manages freight transportation via third-party carriers as well as J.B. Hunt equipment.

	Annual Growth	12/10	12/11	12/12	12/13	12/14
Sales ($ mil.)	12.9%	3,793.5	4,526.8	5,055.0	5,584.6	6,165.4
Net income ($ mil.)	17.1%	199.6	257.0	310.4	342.4	374.8
Market value ($ mil.)	19.9%	4,757.4	5,254.0	6,960.7	9,011.3	9,821.5
Employees	5.6%	16,233	15,631	16,475	18,467	20,158

HUNTER DOUGLAS INC.

1 Blue Hill Plaza
Pearl River NY 10965
Phone: 845-664-7000
Fax: 914-381-6601
Web: www.castleoil.com

CEO: Marvin B Hopkins
CFO: Leen Reijtenbagh
HR: –
FYE: December 31
Type: Subsidiary

Don't move Hunter Douglas has got you covered — well at least it has your "windows" covered. Hunter Douglas the North American subsidiary of Netherlands-based Hunter Douglas N.V. makes a variety of blinds shades and shutters. The company markets its window coverings under such brand names as Country Woods and Chalet Woods (wood blinds) Silhouette (shades) Palm Beach (custom shutters) Vignette (Roman shades) Luminette (privacy sheers) and Duette (honeycomb shades). In addition to its own sales outlets and specialty blind and home decor stores Hunter Douglas sells its window products through independent dealers in the US and Canada.

HUNTINGTON BANCSHARES, INC

NMS: HBAN

41 South High Street
Columbus, OH 43287
Phone: 614 480-8300
Fax: –
Web: www.huntington.com

CEO: Stephen D. (Steve) Steinour
CFO: Howell D. (Mac) McCullough
HR: Rob Nussbaum
FYE: December 31
Type: Public

Huntington Bancshares is the holding company for The Huntington National Bank which operates about 700 branches in Ohio Michigan and four other Midwestern and Northeastern states. In addition to traditional retail and commercial banking services the bank offers mortgage banking capital market services equipment leasing brokerage services wealth and investment management trust and estate services and personal and business insurance. The company's automobile finance business provides car loans to consumers and real estate and inventory finance to car dealerships throughout the Midwest and Northeast. Founded in 1966 the company boasts total assets of more than $65 billion.

	Annual Growth	12/10	12/11	12/12	12/13	12/14
Assets ($ mil.)	5.4%	53,819.6	54,450.7	56,153.2	59,476.3	66,298.0
Net income ($ mil.)	19.3%	312.3	542.6	641.0	638.7	632.4
Market value ($ mil.)	11.2%	5,574.7	4,454.9	5,185.2	7,830.5	8,536.5
Employees	1.2%	11,341	11,245	11,806	11,964	11,873

HUNTINGTON HOSPITAL

270 Park Ave.
Huntington NY 11743
Phone: 631-351-2000
Fax: 631-351-2586
Web: www.hunthosp.org

CEO: Michael J Dowling
CFO: Kevin Lawlor
HR: –
FYE: December 31
Type: Subsidiary

Even the wealthy residents of the Gold Coast feel a little poor from time to time. When they do Huntington Hospital is there to help. Part of the North Shore-Long Island Jewish Health System Huntington Hospital is a 408 bed not-for-profit tertiary care center providing a comprehensive range of medical services to residents of Huntington New York and Long Island's North Shore. Along with general surgical services the hospital provides specialty cardiac cancer and pediatric care. Huntington also operates a number of outpatient diagnostic and community clinics where patients can turn for primary care physical rehabilitation or specialized care for other ailments. The hospital was established in 1916.

HUNTINGTON INGALLS INDUSTRIES INC.

NYSE: HII

4101 Washington Ave.
Newport News VA 23607-2770
Phone: 757-380-2000
Fax: 757-380-4713
Web: www.huntingtoningalls.com

CEO: –
CFO: –
HR: –
FYE: December 31
Type: Public

For 40 years Huntington Ingalls Industries (HII) — formerly Newport News and Ship Systems and most recently a Northrop Grumman sector — has been the sole builder of the US Navy's nuclear aircraft carriers. Rivaling nuclear submarine builder General Dynamics HII is the largest naval shipbuilder in the world; it also maintains refuels and repairs nuclear aircraft carriers and submarines. In addition HII supplies expeditionary warfare ships surface combatants submarines commercial oil hull tankers and Coast Guard surface ships as well as provides aftermarket fleet support. Almost off its offerings are sold to the US government. Northrop Grumman spun off its shipbuilding sector in spring 2011.

HUNTINGTON INGALLS INDUSTRIES, INC. NYS: HII

4101 Washington Avenue
Newport News, VA 23607
Phone: 757 380-2000
Fax: –
Web: www.huntingtoningalls.com

CEO: C. Michael (Mike) Petters
CFO: Barbara A. (Barb) Niland
HR: Edmond Hughes
FYE: December 31
Type: Public

For 40 years Huntington Ingalls Industries (HII) — formerly a Northrop Grumman subsidiary — has been the sole builder of the US Navy's nuclear aircraft carriers. Rivaling nuclear submarine builder General Dynamics HII is the largest naval shipbuilder in the world; it also maintains refuels and repairs nuclear aircraft carriers and submarines. In addition HII supplies expeditionary warfare ships surface combatants submarines commercial oil hull tankers and Coast Guard surface ships as well as provides aftermarket fleet support. Almost off its offerings are sold to the US government. Northrop Grumman spun off HII in spring 2011.

	Annual Growth	12/10	12/11	12/12	12/13	12/14
Sales ($ mil.)	1.9%	–	6,575.0	6,708.0	6,820.0	6,957.0
Net income ($ mil.)	–	–	(94.0)	146.0	261.0	338.0
Market value ($ mil.)	53.2%	–	1,510.8	2,093.3	4,347.5	5,431.8
Employees	(0.6%)	39,000	38,000	37,000	3,800	38,000

HUNTON & WILLIAMS LLP

Riverfront Plaza East Tower 951 E. Byrd St.
Richmond VA 23219-4074
Phone: 804-788-8200
Fax: 804-788-8218
Web: www.hunton.com

CEO: –
CFO: –
HR: –
FYE: March 31
Type: Private - Partnershi

With about 20 offices that span not only the US but also the Asia/Pacific region and Europe law firm Hunton & Williams has expanded well beyond its Virginia home. Overall the firm has more than 800 attorneys. Hunton & Williams focuses primarily on representing clients from industries such as energy financial services and life sciences but the firm has 100 separate practice specialties such as bankruptcy corporate transactions commercial litigation intellectual property and regulatory law. Major clients have included Altria MasterCard Smithfield Foods and Wells Fargo. Henry Anderson Eppa Hunton Beverley Munford and E. Randolph Williams founded Hunton & Williams in 1901.

HUNTSMAN CORP NYS: HUN

500 Huntsman Way
Salt Lake City, UT 84108
Phone: 801 584-5700
Fax: –
Web: www.huntsman.com

CEO: Peter R. Huntsman
CFO: J. Kimo Esplin
HR: Wade Rogers
FYE: December 31
Type: Public

Huntsman Corporation has a long track record of successfully stalking profits in the world's chemical marketplace. The global chemical manufacturer operates its businesses through subsidiary Huntsman International. Its broad range of products include MDI (methylene diphenyl diisocyanate) amines surfactants epoxy-based polymers and polyurethanes. Huntsman's chemicals are sold worldwide to a variety of customers in the adhesives construction products electronics medical and packaging industries. Huntsman operates manufacturing and research and development facilities in more than 30 countries worldwide. It gets 53% of its revenues from the US.

	Annual Growth	12/11	12/12	12/13	12/14	12/15
Sales ($ mil.)	(2.1%)	11,221.0	11,187.0	11,079.0	11,578.0	10,299.0
Net income ($ mil.)	(21.7%)	247.0	363.0	128.0	323.0	93.0
Market value ($ mil.)	3.3%	2,370.8	3,769.6	5,832.2	5,400.7	2,695.6
Employees	5.7%	12,000	12,000	12,000	16,000	15,000

HUNTSMAN INTERNATIONAL LLC

500 Huntsman Way
Salt Lake City UT 84108
Phone: 801-584-5700
Fax: 801-584-5781
Web: www.huntsman.com

CEO: Peter R Huntsman
CFO: J Kimo Esplin
HR: –
FYE: December 31
Type: Subsidiary

Chemistry is key to any successful relationship and good chemistry is what Huntsman is all about. Huntsman International operates in five business segments: polyurethanes advanced materials textile effects performance products and pigments. The company manufactures surfactants (used in cleaning and personal care products) and performance chemicals like polyurethanes propylene oxides and propylene glycol. Its polyurethanes segment is the company's largest representing 39% of 2011 sales. Huntsman ranks among the largest makers of titanium dioxide the most commonly used white pigment with 15% of the world market. Huntsman International operates the business of parent Huntsman Corporation.

HURCO COMPANIES, INC. NMS: HURC

One Technology Way
Indianapolis, IN 46268
Phone: 317 293-5309
Fax: 317 328-2811
Web: www.hurco.com

CEO: Michael Doar
CFO: Sonja K. McClelland
HR: –
FYE: October 31
Type: Public

When it comes to improving automation and productivity Hurco happily helps. The company designs and makes computerized metal cutting and forming machine tools such as vertical machining (mills) and turning (lathes) centers as well as the software that automates the machinery. Its machines are manufactured and assembled by Taiwan subsidiary Hurco Manufacturing using components produced by neighboring contract suppliers. Hurco markets its five-axis machines through its TM/TMM TMX and VMX series and other specialty product lines. It sells to customers in the aerospace/military automotive computers/electronics energy medical equipment and transportation industries spanning about 50 countries.

	Annual Growth	10/11	10/12	10/13	10/14	10/15
Sales ($ mil.)	5.0%	180.4	203.1	192.8	222.3	219.4
Net income ($ mil.)	9.9%	11.1	15.6	8.2	15.1	16.2
Market value ($ mil.)	0.7%	171.1	150.6	160.5	252.4	176.0
Employees	10.3%	520	560	625	617	769

HURLEY MEDICAL CENTER INC.

1 HURLEY PLZ
FLINT, MI 485035902
Phone: 810-257-9000
Fax: –
Web: www.hurleymc.com

CEO: –
CFO: Kevin Murphy
HR: Jay Kitson
FYE: June 30
Type: Private

A community hospital owned by the City of Flint Hurley Medical Center is a teaching hospital serving Genesee Lapeer and Shiawassee counties in eastern Michigan. The 440-bed acute care facility is affiliated with the medical schools of Michigan State University and The University of Michigan. It provides care in areas such as cancer mental health rehabilitation surgery and women's health and it is a regional center for pediatrics. Hurley Medical Center also offers advanced specialty care such as trauma care neonatal intensive care kidney transplantation burn medicine and bariatric (weight loss) surgery. The center was founded in 1908 and is owned by the state of Michigan.

	Annual Growth	03/05	03/06	03/07	03/08*	06/08
Sales ($ mil.)	–	–	–	–	250.1	350.2
Net income ($ mil.)	–	–	–	–	0.2	3.8
Market value ($ mil.)	–	–	–	–	–	–
Employees	–	–	–	–	–	2,884

*Fiscal year change

HURON CONSULTING GROUP INC

NMS: HURN

550 West Van Buren Street
Chicago, IL 60607
Phone: 312 583-8700
Fax: –
Web: www.huronconsultinggroup.com

CEO: James H. Roth
CFO: C. Mark Hussey
HR: –
FYE: December 31
Type: Public

Huron Consulting Group aims to help keep companies sailing smoothly but the firm also will dredge through financial statements to address issues that cause businesses to sink. The firm provides a variety of financial consulting services to corporate clients that are in financial distress or involved in other legal and regulatory disputes. Its more than 1400 consultants offer forensic accounting and economic analysis expertise and often serve as expert witnesses. The firm's operational consulting services are delivered primarily to health care and education enterprises and to law firms.

	Annual Growth	12/10	12/11	12/12	12/13	12/14
Sales ($ mil.)	10.1%	604.6	657.9	681.7	787.8	889.2
Net income ($ mil.)	74.5%	8.5	20.5	36.4	66.4	79.1
Market value ($ mil.)	26.8%	605.2	886.3	770.8	1,433.8	1,564.7
Employees	13.1%	1,757	1,992	2,283	2,596	2,870

HUSCH BLACKWELL LLP

4801 Main St. Ste. 1000
Kansas City MO 64112
Phone: 816-983-8000
Fax: 816-983-8080
Web: www.huschblackwell.com

CEO: Gregory Smith
CFO: –
HR: –
FYE: December 31
Type: Private - Partnershi

Law firm Husch Blackwell focuses on litigation and business services. Within those broad areas the firm maintains practices such as commercial transactions environmental intellectual property labor and employment mergers and acquisitions and real estate. Overall it has about 600 lawyers in more than a dozen offices mainly in the midwestern US but also in Washington DC and in London. Husch Blackwell was formed in 2008 when Kansas City-based Blackwell Sanders merged with St. Louis-based Husch & Eppenberger. The firm has two headquarters based in Kansas City and St. Louis.

HUSSMANN INTERNATIONAL INC.

12999 St. Charles Rock Rd.
Bridgeton MO 63044-2483
Phone: 314-291-2000
Fax: 314-298-4756
Web: www.hussmann.com

CEO: Dennis Gipson
CFO: Tim Figge
HR: –
FYE: December 31
Type: Subsidiary

Refrigeration expert Hussmann International helps supermarkets and convenience stores chill out. The company makes and sells refrigerated display cases and other refrigerated and non-refrigerated systems including beverage coolers walk-in storage coolers and island delis to the commercial food industry. Hussmann was acquired by industrial giant Ingersoll-Rand (IR) in 2000 and along with Thermo King formed IR's Climate Control division. IR sold a 60% stake in Hussmann to turnaround specialist Clayton Dubilier & Rice for $370 million in 2011.

HUSSON UNIVERSITY

1 COLLEGE CIR
BANGOR, ME 044012929
Phone: 207-941-7000
Fax: –
Web: www.husson.edu

CEO: Robert A Clark
CFO: Craig Hadley
HR: –
FYE: June 30
Type: Private

If the hustle and bustle of college life attracts you Husson University is probably not the place for you. The university tucked away on 175 acres of fields and forests primarily caters to rural and small town residents in its home state of Maine. Enrollment is about 2500 students about 20% of whom are seeking graduate degrees. The school has about 70 faculty members and a 19-to-1 student teacher ratio. Husson offers both undergraduate and graduate degreee programs in such academic disciplines as business communications education health language studies and science and humanities. The school was founded in 1898.

	Annual Growth	06/07	06/08	06/09	06/10	06/13
Sales ($ mil.)	–	–	0.0	35.6	40.5	53.2
Net income ($ mil.)	–	–	–	0.0	2.4	4.1
Market value ($ mil.)	–	–	–	–	–	–
Employees	–	–	–	–	–	520

HUTCHESON MEDICAL CENTER INC.

100 GROSS CRESCENT CIR
FORT OGLETHORPE, GA 30742-3669
Phone: 706-858-2000
Fax: –
Web: www.hutcheson.org

CEO: Farrell Hayes
CFO: Bill J Otting
HR: –
FYE: September 30
Type: Private

Hutcheson Medical Center is a community hospital that serves the residents of Catoosa Dade and Walker counties in northwestern Georgia. Founded in 1953 the nearly 200-bed hospital provides specialty services such as emergency medicine orthopedics cancer treatment physical therapy and women's and children's care as well as home health and hospice services. The hospital has more than 200 physicians on its medical staff. Hutcheson Medical Center also operates the 110-bed Parkside Nursing Home an outpatient surgery center and family practice medical clinics.

	Annual Growth	09/05	09/06	09/07	09/08	09/09
Sales ($ mil.)	(4.1%)	–	111.9	115.5	123.2	98.6
Net income ($ mil.)	–	–	(1.0)	0.3	(0.5)	(6.6)
Market value ($ mil.)	–	–	–	–	–	–
Employees	–	–	–	–	–	530

HUTCHINSON TECHNOLOGY INC.

NMS: HTCH

40 West Highland Park Drive N.E.
Hutchinson, MN 55350
Phone: 320 587-3797
Fax: –
Web: www.htch.com

CEO: Richard J Penn
CFO: David P Radloff
HR: –
FYE: September 27
Type: Public

Suspensions at Hutchinson Technology have nothing to do with getting kicked out of school. The company is a top global maker of disk drive suspension assemblies. These support the read-write head above the spinning magnetic disk in hard drives typically at a height of about a millionth of an inch — 3000 times thinner than a piece of paper. The company's products include conventional assemblies trace suspension assemblies and accessories such as base plates and flexures. Hutchinson serves OEMs primarily in Asia which accounts for most of its revenue. The company generates minimal sales from biomeasurment devices for the healthcare market.

	Annual Growth	09/11	09/12	09/13	09/14	09/15
Sales ($ mil.)	(2.4%)	278.1	248.6	249.6	261.1	252.8
Net income ($ mil.)	–	(55.6)	(48.6)	(35.1)	(40.4)	(39.1)
Market value ($ mil.)	(8.4%)	67.1	58.7	118.7	120.7	47.3
Employees	1.0%	2,317	2,060	2,436	2,489	2,412

HUTTIG BUILDING PRODUCTS, INC.
NAS: HBP

555 Maryville University Drive, Suite 400
St. Louis, MO 63141
Phone: 314 216-2600
Fax: –

CEO: Jon P Vrabely
CFO: –
HR: –
FYE: December 31
Type: Public

Hut one! Hut two! Huttig Building Products works to make buying building supplies a snap. Huttig is one of the US's largest distributors of millwork building materials and wood products for new housing construction and remodeling and repair. Huttig sells doors windows moldings trusses wall panels lumber and other supplies through more than 25 distribution centers in some 40 states covering a substantial portion of the US housing market. The centers primarily sell to building materials dealers (such as 84 Lumber Stock Building Supply) buying groups home centers and industrial users. Huttig's products typically end up in the hands of professional builders and contractors.

	Annual Growth	12/10	12/11	12/12	12/13	12/14
Sales ($ mil.)	7.5%	467.7	478.7	520.5	561.5	623.7
Net income ($ mil.)	–	(18.9)	(13.2)	(0.5)	3.2	2.2
Market value ($ mil.)	37.1%	23.3	12.8	39.3	94.8	82.3
Employees	2.7%	900	900	900	1,000	1,000

HY-VEE INC.

5820 WESTOWN PKWY
WEST DES MOINES, IA 502668223
Phone: 515-267-2800
Fax: –
Web: www.hy-vee.com

CEO: Randy Edeker
CFO: Mike Skokan
HR: Leigh Walters
FYE: September 28
Type: Private

Give Hy-Vee a high five for being one of the largest privately owned US supermarket chains despite serving some modestly sized towns in the Midwest. The company runs some 235 stores in eight Midwestern states. About half of its supermarkets are in Iowa as are most of its 20-plus Hy-Vee drugstores. It distributes products to its stores through several subsidiaries including Lomar Distributing (specialty foods) and Perishable Distributors of Iowa (fresh foods). Other activities include construction and specialty pharmacies. Charles Hyde and David Vredenburg founded the employee-owned firm in 1930. It takes its name from a combination of its founders' names.

	Annual Growth	10/10	10/11*	09/12	09/13	09/14
Sales ($ mil.)	–	–	0.0	7,682.0	8,014.2	8,014.2
Net income ($ mil.)	–	–	–	0.0	0.0	0.0
Market value ($ mil.)	–	–	–	–	–	–
Employees	–	–	–	–	–	62,000

*Fiscal year change

HYATT HOTELS CORP
NYS: H

71 South Wacker Drive, 12th Floor
Chicago, IL 60606
Phone: 312 750-1234
Fax: –
Web: www.hyatt.com

CEO: Mark S. Hoplamazian
CFO: Patrick J. (Pat) Grismer
HR: Robert W. K. Webb
FYE: December 31
Type: Public

Travelers interested in luxury lodgings can check in for the Hyatt touch. The company is one of the world's top operators of luxury hotels and resorts with more than 500 managed franchised and owned properties in nearly 50 countries. Its core Hyatt Regency brand offers hospitality services targeted primarily to business travelers and upscale vacationers. The firm also operates the upscale full service Hyatt Grand Hyatt and Andaz brands as well as Park Hyatt (luxury) Hyatt Place (select service) and Hyatt Summerfield Suites (extended stay) brands. Although Hyatt Hotels was formed in 2004 the Hyatt chain traces its roots back to 1957.

	Annual Growth	12/10	12/11	12/12	12/13	12/14
Sales ($ mil.)	5.8%	3,527.0	3,698.0	3,949.0	4,184.0	4,415.0
Net income ($ mil.)	51.1%	66.0	113.0	88.0	207.0	344.0
Market value ($ mil.)	7.1%	6,822.0	5,611.4	5,750.1	7,373.6	8,976.2
Employees	0.0%	45,000	50,000	45,000	45,000	45,000

HYCROFT MINING CORP
NBB: ANVG Q

9790 Gateway Drive, Suite 200
Reno, NV 89521
Phone: 775 358-4455
Fax: 775 358-4458
Web: www.alliednevada.com

CEO: Randy E Buffington
CFO: Stephen M Jones
HR: Rebecca Rivenbark
FYE: December 31
Type: Public

All that glitters is not gold; some of it's silver. That's the story at Allied Nevada Gold a mining company that produces gold primarily and silver as a by-product from its property in Nevada. Its wholly owned Hycroft Mine sitting on 96 sq. mi. has proven and probable mineral reserves of about 3 million ounces of gold and nearly 50 million ounces of silver. The company is conducting feasibility studies for a mill on the property that would process sulfide and other high oxide ores. Allied Nevada Gold also explores for gold silver and other minerals on more than 100 properties in the state. The company was spun off from Vista Gold in 2007 when it acquired its former parent's Nevada mining operations.

	Annual Growth	12/10	12/11	12/12	12/13	12/14
Sales ($ mil.)	24.1%	130.9	152.0	214.6	267.9	310.4
Net income ($ mil.)	–	34.1	36.7	47.7	1.4	(518.9)
Market value ($ mil.)	(57.4%)	3,320.1	3,821.1	3,802.2	448.0	109.8
Employees	18.7%	231	291	742	428	459

HYDROMER, INC.
NBB: HYDI

35 Industrial Parkway
Branchburg, NJ 08876
Phone: 908 722-5000
Fax: 908 526-3633
Web: www.hydromer.com

CEO: –
CFO: Robert Y Lee
HR: Ann Wallin
FYE: June 30
Type: Public

Hydromer would say its products become lubricious when wet. Bon Jovi preferred the term "slippery" but it amounts to the same thing. The company makes lubricating and water-resistant coatings for use in medical pharmaceutical cosmetic industrial and veterinary markets. Its products include lubricated medical devices hydro-gels for drugs anti-fog coatings marine hull protective coatings barrier dips for dairy cows and intermediaries for hair and skin care products. Services include research and development medical device manufacturing (through subsidiary Biosearch Medical Products) and contract coating. Chairman and CEO Manfred Dyck owns a third of Hydromer.

	Annual Growth	06/10	06/11	06/12	06/13	06/14
Sales ($ mil.)	(0.8%)	6.2	5.5	5.7	5.8	6.0
Net income ($ mil.)	–	(0.6)	(0.6)	(0.4)	0.3	0.1
Market value ($ mil.)	(3.4%)	4.7	3.1	6.0	4.8	4.1
Employees	(5.7%)	48	43	36	–	38

HYDRON TECHNOLOGIES INC.
OTC: HTEC

4400 34th St. North Ste. F
St. Petersburg FL 33714
Phone: 727-342-5050
Fax: 727-344-3920
Web: www.hydron.com

CEO: Helen Canetano
CFO: William Lauby
HR: –
FYE: September 30
Type: Public

The magic is in the moisture at Hydron Technologies. The company focuses on developing skin care products that contain microbubbles of pure oxygen used in treating the epidermis and underlying tissues. Hydron Technologies also manufactures personal and oral care products that contain its moisture-attracting ingredient the Hydron polymer. The company distributes about 40 skin hair and sun care products as well as bath and body items through its Web site. It also produces private-label skin care items and ships them to contract manufacturers.

HYNIX SEMICONDUCTOR AMERICA INC.

3101 N. 1st St.
San Jose CA 95134
Phone: 408-232-8000
Fax: 408-232-8103
Web: hsa.hynix.com

CEO: Kun Chul Suh
CFO: –
HR: –
FYE: December 31
Type: Subsidiary

Hynix Semiconductor America (HSA) helps Hynix get a fix on its American markets. The company is the North American branch of Hynix Semiconductor. HSA's scope includes the development sales marketing and distribution of semiconductors as well as R&D activities that support Hynix. DRAMs static RAMs (SRAMs) flash memory devices and application-specific integrated circuits are just some of the product areas that HSA specializes in along with embedded flash drives for MP3 players video-game consoles mobile phones and other consumer electronics. Formerly part of the South Korea-based Hyundai conglomerate Hynix is a leading maker of computer memory chips.

HYPERDYNAMICS CORPORATION   NYSE AMEX: HDY

1 Sugar Creek Center Blvd. Ste. 125
Sugar Land TX 77478-3560
Phone: 713-353-9400
Fax: 713-353-9421
Web: www.hypd.com

CEO: Ray Leonard
CFO: David Wesson
HR: –
FYE: June 30
Type: Public

Not as hyper as it was but still dynamic Hyperdynamics has shifted its business focus from IT consulting services to oil and gas exploration primarily in Africa. Its SCS Corporation subsidiary concentrates on developing an oil and gas concession located offshore in the Republic of Guinea in West Africa. Hyperdynamics' HYD Resources subsidiary and gas exploration and production company focuses on low-risk shallow exploration projects in Louisiana where in 2008 it held proved reserves of 150435 barrels of oil. Chairman Kent Watts who stepped down as CEO in 2009 owns 17% of Hyperdynamics.

HYPERTENSION DIAGNOSTICS INC.   OTC: HDII

2915 Waters Rd. Ste. 108
Eagan MN 55121
Phone: 651-687-9999
Fax: 651-687-0485
Web: www.hdi-pulsewave.com

CEO: Kenneth W Brimmer
CFO: Kenneth W Brimmer
HR: –
FYE: June 30
Type: Public

Hypertension Diagnostics can tell if your cardiovascular system is about to go snap crackle and pop. The company's noninvasive instruments measure the elasticity of arteries helping physicians assess patients' risk for cardiovascular disease. Its CR-2000 Research System is marketed for research purposes to government agencies pharmaceutical companies academic research centers and cardiovascular research centers worldwide; drug heavyweights AstraZeneca and Pfizer are among the system's users. The CVProfilor DO-2020 and the CVProfilor MD-3000 are intended for general physicians cardiologists and other health care practitioners in the US and abroad.

HYSTER-YALE MATERIALS HANDLING, INC.   NYS: HY

5875 Landerbrook Drive, Suite 300
Cleveland, OH 44124-4069
Phone: 440 449-9600
Fax: –
Web: www.hyster-yale.com

CEO: Alfred M. Rankin
CFO: Kenneth C. Schilling
HR: –
FYE: December 31
Type: Public

Hyster-Yale Materials Handling isn't concerned about pleasing your palate but it does want to move your pallets — and containers. A leading lift truck manufacturer the company designs manufactures and sells a variety of forklifts and other lift truck products through its NACCO Materials Handling subsidiary. Its trucks are sold under the Hyster Yale and UTILEV brands and include everything from hand-controlled pallet lifts to heavy-duty container handlers. The company which operates facilities in North America Europe and Asia was spun off from NACCO Industries in 2012 and restructured as an independently operated public company. Hyster and Yale branded products originally made and sold in Japan have been sold worldwide since the early 1970s.

	Annual Growth	12/10	12/11	12/12	12/13	12/14
Sales ($ mil.)	11.3%	1,801.9	2,540.8	2,469.1	2,666.3	2,767.2
Net income ($ mil.)	35.7%	32.4	82.6	98.0	110.0	109.8
Market value ($ mil.)	22.5%	–	–	792.6	1,513.0	1,188.9
Employees	1.9%	5,000	5,300	5,400	5,100	5,400

HYTEK MICROSYSTEMS INC.

400 Hot Springs Rd.
Carson City NV 89706
Phone: 775-883-0820
Fax: 775-883-0827
Web: www.hytek.com

CEO: John Cole
CFO: John Lowri
HR: Roe Borg
FYE: December 31
Type: Private

Funny spelling serious business: Hytek Microsystems makes microelectronic circuits. The company specializes in thick-film hybrid circuits. "Thick-film" refers to the procedure for printing circuits on a ceramic substrate "hybrid" to the fact that they comprise smaller components such as semiconductors. Hytek's custom products and standard circuits are used in medical devices communication and satellite systems oil exploration equipment and military and industrial electronics. Other products include delay lines thermoelectric cooler controllers and laser diode drivers. Established in 1974 Hytek went public in 1983 and was acquired by Natel Engineering in 2005.

I.D. SYSTEMS, INC. (DE)   NMS: IDSY

123 Tice Boulevard
Woodcliff Lake, NJ 07677
Phone: 201 996-9000
Fax: –
Web: www.id-systems.com

CEO: Kenneth S Ehrman
CFO: Ned Mavrommatis
HR: –
FYE: December 31
Type: Public

I.D. Systems has taken its tracking business on the road. The company's products track analyze and control the movements of objects such as packages and vehicles. Its systems use radio-frequency identification (RFID) technology and tiny computers attached to the object to be monitored and users can access tracking data via the Internet. The company is focused on vehicle management rental car package tracking and airport ground security applications. Customers include 3M the FAA Ford Hallmark Cards Target the US Postal Service (42% of sales) and Wal-Mart Stores (41%).

	Annual Growth	12/10	12/11	12/12	12/13	12/14
Sales ($ mil.)	15.3%	25.9	39.3	44.6	39.9	45.6
Net income ($ mil.)	–	(12.6)	(4.0)	(2.6)	(7.5)	(11.6)
Market value ($ mil.)	19.0%	42.8	60.6	74.6	74.2	85.7
Employees	9.4%	86	101	103	104	123

I/OMAGIC CORPORATION
OTC: IOMG

4 Marconi
Irvine CA 92618
Phone: 949-707-4800
Fax: 949-855-3550
Web: www.iomagic.com

CEO: Tony Shahbaz
CFO: –
HR: –
FYE: December 31
Type: Public

I/OMagic has some input regarding computer peripheral output. It designs and markets optical storage products such as CD-ROM and DVD-ROM playback and read-write devices. Other products include audio cards digital photo frames external hard drives headphones and Web cameras. The company also markets LCD-based HDTVs and home theater speakers through its Digital Research Technologies (DRT) division. I/OMagic sells to retailers such as Staples (nearly half of sales) OfficeMax and Costco in the US and Canada. Other significant customers include distributors Tech Data (29% of sales) and D&H Distributing. The company subcontracts the manufacturing of most of its products.

IA GLOBAL INC.
OTC: IAGI

101 California St. Ste. 2450
San Francisco CA 94111
Phone: 415-946-8828
Fax: 415-946-8801
Web: www.iaglobalinc.com

CEO: –
CFO: –
HR: –
FYE: March 31
Type: Public

IA Global has made the call to the Pacific Rim region. The holding company is focused on growing its existing businesses and making strategic acquisitions in Asia. Its primary holdings revolve around Global Hotline a Japanese business process outsourcing (BPO) company that owns two call centers and offers telemarketing services medical insurance and other products to customers in Japan. IA Global also owns call center operations in the Philippines along with parts of Japanese firms GPlus Media (online media) Slate Consulting (executive search) Taicom Securities (financial services) and Australian Secured Financial Limited (private loans and real estate investment). IA Global was formed in 1998.

IAC/INTERACTIVECORP
NMS: IAC

555 West 18th Street
New York, NY 10011
Phone: 212 314-7300
Fax: –
Web: www.iac.com

CEO: Chris Terrill
CFO: Jeffrey W Kip
HR: –
FYE: December 31
Type: Public

IAC/InterActiveCorp (IAC) satisfies inquisitive minds. The Internet conglomerate owns more than 150 brands including search engine Ask.com local guide Citysearch (part of advertising network CityGrid Media) dating site Match.com About.com video service Vimeo and home service provider network HomeAdvisor. Other IAC holdings include Shoebuy.com Dictionary.com and a majority stake in Connected Ventures the parent company of entertainment site CollegeHumor.com. It also operates current affairs Web magazine Daily Beast and publishes Newsweek magazine through its majority-owned The Newsweek/Daily Beast Company.

	Annual Growth	12/10	12/11	12/12	12/13	12/14
Sales ($ mil.)	17.4%	1,636.8	2,059.4	2,800.9	3,023.0	3,109.5
Net income ($ mil.)	42.9%	99.4	174.2	159.3	285.8	414.9
Market value ($ mil.)	20.6%	2,415.0	3,584.6	3,975.2	5,776.7	5,115.2
Employees	11.8%	3,200	3,200	4,200	4,000	5,000

IANYWHERE SOLUTIONS INC.

1 Sybase Dr.
Dublin CA 94568-7976
Phone: 519-883-6898
Fax: 519-747-4971
Web: www.ianywhere.com

CEO: –
CFO: –
HR: –
FYE: December 31
Type: Subsidiary

Information is key and iAnywhere knows that. The company's wireless mobile enterprise platform is used by customers to access and synchronize corporate data web based content and email wherever they're using smart phones PDAs and laptops. Its SQL Anywhere Studio is a similar product aimed at small to medium-sized businesses. iAnywhere has a strong presence in sectors that depend heavily on time-sensitive information such as banks securities firms and pharmaceutical companies. Customers include the FBI and Prudential. iAnywhere is a subsidiary of Sybase.

IASIS HEALTHCARE CORPORATION

117 Seaboard Ln. Bldg. E
Franklin TN 37067
Phone: 615-844-2747
Fax: 615-846-3006
Web: www.iasishealthcare.com

CEO: David R White
CFO: John M Doyle
HR: –
FYE: September 30
Type: Private

If you're sick in the city or have a stomach ache in the suburbs IASIS Healthcare provides a medical oasis. The company owns and operates 18 acute care hospitals and one behavioral health facility (with some 4300 beds total) in Arizona Colorado Florida Louisiana Nevada Texas and Utah. IASIS also operates several outpatient facilities and other centers providing ancillary services such as radiation therapy diagnostic imaging and ambulatory surgery. Its Health Choice subsidiary is a Medicaid and Medicare managed health plan that serves about 200000 individuals in Arizona and Utah. An investor group led by TPG Capital owns the lion's share of the company.

IASO PHARMA INC.

12707 High Bluff Dr. Ste. 200
San Diego CA 92130
Phone: 858-350-4312
Fax: +86-10-5123-8866
Web: www.mienergy.com.cn

CEO: –
CFO: –
HR: –
FYE: December 31
Type: Private

IASO Pharma aims to cure what ails ya. The development-stage drug company focuses on in-licensing potential treatments for bacterial and fungal infections. Its lead candidate is an antibiotic for the treatment of respiratory tract infections. Other potential products include an antifungal used to treat yeast and sinus infections and a process to improve the treatment of nail infections. IASO's candidates are in-licensed from Dong Wha Pharmaceutical UCB Celltech and Santee Biosciences. The company plans to exclusively license pretested candidates; it doesn't conduct any of its own discovery research. It was formed in 2006 as Pacific Beach Biosciences; it changed its name and filed to go public in 2010.

IBERDROLA RENEWABLES INC.

1125 NW Couch Ste. 700
Portland OR 97209
Phone: 503-796-7000
Fax: 503-796-6901
Web: www.iberdrolarenewables.us

CEO: –
CFO: I Merrick Kerr
HR: –
FYE: March 31
Type: Subsidiary

IBERDROLA Renewables (formerly PPM Energy) is a real power player in the energy industry. Part of IBERDROLA's global network IBERDROLA Renewables develops cogeneration power plants and wind farms; it has wind power generating capacity of about 4800 MW in operation (at more than 40 wind farms) and more than 23000 MW under construction or in the product pipeline in more than 20 states primarily in the Midwest and western US. IBERDROLA Renewables also offers solar power projects biomass cogeneration projetcs natural gas transmission storage and marketing and risk and asset management services. The company's customers include utilities industrial companies and other energy marketers.

IBERDROLA USA INC.

52 Farm View Dr.
New Gloucester ME 04260-5116
Phone: 207-688-6300
Fax: 207-688-4354
Web: www.iberdrolausa.com

CEO: Robert D Kump
CFO: Daniel Alcain
HR: –
FYE: December 31
Type: Subsidiary

Iberdrola USA (formerly Energy East) is a major regional player and the leading US operating subsidiary of IBERDROLA. The utility holding company (98% of its assets are in regulated utilities) distributes electricity and natural gas in the US northeast through Central Maine Power New York State Electric & Gas and Rochester Gas and Electric. Iberdrola USA serves about 2.7 million electricity and natural gas customers. Other operations include power generation gas transportation and processing telecommunications and energy infrastructure and management services.

IBERIABANK CORP   NMS: IBKC

200 West Congress Street
Lafayette, LA 70501
Phone: 337 521-4003
Fax: –
Web: www.iberiabank.com

CEO: Daryl G. Byrd
CFO: Anthony J. Restel
HR: Elizabeth A. (Beth) Ardoin
FYE: December 31
Type: Public

IBERIABANK Corp. serves up financial services with a Cajun flare. Through its flagship bank subsidiary also called IBERIABANK the holding company operates some 267 branches in Louisiana and five other southern states. It also has about 21 title insurance offices in Louisiana and Arkansas in addition to some 61 mortgage loan offices in a dozen states. Offering deposit products such as checking and savings accounts CDs and IRAs the bank uses funds gathered mainly to make loans. Commercial real estate and business loans make up nearly three-quarters of the company's loan portfolio which also includes consumer loans and residential mortgages. IBERIABANK Corp. has $13.4 billion in assets.

	Annual Growth	12/10	12/11	12/12	12/13	12/14
Assets ($ mil.)	12.0%	10,026.8	11,757.9	13,129.7	13,365.6	15,758.6
Net income ($ mil.)	21.2%	48.8	53.5	76.4	65.1	105.5
Market value ($ mil.)	2.3%	1,978.1	1,649.3	1,643.2	2,102.5	2,169.5
Employees	6.5%	2,193	2,645	2,758	2,638	2,825

IBW FINANCIAL CORPORATION   PINK SHEETS: IBWC

4812 Georgia Ave. NW
Washington DC 20011
Phone: 202-722-2000
Fax: 202-722-2040
Web: www.industrial-bank.com

CEO: B Doyle Mitchell Jr
CFO: –
HR: –
FYE: December 31
Type: Public

IBW Financial is the holding company for Industrial Bank one of the largest minority-owned banks in the US. Catering to the African-American community in and around Washington DC the bank offers standard personal and commercial services such as checking and savings accounts debit cards and cash management. It primarily writes real estate loans with residential mortgages and commercial mortgages each accounting for nearly 40% of its portfolio. Industrial Bank has about 10 branches and loan production offices in Washington DC and nearby parts of Maryland. The Mitchell family including CEO B. Doyle Mitchell Jr. whose grandfather founded the bank in 1934 holds a controlling stake in IBW Financial.

IC COMPLIANCE LLC

1065 E. Hillsdale Blvd. Ste. 300
Foster City CA 94404
Phone: 650-378-4150
Fax: 650-378-4157
Web: www.gotoicon.com

CEO: Teresa Creech
CFO: Keith Corbin
HR: Lisa Bell
FYE: December 31
Type: Private

IC Compliance (doing business as ICon Professional Services) keeps the IRS off the backs of companies with contingent workforces. The consulting firm ensures that its clients are in compliance with tax rules for independent contractors providing advice on employee classification guidelines IRS audit support tax reporting and invoice submission and other services. Additionally ICon offers outsourced payroll and benefits administration for certain classes of employees including non-independent contractors non-sourced workers and former employees. The firm was established in 1997.

ICAD INC   NAS: ICAD

98 Spit Brook Road, Suite 100
Nashua, NH 03062
Phone: 603 882-5200
Fax: –
Web: www.icadmed.com

CEO: –
CFO: Kevin Burns
HR: Denise Mitchell
FYE: December 31
Type: Public

Early detection is the best prevention in iCAD's eyes. The company targets the breast cancer detection market with its core SecondLook computer-aided detection (CAD) systems. The systems include workstations and analytical software that help radiologists better identify potential cancers in mammography images. iCAD sells models that can be used with film-based and digital mammography systems. In addition the company also makes similar CAD systems that are used with magnetic resonance imaging (MRI) systems to detect breast and prostate cancers. iCAD markets its products directly and through sales partnerships with the likes of GE Healthcare Siemens Medical Solutions Fuji Medical and Agfa.

	Annual Growth	12/10	12/11	12/12	12/13	12/14
Sales ($ mil.)	15.6%	24.6	28.7	28.3	33.1	43.9
Net income ($ mil.)	–	(6.2)	(37.6)	(9.4)	(7.6)	(1.0)
Market value ($ mil.)	61.4%	21.0	8.9	74.5	181.3	142.6
Employees	(0.3%)	146	110	101	102	144

ICAGEN INC.

4222 Emperor Blvd. Ste. 350
Durham NC 27703
Phone: 919-941-5206
Fax: 919-941-0813
Web: www.icagen.com

CEO: P Kay Wagoner PHD
CFO: Richard D Katz
HR: –
FYE: December 31
Type: Private

Icagen wants to set the market for ion channel modulators on fire. The development-stage biotech focuses on treatments for epilepsy asthma pain and inflammation by regulating the inflow into cells of such ions as calcium potassium and sodium. Icagen's lead candidate senicapoc for sickle cell disease died in 2007 following lackluster Phase III clinical trial results. The drug was being developed in a partnership with Johnson & Johnson subsidiary McNeil Consumer & Specialty Pharmaceuticals. Shortly thereafter Icagen announced a deal collaborating with Pfizer on the development of epilepsy and pain treatments. Then in 2011 the company decided to just go ahead and be acquired by Pfizer.

ICAHN ENTERPRISES LP

NMS: IEP

767 Fifth Avenue, Suite 4700
New York, NY 10153
Phone: 212 702-4300
Fax: –
Web: www.ielp.com

CEO: Keith Cozza
CFO: SungHwan Cho
HR: –
FYE: December 31
Type: Public

Icahn Enterprises has a can-do attitude when it comes to making money. The holding company has stakes in firms in a diverse array of industries including metals manufacturing energy real estate gaming and home fashion. Holdings include car parts maker Federal-Mogul; energy refinery and production company CVR; PSC Metals one of the largest scrap yard operators in the US; residential developer Bayswater which is active in Florida and Massachusetts; and WestPoint Home a maker of bed bath and other home products. Billionaire corporate raider Carl Icahn and his affiliates control his namesake firm.

	Annual Growth	12/10	12/11	12/12	12/13	12/14
Sales ($ mil.)	20.4%	9,119.0	11,855.0	15,654.0	20,682.0	19,157.0
Net income ($ mil.)	–	–	199.0	750.0	396.0	1,025.0	(373.0)
Market value ($ mil.)	27.3%	4,340.6	4,407.1	5,502.7	13,468.7	11,383.4
Employees	4.1%	56,647	59,559	60,665	59,565	66,559

ICF INTERNATIONAL INC

NMS: ICFI

9300 Lee Highway
Fairfax, VA 22031
Phone: 703 934-3000
Fax: –
Web: www.icfi.com

CEO: Sudhakar Kesavan
CFO: James C. Morgan
HR: –
FYE: December 31
Type: Public

Consultant ICF International sees opportunity — and most of its business — in government spending. The firm advises government entities and businesses on issues related to health human services and social programs as well as defense and homeland security energy and climate change and the environment. The company groups its consulting and information technology services into three main categories: advice implementation and evaluation and improvement. ICF International has more than 60 offices in Asia Canada Europe and South America. Almost 75% of its total revenue comes from government clients.

	Annual Growth	12/10	12/11	12/12	12/13	12/14
Sales ($ mil.)	8.3%	764.7	840.8	937.1	949.3	1,050.1
Net income ($ mil.)	10.2%	27.2	34.9	38.1	39.3	40.0
Market value ($ mil.)	12.4%	499.7	481.5	455.4	674.4	796.2
Employees	7.8%	3,700	4,000	4,500	4,500	5,000

iCIMS.COM INC

90 MATAWAN RD FL 500
MATAWAN, NJ 077472624
Phone: 732-847-1941
Fax: –
Web: www.icims.com

CEO: –
CFO: –
HR: John Teehan
FYE: December 31
Type: Private

Who says good help is hard to find? iCIMS provides Web-based applicant tracking and recruiting management software for corporate human resources professionals and third-party recruiters. The company's iCIMS Talent Platform which is designed to help businesses make their hiring processes more efficient includes software for screening and storing applicant information enabling online job applications tracking candidates monitoring performance after recruitment and managing post-employment processes. It sells its applications on a Software-as-a-Service basis. iCIMS targets recruiters midsized companies and large corporations. The company was founded in 1999 by Colin Day and George Lieu.

	Annual Growth	12/09	12/10	12/11	12/12	12/13
Sales ($ mil.)	22.7%	–	25.7	30.7	37.3	47.4
Net income ($ mil.)	16.8%	–	–	3.7	(3.4)	5.0
Market value ($ mil.)	–	–	–	–	–	–
Employees	–	–	–	–	–	240

ICL PERFORMANCE PRODUCTS LP

622 Emerson Rd. Ste. 500
St. Louis MO 63141-1160
Phone: 314-983-7500
Fax: 314-983-7638
Web: www.icl-pplp.com

CEO: Mark Volmer
CFO: Paul Schlessman
HR: Michael Bork
FYE: December 31
Type: Subsidiary

ICL Performance Products LP is phosphorific! The North American unit of the performance products segment of Israel Chemicals Limited (ICL) it produces phosphorus chemicals phosphoric acid and phosphate salts. The chemicals are used in foods cleaners water treatment flat-panel displays oral care products paints and coatings and pharmaceuticals. The company also manufactures flame retardants. ICL Performance Products operates plants in Brazil and the US (California Kansas Missouri and New Jersey). It represents about a quarter of its parent's total business.

ICON CAPITAL CORP.

100 5th Ave. 4th Fl.
New York NY 10011
Phone: 212-418-4700
Fax: 212-418-4739
Web: www.iconcapital.com

CEO: Micheal A Reisner
CFO: –
HR: Tamara Lawrie
FYE: March 31
Type: Private

Companies that need expensive equipment often say "I think ICON I think ICON." Specialty finance company ICON Capital buys and manages big-ticket leases through limited partnerships with more than 30000 investors. The partnerships are managed by ICON Capital which acquires pieces of equipment to lease to large corporate customers and provides specialty financing. Customers which have included Continental Airlines BP Wal-Mart J. C. Penney and FedEx rent such equipment as airplanes ocean vessels drilling rigs trailer equipment and telecommunications equipment. ICON has offices in the US Canada and the UK.

ICON HEALTH & FITNESS INC.

1500 S. 1000 West
Logan UT 84321
Phone: 435-750-5000
Fax: 435-750-3917
Web: www.iconfitness.com

CEO: Scott R Watterson
CFO: S Fred Beck
HR: -
FYE: May 31
Type: Private

ICON Health & Fitness has brawn as one of the leading US makers of home fitness equipment. Its products primarily include treadmills elliptical trainers and weight benches. Brands include NordicTrack HealthRider ProForm Image iFit Weslo and Weider. ICON also offers commercial equipment through its FreeMotion Fitness unit. It makes most of its products in Utah but it also has operations in Asia Australia Brazil Europe and Mexico. Products are sold through retailers (such as Sears Wal-Mart and Sports Authority) infomercials and the Web. The company was founded as a housewares importer in 1977. Bain Capital Credit Suisse and founders Scott Watterson and Gary Stevenson collectively own ICON.

ICON IDENTITY SOLUTIONS INC.

1418 ELMHURST RD
ELK GROVE VILLAGE, IL 600076417
Phone: 847-364-2250
Fax: -
Web: www.iconid.com

CEO: Kurt W. Ripkey
CFO: John Callan
HR: -
FYE: December 31
Type: Private

Icon Identity Solutions helps its customers avoid identity crises. The firm provides a variety of services related to the building of a company's brand through the use of signs and exterior graphics. Icon can help clients manage multiple sign projects on a global scale if needed. Its services include sign design permitting and manufacturing. Icon Identity Solutions is one arm of Icon Companies which also operates subsidiaries East Coast Sign Advertising and ImageCare Maintenance Services (IMS). IMS provides sign repair and maintenance. Past clients have included BMW's Mini unit and Citigroup.

	Annual Growth	12/08	12/09	12/11	12/12	12/13
Sales ($ mil.)	(4.0%)	-	116.5	112.4	106.4	98.9
Net income ($ mil.)	(27.2%)	-	-	9.2	6.7	4.9
Market value ($ mil.)	-	-	-	-	-	-
Employees	-	-	-	-	-	450

ICONIX BRAND GROUP INC   NMS: ICON

1450 Broadway
New York, NY 10018
Phone: 212 730-0030
Fax: 212 391-2057
Web: www.iconixbrand.com

CEO: F. Peter Cuneo
CFO: David K. Jones
HR: Aaron Kopelowitz
FYE: December 31
Type: Public

Once a shoemaker Iconix Brand Group has stepped it up as a licensing and brand management company. Its company-owned consumer and home brands are licensed to third parties that make and sell apparel footwear and a variety of other fashion and home products. Consumer brands in the Iconix stable include Badgley Mischka Danskin Ocean Pacific Mossimo London Fog Mudd and Rocawear; among the company's home brands are Cannon Fieldcrest and Waverly. The firm diversified through its high-profile purchase of the Peanuts cartoon brand from E. W. Scripps in 2010. Along with licensing the brands Iconix markets and promotes them through its in-house advertising and public relations services.

	Annual Growth	12/10	12/11	12/12	12/13	12/14
Sales ($ mil.)	8.5%	332.6	369.8	353.8	432.6	461.2
Net income ($ mil.)	11.5%	98.8	126.1	109.4	128.0	152.7
Market value ($ mil.)	15.0%	926.0	781.2	1,070.3	1,903.7	1,620.3
Employees	3.1%	133	129	148	151	150

ICONMA L.L.C.

850 STEPHENSON HWY
TROY, MI 480831152
Phone: 248-583-1930
Fax: -
Web: www.iconma.com

CEO: Claudine S George
CFO: -
HR: -
FYE: December 31
Type: Private

ICONMA offers companies a number of consulting and staffing services with a focus on information technology. Its staffing services include contract contract-to-hire and direct hire IT placement as well as staffing in the areas of engineering accounting/finance and professional. The firm also provides offshore software development services and other IT consulting and has a health care services division dedicated to the technology needs of insurance providers hospitals and other medical companies. Clients include Deutsche Bank Toyota and Anthem. Established in 2000 ICONMA has offices across the US and one in India.

	Annual Growth	12/05	12/06	12/07	12/08	12/09
Sales ($ mil.)	(47.8%)	-	-	195.5	40.5	53.2
Net income ($ mil.)	906.5%	-	-	0.0	1.2	1.7
Market value ($ mil.)	-	-	-	-	-	-
Employees	-	-	-	-	-	1,556

ICU MEDICAL, INC.   NMS: ICUI

951 Calle Amanecer
San Clemente, CA 92673
Phone: 949 366-2183
Fax: -

CEO: George A. Lopez
CFO: Scott E. Lamb
HR: Clay Fradd
FYE: December 31
Type: Public

ICU Medical sees the future of infection prevention. The company's devices protect health care workers and patients from the spread of diseases such as HIV and hepatitis. Its primary products are intravenous (IV) connection devices called Clave needleless connectors that reduce the risk of needle sticks and disconnections. The firm also makes custom IV sets many of which use Clave connectors and other ICU products for third parties. Additionally ICU Medical makes critical care equipment such as angiography kits and heart monitors. ICU Medical sells its products to other equipment makers and distributors throughout the US and internationally.

	Annual Growth	12/10	12/11	12/12	12/13	12/14
Sales ($ mil.)	2.1%	284.6	302.2	316.9	313.7	309.3
Net income ($ mil.)	(3.9%)	30.9	44.7	41.3	40.4	26.3
Market value ($ mil.)	22.4%	569.2	701.8	950.2	993.6	1,277.2
Employees	(1.7%)	2,437	2,128	2,239	2,269	2,280

ID SOFTWARE INC.

3819 Town Crossing #222
Mesquite TX 75150
Phone: 972-613-3589
Fax: 972-686-9288
Web: www.idsoftware.com

CEO: -
CFO: -
HR: -
FYE: December 31
Type: Subsidiary

Under analysis id Software may posit that the virtual boodthirst its players exhibit comes from an instinctual and unconscious part of the psyche. The video game maker is best known for titles in its popular "Doom" and Quake series in which the primary objective is to kill — or frag in gamer parlance — as many opponents as possible. The company continues to develop sequels to its classics as well as new titles. id's games are predominately made for PCs operating Windows; some titles are available for Mac. id Software was acquired in 2009 by ZeniMax Media and will operate as a subsidiary under the direction of founder John Carmack who established the company in 1991.

IDACORP, INC.

NYS: IDA

1221 W. Idaho Street
Boise, ID 83702-5627
Phone: 208 388-2200
Fax: –
Web: www.idacorpinc.com

CEO: Darrel T. Anderson
CFO: Steven R. (Steve) Keen
HR: –
FYE: December 31
Type: Public

Energy is more than small potatoes for IDACORP. The holding company's regulated utility Idaho Power distributes electricity to 616000 residential business agricultural and industrial customers in 80 cities (71 in Idaho and nine in Oregon). The utility's generation assets include 17 hydroelectric plants three gas-fired plants one diesel generator and stakes in three coal-fired plants. Other IDACORP businesses include independent power project developer IDA-WEST ENERGY) affordable housing investments (IDACORP Financial Services) and coal mining (Idaho Energy Resources) a joint venture partner of the Bridger Coal Company which supplies coal to a power plant partly owned by IDACORP.

	Annual Growth	12/10	12/11	12/12	12/13	12/14
Sales ($ mil.)	5.5%	1,036.0	1,026.8	1,080.7	1,246.2	1,282.5
Net income ($ mil.)	7.9%	142.8	166.7	168.8	182.4	193.5
Market value ($ mil.)	15.7%	1,859.0	2,131.9	2,179.2	2,606.0	3,327.4
Employees	(0.1%)	2,051	2,081	2,100	2,042	2,043

IDAHO POWER CO

NL:

1221 W. Idaho Street
Boise, ID 83702-5627
Phone: 208 388-2200
Fax: 208 388-6903
Web: www.idahopower.com

CEO: Darrel T Anderson
CFO: Steven R Keen
HR: –
FYE: December 31
Type: Public

Idaho Power lights up the potato farms and factories in southern Idaho and eastern Oregon. The utility a subsidiary of holding company IDACORP provides electricity to about 508000 residential commercial and industrial customers over more than 31540 miles of transmission and distribution lines. Idaho Power holds franchises in 71 cities in Idaho and nine in Oregon. It also owns power plant interests that give it a generating capacity of 3407 MW. In addition through its Idaho Energy Resources unit the company has a 33% stake in the Bridger Coal Company which supplies fuel to the Jim Bridger generating plant in Wyoming.

	Annual Growth	12/10	12/11	12/12	12/13	12/14
Sales ($ mil.)	5.5%	1,033.1	1,022.7	1,076.7	1,243.1	1,278.7
Net income ($ mil.)	7.7%	140.6	164.8	168.2	176.7	189.4
Market value ($ mil.)	–					
Employees	(0.0%)	2,035	2,068	2,087	2,029	2,031

IDAHO STATE UNIVERSITY

921 S 8TH AVE
POCATELLO, ID 832090001
Phone: 208-282-0211
Fax: –
Web: www.isu.edu

CEO: –
CFO: –
HR: Richard (Dick) Cheatum
FYE: June 30
Type: Private

Even couch potatoes know that Idaho State University (ISU) is the spud state's place to go for a good education. The state institution provides graduate and undergraduate instruction through departments in seven colleges. The school's 14500 students can choose from about 280 certificate and degree programs in a range of subjects including arts and sciences business health professions and technology. ISU is a Carnegie-classified doctoral research and teaching institution and it has student-teacher ratio of 17:1. In addition to its main campus in Pocatello the school also has academic centers in Idaho Falls Meridian and Twin Falls as well as a research institute specialized in natural and physical sciences.

	Annual Growth	06/05	06/06	06/12	06/13	06/14
Sales ($ mil.)	1.7%	–	114.0	129.1	9.5	130.5
Net income ($ mil.)	28.2%	–	–	11.1	2.5	18.2
Market value ($ mil.)	–	–	–	–	–	–
Employees	–	–	–	–	–	1,900

IDEAL INNOVATIONS INC.

950 North Glebe Rd. Ste. 800
Arlington VA 22203
Phone: 703-528-9101
Fax: 703-528-1913
Web: www.idealinnovations.com

CEO: Robert W Kocher Jr
CFO: Richard Syretz
HR: –
FYE: December 31
Type: Private

Ideal Innovations is a perfectionist when it comes to sharing new ideas with government agencies and private organizations. The fast-growing company specializes in offering consulting in scientific managerial security and technological fields. Services areas include research and development training forensics and armor systems for vehicles and personnel. Ideal Innovations operates from offices in Texas Virginia and West Virginia as well as in Afghanistan and Iraq. CEO Bob Kocher established the company in 1998 in order to provide technical consulting related to the health and safety of military personnel and US civilians.

IDEALAB

130 W. Union St.
Pasadena CA 91103
Phone: 626-585-6900
Fax: 626-535-2701
Web: www.idealab.com

CEO: Bill Gross
CFO: Craig Chrisney
HR: Andres Castaneda
FYE: January 31
Type: Private

When entrepreneur Bill Gross wanted to coddle his Internet-related brainchildren he created Idealab. The company which once teetered on the brink of bankruptcy amid the flame-outs of its erstwhile dot-com progeny nurtures business ideas (several generated by Gross) with the hopes of growing them into full-fledged companies by providing money office space strategic advice and other resources. Idealab is increasingly involved in emerging technologies such as renewable energy (eSolar Energy Innovations) automation (Evolution Robotics) and electric and hybrid vehicle development (Aptera Motors) in addition to its traditional focus on Internet companies.

IDENIX PHARMACEUTICALS INC

NMS: IDIX

320 Bent Street
Cambridge, MA 02141
Phone: 617 995-9800
Fax: –
Web: www.idenix.com

CEO: Ronald C Renaud Jr
CFO: –
HR: –
FYE: December 31
Type: Public

Idenix Pharmaceuticals seeks to identify treatments for viral diseases. The firm is busily developing orally administered drugs to combat hepatitis C (HCV). It has one marketed drug for hepatitis B (HBV) Telbivudine sold under the brand names Tyzeka in the US and Sebivo internationally. Idenix's other candidates are in various stages of clinical testing — from preclinical to late stage trials. Most are intended to be taken in combination with other therapeutic agents to improve efficacy and convenience. Idenix's lead HCV drug candidates include IDX184 a nucleotide inhibitor in Phase II clinical testing and IDX719 an NS5A inhibitor to which the FDA granted fast-track status in 2012.

	Annual Growth	12/08	12/09	12/10	12/11	12/12
Sales ($ mil.)	62.3%	10.0	12.6	10.2	7.0	69.7
Net income ($ mil.)	–	(70.2)	(53.2)	(61.6)	(52.0)	(32.4)
Market value ($ mil.)	(4.3%)	775.6	288.0	675.1	997.3	649.7
Employees	(11.3%)	173	144	109	105	107

IDENTIV, INC.
NAS: INVE

39300 Civic Center Drive, Suite 140
Fremont, CA 94538
Phone: 949 250-8888
Fax: -
Web: www.identiv.com

CEO: Steven Humphreys
CFO: Melvin Denton
HR: -
FYE: December 31
Type: Public

Identive Group grants secure access to the digital world. The company makes hardware and software for securely accessing digital content and services. Its products include smart card readers for electronic IDs and driver's licenses as well as health care computer network and facility access cards. Among other purposes Identive's digital media readers are used in digital photo kiosks to transfer data to and from flash media. The company sells to computer makers government contractors systems integrators financial institutions and photo processing equipment makers. Identive has international facilities in Australia Canada Germany Hong Kong India Japan the Netherlands Singapore and Switzerland.

	Annual Growth	12/10	12/11	12/12	12/13	12/14
Sales ($ mil.)	(1.1%)	84.8	102.7	94.6	75.6	81.2
Net income ($ mil.)	-	(9.5)	(9.5)	(50.3)	(34.9)	(17.9)
Market value ($ mil.)	53.2%	26.8	23.7	16.0	6.1	147.8
Employees	(5.5%)	387	436	429	346	308

IDEO LLC

100 Forest Ave.
Palo Alto CA 94301
Phone: 650-289-3400
Fax: 650-289-3707
Web: www.ideo.com

CEO: Tim Brown
CFO: -
HR: -
FYE: February 28
Type: Subsidiary

Ideas are IDEO's stock-in-trade. The company provides product development and branding services for a wide range of clients. It offers packaging design product research and strategic consulting services. Its work has included contributions to TiVo's digital video recorder and the Palm V for Palm. In addition IDEO (pronounced EYE-dee-oh) provides executive training and education services to help enterprises become more innovative. It operates from a network of several offices in the US Europe and the Asia/Pacific region. IDEO is a subsidiary of office furniture manufacturer Steelcase. Chairman David Kelley whose design credits include the first mouse for Apple and Bill Moggridge formed IDEO in 1991.

IDERA PHARMACEUTICALS INC
NAS: IDRA

167 Sidney Street
Cambridge, MA 02139
Phone: 617 679-5500
Fax: -

CEO: Vincent J. (Vinnie) Milano
CFO: Louis J. (Lou) Arcudi
HR: Leslie Fontaine
FYE: December 31
Type: Public

Idera Pharmaceuticals is open to the idea of tinkering with your immune system. The biotech firm is developing DNA and RNA therapies that manipulate the immune system's response to disease. It is focused on Toll-Like Receptors (TLRs) — immune cell receptors that recognize and respond to viral and bacterial invaders. Some of Idera's drugs (such as treatments for infectious disease and cancer) mimic those invaders to stimulate an immune response; others (including treatments for autoimmune and inflammatory diseases) target TLRs to suppress the immune response. The company's lead candidate is a potential treatment for hepatitis C. Idera conducts some of its R&D efforts through partnerships.

	Annual Growth	12/10	12/11	12/12	12/13	12/14
Sales ($ mil.)	(74.1%)	16.1	0.1	0.1	0.0	0.1
Net income ($ mil.)	-	(18.0)	(23.8)	(19.2)	(18.2)	(38.6)
Market value ($ mil.)	11.1%	274.1	99.6	84.4	439.1	418.2
Employees	5.7%	36	26	18	18	45

IDEX CORPORATION
NYS: IEX

1925 West Field Court
Lake Forest, IL 60045
Phone: 847 498-7070
Fax: -
Web: www.idexcorp.com

CEO: Andrew K. Silvernail
CFO: Heath A. Mitts
HR: Jason Clayton
FYE: December 31
Type: Public

The idea at IDEX is to dispense with inefficiencies and pump up profits. The company organized into three business segments that consist of various operating units is a diversified manufacturer of pumps and other engineered products geared at different niche markets around the world. Its largest segment Fluid & Metering Technologies makes pumps flow meters and injectors used to handle or monitor water chemicals and fuels. Health & Science Technologies produces fluidics and pumps used in medical devices analytical instrumentation and photonics. The Fire & Safety/Diversified Products segment manufactures firefighting pumps and rescue tools including the branded Hurst Jaws of Life.

	Annual Growth	12/10	12/11	12/12	12/13	12/14
Sales ($ mil.)	9.2%	1,513.1	1,838.5	1,954.3	2,024.1	2,147.8
Net income ($ mil.)	15.5%	157.1	193.9	37.6	255.2	279.4
Market value ($ mil.)	18.8%	3,081.3	2,923.0	3,665.0	5,816.9	6,131.1
Employees	3.0%	5,966	6,814	6,717	6,787	6,712

IDEXX LABORATORIES, INC.
NMS: IDXX

One IDEXX Drive
Westbrook, ME 04092
Phone: 207 556-0300
Fax: 207 856-0346
Web: www.idexx.com

CEO: Jonathan W. (Jon) Ayers
CFO: Brian P. McKeon
HR: Giovani Twigge
FYE: December 31
Type: Public

IDEXX can identify what's wrong with Fluffy Fido Flossie or Flicka. A leading animal health care company IDEXX makes diagnostic testing kits and machines for cats and dogs as well as cows and horses. Veterinarians use the company's VetTest analyzers for blood and urine chemistry and its SNAP in-office test kits to detect heartworms feline leukemia and other diseases. The company also provides lab testing services and practice management software. In addition IDEXX makes diagnostic products to detect livestock and poultry diseases and to test for contaminants in water and milk. The company sells its products worldwide.

	Annual Growth	12/10	12/11	12/12	12/13	12/14
Sales ($ mil.)	7.7%	1,103.4	1,218.7	1,293.3	1,377.1	1,485.8
Net income ($ mil.)	6.5%	141.3	161.8	178.3	187.8	181.9
Market value ($ mil.)	21.0%	6,558.3	7,291.7	8,792.4	10,078.1	14,048.0
Employees	7.5%	4,800	5,100	5,400	5,700	6,400

IDT CORP.
NYS: IDT

520 Broad Street
Newark, NJ 07102
Phone: 973 438-1000
Fax: -
Web: www.idt.net

CEO: Bill Pereira
CFO: Marcelo Fischer
HR: -
FYE: July 31
Type: Public

IDT keeps international phone calls cheap whether you're calling Argentina or Zambia. The holding company makes most of its money through IDT Telecom which provides prepaid and rechargeable calling cards and other payment services to customers in the US and 30 other countries. As a pioneer in international callback technology (sometimes known as call reorigination) IDT Telecom also offers wholesale termination services to reroute international calls through less expensive US exchanges. In addition the company offers local and long distance services in 11 states under the IDT America brand.

	Annual Growth	07/11	07/12	07/13	07/14	07/15
Sales ($ mil.)	0.7%	1,555.5	1,506.8	1,620.6	1,651.5	1,596.8
Net income ($ mil.)	33.2%	26.8	38.6	11.6	18.8	84.5
Market value ($ mil.)	(8.4%)	562.9	236.1	482.2	363.7	397.1
Employees	(2.3%)	1,370	1,280	1,320	1,570	1,250

IDW MEDIA HOLDINGS INC   NBB: IDWM

11 Largo Drive South   CEO: Marc Knoller
Stamford, CT 06907   CFO: –
Phone: 203 323-5161   HR: –
Fax: –   FYE: October 31
Web: www.ctmholdings.com   Type: Public

CTM Media Holdings is not embarrassed by tourists. The company distributes travel-related print and online advertising and information. Offerings include visitor maps brochures and other destination guides. Its publications are found in strategically located display stands primarily located in hotels attractions restaurants and rest stops along high-traffic throughways and interstates. In addition CTM Media publishes books and comics through its IDW Publishing subsidiary. The company was founded in 1983 as Creative Theatre Marketing. Previously known as IDT Capital the company was spun off from telecommunications firm IDT Corporation in 2009.

	Annual Growth	10/10	10/11	10/12	10/13	10/14
Sales ($ mil.)	–	0.0	0.0	0.0	41.6	45.2
Net income ($ mil.)	–	0.0	0.0	0.0	2.2	5.3
Market value ($ mil.)	–	0.0	0.0	0.0	273.0	414.0
Employees	–	–	–	–	–	–

IEC ELECTRONICS CORP.   ASE: IEC

105 Norton Street   CEO: –
Newark, NY 14513   CFO: Michael T Williams
Phone: 315 331-7742   HR: –
Fax: –   FYE: September 30
Web: www.iec-electronics.com   Type: Public

IEC makes products you may never see. The company is a contract electronics manufacturer of printed circuit boards system-level assemblies extreme-condition cable and wire assemblies and precision sheet metal components. Customers come from the aerospace communications medical and military sectors. Like many contract electronics manufacturers IEC also offers a variety of auxiliary services including systems integration design and prototyping materials procurement and management engineering and testing.

	Annual Growth	09/11	09/12	09/13	09/14	09/15
Sales ($ mil.)	(1.2%)	133.3	145.0	140.9	135.6	127.0
Net income ($ mil.)	–	6.8	7.8	(9.5)	(2.1)	(10.2)
Market value ($ mil.)	(6.7%)	51.8	69.1	37.4	46.0	39.3
Employees	(1.3%)	841	925	951	994	798

IGATE CORP   NMS: IGTE

100 Somerset Corporate Blvd   CEO: Ashok Vemuri
Bridgewater, NJ 08807   CFO: Sujit Sircar
Phone: 908 219-8050   HR: –
Fax: –   FYE: December 31
Web: www.igate.com   Type: Public

iGate is open to all things IT. The company provides business process outsourcing (BPO) and offshore development services including software development and maintenance outsourcing. In addition to IT-related services iGate handles such tasks as mortgage and claims processing and call center operations. The company targets midsized and large corporations in the banking financial services and insurance industries. Its more than 300 active customers include General Electric IBM Royal Bank of Canada and TEKsystems. The majority of iGate's operations are in India but the company earns most of its sales from customers in North America.

	Annual Growth	12/09	12/10	12/11	12/12	12/13
Sales ($ mil.)	56.2%	193.1	280.6	779.6	1,073.9	1,150.9
Net income ($ mil.)	46.0%	28.6	51.8	51.5	95.8	129.8
Market value ($ mil.)	41.6%	584.4	1,151.8	919.2	921.6	2,346.9
Employees	44.0%	6,910	8,338	26,889	27,616	29,733

IGN ENTERTAINMENT INC.

625 2nd St. 3rd Fl.   CEO: Christopher Coy
San Francisco CA 94107   CFO: –
Phone: 415-896-3700   HR: –
Fax: +41-44-271-52-82   FYE: December 31
Web: www.kuoni-group.com   Type: Subsidiary

IGN Entertainment may not stand for International Geek Network but it does court some serious video gamers. The company operates a network of video game and entertainment-related websites that target males aged 18-34. Its flagship gaming site IGN.com (along with GameSpy FilePlanet and TeamXbox) is the US's leading gaming network; IGN also operates lifestyle site AskMen.com. Together its IGN sites attract more than 40 million unique monthly visitors globally (in the US Australia and Germany). IGN also includes GameSpy Technology group which provides technology for online game play. IGN is a subsidiary of News Corp..

IGNITE RESTAURANT GROUP INC   NMS: IRG

9900 Westpark Drive, Suite 300   CEO: Robert S. (Chip) Merritt
Houston, TX 77063   CFO: Jeffrey L Rager
Phone: 713 366-7500   HR: –
Fax: –   FYE: December 29
Web: www.igniterestaurants.com   Type: Public

Foodies with a burning passion for seafood and fun turn to this company. Ignite Restaurant Group operates Joe's Crab Shack a casual dining chain with more than 135 locations. The eateries feature a wide variety of grilled fried and stuffed seafood along with sandwiches and sides. The seafood chain is known for its quirky surf-inspired atmosphere where the servers are often part of the entertainment. In addition to its flagship restaurant brand Ignite Restaurant Group operates a small number of Brick House Tavern + Tap locations. Private equity group J. H. Whitney Capital Partners owns the company.

	Annual Growth	01/11	01/12*	12/12	12/13	12/14
Sales ($ mil.)	33.6%	351.3	405.2	465.1	760.8	837.2
Net income ($ mil.)	–	11.8	11.3	8.7	(6.6)	(53.5)
Market value ($ mil.)	(22.1%)	–	–	340.4	333.8	206.6
Employees	30.6%	–	10,900	9,700	19,800	18,600

*Fiscal year change

IGNITION PARTNERS LLC

11400 SE 6th St. Ste. 100   CEO: –
Bellevue WA 98004   CFO: –
Phone: 425-709-0772   HR: –
Fax: 425-709-0798   FYE: December 31
Web: www.ignitionpartners.com   Type: Private

When first-stage companies need fuel they turn to Ignition. Founded by Microsoft veterans (including founding partner Brad Silverberg who was head of Windows from 1990 to 1995) and former wireless communications executives Ignition invests in its areas of expertise: business information technology software communications infrastructure and consumer services. The firm along with its Chinese affiliate manages some $2.5 billion and invests primarily in early-stage enterprises. Ignition usually acquires large but non-controlling stakes in its portfolio companies and holds onto them long-term. It also makes later-stage investments through Ignition Capital.

IGO INC

17800 N. Perimeter Dr., Suite 200
Scottsdale, AZ 85255
Phone: 480 596-0061
Fax: –
Web: www.igo.com

NBB: IGOI

CEO: Terry R Gibson
CFO: Terry R Gibson
HR: James Doroz
FYE: December 31
Type: Public

iGo has the power to keep electronics running. The company designs power products and chargers for portable consumer electronics such as notebook computers mobile phones digital music players handheld computers and gaming systems. Its product line includes AC DC combination AC/DC and battery-based universal power adapters. iGo tries to differentiate its products by incorporating interchangeable tips which let users charge and power a wide range of electronic products using the same power supply. It sells to computer makers including Dell and Lenovo as well as distributors (D&H Distributing Ingram Micro) and retailers (Wal-Mart RadioShack).

	Annual Growth	12/09	12/10	12/11	12/12	12/13
Sales ($ mil.)	(25.7%)	55.4	43.4	38.4	29.9	16.9
Net income ($ mil.)	–	(0.5)	0.8	(11.5)	(12.0)	(12.6)
Market value ($ mil.)	20.9%	3.6	11.3	2.3	0.8	7.7
Employees	(33.8%)	52	62	64	38	10

IHEARTMEDIA INC

200 East Basse Road, Suite 100
San Antonio, TX 78209
Phone: 210 822-2828
Fax: –
Web: www.iheartmedia.com

NBB: IHRT

CEO: Robert W. (Bob) Pittman
CFO: Richard J. Bressler
HR: Kim Heintz
FYE: December 31
Type: Public

iHeartMedia loves the advertising-supported consumer-focused business of show business. The firm formerly known as CC Media owns and operates more than 850 radio stations in about 150 markets through iHeartCommunications. With more than 245 million listeners a month iHeartMedia is the #1 radio company in the US. The company also owns outdoor advertising giant Clear Channel Outdoor Holdings. Clear Channel Outdoor Holdings sells advertising space on billboards public transportation buildings and other outdoor environments throughout the US and more than 30 other countries.

	Annual Growth	12/10	12/11	12/12	12/13	12/14
Sales ($ mil.)	1.9%	5,865.7	6,161.4	6,246.9	6,243.0	6,318.5
Net income ($ mil.)	–	(479.1)	(302.1)	(424.5)	(606.9)	(793.8)
Market value ($ mil.)	(4.9%)	797.4	389.0	301.3	578.6	651.2
Employees	(1.4%)	20,283	21,200	20,800	20,800	19,200

IHS INC

15 Inverness Way East
Englewood, CO 80112
Phone: 303 790-0600
Fax: –
Web: www.ihs.com

NYS: IHS

CEO: Jerre L. Stead
CFO: Todd Hyatt
HR: Jeffrey (Jeff) Sisson
FYE: November 30
Type: Public

IHS (Information Handling Services) does more than handle information. Its experts process information from a variety of sources to provide analysis business and market intelligence and technical documents which it distributes in electronic formats. Products such as collections of technical specifications and standards regulations parts data and design guides are sold through its four areas of information: Energy Product Lifecycle Security and Environment. The company also offers economic-focused information and analysis through its IHS Global Insight subsidiary. IHS primarily earns revenue through subscription sales.

	Annual Growth	11/11	11/12	11/13	11/14	11/15
Sales ($ mil.)	13.3%	1,325.6	1,529.9	1,840.6	2,230.8	2,184.3
Net income ($ mil.)	15.4%	135.4	158.2	131.7	194.5	240.2
Market value ($ mil.)	8.7%	5,967.8	6,221.7	7,726.8	8,269.0	8,326.4
Employees	11.8%	5,500	6,000	8,000	8,800	8,600

II-VI INC

375 Saxonburg Boulevard
Saxonburg, PA 16056
Phone: 724 352-4455
Fax: –
Web: www.ii-vi.com

NMS: IIVI

CEO: Francis J. Kramer
CFO: Mary Jane Raymond
HR: –
FYE: June 30
Type: Public

II-VI could play a mean game of laser tag but it's more interested in making things. The company (its name is pronounced "two-six") makes lenses mirrors prisms and other optical components and materials. II-VI's clients — drawn from the aerospace health care industrial military and telecom equipment sectors — use these components in lasers and other systems used in precision manufacturing communications networks military targeting and navigation systems and other applications. The company has manufacturing operations throughout the US as well as in Asia and Germany. Customers have included Caterpillar Volkswagen Raytheon and the US government.

	Annual Growth	06/11	06/12	06/13	06/14	06/15
Sales ($ mil.)	10.2%	502.8	534.6	558.4	683.3	742.0
Net income ($ mil.)	(5.5%)	82.7	60.3	50.8	38.4	66.0
Market value ($ mil.)	(7.2%)	1,567.1	1,020.4	995.3	885.2	1,161.9
Employees	8.2%	6,195	6,030	6,185	6,796	8,490

IKANO COMMUNICATIONS INC.

420 E SOUTH TEMPLE # 550
SALT LAKE CITY, UT 841111319
Phone: 801-924-0900
Fax: –
Web: www.ikano.com

CEO: Jim Murphy
CFO: –
HR: –
FYE: June 30
Type: Private

IKANO Communications says "I can" to businesses looking for access to the Web. The company resells wholesale Internet service in North America through agreements with network operators such as Covad enabling customers to resell Internet service under their own private brands. Clients include ISP's as well as customers in such industries as health care marketing and higher education. IKANO serves broadband customers in California through subsidiary DSL Extreme. Other brands include Dialup USA and DNA-Mail. The company operates from satellite offices in Los Angeles Seattle Toronto and Washington DC. Founded in 1999 IKANO has received funding from investors including Insight Venture Partners.

	Annual Growth	06/01	06/02	06/04	06/05	06/08
Sales ($ mil.)	10.4%	–	28.0	–	26.0	50.8
Net income ($ mil.)	–	–	–	–	(1.9)	13.5
Market value ($ mil.)	–	–	–	–	–	–
Employees	–	–	–	–	–	184

IKANOS COMMUNICATIONS INC

47669 Fremont Boulevard
Fremont, CA 94538
Phone: 510 979-0400
Fax: –
Web: www.ikanos.com

NAS: IKAN

CEO: –
CFO: Sanjay Mehta
HR: –
FYE: December 29
Type: Public

Ikanos Communications hopes to become an icon in the field of broadband semiconductors. The fabless semiconductor company designs DSL chipsets for use in modems and other customer premises equipment and communications processors used in gateways (multi-protocol routers). Its products allow networks to achieve fiber-like broadband speeds (up to 100 megabits per second) over copper wires enabling high-speed data features. Besides DSL its products also support wireless broadband passive optical network and Ethernet. Service providers such as AT&T and Orange are Ikanos' end users but its direct customers are manufacturers such as Alcatel-Lucent Sumitomo Electric Industries and ZTE.

	Annual Growth	01/10	01/11	01/12*	12/12	12/13
Sales ($ mil.)	(15.2%)	130.7	191.7	136.6	125.9	79.7
Net income ($ mil.)	–	(37.1)	(49.8)	(7.5)	(17.6)	(30.4)
Market value ($ mil.)	(13.9%)	18.5	13.2	8.0	16.5	11.8
Employees	(23.5%)	588	386	337	263	263

*Fiscal year change

IKONICS CORP   NAS: IKNX

4832 Grand Avenue   CEO: William C Ulland
Duluth, MN 55807   CFO: Jon Gerlach
Phone: 218 628-2217   HR: –
Fax: –   FYE: December 31
                                                   Type: Public

IKONICS makes light-sensitive coatings (emulsions) and films used primarily by the screen printing and abrasive etching markets (to create stencil images for the one and to create architectural glass and art pieces for the other). The company also makes photoresist films and metal etching materials for sign making and ink jet receptive films for creating photopositives and photonegatives. Custom etching services and digital imaging technologies for niche industrial markets is of increasing importance to the company. IKONICS sells its products through about 200 distributors worldwide although the US accounts for more than two-thirds of sales.

	Annual Growth	12/10	12/11	12/12	12/13	12/14
Sales ($ mil.)	2.9%	16.5	16.8	17.3	17.5	18.5
Net income ($ mil.)	(12.6%)	1.1	0.7	0.7	0.7	0.6
Market value ($ mil.)	19.1%	14.6	15.3	16.2	29.8	29.4
Employees	1.0%	72	72	73	75	75

ILITCH HOLDINGS INC.

2211 Woodward Ave.   CEO: Christopher Ilitch
Detroit MI 48201-3400   CFO: Scott Fisher
Phone: 313-471-6600   HR: –
Fax: 313-471-6094   FYE: December 31
Web: www.ilitchholdings.com   Type: Holding Company

This holding company rules over a Caesar tames Tigers and takes flight on the ice. Ilitch Holdings controls the business interests of Mike and Marian Ilitch and their family which includes the Little Caesars pizza chain the Detroit Tigers baseball team and the Detroit Red Wings hockey team. Subsidiary Olympia Entertainment owns Detroit's Fox Theatre and operates Comerica Park Joe Louis Arena and Cobo Arena. Additional holdings include Blue Line Foodservice Distribution a leading supplier of food and equipment to restaurant operators (including Little Caesars operators) and an interest in the MotorCity Casino Hotel. The Ilitches started Little Caesars in 1959 and formed Ilitch Holdings in 1999.

ILLINOIS INSTITUTE OF TECHNOLOGY

10 W 35TH ST   CEO: –
CHICAGO, IL 606163717   CFO: –
Phone: 312-567-3000   HR: Antoinette Murril
Fax: –   FYE: May 31
Web: www.iit.edu   Type: Private

Chicago has some cool architecture due in part to the Illinois Institute of Technology (IIT). The school offers more than 100 undergraduate and graduate degree programs in engineering science psychology architecture business law humanities and design. In addition to three campuses in Chicago IIT also has locations in Summit-Argo (Moffet campus) and Wheaton (Daniel F. and Ada L. Rice campus). The institute has an enrollment of some 8000 undergraduate graduate business school and law school students with a student-to-faculty ratio of 8:1.

	Annual Growth	05/09	05/10	05/11	05/12	05/13
Sales ($ mil.)	(8.0%)	–	333.2	305.1	249.7	259.3
Net income ($ mil.)	106.7%	–	–	8.8	(6.9)	37.5
Market value ($ mil.)	–	–	–	–	–	–
Employees	–	–	–	–	–	1,662

ILLINOIS TOOL WORKS, INC.   NYS: ITW

155 Harlem Avenue   CEO: E. Scott Santi
Glenview, IL 60025   CFO: Michael M. Larsen
Phone: 847 724-7500   HR: –
Fax: –   FYE: December 31
Web: www.itw.com   Type: Public

Illinois Tool Works (ITW) hammers out more than just tools and it operates well beyond the Land of Lincoln. With operations in about 60 countries ITW manufactures and services equipment for the automotive construction electronics food/beverage power system decorative surfaces and medical (adhesives) industries. The largest of its segments is Transportation which provides metal and plastic fasteners fluids and body repair putties as well as truck remanufacturing. Second in sales Power Systems & Electronics churns out arc welding equipment and airport ground support equipment.

	Annual Growth	12/11	12/12	12/13	12/14	12/15
Sales ($ mil.)	(6.8%)	17,786.6	17,924.0	14,135.0	14,484.0	13,405.0
Net income ($ mil.)	(2.1%)	2,071.4	2,870.0	1,679.0	2,946.0	1,899.0
Market value ($ mil.)	18.7%	16,988.9	22,117.2	30,580.7	34,443.3	33,708.6
Employees	(7.3%)	65,000	60,000	51,000	49,000	48,000

ILLINOIS WESLEYAN UNIVERSITY

1312 PARK ST   CEO: –
BLOOMINGTON, IL 617011773   CFO: –
Phone: 309-556-1000   HR: Catherine (Cathy) Spitz
Fax: –   FYE: July 31
Web: www.iwu.edu   Type: Private

The Fightin' Titans of Illinois Wesleyan University cannot be accused of having a one-track mind. The small private university offers 50 majors and programs and is organized into three colleges: liberal arts fine arts and the school of nursing. As an undergraduate university with about 2000 students Illinois Wesleyan also offers pre-professional programs in fields including engineering law and medicine. Traditionally about 80% of the student population is enrolled in the College of Liberal Arts. The school was founded in 1850 by civic and Methodist Church leaders.

	Annual Growth	07/10	07/11	07/12	07/13	07/14
Sales ($ mil.)	(2.1%)	–	97.5	77.5	101.6	91.5
Net income ($ mil.)	136.8%	–	–	2.8	28.6	15.7
Market value ($ mil.)	–	–	–	–	–	–
Employees	–	–	–	–	–	500

ILLUMINA INC   NMS: ILMN

5200 Illumina Way   CEO: Jay T. Flatley
San Diego, CA 92122   CFO: Marc A. Stapley
Phone: 858 202-4500   HR: Paul Bianchi
Fax: –   FYE: December 28
Web: www.illumina.com   Type: Public

Illumina elucidates the human genome. The firm makes tools used by life sciences and drug researchers to isolate and analyze genes. Its systems include the machinery and the software used to sequence pieces of DNA and RNA and the means to put them through large-scale testing of genetic variation and biological function. Its proprietary BeadArray technology uses microscopic glass beads which can carry samples through the genotyping process. The tests allow medical researchers to determine what genetic combinations are associated with various diseases enabling faster diagnosis better drugs and individualized treatment. Customers include pharma and biotech companies research centers and academic institutions.

	Annual Growth	01/11	01/12*	12/12	12/13	12/14
Sales ($ mil.)	27.3%	902.7	1,055.5	1,148.5	1,421.2	1,861.4
Net income ($ mil.)	41.4%	124.9	86.6	151.3	125.3	353.4
Market value ($ mil.)	43.8%	9,097.5	4,377.8	7,863.7	15,853.8	27,031.0
Employees	20.8%	2,100	2,200	2,400	3,000	3,700

*Fiscal year change

IMAGE ENTERTAINMENT INC.

PINK SHEETS: DISK

20525 Nordhoff St. Ste. 200
Chatsworth CA 91311
Phone: 818-407-9100
Fax: 818-407-9151
Web: www.image-entertainment.com

CEO: –
CFO: Drew Wilson
HR: Jacqui Bastock
FYE: March 31
Type: Public

This Image has been altered to fit the format of your home entertainment center. Image Entertainment acquires licenses and distributes the rights to movie and TV titles. The company sells broadcast rights to cable and satellite channels and acquires and distributes digital content through video on demand (VOD) streaming video and download channels. Its media library includes some 3200 exclusive DVD and Blu-ray titles 400 audio titles 300 CD titles and digital rights to 2300 programs. It releases more than 15 titles monthly which include VOD digital and broadcast content. San Francisco-based private equity firm JH Partners owns more than 75% of Image which is being sold to RLJ Acquisition.

IMAGE SENSING SYSTEMS, INC.

NAS: ISNS

500 Spruce Tree Centre, 1600 University Avenue West
St. Paul, MN 55104
Phone: 651 603-7700
Fax: –
Web: www.imagesensing.com

CEO: –
CFO: Dale E Parker
HR: –
FYE: December 31
Type: Public

If you're stuck in traffic you can't blame Image Sensing Systems (ISS). ISS's Autoscope vehicle detection system converts video images into digitized traffic data for traffic management. Unlike traditional embedded wire loop detectors which are buried in the pavement Autoscope enables wide-area detection using video cameras a microprocessor software and a PC. The systems help users to design roads manage traffic signals and determine the environmental impact of gridlock. Royalty income from traffic management company Econolite Control Products accounts for nearly half of sales. The company gets three-quarters of its sales in North America.

	Annual Growth	12/10	12/11	12/12	12/13	12/14
Sales ($ mil.)	(7.6%)	31.7	30.5	25.0	26.3	23.1
Net income ($ mil.)	–	3.0	(10.0)	(3.4)	(15.9)	(9.7)
Market value ($ mil.)	(32.7%)	65.0	32.5	24.8	24.7	13.3
Employees	(3.0%)	123	131	104	124	109

IMAGETREND INC.

20855 KENSINGTON BLVD
LAKEVILLE, MN 550447486
Phone: 952-469-1589
Fax: –
Web: www.imagetrend.com

CEO: –
CFO: –
HR: Joannie Hennen
FYE: December 31
Type: Private

ImageTrend hopes that the trend in your enterprise is towards increased efficiency. The company provides software development services and Web-based software used to address tasks such as content and document management e-commerce development database design and back-office integration. ImageTrend founded in 1998 also provides services including consulting support and training. The company's clients come from fields such as manufacturing health care financial services and education and have included Russell Athletic Goodyear Tire HealthEast Care System the University of Minnesota Cargill and FirstComp Insurance.

	Annual Growth	12/06	12/07	12/08	12/10	12/12
Sales ($ mil.)	10.1%	–	7.9	11.0	11.0	12.7
Net income ($ mil.)	–	–	–	2.4	0.5	(0.9)
Market value ($ mil.)	–	–	–	–	–	–
Employees	–	–	–	–	–	145

IMAGEWARE SYSTEMS, INC.

NBB: IWSY

10815 Rancho Bernardo Road, Suite 310
San Diego, CA 92127
Phone: 858 673-8600
Fax: 858 673-1770
Web: www.iwsinc.com

CEO: S James Miller Jr
CFO: Wayne Wetherell
HR: –
FYE: December 31
Type: Public

Even if your face won't launch a thousand ships ImageWare Systems will remember it. The company's identification products are used to manage and issue secure credentials including national IDs passports driver's licenses smart cards and access-control credentials. Its software creates secure digital images and enables the enrollment and management of unlimited population sizes while its digital booking products provide law enforcement agencies with integrated mug shot fingerprint and investigative capabilities. The company markets its products worldwide to governments public safety agencies and commercial enterprises such as Unisys. The US government accounts for about 15% of revenue.

	Annual Growth	12/10	12/11	12/12	12/13	12/14
Sales ($ mil.)	(8.0%)	5.8	5.5	4.0	5.3	4.2
Net income ($ mil.)	–	(5.0)	(3.2)	(10.2)	(9.8)	(7.9)
Market value ($ mil.)	25.1%	91.6	74.8	79.5	180.5	224.4
Employees	5.5%	50	50	54	61	62

IMAGINE ENTERTAINMENT

9465 Wilshire Blvd. 7th Fl.
Beverly Hills CA 90212
Phone: 310-858-2000
Fax: 310-858-2020
Web: www.imagine-entertainment.com

CEO: –
CFO: –
HR: –
FYE: September 30
Type: Private

Imagine Entertainment has dreamt up a lot of success producing films and TV programs. Hollywood heavy-hitters Brian Grazer (movie producer) and Ron Howard (former child actor turned director) co-chair the studio which has a roster of critically acclaimed and commercially successful movies and TV shows. Among the company's notable films include numerous Howard-directed projects such as "Apollo 13" "A Beautiful Mind" (winner of Best Picture and Best Director Oscars) and The Da Vinci Code as well as films by others such as Eddie Murphy's The Nutty Professor. Imagine Entertainment's TV credits include the series "24" Arrested Development "Felicity" and Sports Night. Its films are distributed by Universal Pictures.

IMAGING BUSINESS MACHINES LLC

2750 Crestwood Blvd.
Birmingham AL 35210
Phone: 205-439-7100
Fax: 205-956-5309
Web: www.ibml.com

CEO: Derrick Murphy
CFO: T Summersell
HR: –
FYE: December 31
Type: Private - Partnershi

Imaging Business Machines (IBML) manufactures and markets high-speed document scanners and related software. Enterprises including airlines banks government agencies and pharmaceutical companies use the company's products to scan and store documents. IBML's Conversion Assistance Services (CAS) division provides on-site and off-site document preparation and scanning services as well as short-term rentals. Customers have included athenahealth Bank of America Mellon Bank and the US federal government. The company has offices in Germany the UK and the US.

IMAGING DIAGNOSTIC SYSTEMS INC.   OTC: IMDS

5307 NW 35th Court
Plantation FL 33309
Phone: 954-581-9800
Fax: 954-581-0555
Web: www.imds.com

CEO: Linda B Grable
CFO: Allan L Schwartz
HR: –
FYE: June 30
Type: Public

Imaging Diagnostic Systems is a medical technology company involved in the research and development of breast-imaging devices used for detecting cancer. Using laser-based technology the company has created a more comfortable radiation-free breast examination that does not require breast compression. Its CTLM (Computed Tomography Laser Mammography) system used in conjuction with X-ray mammography may help improve early diagnosis of cancer. The company is also researching other breast screening systems using fluorescence imaging. It had been developing laser imaging products for research with lab animals but it has licensed the technology to Bioscan in order to focus on the women's health market.

IMG WORLDWIDE INC.

767 5th Ave. 45th Fl.
New York NY 10153
Phone: 646-558-8357
Fax: 646-558-8399
Web: www.imgworld.com

CEO: –
CFO: Arthur J La Fave Jr
HR: Kara Cox
FYE: December 31
Type: Subsidiary

Show me the money! Founded by the late pioneer of sports marketing Mark McCormack IMG Worldwide (previously International Management Group) is the world's largest sports talent and marketing agency operating in some 30 countries. Its IMG Clients represents athletes (Venus Williams) models (Giselle Bundchen) and broadcasters (Bob Costas). IMG also represents corporate clients and offers a variety of related services with divisions devoted to collegiate sports marketing (IMG College); sports programming production and distribution (IMG Media); consumer products licensing (IMG Licensing); and sponsorship and media consulting (IMG Consulting). IMG is owned by investment firm Forstmann Little & Co.

IMATION CORP.   NYS: IMN

1 Imation Way
Oakdale, MN 55128
Phone: 651 704-4000
Fax: –
Web: www.imation.com

CEO: Robert B. (Bob) Fernander
CFO: Barry Kasoff
HR: Patricia A Hamm
FYE: December 31
Type: Public

Imation wants to start fresh with a blank disk. The company is one of the world's top makers of media used to capture process store and distribute information on computers and other electronic devices. Its removable data storage media products include optical disks (CDs DVDs Blu-ray discs) and magnetic storage tapes. It also offers flash memory drives removable storage drives mobile security products and hybrid storage products (sold under the Nexsan brand). The company is shifting its focus from traditional media to more data storage and security products and looking to sell its consumer electronics brands Memorex and XtremeMac.

	Annual Growth	12/10	12/11	12/12	12/13	12/14
Sales ($ mil.)	(15.9%)	1,460.9	1,290.4	1,099.6	860.8	729.5
Net income ($ mil.)	–	(158.5)	(46.7)	(340.7)	(44.4)	(114.7)
Market value ($ mil.)	(22.1%)	435.8	242.2	197.4	197.8	160.2
Employees	(5.0%)	1,115	1,130	1,230	940	910

IMMEDIATE RESPONSE TECHNOLOGIES INC.

7100 Holladay Tyler Rd.
Glenn Dale MD 20769
Phone: 301-352-8800
Fax: 301-352-8818
Web: www.imresponse.com

CEO: –
CFO: Sherri S Voelkel
HR: –
FYE: December 31
Type: Private

Immediate Response Technologies (IRT) helps first responders out of a bad situation. IRT supplies rapid-deploy shelters (including isolation and infection control systems) for the military first-response agencies and law enforcement. It sells related accessories too — tents respirators and filters. IRT's infrared thermal line includes markers targets beacons and reflective material. Products are sold through IRT sales staff and distributors to customers in the US Europe and Australia. Based outside of Washington DC IRT equipment assisted the Pentagon following the 911 attack. The company (formerly TVI Corp.) and its subsidiaries filed for Chapter 11 bankruptcy in April 2009 and exited in December.

IMERYS PIGMENTS INC.

100 Mansell Ct. East Ste. 300
Roswell GA 30076
Phone: 770-594-0660
Fax: 770-645-3384
Web: www.imerys-paper.com

CEO: Susan F Boss
CFO: Jeffrey C Hicks
HR: –
FYE: December 31
Type: Subsidiary

You didn't think paper just came out that brightly white did you? Imerys Pigments for Paper develops the pigments that render that paper in front of you so very white. It produces white mineral pigments manufacturing kaolin ground calcium carbonate and precipitated calcium carbonate. Paper manufacturers use those products for coating and filling applications to improve the quality of paper and paperboard. The division of French chemical company Imerys pulls in about a quarter of the parent company's annual sales and operates globally. Imerys Pigments for Paper was created in 2003.

IMMERSION CORP   NMS: IMMR

30 Rio Robles
San Jose, CA 95134
Phone: 408 467-1900
Fax: –
Web: www.immersion.com

CEO: Victor (Vic) Viegas
CFO: Paul Norris
HR: –
FYE: December 31
Type: Public

Immersion wants to immerse people in digital experiences with its haptics technology. The company develops touch feedback technology called haptics that simulates tactile experiences — such as the feel of an object or the jolt of an explosion during a video game — in order to improve how people interact with digital devices. Immersion licenses its TouchSense technology to companies such as Motorola and Samsung for use in mobile phones and to Logitech and Microsoft which use TouchSense in joysticks mice steering wheels and other peripherals. Its technology backed by more than 2000 issued and pending patents is also used in automotive consumer electronics and medical products.

	Annual Growth	12/10	12/11	12/12	12/13	12/14
Sales ($ mil.)	14.2%	31.1	30.6	32.2	47.5	52.9
Net income ($ mil.)	–	(5.9)	(1.6)	(5.6)	40.2	4.1
Market value ($ mil.)	9.0%	186.0	143.6	190.4	287.7	262.5
Employees	14.5%	82	85	94	105	141

IMMIXGROUP INC.

8444 WESTPARK DR STE 200
MC LEAN, VA 221025112
Phone: 703-752-0610
Fax: –
Web: www.immixgroup.com

CEO: Art Richer
CFO: Noel N Samuel
HR: –
FYE: May 31
Type: Private

immixGroup offers a blend of information technology (IT) business development and consulting services to help tech firms do business with federal state and local government agencies. Through its technology sales division the company is a hardware and software reseller for such manufacturers as IBM Oracle and Hewlett-Packard. It also offers customized public sector channel development programs outsourced government contract management and IT consulting and execution. Other services include market intelligence sales training and recruiting. immixGroup serves more than 250 tech manufacturers and its government partner network includes more than 600 resellers systems integrators and other providers. Arrow Electronics acquired immixGroup in 2015.

	Annual Growth	05/09	05/10	05/11	05/12	05/13
Sales ($ mil.)	(3.5%)	–	563.6	43.6	502.1	505.9
Net income ($ mil.)	(14.3%)	–	–	16.5	13.3	12.1
Market value ($ mil.)	–	–	–	–	–	–
Employees	–	–	–	–	–	201

IMMUCOR INC.

3130 Gateway Dr.
Norcross GA 30091-5625
Phone: 770-441-2051
Fax: 770-441-3807
Web: www.immucor.com

CEO: Jeffrey R Binder
CFO: Dominique Petitgenet
HR: Anthony Howard
FYE: May 31
Type: Private

Immucor makes sure you can feel safe about getting a blood transfusion. The company develops makes and sells manual and automated analysis equipment used by blood banks hospitals and clinical laboratories to test blood prior to transfusions. Its traditional reagents are used to manually test samples for blood type group matching and foreign substance detection while its Galileo Galileo Echo and Galileo NEO automated instrumentation systems use traditional and proprietary Capture reagents to perform multiple blood tests at one time. The company sells its products primarily in North America Western Europe and Japan. Founded in 1982 Immucor is owned by TPG Capital.

IMMTECH PHARMACEUTICALS INC.
PINK SHEETS: IMMP

1 North End Ave. Ste. 1111
New York NY 10282
Phone: 212-791-2911
Fax: 212-791-2917
Web: www.immtech-international.com

CEO: Eric L Sorkin
CFO: –
HR: Helen Reese
FYE: March 31
Type: Public

Immtech Pharmaceuticals has a vendetta against infectious diseases. The development-stage pharmaceutical company has focused its efforts on finding treatments for bacterial viral and fungal infections including hepatitis C and hospital-acquired infections. Much of the company's work is in the early stages of research and development; it halted work on its clinical-stage candidate pafuramidine in 2008 because of safety issues. Immtech has licensed some of its other drug technology from academic researchers at the University of North Carolina at Chapel Hill and Georgia State University.

IMMUNE PHARMACEUTICALS INC
NAS: IMNP

430 East 29th Street, Suite 940
New York, NY 10016
Phone: 646 440-9310
Fax: –
Web: www.epicept.com

CEO: Daniel G Teper
CFO: –
HR: –
FYE: December 31
Type: Public

EpiCept's drug development mission is to help patients avoid pain leukemia remission and other conditions. The company's research pipeline includes AmiKet a topical analgesics for neuropathic pain conditions. Cancer drug candidate Ceplene is a remission maintenance therapy for acute myeloid leukemia (AML) patients; the drug is sold in the EU by Meda and EpiCept is developing Ceplene for additional markets. In 2012 EpiCept agreed to merge with Israeli drug development firm Immune Pharmaceuticals; the transaction will add additional inflammatory disease and cancer candidates to the combined pipeline.

	Annual Growth	12/10	12/11	12/12	12/13	12/14
Sales ($ mil.)	(78.8%)	1.0	0.9	7.8	0.0	0.0
Net income ($ mil.)	–	(15.5)	(15.7)	(2.6)	(5.8)	(23.6)
Market value ($ mil.)	21.3%	20.9	8.4	1.4	55.1	45.3
Employees	(5.9%)	14	11	4	8	11

IMMUCELL CORP.
NAS: ICCC

56 Evergreen Drive
Portland, ME 04103
Phone: 207 878-2770
Fax: –
Web: www.immucell.com

CEO: Michael F Brigham
CFO: –
HR: –
FYE: December 31
Type: Public

Many biotech companies focus on human health but ImmuCell has udder pursuits. The company develops products to help livestock farmers maintain the health of their herds. Its animal-health products include First Defense which prevents diarrhea in calves; MASTiK which diagnoses bovine mammary gland inflammation; rjt a test for highly contagious Johne's Disease in cattle; and Wipe Out Dairy Wipes moist towelettes used to disinfect the teat area of cows prior to milking. ImmuCell makes one product for preventing disease in humans — Isolate (formerly called Crypto-Scan) a test for cryptosporidium in water. When present in municipal drinking water supplies cryptosporidium can cause diarrheal disease in humans.

	Annual Growth	12/10	12/11	12/12	12/13	12/14
Sales ($ mil.)	14.7%	4.4	5.1	5.4	6.0	7.6
Net income ($ mil.)	–	(0.4)	(0.4)	0.1	0.1	(0.2)
Market value ($ mil.)	11.0%	9.7	14.1	12.1	12.9	14.7
Employees	2.3%	32	29	29	30	35

IMMUNOCELLULAR THERAPEUTICS LTD.
NYSE: IMUC

21900 Burbank Blvd. 3rd Fl.
Woodland Hills CA 91367
Phone: 818-992-2907
Fax: 818-992-2908
Web: www.imuc.com

CEO: Andrew Gengos
CFO: David Fractor
HR: –
FYE: December 31
Type: Public

ImmunoCellular Therapeutics primarily targets glioblastoma multiforme (GBM) which can hurt the brain just by trying to say or spell it. However GBM is also regarded as the most aggressive brain cancer affecting humans. The development-stage company is also going after other cancers such as those that attack the ovaries pancreas colon bones and lungs. Its immunotherapy aims not only at normal tumor cells but also the stem cells where cancers grow and recur. ImmunoCellular has a partnership and licensing agreement with Los Angeles' Cedars-Sinai Medical Center to use the latter's technology in its research. The company was founded in 1987 took its current name in 2006 and went public in 2010.

IMMUNOGEN, INC. NMS: IMGN

830 Winter Street
Waltham, MA 02451
Phone: 781 895-0600
Fax: –
Web: www.immunogen.com

CEO: Daniel M Junius
CFO: David B. Johnston
HR: –
FYE: June 30
Type: Public

ImmunoGen really has it out for cancer. Its antibody-drug conjugates (ADC) technology targets tumors delivering an ImmunoGen cell-killing agent specifically to cancer cells. The firm uses its antibodies along with its ADC platform to create product candidates; it also out-licenses the ADC technology to other companies. (Breast cancer drug Kadcyla produced by Roche is the first marketed product using ADC.) ImmunoGen's lead compounds target conditions including lung cancer multiple myeloma and non-Hodgkin's lymphoma. In addition to its proprietary candidates the company has some compounds that are being developed through partnerships and licensing agreements with companies such as Genentech and Amgen.

	Annual Growth	06/11	06/12	06/13	06/14	06/15
Sales ($ mil.)	45.1%	19.3	16.4	35.5	59.9	85.5
Net income ($ mil.)	–	(58.3)	(73.3)	(72.8)	(71.4)	(60.7)
Market value ($ mil.)	4.2%	1,055.4	1,449.3	1,436.3	1,026.0	1,245.0
Employees	6.3%	248	245	280	307	317

IMMUNOMEDICS, INC. NMS: IMMU

300 The American Road
Morris Plains, NJ 07950
Phone: 973 605-8200
Fax: 973 605-8282
Web: www.immunomedics.com

CEO: Cynthia L. Sullivan
CFO: Peter P. Pfreundschuh
HR: –
FYE: June 30
Type: Public

Immunomedics is a MAb scientist mixing up monoclonal antibody (MAb) medicines to treat cancer autoimmune conditions and other diseases. Its lead product epratuzumab is in development for the treatment of lupus; biopharmaceutical firm UCB has licensed the drug for further applications in autoimmune diseases. Immunomedics is also conducting clinical trials for epratuzumab as an oncology treatment for non-Hodgkin's lymphoma. Other drugs in clinical trials aim to treat various cancers including pancreatic cancer and multiple myeloma. It also makes diagnostic imaging products; its majority-owned IBC Pharmaceuticals develops radiotherapeutics for applications in oncology treatments.

	Annual Growth	06/11	06/12	06/13	06/14	06/15
Sales ($ mil.)	(21.3%)	14.7	32.7	5.0	9.0	5.7
Net income ($ mil.)	–	(15.1)	0.8	(12.2)	(35.4)	(48.0)
Market value ($ mil.)	(0.1%)	384.7	336.5	514.1	345.0	383.7
Employees	0.4%	121	124	119	120	123

IMPAC MORTGAGE HOLDINGS, INC. ASE: IMH

19500 Jamboree Road
Irvine, CA 92612
Phone: 949 475-3600
Fax: 949 474-8599
Web: www.impaccompanies.com

CEO: Joseph R Tomkinson
CFO: Todd R Taylor
HR: –
FYE: December 31
Type: Public

Did you feel the impact of the mortgage bust? Impac Mortgage Holdings did. The company was formerly a real estate investment trust that invested in primarily Alt-A (one step above subprime on the creditworthiness scale) residential mortgages second mortgages and mortgage-backed securities. As the credit markets fell and loan defaults rose Impac switched gears and began offering fee-based real estate and asset management services to lenders borrowers servicers and investors. Its Integrated Real Estate Services subsidiary offers mortgage lending portfolio monitoring and title and escrow services. Through Exel Mortgage the company once again began funding conforming residential mortgages in 2010.

	Annual Growth	12/08	12/09	12/10	12/11	12/12
Assets ($ mil.)	(2.8%)	6,715.5	5,872.9	6,153.9	5,612.0	5,986.6
Net income ($ mil.)	–	(44.7)	10.8	10.3	3.2	(3.4)
Market value ($ mil.)	293.2%	0.5	27.9	23.6	17.0	119.5
Employees	43.6%	127	299	376	394	540

IMPAX LABORATORIES INC NMS: IPXL

30831 Huntwood Avenue
Hayward, CA 94544
Phone: 510 240-6000
Fax: –
Web: www.impaxlabs.com

CEO: G. Frederick (Fred) Wilkinson
CFO: Bryan Reasons
HR: Donna Hughes
FYE: December 31
Type: Public

Impax Laboratories is betting that its pharmaceuticals will make a positive impact on the world's health. The company makes specialty generic pharmaceuticals which it markets through its Global Pharmaceuticals division and through marketing alliances with other pharmaceutical firms. It concentrates on controlled-release versions of various generic versions of branded and niche pharmaceuticals that require difficult-to-obtain raw materials or specialized expertise. Additionally the company's branded pharmaceuticals business (Impax Pharmaceuticals) is developing and improving upon previously approved drugs that target Parkinson's disease multiple sclerosis and other central nervous system disorders.

	Annual Growth	12/10	12/11	12/12	12/13	12/14
Sales ($ mil.)	(9.3%)	879.5	512.9	581.7	511.5	596.0
Net income ($ mil.)	(30.8%)	250.4	65.5	55.9	101.3	57.4
Market value ($ mil.)	12.0%	1,432.4	1,436.7	1,459.4	1,790.6	2,256.5
Employees	3.7%	918	1,002	1,125	973	1,061

IMPERIAL INDUSTRIES INC. OTC: IPII

3790 Park Central Blvd. North
Pompano Beach FL 33064
Phone: 954-917-4114
Fax: 954-970-6565
Web: www.imperialindustries.com

CEO: Howard L Ehler Jr
CFO: Steven M Healy
HR: –
FYE: December 31
Type: Public

Imperial Industries manufactures roof tile mortar stucco and plaster adhesive and pool finish products through its Premix-Marbletite Manufacturing subsidiary. Founded in 1968 its primary market is the southeastern US. Its Just-Rite Supply subsidiary which distributed the company's products and such products as gypsum roofing insulation and masonry materials made by other companies ceased operation in mid-2009 and is selling its assets to satisfy creditors. (Just-Rite accounted for about two-thirds of Imperial Industries' sales.) Hardwood flooring company Q.E.P. is buying Imperial Industries.

IMPERIAL IRRIGATION DISTRICT

333 E BARIONI BLVD
IMPERIAL, CA 922511773
Phone: 800-303-7756
Fax: –
Web: www.iid.com

CEO: Keven Kelly
CFO: –
HR: –
FYE: December 31
Type: Private

Imperial Irrigation District (IID) keeps the lights on and the water flowing. A public agency IID is the six largest public power utility in the state of California providing generation transmission and distribution services to more than 145000 residential commercial and industrial customers. It is also the largest irrigation district in the US with more than 3000 miles of canals and drains delivering water to active farmland and providing wholesale water to local municipalities primarily in the Southern California desert corridors of Imperial Valley and Coachella Valley. The district is governed by a five-member board of directors elected by district residents.

	Annual Growth	12/03	12/04	12/05	12/06	12/07
Sales ($ mil.)	12.6%	–	367.7	408.5	503.7	524.2
Net income ($ mil.)	55.8%	–	–	62.6	108.2	151.9
Market value ($ mil.)	–	–	–	–	–	–
Employees	–	–	–	–	–	1,300

IMPERIAL PETROLEUM RECOVERY CORPORATION — PINK SHEETS: IREC

61 S. Concord Forest Cir.
The Woodlands TX 77381
Phone: 281-362-1042
Fax: 281-362-1051
Web: www.iprc.com

CEO: Alan Springer
CFO: –
HR: –
FYE: October 31
Type: Public

Though it sticks to the sludge business Imperial Petroleum Recovery isn't bogged down. The company makes and markets oil sludge remediation equipment for oil producers and refiners pipelines and tankers. Its Microwave Separation Technology system breaks down sludge with heat and recovers hydrocarbon compounds salable oil treatable water and disposable solids. The trailer-mounted system consists of a microwave generator a series of waveguides and tuners and a sludge applicator. Imperial Petroleum Recovery has yet to post a profit and the company's auditors have questioned whether it will be able to stay in business.

IMPERIAL SUGAR COMPANY — NASDAQ: IPSU

1 Imperial Sq. 8016 Hwy. 90A
Sugar Land TX 77478
Phone: 281-491-9181
Fax: 281-490-9530
Web: www.imperialsugarcompany.com

CEO: John C Sheptor
CFO: H P Mechler
HR: –
FYE: December 31
Type: Public

I'm not going to sugar coat this for you: Imperial Sugar is one of the biggest processors and marketers of refined sugar in the US. Its white brown and powdered sugars are sold under name brands — Dixie Crystals Holly and Imperial — and under private labels to retailers. Most refined sugar which generates approximately 85% of the company's sales is sold domestically in bulk and liquid form to industrial markets (mainly food manufacturers of baked goods desserts and beverages) and food service and industrial distributors who sell the sugar to manufacturers restaurants and institutional food service customers. Imperial Sugar was acquired by a subsidiary of Louis Dreyfus Commodities (LDC) in 2012.

IMPERIAL TOY LLC

16641 Roscoe Place
North Hills CA 91343
Phone: 818-536-6500
Fax: 818-536-6501
Web: www.imperialtoy.com

CEO: –
CFO: –
HR: –
FYE: December 31
Type: Private

Even the imperials need their fun. Imperial Toy founded in 1969 is a leading toy manufacturer whose products include bubbles bubble toys girls' role-play toys steel trucks and assorted novelty items. Fred Kort the company's founder and a holocaust survivor came to the US after WWII and created Imperial to bring fun to kids everywhere and to recreate the lost years of his own tumultuous childhood. Imperial's many toys (the catalog of which numbers about 900) are distributed through a global network of distributors (including well-known retailers such as Wal-Mart Kmart and Toys 'R' Us). Co-presidents Peter Tiger and Art Hirsch purchased the company from the Kort family in 2006.

IMPERVA INC. — NYS: IMPV

3400 Bridge Parkway, Suite 200
Redwood Shores, CA 94065
Phone: 650 345-9000
Fax: 650 345-9004
Web: www.imperva.com

CEO: Anthony J. Bettencourt
CFO: Terrence J. (Terry) Schmid
HR: –
FYE: December 31
Type: Public

Imperva aims to create an impervious barrier around corporate data centers. The company's data security platform called SecureSphere protects databases files and Web applications against threats from hackers and insiders and helps its corporate customers maintain regulatory compliance. Subsidiary Incapsula provides cloud-based Web application security services for small and midsized companies. Imperva's security products cater to the energy financial services government health care higher education insurance and retail and e-commerce industries. It was established in 2002.

	Annual Growth	12/10	12/11	12/12	12/13	12/14
Sales ($ mil.)	31.2%	55.4	78.3	104.2	137.8	164.0
Net income ($ mil.)	–	(12.0)	(10.3)	(7.4)	(25.2)	(59.0)
Market value ($ mil.)	12.4%	–	936.2	848.0	1,294.5	1,329.4
Employees	17.8%	375	383	474	580	723

IMPINJ INC.

701 N. 34th St. Ste. 300
Seattle WA 98103
Phone: 206-517-5300
Fax: 206-517-5262
Web: www.impinj.com

CEO: Chris Diorio
CFO: Evan Fein
HR: –
FYE: December 31
Type: Private

Impinj designs semiconductors to adapt to their surroundings. The company's "self-adaptive silicon" technology allows analog circuits — which translate light sound and radio waves into data usable by electronic systems — to be made smaller and more efficient and allow for chip adjustment. The company focuses on designing communications chips particularly UHF Gen 2 radio-frequency identification (RFID) devices for supply chain management/automation (from pharmaceuticals to apparel) and other applications such as food safety and event timing. Impinj was founded in 2000 by chip design legend (and Caltech professor emeritus) Carver Mead and his former student Chris Diorio. The company withdrew its IPO in 2012.

IMPLANT SCIENCES CORP — NBB: IMSC

500 Research Drive, Unit 3
Wilmington, MA 01887
Phone: 978 752-1700
Fax: 978 752-1711
Web: www.implantsciences.com

CEO: William J McGann
CFO: Roger P Deschenes
HR: –
FYE: June 30
Type: Public

Implant Sciences is giving the security industry new technologies to detect explosives. Using its ion implantation know-how the company has developed handheld and tabletop bomb detectors for use in airports and other public places. The firm is developing a walk-through portal through a contract with the Transportation Security Administration. Originally the company applied ion implantation technology into use in medical technology and semiconductor production but has since refocused its operations entirely into security sensors. It is building a customer base in China and the US.

	Annual Growth	06/11	06/12	06/13	06/14	06/15
Sales ($ mil.)	18.2%	6.7	3.4	12.0	8.6	13.0
Net income ($ mil.)	–	(15.6)	(14.6)	(27.4)	(21.0)	(21.5)
Market value ($ mil.)	(1.5%)	63.8	105.1	87.1	78.1	60.1
Employees	18.5%	38	47	57	74	75

IMPRESO INC.
PINK SHEETS: ZCOM
652 Southwestern Blvd.
Coppell TX 75019-4419
Phone: 972-462-0100
Fax: 800-562-5359
Web: www.tstimpreso.com

CEO: –
CFO: –
HR: –
FYE: August 31
Type: Public

Money is just paper to holding company Impreso. Impreso a Spanish word meaning "printed matter" was founded in 1976. Through its primary subsidiary TST/Impreso the company makes and distributes specialty paper and film imaging products. Its paper products include thermal fax copier wide-format continuous-feed and special surface papers such as film transparencies. Impreso operates a number of manufacturing plants and distributes in North America through its warehouses to dealers and other resellers. Impreso owns two other subsidiaries: Hotsheet.com (provides links to popular websites) and Alexa Springs (a custom-label water bottling business). Impreso suspended its SEC reporting obligations in 2006.

IN-N-OUT BURGERS
4199 Campus Dr. 9th Fl.
Irvine CA 92612
Phone: 949-509-6200
Fax: 949-509-6389
Web: www.in-n-out.com

CEO: –
CFO: Annette Neeley
HR: –
FYE: December 31
Type: Private

Made-to-order hamburgers are in and franchising is out at In-N-Out Burger. The company owns and operates about 250 popular burger joints located primarily in California. The chain's menu features just four basic items — hamburgers cheeseburgers the Double-Double (two patties and two slices of cheese) and french fries — but patrons are free to customize how their hamburger is prepared. The chain famously does not use microwaves heat lamps or freezers and it has no franchise operators. In-N-Out does offer on-site catering for parties and events with its In-N-Out Cookout Trailers. Harry and Esther Snyder started the family-owned company in 1948.

IN-Q-TEL INC
2107 WILSON BLVD STE 1100
ARLINGTON, VA 222013079
Phone: 703-248-3000
Fax: –

CEO: Christopher A. R. (Chris) Darby
CFO: Matthew Strottman
HR: Marsha Call
FYE: March 31
Type: Private

Just where do spies go to get their toys? Well James Bond had "Q" and the CIA has In-Q-Tel. While it doesn't deal in exploding pens or cars equipped with missiles this not-for-profit venture capital firm does keep the CIA and the broader US intelligence community equipped with the latest in information technology by investing in innovative high-tech companies. Originally named "Peleus" and renamed after the above-mentioned "007" series character In-Q-Tel was formed in 1999 to help the CIA keep pace with the rapid technological advances of the private sector an increasingly daunting task.

	Annual Growth	05/97	05/98	05/99*	03/10	03/11
Sales ($ mil.)	(11.5%)	–	–	250.3	69.3	57.8
Net income ($ mil.)	72.7%	–	–	0.0	17.6	11.6
Market value ($ mil.)	–	–	–	–	–	–
Employees	–	–	–	–	–	60

*Fiscal year change

INCOME OPPORTUNITY REALTY INVESTORS INC.
NYSE AMEX: IOT
1755 Wittington Place Ste. 340
Dallas TX 75234
Phone: 972-407-8400
Fax: 972-407-8436
Web: www.incomeopp-realty.com

CEO: Daniel J Moos
CFO: Gene S Bertcher
HR: –
FYE: December 31
Type: Public

When opportunity knocks Income Opportunity Realty Investors (IORI) is there to answer. The real estate investment firm owns commercial retail and industrial real estate and land parcels in Texas as well as an apartment complex in Indiana. Transcontinental Realty Investors (TRI) owns about 80% of IORI after buying out the majority stake of Syntek West which had overseen IORI's daily activities. American Realty Investors shares executive officers and board members with both IORI and TRI; affiliates of Prime Income Asset Management manage IORI's properties as well as those of TRI. In 2008 IORI sold six apartment properties in Texas (about half of its assets).

INCONTACT, INC.
NAS: SAAS
7730 S. Union Park Avenue, Suite 500
Salt Lake City, UT 84047
Phone: 801 320-3200
Fax: –
Web: www.incontact.com

CEO: Paul Jarman
CFO: Gregory S. (Greg) Ayers
HR: –
FYE: December 31
Type: Public

inContact keeps customer service agents in touch with customers. The company provides call center software and an enterprise-class telecom network for a complete customer service operation. Small and midsized departments use inContact for handling inbound and outbound customer service calls as well as connectivity services and workforce optimization. Its inCloud Apps allow customers to specify and deploy services that are pre-integrated into the inContact platform. Its products are offered on a pay-as-you-go basis without the costs of premise-based systems. Customers include financial services firms retailers health care organizations utilities and government agencies.

	Annual Growth	12/10	12/11	12/12	12/13	12/14
Sales ($ mil.)	20.3%	82.2	89.0	110.3	130.0	171.8
Net income ($ mil.)	–	(1.1)	(9.4)	(5.4)	(9.0)	(10.6)
Market value ($ mil.)	27.9%	200.1	270.2	316.0	476.4	536.2
Employees	29.5%	330	412	424	547	928

INCYTE CORPORATION
NMS: INCY
1801 Augustine Cut-Off
Wilmington, DE 19803
Phone: 302 498-6700
Fax: –
Web: www.incyte.com

CEO: Herve Hoppenot
CFO: David W Gryska
HR: –
FYE: December 31
Type: Public

Incyte hopes its success with inhibitors is uninhibited. The biotechnology company is focused on discovering and developing drugs that inhibit specific enzymes associated with cancer diabetes blood disorders and inflammatory diseases. The company's lead program is its JAK (Janus associated kinase) inhibitor program which covers treatments for inflammatory diseases and cancers. Its first commercial product JAKAFI is approved for treatment of myelofibrosis (a rare blood cancer). Incyte's other JAK product candidates are in various stages of research and clinical trials partially through partnerships with other drugmakers for conditions including rheumatoid arthritis psoriasis solid tumors and breast cancer.

	Annual Growth	12/10	12/11	12/12	12/13	12/14
Sales ($ mil.)	31.7%	169.9	94.5	297.1	354.9	511.5
Net income ($ mil.)	–	(31.8)	(186.5)	(44.3)	(83.1)	(48.5)
Market value ($ mil.)	45.0%	2,829.7	2,564.9	2,838.3	8,651.5	12,492.8
Employees	24.2%	247	368	413	481	588

INDECK ENERGY SERVICES INC.

600 N. Buffalo Grove Rd. Ste. 300
Buffalo Grove IL 60089
Phone: 847-520-3212
Fax: 847-520-9883
Web: www.indeckenergy.com

CEO: Gerald Forsythe
CFO: Thomas M Capone
HR: –
FYE: November 30
Type: Private

Power plant developer owner and operator Indeck Energy Services tries to make sure it always has a project on deck. The company owns and operates 13 fossil-fueled one hydroelectric and four biomass generation plants located in the US (primarily in the Northeast) and in Canada Guatemala and the UK. Indeck Energy Services operates two plants (400-MW of capacity) in the northeastern US for NRG Energy. Affiliate Indeck Power Equipment rents or leases boilers and generators and Indeck Operations runs and maintains power and steam plants. Chairman and CEO Gerald Forsythe owns Indeck Energy Services which was founded in 1985.

INDEPENDENCE BLUE CROSS

1901 Market St.
Philadelphia PA 19103-1480
Phone: 215-636-9559
Fax: 215-241-0403
Web: www.ibx.com

CEO: Daniel J Hilferty
CFO: –
HR: –
FYE: December 31
Type: Private - Not-for-Pr

Independence Blue Cross (IBC) provides health insurance and related services to some 2.2 million members in southeastern Pennsylvania and through its subsidiaries to more than 3.1 million people nationwide. The company's plans include Personal Choice (PPO) Keystone Health Plan East (HMO and POS) and traditional indemnity options for groups families and individuals. It also offers supplemental Medicare dental vision life and disability insurance. Through subsidiary AmeriHealth Administrators IBC provides third-party administration (TPA) services. It is an independent licensee of the Blue Cross and Blue Shield Association.

INDEPENDENCE FEDERAL SAVINGS BANK — PINK SHEETS: IFSB

1229 Connecticut Ave. NW
Washington DC 20036
Phone: 202-628-5500
Fax: 202-626-7106
Web: www.ifsb.com

CEO: –
CFO: –
HR: –
FYE: December 31
Type: Public

Founded in 1968 to provide loans to African-Americans living in Washington DC Independence Federal Savings Bank continues that mission today. Through three branches in the US capital and nearby Maryland the bank offers standard deposit products such as checking and savings accounts money market accounts and CDs. Mortgages secured by residential and commercial real estate make up almost all of its loan portfolio; the bank ceased providing guaranteed student loans through Sallie Mae in 2008. Chairman Morton Bender owns a majority of Independence Federal. The company withdrew a plan to merge with Maryland-based Colombo Bank after regulatory approvals were delayed indefinitely in 2010.

INDEPENDENCE HOLDING CO. — NYS: IHC

96 Cummings Point Road
Stamford, CT 06902
Phone: 203 358-8000
Fax: 203 348-3103
Web: www.ihcgroup.com

CEO: Roy T.K. Thung
CFO: Teresa A. Herbert
HR: Steven Lapin
FYE: December 31
Type: Public

Independence Holding Company (IHC) wants to hold insurance policies in the US. Through its wholly owned subsidiaries Madison National Life Insurance and Standard Security Life Insurance Company of New York it sells and reinsures health and life insurance to groups and individuals. Though it does offer some major medical plans the company prefers to offer niche coverage such as medical stop-loss insurance (which allows employers to limit their exposure to high health insurance claims) short-term medical coverage critical illness small-group major medical and pet insurance. IHC's majority-owned subsidiary American Independence also writes medical stop-loss insurance.

	Annual Growth	12/10	12/11	12/12	12/13	12/14
Assets ($ mil.)	(3.4%)	1,361.8	1,358.9	1,262.3	1,269.0	1,187.7
Net income ($ mil.)	(7.0%)	21.7	13.0	19.7	13.8	16.3
Market value ($ mil.)	14.5%	141.1	141.2	165.4	234.3	242.3
Employees	(2.0%)	650	580	580	600	600

INDEPENDENT BANK CORP. (MA) — NMS: INDB

2036 Washington Street
Hanover, MA 02339
Phone: 781 878-6100
Fax: –
Web: www.rocklandtrust.com

CEO: Christopher (Chris) Oddleifson
CFO: Robert D. Cozzone
HR: Kathleen Sawyer
FYE: December 31
Type: Public

Independent Bank wants to rock the northeast. Its banking subsidiary Rockland Trust operates almost 75 retail branches as well as investment and lending offices in Eastern Massachusetts and Rhode Island. Serving area individuals and small to midsized businesses the bank offers standard banking services such as checking and savings accounts CDs and credit cards in addition to insurance products financial planning trust services. Commercial loans including industrial construction and small business loans make up more than 70% of Rockland Trust's loan portfolio. Incorporated in 1985 the bank boasts total assets of nearly $7 billion including over $5 billion in deposits and $5 billion in loans.

	Annual Growth	12/10	12/11	12/12	12/13	12/14
Assets ($ mil.)	7.9%	4,695.7	4,970.2	5,757.0	6,099.2	6,364.9
Net income ($ mil.)	10.4%	40.2	45.4	42.6	50.3	59.8
Market value ($ mil.)	12.2%	649.2	654.9	694.8	938.8	1,027.4
Employees	1.6%	919	909	998	984	980

INDEPENDENT BANK CORPORATION (IONIA, MI) — NMS: IBCP

4200 East Beltline
Grand Rapids, MI 49525
Phone: 616 527-5820
Fax: –
Web: www.ibcp.com

CEO: William B Kessel
CFO: Robert N Shuster
HR: Amie Stout
FYE: December 31
Type: Public

Independent Bank Corporation is the holding company for Independent Bank which serves rural and suburban communities of Michigan's Lower Peninsula from more than 100 branches. The bank offers traditional deposit products including checking and savings accounts and CDs. Loans to businesses account for about 40% of the bank's portfolio; real estate mortgages are more than a third. Independent Bank also offers additional products and services like title insurance through subsidiary Independent Title Services and investments through agreement with third-party provider PrimeVest.

	Annual Growth	12/10	12/11	12/12	12/13	12/14
Assets ($ mil.)	(3.0%)	2,535.2	2,307.4	2,023.9	2,209.9	2,248.7
Net income ($ mil.)	–	(16.7)	(20.2)	26.2	77.5	18.0
Market value ($ mil.)	78.1%	29.8	30.5	80.5	275.5	299.6
Employees	(8.3%)	1,240	1,185	934	896	876

INDEPENDENT BANK GROUP INC.   NMS: IBTX

1600 Redbud Boulevard, Suite 400　　　　　　　CEO: David R. Brooks
McKinney, TX 75069-3257　　　　　　　　　　CFO: Michelle S. Hickox
Phone: 972 562-9004　　　　　　　　　　　　　　　　　　　HR: –
Fax: –　　　　　　　　　　　　　　　　　　　　　FYE: December 31
Web: www.ibtx.com　　　　　　　　　　　　　　　　　　Type: Public

It makes sense that a company that calls itself Independent Bank Group (IBG) would do business in a state that was once its own country. The bank holding company does business through subsidiary Independent Bank which operates about 30 branches in Texas. The banks offer standard personal and business accounts and services including some focused on small business owners. IBG has total assets of nearly $2 billion and loans of about $1.4 billion. Most of its branches are in the Dallas-Fort Worth area with a few locations in Central Texas (Waco Austin San Antonio). The company traces its roots back 100 years but was formed in its current incarnation in 2002; it went public in 2013.

	Annual Growth	12/10	12/11	12/12	12/13	12/14
Sales ($ mil.)	24.6%	63.9	67.3	81.1	98.2	153.8
Net income ($ mil.)	21.9%	13.1	13.7	17.4	19.8	29.0
Market value ($ mil.)	(21.3%)	–	–	–	845.8	665.3
Employees	23.5%	–	–	335	340	511

INDEX FRESH INC.

3880 LEMON ST STE 210　　　　　　　　　　　　　　　　CEO: –
RIVERSIDE, CA 925013355　　　　　　　　　　CFO: Merrill Causey
Phone: 909-877-0999　　　　　　　　　　　　　　　　　　HR: –
Fax: –　　　　　　　　　　　　　　　　　　　　　　FYE: October 31
Web: www.indexfresh.com　　　　　　　　　　　　　　　Type: Private

These growers are found in the index under "fresh". Index Fresh is a grower-owned cooperative that packs ships and markets fresh avocados. The produce it sells is grown in California or imported from Mexico and Chile. It markets products to customers across the US. Aside from Index's headquarters near Riverside California it also has three field offices and a fruit delivery station. The company was a grower cooperative dating back to 1929 organized to pack and market lemons and oranges until the 1950s when it absorbed sister cooperative United Avocado Growers. It became a corporation in 1999.

	Annual Growth	10/02	10/03	10/04	10/06	10/07
Sales ($ mil.)	39.5%	–	8.5	11.5	24.7	32.2
Net income ($ mil.)	(68.8%)	–	–	9.6	0.6	0.3
Market value ($ mil.)	–	–	–	–	–	–
Employees	–	–	–	–	–	57

INDIA GLOBALIZATION CAPITAL INC   ASE: IGC

4336 Montgomery Avenue　　　　　　　　　　CEO: Ram Mukunda
Bethesda, MD 20814　　　　　　　　　　　　　CFO: John Clarke
Phone: 301 983-0998　　　　　　　　　　　　　　　　　　HR: –
Fax: –　　　　　　　　　　　　　　　　　　　　　　FYE: March 31
Web: www.indiaglobalcap.com　　　　　　　　　　　　Type: Public

India Globalization Capital (IGC) sounds like a finance firm but its business is much more concrete. It operates mines and quarries that produce cement concrete and other highway and heavy construction materials; builds roads tunnels and other infrastructure projects exports iron ore and provides related logistics. The US-based company serves the infrastructure industry in fast-growing India and China from four offices in India. It operates through three wholly owned subsidiaries all bearing the IGC name and one 77% owned subsidiary Techni Bharathi Ltd that has built highways and tunnels for the National Highway Authority of India and the Indian Railroad.

	Annual Growth	03/11	03/12	03/13	03/14	03/15
Sales ($ mil.)	17.2%	4.1	4.2	8.0	2.3	7.7
Net income ($ mil.)	–	(21.0)	(7.9)	(2.3)	(3.0)	(4.7)
Market value ($ mil.)	(5.1%)	8.0	7.2	4.1	11.5	6.5
Employees	(19.3%)	130	105	110	55	55

INDIANA BOTANIC GARDENS INC

3401 W 37TH AVE　　　　　　　　　　　　　　　　　　CEO: –
HOBART, IN 463421751　　　　　　　　　　　　　　　CFO: –
Phone: 219-947-4040　　　　　　　　　　　　　　　　　　HR: –
Fax: –　　　　　　　　　　　　　　　　　　　　　FYE: December 31
Web: www.botanicchoice.com　　　　　　　　　　　　Type: Private

|Indiana Botanic Gardens makes markets and sells herbal supplements cosmetics and other natural products. Its Botanic Choice and Botanic Spa lines feature such exotic ingredients as hoodia (an African desert plant) Indian Water Hyssop and emu oil. In all it sells about 1700 items to customers throughout the US and abroad. The company does most of its business through its mail-order catalogue and online retail site; it also operates a retail store and offers wholesale sales for other retailers. Joseph E. Meyer author of the classic reference book The Herbalist founded Indiana Botanic Gardens in 1910. His great-grandson Tim Cleland is the company's president.

	Annual Growth	12/07	12/08	12/11	12/12	12/13
Sales ($ mil.)	(2.7%)	–	23.9	21.6	21.3	20.8
Net income ($ mil.)	35.7%	–	–	0.5	(0.1)	1.0
Market value ($ mil.)	–	–	–	–	–	–
Employees	–	–	–	–	–	157

INDIANA HARBOR BELT RAILROAD CO

2721 161ST ST　　　　　　　　　　　　　　　　　　CEO: Jim Roots
HAMMOND, IN 463231099　　　　　　　　　　　CFO: Derek Smith
Phone: 219-989-4703　　　　　　　　　　　　　　　　　　HR: –
Fax: –　　　　　　　　　　　　　　　　　　　　　FYE: December 31
Web: www.ihbrr.com　　　　　　　　　　　　　　　　　Type: Private

Indiana Harbor Belt Railroad provides switching services on its network of more than 50 miles of mainline track in Indiana and Illinois. The company serves the Chicago area which is North America's primary railroad hub. Indiana Harbor Belt handles traffic from industrial customers such as chemical and metal producers and interchanges traffic with about 15 other rail lines. Steel companies account for the largest share of the company's freight traffic. Conrail which is controlled by Norfolk Southern and CSX owns 51% of Indiana Harbor Belt; Canadian Pacific Railway owns 49%. Indiana Harbor Belt Railroad was formed in 1907.

	Annual Growth	12/08	12/09	12/10	12/11	12/12
Sales ($ mil.)	10.9%	–	85.1	107.3	111.1	116.0
Net income ($ mil.)	(33.6%)	–	–	9.7	6.3	4.3
Market value ($ mil.)	–	–	–	–	–	–
Employees	–	–	–	–	–	750

INDIANA INSURANCE COMPANY

6281 Tri-Ridge Blvd.　　　　　　　　　　　　CEO: Richard Bell
Loveland OH 45140　　　　　　　　　　　　　　　　　　CFO: –
Phone: 513-576-3200　　　　　　　　　　　　　　　　　　HR: –
Fax: 800-436-9611　　　　　　　　　　　　　　　FYE: December 31
Web: www.indiana-ins.com　　　　　　　　　　　　Type: Subsidiary

It may have a Hoosier name but Indiana Insurance has a wider regional base. The property/casualty insurer offers products in Illinois Indiana Michigan Minnesota Nebraska North Dakota South Dakota and Wisconsin. The company offers a variety of commercial and personal insurance coverage including automobile homeowners umbrella and workers' compensation policies. It targets individuals and small and midsized businesses as well as schools marketing its products through local independent agents. The company also offers commercial claims and litigation management services as well as loss control programs. Indiana Insurance is a member of the Agency Markets unit of Boston-based Liberty Mutual.

INDIANA MICHIGAN POWER COMPANY

1 Riverside Plaza
Columbus OH 43215-2372
Phone: 614-716-1000
Fax: 614-716-1823
Web: www.indianamichiganpower.com

CEO: Nicholas K Akins
CFO: Brian X Tierney
HR: –
FYE: December 31
Type: Subsidiary

Indiana Michigan Power flips the switch where the Hoosiers and the Wolverines live and work. The utility serves about 582000 electricity customers over its 24220-mile transmission and distribution system in eastern and northern Indiana and southwestern Michigan. The American Electric Power subsidiary also sells power wholesale to other energy market participants and it has some 5930 MW of capacity from its primarily fossil-fueled (61% of total capacity) and nuclear power plants. Indiana Michigan Power owns the Cook Plant in Michigan which consists of two nuclear generating units with a capacity of 2160 MW. Nuclear power accounts for about 36% of Indiana Michigan Power's generating capacity.

INDIANA UNIVERSITY FOUNDATION INC.

1500 N STATE ROAD 46 BYP
BLOOMINGTON, IN 47408
Phone: 812-855-8311
Fax: –
Web: www.iufoundation.iu.edu

CEO: –
CFO: James Perin
HR: –
FYE: June 30
Type: Private

Hoosier favorite fund-raiser? If you're a fan of Indiana University then it might well be the Indiana University Foundation (IUF). The not-for-profit foundation raises more than $100 million annually in donations from individuals corporations and institutional organizations; alumni gifts account for about half of IUF's funds. It manages an endowment of about $1 billion and provides administrative services for gift accounts and scholarship and fellowship accounts. The organization has offices in Bloomington and Indianapolis. IUF was established in 1936.

	Annual Growth	06/09	06/10	06/11	06/12	06/13
Assets ($ mil.)	8.8%	–	1,767.6	2,054.9	2,105.5	2,277.6
Net income ($ mil.)	(35.2%)	–	–	255.3	(11.5)	107.2
Market value ($ mil.)	–	–	–	–	–	–
Employees	–	–	–	–	–	220

INDIANA UNIVERSITY HEALTH BLOOMINGTON INC.

601 W 2ND ST
BLOOMINGTON, IN 474032317
Phone: 812-353-9830
Fax: –
Web: www.bloomingtonhospital.org

CEO: –
CFO: Jim Myers
HR: –
FYE: December 31
Type: Private

Indiana University Health Bloomington wants to put a bloom back in patients' cheeks. The facility operating as IU Health Bloomington provides care in a ten-county region in south central Indiana. The not-for-profit hospital — which includes a 350-bed main campus in Bloomington and a 25-bed rural hospital in Paoli — provides care in a number of medical specialties including cardiovascular disease cancer orthopedics and neuroscience. It also runs home health and hospice urgent care lab and specialty care facilities as well as physician practices under the name Southern Indiana Physicians. IU Health Bloomington is part of the Indiana University Health (IU Health) system.

	Annual Growth	12/08	12/09	12/10	12/11	12/12
Sales ($ mil.)	0.8%	–	346.8	359.4	391.6	355.7
Net income ($ mil.)	45.9%	–	–	30.2	22.4	64.3
Market value ($ mil.)	–	–	–	–	–	–
Employees	–	–	–	–	–	3,200

INDIANA UNIVERSITY HEALTH INC.

1701 N SENATE BLVD
INDIANAPOLIS, IN 462021239
Phone: 317-962-2000
Fax: –
Web: www.iuhealth.org

CEO: Daniel F. (Dan) Evans
CFO: –
HR: –
FYE: December 31
Type: Private

Indiana University Health (IU Health) cares about health care for all in the state of Indiana. As one of the largest health systems in the state not-for-profit IU Health owns or is affiliated with more than 20 hospitals and health centers throughout the state including three major hospitals — Methodist Hospital Indiana University Hospital and Riley Hospital for Children — that serve the downtown Indianapolis area. The largest Methodist Hospital features the Methodist Research Institute which conducts research and clinical trials. The system's hospitals also serve as teaching facilities for Indiana University's medical school.

	Annual Growth	12/03	12/04	12/05	12/06	12/08
Sales ($ mil.)	(12.7%)	–	–	–	2,478.3	1,889.6
Net income ($ mil.)	–	–	–	–	159.1	(24.0)
Market value ($ mil.)	–	–	–	–	–	–
Employees	–	–	–	–	–	17,242

INDIANAPOLIS COLTS INC.

7001 W. 56th St.
Indianapolis IN 46254
Phone: 317-297-2658
Fax: 317-297-8971
Web: www.colts.com

CEO: –
CFO: –
HR: –
FYE: January 31
Type: Private

Fans of this team are can saddle up for football glory. The Indianapolis Colts trace a long and storied history as a franchise in the National Football League boasting five championships since joining the league in 1953. Most of those glory days though took place when the team was the Baltimore Colts and boasted the likes of Johnny Unitas on its roster. The team relocated to Indianapolis in 1984 but fans there had to wait until the 2006 season for the team to make a successful Super Bowl run with the help of such talent as Peyton Manning and Marvin Harrison. Started by Carroll Rosenbloom the team has been owned by CEO James Irsay and his family since 1972.

INDIANAPOLIS MOTOR SPEEDWAY CORPORATION

4790 W. 16th St.
Indianapolis IN 46222-2550
Phone: 317-481-8500
Fax: 513-684-7500
Web: www.burke.com

CEO: Anton H George
CFO: Jeffrey G Belskus
HR: –
FYE: December 31
Type: Private

The Brickyard might be stationary but those who compete there are anything but. Indianapolis Motor Speedway Corporation (IMS) owns and operates the 2.5 mile race track also known as the Brickyard that is home to the famous Indianapolis 500. A spotlight event of the Indy Racing League (IRL) and American motorsports in general the Indy 500 is held every Memorial Day weekend and draws more than 250000 spectators. IMS also hosts the Brickyard 400 an event sanctioned by NASCAR as well as the Red Bull Indianapolis GP. In addition to the track IMS operates a hotel and an 18-hole golf course. The track was built in 1911 and acquired by Tony Hulman in 1945. His family continues to own IMS.

INDUS CORPORATION

1951 KIDWELL DR FL 8
VIENNA, VA 221823930
Phone: 703-506-6776
Fax: –
Web: www.induscorp.us.com

CEO: Shivram Krishnan
CFO: Donald Shoff
HR: Gulay Muslu
FYE: December 31
Type: Private

INDUS hopes to capitalize on technology by providing a variety of information technology (IT) services to the federal government and commercial clients. The company's services include software design consulting application integration systems engineering and enterprise support services. Its areas of expertise include database management data warehousing and data mining; Web development; geographic information systems (GIS); telecommunications; and data security. The company has nine satellite offices in the US. Clients have included NASA the Department of Defense and Homeland Security agencies. INDUS CEO and majority owner Shiv Krishnan founded the company in 1993.

	Annual Growth	12/01	12/02	12/03	12/04	12/14
Sales ($ mil.)	–	–	(153.6)	61.0	75.3	51.4
Net income ($ mil.)	2.2%	–	–	2.6	3.8	3.3
Market value ($ mil.)	–	–	–	–	–	–
Employees	–	–	–	–	–	450

INDUSTRIAL SCIENTIFIC CORPORATION

1001 OAKDALE RD
OAKDALE, PA 150711500
Phone: 412-788-4353
Fax: –
Web: www.indsci.com

CEO: –
CFO: –
HR: Harrold Griffith
FYE: December 31
Type: Private

Detection is a gas for Industrial Scientific. The company makes sells rents and services gas monitoring instruments systems software and related products to detect oxygen and combustible and toxic gases. Its Instrument Network (iNet) tracks the performance of customers' gas monitors and provides status reports as well as instant notification if a problem is detected. Its portable and fixed monitors ("sniffers") calibration stations transmitters controllers and accessories are designed to work alone or together through iNet. The products are used worldwide in work environments such as underground mines and oil refineries as well as by hazardous response units.

	Annual Growth	01/03	01/04	01/05	01/06*	12/07
Sales ($ mil.)	33.6%	–	59.1	63.2	72.7	140.8
Net income ($ mil.)	31.7%	–	–	7.2	8.8	12.5
Market value ($ mil.)	–	–	–	–	–	–
Employees	–	–	–	–	–	700

*Fiscal year change

INDUSTRIAL SERVICES OF AMERICA INC. (FL)   NAS: IDSA

7100 Grade Lane, P.O. Box 32428
Louisville, KY 40232
Phone: 502 368-1661
Fax: 502 368-1440
Web: www.isa-inc.com

CEO: Harry Kletter
CFO: Todd L. Phillips
HR: –
FYE: December 31
Type: Public

Industrial Services of America manages solid waste and scrap metals so its customers don't have to. Its Computerized Waste Systems (CWS) unit doesn't pick up trash but instead arranges waste disposal services for its commercial and industrial customers at 2300 locations. CWS negotiates contracts with service providers and offers centralized billing and dispatching and invoice auditing services. Industrial Services of America's ISA Recycling unit handles ferrous and nonferrous metals and fiber products and the company's Waste Equipment Sales & Service unit sells leases and services waste handling and recycling equipment.

	Annual Growth	12/10	12/11	12/12	12/13	12/14
Sales ($ mil.)	(23.5%)	343.0	276.9	194.2	136.8	117.4
Net income ($ mil.)	–	–	8.1	(3.9)	(6.6)	(13.8)	(7.3)
Market value ($ mil.)	(16.5%)	97.9	42.2	19.1	25.2	47.5
Employees	(15.1%)	185	176	155	108	96

INDYNE INC.

11800 SUNRISE VALLEY DR # 250
RESTON, VA 201915300
Phone: 703-903-6900
Fax: –
Web: www.indyneinc.com

CEO: –
CFO: –
HR: –
FYE: December 31
Type: Private

InDyne offers out-of-this-world technology expertise. The company provides information technology science and engineering and technical and administrative services primarily to US government agencies including NASA. It develops custom software designs Web sites and builds computer networks. InDyne's science and engineering division designs aerospace systems provides space mission support and crew training and offers structural and fluid analysis. Its technical and administrative services unit handles imagery operations data management media services and operations support. InDyne's projects have included the development of custom database software for the CDC and the Department of Transportation.

	Annual Growth	12/06	12/07	12/08	12/09	12/10
Sales ($ mil.)	(57.6%)	–	–	1,449.3	256.0	260.4
Net income ($ mil.)	1951.1%	–	–	0.0	7.7	6.9
Market value ($ mil.)	–	–	–	–	–	–
Employees	–	–	–	–	–	1,700

INFINERA CORP   NMS: INFN

140 Caspian Court
Sunnyvale, CA 94089
Phone: 408 572-5200
Fax: –
Web: www.infinera.com

CEO: Thomas J. (Tom) Fallon
CFO: Brad Feller
HR: –
FYE: December 27
Type: Public

To Infinera and beyond! The buzz on this company is that it designs photonic integrated circuits (PICs) intended to replace much larger components within optical networks. (Optical networks are used to provide high-speed Internet access 3G/4G mobile broadband business Ethernet services cloud-based services and wholesale bandwidth services.) Infinera also offers networking equipment built around these chips which are made from indium phosphide — a specialized compound semiconductor material that offers light-years faster performance than standard silicon. Customers include cable system operators ISPs and telecos such as Cox Communications Interoute Deutsche Telekom Global Crossing and Level 3.

	Annual Growth	12/10	12/11	12/12	12/13	12/14
Sales ($ mil.)	10.1%	454.4	404.9	438.4	544.1	668.1
Net income ($ mil.)	–	(27.9)	(81.7)	(85.3)	(32.1)	13.7
Market value ($ mil.)	9.7%	1,300.7	792.5	731.7	1,235.1	1,881.0
Employees	8.7%	1,072	1,181	1,242	1,318	1,495

INFINITE ENERGY INC.

7001 SW 24TH AVE
GAINESVILLE, FL 326073704
Phone: 352-331-1654
Fax: –
Web: www.infiniteenergy.com

CEO: Darin Cook
CFO: –
HR: –
FYE: December 31
Type: Private

Infinite wisdom? No. Infinite energy? Yes. Infinite Energy does not provide its customers with the natural high of endorphins or with the latest health diet but with the more prosaic commodity of natural gas. The company supplies natural gas to clients in Florida Georgia and New York. Wholesale customers include municipalities institutions and utilities; Infinite Energy also sells to large and small commercial establishments (including restaurants) and to residential customers.

	Annual Growth	12/02	12/03	12/04	12/05	12/09
Sales ($ mil.)	6.0%	–	335.8	474.0	583.9	477.6
Net income ($ mil.)	8.5%	–	–	8.7	4.5	13.0
Market value ($ mil.)	–	–	–	–	–	–
Employees	–	–	–	–	–	250

INFINITE GROUP, INC.   NBB: IMCI

80 Office Park Way
Pittsford, NY 14534
Phone: 585 385-0610
Fax: -
Web: www.igius.com

CEO: James A. (Jim) Villa
CFO: James Witzel
HR: -
FYE: December 31
Type: Public

As far as Infinite Group Inc. (IGI) is concerned it's capacity to handle its clients' IT outsourcing is unlimited — particularly for government clients. The company provides infrastructure management information security systems engineering server and desktop virtualization enterprise architecture and software development. US government contracts account for the majority of IGI's sales and some its government clients are the Department of Homeland Security and the US Navy. The company has offices in New York Colorado and Virginia (which serves its DC customers).

	Annual Growth	12/10	12/11	12/12	12/13	12/14
Sales ($ mil.)	(2.3%)	9.4	9.2	8.7	8.7	8.6
Net income ($ mil.)	-	(1.1)	0.0	0.3	0.1	(0.5)
Market value ($ mil.)	9.6%	0.9	1.7	6.4	2.9	1.3
Employees	1.9%	77	77	74	74	83

INFINITY ENERGY RESOURCES INC.   PINK SHEETS: IFNY

11900 College Blvd. Ste. 204
Overland Park KS 66210
Phone: 913-948-9512
Fax: 913-338-4458
Web: www.infinity-res.com

CEO: Stanton E Ross
CFO: Daniel F Hutchins
HR: -
FYE: December 31
Type: Public

Maybe nothing lasts forever but Infinity Energy Resources hopes that US demand for fossil fuels won't go away for a long long time. The company focuses its oil exploration and production operations in the Fort Worth Basin of Texas in the Rocky Mountain region in the Greater Green River Basin in Wyoming and the Sand Wash and Piceance Basins in Colorado. It is also pursuing an opportunity in offshore Nicaragua. The company has proved reserves of 7.8 billion cu. ft. of natural gas equivalent. Infinity Energy Resources has exited the oil services business.

INFINITY PHARMACEUTICALS INC   NMS: INFI

780 Memorial Drive
Cambridge, MA 02139
Phone: 617 453-1000
Fax: -
Web: www.infi.com

CEO: Adelene Q Perkins
CFO: Lawrence E Bloch
HR: -
FYE: December 31
Type: Public

Infinity Pharmaceuticals acts on the endless possibilities for new cancer treatments. The firm works to discover and develop targeted therapies for different types of cancer including non-small cell lung cancer. Such targeted therapies aim at inhibiting specific disease signaling pathways and proteins. In addition to cancer Infinity Pharmaceuticals has candidates for various inflammatory conditions and autoimmune diseases. The company has multiple programs in preclinical and clinical trial stages; it also investigates candidates through partnerships with other drugmakers.

	Annual Growth	12/08	12/09	12/10	12/11	12/12
Sales ($ mil.)	(13.3%)	83.4	49.5	71.3	92.8	47.1
Net income ($ mil.)	-	23.7	(32.5)	(49.0)	(40.0)	(54.0)
Market value ($ mil.)	44.7%	379.5	293.5	281.7	419.9	1,662.5
Employees	(1.1%)	161	179	168	190	154

INFINITY PROPERTY & CASUALTY CORP   NMS: IPCC

3700 Colonnade Parkway, Suite 600
Birmingham, AL 35243
Phone: 205 870-4000
Fax: -
Web: www.infinityauto.com

CEO: James R. Gober
CFO: Roger Smith
HR: -
FYE: December 31
Type: Public

Infinity Property and Casualty does have its limits but it goes farther than most to cover high-risk drivers. The insurer primarily provides personal non-standard auto policies — Infinity is a leading writer of policies for high-risk drivers in the US. The company also offers standard and preferred personal auto commercial small fleet and classic collector auto insurance. Licensed in all 50 states the company currently focuses its business on targeted urban areas of a handful of states. Personal non-standard auto insurance accounts for more than 90% of its premiums; California accounts for about half of that business. Infinity distributes its products through more than 12900 independent agents.

	Annual Growth	12/10	12/11	12/12	12/13	12/14
Assets ($ mil.)	6.5%	1,852.4	1,936.8	2,303.6	2,317.3	2,384.8
Net income ($ mil.)	(11.1%)	91.5	42.1	24.3	32.6	57.2
Market value ($ mil.)	5.7%	709.7	651.6	668.8	823.9	887.2
Employees	3.7%	1,900	2,100	2,200	2,400	2,200

INFOBLOX INC   NYS: BLOX

3111 Coronado Drive
Santa Clara, CA 95054
Phone: 408 986-4000
Fax: 408 986-4001
Web: www.infoblox.com

CEO: Jesper Andersen
CFO: Janesh Moorjani
HR: -
FYE: July 31
Type: Public

Infoblox thinks its products for managing core network services stack up well against the competition. Customers from various sectors use its products to automate consolidate and more securely operate corporate networks. The company's Trinzic DDI network identity appliances manage such functions as Internet domain name server (DNS) resolution IP address management and network access control. Its NetMRI product line automates network change and configuration management processes. Infoblox works cooperatively with networking equipment vendors including CA Avaya Neustar VMware Cisco and Juniper Networks. The company was founded in 1999 when it released the first hardened DNS appliance.

	Annual Growth	07/11	07/12	07/13	07/14	07/15
Sales ($ mil.)	23.2%	132.8	169.2	225.0	250.3	306.1
Net income ($ mil.)	-	(5.3)	(8.2)	(4.4)	(23.9)	(27.1)
Market value ($ mil.)	3.8%	-	1,236.1	1,923.9	713.1	1,382.6
Employees	11.8%	494	520	603	691	772

INFOGLIDE SOFTWARE CORPORATION

6500 River Place Bldg. 2 Ste. 101
Austin TX 78730
Phone: 512-532-3500
Fax: 512-532-3505
Web: www.infoglide.com

CEO: -
CFO: -
HR: -
FYE: December 31
Type: Private

Infoglide Software wants your quest for information to proceed smoothly. The company's Identity Resolution Engine (IRE) software scans multiple disparate databases for fraud risk and conflicts of interest. IRE makes automated decisions based on an organization's policies and applies them in real time to business processes. Its applications include employment and terrorist screening retail returns management detection of insurance claims fraud and compliance. Established in 1996 the company offers services to customers in the government insurance law enforcement banking and retail sectors.

INFOGROUP INC.

1020 E. 1st St.
Papillion NE 68046
Phone: 402-593-4500
Fax: 402-596-8902
Web: www.infogroup.com

CEO: Michael Iaccarino
CFO: Richard Hanks
HR: –
FYE: December 31
Type: Private

Making business information available for marketing purposes keeps this group together. Formerly infoUSA Infogroup is a provider of data and marketing products and services designed to help businesses with direct marketing and sales prospecting. Clients ranging from local businesses to Fortune 100 companies use Infogroup's data and services to find new customers and grow sales and for telemarketing customer analysis and credit referencing purposes. Infogroup also provides business information through social data solutions. Private equity firm CCMP Capital Advisors owns the company.

INFORMA INVESTMENT SOLUTIONS INC.

4 Gannett Dr.
White Plains NY 10604
Phone: 914-640-0200
Fax: 914-694-6728
Web: www.informais.com

CEO: Leno Toich
CFO: –
HR: –
FYE: December 31
Type: Subsidiary

Keeping investors informed is what Informa Investment Solutions is all about. The company specializes in software for financial institutions investment managers and independent financial advisors. Informa Investment Solutions' products include PSN software for managers of separate accounts Performer software for portfolio performance evaluation and reporting and Wealth Management System software for financial planning. Informa Investment Solutions which traces its roots to the founding of Effron Enterprises in 1976 took its present form in 2004 when parent Informa combined subsidiaries Effron Enterprises Plan Sponsor Network and netDecide into one operating unit.

INFOR GLOBAL SOLUTIONS INC.

641 Avenue of the Americas 4th Fl.
New York NY 10011
Phone: 678-319-8000
Fax: 678-319-8682
Web: www.infor.com

CEO: Charles Phillips
CFO: Kevin Samuelson
HR: –
FYE: May 31
Type: Private

Before manufacturers and distributors get products to the shelf Infor Global Solutions gets software to their computers. The company develops enterprise applications used for a wide range of business purposes that automate and link disparate functions across an organization. Uses for its products include managing inventories tracking shipments and managing customer interactions. Infor targets such industries as automotive chemicals consumer packaged goods food processing and pharmaceuticals. Clients have included Bristol-Myers Squibb Cargill Grohe Heinz and TRW. The company has customers in about 200 countries. Infor is controlled by a group of investors led by Golden Gate Capital and Summit Partners.

INFORMATICA CORP.

NMS: INFA

2100 Seaport Boulevard
Redwood City, CA 94063
Phone: 650 385-5000
Fax: –
Web: www.informatica.com

CEO: Anil Chakravarthy
CFO: Earl E Fry
HR: –
FYE: December 31
Type: Public

Big data is a big opportunity for Informatica. The company provides enterprise data integration software that enables companies to access integrate and consolidate their data across a variety of systems and users. Its PowerCenter platform consolidates codes and moves large data warehouses and its PowerExchange software enables access to bulk or changed data. Other products include Master Data Management (MDM) and the Informatica B2B Data Exchange as well as Fast Clone (data replication) Data Explorer (data quality) and a range of software-as-a-service (SaaS) offerings which integrate data from other business applications into a single hosted platform.

	Annual Growth	12/09	12/10	12/11	12/12	12/13
Sales ($ mil.)	17.3%	500.7	650.1	783.8	811.6	948.2
Net income ($ mil.)	7.7%	64.2	86.3	117.5	93.2	86.4
Market value ($ mil.)	12.5%	2,811.7	4,783.6	4,012.2	3,294.1	4,508.7
Employees	16.5%	1,755	2,126	2,554	2,814	3,234

INFORELIANCE CORPORATION

4050 Legato Rd. Ste. 700
Fairfax VA 22033
Phone: 703-246-9360
Fax: 703-246-9331
Web: www.inforeliance.com

CEO: Andrew J Butler
CFO: Chrissy Bristow
HR: –
FYE: December 31
Type: Private

If you need to rely on information technology services InfoReliance could be the contractor you want. Founded in 2000 the company provides commercial and government customers with custom Web-based software development and IT services such as systems integration portal and network design project management consulting and training. Clients have included the US departments of Agriculture and Commerce; the US Army; the Centers for Disease Control and Prevention; and the Drug Enforcement Administration. Its commercial customers come from industries including financial services health care and manufacturing and have included Epson Microsoft and Diversified Lending Group.

INFORMATION ANALYSIS INC.

NBB: IAIC

11240 Waples Mill Road, Suite 201
Fairfax, VA 22030
Phone: 703 383-3000
Fax: –
Web: www.infoa.com

CEO: Sandor Rosenberg
CFO: Richard S Derose
HR: –
FYE: December 31
Type: Public

Obsolete computer programs goto that great big disk drive in the sky thanks to Information Analysis Incorporated (IAI). The company's software and services help government agencies and corporations migrate from older mainframe-based computer systems to client-server and Web-based applications. IAI offers programming platform migration systems analysis training and maintenance. The company is a Micro Focus partner and uses its modernization software as well as applications by Oracle and SAP. The federal government accounts for the majority of sales but corporate clients include Aleris and Rich Products. IAI was founded in 1979; chairman and CEO Sandor Rosenberg controls 16% of the company's stock.

	Annual Growth	12/10	12/11	12/12	12/13	12/14
Sales ($ mil.)	(4.2%)	6.9	7.8	7.1	7.5	5.8
Net income ($ mil.)	–	0.1	0.2	0.1	(0.1)	(0.0)
Market value ($ mil.)	5.4%	1.7	1.8	1.7	1.9	2.1
Employees	(0.9%)	28	28	32	27	27

INFORMATION BUILDERS INC.

2 Penn Plaza 27th Fl.
New York NY 10121-2898
Phone: 212-736-4433
Fax: 212-967-6406
Web: www.informationbuilders.com

CEO: Gerald D Cohen
CFO: –
HR: –
FYE: December 31
Type: Private

Information Builders Inc. (IBI) wants to help you grow your business intelligently. The company's flagship WebFOCUS software makes it easier to conduct data integration and business intelligence analysis over the Internet intranets and with mobile devices. Customers use IBI's products to collect analyze and distribute a variety of enterprise data. Its iWay Software subsidiary offers middleware technology that helps businesses integrate legacy systems with newer applications. Information Builders also provides consulting training and support services. President and CEO Gerald Cohen helped found IBI in 1975 bootstrapping the company's operations with advance payments from its first two customers.

INFORMATION SERVICES GROUP INC
NMS: III

Two Stamford Plaza, 281 Tresser Boulevard
Stamford, CT 06901
Phone: 203 517-3100
Fax: –
Web: www.isg-one.com

CEO: –
CFO: David E Berger
HR: Martha Preston
FYE: December 31
Type: Public

True to its name Information Services Group's (ISG) service is information. ISG provides technology insights market intelligence and advisory services to companies seeking to outsource their business operations. The company specializes in marketing advertising human resources legal supply chain management and other business services. It targets North American European and Asia/Pacific markets and has operations in some 20 countries. It serves such industries as telecom financial services health care pharmaceutical and utilities. ISG operates through subsidiaries TPI Advisory Services (data and advisory) Compass (benchmarking and analysis) and STA Consulting (public sector IT services).

	Annual Growth	12/10	12/11	12/12	12/13	12/14
Sales ($ mil.)	12.3%	132.0	184.4	192.7	211.0	209.6
Net income ($ mil.)	–	(53.2)	(55.9)	0.6	4.8	6.2
Market value ($ mil.)	19.5%	76.1	37.9	42.3	155.9	155.1
Employees	19.8%	438	699	812	850	902

INFOSONICS CORP
NAS: IFON

3636 Nobel Drive, Suite 325
San Diego, CA 92122-1078
Phone: 858 373-1600
Fax: –
Web: www.infosonics.com

CEO: Joseph Ram
CFO: Vernon A Loforti
HR: –
FYE: December 31
Type: Public

InfoSonics answers the call for phone fulfillment. The company distributes a wide variety of cell phone models and accessories from electronics manufacturers such as LG Electronics and Novatel Wireless. It supplies and supports retailers wireless carriers and distributors in South and Central America India and China from facilities centers in San Diego Miami and Beijing. InfoSonics' services include inspection testing programming software loading and light assembly. Its logistics business includes outsourced supply chain services such as inventory management and customized packaging. InfoSonics also sells its own line of phones under the verykool brand.

	Annual Growth	12/10	12/11	12/12	12/13	12/14
Sales ($ mil.)	(9.7%)	72.5	34.9	34.3	37.9	48.1
Net income ($ mil.)	–	(3.6)	(2.5)	(2.5)	(0.6)	0.3
Market value ($ mil.)	9.1%	11.1	8.9	9.3	22.0	15.7
Employees	(4.6%)	70	88	103	67	58

INFOVISION INC.

800 E CAMPBELL RD STE 388
RICHARDSON, TX 75081-1841
Phone: 972-234-0058
Fax: –
Web: www.infovision.net

CEO: –
CFO: –
HR: Jessi Coleman
FYE: December 31
Type: Private

Infovision's insight is all about computer systems. The company designs and integrates large and small software systems for clients in the telecom manufacturing banking financial services retail pharmaceuticals and energy industries. With expertise in a wide range of technologies — including multi-tier architectures database administration statistical analysis graphical user interfaces and enterprise resource planning — Infovision offers contract services outsourcing engineering services vendor management and offshore software development. The company was co-founded in 1995 by chairman Sean Yalamanchi and director Raman Kovelamudi.

	Annual Growth	12/02	12/03	12/04	12/05	12/11
Sales ($ mil.)	–	–	0.0	29.0	38.2	50.7
Net income ($ mil.)	86.1%	–	0.0	13.3	4.9	2.4
Market value ($ mil.)	–	–	–	–	–	–
Employees	–	–	–	–	–	600

ING BANK FSB

1 S. Orange St.
Wilmington DE 19801
Phone: 302-658-2200
Fax: +44-1753-552-662
Web: www.adler.co.uk

CEO: Ralph Hamers
CFO: Pg Flynn
HR: –
FYE: December 31
Type: Subsidiary

Orange you glad you can count on ING Bank? The company better known as ING Direct offers the Orange Savings Account which boasts higher-than-average interest rates and one of the highest yields in the industry. Doing business in the US via the Internet over the phone by ATM and by mail ING Direct also offers certificates of deposit individual retirement accounts home mortgages and paperless checking accounts. For businesses ING Direct offers savings accounts CDs and 401(k) plans. The bank offers online brokerage services through ING Direct Investing (formerly ShareBuilder) which it acquired in 2007. Capital One bought ING Direct from Amsterdam-based ING Groep for some $9 billion in 2012.

ING DIRECT INVESTING INC.

83 S. King St. Ste. 700
Seattle WA 98104
Phone: 310-244-4000
Fax: 310-244-2626
Web: www.screengems.net

CEO: –
CFO: Dan Greenshields
HR: –
FYE: December 31
Type: Subsidiary

ING DIRECT Investing helps the average individual investor construct a profitable portfolio. Doing business as ShareBuilder the online brokerage arm of online bank ING Direct USA offers real-time trading of more than 7000 stocks options mutual funds and exchange-traded funds over the phone via mobile device and online. Amerstam-based ING Groep sold ING Direct USA and ING DIRECT Investing to Capital One for some $9 billion in 2012. The deal was made to satisfy terms of a restructuring plan from the European Commission and includes a licensing agreement through which Capital One continues to use the ING brand at the online brokerage and the online bank.

ING NORTH AMERICA INSURANCE CORPORATION

5780 Powers Ferry Rd. NW
Atlanta GA 30327-4390
Phone: 770-980-5100
Fax: 770-980-3301
Web: www.ing-usa.com

CEO: Rodney O Martin Jr
CFO: David A Wheat
HR: –
FYE: December 31
Type: Subsidiary

From New York to Los Angeles individuals to institutions ING North America Insurance has a plan. The company offers insurance and financial products including fixed and variable annuities life insurance individual life reinsurance and retirement savings plans. It also provides policy brokerage investment planning mutual funds wealth management and employee benefits administration. ING North America administers and manages the life and accident insurance policies underwritten by affiliates including ReliaStar Life Insurance ING Life Insurance and Annuity Midwestern United Life and Security Life of Denver. ING North America Insurance is a subsidiary of Dutch financial services giant ING Groep.

ING U.S. INC.

230 Park Ave.
New York NY 10169
Phone: 212-309-8200
Fax: 303-532-1642
Web: www.heatwurx.com

CEO: Rodney O Martin Jr
CFO: Ewout L Steenbergen
HR: –
FYE: December 31
Type: Private

ING U.S. is the American arm of Dutch financial services firm ING Groep. It offers retirement investment and insurance (mostly life) services to 13 million individual and corporate customers. Retirement products include IRAs brokerage accounts and annuities; it has about $107 billion in assets under management (AUM) for this segment. ING U.S.'s investment management services with $166 billion AUM include international and domestic equity fixed-income and multi-asset products. Insurance covers individual term and universal life as well as employee benefits (stop loss group life disability) which it sells to midsized and large companies. Formed in 1999 the company filed to go public in 2012.

INGENICO CORP.

6195 Shiloh Rd. Ste. D
Alpharetta GA 30005
Phone: 678-456-1200
Fax: 678-456-1201
Web: www.ingenico-us.com

CEO: Philip Lazar
CFO: –
HR: –
FYE: December 31
Type: Subsidiary

Ingenico Corp. wants to make a swipe across the North American electronic payment market. The company develops and sells electronic payment hardware and software for the finance health care hospitality retail and transportation industries. Its point-of-sale terminals and scanners verify check debit and credit payments. Other products include signature capture devices magnetic strip readers check readers receipt printers and smart cards. Ingenico Corp. is the North American subsidiary of France-based Ingenico a leading European maker of electronic payment systems.

INGERSOLL MACHINE TOOLS INC.

707 FULTON AVE
ROCKFORD, IL 611034069
Phone: 815-987-6000
Fax: –
Web: www.camozzimachinetools.com

CEO: –
CFO: Paul Ballweg
HR: –
FYE: December 31
Type: Private

At Ingersoll Machine Tools folks want to talk shop. The company leads the conversation in global production churning out advanced machine tools for other industries' goods. Products include general purpose equipment (vertical turning lathes scalpers and horizontal boring centers) to one-of-a-kind machines that produce aluminum and hard metal components and structures from composite materials. Ingersoll's contract manufacturing services offer prototype machining and short production runs of windmill hubs to small engine parts. Customers include most of the world's aerospace transportation energy and heavy industry OEMs from Caterpillar to Lockheed Martin. Ingersoll is a company of Italy's Camozzi Group.

	Annual Growth	12/05	12/06	12/07	12/08	12/09
Sales ($ mil.)	–	–	–	(1,099.7)	81.9	56.4
Net income ($ mil.)	3071.9%	–	–	0.0	0.3	0.3
Market value ($ mil.)	–	–	–	–	–	–
Employees	–	–	–	–	–	331

INGLES MARKETS, INC. NMS: IMKT A

P.O. Box 6676
Asheville, NC 28816
Phone: 828 669-2941
Fax: –
Web: www.ingles-markets.com

CEO: Robert P. (Bobby) Ingle
CFO: Ronald B. (Ron) Freeman
HR: Masoud Golriz
FYE: September 26
Type: Public

The Ingalls family could have used an Ingles market near its little house on the prairie. Ingles Markets operates more than 200 supermarkets primarily in suburbs small towns and rural areas of six southeastern states. The stores largely operate under the Ingles name; about 10 do business as Sav-Mor. In addition to brand-name products Ingles has Laura Lynn and Ingles Best private labels. The company also owns a dairy that sells about a third of its products to Ingles stores and the rest to other retailers and distributors. It also owns about 70 shopping centers nearly all of which contain an Ingles store. Robert Ingle founder and CEO of the company died in 2011. He was succeeded by his son.

	Annual Growth	09/11	09/12	09/13	09/14	09/15
Sales ($ mil.)	1.5%	3,559.9	3,709.4	3,738.5	3,836.0	3,778.6
Net income ($ mil.)	11.0%	39.1	43.4	20.8	51.4	59.4
Market value ($ mil.)	33.1%	285.9	331.2	575.8	487.0	898.3
Employees	6.3%	19,600	20,800	23,000	23,000	25,000

INGRAM MICRO INC. NYS: IM

3351 Michelson Drive, Suite 100
Irvine, CA 92612-0697
Phone: 714 566-1000
Fax: 714 566-7604
Web: www.ingrammicro.com

CEO: Alain Moni ⓒ
CFO: William D. Humes
HR: Scott D. Sherman
FYE: December 31
Type: Public

The only things micro about Ingram are some of the smaller electronic components it sells. The world's largest wholesale distributor of information technology products Ingram Micro provides thousands of products — desktop and notebook PCs servers storage devices monitors printers and software — to more than 200000 customers in some 160 countries worldwide. Its sells products from more than 1700 suppliers including many of the world's top manufacturers; Hewlett-Packard is the company's largest supplier. Ingram Micro also offers a wide range of services to its resellers and suppliers including supply chain management business intelligence financing logistics cloud computing and network support services. The company rings up 61% of sales outside North America.

	Annual Growth	01/11*	12/11	12/12	12/13	12/14
Sales ($ mil.)	10.4%	34,589.0	36,328.7	37,827.3	42,553.9	46,487.4
Net income ($ mil.)	(5.7%)	318.1	244.2	305.9	310.6	266.7
Market value ($ mil.)	13.1%	2,982.1	2,841.5	2,583.8	3,652.3	4,317.8
Employees	11.5%	15,650	15,500	20,800	21,800	21,700

*Fiscal year change

INGREDION INC
NYS: INGR

5 Westbrook Corporate Center
Westchester, IL 60154
Phone: 708 551-2600
Fax: 708 551-2700
Web: www.ingredion.com

CEO: Ilene S. Gordon
CFO: Jack C. Fortnum
HR: Becky Tinkham
FYE: December 31
Type: Public

Sweet sodas and diet desserts alike get their taste from Ingredion's ingredients. The company makes food ingredients and industrial products from corn and other starch-based raw materials. It serve 60 markets including food beverage brewing and pharmaceutical companies. More than 40% of sales come from sweeteners including high-fructose corn syrup which is used by just about every beverage maker and a good many food companies to sweeten their products. Ingredion also produces corn starch (a thickener for processed foods) corn oil and corn gluten (for animal feed). Ingredion operates manufacturing plants throughout Africa Asia Europe and North and South America.

	Annual Growth	12/10	12/11	12/12	12/13	12/14
Sales ($ mil.)	6.7%	4,367.0	6,219.0	6,532.0	6,328.0	5,668.0
Net income ($ mil.)	20.4%	169.0	416.0	428.0	396.0	355.0
Market value ($ mil.)	16.5%	3,280.8	3,750.8	4,595.3	4,882.7	6,051.0
Employees	1.6%	10,700	11,100	11,200	11,300	11,400

INJURED WORKERS' INSURANCE FUND

8722 Loch Raven Blvd.
Towson MD 21286-2235
Phone: 410-494-2000
Fax: 410-494-2154
Web: www.iwif.com

CEO: Thomas J Phelan
CFO: -
HR: Nancy Winter
FYE: December 31
Type: Private - Not-for-Pr

The Injured Workers' Insurance Fund (IWIF) has businesses covered in Maryland a state that is said to be the birthplace of workers' compensation benefits. IWIF is a top workers' compensation insurer in the state covering about 25000 employers. The not-for-profit company offers claims processing legal advisement risk management workplace safety and loss control services including consultations and training programs. Though it is an independent entity IWIF serves as the provider of last resort for workers' comp in Maryland and therefore receives oversight from a governor-appointed board of directors. However IWIF is converting into a private entity.

INKSURE TECHNOLOGIES INC.
OTC: INKS

1770 NW 64th St. Ste. 350
Fort Lauderdale FL 33309
Phone: 954-772-8507
Fax: 954-772-8509
Web: www.inksure.com

CEO: Gadi Peleg
CFO: Chanan Morris
HR: -
FYE: December 31
Type: Public

Don't think it ink it; InkSure Technologies makes the mark genuine and permanent. The company markets custom security inks that are designed to prevent counterfeiting. The company also sells readers that use the company's proprietary software to identify and analyze marks printed with its inks which can be used on a variety of paper and plastic materials and have a unique chemical code. Applications for InkSure Technologies systems include financial and government documents pharmaceutical and tobacco product packaging retail gift certificates and travel tickets. Aviation security company ICTS International holds roughly a 30% stake in InkSure Technologies.

INLAND REAL ESTATE CORP
NYS: IRC

2901 Butterfield Road
Oak Brook, IL 60523
Phone: 877 206-5656
Fax: -

CEO: Mark E. Zalatoris
CFO: Brett A. Brown
HR: -
FYE: December 31
Type: Public

Inland Real Estate a member of The Inland Real Estate Group buys leases and operates retail properties mainly in the Midwest with a concentration in the Chicago and Minneapolis/St. Paul metropolitan markets. The self-managed real estate investment trust (REIT) owns about 150 properties most of which are strip shopping centers anchored by a grocery or big-box store. It also invests in single-tenant retail properties and develops properties usually through joint ventures. The REIT's portfolio totals about 14 million sq. ft. of leasable space in a dozen states. Grocery store chain Safeway is the company's largest tenant; other major clients include Roundy's CarMax and Best Buy.

	Annual Growth	12/10	12/11	12/12	12/13	12/14
Sales ($ mil.)	5.2%	167.0	167.2	159.8	183.4	204.8
Net income ($ mil.)	-	(0.3)	(7.2)	17.8	111.7	39.2
Market value ($ mil.)	5.6%	881.3	762.1	839.3	1,053.6	1,096.7
Employees	5.7%	113	111	125	129	141

INNERWORKINGS INC
NMS: INWK

600 West Chicago Avenue, Suite 850
Chicago, IL 60654
Phone: 312 642-3700
Fax: -
Web: www.inwk.com

CEO: Eric D. Belcher
CFO: Jeffrey P. Pritchett
HR: -
FYE: December 31
Type: Public

InnerWorkings has inserted itself into the nuts and bolts of the corporate printing world. The company procures manages and delivers printed products (brochures catalogs and other promotional materials) to companies in the advertising consumer products publishing and retail industries. InnerWorkings' proprietary software application and database PPM4 matches customers' jobs with printing companies' equipment and capacity. The InnerWorkings system submits a job to multiple printers who then bid for the business. Approximately 10000 suppliers participate in the company's network which includes includes printers graphic designers paper mills and merchants digital imaging companies and binders.

	Annual Growth	12/10	12/11	12/12	12/13	12/14
Sales ($ mil.)	20.0%	482.2	633.8	797.7	891.0	1,000.1
Net income ($ mil.)	41.1%	11.2	16.4	19.1	(8.7)	44.5
Market value ($ mil.)	4.4%	346.0	491.9	728.0	411.6	411.6
Employees	21.1%	743	1,034	1,379	1,500	1,600

INNODATA INC
NMS: INOD

Three University Plaza
Hackensack, NJ 07601
Phone: 201 371-8000
Fax: -
Web: www.innodata.com

CEO: Jack S Abuhoff
CFO: O'Neil Nalavadi
HR: Chris Lynch
FYE: December 31
Type: Public

Innodata handles information inundation. The company provides content management and process outsourcing services to businesses and government agencies mainly in the US and Europe. It oversees abstracting and indexing data capture and entry research and analysis and technical writing among other tasks. Innodata manages such tasks as digitizing paper documents into a more manageable electronic form. The company also provides IT services such as consulting systems integration and software and systems engineering. It primarily serves the media publishing and information services industries. Innodata's top clients are Apple Wolters Kluwer Bloomberg and Reed Elsevier.

	Annual Growth	12/10	12/11	12/12	12/13	12/14
Sales ($ mil.)	(1.0%)	61.5	73.9	86.6	64.2	59.1
Net income ($ mil.)	-	(0.7)	4.5	7.5	(10.6)	(1.0)
Market value ($ mil.)	0.5%	72.5	99.8	95.8	62.1	74.0
Employees	0.1%	5,060	7,065	6,060	5,040	5,090

INNOPHOS HOLDINGS INC
NMS: IPHS

259 Prospect Plains Road
Cranbury, NJ 08512
Phone: 609 495-2495
Fax: –
Web: www.innophos.com

CEO: Kim Ann Mink
CFO: Robert Harrer
HR: Gail Holler
FYE: December 31
Type: Public

Innophos Holdings adds a dash of its phosphate products to food beverages toothpaste detergents and asphalt. Innophos manufactures specialty phosphates used in consumer products pharmaceuticals and industrial applications. Customers use the company's phosphates to improve the quality and performance of a broad range of products from electronics and textiles to pharmaceuticals water and detergents. Innophos divides its business into three segments: specialty salts and specialty acids; purified phosphoric acid; and granular triple super phosphates (GSTP) a fertilizer.

	Annual Growth	12/10	12/11	12/12	12/13	12/14
Sales ($ mil.)	4.1%	714.2	810.5	862.4	844.1	839.2
Net income ($ mil.)	9.3%	45.2	86.5	74.2	49.5	64.5
Market value ($ mil.)	12.8%	775.0	1,043.1	998.8	1,043.9	1,255.5
Employees	7.4%	1,087	1,166	1,290	1,427	1,445

INNOSPEC INC
NMS: IOSP

8310 South Valley Highway, Suite 350
Englewood, CO 80112
Phone: 303 792-5554
Fax: –
Web: www.innospecinc.com

CEO: Patrick S. Williams
CFO: Ian P. Cleminson
HR: –
FYE: December 31
Type: Public

After some introspection Innospec has concluded that the company's future lies in growing its specialty chemicals businesses by developing fuel additives and niche performance chemicals. Innospec's Fuel Specialties segment makes chemical additives that enhance fuel efficiency and engine performance and its Performance Chemicals unit makes several products used in the personal care paper detergent and photographic markets. It is also the sole producer of TEL (tetra ethyl lead) product an anti-knock gas additive sold to oil refineries worldwide.

	Annual Growth	12/10	12/11	12/12	12/13	12/14
Sales ($ mil.)	8.9%	683.2	774.4	776.4	818.8	960.9
Net income ($ mil.)	3.4%	73.7	48.9	68.3	77.8	84.1
Market value ($ mil.)	20.3%	495.5	681.8	837.8	1,122.7	1,037.2
Employees	11.2%	850	850	900	1,100	1,300

INNOVARO INC.
NBB: INNI

2109 Palm Avenue
Tampa, FL 33605
Phone: 813 754-4330
Fax: –
Web: www.innovaro.com

CEO: Asa Lanum
CFO: Carole R Wright
HR: –
FYE: December 31
Type: Public

Innovaro's mission in life is to turn innovations into profitable ventures. The company (formerly UTEK) provides consultation services to help clients to locate new markets identify game-changing strategies and develop new platforms; it also facilitates the sale of licensing deals for potential commercial use. Areas of expertise include biotechnology energy geology manufacturing and electronics. Founded in 1997 Innovaro has worked with hundreds of big-name clients such as Disney Johnson & Johnson and Nokia. The former UTEK changed its name to Innovaro in mid-2010 after a UK consulting firm it had acquired in 2008.

	Annual Growth	09/09*	12/09	12/10	12/11	12/12
Sales ($ mil.)	(59.1%)	7.8	3.0	13.1	14.9	0.5
Net income ($ mil.)	–	(9.3)	(0.6)	(19.1)	(4.6)	(10.0)
Market value ($ mil.)	(62.5%)	75.6	68.6	23.1	15.5	4.0
Employees	(51.4%)	–	61	39	31	7

*Fiscal year change

INNOVATION VENTURES LLC

38955 Hills Tech Dr.
Farmington Hills MI 48331
Phone: 248-960-1700
Fax: +81-3-5201-6292
Web: www.kamipa.co.jp

CEO: Manoj Bhargava
CFO: –
HR: –
FYE: December 31
Type: Private

Just because you're tired doesn't mean you're thirsty. Innovation Ventures is a holding company that owns Living Essentials LLC which markets the two-ounce energy drink 5-hour Energy. Unlike other carbonated energy drinks 5-hour Energy doesn't contain any sugar and only has four calories thanks to its small size that packs quite a punch. Five-hour Energy is a blend of vitamins amino acids and caffeine and comes in flavors (berry grape lemon-lime) as well as a decaf and extra-strength formula. Five-hour Energy drinks are strategically placed at the checkout counter not the beverage aisle at most major grocery drug and convenience stores in the US and Canada.

INNOVATIVE CARD TECHNOLOGIES INC.
OTC: INVC

US Bank Tower 633 W. 5th St. Ste. 2600
Los Angeles CA 90071
Phone: 213-223-2145
Fax: 213-223-2147
Web: www.incardtech.com

CEO: Richard J Nathan
CFO: Richard J Nathan
HR: –
FYE: December 31
Type: Public

Innovative Card Technologies (ICT) is almost ready to make your plastic more powerful. The company has developed power inlay technology designed for information-bearing plastic cards. The company's primary product is the ICT DisplayCard which incorporates a battery circuit and display on a card the size of a credit card. The DisplayCard offers increased security by ensuring the card is physically present; at the push of a button the card displays a one-time password that must be used in conjunction with the card for the transaction to be authorized. The DisplayCard can be configured for use as a payment card (debit or credit) or as an RFID access card serving electronic banking or data access needs.

INNOVATIVE SOLUTIONS AND SUPPORT INC
NMS: ISSC

720 Pennsylvania Drive
Exton, PA 19341
Phone: 610 646-9800
Fax: –
Web: www.innovative-ss.com

CEO: –
CFO: Relland M Winand
HR: Jonathan Freiman
FYE: September 30
Type: Public

Pilots use products by Innovative Solutions and Support (IS&S) to gauge their success. The company makes flight information computers electronic displays and monitoring systems that measure flight information such as airspeed altitude and engine and fuel data. IS&S's reduced vertical separation minimum (RVSM) system enables planes to fly closer together; engine and fuel displays help pilots track fuel and oil levels and other engine functions. IS&S offers flat-panel displays which take up less cockpit space than conventional displays. Customers are the US DoD and other government agencies defense contractors and commercial/corporate air carriers.

	Annual Growth	09/11	09/12	09/13	09/14	09/15
Sales ($ mil.)	(6.0%)	25.7	24.6	31.6	44.1	20.1
Net income ($ mil.)	–	0.7	3.0	1.9	0.2	(5.9)
Market value ($ mil.)	(13.5%)	81.7	67.3	134.6	88.2	45.8
Employees	(6.9%)	117	105	141	146	88

INNOVIVA INC
NMS: INVA

951 Gateway Boulevard
South San Francisco, CA 94080
Phone: 650 238-9600
Fax: –
Web: www.thrxinc.com

CEO: Michael W. Aguiar
CFO: Eric d'Esparbes
HR: –
FYE: December 31
Type: Public

Innoviva (formerly Theravance) figures there's no sense in re-inventing the wheel. The biotech takes aim at already proven biological targets taking advantage of existing research to create next-generation treatments. The firm is focused on the discovery development and commercialization of small molecule medicines across a number of therapeutic areas including respiratory disease bacterial infections and central nervous system pain. Its VIBATIV product (an injectable antibiotic approved to treat skin infections and hospital-acquired pneumonia) was successfully developed and commercialized with partner Astellas. It also develops chronic obstructive pulmonary disease (COPD) products with GlaxoSmithKline (GSK).

	Annual Growth	12/10	12/11	12/12	12/13	12/14
Sales ($ mil.)	(23.2%)	24.2	24.5	135.8	4.8	8.4
Net income ($ mil.)	–	(83.9)	(115.3)	(18.5)	(170.7)	(168.5)
Market value ($ mil.)	(13.3%)	2,915.5	2,570.1	2,586.4	4,145.9	1,645.6
Employees	(52.3%)	193	222	226	241	10

INNSUITES HOSPITALITY TRUST
ASE: IHT

InnSuites Hotels Centre, 1625 E. Northern Avenue, Suite 105
Phoenix, AZ 85020
Phone: 602 944-1500
Fax: –
Web: www.innsuitestrust.com

CEO: James F Wirth
CFO: Adam B Remis
HR: –
FYE: January 31
Type: Public

This company trusts you'll have a night full of sweet dreams while staying at one of its hotels. InnSuites Hospitality Trust wholly-owns and operates five studio and two-room suite hotels in Arizona New Mexico and southern California four of which are co-branded as Best Westerns. The company also provides management services for nine hotels and trademark license services for 11 hotels. InnSuites Hospitality Trust primarily operates through the InnSuites Hotels & Suites and InnSuites Boutique Hotel Collection brands. InnSuites Hospitality Trust operates through its majority-owned affiliate RRF Limited Partnership which in turn operates through subsidiary InnSuites Hotels.

	Annual Growth	01/11	01/12	01/13	01/14	01/15
Sales ($ mil.)	(1.7%)	15.7	17.1	15.0	14.9	14.7
Net income ($ mil.)	–	(2.0)	(1.1)	(1.0)	(1.0)	(2.1)
Market value ($ mil.)	20.0%	10.7	18.2	14.2	12.5	22.2
Employees	(5.0%)	368	261	250	300	300

INOGEN, INC
NMS: INGN

326 Bollay Drive
Goleta, CA 93117
Phone: 805 562-0500
Fax: –
Web: www.inogen.com

CEO: Raymond Huggenberger
CFO: Alison Bauerlein
HR: –
FYE: December 31
Type: Public

Combine innovation with oxygen and you've got Inogen. The company makes portable oxygen-concentrators that provide supplemental oxygen by people with chronic respiratory conditions. Oxygen concentrators pull nitrogen from ambient air to supply an oxygen-rich mix through a breathing tube. Its 4.8- and 7-pound models are meant to replace both large in-home concentrators as well as portable tank systems which also eliminates the need for home delivery of oxygen tanks. Unlike most suppliers in the market Inogen sells and rents directly to patients. International customers account for about a third of revenue. Inogen was formed in 2001 and went public in early 2014.

	Annual Growth	12/10	12/11	12/12	12/13	12/14
Sales ($ mil.)	–	0.0	30.6	48.6	75.4	112.5
Net income ($ mil.)	–	0.0	(2.0)	0.6	25.4	6.8
Market value ($ mil.)	–	0.0	–	–	–	597.9
Employees	7.8%	–	–	354	354	411

INOVA HEALTH SYSTEM

8110 GATEHOUSE RD 200E
FALLS CHURCH, VA 22042-1217
Phone: 703-289-2072
Fax: –
Web: www.inovacareers.org

CEO: John Knox Singleton
CFO: –
HR: –
FYE: December 31
Type: Private

Inova Health Foundation provides financial support and assistance to the Inova Health System which operates a network of not-for-profit community hospitals in northern Virginia. It also supports home health services heart care programs clinical research and trials emergency and urgent care centers family practice locations and rehabilitation centers. To raise funds for the hospital system the foundation organizes special events such as galas golf tournaments and silent auctions. Donors can also make contributions through the Inova website. The foundation took in $15.8 million in contributions in 2012.

	Annual Growth	12/03	12/04	12/05	12/06	12/08
Sales ($ mil.)	4.0%	–	–	–	1,978.9	2,140.9
Net income ($ mil.)	1842.2%	–	–	–	0.4	147.9
Market value ($ mil.)	–	–	–	–	–	–
Employees	–	–	–	–	–	16,000

INOVA TECHNOLOGY INC
NBB: INVA

2300 W. Sahara Ave., Suite 800
Las Vegas, NV 89102
Phone: 800 507-2810
Fax: –
Web: www.inovatechnology.com

CEO: Adam Radly
CFO: –
HR: –
FYE: April 30
Type: Public

Inova Technology has innovative ways of keeping track of things. The company provides radio frequency identification (RFID) scanners and tags through its RighTag subsidiary. Its Trakkers subsidiary offers a tracking solution that allows trade show exhibitors to scan badges of attendees to capture contact information then store the data in a specially designated Web site for access from any location. Inova Technology also offers IT consulting and computer network services through its Desert Communications subsidiary. Chairman and CEO Adam Radly controls more than half of the company.

	Annual Growth	04/09	04/10	04/11	04/12	04/13
Sales ($ mil.)	(4.6%)	22.6	21.0	22.1	21.2	18.7
Net income ($ mil.)	–	(2.0)	(7.1)	(3.4)	(1.2)	(6.6)
Market value ($ mil.)	–	2.4	1.9	0.1	0.0	0.0
Employees	–	–	–	–	–	75

INOVIO PHARMACEUTICALS INC.
NMS: INO

660 W. Germantown Pike, Suite 100
Plymouth Meeting, PA 19462
Phone: 267 440-4200
Fax: –
Web: www.inovio.com

CEO: J. Joseph Kim
CFO: Peter D. Kies
HR: –
FYE: December 31
Type: Public

Inovio Pharmaceuticals is electrifying its vaccine delivery process. The firm's electroporation infusion therapy uses electrical pulses to open up cell membranes thus optimizing the delivery of its DNA vaccines that can protect from cancers as well as chronic infectious diseases including HIV and hepatitis C. Its SynCon process identifies shared characteristics among different strains of similar viruses to help develop a universal flu vaccine that will be effective on most influenza strains unlike traditional flu vaccines that are strain-specific. It also has a couple of anti-inflammatory drugs in its pipeline and some DNA-based animal growth hormones for livestock. Partners and collaborators include Roche MedImmune and DARPA.

	Annual Growth	12/10	12/11	12/12	12/13	12/14
Sales ($ mil.)	14.2%	6.1	9.8	4.1	13.5	10.5
Net income ($ mil.)	–	(17.6)	(15.3)	(19.7)	(66.0)	(36.1)
Market value ($ mil.)	68.1%	69.9	26.0	30.3	176.1	557.6
Employees	25.7%	44	53	59	74	110

INPHI CORP

NYS: IPHI

2953 Bunker Hill Lane, Suite 300
Santa Clara, CA 95054
Phone: 408 217-7300
Fax: –
Web: www.inphi.com

CEO: Ford G. Tamer
CFO: John S. Edmunds
HR: Mona Taylor
FYE: December 31
Type: Public

Inphi wants to shift broadband networks into high gear. The fabless semiconductor company offers specialized logic devices modulator drivers and other components used in high-speed optical telecom networks. Key parts of Inphi's more than 170 products are made from indium phosphide (InP; hence the company name) which Inphi touts as running at much higher speeds but with lower power consumption than competing products made from other specialized materials such as silicon germanium. Other elements of the company's designs are made from standard silicon to lower overall costs.

	Annual Growth	12/10	12/11	12/12	12/13	12/14
Sales ($ mil.)	17.0%	83.2	79.3	91.2	102.7	156.1
Net income ($ mil.)	–	26.1	1.9	(20.7)	(13.2)	(22.6)
Market value ($ mil.)	(2.1%)	749.6	446.2	357.4	481.3	689.5
Employees	28.0%	166	165	192	229	446

INRAD OPTICS INC

NBB: INRD

181 Legrand Avenue
Northvale, NJ 07647
Phone: 201 767-1910
Fax: –
Web: www.inradoptics.com

CEO: Amy Eskilson
CFO: William J Foote
HR: –
FYE: December 31
Type: Public

Inrad Optics (formerly Photonic Products Group) manufactures products for use in photonics including custom optics crystals and components and provides thin-film coating services on a contract basis. Its products find applications in laser systems military gear semiconductor production equipment and telecommunications networks. The company's INRAD unit grows and finishes crystals used in commercial laser systems. Its custom optics segment includes waveplates beam displacers rotators and phase-shift plates. Inrad Optics gets about 10% of its sales from overseas customers.

	Annual Growth	12/10	12/11	12/12	12/13	12/14
Sales ($ mil.)	(3.1%)	11.1	13.2	11.4	11.2	9.7
Net income ($ mil.)	–	(0.7)	0.2	(1.4)	(1.7)	(2.5)
Market value ($ mil.)	(35.7%)	11.7	11.7	3.2	2.7	2.0
Employees	(4.2%)	83	81	77	71	70

INSERRA SUPERMARKETS INC.

20 Ridge Rd.
Mahwah NJ 07430
Phone: 201-529-5900
Fax: 201-529-1189

CEO: Lawrence R Inserra
CFO: Theresa Inserra
HR: –
FYE: December 31
Type: Private

The Big Apple need never be short of apples (or oranges for that matter) thanks to Inserra Supermarkets. Inserra owns and operates 20-plus ShopRite supermarkets and superstores in northern New Jersey and southeastern New York State (most are in Westchester and Rockland counties). Inserra's superstores feature bagel bakeries cafes and pharmacies. The regional grocery chain also offers banking services in selected stores through agreements with Poughkeepsie Savings Bank Statewide Savings Bank and others. Owned by the Inserra family the retailer is one of some 45 members that make up cooperative Wakefern Food the owner of the ShopRite name.

INSIGHT ENTERPRISES INC.

NMS: NSIT

6820 South Harl Avenue
Tempe, AZ 85283
Phone: 480 333-3000
Fax: –
Web: www.insight.com

CEO: Kenneth T. (Ken) Lamneck
CFO: Glynis A. Bryan
HR: –
FYE: December 31
Type: Public

With Insight Enterprises around the end of your technology woes could be in sight. The company distributes computer hardware and software and provides IT services for businesses schools and government agencies and departments. Insight offers thousands of products from major manufacturers (including Hewlett-Packard IBM and Cisco) and it provides networking and communications services through subsidiaries Insight Networking in the US and UK-based MINX. The company uses direct telesales field sales agents and an e-commerce site to reach its clients in North America and about 200 other countries across Europe the Middle East Africa and the Asia/Pacific region.

	Annual Growth	12/10	12/11	12/12	12/13	12/14
Sales ($ mil.)	2.5%	4,809.9	5,287.2	5,301.4	5,144.3	5,316.2
Net income ($ mil.)	0.1%	75.5	100.2	92.8	71.0	75.7
Market value ($ mil.)	18.4%	528.3	613.8	697.4	911.7	1,039.4
Employees	1.4%	5,115	5,386	5,045	5,202	5,406

INSIGHT GLOBAL INC.

4170 Ashford Dunwoody Rd. Ste. 250
Atlanta GA 30319
Phone: 404-257-7900
Fax: 404-257-1070
Web: www.insightglobal.net

CEO: Rich Lingle
CFO: Mike Lewis
HR: Jen Roovers
FYE: December 31
Type: Private

Insight Global provides something more tangible than just insight; it provides people. The staff recruiting firm finds and screens candidates to fill temporary and permanent IT positions including applications programmers database administrators network engineers systems analysts technical writers and Web developers. Insight Global also acts as an outside human resources and payroll department for its clients handling references W2s and unemployment and workers compensation insurance. It primarily serves the technology health care energy retail telecom financial services and government sectors and operates through some 25 offices located throughout the US.

INSIGHT HEALTH SERVICES HOLDINGS CORP.

26250 Enterprise Ct. Ste. 100
Lake Forest CA 92630
Phone: 949-282-6000
Fax: 303-254-8343
Web: www.qualmark.com

CEO: Louis E Hallman III
CFO: Keith S Kelson
HR: –
FYE: June 30
Type: Private

InSight Health Services (dba Insight Imaging) knows what lies within the hearts brains and pancreases of men. The company offers diagnostic imaging services to wholesale and retail customers in some 30 states. It mainly provides MRI (magnetic resonance imaging) services but also offers CT (computed tomography) and PET (positron emission tomography) scanning as well as conventional X-ray mammogram and ultrasound services. Customers include hospitals and physicians as well as insurance payers and Medicare or Medicaid programs. InSight restructured and emerged from bankruptcy protection in 2011. It is controlled by investment firm Black Diamond Capital Management.

INSIGNIA SYSTEMS, INC.   NAS: ISIG

8799 Brooklyn Blvd.   CEO: -
Minneapolis, MN 55445   CFO: John C Gonsior
Phone: 763 392-6200   HR: -
Fax: -   FYE: December 31
Web: www.insigniasystems.com   Type: Public

Insignia Systems believes all signs point to greater sales. The company's point of purchase (POP) software and services help retailers and consumer goods manufacturers create promotional signage and in-store advertising that's displayed close to products on store shelving. As part of its POPSign program Insignia Systems creates customized signs based on information from retailers and manufacturers; it generates the majority of its revenue from its POP-Sign program. Its Stylus software suite is used to create signs labels and posters. Insignia Systems also sells specialized cardstock and other printing supplies for its systems. The company was founded in 1990.

	Annual Growth	12/10	12/11	12/12	12/13	12/14
Sales ($ mil.)	(3.2%)	30.0	17.2	20.2	27.8	26.3
Net income ($ mil.)	(59.2%)	7.6	51.1	(1.6)	1.4	0.2
Market value ($ mil.)	(14.1%)	80.0	24.5	20.8	33.3	43.6
Employees	(13.1%)	114	83	71	70	65

INSITE VISION INC.   NBB: INSV

965 Atlantic Avenue   CEO: Timothy Ruane
Alameda, CA 94501   CFO: Louis Drapeau
Phone: 510 865-8800   HR: -
Fax: 510 865-5700   FYE: December 31
Web: www.insitevision.com   Type: Public

InSite Vision provides insight into the murky realm of eye disease. The company develops ophthalmic products using its DuraSite eyedrop-based drug delivery system. Its topical anti-infective product AzaSite is marketed in the US by licensing partner Inspire Pharmaceuticals as a treatment for conjunctivitis (pink eye). Various other AzaSite products are in development to treat eyelid inflammation and other infections. InSite Vision has licensed rights to use azithromycin (the active ingredient in AzaSite) from Pfizer. Inspire markets AzaSite in the US and Canada while international units are supplied by Catalent Pharma Solutions.

	Annual Growth	12/09	12/10	12/11	12/12	12/13
Sales ($ mil.)	33.2%	9.8	11.9	15.9	21.6	30.8
Net income ($ mil.)	-	(14.2)	(9.6)	(6.9)	(8.3)	5.8
Market value ($ mil.)	(6.0%)	50.7	44.2	58.2	40.5	39.6
Employees	34.8%	10	12	25	30	33

INSITUFORM TECHNOLOGIES INC.

17988 Edison Ave.   CEO: Charles R Gordon
Chesterfield MO 63005   CFO: David A Martin
Phone: 636-530-8000   HR: Laura Villa
Fax: 636-519-8010   FYE: December 31
Web: www.insituform.com   Type: Subsidiary

Under many a city lurks a decaying infrastructure and that's what Insituform Technologies takes care of "in situ". Serving industrial and municipal clients the company and its subsidiaries manufacture and install products for rehabilitating and protecting sewers water lines oil pipelines mining pipelines and other types of pipe systems. The heart of its business is its cured-in-place pipe process which allows for pipe rehabilitation without digging or disruption. Insituform which has operations in North America as well as in Asia Europe Australia the Middle East and South America has been expanding both geographically and by product offering. The company is part of infrastructure firm Aegion.

INSMED INCORPORATED   NASDAQ: INSM

8720 Stony Point Pkwy.   CEO: William H Lewis
Richmond VA 23235   CFO: Andrew T Drechsler
Phone: 804-565-3000   HR: -
Fax: 804-565-3500   FYE: December 31
Web: www.insmed.com   Type: Public

Insmed is focused on inhaled medicines. The company is combining its inhaled drug delivery technology with its pharmaceutical findings to create potential therapeutics lung infections and lung diseases. Its inhaled ARIKACE is being investigated for the treatment of chronic lung infections in patients with cystic fibrosis (CF) and non-tuburculous mycobacteria (NTM). Insmed also has its eFlow Nebulizer drug delivery technology in development. Another candidate IPLEX is being investigated for the treatment of neurodegenerative and retinal diseases. Insmed has also conducted research programs for other lung cancer and metabolism drugs.

INSOUND MEDICAL INC.

39660 Eureka Dr.   CEO: David Thrower
Newark CA 94560   CFO: -
Phone: 510-792-4000   HR: -
Fax: 510-792-4050   FYE: December 31
Web: www.insoundmedical.com   Type: Subsidiary

InSound Medical is into making sounds heard. The company develops hearing devices made for continuous wear and that cannot be seen when used. Unlike conventional hearing aids InSound Medical's devices are fitted into the ear by an audiology professional and worn continuously even during sleeping or swimming. Customers pay for a year's worth of devices (a "subscription") and return every two to four months for replacements when the batteries wear out. The FDA-approved Lyric was introduced in 2008 and is marketed to younger consumers with mild to moderate hearing loss. InSound Medical was acquired by Sonova in 2010.

INSPERITY INC   NYS: NSP

19001 Crescent Springs Drive   CEO: Paul J. Sarvadi
Kingwood, TX 77339   CFO: Douglas S. (Doug) Sharp
Phone: 281 358-8986   HR: -
Fax: -   FYE: December 31
Web: www.insperity.com   Type: Public

Insperity handles the payroll so you don't have to. The company provides an array of human resources services to small and midsized companies (employing about 2300 workers) in the US. As a PEO (professional employer organization) Insperity offers payroll and benefits administration workers' compensation programs and personnel records management through its flagship Workforce Optimization product. It also offers what it calls "adjacent businesses" that include performance and expense management employment screening recruiting and organizational planning services. Most of its client companies are engaged in the administration financial manufacturing and computer services industries.

	Annual Growth	12/11	12/12	12/13	12/14	12/15
Sales ($ mil.)	7.1%	1,976.2	2,158.8	2,256.1	2,357.8	2,603.6
Net income ($ mil.)	6.6%	30.5	40.4	32.0	28.0	39.4
Market value ($ mil.)	17.4%	615.1	790.1	876.7	822.3	1,168.4
Employees	3.4%	2,100	2,200	2,300	2,300	2,400

INSPIRE PHARMACEUTICALS INC.

8081 Arco Corporate Dr. Ste. 400　　　　　　　　　　　CEO: –
Raleigh NC 27617　　　　　　　　　　　　　　　　　　CFO: –
Phone: 919-941-9777　　　　　　　　　　　　　　　　HR: –
Fax: 919-941-9797　　　　　　　　　　　　　　FYE: December 31
Web: www.inspirepharm.com　　　　　　　　　　　Type: Subsidiary

Inspire Pharmaceuticals doesn't want to leave a dry eye in the house. The company targets treatments for various ocular diseases. Inspire Pharmaceuticals markets two North American eye products AzaSite (licensed from InSite Vision) which treats bacterial conjunctivitis (eye infections) and Elestat for allergic conjunctivitis (developed and marketed in collaboration with Allergan). The company is also working to find additional applications for AzaSite. The company also sells treatments for dry eye in Japan and the US through licensing agreements. Inspire Pharmaceuticals was acquired by Merck in 2011.

INSTALLED BUILDING PRODUCTS INC   NYS: IBP

495 South High Street, Suite 50　　　　　　　　　CEO: Jeffrey w. Edwards
Columbus, OH 43215　　　　　　　　　　　　　CFO: Michael T. Miller
Phone: 614 221-3399　　　　　　　　　　　　　　　　HR: –
Fax: –　　　　　　　　　　　　　　　　　　　FYE: December 31
Web: www.installedbuildingproducts.com　　　　　　Type: Public

Installed Building Products (IBP) wants to insulate its customers from the elements. The company is a leading new residential insulation installer with more than 100 branches in about 45 states. IBP manages all aspects of the installation process for its customers including direct purchases of materials from national manufacturers to delivery and installation. In addition to insulation IBP installs garage doors rain gutters shower doors shelving fireplaces locksets and hardware and mirrors. The company's primary market is residential new home construction (about three-quarters of sales). Seeking to capitalize on the recovery in new home building IBP went public in 2014.

	Annual Growth	12/10	12/11	12/12	12/13	12/14
Sales ($ mil.)	–	0.0	238.4	301.3	431.9	518.0
Net income ($ mil.)	–	0.0	(9.0)	(1.9)	6.0	13.9
Market value ($ mil.)	–	0.0	–	–	–	562.0
Employees	7.8%	–	–	3,100	3,200	3,600

INSTANT WEB INC.

7951 Powers Blvd.　　　　　　　　　　　　　　CEO: Jim Andersen
Chanhassen MN 55317-9502　　　　　　　　　CFO: Joe Morrison
Phone: 952-474-0961　　　　　　　　　　　　　　　HR: –
Fax: 952-474-6467　　　　　　　　　　　　　　FYE: April 30
Web: www.iwco.com　　　　　　　　　　　　　　Type: Private

You might say this company gets promotional items directly into mailboxes everywhere. Doing business as IWCO Direct Instant Web provides a range of direct-mail marketing services including printing assembling and mailing. The company also makes promotional plastic and printed paper products phone cards and envelopes and it offers customized products with pull tabs peel-apart adhesive messages fragrance patches and photographic-quality images. Other services include database management automated sorting and mailing and bindery services. IWCO Direct was founded in 1969 as Instant Services Inc. Private equity firm Avista Capital Partners acquired the firm in 2007.

INSTEEL INDUSTRIES, INC.   NMS: IIIN

1373 Boggs Drive　　　　　　　　　　　　　　CEO: H. O. Woltz
Mount Airy, NC 27030　　　　　　　　　CFO: Michael C. Gazmarian
Phone: 336 786-2141　　　　　　　　　　　　　　HR: –
Fax: –　　　　　　　　　　　　　　　　　　　FYE: October 03
Web: www.insteel.com　　　　　　　　　　　　　Type: Public

Insteel Industries is part of many concrete victories. The company manufactures steel welded wire reinforcement (WWR) used primarily in concrete construction materials such as pipe (pipe mesh building mesh engineered structural mesh and precast manholes) driveways and slabs. Its prestressed concrete (PC) strand products are the spine for concrete structures from bridges to parking garages. Insteel's customers include concrete pipe and precast and prestressed producers distributors and rebar fabricators. A majority of its sales come from manufacturers of non-residential concrete construction products.

	Annual Growth	10/11*	09/12	09/13	09/14*	10/15
Sales ($ mil.)	7.4%	336.9	363.3	363.9	409.0	447.5
Net income ($ mil.)	–	(0.4)	1.8	11.7	16.6	21.7
Market value ($ mil.)	12.4%	186.0	216.6	295.5	387.2	297.3
Employees	2.2%	725	682	687	847	790

*Fiscal year change

INSTITUTE FOR DEFENSE ANALYSES INC

4850 MARK CENTER DR　　　　　　　　　　　CEO: David S.C. Chu
ALEXANDRIA, VA 223111882　　　　　　　　　　　CFO: –
Phone: 703-845-2000　　　　　　　　　　　　　　HR: –
Fax: –　　　　　　　　　　　　　　　　　　FYE: September 27
Web: www.ida.org　　　　　　　　　　　　　　Type: Private

The Institute for Defense Analyses founded in 1947 to provide technical analyses of weapons is a federally funded organization that works for the US government's defense agencies as well as for other government entities. The institute's focus areas include war and defense systems evaluations materials and information technology assessments resource cost and readiness analyses and force and strategy assessments. The Institute for Defense Analyses' Science and Technology Policy Institute analyzes global science and tech trends to help the US government formula policy.

	Annual Growth	09/09	09/10	09/11	09/12	09/13
Sales ($ mil.)	(1.2%)	–	227.8	226.8	221.8	219.4
Net income ($ mil.)	1628.2%	–	–	0.1	23.3	18.7
Market value ($ mil.)	–	–	–	–	–	–
Employees	–	–	–	–	–	1,500

INSTITUTE OF GAS TECHNOLOGY

1700 S MOUNT PROSPECT RD　　　　　　　　　CEO: David C Carroll
DES PLAINES, IL 600181800　　　　　　　　　CFO: James Ingold
Phone: 847-768-0500　　　　　　　　　　　　　　HR: –
Fax: –　　　　　　　　　　　　　　　　　　FYE: December 31
Web: www.gastechnology.org　　　　　　　　　　Type: Private

Natural gas burns more cleanly and efficiently thanks to the Institute of Gas Technology (dba Gas Technology Institute or GTI) which provides engineering research development and training services for energy and environmental companies consumers and government clients. GTI's research focuses on expanded energy supply reduced energy delivery costs efficient energy use and clean energy systems primarily in the natural gas sector. Natural gas companies as well as large energy consumers and private industry firms comprise the majority of GTI's client base. The not-for-profit company's contract services range from market and technology analysis to product development testing and commercialization.

	Annual Growth	12/04	12/05	12/06	12/07	12/08
Sales ($ mil.)	(32.5%)	–	–	137.4	53.0	62.6
Net income ($ mil.)	–	–	–	0.0	4.8	(32.3)
Market value ($ mil.)	–	–	–	–	–	–
Employees	–	–	–	–	–	250

INSULET CORP

NMS: PODD

600 Technology Park Drive, Suite 200
Billerica, MA 01821
Phone: 978 600-7000
Fax: –
Web: www.myomnipod.com

CEO: Patrick Sullivan
CFO: Michael Levitz
HR: Brad Thomas
FYE: December 31
Type: Public

Insulet wants to isolate an insolent disease. The medical device company manufactures an insulin pump for people with insulin-dependent diabetes. Its disposable waterproof product called the OmniPod Insulin Management System weighs a mere 1.2 ounces and adheres directly to the patient's skin making it more discrete than most insulin infusion systems that typically clip to a belt or fit in a pocket. It also includes a handheld device to wirelessly program the OmniPod with insulin delivery instructions. The company also sells other diabetes treatment and testing supplies.

	Annual Growth	12/10	12/11	12/12	12/13	12/14
Sales ($ mil.)	31.4%	97.0	152.3	211.4	247.1	288.7
Net income ($ mil.)	–	(61.2)	(57.2)	(51.9)	(45.0)	(51.5)
Market value ($ mil.)	31.3%	872.6	1,060.1	1,194.7	2,088.7	2,593.1
Employees	13.8%	310	576	538	478	519

INSURANCE COMPANY OF THE WEST

11455 El Camino Real
San Diego CA 92130-2045
Phone: 858-350-2400
Fax: 856-436-8920
Web: www.icwgroup.com

CEO: Kevin Prior
CFO: –
HR: –
FYE: December 31
Type: Group

Insurance Company of the West reaches as far as Florida and sells earthquake policies in Illinois but always has California in its heart. The company provides commercial property surety bonds and workers' compensation coverage in key markets. It operates alongside its two sister companies Explorer Insurance and Independence Casualty and Surety. Founded in 1972 Insurance Company of the West is the oldest of the three companies that operate together as the ICW Group. The companies distribute their products through a network of more than 2000 independent agents and brokers.

INSYS THERAPEUTICS INC

NMS: INSY

1333 S. Spectrum Blvd, Suite 100
Chandler, AZ 85286
Phone: 602 910-2617
Fax: –

CEO: John N. Kapoor
CFO: Darryl S. Baker
HR: –
FYE: December 31
Type: Public

Insys Therapeutics aims to take the rough edges off of chemo and cancer pain. The drug development company is focused on treating side effects of chemotherapy as well as therapies for pain management. Its lead candidate is a fast-acting oral spray version of cancer pain drug Fentanyl. Its Dronabinol candidate is a generic capsule form of Marinol (a synthetic version of the active chemical in marijuana) for treatment of chemotherapy-induced nausea and vomiting. Both drugs are in late stage development awaiting FDA approval. All of the company's drug candidates are re-formulations of already-approved therapeutic ingredients. Insys filed to go public in 2011 but didn't until 2013.

	Annual Growth	12/06	12/07	12/12	12/13	12/14
Sales ($ mil.)	245.3%	0.0	–	15.5	99.3	222.1
Net income ($ mil.)	–	(33.2)	(11.0)	(24.4)	40.4	38.0
Market value ($ mil.)	49.7%	118.1	41.7	547.9	2,736.9	2,980.8
Employees	28.0%	53	17	–	202	382

INSYS THERAPEUTICS INC.

10220 S. 51st St. Ste. 2
Phoenix AZ 85044-5231
Phone: 602-910-2617
Fax: 602-910-2627
Web: www.insysrx.com

CEO: –
CFO: Darryl S Baker
HR: –
FYE: December 31
Type: Private

Insys Therapeutics aims to take the rough edges off of chemo and cancer pain. The drug development company is focused on treating side effects of chemotherapy as well as therapies for pain management. Its lead candidate is a fast-acting oral spray version of cancer pain drug Fentanyl. Its Dronabinol candidate is a generic capsule form of Marinol (a synthetic version of the active chemical in marijuana) for treatment of chemotherapy-induced nausea and vomiting. Both drugs are in late stage development awaiting FDA approval. All of the company's drug candidates are re-formulations of already-approved therapeutic ingredients. Insys filed to go public in 2011.

INTCOMEX INC.

3505 NW 107th Ave. Ste. A
Miami FL 33178
Phone: 305-477-6230
Fax: 305-477-5694
Web: www.intcomex.com

CEO: Michael Shalom
CFO: Humberto Lopez
HR: –
FYE: December 31
Type: Private

Intcomex is IT in Latin America and the Caribbean. The wholesaler distributes computer systems and components peripherals software accessories networking products mobile devices and digital consumer electronics to more than 42000 customers in 40 countries. Clients are primarily third-party IT distributors resellers and retailers. Intcomex offers more than 13000 products from more than 140 manufacturers including Apple Dell HP Intel Microsoft and Western Digital. Founded in 1988 the company began as a small retail store that sold computer software in South Florida. Today Intcomex operates sales offices in about a dozen countries. The company filed to go public in 2007 but has yet to do so.

INTEGRA LIFESCIENCES HOLDINGS CORP

NMS: IART

311 Enterprise Drive
Plainsboro, NJ 08536
Phone: 609 275-0500
Fax: –
Web: www.integralife.com

CEO: Peter J. Arduini
CFO: Glenn Coleman
HR: –
FYE: December 31
Type: Public

When it comes to regenerative medicine Integra LifeSciences is integral to the healing process. Using its proprietary collagen matrix technology the firm makes biological implants (including grafts and wound dressings) for brain spine and other orthopedic surgeries that eventually become part of a patient's body helping it to generate new bone tissue and nerves to replace damaged elements. In addition Integra makes surgical equipment including bone fixation devices spinal fixation systems tissue ablation equipment and drainage catheters used in neurosurgery and orthopedic reconstruction as well as basic surgical instruments. Its products are marketed worldwide through direct sales and distributors.

	Annual Growth	12/10	12/11	12/12	12/13	12/14
Sales ($ mil.)	6.1%	732.1	780.1	830.9	836.2	928.3
Net income ($ mil.)	(15.2%)	65.7	28.0	41.2	(17.0)	34.0
Market value ($ mil.)	3.5%	1,548.6	1,009.4	1,275.9	1,562.1	1,775.5
Employees	3.2%	3,000	3,400	3,500	3,300	3,400

INTEGRA TELECOM INC.

1201 NE Lloyd Blvd. Ste. 500
Portland OR 97232
Phone: 503-453-8000
Fax: 503-453-8221
Web: www.integratelecom.com

CEO: Mark Willency
CFO: Jesse Selnick
HR: –
FYE: December 31
Type: Private

Integra Telecom wants to be a key component of the US communications network. The facilities-based telecommunications carrier provides local and long-distance telephony and broadband Internet largely to small to midsized businesses as well as some residential customers in 35 metropolitan areas in 11 mostly western states. Its enterprise data services include managed network services data and server colocation and hosted cloud computing services. Integra also sells its products to other carriers on a wholesale basis through its Electric Lightwave division. The company serves the energy food broadcasting and real estate industries among others. Clients have included SolarWorld and the Red Cross.

INTEGRAL VISION INC.   OTC: INVI

49113 Wixom Tech Dr.
Wixom MI 48393
Phone: 248-668-9230
Fax: 248-668-9384
Web: www.iv-usa.com

CEO: –
CFO: –
HR: –
FYE: December 31
Type: Public

Integral Vision wants manufacturers to take a closer look. The company makes machine vision systems that monitor and control manufacturing processes in the small flat-panel display industry. Its systems inspect for both cosmetic and functional defects in display components used in camcorders cell phones digital still cameras computer monitors and handheld video games. Integral Vision also offers software for developing machine vision inspection applications. Customers have included Liquavista QUALCOMM Samsung Electronics and Texas Instruments.

INTEGRAL SYSTEMS INC.

6721 Columbia Gateway Dr.
Columbia MD 21046
Phone: 443-539-5008
Fax: 410-312-2705
Web: www.integ.com

CEO: Paul G Casner Jr
CFO: Christopher Roberts
HR: –
FYE: September 30
Type: Subsidiary

Integral Systems provides high-flying customers with a sense of control. The company designs satellite command and control data processing flight simulation integration and test and signals analysis systems. Military agencies communication service providers and scientific researchers use the company's EPOCH Integrated Product Suite (IPS) to monitor and control their ground systems and satellites and to analyze the data that they gather. Integral Systems counts the US Air Force the US Navy the US NOAA and China's National Space Program Office among its largely US-based customer roster. The company was acquired in 2011 by Kratos Defense & Security in a stock swap transaction.

INTEGRAMED AMERICA INC.   NASDAQ: INMD

2 Manhattanville Rd.
Purchase NY 10577-2113
Phone: 914-253-8000
Fax: 914-253-8008
Web: www.integramed.com

CEO: Jay Higham
CFO: Timothy P Sheehan
HR: –
FYE: December 31
Type: Public

IntegraMed America's specialty is identifying and entering niche medical markets throughout the US. The company operates through two segments: its Attain Fertility Clinics and Vein Clinics. The company's fertility services include in vitro fertilization (IVF) artificial insemination and other reproductive assistance through more than 130 clinics in metropolitan markets. Its Fertility Services division supplies administrative and management support to its clinics and helps guide potential parents through the IVF process. The second division Vein Clinics operates 45 vein treatment centers throughout the US. IntegraMed America was acquired by investment firm Sagard Capital Partners in 2012.

INTEGRAL TECHNOLOGIES INC.   NBB: ITKG

805 W. Orchard Drive, Suite 7
Bellingham, WA 98225
Phone: 360 752-1982
Fax: –
Web: www.itkg.net

CEO: Doug Bathauer
CFO: W Bartlett Snell
HR: –
FYE: June 30
Type: Public

Integral Technologies hopes to discover that technology truly is integral to everyday life. The company has developed what it calls its "ElectriPlast" product an electrically conductive resin-based polymer that can be molded into any shape. The company's "PlasTenna" technology uses ElectriPlast for antenna design and other manufacturing processes. It can become part of the cell phone casing itself. Integral Technologies outsources its manufacturing and is marketing its products to cell phone and other wireless device manufacturers. The development stage company has yet to recognize any appreciable revenues from its products.

	Annual Growth	06/11	06/12	06/13	06/14	06/15
Sales ($ mil.)	–	0.0	0.0	0.0	0.0	0.2
Net income ($ mil.)	–	(2.8)	(3.4)	(3.7)	(4.5)	(4.4)
Market value ($ mil.)	6.1%	57.2	43.4	64.2	34.3	72.6
Employees	–	8	4	–	–	–

INTEGRATED BIOPHARMA INC   NBB: INBP

225 Long Avenue
Hillside, NJ 07205
Phone: 888 319-6962
Fax: –
Web: www.integratedbiopharma.com

CEO: E Gerald Kay
CFO: Dina L Masi
HR: –
FYE: June 30
Type: Public

Integrated BioPharma has taken a bounty of businesses and coalesced them into the cohesive nutraceuticals manufacturer it is today. Through numerous subsidiaries Integrated BioPharma manufactures and distributes vitamins nutritional supplements herbal products and natural chemicals. Subsidiaries include AgroLabs (nutritional drinks vitamins supplements) Chem International (vitamins) IHT Health Products (natural chemicals) Manhattan Drug Company (vitamins and nutritional supplements sold to distributors multi-level marketers and specialized health care providers) and Vitamin Factory (sells private-label Manhattan Drug products online and via mail order catalogue).

	Annual Growth	06/11	06/12	06/13	06/14	06/15
Sales ($ mil.)	10.5%	25.1	36.6	33.6	33.7	37.5
Net income ($ mil.)	–	(2.3)	(2.7)	0.1	0.1	0.7
Market value ($ mil.)	(26.9%)	6.3	6.3	3.2	5.3	1.8
Employees	0.9%	115	108	115	120	119

INTEGRATED DEVICE TECHNOLOGY, INC.
NMS: IDTI

6024 Silver Creek Valley Road
San Jose, CA 95138
Phone: 408 284-8200
Fax: –
Web: www.idt.com

CEO: Gregory L. (Greg) Waters
CFO: Brian C. White
HR: –
FYE: March 29
Type: Public

Integrated Device Technology (IDT) knows about integrating devices. The company offers hundreds of high-performance semiconductors and modules available in thousands of configurations primarily for computers computer peripherals and consumer electronics but also for the networking and communications markets. Much of IDT's sales come from its communications and high-performance logic products which include processors specialized memories logic and clock management products and chipsets and controllers for networking gear. The company gets about three-quarters of its sales from Asia/Pacific.

	Annual Growth	04/11	04/12*	03/13	03/14	03/15
Sales ($ mil.)	(2.2%)	625.7	526.7	487.2	484.8	572.9
Net income ($ mil.)	6.6%	72.6	58.5	(20.2)	88.4	93.7
Market value ($ mil.)	28.1%	1,089.4	1,061.2	1,108.7	1,772.1	2,936.4
Employees	(8.4%)	2,053	1,800	1,748	1,484	1,447

*Fiscal year change

INTEGRATED ELECTRICAL SERVICES, INC.
NMS: IESC

5433 Westheimer Road, Suite 500
Houston, TX 77056
Phone: 713 860-1500
Fax: –
Web: www.ies-corporate.com

CEO: –
CFO: Tracy A McLauchlin
HR: –
FYE: September 30
Type: Public

Lights! Camera! Action! Integrated Electrical Services (IES) has a hand in all three. It installs and maintains electrical and communications systems for residential commercial and industrial customers. Work on commercial buildings and homes includes custom design testing and maintenance on low-voltage systems such as lighting fire alarm audio/video and Internet cabling. On the industrial side IES performs high- and medium-voltage systems installation and construction on power stations oil and gas pipelines and processing plants. It has a network of more than 60 locations serving the continental US. Banking investor Jeffrey Gendell through Tontine Capital Partners owns about 57% of IES.

	Annual Growth	09/11	09/12	09/13	09/14	09/15
Sales ($ mil.)	4.5%	481.6	456.1	494.6	512.4	573.9
Net income ($ mil.)	–	(37.7)	(11.8)	(3.6)	5.3	16.5
Market value ($ mil.)	39.7%	43.5	97.7	87.2	177.2	165.8
Employees	3.3%	2,724	2,583	2,740	2,779	3,106

INTEGRATED MEDICAL SYSTEMS INTERNATIONAL INC.

3316 2ND AVE N
BIRMINGHAM, AL 352221214
Phone: 205-879-3840
Fax: –
Web: www.imsready.com

CEO: Gene Robinson
CFO: David Strevy
HR: –
FYE: December 31
Type: Private

When the surgeon asks for a rongeur and the assistant hands it over Integrated Medical Systems International (IMS) wants to make sure it is in good condition. The company repairs sterilizes and maintains medical ophthalmic and surgical equipment either at the hospital or at one of its own laboratories. IMS also sells products such as instrument cabinets and cleaning devices as well as certified pre-owned surgical equipment. Through its InstrumentReady program the company also offers instrument-tracking software and support services aimed at making sure the right instruments medical devices and equipment are ready when a surgical or minimally invasive procedure begins. IMS is being purchased by STERIS.

	Annual Growth	12/05	12/06	12/07	12/08	12/12
Sales ($ mil.)	10.5%	–	–	–	79.1	117.9
Net income ($ mil.)	26.7%	–	–	–	1.8	4.6
Market value ($ mil.)	–	–	–	–	–	–
Employees	–	–	–	–	–	1,100

INTEGRATED SILICON SOLUTION, INC.
NMS: ISSI

1623 Buckeye Drive
Milpitas, CA 95035
Phone: 408 969-6600
Fax: –
Web: www.issi.com

CEO: Jimmy Lee
CFO: –
HR: –
FYE: September 30
Type: Public

Fabless semiconductor company Integrated Silicon Solution Inc. (ISSI) has the right acronyms for the manufacturing process. ISSI primarily makes SRAMs (static random-access memory) chips and DRAMs (dynamic RAM) chips that are used in cars computers consumer electronics cell phones and networking devices. ISSI sells its chips to dozens of electronics manufacturers from the automotive communications consumer industrial medical and military markets either directly or through distributors and contract manufacturers. Customers include Bosch Cisco GE and Samsung. Most of its sales come from Asia.

	Annual Growth	09/10	09/11	09/12	09/13	09/14
Sales ($ mil.)	6.8%	252.5	270.5	266.0	307.6	329.0
Net income ($ mil.)	(13.8%)	42.2	56.0	(2.7)	17.5	23.3
Market value ($ mil.)	12.4%	265.5	240.8	285.5	335.8	423.6
Employees	6.9%	452	469	552	590	590

INTEGRATED SURGICAL SYSTEMS INC.
PINK SHEETS: ISSM

1433 N. Market Blvd. Ste. 1
Sacramento CA 95834
Phone: 916-285-9943
Fax: 916-285-9104
Web: www.robodoc.com

CEO: Christopher A Marlett
CFO: Gary Schuman
HR: –
FYE: December 31
Type: Public

Integrated Surgical Systems (ISS) wanted to be the hippest company around with its ROBODOC Surgical Assistant System a computer-controlled robot used in hip and knee replacements. However ISS ceased operations in mid-2005 because of lawsuits and lack of funding and it sold its ROBODOC assets to Novatrix Biomedical in 2007. Using those assets Novatrix has set up a new company called Curexo Medical to continue development of ROBODOC which is sold in Europe Asia and other regions and received FDA approval in 2008. Meanwhile ISS used the money from the asset sale to pay its debtors and is looking for acquisition opportunities.

INTEGRYS ENERGY GROUP INC
NYS: TEG

200 East Randolph Street
Chicago, IL 60601-6207
Phone: 312 228-5400
Fax: –
Web: www.integrysgroup.com

CEO: –
CFO: –
HR: –
FYE: December 31
Type: Public

Integrys Energy integrates energy activities in the Windy City and surrounding areas. The energy holding company owns six regulated utilities: Michigan Gas Utilities Corp. (169000 gas customers) Minnesota Energy Resources Corp. (216000 gas customers) North Shore Gas Company (159000 customers in northern Chicago) Peoples Gas Light and Coke Company (831000 natural gas customers in Chicago) Wisconsin Public Service (445000 electric customers and 323000 natural gas customers in Wisconsin and Michigan) and Upper Peninsula Power (52000 electricity customers). The company's nonregulated subsidiary Integrys Energy Services (sold to Constellation in 2014) provided retail energy supply and services.

	Annual Growth	12/09	12/10	12/11	12/12	12/13
Sales ($ mil.)	(6.9%)	7,499.8	5,203.2	4,708.7	4,212.4	5,634.6
Net income ($ mil.)	–	(68.8)	223.7	230.5	284.3	354.8
Market value ($ mil.)	6.7%	3,335.9	3,853.9	4,304.4	4,148.6	4,322.6
Employees	(0.7%)	5,025	4,612	4,619	4,717	4,888

INTEL CORP
NMS: INTC

2200 Mission College Boulevard
Santa Clara, CA 95054-1549
Phone: 408 765-8080
Fax: 408 765-2633
Web: www.intc.com

CEO: Brian M. Krzanich
CFO: Stacy J. Smith
HR: Michael Hill
FYE: December 26
Type: Public

Intel has followed the law — Moore's Law that is — to the top spot in manufacturing and selling semiconductors. Company co-founder Gordon Moore determined in 1965 (making 2015 the 50th anniversary of the law) that microprocessors would regularly get more powerful smaller and less expensive. Intel has followed that formula to grab about 80% of the market share for microprocessors that go into desktop and notebook computers smartphones tablets and computer servers. The company's technology roadmap calls for releasing a new Core processor and a Xeon processor every two years. Most computer makers use Intel processors. In late 2015 Intel bought chipmaker Altera for $16.7 billion.

	Annual Growth	12/11	12/12	12/13	12/14	12/15
Sales ($ mil.)	0.6%	53,999.0	53,341.0	52,708.0	55,870.0	55,355.0
Net income ($ mil.)	(3.1%)	12,942.0	11,005.0	9,620.0	11,704.0	11,420.0
Market value ($ mil.)	–	0.0	0.0	0.0	0.0	0.0
Employees	1.8%	100,100	105,000	107,600	106,700	107,300

INTELIQUENT INC
NMS: IQNT

550 West Adams Street, Suite 900
Chicago, IL 60661
Phone: 312 384-8000
Fax: –
Web: www.inteliquent.com

CEO: Matthew Carter
CFO: Kurt J. Abkemeier
HR: John R. Harrington
FYE: December 31
Type: Public

Inteliquent tries to keep customers in step with smart networking choices. The company provides wholesale interconnectivity services for voice IP transit Ethernet and cloud computing via its multiprotocol label switching (MPLS)/IP network. That network exclusively uses Sonus Networks equipment and has more than 120 points of presence across North America Europe and Asia. Inteliquent's customers are competitive local exchange carriers ISPs large businesses and other telecom content and service providers. Its services are used in more than 80 countries.

	Annual Growth	12/10	12/11	12/12	12/13	12/14
Sales ($ mil.)	2.5%	199.8	268.3	275.5	211.7	220.5
Net income ($ mil.)	4.3%	32.6	27.1	(78.1)	55.7	38.5
Market value ($ mil.)	8.0%	483.1	357.7	86.0	381.8	656.8
Employees	(11.9%)	265	291	290	143	160

INTELLICHECK MOBILISA, INC.
ASE: IDN

100 Jericho Quadrangle, Suite 202
Jericho, NY 11753
Phone: 516 992-1900
Fax: –
Web: www.icmobil.com

CEO: William H Roof
CFO: Bill White
HR: –
FYE: December 31
Type: Public

IntelliCheck Mobilisa will need to see some ID. The company provides handheld electronic card readers and related software for the commercial government and military markets. Used to secure military and federal government locations its Defense ID System can read barcodes magnetic stripes optical character recognition (OCR) and radio frequency identification (RFID) codes. Its ID-Check systems are designed to verify the age and identity of customers who swipe a driver's license military ID or other magnetically encoded ID card. The company has installed systems in airports bars casinos convenience stores hotels and stadiums.

	Annual Growth	12/10	12/11	12/12	12/13	12/14
Sales ($ mil.)	(14.4%)	12.3	12.5	8.8	7.3	6.6
Net income ($ mil.)	–	(2.6)	(0.3)	(2.3)	(2.4)	(7.6)
Market value ($ mil.)	21.0%	6.8	4.4	3.2	2.5	14.6
Employees	(9.9%)	47	40	37	31	31

INTELLICORP INC.

2900 Lakeside Dr. Ste. 221
Santa Clara CA 95054
Phone: 408-454-3500
Fax: 408-454-3529
Web: www.intellicorp.com

CEO: Jerome Klajbor
CFO: –
HR: –
FYE: June 30
Type: Private

IntelliCorp isn't a sap when it comes to good software. The company provides software and services that enable businesses to integrate enterprise customer relationship management (CRM) software made by SAP with back-office functions such as logistics accounting and order processing. Its products include applications for business process management (LivdModel) efficiency monitoring (LiveCompare) and data management (DataWorks). Intellicorp also offers consulting related to software integration and legacy CRM systems migration. Intellicorp has offices in the US and the UK. It sells directly and through systems integrators and other distributors. Customers have included Boeing and General Motors.

INTELLIDYNE L.L.C.

5203 LEESBURG PIKE # 400
FALLS CHURCH, VA 22041-3401
Phone: 703-575-9715
Fax: –
Web: www.intellidynellc.com

CEO: Tony Crescenzo
CFO: Joseph W Kuhn
HR: –
FYE: December 31
Type: Private

IntelliDyne likes to think it takes a smarter approach to solving IT problems. The company consults with US government and commercial customers to help them plan design install lease and manage information technology systems and services. Its areas of expertise include network security cloud computing custom software development business process management and data center consolidation. IntelliDyne primarily serves defense homeland security law enforcement and civilian agencies. The US Department of Defense its largest client uses its services primarily to support medical centers and hospitals. The company was established in 1999 by president Robert Grey.

	Annual Growth	12/01	12/02	12/04	12/05	12/10
Sales ($ mil.)	18.0%	–	14.1	18.7	26.3	53.0
Net income ($ mil.)	17.1%	–	1.4	6.0	1.2	4.9
Market value ($ mil.)	–	–	–	–	–	–
Employees	–	–	–	–	–	275

INTELLIGENT SOFTWARE SOLUTIONS INC.

5450 TECH CENTER DR # 400
COLORADO SPRINGS, CO 809192339
Phone: 719-452-7000
Fax: –
Web: www.issinc.com

CEO: –
CFO: Nikki Herman
HR: –
FYE: December 31
Type: Private

Intelligent Software Solutions is no dummy when it comes to software development and IT systems analysis. The privately-held company develops and integrates custom software used for such applications as data visualization and analysis pattern detection and mission planning for the aerospace defense and maritime industries. It also provides on-site product and development support and training. As a government contractor it serves a range of public sector agencies within the US Department of Defense US Department of Homeland Security and US Air Force. Intelligent Software Solutions corporate clients have included Lockheed Martin Northrop Grumman and Leidos.

	Annual Growth	12/07	12/08	12/09	12/10	12/11
Sales ($ mil.)	39.1%	–	–	86.5	121.3	167.3
Net income ($ mil.)	30647.7%	–	–	0.0	7.5	12.6
Market value ($ mil.)	–	–	–	–	–	–
Employees	–	–	–	–	–	650

INTELLIGENT SYSTEMS CORP.

ASE: INS

4355 Shackleford Road
Norcross, GA 30093
Phone: 770 381-2900
Fax: –
Web: www.intelsys.com

CEO: J Leland Strange
CFO: Bonnie L Herron
HR: –
FYE: December 31
Type: Public

Intelligent Software Solutions (ISS) is no dummy when it comes to software development and IT systems analysis. The privately-held company develops and integrates custom software for data visualization and analysis pattern detection and mission planning for the aerospace defense and maritime industries. Its products include a software tool that counters improvised explosive devices (Dfuze) and public safety management software tool (WebTAS). The company provides on-site product and development support and training. Customers include government military intelligence agencies and local law enforcement in the US and abroad.

	Annual Growth	12/10	12/11	12/12	12/13	12/14
Sales ($ mil.)	(1.4%)	15.4	16.3	16.5	16.3	14.6
Net income ($ mil.)	–	(0.2)	0.7	0.5	1.1	(0.1)
Market value ($ mil.)	5.6%	11.6	14.3	12.3	14.5	14.4
Employees	3.0%	234	255	257	255	263

INTELLIGRATED INC.

7901 Innovation Way
Mason OH 45040
Phone: 513-701-7300
Fax: 513-701-7320
Web: www.intelligrated.com

CEO: Chris Cole
CFO: Ed Puisis
HR: Bernie Hess
FYE: December 31
Type: Private

Intelligrated helps businesses move products — literally. The company makes and installs automated material handling equipment including conveyors sorters and airport baggage handling equipment as well as order fulfillment and warehouse control software. Its InControlWare software system manages conveyor and sortation systems while its Real Time Solutions software aids in order fulfillment. It targets the consumer goods distribution logistics pharmaceutical postal and warehousing markets. Customers have included Dick's Sporting Goods The Hershey Company Big Lots and McKesson. Formed in 2001 Intelligrated was acquired by European private equity firm Permira in mid-2012 for more than $500 million.

INTEPLAST GROUP LTD.

9 Peach Tree Hill Rd.
Livingston NJ 07039
Phone: 973-994-8000
Fax: 973-994-8005
Web: www.inteplast.com

CEO: –
CFO: Robert Wang
HR: –
FYE: December 31
Type: Private

The Inteplast Group is best known for turning plastic into gold. Working through three divisions Inteplast manufactures a diversity of essential plastic products. Its AmTopp division produces biaxially oriented polypropylene (BOPP) film stretch wrap and plastic concentrates and compounds; its World-Pak unit makes fluted boards plastic sheets and foam and cross-laminated film; and its Integrated Bagging Systems (IBS) unit trash can liners produce bags and plastic packaging. Inteplast products are used in construction materials as well as boat building healthcare food and merchandise packaging shipping and more. Founded in 1991 Inteplast operates plants in Texas and Massachusetts Canada and Asia.

INTER PARFUMS, INC.

NMS: IPAR

551 Fifth Avenue
New York, NY 10176
Phone: 212 983-2640
Fax: 212 983-4197
Web: www.interparfumsinc.com

CEO: Philippe Benacin
CFO: Russell Greenberg
HR: –
FYE: December 31
Type: Public

Would a perfumer by any other name smell as sweet? Inter Parfums certainly hopes not. Most of the fragrance developer and manufacturer's revenue is generated by sales of its prestige fragrance brands including Karl Lagerfeld Jimmy Choo Lanvin Montblanc Repetto S.T. Dupont and Van Cleef & Arpels among others. (The company owns the Lanvin and Jean Philippe brand names.) It also sells moderately priced perfumes personal care products and cosmetics for specialty retailers such as The Gap bebe stores Brooks Brothers and Lane Bryant. Customers include specialty shops and department stores mass merchandisers and drugstore chains. Its fragrances are sold in more than 100 countries.

	Annual Growth	12/10	12/11	12/12	12/13	12/14
Sales ($ mil.)	2.0%	460.4	615.2	654.1	563.6	499.3
Net income ($ mil.)	2.6%	26.6	32.3	131.1	39.2	29.4
Market value ($ mil.)	9.9%	583.9	482.0	602.8	1,109.3	850.3
Employees	2.4%	271	283	312	296	298

INTER-AMERICAN DEVELOPMENT BANK

1300 New York Ave. NW
Washington DC 20577
Phone: 202-623-1000
Fax: 202-623-3096
Web: www.iadb.org

CEO: –
CFO: Gustavo De Rosa
HR: –
FYE: December 31
Type: Private - Member-Own

Inter-American Development Bank is like a mutual aid society that packs an economic punch. The institution was founded in 1959 to aid in the social and economic development of Latin America and the Caribbean. It provides grants and loans to help fund public and private projects promote sustainable growth modernize public institutions foster free trade and fight poverty and injustice. The bank is also involved in cross-border issues such as infrastructure and energy. Governments government organizations (such as state banks and universities) civil societies and private-sector companies are all eligible to receive Inter-American Development Bank loans.

INTER-CON SECURITY SYSTEMS INC.

210 S. De Lacey Ave.
Pasadena CA 91105
Phone: 626-535-2200
Fax: 626-685-9111
Web: www.icsecurity.com

CEO: –
CFO: Paul Miller
HR: Shar Pasquini
FYE: December 31
Type: Private

There is no conning Inter-Con Security Systems. The company one of the largest private security consulting firms in the US provides custom-designed security programs for commercial governmental and industrial clients in Asia North and South America Europe and Africa. Inter-Con's services include security consulting investigations and training. The company also provides security guard and fire protection services as well as risk assessment and classified information safeguarding. The company employs more than 25000 security personnel in some 25 countries. Inter-Con's clients have included General Motors Kaiser Permanente NASA and the US Department of State. The company was founded in 1973.

INTERACTIVE BROKERS GROUP INC — NMS: IBKR

One Pickwick Plaza
Greenwich, CT 06830
Phone: 203 618-5800
Fax: –
Web: www.interactivebrokers.com

CEO: Thomas Peterffy
CFO: Paul J. Brody
HR: –
FYE: December 31
Type: Public

Interactive Brokers Group serves investors who interact with world markets. It performs trade order management execution and portfolio management services through its Interactive Brokers subsidiaries and electronic market-maker Timber Hill. The group provides access to about 100 electronic exchanges and trading centers worldwide executing nearly one million trades per day in stocks options futures foreign exchange instruments bonds and mutual funds. It caters to institutional and experienced individual investors. The company also licenses its trading interface to large banks and brokerages through white-label agreements. Founder chairman and CEO Thomas Peterffy controls Interactive Brokers Group.

	Annual Growth	12/10	12/11	12/12	12/13	12/14
Sales ($ mil.)	3.1%	988.3	1,444.6	1,192.5	1,127.9	1,115.5
Net income ($ mil.)	–	(9.3)	61.9	40.7	37.0	44.5
Market value ($ mil.)	13.1%	1,042.0	873.6	799.9	1,423.2	1,705.1
Employees	2.9%	857	874	891	880	960

INTERACTIVE DATA CORPORATION

32 Crosby Dr.
Bedford MA 01730
Phone: 781-687-8500
Fax: 781-687-8005
Web: www.interactivedata.com

CEO: Stephen C Daffron
CFO: Vincent Chippari
HR: –
FYE: December 31
Type: Private

Interactive Data Corporation has something vital to the information superhighway — the information. Its subscription services provide financial market data analytics and related services to financial institutions active traders and individual investors. Interactive Data conducts business through two segments: Institutional Services and Active Trader Services. Products include Interactive Data Fixed Income Analytics (fixed-income portfolio analytics for institutions) Interactive Data Pricing and Reference Data (securities information for institutions) and Interactive Data Desktop Solutions (real-time market data for individuals). Private-equity firms Silver Lake and Warburg Pincus own the company.

INTERACTIVE INTELLIGENCE GROUP INC. — NMS: ININ

7601 Interactive Way
Indianapolis, IN 46278
Phone: 317 872-3000
Fax: –
Web: www.inin.com

CEO: Donald E. Brown
CFO: Stephen R. (Steve) Head
HR: –
FYE: December 31
Type: Public

Interactive Intelligence knows legacy PBX telephone systems are going the way of the telegraph. The company's software manages call center operations for both inbound and outbound applications. Its Customer Interaction Center software can process thousands of interactions per hour across various media channels: telephone calls emails faxes voice mail Internet chat sessions IP telephony calls text messages and social media. Products are available in two dozen languages and have been installed in more than 100 different countries. The company's technology handles the automated call center operations for more than 6000 customers including CarMax IKEA and Walgreens.

	Annual Growth	12/10	12/11	12/12	12/13	12/14
Sales ($ mil.)	19.7%	166.3	209.5	237.4	318.2	341.3
Net income ($ mil.)	–	–	14.9	14.8	0.9	9.5	(41.4)
Market value ($ mil.)	16.3%	556.7	487.7	713.7	1,433.3	1,019.3
Employees	25.7%	849	1,106	1,437	1,848	2,122

INTERACTIVE INTELLIGENCE INC. — NASDAQ: ININ

7601 Interactive Way
Indianapolis IN 46278
Phone: 317-872-3000
Fax: +972-3-976-4040
Web: www.audiocodes.com

CEO: –
CFO: Stephen R Head
HR: –
FYE: December 31
Type: Public

Interactive Intelligence is hoping legacy PBX telephone systems go the way of the telegraph. The company's software helps integrate a wide array of communication systems via VoIP technology from phone calls voice mail and e-mail to faxes and Web-based communications. Its applications integrate with enterprise messaging platforms such as Microsoft Exchange and Lotus Notes and provide tools for connecting mobile and home-based workers to enterprise information systems. The company's technology handles the call center operations for more than 3500 customers including Ceridian InfoCision Vizio and Walgreens. Chairman and CEO Donald Brown founded Interactive Intelligence in 1994; he owns 26% of its stock.

INTERBOND CORPORATION OF AMERICA

3200 SW 42ND ST
FORT LAUDERDALE, FL 333126813
Phone: 954-797-4000
Fax: –
Web: www.prod.brandsmartusa.com

CEO: –
CFO: –
HR: –
FYE: September 24
Type: Private

Interbond Corporation of America (doing business as BrandsMart USA) boasts more than 500 brand names across its nearly 50000 electronics and entertainment products. It sells them in the US and internationally. It offers low-priced appliances computers TVs car stereos mobile phones personal care gadgets movie music games and more. The retailer runs about 10 electronics stores under the BrandsMart USA banner in the South Florida and Atlanta metropolitan areas. Each stocks more than $8 million in merchandise. BrandsMart USA also sells products online providing shipping for orders placed throughout the US Latin America and the Caribbean. Chairman Robert Perlman founded the company in 1977.

	Annual Growth	09/06	09/07	09/08	09/10	09/11
Sales ($ mil.)	32.3%	–	–	320.9	800.0	743.7
Net income ($ mil.)	2377.1%	–	–	0.0	7.2	3.6
Market value ($ mil.)	–	–	–	–	–	–
Employees	–	–	–	–	–	2,400

INTERCALL INC.

8420 W. Bryn Mawr Ave. Ste. 400
Chicago IL 60631
Phone: 773-399-1600
Fax: 773-399-1588
Web: www.intercall.com

CEO: –
CFO: –
HR: Brad Vanacore
FYE: December 31
Type: Subsidiary

It's a small world after InterCall. The company provides audio video and Web conferencing services and software as well as related products from Microsoft and Cisco. Its systems also enable conferencing via mobile devices such as Research In Motion's BlackBerry. The company offers conferencing equipment procurement services for products from Polycom and Westcon among others. Its Web collaboration application Unified Meeting enables online training promotional programs presentations and document sharing. InterCall markets to businesses and government agencies worldwide directly and through resellers and partners. The company is owned by outsourced communication services provider West Corporation.

INTERCEPT PHARMACEUTICALS INC
NMS: ICPT

450 West 15th Street, Suite 505
New York, NY 10011
Phone: 646 747-1000
Fax: –
Web: www.interceptpharma.com

CEO: Mark Pruzanski
CFO: Barbara Duncan
HR: –
FYE: December 31
Type: Public

Intercept Pharmaceuticals looks to cut liver disease off at the pass. A biopharmaceutical company Intercept Pharmaceuticals is developing and seeking to commercialize therapies to treat chronic liver disease. Its lead product candidate obeticholic acid (OCA) is being developed to treat primary biliary cirrhosis an autoimmune liver disease that can lead to liver failure and death. OCA is currently in late-stage clinical development. Intercept also has other candidates in its pipeline in earlier stages of development including treatments for other forms of cirrhosis portal hypertension (pressure in a key vein leading to the liver) fibrosis and Type 2 diabetes. Intercept went public in 2012.

	Annual Growth	12/10	12/11	12/12	12/13	12/14
Sales ($ mil.)	(1.2%)	–	1.8	2.4	1.6	1.7
Net income ($ mil.)	–	(15.1)	(12.7)	(43.6)	(67.8)	(283.2)
Market value ($ mil.)	113.4%	–	–	733.3	1,462.2	3,340.8
Employees	96.2%	–	18	25	50	136

INTERCLOUD SYSTEMS, INC.
NAS: ICLD

1030 Broad Street, Suite 102
Shrewsbury, NJ 07702
Phone: 732 898-6308
Fax: –
Web: www.intercloudsys.com

CEO: Mark Munro
CFO: Timothy A Larkin
HR: –
FYE: December 31
Type: Public

It took a lot of storms to form InterCloud Systems. Formerly real estate firm Genesis Group Holdings the company changed its name to InterCloud Systems in 2013 and now oversees a group of subsidiaries that serve the telecom industry. It owns ADEX Corporation which provides engineering and installation services; structured cabling and DAS installers TNS and Tropical Communications; engineering firm Rives-Monteiro Engineering and equipment provider Rives-Monteiro Leasing; and AW Solutions which provides network systems design and engineering services. Customers include wireless and wireline telcos (Sprint) cable broadband multiple system operators (Verizon) and original equipment manufacturers (Ericsson).

	Annual Growth	12/10	12/11	12/12	12/13	12/14
Sales ($ mil.)	199.1%	1.0	2.8	17.2	51.4	76.2
Net income ($ mil.)	–	(2.1)	(7.4)	(1.2)	(24.4)	(18.8)
Market value ($ mil.)	95.2%	3.6	0.1	0.3	328.8	52.3
Employees	109.7%	25	60	455	354	483

INTERCONNECT DEVICES INC.

5101 Richland Ave.
Kansas City KS 66106-1019
Phone: 913-342-5544
Fax: 913-342-7043
Web: www.idinet.com

CEO: Michael Kirkman
CFO: Mark Deuel
HR: –
FYE: December 31
Type: Subsidiary

Interconnect Devices Inc. (IDI) makes spring-loaded contact probes used in automated test equipment (ATE) as well as semiconductor test probes and sockets. A sister company Synergetix makes connectors sockets and interfaces used by manufacturers in aerospace ATE automobiles medical equipment telecommunications and portable electronics. Synergetix was established in 1994 and constitutes the company's brand name for IDI's test and measurement equipment. IDI was founded in 1979 and was owned by Milestone Partners a private equity firm. In 2010 Smiths Group acquired IDI for $185 million in cash.

INTERCONTINENTAL EXCHANGE INC.
NYS: ICE

5660 New Northside Drive
Atlanta, GA 30328
Phone: 770 857-4700
Fax: 770 937-0020
Web: www.theice.com

CEO: Jeffrey C. (Jeff) Sprecher
CFO: Scott A. Hill
HR: –
FYE: December 31
Type: Public

If there were money to be made in ice futures Intercontinental Exchange (ICE) would probably trade that as well. The firm is a leading provider of online marketplaces and clearing services for global commodity trading primarily of electricity natural gas crude oil refined petroleum products precious metals and weather and emission credits. It manages a handful of global OTC markets and regulated futures exchanges. The firm owns the ICE Futures Europe a leading European energy futures and options platform as well as NYSE Holdings. ICE Data provides real-time daily and historical market data reports. ICE serves clients in more than 120 countries globally.

	Annual Growth	12/11	12/12	12/13	12/14	12/15
Sales ($ mil.)	25.9%	1,327.5	1,363.0	1,674.0	3,092.0	3,338.0
Net income ($ mil.)	25.7%	509.7	551.6	254.0	981.0	1,274.0
Market value ($ mil.)	20.7%	14,345.5	14,733.4	26,765.5	26,095.5	30,494.9
Employees	53.0%	1,013	1,077	4,232	2,902	5,549

INTERCONTINENTALEXCHANGE INC.
NYS: ICE

5660 New Northside Drive
Atlanta, GA 30328
Phone: 770 857-4700
Fax: 770 937-0020
Web: www.theice.com

CEO: Jeffrey C Sprecher
CFO: Scott A Hill
HR: –
FYE: December 31
Type: Public

If there were money to be made in ice futures Intercontinental Exchange (ICE) would probably trade that as well. The firm is a leading provider of online marketplaces and clearing services for global commodity trading primarily of electricity natural gas crude oil refined petroleum products precious metals and weather and emission credits. It manages a handful of global OTC markets and regulated futures exchanges. The firm owns the ICE Futures Europe a leading European energy futures and options platform. ICE Data provides real-time daily and historical market data reports. ICE serves clients in more than 120 countries globally. It acquired NYSE Holdings in late 2013.

	Annual Growth	12/10	12/11	12/12	12/13	12/14
Sales ($ mil.)	28.1%	1,149.9	1,327.5	1,363.0	1,674.0	3,092.0
Net income ($ mil.)	25.3%	398.3	509.7	551.6	254.0	981.0
Market value ($ mil.)	16.5%	13,464.0	13,622.2	13,990.5	25,416.0	24,779.8
Employees	32.8%	933	1,013	1,077	4,232	2,902

INTERDIGITAL INC (PA)
NMS: IDCC

200 Bellevue Parkway, Suite 300
Wilmington, DE 19809-3727
Phone: 302 281-3600
Fax: –
Web: www.interdigital.com

CEO: William J. Merritt
CFO: Richard J. Brezski
HR: –
FYE: December 31
Type: Public

InterDigital is more than just interested in wireless digital telecommunications. The company develops and licenses circuitry designs software and other technology using CDMA (code-division multiple access) and other wireless communications standards. Altogether it holds a patent portfolio of about 1700 US patents and 10300 foreign ones. InterDigital licenses its technology patents to companies that make smartphones tablets notebook computers and wireless personal digital assistants as well as wireless infrastructure equipment such as base stations and components dongles and modules for wireless devices. Top customers include Acer Samsung HTC and other makers of chips software and telecom equipment.

	Annual Growth	12/10	12/11	12/12	12/13	12/14
Sales ($ mil.)	1.3%	394.5	301.7	663.1	325.4	415.8
Net income ($ mil.)	(9.2%)	153.6	89.5	271.8	38.2	104.3
Market value ($ mil.)	6.2%	1,537.3	1,608.6	1,517.0	1,088.8	1,953.1
Employees	1.6%	300	330	290	290	320

INTERFACE INC.

NMS: TILE

2859 Paces Ferry Road, Suite 2000
Atlanta, GA 30239
Phone: 770 437-6800
Fax: –

CEO: Daniel T. Hendrix
CFO: Patrick C. Lynch
HR: –
FYE: December 28
Type: Public

Interface provides a soft place to land. The company is a leading global producer and seller of modular carpet. The tiles and rolls used in offices and many institutional facilities are sold under brand names Interface Heuga and FLOR. Interface's other offerings include an antimicrobial chemical Intersept which it blends in its carpet as well as licenses for use in air filters and the TacTiles carpet tile installation system. Core markets are the Americas Europe and the Asia/Pacific region; the Americas represent more than 50% of sales.

	Annual Growth	01/11	01/12*	12/12	12/13	12/14
Sales ($ mil.)	1.4%	961.8	1,057.1	932.0	960.0	1,003.9
Net income ($ mil.)	44.1%	8.3	38.7	5.9	48.3	24.8
Market value ($ mil.)	1.9%	1,034.4	761.3	1,041.0	1,421.0	1,095.1
Employees	(1.4%)	3,567	3,702	3,277	3,528	3,423

*Fiscal year change

INTERFACE SECURITY SYSTEMS L.L.C.

3773 Corporate Center Dr.
Earth City MO 63045
Phone: 314-595-0100
Fax: 314-595-0376
Web: www.interfacesys.com

CEO: Michael Shaw
CFO: Ken Obermeyer
HR: –
FYE: July 31
Type: Private

Interface Security Systems is a leading provider of security systems and monitoring services for businesses and residential customers. It installs and monitors alarm systems for access control fire and life safety and intrusion detection. The company also offers video monitoring and alarm verification remote managed access monitoring and support and Internet-based alarm monitoring. Interface Security Systems has offices in about a dozen states mostly in the South and Southwest. The company was founded in 1981.

INTERGRAPH CORPORATION

19 Interpro Rd.
Madison AL 35758
Phone: 256-730-2000
Fax: 256-730-2048
Web: www.intergraph.com

CEO: Ola Rollen
CFO: Steven Cost
HR: –
FYE: December 31
Type: Subsidiary

They like wide open spaces at Intergraph — and city streets too. The company provides spatial information management software which enables mapping and design functions for local state and federal government agencies and for businesses in the transportation process plant design power marine public safety and utilities industries. Its systems (a combination of software third-party hardware and services) are used for a wide range of functions including plant design ship construction public safety dispatch aerial photography and geospatial mapping and analysis. In 2010 the company was acquired by Hexagon in a transaction valued at around $2 billion.

INTERGROUP CORP. (THE)

NAS: INTG

10940 Wilshire Blvd., Suite 2150
Los Angeles, CA 90024
Phone: 310 889-2500
Fax: –

CEO: John V Winfield
CFO: –
HR: –
FYE: June 30
Type: Public

InterGroup buys develops and manages affordable housing and other projects with an eye toward social responsibility. The company owns around 20 apartment complexes two commercial real estate properties two single-family residences and through subsidiary Santa Fe Financial majority interest in a San Francisco hotel. Its holdings are primarily concentrated in California and Texas. InterGroup also invests in securities and in real estate portfolios held by other corporations. Chairman and CEO John Winfield owns about 60% of the company. Winfield is also CEO of Santa Fe Financial and its subsidiary Portsmouth Square.

	Annual Growth	06/11	06/12	06/13	06/14	06/15
Sales ($ mil.)	9.7%	50.2	57.0	62.0	67.3	72.7
Net income ($ mil.)	(23.9%)	8.8	(2.3)	(0.7)	(4.7)	2.9
Market value ($ mil.)	(6.0%)	59.5	59.5	50.1	45.6	46.5
Employees	151.3%	8	8	8	7	319

INTERLEUKIN GENETICS, INC.

NBB: ILIU

135 Beaver Street
Waltham, MA 02452
Phone: 781 398-0700
Fax: 781 398-0720
Web: www.ilgenetics.com

CEO: –
CFO: Stephen Dipalma
HR: Rose Villandry
FYE: December 31
Type: Public

Interleukin Genetics counts on the high failure rate of crystal balls. The genetics-based personalized health company develops genetic tests for use in the emerging personalized health market to identify individuals' chances of developing certain diseases. Its PerioPredict product tests for gum disease and is available in the US and Europe. The company also offers predictive tests for heart disease and general nutrition through its partnership with Alticor. Interleukin Genetics has also teamed with Alticor to develop nutritional and skin care products.

	Annual Growth	12/10	12/11	12/12	12/13	12/14
Sales ($ mil.)	(2.4%)	2.0	2.9	2.2	2.4	1.8
Net income ($ mil.)	–	(6.0)	(5.0)	(5.1)	(7.1)	(6.3)
Market value ($ mil.)	(17.3%)	51.8	33.7	53.5	60.4	24.2
Employees	–	–	–	–	–	–

INTERLINE BRANDS INC.

NYSE: IBI

801 W. Bay St.
Jacksonville FL 32204
Phone: 904-421-1400
Fax: 904-358-2486
Web: www.interlinebrands.com

CEO: Michael J Grebe
CFO: Federico Pensotti
HR: –
FYE: December 31
Type: Private

When something breaks bursts or drips you can call Interline Brands a national distributor and direct marketer of repair and maintenance products. The company sells about 100000 plumbing hardware electrical janitorial and related products under private labels such as AmSan CleanSource Hardware Express Maintenance USA Sexauer U.S. Lock and Wilmar. Interline Brands operates 55 regional distribution centers and more than 25 showrooms that serve professional contractors throughout North America. Interline Brands which went public in 2004 was formed in 2000 through the merger of the Wilmar Barnett and Sexauer companies. Two private equity firms acquired the company in 2012.

INTERLINK ELECTRONICS, INC.   NBB: LINK

31248 Oak Crest Dr, Suite 110　　　　　　　　　　　　　CEO: –
Westlake Villag, CA 91361　　　　　　　　　　　　　CFO: Tracy Kern
Phone: 805 484-8855　　　　　　　　　　　　　HR: Patrice Poleto
Fax: 805 484-9457　　　　　　　　　　　　　FYE: December 31
Web: www.interlinkelectronics.com　　　　　　　　　　　　　Type: Public

Interlink Electronics designs electronic signature capture devices and specialty interface products. The company's signature capture products include its ePad line of hardware devices and IntegriSign software. Its sensor interface components enable menu navigation cursor control and character input in devices such as computer mice and mobile phones. Interlink's patented force-sensing technology enables smaller more touch-sensitive input devices. The company also provides design and integration services. Special Situations Technology Fund owns about 40% of the company.

	Annual Growth	12/10	12/11	12/12	12/13	12/14
Sales ($ mil.)	6.4%	8.0	5.0	6.4	7.6	10.3
Net income ($ mil.)	–	(1.1)	(1.6)	0.1	0.0	1.6
Market value ($ mil.)	178.8%	1.6	1.2	52.7	44.0	96.7
Employees	–	–	85	–	–	–

INTERMATIC INCORPORATED

7777 Winn Rd.　　　　　　　　　　　　　CEO: David Schroeder
Spring Grove IL 60081-9698　　　　　　　　　　　　　CFO: –
Phone: 815-675-2321　　　　　　　　　　　　　HR: –
Fax: 815-675-7055　　　　　　　　　　　　　FYE: December 31
Web: www.intermatic.com　　　　　　　　　　　　　Type: Private

From its start in 1891 as a maker of streetcar fare registers Intermatic has evolved to become an integrated manufacturer of energy-control products for both industrial and residential use. The company makes home timers that include pool and spa controls portable burglar alarms and appliance timers. It makes night-lights and portable alarms as well as outdoor lighting systems such as its Malibu brand of low-voltage systems. Other products include industrial surge protectors weatherproof covers for electrical outlets and solar-powered lights. Chairman emeritus Douglas Kinney Sr. and his family own the company.

INTERMETRO COMMUNICATIONS, INC. (NV)   NBB: IMTO

2685 Park Center Drive, Building A　　　　　　　　　　　　　CEO: Charles Rice
Simi Valley, CA 93065　　　　　　　　　　　　　CFO: James Winter
Phone: 805 433-8000　　　　　　　　　　　　　HR: –
Fax: –　　　　　　　　　　　　　FYE: December 31
Web: www.intermetrocomm.net　　　　　　　　　　　　　Type: Public

InterMetro Communications hopes to take over the VoIP market city by city. The company's national private voice-over Internet Protocol (VoIP) network delivers long-distance phone service to telecoms providers and calling card users. InterMetro's more than 200 customers include traditional long-distance carriers broadband companies VoIP service providers and wireless providers. Its VoIP network utilizes proprietary software switching equipment and fiber-optic lines to deliver carrier-quality VoIP services which are typically more cost efficient than circuit-based technologies used in traditional long-distance networks. Chairman and CEO Charles Rice owns almost 40% of the company.

	Annual Growth	12/09	12/10	12/11	12/12	12/13
Sales ($ mil.)	(15.1%)	22.3	28.0	21.3	20.1	11.6
Net income ($ mil.)	–	(4.9)	3.2	3.6	0.7	(2.5)
Market value ($ mil.)	50.5%	0.8	5.0	4.1	8.3	4.1
Employees	(2.9%)	27	29	23	30	24

INTERMOLECULAR INC.   NMS: IMI

3011 N. First Street　　　　　　　　　　　　　CEO: Bruce M McWilliams
San Jose, CA 95134　　　　　　　　　　　　　CFO: C Richard Neely Jr
Phone: 408 582-5700　　　　　　　　　　　　　HR: Roxie Vogt
Fax: –　　　　　　　　　　　　　FYE: December 31
Web: www.intermolecular.com　　　　　　　　　　　　　Type: Public

Intermolecular sees R&D as a service that can be sold to semiconductor and clean energy customers. Through multi-year collaborative development programs (CDPs) customers pay the company service fees to help them develop proprietary technology and intellectual property (IP) so that they can quickly move new devices materials and processes into high-volume production. Intermolecular uses its High Productivity Combinatorial (HPC) platform to reduce the time needed to experiment with and prototype devices. Smaller portions of revenues are made from the sale of its Tempus HPC hardware and software platform and royalty fees from licensing out its IP. Founded in 2004 Intermolecular went public in 2011.

	Annual Growth	12/10	12/11	12/12	12/13	12/14
Sales ($ mil.)	2.8%	42.7	53.8	66.8	67.4	47.7
Net income ($ mil.)	–	(1.8)	(30.0)	(0.8)	(8.8)	(21.8)
Market value ($ mil.)	(39.2%)	–	408.5	423.8	234.3	91.9
Employees	(5.0%)	204	212	232	253	166

INTERMOUNTAIN HEALTH CARE INC

36 S STATE ST STE 1600　　　　　　　　　　　　　CEO: Linda C. Leckman
SALT LAKE CITY, UT 841111441　　　　　　　　　　　　　CFO: Bert R. Zimmerli
Phone: 801-442-2000　　　　　　　　　　　　　HR: Dan Zuhlke
Fax: –　　　　　　　　　　　　　FYE: December 31
Web: www.intermountainhealthcare.org　　　　　　　　　　　　　Type: Private

If you whoosh down the side of one of Idaho's majestic mountains and take a nasty spill Intermountain Health Care (dba Intermountain Healthcare) will pick you up and put you back together. From air ambulance services to urgent care clinics and general hospitals Intermountain has all the tools to mend skiers (and non-skiers alike) in Utah and southern Idaho. With about 1100 physicians the not-for-profit health system operates 22 hospitals and 185 urgent care clinics as well as home health care agencies and rehabilitation centers. Its hospitals have a combined total of about 2700 licensed beds.

	Annual Growth	12/09	12/10	12/11	12/12	12/13
Sales ($ mil.)	4.8%	–	4,381.7	4,049.2	4,700.3	5,041.5
Net income ($ mil.)	1466.7%	–	–	6.3	546.7	1,546.4
Market value ($ mil.)	–	–	–	–	–	–
Employees	–	–	–	–	–	23,000

INTERMUNE INC.   NMS: ITMN

3280 Bayshore Boulevard　　　　　　　　　　　　　CEO: Daniel G Welch
Brisbane, CA 94005　　　　　　　　　　　　　CFO: John C Hodgman
Phone: 415 466-2200　　　　　　　　　　　　　HR: Shauna Lucas
Fax: –　　　　　　　　　　　　　FYE: December 31
Web: www.intermune.com　　　　　　　　　　　　　Type: Public

InterMune develops and sells drugs that interfere with pulmonary and immune system functions. The company's lead candidate Esbriet (pirfenidone) is a treatment for idiopathic pulmonary fibrosis (IPF) that was approved for sale in Europe in 2011. To focus on the development of Esbriet for additional markets InterMune divested its other primary commercial product rare congenital disorder treatment Actimmune (interferon gamma-1b) in 2012. Additional research programs aim to discover treatments for additional pulmonary and fibrotic conditions.

	Annual Growth	12/08	12/09	12/10	12/11	12/12
Sales ($ mil.)	(14.1%)	48.2	48.7	259.3	25.6	26.2
Net income ($ mil.)	–	(97.7)	(116.0)	122.4	(154.8)	(150.1)
Market value ($ mil.)	(2.2%)	698.8	861.3	2,404.2	832.2	640.0
Employees	(1.6%)	130	121	105	201	122

INTERNAP CORP
NMS: INAP

One Ravinia Drive, Suite 1300
Atlanta, GA 30346
Phone: 404 302-9700
Fax: –
Web: www.internap.com

CEO: Michael A. (Mike) Ruffolo
CFO: Kevin M. Dotts
HR: Deborah Levine
FYE: December 31
Type: Public

Internap has a solution for CIOs losing sleep over slow network connections. The company helps businesses bypass congested public network access points (NAPs) — the crossroads where major backbone carriers connect and exchange Internet traffic - with its own private NAPs (P-NAPS). Internap has P-NAPs located in Asia Australia Europe and North America. Internap provides application hosting and other data center services for clients with a need to outsource the housing and management of their networks. It also offers content delivery services to enable streaming audio and video as well as software for clients including media companies broadcasters and providers of Software-as-a Service.

	Annual Growth	12/10	12/11	12/12	12/13	12/14
Sales ($ mil.)	8.2%	244.2	244.6	273.6	283.3	335.0
Net income ($ mil.)	–	(3.6)	(1.7)	(4.3)	(19.8)	(39.5)
Market value ($ mil.)	7.0%	330.8	323.2	376.8	409.2	433.1
Employees	13.9%	416	500	500	700	700

INTERNATIONAL ASSOCIATION OF AMUSEMENT PARKS & ATTRACTIONS INC

1448 DUKE ST
ALEXANDRIA, VA 223143403
Phone: 703-836-3677
Fax: –
Web: www.iaapa.org

CEO: –
CFO: Thomas Fischetti
HR: –
FYE: July 31
Type: Private

Work is just a walk in the park for this group. The International Association of Amusement Parks and Attractions (IAAPA) is the world's largest trade organization for the amusement and theme park industry with 5000 members in 80 countries. The not-for-profit group develops services training products and networking opportunities for its members which include zoo museum arcade and family fun center operators. It holds annual trade shows publishes FUN-WORLD magazine offers management and customer service advice sets safety standards and lobbies government on behalf of the industry. IAAPA was founded in 1918.

	Annual Growth	07/03	07/04	07/05*	06/06*	07/08
Sales ($ mil.)	(72.1%)	–	–	599.7	0.0	13.0
Net income ($ mil.)	241.5%	–	–	0.0	(0.0)	0.7
Market value ($ mil.)	–	–	–	–	–	–
Employees	–	–	–	–	–	33

*Fiscal year change

INTERNATIONAL AUTOMOTIVE COMPONENTS GROUP NORTH AMERICA I

28333 Telegraph Rd.
Southfield MI 48034
Phone: 248-455-7000
Fax: 248-455-7000
Web: www.iacna.com

CEO: Robert Steven Miller
CFO: Dennis E Richardville
HR: Crystal Williams
FYE: December 31
Type: Subsidiary

Automobile interiors: Who doesn't love that new car smell? But when it comes to comfort convenience and safety thank International Automotive Components Group North America. The company doing business as IAC North America designs and produces automobile consoles instrument panels interior trim engineered for storage and safety (side airbags and sensors) exterior trim door panels and flooring. Its customers include such major auto OEMs as Ford GM Honda Toyota and Volkswagen. IAC North America operates more than 30 manufacturing facilities across Canada Mexico and the US. IAC North America is part of IAC Group.

INTERNATIONAL BALER CORP
NBB: IBAL

5400 Rio Grande Avenue
Jacksonville, FL 32254
Phone: 904 358-3812
Fax: 904 358-7013
Web: www.intl-baler.com

CEO: D Roger Griffin
CFO: William E Nielsen
HR: –
FYE: October 31
Type: Public

No need to bail on International Baler. This holding company formerly known as Waste Technology banks on its business being in the dumps. International Baler manufactures about 50 different types of waste baling equipment. It also sells replacement parts for waste haulers. In addition International Baler produces accessories such as conveyor belts and "rufflers" which break down refuse for better compaction. Customers include rubber and polymer makers solid-waste recycling facilities power generating facilities textile and paper mills cotton gins and supermarkets. International Baler makes about three-quarters of its sales in the US.

	Annual Growth	10/11	10/12	10/13	10/14	10/15
Sales ($ mil.)	13.1%	11.0	17.8	16.1	19.8	18.1
Net income ($ mil.)	4.4%	0.7	1.2	0.7	0.7	0.8
Market value ($ mil.)	7.6%	6.5	10.7	8.6	11.9	8.7
Employees	4.6%	56	67	60	68	67

INTERNATIONAL BANCSHARES CORP.
NMS: IBOC

1200 San Bernardo Avenue
Laredo, TX 78042-1359
Phone: 956 722-7611
Fax: –
Web: www.iboc.com

CEO: R. David Guerra
CFO: –
HR: Rosie Ramirez
FYE: December 31
Type: Public

International Bancshares Corp. is leading post-NAFTA banking in South Texas. One of the largest bank holding companies in Texas it does business through International Bank of Commerce (IBC) and Commerce Bank in Texas and Oklahoma through nearly 220 locations. The company facilitates trade between the US and Mexico and serves Texas' growing Hispanic population; about 30% of its deposits come from south of the border. In addition to commercial and international banking services International Bancshares provides retail deposit services insurance and investment products and mortgages and consumer loans. The bulk of the company's portfolio is made up of business and construction loans.

	Annual Growth	12/10	12/11	12/12	12/13	12/14
Assets ($ mil.)	0.5%	11,943.5	11,739.6	11,882.7	12,079.5	12,196.5
Net income ($ mil.)	4.2%	130.0	127.1	107.8	126.4	153.2
Market value ($ mil.)	7.3%	1,331.2	1,218.5	1,202.3	1,751.9	1,763.8
Employees	(3.5%)	3,747	3,388	3,259	3,223	3,256

INTERNATIONAL BROTHERHOOD OF ELECTRICAL WORKERS

900 7TH ST NW BSMT 1
WASHINGTON, DC 200014089
Phone: 202-833-7000
Fax: –
Web: www.ibew.org

CEO: –
CFO: –
HR: –
FYE: June 30
Type: Private

These brothers are held together with wire steel girders fiber optic cable and conveyor belts. The International Brotherhood of Electrical Workers (IBEW) is about a 725000-member labor union for workers in such industries as utilities construction telecommunications and manufacturing in the US and Canada. The union lobbies government on behalf of its members provides training and scholarships maintains an electronic job board and helps members secure higher wages better health care and safer working conditions. The union was formally organized in 1891 at a convention in St. Louis run by the original American Federation of Labor a predecessor to the AFL-CIO with which the union is affiliated.

	Annual Growth	12/07	12/08*	06/09*	08/09*	06/13
Sales ($ mil.)	72.1%	–	9.9	2.2	0.1	149.1
Net income ($ mil.)	–	–	–	0.0	0.0	(10.1)
Market value ($ mil.)	–	–	–	–	–	–
Employees	–	–	–	–	–	970

*Fiscal year change

INTERNATIONAL BROTHERHOOD OF TEAMSTERS

25 LOUISIANA AVE NW
WASHINGTON, DC 200012130
Phone: 202-624-6800
Fax: –
Web: www.teamster.org

CEO: –
CFO: –
HR: Joena Berrios
FYE: December 31
Type: Private

One of the largest and best-known labor unions in the US the International Brotherhood of Teamsters has 1.4 million members. The Teamsters represents workers in some 20 industry sectors including airlines freight parcel delivery industrial trades and public service. More than 200000 of the union's members are employees of package delivery giant United Parcel Service. Besides negotiating labor contracts with employers on behalf of its members the union oversees pension funds and serves as an advocate in legislative and regulatory arenas. The union and its affiliates have about 1900 local chapters in the US and Canada including about 475 Teamsters locals. The Teamsters union was founded in 1903.

	Annual Growth	12/05	12/06	12/07	12/08	12/09
Sales ($ mil.)	–	–	–	(91.4)	155.7	172.8
Net income ($ mil.)	353635.6%	–	–	0.0	(22.3)	12.5
Market value ($ mil.)	–	–	–	–	–	–
Employees	–	–	–	–	–	649

INTERNATIONAL BUILDING TECHNOLOGIES GROUP INC. OTC: INBG

17800 Castleton St. Ste. 638
City of Industry CA 91748
Phone: 626-581-8500
Fax: 626-626-7603
Web: www.ibtgi.com

CEO: Kenneth Yeung
CFO: Kenneth Yeung
HR: –
FYE: December 31
Type: Public

International Building Technologies Group (INBG) has raced from business to business. Formerly a card game developer for casinos and a seller of racing and motorsports accessories and apparel the company changed lanes in 2007. That's when it began a new life as a manufacturer of a specialty panel-based technology that helps buildings withstand earthquakes and hurricane-force winds. INBG also offers other services including site planning engineering contractor services training and supervision. In 2011 a merger plan between INBG and Chinese petroleum storage company FHH Sino New Energies was terminated. The deal would have allowed INBG to move into yet another line of business — the energy sector.

INTERNATIONAL BUSINESS MACHINES CORP. NYS: IBM

One New Orchard Road
Armonk, NY 10504
Phone: 914 499-1900
Fax: 914 765-4190
Web: www.ibm.com

CEO: –
CFO: Martin J. Schroeter
HR: Thomas (Thom) Fleming
FYE: December 31
Type: Public

International Business Machines (IBM) is the world's top provider of computer products and services. Called Big Blue for a reason the company is among the leaders in almost every market in which it competes. It focuses primarily on its services business which accounts for nearly 60% of sales. While IBM made its name in computer hardware (think mainframes) the company's information technology business services and software units are now among the largest in the world. While it has moved from hardware to a large degree the company maintains its industry-leading enterprise server and data storage products lines. IBM is transforming its operations as it deals with a rapidly changing technology environment.

	Annual Growth	12/10	12/11	12/12	12/13	12/14
Sales ($ mil.)	(1.8%)	99,870.0	106,916.0	104,507.0	99,751.0	92,793.0
Net income ($ mil.)	(5.1%)	14,833.0	15,855.0	16,604.0	16,483.0	12,022.0
Market value ($ mil.)	2.3%	145,369.3	182,137.5	189,734.8	185,792.5	158,919.6
Employees	(2.9%)	426,751	433,362	434,246	431,212	379,592

INTERNATIONAL CARD ESTABLISHMENT INC. OTC: ICRD

555 Airport Way Ste. A
Camarillo CA 93010
Phone: 209-946-2344
Fax: 212-261-4286
Web: www.dentsuamerica.com

CEO: William Lopshire
CFO: Candace Mills
HR: –
FYE: December 31
Type: Public

International Card Establishment (ICE) believes that it's cool for every merchant big or small to have the ability to swipe your credit card. More and more customers are using electronic payments to purchase items and ICE is there to provide businesses with the ability to accept transactions. ICE targets small businesses as its core customer base and offers a variety of credit card servicing offerings including processing systems processing services software and loyalty management programs. ICE has used acquisitions to transition away from its previous business of providing Web-based event management software and services.

INTERNATIONAL COFFEE & TEA LLC

1945 S. La Cienega Blvd.
Los Angeles CA 90034
Phone: 310-237-2326
Fax: 310-815-3676
Web: www.coffeebean.com

CEO: John Fuller
CFO: –
HR: –
FYE: December 31
Type: Private

Don't be chai; stand your grounds and espresso yourself over a cup at The Coffee Bean. International Coffee & Tea operates and franchises more than 800 coffee shops under the name The Coffee Bean & Tea Leaf. The outlets which are located primarily in Arizona California Hawaii Nevada and Texas feature a variety of fresh roasted coffees and specialty teas along with baked goods and blended ice drinks. The chain also operates locations in more than 20 countries outside of the US. About 350 locations are company-owned while the rest are franchised. The Coffee Bean & Tea Leaf also sells bagged coffee and tea at a handful of grocery stores including Albertsons and Vons.

INTERNATIONAL COMFORT PRODUCTS LLC

650 Heil Quaker Ave.
Lewisburg TN 37091
Phone: 931-359-3511
Fax: 931-270-3312
Web: www.icpusa.com

CEO: –
CFO: –
HR: –
FYE: December 31
Type: Subsidiary

International Comfort Products (ICP) makes sure you aren't too hot or too cold but just right. A United Technologies subsidiary (and part of its Carrier operating unit) ICP makes oil and gas furnaces heat pumps and central air-conditioning systems for residential and commercial customers. It sells home heating and cooling systems under the Heil Tempstar Comfortmaker Arcoaire Day & Night and KeepRite brands. Its commercial units with up to 20 tons of cooling capacity are sold under the ICP Commercial Heil Arcoaire Tempstar and KeepRite names. ICP produces more than a million units a year at plants in the US Mexico and Canada. Products are sold through distributors primarily in the US.

INTERNATIONAL CREATIVE MANAGEMENT INC.

10250 Constellation Blvd.
Los Angeles CA 90067
Phone: 310-550-4000
Fax: 310-550-4100
Web: www.icmtalent.com
CEO: –
CFO: –
HR: –
FYE: July 30
Type: Private

If anyone can manage creativity internationally it's International Creative Management (ICM). The agency represents film and television actors and directors as well as artists in theater music publishing and new media. A major "tenpercentery" (along with CAA and William Morris Endeavor) ICM represents such A-list clients as Susan Sarandon Al Pacino Robert Duvall Beyonce Knowles Chris Rock and Jay Leno as well as emerging performers. It has offices in Los Angeles New York and London. ICM was formed in 1975 by the merger of Creative Management Associates and The International Famous Agency. Private equity firm Traverse Rizvi Management and Merrill Lynch hold controlling stakes in the agency.

INTERNATIONAL DAIRY QUEEN INC.

7505 Metro Blvd.
Minneapolis MN 55439-0286
Phone: 952-830-0200
Fax: 952-830-0273
Web: www.dairyqueen.com
CEO: Charles W Mooty
CFO: James S Simpson
HR: Debra R Nelson
FYE: December 31
Type: Subsidiary

International Dairy Queen (IDQ) has been supplying brain-freezes for a long long time. The company is a leading franchisor of frozen treat stores with more than 5900 quick-service restaurants most of which operate under the Dairy Queen banner. Popular DQ ice cream treats include Blizzards sundaes and cones. Many of the stores also serve burgers fries and other items. In addition to its flagship chain IDQ has about 700 Orange Julius locations offering blended fruit drinks and a small number of Karmelkorn stands that feature popcorn snacks. Only a small number of units are company-owned. Tracing its roots back to 1938 the company is owned by Warren Buffett's Berkshire Hathaway.

INTERNATIONAL FINANCE CORP. (WORLD CORPORATIONS GOV'T)

2121 Pennsylvania Avenue, N.W.
Washington, DC 20433
Phone: 202 473-3800
Fax: 202 974-4384
Web: www.ifc.org
CEO: Gavin Wilson
CFO: –
HR: –
FYE: June 30
Type: Public

International Finance Corporation (IFC) is the lender known 'round the world. IFC promotes economic development worldwide by providing loans and equity financing for private-sector investment. Boasting $90 billion in assets the IFC typically focuses on small and mid-sized businesses financing projects in several industries including manufacturing agribusiness services infrastructure natural resources financial markets telecom media & technology and venture investing. Established in 1956 the IFC is the private sector arm of the World Bank group. Although it often acts in concert with the World Bank the IFC is legally and financially autonomous. It is owned by some 185 member countries.

	Annual Growth	06/10	06/11	06/12	06/13	06/14
Sales ($ mil.)	0.2%	3,383.0	3,178.0	3,120.0	2,514.0	3,415.0
Net income ($ mil.)	(4.0%)	1,746.0	1,579.0	1,328.0	1,018.0	1,483.0
Market value ($ mil.)	–	–	–	–	–	–
Employees	–	–	–	–	–	–

INTERNATIONAL FLAVORS & FRAGRANCES INC.   NYS: IFF

521 West 57th Street
New York, NY 10019-2960
Phone: 212 765-5500
Fax: –
Web: www.iff.com
CEO: Andreas Fibig
CFO: Alison A. Cornell
HR: Stuart (Stu) Maxwell
FYE: December 31
Type: Public

If you've got a taste for the sweet and a nose for a scent then International Flavors & Fragrances (IFF) is your kind of company. One of the world's leading creators and manufacturers of artificial and natural aromas and flavors IFF produces fragrances used in the manufacture of perfumes cosmetics soaps and other personal care and household products. The company is among the top four companies in its industry. IFF sells its flavors principally to makers of prepared foods dairy foods beverages confections and pharmaceuticals. The company sells its fragrances and flavors in solid and liquid forms in amounts that range from a few pounds to several tons.

	Annual Growth	12/10	12/11	12/12	12/13	12/14
Sales ($ mil.)	4.2%	2,622.9	2,788.0	2,821.4	2,952.9	3,088.5
Net income ($ mil.)	12.0%	263.6	266.9	254.1	353.5	414.5
Market value ($ mil.)	16.2%	4,490.4	4,234.4	5,374.9	6,945.3	8,187.6
Employees	3.0%	5,500	5,600	5,700	6,000	6,200

INTERNATIONAL FLEET SALES INC.

476 MCCORMICK ST
SAN LEANDRO, CA 945771106
Phone: 510-569-9770
Fax: –
Web: www.internationalfleetsales.com
CEO: Michael Libasci
CFO: Peggy King
HR: –
FYE: December 31
Type: Private

By air land or sea International Fleet Sales (IFS) can ship North American cars to international buyers. IFS is an authorized export distributor of General Motors vehicles (including Cadillac Chevrolet and GMC) as well as parts and service. It is also an export distributor of Blue Bird Bus and Volvo Trucks North America parts. Customers include auto retailers and distributors governments individual buyers and humanitarian aid agencies. The company's US office handles sales in Central and South America Asia Africa and the Middle East while its Netherlands office supports sales in Europe. IFS was founded in 1999 by president and CEO Mike Libasci.

	Annual Growth	12/05	12/06	12/07	12/08	12/09
Sales ($ mil.)	–	–	–	(593.2)	37.5	63.4
Net income ($ mil.)	1645.5%	–	–	0.0	2.0	5.0
Market value ($ mil.)	–	–	–	–	–	–
Employees	–	–	–	–	–	15

INTERNATIONAL IMAGING MATERIALS INC.

310 Commerce Dr.
Amherst NY 14228
Phone: 716-691-6333
Fax: 716-691-3395
Web: www.iimak.com
CEO: Douglas Wagner
CFO: Joe Perna
HR: –
FYE: December 31
Type: Private

Talk about a company that's concerned about image. International Imaging Materials (IIMAK) makes inks specialty papers cartridges and cassettes that are used by manufacturers retailers and shipping and distribution companies as well as in medical applications. The company also makes ribbons for fax machines bar-code machines and ID card printers. IIMAK's thermal transfer ribbons are used to print tags and labels in addition to making decals signs and other graphic art. Its customers include OEMs and distributors. Though headquartered in the US IIMAK also has locations in Belgium Brazil and Mexico. IIMAK was founded in 1983 and is owned by management and investment firm Centre Partners.

INTERNATIONAL ISOTOPES INC.
OTC: INIS

4137 Commerce Circle
Idaho Falls ID 83401
Phone: 208-524-5300
Fax: 208-524-1411
Web: www.intisoid.com/

CEO: Steve T Laflin
CFO: Laurie A McKenzie-Carter
HR: –
FYE: December 31
Type: Public

Despite its name International Isotopes is confined to a single US state. The firm operates primarily through subsidiary International Isotopes Idaho where it makes calibration and measurement equipment used with nuclear imaging cameras. Most of its nuclear imaging products including dose measurement devices and testing equipment are made under contract with RadQual a privately held firm that markets the devices; International Isotopes owns a minority stake in RadQual. The company partnered with RadQual in late 2010 to acquire Technology Imaging Services. The joint venture called TI Services LLC distributes products and services for nuclear medicine nuclear cardiology and PET imaging.

INTERNATIONAL MINERALS CORPORATION
TORONTO: IMZ

7950 E. Acoma Dr. Ste. 211
Scottsdale AZ 85260
Phone: 480-483-9932
Fax: 480-483-9926
Web: www.intlminerals.com

CEO: Stephen J Kay
CFO: Scott M Brunsdon
HR: –
FYE: June 30
Type: Public

International Minerals is working to develop gold and silver properties in South America. The company's primary projects include the Rio Blanco Gaby and Ca?icapa properties in Ecuador and the Antabamba and Pallancata properties in Peru. Through a 2010 purchase of Ventura Gold International Minerals owns a 51% interest in the Peruvian Inmaculada gold/silver project. Hochschild Mining owns the remaining stake. It also bought Metallic Ventures that same year winning a bidding contest with Solitario Exploration to add to its Goldmine and Converse operations in Nevada. The company continues to look to acquire low-cost gold and silver mining operations in the Americas.

INTERNATIONAL LEASE FINANCE CORP.
NYS: AIG 09

10250 Constellation Blvd., Suite 3400
Los Angeles, CA 90067
Phone: 310 788-1999
Fax: –
Web: www.ilfc.com

CEO: Henri Courpron
CFO: Elias Habayeb
HR: –
FYE: December 31
Type: Public

John Travolta bought his own Boeing; if your company's cash flow is more limited International Lease Finance Corporation (ILFC) will lease you one. The company which leases the entire range of Boeing and Airbus commercial aircraft is the world's second-largest lessor of new aircraft and widebody carriers. It boasts of owning the world's most valuable fleet of leasable aircraft — about 930 planes. ILFC's airplane-parts management business maintains the aging aircraft in its fleet. Commercial airlines outside the US generate more than 95% of revenue; ILFC counts most of the world's airlines as customers. Parent AIG (American International Group) spun off ILFC's holding company ILFC Holdings as an IPO in 2011.

	Annual Growth	12/09	12/10	12/11	12/12	12/13
Sales ($ mil.)	(4.5%)	5,321.7	4,798.9	4,526.7	4,504.2	4,417.4
Net income ($ mil.)	–	895.6	(383.8)	(723.9)	410.3	(517.1)
Market value ($ mil.)	–	–	–	–	–	–
Employees	36.9%	180	194	497	564	632

INTERNATIONAL MONETARY FUND

700 19th St. NW
Washington DC 20431
Phone: 202-623-7000
Fax: 202-623-4661
Web: www.imf.org

CEO: –
CFO: –
HR: –
FYE: April 30
Type: Private - Associatio

The International Monetary Fund (IMF) is an organization dedicated to promoting global monetary cooperation and the health and stability of the international financial system. Each member of the IMF contributes through the payment of quotas which reflect that country's size in the world economy and determine its voting power. The IMF supports worldwide economic growth by granting loans and technical assistance to countries in need. The IMF and sister institution the World Bank were formed by 45 countries in Bretton Woods New Hampshire in 1944 in an attempt to avoid the kinds of problems brought about by the Great Depression of the 1930s.

INTERNATIONAL LOTTERY & TOTALIZATOR SYSTEMS, INC.
NBB: ITSI

2310 Cousteau Court
Vista, CA 92081-8346
Phone: 760 598-1655
Fax: –
Web: www.ilts.com

CEO: –
CFO: –
HR: –
FYE: April 30
Type: Public

Designing systems for gambling and the ballot booth maybe this company should be called Tote & Vote. International Lottery & Totalizator Systems (ILTS) is a leading manufacturer of computerized wagering systems used by pari-mutuel racing operators off-track betting centers and lottery operators. It also provides consulting and training services along with its software and hardware. In addition to wagering ILTS markets electronic voting systems through its Unisyn Voting Solutions subsidiary. Berjaya Lottery Management a subsidiary of Malaysia-based Berjaya Group owns more than 70% of ILTS.

	Annual Growth	04/09	04/10	04/11	04/12	04/13
Sales ($ mil.)	12.9%	6.5	7.1	5.9	12.1	10.6
Net income ($ mil.)	–	(0.9)	(0.6)	(1.0)	1.2	3.1
Market value ($ mil.)	50.9%	2.7	3.1	3.4	7.8	14.0
Employees	(0.7%)	36	36	32	36	35

INTERNATIONAL MONETARY SYSTEMS LTD.
NBB: ITNM

16901 West Glendale Drive
New Berlin, WI 53151
Phone: 262 780-3640
Fax: 262 780-3655
Web: www.internationalmonetary.com

CEO: John E Strabley
CFO: David A Powell
HR: –
FYE: December 31
Type: Public

Who says the barter system is dead? Not International Monetary Systems (IMS). IMS runs one of the world's largest trade exchanges or barter networks allowing businesses and professionals to convert excess inventory into goods and services. Its IMS Barter Network serves approximately 17000 clients in major markets in the US and Canada. Users swap excess goods or services electronically with trade dollars IMS' electronic currency. Founded in 1985 the company has expanded by acquiring other trade exchanges.

	Annual Growth	12/10	12/11	12/12	12/13	12/14
Sales ($ mil.)	(2.6%)	13.7	13.5	13.8	13.0	12.3
Net income ($ mil.)	–	(0.5)	0.2	0.0	(0.1)	(0.0)
Market value ($ mil.)	74.4%	0.4	1.8	0.5	4.6	3.7
Employees	–	–	–	–	–	–

INTERNATIONAL PAPER CO
NYS: IP

6400 Poplar Avenue
Memphis, TN 38197
Phone: 901 419-7000
Fax: –
Web: www.internationalpaper.com

CEO: Mark S. Sutton
CFO: Carol L. Roberts
HR: Thomas G. (Tom) Kadien
FYE: December 31
Type: Public

For International Paper (IP) business is a global paper chase. It is one of the world's largest manufacturers of printing papers. Products include uncoated paper used in printers market pulp for making towels and tissues and coated paper and uncoated bristols (heavyweight art paper). In the US IP is #1 in containerboard production 70% of which is used in industrial corrugated boxes. A consumer packaging arm makes board to box cosmetics and food. IP owns recycling plants mainly in the US and a pulp and paper business in Russia via a 50/50 venture with Ilim Holding.

	Annual Growth	12/10	12/11	12/12	12/13	12/14
Sales ($ mil.)	(1.6%)	25,179.0	26,034.0	27,833.0	29,080.0	23,617.0
Net income ($ mil.)	(3.7%)	644.0	1,341.0	794.0	1,395.0	555.0
Market value ($ mil.)	18.4%	11,445.3	12,436.9	16,739.4	20,600.7	22,512.5
Employees	(0.6%)	59,500	61,500	70,000	69,000	58,000

INTERNATIONAL RECTIFIER CORP.
NYS: IRF

101 N. Sepulveda Blvd.
El Segundo, CA 90245
Phone: 310 726-8000
Fax: 310 322-3332
Web: www.irf.com

CEO: Oleg Khaykin
CFO: Ilan Daskal
HR: –
FYE: June 30
Type: Public

International Rectifier (IR) is a top maker of power management semiconductors which refine the electricity flowing into a device from a battery or a power grid enabling more efficient operation. Its products — including MOSFETs (metal oxide semiconductor field-effect transistors) diodes relays and rectifiers — are used in appliances automobiles computers communication devices lighting and displays gaming consoles industrial motors and military equipment. IR sells its products through distributors OEMs and contract manufacturers. Most of the global company's sales come from Asian customers.

	Annual Growth	06/09	06/10	06/11	06/12	06/13
Sales ($ mil.)	7.2%	740.4	895.3	1,176.6	1,050.6	977.0
Net income ($ mil.)	–	(247.4)	80.8	166.5	(55.1)	(88.8)
Market value ($ mil.)	9.3%	1,034.2	1,419.9	1,836.7	1,403.8	1,474.2
Employees	1.4%	3,939	4,534	4,920	4,911	4,162

INTERNATIONAL SHIPHOLDING CORP.
NBB: ISHC

11 North Water Street, Suite 18290
Mobile, AL 36602
Phone: 251 243-9100
Fax: –
Web: www.intship.com

CEO: Niels M Johnsen
CFO: Manuel G Estrada
HR: Sheryl Wainwright
FYE: December 31
Type: Public

International Shipholding helps put the "car" in cargo. Most of the company's sales come from its time-charter vessels including car and truck carriers ships with strengthened hulls (used in polar regions) and coal and sulfur carriers. Its fleet consists of some nearly 40 US and international-flag vessels. International Shipholding's primary subsidiaries include Central Gulf Lines Waterman Steamship Corp. LCI Shipholdings CG Railway and East Gulf Shipholding. The company has offices in Mobile Alabama; New York City; Singapore; and Shanghai. Customers have included such big names as Toyota Hyundai Motor International Paper and the US Navy's Military Sealift Command.

	Annual Growth	12/10	12/11	12/12	12/13	12/14
Sales ($ mil.)	0.4%	290.0	263.2	243.5	310.2	294.8
Net income ($ mil.)	–	15.3	31.5	22.0	18.2	(54.7)
Market value ($ mil.)	(12.5%)	185.5	136.5	120.3	215.4	108.8
Employees	4.3%	501	424	561	625	593

INTERNATIONAL SPEEDWAY CORP
NMS: ISCA

One Daytona Boulevard
Daytona Beach, FL 32114
Phone: 386 254-2700
Fax: –
Web: www.internationalspeedwaycorporation.com

CEO: Lesa France Kennedy
CFO: Daniel W. (Dan) Houser
HR: –
FYE: November 30
Type: Public

International Speedway Corporation (ISC) doesn't believe in slow and steady. The company is the top motorsports operator in the US with more than a dozen racetracks hosting more than 100 events annually. Its race facilities include Daytona International Speedway (home of the Daytona 500) Talladega Superspeedway and Michigan International Speedway. In addition ISC operates the Daytona 500 EXperience theme park and museum and it owns 50% of motorsports merchandiser Motorsports Authentics with rival Speedway Motorsports. Former CEO James France and his family own about 70% control of the company. Events sanctioned by NASCAR also controlled by the France family account for about 90% of sales.

	Annual Growth	11/11	11/12	11/13	11/14	11/15
Sales ($ mil.)	0.6%	629.7	612.4	612.6	651.9	645.4
Net income ($ mil.)	(5.0%)	69.4	54.6	45.3	67.4	56.6
Market value ($ mil.)	9.7%	1,138.7	1,242.0	1,589.1	1,448.0	1,647.5
Employees	(2.1%)	880	840	840	845	807

INTERNATIONAL TEXTILE GROUP, INC.
NBB: ITXN

804 Green Valley Road, Suite 300
Greensboro, NC 27408
Phone: 336 379-6299
Fax: –
Web: www.itg-global.com

CEO: Joseph L. Gorga
CFO: Gail A. Kuczkowski
HR: Robert E Garren
FYE: December 31
Type: Public

The totally material group — International Textile (ITG) — asks dress uniform or jeans? ITG makes a range of apparel and technical fabrics military garb as well as specialty textiles and less so auto safety fabrics. It stands as the world's #1 producer of better denim fabrics including premium brand Cone Denim used in retail goods. Other business units include Burlington Safety Components Narricot and Carlisle Finishing. ITG is also one of North America's top manufacturers of worsted wool and commission printers and finishers. The US and Mexico are its largest markets.

	Annual Growth	12/10	12/11	12/12	12/13	12/14
Sales ($ mil.)	(0.9%)	616.1	694.4	619.1	624.2	595.4
Net income ($ mil.)	–	(37.6)	(59.1)	(64.7)	23.3	0.4
Market value ($ mil.)	38.8%	0.7	0.5	0.1	2.1	2.6
Employees	(14.5%)	8,700	7,800	4,800	4,800	4,650

INTERNATIONAL WIRE GROUP INC.
PINK SHEETS: ITWG

12 Masonic Ave.
Camden NY 13316
Phone: 315-245-3800
Fax: 315-245-0737
Web: itwg.client.shareholder.com

CEO: –
CFO: Glenn J Holler
HR: Roy Plumley
FYE: December 31
Type: Public

International Wire Group (IWG) bares it all in the wire business. Through three divisions — Bare Wire Products Engineered Products - Europe and High Performance Conductors — IWG makes multi-gauge bare silver- nickel- and tin-plated copper wire as well as engineered wire products and performance conductors. Customers — General Cable is one of its largest — include suppliers and OEMs. IWG's wire is used in industrial/energy consumer electronics aerospace and defense medical electronics automotive and appliance applications. The company maintains 16 facilities located in the US and Europe (France and Italy). International Wire Group makes the majority of its sales in the US.

INTERNET AMERICA INC.
NBB: GEEK

6210 Rothway Street, Suite 100
Houston, TX 77064
Phone: 713 968-2500
Fax: –
Web: www.internetamerica.com

CEO: William E Ladin Jr
CFO: Randall J Frapart
HR: Victor Joseph
FYE: June 30
Type: Public

Internet America is changing its "lines" of business. Traditionally a provider of dial-up Internet access and to a lesser degree of wire-line DSL broadband Internet access to rural and suburban markets in Texas the company is battling dwindling subscriber numbers by expanding its wireless broadband Internet business. Total subscribers number more than 30000 with about one quarter of those connecting wirelessly. Internet America also provides installation and maintenance services from its three Texas operational centers in Corsicana San Antonio and Stafford (near Houston). The ISP founded in 1995 is known regionally for its 1-800-BE-A-GEEK sign-up number.

	Annual Growth	06/10	06/11	06/12	06/13	06/14
Sales ($ mil.)	2.2%	7.4	7.0	7.3	7.8	8.1
Net income ($ mil.)	–	(1.0)	(0.3)	0.6	4.5	5.9
Market value ($ mil.)	31.6%	4.2	4.2	4.9	6.7	12.6
Employees	7.5%	39	35	44	48	52

INTERNET BRANDS INC.

909 N. Sepulveda Blvd. 11th Fl.
El Segundo CA 90245
Phone: 310-280-4000
Fax: 310-280-4868
Web: www.internetbrands.com

CEO: Robert N Brisco
CFO: Scott Friedman
HR: –
FYE: December 31
Type: Private

Looking for a car or a career change? Internet Brands can fill you in on all you need to know. The company owns and operates 100-plus websites that provide information on automobiles careers health home-related activities money and business shopping and travel and leisure. Sites feature news articles reviews forums how-to's directories and coupons and they generate the majority of Internet Brands' revenue through sales of online advertising. The company also licenses auto-related technology products via its Autodata Solutions subsidiary and develops community bulletin board software through vBulletin Solutions. Funds managed by Hellman & Friedman acquired Internet Brands for $640 million in 2010.

INTERNET CORPORATION FOR ASSIGNED NAMES AND NUMBERS

12025 WATERFRONT DR # 300
LOS ANGELES, CA 900942536
Phone: 310-823-9358
Fax: –
Web: www.icann.org

CEO: Fadi Chehad
CFO: –
HR: –
FYE: June 30
Type: Private

Can anyone manage the Internet? This group says "ICANN." The Internet Corporation for Assigned Names and Numbers (ICANN) is a not-for-profit organization responsible for the management of the Internet's domain name system (DNS) allocation of Internet protocol (IP) addresses and assignment of protocol parameters. The DNS allows people to type in an address like "www.hoovers.com" rather than the string of numbers that represents the underlying IP address. Internet users register some 20 domain names ending in .com .org .info and .net among others through ICANN-accredited DNS registrars. The group is also managing the application process for a slew of new generic top-level domains (gTLDs).

	Annual Growth	06/07	06/08	06/09	06/10	06/13
Sales ($ mil.)	(33.7%)	–	1,841.9	59.9	68.3	236.2
Net income ($ mil.)	–	–	–	0.0	9.4	85.8
Market value ($ mil.)	–	–	–	–	–	–
Employees	–	–	–	–	–	160

INTERPACE DIAGNOSTICS GROUP INC
NAS: IDXG

Morris Corporate Center 1, Building A, 300 Interpace Parkway
Parsippany, NJ 07054
Phone: 800 242-7494
Fax: –
Web: www.pdi-inc.com

CEO: Jack E. Stover
CFO: Graham G. Miao
HR: Jennifer Leonard
FYE: December 31
Type: Public

PDI handles sales and marketing for pharmaceutical companies that would rather focus on product development. As a contract sales organization (CSO) the company provides sales teams dedicated to a single client and teams that represent multiple non-competing brands. Sales teams typically are assigned to geographic territories on a client's behalf. Each year contract sales services account for about 90% of PDI's revenue. The company's marketing and strategic consulting services operations are represented by its Pharmakon Interactive Healthcare Communications unit. PDI was established in 1987.

	Annual Growth	12/10	12/11	12/12	12/13	12/14
Sales ($ mil.)	(4.6%)	144.7	157.3	126.9	150.8	119.9
Net income ($ mil.)	–	(6.8)	(11.9)	(25.5)	(4.6)	(16.1)
Market value ($ mil.)	(35.8%)	161.9	98.6	116.7	73.9	27.5
Employees	(7.6%)	1,550	870	1,194	830	1,129

INTERPLASTIC CORPORATION

1225 Willow Lake Blvd.
St. Paul MN 55110-5145
Phone: 651-481-6860
Fax: 651-481-9836
Web: www.interplastic.com

CEO: James D Wallenfelsz
CFO: Steven Dittel
HR: –
FYE: December 31
Type: Private

Why start a business in the chemicals industry? Interplastic has its resins er reasons including its resins esters gel coats and additives as well. The company's Thermoset Resins Division manufactures high-performance materials for the composites and cast polymer industries. The Molding Products Division makes molding compounds for automotive industrial and marine applications. Its North American Composites unit provides international distribution services. Interplastic markets its products to makers of everything from marine coatings to shower stalls.

INTERPORE SPINE LTD.

181 Technology Dr.
Irvine CA 92618-2402
Phone: 949-453-3200
Fax: 949-453-3225
Web: www.interpore.com

CEO: –
CFO: Greg Hartman
HR: –
FYE: May 31
Type: Subsidiary

Interpore Spine has biomaterials deep in its bones. The company which operates as Interpore Cross makes synthetic tissue bone products and implant systems for spinal and orthopedic procedures. Interpore also makes biological grafting products that encourage bone growth. Interpore Spine also manufactures minimally invasive surgery systems used by orthopedic surgeons and neurologists. Brands include Pro Osteon InterGro and BioPlex. The company is a subsidiary of Biomet; other sister company products include dental implants sports medicine devices and bracing equipment.

INTERPUBLIC GROUP OF COMPANIES INC. NYS: IPG

1114 Avenue of the Americas
New York, NY 10036
Phone: 212 704-1200
Fax: –
Web: www.interpublic.com

CEO: Michael I. Roth
CFO: Frank Mergenthaler
HR: –
FYE: December 31
Type: Public

Subsidiaries of this company come between brands and the general public. The Interpublic Group of Companies is one of the world's largest advertising and marketing services conglomerates. Its flagship creative agencies include McCann Worldgroupand Lowe & Partners while such firms as Campbell-Ewald Deutsch and Hill Holliday are leaders in the US advertising business. Interpublic also offers direct marketing media services and public relations through such agencies as Initiative and Weber Shandwick. Its largest have clients included General Motors Johnson & Johnson Microsoft Samsung and Unilever.

	Annual Growth	12/10	12/11	12/12	12/13	12/14
Sales ($ mil.)	3.6%	6,531.9	7,014.6	6,956.2	7,122.3	7,537.1
Net income ($ mil.)	16.3%	261.1	532.3	446.7	267.9	477.1
Market value ($ mil.)	18.3%	4,394.6	4,026.3	4,560.1	7,324.3	8,594.6
Employees	3.7%	41,000	42,000	43,300	45,400	47,400

INTERSECTIONS INC NMS: INTX

3901 Stonecroft Boulevard
Chantilly, VA 20151
Phone: 703 488-6100
Fax: –
Web: www.intersections.com

CEO: Michael R Stanfield
CFO: Ronald L Barden
HR: –
FYE: December 31
Type: Public

Robert Johnson went to the crossroads to get the blues; consumers can go to Intersections to make sure they don't. Intersections provides credit management and identity theft protection to subscribers in North America. Its offerings include credit reports and ongoing record monitoring through major reporting agencies Equifax Experian and TransUnion. Its Intersections Insurance Services unit offers customers discounts on insurance products. Bank of America is the firm's #1 client accounting for more than 40% of its revenue. Amid declining sales and profits Intersections has exited the bail bonds and market intelligence businesses to focus on its core consumer protection services business.

	Annual Growth	12/10	12/11	12/12	12/13	12/14
Sales ($ mil.)	(9.3%)	364.1	373.0	349.2	310.3	246.6
Net income ($ mil.)	–	20.4	18.6	19.7	2.4	(30.7)
Market value ($ mil.)	(21.8%)	198.5	210.5	179.9	147.8	74.2
Employees	(11.7%)	787	987	817	644	478

INTERSIL CORP. NMS: ISIL

1001 Murphy Ranch Road
Milpitas, CA 95035
Phone: 408 432-8888
Fax: 408 434-5351
Web: www.intersil.com

CEO: Necip Sayiner
CFO: Richard D. (Rick) Crowley
HR: Vern Kelley
FYE: January 02
Type: Public

Intersil makes transfer of power an orderly process at least in electronics. Its line of semiconductor devices for power management include power regulators converters and controllers power modules amplifiers and buffers proximity and light sensors data converters video decoders and interfaces. Its products are components in data centers computers smartphones autos and a range of other applications. Almost three-quarters of its sales are to customers in Asia.

	Annual Growth	12/10	12/11	12/12*	01/14	01/15
Sales ($ mil.)	(7.3%)	822.4	760.5	607.9	575.2	562.6
Net income ($ mil.)	15.7%	26.4	67.2	(37.6)	2.9	54.8
Market value ($ mil.)	(0.7%)	1,988.4	1,359.5	1,054.8	1,442.8	1,916.8
Employees	(10.2%)	1,762	1,643	1,488	1,017	1,031

*Fiscal year change

INTERSTATE DISTRIBUTOR CO.

11707 21st Ave. S.
Tacoma WA 98444-1236
Phone: 253-537-9455
Fax: 800-845-7074
Web: www.intd.com

CEO: –
CFO: –
HR: –
FYE: December 31
Type: Subsidiary

Driving on interstate highways as well as less-traveled roads Interstate Distributor provides truckload freight transportation and a full set of complementary offerings. The company's services include temperature-controlled and heavy cargo hauling logistics and intermodal marketing (arrangement of freight transportation by multiple methods such as truck and train). Interstate Distributor's fleet consists of some 1900 tractors and 7100 trailers. The company operates primarily in the western US but it provides service throughout the 48 contiguous states and in Canada and Mexico. Owned by Saltchuk Resources Interstate Distributor was founded in 1933.

INTERSTATE NATIONAL DEALER SERVICES INC.

6120 Powers Ferry Rd. NW Ste. 200
Atlanta GA 30339
Phone: 678-894-3500
Fax: 770-952-9284
Web: www.inds.com

CEO: Mark H Mishler
CFO: Geoffrey Tirone
HR: –
FYE: October 31
Type: Private

Through Interstate National Dealer Services car dealers can offer extended warranties and service contracts to their customers. Available through new and used car dealers in the US and Canada the contracts supplement or replace manufacturers' warranties and range in length from three months to seven years. The firm markets to dealers leasing firms and finance companies across the US through a network of independent agents; the company also sells warranties directly to vehicle owners. Interstate National Dealer Services also offers policies that cover RVs watercraft and motorcycles.

INTERSTATE POWER & LIGHT CO NYS: IPL PRD

Alliant Energy Tower
Cedar Rapids, IA 52401
Phone: 319 786-4411
Fax: –
Web: www.alliantenergy.com

CEO: –
CFO: –
HR: –
FYE: December 31
Type: Public

Interstate Power and Light (IP&L) got the bright idea of providing electricity and has hit the road to make it happen. The company provides energy in a tri-state area of the Midwest (portions of Minnesota Iowa and Wisconsin). The Alliant Energy utility subsidiary serves more than 528355 electricity customers and more than 234560 natural gas customers in more than 700 communities. In addition IP&L has 2409 MW of generating capacity from fossil-fueled and nuclear power plants; it provides steam to two customers in Cedar Rapids; and it offers other energy-related services across its service area.

	Annual Growth	12/10	12/11	12/12	12/13	12/14
Sales ($ mil.)	0.7%	1,795.8	1,740.1	1,650.3	1,818.8	1,848.1
Net income ($ mil.)	7.9%	143.4	139.3	150.2	189.9	194.6
Market value ($ mil.)	19.8%	–	–	–	279.2	334.5
Employees	11.2%	1,157	1,652	1,651	1,676	1,766

INTERSYSTEMS CORPORATION

1 Memorial Dr.
Cambridge MA 02142
Phone: 617-621-0600
Fax: 617-494-1631
Web: www.intersystems.com

CEO: –
CFO: –
HR: –
FYE: December 31
Type: Private

InterSystems serves healthcare firms and other corporate and government clients with its flagship database software and associated products. Cache is an object database designed for high-performance handling of large volumes of transactional data. The company also offers an embeddable business intelligence product (DeepSee) for use with Cache as well as an integration platform (Ensemble). Its two healthcare-specific offerings include HealthShare which enables the creation of electronic health records and TrakCare a unified healthcare information system for use outside the US. The company which was founded in 1978 serves clients worldwide from offices in about two dozen countries.

INTERTRUST TECHNOLOGIES CORPORATION

955 Stewart Dr.
Sunnyvale CA 94085
Phone: 408-616-1600
Fax: 408-616-1626
Web: www.intertrust.com

CEO: Talal G Shamoon
CFO: –
HR: –
FYE: December 31
Type: Private

Trust Intertrust Technologies' technology to protect your digital content. The company's digital rights management and trusted computing technology helps protect and manage content rights for companies that distribute music movies information and other digital content. Intertrust's software covers Internet wireless and cable distribution as well as content burned on disks. Intertrust's technology delivers authorization access in RightsPacks digital packages that allow users to access files according to the level of access specified. The company is a subsidiary of Fidelio Acquisition Company a firm whose investors include Royal Philips Electronics and Sony Corporation of America.

INTERVAL LEISURE GROUP INC   NMS: IILG

6262 Sunset Drive
Miami, FL 33143
Phone: 305 666-1861
Fax: –
Web: www.iilg.com

CEO: Craig M. Nash
CFO: William L. (Bill) Harvey
HR: –
FYE: December 31
Type: Public

Your vacation time is worth something to Interval Leisure Group. The timeshare exchange broker offers services to some 2 million member-property owners. Its primary Interval Network is an exchange program that lets owners trade their timeshare intervals for accommodations at more than 2900 resorts in approximately 80 countries. In addition the company provides exchange services to owners at timeshare properties managed by vacation services subsidiary Trading Places International (TPI) while its Preferred Residences is a luxury branded membership program with Preferred Hotel Group. The company also provides resort management services.

	Annual Growth	12/10	12/11	12/12	12/13	12/14
Sales ($ mil.)	10.7%	409.4	428.8	473.3	501.2	614.4
Net income ($ mil.)	16.8%	42.4	41.1	40.7	81.2	78.9
Market value ($ mil.)	6.7%	921.6	777.1	1,107.2	1,764.8	1,192.8
Employees	20.4%	2,900	3,000	3,800	5,000	6,100

INTERVEST BANCSHARES CORP.   NMS: IBCA

One Rockefeller Plaza, Suite 400
New York, NY 10020-2002
Phone: 212 218-2800
Fax: –
Web: www.intervestnatbank.com

CEO: –
CFO: –
HR: –
FYE: December 31
Type: Public

Intervest Bancshares is the holding company for Intervest National Bank which operates one branch in New York City and six other branches in Pinellas County Florida. Most of the company's lending activities are real estate-related: Commercial mortgages make up more than half of its loan portfolio while multifamily residential mortgages account for another 40%. Some of the company's lending has historically been carried out by its Intervest Mortgage Corporation arm. However the subsidiary drastically scaled back its lending practices as market conditions deteriorated in 2008. The family of chairman and CEO Lowell Dansker controls Intervest Bancshares.

	Annual Growth	12/08	12/09	12/10	12/11	12/12
Assets ($ mil.)	(7.5%)	2,271.8	2,401.2	2,070.9	1,969.5	1,665.8
Net income ($ mil.)	13.9%	7.3	3.1	(53.3)	11.2	12.2
Market value ($ mil.)	(0.6%)	86.1	70.8	63.3	57.2	84.0
Employees	2.3%	72	72	73	75	79

INTERWEST PARTNERS LLC

2710 Sand Hill Rd. 2nd Fl.
Menlo Park CA 94025
Phone: 650-854-8585
Fax: 650-854-4706
Web: www.interwest.com

CEO: –
CFO: –
HR: –
FYE: March 31
Type: Private

InterWest Partners provides venture capital to development-stage information technology (IT) and life sciences companies. Targeted sectors include communications digital media datacenter infrastructure software semiconductors and wireless services as well as biopharmaceuticals medical devices and health care IT. Usually acting as lead investor the firm typically provides up to $15 million over various stages of a company's development. InterWest is an active investor often assigning one of its general partners to a seat on a portfolio company's board and providing strategic advice and operations support over the duration of the investment which usually lasts more than five years.

INTEST CORP.   ASE: INTT

804 East Gate Drive, Suite 200
Mt. Laurel, NJ 08054
Phone: 856 505-8800
Fax: 856 505-8801
Web: www.intest.com

CEO: Robert E Matthiessen
CFO: Hugh T Regan Jr
HR: –
FYE: December 31
Type: Public

When semiconductor makers are testing their chips inTEST handles the trickiest chores. The semiconductor test equipment supplier offers test head manipulators docking hardware and systems for managing temperatures during integrated circuit (IC) production and testing. inTEST's products facilitate testing procedures by quickly moving and connecting IC components to handling and testing equipment. The company's clients include Analog Devices Freescale Semiconductor Intel Sony STMicroelectronics and Texas Instruments (14% of sales). inTEST built up its product line through a series of acquisitions. The company gets most of its sales in the US.

	Annual Growth	12/10	12/11	12/12	12/13	12/14
Sales ($ mil.)	(2.5%)	46.2	47.3	43.4	39.4	41.8
Net income ($ mil.)	(17.0%)	7.3	9.9	2.2	3.1	3.4
Market value ($ mil.)	13.7%	26.9	29.4	29.2	40.1	44.9
Employees	(0.6%)	128	131	131	127	125

INTEVAC, INC.

NMS: IVAC

3560 Bassett Street
Santa Clara, CA 95054
Phone: 408 986-9888
Fax: –
Web: www.intevac.com

CEO: Wendell T. Blonigan
CFO: James P. (Jim) Moniz
HR: –
FYE: January 03
Type: Public

Intevac's sputtering doesn't stem from a speech impediment. The company's Equipment division manufactures sputtering systems that deposit alloy films onto hard-disk drives; the films magnetize the drives enabling them to record information. The Equipment division also makes disk lubrication systems used in disk drive manufacturing and processing equipment used to manufacture solar cells. Intevac's Photonics division develops electro-optical devices used in night vision and materials identification applications. Top customers include Seagate Fuji Electric and Hitachi Global Storage Technologies which collectively account for more than half of sales.

	Annual Growth	12/10	12/11	12/12	12/13*	01/15
Sales ($ mil.)	(20.2%)	202.5	83.0	83.4	69.6	65.6
Net income ($ mil.)	–	28.0	(22.0)	(55.3)	(15.7)	(27.4)
Market value ($ mil.)	(12.0%)	326.1	172.2	106.4	172.9	171.8
Employees	(9.4%)	445	429	387	302	271

*Fiscal year change

INTL FCSTONE INC.

NMS: INTL

708 Third Avenue, Suite 1500
New York, NY 10017
Phone: 212 485-3500
Fax: –
Web: www.intlfcstone.com

CEO: Sean M. O'Connor
CFO: William J. (Bill) Dunaway
HR: –
FYE: September 30
Type: Public

Going global is the name of the game for securities broker INTL FCStone and its subsidiaries. The company specializes in niche international markets offering commodity risk management consulting and international securities. It offers clearing and execution services of listed futures and options on futures. Its INTL FCStone Securities subsidiary is a wholesale market-maker for some 800 foreign securities. The company also offers asset management and commodity financing and facilitation. INTL FCStone serves financial institutions corporations charitable organizations and other institutional investors in the US and abroad.

	Annual Growth	09/11	09/12	09/13	09/14	09/15
Sales ($ mil.)	(17.7%)	75,486.3	69,249.0	43,755.8	34,011.9	34,676.1
Net income ($ mil.)	10.5%	37.3	15.0	19.3	19.3	55.7
Market value ($ mil.)	4.4%	390.6	358.6	384.7	325.8	464.5
Employees	8.0%	904	1,074	1,094	1,141	1,231

INTRALINKS HOLDINGS INC

NYS: IL

150 East 42nd Street, 8th Floor
New York, NY 10017
Phone: 212 543-7700
Fax: –
Web: www.intralinks.com

CEO: Ronald W. (Ron) Hovsepian
CFO: Derek Irwin
HR: Russell C. Poole
FYE: December 31
Type: Public

IntraLinks can keep a secret. The company provides hosted software known as virtual data rooms. The IntraLinks platform is used by businesses to create secure collaborative online digital workspaces for conducting financial transactions managing mergers and acquisitions exchanging documents and collaborating with advisers customers and suppliers. While it has a strong position within the banking industry IntraLinks has branched out into other fields and tailors industry-specific versions of its products for use in markets such as life sciences legal private equity investing media and real estate. Customers have included Citigroup KPMG and Pfizer.

	Annual Growth	12/10	12/11	12/12	12/13	12/14
Sales ($ mil.)	8.5%	184.3	213.5	216.7	234.5	255.8
Net income ($ mil.)	–	(12.4)	(1.2)	(17.4)	(15.3)	(26.5)
Market value ($ mil.)	(10.7%)	1,068.0	356.2	352.2	691.3	679.3
Employees	15.6%	454	601	635	666	810

INTRAWEST RESORTS HOLDINGS INC

NYS: SNOW

1621 18th Street, Suite 300
Denver, CO 80202
Phone: 303 749-8200
Fax: –
Web: www.intrawest.com

CEO: Thomas F. Marano
CFO: Travis Mayer
HR: –
FYE: June 30
Type: Public

Intrawest Resorts Holdings wants to snow you a good time. The company owns six North American ski mountain resorts including well-known spots Mammoth Mountain Snowshoe Steamboat and Winter Park. Instrawest also runs a real estate business and an adventure travel business. Its mountain resorts offer activities combining outdoor adventure and fitness with services and amenities such as retail equipment rental dining lodging ski school spa services golf mountain biking and other summer activities. All told the company's six resort areas offer a total of about 8000 skiable acres and more than 1100 acres of land available for real estate development. In early 2014 Instrawest went public.

	Annual Growth	06/11	06/12	06/13	06/14	06/15
Sales ($ mil.)	–	0.0	513.4	524.4	527.1	587.6
Net income ($ mil.)	–	0.0	(336.1)	(296.0)	(188.6)	(6.9)
Market value ($ mil.)	–	0.0	–	–	518.3	525.6
Employees	35.0%	–	–	–	4,000	5,400

INTREPID POTASH INC

NYS: IPI

707 17th Street, Suite 4200
Denver, CO 80202
Phone: 303 296-3006
Fax: –
Web: www.intrepidpotash.com

CEO: –
CFO: Brian D Frantz
HR: James N. Whyte
FYE: December 31
Type: Public

Hungry plants turn to Intrepid Potash for their food supply. The mining company produces two potassium-containing minerals potash and langbeinite that are essential ingredients in plant and crop fertilizer. Intrepid culls these minerals from a handful mines in New Mexico and Utah where it also operates production facilities. The company has the capacity to annually produce about 1.1 million tons of potash and 200000 tons of langbeinite and sells its products primarily in the US to the agricultural industrial and feed markets. It markets langbeinite under the brand Trio. Intrepid Potash is the largest producer of muriate of potash (potassium chloride) in the US the second-largest consuming country of potash.

	Annual Growth	12/10	12/11	12/12	12/13	12/14
Sales ($ mil.)	3.4%	359.3	443.0	451.3	336.3	410.4
Net income ($ mil.)	(31.9%)	45.2	109.4	87.4	22.3	9.8
Market value ($ mil.)	(21.9%)	2,816.8	1,709.4	1,608.2	1,196.5	1,048.5
Employees	3.7%	803	871	935	993	928

INTREXON CORP

NYS: XON

20374 Seneca Meadows Parkway
Germantown, MD 20876
Phone: 301 556-9900
Fax: –
Web: www.dna.com

CEO: Randal J Kirk
CFO: Rick L Sterling
HR: –
FYE: December 31
Type: Public

One man's frankenfood is another man's solution to world hunger. Intrexon is developing technology that uses synthetic biology or biological engineering to make advances in everything from pharmaceuticals to genetically modified plants and animals. The company has development agreements with AmpliPhi (antibacterial medication) AquaBounty (genetically modified salmon) BioLife (genetic disease) Eli Lilly (animal medication) Fibrocell (dermatology medication) Genopaver (pharmaceutical ingredients) Oragenics (antibiotics) Soligenix (antibiotics) Synthetic Biologics (antibiotics) and ZIOPHARM (cancer medicine). Intrexon went public in 2013 raising $160 million in its IPO.

	Annual Growth	12/10	12/11	12/12	12/13	12/14
Sales ($ mil.)	–	0.0	8.2	13.9	23.8	71.9
Net income ($ mil.)	–	0.0	(85.3)	(81.9)	(39.0)	(81.8)
Market value ($ mil.)	–	–	–	–	2,393.3	2,768.4
Employees	66.6%	–	–	201	208	558

INTRICON CORP
NMS: IIN

1260 Red Fox Road
Arden Hills, MN 55112
Phone: 651 636-9770
Fax: 651 636-9503
Web: www.intricon.com

CEO: Mark S Gorder
CFO: Scott Longval
HR: –
FYE: December 31
Type: Public

IntriCon hears its future calling and that future is in precision microminiature components and molded plastic parts such as volume controls and switches primarily used in hearing aids. IntriCon's components are also used in professional audio equipment such as headsets and microphones and in biotelemetry devices for such uses as diagnostic monitoring and drug delivery. The company has concentrated its product portfolio on what it terms "body-worn devices" through a series of acquisitions and divestitures including the 2010 sale of its RTI Electronics business line to Shackleton Equity Partners.

	Annual Growth	12/10	12/11	12/12	12/13	12/14
Sales ($ mil.)	3.9%	58.7	56.1	63.9	53.0	68.3
Net income ($ mil.)	58.0%	0.4	(1.4)	0.7	(6.2)	2.2
Market value ($ mil.)	15.2%	22.8	36.6	23.7	22.5	40.1
Employees	2.7%	504	599	569	572	561

INTRUSION INC
NBB: INTZ

1101 East Arapaho Road, Suite 200
Richardson, TX 75081
Phone: 972 234-6400
Fax: –
Web: www.intrusion.com

CEO: G Ward Paxton
CFO: Michael L Paxton
HR: –
FYE: December 31
Type: Public

Think of Intrusion as a virtual police force protecting and serving your network. The security specialist sells network intrusion detection and security monitoring systems. Its products include software and stand-alone security appliances that guard against misuse of classified or private information and aid law enforcement agencies in battling cyber crimes. Intrusion also provides consulting design installation and technical support services. The company sells its products directly and through distributors and resellers. Intrusion markets its products to government agencies as well as businesses ranging from health care providers to telecommunications service operators.

	Annual Growth	12/10	12/11	12/12	12/13	12/14
Sales ($ mil.)	6.6%	5.6	5.3	6.7	7.7	7.2
Net income ($ mil.)	–	0.2	(0.9)	(0.2)	0.6	(0.3)
Market value ($ mil.)	75.5%	3.7	3.7	6.1	16.4	35.1
Employees	7.5%	27	31	31	33	36

INTRUST FINANCIAL CORPORATION

105 N. Main St.
Wichita KS 67202
Phone: 316-383-1111
Fax: 316-383-5765
Web: www.intrustbank.com

CEO: Charles Q Chandler III
CFO: Jay L Smith
HR: –
FYE: December 31
Type: Private

INTRUST Financial wants to be entrusted with your cash. The holding company owns INTRUST Bank which is the largest bank headquartered in Kansas. The bank operates about 40 branches in the Sunflower State in addition to a handful of locations in Oklahoma and Arkansas. Serving consumers and small businesses the bank offers a range of financial products including savings checking and retirement accounts; CDs; credit cards; and loans and mortgages. INTRUST Bank was founded in 1876 as the Farmers and Merchants Bank. It has been run by the Chandler family for more than a century.

INTUIT INC
NMS: INTU

2700 Coast Avenue
Mountain View, CA 94043
Phone: 650 944-6000
Fax: –
Web: www.intuit.com

CEO: Brad D. Smith
CFO: R. Neil Williams
HR: –
FYE: July 31
Type: Public

Intuit knows that good accounting takes more than a pocket calculator. The company is a leading developer of software used for small business accounting (QuickBooks) and consumer tax preparation (TurboTax). It also helps manage personal finances and budgeting with its online Mint service. Customers include individual consumers accountants and small businesses; Intuit claims more than 45 million users for its products and services. Other offerings include payroll and payment software for small businesses financial supplies (paper checks invoices deposit slips) and online marketing and communications products. It generates most of its sales in the US.

	Annual Growth	07/11	07/12	07/13	07/14	07/15
Sales ($ mil.)	2.1%	3,851.0	4,151.0	4,171.0	4,506.0	4,192.0
Net income ($ mil.)	(12.9%)	634.0	792.0	858.0	907.0	365.0
Market value ($ mil.)	22.7%	12,968.9	16,112.5	17,751.0	22,763.6	29,373.0
Employees	(1.0%)	8,000	8,500	8,000	8,000	7,700

INTUITIVE SURGICAL INC
NMS: ISRG

1020 Kifer Road
Sunnyvale, CA 94086
Phone: 408 523-2100
Fax: –
Web: www.intuitivesurgical.com

CEO: Gary S. Guthart
CFO: Marshall L. Mohr
HR: Heather Hand
FYE: December 31
Type: Public

Intuitive Surgical gives an artistic flair to advanced surgical equipment. Employing haptics (the science of computer-aided touch sensitivity) the firm developed the da Vinci Surgical System a combination of software hardware and optics that allows doctors to perform robotically aided surgery from a remote console. The da Vinci system reproduces the doctor's hand movements in real time during minimally invasive surgery performed by tiny electromechanical arms and instruments. The company manufactures its systems and relies upon contract manufacturers to supply the instruments and accessories used with the systems.

	Annual Growth	12/11	12/12	12/13	12/14	12/15
Sales ($ mil.)	7.9%	1,757.3	2,178.8	2,265.1	2,131.7	2,384.4
Net income ($ mil.)	4.4%	495.1	656.6	671.0	418.8	588.8
Market value ($ mil.)	4.2%	17,316.6	18,339.8	14,364.6	19,782.4	20,426.4
Employees	13.7%	1,924	2,362	2,792	2,978	3,211

INUVO INC
ASE: INUV

1111 Main St., Ste. 201
Conway, AR 72032
Phone: 501 205-8508
Fax: –
Web: www.inuvo.com

CEO: Richard K Howe
CFO: Wally Ruiz
HR: –
FYE: December 31
Type: Public

As consumers surf the Web Inuvo wants to help advertisers ride the waves alongside them. Inuvo provides online marketing and advertising services through its Exchange segment which includes technology and analytics and its Direct segment which consists of websites designed to drive traffic to advertisers. Included in the Exchange segment is the Inuvo Platform which offers affiliate marketing search engine marketing and lead generation services helping customers drive Web traffic and convert that traffic into sales. Its Inuvo Search platform acts as a pay-per-click marketplace. Inuvo's Direct segment websites include BabytoBee (pregnancy advice) and Kowabunga (daily deals).

	Annual Growth	12/10	12/11	12/12	12/13	12/14
Sales ($ mil.)	0.3%	49.0	35.8	53.4	55.0	49.6
Net income ($ mil.)	–	(5.0)	(9.0)	(7.0)	0.5	2.1
Market value ($ mil.)	(29.0%)	121.4	16.8	22.1	31.1	30.8
Employees	(7.3%)	46	49	46	34	34

INVACARE CORP
NYS: IVC

One Invacare Way, P.O. Box 4028
Elyria, OH 44036
Phone: 440 329-6000
Fax: –

CEO: Gerald B. Blouch
CFO: Robert Gudbranson
HR: Audrey White
FYE: December 31
Type: Public

Invacare helps those with disabilities stay on the move. The company is a leading maker of wheelchairs including manual powered custom-made and the ultra-zippy chairs used by athletes. It also makes other medical equipment including crutches patient handling equipment bed systems respiratory devices and motorized scooters as well as home care durables such as bathing equipment cushions and slings. It manufactures and sells its products to health care providers consumers and medical equipment dealers in North America Europe and the Asia/Pacific region.

	Annual Growth	12/10	12/11	12/12	12/13	12/14
Sales ($ mil.)	(7.3%)	1,722.1	1,801.1	1,455.5	1,352.4	1,270.2
Net income ($ mil.)	–	25.3	(4.1)	1.8	33.1	(56.1)
Market value ($ mil.)	(13.7%)	968.6	491.1	523.5	745.4	538.3
Employees	(4.7%)	6,300	6,200	6,200	5,400	5,200

INVENSENSE, INC.
NYS: INVN

1745 Technology Drive, Suite 200
San Jose, CA 95110
Phone: 408 501-2200
Fax: –
Web: www.invensense.com

CEO: Behrooz Abdi
CFO: Mark P. Dentinger
HR: Leon Bezdikian
FYE: March 29
Type: Public

InvenSense is ready to move technology beyond point and click. A semiconductor manufacturer the company offers motion interface sensors used to detect track and assess a user's position. Its MotionTracking sensors which include MEMS (microelectronic) gyroscopes and motion measurement processing units are used in many consumer devices such as smartphones tablets wearable devices gaming consoles and smart TVs to provide a more immersive user interface. As a fabless company InvenSense outsources manufacturing to TSMC and GLOBALFOUNDRIES. It generates the majority of sales in Asia.

	Annual Growth	04/11	04/12*	03/13	03/14	03/15
Sales ($ mil.)	40.1%	96.5	153.0	208.6	252.5	372.0
Net income ($ mil.)	–	9.3	36.9	51.7	6.1	(1.1)
Market value ($ mil.)	(5.5%)	–	1,645.2	970.7	2,063.3	1,387.0
Employees	34.8%	–	263	326	476	644

*Fiscal year change

INVENSYS RAIL CORPORATION

2400 Nelson Miller Pkwy.
Louisville KY 40223
Phone: 502-618-8800
Fax: 502-618-8810
Web: www.invensysrail.com

CEO: Nick Crossfield
CFO: Paul Kerr
HR: –
FYE: March 31
Type: Subsidiary

Invensys Rail Corp. is the products segment of Invensys Rail which is one of three divisions within parent Invensys plc. It manufactures railroad switch signal and railroad-highway crossing warning systems. Its customers include the National Railroad Passenger Corporation (better known as AMTRAK) and the transit operations of Atlanta Boston Chicago Los Angeles and New York City. Invensys Rail Corp.'s products represent about 20% of the annual revenues of the rail division which generates more than 30% of its parent's revenues. It has core markets in Australia Iberia and North America. In late 2012 Invensys agreed to sell Invensys Rail to global manufacturing giant Siemens AG.

INVENTERGY GLOBAL INC
NAS: INVT

900 E. Hamilton Avenue #180
Campbell, CA 95008
Phone: 408 389-3510
Fax: –
Web: www.inventergy.com

CEO: Joseph W Beyers
CFO: John Niedermaier
HR: –
FYE: December 31
Type: Public

eOn Communications knows it's been ages since you've had a good customer service experience. The company's products integrate voice and Internet communications for large call centers and e-commerce customer contact centers. eOn's communications servers feature automatic call distribution e-mail queuing and customer identification. It also sells the Millennium voice switching hardware platform a private branch exchange (PBX) system with computer telephony integration. Customers include Lillian Vernon and Rockhurst University. eOn gets more than 90% of sales from the US. Chairman David Lee owns about 27% of the company.

	Annual Growth	07/10	07/11	07/12	07/13*	12/14
Sales ($ mil.)	(54.7%)	17.1	23.4	22.5	20.6	0.7
Net income ($ mil.)	–	0.5	(1.3)	0.5	0.2	(20.1)
Market value ($ mil.)	(17.9%)	4.4	4.6	2.5	2.5	2.0
Employees	(38.4%)	104	86	82	75	15

*Fiscal year change

INVENTIV HEALTH INC.

1 Van de Graaff Dr.
Burlington MA 01803
Phone: 800-416-0555
Fax: 616-776-2776
Web: www.meritagehospitality.com

CEO: Michael Bell
CFO: Jonathan E Bicknell
HR: –
FYE: December 31
Type: Private

To sell a new drug it may be time to get inVentiv. inVentiv Health provides commercial clinical communications and patient assistance services for 550 customers in the life sciences biotech and pharmaceutical industries. Its Commercial segment provides outsourced sales and marketing services market research data collection and management recruitment and training. The Clinical segment provides clinical staffing clinical research and statistical analysis and executive placement. It has served such notable clients as Johnson and Johnson Bristol-Myers Squibb and Novartis Pharmaceuticals. In mid-2010 private equity firm Thomas H. Lee Partners (THL) bought inVentiv Health for $1.1 billion.

INVENTURE FOODS INC.
NMS: SNAK

5415 East High Street, Suite #350
Phoenix, AZ 85054
Phone: 623 932-6200
Fax: –
Web: www.inventurefoods.com

CEO: Terry McDaniel
CFO: Steve Weinberger
HR: Kirk Roles
FYE: December 27
Type: Public

Inventure Foods caters to avid snackers and the more health conscious alike. The company's Rader Farms business grows and processes berries and produces frozen fruits vegetables and beverages for sale primarily to grocery and club stores and mass merchandisers. The snack business makes potato and other snack chips pretzels and more under Bob's Texas Style Braids Poore Brothers Boulder Canyon Natural Foods to name a few. Inventure Foods also makes salted snacks branded with the T.G.I. Friday's and Nathan's Famous names and manufactures private label snacks for food stores in the US. Costco is the company's #1 customer. With roots in salty snacks Inventure is now focused on healthier fare.

	Annual Growth	12/10	12/11	12/12	12/13	12/14
Sales ($ mil.)	20.8%	134.0	162.2	185.2	215.6	285.7
Net income ($ mil.)	24.0%	4.5	2.8	7.4	6.6	10.6
Market value ($ mil.)	30.0%	84.6	73.3	123.6	263.9	241.4
Employees	20.5%	389	448	497	785	821

INVESCO LTD.

NYSE: IVZ

1555 Peachtree St. NE Ste. 1800
Atlanta GA 30309
Phone: 404-479-1095
Fax: 510-492-1098
Web: www.esstech.com

CEO: Martin L Flanagan
CFO: Loren M Starr
HR: –
FYE: December 31
Type: Public

Invesco offers a range of investment products and services including mutual funds exchange-traded funds separately managed accounts and savings plans. Invesco serves retail and institutional clients in more than 20 countries in North America Europe the Middle East and the Asia/Pacific region. It operates under the Invesco Invesco Perpetual and Powershares brands (it dropped the AIM brand in 2010). Subsidiary Atlantic Trust offers private wealth management services. Invesco and its subsidiaries have more than $660 billion of assets under management. The company also owns turnaround firm WL Ross.

INVESTORS BANCORP INC (NEW)

NMS: ISBC

101 JFK Parkway
Short Hills, NJ 07078
Phone: 973 924-5100
Fax: –
Web: www.myinvestorsbank.com

CEO: Kevin Cummings
CFO: Sean Burke
HR: –
FYE: December 31
Type: Public

Investors Bancorp is the holding company for Investors Savings Bank which serves New Jersey and New York from more than 130 branch offices. Founded in 1926 the bank offers such standard deposit products as savings and checking accounts CDs money market accounts and IRAs. Nearly 40% of the bank's loan portfolio is made up of residential mortgages while multi-family loans and commercial real estate loans make up more than 50% combined. The bank also originates business industrial and consumer loans. Founded in 1926 Investors Bancorp's assets now exceed $20 billion.

	Annual Growth	12/10	12/11	12/12	12/13	12/14
Assets ($ mil.)	18.2%	9,602.1	10,701.6	12,722.6	15,623.1	18,773.6
Net income ($ mil.)	20.7%	62.0	78.9	88.8	112.0	131.7
Market value ($ mil.)	(3.8%)	4,697.1	4,826.0	6,365.5	9,158.0	4,018.7
Employees	17.6%	892	982	1,219	1,597	1,708

INVESCO MORTGAGE CAPITAL INC.

NYS: IVR

1555 Peachtree Street, N.E., Suite 1800
Atlanta, GA 30309
Phone: 404 892-0896
Fax: –
Web: www.invescomortgagecapital.com

CEO: Richard J. King
CFO: Richard Lee Phegley
HR: –
FYE: December 31
Type: Public

Invesco Mortgage Capital is ready to roll now that the mortgage industry has finally reversed its course. Invesco Mortgage is a real estate investment trust (REIT) that finances and manages residential and commercial mortgage-backed securities and mortgage loans. It purchases agency-backed mortgages secured by the likes of Fannie Mae and Freddie Mac and is managed and advised by sibling Invesco Institutional a subsidiary of Invesco Ltd. The firm's mortgage-backed securities portfolio is concentrated within the four populous states of California Florida Texas and New York. Invesco Mortgage Capital began operations and went public in 2009.

	Annual Growth	12/10	12/11	12/12	12/13	12/14
Sales ($ mil.)	(2.2%)	145.4	472.2	621.1	529.4	132.9
Net income ($ mil.)	–	98.4	281.9	339.9	141.6	(199.4)
Market value ($ mil.)	(8.3%)	2,688.7	1,729.7	2,426.5	1,807.3	1,903.3
Employees	–	–	–	–	–	–

INVESTORS CAPITAL HOLDINGS, LTD.

ASE: ICH

Six Kimball Lane, Suite 150
Lynnfield, MA 01940
Phone: 781 593-8565
Fax: –
Web: www.investorscapital.com

CEO: Timothy B Murphy
CFO: Kathleen L Donnelly
HR: –
FYE: March 31
Type: Public

The name pretty much says it all. Investors Capital Holdings offers brokerage and investment advisory services to clients across the US through more than 500 registered independent advisors. The company provides marketing technology and compliance support as well as approved investment products to its representatives in exchange for a negotiated percentage of commissions. Its Investors Capital Corporation (ICC) broker-dealer subsidiary provides securities trading research online brokerage and other services. Subsidiary ICC Insurance Agency sells variable life insurance and annuities. The company's Investors Capital Advisory business surpassed $1 billion in assets under management in 2010

	Annual Growth	03/09	03/10	03/11	03/12	03/13
Sales ($ mil.)	1.0%	81.6	79.2	85.3	81.0	84.9
Net income ($ mil.)	–	(1.8)	0.3	(0.9)	(2.3)	0.4
Market value ($ mil.)	28.7%	9.7	10.4	43.4	28.3	26.6
Employees	(3.8%)	69	81	83	57	59

INVESTMENT TECHNOLOGY GROUP INC.

NYS: ITG

165 Broadway
New York, NY 10006
Phone: 212 588-4000
Fax: –
Web: www.itginc.com

CEO: Frank Troise
CFO: Steven R. (Steve) Vigliotti
HR: Peter A. Goldstein
FYE: December 31
Type: Public

As its name implies Investment Technology Group (ITG) combines technology with investing. The company provides automated equity option and derivative trading products and services related to order and execution management; it is involved throughout the trading process from analysis before the trade to post-transaction processing and evaluation. The company also offers tools to assist in portfolio modeling and construction compliance monitoring and asset valuation. ITG serves institutional investors brokerages alternative investment funds and asset managers in North America Europe and the Asia/Pacific region; international operations account for roughly 45% of sales.

	Annual Growth	12/10	12/11	12/12	12/13	12/14
Sales ($ mil.)	(0.5%)	570.8	572.0	504.4	530.8	559.8
Net income ($ mil.)	20.7%	24.0	(179.8)	(247.9)	31.1	50.9
Market value ($ mil.)	6.2%	560.3	370.0	308.1	703.8	712.7
Employees	(2.2%)	1,186	1,118	1,047	1,001	1,087

INVESTORS HERITAGE CAPITAL CORP.

NBB: IHRC

200 Capital Avenue
Frankfort, KY 40602
Phone: 502 223-2361
Fax: –

CEO: Harry Lee Waterfield II
CFO: Larry J Johnson II
HR: –
FYE: December 31
Type: Public

Investors Heritage Capital puts its money into insurance. The company (formerly Kentucky Investors) operates through primary subsidiary Investors Heritage Life Insurance which provides group and individual life insurance burial insurance credit insurance and similar products which are sold through independent agents and through funeral homes in about 30 states. Investors Heritage Life Insurance does most of its business in the East Midwest and Southeast. Investors Heritage Capital also owns non-insurance subsidiaries which offer commercial printing investment holding services and funeral lending services.

	Annual Growth	12/10	12/11	12/12	12/13	12/14
Assets ($ mil.)	8.0%	430.6	551.8	576.0	563.6	585.2
Net income ($ mil.)	(15.1%)	2.4	0.6	2.1	1.8	1.3
Market value ($ mil.)	3.8%	20.8	18.0	19.9	23.3	24.1
Employees	(7.1%)	2,594	1,874	1,905	2,058	1,936

INVESTORS REAL ESTATE TRUST
NYS: IRET

1400 31st Avenue S.W., Suite 60, P.O. Box 1988
Minot, ND 58702-1988
Phone: 701 837-4738
Fax: –
Web: www.iret.com

CEO: Timothy P. Mihalick
CFO: Ted E. Holmes
HR: –
FYE: April 30
Type: Public

Investors Real Estate Trust (IRET) is a self-advised umbrella partnership real estate investment trust (UPREIT) that invests in develops and maintains a portfolio of office retail and multifamily residential properties. IRET owns some 250 properties in the Upper Midwest including around 100 apartment communities composing nearly 12000 individual units more than 50 office properties about 25 retail properties over 65 medical properties (including senior housing and assisted living facilities) and more than five industrial properties. More than 40% of its revenue comes from multi-family residential properties while healthcare properties bring in nearly 30%.

	Annual Growth	04/11	04/12	04/13	04/14	04/15
Sales ($ mil.)	4.5%	237.4	241.8	259.4	265.5	283.2
Net income ($ mil.)	4.7%	20.1	8.2	25.5	(13.2)	24.1
Market value ($ mil.)	(6.6%)	1,171.1	898.6	1,211.0	1,085.3	892.3
Employees	3.1%	383	400	422	445	433

INVESTORS TITLE CO.
NMS: ITIC

121 North Columbia Street
Chapel Hill, NC 27514
Phone: 919 968-2200
Fax: –
Web: www.invtitle.com

CEO: –
CFO: Richard (Dick) Fine
HR: Mitchell (Mitch) Warren
FYE: December 31
Type: Public

Investors Title insures you in case your land is well not completely yours. It's the holding company for Investors Title Insurance and Northeast Investors Title Insurance which underwrite land title insurance and sell reinsurance to other title companies. (Title insurance protects those who invest in real property against loss resulting from defective titles.) Investors Title Insurance serves customers from about 30 offices in North Carolina South Carolina Michigan and Nebraska and through branches or agents in 20 additional states. Northeast Investors Title operates through an agency office in New York. Founder and CEO J. Allen Fine and his family own more than 20% of Investors Title.

	Annual Growth	12/10	12/11	12/12	12/13	12/14
Assets ($ mil.)	6.6%	153.5	158.0	171.9	188.3	198.0
Net income ($ mil.)	10.9%	6.4	6.9	11.1	14.7	9.6
Market value ($ mil.)	24.3%	61.7	72.4	121.4	163.8	147.5
Employees	7.6%	196	199	212	233	263

INVISTA B.V.

4123 E. 37th St. N.
Wichita KS 67220
Phone: 316-828-1000
Fax: 316-828-1801
Web: invista.com

CEO: –
CFO: –
HR: –
FYE: December 31
Type: Subsidiary

As one of the word's largest makers of spandex INVISTA's business model surveys an expanding vista of spandex nylon and polyester product users. The Koch Industries company is a global leader in polymer and fiber manufacturing. INVISTA consists of four major business units — Apparel Intermediates Performance Surfaces and Materials and Polymers and Resins — and its portfolio includes brand names CoolMax Dacron Lycra Polyclear Stainmaster and Thermolite. The company's products are used in clothing plastic packaging automobile airbags and pharmaceutical ingredients.

IOMEGA CORPORATION

3721 Valley Centre Dr. Ste. 200
San Diego CA 92130
Phone: 858-314-7000
Fax: 858-314-7001
Web: www.iomega.com

CEO: Jonathan S Huberman
CFO: Brooke Beers
HR: –
FYE: December 31
Type: Subsidiary

Iomega carved a space for itself in the data storage market with a slash-and-burn strategy. The company provides rewritable optical DVD drives desktop and portable PC hard drives as well as wireless-capable drives for the consumer market. Its business products include network attached storage (NAS) equipment and its REV line of removable hard disk drives. Iomega also provides online storage and data recovery services for the consumer and professional markets through its iStorage unit. The company sells its products worldwide through such distributors as Ingram Micro CDW and Tech Data and retailers including Best Buy and Fry's Electronics. Iomega is a subsidiary of data storage giant EMC.

ION GEOPHYSICAL CORP
NYS: IO

2105 CityWest Blvd., Suite 400
Houston, TX 77042-2839
Phone: 281 933-3339
Fax: 281 879-3626
Web: www.iongeo.com

CEO: R. Brian Hanson
CFO: Steve Bate
HR: Larry Burke
FYE: December 31
Type: Public

There's a whole lotta shakin' goin' on at ION Geophysical. The seismic data-acquisition imaging and software systems company helps worldwide petroleum exploration contractors identify and measure subsurface geological structures that could contain oil and gas. Its data acquisition products are capable of processing 3-D 4-D and multi-component 3-C seismic data for land marine and transition areas (such as swamps shoreline marsh and jungle). ION Geophysical also makes other products such as geophysical software helicopter-transportable enclosures seismic sensors specialty cables and connectors and radio telemetry systems. Its marine positioning systems map the geography of the ocean's floor.

	Annual Growth	12/11	12/12	12/13	12/14	12/15
Sales ($ mil.)	(16.5%)	454.6	526.3	549.2	509.6	221.5
Net income ($ mil.)	–	24.8	63.3	(245.9)	(128.3)	(25.1)
Market value ($ mil.)	(46.4%)	65.6	69.7	35.3	29.4	5.4
Employees	(12.1%)	937	1,071	1,072	879	560

IONIS PHARMACEUTICALS INC
NMS: IONS

2855 Gazelle Court
Carlsbad, CA 92010
Phone: 760 931-9200
Fax: –
Web: www.isispharm.com

CEO: Stanley T Crooke
CFO: Elizabeth L Hougen
HR: –
FYE: December 31
Type: Public

Ionis (formerly Isis) Pharmaceuticals is trying to make sense out of antisense. The biotech develops drugs based on its antisense technology in which drugs attach themselves to strands of RNA in order to prevent them from producing disease-causing proteins; the hoped-for end result is a therapy that fights disease without harming healthy cells. Ionis has nearly 40 pipeline drugs under development in areas including cardiovascular metabolic and severe and rare diseases (including cancer and neurological disorders). Its lead product is the cholesterol-lowering drug Kynamro which Ionis has licensed to Genzyme; it is marketed in the US and other countries for the treatment of genetic disorder homzygous FH.

	Annual Growth	12/10	12/11	12/12	12/13	12/14
Sales ($ mil.)	18.5%	108.5	99.1	102.0	147.3	214.2
Net income ($ mil.)	–	(61.3)	(84.8)	(65.5)	(60.6)	(39.0)
Market value ($ mil.)	57.2%	1,198.6	854.0	1,236.5	4,718.8	7,312.7
Employees	9.6%	270	281	288	304	390

IOWA HEALTH SYSTEM

1776 WEST LAKES PKWY # 400
WEST DES MOINES, IA 502668239
Phone: 515-241-6161
Fax: –
Web: www.unitypoint.org

CEO: Eric Crowell
CFO: Mark Johnson
HR: Joyce McDanel
FYE: December 31
Type: Private

The land where the tall corn grows is also the land of Iowa Health System (IHS) which does business as UnityPoint. The integrated health care system operates some 15 acute care hospitals that serve large communities throughout Iowa as well as parts of western Illinois and Madison Wisconsin. UnityPoint also supports about a dozen rural hospitals and it manages about 300 physician clinics located in rural and suburban areas. The system's hospitals provide general medical-surgical care as well as care in a number of medical specialties such as cardiovascular disease and home health services. Founded in 1993 UnityPoint has about 3700 licensed beds.

	Annual Growth	12/08	12/09	12/11	12/12	12/13
Sales ($ mil.)	125.7%	–	109.4	2,380.2	2,732.5	2,841.5
Net income ($ mil.)	52.3%	–	–	159.2	220.6	369.3
Market value ($ mil.)	–	–	–	–	–	–
Employees	–	–	–	–	–	18,923

IOWA INTERSTATE RAILROAD LTD.

5900 6th St. SW
Cedar Rapids IA 52404
Phone: 319-298-5400
Fax: 319-298-5457
Web: www.iaisrr.com

CEO: –
CFO: –
HR: –
FYE: December 31
Type: Private

Regional freight carrier Iowa Interstate Railroad (IAIS) operates over about 600 miles of track running from Omaha Nebraska to Chicago passing through Iowa along the way. IAIS hauls cargo such as agricultural products chemicals coal ethanol forest products intermodal containers and trailers and steel. Because of its central location the IAIS system connects with all of North America's largest railroads. IAIS has intermodal facilities in Blue Island Illinois and Council Bluffs Iowa. The company is a subsidiary of Pittsburgh-based railroad management and investment company Railroad Development Corp. (RDC). IAIS was formed in 1984 and acquired by RDC in 2004.

IPASS INC
NMS: IPAS

3800 Bridge Parkway
Redwood Shores, CA 94065
Phone: 650 232-4100
Fax: –
Web: www.ipass.com

CEO: Gary A Griffiths
CFO: Darin R Vickery
HR: –
FYE: December 31
Type: Public

On the information superhighway iPass is in the passing lane. The company provides mobile employees with remote access to their company's internal networks and data. Through agreements with telecom carriers ISPs and other network service providers its mobile offerings create a virtual network in more than 120 countries. The network includes dial-up Ethernet and Wi-Fi access points. The cloud-based Open Mobile platform lets users connect from mobile devices over a wide range of carrier-independent networks. iPass also offers managed network services that allow enterprises to offer in-store and in-office Wi-Fi for employees and customers. It generates more than half of its sales in the US.

	Annual Growth	12/10	12/11	12/12	12/13	12/14
Sales ($ mil.)	(18.2%)	156.1	140.8	126.1	111.1	69.8
Net income ($ mil.)	–	(3.1)	(3.0)	(4.4)	(12.3)	7.0
Market value ($ mil.)	2.3%	80.9	92.0	118.5	101.7	88.7
Employees	(8.9%)	363	366	358	350	250

IPAYMENT INC.

40 Burton Hills Blvd. Ste. 415
Nashville TN 37215
Phone: 615-665-1858
Fax: 847-391-2253
Web: www.uop.com

CEO: Carl A Grimstad
CFO: Mark C Monaco
HR: –
FYE: December 31
Type: Private

iPayment doesn't want small businesses to pay an arm and a leg for credit and debit card processing. The company's approximately 133000 clients are mostly small US merchants firms taking money over the phone or Internet and those that previously may have accepted only cash or checks as payment. iPayment markets through independent sales organizations and has grown by consolidating its niche buying a dozen competitors and merchant portfolios since 2003. A typical iPayment merchant generates less than $185000 of charge volume per year with an average transaction value of about $70. Company co-founder Greg Daily sold his two-thirds' stake and stepped down as CEO in 2011.

IPC HEALTHCARE, INC.
NMS: IPCM

4605 Lankershim Boulevard, Suite 617
North Hollywood, CA 91602
Phone: 888 447-2362
Fax: –

CEO: Adam D Singer
CFO: Richard H Kline III
HR: –
FYE: December 31
Type: Public

IPC The Hospitalist Company (IPC) is on the leading edge of a growing US trend toward hospitalist specialization. The staffing firm provides 1800 hospitalists to more than 400 hospitals and 1200 post-acute care facilities facilities in about 30 states. Hospitalists are health care providers (physicians nurses and physicians assistants) who oversee all of a patient's treatment from the beginning to the end of their stay. They answer questions and coordinate treatment programs to improve the quality of care and reduce the length of a patient's hospital stay. In addition to providing staff IPC offers training data management billing and risk management services for its medical professionals and clients.

	Annual Growth	12/09	12/10	12/11	12/12	12/13
Sales ($ mil.)	18.4%	310.5	363.4	457.5	523.5	609.5
Net income ($ mil.)	22.1%	18.6	24.3	29.3	32.6	41.4
Market value ($ mil.)	15.6%	565.8	663.8	778.0	675.7	1,010.6
Employees	17.5%	1,451	1,792	2,030	2,381	2,769

IPC SYSTEMS INC.

Harborside Financial Center 1500 Plaza 10 15th Fl.
Jersey City NJ 07311
Phone: 201-253-2000
Fax: 201-253-2361
Web: www.ipc.com

CEO: Neil Barua
CFO: William J McHale Jr
HR: –
FYE: September 30
Type: Private

IPC Systems makes and services "turret" communications systems also called dealerboards that combine PBX data switching computer telephony voice recording and multimedia capabilities. Its products are used by financial institutions for voice and data transmission and routing in their trading environments. These products are designed to integrate with products from technology vendors such as Avaya and Cisco. With more than 115000 dealerboards worldwide IPC's financial extranet includes some 4000 locations in more than 700 cities. Its offerings also include enhanced voice services business continuity and support. IPC Systems is owned by Silver Lake Partners.

IPG PHOTONICS CORP

NMS: IPGP

50 Old Webster Road
Oxford, MA 01540
Phone: 508-373-1100
Fax: –
Web: www.ipgphotonics.com

CEO: Valentin P. Gapontsev
CFO: Timothy P. V. Mammen
HR: John (Jack) Weaver
FYE: December 31
Type: Public

IPG Photonics has a laser focus. The company makes fiber lasers and amplifiers and diode lasers which are primarily used in materials processing applications (nearly 90% of sales) such as welding cutting marking and engraving. Its fiber lasers also have applications in medicine and in telecommunications networks from enabling data signal transmission to surgical cosmetic urological and dental procedures. The company's customers have included BAE SYSTEMS Mitsubishi Heavy Industries and Nippon Steel. Deriving more than 80% of its sales outside North America IPG Photonics operates sales offices in about a dozen countries in Asia and Europe.

	Annual Growth	12/10	12/11	12/12	12/13	12/14
Sales ($ mil.)	26.6%	299.3	474.5	562.5	648.0	769.8
Net income ($ mil.)	38.8%	54.0	117.8	145.0	155.8	200.4
Market value ($ mil.)	24.1%	1,655.9	1,773.8	3,490.4	4,064.4	3,923.5
Employees	17.6%	1,760	2,137	2,400	2,800	3,370

IPREO HOLDINGS LLC

1359 Broadway 2nd Fl.
New York NY 10018
Phone: 212-849-5000
Fax: 212-812-4447
Web: www.ipreo.com

CEO: –
CFO: Brian Dockray
HR: –
FYE: December 31
Type: Private

Ipreo provides software and services for entities involved in the global capital markets including investments banks and underwriters trading desks and analysts and publicly traded corporations. It offers new-issuance software investor prospecting tools event management systems investor relations software and a host of research data and analytics applications (including the Bigdough database of institutional investor contacts and profiles). Ipreo which serves customers in the Americas the Asia-Pacific region Europe and the Middle East and North Africa is owned by investment firm KKR & Co.

IPSWITCH INC

83 Hartwell Ave.
Lexington MA 02421
Phone: 781-676-5700
Fax: 781-676-5710
Web: www.ipswitch.com

CEO: Joe Krivickas
CFO: David Stott
HR: –
FYE: December 31
Type: Private

Ipswitch would like to see people make the change to its software for corporate and personal communications. The company provides applications used for e-mail and instant messaging (IMail Server) network management (WhatsUp) and file transfering (WS_FTP). Ipswitch sells to both corporations and individual consumers. The company has research and development offices in Georgia and Wisconsin and a customer support facility in Amsterdam. Ipswitch sells its products through distributors resellers and OEMs in the North America Latin America Europe and the Pacific Rim. The company was founded in 1991.

IQOR US INC.

335 Madison Ave. 27th Fl.
New York NY 10017
Phone: 646-274-3030
Fax: 646-274-6032
Web: www.iqor.com

CEO: Norm Merritt
CFO: Margaret M Cowherd
HR: –
FYE: December 31
Type: Private

When iQor comes a-ringin' you'd better come a-bringin'. One of the world's largest business process outsourcing and a top collection agency iQor provides third-party collections accounts receivable management and customer service. Its clients represent a wide swath of sectors ranging from commercial groups and financial services companies to utilities and government agencies. The company operates about 40 call centers in North America Europe and Asia. Investment firm Huntsman Gay Global Capital acquired a majority stake in iQor in 2010.

IRELL & MANELLA LLP

1800 Avenue of the Stars Ste. 900
Los Angeles CA 90067-4276
Phone: 310-277-1010
Fax: 310-203-7199
Web: www.irell.com

CEO: –
CFO: –
HR: –
FYE: December 31
Type: Private - Partnershi

Law firm Irell & Manella is known for its work related to the entertainment industry and over the years its clients have included big movers and shakers like Pinnacle Entertainment TiVo and Viacom. The firm employs about 200 attorneys that maintain a wide range of practices including antitrust employee benefits and compensation intellectual property transactions mergers and acquisitions securities litigation taxation and white collar defense. Irell & Manella operates from two Los Angeles-area offices. The firm was founded in 1941.

IRIDEX CORP.

NMS: IRIX

1212 Terra Bella Avenue
Mountain View, CA 94043-1824
Phone: 650 940-4700
Fax: –
Web: www.iridex.com

CEO: William M Moore
CFO: William M Moore
HR: –
FYE: January 03
Type: Public

A meeting with IRIDEX can be an eye-opening experience. The company makes laser systems and peripheral devices used to treat serious eye conditions including the three major causes of blindness: macular degeneration glaucoma and diabetic retinopathy. The company markets its products under such brands as IQ and OcuLight through a direct sales staff in the US and through distributors in more than 100 countries worldwide. Its ophthalmic systems including laser consoles delivery devices and disposable probes are used by ophthalmologists in hospitals surgery centers and physician practice centers. IRIDEX exited its aesthetics business (lasers for dermatology and plastic surgery procedures) in 2012.

	Annual Growth	01/11*	12/11	12/12	12/13*	01/15
Sales ($ mil.)	(0.5%)	43.7	33.2	33.9	38.3	42.8
Net income ($ mil.)	34.7%	3.0	2.6	1.4	2.2	10.0
Market value ($ mil.)	21.7%	38.4	36.6	36.8	94.6	84.3
Employees	(6.4%)	167	133	125	118	128

*Fiscal year change

IRIDIUM COMMUNICATIONS INC   NMS: IRDM

1750 Tysons Boulevard, Suite 1400
McLean, VA 22102
Phone: 703 287-7400
Fax: –
Web: www.iridium.com

CEO: Matthew J. (Matt) Desch
CFO: Thomas J. Fitzpatrick
HR: –
FYE: December 31
Type: Public

If you want to make a phone call from the North Pole you want Iridium Communications (formerly Iridium Satellite). The company offers mobile voice data and Internet services worldwide targeting companies that operate in remote areas. While Iridium focuses on such commercial industries as energy defense maritime and mining its main customer is the US Department of Defense. Boeing primarily operates and maintains the Iridium satellite system which consists of 66 low-earth-orbit satellites linked to ground stations (the world's largest commercial satellite operation). The mobile satellite communications company has operations centers in the US Canada and Europe.

	Annual Growth	12/10	12/11	12/12	12/13	12/14
Sales ($ mil.)	4.1%	348.2	384.3	383.5	382.6	408.6
Net income ($ mil.)	34.8%	22.7	39.7	64.6	62.5	75.0
Market value ($ mil.)	4.3%	774.7	724.0	631.0	587.0	915.6
Employees	7.6%	174	197	211	224	233

IRIDIUM COMMUNICATIONS INC.   NASDAQ: IRDM

1750 Tysons Blvd. Ste. 400
McLean VA 22102
Phone: 703-287-7400
Fax: 703-287-7450
Web: www.iridium.com

CEO: Matthew J Desch
CFO: –
HR: –
FYE: December 31
Type: Public

If you want to make a phone call from the North Pole you want Iridium Communications (formerly Iridium Satellite). The company offers mobile voice data and Internet services worldwide targeting companies that operate in remote areas. While Iridium focuses on such commercial industries as energy defense maritime and mining its main customer is the US Department of Defense. Boeing primarily operates and maintains the Iridium satellite system which consists of 66 low-earth-orbit satellites linked to ground stations (the world's largest commercial satellite operation). The company has operations centers in Arizona and Virginia.

IRIS INTERNATIONAL INC.   NASDAQ: IRIS

9172 Eton Ave.
Chatsworth CA 91311-5874
Phone: 818-709-1244
Fax: 818-700-9661
Web: www.proiris.com

CEO: Cesar M Garcia
CFO: Amin I Khalifa
HR: –
FYE: December 31
Type: Public

To really know a person IRIS International doesn't look deep into their eyes. Instead the company manufactures automated in-vitro diagnostic systems that analyze bodily fluids. Beginning with urinalysis technology the company has expanded to include blood (hematology) and other fluids. Its Iris Diagnostics division develops the iQ family of automated imaging systems used in urinalysis and microscopic analysis as well as related consumables (reagents and test strips) and services. The Iris Sample Processing division markets centrifuges small instruments and laboratory supplies for specimen processing. The company was acquired by industrial and medical conglomerate Danaher in October 2012.

IROBOT CORP   NMS: IRBT

8 Crosby Drive
Bedford, MA 01730
Phone: 781 430-3000
Fax: –
Web: www.irobot.com

CEO: Colin M. Angle
CFO: Alison Dean
HR: Russell J. (Russ) Campanello
FYE: December 27
Type: Public

Fans of The Jetsons appreciate iRobot. The company makes robots for home cleaning use with its Roomba FloorVac and Scooba being the first of their kind to automatically clean floors. iRobot has sold more than 13 million home care robots along with 4500 robots to military and civil defense forces including PackBots to the US Army. iRobot sold its struggling defense and security robot business (which performed tasks such as battlefield reconnaissance and bomb disposal) to Arlington Capital Partners in 2016. Founded in 1990 by robot engineers from the Massachusetts Institute of Technology iRobot has offices in the US UK China and Hong Kong and sells its home products worldwide through retailers.

	Annual Growth	01/11*	12/11	12/12	12/13	12/14
Sales ($ mil.)	11.6%	401.0	465.5	436.2	487.4	556.8
Net income ($ mil.)	14.0%	25.5	40.2	17.3	27.6	37.8
Market value ($ mil.)	11.8%	737.6	884.9	551.1	1,049.7	1,031.9
Employees	(4.5%)	657	619	534	528	572

*Fiscal year change

IRON MOUNTAIN INC (NEW)   NYS: IRM

One Federal Street
Boston, MA 02110
Phone: 617 535-4766
Fax: –
Web: www.ironmountain.com

CEO: William L. Meaney
CFO: Roderick (Rod) Day
HR: Lynda Dec
FYE: December 31
Type: Public

Iron Mountain? It's more like paper mountain at Iron Mountain one of the world's largest records storage and information management companies. The firm stores paper and other media including microfilm and microfiche audio and video files film and X-rays. It also provides such services as records filing database management fulfillment (through Iron Mountain Fulfillment Services) disaster recovery and information destruction. The company serves about 155000 corporate clients in North America Europe Latin America and Asia/Pacific. Iron Mountain traces its paper trail back to 1951 when it was established in an underground facility near Hudson New York.

	Annual Growth	12/10	12/11	12/12	12/13	12/14
Sales ($ mil.)	(0.1%)	3,127.5	3,014.7	3,005.3	3,025.9	3,117.7
Net income ($ mil.)	–	(53.9)	395.5	171.7	97.3	326.1
Market value ($ mil.)	11.5%	5,247.6	6,462.4	6,514.9	6,368.0	8,111.6
Employees	0.8%	19,400	17,000	17,500	8,500	20,000

IRONPLANET INC.

4695 Chabot Dr. Ste. 102
Pleasanton CA 94588-2756
Phone: 925-225-8800
Fax: 925-225-8610
Web: www.ironplanet.com

CEO: Gregory J Owens
CFO: –
HR: –
FYE: December 31
Type: Private

Need to auction off heavy equipment but don't feel like sweating it out in an auction house? An online marketplace operator IronPlanet provides virtual auctions through which customers buy and sell a variety of heavy construction mining and agricultural equipment including bulldozers dump trucks excavators tractors and harvesters. The company which operates on a consignment basis offers weekly public auctions as well as private and daily auctions; it also provides equipment inspection services. It serves customers — from sole proprietors to large corporations — in North America and to a lesser extent the Asia-Pacific region. Founded in 1999 IronPlanet withdrew its initial public offering in 2012.

IRONWOOD PHARMACEUTICALS INC.

NMS: IRWD

301 Binney Street
Cambridge, MA 02142
Phone: 617 621-7722
Fax: –
Web: www.ironwoodpharma.com

CEO: Peter M. Hecht
CFO: Thomas Graney
HR: –
FYE: December 31
Type: Public

Ironwood Pharmaceuticals takes an iron fist to gastrointestinal ailments and other medical conditions. The firm develops internally discovered gastrointestinal drugs. Its first commercial product Linzess (or linaclotide) a treatment for irritable bowel syndrome (IBS) and chronic constipation is sold in the US and in Canada under the brand name Constella. Linzess was developed with partner Forest Laboratories which shares US marketing rights. Outside of the US Ironwood licensed development and commercialization rights for the drug to Almirall in Europe and other partners in Asia. The firm also has products in development for other gastrointestinal central nervous system (CNS) and inflammatory conditions.

	Annual Growth	12/10	12/11	12/12	12/13	12/14
Sales ($ mil.)	14.9%	43.9	65.9	150.2	22.9	76.4
Net income ($ mil.)	–	(53.0)	(64.9)	(72.6)	(272.8)	(189.6)
Market value ($ mil.)	10.3%	1,457.5	1,685.7	1,560.3	1,635.0	2,157.4
Employees	20.9%	217	276	530	534	464

IRVINE SENSORS CORPORATION

OTC: IRSN

3001 Red Hill Ave. Bldg. 4 Ste. 108
Costa Mesa CA 92626-4526
Phone: 714-549-8211
Fax: 714-444-8773
Web: www.irvine-sensors.com

CEO: –
CFO: –
HR: –
FYE: September 30
Type: Public

Irvine Sensors puts its hopes in big returns from tiny products. Much of the company's sales come from research and development contracts related to its minute solid-state microcircuitry technology in which circuits are assembled in 3-D stacks (rather than flat layouts) to lower weight and boost performance. Irvine Sensors also develops and manufactures miniaturized infrared and electro-optical cameras and image processors as well as products incorporating the components primarily for defense and security applications. The US government and its contractors account for nearly all of the company's sales. Leading customers include the US Air Force US Army and Optics 1 a defense contractor.

IRVING MATERIALS INC.

8032 N. State Rd. 9
Greenfield IN 46140
Phone: 317-326-3101
Fax: 317-326-7727
Web: www.irvmat.com

CEO: Earl G Brinker
CFO: –
HR: –
FYE: December 31
Type: Private

Irving Materials Inc. (IMI) digs deep for business. One of the largest privately held concrete suppliers the company produces stone sand gravel and concrete materials for customers in Alabama Illinois Indiana Ohio Kentucky and Tennessee. It operates four regional operations centers and more than 150 ready-mix plants about 15 asphalt plants and 10 stone quarries. IMI also sells used equipment ranging from haul trucks and fleet cars to portable crushing equipment and other heavy equipment. C. C. "Skunk" Irving founded the company in 1946. It is employee owned.

ISAGENIX INTERNATIONAL LLC

2225 S. Price Rd.
Chandler AZ 85286
Phone: 480-889-5747
Fax: 503-443-2423
Web: www.buenavistahomes.com

CEO: –
CFO: –
HR: –
FYE: December 31
Type: Private

Isagenix promotes the belief that a "clean" body is a healthy body. The company develops and manufactures a range of health and wellness products from nutritional and dietary supplements its offerings include weight loss solutions energy and performance products healthy aging products shakes soups sars vitamins nutritional supplements healthy snacks sports drinks and personal care items.Isagenix's line of "Nutritional Cleansing and Replenishing" products help improve health by accelerating the removal of impurities from the body and replacing them with nutrients to revive health. The company also offers dietary supplements to help customers lose weight and increase energy.

ISG TECHNOLOGY LLC

127 N 7TH ST
SALINA, KS 674012603
Phone: 785-823-1555
Fax: –
Web: www.isgtech.com

CEO: Scott Cissna
CFO: Scott Cissna
HR: –
FYE: March 31
Type: Private

ISG Technology hopes to help you capitalize on all of your technology operations. The company which does business as Integrated Solutions Group provides information technology (IT) and telecommunications services primarily to small and midsized businesses in the midwestern US. ISG services include network design hardware and software procurement web development and hosting and training. Clients come from fields such as financial services manufacturing telelcommunications and health care. The company has seven locations in the Midwest including offices in Kansas Missouri and Oklahoma.

	Annual Growth	03/04	03/05	03/06	03/07	03/08
Sales ($ mil.)	(75.9%)	–	–	954.3	44.4	55.3
Net income ($ mil.)	77119.0%	–	–	0.0	0.2	12.5
Market value ($ mil.)	–	–	–	–	–	–
Employees	–	–	–	–	–	118

ISIGN SOLUTIONS INC

NBB: ISGN D

275 Shoreline Drive, Suite 500
Redwood Shores, CA 94065-1413
Phone: 650 802-7888
Fax: –
Web: www.cic.com

CEO: Philip S Sassower
CFO: Andrea Goren
HR: –
FYE: December 31
Type: Public

If your intelligent communication involves hunting and pecking try Communication Intelligence Corp. (CIC). The company's handwriting recognition software including its SignatureOne Sign-it and iSign products recognizes character strokes of words from English Chinese and Western European languages and converts them to digital text. Industries served by CIC include banking insurance and financial services which often require electronic signatures for legal documents. Customers have included Charles Schwab and Wells Fargo. CIC was founded in 1981 in conjunction with Stanford University's Research Institute. Phoenix Ventures is the company's largest shareholder with a 37% stake.

	Annual Growth	12/10	12/11	12/12	12/13	12/14
Sales ($ mil.)	15.5%	0.9	1.5	2.4	1.4	1.5
Net income ($ mil.)	–	(4.2)	(4.5)	(3.1)	(4.8)	(4.0)
Market value ($ mil.)	–	0.0	0.0	0.0	0.0	0.0
Employees	6.8%	20	21	21	24	26

ISILON SYSTEMS INC.

3101 Western Ave.
Seattle WA 98121
Phone: 206-315-7500
Fax: 206-315-7501
Web: www.isilon.com

CEO: -
CFO: -
HR: -
FYE: December 31
Type: Business Segment

Isilon Systems isn't daunted by the ever-expanding digital world. The company's network-attached storage (NAS) systems are designed for businesses with digital imaging and content delivery operations. Its modular Isilon IQ nodes which use the proprietary OneFS operating software store and deliver large digital files such as photos video and audio content. Many of its customers are media companies but Isilon also markets to health care providers oil and gas firms and government agencies among others. Isilon designs its storage systems in the US but the hardware is made by contract manufacturers. Customers have included The Associated Press Sony NASA NBC and Paramount Pictures. Isilon is a division of EMC.

ISOLA GROUP LTD.

3100 W. Ray Rd. Ste. 301
Chandler AZ 85226
Phone: 480-893-6527
Fax: 480-893-1409
Web: www.isola-group.com

CEO: Ray Sharpe
CFO: Gordon Bitter
HR: Charles Englebert
FYE: December 31
Type: Private

Isola puts the "board" in printed circuit board (PCB). The company manufactures base materials used to make PCBs at more than a dozen facilities around the globe. Its manufacturing processes for laminates and other materials such as glass cellulose and epoxy use state-of-the-art technologies (closed-loop feed-forward and feed-back cure and thickness control systems) to ensure composite integrity. Other technical innovations ensure tight dielectric thickness control. End users include customers in the automotive computer medical military and wireless communications markets. Nearly 80% of sales come from outside the US. Investment firm TPG Capital owns Isola which filed to go public in late 2011.

ISLE OF CAPRI CASINOS INC

NMS: ISLE

600 Emerson Road, Suite 300
Saint Louis, MO 63141
Phone: 314 813-9200
Fax: -
Web: www.islecorp.com

CEO: Virginia M. McDowell
CFO: Eric L. Hausler
HR: Robert (Bob) Boone
FYE: April 26
Type: Public

Rollin' on the river takes on new meaning when you're talking about Isle of Capri Casinos. The company owns and operates about 15 dockside riverboat and land-based casinos in Colorado Iowa Louisiana Mississippi and Missouri. In addition the company has a pari-mutuel harness racetrack and casino in Pompano Beach Florida. Most of the company's casinos have hotels and feature restaurants live entertainment and private lounges for high-rollers. Altogether Isle of Capri's properties feature approximately 14000 slot machines and 350 table games (including some 90 poker tables) as well as more than 3000 hotel rooms and 45 restaurants.

	Annual Growth	04/11	04/12	04/13	04/14	04/15
Sales ($ mil.)	(0.2%)	1,005.0	977.4	965.2	954.6	996.3
Net income ($ mil.)	3.3%	4.5	(129.8)	(47.6)	(127.7)	5.2
Market value ($ mil.)	10.7%	400.5	260.4	285.5	273.4	601.4
Employees	(4.7%)	8,600	7,700	7,500	7,000	7,100

ISOMET CORP.

NBB: IOMT

5263 Port Royal Road
Springfield, VA 22151
Phone: 703 321-8301
Fax: 703 321-8546
Web: www.isomet.com

CEO: -
CFO: Jerry Rayburn
HR: -
FYE: December 31
Type: Public

Isomet never met a laser beam it couldn't control. The company makes acousto-optic systems that manipulate interactions between light and sound to control laser beams especially in color image reproduction applications such as laser printing and phototypesetting. Isomet had long made graphic arts systems of its own — including digital scanners and graphics plotters — but has been winding down that business as it expands its production of birefringent materials (such as lead molybdate) used in fiber-optic applications. The company also offers components such as athermal filters anti-reflection coatings tunable filters and optical switches.

	Annual Growth	12/01	12/04	12/05	12/13	12/14
Sales ($ mil.)	(1.6%)	4.7	3.7	3.6	4.1	3.9
Net income ($ mil.)	-	(0.7)	(1.4)	(1.0)	0.2	0.1
Market value ($ mil.)	-	0.0	0.0	0.0	0.0	0.0
Employees	(9.0%)	51	36	35	-	-

ISO NEW ENGLAND INC.

1 SULLIVAN RD
HOLYOKE, MA 010402841
Phone: 413-535-4000
Fax: -
Web: www.isonewengland.com

CEO: Gordon van Welie
CFO: Robert C. Ludlow
HR: Janice S Dickstein
FYE: December 31
Type: Private

The transmission lines in the Northeast power grid keep humming because of ISO New England. The not-for-profit corporation is responsible for electricity generation and transmission throughout Connecticut Maine Massachusetts New Hampshire Rhode Island and Vermont. The independent systems operator (ISO) runs the 31000 MW generating capacity grid that is owned by utilities of the New England Power Pool and manages the wholesale electric market. The power grid is made up of hundreds of generating units (about 350 under direct ISO New England control) connected by some 8500 miles of high-voltage transmission lines. It provides power to more than 6.5 million households and businesses.

	Annual Growth	12/07	12/08	12/09	12/10	12/13
Sales ($ mil.)	-	-	(1,008.2)	123.5	128.1	157.3
Net income ($ mil.)	-	-	-	0.0	0.0	0.0
Market value ($ mil.)	-	-	-	-	-	-
Employees	-	-	-	-	-	560

ISORAY, INC.

ASE: ISR

350 Hills Street, Suite 106
Richland, WA 99354
Phone: 509 375-1202
Fax: -
Web: www.isoray.com

CEO: William A. Cavanagh
CFO: Brien Ragle
HR: -
FYE: June 30
Type: Public

IsoRay hopes its medical device is a seed of change for cancer patients. Through subsidiary IsoRay Medical the company produces and sells FDA-approved Proxcelan Cs-131 brachytherapy seeds which are mainly used in the treatment of prostate cancer. Brachytherapy is a procedure that implants anywhere from eight to 125 small seed devices containing therapeutic radiation as close as possible to a cancerous tumor. The seeds can be used alone or in combination with external beam radiation surgery or other therapies. Proxcelan Cs-131's application is also expanding to other areas of the body with US approval for use in the treatment of head and neck tumors as well as eye lung colorectal and chest wall cancers.

	Annual Growth	06/11	06/12	06/13	06/14	06/15
Sales ($ mil.)	(3.2%)	5.2	5.1	4.5	4.2	4.6
Net income ($ mil.)	-	(2.8)	(3.5)	(3.9)	(6.0)	(3.7)
Market value ($ mil.)	12.2%	51.4	55.5	26.4	171.5	81.4
Employees	(0.7%)	37	37	38	39	36

ISRAEL DISCOUNT BANK OF NEW YORK

511 5th Ave.
New York NY 10017
Phone: 212-551-8500
Fax: 212-551-8540
Web: www.idbny.com

CEO: Arie Sheer
CFO: –
HR: –
FYE: December 31
Type: Subsidiary

Israel Discount Bank of New York (IDB Bank) is all over the map. The institution offers personal commercial and private banking services in the US and abroad. Focusing on middle-market businesses the bank provides lending services such as working capital commercial real estate loans construction and land development loans asset-based lending and factoring. It specializes in serving accounting law and professional services firms and not-for-profit organizations. International services include import financing letters of credit and foreign exchange. A subsidiary of Israel Discount Bank Limited IDB Bank has about 10 locations in the US Israel and South America.

ISRAMCO, INC.
NAS: ISRL

2425 West Loop South, Suite 810
Houston, TX 77027
Phone: 713 621-5946
Fax: –
Web: www.isramcousa.com

CEO: Haim Tsuff
CFO: Edy Francis
HR: –
FYE: December 31
Type: Public

There may be milk and honey on the other side of the River Jordan but to date not much oil. Because of that Isramco focuses on growing its US operations and is engaged (through subsidiaries) in oil and gas exploration primarily in Colorado Louisiana Oklahoma New Mexico Texas Utah and Wyoming. It also has oil and gas assets in offshore Israel. In 2012 Isramco reported proved reserves of 32.3 million barrels of oil equivalent. Its 2012 production average was 2170 barrels of oil per day. It also operates a well service company serving oil companies and independent oil and natural gas production firms active in the US. Chairman and CEO Haim Tsuff owns about 67% of Isramco.

	Annual Growth	12/10	12/11	12/12	12/13	12/14
Sales ($ mil.)	22.1%	42.2	45.6	50.4	68.7	93.9
Net income ($ mil.)	–	(2.8)	7.4	2.2	(6.7)	5.2
Market value ($ mil.)	13.1%	229.1	243.4	282.6	345.3	375.0
Employees	73.5%	29	62	150	228	263

ISTA PHARMACEUTICALS INC.
NASDAQ: ISTA

50 Technology Dr.
Irvine CA 92618
Phone: 949-788-6000
Fax: 949-788-6010
Web: www.istavision.com

CEO: –
CFO: –
HR: –
FYE: December 31
Type: Public

ISTA Pharmaceuticals has set its sights on treating eye diseases. The pharmaceutical company has products in development and on the market. ISTA's marketed products include Bepreve (for itchy eyes associated with allergic conjunctivitis) Istalol (a glaucoma treatment) and Bromday (used for pain and inflammation following cataract surgery) in the US. Its drug Vitrase is a spreading agent that promotes absorption of injected drugs. The drug candidates in the company's pipeline include treatments for dry eye syndrome ocular pain and inflammation. The company has additional ocular and allergy treatments in research and development stages. ISTA was acquired by global eye health company Bausch & Lomb in 2012.

ISTAR INC
NYS: STAR

1114 Avenue of the Americas, 39th Floor
New York, NY 10036
Phone: 212 930-9400
Fax: 212 930-9494
Web: www.istarfinancial.com

CEO: Jay Sugarman
CFO: David M. DiStaso
HR: –
FYE: December 31
Type: Public

iStar Financial is a real estate investment trust (REIT) that acts as a private banker for owners of high-end commercial real estate in the US and abroad. Its financing activities include first mortgages senior and mezzanine real estate debt and corporate capital net lease financing and equity investments. The REIT's loans typically range in size from $20 million to $150 million and are mainly secured by apartments or other residential properties office complexes land hotels or industrial retail entertainment or mixed-use properties. Office or industrial properties make up 25% of its secured assets while land makes up another 20%.

	Annual Growth	12/10	12/11	12/12	12/13	12/14
Assets ($ mil.)	(12.2%)	9,174.5	7,517.8	6,150.8	5,642.0	5,463.1
Net income ($ mil.)	(32.6%)	79.7	(22.1)	(239.9)	(112.0)	16.5
Market value ($ mil.)	14.9%	666.2	450.7	694.3	1,215.7	1,162.9
Employees	(2.3%)	200	184	170	175	182

ITA GROUP INC

4600 WESTOWN PKWY STE 100
WEST DES MOINES, IA 502661042
Phone: 515-326-3400
Fax: –
Web: www.itagroup.com

CEO: Thomas J. (Tom) Mahoney
CFO: Brent VanderWaal
HR: –
FYE: August 31
Type: Private

ITA Group (doing business as ITAGroup) bets it can make your company better. Specializing in performance marketing ITAGroup (standing for "Ideas to Action") builds and manages programs that help clients increase sales and customer satisfaction through incentives and training. The company's services include research and program design administration fulfillment and measurement for employee recognition and rewards programs business-to-business loyalty programs and sales incentive programs. ITAGroup also provides business meeting and event planning services.

	Annual Growth	08/09	08/10	08/11	08/12	08/13
Sales ($ mil.)	–	–	0.0	233.1	288.3	288.3
Net income ($ mil.)	–	–	–	0.0	0.0	0.0
Market value ($ mil.)	–	–	–	–	–	–
Employees	–	–	–	–	–	550

ITC HOLDINGS CORP
NYS: ITC

27175 Energy Way
Novi, MI 48377
Phone: 248 946-3000
Fax: –
Web: www.itc-holdings.com

CEO: –
CFO: Rejji P Hayes
HR: Kevin Burke
FYE: December 31
Type: Public

ITC Holdings (ITC) owns and operates 15000 circuit miles of power transmission lines. Through its subsidiaries ITC Transmission Michigan Electric Transmission Company (METC) ITC Great Plains and ITC Midwest ITC operates regulated high-voltage transmission systems in Michigan's Lower Peninsula and portions of Illinois Iowa Kansas Minnesota Missouri and Oklahoma serving a combined peak load of more than 26000 MW. ITC is a member of the Midwest ISO (MISO) a regional transmission organization. The company also operates as ITC Grid Development which invests in transmission infrastructure development. In 2016 Fortis agreed to buy the company for $11.3 billion.

	Annual Growth	12/10	12/11	12/12	12/13	12/14
Sales ($ mil.)	10.1%	696.8	757.4	830.5	941.3	1,023.0
Net income ($ mil.)	13.8%	145.7	171.7	187.9	233.5	244.1
Market value ($ mil.)	(10.1%)	9,615.6	11,772.1	11,931.9	14,865.6	6,272.3
Employees	7.9%	433	452	503	539	587

ITC^DELTACOM INC.

7037 Old Madison Pike
Huntsville AL 35806
Phone: 256-382-5900
Fax: 256-264-9924
Web: www.deltacom.com

CEO: –
CFO: –
HR: –
FYE: December 31
Type: Subsidiary

ITC^DeltaCom keeps businesses in the Southeast connected. Doing business as Deltacom the competitive local-exchange carrier (CLEC) operates in eight states — Alabama Florida Georgia Louisiana Mississippi North Carolina South Carolina and Tennessee — offering integrated voice and data communications including local and long-distance phone service and DSL Internet access mainly to business customers. Deltacom also wholesales transmission capacity to other carriers on its fiber-optic network which spans more than 16000 miles from New York to Florida and as far west as Texas. Deltacom was acquired by ISP EarthLink for $524 million in late 2010 and folded into the company's EarthLink Business segment.

ITERIS INC

NAS: ITI

1700 Carnegie Avenue, Suite 100
Santa Ana, CA 92705
Phone: 949 270-9400
Fax: –
Web: www.iteris.com

CEO: Joe Bergera
CFO: Andrew C. (Andy) Schmidt
HR: –
FYE: March 31
Type: Public

Thanks to the technology and services Iteris provides for traffic management motorcycle cops might have to start using their ticket pads for scribbling shopping lists. The company's roadway sensors business segment includes video vehicle detection systems installed at intersections to help manage traffic flow and traffic data collection; product brands include Vantage Pico and Abacus. Iteris' transportation systems division offers engineering and consulting services and the development of transportation management and information systems. The company generates most of its revenue in the US.

	Annual Growth	03/11	03/12	03/13	03/14	03/15
Sales ($ mil.)	5.0%	59.4	58.4	61.7	68.2	72.3
Net income ($ mil.)	–	(5.2)	2.5	2.4	1.4	(1.1)
Market value ($ mil.)	6.0%	46.7	48.3	59.0	64.2	59.0
Employees	0.8%	276	264	258	266	285

ITEX CORP.

NBB: ITEX

3326 160th Avenue SE, Suite 100
Bellevue, WA 98008-6418
Phone: 425 463-4000
Fax: 425 463-4040
Web: www.itex.com

CEO: Steven White
CFO: John A Wade
HR: –
FYE: July 31
Type: Public

ITEX provides a business-to-business payment system for corporate members through a licensed broker network across the US and Canada. In lieu of cash some 24000 member businesses of the company's ITEX Marketplace barter time-sensitive slow-moving or surplus goods and services valued in ITEX dollars. Members represent a variety of industries including advertising construction dining health care hospitality media printing and professional services. ITEX administers the trade exchange; it (or any of its 95 franchisees or licensed brokers) also acts as a record keeper for member transactions.

	Annual Growth	07/11	07/12	07/13	07/14	07/15
Sales ($ mil.)	(7.5%)	16.4	15.8	14.8	13.5	12.0
Net income ($ mil.)	(0.4%)	0.7	1.0	1.1	0.7	0.7
Market value ($ mil.)	(7.2%)	7.7	7.4	7.1	6.5	5.7
Employees	(17.3%)	30	22	20	16	14

ITRON, INC.

NMS: ITRI

2111 N Molter Road
Liberty Lake, WA 99019
Phone: 509 924-9900
Fax: –
Web: www.itron.com

CEO: Philip C. Mezey
CFO: W. Mark Schmitz
HR: Michel C. Cadieux
FYE: December 31
Type: Public

Itron aims to make meter-reading a desk job. The company is a global supplier of metering products and services for electric natural gas and water utilities. Itron makes radio- and telephone-based automatic meter-reading (AMR) systems handheld meter-reading computers smart meters and meter data acquisition and analysis software in addition to traditional standard (manual-read) meters. Its systems are installed at about 8000 utilities across 100 countries. The company also provides consulting project management and outsourcing services. Customers have included BC Hydro Electrabel Ford Progress Energy and Southern California Edison.

	Annual Growth	12/10	12/11	12/12	12/13	12/14
Sales ($ mil.)	(3.4%)	2,259.3	2,434.1	2,178.2	1,948.7	1,970.7
Net income ($ mil.)	–	104.8	(510.2)	108.3	(146.8)	(22.9)
Market value ($ mil.)	(6.5%)	2,139.9	1,380.4	1,719.2	1,598.8	1,632.0
Employees	(4.2%)	9,500	9,600	8,500	8,200	8,000

ITT CORPORATION

NYS: ITT

1133 Westchester Avenue
White Plains, NY 10604
Phone: 914 641-2000
Fax: –
Web: www.itt.com

CEO: Denise L. Ramos
CFO: Thomas M. (Tom) Scalera
HR: Kelly Noyes
FYE: December 31
Type: Public

ITT Corporation hopes its customers are pumped moved and energized about its products. A diversified manufacturer ITT makes a range of industrial products through four operating segments: industrial process (pumping systems though Goulds Pumps valves and services for oil and gas and chemical companies); motion technologies (brake pads and friction materials for transportation markets); interconnect solutions (ICS connectors for fiber optic RF power and other electronic products); and control technologies (hydraulic valves actuators and switches for aerospace companies).

	Annual Growth	12/10	12/11	12/12	12/13	12/14
Sales ($ mil.)	(29.9%)	10,995.0	2,119.0	2,227.8	2,496.9	2,654.6
Net income ($ mil.)	(30.7%)	798.0	(130.0)	125.4	488.5	184.5
Market value ($ mil.)	(6.1%)	4,742.0	1,759.0	2,134.9	3,951.2	3,681.9
Employees	(30.4%)	40,000	8,500	9,000	9,400	9,400

ITT EDUCATIONAL SERVICES, INC.

NYS: ESI

13000 North Meridian Street
Carmel, IN 46032-1404
Phone: 317 706-9200
Fax: –
Web: www.ittesi.com

CEO: Kevin M. Modany
CFO: Rocco F. Tarasi
HR: –
FYE: December 31
Type: Public

To get a mortarboard from ITT you may need to know a little something about motherboards. One of the largest US providers of technical education ITT Educational Services offers mainly associate and bachelor degree programs to nearly 73000 students at more than 140 ITT Technical Institutes in roughly 40 states. Although the company is known for its technology-focused degrees in such areas as computer-aided design (CAD) engineering technology and information technology it has expanded its offerings to include degrees in business criminal justice design and health sciences. Programs are offered through a combination of classroom and online instruction.

	Annual Growth	12/10	12/11	12/12	12/13	12/14
Sales ($ mil.)	(11.9%)	1,596.5	1,499.9	1,287.2	1,072.3	961.8
Net income ($ mil.)	(47.1%)	374.2	307.8	140.5	(27.0)	29.3
Market value ($ mil.)	(37.7%)	1,493.5	1,334.1	405.9	787.4	225.4
Employees	(5.4%)	11,100	10,000	9,800	9,500	8,900

ITUS CORP
NAS: ITUS

12100 Wilshire Boulevard, Suite 1275
Los Angeles, CA 90025
Phone: 310 484-5200
Fax: –

CEO: Robert A Berman
CFO: Henry P Herms
HR: –
FYE: October 31
Type: Public

CopyTele has an original take on display and communications technology. The company licenses technology used in thin low-voltage phosphor displays. A licensing agreement with Videocon Industries allows the India-based consumer electronics company to develop televisions utilizing CopyTele's technology. CopyTele also provides secure communications products. Its stand-alone devices provide encryption for secure voice fax and data communication. Boeing the exclusive distributor for many of the company's security products uses CopyTele's encryption products on the Thuraya satellite communications network which is employed by the US military.

	Annual Growth	10/11	10/12	10/13	10/14	10/15
Sales ($ mil.)	74.3%	1.0	0.9	0.4	3.7	9.3
Net income ($ mil.)	–	(7.4)	(4.3)	(10.1)	(9.6)	(1.4)
Market value ($ mil.)	119.5%	1.4	2.3	1.7	1.7	32.5
Employees	(36.5%)	37	7	7	9	6

IVEY MECHANICAL COMPANY LLC

514 N WELLS ST
KOSCIUSKO, MS 390903200
Phone: 662-289-8601
Fax: –
Web: www.iveymechanical.com

CEO: –
CFO: Randy Dew
HR: –
FYE: December 31
Type: Private

More blue-collar than Ivy League Ivey Mechanical Company gets an "A" for its slate of mechanical services. The specialty contractor designs fabricates and manufactures sheet metal work as well as air conditioning/heating and medical gas and plumbing/piping systems. It also provides system repairs maintenance and emergency services. With projects covering 30 states Ivey Mechanical drives preconstruction and construction and prefabrication work for commercial and industrial facilities correctional health care and government contracts. The company operates through service offices dotting the Southeast US. It is owned by CEO Larry Terrell along with members of Ivey Mechanical's management team.

	Annual Growth	12/09	12/10	12/11	12/12	12/13
Sales ($ mil.)	(0.3%)	–	124.7	124.7	144.9	123.7
Net income ($ mil.)	–	–	–	0.0	0.0	0.0
Market value ($ mil.)	–	–	–	–	–	–
Employees	–	–	–	–	–	750

IVILLAGE INC.

500 7th Ave. 14th Fl.
New York NY 10018
Phone: 212-664-4444
Fax: 212-664-4085
Web: www.ivillage.com

CEO: –
CFO: –
HR: –
FYE: December 31
Type: Subsidiary

iVillage offers a cyber retreat for the female Web surfer. The NBCUniversal (NBCU)-owned network of websites aims to be the leading online destination for women. The iVillage Network blends expert opinion on a variety of topics (pregnancy and parenting beauty and style home and garden entertainment and food) with community features (message boards and blogs). In addition to its flagship portal iVillage operates sites such as iVillage UK the NBC Digital Health Network GardenWeb and Astrology.com. A majority of revenue comes from online advertising. iVillage was founded in 1995. NBCU acquired the business for $600 million in 2006.

IWATT INC.

675 Campbell Technology Pkwy. Ste. 150
Campbell CA 95008
Phone: 408-374-4200
Fax: 408-341-0455
Web: www.iwatt.com

CEO: Ronald P Edgerton
CFO: James V McCanna
HR: –
FYE: December 31
Type: Private

iWatt makes watts behave inside electronic gear. The fabless semiconductor company designs power management chips used in flat panel displays notebook computers digital cameras and other portable devices. Its chips are designed into high-density low-cost AC/DC and DC/DC power supplies that make more efficient use of electricity saving on operating costs and helping equipment run cooler. iWatt also makes custom power converter modules for computer servers and workstations. Founded in 2000 iWatt has offices in China Hong Kong Japan South Korea Taiwan and the US. Investors include VantagePoint Venture Partners (39% of shares) and Sigma Partners (31%). The company filed for an IPO in 2012.

IXIA
NMS: XXIA

26601 West Agoura Road
Calabasas, CA 91302
Phone: 818 871-1800
Fax: 818 871-1805
Web: www.ixiacom.com

CEO: Bethany J. Mayer
CFO: Brent Novak
HR: Tim Jones
FYE: December 31
Type: Public

Ixia nixes network glitches. The company designs network validation testing hardware and software that provides visibility into traffic performance and also addresses the network applications. Hardware consists of optical and electrical interface cards and the chassis to hold them. Its software tests the functionality of video voice conformance and security across ethernet wi-fi and 3G/LTE equipment and networks. Ixia primarily serves network equipment manufacturers (Cisco) service providers (AT&T) corporate customers (Bloomberg) the federal government (US Army) and its contractors (General Dynamics). Geographically sales are about evenly divided between the US and international customers.

	Annual Growth	12/10	12/11	12/12	12/13	12/14
Sales ($ mil.)	13.8%	276.8	308.4	413.4	467.3	464.5
Net income ($ mil.)	–	11.2	23.8	45.5	11.9	(41.6)
Market value ($ mil.)	(9.5%)	1,318.5	825.8	1,334.2	1,045.8	884.0
Employees	12.4%	1,100	1,300	1,710	1,846	1,755

IXYS CORP.
NMS: IXYS

1590 Buckeye Drive
Milpitas, CA 95035-7418
Phone: 408 457-9000
Fax: –
Web: www.ixys.com

CEO: Nathan Zommer
CFO: Uzi Sasson
HR: –
FYE: March 31
Type: Public

The US Constitution does a pretty good job with transfer of power. So does IXYS in a different context. IXYS (pronounced ike-sys) makes a variety of power semiconductors (including transistors and rectifiers) and power modules which convert and control electric power in electronic gear. They are used in such equipment as power supplies and medical electronics. IXYS also sells microcontroller chips display drivers power management integrated circuits (ICs) gallium arsenide field-effect transistors and proprietary direct copper bond substrate technology. The company's 2500-plus customers include ABB Boston Scientific Emerson Medtronic Schneider Electric and Siemens. Three quarters of the company's sales come from customers outside the US.

	Annual Growth	03/11	03/12	03/13	03/14	03/15
Sales ($ mil.)	(1.7%)	363.3	368.0	280.0	336.3	338.8
Net income ($ mil.)	(10.3%)	36.6	30.3	7.6	6.0	23.7
Market value ($ mil.)	(2.1%)	425.4	418.1	303.8	359.5	390.2
Employees	(6.3%)	1,244	1,173	1,010	1,016	958

IXYS INTEGRATED CIRCUITS DIVISION INC.

78 Cherry Hill Dr.
Beverly MA 01915-1048
Phone: 978-524-6700
Fax: 978-524-4700
Web: www.ixysic.com/index/index.htm

CEO: –
CFO: –
HR: Lisa Legault
FYE: March 31
Type: Subsidiary

Clare wants to promote clear communications. The company makes solid-state relays and high-voltage integrated circuits that are used to maintain connectivity in the worldwide public telecommunications network. Clare's products are also used in the industrial and consumer sectors especially the flat-panel display market. Clare's OptoMOS line protects electronic systems from high voltage. The company has added a line of photovoltaic solar cells. Its products are sold globally through direct sales representatives and distributors. Clare was acquired by chip maker IXYS in 2002.

J. & W. SELIGMAN & CO. INCORPORATED

100 Park Ave.
New York NY 10017
Phone: 212-850-1864
Fax: 212-922-5726
Web: www.jwseligman.com

CEO: William C Morris
CFO: –
HR: Martin Dowling
FYE: December 31
Type: Subsidiary

One of the oldest asset managers in the US J. & W. Seligman & Co. offers a variety of investment products to investors. Founded in 1864 it manages more than 50 mutual funds with prominent holdings in communications information and technology firms as well as municipal debt. It also oversees more than $16 billion in assets for public funds corporations and foundations. Services for individuals include 401(k) plans and IRAs. Seligman also manages the Tri-Continental Corporation one of the oldest and largest closed-end investment funds traded on the NYSE. Ameriprise Financial bought the firm for some $440 million in 2008. RiverSource a subsidiary of Ameriprise is the new manager of the corporation.

J M SMITH CORPORATION

101 W SAINT JOHN ST # 305
SPARTANBURG, SC 293065179
Phone: 864-542-9419
Fax: –
Web: www.qs1.com

CEO: William (Bill) Cobb
CFO: James C. Wilson
HR: Glynda Karabinos
FYE: February 28
Type: Private

J M Smith Corporation has gone from corner drugstore to supplying drugstores and more. The family owned holding company's primary subsidiary is Smith Drug which provides purchasing and distribution services for more than 1000 independent pharmacies in more than 20 US states. It also operates through QS/1 Data Systems and Integral Solutions both of which offer data management software and services for pharmacies care providers and government agencies. Smith Premier provides prescription benefit management while other divisions offer automated dispensing systems for pharmacies and marketing services for drugmakers. Other units include Norgenix and RxMedic Systems.

	Annual Growth	02/10	02/11	02/12	02/13	02/14
Sales ($ mil.)	(0.9%)	–	2,437.4	2,479.6	2,362.8	2,370.0
Net income ($ mil.)	22.2%	–	–	25.7	26.3	38.4
Market value ($ mil.)	–	–	–	–	–	–
Employees	–	–	–	–	–	1,050

J. CREW GROUP INC.

770 Broadway
New York NY 10003
Phone: 212-209-2500
Fax: 212-209-2666
Web: www.jcrew.com

CEO: Millard Drexler
CFO: Joan Durkin
HR: –
FYE: January 31
Type: Private

The crews appearing in the polished catalogs of the J. Crew Group are far from motley. The retailer is known for its preppy fashions including jeans khakis and other basic (but pricey) items sold to young professionals through its catalogs websites and more than 360 retail and factory stores in the US (and now Canada) under the J. Crew crewcuts (for kids) and Madewell banners. Madewell is a women's-only collection of hip casual clothes. CEO Millard "Mickey" Drexler recruited from The Gap to revive J. Crew's ailing fortunes has led a renaissance at the firm capped by a public offering in 2006. In 2011 the company was taken private by TPG Capital and Leonard Green & Partners.

J&J SNACK FOODS CORP.   NMS: JJSF

6000 Central Highway
Pennsauken, NJ 08109
Phone: 856 665-9533
Fax: –
Web: www.jjsnack.com

CEO: Gerald B. Shreiber
CFO: Dennis G. Moore
HR: Harry Fronjian
FYE: September 26
Type: Public

J & J Snack Foods boasts freezers full of goodies. The company offers an assortment of brands including SUPERPRETZEL soft pretzels ICEE frozen drinks Whole Fruit juice treats Tio Pepe's churros and Funnel Cake Factory funnel cakes. J & J also sells snacks made under license such as Cinnabon's CinnaPretzels and Mrs. GoodCookie pastries as well as Minute Maid's frozen lemonade and juice bars. Besides serving foodservice operators and retail food outlets J & J caters to consumers directly too through BAVARIAN PRETZEL BAKERY shops in the mid-Atlantic region of the US. Adding to its offerings J & J acquired the Patio Hand Fulls Villa Taliano and other frozen snack brands from ConAgra Foods in 2011.

	Annual Growth	09/11	09/12	09/13	09/14	09/15
Sales ($ mil.)	7.0%	744.1	830.8	867.7	919.5	976.3
Net income ($ mil.)	6.3%	55.1	54.1	64.4	71.8	70.2
Market value ($ mil.)	25.4%	888.8	1,070.5	1,508.8	1,760.0	2,201.0
Employees	2.3%	3,100	3,200	3,400	3,400	3,400

J. D. STREETT & COMPANY INC.

144 WELDON PKWY
MARYLAND HEIGHTS, MO 630433100
Phone: 314-432-6600
Fax: –
Web: www.jdstreett.com

CEO: Newell A Baker Jr
CFO: James A Schuering
HR: Kristy Meyer
FYE: December 31
Type: Private

Word on the street is that J. D. Streett tries to stay streets ahead of its rivals as it supplies its customers with a wide range of fuels oxygenates lubricants transmission fluids and antifreezes. The company operates more than 20 retail locations (convenience stores and gas stations) under its own ZX label and/or BP brand in Missouri and Illinois. J. D. Streett also serves more than 10 international markets. In addition the company offers terminalling services for distillate ethanol and oil products and owns and operates a chain of discount cigarette shops (most that also sell beer) across Missouri.

	Annual Growth	12/09	12/10	12/11	12/12	12/13
Sales ($ mil.)	0.3%	–	313.2	366.6	342.9	316.5
Net income ($ mil.)	36.1%	–	–	3.1	(11.0)	5.7
Market value ($ mil.)	–	–	–	–	–	–
Employees	–	–	–	–	–	240

J. F. WHITE CONTRACTING COMPANY

10 BURR ST
FRAMINGHAM, MA 01701-4692
Phone: 508-879-4700
Fax: -
Web: www.jfwhite.com

CEO: -
CFO: -
HR: -
FYE: September 30
Type: Private

From excavating the foundation for the Harvard Business School to working on Boston's Big Dig project J.F. White Contracting has been a key player in heavy civil construction in New England for over 80 years. The group has civil design/build mechanical electrical and fiber optic/telecom divisions to provide a large range of engineering construction infrastructure and equipment and wiring installation services. J.F. White also has a diving division (marine construction) to complement its heavy civil construction operations. The company was founded in 1924 by Joseph F. White Sr.

	Annual Growth	09/07	09/08	09/09	09/11	09/12
Sales ($ mil.)	-	-	0.0	251.8	374.5	271.3
Net income ($ mil.)	-	-	0.0	0.0	0.0	0.0
Market value ($ mil.)	-	-	-	-	-	-
Employees	-	-	-	-	-	400

J. H. FINDORFF & SON INC.

300 S BEDFORD ST
MADISON, WI 537033622
Phone: 608-257-5321
Fax: -
Web: www.findorff.com

CEO: -
CFO: Daniel L Petersen
HR: -
FYE: September 30
Type: Private

J.H. Findorff & Son has been building its resume since the 19th century. The company constructs commercial and institutional projects in the US Midwest. It provides general contracting design/build and construction management services. Projects include schools government buildings health care centers hotels condos offices and shopping complexes. Findorff also self-performs trade work including carpentry concrete masonry drywall and steel erection. Among its projects is Madison Wisconsin's Children's Museum and the Overture Center for the Arts. It also built the Wisconsin Institutes for Discovery at The University of Wisconsin-Madison. John Findorff founded the company as J.H. Findorff in 1890.

	Annual Growth	09/05	09/06	09/08	09/11	09/12
Sales ($ mil.)	4.4%	-	248.4	322.0	209.2	320.9
Net income ($ mil.)	2.2%	-	-	3.8	0.3	4.1
Market value ($ mil.)	-	-	-	-	-	-
Employees	-	-	-	-	-	500

J. L. FRENCH AUTOMOTIVE CASTINGS INC.

3101 S. Taylor Dr.
Sheboygan WI 53081
Phone: 920-458-7724
Fax: 920-458-0140
Web: www.jlfrench.com

CEO: Tom Musgrave
CFO: -
HR: -
FYE: December 31
Type: Private

With a cast of customers like Ford General Motors Hyundai Nissan and Renault J. L. French Automotive Castings hopes to get rave reviews. The company provides automotive OEMs and Tier 1 suppliers with aluminum die-cast engine and drivetrain components such as brackets cam covers engine blocks front engine covers oil pans and transmission cases. It has supplied components for a number of Ford models (including such top sellers as the F-Series pickup and the Explorer SUV); it also makes parts for GM's Chevrolet trucks. The company has five manufacturing facilities in Asia Europe and North America. J. L. French's Allotech International subsidiary operates an aluminum smelter.

J. RAY MCDERMOTT INC.

757 N. Eldridge Pkwy.
Houston TX 77079-4526
Phone: 281-870-5000
Fax: 847-381-9424
Web: www.rosepacking.com

CEO: David D Ickson
CFO: -
HR: Cooper Ford
FYE: December 31
Type: Subsidiary

Deeply dependent on the oil industry J. Ray McDermott (JRM) is ocean-deep in projects to design fabricate and install platforms vessels and pipelines for offshore oil and gas production. A subsidiary of engineering group McDermott International the marine construction company's services include design fabrication and installation of spar platforms; design and installation of subsea facilities; design fabrication and installation of new and refurbished bottom-founded offshore platforms; and installation of offshore pipelines for the oil and gas industry. JRM operates a diversified fleet of vessels used for derrick work pipelaying and pipe burying.

J. WALTER THOMPSON COMPANY

466 Lexington Ave.
New York NY 10017-3176
Phone: 212-210-7000
Fax: 212-210-7770
Web: www.jwt.com

CEO: Bob Jeffrey
CFO: -
HR: -
FYE: December 31
Type: Subsidiary

J. Walter Thompson Company doing business as JWT is a leading advertising agency in the US and one of the largest in the world (along with McCann Worldgroup and BBDO Worldwide). It has provided creative ad development campaign management and strategic planning services to such clients as Ford Kimberly-Clark and Shell. JWT also offers brand development and specialized marketing services including customer relationship marketing event marketing and sponsorships. Its Digitaria unit provides digital and new media marketing services. JWT operates in almost 90 countries through more than 200 offices. Founded in 1864 it is one of the flagship agency networks of UK-based media conglomerate WPP.

J.D. ABRAMS L.P.

111 CONGRESS AVE STE 2400
AUSTIN, TX 787014298
Phone: 512-243-3317
Fax: -
Web: www.jdabrams.com

CEO: Jon F. Abrams
CFO: Kelly Gallagher
HR: -
FYE: December 31
Type: Private

J.D. Abrams builds the infrastructure that helps travelers drive across Texas. While highway and bridge construction projects from the Texas Department of Transportation make up the bulk of its construction work the civil engineering and construction firm also works on flood control dams reservoirs waterways railroad test track airport taxiways and other infrastructure projects in Texas and elsewhere in the Sun Belt. J.D. Abrams also operates two subsidiaries Transmountain Equipment and Austin Prestress which runs a concrete casting plant. Founded in 1966 the company operates from four Texas-based offices in Austin Dallas El Paso and Houston.

	Annual Growth	12/07	12/08	12/09	12/12	12/13
Sales ($ mil.)	29.3%	-	42.9	307.8	176.6	155.2
Net income ($ mil.)	-	-	-	15.0	(2.3)	(2.6)
Market value ($ mil.)	-	-	-	-	-	-
Employees	-	-	-	-	-	750

J.D. POWER AND ASSOCIATES INC.

2625 Townsgate Rd. Ste. 100
Westlake Village CA 91361
Phone: 805-418-8000
Fax: 805-418-8900
Web: www.jdpower.com

CEO: –
CFO: –
HR: –
FYE: December 31
Type: Subsidiary

They've got the power. Marketing information firm J.D. Power and Associates (best known for its car ratings) awards badges of excellence in dozens of categories based on yearly customer satisfaction surveys. Its studies are independently financed and then sold for use in marketing. Only top-rated performers can license the use of the awards. J.D. Power also provides its ratings for the financial home building and travel industries. In addition to surveys the firm offers forecasting and other market research services. J.D. Power has half a dozen offices in the US and another 11 internationally. The company was founded in 1968 by its namesake James D. Power III and is owned by publisher McGraw-Hill.

J.M. HUBER CORPORATION

499 Thornall St. 8th Fl.
Edison NJ 08837-2267
Phone: 732-549-8600
Fax: 732-549-7256
Web: www.huber.com

CEO: Mike Marberry
CFO: Michael L Marberry
HR: –
FYE: December 31
Type: Private

As great as toothpaste paint and tires may be J.M. Huber claims to make them even better. The company makes specialty additives and minerals used to thicken and improve the cleaning properties of toothpaste the brightness and gloss of paper the strength and durability of rubber and the flame-retardant properties of wire and cable. The diverse company also makes oriented strand board (a plywood substitute) explores for and produces oil and gas and provides technical and financial services. Huber also makes hydrocolloids (thickeners for gums) among other products through subsidiary CP Kelco.

J.E. DUNN CONSTRUCTION GROUP INC.

1001 Locust St.
Kansas City MO 64106
Phone: 816-474-8600
Fax: 816-391-2510
Web: www.jedunn.com

CEO: Gordon Lansford III
CFO: Beth Soukup
HR: –
FYE: December 31
Type: Private

Owned by descendants of founder John Ernest Dunn J.E. Dunn Construction Group operates as the holding company for a group of construction firms that includes flagship J.E. Dunn Construction and Atlanta-based R.J. Griffin & Company. Founded in 1924 it builds institutional commercial and industrial structures nationwide. It also provides construction and program management and design/build services. J.E. Dunn Construction which is among the largest US general builders was one of the first contractors to offer the construction management delivery method. Some of its major projects have included an IRS facility and the world headquarters for H&R Block both located in Kansas City Missouri.

J.R. SIMPLOT COMPANY

999 Main St. Ste. 1300
Boise ID 83702
Phone: 208-336-2110
Fax: 510-271-6493
Web: www.kaiserpermanente.org

CEO: William Whitacre
CFO: Annette Elg
HR: –
FYE: August 31
Type: Private

J.R. Simplot hopes you'll have fries with that. Potato potentate J. R. "Jack" Simplot simply shook hands with McDonald's pioneer Ray Kroc in the mid-1960s and his company's french fry sales have sizzled ever since. Simplot still remains the major french fry supplier for McDonald's and supplies Burger King and Wendy's as well. Along with potatoes J.R. Simplot produces fruits and vegetables under the RoastWorks and Simplot Classic labels. It owns and operates more than 82000 acres on some 40 farms located primarily in Idaho and Washington. It produces more than 3 billion pounds of frozen french fries and formed potatoes annually making it one of the world's largest processors of frozen potatoes.

J.H. HARVEY CO. LLC

727 S. Davis St.
Nashville GA 31639
Phone: 229-686-7654
Fax: 229-686-2927
Web: www.harveys-supermarkets.com

CEO: –
CFO: –
HR: –
FYE: December 31
Type: Subsidiary

The J.H. Harvey Co. operates about 70 Harveys Supermarkets mostly in Georgia but also in northern Florida and South Carolina. Founded in 1950 the regional grocery chain was acquired in 2003 by international food retailer Delhaize Group and became its Belgian parent's fourth US banner. Under Delhaize's ownership Harveys has grown with about 15 new stores added since the acquisition. The new stores belonged to the Food Lion supermarket chain (also owned by Delhaize) which were converted to the Harveys banner. Most Harveys stores are between 18000 and 35000 square feet. About a third of the grocery chain's Georgia stores have in-store phamacy departments.

J.W. CHILDS ASSOCIATES LIMITED PARTNERSHIP

111 Huntington Ave. Ste. 2900
Boston MA 02199-7610
Phone: 617-753-1100
Fax: 617-753-1101
Web: www.jwchilds.com

CEO: –
CFO: Todd Fitzpatrick
HR: –
FYE: December 31
Type: Private - Partnershi

J.W. Childs Associates (JWC) makes private equity investment look like mere child's play. Established in 1995 by Thomas H. Lee veteran John W. Childs the firm participates in friendly leveraged buyouts (LBOs) and recapitalizations of middle-market companies with strong brands and prospects for growth. It targets firms with enterprise values of $150 million to $600 million in North America and Asia focusing on the consumer products specialty retail asset management and health care sectors. JWC's portfolio includes about a dozen firms including CHG Healthcare Services NutraSweet Mattress Firm Sunny Delight Beverages specialty retailer Brookstone and menswear line Joseph Abboud.

JABIL CIRCUIT, INC.   NYS: JBL

10560 Dr. Martin Luther King, Jr. Street North
St. Petersburg, FL 33716
Phone: 727 577-9749
Fax: –
Web: www.jabil.com

CEO: Mark T. Mondello
CFO: Forbes I. J. Alexander
HR: Scott D. Slipy
FYE: August 31
Type: Public

Jabil Circuit makes a jabillion different kinds of electronics. The company is one of the leading providers of outsourced electronics manufacturing services (EMS) in the world. It makes electronics components and parts on a contract basis for computers smartphones printers and other consumer electronics as well as more complex specialized products for the aerospace automotive and healthcare industries. The company's services range from product design and component procurement to product testing order fulfillment and supply chain management. Jabil Circuit operates some 90 plants in about 25 countries across the Americas Asia and Europe.

	Annual Growth	08/11	08/12	08/13	08/14	08/15
Sales ($ mil.)	2.0%	16,518.8	17,151.9	18,336.5	15,762.1	17,899.2
Net income ($ mil.)	(7.1%)	381.1	394.7	371.5	241.3	284.0
Market value ($ mil.)	3.5%	3,236.3	4,375.3	4,383.0	4,144.8	3,716.5
Employees	7.4%	121,000	141,000	177,000	142,000	161,000

JACK COOPER TRANSPORT CO. INC.

2345 Grand Blvd. Ste. 400
Kansas City MO 64108
Phone: 816-983-4000
Fax: 816-983-5000
Web: www.jackcooper.com

CEO: Robert Griffin
CFO: –
HR: –
FYE: December 31
Type: Private

Your new car's journey from the factory to your garage might include a trip on a Jack Cooper Transport trailer. The company hauls motor vehicles from assembly plants ports and railway terminals to dealers and other locations across the US. Through its Jack Cooper Transport and Pacific Motor Trucking units the company moves more than 1 million new and used vehicles each year including cars light trucks and sport utility vehicles. It maintains a fleet of about 1200 tractor-trailer pairs. The company operates primarily in the western midwestern and southern US. Jack Cooper Transport is owned by Thom Cooper whose grandfather Jack Cooper founded the company in 1928.

JACK HENRY & ASSOCIATES, INC.   NMS: JKHY

663 Highway 60, P.O. Box 807
Monett, MO 65708
Phone: 417 235-6652
Fax: –
Web: www.jackhenry.com

CEO: John F. (Jack) Prim
CFO: Kevin D. Williams
HR: –
FYE: June 30
Type: Public

Jack Henry & Associates (JHA) provides integrated in-house and outsourced software systems for data processing to some 11300 banks credit unions and other financial services companies. Products include core processing systems electronic funds transfer (EFT) systems automated teller machine networking products digital check and document imaging systems Internet banking tools and customer relationship management (CRM) software. The company's three primary brands include Jack Henry Banking Symitar and ProfitStars. JHA also provides electronic bill payment services through iPay Technologies. It primarily serves small and midsized institutions in the US.

	Annual Growth	06/11	06/12	06/13	06/14	06/15
Sales ($ mil.)	6.8%	966.9	1,027.1	1,129.4	1,210.1	1,256.2
Net income ($ mil.)	11.3%	137.5	155.0	176.6	201.1	211.2
Market value ($ mil.)	21.2%	2,426.4	2,791.0	3,810.6	4,805.1	5,231.2
Employees	5.7%	4,667	4,872	5,139	5,499	5,822

JACK IN THE BOX, INC.   NMS: JACK

9330 Balboa Avenue
San Diego, CA 92123
Phone: 858 571-2121
Fax: –
Web: www.jackinthebox.com

CEO: Leonard A. (Lenny) Comma
CFO: Jerry P. Rebel
HR: Kathy Lama
FYE: September 27
Type: Public

Led by an affable "CEO" with a Ping-Pong ball for a head Jack in the Box is among the leading quick-service restaurant businesses in the US. The company operates and franchises about 2250 of its flagship hamburger outlets in California Texas and more than 20 other states. Jack in the Box offers such standard fast-food fare as burgers fries and soft drinks as well as salads tacos and breakfast items. About 415 locations are company-owned while the rest are franchised. In addition to its mainstay burger business the company runs a chain of more than 660 Qdoba Mexican Grill fast-casual eateries through its Qdoba Restaurant subsidiary.

	Annual Growth	10/11*	09/12	09/13	09/14	09/15
Sales ($ mil.)	(8.5%)	2,193.3	1,545.0	1,489.9	1,484.1	1,540.3
Net income ($ mil.)	7.8%	80.6	57.7	51.2	89.0	108.8
Market value ($ mil.)	41.4%	712.8	1,005.8	1,434.8	2,351.9	2,852.2
Employees	(5.3%)	25,700	22,100	19,310	19,150	20,700

*Fiscal year change

JACK MORTON WORLDWIDE INC.

142 Berkeley St.
Boston MA 02116
Phone: 617-585-7000
Fax: 617-585-7171
Web: www.jackmorton.com

CEO: Josh McCall
CFO: William Davis
HR: Cara Antonacci
FYE: December 31
Type: Subsidiary

Jack Morton Worldwide dramatizes marketing. The marketing firm stages more than 1000 multimedia events both live and virtual to promote clients' images and brands annually. It offers creative development planning speaker and entertainment arrangements video production staffing and logistics among other services. Clients have included such big names as Procter & Gamble General Motors eBay IBM and NBCUniversal. Jack Morton Worldwide has 15 offices spanning the US Europe and the Asia/Pacific. Founded by entertainment booking agent Jack Morton the company traces its roots back to 1939. It is a subsidiary of advertising and marketing services conglomerate Interpublic.

JACKSON COUNTY MEMORIAL HOSPITAL AUTHORITY

1200 E PECAN ST
ALTUS, OK 735216141
Phone: 580-482-4781
Fax: –
Web: www.jcmh.com

CEO: Steve Hartgraves
CFO: Nancy Davidson
HR: –
FYE: June 30
Type: Private

If you happen to get hobbled in Hollis get the gout in Gould get tripped up in Tipton or are ailing in Altus chances are your best bet for care is at Jackson County Memorial Hospital Trust Authority (JCMHTA). JCMHTA provides medical care to residents of Southwest Oklahoma and North Texas through its 150-bed Jackson County Memorial Hospital and 55-bed Tamarack Assisted Living Center an assisted-living facility. More than 20 specialized services include home health and hospice care emergency medicine pediatrics and orthopedics. The hospital also offers an outpatient same-day surgery unit a women's center a cancer center and an intensive care unit.

	Annual Growth	06/07	06/08	06/09	06/12	06/13
Sales ($ mil.)	0.5%	–	73.0	70.5	77.2	74.7
Net income ($ mil.)	(28.7%)	–	–	1.8	(1.5)	0.5
Market value ($ mil.)	–	–	–	–	–	–
Employees	–	–	–	–	–	800

JACKSON ELECTRIC MEMBERSHIP CORPORATION

850 COMMERCE RD
JEFFERSON, GA 305493329
Phone: 706-367-5281
Fax: –
Web: www.jacksonemc.com

CEO: Randall Pugh
CFO: Greg Keith
HR: Bill Ormsby
FYE: December 31
Type: Private

Jackson EMC distributes electricity to more than 197800 individual customers (more than 210200 meters) in 10 counties around Atlanta and in northeastern Georgia. The majority of customers are residential with commercial and industrial customers accounting for 42% of fiscal year 2013 revenues. One of the largest nonprofit power cooperatives in the US and the largest electric cooperative in Georgia Jackson EMC is owned by its members. The cooperative's generation and transmission partners include Oglethorpe Power Corp. Georgia Systems Operation and Georgia Transmission Corp.

	Annual Growth	05/10	05/11	05/12	05/13*	12/13
Sales ($ mil.)	1.0%	–	462.7	472.6	475.3	472.0
Net income ($ mil.)	–	–	–	21.9	21.8	0.0
Market value ($ mil.)	–	–	–	–	–	–
Employees	–	–	–	–	–	445

*Fiscal year change

JACKSON ENERGY AUTHORITY

119 E COLLEGE ST
JACKSON, TN 383016201
Phone: 731-422-7500
Fax: –
Web: www.jaxenergy.com

CEO: Danny Wheeler
CFO: –
HR: –
FYE: June 30
Type: Private

Jackson Energy Authority has the power and the authority to provide for all of Jackson Tennessee's energy needs. The municipal utility distributes electricity natural gas and water and provides wastewater services to about 40000 residential commercial and industrial customers in Jackson and surrounding areas. Jackson Energy also sells propane and offers broadband telecommunications services (cable Internet and telephone). Other services provided by Jackson Energy Authority include the sale of outdoor security lights surge protection systems gas grills and decorative lights.

	Annual Growth	06/09	06/10*	12/11*	06/13	06/14
Sales ($ mil.)	3.4%	–	218.6	243.2	244.0	250.3
Net income ($ mil.)	2.3%	–	–	23.0	22.7	24.6
Market value ($ mil.)	–	–	–	–	–	–
Employees	–	–	–	–	–	425

*Fiscal year change

JACKSON HEWITT TAX SERVICE INC.

3 Sylvan Way
Parsippany NJ 07054
Phone: 973-630-1040
Fax: 973-496-2785
Web: www.jacksonhewitt.com

CEO: –
CFO: Daniel N Chicoine
HR: –
FYE: April 30
Type: Private

For Jackson Hewitt there's no season like tax season. The tax preparer ranked #2 in the US behind H&R Block prepares tax returns for primarily low- and middle-income customers. Jackson Hewitt provides full-service individual federal and state income tax preparation through more than 6500 primarily franchised offices including 2800 locations within Wal-Mart Stores and mall kiosks. The firm's tax preparers which use its proprietary ProFiler decision-tree software filed more than 2 million tax returns in the fiscal year ended April 2010. Beset by heavy debt that followed aggressive expansion Jackson Hewitt filed for Chapter 11 bankruptcy protection in 2011 but emerged later that year.

JACKSON STATE UNIVERSITY

1400 J R LYNCH ST STE 206
JACKSON, MS 392170001
Phone: 601-979-2121
Fax: –
Web: www.jsums.edu

CEO: –
CFO: –
HR: Centrus Cilus
FYE: June 30
Type: Private

Jackson State University (JSU) is a public coeducational institution that offers more than 90 undergraduate and graduate degrees. It offers programs through five academic colleges covering business; education and human development; liberal arts; public service; and science technology and engineering. The historically black school now serves a diverse 9000-strong student body. JSU also operates the Mississippi Urban Research Center which analyzes and distributes information relating to public policies and activities that affect urban life. The school was founded as Natchez Seminary in 1877; after multiple name changes it became JSU in 1974 after achieving university status.

	Annual Growth	06/03	06/04	06/05	06/06	06/07
Sales ($ mil.)	–	–	–	0.0	114.8	112.2
Net income ($ mil.)	–	–	–	0.0	(11.9)	0.7
Market value ($ mil.)	–	–	–	–	–	–
Employees	–	–	–	–	–	2,000

JACKSONVILLE BANCORP INC (FL)   NAS: JAXB

100 North Laura Street, Suite 1000
Jacksonville, FL 32202
Phone: 904 421-3040
Fax: –
Web: www.jaxbank.com

CEO: Kendall L Spencer
CFO: Valerie A Kendall
HR: Aubree Rickerson
FYE: December 31
Type: Public

Need to stow some greenbacks in Jax? Check out Jacksonville Bancorp the holding company for Jacksonville Bank which has about 10 branches in and around Jacksonville Florida. The community bank offers standard deposit products including checking and savings accounts money market accounts CDs and IRAs. Commercial mortgages make up more than half of the bank's loan portfolio; residential mortgages account for most of the rest. Subsidiary Fountain Financial sells insurance and investment products. Ameris Bancorp agreed to buy the company in late 2015.

	Annual Growth	12/10	12/11	12/12	12/13	12/14
Assets ($ mil.)	(7.0%)	651.8	561.4	565.1	507.3	488.6
Net income ($ mil.)	–	(11.4)	(24.1)	(43.0)	(1.0)	1.9
Market value ($ mil.)	13.6%	42.8	18.3	4.6	73.0	71.2
Employees	(28.5%)	283	106	100	103	74

JACKSONVILLE BANCORP INC. (MD)   NAS: JXSB

1211 West Morton Avenue
Jacksonville, IL 62650
Phone: 217 245-4111
Fax: –
Web: www.jacksonvillesavings.com

CEO: Richard A Foss
CFO: Diana S Tone
HR: –
FYE: December 31
Type: Public

Jacksonville Bancorp (unaffiliated with the Florida corporation of the same name) is the holding company for Jacksonville Savings Bank which serves consumers and businesses in western Illinois through more than five offices including its Chapin State Bank First Midwest Savings Bank and Litchfield Community Savings divisions. The bank is mainly a real estate lender with residential commercial and agricultural mortgages accounting for more than half of its loan portfolio. Subsidiary Financial Resources Group offers investment and trust services. The company converted from a mutual holding company to a stock holding company structure in mid-2010.

	Annual Growth	12/10	12/11	12/12	12/13	12/14
Assets ($ mil.)	0.9%	301.5	307.3	321.4	318.4	311.9
Net income ($ mil.)	9.5%	2.1	3.3	3.6	3.2	3.0
Market value ($ mil.)	20.9%	19.4	24.7	31.2	35.2	41.4
Employees	(3.0%)	115	112	112	106	102

JACKSONVILLE JAGUARS LTD.

1 ALLTEL Stadium Place
Jacksonville FL 32202
Phone: 904-633-6000
Fax: 904-633-6050
Web: www.jaguars.com

CEO: –
CFO: Bill Prescott
HR: –
FYE: March 31
Type: Private

Gators might come to mind first when you think of Florida sports but these big cats have a following too. The Jacksonville Jaguars joined the National Football League as an expansion franchise in 1995 along with the Carolina Panthers. The team quickly gained respect by securing playoff berths the following four years but the Jags have struggled to be a consistent contender in the years since. The team plays host at Jacksonville Municipal Stadium. Wayne Weaver chairman and majority owner of retailer Shoe Carnival owns 48% of the team while a group of local businessmen owns the rest.

JACKSONVILLE UNIVERSITY

2800 UNIVERSITY BLVD N
JACKSONVILLE, FL 322113394
Phone: 904-256-8000
Fax: –
Web: www.ju.edu

CEO: –
CFO: –
HR: James V William
FYE: June 30
Type: Private

To become a jack of all knowledgeable trades you might head to Jacksonville University. The private liberal arts university has roughly 4000 students and offers 70 undergraduate and about 10 graduate programs through eight colleges and schools. Programs include business fine arts education nursing orthodontics math public policy health science and marine science. Its Accelerated Degree Program is designed for adults to complete a bachelor's degree without putting their career or family on hold.

	Annual Growth	06/07	06/08	06/09	06/10	06/13
Sales ($ mil.)	–	–	–	0.0	78.8	96.2	110.9
Net income ($ mil.)	–	–	–	–	0.0	2.0	0.4
Market value ($ mil.)	–	–	–	–	–	–
Employees	–	–	–	–	–	450

JACLYN INC.

PINK SHEETS: JCLY

197 W. Spring Valley Ave.
Maywood NJ 07607
Phone: 201-909-6000
Fax: 626-568-7144
Web: www.jacobs.com

CEO: Robert Chestnov
CFO: Anthony Christon
HR: –
FYE: February 28
Type: Public

Jaclyn has Jack and Jill covered. The company designs markets and distributes private-label children's wear and women's and some men's apparel. Jaclyn's apparel includes sleepwear loungewear and robes and infants' and children's play clothing marketed under the Jaclyn Apparel and Topsville labels. The company also supplies backpacks handbags cosmetic bags sport bags and travel bags some of which is used in creating promotional products for toiletries through its Premium Incentive and Bonnie Int'l divisions. The apparel and handbags made by outside contractors in Asia are sold in the US through mass merchandise department and specialty stores. Wal-Mart represents more than 40% of Jaclyn's sales.

JACO OIL COMPANY

3101 STATE RD
BAKERSFIELD, CA 933084931
Phone: 661-393-7000
Fax: –
Web: www.jaco.com

CEO: T J Jamieson
CFO: Brian Busacca
HR: –
FYE: December 31
Type: Private

Jaco Oil Company is jockeying for its piece of the convenience store pie. The company's Fastrip Food Stores subsidiary operates more than 50 convenience stores and gas stations primarily in and around Bakersfield California but also in Arizona. Besides offering customers traditional convenience-store fare which includes coffee milk beer snacks tobacco and the like the Fastrip chain stocks a full range of grocery items and provides in-store financial service centers. Financial services include check cashing payday loans wire transfer services via The Western Union Company refund anticipation loans and other services at many locations. Jaco Oil Company was founded in 1970.

	Annual Growth	12/07	12/08	12/10	12/11	12/12
Sales ($ mil.)	12.5%	–	517.8	644.7	794.7	829.7
Net income ($ mil.)	65.7%	–	–	10.5	21.0	28.7
Market value ($ mil.)	–	–	–	–	–	–
Employees	–	–	–	–	–	350

JACOBS ENGINEERING GROUP, INC.

NYS: JEC

155 North Lake Avenue
Pasadena, CA 91101
Phone: 626 578-3500
Fax: 626 568-7144
Web: www.jacobs.com

CEO: Steven J. Demetriou
CFO: Kevin C. Berryman
HR: Mark Cooper
FYE: October 02
Type: Public

Jacobs Engineering fuels its rise up the ladder with oil gas and chemicals. The group provides technical professional and construction services for industrial government and commercial clients primarily in the US the UK and Canada. Jacobs handles project design and engineering construction operations maintenance and scientific consultation. Typical projects include oil refineries manufacturing plants and roads and highways. The company's largest single customer is the US government (about 20% of revenues) for which it chiefly performs aerospace and defense work. Founded in 1947 Jacobs Engineering has more than 200 offices in more than 25 countries.

	Annual Growth	09/11	09/12	09/13	09/14*	10/15
Sales ($ mil.)	3.9%	10,381.7	10,893.8	11,818.4	12,695.2	12,114.8
Net income ($ mil.)	(2.2%)	331.0	379.0	423.1	328.1	303.0
Market value ($ mil.)	3.7%	3,976.6	4,979.1	7,117.0	6,118.2	4,605.9
Employees	0.8%	62,000	63,400	66,500	66,300	64,000

*Fiscal year change

JACOBS ENTERTAINMENT INC.

17301 W. Colfax Ave. Ste. 250
Golden CO 80401
Phone: 303-215-5200
Fax: 303-215-5219
Web: www.bhwk-hr.com

CEO: Jeffrey Jacobs
CFO: Brent Kramer
HR: –
FYE: December 31
Type: Private

Jacobs Entertainment wants you to come out and play. The company operates gaming properties in Colorado Louisiana Nevada and Virginia. Its portfolio includes five casinos: The Lodge Casino and The Gilpin Casino in Black Hawk Colorado and the Gold Dust West casinos in Reno Carson City and Elko Nevada. The firm also has about 20 truck stop video gaming facilities throughout Louisiana. In Virginia it has The Colonial Downs horseracing track which has ten satellite pari-mutuel wagering locations throughout the state. Chairman and CEO Jeffrey Jacobs is also responsible for the Nautica Entertainment Complex a development on the Cleveland Ohio waterfront. He owns Jacobs Entertainment through family trusts.

JACOBS FINANCIAL GROUP INC
NBB: JFGI

300 Summers Street, Suite 970
Charleston, WV 25301
Phone: 304 343-8171
Fax: –
Web: www.thejacobsfinancialgroup.com

CEO: John M Jacobs
CFO: John M Jacobs
HR: –
FYE: May 31
Type: Public

If Jacob needed to bond his ladder Jacobs Financial Group could provide the surety. Through subsidiaries Jacobs Financial provides surety and insurance as well as investment advisory services. The company's FS Investments (FSI) is a holding company that develops surety business by creating companies engaged in the issuance of surety bonds (bonds collateralized by accounts managed by Jacobs & Co.). FSI's wholly owned subsidiary Triangle Surety Agency specializes in placing surety bonds with insurance companies with an emphasis on clients in industries such as coal oil and gas. Jacobs Financial whose background is in energy has been expanding its insurance and surety operations through acquisitions.

	Annual Growth	05/09	05/10	05/11	05/12	05/13
Sales ($ mil.)	3.0%	1.2	1.4	1.6	1.8	1.3
Net income ($ mil.)	–	(1.4)	(1.5)	(1.3)	(1.1)	(2.0)
Market value ($ mil.)	(34.3%)	14.5	1.0	2.0	0.9	2.7
Employees	(3.8%)	7	7	7	7	6

JACOBS MALCOLM & BURTT

18 CROW CANYON CT STE 210
SAN RAMON, CA 945831786
Phone: 415-285-0400
Fax: –

CEO: –
CFO: –
HR: –
FYE: December 31
Type: Private

Jacobs Malcolm & Burtt may sound like a law office but the only argument this company would make is to eat your vegetables. The firm is a California-based wholesaler and distributor of fruits and vegetables such as asparagus oranges and berries. Jacobs and Malcolm founded the company in 1888 and Burtt joined the name in 1969. Leo Rolandelli owns 50% of the capital stock the Wilson Family Trust owns 31% and the rest is controlled by the other officers.

	Annual Growth	12/09	12/10	12/11	12/12	12/13
Sales ($ mil.)	(10.4%)	–	78.1	72.3	57.3	56.1
Net income ($ mil.)	34.6%	–	–	0.1	0.2	0.2
Market value ($ mil.)	–	–	–	–	–	–
Employees	–	–	–	–	–	31

JACOBSEN CONSTRUCTION COMPANY INC.

3131 W. 2210 South
Salt Lake City UT 84119
Phone: 801-973-0500
Fax: 801-973-7496
Web: www.jacobsenconstruction.com

CEO: –
CFO: –
HR: –
FYE: December 31
Type: Private

Jacobsen Construction Company helps to build a strong foundation. The company performs design/build services and general contracting for medical and medical research commercial hospitality institutional residential manufacturing and industrial construction projects mainly in the western US and Mexico. Jacobsen Construction performs earthwork concrete work structural steel and metals erection carpentry and the setting of industrial equipment. The company which is employee-owned makes most of its revenue from negotiated work and from work awarded in negotiated selection processes. Soren Jacobsen founded the enterprise in Salt Lake City in 1922.

JACUZZI BRANDS CORP.

13925 City Center Dr. Ste. 200
Chino Hills CA 91709
Phone: 909-247-2920
Fax: 408-746-5060
Web: solutions.us.fujitsu.com

CEO: Bob Rowen
CFO: Jeffrey B Park
HR: –
FYE: September 30
Type: Private

If hot tubs really were time machines Jacuzzi would be the name brand of hydrotherapeutic time travel. For more than 50 years Jacuzzi Brands has made the eponymous jetted baths spas and showers that soothe the aches and pains of residential and commercial customers around the world. Besides hot tubs baths and showers Jacuzzi also offers luxury mattresses bedding and accessories. The company's bath division also makes toilets sinks and accessories such as bath pillows towel warmers and radiant floor heating systems. Investment firm Apollo Management owns Jacuzzi Brands.

JAGGED PEAK INC.
OTC: JGPK

3000 Bayport Dr. Ste. 250
Tampa FL 33607
Phone: 813-637-6900
Fax: 800-749-4998
Web: www.jaggedpeak.com

CEO: Paul Demirdjian
CFO: Albert Narvades
HR: Jennifer Novak
FYE: December 31
Type: Public

Jagged Peak rises up to help customers reach the peak of supply chain management. The company's E-Business Dynamic Global Engine (EDGE) software is a ready-to-use Web-based application that captures processes and distributes orders from multiple sources sending them in real-time to warehouses. With automated purchases and orders companies can streamline their supply chain processes to improve delivery reduce costs and integrate inventory information. Jagged Peak took its present form in 2005 when publicly traded Absolute Glass Protection acquired the private company and adopted its name officers and operations.

JAKKS PACIFIC INC.
NMS: JAKK

2951 28th Street
Santa Monica, CA 90405
Phone: 424 268-9444
Fax: –

CEO: –
CFO: Joel M. Bennett
HR: Elsa Morgan
FYE: December 31
Type: Public

JAKKS Pacific is a big wheel in toys. The maker of The Original Big Wheel JAKKS is one of the US's top toy companies. It makes and sells action figures (including licenses for Pokémon Ultimate Fighting Champion) die-cast and plastic cars electronic games dolls (such as Cabbage Patch Kids Fancy Nancy) pool toys and floats Halloween costumes and dress-up products children's indoor and outdoor furniture and pet toys (including American Kennel Club Cat Fanciers Association). Its playthings and other products are sold to US mass merchandisers such as Target Toys "R" Us and Wal-Mart; drugstores; supermarkets; and warehouse clubs. The US is the company's largest market.

	Annual Growth	12/10	12/11	12/12	12/13	12/14
Sales ($ mil.)	2.0%	747.3	677.8	666.8	632.9	810.1
Net income ($ mil.)	(17.8%)	47.0	8.5	(104.8)	(53.9)	21.5
Market value ($ mil.)	(21.8%)	413.3	320.0	284.0	152.4	154.2
Employees	(1.4%)	828	865	828	758	783

JAMAICA HOSPITAL MEDICAL CENTER

8900 Van Wyck Expy.
Jamaica NY 11418
Phone: 718-206-6000
Fax: 718-206-8673
Web: www.jamaicahospital.org

CEO: Bruce Flanz
CFO: Mounir F Doss
HR: –
FYE: December 31
Type: Subsidiary

Jamaica Hospital Medical Center has been operating (so to speak) in the Queens Borough of New York since before the nation of Jamaica even was born. Originally founded in 1892 the hospital serves Queens and eastern Brooklyn with general medical pediatric psychiatric and ambulatory services. The facility has about 380 beds. The hospital's specialty services include a coma recovery unit a dialysis center a psychiatric emergency department a rehabilitation center as well as a traumatic brain injury recovery unit. The hospital also operates a nursing home with more than 220 beds as well as a network of family health clinics. Jamaica Hospital Medical Center is a subsidiary of MediSys Health Network.

JAMES R. GLIDEWELL DENTAL CERAMICS INC.

4141 MacArthur Blvd.
Newport Beach CA 92660
Phone: 949-440-2600
Fax: 800-411-9722
Web: www.glidewelldental.com

CEO: James R Glidewell
CFO: Glenn Sasaki
HR: Stephanie Goddard
FYE: December 31
Type: Private

James R. Glidewell Dental Ceramics known by its dba Glidewell Laboratories makes a wide range of restorative reconstructive and cosmetic dental products such as crowns dentures and bridges. Its BDL Prosthetics division makes aesthetic temporary teeth (known as BioTemps) used for provisional restoration until final ceramic restorations are ready. It employs a mail-order business model by which dentists send in dental impressions and receive custom restorative products via the US Postal Service or FedEx. Another unit Glidewell Direct sells clinical and lab products including impression materials via its e-commerce site. Glidewell Laboratories also offers snoring and sleep apnea treatment products.

JAMBA INC   NMS: JMBA

6475 Christie Avenue, Suite 150
Emeryville, CA 94608
Phone: 510 596-0100
Fax: –

CEO: David A. (Dave) Pace
CFO: Karen L. Luey
HR: –
FYE: December 30
Type: Public

This company is blending up business with its fruit-filled drinks. Jamba operates the Jamba Juice chain the leading outlet for blended fruit drinks with about 875 smoothie stands throughout the US and in a handful of other countries. Its menu includes more than 30 varieties of custom smoothies (including Aloha Pineapple Mango-a-go-go and Strawberry Surf Rider) and Jamba Boosts (smoothies made with vitamin and protein supplements) along with other fruit juices and food items. Jamba Juice locations include freestanding units as well as on-site kiosks in high traffic areas including college campuses gyms and airports.

	Annual Growth	12/10*	01/12	01/13*	12/13	12/14
Sales ($ mil.)	(4.5%)	262.7	226.4	228.8	229.2	218.0
Net income ($ mil.)	–	(16.7)	(8.3)	0.3	2.1	(3.6)
Market value ($ mil.)	58.0%	38.9	21.9	37.1	205.9	242.4
Employees	(8.1%)	5,900	4,900	4,300	4,000	4,200

*Fiscal year change

JAMES RIVER COAL CO   NMS: JRCC

901 E. Byrd Street, Suite 1600
Richmond, VA 23219
Phone: 804 780-3000
Fax: –
Web: www.jamesrivercoal.com

CEO: Peter T Socha
CFO: –
HR: –
FYE: December 31
Type: Public

James River keeps the coal flowing. The company operates about 40 mines in Kentucky and West Virginia (in the Central Appalachian Basin) and Indiana (in the Illinois Basin) that produce more than 10 million tons of coal annually. Though a small percentage of the coal it sells comes from independent operators and third-party producers the vast majority of James River's coal is produced from company-operated mines. It controls approximately 362.8 million tons of proved and probable reserves (92% in Appalachia). The company sell its coal to power station in the southern US and to steel producers around the world.

	Annual Growth	12/08	12/09	12/10	12/11	12/12
Sales ($ mil.)	17.9%	568.5	681.6	701.1	1,177.7	1,099.6
Net income ($ mil.)	–	(96.0)	51.0	78.2	(39.1)	(138.9)
Market value ($ mil.)	(32.4%)	549.8	663.2	908.5	248.2	115.1
Employees	4.9%	1,751	1,736	1,746	2,405	2,124

JAMES MADISON UNIVERSITY INC.

800 S MAIN ST
HARRISONBURG, VA 228070002
Phone: 540-568-6211
Fax: –
Web: www.jmu.edu

CEO: –
CFO: John Knight
HR: Kendall Capps
FYE: June 30
Type: Private

James Madison is known as the Father of the Constitution and America's fourth president but he also has a public institution of higher education named after him. James Madison University (JMU) offers some 70 undergraduate and 40 graduate degrees through more than a half-dozen colleges including arts and letters business education visual and performing arts and science and mathematics. The university enrolls about 20000 students mostly undergrads with a faculty of 1200 teachers and a student-to-faculty ratio of 16:1. JMU also has extensive men's and women's athletic programs. JMU was established in 1908 in Harrisonburg Virginia.

	Annual Growth	06/07	06/08	06/11	06/13	06/14
Sales ($ mil.)	5.7%	–	270.4	323.3	365.0	377.7
Net income ($ mil.)	3.4%	–	–	56.5	71.7	62.5
Market value ($ mil.)	–	–	–	–	–	–
Employees	–	–	–	–	–	1,700

JANEL CORP   NBB: JANL

303 Merrick Road, Suite 400
Lynbrook, NY 11563
Phone: 718 527-3800
Fax: 718 527-1689
Web: www.janelgroup.net

CEO: Brendan J Killackey
CFO: Brian Aronson
HR: –
FYE: September 30
Type: Public

Janel World Trade puts it all together for customers that ship by air land or sea. The freight forwarding and logistics management company gets lower bulk shipping rates for its clients by consolidating cargo headed to the same destination. Janel also provides customs brokerage warehousing and distribution and other logistics services. The company primarily handles clothing and textiles household appliances machinery and machine parts and sporting goods shipped to and from the US Europe and the Far East. In addition to offices in the US Janel has franchise operations in China Guatemala Honduras Hong Kong and Thailand; the company works with agents in other parts of the world.

	Annual Growth	09/11	09/12	09/13	09/14	09/15
Sales ($ mil.)	(6.7%)	98.5	98.7	44.7	47.9	74.7
Net income ($ mil.)	–	(0.7)	(2.7)	(2.2)	(0.3)	0.6
Market value ($ mil.)	93.4%	0.1	0.0	0.0	0.0	1.4
Employees	8.1%	79	78	52	75	108

JANSSEN BIOTECH INC.

800 Ridgeview Rd.
Horsham PA 19044
Phone: 610-651-6000
Fax: 610-651-6100
Web: www.janssenbiotech.com

CEO: –
CFO: –
HR: –
FYE: December 31
Type: Subsidiary

Janssen Biotech (formerly Centocor Ortho Biotech) has ways of making your immune system behave itself. The Johnson & Johnson (J&J) subsidiary makes blockbuster biotech drug Remicade a monoclonal antibody used to treat a number of autoimmune conditions or diseases in which the body's immune system attacks its own tissues. It is approved in the US and Europe for several indications including Crohn's disease rheumatoid arthritis ulcerative colitis psoriasis arthritis and ankylosing spondylitis (a type of arthritis of the spine). The company also makes anemia therapy Procrit oncology drugs Doxil and Zytiga psoriasis drug Stelara and rheumatoid arthritis drug Simponi.

JANSSEN PHARMACEUTICALS INC.

1125 Trenton-Harbourton Rd.
Titusville NJ 08560-0200
Phone: 609-730-2000
Fax: 609-730-2323
Web: www.janssenpharmaceuticalsinc.com

CEO: William C Weldon
CFO: Joseph Bondi
HR: –
FYE: December 31
Type: Subsidiary

Janssen Pharmaceuticals jaunts across the drug market offering therapeutics for mental health neurology pain management infectious disease and a number of other ailments. A US-based arm of Johnson & Johnson's global pharmaceuticals segment the company's offerings include Risperdal for schizophrenia anti-infective Levaquin ADHD drug Concerta acid reflux medication Aciphex pain medicine Nucynta and contraceptive Ortho Evra. Janssen Pharmaceuticals markets its products in the US through a direct sales force to doctors and pharmacies as well as through wholesale distributors.

JANUS CAPITAL GROUP INC   NYS: JNS

151 Detroit Street
Denver, CO 80206
Phone: 303 333-3863
Fax: –
Web: www.janus.com

CEO: Richard M. (Dick) Weil
CFO: Jennifer J. McPeek
HR: Tiphani Krueger
FYE: December 31
Type: Public

Named after the Roman god with two faces Janus Capital Group provides investment management and advisory services for institutional and individual customers. Known for its intensive equities research the company manages dozens of mutual funds including its flagship Janus Fund (formed in 1969) as well as separate accounts and sub-advised portfolios. Subsidiary INTECH manages institutional portfolios by utilizing investment strategies based on mathematical analysis of the stock market while Perkins Investment Management focuses on long-term value investments. All told Janus Capital and its subsidiaries have $183 billion of assets under management.

	Annual Growth	12/10	12/11	12/12	12/13	12/14
Sales ($ mil.)	(1.6%)	1,015.7	981.9	850.0	873.9	953.2
Net income ($ mil.)	(0.9%)	159.9	142.9	102.3	114.7	154.4
Market value ($ mil.)	5.6%	2,401.4	1,168.3	1,577.5	2,290.3	2,986.5
Employees	2.0%	1,119	1,125	1,156	1,194	1,209

JARDEN CORP   NYS: JAH

1800 North Military Trail
Boca Raton, FL 33431
Phone: 561 447-2520
Fax: –
Web: www.jarden.com

CEO: James E. (Jim) Lillie
CFO: Alan W. (Al) Lefevre
HR: –
FYE: December 31
Type: Public

More than 120 brands of consumer products for inside and outside the home make Jarden beam. It makes a wide variety of branded consumer products including Sunbeam and Oster appliances Coleman outdoor gear and First Alert home safety products. It also makes Ball canning jars Diamond matches and plastic cutlery Loew-Cornell art supplies K2 snowboards and Bee and Bicycle brand playing cards. Jarden sells its products primarily to retailers such as Wal-Mart Dick's Sporting Goods and Target. It also supplies copper-plated zinc penny blanks to the US Mint and the Royal Canadian Mint. To further diversify its products portfolio Jarden acquired The Yankee Candle Co. in 2013.

	Annual Growth	12/10	12/11	12/12	12/13	12/14
Sales ($ mil.)	8.3%	6,022.7	6,679.9	6,696.1	7,355.9	8,287.1
Net income ($ mil.)	22.8%	106.7	204.7	243.9	203.9	242.5
Market value ($ mil.)	11.6%	5,927.0	5,737.0	9,926.4	11,779.2	9,193.0
Employees	8.3%	24,000	23,000	25,000	33,000	33,000

JASON INCORPORATED

411 E. Wisconsin Ave. Ste. 2120
Milwaukee WI 53202
Phone: 414-277-9300
Fax: 414-277-9445
Web: www.jasoninc.com

CEO: –
CFO: Steve Cripe
HR: –
FYE: December 31
Type: Private

Whether you're making the Sturgis run or just mowing your lawn Jason Incorporated adds cush to your tush. The company's Motor Vehicle products segment has supplied seats for Harley-Davidson motorcycles since the 1930s; it also makes seats for lawn care construction and agricultural equipment makers such as John Deere. This unit also makes fiber insulation for the automotive industry. The company's Industrial segment makes such products as power brushes buffing wheels assembly processes and metal and wire components. Investors in Jason include the company's management team and private equity firm Saw Mill Capital. Jason has operations in the US and 11 countries.

JASON INDUSTRIES, INC   NAS: JASN

411 East Wisconsin Avenue, Suite 2100
Milwaukee, WI 53202
Phone: 414 277-9300
Fax: –
Web: www.jasoninc.com

CEO: Jeffry N Quinn
CFO: Sarah C Sutton
HR: –
FYE: December 31
Type: Public

Whether you're making the Sturgis run or just mowing your lawn Jason Incorporated makes sure you are on a easy rider. The company's Seating businesses segment has supplied seats for Harley-Davidson motorcycles since the 1930s; it also makes seats for lawn care construction and agricultural equipment makers such as John Deere. This unit also makes fiber insulation for the automotive industry. The company's Components and Finishing segments make such products as power brushes buffing wheels assembly processes industrial machine tools and metal and wire components. It agreed to be acquired by Quinpario Acquisition Corp (QPAC) for $539 million in 2014.

	Annual Growth	12/11	12/12	12/13*	06/14*	12/14
Sales ($ mil.)	–	0.0	0.0	–	377.2	325.3
Net income ($ mil.)	–	0.0	0.0	(0.5)	(5.0)	(11.6)
Market value ($ mil.)	–	0.0	0.0	222.1	231.3	216.6
Employees	79900.0%	–	–	5	–	4,000

*Fiscal year change

JASPER ENGINE EXCHANGE INC.

815 Wernsing Rd.
Jasper IN 47546
Phone: 812-482-1041
Fax: 812-634-1820
Web: www.jasperengines.com

CEO: Douglas Bawel
CFO: –
HR: –
FYE: December 31
Type: Private

The maxim "one man's junk is another man's treasure" is a saying Jasper Engine Exchange (dba Jasper Engines & Transmissions; JASPER) takes to the bank. The company is a remanufacturer of automotive drive train parts. JASPER takes worn out auto parts or "cores" and remanufactures them for sale to the automotive aftermarket. Products remanufactured by the company include gasoline and diesel engines transmissions and differentials (gears axel assemblies). It also remanufactures high-performance engines and transmissions marine engines alternative fuel engines and electric motors. Jasper Engine Exchange was founded in 1942 by Alvin Ruxer.

JAVELIN MORTGAGE INVESTMENT CORP   NYS: JMI

3001 Ocean Drive, Suite 201
Vero Beach, FL 32963
Phone: 772 617-4340
Fax: –

CEO: Scott J Ulm
CFO: James R Mountain
HR: –
FYE: December 31
Type: Public

JAVELIN Mortgage Investment is looking to spearhead a new effort in mortgage-related investments. The company formed in June 2012 as a real estate investment trust (REIT) with plans to invest in mortgage securities backed by government-supported enterprises such as Fannie Mae Freddie Mac and Ginnie Mae as well as other mortgage securities. As a REIT JAVELIN Mortgage Investment will be exempt from paying federal income tax as long as it makes a quarterly distribution to shareholders. It will be externally managed by ARMOUR Residential Management LLC the same external manager of sister company ARMOUR Residential REIT Inc. The company went public in 2012.

	Annual Growth	12/10	12/11	12/12	12/13	12/14
Sales ($ mil.)	–	0.0	0.0	8.4	(31.0)	(8.0)
Net income ($ mil.)	–	0.0	0.0	6.1	(43.8)	(21.8)
Market value ($ mil.)	–	0.0	0.0	228.8	167.0	124.3
Employees	–	–	–	–	–	–

JAVO BEVERAGE COMPANY INC.

1311 Specialty Dr.
Vista CA 92081-8521
Phone: 760-560-5286
Fax: 760-560-5287
Web: www.javobeverage.com

CEO: Stanley L Greanias
CFO: Richard A Gartrell
HR: –
FYE: December 31
Type: Private

Javo puts the S-Q-U-E-E-Z-E on coffee. Javo Beverage Company makes and markets coffee and tea concentrates drink mixes iced and hot ready-to-drink beverages and flavor and dispenser systems. Its national and international customers do business in the retail health care oil food and beverage manufacturing and food service industries. Of note is Javo's line of "bag-in-a-box" products that allows restaurants hotels and hospitals to offer fresh-tasting coffee without having to do any actual brewing. In May 2011 Javo emerged from Chapter 11 — after four months in bankruptcy — as a private company; it is majority owned by Coffee Holdings an affiliate of Falconhead Capital.

JAYCO INC.

903 S. Main St.
Middlebury IN 46540
Phone: 574-825-5861
Fax: 574-825-6062
Web: www.jayco.com

CEO: Derald Bontrager
CFO: Kent Yoder
HR: –
FYE: August 31
Type: Private

Jayco's motto could be "have trailer will travel." The company develops and manufactures its line of camping trailers light-weight trailers park and travel trailers fifth-wheels toy haulers and motor homes and markets them through a network of about 300 authorized dealers in the US and Canada. It also makes and distributes aftermarket parts. Product brand names include Eagle Greyhawk Jay Feather Jay Flight Jay Series Sport and Octane ZX. The company also offers roadside assistance through membership to its Customer First program. Chairman and CEO Wilbur Bontrager and his family own Jayco. His father the late Lloyd Bontrager founded the company in 1968 in two chicken houses and a barn.

JDA SOFTWARE GROUP INC.   NASDAQ: JDAS

14400 N. 87th St.
Scottsdale AZ 85260-3649
Phone: 480-308-3000
Fax: 480-308-3001
Web: www.jda.com

CEO: Baljit Dail
CFO: Peter S Hathaway
HR: –
FYE: December 31
Type: Private

JDA Software Group makes software that helps companies manage their supply chains. It offers integrated supply chain planning and execution software as well as a comprehensive set of services to help companies manage everything from raw materials to delivery of finished products. Its services include cloud consulting education and support. JDA Software Group serves a wide variety of industries and companies of all sizes with a particular focus on retail companies like Dr Pepper Snapple Group Kraft Foods and OfficeMax. Manufacturers distributors and logistics service providers are also among its customer base. In December 2012 JDA Software Group was acquired by RedPrairie in a $1.9 billion deal.

JEA

21 W. Church St.
Jacksonville FL 32202
Phone: 904-665-6000
Fax: 904-665-7008
Web: www.jea.com

CEO: Paul McElroy
CFO: –
HR: –
FYE: September 30
Type: Government-owned

As long as sparks are flying in Jacksonville everything is A-OK with JEA. The community-owned not-for-profit utility provides electricity to 420000 customers in Jacksonville and surrounding areas in northeastern Florida. Managing an electric system that dates back to 1895 JEA has a net generating capacity of 3760 MW. It owns an electric system with five primarily fossil-fueled generating plants. JEA also gets 12.8 MW of generating capacity from two methane-fueled landfill plants. The company resells electricity to other utilities including NextEra Energy. JEA also provides water and wastewater services; it serves 300000 water customers and 230000 wastewater customers.

JEFFERSON BANCSHARES INC (TN)

NMS: JFBI

120 Evans Avenue
Morristown, TN 37814
Phone: 423-586-8421
Fax: –
Web: www.jeffersonfederal.com

CEO: –
CFO: –
HR: –
FYE: June 30
Type: Public

Here's a Tennessee bank that will definitely volunteer its services. Jefferson Bancshares is the holding company for Jefferson Federal Bank which has about a dozen locations in eastern parts of the Volunteer State. Founded in 1963 the bank serves individuals and businesses in Hamblen Knox Sullivan and Washington counties offering standard services such as checking and savings accounts CDs and IRAs. Lending activities primarily consist of commercial real estate loans and one- to four-family residential mortgages which together account for a majority of the company's loan portfolio. In 2008 Jefferson Bancshares acquired State of Franklin Bancshares a community bank hurt by the national mortgage crisis.

	Annual Growth	06/09	06/10	06/11	06/12	06/13
Assets ($ mil.)	(6.7%)	662.7	630.8	561.2	522.9	503.0
Net income ($ mil.)	(11.8%)	2.6	(24.0)	0.0	(4.0)	1.6
Market value ($ mil.)	(1.9%)	40.2	26.3	21.4	16.2	37.3
Employees	(4.9%)	175	155	146	142	143

JEFFERSON HEALTH SYSTEM INC.

259 N RADNOR CHESTER RD # 290
RADNOR, PA 19087-5240
Phone: 610-225-6200
Fax: –
Web: www.jeffersonhealth.org

CEO: Joseph Sebastianelli
CFO: Kirk E Gorman
HR: –
FYE: June 30
Type: Private

This health care system's freedom-loving namesake might approve of its work to preserve the people's freedom of choice in health care. Jefferson Health System is a not-for-profit network that includes three health systems with hospitals specialty clinics and other medical facilities serving communities in the greater Philadelphia area. Members include the Thomas Jefferson University Hospital family (one of the system's founders) Main Line Health (the other founding organization) and Magee Rehabilitation. The Jefferson network has some 2435 beds and 3400 medical staff members and is affiliated with Thomas Jefferson University.

	Annual Growth	06/09	06/10	06/11	06/12	06/13
Sales ($ mil.)	1.6%	–	–	2,950.7	3,101.8	3,047.3
Net income ($ mil.)	5.7%	–	–	422.9	(28.3)	472.1
Market value ($ mil.)	–	–	–	–	–	–
Employees	–	–	–	–	–	17,485

JEFFERSON HOMEBUILDERS INC.

501 N MAIN ST
CULPEPER, VA 227012607
Phone: 540-825-5898
Fax: –
Web: www.culpeperwood.com

CEO: Joseph R. (Joe) Daniel
CFO: –
HR: –
FYE: September 30
Type: Private

Culpeper Wood Preservers may sound like the name of an environmental non-profit but this Virginia-based building materials supplier has more commercial interests in mind. The company manufactures and distributes pressure-treated lumber from plants located in the midwestern and northeastern US (pressure treating protects wood from damage by moisture and insects). Products include standard dimensional lumber decking boards plywood and timbers. The company also makes such specialty products as deck accessories lattice fencing moulded products and landscaping items.

	Annual Growth	09/03	09/04	09/05	09/06	09/07
Sales ($ mil.)	(58.5%)	–	–	912.5	166.0	157.2
Net income ($ mil.)	19522.0%	–	–	0.0	5.1	3.2
Market value ($ mil.)	–	–	–	–	–	–
Employees	–	–	–	–	–	177

JEFFERSON HOSPITAL ASSOCIATION INC.

1600 W 40TH AVE
PINE BLUFF, AR 716036301
Phone: 870-541-7100
Fax: –
Web: www.davislifecare.org

CEO: –
CFO: Nathan Van Genderan
HR: Steve Beckman
FYE: June 30
Type: Private

Jefferson Regional Medical Center (JRMC) provides acute care and other health services to residents of Pine Bluff and an 11-county area of southern Arkansas. The not-for-profit community-owned hospital has about 470 acute care beds and offers general medical and surgical care as well as services in a range of specialties including urology orthopedics cardiology and oncology. It also has a 25-bed skilled nursing unit that cares for patients transitioning to long-term care or home care. A network of clinics offers outpatient surgery diagnostic imaging wound care and other ambulatory health services. Additionally the health system operates a nursing school and home health and hospice agencies.

	Annual Growth	06/06	06/07	06/09	06/10	06/13
Sales ($ mil.)	–	–	(941.2)	5.5	199.0	180.6
Net income ($ mil.)	–	–	–	(4.7)	11.2	0.3
Market value ($ mil.)	–	–	–	–	–	–
Employees	–	–	–	–	–	1,700

JEFFERSON REGIONAL MEDICAL CENTER

565 COAL VALLEY RD
CLAIRTON, PA 15025-3703
Phone: 412-469-5000
Fax: –
Web: www.jeffersonregional.com

CEO: John J Dempster
CFO: Joanne Hachey
HR: Jan R Jennings
FYE: June 30
Type: Private

Jefferson Regional Medical Center serves the South Hills area of Pittsburgh. The hospital has about 370 beds. In addition to primary care Jefferson Regional Medical Center offers such specialized services as a heart institute for treating cardiovascular conditions and a physical rehabilitation and sports medicine center. Its emergency department treats more than 55000 patients each year. Jefferson Regional Medical Center also provides home health care and emergency helicopter transportation services and it operates nearby outpatient clinics and physician offices.

	Annual Growth	06/05	06/06	06/07	06/08	06/09
Sales ($ mil.)	(65.7%)	–	–	1,737.0	216.5	204.8
Net income ($ mil.)	–	–	–	0.0	(19.6)	(19.2)
Market value ($ mil.)	–	–	–	–	–	–
Employees	–	–	–	–	–	2,000

JEFFERSONVILLE BANCORP

NBB: JFBC

4866 State Rte. 52
Jeffersonville, NY 12748
Phone: 845-482-4000
Fax: –
Web: www.jeffbank.com

CEO: Wayne V Zanetti
CFO: John A Russell
HR: –
FYE: December 31
Type: Public

Jeffersonville Bancorp is the holding company for The First National Bank of Jeffersonville. The bank serves businesses and consumers through about 10 locations in southeastern New York's Sullivan County. First National Bank of Jeffersonville offers such standard retail services as demand deposit savings and money market accounts; NOW accounts; CDs; and IRAs to fund a variety of loans. Nearly 40% of the bank's loan portfolio consists of residential mortgages while commercial mortgages account for another 35%. The bank also provides home equity business consumer construction and agricultural loans.

	Annual Growth	12/10	12/11	12/12	12/13	12/14
Assets ($ mil.)	0.5%	430.8	433.5	429.1	432.5	440.2
Net income ($ mil.)	22.3%	3.1	3.9	4.4	4.6	7.0
Market value ($ mil.)	5.8%	44.5	43.4	46.6	47.6	55.7
Employees	(20.4%)	131	125	83	–	–

JEL SERT CO.

Rte. 59 and Conde St.
West Chicago IL 60185
Phone: 630-231-7590
Fax: 630-231-3993
Web: www.jelsert.com

CEO: Gary Ricco
CFO: –
HR: –
FYE: October 31
Type: Private

Just call Jel Sert Company the king of freezer pops. The company made its name in the early 1960s with its popular Pop-Ice "stick 'em in the freezer and squeeze 'em out of the tube" treats. Since then it has expanded its products portfolio to include Flavor-Aid and Wyler's powdered drink mixes; Fla-Vor-Ice Otter Pops and Wyler's Italian Ice freezer pops; and MONDO Fruit Squeezers fruit drinks. Jel Sert also makes My*T*Fine and Royal pudding mixes purchased from Nabisco. The company offers contract manufacturing services. Its products are available throughout the US and Canada. Founded in 1926 Jel Sert is still owned by the Wegner family; Charles Wegner (grandson of the founder) is chairman.

JELD-WEN INC.

3250 Lakeport Blvd.
Klamath Falls OR 97601
Phone: 541-882-3451
Fax: 541-885-7454
Web: www.jeld-wen.com

CEO: Kirk Hachigian
CFO: L Brooks Mallard
HR: David Sheil
FYE: December 31
Type: Private

JELD-WEN's business strategy is open and shut. A leading maker of windows and doors the company offers aluminum vinyl and wood windows; interior and exterior doors; garage doors; swinging and sliding patio doors; and door frames and moldings. Tracing its roots to 1960 the company operates more than 100 manufacturing and distribution sites and sells its products in some 20 countries mainly in the Americas Asia Europe and Australia. In late 2011 Canadian private equity firm Onex invested more than $870 million in JELD-WEN gaining a nearly 60% stake in the company.

JELLY BELLY CANDY COMPANY

1 Jelly Belly Ln.
Fairfield CA 94533-6741
Phone: 707-428-2800
Fax: 707-423-4436
Web: www.jellybelly.com

CEO: Robert M Simpson Jr
CFO: –
HR: –
FYE: March 31
Type: Private

This company has cheesecake buttered popcorn orange sherbet and jalape?o on the menu — who could ask for anything more? You could and can. The Jelly Belly Candy Company makes Jelly Belly jelly beans in 50 "official" flavors with new and sometimes startlingly flavored (and named) versions introduced periodically such as Chili Mango. The company's other products include gumballs gummies and sour candies in Jelly Belly flavors. Its more than 100 confections also include candy corn sour candies jellies novelty candy chocolates chocolate-covered nuts cinnamon confections and licorice along with seasonal offerings. Jelly Belly's candy is sold worldwide.

JENNER & BLOCK LLP

353 N. Clark St.
Chicago IL 60654-3456
Phone: 312-222-9350
Fax: 312-527-0484
Web: www.jenner.com

CEO: –
CFO: –
HR: Sheryl Ross
FYE: December 31
Type: Private - Partnershi

Law firm Jenner & Block concentrates on handling corporate transactions and complex litigation. Within those two main practice groups the firm maintains specialties such as bankruptcy intellectual property and mergers and acquisitions along with appellate work and securities litigation. The firm has offices in Chicago Los Angeles New York and Washington DC; overall it has more than 450 lawyers. Clients have included large companies in the construction financial services media real estate and telecommunications industries among others as well as government agencies. Jenner & Block was founded in 1914 as Newman Poppenhusen & Stern.

JENNIFER CONVERTIBLES INC.

419 Crossways Park Dr.
Woodbury NY 11797
Phone: 516-496-1900
Fax: 516-496-0008
Web: www.jenniferfurniture.com

PINK SHEETS: JENNQ

CEO: –
CFO: Rami Abada
HR: –
FYE: August 31
Type: Public

Houseguests are likely to get a good night's sleep thanks to Jennifer Convertibles. The company owns and operates about 80 namesake stores and some 10 Jennifer Leather stores that sell sofa beds loveseats recliners and chairs. The furniture firm also is among one of the top dealers of Sealy sofa beds in the US. Besides its network of Jennifer-branded stores the retailer also boasts half a dozen licensed Ashley Furniture HomeStores. Jennifer Convertibles sells name-brand products as well as the company's private-label: the Bellissimo Collection. In early 2011 Jennifer Convertibles emerged from Chapter 11 bankruptcy protection under new ownership and a new CEO.

JENNY CRAIG INC.

5770 Fleet St.
Carlsbad CA 92008
Phone: 760-696-4000
Fax: 760-696-4009
Web: www.jennycraig.com

CEO: Monty Sharma
CFO: Jim Kelly
HR: –
FYE: December 31
Type: Subsidiary

Jenny Craig would like for everyone to lighten up at least a little. The weight-control company which has provided products and services to more than 5 million clients is one of the world's largest diet firms (along with rival Weight Watchers). It owns or franchises more than 725 centers in the US Canada Australia New Zealand Puerto Rico the UK France and Guam. Its Jenny's Cuisine prepared foods along with DVDs CDs journals and cookbooks are sold to participants at its centers. The program is also available at home through telephone consultations and home delivery of food and support materials. Nestle the world's largest food and drink company owns Jenny Craig.

JEPPESEN SANDERSON INC.

55 Inverness Dr. East
Englewood CO 80112-5498
Phone: 303-799-9090
Fax: 317-398-3675
Web: www.knaufinsulation.us

CEO: Mark Van Tine
CFO: Jepson Fuller
HR: –
FYE: December 31
Type: Subsidiary

This company helps map the way for pilots mariners and railway engineers. Jeppesen Sanderson is a leading publisher of navigation charts reference materials and other information products for the aviation marine and rail transportation industries. It offers printed and electronic navigation data along with computerized tools for planning trips and making other important calculations. Jeppesen also publishes training materials and offers logistics services for the air marine and rail industries. Captain E.B. Jeppesen started the business in 1934 producing the first instrument flying charts in the basement of his Salt Lake City home. Boeing the world's largest aerospace company owns Jeppesen Sanderson.

JER INVESTORS TRUST INC.

1650 Tysons Blvd. Ste. 1600
McLean VA 22102
Phone: 703-714-8000
Fax: 703-714-8100
Web: www.jer.com

PINK SHEETS: JERT
CEO: Joseph E Robert Jr
CFO: –
HR: –
FYE: December 31
Type: Public

A real estate investment trust (REIT) JER Investors Trust manages a portfolio of real estate structured finance products primarily commercial mortgage-backed securities (CMBS) commercial mortgage loans mezzanine loans and other real estate investments. Founded in 2004 the company is managed by an affiliate of real estate investment management firm J.E. Robert Company (JER). It went public the following year. Due to the downturn in the mortgage industry and the credit industry overall JER Investors Trust has turned its focus on managing its portfolio credit risk and maintaining liquidity. The REIT has sold some of its real property assets and CMBS investments.

JERRY BIGGERS CHEVROLET INC.

1385 E CHICAGO ST
ELGIN, IL 601204715
Phone: 847-742-9000
Fax: –
Web: www.biggerschevy.com

CEO: –
CFO: –
HR: –
FYE: December 31
Type: Private

Jerry Biggers Chevrolet (dba Biggers Chevy Heaven) certainly enjoys its size. The company which has been in business for more than 40 years sells Chevy Camaros Corvettes Impalas and Yukons along with Isuzu Rodeos Ascenders and Amigos at a dealership in Elgin Illinois. It also offers a variety of used car models. In addition to cars Biggers Chevrolet sells aftermarket accessories like DVD players and truck bed liners and offers parts service and fleet sales. Its Web site allows customers to apply for financing search new and used inventory and schedule service. Help is available in English Spanish and Polish. The big dog at Biggers is owner Jim Leichter.

	Annual Growth	12/03	12/04	12/05	12/06	12/08
Sales ($ mil.)	(8.0%)	–	80.5	51.5	67.8	57.6
Net income ($ mil.)	–	–	–	(0.3)	0.0	(0.6)
Market value ($ mil.)	–	–	–	–	–	–
Employees	–	–	–	–	–	105

JERSEY CENTRAL POWER & LIGHT CO.

c/o FirstEnergy Corp., 76 South Main Street
Akron, OH 44308
Phone: 800 736-3402
Fax: –

CEO: Donald M Lynch
CFO: Marlene A Barwood
HR: –
FYE: December 31
Type: Public

New Jersey native son Bruce Springsteen may be The Boss but Jersey Central Power & Light (JCP&L) electrifies more fans than he does every day. The company a subsidiary of multi-utility holding company FirstEnergy transmits and distributes electricity to 1.1 million homes and businesses in 13 counties in central and northern New Jersey. JCP&L operates 22670 miles of distribution lines; its 2550-mile transmission system is overseen by regional transmission organization (RTO) PJM Interconnection. The utility also has some power plant interests.

	Annual Growth	12/08	12/09	12/10	12/11	12/12
Sales ($ mil.)	(12.6%)	3,472.3	2,992.7	3,027.1	2,495.0	2,027.0
Net income ($ mil.)	(8.2%)	187.0	170.5	192.1	144.0	133.0
Market value ($ mil.)	–	–	–	–	–	–
Employees	(1.0%)	1,470	1,432	1,434	1,413	1,410

JERSEY CITY MEDICAL CENTER INC

355 GRAND ST
JERSEY CITY, NJ 073024321
Phone: 201-915-2000
Fax: –
Web: www.libertyhealth.org

CEO: Joe Scott
CFO: Donald Parseghin
HR: Ron Brooks
FYE: December 31
Type: Private

With roots extending back to 1882 Jersey City Medical Center (JCMC) may have history but it's not stuck in the past. The 350-bed acute-care hospital serves residents of New Jersey's Hudson County area. Operated by Liberty Healthcare the hospital includes a trauma center a perinatal center and a heart institute. JCMC also offers pediatric women's health rehabilitation and ambulatory care and it is a teaching affiliate for the Mount Sinai School of Medicine. JCMC's modern incarnation came about in the Great Depression when it was constructed by a political ally of Franklin Roosevelt.

	Annual Growth	12/00	12/01	12/02	12/08	12/13
Sales ($ mil.)	(9.2%)	–	1,173.8	202.1	249.3	367.1
Net income ($ mil.)	45.2%	–	–	0.5	8.3	30.2
Market value ($ mil.)	–	–	–	–	–	–
Employees	–	–	–	–	–	1,942

JERVIS B. WEBB COMPANY

34375 W. Twelve Mile Rd.
Farmington Hills MI 48331
Phone: 248-553-1000
Fax: 248-553-1228
Web: www.jervisbwebb.com

CEO: Dina Salehi
CFO: Tetsuya Hibi
HR: –
FYE: December 31
Type: Subsidiary

Jervis B. Webb Company aka Daifuku Webb Group has spun a global web of custom-engineered material-handling systems and maintenance support services. Through facilities located around the world the firm makes equipment used in multiple markets including automotive production bulk and baggage handling automated newsprint handling beverage bottling and furniture manufacturing. Products include conveyors automatic guided vehicles (branded under the SmartCart name) automated storage and retrieval systems and loading vehicles. Webb is a subsidiary of Japanese-based material-handling firm Daifuku Co. Ltd.

JETBLUE AIRWAYS CORP

NMS: JBLU

27-01 Queens Plaza North
Long Island City, NY 11101
Phone: 718 286-7900
Fax: -
Web: www.jetblue.com

CEO: Robin Hayes
CFO: Mark D. Powers
HR: -
FYE: December 31
Type: Public

JetBlue Airways is counting on more than low fares to make its ledgers jet-black. The carrier offers one-class service — with leather seats satellite TV from DIRECTV satellite radio from XM and movies — to more than 32 million passengers a year and taking them to more than 90 cities. It has 825 daily flights in more than 25 US states Puerto Rico Mexico and about a dozen countries in the Caribbean and Latin America. Most of its flights arrive or depart from Boston; Los Angeles; New York; Orlando and Fort Lauderdale Florida; and San Juan Puerto Rico. JetBlue's fleet of more than 190 aircraft consists mainly of Airbus A320s and A321s but also includes Embraer 190s.

	Annual Growth	12/10	12/11	12/12	12/13	12/14
Sales ($ mil.)	11.4%	3,779.0	4,504.0	4,982.0	5,441.0	5,817.0
Net income ($ mil.)	42.6%	97.0	86.0	128.0	168.0	401.0
Market value ($ mil.)	24.5%	2,048.2	1,611.3	1,772.5	2,646.3	4,914.6
Employees	4.3%	12,948	14,022	14,347	14,883	15,334

JEWEL-OSCO

150 Pierce Rd.
Itasca IL 60143
Phone: 630-948-6895
Fax: 630-948-6959
Web: www.jewelosco.com

CEO: -
CFO: -
HR: -
FYE: February 28
Type: Business Segment

Jewel-Osco operates about 180 combination food-and-drug stores mostly in Illinois but also in Indiana and Iowa. The regional chain is the #1 seller of groceries in Chicago with more than 30 stores there and about 31% of the market (triple that of its nearest competitor Safeway-owned Dominick's). Jewel-Osco trails rival Walgreen in pharmacy sales in the Windy City. The company also runs about 30 fuel centers. Started as the Jewel Tea Company in 1899 Jewel-Osco is the largest traditional supermarket chain owned by grocery retailer and wholesaler SUPERVALU. Long accustomed to being #1 in a two-company market Jewel-Osco is fighting to stay on top of an increasingly crowded Chicago grocery scene.

JEWETT-CAMERON TRADING COMPANY LTD.

NASDAQ: JCTCF

32275 NW Hillcrest
North Plains OR 97133
Phone: 503-647-0110
Fax: 503-647-2272
Web: www.jewettcameron.com

CEO: Donald M Boone
CFO: -
HR: -
FYE: August 31
Type: Public

Jewett-Cameron Trading Company (JCTC) puts the lumber in lumberyards the air in pneumatic tools and seeds in the ground. Its Jewett-Cameron Lumber Company (JCLC) subsidiary supplies wood and other building materials to home improvement chains in the western US from distribution centers in Oregon. The MSI-PRO subsidiary imports pneumatic air tools and industrial clamps from Asia. The Jewett-Cameron Seed business distributes processed agricultural seeds and grain along with lawn garden and pet supplies in the US. It also owns plywood panel maker Greenwood Products. Employees own nearly 20% of the company.

JEWISH HOSPITAL & ST. MARY'S HEALTHCARE

200 Abraham Flexner Way
Louisville KY 40202
Phone: 502-587-4011
Fax: 502-587-4598
Web: www.jhsmh.org

CEO: -
CFO: -
HR: -
FYE: December 31
Type: Private

Jewish Hospital & St. Mary's HealthCare (JHSMH) operates a regional network of more than 70 health care facilities with some 1400 beds in Kentucky and southern Indiana. The system has about a dozen hospitals including the Jewish Hospital in Louisville (460 beds) the Sts. Mary & Elizabeth Hospital (330 beds) and Our Lady of Peace a 415-bed psychiatric hospital. JHSMH also includes assisted living and nursing home facilities as well as home health rehabilitation primary care occupational and emergency service centers. Already an affiliate of Catholic Health Initiatives (CHI) the system merged with CHI's Saint Joseph Health System in 2012 under a new CHI-controlled parent organization KentuckyOne Health.

JFK HEALTH SYSTEM INC.

65 JAMES ST
EDISON, NJ 088203947
Phone: 732-321-7000
Fax: -

CEO: Raymond F. Fredericks
CFO: -
HR: Shir Higgins-bouers
FYE: December 31
Type: Private

JFK Health System provides medical services in a tri-county area in central New Jersey through flagship facility JFK Medical Center. The hospital has about 500 acute care beds and is one of the Garden State's major health care facilities. Included in the medical center complex are JFK Johnson Rehabilitation Institute JFK New Jersey Neuroscience Institute and a number of outpatient care and imaging centers. A separate site Muhlenberg Campus consists of a satellite emergency room and outpatient care facilities as well as schools of nursing and medicine. Other JFK Health System facilities provide primary and specialty services as well as senior living home health and hospice care.

	Annual Growth	12/08	12/09	12/10	12/11	12/12
Sales ($ mil.)	(0.5%)	-	488.6	500.8	509.6	481.2
Net income ($ mil.)	-	-	-	(12.4)	11.4	9.9
Market value ($ mil.)	-	-	-	-	-	-
Employees	-	-	-	-	-	6,735

JG WENTWORTH CO (THE)

NYS: JGW

201 King of Prussia Road, Suite 501
Radnor, PA 19087
Phone: 484 434-2300
Fax: -
Web: www.jgwpt.com

CEO: David Miller
CFO: John R. Schwab
HR: -
FYE: December 31
Type: Public

J.G. Wentworth Co. (formerly JGWPT Holdings) is for those who just can't wait for the big payoff. The company purchases the rights of claimants in lawsuits insurance annuities and lotteries so that instead of receiving a series of settlement payments the claimants get a smaller lump sum payment up front. J.G. Wentworth Co. operates under the brands J.G. Wentworth and Peachtree Financial Solutions and advertises its structured settlement services heavily on TV radio and digital media. (Structured settlements became legal in 1982 with the Periodic Payment Settlement Act.) Founded in 1995 J.G. Wentworth went public in 2013 raising $115 million which it will use to pay down debt.

	Annual Growth	12/10	12/11	12/12	12/13	12/14
Sales ($ mil.)	-	0.0	253.3	467.4	459.6	494.4
Net income ($ mil.)	-	0.0	(3.9)	116.7	(5.6)	31.2
Market value ($ mil.)	-	0.0	-	-	424.0	259.9
Employees	8.9%	-	-	346	388	410

JIM PALMER TRUCKING

9730 Derby Dr.
Missoula MT 59808
Phone: 406-721-5151
Fax: 406-728-7376
Web: www.jimpalmertrucking.com

CEO: Joe Kalafat
CFO: Bill Dunn
HR: –
FYE: December 31
Type: Private

This Jim Palmer isn't related to the former Baltimore Orioles pitcher but Jim Palmer Trucking wants to move freight the way the National Baseball Hall of Fame member threw strikes — and to stay as cool in the process. Jim Palmer Trucking offers truckload transportation of temperature-controlled cargo with a fleet of about 350 tractors and 500 trailers. The company operates throughout the US from terminals in Denver; Missoula Montana; and Salina Kansas. After voluntarily filing for Chapter 11 bankruptcy protection in mid-2008 the company emerged from bankruptcy in May 2009. It cited the rising costs of fuel as one of the primary reasons for its financial woes.

JIM WALTER RESOURCES INC.

16243 Hwy. 216
Brookwood AL 35444
Phone: 205-554-6150
Fax: 205-554-6161
Web: www.walterenergy.com/operationscenter/jwr.html

CEO: –
CFO: –
HR: Bobbie Allen
FYE: December 31
Type: Subsidiary

Homes and businesses would have a hard time running their air conditioners and other electrical appliances without the power produced from the coal mined by Jim Walter Resources and its industry peers. A subsidiary of Walter Energy Jim Walter Resources operates two coal mines in Alabama that have total reserves of more than 147 million tons and the capacity to produce about 7 million tons of coal annually. The company sells its coal to steel producers in the US and overseas though sales outside the US account for more than three-quarters of the company's coal revenue.

JIMMY JOHN'S FRANCHISE LLC

2212 Fox Dr.
Champaign IL 61820
Phone: 217-356-9900
Fax: 217-359-2956
Web: www.jimmyjohns.com

CEO: –
CFO: –
HR: –
FYE: December 31
Type: Private

For some sandwich fans the company with two first names is the first choice for subs. Jimmy John's Franchise operates and franchises more than 1 000 quick-service Jimmy John's Gourmet Sandwich Shops in more than 35 mostly midwestern states. The chain's menu features submarine-style sandwiches made with a variety of toppings and carrying such names as Big John J.J. Gargantuan and Vito. Jimmy John's also serves club sandwiches made with whole wheat or French bread. The company's restaurants typically offer carryout and delivery services along with some limited seating. Chairman "Jimmy" John Liautaud started the Jimmy John's chain in 1983.

JIVE SOFTWARE INC

NMS: JIVE

325 Lytton Avenue, Suite 200
Palo Alto, CA 94301
Phone: 650 319-1920
Fax: –

CEO: Elisa Steele
CFO: Bryan J. LeBlanc
HR: –
FYE: December 31
Type: Public

Jive Software brings social networking into the workplace. The company offers its flagship Jive Social Business Platform that allows businesses to communicate collaborate and create and share content through internal social networks for employees and external communities for customers and partners to engage with each other and the business. The core platform can be expanded with optional modules such as analytics ideation (prioritizing ideas) mobile and video. The platform also accommodates cloud and customer-built applications through the Jive Apps Market. Customers include HP SAP and Starbucks. Jive Software was founded in 2001.

	Annual Growth	12/10	12/11	12/12	12/13	12/14
Sales ($ mil.)	40.2%	46.3	77.3	113.7	145.8	178.7
Net income ($ mil.)	–	(27.6)	(50.8)	(47.4)	(75.4)	(56.2)
Market value ($ mil.)	(27.8%)	–	1,182.7	1,074.0	831.6	445.7
Employees	13.8%	392	430	527	673	658

JLG INDUSTRIES INC.

13224 Fountain Head Plaza
Hagerstown MD 21742
Phone: 240-420-2661
Fax: 240-420-8719
Web: www.jlg.com

CEO: –
CFO: –
HR: –
FYE: July 31
Type: Subsidiary

Need a boost? JLG Industries' lift equipment can provide that extra reach. Since 1969 when founder John L. Grove invented the first self-propelled boom lift the company has been providing such products as aerial work platforms telescopic material handlers stock pickers (to access high shelving) and power deck trailers for ground-level loading of everything from heavy construction equipment to vending machines. Products are sold under such names as JLG SkyTrak and Lull. The company supplies customers in the government equipment leasing construction contracting agricultural and military markets. Equipment manufacturer Oshkosh Corp. has owned JLG since 2007.

JLM COUTURE INC.

NBB: JLMC

225 West 37th Street
New York, NY 10018
Phone: 212 921-7058
Fax: 212 768-2902
Web: www.jlmcouture.com

CEO: –
CFO: –
HR: –
FYE: October 31
Type: Public

Here comes the bride and she might be wearing a gown from JLM Couture. The company designs manufactures and markets bridal and bridesmaid gowns veils and related items in the US and the UK. Its bridal gowns which boast price tags of several thousand dollars are made under the Alvina Valenta Jim Hjelm Couture Jim Hjelm Visions Tara Keely and Lazaro names. JLM Couture markets its gowns through bridal magazines trunk shows and catalogs. The company's bridesmaid and flower girl collections are produced under the Jim Hjelm Occasions and Lazaro Bridesmaids labels; they're peddled through bridal boutiques and bridal departments in clothing stores. Its Party by JLM is a collection of evening wear.

	Annual Growth	10/10	10/11	10/12	10/13	10/14
Sales ($ mil.)	9.7%	21.2	24.7	27.3	29.1	30.7
Net income ($ mil.)	–	(0.5)	0.3	0.6	0.1	0.4
Market value ($ mil.)	13.6%	2.7	2.0	2.9	4.4	4.5
Employees		–	–	–	–	–

JM FAMILY ENTERPRISES INC.

100 Jim Moran Blvd.
Deerfield Beach FL 33442
Phone: 954-429-2000
Fax: 954-429-2300
Web: www.jmfamily.com

CEO: Colin Brown
CFO: Brent D Burns
HR: –
FYE: December 31
Type: Private

JM Family Enterprises is a family affair. Owned by the family of founder James Moran JMFE is a holding company (Florida's second-largest private company in fact after Publix Super Markets) with about a dozen automotive-related businesses including the world's largest-volume Lexus retailer JM Lexus in Margate Florida. JMFE's major subsidiary Southeast Toyota Distributors is the nation's largest independent Toyota and Scion distribution franchise delivering vehicles to 170-plus dealers across Alabama Florida Georgia Texas and the Carolinas. As part of its business JMFE also offers financial services insurance inspections dealer IT products and marketing services. It was established in 1968.

JMB REALTY CORPORATION

900 N. Michigan Ave. Ste. 1400
Chicago IL 60611
Phone: 312-440-4800
Fax: 312-915-2310

CEO: –
CFO: Ron Godsey
HR: –
FYE: December 31
Type: Private

JMB Realty wants to make State Street a great street again and bring glitter back to the Steel City's Golden Triangle. A major US commercial real estate investment firm JMB Realty is heavily involved in ambitious retail developments in Chicago's Loop and downtown Pittsburgh. It owns develops and manages projects throughout North America including regional malls hotels (the Chicago Ritz-Carlton) planned communities and office complexes. JMB Realty was founded in 1968 by Robert Judelson Judd Malkin and Neil Bluhm; Judelson (the "J" of JMB) is no longer involved with the company but Malkin remains as chairman and Bluhm is president. Bluhm also owns casino company Midwest Gaming and Entertainment.

JMP GROUP LLC

NYS: JMP

600 Montgomery Street, Suite 1100
San Francisco, CA 94111
Phone: 415 835-8900
Fax: –
Web: www.jmpg.com

CEO: Joseph A Jolson
CFO: Raymond S Jackson
HR: –
FYE: December 31
Type: Public

JMP Group wants to get the jump on the competition. Positioning itself as an alternative to bulge-bracket firms the company provides investment banking services such as strategic advice corporate finance and equity underwriting sales trading and research to small and midsized growth companies. It focuses on the technology health care financial services and real estate sectors. Its research department covers more than 300 small- and mid-cap public companies. JMP Group's Heartland Capital Strategies (HCS) subsidiary manages alternative investments such as equity hedge funds middle-market corporate loans and private equity for institutional and high-net-worth investors.

	Annual Growth	12/10	12/11	12/12	12/13	12/14
Sales ($ mil.)	3.5%	179.7	149.1	143.1	182.0	206.3
Net income ($ mil.)	10.8%	8.9	(2.5)	2.8	3.6	13.4
Market value ($ mil.)	(0.0%)	161.9	151.7	128.8	157.0	161.7
Employees	2.2%	215	217	224	235	235

JOCKEY INTERNATIONAL INC.

2300 60th St.
Kenosha WI 53141
Phone: 262-658-8111
Fax: 262-658-1812
Web: www.jockey.com

CEO: –
CFO: –
HR: –
FYE: December 31
Type: Private

Jockey International has nothing to do with horses and everything to do with the classic men's brief (its invention). The more than 130-year-old company makes men's women's and children's underwear and loungewear. Its products are sold through thousands of department and specialty stores the likes of Bloomingdale's and JCPenney. Jockey International licenses and distributes its apparel in more than 120 countries and holds numerous licensing agreements. Chairman and CEO Debra Waller and her family own the company. Jockey International was founded by Samuel Cooper in 1876 as a hosiery company intended to relieve lumberjacks of blisters and infections resulting from shoddy wool socks.

JOHN BEAN TECHNOLOGIES CORP

NYS: JBT

70 West Madison Street
Chicago, IL 60602
Phone: 312 861-5900
Fax: –
Web: www.jbtcorporation.com

CEO: Thomas W. Giacomini
CFO: Brian A. Deck
HR: Mark K. Montague
FYE: December 31
Type: Public

John Bean Technologies Corporation (dba as JBT Corporation) keeps food cold and jets in the air. JBT Corporation manufactures industrial equipment for the food processing and air transportation industries. Its JBT FoodTech segment makes commercial-grade refrigeration systems freezers ovens canning equipment and food processing systems for fruit poultry meat patties breads pizzas seafood and ready-to-eat meals. JBT AeroTech manufactures and services ground support equipment (plane de-icers aircraft tow vehicles and cargo loading systems) airport gate equipment (Jetway brand) and military equipment.

	Annual Growth	12/10	12/11	12/12	12/13	12/14
Sales ($ mil.)	2.8%	880.4	955.8	917.3	934.2	984.2
Net income ($ mil.)	(4.7%)	37.3	30.5	36.2	33.1	30.8
Market value ($ mil.)	13.0%	585.6	447.1	517.0	853.3	955.9
Employees	1.5%	3,300	3,300	3,200	3,330	3,500

JOHN BROWN UNIVERSITY

2000 W UNIVERSITY ST
SILOAM SPRINGS, AR 727612121
Phone: 479-524-9500
Fax: –
Web: www.jbu.edu

CEO: –
CFO: –
HR: –
FYE: June 30
Type: Private

John Brown University is a non-denominational Christian university with a student body of some 2300 and a student/faculty ratio of 13:1. Enrollment is comprised of about 1300 undergrads some 500 graduate students and about 500 adult degree completion students. Popular undergraduate majors among the 40 offered include engineering graphic and web design family and human services early childhood education and business administration; the university also offers nine graduate degree programs such as international business and school counseling. John Brown University was founded in northwest Arkansas in 1919 by evangelist and broadcaster John E. Brown Sr.

	Annual Growth	06/08	06/09	06/10	06/11	06/13
Sales ($ mil.)	–	–	0.0	68.3	63.2	68.2
Net income ($ mil.)	(24.4%)	–	–	16.3	8.3	7.1
Market value ($ mil.)	–	–	–	–	–	–
Employees	–	–	–	–	–	242

JOHN C. LINCOLN HEALTH NETWORK

2500 E DUNLAP AVE
PHOENIX, AZ 85020
Phone: 602-870-6060
Fax: –
Web: www.jcl.com

CEO: –
CFO: –
HR: Frank Cummins
FYE: December 31
Type: Private

John C. Lincoln Health Network takes care of the health of John Q. Public in Arizona. The not-for-profit health care network serves the northern Phoenix area and is home to two hospitals: John C. Lincoln Deer Valley Hospital with more than 200 beds and John C. Lincoln North Mountain Hospital with roughly 260 beds (the Valley's first Magnet nursing hospital an accredited Chest Pain Center and the host of a Level 1 Trauma Center). The system also features a children's care facility various physician and dental clinics a food bank and assisted living facilities for the elderly all operating under the Desert Mission moniker. John C. Lincoln Health Network is part of the Scottsdale Lincoln Health Network along with Scottsdale Healthcare.

	Annual Growth	12/09	12/10	12/11	12/12	12/13
Sales ($ mil.)	2.0%	–	551.2	486.8	509.2	584.5
Net income ($ mil.)	58.7%	–	–	17.5	32.7	44.1
Market value ($ mil.)	–	–	–	–	–	–
Employees	–	–	–	–	–	3,500

JOHN CARROLL UNIVERSITY (INC)

1 JOHN CARROLL BLVD
UNIVERSITY HEIGHTS, OH 441184581
Phone: 216-397-1886
Fax: –
Web: www.sites.jcu.edu

CEO: –
CFO: –
HR: Charles Stuppy
FYE: May 31
Type: Private

John Carroll University (JCU) is a Roman Catholic school that offers degree programs in more than 40 fields of the liberal arts social sciences natural sciences business and interdisciplinary studies at the undergraduate level and in selected areas at the master's level. Operated by the Society of Jesus — the Jesuits — it provides instruction to about 3600 students (including 2950 undergraduates). The school is one of 28 Jesuit universities in the US and has been listed in U.S. News & World Report magazine's top 10 rankings of Midwest regional universities for more than 20 consecutive years.

	Annual Growth	05/10	05/11	05/12	05/13	05/14
Sales ($ mil.)	2.9%	–	84.0	88.2	92.5	91.5
Net income ($ mil.)	–	–	–	(5.7)	20.9	14.7
Market value ($ mil.)	–	–	–	–	–	–
Employees	–	–	–	–	–	2,343

JOHN D. OIL AND GAS COMPANY

8500 Station St. Ste. 345
Mentor OH 44060
Phone: 440-255-6325
Fax: 440-205-8680
Web: www.johndoilandgas.com

OTC: JDOG

CEO: Richard M Osborne
CFO: Carolyn Coatoam
HR: –
FYE: December 31
Type: Public

John D. Oil and Gas (formerly Liberty Self-Stor) has shed its storage sheds in favor of oil and natural gas extraction in northeastern Ohio and the Appalachian Basin. In 2008 John D. Oil and Gas reported proved reserves of 2.1 billion cu. ft. of natural gas and 17500 barrels of oil. That year it had 49 net productive wells. The company also owns and manages Kykuit Resources LLC which leases natural gas and oil rights to more than 203840 acres in the Montana Breaks region in Montana. Chairman and CEO Richard Osborne owns 46% of John D. Oil and Gas.

JOHN F KENNEDY CENTER FOR THE PERFORMING ARTS

2700 F ST NW
WASHINGTON, DC 205660002
Phone: 202-416-8000
Fax: –
Web: www.kennedy-center.org

CEO: –
CFO: Lynne Pratt
HR: –
FYE: September 30
Type: Private

The John F. Kennedy Center for the Performing Arts also known as The Kennedy Center traces its roots to 1958 when president Dwight Eisenhower signed the National Cultural Center Act calling for a privately funded venture featuring a variety of classic and contemporary programming with an educational focus. The center was a pet project and fund raiser beneficiary of president Kennedy; it was named as a living memorial to him after his death. Located on 17 acres overlooking the Potomac River in Washington D.C. the center opened in 1971 and presents some 2000 events a year including musicals dance performances and jazz and orchestral concerts. It also produces TV programming workshops and lectures.

	Annual Growth	09/07	09/08	09/09	09/10	09/13
Sales ($ mil.)	2.6%	–	186.5	156.8	182.8	211.6
Net income ($ mil.)	–	–	–	(7.2)	21.8	10.7
Market value ($ mil.)	–	–	–	–	–	–
Employees	–	–	–	–	–	1,144

JOHN HANCOCK FINANCIAL SERVICES INC.

601 Congress St.
Boston MA 02210-2805
Phone: 617-663-3000
Fax: 617-572-6015
Web: www.johnhancock.com

CEO: –
CFO: Steven Finch
HR: Diana L Scott
FYE: December 31
Type: Subsidiary

John Hancock the man was a revolutionary but the company that bears his name is a bit less fiery. John Hancock Financial Services offers life insurance wealth management and other services. Its insurance products include variable universal and term life insurance along with long-term care insurance. John Hancock's wealth management products include annuities mutual funds and 401(k)s. One of the US's largest investors John Hancock offers institutional asset management services providing clients with specialty funds in such industries as timber and agriculture. It has more than $185 billion in funds under its management. First established in 1862 John Hancock is owned by Canada's Manulife.

JOHN HINE PONTIAC

1545 CAMINO DEL RIO S
SAN DIEGO, CA 921083575
Phone: 619-297-4251
Fax: –
Web: www.johnhine.com

CEO: –
CFO: –
HR: Deidra Hernandez
FYE: December 31
Type: Private

John Hine Mazda (formerly John Hine Pontiac) sells new and used Mazda brand vehicles to customers in the San Diego area. The dealership also offers parts service and collision repair through its John Hine Auto Body Center. Visitors to its Web site can check new and used inventory get a quote on a vehicle schedule service order parts and apply for financing. The company is a founding member of the California Sales Training Academy a private training program that has become an associates degree program at a local community college. The company was established in 1957. Prior to the discontinuation of the Pontiac brand the dealership sold Dodge and Pontiac vehicles in addition to Mazdas.

	Annual Growth	12/05	12/06	12/07	12/08	12/09
Sales ($ mil.)	(11.6%)	–	69.0	0.0	58.7	47.7
Net income ($ mil.)	–	–	–	0.0	(0.4)	(0.1)
Market value ($ mil.)	–	–	–	–	–	–
Employees	–	–	–	–	–	201

JOHN MORRELL & CO.

805 E. Kemper Rd.
Cincinnati OH 45246-2515
Phone: 513-346-3540
Fax: 513-346-7556
Web: www.johnmorrell.com

CEO: –
CFO: –
HR: Lisa Swaney
FYE: April 30
Type: Subsidiary

Here's one of the top names in meat. John Morrell & Co. is a leading producer of processed-meat and fresh-pork products. It makes bacon fresh pork hams and sausage as well as cold cuts and lunch meats hot dogs and deli meats. The company's brands include E-Z-Cut Farmers Hickory and its flagship John Morrell banner. Most of its products are sold through supermarkets and other retail grocers. John Morrell also sells pork products to convenience stores foodservice suppliers restaurants and other customers in the hospitality industry. Tracing its roots to the UK where it was founded in 1827 John Morrell is a subsidiary of top US pork producer Smithfield Foods.

JOHN MUIR HEALTH

1400 Treat Blvd.
Walnut Creek CA 94597
Phone: 925-939-3000
Fax: 757-631-3659
Web: www.mynavyexchange.com

CEO: Calvin Knight
CFO: –
HR: –
FYE: December 31
Type: Private

Named after famed naturalist and champion of wilderness preservation John Muir John Muir Health provides health care throughout the scenic San Francisco Bay area. The not-for-profit system operates three hospitals 20 outpatient and urgent care centers a physician practice organization and several community health foundations. The John Muir Medical Center Walnut Creek Campus has about 570 beds and specializes in neurological and obstetrics care. The Concord Campus has about 315 beds and specializes in cardiac and cancer care. The John Muir Behavioral Health Center is a 70-bed psychiatric hospital. John Muir Health also offers home health rehabilitation and wellness programs.

JOHN T. MATHER MEMORIAL HOSPITAL OF PORT JEFFERSON NEW YORK INC.

75 N COUNTRY RD
PORT JEFFERSON, NY 117772119
Phone: 631-476-2738
Fax: –
Web: www.matherhospital.org

CEO: –
CFO: –
HR: –
FYE: December 31
Type: Private

Shipbuilder John T. Mather envisioned a legacy that would keep his community of Port Jefferson in good health and John T. Mather Memorial Hospital came to fruition in 1929 one year after it's namesake's death. The not-for-profit hospital has some 250 beds and provides a variety of health care services to the residents of Port Jefferson New York and surrounding areas of Suffolk County. Services include emergency care occupational therapy psychiatry and radiology. Mather Hospital is a member of Long Island Health Network an association of about a dozen affiliated hospitals all serving Long Island. It is also Magnet® recognized hospital by the American Nurses Credentialing Center.

	Annual Growth	12/05	12/06	12/08	12/12	12/13
Sales ($ mil.)	6.2%	–	181.5	192.8	238.0	276.7
Net income ($ mil.)	19.0%	–	–	2.5	(0.9)	6.0
Market value ($ mil.)	–	–	–	–	–	–
Employees	–	–	–	–	–	1,700

JOHN WIELAND HOMES AND NEIGHBORHOODS INC.

1950 Sullivan Rd.
Atlanta GA 30337
Phone: 770-996-1400
Fax: 770-907-3485
Web: www.jwhomes.com

CEO: John Wieland
CFO: Shelly Pruitt
HR: –
FYE: September 30
Type: Private

John Wieland Homes and Neighborhoods develops land and builds cluster homes townhomes and upscale single-family houses in the southeastern US. Target markets include Atlanta Charlotte Charleston Nashville and Raleigh with home prices ranging from around $200000 to more than $1 million. The company also operates New Home Design Studios that provide customizable interior and exterior design services. WFS Mortgage a joint venture with Wells Fargo Home Mortgage offers lending to John Wieland Homes' customers and others. John Wieland also has a commercial division which develops office retail and mixed-use properties. Chairman John Wieland owns his namesake firm which he founded in 1970.

JOHNS HOPKINS BAYVIEW MEDICAL CENTER

4940 Eastern Ave.
Baltimore MD 21224
Phone: 410-550-0100
Fax: 410-550-0178
Web: www.hopkinsbayview.org

CEO: –
CFO: –
HR: –
FYE: June 30
Type: Subsidiary

If you've just been pulled from the bay like an old empty crab trap Johns Hopkins Bayview might be the first place you're taken. One of five member institutions in the Johns Hopkins Health System Johns Hopkins Bayview Medical Center is a community teaching hospital. Its Baltimore-based operations include a neonatal intensive care unit as well as centers devoted to trauma geriatrics sleep disorders and weight management. It also features the state's only regional burn center. The facility includes a meditation labyrinth for patients families and staff to walk. Established in 1773 the medical center has more than 560 beds.

JOHNS HOPKINS HEALTH SYS CORP

600 N WOLFE ST
BALTIMORE, MD 21287-0005
Phone: 410-955-5000
Fax: –
Web: www.jhmi.edu

CEO: –
CFO: Ronald J Werthman
HR: –
FYE: June 30
Type: Private

Named after philanthropist Johns Hopkins the Johns Hopkins Health System (JHHS) gifts Baltimore residents with an array of health care services. The health system is an affiliate of world-renowned Johns Hopkins Medicine and oversees six hospitals: All Children's Hospital Johns Hopkins Hospital Bayview Medical Center Howard County General Hospital Sibley Memorial Hospital and Suburban Hospital. The not-for-profit teaching hospitals offer inpatient and outpatient health services that include general medicine emergency/trauma care pediatrics maternity care senior care and numerous specialized areas of medicine. It also community health and satellite care facilities.

	Annual Growth	06/02	06/03	06/05	06/06	06/07
Sales ($ mil.)	11.1%	–	1,599.3	106.5	0.4	2,438.5
Net income ($ mil.)	54.9%	–	28.4	6.4	0.0	163.1
Market value ($ mil.)	–	–	–	–	–	–
Employees	–	–	–	–	–	13,000

JOHNS HOPKINS MEDICINE INTERNATIONAL L.L.C.

600 N. Wolfe St.
Baltimore MD 21287
Phone: 410-955-2000
Fax: 410-442-1082
Web: www.bshsi.org

CEO: Harris Benny
CFO: -
HR: -
FYE: June 30
Type: Private - Not-for-Pr

Johns Hopkins Medicine has a sterling reputation for health care in Baltimore and beyond. Consisting of Johns Hopkins University School of Medicine and the Johns Hopkins Health System Johns Hopkins Medicine oversees six area hospitals (with a combined total of almost 2680 beds) in addition to the academic offerings of the medical school and and a nursing program. It also operates a pediatric facility in Florida. Other facilities and programs include community clinics a home health care provider and its own managed care plan. The system has educational patient care and management partnerships with neighboring medical centers including Greater Baltimore Medical Center and Anne Arundel Medical Center.

JOHNS MANVILLE CORPORATION

717 17th St.
Denver CO 80202
Phone: 303-978-2000
Fax: 303-978-2318
Web: www.jm.com

CEO: Mary Rhinehart
CFO: -
HR: -
FYE: December 31
Type: Subsidiary

Come rain snow sleet hail and even fire Johns Manville (JM) keeps its customers protected from the elements. JM founded in 1858 makes commercial and industrial roofing systems and formaldehyde-free fiberglass insulation for the commercial and residential building industries. It also manufactures residential building insulation and specialty insulation for the aerospace transportation acoustics appliance and HVAC industries. Other items include fire-protection systems thermal and acoustical insulation glass textile wall coverings and fibers and nonwoven mats used in roofing and flooring. JM operates about 40 plants in China Europe and North America. Warren Buffett's Berkshire Hathaway owns JM.

JOHNSON & JOHNSON

NYS: JNJ

One Johnson & Johnson Plaza
New Brunswick, NJ 08933
Phone: 732 524-0400
Fax: 732 214-0332
Web: www.jnj.com

CEO: Alex Gorsky
CFO: Dominic J. Caruso
HR: Peter (Pete) Fasolo
FYE: December 28
Type: Public

It's difficult to get well without Johnson & Johnson (J&J). The diversified health care giant operates in three segments through more than 265 operating companies located in some 60 countries. Its Medical Devices division offers surgical equipment monitoring devices orthopedic products and contact lenses among other things. J&J's Pharmaceuticals division makes drugs for an array of ailments such as neurological conditions blood disorders autoimmune diseases and pain. Top sellers are psoriasis drug Remicade and cancer medication Velcade. Its Consumer business makes over-the-counter drugs and products for baby skin and oral care as well as first-aid and nutritional uses.

	Annual Growth	01/11	01/12*	12/12	12/13	12/14
Sales ($ mil.)	6.5%	61,587.0	65,030.0	67,224.0	71,312.0	74,331.0
Net income ($ mil.)	7.0%	13,334.0	9,672.0	10,853.0	13,831.0	16,323.0
Market value ($ mil.)	-	0.0	0.0	0.0	0.0	0.0
Employees	3.5%	114,000	117,900	127,600	128,100	126,500

*Fiscal year change

JOHNSON & JOHNSON HEALTH CARE SYSTEMS INC.

425 Hoes Ln.
Piscataway NJ 08855-6800
Phone: 732-562-3000
Fax: 732-214-0332
Web: www.jjhcs.com

CEO: -
CFO: -
HR: -
FYE: December 31
Type: Subsidiary

Health care providers can count on Johnson & Johnson Health Care Systems (JJHCS) to make their lives a little easier. The company provides business support services to large health care clients as well as access to parent Johnson & Johnson's products. It operates through three divisions: contracting (resource and risk management) strategic account management and supply chain (order management and distribution services). Its customers include managed care organizations hospital groups physician networks pharmacies and government customers. The company also provides e-business and supply management services for a number of fellow J&J subsidiaries.

JOHNSON & WALES UNIVERSITY INC

8 ABBOTT PARK PL
PROVIDENCE, RI 029033775
Phone: 401-598-1000
Fax: -
Web: www.jwu.edu

CEO: -
CFO: Joseph J. Greene
HR: Diane D'Ambra
FYE: June 30
Type: Private

Things are a little upside-down at Johnson & Wales University and that's just the way they like it. The private not-for-profit accredited institution provides what it calls an upside-down curriculum allowing students to take courses in their major during the first year so they learn right away if their career choice is right for them. At the end of two years of study students earn an associate's degree and the opportunity to go on to earn a bachelor's degree. Founded in 1914 the school enrolls more than 17000 students across its four campuses in Colorado Florida North Carolina and Rhode Island. It offers degrees in business education foodservice hospitality culinary arts and technology.

	Annual Growth	06/09	06/10	06/11	06/12	06/13
Sales ($ mil.)	(6.6%)	-	427.9	343.3	353.4	349.1
Net income ($ mil.)	(29.9%)	-	-	75.4	4.2	37.0
Market value ($ mil.)	-	-	-	-	-	-
Employees	-	-	-	-	-	1,400

JOHNSON CITY POWER BOARD

2600 Boones Creek Rd.
Johnson City TN 37615
Phone: 423-282-5272
Fax: 513-639-7575
Web: www.deskey.com

CEO: -
CFO: -
HR: Connie Crouch
FYE: June 30
Type: Government-owned

Board members have real power (to dispense) on the Johnson City Power Board. Based in Johnson City Tennessee the Johnson City Power Board provides electricity and related programs services and products to approximately 68000 residential and business customers in Washington County as well as parts of Carter Greene and Sullivan Counties. The company is one of 158 power companies throughout Alabama Georgia Kentucky and Tennessee which purchase electricity from the Tennessee Valley Authority. Johnson City Power Board teams with cities towns governments economic development and Chambers of Commerce to promote business and industry in its service area.

JOHNSON CONTROLS INC

NYS: JCI

5757 North Green Bay Avenue
Milwaukee, WI 53209
Phone: 414 524-1200
Fax: –
Web: www.johnsoncontrols.com

CEO: –
CFO: Brian J. Stief
HR: Susan F. Davis
FYE: September 30
Type: Public

Johnson Controls (JCI) wants to put you in the driver's seat — an environmentally conscious one. The company makes car batteries and interior parts for combustion engine and hybrid electric vehicles as well as energy-efficient HVAC systems for commercial buildings. Products include seating instrument panels and a slew of electronics. OEM customers include GM Daimler and Ford. The battery unit supplies car batteries for retailers such as Advance Auto Parts AutoZone Pep Boys and Wal-Mart. The building efficiency unit makes installs and services mechanical equipment that controls HVAC lighting security and fire systems in commercial buildings. The unit also offers on-site facility management.

	Annual Growth	09/11	09/12	09/13	09/14	09/15
Sales ($ mil.)	(2.3%)	40,833.0	41,955.0	42,730.0	42,828.0	37,179.0
Net income ($ mil.)	(1.0%)	1,624.0	1,226.0	1,178.0	1,215.0	1,563.0
Market value ($ mil.)	11.9%	17,071.1	17,737.9	26,865.7	28,484.2	26,775.1
Employees	(3.8%)	162,000	170,000	170,000	168,000	139,000

JOHNSON MATTHEY INC.

435 Devon Park Dr. Ste. 600
Wayne PA 19087
Phone: 610-971-3000
Fax: 610-971-3191
Web: www.jmusa.com

CEO: Robert Macleod
CFO: –
HR: –
FYE: March 31
Type: Subsidiary

According to Johnson Matthey's math it adds up to serve the precious metals catalysts coatings and pharmaceutical industries in the US. The company also provides contract research and development for the pharmaceutical industry. Its Emission Control Technologies segment makes catalytic systems and emission controls for a range of industries including automotive manufacturing. The Precious Metals segment is engaged in supplying fabricated precious metal alloys chemicals and catalysts as well as medical device components and colors and coatings. The company is the North American unit of UK chemicals and catalysts maker Johnson Matthey plc.

JOHNSON OUTDOORS INC

NMS: JOUT

555 Main Street
Racine, WI 53403
Phone: 262 631-6600
Fax: –
Web: www.johnsonoutdoors.com

CEO: H P Johnson-Leipold
CFO: David W Johnson
HR: W Floyd Wilkinson
FYE: October 03
Type: Public

Johnson Outdoors keeps sports buffs from staying indoors. The company makes markets and sells camping and outdoor equipment (such as Jetboil cooking systems and Eureka! tents and backpacks). It also focuses on supplying equipment for water activities with its diving gear (Scubapro and Uwatec masks fins snorkels and tanks) trolling motors (Minn Kota) fish finders (Humminbird) autopilot systems (Navicontrol) and watercraft (Old Town canoes Necky kayaks). With GPS technologies and electric boat motors Johnson Outdoors' marine electronics unit generates about 55% of the firm's sales. The Johnson family including CEO Helen Johnson-Leipold controls the company.

	Annual Growth	10/10*	09/11	09/12	09/13*	10/14
Sales ($ mil.)	2.7%	382.4	407.4	412.3	426.5	425.4
Net income ($ mil.)	8.7%	6.5	32.6	10.1	19.3	9.1
Market value ($ mil.)	19.2%	127.3	153.5	213.5	265.5	257.3
Employees	(3.2%)	1,255	1,200	1,100	1,200	1,100

*Fiscal year change

JOHNSON SUPPLY AND EQUIPMENT CORPORATION

10151 STELLA LINK RD
HOUSTON, TX 770255398
Phone: 713-830-2300
Fax: –
Web: www.johnsonsupply.com

CEO: Carl I Johnson
CFO: Donald K Wile
HR: –
FYE: March 31
Type: Private

Global warming? Bring it on! Keeping Texas and Louisiana residents cool is no easy task but Johnson Supply does what it can. Through about two dozen locations in hot spots like Houston and Lake Charles Louisiana Johnson Supply distributes air-conditioning and refrigeration equipment controls parts and supplies from more than 200 manufacturers. Since those places also get cold relatively speaking the company sells heating and ventilation equipment as well. Its 200 suppliers include names like York Friedrich Warren Mueller and Johnson Controls. The company was founded in 1953 by Carl I. Johnson Sr.

	Annual Growth	03/02	03/03	03/04	03/05	03/08
Sales ($ mil.)	1.2%	–	97.9	105.8	110.3	103.9
Net income ($ mil.)	2.7%	–	–	22.4	80.0	24.9
Market value ($ mil.)	–	–	–	–	–	–
Employees	–	–	–	–	–	270

JOHNSONVILLE SAUSAGE LLC

N6928 Johnsonville Way
Sheboygan Falls WI 53085
Phone: 920-453-6900
Fax: 920-459-7824
Web: www.johnsonville.com

CEO: Ralph Stayer
CFO: Kristine Dirkse
HR: –
FYE: December 31
Type: Private

Johnsonville Sausage has found the missing link to family meals. The company makes a variety of top-selling fresh pre-cooked and smoked sausage products. Its products portfolio includes bratwurst breakfast links and bulk rolls chorizo and smoked and Italian sausage. Outside mealtime the company offers snack sausages and deli bites. Sold under the Johnsonville and Table for Two brand names the company's more than 50 link and bulk sausage meats are sold primarily through grocery stores and food service operators. Johnsonville's sausage is available in some 30 countries worldwide. Its products are on the menu at more than 4000 US McDonald's restaurants. The privately-owned company was founded in 1945.

JOHNSTON ENTERPRISES INC.

411 W CHESTNUT AVE
ENID, OK 737012057
Phone: 580-233-5800
Fax: –
Web: www.jeinc.com

CEO: Lew Meibergen
CFO: Gary Tucker
HR: –
FYE: April 30
Type: Private

Johnston Enterprises serves the harvesters of America's amber waves of grain. The company offers farmers in Oklahoma and other Midwestern states grain-processing and storage facilities and inland water transportation services through its Johnston Grain and Johnston Port Terminals divisions. Its Johnston Seed subsidiary sells wildflower and turf wild forage and native grass seed and wildlife feed. The company was founded in 1893 by W. B. Johnston and is owned and operated by the founder's descendants president Lew Meibergen and COO Butch Meibergen.

	Annual Growth	04/09	04/10	04/11	04/12	04/13
Sales ($ mil.)	33.6%	–	140.2	289.9	297.8	334.2
Net income ($ mil.)	7.8%	–	–	1.4	1.6	1.7
Market value ($ mil.)	–	–	–	–	–	–
Employees	–	–	–	–	–	280

JOIE DE VIVRE HOSPITALITY INC.

530 Bush St. Ste. 501
San Francisco CA 94108
Phone: 415-835-0300
Fax: 415-835-0317
Web: www.jdvhotels.com

CEO: Niki Leondakis
CFO: Michael J Wisner
HR: –
FYE: December 31
Type: Private

You might say this company has a zest for hotel life. Joie de Vivre Hospitality operates boutique hotels with more than 30 properties in California many of which are in the San Francisco Bay area. Hotels include Hotel Rex featuring a book-lined lounge inspired by 1930s literary salons and Phoenix Hotel a funky San Francisco landmark that is frequented by entertainers and celebrities. (So much so that it is known as the "rock 'n roll hotel.") Some properties feature spa facilities and upscale restaurants. Chip Conley founded Joie de Vivre in 1987. John Pritzker son of Hyatt Hotels Corporation founder Jay Pritzker owns a majority of the firm. The company is joining Thompson Hotels to form JT Hospitality.

JOINT COMMISSION ON ACCREDITATION OF HEALTHCARE ORGANIZATIONS

1 RENAISSANCE BLVD
OAKBROOK TERRACE, IL 60181-4805
Phone: 630-792-5000
Fax: –

CEO: –
CFO: –
HR: –
FYE: December 31
Type: Private

With an eye on improving performance and patient care the Joint Commission on Accreditation of Health Care Organizations is a nonprofit that provides accreditation and certification services. The group evaluates and accredits more than 20000 health care providers in the US. Its board of commissioners includes doctors nurses consumers and administrators. They evaluate hospitals health care networks nursing homes and other long-term care facilities laboratories and health-related groups. The Joint Commission's Quality Check website includes each accredited organization's quality review. The group also known simply as The Joint Commission was founded in 1951.

	Annual Growth	03/00	03/01*	12/01	12/02	12/11
Sales ($ mil.)	(16.1%)	–	1,045.8	122.2	115.4	180.5
Net income ($ mil.)	174.0%	–	0.0	8.9	12.5	8.3
Market value ($ mil.)	–	–	–	–	–	–
Employees	–	–	–	–	–	936

*Fiscal year change

JONES DAY

North Point 901 Lakeside Ave.
Cleveland OH 44114-1190
Phone: 216-586-3939
Fax: 216-579-0212
Web: www.jonesday.com

CEO: –
CFO: –
HR: –
FYE: December 31
Type: Private - Partnershi

Legal leviathan Jones Day ranks as one of the world's largest law firms providing counsel to about half of the "FORTUNE" 500 companies. It has some 2400 attorneys in about 35 offices worldwide. Outside the US Jones Day has offices in Europe the Middle East the Asia/Pacific region and Mexico. The firm's practice areas include capital markets government regulation intellectual property real estate and tax. Jones Day has counted Bridgestone/Firestone General Motors IBM RJR Nabisco and Texas Instruments among its clients. The firm traces its roots to the Cleveland law partnership founded by Edwin Blandin and William Rice in 1893.

JONES GROUP INC

1411 Broadway
New York, NY 10018
Phone: 212 642-3860
Fax: –
Web: www.jonesgroupinc.com

NYS: JNY
CEO: –
CFO: –
HR: –
FYE: December 31
Type: Public

While some are busy keeping up with the Joneses The Jones Group (formerly Jones Apparel Group) is too busy taking stock in its own brand portfolio to take notice. The company provides a wide range of clothing shoes and accessories for men women and juniors. Its brands include Anne Klein Jones New York Gloria Vanderbilt Nine West Evan-Picone and l.e.i. among some 30 others. Through licensing agreements Jones also supplies Givenchy jewelry Rachel Roy designer apparel and Dockers footwear. It is active in both the retail and wholesale sectors. The Jones Group operates about 950 outlet and specialty stores in the US and internationally as well as branded e-commerce sites.

	Annual Growth	12/08	12/09	12/10	12/11	12/12
Sales ($ mil.)	1.2%	3,616.4	3,327.4	3,642.7	3,785.3	3,798.1
Net income ($ mil.)	–	(765.4)	53.8	50.7	(56.1)
Market value ($ mil.)	17.2%	464.1	1,272.0	1,230.8	835.6	876.0
Employees	(1.9%)	12,710	11,535	10,940	12,060	11,790

JONES INTERNATIONAL LTD.

9697 E. Mineral Ave.
Englewood CO 80112
Phone: 303-792-3111
Fax: 303-784-8508
Web: www.jones.com

CEO: Glenn R Jones
CFO: –
HR: Marsha Parent
FYE: December 31
Type: Private

To keep up with these Joneses you'd have to be active in such industries as education entertainment and enterprise software just to name a few. Jones International is a diversified holding company controlled by chairman and founder Glenn Jones. Its units include for-profit education company Jones Knowledge Group which runs online school Jones International University. Its Jones Entertainment Group produces independent films and documentaries while Jones Cyber Solutions provides customer relationship management (CRM) software for communications companies. Other subsidiaries include Jones Banana Network (comedy content for mobile devices) and Jones/NCTI (corporate training and continuing education).

JONES LANG LASALLE INC

200 East Randolph Drive
Chicago, IL 60601
Phone: 312 782-5800
Fax: 312 782-4339
Web: www.jll.com

NYS: JLL
CEO: Colin Dyer
CFO: Christie B. Kelly
HR: Darline Scelzo
FYE: December 31
Type: Public

Jones Lang LaSalle (JLL) provides real estate without borders. Its services include commercial leasing real estate brokerage management advisory and financing through more than 230 corporate offices in more than 80 countries. It focuses on three main geographic areas: the Americas; Europe Middle East and Africa (EMEA); and Asia Pacific. The company's LaSalle Investment Management arm is a diversified real estate management firm with about $50 billion in assets under management. Jones Lang LaSalle has commercial real estate expertise across office retail hotel health care industrial cultural and multifamily residential properties. It manages approximately 3.5 billion sq. ft. worldwide.

	Annual Growth	12/10	12/11	12/12	12/13	12/14
Sales ($ mil.)	16.7%	2,925.6	3,584.5	3,932.8	4,461.6	5,429.6
Net income ($ mil.)	25.9%	153.9	164.4	208.1	269.9	386.1
Market value ($ mil.)	15.6%	3,762.0	2,746.8	3,762.9	4,590.0	6,721.2
Employees	9.6%	40,300	45,500	48,000	52,700	58,100

JONES SODA CO.
NBB: JSDA

66 South Hanford Street, Suite 150
Seattle, WA 98134
Phone: 206 624-3357
Fax: 206 624-6857
Web: www.jonessoda.com

CEO: Jennifer Cue
CFO: Carrie L Traner
HR: –
FYE: December 31
Type: Public

Keeping up with the Joneses at Jones Soda requires an adventurous palate. The beverage company makes markets and sells brightly colored sodas with wacky names and flavors like Fufu Berry and Blue Bubblegum. Seasonal offerings include Turkey and Gravy for Thanksgiving and Chocolate Fudge for Valentine's Day. To keep things interesting it regularly discontinues flavors and introduces new ones; labels also can be customized with photos submitted by customers. Jones Soda also sells Jones Zilch (zero calories) and the WhoopAss Energy Drink an energy beverage that's available with or without sugar. Jones Soda's beverages are distributed throughout North America as well as in Australia the UK and Ireland.

	Annual Growth	12/10	12/11	12/12	12/13	12/14
Sales ($ mil.)	(6.2%)	17.5	17.4	16.4	13.7	13.6
Net income ($ mil.)	–	(6.1)	(7.2)	(2.9)	(1.9)	(1.5)
Market value ($ mil.)	(26.4%)	48.8	15.2	12.3	19.7	14.3
Employees	(13.9%)	40	40	30	26	22

JORDAN CF INVESTMENTS LLP

7700 CF JORDAN DR
EL PASO, TX 799128808
Phone: 915-877-3333
Fax: –

CEO: –
CFO: –
HR: –
FYE: December 31
Type: Private

A high-flier in construction services C.F. Jordan is a top building contractor that offers preconstruction design/build development and project management services. The company has traditionally built hotels and resorts but has diversified into military residential highway and school construction. Its contracts include projects for the Immigration and Naturalization Service for border patrol stations health care centers and detention centers. Other works have included Sea World in San Antonio the Insights Science Museum in El Paso and the Pearl Harbor Commissary and Exchange in Hawaii. Chairman Charles "Paco" Jordan started the Texas-based firm in 1988.

	Annual Growth	12/03	12/04	12/05	12/08	12/09
Sales ($ mil.)	(35.2%)	–	–	1,911.2	337.9	337.9
Net income ($ mil.)	1686.3%	–	–	0.0	3.9	3.9
Market value ($ mil.)	–	–	–	–	–	–
Employees	–	–	–	–	–	500

JORDAN INDUSTRIES INC.

1751 Lake Cook Rd. Ste. 550
Deerfield IL 60015
Phone: 847-945-5591
Fax: 847-945-0198

CEO: John W Jordan II
CFO: Lisa M Ondrula
HR: –
FYE: December 31
Type: Private

Like the River Jordan that touches the lives many people so too Jordan Industries (JII). JII is a holding company that fosters a range of businesses. The conglomerate opens up a financial channel for capital expansion which would otherwise elude businesses relying on their own assets. Operating through Jordan Specialty Plastics JII's subsidiaries include Beemak a maker of point-of-purchase plastic displays for brochures. Safety reflectors for bicycles and commercial vehicles are made by Sate-Lite. Deflecto produces plastic injection-molded hardware and office supply products. Formed by The Jordan Company JII is held by David Zalaznick and chairman and CEO John W. Jordan II each with stakes of about 20%.

JORDAN'S FURNITURE INC.

450 Revolutionary Dr.
E. Taunton MA 02718
Phone: 508-828-4000
Fax: 508-580-8953
Web: www.jordans.com

CEO: Barry Tatelman
CFO: David Stavros
HR: Alicia Healey
FYE: December 31
Type: Subsidiary

"Shoppertainment" continues to be the key to success for Jordan's Furniture. Through several stores in Massachusetts and New Hampshire the company sells furniture to outfit bedrooms dining rooms living rooms and home offices. It also peddles mattresses rugs and home decor. The retailer is extending its reach to Rhode Island by opening an 100000-sq.-ft. store there. Known for taking furniture merchandising to the next level Jordan's Furniture stores feature IMAX theaters a laser light hall and MOM (Motion Odyssey Movie) ride. Founded in 1918 by Samuel Tatelman Jordan's Furniture is owned by billionaire Warren Buffett's Berkshire Hathaway.

JOS. A. BANK CLOTHIERS, INC.
NMS: JOSB

500 Hanover Pike
Hampstead, MD 21074-2095
Phone: 410 239-2700
Fax: –
Web: www.josbank.com

CEO: R Neal Black
CFO: David E Ullman
HR: –
FYE: February 02
Type: Public

When casual Fridays put a wrinkle in the starched selling philosophy of Jos. A. Bank Clothiers the company dressed down. Although it is still best known for making tailored clothing for the professional man including suits sport coats dress shirts and pants it has added casual wear suitable for those dress-down Fridays and weekends. It also launched the David Leadbetter line of golf wear. The company sells its Jos. A. Bank clothes and a few shoe brands through its catalogs website and some 625 company-owned or franchised stores in 40-plus states and the District of Columbia. For corporate customers it offers a credit card that provides users with discounts. Most of its stores house a tailoring shop.

	Annual Growth	01/09	01/10	01/11	01/12*	02/13
Sales ($ mil.)	17.7%	546.4	770.3	858.1	979.9	1,049.3
Net income ($ mil.)	16.5%	43.2	71.2	85.8	97.5	79.7
Market value ($ mil.)	10.5%	767.8	1,171.9	1,173.0	1,343.9	1,144.5
Employees	11.9%	4,040	4,318	4,998	5,883	6,342

*Fiscal year change

JOURNAL COMMUNICATIONS INC
NYS: JRN

333 West State Street
Milwaukee, WI 53203
Phone: 414 224-2000
Fax: –
Web: www.journalcommunications.com

CEO: –
CFO: –
HR: –
FYE: December 29
Type: Public

You might say this company chronicles the news in Milwaukee. Journal Communications is a diversified media company with operations in publishing radio and TV broadcasting and interactive media. Its publishing business is anchored by its flagship paper the Milwaukee Journal Sentinel a leading daily newspaper in Milwaukee with a circulation of about 185000. Its Journal Community Publishing Group also runs about 50 community newspapers and shoppers serving markets in Wisconsin and Florida. Journal Communications owns and operates about 35 radio stations and 15 TV stations in a dozen states through its Journal Broadcast unit. It also operates several websites in conjunction with its media properties.

	Annual Growth	12/09	12/10	12/11	12/12	12/13
Sales ($ mil.)	(2.2%)	433.6	376.8	356.8	400.0	397.3
Net income ($ mil.)	57.0%	4.3	34.4	22.2	33.3	26.2
Market value ($ mil.)	23.4%	200.2	259.1	234.7	262.7	464.3
Employees	(4.2%)	3,200	2,600	2,500	2,500	2,700

JOY GLOBAL INC

100 East Wisconsin Avenue, Suite 2780
Milwaukee, WI 53202
Phone: 414 319-8500
Fax: –
Web: www.joyglobal.com

NYS: JOY
CEO: Edward L. (Ted) Doheny
CFO: James M. Sullivan
HR: Johan S. Maritz
FYE: October 30
Type: Public

Joy Global is happy for a company that builds equipment destined to spend the majority of its life down in a hole. The company makes heavy equipment for the mining industry through two subsidiaries. Its Joy Global Underground Machinery subsidiary makes underground coal-mining equipment that includes armored face conveyors roof supports longwall shearers and shuttle cars. Other operations make electric mining shovels rotary blasthole drills and other equipment used in surface open-pit mining; it also provides parts and service through its P&H MinePro Services network. Joy Global operates manufacturing and service facilities worldwide about half of its sales are made outside of the US.

	Annual Growth	10/11	10/12	10/13	10/14	10/15
Sales ($ mil.)	(7.9%)	4,403.9	5,660.9	5,012.7	3,778.3	3,172.1
Net income ($ mil.)	–	609.7	762.0	533.7	331.0	(1,178.0)
Market value ($ mil.)	(34.1%)	8,899.9	6,007.1	5,669.4	5,136.5	1,676.7
Employees	(2.0%)	14,500	18,019	16,600	15,400	13,400

JOY MINING MACHINERY

177 Thorn Hill Rd.
Warrendale PA 15086
Phone: 724-779-4500
Fax: 724-779-4509
Web: www.joy.com

CEO: –
CFO: –
HR: –
FYE: October 31
Type: Subsidiary

Joy Mining Machinery finds happiness underground. The company manufactures and distributes underground mining equipment and bulk material conveyor systems from multiple service locations located near major mining regions throughout the world. The foundation for Joy Mining Machinery was laid when inventor Joseph F. Joy received a patent for his mechanical gathering arm loader in 1919. Products include bolting systems (used in coal mining) haulage systems and longwall systems (consisting of shearers roof supports face conveyors stageloaders crushers and mobile belt tail pieces). The company is a subsidiary of Joy Global. Sister company P&H Mining Equipment produces surface mining machinery.

JOYCE LESLIE INC.

170 W COMMERCIAL AVE
MOONACHIE, NJ 070741706
Phone: 201-804-7800
Fax: –
Web: www.joyceleslie.com

CEO: Celia Clancy
CFO: Peter Left
HR: –
FYE: January 30
Type: Private

Club-hoppers (and high schoolers) hoping to look like Paris Hilton without spending like her do their shopping at Joyce Leslie. The northeastern retail chain specializes in trendy and inexpensive women's and junior's clothing aimed primarily at teens and tweens. It operates about 50 shops filled with high-fashion knockoffs in Connecticut New Jersey New York and Pennsylvania. Joyce Leslie named after the daughter of the company's founder Julius Gewirtz was established in Brooklyn in 1945 and originally sold women's dresses. In February 2016 after struggling to find a business strategic partner to save the business the company announced it would be closing its stores for good.

	Annual Growth	01/06	01/07	01/08	01/09	01/10
Sales ($ mil.)	(75.3%)	–	–	1,654.7	100.9	101.0
Net income ($ mil.)	786.8%	–	–	0.0	1.2	1.3
Market value ($ mil.)	–	–	–	–	–	–
Employees	–	–	–	–	–	900

JPI PARTNERS LLC

600 E. Las Colinas Blvd. Ste. 1800
Irving TX 75039
Phone: 972-556-1700
Fax: 972-556-3889
Web: www.jpi.com

CEO: –
CFO: –
HR: –
FYE: December 31
Type: Private

JPI may have the keys to your next place. As one of the largest luxury apartment developers in the US JPI has developed or managed more than 200 apartment condo and student housing complexes. The company typically buys underperforming properties in desirable areas and upgrades them with such features as parking garages fitness centers and 24-hour concierge services. JPI's more than 50 student complexes (many of which have "Jefferson" in their name) include game rooms and fitness centers. Founded in 1976 as Jefferson Properties Inc. JPI was a subsidiary of Southland Financial until the early 1990s when Hunt Realty became a major investor.

JPMORGAN CHASE & CO

270 Park Avenue
New York, NY 10017
Phone: 212 270-6000
Fax: –
Web: www.jpmorganchase.com

NYS: JPM
CEO: James (Jamie) Dimon
CFO: Marianne Lake
HR: Jim Odonnell
FYE: December 31
Type: Public

Boasting some $2.6 trillion in assets JPMorgan Chase is the largest bank holding company in the US. With more than 5600 branches in about two dozen states (and counting) it is also among the nation's top mortgage lenders and credit card issuers (it holds some $131 billion in credit card loans). Active in 60 countries the bank also boasts formidable investment banking and asset management operations through its prestigious JPMorgan Private Bank and institutional investment manager JPMorgan Asset Management (with $2.4 trillion in assets under supervision) subsidiaries respectively.

	Annual Growth	12/10	12/11	12/12	12/13	12/14
Assets ($ mil.)	5.0%	2,117,605.0	2,265,792.0	2,359,141.0	2,415,689.0	2,573,126.0
Net income ($ mil.)	5.8%	17,370.0	18,976.0	21,284.0	17,923.0	21,762.0
Market value ($ mil.)	–	0.0	0.0	0.0	0.0	0.0
Employees	2.1%	222,316	260,157	258,965	251,196	241,359

JPS INDUSTRIES INC.

55 Beattie Place, Suite 1510
Greenville, SC 29601
Phone: 864 239-3900
Fax: –

NBB: JPST
CEO: Mikel H Williams
CFO: Charles R Tutterow
HR: –
FYE: November 02
Type: Public

JPS Industries' glass and plastic products can be found surfing the waves and saving lives. Its JPS Composite Materials arm makes high-strength fiberglass and synthetic fabrics for the aerospace military electrical construction and other industries. The products are used in myriad applications including body armor insulation circuit boards and even surfboards. JPS Industries also operates as JPS Elastomerics which includes Stevens Urethane a maker of polyurethane film sheet and tubing used to make an array of goods such as athletic shoes medical devices and scuba equipment. JPS Elastomerics' traces back to the 1863 founding of predecessor Easthampton Rubber Thread.

	Annual Growth	10/09	10/10	10/11	10/12*	11/13
Sales ($ mil.)	1.4%	191.3	186.7	190.3	158.3	202.0
Net income ($ mil.)	38.7%	0.6	3.2	(0.9)	1.3	2.0
Market value ($ mil.)	15.0%	28.8	41.7	69.5	72.0	50.4
Employees	–	–	–	–	–	–

*Fiscal year change

JTH HOLDING INC.

1716 Corporate Landing Pkwy.
Virginia Beach VA 23454
Phone: 757-493-8855
Fax: 800-880-6432
Web: www.libertytax.com

CEO: John T Hewitt
CFO: Mark F Baumgartner
HR: –
FYE: April 30
Type: Private

JTH Holding wants to free you from those tax preparation shackles. Doing business as Liberty Tax Service it is the third-largest income tax preparation chain (behind H&R Block and Jackson Hewitt). Liberty Tax Service provides computerized tax preparation services through about 4200 offices throughout the US and in Canada. More than 98% of the offices are operated by franchises and are easily recognized by the costumed Uncle Sams or Lady Liberties waving out front. The company's eSmart Tax product allows customers to file their taxes online. Liberty Tax also offers tax-preparation courses refund loans audit assistance and related programs and services. CEO John Hewitt founded the company in 1997.

JTM PROVISIONS COMPANY INC.

200 Sales Dr.
Harrison OH 45030
Phone: 513-367-4900
Fax: 513-367-1132
Web: www.jtmfoodgroup.com

CEO: Anthony A Maas
CFO: –
HR: Richard Maltner
FYE: December 31
Type: Private

The lunch lady makes a mean meal with help from JTM Provisions. The company produces some 600 fully cooked meals from traditional to ethic dishes for the foodservice industry. Its mainstay offerings are marketed in North America under name brands including Cecilia's Italian Favorites Cocina Tejada Mexican Favorites Soaring Dragon Asian Sauces and Main Street Cafe American Fare. JTM Provisions also supplies bakery items such as hoagie rolls and prepared meats including meatloaf. It caters to food distributors and institutional buyers for schools restaurants and delis military commissaries and some convenience/grocery stores. The family-owned company has been in business for more than half a century.

JUJAMCYN THEATERS LLC

246 W. 44th St.
New York NY 10036
Phone: 212-840-8181
Fax: 212-944-0708
Web: www.jujamcyn.com

CEO: –
CFO: –
HR: –
FYE: June 30
Type: Private

Jujamcyn Theaters screws in a lot of the light bulbs on the Great White Way. The company owns and operates five theaters in New York City that house plays and musicals such as Tony award winner The Producers and Pulitzer Prize winner Angels in America. Its theaters include the St. James and the August Wilson Theatre (formerly the Virginia). Jujamcyn — along with The Shubert Organization and the Nederlander Producing Company — controls most Broadway productions. Jujamcyn was founded in 1956 by James Binger. It's named after his children Ju[dith] Jam[es] and Cyn[thia]. Former president and producer Rocco Landesman bought Jujamcyn in 2005 for about $30 million but left the company in 2009 to head the NEA.

JUNIATA COLLEGE

1700 MOORE ST
HUNTINGDON, PA 16652-2196
Phone: 814-641-3000
Fax: –
Web: www.juniata.edu

CEO: –
CFO: Andrea M Denkovich
HR: –
FYE: May 31
Type: Private

Brothers and sisters are welcome at Juniata College an independent co-educational school affiliated with the Church of the Brethren. The college offers bachelor of arts (BA) and bachelor of science (BS) degrees in about 100 fields at its two dozen academic departments. Students are encouraged to design their own majors or "programs of emphasis" (POEs); nearly half do just that. Its most popular POEs include biology pre-health accounting business education environmental science psychology chemistry and sociology. Founded in 1876 Juniata College enrolls about 1600 students.

	Annual Growth	05/09	05/10	05/10	05/12	05/13
Sales ($ mil.)	11.3%	–	46.4	61.6	49.9	63.9
Net income ($ mil.)	–	–	(1.6)	11.9	(1.6)	12.9
Market value ($ mil.)	–	–	–	–	–	–
Employees	–	–	–	–	–	500

JUNIATA VALLEY FINANCIAL CORP   OTC: JUVF

Bridge and Main Streets
Mifflintown, PA 17059
Phone: 717 436-8211
Fax: –
Web: www.jvbonline.com

CEO: Marcie A Barber
CFO: Joann N McMinn
HR: Pamela Eberman
FYE: December 31
Type: Public

Juniata Valley Financial is the holding company for Juniata Valley Bank which serves central Pennsylvania from some 15 locations. The bank offers standard products such as checking and savings accounts money market accounts certificates of deposit individual retirement accounts and credit cards. Residential estate mortgages account for about half the company's loan portfolio which also includes commercial construction home equity municipal and personal loans. The bank offers trust and investment services as well. Juniata Valley Bank was established in 1867.

	Annual Growth	12/10	12/11	12/12	12/13	12/14
Assets ($ mil.)	2.5%	435.8	447.4	448.9	448.8	480.5
Net income ($ mil.)	(3.8%)	4.9	4.7	3.6	4.0	4.2
Market value ($ mil.)	1.8%	71.2	76.2	76.4	74.3	76.4
Employees	3.4%	134	154	150	151	153

JUNIPER GROUP INC.   OTC: JUNP

20283 State Rd. 7 Ste. 300
Boca Raton FL 33498
Phone: 561-807-8990
Fax: 516-829-4691
Web: www.junipergroup.com

CEO: –
CFO: –
HR: –
FYE: December 31
Type: Public

The Juniper Group is hoping to turn over a new leaf. The company primarily provides broadband installation and wireless infrastructure construction services through its Tower West Communications subsidiary including tower erection and construction site installation and surveying and antenna installation. Its clients include national providers of wireless voice messaging and data services. Juniper also is involved in film distribution acquiring motion picture rights from independent producers; that business line accounted for less than 2% of revenues in fiscal 2008.

JUNIPER NETWORKS INC

NYS: JNPR

1133 Innovation Way
Sunnyvale, CA 94089
Phone: 408 745-2000
Fax: 408 745-2100
Web: www.juniper.net

CEO: Rami Rahim
CFO: Robyn M. Denholm
HR: –
FYE: December 31
Type: Public

Juniper Networks has cultivated a business in an environment in where the big tree is Cisco. The company designs and sells network infrastructure equipment used to deploy and manage services and applications across Internet protocol (IP) networks. Its products include routers network traffic management software virtual private network and firewall devices data center and WAN acceleration tools and intrusion prevention systems. Juniper sells directly and through resellers to network service providers enterprises government agencies and schools. The company has resale agreements with Ericsson IBM and Nokia Siemens and it counts Ingram Micro and Hitachi among its distribution partners. More than half of sales are made in the US.

	Annual Growth	12/10	12/11	12/12	12/13	12/14
Sales ($ mil.)	3.1%	4,093.3	4,448.7	4,365.4	4,669.1	4,627.1
Net income ($ mil.)	–	618.4	425.1	186.5	439.8	(334.3)
Market value ($ mil.)	(11.8%)	15,366.1	8,494.6	8,186.7	9,393.6	9,289.6
Employees	0.1%	8,772	9,129	9,234	9,483	8,806

JUNIPER PHARMACEUTICALS INC

NMS: JNP

4 Liberty Square
Boston, MA 02109
Phone: 617 639-1500
Fax: –
Web: www.columbialabs.com

CEO: –
CFO: George O Elston
HR: Mark Spencer
FYE: December 31
Type: Public

Columbia Laboratories knows the power hormones have over us. The company develops manufactures and markets hormone therapies. Its products in development include a progesterone product delivered through a propriety bioadhesive technology to reduce the risk of preterm births. Columbia Laboratories already developed two such products PROCHIEVE and CRINONE and is now working on a new generation in agreement with Watson Pharmaceuticals. The company relies upon third-party manufacturers to produce its products.

	Annual Growth	12/10	12/11	12/12	12/13	12/14
Sales ($ mil.)	(8.2%)	45.7	43.1	25.8	29.2	32.5
Net income ($ mil.)	–	(21.8)	20.5	9.9	6.7	3.4
Market value ($ mil.)	25.3%	24.5	26.9	6.8	71.2	60.3
Employees	40.2%	22	21	11	77	85

JUNO LIGHTING LLC

1300 S. Wolf Rd.
Des Plaines IL 60017
Phone: 847-827-9880
Fax: 847-296-4056
Web: www.junolighting.com

CEO: Amelia Huntington
CFO: –
HR: –
FYE: November 30
Type: Subsidiary

Sharing its name with Jupiter's wife Juno Lighting can bask in the light of its own glow. Doing business as Juno Lighting Group the company makes light fixtures for commercial institutional and residential buildings under several brand names. Product lines comprise showcase lighting fixtures fiber optic lighting products and emergency and exit lighting signs using light-emitting diode (LED) technology. Other products include recessed and track-lighting systems. Under the Juno AccuLite and Danalite labels the company offers LED undercabinet and casework lighting products. Founded in 1976 the company is a subsidiary of Paris-based giant Schneider Electric.

JUPITER MEDICAL CENTER INC.

1210 S OLD DIXIE HWY
JUPITER, FL 334587205
Phone: 561-747-2234
Fax: –
Web: www.jupitermed.com

CEO: –
CFO: –
HR: Peter (Pete) Gloggner
FYE: September 30
Type: Private

Nope this hospital is not on the fifth planet from the Sun but by Jupiter it delivers great health care to a number of Floridians. Located just north of West Palm Beach Jupiter Medical Center provides specialty services that include cancer treatment cardiologyorthopedics emergency medicine wound care birthingand pain management. Not-for-profit Jupiter Medical Center consists of more than 205 private acute-care beds and 120 long-term rehab and hospice beds. The hospital is affiliated with the University of Miami's Miller School of Medicine.

	Annual Growth	09/09	09/10	09/11	09/12	09/13
Sales ($ mil.)	0.5%	–	176.6	185.3	174.3	179.2
Net income ($ mil.)	19.3%	–	–	4.7	6.6	6.7
Market value ($ mil.)	–	–	–	–	–	–
Employees						1,500

JUST BORN INC.

1300 Stefko Blvd.
Bethlehem PA 18017
Phone: 610-867-7568
Fax: 610-867-9931
Web: www.justborn.com

CEO: David N Shaffer
CFO: –
HR: –
FYE: December 31
Type: Private

Just Born gave birth to marshmallow treats for all occasions. The company makes the popular Easter candy sold under the name Marshmallow Peeps. These seasonal candy versions of little chick-ettes and bunnies come in such colors as blue lavender pink white green yellow and orange. In addition moviegoers will recognize the company's Hot Tamales and Mike and Ike brands. Other candy treats produced by the company include Just Born Jelly Beans Teenee Beanee Gourmet jelly beans and Peanut Chews. Sam Born founded the company in 1923. The family-owned and -operated company is run by co-CEOs Ross Born (Sam Born's grandson) and David Shaffer (Sam's nephew).

JUSTIN BRANDS INC.

610 W. Daggett Ave.
Fort Worth TX 76104-1103
Phone: 817-332-4385
Fax: 817-348-2037
Web: www.justinboots.com

CEO: Randy Watson
CFO: Herbert Beckwith Jr
HR: –
FYE: December 31
Type: Subsidiary

Once a unit of Justin Industries Justin Brands two-stepped away returning to its cowboy roots. The firm is known as a maker of western boots under the Justin Boots Nocona Boots Chippewa Boots and Justin Original Workboots brands but the company also makes and markets work safety and sports footwear. Its western boots come in a variety of exotic leathers including lizard and ostrich. Justin Brands sells its footwear through department stores shoe chains specialty stores (Academy Cavenders Boot City) catalogs and online (Zappos.com). It also caters to cowboys and fillies who want to learn more about the West through its Northland Publishing unit. Justin Brands is owned by Berkshire Hathaway.

K&G MEN'S COMPANY INC

1225 Chattahoochee Ave. NW
Atlanta GA 30318-3648
Phone: 404-351-7987
Fax: 404-351-8038
Web: www.kgmens.com

CEO: Douglas S Ewert
CFO: Jon W Kimmins
HR: –
FYE: January 31
Type: Subsidiary

The feminization of K&G Men's Company is well underway. The retailer operates about 100 deep-discount career apparel superstores in nearly 30 states. Its stores feature brand-name and private-label tailored and casual clothing footwear and accessories for men women and children. The bargain warehouse-type stores average about 23000 sq. ft. and offer first-run merchandise at prices 30%-60% lower than department stores. Founded in 1989 K&G is a subsidiary of The Men's Wearhouse and accounts for about 18% of its parent company's sales. After purchasing K&G Men's Wearhouse converted most of its outlets to the K&G Fashion Superstores banner and began adding women's and kids' apparel to the racks.

K-SEA TRANSPORTATION PARTNERS L.P.

1 Tower Center Blvd. 17th Fl.
East Brunswick NJ 08816
Phone: 732-339-6100
Fax: 732-339-6140
Web: www.k-sea.com

CEO: –
CFO: Terrence P Gill
HR: –
FYE: June 30
Type: Subsidiary

Not to be confused with the KC & the Sunshine Band tour bus K-Sea Transportation hauls refined petroleum products via its fleet of about 130 tank barges and tugboats. The company's barges have a carrying capacity of more than 4 million barrels. From locations in New York Philadelphia Seattle Honolulu and Norfolk Virginia K-Sea serves major oil companies and refiners along the US east and west coasts and up into coastal Canada and Alaska. Most of its business comes from contracts with customers such as BP ConocoPhillips Exxon Mobil and Tesoro. Kirby Corp. took over K-Sea in a deal valued at approximately $604 million in 2011 from unit holders and general partner K-Sea GP Holdings LP.

K-TRON INTERNATIONAL INC.

Rtes. 55 and 553
Pitman NJ 08071
Phone: 856-589-0500
Fax: 856-589-8113
Web: www.ktron.com

CEO: Edward B Cloues II
CFO: Robert E Wisniewski
HR: –
FYE: September 30
Type: Subsidiary

K-Tron International helps manufacturers watch their weight. Operating via subsidiary companies K-Tron makes feeders that let manufacturers control the flow (by weight or volume) of bulk solids and liquids during manufacturing processes. The group's expertise lies in the building of pneumatic conveying systems that use vacuum and pressure to precisely control the flow of ingredients to make pharmaceutical food chemical and plastic products. These pneumatic conveying systems are branded under the Colormax Limited Premier Pneumatics and Pneumatic Conveying Systems Limited product lines. K-Tron is owned by casket maker Hillenbrand.

K-V PHARMACEUTICAL COMPANY   NYSE: KV.A

1 Corporate Woods Dr.
Bridgeton MO 63044
Phone: 314-645-6600
Fax: 314-646-3751
Web: www.kvpharmaceutical.com

CEO: Gregory Divis
CFO: Thomas S McHugh
HR: Chris Dumm
FYE: March 31
Type: Public

K-V Pharmaceutical hopes to help women feel cooler calmer and healthier. The company's Ther-Rx subsidiary markets branded drugs with a focus on women's health therapies manufactured by third parties through licensing agreements including estrogen spray EvaMist licensed from VIVUS and preterm birth prevention drug Makena from Hologic. Historically the company manufactured and sold a variety of branded and generic drugs in the US market as well as drug delivery technologies used to make its drugs dissolve faster release slower or absorb better. However the company has been struggling financially and has sold off much of its operations. In 2012 it sought Chapter 11 bankruptcy protection.

K-VA-T FOOD STORES INC.

201 Trigg St.
Abingdon VA 24210
Phone: 276-628-5503
Fax: 276-623-5440
Web: www.foodcity.com

CEO: Steven C Smith
CFO: Michael T Lockard
HR: –
FYE: December 31
Type: Private

What do you call a chain of supermarkets in Kentucky Virginia and Tennessee? How about K-VA-T Food Stores? K-VA-T is one of the largest grocery chains in the region with more than 100 supermarkets under the Food City and Super Dollar Discount Foods banners. Originally a Piggly Wiggly franchise with three stores K-VA-T was founded in 1955. It has grown by acquiring stores from other regional food retailers opening new stores and adding services such as about 75 pharmacies 55 Gas'N Go gasoline outlets and banking. Its Food City Distribution Center provides warehousing and distribution services. The founding Smith family owns a majority of K-VA-T; employees own about 14% of the company.

K.V. MART CO.

1245 E. Watson Center Rd.
Carson CA 90745-4228
Phone: 310-816-0200
Fax: 310-816-0201
Web: www.kvmart.com

CEO: Darioush Khaledi
CFO: –
HR: Rent Trauffer
FYE: December 31
Type: Private

K.V. may as well be an acronym for knockout value. K.V. Mart Co. operates some 25 grocery stores primarily under the Top Valu Market and Valu Plus Food Warehouse (membership not required) banners. Other formats include Buy Low Price Rite Grocery Depot and Amar Ranch stores primarily in Los Angeles County California. The stores focus on serving low-income shoppers and catering to their surrounding ethic communities. K.V. Mart was founded in 1977 and is owned and operated by chairman and CEO Darioush Khaledi who fled Iran in the late-1970s. K.V. Mart is one of the leading independent grocery chains in Southern California as well as one of the largest minority-owned companies in the Los Angeles area.

K12 INC

NYS: LRN

2300 Corporate Park Drive
Herndon, VA 20171
Phone: 703 483-7000
Fax: -
Web: www.k12.com

CEO: Stuart J. Udell
CFO: James Rhyu
HR: -
FYE: June 30
Type: Public

K12 isn't a missing element from the periodic table but it could help kids learn about the periodic table. The company offers online educational programs to students in kindergarten through 12th grade through "virtual schools." It also offers online curriculum to public and private schools. It provides course material and product sales directly to parents and individualized supplemental programs offered through schools. K12 also manages and sells its products and services to blended schools (public schools that combine online and face-to-face instruction) and provides services to US school districts and to international partners. K12 was founded in 2000 by former CEO Ron Packard.

	Annual Growth	06/11	06/12	06/13	06/14	06/15
Sales ($ mil.)	16.1%	522.4	708.4	848.2	919.6	948.3
Net income ($ mil.)	(3.7%)	12.8	17.5	28.1	19.6	11.0
Market value ($ mil.)	(21.4%)	1,270.4	893.2	1,007.1	922.7	484.9
Employees	17.7%	2,500	3,300	3,500	4,200	4,800

KAHALA CORP.

9311 E. Via De Ventura Ste. 104
Scottsdale AZ 85258
Phone: 480-362-4800
Fax: 843-216-6100
Web: www.blackbaud.com

CEO: -
CFO: -
HR: -
FYE: December 31
Type: Private

Life is a quick-service beach at Kahala Corp. The company is a leading multi-concept franchisor with about a dozen restaurant brands encompassing about 3500 locations across the US and in a small number of other countries. Its flagship brands include 1500 unit ice cream purveyor Cold Stone Creamery and Blimpie sub sandwiches. Other concepts include Great Steak & Potato Co. (cheesesteak sandwiches) Surf City Squeeze (smoothies) and Samurai Sam's (Asian-inspired cuisine). Most of Kahala's eateries are typically found in mall food courts airports and other high-traffic areas. The company is controlled by chairman Kevin Blackwell and former CFO David Guarino.

KADANT INC

NYS: KAI

One Technology Park Drive
Westford, MA 01886
Phone: 978 776-2000
Fax: -

CEO: Jonathan W. (Jon) Painter
CFO: Thomas M. O'Brien
HR: -
FYE: January 03
Type: Public

Kadant wants to hear the ka-ching of profits being made from its papermaking equipment. The company's papermaking machinery and components which Kadant develops and manufactures can be found in most of the world's pulp and paper mills. Its papermaking products include stock preparation (including pulping screening cleaning and de-inking) doctoring (cleaning of paper rolls) fluid handling (mainly drying) and water management (water cleaning draining and filtering) systems. It also recycles papermaking byproducts into biodegradable fiber-based granules for oil and grease absorption and other uses. Kadant has operations in North America South America Europe and Asia.

	Annual Growth	01/11*	12/11	12/12	12/13*	01/15
Sales ($ mil.)	10.5%	270.0	335.5	331.8	344.5	402.1
Net income ($ mil.)	11.6%	18.5	33.6	31.6	23.4	28.7
Market value ($ mil.)	15.8%	256.1	245.6	285.3	443.1	460.4
Employees	3.0%	1,600	1,700	1,600	1,800	1,800

*Fiscal year change

KAISER ALUMINUM CORP.

NMS: KALU

27422 Portola Parkway, Suite 200
Foothill Ranch, CA 92610-2831
Phone: 949 614-1740
Fax: -
Web: www.kaiseraluminum.com

CEO: Jack A. Hockema
CFO: Daniel J. Rinkenberger
HR: John M. Donnan
FYE: December 31
Type: Public

Kaiser Aluminum may not be the biggest aluminum company on the block but it holds its own in fabricating specialty aluminum products. It operates 11 fabricated product plants in the US and one in Canada. Kaiser manufactures rolled extruded and drawn aluminum products to serve customers in the aerospace automotive general engineering and custom industrial markets. The company purchases primary aluminum ingot and recycled and scrap aluminum from third-party suppliers to make its fabricated products. Some of its facilities supply billet log and other aluminum materials to its other plants for use in production.

	Annual Growth	12/10	12/11	12/12	12/13	12/14
Sales ($ mil.)	5.9%	1,079.1	1,301.3	1,360.1	1,297.5	1,356.1
Net income ($ mil.)	50.2%	14.1	25.1	85.8	104.8	71.8
Market value ($ mil.)	9.3%	881.9	807.8	1,086.2	1,236.7	1,257.7
Employees	3.6%	2,300	2,600	2,600	2,650	2,650

KADLEC REGIONAL MEDICAL CENTER

888 SWIFT BLVD
RICHLAND, WA 993523514
Phone: 509-946-4611
Fax: -
Web: www.kadlecmed.org

CEO: Lane Savitch
CFO: Julie Meek
HR: -
FYE: December 31
Type: Private

Kadlec Regional Medical Center is an acute care hospital facility serving southeastern Washington and northeastern Oregon. In addition to providing comprehensive medical surgical and emergency services the hospital provides neonatal intensive care cardiopulmonary rehabilitation interventional cardiology neurology cancer care and other specialist services. Not-for-profit Kadlec Regional has some 270 inpatient beds including pediatric intensive intermediate and critical care capacity. It also operates outpatient physician offices and clinics in surrounding areas.

	Annual Growth	12/08	12/09	12/10	12/12	12/13
Sales ($ mil.)	10.1%	-	255.9	277.6	312.5	375.4
Net income ($ mil.)	90.6%	-	-	3.7	16.2	25.3
Market value ($ mil.)	-	-	-	-	-	-
Employees	-	-	-	-	-	2,668

KAISER FOUNDATION HEALTH PLAN OF COLORADO

10350 E. Dakota Ave.
Denver CO 80231
Phone: 303-338-3800
Fax: 303-344-7277
Web: www.kaiserpermanente.org

CEO: -
CFO: -
HR: -
FYE: December 31
Type: Subsidiary

Kaiser Foundation Health Plan of Colorado has high hopes for the health of those living in the Mile High City. Also known as Kaiser Permanente Colorado the division of Kaiser Foundation Health Plan provides health care plans and related services to nearly half a million members living in and around the cities of Colorado Spring Denver and Boulder. One of the leading health plan providers in the state Kaiser Permanente Colorado offers its plans to individuals and businesses large and small. Kaiser Foundation Health Plans have an integrated care model offering both hospital and physician care through a vast network of hospitals and physician practices operating under the Kaiser and Exempla name.

KAISER FOUNDATION HEALTH PLAN OF THE NORTHWEST

500 NE Multnomah St. Ste. 100
Portland OR 97232
Phone: 503-813-2800
Fax: 503-813-4235
Web: www.kaiserpermanente.org

CEO: Andrew McCulloch
CFO: -
HR: Deborah Hedges
FYE: December 31
Type: Subsidiary

Kaiser Foundation Health Plan of The Northwest a subsidiary of Kaiser Permanente is an HMO that provides health care insurance and related services to more then 480000 members from nearly 900 doctors at community hospitals and medical centers in Oregon and Southwest Washington state. The company is the only Kaiser organization to also offer dental benefits; its dental network is one of the nation's largest. Kaiser Foundation Health Plans have an integrated care model offering both hospital and physician care through a network of hospitals and physician practices operating under the Kaiser name in 9 states and the District of Columbia.

KAISER FOUNDATION HOSPITALS INC

1 KAISER PLZ STE 2600
OAKLAND, CA 946123673
Phone: 510-271-5800
Fax: -
Web: www.healthy.kaiserpermanente.org

CEO: Bernard J Tyson
CFO: Shawn Freeman
HR: -
FYE: December 31
Type: Private

Kaiser Foundation Hospitals is on a roll. The hospital group operates 38 acute care hospitals and almost 630 medical offices in eight states (California Colorado Georgia Hawaii Maryland Oregon Virginia and Washington) and Washington D.C. The company's largest presence is in California where the majority of its hospitals are located. Hawaii and Oregon are home to one hospital each. Specialty facilities include three behavioral health and chemical dependency clinics the Denver area and more than a dozen dental clinics in Oregon and Washington.

	Annual Growth	12/03	12/04	12/05	12/08	12/09
Sales ($ mil.)	10.7%	-	-	9,852.0	0.2	14,795.3
Net income ($ mil.)	(13.7%)	-	-	774.0	0.2	429.5
Market value ($ mil.)	-	-	-	-	-	-
Employees	-	-	-	-	-	175,668

KAISER-FRANCIS OIL COMPANY

6733 S. Yale Ave.
Tulsa OK 74136-3302
Phone: 918-494-0000
Fax: 918-491-4694
Web: www.kfoc.net

CEO: George B Kaiser
CFO: Don Millican
HR: -
FYE: June 30
Type: Private

King of the Tulsa oil patch oil and gas exploration and production independent Kaiser-Francis Oil Company buys sells and develops oil and gas properties primarily in Arkansas Colorado Kansas Nebraska New Mexico North Dakota Oklahoma Oregon Texas West Virginia and Wyoming. The company teamed up with fellow Tulsa-based energy firm SemGas LP to help build the Wyckoff Gas Storage facility (6 billion cu. ft. of working gas storage) in Steuben County New York. Local billionaire George Kaiser owns and manages Kaiser-Francis Oil. In 2009 Forbes pegged George Kaiser's estimated wealth at $9.5 billion.

KALEIDA HEALTH

726 EXCHANGE ST
BUFFALO, NY 142101484
Phone: 716-859-8000
Fax: -
Web: www.kaleidahealth.org

CEO: -
CFO: -
HR: Daniel (Dan) Farberman
FYE: December 31
Type: Private

Kaleida Health provides a kaleidoscope of services to residents of western New York. The health system operates five acute care hospitals including Buffalo General Hospital and Gates Vascular Institute (combined with about 550 beds) The Women & Children's Hospital of Buffalo (200) DeGraff Memorial Hospital (70) and Millard Fillmore Suburban Hospital (260). Community health needs are met through a network of some 80 medical clinics. Kaleida Health also operates skilled nursing care facilities and provides home health care through its Visiting Nursing Association. To help train future medical professionals Buffalo General Hospital is a teaching affiliate of the State University of New York.

	Annual Growth	12/05	12/06	12/07	12/08	12/09
Sales ($ mil.)	5.0%	-	997.8	1,059.4	1,102.2	1,155.7
Net income ($ mil.)	(3.9%)	-	-	81.7	(209.0)	75.4
Market value ($ mil.)	-	-	-	-	-	-
Employees	-	-	-	-	-	9,000

KALOBIOS PHARMACEUTICALS INC.

260 E. Grand Ave.
South San Francisco CA 94080
Phone: 650-243-3100
Fax: 650-243-3260
Web: www.kalobios.com

NASDAQ: KBIO

CEO: Martin Shkreli
CFO: Chris Thorn
HR: -
FYE: December 31
Type: Private

KaloBios Pharmaceuticals seeks the "good life" (its meaning from the Greek) for patients afflicted with serious medical conditions especially respiratory diseases and certain cancers. It is developing drugs containing antibodies produced via its own technology. The most advanced is in clinical trials and is engineered to fight common bacteria found even in hospitals that cause pneumonia in patients treated by mechanical ventilation. KaloBios has partnered with Sanofi Pasteur to further develop manufacture and market the drug. It also is working on antibodies to treat severe cases of asthma and blood disease. In early 2012 the company went public with an offering valued at $70.6 million.

KAMAN AEROSPACE CORPORATION

Old Windsor Road
Bloomfield CT 06002-0002
Phone: 860-242-4461
Fax: 860-243-7514
Web: www.kamanaero.com

CEO: -
CFO: -
HR: -
FYE: December 31
Type: Subsidiary

Kaman Aerospace is best known for its Super Seasprite (SH-2G) and K-MAX Aerial Truck helicopters but it does much more than make maritime and large transport helicopters. The subsidiary of Kaman Corporation includes Kaman Aerospace and K-MAX Corporation. Its aerospace offerings include electro-optic devices (light detection and ranging systems) fuzes and safety systems (munitions safing and arming devices) aircraft components (wing structures engine doors and machined parts) rugged memory systems (disk and solid state) aerospace bearings (Kamatics) and non-contact position measuring systems (used to measure alignment thickness dimensions pressure and vibration).

KAMAN CORP.
NYS: KAMN

1332 Blue Hills Avenue
Bloomfield, CT 06002
Phone: 860-243-7100
Fax: –
Web: www.kaman.com

CEO: Neal J. Keating
CFO: Robert D. Starr
HR: Nancy L'Esperance
FYE: December 31
Type: Public

Kaman makes fixed and rotary wing aircraft but it's the distribution of four million industrial items to 65000 customers that makes the company fly. The company operates through two segments. Industrial Distribution supplies power transmission/motion control industrial products while the Aerospace segment manufactures Kaman-branded aircraft bearings and components and metallic/composite aerostructures for commercial military and general aviation (fixed and rotary wing) aircraft. It also makes safety arming and fuzing devices for missile and bomb systems for the US and its allies. Customers include such notable names as Airbus BAE Systems Bell Boeing Lockheed Martin Raytheon and Sikorsky.

	Annual Growth	12/10	12/11	12/12	12/13	12/14
Sales ($ mil.)	8.0%	1,318.5	1,498.2	1,592.8	1,681.8	1,795.0
Net income ($ mil.)	10.9%	38.3	51.1	55.0	57.1	57.9
Market value ($ mil.)	8.4%	788.7	741.3	998.5	1,078.0	1,087.7
Employees	3.0%	4,269	4,614	5,007	4,743	4,797

KANA SOFTWARE INC.

840 W. California Ave Ste. 100
Sunnyvale CA 94086
Phone: 650-614-8300
Fax: 408-736-7613
Web: www.kana.com

CEO: Mark Duffell
CFO: Jeff Wylie
HR: –
FYE: December 31
Type: Private

KANA Software knows that a good customer experience can be just a click away. The company's customer relationship management (CRM) software is used by call centers and businesses with e-commerce websites. Its capabilities include customer service interaction through live chat e-mail phone and customer self-service portals. It also offers applications used to assist agents in their conversations with customers. KANA serves companies in the communications financial services retail health care and technology industries as well as government clients in such cities as Boston Brisbane San Francisco Sheffield Toronto and Vancouver.

KANE IS ABLE INC.

Stauffer Industrial Park
Scranton PA 18517
Phone: 570-344-9801
Fax: 570-207-2244
Web: www.kaneisable.com

CEO: Michael J Gardner
CFO: Eugene J Kane Jr
HR: –
FYE: December 31
Type: Private

Kane is Able is able to offer logistics warehousing packaging and freight transportation services to customers in the Northeast US. Through Kane Warehousing and Trucking the company maintains some 8.5 million sq. ft. of dry and temperature-controlled storage facilities in more than 15 distribution locations; it also hauls dry and temperature-controlled freight in both less-than-truckload (LTL) and truckload quantities. (LTL carriers consolidate freight from multiple shippers into a single truckload.) It also operates a fleet of about 925 trailers and a truckload fleet of 200. Edward J. Kane founded the company in 1930; the Kane family still owns and runs it.

KANEMATSU USA INC.

75 Rockefeller Plaza 22nd Fl.
New York NY 10019
Phone: 212-704-9400
Fax: 212-704-9483
Web: www.kanematsuusa.com

CEO: Katsumi Morita
CFO: –
HR: –
FYE: March 31
Type: Subsidiary

Kanematsu USA is a sogo shosa American style. The general trading company helps global industries import and export goods as well as locate suppliers. Its major business groups include food and foodstuffs environment and materials electronics and IT iron and steel and machinery and plant. It assists companies in exporting to unfamiliar markets and in finding high-quality suppliers. Kanematsu USA also helps US manufacturers with such services as logistics financing marketing and research and development. The company is a subsidiary of Japan-based Kanematsu Corporation which was established in 1889.

KANSAS CITY CHIEFS FOOTBALL CLUB INC.

1 Arrowhead Dr.
Kansas City MO 64129
Phone: 816-920-9300
Fax: 816-923-4719
Web: www.kcchiefs.com

CEO: Daniel L Crumb
CFO: –
HR: –
FYE: January 31
Type: Private

These chiefs are trying to lead a tribe of football fans to the Super Bowl. The Kansas City Chiefs Football Club was founded by oilman and sports impresario Lamar Hunt as the Dallas Texans in 1959 a charter member of the American Football League. (Hunt also helped start the AFL and served as its first president.) The franchise moved to Kansas City Missouri in 1963 and was renamed the Chiefs. After winning three league titles and one Super Bowl the franchise joined the National Football League when the rival associations merged in 1970. The Chiefs play host at Kansas City's Arrowhead Stadium. Hunt's family led by his son Clark Hunt continues to own the football franchise.

KANSAS CITY LIFE INSURANCE CO. (KANSAS CITY, MO)
NBB: KCLI

3520 Broadway
Kansas City, MO 64111-2565
Phone: 816-753-7000
Fax: –
Web: www.kclife.com

CEO: R. Philip Bixby
CFO: Tracy W Knapp
HR: –
FYE: December 31
Type: Public

It's not just standing on the corner of 12th Street and Vine... it is moving across America with insurance policies. Kansas City Life Insurance and subsidiary Sunset Life provide insurance products throughout the US to individuals (life and disability coverage and annuities) and to groups (life dental vision and disability insurance). Subsidiary Old American Insurance focuses on burial and related insurance. The insurance companies sell through more than 2500 independent agents brokers and third-party marketers. Kansas City Life also operates its own insurance and investment brokerage network through its Sunset Financial Services unit. Chairman and CEO R. Philip Bixby and his family control the company.

	Annual Growth	12/10	12/11	12/12	12/13	12/14
Assets ($ mil.)	1.3%	4,333.3	4,398.2	4,525.7	4,514.7	4,571.9
Net income ($ mil.)	7.7%	22.3	26.1	39.9	29.6	30.0
Market value ($ mil.)		–	–	–	–	–
Employees	(0.6%)	446	444	443	446	436

KANSAS CITY SOUTHERN   NYS: KSU

427 West 12th Street
Kansas City, MO 64105
Phone: 816 983-1303
Fax: 816 556-0297
Web: www.kcsouthern.com

CEO: David L. Starling
CFO: Michael W. (Mike) Upchurch
HR: John (Jack) Derry
FYE: December 31
Type: Public

Kansas City Southern (KCS) rides the rails of a 6500-mile network that stretches from Missouri to Mexico. The company's Kansas City Southern Railway (KCSR) owns and operates about 3300 miles of track in the midwestern and southern US. KCS offers rail freight service in Mexico through Kansas City Southern de México (KCSM formerly TFM) which maintains more than 3200 miles of track and serves three major ports. Another KCS unit Texas Mexican Railway connects the KCSR and KCSM systems. The KCS railroads transport such freight as industrial and consumer products agricultural and mineral products and chemical and petroleum products.

	Annual Growth	12/11	12/12	12/13	12/14	12/15
Sales ($ mil.)	3.6%	2,098.3	2,238.6	2,369.3	2,577.1	2,418.8
Net income ($ mil.)	10.0%	330.3	377.3	351.4	502.6	483.5
Market value ($ mil.)	2.4%	7,376.4	9,054.3	13,430.7	13,235.5	8,098.8
Employees	2.1%	6,140	6,110	6,260	6,490	6,670

KANSAS ELECTRIC POWER COOPERATIVE INC.

600 SW CORPORATE VW
TOPEKA, KS 666151233
Phone: 785-273-7010
Fax: –
Web: www.kepco.org

CEO: Thuck Terrill
CFO: –
HR: –
FYE: December 31
Type: Private

If Dorothy lived in rural Kansas today she'd probably hear that tornado warning and reach safety thanks to the power supplied by Kansas Electric Power Cooperative (KEPCo). KEPCo operates power plants and purchases additional energy for its 19 member distribution cooperatives which serve more than 110000 rural customers. The generation and transmission utility's assets include a 6% stake in Wolf Creek Nuclear Operating Corporation which operates Kansas' Wolf Creek Generating Station. Subsidiary KSI Engineering provides utility construction and infrastructure services. KEPCo which was formed in 1975 is part of the alliance of Touchstone Energy Cooperatives.

	Annual Growth	12/06	12/07	12/08	12/09	12/10
Sales ($ mil.)	(72.3%)	–	–	1,833.0	122.7	140.5
Net income ($ mil.)	10032.3%	–	–	0.0	9.3	7.6
Market value ($ mil.)	–	–	–	–	–	–
Employees	–	–	–	–	–	24

KANSAS STATE UNIVERSITY

ANDERSON HALL 110
MANHATTAN, KS 66506
Phone: 785-532-6210
Fax: –
Web: www.ksu.edu

CEO: –
CFO: –
HR: –
FYE: June 30
Type: Private

K-State is a big deal in the Little Apple. Located in Manhattan Kansas (aka the Little Apple) Kansas State University (K-State) is a land grant institution that has an enrollment of some 24000 students. It offers more than 250 undergraduate majors 65 master's degrees 45 doctoral degrees and more than 20 graduate certificate programs. Major fields of study include agriculture technology and veterinary medicine. Notable alumni include former White House press secretary Marlin Fitzwater and actor Gordon Jump. Along with the University of Kansas and other universities technical schools and community colleges in the state K-State is governed by The Kansas Board of Regents.

	Annual Growth	06/07	06/08	06/09	06/10	06/13
Sales ($ mil.)	(22.4%)	–	1,988.9	420.6	459.8	558.1
Net income ($ mil.)	54.1%	–	–	10.7	50.5	60.5
Market value ($ mil.)	–	–	–	–	–	–
Employees	–	–	–	–	–	5,168

KANTHAL GLOBAR

495 Commerce Dr. Ste. 7
Amherst NY 14228-2311
Phone: 716-691-4010
Fax: 716-691-7850
Web: www.globar.com

CEO: –
CFO: –
HR: –
FYE: December 31
Type: Subsidiary

Kanthal Globar markets high-temperature ceramic products for industrial and residential applications. The company's product lines serve two main categories including electronic components such as resistors (produce charges) capacitors (store charges) and thermistors; electric heating elements for furnaces comprise the second category. Kanthal Globar is a subsidiary of Sweden's Kanthal AB which in turn is a part of Sandvik AB a manufacturer of tools and materials for the mining and construction industries. Kanthal Globar is part of Sandvik's Materials Technology business area.

KAPSTONE PAPER & PACKAGING CORP   NYS: KS

1101 Skokie Blvd., Suite 300
Northbrook, IL 60062
Phone: 847 239-8800
Fax: 847 205-7551
Web: www.kapstonepaper.com

CEO: Roger W. Stone
CFO: Andrea K. Tarbox
HR: –
FYE: December 31
Type: Public

Rock paper sissors? KapStone Paper and Packaging has the upper hand in the game of unbleached kraft. The company manufactures largely linerboard a type of paperboard that is converted into laminated tier sheets and wrapping material. It also produces kraft paper (industry-speak for strong wrapping paper) for multiwall bags; saturating kraft (sold under the Durasorb brand) to produce mainly high pressure laminates for furniture construction materials and electronics; and unbleached folding carton board (Kraftpak) which is converted into packaging for consumer goods. KapStone counts 3200-plus customers including Graphic Packaging Exopack and other major converters. The US represents about 80% of sales.

	Annual Growth	12/10	12/11	12/12	12/13	12/14
Sales ($ mil.)	30.9%	782.7	906.1	1,216.6	1,748.2	2,300.9
Net income ($ mil.)	27.5%	65.0	124.0	62.5	127.3	171.9
Market value ($ mil.)	17.6%	1,469.5	1,511.8	2,131.3	5,365.2	2,815.1
Employees	30.4%	1,600	2,715	2,760	4,601	4,628

KAR AUCTION SERVICES INC.   NYS: KAR

13085 Hamilton Crossing Boulevard
Carmel, IN 46032
Phone: 800 923-3725
Fax: –
Web: www.karauctionservices.com

CEO: James P. (Jim) Hallett
CFO: Eric M. Loughmiller
HR: Lisa Price
FYE: December 31
Type: Public

As its name suggests KAR Auction Services and its subsidiaries sell nearly 4 million used and salvaged vehicles annually. KAR is a holding company for ADESA a wholesaler of used vehicles at auction; Insurance Auto Auctions a salvage auto auction company; and Automotive Finance Corporation a capital funding business that serves used car dealers. In addition to more than 230 physical auction sites located throughout North America KAR also hosts Internet auctions. The company makes money through auction fees extended to vehicle buyers and sellers and by providing add-on services such as inspections storage transportation reconditioning salvage recovery and titling and financing.

	Annual Growth	12/10	12/11	12/12	12/13	12/14
Sales ($ mil.)	6.8%	1,815.0	1,886.3	1,963.4	2,173.3	2,364.5
Net income ($ mil.)	24.9%	69.6	72.2	92.0	67.7	169.3
Market value ($ mil.)	25.9%	1,950.2	1,907.8	2,860.2	4,175.9	4,896.6
Employees	0.1%	12,558	12,215	12,069	12,300	12,600

KARSTEN MANUFACTURING CORPORATION

2201 W. Desert Cove
Phoenix AZ 85029
Phone: 602-870-5000
Fax: 602-687-4482
Web: www.ping.com/

CEO: John A Solheim
CFO: –
HR: –
FYE: December 31
Type: Private

If there's a PING in your putt it's got to be Karsten Manufacturing. The company designs and produces customized PING golf clubs. (The clubs are named for the sound they make when striking the ball.) The company also supplies golf bags gloves headwear and related gear. Karsten provides club-fitting services systems and training at golf courses and pro shops across the US as well as an online fitting program. Professionals from all over the world swing with PING including Mark Wilson Maria Hjorth Sherri Steinhauer and Angel Cabrera. The company was founded in 1959 after Karsten Solheim designed a revolutionary putter in his garage. His youngest son John leads the family-owned firm.

KARYOPHARM THERAPEUTICS INC

NMS: KPTI

85 Wells Avenue, 2nd Floor
Newton, MA 02459
Phone: 617 658-0600
Fax: –
Web: www.karyopharm.com

CEO: Michael F Kauffman
CFO: Justin A. Renz
HR: –
FYE: December 31
Type: Public

Karyopharm Therapeutics is ready to combat cancer on a chromosomal level. The company is developing an orally administered drug for patients with certain blood and solid tumor cancers. Its lead drug candidate Selinexor is being studied to determine its effectiveness in suppressing a cancer-causing protein. In addition to cancer Karyopharm hopes its compounds have the potential to also combat autoimmune and inflammatory diseases HIV and influenza as well as promote wound healing. The company went public in 2013 raising $108 million with which it plans to fund further clinical development of Selinexor.

	Annual Growth	12/10	12/11	12/12	12/13	12/14
Sales ($ mil.)	–	0.0	0.2	0.6	0.4	0.2
Net income ($ mil.)	–	0.0	(10.3)	(15.9)	(33.9)	(75.8)
Market value ($ mil.)	–	0.0	–	–	749.5	1,223.9
Employees	75.7%	–	–	23	31	71

KATE SPADE LLC

48 W. 25th St.
New York NY 10010-2708
Phone: 212-739-6550
Fax: 212-739-6544
Web: www.katespade.com

CEO: Craig A Leavitt
CFO: –
HR: –
FYE: December 31
Type: Subsidiary

kate spade's story is one of simplicity like the bags it sells and expansion. The company begun in 1993 by designer Kate Spade and her husband Andy to make kate spade handbags has since lent its uncomplicated design for the manufacture of stationery various functional bags (think diaper bags) and licensed products — with lines of homewares (sheets tabletop items and wallpaper) as well as beauty items eyewear and shoes. Women's items are sold under the kate spade name; men's products carry the jack spade moniker. Owned by Fifth & Pacific the firm distributes products in Asia and sells them through more than 70 company-owned specialty and outlet stores upscale US department stores and its website.

KATUN CORPORATION

10951 Bush Lake Rd.
Minneapolis MN 55438
Phone: 952-941-9505
Fax: 952-941-4307
Web: www.katun.com

CEO: Carlyle Singer
CFO: –
HR: –
FYE: December 31
Type: Private

Katun wants you to exercise your options — to not buy OEM parts. The company designs and makes alternative parts and supplies for copiers printers and fax machines. Other sales come from toner cartridges drums and rollers. Also included among Katun's more than 6000 products are ink jet cartridges thermal ribbons ball bearings and tools — many for products made by companies such as Canon IBM and Ricoh. Katun (Mayan for "a period of 20 years") sells its wares to more than 18000 office equipment dealers and distributors in about 150 countries. It also markets products through catalogs and the Internet. Founded in 1979 the company was acquired by equity firm Monomoy Capital Partners (MCP) in 2008.

KATY INDUSTRIES, INC.

NBB: KATY

305 Rock Industrial Park Drive
Bridgeton, MO 63044
Phone: 314 656-4321
Fax: –
Web: www.katyindustries.com

CEO: David J. (Dave) Feldman
CFO: Curt Kroll
HR: Brian G. Nichols
FYE: December 31
Type: Public

Katy Industries gives janitors the tools and supplies to clean up the acts of others. The firm makes and markets commercial cleaning products as well as plastic home storage items. Its Continental Commercial Products (CCP) subsidiary operates multiple divisions including: Container Contico Continental and Wilen. Products are sold under the Continental Kleen Aire Huskee KingKan Unibody SuperKan and Tilt-N-Wheel brands. CCP has operations in Missouri and California as well as Canada. Its customers include janitorial/sanitary and food service distributors that supply restaurants hotels schools and other facilities. Founded in 1967 Katy is restructuring to return to profitability.

	Annual Growth	12/10	12/11	12/12	12/13	12/14
Sales ($ mil.)	(8.3%)	141.0	120.3	100.5	78.3	99.7
Net income ($ mil.)	–	(5.1)	4.8	(15.1)	(1.5)	2.5
Market value ($ mil.)	(0.2%)	11.2	1.3	1.4	3.3	11.1
Employees	(13.4%)	607	533	407	263	341

KATZ MEDIA GROUP INC.

125 W. 55th St.
New York NY 10019-5366
Phone: 212-424-6000
Fax: 212-424-6110
Web: www.katz-media.com

CEO: Stuart O Olds
CFO: Robert Damon
HR: –
FYE: December 31
Type: Subsidiary

As a subsidiary of radio broadcaster Clear Channel Katz Media Group is the leading media representative that sells spot advertising on radio and TV. It represents about 4000 radio stations and 600 TV and digital multicast stations throughout the US. Its Katz Radio Group (including Christal Radio Eastman Radio and Katz Radio) represents such radio broadcasters as Cox Radio Hubbard Broadcasting and CBS Radio while Clear Channel Radio Sales sells spot ads on Clear Channel stations. The company also operates divisions such as Katz Television and Katz Marketing. All total it has about 20 offices throughout the US. Emanuel Katz founded the company in 1888. It was acquired by Clear Channel in 2000.

KAWNEER COMPANY INC.

555 Guthridge Ct. Technology Park/Atlanta
Norcross GA 30092-3503
Phone: 770-449-5555
Fax: 770-734-1560
Web: www.kawneer.com

CEO: –
CFO: Peter Hong
HR: –
FYE: December 31
Type: Subsidiary

Although not really a headbanger Kawneer is definitely into metal. Operating as Kawneer North America the company manufactures architectural aluminum building products and systems for use in commercial and industrial construction. The Alcoa subsidiary's products include sliding and swing entrances framing systems for shopping malls and storefronts hung/sliding and ribbon/fixed windows building panels sun control products and curtain wall systems for stadiums sports facilities schools low-rise offices and high-rise buildings. Kawneer operates manufacturing plants and fabricating service centers throughout the US and Canada. The company also sells products in Europe Asia and the Middle East.

KAYE SCHOLER LLP

425 Park Ave.
New York NY 10022-3598
Phone: 212-836-8000
Fax: 212-836-8689
Web: www.kayescholer.com

CEO: –
CFO: Rod Dolan
HR: –
FYE: December 31
Type: Private - Partnershi

Corporations the world over have trusted Kaye Scholer LLP with their antitrust issues. Founded in 1917 the law firm has specialized in antitrust cases since the 1950s. Kaye Scholer has about 450 attorneys practicing corporate law as well as an extensive litigation practice (almost half of the firm's attorneys specialize in this area). Major corporate clients of the firm have included such big names as Bank of America J.P. Morgan ChaseNovartis Onex Corporation Pfizer and the California State Controller's Office. Kaye Scholer operates six offices in the US and three international outposts.

KAZ INC.

1775 Broadway Ste. 2405
New York NY 10019
Phone: 212-586-1630
Fax: 212-265-9248
Web: www.kaz.com

CEO: Julien Mininberg
CFO: Jon Kosheff
HR: –
FYE: February 28
Type: Subsidiary

Kaz allows customers to blow off a little steam. The company makes humidifiers vaporizers air purifiers and filters thermometers heating pads and portable heaters as well as electronic mosquito traps. Its products made under the Kaz Braun Enviracare Honeywell and Vicks brand names are sold worldwide through drugstore chains and mass merchandisers such as CVS Kmart Target and Wal-Mart and some medical distributors and home improvement stores. Vicks and Braun brands are licensed from Procter & Gamble (P&G) and the Honeywell label from Honeywell International. The company operates as the healthcare/home environment segment of personal care products giant Helen of Troy which acquired Kaz in 2011.

KB HOME

NYS: KBH

10990 Wilshire Boulevard
Los Angeles, CA 90024
Phone: 310 231-4000
Fax: 310 231-4222
Web: www.kbhome.com

CEO: Jeffrey T. (Jeff) Mezger
CFO: Jeff J. Kaminski
HR: Kathleen Knoblauch
FYE: November 30
Type: Public

For a dwelling done your way you might turn to KB Home. As one of the largest homebuilders in the US KB Home constructs single-family (attached and detached) homes townhomes and condominiums suited mainly for first-time move-up and active adult buyers primarily in California Colorado Texas and southeastern US. Its Built to Order brand homes allows buyers to customize their homes by choosing a floor plan as well as exterior and interior features. The homebuilder's average home sold for $354800 in fiscal 2015. To help with the homebuying process KB Home also offers mortgage banking title services and insurance. KB has built 600000 homes since it was founded in 1957.

	Annual Growth	11/11	11/12	11/13	11/14	11/15
Sales ($ mil.)	23.2%	1,315.9	1,560.1	2,097.1	2,400.9	3,032.0
Net income ($ mil.)	–	(178.8)	(59.0)	40.0	918.3	84.6
Market value ($ mil.)	17.7%	752.7	1,470.6	1,795.3	1,799.4	1,443.0
Employees	8.8%	1,200	1,200	1,430	1,590	1,680

KBM GROUP

2050 N. Greenville Ave.
Richardson TX 75082
Phone: 972-664-3600
Fax: 972-664-3656
Web: www.kbmg.com

CEO: Gary Laben
CFO: Jim Pike
HR: –
FYE: December 31
Type: Subsidiary

KBM Group (formerly KnowledgeBase Marketing) aims to put some smarts into your database marketing efforts. The firm provides demographic data used for marketing databases by its client companies. In addition to raw data KBM Group helps its customers integrate their online and offline marketing strategies. It also offers database expertise and data processing services for its clients who typically come from the financial services health care retail and telecommunications sectors. Owning more than 15 offices spread throughout the world the company is part of marketing services firm Wunderman which itself is a key component of the Young & Rubicam Brands unit of UK-based advertising conglomerate WPP Group.

KBR INC

NYS: KBR

601 Jefferson Street, Suite 3400
Houston, TX 77002
Phone: 713 753-3011
Fax: –
Web: www.kbr.com

CEO: Stuart J.B. Bradie
CFO: Brian K. Ferraioli
HR: Ian Mackey
FYE: December 31
Type: Public

KBR builds big projects for the US government. But the engineering and construction services company also lends its capabilities to the hydrocarbon energy minerals civil infrastructure and power and industrial markets. The company is widely known for its service to the government and infrastructure sector; however that figure is slowly declining as the military pulls its presence in the Middle East. KBR is increasingly focused on projects in the oil and gas industry. It has designed many of world's liquefied natural gas production facilities and develops new technologies such as coal gasification. Operations outside the US account for two-thirds of KBR's revenue.

	Annual Growth	12/10	12/11	12/12	12/13	12/14
Sales ($ mil.)	(10.9%)	10,099.0	9,261.0	7,921.0	7,283.0	6,366.0
Net income ($ mil.)	–	327.0	480.0	144.0	229.0	(1,262.0)
Market value ($ mil.)	(13.6%)	4,413.2	4,036.6	4,333.5	4,618.9	2,455.0
Employees	(8.1%)	35,000	27,000	27,000	27,000	25,000

KBS INC.

8050 KIMWAY DR
RICHMOND, VA 232282831
Phone: 804-262-0100
Fax: -
Web: www.kbsgc.com

CEO: -
CFO: James Lipscombe
HR: -
FYE: September 30
Type: Private

You would hit the nail right on the head if you were to call KBS a "regional contractor." The company provides design/build planning general contracting and construction management services for commercial and multifamily residential projects in Virginia. Its projects include office buildings apartment complexes shopping centers hotels schools jails warehouses and senior living facilities. Some 60% of the company's business comes in the form of repeat customers. Clients have included Cousins Properties Forest City Enterprises Ukrop's Best Buy Wal-Mart and Virginia Commonwealth University. President Bill Paulette founded KBS in a sheet metal shop in 1975.

	Annual Growth	09/09	09/10	09/11	09/12	09/13
Sales ($ mil.)	(0.4%)	-	153.2	159.4	192.5	151.5
Net income ($ mil.)	(20.2%)	-	-	2.9	2.1	1.8
Market value ($ mil.)	-	-	-	-	-	-
Employees	-	-	-	-	-	130

KEARNY FINANCIAL CORP

120 Passaic Ave.
Fairfield, NJ 07004-3510
Phone: 973 244-4500
Fax: -

NMS: KRNY
CEO: Craig L Montanaro
CFO: Eric B Heyer
HR: -
FYE: June 30
Type: Public

Kearny Financial is the holding company for Kearny Federal Savings Bank which has some 40 branches in northern New Jersey. Kearny Federal Savings Bank offers such standard services as checking and savings accounts CDs ATM and debit cards IRAs and loans. Residential mortgages make up about two-thirds of its loan portfolio; multifamily and commercial mortgages and home equity loans round out most of the rest. Kearny also invests in mortgage-backed securities government and municipal bonds and other securities. In 2010 the company acquired Central Jersey Bancorp for approximately $72 million adding 13 branches to its network.

	Annual Growth	06/10	06/11	06/12	06/13	06/14
Assets ($ mil.)	10.7%	2,339.8	2,904.1	2,937.0	3,145.4	3,510.0
Net income ($ mil.)	10.6%	6.8	7.9	5.1	6.5	10.2
Market value ($ mil.)	13.4%	616.2	612.8	651.8	705.6	1,018.4
Employees	13.6%	285	436	459	453	474

KECK GRADUATE INSTITUTE

535 WATSON DR
CLAREMONT, CA 917114817
Phone: 909-621-8000
Fax: -
Web: www.kgi.edu

CEO: -
CFO: Robert W Caragher
HR: -
FYE: June 30
Type: Private

Those who attend Keck Graduate Institute (KGI) know good things come in small packages. The institute which enrolls 82 students (and has 21 faculty members for a ratio of approximately 1-to-4) specializes in applied life sciences and is a member of The Claremont Colleges maintained by the Claremont University Consortium. KGI offers a two-year graduate program that culminates in a Master of Bioscience (MBS) degree. Those who earn their MBS may put in an additional three years for a Ph.D. in Applied Life Sciences. Curriculum is designed to prepare students for careers in the biotech medical device and pharmaceutical industries. KGI was founded in 1997 with a $50 million grant from the W.M. Keck Foundation.

	Annual Growth	06/09	06/10	06/11	06/12	06/13
Sales ($ mil.)	5.1%	-	12.3	9.0	16.5	14.3
Net income ($ mil.)	-	-	-	2.7	(0.0)	(2.8)
Market value ($ mil.)	-	-	-	-	-	-
Employees	-	-	-	-	-	65

KEENAN HOPKINS SCHMIDT AND STOWELL CONTRACTORS INC.

5422 BAY CENTER DR # 200
TAMPA, FL 336093437
Phone: 813-628-9330
Fax: -
Web: www.khss.com

CEO: Michael Cannon
CFO: Dennis Norman
HR: -
FYE: December 31
Type: Private

Business is always looking up for KHS&S Contractors which specializes in wall and ceiling construction including interior exterior acoustical and insulation work. KHS&S is one of the largest theme park contractors in the US completing more than 5.5 million square feet of thematic finishes and providing water feature and rockwork technology and concrete/tilt-up construction. The specialty contractor has worked on projects for Universal Studios' Islands of Adventure and Walt Disney Parks & Resorts. KHS&S also works on casinos convention centers health care facilities office buildings laboratories and other commercial projects. Founded in 1984 the company is owned by its employees.

	Annual Growth	12/09	12/10	12/11	12/12	12/13
Sales ($ mil.)	60.5%	-	28.0	73.6	99.7	115.8
Net income ($ mil.)	131.6%	-	-	0.8	2.6	4.3
Market value ($ mil.)	-	-	-	-	-	-
Employees	-	-	-	-	-	350

KEHE DISTRIBUTORS LLC

900 N. Schmidt Rd.
Romeoville IL 60446-4056
Phone: 630-343-0000
Fax: 815-886-1111
Web: www.kehefood.com

CEO: Brandon Barnholt
CFO: Christopher Meyers
HR: -
FYE: April 30
Type: Private

KeHE Distributors plays a key role in getting specialty foods on to grocery store shelves. It is a wholesale supplier of ethnic and gourmet foods serving more than 33000 food retailers across the US Canada Mexico and the Caribbean. It distributes more than 60000 items from 3500 vendors and offers African-American Asian Latin American Mediterranean and kosher food products as well as a wide variety of organic and natural food items. The company's KeHE Direct unit provides online ordering services for its customers. Arthur Kehe founded the employee-owned company in 1952 in the basement of his home.

KEITHLEY INSTRUMENTS INC.

28775 Aurora Rd.
Solon OH 44139
Phone: 440-248-0400
Fax: 440-248-6168
Web: www.keithley.com

CEO: Joseph P Keithley
CFO: Mark J Plush
HR: -
FYE: September 30
Type: Subsidiary

Keithley Instruments wants to be instrumental to the success of engineers scientists and technicians. The company makes some 500 different products used to control measure and trace signals whether they take the form of electrical current light or radio waves. Its offerings include digital multimeters semiconductor parametric test and device characterization systems signal analyzers and generators and plug-in boards that enable PCs to be used for data acquisition. Keithley primarily sells to the precision electronics research and education semiconductor and wireless markets. In 2010 Danaher acquired Keithley in a deal valued at around $300 million.

KELLEY DRYE & WARREN LLP

101 Park Ave.
New York NY 10178-0002
Phone: 212-808-7800
Fax: 212-808-7897
Web: www.kelleydrye.com

CEO: -
CFO: -
HR: -
FYE: December 31
Type: Private - Partnershi

One of the oldest law firms in New York Kelley Drye & Warren has about 400 lawyers in seven offices in the US and Europe. It specializes in areas such as advertising law antitrust and trade regulation bankruptcy and restructuring tax government relations white collar crime and other commercial litigation and has served such blue-chip clients as Dow Chemical and Wells Fargo. During its long history (the firm traces its roots back to 1836) Kelley Drye has defended such high-profile clients as Union Carbide after the Bhopal gas disaster and Hercules Incorporated in Agent Orange litigation.

KELLOGG CO

One Kellogg Square, P.O. Box 3599
Battle Creek, MI 49016-3599
Phone: 269 961-2000
Fax: 616 961-2871
Web: www.kelloggcompany.com

NYS: K
CEO: John A. Bryant
CFO: Ronald L. (Ron) Dissinger
HR: Xavier Boza
FYE: January 03
Type: Public

From the company's home base in Battle Creek Michigan Kellogg Company is in a constant battle for the #1 spot in the US cereal market with its main rival General Mills. Kellogg founded in 1906 boasts many familiar brand names including Kellogg's Corn Flakes Frosted Flakes Corn Pops and Rice Krispies. While the company works to fill the world's cereal bowls it supplements its bottom line with snacks and cookies (Keebler Cheez-It and Famous Amos) along with convenience foods such as Eggo waffles and Nutri-Grain and Bear Naked cereal bars. Its products are sold worldwide.

	Annual Growth	01/11*	12/11	12/12	12/13*	01/15
Sales ($ mil.)	4.1%	12,397.0	13,198.0	14,197.0	14,792.0	14,580.0
Net income ($ mil.)	(15.6%)	1,247.0	1,231.0	961.0	1,807.0	632.0
Market value ($ mil.)	6.4%	18,184.6	18,003.1	19,697.6	21,709.0	23,311.1
Employees	(0.7%)	30,645	30,700	31,006	30,277	29,790

*Fiscal year change

KELLSTROM AEROSPACE LLC

3701 S FLAMINGO RD
MIRAMAR, FL 330272934
Phone: 954-538-2000
Fax: -
Web: www.aerosonic.com

CEO: -
CFO: -
HR: -
FYE: December 31
Type: Private

Does the spell-check at aircraft parts inventory service Kellstrom Aerospace correct "enginuity"? Using its ingenuity to specialize in engines made by CFM International General Electric Pratt & Whitney and Rolls-Royce the company supplies new and overhauled products for military and commercial aircraft. Kellstrom doing business as Kellstrom Industries also provides maintenance for military and commercial aircraft components. Customers include commercial airlines US and foreign military forces and maintenance repair and overhaul facilities. Kellstrom Aerospace was established in 1990 and has been privately owned since 2002.

	Annual Growth	12/08	12/09	12/10	12/11	12/12
Sales ($ mil.)	3.4%	-	163.2	149.4	155.5	180.5
Net income ($ mil.)	54.4%	-	-	2.7	1.0	6.4
Market value ($ mil.)	-	-	-	-	-	-
Employees	-	-	-	-	-	262

KELLWOOD COMPANY

600 Kellwood Pkwy.
Chesterfield MO 63017
Phone: 314-576-3100
Fax: 314-576-3460
Web: www.kellwood.com

CEO: Lynn Shanahan
CFO: Joe Lombardi
HR: -
FYE: January 31
Type: Private

Who would be one of the leading US apparel makers? Kellwood would. The firm generates most of its sales from women's wear including the Rebecca Taylor David Meister and Sag Harbor lines. It also makes and designs juniors and girls clothes and accessories. Its portfolio of about 20 brands also includes My Michelle Baby Phat Phat Farm Rewind Vince and XOXO. The company is a major supplier to department stores as well as mass retailers specialty boutiques and catalogs. Kellwood also operates Vince Lamb & Flag and Rebecca Taylor brand outlet stores across the US. Kellwood has been adding contemporary brands while shedding mainstream brands such as Koret. The company is owned by Sun Capital Partners.

KELLY SERVICES, INC.

999 West Big Beaver Road
Troy, MI 48084
Phone: 248 362-4444
Fax: -
Web: www.kellyservices.com

NMS: KELY A
CEO: Carl T. Camden
CFO: Patricia Little
HR: Dave Charlip
FYE: December 28
Type: Public

These days a lot of "Kelly Girls" are men. Once a business that supplied only female clerical help Kelly Services has expanded to include male and female temporary employees in light industrial technical and professional sectors including information technology specialists engineers and accountants. It also places lawyers (Kelly Law Registry) scientists (Kelly Scientific Resources) substitute teachers (Kelly Educational Staffing) nurses and other medical staff (Kelly Healthcare Resources) and teleservices personnel (KellyConnect). Kelly Services assigns some 555000 temporary employees around the world each year. Chairman Terence Adderley owns a controlling stake in the company.

	Annual Growth	01/11	01/12*	12/12	12/13	12/14
Sales ($ mil.)	4.0%	4,950.3	5,551.0	5,450.5	5,413.1	5,562.7
Net income ($ mil.)	(3.2%)	26.1	63.7	50.1	58.9	23.7
Market value ($ mil.)	(3.3%)	709.2	516.1	586.6	954.1	641.3
Employees	1.5%	538,000	558,200	568,100	548,100	563,300

*Fiscal year change

KELLY-MOORE PAINT COMPANY INC.

987 Commercial St.
San Carlos CA 94070
Phone: 650-592-8337
Fax: 707-569-0105
Web: www.kj.com

CEO: -
CFO: Roy George
HR: -
FYE: December 31
Type: Private

You'd call them red yellow and green. Kelly-Moore Paint Company might dub them Gatsby Brick Sunlit Plaza and Emerald Lights. By whatever hue Kelly-Moore aims to show that the paint business isn't entirely run by multinational big brushes like Sherwin-Williams and DuPont. The company produces about 1.8 million gallons of paint per year in three regional warehouses and owns and operates about 140 stores in several states west of the Mississippi River. Kelly-Moore sells about 400 types of paints finishes and sundries to professional contractors and painters and to the do-it-yourself market.

KELSO & COMPANY

320 Park Ave. 24th Fl.
New York NY 10022
Phone: 212-751-3939
Fax: 212-223-2379
Web: www.kelso.com

CEO: –
CFO: –
HR: –
FYE: December 31
Type: Private

They're the softer side of private equity. Kelso & Company is a private equity firm that specializes in supporting management buyouts. It eschews hostile takeovers and liquidations and is often a "white knight" investor that helps companies dodge unsolicited bids. The firm's investments generally center around industrial and consumer products concerns. Kelso & Company's most recent investment fund its eighth garnered more than $5 billion in investment capital. The firm was founded in 1971 by the late renowned economist Louis O. Kelso and has invested in more than 100 companies with a total capitalization of about $35 billion since establishing its first investment partnership in 1980.

KEMET CORP.   NYS: KEM

2835 Kemet Way
Simpsonville, SC 29681
Phone: 864 963-6300
Fax: –
Web: www.kemet.com

CEO: Per-Olof Loof
CFO: William M. Lowe
HR: –
FYE: March 31
Type: Public

KEMET is one of the world's largest makers of tantalum and multilayer ceramic capacitors — devices that store filter and regulate electrical energy and that are used in virtually all electronic devices. KEMET makes about 35 billion capacitors a year; its focus is on surface-mount capacitors including specialized units for aerospace automotive communications systems computers and military equipment. The company also makes solid aluminum capacitors for high-frequency applications. More than 70% of its sales come from outside the US.

	Annual Growth	03/11	03/12	03/13	03/14	03/15
Sales ($ mil.)	(5.2%)	1,018.5	984.8	843.0	833.7	823.2
Net income ($ mil.)	–	63.0	6.7	(82.2)	(68.5)	(14.1)
Market value ($ mil.)	(27.3%)	674.1	425.4	284.1	264.1	188.2
Employees	70.2%	1,100	9,700	9,800	9,625	9,225

KEMIRA CHEMICALS INC.

1950 Vaughn Rd.
Kennesaw GA 30144
Phone: 770-436-1542
Fax: 770-436-3432
Web: www.kemirachemicals.com

CEO: Carolina Den Brok-Perez
CFO: Belinda Rosario
HR: –
FYE: December 31
Type: Subsidiary

Kemira Chemicals brings a Nordic approach to the chemical industry in the New World. The company is the North American subsidiary of Finnish international specialty chemical maker Kemira Oyj. It manufactures specialty and process chemicals for the pulp and paper water treatment mineral slurries and chemical industries. Products include biocides colloidal silica de-foamers dispersants hazardous waste stabilizers polishing slurries sodium aluminate and water treatment polymers. It also produces bleaching agents for detergents and titanium dioxide as well as organic acids salts and blends.

KEMPER CORP. (DE)   NYS: KMPR

One East Wacker Drive
Chicago, IL 60601
Phone: 312 661-4600
Fax: –
Web: www.kemper.com

CEO: Joseph P. (Joe) Lacher
CFO: Eric Draut
HR: Edward (Ed) Konar
FYE: December 31
Type: Public

Kemper is among the largest property and casualty insurance groups in the nation. The company operates through two operating segments: Property and Casualty Insurance and Life and Health Insurance. The Property and Casualty Insurance segment's principal products are personal automobile insurance both standard and non-standard risk homeowners insurance other personal insurance and commercial automobile insurance. The Life and Health Insurance segment's principal products are individual life accident health and property insurance. The company operates in the southern midwestern and western US.

	Annual Growth	12/11	12/12	12/13	12/14	12/15
Assets ($ mil.)	(0.2%)	8,085.9	8,009.1	7,656.4	7,833.4	8,036.1
Net income ($ mil.)	0.6%	83.7	103.4	217.7	114.5	85.7
Market value ($ mil.)	6.3%	1,499.3	1,514.1	2,098.2	1,853.4	1,911.9
Employees	(2.7%)	–	6,075	6,100	5,350	5,600

KEN'S FOODS INC.

1 D'angelo Dr.
Marlborough MA 01752-3066
Phone: 508-485-7540
Fax: 570-473-4303
Web: www.keystoneinsgrp.com

CEO: Frank A Crowley III
CFO: James Sutherby
HR: –
FYE: April 30
Type: Private

Having some leafy greens with that steak? Ask Ken's Foods for some dressing. The condiments company manufactures and markets more than 400 varieties of bottled salad dressings marinades and sauces under the Ken's Steak House brand name. Its products are distributed to retail food companies such as Albertsons Wal-Mart Hy-Vee Kroger Meijer HEB and others and to foodservice operators throughout most of the US. As part of its business Ken's Foods which is family owned and operated also offers production labeling and packaging services for other food manufacturers. The dressings manufacturer owns and operates production facilities in Massachusetts Georgia and Nevada.

KENERGY CORP.

6402 OLD CORYDON RD
HENDERSON, KY 424209392
Phone: 270-926-4141
Fax: –
Web: www.kenergycorp.com

CEO: Stanford Noveick
CFO: –
HR: –
FYE: December 31
Type: Private

Kenergy kens energy as the Scots might say. Electric distribution cooperative Kenergy serves about 55000 customers in 14 counties (Breckinridge Caldwell Crittenden Daviess Hancock Henderson Hopkins Livingston Lyon McLean Muhlenberg Ohio Union and Webster) in Western Kentucky. Kenergy serves its customer base of households commercial enterprises and industries via more than 6700 miles of power lines. The customer-owned company is part of Touchstone Energy Cooperatives a national alliance of more than 600 local consumer-owned electric utility cooperatives.

	Annual Growth	12/09	12/10	12/11	12/12	12/13
Sales ($ mil.)	8.0%	–	402.2	426.6	496.0	506.9
Net income ($ mil.)	6.9%	–	–	0.1	0.1	0.1
Market value ($ mil.)	–	–	–	–	–	–
Employees		–	–	–	–	155

KENEXA CORPORATION

NASDAQ: KNXA

650 E. Swedesford Rd. 2nd Fl.
Wayne PA 19087
Phone: 610-971-9171
Fax: 610-971-9181
Web: www.kenexa.com

CEO: Nooruddin S Karsan
CFO: Donald F Volk
HR: –
FYE: December 31
Type: Public

Kenexa can execute on HR functions. The company develops integrated and Web-based or cloud applications that automate human resources activities such as recruitment skills testing and employee development tracking. Kenexa also offers outsourcing options to clients taking over part or all of the recruitment and hiring process. In addition the company conducts employee surveys for its customers. It sells its services and software products mostly on a subscription basis to about 9000 large and midsized corporations such as Eli Lilly and KPMG. In 2012 Kenexa agreed to be acquired by IBM in a cash transaction valued at around $1.3 billion.

KENNAMETAL INC.

NYS: KMT

600 Grant Street, Suite 5100
Pittsburgh, PA 15219-2706
Phone: 412 248-8000
Fax: –
Web: www.kennametal.com

CEO: Ronald M. DeFeo
CFO: Jan Kees van Gaalen
HR: –
FYE: June 30
Type: Public

Kennametal offers a host of metal-cutting tools and tooling supplies for machining steel equipment for mining and highway construction and engineering services for production processes. Its lines include cutting milling and drilling tools used in metalworking; drums bits and accessories used in mining; and grader blades used in construction. The company which sells its products globally serves customers in the aerospace defense transportation engineering energy and mining sectors. Its customers have included such giants as Honda Caterpillar and Pratt & Whitney Canada. More than half of sales come from outside of the US.

	Annual Growth	06/11	06/12	06/13	06/14	06/15
Sales ($ mil.)	2.4%	2,403.5	2,736.2	2,589.4	2,837.2	2,647.2
Net income ($ mil.)	–	229.7	307.2	203.3	158.4	(373.9)
Market value ($ mil.)	(5.2%)	3,350.4	2,631.3	3,082.1	3,673.5	2,708.3
Employees	2.3%	11,600	12,900	12,600	13,500	12,700

KENNEDY HEALTH SYSTEM INC.

1099 WHITE HORSE RD
VOORHEES, NJ 080434405
Phone: 856-488-6500
Fax: –
Web: www.kennedyhealth.org

CEO: Joseph W. Devine
CFO: Gary Perrinoni
HR: –
FYE: September 30
Type: Private

Like its namesake The Kennedy Health System is all about service to the public. The system operates three acute care hospitals with more than 600 beds in southern interior New Jersey. Its operations include several outpatient centers and wellness programs cancer care dialysis centers primary care facilities and a nursing home. Its outpatient services are vast and varied ranging from behavioral and occupational health centers to balance centers (to treat dizziness and balance problems) and sleep centers. Affiliated with the Rowan University School of Osteopathic Medicine Kennedy Health System was founded in 1965 as John F. Kennedy Hospital. It plans to merge with Thomas Jefferson University Hospitals.

	Annual Growth	12/05	12/06	12/07	12/08*	09/09
Sales ($ mil.)	–	–	–	(16.8)	455.8	355.3
Net income ($ mil.)	23787.8%	–	–	0.0	(15.1)	11.0
Market value ($ mil.)	–	–	–	–	–	–
Employees	–	–	–	–	–	3,030

*Fiscal year change

KENNEDY KRIEGER INSTITUTE INC.

707 N BROADWAY
BALTIMORE, MD 212051888
Phone: 443-923-9200
Fax: –
Web: www.kennedykrieger.org

CEO: –
CFO: Michael Neuman
HR: Michael Loughran
FYE: June 30
Type: Private

Kennedy Krieger Institute is dedicated to the research education and treatment of children with brain disorders spinal cord injuries and developmental disabilities. It operates more than 55 outpatient clinics that provide services in behavioral psychology family support occupational and physical therapies and speech pathology among others. Altogether the institute serves more than 20000 individuals each year. Its 70-bed inpatient pediatric hospital caters to children who suffer from feeding problems and severe behaviors such as self-injury and aggression. Kennedy Krieger also runs a school for special-education students ages 3 to 21 to help prepare them for integration into their communities.

	Annual Growth	06/06	06/07	06/08	06/09	06/13
Sales ($ mil.)	1.6%	–	–	–	200.4	213.5
Net income ($ mil.)	–	–	–	–	(23.6)	13.9
Market value ($ mil.)	–	–	–	–	–	–
Employees	–	–	–	–	–	2,200

KENNEDY-WILSON HOLDINGS INC

NYS: KW

151 S El Camino Drive
Beverly Hills, CA 90212
Phone: 310 887-6400
Fax: –

CEO: William J. McMorrow
CFO: Justin Enbody
HR: –
FYE: December 31
Type: Public

Kennedy-Wilson doesn't run for office it invests in them. The international real estate company provides investment and property services in the US UK Ireland Spain and Japan. Kennedy-Wilson operates through two core practices real estate services and investments. In addition to office space the company's KW Investments unit acquires and manages portfolios of multifamily loans retail space hotels condos and land. Its KW Services division provides property and asset management auction and residential sales and brokerage services. Kennedy-Wilson which has about $15 billion in assets under management manages more than 40 million sq. ft. of property.

	Annual Growth	12/10	12/11	12/12	12/13	12/14
Sales ($ mil.)	67.6%	50.5	62.6	64.1	121.2	398.6
Net income ($ mil.)	125.2%	3.5	6.3	4.3	(6.4)	90.1
Market value ($ mil.)	26.1%	960.0	1,016.6	1,343.4	2,138.0	2,431.1
Employees	10.7%	300	300	340	400	450

KENNESAW STATE UNIVERSITY

1000 CHASTAIN RD NW
KENNESAW, GA 301445591
Phone: 770-423-6000
Fax: –
Web: www.kennesaw.edu

CEO: –
CFO: –
HR: –
FYE: June 30
Type: Private

Kennesaw State University (KSU) is a stomping ground for higher education students in northwest Georgia. The college offers about 80 undergraduate and graduate degree programs including bachelor's master's and doctorate programs in the core areas of nursing business and education as well as such subjects as public administration information technology and social work. KSU enrolls more than 24000 students at its 380-acre campus which is located near Kennesaw Mountain in the Atlanta metropolitan area. The university is the third largest member of the University System of Georgia after University of Georgia and Georgia State.

	Annual Growth	06/05	06/06	06/07	06/08	06/09
Sales ($ mil.)	10.4%	–	86.5	99.6	113.9	116.5
Net income ($ mil.)	–	–	–	10.2	10.8	(0.7)
Market value ($ mil.)	–	–	–	–	–	–
Employees	–	–	–	–	–	3,000

KENNETH COLE PRODUCTIONS INC.   NYSE: KCP

603 W. 50th St.
New York NY 10019
Phone: 212-265-1500
Fax: 866-741-5753
Web: www.kennethcole.com

CEO: Marc Schneider
CFO: David P Edelman
HR: –
FYE: December 31
Type: Private

Kenneth Cole is a trendy old sole. Known for its shoes Kenneth Cole Productions makes stylish apparel and accessories under the Kenneth Cole New York Kenneth Cole Reaction Unlisted and Gentle Souls names. Kenneth Cole licenses its name for hosiery luggage watches and eyewear. It continues to expand adding new lines for women and children as well as fragrances. About 4700 department and specialty stores carry its products. Kenneth Cole operates about 100 retail and outlet stores and sells through catalogs and websites. Chairman Kenneth Cole who effective September 2012 owns the namesake company took Kenneth Cole Productions private through a merger with his KCP Holdco Inc.

KENNYWOOD ENTERTAINMENT COMPANY INC.

4800 Kennywood Blvd.
West Mifflin PA 15122
Phone: 412-461-0500
Fax: 412-464-0719
Web: www.kennywoodentertainment.com

CEO: –
CFO: –
HR: –
FYE: December 31
Type: Subsidiary

Kennywood is not the Islands in the Stream counterpart to singer Dolly Parton's Dollywood. (Turn to Herschend Family Entertainment for that distinction). It does own and operate four amusement parks in Pennsylvania: Kennywood Park Idlewild & Soak Zone Sandcastle Waterpark and Pittsburgh's Riverplex a traditional picnic-type park located next to Sandcastle. The company markets its parks for group outings and offers event planning and catering services. Kennywood Entertainment was founded in 1898. It is a subsidiary of Spanish theme park company Parques Reunidos.

KENSEY NASH CORPORATION   NASDAQ: KNSY

735 Pennsylvania Dr.
Exton PA 19341
Phone: 484-713-2100
Fax: 484-713-2900
Web: www.kenseynash.com

CEO: Joseph W Kaufmann
CFO: Michael Celano
HR: –
FYE: June 30
Type: Public

Kensey Nash takes heart in its surgical sucesses. The firm developed the Angio-Seal a bio-absorbable material to seal arterial punctures which can occur during cardiovascular procedures. St. Jude Medical has licensed the rights to manufacture and market Angio-Seal worldwide. Kensey Nash manufactures biomaterial components for the Angio-Seal system including collagen plugs and polymer anchors. The company also makes other biomaterial products including tissue and bone grafting material and fixation devices for orthopedic surgeries collagen-based burn treatments and wound dressings and dental surgery aids. In 2012 Kensey Nash was acquired by global life sciences and materials sciences company Royal DSM.

KENSINGTON PUBLISHING CORP.

119 W 40TH ST FL 21
NEW YORK, NY 100182522
Phone: 212-407-1500
Fax: –
Web: www.kensingtonbooks.com

CEO: Steven Zacharius
CFO: Michael Rosamilia
HR: –
FYE: September 30
Type: Private

Kensington Publishing holds court with readers. The independent publisher sells hardcover trade and mass market fiction and non-fiction books through its Kensington Zebra Pinnacle and Citadel imprints. The company publishes about 600 titles a year and has a backlist of more than 3000. Romance and women's fiction account for more than half of its titles published each year. Other niche topics covered include wicca gambling gay & lesbian and military history. Readers can turn to the company's Rebel Base Books Web site to order titles such as I Hope They Serve Beer in Hell by Tucker Max which sold more than 70000 copies its first year and made the New York Times Bestseller list in 2006 2007 and 2008.

	Annual Growth	09/03	09/04	09/05	09/06	09/11
Sales ($ mil.)	(36.4%)	–	–	980.9	57.0	64.7
Net income ($ mil.)	544.4%	–	–	0.0	1.9	3.2
Market value ($ mil.)	–	–	–	–	–	–
Employees						81

KENT COUNTY MEMORIAL HOSPITAL

455 TOLL GATE RD
WARWICK, RI 028862770
Phone: 401-737-7000
Fax: –
Web: www.kentri.org

CEO: –
CFO: –
HR: Dave Campbell
FYE: September 30
Type: Private

As one of Rhode Island's largest hospitals Kent County Memorial Hospital offers Ocean Staters a sea of medical care options. The healthcare facility provides inpatient acute care as well as outpatient services (such as diagnostic imaging) and primary care. It also offers a range of specialties including cardiology orthopedics oncology surgery pediatrics and women's health. A member of the Care New England Health System Kent Hospital opened in 1951 with 90 beds; today the hospital has about 360 beds and a staff of some 600 doctors.

	Annual Growth	09/03	09/04*	12/05	12/09*	09/13
Sales ($ mil.)	6.0%	–	200.7	0.4	0.6	339.9
Net income ($ mil.)	–	–	–	0.0	(0.0)	(0.6)
Market value ($ mil.)	–	–	–	–	–	–
Employees	–	–	–	–	–	1,850

*Fiscal year change

KENT FINANCIAL SERVICES INC.   NASDAQ: KENT

10911 Raven Ridge Rd. Ste. 103-45
Raleigh NC 27614
Phone: 919-847-8710
Fax: 201-791-8015
Web: www.kreisler-ind.com

CEO: Bryan P Healey
CFO: Sue Ann Merrill
HR: –
FYE: December 31
Type: Public

Kent Financial Services (once known as Texas American Energy) has moved from the oil patch to the financial services field. The firm holds a majority stake in publicly traded Kent International Holdings (formerly Cortech) which scrapped its pharmaceutical research and is seeking new business opportunities in the US and China. The company in 2010 also scrapped subsidiary Kent Educational Services which controlled The Academy for Teaching and Leadership a provider of educational programs for school administrators and teachers. Chairman and CEO Paul Koether owns approximately 60% of Kent Financial Services.

KENTROX INC.

5800 Innovation Dr.
Dublin OH 43016
Phone: 614-798-2000
Fax: 212-232-0309
Web: www.mosaicaeducation.com

CEO: –
CFO: –
HR: –
FYE: December 31
Type: Private

Kentrox keeps telecommunications networks under control. The company manufactures and distributes site monitoring management and control solutions enabling service providers to reduce network and operating costs while improving network performance. Its products include data service unit/channel service unit (DSU/CSU) equipment quality of service (QoS) routers cell site aggregation equipment remote site management software and access concentrators. Kentrox's customers include government agencies enterprises and telecom carriers. It sells through distributors and resellers worldwide and also provides installation support and training services.

KENTUCKY POWER COMPANY

1 Riverside Plaza
Columbus OH 43215-2372
Phone: 614-716-1000
Fax: 614-716-1823
Web: www.kentuckypower.com

CEO: –
CFO: Holly K Koeppel
HR: –
FYE: December 31
Type: Subsidiary

The sun may shine bright on old Kentucky homes but Kentucky Power provides light regardless of the sun's hue. Organized in 1919 the utility distributes electricity to about 175000 homes and businesses across 20 counties in eastern Kentucky. An operating unit of holding company American Electric Power (AEP) Kentucky Power also sells electricity to wholesale customers and has coal-fired power plant interests that combined have a generating capacity of more than 1060 MW. The company operates more than 11040 miles of overhead transmission and distribution power lines.

KENTUCKY FIRST FEDERAL BANCORP

NMS: KFFB

216 West Main Street
Frankfort, ME 40601
Phone: 502 223-1638
Fax: –
Web: www.ffsbfrankfort.com/kffb.html

CEO: Don D Jennings
CFO: R Clay Hulette
HR: –
FYE: June 30
Type: Public

Kentucky First Federal wants to be second to none for banking in the Bluegrass State. Formed in 2005 to be the holding company for First Federal Savings and Loan of Hazard and First Federal Savings Bank of Frankfort which operate three branches in the state's capital and one in the town of Hazard. The banks offer traditional deposit products such as checking and savings accounts NOW and money market accounts and CDs. Lending is focused on residential mortgages but the banks also offer loans secured by churches and commercial real estate as well as consumer and construction loans. Kentucky First Federal which has received final regulatory approval is merging with CKF Bancorp.

	Annual Growth	06/11	06/12	06/13	06/14	06/15
Assets ($ mil.)	7.0%	226.1	222.9	324.1	299.7	296.3
Net income ($ mil.)	4.2%	1.8	1.7	2.9	1.9	2.1
Market value ($ mil.)	(1.8%)	76.4	72.0	68.4	74.2	71.1
Employees	16.9%	38	40	67	72	71

KENWAL STEEL CORP.

8223 W. Warren
Dearborn MI 48126
Phone: 313-739-1000
Fax: 313-739-1001
Web: www.kenwal.com

CEO: –
CFO: Frank Jerneycic
HR: –
FYE: December 31
Type: Private

After more than 60 years Kenwal Steel is still forging ahead. The flat-rolled steel supplier and processor targets automotive appliance and electronics industries and other major OEMs concentrated in the Midwest and Southeast US and Ontario. Through its collection of companies Kenwal allies with steel mills to broker carbon and alloy steel products and services. Its lineup includes hot and cold rolled pickled aluminized galvanized stainless and high-strength grades flat and sheet steel. Processing and distribution facilities neighbor many of its partner mills linking to customers via the company's rail and truck line. Kenwal Steel is owned and led by descendants of Sol Eisenberg company founder.

KENTUCKY MEDICAL SERVICES FOUNDATION INC.

2333 ALUMNI PARK PLZ # 200
LEXINGTON, KY 405174022
Phone: 859-257-7910
Fax: –
Web: www.kmsf.org

CEO: –
CFO: –
HR: –
FYE: June 30
Type: Private

Does the mailbox at your old Kentucky home contain doctors' bills? They might be from Kentucky Medical Services Foundation. The physician's practice group provides billing and other administrative services for the more than 600 physicians and other health care providers affiliated with the University of Kentucky's health system UK HealthCare. The network provides more than 80 specialty services offers educational programs and operates acute medical centers including Chandler Hospital Good Samaritan Hospital and Kentucky Children's Hospital.

KENYON COLLEGE

1 KENYON COLLEGE
GAMBIER, OH 430229623
Phone: 740-427-5000
Fax: –
Web: www.athletics.kenyon.edu

CEO: –
CFO: –
HR: –
FYE: June 30
Type: Private

Kenyon College is a small liberal arts school located approximately 45 miles northeast of Columbus Ohio. With an enrollment of some 1600 students the school offers bachelor's degrees in more than 30 majors in fields such as fine arts humanities natural sciences and social sciences. Notable alumni include actor Paul Newman and poet Robert Lowell. The college also produces renowned literary journal The Kenyon Review. The oldest private institution of higher education in Ohio Kenyon College was founded in 1824 by Philander Chase an Episcopal bishop.

	Annual Growth	06/07	06/08	06/09	06/10	06/13
Sales ($ mil.)	(31.8%)	–	1,523.5	190.0	196.6	225.1
Net income ($ mil.)	–	–	–	2.7	(4.6)	(0.4)
Market value ($ mil.)	–	–	–	–	–	–
Employees	–	–	–	–	–	150

	Annual Growth	06/03	06/04	06/05	06/06	06/08
Sales ($ mil.)	–	–	–	0.0	131.9	123.7
Net income ($ mil.)	4225.4%	–	–	0.0	58.6	24.6
Market value ($ mil.)	–	–	–	–	–	–
Employees	–	–	–	–	–	450

KERR DRUG INC.

3220 Spring Forest Rd.
Raleigh NC 27616
Phone: 919-544-3896
Fax: 919-544-3796
Web: www.kerrdrug.com

CEO: Anthony N Civello
CFO: -
HR: -
FYE: December 31
Type: Private

Oh you can buy knick-knacks and doo-dads at a Kerr Drug store but the company that bills itself as "North Carolina's Drugstore" puts its primary focus on pharmacy operation which accounts for about two-thirds of sales. Kerr Drug operates some 80 stores in North Carolina in several formats ranging from large health care centers to smaller clinical hubs and traditional drugstores. In addition to dispensing prescriptions and over-the-counter medications its pharmacists dispense health care advice and patient information. Founded by Banks Kerr in 1951 the North Carolina drugstore chain is owned by a management group led by Kerr CEO Anthony Civello.

KERYX BIOPHARMACEUTICALS INC.   NAS: KERX

750 Lexington Avenue
New York, NY 10022
Phone: 212 531-5965
Fax: -
Web: www.keryx.com

CEO: Gregory P. (Greg) Madison
CFO: Scott A. Holmes
HR: -
FYE: December 31
Type: Public

Drugs are a life-or-death business for Keryx Biopharmaceuticals. The company specializes in developing treatments for life-threatening ailments such as cancer and kidney disease. Its lead candidates are Zerenex a compound that may reduce high phosphate levels in patients with end-stage renal disease. The drug has been approved for sale in Japan under the name Riona to treat elevated phosphate levels in patients with chronic kidney disease. Marketing rights there have been granted to partner Japan Tobacco. Keryx is also testing Zerenx as a treatment for elevated phosphorous levels and iron deficiency in patients with kidney disease.

	Annual Growth	12/10	12/11	12/12	12/13	12/14
Sales ($ mil.)	29.4%	-	5.0	-	7.0	10.8
Net income ($ mil.)	-	(20.3)	(28.1)	(22.7)	(46.7)	(111.5)
Market value ($ mil.)	32.6%	424.5	234.5	242.8	1,200.2	1,311.4
Employees	57.8%	25	29	25	41	155

KETTERING MEDICAL CENTER

3535 SOUTHERN BLVD
KETTERING, OH 454291298
Phone: 937-298-4331
Fax: -
Web: www.ketteringhealth.org

CEO: Fred Manchur
CFO: Russ Wetherell
HR: Beverly Morris
FYE: December 31
Type: Private

Kettering Health Network keeps Ohio in a healthy state. The network named for famed inventor Charles F. Kettering is an Ohio-based healthcare system that comprises about 75 outpatient facilities including seven acute care hospitals: Kettering Medical Center Grandview Medical Center Sycamore Medical Center Southview Medical Center Fort Hamilton Hospital Greene Memorial Hospital and Soin Medical Center. Other facilities include a mental health hospital (Kettering Behavioral Hospital) and multiple outpatient diagnostic senior care and urgent care clinics. Among its specialized services are heart care rehabilitation orthopedics women's health and emergency medicine.

	Annual Growth	12/01	12/02	12/03	12/04	12/09
Sales ($ mil.)	1.0%	-	496.4	568.9	628.3	531.9
Net income ($ mil.)	(35.4%)	-	-	561.1	40.3	40.7
Market value ($ mil.)	-	-	-	-	-	-
Employees	-	-	-	-	-	3,100

KETTERING UNIVERSITY

1700 UNIVERSITY AVE
FLINT, MI 485044898
Phone: 810-762-9925
Fax: -
Web: www.my.kettering.edu

CEO: -
CFO: -
HR: -
FYE: June 30
Type: Private

Sometimes referred to as the "West Point of Industry" Kettering University specializes in engineering science and mathematics programs. Other academic fields include business pre-law pre-med and computer gaming. The private school offers about 15 undergraduate degrees and five graduate degrees to a small student body of more than 1680. As part of its cooperative educational framework the school provides academic credit for structured job experience. Kettering's students work with employers in aerospace accounting government law medical and not-for-profits and research firms in addition to companies in the manufacturing sector. Its student/faculty ratio is 13:1.

	Annual Growth	06/10	06/11	06/12	06/13	06/14
Sales ($ mil.)	1.4%	-	54.9	49.3	53.8	57.3
Net income ($ mil.)	-	-	-	(5.1)	10.5	13.3
Market value ($ mil.)	-	-	-	-	-	-
Employees	-	-	-	-	-	425

KEUKA COLLEGE

141 CENTRAL AVE
KEUKA PARK, NY 144789764
Phone: 315-279-5000
Fax: -
Web: www.keuka.edu

CEO: -
CFO: Jerry Hiller
HR: -
FYE: June 30
Type: Private

In 1890 Emily Dickinson's first volume of poetry was published the Battle of Wounded Knee took place Otto von Bismarck resigned as Germany's prime minister and Keuka College was founded in New York's Finger Lakes region. Today the liberal arts school has about 1600 students working toward around 35, undergraduate and graduate degrees; its focus is on experiential learning which includes annual internship periods. An additional 3000 Chinese students attend Keuka College in mainland China.

	Annual Growth	06/10	06/11	06/12	06/13	06/14
Sales ($ mil.)	3.8%	-	37.2	37.0	40.9	41.6
Net income ($ mil.)	-	-	-	(0.1)	2.4	2.0
Market value ($ mil.)	-	-	-	-	-	-
Employees	-	-	-	-	-	253

KEURIG GREEN MOUNTAIN INC   NMS: GMCR

33 Coffee Lane
Waterbury, VT 05676
Phone: 802 244-5621
Fax: -
Web: www.gmcr.com

CEO: Brian P. Kelley
CFO: Peter G. Leemputte
HR: -
FYE: September 26
Type: Public

Keurig Green Mountain's business amounts to far more than a hill of beans. The company (formerly Green Mountain Coffee Roasters) is a leader in the specialty coffee and coffeemaker business in North America. Its Keurig subsidiary makes single-cup brewing systems for home and office use and roasts coffee for its K-Cups and Vue portion packs. Green Mountain also roasts and packages whole bean and ground coffee and supplies apple cider teas cocoa and other beverages wholesale to food stores resorts and office-delivery services. The company markets coffee under the Newman's Own Organics Tully's and Green Mountain Coffee labels. In Canada it owns the Van Houtte gourmet coffee and coffee-service business.

	Annual Growth	09/11	09/12	09/13	09/14	09/15
Sales ($ mil.)	14.3%	2,650.9	3,859.2	4,358.1	4,707.7	4,520.0
Net income ($ mil.)	25.7%	199.5	362.6	483.2	596.5	498.3
Market value ($ mil.)	(14.6%)	15,973.6	3,637.2	11,472.3	20,013.7	8,506.2
Employees	1.7%	5,600	5,800	6,300	6,600	6,000

KEURIG INCORPORATED

55 Walkers Brook Dr.
Reading MA 01867
Phone: 781-928-0162
Fax: 562-345-6084
Web: www.razor.com

CEO: –
CFO: –
HR: –
FYE: December 31
Type: Subsidiary

Keurig knows that time is of the essence. The company makes a hot beverage system that brews a single cup of coffee or tea in less than a minute. The system uses portioned-product "K-Cups" designed for use with its machines. Some 200000 of its systems are located in offices foodservice outlets and homes in North America. The system was developed in 1998 when the firm licensed Green Mountain Coffee Roasters (GMCR) to pack its specialty coffees in Keurig's patented K-Cup. (GMCR acquired Keurig in 2006 for about $104 million.) Other partnerships include coffee roasters Gloria Jean's Timothy's World Coffee specialty tea makers Bigelow and Celestial Seasonings and GMCR-owned Diedrich and Van Houtte.

KEY ENERGY SERVICES, INC.
NYS: KEG

1301 McKinney Street, Suite 1800
Houston, TX 77010
Phone: 713 651-4300
Fax: –
Web: www.keyenergy.com

CEO: Richard J. (Dick) Alario
CFO: J. Marshall Dodson
HR: Joe Halsey
FYE: December 31
Type: Public

Energy is the key to growth for Key Energy Services one of the US's largest well-servicing and workover companies. The company provides maintenance workover and recompletion of wells primarily for onshore drilling. It provides services such as contract drilling well completion oilfield fluid transportation production testing and storage and disposal services to major and independent oil companies. Key Energy Services has a fleet of 987 well service rigs in the US. It also operates in Colombia Mexico and the Middle East and has stakes in a Canada-based drilling and production services company and a Russia-based drilling and workover services firm.

	Annual Growth	12/10	12/11	12/12	12/13	12/14
Sales ($ mil.)	5.5%	1,153.7	1,846.9	1,960.1	1,591.7	1,427.3
Net income ($ mil.)	–	73.5	101.5	7.6	(21.8)	(178.6)
Market value ($ mil.)	(40.1%)	1,993.2	2,375.5	1,067.2	1,213.1	256.4
Employees	(8.7%)	9,630	8,000	9,600	8,400	6,700

KEWAUNEE SCIENTIFIC CORPORATION
NMS: KEQU

2700 West Front Street
Statesville, NC 28677-2927
Phone: 704 873-7202
Fax: 704 873-5160
Web: www.kewaunee.com

CEO: David M. Rausch
CFO: Thomas D. Hull
HR: –
FYE: April 30
Type: Public

The nutty professor once wreaked havoc on furniture like that made by Kewaunee Scientific. The company makes furniture for laboratories including wood and steel cabinets fume hoods and work surfaces. It also makes technical workstations workbenches and computer enclosures for local area networking applications. Kewaunee's primary customers are schools health care institutions and labs (pharmaceutical biotech industrial chemical and commercial research). The company's products are sold through VWR International a school and lab products supplier as well as through designated Kewaunee dealers. Kewaunee's subsidiaries in Singapore and India handle sales in the Asian and Middle Eastern markets.

	Annual Growth	04/11	04/12	04/13	04/14	04/15
Sales ($ mil.)	4.4%	100.0	102.8	117.1	111.2	118.8
Net income ($ mil.)	17.5%	1.9	1.0	3.0	3.9	3.5
Market value ($ mil.)	9.3%	29.2	22.6	34.3	44.2	41.6
Employees	1.9%	598	558	587	619	645

KEY FOOD STORES CO-OPERATIVE INC.

1200 SOUTH AVE
STATEN ISLAND, NY 103143413
Phone: 718-370-4200
Fax: –
Web: www.keyfoods.com

CEO: Dean Janeway
CFO: –
HR: –
FYE: April 26
Type: Private

Key Food Stores Co-Operative is a friend to independent New York area grocers. The co-op provides retail support and other services to 150 independently owned food retailers in the New York City area. Key Food's member-owners run stores mainly in Brooklyn and Queens but also in the other boroughs and surrounding counties. It operates stores primarily under the Key Food banner but it also has Key Food Marketplace locations that feature expanded meat deli and produce departments. In addition the co-op supplies Key Foods-branded products to member stores. Among its members are Pick Quick Foods Dan's Supreme Super Markets Gemstone Supermarkets and Queens Supermarkets. Key Foods was founded in 1937.

	Annual Growth	04/08	04/09	04/10	04/11	04/14
Sales ($ mil.)	–	–	–	0.0	537.7	753.4
Net income ($ mil.)	–	–	–	0.0	(0.0)	0.0
Market value ($ mil.)	–	–	–	–	–	–
Employees	–	–	–	–	–	66

KEY CITY FURNITURE COMPANY INC

1804 RIVER ST
WILKESBORO, NC 286977633
Phone: 336-838-4191
Fax: –

CEO: –
CFO: –
HR: –
FYE: January 01
Type: Private

Family-owned and -operated since 1927 Key City Furniture has a lock on handcrafting furniture. The company operates facilities in Wilkesboro and North Wilkesboro North Carolina. More than 400 types of furniture are made to order including sleeper sofas sectionals rockers and ottomans. The company offers its customers some 1200 different fabrics and leathers. Key City Furniture founded by James E. Caudill is run by his grandsons F.D. Forester III and James Caudill Forester.

	Annual Growth	12/05	12/06	12/07*	01/09	01/10
Sales ($ mil.)	(70.8%)	–	–	384.0	13.1	9.5
Net income ($ mil.)	–	–	–	0.0	(2.2)	(0.8)
Market value ($ mil.)	–	–	–	–	–	–
Employees	–	–	–	–	–	105

*Fiscal year change

KEY PLASTICS L.L.C.

21700 Haggerty Rd. Ste. 150 North
Northville MI 48167
Phone: 248-449-6100
Fax: 248-449-4105
Web: www.keyplastics.com

CEO: Terry Gohl
CFO: Jonathan Ball
HR: –
FYE: December 31
Type: Private

Key Plastics has a grip on car parts; it is one of the leading North American manufacturers of exterior door handles for the auto industry. Other exterior and engineered plastic components include cladding (covering one material with another) and mirror shells. Look under the hood and you'll find pressurized coolant and power steering bottles made by the company. Interior and trim products round out its portfolio. Major customers include Chrysler Mitsubishi Nissan and Volkswagen as well as suppliers to the world's top carmakers. Key Plastics operates more than 10 locations in seven countries throughout Asia Europe and North America. Minnesota-based Wayzata Investment is its controlling stakeholder.

KEY TECHNOLOGY INC
NMS: KTEC

150 Avery Street
Walla Walla, WA 99362
Phone: 509 529-2161
Fax: 509 522-3378
Web: www.key.net

CEO: John J Ehren
CFO: Jeffrey T Siegal
HR: –
FYE: September 30
Type: Public

When good french fries go bad Key Technology can sort out the problem. The company makes food and material processing automation equipment under brand names such as Manta Tegra and Optyx. Its electro-optical automated inspection sorting and product preparation systems can be used to evaluate fresh fruits and vegetables beans potato chips and other snacks. Items can be sorted by color size and shape to identify defective or inconsistent products for removal. The company also makes conveyor and sorting systems for the tobacco pharmaceutical nutraceutical and coffee industries.

	Annual Growth	09/11	09/12	09/13	09/14	09/15
Sales ($ mil.)	(3.0%)	116.3	115.2	136.8	118.3	102.9
Net income ($ mil.)	–	1.5	0.4	4.0	(5.4)	(5.0)
Market value ($ mil.)	1.0%	72.1	61.8	88.1	84.5	75.1
Employees	(0.0%)	556	512	602	559	555

KEY TRONIC CORP.
NMS: KTCC

N. 4424 Sullivan Road
Spokane Valley, WA 99216
Phone: 509 928-8000
Fax: –
Web: www.keytronicems.com

CEO: Craig D Gates
CFO: Brett R Larsen
HR: –
FYE: June 27
Type: Public

Contract electronics manufacturing is key for Key Tronic. The company which does business as KeyTronicEMS to highlight its focus on electronics manufacturing services provides printed circuit board assembly tooling and prototyping box build (completely built) systems and plastic injection molding. In addition Key Tronic offers such services as product design engineering materials management and in-house testing. The company also makes customized and standard keyboards for PCs terminals and workstations.

	Annual Growth	07/11*	06/12	06/13	06/14	06/15
Sales ($ mil.)	14.3%	253.8	346.5	361.0	305.4	434.0
Net income ($ mil.)	(6.9%)	5.7	11.6	12.6	7.6	4.3
Market value ($ mil.)	23.9%	48.4	88.2	110.8	114.9	114.1
Employees	24.9%	1,997	2,700	2,584	3,343	4,866

*Fiscal year change

KEYCORP
NYS: KEY

127 Public Square
Cleveland, OH 44114-1306
Phone: 216 689-3000
Fax: –
Web: www.key.com

CEO: Christopher M. (Chris) Gorman
CFO: Donald R. Kimble
HR: Katie Ladd
FYE: December 31
Type: Public

Financial services giant KeyCorp unlocks its customers' monetary potential. With a focus on retail operations flagship subsidiary KeyBank operates nearly 1000 branches and 1300 ATMs in a dozen states in the Northeast the Midwest the Rocky Mountains and the Pacific Northwest including Alaska. Its operations are divided into two groups: Key Community Bank offers traditional services such as deposits loans credit cards and financial planning; while Key Corporate Bank provides investment banking services real estate capital equipment financing and capital markets services to large corporate clients nationwide.

	Annual Growth	12/10	12/11	12/12	12/13	12/14
Assets ($ mil.)	0.5%	91,843.0	88,785.0	89,236.0	92,934.0	93,821.0
Net income ($ mil.)	12.9%	554.0	920.0	858.0	910.0	900.0
Market value ($ mil.)	11.9%	7,605.7	6,608.8	7,236.2	11,533.6	11,945.7
Employees	(2.9%)	15,610	15,381	15,589	14,783	13,853

KEYSTONE MERCY HEALTH PLAN

200 Stevens Dr.
Philadelphia PA 19113
Phone: 215-937-8000
Fax: 215-863-5673
Web: www.keystonemercy.com

CEO: –
CFO: –
HR: –
FYE: December 31
Type: Private

Keystone Mercy Health Plan thinks the key to good health is proper medical care. The firm provides health care benefits to more than 300000 Medicaid recipients in southeastern Pennsylvania. Operating as a health maintenance organization (HMO) the company manages care for its members through a network of primary care physicians specialists hospitals and pharmacies. It provides benefits including dental vision and prescription coverage pregnancy programs and assistance with transportation needs. Keystone Mercy Health Plan is controlled by majority owner Independence Blue Cross (IBC) and minority shareholder Blue Cross Blue Shield of Michigan (BCBSM).

KEYW HOLDING CORP
NMS: KEYW

7740 Milestone Parkway, Suite 400
Hanover, MD 21076
Phone: 443 733-1600
Fax: –
Web: www.keywcorp.com

CEO: William (Bill) Weber
CFO: Philip L. (Phil) Calamia
HR: –
FYE: December 31
Type: Public

KEYW is a key player in US cybersecurity. Operating through contractor KEYW Corporation and its subsidiaries the company is an IT contractor to the federal government. Its main areas of expertise include engineering services specialized training field support and testing services; and collecting processing and analyzing data in order to help customers make intelligent decisions around preventing and responding to threats. The company also owns a fleet of a half-dozen aircraft used for surveillance and to collect data. Customers include US government intelligence and defense agencies like the National Security Agency and the US Department of Defense.

	Annual Growth	12/10	12/11	12/12	12/13	12/14
Sales ($ mil.)	28.1%	108.0	190.6	243.5	298.7	290.5
Net income ($ mil.)	–	10.9	0.5	1.0	(10.6)	(12.9)
Market value ($ mil.)	(8.3%)	551.6	278.3	477.2	505.4	390.3
Employees	10.8%	722	827	1,104	1,068	1,087

KFC CORPORATION

1441 Gardiner Ln.
Louisville KY 40213
Phone: 502-874-8300
Fax: 770-955-0302
Web: www.manh.com

CEO: David Novak
CFO: –
HR: –
FYE: December 31
Type: Subsidiary

KFC rules the roost when it comes to serving chicken. One of the world's largest fast-food chains the company owns and franchises more than 16200 outlets in about 100 countries. (More than 5100 locations are in the US.) The restaurants offer the Colonel's trademark fried chicken (in both Original Recipe and Extra Crispy varieties) along with chicken sandwiches chicken pot pies crispy chicken strips mashed potatoes and gravy and potato wedges. Its locations can be found operating as free-standing units and kiosks in high-traffic areas. More than 25% of the restaurants are company-operated. KFC is a unit of fast-food franchisor YUM! Brands which also operates Pizza Hut and Taco Bell.

KFORCE INC.

NMS: KFRC

1001 East Palm Avenue
Tampa, FL 33605
Phone: 813 552-5000
Fax: –
Web: www.kforce.com

CEO: David L. Dunkel
CFO: David M. Kelly
HR: –
FYE: December 31
Type: Public

Kforce is a corporate matchmaker placing highly skilled workers with the companies that need them. The specialty staffing firm provides primarily temporary staffing services (and to a lesser extent permanent placement) in such areas as information technology accounting and government. It additionally offers Web-based services such as online resumes job postings career management information and interactive interviews. Clients include FORTUNE 1000 corporations as well as small and midsized firms nationwide. The company caters to about 40 different US markets.

	Annual Growth	12/10	12/11	12/12	12/13	12/14
Sales ($ mil.)	5.3%	990.8	1,110.9	1,082.5	1,151.9	1,217.3
Net income ($ mil.)	44.9%	20.6	27.2	(13.7)	10.8	90.9
Market value ($ mil.)	10.5%	475.9	362.7	421.8	601.8	709.7
Employees	2.3%	12,400	13,300	13,200	14,500	13,600

KGBO HOLDINGS INC

4289 IVY POINTE BLVD
CINCINNATI, OH 452450002
Phone: 513-831-2600
Fax: –
Web: www.tql.com

CEO: –
CFO: –
HR: Jackie Hatchett
FYE: December 30
Type: Private

Total Quality Logistics sets a high standard for moving merchandise. The third-party logistics (non-asset based) provider specializes in arranging freight transportation using reefers (refrigerated trucks) vans and flatbeds — moving in excess of 500000 loads each year. The trucking brokerage company serves more than 7000 clients across the US Canada and Mexico ranging from small businesses to Fortune 500 organizations. Founded in 1997 by company president Ken Oaks Total Quality Logistics (TQL) has contracts with carriers that include single owner operators and large fleets. Customers have included Kroger Dole Food and Laura's Lean Beef.

	Annual Growth	12/08	12/09	12/10	12/11	12/12
Sales ($ mil.)	34.9%	–	–	762.1	1,046.7	1,387.4
Net income ($ mil.)	–	–	–	0.0	0.0	0.0
Market value ($ mil.)	–	–	–	–	–	–
Employees	–	–	–	–	–	2,150

KID BRANDS, INC.

NBB: KIDB Q

301 Route 17 North, 6th Floor
Rutherford, NJ 07070
Phone: 201 405-2400
Fax: 204 405-7355
Web: www.kidbrands.com

CEO: –
CFO: –
HR: –
FYE: December 31
Type: Public

Kid Brands sells products for brand-new people: newborns to 3-year-olds. Through its subsidiaries the company designs imports and markets infant and juvenile bedding and furniture as well as related nursery accessories. It also peddles infant-development toys and teething feeding and bath and baby care products. Kid Brands' principal subsidiaries include Sassy Kids Line LaJobi and CoCaLo. The company also makes juvenile products under license from Carters Disney Graco and Serta. Founded in 1963 by the late Russell Berrie the company (formerly Russ Berrie and Co.) changed its name to Kid Brands in 2009 to underscore its shift to infant and juvenile products.

	Annual Growth	12/09	12/10	12/11	12/12	12/13
Sales ($ mil.)	(6.3%)	243.9	275.8	252.6	229.5	188.2
Net income ($ mil.)	–	11.7	34.7	(38.6)	(54.1)	(28.8)
Market value ($ mil.)	(30.5%)	96.7	188.8	69.8	34.2	22.5
Employees	(3.1%)	340	304	320	300	300

KIDS II INC.

555 N. Point Center East Ste. 600
Alpharetta GA 30022-8234
Phone: 770-751-0442
Fax: 770-751-0543
Web: www.kidsii.com

CEO: Ryan Gunnigle
CFO: –
HR: Patti Plouff
FYE: December 31
Type: Private

Kids II wants to take playtime to a more advanced level. The company which got its start making The Original Infant Foam Bath Aid in 1969 designs and produces nursery items and developmental toys for infants and children up to 2 years old. It makes toys under its proprietary Bright Starts brand and under license with Disney for the Baby Einstein and Disney Baby names. Kids II's product offerings including bouncers play gyms and mats mobiles swaddling blankets and travel toys are sold in toy stores children's specialty shops and department stores (such as Mothercare Target Toys "R" Us and Wal-Mart) in more than 60 countries worldwide. It also sells its products through its website.

KIEHL'S SINCE 1851 LLC

435 Hudson St. 5th Fl.
New York NY 10014
Phone: 917-606-2740
Fax: 917-606-9536
Web: www.kiehls.com

CEO: Joseph J Campinell
CFO: –
HR: –
FYE: December 31
Type: Subsidiary

Kiehl's Since 1851 makes natural hair and skin care products and lipstick and sells them strictly by word of mouth. Pretty strictly anyway. Kiehl's doesn't advertise much or go door-to-door and its rigid marketing policy keeps its luxury products out of all but a few exclusive retailers — stores such as Barneys and Bergdorf Goodman. The company's East Village location in Manhattan is frequented by celebrity hairdressers entertainers and others willing to brave long checkout lines. Its products are also available at Kiehl's stores nationwide and overseas. Customers can order online by catalog and by phone. Founded more than 150 years ago Kiehl's is owned by the French cosmetics giant L'Oreal.

KIEWIT OFFSHORE SERVICES LTD.

2440 Kiewit Rd.
Ingleside TX 78362
Phone: 361-775-4399
Fax: 361-775-4433
Web: www.kiewit.com/offshore

CEO: Bruce Grewcock
CFO: –
HR: –
FYE: December 31
Type: Subsidiary

Going off the deep end is all in a day's work for Kiewit Offshore Services. Founded in 2001 the company is a subsidiary of employee-owned Peter Kiewit Sons' that primarily acts as a contractor for oil and gas production customers operating off the coast of the Gulf of Mexico. It primarily manufactures and repairs offshore oil and gas platforms and large structural steel components. In addition to deepwater projects Kiewit Offshore Services also builds small platforms modules suction piles and tendons. After partnering with Bullwinkle Constructors to build the Bullwinkle Jacket (the largest oil-production platform and the time of its completion) Peter Kiewit Sons' formed Kiewit Offshore Services.

KILLBUCK BANCSHARES, INC. NBB: KLIB

165 North Main Street, P.O. Box 407
Killbuck, OH 44637
Phone: 330 276-2771
Fax: 330 276-0216
Web: www.killbuckbank.com

CEO: Craig A Lawhead
CFO: Lawrence Cardinal
HR: –
FYE: December 31
Type: Public

Interestingly enough if you want to save a buck you can take your doe to Killbuck. Killbuck Bancshares is the holding company for The Killbuck Savings Bank which operates about 10 branches in northeast Ohio. It offers traditional retail products to individuals and small to midsized businesses including checking and savings accounts credit cards and IRAs. Residential and commercial mortgages make up about two-thirds of its loan portfolio which also includes business loans and consumer loans. Killbuck Bancshares is the #1 financial institution in Holmes County where most of its offices are located. It also has branches in Knox and Tuscarawas counties.

	Annual Growth	12/10	12/11	12/12	12/13	12/14
Assets ($ mil.)	4.3%	405.1	436.5	460.4	461.8	479.8
Net income ($ mil.)	8.3%	3.0	2.9	3.3	3.6	4.1
Market value ($ mil.)	2.1%	62.2	66.1	65.9	62.6	67.7
Employees	(1.6%)	123	121	–	–	–

KILROY REALTY CORP NYS: KRC

12200 W. Olympic Boulevard, Suite 200
Los Angeles, CA 90064
Phone: 310 481-8400
Fax: –
Web: www.kilroyrealty.com

CEO: John B. Kilroy
CFO: Tyler H. Rose
HR: –
FYE: December 31
Type: Public

Kilroy is still here especially if you're referring to the West Coast. A self-administered real estate investment trust (REIT) Kilroy Realty owns manages and develops Class A office space mostly in suburban Southern California's Orange County San Diego and Los Angeles but it has since expanded to the San Francisco Bay and greater Seattle area to woo technology companies as tenants. Its portfolio includes about 115 office properties encompassing more than 13 million square feet of leasable space. A majority of Kilroy Realty's 500-plus tenants are involved in technology media financial services and real estate.

	Annual Growth	12/11	12/12	12/13	12/14	12/15
Sales ($ mil.)	12.2%	367.1	404.9	465.1	521.7	581.3
Net income ($ mil.)	37.2%	66.0	270.9	43.9	183.5	234.1
Market value ($ mil.)	13.5%	3,512.3	4,370.3	4,629.5	6,372.3	5,838.1
Employees	8.2%	169	201	219	226	232

KIMBALL ELECTRONICS GROUP INC.

1600 Royal St. G0-149
Jasper IN 47549
Phone: 812-634-4200
Fax: 812-634-4600
Web: www.kegroup.com

CEO: –
CFO: Michael K Sergesketter
HR: Julie Dutchess
FYE: June 30
Type: Subsidiary

Kimball Electronics Group (a subsidiary of Kimball International) makes printed circuit boards and electronic assemblies along with offering such services as design engineering prototyping testing and packaging. The company was established in 1961 to build electronic organs for its parent firm then transitioned into the contract electronics manufacturing services business in 1985. Customers have included FLIR Systems Johnson Controls TRW Automotive Holdings and Xhale Innovations. Kimball Electronics has facilities in China Mexico Poland Thailand and the US.

KIMBALL INTERNATIONAL, INC. NMS: KBAL

1600 Royal Street
Jasper, IN 47549-1001
Phone: 812 482-1600
Fax: –

CEO: Robert F. (Bob) Schneider
CFO: Michelle R. Schroeder
HR: –
FYE: June 30
Type: Public

No odd coupling: Furniture and electronic manufacturing services bring out the best in Kimball International. The company's Kimball Electronics business produces electronics and electro-mechanical products (electronic assemblies) on a contract basis for customers in the auto industrial control medical and public safety markets. Kimball's services include prototype product development and launch supply chain management testing assembly and repair and return. The Furniture business makes desks cubicles credenzas and cabinets under the Kimball Office and National brand names for the office and hospitality industries. Kimball is 52% owned by the founding Habig and Thyen families.

	Annual Growth	06/11	06/12	06/13	06/14	06/15
Sales ($ mil.)	(15.9%)	1,202.6	1,142.1	1,203.1	1,285.3	600.9
Net income ($ mil.)	42.5%	4.9	11.6	19.9	33.5	20.3
Market value ($ mil.)	17.3%	243.8	291.9	368.1	633.9	461.0
Employees	(17.9%)	6,362	6,295	6,426	6,666	2,894

KIMBALL MEDICAL CENTER INC.

600 RIVER AVE
LAKEWOOD, NJ 087015281
Phone: 732-363-1900
Fax: –

CEO: Michael Mimoso
CFO: Paul Rouvell
HR: –
FYE: December 31
Type: Private

Kimball Medical Center knows that life on the Jersey Shore isn't always as beachy as it's cracked up to be. Kimball Medical Center is a 350-bed acute care hospital and part of the Saint Barnabas Health Care System. Located in Lakewood the medical center serves the southern Monmouth and Ocean counties of New Jersey. Services include cancer treatment rehabilitation emergency care maternity and pediatrics and occupational medicine. The hospital also offers wellness and health education programs and support groups at its Center For Healthy Living.

	Annual Growth	12/01	12/02	12/03	12/08	12/12
Sales ($ mil.)	(1.1%)	–	158.7	129.9	147.9	141.8
Net income ($ mil.)		–	–	0.5	(18.0)	(3.3)
Market value ($ mil.)		–	–	–	–	–
Employees		–	–	–	–	1,500

KIMBERLY-CLARK CORP. NYS: KMB

P.O. Box 619100
Dallas, TX 75261-9100
Phone: 972 281-1200
Fax: –
Web: www.kimberly-clark.com

CEO: Thomas J. (Tom) Falk
CFO: Maria Henry
HR: Rick Purdy
FYE: December 31
Type: Public

Nobody knows noses and bottoms better than Kimberly-Clark. One of the world's largest makers of personal paper products the company operates through three business segments: personal care consumer tissue and K-C Professional. Kimberly-Clark's largest unit personal care makes products such as diapers (Huggies Pull-Ups) feminine care items (Kotex) and incontinence care products (Poise Depend). Through its consumer tissue segment the manufacturer offers facial and bathroom tissues paper towels and other household items under the names Cottonelle Kleenex Viva and Scott (plus the Scott Naturals line). Kimberly-Clark's professional unit makes WypAll commercial wipes among other items.

	Annual Growth	12/11	12/12	12/13	12/14	12/15
Sales ($ mil.)	(2.8%)	20,846.0	21,063.0	21,152.0	19,724.0	18,591.0
Net income ($ mil.)	(10.7%)	1,591.0	1,750.0	2,142.0	1,526.0	1,013.0
Market value ($ mil.)	14.7%	26,547.8	30,470.8	37,699.6	41,698.4	45,942.6
Employees	(6.8%)	57,000	58,000	57,000	43,000	43,000

KIMCO REALTY CORP. NYS: KIM

3333 New Hyde Park Road
New Hyde Park, NY 11042
Phone: 516 869-9000
Fax: –
Web: www.kimcorealty.com

CEO: Conor C. Flynn
CFO: Glenn G Cohen
HR: –
FYE: December 31
Type: Public

Kimco Realty is the real deal. The self-managed and self-administered real estate investment trust (REIT) owns or has interests in about 750 community shopping centers with 110 million sq. ft. of leasable space in metropolitan areas in nearly 40 states as well as in Canada Mexico Puerto Rico and Chile. Kimco properties are usually anchored by a supermarket or a big-box store that sells day-to-day necessities rather than big-ticket items. Home Depot Kohl's TJX Sears and Wal-Mart are its largest tenants. Through subsidiaries the company also develops shopping centers and provides real estate management and disposition services to retailers.

	Annual Growth	12/10	12/11	12/12	12/13	12/14
Sales ($ mil.)	4.0%	849.5	873.7	922.3	946.7	993.9
Net income ($ mil.)	31.3%	142.9	169.1	266.1	236.3	424.0
Market value ($ mil.)	8.7%	7,429.2	6,688.0	7,956.4	8,133.4	10,353.2
Employees	(4.1%)	687	685	635	597	580

KIMPTON HOTEL & RESTAURANT GROUP LLC

222 Kearney St. Ste. 200
San Francisco CA 94108
Phone: 415-397-5572
Fax: 415-296-8031
Web: www.kimptonhotels.com

CEO: Mike Depatie
CFO: Ben Rowe
HR: –
FYE: December 31
Type: Private

Kimpton Hotel & Restaurant Group hopes a little style can help it stand out in the crowded leisure industry. The company owns some 12 boutique hotels and manages about 40 others in more than 20 markets across the US. Kimpton buys older buildings in urban areas and transforms them into four-star hotels hotels that feature mostly smaller European-style accommodations. Upscale Kimpton Restaurants are located next to most hotels. The company's management services include strategic planning sales and marketing human resources and administration support. Investment banker and founder Bill Kimpton opened the company's first hotel the Clarion Bedford in San Francisco in 1981.

KINDER MORGAN ENERGY PARTNERS, L.P. NYS: KMP

1001 Louisiana Street, Suite 1000
Houston, TX 77002
Phone: 713 369-9000
Fax: –
Web: www.kindermorgan.com

CEO: Richard D Kinder
CFO: Kimberly A Dang
HR: –
FYE: December 31
Type: Public

Kinder Morgan Energy Partners (KMP) keeps energy on the move throughout the North America. The company holds stakes in more than 37000 miles of natural gas and petroleum product pipelines and owns 180 bulk terminals and rail transloading facilities with 200 millions barrels of storage capacity that handle 100 million tons of coal petroleum coke and bulk products annually. KMP transports refined petroleum products (gasoline diesel and jet fuel) through 8400 miles of pipelines and stores the products in 60 terminals in the US. Through its CO2 subsidiary KMP transports carbon dioxide. Kinder Morgan owns about 13% of KMP and through its Kinder Morgan Management unit acts as general partner.

	Annual Growth	12/08	12/09	12/10	12/11	12/12
Sales ($ mil.)	(7.4%)	11,740.3	7,003.4	8,077.7	8,211.2	8,642.0
Net income ($ mil.)	0.6%	1,304.8	1,267.5	1,316.3	1,257.8	1,339.0
Market value ($ mil.)	14.9%	17,073.4	22,757.0	26,220.2	31,702.3	29,776.7
Employees	31.6%	–	–	–	8,120	10,685

KINDER MORGAN INC. NYS: KMI

1001 Louisiana Street, Suite 1000
Houston, TX 77002
Phone: 713 369-9000
Fax: –
Web: www.kindermorgan.com

CEO: Steven J. (Steve) Kean
CFO: Kimberly Allen (Kim) Dang
HR: Lisa M. Shorb
FYE: December 31
Type: Public

Kinder Morgan Inc. (KMI formerly Kinder Morgan Holdco) is the top layer of a large oil and gas cake. The company owns Kinder Morgan Management which manages the general partner of Kinder Morgan Energy Partners (KMP). KMP operates pipeline that transport natural gas crude oil gasoline and other products along with terminals used to store chemicals and petroleum products and other items (including coal and steel). It produces carbon dioxide (CO2) which is used in oil field production. KMI owns stakes in or operates 84000 miles of pipelines and 180 terminals. It also holds 51% of El Paso Pipeline Partners.

	Annual Growth	12/11	12/12	12/13	12/14	12/15
Sales ($ mil.)	14.9%	8,264.9	9,973.0	14,070.0	16,226.0	14,403.0
Net income ($ mil.)	(19.2%)	594.4	315.0	1,193.0	1,026.0	253.0
Market value ($ mil.)	–	0.0	0.0	0.0	0.0	0.0
Employees	8.6%	8,120	10,685	11,075	11,535	11,290

KINDRED HEALTHCARE INC NYS: KND

680 South Fourth Street
Louisville, KY 40202-2412
Phone: 502 596-7300
Fax: –
Web: www.kindredhealthcare.com

CEO: Benjamin A. Breier
CFO: Stephen D. Farber
HR: Jeffrey (Jeff) Jasnoff
FYE: December 31
Type: Public

Families unable to provide 24-hour care to their kin can at least turn to Kindred Healthcare. As a leading provider of long-term health care Kindred operates more than 100 nursing and rehabilitation centers and some 100 long-term acute care hospitals in the US. In addition Kindred's RehabCare business provides contract rehabilitation therapy services at more than 1900 facilities. The firm also runs sub-acute and inpatient rehabilitation centers as well as home health and hospice agencies. Its facilities have a combined capacity of more than 35000 beds and span 47 states. In 2015 the company bought Gentiva Health Services in a $1.8 billion transaction; the deal nearly doubled Kindred's size.

	Annual Growth	12/10	12/11	12/12	12/13	12/14
Sales ($ mil.)	3.6%	4,359.7	5,521.8	6,181.3	4,900.5	5,027.6
Net income ($ mil.)	–	56.5	(53.5)	(40.4)	(168.5)	(79.8)
Market value ($ mil.)	(0.3%)	1,285.5	823.6	757.2	1,381.3	1,272.2
Employees	2.0%	56,800	77,800	78,000	63,300	61,500

KINECTA FEDERAL CREDIT UNION

1440 Rosecrans Ave.
Manhattan Beach CA 90266
Phone: 310-643-5458
Fax: 310-643-8350
Web: www.kinecta.org

CEO: Keith Sultemeier
CFO: –
HR: Brian E Cote
FYE: December 31
Type: Private - Not-for-Pr

Kinecta Federal Credit Union provides retail financial services to more than 225000 member-owners in Southern California where it operates about two dozen branches. Members also have access to more than 4000 branches worldwide through a network of affiliated credit unions. Kinecta's offerings include checking and savings accounts IRAs savings bonds and credit cards. The credit union with about $3.5 billion in assets originates residential mortgages in some 25 states. Other lending activities include automobile and home equity loans. Retirement investment and insurance products are offered through subsidiaries Kinecta Financial & Insurance Services and Apollo Insurance Services.

KINETEK INC.

ArborLake Center 1751 Lake Cook Rd. Ste. 550
Deerfield IL 60015
Phone: 847-267-4473
Fax: 847-945-9645
Web: www.kinetekinc.com

CEO: –
CFO: Daniel D Drury
HR: –
FYE: December 31
Type: Subsidiary

Kinetek's motors keep elevators and escalators on the up and up. The holding company owns about 15 subsidiaries that manufacture a range of motor control and drive systems including controllers found in elevators. Other products include electric motors (AC and DC) gearboxes gear motors gears and transaxles. Its motors are used in appliances electric bikes floor-care equipment golf carts lift trucks surgical hand devices vending machines and wheelchairs. Kinetek was acquired by Nidec a major producer of spindle motors in 2012.

KINETIC CONCEPTS INC.

8023 Vantage Dr.
San Antonio TX 78230-4726
Phone: 210-524-9000
Fax: 210-255-6998
Web: www.kci1.com

CEO: Joseph F Woody
CFO: Robert Hureau
HR: –
FYE: December 31
Type: Private

Kinetic Concepts Inc. (KCI) exudes positive energy for wound-healing purposes. The company's active healing solutions (AHS) business makes vacuum-assisted wound care systems (including the V.A.C. Via system) which use KCI's negative pressure technology to speed patient recovery from complex wounds. The unit also makes negative pressure systems to aid in the healing of surgical incisions. Its LifeCell business develops tissue regeneration products used in reconstructive surgical procedures. The firm is selling its therapeutic support systems (TSS) business which makes hospital beds specialized mattresses and patient mobility assistance devices. KCI is owned by a consortium of private-investors.

KINETIC SYSTEMS INC.

48400 Fremont Blvd.
Fremont CA 94538
Phone: 510-683-6000
Fax: 510-683-6001
Web: www.kinetics.net

CEO: Peter Maris
CFO: Martin Kaus
HR: –
FYE: December 31
Type: Private

Kinetic Systems stays in motion. The company (known as Kinetics) provides process and mechanical systems primarily to the microelectronics solar energy and biopharmaceutical industries in the Americas Asia and Europe. It installs gas chemical water and utility systems as well as fabricated steel pipe HVAC and plumbing systems. While most of its work is done designing and constructing laboratories and manufacturing facilities Kinetics also installs systems for data centers condominiums schools and water treatment plants. Kinetics has served clients including AMD Merck and Pepsi. Founded in 1973 the firm is controlled by Ares Management.

KING KULLEN GROCERY CO. INC.

185 Central Ave.
Bethpage NY 11714
Phone: 516-733-7100
Fax: 516-827-6325
Web: www.kingkullen.com

CEO: Ronald Conklin
CFO: –
HR: –
FYE: September 30
Type: Private

How's this for a crowning achievement? King Kullen Grocery claims to have been the originator of the supermarket format. Heralding itself as "America's first supermarket" the firm operates some 40 grocery stores on Long Island New York. King Kullen also owns four Wild By Nature natural foods stores and offers a line of vitamins and supplements under the same name in some King Kullen stores. Most outlets average about 35000 sq. ft. but it has a 62000-sq.-ft. upscale market with features such as ethnic fare catering and a Wild By Nature section. Started in a Queens New York warehouse in 1930 by Michael Cullen the firm is owned and operated by Cullen's descendants.

KING RANCH INC.

3 River Way Ste. 1600
Houston TX 77056
Phone: 832-681-5700
Fax: 404-572-5100
Web: www.kslaw.com

CEO: –
CFO: Bill Gardiner
HR: –
FYE: December 31
Type: Private

Meanwhile back at the ranch ... the quite-sprawling King Ranch to be exact. Founded in 1853 King Ranch's operations extend beyond its original 825000 Texan cattle-raising acres. The ranch is still home to cattle and horses of course. However King Ranch oversees considerable farming interests in its home state and elsewhere (cotton sorghum sod citrus pecans vegetables and cane sugar). It also has various retail operations (hardware designer saddles and other leather goods publishing and printing). In addition King Ranch also beefs up revenues with tourist dollars from birdwatchers hunters and sightseers who visit its Texas ranch lands. The descendants of founder Richard King own King Ranch.

KING"S COLLEGE

133 N RIVER ST
WILKES BARRE, PA 187110801
Phone: 570-208-5900
Fax:
Web: www.kings.edu

CEO: –
CFO: –
HR: –
FYE: June 30
Type: Private

King's College emphasizes intelligence over royalty. The school is a Catholic university offering more than 35 majors in allied health business education natural science and humanities and social sciences. King's enrolls about 2700 undergraduate and graduate students. The school also offers about a dozen pre-professional programs as well as special concentration programs in ethics forensic studies and other fields. Founded in 1946 by the Holy Cross congregation from the University of Notre Dame the school is part of a national network of Holy Cross colleges and universities.

	Annual Growth	06/09	06/10	06/11	06/12	06/13
Sales ($ mil.)	15.9%	–	53.7	52.7	83.1	83.5
Net income ($ mil.)	(0.1%)	–	–	4.3	1.6	4.3
Market value ($ mil.)	–	–	–	–	–	–
Employees	–	–	–	–	–	500

KINGOLD JEWELRY INC
NAS: KGJI

15 Huangpu Science and Technology Park, Jiang'an District
Wuhan, Hubei Province 10170
Phone: (86) 27 65694977
Fax: –
Web: www.kingoldjewelry.com

CEO: –
CFO: –
HR: –
FYE: December 31
Type: Public

Kingold Jewelry would like to corner the market on the shiny gold stuff in central China. The company through subsidiary Dragon Lead designs and manufactures 24 karat gold jewelry and accessories in Hubei Hunan Henan Jiangxi Anhui and Sichuan provinces. It creates nearly 900 new necklaces bracelets rings earrings and pendants each month and sells them to wholesalers and distributors. The finished products under the Kingold or Jin Huang brand are sold in department and jewelry stores in China's most populous areas. The company began in 1995 as a software firm became a shell in 2002 completed a reverse merger with Dragon Lead in 2009 and took its current name in early 2010.

	Annual Growth	12/10	12/11	12/12	12/13	12/14
Sales ($ mil.)	20.6%	523.0	789.0	915.7	1,189.9	1,107.6
Net income ($ mil.)	27.1%	18.2	26.2	32.7	28.3	47.3
Market value ($ mil.)	(31.7%)	269.1	75.2	75.9	110.8	58.7
Employees	2.1%	507	661	620	532	550

KINGSTONE COMPANIES INC
NAS: KINS

15 Joys Lane
Kingston, NY 12401
Phone: 845 802-7900
Fax: –
Web: www.kingstonecompanies.com

CEO: Barry B Goldstein
CFO: Victor Brodsky
HR: –
FYE: December 31
Type: Public

Kingstone Companies (formerly DCAP Group) keeps things covered. While the company has transformed itself from a broker into an underwriter its main business is still insurance. Its Kingstone Insurance Company (formerly Commercial Mutual Insurance Company) provides property/casualty insurance policies for individuals and businesses in New York State. Its products including auto business and homeowners' policies are sold through independent agents. The company has divested its former insurance brokerage business which offered life and property/casualty policies through owned and franchised retail locations in New York and eastern Pennsylvania.

	Annual Growth	12/10	12/11	12/12	12/13	12/14
Sales ($ mil.)	23.4%	21.6	27.7	29.1	36.6	50.1
Net income ($ mil.)	52.6%	1.0	2.5	0.8	2.0	5.3
Market value ($ mil.)	23.5%	25.6	26.2	35.6	53.1	59.6
Employees	11.3%	43	49	54	59	66

KINGS FOOD MARKETS

700 Lanidex Plaza
Parsippany NJ 07054-2705
Phone: 973-463-6300
Fax: 973-463-6512
Web: www.kingswebsite.com

CEO: –
CFO: –
HR: –
FYE: March 31
Type: Private

Kings Food Markets aims to serve food fit for a king. The regional supermarket chain operates about 25 upscale grocery stores in northern New Jersey on Long Island New York and now in Connecticut. It also operates six Balducci's food stores. Once owned by UK department store operator Marks and Spencer which first put Kings up for sale in 1999 the chain was finally sold — after several unsuccessful attempts — to a pair of New York-based private equity firms (Angelo Gordon & Co. and MTN Capital Partners) and Bruce Weitz a former CEO of Duane Reade for about $61 million. The company was founded in 1936 as Kings Super Markets.

KINRAY INC.

152-35 10th Ave.
Whitestone NY 11357
Phone: 718-767-1234
Fax: 718-767-4388
Web: www.kinray.com

CEO: –
CFO: –
HR: –
FYE: December 31
Type: Subsidiary

Kinray one of the US's top private wholesale drug distributors provides generic branded and repackaged drugs health and beauty products medical equipment vitamins and diabetes-care products to 2000 independent pharmacies long-term care facilities and specialty pharmacies along the Eastern Seaboard. It also offers about 800 private label products under the Preferred Plus Pharmacy brand. Kinray's stock of goods doesn't stop at medical supplies and prescription drugs; other products include DVDs fragrances and household items (both branded and private label). The company is a subsidiary of Cardinal Health.

KINGSBROOK JEWISH MEDICAL CENTER INC

585 SCHENECTADY AVE STE 2
BROOKLYN, NY 112031809
Phone: 718-604-5000
Fax: –
Web: www.kingsbrook.org

CEO: Linda Brady
CFO: John Schmitt
HR: –
FYE: December 31
Type: Private

Kingsbrook Jewish Medical Center (KJMC) cares for the health needs of all Brooklyn residents. Founded in 1925 to serve the area's Jewish community the campus includes an acute care hospital with about 320 inpatient beds and an adult and pediatric long-term care facility with 540 beds. KJMC provides emergency surgical cardiology gastroenterology pulmonary wound care and diagnostic imaging services as well as skilled nursing services. The hospital also serves as a training facility for medical dental and pharmacy residents. It also operates a primary and specialty care outpatient center and a rehabilitation institute.

	Annual Growth	12/00	12/01	12/02	12/05	12/08
Sales ($ mil.)	–	–	–	0.0	227.7	241.8
Net income ($ mil.)	–	–	–	0.0	(14.7)	(3.8)
Market value ($ mil.)	–	–	–	–	–	–
Employees	–	–	–	–	–	2,100

KINSLEY CONSTRUCTION INC.

2700 Water St.
York PA 17403
Phone: 717-741-3841
Fax: 717-741-9054
Web: www.rkinsley.com

CEO: Robert A Kinsley
CFO: –
HR: –
FYE: December 31
Type: Private

Kinsley Construction provides general contracting design/build and construction management services primarily in Pennsylvania and the mid-Atlantic. The company builds commercial institutional health care manufacturing and distribution facilities in addition to highways bridges and other infrastructure projects. Kinsley also operates a concrete plant with a fleet of mixer trucks. Other operations include asphalt plants demolition construction materials recycling and metal fabrication. Another unit specializes in site work. Chairman and CEO Bob Kinsley founded the firm as a concrete services subcontractor in 1963; he and his family still control the company.

KINTETSU WORLD EXPRESS (U.S.A.) INC.

100 Jericho Quadrangle Ste. 326
Jericho NY 11753
Phone: 516-933-7100
Fax: 516-933-7731
Web: www.kweusa.com

CEO: Takashi Chris Bamba
CFO: –
HR: –
FYE: March 31
Type: Subsidiary

Kintetsu World Express (U.S.A.) helps move freight in and out of the US — and the rest of the world. The company specializes in international airfreight and ocean freight forwarding and customs brokerage services. (As a freight forwarder Kintetsu World Express (U.S.A.) buys transportation capacity from carriers and resells it to customers.) Other services include consulting inventory management and warehousing and distribution as well as handling perishable or dangerous cargo. The company operates from a network of about 40 offices in major trade gateways throughout the US. Kintetsu World Express (U.S.A.) is a unit of Japan-based Kintetsu World Express which launched its US operations in 1969.

KIOR, INC.   NBB: KIOR Q

13001 Bay Park Road
Pasadena, TX 77507
Phone: 281 694-8700
Fax: –
Web: www.kior.com

CEO: Fred Cannon
CFO: Christopher A Artzer
HR: –
FYE: December 31
Type: Public

Renewable crude oil. Wait - what? KiOR makes actual crude oil using renewable non-food biomass like wood chips and switch grass. It also makes gasoline and diesel as well as blends for standard gasoline from its crude. Refined in standard petrochemical refinery equipment the development stage company's products can be transported using existing oil and gas transportation infrastructure. Unlike ethanol and biodiesel KiOR's fuel is completely interchangeable with fossil fuels and can be "dropped in" to engines. The company claims it can produce a gallon of gas for $1.80 with an 80% reduction in greenhouse gas emissions compared to standard gasoline.

	Annual Growth	12/09	12/10	12/11	12/12	12/13
Sales ($ mil.)	1997.7%	–	–	–	0.1	1.8
Net income ($ mil.)	–	(14.1)	(45.9)	(64.1)	(96.4)	(347.5)
Market value ($ mil.)	(59.4%)	–	–	1,121.8	706.4	185.1
Employees	19.6%	–	107	163	212	183

KIPS BAY MEDICAL INC.   NBB: KIPS

3405 Annapolis Lane North, Suite 200
Minneapolis, MN 55447
Phone: 763 235-3540
Fax: –
Web: www.kipsbaymedical.com

CEO: Scott Kellen
CFO: –
HR: –
FYE: December 31
Type: Public

Kips Bay Medical makes medical devices that help veins do their jobs in patients with coronary artery disease. The company is focused on developing and commercializing a vein support device called eSVS MESH a mesh sleeve implanted by surgeons in coronary artery bypass grafting (CABG) that when placed over a patient's vein graft improves the graft's structure and long-term performance. It is designed to mimic the artery's job of constricting the vein and preventing harmful vessel expansion. The company began selling the eSVS MESH in Europe and other international markets in 2010 and it plans to seek marketing approval in the US as well. Kips Bay Medical completed an IPO in 2011.

	Annual Growth	12/09	12/10	12/11	12/12	12/13
Sales ($ mil.)	(16.5%)	–	0.2	0.3	0.2	0.1
Net income ($ mil.)	–	(3.3)	(10.9)	(4.3)	(5.5)	(6.1)
Market value ($ mil.)	(26.8%)	–	–	36.2	16.9	19.4
Employees	1.9%	13	13	15	13	14

KIRBY CORP.   NYS: KEX

55 Waugh Drive, Suite 1000
Houston, TX 77007
Phone: 713 435-1000
Fax: 713 435-1010
Web: www.kirbycorp.com

CEO: David W. Grzebinski
CFO: C. Andrew (Andy) Smith
HR: –
FYE: December 31
Type: Public

Where Kirby hauls cargo the only curbs are riverbanks — the company is the largest inland tank barge operator in the US. Its fleet operated by subsidiary Kirby Inland Marine consists of over 860 barges and about 250 inland towboats with a transportation capacity of 17.8 million barrels. The vessels are used to transport liquid bulk cargo: petrochemicals crude and refined petroleum products and agricultural chemicals. Its Marine Transportation segment (inland/offshore operations) is joined by its Diesel Engine Services segment which is a leading provider of diesel engine services and parts for marine rail and power generation customers.

	Annual Growth	12/10	12/11	12/12	12/13	12/14
Sales ($ mil.)	23.3%	1,109.6	1,850.4	2,112.7	2,242.2	2,566.3
Net income ($ mil.)	24.8%	116.2	183.0	209.4	253.1	282.0
Market value ($ mil.)	16.4%	2,505.1	3,744.3	3,519.7	5,644.3	4,591.7
Employees	16.7%	2,520	4,100	4,575	4,450	4,675

KIRBY INLAND MARINE LP

55 Waugh Dr. Ste. 1000
Houston TX 77007
Phone: 713-435-1000
Fax: 713-435-1464
Web: www.kirbycorp.com/2_inland/index.cfm

CEO: –
CFO: –
HR: –
FYE: December 31
Type: Subsidiary

Avoiding highways and railways Kirby Inland Marine uses waterways to carry liquid bulk cargo. The primary subsidiary of Kirby Corp. Kirby Inland Marine operates a fleet of about 915 tank barges and 240 towing vessels. Hauling petrochemicals accounts for the majority of the company's sales; other freight carried by Kirby Inland Marine includes crude and refined petroleum products and agricultural chemicals. The company's operations span the major inland waterway systems of the US including the Mississippi River and its tributaries the Gulf Intracoastal Waterway the Illinois River and the Ohio River.

KIRBY RISK CORPORATION

1815 SAGAMORE PKWY N
LAFAYETTE, IN 479041765
Phone: 765-448-4567
Fax: –
Web: www.kirbyrisk.com

CEO: James K. (Jim) Risk
CFO: Jason Bricker
HR: Doug Gutridge
FYE: December 31
Type: Private

Kirby Risk sees nothing risky about helping harness a little electrical energy. The company named after one of its co-founders supplies electrical products (process automation products drives and motors lighting fuses wire and cable) and services to the Midwestern US. The company operates through four business units comprising Electrical Supply Service Center Mechanical Solutions and Service and Precision Machining. The Electrical Supply distribution unit handles more than 20000 products from some 500 manufacturers including GE Thomas & Betts and Rockwell Automation. Other operations include ARCO Electric Products (phase converters). CEO James Risk III owns the company that was founded in 1926.

	Annual Growth	12/09	12/10	12/11	12/12	12/13
Sales ($ mil.)	0.1%	–	399.6	377.9	398.4	401.3
Net income ($ mil.)	–	–	–	–	0.0	0.0
Market value ($ mil.)	–	–	–	–	–	–
Employees	–	–	–	–	–	950

KIRKLAND & ELLIS LLP

300 N. LaSalle St.
Chicago IL 60654
Phone: 312-862-2000
Fax: 312-862-2200
Web: www.kirkland.com

CEO: –
CFO: Nicholas J Willmott
HR: –
FYE: January 31
Type: Private - Partnershi

Known for its work in cases that go to trial law firm Kirkland & Ellis maintains a variety of practices aimed mainly at corporate clients. Besides litigation the firm's core practice areas include corporate transactions intellectual property restructuring and tax. Kirkland & Ellis represents public and private companies from a wide range of industries as well as individuals and government agencies. Over the years its clients have included companies such as Bank of America General Motors McDonald's and Siemens. The firm was founded in 1908.

KIRKLAND'S INC

NMS: KIRK

5310 Maryland Way
Brentwood, TN 37027
Phone: 615 872-4800
Fax: –
Web: www.kirklands.com

CEO: Robert E. Alderson
CFO: Adam C Holland
HR: –
FYE: January 31
Type: Public

When you just deplore your bare wood floor and feel the need to improve your home's décor Kirkland's hopes you'll explore its stores for affordable rugs art lamps and more. The company operates about 325 stores (down from 350 in 2007) throughout 35 US states. It is known for stocking decorative home accessories and gifts including framed art mirrors candles lamps picture frames artificial flowers rugs garden accessories and coffee-table books. Kirkland's also adds holiday items during Christmas and Easter to its merchandise mix. The retailer has operated its growing kirklands.com e-commerce business since late 2010. Kirkland's was founded in 1966 by Carl Kirkland.

	Annual Growth	01/11	01/12*	02/13	02/14*	01/15
Sales ($ mil.)	5.1%	415.3	430.3	448.4	460.6	507.6
Net income ($ mil.)	(9.4%)	26.4	19.1	13.8	14.5	17.8
Market value ($ mil.)	14.6%	230.9	244.8	194.1	322.5	398.6
Employees	12.4%	3,948	4,392	4,866	4,395	6,312

*Fiscal year change

KISSIMMEE UTILITY AUTHORITY

1701 W. Carroll St.
Kissimmee FL 34741
Phone: 407-933-7777
Fax: 407-933-7715
Web: www.kua.com

CEO: –
CFO: –
HR: –
FYE: September 30
Type: Government-owned

Kissimmee Utility Authority (KUA) is committed to redoubling efforts to serve this Florida city with three double letters in its name. KUA operates the municipal power distribution system serving 64000 commercial and industrial and residential customers in Kissimmee and surrounding areas. It also offers its customers internet telephone and security services. In addition the community-owned utility has stakes in and handful of power plants and has a total generating capacity of 410 MW. The venerable company is used to managing operations in a hurricane-prone area and is equipped to mobilize maintenance crews to quickly restore power in the wake of infrastructure damage caused by severe storms.

KITCHELL CORPORATION

1707 E HIGHLAND AVE # 100
PHOENIX, AZ 850164668
Phone: 602-264-4411
Fax: –
Web: www.kitchell.com

CEO: James T (Jim) Swanson
CFO: –
HR: Sara Stewart
FYE: December 31
Type: Private

From the first structure design sketch to the last brick laid Kitchell builds the whole kit and caboodle. The employee-owned company which operates through half a dozen subsidiaries offers general contracting project and construction management engineering and architectural services and environmental services. Its projects run the gamut of public- and private-sector work and include bioscience labs casinos student housing hotels jails custom homes and performing arts centers. Kitchell is also active in facility and project management and real estate development as well as fleet management and air conditioning equipment wholesale supply. While the western US is its primary area of focus Kitchell boasts projects in about two dozen US states.

	Annual Growth	12/06	12/07	12/08	12/09	12/10
Sales ($ mil.)	(31.6%)	–	–	1,027.8	677.8	480.8
Net income ($ mil.)	–	–	–	0.0	0.0	0.0
Market value ($ mil.)	–	–	–	–	–	–
Employees	–	–	–	–	–	946

KITE REALTY GROUP TRUST

NYS: KRG

30 S. Meridian Street, Suite 1100
Indianapolis, IN 46204
Phone: 317 577-5600
Fax: –
Web: www.kiterealty.com

CEO: John A. Kite
CFO: Daniel R. Sink
HR: –
FYE: December 31
Type: Public

A real estate investment trust (REIT) Kite Realty Group Trust acquires develops and operates retail properties. It owns more than 70 strip malls and anchored shopping centers with some 12.4 million sq. ft. of leasable space in about a dozen states with about a third in Indiana. The REIT also has interests in three commercial properties a parking garage several retail sites under development and nearly 100 acres of land held for possible future development. Kite Realty also provides third-party management development and construction services. Its largest tenants include Florida grocer Publix and TJX Cos. though no single tenant accounts for more than 5% of the company's rental income.

	Annual Growth	12/10	12/11	12/12	12/13	12/14
Sales ($ mil.)	26.5%	101.4	101.9	101.1	129.5	259.5
Net income ($ mil.)	–	(8.3)	5.0	(4.3)	(2.8)	(5.7)
Market value ($ mil.)	51.8%	451.7	376.5	466.7	548.5	2,399.5
Employees	17.5%	74	77	84	95	141

KIWANIS INTERNATIONAL

3636 Woodview Trace
Indianapolis IN 46268-3196
Phone: 317-875-8755
Fax: 317-879-0204
Web: www.kiwanis.org

CEO: Stan Soderstrom
CFO: –
HR: Erin Sloan
FYE: September 30
Type: Private - Not-for-Pr

Kiwanians focus on kids. Kiwanis International unites local clubs that serve children and young adults through various service projects. These projects are targeted to address one or more of the club's six permanent "Objects of Kiwanis" which include fostering spiritual values and higher social standards developing a more aggressive citizenship and increasing patriotism and goodwill. Kiwanis' Circle K is its collegiate club Key Club is for high schoolers Builders Club serves junior high and middle school students K-Kids is for elementary kids and Aktion Club helps adults with disabilities do service projects. Founded in 1915 Kiwanis International operates more than 8000 clubs in about 95 countries.

KIWIBOX.COM, INC.

NBB: KIWB

330 West 42nd Street, Suite 3210
New York, NY 10036
Phone: 212 239-8210
Fax: –

CEO: Andre Scholz
CFO: –
HR: –
FYE: December 31
Type: Public

Kiwibox.com (formerly Magnitude Information Systems) offered a line of ergonomic software tools that helped employees avoid repetitive stress injuries in their use of computers. In 2007 Magnitude acquired Kiwibox Media which operates a social networking site for teenagers. In late 2009 the company changed its name to Kiwibox.com as part of a shifting strategy to focus on its social networking operations. With social media only getting stronger in 2012 it completed its purchase of European social network site KWICK! based near Stuttgart Germany for about €6.4 million ($8.3 million). KWICK! reports more than 10 million registered users and 1 million active users.

	Annual Growth	12/10	12/11	12/12	12/13	12/14
Sales ($ mil.)	106.1%	0.0	0.6	1.5	0.9	0.0
Net income ($ mil.)	–	(4.0)	(5.9)	(14.0)	(7.0)	(4.7)
Market value ($ mil.)	(48.4%)	11.3	23.9	4.6	3.1	0.8
Employees	(13.1%)	7	22	13	3	4

KLA-TENCOR CORP.

NMS: KLAC

One Technology Drive
Milpitas, CA 95035
Phone: 408 875-3000
Fax: –
Web: www.kla-tencor.com

CEO: Richard P. (Rick) Wallace
CFO: Bren Higgins
HR: –
FYE: June 30
Type: Public

Don't feel bad if KLA-Tencor points out your flaws. It's probably going to save you a ton of money — if you make computer chips. The company is one of the world's largest makers of process control equipment for the semiconductor and related nanoelectronics as well as other high tech industries. It makes offers yield management systems that monitor and analyze materials during the entire fabrication process inspecting reticles (which make circuit patterns) and measuring microscopic layers. KLA-Tencor has long dominated the market for equipment that inspects semiconductor photomasks and reticles. The company agreed to be bought by Lam Research which makes semiconductor manufacturing equipment for $10.6 billion.

	Annual Growth	06/11	06/12	06/13	06/14	06/15
Sales ($ mil.)	(3.0%)	3,175.2	3,171.9	2,842.8	2,929.4	2,814.0
Net income ($ mil.)	(17.6%)	794.5	756.0	543.1	582.8	366.2
Market value ($ mil.)	8.6%	6,389.8	7,774.2	8,797.0	11,466.3	8,872.8
Employees	1.7%	5,500	5,710	5,820	6,060	5,880

KKR & CO. L.P.

9 W. 57th St. Ste. 4200
New York NY 10019
Phone: 212-750-8300
Fax: 212-750-0003
Web: www.kkr.com

CEO: Henry R Kravis
CFO: –
HR: –
FYE: December 31
Type: Public

Have the barbarians at the gate become civilized? KKR & Co. the master of the leveraged buyout has ditched its hostile takeover image for a kinder gentler buy-and-build strategy. The global investment firm has some $59 billion in assets under management including significant stakes in such companies as Del Monte Foods Samson Investment and Go Daddy. An active owner it often supervises or installs new management and revamps strategy and corporate structure selling underperforming units or adding new ones. KKR tends to hold onto its investments for the long term. The company has offices in major business centers in Asia Australia Europe and the US. KKR went public via a nearly $2 billion IPO in 2010.

KLAUSSNER FURNITURE INDUSTRIES INC.

405 Lewallen Rd.
Asheboro NC 27205
Phone: 336-625-6174
Fax: 336-626-0905
Web: www.klaussner.com

CEO: Bill Wittenberg
CFO: David O Bryant
HR: Mark Walker
FYE: December 31
Type: Private

Klaussner Furniture Industries makes accoutrements for the American dream. As one of the nation's largest makers of home furniture Klaussner sells fabric- and leather-upholstered sofas and recliners chairs ottomans occasional tables home entertainment and dining furniture under the Distinctions and Klaussner names. It also licenses such brand names as Sealy and Dick Idol. The furniture company boasts manufacturing and distribution facilities in North Carolina and Iowa as well as a handful of licensed Klaussner home stores and about 150 Klaussner Home Furnishings Galleries. Founded in 1963 the company was owned by Hans Klaussner from 1979 to 2011 when it was bought out by management.

KKR FINANCIAL HOLDINGS LLC

NYS: KFN

555 California Street, 50th Floor
San Francisco, CA 94104
Phone: 415 315-3620
Fax: 415 391-3077
Web: www.ir.kkr.com/kfn_ir/kfn_overview.cfm

CEO: William J Janetschek
CFO: Thomas N Murphy
HR: –
FYE: December 31
Type: Public

KKR Financial Holdings is a specialty finance company that invests in a variety of financial products primarily below-investment-grade corporate debt as well as public and private equity. Its portfolio which weighs in at more than $8 billion includes syndicated bank loans mezzanine loans high-yield corporate bonds asset-backed securities commercial real estate and debt and equity securities. KKR Financial Holdings is externally managed by KKR Financial Advisors; both firms are affiliates of private equity and leveraged buyout giant KKR & Co.

	Annual Growth	12/08	12/09	12/10	12/11	12/12
Assets ($ mil.)	(9.6%)	12,515.1	10,300.0	8,418.4	8,647.2	8,358.9
Net income ($ mil.)	–	(1,075.0)	76.9	371.1	318.1	348.2
Market value ($ mil.)	60.8%	281.9	1,034.9	1,659.5	1,557.8	1,884.3
Employees						

KLEIN TOOLS INC.

450 Bond St.
Lincolnshire IL 60069
Phone: 847-821-5500
Fax: 847-478-0625
Web: www.klein-tools.com

CEO: –
CFO: Verne Tuite
HR: –
FYE: December 31
Type: Private

Five generations of Kleins have had a grip on Klein Tools a maker of non-powered hand tools. The company's products can be found in the tool pouches of professionals in the construction electronics mining telecommunications and general industries. (Klein makes their pouches too.) Its lineup includes cable cutters chisels drill bits hammers pliers saws screwdrivers wire strippers and wrenches. Klein also sells diagnostic equipment occupational protective gear and specialty chemicals. Products are distributed worldwide and sold by tool retailers and building supply stores including Home Depot Ace and Grainger. Founded by Mathias Klein in 1857 the company is still owned by the Klein family.

KLEINER PERKINS CAUFIELD & BYERS

2750 Sand Hill Rd.
Menlo Park CA 94025
Phone: 650-233-2750
Fax: 650-233-0300
Web: www.kpcb.com

CEO: -
CFO: -
HR: -
FYE: December 31
Type: Private

Let Kleiner Perkins Caufield & Byers (KPCB) beware — or at the very least be on the lookout. The venture capital firm invests money time and intellect in innovative early-stage companies that sometimes become the foundations for new industries. KPCB has invested in such notable outfits as AOL Amazon Genentech Google Groupon Sun Microsystems and Twitter. The firm focuses its energies on information technology life sciences social networking iPhone and iPad applications (apps) and green technology investments. (Al Gore is one of its partners.) Since its inception in 1972 KPCB has invested in more than 500 companies; it has taken more than 150 of them public.

KNAPE & VOGT MANUFACTURING COMPANY

2700 Oak Industrial Dr. NE
Grand Rapids MI 49505
Phone: 616-459-3311
Fax: 616-459-3467
Web: www.knapeandvogt.com

CEO: Peter Martin
CFO: -
HR: -
FYE: June 30
Type: Private

Knape & Vogt Manufacturing (KV) believes in easy access to your drawers — and all your stuff — whether it's at home or the office. The company makes drawer slides shelving systems closet rods and other storage-related hardware items. It also offers kitchen and bath storage products from its Real Solutions for Real Life brand and ergonomic office products from its idea@WORK brand. KV sells mostly to original equipment manufacturers office furniture retailers hardware chains and specialty distributors in the US and Canada but it also sells directly to consumers and government agencies. The company is owned by private equity firm Wind Point Partners.

KMART CORPORATION

3333 Beverly Rd.
Hoffman Estates IL 60179
Phone: 847-286-2500
Fax: 847-286-5500
Web: www.kmart.com

CEO: -
CFO: -
HR: -
FYE: January 31
Type: Subsidiary

Attention Kmart shoppers: Kmart is the #3 discount retailer in the US behind Wal-Mart and Target. It sells name-brand and private-label goods (including its Joe Boxer and Jaclyn Smith labels) mostly to low- and mid-income families. It runs about 1300 off-mall stores (including 30 Supercenters) in 49 US states Puerto Rico Guam and the US Virgin Islands. About 270 Kmart stores sell home appliances (including Sears' Kenmore brand) and some 980 locations house in-store pharmacies. Poor sales have forced its parent Sears Holdings Corp. to close 100 to 120 Kmart and sister subsidiary Sears Roebuck stores. Kmart also operates the kmart.com website which includes merchandise from Sears.

KNIGHT TRANSPORTATION INC.

NYS: KNX

20002 North 19th Avenue
Phoenix, AZ 85027
Phone: 602 269-2000
Fax: -
Web: www.knighttrans.com

CEO: David A. (Dave) Jackson
CFO: Adam Miller
HR: Glen Palmer
FYE: December 31
Type: Public

Knight Transportation drivers don't drive long hours into the night. The truckload carrier instead focuses on short- to medium-haul trips averaging about 500 miles. From some 35 regional operations centers mainly in the southern midwestern and western US Knight carries such cargo as consumer goods food and beverages and paper products. It has a fleet of more than 4100 tractors and 9700 trailers including nearly 900 refrigerated trailers. Besides for-hire hauling Knight provides dedicated contract carriage in which drivers and equipment are assigned to a customer long-term. It also offers freight brokerage services.

	Annual Growth	12/10	12/11	12/12	12/13	12/14
Sales ($ mil.)	10.8%	730.7	866.2	936.0	969.2	1,102.3
Net income ($ mil.)	14.9%	59.1	60.2	64.1	69.3	102.9
Market value ($ mil.)	15.4%	1,555.0	1,280.0	1,197.3	1,501.0	2,754.8
Employees	4.9%	4,526	4,682	5,176	5,177	5,485

KMG CHEMICALS, INC.

NYS: KMG

9555 West Sam Houston Parkway South, Suite 600
Houston, TX 77099
Phone: 713 600-3800
Fax: -
Web: www.kmgchemicals.com

CEO: J. Neal Butler
CFO: John V. Sobchak
HR: Jody Manzon
FYE: July 31
Type: Public

KMG Chemicals protects wood and helps make chips though it has nothing to do with wood chips. Its electronic chemicals are used in the manufacture of semiconductors. KMG's largest customer is silicon chip kingpin Intel which regularly accounts for about 10% of total sales. Its wood preservatives are pentachlorophenol (penta) sodium penta and creosote. KMG sells penta and creosote in the US primarily to the railroad construction and utility industries. Sodium penta is sold in Latin America. Creosote customer Stella-Jones accounted for 10% or more of total sales in 2011 and 2012. To focus on its core businesses in 2012 the company agreed to sell its animal health business to Bayer HealthCare.

	Annual Growth	07/11	07/12	07/13	07/14	07/15
Sales ($ mil.)	4.7%	266.4	272.7	263.3	353.4	320.5
Net income ($ mil.)	5.7%	9.7	13.8	9.3	(1.0)	12.1
Market value ($ mil.)	6.8%	195.9	209.0	264.0	196.0	255.2
Employees	18.3%	336	331	740	733	657

KNIGHTS OF COLUMBUS

1 COLUMBUS PLZ STE 1700
NEW HAVEN, CT 065103326
Phone: 203-752-4000
Fax: -
Web: www.eastonkofc.org

CEO: -
CFO: -
HR: -
FYE: December 31
Type: Private

Good Knight! The Knights of Columbus is a formidable volunteer group boasting 15000 councils made up of 1.9 million Roman Catholic male members in the US Canada Mexico Cuba the Philippines Poland and several other countries. The fraternal organization is also a force to be reckoned with in the insurance world providing life insurance annuities and long-term care insurance to its members and their families. In addition the group manages the Knights of Columbus Museum in New Haven Connecticut featuring exhibits of religious art and history.

	Annual Growth	12/09	12/10	12/11	12/12	12/13
Assets ($ mil.)	6.8%	-	16,862.0	18,026.6	19,401.7	20,534.4
Net income ($ mil.)	18.5%	-	-	81.0	127.7	113.7
Market value ($ mil.)	-	-	-	-	-	-
Employees	-	-	-	-	-	2,300

KNOLL INC

NYS: KNL

1235 Water Street
East Greenville, PA 18041
Phone: 215 679-7991
Fax: –
Web: www.knoll.com

CEO: Andrew B. Cogan
CFO: Craig B. Spray
HR: Karen Clary
FYE: December 31
Type: Public

From the Bauhaus style to business chic Knoll has designs on the furniture market. The company makes a variety of distinctively designed curvilinear office furniture and related accessories including office systems (aka cubicles). Its products are sold under such names as Equity Antenna AutoStrada Reff Profiles Morrison Template and Currents. Other items include ergonomic seating tables and desks and filing systems. Founded in 1938 it offers an upscale line of designed furniture (KnollStudio) computer and desk accessories (KnollExtra) and fabric and leather upholstery (KnollTextiles). The company markets its products directly and through some 300 independent dealers in North America and Europe.

	Annual Growth	12/10	12/11	12/12	12/13	12/14
Sales ($ mil.)	6.7%	809.5	922.2	887.5	862.7	1,050.3
Net income ($ mil.)	13.6%	28.0	58.0	50.0	23.1	46.6
Market value ($ mil.)	6.1%	794.5	705.2	729.4	869.5	1,005.3
Employees	2.7%	3,006	3,121	3,211	3,167	3,343

KNOUSE FOODS COOPERATIVE INC.

800 PACH GLEN IDAVILLE RD
PEACH GLEN, PA 173750001
Phone: 717-677-8181
Fax: –
Web: www.knousefoodservice.com

CEO: –
CFO: –
HR: –
FYE: June 30
Type: Private

Is there a Knouse in the house? Might be. With retail brand names such as Apple Time Lucky Leaf Musselman's Lincoln and Speas Farm Knouse Foods Cooperative's apple products are in many a pantry. The company is a growers' co-op made up of some 150 Appalachian Mountain and Midwestern grower/members. It processes its members' apples for sale as canned and bottled applesauce juice cider vinegar apple butter pie fillings and snack packs all of which are available nationwide. In addition to stocking supermarket shelves Knouse founded in 1949 supplies foodservice operators and industrial-ingredient companies with bulk apple and other fruit products. It also offers private-label and co-packing services.

	Annual Growth	06/04	06/05	06/06	06/07	06/08
Sales ($ mil.)	4.2%	–	239.5	248.1	259.7	270.6
Net income ($ mil.)	76.9%	–	–	2.5	2.1	7.7
Market value ($ mil.)	–	–	–	–	–	–
Employees	–	–	–	–	–	1,200

KNOWLES CORP

NYS: KN

1151 Maplewood Drive
Itasca, IL 60143
Phone: 630 250-5100
Fax: 630 250-0575
Web: www.knowles.com

CEO: Jeffrey S Niew
CFO: John S. Anderson
HR: –
FYE: December 31
Type: Public

Knowles knows electrical products and components. Developing the microphone and receiver for hearing aids in 1954 Knowles Corporation continues to make those products along with volume controls trimmers switches telecoils and other components used in aerospace computer instrumentation medical military and telecommunications applications. The company also makes speakers and receivers used in mobile handsets smartphones and tablets. Its operations are divided across two segments: Mobile Consumer Electronics (MCW) and Specialty Components (SC).

	Annual Growth	12/10	12/11	12/12	12/13	12/14
Sales ($ mil.)	–	0.0	983.3	1,118.0	1,214.8	1,141.5
Net income ($ mil.)	–	0.0	98.5	79.1	105.8	(87.0)
Market value ($ mil.)	–	0.0	–	–	–	2,003.2
Employees	30.0%	–	–	–	10,000	13,000

KNOX COUNTY HOSPITAL

520 S 7TH ST
VINCENNES, IN 475911038
Phone: 812-882-5220
Fax: –
Web: www.gshvin.org

CEO: –
CFO: –
HR: Emily Heineke
FYE: December 31
Type: Private

Good Samaritan Hospital provides a full slate of healthcare services to both southwest Indiana and southeast Illinois. Its services include cardiology emergency care orthopedics women's health and pediatrics among others. The 230-bed hospital is located a few blocks from the Wabash River which forms the border between the Hoosier and Prairies states. Good Samaritan operates specialty units as well including same-day surgery breast care behavioral health radiology sleep cancer care and rehabilitation centers. It also provides home health and hospice services. Established in 1908 with 25 beds Good Samaritan was Indiana's first county hospital.

	Annual Growth	12/09	12/10	12/11	12/12	12/13
Sales ($ mil.)	8.2%	–	156.6	175.0	191.9	198.1
Net income ($ mil.)	(30.3%)	–	–	8.4	12.7	4.1
Market value ($ mil.)	–	–	–	–	–	–
Employees	–	–	–	–	–	1,850

KOCH ENTERPRISES INC.

14 S 11TH AVE
EVANSVILLE, IN 47712-5020
Phone: 812-465-9800
Fax: –
Web: www.kochenterprises.com

CEO: –
CFO: Susan E Parsons
HR: –
FYE: December 31
Type: Private

Koch gets straight A's for diversification; it's a private holding company active in automobile parts manufacturing metals recycling wholesale distribution and equipment design and construction. Subsidiaries include Audubon Metals (processes aluminum) George Koch Sons (engineers installs and services auto finishing systems) Koch Air (distributes Carrier HVAC equipment) Gibbs Die Casting (parts for making cars lighter) Brake Supply (repairs brakes and hydraulic systems for auto and mining equipment) and Uniseal (makes structural adhesives thermoplastics and sealant systems for industrial and auto markets). George Koch founded the company in 1873.

	Annual Growth	12/08	12/09	12/10	12/11	12/12
Sales ($ mil.)	4.3%	–	830.9	851.1	915.6	942.6
Net income ($ mil.)	–	–	0.0	22.7	0.0	0.0
Market value ($ mil.)	–	–	–	–	–	–
Employees	–	–	–	–	–	2,482

KOCH FOODS INCORPORATED

1300 W. Higgins Rd.
Park Ridge IL 60068
Phone: 847-384-5940
Fax: 847-384-5961
Web: www.kochfoods.com

CEO: –
CFO: Mark Kaminsky
HR: Tom Downard
FYE: December 31
Type: Private

Why did the chicken cross the road? To escape "America's Chicken Specialist" Koch Foods no doubt. The vertically-integrated poultry processor makes commodity and value-added fresh and frozen chicken products such as chicken tenderloins tenders strips boneless breasts and wings along with diced and pulled white and dark meat and whole and whole cut-up chickens. Koch's customers include companies in the retail food and foodservice sectors throughout the US as well as overseas. The company sells its value-added poultry products under the Antioch and Cravers retail brands. Koch Foods began as a one-room chicken de-boning and cutting operation in 1985.

KOCH INDUSTRIES INC.

4111 E. 37th St. North
Wichita KS 67220-3203
Phone: 316-828-5500
Fax: 316-828-5739
Web: www.kochind.com

CEO: Charles G Koch
CFO: –
HR: –
FYE: December 31
Type: Private

Koch (pronounced "coke") Industries is the real thing one of the largest (if not the largest) private companies in the US. Koch's operations are diverse including refining and chemicals process and pollution control equipment and technologies; fibers and polymers; commodity and financial trading; and forest and consumer products (led by Georgia-Pacific). Its Flint Hills Resources subsidiary owns three refineries that together process more than 800000 barrels of crude oil daily. Koch operates crude gathering systems and pipelines across North America as well as cattle ranches with more than 15000 head of cattle in Kansas Montana and Texas. Brothers Charles and David Koch control the company.

KOHLBERG CAPITAL CORPORATION   NASDAQ: KCAP

295 Madison Ave. 6th Fl.
New York NY 10017
Phone: 212-455-8300
Fax: 212-983-7654
Web: www.kohlbergcapital.com

CEO: Dayl W Pearson
CFO: Edward U Gilpin
HR: –
FYE: December 31
Type: Public

Kohlberg Capital acts as the middleman for companies in need of a loan. The internally managed investment firm provides loans to middle market companies earning between $10 million to $50 million with debt of $25 million to $150 million. It originates junior and senior secured term loans mezzanine debt and equity securities. Its Katonah Debt Advisors which has more than $2 billion of assets under management manages collateralized loan obligation funds that invest in syndicated loans and high-yield bonds. Organized as a business development company Kohlberg Capital pays 4% in income tax as long as it distributes 90% of its profits back to shareholders. The company was spun off from Kohlberg & Co. in 2006.

KODIAK OIL & GAS CORP.   NYSE AMEX: KOG

1625 Broadway Ste. 330
Denver CO 80202
Phone: 303-592-8075
Fax: 303-592-8071
Web: www.kodiakog.com

CEO: James J Volker
CFO: Michael J Stevens
HR: –
FYE: December 31
Type: Public

Kodiak Oil & Gas bears the responsibility for exploration development and production of oil and natural gas in the Rockies. The company which focuses on assets in the Vermillion Basin of the Green River Basin and the Williston Basin (located in Montana and North Dakota) has proved reserves of 1.2 billion cu. ft. of natural gas and 344000 barrels of oil. Kodiak Oil & Gas has 99434 net acres of land holdings. In the Green River Basin it is exploring for unconventional gas through the exploitation of coalbed methane over-pressured shales and tight-gas-sands. In recent years the company has increased its holdings in the Williston Basin to 110000 acres through deals worth $345 million.

KOHLER CO.

444 Highland Dr.
Kohler WI 53044
Phone: 920-457-4441
Fax: 920-457-1271
Web: kohlerco.com

CEO: K David Kohler
CFO: –
HR: –
FYE: December 31
Type: Private

When profits go down the drain at Kohler that's not necessarily a bad thing. The company makes bathroom and kitchen products — from toilets and baths to showers and sinks — under names including Jacob Delafon Karat Kohler Kallista Mira and Sterling. It also makes furniture under the Baker and McGuire brands and tile under the Ann Sacks brand. Lesser-known operations include Kohler's manufacturing of small engines generators and power supplies for both consumer and industrial applications under the Kohler and Lombardini names. Kohler also owns golf courses and resorts in Wisconsin and The Old Course Hotel Golf Resort and Spa in Scotland. The Kohler family controls the company.

KOHL'S CORP.   NYS: KSS

N56 W17000 Ridgewood Drive
Menomonee Falls, WI 53051
Phone: 262 703-7000
Fax: 262 703-6373
Web: www.kohls.com

CEO: Kevin B. Mansell
CFO: Wesley S. (Wes) McDonald
HR: Genny Shields
FYE: January 31
Type: Public

Kohl's wants its prices to be easy on shoppers and tough on competition. The clothing retailer operates about 1160 department stores in 49 states with nearly half of stores in the Midwest and West. Competing with discount and mid-level department stores it sells moderately priced name-brand and private-label apparel shoes accessories and housewares through centrally located cash registers designed to speed checkout and keep staff costs down. Merchandising relationships allow Kohl's to carry top brands (NIKE Levi's OshKosh B'Gosh) not always available to discounters; it's able to sell them for lower prices by controlling costs. A typical store spans 88000 sq. ft. and serves markets with 150000 to 200000 people.

	Annual Growth	01/11	01/12*	02/13	02/14*	01/15
Sales ($ mil.)	0.8%	18,391.0	18,804.0	19,279.0	19,031.0	19,023.0
Net income ($ mil.)	(6.1%)	1,114.0	1,167.0	986.0	889.0	867.0
Market value ($ mil.)	3.9%	10,291.2	9,384.7	9,248.0	10,176.6	12,003.7
Employees	0.2%	136,000	142,000	135,000	137,000	137,000

*Fiscal year change

KOHN PEDERSEN FOX ASSOCIATES PC

11 W 42ND ST STE 8A
NEW YORK, NY 100368002
Phone: 212-977-6500
Fax: –
Web: www.kpf.com

CEO: –
CFO: Peter Catalano
HR: Denise Norsted
FYE: December 31
Type: Private

Kohn Pedersen Fox Associates (KPF) puts its stamp on buildings around the world. One of the top 10 architectural and planning firms in the US the company offers services such as master planning urban design space planning programming building analysis graphic and product and interior design. It specializes in such projects as corporate headquarters government offices health care facilities hotels and educational facilities. KPF's structures range from small pavilions to entire cities. The firm operates from offices in New York London and Shanghai. Architects A. Eugene Kohn William Pedersen and Sheldon Fox founded the firm in 1976.

	Annual Growth	12/02	12/03	12/04	12/05	12/07
Sales ($ mil.)	5.3%	–	–	62.4	64.1	72.8
Net income ($ mil.)	142.4%	–	–	0.4	22.2	6.3
Market value ($ mil.)	–	–	–	–	–	–
Employees	–	–	–	–	–	350

KOHR BROTHERS INC.

2151 RICHMOND RD STE 200
CHARLOTTESVILLE, VA 229113636
Phone: 434-975-1500
Fax: –
Web: www.kohrbros.com

CEO: –
CFO: –
HR: –
FYE: October 31
Type: Private

Kohr Brothers operates and franchises more than 30 Kohr Bros. Frozen Custard outlets in about 10 states a majority of which are in New Jersey. Most of its shops are in high traffic areas such as shopping malls airports and sports arenas. School teacher Archie Kohr started the chain with his brothers in 1919 in order to sell more cream from the family's dairy business. The brothers began with a single ice cream shop on Coney Island's boardwalk.

	Annual Growth	10/10	10/11	10/12	10/13	10/14
Sales ($ mil.)	4.5%	–	10.9	11.3	11.3	12.4
Net income ($ mil.)	5.4%	–	–	0.6	0.5	0.6
Market value ($ mil.)	–	–	–	–	–	–
Employees	–	–	–	–	–	250

KOLBE & KOLBE MILLWORK CO. INC.

1323 S. 11th Ave.
Wausau WI 54401-5998
Phone: 715-842-5666
Fax: 715-842-2863
Web: www.kolbe-kolbe.com

CEO: Mike Salsieder
CFO: –
HR: –
FYE: December 31
Type: Private

You won't find anyone milling around at Kolbe & Kolbe Millwork. Instead workers are busy making wooden and aluminum-clad windows and doors in a variety of styles. The family-owned company also includes Kolbe Vinyl Windows & Doors and Pointe Five which offer custom-made and Craftsman-style doors and garden windows. The company provides installation and maintenance through its ServicePro unit. Sales and distribution of Kolbe & Kolbe products is handled by K-K Sales and K-K Way. Kolbe & Kolbe sells its products to distributors and dealers throughout the US and in Canada China Ireland the Netherlands South Korea and the UK. The building products company is led by CEO Judith Kolbe Gorski.

KOMATSU AMERICA CORP.

1701 W. Golf Rd.
Rolling Meadows IL 60008
Phone: 847-437-5800
Fax: 847-437-5814
Web: www.komatsuamerica.com

CEO: –
CFO: –
HR: –
FYE: March 31
Type: Subsidiary

You would need a very big sandbox to play with Komatsu America's dump trucks and dozers. The company a subsidiary of Japanese construction equipment giant Komatsu (#2 worldwide after Caterpillar) manufactures sells and maintains earthmoving machinery for the North American construction and mining markets. Komatsu America divides its operations into utility equipment (compact construction equipment) and mining systems. Its products include dump trucks backhoes crushers graders hydraulic excavators crawler carriers wheel loaders bulldozers and a computer-based mine management system. The company also provides financing and rents and sells equipment through its sales subsidiaries and distributors.

KONA GRILL INC

NMS: KONA

7150 East Camelback Road, Suite 333
Scottsdale, AZ 85251
Phone: 480 922-8100
Fax: –
Web: www.konagrill.com

CEO: Berke Bakay
CFO: Christi Hing
HR: Carrie Remarke
FYE: December 31
Type: Public

This company is pinning its hopes on the flavor of the Big Island to draw a few mainlanders into its restaurants. Kona Grill operates about 30 upscale casual-dining restaurants offering both seafood and American dishes with an island twist. The restaurants serve both lunch and diner menus and they offer a wide selection of sushi. In addition to dining each location typically has a bar area for happy hour with margaritas and martinis. The restaurants are typically found near upscale shopping areas in Arizona Texas and more than 16 other states.

	Annual Growth	12/10	12/11	12/12	12/13	12/14
Sales ($ mil.)	8.0%	87.6	93.7	96.0	98.3	119.1
Net income ($ mil.)	–	(1.6)	2.0	4.8	2.7	0.7
Market value ($ mil.)	54.0%	46.0	68.6	97.5	207.6	258.8
Employees	8.4%	1,986	1,898	1,884	2,575	2,743

KOPIN CORP.

NMS: KOPN

125 North Drive
Westborough, MA 01581-3335
Phone: 508 870-5959
Fax: –
Web: www.kopin.com

CEO: John C. C. Fan
CFO: Richard A. Sneider
HR: –
FYE: December 27
Type: Public

A pioneer of wearable technology Kopin Corp. makes headset computers for hands-free mobile computing based on its proprietary Golden-i technology. The company's newest GEN 3.8D headset enables wearers — typically workers in light industry — to control the devices with their voices and movements. The company's other wearable technology products are based on CyberDisplay transmissive LCDs that use high-quality single-crystal silicon transistors. Kopin's display devices used in consumer electronics eyewear and military products. Kopin was founded in 1984 by engineers from the Massachusetts Institute of Technology's Electronic Materials Group including co-founder and CEO John Fan.

	Annual Growth	12/10	12/11	12/12	12/13	12/14
Sales ($ mil.)	(28.3%)	120.4	131.1	34.6	22.9	31.8
Net income ($ mil.)	–	8.9	3.6	(18.4)	(4.7)	(28.2)
Market value ($ mil.)	(4.4%)	270.6	244.7	198.7	264.9	226.4
Employees	(13.7%)	357	370	304	180	198

KOPPERS HOLDINGS INC

NYS: KOP

436 Seventh Avenue
Pittsburgh, PA 15219
Phone: 412 227-2001
Fax: –

CEO: Leroy M. Ball
CFO: Michael J. (Mike) Zugay
HR: –
FYE: December 31
Type: Public

Koppers Holdings treats wood right. The company makes carbon compounds and treated-wood products for the chemical railroad aluminum utility construction and steel industries around the world. Its carbon materials and chemicals unit makes materials for producing aluminum polyester resins plasticizers and wood preservatives. The railroad and utility products unit supplies treated crossties and utility poles and treats wood for vineyard construction and other uses. Koppers Holdings owns 50% of KSA Limited (subsidiaries of Heidelberg Cement own the other half) which produces concrete crossties.

	Annual Growth	12/10	12/11	12/12	12/13	12/14
Sales ($ mil.)	5.7%	1,245.5	1,538.9	1,555.0	1,478.3	1,555.0
Net income ($ mil.)	–	44.1	36.9	65.6	40.4	(32.4)
Market value ($ mil.)	(7.7%)	733.3	704.2	781.9	937.6	532.5
Employees	5.5%	1,729	1,711	1,660	1,589	2,142

KORN/FERRY INTERNATIONAL (DE) NYS: KFY

1900 Avenue of the Stars, Suite 2600
Los Angeles, CA 90067
Phone: 310 552-1834
Fax: –
Web: www.kornferry.com

CEO: Gary D. Burnison
CFO: Robert P. Rozek
HR: Linda Hyman
FYE: April 30
Type: Public

High-level executives can jump ship via Korn/Ferry International. The world's largest executive recruitment firm Korn/Ferry has almost 75 offices in more than 35 countries. The company's more than 600 consultants help prominent public and private companies as well as government and not-for-profit organizations find qualified job applicants for openings in a variety of executive level positions (including CEOs CFOs and other senior-level jobs). Through Futurestep job seekers use the Internet and videotaped job interviews to find mid-level management positions. In addition the company provides management assessment as well as coaching and executive development services. Korn/Ferry was founded in 1969.

	Annual Growth	04/11	04/12	04/13	04/14	04/15
Sales ($ mil.)	8.3%	776.3	826.8	849.7	995.6	1,066.1
Net income ($ mil.)	10.7%	58.9	54.3	33.3	72.7	88.4
Market value ($ mil.)	11.1%	1,047.4	816.8	837.0	1,469.1	1,594.6
Employees	10.6%	2,463	2,654	3,272	3,396	3,687

KORN/FERRY INTERNATIONAL FUTURESTEP INC.

1900 Avenue of the Stars Ste. 2600
Los Angeles CA 90067
Phone: 310-552-1834
Fax: 310-553-6452
Web: www.futurestep.com

CEO: Byrne Mulrooney
CFO: –
HR: –
FYE: April 30
Type: Subsidiary

Futurestep connects mid-level managers with jobs. A subsidiary of executive search giant Korn/Ferry the company combines traditional search techniques with Internet-based recruiting to provide a range of opportunities globally. The company maintains a database of more than one million pre-screened candidates in order to quickly match up jobs with employees. In addition to middle management recruiting Futurestep offers specialized talent consulting services project-based recruitment recruitment outsourcing and recruitment for interim positions. Founded in 1998 the company has nearly 40 locations in 17 countries and is headquartered in Los Angeles.

KORTE CONSTRUCTION COMPANY

5700 OAKLAND AVE STE 200
SAINT LOUIS, MO 631101355
Phone: 314-231-3700
Fax: –
Web: www.korteco.com

CEO: Todd Korte
CFO: William D Bououris
HR: –
FYE: December 31
Type: Private

The Korte Company provides design/build design/build/furnish construction management and interior design services for a variety of commercial and industrial construction projects. The group works on projects that include warehouse/distribution centers recreational centers schools office complexes churches and facilities for local state and federal government agencies including Department of Defense. The Korte Company which was founded in 1958 operates from offices in Las Vegas St. Louis and Highland Illinois.

	Annual Growth	12/09	12/10	12/11	12/12	12/13
Sales ($ mil.)	(26.5%)	–	267.5	240.9	148.3	106.4
Net income ($ mil.)	–	–	–	1.8	(1.5)	(2.4)
Market value ($ mil.)	–	–	–	–	–	–
Employees	–	–	–	–	–	170

KOSS CORP NAS: KOSS

4129 North Port Washington Avenue
Milwaukee, WI 53212
Phone: 414 964-5000
Fax: –
Web: www.koss.com

CEO: Michael J Koss
CFO: David D Smith
HR: –
FYE: June 30
Type: Public

Koss makes sure you can turn up the volume without disturbing the neighbors. The company makes stereo headphones or "stereophones" and related accessories for consumers and audio professionals. Its lineup includes full-size noise-cancellation portable earbud and wireless headphones. Products are sold through more than 17000 US retail outlets including specialty audio stores discount stores and mass merchandisers as well as by catalogs and online merchants. The company also produces classical music recordings through its Koss Classics subsidiary. In addition to its US operations Koss has an international sales office in Switzerland. Founded by John Koss the firm has roots reaching back to the 1950s.

	Annual Growth	06/11	06/12	06/13	06/14	06/15
Sales ($ mil.)	(12.6%)	41.5	37.9	35.8	23.8	24.2
Net income ($ mil.)	(42.4%)	4.4	2.9	5.4	(5.6)	0.5
Market value ($ mil.)	(21.8%)	45.8	39.3	36.8	23.6	17.1
Employees	(4.5%)	65	60	61	60	54

KPH HEALTHCARE SERVICES INC.

520 E MAIN ST
GOUVERNEUR, NY 136421561
Phone: 315-287-1500
Fax: –
Web: www.kinneydrugs.com

CEO: –
CFO: –
HR: –
FYE: December 31
Type: Private

Founded by Burt Orrin Kinney who opened the company's first drugstore in 1903 Kinney Drugs has grown to number about 100 stores in central and northern New York and Vermont. Most of the company's stores are free-standing units with pharmacies one-hour photo developing services and a growing selection of convenience foods. The 100%-employee-owned company maintains its own distribution warehouse and offers about 800 different products including Kinney-branded over-the-counter medicines. Pharmacy accounts for 75% of sales. Besides retail stores the firm operates ProAct prescription benefit management firm HealthDirect institutional pharmacy services and HealthDirect mail order pharmacy services.

	Annual Growth	12/04	12/05	12/06	12/07	12/08
Sales ($ mil.)	10.6%	–	525.5	606.5	666.9	711.3
Net income ($ mil.)	2.2%	–	–	9.9	11.7	10.4
Market value ($ mil.)	–	–	–	–	–	–
Employees	–	–	–	–	–	3,000

KPMG L.L.P.

3 Chestnut Ridge Rd.
Montvale NJ 07645-0435
Phone: 201-307-7000
Fax: 201-930-8617
Web: www.us.kpmg.com

CEO: John Veihmeyer
CFO: –
HR: –
FYE: September 30
Type: Private - Partnershi

KPMG L.L.P. is the US member firm of KPMG International a global network of accountancies with a 300-year history. Today parent KPMG is one of the industry's Big Four (alongside Deloitte Touche Tohmatsu Ernst & Young and PricewaterhouseCoopers). The US-centric business of KPMG provides audit tax and advisory services through approximately 90 offices located nationwide. As part of its business focus KPMG L.L.P. targets several industries such as financial services media and entertainment consumer products chemicals and healthcare and pharmaceuticals. KPMG L.L.P. is part of KPMG's Americas division which accounts for about a third of the group's global revenues.

KPS CAPITAL PARTNERS LP

485 Lexington Ave. 31st Fl.
New York NY 10017
Phone: 212-338-5100
Fax: 646-307-7100
Web: www.kpsfund.com

CEO: –
CFO: –
HR: –
FYE: December 31
Type: Private

KPS Capital Partners delivers a little CPR to struggling businesses. The firm manages the KPS Special Situations Funds which are invested in troubled companies with annual revenues of at least $250 million in the manufacturing transportation and service industries. Specializing in restructurings and turn-arounds it is a hands-on investor taking controlling stakes in its portfolio companies working with management and providing oversight and advice. KPS which usually invests $25 million to $200 million per transaction has some $2.7 billion of committed capital. Investors in its funds include pension funds financial corporations and trusts.

KQED INC.

2601 MARIPOSA ST
SAN FRANCISCO, CA 941101426
Phone: 415-864-2000
Fax: –
Web: www.kqed.org

CEO: –
CFO: Mitzie Kelley
HR: Joseph B Runs
FYE: September 30
Type: Private

Public interest is a big concern for this West Coast broadcasting company. Publicly financed TV and radio broadcaster KQED serves the Northern California area through its flagship KQED Public Television 9 station. KQED produces and broadcasts educational programming focused on arts science and the humanities as well as public interest shows highlighting local national and international issues. It creates most of its own programming but also specializes in broadcasting independent films and programs from PBS and other distributors. In addition KQED Public Radio broadcasts to listeners across San Francisco and Sacramento and its website provides event listings resources polls podcasts and blogs.

	Annual Growth	09/10	09/11	09/12	09/13	09/14
Sales ($ mil.)	3.3%	–	62.6	67.0	66.0	69.0
Net income ($ mil.)	(32.7%)	–	–	11.3	11.7	5.1
Market value ($ mil.)	–	–	–	–	–	–
Employees	–	–	–	–	–	266

KRAFT FOODS GROUP INC   NMS: KRFT

Three Lakes Drive
Northfield, IL 60093-2753
Phone: 847 646-2000
Fax: –
Web: www.kraftfoodsgroup.com

CEO: John T Cahill
CFO: James Kehoe
HR: –
FYE: December 28
Type: Public

What's old is new again at Kraft Foods Group. The newly-independent company was spun off by Mondelez International (formerly Kraft Foods Inc.) separating the North American grocery from the global snacks business in 2012. Kraft Foods Group is one of the largest consumer packaged food and beverage companies in North America. Its familiar brands include Kraft natural/processed cheeses beverages (Maxwell House coffee Kool-Aid drinks) convenient meals (Oscar Mayer meats and Kraft mac 'n cheese) grocery fare (Cool Whip topping Shake N' Bake coatings) and nuts (Planters). While globe-trotting Mondelez is focused on growth overseas Kraft Foods Group is looking to revive its business in North America.

	Annual Growth	12/09	12/10	12/11	12/12	12/13
Sales ($ mil.)	1.3%	17,278.0	17,797.0	18,655.0	18,339.0	18,218.0
Net income ($ mil.)	5.8%	2,170.0	3,531.0	1,839.0	1,642.0	2,715.0
Market value ($ mil.)	20.9%	–	–	–	26,478.8	32,020.8
Employees	(2.2%)	–	–	23,500	23,000	22,500

KRAMER LEVIN NAFTALIS & FRANKEL LLP

1177 Avenue of the Americas
New York NY 10036
Phone: 212-715-9100
Fax: 212-715-8000
Web: www.kramerlevin.com

CEO: –
CFO: –
HR: –
FYE: December 31
Type: Private - Partnershi

Law firm Kramer Levin Naftalis & Frankel serves clients through offices in New York City Paris and Silicon Valley. It employs more than 350 attorneys in about 20 practice areas including banking and finance business immigration corporate restructuring and bankruptcy employment and labor intellectual property and real estate. The internationally-focused firm also handles initial public offerings and acquisitions representing both emerging companies and major corporations. Kramer Levin Naftalis & Frankel was founded in 1968 starting off with only 20 lawyers.

KRATON PERFORMANCE POLYMERS INC   NYS: KRA

15710 John F. Kennedy Blvd., Suite 300
Houston, TX 77032
Phone: 281 504-4700
Fax: –
Web: www.kraton.com

CEO: Kevin M. Fogarty
CFO: Stephen E. Tremblay
HR: Melinda Conley
FYE: December 31
Type: Public

If you brushed your teeth or shaved this morning you probably touched a Kraton Performance Polymers product. Through operating subsidiary Kraton Polymers the company makes styrenic block copolymers (SBCs) a material it invented in the 1960s and other engineered polymers. SBCs are used in adhesives coatings sealants lubricants packaging and other applications across a range of industries such as paving and roofing automotive and personal care products (the rubbery grip on your toothbrush or razor handle for example). Under its Caroflex brand it sells isoprene rubber latex products (synthetic substitutes for rubber latex). In 2016 the company sold its compounding business to PolyOne for $72 million.

	Annual Growth	12/10	12/11	12/12	12/13	12/14
Sales ($ mil.)	0.0%	1,228.4	1,437.5	1,423.1	1,292.1	1,230.4
Net income ($ mil.)	(60.2%)	96.7	90.9	(16.2)	(0.6)	2.4
Market value ($ mil.)	(9.5%)	985.2	646.2	764.9	733.7	661.8
Employees	1.4%	884	916	941	936	934

KRATON POLYMERS LLC

15710 John F. Kennedy Blvd. Ste. 300
Houston TX 77032
Phone: 281-504-4700
Fax: 281-504-4817
Web: www.kraton.com

CEO: Kevin M Fogarty
CFO: Stephen E Tremblay
HR: –
FYE: December 31
Type: Subsidiary

When the rubber meets the road Kraton Polymers is responsible for both ends of the equation. It makes chemical ingredients used in both autos and in asphalt for road-building. As the operating subsidiary of holding company Kraton Performance Polymers it is a leading global producer of styrenic block copolymers (SBCs). SBCs are a kind of polymer used in a variety of plastic rubber and chemical products as well as for improving the stability of asphalt. Kraton splits its operations into four main end-use markets: Adhesives Sealants and Coatings; Advanced Materials; Paving and Roofing; and Cariflex its brand for isopene rubber latex products. Kraton Polymers sells its products worldwide.

KRATOS DEFENSE & SECURITY SOLUTIONS, INC. NMS: KTOS

4820 Eastgate Mall, Suite 200
San Diego, CA 92121
Phone: 858 812-7300
Fax: –
Web: www.kratosdefense.com

CEO: Eric M. DeMarco
CFO: Deanna H. Lund
HR: Marc Shapiro
FYE: December 28
Type: Public

Kratos Defense & Security Solutions is a government contractor that designs and implements information technology systems and provides engineering and other technical services to federal intelligence military and security agencies as well as state and local agencies. The company also creates and maintains in-building IT networks that integrate voice data security and building automation. Additionally it provides program requirement development operational testing and software customization services. The US Navy and US Army are key customers. Kratos was founded in 1995 and initially focused on commercial clients.

	Annual Growth	12/10	12/11	12/12	12/13	12/14
Sales ($ mil.)	20.7%	408.5	723.1	969.2	950.6	868.0
Net income ($ mil.)	–	14.5	(24.2)	(114.4)	(37.2)	(78.0)
Market value ($ mil.)	(19.8%)	712.1	357.8	277.4	414.2	294.8
Employees	5.6%	2,900	4,000	4,300	3,800	3,600

KRAUSE GENTLE CORP.

6400 Westown Pkwy.
West Des Moines IA 50266
Phone: 515-226-0694
Fax: 515-226-0995
Web: www.kumandgo.com

CEO: William A Krause
CFO: Craig A Bergstrom
HR: Steve Kimmes
FYE: December 31
Type: Private

If you're in a hurry in Iowa Krause Gentle provides an assist. The company runs more than 400 Kum & Go convenience stores mostly in Iowa but also in a dozen other Midwestern and western states. The stores provide basic gas station amenities as well as the company's private-label line (Hiland) of coffee potato chips sandwiches and other foods. The company has more than doubled its Kum & Go store count since 1997 mostly through acquisitions. Solar Transport a petroleum products and fertilizer hauler Liberty Bank and the Des Moines Menace soccer team are affiliated with Krause Gentle which was founded in 1959. The founding Krause and Gentle families still own and run Krause Gentle.

KREISLER MANUFACTURING CORP. NBB: KRSL

180 Van Riper Avenue
Elmwood Park, NJ 07407
Phone: 201 791-0700
Fax: –
Web: www.kreislermfg.com

CEO: –
CFO: Edward A Stern
HR: Michael (Mel) Stern
FYE: June 30
Type: Public

Your Chrysler might have a hemi under the hood but this Kreisler focuses on bigger engines. Kreisler Manufacturing through subsidiary Kreisler Industrial makes precision metal components for commercial and military aircraft engines and industrial gas turbines. Tube assemblies — used to transfer fuel for combustion hydraulic fluid for thrust reversers and oil for lubrication — account for most of the company's sales. A second subsidiary Kreisler Polska supplies machined components to Kreisler Industrial from a manufacturing plant in Krakow Poland.

	Annual Growth	06/11	06/12	06/13	06/14	06/15
Sales ($ mil.)	2.7%	27.4	37.5	30.4	30.6	30.5
Net income ($ mil.)	–	(0.8)	(2.3)	1.8	2.7	1.0
Market value ($ mil.)	32.4%	6.6	10.4	15.8	24.4	20.3
Employees	–	–	–	–	–	–

KRISPY KREME DOUGHNUTS INC NYS: KKD

370 Knollwood Street
Winston-Salem, NC 27103
Phone: 336 725-2981
Fax: 336 733-3794
Web: www.krispykreme.com

CEO: Anthony N. (Tony) Thompson
CFO: Douglas R. (Doug) Muir
HR: Cathleen D Allred
FYE: February 01
Type: Public

You might say these sweet treats are wholly delicious. Krispy Kreme Doughnuts operates a leading chain of doughnut outlets with more than 1000 locations throughout the US and in about 25 other countries. The shops are popular for their glazed doughnuts that are served fresh and hot out of the fryer. In addition to its original glazed variety Krispy Kreme serves cake and filled doughnuts crullers and fritters as well as hot coffee and other beverages. The company owns and operates 114 locations and franchises the rest. Krispy Kreme also markets its doughnuts through grocery stores and supermarkets.

	Annual Growth	01/11	01/12*	02/13	02/14	02/15
Sales ($ mil.)	7.9%	362.0	403.2	435.8	460.3	490.3
Net income ($ mil.)	41.0%	7.6	166.3	20.8	34.3	30.1
Market value ($ mil.)	32.1%	414.9	496.7	842.7	1,120.0	1,264.1
Employees	10.4%	3,370	3,800	4,300	4,300	5,000

*Fiscal year change

KROGER CO (THE) NYS: KR

1014 Vine Street
Cincinnati, OH 45202
Phone: 513 762-4000
Fax: 513 762-1400
Web: www.thekrogerco.com

CEO: W. Rodney McMullen
CFO: J. Michael Schlotman
HR: Kathleen Barclay
FYE: January 31
Type: Public

Kroger is still the US's largest traditional grocer despite Wal-Mart overtaking the chain as the nation's largest seller of groceries years ago. It operates some 3800 stores including 2600-plus supermarkets and multi-department stores under two dozen banners across 35 states. It also runs 780-plus convenience stores (under the Quik Stop Kwik Shop and other brands) around 330 jewelry stores and nearly 40 food processing plants in the US. Kroger's Fred Meyer Stores subsidiary operates around 130 supercenters that offer groceries merchandise and jewelry in the western US. While Kroger has added other amenities to its mix groceries still make up over 70% of its sales while fuel sales make up another 20%.

	Annual Growth	01/11	01/12*	02/13	02/14*	01/15
Sales ($ mil.)	7.2%	82,189.0	90,374.0	96,751.0	98,375.0	108,465.0
Net income ($ mil.)	11.6%	1,116.0	602.0	1,497.0	1,519.0	1,728.0
Market value ($ mil.)	34.2%	20,736.5	23,668.2	27,164.9	35,161.4	67,254.7
Employees	4.3%	338,000	339,000	343,000	375,000	400,000

*Fiscal year change

KROLL BACKGROUND AMERICA INC.

100 Centerview Dr. Ste. 300
Nashville TN 37214
Phone: 615-320-9800
Fax: 615-321-9585
Web: www.krollbackgroundscreening.com

CEO: –
CFO: Rick King
HR: Donna Wells
FYE: December 31
Type: Subsidiary

Hiring is risky business so Kroll Background America weeds out the good from the bad. The company is the background screening division of risk consulting firm Kroll. Kroll Background America provides vetting services that include employee pre-screening drug testing physical exams identity fraud investigation and other services to customers ranging from small businesses to large multinational corporations. Its screening services check the credit criminal and education histories of prospective and current employees as well as public records on business suppliers and vendors. It also verifies employees' legal right to work in the US.

KROLL FACTUAL DATA INC.

5200 Hahns Peak Dr.
Loveland CO 80538
Phone: 970-663-5700
Fax: 302-283-6090
Web: www.delmarva.com

CEO: –
CFO: –
HR: –
FYE: December 31
Type: Subsidiary

If you need a bucket of business information with a side of credit data and skip tracing you need KFD. Kroll Factual Data (KFD) resells business data delivering it primarily to mortgage lenders via Web-based reports. KFD performs credit and background screening for lenders employers leasing agents and landlords. Business information services offered include credit verification criminal history checks collateral fraud analysis and personal credit history of company executives. KFD is a subsidiary of risk consulting group Kroll itself a subsidiary of Marsh & McLennan Companies. Marsh & McLennan is seeking a buyer for KFD one of its underperforming units.

KROLL INC.

600 3rd Ave.
New York NY 10016
Phone: 212-593-1000
Fax: 212-593-2631
Web: www.krollworldwide.com

CEO: –
CFO: Ken Roche
HR: Gabriela Ojeda
FYE: December 31
Type: Subsidiary

Kroll could tell you what it does but then it would have to charge you. The risk consulting company offers advisory services in a number of key areas: business intelligence data security and recovery due diligence employee background screening (through Kroll Background America) investigations and disputes litigation technology (through Kroll Ontrack) risk and compliance and security consulting and systems design and engineering (through Kroll Security Group). Founded in 1972 by Jules Kroll the firm has offices in more than 55 cities in 27 countries. Altegrity acquired Kroll in 2010 from insurance broker Marsh & McLennan Companies in a deal valued in excess of $1 billion.

KROLL ONTRACK INC.

9023 Columbine Rd.
Eden Prairie MN 55347-4182
Phone: 952-937-5161
Fax: 952-937-5750
Web: www.krollontrack.com

CEO: Mark R Williams
CFO: –
HR: Steve Wood
FYE: December 31
Type: Subsidiary

Kroll Ontrack helps keep data on the straight and narrow. The company a subsidiary of Kroll provides data recovery and legal software and services. With applications for document review case management interactive filing and trial preparation its legal division handles electronic discovery computer forensics and consulting services. Kroll's Verve software product enables such functions as e-discovery and legal data assessment. The company also specializes in email recovery and data erasure. Its Engenium application is tailored for data search and analysis. Kroll Ontrack serves consumer and enterprise customers law firms and government agencies.

KRONES INC.

9600 S 58TH ST
FRANKLIN, WI 53132-9107
Phone: 414-409-4000
Fax: –
Web: www.kronesusa.com

CEO: Holger Beckmann
CFO: –
HR: –
FYE: December 31
Type: Private

Krones is in the business of keeping things all bottled up. The company develops manufactures and installs packaging machinery and systems that design clean rinse and fill bottles cans and plastic containers. Its offerings include labeling and sealing machines inspection and monitoring systems and mixing and carbonating systems. Krones caters to companies in North and Central America and the Caribbean in the food and beverage beer wine and spirits health and cosmetic pharmaceutical and household goods industries. Established in 1966 Krones is a subsidiary of KRONES owned largely by the founding Kronseder family.

	Annual Growth	12/04	12/05	12/06	12/07	12/08
Sales ($ mil.)	(1.7%)	–	383.1	364.4	359.7	363.9
Net income ($ mil.)	58.2%	–	1.5	2.3	6.8	6.0
Market value ($ mil.)	–	–	–	–	–	–
Employees	–	–	–	–	–	499

KRONOS INCORPORATED

297 Billerica Rd.
Chelmsford MA 01824
Phone: 978-250-9800
Fax: 978-367-5900
Web: www.kronos.com

CEO: Aron J AIN
CFO: Mark Julien
HR: –
FYE: September 30
Type: Private

Kronos knows time is money for its customers. The company makes and implements workforce management software particularly for organizations with large complex workforces. With a goal of controlling labor costs and improving employee productivity its software products automatically collect time and attendance data manage scheduling and absence oversee administrative HR payroll and hiring processes and provide data analytics on cost and performance problems. Serving more than half of the Fortune 1000 it focuses on the education health care hospitality manufacturing retail and government markets among others. Kronos is owned by an investment group led by private equity firm Hellman & Friedman.

KRONOS WORLDWIDE INC

5430 LBJ Freeway, Suite 1700
Dallas, TX 75240-2697
Phone: 972 233-1700
Fax: –

NYS: KRO
CEO: Bobby D O'Brien
CFO: Gregory M. (Greg) Swalwell
HR: –
FYE: December 31
Type: Public

Kronos Worldwide produces pigments that impart whiteness brightness and opacity to everything from plastics paper and coatings to inks food and cosmetics. Controlled by Valhi Kronos is a leading manufacturer of a commercially used base white inorganic pigment known as titanium dioxide (TiO2). TiO2 is designed based on specific end-use applications. Kronos makes and sell some 40 different TiO2 grades; the company and its distributors and agents also provide technical services for its products in some 100 countries mainly in Europe and North America.

	Annual Growth	12/10	12/11	12/12	12/13	12/14
Sales ($ mil.)	3.3%	1,449.7	1,943.3	1,976.3	1,732.4	1,651.9
Net income ($ mil.)	(6.6%)	130.6	321.0	218.5	(102.0)	99.2
Market value ($ mil.)	(25.6%)	4,924.6	2,090.8	2,260.1	2,207.9	1,509.0
Employees	0.5%	2,440	2,470	2,555	2,450	2,485

KRUEGER INTERNATIONAL INC.

1330 BELLEVUE ST
GREEN BAY, WI 543022197
Phone: 920-468-8100
Fax: –
Web: www.ki.com

CEO: Richard J. (Dick) Resch
CFO: Kelly Andersen
HR: –
FYE: December 31
Type: Private

Krueger International can be found in cubicles classrooms cafeterias and college dorms. The company which does business as KI makes ergonomic seating cabinets and other furniture used by businesses healthcare organizations government agencies and educational institutions. The company offers everything from benches and beds to desks and tables not to mention shelving filing systems movable walls and trash bins. KI markets its products through sales representatives furniture dealers architects and interior designers worldwide. Founded in 1941 KI was purchased in the 1980s by its managers who later allowed employees to buy stock. Today KI is 100% employee owned.

	Annual Growth	12/06	12/07	12/08	12/10	12/11
Sales ($ mil.)	(22.2%)	–	–	1,377.8	615.5	649.7
Net income ($ mil.)	4991.3%	–	–	0.0	59.0	56.9
Market value ($ mil.)	–	–	–	–	–	–
Employees	–	–	–	–	–	2,300

KSW INC.

37-16 23rd St.
Long Island City NY 11101
Phone: 718-361-6500
Fax: 718-784-1943
Web: www.kswmechanical.com

NASDAQ: KSW
CEO: –
CFO: Richard Lucas
HR: –
FYE: December 31
Type: Public

KSW may have a need to vent on occasion but the company still knows how to keep its cool. Its KSW Mechanical Services subsidiary installs HVAC and process piping systems for large-scale industrial commercial institutional public and residential projects. The company also provides mechanical trade management services and engineering assistance. KSW primarily works in the New York metropolitan area but hopes to expand in the Northeast. Much of KSW's business comes from repeat customers; the company is an authorized bidder for agencies including the New York City Transit Authority and the Port Authority of New York and New Jersey. Real estate developer Related Companies is buying KSW in a $32 million deal.

KUNI AUTOMOTIVE GROUP

203 SE Park Plaza Dr. Ste. 290
Vancouver WA 98684
Phone: 503-372-7457
Fax: 360-567-0970
Web: www.kuniauto.com

CEO: Greg Goodwin
CFO: –
HR: –
FYE: December 31
Type: Private

Kuni Automotive has the right wheels for the Left Coast. The auto group annually sells new BMW Buick Honda Land Rover Lexus Smart and Volkswagen cars at about eight dealerships in California Colorado Oregon and Washington. The dealership group also sells used cars. Kuni Automotive's dealerships provide parts and services and some of them also perform collision repair. On the group's Web site car shoppers can browse for new and used offerings order parts schedule service or apply for financing. With Burt Automotive Kuni operates Burt-Kuni Honda near Denver Colorado.

KURT MANUFACTURING COMPANY INC.

5280 MAIN ST NE
MINNEAPOLIS, MN 554211594
Phone: 763-572-1500
Fax: –
Web: www.kurt.com

CEO: –
CFO: Paul Lillyblad
HR: Laura Erickson
FYE: October 31
Type: Private

Kurt Manufacturing helps you provide decisions on precision when it comes to the manufacturing process. It makes precision-machined parts and components on a contract basis for the aerospace automotive oil and defense markets. Kurt operates through divisions including Hydraulics Engineered Systems Kinetic and Workholding. These divisions make gauging systems hydraulic coupling and hoses vises and other workholding tools to a list of clients that have included such big names as ATK Deere & Co. General Dynamics General Electric General Motors Honeywell IBM and Lockheed Martin. Kurt is an employee owned company.

	Annual Growth	10/05	10/06	10/07*	11/08*	10/09
Sales ($ mil.)	(79.6%)	–	–	1,623.2	108.9	67.8
Net income ($ mil.)	–	–	–	0.0	3.3	(1.3)
Market value ($ mil.)	–	–	–	–	–	–
Employees	–	–	–	–	–	410

*Fiscal year change

KUSHNER COMPANIES

18 Columbia Tpke.
Florham Park NJ 07932
Phone: 973-822-0050
Fax: 973-822-2507
Web: www.kushnercompanies.com

CEO: –
CFO: –
HR: Daniel Poray
FYE: December 31
Type: Private

The one-time king of New Jersey apartment real estate has shifted its focus from multifamily to office and retail properties in New York City. The effort is being lead by Jared Kushner son of the company's founder Charles Kushner who went to prison for tax fraud and campaign contribution charges. The company's subsidiary Kushner Properties which once owned and managed some 8 million sq. ft. of property drastically reduced its apartment holdings by selling more than 17000 units in 2007. The company's hotel division continues to be run by Westminster Hospitality. Westminster Communities the firm's construction division develops property in the Northeast.

KUTAK ROCK LLP

The Omaha Building 1650 Farnam St.
Omaha NE 68102-2186
Phone: 402-346-6000
Fax: 402-346-1148
Web: www.kutakrock.com

CEO: –
CFO: Vicki L Young
HR: –
FYE: December 31
Type: Private - Partnershi

Kutak Rock is not the latest genre of music your kids are listening to on iTunes these days. Instead Kutak Rock is a national law firm with more than 450 attorneys. The firm's practice areas include corporate law public and corporate finance and litigation. Through a founding partnership featuring Robert Kutak and Harold Rock Kutak Rock first opened its doors in Omaha in 1965 and has now grown to include more than 15 offices nationwide. Clients have included state and local governments investment banking firms insurance companies and real estate developers and investors.

KVH INDUSTRIES, INC.

NMS: KVHI

50 Enterprise Center
Middletown, RI 02842
Phone: 401-847-3327
Fax: –

CEO: Martin A. Kits van Heyningen
CFO: Peter A. Rendall
HR: Chris Holm
FYE: December 31
Type: Public

KVH Industries makes communications products for people (or boats or armies) on the go. The company's mobile satellite communications products include antennas and compasses for yachts and commercial ships (CommBox) and mobile satellite TVs telephones and high-speed Internet antennas (TracVision and TracPhone) for automobiles boats small planes and RVs. It sells to distributors as well as boat and other vehicle manufacturers. KVH's guidance and stabilization products — sold mainly to US and allied governments and defense contractors — include digital compasses fiber optic gyros for tactical navigation and guidance systems for torpedoes and unmanned aerial vehicles. The company has branched out to transmit various kinds of content including educational services.

	Annual Growth	12/10	12/11	12/12	12/13	12/14
Sales ($ mil.)	11.4%	112.2	112.5	137.1	162.3	172.6
Net income ($ mil.)	(73.5%)	8.3	0.9	3.6	4.5	0.0
Market value ($ mil.)	1.4%	185.2	120.5	216.6	201.9	196.0
Employees	7.6%	390	368	355	471	523

KWIK TRIP INC.

1626 OAK ST
LA CROSSE, WI 546032308
Phone: 608-793-6331
Fax: –
Web: www.kwiktrip.com

CEO: Donald P. (Don) Zietlow
CFO: Scott Teigen
HR: –
FYE: September 27
Type: Private

Midwesterners who need to make a quick trip to get gas or groceries cigarettes or donuts race on over to Kwik Trip stores. Kwik Trip owns and operates about 500 Kwik Trip Kwik Star Hearty Platter and Tobacco Outlet Plus convenience stores in Iowa Minnesota and Wisconsin. The company also runs about a dozen Hearty Platter restaurants and cafes some 40 Tobacco Outlet Plus (TOP) cigar stores and car washes at some Kwik Trip store locations. All Kwik Trip stores built since 1990 are owned by Convenience Store Investments a separate firm which leases the land and stores to Kwik Trip. Kwik Trip which opened its first store in 1965 in Eau Claire Wisconsin is owned by the family of CEO Don Zietlow.

	Annual Growth	09/01	09/02	09/03	09/04	09/08
Sales ($ mil.)	17.9%	–	–	–	1,887.1	3,640.4
Net income ($ mil.)	(0.8%)	–	–	–	24.7	23.9
Market value ($ mil.)	–	–	–	–	–	–
Employees	–	–	–	–	–	10,500

KWIKSET CORPORATION

19701 DaVinci
Lake Forest CA 92610
Phone: 949-672-4000
Fax: 949-672-4001
Web: www.kwikset.com

CEO: David R Lumley
CFO: –
HR: –
FYE: December 31
Type: Subsidiary

Without hardware doors are just pieces of wood; Kwikset makes the devices that turn those pieces into doors. A subsidiary of Stanley Black & Decker (formerly Black & Decker) Kwikset manufactures handlesets levers knobs as well as deadbolts and electronic keyless entry locks for light commercial and residential use. Its products are marketed in primarily in Europe and North America under brands Kwikset Kwikset Signature Series and SmartSeries. SmartSeries comprises several trademark electronically controlled access mechanisms. Customers are retailers wholesalers distributors and jobbers; Home Depot and Lowe's are Kwikset's largest. Kwikset is part of Stanley Black & Decker's security business segment.

KYOCERA DOCUMENT SOLUTIONS AMERICA INC.

225 Sand Rd.
Fairfield NJ 07004
Phone: 973-808-8444
Fax: 973-882-6000
Web: www.kyoceradocumentsolutions.com/us

CEO: Norihiko INA
CFO: Nicholas Maimone
HR: –
FYE: March 31
Type: Subsidiary

Need a copy machine? Meet Kyocera Document Solutions America (formerly Kyocera Mita America). The company sells printers fax machines and combination machines to offices in the US. It offers about 70 different printer models including wide-format ranging from desktop-size to floor-standing models. The company also provides document management software and support services. From five US locations and with distribution out of Memphis it sells directly and through more than 400 independent dealers and resellers to enterprise and public sectors clients. Kyocera Document Solutions America is the US arm of Kyocera Document Solutions a subsidiary of electronic equipment and component manufacturing giant Kyocera.

KYOCERA INTERNATIONAL INC.

8611 Balboa Ave.
San Diego CA 92123-1580
Phone: 858-576-2600
Fax: 858-492-1456
Web: americas.kyocera.com/index.cfm

CEO: John Rigby
CFO: Mark Umemura
HR: Jennifer Trttino
FYE: March 31
Type: Subsidiary

Kyocera International the holding company for the North American operations of Japan's Kyocera Corporation makes ceramic products (the "cera" in Kyocera) ranging from mobile phones to kitchen utensils. Having expanded through acquisitions beyond its origins in specialty ceramics Kyocera International also makes LCD panels thin-film devices printers industrial cutting tools and solar energy systems. Its Kyocera Communications unit provides sales marketing and customer support for Kyocera and SANYO brand wireless phones in the US. Kyocera International's Kyocera Solar subsidiary is one of the world's largest producers of photovoltaic solar cells.

KYOCERA SOLAR INC.

7812 E. Acoma Dr.
Scottsdale AZ 85260
Phone: 480-948-8003
Fax: 480-483-6431
Web: www.kyocerasolar.com

CEO: –
CFO: –
HR: –
FYE: March 31
Type: Subsidiary

Kyocera Solar turns daylight into more than night lights. A subsidiary of Kyocera International the company makes sells and installs solar-powered electric systems to residential and commercial customers in the US. Its solar modules are also manufactured by Kyocera Corporation companies in China and the Czech Republic. Kyocera Solar has worked on projects for thousands of customers including a 500 kW Gatorade distribution center and a 1186 kW installation at the University of California San Diego. Altogether Kyocera produces solar panels totaling 650 MW each year.

L & S ELECTRIC INC.

5101 MESKER ST
SCHOFIELD, WI 544763056
Phone: 715-359-3155
Fax: –
Web: www.lselectric.com

CEO: –
CFO: David Krause
HR: –
FYE: December 31
Type: Private

L&S Electric isn't a run of the mill distributor even if its products run the mill. The company specializes in selling motors controls drives and integrated systems used in power generation railway pulp and paper mill mining and other industrial applications. It also offers engineering and repair services worldwide through an engineering division and its L&S Electric of Canada subsidiary. L&S Electric has about eight locations in Wisconsin Minnesota and Michigan. The company was formed in the 1983 merger of Leverence Electric and Snapp Electric two motor repair shops that dated back to the 1930s. L&S Electric is owned by the Lewitzke family.

	Annual Growth	12/09	12/10	12/11	12/12	12/13
Sales ($ mil.)	5.0%	–	72.5	79.3	85.2	84.0
Net income ($ mil.)	42.9%	–	–	2.8	6.3	5.8
Market value ($ mil.)	–	–	–	–	–	–
Employees		–	–	–	–	335

L BRANDS, INC

Three Limited Parkway
Columbus, OH 43230
Phone: 614 415-7000
Fax: –
Web: www.lb.com

NYS: LB
CEO: Leslie H. Wexner
CFO: Stuart B. Burgdoerfer
HR: Dominique Jakobowski
FYE: January 31
Type: Public

L Brands (formerly Limited Brands) is as much of a shopping-mall mainstay as food courts and teenagers. The company operates nearly 3000 specialty stores in North America and the UK primarily under the Victoria's Secret Bath & Body Works (BBW) and La Senza (in Canada) banners as well as corresponding websites and catalogs. Originally focused on apparel L Brands sold its ailing Limited and Express chains — leaving the company free to focus on two core businesses: Victoria's Secret and BBW. L Brands also owns apparel importer MAST Industries accessories boutique operator Henri Bendel apothecary C.O. Bigelow and The White Barn Candle Co. Founded in 1963 the company changed its name to L Brands in 2013.

	Annual Growth	01/11	01/12*	02/13	02/14*	01/15
Sales ($ mil.)	4.5%	9,613.0	10,364.0	10,459.0	10,773.0	11,454.0
Net income ($ mil.)	6.7%	805.0	850.0	753.0	903.0	1,042.0
Market value ($ mil.)	30.8%	8,444.6	12,106.3	13,797.0	15,289.1	24,712.0
Employees	(4.5%)	96,500	97,000	99,400	94,600	80,100

*Fiscal year change

L&L ENERGY INC

130 Andover Park East, Suite 200
Seattle, WA 98188
Phone: 206 264-8065
Fax: 206 838-0488
Web: www.llenergyinc.com

NBB: LLEN
CEO: –
CFO: Ian G Robinson
HR: Youwei Cramer
FYE: April 30
Type: Public

You'll excuse L & L Energy (formerly L & L International) if it's a bit jet lagged. Incorporated in Nevada with headquarters in Seattle the company mines coal in China. Granted a license by the government to extract a set amount of coal in exchange for up-front fees L & L owns mines in China's Yunnan and Guizhou provinces. The company currently extracts more than 630000 tons of coal per year from the mines. It also processes coal to produce coke used in steel production medium coal used for heating and coal slurries used as a lower quality fuel. L & L is swapping a stake in a coking mine with Singapore-based Union Energy to acquire a 50% stake in the LuoZhou coal mine.

	Annual Growth	04/09	04/10	04/11	04/12	04/13
Sales ($ mil.)	48.5%	40.9	109.2	223.9	143.6	199.0
Net income ($ mil.)	40.1%	10.0	32.9	36.8	14.2	38.4
Market value ($ mil.)	21.1%	68.6	411.5	264.8	85.7	147.4
Employees	3.3%	1,200	1,400	1,600	1,330	1,364

L&W SUPPLY CORPORATION

550 W. Adams St.
Chicago IL 60606
Phone: 312-606-4000
Fax: 831-460-3335
Web: www.beachboardwalk.com

CEO: –
CFO: –
HR: Andy Paasch
FYE: December 31
Type: Subsidiary

At the construction job site A&W can supply the root beer while L&W can deliver the gypsum wallboard and other building materials. L&W Supply distributes more than 40000 building products made by parent company USG and other manufacturers through about 165 locations in some 35 states. Besides wallboard (which accounts for about 30% of sales) L&W Supply's products include ceilings insulation joint treatment and texture products metal framing and roofing supplies. It also offers such services as delivery of less-than-truckload quantities stocking and lending. The company's customers are primarily builders and contractors. USG organized L&W Supply in 1971.

L-3 COMMUNICATIONS HOLDINGS, INC.

600 Third Avenue
New York, NY 10016
Phone: 212 697-1111
Fax: –
Web: www.l-3com.com

NYS: LLL
CEO: Michael T. Strianese
CFO: Ralph G. D'Ambrosio
HR: –
FYE: December 31
Type: Public

L-3's good defense is its best commercial offense. L-3 Communications Holdings provides products and services to the government based on Command Control Communications Intelligence Surveillance and Reconnaissance (C3ISR) including systems for satellite avionics (aircraft electronics) security and marine communications. It also provides aircraft maintenance and modernization. The US government primarily the Department of Defense (DoD) accounts for nearly 70% of its business but L-3 is expanding its commercial offerings. The company derives all of its income from operating subsidiary L-3 Communications Corporation (L-3).

	Annual Growth	12/10	12/11	12/12	12/13	12/14
Sales ($ mil.)	(6.2%)	15,680.0	15,169.0	13,146.0	12,629.0	12,124.0
Net income ($ mil.)	(8.7%)	955.0	956.0	810.0	778.0	664.0
Market value ($ mil.)	15.7%	5,783.0	5,470.5	6,285.9	8,766.9	10,354.3
Employees	(8.1%)	63,000	61,000	51,000	48,000	45,000

L-3 COMMUNICATIONS VERTEX AEROSPACE LLC

555 Industrial Dr. South
Madison MS 39110
Phone: 601-856-2274
Fax: 601-856-8006
Web: www.l-3vertex.com

CEO: Michael T Strianese
CFO: Ralph G D'Ambrosio
HR: Robert James
FYE: December 31
Type: Subsidiary

L-3 Communications Vertex Aerospace a subsidiary of battlefield communications systems giant L-3 Communications does business as L-3 Communications Systems Field Support Vertex Aerospace (SFS Vertex). The business primarily serves the US government by providing contract field services; depot operations (avionics installation and retrofit); engineering; aircraft logistics; maintenance repair and overhaul (MRO); supply chain management; and pilot services. Its client list includes the armed forces Customs and Border Protection the DEA and NASA. SFS Vertex has 300 locations worldwide and supports almost 90 distinct aircraft types as well as 3500 military and government aircraft systems.

L. & R. DISTRIBUTORS INC.

9301 AVENUE D
BROOKLYN, NY 11236-1899
Phone: 718-272-2100
Fax: –
Web: www.lrdist.com

CEO: Marc Bodner
CFO: Edward Musantry
HR: –
FYE: December 31
Type: Private

Stocking shelves? L&R Distributors (formerly Allied Supply) is a wholesale distributor of a wide variety of household and personal care products stationery items toys and sundries to supermarkets independent pharmacies and discount and stationery stores. Its offerings have ranged from ACE bandages to Zippo lighters and from Wiffle balls to baby wipes. The company operates throughout the US; among its key partners have been pharmaceutical distributors such as McKesson and Cardinal Health. L&R Distributors has been assembled via a string of transactions dating to the 1950s including the 1986 merger of E&N Sales Corp. and Ortner Drug Co.

	Annual Growth	12/00	12/01	12/02	12/06	12/10
Sales ($ mil.)	14.0%	–	44.6	43.3	76.5	145.1
Net income ($ mil.)	17.5%	–	0.3	0.7	0.8	1.4
Market value ($ mil.)	–	–	–	–	–	–
Employees						550

L.A. DARLING COMPANY

1401 Hwy. 49B
Paragould AR 72450
Phone: 870-239-9564
Fax: 870-239-6427
Web: www.ladarling.com

CEO: –
CFO: Bobby Wallis
HR: Mark Niemeier
FYE: December 31
Type: Subsidiary

L.A. Darling Company (LAD) gives shoppers their retail therapy. LAD manufactures and markets an array of wood and metal store fixtures shelves racks and point-of-purchase displays. For over a century the company has customized displays to the unique needs of retailers; services range from metal and tube and roll forming and stamping to various welding machining finishing and assembly processes. With facilities and service centers in the US and Mexico LAD caters to discount department and specialty retailers worldwide including Wal-Mart and Best Buy. Founded as the Ideal Fixture Company and subsequently acquired and renamed by Lewis Archer Darling LAD operates under the Marmon Group of companies.

LA FRANCE CORP.

1 LAFRANCE WAY
CONCORDVILLE, PA 19331
Phone: 610-361-4300
Fax: –
Web: www.lafrancecorp.com

CEO: –
CFO: Thomas Sheehan
HR: –
FYE: December 31
Type: Private

Viva LaFrance! would make a nice nameplate and this company could design it. LaFrance Corp. makes nameplates trim plastic enclosures metal letters and other products through several divisions. Its Benmatt Industries unit makes a range of customized products including key fobs license plate frames and trailer hitch covers that are used as promotional items by auto dealerships. The company's J.A.T. Creative Products division provides products like bottle openers bottle and can huggers and keychains to promote and advertise companies and special events. PacTec is a producer of standard and custom modified plastic electronic enclosures.

	Annual Growth	12/09	12/10	12/11	12/12	12/13
Sales ($ mil.)	14.1%	–	–	–	115.1	131.4
Net income ($ mil.)	(5.8%)	–	–	–	10.9	10.3
Market value ($ mil.)	–	–	–	–	–	–
Employees						1,827

LA JOLLA PHARMACEUTICAL COMPANY
PINK SHEETS: LJPC

6455 Nancy Ridge Dr.
San Diego CA 92121-2249
Phone: 858-452-6600
Fax: 858-626-2851
Web: www.ljpc.com

CEO: George F Tidmarsh
CFO: Dennis M Mulroy
HR: –
FYE: December 31
Type: Public

La Jolla Pharmaceutical aims to eliminate tissue damage. The company is working to develop tissue-repair compounds based on a cell-stimulating regenerative medicine technology. It is focused on skin and lung tissue cardiac muscle cartilage and bone repair. La Jolla Pharmaceutical had previously ceased most of its operations after trials of lupus candidate Riquent failed in 2009. After exploring its options the firm began searching for new potential pharmaceutical candidates to develop. In 2011 La Jolla found a new focus when it acquired a regenerative medicine program for tissue repair from private research firm GliaMed.

LA MADELEINE OF TEXAS INC.

12201 Merit Dr. Ste. 900
Dallas TX 75251
Phone: 214-696-6962
Fax: 214-696-0485
Web: www.lamadeleine.com

CEO: –
CFO: –
HR: –
FYE: June 30
Type: Private

This company hopes its creme brulee croissants and quiche prove as memorable as Proust's famous teacake. La Madeleine operates 60 la Madeleine Bakery Cafe & Bistro casual dining locations mostly in Texas Georgia and Louisiana offering French country cuisine for breakfast lunch and dinner. The restaurants which welcome patrons with such interior appointments as a stone hearth and handcrafted wood tables use a cafeteria-style serving line and limited table service. Each location also sells a variety of fresh baked goods. French native Patrick Leon Esquerre started the business in 1983. La Madeleine is owned by a group of investors including restaurant operator Groupe Le Duff.

LA-Z-BOY INC.
NYS: LZB

One La-Z-Boy Drive
Monroe, MI 48162-5138
Phone: 734 242-1444
Fax: –

CEO: Kurt L. Darrow
CFO: Louis M. (Mike) Riccio
HR: Kathy Till
FYE: April 25
Type: Public

La-Z-Boy works so that its customers can kick back and relax. A top US maker of upholstered furniture La-Z-Boy sells its ubiquitous recliners plus chairs sofas tables and modular seating units. One recliner boasts a drink cooler phone and massage and heat system. Its brands include La-Z-Boy England Hammary American Drew Lea and Kincaid. La-Z-Boy sells its products through about 110 company-owned stores some 325 independent La-Z-Boy Furniture Galleries and 570-plus Comfort Studios (about 5000 sq. ft. of dedicated La-Z-Boy space hosted by an independent retailer). La-Z-Boy also makes wood desks and bedroom items and licenses its name for use on furniture for the health care industry.

	Annual Growth	04/11	04/12	04/13	04/14	04/15
Sales ($ mil.)	4.7%	1,187.1	1,231.7	1,332.5	1,357.3	1,425.4
Net income ($ mil.)	31.0%	24.0	88.0	46.4	55.1	70.8
Market value ($ mil.)	23.6%	596.8	778.5	897.7	1,245.8	1,395.0
Employees	1.1%	7,910	8,160	8,185	8,300	8,270

LABORATORY CORPORATION OF AMERICA HOLDINGS — NYS: LH

358 South Main Street
Burlington, NC 27215
Phone: 336 229-1127
Fax: –
Web: www.labcorp.com
CEO: David P. (Dave) King
CFO: Glenn A. Eisenberg
HR: –
FYE: December 31
Type: Public

This company pricks and prods for profit. Laboratory Corporation of America (LabCorp) is a top provider of clinical laboratory services performing tests on more than 470000 patient specimens each day on behalf of managed care organizations hospitals doctors government agencies drug companies and employers. Its services range from routine urinalyses HIV tests and Pap smears to specialty testing for diagnostic genetics disease monitoring forensics identity clinical drug trials and allergies. Through Covance the company provides end-to-end drug development support. LabCorp operates more than 1700 service sites that collect specimens and some 40 primary labs where tests are performed.

	Annual Growth	12/10	12/11	12/12	12/13	12/14
Sales ($ mil.)	4.7%	5,003.9	5,542.3	5,671.4	5,808.3	6,011.6
Net income ($ mil.)	(2.2%)	558.2	519.7	583.1	573.8	511.2
Market value ($ mil.)	5.3%	7,438.0	7,273.1	7,328.1	7,729.9	9,128.3
Employees	3.8%	31,000	31,000	34,000	34,000	36,000

LACKS ENTERPRISES INC.

5460 Cascade Rd. SE
Grand Rapids MI 49546
Phone: 616-949-6570
Fax: 616-285-2367
Web: www.lacksenterprises.com
CEO: –
CFO: –
HR: –
FYE: July 31
Type: Private

It's not "hipp" if your car lacks a wheel cover or has a rusty grille. Lacks Enterprises makes high-impact plated plastic (HIPP) alternatives to die-cast and stainless steel automotive products such as wheel covers and grilles. The company's HIPP parts plated with copper nickel chrome are lighter and cheaper than all-metal alternatives as well as resistant to dents and rust. Other products include molding rocker panels and trim. Automotive OEM customers have included Ford General Motors Honda Nissan and Toyota. Its Plastic-Plate subsidiary makes items such as cell phone face plates for manufacturers of consumer electronics and telecommunications equipment. The Lacks family owns Lacks Enterprises.

LACLEDE GROUP INC — NYS: LG

700 Market Street
St. Louis, MO 63101
Phone: 314 342-0500
Fax: –
Web: www.thelacledegroup.com
CEO: Suzanne Sitherwood
CFO: Steven P. Rasche
HR: –
FYE: September 30
Type: Public

In the "Show Me" state The Laclede Group is saying "Show me the money." The group's main revenue source is utility Laclede Gas which distributes natural gas to approximately 631000 customers in eastern Missouri including St. Louis. Laclede Group's nonregulated businesses provide gas transportation and other services and operate underground gas storage fields. Operations include wholesale gas marketing (Laclede Energy Resources) a propane pipeline (Laclede Pipeline) insurance (Laclede Gas Family Services) real estate development (Laclede Development) and natural gas compression services (Laclede Venture).

	Annual Growth	09/11	09/12	09/13	09/14	09/15
Sales ($ mil.)	5.4%	1,603.3	1,125.5	1,017.0	1,627.2	1,976.4
Net income ($ mil.)	21.0%	63.8	62.6	52.8	84.6	136.9
Market value ($ mil.)	8.9%	1,679.2	1,863.4	1,950.1	2,010.7	2,363.1
Employees	17.1%	1,638	1,656	2,326	3,152	3,078

LACROSSE FOOTWEAR INC. — NASDAQ: BOOT

17634 NE Airport Way
Portland OR 97230
Phone: 503-262-0110
Fax: 503-262-0115
Web: www.lacrossefootwear.com/
CEO: Joseph P Schneider
CFO: David P Carlson
HR: –
FYE: December 31
Type: Public

If customers are wearing its protective boots LaCrosse Footwear doesn't care who steps on their toes. The company offers sturdy footwear for outdoor pursuits (hunting snowmobiling) and occupations such as farming general utility and construction. LaCrosse makes rubber vinyl and leather footwear as well as rainwear and protective clothing for adults and children. Its brands include LaCrosse Danner Burly Camohide and Iceman among other names. LaCrosse's products are sold throughout North America to catalog and online merchants retailers wholesalers and the US government as well as through company websites and outlet stores. The company's Danish subsidiary supplies retailers in Asia and Europe.

LADENBURG THALMANN FINANCIAL SERVICES, INC. — ASE: LTS

4400 Biscayne Boulevard, 12th Floor
Miami, FL 33137
Phone: 305 572-4100
Fax: –
Web: www.ladenburg.com
CEO: Richard J. (Dick) Lampen
CFO: Brett H. Kaufman
HR: –
FYE: December 31
Type: Public

Laden with cash? You might want to call Ladenburg Thalmann Financial Services. The company provides brokerage asset management and investment banking services to corporate institutional and individual clients throughout the US. Subsidiaries Triad Advisors Investacorp and Securities America are independent broker-dealers primarily serving retail clients; together they have some 2700 registered representatives and manage more than $80 billion in assets. Another subsidiary Ladenburg Thalmann & Co. is an investment bank providing capital raising and advisory services to middle-market companies. Ladenburg Thalmann Asset Management offers mutual funds alternative investments and investment counseling.

	Annual Growth	12/10	12/11	12/12	12/13	12/14
Sales ($ mil.)	47.5%	194.5	273.6	650.1	793.1	921.3
Net income ($ mil.)	–	(11.0)	3.9	(16.4)	(0.5)	33.4
Market value ($ mil.)	35.6%	216.4	458.7	259.0	579.0	730.6
Employees	64.4%	152	618	686	715	1,109

LADIES PROFESSIONAL GOLF ASSOCIATION

100 INTERNATIONAL GOLF DR
DAYTONA BEACH, FL 321241082
Phone: 386-274-2073
Fax: –
Web: www.lpga.com
CEO: –
CFO: –
HR: –
FYE: December 31
Type: Private

This organization has chipped out a place for itself in the male-dominated sports world. The Ladies Professional Golf Association (LPGA) is the organizing body for women's golf overseeing development and promotion of the game and its star players. It operates the LPGA Tour consisting of about 30 events a year. In addition to its high-profile golf tournaments the organization runs the LPGA Teaching & Club Professional Division which is the golf education and development subsidiary for its 1200 members. The LPGA was founded in 1950 making it one of the oldest women's sports organizations in the world.

	Annual Growth	12/06	12/07	12/08	12/09	12/12
Sales ($ mil.)	2.6%	–	–	–	82.5	89.1
Net income ($ mil.)	–	–	–	–	(3.2)	0.2
Market value ($ mil.)	–	–	–	–	–	–
Employees	–	–	–	–	–	85

LAFAYETTE COLLEGE

316 MARKLE HALL
EASTON, PA 180421729
Phone: 610-330-5000
Fax: -
Web: www.me.lafayette.edu

CEO: -
CFO: -
HR: -
FYE: June 30
Type: Private

Lafayette College has a revolutionary background. Named after the French hero of the American Revolution the school offers bachelor's degrees in about 45 areas of study in engineering sciences and the arts. Some 2400 students — all undergraduates— are enrolled on the campus located about 70 miles west of New York City and 60 miles north of Philadelphia. Students come from 42 US states and territories and from 37 other countries. Lafayette is a member of the Lehigh Valley Association of Independent Colleges which also includes Cedar Crest College DeSales University Lehigh University Moravian College and Muhlenberg College.

	Annual Growth	06/07	06/08	06/12	06/13	06/14
Sales ($ mil.)	(4.4%)	-	191.1	134.5	142.1	145.6
Net income ($ mil.)	-	-	-	(25.8)	69.6	97.8
Market value ($ mil.)	-	-	-	-	-	-
Employees	-	-	-	-	-	675

LAFAYETTE GENERAL MEDICAL CENTER INC

1214 COOLIDGE BLVD
LAFAYETTE, LA 705032621
Phone: 337-289-7991
Fax: -
Web: www.lafayettegeneral.com

CEO: -
CFO: -
HR: -
FYE: September 30
Type: Private

Serving the people of Acadiana (southern Louisiana) Lafayette General Medical Center (LGMC) provides general inpatient medical and surgical care as well as specialized trauma care and neonatal intensive care. The not-for-profit hospital which has more than 365 beds also offers home health services outpatient care occupational medicine and mental health care. As part of umbrella group Lafayette Health LGMC is affiliated with Lafayette General Surgical Hospital St. Martin Hospital Acadia General Hospital University Hospital and Clinics and Abrom Kaplan Memorial Hospital. It's also a teaching hospital for LSU. Non-profit foundation Lafayette General Foundation supports and governs Lafayette Health.

	Annual Growth	09/07	09/08	09/09	09/12	09/13
Sales ($ mil.)	14.1%	-	177.0	182.0	268.1	342.5
Net income ($ mil.)	119.2%	-	-	1.9	25.7	44.2
Market value ($ mil.)	-	-	-	-	-	-
Employees	-	-	-	-	-	1,626

LAIRD TECHNOLOGIES INC.

3481 Rider Trail South
Earth City MO 63045
Phone: 636-898-6000
Fax: 636-898-6100
Web: www.lairdtech.com

CEO: David Lockwood
CFO: -
HR: -
FYE: December 31
Type: Subsidiary

Laird Technologies feels that the shield is mightier than the sword. The company manufactures electromagnetic interference (EMI) shielding materials such as custom metal stampings signal integrity components thermal management products wireless antennas and radio frequency modules. It also produces metalized fabric and conductive tape and offers product engineering and testing services. Laird Technologies has two divisions: Performance Materials (handset metals) which includes EMI shields signal integrity products and thermal management products; and Wireless Systems such as telematics and satellite radio antennas handset antennas and other wireless systems. Laird Technologies is an operating unit of Laird PLC.

LAKE AREA CORN PROCESSORS CO-OPERATIVE

46269 SD HIGHWAY 34
WENTWORTH, SD 570756934
Phone: 605-483-2676
Fax: -
Web: www.dakotaethanol.com

CEO: -
CFO: -
HR: -
FYE: December 31
Type: Private

Lake Area Corn Processors produces ethanol and its byproduct distillers grains which are used in livestock feed. Through its Dakota Ethanol unit the company produces about 48 million gallons of ethanol per year. Dakota Ethanol had worked in tandem with Broin Companies a manufacturer of ethanol processing plants until Lake Area Corn Processors bought out Broin's minority stake in Dakota Ethanol in 2006. The following year the company acquired a stake in its ethanol distributor Renewable Products Marketing Group. Lake Area Corn Processors is owned by its 1000 members.

	Annual Growth	12/04	12/05	12/06	12/07	12/10
Sales ($ mil.)	3.8%	-	80.0	103.9	103.7	96.4
Net income ($ mil.)	(37.5%)	-	-	46.0	18.0	7.0
Market value ($ mil.)	-	-	-	-	-	-
Employees	-	-	-	-	-	40

LAKE FOREST COLLEGE

555 N SHERIDAN RD
LAKE FOREST, IL 600452399
Phone: 847-234-3100
Fax: -
Web: www.lakeforest.edu

CEO: -
CFO: -
HR: -
FYE: May 31
Type: Private

Living up to its name Lake Forest College is a liberal arts school near the shores of Lake Michigan just north of Chicago. The school sits on about a 100 acre campus 30 miles north of downtown Chicago and offers undergraduate and graduate programs to its approximately 1500 students. With nearly 20 departmental and about 10 interdisciplinary majors its subjects include economics international studies neuroscience and pre-law. The College's Center for Chicago Programs facilitates research and internships at Chicago institutions as well as brings Chicago-based artists and artisans alike to the campus for lectures and performances.

	Annual Growth	05/08	05/09	05/10	05/11	05/13
Sales ($ mil.)	-	-	0.0	63.7	73.9	83.0
Net income ($ mil.)	-	-	-	(4.7)	0.0	0.1
Market value ($ mil.)	-	-	-	-	-	-
Employees	-	-	-	-	-	385

LAKE HOSPITAL SYSTEM INC.

7590 AUBURN RD
PAINESVILLE, OH 440779176
Phone: 440-354-2400
Fax: -
Web: www.lakehealth.org

CEO: Cynthia Moore-Hardy
CFO: -
HR: -
FYE: December 31
Type: Private

The aptly named Lake Hospital System (doing business as Lake Health) serves several northeast Ohio communities located along Lake Erie and throughout Lake County. The not-for-profit health system comprises two main hospital campuses (TriPoint Medical Center and West) which together house more than 350 beds as well as a dozen ancillary facilities offering rehabilitative care outpatient surgery urgent care services primary care and specialist doctors' offices and diagnostic imaging. The system's Lake Health Physician Group includes physicians ranging from family practitioners to vascular surgeons.

	Annual Growth	12/01	12/02	12/08	12/11	12/12
Sales ($ mil.)	5.5%	-	185.0	278.4	360.0	315.0
Net income ($ mil.)	-	-	-	(31.1)	23.2	5.4
Market value ($ mil.)	-	-	-	-	-	-
Employees	-	-	-	-	-	2,200

LAKE SHORE BANCORP INC
NMS: LSBK

31 East Fourth Street
Dunkirk, NY 14048
Phone: 716 366-4070
Fax: –
Web: www.lakeshoresavings.com

CEO: Daniel P Reininga
CFO: Rachel A Foley
HR: –
FYE: December 31
Type: Public

Money washes up along this shore. Lake Shore Bancorp is the holding company for Lake Shore Savings Bank which serves consumers and businesses through 11 branches in Chautauqua and Erie counties in western New York near Lake Erie. Founded in 1891 the community oriented savings bank focuses on residential real estate lending with one- to four-family mortgages accounting for a majority of its loan portfolio. Lake Shore Savings Bank also offers home equity loans and commercial and consumer loans as well as checking and savings accounts CDs and IRAs. Mutual holding company Lake Shore MHC owns about 60% of Lake Shore Bancorp.

	Annual Growth	12/10	12/11	12/12	12/13	12/14
Assets ($ mil.)	0.4%	479.0	488.6	482.4	482.2	487.5
Net income ($ mil.)	0.9%	3.0	3.7	3.6	3.7	3.2
Market value ($ mil.)	10.1%	55.3	57.2	61.6	73.1	81.2
Employees	(0.2%)	123	121	121	119	122

LAKE SUNAPEE BANK GROUP
NMS: LSBG

9 Main Street, P.O. Box 9
Newport, NH 03773
Phone: 603 863-0886
Fax: –
Web: www.nhthrift.com

CEO: Stephen R Theroux
CFO: Laura Jacobi
HR: Frances E Clow
FYE: December 31
Type: Public

New Hampshire Thrift Bancshares is the holding company for Lake Sunapee Bank which operates nearly 30 branches in western and central New Hampshire and western Vermont. Targeting individuals and local businesses the bank mainly uses funds from deposits to originate a variety of loans mainly residential and commercial mortgages. It also offers investment insurance and trust services. New Hampshire Thrift Bancshares expanded into Vermont with the 2007 acquisition of First Brandon National Bank which now operates as a division of Lake Sunapee Bank. The company bought insurance agency McCrillis & Eldredge in 2011. It now plans to buy the single-branch Nashua Bank.

	Annual Growth	12/10	12/11	12/12	12/13	12/14
Assets ($ mil.)	10.9%	995.1	1,041.8	1,270.5	1,423.9	1,503.8
Net income ($ mil.)	6.0%	7.9	7.7	7.8	8.4	10.0
Market value ($ mil.)	5.6%	103.6	93.3	104.9	125.9	129.0
Employees	11.3%	249	274	304	382	382

LAKELAND BANCORP, INC.
NMS: LBAI

250 Oak Ridge Road
Oak Ridge, NJ 07438
Phone: 973 697-2000
Fax: –
Web: www.lakelandbank.com

CEO: Thomas J. Shara
CFO: Joseph F. Hurley
HR: –
FYE: December 31
Type: Public

Lakeland Bancorp is shoring up in the Garden State. It's the holding company for Lakeland Bank which serves northern New Jersey from more than 50 branch offices. Targeting individuals and small to midsized businesses the bank offers standard retail products such as checking and savings accounts money market and NOW accounts and CDs. It also offers financial planning and advisory services for consumers. The bank's lending activities primarily consist of commercial loans and mortgages (more than half of the company's loan portfolio) and residential mortgages. Lakeland also offers commercial lease financing for office systems and heavy equipment. Lakeland Bancorp plans to acquire Somerset Hills Bancorp.

	Annual Growth	12/10	12/11	12/12	12/13	12/14
Assets ($ mil.)	6.1%	2,792.7	2,826.0	2,918.7	3,317.8	3,538.3
Net income ($ mil.)	12.8%	19.2	19.9	21.7	25.0	31.1
Market value ($ mil.)	1.6%	415.9	326.8	385.9	469.0	443.6
Employees	1.7%	529	527	522	550	566

LAKELAND FINANCIAL CORP.
NMS: LKFN

202 East Center Street, P.O. Box 1387
Warsaw, IN 46581-1387
Phone: 574 267-6144
Fax: –
Web: www.lakecitybank.com

CEO: Michael L. Kubacki
CFO: David M. Findlay
HR: –
FYE: December 31
Type: Public

American dollars are preferred over Polish zloty in this Warsaw bank. Lakeland Financial is the holding company for Lake City Bank which serves area business customers and individuals through more than 40 branches scattered across about a dozen northern Indiana counties. Founded in 1872 in Warsaw Indiana the bank offers such standard retail services as checking and savings accounts money market accounts and CDs. Commercial loans including agricultural loans and mortgages make up about 80% of the bank's loan portfolio. Lake City Bank also offers investment products and services such as corporate and personal trust brokerage employee benefit plans and estate planning.

	Annual Growth	12/10	12/11	12/12	12/13	12/14
Assets ($ mil.)	6.4%	2,681.9	2,889.7	3,064.1	3,175.8	3,443.3
Net income ($ mil.)	15.6%	24.5	30.7	35.4	38.8	43.8
Market value ($ mil.)	19.3%	353.4	426.0	425.5	642.2	715.8
Employees	1.5%	467	482	493	497	496

LAKELAND INDUSTRIES, INC.
NMS: LAKE

3555 Veterans Memorial Highway, Suite C
Ronkonkoma, NY 11779
Phone: 631 981-9700
Fax: 631 981-9751
Web: www.lakeland.com

CEO: Christopher J Ryan
CFO: Gary Pokrassa
HR: –
FYE: January 31
Type: Public

The wrong clothing can be hazardous to your health — not based on style but by OSHA and EPA standards. Lakeland makes protective clothing for on-the-job hazards. It uses DuPont specialty fabrics such as Kevlar TyChem and Tyvek as well as its own fabrics to make industrial disposable garments toxic-waste cleanup suits fire- and heat-resistant apparel (including Fyrepel gear for firefighters) industrial work gloves high-visibility garments and industrial/medical garments. Lakeland manufactures its products in Brazil China India Mexico and the US. Customers — nearly 65% are outside of the US — include high tech electronics manufacturers construction companies hospitals and laboratories.

	Annual Growth	01/11	01/12	01/13	01/14	01/15
Sales ($ mil.)	(0.4%)	101.2	96.3	95.1	91.4	99.7
Net income ($ mil.)	71.4%	1.0	(0.4)	(26.3)	(0.1)	8.4
Market value ($ mil.)	(1.0%)	62.5	66.5	35.6	46.3	60.0
Employees	(10.1%)	2,000	1,912	1,652	1,427	1,304

LAKELAND REGIONAL MEDICAL CENTER INC.

1324 LAKELAND HILLS BLVD
LAKELAND, FL 338054500
Phone: 863-687-1100
Fax: –
Web: www.lrmc.com

CEO: –
CFO: –
HR: Amy Barry
FYE: September 30
Type: Private

In the land o' lakes Lakeland Regional Medical Center (LRMC) cares for residents' physical ailments. LRMC serves Florida's Polk County (roughly between Kissimmee and Tampa) through an acute care hospital with approximately 850 beds. Among its specialty services are cardiac care cancer treatment senior care urology emergency medicine orthopedics women's and children's health care and surgery. LRMC also operates general care and specialty outpatient clinics. Additionally the hospital provides medical training programs for radiology specialists. Its LRMC Foundation offers financial support for indigent patients facing ongoing treatment.

	Annual Growth	09/08	09/09	09/10	09/11	09/13
Sales ($ mil.)	0.7%	–	567.5	612.5	0.6	584.2
Net income ($ mil.)	36.9%	–	–	21.5	0.0	55.1
Market value ($ mil.)	–	–	–	–	–	–
Employees	–	–	–	–	–	3,100

LAKESHORE STAFFING GROUP INC.

1 N. Franklin St. Ste. 600
Chicago IL 60606
Phone: 312-251-7575
Fax: 312-251-7580
Web: www.lakeshorestaffing.com

CEO: -
CFO: Erin Robinson
HR: Amy Brenchley
FYE: December 31
Type: Private

When it comes to landing a job Lakeshore Staffing can provide both temporary and permanent relief. The company provides temporary and permanent employment for workers in areas such as technology administration legal health care and finance and accounting. Through its Web site the company offers various resources and information such as job openings job fairs salary data and online application processing. Staffing consultants provide both job placement services to applicants and strategic advice to employers. Its clients include "FORTUNE" 500 companies not-for-profits law firms and universities. Denver-based PeoplePartners owns Lakeshore Staffing.

LAKESIDE FOODS INC.

808 Hamilton St.
Manitowoc WI 54220
Phone: 920-684-3356
Fax: 920-686-4033
Web: www.lakesidefoods.com

CEO: David J Yanda
CFO: -
HR: -
FYE: April 30
Type: Private

Lakeside Foods is full of beans — green wax lima and more. The company specializes in the production of private-label canned and frozen vegetables and beans. Lakeside's customers are retail food industry companies including Roundy's and IGA located in the Midwest. The food manufacturer and marketer also offers other food items such as canned meat and stews; jams jellies and preserves; frozen and shelf-stable meals; salsa and other sauces; and whipped toppings. The food maker operates more than a dozen plants and about 10 distribution centers in both Minnesota and Wisconsin. Lakeside exports its food products to nearly 15 countries overseas.

LAKESIDE INDUSTRIES INC.

6505 226TH PL SE STE 200
ISSAQUAH, WA 980278905
Phone: 425-313-2600
Fax: -
Web: www.lakesideind.com

CEO: Timothy Lee Jr
CFO: Hank Waggoner
HR: Tammy Vibbert
FYE: November 30
Type: Private

Lakeside Industries is one of the largest highway contractors in the Pacific Northwest. A leading asphalt paving contractor and manufacturer the company works on municipal commercial and industrial sites as well as residential projects. It also sells hot-mix and cold asphalt to other paving contractors. It has about a dozen offices in western Washington northwestern Oregon and central Idaho. Owned by the founding Lee family Lakeside Industries was established when the family combined their mining sand and gravel asphalt and trucking businesses in 1972.

	Annual Growth	11/02	11/03	11/04	11/05	11/07
Sales ($ mil.)	10.9%	-	136.1	0.0	147.5	206.0
Net income ($ mil.)	-	-	-	0.0	6.0	0.0
Market value ($ mil.)	-	-	-	-	-	-
Employees	-	-	-	-	-	750

LAM RESEARCH CORP   NMS: LRCX

4650 Cushing Parkway
Fremont, CA 94538
Phone: 510 572-0200
Fax: 510 572-6454
Web: www.lamresearch.com

CEO: Martin B. Anstice
CFO: Douglas R. (Doug) Bettinger
HR: -
FYE: June 28
Type: Public

It's not uncommon for chip makers in need of critical manufacturing equipment to go on the Lam. Lam Research is a top maker of the equipment used to make semiconductors. The company's products address two key steps in the chip-making process. Its market-leading plasma etch machines are used to create tiny circuitry patterns on silicon wafers. Lam also makes cleaning equipment that keeps unwanted particles from contaminating processed wafers. The company's Customer Support Business Group provides products and services to maximize installed equipment performance. Lam's customers include many of the world's large chip makers; customers outside the US primarily in Asia represent the majority of sales. The company is buying KLA-Tencor for about $10.6 billion.

	Annual Growth	06/11	06/12	06/13	06/14	06/15
Sales ($ mil.)	12.9%	3,237.7	2,665.2	3,598.9	4,607.3	5,259.3
Net income ($ mil.)	(2.4%)	723.7	168.7	113.9	632.3	655.6
Market value ($ mil.)	17.7%	6,851.7	6,016.3	7,029.3	10,613.7	13,135.9
Employees	18.5%	3,700	6,600	6,600	6,500	7,300

LAMAR ADVERTISING CO (NEW)   NMS: LAMR

5321 Corporate Blvd.
Baton Rouge, LA 70808
Phone: 225 926-1000
Fax: -
Web: www.lamar.com

CEO: Sean E. Reilly
CFO: Keith A. Istre
HR: -
FYE: December 31
Type: Public

Here's a company that shows all the signs of being a successful outdoor advertising business. Lamar Advertising is one of the top billboard operators in the US along with CBS Outdoor and Clear Channel Outdoor. The company maintains more than 144000 billboards in about 45 states plus Canada and Puerto Rico. It also sells advertising space on almost 41000 signs placed on buses and at bus stops in more than 15 states and it maintains more than 132000 logo signs (highway exit signs with logos of nearby hotels and restaurants) along interstates in about 20 states and Canada. Chairman Kevin Reilly Jr. together with members of his family controls a 66% voting stake in the company.

	Annual Growth	12/10	12/11	12/12	12/13	12/14
Sales ($ mil.)	4.2%	1,092.3	1,133.5	1,182.9	1,245.8	1,287.1
Net income ($ mil.)	-	(40.1)	8.6	9.8	40.1	253.5
Market value ($ mil.)	7.7%	3,806.5	2,627.4	3,702.3	4,992.1	5,124.9
Employees	1.6%	3,000	3,000	3,000	3,000	3,200

LANCASTER COLONY CORP.   NMS: LANC

37 West Broad Street
Columbus, OH 43215
Phone: 614 224-7141
Fax: 614 469-8219
Web: www.lancastercolony.com

CEO: John B. Gerlach
CFO: Douglas A. Fell
HR: -
FYE: June 30
Type: Public

Lancaster Colony provides some of the necessary ingredients — caviar candles and wine glasses — practically guaranteed to result in a romantic meal. The company makes specialty foods including Romanoff caviar Marzetti salad dressings Chatham Village croutons Texas Toast and other specialty bread pasta and sauce products. Lancaster Colony's food products are available through US food retailers and foodservice operators mainly restaurants. The company also offers private-label services. In addition to food the company supplies other amenities by making and selling candles and associated glassware and accessories under the Candle-lite brand name.

	Annual Growth	06/11	06/12	06/13	06/14	06/15
Sales ($ mil.)	0.3%	1,089.9	1,131.4	1,165.9	1,041.1	1,104.5
Net income ($ mil.)	(1.1%)	106.4	95.8	109.2	75.0	101.7
Market value ($ mil.)	10.6%	1,664.1	1,948.3	2,133.9	2,603.6	2,485.7
Employees	(4.3%)	3,100	3,100	3,100	2,500	2,600

LAND O' LAKES INC

4001 Lexington Avenue North
Arden Hills, MN 55126
Phone: 651 481-2222
Fax: –
Web: www.landolakesinc.com

CEO: Christopher J. (Chris) Policinski
CFO: Daniel E. (Dan) Knutson
HR: Karen Grabow
FYE: December 31
Type: Public

Best known for its #1 US butter brand Land O'Lakes looks to butter everyone's bread to boost its bottom line. One of the largest dairy co-ops in the nation it's owned by roughly 4400 dairy farmer/members and some 900 member associations. It markets dairy-based consumer food service and food ingredient items. The co-op makes more than 300 dairy products from the 12 billion pounds of milk that members supply annually. Land O'Lakes produces animal feed through Land O'Lakes Purina Feed. The co-op also offers members seed and crop protection products animal feed and agricultural assistance. It operates dairy facilities in the US and does business in all 50 states and 60-plus countries.

	Annual Growth	12/10	12/11	12/12	12/13	12/14
Sales ($ mil.)	7.6%	11,146.4	12,849.3	14,116.2	14,236.4	14,965.5
Net income ($ mil.)	10.6%	178.1	182.2	240.4	306.0	266.5
Market value ($ mil.)	–	–	–	–	–	–
Employees	–	–	–	–	10,000	–

LAND O'LAKES PURINA FEED LLC

1080 County Rd. F
Shoreview MN 55126
Phone: 651-481-2222
Fax: 518-862-9525
Web: www.iplogic.com

CEO: –
CFO: –
HR: –
FYE: December 31
Type: Subsidiary

Old MacDonald's farm of cows and pigs is likely to have depended upon Land O'Lakes Purina Feed. As the largest US producer of animal feeds the company manufactures and markets feed for both commercial dairy and beef cattle and swine and the "lifestyle" animal market. Commercial feed is purchased by farmers and livestock producers; by contrast lifestyle feed is used by consumers that don't intend to sell their animals. In addition to livestock feed the company makes milk-replacer products for young animals premixes supplements and custom-mixed feeds as well as offers farm-management advice. Land O'Lakes Purina Feed is a subsidiary of dairy co-op and the nation's top-selling brand of butter Land O'Lakes.

LANDAUER, INC.

NYS: LDR

2 Science Road
Glenwood, IL 60425
Phone: 708 755-7000
Fax: –
Web: www.landauerinc.com

CEO: Michael P. Kaminski
CFO: Dan Fujii
HR: –
FYE: September 30
Type: Public

If your employees are glowing — and not with joy — Landauer can tell you why. Through its subsidiaries Landauer manufactures and markets dosimeters (radiation detection monitors) used in nuclear plants hospitals and university and government laboratories. Landauer's services include distribution and collection of radiation monitors and exposure reporting. Its HomeBuyer's Preferred subsidiary provides residential radon monitoring services. Landauer also offers medical physics services to hospitals and radiation therapy centers through its GPS subsidiary.

	Annual Growth	09/11	09/12	09/13	09/14	09/15
Sales ($ mil.)	5.9%	120.5	152.4	150.2	155.1	151.3
Net income ($ mil.)	(12.3%)	24.5	19.3	4.8	(25.2)	14.5
Market value ($ mil.)	(7.0%)	477.6	575.8	494.1	318.3	356.6
Employees	1.7%	560	660	650	600	600

LANDEC CORP.

NMS: LNDC

3603 Haven Avenue
Menlo Park, CA 94025
Phone: 650 306-1650
Fax: 650 368-9818
Web: www.landec.com

CEO: Ronald L. (Ron) Midyett
CFO: Gregory S. (Greg) Skinner
HR: Jennifer Byer
FYE: May 31
Type: Public

Landec's products don't turn into pumpkins at midnight but the changes are nearly as sudden and much more practical. The company has developed a technology that allows polymers to change physical characteristics when exposed to temperature changes. Its BreatheWay permeable membrane packaging allows oxygen and carbon dioxide to enter and escape from sealed fresh-cut produce packages to keep produce fresh. It's used primarily by subsidiary Apio which grows and packages fresh vegetables. Landec's Lifecore Biomedical subsidiary is a leading supplier of premium hyaluronan-based biomaterials for the ophthalmic and orthopedic markets. Landec has licensing deals with Air Products and Chemicals and Monsanto.

	Annual Growth	05/11	05/12	05/13	05/14	05/15
Sales ($ mil.)	18.2%	276.7	317.6	441.7	476.8	539.3
Net income ($ mil.)	34.0%	4.3	13.1	22.8	19.3	13.7
Market value ($ mil.)	25.1%	157.4	190.8	374.6	324.2	385.7
Employees	21.2%	255	532	526	531	550

LANDMARK BANCORP INC

NMS: LARK

701 Poyntz Avenue
Manhattan, KS 66502
Phone: 785 565-2000
Fax: –
Web: www.landmarkbancorpinc.com

CEO: Michael E Scheopner
CFO: Mark A Herpich
HR: –
FYE: December 31
Type: Public

Landmark Bancorp is a tourist attraction for Kansas money. It is the holding company for Landmark National Bank which has about 15 branches in communities in central eastern and southwestern Kansas. The bank provides standard commercial banking products including checking savings and money market accounts as well as CDs and credit and debit cards. It primarily uses funds from deposits to write residential and commercial mortgages and business loans. Landmark National Bank offers non-deposit investment services through its affiliation with Investment Planners.

	Annual Growth	12/10	12/11	12/12	12/13	12/14
Assets ($ mil.)	11.4%	561.5	598.2	614.1	828.8	863.5
Net income ($ mil.)	40.9%	2.0	4.5	6.4	4.7	8.0
Market value ($ mil.)	5.8%	59.2	65.4	69.6	68.6	74.1
Employees	5.8%	221	216	215	292	277

LANDMARK GRAPHICS CORPORATION

2107 CityWest Blvd. Bldg. 2
Houston TX 77042-3051
Phone: 713-839-2000
Fax: 713-839-2015
Web: www.lgc.com

CEO: Peter Bernard
CFO: –
HR: Pamela Jolly
FYE: December 31
Type: Subsidiary

As you look for oil keep an eye out for Landmark Graphics. The company develops software used by high-tech wildcatters to find oil drill for it and analyze economic return. Databases built with Landmark software store information used by seismic analysis programs to simulate reservoirs and other geological structures. Well planning and drilling applications calculate how to get the oil while reservoir management software track the amount left. Throughout the process Landmark's production and economic applications manage risk and measure returns. Customers include BP Chevron and Statoil. Founded in 1982 Landmark Graphics was acquired by Halliburton in 1996.

LANDRY'S INC.

1510 W. Loop South
Houston TX 77027
Phone: 713-850-1010
Fax: 713-850-7205
Web: www.landrysinc.com

CEO: Tilman J Fertitta
CFO: Richard H Liem
HR: –
FYE: December 31
Type: Private

Landry's Restaurants is a leading full-service restaurant operator with more than 275 locations throughout the US. The company's estate of eateries is anchored by its flagship Landry's Seafood House chain; other concepts include Rainforest Cafe McCormick & Schmick's Saltgrass Steak House and Bubba Gump Shrimp. Through an agreement with an affiliate Landry's manages the Claim Jumper chain of about 35 restaurants. The company also owns and operates the iconic Golden Nugget Hotel & Casino in Las Vegas along with a number of other entertainment properties including aquariums hotels and other tourist attractions. CEO Tilman Fertitta led a buyout of Landry's in 2010 taking the company private.

LANDSTAR SYSTEM, INC.

13410 Sutton Park Drive South
Jacksonville, FL 32224
Phone: 904 398-9400
Fax: –
Web: www.landstar.com

NMS: LSTR
CEO: James B. (Jim) Gattoni
CFO: L. Kevin Stout
HR: –
FYE: December 27
Type: Public

Truckload freight carrier Landstar System has hitched its star to an asset-light business model. The company's fleet of almost 13000 trailers (including flatbed refrigerated and standard dry vans) is operated primarily by independent contractors and the company's services are marketed by sales agents. Landstar's freight carrier units transport general commodities and goods such as automotive products building materials chemicals and machinery as well as ammunition and explosives. Customers include third-party logistics providers and government agencies such as the US Department of Defense. In addition to truckload transportation Landstar offers logistics and warehousing services.

	Annual Growth	12/10	12/11	12/12	12/13	12/14
Sales ($ mil.)	7.3%	2,401.7	2,650.8	2,795.0	2,666.3	3,186.2
Net income ($ mil.)	12.2%	87.5	113.0	129.8	146.0	138.8
Market value ($ mil.)	16.2%	1,825.4	2,146.6	2,312.3	2,576.1	3,332.7
Employees	(2.7%)	1,353	1,351	1,369	1,217	1,211

LANE BRYANT INC.

3344 Morse Crossing
Columbus OH 43219
Phone: 614-463-5200
Fax: 614-463-5240
Web: www.lanebryant.com

CEO: Linda Heasley
CFO: –
HR: –
FYE: January 31
Type: Subsidiary

Lane Bryant is a big name in women's plus-size fashion. The nation's #1 plus-size clothing chain operates some 800 full-line and outlet stores in about 45 states that sell moderately-priced private label and select name brand career and casual apparel (in sizes 12 to 32) accessories hosiery and intimate apparel for women ages 35 to 55. Lane Bryant stores are found in malls and strip shopping centers and average about 5500 square feet. Women can also shop online at lanebryant.com. Founded in 1904 by Lena Bryant (she misspelled her name on a bank loan) Lane Bryant is owned by Ascena Retail Group.

LANE POWELL PC

1420 5TH AVE STE 4100
SEATTLE, WA 981012375
Phone: 206-223-7000
Fax: –
Web: www.lanepowell.com

CEO: –
CFO: –
HR: –
FYE: December 31
Type: Private

Lane Powell PC brings the power of attorney to the Pacific Northwest. Operating out of offices in Washington Oregon Alaska and internationally in London the law firm specializes in a range of legal services including corporate finance intellectual property regulation and taxation real estate labor relations and commercial litigation. Lane Powell employs more than 200 attorneys and around 300 support personnel handling local national and international clientele. The law firm traces its roots back to 1889 when it was named Strudwick Peters & Collins. (John Powell arrived that same year while W. Byron Lane joined the firm in 1929.)

	Annual Growth	12/08	12/09	12/11	12/12	12/13
Sales ($ mil.)	4.8%	–	78.1	93.2	95.3	94.3
Net income ($ mil.)	(0.3%)	–	–	0.2	0.1	0.2
Market value ($ mil.)	–	–	–	–	–	–
Employees	–	–	–	–	–	410

LANGSTON SNYDER L P

17962 COWAN
IRVINE, CA 926146026
Phone: 949-863-9200
Fax: –
Web: www.snyder-langston.com

CEO: Stephen Jones
CFO: Paul Pfeiffer
HR: –
FYE: December 31
Type: Private

No Snyder Langston isn't the name of a "wacky neighbor" sitcom character but it might have built the property next door. Snyder Langston develops and builds commercial industrial and multifamily residential properties. Serving business clients ranging from start-ups to Fortune 500 firms the company provides a range of services such as planning design financing government relations general contracting and construction management. Properties that Snyder Langston has developed include business parks retail centers office buildings manufacturing facilities parking garages car dealerships condominiums churches schools and hotels. The firm was founded in 1959 by Donald Snyder and William Langston.

	Annual Growth	12/05	12/06	12/07	12/09	12/10
Sales ($ mil.)	(38.3%)	–	–	238.6	78.9	56.0
Net income ($ mil.)	–	–	–	0.0	(1.5)	(1.7)
Market value ($ mil.)	–	–	–	–	–	–
Employees	–	–	–	–	–	91

LANIER PARKING HOLDINGS INC.

233 PEACHTREE ST
ATLANTA, GA 30303
Phone: 404-523-0864
Fax: –
Web: www.lanierparking.com

CEO: Jerry Skillett
CFO: David A Klarman
HR: –
FYE: December 31
Type: Private

Lanier Parking offers more than just a spot to park your car. It offers a full array of parking and transportation services from shuttle and valet to design/build and financial consulting at more than 300 locations throughout the Southeast. In addition to providing traditional parking management and facility operations the company touts its planning capabilities at sites where there is likely to be insufficient space or heavy congestion such as hospitals hotels municipalities sports and entertainment venues and universities. Its consulting services include feasibility site selection and master planning. The company was founded by J. Michael Robison in 1989.

	Annual Growth	12/07	12/08	12/09	12/10	12/12
Sales ($ mil.)	9.3%	–	59.1	59.6	61.3	84.3
Net income ($ mil.)	19.1%	–	–	2.3	2.1	3.9
Market value ($ mil.)	–	–	–	–	–	–
Employees	–	–	–	–	–	2,000

LANNETT CO., INC.
NYS: LCI

9000 State Road
Philadelphia, PA 19136
Phone: 215 333-9000
Fax: –
Web: www.lannett.com

CEO: Arthur P. Bedrosian
CFO: Martin P. Galvan
HR: –
FYE: June 30
Type: Public

Lannett banks on the designation of "bioequivalent" for its products. The firm develops manufactures packages markets and distributes generic prescription drugs in the US including thyroid treatment levothyroxine digoxin for congestive heart failure migraine drug butalbital and ursodiol for gallstones. Such medicines are pharmaceutical equivalents or bioequivalents of branded medicines made by other drug companies. While Lannett maintains two plants it also relies on manufacturer Jerome Stevens Pharmaceuticals for a significant portion of its inventories. The company produces medicines in oral solid (tablets liquids and capsules) and topical dosages forms.

	Annual Growth	06/11	06/12	06/13	06/14	06/15
Sales ($ mil.)	39.7%	106.8	123.0	151.1	273.8	406.8
Net income ($ mil.)	–	(0.3)	3.9	13.3	57.1	149.9
Market value ($ mil.)	85.9%	180.6	153.8	431.9	1,799.4	2,155.6
Employees	12.8%	310	324	356	399	502

LANSING BOARD OF WATER AND LIGHT

1201 S WASHINGTON AVE
LANSING, MI 489101650
Phone: 517-702-6000
Fax: –
Web: www.lbwl.com

CEO: J Peter Lark
CFO: Susan Devon
HR: Dan Barnes
FYE: June 30
Type: Private

Letting off a little steam is a good thing for Lansing Board of Water and Light which provides electricity to 95000 residential commercial and industrial customers and water to about 55000 customers in Lansing Michigan. The city-owned utility also produces and distributes steam to 162 customers along 14 miles of steam line. Lansing Board of Water and Light can chill out too. Its chilled water system delivers up to 10000 tons of chilled water capacity to 16 customers to cool the interior of buildings in the downtown area. Lansing Board of Water and Light is the largest municipally owned utility in the state. It is also a major employer in the Lansing area.

	Annual Growth	06/07	06/08	06/09	06/10	06/11
Sales ($ mil.)	1567.1%	–	–	–	18.4	306.1
Net income ($ mil.)	(57.2%)	–	–	–	17.9	7.6
Market value ($ mil.)	–	–	–	–	–	–
Employees	–	–	–	–	–	740

LANTRONIX INC.
NAS: LTRX

7535 Irvine Center Drive, Suite 100
Irvine, CA 92618
Phone: 949 453-3990
Fax: 949 453-3995
Web: www.lantronix.com

CEO: Jeffrey W. (Jeff) Benck
CFO: Jeremy Whitaker
HR: Tom Morton
FYE: June 30
Type: Public

Lantronix specializes in M2M communication technology. The company designs develops markets and sells smart machine-to-machine connectivity products that enable data sharing between devices and applications. Lantronix products remotely and securely connect devices via networks and the Internet. It also provides products for remote management of data centers and IT equipment. Lantronix which outsources its manufacturing sells primarily through OEMs resellers system integrators and distributors. Its products are geared at a wide range of global markets from industrial automation and security to medical and transportation. Ingram Micro and Acal plc are its largest customers.

	Annual Growth	06/11	06/12	06/13	06/14	06/15
Sales ($ mil.)	(3.4%)	49.3	45.4	46.7	44.5	42.9
Net income ($ mil.)	–	(5.3)	(3.0)	(2.8)	(0.9)	(2.8)
Market value ($ mil.)	(10.1%)	38.2	30.8	23.8	29.7	24.9
Employees	(3.9%)	129	114	109	112	110

LAPOLLA INDUSTRIES INC
NBB: LPAD

Intercontinental Business Park, 15402 Vantage Parkway East, Suite 322
Houston, TX 77032
Phone: 281 219-4700
Fax: –
Web: www.lapolla.com

CEO: Douglas J Kramer
CFO: Jomarc C Marukot
HR: –
FYE: December 31
Type: Public

LaPolla Industries would hate for its customers to have leaky roofs over their heads or insufficiently protected exterior walls. The company makes foam products used to protect roofs and the "building envelope" which is the separation of the exterior and interior parts of a building. It also makes coatings for weatherproofing concrete and metal roofing and other materials. The company changed its name in 2005 when it absorbed subsidiary LaPolla Industries a provider of roof coatings and polyurethane foam construction systems. The former IFT Corp. which had previously been called Urecoats acquired LaPolla in 2005. Chairman Richard Kurtz owns 57% of LaPolla.

	Annual Growth	12/10	12/11	12/12	12/13	12/14
Sales ($ mil.)	0.6%	70.5	86.2	70.4	71.2	72.1
Net income ($ mil.)	–	2.1	(3.5)	(4.4)	(2.0)	(3.7)
Market value ($ mil.)	(9.1%)	71.9	59.9	21.6	89.9	49.1
Employees	(5.9%)	79	88	71	73	62

LAREDO PETROLEUM HOLDINGS INC.
NYSE: LPI

15 W. Sixth St. Ste. 1800
Tulsa OK 74119
Phone: 918-513-4570
Fax: 918-513-4571
Web: www.laredopetro.com

CEO: Randy A Foutch
CFO: –
HR: –
FYE: December 31
Type: Public

Only in Oklahoma would a company named Laredo Petroleum be based in Tulsa. Laredo Petroleum drills for oil and natural gas across 338000 net acres in the abundant Wolfberry plan in the Permian Basin in West Texas and Granite Wash in the Anadarko Basin located along the Texas Panhandle and into western Oklahoma. The company reported proved reserves of 137000 million barrels of oil equivalent for the first six months of 2011 and has interests in about 1000 gross producing wells. It generated 52% of sales from oil and 47% from gas in 2010. Laredo Petroleum is owned by investment firm Warburg Pincus. It filed an initial public offering in August 2011 and went public ($298 million in proceeds) in December.

LARKIN COMMUNITY HOSPITAL INC.

7031 SW 62ND AVE
SOUTH MIAMI, FL 331434701
Phone: 305-284-7500
Fax: –
Web: www.larkinhospital.com

CEO: –
CFO: Estephany Giraldo
HR: –
FYE: December 31
Type: Private

Larkin Community Hospital may be small but it doesn't skimp on its array of health care services. The 110-bed hospital provides general medical and surgical services to the sun-drenched residents of the Miami-Dade County area of Florida. Larkin Community Hospital offers more than 40 specialties including diagnostic radiology intensive care arthritis services an inpatient psychiatric ward surgery cardiovascular care and rehabilitation (including physical occupational and speech therapy). President and CEO Jack Michel owns the health care facility.

	Annual Growth	12/01	12/02	12/03	12/04	12/12
Sales ($ mil.)	–	–	(1,456.1)	33.8	37.3	74.4
Net income ($ mil.)	(25.4%)	–	–	32.1	2.5	2.3
Market value ($ mil.)	–	–	–	–	–	–
Employees	–	–	–	–	–	525

LAS VEGAS SANDS CORP

NYS: LVS

3355 Las Vegas Boulevard South
Las Vegas, NV 89109
Phone: 702 414-1000
Fax: –
Web: www.lasvegassands.com

CEO: Sheldon G. Adelson
CFO: –
HR: Dave Newton
FYE: December 31
Type: Public

Las Vegas Sands brings a touch of Venice to the US and China. Replete with gondoliers and a replica of the Rialto Bridge the company's Venetian Las Vegas Hotel Resort & Casino offers a 120000-sq.-ft. casino and a 4000-suite hotel as well as a shopping dining and entertainment complex. Through its majority-owned Sands China subsidiary the firm operates The Venetian Macau on the Cotai Strip (the Chinese equivalent of the Las Vegas Strip) as well as two other properties in Macao. Properties also include the Marina Bay Sands in Singapore and the partially-owned Sands Bethlehem in Bethlehem Pennsylvania.

	Annual Growth	12/10	12/11	12/12	12/13	12/14
Sales ($ mil.)	20.8%	6,853.2	9,410.7	11,131.1	13,769.9	14,583.8
Net income ($ mil.)	47.5%	599.4	1,560.1	1,524.1	2,306.0	2,840.6
Market value ($ mil.)	6.1%	36,680.0	34,109.6	36,847.6	62,958.6	46,426.7
Employees	9.3%	34,000	40,000	46,000	48,500	48,500

LAS VEGAS VALLEY WATER DISTRICT

1001 S. Valley View Blvd.
Las Vegas NV 89153
Phone: 702-870-2011
Fax: 702-258-3900
Web: www.lvvwd.com

CEO: –
CFO: –
HR: –
FYE: June 30
Type: Government Agency

If casinos can bloom in the desert why can't water flow? It can thanks to the Las Vegas Valley Water District (LVVWD) which provides water to some one million residents living in one of the driest places in the US. In addition to Las Vegas the LVVWD serves residents of Blue Diamond Coyote Springs Jean Kyle Canyon Laughlin Searchlight and other parts of Clark County in Southern Nevada. The district delivers water to customers through some 4500 miles of water transmission pipeline connected to 65 pumping stations 76 wells and 68 reservoirs and tanks. (Its tanks and reservoirs have the capacity to store more than 900 million gallons.) The LVVWD sources 90% of its water to the Colorado River.

LASALLE HOTEL PROPERTIES

NYS: LHO

7550 Wisconsin Avenue, 10th Floor
Bethesda, MD 20814
Phone: 301 941-1500
Fax: 301 941-1553
Web: www.lasallehotels.com

CEO: Michael D. (Mike) Barnello
CFO: Bruce A. Riggins
HR: –
FYE: December 31
Type: Public

LaSalle Hotel Properties is a self-administered and self-managed real estate investment trust (REIT) that invests in renovates and leases full-service luxury hotels in the US. It owns more than 45 properties in 10 states and the District of Columbia. LaSalle Hotel Properties' holdings which altogether boast about 11400 rooms are typically located in major urban markets near convention centers business districts and resorts. The properties are managed by outside hotel companies that operate under such names as Marriott Sheraton Hilton and Hyatt. LaSalle Hotel Properties became self-managing in 2001 after three years under the wing of Jones Lang LaSalle.

	Annual Growth	12/10	12/11	12/12	12/13	12/14
Sales ($ mil.)	16.6%	600.4	719.0	867.1	977.3	1,109.8
Net income ($ mil.)	222.8%	2.0	43.6	71.3	89.9	212.8
Market value ($ mil.)	11.3%	2,978.6	2,731.5	2,864.6	3,481.8	4,566.0
Employees	4.8%	29	31	33	36	35

LASALLE UNIVERSITY

1900 W OLNEY AVE
PHILADELPHIA, PA 191411199
Phone: 215-951-1000
Fax: –
Web: www.lasalle.edu

CEO: –
CFO: –
HR: Susan Rohanna
FYE: May 31
Type: Private

La Salle University is an independent Catholic institution of higher learning with an enrollment of more than 7000 students. It offers about 40 undergraduate majors and 15 minors as well as 15 graduate programs (including a doctoral program in Clinical Psychology) and about 40 certificate programs. The liberal arts university consists of three schools: arts and sciences business and nursing and health sciences plus a College of Professional and Continuing Studies. Nursing psychology education accounting and communications are among the school's most popular undergraduate areas of study.

	Annual Growth	05/10	05/11	05/12	05/13	05/14
Sales ($ mil.)	(0.6%)	–	134.0	132.6	131.0	131.5
Net income ($ mil.)	–	–	–	(0.6)	20.6	12.5
Market value ($ mil.)	–	–	–	–	–	–
Employees	–	–	–	–	–	900

LASERLOCK TECHNOLOGIES INC.

OTC: LLTI

837 Lindy Ln.
Bala Cynwyd PA 19004
Phone: 610-668-1952
Fax: 610-668-2771
Web: www.laserlocktech.com

CEO: Paul Donfried
CFO: Scott McPherson
HR: –
FYE: December 31
Type: Public

Willy Wonka could have used LaserLock Technologies to help ensure that each Golden Ticket was the genuine article. A development-stage company LaserLock plans to license an invisible ink to third parties that can be used to authenticate documents. The company's system is targeted to the gambling industry where uses could include verification of cashless tickets from slot machines and detection of counterfeit cards chips or dice. LaserLock has plans to raise additional capital and/or enter into strategic alliances or partnerships with other companies in order to do business.

LATHAM & WATKINS LLP

355 S. Grand Ave.
Los Angeles CA 90071-1560
Phone: 213-485-1234
Fax: 213-891-8763
Web: www.lw.com

CEO: –
CFO: –
HR: –
FYE: December 31
Type: Private - Partnershi

Latham & Watkins' founders Dana Latham and Paul Watkins flipped a coin in 1934 to determine which of their names would go first on the law firm's shingle. From that coin toss the firm has grown into one of the largest in the US and boasts more than 2000 lawyers in about 30 offices around the world from Europe to Asia. Latham & Watkins organizes its practices into five main areas: corporate; environment land and resources; finance; litigation; and tax. The firm has counted companies such as Amgen Time Warner Inc. and Morgan Stanley among its clients.

LATINWORKS MARKETING INC.

206 E. 9th St.
Austin TX 78701
Phone: 512-479-6200
Fax: 512-479-6024
Web: www.latinworks.com

CEO: Manny Flores
CFO: –
HR: –
FYE: December 31
Type: Private

Sometimes just plain advertising works and sometimes you need LatinWorks. LatinWorks Marketing provides advertising and marketing services to FORTUNE 1000 clients seeking to tap into the growing Hispanic market. Its portfolio includes TV print and digital work for such brands as Anheuser-Busch Mars ESPN and Burger King. Renouncing stereotypes in its creative work the agency has instead based its strategic development process on an understanding of how generational differences influence the Hispanic worldview — from acculturation through assimilation. The Diversified Agency Services unit of Omnicom Group the world's largest media services conglomerate is an investor in LatinWorks.

LATTICE INC

NBB: LTTC

7150 N. Park Drive
Pennsauken, NJ 08109
Phone: 856 910-1166
Fax: 856 910-1811
Web: www.latticeincorporated.com

CEO: Paul Burgess
CFO: Joe Noto
HR: –
FYE: December 31
Type: Public

Government IT contractor Lattice has constructed a diverse product framework. The company provides data management applications Internet server technology and information systems for federal agencies. Deriving the majority of its revenue from Dept. of Defense it develops applications related to business management geographic information systems (GIS) Web services and geospatial systems. In addition the company's Nexus Call Control System provides technology that allows correctional facilities to monitor and control inmate collect-only phone calls. Lattice which began in the 1970s as a telephone services company also offers direct telecom services to correctional facilities.

	Annual Growth	12/10	12/11	12/12	12/13	12/14
Sales ($ mil.)	(9.9%)	13.5	11.4	10.8	8.3	8.9
Net income ($ mil.)	–	(1.4)	(6.1)	(0.6)	(1.0)	(1.8)
Market value ($ mil.)	(6.3%)	7.0	6.5	4.3	8.9	5.4
Employees	(15.0%)	44	44	37	26	23

LATTICE SEMICONDUCTOR CORP.

NMS: LSCC

111 SW Fifth Ave, Suite 700
Portland, OR 97204
Phone: 503 268-8000
Fax: 503 268 8347
Web: www.latticesemi.com

CEO: Darin G. Billerbeck
CFO: Joe Bedewi
HR: –
FYE: January 03
Type: Public

The garden that grows on this Lattice is made up of silicon. Lattice Semiconductor is a top developer of programmable logic devices (PLDs). Lattice also makes low-density logic devices and sells software used to customize its chips which are used in communications computing industrial military consumer and automotive applications. The fabless chipmaker has expanded into the market for field-programmable gate arrays (FPGAs) another type of programmable chip. The majority of sales come from Asia.

	Annual Growth	01/11*	12/11	12/12	12/13*	01/15
Sales ($ mil.)	5.3%	297.8	318.4	279.3	332.5	366.1
Net income ($ mil.)	(3.9%)	57.1	78.2	(29.6)	22.3	48.6
Market value ($ mil.)	3.3%	710.8	696.7	449.2	629.8	810.5
Employees	1.1%	749	852	739	783	784

*Fiscal year change

LAUREN ENGINEERS & CONSTRUCTORS INC.

901 S 1ST ST
ABILENE, TX 796021502
Phone: 325-670-9660
Fax: –
Web: www.laurenec.com

CEO: C. Cleve Whitener
CFO: Tom Modisett
HR: –
FYE: December 31
Type: Private

Lauren Engineers & Constructors is a contractor that targets the power chemical special metals and oil refining industries. In addition to its core engineering procurement and construction capabilities the company offers fabrication project management and mechanical and electrical maintenance services. With offices in Georgia Tennessee and Texas Lauren Engineers & Constructors serves about 25 states. It also operates in Canada with a presence in Calgary. Some of its power and chemical customers include Flying J Florida Power & Light General Electric Company and Procter & Gamble. The company was originally established in 1984 as a subsidiary of Comstock Mechanical.

	Annual Growth	12/09	12/10	12/11	12/12	12/13
Sales ($ mil.)	0.1%	–	162.7	249.9	129.2	163.3
Net income ($ mil.)	–	–	–	(0.1)	(13.7)	(3.4)
Market value ($ mil.)	–	–	–	–	–	–
Employees	–	–	–	–	–	1,000

LAUREN MANUFACTURING COMPANY

2228 Reiser Ave. SE
New Philadelphia OH 44663
Phone: 330-339-3373
Fax: 330-339-1515
Web: www.lauren.com

CEO: Kevin E Gray
CFO: –
HR: –
FYE: December 31
Type: Private

Extruding confidence in the face of difficult environments Lauren Manufacturing lets its products seal the deal. The custom extrusion company uses organic silicone and specialty polymer materials (butyl rubber and neoprene for example) to mold products such as weather stripping high performance (UV and ozone resistant) synthetic rubber sponges automotive gaskets and seals. Supplying industries from vehicle and transportation to building and construction and container manufacturers its 1000-plus customers include General Motors Harley-Davidson IBM and Pella Windows. Lauren International acts as parent company of Lauren Manufacturing and divisions Edgetech Lauren AgriSystems and LMI Custom Mixing.

LAURENS COUNTY HEALTH CARE SYSTEM

22725 Hwy. 76 East
Clinton SC 29325
Phone: 864-833-9100
Fax: 864-833-9142
Web: www.lchcs.org

CEO: Michael C Riordan
CFO: –
HR: –
FYE: October 31
Type: Government-owned

It may be on the small side but that doesn't keep Laurens County Health Care System from keeping Lauren County South Carolina's residents hearty and hale. Operating as Laurens County Hospital the 90-bed facility provides general acute care medical services as well as specialty care for diabetes breast cancer emergency medicine pediatrics and wound care. Laurens County Health Care System founded in 1990 also provides a range of community wellness programs and classes on subjects such as smoking cessation and prenatal care. The hospital's 14-bed skilled nursing facility administers rehabilitation care to patients in recovery from accident or illness.

LAWRENCE & MEMORIAL HOSPITAL INC.

365 MONTAUK AVE
NEW LONDON, CT 063204769
Phone: 860-442-0711
Fax: –
Web: www.lmhospital.org

CEO: –
CFO: –
HR: Donna Epps
FYE: September 30
Type: Private

Lawrence & Memorial Hospital (L&M) connects residents of Connecticut with health care whether they're near the Rhode Island border or enjoying the Connecticut River. The not-for-profit hospital founded in 1912 provides services to a 10-town region on the Connecticut shoreline and neighboring areas in the Northeast. L&M has roughly 280 beds and provides general acute care including medical surgical rehabilitative pediatric psychiatric and obstetrical services. The hospital also runs about a dozen community physician practices and specialty clinics.

	Annual Growth	09/07	09/08	09/09	09/10	09/13
Sales ($ mil.)	(22.5%)	–	1,125.1	293.3	324.5	315.4
Net income ($ mil.)	–	–	–	(11.7)	8.3	10.8
Market value ($ mil.)	–	–	–	–	–	–
Employees	–	–	–	–	–	2,200

LAWSON PRODUCTS, INC. NMS: LAWS

8770 W. Bryn Mawr Avenue, Suite 900
Chicago, IL 60631
Phone: 773 304-5050
Fax: –
Web: www.lawsonproducts.com

CEO: Michael G. DeCata
CFO: Ronald J. (Ron) Knutson
HR: Lawrence Krema
FYE: December 31
Type: Public

Lawson Products' stock in trade may sound boring to some but to manufacturers it's positively riveting. The company offers more than 4500 different MRO (maintenance repair and overhaul) items — in addition to rivets screws and nuts — from more than 2000 suppliers. It also manufactures sells and distributes specialized component and production parts to OEMs in the automotive appliance aerospace construction oil and gas and transportation markets. Sales are mainly generated in the US via 1100 independent sales agents and its website and catalogs.

	Annual Growth	12/10	12/11	12/12	12/13	12/14
Sales ($ mil.)	(2.5%)	316.8	315.0	290.5	269.5	285.7
Net income ($ mil.)	–	–	6.9	(4.6)	(62.6)	(5.1)	(4.4)
Market value ($ mil.)	1.8%	216.7	134.3	86.2	106.7	232.6
Employees	12.9%	930	950	1,550	1,540	1,510

LAYNE CHRISTENSEN CO. NMS: LAYN

1800 Hughes Landing Blvd. Ste. 800
The Woodlands, TX 77380
Phone: 281 475-2600
Fax: 281 475-2733
Web: www.layne.com

CEO: Michael J. (Mike) Caliel
CFO: Andrew Atchison
HR: Robin Cheng
FYE: January 31
Type: Public

Layne Christensen cuts its way through the upper crust. The company provides drilling and construction services related to water wastewater treatment and mineral exploration. Its clients include public and private water utilities industrial companies mining firms and heavy civil construction contractors. The group has operations throughout North America and in Africa Australia Europe and Brazil. Layne Christensen's water and wastewater operations account for about three-fourths of total sales while its mineral exploration operations comprise most of the rest. The Energy Division sold its exploration and production assets in 2012. Layne Christensen has some 100 sales and operations offices worldwide.

	Annual Growth	01/11	01/12	01/13	01/14	01/15
Sales ($ mil.)	(6.1%)	1,025.7	1,133.1	1,075.6	859.3	797.6
Net income ($ mil.)	–	30.0	(56.1)	(36.7)	(128.6)	(110.2)
Market value ($ mil.)	(28.9%)	635.4	467.6	456.1	341.2	162.8
Employees	(6.4%)	4,400	4,600	4,600	4,100	3,380

LCA-VISION INC. NMS: LCAV

7840 Montgomery Road
Cincinnati, OH 45236
Phone: 513 792-9292
Fax: 513 792-5620
Web: www.lca-vision.com

CEO: Craig Joffe
CFO: –
HR: –
FYE: December 31
Type: Public

LCA-Vision thinks its services are a sight better than glasses. The company provides laser vision correction procedures at about 55 Lasik"Plus" freestanding facilities. LCA-Vision's facilities treat nearsightedness farsightedness and astigmatism primarily using laser-assisted in situ keratomileusis (LASIK) which reshapes the cornea with a computer-guided excimer laser. Additionally the company's centers offer photorefractive keratectomy (PRK) and other corrective procedures. LCA-Vision operates through centers located in major cities across North America.

	Annual Growth	12/08	12/09	12/10	12/11	12/12
Sales ($ mil.)	(16.1%)	205.2	129.2	99.8	103.0	101.5
Net income ($ mil.)	–	(6.6)	(33.2)	(20.6)	(6.2)	(8.5)
Market value ($ mil.)	(8.7%)	78.3	97.5	109.5	55.2	54.3
Employees	(9.5%)	568	450	365	380	381

LCNB CORP NAS: LCNB

2 North Broadway
Lebanon, OH 45036
Phone: 513 932-1414
Fax: –
Web: www.lcnb.com

CEO: Steve P. Foster
CFO: Robert C. Haines
HR: –
FYE: December 31
Type: Public

It just makes cents that LCNB counts bucks in the Buckeye State. The firm is the holding company for LCNB National Bank which operates some 36 offices across southwestern Ohio. The bank serves about 10 Ohio counties offering personal and commercial banking services. such as checking and savings accounts money markets IRAs and CDs. Residential mortgages account for nearly half of the company's loan book. Other offerings include commercial mortgages consumer loans including credit cards and business loans. It also provides trust services. LCNB's subsidiary Dakin Insurance Agency sells commercial and personal property/casualty insurance.

	Annual Growth	12/10	12/11	12/12	12/13	12/14
Assets ($ mil.)	9.9%	760.1	791.6	788.6	932.3	1,108.1
Net income ($ mil.)	1.3%	9.4	8.1	8.3	8.8	9.9
Market value ($ mil.)	6.0%	111.3	120.6	127.6	166.4	140.3
Employees	4.9%	230	235	217	248	278

LDI LTD. LLC

54 Monument Cir. Ste. 800
Indianapolis IN 46204-2949
Phone: 317-237-5400
Fax: 317-237-3444
Web: www.ldiltd.com

CEO: Ja Lacy
CFO: Jon Black
HR: –
FYE: December 31
Type: Private

At LDI the "D" could stand for "diversified." The investment company has interests in firms that deal in clothing motorcycle parts logistics and distribution. Focusing on long-term investments it typically is a cash buyer of controlling stakes in companies and holds onto investments for an average of more than 15 years. LDI's holdings include Tucker Rocky a distributor of aftermarket parts apparel and accessories for the power sports industry. It sells more than 100000 items for street and off-road motorcycles and all-terrain vehicles internationally through seven distribution centers across the US. Founded in 1912 as Corrugated-Fibre Box Company LDI is owned by the Lacy family as it always has been.

LDR HOLDING CORP
NMS: LDRH

13785 Research Boulevard, Suite 200
Austin, TX 78750
Phone: 512 344-3333
Fax: –
Web: www.ldrholding.com

CEO: Christophe Lavigne
CFO: Robert E. McNamara
HR: –
FYE: December 31
Type: Public

LDR Holdings is at the spinal frontier of medical devices. The company makes cervical disc replacements used in spinal implant surgeries. Its VerteBRIDGE fusion device is affixed to discs without using screws and its Mobi-C non-fusion device is the only FDA approved implant for one- and two-level cervical disc surgeries. Mobi-C received FDA approval in 2013. LDR Holdings also makes and sells traditional fusion products under the brands C-Plate Easyspine MC+ ROI and SpineTune. Its products are sold in more than 25 countries but the US accounts for about 70% of sales. Founded in France in 2000 LDR Holdings went public in 2013 raising $75 million in its IPO which it will use to launch Mobi-C in the US.

	Annual Growth	12/10	12/11	12/12	12/13	12/14
Sales ($ mil.)	–	0.0	78.0	90.9	111.6	141.3
Net income ($ mil.)	–	0.0	(1.8)	(9.7)	(27.9)	(11.0)
Market value ($ mil.)	–	–	–	–	624.4	867.3
Employees	24.8%	–	–	290	323	452

LE MOYNE COLLEGE

1419 SALT SPRINGS RD
SYRACUSE, NY 132141301
Phone: 315-445-4100
Fax: –
Web: www.lemoyne.edu

CEO: –
CFO: –
HR: –
FYE: May 31
Type: Private

Le Moyne College offers more than 700 courses leading to Bachelor of Arts or Bachelor of Science degrees in 24 different majors. A Jesuit Catholic school Le Moyne has approximately 2200 undergraduate students and 700 students in the graduate program which offers degrees in business administration and education. It has a 13-1 ratio of students to faculty. Le Moyne was founded in 1946.

	Annual Growth	05/09	05/10	05/11	05/12	05/13
Sales ($ mil.)	2.9%	–	99.4	102.2	108.6	108.3
Net income ($ mil.)	(18.9%)	–	–	10.3	9.6	6.7
Market value ($ mil.)	–	–	–	–	–	–
Employees	–	–	–	–	–	500

LEAP WIRELESS INTERNATIONAL INC
NMS: LEAP

5887 Copley Drive
San Diego, CA 92111
Phone: 858 882-6000
Fax: –
Web: www.leapwireless.com

CEO: S Douglas Hutcheson
CFO: R Perley McBride
HR: –
FYE: December 31
Type: Public

Leap Wireless wants to hurdle the competition. Through its Cricket Communications subsidiary the company provides wireless voice and data services to some 5.3 million customers (down from 6 million in 2012) in 48 US states and the District of Columbia. It primarily targets the youth and minority markets with no-contract flexible payment plans that are a key component of its marketing message. Leap's service features unlimited flat-rate local calling a prepaid roaming option multimedia music and wireless data as well as mobile Web access through its Cricket Broadband service. The company makes sales through its chain of 195 retail locations via partnerships with distributors and resellers and on the Internet. It is being acquired by AT&T.

	Annual Growth	12/08	12/09	12/10	12/11	12/12
Sales ($ mil.)	12.5%	1,958.9	2,383.2	2,697.2	3,071.1	3,142.3
Net income ($ mil.)	–	(147.8)	(238.0)	(785.1)	(317.7)	(187.3)
Market value ($ mil.)	(29.5%)	2,129.5	1,389.9	970.9	735.7	526.6
Employees	(1.0%)	3,423	4,202	4,362	3,891	3,292

LEAPFROG ENTERPRISES INC
NYS: LF

6401 Hollis Street, Suite 100
Emeryville, CA 94608-1463
Phone: 510 420-5000
Fax: –
Web: www.leapfroginvestor.com

CEO: John Barbour
CFO: Raymond L Arthur
HR: Shannon Walden
FYE: March 31
Type: Public

If putting pen to interactive paper helps your little Einstein learn LeapFrog Enterprises wants to spend some time with your pint-sized genius. The toy maker develops interactive reading systems educational games books and learning toys in five languages covering subjects from math to music. Its bestselling brands include LeapPad Leapster LeapBand Learning Path and Tag. Products are sold to retailers distributors and schools worldwide as well as to consumers via the company's website. LeapFrog's target market is infants and children through age nine. Former vice chairman and CEO Michael Wood founded LeapFrog in 1995 because he felt the toy market offered nothing to help his 3-year-old learn phonics. Vtech Holdings agreed to buy LeapFrog in February 2016 for $72 million.

	Annual Growth	12/11	12/12	12/13*	03/14	03/15
Sales ($ mil.)	(7.1%)	455.1	581.3	553.6	56.9	339.1
Net income ($ mil.)	–	19.9	86.5	84.0	(11.8)	(218.8)
Market value ($ mil.)	(21.0%)	394.0	608.2	559.6	528.6	153.6
Employees	1.5%	494	552	579	–	524

*Fiscal year change

LEAR CORP.
NYS: LEA

21557 Telegraph Road
Southfield, MI 48033
Phone: 248 447-1500
Fax: 248 447-5250
Web: www.lear.com

CEO: Matthew J. Simoncini
CFO: Jeffrey H. Vanneste
HR: Patricia (Pat) Krinock
FYE: December 31
Type: Public

Lear doesn't take a back seat to anyone when it comes to manufacturing automotive seats. The company's Seating business by far its most lucrative segment is a leader in the global market for manufacturing car seat systems and their components. The company's Electrical Power Management Systems (EPMS) segment produces automotive electronics including the manufacture of wire harnesses junction boxes terminals and connectors and body control modules. It operates from 219 facilities in 34 countries. Its largest customers include BMW Ford and General Motors Fiat and Volkswagen. Lear traces its history back to 1917 when it was founded in Detroit as American Metal Products.

	Annual Growth	12/11	12/12	12/13	12/14	12/15
Sales ($ mil.)	6.5%	14,156.5	14,567.0	16,234.0	17,727.3	18,211.4
Net income ($ mil.)	8.4%	540.7	1,282.8	431.4	672.4	745.5
Market value ($ mil.)	32.5%	2,963.7	3,487.9	6,029.4	7,303.5	9,146.4
Employees	8.6%	97,800	113,400	122,300	125,200	136,200

LEARJET INC.

1 Learjet Way
Wichita KS 67209
Phone: 316-946-2000
Fax: 316-946-2200
Web: www.learjet.com

CEO: –
CFO: Sylvie Desjardins
HR: Brenda Wiechman
FYE: January 31
Type: Subsidiary

A pioneer in the aerospace industry Learjet Inc. builds high-performance business jets — the limos of the sky. The company has produced more than 2000 aircraft at its Wichita Kansas plant since its first jet rolled off the assembly line in 1964. Current Learjet models — light business aircraft including the 40 XR 45 XR 60 XR and 85 — tout superior cruise velocities the highest operating ceilings ascent rates and operating maximums and competitive operating costs. In addition to private businesses Learjet occasionally wins work with the US Air Force. The company has operated as a subsidiary of Canada's Bombardier since 1990.

LEARNING TREE INTERNATIONAL INC   NBB: LTRE

1831 Micheal Faraday Dr.
Reston, VA 20190
Phone: 703 709-9119
Fax: –
Web: www.learningtree.com

CEO: Richard A Spires
CFO: Jamie Donelan
HR: –
FYE: October 02
Type: Public

This tree of knowledge won't trick you into eating evil apples. It will however further your knowledge of information. Information technology that is. The Learning Tree offers more than 180 courses including professional certification programs to IT managers in corporations and government agencies. The bulk of the company's course library focuses on IT topics such as Web development programming languages network security and operating systems. Learning Tree has a growing list of management training offerings as well with courses in business skills leadership development and project management. It offers its classes in Japan Europe and North America and online.

	Annual Growth	09/11	09/12	09/13*	10/14	10/15
Sales ($ mil.)	(8.2%)	133.8	129.0	116.8	118.2	94.9
Net income ($ mil.)	–	3.2	(11.9)	(8.7)	0.0	(12.6)
Market value ($ mil.)	(35.7%)	97.7	67.3	48.0	30.9	16.7
Employees	(3.3%)	1,084	1,060	972	1,006	948

*Fiscal year change

LEBHAR-FRIEDMAN INC.

425 Park Ave.
New York NY 10022
Phone: 212-756-5000
Fax: 212-756-5290
Web: www.lf.com

CEO: –
CFO: Daniel J Mills
HR: –
FYE: December 31
Type: Private

This company knows a thing or two about the world of five and dimes. Lebhar-Friedman publishes industry-specific content for the retail market. Its two flagship brands include trade magazines Chain Store Age and Drug Store News and their related websites. It also offers research and analysis through Retailing Today which publishes eight weekly e-newsletters. In addition the company operates RetailNet.com a database of articles reports and digital information on the various sectors of the retail market including apparel grocery drug store and home improvement. Lebhar-Friedman was founded in 1925 when Arnold Friedman and his partners Godfrey Lebhar and John Stern started Chain Store Age.

LEE COUNTY ELECTRIC COOPERATIVE INC.

4980 BAYLINE DR
FORT MYERS, FL 339173998
Phone: 800-599-2356
Fax: –
Web: www.lcec.net

CEO: Dennie Hamilton
CFO: Donald Schleicher
HR: Jane Hillabrant
FYE: December 31
Type: Private

If you are a Floridian who is a really early riser or a night owl Lee County Electric Cooperative (LCEC) may help light your way. The electric cooperative provides power to more than 198880 residential and commercial customers across five counties in southwestern Florida (Lee County and parts of Collier Hendry Charlotte and Broward counties. The member-owned non-profit electric utility operates more than 8000 miles of transmission and distribution lines and more than 20 substations. Tampa-based Seminole Electric Cooperative serves as LCEC's wholesale power supplier.

	Annual Growth	12/09	12/10	12/11	12/12	12/13
Sales ($ mil.)	0.3%	–	–	–	404.5	405.9
Net income ($ mil.)	(12.7%)	–	–	–	2.5	2.2
Market value ($ mil.)	–	–	–	–	–	–
Employees	–	–	–	–	–	400

LEE ENTERPRISES, INC.   NYS: LEE

201 N. Harrison Street, Suite 600
Davenport, IA 52801
Phone: 563 383-2100
Fax: –
Web: www.lee.net

CEO: Kevin D. Mowbray
CFO: Ronald A Mayo
HR: Astrid Garcia
FYE: September 27
Type: Public

This Lee commands an army of newspapers. Lee Enterprises owns or has stakes in about 50 daily newspapers and nearly 300 weekly papers and niche publications. Its papers serve primarily small and midsized markets in some 20 states. Its portfolio is anchored by the St. Louis Post Dispatch; it also owns 50% of Madison Newspapers publisher of the Wisconsin State Journal. The eighth-largest newspaper publisher in the US Lee serves a daily circulation of more than 1.3 million readers. It additionally operates several websites in conjunction with its newspapers and it has commercial printing facilities. Lloyd Schermer and his family have nearly 30% voting control of the firm which filed for bankruptcy in 2011.

	Annual Growth	09/11	09/12	09/13	09/14	09/15
Sales ($ mil.)	(3.8%)	756.1	710.5	674.7	656.7	648.5
Net income ($ mil.)	–	(146.9)	(16.7)	(78.3)	6.8	23.3
Market value ($ mil.)	20.5%	45.9	80.9	147.6	183.2	96.8
Employees	(5.7%)	5,700	5,200	4,600	4,500	4,500

LEE HECHT HARRISON LLC

50 Tice Blvd.
Woodcliff Lake NJ 07677
Phone: 201-930-9333
Fax: 201-307-0878
Web: www.lhh.com

CEO: –
CFO: Karine Storm
HR: –
FYE: December 31
Type: Subsidiary

Lee Hecht Harrison a unit of the world's #1 employment services firm Adecco provides career and leadership consulting through its more than 270 offices covering 60 countries around the globe. The company offers services in areas such as career and leadership development outplacement and executive coaching. Clients include organizations individuals and recruiters. It additionally offers clients the opportunity to access career information from home. Lee Hecht Harrison sponsors events featuring experts on human resources topics. The company was founded in 1974 and resides within its parent company's Human Capital Solutions division.

LEE LEWIS CONSTRUCTION INC.

7810 ORLANDO AVE
LUBBOCK, TX 794231942
Phone: 806-797-8400
Fax: –
Web: www.leelewis.com

CEO: Lee Lewis
CFO: –
HR: –
FYE: June 30
Type: Private

General builder Lee Lewis Construction has waltzed across Texas and beyond to keep in step with the top US contractors. The company provides construction-related services and construction management for commercial institutional and industrial projects. Among its projects is the Garland ISD Special Events Center in Garland Texas; it also worked on the Grand Floridian Resort at Walt Disney World. The company earns much of its revenue from projects for Texas school systems. Projects for hometown neighbor Texas Tech University have generated a significant portion of the company's business. CEO Lee Lewis founded the company in 1976.

	Annual Growth	06/03	06/04	06/05	06/06	06/09
Sales ($ mil.)	10.6%	–	138.8	176.5	245.1	229.5
Net income ($ mil.)	29.0%	–	–	2.3	4.3	6.3
Market value ($ mil.)	–	–	–	–	–	–
Employees	–	–	–	–	–	200

LEE UNIVERSITY

1120 N OCOEE ST STE 102
CLEVELAND, TN 373114475
Phone: 423-614-8000
Fax: –
Web: www.leeuniversity.edu

CEO: –
CFO: –
HR: –
FYE: June 30
Type: Private

Lee University is a Christian liberal arts college located in southeastern Tennessee. Boasting an enrollment of more than 4250 students the university offers academic programs at both baccalaureate and master's levels. Religion courses are a requirement of each student. Lee University is owned and operated by the Church of God. It was founded in 1918.

	Annual Growth	06/07	06/08	06/09	06/10	06/11
Sales ($ mil.)	–	–	–	0.0	74.8	75.2
Net income ($ mil.)	1576.6%	–	–	0.0	9.7	4.6
Market value ($ mil.)	–	–	–	–	–	–
Employees	–	–	–	–	–	635

LEGACY EMANUEL HOSPITAL & HEALTH CENTER

2801 N GANTENBEIN AVE
PORTLAND, OR 972271623
Phone: 503-413-2200
Fax: –
Web: www.legacyhealth.org

CEO: George J Brown
CFO: –
HR: –
FYE: March 31
Type: Private

Legacy Emanuel Hospital and Health Center part of the Legacy Health System provides acute and specialized health care to residents of Portland Oregon and surrounding communities. The 420-bed teaching hospital's operations include centers devoted to trauma treatment burn care oncology birthing neurosurgery orthopedics and cardiology. It also houses a pediatric hospital and operates the region's Life Flight Network service which is owned by a consortium of local hospitals. Legacy Emanuel's emergency department handles more than 15600 visits every year.

	Annual Growth	03/09	03/10	03/12	03/13	03/14
Sales ($ mil.)	3.2%	–	573.2	571.3	566.1	649.8
Net income ($ mil.)	–	–	–	(6.4)	6.4	31.0
Market value ($ mil.)	–	–	–	–	–	–
Employees	–	–	–	–	–	3,619

LEGACY HEALTH

1919 NW LOVEJOY ST
PORTLAND, OR 972091503
Phone: 503-415-5600
Fax: –
Web: www.legacyhealth.org

CEO: George J. Brown
CFO: –
HR: Sonya Steves
FYE: March 31
Type: Private

Legacy Health System strives to create a legacy of positive health in the Portland/Vancouver metropolitan area. A not-for-profit provider of health care services in Oregon and Washington the health system operates half a dozen hospitals including Legacy Emanuel Hospital and Legacy Good Samaritan Hospital all founded by a variety of secular organizations. Legacy Health has more than 1100 total beds and its facilities provide such services as acute and critical care behavioral health and outpatient and health education programs. It also operates home health hospice and research facilities; emergency transportation helicopters; and a number of regional clinics and labs.

	Annual Growth	03/09	03/10*	08/10*	03/12	03/14
Sales ($ mil.)	(38.1%)	–	1,249.5	1,249.5	1,326.4	183.1
Net income ($ mil.)	(52.8%)	–	–	192.6	(0.6)	9.5
Market value ($ mil.)	–	–	–	–	–	–
Employees	–	–	–	–	–	8,000

*Fiscal year change

LEGACY PARTNERS INC.

4000 E. 3rd Ave. Ste. 600
Foster City CA 94404-4805
Phone: 650-571-2200
Fax: 650-571-2222
Web: www.legacypartners.com

CEO: Barry S Diraimondo
CFO: –
HR: –
FYE: December 31
Type: Private

Legacy Partners specializes in the acquisition development and management of commercial and residential real estate in the western US. Legacy Partners manages more than 35 million sq. ft. of commercial space as well as some 150 apartment communities. All told the firm's real estate holdings are valued at more than $7 billion. In addition to investment and asset management Legacy Partners provides property management disposition services design and construction technology and marketing and leasing services. The firm has offices in California Texas Colorado and Washington. Founded by Lincoln Property in 1972 Legacy was spun off in 1998.

LEGACY RESERVES LP   NMS: LGCY

303 W. Wall, Suite 1800
Midland, TX 79701
Phone: 432 689-5200
Fax: –
Web: www.legacylp.com

CEO: Paul T Horne
CFO: –
HR: –
FYE: December 31
Type: Public

Legacy Reserves has its sights set on creating its very own prosperous legacy. The independent oil and gas company explores for oil and gas deposits in the Permian Basin of West Texas and southeast New Mexico and exploits those resources. In 2013 Legacy Reserves had proved reserves of 87.6 million barrels of oil equivalent (70% oil and natural gas liquids; 85% proved developed). The company owns interests in producing oil and natural gas properties in 664 fields in the Permian Basin Texas Panhandle Wyoming North Dakota Montana Oklahoma and several other states. In 2013 it had 664 fields and 8071 gross productive wells of which 3734 were operated and 4337 non-operated.

	Annual Growth	12/10	12/11	12/12	12/13	12/14
Sales ($ mil.)	25.2%	216.4	336.9	346.5	485.5	532.3
Net income ($ mil.)	–	10.8	72.1	68.6	(35.3)	(283.6)
Market value ($ mil.)	(20.6%)	1,982.0	1,948.9	1,642.5	1,943.3	788.8
Employees	21.0%	140	163	206	254	300

LEGACYTEXAS FINANCIAL GROUP INC   NMS: LTXB

5851 Legacy Circle
Plano, TX 75024
Phone: 972 578-5000
Fax: –
Web: www.viewpointfinancialgroup.com

CEO: Kevin J. Hanigan
CFO: Kari J Anderson
HR: –
FYE: December 31
Type: Public

With its eye on the Lone Star State LegacyTexas Financial (formerly ViewPoint Financial) provides retail and commercial banking through its LegacyTexas Bank subsidiary which operates about 50 branches located mostly in the Dallas/Fort Worth area. LegacyTexas offers standard deposit products such as checking and savings accounts and CDs and uses deposit funds to originate primarily real estate loans: Commercial Real Estate loans account for nearly 50% of its lending portfolio while consumer real estate loans make up another nearly 20%. Non-real estate commercial loans make up almost 30% of its loan portfolio.

	Annual Growth	12/10	12/11	12/12	12/13	12/14
Assets ($ mil.)	9.1%	2,942.0	3,180.6	3,663.1	3,525.2	4,164.1
Net income ($ mil.)	15.1%	17.8	26.3	35.2	31.7	31.3
Market value ($ mil.)	19.5%	467.8	520.6	837.9	1,098.4	954.4
Employees	(3.6%)	613	598	572	576	530

LEGALSHIELD
NYSE: PPD

1 Pre-Paid Way
Ada OK 74820
Phone: 580-436-1234
Fax: 580-421-6305
Web: www.legalshield.com

CEO: Jeff Bell
CFO: Steve Williamson
HR: –
FYE: December 31
Type: Private

LegalShield (formerly Pre-Paid Legal Services) wants to help see that justice is done. The company's membership plans which are similar to insurance give participants access to an independent network of attorneys and other legal professionals at provider law firms for a monthly fee. Covered services include IRS audit protection traffic violation defense and will preparation. LegalShieldhas about 1.5 million members mainly in the US but also in Canada. Private equity company MidOcean Partners acquired the company in 2011 and took it private.

LEGALZOOM.COM INC.

101 N. Brand Blvd. 11th Fl.
Glendale CA 91203
Phone: 323-962-8600
Fax: 323-962-8300
Web: www.legalzoom.com

CEO: –
CFO: –
HR: –
FYE: December 31
Type: Private

Where there's a will (or a trust or business entity) LegalZoom.com looks to find a virtual way. A provider of online legal services in the US LegalZoom.com offers small businesses and consumers access to a portfolio of self-help interactive legal documents which can be purchased on a transactional basis. Business clients use the company's services to set up legal entities (e.g. LLC Inc.) and apply for trademarks while consumers may set up wills living trusts powers of attorney and even file for divorce. For customers in need of legal advice the company offers access to a network of independent attorneys via subscription. Formed in 1999 LegalZoom filed to go public in mid-2012.

LEGEND OIL & GAS LTD
NBB: LOGL

555 Northpoint Center East, Suite 400
Alpharetta, GA 30022
Phone: 678 366-4587
Fax: –
Web: www.legendoilandgas.com

CEO: Andrew Reckles
CFO: Warren Binderman
HR: –
FYE: December 31
Type: Public

SIN Holdings owns and operates Senior-Inet.com (The Senior Information Network) a Web portal for senior citizens throughout the US seeking information about support services for senior citizens in ten cities in Colorado as well as for the City of Houston. Information categories include health housing senior centers travel services rehabilitation Alzheimer's hospice and adult day care and funeral services. James Vandeberg an attorney from Seattle acquired controlling interest in SIN Holdings from founder and former company president Steve Sinohui.

	Annual Growth	12/10	12/11	12/12	12/13	12/14
Sales ($ mil.)	155.1%	0.0	0.9	2.5	2.0	0.7
Net income ($ mil.)	–	(0.2)	(6.0)	(9.3)	(12.3)	(2.4)
Market value ($ mil.)	(82.0%)	384.5	195.1	11.3	6.6	0.4
Employees			4	5	4	

LEGG MASON, INC.
NYS: LM

100 International Drive
Baltimore, MD 21202
Phone: 410 539-0000
Fax: –
Web: www.leggmason.com

CEO: Joseph A. Sullivan
CFO: Peter H. (Pete) Nachtwey
HR: Brad Truffer
FYE: March 31
Type: Public

Legg Mason specializes in wealth management and mutual fund management. The financial services firm has several subsidiaries that offer asset management trust services and annuities to retail and institutional investors. Managing more than $700 billion in assets across 150 mutual funds under the Legg Mason Western Asset and Royce Funds banners the firm also manages closed-end funds and separately managed accounts. Legg Mason distributes its products through its own offices retirement plans and financial intermediaries as well as through an agreement with Morgan Stanley Smith Barney. The company mostly has offices in North America and the UK but also has a presence in more than 30 other countries.

	Annual Growth	03/11	03/12	03/13	03/14	03/15
Sales ($ mil.)	0.3%	2,784.3	2,662.6	2,612.7	2,741.8	2,819.1
Net income ($ mil.)	(1.7%)	253.9	220.8	(353.3)	284.8	237.1
Market value ($ mil.)	11.2%	4,022.9	3,113.3	3,583.7	5,466.4	6,153.1
Employees	(3.2%)	3,395	2,979	2,975	2,843	2,982

LEGGETT & PLATT, INC.
NYS: LEG

No. 1 Leggett Road
Carthage, MO 64836
Phone: 417 358-8131
Fax: –
Web: www.leggett.com

CEO: Karl G. Glassman
CFO: Matthew C. (Matt) Flanigan
HR: John Hale
FYE: December 31
Type: Public

That spring in your step after a good night's sleep may be there courtesy of Leggett & Platt (L&P) — the pioneer of steel coil bedsprings. Using primarily aluminum and steel the company makes residential furnishings (such as innersprings and bed frames) industrial materials (wire steel tubing) and specialized items (quilting machines automotive seating docking stations for electronic devices). It also makes commercial fixtures (shelves and work furniture). Customers include furniture retailers telecommunications firms and makers of automobiles construction products bedding and lawn gear. L&P operates about 130 manufacturing facilities in 18 countries.

	Annual Growth	12/10	12/11	12/12	12/13	12/14
Sales ($ mil.)	3.0%	3,359.1	3,636.0	3,720.8	3,746.0	3,782.3
Net income ($ mil.)	(13.7%)	176.6	153.3	248.2	197.3	98.0
Market value ($ mil.)	17.0%	3,136.3	3,174.9	3,750.9	4,263.5	5,871.7
Employees	0.0%	19,000	18,300	18,300	18,800	19,000

LEHIGH UNIVERSITY

27 MEMORIAL DR W UNIT 8
BETHLEHEM, PA 180153005
Phone: 610-758-3000
Fax: –
Web: www.lehigh.edu

CEO: –
CFO: –
HR: –
FYE: June 30
Type: Private

Lehigh University (LU) nestled in eastern Pennsylvania's Lehigh Valley offers about 90 undergraduate programs and majors at colleges of arts and sciences business and economics engineering and applied sciences and education. It also offers more than 40 masters and doctoral degree programs as well as certificate programs. Tuition is more than $40000 per year; more than half of students receive financial aid. LU has an enrollment of nearly 7000 undergraduate and graduate students. The university was founded in 1865 by entrepreneur and philanthropist Asa Packer.

	Annual Growth	06/06	06/07	06/12	06/13	06/14
Sales ($ mil.)	2.2%	–	316.3	423.5	357.7	367.3
Net income ($ mil.)	159.2%	–	–	23.3	114.6	156.4
Market value ($ mil.)	–	–	–	–	–	–
Employees	–	–	–	–	–	4,000

LEHIGH VALLEY HEALTH NETWORK INC.

1247 S CEDAR CREST BLVD
ALLENTOWN, PA 181036298
Phone: 610-402-8000
Fax: –
Web: www.lvhn.org

CEO: Brian Nester
CFO: Edward O'Dea
HR: Debby Patrick
FYE: June 30
Type: Private

Residents of the Lehigh Valley seeking medical care head uptown to facilities operated by the Lehigh Valley Health Network (LVHN). The not-for-profit health care provider operates through four full-service hospital campuses housing a total of about 1000 licensed beds. The medical center serves as a regional referral center for trauma and burn care and organ transplantation as well as specialty care in numerous areas such as cardiology women's health and pediatric surgery. LVHN also boasts a network of physician practices and community health centers as well as home health and hospice units.

	Annual Growth	06/09	06/10	06/11	06/12	06/14
Sales ($ mil.)	4.9%	–	1,399.3	1,524.5	1,620.5	1,694.2
Net income ($ mil.)	(10.6%)	–	–	314.2	(63.7)	224.8
Market value ($ mil.)	–	–	–	–	–	–
Employees	–	–	–	–	–	12,000

LEHMAN TRIKES USA INC.

125 Industrial Dr.
Spearfish SD 57783
Phone: 605-642-2111
Fax: 605-642-1184
Web: www.lehmantrikes.com

TSX VENTURE: LHT
CEO: Ken Hines
CFO: Timothy Kling
HR: –
FYE: November 30
Type: Private

Lehman Trikes proudly proclaims that it is the "leader of the three-world." Through its US subsidiary the company builds motorized tricycles by converting heavy-cruiser motorcycles manufactured by Honda Victory and Suzuki. In 2010 Lehman Trikes ended its supply agreement with Harley-Davidson a customer that represented approximately 80% of the tricycle maker's sales. The company also produces and wholesales the kits for do-it-yourselfers to convert traditional two-wheelers into motor trikes. In addition the company offers a line of accessories including custom wheels lights racks and running boards. The company's products are sold in the US and Canada through a dealer network located in the US.

LEIDOS HOLDINGS INC

11951 Freedom Drive
Reston, VA 20190
Phone: 571 526-6000
Fax: –
Web: www.leidos.com

NYS: LDOS
CEO: Roger A. Krone
CFO: James C. (Jim) Reagan
HR: Sarah K. Allen
FYE: January 30
Type: Public

Leidos Holdings (formerly SAIC) provides a host of national security services to civil agencies of the US government all branches of the military and the intelligence community. Areas of expertise include cybersecurity; mission support; logistics; and intelligence surveillance and reconnaissance. It also operates one of the country's largest health system integrators and offers engineering services for energy (oil gas and electric) and industrial clients. In early 2016 Leidos agreed to a $5 billion combination with Lockheed Martin's Information Systems & Global Solutions segment to form a company focused on providing IT and intelligence services.

	Annual Growth	01/11	01/12	01/13	01/14	01/15
Sales ($ mil.)	(17.9%)	11,117.0	10,587.0	11,173.0	5,772.0	5,063.0
Net income ($ mil.)	–	618.0	59.0	525.0	164.0	(323.0)
Market value ($ mil.)	25.7%	1,226.2	951.6	895.4	3,355.2	3,063.6
Employees	(18.7%)	43,400	41,100	40,000	22,000	19,000

LEMAITRE VASCULAR INC

63 Second Avenue
Burlington, MA 01803
Phone: 781 221-2266
Fax: –
Web: www.lemaitre.com

NMS: LMAT
CEO: George W. LeMaitre
CFO: Joseph P. Pellegrino
HR: Cornelia Lemaitre
FYE: December 31
Type: Public

LeMaitre Vascular makes the veins run on time. The company makes both disposable and implanted surgical vascular devices including catheters and stents under such brands as AnastoClip EndoFit and Pruitt-Inahara. Originally founded by a vascular surgeon to develop a valvulotome to prepare veins for arterial bypass surgery the company has since expanded its offerings to include a device to create dialysis access sites and another to treat aortic aneurysms. Le Maitre sells 12 product lines most of which are used in open vascular surgery and some of which are used in endovascular procedures. Its products are sold to hospitals in North America Europe and Japan through a direct sales force.

	Annual Growth	12/10	12/11	12/12	12/13	12/14
Sales ($ mil.)	6.1%	56.1	57.7	56.7	64.5	71.1
Net income ($ mil.)	(10.2%)	6.0	2.1	2.6	3.2	3.9
Market value ($ mil.)	3.1%	117.6	102.8	99.7	139.1	132.9
Employees	7.5%	255	276	301	334	341

LENDINGTREE INC (NEW)

11115 Rushmore Drive
Charlotte, NC 28277
Phone: 704 541-5351
Fax: –
Web: www.tree.com

NMS: TREE
CEO: Douglas R. (Doug) Lebda
CFO: Alexander Mandel
HR: Colleen Forness
FYE: December 31
Type: Public

LendingTree (formerly Tree.com) helps consumers cut through a forest of options in financing education insurance home services and more. The company allows users to comparison shop for home loans through its most prominent branch LendingTree which helps match home buyers with lenders. Its lending network includes over 350 banks and other lenders. Other subsidiaries help consumers choose between colleges and home service providers. LendingTree also markets auto loans and credit cards. Services are free to consumers as the firm collects fees from the companies to which it refers business.

	Annual Growth	12/10	12/11	12/12	12/13	12/14
Sales ($ mil.)	(4.1%)	198.2	54.6	77.4	139.2	167.4
Net income ($ mil.)	–	(17.6)	(59.5)	46.6	3.9	9.4
Market value ($ mil.)	50.4%	107.6	63.6	205.3	373.9	550.4
Employees	(29.8%)	900	135	174	192	218

LENNAR CORP.

700 Northwest 107th Avenue
Miami, FL 33172
Phone: 305 559-4000
Fax: –
Web: www.lennar.com

NYS: LEN
CEO: Stuart A. Miller
CFO: Bruce E. Gross
HR: –
FYE: November 30
Type: Public

Lennar is one of the largest homebuilding land-owning loan-making leviathans in the US along with D.R. Horton and Pulte Homes. The company builds single-family attached and detached homes in 18 states under brand names including Lennar Camelot NuHome and Greystone. Lennar targets first-time move-up and active adult buyers and markets its homes as "everything included." The company also provides financial services including mortgage financing title and closing services. During fiscal 2015 (ended November) Lennar delivered more than 24200 homes at an average price of $344000.

	Annual Growth	11/11	11/12	11/13	11/14	11/15
Sales ($ mil.)	32.3%	3,095.4	4,104.7	5,935.1	7,779.8	9,474.0
Net income ($ mil.)	71.8%	92.2	679.1	479.7	638.9	802.9
Market value ($ mil.)	29.1%	3,887.2	8,032.0	7,550.6	9,974.5	10,812.8
Employees	17.5%	4,062	4,722	5,741	6,825	7,749

LENNOX INTERNATIONAL INC

NYS: LII

2140 Lake Park Blvd.
Richardson, TX 75080
Phone: 972 497-5000
Fax: –
Web: www.lennoxinternational.com

CEO: Todd M. Bluedorn
CFO: Joseph W. Reitmeier
HR: James (Jamie) Newby
FYE: December 31
Type: Public

Lennox International makes sure the temperature is just right. The company makes climate control equipment such as heating ventilation air conditioning and refrigeration (HVACR) units for residential and commercial uses. It sells furnaces heat pumps fireplaces and air conditioners under such brands as Lennox Armstrong Air and Aire-Flo; chillers and condensing units are sold under the Bohn and Larkin names. The heating-and-cooling maker's products are sold through some 7000 dealers in the US and Canada. Lennox has operations in Asia Australia Europe and South America. Named after inventor Dave Lennox the company was founded in 1895.

	Annual Growth	12/11	12/12	12/13	12/14	12/15
Sales ($ mil.)	1.2%	3,303.6	2,949.4	3,199.1	3,367.4	3,467.4
Net income ($ mil.)	20.6%	88.3	90.0	171.8	205.8	186.6
Market value ($ mil.)	38.7%	1,507.9	2,346.5	3,800.3	4,247.6	5,580.3
Employees	(5.2%)	12,400	12,000	9,700	9,800	10,000

LEO A. DALY COMPANY

8600 INDIAN HILLS DR
OMAHA, NE 681144039
Phone: 808-521-8889
Fax: –
Web: www.leodaly.com

CEO: Leo A Daly III
CFO: –
HR: –
FYE: February 28
Type: Private

Firmly ensconced among the lions of design Leo A Daly takes great pride in its work. The company provides architecture engineering design and program management services for commercial industrial and public projects in more than 85 countries. Its project portfolio includes the award-winning First National Tower in its home state of Nebraska and the Lockheed Martin Center for Leadership Excellence in Maryland. Leo A Daly also owns engineering group Lockwood Andrews & Newnam which specializes in infrastructure management and consulting. Leo A Daly and its subsidiaries have more than 30 offices worldwide. Established in 1915 by Leo A. Daly Sr. the company is now led by his grandson Leo A. Daly III.

	Annual Growth	02/10	02/11	02/12	02/13	02/14
Sales ($ mil.)	(4.3%)	–	–	114.9	132.0	162.7	100.6
Net income ($ mil.)	–	–	–	–	(5.1)	1.1	(3.3)
Market value ($ mil.)	–	–	–	–	–	–
Employees	–	–	–	–	–	750

LESCARDEN, INC.

NBB: LCAR

420 Lexington Avenue, Suite 212
New York, NY 10170
Phone: 212 687-1050
Fax: 212 687-1051
Web: www.lescarden.com

CEO: William E Luther
CFO: William E Luther
HR: –
FYE: May 31
Type: Public

Lescarden lessens scarring when it can. The company develops clinical dermatological osteoarthritis and wound care products. Lescarden focuses on developing natural therapies. Many of its products utilize bovine cartilage which is said to possess beneficial healing qualities. Its lead product the bovine-based and FDA-approved Catrix is sold as a dressing for non-healing wounds such as diabetic ulcers. Lescarden also markets a line of Catrix-based skin care products targeting the plastic surgery dermatology and medical spa markets. Other products include Poly-Nag an anti-arthritic compound made from chitin a material found in the shells of invertebrates and BIO-CARTILAGE a nutritional supplement.

	Annual Growth	05/11	05/12	05/13	05/14	05/15
Sales ($ mil.)	(17.9%)	0.6	0.4	0.4	0.4	0.3
Net income ($ mil.)	–	(0.1)	(0.2)	(0.3)	(0.2)	(0.2)
Market value ($ mil.)	0.0%	1.6	1.1	1.9	1.7	1.6
Employees	0.0%	1	1	1	1	1

LESTER E. COX MEDICAL CENTERS

1423 N JEFFERSON AVE
SPRINGFIELD, MO 658021917
Phone: 417-269-3000
Fax: –
Web: www.coxhealth.com

CEO: Steven D. (Steve) Edwards
CFO: Jacob McWay
HR: –
FYE: September 30
Type: Private

Where health care in the Ozarks is concerned Lester is more. Lester E. Cox Medical Centers (dba CoxHealth) provides a myriad of medical services to people in Missouri and Arkansas. CoxHealth's network includes five acute care hospitals (with more than 950 beds) and more than 80 physician clinics. Centers for cardiac care cancer treatment orthopedics mental health and women's health are among CoxHealth's specialized care options. Other operations include an ambulance service offering both ground and air transportation the Cox Health Systems HMO the Oxford HealthCare home health agency and educational programs. The organization was named after its primary fundraiser in the 1940s.

	Annual Growth	09/07	09/08	09/09	09/12	09/13
Sales ($ mil.)	(1.0%)	–	900.6	876.5	843.2	858.3
Net income ($ mil.)	37.1%	–	–	30.0	66.9	106.0
Market value ($ mil.)	–	–	–	–	–	–
Employees	–	–	–	–	–	9,100

LET'S GO PUBLICATIONS INC.

67 Mt. Auburn St.
Cambridge MA 02138
Phone: 617-495-9659
Fax: 617-496-7070
Web: www.letsgo.com

CEO: –
CFO: –
HR: –
FYE: December 31
Type: Subsidiary

Let's Go Publications are travel guides written by students who venture off the beaten path. The company employs students of Harvard University to revise and update the publisher's nearly 50 travel guides each year. Its staff includes more than 150 young editors associate editors and researcher/writers. The budget travel guides are published through a relationship with St. Martin's Press and include titles such as Let's Go Europe Let's Go Mexico and Roadtripping USA. Let's Go also offers travel information on its Web site through its free online travel guides.

LETTS INDUSTRIES INC.

1111 Bellevue Ave.
Detroit MI 48207
Phone: 313-579-1100
Fax: 313-579-2379
Web: www.dzyneloft.com/letts/about.htm

CEO: –
CFO: –
HR: –
FYE: December 31
Type: Private

Letts Industries is engaged in metal part fabrication and industrial equipment sales through its two groups (four divisions). Manufacturing is comprised of Powers and Sons and Trek; Product Services includes Pioneer Forge and Letts Equipment. Powers and Sons unit makes steering and suspension parts for cars and light- medium- and heavy-duty trucks. Products include pitman and idler arms track bars and rear tow links. Letts Industries also serves as a US sales outlet for solid metal forming and powder metal compacting equipment made by Germany-based LASCO. Letts Industries can trace its origins back to 1915 when Charles Letts Sr. delivered his metal forgings to Henry Ford's factory by horse-drawn wagon.

LETTUCE ENTERTAIN YOU ENTERPRISES INC.

5419 N. Sheridan Rd.
Chicago IL 60640
Phone: 773-878-7340
Fax: 773-878-1205
Web: www.leye.com

CEO: Kevin Brown
CFO: –
HR: Susan Southgate-Fox
FYE: December 31
Type: Private

With such names as R.J. Grunts Cafe Ba-Ba-Reeba and Mity Nice Grill it's clear that these restaurants serve up a helping of humor along with the food. Lettuce Entertain You Enterprises (LEYE) operates more than 70 upscale and casual-dining restaurants mostly in the Chicago area encompassing more than 35 concepts. At the high end LEYE operates the sophisticated Everest (located in the Chicago Stock Exchange building) one of the top-rated dining rooms in Chicago. At the lower end the company offers quick bites from foodlife and Wow Bao. In addition to the Windy City LEYE has operations in Atlanta Las Vegas Minneapolis and Washington DC. Richard Melman started the company in 1971.

LEUCADIA NATIONAL CORP.   NYS: LUK

520 Madison Avenue
New York, NY 10022
Phone: 212 460-1900
Fax: 212 598-4869
Web: www.leucadia.com

CEO: Richard B Handler
CFO: Teresa S. Gendron
HR: –
FYE: December 31
Type: Public

Holding company Leucadia National owns stakes in a variety of firms involved in manufacturing medical products gaming and beef processing. The investment firm typically seeks out troubled companies that it believes are undervalued. Some of its largest holdings include the National Beef Packaging Company; global securities and investment bank Jefferies Group; Leucadia Asset Management; Home-Fed Corporation; a 50% stake in Berkadia Commercial Mortgage; Idaho Timber; Conwed Plastics; and Crimson Wine Group among others. It also has interests in gold and silver mining companies telecommunication services business in Italy and automobile dealerships.

	Annual Growth	12/10	12/11	12/12	12/13	12/14
Sales ($ mil.)	71.8%	1,320.0	1,570.8	9,193.7	10,429.5	11,486.5
Net income ($ mil.)	(43.4%)	1,939.3	25.2	854.5	362.2	199.0
Market value ($ mil.)	(6.4%)	10,723.6	8,356.9	8,742.8	10,414.9	8,239.3
Employees	52.6%	2,414	11,711	10,943	14,647	13,082

LEVEL 3 COMMUNICATIONS, INC.   NYS: LVLT

1025 Eldorado Blvd.
Broomfield, CO 80021-8869
Phone: 720 888-1000
Fax: –
Web: www.level3.com

CEO: Jeffrey K. (Jeff) Storey
CFO: Sunit S. Patel
HR: –
FYE: December 31
Type: Public

Level 3 Communications makes valuable connections through its networking efforts. Operator of one of the world's largest fiber-optic communications networks the firm connects customers in 60 countries. Its services include broadband Internet access wholesale voice origination and termination enterprise voice content distribution broadband transport and colocation. Wholesale customers include ISPs telecom carriers cable-TV operators wireless providers and the US government. The company markets its products and services directly to businesses state agencies and schools. Its content delivery unit targets video distributors Web portals online gaming and software companies and social networking sites.

	Annual Growth	12/10	12/11	12/12	12/13	12/14
Sales ($ mil.)	16.7%	3,651.0	4,333.0	6,376.0	6,313.0	6,777.0
Net income ($ mil.)	–	(622.0)	(756.0)	(422.0)	(109.0)	314.0
Market value ($ mil.)	166.4%	334.5	5,799.7	7,888.9	11,323.0	16,856.4
Employees	25.2%	5,500	10,900	10,800	10,000	13,500

LEVENGER COMPANY

420 S. Congress Ave.
Delray Beach FL 33445-4696
Phone: 561-276-2436
Fax: 561-266-2181
Web: www.levenger.com

CEO: –
CFO: –
HR: Diana Sutton
FYE: December 31
Type: Private

Levenger began when Lori Granger Leveen and her husband Steve said: "Let there be lighting!" The company which got its start in 1987 by selling halogen lights for reading has fashioned itself into the provider of "Tools for Serious Readers." It offers an assortment of home and office accessories and furniture including briefcases leather armchairs lap desks pens stationery and of course lighting products. The company also operates a publishing division Levenger Press. Levenger (which derives its name from combining Leveen and Granger) sells its merchandise through its catalog website and retail stores in Boston Chicago and the Washington DC area.

LEVI STRAUSS & CO.

1155 Battery Street
San Francisco, CA 94111
Phone: 415 501-6000
Fax: –

CEO: Charles V. (Chip) Bergh
CFO: Harmit J. Singh
HR: Edel Keville
FYE: November 30
Type: Public

Pioneering American apparel maker Levi Strauss & Co. (LS&CO.) has jeans in its genes. A global manufacturer of brand-name clothing LS&CO. sells jeans and sportswear under the Levi's Dockers Signature by Levi Strauss and Denizen labels in more than 110 countries. It also markets men's and women's underwear and loungewear. Levi's Red Tag jeans department store staples and once the uniform of America's youth have expanded outside to markets beyond the US. LS&CO. has further transformed its products portfolio to include wrinkle-free and stain-resistant fabrics used in making some of its Levi's and Dockers slacks. The Haas family (descendants of founder Levi Strauss) controls LS&CO.

	Annual Growth	11/10	11/11	11/12	11/13	11/14
Sales ($ mil.)	1.9%	4,410.6	4,761.6	4,610.2	4,681.7	4,754.0
Net income ($ mil.)	(9.3%)	156.5	138.0	143.9	229.2	106.1
Market value ($ mil.)	–	–	–	–	–	–
Employees	(1.9%)	16,200	17,000	17,000	16,000	15,000

LEVINDALE HEBREW GERIATRIC CENTER AND HOSPITAL INC.

2434 W BELVEDERE AVE # 1
BALTIMORE, MD 212155267
Phone: 410-601-2400
Fax: –
Web: www.levindale.com

CEO: Ronald Rothstein
CFO: Raul Lujuan
HR: –
FYE: June 30
Type: Private

Levindale Hebrew Geriatric Center and Hospital is a Jewish-sponsored nursing home that also operates a specialty hospital. In addition to traditional skilled nursing services the hospital provides subacute (short-term) medical care inpatient and outpatient mental health care and adult day-care services. Founded in 1890 the medical center has more than 290 beds. Among its specialized services are rehabilitation pain management and wound care as well as hospice care. Levindale Hebrew is part of the LifeBridge Health network of facilities in the Baltimore area and is sponsored by the Jewish Community Federation of Baltimore.

	Annual Growth	06/09	06/10	06/11	06/12	06/13
Sales ($ mil.)	0.7%	–	78.7	73.0	72.9	80.3
Net income ($ mil.)	–	–	–	(1.1)	0.5	0.9
Market value ($ mil.)	–	–	–	–	–	–
Employees	–	–	–	–	–	461

LEVITON MANUFACTURING CO. INC.

201 North Service Rd.
Melville NY 11747
Phone: 800-323-8920
Fax: 800-832-9538
Web: www.leviton.com
CEO: Donald J Hendler
CFO: Mark Baydarian
HR: Brenda Placek
FYE: December 31
Type: Private

Its more than 25000 products make Leviton Manufacturing a leviathan of electrical and electronic components but it's certainly no dinosaur. In addition to components such as switches plugs and connectors for home and commercial uses the family-owned business has added data center connectivity and energy-efficient lighting systems lighting controls and voice and data equipment. Its Wiring Device division makes everything from basic switches to receptacles including the designer Decora and Acenti collections. Products are sold in North America to distributors manufacturers and retail outlets such as Home Depot and Wal-Mart.

LEWIS TREE SERVICE INC.

300 Lucius Gordon Dr.
West Henrietta NY 14586
Phone: 585-436-3208
Fax: 585-235-5864
Web: www.lewistree.com
CEO: –
CFO: Joseph L Redman
HR: –
FYE: December 31
Type: Private

Lewis Tree Service really keeps trees in line with its vegetation management services. The employee-owned company helps utilities and government agencies throughout the eastern US distribute remove and maintain vegetation near construction sites pipelines substations and billboards. It also provides storm emergency response services to clear fallen vegetation from roads and right-of-ways so that power can be restored. In addition Lewis Tree Service sells its retired automotive equipment including both gas and diesel pick-up trucks lift trucks and chip trucks. Connecticut Light and Power is among the company's customers.

LEVY RESTAURANT HOLDINGS LLC

980 N. Michigan Ave. Ste. 400
Chicago IL 60611
Phone: 312-664-8200
Fax: 312-280-2739
Web: www.levyrestaurants.com
CEO: Andy Lansing
CFO: –
HR: –
FYE: December 31
Type: Subsidiary

This company's menu of operations feeds people out on the town and at the game. Levy Restaurants is a leading restaurant operator and contract foodservices provider. Its fine dining spots found mostly in Chicago include Fulton's on the River and Spiaggia. Most of the company's business though comes from running foodservice operations at more than 75 sports stadiums convention centers and race tracks including Churchill Downs (Louisville Kentucky) Lambeau Field (Green Bay Wisconsin) and Wrigley Field (Chicago). Levy Restaurants also runs dining locations at Walt Disney's Disney World resort and theme park in Orlando. The company is a subsidiary of UK-based Compass Group.

LEXAR MEDIA INC.

47300 Bayside Pkwy.
Fremont CA 94538
Phone: 510-413-1200
Fax: 510-440-3499
Web: www.lexar.com
CEO: –
CFO: –
HR: –
FYE: December 31
Type: Subsidiary

Lexar Media is banking on a digital picture being worth more than a thousand words. The company a subsidiary of Micron Technology designs and markets USB flash drives memory cards card readers computer memory and solid state drives for the digital photography consumer electronic and communications markets. Its NAND flash and DRAM memory products are sold under the Lexar and Crucial brands. Lexar's products are made by third parties and sold mostly in the US (which accounts for more than half of sales) as well as in Canada Europe and the Asia/Pacific region. Customers include retailers OEMs and licensees. Lexar has a licensing agreement with Kodak to make and distribute Kodak-branded memory cards.

LEWIS & CLARK COLLEGE

0615 SW PALATINE HILL RD
PORTLAND, OR 972197879
Phone: 503-768-7000
Fax: –
Web: www.graduate.lclark.edu
CEO: –
CFO: –
HR: –
FYE: May 31
Type: Private

Lewis & Clark College sends students on an expedition to higher learning. The private university offers bachelor's degrees in more than two dozen majors through its College of Arts and Sciences. Fields of study include the humanities art history communications psychology natural sciences and mathematics. The school also offers master's and doctoral degrees at its Graduate School of Education and Counseling and its School of Law. Lewis & Clark has an enrollment of more than 3700 students. Founded as Albany Collegiate Institute in 1867 the college changed its name to Lewis & Clark when it moved to Portland Oregon in 1942.

	Annual Growth	05/10	05/11	05/12	05/13	05/14
Sales ($ mil.)	(12.6%)	–	173.6	113.3	116.7	115.8
Net income ($ mil.)	–	–	–	(19.0)	29.1	11.8
Market value ($ mil.)	–	–	–	–	–	–
Employees	–	–	–	–	–	800

LEXICON PHARMACEUTICALS, INC. NMS: LXRX

8800 Technology Forest Place
The Woodlands, TX 77381
Phone: 281 863-3000
Fax: –
Web: www.lexgen.com
CEO: Arthur T. Sands
CFO: Jeffrey L. Wade
HR: –
FYE: December 31
Type: Public

Lexicon Pharmaceuticals works with some of the biggest words in the dictionary — words like deoxyribonucleic acid. The drug development company is focused on a handful of potential medicines in clinical and pre-clinical research stages. Its candidates have been identified by its gene knockout technology and aim to treat conditions such as diabetes irritable bowel syndrome carcinoid syndrome rheumatoid arthritis and glaucoma some of which are being researched through partnerships with other drugmakers. The company got its start with the development of knockout mice — mice with DNA modified to disrupt or "knock out" certain gene functions — to study the potential effects of drugs on various genetic targets.

	Annual Growth	12/10	12/11	12/12	12/13	12/14
Sales ($ mil.)	46.9%	4.9	1.8	1.1	2.2	22.9
Net income ($ mil.)	–	(101.8)	(116.2)	(110.2)	(104.1)	(100.3)
Market value ($ mil.)	(10.8%)	149.0	133.5	228.7	186.2	94.2
Employees	(22.2%)	290	225	230	149	106

LEXINGTON REALTY TRUST
NYS: LXP

One Penn Plaza - Suite 4015
New York, NY 10119
Phone: 212 692-7200
Fax: 212 594-6600
Web: www.lxp.com

CEO: T. Wilson Eglin
CFO: Patrick Carroll
HR: Irfan Butt
FYE: December 31
Type: Public

Lexington Realty Trust is a self-managed real estate investment trust (REIT) that owns and manages more than 220 commercial properties across nearly 40 states. Its diverse portfolio of properties includes single-tenant offices warehouses manufacturing facilities and retail sites totaling 41 million sq. ft. of rentable space. The trust also provides financing for mortgage and mezzanine loans. Most properties are rented under triple net leases in which tenants are responsible for expenses such as real estate taxes and repairs. Its occupancy rate is more than 97%. Prominent tenants include Michelin UTC and Sears — their warehouses and industrial buildings alone account for more than 4 million sq. ft. of space.

	Annual Growth	12/10	12/11	12/12	12/13	12/14
Sales ($ mil.)	5.5%	342.9	326.9	344.9	398.4	424.4
Net income ($ mil.)	–	(33.0)	(79.6)	180.3	1.6	93.1
Market value ($ mil.)	8.4%	1,854.6	1,747.3	2,437.8	2,381.8	2,561.4
Employees	(2.4%)	53	54	50	47	48

LEXISNEXIS GROUP

9443 Springboro Pike
Dayton OH 45342
Phone: 937-865-6800
Fax: 937-847-3090
Web: www.lexisnexis.com

CEO: Kurt Sanford
CFO: –
HR: –
FYE: December 31
Type: Subsidiary

LexisNexis Group flexes its information muscles. The company offers subscribers access to thousands of sources — including public records and newspaper magazine and journal articles through its LexisNexis Legal & Professional business. The bulk of content focuses on legal tax business government and academic information. Flagship research service LexisNexis.com offers online access to documents from some 45000 sources. The company also offers risk management and fraud prevention services via LexisNexis Risk Solutions. The news and business information research service was launched in 1979; it became part of publishing giant Reed Elsevier Group in 1994.

LEXMARK INTERNATIONAL, INC.
NYS: LXK

One Lexmark Centre Drive, 740 West New Circle Road
Lexington, KY 40550
Phone: 859 232-2000
Fax: –
Web: www.lexmark.com

CEO: Paul A. Rooke
CFO: David Reeder
HR: –
FYE: December 31
Type: Public

Increasingly Lexmark is about what ends up on a printed page than it is about the printing. Still a leading maker of printers and related supplies the company has been adding software for capturing and managing data and images to its business. Its printer business Imaging Solutions and Services (ISS) offers laser and dot matrix printers multifunction devices and related products. Through its Perceptive Software segment the company offers content document output and business process management services. Lexmark expects to double the size of its software business with its $1 billion acquisition of Kofax. The company markets worldwide to individual consumers as well as large organizations in the financial services government health care manufacturing and retail sectors.

	Annual Growth	12/10	12/11	12/12	12/13	12/14
Sales ($ mil.)	(3.0%)	4,199.7	4,173.0	3,797.6	3,667.6	3,710.5
Net income ($ mil.)	(30.5%)	340.0	320.9	106.3	261.8	79.1
Market value ($ mil.)	4.3%	2,134.5	2,027.2	1,421.5	2,177.4	2,529.9
Employees	(1.0%)	13,200	13,300	12,200	12,000	12,700

LGI HOMES, INC.
NMS: LGIH

1450 Lake Robbins Drive, Suite 430
The Woodlands, TX 77380
Phone: 281 362-8998
Fax: –
Web: www.lgihomes.com

CEO: Eric Lipar
CFO: Charles Merdian
HR: –
FYE: December 31
Type: Public

LGI Homes wants everyone to stop wasting money on rent. The residential builder develops entry-level properties that appeal to renters looking to buy an affordable home in an affordable area. LGI has developed about 30 suburban communities in Arizona Florida Georgia and Texas. Targeting first-time homebuyers its homes are priced between $115000 and $260000 and range from 1200 to 3000 sq. ft. Founded in 2003 LGI Homes went public in 2013 raising $99 million which it plans to use to buy back stock from investment firm GTIS Partners. Any remainder will be used to buy land develop lots and build more homes.

	Annual Growth	12/10	12/11	12/12	12/13	12/14
Sales ($ mil.)	–	0.0	50.5	76.2	162.8	383.3
Net income ($ mil.)	–	0.0	3.4	9.7	22.3	28.2
Market value ($ mil.)	–	0.0	–	–	353.1	296.1
Employees	42.9%	–	–	191	253	390

LGL GROUP INC
ASE: LGL WS

2525 Shader Road
Orlando, FL 32804
Phone: 407 298-2000
Fax: –
Web: www.lglgroup.com

CEO: Michael J. Ferrantino
CFO: Patti A. Smith
HR: –
FYE: December 31
Type: Public

The LGL Group is hoping that one isn't the loneliest number. Previously made up of two separate businesses the company has a sole remaining line of business: its MtronPTI subsidiary. The subsidiary produces frequency control devices such as crystals and oscillators used primarily in communications equipment. MtronPTI was formed in the 2004 merger of M-tron Industries and Piezo Technology Inc. In 2007 The LGL Group sold certain assets of its unprofitable Lynch Systems subsidiary for about $3 million. The company's sales are roughly split between the US and other countries.

	Annual Growth	12/10	12/11	12/12	12/13	12/14
Sales ($ mil.)	(16.2%)	46.7	35.7	29.7	26.2	23.0
Net income ($ mil.)	–	9.4	0.4	(1.3)	(8.2)	(2.8)
Market value ($ mil.)	–	–	–	–	0.2	0.0
Employees	(11.6%)	233	199	184	153	142

LHC GROUP INC
NMS: LHCG

901 Hugh Wallis Road South
Lafayette, LA 70508
Phone: 337 233-1307
Fax: 337 235-8037
Web: www.lhcgroup.com

CEO: Keith G. Myers
CFO: Dionne E. Viator
HR: –
FYE: December 31
Type: Public

The injured and ailing in need of a little TLC need look no further than LHC. LHC Group administers post-acute health care services through home nursing agencies hospices and long-term acute care hospitals (LTACH). The company operates through two segments: home-based services and facility-based services in rural areas in about 25 US states. LHC's home health nursing agencies provide care to Medicare beneficiaries offering such services as private duty nursing physical therapy and medically-oriented social services. Its hospices provide palliative care for terminal patients while its LTACHs serve patients who no longer need intensive care but still require complex care in a hospital setting.

	Annual Growth	12/10	12/11	12/12	12/13	12/14
Sales ($ mil.)	3.7%	635.0	633.9	637.6	658.3	733.6
Net income ($ mil.)	(12.4%)	48.8	(13.2)	27.4	22.3	28.8
Market value ($ mil.)	1.0%	518.4	221.7	368.1	415.4	538.8
Employees	7.8%	7,973	7,571	7,903	8,186	10,767

LIBBEY INC.
ASE: LBY

300 Madison Avenue
Toledo, OH 43604
Phone: 419 325-2100
Fax: 419 727-2473
Web: www.libbey.com

CEO: William A. Foley
CFO: Sherry L. Buck
HR: Tim Page
FYE: December 31
Type: Public

The sound of breaking glass is music to Libbey's ears. It signals potential sales for the company which is a leading maker and seller of glassware tableware and flatware to the foodservice industry and to retailers (Bed Bath & Beyond Target Wal-Mart) in the US and Canada. Libbey's products are made in five countries including the US Mexico and China and are sold in more than 100 others. Its brands include Libbey Crisa and Royal Leerdam among others. Subsidiary World Tableware imports metal flatware serveware and ceramic dinnerware for resale. Libbey owns Crisa the largest Mexican glass tableware maker. Libbey's roots reach back to 1888 when The W.L. Libbey & Son Company was founded.

	Annual Growth	12/10	12/11	12/12	12/13	12/14
Sales ($ mil.)	1.7%	801.6	819.5	828.5	822.2	855.9
Net income ($ mil.)	(48.4%)	70.1	23.6	7.0	28.5	5.0
Market value ($ mil.)	19.4%	337.9	278.3	422.7	458.7	686.8
Employees	(1.7%)	7,005	6,907	6,663	6,437	6,553

LIBERTY BANCORP INC (MO)
OTC: LBCP

16 West Franklin Street
Liberty, MO 64068
Phone: 816 781-4822
Fax: –
Web: www.banklibertykc.com

CEO: Brent M Giles
CFO: Marc J Weishaar
HR: –
FYE: December 31
Type: Public

Liberty Bancorp was formed in 2006 to be the holding company for BankLiberty (formerly Liberty Savings Bank) which operates about 10 branches in the Kansas City area. It offers traditional deposit services such as checking and savings accounts CDs and IRAs in addition to newfangled offerings like Internet banking bill payment and cash management services. Commercial real estate loans account for the largest portion of the company's loan portfolio (around 40%) followed by construction loans mainly to custom homebuilders. However citing depressed market conditions the bank has decreased its volume of construction loans. It also offers business residential real estate and consumer loans.

	Annual Growth	09/10	09/11*	12/12	12/13	12/14
Assets ($ mil.)	(0.0%)	458.0	462.4	413.8	510.1	457.3
Net income ($ mil.)	(3.6%)	4.7	3.7	3.7	3.1	4.1
Market value ($ mil.)	14.4%	44.9	49.6	52.1	61.5	76.8
Employees	–	–	–	–	–	–

*Fiscal year change

LIBERTY DIVERSIFIED INTERNATIONAL INC.

5600 N. Hwy. 169
New Hope MN 55428-3096
Phone: 763-536-6600
Fax: 763-536-6685
Web: www.libertydiversified.com

CEO: Michael Fiterman
CFO: Byron Wieberdink
HR: –
FYE: May 31
Type: Private

Give me Liberty or give me Diversity — Liberty Diversified International (LDI; formerly Liberty Diversified Industries) gives you both. Its companies provide products and services for key markets including health care (Ergolet); precision machining (Milltronics and Takumi); paper packaging and recycling (Presentation Packaging Liberty Carton and Liberty Paper); building and construction (Diversi-Plast); office products and furniture (Safco); and hauling (LDI Transport). It also manufactures corrugated and plastic pallets for the shipping industry material handling products and graphic arts products. Family-owned LDI is led by its founder's grandson CEO Mike Fiterman.

LIBERTY INTERACTIVE CORP
NMS: QVCA

12300 Liberty Boulevard
Englewood, CO 80112
Phone: 720 875-5300
Fax: –
Web: www.libertyinteractive.com

CEO: Gregory B. (Greg) Maffei
CFO: Christopher W. Shean
HR: –
FYE: December 31
Type: Public

Liberty Interactive Corp. (formerly Liberty Media Corp.) stands by your right to shop at home and online. The company focuses on television and e-commerce sales through its QVC home-shopping subsidiary and numerous online businesses including CommerceHub Backcountry.com Bodybuilding.com and the online invitation site Evite. It also holds equity stakes in companies like Internet travel service Expedia HSN and LendingTree among others. Liberty Interactive Corp. was formed in 2011 when its predecessor restructured by merging and splitting off its Liberty Capital and Liberty Starz businesses under a newly-formed holding company also called Liberty Media.

	Annual Growth	12/10	12/11	12/12	12/13	12/14
Sales ($ mil.)	(1.1%)	10,982.0	9,616.0	10,054.0	11,252.0	10,499.0
Net income ($ mil.)	(27.0%)	1,892.0	912.0	1,530.0	501.0	537.0
Market value ($ mil.)	16.9%	9,743.4	10,018.4	12,159.2	18,133.8	18,177.0
Employees	(4.4%)	24,073	22,077	22,078	23,079	20,078

LIBERTY MUTUAL AGENCY CORPORATION

10 St. James Ave.
Boston MA 02117
Phone: 617-654-3600
Fax: 615-622-2302
Web: www.vistaproauto.com

CEO: Gary R Gregg
CFO: Michael J Fallon
HR: –
FYE: December 31
Type: Subsidiary

Liberty Mutual has stitched together a quilt of regional insurance providers and thrown them into Liberty Mutual Agency which blankets the entire country. The company offers property/casualty and specialty insurance products throughout the US. The company offers individual auto homeowners and other property/casualty insurance products under the Safeco name as well as commercial coverage like workers' compensation peril liability and fleet insurance to small and midsized businesses. The company is also a leading writer of surety bonds in the US.

LIBERTY MUTUAL HOLDING COMPANY INC.

175 Berkeley St.
Boston MA 02116
Phone: 617-357-9500
Fax: 617-350-7648
Web: www.libertymutual.com

CEO: David H Long
CFO: Dennis J Langwell
HR: –
FYE: December 31
Type: Private - Mutual Com

Liberty Mutual Holding defends our freedom to buy car insurance. As the parent company of Liberty Mutual Group and its operating subsidiaries Liberty Mutual is one of the top property/casualty insurers in the US and among the top 10 providers of automobile insurance. The company also offers homeowners' insurance workers compensation general liability group disability fire and surety and commercial lines for small to large companies. Liberty Mutual operates through four business divisions: Liberty Mutual Agency Corporation (LMAC) International Personal Markets and Commercial Markets. It distributes its products through a diversified blend of independent and exclusive agents brokers and direct sales.

LIBERTY ORCHARDS COMPANY INC.

117 MISSION AVE
CASHMERE, WA 988151007
Phone: 509-782-4088
Fax: –
Web: www.libertyorchards.com

CEO: –
CFO: –
HR: –
FYE: December 31
Type: Private

Liberty Orchards exercises its freedom to manufacture candies and baked goods. The company's signature products are aplets and cotlets — jellied fruit candies made from apples and apricots. It also makes and sells chocolates and fruity breads and cookies. Liberty Orchards products are sold online and by major chain retail stores. The candy maker was founded in 1919 as a fruit dehydration and canning enterprise by Armenian immigrants Mark Balaban and Armen Tertsagian.

	Annual Growth	12/02	12/03	12/05	12/06	12/07
Sales ($ mil.)	1.2%	–	13.5	15.4	14.4	14.2
Net income ($ mil.)	16.2%	–	–	0.1	0.2	0.2
Market value ($ mil.)	–	–	–	–	–	–
Employees	–	–	–	–	–	80

LIBERTY PROPERTY TRUST

500 Chesterfield Parkway
Malvern, PA 19355
Phone: 610 648-1700
Fax: –
Web: www.libertyproperty.com

NYS: LPT
CEO: –
CFO: George J. Alburger
HR: Caren Hosansky
FYE: December 31
Type: Public

There's the "Land of the Free" but no such thing as "free land" to Liberty Property Trust. The self-managed real estate investment trust (REIT) owns leases manages and has interests in nearly 500 industrial properties including distribution warehouse light manufacturing and research and development facilities and some 180 office buildings. The company's properties encompass some 90 million sq. ft. of space mainly in the mid-Atlantic southeastern and Midwestern regions of the US as well as the UK. The REIT also owns nearly 1500 acres of developable land. Liberty Property has some 1900 tenants; The Vanguard Group and GlaxoSmithKline are the two largest.

	Annual Growth	12/10	12/11	12/12	12/13	12/14
Sales ($ mil.)	1.5%	746.8	667.6	685.6	645.9	792.6
Net income ($ mil.)	14.3%	127.8	184.0	137.4	209.7	217.9
Market value ($ mil.)	4.2%	4,855.4	4,697.2	5,444.0	5,152.0	5,723.9
Employees	(1.6%)	479	462	452	471	449

LIBERTY TAX INC

1716 Corporate Landing Parkway
Virginia Beach, VA 23454
Phone: 757 493-8855
Fax: –
Web: www.libertytax.com

NMS: TAX
CEO: John T Hewitt
CFO: Mark F. Baumgartner
HR: –
FYE: April 30
Type: Public

Liberty Tax (formerly JTH Holding) wants to free you from those tax preparation shackles. It is the third-largest income tax preparation chain (behind H&R Block and Jackson Hewitt). Liberty Tax provides computerized tax preparation services through about 4200 offices throughout the US and in Canada. More than 98% of the offices are operated by franchises and are easily recognized by the costumed Uncle Sams or Lady Libertys waving out front. The company's eSmart Tax product allows customers to file their taxes online. Liberty Tax also offers tax-preparation courses refund loans audit assistance and related programs and services. CEO John Hewitt founded the company in 1997.

	Annual Growth	04/11	04/12	04/13	04/14	04/15
Sales ($ mil.)	14.1%	95.5	109.1	147.6	159.7	162.2
Net income ($ mil.)	(13.8%)	15.8	17.4	17.6	22.0	8.7
Market value ($ mil.)	26.7%	–	–	220.9	348.3	354.7
Employees	15.2%	–	788	950	645	1,206

LIBERTY TRAVEL INC.

69 Spring St.
Ramsey NJ 07446
Phone: 201-934-3500
Fax: 201-934-3651
Web: www.libertytravel.com

CEO: Dean Smith
CFO: Kathryn Atwell
HR: –
FYE: December 31
Type: Private

Give me liberty or give me ... travel? Liberty Travel gives you both. The company offers leisure and corporate travel services to consumers mainly in the Northeast and Florida. From its roughly 160 offices Liberty offers complete vacation packages such as Colorado Rockies ski excursions Alaskan cruises and family vacations to Walt Disney World. Travel agents can also book customized land-only and air-inclusive travel packages through Liberty's wholesale travel business GOGO Worldwide Vacations which operates about 40 offices in 20 states. The company was founded in 1951 and was acquired by Australian-based travel agency Flight Centre in early 2008 for about $135 million.

LICKING MEMORIAL HEALTH SYSTEMS

1320 W MAIN ST
NEWARK, OH 430551822
Phone: 740-348-4000
Fax: –
Web: www.lmhealth.org

CEO: –
CFO: Rob Montagnese
HR: –
FYE: December 31
Type: Private

Here to help Buckeye Staters lick disease is Licking Memorial Health Systems. The the not-for-profit health care provider operates the 230-bed Licking Memorial Hospital. Specialty services at the hospital include cancer care home health occupational health cardiology rehabilitation and obstetrics. Licking Memorial Hospital administers behavioral health care (including substance abuse treatments) through its Shepherd Hill department. The health system also includes area outpatient medical practices largely through the multi-specialty physician group Licking Memorial Health Professionals which has 100-plus physicians in various practices.

	Annual Growth	12/08	12/09	12/10	12/11	12/13
Sales ($ mil.)	1.2%	–	199.6	199.0	184.2	209.7
Net income ($ mil.)	108.7%	–	–	4.4	(7.7)	39.7
Market value ($ mil.)	–	–	–	–	–	–
Employees	–	–	–	–	–	1,700

LIEBERT CORPORATION

1050 Dearborn Dr.
Columbus OH 43085
Phone: 614-841-6700
Fax: 614-841-6022
Web: www.emersonnetworkpower.com/en-us/brands/liebe

CEO: –
CFO: –
HR: –
FYE: September 30
Type: Subsidiary

Liebert keeps its cool in the face of a power meltdown. The company designs makes and markets surge suppressors uninterruptable power supply (UPS) units precision cooling equipment enclosures and monitoring equipment that helps protect and support IT environments. Its products are used by companies in the communications government industrial and utilities sectors. Liebert which also provides support services sells directly and through independent and factory-direct representatives distributors and resellers. Customers have included BayCare Health System Terminix and Hess Corporation. Founded in 1965 Liebert is part of Emerson Network Power a business segment of Emerson Electric.

LIFE CARE CENTERS OF AMERICA INC.

3570 KEITH ST NW
CLEVELAND, TN 373124309
Phone: 423-472-9585
Fax: –
Web: www.lcca.com

CEO: Forrest L. Preston
CFO: Steve Ziegler
HR: –
FYE: September 30
Type: Private

If you or a loved one has reached the Golden Age of retirement there's a good chance Life Care Centers of America offers a service you can use. The company is a privately owned operator of more than 260 retirement and health care centers in 28 states across the US. Its offerings include retirement communities assisted-living facilities and nursing homes (and even some campuses that provide all three in a continuum of care). In addition Life Care operates centers specifically for people with Alzheimer's disease or related dementia. Some of Life Care's specialized services include home health care adult day care hospice and wound care.

	Annual Growth	12/01	12/02*	09/05	09/06	09/08
Sales ($ mil.)	–	–	0.0	0.0	40.8	82.9
Net income ($ mil.)	–	–	–	0.0	6.2	3.2
Market value ($ mil.)	–	–	–	–	–	–
Employees	–	–	–	–	–	29,000

*Fiscal year change

LIFE FITNESS INC.

5100 N. River Rd.
Schiller Park IL 60176
Phone: 847-288-3300
Fax: 847-288-3703
Web: www.lifefitness.com

CEO: –
CFO: –
HR: –
FYE: December 31
Type: Business Segment

Life Fitness thinks life is better when you're fit. It makes fitness equipment for the consumer and commercial markets under the Life Fitness Life Fitness Sport and Hammer Strength names. The fitness firm's products include strength systems stationary exercise bikes treadmills cross-trainers and stair-climbers. Founded in 1977 as Lifecycle the company distributes its products through dealers in more than 120 countries. Recreational products maker Brunswick Corporation has owned Life Fitness since 1997. To boost the business Life Fitness has bulked up through the acquisitions of Hammer Strength (maker of plate-loaded equipment) and ParaBody (home strength training equipment maker).

LIFE PARTNERS HOLDINGS INC

NBB: LPHI Q

204 Woodhew Drive
Waco, TX 76712
Phone: 254 751-7797
Fax: –
Web: www.lphi.com

CEO: Colette C Pieper
CFO: Colette C Pieper
HR: –
FYE: February 28
Type: Public

Life Partners Holdings parent company of Life Partners Inc. makes its bucks by helping its customers make a buck. The company facilitates viatical and life settlement transactions in which an institution or wealthy investor purchases individual life insurance policies (at a discount) and becomes the beneficiary of those policies when they mature. Viatical settlements involve terminally ill policyholders with only a couple of years to live; life settlement transactions involve sellers with longer life expectancies. Life Partners makes its money from fees earned by facilitating viatical and life settlements. Nearly all of the company's business is done through life settlement brokers. It filed for Chapter 11 bankruptcy in early 2015.

	Annual Growth	02/10	02/11	02/12	02/13	02/14
Sales ($ mil.)	(39.0%)	113.0	101.6	32.9	18.9	15.7
Net income ($ mil.)	–	29.4	23.4	(3.1)	(2.9)	(2.5)
Market value ($ mil.)	(41.5%)	383.8	154.0	79.3	74.2	44.9
Employees	(26.9%)	6,454	1,885	1,806	1,823	1,844

LIFE QUOTES INC.

8205 S. Cass Ave. Ste. 102
Darien IL 60561
Phone: 630-515-0170
Fax: 630-515-0270
Web: www.lifequotes.com

CEO: Robert Bland
CFO: Phillip A Perillo
HR: –
FYE: December 31
Type: Private

No pithy or inspirational sentiments here Life Quotes is in the insurance business. Formerly known as Insure.com the company offers comparative shopping for insurance products from more than two dozen carriers through its Life Quotes and Consumer Insurance Guide brands. Customers access Life Quote online or by phone. Life Quotes provides information on personal and commercial life insurance. The company earns commissions on the policies it sells through its website or call centers. It also receives fees for passing on qualified leads to property/casualty insurance companies. Chairman and founder Robert Bland controls Life Quotes.

LIFE SCIENCES RESEARCH INC.

Mettlers Road
East Millstone NJ 08875-2360
Phone: 201-525-1819
Fax: +44-1530-257-457
Web: www.ibstock.uk.com

CEO: Andrew Baker
CFO: Richard Michaelson
HR: –
FYE: December 31
Type: Private

Life Sciences Research stands ready to test everything that humans animals and the environment eat use and are exposed to. The contract research organization (CRO) performs safety and efficacy tests on pharmaceutical and chemical compounds used in products being developed by drug agricultural industrial and veterinary companies. Life Sciences Research and its subsidiaries provide both large and start-up drugmaker clients worldwide with toxicology metabolism and stability studies for preclinical candidates that are applying for product approval. The company is owned by Lion Holdings.

LIFE-TIME FITNESS INC

NYS: LTM

2902 Corporate Place
Chanhassen, MN 55317
Phone: 952 947-0000
Fax: –
Web: www.lifetimefitness.com

CEO: Bahram Akradi
CFO: Eric J Buss
HR: –
FYE: December 31
Type: Public

Life Time Fitness wants to help you keep your New Year's resolutions. The company operates more than 100 exercise and recreation centers. Life Time Fitness facilities offer swimming pools basketball and racquet courts child care centers spas dining services and climbing walls in addition to some 400 pieces of exercise equipment. Most facilities are open 24 hours a day seven days a week and average around 100000 sq. ft. in size. They target a membership of about 7500 to 11000 and are designed to serve as an all-in-one sports and athletic club professional fitness facility family recreation center and spa and resort.

	Annual Growth	12/09	12/10	12/11	12/12	12/13
Sales ($ mil.)	9.6%	837.0	912.8	1,013.7	1,126.9	1,205.9
Net income ($ mil.)	13.9%	72.4	80.7	92.6	111.5	121.7
Market value ($ mil.)	17.2%	1,049.9	1,726.3	1,968.9	2,072.5	1,979.4
Employees	6.6%	17,400	19,000	20,000	21,700	22,500

LIFEBRIDGE HEALTH INC.

2401 W BELVEDERE AVE
BALTIMORE, MD 212155216
Phone: 410-601-5653
Fax: –
Web: www.lifebridgeblogs.org

CEO: Neil M Meltzer
CFO: David Krajewski
HR: –
FYE: June 30
Type: Private

Like a bridge over troubled waters LifeBridge Health links ailing patients to care and healing. Serving the Baltimore region the not-for-profit company operates two general hospitals — Sinai Hospital of Baltimore and Northwest Hospital — with specialties including oncology neurology pediatrics and sports medicine. The LifeBridge Health network also provides long-term care at the Levindale Hebrew Geriatric Center and Hospital (nursing subacute and adult day care services) and the Courtland Gardens Nursing & Rehabilitation Center. Altogether the health system boasts some 1190 beds. LifeBridge's Health Wellness division includes a health and fitness program and community fitness center.

	Annual Growth	06/08	06/09	06/10	06/11	06/13
Sales ($ mil.)	121.0%	–	–	95.8	99.9	1,034.0
Net income ($ mil.)	–	–	–	(2.5)	(3.2)	53.7
Market value ($ mil.)	–	–	–	–	–	–
Employees	–	–	–	–	–	6,000

LIFECORE BIOMEDICAL INC.

3515 Lyman Blvd.
Chaska MN 55318-3051
Phone: 952-368-4300
Fax: 952-368-3411
Web: www.lifecore.com

CEO: –
CFO: Scott Collins
HR: –
FYE: May 31
Type: Subsidiary

Lifecore Biomedical aims to help bodies plump up smooth out and keep moving. Lifecore manufactures hyaluronan a natural lubricating compound found in animal and human connective tissues. The hyaluronan is then turned into products used in ophthalmic surgeries during bone grafting as pain treatments for osteoarthritis and in veterinary orthopedics. Hyaluronan might eventually be used in cosmetic procedures as a dermal filler (to smooth out wrinkles). Lifecore has supply agreements with Alcon to use its hyaluronan solution in cataract surgery products. Landec Corporation acquired Lifecore in 2010.

LIFELOCK INC

NYS: LOCK

60 East Rio Salado Parkway, Suite 400
Tempe, AZ 85281
Phone: 480 682-5100
Fax: –
Web: www.lifelock.com

CEO: Larry McIntosh
CFO: Chris Power
HR: Natalie Dopp
FYE: December 31
Type: Public

LifeLock is trying to put a choke hold on identity theft. One of the fastest growing privately-held companies in the US and a leader in the security industry LifeLock serves consumers and businesses in the US Puerto Rico and the Virgin Islands with its identity theft protection and detection services. Members pay annual or monthly subscription fees to receive alerts about potentially fraudulent credit applications made in their names. Its eRecon and TrueAddress services search the Web for illegal selling and trading of personal information as well as fraudulent address change attempts. LifeLock was founded in 2005 and went public through a 2012 IPO.

	Annual Growth	12/10	12/11	12/12	12/13	12/14
Sales ($ mil.)	30.9%	162.3	193.9	276.4	369.7	476.0
Net income ($ mil.)	–	–	(15.4)	(4.3)	23.5	52.5	2.5
Market value ($ mil.)	50.9%	–	–	763.4	1,540.9	1,738.1
Employees	2.8%	–	616	644	675	669

LIFEPOINT HEALTH INC

NMS: LPNT

330 Seven Springs Way
Brentwood, TN 37027
Phone: 615 920-7000
Fax: –
Web: www.lifepointhospitals.com

CEO: William F. (Bill) Carpenter
CFO: Leif M. Murphy
HR: Marianne Freeman
FYE: December 31
Type: Public

LifePoint Health (formerly LifePoint Hospitals) hopes that folks who get sick in the country won't head to the city to get well. The company operates about 65 hospitals located in non-urban areas. In most cases the hospitals (which house more than 8000 beds combined) are the only available acute care facilities in the region. LifePoint operates its hospitals in some 21 states through its subsidiaries with a concentration in the southeastern US. In many markets LifePoint also operates outpatient clinics that provide family care diagnostic surgical and therapeutic services. The company has 4100 physician partners.

	Annual Growth	12/11	12/12	12/13	12/14	12/15
Sales ($ mil.)	14.6%	3,026.1	3,391.8	3,678.3	4,483.1	5,214.3
Net income ($ mil.)	2.8%	162.9	151.9	128.2	126.1	181.9
Market value ($ mil.)	18.6%	1,602.4	1,628.3	2,279.1	3,101.7	3,166.0
Employees	14.8%	23,000	28,000	31,000	38,000	40,000

LIFEQUEST WORLD CORPORATION

OTC: LQWC

1181 Grier Dr. Ste. C
Las Vegas NV 89119-3746
Phone: 702-914-9688
Fax: 702-914-9625
Web: www.lifequestworld.com

CEO: –
CFO: –
HR: –
FYE: May 31
Type: Public

Tired? Run-down? Listless? Do you poop out at parties? Time to call Tonicman! LifeQuest World uses its Tonicman radio shows to help get the word out about its Jurak Classic Whole Body Tonic but its main distribution is through multilevel marketing. The company's primary product is a liquid herbal formula created in 1943 by Carl Jurak father of CEO Anthony Jurak (who owns 41% of the company). LifeQuest has acquired ImmunXT for about $2 million and since has invested heavily in marketing the immune stimulating dietary supplement (even hiring actor and body builder Peter Lupus as its spokesman). The company expects ImmunXT — which is an algae-based botanical complex — to become its flagship product.

LIFESPAN CORPORATION

167 Point St.
Providence RI 02903
Phone: 401-444-3500
Fax: 401-444-5433
Web: www.lifespan.org

CEO: Timothy J Babineau
CFO: –
HR: –
FYE: September 30
Type: Private

From the youngest babies to the most golden oldies Lifespan Corporation has the health of Rhode Islanders covered through every stage of life. Founded in 1994 the multi-hospital health system includes the state's largest acute care facility Rhode Island Hospital. Rhode Island Hospital has about 720 beds and provides general and advanced medical-surgical care in a wide range of specialties including organ transplantation neurosurgery and orthopedics. Rhode Island Hospital and its sister facility the 250-bed Miriam Hospital serve as teaching facilities for Brown University's medical school. Lifespan was formed through the partnership of Rhode Island Hospital and the Miriam Hospital in 1994.

LIFESTORE FINANCIAL GROUP

PINK SHEETS: LSFG

21 E. Ashe St.
West Jefferson NC 28694
Phone: 336-246-4344
Fax: 336-246-3966
Web: www.golifestore.com

CEO: Robert E Washburn
CFO: Melanie Paisley Miller
HR: –
FYE: June 30
Type: Public

LifeStore helps you prepeare for whatever life has in store. Formerly AF Financial Group LifeStore Financial Group provides good ol' traditional banking and insurance services through subsidiaries LifeStore Bank and LifeStore Insurance Services. The bank operates seven offices in northwestern North Carolina's Alleghany Ashe and Watauga counties. It provides standard deposit products such as checking and savings accounts and CDs. Residential mortgages make up about half of its loan portfolio. The bank also offers investment products and services through a pact with a third-party provider. LifeStore Insurance Services sells bonds and auto homeowners health and life insurance.

LIFETIME BRANDS INC

NMS: LCUT

1000 Stewart Avenue
Garden City, NY 11530
Phone: 516 683-6000
Fax: –

CEO: Jeffrey (Jeff) Siegel
CFO: Laurence Winoker
HR: Anna Dee
FYE: December 31
Type: Public

Take-out meals eaten from the carton? Not in this lifetime. Lifetime Brands designs and distributes cutlery cutting boards cookware dinnerware kitchen utensils and tools and home décor under 30-plus brands (both owned and licensed) including Cuisinart Farberware KitchenAid Mikasa Pfaltzgraff Pedrini and Wallace. The company sells its varied lines in the US Canada Mexico Central and South America and Europe through high-end retailers supermarkets department stores and discount chains (including Bed Bath & Beyond Wal-Mart and Target) as well as online and by catalog.

	Annual Growth	12/10	12/11	12/12	12/13	12/14
Sales ($ mil.)	7.2%	443.2	444.4	486.8	502.7	586.0
Net income ($ mil.)	(47.5%)	20.3	14.1	20.9	9.3	1.5
Market value ($ mil.)	5.2%	192.5	166.5	145.5	215.7	235.8
Employees	10.6%	1,100	1,209	1,298	1,295	1,643

LIFETIME HEALTHCARE INC.

165 Court St.
Rochester NY 14647
Phone: 585-454-1700
Fax: 419-782-0148
Web: www.defiancemetal.com

CEO: David H Klein
CFO: –
HR: –
FYE: December 31
Type: Private

Lifetime Healthcare wants good health to last a lifetime for New Yorkers. The company which operates as The Lifetime Healthcare Companies is a not-for-profit holding company that provides health insurance and delivers health care services to some 1.7 million members in New York State through its various subsidiaries. The company's core products are the health insurance plans offered through its Excellus BlueCross BlueShield subsidiary. Long-term care insurance is provided through the company's MedAmerica subsidiary. Primary care is provided to members via the company's Lifetime Health Medical Group. The company also provides third-party administration services through its EBS-RMSCO subsidiary.

LIFETIME PRODUCTS INC.

Freeport Center Bldg. D-11
Clearfield UT 84016-0010
Phone: 801-776-8993
Fax: 801-728-1959
Web: www.lifetime.com

CEO: –
CFO: –
HR: –
FYE: December 31
Type: Private

Lifetime Products wants its goods to stand the test of time (and in many cases the elements). The company makes plastic folding tables and chairs storage sheds and cabinets patio furniture gardening products and sporting goods. Its products are manufactured in Utah and sold through half a dozen factory stores in the state as well as by major retailers (such as Wal-Mart and Costco) in about 60 countries worldwide. Lifetime also sells its products online. Lifetime Products was founded in 1973 as American Playworld a manufacturer of playground equipment.

LIFEWAY CHRISTIAN RESOURCES OF THE SOUTHERN BAPTIST CONVENTION

1 LIFEWAY PLZ
NASHVILLE, TN 372341001
Phone: 615-251-2000
Fax: –
Web: www.lifeway.com

CEO: Thom S. Rainer
CFO: Jerry Rhyne
HR: –
FYE: September 30
Type: Private

LifeWay Christian Resources of the Southern Baptist Convention helps to spread the teachings of Jesus. The company is a not-for-profit Christian publisher. It also sells Bibles CDs gifts software church furniture signs and other supplies. In addition to its roughly 200 LifeWay Christian Stores located in more than 25 states the retailer sells products online and through its catalog. LifeWay operates two of the nation's largest Christian conference facilities and summer camps. LifeWay Ridgecrest Conference Center in North Carolina and LifeWay Glorieta Conference Center in New Mexico together welcome some 2000 conference and overnight guests each year. LifeWay was founded in 1891 by Dr. J.M. Frost.

	Annual Growth	09/10	09/11	09/12	09/13	09/14
Sales ($ mil.)	2.2%	–	468.8	488.9	481.5	500.2
Net income ($ mil.)	–	–	–	(35.5)	79.4	(25.4)
Market value ($ mil.)	–	–	–	–	–	–
Employees	–	–	–	–	–	2,477

LIFEWAY FOODS, INC.

NMS: LWAY

6431 West Oakton
Morton Grove, IL 60053
Phone: 847 967-1010
Fax: –
Web: www.lifeway.net

CEO: Julie Smolyansky
CFO: Edward P. (Ed) Smolyansky
HR: –
FYE: December 31
Type: Public

Kefir is not milk with a pedigree but it is cultured and it's the lifeblood of Lifeway Foods. In addition to the yogurt-like dairy beverage called Kefir (sold under the Tuscan Lassi and BasicsPlus brands) the company's products include farmer and cream cheeses Sweet Kiss (a sweetened cheese spread) and a vegetable-based seasoning called Golden Zesta. Its ProBugs offering a flavored drink with live kefir cultures packaged in pouches is aimed at children. A longtime staple in the dairy cases of health-food stores Lifeway's products are available throughout the US as well as internationally. The dairy products company has been expanding its menu of products with additional children's items.

	Annual Growth	12/10	12/11	12/12	12/13	12/14
Sales ($ mil.)	19.4%	58.5	70.0	81.4	97.5	119.0
Net income ($ mil.)	(14.3%)	3.6	2.9	5.6	5.0	2.0
Market value ($ mil.)	18.0%	156.1	157.6	142.9	261.2	302.9
Employees	3.4%	315	330	330	350	360

LIGAND PHARMACEUTICALS INC
NMS: LGND

11119 North Torrey Pines Rd, Suite 200
La Jolla, CA 92037
Phone: 858 550-7500
Fax: –
Web: www.ligand.com

CEO: John L. Higgins
CFO: Nishan Silva
HR: –
FYE: December 31
Type: Public

Biopharmaceutical firm Ligand Pharmaceuticals seeks to discover disease-curing molecules. The drug development company works with gene transcription technology to address assorted illnesses. Its research and development projects include treatments for thrombocytopenia (low blood platelet count) osteoporosis Alzheimer's disease hepatitis C muscular conditions asthma and diabetes. Ligand conducts many of its programs through partnerships with other drugmakers including CyDex Pharmaceuticals GlaxoSmithKline (GSK) Pfizer and Lilly. The company is focused on expanding its development pipeline through additional partnerships and technology licensing agreements as well as via acquisitions.

	Annual Growth	12/10	12/11	12/12	12/13	12/14
Sales ($ mil.)	28.7%	23.5	30.0	31.4	49.0	64.5
Net income ($ mil.)	–	(10.4)	10.2	(0.5)	11.4	12.0
Market value ($ mil.)	56.3%	174.6	232.4	406.0	1,029.7	1,041.6
Employees	(11.5%)	31	21	21	20	19

LIGHTING SCIENCE GROUP CORP
NBB: LSCG

1830 Penn Street
Melbourne, FL 32901
Phone: 321 779-5520
Fax: –

CEO: Edward D. (Ed) Bednarcik
CFO: Thomas C. Shields
HR: –
FYE: December 31
Type: Public

Going green turns on Lighting Science (LSGC). The company designs manufactures and markets eco-friendly light-emitting diode (LED) technologies that conserve energy and eliminate the use of hazardous materials. It products use LED chips to integrate power sources with thermal management optic and control systems. The company sells optimized digital lighting (ODL) and LED replacement lamps fixtures and bulbs for streets garages stages and retail displays. While most of its customers are in retail commercial industrial and public sectors LSGC also customizes ambiance and lighting systems for entertainment venues and nightclubs.

	Annual Growth	12/10	12/11	12/12	12/13	12/14
Sales ($ mil.)	14.5%	53.2	109.0	127.1	83.2	91.3
Net income ($ mil.)	–	(295.1)	(90.4)	(111.3)	(89.8)	(65.6)
Market value ($ mil.)	(59.0%)	682.3	325.4	117.6	65.1	19.3
Employees	(21.1%)	243	1,455	377	177	94

LIGHTBRIDGE CORP
NAS: LTBR

1600 Tysons Boulevard, Suite 550
Mclean, VA 22102
Phone: 571 730-1200
Fax: –
Web: www.ltbridge.com

CEO: Seth Grae
CFO: Linda Zwobota
HR: –
FYE: December 31
Type: Public

Lightbridge is ready to illuminate the wonders of using thorium as a possible nuclear fuel. The development-stage company has been working on a new kind of nuclear fuel that uses thorium a less radioactive element than uranium to power nuclear reactors. Thorium's lessened radioactivity also means it doesn't produce enough plutonium to make nuclear weapons unlike uranium. The company's ideas for thorium were developed by the late nuclear engineer Dr. Alvin Radkowsky who co-founded Lightbridge's predecessor Thorium Power in 1992. While Lightbridge's plans for thorium power plants are not ready for commercialization the company has earned some revenue as a nuclear energy consultant.

	Annual Growth	12/10	12/11	12/12	12/13	12/14
Sales ($ mil.)	(35.5%)	7.6	6.4	3.7	1.9	1.3
Net income ($ mil.)	–	(7.6)	(5.9)	(4.1)	(4.9)	(4.8)
Market value ($ mil.)	(26.7%)	96.9	36.9	25.5	26.2	28.0
Employees	(12.0%)	20	15	15	12	12

LIGHTPATH TECHNOLOGIES, INC.
NAS: LPTH

2603 Challenger Tech Court, Suite 100
Orlando, FL 32826
Phone: 407 382-4003
Fax: 407 382-4007
Web: www.lightpath.com

CEO: J James Gaynor
CFO: Dorothy Cipolla
HR: –
FYE: June 30
Type: Public

LightPath Technologies is lighting the optical networking way. The company which has traditionally used its patented GRADIUM glass to make distortion-reducing lenses for inspection equipment is developing new applications for its technologies in the optoelectronics and fiber-optic communications fields. Its optoelectronics products include collimators (optical network components) and optical isolators (filters that prevent light waves from reflecting backwards). LightPath serves such customers as CyOptics Intel Santur ThorLabs and T-Networks. The company targets aerospace telecommunications health care instrumentation and the military. LightPath gets about two-thirds of its sales in the US.

	Annual Growth	06/11	06/12	06/13	06/14	06/15
Sales ($ mil.)	8.1%	10.0	11.3	11.8	11.8	13.7
Net income ($ mil.)	–	(1.6)	(0.9)	0.2	(0.3)	(0.7)
Market value ($ mil.)	3.3%	23.5	15.7	18.9	20.7	26.8
Employees	(3.6%)	200	169	171	175	173

LIGHTHOUSE COMPUTER SERVICES INC.

6 BLACKSTONE VALLEY PL # 205
LINCOLN, RI 028651179
Phone: 401-334-0799
Fax: –
Web: www.lighthousecs.com

CEO: –
CFO: Tony Fiore
HR: Telly Henan
FYE: December 31
Type: Private

Lighthouse Computer Services shines a light on companies' IT needs. The firm provides IT services to businesses primarily FORTUNE 1000 and midsized companies in the New England region. Lighthouse's services include customization implementation data migration network design and systems administration. It also refurbishes and sells computer equipment from IBM and other vendors. The company's consultants employ products from a variety of software and hardware partners including Cisco Systems Microsoft NetApp STORServer Symantec and VMware. CEO Tom Mrva controls Lighthouse Computer Services which he founded in 1995.

	Annual Growth	12/02	12/03	12/04	12/06	12/07
Sales ($ mil.)	17.8%	–	62.1	51.8	97.5	119.7
Net income ($ mil.)	235.9%	–	–	0.1	2.6	2.7
Market value ($ mil.)	–	–	–	–	–	–
Employees	–	–	–	–	–	105

LIGHTSPEED ONLINE RESEARCH INC.

180 Mt. Airy Rd. Ste. 100
Basking Ridge NJ 07920
Phone: 908-630-0542
Fax: 908-630-9436
Web: www.lightspeedresearch.com

CEO: David Day
CFO: Mich McCauley
HR: –
FYE: December 31
Type: Subsidiary

Lightspeed Online Research provides market research in the US and Europe as part of the Kantar Group the market research arm of advertising giant WPP Group. Working in tandem with GMI another Kantar unit Lightspeed gathers its data through online panels and provides custom research for clients. Throughout its paneling networks the company can access more than four million household members across more than 35 countries in the Asia/Pacific region Europe and North America. Established in 2000 Lightspeed conducts a variety of studies including customer satisfaction and retention attitude and awareness tests website evaluations new product and concept tests brand awareness and in-home product tests.

LIGHTSPEED VENTURE PARTNERS

2200 Sand Hill Rd.
Menlo Park CA 94025
Phone: 650-234-8300
Fax: 650-234-8333
Web: www.wpgvp.com

CEO: –
CFO: Dave Markland
HR: –
FYE: December 31
Type: Private

Companies that Lightspeed Venture Partners invests in might not operate at the speed of light but their products sure come close. The venture capital firm makes lead investments in early-stage software digital media semiconductor e-commerce clean technology and communications infrastructure startups and growth companies. Most are in the US but the company also has investments in Israel India and China. Working closely with its portfolio firms Lightspeed provides not only debt and equity funding but also advice on strategy recruiting raising capital and mergers and acquisitions.

LIGHTSQUARED INC.

10802 Parkridge Blvd.
Reston VA 20191-4334
Phone: 703-390-1899
Fax: 703-390-1893
Web: www.lightsquared.com

CEO: –
CFO: Marc Montagner
HR: –
FYE: December 31
Type: Private

LightSquared's plans to bring more choice to the North American broadband wireless market are up in the air. The company was building a network to offer high-speed wireless service on a wholesale basis through a group of about 40 dealers and resellers in North America. It planned to supplement services offered over its network through agreements with other carriers in the Americas and Caribbean regions including Stratos Global and Waveburst. LightSquared was dealt a blow by the FCC in 2012 when the agency withdrew preliminary approval of the network on the grounds that it interfered with GPS receivers. The company responded by filing for Chapter 11 bankruptcy protection later that year.

LILLY (ELI) & CO.

Lilly Corporate Center
Indianapolis, IN 46285
Phone: 317 276-2000
Fax: –
Web: www.lilly.com

NYS: LLY

CEO: John C. Lechleiter
CFO: Derica W. Rice
HR: Raymond Muller
FYE: December 31
Type: Public

Healthwise Eli Lilly hopes everything will come up roses for you. Best known for its neuroscience products the pharmaceutical company also makes endocrinology oncology and cardiovascular care medicines. Its top-selling drugs include Cymbalta for depression and pain Alimta for lung cancer Humalog and Humulin insulin for diabetes and Cialis for erectile dysfunction. Lilly also makes medications to treat schizophrenia and bipolar disorder (Zyprexa) osteoporosis (Evista and Forteo) heart conditions (Effient) and ADHD (Strattera) as well as anti-infective agents and a growing line of animal health products.

	Annual Growth	12/10	12/11	12/12	12/13	12/14
Sales ($ mil.)	(4.0%)	23,076.0	24,286.5	22,603.4	23,113.1	19,615.6
Net income ($ mil.)	(17.1%)	5,069.5	4,347.7	4,088.6	4,684.8	2,390.5
Market value ($ mil.)	18.5%	38,916.4	46,157.7	54,776.1	56,642.0	76,622.2
Employees	0.5%	38,350	38,080	38,350	37,925	39,135

LIME ENERGY CO

3 Convery Blvd., Suite 600
Woodbridge, NJ 07095
Phone: 732 791-5380
Fax: –
Web: www.lime-energy.com

NAS: LIME

CEO: C Adam Procell
CFO: Mary Colleen Brennan
HR: Maria Medrano
FYE: December 31
Type: Public

Being green is easy with help from Lime Energy. The company designs and installs programs for small businesses mostly utility companies that analyze energy use and develop a plan to reduce energy consumption and maintenance costs. Lime Energy helps its customers identify multiple energy-consuming points of a building and redesigns lighting systems to help them cost save and also reduce harmful emissions of carbon dioxide sulfur dioxide and nitric dioxide. The company works on all types of buildings including factories high rises retail data centers banks government facilities schools and hospitals.

	Annual Growth	12/10	12/11	12/12	12/13	12/14
Sales ($ mil.)	(11.5%)	95.7	120.1	43.4	51.6	58.8
Net income ($ mil.)	–	(5.2)	(11.6)	(31.8)	(15.6)	(2.6)
Market value ($ mil.)	(7.7%)	38.2	30.1	5.5	27.3	27.7
Employees	(18.1%)	364	342	167	125	164

LIMELIGHT NETWORKS INC

222 South Mill Avenue, 8th Floor
Tempe, AZ 85281
Phone: 602 850-5000
Fax: –
Web: www.limelight.com

NMS: LLNW

CEO: Robert Lento
CFO: Sajid Malhotra
HR: –
FYE: December 31
Type: Public

Limelight Networks helps put its clients' online presence in the spotlight. The company's cloud-based Orchestrate Digital Presence Platform suite enables the management and optimization of a customer's entire digital presence including its website mobile and social initiatives and large-screen channels. Services include website personalization web content management online video publishing mobile device delivery and cloud storage. Limelight's platform is powered by a private delivery network with more than 75 locations across the globe. It serves about 1300 customers including such well-known names as Amazon QVC Swiss Re Electronic Arts NetApp Ciena HBO Netflix and PSA Peugeot Citroen.

	Annual Growth	12/10	12/11	12/12	12/13	12/14
Sales ($ mil.)	(3.0%)	183.3	171.3	180.2	173.4	162.3
Net income ($ mil.)	–	(20.4)	(25.3)	(32.9)	(35.4)	(24.6)
Market value ($ mil.)	(16.9%)	571.8	291.3	218.5	194.8	272.6
Employees	(6.8%)	689	482	511	482	520

LIMONEIRA CO.

1141 Cummings Road
Santa Paula, CA 93060
Phone: 805 525-5541
Fax: 805 525-8211
Web: www.limoneira.com

NMS: LMNR

CEO: Harold S. Edwards
CFO: Joseph Rumley
HR: –
FYE: October 31
Type: Public

When life gives you lemons you name your company Limoneira. The agriculture and real estate development business grows you guessed it lemons in three counties in California's fertile San Joaquin Valley. It also grows avocados oranges and other crops on a total of about 11000 acres. The company one of the state's oldest citrus growers is a leading producer of both lemons and avocados. Limoneira packs its own lemons and those of other growers; its products are marketed through agreements with Sunkist (oranges) and Calavo (avocados). Real estate holdings include residential commercial and agricultural rental properties and land holdings in California and Arizona. Limoneira traces its roots to 1893.

	Annual Growth	10/11	10/12	10/13	10/14	10/15
Sales ($ mil.)	17.6%	52.5	65.8	84.9	103.5	100.3
Net income ($ mil.)	45.1%	1.6	3.2	4.9	7.0	7.1
Market value ($ mil.)	(2.2%)	245.2	317.6	372.3	362.7	224.2
Employees	13.2%	203	226	254	331	333

LINBECK GROUP LLC

3900 Essex Ln. Ste. 1200
Houston TX 77027
Phone: 713-621-2350
Fax: 713-341-9436
Web: www.linbeck.com

CEO: David Stueckler
CFO: -
HR: -
FYE: March 31
Type: Private

The Linbeck Group lands landmark construction projects in Texas and beyond. The commercial and institutional construction company offers project management construction management real estate services and design/build services. It serves clients in several sectors: education health care biotech/pharmaceutical retail entertainment and corporate. The company's projects include Reliant Stadium in Houston; the Modern Art Museum of Fort Worth; the Federal Express headquarters in Tennessee; and MIT's School of Architecture in Massachusetts. The company was founded in 1938 by Leo E. Linbeck who was the grandfather of current chairman Leo E. Linbeck III.

LINC LOGISTICS COMPANY

11355 Stephens Rd.
Warren MI 48089
Phone: 586-467-1500
Fax: 704-499-9301
Web: www.portraitinnovations.com

CEO: -
CFO: -
HR: -
FYE: December 31
Type: Private

LINC Logistics is a not-so-missing link between car manufacturers and car buyers. A third-party logistics company LINC provides a variety of supply chain and freight transportation services including material handling and packaging warehousing freight delivery and international freight forwarding services (where companies purchase transportation capacity from carriers and resell it to customers). It serves primarily auto manufacturers including the "Big Three" — Ford GM and Chrysler as well as industrial technology and aerospace companies. LINC in late 2012 was acquired by Universal Truckload Services for about $350 million which included the assumption of debt.

LINCARE HOLDINGS INC.

NASDAQ: LNCR

19387 US 19 North
Clearwater FL 33764
Phone: 727-530-7700
Fax: 727-532-9692
Web: www.lincare.com

CEO: John P Byrnes
CFO: Paul G Gabos
HR: -
FYE: December 31
Type: Public

There are some things you shouldn't have to leave the house to get Lincare Holdings believes oxygen therapy is one of them. The company helps some 800000 patients with chronic obstructive pulmonary diseases (including emphysema and severe asthma) by providing oxygen therapy services through a network of offices. Lincare's local service centers deliver oxygen equipment to patients in their homes trains them and monitors use of the equipment. Lincare offers positive airway pressure (PAP) machines for sleep apnea as well as other home medical equipment. It also provides home infusion such as chemotherapy pain therapy and parenteral nutrition. Global gases firm Linde owns Lincare.

LINCOLN CENTER FOR THE PERFORMING ARTS INC.

70 LINCOLN CENTER PLZ # 9
NEW YORK, NY 10023-6548
Phone: 212-875-5000
Fax: -
Web: www.nyphil.org

CEO: -
CFO: Daniel Rubin
HR: -
FYE: June 30
Type: Private

One of the world's largest cultural hubs Lincoln Center presents live music theater dance and opera performances from its 16-acre complex in New York City. The Center also offers educational programming and provides a home base for such organizations as the School of American Ballet the New York Philharmonic the Metropolitan Opera and The Film Society of Lincoln Center. More than 5000 performances and educational programs are presented and more than 5 million people visit each year. The Lincoln Center was conceived by New York City movers and shakers including Robert Moses Robert F. Wagner Jr. and John D. Rockefeller III; construction of the complex took place between 1959 and 1972.

	Annual Growth	06/05	06/06	06/09	06/10	06/11
Sales ($ mil.)	(2.8%)	-	196.2	246.4	205.6	169.9
Net income ($ mil.)	-	-	78.5	0.0	(28.8)	(17.2)
Market value ($ mil.)	-	-	-	-	-	-
Employees	-	-	-	-	-	525

LINCOLN EDUCATIONAL SERVICES CORP

NMS: LINC

200 Executive Drive, Suite 340
West Orange, NJ 07052
Phone: 973 736-9340
Fax: -
Web: www.lincolnedu.com

CEO: -
CFO: Brian K Meyers
HR: Stephen (Steve) Ace
FYE: December 31
Type: Public

Lincoln hopes its graduates are better "Abe-l" to get a career. Lincoln Educational Services provides vocational programs from schools including Lincoln Technical Institute and Nashville Auto-Diesel College. It offers programs in automotive technology and skilled trades (including HVAC and electronics). Some 14000 students are enrolled at more than 30 campuses and five training sites more than 15 states throughout the US. Lincoln tends to grow by buying smaller schools and by opening campuses in new markets. It also expands its campus facilities to accommodate higher enrollment numbers. The company announced plans to divest its health care and other professions business in 2015.

	Annual Growth	12/10	12/11	12/12	12/13	12/14
Sales ($ mil.)	(15.6%)	639.5	512.6	402.7	345.0	325.0
Net income ($ mil.)	-	69.7	17.5	(37.2)	(51.3)	(56.1)
Market value ($ mil.)	(34.8%)	372.6	189.8	134.3	119.6	67.3
Employees	(13.1%)	4,500	3,800	3,570	3,085	2,572

LINCOLN ELECTRIC HOLDINGS, INC.

NMS: LECO

22801 St. Clair Avenue
Cleveland, OH 44117
Phone: 216 481-8100
Fax: 216 486-1751
Web: www.lincolnelectric.com

CEO: Christopher L. Mapes
CFO: Vincent K. Petrella
HR: -
FYE: December 31
Type: Public

Wielding great welding power Lincoln Electric the world's largest maker of arc welders and welding gear by sales is a global manufacturer of welding and cutting products including arc welding power sources consumable electrodes fluxes fume extraction equipment robotic welding systems and wire feeders; other welding products include regulators and torches. The company also has a leading global position in the brazing and soldering alloys market. In North America which accounts for nearly 50% of its sales products are sold through a network of industrial distributors. In addition Lincoln Electric has an international sales organization that sells to 160 countries.

	Annual Growth	12/10	12/11	12/12	12/13	12/14
Sales ($ mil.)	8.0%	2,070.2	2,694.6	2,853.7	2,852.7	2,813.3
Net income ($ mil.)	18.3%	130.2	217.2	257.4	293.8	254.7
Market value ($ mil.)	1.4%	5,025.6	3,012.1	3,748.2	5,493.0	5,319.7
Employees	1.4%	9,472	9,929	10,000	10,000	10,000

LINCOLN INDUSTRIES

600 W. E St.
Lincoln NE 68522
Phone: 402-475-3671
Fax: 402-475-9565
Web: www.lincolnindustries.com

CEO: Marc Le Baron
CFO: Andy Hunzeker
HR: –
FYE: September 30
Type: Private

Two score and fifteen years ago Lincoln Industries brought forth on this continent a metal finishing company; its capabilities include anodizing chromate conversion coating and nickel plating. The company specializes in the functional and decorative finishing of steel aluminum and brass operating more than 20 automated and manual lines capable of more than 40 finishing processes. Lincoln's integrated finishing services include sourcing materials management manufacturing and assembly polishing packaging inventory management and design and engineering support.

LINCOLN NATIONAL CORP.   NYS: LNC

150 N. Radnor Chester Road, Suite A305
Radnor, PA 19087
Phone: 484 583-1400
Fax: –
Web: www.lfg.com

CEO: Dennis R. Glass
CFO: Randal J. Freitag
HR: Lisa M. Buckingham
FYE: December 31
Type: Public

Who better to trust with your nest egg than the company that took its name from Honest Abe? Lincoln National which operates as Lincoln Financial Group provides retirement planning and life insurance to individuals and employers in the form of annuities 401k and savings plans and a variety of life dental and disability insurance products. It does business through such subsidiaries as Lincoln National Life Insurance and Lincoln Life & Annuity Company of New York. The company is also active in the investment management business offering individual and institutional clients such financial services as pension plans trusts and mutual funds through its subsidiaries.

	Annual Growth	12/10	12/11	12/12	12/13	12/14
Assets ($ mil.)	6.9%	193,824.0	202,906.0	218,869.0	236,945.0	253,377.0
Net income ($ mil.)	11.5%	980.0	294.0	1,313.0	1,244.0	1,515.0
Market value ($ mil.)	20.0%	7,134.7	4,982.2	6,644.7	13,243.2	14,795.3
Employees	3.8%	9,500	9,723	9,742	10,539	11,046

LINCOLN PROVISION INC.

824 W. 38th Place
Chicago IL 60609
Phone: 773-254-2400
Fax: 773-254-2405
Web: www.chigourmetsteaks.com

CEO: –
CFO: Niteen Joshi
HR: Gail Glowacki
FYE: December 31
Type: Private

Chicago has a loop around some of the best steer in the herd. Chicago Gourmet Steaks offers a plateful of the best cuts of beef including chateaubriand filet mignon and porterhouse steaks to hungry eaters. It sells its premium flash-frozen packed-in-ice meats through its website or by telephone or fax. The company also supplies foodservice establishments mainly high-end restaurants. CEO James Stevens acquired the company in 1990 from the late Walter Mander a longtime fixture in the Chicago meatpacking industry. Mander's Lincoln Meat Company which closed that same year was one of the last surviving slaughterhouses in the city.

LINDAL CEDAR HOMES INC.

4300 S. 104th Place
Seattle WA 98178
Phone: 206-725-0900
Fax: 206-725-1615
Web: www.lindal.com

CEO: Michael Harris
CFO: Dennis Greg
HR: –
FYE: December 31
Type: Private

This is surely not Abe Lincoln's log cabin. Lindal Cedar Homes makes custom cedar homes and sunrooms. Customers choose from more than 3000 floor plans and Lindal ships homebuilding packages to customers' sites. The houses have solid cedar log post-and-beam or conventional framing construction and are made with western red cedar. Lindal also offers solid wood and wood clad windows. The company operates through about 150 independent dealers and sells its products worldwide. Former US President Lyndon Johnson had two Lindal homes built on his ranch near Johnson City Texas. Sir Walter Lindal founded the company in 1945. Lindal and his family control the company which has produced more than 50000 homes.

LINDSAY CORP   NYS: LNN

2222 North. 111th Street
Omaha, NE 68164
Phone: 402 829-6800
Fax: 402 829-6834
Web: www.lindsay.com

CEO: –
CFO: James C Raabe
HR: Reuben Srinivasan
FYE: August 31
Type: Public

Liquid resources are big assets at Lindsay Corp. The company designs and manufactures irrigation systems primarily for farmers. The Zimmatic brand irrigation system a self-propelled center-pivot and lateral-move lineup is designed to use water energy and labor more efficiently than traditional flood or surface irrigation equipment. Touting better-to-bumper crop yields a dealer network sells to farmers in key markets worldwide. (The US represents more than 60% of sales.) Lindsay offers chemical injection systems water pumping stations (via subsidiary Watertronics) as well as replacement parts. An infrastructure division supplies movable barriers for traffic control and crash cushions for road safety.

	Annual Growth	08/11	08/12	08/13	08/14	08/15
Sales ($ mil.)	4.0%	478.9	551.3	690.8	617.9	560.2
Net income ($ mil.)	(8.0%)	36.8	43.3	70.6	51.5	26.3
Market value ($ mil.)	5.2%	702.2	737.9	858.3	878.1	860.6
Employees	7.3%	999	1,082	1,262	1,202	1,324

LINE 6 INC.

29901 Agoura Rd.
Agoura Hills CA 91301-2513
Phone: 818-575-3600
Fax: 818-575-3601
Web: www.line6.com

CEO: Paul Foeckler
CFO: Mary Ellen Broganer
HR: –
FYE: December 31
Type: Private

You can bet the music is turned all the way up at Line 6 a leading maker of electric guitar amplifiers. The firm focuses on integrating technology with music products such as its digital modeling amps that are designed to reproduce the distinctive sounds of a wide range of traditional tube amps and much more. Beyond an array of amps Line 6 makes and sells Variax guitars stomp boxes pedals and other accessories. Its amps are sold in more than 60 countries through major music retailers such as Guitar Center and Sam Ash as well as on the company's website. Executives Marcus Ryle and Michel Doidic established Line 6 in 1996 when they spun it off from their earlier venture: Fast Forward Designs.

LINEAGE POWER CORPORATION

601 Shiloh Rd.
Plano TX 75149-7507
Phone: 972-244-9288
Fax: 703-273-7011
Web: www.spacequest.com

CEO: Craig A Witsoe
CFO: Roxi Wen
HR: –
FYE: December 31
Type: Subsidiary

Lineage Power has a tradition of serving those in power. The company makes power converters filter modules inverters power bays and cabinets power supplies and rectifiers for electrical power conversion equipment. Customers have included telecommunications network operator Verizon Communications. Lineage sells directly and through distributors resellers and systems intgrators. The company also offers a range of services including systems engineering installation facility design project management and energy auditing. Lineage was acquired by GE in 2011 for about $520 million. GE used the deal to expand its high-efficiency energy products for telecom and data center applications to keep pace with demand.

LINKSHARE CORPORATION

215 Park Ave. South 9th Fl.
New York NY 10003
Phone: 646-943-8200
Fax: 646-943-8204
Web: www.linkshare.com

CEO: Yaz Iida
CFO: Bodie Gavnon
HR: –
FYE: June 30
Type: Subsidiary

Turning clicks into commerce has been LinkShare's plan since 1996. The company doing business as Rakuten LinkShare operates a performance-based affiliate marketing network. Clients which have included retailers Dell and Land's End market their products through promotional links placed on affiliate websites. Rakuten LinkShare charges clients based on volume of traffic and purchases made. The firm also offers tools that help clients manage track and analyze affiliate search and e-mail marketing campaigns. It has offices throughout the US as well as in the UK and Japan. LinkShare was founded in 1996 by brother and sister Stephen and Heidi Messer. Today it is part of Japanese online retailer Rakuten.

LINEAR TECHNOLOGY CORP.

NMS: LLTC

1630 McCarthy Boulevard
Milpitas, CA 95035
Phone: 408 432-1900
Fax: 408 434-0507
Web: www.linear.com

CEO: Lothar Maier
CFO: Paul Coghlan
HR: Bruce Vakiener
FYE: June 28
Type: Public

Linear Technology's high performance linear integrated circuits (ICs) create a connection from the analog world to the digital one. Its chips convert temperature pressure sound speed and other information into a digital form that can be read by digital devices. Linear Technology also makes linear devices that control power and regulate voltage in electronic systems. The company's products are used in a myriad of equipment from PCs to radar systems satellites and industrial instrumentation. It caters largely to communications and industrial markets as well as to the computer consumer goods aerospace and automotive markets. Linear generates roughly 70% of its sales outside of the US.

	Annual Growth	07/11	07/12*	06/13	06/14	06/15
Sales ($ mil.)	(0.1%)	1,484.0	1,266.6	1,282.2	1,388.4	1,475.1
Net income ($ mil.)	(2.7%)	580.8	398.1	406.9	460.0	521.0
Market value ($ mil.)	7.9%	8,014.9	7,511.4	8,832.4	11,191.6	10,877.5
Employees	2.0%	4,505	4,365	4,306	4,661	4,868

*Fiscal year change

LINN ENERGY LLC

NMS: LINE

600 Travis, Suite 5100
Houston, TX 77002
Phone: 281 840-4000
Fax: –
Web: www.linnenergy.com

CEO: Mark E. Ellis
CFO: David B. Rottino
HR: –
FYE: December 31
Type: Public

It's a Linn-Linn situation. Founder and chairman Michael Linn's namesake company Linn Energy has successfully drilled for oil and natural gas across the US although in recent years the company has narrowed its focus to exploiting assets in the Mid-Continent California and the Permian Basin. In 2012 the company reported proved reserves of 4.8 trillion cu. ft. of natural gas equivalent. The company operates about 70% of its more than 15800 gross productive wells. In addition to its core oil and gas activities Linn Energy pursues an aggressive hedging strategy to reduce the effects of oil price volatility on its annual income.

	Annual Growth	12/10	12/11	12/12	12/13	12/14
Sales ($ mil.)	59.4%	772.3	1,622.5	1,774.2	2,331.7	4,983.3
Net income ($ mil.)	–	(114.3)	438.4	(386.6)	(691.3)	(451.8)
Market value ($ mil.)	(27.9%)	12,445.7	12,585.2	11,698.8	10,221.5	3,362.9
Employees	26.6%	700	824	1,136	1,645	1,800

LINKEDIN CORP

NYS: LNKD

2029 Stierlin Court
Mountain View, CA 94043
Phone: 650 687-3600
Fax: –
Web: www.linkedin.com

CEO: Jeffrey (Jeff) Weiner
CFO: Steven J. (Steve) Sordello
HR: –
FYE: December 31
Type: Public

Feeling a bit disconnected to the business world? LinkedIn wants to help. The firm operates an online professional network designed to help members find jobs connect with other professionals and locate business opportunities. The site has grown to reach more than 340 million users in some 200 countries since its launch in 2003. LinkedIn is free to join; it offers a paid premium membership with additional tools and sells advertising. It additionally earns revenue through its job listing service which allows companies to post job openings and search for candidates on LinkedIn.

	Annual Growth	12/11	12/12	12/13	12/14	12/15
Sales ($ mil.)	54.7%	522.2	972.3	1,528.5	2,218.8	2,990.9
Net income ($ mil.)	–	11.9	21.6	26.8	(15.3)	(164.8)
Market value ($ mil.)	37.5%	8,320.4	15,161.9	28,632.2	30,333.0	29,721.6
Employees	45.1%	2,116	3,458	5,045	6,897	9,372

LINNCO LLC

NASDAQ: LNCO

600 Travis Ste. 5100
Houston TX 77002
Phone: 281-840-4000
Fax: 303-625-2710
Web: www.globeimmune.com

CEO: Mark E Ellis
CFO: Kolja Rockov
HR: –
FYE: December 31
Type: Private

LinnCo. LLC knows the drill on how to raise money. The company formed in April 2012 in order to buy shares of stock in Linn Energy LLC an oil and natural gas concern focused on production in the Mid-Continent California and the Permian Basin. LinnCo. LLC filed a $1 billion initial public offering in June 2012 with plans to buy stock in Linn Energy and become a major shareholder. (Linn Energy completed its IPO in January 2006 and doesn't have any significant shareholders.) While LinnCo. LLC doesn't have any operations or assets of its own as an investment vehicle its IPO (which took place in October 2012) helped raise additional equity capital for Linn Energy.

LIONBRIDGE TECHNOLOGIES INC.   NMS: LIOX

1050 Winter Street
Waltham, MA 02451
Phone: 781-434-6000
Fax: –
Web: www.en-gb.lionbridge.com

CEO: Rory J. Cowan
CFO: Marc Litz
HR: Michele Erwin
FYE: December 31
Type: Public

Lionbridge Technologies wants to be king of the jungle at bridging the language gap. The company offers translation (or localization) of software user manuals Web content and other content. It prepares materials for international use by tailoring them to individual languages and cultures. The firm sells subscriptions to access its branded Web-based translation software; it also supplies human interpreters to government agencies and businesses. Additionally Lionbridge provides testing services under its VeriTest brand through which it checks websites software and hardware to ensure their quality. Among its more than 400 clients include Microsoft Google Adobe Systems and Samsung Group.

	Annual Growth	12/10	12/11	12/12	12/13	12/14
Sales ($ mil.)	4.9%	405.2	427.9	457.2	489.2	490.6
Net income ($ mil.)	–	(1.3)	1.7	11.3	11.6	8.1
Market value ($ mil.)	11.7%	234.3	145.4	255.3	378.5	365.1
Employees	5.1%	4,500	4,500	5,000	4,800	5,500

LIONS GATE ENTERTAINMENT CORP.   NYSE: LGF

2700 Colorado Ave. Ste. 200
Santa Monica CA 90404
Phone: 310-449-9200
Fax: 310-255-3870
Web: www.lionsgate.com

CEO: Jon Feltheimer
CFO: James Keegan
HR: –
FYE: March 31
Type: Public

Independent films are the cat's meow at Lions Gate Entertainment. The firm which operates as Lionsgate is a leading producer and distributor of films such as Warrior and the horror title Saw 3D as well as the most-talked about film of 2012 The Hunger Games. It produces TV content (including Nurse Jackie for Showtime Networks) through Lionsgate Television. Lionsgate also releases films under the Trimark brand and owns a library of more than 1300 movie and TV titles that it distributes to retailers rental kiosks and TV channels. In addition it owns 43% of production studio Roadside Attractions. In 2012 Lionsgate acquired Summit Entertainment producer of the lucrative Twilight series of movies.

LIPPERT COMPONENTS INC.

2703 College Ave.
Goshen IN 46528
Phone: 574-535-1125
Fax: 574-534-3475
Web: www.lci1.com

CEO: Jason Lippert
CFO: Joshua Lippert
HR: –
FYE: December 31
Type: Subsidiary

For Lippert Components making chassis brings the company both cachet and cha-ching. A subsidiary of Drew Industries Lippert Components is a manufacturer of chassis for manufactured and modular homes. It also makes chassis for recreational vehicles (RVs) as well as galvanized roofing and utilitycargo and horse trailers. Lippert Components fabricates parts for more than 150 customers. The company process more than 90 tons of hot-rolled sheet steel per day in its fabrication operations. Using environmentally friendly powder coating technology Lippert Components powder coats more than 5000 chassis per month.

LIPSCOMB UNIVERSITY

1 UNIVERSITY PARK DR
NASHVILLE, TN 372043956
Phone: 615-966-1000
Fax: –
Web: www.lipscomb.edu

CEO: –
CFO: Danny Taylor
HR: –
FYE: May 31
Type: Private

Lipscomb University was founded in 1891 as the Nashville Bible School by David Lipscomb and James A. Harding; it was renamed in Lipscomb's honor in 1918. The coeducational Christian school offers more than 150 programs of study in about 80 majors leading to bachelor's degrees about eight of them at colleges of arts and humanities Bible and ministry business education engineering pharmacy and health sciences and professional studies. It also offers graduate degrees in areas such as theology accountancy business administration conflict management counseling and education in addition to a doctorate degree in pharmacy. Lipscomb has an annual enrollment of approximately 4500 students.

	Annual Growth	05/06	05/07	05/11	05/12	05/13
Sales ($ mil.)	12.7%	–	71.9	115.3	132.6	147.1
Net income ($ mil.)	79.6%	–	–	3.3	2.1	10.8
Market value ($ mil.)	–	–	–	–	–	–
Employees	–	–	–	–	–	550

LIQUID INVESTMENTS INC.

3840 VIA DE LA VALLE # 300
DEL MAR, CA 920144268
Phone: 858-509-8510
Fax: –
Web: www.lqdinv.com

CEO: Ron L Fowler
CFO: –
HR: –
FYE: December 31
Type: Private

Liquid Investments has nothing to do with your bank accounts your retirement fund or your broker. The company supplies beer malt beverages soda energy drinks and water to customers in parts of California and Colorado. It owns the Mesa Beverage Co. in Santa Rosa California which handles over 1500 accounts in Sonoma and Marin counties. It also serves 475 accounts in the western slope area of Colorado through Colorado Beverage Distribution which has locations in Grand Junction and Montrose Colorado. Liquid distributes imported domestic and craft beers. It also offers regional and local beers along with soda and bottled water. Its latest addition to its craft labels is Victoria lagers.

	Annual Growth	12/07	12/08	12/09	12/10	12/11
Sales ($ mil.)	(0.5%)	–	95.3	93.2	91.8	93.8
Net income ($ mil.)	83.2%	–	–	0.4	(0.1)	1.2
Market value ($ mil.)	–	–	–	–	–	–
Employees	–	–	–	–	–	629

LIQUIDITY SERVICES INC   NMS: LQDT

1920 L Street N.W., 6th Floor
Washington, DC 20036
Phone: 202 467-6868
Fax: –
Web: www.liquidation.com

CEO: William P. (Bill) Angrick
CFO: Jorge A. Celaya
HR: –
FYE: September 30
Type: Public

Hey bidder bidder. Take a swing at Liquidity Services (LSI). The online auction firm provides manufacturers retailers corporations and governments with an electronic marketplace to dispose of liquidate and track goods in the reverse supply chain. More than one million professional buyers are registered on the firm's online marketplaces through which they can bid for wholesale surplus and salvage items like retail customer returns overstock products and end-of-life goods. LSI founded in 1999 also offers valuation appraisal inventory marketing sale and logistical management of assets; warehousing and inspection of inventory; and transaction support such as collections and dispute mediation.

	Annual Growth	09/11	09/12	09/13	09/14	09/15
Sales ($ mil.)	4.9%	327.4	475.3	505.9	495.7	397.1
Net income ($ mil.)	–	8.5	48.3	41.1	30.4	(104.8)
Market value ($ mil.)	(30.7%)	962.9	1,507.6	1,005.9	412.9	221.9
Employees	14.2%	694	965	1,302	1,049	1,179

LIQUIDMETAL TECHNOLOGIES INC
NBB: LQMT

30452 Esperanza
Rancho Santa Margarita, CA 92688
Phone: 949 635-2100
Fax: –
Web: www.liquidmetal.com

CEO: Thomas Steipp
CFO: Tony Chung
HR: –
FYE: December 31
Type: Public

It's not liquid it's not metal — well OK it is metal. Still Liquidmetal Technologies has built on research done at the California Institute of Technology by company officers William Johnson and Atakan Peker to sell amorphous metal alloys. Those products include an alloy that's lighter than titanium but twice as strong as conventional titanium alloys. The company's products are sold as bulk alloys coatings composites and powders. Applications include casings for cell phones defense products (armor-piercing ammunition) industrial coatings and sporting goods (baseball bats tennis rackets). Electronics giant Samsung is among the company's largest customers.

	Annual Growth	12/10	12/11	12/12	12/13	12/14
Sales ($ mil.)	(63.3%)	33.3	1.0	0.7	1.0	0.6
Net income ($ mil.)	–	(1.9)	6.2	(14.0)	(14.2)	(6.5)
Market value ($ mil.)	(36.3%)	353.0	353.0	58.1	58.1	58.1
Employees	(8.6%)	33	15	19	18	23

LIRO PROGRAM AND CONSTRUCTION MANAGEMENT P.C.

3 AERIAL WAY
SYOSSET, NY 11791-5501
Phone: 516-938-5476
Fax: –
Web: www.liro.com

CEO: Luis Tormenta
CFO: Lawrence Roberts
HR: –
FYE: December 31
Type: Private

The LiRo Group does construction with a New York accent. Through its operating companies LiRo provides engineering architectural and construction management services to mostly public sector clients in New York New Jersey and Connecticut. It offers a wide range of engineering and inspection services including civil structural mechanical electrical traffic and environmental. Its projects have included renovation of municipal buildings such as schools correctional facilities fire stations and court houses as well as reconstruction of highways bridges and subways and capital improvements at professional sports facilities like Yankee Stadium. LiRo was co-founded in 1983 by owner Rocco L. Trotta.

	Annual Growth	12/0-1	12/00	12/01	12/02	12/10
Sales ($ mil.)	20.5%	–	11.7	14.7	12.9	75.6
Net income ($ mil.)	17.2%	–	1.6	2.5	2.9	7.8
Market value ($ mil.)	–	–	–	–	–	–
Employees	–	–	–	–	–	200

LITEHOUSE INC.

1109 N ELLA AVE
SANDPOINT, ID 838642202
Phone: 208-263-7569
Fax: –
Web: www.litehousefoods.com

CEO: Jim Frank
CFO: Kelly Prior
HR: –
FYE: December 28
Type: Private

This company shines its light on salads. Litehouse is a leading maker of salad dressings sauces and vegetable dips under the Litehouse label. It produces a variety of dressings including blue cheese ranch and vinaigrette along with low fat and organic products. The company also makes fruit dips glazes and cheese crumbles as well as apple cider marinades and freeze-dried herbs. With manufacturing facilities in Idaho Utah and Michigan Litehouse products are sold through supermarkets and warehouse clubs in the US and Canada. Litehouse also supplies dressings and other products to food service distributors and restaurants. Founded by Edward Hawkins in 1963 Litehouse is run by the Hawkins family.

	Annual Growth	12/09	12/10	12/11	12/12	12/13
Sales ($ mil.)	5.1%	–	132.6	142.8	142.8	153.9
Net income ($ mil.)	–	–	–	(3.1)	(3.1)	6.4
Market value ($ mil.)	–	–	–	–	–	–
Employees	–	–	–	–	–	450

LITHIA MOTORS, INC.
NYS: LAD

150 N. Bartlett Street
Medford, OR 97501
Phone: 541 776-6401
Fax: –
Web: www.lithia.com

CEO: Bryan B. DeBoer
CFO: Christopher (Chris) Holzshu
HR: –
FYE: December 31
Type: Public

Acquisitive Lithia Motors is a big hungry fish among US auto retailers. The company operates about 130 stores in select markets in more than a dozen states. The firm sells 30 brands of new domestic and imported vehicles and all brands of used cars and trucks through its stores and online. Chrysler (Dodge Jeep) and GM (Chevrolet Cadillac Saab) are the top sellers. Lithia Motors also offers financing and replacement parts and operates about 18 collision-repair centers. Unlike most consolidators it prefers to pay cash (rather than stock) for dealerships in smaller markets. Chairman Sidney DeBoer through Lithia Holding Co. controls Lithia Motors which was founded in 1946 by his father Walt.

	Annual Growth	12/10	12/11	12/12	12/13	12/14
Sales ($ mil.)	26.1%	2,131.6	2,699.4	3,316.5	4,005.7	5,390.3
Net income ($ mil.)	78.3%	13.7	58.9	80.4	106.0	138.7
Market value ($ mil.)	56.9%	374.9	573.5	981.6	1,821.1	2,274.1
Employees	21.6%	4,039	4,397	5,403	5,700	8,827

LITITZ MUTUAL INSURANCE COMPANY

2 N. Broad St.
Lititz PA 17543
Phone: 717-626-4751
Fax: 717-626-0970
Web: www.lititzmutual.com

CEO: –
CFO: –
HR: –
FYE: December 31
Type: Private - Mutual Com

Lititz Mutual provides a variety of individual and commercial property/casualty insurance products primarily in the heart of Pennsylvania Dutch country but also in surrounding states. Its offerings include businessowners farmowners personal umbrella and homeowners' insurance. A network of independent agents sell the company's products. Along with Livingston Mutual Insurance Farmers & Mechanics Mutual Insurance and Penn Charter Mutual the firm is a member of the Lititz Mutual Group. Lititz Mutual was founded by area residents as The Agricultural Mutual Fire Company of Lancaster County in 1888.

LITLE & CO. LLC

900 Chelmsford St.
Lowell MA 01851
Phone: 978-275-6500
Fax: 978-937-7250
Web: www.litle.com

CEO: –
CFO: –
HR: –
FYE: December 31
Type: Private

Litle & Co. sees eye-to-eye with non-face-to-face merchants. The company provides credit card payment processing services to direct marketers e-commerce merchants and other participants in card-not-present (CNP) transactions. Its products include e-check and international payment processing mobile payments recovery services and fraud protection. It also offers customers a chargeback management system and a proprietary online reporting and analytics platform. Other clients include catalogs TV shopping networks and not-for-profits. The company is a subsidiary of payment processing firm Vantiv.

LITTELFUSE, INC.

NMS: LFUS

8755 West Higgins Road, Suite 500
Chicago, IL 60631
Phone: 773 628-1000
Fax: –
Web: www.littelfuse.com

CEO: Gordon B. Hunter
CFO: Philip G. (Phil) Franklin
HR: Elizabeth Calhoun
FYE: December 27
Type: Public

Littelfuse is big on circuit protection. The company is one of the world's largest fuse makers. In addition to its fuses Littelfuse's other circuit protection devices include positive temperature coefficient devices that limit current when too much is being supplied and electrostatic discharge suppressors that redirect transient high voltage. The company's thyristors protect telecommunications circuits from transient voltage caused by lightning strikes. Littelfuse's 5000-plus customers include electronics manufacturers (Hewlett-Packard and Samsung) automakers (Ford and GM) and the automotive aftermarket (O'Reilly Automotive and Pep Boys).

	Annual Growth	01/11*	12/11	12/12	12/13	12/14
Sales ($ mil.)	11.9%	608.0	665.0	667.9	757.9	852.0
Net income ($ mil.)	8.1%	78.7	87.0	75.3	88.8	99.4
Market value ($ mil.)	28.0%	1,062.9	970.7	1,354.5	2,093.0	2,230.5
Employees	9.6%	6,000	6,000	6,000	7,400	7,900

*Fiscal year change

LITTLE CAESAR ENTERPRISES INC.

2211 Woodward Ave.
Detroit MI 48201
Phone: 313-983-6000
Fax: 313-983-6390
Web: www.littlecaesars.com

CEO: Christopher Ilitch
CFO: Scott Fischer
HR: –
FYE: December 31
Type: Subsidiary

I came I saw I bought a pizza. Little Caesar Enterprises operates and franchises more than 2500 Little Caesars carryout pizza restaurants throughout the US and in about ten other countries. The chain offers a variety of original and deep-dish pizzas along with cheese bread salads and sandwiches. While some stores are stand-alone units many Little Caesars locations can be found in strip malls and other high-traffic areas; the units typically do not offer dine-in seating. About 80% of the chain's outlets are run by franchisees. Little Caesars was founded in 1959 by Mike and Marian Ilitch who also control a sports and entertainment empire through Ilitch Holdings.

LITTLE LADY FOODS INC.

2323 Pratt Blvd.
Elk Grove Village IL 60007
Phone: 847-806-1440
Fax: 847-806-0026
Web: www.littleladyfoods.com

CEO: John Geocaris
CFO: James Sharwarko
HR: Ruth Gilman
FYE: December 31
Type: Private

This Little Lady serves up man-sized portions of frozen food. Little Lady Foods is a leading supplier of frozen food products for the foodservice and retail food industries. With facilities in the greater Chicago area the company makes stone-fired and kid-sized pizzas and a line of sandwiches that includes breakfast sandwiches paninis and wrap-style sandwiches on tortillas and flatbreads. The company markets its sandwiches for restaurants lunch stands and retail operators worldwide. It also offers sweet goods including an apple pancake muffins and turnovers. Little Lady Foods founded in 1961 provides custom product design creation and marketing services for private-label customers.

LITTLE SIOUX CORN PROCESSORS LLC

4808 F AVE
MARCUS, IA 510357070
Phone: 712-376-2800
Fax: –
Web: www.littlesiouxcornprocessors.com

CEO: –
CFO: Gary Grotjohn
HR: –
FYE: September 30
Type: Private

Pursuing the corny American Heartland dream of profitable renewable energy Little Sioux Corn Processors operates an ethanol plant in northwest Iowa. (It actually owns a 60% interest in the limited partnership that owns the ethanol facility.) The company converts bushels of corn into ethanol distiller grains (used as feed for the dairy and beef industries) and corn oil. Ethanol is used as an additive to gasoline as well as a fuel enhancer for high-octane motors and it burns more cleanly than normal gasoline thereby reducing carbon monoxide emissions. Little Sioux's production capacity is about 90 million gallons of ethanol annually more than double its orginal capacity after successive expansions.

	Annual Growth	09/02	09/03	09/10	09/11	09/13
Sales ($ mil.)	27.0%	–	31.8	–	329.7	346.7
Net income ($ mil.)	(30.2%)	–	–	–	9.5	4.6
Market value ($ mil.)	–	–	–	–	–	–
Employees	–	–	–	–	–	45

LITTLER MENDELSON P.C.

650 California St. 20th Fl.
San Francisco CA 94108-2693
Phone: 415-433-1940
Fax: 415-399-8490
Web: www.littler.com

CEO: Thomas J Bender
CFO: –
HR: –
FYE: December 31
Type: Private - Partnershi

Most national law firms aim to be full-service shops but Littler Mendelson concentrates on the law of the workplace. With about 800 lawyers Littler Mendelson is one of the largest employment law firms in the US. Its specialty is representing management in all types of labor disputes and employee lawsuits. Practice areas include appellate work business restructuring employment litigation unfair competition and workplace safety. Littler Mendelson has more than 50 offices spanning cities from New York to Seattle. The firm was founded in San Francisco in 1942; it began expanding beyond California in the 1990s.

LIVE NATION ENTERTAINMENT, INC.

NYS: LYV

9348 Civic Center Drive
Beverly Hills, CA 90210
Phone: 310 867-7000
Fax: –
Web: www.livenationentertainment.com

CEO: Michael (Mike) Rapino
CFO: Kathy Willard
HR: Tracy Wagner
FYE: December 31
Type: Public

Live Nation Entertainment holds center stage as the world's largest ticket seller and promoter of live entertainment. The company significantly expanded its ticketing services with the purchase of Ticketmaster Entertainment. The 2010 deal worth some $889 million created a powerful live-music conglomerate. The firm owns or operates about 160 venues in North America and Europe. Annually about 520 million people attend some 250000 Live Nation events. Live Nation also owns House of Blues venues through HOB Entertainment and dozens of prestigious concert halls. In addition Live Nation owns a stake in about 280 artists' music including albums tours and merchandise.

	Annual Growth	12/10	12/11	12/12	12/13	12/14
Sales ($ mil.)	7.9%	5,063.7	5,384.0	5,819.0	6,478.5	6,867.0
Net income ($ mil.)	–	(228.4)	(83.0)	(163.2)	(43.4)	(90.8)
Market value ($ mil.)	23.0%	2,297.6	1,671.9	1,873.1	3,975.6	5,253.2
Employees	21.1%	6,500	6,600	7,100	7,400	14,000

LIVE VENTURES INC   NAS: LIVE

325 E. Warm Springs Road, Suite 102
Las Vegas, NV 89119
Phone: 702 939-0231
Fax: –
Web: www.livedeal.com
CEO: Jon Isaac
CFO: Jon Isaac
HR: –
FYE: September 30
Type: Public

LiveDeal (formerly YP Corp.) is an Internet yellow pages and local online classifieds provider. The company offers goods and services listed for sale through its online classified marketplace at classifieds.livedeal.com; LiveDeal also publishes about 17 million business listings via its business directory at yellowpages.livedeal.com. Sources of revenue include advertising sales a pay-per-lead program with major auto dealers and optional listing upgrade and e-commerce/fraud prevention fees. The company changed its name from YP Corp. after its 2007 purchase of online local classifieds marketplace LiveDeal.

	Annual Growth	09/11	09/12	09/13	09/14	09/15
Sales ($ mil.)	69.1%	4.1	3.1	2.4	7.3	33.4
Net income ($ mil.)	–	(5.5)	(1.6)	(5.7)	(4.7)	(14.7)
Market value ($ mil.)	1.3%	27.0	87.4	58.1	50.4	28.4
Employees	124.0%	12	38	22	112	302

LIVEPERSON INC   NMS: LPSN

475 Tenth Avenue, 5th Floor
New York, NY 10018
Phone: 212 609-4200
Fax: –
Web: www.liveperson.com
CEO: Robert P. LoCascio
CFO: Daniel R. (Dan) Murphy
HR: –
FYE: December 31
Type: Public

The message from LivePerson is that messaging is the effective way to connect with customers. The company's messaging apps and other software tools help companies provide information and service to customers and provide information about customers to companies. Primarily serving retailers and other companies with intensive customer interactions LivePerson's software enhances communications through multiple channels including messaging apps text-based chat e-mail and customer self-service tools. LivePerson's LiveEngage product allows companies to communicate with customes via mobile social media and messaging for e-commerce and service. Customers in the US make up about two-thirds of sales. In late 2014 LivePerson in its biggest deal acquired Contact At Once for $65 million.

	Annual Growth	12/10	12/11	12/12	12/13	12/14
Sales ($ mil.)	17.6%	109.9	133.1	157.4	177.8	209.9
Net income ($ mil.)	–	–	9.3	12.0	6.4	(3.5)	(7.3)
Market value ($ mil.)	5.7%	634.6	704.8	737.9	832.2	791.8
Employees	21.8%	481	524	748	796	1,058

LIVEWORLD, INC.   NBB: LVWD

4340 Stevens Creek Blvd., Suite 101
San Jose, CA 95129
Phone: 408 871-5200
Fax: –
Web: www.liveworld.com
CEO: Peter H Friedman
CFO: David Houston
HR: –
FYE: December 31
Type: Public

LiveWorld hopes that online collaboration is the key to its livelihood. Promoting itself as a "social brand flow" manager the company designs websites and offers applications that can be added to a customers' existing site. It also offers customized pages on popular social media sites including Twitter and Facebook as well as moderators and community managers on these sites to keep the discussion headed in the right direction. LiveWorld has created online communities for prominent companies including HSBC Johnson & Johnson The Campbell Soup Company and Warner Brothers. Chairman and CEO Peter Friedman and EVP Jenna Woodul founded LiveWorld in 1996 from remnants of Apple's now-defunct eWorld online service.

	Annual Growth	12/06	12/07	12/12	12/13	12/14
Sales ($ mil.)	4.3%	9.8	10.9	13.6	14.5	13.8
Net income ($ mil.)	–	(1.0)	(2.4)	1.8	0.8	(0.4)
Market value ($ mil.)	(14.4%)	19.7	11.0	8.5	7.9	5.7
Employees	17.7%	62	73	–	–	–

LKQ CORP   NMS: LKQ

500 West Madison Street, Suite 2800
Chicago, IL 60661
Phone: 312 621-1950
Fax: –
Web: www.lkqcorp.com
CEO: John S. Quinn
CFO: Dominick P. (Nick) Zarcone
HR: –
FYE: December 31
Type: Public

Not just any part will do for LKQ. The company specifically distributes replacement parts and components needed to repair passenger cars and trucks. It's one of the leading aftermarket parts suppliers in the US through subsidiary Keystone Automotive (acquired in 2007). LKQ also offers reconditioned remanufactured and refurbished parts including wheels bumpers mirrors and engines as well as recycled parts that are reclaimed from salvage vehicles. Customers include collision repair and mechanical repair shops. Additionally LKQ operates self-service retail yards that allow customers to come in search through and buy recycled auto parts. To diversifyacquisitive LKQ is expanding internationally.

	Annual Growth	12/10	12/11	12/12	12/13	12/14
Sales ($ mil.)	28.5%	2,469.9	3,269.9	4,122.9	5,062.5	6,740.1
Net income ($ mil.)	22.6%	169.1	210.3	261.2	311.6	381.5
Market value ($ mil.)	5.5%	6,894.4	9,127.9	6,402.9	9,983.6	8,533.1
Employees	25.2%	12,000	17,900	20,300	23,800	29,500

LMI AEROSPACE, INC.   NMS: LMIA

411 Fountain Lakes Blvd.
St. Charles, MO 63301
Phone: 636 946-6525
Fax: –
Web: www.lmiaerospace.com
CEO: Daniel G Korte
CFO: Clifford C Stebe Jr
HR: –
FYE: December 31
Type: Public

LMI Aerospace doesn't have to "just wing it." The company makes key airplane structures such as cockpit window frames fuselage skins and interior components. Its aerostructures segment fabricates machines finishes and integrates more than 40000 aluminum and specialty alloy components for commercial corporate and military aircraft. The engineering services unit (D3 Technologies) provides design engineering and program management services for aircraft. The Intec division designs and tests composites for production parts. The company also makes components for laser equipment used by semiconductor makers and reusable containers with industrial and military applications.

	Annual Growth	12/10	12/11	12/12	12/13	12/14
Sales ($ mil.)	14.8%	223.4	254.0	278.6	412.6	387.8
Net income ($ mil.)	–	12.9	16.4	16.5	(58.5)	(29.0)
Market value ($ mil.)	(3.1%)	208.8	229.2	252.6	192.5	184.2
Employees	10.3%	1,330	1,480	2,420	2,330	1,970

LNB BANCORP, INC.   NMS: LNBB

457 Broadway
Lorain, OH 44052-1769
Phone: 440 244-6000
Fax: 440 244-4815
Web: www.4lnb.com
CEO: –
CFO: –
HR: –
FYE: December 31
Type: Public

LNB Bancorp is the holding company for The Lorain National Bank which operates more than 20 branches in Ohio's Cuyahoga Erie Lorain and Summit counties. The bank serves local businesses and individuals offering such deposit products as checking and savings accounts money market accounts CDs and IRAs. It also offers trust services and credit cards. The bank's lending activities primarily consist of commercial loans (approximately 60% of its portfolio) and real estate mortgages as well as installment and home equity loans. The Lorain National Bank offers brokerage and investment services to customers through an agreement with Investment Centers of America.

	Annual Growth	12/09	12/10	12/11	12/12	12/13
Assets ($ mil.)	1.7%	1,149.5	1,152.5	1,168.4	1,178.3	1,230.3
Net income ($ mil.)	–	(2.0)	5.4	5.0	6.1	6.2
Market value ($ mil.)	23.5%	41.7	48.1	45.5	57.1	97.0
Employees	(0.5%)	272	272	260	262	267

LNR PROPERTY LLC

1601 Washington Ave. Ste. 800
Miami Beach FL 33139
Phone: 305-695-5500
Fax: 305-695-5589
Web: www.lnrproperty.com

CEO: Jeffrey P Krasnoff
CFO: –
HR: –
FYE: November 30
Type: Private

LNR Property looks left 'n' right 'n' all around to find the best real estate opportunities. The company invests in finances and manages real estate and related assets including income-producing properties commercial mortgage-backed securities (CMBS) high-yield mortgage loans and mezzanine financing. LNR Property is the world's largest CMBS special servicer managing about a fourth of all distressed securities that have been turned over to a servicing firm. Homebuilding giant Lennar spun its investment operations off as LNR Property in 1997. Today the company is controlled by investment firm Cerberus Capital Management.

LOCKE LORD LLP

2200 Ross Ave. Ste. 2200
Dallas TX 75201
Phone: 214-740-8000
Fax: 214-740-8800
Web: www.lockelord.com

CEO: –
CFO: Mary Ann Jay
HR: –
FYE: December 31
Type: Private - Partnershi

Whether its involves filing for acquittals sanctions or subpoenas this law firm maintains a strong presence across the country. Employing about 650 lawyers spanning a dozen offices across the US Hong Kong and London Locke Lord Bissell & Liddell specializes in complex litigation regulatory and transactional work. The firm's other practice areas include appellate corporate energy litigation and real estate finance. In addition the firm has a dedicated Troubled Asset Relief Practice (TARP) Group which assists financial institutions insurance companies and broker dealers with adhering to the legal polices and procedures stemming from the government program introduced during the recession in 2008.

LOCAL CORP

7555 Irvine Center Drive
Irvine, CA 92618
Phone: 949-784-0800
Fax: 949-784-0880
Web: www.localcorporation.com

NBB: LOCM Q
CEO: Fred Thiel
CFO: Kenneth S. (Ken) Cragun
HR: –
FYE: December 31
Type: Public

Local.com traffics in keywords. Specializing in paid-search advertising the company connects businesses to consumers online. It attracts more than 30 million visitors per month through its Local.com search site its network of more than 1000 regional media websites and ones that distribute its advertising feeds to third-party sites. It makes money from direct advertisers who bid for placement (based on keywords) and pay per click and from indirect advertising subscribers that gain inclusion on the network through paid-search firms including Yahoo! and SuperMedia. Local.com also offers search engine optimization and other advertising support services.

LOCKHEED MARTIN COMMERCIAL SPACE SYSTEMS

100 Campus Dr.
Newtown PA 18940
Phone: 215-497-1100
Fax: 215-497-4004
Web: www.lmcommercialspace.com

CEO: –
CFO: –
HR: –
FYE: December 31
Type: Business Segment

The Russians launched Sputnik in 1957; it was only a year later that Lockheed Martin launched the world's first communications satellite. Today Lockheed Martin Commercial Space Systems still makes telecommunications scientific and environmental satellites. Its satellites are used for direct broadcast broadband fixed satellite and mobile applications. Lockheed which also makes satellite support and control centers has launched more than 875 satellites since inception. Customers include AsiaSat ASTROLINK Cablevision Systems DISH Network (formerly EchoStar Communications) IKONOS Intelsat Iridium Satellite and Telesat Canada.

	Annual Growth	12/10	12/11	12/12	12/13	12/14
Sales ($ mil.)	(0.3%)	84.1	78.8	97.8	94.4	83.1
Net income ($ mil.)	–	4.2	(14.6)	(24.2)	(10.4)	(5.5)
Market value ($ mil.)	(36.7%)	151.2	49.4	47.8	36.8	24.2
Employees	(11.9%)	116	227	146	88	70

LOCAL MATTERS INC.

1221 Auraria Pkwy.
Denver CO 80204
Phone: 303-572-1122
Fax: 303-572-1123
Web: www.localmatters.com

CEO: Mat Stover
CFO: Marty Katz
HR: –
FYE: December 31
Type: Private

Local Matters speaks to those seeking the higher truths of online directory publishing. The company (formerly Aptas) provides software and media services that enable Yellow Pages print publishers to convert their offerings into Web-based directories. Local Matters also serves more than 400 service providers offering its FlexiQ platform that enables operators to conduct queries and locate local business information. The company's media services include Web site development search engine optimization and search engine marketing. Local Matters which has operations in the Americas Europe and Asia/Pacific was formed from the 2005 merger of Aptas Information Services Extended and YP Web Partners.

LODGIAN INC.

3445 Peachtree Rd. NE Ste. 700
Atlanta GA 30326
Phone: 404-364-9400
Fax: 404-364-0088
Web: www.lodgian.com

CEO: Daniel E Ellis
CFO: James A Maclennan
HR: –
FYE: December 31
Type: Private

If you're living in hotel lodgings does that make you a Lodgian? Lodgian is a multi-brand hospitality franchisee that operates 12 hotels spanning 10 US states. The company's portfolio is focused mostly on the mid-market segment serving both leisure and business travels with full-service brands franchised from Inter-Continental Hotels (including Crowne Plaza and Holiday Inn) and Marriott (Courtyard by Marriott and Residence Inn by Marriott). It also runs a handful of unaffiliated and other branded hotels (Hilton and Doubletree). An affiliate of Lone Star Funds owns Lodgian.

LOEB & LOEB LLP

10100 Santa Monica Blvd. Ste. 2200
Los Angeles CA 90067
Phone: 310-282-2000
Fax: 310-282-2200
Web: www.loeb.com

CEO: –
CFO: –
HR: –
FYE: January 31
Type: Private - Partnershi

Law firm Loeb & Loeb offers counsel in areas such as commercial finance entertainment intellectual property litigation real estate and tax. The firm has five US offices and international offices in Beijing and Hong Kong. Loeb & Loeb has more than 300 lawyers overall including former California governor Gray Davis. Clients have included classic rock 'n' roll band The Grateful Dead the estate of late actress Marilyn Monroe and the Motion Picture Association as well as corporate titans such as Bertelsmann Merrill Lynch and Prudential Securities.

LOEBER MOTORS INC.

4255 W TOUHY AVE
LINCOLNWOOD, IL 607121933
Phone: 847-675-1000
Fax: –
Web: www.loebermotors.com

CEO: –
CFO: –
HR: Kris Colelle
FYE: December 31
Type: Private

Want to buy a car from a son of a son of a salesman? Go to Loeber Motors family-owned and -operated for three generations. The company sells Mercedes-Benz Porsche and smart cars vans and trucks from its dealerships in Lincolnwood Illinois. Loeber Motors also sells used cars and maintains parts and service departments. Loeber's Web site allows visitors to get quick quotes on new cars schedule service appointments order parts apply for finance and search for used vehicles. The site also provides a forum for owners to chat about their cars. Martin Loeber founded Loeber Motors in 1938.

	Annual Growth	12/09	12/10	12/11	12/12	12/13
Sales ($ mil.)	(45.3%)	–	120.8	139.0	138.9	19.8
Net income ($ mil.)	(19.7%)	–	–	2.2	1.7	1.4
Market value ($ mil.)	–	–	–	–	–	–
Employees	–	–	–	–	–	110

LOEHMANN'S HOLDINGS INC.

2500 Halsey St.
Bronx NY 10461
Phone: 718-409-2000
Fax: 718-518-2766
Web: www.loehmanns.com

CEO: Steven Newman
CFO: –
HR: –
FYE: January 31
Type: Private

Humorist Erma Bombeck claimed that "All I Know About Animal Behavior I Learned in Loehmann's Dressing Room" --- and if you've ever tussled over the last discounted Donna Karan blouse at one of this retailer's stores you know what she was talking about. With some 40 Loehmann's stores in about a dozen states and the District of Columbia Loehmann's stores sells designer and brand-name women's and men's apparel accessories intimate apparel fragrances shoes and gifts at deep discounts. But caution to the shy: Loehmann's is famous for its communal dressing rooms. Founded in Brooklyn in 1921 by Frieda Loehmann the company was acquired by Dubai-based Istithmar PJSC in 2006. It emerged from Chapter 11 in 2011.

LOEWS CORP.

NYS: L

667 Madison Avenue
New York, NY 10065-8087
Phone: 212 521-2000
Fax: –
Web: www.loews.com

CEO: Thomas F. (Tom) Motamed
CFO: David B. Edelson
HR: –
FYE: December 31
Type: Public

When it comes to diversification Loews definitely has the low-down. The holding company's main interest is insurance through publicly traded subsidiary CNA Financial which offers commercial property/casualty coverage. Other wholly owned and partially owned holdings include hotels in the US and Canada through its Loews Hotels subsidiary. Its energy holdings include contract oil-drilling operator Diamond Offshore Drilling (which operates roughly 35 offshore oil rigs) and interstate natural gas transmission pipeline systems operator Boardwalk Pipeline. Loews is controlled and run by the Tisch family including co-chairmen and cousins Andrew and Jonathan.

	Annual Growth	12/10	12/11	12/12	12/13	12/14
Assets ($ mil.)	0.7%	76,277.0	75,375.0	80,021.0	79,939.0	78,367.0
Net income ($ mil.)	(17.7%)	1,288.0	1,064.0	568.0	595.0	591.0
Market value ($ mil.)	1.9%	14,510.9	14,041.0	15,197.1	17,990.4	15,670.7
Employees	(1.2%)	18,400	18,250	18,300	18,175	17,510

LOGANSPORT FINANCIAL CORP.

NBB: LOGN

723 East Broadway
Logansport, IN 46947
Phone: 574 722-3855
Fax: 574 722-3857
Web: www.logansportsavings.com

CEO: –
CFO: Dottye Robeson
HR: –
FYE: December 31
Type: Public

Community banking is the main sport at Logansport. Logansport Financial is the holding company for Logansport Savings Bank which serves customers in Cass County Indiana. From a single office in Logansport the bank offers individuals and businesses a variety of financial services including such deposit products as checking savings and NOW accounts as well as IRAs and certificates of deposit. Logansport Savings Bank uses funds from deposits to originate residential mortgages which account for almost half of its loan portfolio. The bank originally chartered in 1925 also offers home equity home improvement commercial real estate business and consumer loans.

	Annual Growth	12/05	12/06	12/07	12/13	12/14
Assets ($ mil.)	0.1%	157.8	159.9	156.8	166.0	159.7
Net income ($ mil.)	5.7%	1.1	1.0	0.8	1.7	1.8
Market value ($ mil.)	5.6%	11.4	10.9	10.2	16.4	18.6
Employees	–	–	–	–	–	–

LOGIC DEVICES INCORPORATED

PINK SHEETS: LOGC

1375 Geneva Dr.
Sunnyvale CA 94089
Phone: 408-542-5400
Fax: 408-542-0080
Web: www.logicdevices.com

CEO: Bill Volz
CFO: Kimiko Milheim
HR: –
FYE: September 30
Type: Public

LOGIC Devices doesn't produce philosophical machines. Rather LOGIC specializes in high-end digital signal processor (DSP) chips used in applications including medical imaging instrumentation telecommunications and military weapons systems. The company outsources production of its chips to Asian foundries primarily Taiwan Semiconductor Manufacturing. LOGIC works with sales representatives and international distributors and also sells directly to OEMs including Lockheed Martin QUALCOMM Raytheon Sony Teradyne and Texas Instruments.

LOGICALIS INC.

1 PENN PLZ STE 5130
NEW YORK, NY 10119-5160
Phone: 212-596-7160
Fax: –
Web: www.us.logicalis.com

CEO: Vince Deluca
CFO: –
HR: –
FYE: February 29
Type: Private

Logicalis believes enterprise technology should operate in a straightforward fashion. The company provides a variety of IT services such as consulting implementation systems integration staffing network design and training. Logicalis also offers managed services for tasks such as network security IT infrastructure management and monitoring and application management. Customers come from a variety of fields including manufacturing financial services and health care. In the US Logicalis operates from more than 20 offices. It is a subsidiary of UK-based Logicalis Group. Both are owned by South Africa-based Datatec Limited.

	Annual Growth	02/08	02/09	02/10	02/11	02/12
Sales ($ mil.)	(2.1%)	–	409.3	338.5	357.7	384.3
Net income ($ mil.)	(21.3%)	–	8.7	0.7	5.0	4.3
Market value ($ mil.)	–	–	–	–	–	–
Employees	–	–	–	–	–	700

LOGICQUEST TECHNOLOGY INC

NBB: LOGQ

410 Park Avenue, 15th Floor #31,
New York, NY 10022
Phone: 212 231-0033
Fax: –
Web: www.bluegate.com

CEO: Ang Woon Han
CFO: Cheng Yew Siong
HR: –
FYE: December 31
Type: Public

Bluegate holds the keys to the gates of medical information. The company provides information technology (IT) services to the health care industry. It specializes in medical-grade network and managed services that meet HIPAA compliance regulations. It serves hospitals medical practices and other centralized health care providers. The company operates a leading Medical Grade Network dedicated to health care-related security and privacy concerns; Bluegate markets it as the only such network in the US. Memorial Hermann Health Net Providers a subsidiary of the Memorial Hermann Healthcare System is a client; Bluegate also provides services to the Texas-based Renaissance Healthcare Systems.

	Annual Growth	12/10	12/11	12/12	12/13	12/14
Sales ($ mil.)	(40.0%)	0.3	0.2	0.1	0.1	0.0
Net income ($ mil.)	–	(0.2)	(0.5)	(0.5)	(0.6)	(0.5)
Market value ($ mil.)	–	0.0	0.0	0.0	0.0	0.0
Employees	–	–	–	–	–	–

LOGISTICARE INC.

1800 Phoenix Blvd. Ste. 120
Atlanta GA 30349
Phone: 770-907-7596
Fax: 770-907-7598
Web: www.logisticare.com

CEO: Herman Schwarz
CFO: Thomas E Oram
HR: –
FYE: December 31
Type: Subsidiary

LogistiCare is a go-between for getting from your house to the doctor's office and back. The company brokers non-emergency transportation services for commercial health plans government entities (such as state Medicaid agencies) and hospitals throughout the US. Using its nearly 20 call centers and a network of some 1500 independent contracted transportation providers the company coordinates the medical-related travel arrangements of its clients' members. In addition it contracts with local school boards to coordinate transportation for special needs students. The company provides more than 26 million trips each year for clients in some 40 states. LogistiCare is a subsidiary of Providence Service.

LOGISTICS MANAGEMENT SOLUTIONS L.C.

1 CITYPLACE DR STE 415
SAINT LOUIS, MO 63141-7066
Phone: 314-692-8886
Fax: –
Web: www.lmslogistics.com

CEO: Dennis Schoemehl
CFO: Scott Hunt
HR: –
FYE: December 31
Type: Private

Logistics Management Solutions (LMS) ensures a speedy delivery. The company provides a variety of third-party logistics and supply chain management services from process optimization consulting to shipment execution and transportation management. LMS also offers TOTAL a Web-based software package designed to work with customers' enterprise resource planning (ERP) systems. The company operates through a network of independent shippers to safely efficiently and cost-effectively manage the transportation of freight for manufacturers as well as wholesalers and retailers. Its roster of customers has included Monsanto (former parent) BASF Sara Lee Honeywell and American Railcar.

	Annual Growth	12/05	12/06	12/07	12/08	12/09
Sales ($ mil.)	–	–	–	(371.3)	108.4	97.5
Net income ($ mil.)	1353.8%	–	–	0.0	2.6	3.5
Market value ($ mil.)	–	–	–	–	–	–
Employees	–	–	–	–	–	146

LOGMEIN INC

NMS: LOGM

320 Summer Street, Suite 100
Boston, MA 02210
Phone: 781 638-9050
Fax: 781 437-1803
Web: www.logmein.com

CEO: William R. Wagner
CFO: Edward K. (Ed) Herdiech
HR: –
FYE: December 31
Type: Public

LogMeIn wants to help you stay productive even on the go. The company provides Web-based remote access software and services to consumers small and midsized businesses and IT service providers. Its user access and remote collaboration offerings serve consumers and business users while businesses and IT service providers use LogMeIn's technology to provide remote management and support. LogMeIn offers both free and subscription-based services. Its paid services add advanced features such as file transfer remote printing and drive mapping. Corporate customers include 3M AMD and IBM. Although LogMeIn's services are sold around the world about two-thirds of sales come from US clients.

	Annual Growth	12/10	12/11	12/12	12/13	12/14
Sales ($ mil.)	21.7%	101.1	119.5	138.8	166.3	222.0
Net income ($ mil.)	(21.6%)	21.1	5.8	3.6	(7.7)	8.0
Market value ($ mil.)	2.7%	1,082.7	941.3	547.2	819.2	1,204.8
Employees	18.0%	415	482	575	613	804

LOJACK CORP

NMS: LOJN

40 Pequot Way
Canton, MA 02021
Phone: 781 302-4200
Fax: –
Web: www.lojack.com

CEO: –
CFO: Kenneth L Dumas
HR: Jeannine Lombardi-Sheehan
FYE: December 31
Type: Public

LoJack's signature product helps police recover stolen vehicles — a chilling thought for those driving hot cars. When a car equipped with a LoJack transmitter is stolen its signal is activated and tracked by police. The company rents tracking computers to law enforcement agencies then markets transponders to dealers and operators in 28 states and the District of Columbia and roughly 30 countries internationally. It also sells products for tracking people personal electronics cargo data and commercial equipment. LoJack provides installation and maintenance of its units which are manufactured by third parties.

	Annual Growth	12/10	12/11	12/12	12/13	12/14
Sales ($ mil.)	(2.3%)	146.6	140.8	132.5	140.2	133.6
Net income ($ mil.)	–	(18.3)	1.4	(8.4)	3.2	(17.9)
Market value ($ mil.)	(20.8%)	121.2	57.6	52.3	67.7	47.6
Employees	1.8%	624	607	636	685	670

LONG BEACH MEDICAL CENTER

455 E BAY DR
LONG BEACH, NY 11561-2301
Phone: 516-897-1000
Fax: –
Web: www.lbmc.org

CEO: –
CFO: –
HR: –
FYE: December 31
Type: Private

After crisping on one of Long Island's south coast beaches one might just need to go to Long Beach Medical Center (LBMC) to have that nasty burn treated. LBMC serves half a dozen Long Island communities. The facility has more than 160 acute care beds at the main center as well as 200 subacute care beds at The Komanoff Center for Geriatric and Rehabilitative Medicine and provides certified Home Care Agency and numerous outpatient programs. LBMC also provides behavioral health family health care emergency and rehabilitation services. Its Family Care Center offers health care to those with inadequate financial resources. LBMC has teaching affiliations with the New York College of Podiatric Medicine and the New York College of Osteopathic Medicine.

	Annual Growth	12/03	12/04	12/05	12/06	12/08
Sales ($ mil.)	–	–	–	(775.1)	73.3	78.0
Net income ($ mil.)	–	–	–	0.0	(1.1)	(2.3)
Market value ($ mil.)	–	–	–	–	–	–
Employees	–	–	–	–	–	830

LONG BEACH MEMORIAL MEDICAL CENTER

2801 ATLANTIC AVE
LONG BEACH, CA 908061701
Phone: 562-933-2000
Fax: –
Web: www.supportlongbeach.memorialcare.org

CEO: Barry Arbuckle
CFO: Wendy Dorchester
HR: Jonathan S Berek
FYE: June 30
Type: Private

Long Beach Memorial Medical Center (LBMMC) is an old-timer in the Long Beach health care market. A subsidiary of Memorial Health Services LBMMC provides a full range of health services to residents of the Long Beach California area. The medical center a 420-bed acute-care hospital was founded in 1907 and is one of the largest private hospitals on the West Coast. Services include primary emergency diagnostic surgical therapeutic and rehabilitative care. The hospital is home to centers for treatment of cancer heart stroke and women's and children's health concerns. It also provides home and hospice care programs as well as occupational health services.

	Annual Growth	06/06	06/07	06/08	06/09	06/11
Sales ($ mil.)	55.8%	–	–	–	446.2	1,083.1
Net income ($ mil.)	8.8%	–	–	–	53.7	63.5
Market value ($ mil.)	–	..	–	–	–	–
Employees	–	–	–	–	–	–

LONG ISLAND UNIVERSITY

700 NORTHERN BLVD
GREENVALE, NY 115481327
Phone: 516-299-2535
Fax: –
Web: www.liu.edu

CEO: –
CFO: Robert Altholz
HR: –
FYE: August 31
Type: Private

Long Island University (LIU) helps students see a long future in professional fields including medicine and business. LIU has an enrollment of more than 24000 students at multiple locations in New York State. The university employs more than 600 full-time faculty members and has a 12:1 student-to-teacher ratio. LIU offers 575 degree programs and certificates in fields including pharmacy nursing health sciences education liberal arts sciences business and information studies. The school traces its roots to 1886 when the Brooklyn College of Pharmacy was founded.

	Annual Growth	08/08	08/09	08/10	08/11	08/12
Sales ($ mil.)	10.0%	–	363.6	370.7	468.6	484.1
Net income ($ mil.)	–	–	–	(1.1)	2.5	4.6
Market value ($ mil.)	–	–	–	–	–	–
Employees	–	–	–	–	–	3,300

LONG JOHN SILVER'S LLC

9505 Williamsburg Plz.
Louisville KY 40222
Phone: 502-815-6100
Fax: 214-740-8800
Web: www.lockelord.com

CEO: –
CFO: –
HR: –
FYE: December 31
Type: Private

Avast ye and prepare to board the largest quick-service seafood restaurant chain on the US mainland. Taking its name from a character in Robert Louis Stevenson's "Treasure Island" Long John Silver's franchises more than 1200 nautically themed eateries offering such menu items as batter-dipped fish chicken shrimp and hushpuppies. Patrons can also select from sandwiches and salads as well as chicken items and family-size meals. The Long John Silver's chain operates primarily in the US though it does have a small number of international locations. The seafood chain traces its roots back to 1929; it was part of the YUM! Brands fast food empire that includes KFC Pizza Hut and Taco Bell until late 2011.

LONGVIEW FIBRE COMPANY

300 Fibre Way
Longview WA 98632
Phone: 360-425-1550
Fax: 360-575-5935
Web: www.longviewfibre.com

CEO: Roger W Stone
CFO: Andrea K Tarbox
HR: Mike R Fitzpatrick
FYE: December 31
Type: Subsidiary

"Paper or plastic?" is not an option at Longview Fibre. The company owns and manages tree farms one of the largest pulp and paper mills in North America. Its mill and plants produce specialty kraft paper (FibreShield and TEA-Kraft brands) recycled bag and wrapping paper (FibreGreen) containerboard (FibreLok) and converted goods such as corrugated containers packaging and point-of-purchase displays. No shortage of lumber Longview Fibre's timberland spans more than 580000 acres in Oregon and Washington and its unprocessed logs are sold to saw mills and plywood plants. Longview Fibre is owned by Brookfield Asset Management.

LOOKSMART LTD.

NAS: LOOK

50 California Street, 16th Floor
San Francisco, CA 94108
Phone: 415 348-7000
Fax: –
Web: www.looksmart.com

CEO: –
CFO: –
HR: –
FYE: December 31
Type: Public

It's hard to find anything online without looking unless you're talking about ads. LookSmart helps publishers advertisers and consumers see what they want when it comes to online advertising. The company earns most of its revenue through its Advertiser Networks offering (AdCenter) which provides advertisers with targeted pay-per-click search advertising contextual advertising and banner products. It also offers Publisher Solutions that help content publishers maintain advertiser relationships online. LookSmart completed its transition to a full-on provider of advertising and publishing services after a couple of years spent divesting its non-core consumer website assets.

	Annual Growth	12/09	12/10	12/11	12/12	12/13
Sales ($ mil.)	(40.1%)	51.8	47.5	27.6	15.7	6.7
Net income ($ mil.)	–	(6.2)	1.0	(2.5)	(11.0)	(5.4)
Market value ($ mil.)	18.9%	5.9	12.2	7.4	5.1	11.8
Employees	(20.5%)	65	52	50	38	26

LOOP LLC

137 NORTHPARK BLVD
COVINGTON, LA 704335071
Phone: 985-632-6970
Fax: –
Web: www.loopllc.com

CEO: –
CFO: –
HR: –
FYE: December 31
Type: Private

LOOP (Louisiana Offshore Oil Port) offloads crude oil from tankers stores it and routes it to pipelines and refineries along the Gulf Coast and the Midwest. It is also the storage and terminalling facility for the MARS pipeline system and its supply of offshore Gulf of Mexico crude oil. Oil is stored in eight underground caverns leached out of a naturally occurring salt dome. These caverns are capable of storing about 50 million barrels of crude oil. The company is owned by Marathon Ashland Pipe Line Murphy Oil and Shell Oil. In addition to other services LOOP has an above-ground tank farm made up of six 600000 barrel tanks.

	Annual Growth	12/04	12/05	12/06	12/08	12/09
Sales ($ mil.)	7.3%	–	184.0	235.8	265.3	243.6
Net income ($ mil.)	(5.8%)	–	–	104.3	79.2	87.3
Market value ($ mil.)	–	–	–	–	–	–
Employees	–	–	–	–	–	128

LOOPNET INC.

NASDAQ: LOOP

185 Berry St. Ste. 4000
San Francisco CA 94107
Phone: 415-243-4200
Fax: 415-764-1622
Web: www.loopnet.com

CEO: Richard J Boyle Jr
CFO: Brent Stumme
HR: –
FYE: December 31
Type: Subsidiary

Feeling out of the loop when it comes to commercial real estate? LoopNet provides information services to the commercial real estate market through LoopNet.com. Its flagship LoopNet Marketplace includes some 788000 property listings; it offers a free basic membership as well as a subscription-based premium membership. LoopNet has more than 4 million registered members and about 68000 premium members. The firm also offers LoopLink which helps real estate brokers integrate LoopNet listings into their own websites; BizBuySell and BizQuest online marketplaces for businesses that are for sale; and commercial real estate network CityFeet.com. Real estate data firm CoStar Group owns LoopNet.

LORILLARD, INC.

NYS: LO

714 Green Valley Road
Greensboro, NC 27408-7018
Phone: 336 335-7000
Fax: –
Web: www.lorillard.com

CEO: –
CFO: –
HR: –
FYE: December 31
Type: Public

Money smells of menthol at Lorillard the #3 cigarette maker in the US (behind Philip Morris and Reynolds American). Flagship brand Newport is its best-selling menthol cigarette and #2-top selling cigarette name in the US accounting for about 85% of sales. Other brands include the premium and discount lines of Kent Old Gold True and Maverick as well as the blu e-cigarette. The company sells its lineup to wholesale distributors (who supply retail and chain stores and government agencies). Lorillard was known as the Carolina Group until 2008 when it split from former parent Loews. Founded in 1760 by French immigrant Pierre Lorillard it is the nation's oldest continuously operating tobacco business.

	Annual Growth	12/10	12/11	12/12	12/13	12/14
Sales ($ mil.)	4.2%	5,932.0	6,466.0	6,623.0	6,950.0	6,990.0
Net income ($ mil.)	3.6%	1,029.0	1,116.0	1,099.0	1,180.0	1,187.0
Market value ($ mil.)	(6.4%)	29,541.6	41,040.0	42,001.2	18,244.8	22,658.4
Employees	1.8%	2,700	2,800	2,900	2,900	2,900

LOS ANGELES COUNTY DEPARTMENT OF HEALTH SERVICES

313 N. Figueroa St.
Los Angeles CA 90012
Phone: 213-240-8101
Fax: 213-250-4013
Web: www.ladhs.org

CEO: –
CFO: –
HR: –
FYE: June 30
Type: Government Agency

Los Angeles County Department of Health Services is one of the US's largest publicly supported health systems. The department includes three general acute care hospitals a rehabilitation hospital (Rancho Los Amigos National Rehabilitation Center which has some 400 beds) two ambulatory care centers and several community health clinics. The system is the main provider of health care for the area's poor and uninsured. It provides general medical and surgical care and is affiliated with the medical school at USC. The system also manages the Emergency Medical Services (EMS) Agency and the Community Health Plan HMO a low-cost managed care plan for members of Medicaid and other state-funded programs.

LOS ANGELES COUNTY METROPOLITAN TRANSPORTATION AUTHORITY

1 Gateway Plaza
Los Angeles CA 90012-2952
Phone: 213-922-6000
Fax: 213-922-2704
Web: www.metro.net

CEO: Arthur Leahy
CFO: Nalini Ahuja
HR: –
FYE: June 30
Type: Government-owned

In the City of Angels it takes more than wings to get around. Thanks to the bus and rail systems of the Los Angeles County Metropolitan Transportation Authority (LACMTA or Metro) millions of passengers are carried through one of the most populous counties in the US via Metro Bus Metrolink (commuter rail) and Metro Rail (subway and light rail). Together they cover an extensive freeway network four airports and various ports. LACTMA operates these systems and it serves as a transportation planner designer and builder. A 14-member board consisting of elected officials (including the mayor) and appointees secures the budget (approximately $4 billion) and selects the projects for Metro.

LOS ANGELES DEPARTMENT OF WATER AND POWER

111 N HOPE ST
LOS ANGELES, CA 900122607
Phone: 213-367-4211
Fax: –
Web: www.ladwp.com

CEO: –
CFO: Phil Leiber
HR: –
FYE: June 30
Type: Private

The Los Angeles Department of Water and Power (LADWP) keeps the movie cameras running and the swimming pools full. The largest municipally owned utility in the US LADWP provides electricity to 1.4 million residential and business customers and water to 666000 customers. The company has power plant interests that give it more than 7220 MW of generating capacity; it also buys and sells wholesale power. Most of the city's water supply is transported through two aqueduct systems from the Sierra Nevada Mountains; other water sources include wells and local groundwater basins. Because LADWP is city-owned its retail monopoly status has been unaffected by utility deregulation in California.

	Annual Growth	06/07	06/08	06/09	06/10	06/11
Sales ($ mil.)	284.8%	–	–	–	812.4	3,126.0
Net income ($ mil.)	(14.4%)	–	–	–	67.3	57.6
Market value ($ mil.)	–	–	–	–	–	–
Employees	–	–	–	–	–	8,000

LOS ANGELES DODGERS INC.

1000 Elysian Park Ave.
Los Angeles CA 90012-1199
Phone: 323-224-1500
Fax: 323-224-1269
Web: losangeles.dodgers.mlb.com

CEO: Ron Wheeler
CFO: -
HR: -
FYE: October 31
Type: Private

These Dodgers try to be artful on the baseball diamond. The Los Angeles Dodgers sports franchise is one of the oldest and most storied franchises in Major League Baseball boasting six World Series championships and 21 National League pennants. The team started in Brooklyn New York in 1884 but moved west to Los Angeles in 1957. The Dodgers were the first team to break the color barrier with the signing of Jackie Robinson. The team plays home games at Dodger Stadium. In April 2012 a group led by former Los Angeles Lakers star Magic Johnson acquired the iconic Dodgers franchise from Frank McCourt for a record $2.15 billion.

LOUIS VUITTON NORTH AMERICA INC.

19 E. 57th St.
New York NY 10022
Phone: 212-931-2000
Fax: 212-931-2730
Web: www.lvmh.com

CEO: Antonio Belloni
CFO: Patrice Pfistner
HR: Stella Ietta
FYE: December 31
Type: Subsidiary

Louis Vuitton North America knows fashion and leather retailing. The company is the North American operating subsidiary of French luxury goods giant LVMH Moet Hennessy Louis Vuitton which boasts more than 60 luxury brands including Clicquot Dom Perignon Moet & Chandon Christian Dior Givenchy Donna Karan (DKI) Sephora and TAG Heuer. Louis Vuitton North America runs the Louis Vuitton fashion and leather goods business in the US. The company also dabbles in duty free shopping. Louis Vuitton North America operates more than 530 US stores including a four-story emporium on New York's Fifth Avenue. The North American arm of the Maison contributed about 20% of its parent company's 2012 sales.

LOS ANGELES PHILHARMONIC ASSOCIATION

151 S GRAND AVE
LOS ANGELES, CA 900123034
Phone: 213-972-7300
Fax: -
Web: www.hollywoodbowl.com

CEO: Deborah Borda
CFO: -
HR: -
FYE: September 30
Type: Private

The Los Angeles Philharmonic Association promotes its orchestra which is one of Southern California's leading performing arts institutions. The orchestra often known simply as the LA Phil performs orchestral and chamber music jazz world music and holiday concerts at the Walt Disney Concert Hall (in winter) and the Hollywood Bowl (in summer). The orchestra that would become the Los Angeles Philharmonic was originally founded and financed back in 1919 by copper baron and music enthusiast William Andrews Clark Jr. The Association was officially formed in 1976 but traces its roots to the beginning of the orchestra.

	Annual Growth	09/01	09/02	09/07	09/08	09/13
Sales ($ mil.)	-	-	0.0	0.0	103.2	124.8
Net income ($ mil.)	-	-	-	0.0	14.2	14.5
Market value ($ mil.)	-	-	-	-	-	-
Employees	-	-	-	-	-	2,000

LOUISIANA BANCORP INC

NMS: LABC

1600 Veterans Memorial Boulevard
Metairie, LA 70005
Phone: 504 834-1190
Fax: -
Web: www.bankofneworleans.com

CEO: -
CFO: -
HR: -
FYE: December 31
Type: Public

Louisiana Bancorp's vault isn't filled with Mardi Gras doubloons ch ire. The holding company owns the Bank of New Orleans which offers standard retail banking products to individuals and small businesses including deposit accounts loans and mortgages and credit cards. Residential mortgages represent about half of the bank's loan portfolio; commercial mortgages and land loans make up most of the rest. Bank of New Orleans operates three locations and a loan office in the Crescent City; a fourth branch has been closed since being damaged by Hurricane Katrina in 2005. The bank was founded in 1909 as Greater New Orleans Homestead.

	Annual Growth	12/09	12/10	12/11	12/12	12/13
Assets ($ mil.)	(1.0%)	329.8	320.9	313.1	311.9	316.7
Net income ($ mil.)	1.7%	2.5	2.6	2.1	2.5	2.7
Market value ($ mil.)	5.9%	41.9	42.1	45.8	49.0	52.6
Employees	0.7%	68	65	64	72	70

LOTUS DEVELOPMENT CORPORATION

55 Cambridge Pkwy.
Cambridge MA 02142-1234
Phone: 617-577-8500
Fax: +47-67-12-64-99
Web: www.navico.com

CEO: -
CFO: -
HR: -
FYE: December 31
Type: Subsidiary

This lotus helps employee collaboration bloom. Lotus Development an IBM subsidiary that does business as Lotus Software develops business applications that help people collaborate across corporate networks. Its main offering is the communication and collaboration platform Lotus Notes. Other products include messaging and scheduling applications (Domino) collaboration management (LotusLive) and corporate social networking software (Connections). The company also offers consulting support and training. Lotus products are marketed through IBM's vast sales organization and via an extensive collection of global partners and distributors. Clients have included leading Israeli bank Bank Hapoalim and Bayer.

LOUISIANA HEALTH SERVICE AND INDEMNITY COMPANY

5525 Reitz Ave.
Baton Rouge LA 70809
Phone: 225-295-3307
Fax: 225-295-2054
Web: www.bcbsla.com

CEO: Mike Reitz
CFO: Adam Short
HR: -
FYE: December 31
Type: Private - Not-for-Pr

The Bayou State's largest health insurer Louisiana Health Service and Indemnity operates as Blue Cross and Blue Shield of Louisiana (BCBSLA) an independent licensee of the Blue Cross and Blue Shield Association. It provides health insurance products and related services to more than 1.1 million members from offices across the state. BCBSLA offers HMO PPO supplemental Medicare and traditional indemnity plans as well as the BlueSaver high-deductible plan with a health savings account. Its HMO Louisiana subsidiary offers a point-of-service (POS) plan that provides some out-of-network benefits. Customers include both individuals and employer groups. BCBSLA is a mutual insurance firm owned by its customers.

LOUISIANA-PACIFIC CORP.   NYS: LPX

414 Union Street
Nashville, TN 37219
Phone: 615-986-5600
Fax: 615-986-5666
Web: www.lpcorp.com

CEO: Curtis M. (Curt) Stevens
CFO: Sallie B. Bailey
HR: –
FYE: December 31
Type: Public

Louisiana-Pacific (LP) has you surrounded. The building materials company specializes in manufacturing products for floors walls and roofs. LP produces oriented strand board (OSB) siding products and engineered wood products. It also makes decorative molding and cellulose insulation. Products are used in new home and manufactured housing construction and for repair and remodeling. The company sells its products to distributors dealers professional lumberyards and retail home centers including The Home Depot. It has production facilities throughout North and South America. After a difficult period during the recession and housing crisis LP is poised to capitalize on the uptick in housing starts.

	Annual Growth	12/10	12/11	12/12	12/13	12/14
Sales ($ mil.)	8.7%	1,383.6	1,356.9	1,715.8	2,085.2	1,934.8
Net income ($ mil.)	–	(39.0)	(181.3)	28.8	177.1	(75.4)
Market value ($ mil.)	15.0%	1,345.5	1,147.8	2,747.8	2,632.6	2,355.3
Employees	4.3%	3,800	3,900	3,900	4,200	4,500

LOVE'S TRAVEL STOPS & COUNTRY STORES INC.

10601 N. Pennsylvania Ave.
Oklahoma City OK 73120
Phone: 405-751-9000
Fax: 405-749-9110
Web: www.loves.com

CEO: Tom E Love
CFO: Doug Stussi
HR: –
FYE: December 31
Type: Private

If you're a trucker or RVer on the road all you need is Love's. Love's Travel Stops & Country Stores operates more than 290 travel stop locations and 150 truck tire care centers throughout a swath of about 40 states from California to Virginia including convenience stores in Colorado Kansas New Mexico Oklahoma and Texas. Each travel stop includes a convenience store; a fast-food restaurant such as Taco Bell or Subway; and gas outlets for cars trucks and RVs. The travel stops also provide shower rooms laundry facilities game rooms and mail drops. Love's Travel Stops & Country Stores is owned by the family of CEO Tom Love who founded the company in 1964.

LOW TEMP INDUSTRIES INC.

9192 TARA BLVD
JONESBORO, GA 302364913
Phone: 678-379-0913
Fax: –
Web: www.lowtempind.com

CEO: William E Casey
CFO: Richard V Priegel
HR: Angie Norris
FYE: October 31
Type: Private

Bam! Cooks kick it up a notch on Low Temp Industries' commercial chef's counters and dish tables. Constructed of stainless steel the tables and counters outfit the kitchens of restaurants hospitals schools and cafeterias. The chef's counter can be custom built for the customer to include a variety of food warmers shelves self-contained sandwich units cutting boards and a sink. Low Temp also manufactures custom serving counters for dining areas and automatic dish conveyors with washing systems., Low Temp's, Colorpoint division builds mobile fiberglass serving line equipment while its Visions division designs and builds specialty counters booths window treatments signage and menu boards.

	Annual Growth	10/02	10/03	10/04	10/06	10/07
Sales ($ mil.)	4.7%	–	19.6	20.3	24.4	23.5
Net income ($ mil.)	–	–	–	0.0	0.0	0.0
Market value ($ mil.)	–	–	–	–	–	–
Employees	–	–	–	–	–	150

LOWE ENTERPRISES INC.

11777 San Vicente Blvd. Ste. 900
Los Angeles CA 90049
Phone: 310-820-6661
Fax: 310-207-1132
Web: www.loweenterprises.com

CEO: –
CFO: William Raphae
HR: –
FYE: December 31
Type: Private

Lowe knows how to navigate the property market. Through subsidiaries Lowe Enterprises invests in develops renovates and manages commercial real estate primarily in the western US. It operates through three divisions: Lowe Hospitality Group a hotel development and management firm and parent of Destination Hotels & Resorts; Lowe Enterprises Investors which invests on the behalf of pension plans; and Lowe Enterprises Real Estate which develops and manages commercial and residential real estate. Notable properties include Inverness Hotel in Denver and Teton Mountain Lodge in Jackson Hole Wyoming. Founded in 1972 by CEO Robert Lowe the firm is owned by about 50 shareholders and has about 15 offices.

LOWE'S COMPANIES INC   NYS: LOW

1000 Lowe's Blvd.
Mooresville, NC 28117
Phone: 704-758-1000
Fax: –
Web: www.lowes.com

CEO: –
CFO: Robert A. Niblock
HR: Maureen K. Ausura
FYE: January 30
Type: Public

No longer a low-profile company Lowe's Companies has evolved from a regional hardware store operator into a nationwide chain of home improvement superstores bent on international expansion. The #2 US home improvement chain (after The Home Depot) Lowe's operates nearly 1800 stores in the US along with some 40 stores in Canada 10 stores in Mexico and an e-commerce site. Its stores sell roughly 36000 products for do-it-yourselfers and professionals for home improvement and repair projects such as lumber paint plumbing and electrical supplies tools and gardening products as well as appliances lighting and furniture. Lowe's is also the second-largest US home appliance retailer after Sears.

	Annual Growth	01/11*	02/12	02/13*	01/14	01/15
Sales ($ mil.)	3.6%	48,815.0	50,208.0	50,521.0	53,417.0	56,223.0
Net income ($ mil.)	7.6%	2,010.0	1,839.0	1,959.0	2,286.0	2,698.0
Market value ($ mil.)	28.0%	24,240.0	26,112.0	37,017.6	44,438.4	65,049.6
Employees	3.3%	234,000	248,000	245,000	262,000	266,000

*Fiscal year change

LOWE'S FOOD STORES INC.

1381 Old Mill Circle Ste. 200
Winston-Salem NC 27114
Phone: 336-659-0180
Fax: 336-768-4702
Web: www.lowesfoods.com

CEO: –
CFO: –
HR: Paula Mitchell
FYE: September 30
Type: Subsidiary

Lowe's Food Stores operates a chain of more than 100 supermarkets in North Carolina South Carolina and Virginia. The stores offer traditional supermarket fare including fresh meat seafood deli and bakery departments in addition to natural foods and supplements. The regional grocery chain's Lowe's-Foods-to-Go program lets customers shop online and either pick up their groceries at their local Lowe's Food store or have them delivered. The company's Just$ave division operates more than 15 discount food stores in North Carolina as well as more than half a dozen fuel stations. Founded in 1954 Lowe's Food Stores is owned by food wholesaler Alex Lee.

LOWENSTEIN SANDLER PC

65 Livingston Ave.
Roseland NJ 07068-1791
Phone: 973-597-2500
Fax: 973-597-2400
Web: www.lowenstein.com

CEO: Gary M Wingens
CFO: William B Farrell
HR: –
FYE: December 31
Type: Private - Partnershi

Lowenstein Sandler a New Jersey law firm of nearly 300 attorneys offers a full range of legal services. Its core practice areas include corporate employment and employee benefits life sciences litigation real estate and trusts. Lowenstein Sandler is also affiliated with Issues Management a lobbying firm run by lawyers and public policy advocates. Lowenstein Sandler operates from offices in New York; Palo Alto California; and Roseland New Jersey. The firm has represented clients including celebrity photographer Annie Leibovitz pharmaceuticals giant Schering-Plough Ivy League pillar Princeton University and utilities holding company PSEG Global.

LOWER COLORADO RIVER AUTHORITY

3700 Lake Austin Blvd.
Austin TX 78703
Phone: 512-473-3200
Fax: 703-907-5528
Web: www.nreca.org

CEO: –
CFO: –
HR: –
FYE: June 30
Type: Government-owned

The stars at night may be big and bright but more than 1 million people deep in the heart of Texas still need electricity from the Lower Colorado River Authority (LCRA). Serving 55 counties along the lower Colorado River between Central Texas and the Gulf of Mexico the not-for profit state-run entity supplies wholesale electricity to more than 40 retail utilities (primarily municipalities and cooperatives). It operates three fossil-fuel powered plants and six hydroelectric dams that give it a production capacity of about 3800 megawatts; it also purchases electricity from Texas wind farms. The LCRA provides water and wastewater utility services to more than 30 communities as well.

LOYOLA MARYMOUNT UNIVERSITY INC

1 LMU DR STE 100
LOS ANGELES, CA 900452677
Phone: 310-338-3055
Fax: –
Web: www.lmu.edu

CEO: –
CFO: –
HR: –
FYE: May 31
Type: Private

Loyola Marymount University (LMU) in Los Angeles is a Jesuit (Catholic) institution with an enrollment of more than 9500 students. It offers more than 115 graduate and undergraduate programs through four colleges: Bellarmine College of Liberal Arts College of Business Administration College of Communication and Fine Arts and Seaver College of Science and Engineering. There is also the School of Education and School of Film and Television. Other programs include the Graduate Division Continuing Education Program and Loyola Law School. LMU has an 11:1 student-to-faculty ratio. The university was formed in 1973 by the merger of Loyola College (founded in 1911) and Marymount Junior College.

	Annual Growth	05/05	05/06	05/07	05/12	05/13
Sales ($ mil.)	4.9%	–	234.9	254.3	320.2	328.7
Net income ($ mil.)	(6.4%)	–	–	93.4	(16.3)	62.9
Market value ($ mil.)	–	–	–	–	–	–
Employees	–	–	–	–	–	1,449

LOYOLA UNIVERSITY MARYLAND INC.

4501 N CHARLES ST
BALTIMORE, MD 212102601
Phone: 410-617-2000
Fax: –
Web: www.loyola.edu

CEO: –
CFO: –
HR: –
FYE: May 31
Type: Private

Loyola University in Maryland is a Jesuit Catholic university that offers studies in liberal arts and sciences. In addition to its undergraduate programs Loyola has graduate degree programs in education speech pathology finance psychology modern studies pastoral counseling and engineering science. The university annually enrolls about 3500 undergraduate and some 2600 graduate students. The school has more than 300 full-time faculty and a student-teacher ratio of about 12:1. Loyola was founded in 1852 by Father John Early and eight other Jesuits.

	Annual Growth	05/09	05/10	05/11	05/12	05/13
Sales ($ mil.)	5.8%	–	222.0	238.4	185.2	263.0
Net income ($ mil.)	27.9%	–	–	11.9	(2.3)	19.5
Market value ($ mil.)	–	–	–	–	–	–
Employees	–	–	–	–	–	2,066

LOYOLA UNIVERSITY NEW ORLEANS INC

6363 SAINT CHARLES AVE
NEW ORLEANS, LA 701186195
Phone: 504-865-2011
Fax: –
Web: www.loyno.edu

CEO: –
CFO: Rhonda Cartwright
HR: –
FYE: July 31
Type: Private

Loyola University New Orleans provides legal medical and fine arts education programs in the Big Easy. The university is part of US network of Jesuit universities and enrolls roughly 5000 students. The liberal arts university offers some 65 undergraduate and 15 graduate degree programs through five colleges: Business Humanities and Natural Science Law Music and Fine Arts and Social Sciences. Loyola University New Orleans has about 500 full-time and part-time faculty members and it has a student-to-teacher ratio of 11:1.

	Annual Growth	07/10	07/11	07/12	07/13	07/14
Sales ($ mil.)	1.4%	–	129.4	126.7	154.3	135.0
Net income ($ mil.)	–	–	–	(16.0)	26.3	3.2
Market value ($ mil.)	–	–	–	–	–	–
Employees	–	–	–	–	–	1,000

LPL FINANCIAL HOLDINGS INC.

NMS: LPLA

75 State Street
Boston, MA 02109
Phone: 617 423-3644
Fax: –
Web: www.lpl.com

CEO: Mark S. Casady
CFO: Thomas D. Lux
HR: –
FYE: December 31
Type: Public

LPL Financial (formerly LPL Investment Holdings) is one of the largest independent brokerage firms in the US. The firm offers technology training infrastructure and research as well as stocks bonds mutual funds annuities insurance and other investment products and services. Its clients include some 14100 self-employed advisers nationwide. LPL doesn't create or sell its own investment products but it provides access to those of other firms. The brokerage firm provides similar services to about 700 US community banks and credit unions. It also performs clearing and custody services for financial professionals and institutions. LPL was formed in 1989 by the merger of Linsco and Private Ledger.

	Annual Growth	12/10	12/11	12/12	12/13	12/14
Sales ($ mil.)	8.9%	3,113.5	3,479.4	3,661.1	4,140.9	4,373.7
Net income ($ mil.)	–	(56.9)	170.4	151.9	181.9	178.0
Market value ($ mil.)	5.2%	3,533.2	2,966.8	2,735.6	4,570.7	4,327.8
Employees	7.0%	2,583	2,726	2,917	3,185	3,384

LQ MANAGEMENT LLC

909 Hidden Ridge Ste. 600
Irving TX 75038
Phone: 214-492-6600
Fax: 214-492-6616
Web: www.lq.com

CEO: –
CFO: Keith Cline
HR: –
FYE: December 31
Type: Subsidiary

La Quinta...Spanish for "Next to Denny's?" LQ Management is owner of the La Quinta (which is Spanish for the villa) hotel brand. The company has hotels throughout the US (about 45 states) Canada and Mexico under the La Quinta Inns and La Quinta Inn & Suites brands. LQ Management franchises the majority of its properties. The growing company has more than 800 hotels which encompass some 65000 guest rooms; in addition it has some 200 properties in the development pipeline. La Quinta hotels operate in the limited service midscale segment. It targets a mix of corporate and leisure travelers. LQ Management is owned by investment firm The Blackstone Group.

LRAD CORP NAS: LRAD

16990 Goldentop Road
San Diego, CA 92127
Phone: 858 676-1112
Fax: –
Web: www.lradx.com

CEO: Thomas R Brown
CFO: Katherine H McDermott
HR: –
FYE: September 30
Type: Public

High-tech sound may drive development for LRAD (formerly American Technology Corporation) but the firm is also banking on it to drive its bottom line. LRAD whose past sales largely came from its portable radios discontinued its portable consumer electronics division to make products that transmit sound over short and long distances. The company's Long Range Acoustic Devices generate the majority of revenues nowadays and they have been deployed by the US military and used by public safety agencies worldwide. To strengthen its identity as a global provider of long-range acoustic technology systems the company changed its name to LRAD in 2010.

	Annual Growth	09/11	09/12	09/13	09/14	09/15
Sales ($ mil.)	(10.8%)	26.5	14.8	17.1	24.6	16.8
Net income ($ mil.)	17.8%	5.0	1.5	1.3	3.3	9.7
Market value ($ mil.)	(2.6%)	60.9	45.7	47.7	89.2	54.9
Employees	3.1%	39	36	38	41	44

LRI HOLDINGS INC.

3011 Armory Dr. Ste. 300
Nashville TN 37204
Phone: 615-885-9056
Fax: 615-885-9057
Web: www.logansroadhouse.com

CEO: Samuel N Borgese
CFO: Edmund J Schwartz
HR: –
FYE: July 31
Type: Private

LRI Holdings earns a lot of peanuts even though it gives them away for free. The company operates Logan's Roadhouse a chain of casual restaurants that serve generous-sized plates of grilled steaks chicken barbecued ribs and hamburgers. The chain prides itself on its affordable prices (the average bill is less than $15) while also offering free all-you-can-eat buckets of shelled peanuts and rolls. LRI Holdings has 185 company-owned locations of Logan's Roadhouse across 20 states and 26 franchises in four states. LRI Holdings was formed in 2006 by a private investor group. The company agreed to be acquired by private equity firm Kelso & Co. in 2010.

LRR ENERGY, L.P. NYS: LRE

Heritage Plaza, 1111 Bagby, Suite 4600
Houston, TX 77002
Phone: 713 292-9510
Fax: –

CEO: Scott W Smith
CFO: Richard A Robert
HR: –
FYE: December 31
Type: Public

What do Texas Oklahoma and New Mexico have in common? Oil gas and LRR Energy. An oil and natural gas producer LRR Energy owns assets in the Permian Basin in West Texas and southern New Mexico the Mid-Continent region in Oklahoma and East Texas and along the Gulf Coast in Texas. The company's properties have proved reserves of more than 30 million barrels of oil equivalent. It operates more than 850 oil or gas-producing wells. Formed in April 2011 from assets held by investment fund Lime Rock Resources LRR Energy and went public in November 2011.

	Annual Growth	12/09	12/10	12/11	12/12	12/13
Sales ($ mil.)	–	0.0	0.0	21.8	105.5	115.1
Net income ($ mil.)	–	0.0	0.0	12.2	(0.0)	(48.7)
Market value ($ mil.)	–	0.0	0.0	515.8	452.1	447.9
Employees	–	–	–	–	–	–

LSB FINANCIAL CORP. NMS: LSBI

101 Main Street
Lafayette, IN 47901
Phone: 765 742-1064
Fax: –
Web: www.lsbank.com

CEO: Randolph F Williams
CFO: Mary Jo David
HR: –
FYE: December 31
Type: Public

There's nothing psychedelic about LSB. Straight-laced LSB Financial is the holding company for Lafayette Savings Bank which has been serving northern Indiana since 1869. Today the bank has a handful of branches in the communities of Lafayette and West Lafayette offering checking savings and money market accounts NOW accounts and CDs. It primarily writes real estate loans with residential mortgages making up about half of the company's loan portfolio. It also writes commercial and multifamily residential mortgages real estate construction loans and land development loans.

	Annual Growth	12/08	12/09	12/10	12/11	12/12
Assets ($ mil.)	(0.6%)	373.0	371.1	371.8	364.3	364.6
Net income ($ mil.)	11.2%	1.7	0.5	2.1	0.5	2.7
Market value ($ mil.)	18.6%	15.5	15.2	21.1	21.0	30.7
Employees	1.3%	91	97	93	100	96

LSB INDUSTRIES, INC. NYS: LXU

16 South Pennsylvania Avenue
Oklahoma City, OK 73107
Phone: 405 235-4546
Fax: 405 235-5067
Web: www.lsbindustries.com

CEO: Daniel D Greenwell
CFO: Mark T. Behrman
HR: –
FYE: December 31
Type: Public

LSB Industries makes a wide variety of chemicals (including nitric acid) and climate-control products. Its Chemical business segment makes nitrate fertilizers and acids for agricultural mining and industrial markets. The Climate Control division makes hydronic fan coils and a variety of heat pumps and other heating ventilation and air conditioning (HVAC) products. LSB Industries also sells industrial machinery and related parts to machine tool dealers and other customers in North America. The company's Chemical unit accounted for 62% of the company's 2014 revenues; geographically most of its sales are within the US.

	Annual Growth	12/10	12/11	12/12	12/13	12/14
Sales ($ mil.)	4.7%	609.9	805.3	759.0	679.3	732.5
Net income ($ mil.)	(9.7%)	29.6	83.8	58.6	55.0	19.6
Market value ($ mil.)	6.7%	549.4	634.8	802.2	929.0	712.0
Employees	2.3%	1,780	1,841	1,881	1,885	1,949

LSI CORP

NMS: LSI

1320 Ridder Park Drive
San Jose, CA 95131
Phone: 408 433-8000
Fax: –
Web: www.lsi.com

CEO: Abhijit Y Talwalkar
CFO: Bryon Look
HR: –
FYE: December 31
Type: Public

LSI can show you around the circuit. The fabless semiconductor developer provides standard integrated circuits (ICs) and custom-designed application-specific ICs (ASICs) focusing on broadband and wireless communications data storage personal computer and networking markets. LSI (an acronym for large-scale integration) was a pioneer of system-on-a-chip (SoC) devices which combine elements of an electronic system — essentially a microprocessor memory and logic — onto a single chip. LSI also provides hardware and software for storage area networks. Customers located in the Asia/Pacific region account for most of the company's sales. LSI has agreed to be acquired by Avago Technologies for $6.6 billion.

	Annual Growth	12/08	12/09	12/10	12/11	12/12
Sales ($ mil.)	(1.6%)	2,677.1	2,219.2	2,570.0	2,044.0	2,506.1
Net income ($ mil.)	–	(622.3)	(47.7)	40.0	331.5	196.2
Market value ($ mil.)	21.1%	1,812.4	3,310.9	3,299.9	3,277.8	3,894.8
Employees	(1.9%)	5,488	5,397	5,718	4,588	5,080

LSI INDUSTRIES INC.

NMS: LYTS

10000 Alliance Road
Cincinnati, OH 45242
Phone: 513 793-3200
Fax: –
Web: www.lsi-industries.com

CEO: Dennis W. Wells
CFO: Ronald S. Stowell
HR: Sharon Martin
FYE: June 30
Type: Public

LSI Industries will dance sing and do just about anything to get your name in lights. The company makes lighting graphics and menu boards for various commercial markets primarily in the US and Canada. LSI operates via several business segments. Its lighting unit makes LED light fixtures for outdoor/indoor/landscape use such as convenience and chain store lighting. A graphics arm produces indoor/outdoor graphics lighting and menu boards including digital signage canopy graphics and shelf talkers. Design and production of LED video screens is led by its technology and electronic components units. The company sells to a diverse group of customers like ExxonMobil Burger King Ford and Wal-Mart.

	Annual Growth	06/11	06/12	06/13	06/14	06/15
Sales ($ mil.)	1.2%	293.5	268.4	280.8	299.5	307.9
Net income ($ mil.)	(17.0%)	10.8	3.2	(0.1)	0.9	5.2
Market value ($ mil.)	4.1%	193.7	173.7	197.3	194.7	227.8
Employees	1.6%	1,482	1,456	1,467	1,617	1,579

LTC PROPERTIES, INC.

NYS: LTC

2829 Townsgate Road, Suite 350
Westlake Village, CA 91361
Phone: 805 981-8655
Fax: –
Web: www.ltcproperties.com

CEO: Wendy L. Simpson
CFO: Pamela J. (Pam) Shelley-Kessler
HR: –
FYE: December 31
Type: Public

Specializing in TLC LTC Properties sees real estate as a healthy investment. The self-administered real estate investment trust (REIT) primarily invests in health care and long-term care facilities. Its portfolio includes about 90 assisted living centers (homes for elderly residents not requiring constant supervision) more than 100 skilled nursing facilities (which provide rehabilitative and restorative nursing care) a dozen other health care properties (such as independent living or memory care) and even a couple of schools. It owns properties in more than 25 states. Top tenants include Brookdale Senior Living Extendicare and Prestige Care.

	Annual Growth	12/10	12/11	12/12	12/13	12/14
Sales ($ mil.)	12.5%	74.3	85.2	94.0	105.0	119.0
Net income ($ mil.)	12.5%	45.9	49.3	51.3	57.8	73.4
Market value ($ mil.)	11.4%	996.3	1,094.9	1,248.5	1,255.6	1,531.7
Employees	10.0%	13	17	18	18	19

LUBY'S, INC.

NYS: LUB

13111 Northwest Freeway, Suite 600
Houston, TX 77040
Phone: 713 329-6800
Fax: 210 654-3211
Web: www.lubys.com; www.lubysinc.com

CEO: Christopher J Pappas
CFO: K Scott Gray
HR: –
FYE: August 26
Type: Public

This company has a spot in the cafeteria line and behind the burger grill. Luby's is a multi-concept restaurant operator with two flagship brands: Luby's and Fuddruckers. Its namesake chain includes about 90 cafeteria-style restaurants found almost entirely in Texas that offer dozens of different entrees salads vegetable dishes and desserts. Its menu is heavy on such comfort foods as mashed potatoes macaroni and cheese and fried chicken. Luby's also operates and franchises about 60 Fuddruckers locations in more than 30 states that specialize in gourmet made-to-order hamburgers. In addition the company owns several smaller chains and provides contract foodservices to clients mostly in Houston.

	Annual Growth	08/11	08/12	08/13	08/14	08/15
Sales ($ mil.)	3.1%	348.7	350.1	390.4	394.4	394.1
Net income ($ mil.)	–	3.0	6.9	3.3	(3.4)	(2.1)
Market value ($ mil.)	0.6%	130.3	180.7	207.6	155.2	133.4
Employees	3.3%	7,348	7,320	9,100	8,490	8,352

LUCAS ENERGY INC

ASE: LEI

450 Gears Road, Suite 780
Houston, TX 77067
Phone: 713 528-1881
Fax: 713 337-1510
Web: www.lucasenergy.com

CEO: –
CFO: Anthony C Schnur
HR: –
FYE: March 31
Type: Public

Lucas Energy puts a good amount of energy into drilling. The independent crude oil and gas company owns and operates about 35 production wells and holds more than 1.5 million barrels of oil in proved reserves. Its operations are spread over some 11000 acres primarily in the Austin Chalk region of Texas. The company leases its well-producing properties from local landowners and small operators and is building up its reserve base by acquiring and re-drilling older or underperforming wells that have been overlooked by larger oil and gas companies. Most of Lucas Energy's revenue comes from sales of crude oil to customers such as Gulfmart and Texon with the remainder derived from natural gas sales.

	Annual Growth	03/11	03/12	03/13	03/14	03/15
Sales ($ mil.)	(0.2%)	3.0	5.3	8.2	5.2	3.0
Net income ($ mil.)	–	(4.5)	(7.6)	(6.8)	(4.7)	(5.1)
Market value ($ mil.)	(50.5%)	5.0	3.5	1.9	1.1	0.3
Employees	(24.9%)	22	26	18	17	7

LUCASFILM ENTERTAINMENT COMPANY LTD.

1110 Gorgas Ave.
San Francisco CA 94129
Phone: 415-746-8000
Fax: +82-2-3773-2292
Web: www.lg.co.kr

CEO: –
CFO: –
HR: –
FYE: April 30
Type: Subsidiary

Not so long ago in a galaxy not so far away filmmaker George Lucas founded a software company to entertain audiences with something other than movies. Lucasfilm Entertainment (which does business as LucasArts) produces games for computers and home video game consoles. Much of that source material is of course the "Star Wars" films created by Lucas. LucasArts has more "Star Wars" games than you can shake a lightsaber at and it also produces games based on Lucasfilm's successful trilogy of "Indiana Jones" films as well as other titles such as the popular and acclaimed Monkey Island series. LucasArts' products are distributed in about 60 countries worldwide through its own distribution efforts and those of partners.

LUCID INC.

2320 Brighton Henrietta Town Line Rd.
Rochester NY 14623
Phone: 585-239-9800
Fax: 585-239-9806
Web: www.lucid-tech.com

CEO: L Michael Hone
CFO: Richard J Pulsifer
HR: –
FYE: December 31
Type: Private

Lucid Inc. hopes to have a clear understanding of skin cancer. The company's medical imaging device the VivaScope cuts down on the ouch factor for skin biopsies. The VivaScope takes a microscopic-resolution picture of a skin lesion a less painful alternative to the traditional method of cutting out a portion of the lesion to ship off to the lab. Lucid Inc. has also developed a complementary network called VivaNet that allows immediate transfer of the images over the Internet for pathologists to diagnose melanoma and give patients same-day results. The VivaScope is cleared for sale and use in Australia China the European Union and the US. Lucid Inc. filed a modest $28.75 million IPO in April 2011.

LUMBER LIQUIDATORS HOLDINGS INC   NYS: LL

3000 John Deere Road
Toano, VA 23168
Phone: 757 259-4280
Fax: –
Web: www.lumberliquidators.com

CEO: John M. Presley
CFO: Gregory A. Whirley
HR: –
FYE: December 31
Type: Public

Customers are floored by Lumber Liquidators Holdings if the sales staff does its job. Known for its low prices Lumber Liquidators is one of the nation's largest retailers of hardwood flooring. It sells more than 25 domestic and exotic species of hardwoods from more than 340 Lumber Liquidators stores in about 46 states and Canada online by catalog and from its Virginia call center. The company also offers antique and reclaimed boards laminate flooring moldings and installation products. Its brands include Bellawood Builder's Pride Schön Morning Star and Virginia Mill Works. Homeowners represent about 90% of Lumber Liquidators' customer base. The company was founded in 1994 by chairman Tom Sullivan.

	Annual Growth	12/10	12/11	12/12	12/13	12/14
Sales ($ mil.)	14.0%	620.3	681.6	813.3	1,000.2	1,047.4
Net income ($ mil.)	24.6%	26.3	26.3	47.1	77.4	63.4
Market value ($ mil.)	27.7%	674.3	478.0	1,430.1	2,785.2	1,795.0
Employees	12.3%	1,191	1,302	1,420	1,750	1,891

LUCKEY FARMERS INC.

1200 W MN ST
WOODVILLE, OH 43469
Phone: 419-849-2711
Fax: –
Web: www.luckeyfarmers.com

CEO: Daniel Walski
CFO: –
HR: –
FYE: January 31
Type: Private

You don't have to be lucky to be a grain farmer in northwestern Ohio but the members of Luckey Farmers agricultural cooperative might feel fortunate just the same. The co-op offers services such as grain storage and marketing for the corn soybean and wheat crops of its member-farmers. It supplies its members with grain marketing and agronomy services and information feed and seed processing facilities gas stations and fuel-delivery services. Luckey Farmers which has approximately 2000 member/farmers was established in 1919.

	Annual Growth	01/03	01/04	01/05	01/06	01/07
Sales ($ mil.)	(7.7%)	–	–	95.6	72.3	81.4
Net income ($ mil.)	7019.8%	–	–	0.0	0.9	0.7
Market value ($ mil.)	–	–	–	–	–	–
Employees	–	–	–	–	–	115

LUMINESCENT SYSTEMS INCORPORATED

130 Commerce Way
East Aurora NY 14052
Phone: 716-655-0800
Fax: 716-655-0309
Web: www.lumsys.com

CEO: –
CFO: Dave Burner
HR: Jill Draper
FYE: December 31
Type: Subsidiary

When you're flying you want the pilot to see everything he or she needs to see and so does Luminescent Systems. A unit of Astronics Luminescent Systems makes high-performance lighting systems for commercial aircraft which represents approximately 60% of sales; it also makes systems for private/business and military aircraft — each accounting for about 20% of sales. Products include cabin emergency lighting cockpit lighting and formation lighting systems. Luminescent Systems operates two manufacturing facilities in the US (East Aurora New York; and Lebanon New Hampshire) and one in Canada (Quebec). Customers include the US military as well as Panasonic Avionics Bombardier (Learjet) and Boeing.

LULULEMON ATHLETICA INC   NMS: LULU

1818 Cornwall Avenue
Vancouver, British Columbia V6J 1C7
Phone: 604 732-6124
Fax: 604 874-6124
Web: www.lululemon.com

CEO: –
CFO: –
HR: –
FYE: February 01
Type: Public

lululemon athletica designs and sells yoga-inspired apparel under the lululemon athletica and ivivva athletica brands to the limber and athletically hip. It operates some 250 company-owned stores primarily located in North America. The rest are in Australia and New Zealand where lululemon operates through a joint venture. While it specializes in making women's clothing for yoga dance and running the company also offers men's apparel. Third-party mostly Taiwanese vendors make its clothing which is distributed from facilities in Canada the US and Australia. The fast-growing company was founded in 1998 by Chairman Dennis "Chip" Wilson.

	Annual Growth	01/11	01/12*	02/13	02/14	02/15
Sales ($ mil.)	26.1%	711.7	1,000.8	1,370.4	1,591.2	1,797.2
Net income ($ mil.)	18.3%	121.8	184.1	270.6	279.5	239.0
Market value ($ mil.)	(0.9%)	9,738.8	9,101.5	9,632.4	6,485.5	9,402.4
Employees	17.2%	4,572	5,807	6,383	7,622	8,628

*Fiscal year change

LUMINEX CORP   NMS: LMNX

12212 Technology Blvd.
Austin, TX 78727
Phone: 512 219-8020
Fax: –
Web: www.luminexcorp.com

CEO: Nachum Shamir
CFO: Harriss T Currie
HR: Nancy Capezzuti
FYE: December 31
Type: Public

William Blake could "see a world in a grain of sand" and Luminex can reveal hundreds of secrets in a drop of fluid. Its xMAP (Multi-Analyte Profiling) technology allows simultaneous analysis of up to 500 bioassays or tests from a single drop of fluid. xMAP consists of instruments software and disposable microspheres (microscopic polystyrene beads on which tests are performed). Luminex also uses Multi-Code real-time polymerase chain reaction and xTAG technology. Luminex's systems are used by clinical and research laboratories and are distributed through strategic partnerships with other life sciences firms. Luminex also develops testing assays and disposable testing supplies for the clinical diagnostics market.

	Annual Growth	12/10	12/11	12/12	12/13	12/14
Sales ($ mil.)	12.5%	141.6	184.3	202.6	213.4	227.0
Net income ($ mil.)	65.3%	5.2	14.5	12.4	7.1	39.0
Market value ($ mil.)	0.7%	764.2	887.5	702.3	811.0	784.3
Employees	9.1%	525	614	687	731	745

LUMMUS TECHNOLOGY INC.

1515 Broad St.
Bloomfield NJ 07003-3096
Phone: 973-893-1515
Fax: 973-893-2000
Web: www.cbi.com/lummus

CEO: Philip K Asherman
CFO: Ronald A Ballschmiede
HR: –
FYE: December 31
Type: Subsidiary

Lummus Technology looms large across the globe in engineering projects. The company provides engineering procurement and construction-related services for the petrochemical refining and gas processing industries. The subsidiary of Chicago Bridge & Iron Company (CB&I) oversees the construction of process plants and offshore facilities performing a range of services including process design project management project financing engineer training and technical support. Its Lummus Heat Transfer unit supplies and designs specialized heat transfer equipment. Major clients include Chevron Shell and ExxonMobil.

LUMOS NETWORKS CORP.

NMS: LMOS

One Lumos Plaza
Waynesboro, VA 22980
Phone: 540 946-2000
Fax: –
Web: www.lumosnetworks.com

CEO: Timothy G. Biltz
CFO: Johan G. Broekhuysen
HR: –
FYE: December 31
Type: Public

Lumos Networks hopes your every telephone conversation is illuminating. The company spun off from wireless operator NTELOS in 2011 comprises NTELOS' wireline business. Lumos Networks provides data voice and IP service to carrier business government and residential customers over a 7800-mile fiber network in the Mid-Atlantic region (Virginia West Virginia and portions of Kentucky Maryland Ohio and Pennsylvania). Its network allows it to offer bundled cable Internet and phone service. It also operates as a rural local-exchange carrier (RLEC) in the rural Virginia cities of Waynesboro and Covington and portions of Alleghany Augusta and Botetourt counties.

	Annual Growth	12/10	12/11	12/12	12/13	12/14
Sales ($ mil.)	8.4%	146.0	207.4	206.9	207.5	201.5
Net income ($ mil.)	0.8%	20.8	(43.9)	16.3	17.8	21.5
Market value ($ mil.)	3.1%	–	345.8	225.9	473.4	379.2
Employees	4.9%	–	524	602	579	604

LUNA INNOVATIONS INC

NAS: LUNA

301 First Street SW, Suite 200
Roanoke, VA 24011
Phone: 540 769-8400
Fax: –
Web: www.lunainc.com

CEO: –
CFO: Scott A. Graeff
HR: Jonathan (Jon) Murphy
FYE: December 31
Type: Public

R&D firm Luna Innovations endeavors to make practical use of cutting-edge technologies in the areas of molecular technology and sensing. Its molecular technology efforts focus on materials (including polymers reagents and nanomaterials) with enhanced performance characteristics; Luna has developed contrast agents for MRI testing nanomaterials used in solar cells and protective coatings. It has also created sensing technologies used in medical monitoring equipment as well as wireless and fiber-optic monitoring systems for defense and industrial instrumentation. In mid-2015 Luna Innovations merged with Advanced Photonix.

	Annual Growth	12/10	12/11	12/12	12/13	12/14
Sales ($ mil.)	(11.4%)	34.5	35.6	32.3	22.0	21.3
Net income ($ mil.)	–	(2.6)	(1.4)	(1.4)	(0.8)	6.0
Market value ($ mil.)	(4.0%)	25.2	26.1	18.1	21.1	21.4
Employees	(11.8%)	187	185	170	138	113

LUND INTERNATIONAL INC.

4325 Hamilton Mill Rd. Ste. 400
Buford GA 30518
Phone: 678-804-3767
Fax: 952-937-4515
Web: www.mts.com

CEO: George Scherff
CFO: Glenn A Hollis
HR: –
FYE: December 31
Type: Private

Whether you favor form or function Lund manufactures accessories to make your car or truck stand out while it holds up. The company sells more than 150 vehicle-accessory product lines to both OEMs and the automotive aftermarket. Lund's aftermarket products are sold through a network of dealers warehouse distributors specialty chain stores and catalog companies. The company's products include such indispensables as bug deflectors external windshield visors grill and brush guards hood shields rear-window air deflectors rock guards running boards taillight and headlight covers and tonneau covers for pickup beds.

LUNDBECK INC.

4 Parkway North Ste. 200
Deerfield IL 60015
Phone: 847-282-1000
Fax: 847-282-1001
Web: www.lundbeckinc.com

CEO: Sean Nolan
CFO: Curtis Rhine
HR: Patty Adams
FYE: December 31
Type: Subsidiary

Lundbeck Inc. (formerly Ovation Pharmaceuticals) is staying on the look-out for niche pharmaceuticals that larger drugmakers cast aside. The company's focus is on marketing and developing drugs for central nervous system (CNS) disorders as well as cancer drugs and hospital-based therapies for rare conditions. Its FDA-approved products for neurological conditions include treatments for ADHD anxiety and seizures. The company's pipeline includes several CNS products including epilepsy drugs drug addiction therapies and seizure medications. Among its other marketed products are several oncology drugs as well as a treatment for lead poisoning. The company was acquired by Denmark-based H. Lundbeck in 2009.

LUSTER PRODUCTS CO.

1104 W. 43rd St.
Chicago IL 60609
Phone: 773-579-1800
Fax: 773-579-1912
Web: www.lusterproducts.com

CEO: Jory Luster
CFO: –
HR: –
FYE: December 31
Type: Private

Luster Products wants its customers to win the best tressed award. The African-American-owned company makes professional and consumer hair care products for people of African descent. Its products are sold to men and women under several brand names including Renutrients Pink and S-Curl. Luster Products sells children's items under the PCJ Pretty-n-Silky & Smooth Roots name and products for stylists under the Designer Touch line. It sells its products worldwide through its own sales force and through specialty retailers. The hair care firm operates manufacturing facilities in Illinois and international branch offices in South Africa and the UK. The company was founded in 1957 by hairstylist Fred Luster Sr.

LUTHER COLLEGE

700 COLLEGE DR
DECORAH, IA 521011041
Phone: 563-387-1372
Fax: –
Web: www.english.luther.edu

CEO: –
CFO: –
HR: –
FYE: May 31
Type: Private

Luther College is an independent liberal arts school offering undergraduate and graduate programs to about 2500 students from about 35 states and 40 countries. The college provides more than 60 majors and professional certificate programs. The Luther student body has more than 110 student-run clubs and organizations 19 athletic teams and 15 student music ensembles. Courses are conducted by 181 full-time teaching faculty members 89% with Ph.D. or equivalent. The ratio of students to faculty is 12:1. Luther College is affiliated with the Evangelical Lutheran Church in America.

	Annual Growth	05/10	05/11	05/12	05/13	05/14
Sales ($ mil.)	2.9%	–	79.0	76.4	80.8	85.9
Net income ($ mil.)	–	–	–	(1.8)	19.0	16.3
Market value ($ mil.)	–	–	–	–	–	–
Employees	–	–	–	–	–	550

LUTHERAN MEDICAL CENTER

150 55th St.
Brooklyn NY 11220
Phone: 718-630-7000
Fax: 317-848-0713
Web: www.deltafaucet.com

CEO: –
CFO: –
HR: –
FYE: December 31
Type: Private - Not-for-Pr

Unlike the Dodgers Lutheran Medical Center isn't leaving Brooklyn. The health care system serves patients in the New York City borough through a network that includes its primary Lutheran Medical Center (LMC) as well as the 240-bed skilled nursing facility Lutheran Augustana Center for Extended Care and Rehabilitation and several neighborhood clinics and nursing homes. LMC is a 470-bed tertiary care teaching hospital affiliated with the State University of New York Health Science Center at Brooklyn and other university medical programs. Lutheran Medical Center also operates a home health program under the Community Care Organization name. It's a social ministry of the Evangelical Lutheran Church in America.

LUXOTTICA RETAIL

4000 Luxottica Place
Mason OH 45040
Phone: 513-765-6000
Fax: 513-765-6249
Web: www.luxottica.com

CEO: –
CFO: –
HR: –
FYE: December 31
Type: Business Segment

If you need glasses Luxottica Retail has you in its sights. The retail arm of Italian eyewear giant Luxottica Group Luxottica Retail is one of the world's leading operators of optical stores. The company has more than 6200 locations in North America Europe China the Asia/Pacific region the Middle East and Africa. Its chains include LensCrafters Oakley Oliver Peoples Pearle Vision and Sunglass Hut as well as more than 1200 in-store businesses Sears Optical and Target Optical. About 5675 of Luxottica Retail's stores are company-owned; the rest are franchised. In addition Luxottica Retail oversees a leading US managed vision care plan EyeMed Vision Care which serves some 3400 corporations.

LUXOTTICA RETAIL NORTH AMERICA INC.

4000 Luxottica Place
Mason OH 45040
Phone: 513-765-6000
Fax: 513-765-6249
Web: www.lenscrafters.com

CEO: –
CFO: Jack Dennis
HR: –
FYE: December 31
Type: Subsidiary

LensCrafters brings eyewear and malls together. Part of the growing retail arm (Luxottica Retail) of Italy's Luxottica Group LensCrafters is North America's largest seller of eyewear and related services (based on sales) with about 955 stores in the US Canada and Puerto Rico. The company-owned stores mainly located in shopping malls offer prescription frames and sunglasses (most made by Luxottica) contact lenses and vision exams by an on-site optometrist. Most of the locations house in-store lens finishing labs. Beyond North America Luxottica operates some 260 LensCrafters stores in China and Hong Kong. Founded in 1983 LensCrafters was acquired by Luxottica to increase its retail presence.

LYDALL, INC.

NYS: LDL

One Colonial Road
Manchester, CT 06042
Phone: 860 646-1233
Fax: 860 646-4917
Web: www.lydall.com

CEO: Dale G. Barnhart
CFO: Robert K. Julian
HR: William (Bill) Lachenmeyer
FYE: December 31
Type: Public

Lydall's products help to beat the heat nix the noise and filter the rest. The company makes thermal and acoustical barriers automotive heat shields and insulation products that offer protection in extreme temperatures. Lydall's thermal and acoustical products are used by the appliance and automotive industries and in industrial kilns and furnaces. The company rounds out its offerings with industrial and commercial air and liquid filtration products and — through its subsidiary Charter Medical — fluid management systems for the medical and biopharmaceutical markets. Export sales represent about 45% of the company's annual net sales.

	Annual Growth	12/10	12/11	12/12	12/13	12/14
Sales ($ mil.)	12.2%	338.0	383.6	378.9	398.0	535.8
Net income ($ mil.)	68.1%	2.7	13.8	16.8	19.2	21.8
Market value ($ mil.)	42.1%	139.4	164.4	248.4	305.2	568.4
Employees	7.0%	1,600	1,600	1,600	1,600	2,100

LYNCHBURG COLLEGE

1501 LAKESIDE DR
LYNCHBURG, VA 245013113
Phone: 434-544-8100
Fax: –
Web: www.lynchburg.edu

CEO: –
CFO: –
HR: –
FYE: June 30
Type: Private

In Lynchburg Tennessee they make whiskey. In Lynchburg Virginia they make graduates. Lynchburg College is an independent residential college with more than 170 full-time faculty members and about 2300 undergraduate and graduate students across some 40 majors. It consists of six schools: Business and Economics Communication and the Arts Education and Human Development Health Sciences and Human Performance Humanities and Social Sciences and Sciences. Tuition is about $14000 per semester; however virtually all students receive financial aid. The college was founded in 1903 by Dr. Josephus Hopwood a Christian Church (Disciples of Christ) minister and his wife Sarah.

	Annual Growth	06/10	06/11	06/12	06/13	06/14
Sales ($ mil.)	(9.8%)	–	87.3	62.0	62.5	64.1
Net income ($ mil.)	–	–	–	(2.6)	11.2	21.5
Market value ($ mil.)	–	–	–	–	–	–
Employees	–	–	–	–	–	1,077

LYNDEN INCORPORATED

18000 International Blvd. Ste. 800
Seattle WA 98188-4255
Phone: 206-241-8778
Fax: 206-243-8415
Web: www.lynden.com

CEO: -
CFO: Brad McKeown
HR: -
FYE: December 31
Type: Private

Lynden lends you a hand by sendin' your freight by truck barge train or airplane. With some 15 subsidiaries Lynden transports truckload (TL) and less-than-truckload (LTL) shipments primarily to Alaska Canada and the northwestern US. It also arranges international air and ocean forwarding as well as customs brokerage and multi-modal logistics. The company carries dry freight bulk chemicals and refrigerated cargo for companies in the oil/gas mining construction retail and manufacturing sectors. Lynden's offers barge service between Seattle and southeastern Alaska and airfreight service within Alaska. The company traces its roots to 1907 and is owned by CEO Jim Jansen's family.

LYNTEGAR ELECTRIC COOPERATIVE INC.

1807 MAIN ST
TAHOKA, TX 79373
Phone: 806-561-4588
Fax: -
Web: www.lyntegar.coop

CEO: Greg Henley
CFO: -
HR: Jana Bishop
FYE: December 31
Type: Private

Lyntegar Electric Cooperative is based in the agricultural heart of the Texas Panhandle where the summer heat sizzles and the winter ice storms freeze. The rural power cooperative provides electric utility services to customers in Borden Dawson Gaines Garza Hockley Lynn Martin Terry and Yoakum counties. The cooperative also sells electric grills and provides internet and television services. In addition Lyntegar Electric Cooperative produces Typically Texas Cookbooks which share collections of recipes used by cooperative member-consumers.

	Annual Growth	12/09	12/10	12/11	12/12	12/13
Sales ($ mil.)	7.3%	-	58.3	73.0	63.8	71.9
Net income ($ mil.)	(12.7%)	-	-	10.0	9.4	7.7
Market value ($ mil.)	-	-	-	-	-	-
Employees	-	-	-	-	-	103

LYNUXWORKS INC.

855 Embedded Way
San Jose CA 95138-1018
Phone: 408-979-3900
Fax: 408-979-3920
Web: www.lynuxworks.com

CEO: Gurjot Singh
CFO: -
HR: Gurjot L Singh Rajpa
FYE: April 30
Type: Private

LynuxWorks works hard to make Linux work for its clients. The company's LynxOS and BlueCat operating systems power miniaturized computers known as embedded systems that are built into hardware for airplanes cellular phone switches copiers and other products. LynuxWorks caters to embedded systems developers working with Linux the open-source operating system that has found some favor over Microsoft operating systems for speed and flexibility. The company also provides consulting technical training and support services as well as its LynxSecure technology which is used for securely running multiple operating systems simultaneously.

LYON (WILLIAM) HOMES

NYS: WLH

4695 MacArthur Court, 8th Floor
Newport Beach, CA 92660
Phone: 949 833-3600
Fax: 949 476-2178
Web: www.lyonhomes.com

CEO: William H. (Bill) Lyon
CFO: Colin T. Severn
HR: -
FYE: December 31
Type: Public

William Lyon's compass is pointed due west. That's where the homebuilder and its joint venture partners design and build single-family detached and attached houses. California accounts for about 80% of the company's home closings; William Lyon also builds and sells homes in Arizona and Nevada. The company targets entry-level and move-up buyers; its homes range from $110000 to $700000 averaging some $350000. William Lyon owns about 10000 development lots and holds options to buy more than 400 additional lots. The company assists with financing through William Lyon Mortgage. Chairman William Lyon and his family control the company which went public in 2013.

	Annual Growth	12/11*	02/12*	12/12	12/13	12/14
Sales ($ mil.)	58.1%	226.8	25.6	372.8	572.5	896.7
Net income ($ mil.)	-	(193.3)	228.4	(8.9)	129.1	44.6
Market value ($ mil.)	(8.4%)	-	-	-	693.0	634.5
Employees	50.3%	-	-	259	350	585

*Fiscal year change

LYRIS, INC.

NBB: LYRI

6401 Hollis Street, Suite 125
Emeryville, CA 94608
Phone: 800 768-2929
Fax: -
Web: www.lyris.com

CEO: Scott Brighton
CFO: -
HR: Barron Cox
FYE: June 30
Type: Public

Lyris sings a song of SaaS-pence. The company provides a variety of Software-as-a-Service (Saas) online marketing applications and services. Its more than 8000 clients use the company's products to manage email lists and to create and monitor email marketing campaigns. More than three quarters of its revenues come from subscriptions to its cloud-based Lyris HQ hosted software application. Customers come from a wide range of industries including financial services consumer goods health care retail media and transportation. The company also provides professional services such as consulting support and training. Formerly called J. L. Halsey the company took its present name in 2007.

	Annual Growth	06/10	06/11	06/12	06/13	06/14
Sales ($ mil.)	(8.3%)	44.2	40.1	38.8	36.2	31.3
Net income ($ mil.)	-	(2.7)	(7.0)	(10.5)	(0.3)	(5.0)
Market value ($ mil.)	40.3%	3.3	2.7	26.3	18.8	12.8
Employees	(15.3%)	272	233	162	150	140

This Page left intentionally blank